First edition written by the Editors at FL Memo with assistance from:
Clive Borthwick and Patrick McGrath, Taylor Walton Solicitors (Debt finance, Buying and Selling a Company)
Sean Williams, Fortune Law (Corporate Restructuring and Development)
Subsequent editions written, updated and revised by the Editors at FL Memo

FL Memo Limited

Important Disclaimer

This publication is sold on the understanding that the information provided within it is for guidance only, and that the publisher is not in business to provide legal or accounting advice or other professional services. Readers entering into transactions on the basis of, or otherwise relying on, such information should seek the services of a competent professional adviser.

Whilst every care has been taken to ensure the accuracy of the contents, the editors and the publishers cannot accept responsibility for any loss occasioned to any person acting or refraining to act as a result of any statement in it.

ISBN : 978-0-9557190-0-4

FL MEMO LTD
185 Park Street
Bankside
London SE1 9DY

Telephone: (020) 7803 4666; Fax: (020) 7803 4699
Email: flm@flmemo.co.uk
Website: www.flmemo.co.uk

© 2008 FL Memo Limited
All rights reserved. No part of this work covered by the publisher's copyright may be reproduced or copied in any form or by any means without written permission from the publisher.
British Library Cataloguing in Publication Data.
A catalogue record for this book is available from the British Library.

FL MEMO

Company Law

2008

Contents

All references in *Company Law Memo* are to paragraphs

1: Types of business and corporate structures 1
Unincorporated 8
Incorporated 39
Choice of business structure 130
Overseas companies 140
Group structures 194

2: Company and business names 240

3: Company formation and constitution 340

4: Shares and share capital 700
Types of share 740
Share issues and allotments 889
Variation of class rights 1270
Alteration of share capital 1312
Own share purchase and redemption 1337
Reduction of share capital 1435

5: Dividends and distributions 1600

6: Transfer and transmission of shares 1825

7: Shareholders 2000

8: Directors 2160
Appointment 2230
Duties 2317
Service contract 2627
Remuneration 2696
Loans to directors 2804
Termination 2912
Disqualification 3000

9: Company management and decision making 3110
Management roles 3118
Board decisions 3217
Shareholder decisions 3513

Company registers	3888
Companies House	4040

10: Company secretary 4115

11: Company accounts 4185

12: Company finance 4500
Debt finance	4504
Private equity finance	4800

13: Buying and selling a company 5200

14: Corporate restructuring and development 6400
Hive-down	6415
Share for share exchange	6453
Section 110 reorganisation	6465
Scheme of arrangement	6500
Joint ventures	6550
Takeovers	6675

15: Litigation and investigations 7115

16: Introduction to corporate insolvency 7300
Informal solutions	7323
Formal solutions	7334
General principles	7360
Dissolution, striking off and restoration	7491

17: Compulsory liquidation 7570

18: Voluntary liquidation 8425
Creditors' voluntary liquidation	8437
Members' voluntary liquidation	8594

19: Administration 8690

20: Receivership 9195

21: Company voluntary arrangements 9435

Appendix
Companies House forms and filing deadlines	9900
Useful contacts	9905
Table B 1985	9910
Table A 1985	9915
Comparison between Table A 1985 and Table A 1948	9920
Sample director's service contract	9925
Definition of "connected person"	9930
Table of criminal offences	9935

Glossary 9940

Index (p. 1235)

Preface

Company Law Memo 2008 provides **practical guidance** and **up to date commentary** on company law and practice. It is based on an internationally successful formula, which is accessible and easy to navigate, whilst retaining depth of coverage on a wide range of company law issues.

Company Law Memo 2008 takes the reader through the full life-span of a company, **covering** day to day management and administrative matters as well as the key transactions and insolvency procedures in which a company may become involved. It also looks at the duties and liabilities of the individuals associated with a company, principally its shareholders and directors. The handbook focuses on private and public companies limited by shares, but also discusses those limited by guarantee and unlimited companies. Listed/quoted companies, partnerships and banking or insurance companies are, however, outside the scope of this work.

This edition has been extensively updated to include commentary on the **Companies Act 2006**. *Company Law Memo 2008* reflects the law at the time of writing, which is currently set out in a mixture of the 1985 and 2006 Acts. Although the new Act received Royal Assent on 8 November 2006, it is being brought into force in stages. At the time of writing, a significant proportion is already in force, most notably many of the provisions relating to shareholder decisions and directors. The next implementation stage will occur on 6 April 2008. The Government announced in mid-November that the final tranche of provisions would not be implemented in October 2008 as expected, but would be postponed. Implementation of most of these provisions is now expected by October 2009, although the final date for some provisions is currently still subject to consultation. Readers will be kept informed of all implementation matters in updates and newsletters.

Company Law Memo 2008 also includes commentary on the **new model articles**, which will replace Table A for companies incorporated from October 2009. The references are to the latest draft at the time of writing, as set out in the draft Companies (Model Articles) Regulations 2007 (July 2007 version). Transitional amendments have been made to Table A to reflect some of the provisions of the new Act which were brought into force on 1 October 2007. They apply to companies incorporated on or after this date. They are noted in the text where relevant and included in the version of Table A reproduced in the appendix.

Company Law Memo 2008 covers the **law applying to** England and Wales. Whilst much of the law applicable in Scotland and Northern Ireland is similar, there are important differences and specialist advice should be sought.

This work is intended to reflect law and practice as at 1 December 2007, although later amendments have been noted where possible. *Company Law Memo 2008* provides a reliable source of information throughout the year using:
– an **online updating facility**, giving detailed updates to individual paragraphs reflecting the latest developments. This is available via our website (*www.flmemo.co.uk*);
– an **online product updating facility** whereby the online updates are automatically incorporated into the text of the online version of *Company Law Memo 2008*; and

– **regular newsletters**, which highlight and explore developments in the law and other subjects of interest. Readers are notified via email when newsletters are published on the website.

The editors are always interested in feedback from readers, who are welcome to contact them at *companyeditors@flmemo.co.uk*.

FL Memo Ltd
December 2007

Abbreviations

The following abbreviations are used in *Company Law Memo*

ACT	Advance Corporation Tax	ICAEW	Institute of Chartered Accountants of England and Wales
AGM	Annual General Meeting		
ASB	Accounting Standards Board	ICANN	Internet Corporation for Assigned Names and Numbers
BERR	Department for business, enterprise and regulatory reform	ICSA	Institute of Chartered Secretaries and Administrators
BNA 1985	Business Names Act 1985	ICTA 1988	Income and Corporation Taxes Act 1988
CA	Companies Act	IFRS	International Financial Reporting Standard
CC(CP)A 1985	Companies Consolidation (Consequential Provisions) Act 1985	IR 1986	Insolvency Rules 1986
CDDA 1986	Company Directors Disqualification Act 1986	IRC	Inland Revenue Commissioners
		ITEPA 2003	Income Tax (Earnings and Pensions) Act 2003
CIB	Companies Investigation Branch	ITTOIA 2005	Income Tax (Trading and Other Income) Act 2005
CIC	Community Interest Company		
CPR	Civil Procedure Rules		
CVA	Company Voluntary Arrangement	IVA	Individual voluntary arrangement
CVL	Creditors' Voluntary Liquidation		
		JVC	Joint Venture Company
DPA 1998	Data Protection Act 1998		
		LLP	Limited Liability Partnership
EA 2002	Enterprise Act 2002	LPA 1925	Law of Property Act 1925
EC	European Community	Ltd	Limited
EEA	European Economic Area		
EEC	European Economic Community	MVL	Members' Voluntary Liquidation
EEIG	European Economic Interest Grouping		
EIS	Enterprise Investment Scheme	NICs	National Insurance Contributions
ESC	Extra Statutory Concession		
EU	European Union	OFT	Office of Fair Trading
		PAYE	Pay As You Earn
FA	Finance Act	PD	Practice Direction
FII	Franked Investment Income	plc	Public limited company
FRED	Financial Reporting Exposure Draft		
FRS	Financial Reporting Standard	RPI	Retail Price Index
FRSSE	Financial Reporting Standard for Smaller Entities		
		SDLT	Stamp Duty Land Tax
FSA	Financial Services Authority	SORP	Statement of Recommended Practice
FSMA 2000	Financial Services and Markets Act 2000	SSAP	Statements of Standard Accounting Practice
GAAP	Generally Accepted Accounting Principles	TA	Table A
		TCGA 1992	Taxation of Chargeable Gains Act 1992
		TR	Technical Release
HSWA 1974	Health and Safety at Work etc Act 1974	TUPE	Transfer of Undertakings (Protection of Employment) Regulations
IA 1986	Insolvency Act 1986		
IAS	International Accounting Standards	UKLA	United Kingdom Listings Authority
IASB	International Accounting Standards Board		
		VAT	Value Added Tax

The following case report citations are referred to in *Company Law Memo*

AC	Appeal Cases (3rd Series)	KB	King's Bench
ACLR	Australian Company Law Reports		
ACSR	Australian Corporations and Securities Reports	LJ Ch	Law Journal Reports, Chancery New Series
All ER	All England Reports	LJQB	Law Journal Reports, Queen's Bench New Series
All ER (D)	All England Direct Law Reports (Digests)		
All ER Rep	All England Law Reports Reprint	Lloyd's Rep	Lloyd's Reports
App Cas	Appeal Cases (2nd Series)	LR Eq	Law Reports, Equity Cases
		LT	Law Times Reports
BCC	British Company Cases	LTL	Lawtel Transcripts
BCLC	Butterworths Company Law Cases		
Beav	Beavan's Rolls Court Reports	NZCLC	New Zealand Company Law Cases
BPIR	Bankruptcy and Personal Insolvency Reports		
		QB	Queen's Bench
Ch	Chancery Division (3rd Series)		
Ch App	Chancery Appeal Cases	RPC	Reports of Patent, Design and Trade Mark Cases
Ch D	Chancery Division (2nd Series)		
CMLR	Common Market Law Reports	Russ	Russell's Chancery Reports tempore Eldon
Cr App Rep	Criminal Appeal Reports		
De G&J	De Gex & Jones, Chancery Reports	SC	Session Cases
DLR	Dominion Law Reports	SCCR	Scottish Criminal Case Reports
		STC	Simon's Tax Cases
ECR	European Court Reports		
EWCA	England & Wales Court of Appeal (neutral citation)	TLR	Times Law Reports
EWHC	England & Wales High Court (neutral citation)	UKHL	United Kingdom House of Lords (neutral citation)
Ex D	Law Reports, Exchequer Division		
Exch	Exchequer Reports	VR	Victorian Reports
ICR	Industrial Case Reports		
IR	Irish Reports	WLR	Weekly Law Reports
IRLR	Industrial Relations Law Reports	WN	Weekly Notes of Cases

CHAPTER 1
Types of business and corporate structures

OUTLINE

SECTION 1 **Types of business** 8	SECTION 2 **Choice of business structure** 130
A Unincorporated structures 8	
1 Sole trader............. 12	
2 Partnership............. 17	SECTION 3 **Overseas companies** 140
3 Unincorporated association...... 24	
4 Co-operative............ 29	1 Registration of branch 145
B Incorporated structures......... 39	2 Registration of established place of business............ 151
1 Company limited by shares...... 45	
2 Company limited by guarantee...... 52	3 Overseas company names........ 158
3 Unlimited company............ 57	4 Ongoing filing and disclosure 163
4 Community Interest Company (CIC)...... 62	
5 Limited Liability Partnership (LLP) 77	SECTION 4 **Group structures** 194
6 European Company (Societas Europaea) 88	
7 European Economic Interest Grouping (EEIG)................ 104	1 Holding companies and subsidiaries..... 199
8 Industrial and provident society 121	2 Parent and subsidiary undertakings 213

There are many different ways in which a business can be structured in the UK. The types of structure can broadly be divided into two categories: unincorporated and incorporated.

An **unincorporated** business is one without its own legal identity, often referred to as a "legal personality". This means that the business is just the people who run it. Many small businesses are run in this manner, as the administrative costs of incorporation are too high for them. An outline of the main types of unincorporated business structures is at ¶8+. The most common type of unincorporated business is a sole trader. BERR estimates that there were 2.8 million sole trader businesses in the UK at the beginning of 2006.

An **incorporated** business is one with its own legal personality. This means that it has a legal identity which is distinct from that of its owners or managers. This has many benefits in business but is accompanied by higher regulation. An outline of the many types of incorporated business structures is at ¶39+. The most common type of incorporated business structure is a company. BERR's figures show that there were 1.145 million companies in the UK at the beginning of 2006.

There are several different **types of company**. The most common type is a private limited company, the formal name for which is a "private company limited by shares". The other types of company are:
– a public company limited by shares, usually referred to as a plc or public company;
– a company limited by guarantee, often referred to as a guarantee company; and
– an unlimited company.

A summary of the factors which impact upon the **choice** between an unincorporated or incorporated business format is at ¶130.

One advantage of trading through a company is that different businesses can be operated separately but under the same family or group of companies. **Group structures** are examined at ¶194+.

3   **Overseas companies** which establish a branch or place of business in GB are required to register at Companies House (the UK company registration body). The regime governing overseas companies operating in GB is considered at ¶140+.

SECTION 1
Types of business

A. Unincorporated structures

8   An unincorporated business does not have its own legal personality, so the business is, in effect, the people who run it. The unincorporated business structures discussed here are:
- sole trader (¶12);
- partnership (¶17+);
- unincorporated association (¶24); and
- co-operative (¶29).

1. Sole trader

12   A sole trader enterprise is a **business run by** an individual in his own name or under a trade name (for example, John Smith trading as JS Builders). The business itself does not have a separate legal personality. Many small businesses are run by sole traders.

The basic characteristics of a sole trader business are that the sole trader:
- has personal **liability** for the business' debts and obligations;
- personally owns the **assets** of the business; and
- is **taxed** personally on the business' income and capital gains.

2. Partnership

17   A partnership is a **business run by** two or more persons (individuals or companies) "in common with a view to profit" (s 1 Partnership Act 1890). In other words, at least two people have to be acting together in a business venture. The partnership itself does not have a legal personality. Instead, each partner acts as agent for the other partners and the partnership (s 5 Partnership Act 1890). Many professional businesses (for example, accountants and solicitors) are conducted through partnerships. Partnerships are often named after the founding partners (e.g. Adams, Bassett and Cardinal) but it is equally possible for the partnership business to operate under a trading name.

Partners are **taxed** individually on their share of the partnership's profits and losses.

> MEMO POINTS   A partnership is distinct from a **limited liability partnership** (see ¶77+), and the far rarer **limited partnership**. Under a limited partnership, the liability of one or more of the partners for the partnership debts is limited to the amount contributed by him when he joined the partnership. Such partners are termed "limited partners". They may not participate in the

management of the partnership and do not have the power to bind the partnership (s 6 Limited Partnership Act 1907). However, they are still expected to share in partnership losses (*Reed (Inspector of Taxes) v Young* [1986] 1 WLR 649). A limited partnership is only permitted if at least one partner has unlimited liability for the partnership's debts (s 4 Limited Partnership Act 1907). Such partners are termed "general partners". Limited partnerships must be registered at Companies House on Form LP5. The registration fee is £2.

Most partnerships are governed by a written **partnership agreement** but this is not a prerequisite. A partnership can arise under an oral agreement or even be implied by a course of dealing. The basic characteristics of a partnership are that each partner has:

a. personal joint **liability** for the debts and obligations of himself and the other partners which are incurred either in the ordinary course of partnership business or with the authority of the partners (ss 5-10 Partnership Act 1890). This liability will continue even after a partner has left a partnership, at least in respect of liabilities incurred before exit (s 17 Partnership Act 1890);

b. the right to share in the **profits and assets** of the partnership business. Unless there is an agreement to the contrary, the partners will be entitled to an equal share (s 24 Partnership Act 1890); and

c. the right to take part in the **management** of the business, although there is no obligation to do so. Unless there is an agreement to the contrary, most decisions will be made by a simple majority. The exceptions are decisions on changing the nature of the partnership business or the introduction of a new partner, which require unanimity (s 24 Partnership Act 1890).

Where there is no express agreement as to **how it can be brought to an end** (known as "dissolution"), the partnership can be dissolved at any time by any partner giving notice to the others. This type of partnership is known as a "**partnership at will**". This is avoided in practice because of the insecurity inherent in a business which can be terminated at any time. As a result, a written partnership agreement will normally set out in detail the ways in which a partner may **exit the partnership**. It will also normally state that, even if some partners leave, the partnership will continue for so long as there are at least two partners. An exiting partner should give notice to all those who have dealt with the partnership before he left and advertise his exit in the *Gazette*, otherwise he will continue to be liable for the acts of his former partners that are carried out after he has left (s 36 Partnership Act 1890).

3. Unincorporated association

An unincorporated association is an **organisation of** a group of people (called the "members") who have agreed to co-operate with each other for a particular purpose and who all have a say in the organisation's administration. Many smaller charities and most voluntary or community groups are run as unincorporated associations because they are quick and easy to set up and are not answerable to any agencies (although charitable associations may have to register with the Charities Commission).

The agreement to co-operate does not have to be in writing, but usually the association is governed by a **constitution** which may be known by another name, such as "rules". The basic characteristics of an unincorporated association are:

– all **assets** and contracts are held in the name of individual members (known as trustees), who hold them on trust for the people who will benefit from the objects of the organisation;
– the trustees can be held personally **liable** for the debts and obligations of the organisation; and
– the association is usually run by a **management** committee elected by its members.

4. Co-operative

A co-operative is **defined as** an autonomous association of persons united voluntarily to meet their common economic, social and cultural needs and aspirations through a jointly-owned and democratically controlled enterprise. Business co-operatives are **owned and controlled by** their employees. The legal structure of a co-operative can take the form of an unincorporated association (¶24), limited company or, more commonly, an industrial and provident society (¶121).

Further information on co-operatives can be obtained from Co-operatives[UK], the union for the co-operative sector in the UK.

B. Incorporated structures

39 An **incorporated** vehicle is one with its own legal personality, which is distinct from that of its owners or managers. The incorporated vehicles discussed here are as follows:
- company limited by shares (¶45+);
- company limited by guarantee (¶52);
- unlimited company (¶57);
- Community Interest Company (CIC) (¶62+);
- Limited Liability Partnership (LLP) (¶77+);
- European Company (Societas Europaea) (¶88+);
- European Economic Interest Grouping (EEIG) (¶104+); and
- Industrial and provident society (¶121+).

> MEMO POINTS In 2007, the European Commission consulted on its plans to introduce a **European Private Company** (this would be in addition to the European Company and EEIG). The purpose of this new corporate vehicle would be to make it easier for small and medium-sized companies to conduct cross-border business by having a type of company which would be governed by one set of rules no matter which member state it was set up in. The Commission consulted on the possible model of this new type of company and the forms that the statute governing it might take. It also asked consultees to comment on the legal and other obstacles facing companies doing cross-border business by establishing subsidiaries or branches in other member states. One of the aims of the consultation was to ascertain whether or not there is a need for a European Private Company. At the time of writing, the Commission has not yet published its response to this consultation.

40 The first four types of company are subject to company law and are the topic of this publication. A wholesale reform of company law in the UK will occur over the course of the next year as the **new Companies Act** is implemented. Under the new law, there will be no changes to the types of company which may be incorporated. However, there will be substantial changes to the way in which these companies are regulated and these are detailed at the appropriate place in each chapter.

1. Company limited by shares

45 A company limited by shares is the most common type of incorporated business structure. Such companies are **owned by** their shareholders but **managed by** their directors. The **rules** of the company are set out in its constitutional document known as the "memorandum and articles of association".

> MEMO POINTS Under the **new Companies Act**, a company's constitution will be its "articles of association" together with any resolutions or agreements affecting its constitution (s 18 CA 2006, expected to come into force by 1 October 2009). The memorandum will simply evidence the subscribers' intention to form a company. The objects in existing memoranda will be treated as being in the articles instead. See ¶394+ for more on these changes.

46 The identifying feature of a company limited by shares is that the **liability of the shareholders** for the debts of the company is limited to the amount unpaid on the shares held by them (s 1(2)(a) CA 1985; restated at s 3 CA 2006 by 1 October 2009). Since shareholders normally fully pay for their shares when they are issued, they are rarely held liable for the company's debts.

A company limited by shares has a separate **legal personality** from its shareholders and directors. This means that it can enter into contracts in the name of the company, sue and be sued. Only in rare circumstances will persons who deal with the company be able to hold the shareholders and/or directors liable for the company's actions. Conversely, because the company is a legal person in its own right, the directors must manage it in a way that promotes the success of the company for the benefit of the shareholders as a whole, not in the interests of themselves and/or individual shareholders.

A company limited by shares can be a **private company** or a **public company**. Private companies limited by shares can be identified by the word "limited" or abbreviation "Ltd" at the end of their name. Public companies limited by shares can be identified by the words "public limited company" or abbreviation "plc" at the end of their name.

The main **differences between a public and private** company are that:
– public companies can offer their shares to the public, but private companies are prohibited from doing so; and
– public companies have minimum share capital requirements.

Public companies are subject to greater restrictions than private companies so most companies limited by shares are private. On the other hand, because of those restrictions, investors have greater confidence in public companies. For this reason, many large companies are public.

> MEMO POINTS A company whose shares are listed on the official list of the London Stock Exchange or dealt with on a regulated stock market is known as a **listed company**. "**Quoted company**" has a narrower definition: it refers to a company on the official list of the London Stock Exchange, an EEA state, or one that is admitted to dealing on either the New York Stock Exchange or Nasdaq. Although a listed or quoted company must be a public company, it is not necessary for a public company to be listed/quoted. There are specific rules governing listed/quoted companies, which are outside the scope of this book.

2. Company limited by guarantee

A company limited by guarantee is in many respects the same as a company limited by shares, although not as common. Those with a stake in the company are referred to as "members" rather than "shareholders". The main feature of a company limited by guarantee is that the **liability of its members** for the debts of the company is limited to the amount which they have undertaken to guarantee (s 1(2)(b) CA 1985; restated at s 3 CA 2006 by 1 October 2009). The guaranteed amount is stated in the company's memorandum and is usually only a nominal sum, for example, £1 per member.

Companies limited by guarantee are often used by not-for-profit organisations such as charities, clubs and associations, which are run on a one-member, one-vote system.

A company limited by guarantee can now only be incorporated as a **private company**, although some historical public companies limited by guarantee may still be in existence (s 1(3), (4) CA 1985; restated at ss 4, 5 CA 2006 by 1 October 2009).

> MEMO POINTS 1. Since 22 December 1980, a company cannot be formed as, or become, a company limited by guarantee and have **share capital** (s 1(4) CA 1985; restated at s 5 CA 2006 by 1 October 2009). Any such company is therefore a rare historical overhang.
> 2. Under the **new Companies Act**, the guaranteed amount will be stated in the company's "statement of guarantee" which it will have to file at Companies House as part of the incorporation process (s 11 CA 2006, expected to come into force by 1 October 2009). It will also have to state the names and addresses of the subscribers to the memorandum (reg 4 draft Companies (Registration) Regulations 2007, also expected to come into force on 1 October 2009).

3. Unlimited company

An unlimited company is a company with no limit on the **liability of its members** (s 1(2)(c) CA 1985; restated at s 3 CA 2006). An unlimited company may or may not have share capital but can only be registered as a private company (s 1(3) CA 1985; restated at ss 3, 4 CA 2006).

Since its members can be liable for the company's debts, unlimited companies are an unpopular and rare corporate format.

4. Community Interest Company (CIC)

62 CICs are limited companies **designed for use by** social enterprises that want to use their profits and assets for the public good (for example, environmental improvement, community transport, fair trade, etc). A company cannot be both a CIC and a charity, even if its objects are entirely charitable in nature. However, a charity can own a CIC so, for example, a CIC could be set up by a charity to run a charity shop and distribute its profits back to the charity.

The following is a brief overview of CICs. The **relevant law** is set out in legislation (Pt 2, Sch 3-8 Companies (Audit, Investigations and Community Enterprise) Act 2004 and SI 2005/2625). CICs are also subject to general company law.

Further information about CICs can be obtained from the Office of the Regulator of Community Interest Companies.

> MEMO POINTS   The CIC is a relatively **new** type of company; it has only been possible to form one since 1 July 2005. Since 6 April 2007, it has been possible to form a CIC in **Northern Ireland** as well (s 1284(1) CA 2006; art 2 SI 2007/1093).

Structure

64 A CIC must be structured as one of the following conventional limited company **formats** and is subject to the same regulation as any other company in that format:
- company limited by guarantee;
- private company limited by shares; or
- public company limited by shares.

However, a CIC has the following additional **special features**:
- it is subject to an "asset lock";
- it must file an annual CIC report; and
- it is subject to regulation by the Office of the Regulator of Community Interest Companies.

65 An "**asset lock**" means that:
a. the CIC can only transfer assets at full market value or to another asset-locked body (for example, another CIC or a charity);
b. dividends must be declared by shareholders (not by the directors alone). Where a CIC's memorandum and articles allow it to pay dividends to non-asset locked bodies, the dividend is subject to a cap. The maximum dividend per share is 5% above the Bank of England's Repo Rate at the time the share was issued. Unused dividend capacity can be carried forward for 4 years. This is subject always to a maximum aggregate dividend per year of 35% of distributable profits;
c. there is a cap of 4% above the Bank of England's Repo Rate on interest on loans where the rate of interest is linked to the CIC's performance; and
d. on dissolution, any surplus assets must be transferred to another asset locked body.

66 The purpose of the **annual CIC report** is to show that the CIC is still satisfying the community interest test (see ¶70 below) and is carrying out activities which benefit the community. The minimum required contents include:
- details of what the CIC has done to benefit the community;
- details of how it has involved its stakeholders in its activities;
- information about the remuneration of directors (unless this duplicates information in the accounts);
- details of declared or proposed dividends, performance related interest on loans paid and compliance with the asset lock cap referred to above; and
- information on the transfer of assets.

The report must be filed with the CIC's annual accounts and will be placed on the public record by Companies House. There is a £15 filing fee. Although the report is separate from the accounts, the regulator recommends that it be sent to shareholders and other stakeholders with the annual accounts.

The **CIC regulator** is an independent public officer appointed by the secretary of state for business, enterprise & regulatory reform. CICs are to be regulated using a "light touch". The regulator's main tasks are to encourage the formation of CICs, develop the CIC brand, and provide guidance and assistance on matters relating to CICs. Where necessary, he will consider complaints and take enforcement action. His enforcement powers include: bringing civil proceedings in the name of the CIC; appointing or removing directors; and appointing a manager to take control of the CIC in appropriate circumstances (for example, where a CIC is being mismanaged). Appeals from decisions or orders of the regulator are heard by a specially appointed Appeal Officer.

Formation

A new CIC is formed in the same way as a limited company (see ¶340+). Its **name** must end with "community interest company" or "c.i.c." if it is to be a private company, or "community interest public limited company" or "community interest plc" if it is to be a public company. Welsh language alternatives are also acceptable.

A CIC must also provide the regulator with evidence that it satisfies the "**community interest test**". This means that it must show that a reasonable person might consider that the ultimate purpose of its activities is the provision of benefits for the community, or a section of the community. However, certain activities are excluded from being in the community's interest. These are political campaigning, and activities which only benefit the members of a particular body or the employees of a particular employer.

In order to satisfy the regulator, the following **additional documents** will have to be filed at Companies House when the application for registration is made:
– a Community Interest Statement which confirms that the company will benefit the community, describes its intended activities and shows how they will benefit the community; and
– an Excluded Company Declaration to confirm that the company is not an excluded company (currently these are political parties, political campaigning organisations and their subsidiaries).
These documents are both contained in Form CIC 36 "Declarations on Formation of a Community Interest Company", available from the CIC regulator. There is an additional filing fee of £15, on top of the normal incorporation fee charged by Companies House.
In addition, the **memorandum and articles** must comply with the CIC regulations (SI 2005/2625). A CIC cannot rely on Table A as its default form of articles but a model form of articles is available from the CIC regulator.

Existing companies can also **convert into CICs** by passing a special resolution, amending their memorandum and articles and filing Form CIC 36. In addition, existing companies have to file a declaration that the company is not a charity (the form of declaration is available from the CIC regulator). Again, there is an additional filing fee of £15, on top of the normal incorporation fee charged by Companies House. Note that if the decision to convert into a CIC is not unanimous, the dissenting minority shareholders may be able to bring a court claim for unfair prejudice (see ¶2105+) and/or apply to prevent any change to the company's objects clause. Companies which are **charities** may need the consent of the Charities Commission.

5. Limited Liability Partnership (LLP)

A limited liability partnership (LLP) is a relatively new form of business structure with a separate legal personality. It has the management organisation of a partnership but the partners (known as members) have limited liability. In return for limited liability, the organisation has the public reporting obligations of a company. LLPs are taxed as partnerships. They must be formed by two or more persons for the purpose of carrying on business with a view to a profit; they are not available for non-profit activities.

The following is a brief overview of LLPs. The **relevant law** is set out in legislation (Limited Liability Partnerships Act 2000 and SI 2001/1090); the law of partnerships (see ¶17+) does not apply to LLPs.

> MEMO POINTS The Government has issued a consultation paper on the application of the new Companies Act to LLPs ("Proposals for the application of the Companies Act 2006 to Limited Liability Partnerships (LLPs)" (November 2007)). The consultation also proposes to simplify SI 2001/1090. It is due to close on 6 February 2008.

Management

79 An LLP is managed by its **members** and every member is an agent of the LLP. This means the LLP is bound by the actions of any member, unless he has no authority to act and the person with whom the member is dealing knows that he does not have that authority.

At least two members must be specified as "**designated members**", or the incorporation document can specify that all members are designated members. In addition to the rights and duties of ordinary members, the designated members have the following extra **administrative responsibilities**:
- signing the accounts and filing them at Companies House;
- notifying Companies House of any changes to the membership, registered office address or LLP name;
- filing the annual return (Form LLP 363); and
- appointing an auditor (if one is needed).

> MEMO POINTS The name of Form LLP 363 is adapted from the **Companies House form** for companies, which is taken from the relevant section number of the legislation. As all of the section numbers will change under the new Companies Act, Companies House proposes to change the names of all of its forms to reflect their function rather than the relevant section number ("Working with Companies House: a consultation on the registrar's rules and related provisions which will apply under the Companies Act 2006"). At the time of writing, the new form names are not yet available.

80 The mutual rights and duties of the LLP and its members can be agreed between themselves in an **LLP agreement**. Certain default rights and duties are prescribed by law, unless excluded by the LLP agreement (reg 7 SI 2001/1090). These are similar to those found in general partnership law, for example:
- the members are entitled to share equally in the capital and profits;
- every member is entitled to take part in the management of the LLP; and
- decisions can be made on a simple majority, except for the introduction of a new member or a change in the nature of the LLP's business, which require unanimity.

81 An LLP has **obligations to report** matters to Companies House, similar to those of a company. For example, an obligation:
- to prepare and file annual accounts. These accounts will have to be audited unless the LLP qualifies as "small" (the same thresholds apply as for companies, see ¶4362+);
- to notify Companies House when a member is appointed, when someone ceases to be a member or when a member's details change (including if his status changes from ordinary member to designated member, or vice versa);
- to register mortgages and charges;
- to notify any change to the registered office; and
- to file an annual return.

Formation

83 An LLP is formed by filing Form LLP2, known as the "**incorporation document**", together with a **fee** of £20. Registration takes approximately 5 working days. For same-day registration, the fee is £50.

Form LLP2 **sets out**:
- the LLP's name (this must end with either "limited liability partnership" or "LLP");
- where the registered office is situated (either "England and Wales", "Wales" or "Scotland");
- the registered office address; and

– the details of the initial members (continuation sheets are available if there are to be more than two initial members) specifying which are to be designated members.

Note that there is no requirement to file the LLP agreement, which remains a private document.

6. European Company (Societas Europaea)

The intended **benefit** of a European Company (the formal name for which is a "Societas Europaea", or SE) is the management and administrative savings that can be made if a pan-European business is registered in just one member state. It can then operate throughout the EU without the need to register branches or set up a complex series of subsidiaries in different EU jurisdictions. A European Company must be registered in the same EU member state in which its head office is registered.

A European Company is **treated as** if it is a public limited company formed in accordance with the law of the EU member state in which it has its registered office. Therefore, the GB laws applicable to public limited companies also apply to European Companies registered in GB.

One feature of the European Company is the **involvement of employees**. This may not be as revolutionary as it first appears; the employees may in any event have information and consultation rights under employment legislation (see *Employment Memo*).

The following is a brief overview of European Companies registered in GB. The **relevant law** is contained in SI 2004/2326 which implements EC Regulation 2157/2001, and EC Directive 2001/86, regarding the involvement of employees in European Companies. Similar national legislation exists in other EU member states.

> MEMO POINTS The European Company is a relatively **new** type of company; it has only been possible to form one since 8 October 2004.
>
> Under the new Companies Act, it will also be possible to form a European Company in **Northern Ireland** (s 1285 CA 2006, expected to come fully into force by 1 October 2009).

Structure

A European Company has **shareholders**, like other public limited companies. The minimum amount of subscribed **share capital** is the equivalent of at least €120,000. The relevant conversion rate is that on the last day of the month before formation. Of this amount, at least £50,000 must be denominated in pounds sterling. The remainder can be denominated in any currency. The usual rules for the paying up, maintenance, allotment and restructuring of share capital in a public limited company apply.

A European Company's rules and procedures are set out in its "**statute**". There is no standard format for the statute but it must contain matters relating to the company's management. Statutes can normally only be changed with the approval of 75% of the shareholders. Amendments must be registered with Companies House within 14 days using Form SE82(1)(a).

> MEMO POINTS The name of Form SE82(1)(a), like the names of other **Companies House forms**, is taken from the relevant section number of the legislation. As all of the section numbers will change under the new Companies Act, Companies House proposes to change the names of all of its forms to reflect their function rather than the relevant section number ("Working with Companies House: a consultation on the registrar's rules and related provisions which will apply under the Companies Act 2006"). At the time of writing, the new form names are not yet available.

The day to day **management** of a European Company depends upon whether it has chosen to operate a one-tier or two-tier management system. Under a **one-tier system**, an "administrative organ" manages the company. It must meet at least once every 3 months. Under a **two-tier system**, a "management organ" manages the company and it must report at least every 3 months to a separate "supervisory organ", which oversees it (this two-tier system is used in German company law). The supervisory organ is responsible for appointing the members of the management organ but cannot exercise any management powers itself. In both cases, there is no maximum number of members of each organ, but the minimum number is two.

93 For the purposes of legislation relating to public limited companies, the members of the administrative, supervisory and management organ are "**directors**" and each of those organs is a "**board of directors**". There is no equivalent of a company secretary. Appointments, resignations and changes to details of the members of the administrative or management organ must be registered at Companies House in the same way as for directors: by using Forms 288a, 288b and 288c, respectively. For the supervisory organ, appointments must be registered using Form SE79A, termination of appointments using Form SE79B and changes to particulars using Form SE79C.

> MEMO POINTS The names of these forms, like the names of other **Companies House forms**, are taken from the relevant section number of the legislation. As all of the section numbers will change under the new Companies Act, Companies House proposes to change the names of all of its forms to reflect their function rather than the relevant section number ("Working with Companies House: a consultation on the registrar's rules and related provisions which will apply under the Companies Act 2006"). At the time of writing, the new form names are not yet available.

Employee involvement

95 Every European Company must have in place an arrangement for the involvement of employees. There are three aspects to employee involvement:
- **information** rights: the rights of employee representatives to be informed of matters concerning the company;
- **consultation** rights: the rights of employee representatives to express their opinion on company proposals; and
- **participation** rights: the rights of employees to elect, appoint, recommend or oppose the appointment of some members of the supervisory organ (in a two-tier system) or administrative organ (in a one-tier system).

96 The detailed provisions of how employees are to be involved can be set out in an **agreement** negotiated between the companies forming the European Company (see below) and a "special negotiating body" elected by and representative of those companies' employees. It is the responsibility of the participating companies to start this process.

Default standard provisions will apply if **agreement cannot be reached** within 12 months, or if the parties choose that they should apply. Under the standard provisions, the European Company must inform and consult with a "representative body" elected by and representative of employees. Employees will only have participation rights if at least one of the companies was previously governed by participation rules.

If the special negotiating body **decides not to open or terminates negotiations**, then the national rules relating to information and consultation with employees will apply (e.g. European Works Councils, see *Employment Memo* for further information).

Formation

98 There are **four ways** to form a European Company as set out in the table below. The **registration fee** in each case is £20.

> MEMO POINTS 1. A European Company can only be formed after the issue of **employee involvement** (see ¶95+ above) has been resolved.
> 2. All the bodies participating in the formation must have their registered office in the EU and there must be a **cross-border element**. In the case of a merger, the public limited bodies must be registered in at least two EU member states. In the case of a holding European Company or subsidiary European Company, at least two of the participating bodies must be registered in different EU member states or for 2 years have had a subsidiary or branch in another EU member state. This does not apply when a European Company is itself forming a subsidiary European Company. In the case of a public limited company transforming into a European company, it must have had a subsidiary company registered in another EU member state for 2 years.
> 3. The names of these forms, like the names of other **Companies House forms**, are taken from the relevant section number of the legislation. As all of the section numbers will change under the new Companies Act, Companies House proposes to change the names of all of its forms to reflect their function rather than the relevant section number ("Working with Companies House: a consultation on the registrar's rules and related provisions which will apply under the Companies Act 2006"). At the time of writing, the new form names are not yet available.

TYPES OF BUSINESS AND CORPORATE STRUCTURES

Method	Participating bodies	Process	Companies House filing
Merger	2 or more plcs (including SEs)	a. The **method** of merger can be by **acquisition** (with the acquiring company becoming an SE) or formation of **new company** (with the merging companies ceasing to exist)	-
		b. **Draft terms** of the merger must be **approved by** a general meeting of each plc's shareholders	-
		c. **High Court** must issue **certificate** that all pre-merger acts and formalities have been completed	-
		d. **Registration** at Companies House	– Form SE5 – Statutes – Office copy of court certificate
Holding SE	2 or more private or public limited companies (including SEs)	a. Participating bodies must become **majority-owned** by SE	-
		b. **Draft terms** of formation prepared by directors must be **approved by** general meeting of each participating body's shareholders. Draft terms must include an **explanatory report** by an independent expert.	– Form SE68(2)(a) (draft terms of formation) at least 1 month before meeting
		c. **Shareholders** have 3 months from approval to notify the relevant participating body whether they intend to **contribute their shares** to the formation of the holding SE. Formation can only proceed if minimum proportion of shareholders in each company, as set out in draft terms, agree to contribute their shares. Remaining shareholders have further 1 month to indicate whether they intend to contribute their shares.	– Form SE70(1) (notice that minimum conditions achieved) within 14 days
		d. **Registration** at Companies House	– Form SE6 – Statutes – Expert's explanatory report – Copy of shareholder resolutions from each participating body

Method	Participating bodies	Process	Companies House filing
Subsidiary SE	2 or more companies (including SEs), firms or other legal bodies	**Registration** at Companies House	– Form SE7 – Statutes
	Existing SE	**Registration** at Companies House	– Form SE9(1) – Statutes
Transformation	Existing plc	a. Directors must prepare **draft terms** of conversion for **approval by** special resolution at general meeting of shareholders. Draft terms must include an **explanatory report** by directors.	– Form SE68(3)(a) (draft terms of conversion) at least 1 month before meeting
		b. Before general meeting, an **expert's certificate** must state that the company has net assets at least equivalent to its capital plus undistributable reserves	
		c. **Registration** at Companies House	– Form SE8 – Statutes – Copy of shareholder resolution – Copy of expert's certificate – Copy of directors' explanatory report

A European Company can **transfer** its **registration** from one EU member state to another but it cannot transfer its registration from England/Wales to Scotland or Northern Ireland, or vice versa.

7. European Economic Interest Grouping (EEIG)

A European Economic Interest Grouping (EEIG) is a form of **association between** legal persons (including companies) from two or more EU member states. An EEIG has a legal personality of its own. It therefore allows it members to facilitate or develop their economic activities without losing their individual identity and independence.

The EEIG's activities cannot replace the **economic activities** of its members, but must be ancillary to them. For example, an EEIG may be used for a joint marketing operation or to carry out research in an area of common interest. An EEIG may be registered in any one member state and can operate in any part of the EU. It can enter into arrangements with non-EU organisations or people, but they cannot become members of the EEIG. It cannot exercise management control over its members' activities or those of another undertaking, nor can it be a member of another EEIG.

The following is a brief overview of EEIGs. In the UK, the relevant law is contained in SI 1989/638 which implemented EC Regulation 2137/1985.

Structure

An EEIG is structured in a similar way to a company. It must be formed by at least two **members** (analogous to shareholders) with their central administrations or principal activities based in different EU member states. The main requirement is that each member must have been engaged in an economic activity in the EU before becoming a member of the EEIG. EEIGs are therefore not appropriate for business start-ups but may be appropriate for a joint venture. For example, three diesel engine manufacturers have entered into an EEIG to develop new engines.

The day to day management of an EEIG is conducted by **managers** (analogous to directors). Managers are appointed by the members, who can set limits on their powers. Nevertheless, as far as third parties are concerned, the actions of the managers are binding on the EEIG and the members are jointly liable for those actions.

The rules of the EEIG are contained in its **formation contract** (similar to a company's memorandum and articles). The EEIG is free to decide its own rules and procedures, but the formation contract must at least set out:
– its full **name** (which must include either "European Economic Interest Grouping" or "EEIG" but not any official company name ending such as "limited", "public limited company", "SE" or "unlimited");
– its official **address**;
– the **objects** for which it was formed (this cannot be to make a profit, although it may do so as a by-product of its normal operations);
– each **member's** name, business name, legal form, permanent address or registered office, and the number and place of registration (if any); and
– the **duration** of the EEIG, if it is for a definite period.

There is no requirement for regular **meetings**; the members can specify how decisions can be taken, for example, by telephone or in writing. Each member has at least one vote. No member can hold a majority of the votes, but members can have proportionately higher **voting rights** (for example, if one has contributed more than the others). Decisions can be made on the majority agreed between the members, except for the following decisions which require **unanimity**:
– alteration of the objects;
– alteration of the number of votes allotted to each member;
– extension of the EEIG's duration;
– alteration of the members' contributions to the EEIG's financing;

- alteration of the members' obligations, unless otherwise provided by the formation contract;
- alteration of the formation contract, unless provision for the alteration is contained within the contract itself; and
- transfer of the official address to another EU member state.

110 An EEIG has the following basic characteristics:
- it has its own legal personality and so can own **assets** and enter into contracts in its own name;
- there are no **capital** requirements, so some members can contribute services and skills rather than money;
- the members have joint and several unlimited **liability** for the EEIG's activities. This is one of the main disadvantages when compared to a company;
- it can be **funded by** capital from its members or loans but it cannot seek funds from the public (in contrast to a public limited company); and
- it cannot **employ** more than 500 people.

Registration

112 An EEIG must **register in**:
- the EU member state where its official address is situated. Its official address is either where the EEIG has its central administration or where one of its members has its central administration, provided that the EEIG carries on an activity there; and
- every EU member state where it opens an establishment.

113 In the UK, EEIGs must be **registered at** the relevant Companies House, depending upon whether the official or establishment address is in England and Wales, Scotland or Northern Ireland.

Registration of a **new EEIG** with an official address in the UK must be made on Form EEIG1, together with the formation contract (and an English translation if it is not in English).

Registration of a **UK establishment** of an EEIG with an official address elsewhere in the EU must be made on Form EEIG2, together with certified copies of all documents which were submitted to the registering authority where the EEIG has its official address (and an English translation if the documents are not in English).

The registration **fee** in both cases is £20.

114 An EEIG is able to **transfer its official address** within the EU.

In order to **transfer to the UK**, a transfer proposal must be published in accordance with the laws of the EU member state of the current official address. No decision to transfer can be taken until 2 months after publication. An application to transfer the official address must then be made to Companies House as if a new EEIG were being registered, together with evidence of publication of the transfer proposal and a statement that no competent authority has opposed the transfer.

In order to **transfer out of the UK**, a transfer proposal must be filed at Companies House, which will be responsible for publication in the London, Edinburgh or Belfast *Gazette*, as appropriate, and also in the *Official Journal* of the European Union within 1 month of the *Gazette* notice. It will be the EEIG's responsibility to obtain a copy of the relevant *Gazette* as proof of publication, which will be required by the relevant registry for the EEIG's new address. Registration of the new official address must then be carried out in accordance with the law of the relevant EU member state.

Tax and accounting

116 EEIGs operate under a system of fiscal transparency. Any **profits and losses** are apportioned between the members in accordance with their shares. These are then taxed in the hands of the members according to the national law applicable to them individually (in the UK, see s 510A ICTA 1988).

In the UK, an EEIG is not subject to any accounting or auditing requirements and does not have to file an **annual return** at Companies House. However, it does have to file an annual tax return to Revenue and Customs (s 12A Taxes Management Act 1970). If the EEIG has employees, it is responsible for operation of the PAYE system.

8. Industrial and provident society

121 An industrial and provident society is a registered organisation conducting an industry, business or trade, either:
– as a **co-operative** (that is for the mutual benefit of its members); or
– for the **benefit of the community** (that is to provide services for people other than its members), although the organisation will have to provide special reasons why it should be registered as a society rather than as a company.

Industrial and provident societies are governed by the Industrial and Provident Societies Act 1965 and are **registered with** the Financial Services Authority rather than at Companies House. A registered society has a legal personality of its own.

The basic characteristics of an industrial and provident society are that:
– the society's **assets** are held in its own name;
– the personal **liability** of its members is limited to the amount of their unpaid share capital;
– the **management** of the society is controlled by its members, generally on the principle of "one member, one vote". In many cases, the day to day management is conducted by officers who are elected by the members and may also be removed by them; and
– the **profits** of the society must generally be used to further its objects or be ploughed back into the business. Profits can only be distributed to members if the society is a co-operative, in which case each member should receive an amount that reflects the extent to which they have traded with the society or taken part in its business.

Further information can be obtained from the Mutual Societies Registration department of the FSA.

SECTION 2

Choice of business structure

130 When a new business is being set up, the choice of business structure is usually between a **sole trader/partnership** (depending on the number of proprietors) or a **company limited by shares**. The table below summarises the various factors to be taken into consideration.

Factor	Sole trader/partnership	Company limited by shares
Legal status of business	– No separate legal identity – Business' assets held by the proprietors	– Separate legal identity. Business run in the name of the company – Business' assets belong to the company not the directors/shareholders (even if there is only one director/shareholder) – Directors/shareholders are bound by restrictions which protect the company's capital and assets, e.g. restrictions on loans to directors (¶2804+), changes to share capital (¶1310+) and payment of dividends (¶1600+)
Personal liability of proprietor	Proprietor(s) personally liable for debts of business	Shareholders have limited liability for debts of business but: – directors could be personally liable for breach of duty (¶2317+) or in the event of insolvency (¶7439+); – directors or shareholders could be asked by a bank to personally guarantee repayment of any loans made to the company (¶4698+); – directors or shareholders could be asked by a landlord to guarantee obligations of company under a lease of its premises; and – shareholders could be liable if the corporate veil is lifted (¶7125)

Factor	Sole trader/partnership	Company limited by shares
Publication of business information	No requirement to make information public (although some professional partnerships require names of partners to be displayed at place of business and/or on stationery)	Certain business information must be filed at Companies House and is available for inspection by the public including: – personal details of directors and company secretary; – names and addresses of shareholders and their shareholding; and – company's annual accounts (including profit and loss account and balance sheet)
Management	Business owned and managed by proprietors/partners	Company managed by directors but owned by shareholders who can be: – the same people (as is the case in an owner-managed company); – a wider group of people (e.g. directors and employees); or – a different group of people (e.g. if the shareholders are purely investors)
Regulatory expenses	– No necessary formation expenses although, in the case of a partnership, professional fees may be incurred if a partnership agreement is required – Professional accountancy advice normally required to prepare business accounts – Administrative expenses of VAT registration, if required	– Formation expenses (¶474+) – Administrative expense and professional fees to ensure compliance with formalities of company law (e.g. preparation of board minutes, shareholder resolutions, payment of dividends) – Administrative expense of ongoing requirement to file information at Companies House, including Companies House fees for certain filings (e.g. annual return (¶4060+), registration of a charge (¶4641+)) – Administrative expense of maintaining registers of company information at company's registered office (¶3888+) – Professional accountancy advice required to prepare company accounts. Accounts may need to be audited (¶4209+) – Administrative expenses of VAT registration, if required
Finance	Debt, normally secured on particular assets of business/proprietor	– Debt, normally secured on particular company assets or a floating charge over all the company's business and assets – Investment in exchange for shares (e.g. from venture capitalist, offer of shares to the public and/or flotation on a stock market)
Profit extraction	– Share of business profits – Salary, benefits, pension contributions	– Profits can be distributed to shareholders by way of a dividend – Directors can be paid a salary, with benefits and pension contributions
Exit strategy	Sale of business or share of business	– Sale of company – Sale of shares either by an individual shareholder or by all shareholders to pass control of company to purchaser – Flotation on stock market
Tax	Business profits and capital gains taxed once in hands of proprietor/partner (i.e. subject to income tax and capital gains tax)	– Company's profits and capital gains are first taxed in the hands of the company (i.e. subject to corporation tax) – Any income of the directors/shareholder derived from the company (e.g. salary, dividends) taxed again in the hands of the director/shareholder (i.e. subject to income tax and capital gains tax)

SECTION 3

Overseas companies

140 There are two mutually exclusive registration regimes for overseas companies with a presence in GB:
- registration of a branch; and
- registration of an established place of business.

> *MEMO POINTS* The **new Companies Act** will allow the government to standardise the regime for overseas companies and the new regime is expected to apply from 1 October 2009 (ss 1044-1059 CA 2006). "Overseas company" will be defined as a company incorporated outside of the UK (s 1044 CA 2006). The details of the new regime will be set out in separate regulations. No draft has yet been published but the Government has stated that it intends to apply the new overseas company registration regime to branches only, so that companies operating a place of business in the UK but not a branch would not be required to register at Companies House ("Companies Act 2006 – A Consultative Document" (February 2007)). This would be consistent with the requirements of EC law on the subject, from which the branch registration regime derives (EC Directive 1989/666).

1. Registration of branch

145 A branch must be **registered by** limited companies incorporated outside GB or Gibraltar whose presence in GB qualifies as a branch (s 690A CA 1985). A "**branch**" is an establishment which allows business to be conducted through local representatives rather than being referred to an overseas office. The organisation must appear to be permanent and must be capable of dealing with business itself (e.g. through appropriate management and physical equipment) (*Etablissements Somafer SA v Saar-Ferngas AG*, Case 33/78 [1979] CMLR 490).

If the branch registration regime does not apply, the established place of business registration regime may apply instead (see ¶151+).

146 Each branch established in GB must be **registered within** 1 month of it being established. To register, the following **documents** must be filed at Companies House:
– Form BR1;
– certified copies of the company's constitutional documents (i.e. the equivalent of the memorandum and articles) together with a certified translation if they are not in English; and
– a copy of the latest set of accounts required to be published under the company's national law.

The **registration fee** is £20 and must be paid at the time of filing.

> *MEMO POINTS* If an overseas company **fails to register** its branch, the company and every officer or agent of it who knowingly and wilfully authorises or permits the default is liable to a fine (s 697(3) CA 1985; ¶9935).

2. Registration of established place of business

151 A "**place of business**" is established if the business has a physical or visible connection with premises (e.g. a sign outside an office), or if business is regularly carried out at particular premises. A place of business is not established if the business is carried out through a subcontractor or independent agent. Nor is it established if the premises are used only occasionally (e.g. a hotel used by a director on his visits). A place of business is therefore less significant than a branch.

152 Each established place of business in GB must be **registered by** a company which cannot register a branch because it is:
– a limited company incorporated outside of GB whose place of business in GB does not qualify as a branch;

– an unlimited company incorporated outside of GB; or
– a company incorporated in Northern Ireland or Gibraltar.

153 A place of business must be **registered within** 1 month of it being established (s 691 CA 1985). To register, the following **documents** must be filed at Companies House:
– Form 691; and
– certified copies of the company's constitutional documents (i.e. the equivalent of the memorandum and articles) together with a certified translation if they are not in English.

The **registration fee** is £20 and must be paid at the time of filing.

> MEMO POINTS 1. If an overseas company **fails to register** its place of business, the company and every officer or agent of it who knowingly and wilfully authorises or permits the default is liable to a fine (s 697(1) CA 1985; ¶9935).
> 2. The name of Form 691, like the names of other **Companies House forms**, is taken from the relevant section number of the legislation. As all of the section numbers will change under the new Companies Act, Companies House proposes to change the names of all of its forms to reflect their function rather than the relevant section number ("Working with Companies House: a consultation on the registrar's rules and related provisions which will apply under the Companies Act 2006"). At the time of writing, the new form names are not yet available.

3. Overseas company names

158 An overseas company must register in its **corporate name**. However, it then becomes subject to the same regulations on company names as English and Welsh companies (see ¶242+).

If the overseas company's **corporate name is unacceptable** under those regulations (for example, because it is too similar to an existing company's name), Companies House will notify the company within 12 months of registration (s 694 CA 1985). Two months after having received such a notice (or any longer period which may be specified in the notice), the overseas company will not be able to use its corporate name to carry on business in GB. However, the overseas company may instead notify Companies House on Form 694(4)(a) of a suitable name, other than its corporate name, under which it proposes to carry on business in GB. Any subsequent changes to this trading name must be notified to Companies House on Form 694(4)(b).

> MEMO POINTS 1. If an overseas company continues to **use an unacceptable corporate name**, the company and every officer or agent who knowingly and wilfully authorises or permits the contravention is guilty of an offence and liable to a fine (s 697(2) CA 1985; ¶9935).
> 2. Under the **new Companies Act**, instead of its original corporate name, an overseas company will be able to choose to register an alternative name under which it proposes to carry on business in the UK (s 1048 CA 2006, expected to come into force by 1 October 2009). The alternative name will have to comply with the UK rules governing corporate names. Once registered, this alternative name will, for all purposes, be deemed to be the overseas company's corporate name in the UK. So, for example, it will be able to enter into contracts using that name.
> 3. The names of these forms, like the names of other **Companies House forms**, are taken from the relevant section number of the legislation. As all of the section numbers will change under the new Companies Act, Companies House proposes to change the names of all of its forms to reflect their function rather than the relevant section number ("Working with Companies House: a consultation on the registrar's rules and related provisions which will apply under the Companies Act 2006"). At the time of writing, the new form names are not yet available.

4. Ongoing filing and disclosure

163 Overseas companies, whether registered with a place of business or a branch, are subject to ongoing filing and disclosure requirements in the following **areas**:
– changes to registered details;
– stationery and signs;
– accounts;
– mortgages and charges;

– insolvency; and
– increasing or decreasing activities in GB.

Changes to registered details

An overseas company with either a registered place of business or branch must notify Companies House if any changes occur to its registered details. The requirements are more extensive for registered branches. All notifications must be filed within 21 days. The changes which must be notified and the forms required are set out in the table below.

Change to be registered	Place of business Form	Branch Form
Change to constitutional documents	692(1)(a)	BR2
Change to director or secretary details	692(1)(b)	BR4
Change to name or address of persons authorised to accept service on behalf of overseas company	692(1)(c)	BR6
Change to corporate name	692(2)	BR3
Change to other registered details about the company (e.g. legal form)	n/a	BR3
Change to registered details about the branch (e.g. address, nature of business, trading name)	n/a	BR5
Change of branch against which the constitutional documents and accounts of the company are registered	n/a	BR7

MEMO POINTS 1. If an overseas company **fails to update** its registered details, the company and every officer or agent of it who knowingly and wilfully authorises or permits the default is liable to a fine (s 697(1) CA 1985; ¶9935).
2. The **new Companies Act** envisages that the documents which an overseas company will have to file at Companies House when there has been a change in its registered particulars will be set out in regulations (s 1046 CA 2006, expected to come into force by 1 October 2009). No draft regulations have yet been published.
3. The names of the forms for place of business registrations, like the names of other **Companies House forms**, are taken from the relevant section number of the legislation. As all of the section numbers will change under the new Companies Act, Companies House proposes to change the names of all of its forms to reflect their function rather than the relevant section number ("Working with Companies House: a consultation on the registrar's rules and related provisions which will apply under the Companies Act 2006"). At the time of writing, the new form names are not yet available.

Stationery and signs

In **every place where it carries on business** in GB, any overseas company with either a registered place of business or branch must (s 693(1) CA 1985):
– exhibit its **name and country** of incorporation; and
– display a notice that the shareholders of the company have **limited liability**, if that is the case.

Overseas companies must also display certain information on their **stationery**. The information to be displayed depends upon whether the overseas company has registered a place of business or a branch and, in the latter case, whether the overseas company is incorporated within or outside the EEA. The **information to be displayed** is detailed in the table below (s 693 CA 1985).

	Registered place of business	Registered branch (overseas company incorporated in EEA)	Registered branch (overseas company incorporated outside EEA)
Minimum requirements on every bill, letterhead, notice and other official publication (including any share prospectus issued in GB)	– Company name – Country of incorporation – Notice that shareholders have limited liability, if that is the case		
Additional requirements on all letter paper and order forms	n/a	– Place of registration of branch – Registered number of branch	– Place of registration of branch – Registered number of branch – Legal form of company – Head office location – Registry in which company is registered in its country of incorporation [1] – Registration number in country of incorporation [1] – If applicable, the fact it is being wound up
Note: [1] Only if the company must be registered in its country of incorporation under the local law of that country.			

MEMO POINTS 1. If an overseas company **fails** to state its name and other particulars as required, the company and every officer or agent who knowingly and wilfully authorises or permits the default is liable to a fine (s 697(1) CA 1985; ¶9935).

2. The **new Companies Act** envisages that the disclosures which an overseas company must make on its stationery and signs will be set out in regulations (s 1051 CA 2006, expected to come into force by 1 October 2009). No draft regulations have yet been published, but the latest consultation paper indicates that overseas companies, including those incorporated outside the EU, will be required to disclose their names and registration details in their business letters and order forms (whether in hard copy, electronic or any other form) and also in any .uk websites ("Companies Act 2006 – A Consultative Document" (February 2007)).

Accounts

172 All registered overseas companies must file accounts at Companies House. A filing **fee** of £30 must be paid with each set of accounts.

MEMO POINTS The **new Companies Act** envisages that the accounts which an overseas company will have to file will be set out in regulations (s 1053 CA 2006, expected to come into force by 1 October 2009). No draft regulations have yet been published.

173 An overseas company with a **registered branch** which is required by the law of its country of incorporation to prepare, have audited and disclose accounts must file a copy of those accounts at Companies House within 3 months from the date on which the accounts are first disclosed. If the laws of the country of incorporation allow the company to disclose modified and/or unaudited accounts (e.g. because it is a small company) then a copy of those accounts should be filed instead (s 699AA; Pt 1 Sch 21D CA 1985).

MEMO POINTS If an overseas company **fails to deliver** a copy of its accounts to Companies House, the company and every person who was a director immediately before the end of the period allowed for compliance is guilty of an offence and liable to be fined. A person can defend such a charge on the basis that he took all reasonable steps to secure compliance (para 5 Pt I Sch 21D CA 1985; ¶9935).

174 An overseas company with a **registered place of business** or a registered branch, where the law of its country of incorporation does not require it to prepare, have audited and disclose accounts, must file "**Section 700 accounts**" within 13 months of the company's accounting reference date (ss 699AA, 700; Sch 21D CA 1985). These are the accounts which a company registered

in GB would have to prepare (see ¶4209+) subject to significant modifications (SI 1990/440). The effect of the modifications is that Section 700 accounts are far less detailed that those required for GB-registered companies, although the accounts must relate to the company as a whole and not just that part of the company that operates in GB. In particular:
– no formats are prescribed for the balance sheet or profit and loss account;
– there is no requirement to disclose loans to and other transactions with directors, details of UK tax liability or turnover; and
– there is no requirement for a directors' or auditor's report.

Overseas companies which have to file Section 700 accounts are subject to the same rules regarding their financial year and **accounting reference date** as companies incorporated in GB (see ¶4217+) (s 701 CA 1985). The accounting reference date is set with reference to the date of establishment in GB. Any change to such an overseas company's accounting reference date must be notified to Companies House on Form 225.

MEMO POINTS 1. Overseas **unlimited companies** are treated in the same way as unlimited companies registered in GB. They are not required to file Section 700 accounts if they fall within the exemption from the requirement to file accounts granted to domestic unlimited companies (see ¶4278/mp).
2. An overseas company which **fails to prepare and file** Section 700 accounts properly, and every person who was a director immediately before the end of the period allowed for filing the accounts, is guilty of an offence and liable to be fined. A person can defend such a charge on the basis that he took all reasonable steps to secure compliance, but it is not a defence to prove that the accounts were not in fact prepared (s 703; para 13 Pt II Sch 21D CA 1985; ¶9935).
3. The name of Form 225, like the names of other **Companies House forms**, is taken from the section number of the legislation. As all of the section numbers will change under the new Companies Act, Companies House proposes to change the names of all of its forms to reflect their function rather than the relevant section number ("Working with Companies House: a consultation on the registrar's rules and related provisions which will apply under the Companies Act 2006"). At the time of writing, the new form names are not yet available.

Mortgages and charges

All registered overseas companies must register a mortgage or charge created over property in GB with Companies House (s 409 CA 1985). The **registration regime** is the same as for GB companies (see ¶4636+).

The requirement to register may also extend to "**Slavenburg**" **companies** (i.e. an overseas company operating in GB which has not registered a branch or established place of business) (N V Slavenburg's Bank v Intercontinental Natural Resources Ltd [1980] 1 All ER 955). As a result, a precautionary registration of mortgages or charges given by such companies should also be made (see ¶4644).

MEMO POINTS The **new Companies Act** envisages that the regime for the registration of mortgages and charges over the UK assets of registered overseas companies will be set out in regulations (s 1052 CA 2006, expected to come into force by 1 October 2009). At the time of writing, draft regulations have not yet been published. However, the latest consultation paper indicated that ("Companies Act 2006 – A Consultative Document" (February 2007)):
– only overseas companies registered with Companies House will have to register their mortgages and charges (so, if a company is not required to register or has failed to do so, it will not have to give notice of its charges);
– only certain types of mortgages and charges will have to be registered, including: all floating charges; and mortgages or charges over property located in the UK (including where it has subsequently been moved out of the UK, or where it was not originally in the UK but has been relocated here), book debts entered into under English or Scots law, and property for which there is a specialist register in the UK; and
– like domestic companies, the mortgage or charge will have to be registered within 21 days of creation.

Insolvency

An overseas company with a **registered branch** must make certain filings at Companies House if it is subject to (ss 703P, 703Q CA 1985):
– winding up proceedings; or
– other insolvency proceedings, arrangements, compositions or analogous proceedings.

The filing requirements are summarised in the table below. A filing should be made in respect of each branch which the company has in GB, although it is permitted to include the branch numbers of two or more branches on one form.

An overseas company with a **registered established place of business** is not subject to these filing requirements.

Form	Content	Time limit (ss 703P, 703Q CA 1985)	Filed by
703P(1)	Notice of winding up of an overseas company	Within 14 days of commencement of winding up	Company
703P(3)	Notice of the appointment of a liquidator	Within 14 days of appointment	Liquidator
703P(5)	Notice of the cessation of liquidation	Within 14 days of termination of winding up or company ceasing to be registered	Liquidator
703Q(1)	Notice of insolvency proceedings	Within 14 days of the company becoming subject to the proceedings concerned	Company
703Q(2)	Notice of cessation of insolvency proceedings	Within 14 days of the company ceasing to be subject to the proceedings concerned	Company

MEMO POINTS 1. **Failure to file** these forms as required renders the defaulting company, officer or liquidator liable to a fine (s 703R CA 1985; ¶9935).

2. The **new Companies Act** envisages that the documents which an overseas company will have to file at Companies House if it is wound up or subject to other insolvency proceedings will be set out in regulations (s 1053 CA 2006, expected to come into force by 1 October 2009). At the time of writing, no draft regulations have been published.

3. The names of these forms, like the names of other **Companies House forms**, are taken from the section number of the legislation. As all of the section numbers will change under the new Companies Act, Companies House proposes to change the names of all of its forms to reflect their function rather than the relevant section number ("Working with Companies House: a consultation on the registrar's rules and related provisions which will apply under the Companies Act 2006"). At the time of writing, the new form names are not yet available.

Increasing or reducing activities in GB

183 Where an overseas company **increases its activities** so that it has a branch presence, rather than an established place of business presence, it must re-register as such by filing Form BR1 at Companies House with the registration fee (see ¶145+).

Where an overseas company with a registered branch in GB **reduces its activities** so that it has an established place of business presence, rather than a branch presence, it must re-register as such by filing Form 691 at Companies House with the registration fee (see ¶151+).

In both cases, there is no need to re-file the constitutional documents and directors' details if these are up to date.

MEMO POINTS 1. An overseas company will not be able to re-register an established place of business in GB if it has a branch registration in Northern Ireland. Similarly, it will not be able to re-register a place of business as a branch if it has another registered place of business in the UK. This is because a company cannot have **both a place of business registration and a branch registration** in the UK at the same time. In order to convert to a branch registration, all places of business will either have to be re-registered as a branch or have their registrations terminated. In order to convert to a place of business registration, the original branch registration in Northern Ireland would have to be registered as a place of business.

2. If an overseas company **fails to update** its registration, the company and every officer or agent who knowingly and wilfully authorises or permits the default is liable to a fine (s 697(1) CA 1985; ¶9935).

3. Since the **new Companies Act** envisages a standard regime for all overseas companies established in the UK, presumably there will be no need for it to re-register if it increases or decreases its activities.

4. The name of Form 691, like the names of other **Companies House forms**, is taken from the section number of the legislation. As all of the section numbers will change under the new Companies Act, Companies House proposes to change the names of all of its forms to reflect their function rather than the relevant section number ("Working with Companies House: a consultation on the registrar's rules and related provisions which will apply under the Companies Act 2006"). At the time of writing, the new form names are not yet available.

184

Where a company **closes a place of business or a branch** or moves it to another part of GB, it must give notice of that fact to Companies House (s 695A(3), (4) CA 1985). There is no particular form of notice; a letter signed by an officer or authorised person of the company is sufficient. All obligations of the company to deliver documents to Companies House will cease from the date of receipt of the notice.

MEMO POINTS 1. If an overseas company closes its principal branch in GB but retains one or more **other branches**, it will need to file Form BR7 to notify Companies House of the branch at which the constitutional documents and accounts are kept.
2. As the **new Companies Act** is likely to require only the registration of branches, companies increasing their activities will have to register as a branch but those decreasing their activities will simply have to give notice that the branch has closed. The procedure which an overseas company must follow if it closes a registered establishment, or relocates to another location in the UK, will be set out in regulations (ss 1058, 1059 CA 2006); no draft regulations have been published at the time of writing.

SECTION 4

Group structures

A "group" is a **family of companies** linked together by their shareholdings in each other.

194

In broad terms, a company which is controlled by another is termed a "**subsidiary**" company and a company which controls another is termed a "**holding**" company. For accounting purposes, the "holding company" concept is replaced by the concept of a "**parent company**". These concepts are explained further below. The important point to remember is that each company in a group remains a legal entity in its own right.

Groups are a common feature of corporate structures as subsidiaries are often used to undertake different business activities or hold assets. Alternatively, a group structure may arise through company acquisitions.

1. Holding companies and subsidiaries

Definitions

A company is a "subsidiary" of another company, its "holding company", if that other company meets at least one of the following **conditions** (s 736(1) CA 1985; restated at s 1159 CA 2006, a provision which is in force as far as necessary to interpret the other provisions of the new Act already in force):
– it holds more than 50% of the subsidiary's voting rights;
– it is a legal shareholder and on its own it controls more than 50% of the subsidiary's voting rights under an agreement with the other shareholders; or
– it is a legal shareholder and has the right to appoint or remove a majority of the subsidiary's board of directors.

199

MEMO POINTS 1. The references to **voting rights** are to voting rights conferred on shareholders in respect of their shares. In the case of a company without a share capital, the reference is to the rights of members to vote at a general meeting of the company on all, or substantially all, matters (s 736A(2) CA 1985; restated at para 2 Sch 6 CA 2006, in force for the interpretation of other provisions of the new Act already in force). Rights which are only exercisable in particular circumstances will only be taken into account when those circumstances have arisen (and for as long as they continue) or when the circumstances are within the control of the person with the rights. Rights which are normally exercisable but are temporarily incapable of exercise will continue to be taken into account (s 736A(4) CA 1985; restated at para 4 Sch 6 CA 2006, in force for the interpretation of other provisions of the new Act already in force).

2. The reference to the **right to appoint or remove a majority of the board** of directors is to the right to remove directors holding a majority of the voting rights at board meetings on all, or substantially all, matters. A company (H) will be treated as having the right to appoint a director of another company (S) if H is a director of S, or if an appointment to the board of S necessarily follows from an appointment to the board of H. However, a right to appoint or remove which is exercisable only with the consent of another person will be disregarded, unless no other person has the right to appoint or remove that director (s 736A(3) CA 1985; restated at para 3 Sch 6 CA 2006, in force for the interpretation of other provisions of the new Act already in force). It should be noted that the right to appoint or remove directors is not sufficient in itself to create a subsidiary relationship; the potential holding company must also be a shareholder of the potential subsidiary (or a member of the potential subsidiary in the case of a company without share capital).

200 These definitions mean that it is possible to form **chains of companies**. For example, a company (B Ltd) could have a subsidiary (C Ltd) and at the same time be the subsidiary of another company (A Ltd). In such a case, C Ltd will also be the subsidiary of A Ltd. Sometimes, A Ltd is referred to as C Ltd's "**ultimate holding company**" to differentiate it from B Ltd, but this is not a legal definition.

EXAMPLE

A Ltd	A Ltd is the holding company of B Ltd and C Ltd
51%	
B Ltd	B Ltd is the holding company of C Ltd and a subsidiary of A Ltd
51%	
C Ltd	C Ltd is a subsidiary of A Ltd and B Ltd

Special circumstances

202 It is possible for more than one person to have rights over the same shares. For example, one person could be the legal shareholder and another could be the beneficial shareholder (see ¶1829 for an explanation of these terms). In these circumstances, it can become difficult to decide who holds the rights for the purpose of determining a holding company/subsidiary relationship.

The **general rule** is that only the legal shareholder holds the rights conferred by his shares. The **exceptions** to this rule are where:
– the legal shareholder is a nominee;
– the legal shareholder is a fiduciary;
– the shareholder has granted security over the shares; or
– the shareholder is a subsidiary.

203 Where a right is held by a person acting as a **nominee** for another, that other person will be treated as holding those rights (s 736A(6) CA 1985; restated at para 6 Sch 6 CA 2006, in force for the interpretation of other provisions of the new Act already in force). A right will be regarded as held by a nominee for another if they are exercisable only on the other person's instructions, or with his consent or agreement.

Similarly, rights held by a person acting as a **fiduciary** will be treated as not held by him (s 736A(5) CA 1985; restated at para 5 Sch 6 CA 2006, in force for the interpretation of other provisions of the new Act already in force). A "fiduciary" means someone who has undertaken to act for or on behalf of another in circumstances which give rise to a relationship of trust and confidence (*Bristol and West Building Society v Mothew (t/a Stapley & Co)* [1996] 4 All ER 698). So, for example, trustees act as fiduciaries.

The **effect** of these two provisions is that it is not possible for someone to avoid the holding company/subsidiary relationship by putting legal ownership of the subsidiary's shares into the hands of another whilst still exercising control behind the scenes.

Comment: The legislation does not specify who will be treated as holding rights that are held by a fiduciary. It is likely that they will be treated as held by the person for whom the fiduciary is acting.

When a shareholder grants **security over his shares**, he gives the security holder a legal or beneficial interest in those shares (the type of interest depends upon the type of security granted). In such a case, the **general rule** is that the rights of the secured shares are treated as held by the security holder.

There are two **exceptions** to this rule when the rights continue to be treated as held by the shareholder (s 736A(7) CA 1985; restated at para 7 Sch 6 CA 2006, in force for the interpretation of other provisions of the new Act already in force). These are where the rights of the shares, apart from the right to exercise them for the purpose of preserving or realising the value of the shares, are exercisable only:
– in accordance with the instructions of the shareholder; or
– in the interests of the shareholder where the shares are held in connection with the granting of loans as part of normal business activities.

 MEMO POINTS Rights will be treated as being exercisable in accordance with the **instructions**, or in the **interests**, of a company if they are exercisable in accordance with the instructions, or in the interests, of (s 736A(9) CA 1985; restated at para 8 Sch 6 CA 2006):
– its subsidiary;
– its holding company; or
– another subsidiary of its holding company.

Rights **held by a subsidiary** will be treated as held by its holding company (s 736A(8) CA 1985; restated at para 9 Sch 6 CA 2006, in force for the interpretation of other provisions of the new Act already in force).

Wholly-owned subsidiary

A company is a "**wholly-owned subsidiary**" of another company if the only shareholders in the subsidiary are that other company and either (s 736(2) CA 1985; restated at s 1159 CA 2006, in force for the interpretation of other provisions of the new Act already in force):
– that other company's wholly-owned subsidiaries; or
– persons acting on behalf of that other company or its wholly-owned subsidiaries.

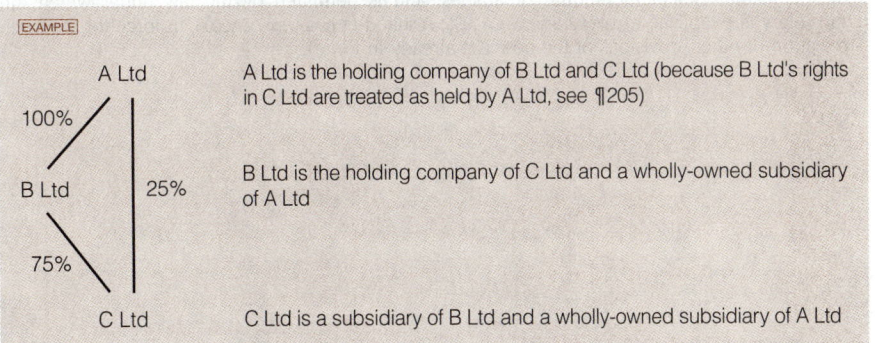

EXAMPLE

A Ltd is the holding company of B Ltd and C Ltd (because B Ltd's rights in C Ltd are treated as held by A Ltd, see ¶205)

B Ltd is the holding company of C Ltd and a wholly-owned subsidiary of A Ltd

C Ltd is a subsidiary of B Ltd and a wholly-owned subsidiary of A Ltd

2. Parent and subsidiary undertakings

The concept of parent and subsidiary undertakings technically only applies to the **law relating to accounts** (s 258(1) CA 1985), although, "parent" company is frequently used as a synonym for "holding" company by practitioners.

The concept of a parent is broader than that of a holding company in two ways:
a. as well as companies, "**undertakings**" includes partnerships and unincorporated associations carrying on a trade or business (with or without a view to a profit) (s 259(1) CA 1985; restated at s 1161 CA 2006, in force for the interpretation of other provisions of the new Act already in force); and
b. as well as the tests to determine a holding company/subsidiary relationship (see ¶199+), a parent/subsidiary relationship can **arise in two additional circumstances**.

> MEMO POINTS 1. When applying the holding company/subsidiary tests to a parent undertaking/subsidiary, the **interpretation** of voting rights, the right to appoint or remove a majority of directors, rights held as nominee or fiduciary, rights attached to shares held by way of security and rights held by a subsidiary, are the same (see ¶199+) (s 258(6); Sch 10A CA 1985; restated at s 1162; Sch 7 CA 2006, in force for the interpretation of other provisions of the new Act already in force).
> 2. Under the **new Companies Act**, the definitions of parent and subsidiary are not necessarily limited to the law relating to accounts (s 1162 CA 2006, in force for the interpretation of other provisions of the new Act already in force).

214 The two additional circumstances are (s 258(2)(c), (4) CA 1985; restated at s 1162 CA 2006, in force for the interpretation of other provisions of the new Act already in force):
a. when one undertaking (the parent) has the right to exercise a **dominant influence** over another (the subsidiary) by virtue of either:
– provisions contained in the subsidiary's memorandum or articles; or
– a control contract; and
b. when one undertaking (the parent) in relation to another undertaking (the subsidiary):
– has the power to exercise, or actually exercises, dominant influence or control over the subsidiary; or
– it and the subsidiary undertaking are managed on a unified basis.

> MEMO POINTS 1. A right or power to exercise "**dominant influence**" **means** that the parent has the right to give directions to the subsidiary with respect to its operating and financial policies and the directors of the subsidiary are obliged to comply with those directions, whether or not they are for the benefit of the subsidiary (para 4(1) Sch 10A CA 1985; restated at para 4 Sch 7 CA 2006, in force for the interpretation of other provisions of the new Act already in force). This definition does not apply to the expression "actually exercises dominant influence" which is left undefined (para 4(3) Sch 10A CA 1985; restated at para 4 Sch 7 CA 2006, in force for the interpretation of other provisions of the new Act already in force). Guidance by the Accounting Standards Board indicates that the test is a matter of fact (i.e. actual dominant influence can be exercised even if there is no legal right to do so) and that the full relationship between the undertakings needs to be considered (FRS 2).
> 2. A "**control contract**" **means** a written contract conferring a right on the parent which is authorised by the subsidiary's memorandum or articles, and is permitted by the law under which the subsidiary is established (para 4(2) Sch 10A CA 1985; restated at para 4 Sch 7 CA 2006, in force for the interpretation of other provisions of the new Act already in force).

CHAPTER 2

Company and business names

OUTLINE

		¶¶				¶¶
A	Company names	242	5	Changing names		273
1	Prohibited names	247	B	Business names		285
2	Names requiring consent	254	1	Names requiring consent		290
3	Disclosure of name	259	2	Disclosure of name		296
4	Use of name after insolvency	264	C	Protection of name		305

Choosing a name is one of the most important commercial decisions to be made about a company, and can affect how well it performs in its field of business. Each company will have to consider different factors appropriate to its own circumstances in reaching this decision, such as:
– whether the name will reflect those of the individuals involved or the product or service;
– whether the company can utilise the existing goodwill in a name, such as when a partnership or sole trader is incorporated;
– how the chosen name will fit into the relevant market; and
– what steps the company can take to protect any intellectual property in its name, for example by registering a trade mark or domain name (¶645).

240

Companies will often be incorporated and trade under the same name, but they will sometimes trade under a different name to that registered at Companies House. This may occur for several reasons, for instance because the trading name has more goodwill in it, or the company name denotes its position in the group whereas it does business under a more descriptive name.

The name a company registers at Companies House is referred to as its "**company name**", and the one it trades under as its "**business name**". They do not have to be different, but often it suits a company to use both types of name, for example to retain the goodwill in the trading name that it used prior to incorporation. Statute imposes requirements on the use of both types of name, to avoid confusion and to ensure that those with whom the company does business and the general public are aware of the company's registered name, office and registration number, so that a company cannot "disappear" behind different names.

A. Company names

There are some **basic requirements** relating to company names, which ensure that the company's status is correctly identified:
a. a private limited company must end its name with the word "limited" (s 25(2) CA 1985);
b. a public company must end its name with the words "public limited company" (s 25(1) CA 1985); and
c. an unlimited company cannot use the word "limited" in its name (s 34 CA 1985).

242

The **abbreviations** "ltd" or "plc" can be used instead (s 27 CA 1985).

> MEMO POINTS 1. If a company's memorandum states that its registered office is situated in Wales, it can use the **Welsh** translation of "limited" or "public limited company" instead: respectively, "cyfyngedig" and "cwmni cyfyngedig cyhoeddus" (s 25 CA 1985). The Welsh abbreviations are "cyf" and "ccc" (s 27 CA 1985).
> 2. There is an **exception for a company limited by guarantee**. Such a company does not have to have "limited" or "ltd" in its name, provided (s 30 CA 1985):
> – its objects are for (or incidental or conducive to) the promotion of commerce, art, science, education, religion, charity or any profession; and
> – its memorandum or articles requires any profits to be applied towards promoting the company's objects, prohibits dividends being paid to its members, and requires its assets to be transferred to a company with similar (or at least charitable) objects.
> To benefit from this exception, a statutory declaration must be sent to Companies House with the incorporation or change of name documents. Making a false declaration renders the deponent liable to a fine and/or imprisonment (s 30(5C) CA 1985; ¶9935). If the secretary of state considers that the company has failed to comply with the provision, he can require it to change its name to include "limited" or "ltd" (s 31 CA 1985). Once the secretary of state has served such a notice, his permission will be required in the future to re-register the company with a name that does not include the word "limited". If Companies House allows the name to be registered without "limited", the company does not have to comply with the requirements to publicise its name (¶259) or to file lists of shareholders at Companies House with its annual return (¶4060+). Such a company cannot alter its memorandum or articles so that it no longer complies with this exception. If it does, the secretary of state can require it to change its name and the company and any officers in default are liable to a fine (s 31 CA 1985; ¶9935). If the company receives such a direction from the secretary of state, the board can pass a resolution to change the company's name. It must then notify Companies House of the change, which will issue an amended certificate of incorporation if the new name is valid (s 31(2A)-(2C) CA 1985, inserted by para 1 Sch 4 SI 2007/2194). This change of name does not affect the company's rights or obligations, and any litigation commenced by or against it under its old name can be continued under the new one.
> 3. These provisions will be restated in the **new Companies Act** (ss 58, 59 CA 2006, expected to come into force by 1 October 2009). The exception for a company limited by guarantee will continue to be available (reg 4 draft Companies (Company and Business Names) (Miscellaneous Provisions) Regulations 2007; ss 60-62 CA 2006, expected to come into force by 1 October 2009). Further, an exempt company will not be able to change its articles in such a way that it no longer meets the requirements for the exemption (s 63 CA 2006, expected to come into force by 1 October 2009).

1. Prohibited names

247 A company cannot be incorporated using a name which is **already on the register** at Companies House. The register can be searched by contacting Companies House or by using its website (¶4090).

The name should not be the same as or similar to one **already in use** by a company or business either, as this may put the company at risk of having action taken against it for passing off (¶305+) or infringing another's intellectual property (summarised at ¶645, domain names and trade or service marks being particularly relevant to names).

> MEMO POINTS The **new Companies Act** will introduce new provisions which could compel a company to change its name if it was one in which someone had already acquired goodwill (see ¶278/mp).

248 A company **name cannot** (s 26 CA 1985):
a. contain the words "limited", "unlimited", "public limited company", "community interest company" or "community interest public company", other than at the end of the name;
b. contain the abbreviations "ltd" or "plc", other than at the end of the name;
c. contain the expressions "investment company with variable capital", "open-ended investment company" or "limited liability partnership" (such companies must be registered under separate provisions);
d. be the same as a name already on the register at Companies House;
e. constitute a criminal offence; or
f. be offensive.

MEMO POINTS Regulations under the **new Companies Act**, which are likely to come into force by 1 October 2009, will stipulate (ss 57, 65 CA 2006; draft Companies (Company and Business Names) (Miscellaneous Provisions) Regulations 2007):
– what characters (i.e. letters, symbols etc) can be used in a company's name;
– that a company's registered name cannot be longer than 160 characters (including spaces between words);
– that neither a company nor a business name can include words indicating that it is a particular type of company when it is not (these are the same situations as a-c in the list above);
– that the name cannot be the same as one already on the register. The regulations include a list of words, abbreviations and symbols that will be ignored or regarded as the same when deciding whether one name is the same as another. A company is only permitted to have the same name as another if it can prove to Companies House that it has the permission of the other company and is in the same group. For example, this will allow a parent company to be called "Smiths Builders Group Ltd" and one of its subsidiaries to be called "Smiths Builders UK Ltd", whereas without this exception "group" and "UK" are two of the words to be ignored when deciding whether two names are the same or not.

A **criminal offence** is committed if:

249

a. a person carries on a business under a name which includes "public limited company" (or its Welsh equivalent) at the end when the business is not registered as a public company (s 33(1) CA 1985);
b. a public company uses a name which implies that it is a private company in circumstances where the company's status is likely to be of material importance (s 33(2) CA 1985);
c. a person carries on a business under a name which includes "limited" (or its Welsh equivalent) or an abbreviated version at the end when the business is not registered as a company with limited liability (s 34 CA 1985); or
d. a company or person carries on a business under a name which includes "community interest company" or "community interest public company" (or their Welsh equivalents) when it is not a community interest company (unless that name was registered to the person using it as a trade mark or Community trade mark on or before 4 December 2003) (s 34A CA 1985).

It is also an offence to use certain words (usually denoting a regulated profession, e.g. solicitor, dentist) in a company name without the permission of the relevant body and the secretary of state (see the table at ¶254).

The individuals, companies and/or officers in default are **liable to** fines for the commission of these offences (see ¶9935).

MEMO POINTS The rules governing what may be included in a company's name under the **new Companies Act** will be set out in regulations (see ¶248/mp above). If these rules are breached, the person in breach, or officer in default if the offence is committed by a company, will be liable to a fine (s 1197 CA 2006, expected to come into force by 1 October 2009; ¶9935).

2. Names requiring consent

There are various **categories** of words which can only be used with the consent of the secretary of state or relevant body. The list below is not exhaustive; readers should consult Companies House's guidance booklet "Company Names" or the relevant secondary legislation (SI 1981/1685, as amended) for further details.

254

Failure to obtain the requisite **consent** will result in Companies House refusing to register the chosen name and/or criminal sanctions.

Category	Examples	Consent required
Words implying national or international pre-eminence	British Scottish European International United Kingdom	Secretary of state for business, enterprise & regulatory reform
Words implying a connection with government or local authority	Government[1]	Secretary of state for business, enterprise & regulatory reform

Category	Examples	Consent required
Words implying business pre-eminence or representative or authoritative status	Association Institution Society	Secretary of state for business, enterprise & regulatory reform
Words implying specific functions	Chartered Group Holding Insurance Registered Trust	Secretary of state for business, enterprise & regulatory reform
Words linked to particular professions and organisations	Charity Health Centre Police Royal University	– Written permission of the relevant body (e.g. Charity Commission); and – Secretary of state for business, enterprise & regulatory reform
Words carrying criminal penalties for improper use under other legislation	Architect Solicitor Olympic Building Society[2] Chamber of Commerce	– Written permission of relevant body (e.g. Architects Registration Board); and – Secretary of state for business, enterprise & regulatory reform

Note:
1. Use of the word "**Government**" in a company name without the permission of the secretary of state has been prohibited since 10 July 2007 (SI 2007/1947, since replaced by SI 2007/3152). There is an exception for those already carrying on business under a name which includes the word. A person to whom such a business is transferred may continue to use the name for up to 12 months after the transfer. SI 2007/3152 also restricts the use of HPSS, HSC and NHS.
2. Permission used to be required for the terms "bank", "banker", "banking" and "deposit". Now, it is an offence to carry on a banking business (including accepting deposits) without being an authorised person or falling within one of the exemptions to this prohibition (s 24 FSMA 2000).

3. Disclosure of name

259 A company's **name must be included**:
a. in the memorandum (s 2(1)(a) CA 1985);
b. outside every office and place of business (s 348 CA 1985);
c. in the following company documents (whether in hard copy, electronic or any other form) (s 349 CA 1985):
– business letters;
– order form;
– notices and official publications;
– orders for goods/money made by the company;
– invoices;
– receipts;
– cheques; and
– other financial documents, such as bills of exchange and promissory notes; and
d. on all its websites.

> **MEMO POINTS** Under the **new Companies Act**, a company will have to publish its name (draft Companies (Trading Disclosures) Regulations 2008. The implementation date for these regulations is yet to be announced at the time of writing):
> – at its registered office, any other location at which it is allowed to keep its company records, and any other business location (other than somewhere that is used primarily as a dwelling or is a director's residential address). If 6 or more companies use the same address, the name must be displayed for at least 20 seconds in every 4 minutes (e.g. on an electronic display). Otherwise, the name must be displayed continuously; and
> – on all business documents and correspondence, including all of the documents listed above and the company's websites.
> Instead of having to state the name in the memorandum, prospective companies will have to notify Companies House of their names in their registration application (s 9 CA 2006, expected to come into force by 1 October 2009; also see ¶517+).

Companies will also have to provide specified information on request to those with whom they deal in the course of their business. A new provision will allow minor variations in the form of the name (e.g. the disclosed name may vary in the case of its letters, the use of punctuation, accents etc and formatting). As far as penalties for breach are concerned, in addition to the criminal penalty imposed on the company and its officers, if a company fails to disclose information as required, it may not be able to bring a claim against a person dealing with it at the time it was in breach. The defendant will have to show that he either has a claim against the company which he has not been able to pursue because of the company's breach, or that he has suffered financial loss as a result of the company's breach. However, the court will still be able to allow the proceedings to continue if it is just and equitable to do so in the circumstances. These provisions mirror the existing civil penalties in the Business Names Act 1985 (see ¶297) (ss 82-85 CA 2006, the implementation date for these provisions is yet to be announced at the time of writing).

260 A memorandum without the company name will not be accepted by Companies House. If the company or its officers **breach** the requirements in b, c. or d. above, they are liable to a fine (¶9935). If the breach relates to a failure to have the company name on the company's cheque or other financial document, the officer who signed or authorised the signature of the document is personally liable to the holder of the cheque or other document if the company fails to pay.

> MEMO POINTS   Like the memorandum, an incomplete registration application under the **new Companies Act** will be rejected. Breach of the other disclosure requirements will render the company and any officer in default liable to a fine (reg 9 draft Companies (Trading Disclosures) Regulations 2008).

4. Use of name after insolvency

264 If a company has gone into insolvent liquidation, there are **restrictions** on its management being involved in another company or business with the same or a similar name (s 216 IA 1986).

The restrictions **apply for** a period of 5 years from the commencement of the liquidation.

The restrictions **apply to** any person who was a director or shadow director of the insolvent company in the 12 months before it went into liquidation.

Subject to the exceptions at ¶267, such persons need the consent of the court to carry out the following **restricted activities**:
– to be a director, or be concerned in the promotion, formation or management, of any other company known by a prohibited name; or
– to be involved in carrying on a non-incorporated business under a prohibited name.

The following are **prohibited names**:
– the name of the company when it went into liquidation;
– any name by which the company was known in the 12 months before it went into liquidation; and
– a name so similar to any of those names that it suggests a connection with the insolvent company.

265 The purpose of the restriction is to protect the general public from "**phoenix companies**", when those involved in an insolvent company start trading with the same or a similar name but from a new "clean" company. This allows the management to exploit the goodwill and opportunities of the insolvent business whilst concealing its previous failure from the public and leaving the creditors of the insolvent company to pursue a valueless shell.

However, despite the purpose of the legislation, the offence is one of strict liability. This means that the **intention of the directors** when using a prohibited name is irrelevant (*Thorne v Silverleaf* [1994] 1 BCLC 637). A director will be liable for using a name which suggests an association with the insolvent company, even if there is no proof that there has been any express misrepresentation or that anyone has actually been deceived or confused into thinking that there was an association between the insolvent company and the new company (*Ad Valorem Factors Ltd v Ricketts* [2004] 1 All ER 894).

266 In order to **avoid liability**, a director must apply to court for leave to use the prohibited name (see ¶7380+). The court can require the (former) liquidator to report on the circumstances of the company's insolvency and the applicant's role in it (r 4.227 IR 1986). In considering the application, the court should not approach it from the point of view that the director has engaged in any misconduct unless there is evidence that this is the case (*Penrose v Official Receiver* [1996] 2 All ER 96).

267 There are **three exceptions** from the need to apply to court for consent to use the insolvent company's name, each requiring particular rules to be followed for the director to benefit from the exception.

Exception	Procedure/rules	Reference (IR 1986)
Insolvency practitioner arranges for whole, or substantially whole, of insolvent company's (A Ltd) business to be acquired by another company (B Ltd) and B Ltd wishes to use A Ltd's name[1]	B Ltd must give notice to A Ltd's creditors within 28 days of completion of acquisition, stating: – A Ltd's name and registered number; – circumstances of acquisition; – name B Ltd has assumed or proposes to assume; – any change of name it has made or proposes to make to assume new name; and – name of the director(s) of A Ltd who will be director(s) or involved in management of B Ltd. Those named in notice can then be involved in B Ltd without contravening restriction.	r 4.228
Director's application for leave is pending	If director applies for leave within 7 days of commencement of liquidation, he will not be in breach for 6 weeks after commencement of liquidation. If his application is dealt with sooner, period of grace ends.	r 4.229
Existing name	Director is involved in a company which has been known by a prohibited name for at least the 12 months preceding commencement of liquidation and has not been dormant (¶4407) at any time during that period[2]	r 4.230

Note:
1. This exception only used to be available if, at the time B Ltd acquired A Ltd's business, the directors were not already directors of B Ltd, or otherwise already involved in its management (*Churchill v First Independent Factors and Finance Ltd* [2006] EWCA Civ 1623). However, r 4.228 IR 1986 was amended as of 6 August 2007 to enable the name to be used where the directors were involved with B Ltd (SI 2007/1974).
2. It is not necessary for the prohibited name to be the **only name** by which the company was known. This means that the company would be within the exception if:
– only part of its business was carried on under the prohibited name;
– it was known by more than one name, one of which was the prohibited name; or
– it was known by more than one prohibited name during the 12-month period (e.g. because it changed its name from one prohibited name to another).
In addition, it is not necessary for the prohibited name to have been used by the company as a **formal name** (e.g. its registered company name or trading name). What is required is for the company to have carried on business under the prohibited name, i.e. the prohibited name was used by third parties dealing with the company (*ESS Production Ltd (In Administration) v Sully* [2005] EWCA Civ 554).

Breach

270 Failure to obtain the requisite consent or follow the correct exception procedure will result in the offending director being **personally responsible for the company's debts** that were incurred whilst he was involved in its management. This liability is shared jointly and severally with any other person who was also involved in the management of the company and who acted or was willing to act on the instructions of the offending director, whilst knowing that he was prohibited from being involved with the company (s 217 IA 1986). This provision is particularly useful for creditors who are able to pierce the "corporate veil" if the company fails to meet its liabilities.

In addition, the offending director is liable to **imprisonment and/or a fine** (s 216(4) IA 1986) (¶9935).

> **EXAMPLE** Mr W had been the director of SG & T Walsh Company Ltd which went into insolvent liquidation. He then became a director of a new company named Walsh Construction Limited. He had not obtained the court's consent to that directorship, nor did he come within any of the exceptions. Revenue and Customs brought a claim against Mr W for £268,425 in respect of money owed to them by Walsh Construction Limited. The two companies operated in similar fields (the former in carpentry and maintenance and the latter in groundworks and heavy construction). In addition, for a period of time, they had the same trading address and similar letterheads. The court held that these factors would lead a reasonable customer or member of the public to associate the two companies. The fact that the name "Walsh" was common or ordinary did not preclude such a finding. Mr W was accordingly personally liable for the debts of Walsh Construction Limited and would have to pay Revenue and Customs the sum claimed (*Revenue and Customs Commissioners v Walsh* [2005] All ER (D) 46 (Jun)).

5. Changing names

Companies can change their name for any **reason**, from stamping a new owner's identity on it or re-branding to improve its image, to being compelled to do so (¶278). **273**

A change of name includes not only entirely new names, but also more **minor changes** such as "ABC Beverages Ltd" to "ABCD Beverages Ltd" or "ABC Drinks Ltd". However, a change from "ABC Beverages Ltd" to "ABC Beverages plc" (and vice versa) requires a status, rather than a name, change (¶662+, ¶673+).

Changing the name of the company does not alter its **legal personality** as it retains the same unique company registration number, allowing third parties to trace the same company through different name changes.

> **MEMO POINTS** It is possible to **change the name and status** of a company at the **same time**, provided the correct resolutions are passed, documents filed at and fees paid to Companies House.

Procedure

A company can change its name by special resolution (s 28(1) CA 1985), provided the new name **complies with** the rules relating to company names. The special resolution must be **filed** at Companies House, together with a reprint of the memorandum containing the new name within 15 days of passing the resolution (s 18(2) CA 1985). The **fee** for a change of name is currently £10 and must be sent to Companies House with the documents. Companies House will then issue a certificate of incorporation on change of name. The name change takes effect from the date of this certificate, so the company must ensure that its stationery and publicity **obligations** are updated from that time (s 28(6) CA 1985; ¶259). **275**

> **MEMO POINTS** 1. Companies House offers an express service, changing a company's name on the **same day** as receipt of the documents for a **fee** of £50.
> 2. If **two companies** need to **swap names**, which may occur in a group reorganisation, they should contact Companies House setting out what they want to do and when in order to ensure that the swap is simultaneous.
> 3. Under the **new Companies Act**, the default statutory provision for changing a name by special resolution will be retained. However, the company will have to notify Companies House of a special resolution for a change of name (probably on a new form) as well as filing a copy of the resolution. New provisions will apply when a special resolution has been passed but the change is not to take place until some other event has occurred (e.g. a merger). A company will also be able to change its name voluntarily by whatever means are provided in the company's articles. This means that a company will be able to determine the procedures for changing its own name. If it exercises this right, the company will have to file at Companies House both a notice of the name change and a statement that the change has been made in accordance with the company's articles (ss 77-81 CA 2006, expected to come into force by 1 October 2009).

Compulsory change of name

278 A company may be obliged to change its name in **three situations**.

Situation	Time limit	Reference (CA 1985)
Company's name is the same as or too similar to a name already on the register (or which should have appeared on the register)	12 months from registration	s 28(2)
Misleading information was presented to Companies House to register the company	5 years from registration	s 28(3)
Name gives such a misleading impression of the company's activities that it is likely to cause harm to the public	Any time after registration	s 32

Failure to comply with such an obligation renders the company and any officer in default liable to a fine (ss 28(5), 32(4) CA 1985; ¶9935).

> MEMO POINTS 1. An **overseas company** may be obliged by the secretary of state to use a different name in this country if its company name would not be allowed to be registered here (¶158).
> 2. The above provisions will be restated in the **new Companies Act** (ss 67, 68, 75, 76 CA 2006, expected to come into force by 1 October 2009).
> The new Companies Act contains new provisions which will allow a person to **apply for a company to be directed to change its name** if the applicant can show that he had previously acquired goodwill in the name or it was sufficiently similar so as to mislead by suggesting a connection between the company and the applicant. Any person who wishes to object to a company name for this reason will be able to apply to a new **company names adjudicator**. The procedure for doing so is set out in regulations (draft Company Names Adjudicator Rules 2007, the implementation date for these regulations is yet to be announced at the time of writing). There is a list of circumstances under which the respondent will be presumed to have legitimately adopted the name. However, these could be rebutted if the applicant shows that the respondent's main purpose was to obtain money from the applicant or prevent him from registering the name. If the applicant succeeds, the company names adjudicator will have to order the respondent to change its name by a specified date, and he may also specify the new name. All decisions of the company names adjudicator will be published. The respondent will have the right to appeal the decision (ss 69-74 CA 2006, the implementation date for these provisions is yet to be announced at the time of writing).

B. Business names

285 Companies will often be incorporated under one name, but trade under another. There can be many **commercial reasons** for this, for example, a company which carries out different trading activities can do so under different trading names without having to set up a group of separate companies, or a sole trader or partnership may choose to incorporate itself but still trade under its old name in order to retain the goodwill in it.

Where a company's trading or business name differs from the name on its certificate of incorporation (as changed, if applicable), **special rules** apply to the names it can use. These are currently set out in the Business Names Act 1985.

When the relevant provisions come into force (expected to be by 1 October 2009), the special rules will be set out in the **new Companies Act** instead of the Business Names Act 1985, which will be repealed (Sch 16 CA 2006). Any significant differences between the current and new provisions are highlighted in the text below.

> MEMO POINTS Currently, the special rules **do not apply** where the company name is added to in order to show that the company is carrying on a business which was previously known as something else (s 1 BNA 1985). For example, "ABC Beverages Ltd, formerly AB Beverages". Under the **new Companies Act**, this exception will only be available to individuals and partnerships, not to companies (s 1192(3) CA 2006, expected to come into force by 1 October 2009).

In contrast to the regulations on company names, there is no statutory prohibition on using business **names** which are **already in use** (for example, on the register of companies at Companies House). However, companies should avoid this where possible, not only because of the potential damage to its own business (e.g. as a result of customer confusion), but also because choosing the same name as another company or business can lead to a claim for passing off (¶305+) or intellectual property infringement (¶645).

286

1. Names requiring consent

The restrictions on business names mirror those for company names. A business name **requires written approval** of the secretary of state if it (s 2 BNA 1985):
a. indicates a connection with the government, any part of the Scottish administration or any local authority; or
b. includes a word or expression which would require permission were it used in a company name (¶254).
A business needs the consent of the court to use the name of a company, or one similar to it, which went into insolvent liquidation in the previous 5 years if a person involved in the business' management was also involved in the insolvent company's management (see ¶264+).

290

> MEMO POINTS 1. Written **approval** from the secretary of state is **not required** if the business name is one which the company (s 2 BNA 1985):
> – has been using since before 26 February 1982, and it was lawful at that time; or
> – is using for up to 12 months after having acquired a business which lawfully used that name (the new owner must obtain permission to use the name after this time).
> 2. These provisions are essentially restated in the **new Companies Act**. In addition, the secretary of state will have the express right to withdraw his approval if there are overriding considerations of public policy (ss 1192-1199 CA 2006, expected to come into force by 1 October 2009).

It is a criminal offence to use a business name which requires approval without obtaining it. The company can be held liable for the offence, as well as any officer or shareholder (who manages the company) who assisted the company in committing the offence by his consent, connivance or neglect (¶9935).

291

2. Disclosure of name

Where a company uses a business name, it must publicise its **company name and address** for service by (s 4 BNA 1985):
a. quoting them on a sign which is easily read and in a prominent position at all premises from which the business is conducted and to which customers and/or suppliers have access;
b. including them on all:
– business letters;
– written orders for goods or services;
– invoices;
– receipts; and
– written demands for payment of debts; and
c. providing them (immediately) in writing to any person with whom it deals in the course of business, on request.

296

> EXAMPLE
> **1. Company letterhead** (to comply with company name publicity and other stationery requirements):
> [Top of letter]
> AB Beverages
> 1 Street
> Town
> County
> AA1 1BB

> [Bottom of letter]
> ABC BEVERAGES LTD registered in England and Wales
> Company registration number: 0012345
> Registered office: 8, Company's solicitors, Street, Town, County, AA2 3CC
>
> **2. Company sign** placed in a prominent position at business premises:
> ABC BEVERAGES LTD, trading as AB Beverages
> 1 Street
> Town
> County
> AA1 1BB

297 **Failure to comply** with these publicity requirements is a criminal offence, for which the company and any officer or shareholder (who manages the company) who assisted the company in committing the offence by his consent, connivance or neglect can be prosecuted (¶9935). Any claim by the company against a person dealing with it at the time it was in breach may also be at risk of being dismissed if the defendant can show that he has (s 5 BNA 1985):

a. a claim against the company which he has not been able to pursue because of the company's breach; or

b. suffered financial loss as a result of the company's breach.

However, the court may still allow the proceedings to continue if it is just and equitable to do so in the circumstances.

298 The **new Companies Act** will abolish these requirements as far as companies are concerned. Companies will be subject to one set of regulations regarding the disclosure of their company and business names (see ¶259/mp).

C. Protection of name

305 As well as registering the company's name at Companies House, companies may need to consider other **methods** of protecting their name in order to preserve their existing or projected goodwill. This includes considering matters such as:
- registering domain names;
- obtaining trade or service marks if the company's name distinguishes its product or service from others'; and
- having a policy for taking action if another business makes use of the company's name.

A summary of intellectual property protection in general is at ¶645.

> MEMO POINTS   Under new provisions in the **new Companies Act**, a person will be able to apply to the Company Names Adjudicator to compel a company to change its name if it was one in which he already had acquired goodwill (see ¶278/mp).

306 A particular course of action available to companies which find that their names are being used by another business is to sue for **passing off**. A potential passing off action often comes to light as a result of customer feedback (for example, when customers tell the company that they thought that a similarly named company was connected to it) or when customers are lost to the other business. Companies should try to pre-empt these consequences of passing off, for example by keeping up to date with competitors' activities and new entrants into the market, and searching the internet regularly for any uses of its name.

A common law action for "passing off" can be brought against a company or business which **uses another's name**, **or one confusingly similar** to it. This has a much wider application than just the use of company and business names, for example, it applies to products, services, packaging and internet domain names as well, and an action may be based on a defendant's use of a number of the claimant's identifying features (for example, using a similar name and logo).

However, passing off actions are very expensive to run, not least because they require the claimant to undertake extensive surveys of customers, and/or to use of expert witnesses from the trade in question. The outcome of passing off actions is also notoriously uncertain.

308 An action for passing off may overlap with an action for **infringement of a registered trade mark**, if the company's name is registered as such. Although passing off is wider (because it covers every way in which the claimant's business is identified, rather than just its name or logo), it is more difficult to prove and is very expensive. To prove trade mark infringement the claimant will just need to show that the mark was infringed (although there are a number of statutory defences) (ss 10, 11 Trade Marks Act 1994).

Infringement includes (s 10 Trade Marks Act 1994):
– use of the same trade mark on similar goods;
– use of a similar trade mark on similar goods; and
– use of a similar trade mark on any goods, even dissimilar ones.

However, the basic stumbling block many companies will face is that in order to seek protection from trade mark infringement, the relevant name or logo has to be registered as a trade mark in the first place.

> *MEMO POINTS* It is more difficult to establish passing off or a trade mark infringement where the **name** in question is purely **descriptive of the goods or services** in question, since the claimant must show that the name has become so closely connected with the claimant's goods or services that the defendant's use of it amounts to a misrepresentation.

310 A successful action can lead to a number of different **remedies**, as appropriate in the circumstances, including:
a. a company being prevented from using the name in question by injunction, even if it has already been registered at Companies House;
b. being liable in damages for the claimant's loss of sales and/or damage to goodwill and reputation;
c. being liable to account for profits;
d. search and seize orders to take possession of infringing items (e.g. publicity material containing the offending name) or to obtain evidence; and
e. delivery up or destruction orders relating to infringing items.

311 A company can base a **defence** to a passing off or trade mark infringement action on a number of grounds, including:
a. it is using the name or address of an individual who is closely connected with the company (e.g. the majority shareholder);
b. the claimant's use of the name is only descriptive and has not acquired distinctiveness through use;
c. the claimant consented or acquiesced (e.g. by not taking action promptly enough) in the company's use of the name; and
d. the claimant is not using the name and has therefore abandoned it.

CHAPTER 3
Company formation and constitution

OUTLINE ¶¶

A	Pre-incorporation acts	345
	Capacity	350
	Contracts	356
B	Company constitution	367
1	Effect of constitutional documents	372
2	Memorandum	394
	Contents	399
	Subscribers	405
	Alterations	410
3	Articles	435
	Table A	441
	Alterations	450
C	Management structure	462
D	Methods of incorporation	474
1	Self-incorporation	479
	a Incorporations before 1 October 2009	479
	b Incorporations on or after 1 October 2009	517
2	Off-the-shelf company	546
3	Business incorporations	550
E	Post-incorporation considerations	565

1	Company administration and management	570
	Registered office	570
	Accounts and audit	575
	Appointing bankers and other advisers	580
	Company stationery and publicity	585
	First board meeting	590
2	Commercial considerations	600
	Tax and other financial matters	605
	Insurance	613
	Employment	618
	Health and safety	623
	Contracts	628
	Intellectual property	645
	Competition law	651
	Document retention and data protection	656
F	Changing company status	660
1	Private company to public company	662
2	Public company to private company	673
3	Private limited company to unlimited private company	681
4	Unlimited private company to limited private company	684

340

Setting up and registering a company is a relatively simple **process**. It involves preparing and filing certain documents at Companies House for a fee. However, actions and decisions which are taken on behalf of the unformed company **before incorporation** may have legal consequences on the person acting on its behalf, as the company has no legal status at this stage (¶345+).

Once incorporated, the subscribers and future shareholders become part of a body corporate (s 13(3) CA 1985; restated at s 16 CA 2006 by 1 October 2009), a legal entity in its own right capable of making its own decisions and taking responsibility for its acts independently of the individuals involved in it (*Salomon v A Salomon & Co Ltd* [1897] AC 22). The company can now enter into transactions, own property, and bring and defend court actions in its own name, without the shareholders incurring personal liability for its acts or debts. This separation between the identities of the company and the individuals running it is referred to as the "**corporate veil**"; the situations in which this veil may be "lifted" are discussed at ¶7125.

The new company will have to make a number of decisions relating to **administrative** and **commercial matters**. The common issues are considered in overview at ¶565+.

A. Pre-incorporation acts

345 Until it comes into existence, the company has no legal capacity, so pre-incorporation acts such as registering the incorporation documents with Companies House, need to be carried out by others for its benefit. Typically, these acts will be **carried out by** the subscriber(s), his/their solicitor or accountant, or by a "deal maker" or "promoter" who sets up the company to facilitate a wider project.

Capacity

350 The person who acts for the benefit of the company before it is incorporated does so in his personal capacity as an **individual**, and will be liable for the consequences of any pre-incorporation acts.

Persons such as solicitors, accountants and company formation agents, who act in a **professional** capacity, act as the agents of the client from whom they took instructions (usually the subscriber(s)). Therefore, they will not take on personal liability for their acts as long as they act within their professional remit.

> MEMO POINTS Since an unformed company does not have the legal capacity to be a principal or beneficiary, the person acting on its behalf at this stage cannot claim to be its **agent** or **trustee**.

351 A **promoter** is a person who plays a specific role at the pre-incorporation stage, and is usually only involved in setting up a public company. A promoter can be distinguished from other individuals involved in setting up a company because he will receive some sort of personal benefit (usually financial) from the incorporation, for example someone who:
– procures the formation of a company to buy property from him or to bring about the transfer of property to him, or otherwise influences the directors to act for his benefit;
– procures the underwriting of the company's capital (for which he is rewarded); or
– forms a company at the request of a vendor to the company, and is paid for his services out of the purchase price.

A **promoter is not**:
– a person selling goods to the company without procuring its formation or having some other interest in it;
– a solicitor setting up the company;
– the company's brokers or bankers; or
– the company's underwriters.

It is important to distinguish promoters from other types of individuals involved in forming a company because promoters owe fiduciary **duties** to the new company and can also incur statutory liability if, for example, they make an unauthorised financial promotion (¶4825+), or they fail to inform a prospective officer that his liability is unlimited (¶464/mp).

Contracts

356 It may be necessary for a company to enter into contracts before it is incorporated, for example, to secure key personnel, premises or a business opportunity. A person who enters into a contract on the company's behalf is personally **liable** under that contract in order to protect the other contracting party/parties from not being able to enforce it (s 36C(1) CA 1985; restated at s 51 CA 2006 by 1 October 2009). This is the case no matter how that person:
– represents himself (for example, even if he makes it clear that the company has not yet been formed and that he is only acting for it at the pre-incorporation stage); or
– signs the contract (for example, even if he signs it "for and on behalf of X Ltd").

Just as the signatory is liable under the contract, he, not the company, has the right to **enforce** it against the other party/parties if that becomes necessary (*Braymist Ltd v Wise Finance Co Ltd* [2002] 1 BCLC 415).

> MEMO POINTS 1. This also applies where the contract is executed as a **deed** (s 36C(2) CA 1985; restated at s 51 CA 2006 by 1 October 2009).
> 2. This also applies to companies **incorporated outside GB** (SI 1994/950).

357 It is possible for the parties to the contract to agree that the person contracting on behalf of the pre-incorporation company will **not** be personally **liable** (s 36C(1) CA 1985; restated at s 51 CA 2006 by 1 October 2009). However, this would be unusual, especially in commercial contracts, as it would leave vulnerable the party/parties with whom the pre-incorporation company has contracted.

Therefore, the practical options open to the signatory to **evade** personal **liability** are:
a. to include a provision in the memorandum that the company will adopt the contract on incorporation. A new contract, called a deed of **novation**, will have to be entered into so that the signatory's liability is superseded. The signatory bears the risk that he will still be liable under the contract if incorporation does not occur; or
b. to prepare a **draft contract** for the company to sign when it is incorporated, which is signed only by the other party/parties before incorporation takes place. The contract will then be held, as yet undated, in "escrow" (usually by a solicitor) until incorporation. A provision is included in the memorandum that the company will execute the contract on incorporation, and the contract comes into existence at the same time as the company. If incorporation does not occur, the contract is returned or destroyed.

> MEMO POINTS 1. An agreement between the parties to the effect that the signatory is **not** personally **liable** cannot be **implied** from the signatory stating that he is signing on the company's behalf.
> 2. Pre-incorporation contracts cannot be adopted by the company by **ratification** after incorporation (*Kelner v Baxter* (1866) LR 2 CP 174). A deed of novation is required for the company to take on all of the liabilities and benefits under the contract.

B. Company constitution

367 The terms which **govern** how a company is run are contained in its memorandum and articles of association. The memorandum is the fundamental basis of the company, containing the basic information about the company's name, type and domicile, as well as setting out its broad rights and powers. The articles deal with managerial and administrative matters, and companies have more freedom to tailor them to their needs. Both documents are **registered** at Companies House and are **available to the public**, therefore, third parties dealing with the company are deemed to have constructive notice of their terms (*Ernest v Nicholls* (1857) 6 HL Cas 401).

> MEMO POINTS 1. The doctrine of **constructive notice** has been eroded by statute so that companies remain liable to third parties where they act outside of their powers set out in the memorandum (see ¶2554+).
> 2. Under the **new Companies Act**, companies will be governed by one constitutional document, the articles (together with any resolutions or agreements affecting it, which have to be filed at Companies House) (s 17 CA 2006, due to be brought fully into force by 1 October 2009). The memorandum will be preserved, but only as a historical snapshot of the company on incorporation. s 17 CA 2006 is in force as far as is necessary for the interpretation of other provisions of the new Act which are already in force. However, as a transitional measure, it has been amended so that references in the new Act to the "articles" include the memorandum, because existing companies will still have memoranda setting out the scope of their powers for the time being (para 1 Sch 1 SI 2007/2194).

1. Effect of constitutional documents

372 Once the constitutional documents are registered, they **bind the shareholders** of the company to follow all of their provisions, as if each had signed and sealed the documents (s 14(1) CA 1985; restated at s 33 CA 2006 by 1 October 2009).

373 The **memorandum defines** the parameters of the company's powers, and any action it takes in contravention of the memorandum may be liable to be set aside (see ¶2554+), although its purpose under the new Companies Act will change completely (see ¶367/mp above). The **articles set out** the terms of the company's relationship with the shareholders, as well as the relationship between shareholders.

As between the two constitutional documents, the memorandum **takes precedence** over the articles (*Re Duncan Gilmour & Co Ltd* [1952] 2 All ER 871). If the terms of the memorandum are ambiguous on a particular point, the articles may be referred to for clarification but not to expand the scope of the memorandum (*Angostura Bitters (Dr JB Siegert & Sons) Ltd v Kerr* [1933] AC 550).

374 All shareholders are entitled to a **copy** of the memorandum and articles for a maximum fee of 5p (s 19(1) CA 1985); a lower fee can be specified in the articles. Failure to provide copies on request renders the company and every officer in default liable to a fine (¶9935).

> MEMO POINTS Under the **new Companies Act**, if requested to do so, the company will have to send any shareholder a copy of the following documents free of charge (s 32 CA 2006, expected to come into force by 1 October 2009):
> – an up to date copy of the articles incorporating any alterations;
> – a copy of any resolution which had to be filed at Companies House;
> – a copy of the company's current certificate of incorporation and any past certificates;
> – in the case of a company with share capital, its current statement of capital (see ¶517+);
> – in the case of a company limited by guarantee, the statement of guarantee; and
> – a copy of any notice sent to Companies House because the company's constitution has been altered by legislation, or a court or other authority's order.

Effect on company and shareholders

379 The articles provide written evidence of the contract between the company and its shareholders in their capacity as shareholders, and therefore **obliges the company** to comply with its terms only as far as they affect the rights and obligations of its shareholders as shareholders (*Hickman v Kent or Romney Marsh Sheep-Breeders' Association* [1914-15] All ER Rep 900). By the same token, the **shareholders are obliged** to the company to comply with the terms of the articles. Therefore, a shareholder can **enforce** the terms of the articles against the company which affect him in this capacity.

> EXAMPLE
> **Shareholder could rely on articles**
> A shareholder obtained an injunction from the court to prevent an ordinary resolution of the shareholders to distribute debenture bonds instead of cash dividends, contrary to the articles (*Wood v Odessa Waterworks Co* (1889) 42 Ch D 636).
>
> **Shareholder could not rely on articles**
> A shareholder could not rely on a provision in the articles giving him the right to be the company's solicitor for life because it did not affect him in his capacity as a shareholder (*Eley v Positive Government Security Life Assurance Co* (1876) 1 Ex D 88).
> A regulation providing for arbitration did not apply to a dispute between the company and a shareholder in his capacity as director, because the articles only governed the company's relationship with him as a shareholder (*Beattie v E & F Beattie Ltd* [1938] 3 All ER 214).

> MEMO POINTS Although the memorandum and articles create a contractual relationship between the company and its shareholders, they are statutory documents. They can only be **rectified or have terms implied** into them by the court on rare occasions (*Folkes Group plc v Alexander* [2002] 2 BCLC 254; *Bratton Seymour Service Company Ltd v Oxborough* [1992] BCLC 693).

Effect between shareholders

384 The articles also govern the relationship between the shareholders, although there have been conflicting judicial decisions as to whether a shareholder can **enforce** the articles directly against another shareholder or whether he must do so through the company. A shareholder can enforce the articles by commencing proceedings **in the company's name** (see ¶7124+). For him to be able to enforce the articles **directly**, he must establish that the other shareholder specifically accepted an obligation in the articles towards him personally (as if that term was contained in a collateral contract to the articles) (*Rayfield v Hands* [1958] 2 All ER 194). This will depend on the circumstances of each case and may arise, for example, where the company is run on a quasi-partnership basis or in relation to pre-emption provisions (¶1842+).

> MEMO POINTS For the purpose of enforcing articles **out of the jurisdiction** under the Brussels Convention, it has been held that the articles bind the shareholders to each other, as well as the company and the shareholders (*Powell Duffryn plc v Petereit* [1992] ECR 1-1745).

2. Memorandum

394 A company cannot exist without a memorandum of association (s 1(1) CA 1985). It **sets out** the fundamental information about the company, so that third parties and shareholders dealing with it know what it is empowered to do.

> MEMO POINTS Under the **new Companies Act**, the memorandum will serve a more limited purpose. It will evidence the intention of the subscribers to the memorandum to form a company and become its members/shareholders on formation. In the case of a company limited by shares, it will also provide evidence of the shareholders' agreement to take at least one share each in the company (s 8 CA 2006, expected to come into force by 1 October 2009). Any limits on the company's powers will have to be included in the articles instead (see ¶399/mp below).

Contents

399 The memorandum **must contain** (s 2 CA 1985):

Clause	Information[1]	Content	¶¶
1	Company's name	Exactly as company wants to be referred to, e.g. Ltd or Limited, capital letters and punctuation in the correct places, as the certificate of incorporation will replicate the name stated here and the company will not be entitled to use any other name, e.g. on stationery, registered office plaque[2]	¶242+
2	Domicile	Either: – England and Wales; – Scotland; or – Wales	–
3	Objects	Sets out the limits of the company's actions and the conduct of its business[3]	–
4	If liability of shareholders is limited, statement to that effect	–	–
5	Statement of share capital[4, 5]	Amount and structure of authorised share capital	¶712
Attestation	Subscriber(s)	– Name, address, description/occupation and signature – Number of shares to which he has subscribed (must be at least one per subscriber)[5]	–
	Witness(es)	– Name, address, description/occupation and signature	

Note:
1. **Public companies** must include a statement at clause 3 that the company is public (s 1(3) CA 1985) (so clause 3 above becomes 4, and so on).
Companies limited by guarantee must include a statement that each member undertakes to contribute up to a stated sum to the company's assets (and to the costs etc of winding up) if the company is wound up while he is member, or within 1 year of leaving (s 2(4) CA 1985).
2. Companies who state they are **situated in Wales** can use Welsh equivalents of limited and public limited company: "cyfyngedig" and "cwmni cyfyngedig cyhoeddus". See ¶4049 for filing Welsh language company documents.
3. The **objects clause** can take a number of forms. The statutory prescribed forms are minimal and can be tailored to a company's business. Statute also allows companies to state that their objects are to carry on business as a "general commercial company". This gives flexibility (e.g. to change business direction) and includes the power to do anything incidental or conducive to that business. However, legal professionals usually favour a more comprehensive objects clause setting out the company's business followed by specific powers to borrow, engage in mergers and acquisitions, give charitable donations etc, to avoid potential problems as to what is "incidental or conducive" to business. The objects clause may end with an "independent objects" clause, stating that each object stands independently, to prevent some objects being interpreted as being subordinate to the "main" ones.
4. **Public companies** must have a minimum authorised share capital of £50,000, and at least one quarter plus any premium must be paid up on each share (see ¶720, ¶1137). There is nothing to prevent private companies from registering share capital in a **denomination** other than pounds sterling, although public companies must hold the authorised minimum in pounds sterling.
5. This clause can be omitted if the company is **unlimited** or **does not have share capital**.

> **MEMO POINTS** Under the **new Companies Act**, the matters currently set out in the memorandum, except for the objects clause, will be contained in the "application for registration" (s 9 CA 2006, expected to come into force by 1 October 2009). Instead of the objects clause, companies will have unlimited objects unless these are specifically restricted by their articles (s 31 CA 2006, expected to come into force by 1 October 2009). The objects clauses in existing companies' memoranda will be treated as being in their articles by 1 October 2009, which means that they will be able to be altered in the same way as other provisions in the articles (s 28 CA 2006). However, companies will be able to "entrench" certain provisions to prevent them from being changed so easily (see ¶450/mp).

400 Although rare in practice, the memorandum can also contain **optional clauses** relating to matters which would usually be contained in the articles of association (s 17 CA 1985). For example, a company may wish to include certain rights in the memorandum as this enables minority shareholders to object to a variation (see ¶428, ¶1270+). If a company wants to entrench a particular right, it can prohibit any alteration to that clause (which is not possible in the articles). A company can also include a statement in its memorandum that the liability of its directors, managers or a managing director is unlimited (s 306(1) CA 1985).

> **MEMO POINTS** Under the **new Companies Act**, it will not be possible or necessary to include optional clauses in the memorandum or application for registration. Instead, companies will be able to entrench elements of their constitution in their articles (see ¶450/mp).

401 The **form** of memorandum is prescribed by regulations (s 3 CA 1985, SI 1985/805). Different types of company have different forms, each of which are given an alphabetical designation. Private companies limited by shares should use Table B which is reproduced in the Appendix at ¶9910. Public companies limited by shares should use Table F.

> **MEMO POINTS** 1. The form of memorandum for **other types of company** is as follows (SI 1985/805):
> – company limited by guarantee with no share capital: Table C;
> – private company limited by guarantee with share capital: Table D Pt II;
> – public company limited by guarantee with share capital: Table D Pt I; and
> – unlimited company with share capital: Table E.
> 2. The form of the memorandum under the **new Companies Act** will also be prescribed in regulations (s 8 CA 2006, due to come fully into force by 1 October 2009). At the time of writing, draft regulations have been published which set out separate forms for companies with a share capital and for those without (draft Companies (Registration) Regulations 2007 (August 2007 version), also expected to come into force by 1 October 2009).

Subscribers

405 The subscribers to the memorandum are the **first shareholder(s)** of the company. By signing the memorandum, they contract to take and pay for (subject to the company's articles) the number of shares shown against their names. They automatically become the holders of those shares, even if the company has not yet allotted and registered them (s 13(3) CA 1985; restated at s 16(2) CA 2006 by 1 October 2009).

> **MEMO POINTS** 1. Subscribers to the memorandum of a public company must pay for their shares in cash (s 106 CA 1985; restated at s 584 CA 2006 by 1 October 2009), but there is no such restriction on **how shares should be paid for** by subscribers of private companies.
> 2. Subscribers do **not have to pay** for the shares or be liable as contributories in the event of insolvency if the company allots the entire share capital to others (*Re Taly Drws Slate Company, Mackley's Case* (1875) 1 Ch D 247). This may occur, for example, in an "off-the-shelf" company.

Alterations

410 Since the memorandum is such a crucial document, its terms can only be varied as specified in the legislation and by making the correct **filings** at Companies House to record the change, which will be advertised in the *Gazette* by the registrar (s 1077 CA 2006).

Once the memorandum has been changed it is an offence to issue an **out-of-date version**, rendering the company and any officers in default liable to a fine (s 20 CA 1985; ¶9935).

> **MEMO POINTS** 1. To change the clause in a **public company**'s memorandum relating to the company's public status, the company must be re-registered as a private company (¶673+).

2. Under the **new Companies Act**, it will not be possible to amend or update the memorandum of a company formed under the Act. The memorandum of such a company will essentially be a snapshot of part of the company's constitution at the point of registration. Provisions in existing companies' memoranda which would not be included in the new form will be treated as if they were in the articles instead. Existing companies will, therefore, be able to alter or update provisions in their constitution which are now set out in their memoranda by amending their articles (s 28 CA 2006, expected to come into force by 1 October 2009). However, companies will be able to "entrench" certain provisions in the articles, making it more difficult to amend them (see ¶450/mp).

Company name

Companies frequently change their names. This topic is dealt with at ¶273+.

413

Domicile

The company's domicile determines its nationality and where its statutory documents should be filed. Once a company has stated that it is situated in a particular jurisdiction, this cannot be changed and its registered office can only move within that jurisdiction.

415

Domicile	Nationality	Where documents filed
England and Wales	English/Welsh	Companies House in Cardiff
Wales	Welsh	Companies House in Cardiff
Scotland	Scottish	Companies House in Edinburgh

MEMO POINTS 1. The only **exception** to this is that a company situated in Wales whose memorandum states that it is situated in England and Wales can amend its memorandum to state that it is situated in Wales (s 2(2) CA 1985). Although this would curb the company's freedom to move its registered office to England, it will enable it to file documents at Companies House in Welsh (¶4049). The company cannot later change its domicile back to England and Wales.
2. Under the **new Companies Act**, a company whose registered office is in Wales will be able to change its domicile between "Wales" and "England and Wales" by passing a special resolution and filing it at Companies House (s 88 CA 2006, expected to come into force by 1 October 2009).

Objects

A company would rarely be required to change its objects. This is because modern objects clauses are widely drafted so that all normal commercial activities are within the company's powers. If a company does wish to alter its objects it may do so by **special resolution** (s 4 CA 1985).

417

Shareholders can **challenge a change** in the objects, by applying to court to have the resolution cancelled within 21 days of it being passed (s 5 CA 1985). This reflects the importance of the memorandum by giving added protection to minority shareholders, who may be outvoted on a special resolution.

418

MEMO POINTS An **application** to object to the change may be **made by** (s 5(2) CA 1985):
– in the case of a company limited by shares, shareholders who hold at least 15% of the nominal value of the issued share capital (or the relevant class, where the variation only affected class rights) who did not vote in favour of the resolution;
– in the case of a company not limited by shares, 15% or more of its members who did not vote in favour of the resolution; or
– in either case, 15% of debenture holders, where the debentures are secured by a floating charge and were first issued before 1 December 1947.
If an application is filed, the company must **notify** Companies House straight away (s 6(1)(b), (4) CA 1985). The **court order** can, as appropriate in the circumstances (s 5(1), (4) CA 1985):
– confirm the resolution entirely or partially;
– impose conditions on the resolution being implemented;
– cancel the resolution;
– adjourn the proceedings so the applicant's shares can be bought; or
– order the purchase of any shareholder's shares, a reduction of capital, or that the memorandum or articles be altered.

The company must **file** an office copy of the court order at Companies House within 15 days of it being made, together with a copy of the amended memorandum if the resolution was confirmed. If the resolution is cancelled, the company will have to apply for the court's consent to make the same alteration at a later date (s 5(6) CA 1985).

419 Assuming no objection is made, the resolution to change the memorandum must be **filed** at Companies House within 15 days of the end of the period for objection (s 6(1)(a) CA 1985). Statute requires an updated copy of the memorandum to be filed (s 6(1)(a) CA 1985), as well as a copy of the special resolution (ss 29, 30 CA 2006).

Failure to comply with the filing requirements renders the company and every officer in default liable to a fine (¶9935).

> MEMO POINTS Under the **new Companies Act**, companies formed under the Act will have unlimited objects unless these are specifically restricted by their articles (s 31 CA 2006, expected to come into force by 1 October 2009). The objects clauses of existing companies will form part of their articles and operate as restrictions on the companies' objects rather than as a list of what the company can do (s 28 CA 2006, expected to come into force by 1 October 2009). The Government's current thinking is that no further specific provision will be made for existing companies. Any existing company that wishes in future to have unrestricted objects will be able to amend its articles to remove the restrictions (see ¶451). There will be no special procedure to allow shareholders to object to the change.

Liability of shareholders

422 The liability of the shareholders can be **changed by** converting from a limited to an unlimited company (¶681+).

Share capital

425 The authorised share capital of the company can be **changed by** following the procedure explained at ¶900+.

Optional clauses

428 These can usually be **changed by** special resolution, although, as with changes to the objects clause, the shareholders have a statutory right to object (s 17(1) CA 1985). The memorandum can set out an alternative procedure by which these clauses may be altered, or it may prohibit their alteration altogether (s 17(2) CA 1985). If the optional clause in question provides for shareholders' class rights, these can only be changed by following the correct procedure (see ¶1270+).

The **filing** requirements relating to alterations to the objects also apply to changes to optional clauses (s 17(3) CA 1985).

3. Articles

435 A company's articles of association **set out** regulations governing, mainly, managerial and administrative matters. They also contain provisions dealing with shareholders' rights, although sometimes these are contained in a separate shareholders' agreement (see ¶2079+).

> MEMO POINTS Under the **new Companies Act**, a company's constitution will comprise its articles and any resolution or agreement which affects it (s 17 CA 2006, due to come fully into force by 1 October 2009). s 17 CA 2006 is in force as far as is necessary for the interpretation of other provisions of the new Act which are already in force. However, as a transitional measure, it has been amended so that references in the new Act to the "articles" include the memorandum, because existing companies will still have memoranda for the time being (para 1 Sch 1 SI 2007/2194).

436 The **form** of the articles is more flexible than that of the memorandum, giving companies the freedom to use it to address whatever matters they see fit. The only **compulsory aspects** are that they are (s 7(3) CA 1985):
– printed;
– divided into consecutive numbered paragraphs; and

– signed by each subscriber to the memorandum (the signatures are attested in the same way as the memorandum).

> **MEMO POINTS** Under the **new Companies Act**, the only compulsory aspects will be that the articles are (s 18 CA 2006, expected to come into force by 1 October 2009):
> – contained in a single document; and
> – divided into consecutive numbered paragraphs.

Table A

Table A is the statutorily prescribed **default set of articles** for private and public companies limited by shares. The current form is Table A 1985, which is reproduced in the Appendix at ¶9915. Companies limited by shares do not have to adopt Table A on incorporation, but it will apply unless it is expressly excluded (s 8(2) CA 1985).

441

Usually, companies will state that Table A applies except for particular regulations, which are expressly excluded or modified. These are known as "**short form**" articles. If a Table A regulation is modified, the articles must state to what extent it is modified. However, it is usually clearer to exclude the relevant Table A regulation altogether and replace it with the modified wording. The company will also usually set out additional regulations.

If a lot of exclusions and/or modifications would be required, companies do not use Table A and set out their own amended version instead. These are known as "**long form**" articles.

The various possibilities are summarised in the table below.

Company's articles	Extent to which Table A is relied upon
Company's own articles exclude Table A	Not at all
Company's own articles do not exclude Table A	Both Table A and company's own articles are applicable (can lead to conflict) – own articles will apply if matter not dealt with in Table A
Company's own articles exclude/modify Table A	Company's articles prevail as far as Table A is excluded or they deal with matters not in Table A
Company does not have own articles or own articles state that Table A applies	Table A applies

> **MEMO POINTS** 1. The form of articles for other **types of company** are as follows:
> – company limited by guarantee with share capital: Table A;
> – company limited by guarantee without share capital: Table C; and
> – unlimited company with share capital: Table E.
>
> **Companies not limited by shares** are obliged to file articles of association in the appropriate form (s 7(1) CA 1985) (and so cannot choose to file no articles and automatically rely on the relevant Table), but they can modify, exclude and add to the relevant Table as necessary provided they still comply with the compulsory requirements (*Gaiman v National Association for Mental Health* [1970] 2 All ER 362).
>
> 2. The **new Companies Act** gives the secretary of state the power to prescribe **new model articles** for different types of company (s 19 CA 2006, expected to come into force by 1 October 2009). Table A will be replaced with different model articles for private companies limited by shares, public companies limited by shares and private companies limited by guarantee. Drafts have been published for all three types of company (draft Companies (Model Articles) Regulations 2008). In brief, the draft new model articles for public companies limited by shares essentially follow Table A. By contrast, the draft new model articles for private companies limited by shares are simpler. They are written in a plain English with a more practical emphasis, for example, they concentrate more on board, rather than shareholder, decision making. Readers are alerted to the equivalent provisions in the draft model articles of private companies limited by shares and public companies where relevant. These references are to the July 2007 draft, which is the latest one at the time of writing, and will be updated as and when necessary.

Table A has evolved in line with legislative changes. If a company's articles incorporate Table A, the **applicable form** of articles is that which was in force when the company was incorporated or when it adopted Table A. Any subsequent changes to Table A will not affect the company, unless it specifically adopts the change as it would any other change to its

442

articles. The table below can be used to check which default Table A is to be used. The most common historical Table A is **Table A 1948**. The differences between Table A 1948 and Table A 1985 are summarised ¶¶9920+, and significant differences are highlighted within each topic as relevant.

Date of incorporation	Default set of articles[1]	Reference
01/07/85 – date	Table A 1985[2]	SI 1985/805
22/12/80 – 30/06/85	Table A 1948, Pt I	Pt I, Sch 1, CA 1948
01/07/48 – 21/12/80	Private company – Table A 1948, Pt II Public company – Table A 1948, Pt I	Pt II, Sch 1, CA 1948 Pt I, Sch 1, CA 1948
01/11/29 – 30/06/48	Table A 1929	Sch 1, CA 1929

Note:
1. For **more historical** Tables A, see CA 1908 and CA 1862.
2. Table A 1985 has been **updated** further on:
– 1 August 1985 (SI 1985/1052);
– 22 December 2000 (SI 2000/3373); and
– 1 October 2007 (SI 2007/2541 and SI 2007/2826). These amendments make specific changes in line with provisions of the new Companies Act already in force, with different changes applicable to private and public companies. These are noted where relevant and at ¶¶9915.
As with the different versions of Table A, these amendments only apply to a company where it was incorporated on or after the date on which they came into force. So, for example, only a company incorporated on or after 1 October 2007 needs to consider the transitional amendments made to fit in with the new Companies Act. The specific amendments, and the dates on which they came into force, can be seen at ¶¶9915.

<u>MEMO POINTS</u>   There will be no change to this principle under the **new Companies Act**. The model articles which are in force when a company is incorporated under the Act will apply to that company and any subsequent changes by the secretary of state will not affect it (s 19 CA 2006, expected to come into force by 1 October 2009). The new model articles will, therefore, only apply to companies incorporated on or after 1 October 2009, or those existing companies which choose to adopt them specifically.

443   Table A covers many of the issues which are useful to regulate by the articles. However, it will not suit every company and it is common for companies to alter at least some of the regulations, usually when drafting its articles for incorporation. The **common alterations** are summarised below.

Alteration	Reference[1]	¶¶
Grant **authority** to board **to allot shares** for up to 5 years	n/a	¶921+
Attach **class rights** to particular shares	n/a	¶914+
Pre-emption rights giving existing shareholders first refusal of allotments or transfers. Common in small and joint-venture companies	s 89 CA 1985	¶940+ ¶1842+
Give directors wider/narrower power to **refuse to register transfers of shares**	reg 24 TA 1985	¶1891+
Directors: – change minimum/maximum number – exclude retirement by rotation – provide for appointment and removal by particular class of shareholders (e.g. where company is controlled by parent) – additional automatic removal provisions (e.g. on conviction of criminal offence with custodial sentence) – provide for sole director – place restriction on directors' power to borrow	 – reg 64 TA 1985 – regs 73-80 TA 1985[2] – n/a – reg 81 TA 1985 – regs 89, 64, 94-98 TA 1985 – n/a	 ¶2230+ ¶2925+ – ¶2939 ¶3460+ ¶4762
Board decisions: – meetings held by tele-/video-conference – change quorum, or provide that directors present by tele-/video-conference count in quorum – directors can count in quorum and vote on matters in which they have an interest	 – n/a – reg 89 TA 1985 – regs 94-98 TA 1985	 ¶3255+ ¶3258+ ¶3341+

Alteration	Reference[1]	¶¶
Shareholder decisions: – alternative written resolution procedure – certain decisions require special resolution – change quorum	– s 381A CA 1985 – n/a – reg 40 TA 1985[2]	¶3580+ ¶3554 ¶3747
Document retention: companies increasingly use electronic storage methods and so include an article specifically allowing them to destroy original documents after a certain length of time, e.g. stock transfer forms, cancelled share certificates etc	n/a	–

Note:
1. These references will change under the **new Companies Act** and the model articles of companies incorporated under that Act. Follow the cross references to other paragraphs for further details on particular topics.
2. For companies **incorporated on or after 1 October 2007** that adopt Table A, amendments have been made to certain provisions of Table A to correspond with the provisions of the new Companies Act which were in force by that date. Different amendments have been made for private and public companies. See ¶9915 for the details of these changes.

Alterations

450 A company has the power, subject to certain constraints, to change its articles, ensuring that these managerial and administrative regulations reflect its needs as the company changes. The company's ability to do so is **restricted** in four main ways:

a. a clause in the **memorandum** may prohibit or contain special rules for changing the articles (s 9(1) CA 1985);

b. the proposed change may circumvent procedures required by **legislation**, for example:
– a company cannot change rights attaching to a class of shares without following the proper procedure (see ¶1270+); or
– a company which has permission to omit the word "limited" from its name cannot change its articles so that it no longer qualifies to do so (¶242/mp);

c. the company may be subject to a **court order** prohibiting it from making the change following an application for relief from unfair prejudice (s 996 CA 2006); or

d. the change may be challenged if it is **unfairly prejudicial** to minority shareholders (see ¶2105+). This restriction should not be overstated. It is for the company to decide whether the change is for its benefit; the court will only overrule the company's decision if it is clearly unreasonable (*Shuttleworth v Cox Bros & Co (Maidenhead) Ltd* [1927] 2 KB 9). It does not automatically follow that a change which benefits one group of shareholders over another will be invalid.

> **MEMO POINTS** Under the **new Companies Act**, instead of placing restrictions in the memorandum, the shareholders will be able to entrench elements of the constitution in the articles if they wish. An "entrenched" provision is one that may only be changed if certain conditions are met which are more restrictive than a special resolution. Provision for entrenchment may only be made on formation of the company or subsequently by unanimous consent of all of the shareholders. Notice will have to be given to Companies House when provisions are entrenched or entrenched provisions are removed (ss 22-24 CA 2006, expected to come into force by 1 October 2009).

451 Assuming that none of the above restrictions apply, the articles can be formally **changed by** special resolution (s 9(1) CA 1985; restated at s 21 CA 2006 by 1 October 2009), which must be **filed** at Companies House within 15 days of being passed (ss 29, 30 CA 2006) together with a copy of the articles as amended (s 18(2) CA 1985). The registrar will then **publish** a notice of the change in the *Gazette* (s 1077 CA 2006). Failure to file alterations to the articles is a criminal offence (see ¶9935).

Once an amendment has been registered, any **copy of the articles** must be the up to date version, or at least have all resolutions or agreements amending them attached (s 380(2) CA 1985 amended by para 1 Sch 4 SI 2007/2194; restated at s 36 CA 2006 by 1 October 2009). Failure to do so renders the company and any officer in default liable to a fine (¶9935; s 380(6) CA 1985; restated at s 36 CA 2006 by 1 October 2009).

> **MEMO POINTS** 1. Alternatively, the **written resolution procedure** can be used (see ¶3580+). The articles can also be **informally altered**, either by the express agreement of all shareholders, or by the acquiescence of all shareholders to a change over a period of time (¶3590+). However,

since the legislation requires a special resolution, the memorandum cannot allow the articles to be changed on the approval of a **lower majority** (e.g. by ordinary resolution).

2. Under the **new Companies Act**, a company will have to file a copy of the articles as amended within 15 days of the amendment taking effect, rather than within 15 days of the resolution being passed (s 26 CA 2006, expected to come into force by 1 October 2009). (However, note that the resolution itself must still be filed within 15 days of being passed (ss 29, 30 CA 2006), so in reality the two will still be filed together.) If a company fails to file the special resolution or amended articles at Companies House, Companies House will be able to serve a notice on the company requiring it to rectify the breach within 28 days. If the company does not comply, in addition to the existing criminal penalties, it will be liable to an automatic penalty of £200 levied by Companies House (s 27 CA 2006, expected to come into force by 1 October 2009).

452 A company **cannot restrict** its ability to alter its articles by special resolution in any other way, for example, in its articles or in another contract such as a shareholders' agreement, as to do so would fetter its statutory powers. Therefore, a regulation **in the articles** stating that certain regulations cannot be changed, or imposing a more restrictive procedure, is void (*Allen v Gold Reefs of West Africa Ltd* [1900] 1 Ch 656). A provision **in another contract** whereby the company agrees not to change certain regulations in its articles would not be enforceable in terms of preventing a change (*Russell v Northern Bank Development Corp Ltd* [1992] 3 All ER 161), although damages may be obtainable for breach of that other contract (*Southern Foundries (1926) Ltd v Shirlaw* [1940] 2 All ER 445).

> MEMO POINTS The **new Companies Act** will provide an exception to this principle since a company will be able to entrench constitutional provisions in its articles, see ¶450/mp.

C. Management structure

462 The management structure of a company **comprises** its shareholders, the board and other officers. Usually, the board and other officers undertake the daily running of a company, with only significant decisions being reserved to the shareholders. For a detailed discussion of the **management roles** undertaken by these different bodies, and the roles of other officers, see ¶3118+.

463 The **initial shareholders** in a company are called "subscribers", because they subscribe to the terms of the memorandum and articles and accept a certain number of shares. A private limited company must have a **minimum** of one subscriber on incorporation. For who can be a shareholder, see ¶2020+.

> MEMO POINTS 1. **Subsequent shareholders** normally join the company by acquiring shares through allotment (¶889+), transfer (¶1827+), or transmission (¶1962+).
> 2. **Public companies** and **unlimited companies** must have a minimum of two subscribers (s 1 CA 1985). Under the **new Companies Act**, it will be possible to form all types of company with only one subscriber (s 7 CA 2006, expected to come into force by 1 October 2009).

464 Companies must also choose their **initial directors and company secretary** in order to become incorporated. A private company needs a **minimum** of one director (s 154 CA 2006) and one secretary on incorporation and throughout its life (s 283(1) CA 1985).

Related information can be found elsewhere in this book, as set out below.

Topic	¶¶
Who can be a director?	¶2241+
Who can be a secretary?	¶4120+
Special rules applying to sole directors	¶3460+
Qualification requirements of secretaries of public companies	¶4124
Changing directors	¶2230+, ¶2912+
Changing secretaries	¶4151+

Comment: From 6 April 2008, when the relevant provisions of the **new Companies Act** come into force, private companies will no longer be required to have a company secretary, although they will be able to do so if they wish. See ¶4116 for further details.

> **MEMO POINTS** 1. **Public companies** need a minimum of two directors (s 154 CA 2006).
> 2. If the memorandum states that the company's directors, managers or a managing director have **unlimited liability**, the promoters of the company must give the proposed appointees to these positions notice of this fact (s 306(3) CA 1985). Failure renders them liable to a fine (¶9935) and for any damage suffered by the new director/manager as a result, but will not affect the validity of the appointment or the appointee's unlimited liability. This provision has not been restated in the new Companies Act.

D. Methods of incorporation

474 Formation of a new company is a relatively easy affair. Persons wishing to form a new company may either **self-incorporate** (meaning that they prepare and file the incorporation documents at Companies House themselves) (see ¶479+) or they may purchase an "**off-the-shelf company**" from formation agents (see ¶546).

In both cases, they should first check that the intended **company name** is available and appropriate (see ¶240+).

The **new Companies Act** will completely change the way in which companies will be formed from 1 October 2009 (see ¶517+).

Many businesses start life as a sole trader business or partnership because of lower set up costs and less regulation. The differences between such businesses and a company is considered at ¶130. However, once the business develops, the proprietors may wish to convert it into a company. This is known as a **business incorporation** (see ¶550+).

1. Self-incorporation

a. Incorporations before 1 October 2009

479 In order to incorporate a new company, the following documents must be filed at Companies House.

Document	¶¶
Memorandum	¶394+
Articles [1]	¶435+
Form 10	¶482
Form 12	¶485
Note: 1. There is no need to file articles if company is **limited by shares** and adopts Table A without amendment.	

Public companies must obtain a trading certificate before they start to trade (see ¶510+).

> **MEMO POINTS** If a company **limited by guarantee** is exempt from the obligation to include the word "limited" in its name, it will also have to file Form 30(5)(A), giving a statutory declaration of that fact (see ¶242/mp).

480 The documents must be accompanied by the appropriate fee, payable to "Companies House".

Service	Fee	¶¶
Standard service	£20	¶493+
Same-day service	£50	¶500
Electronic service	£15	¶505
Electronic same-day service	£30	

The contact details for Companies House can be found at ¶9905.

Form 10

482 Form 10 records the details of the first director(s) and secretary, as well as the registered office of the company.

The **registered office** is the address to which documents can be served on a company (for example, in legal proceedings) and the address to which Companies House will send all correspondence. The registered office can be changed after the company has been incorporated (¶570).

In addition, Form 10 requires the information set out below about the **initial director(s) and company secretary** (s 10 CA 1985).

Details	Director		Secretary	
	Individual	Corporate	Individual	Corporate
Current name	✓	✓	✓	✓
Former name	✓		✓	
Residential address	✓		✓	
Registered or principal office		✓		✓
Occupation	✓			
Details of previous directorships [1]	✓			
Date of birth	✓			
Nationality	✓			
Signatures to confirm consent to act	✓	✓ [2]	✓	✓ [2]

Note:
1. Individual directors are required to provide details of all directorships held by them **within** the last 5 years, **except** those in dormant companies, or companies on the same group statement as the one being incorporated.
2. Signature must be by a person authorised by the **corporate director/secretary** to sign on its behalf, usually a director or secretary of that body corporate.

Form 12

485 The second form which must be filed on incorporation is Form 12. This is a **statutory declaration** confirming that the incorporation documents have been properly constituted. The declaration must be made by a solicitor acting for the company, or by one of the directors or the secretary named on Form 10, and it must be sworn in front of one of the following independent persons, who will charge a small fee:
- solicitor;
- commissioner for oaths;
- notary public; or
- justice of the peace.

If the solicitor, director or secretary swears a false statutory declaration, knowing it to be untrue, he commits a criminal offence (s 4 Perjury Act 1911). Since it confirms the company's compliance with the other requirements, it should be sworn, signed and dated after the other documents to be filed at Companies House.

> MEMO POINTS Alternatively, Companies House may accept a **statement of compliance** by the company's solicitor or person named as a director or secretary on Form 10 as evidence that the incorporation documents have been properly constituted (s 12(3A) CA 1985). A person who knowingly makes a false statement, or does not believe his statement to be true, is liable to a fine and/or imprisonment (s 12(3B) CA 1985; ¶9535).

Standard incorporation

493 For a standard incorporation, the documents should be **sent to** the Registrar of Companies, for the attention of the "New Companies Section" at either Companies House in Cardiff or Edinburgh, depending on whether the company is incorporated in England and Wales (or Wales), or Scotland. See ¶480 for the **fee** for this service.

494 Once the documents are received by Companies House, they are checked to ensure that all of the information has been provided and that the following **statutory regulatory requirements** have been met:
- the memorandum is signed by the subscriber(s);
- the purpose for which the company is formed is lawful;
- the memorandum complies with the statutory requirements;
- the name of the company is permitted;
- the articles, if submitted, comply with the statutory requirements;
- the proposed officers of the company are not disqualified from acting; and
- if the company is to be registered as a public company, its authorised share capital complies with the statutory minimum.

In order to ensure that filed documents are not returned, companies must ensure that they:
- are in the correct format;
- are legible;
- are correct;
- do not use a prohibited name (¶247+); and
- are accompanied by the relevant fee.

495 If all of the requirements are satisfied, the registrar can **register** the company and issue a **certificate** of incorporation (s 13(1) CA 1985). The certificate is conclusive evidence that the company is duly registered under the legislation and that all of the requirements have been met (s 13(7) CA 1985). It records the date on which the company is created, and a private company can carry on business and function as a company from that date (s 13(3), (4) CA 1985). It also states the "**company registration number**", which is a unique reference number used in all correspondence with Companies House and on the company's letterhead, website and order forms.

There is usually a **period** of about 7 days between documents being filed at Companies House and the certificate being issued.

> MEMO POINTS 1. Once incorporated, a **public company** must apply for an additional certificate relating to its share capital before it can carry on business or borrow (¶510+).
> 2. Once incorporated, a company's **registration** can only be **challenged** by the Attorney General (*R v Registrar of Companies, ex parte Central Bank of India* [1986] 1 All ER 105).

Same day incorporation

500 If a company needs to be incorporated quickly, it can use Companies House's express service. If the incorporation documents are delivered **by hand** to Companies House in Cardiff, London or Edinburgh by 3pm on a business day, the incorporation certificate can be collected or posted to the new company or its representative the same day. If the documents are delivered **by post** to Companies House in Cardiff or Edinburgh, the application will be processed on the date of receipt. The envelope should be clearly marked for the attention of the "New Companies Section, Same Day Service". See ¶480 for the **fee**.

Electronic incorporation

505 The incorporation process can be carried out electronically if the company, or its representatives, has the appropriate **software**, see ¶4074 for further details. See ¶480 for the **fees** for this service.

This is by far the most popular incorporation method with more than 85% of incorporations being carried out electronically.

Public company trading certificate

510 Before a public company is allowed to do business or borrow, it must obtain a **trading certificate** from Companies House confirming that the nominal value of its allotted share capital amounts to at least £50,000 (s 117 CA 1985; restated at s 761 CA 2006 as of 6 April 2008).

At least one quarter of the nominal value, and the whole of any premium, on those shares will have to have been paid by the relevant shareholder (see ¶1137).

MEMO POINTS Shares issued under an **employee share scheme** only count towards the public company's minimum share capital if each share is also paid up to at least one quarter of its nominal value and the full premium is paid (s 117(4) CA 1985; restated at s 761 CA 2006 as of 6 April 2008).

511 To obtain the certificate, a director or secretary of the company must **file** a statutory declaration at Companies House on **Form 117**, which states:
– that the company's authorised share capital meets the statutory minimum;
– the amount paid up on the allotted share capital at the time of the application;
– the amount of the company's preliminary expenses, and by whom they are paid/payable; and
– the amount of any benefit or fee to be paid to any promoter, and the consideration received by the company for such benefit.

Therefore, if a company is incorporated as a public company, it must be incorporated with an authorised share capital of at least £50,000, allot the requisite number of shares after incorporation and receive the requisite money due (at least £12,500), before it applies for the trading certificate.

MEMO POINTS 1. As an **alternative** to the statutory declaration, a director or secretary may submit a statement to Companies House electronically confirming the same information (s 117(3A) CA 1985). If he knowingly makes a false statement or does not believe it to be true, he is liable to imprisonment and/or a fine (s 117(7A) CA 1985; ¶9935).
2. Under the **new Companies Act**, instead of a statutory declaration, the application will have to be supported by a statement of compliance, which confirms that the company meets the requirements for the issue of the certificate. The statement will not have to be witnessed and may be in paper or electronic form (s 762 CA 2006, expected to come into force as of 6 April 2008).
3. The name of Form 117, like the names of other **Companies House forms**, is taken from the section number of the legislation. As all of the section numbers will change under the new Companies Act, Companies House proposes to change the names of all of its forms to reflect their function rather than the relevant section number ("Working with Companies House: a consultation on the registrar's rules and related provisions which will apply under the Companies Act 2006"). At the time of writing, the new form names are not yet available.

512 **Failure** to obtain a trading certificate before doing business or borrowing renders the company and any officer in default liable to a fine (s 117(7) CA 1985; ¶9935; restated at s 767(2) CA 2006 as of 6 April 2008). If the company has **entered into a transaction** before obtaining the certificate, and fails to comply with this obligation within 21 days of being required to do so, the directors are jointly and severally liable to indemnify the other party/parties for any loss or damage suffered as a result of this failure (s 117(8) CA 1985; restated at s 767(3) CA 2006 as of 6 April 2008). However, the transaction itself is still valid.

b. Incorporations on or after 1 October 2009

517 From 1 October 2009, a company will be able to be formed by filing the following **documents**, which are explained in further detail below:
– a memorandum;
– an application for registration;
– the proposed articles (unless the company intends to rely on the applicable model articles); and
– a statement of compliance.

Applications must be **filed at** the Companies House corresponding to the proposed domicile of the company. The methods of incorporation (standard, same day and electronic) are likely to remain the same.

Public companies will still have to obtain a trading certificate, see ¶510+ above.

Memorandum

The memorandum must state that the subscribers wish to form a company and agree to become shareholders on formation. In the case of a company with share capital, the subscribers agree to take at least one share each. The memorandum must be authenticated by each subscriber (s 8 CA 2006, expected to come into force by 1 October 2009). The form of the memorandum will be set out in regulations (at the time of writing, the regulations are still in draft form: Schs 1, 2 draft Companies (Registration) Regulations 2007 (August 2007 version)).

519

Application for registration

The application for registration is an amalgam of the current memorandum and Form 10. It states the following **basic information** (s 9 CA 2006, expected to come into force by 1 October 2009):
– the company's proposed name;
– whether the company's registered office is to be situated in England and Wales (or Wales), Scotland or Northern Ireland;
– the intended address of the company's registered office;
– whether the liability of the members is to be limited by shares or guarantee;
– whether the company is to be a private or public company; and
– if the application is delivered by the subscribers' agent, his name and address.

524

> MEMO POINTS Incorporations in **Northern Ireland** are currently governed by different legislation, but they will also be covered by the new Companies Act when it comes into force.

The application for all companies also contains a statement of **proposed officers** (s 12 CA 2006, expected to come into force by 1 October 2009). This requires the same details of the company's first directors and secretary (if appropriate) as is required when a new person is appointed to these roles. For directors see ¶3896/mp and for secretaries see ¶3899.

525

For companies with a share capital, the application for registration also contains a **statement of capital and initial shareholdings** (s 10 CA 2006, expected to come into force by 1 October 2009). This states:
a. the total number of shares of the company to be taken on formation by the subscribers;
b. the aggregate nominal value of those shares;
c. for each class of shares:
– prescribed particulars of the rights attached to the shares;
– the total number of shares of that class; and
– the aggregate nominal value of shares of that class;
d. the amount to be paid up and the amount (if any) to be unpaid on each share (whether on account of the nominal value of the share or by way of premium), in respect of each subscriber and in total; and
e. the name and address of each subscriber to the memorandum (reg 3 draft Companies (Registration) Regulations 2007 (August 2007 version)).

526

For companies limited by guarantee, the application for registration also contains a **statement of guarantee** (s 11 CA 2006, expected to come into force by 1 October 2009). This is essentially an undertaking from the subscribers to contribute to the assets of the company up to a specified amount in the event of it being wound up. It must also contain the name and address of each subscriber to the memorandum (reg 4 draft Companies (Registration) Regulations 2007 (August 2007 version)). The statement will also bind new members.

527

Articles

The default **model articles** for different types of companies are set out in regulations (draft Companies (Model Articles) Regulations 2007; s 19 CA 2006, expected to come into force by 1 October 2009). All new companies will be able to choose either to file bespoke articles on formation or rely on the applicable default articles.

531

Drafts have been published for private companies limited by shares, public companies and private companies limited by guarantee. In brief, the draft new model articles for public companies limited by shares essentially follow Table A. By contrast, the draft new model articles for private companies limited by shares are simpler. They are written in a plain English with a more practical emphasis, for example, they concentrate more on board, rather than shareholder, decision making. Readers are alerted to the equivalent provisions in the draft model articles of private companies limited by shares and public companies where relevant. These references are to the July 2007 draft, which is the latest one at the time of writing, and will be updated as and when necessary.

Statement of compliance

536 The statement of compliance replaces Form 12. It is a statement that the statutory requirements as to registration have been complied with. Unlike Form 12, it does not need to be witnessed. As with all documents delivered, or statements made, to Companies House, it will be an offence to make a false statement of compliance (s 13 CA 2006, expected to come into force by 1 October 2009).

2. Off-the-shelf company

546 "Off-the-shelf", or "shelf", companies are **formed by** company formation agents, solicitors and accountants. They incorporate a number of standard companies and sell them on to prospective companies, who then tailor them to their needs. The **advantage** of this is the convenience and speed, since the standard paperwork outlined above is already completed, and the company is ready to trade (if it is a private company). The **cost** of buying an off-the-shelf company is typically between £100 and £400.

There are a number of **administrative matters** which need to be dealt with immediately after purchasing an off-the-shelf company and before trading it.

Matter [1]	Formalities [2]	¶¶
Check company has not traded or incurred any liabilities	None – but obtain written confirmation/undertaking from agents	–
Consider date of incorporation – how long will first accounting reference period be? [3]	File Form 225 before end of period for filing accounts to change accounting reference date	¶4217+
Change director(s) and secretary	File Forms 288a (appointments) and 288b (resignations) within 14 days	¶2288+ ¶2957+ ¶4151+ ¶4158+
Change registered office	File Form 287 as soon as possible (change takes effect once filed)	¶570
Change company name	File special resolution within 15 days Fee – £10	¶273+
Transfer shares	– Stock transfer forms – Subscriber shares are not usually paid up by the agent, so if Table A applies, new shareholders will have to sign transfer form as well (reg 23 TA 1985) – Enter new shareholders in register – Issue certificates – Stamp duty usually paid by agents	¶1827+
First board meeting	To record above changes – may be undertaken by agents	¶590
New directors obtain company books	None	–

Note:
1. **Other matters** which may need to be addressed, depending on needs of company are: to tailor share capital and structure (¶1310+), alter articles (¶443+), and, if public company, apply for trading certificate (¶510+).
2. The names of these forms, like the names of other **Companies House forms**, are taken from the section number of the legislation. As all of the section numbers will change under the new Companies Act, Companies House proposes to change the names of all of its forms to reflect their function rather than the relevant section number ("Working with Companies House: a consultation on the registrar's rules and related provisions which will apply under the Companies Act 2006"). At the time of writing, the new form names are not yet available.
3. Purchase recently incorporated company for longest **first accounting reference period**.

3. Business incorporations

550 The **incorporation of a business** run by a sole trader or individuals in partnership essentially involves a transfer of the undertaking and assets of the business from the sole trader or partnership to a newly incorporated company. There are therefore two stages to the process:
a. formation of a new company with the business proprietor as director and holder of the subscriber shares (see ¶474+); and
b. transfer of the business by the proprietor to the newly formed company, wholly or partly in exchange for an allotment of shares in that company.

EXAMPLE Mr A is a sole trader with a painting and decorating business. He wishes to incorporate the business so that he has the benefit of limited liability and incorporates B Ltd for this purpose.

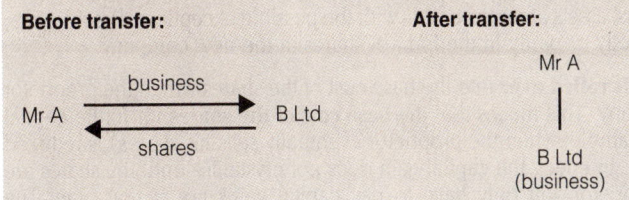

551 There is no requirement for the transfer to be in writing and a **written agreement** may appear to be unnecessary because the parties are connected. However, it is advisable for the proprietors and company to enter into a short-form asset sale and purchase agreement (see ¶5750+). This will at least document the assets transferred, their values, the consideration paid and the apportionment of the consideration for tax purposes.

552 It should be remembered that although the **company is connected** to the proprietor, it is a separate legal person. It is advisable that the purchase of the business by the company be approved by a formal board meeting and recorded in board minutes, even if the proprietor is a sole trader and therefore the only director/shareholder of the company.

As a director/shareholder of the company, the proprietor will need to:
– consider whether the transfer will **promote the company's success** (¶2379+);
– **check the articles** of the company to ensure that he will count in the quorum for a board meeting and that he will be able to vote on a resolution in which he has an interest. If necessary, the articles will need to be amended. In practice, off-the-shelf articles will be used which are appropriate for a sole director to be able to pass resolutions and count in the quorum even if he has an interest;
– consider whether the purchase amounts to a **substantial property transaction** and therefore requires formal shareholder approval (¶2567+); and
– **declare his interest** in the transaction at the board meeting to approve the purchase (¶3317+).

Tax consequences

553 Sole traders, individuals in partnership and companies are all separate legal persons. The incorporation of a business therefore involves a transfer of assets between connected persons, which for tax purposes is treated as a disposal at market value (s 18 TCGA 1992). A transfer of assets on incorporation of a business would therefore normally trigger a **capital gains tax** liability. There are, however, two **reliefs** available which may be available in this situation and they are considered in further detail below:
– incorporation relief; and
– gift relief.

The **stamp tax** liability on incorporation of a business is effectively the same as on a sale of assets (see ¶5297+).

VAT will not be charged on the transfer provided it is a "**transfer as a going concern**", which is likely to be the case. In most cases, it would be preferable to transfer the business' **VAT registration** to the company. The company will then take on the business' VAT liability but this is rarely a cause for concern in practice. The practical advantage is that there is no need to change VAT arrangements. The conditions for a transfer as a going concern are dealt with at ¶5321+ and transferring a VAT number is dealt with at ¶5788+.

The tax consequences of a business incorporation are considered in overview here. For more detail, see *Tax Memo*.

Incorporation relief

554 Incorporation relief is **available if** (ss 162, 162A TCGA 1992):
– the business is transferred as a going concern;
– the whole of the business' assets are transferred (with the possible exception of cash); and
– the consideration is wholly or partly in the form of shares in the new company.

555 Under this relief, the **gain is rolled over** into the base cost of the shares which the proprietor has received in the company. This means that the **base cost of the shares** for future capital gains tax purposes (for example, when the proprietor eventually sells his shares) is reduced by the amount of the gain. In effect, the capital gain does not crystallise until the shares are disposed of and the proprietor will only have to pay capital gains tax at that time. The company, on the other hand, will acquire the assets at market value and this will be the **base cost of the assets** on a subsequent disposal. Contrast this with gift relief below where the tax will eventually have to be paid by the company, not the proprietor.

The drawback is that any accumulated indexation allowance or **taper relief** up to the date of incorporation will be lost and the taper relief clock will begin again by reference to the length of time for which the shares are held (although this is less important since full business asset taper relief can now be accrued in only 2 years). If the proprietors wish to utilise their accrued taper relief, they can **elect for incorporation relief not to apply**. The election must be made no later than the second anniversary of 31 January following the tax year in which the transfer took place.

> MEMO POINTS   The Finance Bill before parliament at the time of writing proposes to **withdraw** indexation allowance for assets acquired before 6 April 1998 and to withdraw taper relief.

556 Incorporation relief is not available if the **sole trader/partners retain any business assets**. One asset which business proprietors often wish to retain is land and buildings. This is because they usually appreciate in value and it will be harder for the proprietors to extract any profit on a future sale if they are held by the company (for example, because of the double-charge to tax for shareholders (¶5292)).

If property is to be retained and incorporation relief is going to be sought, the property must be withdrawn from the business and leased back to it at market rent prior to incorporation. Note that a sole trader cannot grant a lease to himself because the landlord and tenant must be different (*Rye v Rye* [1962] 1 All ER 146). He will therefore either have to transfer the property into joint names and then lease it back to himself or keep the property in his sole name, go into partnership with another person and lease the property back to the partnership (which could have stamp duty land tax consequences). An alternative is to forego incorporation relief and consider gift relief for business assets instead (¶558+).

557 The **consideration** for the transfer can be wholly or partly in the form of shares, so for example, the company could pay some of the consideration in cash (which would be left outstanding on the company's loan account and eventually paid to the proprietor). However, in practice, the consideration is normally **wholly paid in shares**. This is because the amount of gain which can be rolled over is the proportion attributable to the value of the shares received. If some of the consideration is paid in cash (for example, that proportion of the gain is immediately chargeable to capital gains tax. Nevertheless, in some cases, a **mixture of consideration** may be attractive because gift relief for business assets may be still be available in respect of the gain (¶558+) or it may be extinguished by the proprietor's annual exemption (see ¶5343+).

Gift relief

Gift relief on the transfer of any business assets is **available if** the assets are transferred otherwise than under a bargain at arm's length (s 165 TCGA 1992). It is therefore available on incorporation of a business if the proprietor and company are connected (which will be the case where the proprietor holds the subscriber shares in the newly formed company before the transfer takes place). It is not necessary for all of the business' assets to be transferred and therefore gift relief is a useful alternative if incorporation relief is not available.

558

Under this relief, the **gain is held over** into the assets being transferred to the company. This means that the **base cost of the asset** for the company on a future disposal is the market value of the asset less the held-over gain. In effect, the capital gain does not crystallise until the asset is disposed of and the company will have to pay tax on the capital gain at that time. The proprietor on the other hand will acquire the shares at the lower of their market value and the value of the assets transferred and this will be the **base cost of the shares** in the event of a subsequent disposal. Contrast this with incorporation relief above, where the tax on the held-over gain will eventually have to be paid by the proprietor not the company.

559

> MEMO POINTS The amount of gain which can be held over will be **restricted** where the consideration received by the proprietor is more than the base cost of the asset at the time of the transfer.

E. Post-incorporation considerations

A new company will have to consider a number of important matters on incorporation to ensure that it **complies with** companies' administrative requirements, as well as other legal and practical issues and obligations. Here, the considerations that most companies need to take into account are considered, although matters specific to the company's business will often also be an issue, upon which companies may need to take advice from their solicitor or business adviser.

565

1. Company administration and management

Registered office

A company can **change** its registered office within its stated domicile by submitting Form 287 to Companies House (s 287(3) CA 1985).

570

The change **takes effect when** it is registered by Companies House, although documents can validly be served on the company at the old address up to 14 days after this date (s 287(4) CA 1985), so it is important that the company is able to check its mail at the old address for at least this period of time. Following a change of address, the company will have to **update** all documents which refer to the registered office (for example, its company letterhead), and ensure that the company's registers (¶3888+) are moved (or kept at another permitted place).

> MEMO POINTS These provisions are restated in the **new Companies Act**, although the form number is likely to change (s 87 CA 2006, expected to come into force by 1 October 2009; "Working with Companies House: a consultation on the registrar's rules and related provisions which will apply under the Companies Act 2006").

Accounts and audit

Companies have strict requirements with regards to their financial record keeping and preparation of accounts. Some companies have to have their accounts audited. These issues are considered in detail at ¶4185+.

575

Appointing bankers and other advisers

580 The company's **bankers** are usually appointed at one of the first board meetings, when resolutions will also be passed to authorise signatories and open accounts. Most banks will suggest the appropriate resolutions, and will require the following documents in order to open an account:
- the certificate of incorporation (or a certified copy of it);
- any certificate(s) of incorporation on change of name (or certified copies of them);
- copies of the memorandum and articles (complete with any amendments);
- a copy of the board meeting minutes resolving to open the account and authorise the signatories; and
- its own paperwork (completed).

The board may also need to appoint **other advisers** at its first (or a subsequent) meeting, such as a solicitor, accountant, actuary or patent agent, depending on its circumstances.

Company stationery and publicity

585 The legislation requires certain information to be set out on the company's business letters and other documents as well as at its offices.

Information	Where required	Reference (CA 1985)
Company name as it appears in memorandum	– Every office and place of business [1] – Business letters – Websites – Orders for goods/money made by company – Invoices – Receipts – Cheques – Other financial documents [2]	s 348 s 349
Place of registration	– Business letters – Order forms of company – Websites	s 351
Company registration number		
Registered office		
If company is exempt from including "limited" in name, fact it is a limited company		
Note: 1. Company's name can be painted or affixed, but must be legible and conspicuous. 2. Other financial documents are: bills of exchange, promissory notes, bills of parcels and letters of credit.		

The company may also include the **names of its directors** on its business letters, but if it includes the name of one, it must include them all (s 305 CA 1985). If the company states its **share capital** in business letters or order forms it must refer to the paid up share capital (s 351(2) CA 1985).

Failure to meet these requirements renders the company and every officer in default liable to a fine (¶9935).

> MEMO POINTS 1. **Directors' names** can be stated in the text of the letter, or as a signatory to the letter without invoking the requirement to state all of the directors' names (s 305(1) CA 1985).
> 2. Under the **new Companies Act** these "trading disclosure" requirements will be practically the same. A company will have to display (s 82 CA 2006; draft Companies (Trading Disclosures) Regulations 2008; the implementation date for this provision and the regulations is yet to be announced at the time of writing):
> **a.** its name on all:
> – business letters and all other business documents and correspondence;
> – order forms;
> – orders for goods and services;
> – cheques;
> – invoices and other demands for payment;

- receipts;
- bills of exchange;
- letters of credit;
- applications for licences to carry on a trade or activity;
- promissory notes;
- endorsements;
- bills of parcel;
- notices and other official publications; and
- websites; and

b. its domicile (i.e. England and Wales, Wales or Scotland), registered number and registered office address on all business letters, websites and order forms.
Companies exempt from having the word "limited" in their name, and CICs which are not public companies will also have to state that they are limited companies on their business letters, websites and order forms.
The same rules about the disclosure of directors' names and the company's share capital will apply.

First board meeting

The first board meeting should be called as soon as possible after incorporation to **deal with** initial matters, principally:

a. to produce the **documents** filed at Companies House and the certificate of incorporation;
b. to note the **director**(s) and **secretary** named on Form 10 and resolve to enter their details in the registers of directors and secretaries;
c. to note the names of the **subscribers** and resolve to enter their details in the company's register of shareholders;
d. to allot any further shares necessary (if the articles allow; if they do not, it will have to call a shareholder meeting to obtain authority);
e. to change the **accounting reference date**, if necessary;
f. to appoint the **chairman**;
g. to appoint **auditors**, **bankers** and other advisers as necessary;
h. to consider and approve any directors' **service contracts**;
i. to consider and approve any **transactions** with third parties such as leases, hire purchase agreements etc;
j. if the company is a subsidiary, to consider whether a group election for **taxation** purposes needs to be made;
k. to consider the roles of the different officers and whether specific **authority** needs to be delegated to individuals/committees, and resolve to confer authority as necessary;
l. to consider other **management/administrative** matters, e.g:
- the frequency of board meetings;
- allocating responsibility for setting up and maintaining the company's books and registers;
- ordering company stationery;
- setting up insurance policies; and
- adopting a company seal if the company wishes to have one;

m. to consider whether a **shareholder meeting** (or written resolution) is needed, e.g. to alter the memorandum and articles, to give directors authority to allot shares or to approve any decisions that need to be referred to them. If this is required, the board needs to resolve to call a meeting, draft the necessary resolutions and instruct the secretary to convene it; and
n. to instruct the secretary to prepare minutes of the meeting, and deal with any follow-up paperwork (e.g. filing forms at Companies House, see ¶9900).

In the case of an **off-the-shelf company**, the first board meeting will also have to deal with the issues outlined at ¶546 and formulate shareholder resolutions to deal with the following matters at a shareholder meeting (or by the written resolution procedure):
- changing the company's name;
- changing the memorandum and articles to tailor them to the company's needs; and
- altering the share capital.

Comment: From 6 April 2008, private companies will no longer be obliged to have a **company secretary**. If a company chooses not to have a secretary, it will have to ensure that

590

responsibility for tasks that would otherwise fall to the secretary is allocated to another director, officer or employee (see ¶4115+).

MEMO POINTS **Public companies** also need to apply to Companies House for a trading certificate before they can trade and/or borrow money (¶510+).

2. Commercial considerations

600 There are many other practical and legal matters which a company needs to consider once it has been incorporated. The issues highlighted below are those common to most companies, but specialist advice may be required.

Tax and other financial matters

605 Companies must ensure that they have a suitable bookkeeping and tax **records system** in place. Generally, financial records, including tax returns and calculations, need to be kept for 6 years after the end of the accounting period to which they relate. The principal **categories of tax** to which a company is likely to be liable are summarised below. Each tax is considered in detail in *Tax Memo*.

606 Companies resident in the UK are liable to **corporation tax**, which is charged on its profits and gains in an accounting period (usually the same as the company's accounting reference period). Companies must:
– tell Revenue and Customs that they exist and are liable to tax;
– calculate their own liabilities;
– pay the amount due by the deadline;
– file a company tax return; and
– keep accurate records of all expenditure and income.

MEMO POINTS Companies **not resident in the UK** may be subject to income or corporation tax, depending on the nature of their activities.

607 A company must register with Revenue and Customs for **VAT** if it:
– has supplied taxable goods and services amounting to more than the registration threshold in the last 12 months; or
– expects to supply taxable goods and services amounting to more than the registration threshold in the next 30 days alone.

The registration threshold is reviewable every year. From 1 April 2007 it is £64,000 (unless turnover for the next year will not exceed £62,000). Even if a company's turnover does not reach this threshold, it can register voluntarily, although those which only supply VAT exempt goods and services cannot register. VAT-registered businesses which charge more output tax from sales than they pay in input tax on purchases must pay the difference to Revenue and Customs. If they charge less output tax than they pay in input tax, Revenue and Customs refund the difference to them.

VAT-registered companies will have to ensure that they:
– keep a record of the VAT charged and paid;
– issue VAT invoices;
– obtain VAT invoices for purchases; and
– charge the correct rate of VAT (either a standard, reduced or zero rate, depending on the type of goods and services; some goods and services are VAT exempt).

VAT returns and payments are usually due quarterly, 1 month after the end of the company's tax period (which is assigned to the company when it registers for VAT).

608 Companies with employees (including directors) are responsible for calculating and paying appropriate **income tax** and **National Insurance contributions** (NICs) for them. The "Pay As You Earn" (**PAYE**) system is used to collect these taxes, obliging employers to:
– calculate and deduct the correct amount of tax;
– pay the amount due by the deadline;

– keep detailed records for each employee; and
– provide each employee with the appropriate information to enable them to complete their tax returns properly.

All employers with a presence in the UK must operate the PAYE system, and set up a **payroll system** which facilitates it. New employers should notify Revenue and Customs, which will send them a New Employer's starter pack, containing all of the necessary information.

Insurance

The types of insurances which a company should consider are: **613**
– insurance over its **buildings and assets** against risks such as fire and theft;
– **employers' liability** insurance, to cover the company for employees' claims against it for any injuries or illnesses suffered through their employment;
– **public liability** insurance, to meet the cost of claims from members of the public (e.g. customers, visitors to company premises) arising from the company's activities;
– **product liability** insurance, to cover the cost of legal action arising out of damage caused by the company's products; and
– **directors' and officers' liability** insurance (also known as "D&O" liability insurance), to cover the company's directors, secretary and other officers against personal liability (¶2515).

Employment

One of the first issues a new company is likely to face is **hiring new staff**. *Employment Memo* **618** discusses all of the relevant considerations in full, but the principle issues include:
a. in what **capacity** is the person hired: employee, commercial agent, independent contractor?
b. advertising and **interviewing** for the position(s) effectively and non-discriminatorily;
c. ensuring that the employee has the **right to work** in the UK;
d. written **statement of employment**: statutory information must be provided in writing to the employee within 2 months of starting work;
e. an appropriate employment **contract** (depending upon the person's capacity);
f. financial arrangements: payroll system and payment of salary, pension, PAYE and NICs, minimum wage, statutory payments (e.g. sick, maternity, adoption and paternity pay), and equal pay for male and female employees in comparable positions;
g. health and safety: for example, it is the employer's obligation to provide a safe place and system of work (¶623) and to comply with the Working Time Regulations 1998;
h. policies to draft, implement and make available to staff. They should deal with issues such as discipline and grievances, absence, parental rights, anti-discrimination and so on; and
i. the organisational **structure** of the company: responsibility for employment matters, reporting lines etc.

Health and safety

Health and safety is a highly regulated area, and different rules will apply to companies **623** depending on the type of business they operate. Companies' liability for breach of health and safety law is summarised at ¶7178.

Companies are legally **responsible for** the health and safety of those affected by its premises, business and activities. This includes:
– employees;
– visitors; and
– people, including members of the public and customers, affected by its activities, products and services (even at other premises).

All companies must carry out regular health and safety **risk assessments**, and develop a **policy** for dealing with this area. If a company has more than five employees, the policy must be in writing.

Most companies will have to **register** with either the Health and Safety Executive (HSE) or their local authority for health and safety purposes, depending upon the type of premises from which the business operates. Those which must register with their local authority include:
– those with employees in an office or shop;

- caterers and restaurants;
- hotels; and
- wholesale warehouses.

Those which must register with the HSE include:
- manufacturers based in factories;
- engineering workshops; and
- car repair businesses.

A company will need additional **environmental licences** if it creates an environmental risk, for example, by producing emissions into the air, or discharging wastewater or trade effluent. Further special rules relate to specific potentially **hazardous substances**, dealing with how they must be handled, stored, used and disposed of.

Contracts

628 Since a company is a legal person in its own right, it has the capacity to enter into contracts on its own behalf. Most of a company's contracts with third parties will relate to **sales and marketing**. Other contracts the company may need to enter into include:
- those relating to its **premises** (e.g. lease or purchase documents); and
- **hire/purchase** contracts relating to goods and equipment.

In each case, the contract must be considered by the board and, if it is within the company's powers, **approved by** the board or shareholders as appropriate.

> MEMO POINTS **Directors** who have an **interest** in a contract before the board must disclose their interest and may be restricted in participating in the meeting (see ¶3308+).

Standard terms and conditions

633 Any company dealing in goods or services should have a set of standard terms and conditions, setting out the terms on which it deals with third parties. Terms and conditions should be **drafted by** a solicitor, and the employees who enter into contracts using them need to be **trained** properly to prevent unauthorised variations to the terms and to ensure that they apply to every transaction. Terms should be **tailored** to meet the company's requirements (for example, different sets of terms will be needed for supplying and for purchasing, for dealing with consumers or with trade).

Terms and conditions **typically include** the following matters:
- a description of the goods/services;
- the price and payment (e.g. timescale, credit terms);
- logistics (e.g. delivery);
- liability (e.g. for faulty or wrong goods, returns policy) and indemnity (to what extent the company will compensate the customer); and
- legal "boiler plate" clauses (e.g. giving notices, applicable law).

Potential problem areas for companies include:
- exclusion clauses (by which the company tries to exclude or limit its liability);
- retention of title clauses (by which the company tries to assert ownership over the goods until the customer has paid for them in full, even if they have already been delivered or sold on); and
- dealing with consumers (to whom an additional set of protective rules apply).

Once drafted, the terms should be **approved by** the board and resolved to be used. It is advisable to monitor their use by staff (to prevent unauthorised variations) and to keep them under **review**, as the company's needs or the law in this area may well change from time to time.

The terms should be **printed on** all contractual documentation (e.g. orders, invoices, delivery notes and receipts), and so are usually drafted to fit onto one side of A4 paper. This helps (but does not necessarily guarantee) to ensure that contracts are based on the company's terms, even if it is dealing with another business which also tries to incorporate its terms.

MEMO POINTS   Several sets of **statutes and regulations** apply to contracts, principally, the Sale of Goods Act 1979, the Supply of Goods and Services Act 1982 and the Sale of Goods (Implied Terms) Act 1973, which imply basic default terms into any contract for goods or services as well as providing basic protection for consumers (broadly, non-trade customers). Consumers are further protected by the Unfair Contract Terms Act 1977 and the Unfair Terms in Consumer Contract Regulations 1999 (SI 1999/2083). Companies that contract through electronic media (e.g. online, over the telephone or advertising on interactive television, via mobile telephones etc) are also governed by the Consumer Protection (Distance Selling) Regulations 2000 (SI 2000/2334), the Electronic Commerce (EC Directive) Regulations 2002 (SI 2002/2013) and the Electronic Communications Act 2000. Further information can be obtained from the Office of Fair Trading, and professional advice should be sought.

Agency and distribution agreements

638 Companies may need to enter into commercial agency or distribution agreements as part of their sales and marketing strategy.

MEMO POINTS   Other types of marketing agreement which may suit a company include:
a. franchising, which can be used to exploit a business format and gives the company close control over how its product/services are marketed. A block exemption (EC Regulation 2790/1999) can be used to ensure that such agreements do not breach competition law; and
b. licensing, which permits a third party to exploit the company's intellectual property to use a process or manufacture a product.

639 Under an **agency agreement**, the agent deals with customers on behalf of the company, and the company supplies the goods directly to customers. A true agent never owns the goods, but he receives a commission on the sales he facilitates. Agency agreements are appropriate for both goods and services. There are two main **types** of commercial agent:
a. sales agent: where the company authorises the agent to enter into contracts with customers on its behalf; and
b. marketing agent: where the company authorises the agent to introduce customers to it (and the company then contracts with the customer directly).

Agency contracts are **regulated by** the Commercial Agents (Council Directive) Regulations 1993 (SI 1993/3053), which deal with matters such as the exchange of information between the parties, commission, compensation for the agent on termination of the agreement and restraint of trade. Agency agreements are usually used where the company wants or needs to supervise the agent, and to contract directly with the customer.

MEMO POINTS   A **del credere agent** guarantees the customer's performance of the contract to the company for extra commission.

640 Under a **distribution arrangement**, on the other hand, the company does not contract directly with the customer; instead it sells the goods to the distributor who then sells them on to the customer. The distributor owns the goods. He does not receive a commission, rather his income is derived from the profit margin between his purchase and resale prices. Distribution agreements are only generally suitable for marketing goods. There are four main **types** of distribution agreement:
a. exclusive: where there is only one distributor of the company's goods in a defined geographical area, and the company itself may still sell the goods passively (i.e. if approached by the customer) in that area;
b. sole: again, where there is one distributor in an area, but the company may actively sell the goods in the same area;
c. selective: where the company retains more control over the distributor's sales; and
d. exclusive purchasing: where the distributor only purchases the goods from the company (rather than from a number of suppliers), in return for the company granting him control over an exclusive geographical area in which to sell the goods.

Distribution agreements, especially those which assign territory to a distributor, are at risk of breaching UK and EC **competition law** and must be carefully drafted. Some agreements which infringe competition law may be permitted if they are of "minor importance" or fall within a block or parallel exemption, but specialist legal advice should be sought before relying on such exceptions (see ¶651).

Intellectual property

645 "Intellectual property" **refers to** the ownership of ideas and their tangible or virtual representation(s). Therefore, it can exist in representations of ideas from original written material, designs for products and logos to database structures and inventions. The **principal** intellectual property **rights** and how to protect them are summarised in the table below.

Intellectual property right	What is covered?	Protected only when registered?	Effective period	Does disclosure affect right?[1]	Reference
Copyright	Protects expression of an idea: e.g. literary, dramatic, musical, artistic works; films; and computer programs	✗	70 years from end of year author dies[2]	✗	Copyright, Designs and Patents Act 1988, Part I
Moral right	Right applies to literary etc works and films: – to be acknowledged as author and not have works wrongly attributed; – not to have works subjected to derogatory treatment	✗	As for copyright	✗	Copyright, Designs and Patents Act 1988, Part I
Copyright in databases/ database right	Database "structure" is protected, i.e. the collections of information, not its contents 2 levels:				SI 1997/3032
	– full copyright protection if original and author's own intellectual creation under copyright (unlikely)	✗	– As for copyright	✗	
	– database right if substantial investment in quality/quantity in obtaining, verifying or presenting data (prevents extraction/re-utilisation of all or substantial part of database without consent)	✗	– 15 years from end of year completed/ made available to public (can renew)	✗	
Domain name (can also be registered as trade mark)	Protects website and email addresses from cybersquatters and cyberpirates	✓ – .com .net .org .biz .info: register with registrars accredited by ICANN – .uk: register with Nominet	– As long as registration maintained – 2 years (can renew)	✗	n/a

Intellectual property right	What is covered?	Protected only when registered?	Effective period	Does disclosure affect right?[1]	Reference
Design right	Protects 3D designs for articles	✗	Shorter of: – 15 years from end of year of creation; and – 10 years from end of year articles on sale	✗	Copyright, Designs and Patents Act 1988, Part III
Registered design right	Protects designs for articles which are new and have individual character, i.e. appeal to customers aesthetically	✓	5 years (can renew up to 25)	✗	Registered Designs Act 1949
Patent	Protects inventive kernel of product/process. Must be new and not already in public domain	✓	20 years from filing application	✓	Patents Act 1977
Trade and service marks	Protects symbol/logo/name which distinguishes a company's product/service from others	✓	10 years (can renew indefinitely)	✗	Trade Marks Act 1994
Passing off	Right not to have another's goods/services represented as yours	✗	No limit, but delay in enforcing can prevent action	✗	Case law [3]
Confidential information	Prevents disclosure, e.g. trade and industrial secrets	✗	No limit, but cannot be relied on if information in public domain	✓	Case law [4]

Note:
1. This column indicates whether disclosure of the intellectual property before steps are taken to protect it (usually by registration) will prevent protection of the rights associated with it.
2. Copyright in a TV or film broadcast lasts for 50 years. Copyright in a sound recording lasts for 50 years from the end of the year in which it was made or, if published in this time, 50 years from the end of the year of publication. If it is not published during that 50-year period, but it is played in public or communicated to the public during that period, then copyright will last for 50 years from when this happens. Copyright in the typographical arrangement of a published literary work lasts for 25 years.
3. See *Sir Robert McAlpine Ltd v Alfred McAlpine plc* [2004] EWHC 630.
4. *Coco v AN Clark (Engineers) Ltd* [1969] RPC 41 sets out the test that is usually applied.

646

Since intellectual property covers such a wide range of "products", it is often a company's greatest asset and needs to be **protected** in a number of ways:
a. in employment contracts, by ensuring that employees, agents, contractors and officers who create intellectual property in the course of working for the company assign ownership (or, if this is not possible (e.g. with an independent contractor) at least grant a licence to use it) to the company. The contract should also restrict the person's ability to use the intellectual property after he leaves the company, and protect confidential information during and after his association with the company;
b. from third parties, by registering any registerable rights, and ensuring that penalties for breaching the company's intellectual property rights are included in contracts with third parties where appropriate; and
c. by the company having a policy of enforcing its rights where necessary.

Companies should take an **inventory** of intellectual property rights they may own and obtain a valuation of them. This will help the company formulate its policy, and can be used as evidence of the damage suffered if the company has to enforce any of its rights.

Companies must also be sure not to breach third parties' intellectual property rights, as actions for infringement can be costly in terms of legal fees and damages, as well as being harmful to the company's reputation.

Competition law

651 Competition law seeks to create a level playing field in business by prohibiting anti-competitive practices. In some countries, such as the USA, this is referred to as "anti-trust" law. The following summary highlights activities prohibited in the UK and the consequences of infringement. Comparable prohibitions also exist at EU level. Specialist advice should be sought if a company is engaged in, or considering entering into, potentially anti-competitive agreements or practices.

Prohibition [1]	Consequences of infringement	Reference [2]
– Agreement, decision, or concerted practice (i.e. no actual agreement required); – between two or more businesses; – which prevents, restricts or distorts competition within the UK E.g: – fixing prices – fixing trading conditions – limiting/ controlling production, markets, technical development or investment – sharing markets/suppliers – applying different conditions to equivalent transactions with other trading parties – imposing unconnected conditions to completion of contracts	– OFT investigation and publication of findings [3] – Agreement is void (but possible to sever offending term) – Fine of up to 10% company's turnover for up to 3 business years – Company can be open to claims for damages by third parties	Chapter I Competition Act 1998
– Abuse of dominant position in the market; – by one or more undertakings; – which affects trade within the UK Market share of 40% or more usually indicates dominance. Markets can be defined narrowly or widely, and are evaluated geographically and by product market		Chapter II Competition Act 1998
Two or more persons entering into agreements relating to at least two undertakings to: – fix prices – limit/prevent supply of products/services – limit/prevent production – divide supply of product/service to customer – divide customers for supply of product/service – bid-rig Known as the "cartel" offence	– OFT investigation and publication of findings [3] – Agreement will usually breach prohibitions on anti-competitive agreements (see consequences above) – Competition disqualification order against individual(s) (¶3000+) – Imprisonment of up to 5 years of individual(s) – Individual(s) fined	s 188 Enterprise Act 2002

Note:
1. It is possible, under both the UK and EC competition regimes, to obtain specific **exemptions**, to draft an agreement so that it falls within a general exemption or to obtain a degree of confirmation that the agreement does not infringe competition law.
2. **EC law** equivalents of the first two prohibitions are found in Articles 81 and 82 of the EC Treaty. They apply to prohibited agreements or abuse of a dominant position which affects trade within the EU.
3. **Individuals who do not co-operate** with the OFT investigation (e.g. by not providing information when requested) can also be punished.

Document retention and data protection

656

Companies should develop a **document retention policy** to:
a. comply with legal obligations (in important areas such as company law, accounting and tax, employment and pensions, health and safety, insurance and money laundering);
b. assist in preparing accounts, tax returns, annual returns and other reports;
c. assist the company if it needs to take (or has to defend) legal action; and
d. save money in terms of storage and retrieval costs (e.g. by transferring documents which do not have to be kept in paper form into electronic form, and destroying those which no longer need to be retained).

The policy should deal with aspects such as how long documents should be kept, where, in what format (e.g. in originals or copies, electronic or paper) and procedures for retrieval and disposal.

The **destruction of documents** can have legal implications, and so appropriate advice should be sought when developing a policy. For example, contracts and documents relating to them should be kept for the life of the contract (that is until it has been fully performed by both parties), and for at least a further 6 years (the limitation period within which contractual claims may be brought). Contracts executed as a deed and those relating to land carry a longer limitation period of 12 years. This will ensure that the company will have the relevant information if it needs to bring/defend legal action based on a contract.

657

The **retention of information** about living individuals from which they can be identified is regulated by the **Data Protection** Act 1998 (DPA 1998). Examples of information to which this legislation applies includes lists of customers' names, addresses and shopping habits. It does not apply to such information about companies or businesses. Most companies will therefore hold some personal information, as they are obliged to maintain records of their shareholders and officers, at least some of which will be individuals.

A company is therefore a "**data controller**" and must comply with the DPA 1998 whether it obtains, holds, discloses or destroys the data (so that the company has to comply whether it uses the information or not). Data controllers must **notify** the Information Commissioner that they process data.

Data controllers must comply with eight **data protection principles**:
a. process personal data fairly and lawfully;
b. only obtain personal data for specified lawful purposes and ensure that the data is only processed in a manner appropriate to those purposes;
c. ensure that the personal data is not excessive for the purposes for which it was obtained;
d. ensure that the personal data is accurate and updated;
e. do not keep personal data for longer than is necessary to carry out the purpose for which it was obtained;
f. process the data in accordance with the subject's rights;
g. ensure that the data is secure; and
h. ensure that the data is not transferred to a non-EEA country, unless that country imposes an adequate level of protection for the subject's rights or the information is adequately protected by other means.

Processing is only permitted without the data subject's consent if it is necessary to (Sch 2 DPA 1998):
a. perform or enter into a contract with him;
b. comply with a legal obligation (e.g. providing shareholders' names and addresses to Companies House in the annual return); or
c. protect the vital interests of the data subject (e.g. providing information to the emergency services).

Disclosure for any other purpose requires the data subject's properly informed and freely given consent.

> MEMO POINTS 1. A company is **not a data controller** if it processes information on instructions from a third party, since it does not control how or why the data is processed.

2. The EC has so far recognised the following **non-EEA countries**/organisations as providing adequate protection: Switzerland, Canada, Argentina, Guernsey, Isle of Man, organisations which adhere to the US Department of Commerce's safe harbour privacy principles, and the transfer of air passenger name records to the United States' Bureau of Customs and Border Protection.

3. More restrictive conditions are imposed on the processing of **sensitive personal data** (Sch 3 DPA 1998), which companies may hold in relation to their employees for example. Such data includes information about a person's racial or ethnic origins, whether he is a member of a trade union, his health and any criminal proceedings against him. Broadly, processing requires the data subject's express consent, unless the information is processed according to a right or obligation of the company in relation to the employment of the data subject.

F. Changing company status

660 Sometimes, an incorporated company may wish to change its status. For example:
- a private company may wish to become a public company;
- a public company may wish to become a private company;
- a private limited company may wish to become unlimited; or
- an unlimited private company may wish to become limited.

> MEMO POINTS The **new Companies Act** contains a new procedure which will allow a public company to re-register as private and unlimited (ss 109-111 CA 2006, expected to come into force by 1 October 2009). The procedure will be the same as that under the new Act for private companies to re-register as unlimited (see ¶681+) except that it will only be available to public companies who have never re-registered as limited or unlimited before. It is likely that the Takeover Code will apply to such re-registrations (see ¶675).

1. Private company to public company

662 The **formation** of a public company is dealt with at ¶474+. The main **differences** between a public and private company are considered at ¶47. This section deals with an already incorporated private company that wishes to **change status** to a public company. Note that the change does not involve a transfer of the business and so there are no tax consequences.

Only a company with share capital can re-register as a public company. This means that a private company **limited by shares** (and an unlimited company with share capital) can re-register, but a private company **limited by guarantee** cannot.

Before re-registration, the company must ensure that it meets the **share capital requirements**. There are then two steps to re-registration (s 43(1) CA 1985):
- passing a **special resolution**; and
- sending an **application to Companies House**.

> MEMO POINTS The **new Companies Act** will largely replicate the current re-registration regime (ss 90-96 CA 2006, expected to come into force by 1 October 2009). Any significant differences between the current and proposed regimes are highlighted in the text below.

Share capital requirements

664 Before the special resolution referred to below is passed, the nominal value of the company's allotted share capital must be at least $50,000, which is the "**authorised minimum**" (see ¶720). (s 45(2)(a) CA 1985; restated at s 91(1)(a) CA 2006 by 1 October 2009).

In addition, at least a quarter of the nominal value of any allotted shares plus the whole of any premium must be paid up (s 45(2)(b) CA 1985; restated at s 91(1)(b) CA 2006 by 1 October 2009). For example, if a share with a nominal value of £1 is allotted for a consideration of £6, at least £5.25 must be paid up. This does not apply to shares allotted under an employees' share scheme, although if those shares are disregarded, they will not count towards the authorised minimum (s 45(5)(b), (7) CA 1985; restated at s 91(2)(b), (3) CA 2006 by 1 October 2009).

If all or part of the consideration for an allotment was paid up **by way of an undertaking** either (s 45(3), (4) CA 1985; restated at s 91(1)(c), (d) CA 2006 by 1 October 2009):
– the undertaking must have been performed or otherwise discharged; or
– provided it was not an undertaking to do work or perform services, there must be a contract with the company which requires the undertaking to be performed within 5 years from the time the resolution to re-register the company is passed.

> MEMO POINTS The paying up requirements do not apply to **shares allotted before 22 June 1982**, provided that they do not exceed 1/10th of the nominal value of the company's allotted share capital (excluding any employee scheme shares which are being disregarded). Such shares will not count towards the authorised minimum (s 45(6), (7) CA 1985; restated at s 91(2)(a), (3) CA 2006 by 1 October 2009).

Special resolution

665 The first step in the process is for the shareholders to pass a special resolution which **resolves that** the company should be re-registered as a public company. Resolutions will also have to be passed to (s 43(2) CA 1985; restated at s 90 CA 2006 by 1 October 2009):
– alter the memorandum so that it states the company is a public company;
– amend the name of the company so that it ends with the words "public limited company" or "plc"; and
– make any other amendments to the memorandum or articles so that they conform to the requirements for a public limited company.

> MEMO POINTS In addition to the above, an **unlimited company** must (s 48 CA 1985; restated at s 90 CA 2006 by 1 October 2009):
> – include a statement in the resolution that the liability of the shareholders is limited and what the company's share capital will be; and
> – make such alterations to the memorandum and articles of association as are necessary for them to conform to those of a company limited by shares.

Application to Companies House

666 The second step of the re-registration process is to apply to Companies House, which will issue the company with a **new certificate** of incorporation stating that the company is a public company limited by shares (s 47 CA 1985; restated at s 96 CA 2006 by 1 October 2009).

667 The application must be on **Form** 43(3), signed by a director or secretary of the company. The application must be **accompanied by** the following documents (s 43(3) CA 1985):
– a copy of the memorandum and articles of association of the company altered in accordance with the resolution above (¶665);
– a copy of the company's balance sheet prepared not more than 7 months before the application date and containing an unqualified report by the company's auditors;
– a written statement by the company's auditors that, in their opinion, at the balance sheet date the amount of the company's net assets was not less than the aggregate of its called-up share capital and undistributable reserves;
– a valuation report on any shares issued as fully or partly paid up other than in cash after the balance sheet date; and
– a statutory declaration on Form 43(3)(e) confirming that the resolution has been passed, and that there has been no change in the company's financial position that has resulted in its net assets becoming less than its called-up share capital and undistributable reserves.

> MEMO POINTS 1. The **valuation report** must be **prepared** as set out at ¶1158+ in the 6 months before the allotment (s 44 CA 1985; restated at s 93 CA 2006 by 1 October 2009). A valuation is **not required** if the allotment was:
> – a bonus issue which capitalised a credit in the company's reserve accounts or profit or loss account;
> – in connection with a proposed merger with another company, i.e. where one company proposes to acquire all the assets and liabilities of another in exchange for an issue of shares; or
> – in connection with an arrangement (including a court approved scheme of arrangement (¶6500+) or a section 110 reorganisation (¶6465+)) that is open to all of the shareholders and under which the shares are paid up by the transfer or cancellation of shares in another company.

2. As an **alternative to** the **statutory declaration**, a statement confirming the same matters can be sent electronically to Companies House (s 43(3A) CA 1985). If the deponent knowingly makes a false statement or does not believe the statement to be true, he is liable to a fine and/or imprisonment (s 43(3B) CA 1985; ¶9935).

3. The **new Companies Act** sets out an equivalent process (s 94 CA 2006, expected to come into force by 1 October 2009). Since the new Act will abolish the requirement for private companies to have a company secretary from 6 April 2008, where a private company does not already have a company secretary, the application will also have to include a statement of the proposed secretary signed by that person to show his consent (s 95 CA 2006, expected to come into force by 1 October 2009). In addition, the application will have to include a statement of the company's proposed name on re-registration and, instead of a statutory declaration, the application will have to be accompanied by a statement of compliance, which does not have to be sworn under oath or witnessed (s 94 CA 2006, expected to come into force by 1 October 2009).

4. The names of these forms, like the names of other **Companies House forms**, are taken from the section number of the legislation. As all of the section numbers will change under the new Companies Act, Companies House proposes to change the names of all of its forms to reflect their function rather than the relevant section number ("Working with Companies House: a consultation on the registrar's rules and related provisions which will apply under the Companies Act 2006"). At the time of writing, the new form names are not yet available.

668 The application must be accompanied by the correct **fee**, as set out in the table below.

Service	Fee
Standard re-registration	£20
Same-day re-registration	£50
Standard re-registration and change of name [1]	£30
Same-day re-registration and change of name [1]	£100
Note: 1. Deleting the words "company" or "and company", or their abbreviations from a company name does not amount to a **change of name** on re-registration. Other changes may amount to a change of name requiring the higher fee. Companies House should be contacted before filing the application if there is any doubt.	

2. Public company to private company

673 The **formation** of a private company is dealt with at ¶474+. The main differences between a private and public company are considered at ¶47. This section deals with an already incorporated public company which wishes to **change status** to a private company and/or must change its status because its issued share capital has fallen below the authorised minimum (which may happen, for example, on a redemption or own-share purchase). Note that the change does not involve a transfer of the business and so there are no tax consequences.

Before the re-registration, the company must ensure that the requirements of the Takeover Code are met. There are two steps to the actual re-registration (s 43(1) CA 1985):
– passing a **special resolution**; and
– sending an **application to Companies House**.
However, the **shareholders can object** to the re-registration.

> MEMO POINTS 1. A court has the power to order a public company to re-register as private on approving a **reduction of share capital** (¶1435+) that results in the issued share capital falling below the authorised minimum. In such a case the court will also specify alterations to the company's memorandum and articles. A special resolution to re-register is not required.
> 2. The **new Companies Act** largely replicates the current re-registration regime (ss 97-101 CA 2006, expected to come into force by 1 October 2009). Any significant differences between the current and proposed regimes are highlighted in the text below.

Takeover Code

675 The change of status from public company to private company will, unless the company has been publicly listed or has issued a prospectus, result in the company falling outside of the scope of the City Code on Takeovers and Mergers (¶6675+). If the company has been publicly listed the Code will apply for 10 years after the re-registration. If it has issued a prospectus the Code will apply for 10 years following the date of the issue of the prospectus. As a result, if the company has more than one shareholder, the Takeover Panel Executive expects shareholders to be given an adequate **explanation of the Code** and the protection that they will be giving up if the re-registration becomes effective.

The recommended **procedure** is for the company's advisers:
– to contact the Executive to inform it of the proposed re-registration;
– to confirm to the Executive whether or not the company will fall outside of the scope of the Code upon registration (see ¶6755);
– assuming that it will fall outside the scope of the Code, to prepare a draft explanatory statement to shareholders (using the template recommended by the Executive and available to download from the Panel's website) and send it to the Executive for approval; and
– to send the approved statement to the shareholders in good time so that they have an adequate opportunity to consider the Code implications of passing the resolution.

Special resolution

The first step in the re-registration process is for the shareholders to pass a special resolution which **resolves that** the company be re-registered as a private company. Resolutions will also have to be passed to (s 53(1)(a), (2) CA 1985; restated at s 97 CA 2006 by 1 October 2009):
– alter the memorandum so that it no longer states that the company is a public company; and
– make any other necessary amendments to the memorandum or articles (e.g. changing the name so that it no longer ends with the words "public limited company").

676

Application to Companies House

The second stage in the re-registration procedure is to send an **application to Companies House** on Form 53, signed by a director or secretary (s 53(1)(b) CA 1985). The form must be accompanied by:
– a copy of the resolutions referred to above; and
– a copy of the amended memorandum and articles.

The application must be accompanied by the correct **fee**. The fee scale is the same as for a private company re-registering as a public company (see ¶668).

677

> MEMO POINTS 1. Under the **new Companies Act**, consistent with the approach taken regarding other forms of re-registration, the application will have to be accompanied by a statement of compliance, which does not have to be sworn under oath or witnessed. In addition, the application will have to contain a statement of the company's proposed name on re-registration (s 100 CA 2006, expected to come into force by 1 October 2009).
> 2. The name of Form 53, like the names of other **Companies House forms**, is taken from the section number of the legislation. As all of the section numbers will change under the new Companies Act, Companies House proposes to change the names of all of its forms to reflect their function rather than the relevant section number ("Working with Companies House: a consultation on the registrar's rules and related provisions which will apply under the Companies Act 2006"). At the time of writing, the new form names are not yet available.

Shareholder objection

Since the controls over a private company are less stringent than those over a public company, if the minority shareholders object to the re-registration, they can **apply to court** to cancel the resolution (s 54 CA 1985; restated in s 98 CA 2006 by 1 October 2009).

The shareholders' application must be **made within** 28 days of the resolution being passed (s 54(3) CA 1985). It can be **made by** any persons who did not vote in favour of the resolution as long as they are (s 54(2) CA 1985):
– shareholders who together hold at least 5% by nominal value of the company's issued share capital, or of any share class;
– if the company is not limited by shares, at least 5% of its members; or
– at least 50 shareholders of the company.

678

The applicants can appoint one or more of their number to make the application on behalf of the group.

Once the company receives notice of an application, it must immediately **notify Companies House** on Form 54(4). Failure to do so renders the company and any officers in default liable to a fine (¶9935).

Once the application is heard, the **court order** can either cancel or confirm the resolution. Even if the resolution is confirmed, the court can make an order for the minority shareholders to be bought out, or for the company to purchase their shares and for its share capital to be reduced accordingly. The company must file a copy of the order at Companies House within 15 days, or such longer period as the court may direct. Failure to do so renders the company and any officers in default liable to a fine (¶9935).

> MEMO POINTS 1. Under the **new Companies Act**, there will be a new obligation on the applicants, or the persons making the application on their behalf, to notify Companies House immediately when they make the application (s 99(1) CA 2006, expected to come into force by 1 October 2009).
> 2. The name of Form 54(4), like the names of other **Companies House forms**, is taken from the section number of the legislation. As all of the section numbers will change under the new Companies Act, Companies House proposes to change the names of all of its forms to reflect their function rather than the relevant section number ("Working with Companies House: a consultation on the registrar's rules and related provisions which will apply under the Companies Act 2006"). At the time of writing, the new form names are not yet available.

Certificate of re-registration

679 If **no court application** is made by the minority shareholders, Companies House will issue the company with a new certificate of incorporation appropriate to a private company 28 days after the date of the resolution (ss 53(1)(c), 55 CA 1985; restated at s 97(2)(a) CA 2006 by 1 October 2009).

If an **application is made**, the new certificate will not be issued until either the court application is withdrawn or the resolution is confirmed by the court and a copy of the court order has been filed at Companies House (s 53(1)(d) CA 1985; restated at s 97(2)(b) CA 2006 by 1 October 2009).

3. Private limited company to unlimited private company

681 A private limited company can convert to an unlimited company, provided the following **conditions** are met:
– it has not been unlimited before (s 49(1), (2) CA 1985; restated at s 102(2) CA 2006 by 1 October 2009); and
– the conversion is approved by all of the members/shareholders (s 49(8)(a) CA 1985; restated at s 102(1)(a) CA 2006 by 1 October 2009).

Before the company makes the application, it must **amend its memorandum and articles** so that they conform to the requirements of the memorandum and articles of an unlimited company with or without share capital, as appropriate (s 49(5)-(7) CA 1985; restated as far as the company's name and articles are concerned at s 102(3) CA 2006 by 1 October 2009).

682 The **application for re-registration** is made on Form 49(1) which must be signed by a director or the company secretary. It must be accompanied by (s 49(8) CA 1985):
– assents from all of the members/shareholders on Form 49(8)(b);
– a printed copy of the memorandum incorporating the alterations;
– a printed copy of the articles incorporating the alterations; and
– a statutory declaration by the directors that assents have been obtained from the entire membership of the company and that the directors have taken reasonable steps to satisfy themselves that any person who signed an assent on behalf of a member was lawfully empowered to do so.

On receipt of a proper application, Companies House will issue a **new certificate of incorporation** and the company will acquire its new status from the date of that certificate (s 50 CA 1985; restated at s 104 CA 2006 by 1 October 2009).

> **MEMO POINTS** 1. Under the **new Companies Act**, the application will only have to be accompanied by assents from all of the members/shareholders and a copy of the proposed amended articles. Instead of a statutory declaration, the directors will have to provide a statement of compliance which will not have to be sworn under oath or witnessed (s 103 CA 2006, expected to come into force by 1 October 2009). The form of assent is set out in regulations (Sch 3 draft Companies (Registration) Regulations 2007 (August 2007 version)).
> The new Act sets out an equivalent procedure for **public companies** to re-register as private and unlimited (ss 109-111 CA 2006, expected to come into force by 1 October 2009). The procedure will be the same as that under the new Act for private companies to re-register as unlimited, except that it will only be available to public companies who have never re-registered as limited or unlimited before. It is likely that the Takeover Code will apply to such re-registrations (see ¶675). The form of assent is also set out in regulations (Sch 4 draft Companies (Registration) Regulations 2007 (August 2007 version)).
> 2. The names of these forms, like the names of other **Companies House forms**, are taken from the section number of the legislation. As all of the section numbers will change under the new Companies Act, Companies House proposes to change the names of all of its forms to reflect their function rather than the relevant section number ("Working with Companies House: a consultation on the registrar's rules and related provisions which will apply under the Companies Act 2006"). At the time of writing, the new form names are not yet available.

4. Unlimited private company to limited private company

684

An unlimited private company can become a limited private company, provided the following **conditions** are met:
– it has not been limited before (s 51(1), (2) CA 1985; restated at s 105(2) CA 2006 by 1 October 2009); and
– the conversion is approved by a special resolution, which states whether the company is to be limited by shares or guarantee (s 51(3) CA 1985; restated at s 105(3) CA 2006 by 1 October 2009).

Before the company makes the application, it must **amend its memorandum and articles** so that they conform to the requirements of the memorandum and articles of a company limited by shares or by guarantee, as appropriate (s 51(3) CA 1985; restated as far as the company's name and articles are concerned at s 105(4) CA 2006 by 1 October 2009).

685

The **application for re-registration** is made on Form 51 which must be signed by a director or the company secretary. It must be accompanied by (s 51(4), (5) CA 1985, as amended by para 1 Sch 4 SI 2007/2194):
– a printed copy of the memorandum incorporating the alterations;
– a printed copy of the articles incorporating the alterations; and
– a copy of the special resolution (which must be filed under the new Companies Act at Companies House within 15 days of it being passed).

On receipt of a proper application, Companies House will issue a **new certificate of incorporation** and the company will acquire its new status from the date of that certificate (s 52 CA 1985; restated at s 107 CA 2006 by 1 October 2009).

> **MEMO POINTS** 1. Under the **new Companies Act**, the application will have to contain a statement of the company's proposed name on re-registration (s 106(1) CA 2006, expected to come into force by 1 October 2009). It will have to be accompanied by (s 106(2) CA 2006, expected to come into force by 1 October 2009):
> – a copy of the articles as proposed to be amended;
> – a copy of the special resolution (unless it has already been filed);
> – if the company is to be limited by guarantee, a statement of guarantee; and
> – a statement of compliance by the directors that the statutory provisions governing the re-registration have been complied with.
> The new Act also contains a new provision that within 15 days of re-registration, the company will have to file a statement of capital at Companies House if it had already allotted share capital on the date of the re-registration (s 108 CA 2006, expected to come into force by 1 October 2009).

2. The name of Form 51, like the names of other **Companies House forms**, is taken from the section number of the legislation. As all of the section numbers will change under the new Companies Act, Companies House proposes to change the names of all of its forms to reflect their function rather than the relevant section number ("Working with Companies House: a consultation on the registrar's rules and related provisions which will apply under the Companies Act 2006"). At the time of writing, the new form names are not yet available.

CHAPTER 4

Shares and share capital

OUTLINE ¶¶

SECTION 1 **General concepts**	703
1 Doctrine of capital maintenance	703
2 Share capital	709
3 The role of shares	727

SECTION 2 **Types of share**	740
A Ordinary shares	743
B Non-voting shares	749
C Redeemable shares	760
D Preference shares	780
1 Preference share rights	783
a Dividends	786
b Return of capital	803
c Voting	812
2 Redeemable preference shares	817
3 Convertible preference shares	822
4 Participating preference shares	829
E Employee shares	847
F Master shares	860
G Subscriber shares	872
H Deferred shares	877

SECTION 3 **Share issues and allotments**	889
I Methods of issue	896
A Pre-issue considerations	898
1 Alteration of authorised share capital	900
2 New share rights	914
3 Directors' authority	921
4 Pre-emption rights	940
5 Regulatory compliance	984

B Specific types of issue	1008
1 Bonus issue	1013
2 Rights issue	1042
3 Loan capitalisation	1053
C Issue procedure	1068
1 Pre-issue checks	1070
2 Shareholder resolutions	1073
3 Allotment	1079
4 Post allotment	1086
D Failure to allot or issue	1097
II **Payment**	1110
A General principles	1115
Share values	1115
Paying up	1117
Discounts	1121
Method of payment	1123
B Restrictions on public companies	1135
1 Paying up	1137
2 Allotments for non-cash consideration	1142
3 Transfer of non-cash asset	1171
4 Breach of restrictions	1185
C Shareholder calls	1205
1 Making a call	1205
2 Failure to meet a call	1215
D Commission payments	1237
E Share premium account	1245

SECTION 4 **Variation of class rights**	1270
A Key concepts	1273
B Variation procedure	1288
C Shareholders' objection	1297

SECTION 5	**Changes to share capital** 1310	7 Summary..............................	1424
		8 Failure to purchase or redeem	1427
I	Alteration of share capital.............	1312	**III Reduction of share capital**............ 1435
1	Consolidation and sub-division..........	1314	A Key concepts 1438
2	Redenomination.............................	1325	1 Purpose of reduction....................... 1438
II	**Own share purchase and redemption**	1337	2 Form of reduction 1445
		3 Position of third parties..................... 1458
1	Purpose	1344	B Procedure.. 1469
2	Effects..	1351	1 Authority... 1472
3	Financing..	1356	2 Shareholder approval 1475
4	Procedure: redemption.....................	1374	3 Court approval................................. 1483
5	Procedure: off-market purchase.........	1383	4 Registration 1493
6	Additional procedure: purchase or redemption out of capital...............	1400	C Summary and checklist.................. 1500

700 Shares can be held in the two most common types of company: private and public companies limited by shares. A person who holds shares in a company does not own a share of the assets of that company. Instead, the shares carry certain rights from which the holder can benefit (for example, voting and dividend rights). The exact nature of those rights will depend upon the "class" of share. The total face value of a company's shares is known as its "share capital".

A minimum number of shares is issued at incorporation (¶872). Whilst it is not strictly necessary for a company to **issue and allot** further shares, most companies do, resulting in an increase in share capital. Once shares have been issued, it is possible to **vary the rights** attached to them and to **alter the share capital** that they constitute. It is also possible to **decrease share capital** (and cancel the corresponding shares) but this is a much more difficult proposition.

Shares are a valuable personal asset and, once in the hands of a shareholder, they may be transferred by him or automatically transmitted to a third person (for example, on death or bankruptcy). The **transfer and transmission** of shares is dealt with at ¶1825+. A company can change hands by selling all of its shares to a new owner (see ¶5280+). However, companies are generally prohibited from giving financial assistance for the purpose of an acquisition of its own shares (a restriction that will be lifted for private companies when the relevant provisions of the new Companies Act come into force), see ¶5557+.

Shareholders also have general rights and powers as a consequence of holding shares in a company. A detailed explanation of the nature, rights and powers of shareholders (as opposed to the shares they hold) is provided at ¶2000+.

MEMO POINTS 1. It is possible to have shares in a **company limited by guarantee** having share capital and an **unlimited company** having share capital but these types of company are highly unusual. It has not been possible to form a company limited by guarantee with share capital since 22 December 1980 (s 1(4) CA 1985. The new Companies Act will also prevent companies being formed or becoming limited by guarantee with a share capital, s 5 CA 2006, expected to come into force by 1 October 2009).

2. The **new Companies Act** will change many of the statutory provisions regarding shares and share capital when the relevant changes come into force. Differences between the current and new provisions are highlighted in the text below; where the new Act simply restates the current law, the future statutory reference is given.

SECTION 1

General concepts

1. Doctrine of capital maintenance

703 The doctrine of capital maintenance is a judge-made doctrine that **concerns** protecting the level of capital investment in a company by its shareholders (*Trevor v Whitworth* [1886-90] All ER 90; *Aveling Barford v Perion Ltd* [1989] BCLC 626).

The traditional **rationale** for the doctrine is that share capital constitutes creditors' security and must be maintained to protect them. The doctrine can also be looked at in more economic terms: it increases the efficiency with which a company is run by reducing the competition between the shareholders and creditors for a company's assets (shareholders tend to want assets to be liquidated and returned to them; creditors tend to want assets to remain with the company to ensure that they are repaid). The cost of compensating creditors for the risk that assets may be removed from the company and returned to the shareholders (for example, by factoring that cost into the price of their loan to the company) would be high; a better solution would be to impose some restriction on the freedom of shareholders to transfer company assets to themselves.

The doctrine is the **framework** for much of company law. Firstly, it assumes that shareholders have actually made an investment into the company in the first place (i.e. that there is something to be protected). Accordingly, there are various legislative provisions to ensure that a company receives payment for its shares (see ¶1110+). Secondly, once capital has been put into the company, there are strict rules on its maintenance. In particular, there are restrictions on a company acquiring its own shares by way of purchase or redemption (¶1337+) and on reducing its share capital (¶1435+). In order to prevent the circumvention of these provisions, there is also a prohibition on companies giving financial assistance for the acquisition of their shares (¶5557+).

> MEMO POINTS The **new Companies Act** will abolish the prohibition on private companies giving financial assistance for the acquisition of their shares. The implementation date for this change is yet to be announced at the time of writing. There has been concern amongst commentators that this will take us back to the common law position that existed prior to the statutory restrictions, when the doctrine of capital maintenance prevented companies from giving financial assistance in some circumstances. Therefore, the government intends to insert a saving provision into the commencement order which will bring the repeal of the financial assistance provisions of CA 1985 into force to clarify that the law will not revert to the common law position (Appendix B, Chapter 4, "Implementation of Companies Act 2006: a consultative document" (February 2007)).

Reforms

704 The capital maintenance regime enshrined in current law has been criticised for failing to put theory into practice in an efficient manner. The **main criticism** is that the regime protects funds which are historic in nature. For example, the level of called-up share capital represents how much was paid for the shares at the time of issue and may bear no relation to the actual assets of the company. In addition, it is not necessarily the case that a company's share capital has any impact upon the size or success of its business. Most private companies have a share capital of £100 or less.

706 The criticisms led to proposals for reforms in the area, some of which have been implemented for **private companies** by the new Companies Act. These reforms (such as the abolition of the prohibition on financial assistance and the new reduction of share capital procedure) are discussed within the relevant topic.

The scope for reform for **public companies** had been restricted by the requirements of the Second Company Law Directive (EEC Directive 1977/91). This directive was amended on

15 October 2006 by a new EU directive (EC Directive 2006/68), which member states will have to incorporate into national law by 15 April 2008. Under the new provisions:
a. public companies will be able to allot shares for non-cash consideration without a valuation report in cases in which there is a clear point of reference for the valuation. Minority shareholders will have the right to require a valuation if they wish;
b. public companies will be able to purchase their own fully paid shares up to the limit of the company's distributable reserves (this is already permitted under English company law, but the new provisions will allow shareholders to authorise purchases for up to 5 years in the future instead of 18 months as at present);
c. public companies will also be able to give financial assistance for the acquisition of their shares by a third party up to the limit of the company's distributable reserves; and
d. material off-balance sheet arrangements and related party transactions will need to be presented in company accounts.

> MEMO POINTS 1. Draft regulations have been issued with a view to **implement the amendments** to the Second Company Law Directive (EC Directive 2006/68; the draft Companies (Reduction of Capital) Regulations 2008). These regulations will only allow creditors to object to a proposed reduction in the company's capital if they can "credibly demonstrate that due to the reduction in the subscribed capital the satisfaction of their claims is at stake, and that no adequate safeguards have been obtained from the company". Therefore, creditors will have to show that the proposed reduction is likely to put the payment of their debt at risk. When they come into force on 6 April 2008, the regulations will amend the relevant statutory provisions to add in this new requirement and to remove associated provisions such as the publicity requirements (ss 136, 137 CA 1985, ss 645–648 CA 2006).
> 2. In addition to these reforms, an **alternative to the capital maintenance regime** based on a company's solvency was proposed by the EU Company Law Action Plan in May 2003 (COM (2003) 284). The feasibility of this proposal, along with other alternative regimes, is being examined by KPMG in Berlin, who were appointed to do so by the EU Commission in October 2006.

2. Share capital

Definitions

709 "**Share capital**" is a figure expressed in monetary terms which, broadly speaking, represents the shareholders' investment in a company. Share capital is divided into units with a fixed value; these units are known as "**shares**". For example, a company may have a share capital of £100 divided into 100 shares of £1 each. This means that shareholders can invest up to £100 in the company by buying one or more units which have a value of £1 each.

> MEMO POINTS 1. A company's share capital need not be in pounds sterling; any one or more **denominations** are permitted (Re Scandinavian Bank Group plc [1987] 2 All ER 70). This may be particularly useful for companies with overseas shareholders who wish to hold shares in their own currency. The redenomination of shares is dealt with at ¶1325+. Public companies should note that they must hold the authorised minimum in pounds sterling, although the new Companies Act will also allow this to be in euros (¶720).
> 2. A company's share capital need not be divided into amounts that are **legal tender** (for example, 0.5p shares are permitted even though the halfpenny has been withdrawn) (Re Scandinavian Bank Group plc [1987] 2 All ER 70).
> The new Companies Act will require shares to have a **fixed nominal value** (for example, 1p), but does not set a minimum value (s 542 CA 2006, expected to come into force by 1 October 2009). A share without a fixed nominal value will be void.
> 3. Each share in a company must be given a **distinctive number**, unless all of the shares or all of the shares in one particular class have been paid for in full (s 182(2) CA 1985; restated at s 543 CA 2006 by 1 October 2009).
> 4. A company may treat its share capital as "**stock**" rather than shares. Instead of being divided into single units like shares, stock is expressed as a total value (in other words, a person may hold 100 shares of £1 each or stock worth £100). This used to be useful for larger companies when all shares had to be distinctively numbered, as record keeping was difficult. Now that the requirement for numbering has been limited, the use of stock is rarer. The term "share" includes "stock", unless a company has expressly or impliedly made a distinction between them

(s 744 CA 1985; restated at s 540(4) CA 2006 by 1 October 2009 when the provision comes fully in to force (it came into force as far as necessary for the interpretation of other provisions of the new Act already in force on 1 October 2007). However, under the new Companies Act, a company will no longer be able to convert its shares into stock (s 540(2) CA 2006, expected to come into force by 1 October 2009)).

The term "share capital" is used in a wide variety of contexts, both in the legal and accountancy world. In company law, the term can refer to any or all of the **meanings** below. For the difference between equity and non-equity share capital, see ¶727/mp.

Authorised share capital

The authorised share capital is the **maximum level** of share capital that a particular company may issue. It is decided upon by the company itself and may be increased quite easily. There is no upper limit on what a company may choose to set as its authorised share capital. The level chosen (e.g. £100) and how that capital has been divided (e.g. into 100 shares of £1 each) must be stated in the company's memorandum (s 2(5)(a) CA 1985). For the alteration of authorised share capital, see ¶900+.

Authorised share capital is also referred to as **nominal share capital**. For the sake of consistency, and to avoid confusion with the nominal value of shares (see ¶1115), the former term is preferred here.

> MEMO POINTS The **new Companies Act** will abolish the concept of authorised share capital for new companies by 1 October 2009. For existing companies, the concept of authorised share capital will remain, but it will operate as a restriction set out in the company's articles rather than its memorandum. This means that the shareholders will be able to remove the restriction by passing a special resolution to that effect. However, it is anticipated that transitional arrangements will be put in place when the relevant provisions come into force to allow shareholders to remove it by ordinary resolution for a time.
> If a company wishes to be incorporated with an authorised share capital, it will need to send a statement of capital and details of initial shareholdings to Companies House upon formation (see ¶526).

Issued and allotted share capital

The issued and allotted share capital is the total amount of share capital that is actually in the hands of shareholders. For the issue and allotment procedure, see ¶889+. The amount can be calculated by multiplying the number of issued (or allotted) shares by their face value. In practice, since issue and allotment take place almost simultaneously, a company's issued and allotted share capital is usually the same.

Called-up and uncalled share capital

A company is allowed to issue shares on the basis that payment for them will be made on a later unspecified date of the company's choosing, that is to say, on the basis that it will "call" for payment in the future (see ¶1205+). The total amount of share capital which has actually been paid, is to be paid on a specific future date, or has been called (even if the call has not yet been paid by the shareholder) is known as "called-up share capital" (s 737 CA 1985; restated at s 547 CA 2006 by 1 October 2009). "Uncalled share capital" is any share capital that falls outside this definition. In practice, shares are usually issued and paid for in full on issue so there is usually no **distinction between called-up and issued** share capital. It follows that most companies do not have any uncalled share capital.

Paid up share capital

The total value that has been paid to a company in return for its shares is known as its "paid up share capital". "Paid" in this context means where actual payment has been received by the company or where the company has received an undertaking to pay for the shares on a future date. Therefore, the **distinction between paid up and called-up** share capital is very slight (it is the amount of any unpaid share capital that has not yet been called). Since most shares are issued fully paid, the distinction is usually academic.

82 SHARES AND SHARE CAPITAL © FL Memo Ltd

> EXAMPLE A Ltd has an **authorised** share capital of £100 divided into 100 shares of £1 each. Of these, it has issued 50 shares to Mr X. It therefore has an **issued** share capital of £50.
> Mr X has paid 80p per share. A Ltd therefore has a **paid up** and **called-up** share capital of £40.
> **A Ltd makes a call** on Mr X to pay the amount outstanding on his shares. Before Mr X pays the call, A Ltd has a called-up share capital of £50 and a paid-up share capital of £40. After Mr X pays the call, A Ltd has a called-up and paid up share capital of £50 (i.e. the same as its issued share capital).

Authorised share capital $\geq$ Allotted share capital $\geq$ Issued share capital $\geq$ Called-up share capital $\geq$ Paid up share capital

Limits on share capital

720 Private companies are not subject to any **minimum** share capital requirements. However, public companies must have a minimum allotted share capital of £50,000 (ss 117, 118 CA 1985). Any additional capital can be in other currencies (*Re Scandinavian Bank Group plc* [1987] 2 All ER 70). Public companies are also subject to minimum requirements on their paid up share capital (¶1137). In contrast, all companies have a self-imposed **maximum** share capital, which is their authorised share capital (see ¶712).

> MEMO POINTS 1. Where the **net assets of a public company fall** to half or less than half of its called-up share capital, the directors must convene a general meeting of the shareholders for the purpose of considering what steps, if any, should be taken to deal with the situation. Notice for the meeting must be given within 28 days of the earliest day on which a director becomes aware that the net assets of the company have fallen to an unacceptably low level. The meeting must take place within 56 days of that same day. If the directors fail to convene the general meeting as required, each director who knowingly and wilfully authorises or permits the failure is liable to a fine (s 142 CA 1985; restated at s 656 CA 2006 by 1 October 2009; ¶9935).
> 2. A public company's ability to meet its **minimum** allotted share capital requirements may be **affected by** redenomination and reductions of share capital (respectively, ¶1325+, ¶1435+).
> 3. Under the **new Companies Act**, public companies will still be required to have a minimum allotted share capital (s 761 CA 2006, expected to come into force by 6 April 2008). It will be able to be in sterling or euros (s 763 CA 2006; reg 2 draft Companies (Shares, Share Capital and Authorised Minimum) Regulations 2007):
> – £50,000; or
> – €75,000.
> 4. Private companies incorporated in some **EU** member states are required to have a **minimum share capital** (for example Denmark, Austria and Germany). Private companies incorporated in the UK may establish an overseas branch (see ¶145+) in any EU state, free from any minimum share capital requirements that apply to local companies. However, overseas businesses cannot set up a company in the UK and then register a branch in their own country in order to avoid their domestic minimum share capital requirements (*Centros Ltd v Erhvervs-og Selskabsstyrelsen* [2000] 2 BCLC 68).

Share capital and company accounts

722 An understanding of the relationship between share capital and a company's balance sheet is particularly useful for putting the rules on share capital into context. The top part of a balance sheet sets out the company's assets and liabilities, eventually stating its **net asset value** (which is the value of the company's assets less its liabilities). The bottom part of a balance sheet sets out the company's capital and reserves (also referred to as "**shareholder funds**"). The items listed under this bottom section are: called-up share capital; the share premium account; the capital redemption reserve; the revaluation reserve; other reserves; and the profit and loss account (although not all of these items will be applicable to all companies) (Pt I Sch 4 CA 1985). A balance sheet is so called because the top part balances the bottom part; in other words, the net assets of a company equal its shareholder funds.

The items listed under "shareholder funds" can be divided into three broad categories. The first category contains items that represent **shareholder investment** namely, called-up share capital, the share premium account and the capital redemption reserve. These items are all subject to restrictions under company law. The second category comprises items that represent **reserves** which are not the subject of restriction under general company law (although they must be treated in accordance with usual accounting practice and may be subject to restrictions in the company's articles). This category includes the revaluation reserve (which is created on the revaluation of a company's assets) and other reserves created through accounting practice. The existence and amounts of these reserves have no relevance for the purposes of share capital. The final category is made up of the **profit and loss account** which, broadly speaking, is the profit retained (or loss made) by the company.

The general principle of capital maintenance hinges on the concept that the items under the first category of shareholder investment must be preserved. If the second category, reserves, is disregarded, this leaves the profit and loss account as the only amount which a company should be free to distribute to shareholders during the life of a company (by way of dividends). As a result, there are strict rules governing the calculation of "**distributable profits**" and when a company can pay a dividend to its shareholders (see ¶1610+).

3. The role of shares

727

In strict terms, shares are a form of **company funding**; a shareholder invests in a company and gets shares in return (see ¶4800+ for more on this type of company funding).

Shares do not entitle the holder to a share of the company as such. Instead, they carry a **collection of rights**, the exact nature of which are determined by the company that issues them. The three main rights which could attach to a share are:
– voting rights;
– the right to receive a dividend (that is, income from the company); and
– the right to receive a return of capital (that is, a capital payment from the company).

It is these rights that produce the unique relationship between a company and its shareholders and which are important factors in determining the monetary and non-monetary **value** of a company's shares. From a shareholder's point of view, shares allow them to participate in the company. From a company's point of view, shareholders have a vested interest in seeing it develop. As a result, in many companies, there is strong correlation between the management of a company and its shareholders.

> MEMO POINTS   A distinction is sometimes made between **equity** and **non-equity** shares and share capital. This division rests on the rights of the shares into which the share capital has been divided. Shares which have a specified limit on their right to participate in dividends or on a return of capital are non-equity shares and constitute non-equity share capital (this includes most preference shares). Shares which are not restricted in that way are equity shares and constitute equity share capital (e.g. ordinary shares) (s 744 CA 1985; restated at s 548 CA 2006 by 1 October 2009 when the provision comes fully into force (this provision is already in force as necessary for the interpretation of other provisions of the new Act already in force)).

SECTION 2

Types of share

740

The rights attaching to shares can vary considerably. However, certain share rights have been grouped together by convention and, in some cases, by statute. The following is a discussion in respect of the most common bundles of share rights (called "**share classes**") and an explanation of other terms commonly used to describe certain types of share. It must be noted that the actual rights of any share will differ from company to company and share to share, and reference must always be made to the particular share rights in each case (for example, in the articles).

Share rights are often tailored to fit the reasons for the share issue and the person to whom the issue is being made. However, if no particular rights are conferred on them, shares rank equally with and have the same rights as each other. The term "**pari passu**" is often used to denote shares that have been ranked equally whether in respect of all or particular rights.

> MEMO POINTS   A type of share that is not dealt with in this work in detail that readers may come across elsewhere is **treasury shares**. A share is held "in treasury" if the company has bought it

back out of distributable profits but has not cancelled it (in contrast to the treatment of other types of shares which are bought back by the company, see ¶1337+). It can then be held by the company for future sale, transfer or cancellation. Treasury shares are permitted by statute in particular circumstances (ss 162A-162F CA 1985; restated at ss 724-727, 729, 731 CA 2006; SI 2003/1116):
– they must be "qualifying shares", i.e. listed on the official list, traded on AIM, officially listed in or traded on a regulated market in an EEA state;
– a company can only hold up to 10% of its issued share capital, or up to 10% of any class of shares, as treasury shares; and
– where shares are held as treasury shares, the company cannot exercise any rights in respect of them (e.g. the right to vote at meetings). They are shown on the register of shareholders as being owned by the company and still form part of the share capital.
There are certain benefits to holding treasury shares, such as tax advantages (see *Tax Memo* for details) and the fact that the proceeds of sale from treasury shares are treated as realised profit for the purposes of determining the profits available for distribution.

A. Ordinary shares

743 This is the most **basic type** of share. It **entitles** the holder to:
– vote on shareholder resolutions (¶3513+);
– receive dividends if they are declared (¶1660+); and
– participate in any return of capital by the company to its shareholders (for example, on a winding up (¶8087+) or a reduction of share capital (¶1435+)).

There is no need for the share rights to be expressly stated. They are **conferred automatically** on any ordinary share **unless** the share rights specifically state otherwise. If no particular description is given to a company's shares upon their creation and no particular rights are conferred upon them, they will be deemed to be ordinary shares.

The term "ordinary share" is used to describe the standard shares of a company, as they are the **reference point** for all other shares. For example, a preference share (¶780+) is so called because it has rights in preference to those of ordinary shares. Similarly, a deferred share (¶877) is so called because its rights are deferred to those of ordinary shares.

744 Some companies designate their ordinary shares to be "**A**" **ordinary** and "**B**" **ordinary shares**. This makes it easier to set out different rights attaching to those shares. For example, the "A" ordinary shares may have pre-emption rights over the "B" ordinary shares.

Alternatively, "A" ordinary shares and "B" ordinary shares may be created to allow a company to declare dividends in respect of one type of share but not the other. For example, a company could issue "A" ordinary shares to its directors and "B" ordinary shares to employees. The company could then declare a dividend on the "A" ordinary shares whenever it wished to distribute profits to its directors and on the "B" ordinary shares whenever it wished to distribute profits to its employees.

"A" ordinary shares and "B" ordinary shares can also have **differing nominal values** (for example, £1 "A" ordinary shares and 10p "B" ordinary shares). Voting rights are not proportionate to the nominal value of a share and so each ordinary share will have one vote on a poll or a written resolution unless the share rights state otherwise (s 284 CA 2006). On a show of hands, every shareholder has one vote.

B. Non-voting shares

749 The term "non-voting share" is used to describe a share without voting rights.

750 Non-voting shares are usually created and issued to **allow** for the holder to participate in the profits and capital surplus of the company without that holder being able to exercise any powers of control. For this reason, shares without voting rights usually specify that the holder is not entitled to receive notice of **shareholder meetings** or attend them. If the non-voting share rights are silent about receiving notice of shareholder meetings, depending upon the articles, the shares may carry that entitlement even though they are non-voting (see ¶3692). However, if non-voting shareholders are to attend general meetings, the share rights or articles need to allow them to do so specifically *(Re Mackenzie & Co Ltd [1916-17] All ER 1018)*.

Regardless of how the non-voting share rights are expressed, non-voting shareholders will always have the right to vote on resolutions that **vary** their **class rights** at meetings or in writing (and therefore they have the attendant rights to receive notice of such meetings, attend them or receive such written resolutions).

751 Non-voting shares are more commonly found in **private companies**. For example, an owner-managed private company may wish to issue non-voting shares to the spouse, children or other family members of the director/shareholders so that management control is kept in the hands of those actually working in the company but profit is shared amongst their entire family. This can have tax advantages as income and capital gains are spread across as many individuals in a family as possible who are each able to utilise their tax allowances in full. Alternatively, a small private company may issue non-voting shares to incentivise key employees, whether as part of a specific employee share scheme or as a straightforward share issue.

752 Non-voting shares are discouraged in listed companies as they disenfranchise shareholders and any **company aiming for listing** should bear this in mind.

C. Redeemable shares

760 Redeemable shares are shares which are to be "cashed in" by the holder in return for payment to him by the company (s 159(1) CA 1985; restated at s 684(1) CA 2006 by 1 October 2009). The issue and redemption of redeemable shares is governed by statute. Their issue is considered below and their redemption is dealt with at ¶1337+.

> MEMO POINTS An **unlimited company** with share capital may not issue redeemable shares (s 159(1) CA 1985; restated at s 684(1) CA 2006 by 1 October 2009).

761 Redeemable shares are often issued to:
a. private funders of a company, such as a venture capitalist (who will usually want to realise his investment, take his profit and leave the company within 5-7 years of making the investment) or a parent company. They are suitable for investors as they provide a mechanism by which financing may be repaid to them. For this reason, redeemable shares are referred to as "loan capital"; or
b. a **shareholder involved in** the **management** of a company, with redemption to occur upon him ceasing to be involved. This allows the shareholder to realise value from his shares upon his exit from the company's management (for example, on retirement) whilst avoiding the problems of procuring a sale to a third party.

Issue

763 To issue redeemable shares, a company must have a **minimum** of one non-redeemable share in issue (s 159 CA 1985; restated at s 684(4) CA 2006 by 1 October 2009). In addition, redeemable shares may only be **created** out of a fresh issue of shares and so it is not possible to **convert** existing issued shares into redeemable shares. If a company wishes to issue redeemable shares to an existing shareholder in place of his non-redeemable shares, those shares must either be cancelled under a scheme of arrangement (¶6500+) or purchased by the company (¶1337+). The redeemable shares may then be created and issued to the holder of the cancelled/purchased non-redeemable shares.

764 Redeemable shares may be issued **partly paid** but may only be redeemed if they are fully paid (s 159(3) CA 1985; restated at s 686(1) CA 2006 by 1 October 2009).

765 A company is able to issue redeemable shares in any class provided it is **authorised** to do so by its articles (s 159(1) CA 1985). Companies incorporated under Table A 1985 will be authorised but those incorporated under Table A 1948 that have not updated their articles may have a restricted authority, as the table below summarises.

If a company is **not authorised** by its articles, it will need to amend them prior to the issue.

Date of Incorporation	Form of Articles	Ambit of Authority
On or after 1 Jul 1985	Table A 1985	Authority to issue redeemable shares in any class (reg 3 TA 1985)
3 Dec 1981 – 30 Jun 1985 (inc.)	Table A 1948	Authority to issue redeemable shares in any class (reg 3 TA 1948 as amended by CA 1981)
On or before 2 Dec 1981	Table A 1948	Authority to issue redeemable preference shares only (reg 3 TA 1948)

MEMO POINTS 1. Under the **new Companies Act**, only a public company will need to have prior authorisation in its articles to issue redeemable shares, although the articles of all types of company will be able to exclude or restrict their issue (s 684 CA 2006, expected to come into force by 1 October 2009).
2. Draft **new model articles** under the new Companies Act have been published for private companies limited by shares and public companies. They will restate reg 3 TA 1985 (private companies limited by shares: art 22; public companies: art 42).

Terms and manner of redemption

768 Redeemable shares can be **redeemed on** a fixed date, over a certain period of time, upon satisfaction of certain conditions, or upon the occurrence of certain events. They can be redeemed at one time or in stages. Further, they can be issued on the basis that they **must** be redeemed, or that they are liable to be redeemed at the **option** of the company or the shareholder (s 159 CA 1985; restated at s 684 CA 2006 by 1 October 2009).

769 The terms and manner of redemption must be **set out** in the company's articles, but there is no prohibition on the articles leaving matters (such as the timing of the redemption or the amount payable on redemption) to the discretion of the directors (s 160(3) CA 1985).

In practice, the articles set out the particulars of redemption in some detail **prior to issue** as, understandably, redeemable shareholders prefer to have certainty as to their redemption rights. After the shares have been issued, there is no restriction on **changing** the terms and manner of redemption (subject to the agreement of the redeemable shareholders to the variation of their class rights and of the shareholders in general to an alteration of the articles).

Comment: Although there is also arguably no restriction on issuing the shares and leaving the terms and manner of redemption to be inserted into the articles at a later date, this course of action is not recommended due to the period of uncertainty until the articles are amended and the problems that would arise if no amendments were ever made.

MEMO POINTS Under the **new Companies Act**, the terms and manner of redemption will either have to be determined by the directors before allotment, or set out in the company's articles. If they are to be determined by the directors, the directors will need to be authorised by an ordinary resolution or through the articles and the terms and manner of redemption will have to be stated in the statement of capital filed when the new shares are created (see ¶1087/mp) (s 685 CA 2006, expected to come into force by 1 October 2009).

770 Usually, the **payment** on redemption is a fixed amount (for example, the nominal or subscription value of the share) or an amount calculated by reference to a formula. In all cases, the payment must occur on the date of redemption; it cannot be deferred (s 159(3) CA 1985).

MEMO POINTS The **new Companies Act** will remove the requirement for payment on redemption. Instead, subject to agreement between the company and the holder of the redeemable shares, the company will be able to make the payment after the redemption date (s 685 CA 2006, expected to come into force by 1 October 2009).

Accounts

772 Details of any allotted redeemable shares must be included in the **notes** to the company's accounts (para 38(2) Pt III Sch 4 CA 1985).

Comment: This will still be the case when the accounts provisions of the **new Companies Act** are due to come into force, which will apply to financial years starting on or after 6 April 2008 (the relevant regulations are in draft form at the time of writing: para 46 Sch 1 draft Small Companies and Groups (Accounts and Directors' Report) Regulations 2008; para 47 Sch 1 draft Large and Medium-sized Companies and Groups (Accounts and Reports) Regulations 2008).

> MEMO POINTS Redeemable shares used to be an attractive form of raising finance because they were **classified on the company's balance sheet** as equity rather than debt. However, now such shares have to be treated as a financial liability (i.e. as debt) where the terms of redemption provide for mandatory redemption by the company, or give the holder the right to require the company to redeem the shares. They will only be treated as equity where the terms of redemption do not require the company the redeem the shares, for example, if redemption can only ever occur at the company's option (FRS 25(17), (18)).

D. Preference shares

780 These are shares which have rights in preference to the ordinary shares of a company. They normally:
– carry the right to receive **dividends** in preference to any other share (the right is usually capped at a specific rate);
– either carry no rights on a **return of capital** (which can occur on a winding up or reduction of share capital) other than payment of dividend arrears and repayment of the capital paid on the shares, or carry preferential rights on a return of capital; and
– are non-**voting**, except in special circumstances.

It is entirely possible for a company to issue different preference shares at different times, each with different **rights** as regards dividends, voting and the return of capital.

There are four main rights that are commonly attached to or excluded from preference shares:
– for any unpaid dividend in one year to accumulate to the next year (¶793);
– for the shares to be redeemed (¶817);
– for the shares to be converted into ordinary shares (¶822+); and
– to participate in a return of capital and/or dividends (¶829+).

Two or more of these rights can be combined in a class of preference shares.

781 Preference shares are often used to meet a company's funding requirements as there are advantages for both funders and the company.

Preference shares are **attractive to funders** because they can:
– obtain a specific return (which is the preferential dividend) on their capital investment (which is the amount that they paid for the shares), subject always to the risk of insufficient distributable profits; and/or
– obtain a preferential return of capital in a solvent winding up or reduction in share capital.

Preference shares are **attractive to a company** because:
– management control of the company is not diluted as, in most circumstances, the shares are non-voting;
– the preferential dividend may be lower than if the company had to pay interest on a loan; and
– in most cases, the statutory pre-emption provisions on allotment do not apply (¶946).

782 Preference shares are also used in **smaller private companies** to guarantee the top slice of any dividends to certain shareholders. For example, they are commonly issued to:
– key directors or employees as an alternative to an employee bonus scheme;
– an exiting director as a mechanism for paying him a regular "pension"; or
– directors/shareholders so that part of their remuneration is paid by way of preferential dividend rather than salary (which has tax advantages).

1. Preference share rights

783 Once issued, except for certain rebuttable presumptions mentioned below, the **rights** expressed to attach to preferential shares are **exhaustive** (*Scottish Insurance Corp Ltd v Wilsons and Clyde Coal Co Ltd* [1949] 1 All ER 1068). It is, therefore, good practice to set out their rights in considerable detail, either in the articles or in the resolution by which they are created. The actual rights will depend upon the way in which the share rights are construed. Consequently, preferential share rights must be drafted with a high degree of accuracy to ensure that they reflect the intentions of the parties.

a. Dividends

786 The right to receive dividends in preference to any other share means that in each year, any profits available for distribution must first be paid on the preference shares at the specified dividend rate before distributing any surplus profits to the other shareholders. For a general discussion of dividends and distributions, see ¶1600+.

787 The specific **dividend rate** on any particular preference share is as set out in the share rights (for example, in the articles). It is usually:
a. a fixed **percentage of** the **share's value** (for example, "5% preference shares" where the preference shares have a nominal value of £1 would give a dividend rate of 5p per share). The presumption is that the dividend will be calculated by reference to the nominal value, unless the share rights specifically state that the dividend should be calculated by reference to the subscription value. This fixed percentage is sometimes referred to as the "**coupon rate**"; or
b. a fixed **percentage of profits** available for distribution. In such a case, the actual amount of dividend paid on each preference share will depend on the number of preference shares in issue. This is because dividends must be paid pro rata on each share type, so the total dividend (say, 10% of distributable profits) will need to be divided amongst all of the issued preference shares.

Since preferential share rights are exhaustive, unless the share rights state otherwise, the right to a **dividend is capped** at the preferential rate (*Will v United Lankat Plantations Co Ltd* [1911-13] All ER Rep 165). Preference shares which are framed in such a way that the holder is entitled to participate in **additional dividends** are known as "participating preference shares" (see ¶829+).

Payment

789 It should be noted that preference shares do not guarantee that a dividend will be paid. In order for this to occur, the company must have **sufficient distributable profits** and the dividend must be **declared**. Therefore, preference shares in a poorly performing company do not necessarily give the preference shareholder any more comfort than ordinary shares give the other shareholders.

Ordinarily, there is no obligation on a company to declare a dividend. If a company **fails to declare** a preferential dividend when it has sufficient distributable profits, the directors may be in breach of their duties if that failure is a result of their actions. However, although the company may have a claim against the directors for breach of their duties, the preference shareholders are likely to find it difficult to bring such a claim as it must usually be brought in the name of the company and not the individual shareholders. The new derivative claim procedure should make it easier for shareholders to take action (see ¶7127+).

To give preferential shareholders more security, preference share rights can be expressed in such a way that the company is **compelled to declare** the preferential dividend if it has sufficient distributable profits. It may also be appropriate to specify exactly when the declaration should be made (for example, on the first day of every month). If the share rights are framed in such a way and the preferential dividend is still not declared when the company has sufficient distributable profits, the preference shareholders may be entitled to bring unfair prejudice proceedings or apply for the company to be wound up (see ¶2100+).

790

It will be appreciated that these are drastic remedies and a preferential shareholder would rather have a right to claim his dividend instead. Therefore, it is common for preference share rights to state that, subject to there being sufficient distributable profits, preferential dividends are deemed to become due either at the end of the accounting reference period or on certain dates even if no declaration has been made. These are known as "**fixed dividends**". In such a case, the preferential shareholder could claim the unpaid dividend as a debt owed to him by the company. It is even possible for the share rights to state that interest is payable on late dividends.

Cumulative or non-cumulative

Preferential dividend rights can be cumulative or non-cumulative. **Cumulative** dividend rights mean that if a full dividend is not declared in accordance with the preference share rights because the company has insufficient distributable profits in that year, the right to the unpaid dividend rolls forward to the next year, that is to say, it accumulates. Once the company has sufficient distributable profits, it would first have to satisfy its liabilities in respect of undeclared accumulated dividend rights from previous years before it could declare a dividend on any other shares. **Non-cumulative** preference shares lose their right to receive the preferential dividend payable in any year when the company has insufficient distributable profits.

793

Unless the share rights state otherwise, the **presumption** is that dividend rights are cumulative (*Henry v Great Northern Railway Co* (1857) 1 De G & J 606). This presumption is rebuttable so, for example, if the preferential dividend is restricted to a fixed percentage of profits in each year, the dividend will be calculated on the distributable profits of that year and not carried forward to future years. This means the dividend will be non-cumulative (*Staples v Eastman Photographic Materials Co* [1896] 2 Ch 303). It is therefore usual to expressly state that the dividend right is cumulative; non-cumulative preference shares are unusual.

Arrears

The terms "**arrears of dividend**" or "**back dividends**" are sometimes used to describe accumulated preferential dividends that have yet to become due (for example, because the company had insufficient distributable profits). These expressions can be misleading as, technically, there is no right to a dividend until it has been declared and/or becomes due. Prior to this time, the dividend right is simply accruing or accumulating and cannot be enforced. It is only after this time that the dividend falls into "arrears" and the shareholder has a claim against the company (*Re Wakley* [1920] All ER Rep 749).

796

It is possible for accruals of preferential dividends to accumulate on preference shares which have been **issued at different times**. In such a case, the preferential dividend, when paid, should not be paid against the earliest accrual first but should be apportioned amongst all the accrued preferential dividends (*Weymouth Waterworks Co v Coode and Hasell* [1911] 2 Ch 520; *First Garden City v Bonham-Carter* [1928] Ch 53).

797

EXAMPLE A Ltd issues 100 preference shares in Year 1 which together have the right to a preferential dividend of £10,000 per year.

Year 1   There are no distributable profits. The preferential dividend of £10,000 accumulates to the next year.

> A Ltd then issues a further 100 preference shares in Year 2 which together also have the right to a preferential dividend of £10,000 per year.
>
> Year 2   There are no distributable profits. The accrued preferential dividend rights on the Year 1 shares of £20,000 and the preferential dividend rights on the Year 2 shares of £10,000 accumulate to the next year.
>
> Year 3   There are sufficient distributable profits to declare a dividend of £10,000. The accumulated preferential dividend rights of the Year 1 and Year 2 shares stand at £30,000 and £20,000 respectively. The dividend is apportioned between the Year 1 and Year 2 shares so that £6,000 is paid on the Year 1 shares and £4,000 on the Year 2 shares.

798 If a preferential dividend is eventually paid in respect of arrears or back dividends, it must be **treated as income** in the year in which it was paid and not carried back to the years in which the right to that dividend accumulated or the date when it was deemed due (*Re Wakley* [1920] All ER Rep 749).

Payment of dividend arrears and accruals on a winding up or other return of capital depend upon how the preferential share rights on a return of capital have been expressed (see below).

b. Return of capital

803 A return of capital to the shareholders may arise on a winding up or on a reduction of share capital. Unless the share rights state otherwise, the **presumption** is that preference shares carry no rights on a return of capital (*Scottish Insurance Corp Ltd v Wilsons and Clyde Coal Co Ltd* [1949] 1 All ER 1068).

The actual rights on a return of capital, therefore, depend entirely upon the express rights attached to the share. Normally, preference shares will be expressed to carry the right to receive:
– **payment of any arrears of dividend**; and
– **repayment of the capital paid** up on each share (which in the case of a fully paid share is its nominal value).

Payment of dividend arrears

805 Unless otherwise specified in the share rights, preferential dividend rights will be lost **on a winding up**. This is because once a winding up has started, the provisions concerning dividend rights come to an end and, after the debts of the company have been paid, the provisions with regard to the return of capital apply (*Re Crichton's Oil Co* [1900-3] All ER Rep Ext 1378; *Re W Foster & Son Ltd* [1942] 1 All ER 314). In addition, **on other returns of capital** (for example, following a reduction in share capital), there is no requirement to clear preferential dividend arrears in priority to the return of capital.

For this reason, preferential share rights often state that on a winding up or other return of capital, all arrears and accruals of preferential dividend rights must be paid in **priority** to payments to the other shareholders, even if they have not been declared as due or earned. In a winding up, unless the share rights state otherwise, the entitlement will be to arrears and accruals up to the date of the winding up rather than the date of the actual payment to the shareholders (*Re E W Savory Ltd* [1951] 2 All ER 1036).

806 Even if the right to preferential dividend arrears is preserved if the company goes into liquidation, any arrears would **rank** behind the other creditors (see ¶8089 for preferential shareholders' entitlements in a liquidation). This means that they would only be paid once all other creditors had been satisfied (s 74(2)(f) IA 1986). However, the arrears of dividend would be taken into account in deciding upon the rights of the shareholders to any surplus capital.

Repayment of capital paid

808 Normally, preference share rights specify that preferential shareholders are entitled to have their capital repaid in **priority** to payments to other shareholders.

> EXAMPLE A Ltd has been wound up. It has £100,000 to be returned to shareholders. It has an issued share capital of £200,000 divided into 150,000 ordinary shares of £1 each and 25,000 preference shares of £2 each. All shares are fully paid up.
> 1. Suppose the preference shares have **no entitlements** on a return of capital. The £100,000 is paid out on the ordinary shares only. Each ordinary shareholder will receive 66p per share.
> 2. Suppose the preference shares are entitled to the **repayment of capital** paid up on the shares but **not in priority** to the ordinary shares. The £100,000 is apportioned between the ordinary shares and preference shares on a pro rata basis, in other words each share will receive a return of 50p for every £1 of nominal value. Each preference shareholder will therefore receive £1 per share and each ordinary shareholder will receive 50p per share.
> 3. Suppose the preference shares are entitled to the **repayment of capital** paid up on the shares **in priority** to the ordinary shares. Therefore, the preference shareholders will first be paid the full nominal value of their shares, leaving £50,000 to be distributed amongst the ordinary shareholders. Each preference shareholder will therefore receive £2 per share and each ordinary shareholder will receive 33p per share.

809 Sometimes, preference shares are also expressed to have **rights to the surplus assets** of the company on a return of capital. These are known as "participating preference shares" (see ¶829+).

c. Voting

812 Usually, preference shares are **non-voting** and do not carry the right to vote at, receive notice of or attend shareholder meetings **except**:
– in the event that dividends are in arrears;
– on a resolution to wind up the company; and
– on a variation of their class rights.

2. Redeemable preference shares

817 These are preference shares which are to be redeemed or are liable to be redeemed (see ¶760+). They are the most common form of preference share as they combine the benefits of redeemable and preference shares. They are particularly useful in arm's length **private funding** scenarios as they provide the funder with a continuing income from his investment (by way of the preferential dividend), together with the certainty that his capital investment will be returned (by way of the redemption).

> MEMO POINTS Redeemable preference shares used to be an attractive form of raising finance because they were **classified on the company's balance sheet** as equity rather than debt. However, now such shares have to be treated as a financial liability (i.e. as debt) where the terms of redemption provide for mandatory redemption by the company, or give the holder the right to require the company to redeem the shares. They will only be treated as equity where the terms of redemption do not require the company to redeem the shares, for example, if redemption can only ever occur at the company's option (FRS 25(17), (18)).

3. Convertible preference shares

822 When issued, preference shares are sometimes expressed to be convertible into ordinary shares immediately before the occurrence of certain **trigger events**.
The most common trigger events are:
– an arm's length **sale** of the company to a third party at market value (either the sale of a controlling interest in the company's issued share capital or a sale of the whole or substantially the whole of the company's business and assets); or
– a **listing** of the company's ordinary shares on a public exchange (such as the London Stock Exchange or the Alternative Investment Market).

823 The **purpose of the conversion** is so that preference shareholders can benefit from the sale or listing as ordinary shareholders. In a successful company, the dividend potential on ordinary shares is uncapped so they generally have a higher market value than preference shares when a company is performing well. In addition, ordinary shares have full voting rights and so give their holders greater control over the company. Consequently, ordinary shareholders are likely to realise a higher value for their shares upon a sale or listing (or in the case of a sale of a company's business and assets, a higher dividend rate when the proceeds of sale are distributed to the company's shareholders). Convertible preference shares therefore allow funders of a company to enjoy the best of both worlds and so are popular with professional investors such as venture capitalists (¶4800+). For this reason, convertible preference shares are often issued in companies which are being groomed for sale or listing.

824 Convertible preference shares can be **converted** at a **fixed rate** (for example, one ordinary share for every ten preference shares) or can be converted by reference to a **formula** based upon the company's financial performance. This is sometimes described as the "**ratchet**". Normally, the intention on a conversion is that the converted preference shares should amount to a certain percentage of the total number of ordinary shares. The converted shareholders would then receive that percentage of the total value of the sale or listing. In such a case, the drafting of the conversion provisions must take account of the effect of bonus issues, rights issues or other **capital reorganisations** between issue and conversion. Such capital reorganisations could result in the issue of further ordinary shares which would dilute their market value.

4. Participating preference shares

829 In addition to the normal preference share rights, participating preference shares allow the holder to participate in:
– the surplus assets of a company on a **return of capital** on a winding up (specifically rebutting the presumption that preference shares do not carry such a right); and/or
– **dividends** in addition to the preferential dividend rate (which means that the shares are uncapped with regard to dividends).

830 Participating preference shares are often issued in companies which anticipate a **solvent winding up**. For example, a single purpose company set up to hold property that plans to be wound up when the property is sold. Alternatively, the company may be a trading company that, having sold its entire business and assets, intends to wind up and distribute the proceeds of sale to the shareholders by way of a return of capital.

Return of capital

833 There are **two issues** to consider on a return of capital on a winding up:
a. repayment of capital paid (in the case of fully paid shares, this means the repayment to the shareholders of the nominal value of their shares). As noted above, most preference shares carry the entitlement to repayment of capital paid on the shares in priority to payments to the other shareholders; and
b. distribution of any surplus assets (this is the distribution to the shareholders of any assets remaining after payment of the company's debts, costs and repayment of capital paid). Participating preference shares carry this additional entitlement.

Subject to any provision in the articles or any particular share rights, the **fund available** when considering a return of capital (whether a repayment of capital paid or distribution of the surplus) is not just the surplus capital upon the winding up (which is the amount left after all the assets of the company have been sold and its debts paid) but also includes any undistributed profits of the company on the date of the winding up (*Dimbula Valley (Ceylon) Tea Co Ltd v Laurie* [1961] 1 All ER 769).

On a distribution of surplus assets, participating preference shares are usually expressed: **834**
- to **rank equally** with ordinary shares; and/or
- to be entitled to a **fixed additional payment** in priority to payments to other shareholders.

> EXAMPLE B Ltd has an issued share capital of £200,000 divided into 150,000 ordinary shares of £1 each and 25,000 **preference shares** of £2 each with all shares being fully paid up. B Ltd has been wound up and has £400,000 to be returned to the shareholders.
>
> 1. Suppose the preference shares' entitlement is **limited to the repayment of capital** paid up on the shares in priority to the ordinary shares (i.e. they are non-participating). All shareholders will be repaid the full nominal value of their shares leaving £200,000 to be distributed amongst the ordinary shareholders. Each preference shareholder will therefore receive a total of £2 per share and each ordinary shareholder will receive a total of £2.33 per share.
> 2. Suppose the preference shares **rank equally** with the ordinary shares on a return of capital pro rata to their nominal values (i.e. they are participating shares). All shareholders will first be repaid the full nominal value of their shares, leaving £200,000 to be distributed proportionately amongst all the shareholders (i.e. £1 per £1 of nominal value). Each preference shareholder will therefore receive a total of £4 per share and each ordinary shareholder will receive a total of £2 per share.
> 3. Suppose the preference shares are entitled to the **repayment of capital** paid up on the shares in priority to the ordinary shares and a **further payment** of the first £100,000 of any surplus assets in priority to payments to other shareholders. The preference shareholders will be repaid the nominal value of their shares and paid another £100,000, leaving £250,000 to be distributed to the ordinary shareholders. Each preference shareholder will receive a total of £6 per share and each ordinary shareholder will receive a total of £1.67 per share.
> 4. Same as 3 but with the preference shares **ranking equally** with the ordinary shareholders pro rata to the nominal value of each share as to the payment of any remaining surplus assets. In this case, the surplus of £250,000 must be distributed proportionately amongst all shareholders (i.e. £1.25 per £1 of nominal value). Each preference shareholder will receive a total of £8.50 per share and each ordinary shareholder will receive a total of £1.25 per share.

If different rights are intended to apply on a winding up and on another return of capital (such as on a reduction of capital) this will need to be specified in the share rights as the assumption will be that the same rights will apply to both (*Re Saltdean Estate Co Ltd* [1968] 3 All ER 829).

Dividends

A preference share that carries participating dividend rights can be **expressed in** several ways. The declaration of further dividends could be: **837**
- left to the discretion of the company;
- made mandatory at the level declared on the ordinary shares; or
- set at a percentage of distributable profits available after the first preferential dividend has been paid.

> MEMO POINTS   It may be appropriate to state that on a **bonus issue**, the participating preference shares will only rank for further shares in the same class in order to avoid shares of another class being unfairly issued to them (see ¶1013).

E. Employee shares

The term "employee share" **describes** shares issued to employees rather than a particular bundle of share rights. Shares are often issued to employees: **847**
- as part of an unapproved scheme, or an employee scheme that is approved by Revenue and Customs; or
- on an ad hoc basis to give the employee a stake in the company that employs him.

Some companies issue ordinary shares to their employees, others issue preference shares in lieu of a bonus scheme. The actual rights attaching to the shares will vary from case to case.

MEMO POINTS For an overview of employee share schemes, see ¶2724+. For further details on approved and unapproved schemes, see *Tax Memo*.

848 Shares issued under an **employees' share scheme** (whether approved or unapproved) are subject to particular statutory provisions and deemed to be "employee shares" for certain purposes. An "employees' share scheme" for these purposes is a scheme for encouraging or facilitating the holding of shares in a company by or for the **benefit of** (s 743 CA 1985; restated at s 1166 CA 2006, which will be brought into force as necessary for the interpretation of other provisions of the new Act):
a. employees or former employees of:
– the company;
– the company's subsidiary or holding company; or
– a subsidiary of the company's holding company; or
b. the spouses, civil partners, surviving spouses, surviving civil partners, children or step-children under the age of 18 of such employees or former employees.

Since the definition includes shares held for the benefit of employees, it includes shares held in an **employee trust**.

The scheme need not be **open to** all employees to qualify as an employees' share scheme but a scheme that is restricted to the directors of a company is unlikely to be sufficient. It is also unlikely that shares issued to employees on an ad hoc basis, rather than as part of a structured scheme, will fall into the definition.

849 Subject to the articles of the company, the **particular statutory provisions** which apply to shares allotted under an employees' share scheme are summarised below.

Statutory provision	¶¶	Reference (CA 1985)[1]
Directors do not need authority to allot those shares	¶921+	s 80(2)(a)
Statutory pre-emption provisions do not apply to allotments of those shares	¶945+	s 89(5)
Company may give financial assistance to acquire those shares	¶5580	s 153(4)(b)
For public companies and private companies re-registering as public companies: – one-quarter of nominal value and premium does not have to be paid up on those shares; and – those shares will not be taken into account in determining nominal value of company's allotted share capital until such sums have been paid	¶1137	s 45 s 101(2) s 117(4)
Note: 1. These references will change under the **new Companies Act**. Follow the cross-references to the discussion on specific topics for further details.		

850 Shares allotted to employees but **not** as **part of an employees' share scheme** are treated in the same way as other shares, although there may still be tax consequences for both the company and the employee.

F. Master shares

860 The "master share" (sometimes referred to as the "golden share") is a share with special rights that effectively give the holder **control** over certain shareholder decisions. There is usually only one master share.

Since the intention is usually that such powers of control should only be given to a particular person or persons, the articles normally provide that the master share will lose its special rights **if transferred** by that person or if transferred outside of a particular group of people.

861 It is not possible for the share rights simply to state that approval of the master shareholder is required for a particular action to take place (*Southern Foundries (1926) Ltd v Shirlaw* [1940] 2 All ER 445). Instead, the special rights must be expressed as some form of **enhanced voting right** (*Russell v Northern Bank Development Corp Ltd* [1992] 3 All ER 161; *Bushell v Faith* [1970] 1 All ER 53). For example, on a shareholder vote on a particular issue (such as putting the company into voluntary liquidation), the master share's vote could automatically equal one more than the total votes of the other shares or have a multiplied number of votes, thereby always giving the master shareholder ultimate control over that issue. Alternatively, the articles could state that particular decisions (for example, the issue of shares, the granting of security over the company's assets, a sale of a material part of the company's business or assets, etc) amount to a variation of the master share's rights and the master shareholder's consent would therefore be required for the variation to take place.

862 A master share can be used in any company where one shareholder is intended to have control. A **typical example** is in property development where the concept of a master share can be used in different ways. For example, if land is being developed into multiple units with common or shared parts, the common parts are often owned by a single purpose company, the shares in which are initially held by the developer. Each purchaser of a unit is given a share in the single purpose company so that they together control the common parts but the developer retains a master share (and therefore ultimate control) until the last unit is sold.

G. Subscriber shares

872 The "subscriber shares" (sometimes referred to as the "**founder shares**") are those allotted upon the formation of a company to the subscriber(s) to the memorandum. A **minimum** of one share must be allotted to each subscriber (s 2(5) CA 1985; restated at s 8(1) CA 2006 by 1 October 2009) and, in practice, only this minimum is actually allotted. There is no particular bundle of rights that attaches to such a share and after allotment they are not subject to any special provisions.

H. Deferred shares

877 These are shares whose **rights** are deferred to the other issued shares in a company. Deferred shares usually carry full voting rights but their rights to participate in dividends or on a return of capital (for example, on a winding up or reduction of share capital) are deferred to the other shares of the company. Sometimes, the deferred rights have a **time limit** after which the shares will rank equally with the ordinary shares.

> MEMO POINTS It is unusual to find deferred shares in modern capital structures. They were popular in the past for **inheritance tax planning** purposes, the basic idea of which was that the deferred shares would be transferred out of an individual's estate during his lifetime and since they had a low value, the potential inheritance tax charge would be minimised. Once in the hands of the person to whom the shares had been transferred, the deferred rights would be amended so that the shares ranked equally with the ordinary shares once more. There are now tax anti-avoidance provisions which could lead to a tax charge when the deferred share rights are amended and therefore their use has greatly declined.

SECTION 3
Share issues and allotments

889 The terms "issue" and "allotment" are used to describe the granting of new shares in a company. Although they seem to be used interchangeably, the terms do in fact have slight distinctions in meaning.

"**Allotment**" refers to the moment when a person acquires the unconditional right to be a shareholder (for example, when the directors declare that certain shares have been conferred on a particular person) (s 738(1) CA 1985; restated at s 558 CA 2006 by 1 October 2009). At this stage, the person merely has a contractual right to those shares; they have been allocated to him but he is not yet a shareholder.

"**Issue**" refers to the process by which a shareholder takes shares in a company and this is complete at the moment when the person's name is entered in the register of shareholders (even if no share certificate has been given to him yet). It is at this moment that legal title to the shares is acquired and the person can exercise his rights as a shareholder (*National Westminster Bank plc v IRC* [1994] 3 All ER 1).

In practice, a share is often allotted and issued almost simultaneously. However, the distinction can be relevant. For example, directors require authority to allot shares (s 80 CA 1985; restated at s 549 CA 2006 by 1 October 2009) but the shares must have been issued and not just allotted in order to obtain certain stamp duty tax reliefs (ss 75, 76 FA 1986; *Crane Fruehauf Ltd v IRC* [1975] 1 All ER 429). For the relevance of the distinction in relation to bonus shares see ¶1030.

> MEMO POINTS For **capital gains tax purposes**, shares are treated as issued when they are allotted under a letter of allotment, unless the right to the shares conferred by the letter remains provisional until accepted and there has been no acceptance (s 288(5) TCGA 1992).

890 At the **formation** of a company, at least one share will automatically be allotted to the "subscribers" to the memorandum and articles. These are known as the subscriber shares. There is no requirement to issue further shares and a company can continue indefinitely with the subscriber shares being the only shares in issue. However, it is likely that at some point a company will need or wish to issue further shares.

New shares are **created** by shareholders, but the **power** to issue and allot those shares rests with the directors. This power is not unlimited; shares must be issued for a proper purpose (see ¶929). In practice, shares are issued with a variety of consequences. For example, shares can be issued to:
– directors/employees giving them a stake in the growth of the company;
– funders in return for them financing the company; or
– family members of existing shareholders spreading wealth across a family.

891 Subject to its articles and observance of the relevant statutory and regulatory provisions, a company can allot and issue shares with whatever rights and restrictions it may wish at any time from incorporation to winding up (for example, see reg 2 TA 1985).

> MEMO POINTS Draft **new model articles** under the **new Companies Act** have been published for private companies limited by shares and public companies. They will include an equivalent provision (private companies limited by shares: art 22; public companies: art 42).

I. Methods of issue

896 There are certain **statutory provisions** and procedures to which a company must have regard when allotting and issuing any shares. It is always possible for further procedural provisions to be set out in the **memorandum**, **articles** or in a **shareholders' agreement** and so reference must always be made to these documents.

A. Pre-issue considerations

898

Subject to any additional provisions in the company's memorandum, articles or in any shareholder resolutions or agreement to which the company is a party, there are five issues with which a company must be concerned before an issue or allotment can occur:
– whether the company has sufficient **authorised share capital** divided into the appropriate classes (¶900+);
– if **new classes** are to be created, whether the shares have the appropriate rights (¶914+);
– whether the **directors** have **authority** to allot the shares (¶921+);
– whether any **pre-emption rights** apply to the allotment (¶940+); and
– whether the issue conforms to the **regulatory requirements** concerning offers to the public, prospectuses and financial promotions (¶984+).

> MEMO POINTS The **new Companies Act** will change the law relating to authorised share capital and directors' authority to allot shares in particular. Follow the relevant cross-references for details.

1. Alteration of authorised share capital

900

A company is not permitted to issue shares over the level of its authorised share capital (see ¶712). So, if a company had an authorised share capital of £100 divided into 100 shares of £1 each and had already issued 100 shares, it would not have enough authorised share capital to issue any more. If the level of authorised share capital is insufficient for new shares to be issued, it will need to be **increased** and, if it is not **divided** into the appropriate classes of share, the increase will have to take this into account.

> EXAMPLE A Ltd's authorised share capital is £100 divided into 100 ordinary shares of £1 each. The authorised share capital could be changed in a number of ways, such as:
>
> 1. Increased to £1,000 by the creation of 900 ordinary shares of £1 each. The authorised share capital would then be £1,000 divided into 1000 ordinary shares of £1 each; or
> 2. Increased to £1,000 by the creation of 9,000 preference shares of 10p each. The authorised share capital would then be £1,000 divided into 100 ordinary shares of £1 each and 9,000 preference shares of 10p each.

> MEMO POINTS The **new Companies Act** will abolish the concept of authorised share capital for new companies, by 1 October 2009. For existing companies, the concept of authorised share capital will remain, but it will operate as a restriction set out in the company's articles rather than its memorandum. This means that the shareholders will be able to remove the restriction by passing a special resolution to that effect. However, it is anticipated that transitional arrangements will be put in place when the relevant provisions come into force to allow shareholders to remove it by ordinary resolution.

An **undertaking** by the company **not to exercise** its **statutory powers** to increase its share capital is unenforceable (*Russell v Northern Bank Development Corp Ltd* [1992] 3 All ER 161). However, there is nothing to prevent existing shareholders from contracting to this effect between themselves (for example, in a shareholders' agreement), as the increase can only occur if the shareholders pass the required resolution.

901

Procedure

904

A company may increase its authorised share capital if it is **authorised by** its articles to do so (s 121(1) CA 1985) and companies incorporated under Table A have the requisite authority (reg 32 TA 1985). The increase must be **approved by** the shareholders passing an ordinary resolution (s 121(2)(a) CA 1985).

> MEMO POINTS Private companies may use the statutory **written resolution** procedure in lieu of a meeting (¶3580+). Private and public companies may not be able to rely on a written resolution procedure in their articles, as the resolution must be passed at a general meeting of the

shareholders (see ¶3588) (s 121(4) CA 1985). In the absence of a meeting or written resolution, the **informal unanimous consent** of the shareholders will be sufficient (see ¶3590+).

Filing

907 A company must file Form 123 at Companies House within 15 days of passing a resolution to increase its authorised share capital (s 123 CA 1985). This will notify Companies House of the increase, the classes of share affected and any conditions to which the shares are subject when issued. Form 123 must be accompanied by:
– a copy of the resolution (this is one of the few occasions when an ordinary resolution has to be filed at Companies House) (s 123(3) CA 1985); and
– a copy of the revised memorandum setting out the new share capital (s 18(2) CA 1985).

909 **Failure** to comply with the filing requirements renders the company and any officers in default liable to a fine (see ¶9935).

2. New share rights

914 If the new shares are intended to have **different rights** from the company's existing shares, it will be necessary to specify the rights attached to those shares.

Share rights can be **set out in** one or more of the memorandum, the articles or a resolution of the shareholders (such as the resolution to alter/increase the authorised share capital). In practice, share rights are usually set out in the articles but, if there is a conflict between the rights set out in the memorandum and any other document, the rights set out in the memorandum prevail (*Guinness v Land Corporation of Ireland Ltd* (1882) 22 Ch D 349).

> MEMO POINTS When the relevant provisions of the **new Companies Act** come into force (expected to be by 1 October 2009), the memorandum will no longer contain this sort of information. For existing companies, any share rights set out in the memorandum will be treated as if they were included in the articles (s 28 CA 2006). Therefore, any conflicts between the memorandum and articles will no longer be an issue.

915 The **memorandum and articles** are public documents and each amendment to them must be filed at Companies House. If special rights attached to a share are not contained in the memorandum, articles or resolutions filed at Companies House, a statement of those special rights must be filed on Form 128(1) each time the shares are allotted (s 128(1) CA 1985 as amended by para 1 Sch 4 SI 2007/2194). This means that a company will have to make a filing when it creates the shares and again each time it makes an allotment. In addition, Form 128(3) will have to be filed each time those rights are varied and Form 128(4) each time the share class is renamed (s 128(3), (4) CA 1985).

In order to avoid multiple filings, it is common to amend the articles to incorporate the new share rights at the same time as the shares are created.

In any event, the result is that share rights should easily be determined by carrying out the appropriate searches at Companies House.

> MEMO POINTS 1. **Failure** to comply with the requirements relating to registering the particulars of special rights at Companies House renders the company and every officer in default liable to a fine (¶9935).
> 2. Similar requirements and penalties apply where a **company without a share capital** creates a class of members by giving them special rights (s 129 CA 1985 as amended by para 1 Sch 4 SI 2007/2194; restated at ss 638-640 CA 2006) by 1 October 2009).
> 3. Under the **new Companies Act** limited companies will have to notify Companies House of each new allotment and, amongst other matters, the rights attaching to those shares (s 555 CA 2006, expected to come into force by 1 October 2009; regs 10, 11 draft Companies (Shares, Share Capital and Authorised Minimum) Regulations 2007). An unlimited company will only have to notify Companies House if the new allotted shares have different rights to any previously allotted shares (s 556 CA 2006, expected to come into force by 1 October 2009).
> 4. The name of Forms 128(1), 128(3) and 128(4), like the names of other **Companies House forms**, are taken from the section numbers of the legislation. As all of the section numbers will change under the new Companies Act, Companies House proposes to change the names of all

Where there is a desire or need to keep the nature of share rights private, a **shareholders' agreement** is often drawn up. A shareholders' agreement is a contract between named shareholders (and often also the company) and is, therefore, only really practical in a small private limited company with few shareholders and a minimum likelihood of share transfers. They are particularly common in joint venture companies, to protect the shareholders' investment and involvement in the company's management (see ¶6600+ for a discussion of shareholders' agreements in this context). The provisions within it can only be enforced by and against those parties that have agreed to be contractually bound by it. It is therefore common practice for the articles and shareholders' agreement to mirror each other in terms of rights that attach to particular shares and are intended to transfer with them (for example, the right to dividends, pre-emption rights etc) but leave provisions that are personal to the parties (for example, the right to be a director, the business of the company etc) solely to the shareholders' agreement (see ¶2086+).

916

3. Directors' authority

When is authority required?

The actual allotment of shares is carried out by the directors, provided they are authorised to do so. The **general rule** is that authority is required for all allotments of shares or the grant of any right to subscribe for, or convert any security into, shares.

921

The only **exceptions** are (s 80(2)(a) CA 1985; restated at s 549 CA 2006 by 1 October 2009):
a. allotments of shares under an employees' share scheme (or any right to subscribe for or convert any security into such shares). However, it would be prudent to assume that the directors will require authority if the allotment (or rights) are renounced or assigned;
b. allotments pursuant to a right to subscribe for shares or convert any security into shares where the grant of that right was authorised; and
c. allotment of the subscriber shares(s).

Comment: The circumstances in which the directors require authority to allot are the same as when the statutory pre-emption provisions apply. There is also some similarity in the situations in which they do not apply. See ¶945+.

> MEMO POINTS 1. The usual **meaning of "subscribe"** is to take shares for cash (*Government Stock and Other Securities Investment Co v Christopher* [1956] 1 All ER 490). Therefore, authority is not required where the right to subscribe for shares is granted in return for non-cash consideration. However, the directors would need to be authorised to allot those shares when the right was exercised. It would therefore be prudent to ensure that the authority covered both the grant of a right and the allotment pursuant to that grant (see also ¶931).
> 2. Under the **new Companies Act**, the directors of a private company with only one share class will be able to allot shares, grant rights to subscribe for those shares, or grant rights to convert any security into those shares, without prior authority, subject only to any prohibition in the articles (s 550 CA 2006, expected to come into force by 1 October 2009). However, it is anticipated that transitional arrangements will be put in place so that any authorities which exist when the Act comes into force will continue to have legal effect.

Form of authority

The authority can be general or specific, unconditional or conditional (s 80(3), (4) CA 1985; restated at s 551 CA 2006 by 1 October 2009):
– the **maximum amount** of shares to which the authority relates; and
– **when** the authority **expires**.

923

The **length of time** for which the directors may be authorised cannot be more than 5 years from when the authority is given. In the case of companies whose articles contain the authority from incorporation, it is treated as having been given on the date of incorporation. In all other situations, it is treated as having been given on the day on which the authorising resolution is passed.

Private companies can decide that alternative provisions apply regarding the length of time for which the authority may be given by passing an elective resolution to that effect (s 80A(1) CA 1985) (see ¶3562+). If a private company has made such an election, its directors can be authorised for an indefinite period or for any fixed length of time as stated in the authority (s 80A(2) CA 1985). It appears that a two stage process is envisaged; firstly, the company must pass the elective resolution and secondly, the directors can be given authority for a longer period of time.

Comment: This is the only remaining elective resolution. Companies will not have the option to pass an elective resolution under the **new Companies Act**, but it is anticipated that transitional arrangements will preserve any existing elective resolutions when the relevant provisions come into force (expected to be by 1 October 2009).

MEMO POINTS In so far as the authority relates to the **granting of rights** rather than an actual allotment, the relevant maximum amount is the amount of shares to be allotted pursuant to those rights (s 80(6) CA 1985; restated at s 551 CA 2006 by 1 October 2009). There may be a practical problem where the amount of shares to be allotted under a right is not certain (for example, it is to be calculated on the basis of a formula). The exact amount of shares may not be known until the date of allotment and so it may not be possible to determine whether the granting of the right comes within the maximum amount of the authority. In such circumstances, it would be prudent to ensure that either the maximum was well in excess of the estimated amount of shares to be allotted or that there was a cap on the amount of shares which could be allotted pursuant to the right.

Authorisation procedure

925 The directors must be **authorised by** either the shareholders in a general meeting or the articles (s 80(1) CA 1985; restated at s 549 CA 2006 by 1 October 2009). Therefore, the authority can be:
– set out in the articles of the company from incorporation;
– contained in any new articles adopted by the company after incorporation; or
– given by the shareholders passing an ordinary resolution (even if the ordinary resolution alters the articles (s 80(8) CA 1985; restated at s 551 CA 2006 by 1 October 2009)).

MEMO POINTS See ¶921/mp for changes under the **new Companies Act** for private companies with only one share class. For other existing companies, it is anticipated that transitional arrangements will preserve any authority that is already in place when the relevant provisions come into force (expected to be by 1 October 2009).

926 In all cases, the shareholders can also by ordinary resolution **vary** or **revoke** an authority at any time or **renew** an authority on its expiry (s 80(4)-(5) CA 1985; restated at s 551 CA 2006 by 1 October 2009). The renewal must state or restate the maximum amount of shares to which it relates or, as the case may be, the amount remaining to be allotted under it. It must also state when the renewed authority expires (or if relevant, that it is for an indefinite period).

927 Any ordinary resolution to give, vary, revoke or renew the directors' authority **must be filed** at Companies House within 15 days of the resolution being passed (s 80(8) CA 1985 as amended by para 1 Sch 4 SI 2007/2194; restated at s 551 CA 2006 by 1 October 2009.).

Exercise of authority

929 Where the directors are authorised to make the allotment, they are under **duties** to promote the company's success for the benefit of the shareholders as a whole and to act within their powers, exercising them for a proper purpose (see ¶2376+, ¶2378+). The court has not strictly defined the meaning of "**proper purpose**", as this could place inappropriate restrictions on the directors' powers. The question will therefore be decided upon the facts of each case and what is found to be the substantial purpose of the particular allotment, giving credit to the management opinions of the directors (*Howard Smith Ltd v Ampol Petroleum Ltd* [1974] 1 All ER 1126). However, case law has given some guidance.

Primarily, the power to allot is given to directors to enable them to raise capital for the company's use, but it can be used for **other purposes**. For example in *Teck Corporation Ltd v Millar* ((1973) 33 DLR (3d) 288), a Canadian case approved in *Howard Smith Ltd v Ampol Petroleum Ltd*

([1974] 1 All ER 1126)), Teck had acquired the majority shareholding in Afton Mines Ltd and had the intention of replacing Afton's board with its own nominees so that the two companies could sign a joint venture contract which would be extremely lucrative for Teck. The board of Afton, in order to prevent this, signed a joint venture contract with another company and, as was common in such deals, issued that company with a number of shares in Afton, the effect of which was to remove Teck's majority. The court found that the directors had not acted improperly because their motive was to prevent Teck from obtaining the lucrative contract for itself, not to defeat Teck's attempts to obtain control.

An issue of shares purely for the purpose of **creating voting power** or defeating the wishes of the existing majority is an improper exercise of powers (*Punt v Symons & Co Ltd* [1900-3] All ER Rep Ext 1040; *Hogg v Cramphorn Ltd* [1966] 3 All ER 420) unless, as in *Teck Corporation Ltd v Millar* above, protecting the interests of the company is at the core of the decision (*Cayne v Global Natural Resources plc* [1984] 1 All ER 225).

Directors' self-interest is not a proper purpose. Where there is self-interest, the directors cannot assert that they thought in good faith that the allotment was in the best interests of the company (*Hogg v Cramphorn Ltd* [1966] 3 All ER 420). However, the mere fact that the directors derived some benefit from the allotment would not invalidate one that was made in good faith (*Mills v Mills* (1938) 60 CLR 150; *Teck Corporation Ltd v Millar* (1973) 33 DLR (3d) 288; *Cayne v Global Natural Resources plc* [1984] 1 All ER 225). At the same time, even though most successful cases alleging an improper purpose involve self-interest, an allotment made where there is no self-interest will not automatically be for a proper purpose (*Howard Smith Ltd v Ampol Petroleum Ltd* [1974] 1 All ER 1126).

In practice, directors should always take care to ensure that they address their minds to the reasons for the allotment, that those reasons are an appropriate exercise of their powers and that their proper motives are recorded, for example, in the minutes of the board meeting at which the allotment is approved.

> MEMO POINTS   Note that although these directors' duties are now codified into statute, case law on the **interpretation** of the common law versions of the duties is still relevant to interpreting the codified versions (s 170 CA 2006).

Exceeding authority

Non-renewal

If an allotment is made (or subscription or conversion rights are granted) after an authority has **expired** and not been renewed, the directors will still be **deemed** to have had the required authority, provided (s 80(7) CA 1985; restated at s 551 CA 2006 by 1 October 2009):
a. the allotment (or the granting of the right) is made pursuant to an offer or agreement to allot shares (or grant rights) that was made by the company before the authority expired; and
b. the expired authority allowed the directors to make an offer or agreement which would or might require shares to be allotted (or rights granted) after the authority expired.

Presumably, the amount of shares to be allotted would also have to fall within the limits of the expired authority.

The concept of deemed authority does not expressly extend to situations where the directors' authority has been **revoked**. It is therefore considered that the directors would not be authorised to allot shares under a prior offer or agreement if their authority was revoked (in other words, through positive action by the shareholders) rather than if the authority simply lapsed through non-renewal (that is, through lack of action by the shareholders).

931

Breach of legislation

If the legislative requirements are breached (that is, if an allotment is made without the necessary directors' authority or if the appropriate resolutions are not passed and filed at Companies House), any **director** that knowingly or wilfully committed the breach or permitted or authorised it is guilty of a criminal offence and is subject to a fine (s 80(9) CA 1985; restated at s 549 CA 2006 by 1 October 2009) (¶9935).

In such a situation, the **validity of the allotment** itself would not be affected (s 80(10) CA 1985; restated at s 549 CA 2006 by 1 October 2009). Nevertheless, an allotment of shares without

933

Improper purpose

935 An allotment of shares by the directors that is made for improper purposes (for example, to dilute a minority shareholding) may result in the following **consequences**:
a. it may be set aside on an application by an aggrieved shareholder (*Bamford v Bamford* [1969] 1 All ER 969; *Howard Smith Ltd v Ampol Petroleum Ltd* [1974] 1 All ER 1126) unless:
– the allotment is subsequently ratified by the shareholders (which must not itself be a misuse of majority powers (*Clemens v Clemens Bros Ltd* [1976] 2 All ER 268)); or
– the allotment has been made to a person who has subscribed for the shares in good faith and without notice of the breach by the directors of their fiduciary duties;
b. it may form the basis of a claim for unfair prejudice by an aggrieved shareholder (¶2105+); and/or
c. it may lead to the disqualification of a director (*Re Looe Fish Ltd* [1993] BCLC 1160).

4. Pre-emption rights

940 The term "pre-emption rights" refers to the **rights of existing shareholders** to be offered shares in a company before they are offered to an external party. Accordingly, prior to any allotment, the directors must consider whether any pre-emption rights apply, in which case the shares they are proposing to allot would first need to be offered to the existing shareholders in accordance with the relevant pre-emption provisions.

a. Basis of rights

942 Pre-emption provisions are prescribed by **legislation** (ss 89-94 CA 1985; restated at ss 560-577 CA 2006 by 1 October 2009). The statutory provisions apply to most allotments but all companies can exclude them (see table at ¶958). In practice, such exclusions are common as the statutory provisions are considered to be cumbersome. Frequently, where they have been excluded (whether in relation to all or part of an allotment), alternative pre-emption provisions can be found in the **articles** which must be followed instead.

Shareholders' agreements also commonly set out pre-emption provisions. Such provisions are usually intended to take precedence over both the statutory provisions and any provisions in the articles (if they are different from the shareholders' agreement). In order to give effect to the provisions in a shareholders' agreement, the shareholders will have to exclude their statutory pre-emption rights formally and waive any pre-emption rights under the articles. Such a waiver is usually found in the shareholders' agreement.

Statutory pre-emption rights

Application

945 Except as set out below, the statutory pre-emption provisions apply to all **allotments** of shares (s 94(2) CA 1985; restated at s 560 CA 2006 by 1 October 2009). They also apply to the **granting of a right** to subscribe for shares (which means take shares for cash) and a right to convert securities into shares.

Comment: These are the same circumstances as those in which the directors require authority to allot shares (¶921).

946 The statutory provisions **do not apply** to an allotment (or grant of subscription or conversion rights):
a. for **non-cash consideration** (s 89(4) CA 1985; restated at s 565 CA 2006 by 1 October 2009) (see ¶1123+ for the distinction between cash and non-cash consideration);

b. of shares whose rights to dividends and on a return of capital are capped at a specified amount and are not convertible into shares with uncapped rights (s 94(5)(a) CA 1985). This includes most non-convertible **preference shares**. Under the **new Companies Act**, the statutory pre-emption provisions will not apply to convertible preference shares either (s 560 CA 2006, expected to come into force by 1 October 2009);
c. of shares under an **employees' share scheme** (s 94(5)(b) CA 1985; restated at s 566 CA 2006 by 1 October 2009). The exclusion applies even if the right is renounced or assigned to another person (s 89(5) CA 1985; restated at s 566 CA 2006 by 1 October 2009);
d. of **bonus shares** (s 94(2) CA 1985; restated at s 564 CA 2006 by 1 October 2009); and
e. of the **subscriber shares** (s 94(2) CA 1985; restated at s 577 CA 2006 by 1 October 2009).

> MEMO POINTS 1. Where **shares are allotted for non-cash consideration**, the payment structure should be made in good faith. If it was adopted for the sole purpose of avoiding the statutory provisions (for example, by specifying a minimal non-cash element to the payment or by use of a "cash box company", in other words by carrying out a share for share exchange with a shell company for whose shares the proposed allottee subscribed instead), the allotment (or granting of rights) runs the risk of being successfully **challenged**. The court may find that it was entitled to:
> – pierce the corporate veil of any cash box company (*Adams v Cape Industries plc* [1991] 1 All ER 929; *Acatos & Hutcheson plc v Watson* [1995] 1 BCLC 218);
> – set aside the transaction as a sham (*Furniss v Dawson* [1984] 1 All ER 530; *Gisborne v Burton* [1988] 3 All ER 760); and/or
> – find that an aggrieved shareholder was unfairly prejudiced.
> 2. The statutory pre-emption provisions apply to **preference shares with uncertain participation rights** because the rights are not capped at a "specified amount". For example, preference shares with a preferential dividend rate of 10% of distributable profits are not capped to a specified amount, as the actual amount could vary without limit. Where share rights are uncertain in this way, it is possible to bring them within the exception by specifying a maximum monetary limit to the share right.
> 3. There is another exception to the statutory pre-emption provisions for **public companies** which are subject to pre-emption provisions imposed on them before either 22 June 1982 or the date of their application to register/re-register the company as a public company (if the application was made before 22 June 1982). The pre-1982 pre-emption requirements can be contained in any document (for example, memorandum, articles or shareholders' agreement). The statutory pre-emption requirements do not apply to shares that are subject to pre-1982 pre-emption requirements (apart from those relating to how the pre-emption offers must be made and how long they must be kept open for acceptance) (s 96(1)-(2) CA 1985; restated at s 576 CA 2006 by 1 October 2009).

Procedure

948 If the statutory provisions apply, before the directors may allot shares or grant a relevant right in respect of any shares, as appropriate, they must first offer them to the existing shareholders.

The first step is to decide **when** the pre-emption offer should be sent out. Secondly, the directors must determine **to whom** the pre-emption offer should be made. A company is entitled to choose a date up to 28 days before the offer to determine which shareholders are entitled to receive it. For example, if an offer is to be made on 1 April, the company could choose any date between 5 March and 1 April (inclusive). Supposing the date of 10 March were chosen, the shareholdings as at 10 March would determine who was entitled to receive the offer (s 94(7) CA 1985; restated at s 574 CA 2006 by 1 October 2009).

949 Thirdly, the **proportionate entitlements** of the shareholders as at that date must be determined. The pre-emption offer must be made to holders of all shares (excluding those whose rights to dividends and on a return of capital are capped to a specified amount) pro rata to the nominal value of the shares held by them as a proportion of the total nominal value of all of the shares with uncapped rights. If the shares cannot be divided exactly, the entitlements can be rounded so that the division is as proportionate as practicable (s 89(1)(a) CA 1985; restated at s 561 CA 2006 by 1 October 2009).

> EXAMPLE A Ltd wishes to allot 100 "C" ordinary shares. The statutory pre-emption provisions apply. The existing shareholders at the relevant date are:
> – Mr X who holds 200 "A" ordinary shares of £1 each;
> – Mr Y who holds 150 "B" ordinary shares of 50p each; and
> – Mr Z who holds 50 preference shares of £2 each.

1. Identity of offeree
The 100 "C" ordinary shares should be apportioned between Mr X and Mr Y only; as a holder of shares with capped rights, Mr Z is not entitled to any of the "C" ordinary shares.

2. Proportionate entitlements
Mr X's shares have a nominal value of £200 and Mr Y's shares have a nominal value of £75. The total relevant nominal value is therefore £275.
The 100 "C" ordinary shares are divided between Mr X and Mr Y on a pro rata basis using the following formula.

$$\frac{\text{Nominal value of individual's shares}}{\text{Total nominal value of relevant shares}} \times \text{Total no. of shares to be allotted} = \text{Pro rata entitlement}$$

For Mr X: $\frac{£200}{£275} \times 100 = 72.7 = 73$ "C" ordinary shares

For Mr Y: $\frac{£75}{£275} \times 100 = 27.3 = 27$ "C" ordinary shares

950 The offer must be made **in writing** and sent to the relevant shareholder. If the shares are jointly owned, the offer should be sent to the first name in the register of shareholders. If the shareholder has died or been declared bankrupt, the offer should be sent to the person claiming to be entitled to the shares, such as the shareholder's personal representative or trustee in bankruptcy (s 90(4)(a) CA 1985).

Communication of a pre-emption offer to a shareholder can be made:
a. by personal delivery (s 90(2) CA 1985);
b. by post (s 90(2) CA 1985);
c. in electronic form (Pt 3 Sch 5 CA 2006);
d. by means of a website (Pt 4 Sch 5 CA 2006);
e. in any other way agreed with the intended recipient (Pt 5 Sch 5 CA 2006); or
f. by publication in the *Gazette* (s 90(5) CA 1985) if it cannot be made in electronic form, by means of a website or in any other agreed way and:
– the shareholder has not provided the company with an address; or
– the shareholder is a company without a UK registered office.

See ¶3695+ for details of how companies can communicate with shareholders, explained in the context of giving notice of shareholder meetings.

> MEMO POINTS When the provisions of the **new Companies Act** governing pre-emption offers come into force (expected to be by 1 October 2009), a company will be able to make the offer in hard copy or electronic form using the methods described at ¶3695+ (ss 562, 1168, 1144(2), Sch 5 CA 2006). In addition, the company will be able to make an offer by publishing it in the *Gazette* (or publishing a notice specifying where a copy of the offer can be obtained or inspected) if the offer is to be made to (s 562(3) CA 2006):
> – a shareholder who does not have registered address in an EEA state and has not given the company an address in an EEA state for the service of notices on him; or
> – the holder of a share warrant.
> The new Companies Act also requires any documents to be sent to a shareholder's personal representative or trustee in bankruptcy in the event of his death or bankruptcy (para 17 Sch 5 CA 2006).

951 The **address** of the shareholder for the purposes of **personal or postal** delivery is (s 90(2) CA 1985):
– in the case of corporate shareholders, its registered office in the UK; and
– in all other cases and if the corporate shareholder has no registered office in the UK, whatever address has been supplied by the shareholder for the giving of notices.

If the shareholder does not have a UK registered office and/or has not provided the company with an address, a notice of the offer should be placed in the *Gazette* (s 90(5) CA 1985).

In the case of offers following a shareholder's death or bankruptcy, if no address has been provided by the person claiming to be entitled to the shares, the offer must be sent to the appropriate address of the original shareholder (s 90(4) CA 1985).

If the offer is made by post, **service** of the notice is deemed to take place at the time at which the letter would be delivered in the ordinary course of post (s 90(2) CA 1985; restated at s 562 CA 2006 by 1 October 2009). If the offer is made personally, service of the notice will take place at the time of delivery and presumably, if notice is given in the *Gazette*, service will be deemed to have taken place on the date of publication.

> **MEMO POINTS** 1. The **deemed postal service** provision is vague, in that it is not clear when a letter would be delivered in the "ordinary course of post". However, the new Act specifies that, subject to any contrary provisions in the articles, service by post is deemed to occur 48 hours after posting (not counting non-working days) (s 1147(2) CA 2006). It is likely that the CA 1985 rules will be interpreted in accordance with this new provision even though it does not specifically apply until the provisions of the new Act dealing with pre-emption offers come into force (expected to be by 1 October 2009).
> 2. The presumption that service by post has occurred is normally rebuttable if the actual facts show that **service had not occurred** (see s 7 Interpretation Act 1978; *Re Thundercrest Ltd* [1995] 1 BCLC 117). However, in the case of a pre-emption notice, the presumption may be irrebuttable, i.e. service will be deemed to have occurred even if the shareholder can prove that the letter was never received (*R v Westminster Unions Assessment Committee, ex parte Woodward and Sons* [1917] 1 KB 832).

The offer must state the **length of time** for which it is **open for acceptance**, which must be at least 21 days, not including the date the offer is made or deemed to have been made (s 90(6) CA 1985; restated at s 562(4), (5) CA 2006 by 1 October 2009). **952**

The persons to whom a pre-emptive offer has been made are entitled to **accept** the offer, **reject** it (either expressly or by not responding to it) or, depending upon the terms of the offer, **renounce** it in favour of another person. If an offer is accepted or renounced, the company can allot the shares to the relevant person without delay (s 89(4) CA 1985; restated at s 561(2) CA 2006 by 1 October 2009). Other than those allotments, the company must wait for the close of the acceptance period or for all offers to be accepted or expressly rejected before any allotments to other parties can be made (s 89(1)(b) CA 1985; restated at s 561(1)(b) CA 2006 by 1 October 2009). **953**

b. Exclusion of pre-emption provisions

Statutory provisions

Companies may **exclude or disapply** the statutory provisions using the methods set out in the table below (not all of the methods are available to public companies). In practice, most **private companies** expressly exclude the statutory provisions in their articles as this is the easiest method of exclusion. For all **public companies** and for private companies where a blanket exclusion is not appropriate, the statutory provisions can be disapplied in particular cases instead. The disapplication is linked to the directors' authority to allot or grant rights in shares, that is, the directors are given authority and the statutory provisions are disapplied in respect of allotments made under that authority. **958**

Method	Private Companies	Public Companies	Reference (CA 1985)[1]	¶¶
Express exclusion in memorandum or articles	✓	✗	s 91(1)	¶960
Exclusion implied by alternative provisions in articles	✓	✗	s 91(2)	¶962
Directors given power to disapply statutory provisions (where directors generally authorised to allot or grant rights in shares)	✓	✓	s 95(1)	¶964
Shareholders disapply statutory provisions for particular allotment (where directors generally or specifically authorised to allot or grant rights in shares)	✓	✓	s 95(2)	¶966+

Note:
1. By 1 October 2009, when the relevant provisions of the **new Companies Act** are expected to come into force, these references will be ss 567, 570, 571 CA 2006.

> *MEMO POINTS* 1. As to each shareholder's entitlement to **waive** their statutory pre-emption rights, see ¶973+.
> 2. Under the **new Companies Act**, the directors of a private company that has only one class of shares may be given power by the articles or by a special resolution to allot shares of that class as if the statutory pre-emption provisions did not apply, or applied with modifications (s 569 CA 2006, expected to come into force by 1 October 2009).

Express exclusion

960 Private companies **can exclude** the statutory provisions concerning (s 91(1) CA 1985; restated at s 567 CA 2006 by 1 October 2009):
- the requirement to make a pro rata pre-emption offer;
- the way in which the offer is communicated; and/or
- the length of time for which the offer must be open for acceptance.

The express exclusion **can apply to** all allotments or to allotments of a particular description (for example, all allotments of ordinary shares).

The exclusion is **made by** a provision to that effect in the articles (although it could be included the memorandum). Many private companies do in fact exclude the statutory provisions in this way and substitute alternative pre-emption rights can often be found in the articles instead.

Implied exclusion

962 Sometimes, the statutory provisions are entirely or partly substituted by pre-emption **provisions in** the **articles** without an express exclusion of the statutory provisions. In private companies, to the extent that there are any inconsistencies between the articles and the statutory provisions, the articles prevail and the relevant statutory provisions are treated as being excluded (s 91(2) CA 1985; restated at s 567 CA 2006 by 1 October 2009).

> *MEMO POINTS* For private companies, any pre-emption provisions contained in documents other than the memorandum and articles (such as a shareholders' agreement or resolution) that had been imposed on the company **before 22 June 1982** are treated as if they were contained in the memorandum and articles (s 96(3) CA 1985; restated at s 576(3) CA 2006 by 1 October 2009). The same applies to public companies that were not incorporated as such, but only in so far as the provision requires offers to be made to holders of shares in the same class (s 96(4) CA 1985; restated at s 576(4) CA 2006 by 1 October 2009).

Directors' power to disapply

964 Where the directors are **generally authorised** to allot (or grant rights in) shares, they can be empowered to make allotments (or grant rights) under that authority as if the statutory provisions did not apply (s 95(1) CA 1985; restated at s 570 CA 2006 by 1 October 2009). The directors can be given the power to disapply the statutory provisions in their entirety or with whatever modifications the directors think fit. They can be given this power in the articles or by special resolution. Usually the articles are modified or the resolution is passed at the same time as the directors are given the authority to allot (or grant rights in) the shares.

Shareholder resolution to disapply

966 This route is most relevant to **public companies** because it is too procedurally complex for private companies in most cases.

Where the directors are generally or specifically authorised to allot (or grant rights in) shares, shareholders can by special resolution resolve that the statutory provisions do not apply to a **particular allotment** (or granting of rights) (s 95(2) CA 1985; restated at s 571 CA 2006 by 1 October 2009). The resolution can disapply the statutory provisions in their entirety or can apply them with specified modifications.

The special resolution must be recommended by the directors who must circulate a **written statement** with the notice of the meeting at which the resolution is to be proposed. In a private company, if the resolution is to be passed using the written resolution procedure, the statement must be supplied to each shareholder signing the written resolution at the same time or before he is given the resolution for signature (para 3 Sch 15A CA 1985; restated at s 571(7)

CA 2006 by 1 October 2009). The statement must set out (s 95(5) CA 1985; restated at s 571(6) CA 2006 by 1 October 2009):
– the reasons for the directors' recommendation;
– the amount to be paid to the company for the shares that they propose to allot; and
– their justification of that amount.

967 Any disapplication ceases to have effect when the relevant **directors' authority** is **revoked** or **expires**. If the directors' authority is **renewed**, the disapplication of the statutory provisions can also be renewed by special resolution for up to the same length of time for which the directors' authority is renewed (s 95(3) CA 1985; restated at s 571(3) CA 2006 by 1 October 2009). If the renewal is of a special resolution which required the directors' recommendation, the special resolution to renew must also be recommended by the directors and a written statement setting out the same items as before must again be circulated (s 95(5) CA 1985; restated at s 571(5) CA 2006 by 1 October 2009).

Normally, if any disapplication of the statutory requirements ceases to have effect and is **not renewed**, allotments must be made in accordance with the statutory provisions. However, the disapplication is still deemed to have effect if the allotment (or right granted) is (s 95(4) CA 1985; restated at s 571(4) CA 2006 by 1 October 2009):
– made pursuant to an offer or agreement to allot (or grant rights in) shares that was made by the company before the disapplication ceased to have effect; and
– the disapplication allowed the directors to make an offer or agreement which would or might require shares to be allotted (or rights granted) after the disapplication ceased to have effect.

Provisions in the articles

970 Where alternative provisions are contained in the articles, they can be **amended by** special resolution (see ¶450+). If the pre-emption rights differentiate between classes of shares, they will amount to a class right (*Re Smith of Smithfields Ltd* [2003] EWHC 568 (Ch)). The amendment of provisions in the articles will therefore need to be approved by each class of shareholder.

Waiver

973 It is always open to a particular shareholder to waive his **contractual** pre-emption rights (for example, rights in the articles or in a shareholders' agreement) by notice to the company. The waiver can relate to a particular allotment or can be a more general waiver of all future pre-emption rights of that shareholder.

> MEMO POINTS Since, the articles take effect as a **deed** (s 14(1) CA 1985; restated at s 33(1) CA 2006 by 1 October 2009), it is recommended that the waiver is also executed as a deed (insofar as it relates to pre-emption provisions in the articles).

974 It is considered that a waiver is not sufficiently effective to exclude or disapply the **statutory** provisions, although it is debatable whether a shareholder who does waive his statutory entitlements would later be entitled to rely on any technical breach by the company of the statutory requirements. Therefore, shareholders wishing to waive their statutory requirements should simply reject the statutory pre-emption offer when made.

If all shareholders intend to waive their statutory entitlements, the statutory provisions should be excluded or disapplied in accordance with the procedure set out above (¶958+). However, even if the statutory provisions are not properly excluded or disapplied, it may still be sufficient to show that all of the shareholders consented to the exclusion or disapplication (see ¶3590+).

c. Breach

978 If an allotment is made in breach of the **statutory** pre-emption provisions, the company and every officer who knowingly authorised or permitted the allotment are jointly and severally liable to compensate any person for any loss, damage, costs or expenses suffered by them as a result of the breach (s 92 CA 1985; restated at s 563 CA 2006 by 1 October 2009).

Any person who knowingly or recklessly permits the inclusion of **misleading, false or deceptive material in a statement** that is circulated by the directors to support a special resolution to disapply the statutory provisions is liable to imprisonment or a fine, or both (s 95(6) CA 1985; restated at s 572 CA 2006 by 1 October 2009; ¶9935).

979 If an allotment is made in breach of pre-emption provisions in the **articles and/or** of the **statutory** pre-emption provisions, other remedies may also be available. For example:
– the allotment could be held to be invalid (*Re a Company (No 005134 of 1986), ex parte Harries* [1989] BCLC 383);
– an aggrieved shareholder could apply for rectification of the register of shareholders (*Re Thundercrest Ltd* [1995] 1 BCLC 117); and/or
– the allotment could form the basis of a claim for unfair prejudice by a shareholder (*Re a Company (No 005134 of 1986), ex parte Harries*, above).

5. Regulatory compliance

984 The regulatory framework governing issues of shares to non-shareholders is complex and is dealt with at ¶4800+. There are three quite separate regulatory concerns to be considered, governed by three different pieces of legislation and companies must ensure that each has been individually satisfied. The three concerns are:
a. private companies may not **offer shares to the public** (¶986+);
b. all companies must consider whether the proposed share issue amounts to an offer to the public that requires the preparation of a **prospectus** (¶995). An "offer to the public" in this context is defined by another piece of legislation and is different from the definition that private companies need to consider in point a. above. It is an unlikely but theoretical possibility that a private company could legitimately make an offer to the public that required the preparation of a prospectus; and
c. in all cases, an issue of shares in a company, whether or not to the public, is likely to involve a "**financial promotion**" (¶998). In some circumstances, it will need to be approved by an authorised person.

These regulatory requirements are primarily designed to catch large issues to perhaps unsophisticated investors. They do not apply where an issue is made to **existing shareholders**.

Offers to the public

986 **Private companies** are prohibited from directly or indirectly offering shares to the public (s 81(1) CA 1985; restated at s 755(1) CA 2006 as of 6 April 2008). Generally, offers to one or more **existing shareholders, employees, and their families** do not constitute an "offer to the public". Most approaches by private companies to potential subscribers of shares fall within these narrow categories. **Offers to other persons** falling outside these groups, for example, as payment for the purchase of an asset (for example, shares in another company, land or a business) or in return for venture capital finance are acceptable if the offer is made only to one person or is non-renouncable and may not be sold in the short term.

Comment: From 6 April 2008, when the relevant provisions of the **new Companies Act** are due to come into force, a private company will not be in breach of these restrictions if (s 755(3) CA 2006):
– it acts in good faith in pursuance of arrangements under which it is to re-register as a public company before the securities are allotted; or
– it undertakes, as part of the offer, to re-register as a public company within 6 months of the offer first being made and complies with that undertaking.

Direct offers

988 The offer could be as simple as a letter inviting someone to subscribe for shares but there is no actual requirement for it to be **in writing** and, therefore, an **oral** offer would appear to be sufficient.

In this context, an "offer to the public" is one that is **made to** more than one person. The offer does not have to be made to the public at large; it can be restricted to a section of the public or to particular persons. However, it is considered that a single person does not constitute a "section" of the public (s 742A(1) CA 1985; restated at s 756(2) CA 2006 as of 6 April 2008; *Nash v Lynde* [1929] AC 158).

The following are not offers to the public:
a. an offer to **persons connected** with the company making the offer, provided that if it is renounceable, it can only be renounced in favour of another connected person. The relevant connected persons are:
– an existing shareholder;
– an existing employee;
– the widow, widower, civil partner (current or surviving), spouse or child (including step-children) of an existing or past shareholder or employee and their descendants;
– the trustee of a trust, the beneficiaries of which are any of the above people; or
– an existing debenture holder;
b. an offer to subscribe for shares to be held under an **employees' share scheme** provided that if renouncable, the offer may only be renounced in favour of another person entitled to hold shares under the scheme; or
c. an offer where the **shares remain unavailable** for subscription or purchase (whether directly or indirectly) by a person other than the one receiving the offer, e.g. a non-renouncable offer for shares that may not be sold in the short term.

Comment: From 6 April 2008, when the relevant provisions of the **new Companies Act** are due to come into force, an offer will not be an "offer to the public" if (s 756 CA 2006):
– it is not calculated to result in shares or other securities of the company becoming available to anyone other than those receiving the offer;
– it is the private concern of the person receiving it and the person making it;
– the shares are to be held under an employees' share scheme, and the offer may only be renounced in favour of another person entitled to hold shares under the scheme or a person already connected with the company; or
– it is made to persons connected to the company and it may only be renounced in favour of another connected person (see ¶9931).

Indirect offers

It can be seen that it would be quite easy to circumvent the prohibition by use of an intermediary, such as an existing shareholder. Instead of making an offer to the public, a private company could allot shares to the intermediary who could then sell those shares to the public. In order to prevent this, legislation also prohibits allotments of shares or agreements to allot shares to someone with a view to those shares being sold to the public (s 81(1)(b) CA 1985; restated at s 755(1)(b) CA 2006 as of 6 April 2008).

There is a rebuttable **presumption** that an allotment of shares or agreement to allot shares had been made with a view to the shares being offered for sale to the public if it is shown that (s 58(3) CA 1985; restated at s 755(2) CA 2006 as of 6 April 2008):
– an offer for the sale of the shares to the public was made within 6 months after the allotment or agreement to allot; or
– at the date when the offer for the sale of the shares to the public was made, the company had not yet received all of the payment for the shares.

Breach

An **allotment** by a private company in breach of these provisions remains valid, as does any agreement to allot or sell shares (s 81(2) CA 1985; restated at s 760 CA 2006 as of 6 April 2008). However, the **company** and any **officer** in default are liable to a fine (¶9935). In addition, the company may be wound up by the court on the grounds of public interest on a petition by the secretary of state (*Re UK-Euro Group plc* [2006] EWHC 2102 (Ch)).

Comment: From 6 April 2008, when the relevant provisions of the **new Companies Act** come into force, a private company will no longer commit an offence if it offers its securities to the public. Instead, it may be compelled to re-register as a public company or be wound up (s 758 CA 2006). In addition, shareholders, creditors or the secretary of state may apply to court for an order to restrain the company from carrying out any proposed allotment in contravention of the prohibition (s 757 CA 2006). The court will also have the power to make "remedial orders" to put any person affected by the contravention back into the position they would have been in had it not occurred (s 759 CA 2006). This includes ordering any person involved in the contravention (such as a director or the company itself) to purchase the shares themselves. If the company is ordered to purchase the shares, the court will be able to provide for a reduction in share capital.

Requirement for prospectus

995 Regardless of whether or not it is listed, **any company** that offers shares to the public in the UK may be required to issue a "prospectus". An "offer to the public" in this context is much wider than in the context of the prohibition on private companies and will incorporate most offers.

There are, however, a number of available **exemptions** which most unlisted companies will be able to utilise. In particular, a prospectus is not required if the offer:
– it is made to less than 100 persons; or
– is for a bonus issue or stock dividend.

The requirement for a prospectus is dealt with in more detail at ¶4845+.

Financial promotions

998 An offer to take shares in a company may need to be approved by an authorised person. Approval is required of "financial promotions" which, in this context, is any **communication** that invites or induces a person to take shares in a company (s 21 FSMA 2000). This would cover any letter or application form sent to potential allottees and any written or oral representations made to encourage a person to take shares.

Again, there are a number of detailed **exemptions** which should be available in most cases (SI 2005/1529). The exemptions are complex and should be referred to carefully to ensure that they apply to the particular circumstances. In broad terms, they include where the communication is made:
– to an investment professional (reg 19 SI 2005/1529);
– to existing creditors or shareholders (reg 43 SI 2005/1529);
– for the purposes of an employees' share scheme (reg 60 SI 2005/1529); or
– in connection with the sale or purchase of a controlling interest in a company with connected shareholders (reg 62 SI 2005/1529).

The rules governing financial promotions are dealt with at ¶4825+.

B. Specific types of issue

1008 A share issue is the process by which shares in a company are allotted and issued to shareholders. It can take a variety of **forms** dictated by the circumstances in which the issue is taking place. It is not possible to list all of them but, for example, a relatively straight-forward issue would consist of an issue of ordinary shares to an existing shareholder in return for cash. A more complex issue would consist of different classes of shares being issued to several non-shareholders in return for some sort of non-cash consideration, such as shares in another company.

Share issues often take place in the context of a larger transaction such as the re-financing of a company, the acquisition of another business or an employee incentive plan. These may involve consideration of other factors and procedures. However, regardless of complexity or context, the procedure for the issue itself follows the same path and depends on whether the consideration is to be cash or non-cash.

The **procedure** is dealt with at ¶1068+.

Although the rules governing an issue are uniform, there are some particularities if the issue is being carried out by way of a **bonus issue** (¶1013+), **rights issue** (¶1042+) or **loan capitalisation** (¶1053+).

1. Bonus issue

a. What is a bonus issue?

1013

A bonus issue is an issue of shares by a company, usually to its existing shareholders and usually on the basis that no payment is or will be required from the allottee.

The term "bonus" may imply a gift by the company but this is not the case; a company may not give its shares away. Instead, the company **capitalises its available reserves and profits**. This means that it uses its reserves and undistributed profits to pay towards all or part of the subscription value of the bonus shares which will, when issued, form part of its share capital. Another term for a bonus issue is therefore a "**capitalisation issue**" and sometimes the term "**scrip issue**" is used. In effect, a bonus issue allows the issued share capital to be increased without any actual cash or non-cash assets being paid into the company.

There is no limit on the class of shares that may be issued, nor is there a requirement for the bonus shares to be of the same class as the shares that are already issued (*White v Bristol Aeroplane Co Ltd* [1953] 1 All ER 40).

The **procedure** for a bonus issue is dealt with at ¶1068+.

> MEMO POINTS In certain circumstances, a company may also capitalise its available profits to pay towards the nominal value of **existing partly paid shares** (see ¶1029). This would be outside of the definition of "capitalisation" for the purposes of calculating distributable profits (s 280(2) CA 1985; restated at s 853 CA 2006 as of 6 April 2008; see ¶1612).

b. Reasons for a bonus issue

1018

A bonus issue is useful in a number of situations:
a. a bonus issue of ordinary shares can be used to make sure that a company's share capital more accurately **reflects** its **asset value**. It will have the effect of diluting the market value of each ordinary share but each shareholder will still retain his proportionate shareholding provided the bonus issue is made on a pro rata basis. The result is that the shares may be more marketable;
b. a bonus issue of preference shares can **transfer value** out of the ordinary shares. Ordinary shares can therefore be issued at par or at a much lower premium than would otherwise have been the case;
c. a bonus issue of redeemable shares is a way of **returning capital** to the shareholders;
d. a bonus issue of preference shares which are renounced in favour of third parties for cash or sold to a third party following the issue can allow shareholders to **raise finance** without diluting control of the company; or
e. a company may need to increase its issued share capital for **trading reasons**. For example, a private company may be considering changing its status to a public company and therefore needs to increase its issued share capital.

c. Pre-issue checks

1023

A bonus issue requires consideration of all the standard pre-issue checks (see ¶898+). In addition, a company will need to check:
– the availability of reserves and profits;
– that the company has the power to capitalise;

Availability of reserves and profits

1025 A company may only capitalise available reserves and profits. There are four funds which could constitute available reserves or profits:
- **distributable profits** (s 263(3) CA 1985; restated at s 830 CA 2006 as of 6 April 2008) (see ¶1612+);
- **non-distributable profits**;
- **share premium account** (s 130(2) CA 1985; restated at s 610 CA 2006 by 1 October 2009) (see ¶1245+); and
- **capital redemption reserve** (s 170(4) CA 1985; restated at s 733 CA 2006 by 1 October 2009) (see ¶1360+).

A company must identify that it has sufficient profits or reserves before a capitalisation. If, by mistake, a company attempts to capitalise profits or reserves which do not exist, the bonus issue will be void (*Re Cleveland Trust plc* [1991] BCLC 424).

> MEMO POINTS 1. **Non-distributable profits** could be created by a revaluation of fixed assets. The revaluation would have to have been made in good faith by competent valuers and should not be liable to short term fluctuations (*Dimbula Valley (Ceylon) Tea Co Ltd v Laurie* [1961] 1 All ER 769). Such a revaluation could be particularly useful in a company with insufficient distributable profits but an undervalued asset base.
> 2. Under the **new Companies Act**, a company which has redenominated and renominalised its shares resulting in the creation of a "redenomination reserve" will be able to capitalise that reserve (s 628(2) CA 2006, expected to come into force by 1 October 2009) (see ¶1326/mp).

Power to capitalise

1027 A company must be **authorised** to capitalise its profits and/or reserves by its articles (*IRC v Blott* [1921] 2 AC 171; *IRC v Wright* [1927] 1 KB 333). If a company is **not authorised**, its articles will need to be amended to include express authority.

Companies incorporated under Table A, assuming their articles have not been updated, are authorised to capitalise certain funds, as summarised below.

Date of incorporation	Reference	Funds
On or after 1 Jul 1985	reg 110 TA 1985	Distributable and non-distributable profits (to the extent not required to pay preferential dividend) Share premium account Capital redemption reserve
22 Dec 1980 – 30 Jun 1985 (inc.)	regs 128, 128A, 129 TA 1948 as amended by CA 1980	Distributable and non-distributable profits and reserve accounts (including share premium account and capital redemption reserve)
On or before 21 Dec 1980	regs 128, 129 TA 1948	Distributable profit and reserve accounts (including share premium account and capital redemption reserve)

> MEMO POINTS The same provision providing authorisation for a company to capitalise its profits and/or reserves will be included in the draft **new model articles** (private companies limited by shares: art 36; public companies: art 77).

Form of capitalisation

1029 A capitalisation may take the form of a bonus issue of **fully or partly paid shares** to existing or new shareholders. Usually, a bonus issue consists of fully paid shares being issued to existing shareholders. In such a case, under Table A, any of the four funds may be capitalised although there are limits on other forms of capitalisation.

Distributable profits may only be used to fully pay up bonus shares which are to be allotted to existing shareholders and/or towards paying up any amounts unpaid on the shares of existing shareholders. If required, the articles may be amended to allow for the bonus issue of partly paid shares to existing shareholders (but not to new shareholders) (ss 263(2), 280(2)(a) CA 1985; restated at ss 829(2), 853(3) CA 2006 as of 6 April 2008).

Non-distributable profits may only be used to fully pay up bonus shares which are to be allotted to existing shareholders. However, the articles may be amended so that non-distributable profits could be used for other purposes, for example, to partly pay for bonus shares and/or for those shares to be allotted to non-shareholders.

The **share premium account** and **capital redemption reserve** may also only be used to fully pay up bonus shares which are to be allotted to existing shareholders. However, these provisions reflect statutory restrictions which cannot be derogated from by an amendment to the articles.

MEMO POINTS   Under the **new Companies Act**, a company will be able to use its "redenomination reserve" (see ¶1326/mp) to allot fully paid up bonus shares to existing shareholders (s 628(2) CA 2006, expected to come into force by 1 October 2009).

The **differentiation between allotment and issue** is significant for bonus issues. A company only needs the power to pay up shares which are to be allotted to existing shareholders rather than necessarily also being issued to them. This means that a company may pay up shares to which existing shareholders become unconditionally entitled to be allotted under a bonus issue (i.e. shares which are allotted to them) even if the existing shareholders renounce those shares in favour of another person (i.e. the shares are actually issued to another person). **1030**

MEMO POINTS   For companies incorporated on or before 21 December 1980 and operating under an unamended **Table A 1948** the share premium account and capital redemption reserve may only be used to fully pay up bonus shares which are to be issued to existing shareholders.

Where a bonus issue is made of **partly paid shares**, the allottee must be able to decline the bonus issue if he wishes to do so. This is because the holder of partly paid shares is liable to pay the remainder of the nominal value to the company, for example if there were a shareholder call or on a winding up. The proposed allottee of a partly paid bonus issue must be given the option as to whether or not he wishes to assume this liability. **1031**

Procedural limitations

The power to capitalise as set out in **Table A** is also subject to the following procedural limitations but in all cases, the particular **articles** of a company should be consulted to see if different or further limitations have been imposed: **1033**

a. the capitalisation must be **approved** by an ordinary resolution of the shareholders. However, there is nothing to prevent the articles of a company from being amended to give the directors authority to capitalise without the need for shareholder approval or the need for a special resolution instead; and

b. the capitalised sum must be **apportioned** between the existing shareholders as if it were being distributed by way of dividend. This too may be altered by an amendment of the articles.

d. Tax considerations

Specific tax considerations may arise on a bonus issue as follows: **1037**

a. in general, a bonus issue is not a **distribution** for the purposes of company or tax law (see ¶1769+ for further detail on the taxation of distributions). However, for tax purposes, a bonus issue may be treated as a distribution if:
– the company repays share capital and subsequently or simultaneously makes a bonus issue of shares (s 210(1) ICTA 1988);
– the company makes a bonus issue and subsequently makes a distribution in respect of the same type of share capital (s 209(2)(b) ICTA 1988); or
– it is a bonus issue of redeemable share capital (s 209(2)(c) ICTA 1988);

b. a bonus issue to employees of the company (including directors who work for it) may be considered to be an issue of "**employment related securities**" and so may be subject to income tax (Pt 7 ITEPA 2003);

c. there will be a **capital gains tax** disposal if a proposed allottee sells his rights nil paid (i.e. before they are allotted to him); and
d. there may be an **income tax** charge under the transactions in securities tax legislation (ss 703-709 ICTA 1988).

2. Rights issue

What is a rights issue?

1042 A rights issue is usually an issue of ordinary shares made to existing shareholders in proportion to their existing shareholdings and, in contrast to a bonus issue, the allottees are required to pay cash for the shares. In other words, the existing shareholders are given the "right" to subscribe for shares.

In order to encourage shareholders to take up their "rights", the **subscription price** (i.e. the amount that must be paid to the company for each share) is usually lower than the market price of the share.

The **procedure** for a rights issue is dealt with at ¶1068+.

Reasons for a rights issue

1044 A rights issue is carried out to raise funds for the company's use. It is therefore usually found in larger companies with a wide shareholder base. However, it should be remembered that share issues must be carried out for a **proper purpose** (¶929). A rights issue, even though offered to all shareholders on a proportionate basis, may be challenged if it was being carried out for an improper purpose. For example, this could be to dilute a minority shareholding where it was known that certain shareholders could not afford to take up their rights or to reduce the funds of a shareholder when he needed money to pursue a claim against the company (Re a Company [1985] BCLC 80).

Typically, **funds** raised by way of a rights issue are **used to**: pay off borrowings; provide working capital; or, pay for acquisitions of other companies and/or businesses.

Excess applications

1046 On a rights issue, it is possible to give shareholders the ability to apply for any excess shares (i.e. any shares that are not taken up by other shareholders). There are legitimate **reasons** for a rights issue to be conducted in this manner. The company is usually aware that a particular shareholder or group (e.g. the director/shareholders) is willing to apply for the excess and it can therefore be confident that all of the rights will be taken up and the company will raise the full amount that it requires. On the other hand, where excess applications are accepted, the shares will not be issued on a proportionate basis. In some circumstances, there may be scope to argue that the rights issue had not been carried out for a proper purpose (¶929).

Pre-issue checks

1048 A rights issue requires the standard pre-issue checks (¶898+). This includes a check of any **pre-emption provisions**, even though a rights issue is normally made to existing shareholders on a proportionate basis.

3. Loan capitalisation

What is a loan capitalisation?

1053 The term "loan capitalisation" refers to the conversion of borrowing to equity, in other words, when a company turns its loans into share capital. This has an improving effect on the balance sheet as it reduces borrowings.

[MEMO POINTS] Capitalisation in this context does not fall within the definition in the legislation dealing with **dividends and distributions** (s 280(2) CA 1985, restated at s 853 CA 2006 as of 6 April 2008; see ¶1612).

Procedure

The "conversion" is brought about simply by allotting shares to the company's creditor in return for that creditor releasing the company from its liability to repay the loan. The **class of shares** to be allotted will depend upon the degree of involvement the creditor requires. For example, if the loan being capitalised is from a director who is already an ordinary shareholder, it may be appropriate to allot further ordinary shares. If the loan is from an outside investor, it may be more appropriate to allot **non-redeemable preference shares** as they do not affect control of the company.

1055

[MEMO POINTS] **Redeemable preference shares** used to be an attractive form of raising finance because they were classified on the company's balance sheet as equity rather than debt. However, now such shares have to be treated as a financial liability (i.e. as debt) where the terms of redemption provide for mandatory redemption by the company, or give the holder the right to require the company to redeem the shares. They will only be treated as equity where the terms of redemption do not require the company the redeem the shares, for example, if redemption can only ever occur at the company's option (FRS 25(17), (18)).

The loan capitalisation process is the same as a standard issue of shares; however, the consideration in this case is release from the loan. This would normally mean that the procedure would follow an issue for non-cash consideration which is more complex, particularly for public companies (see ¶1142+). It is therefore common to **structure** the procedure so that it is actually an issue for cash consideration. This is done by an exchange of payment between the company and the creditor: the company repays the loan at the same time as the creditor pays the subscription price for the shares.

1056

Tax considerations

Special rules apply when property (for example, shares) is received in satisfaction of a debt. The original creditor is treated as disposing of his debt, which will generally not give rise to any **capital gains tax** and the base cost of the shares will be limited to the lower of the value of the loan or the market value of the shares.

1058

If, on a subsequent disposal of the shares, the shareholder realises a gain, the chargeable gain will be restricted to the gain that would have accrued if he had acquired the property for consideration equal to the debt.

C. Issue procedure

There are four main stages to a share issue:
– **pre-issue checks** (¶1070);
– passing **shareholder resolutions** (¶1073+);
– **allotment** (¶1079+); and
– **post-allotment** administration (¶1086+).

1068

The procedure is slightly different, depending upon whether it is being carried out for **cash or non-cash consideration** (see ¶1123+ for the distinction between the two). The cash consideration procedure applies only when all of the shares are to be paid for in cash; if even part of the consideration is not cash then the non-cash consideration procedure applies. There are also particularities for **bonus** and **rights issues** which are referred to below.

1. Pre-issue checks

1070 The pre-issue checks which must be carried out **depend upon** the type of issue that is being undertaken, as the following table illustrates.

	¶¶	Cash issue	Non-cash issue[1]	Bonus issue	Rights issue
Does the company have sufficient **authorised share capital** divided into the appropriate classes?[2]	¶900+	✓	✓	✓	✓
If new shares are created, do they have appropriate **class rights**?	¶914+	✓	✓	✓	✓
Are the **directors authorised** to allot the shares?	¶921+	✓	✓	✓	✓
Do any **pre-emption provisions** apply and are the allotments going to be made in accordance with them?[3]	¶940+	✓	✓	✓[2]	✓
Is an "**offer to the public**" going to be made, is a **prospectus** required or are any **financial promotions** being made that require approval?	¶984+	✓	✓	✓	✓
Are there **sufficient profits and/or reserves**?	¶1025			✓	
Is the **company authorised** to make the issue by its articles and is the form of the issue within that authority?	¶1027 ¶1029+			✓	
Does the issue need specific **shareholder approval**?	¶1033			✓	
Does the allotment to a director or person connected to him require **disclosure of director's interest**?	¶3308+	✓	✓	✓	✓
Does the allotment to a director or person connected to him amount to a **substantial property transaction**?	¶2567+		✓		

Note:
1. There are particular restrictions on **public companies** allotting shares for non-cash consideration. In certain cases, an independent valuation of the non-cash consideration may be required and the valuation may need to be approved by an ordinary resolution of the shareholders, see ¶1142+.
2. The **new Companies Act** will abolish the concept of authorised share capital by 1 October 2009.
3. Only need to consider contractual **pre-emption provisions** in the company's articles or other agreement; there is no need to consider statutory pre-emption provisions.

2. Shareholder resolutions

1073 Once the pre-issue checks have been carried out, it may become apparent that certain shareholder resolution(s) will have to be passed before the allotment can occur.

If all of the shareholders are contactable and agree to the resolution(s), the company may be able to use the **written resolution procedure** (¶3580+). In all other cases, the board will need to convene a **general meeting** of the shareholders in order that the required resolutions can be put to them (¶3620+). To save time, it may be possible to call the meeting on short notice (¶3681+).

> MEMO POINTS 1. In the case of an issue for non-cash consideration by a public company, the company may need to obtain a **valuation of the non-cash** asset which in some circumstances may also need to be approved by the shareholders (see ¶1142+).
> 2. As well as passing the relevant shareholder resolutions, the directors may also need to procure that the shareholders **waive** their **pre-emption rights** (see ¶973+).

1074 After the meeting (assuming the resolutions are passed) or after the written resolutions are signed, the following **administrative matters** will need to be dealt with:
a. the minutes of the general meeting (or original written resolutions) will need to be filed with the company's records;

b. the following Companies House filings, as appropriate, will need to be made within 15 days of the resolution(s) being passed:
– Form 123 (increase in share capital);
– ordinary resolution to increase authorised share capital;
– print of memorandum showing new authorised share capital;
– elective resolution to increase duration of directors' authority;
– ordinary resolution to give directors authority to allot;
– special resolution to disapply statutory pre-emption provisions;
– special resolution to adopt new articles;
– print of amended articles;
c. any resolution which amended the articles must be incorporated into future prints of the articles. It is recommended that copies of the resolutions are also attached to existing prints; and
d. copies of any resolution to alter/increase the share capital must be attached to existing prints of memorandum and the resolutions must be incorporated into future prints.

> MEMO POINTS   When the relevant provisions of the **new Companies Act** come into force (expected to be by 1 October 2009), the requirements relating to increasing the authorised share capital will no longer be relevant.

3. Allotment

An allotment is usually **initiated by** the board, either by making an offer to the proposed allottee(s) to allot shares to them or by inviting them to apply for shares.

1079

In the most straightforward of cases (such as a small company with identical directors and shareholders making an allotment to existing shareholders for cash), this process will only be implicit; the parties will agree **orally** what allotments are to be made and simply proceed with issuing the shares.

In less straightforward situations, it is best practice (and sometimes necessary) to record the process **in writing**. The terminology used to describe the documents in the process varies depending upon the circumstances:
a. an **application form** is a short form used for cash and rights issues. It is sent to the allottee by the board for him to complete and return, together with payment for the shares;
b. an **allotment letter** is used for bonus issues. It is a letter from board which informs the allottee that a specific number of shares have been allotted to him. The letter may indicate that the allotment is renounceable or is provisional upon the proposed allottee's acceptance (in the case of partly paid bonus shares);
c. a **circular** is a detailed document setting out the reasons for an issue, financial information about the company and an explanation of the rights of the issue shares (e.g. dividend expectations). It is appropriate for issues by larger companies when a prospectus is not required; and
d. in cases involving non-cash consideration, a bespoke **contract** between the allottee and the company is normally required.

> MEMO POINTS   A **renounceable allotment** means that the proposed allottee is permitted to nominate another person to whom the shares should be issued instead of himself. Renounceable allotments are more usual in public companies. Private companies that make an allotment on a renouncable basis should take care to limit the group of persons in whose favour the shares can be renounced (see ¶986+).

Allotments can only be **made after** the necessary shareholder resolutions have been passed. However, where there is some urgency (for example, in the case of a rights issue being carried out to provide the company with a crucial cash injection), the process to obtain the necessary shareholder resolutions is often run together with the allotment process. This means that the proposed allottees are sent their documentation at the same time as the notice of the general meeting/written resolutions are sent to the shareholders. If this option

1080

118   SHARES AND SHARE CAPITAL   © FL Memo Ltd

is taken, the documents sent to the proposed allottees will need to make clear that the allotment is conditional upon all the relevant shareholder resolutions being passed. If the shareholder approvals are not obtained, the board will need to return any payments received to the proposed allottees. This will not be treated as a return of capital to shareholders as no allotment would actually have been made.

1081 This table summarises the procedure to be followed depending upon the type of issue under consideration.

Cash issue	Non-cash issue	Bonus issue		Rights issue
		Non-renounceable	Renounceable	
Board sends application forms to proposed allottees ↓	Board sends contract to proposed allottees for signature ↓	↓	Board sends renounceable allotment letters to proposed allottees ↓	Board sends application forms to proposed allottees (and, if appropriate, invites excess applications)[2] ↓
On return of forms, board meeting to approve allotments	On return of contract, board meeting to: – authorise director(s)/ secretary to execute contract on behalf of company; and – approve allotments	Board meeting to approve allotments. Board sends allotment letters to allottees.[1]	At end of renunciation period, board meeting to approve allotments	At end of acceptance period, board makes allotments taking account of original allotments, renunciations and excess applications

Note:
1. Where the **bonus issue is of partly paid shares**, the allottee will need to accept the allotment (see ¶1031). In such cases, a provisional allotment letter should be sent out and the board meeting to approve the allotments should be held at the end of the acceptance period.
2. In rare cases, a **prospectus** may be required instead (¶995). In larger companies, even where a prospectus is not required, it usual to send shareholders a "**circular**" which sets out more information such as the reasons for the rights issue, the financial and trading state of the company, dividend expectations etc.

1082 **Notice of meetings** must be given to all those entitled to receive it, in hard copy, electronic form or on a website (s 308 CA 2006; ¶3695+). In **other situations**, the company can communicate with shareholders and others in hard copy, electronic form, via a website or by any other method agreed with the recipient (in which case, the information will be validly supplied to the recipient if it is sent as agreed (para 15 Sch 5 CA 2006). See ¶3628 for a discussion on how proposed allottees can communicate with the company.

4. Post-allotment

1086 Within 2 months of the board making the allotments, appropriate **share certificates** should be sent to the allottees and their details should be entered in the **register of allotments** and **register of shareholders**.

1087 Depending upon the type of issue, the documents in the table below will need to be **filed at Companies House**.

All of the forms must be filed **within** 1 month of the date that the first allotment is made. If the allotments are going to take place over longer than a month (for example, if there is a longer renunciation period), it will be necessary to file one form per month to cover the allotments made in each month.

	Cash issue	Non-cash[1] issue	Bonus issue	Rights issue
Form 88(2) (return of allotment)	✓	✓	✓	✓
Form 88(3) (particulars of contract)		✓[2]	✓	
A certified copy of the written contract of allotment		✓[3]		
Form 128(1) (registration of special rights)[4]	✓	✓	✓	✓

Note:
1. The company will need to pay **stamp duty** if the consideration for the issue is shares in another company (see ¶1875+) or **stamp duty land tax** if the consideration for the issue is an estate, interest, right or power in or over land in the UK (see ¶5298+).
2. Only if no written contract.
3. Only if there is a written contract. Companies House will also accept the original contract but it is likely that the parties will wish to retain this for their own records.
4. Only if the allotted shares have rights that are not contained in the memorandum, articles or any resolution required to be filed at Companies House.

MEMO POINTS 1. In the case of **public companies**, where a valuation of non-cash consideration is required but does not need shareholder approval, the valuation report must be filed with Form 88(2) or 88(3) as appropriate.
2. Under the **new Companies Act**, the return of allotment will have to include (s 555 CA 2006, expected to come into force by 1 October 2009; reg 11 draft Companies (Shares, Share Capital and Authorised Minimum) Regulations 2007):
– the number of shares allotted;
– how much is paid up and how much is not (if any); and
– if the shares are allotted as fully or partly paid up in non-cash consideration, the consideration for the allotment.
The return will have to be accompanied by a "statement of capital", which will provide a "snapshot" of the company's total issued share capital at a particular point in time (in this context, the date to which the return of allotment is made up). The statement will have to include details of any (reg 10 draft Companies (Shares, Share Capital and Authorised Minimum) Regulations 2007):
– voting rights;
– rights to participate in dividends;
– rights to a return of capital in a winding up; and
– terms and manner of redemption.

D. Failure to allot or issue

An allotment of shares involves a **contract of allotment** between the company and the allottee. The contractual relationship can be initiated by the company sending the allottee an application form, circular or prospectus inviting applications for shares. The nature of the document (and whether the terms are open to negotiation) of course depends upon the circumstances. In any case, in contractual terms, by advertising that it is open to accepting applications for shares, the company is making an "invitation to treat". This means that it is inviting people to make it an offer.

When the allottee makes an application for shares, whether or not in response to an invitation to treat, the **allottee makes an offer**. It is only when this offer is accepted by the company that the contract for allotment is made and becomes contractually enforceable. The allottee has no right to have shares allotted to him by the company unless and until his offer is accepted.

Usually, the company accepts the offer through performance, that is to say by actually making the allotment. However, if no **time limit for acceptance** has been specified, a company cannot wait too long between receiving the application and making the allotment. Applications are made on the understanding that they will be answered promptly and if they are not, the party applying will not be bound by the application (*Re Irish West Coast Railway Co, Carmichael's Case* (1850) 20 LJ Ch 12). It has been held that a gap of 4 months between receipt of

1097

an application form and the actual allotment by the company was too long and the allottee was not obliged to take the shares allotted to him (*Re Bowron, Baily & Co, ex parte Baily* (1868) 3 Ch App 592).

1098 Alternatively, the contractual relationship can be initiated by the **company making an offer** to allot shares, for example, by sending a provisional allotment letter. In such a case, the contract for allotment is formed by the allottee accepting the offer within the required time period, for example, by returning the allotment letter with payment for the shares.

If no **time limit for acceptance** is specified, as where the offer is made by the allottee, the potential allottee should not wait too long before accepting it as it may be withdrawn or be deemed to have lapsed.

In cases where the company has made an **unconditional offer**, acceptance by the allottee gives him the unconditional right to those shares. Technically, this is when the allotment is made (see definition of allotment at ¶889) but in practice, such allotments are usually formally confirmed at a subsequent board meeting.

> MEMO POINTS Inaccurate or incorrect statements made by a company to induce someone to enter into a contract for allotment could amount to an actionable **misrepresentation**.

1099 Once an allotment has been made, the allottee has a contractual right to be issued with the shares in accordance with the terms of the contract. If the **shares are not issued** following an allotment, the allottee can claim specific performance and/or damages. Damages may also be available if there is a **delay in the issue** as this amounts to a delay in the performance of the contract of allotment (*Sri Lanka Omnibus Co Ltd v Perera* [1952] AC 76).

If the allottee is **not sent a share certificate** within 2 months of an allotment, he can serve notice on the company requiring one to be sent to him (s 185(6)-(7) CA 1985; restated at s 769 CA 2006 as of 6 April 2008). If the company fails to send a share certificate within 10 days of receiving a notice, the allottee can apply for a court order. The court has the discretion to order that the costs of the application should be borne by the company or by any defaulting officer.

II Payment

1110 One of the consequences of the doctrine of capital maintenance (¶703) is that a company must be able to obtain value for its issued shares. Taking shares in a company therefore incurs the **liability to pay up** those shares using an appropriate **method of payment**. One of the marked differences between public and private companies is that **public companies** have tighter restrictions on the paying up of their shares and the methods of payment which may be used (¶1135+). This gives investors and other creditors added confidence as the company is likely to have a more secure financial base.

In keeping with the idea of obtaining value, where value is not received by a company on allotment, it must be able to obtain that value at a later date. The mechanism which enables a company to do this is known as a "**shareholder call**" and is dealt with at ¶1205+.

It will readily be seen that if a company is to obtain value for its shares, it must not give that value away through the back door. This has lead to the general prohibition on a company giving financial assistance for the acquisition of its shares (¶5557+). There are minor exceptions to this rule relating to brokerage fees and commission payments (¶1237+).

The face value of each share (that is its nominal value) is part of a company's share capital. If a higher value is obtained for a share, the excess forms part of the "**share premium account**" over which there are certain restrictions (¶1245+).

> MEMO POINTS Under the **new Companies Act**, the restriction on private companies giving financial assistance will be lifted. The implementation date for this change is yet to be announced at the time of writing.

A. General principles

Share values

1115 There are a number of different terms used to describe the value of a share. The value attributable to the proportion of share capital is referred to as the "**nominal**" or "**par**" value. For example, if the share capital of a company is £100 divided into 100 shares of £1, each share has a nominal or par value of £1. Since the terms are essentially synonymous, for the sake of consistency, the term "nominal value" is used throughout.

When a share is allotted, the shareholder may pay or agree to pay just the nominal value or a sum above that value. Any extra payment above the nominal value of the share is known as the "**premium**". The nominal value together with any premium is the "**subscription**" price of the share.

The **market value** of a share (which is the amount a willing arm's length purchaser would pay for the share) may, of course, be higher or lower than the nominal value. For listed companies, the market value can be readily ascertained by reference to the relevant stock exchange. For unlisted companies, a market valuation is more difficult and professional accountancy advice will be required.

Paying up

1117 The expression "paying up" **means** paying all or part of the subscription price of a share to the company that issued it. Shares can be:
– "**fully paid up**", where the full subscription price of a share has been paid;
– "**partly paid up**", where only some of the subscription price has been paid; or
– "**nil paid**", where none of the subscription price has been paid.

> MEMO POINTS The draft **new model articles** for private companies limited by shares will require all issued shares to be fully paid (except for subscriber shares) (art 21). There are therefore no provisions relating to shares which are not fully paid, such as calls, liens and forfeiture. Public companies, however, will still be allowed to issue partly paid shares and so associated provisions are included (arts 51-61).

1118 Perhaps surprisingly, there is no obligation that shares must be fully **paid on allotment**; the liability to pay can be left to be fulfilled in the future. There is also no obligation to specify when this liability will crystalise, although sometimes this will be decided at the time of issue by setting out the terms of shareholder calls (see ¶1205+). However, although shares can be issued as partly or nil paid, it is recommended that shares are fully paid up on allotment, unless there is a particular reason not to do so. This does not necessarily mean that the full subscription price has to be paid or satisfied at that time; a contractual obligation to satisfy the full subscription price in the future is sufficient. Shares allotted on the basis that a future contractual obligation will be performed in return for the allotment may be **treated as fully paid up**.

> MEMO POINTS 1. There are certain minimum paying up requirements for **public companies** (see ¶1137).
> 2. A contract that provides for **future payment** will terminate on a winding up and the liquidator can make an immediate call for the unpaid amount (s 80 IA 1986; *Re Cordova Union Gold Co* [1891] 2 Ch 580).

1119 The **benefits of fully paying up** a share are twofold. Firstly, the liability to pay up their shares is the limit of each shareholder's liability with respect to the company (hence the term "company limited by shares"). It follows that a holder of fully paid shares has no further liability in relation to his holding. Shareholders with partly or nil paid shares remain liable to pay the amount unpaid. This liability could crystalise on a shareholder call or a winding up.

The second benefit is that partly or nil paid shares may have restricted share rights as these sometimes depend upon the amount paid up on the share. For example, dividends are usually declared pro rata on the amounts paid up on each share. This means that a share with a nominal value of £1 where only 50p had been paid up would be entitled to half the dividend declared on that share and a nil paid share would not be entitled to any dividend at all.

Discounts

1121 It is **unlawful** to allot a share at a discount (that is, on the basis that the shareholder is liable to pay less than the share's nominal value) (s 100 CA 1985; restated at s 580 CA 2006 by 1 October 2009). The allotment of shares at a discount can be distinguished from allotting shares at their nominal value when a premium could be obtained or allotting shares for less than the maximum premium available. The latter two situations are **lawful** (*Hilder v Dexter* [1902] AC 474). However, when allotting shares, the directors have to be aware of their **fiduciary duty** to obtain the best price they can.

Any **allottee** of a discounted share is liable to pay the company the amount of the discount plus interest at a rate of 5% per year (ss 100(2), 107 CA 1985; restated at ss 580(2), 592 CA 2006 by 1 October 2009). Any **subsequent holder** of the share will become jointly and severally liable with the allottee to pay this amount unless he purchased the share and at the time of the purchase he did not actually know that the shares had been issued at a discount (s 112(1)(a), (3) CA 1985; restated at s 605 CA 2006 by 1 October 2009). Once the shares are purchased by an unknowing third party, the chain of liability is broken. This means that the liability will not pass to future holders of the shares. In addition to the shareholders' liability, the **company** and any **officers** in default are liable to be fined (s 114 CA 1985; restated at s 607 CA 2006 by 1 October 2009) (¶9935).

> EXAMPLE A Ltd has unissued ordinary shares with a nominal value of £1 each and a market value of £2 each, which is the maximum amount that the company could obtain for each share. An issue at:
> 1. Less than £1 is an unlawful issue at a discount.
> 2. £1 is a lawful issue at nominal value when a premium could be obtained, although the directors may be in breach of their fiduciary duties.
> 3. More than £1 but less than £2 is a lawful issue at less than the maximum premium, although the directors may be in breach of their fiduciary duties.
> 4. £2 is a lawful issue at a premium of £1.

> MEMO POINTS The obligation on directors to obtain the best price must be considered in context. For example, on a **rights issue**, it is in fact common practice to issue shares at less than market value.

Method of payment

1123 Both the nominal value of shares and any premium can be paid for in cash consideration, non-cash consideration, or a mixture of the two (s 99 CA 1985; restated at s 582 CA 2006 by 1 October 2009). **Cash consideration** includes payment in a foreign currency and is any payment where (s 738(2), (4) CA 1985):
– cash is actually received by the company;
– payment is made by cheque to the company which the directors in good faith believe will be honoured;
– the company is released from a liability for a specified sum of money; or
– the allottee promises to pay cash to the company.

> MEMO POINTS When the relevant provisions of the **new Companies Act** come into force (expected to be by 1 October 2009), these types of cash consideration will still be valid, along with a payment by any other means giving rise to a present or future entitlement (of the company or a person acting on the company's behalf) to a payment, or credit equivalent to payment, in cash. The categories of payment falling within this definition will be specified by the secretary of state in an order (s 583 CA 2006).
> Except when an allotment is made to existing shareholders under their statutory pre-emption rights, the following payments will be treated as non-cash consideration:
> – the payment of cash to a person other than the company; or
> – an undertaking to pay cash to a person other than the company.

1124 **Non-cash consideration** is a valuable payment in any other form. The term "valuable" in this context does not mean that it must be worth a lot of money; it just means that it must be worth something. Non-cash consideration can consist of tangible assets such as property or shares in another company, or intangible assets such as goodwill, intellectual property or services to the company.

Private companies do not have to obtain an independent **valuation** of any non-cash consideration and, provided that it is not obviously inadequate (which may indicate an issue at a discount or a breach of a director's duties), the directors' decision as to what it is worth will not be open to challenge (*Re Theatrical Trust Ltd, Chapman's case* [1895] 1 Ch 771). In practice, prudent directors of private companies obtain independent valuations, particularly where the consideration has a high value. The consideration will also need to be given a fair and accurate value for the purposes of the company's accounts and valuations may need to be obtained for these purposes.

MEMO POINTS There are restrictions on **public companies** allotting shares for non-cash consideration (see ¶1142+).

The consideration for an allotment cannot be paid by the company nor can it assist the allottee in paying for the shares (for example, by lending money to him). This would be in breach of the general prohibition on a company giving **financial assistance** for the acquisition of its own shares. Private companies can circumvent the prohibition in some circumstances (see ¶5557+).

1125

MEMO POINTS The **new Companies Act** will abolish the prohibition on private companies giving financial assistance and so they will be able to assist the allottee in paying for the shares. The implementation date for this change is yet to be announced at the time of writing.

B. Restrictions on public companies

There are many restrictions on the paying up of shares in public companies. They also apply to **private companies** which have passed a resolution to **re-register as** a **public** company (s 116(a) CA 1985; restated at s 90(1) CA 2006 by 1 October 2009; see ¶662+) and any reference here to public company will include such a private company.

1135

1. Paying up

All public companies are subject to **minimum** paying up requirements so that at least a quarter of the nominal value and the whole of any premium on a share in a public company must be paid up on allotment; it is not possible to leave this liability to be met in the future (s 101 CA 1985; restated at s 586 CA 2006 by 1 October 2009).

1137

If the minimum amount is **not paid up** on allotment, the shares should be treated as if it had been (for example, in the company's accounts and for the purposes of any share rights which depend upon the amount paid up). However, the allottee is still liable to pay the amount unpaid and the company and its officers are liable to be fined (¶9935).

MEMO POINTS The minimum paying up requirements do not apply to an allotment of shares under an **employees' share scheme** (¶847+) (s 101(2) CA 1985; restated at s 586(2) CA 2006 by 1 October 2009).

2. Allotments for non-cash consideration

Public companies have several **restrictions** on their ability to issue shares for non-cash consideration. These restrictions relate firstly to the **type of non-cash consideration** for which shares may be allotted (¶1148) and secondly to the procedural steps which must be taken to **value any non-cash consideration** to be received (¶1152+).

1142

As a result of these restrictions, public companies may be tempted to structure the allotment into a two stage process so that the actual allotment is for cash as in the examples below.

1143

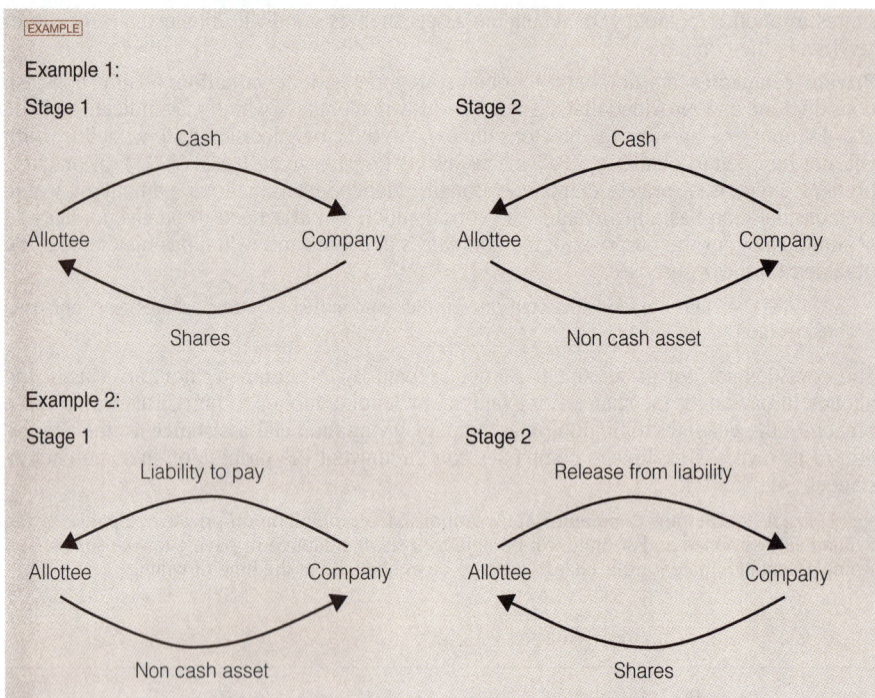

Example 1 shows a two stage process where the cash that the company received for the allotment at stage one is immediately used to purchase the non-cash asset at stage two. Such a structure appears to be accepted in practice (for example in loan capitalisations, see ¶1053+). By contrast, **example 2** envisages that, at stage one, the company purchases the non-cash asset and at stage two, it is released from the liability to pay for it in consideration for the allotment (release from a liability to pay a specified amount of money constitutes cash consideration (see ¶1123)).

Any such split in the process should be carried out with caution. At the very least, two **separate transactions** would have to take place; it would not do to combine them in one set of documentation. However, even then a court may find that it was entitled to look beyond the documentation where the restrictions had been artificially avoided (*Re Bradford Investments plc (No 2)* [1991] BCLC 688).

a. Types of non-cash consideration

1148 The **subscriber shares** together with any premium on them must be paid for in cash (s 106 CA 1985; restated at s 584 CA 2006 by 1 October 2009).

The consideration for **all other shares** cannot:
a. be an **undertaking to work or perform services** for the company or for any other person (s 99(2) CA 1985; restated at s 585 CA 2006 by 1 October 2009); or
b. be or include a **long term undertaking**. A "long term undertaking" is one which is to be, or may be, performed more than 5 years after the date of the allotment (s 102 CA 1985; restated at s 587 CA 2006 by 1 October 2009). Any attempt to vary an otherwise valid contract of allotment to include a long term undertaking is void and the original contract will stand.

For the **consequences of breaching** the above provisions see ¶1185+.

> MEMO POINTS There are similar consequences if an allotment is made in return for a **short term undertaking** which is not in fact performed within the period allowed by the contract between the company and the allottee (see ¶1187/mp).

b. Valuations of non-cash consideration

When is a valuation required?

If a public company proposes to issue shares for non-cash consideration, the consideration must be independently valued **before** the allotment takes place (s 103(1)(a) CA 1985; restated at s 593(1)(a) CA 2006 by 1 October 2009).

The consequences of **failing** to obtain an appropriate valuation are dealt with at ¶1185+.

The allotting company (A Ltd) is **not required** to obtain a valuation:
a. where all or part of the consideration is a **transfer or cancellation of shares** in another company (B Ltd). This includes "share for share exchanges" which are common in acquisition transactions (s 103(3), (4) CA 1985; restated at s 594 CA 2006 by 1 October 2009);
b. where the allotment is made in connection with a **proposed merger** with B Ltd (s 103(5) CA 1985; restated at s 595 CA 2006 by 1 October 2009); or
c. on a **bonus issue** (s 103(2) CA 1985; restated at s 593(2) CA 2006 by 1 October 2009).

1152

1153

MEMO POINTS 1. In the case of a **transfer or cancellation of shares**, the number and class of shares in B Ltd which are transferred to A Ltd (or which are cancelled) in return for the allotment are immaterial. However, all of B Ltd's shareholders must have been entitled to take part in the arrangement to transfer or cancel their shares (or if the transfer/cancellation relates only to a particular class of B Ltd's shares, all of the shareholders in that class must have been so entitled). In determining whether all shareholders have been entitled to take part, shares held by A Ltd, its holding company, subsidiary, holding company's subsidiary or any of their nominees can be disregarded.
2. A **merger** in this context means where A Ltd proposes to acquire all the assets and liabilities of B Ltd in exchange for an issue of shares to the shareholders of B Ltd. Whether or not B Ltd's shareholders also receive a cash payment is immaterial. This type of merger is fairly rare as usually the shares would be allotted to B Ltd rather than its shareholders. It would therefore only usually be found in a scheme of arrangement (¶6500+) or a section 110 reorganisation (¶6465+).

Valuation procedure

Preparing report

The valuation report must be **made to** the company in the 6 months before the allotment (s 103(1)(b) CA 1985; restated at s 593(1)(b) CA 2006 by 1 October 2009) and must be **made by** an independent person qualified to be an auditor of the company (s 108(1) CA 1985; restated at s 1150(1) CA 2006 by 1 October 2009).

1158

The independent person can commission or accept the valuation of an **expert** in respect of all or part of the consideration. However, the expert cannot be connected to the company. In this context, connected means that the expert cannot be an officer or servant of the company or its subsidiaries, or the company's holding company or its subsidiaries, or the partner or employee of such an officer or servant (s 108(2) CA 1985; restated at s 1150(2) CA 2006 by 1 October 2009).

If the company has an **auditor**, he may act as the independent person or as the expert (s 108(1), (3) CA 1985; restated at s 1150 CA 2006 by 1 October 2009).

MEMO POINTS 1. There is no statutory **definition of servant**. It is usually used to describe employees but also extends to agents of the company although not to persons merely engaged to provide services to the company (Re Beeton & Co Ltd [1911-13] All ER Rep Ext 1457).
2. An **example** of a valuation report is available from the Auditing Practices Board, and may be freely downloaded from its website (Bulletin 2007/1, published January 2007).

The independent person and/or expert may **obtain** whatever **information and explanations** he deems necessary from the officers of the company to assist him in carrying out a valuation or preparing the report. Any officer giving false, misleading or deceptive statements to the independent person or expert is guilty of a criminal offence (s 110 CA 1985; restated at s 1153 CA 2006 by 1 October 2009; ¶9935).

1159

Contents of report

1161 Surprisingly, the report need not state the actual value of the non-cash consideration. This is because the **purpose** of the report is to demonstrate that the value being received by the company is adequate. If the value of the non-cash consideration is at least as much as the amount of the nominal value and any premium payable, that is sufficient.

> *MEMO POINTS* The report is only required to refer to the adequacy of the non-cash consideration as against any premium if that **premium** is "**payable**". For example, if shares were to be allotted with a premium of £10 each to be satisfied by the transfer of some property, the premium "payable" would clearly be £10 per share. However, if, as is normally the case, the shares are to be allotted in consideration for the transfer of some property, without the mention of any premium, no premium is "payable" for these purposes. All that the report has to demonstrate in those circumstances is that the non-cash consideration is worth at least the nominal value of the allotted shares.

1162 The independent person's **report must state** (s 108(4), (6) CA 1985; restated at s 596 CA 2006 by 1 October 2009):
– the nominal value of the shares to be allotted;
– the amount of any premium payable;
– a description of the non-cash consideration;
– a description of the non-cash consideration that he valued (if any) and the method and date of valuation;
– the extent to which the nominal value and any premium payable is to be treated as paid up by non-cash consideration and the extent to which it is to be treated as paid up in cash;
– that the independent person considers that the method of valuation was reasonable in all the circumstances;
– that it appears to him that there has been no material change in the value since the valuation; and
– that the value of the consideration together with any cash is not less than the total amount that is to be treated as paid up on the shares.

1163 If an **expert's valuation** has been obtained, the report must also state (s 108(5) CA 1985):
– that an expert's valuation was carried out;
– the name of the expert and his knowledge and experience;
– a description of the non-cash consideration that he valued and the method and date of valuation; and
– that it appeared reasonable to the independent person that the expert's valuation should be made and accepted.

> *MEMO POINTS* When the relevant provisions of the **new Companies Act** come into force (expected to be by 1 October 2009), where an expert's valuation has been obtained, the valuer's report will only have to state that it appeared to the valuer that it was reasonable to arrange for an expert's valuation to be made or to accept a valuation so made by way of additional information (s 596(3) CA 2006).

1164 **If only part of** the non-cash **consideration relates to** the **shares** then the independent person must decide upon the proportion that is attributable to them and he must carry out or arrange for any other valuations that will enable him to make that decision. Any such valuations, the reasons for them, the method and date of valuation and any other matters relevant to his decision must also be set out in the report (s 108(7) CA 1985; restated at s 596 CA 2006 by 1 October 2009).

Distribution and filing

1166 A copy of the report must be **sent to** the allottee before the allotment (s 103 CA 1985; restated at s 593(1)(c) CA 2006 by 1 October 2009). Further, after the allotment, the company must **file** a copy of the report at Companies House with Form 88(2) or 88(3) as appropriate (s 111 CA 1985; restated at s 597 CA 2006 by 1 October 2009). Every officer of a company who breaches this requirement is liable to be fined, although the court does have the power to waive this liability on an application by the officer (¶9935).

> *MEMO POINTS* The name of Forms 88(2) and 88(3), like the names of other **Companies House forms**, are taken from the section number of the legislation. As all of the section numbers will change under the new Companies Act, Companies House proposes to change the names of all of its forms to reflect

their function rather than the relevant section number ("Working with Companies House: a consultation on the registrar's rules and related provisions which will apply under the Companies Act 2006"). At the time of writing, the new form names are not yet available.

3. Transfer of non-cash asset

In certain circumstances, where a public company enters into an agreement with a shareholder for the transfer of a non-cash asset, it must obtain: **1171**
- shareholder approval for the agreement; and
- a valuation report in respect of the asset.

The consequences of failing to obtain a valuation report and/or shareholder approval are dealt with at ¶1185+.

> MEMO POINTS The procedure must be followed whether or not the transfer is made **in consideration of an allotment** of shares, although this is one of the more common reasons for such a transfer to occur. For example, a company could enter into an agreement with one of its shareholders under which the shareholder agreed to transfer a property to the company's subsidiary in return for an allotment of shares in the company. The procedure is similar, though not identical, to those on allotments for non-cash consideration and, of course, there may be situations when both procedures apply.

When do the provisions apply?

Shareholder approval and a valuation report are needed when (s 104(1)-(3) CA 1985; restated at s 598 CA 2006 by 1 October 2009): **1173**

a. the **transfer** is **made by** particular shareholders (or former shareholders). In the case of a public company registered as such from incorporation, these are the subscribers to the memorandum. In the case of a public company which re-registered as such, these are the persons who were shareholders at the date of re-registration;
b. the transfer is **made within** 2 years from the date of its trading certificate; and
c. the **value of** the **consideration** which the company will give to the shareholder in return for the transfer (e.g. the shares which the company will allot him) equals or is more than 10% of the nominal value of the company's issued share capital at the time of the agreement.

> MEMO POINTS Even if the above circumstances are satisfied, the **procedure will not apply** if the acquisition of the asset forms part of the company's ordinary course of business or if it occurs pursuant to a court-authorised agreement (s 104(6) CA 1985; restated at s 598(4) CA 2006 by 1 October 2009).

Procedural requirements

Shareholder approval

Before a public company can enter into an agreement which contemplates a transfer that satisfies the above circumstances, the terms of the **agreement must be approved by** an ordinary resolution of the shareholders (s 104(4)(c) CA 1985; restated at s 601 CA 2006 by 1 October 2009). **1175**

Valuation

In addition, the company must obtain a **valuation report** in respect of both the consideration to be received by the company and any non-cash consideration to be given by the company in return (s 104(4)(a) CA 1985; restated at s 599 CA 2006 by 1 October 2009). In most cases, the asset will be transferred to the company and this will be the consideration it will receive. However, if the asset is actually going to be transferred to another person, the consideration will be the advantage that the company will gain from that transfer (s 104(5)(a) CA 1985; restated at s 599 CA 2006 by 1 October 2009). As with the valuation report that must be obtained on an allotment for non-cash consideration, the actual values need not be stated in the report. The important issue is to confirm that the company is not proposing to give more than it receives. **1177**

> MEMO POINTS An **example** of a valuation report is available from the Auditing Practices Board, and may be freely downloaded from its website (Bulletin 2007/1, published January 2007).

1178 The valuation report must be **prepared** as set out at ¶1158 (ss 104(4)(b), 109(1) CA 1985; restated at s 600(1) CA 2006 by 1 October 2009). The **contents** of the report must state (s 109(2) CA 1985; restated at s 600(2), (3) CA 2006 by 1 October 2009):
– the consideration to be received by the company, describing the asset that will be transferred and specifying any amount that it will receive in cash;
– the consideration to be given by the company in return, specifying any amount to be given in cash;
– the method and date of the valuation;
– that the independent person considers that the method of valuation was reasonable in all the circumstances;
– that it appears to the independent person that there has been no material change in the value since the valuation; and
– that the value of the consideration to be received by the company is not less than the value to be given by it in return.

If an **expert** has been used, then the report must also state the matters referred to at ¶1163 (s 109(1) CA 1985; restated at s 600 CA 2006 by 1 October 2009).

If only part of the consideration to be given by the company relates to the transfer of the asset, then the independent person must decide upon the **proportion** that is attributable to the transfer and he must carry out or arrange for any other valuations that will enable him to make that decision. Any such valuations, the reasons for them, the method and date of valuation and any other matters relevant to his decision must also be set out in the report (s 109(3) CA 1985; restated at s 600(5) CA 2006 by 1 October 2009).

Distribution and filing

1180 A **copy** of the valuation report **must be provided to** the shareholders (and to the person transferring the asset if he is not already a shareholder) before or at the same time as the notice of the shareholder meeting at which the ordinary resolution is proposed (s 104(4)(d) CA 1985; restated at s 599(1)(c) CA 2006 by 1 October 2009).

A copy of the ordinary resolution approving the agreement together with a copy of the valuation report must be **filed at Companies House** within 15 days of it being passed (s 111(2) CA 1985; restated at s 602(2) CA 2006 by 1 October 2009). Every officer of a company who breaches this requirement is liable to be fined (s 111(4) CA 1985; restated at s 602(1) CA 2006 by 1 October 2009; ¶9935).

---

4. Breach of restrictions

1185 A breach of any of the restrictions on public companies has **consequences** for:
– the allottee;
– any subsequent holder of the allotted shares;
– the company and its officers; and
– the enforceability of any related undertaking or agreement.

In some cases, **relief** from liability may be available (¶1192+).

Consequences of breach

1187 An **allottee** who receives shares in breach of any of the restrictions (except for the requirement to pay for the subscriber shares in cash) is **liable to pay** the amount outstanding on the shares (ss 99(3), 101(4), 102(2), 103(6), 105(3) CA 1985; restated at ss 585(2), 586(3), 587(4), 593(3), 604(3) CA 2006 by 1 October 2009). He will also have to pay interest at a rate of 5% per annum from the date of allotment (s 107 CA 1985; restated at s 609 CA 2006 by 1 October 2009). It should be noted that this liability will remain with the allottee even if he subsequently transfers his shares.

The "**amount outstanding**" will depend upon the nature of the breach. Where the minimum paying up requirements have been breached, the amount will be any of the minimum that is left unpaid (except on an allotment of bonus shares where the allottee did not know and should not have known that the minimum had not been paid). Where the restrictions on allotments for non-cash consideration or transfers of non-cash assets have been breached, the amount will be however much of the nominal value and/or premium was to be treated as paid up by the non-cash consideration or non-cash assets, as appropriate. However, the allottee will only be liable if he did not receive a copy of the valuation report or if he knew or ought to have known about any other breach.

> MEMO POINTS 1. Where an allotment is made in return for a permitted **short term undertaking**, and the undertaking is **not performed** within the period allowed by the contract between the company and the allottee, the allottee will also become liable to pay up the amount to be treated as paid up by that undertaking.
> 2. In the case of a breach of the restrictions on **transfers of non-cash assets**, the allottee's liability will obviously only arise where the company has made an allotment in return for the transfer, not when the shareholder has transferred the asset for another reason.

1188 If the original allottee is liable to pay an amount outstanding on the share, any **subsequent holder** will also, with the original allottee and any intermediate holders, be jointly and severally liable unless he purchased the share and, at the time of the purchase, did not actually know that it had been issued in breach of the relevant provision. However, once the share is transferred to an unknowing purchaser, the chain of liability is broken, which means that liability will not pass to future holders of the shares (s 112 CA 1985; restated at s 605 CA 2006 by 1 October 2009).

1189 In addition to the liabilities of the allottee and any subsequent holder, the **company** itself and any **officers** in default are liable to be fined (s 114 CA 1985; restated at s 590 CA 2006 by 1 October 2009; ¶9935).

1190 Any **relevant undertaking or agreement** (that is an undertaking to perform work or services for the company, a long-term undertaking, an undertaking to pay non-cash consideration to the company or an agreement to transfer a non-cash asset in return for an allotment) remains enforceable by the company (s 115 CA 1985; restated at s 591 CA 2006 by 1 October 2009).

> MEMO POINTS In the case of a **prohibited agreement to transfer a non-cash asset** which did not involve an allotment, the company is instead entitled to recover any consideration it gave under the agreement (or an amount equal in value to that consideration) and the agreement, so far as it has not been carried out, is void (s 105(2) CA 1985; restated at s 591 CA 2006 by 1 October 2009).

Relief from liability

1192 It will readily be seen that **unjust consequences** could arise from a breach. For example, an allottee may, in good faith, have transferred a valuable asset to the company in return for an allotment. He would then find out that he is liable to pay further money to the company because of a procedural breach of legislation, of which he may not even have been aware. Alternatively, an allottee may find that he is liable to pay money to a company in respect of an allotment made to him. At the same time he is still liable to perform the undertaking which he gave to the company in consideration for the allotment. For this reason, there are various reliefs available to allottees or subsequent holders of shares who find themselves liable as referred to above.

1193 An allottee or subsequent holder can apply to the court in order to obtain an **exemption** from the liability to pay for the allotted shares or for an exemption from the obligation to perform an undertaking.

The **court** has the **power** to grant either or both exemptions if it would be just and equitable to do so (s 113(2) CA 1985; restated at s 589 CA 2006 by 1 October 2009). In coming to its decision, the **court will consider**:
– whether the applicant has already paid or is liable to pay for the shares under some other obligation. In other words, the applicant should not be charged twice;
– whether another person has paid or is liable to pay for the shares; and
– in the case of relief from the liability to pay for the shares, whether the applicant has performed or partly performed the undertaking (including whether he has transferred assets in exchange for the shares).

1194 In coming to its decision, the court must have regard to the following **overriding principles**:
– that the consideration received by the company should at least equal the total of the nominal value and premium which is to be treated as paid up on the allotted shares; and
– if the company has more than one remedy against the applicant, it is for the company to decide which remedy to pursue.

Although these are principles rather than binding rules, an applicant would need very strong arguments to persuade the court that it should exercise its discretion in a contrary manner (*Re Bradford Investments plc (No 2)* [1991] BCLC 688; *System Control plc v Munro Corporate plc* [1990] BCLC 659; *Re Ossory Estates plc* [1988] BCLC 213).

> MEMO POINTS The court can exempt a person from his liability to repay the consideration he received from the company under a **prohibited agreement to transfer a non-cash asset** if it is just and equitable to do so, having regard to any benefit the company gained as a result of anything done by the person towards carrying out the agreement.

1195 In situations where more than one person is liable to the company, instead of or as well as seeking relief from the court, the applicant may bring proceedings against other liable persons for a **contribution** towards the total liability to the company. In such circumstances, if it is just and equitable to do so, the court could order that the other liable person makes higher or lower contributions than they would otherwise be liable to make, or the court could exempt the contributory from liability altogether (s 113(6) CA 1985; restated at s 589(6) CA 2006 by 1 October 2009).

C. Shareholder calls

1. Making a call

What is a call?

1205 A company can "call" on the holder of any **partly or nil paid shares** to pay all or some of the nominal value or premium that remains unpaid, provided it has not been designated as "reserve capital".

> MEMO POINTS The creation of **reserve capital** is rare. A company may designate any proportion of its unpaid share capital to be reserve capital by passing a special resolution to that effect (s 120 CA 1985). Reserve capital is capital that is not capable of being called up except on a winding up. In addition, reserve capital is outside the directors' control; they may not create a charge over or dispose of it (*Re Mayfair Property Co, Bartlett v Mayfair Property Co* [1898] 2 Ch 28). Once created, it appears that reserve capital may only be cancelled on a reduction of share capital; the special resolution to create it may be irrevocable (*Re Midland Railway Carriage and Wagon Co* (1907) 23 TLR 661). The **new Companies Act** will repeal the current statutory provisions so that it will not be possible for a company to create reserve capital. At the time of writing, it is anticipated that the provisions will be repealed by 1 October 2009 and that transitional arrangements will be put in place for existing companies which have created reserve capital.

Procedure

1207 The **power** of a company to make calls is **set out** in its articles. In companies incorporated under Table A 1985, subject to any terms decided at the time of issue, the directors have a complete discretion to make a call whenever and for whatever amount they wish, including for it to be paid in instalments (reg 12 TA 1985). In companies incorporated under Table A 1948, calls cannot exceed a quarter of the nominal value of the share and, although there is nothing to stop several calls being made on the same day, there must be at least a month's gap between the dates of payment.

> MEMO POINTS The draft **new model articles** for private companies limited by shares will not empower the company to make calls, but those for public companies will contain the same powers as Table A 1985 (arts 53-56).

1208 In both cases, the shareholder to whom the call is being made must be given at least 14 days' clear **notice** of when and where the payment is to be made (that is, not including the date on which the notice is served and the date the first payment is to be made). The call is **made by** the directors passing a board resolution which states the amount and date(s) of payment (reg 13 TA 1985; *Re Cawley & Co* (1889) 42 Ch D 209).

1209 Normally, a call is **carried out pro rata** on all of the shareholders or all of the shareholders in the same class. However, companies incorporated under Table A are authorised to make **different arrangements** between shareholders as to the amounts and times of call payments (reg 17 TA 1985). Other companies will need to amend their articles to include this authority if they wish to impose different arrangements (s 119(1)(a) CA 1985; restated at s 581 CA 2006 by 1 October 2009). If different arrangements were not made at the time of issue, a call that was made on certain shareholders over others would, on the face of it, be invalid (*Galloway v Halle Concerts Society* [1914-15] All ER Rep 543).

> MEMO POINTS 1. **Joint holders** of a share are jointly and severally liable for calls (reg 14 TA 1985; restated in the draft **new model articles** for public companies at art 54(2)).
> 2. The directors may **revoke** or **postpone** payment of all or part of a call at any time before they receive money in respect of the call (reg 12 TA 1985; restated in the draft **new model articles** for public companies at art 53(4)).
> 3. If a **share** is **transferred** following a call, the original shareholder remains liable for the call. In other words, liability does not pass with the transfer (reg 12 TA 1985; restated in the draft new model articles for public companies at art 54(1)).
> 4. In addition to actual calls, any **sum payable for an allotment** is deemed to be a call. Any failure to pay such a sum in accordance with the terms of issue would therefore result in the call being treated as if it has not been met (reg 16 TA 1985; restated in the draft new model articles for public companies at art 55).

1210 The directors must **exercise** their **power** to make a call in good faith and for the benefit of the company, to meet funding requirements. A call that is made to put pressure on a shareholder could form the basis of a claim for unfair prejudice (*Re Hailey Group Ltd* [1993] BCLC 459).

2. Failure to meet a call

1215 Failure to meet a call can lead to three possible independent **consequences**:
– an enforceable debt;
– forfeiture; and
– exercise of a lien.

Debt

1217 A shareholder call gives rise to a debt due from the shareholder to the company which the company is entitled to enforce. The debt is a specialty debt which means that a 12-year **limitation period** applies. This means that the company has 12 years from the date payment becomes due to bring a claim against the defaulting shareholder (s 14(2) CA 1985). In addition, in the case of companies incorporated under Table A 1985, **interest** will accrue from the date payment becomes due until actual payment at the rate fixed by the terms of allotment, the rate fixed in the notice of the call or, if no rate is fixed, at a rate of 5% per year (reg 15 TA 1985; s 107 CA 1985 (restated at s 592 CA 2006 by 1 October 2009)). The directors can waive payment of interest if they wish (reg 15 TA 1985).

> MEMO POINTS 1. For companies **incorporated under Table A 1948**, the level of interest is fixed by the directors but it cannot be more than 5% per year (reg 18 TA 1948).
> 2. Under the **new Companies Act**, a debt due from a shareholder to a company will be an ordinary contract debt. This means that the company will only have 6 years from the date payment becomes due to bring a claim against the defaulting shareholder (s 33(2) CA 2006, expected to come into force by 1 October 2009).
> 3. The draft **new model articles** under the new Companies Act for private companies will not empower the company to make calls and therefore there is no provision for interest on late calls. Those for public companies will impose the same liability to pay interest on unpaid calls (art 56).

Forfeiture

1219 Failure to meet a call could also result in the defaulting shareholder forfeiting the shares upon which the call remained unpaid, provided the **power of forfeiture** was included in the company's articles. A company is not obliged to exercise its power but if it does, the power must be exercised in good faith and for the benefit of the company, not to release the shareholder from liability. Therefore, a forfeiture cannot be arranged in **collusion with the shareholder**. For example, shares taken by a person in order to meet the minimum share capital requirements for a public company cannot later be forfeited in order to release him from the liability to pay for them in full (Re London and County Assurance Co, ex parte Jones (1858) 27 LJ Ch 666). A shareholder who has colluded in the forfeiture of his shares runs the risk of still being liable to contribute to the company on a winding up.

1220 An **invalid forfeiture** will normally be challengeable regardless of how much time has passed. However, if all of the shareholders have or should have had knowledge of the forfeiture and it is left unchallenged for some time (for example, 17 months), the shareholders will be deemed to have acquiesced to it and despite the invalidity, it will not be set aside on their application (Re Financial Corporation, Feiling's & Rimington's Case, King's Case, Holmes's, Pritchard's and Adam's Case (1867) 2 Ch App 714).

1221 Companies incorporated under Table A are empowered to cause shares to be forfeited for non-payment of calls. Before a share can be treated as forfeited, the directors must write to the shareholder giving him 14 clear days' **notice** that payment of the amount unpaid is required together with any interest which may have accrued. The notice must state the place where payment is to be made and warn the shareholder that non-compliance will result in the relevant shares being liable to forfeiture (reg 18 TA 1985).

If the **notice is not complied with**, the directors may at any time after the notice expires declare by a board resolution that the relevant shares have been forfeited (the shareholder would also forfeit any dividends payable in respect of those shares which had not been paid before the forfeiture). However, the board resolution cannot be passed if payment for the call is subsequently received by the company, even though the payment was late (reg 19 TA 1985).

> MEMO POINTS   The draft **new model articles** under the new Companies Act for private companies will not empower the company to cause shares to be forfeited for non-payment of calls. Those for public companies will contain the substantially the same powers as are present in Table A 1985; any differences are highlighted in text below (arts 56-61).

1222 **Once forfeited**, the directors are free to sell, re-allot or dispose of the shares on whatever terms and to whomever they wish (including back to the shareholder who forfeited them in the first place) and they can authorise an appropriate person (such as a particular director) to execute the appropriate transfer documents (reg 20 TA 1985). Subject to the execution of any necessary transfer documents, a statutory declaration by a director or the company secretary that the shares were forfeited on a particular date is all the evidence required to give good **title in the forfeited shares** to the person in whose favour the disposal occurred. That person's title will not be affected by any irregularity or invalidity in the forfeiture or disposal procedure (reg 22 TA 1985).

> MEMO POINTS   1. The directors can **cancel** the **forfeiture** on whatever terms they think fit prior to a disposal of the forfeited shares (reg 20 TA 1985).
> 2. A **public company** must cancel any forfeited shares within 3 years of forfeiture (if the shares are not disposed of earlier) and reduce its authorised and issued share capital accordingly (s 146 CA 1985). Failure to do so renders the company and every officer in default subject to a fine (s 149 CA 1985; ¶9935). The company does not have to obtain court approval for the reduction. However, if the reduction takes the company's allotted share capital below the authorised minimum, the company must re-register as a private company. Re-registration is effected by passing a resolution to amend the memorandum and articles and by filing a copy of the resolution, amended constitution and Form 147 at Companies House within 15 days of the resolution.
> This duty will still apply under the new Companies Act (s 662 CA 2006, expected to come into force by 1 October 2009). Within 1 month, the company will have to file a notice of the reduction and a statement of capital (which records details about the company's share capital at that point in

time) at Companies House (s 663 CA 2006 expected to come into force by 1 October 2009; reg 10 draft Companies (Shares, Share Capital and Authorised Minimum) Regulations 2007). Again, if the public company no longer meets the authorised minimum share capital requirement, it will have to re-register as a private company (ss 664-668 CA 2006 expected to come into force by 1 October 2009; regs 2-8 draft Companies (Shares, Share Capital and Authorised Minimum) Regulations 2007).
3. The **draft new model articles** for public companies provide that if the company sells a forfeited share, it must pay the net proceeds of sale to the person who held it before its forfeiture. The company will not be obliged to pay interest on those proceeds or account for any money earned on them (art 60(4)).

1223 As far as the **shareholder whose shares have been forfeited** is concerned, he ceases to be a shareholder in respect of those shares and is required to return his share certificate(s) to the company for cancellation. However, he is still liable to pay the company any sums that remained owing in respect of those shares (such as the call), together with any accrued interest (reg 21 TA 1985). The directors are entitled to waive all or part of the payment but, in the case of companies incorporated under Table A 1985, if they wish, they can claim the whole debt from the original shareholder without any allowance for the value of the shares at the time of forfeiture or for any consideration the company received on their disposal (reg 21 TA 1985). For companies incorporated under Table A 1948, payments received from the new holder must be set off against the original holder's liability (reg 37 TA 1948).

1224 Any **new holder of the forfeited shares** is not obliged to meet the previous call but he is still liable to meet the amounts unpaid on the share, including the amount of the unpaid call that led to the forfeiture. He is, however, entitled to be credited if payment for the call is recovered from the original holder (*New Balkis Eersteling v Randt Gold Mining Co* [1904] AC 165).

Lien

1227 A "lien" **means** that a creditor (e.g. a company) is entitled to particular rights over a debtor's asset (e.g. a shareholder's shares in the company) in order to protect its interest in an unpaid debt (e.g. the amount payable in respect of the shares) due from the debtor (e.g. the shareholder). The company's lien over its shares is set out in its articles. Companies incorporated under Table A have a first lien over any partly or nil paid shares for any amount called or otherwise payable in respect of them (reg 8 TA 1985). If any such amount is not paid when due (for example, if a call is not met), the company is entitled to sell the share (reg 9 TA 1985).

> MEMO POINTS 1. **Public companies** are not usually permitted to create a charge over their shares, but a lien in these circumstances is expressly permitted by statute (s 150(2) CA 1985; restated at s 670(2) CA 2006 by 1 October 2009).
> 2. In companies incorporated under **Table A 1948** before 22 December 1980, the lien extends to cover all money payable by the shareholder or his estate to the company, whether or not that money was payable in respect of the share.
> 3. The draft **new model articles** for private companies limited by shares do not expressly give the company a lien over any partly or nil paid shares because they require all shares to be fully paid up (art 21). Those for public companies essentially contain the same powers as Table A 1985 (arts 51-52).

1228 If a company wishes to exercise its lien (by selling the share), it must give the shareholder 14 clear days' **notice** that payment of the amount unpaid is required and must warn that non-compliance will result in the relevant shares being sold (reg 9 TA 1985). If the shareholder is dead or bankrupt and someone else (for example, the personal representatives or trustee in bankruptcy) is entitled to the shares, the notice must be sent to that person instead.

1229 If the **amounts** remain **unpaid following** expiry of the **notice**, the directors have a discretion to sell the shares on whatever terms they wish (reg 9 TA 1985). The directors can authorise any appropriate person (such as a particular director) to execute the stock transfer form and the buyer's title to the shares will not be affected by any irregularity or invalidity in the sale process (reg 10 TA 1985).

The **net proceeds of** the **sale** will be set off against the amounts owing to the company. Any surplus will be returned to the person entitled to the shares at the date of the sale (reg 11

TA 1985). In the case of companies incorporated under Table A 1985 (but not under Table A 1948), the return of any surplus is subject to the relevant share certificate being returned to the company for cancellation.

> MEMO POINTS   If further amounts would have become payable on the shares in the future (for example, under subsequent calls), the company will retain a lien over the sale surplus to the extent of that **future liability** (reg 11 TA 1985).

D. Commission payments

1237 On a share issue, as an incentive, a company may consider paying a commission to a person in return for him subscribing for shares or in return for him finding other people to subscribe for shares. The engagement of intermediaries to find subscribers for shares is common in large public issues in which they act as **underwriters**. This means that they agree to take up all or a specified number of shares if they fails to find applications for those shares. In determining whether a payment is a commission or not, the substance of the transaction must be looked at. So, for example, a payment will be treated as a commission even if it has been included in the purchase price of a property or the contract price of any work being carried out for the company (s 98(2) CA 1985; restated at s 552 CA 2006 by 1 October 2009). In **unlisted companies**, the use of underwriters and the payment of commission are rare.

Commissions should be distinguished from **brokerage fees**, which companies are expressly permitted to pay (s 98(3) CA 1985; restated at s 552 CA 2006 by 1 October 2009). Most brokers only deal with large public issues and so brokerage fees are rarely relevant for unlisted companies.

1238 Payment of a commission to subscribers and/or intermediaries (whether or not they act as underwriters) is **only permitted if** (s 97(2), 98 CA 1985; restated at s 553 CA 2006 by 1 October 2009):
a. it is authorised by the company's articles (authority in the memorandum or any other document is not sufficient);
b. the amount paid or agreed to be paid does not exceed 10% of the price at which the shares are to be issued or the amount or rate authorised under the articles, whichever is the lower; and
c. disclosures are made of the amount or rate of commission and the number of shares for which unconditional subscriptions are to be made in return for a commission.

Comment: Although not stated in the legislation, it is thought that since such commission payments are explicitly permitted by statute, they would not constitute **financial assistance** by the company for the acquisition of its shares. In addition, payment of a lawful commission will be permitted even if this effectively results in the shares being issued at a **discount**.

> MEMO POINTS   1. The restriction on commissions only applies to payments in return for "**subscriptions**" for shares, the usual meaning of which is to take shares for cash (*Government Stock and Other Securities Investment Co v Christopher* [1956] 1 All ER 490). Although it could be inferred from this that commission payments can be made to those taking shares for non-cash consideration, it is likely that such payments would constitute unlawful financial assistance.
> 2. Commission may be paid using money from any **source**, including profits, money obtained from an issue or by way of extra shares.
> 3. Where commission is **paid to a director**, he must have performed special services which the articles must authorise as deserving of payment over and above his usual remuneration (*Ural Caspian Oil Corporation Ltd v Hume-Schewedar* (1913) Times, 31 July).
> 4. In the case of **public offers**, the disclosure must be made in the prospectus. In all other cases, it must be made in any circular or notice inviting applications for shares and also in a statement signed by every director which must be filed at Companies House before the commission is paid (s 97(3) CA 1985). If the statement is not filed, the company and every officer in default is currently liable to a fine (¶9935+). (There is no equivalent requirement under the new Companies Act.)
> 5. Commission paid must not be treated as assets in the company's **balance sheet** (para 3(2) Sch 4 CA 1985; restated at para 3 Sch 1 in both the draft Small Companies and Groups (Accounts and Directors' Report) Regulations 2008 and draft Large and Medium-sized Companies and Groups (Accounts and Reports) Regulations 2008).

1239 If commission is paid in **breach** of the prohibition, it can only be recovered from the recipient of the commission if he had actual or constructive knowledge of the breach (*Andreae v Zinc Mines of Great Britain Ltd* [1918] 2 KB 454).

E. Share premium account

1245 In all situations (except for on certain mergers and group reconstructions, ¶1250+), if a company issues shares at a premium, whether for cash or otherwise, the total amount or, in the case of non-cash consideration, the value of the premium, must be transferred into the company's "share premium account" (s 130(1) CA 1985; restated at s 610(1) CA 2006 by 1 October 2009). The value of the premium is that actually received by the company and not the market value of the issued shares (*Shearer v Bercain Ltd* [1980] 3 All ER 295).

The transfer into the share premium account is not a physical transfer of money into a particular bank account but a notional transfer on the company's balance sheet.

Restrictions on share premium account

1247 The share premium account can only be used for the following **limited purposes** (s 130(2) CA 1985):
– allotting shareholders fully paid bonus shares (but not in allotting partly paid bonus shares or paying up partly paid shares);
– writing off a company's preliminary expenses;
– writing off expenses incurred on any issue of shares or debentures of the company, including any commission or brokerage fees paid; or
– paying the premium payable on the redemption of any debentures.

If a company wishes to use the share premium account for **other purposes**, for example, to transfer to distributable reserves or set off against losses, the share premium account must be reduced under the reduction of share capital procedure (s 130(3) CA 1985; restated at s 610(4) CA 2006) (see ¶1435+).

> MEMO POINTS 1. Under the **new Companies Act**, companies will only be able to use the share premium account (s 610(3), (4) CA 2006, expected to come into force by 1 October 2009):
> – to allot shareholders fully paid bonus shares (but not to allot them partly paid bonus shares or paying up partly paid shares);
> – where an issue of shares resulted in a transfer to the share premium account, to write off expenses incurred on that issue; or
> – where an issue of shares resulted in a transfer to the share premium account, to write off any commission paid on that issue.
> 2. The restrictions on the share premium account are a result of the modern tendency to issue shares with a low nominal value and a high premium. **Historically**, shares had a high nominal value which more closely resembled the amount that the company obtained on their allotment. There was therefore a greater correspondence between the value of a company's share capital and the amount raised on a share issue. The tendency towards shares with a low nominal value arose as these were seen to be more marketable. Of course, the shares themselves did not become less valuable in the marketplace and so companies continued to obtain the same amount for their allotment, i.e. the shares were issued at a premium. This led to a disparity between the value of a company's share capital and the amount raised on a share issue. Since the doctrine of capital maintenance protected a company's share capital and not the amount obtained on a share issue, the disparity led to an erosion of those protections. As a result, since 1985, restrictions have also been placed on the share premium account.

Exceptions on transfer of whole premium

1250 The whole premium does not have to be transferred into the share premium account on an allotment pursuant to:
– a **merger** with or acquisition of another company; or
– a **group reconstruction**.

If the circumstances are such that both situations apply, group reconstruction relief has precedence (s 132(8) CA 1985; restated at s 612(4) CA 2006 by 1 October 2009). Where either relief applies, the premium may also be disregarded for the purposes of determining the amount at which the consideration for the issued shares is to be included in the company's balance sheet (s 133 CA 1985; restated at s 629 CA 2006 by 1 October 2009).

Merger relief

1251   The value of the premium paid to A Ltd on an allotment of shares by it which results in its merger with or acquisition of B Ltd does not have to be transferred into the share premium account (s 131 CA 1985; restated at ss 612, 613 CA 2006 by 1 October 2009). A Ltd must make the **allotment pursuant to an arrangement** under which it agrees to allot shares (some of which must be equity shares, which are shares with uncapped rights to dividends and on a return of capital) in return for the issue or transfer to it of shares in B Ltd or the cancellation of any shares in B Ltd which are not held by A Ltd.

As a result of the arrangement, A Ltd **must secure more than** 90% (by nominal value) of B Ltd's share capital (excluding shares with capped rights). If B Ltd has different classes of share capital, A Ltd must secure 90% (by nominal value) of each class. For these purposes, shares in B Ltd held by A Ltd's holding company (C Ltd), subsidiary, holding company's subsidiary (D Ltd) or their nominees are treated as being held by A Ltd. Some of the 90% can have been acquired under previous arrangements. However, it is only the value of the premium paid under the arrangement that takes A Ltd's equity shareholding in B Ltd to over 90% that does not have to be transferred into the share premium account.

EXAMPLE   A Ltd has an issued share capital of 5,000 ordinary shares of £1 each and is in a group with C Ltd and D Ltd.
B Ltd has an issued share capital of:
10,000 "A" ordinary shares of £1 each – market value of £5 each
10,000 "B" ordinary shares of £1 each – market value of £5 each
50,000 7% preference shares of £10 each
Prior to the arrangement, B Ltd's shares are held as follows:

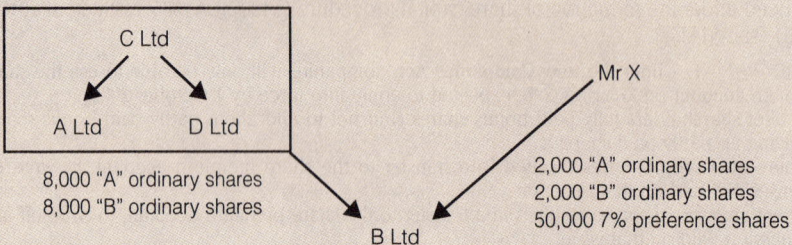

A Ltd and Mr X enter into a share for share exchange arrangement as follows:

allot 2,000 ordinary shares in A Ltd (nominal value: £2,000)

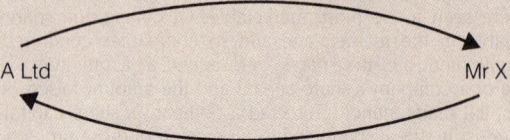

transfer 1,000 "A" ordinary shares and 1,000 "B" ordinary shares in B Ltd (total value: £10,000)

Following the arrangement, B Ltd's shares are held as follows:

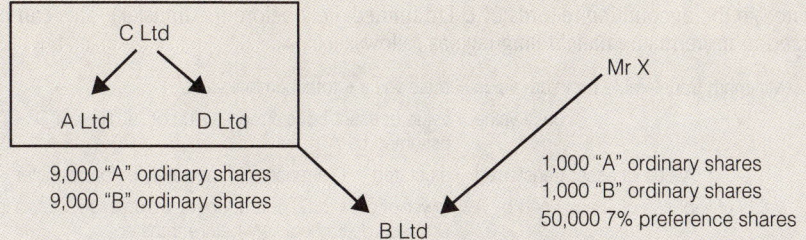

Since the arrangement meets the requirements for merger relief, the premium of £8,000 on the allotment by A Ltd does not have to be transferred into the share premium account.

Group reconstruction relief

The value of any premium over the "minimum transferable value" does not have to be transferred into the share premium account where the following **circumstances** are fulfilled (s 132 CA 1985; restated at s 611 CA 2006 by 1 October 2009):
– A Ltd is the wholly owned subsidiary of B Ltd;
– a group reconstruction is carried out so that A Ltd allots shares to B Ltd or to another wholly owned subsidiary of B Ltd (C Ltd); and
– the consideration for the allotment is the non-cash assets of any company (D Ltd), in the same group as A Ltd, B Ltd and C Ltd, including B Ltd or C Ltd.

As the following examples demonstrate, B Ltd is the parent of both A Ltd and C Ltd but D Ltd can be any other company in the group.

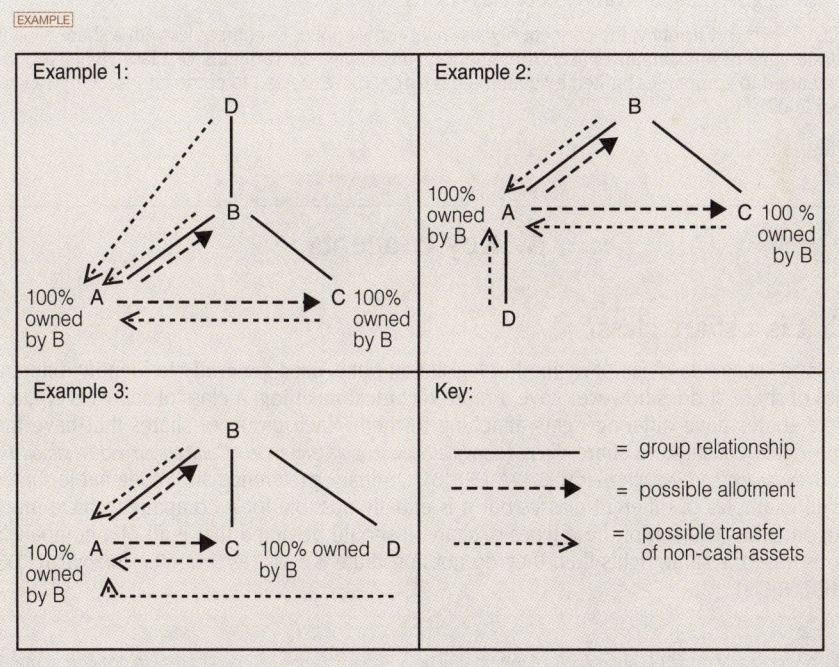

The **minimum transferable value** (that is, the value which must be transferred into the share premium account) is the amount by which the base value of the consideration exceeds the total nominal value of the shares. The base value is calculated by deducting the value of any liabilities of D Ltd assumed by A Ltd (which is the amount at which the liabilities are stated in D Ltd's accounting records immediately before the transfer) from the value of the asset transferred (which is the lower of the cost to D Ltd or the amount at which the asset was stated in the accounting records of D Ltd immediately before the transfer). This can be expressed in more mathematical language as follows:

Minimum transferable premium value = base value − total nominal value
Base value = value of asset transferred − value of liabilities of D assumed by A
Value of asset transferred = as stated in D's records immediately before transfer
Value of liabilities of D assumed by A = lower of cost to D, or amount at which asset stated in D's records immediately before transfer

SECTION 4
Variation of class rights

1270 Once a share has been issued, the holder is entitled to enjoy the rights that attach to it. However, there must be flexibility and a company should be able to vary its share rights to match circumstances. Usually, share rights are set out in the articles and a change to those rights would be achieved by an amendment to the articles (¶450+) or a scheme of arrangement between the company and its shareholders (¶6500+). The law recognises, however, that it would be unfair to impose the will of the majority on all shareholders where there are different share classes, as each class may have competing interests, and so there are special provisions governing the variation of class rights.

> MEMO POINTS Currently, the concept of class rights only applies to companies with a share capital. Under the **new Companies Act**, the statutory provisions on variation of class rights will be extended to companies limited by guarantee (s631 CA 2006, expected to come into force by 1 October 2009).

A. Key concepts

What is a share class?

1273 The term "share class" is not defined in legislation but is **used generally** to identify different types of share. It does however have a more **technical meaning**; a class of shares is created where shares have differing rights attaching to them. Each group of shares that have the same rights constitute a share class (*Cumbrian Newspapers Group Ltd v Cumberland and Westmorland Herald Newspaper and Printing Co Ltd* [1986] 2 All ER 816). Ordinary, preference and redeemable shares are all examples of different classes but it is equally possible for a company to have more than one class of each of these types of share. It should be noted that if all of a company's shares have the same rights then they do not constitute a class (*Re Smith of Smithfields Ltd* [2003] EWHC 568 (Ch)).

> EXAMPLE
> 1. A Ltd has issued 100 shares. All of the shares have the same rights. The shares do not constitute a class.
> 2. B Ltd has issued 50 ordinary shares and 50 preference shares. The shares constitute two classes.
> 3. C Ltd has issued 50 ordinary shares, 25 5% preference shares and 25 10% preference shares. The shares constitute three classes.

> 4. D Ltd has issued 50 "A" ordinary shares and 50 "B" ordinary shares.
> a. All of the shares have the same rights. The shares do not constitute different classes.
> b. The "A" shares have pre-emption rights over the "B" shares. The "A" shares and "B" shares constitute different classes of shares.

> MEMO POINTS   See ¶744 for a discussion on why a company may create "A" shares and "B" shares with the same rights.

What is a class right?

1275 It has been held that class rights are those which (*Cumbrian Newspapers Group Ltd v Cumberland and Westmorland Herald Newspaper and Printing Co Ltd* [1986] 2 All ER 816):
– **attach to a particular share** and remain attached even if the share is transferred to another person (for example, the right to receive dividends); or
– are **conferred on a person** (not necessarily named) in that person's capacity as a holder of shares, although the right is not attached to any particular share and may fall away in the event that the share is transferred.

> MEMO POINTS   For example, in *Bushell v Faith* ([1970] 1 All ER 53), the articles of a company provided that a particular shareholder, who was also a director, would have three votes for every share he held (instead of the usual one vote per share) if there was a shareholder vote to remove him from office as a director. Such a **weighted voting right** constitutes a class right even though it belongs to the shareholder rather than the share and it constitutes a class right whether it is conferred on a particular shareholder, as in *Bushell v Faith*, or whether it is conferred on unspecified shareholders, such as all shareholders who are directors.

1276 **Class rights are not** rights conferred on a person in a capacity other than as a holder of shares (for example, in *Re Blue Arrow plc* ([1987] BCLC 585), the right conferred on a shareholder to be the chairman of a company was held not to be a class right as he would have had that right regardless of whether or not he was a shareholder).

What is a variation?

1278 A variation of class rights **means** a variation of the legal rights attaching to that class of shares.

> MEMO POINTS   An **alteration of a procedure** in the articles which sets out how a particular class' rights may be varied also constitutes a variation of that class' rights (s 125(7) CA 1985; restated at s 630(5) CA 2006 by 1 October 2009).

1279 However, the situations which amount to a "variation" are more limited than may be thought at first. In particular, the following situations are **not a variation**:
a. an action which merely **affects** the **market value** of the shares. For example, an issue of further shares would normally reduce the market value of existing shares but this does not amount to a variation of their rights (*White v Bristol Aeroplane Co Ltd* [1953] 1 All ER 40);
b. an action taken in respect of one class of shares which has a **consequential effect** on another class of shares. For example, where a company had ordinary shares of £1 each and £10 each, a division of the £10 shares into ten shares of £1 did not amount to a variation of the original £1 shares even though their voting power had been reduced (*Greenhalgh v Arderne Cinemas Ltd and Mallard* [1946] 1 All ER 512); and
c. where shares are dealt with **in accordance with** the **articles or statute**. For example, a reduction of share capital or a cancellation or redemption of shares if capital was returned to the shareholders in accordance with their class rights would not constitute a variation of the rights of the affected shares (*Re Saltdean Estate Co Ltd* [1968] 3 All ER 829; *House of Fraser plc v ACGE Investments Ltd* [1987] AC 387; *Re Northern Engineering Industries plc* [1994] 2 BCLC 704).

1280 Because of this narrow ambit, it is common to find that the **articles specify situations** which are to be construed as a variation of class rights. Common examples are:
– an issue of shares;
– a variation of the rights of other classes;
– a reduction of share capital; and
– a resolution to wind up the company.

Situations which may not have a detrimental or indeed any appreciable effect on the shares can also be included (for example, a sale of the business or an alteration in the authorised share capital). In effect, the device can be used to give a particular class **control over key decisions**. It is therefore common to find such a list where outside investors are involved as they often wish to have the last say over important matters in order to protect the value of their investment.

B. Variation procedure

1288 There are minimum procedures which must be followed in order for a variation of class rights to be effective.

The **statutory procedure** will apply where, as in the majority of cases, there is no alternative procedure in the articles (Table A 1985 does not contain an alternative variation procedure). Under the statutory procedure, a class right can only be varied either (s 125(2) CA 1985 as amended by para 2 Sch 4 SI 2007/2194; restated at s 630(4) CA 2006 by 1 October 2009):
– with the written consent of at least 75% by nominal value of the shareholders in that class; or
– by a special resolution passed at a separate class meeting (for class meetings, see ¶3794+).

The company will also have to comply with any other requirement in relation to the variation, to the extent that it does not conflict with the statutory procedure.

Where there is an alternative variation **procedure in the articles**, that procedure will apply instead (s 125(4) CA 1985).

Comment: The alternative variation procedure in **Table A 1948** is the same as the statutory procedure.

MEMO POINTS 1. In the unusual circumstances of the **class right** being **in the memorandum**:
– if there is a variation procedure in the articles and it has been there since incorporation, that procedure should be followed (s 125(4) CA 1985);
– if there is no variation procedure in the memorandum or articles, the unanimous consent of all the shareholders is required (s 125(5) CA 1985); and
– in all other situations, there is no statutory provision for the appropriate procedure and a scheme of arrangement may be required (¶6500+).
2. Where a variation is connected to the **directors' authority to allot shares** or a **reduction of share capital**, and there is a variation procedure in the memorandum or articles, the statutory procedure must be followed in preference. A variation connected to either of these circumstances is rare in practice (as referred to in ¶1279, a reduction of share capital does not necessarily constitute a "variation") (s 125(3) CA 1985).
3. When the relevant provisions of the **new Companies Act** come into force (expected to be by 1 October 2009), if the company's articles contain alternative provisions (such as requiring unanimous consent) to statute, the company must comply with the provisions contained in the articles instead (ss 630, 631 CA 2006). There is no particular saving if the company has entrenched class rights in the articles (see ¶450/mp), but it should be assumed that shareholders will not able to circumvent entrenched provisions by following the statutory procedure for variation of class rights.
The new Act will require companies to notify Companies House within 1 month of:
a. in the case of a company limited by shares:
– assigning a name or designation to any class of shares (s 636 CA 2006); and
– varying the rights attaching to any shares (s 637 CA 2006); and
b. in the case of a company limited by guarantee:
– creating a new class of members (s 638 CA 2006);
– assigning a name or designation to any class of members (s 639 CA 2006); and
– varying the rights of any class of members (s 640 CA 2006).

1289 It is also possible for class rights to be varied as part of a **scheme of arrangement** between a company and its shareholders, or a particular class of them (¶6500+) (s 126 CA 1985; restated at s 632 CA 2006 by 1 October 2009). This is more complicated as a court order is required. However, it would be the only way of achieving a variation if the class rights were contained in the memorandum and there was an express prohibition in the memorandum on varying those rights (s 17 CA 1985).

> MEMO POINTS   Under the **new Companies Act**, although class rights will never be contained in the memorandum, a scheme of arrangement may still be the only way to vary class rights which have been entrenched in the articles (see ¶450/mp).

C. Shareholders' objection

1297 Where a variation has taken place with the consent of the appropriate proportion of shareholders in the relevant class (whether pursuant to provisions in the memorandum, articles or statute), there is still an opportunity for the minority shareholders to object to the variation. An **application** to the court to have a variation cancelled can be **brought by** holders of more than 15% of the total issued shares in the class (provided they did not vote in favour of the resolution to vary their rights). If such an application is made, the variation does not have effect unless and until it is confirmed by the court (s 127(2) CA 1985; restated at s 633(2), (3) CA 2006 by 1 October 2009).

Alternatively, any shareholder could bring an action for **unfair prejudice** for which there is no minimum threshold (see ¶2105+). The remedies available under this action are also much wider and it would therefore be more usual to see an objection to a variation raised in this way.

> MEMO POINTS   1. It is the individual **applicant** who cannot have voted in favour of the resolution. Therefore, if he holds his shares as nominee for more than one person and he approves the variation on the instructions of one of them, he will not be able to bring an application to object to the variation on behalf of any other.
> 2. When the relevant provisions of the **new Companies Act** come into force (expected to be by 1 October 2009), members of a company limited by guarantee will be able to object to a variation of their class rights. The application will have to be brought by at least 15% of the members of the class in question. If an application is made, the variation will not have effect unless and until it is confirmed by the court (s 634(2), (3) CA 2006).

1298 The **application** must be **made within** 21 days after the variation. If the application is going to be brought by more than one shareholder, they can appoint one amongst themselves to make the application on behalf of the whole group (s 127(3) CA 1985; restated at s 648(4) CA 2006 by 1 October 2009). The nominated shareholder must be appointed in writing and he must have been notified of his written appointment by the specific shareholders who have appointed him before bringing the application. He is not permitted to obtain his authority retrospectively (*Re Suburban & Provincial Stores Ltd* [1943] 1 All ER 342; *Re Sound City (Films) Ltd* [1946] 2 All ER 521).

1299 The **court** has the **discretion** to disallow the variation if it finds that it was unfairly prejudicial to the minority shareholders in the relevant class (s 127(3) CA 1985; restated at ss 633(5), 634(5) CA 2006 by 1 October 2009). The burden is on the applicant to demonstrate this to the court. Unfairly prejudicial conduct in this case will normally arise because the majority class shareholders had conflicting interests and, in voting for the variation, did not act in good faith for the benefit of the class. For example, a variation approved by a majority of shareholders in the class whose rights were being varied who were also the majority of shareholders in another class was held to be unfairly prejudicial to the minority shareholder because the majority had voted for the variation in the interests of the other class (*Re Hellenic & General Trust Ltd* [1973] 3 All ER 382).

The **court's decision** is final and, provided a hearing of the merits has occurred, it may not be appealed (s 127(4) CA 1985; restated at ss 633(5), 634(5) CA 2006 by 1 October 2009; *Re Suburban & Provincial Stores Ltd* [1943] 1 All ER 342 which was an appeal against the striking out of the application).

1300 The court's decision will finally be set out in a written court order. The company must **file a copy** of the order at Companies House within 15 days of it having been made. If the company fails to do so, it and every officer in default will be liable to be fined (¶9935).

SECTION 5
Changes to share capital

1310 A company may need to make changes to its issued or unissued share capital by:
– increasing it;
– altering it (without changing the total nominal value); or
– decreasing it.

Changes which do not affect the total amount of issued share capital can be achieved relatively easily upon the appropriate resolution being passed.

On the other hand, changes which result in a decrease in the total amount of issued share capital are generally more complex due to the doctrine of capital maintenance which requires that a company maintains its issued share capital for the protection of creditors (¶703).

The chart below summarises the changes which a company may wish to make to its share capital and the appropriate cross-reference.

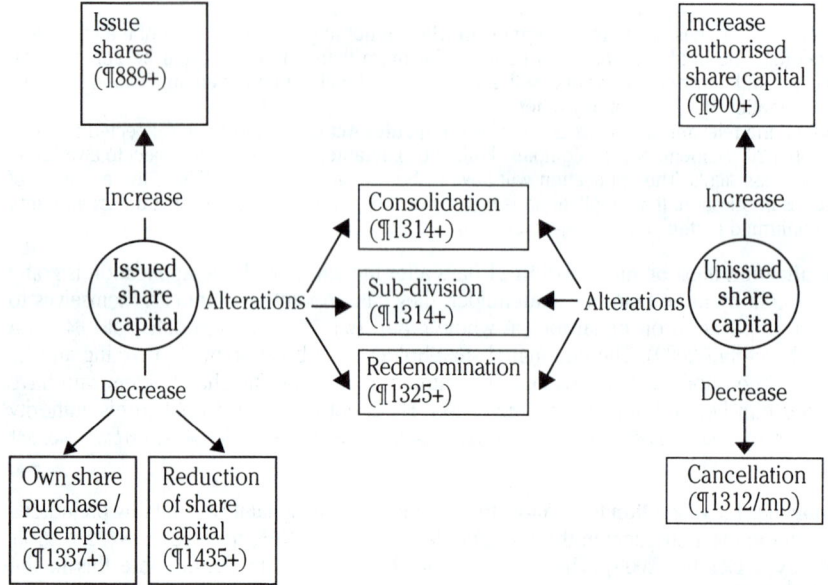

MEMO POINTS 1. Issued and unissued share capital can also be changed as part of a court approved **scheme of arrangement** (¶6500+).
2. **Unlimited companies** with share capital are free to change their share capital by a special resolution to amend their articles (ss 7(2), 9(1) CA 1985). Under the **new Companies Act**, companies will not be required to have an authorised share capital by 1 October 2009 (see ¶712/mp).

I. Alteration of share capital

1312

"Alteration of share capital" is an expression used to describe changes to share capital of a company which do not affect the total amount of issued share capital. The most common alterations to share capital are **consolidation** and **subdivision**.

The **redenomination** of share capital is more difficult as there is not yet any statutory provision for this to occur (¶1325+).

> MEMO POINTS   Other alterations, which are rare in practice, are:
> **a.** a **cancellation of unissued share capital**. If it wishes to do so, a company may cancel any authorised share capital that has not yet been allotted, that is any shares which the company has not contractually agreed to issue (s 121(2)(e) CA 1985; *Re Swindon Town Football Club Ltd* [1990] BCLC 467). Note that where a cancellation of unissued share capital is proposed as part of a general scheme for a reduction in share capital, the cancellation should be dealt with under that procedure instead (*Re Castiglione, Erskine & Co Ltd* [1958] 2 All ER 455). The **new Companies Act** will abolish the concept of authorised share capital, so this provision of CA 1985 is expected to be repealed by 1 October 2009 when the provisions of the new Act dealing with share capital are due to come into force; and
> **b.** a conversion of fully paid issued share capital into **stock or a reconversion of stock** back into shares (s 121(2)(c) CA 1985). It is not possible to issue stock directly and therefore the conversion of fully paid shares into stock is the only method by which stock can be placed in the hands of shareholders. The conversion of shares into stock is rare in practice (for more on stock see ¶709/mp). Under the new Companies Act, companies will no longer be able to convert shares into stock. However, the procedure to reconvert stock back into shares will be retained for those companies that already have stock (s 620 CA 2006, expected to come into force by 1 October 2009). In both cases, the procedure is the same as if the company were consolidating or sub-dividing its shares.

1. Consolidation and sub-division

1314

A **consolidation means** the combination of some or all of a company's share capital and its re-division into shares with a larger nominal value. A **sub-division means** a division of some or all of a company's shares into shares with a smaller nominal value.

> EXAMPLE   A Ltd has a share capital of £100 divided into 100 shares of £1 each. It could:
> – consolidate and divide its share capital into 10 shares of £10 each; or
> – sub-divide each £1 share into 4 shares of 25p each.

The consolidation and sub-division of shares is often **used to** tidy up shareholdings or ensure that certain proportions of shareholdings are maintained.

1315

> EXAMPLE   B Ltd has an issued share capital of £100 divided into 100 shares of £1 each. Mr X, Mr Y and Mr Z each respectively hold 15, 25 and 60 shares. Mr Z is retiring from the business and wishes to transfer all his shares to Mr X and Mr Y. Mr X and Mr Y wish to maintain the proportions of their shareholdings going forward (i.e. 3:5). This would require Mr Z to transfer 22.5 shares to Mr X and 37.5 shares to Mr Y.
> To enable a proportionate transfer to take place, each of B Ltd's shares is sub-divided into 2 shares of 50p each. After the sub-division, Mr X, Mr Y and Mr Z each respectively hold 30, 50 and 120 shares of 50p each. Mr Z is therefore able to transfer 45 shares to Mr X and 75 shares to Mr Y. After the transfers Mr X and Mr Y respectively hold 75 and 125 shares of 50p each (i.e. in the proportion 3:5).

Procedure

1317

Any company may consolidate or sub-divide its authorised and issued share capital if (s 121(1), (2)(b), (2)(d) CA 1985; restated at s 618 CA 2006 by 1 October 2009):
– it is **authorised by** its articles to do so. A company incorporated under Table A has the requisite authority (reg 32 TA 1985); and

– the consolidation or sub-division is **approved by** an ordinary resolution of the shareholders.

> MEMO POINTS 1. Statute requires the resolution to be passed at a shareholder meeting (s 121(4) CA 1985). Despite this, a **written resolution** can be passed by private companies using the new statutory procedure (¶3580+).
> 2. Where a consolidation or sub-division is proposed as **part of a wider scheme for a reduction of share capital**, the consolidation or sub-division should be carried out through that procedure instead and the resolution to consolidate or sub-divide should be expressed to "take effect on the reduction taking effect" (*Re Castiglione, Erskine & Co Ltd* [1958] 2 All ER 455).
> 3. For companies incorporated under Table A 1985 (but not Table A 1948), where the **consolidation of issued share capital results in fractions**, the directors can sell those fractions and distribute the proceeds of sale amongst the shareholders instead (reg 33 TA 1985). For example, C Ltd has an issued share capital of £100 divided into 100 shares of £1 each. Mr X and Mr Y each respectively hold 51 and 49 shares. If C Ltd consolidates its shares into 80 shares of £1.25 each, Mr X and Mr Y should receive 0.8 shares for every share previously held, i.e. Mr X should receive 40.8 shares and Mr Y should receive 39.2 shares. In such circumstances, the total of the fractional entitlements (i.e. 1 share) could be sold to a third party (including to C Ltd itself upon observance of the own share purchase rules) at the best price reasonably obtainable and the proceeds distributed to Mr X and Mr Y in the appropriate proportions.
> This provision is retained in the draft new model articles under the new Companies Act for public companies (art 68) but not in those for private companies limited by shares.
> 4. Ordinarily, **in a sub-division, the proportion paid and unpaid on each share** must not change (s 121(2)(d) CA 1985). However, differing proportions are permitted where the sub-division occurs as part of a scheme of arrangement or reduction of share capital (*Re Vine and General Rubber Trust* (1913) 108 LT 709; *Re Doloswella Rubber and Tea Estates Ltd* [1916-17] All ER Rep 769).
> 5. Table A does not contain authority for a company to convert its shares into **stock** and vice versa and so a specific amendment to the articles is required if this procedure is being used for that purpose.
> 6. Under the **new Companies Act**, a company will not have to be authorised by its articles to sub-divide or consolidate its shares; only an ordinary resolution will be required. The remaining provisions will be unaltered (s 618 CA 2006, expected to come into force by 1 October 2009).

1318 Once the resolution has been passed, insofar as it affects issued shares, shareholders will need to return their **share certificates** to the company for cancellation and new share certificates will need to be issued to them showing the new shareholdings. In addition, the **register of shareholders** will need to be updated.

The company must also file Form 122 at **Companies House** within 1 month of passing a resolution to consolidate or sub-divide its share capital (s 122 CA 1985). This will notify Companies House of the nature of the alteration and the affected shares. Form 122 must be accompanied by a copy of the revised memorandum setting out the new authorised share capital (s 18(2) CA 1985).

> MEMO POINTS Under the **new Companies Act**, the company will have to notify Companies House of a sub-division or consolidation. There will be no need to file a revised memorandum, but companies will have to file a new "statement of capital", showing the company's total issued share capital at a particular point in time, in this case following the consolidation or sub-division (s 619 CA 2006, expected to come into force by 1 October 2009; reg 10 draft Companies (Shares, Share Capital and Authorised Minimum) Regulations 2007).

1320 The company and any officers in **default** of the filing requirements will be subject to a fine (see ¶9935).

2. Redenomination

1325 It is possible for unissued share capital to be created in any **currency** denomination (see ¶709/mp). Foreign currency shares are issued in the normal way. However, there is currently no legislation which deals specifically with the redenomination of issued share capital.

> MEMO POINTS By 1 October 2009, a new procedure will be introduced by the **new Companies Act** to allow a company limited by shares to redenominate its share capital by its shareholders passing an ordinary resolution. The conversion rate will have to be specified in the resolution and can either be the rate on the date of the resolution or the average rate over up to 28 days

before it. The new nominal values of the shares will be arrived at by aggregating the old nominal values of shares in a class, converting the aggregate into the new currency and dividing this by the total number of shares in the class. A company will be free to pass a conditional resolution but it will lapse if the redenomination has not taken effect within 28 days of the resolution. The redenomination will have no effect on the rights or obligations of the shareholders (in particular, any shareholder's liability to pay for partly paid shares will remain in the currency in which the share was originally denominated). Notice of the redenomination, together with a "statement of capital" a copy of the shareholder resolution will have to be filed at Companies House (ss 622-625 CA 2006; reg 10 draft Companies (Shares, Share Capital and Authorised Minimum) Regulations 2007).

If a public company's share capital falls below the authorised minimum (see ¶720) as a result of redenomination, it will have to re-register as a private company within 1 year of the resolution (regs 4-8 draft Companies (Shares, Share Capital and Authorised Minimum) Regulations 2007). Failure to do so will mean that the company will not be able to offer its shares to the public (see ¶986+), but in all other respects it will be treated as a public company. Failure will also render the company and every officer in default liable to a fine.

1326 The redenomination of issued share capital is complex as it normally requires some form of **renominalisation** (that is a change in the nominal value of each share). Share capital is generally divided into shares with round amounts (such as £1, 50p, 10p etc). If a company wished to redenominate its share capital into a different currency, it would find that an equivalent amount in the new currency would create shares with an odd nominal value. In order to create shares in the new denomination with rounded numbers, the company would need to renominalise its shares as well.

EXAMPLE B Ltd wishes to redenominate £20 of its issued share capital into US$. Assuming an exchange rate of £1 = $1.7201, each £1 share will be worth $1.7201 in the new denomination. B Ltd wishes to have shares rounded to the nearest $0.50. Therefore, it will either need to renominalise the new shares upwards by $0.2799 per share to $2 each or downwards by $0.2201 to $1.50 each.

MEMO POINTS The **new Companies Act** will introduce a procedure for the renominalisation of shares following a redenomination by 1 October 2009. A company will be able to reduce its share capital by cancelling part of its share capital. This will require a special resolution of the shareholders passed within 3 months of the resolution to redenominate (but there will be no need for the company to go to court or for the directors to make a solvency statement as with a usual reduction of share capital). The amount by which a company will be able to reduce its share capital using this provision is capped at 10% of the nominal value of the company's share capital immediately after the reduction. The company will have to file a copy of the resolution to reduce its share capital and a statement of capital at Companies House in order for the reduction to take effect. The amount by which the capital is reduced will have to be transferred to a new non-distributable reserve called "the redenomination reserve". A company will be able to use the redenomination reserve to allot fully paid up bonus shares to existing shareholders (ss 626-628 CA 2006; reg 10 draft Companies (Shares, Share Capital and Authorised Minimum) Regulations 2007).

1327 The cancellation of issued shares and an issue of new shares with a different denomination and nominal value can currently only be carried out under a scheme of arrangement between a company and its shareholders (¶6500+) or a formal reduction in share capital (¶1435+) (*Re Scandinavian Bank Group plc* [1987] 2 All ER 70). Both require court and shareholder approval and there would also be a high administrative cost, for example, in the issue of new documentation.

II. Own share purchase and redemption

1337 In accordance with the doctrine of capital maintenance, the **general rule** is that a company cannot acquire an interest in its own shares (s 143(1) CA 1985; restated at s 658 CA 2006 by 1 October 2009; *Trevor v Whitworth* [1886-90] All ER 46). This means that a company cannot hold or have a beneficial interest in its own shares. This rule is intended to protect not just the existing shareholders but all persons dealing with the company, for example, future shareholders and creditors.

> **MEMO POINTS** There is nothing however in principle to prevent a company, A Ltd, from acquiring **shares in another company**, B Ltd, when B Ltd's main or only asset is shares in A Ltd (provided that B Ltd is not A Ltd's holding company). Note that the court will probably feel justified in piercing the corporate veil (¶7125) if an acquisition is structured this way just to avoid the prohibition on own share acquisitions. However if the acquisition is made in good faith, A Ltd's directors act solely in the best interests of A Ltd (and not, for example, in their own interests) and they fulfil their fiduciary duties to safeguard the interests of shareholders and creditors, then such an acquisition will not breach the general rule. Note that B Ltd's shares in A Ltd would become non-voting (*Acatos & Hutcheson plc v Watson* [1995] 1 BCLC 218; s 23(1), (5) CA 1985; restated at s 136 CA 2006 by 1 October 2009).

1338 The most important **exception** to this general rule is a statutory one, namely, that a company can purchase or redeem its own fully paid shares if it follows the appropriate procedure (s 143(3) CA 1985; restated at s 659 CA 2006 by 1 October 2009).

Share redemptions are procedurally light: they must be carried out in accordance with the terms of redemption (see ¶760+), financed appropriately and the relevant filings must be made at Companies House. The process is explained at ¶1374+.

Own share purchases on the other hand are more heavily regulated; in particular, the terms of the own share purchase contract must be approved by the shareholders. The procedure is explained at ¶1383+.

Additional steps must be taken if the redemption or own share purchase is to be **financed out of capital** to allow shareholders and creditors to challenge the payment in court if it would be prejudicial to their interests. The procedure is explained at ¶1400+.

> **MEMO POINTS** 1. A company may **purchase its redeemable shares** (as well as redeem them) in which case it must follow the own share purchase procedure rather than the procedure for redemption (s 162(1) CA 1985; restated at s 690(1) CA 2006 by 1 October 2009).
> 2. **Other exceptions** by which a company could lawfully acquire an interest in its own shares are:
> – as part of scheme for a reduction in its share capital (¶1435+);
> – pursuant to a court order to purchase its shares (for example, following an action for unfair prejudice (¶2105+));
> – following forfeiture or surrender in lieu of forfeiture of shares in accordance with a company's articles (provided the company did not give any consideration for the surrender); and
> – as a gift to nominees to hold on trust for the company (s 144 CA 1985; restated at s 660 CA 2006 by 1 October 2009; *Re Castiglione's Will Trust* [1958] 1 All ER 480; *Kirby v Wilkins* [1929] 2 Ch 444).

1339 If a company illegally acquires an interest in its own shares, the **sanctions** can be severe. Most importantly, the transaction under which the company purported to acquire its shares is void. Additionally, the company itself is liable to be fined and any officers in default are liable to be imprisoned and/or fined (¶9935) (s 143(2) CA 1985; restated at s 658 CA 2006 by 1 October 2009).

It is therefore essential that the appropriate steps are taken to ensure that any acquisition by a company of its own shares falls within the permitted exceptions to the general rule. Generally, where an illegal acquisition has taken place, the defect is more than procedural and cannot be cured by the unanimous consent of the shareholders (*Re R W Peak (Kings Lynn) Ltd* [1998] 1 BCLC 193; contrast with *BDG Roof-Bond Ltd v Douglas* [2000] 1 BCLC 401).

1. Purpose

1344 A purchase or redemption by a company of its own shares serves a useful purpose in allowing a company to return capital to its shareholders prior to a winding up. However, the circumstances in which either situation may arise are quite different.

1345 An **own share purchase** is a useful device when a return of capital has not been specifically planned because a company is permitted to purchase any class of share. Own share purchases are particularly useful for shareholders of unlisted companies. Such shareholders may find it difficult to find a market for their shares outside of persons involved in the company, for example, because a third party may expect disclosure of information about the prospects of the company which may be confidential or to which the shareholders may not have access. Further, the shareholders may be restricted in their ability to transfer their shares by the company's articles or a shareholders' agreement.

Consequently, one of the main reasons to carry out an own share purchase is to allow a shareholder to exit a company and realise value from his shareholding without the remaining shareholders having their own shareholdings diluted, without them having to find funds to buy him out themselves, and without the shares being transferred to an unknown third party. The situation may have arisen because the exiting shareholder works in the business and is retiring or because the shareholders have had a disagreement and one has agreed to leave.

In contrast, a company may only redeem redeemable shares (see ¶760+). Consequently, the act of **redemption** must have been contemplated at the time the shares were issued. Therefore, the **reason** for redemption is usually because the capital which had been provided to the company by the holder of redeemable shares is either no longer required or was only ever intended to be available for a fixed period of time. Such a shareholder is usually a short to medium term investor, such as a venture capitalist (¶4800+), and the redemption of his shares is the device used to repay his capital investment.

1346

2. Effects

A purchase or redemption has a number of effects upon a company:

a. the shares concerned are **cancelled** (the company does not therefore actually become a shareholder of itself). This reduces the issued share capital of the company, but the authorised share capital is not affected (ss 160(4), 162(2) CA 1985; restated at ss 688, 706 CA 2006 by 1 October 2009);

b. the change in the proportion of shareholdings can affect **voting control** and this should be considered prior to any purchase or redemption. An increase in a corporate shareholder's control over the company could result in the creation of a group (see ¶194+). In the case of a public company, the increase in control could trigger the requirement to make a mandatory cash offer for the remaining shares (see ¶6805+);

c. a **capital redemption reserve** (¶1360+) will be created or, if one is already in existence, increased; and

d. the **share premium account** will be reduced if the premium payable on a purchase or redemption is financed out of a fresh issue of shares (see example 2 at ¶1364 and example 4 at ¶1366).

1351

3. Financing

Payment

Own share purchases and redemptions result in a return of capital to shareholders in contradiction to the doctrine of capital maintenance. To minimise the impact of this return, the general rule is that the purchase or redemption must be financed out of (ss 160(1), (2), 162(2) CA 1985; restated at ss 687(2), 692(2) CA 2006 by 1 October 2009):

– **distributable profits** (see example 1 at ¶1363) (see ¶1612+ for the definition of distributable profits); or

– the **proceeds of a fresh issue of shares** (see example 2 at ¶1364).

1356

> MEMO POINTS Where the company is to pay a **premium on the purchase or redemption** (i.e. pay the shareholder more than the nominal value of the shares), the company can only use the proceeds of a fresh issue to pay that premium if the shares were issued at a premium in the first place. The maximum amount of the proceeds which the company can put towards the premium is the lower of the amount of the share premium account, or the amount of premium paid on the shares to be redeemed or purchased when they were issued.

1357 **Private companies** can also finance a purchase or redemption **out of capital** (s 171 CA 1985; restated at s 709 CA 2006 by 1 October 2009), provided it complies with specific additional procedures (see ¶1400+). A payment out of capital can be used as a last resort if the private company does not have enough money after using its "available profits" and the proceeds of any fresh issue of shares (although there is no obligation to raise money by a fresh issue). The amount of capital the company can pay is whatever is required to meet the shortfall (known as the "**permissible capital payment**") (see examples 3 and 4 at ¶1365+).

> MEMO POINTS In order to determine the company's "**available profits**", it must prepare accounts made up to a date within the 3 months before the statutory declaration that must be declared by the directors as part of the procedure to purchase or redeem shares out of capital (¶1404+). The "available profits" are the company's distributable profits calculated by reference to those accounts less any lawful distributions made between the date of the accounts and the date of the directors' statutory declaration. "Lawful distributions", as well as including ordinary dividends, includes any lawful payment made out of distributable profits: for financial assistance by the company; for an own share purchase or redemption; or in consideration for entering into, varying or releasing an own share purchase contract (s 172 CA 1985; restated at s 712 CA 2006 by 1 October 2009).

1358 It had been thought that payment for an own share purchase or redemption had to be in **cash** but case law now suggests that **non-cash** consideration would also be acceptable (*BDG Roof-Bond Ltd v Douglas* [2000] 1 BCLC 401).

Whatever the form of payment, it must be **made on** the purchase or redemption, as appropriate: it is currently not possible for it to be deferred (ss 159(3), 162(2) CA 1985). Therefore, if a company does wish to **stagger or defer** payments (for example, for cash flow reasons) the purchase/redemption will have to be carried out in tranches with staggered completion dates. It is unlikely that an alternative, such as a loan back to the company, would be attractive as this would have adverse tax consequences for the shareholder (who would be treated as having received all of the proceeds even though in reality they remained with the company in the form of a loan) and could amount to financial assistance if the company gave security for the loan.

> MEMO POINTS When the relevant provisions of the **new Companies Act** come into force (expected to be by 1 October 2009), a company will be able to defer payment on redemption (s 686(2) CA 2006) but will continue to have to pay for a purchase on the day of purchase (s 691(2) CA 2006).

Capital redemption reserve

1360 Upon an own share purchase or redemption, a company must make a transfer to its capital redemption reserve which is a special shareholder reserve that forms part the bottom part of a company's balance sheet (s 170 CA 1985; restated at s 733 CA 2006 by 1 October 2009). The **purpose** of this reserve, in keeping with the doctrine of capital maintenance, is to minimise the impact of a purchase or redemption on the overall level of shareholders' funds.

The capital redemption reserve has a particular **status** so that it is treated in many ways as if it was part of the issued share capital of a company. A reduction in the capital redemption reserve must be carried out in the same way as if it was part of the company's paid up share capital (see ¶1435+). It is an undistributable reserve and so cannot be used to pay dividends to shareholders (s 264(3)(b) CA 1985; restated at s 831 CA 2006 as of 6 April 2008). However, it can be used to pay up shares which are to be allotted as fully paid bonus shares (s 170(4) CA 1985; restated at s 733 CA 2006 by 1 October 2009).

1361 The **amount which must be transferred** to the capital redemption reserve depends upon how the purchase or redemption is financed.

If the purchase or redemption is financed wholly **out of distributable profits**, the amount to be transferred is the amount by which the called up share capital has reduced (see ¶1363) (s 170(1) CA 1985; restated at s 733 CA 2006 by 1 October 2009).

If it is financed wholly or partly **out of a fresh issue** of shares (provided the rest, if any, has been financed out of distributable profits and not out of capital), the amount to be transferred is the amount by which the nominal value of the purchased/redeemed shares exceeds the proceeds of the fresh issue (see ¶1364). If the proceeds of the fresh issue exceed the nominal value of the purchased/redeemed shares then no transfer is required (s 170(2), (3) CA 1985; restated at s 733 CA 2006 by 1 October 2009).

If the purchase or redemption is financed **out of capital** and the permissible capital payment plus the proceeds of any fresh issue of shares used to finance the purchase or redemption is less than the nominal value of the purchased/redeemed shares, the amount to be transferred is the difference between those two sums (see ¶1365). If the permissible capital payment plus the proceeds of any fresh issue is more than the nominal value of the purchased/redeemed shares, the excess can be set off against any one or more of the fully paid share capital, share premium account, capital redemption reserve or revaluation reserve (see ¶1366) (s 171(4)-(6) CA 1985; restated at s 734 CA 2006 by 1 October 2009).

Example

A Ltd has an issued share capital of £450,000 divided into 300,000 ordinary shares of £1 each and 150,000 redeemable preference shares of £1 each, all of which are fully paid. The ordinary shares were issued for a total of £328,000 (in other words, for a total premium of £28,000) and the redeemable preference shares were issued for a total of £157,000 (that is, a premium of £7,000). A Ltd intends to redeem the redeemable preference shares for a total of £180,000 (that is, at a premium of £30,000).

1362

The following four scenarios are dealt with below, where the redemption is financed:
– wholly out of distributable profits;
– partly out of the proceeds of a fresh issue of shares and partly out of distributable profits;
– partly out of distributable profits and partly out of capital; and
– partly out of distributable profits, partly out of the proceeds of a fresh issue of shares and partly out of capital.

The situation would be the same if the company proposed an own share purchase rather than a redemption.

Example 1: Financed wholly out of distributable profits

Suppose that A Ltd has distributable profits of £300,000. The amount to be transferred to the capital redemption reserve is the amount by which the called up share capital reduces, namely, the nominal value of the redeemed shares (i.e. £150,000).

1363

	Before redemption	After redemption
	£	£
Distributable profits	300,000	120,000
Called up share capital	450,000	300,000
Share premium account	35,000	35,000
Capital redemption reserve	0	150,000
Total	485,000	485,000

MEMO POINTS The overall level of called up share capital, share premium account and capital redemption reserve is unchanged. Distributable profits have reduced by £180,000.

Example 2: Financed out of a fresh issue of shares and distributable profits

Suppose that A Ltd still has distributable profits of £300,000 but wishes to finance part of the redemption out of a fresh issue of 75,000 ordinary shares of £1 for a total of £100,000 (i.e. for a total premium of £25,000).

1364

The premium on redemption (i.e. £30,000) may be funded out of the fresh issue to the extent of the premium originally received (i.e. £7,000) or the balance on the share premium account after the new issue (i.e £35,000 + £25,000 = £60,000), whichever is the lower. Therefore, the remaining premium on redemption (i.e. £30,000 – £7,000 = £23,000) will need to be financed out of distributable profits.

Since £7,000 of the proceeds of fresh issue have been used to pay the premium on redemption, £93,000 is left to pay towards the nominal value of the redeemable shares. The remaining nominal value (i.e. £57,000) will need to be financed out of distributable profits.

The amount to be transferred into the capital redemption reserve is the amount by which the nominal value of the redeemed shares exceeds the amount raised by the fresh issue (i.e. £150,000 – £100,000 = £50,000).

	Before issue	After issue/ Before redemption	After redemption
	£	£	£
Distributable profits	300,000	300,000	220,000
Called up share capital	450,000	525,000	375,000
Share premium account	35,000	60,000	53,000
Capital redemption reserve	0	0	50,000
Total	485,000	585,000	478,000

MEMO POINTS The overall level of the called up share capital, share premium account and capital redemption reserve has fallen by £7,000 i.e. £7,000 of "protected capital" has been returned to the shareholders (see ¶722). Distributable profits have reduced by £80,000 (£57,000 + £23,000).

Example 3: Financed out of distributable profits and capital

1365 Suppose that A Ltd only had distributable profits of £50,000 and wished to finance the remainder of the redemption out of capital.

Permissible capital payment Assume for the purposes of calculating the permissible capital payment that there are no distributions to be taken into account. The available profits are therefore £50,000. The permissible capital payment would be the price of the redemption less available profits (that is, £180,000 – £50,000 = £130,000).

The amount to be transferred into the capital redemption reserve would be the nominal value of the redeemed shares less the permissible capital payment (that is, £150,000 – £130,000 = £20,000).

	Before redemption	After redemption
	£	£
Distributable profits	50,000	0
Called up share capital	450,000	300,000
Share premium account	35,000	35,000
Capital redemption reserve	0	20,000
Total	485,000	355,000

MEMO POINTS The overall level of the called up share capital, share premium account and capital redemption reserve has fallen by £130,000, in other words, the amount of the permissible capital payment. All of the distributable profits have been used, so this value has been reduced to zero.

Example 4: Financed out of distributable profits, proceeds of fresh issue and capital

1366 Suppose that A Ltd had distributable profits of only £20,000 but that it also intended to raise a further £50,000 through a fresh issue of 45,000 ordinary shares of £1 each (i.e. for a total premium of £5,000) and finance the remainder of the redemption out of capital.

Permissible capital payment Again, as in example 3, assume that there are no distributions to be taken into account. The available profits are therefore £20,000. The permissible capital payment would be the price of the redemption less available profits and the proceeds of the fresh issue (i.e. £180,000 – (£20,000 + £50,000) = £110,000).

Since the permissible capital payment plus the proceeds of the fresh issue (i.e. £110,000 + £50,000 = £160,000) exceeds the nominal value of the redeemed shares (i.e. £150,000), A Ltd chooses to set off the amount of the excess (i.e. £10,000) against the share premium account.

	Before issue	After issue/ Before redemption	After redemption
	£	£	£
Distributable profits	20,000	20,000	0
Called up share capital	450,000	495,000	345,000
Share premium account	35,000	40,000	30,000
Capital redemption reserve	0	0	0
Total	485,000	540,000	375,000

MEMO POINTS   The overall level of the called up share capital, share premium account, capital redemption reserve has fallen by £110,000, i.e. the amount of the permissible capital payment. All of the distributable profits have been used so this value has been reduced to zero.

Disclosure in annual accounts

1367 The **directors' report** to the company's accounts will need to disclose that the company purchased or redeemed its own shares in the preceding financial year (s 234(4), Sch 7 Pt II CA 1985; restated at s 416(4) CA 2006 as of 6 April 2008).

Tax implications

1369 Revenue and Customs will generally treat the purchase or redemption payment as a **distribution** for corporation tax purposes (s 225 ICTA 1988). The taxation of distributions is considered at ¶1769+.

1370 In some circumstances, where a company carries out an own share purchase, it will be treated as having made a capital payment instead. **Capital treatment** will automatically apply where:
– the company is a UK-resident unquoted trading company (or the holding company of a trading group); and
– the purchase is made either for the benefit of the trade, or to enable inheritance tax to be paid on the death of a shareholder (where undue hardship would otherwise arise).

Capital treatment will not apply where the transaction is carried on for the purpose of avoiding tax, or to enable the seller to share in the profits of the company without receiving a dividend.

Clearance can be obtained from Revenue and Customs as to whether the capital treatment does or does not apply to a particular transaction (s 225 ICTA 1988).

The **effect** of capital treatment is that the recipient will be liable to capital gains tax instead of income tax.

MEMO POINTS   A purchase would be for the **benefit of the trade** in the case of a shareholder who is unwilling to hold his shares and therefore could disrupt the operation of the business. Typical examples include:
– an outside shareholder who wishes to withdraw his equity finance;
– a controlling shareholder retiring to make way for new management;
– the personal representatives of a deceased shareholder wishing to realise the value of the holding; and
– the beneficiary of a deceased shareholder who does not want to hold shares in the company.

1371 Normally, the entire holding of the selling shareholder must be purchased, but Revenue and Customs may accept a **partial purchase** if:
– insufficient funds are available to purchase the full holding in one tranche; or
– for sentimental reasons, a retiring controlling shareholder wishes to retain a small stake in the company.

1372 The **selling shareholder** must also satisfy the following conditions, he must:
- be UK-resident and ordinarily resident in the year of the sale;
- have held the shares for at least 5 years (3 years if the shares were inherited); and
- not be connected with the company immediately after it purchases his shares.

> *MEMO POINTS* For these purposes, a person is **connected** with the company if, immediately following the purchase of his shares, he:
> **a.** controls it; or
> **b.** owns, or is entitled to acquire (together with his associates), more than 30% of its:
> - voting power;
> - issued share capital;
> - issued share and loan capital; or
> - assets on a winding up.

4. Procedure: redemption

Pre-redemption checks

1374 Prior to any redemption a company must check:
a. how the redemption is to be **financed** (see ¶1356+);
b. if the redemption is to be out of capital, that it is specifically **authorised by its articles** to finance the redemption in that manner (s 171(1) CA 1985). Companies incorporated under Table A 1985 (but not Table A 1948) are authorised to finance a redemption out of capital (reg 35 TA 1985). Companies without the necessary authority will need to amend their articles;
c. the articles/share rights for the **terms of redemption**;
d. that **at least one non-redeemable share** will be left in issue after the redemption (s 159(3) CA 1985; restated at s 684(4) CA 2006 by 1 October 2009); and
e. that the shares to be redeemed are **fully paid** (s 159(3) CA 1985; restated at s 686(1) CA 2006 by 1 October 2009).

> *MEMO POINTS* Under the **new Companies Act** a private company will not need to be authorised by its articles to finance a redemption out of capital, although the articles may restrict or prohibit such payment (s 709 CA 2006, expected to come into force by 1 October 2009).

Redemption

1376 Where the terms of redemption require or permit the redemption to be **initiated by the company**, the board should resolve to redeem the relevant shares in accordance with the terms of issue. The company should then send a redemption notice to the relevant shareholder(s) in accordance with the articles, setting out when and how the redemption will take place. Sometimes, the terms of redemption require or permit the redemption to be **initiated by the shareholder** in which case, the shareholder will serve a similar redemption notice on the company.

The redemption price is then paid by company to the shareholder(s) in accordance with the notice and on return of the relevant share certificates.

> *MEMO POINTS* The **new Companies Act** will remove the requirement for payment on redemption. Instead, subject to agreement between the company and the holder of the redeemable shares, payment may be made after the redemption date (s 685 CA 2006, expected to come into force by 1 October 2009).

Post redemption formalities

1378 A company must **notify Companies House** within 1 month of the redemption by filing Form 122, specifying the shares that have been redeemed. In addition, the relevant share certificates will need to be marked as "cancelled" and the register of shareholders will need to be updated.

MEMO POINTS Under the **new Companies Act**, there will be a new additional requirement to file a statement of capital. This is a "snapshot" of the company's total issued share capital at a particular point in time, in this case following the redemption (s 689 CA 2006, expected to come into force by 1 October 2009; reg 10 draft Companies (Shares, Share Capital and Authorised Minimum) Regulations 2007).

5. Procedure: off-market purchase

1383

An "off-market purchase" is the term used to describe a purchase by a company of its own shares that is not on a recognised investment exchange or where the shares are not subject to a marketing arrangement on a recognised investment exchange (s 163 CA 1985; restated at s 693 CA 2006 by 1 October 2009). All own share purchases by **private companies** are therefore carried out "off-market".

MEMO POINTS 1. A "**recognised investment exchange**" is one recognised by the FSA under Pt 18 FSMA 2000. There are currently seven recognised investment exchanges but for these purposes only the London Stock Exchange and virt-x Exchange are relevant as they are the only recognised exchanges on which shares can be purchased.
2. An own share purchase by a **public company** whose shares are not publicly traded will be "off-market". If the shares are publicly traded, the purchase will be "on-market" only if the shares are purchased on the London Stock Exchange or virt-x Exchange. Note that an AIM company, although not technically "listed", could carry out an "on-market" own share purchase as AIM is a market provided by the London Stock Exchange.

Pre-purchase checks

1385

Prior to any purchase, a company must check:
a. how the purchase is to be **financed** (see ¶1356+);
b. that it is **authorised by its articles** to purchase its shares (s 162(1) CA 1985) and if the purchase is to be made out of capital, that it is specifically authorised to finance the purchase in that manner (s 171(1) CA 1985). Companies incorporated under Table A 1985 (but not Table A 1948) are authorised both to purchase their shares and to finance the purchase out of capital (reg 35 TA 1985). Companies without the necessary authority will need to amend their articles;
c. whether any **pre-emption provisions** apply on a transfer of shares. If so, the pre-emption rights will need to be excluded and/or waived (¶958+);
d. that **at least one non-redeemable share** will be left in issue after the purchase (s 159(3) CA 1985; restated at s 684(4) CA 2006 by 1 October 2009);
e. that the shares to be purchased are **fully paid** (s 159(3) CA 1985; restated at s 691(1) CA 2006 by 1 October 2009); and
f. if the shares are being purchased from a director or a person connected with a director, whether the purchase is a **substantial property transaction** requiring the approval of the shareholders by an ordinary resolution (see ¶2567+).

MEMO POINTS 1. **Public companies** should also be mindful of the minimum shareholder and issued share capital requirements for a public company (see ¶2012 and ¶720 respectively).
2. Under the **new Companies Act**, a company will not need to be authorised by its articles to carry out an own share purchase and a private company will not need to be authorised by its articles to finance an own share purchase out of capital, although the articles may restrict or prohibit the purchase or payment, as appropriate (ss 690(2), 709 CA 2006, expected to come into force by 1 October 2009).

Approval of purchase contract

1387

The terms of the own share purchase must be **approved in advance** of the contract being entered into (and not at the same time (*Re R W Peak (Kings Lynn) Ltd* [1998] 1 BCLC 193)) by a special resolution of the shareholders (s 164(1), (2) CA 1985; restated at s 694 CA 2006 by 1 October 2009). If the company has different classes of shares, the class rights may require that separate class meetings are called to approve the purchase.

MEMO POINTS The shareholders' authority can be **varied**, **revoked** or **renewed** by passing another special resolution (s 164(3) CA 1985; restated at s 694(4) CA 2006 by 1 October 2009).

1388 The written contract or a memorandum of its terms (including the names of the shareholders whose shares are going to be purchased) must be available for **inspection** by shareholders at the company's registered office for at least 15 days before the meeting to consider the special resolution as well as at the meeting itself (s 164(6) CA 1985; restated at s 696 CA 2006 by 1 October 2009).

1389 Particular **voting rules** apply in considering whether or not the special resolution to approve the contract has been properly passed. The voting rights of the shares in question must be disregarded in deciding whether or not the resolution has been passed (s 164(5) CA 1985; restated at s 695 CA 2006 by 1 October 2009).

> MEMO POINTS   Private companies can use the **written resolution procedure**, in which case the contract or memorandum of terms must be supplied to the shareholders at the same time as the written resolution (s 300C CA 2006 inserted by para 13 Sch 1 SI 2007/2194). If this is not done, exceptionally, case law suggests that the informal unanimous agreement of the shareholders may be sufficient to cure this procedural defect (*BDG Roof-Bond Ltd v Douglas* [2000] 1 BCLC 401). Further, the shareholder whose shares are being purchased is treated as not being entitled to vote. In other words, his signature to the resolution is not required, even if only some of his shares are being purchased (s 289 CA 2006). The written resolution procedure is therefore not open to single shareholder companies.

1390 A contract can be **contingent** upon the occurrence of a particular event or events. A contingent contract must also be approved in advance. Once it has been approved, it is not necessary for another approval to be obtained for the actual purchase (s 165 CA 1985; restated at s 694 CA 2006 by 1 October 2009).

> MEMO POINTS   1. **Public companies** must state the date on which the shareholders' authority expires, which cannot be later than 18 months after the resolution (s 164(4) CA 1985; restated at s 694(5) CA 2006 by 1 October 2009). A contingent contract (for example, an option to purchase) can be used to extend this period as there is no requirement that the purchase must take place within 18 months, only that the contract must be entered into within that time.
> 2. Any payment made by the company in **consideration for** the other party entering into the **contingent contract** (as opposed to the consideration that the company pays for the shares itself) must be made out of distributable profits. If it is not, the purchase under that contract will be unlawful (s 168 CA 1985; restated at s 705 CA 2006 by 1 October 2009).

Changes to contract

1392 Any **variation to the terms** of the contract must be approved by the shareholders in the same way as the original contract, except that both the original and varied contract or memorandum must be made available to the shareholders 15 days before the meeting and at the meeting itself (s 164(7) CA 1985; restated at s 697 CA 2006 by 1 October 2009).

Similarly, a company can only agree to **release** its rights under the contract (that is, excuse the other party from his obligations) if the terms of the release are approved by the shareholders in the same way as the original contract (s 167(2) CA 1985; restated at s 700 CA 2006 by 1 October 2009). Again, both the original contract and the terms of release must be made available to the shareholders 15 days before the meeting and at the meeting itself.

> MEMO POINTS   1. A company's **payment in consideration for a variation or release** of an own share purchase contract must be made out of distributable profits. If it is not, the purchase following the purported variation will be unlawful or the purported release will be void (s 168 CA 1985; restated at s 705 CA 2006 by 1 October 2009).
> 2. An own share purchase contract cannot be **assigned** (s 167(1) CA 1985; restated at s 704 CA 2006 by 1 October 2009).

Post purchase formalities

1394 A company must file a copy of the **special resolution** approving the terms of the own share purchase contract within 15 days of it being passed.

Additionally, it must notify Companies House of the actual purchase within 28 days of completion by filing **Form 169** specifying the number and nominal value of each class of shares purchased and the date on which the purchase was completed. Purchases completed over a 28-day period can be included on the same form. However, if the own share purchase is completed in tranches with more than a 28-day gap between completion of each tranche, a separate Form 169 will be needed in each case (s 169 CA 1985; restated at s 707 CA 2006 by 1 October 2009). Any officer in default of this requirement is subject to a fine (s 169(6) CA 1985; restated at s 707 CA 2006 by 1 October 2009; ¶9935).

The company will also need to pay **stamp duty** on the purchase (see ¶1875+ for the payment of stamp duty on share transfers). Companies House will only accept Form 169 if it has been properly stamped.

> MEMO POINTS 1. **Public companies** must also state the total amount paid for the purchase and the maximum and minimum amount paid for shares in each class on Form 169.
> 2. Under the **new Companies Act**, companies will be subject to a new additional requirement to file a statement of capital. This is a "snapshot" of the company's total issued share capital at a particular point in time, in this case after the own share purchase (s 708 CA 2006, expected to come into force by 1 October 2009; reg 10 draft Companies (Shares, Share Capital and Authorised Minimum) Regulations 2007).

The **share certificates** will need to be returned to the company for cancellation and the **register of shareholders** will need to be updated.

1395

Further, a copy of the **own share purchase contract** (or if there is no written contract, the memorandum of its terms), including any variations, must be kept at the company's registered office for 10 years after the purchase or the date on which the contract otherwise ended, whichever is the later. The copy must be available for free inspection by the shareholders (s 169(4) CA 1985; restated at s 702 CA 2006 by 1 October 2009). Any company or officer in default of these requirements is subject to a fine (s 169(7) CA 1985; restated at s 703 CA 2006 by 1 October 2009; ¶9935).

> MEMO POINTS 1. Anyone (not just the shareholders) is entitled to inspect a copy of the own share purchase contract or memorandum of terms in relation to a **public company**.
> 2. Draft regulations have been published under the new Companies Act which will allow companies to keep their records, including copies of own share purchase contracts, at the registered office or at one alternative **location** that is situated in the same part of the UK as the registered office (reg 5 draft Companies (Company Records and Fees) Regulations 2007). This part of the draft regulations is likely to come into force by 1 October 2009. For the proposed regulations on how a person can inspect company records, see ¶3869/mp.
> 3. However, a company can keep certain types of shares as **treasury shares** (see ¶740/mp), in which case the shares are not cancelled and the company is entered on the register as the shareholder.

Where **tax clearance** for the purchase has been obtained, Revenue and Customs must be notified of the full particulars of the transaction within 60 days of making the payment.

1396

6. Additional procedure: purchase or redemption out of capital

As a last resort, if a company does not have enough distributable profits or enough from the proceeds of a fresh issue, a **private company** can purchase or redeem shares out of capital (¶1356+). Where it decides to do so, it must comply with further procedures (in addition to the relevant procedure above) that ensure the protection of creditors and shareholders. References below to a "company" are to a private company only.

1400

Pre-purchase/redemption

In order to determine the permissible capital payment, the company will need to **prepare accounts** as at a date within the 3 months before the directors' statutory declaration referred to below. To circumvent the expense of preparing a set of accounts in the middle of an accounting period, a redemption or purchase out of capital should be timed so that the directors' statutory declaration occurs within 3 months of the end of the company's accounting period, if possible.

1402

Directors' statutory declaration

1404 Before a company can purchase or redeem shares out of capital, all of the directors must make a joint statutory declaration on Form 173 which **sets out** (s 173(3), (5) CA 1985):
– whether the company is recognised or licensed as a bank or is an insurance company;
– the amount of the permissible capital payment (see ¶1357); and
– a statement regarding the solvency of the company in the terms set out below.

> MEMO POINTS Under the **new Companies Act**, the directors will have to make a statement to the same effect (s 714 CA 2006, expected to come into force by 1 October 2009; reg 14 draft Companies (Shares, Share Capital and Authorised Minimum) Regulations 2007).

1405 The declaration takes the following form:
"We have made full enquiry into the affairs and prospects of the company, and we have formed the opinion:
a. as regards its initial situation immediately following the date on which the payment out of capital is proposed to be made, that there will be no grounds on which the company could then be found unable to pay its debts, and
b. as regards its prospects for the year immediately following that date, that, having regard to our intentions with respect to the management of the company's business during that year and to the amount and character of the financial resources which will in our view be available during that year, the company will be able to continue to carry on business as a going concern (and will accordingly be able to pay its debts as they fall due) throughout that year."

1406 In deciding whether or not the company is able to pay its debts, the directors **must take into account** the company's prospective and contingent liabilities, as would be relevant if the company was being wound up by the court (s 173(4) CA 1985). In addition, the reference to the "management of the company's business during [the following] year" implies that the directors must intend to carry on business for at least a year after the payment out of capital.

> MEMO POINTS The **new Companies Act** will require the directors, when making the solvency statement, to take account of all contingent and prospective liabilities, not just those that would be relevant if the company were being wound up by the court (s 714(4) CA 2006, expected to come into force by 1 October 2009).

1407 **If the opinion** of the directors later turns out to have been **wrong** (that is, if the company becomes insolvent within a year of the payment out of capital), the directors and the shareholder whose shares were purchased or redeemed could be jointly and severally liable to contribute towards the debts and liabilities of the company and the expenses of a subsequent liquidation, up to the amount of capital paid out (see ¶7863+). The actual **liability** would of course depend upon the shortfall in the assets of the company (s 76 IA 1986). In addition, the directors could be liable to a fine, imprisonment or both (s 173(6) CA 1985; restated at s 715 CA 2006 by 1 October 2009; ¶9935).

The directors can **defend** the claim on the basis that their opinion was based on reasonable grounds (s 173(6) CA 1985, restated at s 715(1) CA 2006 by 1 October 2009; s 76(2)(b) IA 1986). The burden of proof is on the directors but, if they are successful in their defence, the ex-shareholder alone is liable to contribute as a result of the inaccurate statutory declaration. The defence does not extend to him and he cannot obtain a contribution from the directors.

> MEMO POINTS The directors and ex-shareholder are able to **petition for a winding up** of the company if it is unable to pay its debts as they fall due or on just and equitable grounds in order to minimise their future potential liability (ss 122(1)(f), (g), 124(3) IA 1986).

Auditor's report

1409 The directors' statutory declaration must have attached to it an auditor's report addressed to the directors (not to the company or shareholders) which **states that** (s 173(5) CA 1985; restated at s 714(6) CA 2006 by 1 October 2009):
– he has enquired into the affairs of the company;

– the amount stated in the declaration as the permissible capital payment is in his view properly determined; and
– he is not aware of anything to indicate that the opinion expressed by the directors is unreasonable in all of the circumstances.

> MEMO POINTS An **example** of an auditor's report is available from the Auditing Practices Board, and may be freely downloaded from its website (Bulletin 2007/1, published January 2007).

The auditor must make sure that his report is accurate as he could be liable to the directors (as the intended recipients of the report) for any **negligent misstatements**. The auditor could also be liable to the shareholders as it is reasonably foreseeable that they would rely on the report, since the statutory procedure requires that the shareholders are given the opportunity to inspect it when considering whether or not to approve the payment out of capital (*Caparo Industries plc v Dickman* [1990] 1 All ER 568; *Galoo v Bright Grahame Murray* [1995] 1 All ER 16). **1410**

Shareholder approval

The payment out of capital must be **approved by** a special resolution of the shareholders passed **within** 1 week of the directors' statutory declaration (ss 173(2), 174(1) CA 1985; restated at s 716 CA 2006 by 1 October 2009). If the company has different classes of shares, the class rights may require that separate class meetings are called to approve the payment out of capital; the articles should be checked in this regard. **1412**

Both the statutory declaration and auditor's report must be available for **inspection** at the meeting for the resolution to be effective (s 174(4) CA 1985; restated at s 718 CA 2006 by 1 October 2009).

As with the special resolution to approve an own share purchase contract, the **voting** rights of the shares in question must be disregarded in deciding whether or not the special resolution has been passed (s 174(2), (3) CA 1985; restated at s 717 CA 2006 by 1 October 2009).

> MEMO POINTS Companies can use the **written resolution** procedure instead, although there may be difficulties in ensuring that the resolutions are signed and returned within a week. If they do so, the statutory declaration and auditor's report must be supplied to the shareholders at the same time as the resolution (s 300D CA 2006 inserted by para 13 Sch 1 SI 2007/2194). The shareholder whose shares are being purchased or redeemed is treated as not being entitled to vote, therefore his signature to the resolution is not required (even if only part of his shares are to be purchased or redeemed) (s 289 CA 2006). The written resolution procedure is therefore not open to single shareholder companies.

Publicity

Within 1 week of the special resolution having been passed, the company must publicise the proposed payment out of capital by (s 175(1)-(3) CA 1985; restated at s 719 CA 2006 by 1 October 2009): **1414**
– **publishing** a notice in the *Gazette*; and
– publishing a notice in a national newspaper; or
– giving **notice** in writing to all of the creditors of the company.

Before any of the notices are published, the company must also **file** a copy of the statutory declaration and auditor's report **at Companies House** (s 175(5) CA 1985; restated at s 719(4) CA 2006 by 1 October 2009).

The **notices must state** (s 175(1) CA 1985; restated at s 719(1) CA 2006 by 1 October 2009):
– that the company has approved a payment out of capital for the purpose of a purchase, redemption or both as appropriate;
– the amount of the permissible capital payment (see ¶1357);
– the date of the special resolution that approved the payment out of capital;
– that the statutory declaration and auditor's report are available for inspection at the registered office of the company; and
– that any creditor may apply to court for an order prohibiting the payment in the 5 weeks immediately following the date of the special resolution that approved the payment.

1415 In accordance with the notices, a copy of the statutory declaration and auditor's report must be kept at the registered office for free **inspection** by any shareholder or creditor from the date on which a notice is first published to 5 weeks after the date of the resolution approving the payment out of capital (s 175(4), (5) CA 1985; restated at s 720 CA 2006 by 1 October 2009).

> MEMO POINTS If a copy is not kept at the registered office and/or is not made available for inspection, the company and any officer in **default** will be subject to a fine and a daily default fine (see ¶9935). Further, the court is able to order an immediate inspection of the documents (s 175(7), (8) CA 1985; restated at s 720(7) CA 2006 by 1 October 2009).
>
> Draft regulations have been published under the **new Companies Act** which will allow companies to keep their records, including the statutory declaration and auditor's report, at the registered office or at one alternative location that is situated in the same part of the UK as the registered office (reg 5 draft Companies (Company Records and Fees) Regulations 2007). This part of the draft regulations is likely to come into force by 1 October 2009. For the proposed regulations on how a person can inspect company records, see ¶3869/mp.

Right to object

1417 Any creditor or shareholder **who** did not vote in favour of the special resolution to approve the payment out of capital can object to the payment by applying to court for the resolution to be cancelled. The application to object must be made **within** 5 weeks of the date on which that resolution was passed (s 176(1) CA 1985; restated at s 721 CA 2006 by 1 October 2009).

The **court** can (and generally will be minded to) adjourn the **hearing** to allow for negotiation between the company and the dissenting creditor or shareholder, for example, so that the creditor's claims are protected or the shareholder's shares are purchased. At the hearing, the court can order that the company purchases any shareholder's shares (not just the shares of the dissenting shareholder, although it would be highly unusual for the court to order that another shareholder's shares are purchased) and for an appropriate reduction in the capital of the company. The court can also make appropriate amendments to the memorandum and articles of the company; the company is not permitted to make these amendments itself. If the court does confirm the resolution, it can extend the time limits in the resolution and statute (s 177 CA 1985; restated at s 721 CA 2006 by 1 October 2009).

1418 If an application objecting to the resolution is made, the company must notify Companies House straight away by **filing** Form 176. In addition, once the court makes its order, the company must file a copy of it at Companies House within 15 days of the date of the order (or any longer period that the court may specify) (s 176(2), (3) CA 1985; restated at s 722 CA 2006 by 1 October 2009).

If a company fails to make the appropriate filings, the company and any officers in default will be liable to a fine (¶9935).

Completion

1420 A purchase or redemption out of capital must take place **between** 5 and 7 weeks after the date of the special resolution approving the payment, unless the court has ordered otherwise (s 174(1) CA 1985; restated at s 723 CA 2006 by 1 October 2009).

These strict time limits mean that the facts upon which the statutory declaration and auditor's report are based are likely to still be accurate at the time of purchase or redemption, as appropriate. However, **if the financial circumstances of the company deteriorate** in that period, it should not proceed with the payment. Note that the company will be protected from its liability for breach of contract (see ¶1427+).

Filing requirements

1422 In addition to the usual Companies House filings on redemption or purchase and any filings to be made if a shareholder objects to the payment (¶1418), a copy of a **special resolution** to approve a payment out of capital must be filed at Companies House within 15 days of it being passed.

SHARES AND SHARE CAPITAL 159

7. Summary

The following table summarises the procedure that must be followed in each case.

1424

Time	Redemption	Own share purchase	Purchase/redemption out of capital
	Pre-redemption/purchase checks		
− 3 months	−	−	Prepare accounts to determine permissible capital payment
− 1 month	Obtain tax clearance if relevant		
− 23 days	−	Circulate notice of general meeting to pass relevant resolutions i.e: − special resolution to approve own share purchase contract; − special resolution to approve payment out of capital; and/or − ordinary resolution to approve substantial property transaction	
− 15 days	−	Keep copy of written contract or memorandum of terms for inspection at registered office	−
− 7 days	−	−	Directors' statutory declaration with attached auditors' report
MEETING	−	General meeting to pass relevant resolutions	
+ 6 days	−	−	File directors' statutory declaration and auditors' report at Companies House
+ 7 days	−	−	Publish notices
+ 7 to 35 days	−	−	Keep copy of directors' statutory declaration and auditors' report for inspection at registered office. If court application, file Form 176 at Companies House straight away and copy of court order within 15 days of it being made[1]
+ 15 days	−	File special resolutions at Companies House	
+ 18 months	−	Public companies only − renew shareholder approval if purchase not completed	−
COMPLETE (+ 35 to 49 days if financed out of capital)	Complete purchase/redemption and make payment at the same time		
+ 1 day	Update register of shareholders		
+ 28 days	−	File Form 169 at companies House[1]	−
+ 1 month	File Form 122 at Companies House[1]	−	−
+ 60 days	If tax clearance obtained, notify Revenue and Customs of completion		−
+ 0 to 10 years	−	Keep copy of written contract or memorandum of terms at registered office	−

Note:
1. The names of Forms 176, 169 and 122, like the names of other **Companies House forms**, are taken from the section numbers of the legislation. As all of the section numbers will change under the new Companies Act, Companies House proposes to change the names of all of its forms to reflect their function rather than the relevant section number ("Working with Companies House: a consultation on the registrar's rules and related provisions which will apply under the Companies Act 2006"). At the time of writing, the new form names are not yet available.

8. Failure to purchase or redeem

1427 Failure to purchase or redeem shares in accordance with an own share purchase contract or the terms of redemption constitutes a **breach of contract**. The company is able to sue the other contracting party (i.e. the shareholder selling or redeeming his shares) for that breach and claim damages or specific performance (this is an order that the party in default complies with the terms of the contract). However, the remedies available to a shareholder suing a company are limited by statute (s 178 CA 1985; restated at s 735 CA 2006 by 1 October 2009). A company cannot be sued for damages. Further, a court can only order specific performance if the company can meet the costs of the purchase or redemption out of distributable profits.

> MEMO POINTS   The terms of redemption or purchase can be enforced by the shareholder as usual **if the company is wound up** after the contractual date of redemption or purchase has passed and the company had sufficient distributable profits to purchase or redeem the shares on that date. The shareholder will be able to prove in the company's liquidation (i.e. have his claim considered by the liquidator).

1428 There are however **other remedies** available to the shareholder who expects his shares to be purchased or redeemed. He can:
a. obtain an injunction to prevent the company paying a dividend that would result in it having insufficient distributable profits to complete a purchase or redemption (*Re Holders Investment Trust Ltd* [1971] 2 All ER 289); or
b. sue on another related contract and claim damages, even if the damages amount to what would have been claimed if he could have sued for breach of the purchase or redemption contract (*Barclays Bank plc v British & Commonwealth Holdings plc* [1996] 1 BCLC 1).

III. Reduction of share capital

1435 The term "reduction of share capital" refers to a statutory procedure which can be **used to** bring about any sort of diminution in the share capital of a company. This can include:
– extinguishing or reducing the liability on any of its shares in respect of unpaid share capital;
– cancelling any paid-up share which is lost or unrepresented by available assets;
– paying off any paid-up share capital which is in excess of the company's needs;
– reducing the share premium account; or
– reducing the capital redemption reserve.

A private company can also purchase its own shares out of capital.

Generally speaking the reduction can take any **form** but it must be carried out for a discernible **purpose**. The purposes can include

> MEMO POINTS   1. A reduction of share capital (in the wider sense of the term) can also be brought about as a result of the following, and in these cases there is no need to also follow the formal statutory procedure:
> – a reduction on a **forfeiture** of shares or a surrender to avoid forfeiture (see ¶1219+);
> – permitted **uses of the share premium account** (see ¶1247);
> – a permitted **purchase or redemption** by the company of its own shares (see ¶1337+);
> – a purchase by the company of its shares and a corresponding reduction in capital as a result of a **court order** (for example, in an action for unfair prejudice);

– a **cancellation of unissued** share capital (see ¶1312/mp); and.
– a **cancellation of treasury shares** (see ¶740/mp for an explanation of this type of share).
2. The **new Companies Act** will introduce important de-regulatory provisions, notably allowing private companies to effect a reduction of capital without the court's approval or a power to do so in its articles (¶1469/mp; ¶1472/mp). A company will also be able to reduce its redenomination reserve (see ¶1326) by following the statutory reduction of share capital procedure (s 628(3) CA 2006, expected to come into force by 1 October 2009).

1436

Most reductions in share capital have a significant impact upon the shareholders and creditors of a company: shareholders may lose their shareholdings and, according to the doctrine of capital maintenance, a diminution in the share capital of a company may prejudice creditors. Accordingly, the protection of these two groups' interests underlies the whole **procedure** which requires:
– authority in the articles;
– shareholder approval;
– court approval; and
– registration.

> MEMO POINTS 1. The restrictions do not apply to **unlimited companies** with a share capital. These companies may reduce their share capital in whatever manner is permitted by their memorandum and articles (*Re Borough Commercial & Building Society Ltd* [1893] 2 Ch 242).
> 2. When the relevant provisions of the **new Companies Act** come into force (expected to be by 1 October 2009), a private company limited by shares will be able to reduce its share capital using a new solvency statement procedure for capital reductions (see ¶1469/mp).

A. Key concepts

1. Purpose of reduction

A reduction in share capital must have a discernible purpose; it must not be a "pointless or hollow act" (*Re Thorn EMI plc* [1989] BCLC 612; *Re Ratners Group plc* [1988] BCLC 685).

1438

Common purposes for a reduction in share capital are:
a. to **eliminate a deficit on the profit and loss account** and enable a company to declare dividends to its shareholders;
b. to **create a distributable reserve** which could be used, for example, to make a distribution in specie to the shareholders thereby transferring an asset of the company to them. Such a device is sometimes used in a group to transfer property or subsidiaries from one holding company to another (for example, *Re Ransomes plc* [1999] 2 BCLC 591);
c. to **repay capital that is in excess of a company's needs** (s 135(2)(c) CA 1985; restated at s 641(4)(b)(ii) CA 2006 by 1 October 2009). Capital can be repaid by way of cash or assets of the company (even if the value of the assets transferred exceeds the amount by which the capital has been reduced); or
d. to **reduce the nominal value of a company's shares** so they more closely reflect their market value (*Forsayth Oil and Gas NL v Livia Pty Ltd* [1985] BCLC 378).

Another reason for a reduction is because **capital has been lost or is unrepresented by available assets** (s 135(2)(b) CA 1985; restated at s 641(4)(b)(i) CA 2006 by 1 October 2009). For example, suppose A Ltd acquires the entire issued share capital of B Ltd for £1 million and satisfies the consideration by issuing the shareholders of B Ltd with 250,000 £1 shares (that is, at a premium of £3 per share). If the subsidiary were to completely collapse, A Ltd would be able to apply for the share capital and share premium account to be reduced by £250,000 and £750,000 respectively as being lost.

1439

> MEMO POINTS 1. When considering whether capital is or is not represented by "**available assets**", both tangible and intangible assets (including goodwill) must be considered together with assets

representing a reserve fund and any amount credited to the profit and loss account (*Re Barrow Haematite Steel Co* (1888) 39 Ch D 582).

2. If the company has reserve funds created out of profits, the **loss of capital should be apportioned** between the reserves and called up share capital (although the company can choose to attribute more to the reserve funds if it wishes to do so). The amount "lost" is the amount apportioned to the share capital (*Re Hoare & Co Ltd and Reduced* [1904-7] All ER Rep 635).

3. Generally, the **nature of the loss** must be permanent; a temporary fall in the value of an asset or the balance of the profit and loss account will not be sufficient (*Re Welsbach Incandescent Gas Light Co Ltd* [1904] 1 Ch 87). However, in some cases of temporary loss the court has agreed to the reduction on the basis of an undertaking from the company that if the loss is recovered or if the value of the company's assets increase, the amount of the recovery (up to the amount by which the capital is reduced) will be transferred to a capital reserve which would not be available to be distributed by way of dividend (*Re Jupiter House Investments (Cambridge) Ltd* [1985] 1 BCLC 222; *Re Grosvenor Press plc* [1985] BCLC 286).

1440 A reduction with a discernible purpose will not necessarily be approved by the court; in some cases **another method of achieving that purpose** should be preferred. In particular, the court has expressed reluctance to approve a reduction which:

a. involved paying off part of the ordinary shares when not all of the ordinary shareholders had consented because the dissenting shareholders would have been better protected if the proposal had been submitted as a scheme of arrangement rather than a reduction in share capital (*Re Robert Stephen Holdings Ltd* [1968] 1 All ER 195);

b. was almost a sham transaction for the purposes of avoiding stamp duty and could have been carried out by means of a contractual arrangement between the parties, as was the usual practice (*Re Rylands Whitecross Ltd*, 21 December 1973, unreported); or

c. involved a cancellation of unissued share capital and did not form part of a general scheme of reduction (*Re Castiglione, Erskine & Co Ltd* [1958] 2 All ER 455).

2. Form of reduction

1445 A reduction in share capital can take many different forms.

> EXAMPLE
> 1. Transferring any paid up share capital or any of the share premium account or capital redemption reserve into a reserve account (*Re Thorn EMI plc* [1989] BCLC 612).
> 2. Repaying any paid up share capital or any of the share premium account or capital redemption reserve to the shareholders (s 135(2)(c) CA 1985; restated at s 641(4)(b)(iii) CA 2006 by 1 October 2009).
> 3. Cancelling any paid up share capital or any of the share premium account or capital redemption reserve (s 135(2)(b) CA 1985; restated at s 641(4)(b)(i) CA 2006 by 1 October 2009).
> 4. Extinguishing or reducing the liability to pay up shares which are not yet fully paid (s 135(2)(a) CA 1985; restated at s 641(4)(a) CA 2006 by 1 October 2009).
> 5. Converting ordinary shares into redeemable shares (so that the reduction is "deferred" to when the shares are redeemed) (*Re Forth Wines Ltd* [1991] BCC 638).
> 6. Cancelling shares in one denomination in return for the issue of shares in another denomination (*Re Scandinavian Bank Group plc* [1987] 2 All ER 70).

1446 Normally, the **reduction must relate to** capital which the company has at the date of the shareholder resolution to approve the reduction (*Re Transfesa Terminals Ltd*, 27 July 1987, unreported). However, the reduction can relate to future capital provided it is conditional upon the creation of that capital and the creation takes effect prior to the presentation of the petition to court to approve the reduction. The court cannot validly confirm a resolution for a reduction which remains conditional at the time of confirmation (*Re Tip-Europe Ltd* [1988] BCLC 231).

Reduction fair and equitable to shareholders

1448 Although statute allows a company to reduce its share capital in any way, the court will only approve a reduction if it is fair and equitable to the shareholders. However, the concept of **fairness and equity is construed** narrowly; the wider issue of whether a particular reduction is favourable to the shareholders or whether it is the best way to achieve the desired result is not one for the court to consider. This is because generally the court will not interfere with the internal management of a company (*Poole v National Bank of China Ltd* [1904-7] All ER Rep 138).

In general, a reduction will be fair and equitable if all of the shareholders are **treated equally**. For example, if A Ltd has an issued share capital of 1,000 ordinary shares of £1 each, of which 200 are held by Mr X and 800 are held by Mr Y, and A Ltd proposes a reduction that will result in a cancellation of 100 shares, the reduction will be fair and equitable if 20 of Mr X's shares and 80 of Mr Y's shares are cancelled. It is however possible for shareholders to agree to **unequal treatment**. In that case, the reduction will still satisfy the "equitable" requirement.

A particular problem arises when a company has **different classes** of shares. In general, a reduction in a company with different classes will be equitable if any loss and/or return of capital to the shareholders is apportioned in accordance with their class rights. This has led to some surprising results, particularly as regards the treatment of preference shareholders, as illustrated by the cases discussed below.

1449

Paying off one class

It is equitable to pay off just one class, provided that the shareholders' rights on a return of capital are respected. Accordingly, if a company's preference shares do not carry a specific right to vote on the matter, it is perfectly possible for the ordinary shareholders to vote to pay off the **preference shares in accordance with their class rights** without the consent of the preference shareholders.

1450

The **reason** for this position is that most preference shares do not carry a right to participate in the surplus capital of a company on winding up over and above the capital paid on each share. Providing the share rights do not contain any protection against early repayment, preference shareholders cannot object to a scheme of reduction which simply returns their capital to them earlier, even though this would result in them losing the income derived from their preferential dividend. This is because, in the court's view, preference shares are deemed to be analogous to loans and just as a lender could not complain about lost interest if a loan were repaid, so preference shareholders cannot complain about their lost dividends if their capital is repaid. Such reasoning would apply even if the preference share carried the right to participate in dividends over and above the fixed rate; the important issue is the right to capital not the right to income (*Scottish Insurance Corp Ltd v Wilsons and Clyde Coal Co Ltd* [1949] 1 All ER 1068; *Re Saltdean Estate Co Ltd* [1968] 3 All ER 829; *House of Fraser plc v ACGE Investments Ltd* [1987] AC 387).

The requirement for equitable treatment therefore provides little protection for the preference shareholder. The court's view is that "this vulnerability is, and has always been, a characteristic of the preferred shares" (*Re Saltdean Estate Co Ltd* [1968] 3 All ER 829). The court will even be prepared to agree to a repayment of preference shares when there are **arrears of dividend** on the basis that the arrears are paid off before registration of the order. More usually, the company would simply arrange for the reduction to take effect immediately after payment of the accrued dividend.

It should be noted that a reduction which involves **paying off** the preference shareholders but **not in accordance with their class rights** will not necessarily be unfair. The court will then go on to examine the proposal and the burden will fall on those supporting the reduction to prove it is fair. This is a difficult burden to discharge; it may be fair to pay off the preference shareholders with an equivalent (such as loan stock) but the court would be inclined to find that the reduction was unfair if the consideration given to the preference shareholders was not adequate compensation (*Re Thomas de la Rue & Co Ltd* [1911] 2 Ch 361; *Re Holders Investment Trust Ltd* [1971] 2 All ER 289).

1451

Of course, the converse situation could also arise, namely, that the ordinary shareholders vote to pay off part of their own **ordinary shares** but not the preference shares. The preference shareholders could then have cause to object because they too wanted to receive a partial payment. In such circumstances, the court appears to be more willing to look into the inherent

1452

fairness of the proposal although the mere fact that the proposal would result in non-payment to the preference shareholders would not make it unfair (*Re Ransomes plc* [1999] 1 BCLC 775; *Re Ransomes plc* [1999] 2 BCLC 591; *Re Fowlers Vacola Manufacturing Co Ltd* [1966] VR 97).

Apportioning loss to one class

1453 The effect is slightly different where there are different classes and the reduction will result in a loss of capital (rather than a repayment). If a company's share classes have the **same rights on a return of capital**, a reduction which results in a loss of capital for the shareholders will only be permitted if it is carried out on a proportionate basis (*Re Mackenzie & Co Ltd* [1916-17] All ER 1018). However, if a company's share classes have **different rights on a return of capital**, the loss ought to fall on those who would bear the loss on a winding up (*Re Floating Dock Co of St Thomas Ltd* [1895] 1 Ch 691). For example, in a company with ordinary shares and preference shares with the right to have their capital repaid to them in priority to the ordinary shares, the loss ought to fall on the ordinary shareholders.

> EXAMPLE   A Ltd has an issued share capital of £75,000 divided into 50,000 ordinary shares of £1 each and 5,000 preference shares of £5, all of which are fully paid. On a return of capital, the preference shares carry the right to receive repayment of the capital paid on each share in preference to the ordinary shares but no further right to participate in the surplus capital of the company. It would be equitable for A Ltd to propose a reduction of:
> – £25,000 which was in excess of its needs by the cancellation of all its preference shares and the repayment to the preferential shareholders of £5 per share held; or
> – £5,000 which had been lost by the cancellation of 5,000 ordinary shares.

> MEMO POINTS   It is unlikely that a reduction in share capital will amount to a **variation of class rights** unless this is specified as a share right (see ¶1279).

3. Position of third parties

Creditors

1458 According to the doctrine of capital maintenance, a reduction in share capital may have a prejudicial effect on creditors. As a result, before the court will confirm the reduction, it must be satisfied that the interests of the creditors have been **protected** (*Re Ratners Group plc* [1988] BCLC 685). In particular, the court must consider the interests of creditors when the reduction involves (s 136(2) CA 1985; restated at s 645 CA 2006 by 1 October 2009):
– a repayment to shareholders of paid up share capital; or
– a diminution in the liability of shareholders to pay up any unpaid share capital.

The court is also permitted to take the interest of creditors into account in any other case which it thinks fit but this rarely occurs in practice; the court will usually accept that the company's creditors are not affected when considering other reductions.

Comment: New regulations expected to come into force on 6 April 2008 will allow creditors to object to a reduction of capital if they can show that it is likely to put the repayment of their debt at risk (draft Companies (Reduction of Capital) Regulations 2008; see ¶704+ for more on this reform).

> MEMO POINTS   The court is concerned with the **existing creditors** as at the date of the reduction; special circumstances (such as the reduction being based on a temporary loss) must exist to require the court to safeguard the **future creditors** of the company (*Re Grosvenor Press plc* [1985] BCLC 286).

1459 There is a **statutory** mechanism which the court can adopt to ensure the protection of creditors (¶1486) but the court is also able to disregard that mechanism if appropriate in the circumstances (s 136(6) CA 1985; restated at s 645 CA 2006 by 1 October 2009). In practice, since the statutory mechanism could lead to delays, other **non-statutory** methods are usually presented to the court by the company to demonstrate that the interests of creditors have been protected. The court will usually accept these as sufficient evidence that the interests of creditors whose consent to the reduction has not been obtained are protected and exercise its discretion to disregard the statutory mechanism.

The most usual non-statutory methods used by companies are:
a. evidence that the company has **sufficient cash and liquid assets** to satisfy creditors' claims. If warranted by the nature and strength of the company's business and/or an independent valuation of it, the court may consider the value of the company's unlisted subsidiaries, as well as its cash, gilt-edged and listed securities (*Re Martin Currie Ltd* [2006] CSOH 77);
b. a **bank guarantee** guaranteeing payment of creditors' claims on default by the company; or
c. the company paying money into a **trust account** for the benefit of creditors.

Other third parties

The position of other third parties is not considered by the court. However, it would be prudent for a company to check whether any **contractual obligations** prevent it from carrying out a reduction of share capital or whether it must obtain consent from a third party. For example, some loan agreements prevent a company from carrying out a reduction of share capital without the lender's consent. Similarly, a shareholders' agreement may require the consent of certain shareholders to be obtained. **1460**

In addition, the company should have regard to the position of **share option** holders as there may need to be a corresponding change in the rights attaching to their options. Normally, the terms of the option itself will expressly provide for how it will be affected by a reduction or other reorganisation of share capital. If it does not, an express variation of the option may be required. Changes to the terms of a share option will not be implied by a reduction and this could lead to unintended consequences when it is exercised (*Forsayth Oil and Gas NL v Livia Pty Ltd* [1985] BCLC 378). **1461**

B. Procedure

There is a **four stage** procedure to effect a reduction of share capital: **1469**
– authority;
– shareholder approval;
– court approval; and
– registration at Companies House.

> MEMO POINTS When the relevant provisions of the **new Companies Act** come into force (expected to be by 1 October 2009), a private company limited by shares will be able to reduce its share capital using a new solvency statement procedure. Under this procedure, the reduction will have to be approved by a special resolution of the shareholders. In addition, all of the directors will have to make a statement regarding the solvency of the company for the following 12 months, similar to the solvency statement required for an own share purchase out of capital (see ¶1404+; reg 13 draft Companies (Shares, Share Capital and Authorised Minimum) Regulations 2007). The solvency statement will have to be made no more than 15 days before the date on which the resolution to reduce capital will be passed and will have to be made available to the company's shareholders before they vote on that resolution. Within 15 days of the resolution being passed, the company will have to file the solvency statement, the resolution and a "statement of capital" at Companies House. A statement of capital will be a "snapshot" of the company's total issued share capital at a particular point in time, in this case following the reduction. The reduction will take effect upon registration of those documents. In addition to making a solvency statement, the directors will also have to make a statement confirming that the solvency statement was made not more than 15 days before the date on which the resolution to reduce capital was passed and that the statement was provided to the company's shareholders (ss 642-644 CA 2006; reg 10 draft Companies (Shares, Share Capital and Authorised Minimum) Regulations 2007).
> Reserves created by a reduction of capital using the new solvency statement procedure will only be distributable (s 654 CA 2006; reg 9 draft Companies (Shares, Share Capital and Authorised Minimum) Regulations 2007):
> – if the reduction was confirmed by the court; or
> – to the extent that the reserve is treated as realised profit, where the reduction was made using the new solvency statement procedure.

This is to protect creditors, whose consent is not required under the new procedure and for whom the company does not have to provide security. Unlimited companies will be able to distribute any reserves created by a reduction of capital.

1. Authority

1472 A company must be **authorised by** its articles to reduce its share capital, capital redemption reserve or share premium account, as appropriate (s 135(1) CA 1985). Companies incorporated under Table A are authorised to do so in any way (reg 34 TA 1985). If the articles do not contain the required authority, they will need to be amended accordingly before the reduction is carried out.

> MEMO POINTS By 1 October 2009, the **new Companies Act** will not require a company to be authorised by its articles, although the articles may restrict or prohibit a reduction (s 641(6) CA 2006).

2. Shareholder approval

1475 A reduction of share capital must be **approved by** a special resolution of the shareholders who must have been **given an explanation** of the purpose of the reduction and the facts behind it.

Explanation to shareholders

1477 An explanation of the cause and **purpose** of the reduction and the **facts** behind it must be given to the shareholders so that they can make an informed decision as to whether or not to approve it. The explanation should be as full as possible and evidence that this has occurred will need to be shown to the court before it will approve the reduction.

1478 Generally, the **latest** that the explanation should be given is with the notice of the meeting at which the special resolution to approve the reduction is proposed (or, if the written resolution procedure is to be used, when the resolution is circulated amongst the shareholders). This gives the shareholders the information they need to decide whether or not to approve the resolution.

1479 If there is a **change in circumstances** between the giving of the explanation and the meeting, it is the duty of the directors to bring this change to the attention of all of the shareholders to whom the explanation has already been sent. The directors cannot wait until the meeting to inform shareholders of the correction because those not present at the meeting may have decided to attend and exercise their vote if they had been aware of the change in circumstances. However, the overall objective is to allow shareholders to make an informed decision. Therefore, any change in circumstances must be material; the court will not be concerned if the change is so small that it would not influence the reasonable shareholder. Equally, though more reluctantly, the court may be persuaded to overlook procedural irregularities or shortcomings concerning the provision of an explanation where they had no effect on the outcome (for example, because the resolution would have been passed anyway) (Re European Home Products plc [1988] BCLC 690; Re Jessel Trust Ltd [1985] BCLC 119; Re Minster Assets plc [1985] BCLC 200; Re Ransomes plc [1999] 1 BCLC 775; Re Ransomes plc [1999] 2 BCLC 591).

Special resolution

1481 The reduction must be approved by a special resolution of the shareholders. This is a statutory requirement and so the articles of the company cannot be changed to require an ordinary resolution instead.

The resolution can be **passed at** a shareholder meeting or by way of the written resolution procedure. However, it is unlikely that the shareholders' informal unanimous consent will be sufficient because it will be difficult to satisfy the court that the shareholders approved the reduction in full knowledge of the cause and its purpose. In addition, it would be difficult to arrange for the reduction to be registered without a minute of the resolution.

It is however possible for a **defective resolution** that was passed either at a meeting or by way of the written resolution procedure to be subsequently ratified by the unanimous consent of the shareholders who were entitled to vote on the resolution (*Re Pearce Duff & Co Ltd* [1960] 3 All ER 222).

3. Court approval

Court approval is **sought by** applying to the Companies Court by Part 8 claim form (Part 49 CPR; CPR PD 49). The applicant is the company; there are no respondents (for more on company applications, see ¶7143+). It will normally be necessary to instruct solicitors to act for the company.

1483

Making the application

In order to commence proceedings, the company must submit a Part 8 **claim form** supported by **witness statement**(s) setting out:
– the form and purpose of the reduction;
– whether or not the creditors are affected and if they are, how they are to be protected;
– how the approval of the shareholders was obtained; and
– the form of minute which the court is asked to approve.

1484

The witness statement should exhibit any necessary documentary evidence, such as the memorandum and articles of the company and any explanatory circular that was sent to the shareholders. The statement is usually made by the chairman of the board who also chaired the shareholder meeting at which the resolution to approve the reduction was passed. He is then able to deal with all aspects of the reduction in one statement.

Upon receipt of the claim form and evidence, the court office will check that the company's share capital has been correctly stated, that the special resolution was properly passed and that the form of minute sought is correct.

> MEMO POINTS   If the **shares** were **issued for non-cash consideration**, the application must set out the extent to which the shares are, or are treated as being, paid up (para 19 CPR PD 49).

Directions from the court

Once the claim form has been issued, the matter will be listed for a **directions hearing** before the Companies Court registrar in chambers (i.e. not in open court). This is a purely procedural hearing to ensure that the matter proceeds smoothly when the petition comes before the court. Depending upon the circumstances, the registrar will give directions as to:
– any further evidence that he considers should be provided to the court;
– the date upon which the petition will be listed for a hearing; and
– the advertisement of the petition hearing date in a national newspaper (in order to notify all creditors and shareholders of the proposed reduction).

1485

The registrar will also consider the **position of creditors**. If the reduction does not affect creditors (or if it does affect them, but the company has put adequate non-statutory protections in place, see ¶1459) he will usually direct that the statutory mechanism for the protection of creditors does not apply to the reduction. Unusually, if the reduction does affect creditors and the company has not put adequate protection in place, the registrar will give directions to implement the statutory mechanism.

1486

The basis of the **statutory mechanism** is that any creditor who, at a date fixed by the court, would be entitled to have his claim considered in a winding up of the company is entitled to object to a reduction of share capital (s 136(3) CA 1985; restated at s 646 CA 2006 by 1 October 2009). The registrar will therefore make directions for an enquiry to establish the debts of, and claims against, the company and the proceedings to be taken to settle the list of creditors entitled to object to the reduction (which may include requiring the company to provide the court with any relevant information). The registrar will also fix the date by reference to which the list is to be made. To this end, the registrar will usually direct that the newspaper advertisement should ask creditors to come forward by a particular date and that any creditors who do not will be excluded from the right to object (s 136(4) CA 1985; restated at s 646 CA 2006 by 1 October 2009).

Comment: New regulations expected to come into force on 6 April 2008 will allow creditors to object to a reduction of capital if they can show that it is likely to put the repayment of their debt at risk (draft Companies (Reduction of Capital) Regulations 2008; see ¶704+ for more on this reform).

> MEMO POINTS 1. It is a criminal offence for an officer of the company to (s 141 CA 1985; restated at s 647 CA 2006 by 1 October 2009; ¶9935):
> – wilfully **conceal** the name of a creditor who is entitled to object to the reduction;
> – wilfully **misrepresent** the nature or amount of any creditor's claim against the company; or
> – aid, abet or be privy to any such concealment or misrepresentation.
> 2. Where a reduction results in a diminution in the **liability of shareholders** to pay up any unpaid share capital, that liability will be restored if a list of creditors is compiled and a creditor who would have been entitled to object to the reduction was omitted from it because he was unaware of the proceedings or the way those proceedings would have affected his claim and the company is unable to pay the amount of his claim after the reduction (using the test under insolvency proceedings, see ¶7593+). In such a case, the shareholders will still be liable to pay the amount that they would have had to pay if the company had been wound up on the day before the reduction was registered (that is, the amount they would have had to contribute if the reduction had not occurred) (s 140(2)-(3) CA 1985; restated at s 653 CA 2006 by 1 October 2009).

1487 After the **directions hearing**, the company must comply with any directions given, including arranging for the advertisement of the petition.

Hearing

1488 The actual hearing will take place in open court before the Companies Court registrar. Most applications are **unopposed** and are decided by the registrar at this stage.

Any creditors or shareholders who object to the reduction can attend to oppose the application. If the application is **opposed**, the registrar will usually adjourn the hearing for listing before a Companies Court judge and make any necessary directions regarding the filing of further evidence. The judge will hear arguments from both the company and the objecting shareholder or creditor. In the case of an objecting creditor, the court can disregard his objections if the company secures payment of that creditor's claim. The company can agree to secure the full amount of the claim. If it does not, or if the amount is unascertained or contingent, the amount to be secured is determined by the court in the way that it would if the company were being wound up (s 136(5) CA 1985; restated at s 646 CA 2006 by 1 October 2009).

1489 In the cases of both opposed and unopposed applications, the **court** has complete **discretion** as to whether or not to approve the proposed reduction and if it does, it can do so on whatever terms and conditions it thinks fit (s 137(1) CA 1985; restated at s 648 CA 2006 by 1 October 2009). For example, the court could approve the reduction on the basis that the company creates a special reserve account which could not be distributed to the shareholders without the court's permission. However, the court will habitually exercise its discretion in favour of the reduction, provided that (*Re Ratners Group plc* [1988] BCLC 685):
– it has a discernible purpose (¶1438+);
– the shareholders have had the facts explained to them (¶1477+);
– the special resolution has been properly passed (¶1481);
– the shareholders have been treated equitably (¶1448+); and
– the creditors are protected (¶1458+).

1490 Assuming that the **application is granted**, the court will make an order that the reduction and the minute set out in the application (subject to any minor errors which may need correction) are approved. The court will also usually order that the registration of the order and minute at Companies House is advertised in the same newspaper in which the hearing was advertised.

MEMO POINTS 1. The court has particular discretion to make an order requiring a company to **publish the reasons for a reduction** or such other information which the court believes should be made available to the public, or to order that a company adds the words "and reduced" after its name (s 137(2) CA 1985; restated at s 648 CA 2006 by 1 October 2009). These powers are rarely used now.

2. There is no statutory bar on the court approving a reduction in the share capital of a **public company** that will take its share capital below the authorised minimum although this is a bar to registration of the reduction at Companies House (see ¶1494/mp). Where the articles of a public company prohibit a reduction to a level below the authorised minimum, the court will approve it provided that the reduction is immediately followed by a resolution to increase its capital above the authorised minimum (*Re MB Group plc* [1989] BCLC 672).

3. A reduction which involves a repayment to shareholders constitutes a **contractual right of each shareholder** against the company. A shareholder therefore has the usual 6 years to enforce that right (*Re Compania de Electricidad de la Provincia de Buenos Aires Ltd* [1978] 3 All ER 668).

4. Once a reduction has been approved and registered, a creditor or shareholder may still **appeal** against the reduction provided there are grounds to do so. The failure of the company to fulfil the purpose of the reduction as stated to the court is not necessarily grounds for appeal. The requirement for a discernible purpose is mainly to ensure full and frank disclosure before the court in order that it can decide whether or not to give its approval. Therefore, the court will not generally be minded to grant an appeal simply because the purpose of the reduction has changed, provided there is still some use in the reduction and that there is no increased risk of prejudice to the opposing party (*Re Ransomes plc* [1999] 2 BCLC 591).

4. Registration

A reduction of share capital only takes effect once it has been registered at Companies House (s 138(2) CA 1985). In order to obtain the registration, the company must file a copy of the **court order and minute** (approved by the court) at Companies House stating (s 138 CA 1985):
– the amount of share capital, capital redemption reserve or share premium account before and after the reduction;
– the number of shares into which it is to be divided and the amount per share; and
– the amount (if any) that is deemed to be paid up on each share at the date of registration.

There is **no minute** for the court to approve or which must be registered in relation to a reduction solely of the capital redemption reserve or share premium account (*Re Ransomes plc* [1999] 1 BCLC 775; *Re Ransomes plc* [1999] 2 BCLC 591).

The company will then have to **advertise** the registration of the order and minute in accordance with the court's order.

MEMO POINTS Under the **new Companies Act**, companies will be required to file a "statement of capital" rather than a minute. This will be a "snapshot" of the company's total issued share capital at a particular point in time, in this case following the reduction (s 649(1) CA 2006, expected to come into force by 1 October 2009; reg 10 draft Companies (Shares, Share Capital and Authorised Minimum) Regulations 2007). The reduction will take effect from registration of the documents at Companies House, as is currently the case, unless the reduction is part of a court approved scheme of arrangement, in which case the reduction will take effect upon delivery of the documents to Companies House (s 649(3) CA 2006, expected to come into force by 1 October 2009).

In addition, a copy of the **special resolution** approving the reduction will need to be filed at Companies House within 15 days of it being passed (s 30 CA 2006). Any alteration to the company's authorised share capital will need to be reflected in future prints of the **memorandum** (s 20(1) CA 1985) but there is no need to send an amended copy to Companies House (s 18(2) CA 1985).

MEMO POINTS 1. A reduction in the share capital of a **public company** that takes the company's share capital below the authorised minimum will not be registered by Companies House unless either the court directs otherwise or the company is first re-registered as a private company (s 139 CA 1985; restated at s 650 CA 2006 by 1 October 2009). The company can re-register as a private company following the usual procedure (see ¶673+) or, at the same time as confirming the reduction, the court can authorise the re-registration and specify the changes that the company will need to make to its memorandum and articles. The company can then re-register by filing

Form 139, a copy of the memorandum and articles as amended by the court, and the fee at Companies House (see ¶668). Upon re-registration, the company will be issued with a new certificate of incorporation which will be conclusive evidence that the company has complied with the requirements of re-registration and that the company is a private company. When the relevant provisions of the new Companies Act come into force (expected to be by 1 October 2009), public companies will be able to comply with the authorised minimum in sterling or euros (see ¶720). Regulations under the new Act will set out a method for calculating whether a public company's share capital has dropped below the authorised minimum on a reduction of capital, whichever currency it share capital comprises (reg 3 draft Companies (Shares, Share Capital and Authorised Minimum) Regulations 2007).

The name of Form 139, like the names of other **Companies House forms**, is taken from the section number of the legislation. As all of the section numbers will change under the new Companies Act, Companies House proposes to change the names of all of its forms to reflect their function rather than the relevant section number ("Working with Companies House: a consultation on the registrar's rules and related provisions which will apply under the Companies Act 2006"). At the time of writing, the new form names are not yet available.

2. The **new Companies Act** will abolish the concept of authorised share capital. There will be no need to amend the memorandum or send a copy to Companies House (see ¶712). This change is expected to be implemented by 1 October 2009.

C. Summary and checklist

1500

	Step
1	Decide upon the purpose of the reduction
2	Consider the proposed form of reduction and ensure that it is fair and equitable to the shareholders
3	Check whether the creditors are affected and if so, consider whether to put any non-statutory methods for their protection into place
4	Check the position of any other affected third parties
5	Check that the company is authorised by its articles
6	Prepare an explanation of the reduction for the shareholders
7	Send out notices of a general meeting to consider a special resolution to approve the reduction or use the written resolution procedure. Send an explanation of the reduction to the shareholders at the same time
8	Hold the general meeting and pass special resolution or obtain signed written resolutions
9	Obtain provisional timetable from court
10	File petition, witness statement in support and application notice for directions
11	Attend directions hearing
12	Comply with directions including arranging for advertisement of petition hearing
13	Attend hearing of petition
14	Arrange for appropriate registration and filings at Companies House
15	Advertise registration in accordance with court order

CHAPTER 5

Dividends and distributions

OUTLINE

SECTION 1 **General concepts** ... 1603	1 Recipient 1702
	2 Form 1708
A What is a distribution? 1603	Cash dividend 1708
B When can a distribution be made? .. 1610	Distribution of assets 1710
1 Profits available for distribution 1612	Stock dividend 1714
2 Reference to relevant accounts 1620	E Procedure checklist 1722
Last annual accounts 1623	
Interim and initial accounts 1630	SECTION 3 **Unlawful distributions** 1728
3 Other considerations 1639	
4 Public companies 1645	A Liability of shareholder 1730
5 Flowchart: can a distribution be made? 1650	B Liability of directors 1742
	C Avoiding liability 1754
SECTION 2 **Declaration and payment of dividends** 1660	SECTION 4 **Tax treatment** 1769
A Types of dividend 1663	A Recipient 1780
B Right to a dividend 1674	B Distributing company 1795
C Effect of declaration 1690	C Close companies 1805
D Payment 1702	

1600 "Distribution" is the general term used to describe a payment made by a company to its shareholders based on their shareholdings. A "dividend" is a division of profits amongst shareholders. It is the most usual type of distribution, but the term is wider than that. Distributions are usually paid in cash, although other forms of payment are possible. The discussion below relates to distributions made by a company whilst it is solvent. Distributions during insolvency proceedings are dealt with separately, according to the type of proceeding.

There is a strict **statutory framework** which governs the making of distributions (¶1610+). The essential requirement is that a company must have "profits available for distribution", by reference to its "relevant accounts". In addition to the statutory requirements, a company must refer to its **memorandum and articles** and the directors must comply with their **duties**. There are additional statutory requirements for **public companies**.

The **declaration and payment of dividends** is governed largely by the provisions in a company's memorandum and articles (¶1660+). Most articles (including Table A 1985) provide for dividends to be declared by shareholders but give the directors the power to pay interim dividends. Although there is no general right to a dividend, some share classes may have particular dividend rights. Once a dividend becomes due, a shareholder will have the right to enforce it as a debt due to him from the company.

It is important that the statutory, common law and procedural requirements are complied with, as an **unlawful distribution** may have to be repaid to the company by the recipient shareholders and/or the company's directors (¶1728+).

A distribution has **tax consequences** for both the recipient shareholder and the company (¶1769+). The distributing company will generally have to pay corporation tax on the profit distributed. The recipient shareholder will have to pay tax on the distribution he receives. In most cases, he will be taxed as having received a distribution, but distributions to employees and/or directors may be taxed as a benefit in kind instead. Conversely, certain benefits paid by close companies to their participators are treated as distributions for tax purposes.

SECTION 1

General concepts

A. What is a distribution?

1603 A distribution is **defined as** a return of assets by a company to its shareholders, whether in the form of cash or otherwise, except for (s 263(2) CA 1985; restated at s 829 CA 2006 as of 6 April 2008):
– an issue of fully or partly paid bonus shares;
– a redemption or purchase of shares in accordance with the appropriate statutory procedure;
– a reduction of share capital that results in paying off share capital, or reducing the liability of shareholders to pay up unpaid share capital; and
– a distribution of assets to shareholders on a winding up.

These are the only exceptions and any other acquisition of the company's assets by a shareholder in his capacity as a shareholder without paying "full consideration" will be **treated as a distribution**. "Full consideration" does not only mean that something must be given by the shareholder in exchange for the asset; it also means that the arrangement must be entered into for the benefit, and to promote the prosperity, of the company (*Ridge Securities Ltd v IRC* [1964] 1 All ER 275; *MacPherson v European Strategic Bureau Ltd* [2000] 2 BCLC 683).

1604 The most common type of distribution is a **dividend**. This is a division of the company's profits amongst its shareholders. It includes:
– a cash dividend: a dividend satisfied by way of cash; and
– a distribution in specie: a dividend satisfied by way of tangible assets other than cash.

Sometimes, shareholders will be given the option to take **shares** instead of a cash dividend. This is referred to as a "stock dividend", although, strictly speaking it is not a dividend as the company is effectively making a bonus issue.

1605 In addition to dividends, the definition of distribution **can also include**:
– the sale of an asset at an undervalue by a company directly or indirectly to a shareholder (*Aveling Barford Ltd v Perion Ltd* [1989] BCLC 626);
– a company entering into a contractual agreement with a shareholder that provides for the payment of large, uncommercial sums (*Ridge Securities Ltd v IRC* [1964] 1 All ER 275);
– a company paying excessive remuneration to a director who is also a shareholder (*Re Halt Garage (1964) Ltd* [1982] 3 All ER 1016); and
– a company entering into a contractual agreement with its shareholders to distribute its assets as if on a winding up (*Macpherson v European Strategic Bureau Ltd* [2000] 2 BCLC 683).

It does not matter what the parties to the transaction call it; the court will look at the substance rather than any label that has been given to it (*Aveling Barford Ltd v Perion Ltd* [1989] BCLC 626).

EXAMPLE
Sale of an asset at an undervalue:
AB Ltd and P Ltd were both controlled by the same shareholder, Dr L. AB Ltd sold a property to P Ltd for £350,000 which had been valued at £650,000 and £1,150,000 by two different valuers only a few months before the sale. Six months after the sale, P Ltd sold the property to a third party for £1,560,000. The court decided that the sale of the property was a distribution dressed up as a genuine transaction. It did not matter that the distribution was to P Ltd rather than to Dr L himself (*Aveling Barford Ltd v Perion Ltd*, above).

Payment of large, uncommercial sums:
RS Ltd was involved in a tax avoidance scheme under which it granted a debenture to its parent company that required the payment of very large and uncommercial sums as "interest". The court decided that the interest payments were dressed-up gifts of capital to the parent (*Ridge Securities Ltd v IRC*, above).

Excessive director's remuneration:
A non-executive director, who was also a shareholder, was paid £30 per week, supposedly as remuneration. The court decided that £10 per week was the maximum remuneration reasonably payable to someone who merely held the office of director. Any payments over this sum were really returns of capital to the shareholder (*Re Halt Garage (1964) Ltd*, above).

Contractual agreement with effect of winding up:
M, T and L were the shareholders of ESB Ltd. They provided the company with consultancy services, for which they were never paid. After a falling out between them, M, T, L and ESB Ltd entered into an agreement under which, after the payment of certain liabilities, all payments received by ESB Ltd relating to the period up to the date of the agreement would be distributed to M, T and L in proportion to their shareholdings, supposedly for their past and future services to the company. The court decided that the purpose of the agreement was to effect an informal winding up, which was not in the interests of the company. The payments due to M, T and L under the agreement were therefore being made in their capacity as shareholders, not as consultants. Accordingly, the payment was a distribution of assets to ESB Ltd's shareholders (*Macpherson v European Strategic Bureau Ltd*, above).

B. When can a distribution be made?

1610

There are strict rules as to when a company is permitted to make a distribution. This is due to the doctrine of capital maintenance which requires that, for the protection of creditors, a company's capital can only be returned to shareholders in limited circumstances (see ¶703). The **general principle** is that only the profits of the company may be returned to shareholders whilst it is a going concern. This principle was developed by case law and then codified and extended by statute. The statutory framework now sits alongside common law principles and the provisions in the company's memorandum and articles (see ¶1639+).

The essential statutory requirement is that a company can only make a distribution when it has "**profits available for distribution**" by reference to its "**relevant accounts**" (ss 263(1), 270 CA 1985; restated at ss 830, 836 CA 2006 as of 6 April 2008). A company's ability to make a distribution is therefore linked to, and controlled by, very detailed statutory accounting codes. These codes build on the basic need for a company's financial statements to give a true and fair view of its financial affairs, so that it is entirely clear on the face of the relevant accounts whether or not a distribution has been properly made (*Bairstow v Queens Moat Houses plc* [2001] 2 BCLC 531). **Public companies** must also ensure that they have sufficient net assets.

The statutory framework for determining whether a distribution can be made is compulsory and must be strictly followed. See ¶1728+ for the **consequences** of making an unlawful distribution, which include the personal liability of directors.

A **flowchart** to assist a company in determining whether or not a distribution can be made is at ¶1650.

1. Profits available for distribution

1612 Profits available for distribution (also referred to as "distributable profits") are **defined as** a company's accumulated, realised profit (so far as not previously utilised by a distribution or capitalisation) less its accumulated, realised losses (so far as not previously written off in a reduction or reorganisation of capital) (s 263(3) CA 1985; restated at s 830 CA 2006 as of 6 April 2008).

> MEMO POINTS   For these purposes, profits are **capitalised** if they are used, wholly or partly, to pay up bonus shares (¶1013+), or to finance an own share purchase and thereby transferred to the capital redemption reserve (¶1356+) (s 280(2) CA 1985; restated at s 853 CA 2006 as of 6 April 2008). See ¶1435+ for a reduction, and ¶6500+ for a reorganisation, of share capital.

1613 **Realised profits and losses** are those profits and losses that fall to be treated as realised in accordance with the generally accepted accounting principles applicable when the relevant accounts are prepared (ss 262(3), 742(2) CA 1985; restated at s 853 CA 2006 as of 6 April 2008). Profit and loss in this context includes both revenue profits and losses (e.g. from product sales) and capital profits and losses (e.g. from the sale of the company's trading premises) (s 280(3) CA 1985; restated at s 853 CA 2006 as of 6 April 2008). For further information on the accounting principles and standards relevant in calculating realised profit, see *Accountancy and Financial Reporting Memo*.

Detailed guidance on this topic is also available from the Institute of Chartered Accountants of England and Wales and the Institute of Chartered Accountants of Scotland in their Technical Release "Guidance on the determination of realised profits and losses in the context of distributions under the Companies Act 1985" (TR 7/03), which was originally issued in March 2003 and is updated from time to time (the most recent update at the time of writing is TR 2/07).

1614 It should be noted that the definition refers to "**accumulated**" realised profits and losses and therefore the profit/loss for a particular financial year should not be looked at in isolation. As a rough guide, reference is often made to the profit and loss account figure on the bottom part of a company's balance sheet.

> MEMO POINTS   Most balance sheets show accumulated realised profits so far as not previously utilised and accumulated realised profits so far as not previously written off. The definition of distributable profits is more precise: it refers to profits so far as not previously utilised "by a distribution or capitalisation" and losses so far as not previously written off "in a reduction or reorganisation of capital". As a result, an **adjustment to the balance sheet** figure may be required: if realised profits have been utilised other than by a distribution or capitalisation, for example to write off unrealised losses, then those profits can be added back. Similarly, if realised losses have been written off other than in a reduction or reorganisation of capital, for example against unrealised profits, then those losses must be deducted from the balance sheet figure.

1615 A company with a **history of losses** may therefore be unable to pay a dividend, even when it makes a profit in the current year. The problem can be exacerbated by the **application of new accounting standards** which have the effect of reducing distributable profits.

If necessary, a company can take steps to **increase** its **distributable profits**. For example:
a. if it has an excess of share capital, or an excess in its share premium account or capital redemption reserve, it can carry out a reduction or cancellation of any of those items (¶1435+). The amount reduced or cancelled could be used to eliminate a deficit on the profit and loss account, or could result in the creation of another general reserve, which is technically profit and so could potentially be distributable;
b. a company with unrealised profit could carry out a bonus issue to increase its share capital (¶1013+). It could then carry out a reduction or cancellation of that share capital as referred to in a. above; or
c. intra-group transactions (such as a sale of fixed assets or the payment of a dividend from a subsidiary to its parent) can have an effect on distributable profits, although, under accounting standards, artificial arrangements may be discounted.

2. Reference to relevant accounts

Whenever a company wishes to make a distribution, it must look to its "**relevant accounts**" to determine whether or not it has sufficient distributable profits. The relevant accounts of a company that has not yet approved the accounts for its first accounting period are its **initial accounts**. The relevant accounts of all other companies are their **last annual accounts**, unless they show insufficient distributable profits, in which case, they must look to their **interim accounts**.

1620

Distributions are made by individual companies, not groups, and therefore **group accounts** are not relevant. It is not possible for a company to go behind the figures in its own relevant accounts to show that what appeared to be an unlawful distribution, on the face of it, was in fact lawful (for example, because the group had sufficient profits) (*Bairstow v Queens Moat Houses plc* [2001] 2 BCLC 531).

1621

> EXAMPLE **Group accounts not relevant**
> QMH plc paid dividends in two consecutive years which exceeded its distributable profits by about £10.8m and £4.9m respectively. The distributable profits for its group for those two years were £129.8m and £151m respectively. Therefore, QMH plc's wholly-owned subsidiaries could have declared dividends in favour of QMH plc which would have covered the excess dividend payments. However, the court rejected an argument that it should look behind QMH plc's accounts to the accounts of the group. It decided that the statutory requirement to look only to the relevant accounts of the distributing company is strict and mandatory (*Bairstow v Queens Moat Houses plc* [2001] 2 BCLC 531).

Last annual accounts

For most companies, the starting point for considering whether a distribution can be made is the last annual accounts of the company. The last annual accounts are **defined** as the last accounts prepared in respect of the last preceding accounting reference period, which will be (s 270(3) CA 1985 as amended by para 3 Sch 4 SI 2007/2194):
– for private companies, the last accounts sent out to the shareholders (see ¶4265+); and
– for public companies, the last accounts that were prepared and laid before the company in a general meeting (see ¶4273+).

1623

For example, if A Ltd's accounting reference period ended on 31 December and it wished to declare a dividend on 15 January Year 2, the last annual accounts would be for the year ended 31 December Year 1.

> MEMO POINTS The **amendments** to s 270 CA 1985 were made as part of the implementation of the new Companies Act, and **apply to** financial years starting on or after 1 October 2007.

The last annual accounts must comply with certain minimum statutory requirements. The balance sheet and profit and loss account must give a **true and fair view** of the company's financial affairs (see ¶4228). Further, the accounts must have been **properly prepared** in accordance with the applicable statutory requirements (see ¶4209+), subject only to matters that are not material in determining whether the proposed distribution is lawful or not (s 271(2) CA 1985; restated at s 837 CA 2006 as of 6 April 2008). It should be noted that there are very few immaterial items which could be disregarded for these purposes. One example is the requirement that the notes to the accounts must give information relating to employee numbers (para 56 Sch 4 CA 1985; restated at s 411 CA 2006 as of 6 April 2008).

1624

> EXAMPLE ME Ltd mistakenly declared an unlawful dividend to its parent GH Ltd, who in turn mistakenly declared an unlawful dividend to its parent, CT plc. The court decided that the unlawful dividends should not have been properly included as a receipt in the profit and loss account of the recipient companies. Therefore, the accounts of GH Ltd had not been properly prepared, nor did they give a true and fair view, and so could not be the relevant accounts on which to base its dividend to CT plc (*Re Cleveland Trust plc* [1991] BCLC 424).

1625 In addition, as long as the company is not exempt from audit, the auditor must have made his report on the accounts (ss 249E(1)(c), 271(3) CA 1985; restated at s 837 CA 2006 as of 6 April 2008). If the accounts have a **qualified auditor's report** then the auditor must also state in writing (either at the same time or after their report) whether the qualification is material for the purposes of determining the payment of a particular distribution or any distribution in general. A copy of his statement must be made available to the shareholders before the distribution is made and (s 271(3)-(5) CA 1985 amended by para 3 Sch 4 SI 2007/2194; restated at s 837 CA 2006 as of 6 April 2008; *Precision Dippings Ltd v Precision Dippings Marketing Ltd* [1985] BCLC 385):
– for private companies, it must be circulated to the shareholders with the accounts (see ¶4265+); and
– for public companies, it must be laid before the company in a general meeting (see ¶4273+).

Comment: The statutory provisions do not specify how the auditor's statement impacts upon the lawfulness of the distribution, it merely requires that one is made and laid before the company. However, the prudent view is that if the auditor states that his qualification is material, then no distribution should be made by reference to those accounts. On the other hand, if the auditor states that his qualification is not material, then the company may refer to them.

> MEMO POINTS 1. Auditors can find **further guidance** on their statement, and an appropriate form of words, in the Practice Note "Reports by Auditors under Company Legislation in the UK" issued by the Auditing Practices Board (APB) in August 1994. A copy can be obtained for a fee from the APB or freely downloaded from its website.
> 2. The **amendments** to s 271 CA 1985 were made as part of the implementation of the new Companies Act, and **apply to** financial years starting on or after 1 October 2007.

1626 If the last annual accounts show sufficient distributable profits, the company must then take into account any **previous distributions** that were made by reference to those accounts (s 274(1) CA 1985; restated at s 840 CA 2006 as of 6 April 2008). It must also take into account any of the **following payments** that were made since the last annual accounts were prepared (s 274(2) CA 1985; restated at s 840 CA 2006 as of 6 April 2008):
a. any financial assistance given by the company in the acquisition of its own shares; and/or
b. any payment by the company out of distributable profits in respect of:
– a purchase by it of its own shares;
– a purchase of a right to buy its own shares;
– a variation of an own share purchase contract; and/or
– a release of an own share purchase contract.

1627 If the company has **sufficient distributable profits** after taking those previous distributions and payments into consideration, statute allows a distribution up to the level of those profits to be made. However, before making the distribution, the company must also refer to the provisions of its memorandum and articles and the directors must consider their duties towards the company (see ¶1639+).

1628 If the last annual accounts show **insufficient distributable profits**, whether before or after previous distributions and payments have been taken into account, the company should refer to its interim accounts.

Interim and initial accounts

1630 If a company's last annual accounts show insufficient distributable profits, it must look to its "interim accounts" in order to determine whether a distribution can be made. If it has not yet approved the accounts for its first accounting period, it must look to its "initial accounts".

The interim and initial accounts are **defined as** those that are necessary to enable a reasonable judgment to be made about the company's (s 270(2), (4) CA 1985; restated at ss 838, 839 CA 2006 as of 6 April 2008):
a. profits, losses, assets and liabilities (including share capital and reserves, and provisions or amounts written off for any depreciation or diminution in the value of any assets); and

b. contingent liabilities or charges (i.e. provisions for liabilities or charges likely to be incurred or certain to be incurred, but uncertain as to the amount or the date on which they will arise).

The **form** of a company's interim and initial accounts depends upon whether it is a private or public company.

As with the last annual accounts, if the interim or initial accounts show sufficient distributable profits, the company must take into account any **previous distributions**, financial assistance or payments relating to an own share purchase made by reference to those accounts (see ¶1626).

If a company has **sufficient distributable profits** after taking these distributions and payments into account, then statute permits it to make a distribution up to the level of those profits. However, before making the distribution, the company must refer to the provisions of its memorandum and articles and the directors must consider their general duties to the company (see ¶1639+).

If the interim or initial accounts, as appropriate, show **insufficient distributable profits**, either before or after such previous distributions and payments are taken into account, no distribution can be made.

> MEMO POINTS   When the relevant provisions of the **new Companies Act** come into force, it will no longer be unlawful for private companies to provide financial assistance for the acquisition of their own shares (¶5557+). The relevant implementation date is yet to be announced at the time of writing.

1631

Private companies

There are no further statutory provisions relating to the preparation of the interim or initial accounts of private companies and therefore a reference to reliable **management accounts** will be sufficient (para B19 TR 07/03).

1632

Public companies

There are **additional statutory provisions** relating to the preparation of the interim or initial accounts of a public company, which effectively bring them up to the standard of annual accounts (ss 272, 273 CA 1985; restated at ss 838, 839 CA 2006 as of 6 April 2008).

1633

The interim or initial accounts of a public company must have been **properly prepared** in accordance with the usual statutory requirements that apply to the preparation of company accounts (¶4209+), with such modifications as are necessary because the accounts are not being prepared in respect of an accounting reference period. Further:
– the balance sheet and profit and loss account must give a **true and fair view**;
– the balance sheet must have been **signed** by the board; and
– a copy of the accounts must have been **filed** at Companies House.

The accounts will be **treated as properly prepared** if they exclude matters that are not material in determining whether or not the distribution was lawful (ss 272(2), 273(2) CA 1985; restated at ss 838, 839 CA 2006 as of 6 April 2008). Therefore, it is possible for the notes to the interim and initial accounts to refer only to matters that are relevant to a distribution. Further, it is not necessary to include corresponding amounts for previous financial years (para B17 TR 7/03).

Finally, in the case of **initial accounts** only, the company's **auditor** must make a **report** as to whether the accounts have been properly prepared. If the report is qualified, the auditor must state whether or not his qualification is material for the purposes of determining the payment of a distribution (see ¶1625 in the context of annual accounts). The statement must be made available to the shareholders before the distribution, by circulating it (in the case of a private company) or laying it before the company in a general meeting (in the case of a public company).

1634

There is no requirement to audit **interim accounts**.

3. Other considerations

1639 In addition to the requirement that any distribution can only be made out of distributable profits determined by reference to a company's relevant accounts, a company must also be mindful (both at the time the distribution is proposed and the time it is made) of the provisions in its **memorandum and articles** (s 281 CA 1985; restated at s 852 CA 2006 as of 6 April 2008).

For example, the articles may state that an interim dividend cannot be paid to the ordinary shareholders whilst the preference shareholders' dividends are in arrears (reg 103 TA 1985) or there may be a provision in the objects clause of the memorandum that prevents the payment of the proposed dividend (see example below).

A distribution made in **breach** of a provision in the company's memorandum or articles will be void.

> EXAMPLE **Lack of corporate capacity**
> ME Ltd was a property investment company. Its objects clause included a provision under which any surplus from the realisation of the company's property or assets would be dealt with as capital surpluses not available for the payment of dividends. Such a clause was fairly common at one time and was intended to demonstrate that ME Ltd was an investment, rather than a trading, company. ME Ltd declared a dividend of £1,214,000, most of which was met by the capital profit on the sale of one of its properties. The court decided that the dividend was void because ME Ltd lacked the corporate capacity to declare the dividend (*Re Cleveland Trust plc* [1991] BCLC 424).

> MEMO POINTS 1. There may also be restrictions on the payment of dividends in other documents to which the company is a party, such as a **shareholders' agreement** or a **loan document**. These should also be checked to ensure that the proposed dividend can be paid.
> 2. Draft **new model articles** under the **new Companies Act** have been published for private companies limited by shares and public companies. They will include a similar provision restricting a company's ability to pay interim dividends (private companies limited by shares: art 30(5); public companies: art 69(5)).

1641 The directors of a company must also be aware of their **general duties** (see ¶2317+). In particular, they are under a duty to exercise reasonable skill, care and diligence when proposing or paying a dividend.

Consequently, they must ensure that the company will remain solvent after the distribution by:
– considering its **future cash needs**; and
– taking into account any **changes to the balance sheet** since the date to which it was made up that would adversely affect the solvency of the company.

In addition, they must consider whether any **losses incurred after the period of the accounts** would affect the amount of profits available for distribution.

If directors do not fulfill their duties, they can be personally **liable** for the improperly declared or paid dividend, see ¶1742+.

> EXAMPLE
> **Dividend made company insolvent**
> L Ltd paid a dividend without taking into account future liabilities for tax under a particular contract and a lease. The effect of the dividend was to render L Ltd insolvent or potentially insolvent and the directors should have been aware of this. The court decided that the directors did not exercise the requisite level of skill and care in making the dividend payment (*Re Loquitur Ltd, IRC v Richmond* [2003] STC 1394).
>
> **Company insolvent at time of dividend**
> M, T and L were the shareholders of ESB Ltd; M and L were also directors. The three shareholders and the company entered into an agreement that effectively provided for the distribution of the company's assets as if on a winding up, without making proper provision for creditors. The company was insolvent when the agreement was entered into. The court decided that the agreement should not have been entered into because it was done in breach of the directors' duties, or alternatively beyond the powers of the company, and it was beyond the directors' powers because the agreement sought to evade the protection for creditors in the statutory requirement to make distributions out of distributable profits (*Macpherson v European Strategic Bureau Ltd* [2000] 2 BCLC 683).

4. Public companies

In addition to the requirement to have sufficient distributable profits, public companies can only make a distribution if, after the distribution, their net assets exceed the aggregate of their called up share capital and undistributable reserves (s 264(1) CA 1985; restated at s 831(1) CA 2006 as of 6 April 2008). **1645**

The **net asset** figure is the company's total assets (including intangible assets such as goodwill, but not including uncalled share capital) less its total liabilities (including any provision for liabilities or charges) (s 264(2) CA 1985; restated at s 831(2) CA 2006 as of 6 April 2008).

Expressed as a **formula**, the net asset figure is:

(total assets − total liabilities) > (called up share capital + undistributable reserves)

A company's **undistributable reserves** are (s 264(3) CA 1985; restated at s 831(4) CA 2006 as of 6 April 2008): **1646**
- its share premium account;
- its capital redemption reserve;
- its undistributable profits; and
- any other reserve which the company cannot distribute because of a statutory prohibition, or one in its memorandum or articles.

For what constitutes called up and uncalled share capital, see ¶716.

The **main effect** of this provision is that, in order to make a distribution, a public company's accumulated realised profits must cover both its accumulated realised losses (as required by the definition of distributable profits) and its accumulated net unrealised losses. **1647**

5. Flowchart: can a distribution be made?

1650

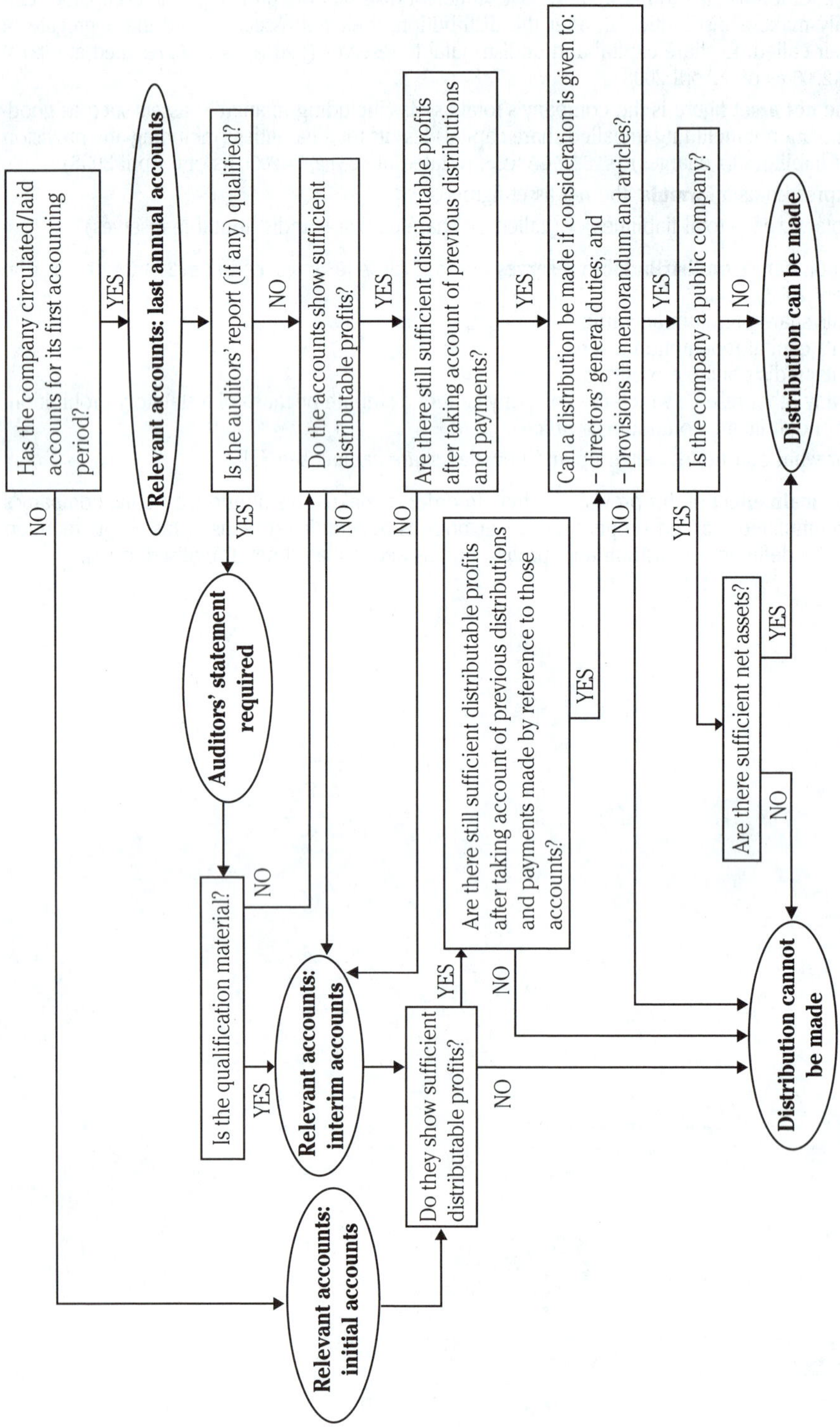

SECTION 2

Declaration and payment of dividends

1660 Most companies divide their profits amongst their shareholders by paying them dividends. The receipt of a dividend is the "income" part of the shareholders' investment in the company. In **smaller companies** in which the shareholders are also the directors, a regular dividend is often paid in lieu of part of the directors' salary because dividends are more tax efficient for both the company and the recipient. In **larger companies**, shareholders expect to be able to participate in the company's profits whilst it is a going concern.

Most dividends are **in the form of** cash (¶1708) but it is also possible for dividends to be satisfied by way of tangible assets, such as property (known as a "distribution in specie") (¶1710+). Sometimes, the shareholders are offered further shares in the company as an alternative to a cash payment (known as a "stock dividend"), although strictly speaking this is not a dividend (¶1714).

Companies have the implied **power** to pay dividends, even if there is no express provision in their articles. In practice, the articles contain extensive provisions relating to the declaration and payment of dividends (e.g. Table A 1985). The **procedure** for declaring and paying dividends is derived from common law and the company's memorandum and articles. In all cases, therefore, reference must be made to the particular provisions in the company's constitution.

A. Types of dividend

Final dividend

1663 The articles of most companies provide for a dividend to be declared by the **shareholders** passing an ordinary resolution (reg 102 TA 1985). However, the **amount** of this dividend is usually capped at the amount recommended by the directors (reg 102 TA 1985). The shareholders' power to declare a dividend is therefore very limited: they can refuse to declare a dividend recommended by the directors (or they can declare a lower dividend) but they cannot declare a dividend unilaterally (that is, without a directors' recommendation) or declare one at a higher level than that which the directors feel should be declared.

There is usually no stipulation as to **when** or **how frequently** the directors can recommend that the shareholders declare a dividend and most companies find the requirement for a shareholder resolution for each dividend is an unnecessary administrative burden. Therefore, dividends are usually declared on an annual basis by companies that hold AGMs (private companies no longer have to hold AGMs), or by written resolution in those that do not (see ¶3777+ for AGMs and ¶3580+ for shareholder written resolutions). Such a dividend is commonly referred to as a "final dividend".

> MEMO POINTS   Draft **new model articles** under the **new Companies Act** have been published for private companies limited by shares and public companies. They will also require a dividend to be based on a recommendation by the directors and declared by the shareholders passing an ordinary resolution (private companies limited by shares: art 30; public companies: art 69).

Interim dividend

1665 Since a company may wish to pay dividends at other times during the year, most articles also allow **directors** to pay interim dividends upon passing a board resolution, if it appears that they are justified in doing so judging from the distributable profits of the company (reg 103 TA 1985).

Again, there is not usually any stipulation as to **when** or **how frequently** the directors may pay interim dividends. In practice, companies use interim dividends to spread payments across a year. For example, a company could pay interim dividends in January, April and July and a final dividend in October so that its dividends are paid quarterly, or it could pay an interim dividend in January and a final dividend in July so that its dividends are paid on a 6-monthly basis.

> MEMO POINTS   1. Since **private companies** are no longer required to hold an annual general meeting, they could pay all of their dividends as interim dividends to avoid having to hold a meeting or circulate a written resolution for the shareholders to declare final dividends.
> 2. Where a final dividend is eventually declared, the usual practice is for the **shareholders** to also **approve any interim dividends** that the directors have paid in the preceding financial year.
> 3. The draft **new model articles** for private companies limited by shares and public companies will allow the directors to declare and pay interim dividends (private companies limited by shares: art 30; public companies: art 69).

Special dividend

1666 Final and interim dividends are usually paid on a periodic basis. However, sometimes a company may decide to pay a special dividend, for example, if the sale of an asset has increased distributable profits above normal trading levels. Such a dividend is also referred to as a "**bonus**" or an "**extraordinary**" dividend. It will usually be paid as an interim dividend, although it can be declared by the shareholders.

> MEMO POINTS   Where the dividend is being paid out of a surplus that has arisen on the sale of a capital asset, it is referred to as a "**capital dividend**" for tax purposes.

B. Right to a dividend

General position

1674 The shareholders do not have a general right to a dividend. There is no requirement on a company to declare dividends, unless its memorandum or articles oblige it to do so (there is no such provision in Table A) or the company has made a contractual commitment to pay dividends, for example, if it is party to a shareholders' agreement. Therefore, in an unlisted company and especially in smaller companies, whether or not a dividend is paid is largely at the **discretion of** the directors. By contrast, the dividend policy of a listed company has a direct impact upon its share value and therefore the market effectively requires the payment of regular adequate dividends.

1675 As is to be expected, the failure of a company to pay dividends (or the payment of what are perceived to be low dividends) is frequently a source of **shareholder discontent**. However the legal rights of shareholders in such a situation are limited. Generally, the court does not have the power to interfere with a company's dividend policy because it is a matter for the company's internal management.

The situation may be different if the **dividend policy is irrational** or if the shareholders have a **legitimate expectation** to receive a dividend (for example, because there was a formal or informal understanding that dividends would be declared on a particular basis). In such cases, the withholding of dividends may give rise to a claim for unfair prejudice (*Re a Company (No 004415 of 1996)* [1997] 1 BCLC 479).

> EXAMPLE
> **Unfair dividend policy**
> A Ltd, G Ltd and R Ltd were controlled both at board and shareholder level by the P family. The petitioners were non-director minority shareholders of the same companies. They brought a claim for unfair prejudice against the companies and individuals in the P family on the grounds that they had been declaring dividends at a lower level than could be justified on any reasonable commercial grounds and, at the same time, had been paying directors' fees to members of the P family at a higher rate than could be justified on any normal commercial or comparative basis. The court agreed that the alleged conduct could amount to unfair prejudice (*Re a Company (No 004415 of 1996)*, above).

> **Not unfair dividend policy**
> Mr H and Mr W were the sole directors and shareholders of MM Ltd; Mr H was the majority shareholder. Mr H had been promised a dividend of £6,000 per month, on account of his share of the profits. When this dividend payment ceased, Mr H alleged unfair prejudice. The court held that since the payments were to be on account of profits, if there were insufficient profits or if the business urgently needed the money, it would not be unfairly prejudicial to Mr H if the dividends to him were stopped (*Hale v Waldock*, *Re Metropolis Motorcycles Ltd* [2006] EWHC 364 (Ch)).

1676 In the absence of any requirement to the contrary, when a dividend is paid, shareholders are entitled to profit in **proportion** to the nominal value of their shareholding in the company; the amount paid up on the share is irrelevant (*Oakbank Oil Co v Crum* (1882) 8 App Cas 65). This can, of course, lead to unfairness between the holders of **fully paid** and **partly or nil paid** shares; an ordinary shareholder who holds 50 fully paid £1 shares will be entitled to the same amount of profit as an ordinary shareholder who holds 50 nil paid £1 shares. Consequently, the articles (including Table A 1985) usually provide that all dividends must be declared and paid according to the amounts paid up on the shares entitled to the dividend (reg 104 TA 1985). Shares that are nil or partly paid therefore will usually not receive their full dividend entitlement.

> MEMO POINTS The draft **new model articles** will not expressly state that dividends must be paid according to the amounts paid up on the shares. Instead, they will require dividends to be paid "in accordance with shareholders' respective rights" (private companies limited by shares: art 30; public companies: art 69). It is not clear whether this wording would be sufficient to require proportionate payments, so companies should adapt their own articles to make it clear if they wish to pay dividends on that basis.

Effect of share classes

Shares with different dividend rights

1678 Different share classes may have different dividend rights. For example, the rights of a share may require the payment of a **regular fixed dividend**. The articles of a company will usually specify that the directors are able to pay regular fixed dividends if it appears that the company has sufficient distributable profits (reg 103 TA 1985), although even without this specific provision, the directors could pay such dividends under their general power to pay interim dividends.

> MEMO POINTS The draft **new model articles** will restate this specific right to pay regular fixed dividends (private companies limited by shares: art 30; public companies: art 69).

1679 Shares with a particular dividend entitlement are most likely to be **preference shares**. For more on the dividend rights of preference shares, see ¶786+. It should be noted that under Table A, interim dividends can be paid on shares with deferred or non-preferred rights (e.g. ordinary shares) as well as on preference shares, provided that there are no arrears of dividends on the preference shares (reg 103 TA 1985). The directors will not incur a liability if, in good faith, they pay interim dividends on shares with deferred or non-preferred rights which result in a loss to the preference shareholders (for example, because subsequently the company fails to have sufficient distributable profits to pay the preferential dividend) (reg 103 TA 1985).

> MEMO POINTS The draft **new model articles** will also absolve the directors from liability in the same circumstances (private companies limited by shares: art 30; public companies: art 69(7)).

Shares with same dividend rights

1681 Share classes are often created and issued with no difference as to their dividend rights. In such cases, dividends may still be declared and paid on one class of share but not on the others. Sometimes, share classes with the same dividend rights are specifically created and issued to different types of shareholder to allow for the declaration of dividends to different groups. For example, a company could create **two classes of ordinary shares** (ordinary A shares and ordinary B shares) and issue:

a. one class to directors and another to other employees, so that a dividend could be paid to either group as and when required to incentivise them;

b. one class to employees and another to non-employees, so that the former could be paid a dividend in lieu of part of their salary which could lead to tax savings; or
c. one class to each joint venturer in a joint venture company, so that dividends could be declared on each class corresponding to the agreed rates of return for each joint venturer.

1682 If a dividend is to be paid on **one class**, it must be paid in respect of all of the shares in that class, not just on some.

Occasionally, a dividend may only be intended for some shareholders in a class, in which case the non-recipient shareholders must waive their entitlement. The waiver can relate to a specific dividend or can be a general waiver of all dividends. It should preferably be made in writing and addressed to the company; an oral waiver made to a director is sufficient but may be difficult to prove in the event of a dispute.

C. Effect of declaration

Creation of debt

Due date

1690 The declaration of a dividend creates a debt due from the company to its shareholders.

When the dividend is **declared by the shareholders** in a general meeting without setting a date for payment, the debt becomes due at the time of the declaration (*Re Severn and Wye and Severn Bridge Railway Co* [1896] 1 Ch 559).

When the **directors recommend** a dividend to the shareholders, they can also stipulate the date on which the dividend is to be paid using their general management powers (*Thairwell v Great Northern Railway Co* [1908-10] All ER Rep 556). If this occurs, and the declared dividend is expressed to be payable at a future date, the debt does not become due until that date (*Re Kidner, Kidner v Kidner* [1929] All ER Rep 551).

Nature of the debt

1691 When a dividend is declared and becomes due either on the date of declaration or on some future date, the nature of the debt is much the same as an **ordinary debt** between a creditor and debtor. For example:
– the shareholder can enforce the debt against the company in the courts in the normal way; and
– the limitation period (that is, the length of time that the shareholder has to bring a claim in the courts) is 6 years.

> MEMO POINTS Companies operating under **Table A 1948** have a limited right of set-off (reg 119 Table A 1948). They can set off money owed to them by a shareholder on account of unpaid calls or otherwise in relation to the company's shares.

1692 However, there are particular characteristics which distinguish this from other debts:
a. on a winding up the debt will be postponed to claims of other creditors (s 74(2)(f) IA 1986), but it will be payable even though the company has insufficient distributable profits (*Marra Developments Ltd v BW Rofe Pty Ltd* (1977) 3 ACLR 185);
b. most articles provide that **interest** is not payable on dividends, unless specifically provided by the share rights (reg 107 TA 1985). However, if a shareholder succeeds in a court claim, he can claim the usual statutory interest for money claimed in court proceedings (s 35A Supreme Court Act 1981); and
c. most articles provide that if a declared dividend has **not been paid or claimed after 12 years**, the directors can resolve that the dividend right has been forfeited (reg 108 TA 1985).

> MEMO POINTS The draft **new model articles** will also provide for a dividend to be forfeited if unclaimed after 12 years (private companies limited by shares: art 33; public companies: art 74).

They will also provide that no interest is payable on dividends, unless otherwise stated in the terms of the share issue or other agreement between the company and shareholder (private companies limited by shares: art 32; public companies: art 73).

Distinguishing declaration from payment

The declaration and payment of a dividend are two separate stages. A dividend is **declared** when the relevant shareholder resolution is passed, following a recommendation from the board. By contrast, the **payment** of a dividend refers to the actual distribution of the company's assets.

1694

This distinction has an important impact on the effect of a directors' resolution to pay an **interim dividend** because directors are usually only authorised by the articles to pay an interim dividend as opposed to declare it (reg 103 TA 1985). Where the directors have resolved to pay an interim dividend, it is open to the board at any time before payment to review its decision and resolve not to pay the dividend after all (*Lagunas Nitrate Co Ltd v Schroeder & Co and Schmidt* (1901) 85 LT 22). Similarly, the directors can, at the time of their resolution or at any time before payment, decide that the interim dividend is to be paid at some future date, in which case the relevant shareholders will not have an enforceable right to demand payment until that date (*Potel v IRC* [1971] 2 All ER 504).

MEMO POINTS The **date of the dividend** (for the purposes of determining whether the company has sufficient distributable profits at the time) is the date of the declaration or, for interim dividends, when the dividend is paid.

D. Payment

1. Recipient

The **general rule** is that a dividend must be paid to the registered holder of the relevant shares on the date of the shareholders' declaration. If the dividend is an interim dividend, it must be paid to the registered holder on the date of the directors' resolution. This is the case even if the relevant shares are transferred between declaration and payment.

1702

MEMO POINTS The articles may allow shares to be issued on terms that they only **rank for dividends** from a particular date **in the future** (reg 104 TA 1985). The draft new model articles for public companies will include an equivalent provision (art 70).

In **large companies** with a wide shareholder base, instead of the general rule, the articles may provide for payment to be made to shareholders registered on a particular date, known as the "**record date**". In such circumstances, the record date as well as the payment date will need to be set out in the resolution declaring the dividend. Table A 1985 does not contain reference to a record date but most modern articles will specify that the record date cannot be more than 28 days prior to payment.

1703

If a share is **transferred** between the record date and the payment date, the right to the dividend remains with the transferring shareholder. The purchaser of shares upon which a dividend has been declared should therefore take care in determining whether or not he will take the right to the dividend with the purchase. "Cum dividend" means that the share is being sold with the right to the dividend and "ex dividend" means the share is being sold without that right.

Date	Effect
Date of declaration	The date on which the resolution declaring the share is passed
Ex-dividend date	A share which is sold on or after this date will transfer without the right to receive the declared dividend. A company must be given time to record a share transfer, so the ex-dividend date will be a few days before the record date

Date	Effect
Record date	The date upon which the company examines its register to determine the identity of the holders of the relevant shares
Payment date	The date on which the company actually pays the dividend. It is usually between 1 and 4 weeks after the record date, so that the company has time to make the correct payments

MEMO POINTS The draft **new model articles** will require dividends to be paid in respect of shareholdings at the date of the shareholder resolution or directors' decision to declare or pay the dividend, unless the resolution/decision or terms of the share issue state otherwise (private companies limited by shares: art 30; public companies: art 69).

2. Form

Cash dividend

1708 In the absence of an express provision to the contrary, dividends must be paid in cash (*Wood v Odessa Waterworks Co* (1889) 42 Ch D 636); these are the most common type of distribution. In most cases, the articles will provide that a company can pay a dividend by cheque, and the despatch of a correctly made out cheque to the correct address will discharge the company's payment obligation (reg 106 TA 1985). The articles will usually state that cheques should be made payable to the entitled shareholder and posted to his registered address (or if a share is held jointly, to the address of the first person named in the register) or to such person and/or address as the entitled person(s) may direct in writing (reg 106 TA 1985).

MEMO POINTS 1. Payment by cheque is not automatically a good discharge of its obligation for companies operating under **Table A 1948**. They may have to prove actual receipt of the dividend.
2. The draft **new model articles** will allow payments to be made by electronic transfer to a bank account, cheque or any other means agreed with the shareholder (private companies limited by shares: art 31; public companies: art 71). Shareholders will still be able to ask the company to pay their dividends to another person.

Distribution of assets

1710 Most articles also provide that a general meeting of the shareholders when declaring a dividend can, upon the recommendation of the directors, direct that it should be satisfied wholly or partly by a distribution of assets (reg 105 TA 1985). This is known as a "**distribution in specie**". If the articles are framed in this way, the directors cannot satisfy an interim dividend by a distribution of assets.

MEMO POINTS The draft **new model articles** will also authorise dividends to be paid by way of a distribution of assets, if approved by an ordinary resolution of the shareholders on the recommendation of the directors (private companies limited by shares: art 34; public companies: art 75).

1711 Whenever a distribution in specie is contemplated, the **tax** advantages and disadvantages should be considered beforehand. For example, depending on the nature of the asset, stamp duty or stamp duty land tax may be payable. Particular **legal formalities** may also have to be observed. For example, if the asset being distributed is shares in another company, a stock transfer form will have to be executed.

In addition, if the distribution is to be made **to directors or persons connected** to the directors, it may need approval as a substantial property transaction (¶2567+).

Subject to those caveats, a distribution in specie can be **useful in** a demerger situation or to return specific assets (such as property) to shareholders.

> EXAMPLE **Demerger**
> B Ltd is the wholly-owned subsidiary of A Ltd, whose shareholders are the Smith family. The two companies wish to demerge. A Ltd therefore declares a dividend to be satisfied by the distribution of all of its shares in B Ltd. Ownership of B Ltd thereby transfers from A Ltd to the Smith family.

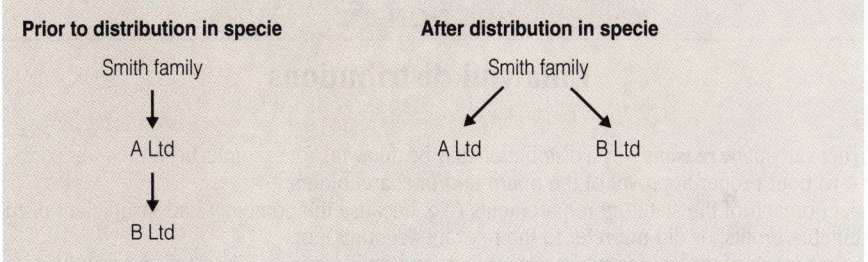

Where a distribution in specie is made, the **value of the returned asset(s)** must be determined in order to be sure that the company has sufficient distributable profits to make the distribution. The correct value to attribute to each asset is cost, less any amounts written off as realised losses (for example, as depreciation).

1712

Stock dividend

Another increasingly common alternative is for a company to give the shareholders the option to take a **dividend of shares** in the distributing company rather than cash. This is known as a "stock dividend" or "scrip dividend". Table A 1985 does not provide for this alternative and so a specific amendment to the articles will be required.

1714

The payment of a stock dividend, in effect, **amounts to a bonus issue** of fully paid shares funded by a company's distributable profits. It therefore does not technically fall within the definition of a distribution (¶1603). Where a stock dividend is proposed, the procedure for a bonus issue should be followed (see ¶1013+). The only difference between a bonus issue and a stock dividend is that the company does not know how many shares will be issued under the stock dividend until all of the options have either been taken up or declined.

MEMO POINTS The draft **new model articles** will allow stock dividends to be paid (private companies limited by shares: art 34; public companies: art 75).

E. Procedure checklist

The following procedure should be used for the declaration of dividends:

1722

Step	Action	¶¶
1.	Establish whether or not the company has **sufficient distributable profits** and that a dividend can be paid	¶1610+
2.	Check the rights of the **different classes of shares**	¶1674+
3.	Check the **articles** to ensure that the company has authority to make the proposed form of dividend	¶1639
4.	Hold a **board meeting** to either resolve to pay an interim dividend or recommend a final dividend to the shareholders	¶3217+
5.	If a final dividend is recommended, obtain shareholder approval by **ordinary resolution** at a general meeting or using the written resolution procedure	¶3513+
6.	Determine **which shareholders are entitled** to the dividend by referring to the register of shareholders either on the date of declaration or the record date and check any waivers	¶1702, ¶1682
7.	**Pay** the dividend on the date of payment. The method of payment will depend upon which form of dividend is proposed.	¶1708+

SECTION 3

Unlawful distributions

1728 There are many **reasons** why a distribution may be unlawful, for example, because it was paid:
– without proper approval of the board and/or shareholders;
– in breach of the statutory requirements (e.g. because the company had insufficient distributable profits, or did not refer to the relevant accounts); or
– in breach of the company's memorandum and articles, or the directors' general duties.

The main **consequence** of an unlawful distribution is that it may have to be repaid by the recipient shareholders and/or the company's directors.

> MEMO POINTS   1. A dividend can be set aside as a **transaction at an undervalue** if it is paid by a company when it is insolvent (or if it becomes insolvent as a result of the payment), and the company goes into insolvent liquidation or administration within 2 years (¶7811+).
> 2. A shareholder, but not a creditor, can apply for an injunction to **prevent payment** of an unlawful dividend (*Hoole v Great Western Railway Co* (1867) 3 Ch App 262; *Mills v Northern Railway of Buenos Ayres Co* (1870) 5 Ch App 621).

A. Liability of shareholder

Liability to company

1730 The recipient of an unlawful distribution has a **statutory liability** to repay it (or the relevant part of it) if he knew or had reasonable grounds for believing that it (or part of it) was unlawful (s 277(1) CA 1985; restated at s 847 CA 2006 as of 6 April 2008). It only applies where the dividend was unlawful because it did not comply with a statutory requirement, for example, if there were insufficient profits available for distribution. It does not apply where the dividend breached a provision of the general law or the company's memorandum and articles (*It's a Wrap (UK) Ltd v Gula* [2006] EWCA Civ 544). The statutory remedy can only be enforced by the company.

> MEMO POINTS   1. If the distribution was **not in cash**, then the shareholder is liable to pay a sum equal in value to the unlawful distribution at the time it was paid.
> 2. The statutory liability to repay does not attach to a distribution which takes the form of **unlawful financial assistance** given by the company in the acquisition of its shares, or any payment made by the company in respect of a **redemption or purchase** of its own shares.

1731 The recipient shareholder may also have a **common law liability** to repay the unlawful distribution as a "constructive trustee". This means that the court may impose a trust relationship between the distributing company and shareholder so that the shareholder is treated as holding the distribution on behalf of the company. The shareholder can be treated as a constructive trustee where he had knowledge of the facts that made the distribution unlawful.

> MEMO POINTS   1. A constructive trustee must also be a **volunteer**. This means that he should not have given any consideration for the money, property or asset which he is said to be holding on trust. This test will always be satisfied in the case of distributions as they are, by their very nature, received by shareholders without the need for any payment in return.
> 2. A shareholder who is deemed to be a constructive trustee may be able to claim **relief from liability** if it appears to the court that he acted honestly and reasonably, and ought fairly to be excused for failing or refusing to repay the dividend (s 61 Trustee Act 1925).

1732 For liability to arise under statute or the common law, the shareholder must know or ought reasonably to know the facts which made the distribution unlawful, that is to say, he must have factual **knowledge** of the unlawful dividend. It is not necessary for the shareholder also to have the legal knowledge that those facts would make the dividend unlawful (*Precision Dippings Ltd v Precision Dippings Marketing Ltd* [1985] BCLC 385; *It's a Wrap (UK) Ltd v Gula* [2006] EWCA Civ 544).

A shareholder can be deemed to have the required knowledge, for example, where:
– he is a director of the distributing company; or
– it is the parent company of the distributing company and the two companies have a common director.

> **EXAMPLE**
>
> 1. PD Ltd was the wholly-owned subsidiary of PDM Ltd. Mr W-J and Mr K were the only directors of both companies and the only shareholders of PDM Ltd. On the advice of its auditors, PD Ltd paid a dividend of £60,000 to PDM Ltd in breach of the statutory requirements. At the time of the dividend, neither Mr W-J nor Mr K were aware of the relevant requirements, or that the dividend was unlawful. A year later, PD Ltd went into liquidation and the liquidator brought a claim against PDM Ltd for return of the dividend plus interest.
> The court decided that PDM Ltd had knowledge of all the facts (through the directorships and shareholdings of Mr W-J and Mr K) and was a volunteer. Accordingly, PDM Ltd held the £60,000 as constructive trustee for PD Ltd and was therefore liable to repay the dividend with interest (*Precision Dippings Ltd v Precision Dippings Marketing Ltd* [1985] BCLC 385).
> 2. ME Ltd declared a dividend of £1,214,000 to its parent, GH Ltd, when it only had sufficient distributable profits to declare a dividend of £1,109,086. GH Ltd in turn declared a dividend to its parent, CT plc, even though it had no distributable profits. All three companies had the same directors and auditors. The court decided that the dividend by ME Ltd was partially unlawful, the whole of the dividend by GH Ltd was unlawful and the directors knew, or ought to have known, that this was the case. Therefore, by virtue of the common directorships, GH Ltd and CT Ltd held the unlawful dividends as constructive trustee for the relevant distributing company (*Re Cleveland Trust plc* [1991] BCLC 424).

MEMO POINTS There is no defence to the statutory liability for a shareholder who has **acted on professional advice**. Instead, the shareholder is left to sue the person who gave him inaccurate advice (if he can). By contrast, under the common law liability, a shareholder may be able to claim that he did not have the requisite knowledge where he acted on professional advice (*It's a Wrap (UK) Ltd v Gula* [2006] EWCA Civ 544).

Liability to directors

1734

Instead of the company bringing a claim for repayment of an unlawful dividend against the shareholders, the directors could be held liable for breach of their duties and be required to repay the distribution instead (see ¶1742+).

In such circumstances, the directors could bring a claim against the shareholders for a **contribution**. The directors' claim would be against the shareholders who received unlawful dividends with notice of the facts; the position of innocent recipients has not been conclusively decided (*Moxham v Grant* [1900] 1 QB 88; *Bairstow v Queens Moat Houses plc* [2001] 2 BCLC 531).

B. Liability of directors

To the company

1742

If the directors recommend or pay an unlawful dividend, the company could bring a claim against them for (*Bairstow v Queens Moat Houses plc* [2001] 2 BCLC 531; *Re Loquitur Ltd*, *IRC v Richmond* [2003] STC 1394; *Re Exchange Banking Co*, *Flitcroft's Case* (1882) 21 Ch D 519):

a. breach of their duty of care, skill and diligence: this duty is now codified into statute, but is pursued as a tortious duty for the purposes of the shareholders' seeking a remedy (see ¶2411+). Executive directors may well have this duty expressly set out in their service contracts, leaving them open to a breach of contract claim; and/or

b. breach of fiduciary duties: the directors owe fiduciary duties to the company and, whilst they are not strictly speaking trustees, they occupy an analogous position (see ¶2373+). Therefore, if they authorise payment of the company's money in unlawful distributions, they are on the face of it in breach of their fiduciary duties and are personally jointly and severally liable to repay them to the company, even if they were not the recipient of the distributions.

1743 If the directors are successfully sued, they could be **required to repay** the unlawful distribution to the company themselves. One potentially problematic consequence of a claim being brought against the directors rather than the shareholders is that it could be seen as unfair to ask the directors to replace money which could later be lawfully distributed to those who received the unlawful distribution; the recipients of the unlawful distribution would receive an unmerited windfall. However, the court has rejected this argument on the basis that the unfairness arises from the original recipients being allowed to keep the unlawful dividend, not from them receiving a second lawful distribution. The directors must therefore rely on their ability to bring a claim for **contribution** against the shareholders (see ¶1734) (*Bairstow v Queens Moat Houses plc* [2001] 2 BCLC 531).

> MEMO POINTS   The directors cannot **set off** any money owed to them by the company against this liability (*Re Exchange Banking Co, Flitcroft's Case* (1882) 21 Ch D 519).

1744 It should be noted that the directors will be liable to **repay the whole** of an unlawful distribution. It does not matter that all or part of the distribution could have been paid lawfully. For example, the full amount will be payable even if:
– sufficient distributable profits were available in the group, if not in the actual distributing company (*Bairstow v Queens Moat Houses plc* [2001] 2 BCLC 531);
– some of the distribution was lawful (*Inn Spirit Ltd v Burns* [2002] 2 BCLC 780); or
– the dividend paid on improperly prepared accounts was the same that would have been paid if the accounts had been properly prepared (*Allied Carpets Group plc v Nethercott* [2001] BCC 81).

During insolvency

1746 The liability of the directors mentioned above is not affected by the insolvency of the company. This means that an insolvent company can still bring an action against the directors for repayment of an unlawful distribution.

However, directors face an **added statutory liability** (called "misfeasance") if the company is insolvent. If a director is found liable for misfeasance, he can be ordered to repay an unlawful dividend (s 212(3) IA 1986; see ¶7457+). In contrast to directors' more general liability to the company explained above, the court has the discretion in an action for misfeasance to determine precisely what, or how much, the director should be ordered to restore to the company. Therefore, it can look at all the circumstances, including why the company became insolvent and whether some or all of the distribution could have been made lawfully (for example, see *Re Loquitur Ltd, IRC v Richmond* [2003] STC 1394, in which the directors only had to repay some of the distribution).

C. Avoiding liability

Consent of shareholders

1754 The scope for obtaining the consent of the shareholders to an unlawful dividend is limited. Most unlawful distributions are made in **breach of the statutory requirements**. These requirements are mandatory and the court views any breach of them strictly. Compliance cannot be waived or dispensed with by the shareholders and an argument that they gave their informal unanimous consent to a distribution in breach of the statutory requirements will not be successful (*Precision Dippings Ltd v Precision Dippings Marketing Ltd* [1985] BCLC 385; *Bairstow v Queens Moat Houses plc* [2001] 2 BCLC 531).

> MEMO POINTS   The court has left open the question of whether something could be done to **restore the situation after a breach** of the statutory requirements has occurred. For example, if the auditors failed to make a statement when one was required, whether they could make their statement afterwards and have this confirmed by a shareholder resolution (*Precision Dippings Ltd v Precision Dippings Marketing Ltd* [1985] BCLC 385).

1756 The consent of the shareholders may be sufficient to rectify the limited cases of **other types of unlawfulness**, for example, a procedural irregularity in the shareholder resolution declaring a dividend. For more on the informal unanimous consent of shareholders, see ¶3590+, and for more on ratification (i.e. retrospective consent), see ¶2497+.

Relief for directors

1758 Often, directors recommend or pay a distribution based on advice given to them by the company's finance director, accountants and/or auditors. It should be noted that directors are not generally able to avoid their liability for an unlawful distribution by claiming that they **relied on** the **advice** of others or **delegated** their functions (*Bairstow v Queens Moat Houses plc* [2001] 2 BCLC 531).

> MEMO POINTS Where distributions are made based on **fraudulent accounts**, a director who had no knowledge or grounds to suspect the fraud will not be liable (even if he was the recipient of the dividend) (*Re Denham & Co* (1883) 25 Ch D 752).

1759 The directors can claim **statutory relief** from their liability on the basis that they acted honestly and reasonably and, having regard to all the circumstances of the case, ought fairly to be excused (see ¶2505+). For the purposes of that relief, acting on professional advice may go towards proving that the directors acted honestly and/or reasonably, although it will not always be sufficient.

> EXAMPLE **Statutory relief refused**
> L Ltd undertook a complicated scheme in order to defer and mitigate a capital gains tax liability. The directors of L Ltd prepared interim accounts on the basis that the scheme would succeed and paid a dividend on the basis of those accounts. The scheme failed and tax became payable. The court decided that the tax liability should have been shown in L Ltd's accounts. The dividend paid by reference to those accounts was therefore unlawful and the directors were liable to repay it. The directors claimed statutory relief on the basis that they acted reasonably on the advice of various professional advisers (accountants, solicitors and counsel). Amongst other reasons, the court decided that the relief was not available because the directors had not properly implemented the advice given to them (and if they thought they had, they were unreasonable in holding that belief) (*Re Loquitur Ltd, IRC v Richmond* [2003] STC 1394).

SECTION 4

Tax treatment

1769 The main tax effect of a distribution is felt by an individual **recipient**; he will have to pay tax on the amount received (¶1780+). Corporate shareholders, on the other hand, do not have to pay tax on distributions they receive (¶1790).

As far as the **distributing company** is concerned, it cannot deduct distributions from its profits chargeable to corporation tax. In addition, the distributing company will have to report certain distributions to Revenue and Customs (¶1795+).

In some cases, benefits paid to the participator of a **close company** will be treated as a distribution for tax purposes (¶1805).

These paragraphs give an overview of the tax position. For full details, see *Tax Memo*.

Definitions

Distribution

1771 A distribution for tax purposes **includes** the following (s 209 ICTA 1988; s 383 ITTOIA 2005):
– a dividend from a UK company satisfied in cash or by a distribution of assets (¶1708+);
– a capital dividend from a UK company (¶1666);

– any other distribution in cash or kind out of the company's assets (such as most transfers at an undervalue and payments for a purchase of its own shares);
– interest payments on a loan in excess of a normal commercial rate (when just the excessive element will be treated as a distribution); and
– benefits paid to a participator of a close company.

A distribution for tax purposes does **not include**:
– a distribution of assets on a winding up;
– a payment for group relief (provided the payment does not exceed the group relief surrendered);
– certain purchases by a company of its own shares (where the distribution is treated as a capital payment instead, see ¶1369+);
– transfers in cash or kind between UK resident companies under common control, or where one is a 51% subsidiary of the other;
– transfers of assets (other than cash) or liabilities between unconnected UK resident companies, neither of which is a 51% subsidiary of a non-resident company; and
– transfers of assets to shareholders who are also employees or directors (which are taxed as a benefit in kind instead, see ¶1785).

> MEMO POINTS Although **stock dividends** (¶1714) are not part of the definition of dividend for tax purposes (s 249 ICTA 1988; s 382(4) ITTOIA 2005), individual recipients do have to pay tax on them (s 410 ITTOIA 2005).

Value of distribution

1773 Where a company makes a distribution, whether in the form of cash or assets, the amount treated as a distribution for tax purposes is the market value of the assets transferred, less:
– any consideration received by the company for the transfer; and
– any amount which represents a repayment of share capital.

Therefore, in the case of most dividends (which are paid in cash), the amount of the distribution is simply the amount of cash paid out.

Qualifying or non-qualifying

1775 Whether a distribution is qualifying or non-qualifying has an impact on its tax treatment.

A non-qualifying distribution is:
– a bonus issue of shares by a UK company;
– a redemption of bonus shares on a winding up; or
– a distribution by a company of shares which it received as a distribution from another company.

All other types of distribution, including a redemption of bonus shares other than in a winding up, are qualifying distributions.

A. Recipient

1. Individuals

Non-employees

1780 For non-employee individuals (including non-executive directors), dividends and other distributions are subject to **income tax** and are deemed to form the top slice of an individual's savings income. Tax is payable on the amount of the distribution plus the tax credit at the following rates:
– basic rate taxpayer: 10%; or
– higher rate taxpayer: 32.5%.

A **tax credit** is an amount of tax that is deemed to have been deducted from a distribution before it is paid to the shareholder. As a general rule, a tax credit is only available in respect of qualifying distributions made to UK resident taxpayers from a UK resident company.

> MEMO POINTS   From April 2008, tax credits will also be available in respect of dividends received from a **non-UK resident company** if the shareholder:
> – owns less than 10% of the company's shares; and
> – receives dividends of less than $5,000 a year from non-UK resident companies.

The tax credit on **qualifying distributions** is 1/9th of the distribution (which equals 10% of the aggregate distribution and tax credit). A lower or basic rate taxpayer will be covered by the tax credit and no further tax will be due (note that a refund is not available if the tax credit exceeds the tax they would have paid). A higher rate taxpayer will have to pay additional tax.

1781

EXAMPLE

Mr A received a qualifying dividend of £3,600.

1. Assuming he also has other taxable income amounting to £50,000 (i.e. he is a higher rate taxpayer), his tax position for the dividend income would be:

	£	£
Dividend		3,600
Add tax credit (1/9th)		400
Total taxable dividend income		4,000
Tax @ 32.5%		1,300
Less tax credit		(400)
Net tax liability		900

2. Assuming he also has other taxable income amounting to £6,000 (i.e. he is a basic rate taxpayer), his tax position in respect of the dividend income would be:

	£	£
Dividend		3,600
Add tax credit (1/9th)		400
Total taxable dividend income		4,000
Tax @ 10%		400
Less tax credit		(400)
Net tax liability		nil

3. Assuming he also has other taxable income amounting to £3,000 (i.e. Mr A is a basic rate taxpayer but has only utilised part of his personal allowance), his tax position in respect of the dividend income would be:

	£	£
Dividend		3,600
Add tax credit (1/9th)		400
		4,000
Less balance of personal allowance (5,225 – 3,000)		(2,225)
Total taxable dividend income		1,775
Tax @ 10%		177.50
Less tax credit (restricted)		(177.50)
Net tax liability (no refund available)		nil

For **non-qualifying distributions**, there is no tax credit but the taxpayer is treated as if he had already paid tax at the dividend rate (currently 10%). This will reduce the tax liability, although it will not be available as a refund.

1782

> MEMO POINTS   Although the issue of bonus shares constitutes a non-qualifying distribution, the **redemption of bonus shares** constitutes a qualifying distribution unless it occurs on a winding up. Where this gives rise to a higher rate tax liability, the amount of the tax will be reduced by the amount of any higher rate tax paid on the original non-qualifying distribution. If the tax paid

on the non-qualifying distribution exceeds the tax liability in respect of the redemption, a refund will not be available.

EXAMPLE In Year 1, Mr B, a higher rate taxpayer, received a non-qualifying distribution of bonus shares of £2,500. His liability in respect of the shares was:

	£
Non qualifying distribution	2,500
Tax thereon:	
2,500 @ 32.5%	812
Less tax deemed to have been paid at the dividend rate	
(2,500 @ 10%)	(250)
Tax liability	562

In Year 2, the shares were redeemed for £2,500 (not on a winding up) which represents a qualifying distribution. The liability in this respect is:

	£
Qualifying distribution	2,500
Add tax credit (1/9th)	278
Total taxable distribution	2,778
Tax thereon:	
2,778 @ 32.5%	902
Less tax credit	(278)
	624
Less excess liability paid on qualifying distribution	(562)
Tax liability	62

Employees

1785 Where an asset (not cash) is distributed to a shareholder who is also a director or employee, this is likely to be subject to tax as a **benefit in kind**, not as a distribution.

For most **directors and other employees earning £8,500 or more** per year, the distribution is valued at the higher of the market value of the asset distributed either:
– at the time of transfer; or
– at the time it was first made available to the employee, less amounts already taxed (both on the employee in question and other employees).

This amount is reduced by any consideration paid by the employee.

For **lower paid employees** (that is, non-director employees earning less than £8,500 p.a.), the amount of the benefit is the second-hand value of the asset.

> MEMO POINTS 1. A **director** is only treated as "**lower paid**" if he:
> – earns less than £8,500 p.a.;
> – has less than a 5% interest in the company as a shareholder; and
> – he is a full-time director, or a director of a non-profit making or charitable company.
> 2. Class 1 **NICs**, which both the company and employee have to pay, are not generally payable on benefits in kind. One exception is if the distribution takes the form of readily convertible assets such as shares capable of being traded on a recognised investment exchange. On the other hand, Class 1A NICs, which just the company has to pay, is almost always payable on benefits in kind. See *Tax Memo* for a detailed discussion of NICs.

2. Corporate shareholders

1790 For corporate shareholders, any income received in the form of distributions from a UK company is **excluded from taxable profit**. This means that they do not have to pay tax on those distributions.

Qualifying distributions received by a company (known as "**franked investment income**" or FII) are relevant in calculating the applicable rate of corporation tax if marginal relief applies (marginal relief aims to smooth the transition from one rate of corporation tax to another). Non-qualifying distributions are not included in FII.

> MEMO POINTS Under UK law, UK companies have to pay tax on **foreign dividends** (i.e. dividends received from a non-UK company). They can claim credit for the amount of foreign tax paid by the non-UK company but this may still result in some UK tax to pay. This dual system has been upheld by the ECJ (*Test Claimants in the FII Group Litigation*, Case C-446/04, 12 December 2006).

B. Distributing company

Distributions

1795 Companies must pay **corporation tax** on their profits, even those that have been distributed to its shareholders (that is to say, a company may not deduct any distributions it paid from its profit chargeable to corporation tax). Distributed profits will be taxed under usual corporation tax rules. For a detailed discussion of corporation tax, see *Tax Memo*.

> MEMO POINTS Historically, companies making qualifying distributions had to deduct **advance corporation tax** (ACT) at source. ACT could be set off against the company's mainstream corporation tax liability up to a limit. Surplus ACT could be carried forward against future corporation tax liabilities. This regime was abolished in 1999 but many companies had surplus ACT which they could still carry forward. A new system, known as shadow ACT, was therefore introduced to limit how this surplus could be used. Under shadow ACT, the amount of surplus ACT that can be set off is the company's ACT capacity (20% of profit chargeable to corporation tax) less the shadow ACT attributable to that period (25% of all distributions made by a company during the accounting period). A company that has fully utilised its surplus ACT no longer needs to worry about the shadow ACT regulations. Further, even if a company has surplus ACT, it can opt out of the shadow ACT regime.

1796 All companies must **notify Revenue and Customs** of any non-qualifying distributions they make, giving (s 234(5) ICTA 1988):
– details of the transaction;
– the name and address of the recipient(s); and
– the value of the distribution received by each recipient.
This information must be provided within 14 days of the end of the accounting period in which the distribution is made.

Own share purchases

1798 Payment by a company to a shareholder in respect of an own share purchase will generally be a distribution. However, in limited circumstances, an **unquoted trading company** will be treated as making a capital payment instead (see ¶1369+).

C. Close companies

1805 A **benefit given to a participator** in a close company, which would have been taxed as a benefit in kind if it had been given to an employee or director, will be treated as a distribution (provided it has not already been taxed as a benefit in kind) (s 418 ICTA 1988).

For the **participator**, this means that he is deemed to have received a distribution, which is calculated by determining the value of an equivalent benefit in kind under the normal provisions and then grossing this amount up at the lower dividend rate. The gross figure is treated as income in the hands of the recipient with a tax credit attached. If the recipient is liable to tax at the higher rate, he will be taxed on the income at the upper dividend rate with a deduction for the tax credit.

For the **company** this means that any expenses incurred in providing the benefit cannot be deducted for corporation tax purposes.

> *MEMO POINTS* A **close company is defined as** any UK resident company which is controlled by five or fewer participators, or any number of participators who are directors (s 414 ICTA 1988). Control is defined as ownership of (or entitlement to acquire) more than 50% of the company's (s 416 ICTA 1988):
> – share capital;
> – voting power;
> – distributable profits; or
> – net assets on a winding up.

CHAPTER 6

Transfer and transmission of shares

OUTLINE

		¶¶
SECTION 1 **Transfer** 1827	2 Legal mortgage............ 1934	
	3 Equitable mortgage......... 1938	
Legal and equitable title........ 1829	4 Priority between lenders....... 1943	
A Restrictions on transfer......... 1836	5 Effect of mortgage on company...... 1950	
Pre-emption provisions....... 1842		
B Transfer instrument.......... 1865		
Stamp duty............ 1875	SECTION 3 **Transmission** 1962	
C Registration............ 1882		
1 Refusal of registration........ 1888	1 Death............ 1964	
2 Share certificates.......... 1902	2 Bankruptcy........... 1976	
	3 Mental incapacity......... 1980	
SECTION 2 **Mortgage of shares** . 1915		
1 Pre-mortgage considerations....... 1920		

1825 The ownership of existing shares can change through two processes: transfer or transmission. In a share **transfer**, a shareholder (who is referred to as the "transferor") sells or gives his shares to another (who is referred to as the "transferee") (¶1827+). In a share **transmission**, ownership changes automatically by operation of the law on the occurrence of a particular event, such as the death or insolvency of a shareholder (¶1962+).

Shareholders can also **mortgage** their shares as security for a personal obligation, normally repayment of a loan (¶1915+). This is sometimes referred to as a "**transfer by way of security**".

SECTION 1

Transfer

1827 Subject to **restrictions** in the articles or any other contract (¶1836+), shareholders are generally free to transfer their shares to whomever they choose and on whatever terms they wish. Shares can be sold for cash or non-cash consideration. They can even be given away, although the position of the recipient of a gift is slightly different to the position of a buyer and, where relevant, this is highlighted in the text below. In addition, although the singular is used throughout, subject to the articles, there is nothing to preclude multiple transferors and transferees.

1828 Once a transferor and transferee have entered into a written or oral contract under which the former agrees to transfer his shares to the latter, there are two main steps which must be taken in order to complete the transfer process:
– the **transfer instrument**, which documents the transfer, must be executed (¶1865+); and
– the transfer must be **registered** with the company, although in some cases the directors may refuse registration (¶1882+).

After the transfer is registered, the company must give the transferee a **share certificate** as evidence of his title to the shares (¶1902+). This share certificate must usually be produced when the shares to which they relate are transferred.

Stamp duty is payable by the transferee on most share transfers (¶1875+).

> MEMO POINTS   1. In the case of a share sale with no special terms, the **contract** is simply that, upon payment of the price, the transferor will deliver genuine share certificates and an executed transfer instrument to the transferee with the rights they convey and will not do anything to prevent the transferee having the full benefit of the transfer. As will be seen, this does not give the transferee much protection and usually he will insist on further express terms (for example, that the shares are transferred with full title guarantee) (see ¶5731). A contract is not necessary where the shares are a **gift**.
> 2. Share transfers are not registered at **Companies House**, although companies provide a list of their current shareholders with their annual return (¶4060+). This means that shareholder information at Companies House may be out of date.
> 3. Listed companies are able to issue shares without paper share certificates and without the need for a paper transfer instrument (s 207 CA 1985; SI 2001/3755). These are known as "**dematerialised**" or "**uncertificated**" shares. At present, all dematerialised shares are held and transferred through the electronic CREST system, which accounts for about 85% by value of shareholdings in listed companies.
> Under the **new Companies Act**, the secretary of state will have the power to introduce mandatory electronic share transfers (ss 783-787 CA 2006 as of 6 April 2008). After consultation, the government expects to exercise this power over listed companies. At the time of writing, draft regulations to this effect have not yet been published, although the draft new model articles (see ¶441/mp) for public companies published under the new Act include provisions dealing with uncertificated shares (particularly: arts 49, 63). The government does not intend to extend compulsory electronic share transfers to non-listed companies, although it has the power to do so in future if there is a demand for it.

Legal and equitable title

1829 In order to understand the transfer process, it is necessary to **distinguish between** the concepts of legal and equitable title. Legal title refers to the strict legal ownership of an asset. Equitable title refers to beneficial ownership or, in other words, ownership of the right to enjoy the benefit of the asset. For example, in relation to a house, the legal owner would be registered as the owner but the beneficial owner would be entitled to live in it.

In most cases, both the legal and equitable title of an asset will belong to the same person. However, in English law, it is possible for them to be **split** so that the legal title is held by one person and the equitable title is held by another. Where this occurs, third parties deal with the legal owner who, on the face of it, exercises all of the rights over that asset. However, the legal owner holds the asset on trust for the beneficial owner and exercises his rights over it in accordance with his obligations as trustee.

This often occurs with **share ownership**. For example, legal title to listed company shares are often held by nominee companies who trade them on behalf of their individual clients, who are the beneficial owners (e.g. Barclays Capital Nominees Ltd, Halifax Share Dealing Ltd). Although the singular has been used here, it is perfectly possible (and indeed quite common) for more than one person to hold the legal title and more than one person to hold the equitable title.

When does title pass?

1830 On a share sale, **equitable title** to the shares that are being transferred passes when the contract for sale is made (regardless of whether the price has been paid). **Legal title** passes when the transfer is registered with the company and the new shareholder is entered in the register of shareholders (*Hawks v McArthur* [1951] 1 All ER 22). Therefore, legal and equitable title are always split on a share transfer.

> MEMO POINTS 1. Shares can be given as a **gift** by a person (the donor) to another (the donee) in three ways. Firstly, the donor can transfer shares to the donee with the intention of them being a gift or, secondly, the donor can transfer them to a third party with the intention that he holds the shares on trust for the donee. In both cases, equitable title passes once the donor has done all he can to perfect the gift. In practical terms, this means the donor must have completed a transfer instrument and delivered it to the donee or trustee, as appropriate, with his share certificates. If the shares are being transferred to a trustee, the donor must also have made a declaration of trust. In both cases, legal title is transferred to the donee or trustee upon registration. The third way in which shares can be gifted is by the donor declaring himself to be the trustee of the shares for the donee. In this case, transfer of the equitable title occurs on the declaration, but legal title remains with the donor and is never transferred (*Pennington v Waine* [2002] 2 All ER 215; *Re Rose* [1952] 1 All ER 1217; *Milroy v Lord* [1861-73] All ER Rep 783).
> 2. It is possible for more than one person to obtain equitable title over the same shares due to the gap between transfer of the equitable and legal titles, for example, if the transferor purported to sell the same shares twice. In practice, **multiple beneficial owners** most commonly occur upon the creation of multiple mortgages over the same shares. The position between such mortgagees is dealt with at ¶1943+.

Rights of transferor and transferee

The rights of the transferor and transferee in the gap between the passing of equitable and legal title are as follows.

1831

Before payment of the price (and assuming the shares are not a gift), as far as voting rights are concerned, the position is not clear cut. The transferor is in a fiduciary position. He has a lien over the shares (as security for the unpaid consideration) and the transferee's equitable title is subject to that lien. Thus, the transferor has not relinquished his rights altogether; he has the right to exercise the voting rights of the shares but he must be mindful of the transferee's interest. What this means in practice is difficult to ascertain, but the transferor does not have to go as far as obeying the transferee's instructions.

Once the price has been paid in full (or, if the shares are a gift, once equitable title has passed) but before the transfer has been registered, the transferor becomes the bare trustee or nominee of the transferee (the terms are interchangeable in this context). This means that he holds the legal title entirely for the transferee's benefit. He must deal with the legal title and exercise his voting rights in accordance with the transferee's instructions and must account to him for any income (dividends or capital) he receives in relation to the shares (*Michaels v Harley House (Marylebone) Ltd* [1999] 1 All ER 356; *JRRT (Investments) Ltd v Haycroft* [1993] BCLC 401; *Musselwhite v C H Musselwhite & Son Ltd* [1962] 1 All ER 201).

> MEMO POINTS The transferor is entitled to all **dividends** declared before transfer, even those that are payable after the sale (*Re Kidner, Kidner v Kidner* [1929] All ER Rep 551). Conversely, the transferee is entitled to all dividends declared after transfer, even those referable to a period before the sale (*Re Wimbush, Richards v Wimbush* [1940] 1 All ER 229). However, the transferor and transferee can agree express contractual terms as to the destination of dividends (see ¶1702+).

A. Restrictions on transfer

Shares are the personal property of shareholders and are freely transferable, subject to the company's **articles** (*Greenhalgh v Mallard* [1943] 2 All ER 234).

1836

> MEMO POINTS 1. **Shareholders** must also be mindful of any other **contractual restrictions** (for example, in a shareholders' agreement). Further, **statutory restrictions** on share transfers may exist (ss 454-457 CA 1985):
> – during a company investigation (s 445 CA 1985; ¶7241); or
> – in relation to a person who fails to give information to a public company when it asks him about his interest in its shares (s 794 CA 2006; ¶2043).

2. A **director** has the same freedom to deal with his shares as any shareholder but:
– if he holds "**qualification shares**" which attach to his directorship, he is not able to deal with those shares without giving up his directorship (¶2254); and
– since he has the power and duty to observe the formalities of a share transfer, any **irregularities** in them will be construed against him.

1837 Most articles give the directors the power to **refuse to register** a transfer. If validly exercised, this power can effectively block a transfer of legal title (see ¶1888+). In addition, the articles of private companies and smaller public companies often contain **pre-emption provisions**.

> MEMO POINTS   Less commonly, and sometimes instead of pre-emption provisions, the articles can require the directors to give their **consent** before a transfer can take place. If the directors **refuse to consent** to a transfer and the transferee brings a claim, the court cannot compel the directors to consent. Instead, it can order the transferor to take whatever steps are required for the transferee to comply with the registration rules of the company, for example, to hand over his share certificate. In the absence of specific performance of the transfer contract, the transferee's only remedy will be damages (*Poole v Middleton* (1861) 54 ER 778; *Langen and Wind Ltd v Bell* [1972] 1 All ER 296).

Pre-emption provisions

1842 Pre-emption provisions can be **described as** provisions in the articles of a company which require a shareholder to offer his shares on a proportionate basis to existing shareholders before being free to transfer them as he pleases. Sometimes the provisions give the company an option to purchase any shares not taken up by existing shareholders. This can be a useful "last resort" where individual shareholders are unlikely to have the money to buy an outgoing shareholder's shares because the company is more likely to be able to fund the purchase. If the company exercises its option, it will have to comply with special rules governing a purchase by a company of its own shares (¶1337+).

Private and unlisted public companies include pre-emption provisions in their articles for the **purpose** of controlling transfers to persons outside the company and maintaining the proportions of existing shareholdings.

There are no pre-emption provisions in Table A and so they must specifically be added to a company's articles. Since pre-emption provisions are essentially a restriction on the transfer of property, they must be expressed in clear language (*Greenhalgh v Mallard* [1943] 2 All ER 234). There are many variations in the drafting of pre-emption provisions and the particular provisions contained in the articles of the relevant company should be referred to in each case.

> MEMO POINTS   1. It may be **unfairly prejudicial** to remove pre-emption provisions from the articles of a company so that a shareholder who had the expectation of gaining control of a company cannot do so (*Re Kenyon Swansea Ltd* [1987] BCLC 514). Conversely, a shareholder may find it difficult to claim unfair prejudice and seek a court order for the purchase of his shares if pre-emption articles exist but are not applied by the complainant (*Re a Company (No 004377 of 1986)* [1987] BCLC 94).
> 2. Pre-emption provisions are not a contravention of **insolvency** law, provided that they require the payment of a fair price for the shares and apply equally to all shareholders, nor are they a contravention of the right to enjoy property enshrined in the European Convention of **Human Rights** (*Borland's Trustee v Steel Bros & Co Ltd* [1901] 1 Ch 579; *Money Markets International Stockbrokers Ltd v London Stock Exchange Ltd* [2001] 2 BCLC 347).

1843 Pre-emption provisions are expressed to be activated upon the occurrence of certain **trigger events** (¶1845+). These can be voluntary (e.g. the desire to transfer) or involuntary (e.g. death or bankruptcy). Most of the provisions concern the **procedure** which must be followed by the transferor, company and other shareholders, such as setting out the time periods within which offers must be sent to the other shareholders and how long they have to accept the offer (¶1850). The **valuation** mechanism is an important provision and sometimes the price of the shares will vary depending upon the reason for the transfer (¶1852+).

1844 If a shareholder wishes to transfer shares without reference to the applicable pre-emption provisions, he will need to obtain a **waiver** from each person entitled to receive a pre-emptive offer. The waiver should be in writing and preferably executed as a deed to avoid problems of consideration and because the articles themselves take effect as a deed.

Trigger events

The most common trigger event is a shareholder's **voluntary** intention to transfer all or part of his shareholding. However, it is also common to include various other acts, which are usually **involuntary**; such as:
– death (otherwise the shares would form part of the deceased shareholder's estate and pass to his personal representatives);
– insolvency (otherwise the shares would pass to the shareholder's trustee in bankruptcy in the case of an individual shareholder, or would be controlled by the relevant insolvency practitioner in the case of a corporate shareholder);
– mental incapacity (otherwise the shares could pass to the shareholder's deputy (formerly known as a receiver));
– the termination of directorship or employment (so that a shareholder who was given shares as part of his directorship or employment cannot keep them once that relationship is over); and/or
– a breach by the shareholder of his obligations to the company, for example under a shareholders' agreement (as a deterrent against such a breach).

1845

When the trigger event occurs is a matter of fact. Involuntary trigger events usually occur on clear cut dates. However, whether or not a shareholder voluntarily intends to transfer his shares is a little more difficult to determine. The act of transfer is not one act, but a series of acts (see ¶1829+) and it is not necessary for all of them to have been completed before the pre-emption provisions are triggered.

1846

Generally speaking, it appears that where the trigger event is a shareholder "proposing to transfer his shares", "desirous of transferring his shares" or something similar, the term "transfer" means only a transfer of the legal title. Such pre-emption provisions are **not triggered** when the intention is only to transfer the equitable interest (*Safeguard Industrial Investments Ltd v National Westminster Bank Ltd* [1982] 1 All ER 449).

1847

Comment: As a result of this uncertainty, modern pre-emption provisions usually expressly state that they apply to transfers of the legal or beneficial interest.

EXAMPLE
1. MWS Ltd's articles stated that no share could be transferred to a non-shareholder as long as a shareholder was willing to purchase it and, in order to ascertain this, a proposing transferor must give notice to the company that he "desires" to transfer his shares. Mr PW, a shareholder, died and Mr PW's executor was registered as the holder of his shares. On completion of the administration of the estate, the executor informed MWS Ltd that it held the shares on trust for the beneficiaries of Mr PW's estate. The beneficiaries stated that they did not want the shares transferred to them and the executor stated that it did not propose to transfer the shares unless and until directed to do so by the beneficiaries. The court decided that the pre-emption provisions had not been triggered because the executor did not have a desire to transfer and in any event the term "transfer" did not apply to a transfer of the beneficial interest (*Safeguard Industrial Investments Ltd v National Westminster Bank Ltd* [1982] 1 All ER 449).

2. R plc's shares were held by GMDC Ltd and four other shareholders. R plc's articles required any shareholder "desiring" to sell his shares to first offer them to the other shareholders. GMDC Ltd undertook to sell its shares to two of the other shareholders provided the pre-emption resolutions were deleted from the articles. A special resolution was passed to delete the pre-emption provisions from the articles so the sale could proceed.
The court decided that the pre-emption provisions had not been triggered prior to their deletion. The required "desire" to sell shares must be present and unequivocal. This was not present in the conditional agreement constituted by the undertaking (*Re a Company (No 005685 of 1988), ex parte Schwarcz (No 2)* [1989] BCLC 427).

3. The shares in T Ltd were held by LT plc, P and M. The articles permitted transfers to other shareholders but imposed pre-emption provisions on any person "proposing to transfer any shares" to an outsider. LT plc wished to sell its shares to an outsider, MB plc, but M objected. Instead, at

MB plc's request, LT plc sold its shares to P. The purchase was financed by MB plc on terms including that (i) P would charge the shares to MB plc as security for the loan and would account for dividends and vote on the shares as directed by MB plc; (ii) P would accept an offer to purchase the shares from MB plc if made and not accept any other offer for any shares in LT plc; and (iii) that the loan was interest free and not repayable until the shares were sold with a proviso limiting P's liability to the amount realised on sale. The court decided that the pre-emption provisions had not been triggered even though the transaction gave MB plc control of the shares and P took no risk. P had validly bought them and charged them to MB plc. Even though he was bound to transfer them if requested, that was not the same as executing a transfer instrument (*Theakston v London Trust plc* [1984] BCLC 390).

1848 Even if the articles do not set out exactly when a voluntary act would trigger the pre-emption provisions, they are likely to be **triggered** where the transferor has done everything necessary for the transfer to be effected (for example, where he has executed a transfer instrument and handed over share certificates).

EXAMPLE
1. The shares in M Ltd and EFC Ltd were held by, amongst others Mr N, Mr M and Mr T. The articles contained pre-emption provisions which stated "a share shall not be transferred" unless first offered to all the other shareholders and any shareholder "desiring to sell a share" had to give notice to the company. Mr N and Mr M entered into an agreement with Mr T to sell him the beneficial interest in their shares and agreed to hold those shares on trust for him. They also executed declarations of trust, and delivered share certificates and executed blank transfer instruments in favour of Mr T. In the declaration of trust, they agreed to transfer their shares and deal with dividends and voting rights as Mr T directed. The court decided that the pre-emption articles had been triggered because Mr N and Mr M had agreed to sell their legal title, despite the wording of the documents. There was nothing further for them to do when Mr T decided to register the shares in his own name (*Re Macro (Ipswich) Ltd*, *Re Earliba Finance Co Ltd*, *Macro v Thompson* [1994] 2 BCLC 354).

2. L & S Ltd's articles stated that no share could be transferred as long as a shareholder was willing to purchase it and a shareholder "desirous of transferring" his shares must give notice to the company. Mr HF, an outsider, made a offer to each shareholder to purchase their shares conditional upon acceptance by at least 75% of the shareholders. S accepted the offer and was later notified that it had become unconditional. S then made Mr HF its proxy, delivered share certificates to his nominee, agreed to execute transfer documents and accepted payment of the price. The court decided that the pre-emption provisions had been triggered (*Lyle & Scott Ltd v Scott's Trustees* [1959] 2 All ER 661).

3. The articles of CB Ltd stated that no share could be transferred unless first offered to the existing shareholders and that any shareholder "desiring to sell a share" must give notice to the company. Mrs A, a shareholder, told the company's auditor that she wished to transfer 400 shares to Mr C. She signed the stock transfer form, the auditor placed it on the company's file and wrote to Mr C to inform him of the gift saying no further action was required from him. The transfer was never registered. The court decided that the pre-emption provisions were triggered (even though it was a gift and not a sale) because where a shareholder goes as far as signing a transfer form he has lost all control over the share. In those circumstances, it was rational and business-like to say that the shareholder had transferred her share (*Hurst v Crampton Bros (Coopers) Ltd* [2003] 1 BCLC 304).

Procedure

1850 Pre-emption procedures are usually quite detailed and should contain **express terms** to deal with:
– the notices that must be given by the transferor and the company and the deadlines for doing so;
– which shareholders are entitled to receive a pre-emption offer to purchase the shares;
– how long they have to accept the pre-emption offer;
– whether they can accept only some of the shares that are offered to them or whether they have to accept all or none of them;
– whether they can apply to take any shares that are rejected by other shareholders;
– the mechanics of purchase, for example, how and when must payment be made, transfer instruments executed and so on;
– what happens if not all of the shares on offer are taken up on pre-emption; and

– what the transferor may do with any shares he has left at the end of the pre-emption process.

> MEMO POINTS   If the pre-emption provisions are lacking in procedural machinery (such as a requirement to give notice of the number of shares on offer) then the court will **imply the minimum term** that is required so as to give effect to the obvious intentions of the parties (*Tett v Phoenix Property and Investment Co Ltd* [1986] BCLC 149).

Valuation

The valuation of the shares on offer is often the most important provision to both the transferor and potential transferees. The pre-emption provisions normally state that the valuation is to be **carried out by** the company's auditors or by an independent valuer appointed by the directors or agreed between the parties. 1852

> MEMO POINTS   Where the articles call for a valuation by an independent valuer, the appointment of a non-independent person could amount to **unfair prejudice** (*Re Benfield Greig Group plc, Nugent v Benfield Greig Group plc* [2002] 1 BCLC 65).

The most common basis for the valuation is **fair market value**. A market valuation can be carried out using many different methods. 1853

One aspect of any market valuation is that a discount will be applied to the valuation of a **minority shareholding**. For example, if a 30% shareholding were being valued, it would be worth less than 30% of the value of the company because, on its own, the shareholding would not give control over the company. The actual amount of the discount will vary from case to case but can be considerable. Shareholders should expect a discount to be applied to each parcel of shares being transferred (even if all or a majority of the company's shares were being acquired by the transferee at the same time) and this will not amount to unfair prejudice (*Re Castleburn Ltd* [1991] BCLC 89). As a result, pre-emption provisions often specify that no discount should be applied when arriving at fair market value.

In some cases, the pre-emption provisions will state that the shares will be valued at **less than market value**. Such a valuation will often follow a trigger event that implies that the shareholder is at fault in some way. For example, an employee who is required to transfer his shares on being dismissed for gross misconduct could have his shares valued at their nominal value instead of fair market value. Alternatively, a shareholder who is required to transfer his shares because he is in breach of an obligation to the company could have the valuation of his shares discounted by the cost to the company of his breach. 1854

> MEMO POINTS   A transfer at less than market value may cause problems where the trigger event relates to the **shareholder's insolvency**. Firstly, generally speaking, a contractual provision that a person's assets pass to another in the event of his insolvency so as to deprive his creditors of the value of those assets is contrary to insolvency principles and void (although this would not be an issue if the shares were transferred for fair market value as the creditors would receive the value of the shares) (*Money Markets International Stockbrokers Ltd v London Stock Exchange Ltd* [2001] 2 BCLC 347). Secondly, such a transaction could be set aside as a transaction at an undervalue (¶7811+).

Normally, the valuer is appointed to act as an expert (not an arbitrator) and his decision is expressed to be final and binding. The circumstances in which such a **valuation can be challenged** are limited to (*Campbell v Edwards* [1976] 1 All ER 785; *Burgess v Purchase & Sons (Farms) Ltd* [1983] 2 All ER 4):
– one that is not made honestly or in good faith;
– where the valuer has materially departed from his instructions (for example, by valuing the wrong number of shares); or
– in the case of a speaking valuation (in other words, where the valuer has given reasons), where it is made on a fundamentally erroneous basis.
Normally, the court will not allow unnecessary analysis of how the result was achieved (*Morgan Sindall plc v Sawston Farms (Cambs) Ltd* (1990) 1 EGLR 90). 1855

> MEMO POINTS   A person (including the company accountant) appointed by the directors to value shares in accordance with pre-emption articles owes a duty of care to the transferor in the conduct of the valuation and will therefore be liable to him for a **negligent valuation** (*Killick v PricewaterhouseCoopers* [2001] 1 BCLC 65).

Breach

1857 A transfer in breach of pre-emption provisions is a **transfer** in breach of the articles. This means that:
- it may be challenged by any shareholder who may also be able to obtain an injunction to prevent a proposed transfer (*Curtis v JJ Curtis & Co Ltd* [1986] BCLC 86); and
- the directors should not register it.

1858 However, the **contract** between the transferor and transferee is not necessarily invalidated by the breach. The transferee can still take equitable title to the shares (¶1829+) and direct the transferor as to how to deal with any rights attaching to them (*Tett v Phoenix Property and Investment Co Ltd* [1986] BCLC 149). In such circumstances, the existing shareholders' pre-emption rights are converted into options over this equitable title.

> MEMO POINTS If a **buyer's equitable interest** is nullified as a result of the exercise by the shareholders of their pre-emption rights, he can recover the purchase price from the seller. If, on the other hand, the shares were a gift, the person to whom the shares were given is entitled to the price that is paid if the pre-emption rights are exercised (*Hurst v Crampton Bros (Coopers) Ltd* [2003] 1 BCLC 304).

B. Transfer instrument

1865 The transfer instrument is the document that records the share transfer. The prescribed form of transfer instrument for transfers of fully paid shares is known as a "**stock transfer form**" (s 1 Stock Transfer Act 1963). Blank stock transfer forms can be purchased from legal stationers.

> MEMO POINTS 1. The stock transfer form applies to the vast majority of transfers. The instrument for **other types of transfer**, for example, transfers of partly paid shares, should be prescribed by the articles.
> 2. Draft **new model articles** under the **new Companies Act** have been published for private companies limited by shares and public companies. Those for private companies will require the transfer instrument to be in "the usual form" or any other form approved by the directors (art 26). Those for public companies make a distinction between certificated and uncertificated shares (see ¶1828/mp). They do not set out the form of transfer instrument uncertificated shares, but they do allow the directors to take any necessary steps to regarding the transfer of such shares which would include setting out a particular form (art 49). The transfer instrument for certificated shares will have to be in "the usual form" or any other form approved by the directors (art 62). The government has not yet indicated whether a new form of stock transfer form will be prescribed.

1866 The table below is a **guide to completing a stock transfer form**. Forms should be typed or completed in block capitals for ease of legibility. Transfers by different transferors (not joint shareholders) to one transferee (e.g. Mr A, Mr B and Mr C all transferring to X Ltd) require separate stock transfer forms (i.e. Mr A to X Ltd, Mr B to X Ltd and Mr C to X Ltd).

Box in form	Guidance
Consideration money	Insert the amount of money being paid for the shares. If the amount is calculated by reference to a contractual formula or is satisfied by non-cash consideration, insert a short description and reference to the relevant contractual provision. If there is no consideration, e.g. because shares are a gift, then insert word "nil"
Name of undertaking	Insert the full name of the company whose shares are being transferred
Description of security	Insert a description of shares including nominal value, e.g. "ordinary shares of £1 each" or "5% preference shares of £7 each". Use a separate stock transfer form for each class of share being transferred
Number of shares	Insert the number of shares being transferred in words and figures
Registered holder(s)	Insert the full name and address of the registered holder (insert only names of holders if the shares are jointly registered). If the transfer is not being executed by the registered holder then also insert the name and capacity of the transferor, e.g. "Mr X, Executor"

Box in form	Guidance
Signature of transferor	Each transferor signs here (space for four signatures, e.g. if joint transferors). If the transferor is a company, the form should be signed by two directors or a director and secretary (or the company can use its seal in accordance with its articles). If the transfer is being signed by someone under a power of attorney, under the attorney's signature insert "Attorney for [name of registered holder]"
Date	Insert the date on which the transfer takes effect: this must be the date on or after the form is executed and delivered to the transferee; never back-date the form
Transferees	Insert the full name and address of the transferee. If shares are to be held jointly, insert the full names of all transferees and the address of the first joint holder

1867 Once the transfer instrument has been executed and delivered to the transferee unconditionally, the transferor cannot **withdraw or revoke** it. A transferee to whom an executed transfer instrument has been delivered with the share certificates is entitled to be registered without recourse to the transferor (*Macmillan Inc v Bishopsgate Investment Trust plc (No 3)* [1995] 3 All ER 747). However, a transferor is entitled to withdraw a signed transfer instrument which is handed over to the transferee subject to conditions which are subsequently not met (*Smith v Charles Building Services Ltd* [2006] All ER (D) 120 (Jan)).

> MEMO POINTS   Where a stock transfer form is executed and delivered to a transferee in order to give effect to a share transfer agreement, the stock transfer form does not have any independent effectiveness to transfer the shares in question if that agreement does not in fact amount to a legally binding contract (*Cox v Cox* [2006] EWHC 1077 (Ch)).

1868 The articles normally require the transfer instrument to be **executed by** or on behalf of the transferor; the transferee only has to execute it if the shares are not fully paid (reg 23 TA 1985). Unless the articles state otherwise, the transfer instrument does not have to be executed as a deed or witnessed; usually just the signature of the transferor (and transferee if required) is sufficient.

> MEMO POINTS   1. The transfer instrument for companies operating under an unamended **Table A 1948** must be executed by both transferor and transferee (reg 22 TA 1948), although if this is not done, the transfer could still lawfully be registered (*Dempsey v Celtic Football and Athletic Co Ltd* [1993] BCC 514).
> 2. The draft new **model articles** for private companies limited by shares will require the transfer instrument to be executed by or on behalf of the transferor (art 26(1)). Those for public companies will mirror Table A (art 62(1)). They will also make a distinction between certificated and uncertificated shares (see ¶1828/mp). No transfer instrument will be required for uncertificated shares, unless the directors exercise their power to require one (art 49).

1869 A transfer instrument is important because a company can only register a transfer upon receipt of an appropriate transfer instrument. It is therefore not possible to transfer shares by an oral agreement or by delivery of share certificates; all transfers must be **in writing** (s 183(1) CA 1985; restated at s 770 CA 2006 as of 6 April 2008). The only exception to this rule is the transfer of uncertificated shares by listed companies (¶1828/mp).

Having said that, **irregularities** in the transfer instrument, such as an error in the denoting numbers of shares or the failure of the transferee to sign the document, do not affect the validity of the transfer and its registration. What is important is that the transfer document sufficiently records the transaction so that it can be stamped (*Nisbet v Shepherd* [1994] 1 BCLC 300). Further, an irregular transfer instrument may not be challenged after a lapse of time (*Re Paradise Motor Co Ltd* [1968] 2 All ER 625).

> EXAMPLE   Mr M transferred his shares to Mr S by way of a stock transfer form which was undated, did not state the consideration money, did not state the address of the transferor or transferee, was not signed by the transferee (as required by the articles) and was never stamped. The court decided that, despite the defects, the transfer document was chargeable with stamp duty. It was therefore a proper instrument and the registration of the transfer was valid (*Nisbet v Shepherd* [1994] 1 BCLC 300).

1870 On the other hand, **forged transfer instruments** cannot be relied upon. A transferee who presents a transfer instrument for registration makes an implied representation that he is entitled to have the transfer registered in his name. A transferor who is removed from the company's register of shareholders on the basis of a forged transfer instrument can demand to be restored. A transferee who is issued with a share certificate on the basis of a forged transfer instrument cannot then rely on that certificate for his title and, if he has wrongly inserted his name into a blank executed transfer instrument as the transferee, he will be liable to the transferor for the tort of injurious falsehood. Any person who presents a forged transfer instrument for registration, including agents or stockbrokers of the purported transferee, will have to indemnify the company for any liability it incurred in registering the forged transfer (*Sheffield Corporation v Barclay* [1905] AC 392; *Royal Bank of Scotland plc v Sandstone Properties Ltd* [1998] 2 BCLC 429; *Lloyd v Popely* [2000] 1 BCLC 19).

MEMO POINTS The only **exception** to this is where an innocent person unknowingly presents a forged transfer instrument for registration accompanied by share certificates issued by the company. In those circumstances, the innocent person is entitled to rely upon the estoppel of the share certificate (¶1906) and the company will be liable for the losses incurred as a result of it registering the forged transfer (*Cadbury Schweppes plc v Halifax Share Dealing Ltd* [2006] EWHC 1184 (Ch)).

Stamp duty

1875 Stamp duty must be **paid by** the transferee on most share transfers at a **rate** of 0.5% of the consideration, rounded up to the nearest £5. This is known as "ad valorem" duty. Stamp duty must be paid to Revenue and Customs **within** 30 days of the transfer, after which time interest and penalties may be imposed. The original stock transfer form will need to be sent to Revenue and Customs' Birmingham Stamp Office with a cheque for the correct duty so the document can physically be stamped (see contact details at ¶9905).

MEMO POINTS 1. If the entire consideration has been paid in **cash**, the appropriate level of duty can easily be calculated. If the shares have been transferred for **non-cash** consideration, an explanation of how the duty has been calculated will need to be sent to Revenue and Customs with the stock transfer form. If the stock transfer form has been executed to give effect to a written contract, the usual practice is to send the contract (including duplicates and counterparts) as well. Revenue and Customs can query the consideration stated on the face of the stock transfer form and the duty paid if it believes it has been understated or underpaid, as appropriate.
2. **Stamp duty reserve tax** at the same rate as stamp duty is payable on agreements to transfer shares unless stamp duty is paid on the transfer.

1876 Certain transfers are **exempt** from stamp duty altogether. These are listed on the back of the stock transfer form and include transfers made:
– as a gift;
– to the beneficiary under a deceased shareholder's will or if he died without a will, to the person entitled to the shares under inheritance law; or
– in consideration of marriage or civil partnership, or in connection with divorce.

If a transfer is exempt, the certificate on the back of the stock transfer form must be completed. However, the document does not then need to be sent to Revenue and Customs.

1877 Certain transfers are exempt from ad valorem duty but are still subject to a **fixed duty** of £5. Such transfers include:
a. a transfer by way of security for a loan or a re-transfer to the original transferor on repayment of a loan (¶1934);
b. a transfer to, from or between nominees where no beneficial interest passes (providing the transfer is not pursuant to any contract or agreement for sale); or
c. a transfer which needs to be adjudicated because an exemption from ad valorem duty is being sought. Such an exemption may be available:
– if the shares are being transferred from one group company to another (s 42 Finance Act 1930); or
– if the transfer is part of a scheme of arrangement or amalgamation (see ¶6500+), including certain share for share exchanges (see ¶6454) (ss 76, 77 Finance Act 1986).

If a transfer is only subject to a fixed duty, the certificate on the back of the stock transfer form should be completed and the form, the amount of duty and a letter of explanation (if an exemption is being sought for which adjudication is required) should be sent to Revenue and Customs' Birmingham Stamp Office.

C. Registration

Once a transfer instrument has been properly executed and stamped, the transferee must deliver it to the company for registration, together with the relevant share certificate (see ¶1905 for the position where a certificate has been lost or damaged).

1882

Registration is the final step in the transfer process but the **purpose** is more than procedural; it perfects the transferee's legal title to the shares (see ¶1829+).

> MEMO POINTS 1. Usually, applying for registration is the **responsibility of** the transferee although the company is required to accept applications from the transferor (s 183(4) CA 1985; restated at s 772 CA 2006 as of 6 April 2008).
> 2. Since registration is so vital to a shareholder, if he feels the register does not properly reflect the shareholdings of the company, he can apply to the court for **rectification of the register** (see ¶4027+).

Although the board must refuse registration in certain situations and has the discretion to refuse it in others (¶1888+), in most cases, applications for registration are approved. In order to **implement** a registration, the company must:
– record the transfer in the register of transfers, if the company keeps such a register (¶4004);
– record the changes to its shareholdings in the register of shareholders (¶3915+); and
– cancel the transferor's share certificate (by crossing it through and marking it cancelled) and issue a new one to the transferee (and one for the balance of the transferor's shares if he has only transferred part of his shareholding).

1883

Comment: From 6 April 2008, when the relevant provision of the **new Companies Act** comes into force, a company will have to register the transfer, or give notice of its refusal to register the transfer, within 2 months of receiving the transfer instrument (s 771 CA 2006).

> MEMO POINTS Companies operating under Table A 1985 cannot charge a **fee** for registration (reg 27 TA 1985). The draft new model articles will restate this provision (private companies limited by shares: art 26(2); public companies: art 62(2)). Those operating under Table A 1948 can (theoretically) charge up to 12.5p (reg 24 TA 1948).

1. Refusal of registration

Obligation to refuse

The board must refuse registration where:
– a transfer has occurred in **breach of the articles** because it would be acting outside of its powers to register it (*Tett v Phoenix Property and Investment Co Ltd* [1986] BCLC 149); or
– stamp duty is payable on the transfer and it has **not received a proper transfer instrument** (meaning one that is appropriate for stamping) (s 183(1) CA 1985; restated at s 770 CA 2006 as of 6 April 2008).

1888

> MEMO POINTS The board can validly register an **unstamped transfer** instrument, provided the transfer instrument is suitable for stamping (*Nisbet v Shepherd* [1994] 1 BCLC 300). However, if the board does so, the secretary or other registration officer is liable to a penalty of up to £300 (s 17 Stamp Act 1891). As a result, the usual practice is for the board to approve registration of a transfer "subject to stamping". However, it should not make the relevant entries in the company's registers or issue the share certificate until the transfer instrument has actually been stamped.

1889 Where the board has no discretion, the secretary (or other officer to whom the transfer instrument has been delivered) need not put the matter of registration before the board because there is no decision to make (*Tett v Phoenix Property and Investment Co Ltd* [1986] BCLC 149).

Discretion to refuse

1891 The articles of most companies also give the directors the discretionary power to refuse to register a transfer. The power can be **restricted** to certain types of transfers, or it can be an **absolute** power to refuse registration of any type of transfer.

Under Table A 1985, the directors have the discretionary power to refuse to register a transfer in the following **circumstances** (reg 24 TA 1985):
– the share is not fully paid;
– the company has a lien over the share;
– the transfer instrument and share certificate or other right of title are not lodged at the company's registered office or other place appointed by the directors;
– the transfer instrument records a transfer of more than one share class; or
– there are five or more transferees.

> MEMO POINTS 1. Under **Table A 1948** (for private companies registered on or after 20 December 1980 and for public companies), the directors can refuse registration when (regs 24, 25 TA 1985):
> – the share is not fully paid;
> – the company has a lien over the shares; or
> – the transfer instrument records a transfer of more than one share class.
> Under Table A 1948 (for companies registered on or before 19 December 1980), the directors have the absolute discretion to refuse registration without giving any reasons (reg 2 Pt II TA 1948).
> 2. Under Table A 1985 and 1948, the directors can **suspend** registrations for up to 30 days in each year (reg 26 TA 1985; reg 27 TA 1948). This power is not replicated in the draft new model articles for companies incorporated under the new Companies Act.
> 3. The draft **new model articles** for private companies limited by shares will give the directors the discretion to refuse registration in any circumstances, but they will be obliged by statute to provide the transferee with reasons for their refusal (art 26(5); see ¶1893 below). The draft new model articles for public companies will give the directors the discretion to refuse registration when (art 62(5)):
> – the share is not fully paid;
> – the transfer is not lodged at the company's registered office or such other place as the directors have appointed;
> – the transfer is not accompanied by the relevant share certificate or other document evidencing ownership of the shares;
> – the transfer is in respect of more than one class of share; or
> – the transfer is in favour of more than four transferees.

1892 The power must be **exercised by** the directors passing a resolution at a board meeting. If no resolution is passed, for example, because there is a deadlock on the board, then the transfer must be registered (*Moodie v W and J Shepherd (Bookbinders) Ltd* [1949] 2 All ER 1044).

1893 The discretionary power to refuse registration is a **fiduciary power**. It must therefore be exercised in good faith and for the benefit of the company. The directors can even refuse to register a transfer to an existing shareholder. However, the directors do not have to give reasons for a refusal unless the articles specifically require them to do so.

If reasons are given, the court will consider whether they are legitimate or not. In doing so, it will adopt a subjective test and will not interfere with the directors' decision on the basis that it was not the decision that the court would have made.

If no reasons are given, the court will only interfere with the decision if the transferee can prove that the directors acted in bad faith or for an improper purpose. Unless the articles state otherwise, the transferee can question the directors as to the grounds for their decision (*Re Smith & Fawcett Ltd* [1942] 1 All ER 542; *Charles Forte Investments Ltd v Amanda* [1963] 2 All ER 940). Further, the court can infer an improper motive from the directors' decision not to give reasons (*Re Hafner, Olhausen v Powderly* [1943] IR 264). On the other hand, the court will not infer bad faith purely because the directors personally dislike the transferee; the transferee must go further and show that the directors' personal feelings overcame their views as to what was in the best interests of the company (*Popely v Planarrive Ltd* [1997] 1 BCLC 8).

Comment: From 6 April 2008, when the relevant provision of the **new Companies Act** comes into force, the directors will have to give reasons for any refusal to register a transfer with the notice of refusal (see ¶1896). They will also have to give the transferee any further information which he may reasonably request, although the transferee will not be entitled to copies of any board minutes (s 771 CA 2006).

> EXAMPLE The shares in P Ltd were owned by the P family. Mrs P and the P children were the directors. A "bitter feud" arose between Mr P on one side and the directors on the other after the discovery by them of Mr P's extra-marital relationships. The directors refused to register a transfer that would give Mr P 55% control of P Ltd. Mrs P's evidence was that if Mr P took control of the company he would replace the board and use the position to his own advantage and to the detriment of the company and its creditors. The court accepted this evidence and decided that the directors had properly exercised their discretion even though the board had strong feelings of personal hostility towards Mr P (*Popely v Planarrive Ltd* [1997] 1 BCLC 8).

Apart from exceptional cases where it is impossible for any reason to constitute a board, the directors must make their decision **within** 2 months of receiving the transfer instrument. If they do not, the court will consider that there has been an unreasonable delay and the directors will lose their power to refuse registration (*Re Swaledale Cleaners Ltd* [1968] 3 All ER 619; *Re Inverdeck Ltd* [1998] 2 BCLC 242). **1894**

Comment: From 6 April 2008, when the relevant provision of the **new Companies Act** comes into force, directors will have to either register a transfer or give the transferee notice of their reasons for refusing to register the transfer within 2 months of receiving the transfer instrument (s 771 CA 2006).

> EXAMPLE **Unreasonable delay**
> Shareholders asked for transfers to be registered in August. The board of SC Ltd had taken no decision by the beginning of December. On 11 December, the shareholders presented a petition for rectification of the register. On 18 December, the directors purported formally to refuse to register the transfer. The court decided that 4 months' delay was unreasonable and the directors had lost their power to refuse registration (*Re Swaledale Cleaners Ltd* [1968] 3 All ER 619).

Consequences of refusal

Notice of a refusal to register a transfer (whether the directors were obliged to refuse or exercised their discretion) must be sent to the transferee within 2 months of the transfer being lodged with the company (s 183(5) CA 1985; reg 25 TA 1985; restated at s 771(1) CA 2006 as of 6 April 2008). **1896**

Failure to give notice within this time leaves the company and every officer in default liable to a fine (s 183(6) CA 1985; restated at s 771(3), (4) CA 2006 as of 6 April 2008) (¶9935). However, failure to give notice does not necessarily affect the decision to refuse registration itself. The refusal will still stand provided the decision was taken within a reasonable time.

> EXAMPLE Mr P presented a transfer for registration on 29 September. The directors decided to refuse registration at a board meeting on 25 October but did not notify the shareholder within 2 months. The court decided that the directors had the power to take the decision at the time they took it and failure to notify did not retrospectively invalidate a proper exercise of their powers (*Popely v Planarrive Ltd* [1997] 1 BCLC 8).

> MEMO POINTS 1. The court has left open the question of whether it would deny the company's right to rely on a refusal if there was a long **delay in notification** coupled with a shareholder taking action based on the assumption that he had been registered (i.e. whether the company could be estopped from relying on the refusal if there were a delay in notification) (*Popely v Planarrive Ltd* [1997] 1 BCLC 8).
> 2. Under Table A 1985 (but not Table A 1948), the **transfer instrument must be returned** to the transferee with the notice of refusal (reg 28 TA 1985). This obligation will be replicated under the draft **new model articles** (private companies limited by shares: art 26(5); public companies: art 62(6)). However, the draft new model articles will allow the directors to keep the transfer instrument if they suspect that the proposed transfer may be fraudulent.

1897 If the directors refuse registration, subject to any express contractual terms, the transferee cannot **recover the price** from the transferor. This is because there is no implied term that the transferor will secure registration; registration is entirely at the transferee's risk.

1898 Directors who **erroneously refuse** to register a transfer (even if they act in good faith) may be held personally liable for the cost of rectifying the register of shareholders (*Morgan v Morgan Insurance Brokers Ltd* [1993] BCLC 676).

2. Share certificates

1902 The **purpose** of a share certificate is to provide evidence that the person named in it holds legal title to the shares to which it relates (s 186 CA 1985; restated at s 768 CA 2006 as of 6 April 2008). The certificate is not concerned with the equitable title which may be held by someone else, so a person who deals with a seller of shares on the basis of the certificate alone should be aware that someone with a prior claim to the equitable title could take precedence (¶1946).

> MEMO POINTS   Instead of a share certificate, if authorised by its articles, a company can issue a **share warrant** in respect of any fully paid shares (s 188(1) CA 1985; restated at s 779(1) CA 2006 as of 6 April 2008). Share warrants are rare in practice. Subject to the articles, the person in possession of a share warrant (known as the bearer) is entitled to be registered as the holder of the shares specified in it when they surrender it to the company for cancellation. The company should only ever register the bearer's right to the underlying shares upon production of the share warrant as otherwise it will be responsible for any loss incurred by any person as a result of the registration. If a share warrant is issued, the company should delete the shareholder's name from the register of shareholders and instead enter the fact that a warrant has been issued, the number of shares in the warrant and the date of issue. When surrendered, the company should enter the date of surrender on the register as well (s 355(1)-(4) CA 1985; restated at s 122 CA 2006 by 1 October 2009). Share warrants are transferable upon delivery (s 188(2) CA 1985; restated at s 779(2) CA 2006 as of 6 April 2008). No stamp duty is payable on transfer but duty is payable on issue at a rate of 1.5% of market value (s 113, Sch 15 Finance Act 1999). The rights of the bearer are as set out in the articles. He can be deemed to be a shareholder to the full extent or for any particular purpose defined in the articles, except for the purposes of directors' share qualification (s 355(5) CA 1985; restated apart from the exception at s 122(3) CA 2006 by 1 October 2009).

Function during transfer

1904 Share certificates are evidence of title to the shares. Therefore, the transferee should ensure that the transferor hands them over to him on the date of the transfer.

> MEMO POINTS   1. A shareholder who wishes to transfer part of his shareholding or transfer his shareholding to more than one party (not as joint holders) usually lodges the share certificate with the company secretary instead of handing it to the transferee(s). The company secretary will put the words "Certificate lodged" in the top right of the stock transfer form to signify that he has seen the share certificate. This is known as "**certification**". Certification of the transfer will prove to any third party that evidence of title to the shares mentioned in the transfer has been produced to the company (s 184 CA 1985; restated at s 775 CA 2006 as of 6 April 2008). Alternatively, the shareholder could obtain **multiple share certificates** to evidence title to each parcel of shareholding. Whether he is able to do this depends upon the articles (*Sharpe v Tophams Ltd* [1939] Ch 373). Usually, a shareholder is entitled to multiple certificates for different shares on payment of a reasonable sum as determined by the directors. A shareholder who transfers part of his shareholding is entitled to a share certificate to cover the balance retained (reg 6 TA 1985; reg 8 TA 1948). These provisions are replicated in the draft **new model articles** for public companies under the new Companies Act (art 47), but those for private companies limited by shares will allow (but will not oblige) the directors to issue multiple certificates (art 24).
> 2. A transferee does not have to produce a share certificate to the company in order to have the **transfer registered**, but the directors may refuse registration if it is not (see ¶1891). Sometimes, a share certificate has noted on it that no transfer of the shares to which it relates will be registered without production of the certificate. This note is a declaration of intention only and the company will not be liable on that basis if it does in fact register a transfer without production of the certificate (*Rainford v James Keith and Blackman Co Ltd* [1905] 1 Ch 296).

1905 If, as frequently occurs, the transferor has **lost** his **share certificate** (or if it is defaced, worn-out or destroyed), he is entitled to a replacement on such terms as the directors determine. The usual practice is for the transferor to provide the company with an indemnity and perhaps payment of a nominal fee. In smaller companies where obtaining a replacement certificate is likely to be a mere formality, the indemnity (and fee, if one is charged) are usually handed to the transferee in lieu of a share certificate and he presents them to the company when he comes to register the transfer.

If the transferor is unable to produce share certificates and there is no dispute as to title to the shares, the breach is not significant enough to entitle the transferee to treat himself as discharged from the contract (*Grant v Cigman* [1996] 2 BCLC 24).

1906 It should be noted that a certificate is not a warranty or representation by the company of the holder's title to the shares. All it signifies is that the person named in the certificate has presented documents to the company which, on the face of them, show legal title to the shares (s 184(1) CA 1985; restated at s 768 CA 2006 as of 6 April 2008). However, the certificate does provide a transferee with some comfort because it operates as an "**estoppel**". This means that the company is prevented from denying that the facts stated on the certificate are true as far as this affects any person acting in good faith who relied upon the certificate to his detriment. For example, the company is estopped from denying the title of a seller to a buyer and will be liable in damages if it refuses to register the transfer (*Royal Bank of Scotland plc v Sandstone Properties Ltd* [1998] 2 BCLC 429).

> MEMO POINTS 1. A person who acquires good title by estoppel cannot necessarily transfer them to a third party, even if that person is aware of all the facts. In practice therefore a transferee who found that the **share certificate** upon which he relied was **incorrect** would seek damages instead, or as well as, registration of the transfer based on estoppel.
> 2. Estoppel does not arise in the case of certificates issued on the basis of a **forged transfer instrument** unless the share certificates are relied upon by an innocent party (¶1870).
> 3. A **director** can rely on an estoppel created against his company, even if he signed the certificate, provided he can prove that he did not know the true facts at the time of signing (*Re Coasters Ltd* [1911] 1 Ch 86).

1907 A company is not estopped by a **forged certificate**, unless the certificate was issued under the directors' authority. It would not be sufficient that the certificate had been forged by the secretary (*Panorama Developments (Guildford) Ltd v Fidelis Furnishing Fabrics Ltd* [1971] 3 All ER 16). However, a purchaser acting in good faith is entitled to rely on a certificate if it purports to have been signed by a director and secretary or two directors (s 36A(6) CA 1985).

Comment: From 6 April 2008, when the relevant provision of the **new Companies Act** comes into force, a purchaser will be entitled to rely on a certificate if it purports to have been signed by two authorised signatories (who are the directors and secretary if there is one) or by a director and a witness (s 44 CA 2006).

Issue of certificate

1909 Companies must issue a share certificate to the transferee **within** 2 months after the date upon which a duly stamped transfer instrument is lodged at the company, unless the directors refuse registration when they are entitled to do so (s 185 CA 1985; restated at s 769 CA 2006 as of 6 April 2008).

The certificate can be given under the official seal of the company or, more commonly, **signed by** two directors or a director and secretary (ss 36A(4), 40 CA 1985). The certificate **sets out** basic information regarding the class of shares, how many are held and their unique reference number(s) (reg 6 TA 1985). Blank share certificates are usually found in the back of the company's registers (and photocopied for repeated use) or can be purchased from legal stationers.

There is no requirement for companies to notify Companies House each time a new shareholder joins the company, as this information is included in the annual return, but companies should keep their own **record** of issued share certificates.

Comment: From 6 April 2008, when the relevant provision of the **new Companies Act** comes into force, a certificate will be able to be signed by two authorised signatories (who are the directors and secretary if there is one) or by a director and a witness, as well as being sealed (s 44 CA 2006).

> MEMO POINTS 1. The directors do **not** need to **issue a certificate** if:
> – the transfer relates to certain gilt-edged securities which can be transferred without a transfer document or share certificate (s 3 Stock Transfer Act 1982). However, if the transferee subsequently becomes entitled to a certificate, he must give the company written notice and the company must provide a certificate within 2 months of that notice; or
> – the transferee is a recognised clearing house acting for a recognised investment exchange, or is the nominee of either type of organisation.
> 2. The draft **new model articles** require that share certificates must be executed under seal or authenticated in accordance with companies legislation (private companies limited by shares: art 24; public companies art 46).

1910 If the company **fails to issue** a certificate within the required time period, the transferee should give notice to the company that it has failed to comply with its statutory obligation. If the company is still in breach 10 days after the notice, the transferee can apply to court for an order that a certificate be provided. The court will normally order that the costs of a successful application be met by the company or the particular officer(s) in default (s 185(6), (7) CA 1985, restated at s 782 CA 2006 as of 6 April 2008). Further, every company and officer in default of the requirement to provide a certificate is liable to a fine (see ¶9935) (s 185(5) CA 1985, restated at s 776(5), (6) CA 2006 as of 6 April 2008).

SECTION 2
Mortgage of shares

1915 A mortgage is a transfer of property from one person to another as **security** for the performance of an obligation on the condition that, if the obligation is performed, the property is transferred back to the first person. If the obligation is not performed (known as "default"), the second person can enforce his security as compensation. Usually, this means that he can sell the property and/or become the absolute legal holder of it. Since shares are the personal property of shareholders, subject to the articles, each shareholder can mortgage his shares to secure a personal obligation owed by him. The most common secured obligation is repayment of a loan.

Mortgages and other types of security for lending are dealt with in **more detail** at ¶4562+. The specific issues relating to mortgages over shares only are dealt with below.

1916 A mortgage over shares commonly occurs in **financed company acquisitions**. For example, if Mr A took out a loan from a bank to buy some shares, he may have to mortgage those shares to the bank as security for the loan.

It is also possible for a person to give a mortgage as security for the repayments of a third party. For example, a holding company could give a mortgage over its shares in its subsidiary to a bank in return for a loan by the bank to the subsidiary. This commonly occurs in **property financing** where the subsidiary is a special purpose vehicle set up to acquire and develop a particular property. The bank can then chose to enforce its security over the shares of the subsidiary rather than the property it owns, which could have tax benefits (the tax on disposals of shares is normally lower than the tax on disposals of property).

> MEMO POINTS 1. Another type of security over shares is known as a **lien**. Most companies have a lien over their unpaid shares (see ¶1227).
> 2. Generally speaking, a charge by a **public company** over its own fully paid shares is void (s 150 CA 1985; restated at s 670 CA 2006 by 1 October 2009). Therefore, a public company cannot lend money to a shareholder and secure its lending by a mortgage over its own fully paid shares.

TRANSFER AND TRANSMISSION OF SHARES 213

1917 There are two types of mortgage: a **legal mortgage** and an **equitable mortgage**. A legal mortgage (also known as an "transfer by way of security" or an "assignment by way of security") is a transfer of the legal title, whereas an equitable mortgage merely gives the lender a beneficial interest in the shares (see ¶1829+ for the difference between legal and equitable title). The distinction between an equitable mortgage and fixed charge is blurred in practice (see ¶4596+) and so references below to an equitable mortgage apply equally to a fixed charge over shares.

1. Pre-mortgage considerations

1920 When considering which type of mortgage is suitable and the implications of taking or granting a mortgage over shares, particular consideration will need to be given to **restrictions in the articles** (¶1922+) and the consequences of a **change in control** (¶1926+). A legal mortgage is better security for the lender but an equitable mortgage is more common as it avoids some of the implications referred to below and does not require the formality of registering the transfer of shares with the company.

> MEMO POINTS 1. In the case of either a legal or equitable mortgage, the company whose shares have been mortgaged will have to be given **notice of the mortgage** by the lender, if the shares are in a public company (see ¶2042+).
> 2. On creation of the mortgage, **stamp duty** is not payable on the value of the shares although a fixed duty will be payable (see ¶1877). Stamp duty at the usual rate will be payable on enforcement if the shares are sold.
> 3. In the rare case of a legal mortgage **over partly or nil paid shares**, the lender will be liable for calls (¶1205+) and as a contributory in the event of the company being wound up (¶7872+). The lender's only remedy against the borrower for repayment of these sums would be under any contractual agreement between them, and, of course, would depend upon the borrower's solvency.

Restrictions in articles

1922 The articles of the company whose shares are being mortgaged may contain restrictions on transfer such as the directors' **power to refuse registration** (see ¶1888+) or **pre-emption provisions** (see ¶1842+). These could be problematic for two reasons. Firstly, they could restrict the ability to create the mortgage, and secondly they could inhibit the lender from enforcing the mortgage.

Since a **legal mortgage** requires registration of the mortgage holder's title to the shares, a legal mortgage holder runs the risk of the directors refusing registration of the transfer. In practice therefore, a legal mortgage holder will want to be certain that the transfer to it and any subsequent transfer by it is going to be registered. A legal mortgage, and any subsequent sale by the lender if it enforces the mortgage, will also breach any pre-emption provisions unless the provisions state that they do not apply to mortgages and sales by mortgage holders.

The directors' power to refuse registration is irrelevant when an **equitable mortgage** is being created, since registration of the transfer is not required. Whether creation of an equitable mortgage is a breach of any pre-emption provisions will depend upon the wording of the trigger events. However, both restrictions could prevent the lender from selling the shares upon enforcement of the security.

1923 In order to circumvent these problems, the lender will usually require:
a. an **undertaking from the directors** that they will not refuse to register a transfer to the lender, its nominees or any person to whom the lender sells the shares; and
b. if the mortgage and a sale by the lender would breach pre-emption provisions, an **amendment to the articles** so that the provisions do not apply to the mortgage. Further, in order to ensure that the articles are not changed back once the mortgage is in effect, such a change will usually be included as an event of default and the shareholders will be required to agree not to exercise their voting rights in favour of such an amendment.

> MEMO POINTS The lender may not accept a mere **waiver of the pre-emption provisions** as this will not assist it if it wishes to enforce its security and the shareholders have changed.

Change of control

1926 One of the lender's primary concerns will be to **preserve the value of its security**. This means that the lender will want to ensure that the value of the mortgaged shares is maintained so that it at least covers the amount of the secured loan. The value of the shares will depend upon the value of the company. The lender will therefore need to exercise control over the company. It can do this by:
- exercising the share rights of the mortgaged shares; and/or
- controlling the business of the company whose shares have been mortgaged.

> MEMO POINTS Consideration should be given to whether the mortgage triggers any **change of control provisions in the contracts** of the company whose shares have been mortgaged.

Exercise of share rights

1927 In the case of a **legal mortgage**, since the lender is the registered holder of the shares, he is free to exercise the share rights without restriction in the absence of any agreement to the contrary between the lender and borrower. In the case of an **equitable mortgage**, the share rights will continue to be exercisable by the borrower. However, since equitable title to the shares has passed to the lender, in the absence of any agreement to the contrary, the borrower must exercise its share rights on behalf of the lender. In practice in both cases, the lender will only be interested in exercising share rights in so far as they protect its security and this is usually specified in the mortgage deed.

1928 As far as **voting** rights are concerned, in the case of a legal mortgage, the mortgage deed will usually require the lender to exercise its voting rights in accordance with the borrower's instructions, except in relation to particular matters which could affect the lender's security. If the lender breaches this requirement, the borrower will be entitled to a mandatory injunction compelling the lender to vote as the borrower directs at future shareholder meetings (*Puddephatt v Leith* [1916] 1 Ch 200). In the case of an equitable mortgage, the borrower will usually be permitted to exercise the voting rights as he thinks fit, except in relation to particular matters which could affect the lender's security.

> MEMO POINTS There can be adverse **implications if the lender has voting control**. In particular:
> **a.** the company could become the lender's subsidiary (see ¶204) or a "quasi-subsidiary" for accounting purposes (FRS 5(7));
> **b.** the lender may be an associated or connected company for the purposes of insolvency legislation (see ¶7808+); and
> **c.** the lender may have control over the company for taxation purposes.

1929 As far as **dividends** are concerned, in the case of a legal mortgage, the borrower and lender can contractually agree for dividends to be passed on to the borrower and, if the articles permit, the lender can send the company a dividend mandate in favour of the borrower. In the case of an equitable mortgage, the mortgage deed can contractually provide for the borrower to retain any dividends paid to it.

Control over company's business

1930 The exercise of share rights alone may, however, be of minimal use. This is because most **decisions** that impact upon the value of the company are made by its directors, not its shareholders.

If the company is driven into insolvency, as a shareholder, the **lender** will **rank** behind all creditors of the company. In order to protect itself, the lender may therefore want the loan or mortgage documents to contain provisions that give the lender some control over the business of the company whose shares are the subject of the mortgage, for example, to prevent the company from giving guarantees, disposing of its assets or materially altering the nature of its business. Whether or not the lender is able to obtain this sort of **contractual commitment** from the company will depend upon the company being connected in some way to the proposed loan, for example, where the company is the subsidiary of the borrower.

2. Legal mortgage

1934

In order to implement a legal mortgage over shares, the borrower and lender have to comply with the usual **transfer formalities** (which comprise completion of a stock transfer form and registration of the transfer with the company). The lender is entered in the register of shareholders and is entitled to a share certificate in the usual way. A legal mortgage only becomes effective when legal title to the shares is transferred to the lender. Underlying this transfer is a separate agreement known as a "**mortgage deed**" which sets out the terms of the mortgage.

3. Equitable mortgage

1938

An equitable mortgage over shares is **implemented by** a deposit of share certificates with the lender (a written agreement is only required when the mortgagor is securing the borrowings of a third party). In practice, however, the lender will always require the borrower to execute a **memorandum of deposit**. The mortgage is created by this document rather than by the deposit of the share certificates (*Re White Rose Cottage* [1965] 1 All ER 11).

> MEMO POINTS If the memorandum of deposit is expressed to confer on the lender an **immediate equitable interest** in the shares and the shares have been adequately identified, the deposit of share certificates is not necessary for the mortgage to be effective. The lender will usually still require the share certificates to be deposited to preserve its priority over third parties.

1939

Sometimes, the borrower is also required to execute a **blank transfer instrument** (normally, a stock transfer form) which the lender can complete upon enforcement. This has the advantage of putting the lender in a better position to take priority (see ¶1943+). However, it can have disadvantages. From the lender's point of view, the transfer instrument will only relate to the shares mortgaged initially and not to any subsequent shares that come within the mortgage (for example, following a bonus issue). From the borrower's point of view, more shares than are necessary to repay the loan may be transferred and, instead of retaining the balance of his shareholding, the borrower will only be entitled to the balance of the proceeds of sale. Further, delivery of an executed transfer document may be sufficient to trigger pre-emption provisions (see ¶1845+).

4. Priority between lenders

1943

The issue of priority is dealt with at ¶4672+. However, there is something more to be said when dealing with priorities of mortgages over shares because of the uncertainty as to when a share has been transferred (see ¶1829+).

> MEMO POINTS **Priority of lien**: a company's lien over its unpaid shares generally takes priority over an equitable interest but probably not over a legal interest. This is because in registering the interest, the company either waives its lien or precludes itself from relying on it. Further, a company's lien will probably not take priority where it has notice of the third party interest before it advances money to a shareholder that is the subject of the lien (*Bradford Banking Co Ltd v Briggs Son & Co Ltd* (1886) 12 App Cas 29).

Transfer of shares is registered

1945

The main difference between a legal and equitable mortgage over shares is when the transfer of the shares under the mortgage is registered. Under a **legal mortgage**, the transfer is registered at the time the mortgage is created. Under an **equitable mortgage**, the transfer is only registered at the time of enforcement.

1946

Generally speaking, the **lender who registers its transfer first** takes priority, provided it did not have notice of any prior equitable interest at the time of the mortgage. However, a problem could arise when more than one lender has taken an equitable mortgage over the shares, the borrower falls into difficulties and each lender attempts to perfect its security (by registering a transfer to itself). In this case, the **first lender to perfect its security** will take priority over any earlier equitable interest of which it did not have notice when the mortgage was created. The first lender will even take priority if it had notice of the earlier equitable interest at the time it registered the transfer, provided that before it had notice it was able to obtain registration without recourse to the legal owner (because the borrower had deposited his share certificates and executed transfer documents). An equitable mortgage holder who is notified of a prior equitable interest before it is in a position to obtain registration is not able to take priority (*Macmillan Inc v Bishopsgate Investment Trust plc (No 3)* [1995] 3 All ER 747).

EXAMPLE

Lender	1 Jan	2 Jan	3 Jan	4 Jan	5 Jan	Result
A Ltd	Mortgage	-	-	-	-	B takes priority
B Ltd	-	Mortgage	Delivery of stock transfer form and share certificates	Notice of A Ltd's mortgage	Registration of transfer	

Lender	1 Jan	2 Jan	3 Jan	4 Jan	5 Jan	Result
A Ltd	Mortgage	-	-	-	-	A takes priority
B Ltd	-	Mortgage	Notice of A Ltd's mortgage	Delivery of stock transfer form and share certificates	Registration of transfer	

Transfer of shares not registered

1947 If more than one lender has taken an equitable mortgage over shares but no transfer of the legal title is registered, generally speaking, the **first equitable mortgage takes priority**.

> MEMO POINTS Rarely, the first equitable mortgage holder's **interest** may be **postponed** to a subsequent equitable interest where (*Macmillan Inc v Bishopsgate Investment Trust plc (No 3)* [1995] 3 All ER 747):
> **a.** the first equitable mortgage holder's actions prevent him from relying on his apparent priority, for example, if he has permitted a subsequent lender to take possession of the share certificates; or
> **b.** a subsequent lender is in a position to obtain registration without recourse to the legal owner (because the borrower has deposited his share certificates and executed transfer documents) and the company cannot prevent the registration (which is unlikely), provided that the subsequent lender was put in this position before he had notice of the prior lender's equitable interest.

5. Effect of mortgage on company

1950 A company is generally not required to take account of any interest apart from that of the registered holder. It may not even be aware that the mortgage has been created. There are two ways in which a company could be required to take notice of an equitable interest: a stop notice or a charging order.

Stop notice

1951 It is possible for equitable holders to protect their position by serving a "stop notice" on the company (r 73.16-73.22 CPR). A "stop notice" is a special type of **notice to the company** of a person's beneficial interest over particular shares. If a company receives a stop notice it must record it against the relevant shares of its registered shareholder. If, after receipt of a stop notice, the company receives a request to register a transfer of those shares or take another step in breach of the stop notice (such as pay dividends to another person), it must give written notice of that fact to the person on whose behalf the stop notice was served. That person has 14 days from the date of the notice to obtain an injunction to prevent the act. If he does not do so within that period, the company must deal with the request as usual.

In order to **obtain a stop notice**, the person with the beneficial interest must file a draft stop notice supported by an affidavit at the High Court. The court will then serve a copy of the notice and affidavit on the company. A central list of stop notices applicable to public companies is kept by the court.

The **use of stop notices** is rare in practice as the costs of obtaining an injunction are high. If this sort of protection is required, a legal mortgage will usually be taken. However, if a legal mortgage is not available or suitable for some reason, a stop notice is the only way to ensure that the company has regard to a beneficial interest.

Charging order

Charging orders are considered at ¶4740. If a company receives notice of an interim charging order over its shares, it is prohibited from permitting any transfer of those shares and from paying any dividend, interest or redemption payment on them (r 73.6 CPR 1998). If the charging order becomes final, the court will usually order that a stop notice be issued with respect to the shares (see ¶1951 above) (r 73.8 CPR 1998).

1952

SECTION 3

Transmission

Transmission is the term used to describe an automatic change in share ownership by operation of the law. It occurs in three **situations**:
- death (¶1964+);
- bankruptcy (¶1976+); and
- mental incapacity (¶1980).

These all apply only to shareholders who are individuals as opposed to other types of legal person (such as corporate shareholders).

These events may also **trigger pre-emption** provisions in the company's articles (see ¶1842+).

1962

---

1. Death

Shares are personal property, so when a shareholder dies (assuming that the shares are not jointly held) they form part of his estate. Title to the shares, as with his other assets, therefore automatically passes to his **personal representatives** (who have authority to administer his estate). The personal representatives are usually entitled to exercise all **rights over the shares**, except for the right to attend or vote at any shareholder meeting. They can only exercise these rights if the shares are registered in their name (reg 31 TA 1985).

Usually, the articles state that upon providing whatever evidence the directors properly require, the personal representatives can **elect** to have the shares registered in their name or they can elect to have the shares transferred to a person nominated by them (for example, the beneficiaries of the will) (reg 30 TA 1985).

1964

> MEMO POINTS 1. If the shares are **jointly owned**, they pass to the surviving joint holder(s) instead of passing to the deceased shareholder's personal representatives.
> 2. Under **Table A 1948**, the directors have the right to compel the personal representatives to make an election and, if they do not do so within 90 days, the directors can withhold payment of dividends until an election has been made (reg 32 TA 1948).
> 3. The new **draft model articles** will restate the provisions of Table A relating to the transmission of shares (private companies limited by shares: arts 27-29; public companies: arts 64-67). The **new Companies Act** will provide the secretary of state with the power to set out further rules relating

to transmission in regulations (s 785(5) CA 2006, due to come fully into force on 6 April 2008). At the time of writing, draft regulations have not yet been published.

Evidence of authority

1966 In order to register the shares in their own name or to transfer them to a third party, the personal representatives must provide the company with evidence of their authority. The articles normally state that the evidence to be provided is whatever the directors properly require (reg 30 TA 1985). As a matter of good practice, the company should insist on **legal proof** that the personal representatives are authorised to deal with the deceased's estate. If such proof is produced, the company must accept this as sufficient evidence despite what the articles require (s 187 CA 1985; restated at s 774 CA 2006 as of 6 April 2008).

> MEMO POINTS   This provision will be restated in the draft **new model articles** at art 27 for private companies limited by shares and art 65 for public companies.

1967 The legal document which proves that a personal representative has authority to deal with an estate is called a "**grant of representation**". There are three types of grant of representation, any of which will be sufficient (the original usually needs to be produced to the company):
– grant of probate: where the shareholder has left a will and has named "executors" to deal with his estate on his death;
– letters of administration (together with the will): where there is a will but no executors have been named or the named executors are unwilling to apply for the grant of representation; and
– letters of administration: where there is no will.

> MEMO POINTS   A grant of representation is a relatively costly and involved affair and it may not be worthwhile obtaining one for a small estate. If the personal representatives **do not obtain a grant of representation** then the company can still register the shares in their name or to a person nominated by them but, in order to protect the company, it should insist on:
> – a certified copy of the death certificate;
> – a letter from Revenue and Customs confirming that no inheritance tax is payable in respect of the estate;
> – the share certificate;
> – a statutory declaration as to the identity and entitlement of the personal representatives; and
> – an indemnity from the personal representatives to the company in respect of any liability which the company may incur by allowing the personal representatives to deal with the shares without a formal grant of administration.

Notice of election

1969 If the personal representatives **elect to register themselves**, they must give the company notice. A letter of request accompanied by the share certificate will be sufficient. It does not matter that the company has not been presented with a proper transfer instrument (s 183(2) CA 1985; restated at s 770(2) CA 2006 as of 6 April 2008).

If the company receives notice of an election, a director or the company secretary should:
– satisfy himself that the evidence produced is genuine;
– check that the identity of the deceased shareholder corresponds to the entry in the register of shareholders;
– update the register of shareholders to show that the shareholder has died and that the personal representatives are now the registered holders;
– endorse the share certificate with the date of death, date of registration and the name and address of the personal representatives; and
– return the original grant of administration and endorsed share certificate to the personal representatives.

1970 If the personal representatives **elect to have the shares transferred** to a third party, they must execute a transfer instrument (such as a stock transfer form) in favour of that person (reg 30 TA 1985). The transferee and company must deal with registration of the transfer as usual. Again, a director or the company secretary will have to satisfy himself that the evidence produced is genuine and that the identity of the deceased shareholder corresponds to the entry in the register of shareholders.

MEMO POINTS   This provision will be restated in the draft **new model articles** as far as certificated shares are concerned (private companies limited by shares: art 28; public companies: art 66). In the case of uncertificated shares in public companies, the personal representative must:
– ensure that all of the appropriate instructions are given to effect the transfer; or
– ensure that the uncertificated share is changed into certificated form and then execute a transfer instrument for it.

Consequences of election

The articles usually state that any election by the personal representative is to be treated as a share transfer (reg 30 TA 1985). This means that any **pre-emption provisions** in the articles and/or the **directors' right to refuse registration** would apply. Note that the provisions are not triggered until the personal representatives make an election.

1972

If the articles do not state that an election by the personal representatives to register themselves is to be treated as a share transfer, they will be able to hold the shares as bare trustees or nominees of the beneficiaries without triggering any pre-emption provisions (*Safeguard Industrial Investments Ltd v National Westminster Bank Ltd* [1982] 1 All ER 449).

MEMO POINTS   The draft **new model articles** will include an equivalent provision (private companies limited by shares: art 28(3); public companies: art 66(4)).

2. Bankruptcy

Upon the bankruptcy of an individual shareholder, the court will make an order to appoint a trustee in bankruptcy to administer the bankrupt's estate. The **position of a trustee in bankruptcy** is the same as that of personal representatives on the death of a shareholder as far as transmission of the bankrupt's shares is concerned (see ¶1964+). The directors should usually insist on seeing the original (or an office copy) of the court order appointing the trustee as evidence of his authority.

1976

If the company receives a **request to register** the trustee in bankruptcy as holder of the shares, a director or the company secretary should:
– satisfy himself that the court order is genuine;
– check that the identity of the bankrupt corresponds to the entry in the register of shareholders;
– update the register of shareholders to show that the shareholder has been declared bankrupt and that the trustee is now the registered holder;
– endorse the share certificate with the date of the bankruptcy order, date of registration and the name and address of the trustee; and
– return the original court order and endorsed share certificate to the trustee in bankruptcy.

1977

3. Mental incapacity

Where a person becomes mentally incapacitated, the court can appoint a **deputy** to make decisions about his welfare, property and affairs (s 16 Mental Capacity Act 2005). If the terms of the court order give the deputy authority to deal with the person's investments, he will register his appointment with the company by lodging an office copy of the court order at the company's registered office. The deputy then becomes entitled to deal with the shares in the manner set out in the order, but beneficial ownership of the shares remains with the original shareholder.

1980

MEMO POINTS   This part of the Mental Capacity Act 2005 came into force on 1 October 2007. Under the previous legislation (the Mental Health Act 1983), deputies were called "**receivers**" and could be appointed to exercise the same powers on behalf of a mentally incapacitated person. Any receivers appointed under the old legislation will be treated as deputies, with the same functions as they had before (Sch 5 Mental Capacity Act 2005).

CHAPTER 7
Shareholders

OUTLINE ¶¶

A	General concepts	2010	B	Rights and remedies	2067
1	What is a shareholder?	2010	1	Standard rights and remedies	2074
2	Who can be a shareholder?	2020	2	Sources and status	2079
	a Individuals	2020		Memorandum and articles	2082
	b Companies	2026		Shareholders' agreements	2086
	c People holding shares on behalf of others	2032	C	Remedies of last resort	2100
	d Joint holders	2048	1	Unfair prejudice	2105
3	How to become a shareholder	2053	2	Wind up the company	2133

2000

Shareholders are vital to a company's existence as both a source of capital and a decision making body. Their role typically varies between companies, with only their basic **rights and powers** being enshrined in statute, which allows companies to tailor any additional rights to suit their circumstances. For example, in a **large company** with many shareholders, their rights will focus on making the most of their investments (such as class rights, entitlements to dividends, etc), whereas in a **small company** operating as a quasi-partnership, the shareholders usually want to have more extensive involvement in management.

The rights set out in the legislation give the shareholders some basic **protection**, for example enabling them to object to significant activities of the company or alterations to its memorandum. Statute also offers additional protection to shareholders who have been taken advantage of by other shareholders and the board.

> MEMO POINTS 1. The wider term "**member**" is often used interchangeably with shareholder; a shareholder is a member of a company limited by shares. Companies not limited by shares only have members. Note that "member" is used by statute to encompass all types of company. However, since this work focuses on companies limited by shares, the term "shareholders" is preferred here.
> For those interested in **companies not limited by shares**, the term "shareholder" should be read as if it was "member"; any differences in the treatment of shareholders and members are highlighted where relevant.
> 2. Shareholders' **management role** is discussed and contrasted with that of the board at ¶3118+.

2001

The **new Companies Act** will impact on the shareholders' role in the company, as well as their rights and remedies. The biggest change shareholders will notice will be in the way in which decisions are made, discussed at ¶3110+. One of the aims of the new Act is to make directors more accountable, and in support of this it sets out a new statutory derivative action that shareholders can take against directors who are in breach of their duties (see ¶7127+). Conversely, they will find that the board does not need their consent for or approval of as many managerial decisions.

Draft **new model articles** under the new Act have been published for private companies limited by shares and public companies. These will apply to companies incorporated once the company formation provisions of the new Act are in force (expected to be by 1 October 2009). At the time of writing, the draft new model articles for private companies limited by shares contain fewer provisions concerning shareholders than are in Table A. This will suit shareholders who do not often need to be involved in decision making, but those who do will need to review the new model articles very carefully and change them as necessary, if they are adopted by their company. The draft new model articles for public companies have more in common with Table A, but should still be reviewed by the shareholders if their company adopts them because they may not reflect the company's intentions.

A. General concepts

1. What is a shareholder?

2010 A shareholder is a member of a company limited by shares (public or private), literally one who holds shares. Statute **defines** a company's members as (s 22 CA 1985; restated at s 112 CA 2006 by 1 October 2009):
– the subscribers to its memorandum; and
– any other person who agrees to be a member and whose name is entered on the register.

A shareholder's **liability** to contribute to the company's assets if it is wound up is limited to any amount remaining unpaid on the shares he holds (s 1(2)(a) CA 1985; restated at s 3(2) CA 2006 by 1 October 2009). When a company is wound up, the shareholders liable to contribute are called "contributories" (¶7863+).

MEMO POINTS If the company is **limited by guarantee**, a member's liability is confined to the amount stated in the memorandum; the members of **unlimited companies** have unlimited liability (s 1(2)(b), (c) CA 1985; restated at s 3(3), (4) CA 2006 by 1 October 2009).

Number of shareholders

2012 A **new company** must have a certain number of subscribers, or initial shareholders:

Type of company	Number of subscribers	Reference (CA 1985)
Private company limited by shares/guarantee	1	s 1(3A)
Public company	2	s 1(1)
Private unlimited company	2	s 1(1)

MEMO POINTS Under the **new Companies Act**, all companies will be able to be formed with only one shareholder (s 7 CA 2006, expected to come into force by 1 October 2009).

2013 Once a company is **incorporated**, there is no requirement for it to maintain a particular number of shareholders. A company has its own legal identity and can therefore exist without shareholders, although it would not be able to make any decisions which require approval at a general meeting, and it would be at risk of being wound up by the court (¶7602+).

MEMO POINTS There would be further problems if, for example, a **sole director/shareholder dies** and his personal representative is not entered in the register of shareholders. In such circumstances, the relevant decisions at board and general meeting levels could not be made to transfer shares, appoint a new director etc, and the company secretary would have to apply to the secretary of state or the court for assistance in calling a general meeting (general meeting: ¶3635+), or rely on the subsequent ratification of unauthorised decisions (¶2497+).

Single shareholder companies

2014 **Private companies** can have a sole shareholder. This is common in small family-run companies and sole traders who incorporate. To facilitate this there are **special rules** which:
– allow the company to make the same decisions as a company with two or more shareholders;

– ensure that records are kept properly; and
– make sure that the company is not taken advantage of by a sole shareholder who is also a director.

These rules **apply** regardless of any provisions to the contrary in the company's articles.

Rule	¶¶
One shareholder who is present in person or by proxy comprises quorum	¶3747
Certain entries must be made in register of shareholders when company: – becomes a single shareholder company; and – ceases to be a single shareholder company	¶3943
A single shareholder must keep written record of all decisions taken at a general meeting	¶3868
If company enters into a contract with a director who is also a sole shareholder, a written memorandum of the contract must be provided, or its terms recorded in board minutes	¶3473

Public companies are required to have at least two shareholders. However, they may also reduce their number of shareholders to one, but this should be avoided because:
a. the provisions listed in the table above only apply to private companies. Therefore, decisions cannot be made at a general meeting of a public company, unless the articles stipulate that the quorum is one;
b. if a public company has one shareholder for more than 6 months, that shareholder (or shareholders, if the shares have changed hands during that time) is liable for the company's debts arising during that period (s 24 CA 1985). This liability is joint and several with the company, and serves to protect third parties dealing with such a public company; and
c. the company can be wound up by the court if its membership falls below two (s 122(1)(e) IA 1986).

2015

> MEMO POINTS 1. The liability at point b. is not attached to **directors**, who can still run the company with fewer than two shareholders. Clearly, this provision will not apply where there are **no shareholders**, as there will be nobody to share liability with the company.
> 2. These consequences also apply to **unlimited private companies**.
> 3. Since the **new Companies Act** will allow any company to have one shareholder, s 24 CA 1985 is expected to be repealed by 1 October 2009 (Sch 16 CA 2006).

2. Who can be a shareholder?

a. Individuals

Any individual can be a shareholder regardless of age, nationality, financial standing or mental capacity (ss 1, 22 CA 1985).

2020

Table A gives the directors a limited discretion to refuse to register transfers of shares to people of whom they disapprove without giving reasons, so they can effectively **restrict membership** to particular types of shareholders (reg 24 TA 1985). However, they can only do so in specified circumstances, such as where the shares are not fully paid up (see ¶1891).

In practice, many companies replace this with an even more limited discretion to refuse to register transfers on certain grounds, or exclude it altogether. Alternatively, the articles may state that certain categories of people cannot be shareholders, for example, minors or those outside the family business, or that shareholders must possess certain qualifications, for example, in the case of a professional body in the form of a company. A shareholders' agreement can also be used to set out who can be a shareholder, in which case the directors should exercise any discretion to refuse to register shares to reflect the agreement. For a more detailed discussion about directors' ability to refuse to register share transfers, see ¶1888+.

MEMO POINTS 1. The **new Companies Act** will not impose any restriction on who can be a shareholder either, although directors will have to give reasons for refusing the register a transfer of shares regardless of what its articles may allow (s 771 CA 2006, due to come into force on 6 April 2008).
2. The draft **new model articles** will contain equivalent provisions giving directors a limited discretion to refuse to register a transfer of shares (private companies limited by shares: art 26(5); public companies: art 62(5)). The public company provision is subject to conditions, for example the directors can only refuse to register a transfer if the share is not fully paid or the transfer is to more than four transferees.

Minors

2022 Although a person under the age of eighteen can hold shares in a company (unless its articles state otherwise), his contract of membership is voidable and **can be repudiated** before or within a reasonable time of his 18th birthday (s 3 Minors' Contracts Act 1987). Repudiation of the contract will only affect the company's and the minor's future rights and liabilities, so the purchase price will not be repaid, but he will be able to avoid future liability for any calls. The company has the power to refuse to accept minors as shareholders, and should do so if liability (for example, payment of calls) is attached to them.

MEMO POINTS 1. Minors can also be **subscribers** to a company's memorandum (*Re Nassau Phosphate Co* (1876) 2 Ch D 610).
2. If a **minor repudiates** his membership, the name of the person who transferred the shares to him should be entered in the register again (*Re Asiatic Banking Corpn, Symons' Case* (1870) 5 Ch App 298). It is this transferor who will be liable for any future calls on the shares, even if he did not know that the transferee was a minor.

Bankrupts

2024 A bankrupt's name can remain on the **register** of shareholders, although the beneficial ownership of his shares has passed to his estate in the hands of his trustee in bankruptcy. If his name remains on the register, he will still be entitled to attend and vote at meetings, but he must **vote** according to his trustee in bankruptcy's instructions (*Morgan v Gray* [1953] 1 All ER 213). Alternatively, his trustee in bankruptcy may elect to have the shares registered in his name or have them transferred to someone else, see ¶2038+.

b. Companies

2026 A company can be a shareholder **in another company**, provided this is authorised by the objects clause in its memorandum (*Re Barned's Banking Co Ltd, ex parte Contract Corporation* [1861-73] All ER Rep Ext 2068). It will appoint a corporate representative to attend meetings, vote and exercise other rights attached to the shares on its behalf (¶3743+).

MEMO POINTS 1. "**Company**" includes foreign companies, but not corporations sole or Scottish firms.
2. Under the **new Companies Act**, companies will have unlimited objects unless they are specifically restricted by their articles (see ¶419/mp).

Shares in its holding company

2028 A company cannot hold shares in its holding company, unless it falls within one of the following exceptions.

Exception	Status of shares	Reference (CA 1985)[1]
The subsidiary holds shares as a personal representative/trustee, provided its holding company/another subsidiary of the same holding company is not a beneficiary[2]	Normal	s 23(2)
The subsidiary acts as professional intermediary ("market maker") and holds shares in that capacity[3]		s 23(3)

Exception	Status of shares	Reference (CA 1985)[1]
The shares were acquired before 20 October 1997	Non-voting if would have been prohibited if it was not for the date on which they were acquired. Other benefits (dividends, etc) remain intact	s 23(4)
Shares (acquired on/after 20 October 1997) were permitted when acquired but subsequently become prohibited		s 23(5)

Note:
1. These provisions (s 23, Sch 2 CA 1985) will be restated in the **new Companies Act** at ss 136-144 CA 2006, expected to come into force by 1 October 2009.
2. Where a **subsidiary is personal representative/trustee**, its holding company or another subsidiary of the same holding company can have a beneficial interest in the shares in limited circumstances: usually, where the company has a residual interest in shares held in a pension/employees' share scheme, or where the holding company has taken security over the shares in the normal course of its business (for example, money-lending company) (s 23(2)(a), paras 1, 3, Sch 2 CA 1985).
3. To **qualify as an intermediary**, a subsidiary must deal in securities as its business, be a member of a recognised exchange and not undertake certain types of business (ss 23(3), (3A), para 4, Sch 2 CA 1985).

Any **allotment or transfer** of shares by a holding company to its subsidiary other than in these exempt circumstances is void.

<u>MEMO POINTS</u> A subsidiary cannot evade this prohibition by holding shares in its holding company through a **nominee**.

Own shares

The doctrine of capital maintenance (see ¶703) **prevents** a company holding its own shares in principle. However, there are some **limited circumstances** in which a company can acquire its own shares, provided it follows the correct procedural safeguards.

2030

Situation	¶¶
Shares fully paid up and acquired for no consideration, e.g. a gift or bequest	¶1338/mp
Shares redeemed or purchased in accordance with legislation	¶1337+
Shares acquired as a result of a lawful reduction of capital	¶1435+
Shares acquired as result of a court order: – to alter objects clause in memorandum – following objection to company becoming private – relating to unfair prejudice application	¶417+ ¶678 ¶2122+
Shares forfeited or surrendered in lieu of forfeiture under the company's articles (provided that the company did not give any consideration for the surrender)	¶1219+

<u>MEMO POINTS</u> 1. See ¶2034+ for the position of a **company's nominee**.
2. In addition, there is a general prohibition on a company providing financial **assistance to another party acquiring its shares**, although there is a process by which private companies can give such financial assistance (¶5557+). The **new Companies Act** will remove the prohibition on private companies providing financial assistance for the acquisition of their own shares. However, the implementation date for this change is yet to be announced at the time of writing.

c. People holding shares on behalf of others

2032 It is relatively common for the person whose name is entered on the register as the shareholder to hold those shares on behalf of another person. This may happen, for example:
a. where investors hold shares through a professional **nominee** for ease of administration, so the nominee deals with any paperwork, attends meetings etc, but the investor receives the benefits of dividends and any increase in value;
b. where the shares form part of a **trust**, which the trustee administers for the benefit of beneficiaries; or
c. where a shareholder **dies** or becomes **bankrupt**, his shares pass to his personal representative or trustee in bankruptcy who will deal with them on behalf of the estate (this process is called "transmission" and is dealt with at ¶1962+).

In addition, a shareholder can now nominate another person to enjoy or exercise any or all of his rights as a shareholder, if the company's articles allow. This is a **new power** introduced by the new Companies Act (s 145 CA 2006). Therefore, a shareholder could nominate someone to attend and vote at meetings in his place, or he could nominate a relative to receive his dividends if he wishes. This could be useful in different situations, for example where a shareholder wants to use a nominee to undertake the administrative side of being a shareholder while still receiving the income from the shares, or as an alternative to granting a power of attorney where he cannot be involved in the company due to absence or illness.

> **MEMO POINTS** 1. If **shares** are **transferred** but the transferee's name is **not recorded** in the register until a later date, the transferor remains registered as the shareholder. He holds them for the benefit of the transferee and must deal with them according to the transferee's instructions (for example, on voting, dealing with dividends, selling the shares and other matters).
> 2. Shares can also be held in the form of **share warrants** (¶1902/mp), where the warrant-holder is not named on the register of shareholders.
> 3. The shares of a **mentally incapacitated person** can be transmitted to the deputy of his estate (¶1980).
> 4. Where a shareholder holds shares on behalf of more than one person, he can **exercise** the **share rights** in different ways to reflect the different interests of the beneficial owners (s 152 CA 2006). For example, on a poll vote, he could cast some votes in one way and some in another. However, the shareholder must inform the company of the extent to which he is exercising the rights and the different ways in which he is doing so, otherwise the company will be entitled to assume that he is exercising all of them in the same way. Special rules apply where a person holding shares on behalf of others joins in a **shareholder requisition** (for example, for a general meeting to be held) so that the company can be sure that the correct number of requests have been made (s 153 CA 2006).
> 5. The Institute of Chartered Secretaries and Administrators (ICSA) has published new **guidance** on shareholder voting, including shareholders' new nomination rights (ICSA guidance note 071017). It is available on ICSA's website.

2033 In these situations, the share's **legal interest** is held by the nominee, trustee, personal representative or trustee in bankruptcy, while its **beneficial interest** is held by the investor, beneficiary of the trust or estate of the shareholder. Such shares are described as being held "on trust".

> **MEMO POINTS** The **"legal" owner** is the person who, to the world at large, owns the shares: his name appears on the register, the company sends notices and correspondence to him, he attends meetings, votes and receives any payments due on the shares. The **"beneficial" owner** is the hidden owner of the shares: he can instruct the legal owner how to deal with them and is entitled to receive payments and any appreciation in value.

The position can be different for a **personal representative** or **trustee in bankruptcy** (¶2038+).

Nominees

2034 Nominees are often **used by** investors because it removes the administrative burden of dealing with shares (which may be held in a variety of companies or by a group of investors) from the individuals.

> **MEMO POINTS** Historically, private companies as well as public companies had to have two subscribers. It was common in **small owner-managed companies** for the director to hold all of

the shares bar one, which was allotted to a nominee to hold on the director's behalf. There are still private companies structured in this way to comply with the old law, and it is a way in which **small public companies** can comply with their minimum subscribers requirement. However, by 1 October 2009, this will not be necessary since the **new Companies Act** will allow all companies to be formed with just one shareholder (s 7 CA 2006).

Where a nominee acts for a company by **holding the company's own shares**, certain rules apply (see ¶2030 for the limited circumstances in which a company can hold its own shares). If shares are issued to him (or he acquires them from a third party) partly paid, they are treated as belonging to the nominee beneficially, as if the company has no interest in them (s 144(1) CA 1985). If the nominee is called upon to **pay up** the **shares** and he fails to do so within 21 days, the directors are jointly and severally liable to meet the debt (s 144(2) CA 1985). A director may be relieved from liability if he can show that he acted honestly and reasonably and that he ought to be excused (s 144(3) CA 1985).

2035

> MEMO POINTS 1. If the shares were **issued** to him **under the memorandum**, the other subscribers will be jointly and severally liable to meet the debt (s 144(2) CA 1985).
> 2. This provision **does not apply** if the company has no beneficial interest in the shares issued or transferred to the nominee (s 145(2) CA 1985).
> 3. In the case of **public companies**, if the nominee acquires partly paid up shares (in which the company has a beneficial interest) with the company's **financial assistance**, he is not treated as the beneficial owner and the company's interest is not ignored (s 145(1) CA 1985). In practice, this situation will be rare because financial assistance by a public company is prohibited unless it falls within the statutory exceptions (¶5557+).
> 4. These rules also apply to **companies limited by guarantee**.
> 5. The **new Companies Act** will restate the restrictions on a company holding its own shares through a nominee (ss 658-699 CA 2006, expected to come into force by 1 October 2009).

Trustees

Trusts usually **arise where** shares are left to a beneficiary in a will, or where they are given or bequeathed to a minor to be held on trust until he reaches a certain age. The trustee is registered as the legal owner and must deal with the shares for the benefit of the trust. He usually has a wide discretion to make decisions relating to the shares, e.g. voting at meetings and transferring them.

2037

Personal representatives and trustees in bankruptcy

A personal representative will be appointed to manage a **deceased shareholder**'s estate, either according to the will or the rules of intestacy. Legal ownership of any shares transmits to the personal representative automatically on the shareholder's death, until he passes it on to the beneficiary of the will/intestacy.

2038

A trustee in bankruptcy will be appointed to manage a **bankrupt shareholder**'s estate. Legal ownership of any shares transmits to the trustee in bankruptcy (for the benefit of the bankrupt's estate) automatically when the bankruptcy order is made, until either:
– the shares are transferred and the proceeds used to pay off the bankrupt's creditors; or
– the bankruptcy is discharged and ownership reverts to the former bankrupt.

> MEMO POINTS 1. The **transmission process** is dealt with at ¶1962+.
> 2. In the case of an **insolvent corporate shareholder**, the insolvency practitioner dealing with the company usually has control of the company's assets, including any shares it holds, and can deal with them for the benefit of the company's creditors.

The position of personal representatives and trustees in bankruptcy is different to other types of legal owner in the way in which they are **registered**. Although legal ownership vests in them automatically, their names are only entered onto the register of shareholders if they elect (regs 29-31 TA 1985).

2039

The various situations and their consequences are explained in the table below. Personal representative is abbreviated to "PR" and trustee in bankruptcy to "TIB".

Situation	Who is registered as shareholder?	Consequences	Reference[1]
PR/TIB **not registered** as shareholder	Deceased/bankrupt	– Deceased's/bankrupt's name remains on register[2]	
		– PR/TIB cannot attend meetings or vote	reg 31 TA 1985
		– Bankrupt must vote and deal with shares in accordance with TIB's instructions	
		– PR/TIB can receive notice of meetings, provided he notifies company of address for service[3]	s 310 CA 2006; regs 38, 116 TA 1985[4]
		– PR/TIB can exercise all other rights attached to shares	reg 31 TA 1985
PR/TIB notifies company that he wants to be **registered**[5, 6]	PR/TIB	– PR/TIB has to produce evidence of entitlement to be registered	reg 30 TA 1985
		– PR/TIB can exercise all rights attached to shares, including attending meetings and voting	reg 31 TA 1985
		– PR/TIB is subject to all liabilities attached to shares, e.g. to pay calls, to contribute in winding up	reg 31 TA 1985
PR/TIB **not registered and transfers shares** according to will/intestacy or for the benefit of bankrupt's estate	Beneficiary or other transferee	– PR/TIB entitled to transfer shares without being registered	PR: s 183(3) CA 1985; TIB: s 83 IA 1986
		– Transfer in usual way	reg 30 TA 1985
PR/TIB **registered and transfers shares** according to will/intestacy or for the benefit of bankrupt's estate	Beneficiary or other transferee	– Transfer in usual way	reg 30 TA 1985

Note:
1. The **new Companies Act** will restate s 183(3) CA 1985 (s 770 CA 2006, expected to come into force by 1 October 2009). Draft **new model articles** under the new Companies Act have been published for private companies limited by shares and public companies. They will include similar transmission provisions (private companies limited by shares: art 27; public companies: arts 64, 65).
2. However, because the estate has automatically passed to PR/TIB, he is beneficial owner. The **estate** is **treated as a shareholder** by the company where distributions are made, for example, on bonus issues (*James v Buena Ventura Nitrate Grounds Syndicate Ltd* [1896] 1 Ch 456), but not for administrative matters such as counting the number of shareholders in the company (*Re Bowling & Welby's Contract* [1895] 1 Ch 663).
3. If PR/TIB does not notify the company of his **address for service**, the company can serve notice as if shareholder had not died/become bankrupt (para 17 Sch 5 CA 2006; reg 116 TA 1985).
4. For companies **incorporated on or after 1 October 2007** that adopt Table A, amendments have been made to certain provisions of Table A to correspond with the provisions of the new Companies Act which were in force by that date. reg 38 TA 1985 has been amended in different ways for private and for public companies. See ¶9915 for the details of these changes.
5. If the company's **articles are silent**, a PR can insist on his name being registered (*Scott v Frank F Scott (London) Ltd* [1940] 3 All ER 508). The articles may compel PR/TIB to elect within a certain period whether he wishes to be registered or is going to transfer the shares. **Table A 1948** contained such a provision (reg 32 TA 1948).
6. A transfer into the PR/TIB's name will have to follow any general **rules** in the company's articles on **transfers and transmissions** of shares, for example, the directors may be able to refuse to register the PR/TIB, or pre-emption rights may apply.

Position of the company

2041 The company in which the shares are held only has to **deal with** the person whose name is entered on the register of shareholders. That person will therefore receive notices, attend meetings, vote, receive dividends, sign share transfers, and be liable for calls and to contribute on winding up.

The company does not need to concern itself with whether or **how the shares are held** on trust. Trusts in shares cannot be noted on the register (s 360 CA 1985; reg 5 TA 1985). This is to prevent the company being held liable by the beneficiary if the shares are not dealt with properly by the trustee.

> MEMO POINTS   1. **Trustees** usually obtain an **indemnity** from beneficiaries in respect of any liabilities they incur as shareholders (*Hardoon v Belilios* [1901] AC 118, 127).
> 2. The **new Companies Act** will also state that trusts cannot be included on the register of shareholders (s 126 CA 2006, expected to come into force by 1 October 2009). The draft **new model articles** contain an equivalent of reg 5 TA 1985 (private company limited by shares: art 44; public companies: art 23).

Public companies

2042 Shareholders in public companies are no longer required to **disclose** their interests in shares to the company once their shareholding reaches a certain level. Instead, public companies can require their shareholders to provide details of their interests in shares and will have to keep a register of any information disclosed (the register is discussed at ¶3990+) (ss 791-807 CA 2006).

> MEMO POINTS   These provisions only **apply to** issued shares in a public company which carry the right to vote at general meetings on all resolutions (s 792 CA 2006). If voting rights have only been temporarily suspended, the provisions will still apply.

2043 A public company can require a **person** to disclose information about interests in its shares if it knows or has reasonable cause to believe that he either has an interest in its shares or has had such an interest within the last 3 years.

The company's **notice can require** the person to:
– confirm the fact that he has or has had an interest in its shares in the last 3 years;
– give details of his own past or present interest;
– give details of any other interest in those shares, if he shares his interest or has shared it at any time in the last 3 years; and
– identify the person to whom he transferred his interest, if he no longer holds it.

The details required to be given of interested persons include whether they were parties to any agreement or arrangement relating to the exercise of any rights conferred by holding the shares, or to certain share acquisition agreements (defined in s 824 CA 2006).

The notice can be **sent** in hard copy, electronic form or via a website, provided the correct consents have been obtained (ss 1143, 1144, Sch 5 CA 2006). The rules for a company communicating with its shareholders are discussed in the context of giving notice of shareholder meetings at ¶3695+.

The person to whom the notice is sent **must comply** within the reasonable period specified in the notice. If he **fails** to provide the information required, the company can apply to court for an order placing restrictions on the shares in question, preventing (subject to the court ordering otherwise, e.g. to protect the rights of a third party):
– their transfer;
– the voting rights attached to the shares from being exercised;
– any more shares being issued to the shareholder; and
– any payment being made in respect of the shares, except in a liquidation.

The person who failed to comply is also guilty of an offence, for which he can be imprisoned and/or fined. It is also an offence to make a false statement deliberately or recklessly in response to a request.

> MEMO POINTS   1. The secretary of state can **exempt** a person **from having to comply** with a notice (s 796 CA 2006). Such exemptions will, however, be rare.
> 2. The company or any aggrieved person can apply to court to have a **restrictions order relaxed** on the ground that it unfairly prejudices the rights of a third party in respect of the shares (s 799 CA 2006). The court can also order that the restrictions are **removed** altogether, if the relevant information about the shares has been disclosed or the shares are to be transferred and the court approves the transfer (s 800 CA 2006). The company can also apply for an order that shares subject to a restrictions order are **sold**, the proceeds of which will have to be paid into court for the benefit of the persons who are beneficially interested in the shares (ss 801, 802 CA 2006).

2044 The **shareholders** can also **require** the company to exercise its power to obtain disclosure of interests in its shares (s 803 CA 2006). The requisition must be made by shareholders who hold at least 10% of the paid-up share capital of the company with the right to vote at a general meeting. Any such request can be in hard copy or electronic form, and must be authenticated by every person putting his name to it. It must state:
- that the company is being requested to exercise its powers under s 793 CA 2006;
- the manner in which the company should exercise its powers; and
- the reasonable grounds for the request.

The rules for shareholders sending documents to the company are set out at ¶3628 in the context of shareholders requisitioning a general meeting.

On receipt of a valid request, the **company has to** (ss 804, 805 CA 2006):
- send a notice to the person(s) in question requiring them to disclose their interests in shares, as described above; and
- report to the shareholders within 15 days of the conclusion of the investigation, or every 3 months if the investigation is not concluded within 3 months. These reports must be available for inspection at the company's registered office or any other permitted place (to be set out in regulations by the secretary of state in due course). The company must inform the requisitioning shareholders that they are available for inspection within 3 days, and notify Companies House of their whereabouts (unless they have always been kept at the registered office). Each report must be kept for at least 6 years from when it was first made available.

If the company **fails** to comply in the following respects, any officer in default will be liable to a fine (¶9935):
- comply with the request;
- report on the outcome of the investigation at the appropriate times; or
- make the reports available for inspection.

If Companies House is not notified of the location of the reports as required, the company and every officer in default is liable to a fine (¶9935).

Any person can **inspect** the reports on investigations into interests in shares without charge (s 807 CA 2006). **Copies** must be provided within 10 days of a request. Companies can charge a fee of 10p per 500 words or part of 500 words copied, plus the reasonable costs of sending out the copies (reg 4 SI 2007/2612). If the company fails to allow inspection or provide copies of a report, it and every officer in default is liable to a fine and the court may order the company to allow inspection or provide copies.

MEMO POINTS 1. By 1 October 2009, the **fees** that a company can charge for copies of documents will be set out in a different set of regulations (draft Companies (Company Records and Fees) Regulations 2007). These regulations will restate the current fee (reg 19).
2. Draft regulations have been published under the new Companies Act which will allow companies to keep their records, including copies of reports, at the registered office or at one alternative **location** that is situated in the same part of the UK as the registered office (reg 5 draft Companies (Company Records and Fees) Regulations 2007). This part of the draft regulations is likely to come into force by 1 October 2009. For the proposed regulations on how a person can inspect company records, see ¶3869/mp. Copies will be able to be provided in hard copy or electronic form, as requested, but the company will not have to present them in a different way to that in which the records are kept (regs 11-13 draft Companies (Company Records and Fees) Regulations 2007).

Position of the beneficiary

2046 Since the company is effectively entitled to ignore the beneficiary's interest, the beneficiary will want to set out the **terms** of the relationship between him and the legal owner. As well as confirming ownership, the trust document should deal with matters such as voting, attending meetings, notices and so on.

Although the company only deals with the legal owner, the beneficiary cannot escape **liability** entirely. Unless the trust document states otherwise, the beneficiary is under a duty to indemnify the trustee for any liabilities he incurs as a result of owning the shares.

MEMO POINTS 1. The relationship between **nominee and investor** is usually documented to clarify points such as whether the nominee is given a discretion to vote, or whether he has to take instructions from the investor each time. It usually contains a power of attorney. The investor often keeps a blank share transfer form signed by the nominee so he can transfer the shares into his own name at will.

2. A beneficiary may apply to court to have a **stop notice** served on the company to prevent a transfer of his shares being registered without notice to him (see ¶1951).

d. Joint holders

Shares may be held by more than one person, in which case the joint holders will be **registered** as shareholders. The shares will carry the same **rights** as any others, and so it is for the joint holders to agree between them how to use their votes, who will attend meetings and so on.

2048

The articles may limit the **number of joint holders** permitted per share. For administrative purposes, the articles usually provide that the **company deals** with the first-named joint holder, as summarised in the table below.

Situation	¶¶
Where more than one joint holder votes at meeting, first-named holder's vote is counted (whether he votes in person or by proxy)	¶3816
Dividends or other moneys payable to shareholders will be sent to first-named holder's address on register of shareholders, unless joint holders direct company to do otherwise	¶1708
Notices will be given to first-named holder	¶3692/mp

3. How to become a shareholder

The **two essential components** of membership are that a person agrees to become a shareholder in the company, and his name is entered on the register of shareholders (s 22 CA 1985; restated at s 112 CA 2006 by 1 October 2009).

2053

Agreement

The relationship between a shareholder and the company is a contractual one so, as with entering into any other contract, there must be an **offer** to become a shareholder which is **accepted** and there must be **consideration** for the contract (¶372+).

2054

There are various **methods** by which a person can **agree** to become a shareholder:
– agreeing to purchase shares from an existing shareholder;
– agreeing to accept an allotment of shares from the company;
– subscribing to the memorandum; or
– if a shareholder dies or is declared bankrupt, his personal representative or trustee in bankruptcy can take the shareholder's place by agreeing to have his name registered (see ¶2038+).

2055

In the case of **allotment or subscription**:
a. the shareholder can offer to become a shareholder by applying for an allotment of shares, which is accepted by the company when it makes the allotment; or
b. the company can offer membership by allotting shares, which is accepted by the person taking the shares.

The **company may specify** how a person can agree to become a shareholder, for example by stating in the articles that a particular consent form must be signed, in which case these rules should be followed.

> *MEMO POINTS* 1. **Subscribing** usually occurs when the company is formed, but subsequent subscribers may be added by altering the memorandum (¶405, ¶410+).
> 2. **Purchases** of shares from existing shareholders must comply with the company's rules on transfers (¶1827+).

3. A person can be **deemed to agree** to become a shareholder in two ways:
– through his conduct, for example where his name is accidentally entered on the register, but rather than apply for rectification, he acts like a shareholder by voting, attending meetings, accepting dividends etc; or
– through the articles, for example where they state that a director is deemed to accept qualification shares on taking up office.
4. A shareholder can **communicate with the company** by sending any necessary documents or information in hard copy, electronic form or other agreed form (ss 1143, 1144, Sch 4 CA 2006). The rules for doing so are discussed in the context of shareholders requisitioning a general meeting at ¶3628.

2056 There must also be **consideration** for the contract, which will be the price paid for the shares. Shares cannot be issued for less than their nominal value, see ¶1110+ for more on payment for issued shares.

Formalities

2057 Once a person has agreed to become a shareholder, there may be **further procedural steps** to take before his name can be entered on the register. Usually, the company specifies that the prospective shareholder must be **approved** by the board before his name is registered. Table A effectively requires the board's approval by giving it the power to refuse to register share transfers in certain situations. Once approved, the shareholder's name can be entered in the company's **register of shareholders**. The date of the entry is taken as the commencement of his membership, even if the shares were transferred to him earlier.

Shareholders will then be issued with a **certificate**, dealt with at ¶1902+.

> MEMO POINTS   1. If shares are **transferred** but the transferee's name is **not recorded** in the register until a later date, the transferor remains the registered holder of the shares. He holds them for the benefit of the transferee and must deal with them according to his instructions (for example, voting, dealing with dividends, selling the shares).
> 2. The register of shareholders is **evidence** of who is a shareholder in the company unless it can be proved otherwise (s 361 CA 1985; restated at s 127 CA 2006 by 1 October 2009), although it is not always conclusive, as mistakes can be rectified, including adding and removing names of shareholders (¶4027+).
> 3. The **new Companies Act** will oblige directors to give reasons for refusing to register a transfer of shares (s 771 CA 2006, due to come into force on 6 April 2008). The company and every officer in default will be liable to a fine if they do not.

B. Rights and remedies

2067 Shareholders' rights and powers principally **derive from** statute (applying to all shareholders) and the articles (which can vary between companies). Many shareholders also sign a shareholders' agreement, which defines their rights and liabilities further. These rights ensure that a balance is maintained between the board's general management of the company and the shareholders' control over significant decisions. Their **status** and enforceability depend upon their source.

2068 Despite their rights and powers, shareholders may still feel that they are being **taken advantage of** in certain situations. Even minority shareholders have a number of options available to them if they feel that the company is being run, or decisions have been taken, to their detriment. They can **protect** their interests by taking preventative action such as blocking resolutions or restraining acts which are not within the company's powers (¶2554+). Statute provides added protection where shareholders could be particularly vulnerable, for example by requiring the court to approve schemes of arrangement (¶6500+). Shareholders can also **take remedial action**, such as removing a director from office or objecting to specific decisions through the court. The last section of the table below summarises shareholders' remedies and actions.

It may be appropriate for shareholders to **take court action** on behalf of, or against, the company if, for example, the company has a claim against its directors for breach of duty which the board will not pursue on the company's behalf. The situations in which shareholders can take action in their own name and in that of the company are dealt with at ¶7124+ and ¶7126+.

Sometimes these protections and remedies are not enough to shield shareholders (particularly those in a minority) from others involved in running the company taking advantage of their position. Therefore, statute provides three **remedies of "last resort"**:
– for a shareholder to issue a **derivative action** in the company's name in the event that a director is in breach of his duties;
– for a shareholder who has been **unfairly prejudiced** by how the company's affairs have been conducted; and
– allowing a shareholder to apply for a **winding up** order on "just and equitable" grounds.

1. Standard rights and remedies

This table **summarises** the rights and remedies granted to shareholders by statute and Table A, most of which impose qualification requirements (chiefly, to hold a certain percentage of the shares in the company) on the shareholder(s) exercising them. Each right/remedy is discussed within its appropriate topic at the cross-reference given. Companies often provide for **additional** rights, or **alter standard** rights where this is possible (marked with a * in the table) in their constitutions or shareholders' agreements, therefore these documents should be consulted for a full picture of shareholder rights applying to a particular company. Where additional or altered rights are set out, there may be conflict between different documents and the right that takes precedence depends upon the source document's status; this is discussed below (¶2079+).

2074

Many of these rights and remedies will be altered by the **new Companies Act**. Readers should follow the cross-references for details.

Right	Qualification [1]	¶¶
Meetings		
Have item placed on public company AGM agenda	At least 5% with right to vote at meeting [2]	¶3780+
Refuse consent to public company AGM on short notice	None	¶3785
Requisition general meeting	At least 10% of paid up share capital with right to vote at meeting	¶3625+
Apply to court for order for general meeting	Any shareholder entitled to vote at meeting	¶3635+
Refuse consent to a general meeting on short notice * [3]	Private companies: more than 10% voting on resolution (can be reduced to 5% depending on articles) Public companies: more than 5% voting on resolution	¶3681+
Receive notice *	None (unless non-voting shares or voting rights suspended)	¶3692+
Circulate written statement	At least 5% with right to vote at meeting	¶3663+
Vote *	Hold shares with right to vote	¶3815+
Demand a poll *	On most resolutions: – at least 10% voting rights at meeting; or – 2 shareholders with right to vote Right can be restricted on resolutions to appoint chairman or adjourn meeting	¶3842+

Right	Qualification[1]	¶¶
Block elective resolution to give directors authority to allot shares for more than 5 years (this last elective resolution will be obsolete by 1 October 2009)	Any shareholder at meeting entitled to vote	¶3562+
Block special/extraordinary resolution *[4]	More than 25% voting on resolution	¶3553+/ ¶3544
Block ordinary resolution *	50% voting on resolution	¶3530+
Block written resolution (new statutory procedure)	Ordinary written resolution: 50% voting on resolution Special written resolution: more than 25% voting on resolution	¶3580+
Inspect general meeting minutes	None	¶3869
Shares		
Right to dividend *	None	¶1674+
Right to benefit from increase in value of shares *	None	–
Right to dispose of shares subject to restrictions *	None	¶1827+
Share certificate *	None	¶1902+
Name entered on register	None	¶3915+
Receive copy annual accounts	None	¶4261+
Requisition public company to exercise power to require information regarding interests in its shares	At least 10% paid-up share capital with voting rights	¶2042+
Obtain remedies/take action		
Remove director from office *	– More than 50% voting on resolution – May be subject to weighted voting rights	¶2946+
Object to alteration of objects	At least 15% issued share capital[5]	¶417
Object to alteration of conditions in memorandum that could have been put in articles *	At least 15% issued share capital[5]	¶428
Apply for rectification of register of shareholders	Person aggrieved	¶4027+
Object to variation of class rights	– At least 15% issued shares of relevant class; and – did not approve variation	¶1297+
Apply to court for special resolution to re-register the company as private to be cancelled	– Did not approve resolution; and – at least 5% share capital; – at least 5% any class; or – 50 shareholders	¶678
Restrain act beyond company's powers in memorandum	None	¶2555
Not to be unfairly prejudiced	Minority or 50/50 shareholders	¶2105+
Have company wound up	None	¶2133+
Bring a derivative claim	None	¶7127+
Apply to CIB for inspectors to investigate affairs or ownership of company[6]	– At least 10% issued shares – 200 shareholders; or – the company (i.e. action is either approved by ordinary resolution, or shareholders have instructed directors by special resolution to make application)[7]	¶7221, ¶7239

Right	Qualification[1]	¶¶
Block approval of loan to director	50% voting on the resolution	¶2804+
Declare unauthorised loan to director void	More than 50% voting on the resolution	¶2886
Declare unauthorised transaction to which a director is a party void	More than 50% voting on the resolution	¶2559+
Declare unauthorised transaction void	More than 50% voting on the resolution	¶2483
Block approval of substantial property transaction	50% voting on the resolution	¶2567+
Apply to court to have resolution approving financial assistance cancelled (this will not be applicable once private companies are allowed to give financial assistance (¶5557/mp))	– At least 10% issued share capital (or any class); and – did not approve resolution	¶5616+
Apply to court to have resolution approving payment out of capital or redemption/purchase of own shares cancelled	Any shareholder who did not approve resolution[8]	¶1417+
Right of minority shareholder to be bought out where takeover offer has been made for all shares in company	– Shareholder did not accept offer; and – offeror has acquired 90% of company's shares, together with 90% of the voting rights carried by those shares[9]	¶6965+

* Companies can **change** these shareholder rights, but restrictions usually apply. See any cross-references for details.

Note:
1. Where a percentage shareholding is required, shareholder(s) exercising power must hold that % of type of shares stated. If company is not limited by shares, figure should be read as referring to a % of number of members.
2. Alternatively, at least 100 shareholders who have right to vote at meeting to which requisition relates can have item placed on agenda, provided they have paid up an average of at least £100 each.
3. Transitional amendments to Table A applying to private companies incorporated on or after 1 October 2007 that adopt Table A reduce the threshold for consent to short notice to the statutory 90% (reg 9 SI 2007/2541).
4. Extraordinary resolutions are no longer required by statute, but if a company's articles or another agreement can still require a decision to be made in this form.
5. Alternatively, holders of at least 15% of certain debentures can make application.
6. Anonymous complaints can also be made through the complaints section of the CIB website.
7. If company does not have a share capital, 20% in number of registered members can apply.
8. An application can also be made by any creditor.
9. If the offer relates to different classes of shares, both thresholds will have to be met in relation to each class.

2. Sources and status

2079

Companies often deal with additional shareholder rights or alter standard ones in their articles or shareholders' agreements (these matters can be dealt with in the memorandum as well, but this is unusual). The **choice of source** can depend upon different factors, most importantly:
a. publicity: the articles are a public document;
b. enforceability: shareholders' agreements can be enforced by and against whoever is made party to them, whereas the articles bind the shareholders as shareholders but not in other capacities; and
c. ease of amendment: altering the articles requires a special resolution, whereas altering a shareholders' agreement requires the consent of all of the parties to the agreement.

Often, the articles deal with more administrative and managerial matters, while a shareholders' agreement deals with personal rights (for example, to appoint a director, agreements between the shareholders as to how they will vote on certain matters and so on). Shareholders' agreements are therefore more common either in smaller companies which are run as quasi-partnerships, to ensure that personal interests do not impact on the company, or in joint venture companies where shareholders may have competing interests (¶6550+). Note that even certain matters in a shareholders' agreement will be a matter of public record if the company is under an obligation to notify them to Companies House, for example, class rights (¶914+), although in general the agreement itself can be kept private (see ¶2086).

2080 Shareholders' ability to **rely on, vary** and **enforce** their rights depends upon the status of the source of the right in question. There can sometimes be an overlap between a right that is originally contained in statute, but modified in the articles and further amended in a shareholders' agreement, for example. Here, the issues relating to the status of the **memorandum, articles and shareholder agreements** as they relate to shareholders are addressed; there is a wider discussion (including to what extent the company is bound) at ¶367+.

Some rights and remedies contained in **statute** can be modified by the company in its articles (marked with a * in the table at ¶2074), but many cannot. If a statutory right cannot be modified, any provision in the articles purporting to change it will be invalid. A provision in a shareholders' agreement which tries to modify such a right will not prevent the shareholder from relying on the right as set out in the legislation, but the other parties to the shareholders' agreement could still sue him for breach of contract.

Memorandum and articles

2082 A **shareholder's relationship with** the **company** is a contractual one, governed by the memorandum and articles (*Prudential Assurance Co Ltd v Newman Industries Ltd (No 2)* [1982] 1 All ER 354).

Once registered at Companies House, the memorandum and articles contractually **bind** the shareholders as if they had all personally signed and sealed the documents. Although the contract is between the company and its shareholders, the company is not deemed to have executed the memorandum and articles in the same way. Therefore, the shareholders are bound to each other by the constitution, but the company and shareholders are only bound in relation to each shareholder's rights as a shareholder of the company. This means that a shareholder can only rely on the memorandum and articles to **protect** his rights as a shareholder; a director/shareholder, for example, could not rely on the articles to enforce his rights as a director (for example, to be paid for his services).

> MEMO POINTS Under the **new Companies Act**, the memorandum will serve a different purpose. Rather than setting out the company's powers, it will simply provide a record of basic information about the company (name, subscribers etc) on incorporation (s 8 CA 2006, expected to come into force by 1 October 2009). Instead, companies will be able to state their powers in their articles if they wish. Any objects in an existing memorandum will be treated as if they are included in the articles (and therefore will be able to be amended in the same way as other provisions in the articles) when the relevant provisions of the new Act come into force, expected to be by 1 October 2009 (s 28 CA 2006). If a company does not include any restrictions on its objects in its articles, it will have unlimited objects (s 31 CA 2006).

2083 The terms of the memorandum and articles can be **varied by** special resolution.

Variation	Restrictions	¶¶
To objects clause in memorandum	Procedure for objecting to alteration	¶417+
To articles	– In memorandum; – in legislation; and – common law	¶450+
To clause in memorandum which could have been dealt with in articles (for example, dealing with management)	Procedure for objecting to alteration	¶428

The **articles** can also be **varied by**:
– written resolution;
– the express agreement of all shareholders; or
– the acquiescence of all shareholders to a change over a period of time.

> MEMO POINTS 1. Therefore, if a **shareholders' agreement** which is executed by all of the shareholders **contradicts** a regulation in the **articles**, provided it would have been a valid alteration to the articles, the amended version in the shareholders' agreement will take precedence over

the articles, because it is a change to which all shareholders have expressly consented (although the agreement would then have to be registered at Companies House, ss 29, 30 CA 2006).
For **examples of changes** which companies often make to Table A, see ¶443.
2. See memo point to ¶2082 above for a summary of how the memorandum will change by 1 October 2009 when the relevant provisions of the **new Companies Act** come into force.

2084

If the terms of the memorandum or articles are breached, shareholders can take action to **enforce** the contract, provided their rights as shareholders have been affected (for example, pre-emption rights).

> MEMO POINTS 1. The constitution cannot be enforced by a **third party**, even if he is affected by the breach.
> 2. Particular **rules** apply to **actions by shareholders** (whether brought individually or on behalf of the company), see ¶7124+, ¶7126+.

Shareholders' agreements

2086

Many companies choose to have a shareholders' agreement as well as articles because it has a number of **advantages**, principally:
a. certainty about who can enforce the agreement, as the usual rules of contract will apply. Therefore, shareholders will be able to enforce any term (whether it relates to their status as shareholders or not);
b. the company and/or individual directors can also be made parties, in which case the agreement can be enforced against (and by) them. This is useful if the agreement deals with managerial matters, such as what the board can decide and what it will refer to the shareholders;
c. it is not a matter of public record (unlike the memorandum and articles), unless its terms alter the articles or it sets out class shareholder rights (¶3600); and
d. it gives minority shareholders more power and security since they may have a better chance of negotiating matters into a shareholders' agreement than changing the articles.

> MEMO POINTS 1. Shareholders' agreements are often used in **quasi-partnerships** and joint ventures to record the intentions of the parties as to how the business is run and how much managerial involvement the shareholders should have. This can help where the parties are in dispute, particularly if one party applies for the company to be wound up or for relief from unfair prejudice because the company is not being managed as agreed.
> 2. **Alternatives** to a shareholders' agreement are irrevocable undertakings (which tend to be used in takeover situations to ensure that shareholders vote in favour of the takeover) and voting trusts (which are rare).
> 3. If the shareholders' agreement **creates class rights**, Companies House must be notified (¶915). Similarly, if the shareholders' agreement, or a variation to it, **varies class rights**, Companies House must be informed within 1 month using Form 128(3) (s 128(3) CA 1985). Failure to do so renders the company and any officer in default liable to a fine (¶9935). In practice, many class rights are incorporated into the articles at the same time (by an amendment to them) and the new articles are filed at Companies House instead.
> Variations will still have to be registered at Companies House under the **new Companies Act** (s 637 CA 2006, expected to come into force by 1 October 2009).
> The name of Form 128(3), like the names of other **Companies House forms**, is taken from the section number of the legislation. As all of the section numbers will change under the new Companies Act, Companies House proposes to change the names of all of its forms to reflect their function rather than the relevant section number ("Working with Companies House: a consultation on the registrar's rules and related provisions which will apply under the Companies Act 2006"). At the time of writing, the new form names are not yet available.

2087

A shareholders' agreement can **deal with** any matters at all, commonly addressing any combination of:
– management issues;
– corporate objectives, social responsibility and similar issues;
– funding;
– rules of membership, such as qualification and exit routes;
– class rights (including weighted voting rights on resolutions such as altering the articles or removing a director);

– transactions which cannot be approved without shareholder consent. These will usually be significant matters such as acquisitions, mergers, borrowing or disposing of company assets;
– the appointment and remuneration of the directors and secretary;
– the appointment of auditors and bankers;
– pre-emption rights (whether in addition to those in the articles, or a statement as to how the shareholders will exercise those rights); and
– dividends (for example, regulating their payment at certain intervals).

2088 The agreement **operates by** the shareholders agreeing to use their voting power in accordance with it, for example, to approve certain types of resolution, or to instruct the board to act in a particular way by special resolution.

Just as a shareholder is free to **use his vote** as he wishes (¶3824+), he is free to bind himself to use it in a particular way. An exception to this is where a **director/shareholder** binds himself to act contrary to the best interests of the company, as this would breach his fiduciary duties as a director. Similarly, if the **company is a party** to the agreement, it cannot bind itself to fetter its statutory powers (for example, by agreeing not to change the memorandum or articles, or agreeing not to increase the share capital of the company) (Russell v Northern Bank Development Corp Ltd [1992] 3 All ER 161). Therefore, if such terms are included in a shareholders' agreement, the parties should be aware that they are not enforceable against the company or a director and should consider whether the company or directors need to be parties to the agreement at all.

2089 Like other contracts, a shareholders' agreement only binds the parties to it. Therefore, **existing shareholders** are usually required to sign it. The **company** and/or its **directors** may also need to be parties to the agreement if it imposes obligations on them (however, note that some obligations will not be enforceable against them (¶2088 above)).

The agreement should contain a provision which ensures that all **new shareholders** entering the company sign a "deed of adherence" before their shares are transferred to them, so that they are bound by the same agreement.

If the agreement is just between shareholders who are being allotted shares, the consideration paid for the shares can be valid consideration for the agreement and it can be **executed** as a contract. If there is any doubt as to consideration, such as where the company or its non-shareholding directors are parties, it can be executed as a deed.

> MEMO POINTS Often **small shareholders**, particularly employees who have received shares as part of their remuneration, do not sign a shareholders' agreement for practical and administrative reasons.

2090 Shareholders' agreements can be **varied** with the consent of all parties to it, in the same way as other contracts. Therefore, a contract documenting the changes or a deed of variation should be entered into, or a new shareholders' agreement drawn up and executed by all of the parties.

2091 If the agreement is **breached**, the usual remedy will be to apply to court for an injunction either to order the defaulting party to act in accordance with the terms, or to prevent him from breaching the agreement. As with any other contract, if a breach has resulted in loss to the innocent party, damages may also be awarded (although a shareholder's ability to recover his losses will be limited if they merely reflect the losses of the company, see ¶2464/mp).

C. Remedies of last resort

2100 The table at ¶2074 above summarises the remedies available to shareholders if actions are taken by the company to their detriment, or proper procedures are not followed. Most of these remedies can be employed by a shareholder with no need to apply to court (or, only a simple application is required) and are therefore reasonably simple and cost-effective. However, a shareholder, particularly one who is in the minority, may feel that he has been taken advantage of and has **exhausted** the relevant "**self-help**" **remedies**, or his **relationship with the company** has **deteriorated** to the extent that the situation cannot be resolved. It may even be the case that he feels that the company has manipulated its legal powers to prejudice him, so it is not possible for him to object to the company's conduct via internal channels. In such cases, there are three remedies of last resort that can be relied on by the shareholder:

– commencing a **derivative action**, by which a shareholder brings a claim that the company should have brought (e.g. against a director for breach of duty). The remedy sought must therefore be for the benefit of the company, rather than the individual shareholder. Derivative actions are discussed at ¶7127+ in the context of litigation;

– an application for **relief from unfair prejudice**, by which a shareholder seeks the court's assistance to rectify the unfair treatment he has suffered. This often results in the court providing the aggrieved shareholder with a fair exit strategy, with the company carrying on without him; and

– **winding the company up**, by which the shareholder can ensure that the conduct of the company is investigated and that he receives anything to which he is entitled on exiting the company. However, the company will ultimately be dissolved.

These are only used as a last resort because the court proceedings can be expensive, time-consuming and complex, and the outcome often provides the disadvantaged shareholder with an exit route from the company.

MEMO POINTS   Applying for relief from unfair prejudice and to wind the company up are often referred to as "**minority shareholder remedies**". However, this term has not been used here because they are not specifically restricted to minority shareholders (for example, applications are just as likely to be made in the case of a deadlocked company in which the shareholding is split equally between two shareholders), and to avoid the impression that these are the only remedies available to minority shareholders (whereas most of those summarised in the table at ¶2074 can also be employed by them).

1. Unfair prejudice

2105

Shareholders can apply to court for a remedy if they have suffered "unfair prejudice" to their interests as shareholders because of the way in which the company has been run (s 994 CA 2006). This remedy **protects** shareholders who do not have the power to rectify or object to unfairly prejudicial conduct internally.

These applications are **most commonly used** where disputes arise in small owner-managed companies, since the success of the company depends on the personalities involved. Such companies are often run on a quasi-partnership basis by director/shareholders who had some kind of agreement (whether in writing or not) that each "partner" would be involved in running the business. When one "partner" is excluded and he does not have a majority shareholding (or there is a deadlock), he may have no choice but to apply to the court for a fair resolution of the dispute. Court action is usually expensive and time-consuming, and so this shareholder remedy is only used as a last resort when relations have broken down between the parties. Therefore, the remedy usually awarded by the court is to provide the excluded director/shareholder with a fair exit route from the company.

MEMO POINTS   1. Applications can also be made by **personal representatives**, **trustees in bankruptcy** and **transferees** whose transfers have not yet been registered (s 994(2) CA 2006). Since the remedy can be used by those to whom shares have been transferred by operation of law, they do not have to elect to have their names registered as shareholders in order to make the application. Even a transferor of shares which have been transferred but not yet registered has standing to petition for unfair prejudice, since he still falls within the statutory definition of "shareholder" (found in s 22 CA 1985; restated at s 112 CA 2006 by 1 October 2009) (*Re McCarthy Surfacing Ltd, Hequet v McCarthy* [2006] EWHC 832 (Ch)).

2. **Majority shareholders** are not usually protected by this remedy because they have the power to correct unfair prejudice, for example, by removing a director or declaring an unauthorised transaction void (*Baker v Potter* [2004] EWHC 1422 (Ch)).

3. The **secretary of state** can also make such an application if the company has been investigated by the CIB or FSA (s 995 CA 2006).

a. Elements of the application

2107 A shareholder's application must **establish** three aspects in order to succeed:
– unfair prejudice;
– relating to the conduct of the company's affairs; and
– which affects his interests as a shareholder.

Unfairly prejudicial conduct

2109 The interpretation of what is unfairly prejudicial conduct has evolved through case law, with **two main types** emerging (*Re a Company (No 000709 of 1992)*, *O'Neill v Phillips* [1999] 2 BCLC 1):
– **breach of an agreement** as to how the company was to be run; and
– use of the rules governing the company in **bad faith**.

> MEMO POINTS 1. An application can be based on **proposed unfairly prejudicial acts** (*Re Kenyyon Swansea Ltd* [1987] BCLC 514), although it should not be made prematurely (for example, where there are still internal methods of opposition that the shareholder can pursue, or where the proposed act is just a possibility) (*Re Astec (BSR) plc* [1998] 2 BCLC 556; *Re a Company (No 005685 of 1988), ex parte Schwarcz (No 2)* [1989] BCLC 427). An application can also be based on unfairly prejudicial conduct that **occurred in the past**, even if it has been remedied by the time of the petition (*Re Kenyon Swansea Ltd*, above).
> 2. The court will take the **petitioner's conduct** into account when assessing whether or not the company's conduct has been unfair. For example, where the parties agreed that the petitioner would contribute to the management of the company but he failed to do so, the company was justified in excluding him from running the business and his petition failed (*Re Wondoflex Textiles Property Ltd* [1951] WLR 458).

Breach of an agreement

2110 Cases falling into this category usually involve the **directors abusing their powers** resulting in an infringement of shareholders' rights under the company's constitution or the legislation. In many companies, the situation can be resolved by removing the director in question, or by the company taking action against him for breach of his duties (¶2936+, ¶2434+). However, where the majority shareholders are also the directors who commit the abuse, the minority will not have enough voting power to invoke such action and will have to resort to an unfair prejudice application.

> EXAMPLE
> 1. Where the company's **assets are misappropriated**, such as where the director/shareholder majority runs the business down to devalue the minority's shareholding, and/or transfers the business and/or assets to a separate company run by the majority.
> 2. Where the board makes **improper allotments** of shares in order to dilute the minority's shareholding further (*Re Coloursource Ltd*, *Dalby v Bodily* [2004] EWHC 3078 (Ch), in which a director/50% shareholder allotted himself shares to dilute the other 50% shareholder's holding).
> 3. Although the courts do not usually interfere in commercial/management decisions, if **serious mismanagement** (e.g. over a number of years) results in financial loss (thereby devaluing the shares), the court may grant relief to the minority shareholders (*Re Macro (Ipswich) Ltd*, *Re Earliba Finance Co Ltd*, *Macro v Thompson* [1994] 2 BCLC 354). Even where the articles have been informally relaxed by conduct, a shareholder may rely on them as written to demonstrate mismanagement (*Fisher v Cadman and others* [2005] EWHC 377 (Ch)).
> 4. Where the shareholders' **statutory rights have been breached**, such as not laying accounts before them, or not following the statutory pre-emption procedure where necessary. If a shareholder is to obtain relief from unfair prejudice on this footing, the infringement must be significant (i.e. more than a technical infringement of the legislation) and not curable by the minority (for example, if a general meeting has not been called because it was impractical, a shareholder can apply to court to order a meeting (¶3635+)).

> MEMO POINTS 1. Failure to comply with **non-statutory codes** relating to **public companies** (for example, the Listing Rules and the City Code on Takeovers and Mergers) has been held, in the circumstances of the case in question, not to amount to unfair prejudice (*Re Astec (BSR) plc* [1998] 2 BCLC 556).
> 2. **Poor management** is not, in itself, enough to form the basis of an application for unfair prejudice because the court will not resolve commercial decisions for the company, and poor

management is part of the risk of being a shareholder (hence the shareholders' powers to deal with this problem, ¶3130+). On the other hand, if poor management amounts to a **breach of the director's duty of skill and care** (now called the duty of care, skill and diligence), his actions can form the basis of a petition (*Re Elgindata Ltd* [1991] BCLC 959).

Bad faith

If one or more of the director/shareholders uses his position to **take advantage** of the other(s), the injured party may be able to claim that he has been unfairly prejudiced. This type of unfair prejudice can be distinguished from breach of an agreement, because the director/shareholder's actions are legal, but in bad faith and therefore inequitable in the circumstances. Usually, in such cases, the petitioner claims that the memorandum and articles have been qualified by an agreement or understanding between the parties (typically in **quasi-partnership** companies), which was then unfairly breached.

2111

The most common basis for these applications is that one of the **director**/shareholders has been **removed from office** by other shareholders using their statutory power (¶2946+) in contravention of an agreement that all or certain shareholders would be involved in the management of the company. The shareholder will be unfairly prejudiced if he has been excluded from management and **cannot resign his membership** because he has not been given a fair offer for his shares (¶2126 below) and, usually, cannot transfer them freely either, because of restrictions in the articles or a shareholders' agreement (*Re a Company (No 000709 of 1992)*, *O'Neill v Phillips* [1999] 2 BCLC 1; *Re Phoenix Office Supplies Ltd, Phoenix Office Supplies Ltd v Larvin* [2003] 1 BCLC 76). Although the shareholders are legally entitled to remove a director and insist on restrictions on transfer, the court may grant the excluded shareholder a remedy on the equitable ground that it was unfair of them to do so.

MEMO POINTS   Another way in which a shareholder can be excluded is if he has effectively been **denied dividends** because the board has not been declaring them while the remuneration packages of the director/shareholders have been structured so that they receive what would have been dividends as salary/bonuses, in contravention of an agreement that all shareholders would share equally in the profits (*Quinlan v Essex Hinge Co Ltd* [1996] 2 BCLC 417).

For this argument to succeed, the prejudiced party must **show that**:
– there was an agreement as to how the company was run (which can be evidenced by a shareholders' agreement, for example, or the parties' conduct);
– which he relied upon; and
– the use by the other "partner" of his legal powers contravened the agreement.

2113

The court will determine whether or not there was such an agreement by examining the circumstances, looking in particular for one or more of the following **characteristics**:
a. the business relies on a personal relationship between the parties which is based on mutual trust and confidence;
b. there is an agreement, or at least an unwritten understanding, that all or some of the shareholders will play an active role in managing the business and will benefit from its profits; and/or
c. there are restrictions on transfers of shares, preventing a shareholder from selling them to an outsider.

MEMO POINTS   1. Factors which would indicate to the court that the company is **not** run on a **quasi-partnership** basis are those which demonstrate a more commercial outlook, such as very detailed directors' service agreements which have been drafted on legal advice (*Re a Company (No 005685 of 1988), ex parte Schwarcz (No 2)* [1989] BCLC 427).
2. It would not be sufficient to claim unfair prejudice simply because the **relationship** of trust and confidence between the parties has **broken down**, without some further abuse of the rules and lack of a fair offer to buy the prejudiced party out. The appropriate remedy in this situation would be a winding up by the court on the just and equitable ground.

Conduct of the company's affairs

The actions upon which the application is based must relate to the conduct of the company's affairs (whether by the company, or by those empowered to act on its behalf), not on the actions of a shareholder in his individual capacity.

2115

> **EXAMPLE**
> Actions **not** in **conduct of the company's affairs** include:
> 1. Enforcement of a shareholders' agreement (*Re Leeds United Holdings plc* [1996] 2 BCLC 545), unless the agreement specifically dealt with how the company was to be managed (*Re Phoneer Ltd* [2002] 2 BCLC 241).
> 2. An offer by one shareholder to another to buy his shares (*Re Estate Acquisition and Development Ltd* [1995] BCC 338).
> 3. A pessimistic opinion stated by a majority shareholder which led to a dip in the share price (*Re Astec (BSR) plc* [1998] 2 BCLC 556).
> 4. Majority shareholders lending money to the company at a high interest rate related to their conduct as lenders only (*Arrow Nominees Inc v Blackledge* [2000] 2 BCLC 167).
> 5. A shareholder who had also been a director and employee of the company but had been dismissed did not unfairly prejudice the others by refusing to sell his shares to them because he was exercising his rights as a shareholder (*Re Legal Costs Negotiators Ltd* [1999] 2 BCLC 171).

MEMO POINTS   The **actions of a holding company**, which was the majority shareholder in its subsidiary and also had nominee directors on the subsidiary's board, could form the basis of an unfair prejudice application regarding the subsidiary (*Scottish Co-operative Wholesale Society Ltd v Meyer* [1958] 3 All ER 66; *Nicholas v Soundcraft Electronics Ltd* [1993] BCLC 360). Similarly, the **actions of a subsidiary company**, which was controlled by its holding company with directors in common, could amount to unfair prejudice in the parent company (*Re Citybranch Ltd, Gross v Rackind* [2005] 1 WLR 3505).

Interests as a shareholder

2117 Unfair prejudice to a shareholder's interests as shareholder clearly **includes** his interests as set out in the articles. The phrase is widely construed by the court to include interests arising from agreements or understandings about how the company should be run (for example, that the shareholder would be appointed as a director), provided the shareholder proves that his interests go further than those set out in the articles (*Re Posgate & Denby (Agencies) Ltd* [1987] BCLC 8) (see ¶372+ for how a shareholder can enforce those interests confined to the articles).

MEMO POINTS   1. A **nominee** shareholder can petition for relief from unfair prejudice, even if he has no interest in the shares, because his ownership encompasses the beneficial owner's economic and contractual interests (*Atlasview Ltd v Brightview Ltd* [2004] 2 BCLC 191).
2. A shareholder's **interests as an employee** cannot form the basis of a petition (*Re Alchemea Ltd* [1998] BCC 964).
3. The court can order a company's directors to pay damages to the company for breaches of duty owed to it, even where the **petitioner would not benefit** from the payment as a shareholder if, for example, the company was insolvent and the payment of damages would not immediately restore the company to a solvent trading position (*Gamlestaden Fastigheter AB v Baltic Partners Limited and others* [2007] UKPC 26).

b. Procedure

2119 The application must be made in the **form** of a petition to court (s 994 CA 2006). The petition must **contain** details of:
– the ground(s) upon which it is presented; and
– the nature of the relief sought by the petitioner.

The applicant is referred to as the **petitioner**; the company and each shareholder should be joined as **respondents** (apart from those shareholders who will not be affected, for example, if they do not belong to the relevant class). Although the application usually concerns a dispute between shareholders, the company needs to be joined into the action to ensure that it is bound by any order of the court (since the relief granted will usually require the company to take some action).

MEMO POINTS   1. The **general rules** relating to Companies Act applications also apply to those for relief from unfair prejudice (¶7143+). **Specific rules** contained in the Companies (Unfair Prejudice Applications) Proceedings Rules 1986 (SI 1986/2000) also apply and include a sample petition in the Schedule. These rules were made with reference to the 1985 Act unfair prejudice provisions. There is a power under the new Companies Act for rules to be made, but at the time of writing no such rules have yet been made. Therefore, the discussion below refers to the rules made under the old provisions in the absence of a new version. Given the similarity of the 1985 and 2006 statutory provisions, it is likely that any new rules will be similar in any event.

2. The application must be in the form of a petition; the court cannot accept applications in other **forms**, such as claim forms (*Bamber v Eaton* [2005] 1 All ER 820).

The petition undergoes the following **process**: **2120**

Action	Timing	Reference[1]
The petitioner files enough copies of petition at court for court and each respondent	n/a	r 3(2) SI 1986/2000
The court: – fixes a date for the directions hearing ("return day"); and – seals copies of the petition to be served on the respondents and sends them to the petitioner	n/a	r 3(3), (4) SI 1986/2000
The petitioner serves sealed copies of petition on the company and every other named respondent	At least 14 days before directions hearing	r 4 SI 1986/2000
Directions hearing.[2] The court can give any directions, including: – the service of petition on any person; – whether the particulars of claim and defence are necessary; – whether the petition needs to be advertised; and – how to deal with any evidence[3]	As notified by court	r 5 SI 1986/2000
The parties follow the court's directions	As directed by court	–
The petition is heard and an order is made	As notified by court	r 6 SI 1986/2000
The order is advertised if it is so required by court[4]	Time limit stated in order	r 6(3) SI 1986/2000

Note:
1. See ¶2119/mp above for these rules.
2. These applications used to be automatically **allocated to** the multi-track, but the new CPR practice direction dealing with companies applications does not include an equivalent provision where the application must be by petition (CPR PD 49). However, it is likely that they will still be allocated to the multi-track. Track allocation and the management of cases (including giving directions) are dealt with in Parts 26-29 CPR.
3. Petitioners can obtain **disclosure of board documents**, including advice and guidance which the board has received on relevant transactions. Such documents will not be protected by legal professional privilege because the company is a nominal defendant (*CAS (Nominees) Ltd v Nottingham Forest plc* [2001] 1 All ER 954).
4. The petition or any order must not be **advertised** without the court's direction.

MEMO POINTS   The court may **strike out the application** on a number of grounds, including where:
– it is unreasonable to pursue the application because alternative relief is available (for example, a fair offer for shares is made, ¶2126 below);
– the relief sought is inappropriate; or
– the application was used to exert pressure on the other side to achieve an ulterior motive.

c. Remedies

If the court decides in favour of the petitioner, it will grant a remedy by making whatever sort of **court order** it sees fit (s 996(1) CA 2006). **2122**

Buy out

Usually, by the time the petitioner has resorted to court action, the relationship between the parties has deteriorated to such an extent that it is not feasible for them to carry on in the company together, and so the **most common order** is for the respondent to buy out the petitioner as shareholder. However, even in quasi-partnerships, there is no right for one "partner" to withdraw from the business and expect the others to buy him out and so such an order will **only be made** if it is a fair solution to the unfair prejudice (*Re a Company* **2124**

(No 000709 of 1992), O'Neill v Phillips [1999] 2 BCLC 1; Re Phoenix Office Supplies Ltd, Phoenix Office Supplies Ltd v Larvin [2003] 1 BCLC 76).

> MEMO POINTS   The court may order that the **petitioner purchases** the **respondent's shares** if, for example, the petitioner and respondent hold the shares equally and the respondent's conduct makes it fair for the petitioner to carry on running the company *(Re Planet Organic Ltd [2000] 1 BCLC 366)*, or the respondent used the company's assets for his own benefit and to the detriment of the petitioners *(Re Brenfield Squash Raquets Club Ltd [1996] 2 BCLC 184)*.

2125 If the court makes such an order, it will determine the **valuation** of the shares, or order that a particular type of expert be appointed to do so, taking into account factors such as the conduct of the parties and whether there should be a discount to reflect a minority holding. Ordinarily, a minority shareholding should be discounted, even if the minority is slight *(Irvine v Irvine [2006] EWHC 583 (Ch))*.

The **date** of the valuation is usually the date of the order, although an earlier date may be chosen in appropriate circumstances *(Profinance Trust SA v Gladstone [2002] 1 BCLC 141)*. For instance, in one case, the parties had agreed heads of terms as to how the company's business and assets should be split but they had subsequently fallen out again. The respondent had gone on to conduct the company in an unfairly prejudicial manner, so the court ordered that the valuation be carried out as at the date of that agreement, or a convenient date after that *(Re Adlink Ltd [2006] All ER (D) 198 (Oct))*.

Interest is not usually awarded on the purchase price, but it is in the court's power to do so, and may be appropriate if, for example, an early valuation date has been set.

2126 The court encourages the **parties** to **resolve** the situation on their own, and if a fair offer for the shares is made during the proceedings, it will usually strike out the petition (there is no point in continuing because the petitioner has already gained his relief). It is therefore in all of the parties' interests for a fair offer to be made. If an unfair offer is made, it will be declined by the other party and the issue will have to be referred to court to decide whether or not the offer should have been accepted, which will increase legal costs and will take more time to resolve *(Callard v Pringle and others [2007] All ER (D) 91 (Aug))*.

A **fair offer** is one *(Re a Company (No 000709 of 1992), O'Neill v Phillips [1999] 2 BCLC 1)*:
a. at a fair value, usually a suitable proportion of the total issued share capital of the company, with a discount to reflect any applicable minority;
b. which, if not agreed between the parties, will be independently assessed by an expert;
c. the object of which is economy and expedition, and does not provide for a protracted expert assessment or arbitration;
d. in which both parties have had equal access to information and any expert used; and
e. which addresses the question of litigation costs (if made during the proceedings).

Other remedies

2128 The court has the power to make whatever order it sees fit, including:
a. placing conditions on the purchase of shares, for example, that repayment of a loan forms part of the package *(Re Nuneaton Borough AFC Ltd (No 2) [1991] BCC 44)*;
b. regulating the company's conduct in future, for example ordering that the company repays loans made by the petitioner as soon as possible *(Re Haden Bill Electrical Ltd, R & H Electrical Ltd v Haden Bill Electrical Ltd [1995] 2 BCLC 280)*;
c. requiring the company to act (or not act) in a particular way, such as holding a general meeting on a certain date *(McGuinness v Bremner plc [1988] BCLC 673)*;
d. authorising civil proceedings in the name or on behalf of the company by way of a derivative action (¶7127+); and
e. ordering the company's directors to pay damages to the company for breaches of duty owed to it, even where the petitioner would not benefit from the payment as a shareholder *(Gamlestaden Fastigheter AB v Baltic Partners Limited and others [2007] UKPC 26)*.

The court can take the past, present and future circumstances of the case into account when deciding on the appropriate remedy

> **EXAMPLE** Mr G was a shareholder and director of TEP Ltd. He complained of unfair prejudice on the grounds that he had been excluded from dividends and dismissed from the board contrary to an agreement that he would be involved in management. The court found that his dismissal was justified, but the failure to pay dividends was unfairly prejudicial. At first instance, the court ordered payment of the unpaid dividends but not that the respondents purchase Mr G's shares. Among other things, the court held that this was a one-off instance of unfair prejudice which would not necessarily be repeated and therefore there was no need to give Mr G an exit route from the company. On appeal, the court made the buy-out order because the lengths to which the respondents were prepared to go to avoid paying Mr G the dividend indicated that they would do so again, and Mr G was no longer on the board to prevent this from occurring. The court could have used its discretion to order payment of the dividends, but in the circumstances it was not appropriate to do so (*Grace v Biagioli and others* [2005] EWCA Civ 1222).

> **MEMO POINTS** 1. The **order** can be made **against third parties**. For example, where a director had made unauthorised payments into a pension fund, the court traced the payments into the pension fund's hands and ordered their return (*Clark v Cutland* [2003] 4 All ER 73).
> 2. The court can also order **interim relief** (under r 25.6 CPR), for example for an interim payment to be made to the petitioner (*Re Clearsprings (Management) Ltd*, *Billems v King* [2003] EWHC 2516 (Ch)).
> 3. The court can also make a **winding up order**, if appropriate on the particular facts of the case (*Re Phoneer Ltd* [2002] 2 BCLC 241). However, petitioners should not ask the court to wind the company up as a matter of course. If they genuinely want to put the company into liquidation, they should just petition for a winding up (para 1 CPR PD 49B; ¶2133+ below).
> 4. The court can also order that **alterations** must be made to the company's **memorandum or articles**, which have effect as though they had been made by shareholder resolution. Conversely, the court can order the company not to alter its memorandum or articles without the court's permission. A copy of a court order altering, or giving leave to alter, the memorandum and articles must be filed at Companies House within 14 days (or a longer period specified by the court). The company and any officer in default of this requirement is liable to a fine (ss 998, 999 CA 2006; ¶9935).

2. Wind up the company

2133 Another course of action open to shareholders is to apply to the court to have the company wound up, where the **relationship** between the parties has **broken down**. Since the end result of this remedy is so drastic, it will usually only be used where an action for unfair prejudice cannot be made out. The situations in which it applies are similar to those for unfair prejudice, which gives the petitioner a more financially secure exit route (since, if the company is wound up, the petitioner may not recoup all of his investment, depending on the company's financial position). However, if money is not an issue to the petitioner and he can persuade the court that it is "just and equitable" in the circumstances to wind the company up, he may prefer this remedy so that the other directors and shareholders are not able to continue running the company without him and to ensure that the company's affairs are thoroughly investigated.

The **procedure** for petitioning to wind a company up is discussed in detail at ¶7585+.

> **MEMO POINTS** 1. This remedy is also open to **other petitioners**: creditors, directors, the company and BERR (where it is in the public interest that the company is wound up) (¶7629).
> 2. It is possible to ask the court to wind the company up as an **alternative to** seeking relief from **unfair prejudice**, if the case for unfair prejudice is weaker than it should be (for example, there is doubt as to the terms of the agreement upon which the company was run), it may be easier for the petitioner to obtain a winding up order (*Re Noble & Sons (Clothing) Ltd* [1983] BCLC 273, where an unfair prejudice application was turned down, but winding up was granted on the same facts). However, the court has since stressed that shareholders should only petition for winding up if this is genuinely the remedy that they prefer, not just as an alternative to unfair prejudice (para 1 CPR PD 49B).

2134 The application should be made **on the basis** that it is "just and equitable" that the company is wound up by the court. The shareholder should be able to show that he would have an interest in the liquidation, and therefore the company should have **assets** that would be distributed to the shareholders.

[MEMO POINTS] The court may still, in exceptional circumstances, wind the company up on this ground if it has **no assets**. For example, even where a company had a deficiency of over £366m, the court made a winding up order because this would enable the liquidator to strike out securities (*Bell Group Finance (Pty) Ltd (in liquidation) v Bell Group (UK) Holdings Ltd* [1996] 1 BCLC 304). Similarly, the court will not strike out an application if a petitioner **cannot establish an interest** because the company will not provide the relevant financial information (*Re a Company (No 007936 of 1994)* [1995] BCC 705).

2135 The court's decision will depend upon a consideration of the **circumstances**, particularly in the light of any agreement between the parties as to how the company was to be run. The court will look for similar factors to those in an unfair prejudice application (*Re a Company (No 007936 of 1994)* [1995] BCC 705):
– a company formed on the basis of a personal relationship;
– with an understanding/agreement that the shareholders would participate in the business beyond their usual involvement; and
– transfers on shares may be restricted so the petitioning shareholder cannot sell up.

[EXAMPLE] A partnership incorporated itself, with the two partners, Mr A and Mr B, becoming director/shareholders. Mr A brought in his son as a third director/shareholder, leaving Mr B in the minority. Mr B was removed as a director, and the board stopped declaring dividends. Although these actions were legal, the court made a winding up order because the parties' legal rights were subject to the equitable considerations of the quasi-partnership agreement/understanding that Mr A and Mr B would both be involved in management and share the profits (*Ebrahimi v Westbourne Galleries Ltd* [1972] 2 All ER 492).

[MEMO POINTS] The petitioner can **rely on** actions which do not necessarily breach his rights as a shareholder, for example dismissal (or non-appointment) as a director (*Re Zinotty Properties Ltd* [1984] 3 All ER 754). However, he **cannot rely on** actions against his interests outside the company, such as his rights as a freeholder, because this strays too far from the agreement as to how the company is run (*Re J E Cade & Son Ltd* [1992] BCLC 213).

2136 The court will **not make an order** where there has been a fair offer to buy out one party's shares, usually the petitioner's. The petitioner is entitled to refuse an offer if it is unfair, for example, in a case in which there was a dispute over the beneficial ownership of the shares, it was reasonable for the petitioner to refuse an offer which did not take all of the shares into account (*Re a Company (No 001363 of 1988), ex parte S-P* [1989] BCLC 579). In such cases, the court will balance the advantages of winding up (for example, that the liquidator can resolve disputes over shares and other property) against the offer to purchase the shares.

CHAPTER 8

Directors

OUTLINE

SECTION 1 **General concepts** 2175	
A	What is a director? 2180
B	Different categories of director 2197
	Executive directors 2200
	Non-executive directors 2204
	Nominee directors 2206
	Alternate directors 2208
	De facto directors 2210
	Shadow directors 2212

SECTION 2 **Appointment** 2230	
A	Who can be a director? 2241
1	Personal factors 2244
2	Objective qualifications 2253
B	Who appoints directors? 2266
C	Formalities of appointment 2288
D	Defects in appointment 2300

SECTION 3 **Directors' duties** 2317	
I	General duties 2333
A	Duties 2333
1	Act within authority 2348
2	Fiduciary duties 2373
	a Act within powers 2376
	b Promote the company's success 2379
	c Exercise independent judgment 2389
	d Avoid conflicts of interest and duty 2390
	e Account for profits 2398
	f Not misuse company property and/or information 2405
3	Care, skill and diligence 2411
B	Remedies for and consequences of breach of duty 2434
1	Availability of remedies 2438
2	Types of remedy 2463
	a Damages 2463

	b Injunctions 2467
	c Account for profits 2471
	d Restitution of property and tracing 2476
	e Removal of the director 2480
	f Consequences on transactions 2483
C	Relief from liability 2494
1	Ratification 2497
2	Relief provided by statute 2505
3	Indemnity and insurance 2512
II	Specific duties 2532
A	Management duties 2548
1	General 2548
2	Act within limitations 2554
3	Substantial property transactions 2567
4	Liability for defrauding creditors 2577
5	Liability for company cheques etc 2580
B	Employment duties 2590
1	Health and safety 2590
2	Other employment duties 2596
C	VAT 2606
D	Insolvency 2612

SECTION 4 **Service contract** 2627	
A	Form and content 2635
B	Approval 2652
C	Retention and inspection obligations 2668
D	Breach of service contract 2678

SECTION 5 **Remuneration** 2696	
A	Elements of remuneration 2710
B	Taxation 2735
1	National insurance contributions 2740
2	Income tax 2745
C	Disclosure of remuneration in the accounts 2761

1	Disclosure generally	2766
2	Disclosure of particular aspects of remuneration	2778

SECTION 6 Loans to directors ... 2804

A	Restricted transactions	2810
B	Exceptions to the restrictions	2826
C	Consequences of entering into prohibited transactions	2880
D	Disclosure of loans in the accounts	2897

SECTION 7 Termination ... 2912

A	Termination of office	2920
1	Resignation	2920
2	Retirement	2925

3	Removal	2936
4	Administrative requirements	2957
5	Compensation for loss of office	2962
B	Termination of service contract	2977

SECTION 8 Disqualification ... 3000

A	General concepts	3008
	Who can be disqualified?	3010
	Grounds for and length of disqualification	3012
B	The concept of unfitness	3021
C	Procedure	3042
D	Disqualification orders and undertakings	3070
	Leave of the court to act as a director	3074
	Register	3080
	Breach of an order or undertaking	3082

2160 Directors form the **managerial body** of a company, the board. They are **appointed** by the shareholders to run the company on a daily basis and to act on its behalf when dealing with third parties. Although directors are to exercise these powers as a board, on a practical level the board cannot conduct every matter as a unit. Therefore, individual directors often act on behalf of the company. The **conduct** of directors is regulated in a number of ways. Duties are imposed on them by legislation, the company's memorandum and articles of association and by case law.

Breach of these duties can have various consequences on the director, including personal **liability** and criminal sanctions (although relief from liability may be available). **Disqualification** from acting as a director may also arise from directors' breaches of duty, especially in insolvency situations.

For the wider issues of the respective management roles of the board and the shareholders, see ¶3130+; and for a detailed discussion of board decisions and meetings, see ¶3217+.

MEMO POINTS The principal **legislation** governing directors is found in the Companies Acts 1985 and 2006. Many of the provisions of the new Companies Act relating to directors were brought into force on 1 October 2007. Any changes that are yet to be made as well as transitional measures are noted where relevant. Disqualification of an individual from being appointed, or continuing to act, as a director is covered by the Company Directors Disqualification Act 1986. Further legislation relevant to company directors is found in the Insolvency Act 1986 and the Financial Services and Markets Act 2000.

The **articles** deal with procedural aspects of directors' appointment, termination and so on, as well as refining the common law restrictions on directors relating to conflicts and profits (¶3308+). The position discussed here is that set out in Table A, but individual companies' articles must always be consulted because they may well contain alternative provisions. Draft new model articles under the new Companies Act have been published. Where relevant, the proposed provisions for private companies limited by shares and public companies are discussed in the memo points.

Directors' general duties to their companies used to be found only in case law. They are now set out in statute in order to make directors' obligations clearer, see ¶2333+. However, the existing **case law** concerning directors' duties remains applicable, which can make it difficult for directors to ascertain their position, since cases are decided on their own facts which may differ from a director's own circumstances.

2161 The **new Companies Act** makes a number of important changes to the law relating to directors. The most significant is that their common law duties will be codified in order to make it easier for them to understand their obligations and so that companies and third parties will know what to expect from them. At the time of writing, most, but not all, of these codifying provisions have been brought into force (see ¶2333+). The new Act will also require every company to have at least one director who is an individual, as opposed to a corporation or firm, to ensure that an identifiable individual can be held accountable. By way of changes which specifically benefit directors, they will no longer be required to have their residential addresses on the register at Companies House or in the company's own registers which are open to general inspection (¶3896+). Specific changes are noted as relevant to the topics discussed in this chapter.

SECTION 1

General concepts

2175 Before discussing who can be a director, it is necessary to ascertain exactly what a director is. Although there is a statutory **definition** of the term, it is wide enough to encompass more than just formally appointed directors.

Many different **terms** are used to describe directors, most of which are not defined by statute. As part of the discussion of what a director is, the various types of director will be looked at, as well as a summary of the different roles he fulfils within a company. This sets the scene for the various duties and liabilities of a director (discussed at ¶2317+), most of which arise out of one or other of these roles.

A. What is a director?

2180 A director is **defined** in the legislation as "any person occupying the position of director, by whatever name called" (s 250 CA 2006).

The **purpose** behind such a loose definition is to include as directors people who behave as such but have not been formally appointed, or have simply been given a different title (e.g. companies can refer to their directors by whatever title they wish, such as "managers" or "governors"). Therefore, whether or not a person is a director is **determined by** his status and what he does within a company rather than by simply looking at his job title. A director's functions will vary from one company to another, influenced by factors such as:
– the nature of the company (e.g. its size and structure);
– its constitution (i.e. the memorandum and articles); and
– any relevant contractual documentation (e.g. the director's service contract).

> MEMO POINTS 1. The **same** statutory **definition** is adopted by IA 1986 and CDDA 1986 and is expressly **extended** by FSMA 2000 to include shadow directors (¶2212+), although both IA 1986 and CDDA 1986 include identical, separate definitions of "shadow director" (s 251 IA 1986; s 22(4), (5) CDDA 1986; s 417(1) FSMA 2000).
> 2. In corporate charities, the directors are often referred to as "**trustees**". Although all directors owe fiduciary duties to their companies (these are discussed in detail at ¶2373+), they cannot be described as trustees of the company in a legal sense (see ¶2186 below).

2181 A director is not usually **liable** for the company's debts and defaults, unless they have been caused by his own breach of duty (see ¶2317+). A company can, however, provide in its memorandum that the liability of its directors, or any managing director, is unlimited (s 306(1) CA 1985), which gives rise to additional requirements when appointing a new director

(¶2278). Even if the memorandum does not contain such a statement, the shareholders may include one by using a special resolution to alter the memorandum (¶410+).

> MEMO POINTS 1. The liability of the company's "**managers**" can also be stated as unlimited in the memorandum (s 306(1) CA 1985). A manager is an officer of the company and therefore subject to the duties and liabilities of an officer (s 744 CA 1985; ss 1121, 1173 CA 2006, which apply for the purposes of interpreting other provisions already in force). He is a person who conducts the management of the whole of the company's affairs (*Gibson v Barton* (1875) LR 10 QB 329). As in the case of directors, his role, functions and powers must be considered along with his job title/description to ascertain whether he is truly a manager (*Re B Johnson & Co (Builders) Ltd* [1955] 2 All ER 775).
> 2. s 306 CA 1985 will be repealed by the **new Companies Act**, because the memorandum will no longer contain such information (Sch 16 CA 2006). This repeal is expected to take effect by 1 October 2009, when the provisions relating to a company's constitution come into force.

The roles of a director

2183 The position of director can be seen as a composite of a number of different roles. This is a result of a combination of functions being assigned to directors through statute and case law, much of the case law arising out of directors' breaches of duty.

Officer

2184 A director is an office-holder and is, therefore, an officer of the company. This is a generic term which also includes a company's secretary and any managers (s 744 CA 1985; restated at s 1173 CA 2006, which applies for the purposes of interpreting other provisions of the new Act already in force).

> MEMO POINTS 1. Several provisions of the legislation refer to the **duties and liabilities of officers**, rather than directors specifically, bringing these other categories of officers within the scope of liability (¶9935).
> 2. Under the **new Companies Act**, the definition of an "officer in default" also includes any other person which is to be treated as an officer for the purposes of the relevant provision (s 1121 CA 2006, which also applies for the purposes of interpreting other provisions of the new Act already in force).

Agent

2185 The relationship between a company and its director(s) has been described as that of principal and agent (*Ferguson v Wilson* (1866) 2 Ch App 77). This role arises out of the company's status as an artificial legal person: it can only enter into legal relationships with third parties by acting through the directors, to whom management of the company has been delegated.

Although the general **rules of agency** can be applied to the relationship between a director and his company (for example, a director will generally not be held personally liable for the company's debts or defaults), they do not describe it entirely: the relationship is in fact much wider. **Statute** and **common law** have increased the number of circumstances in which a director will be held personally liable compared to a normal agent.

Fiduciary

2186 A director occupies a fiduciary position in relation to the company because of his special relationship with it (*Regal (Hastings) Ltd v Gulliver* [1942] 1 All ER 378). This role **arises out of** his position of trust and his control over the property of others (i.e. the shareholders' property). Under equitable law, fiduciaries are subject to certain restrictions and obligations, which give rise to liabilities if breached.

> MEMO POINTS He cannot, however, be described as a **trustee** in relation to the company because different duties are imposed on a director than on a trustee, for example, directors do not hold the legal title to the company's property, they are subject to a lower standard of care, and are expected to take the usual commercial risks in running the company (*Selangor United Rubber Estates Ltd v Cradock (a bankrupt) (No 3)* [1968] 2 All ER 1073). Even so, directors of corporate charities are often referred to as "trustees".

Employee

2187 A director's tenure of office does not automatically confer the status of employee on him, although it is usual for directors who work full time in managing the company to be employees as well. This is a separate matter, dealt with in any service contract or arising out of the nature of the relationship between him and the company. Company law makes no distinction in its treatment of directors who are employed by the company and those who are not, although in practice there are employment law implications.

> MEMO POINTS   The company will usually be in the position of **employer** with respect to its staff. This position imposes a set of duties and liabilities on it which are dealt with in depth in *Employment Memo*. Directors are also subject to certain duties personally in this regard, see ¶2590+.

B. Different categories of director

2197 All directors are subject to the same **duties and liabilities**, and so references to "directors" are references to all types of director, unless stated otherwise. Most companies do not distinguish between the different types of director, as they are more concerned with what a director does than what he is called. Titles, where they are given, merely assist in ascertaining what duties a director may have.

Common **titles** given to directors are listed below. These titles are not mutually exclusive, for example, an alternate director can be appointed to stand in for a managing director. However, certain types often go together, for instance managing directors are usually executive directors, while nominees are often non-executive. Similarly, the titles are not exclusively applied to directors who have been formally appointed, e.g. a de facto director may be a managing director. Shadow directors, on the other hand, should be treated as a separate case because they act behind the scenes and will not fall into these other types.

2198 Directors broadly fall into **two categories**: those who have been formally appointed to office and those who have not.

The majority of directors are **formally appointed** in accordance with the necessary requirements (¶2241+ and ¶2288+). They are known as "de jure" directors, a term which means "by law" and describes a director who has:
– been appointed in accordance with the rules relating to appointment;
– agreed to hold office;
– not been disqualified; and
– has not vacated office.

Directors who have **not** been **formally appointed** to office but who are deemed to fall within the scope of the definition of a "director" (and are therefore subject to the same duties and restrictions as formally appointed directors) will either be "de facto" (a term which means "in fact") directors or shadow directors.

Executive directors

2200 Executive directors devote substantially all of their working time to the company and are actively **involved in** management. They are usually employed by the company, and will often have a service contract setting out the terms and conditions of their dual status as director and employee (¶2627+).

The **distinction** between executive and non-executive directors is not one made by statute, but is often made by companies in their articles and in practice. For example, Table A makes the distinction in its delegation provision and the ability to appoint directors to executive positions (regs 72, 84 TA 1985).

> MEMO POINTS   Draft **new model articles** under the **new Companies Act** have been published for private companies limited by shares and public companies. They will not make this distinction.

2201 A company's articles usually allow the board to appoint and delegate functions to a **managing director** (regs 72, 84 TA 1985). The title does not automatically confer any additional **rights, duties** or **liabilities** on the director and statute does not set out any duties or functions specific to the role. Such matters are left to individual companies to decide and will usually be set out in the managing director's service contract. The delegation must be made specifically (¶3404+).

A managing director will usually **supervise** the running of the company, sometimes acting as a figurehead and, for example, sitting as chairman of the board. How involved the managing director is in the day to day management of the company will depend on the size of the company: it will be a full time job in a large company to organise and co-ordinate the activities of the board, whereas the managing director of a small company will be far more involved in the daily business and may well be the sole director.

> MEMO POINTS The draft **new model articles** will not contain a specific power to appoint and delegate functions to a managing director. However, the delegation provisions will be wide enough to enable such an appointment (private companies limited by shares: arts 4, 19; public companies: arts 4, 22).

2202 It is usually large companies which need to divide management responsibilities into different areas, and they may wish to appoint directors with relevant expertise and experience to **specific executive positions**. Commonly, companies will have a "finance director" and a "sales director", or use geographical locations to denote a director's ambit of responsibility, e.g. European director. As with the position of managing director, such appointments can be made and functions delegated to them, but the terms of the appointment must specifically deal with any matters such as duties or remuneration (respectively, regs 84, 73 TA 1985).

> MEMO POINTS 1. Again, the draft **new model articles** will enable directors to be appointed to specific executive positions (private companies limited by shares: arts 4, 19; public companies: arts 4, 24).
> 2. Transitional amendments to Table A which apply to **companies incorporated on or after 1 October 2007** that adopt Table A omit reg 73 TA 1985 (reg 13 SI 2007/2541).

Non-executive directors

2204 Non-executive directors only devote a small part of their time to the company. They are not employees and are not usually actively involved in managing the company. Their **function** tends to be to monitor the management activities of the executive directors and provide an independent voice on the board. Although non-executive directors are not involved in the day to day management, they have the same **obligations** and **liabilities** as any executive director. Non-executive directors will often hold a number of such directorships with several different companies, and will not usually be employees of any one company in particular.

Non-executive directors are more commonly found in large companies, especially listed **public companies**. The Combined Code, which regulates listed companies, advocates non-executive directors as an important tool in self-regulation.

Nominee directors

2206 A nominee director is **appointed by** a particular shareholder or group of shareholders.

They are often found in **group companies** where the holding company will nominate one of its own directors (or the holding company itself) to sit on the board of its subsidiary to monitor the subsidiary's activities. Nominees are also commonly found in companies with different **classes of shares**. For example, each class may have been given the right to appoint a director to represent its rights on the board, or a shareholder who has made a substantial investment in the company may be allowed to nominate a director to maintain some control over his investment.

Nominee directors may find themselves in a position of **conflict** where the interests of the company clash with those of his nominator (¶2390+).

> MEMO POINTS Simply giving one shareholder or group of shareholders the right to appoint a nominee creates a class of shares. Therefore, any **changes to that right** will have to conform to the procedure for varying class rights (¶1270+).

Alternate directors

A director can appoint an alternate director to take his place on the board, if permitted by the company's articles or by law (¶3438+).

2208

De facto directors

A de facto director is a person who **claims** or **purports** to act as a director, but who has either not been validly appointed or who continues to act as a director after he has been removed from office. Often a person will be a de facto director because the company has attempted to appoint him as a director in the usual way, but there is some **defect in his appointment**, for instance his name has not been entered in the register of directors. As to the validity of such a director's acts, see ¶2300+. De facto directors are treated for most purposes as de jure directors; for example, they are subject to the same duties and liabilities and can be disqualified (*Re Lo-Line Electric Motors Ltd* [1988] BCLC 698).

2210

The principal difference between a de facto director and a shadow director is that a de facto director openly acts and holds himself out as a director of the company. He will carry out the same functions and duties as the other directors, but there is a defect in his appointment or even no formal appointment at all. When determining whether a person is a de facto director or not, the court will assess whether or not he is part of the governing structure, i.e. whether he participates in collective decision making on corporate policy (*Secretary of State for Trade and Industry v Hollier and others* [2006] EWHC 1804 (Ch)). He does not have to be involved in all of the company's affairs or activities, just as a de jure director does not. Therefore, it is possible for him to be a de facto director in relation to some of the company's activities and a shadow director in relation to another (*Re Mea Corporation Ltd, Secretary of State for Trade and Industry v Aviss and others* [2006] EWHC 1846 (Ch)).

Shadow directors

A shadow director is a person in accordance with **whose directions** or **instructions** the directors of a company are accustomed to act (s 251 CA 2006 and see ¶2180/mp for the references in other statutes). A shadow director is neither de jure nor de facto; he is someone who controls the board from behind the scenes (*Re Hydrodam (Corby) Ltd* [1994] 2 BCLC 180).

2212

Guidance on **how to interpret** the statutory definition has been given in case law, indicating that the definition is to be widely construed:
a. it requires the "directors of the company" to follow the alleged shadow director's instructions. Therefore, if just a **minority of the board follows** his **instructions**, he will not be deemed to be a shadow director (*Kuwait Asia Bank EC v National Mutual Life Nominees Ltd* [1990] 3 All ER 404);
b. for the directors to be "accustomed to act" in accordance with his instructions, they must do so over a **period of time** as their regular practice (*Re Unisoft Group Ltd (No 3)* [1994] 1 BCLC 609);
c. the court should look at **communications** between the alleged shadow director and the other directors objectively, i.e. whether they would be viewed as instructions by an outsider, rather than only looking at how the company and alleged shadow director regarded them (*Secretary of State for Trade and Industry v Deverell* [2000] 2 All ER 365);
d. instructions do not need to cover every aspect, or even most aspects, of the company's activities, nor do they have to be overt instructions (*Secretary of State for Trade and Industry v Deverell*, above);
e. instructions can include non-professional **advice** (*Secretary of State for Trade and Industry v Deverell*, above);
f. it is not necessary to show that the **other directors** were **compelled** to follow the alleged director's instructions (*Secretary of State for Trade and Industry v Deverell*, above); and
g. although the term "shadow director" implies that the alleged shadow director **acted in secret**, the court has held that this is not necessary (*Secretary of State for Trade and Industry v Deverell*, above).

> MEMO POINTS This rule does not apply to those who give **professional advice** to a company (s 251(2) CA 2006). Therefore, lawyers, accountants, insolvency practitioners and so on will not become shadow directors because they have advised a company and their client company follows their advice. This does depend on the degree of involvement the professional has with the company. If he steps outside of his role as professional adviser and becomes more directly involved in management, he could well be deemed to be a shadow director (*Re Tasbian Ltd (No 3)*,

Official Receiver v Nixon [1993] BCLC 297, in which leave was granted to the official receiver to commence disqualification proceedings out of time against a chartered accountant employed by the company as a consultant because there was an arguable case that he was a shadow or de facto director as a result of his involvement in the company's management and key decisions.

2213 A **holding company** may be deemed to be a shadow director of its subsidiary if the directors of the subsidiary are accustomed to act in accordance with the instructions of the holding company (i.e. if the usual conditions are fulfilled, not just by virtue of the fact that it is a holding company). If a holding company is found to be a shadow director of its subsidiary, the **directors of the holding company** will not automatically also be shadow directors of the subsidiary unless they have individually behaved in a way that puts them in that position (*Re Hydrodam (Corby) Ltd* [1994] 2 BCLC 180).

MEMO POINTS   Statute contains some **specific exceptions** to this rule (s 251(3) CA 2006). Holding companies will not be deemed to be shadow directors of their subsidiaries for the purposes of the following statutory circumstances: directors' general duties (¶2333+); directors' service contracts for a fixed term longer than 5 years (¶2655+); payments to directors for loss of office (¶2962+); substantial property transactions (¶2567+); contracts between the company and its sole shareholder who is also a director (¶3473); and prohibitions on loans (¶2804+).

SECTION 2

Appointment

2230 Every **private company** must have a minimum of one director (s 154(1) CA 2006). However, Table A requires a minimum of two directors (reg 64 TA 1985). Many companies adapt Table A to allow a sole director to act, in which case ancillary changes to the articles need to be made to ensure that he can carry out certain actions alone (¶3460+). There are also restrictions on bodies corporate acting as sole directors to ensure that at least two separate legal persons run every company, which will remain in force until 6 April 2008.

Public companies, on the other hand, must have at least two directors (s 154(2) CA 2006). Public companies registered before 1 November 1929 used to be allowed to have one director, but this exception was repealed on 1 October 2007 when the relevant provisions of the new Companies Act came into force.

MEMO POINTS   Under the **new Companies Act**, every company will have to have at least one director who is an individual (s 155 CA 2006). If a company does not have the minimum number of directors, or does not have an individual in that office, the secretary of state will be able to order the company to make such an appointment (s 156 CA 2006). The implementation date for these provisions is yet to be announced at the time of writing.

2231 The number of directors is not subject to any **maximum**, although a limit may be imposed by the company's articles. **Table A** does not provide for a maximum, but allows the shareholders to impose one by ordinary resolution (reg 64 TA 1985).

MEMO POINTS   1. The minimum and maximum numbers of directors affect **board meetings**, particularly issues such as the quorum (¶3252+).
2. The draft **new model articles** will not contain a maximum number of directors.

A. Who can be a director?

2241 Any natural or legal person may hold the position of director, provided he is not prevented from acting by statute or the company's articles. There are various **factors** to consider in deciding whether or not a person can be a director. Some of these are personal, others relate to qualifications which a company requires its directors to have before they can hold office.

2242 Directors are usually **individuals**. It is also possible for a **corporation**, limited liability partnership or local authority to hold a directorship (*Re Bulawayo Market and Offices Co Ltd* [1907] 2 Ch 458). There are certain restrictions on a corporation holding office in another company relating to the company having a sole director (see ¶3460+).

> MEMO POINTS The **new Companies Act** will require every company to have at least one director who is an individual (s 155 CA 2006; the implementation date for this provision is yet to be announced at the time of writing). This is to address the difficulties of applying sanctions to corporate directors and to make it easier for third parties to identify who runs the company. The individual will be able to be a corporation sole or a person appointed because of another office he holds. If a company does not have an individual director, the secretary of state will be able to order it to make an appropriate appointment (s 156 CA 2006; the implementation date for this provision is yet to be announced at the time of writing). These provisions of the new Act will come into force later than the other provisions relating to directors to give companies time to appoint new directors where necessary.

1. Personal factors

2244 A **shareholder** of the company may also be a director and it is common for small family companies to be run by director/shareholders. The articles may restrict shareholders' ability to be directors, for example, by requiring that directors hold a certain number or type of shares (¶2254+).

The company **secretary** may also be a director, provided he is not the sole director (s 283(2) CA 1985). Further restrictions apply where the secretary and/or sole director are corporations (see ¶3460+).

The **auditor** of a company cannot also be its officer (s 27(1) CA 1989).

Comment: The **new Companies Act** will require statutory auditors to meet an "independence requirement" in order to be able to act from 6 April 2008. They will not meet this requirement if they are officers or employees of the company, amongst other things (s 1214 CA 2006).

> MEMO POINTS 1. The **new Companies Act** will not prohibit a company secretary from being the sole director. This is because companies will have to have at least one director who is a natural person to ensure that an identifiable person is responsible for the company (however, the implementation date for this provision is yet to be announced at the time of writing) and, from 6 April 2008, private companies will no longer be required to have a secretary (ss 155, 270 CA 2006). Public companies are obliged to have two directors in any event (s 154 CA 2006).
> 2. A **member of the Church of England clergy** cannot be a director of a company which carries on trade for a profit or gain (with the exception of companies which provide instruction or education for a profit) (ss 29, 30 Pluralities Act 1838 and s 11 Clergy (Ordination and Miscellaneous Provisions) Measure 1964, 1964 No. 6).

2245 A person (or corporate director) who is **disqualified** from acting as a director cannot be appointed as a director or be otherwise involved in the management of a company without the consent of the court. A **bankrupt** is automatically disqualified from acting as a director for the period of his bankruptcy (ss 11, 13 CDDA 1986). Table A provides that a director's office is automatically vacated if he becomes bankrupt or makes any arrangement or composition with his creditors, which widens the restriction to include directors subject to individual voluntary arrangements and informal agreements with their creditors as well.

Age

2246 Companies may include a **minimum age** limit in their articles, but this is not usual as they are more likely to require that their directors possess relevant experience if they want to impose such a restriction.

They may also impose a **maximum age** limit or related conditions on directors in their articles. Special rules regarding the appointment (or reappointment) of a director who is aged 70 or more used to apply to public companies and their private subsidiaries (ss 293, 294

CA 1985). These rules were repealed on 6 April 2007 when some provisions of the new Companies Act came into force (art 4 SI 2006/3428).

> *MEMO POINTS* 1. There is no specific prohibition on a **minor** acting as a director, but in practice he would not have the legal capacity to sign his consent to act. A minor is a person under 18 (s 1 Family Law Reform Act 1969), and they can enter into contracts, but the contracts are voidable before or within a reasonable period after they reach 18 (s 3 Minors' Contracts Act 1987).
> 2. The **new Companies Act** will introduce a minimum age of 16 for individual directors, although the secretary of state will be able to make regulations allowing under 16s to act as directors in certain circumstances (ss 157, 158 CA 2006; the implementation date for these provisions is yet to be announced at the time of writing). Any existing directors under 16 will automatically vacate office when this provision comes into force (s 159 CA 2006; the implementation date for this provision is yet to be announced at the time of writing). The new Act will also specify that if an underage director were to act, he would have the same duties and liabilities as a director of age.
> 3. Although direct and indirect **age discrimination** is unlawful, there is an exception from the prohibition of age-related limitations on employment for restrictions under statutory authority (reg 27 SI 2006/1031). Therefore, the minimum age limit in the new Companies Act will not breach these Regulations. However, companies must ensure that their own rules (whether in their articles, service contracts or employment policies) do not breach the prohibition. Companies would be better either to omit any such restrictions altogether, and assess prospective directors on their individual merits, or to place other objective qualification requirements on holding the office if this is absolutely necessary due to the type of work involved.
> For further details on age discrimination, see *Employment Memo*.

Nationality and place of residence

2250 There is no statutory requirement for a director to be of a particular nationality or resident in the UK. Directors are required to **declare** their nationality on the forms recording their appointment, as well as their usual residential address, unless they have obtained a confidentiality order (¶3907). The articles of a company may contain special provisions relating to a director's place of residence, for example requiring that he lives in the UK for at least a certain period of the year.

Directors who are **resident abroad** must ensure that they are able to discharge their duties to the company, otherwise they could be found to be liable to it in a number of ways (¶2317+). Articles often require directors to attend a certain proportion of board meetings as a minimum and/or provide for termination of a director's office if he is absent from board meetings for a certain period (see ¶2939+). Table A provides that a director who is not resident in the UK is not entitled to receive notices of board meetings (¶3238).

> *MEMO POINTS* 1. Some **non-British nationals** may be restricted as to the work they can do in this country. If there is any doubt as to whether such a person can take up office as a director, this should be checked with the Home Office Border and Immigration Agency.
> 2. The **new Companies Act** will allow directors to disclose an address for service to go on the public record, although the company will still have to keep a record of their residential addresses as well (¶3896/mp). These changes are expected to come into force by 1 October 2009.

Mental capacity

2251 There is no statutory requirement for directors to be of sound mind, but a **person of unsound mind** will not be capable of consenting to his appointment, as was held in a case in which a drug addict had purportedly consented to being appointed as a director (*Re CEM Connections Ltd* [2000] BCC 917).

Table A, on the other hand, stipulates that a director's office will **automatically** be **vacated** if he is or may be of unsound mind and is either (reg 81 TA 1985):
– admitted to a hospital for treatment under the Mental Health Act 1983; or
– a court order is made relating to his mental disorder for his detention or the appointment of a person to manage his property or affairs (e.g. a deputy).

Clearly, there is no point in appointing such a director as his office will be immediately vacated.

> *MEMO POINTS* 1. The draft **new model articles** will include similar provisions, allowing a director's appointment to be terminated where a doctor certifies that he is incapable of acting and will remain so for at least 3 months, or where a court order is made for the conduct of the

director's affairs on his behalf due to his mental incapacity (private companies limited by shares: art 18; public companies: art 21).

2. The **legislation** regarding mental incapacity has been altered recently. The part of the Mental Capacity Act 2005 dealing with the appointment of deputies came into force on 1 October 2007. Under the previous legislation (the Mental Health Act 1983), deputies were called "receivers" and could be appointed to exercise the same powers on behalf of a mentally incapacitated person. Any receivers appointed under the old legislation will be treated as deputies, with the same functions as they had before (Sch 5 Mental Capacity Act 2005). The parts of the Mental Health Act 1983 dealing with compulsory admission to hospital and guardianship and with patients subject to criminal proceedings or under sentence are still in force, as amended by the Mental Health Act 2007. However, Table A has not yet been amended to reflect these changes.

2. Objective qualifications

2253 There are no qualifications **required** of directors by the legislation. A company's articles may impose such requirements, for example by stipulating that directors hold certain certificates or have certain experience. More usually, this will be a matter of **policy** for the company or decided on a case by case basis. For example, if a company seeks to appoint a director who will have responsibility for financial matters, they will look for a candidate with appropriate experience, as if they were appointing an ordinary employee.

> MEMO POINTS   The Institute of Directors runs courses for directors enabling them to qualify as **chartered directors**. This qualification is increasingly a requirement of directors of large companies, particularly listed public companies. For more information on the qualification and other courses run by the Institute, see its website.

Requirement to hold shares

2254 A company's articles **may compel** its directors to hold a certain number of shares in the company as a condition of appointment to office, although it is not common in modern articles.

If the shareholding is a **condition precedent** to holding office, then the director's appointment will be void if he does not hold the requisite number of shares in the company prior to his appointment, even if he later obtains the required shareholding (*Re Percy & Kelly Nickel, Cobalt & Chrome Iron Mining Co, Jenner's Case* (1877) 7 Ch D 132). If the articles state that the shares must be **obtained within** a **certain period** of time, then the director can obtain the shares after he has been appointed, provided he does so within 2 months of his appointment or such shorter period as the articles provide (s 291(1) CA 1985).

> MEMO POINTS   The **new Companies Act** will not make any provision for directors' share qualification and will repeal the existing provision (Sch 16 CA 2006). Therefore, if companies wish to impose such a requirement, they will have to deal with it in their articles.

2255 Subject to any contrary provision in the articles, if a director **fails to acquire** or if he **ceases to hold** the requisite shareholding, he must vacate his office and can only be reappointed when he has obtained the qualifying shares (s 291(3), (4) CA 1985). A director who continues to act without fulfilling the share qualification commits an offence and is liable to a fine (¶9935).

B. Who appoints directors?

2266 **First appointments** made on incorporation are dealt with at ¶462 and ¶482. **Subsequent directors** can be appointed either to fill one or more vacancies which have been left by departing director(s) or to increase the number of directors who sit on the board (referred to as "additional directors"). Directors who are obliged to retire by rotation can also be **reappointed** (¶2927+). The **procedure** for appointing directors is normally set out in the company's articles of association.

> MEMO POINTS   Many companies are originally incorporated by a third party (such as a company formation agent) and bought "off-the-shelf" by those intending to run them (see ¶546). In the

case of these **shelf companies**, the first appointment of the "real" directors who will manage the company will be made in the same way as subsequent appointments for other companies, since officers will already have been appointed when the company was incorporated.

2267 For companies governed by Table A, the **power to appoint** a person either to fill a vacancy on the board or as an additional director is vested in both the shareholders and the existing board (regs 78, 79 TA 1985).

> MEMO POINTS 1. Ultimately in such companies, the shareholders have the final say as to who is appointed since any directors appointed by board resolution must retire at the next AGM and have to be **reappointed** (either actively or automatically by the shareholders (¶2927+)).
> 2. The draft **new model articles** will enable directors to be appointed either by ordinary resolution of the shareholders, or by the board (private companies limited by shares: art 17; public companies: art 19). Since private companies do not have to hold AGMs, directors appointed by the board will not have to retire at the next AGM. Instead, shareholders will have to remove such a director by ordinary resolution (which will not be able to occur by written resolution, because of the requirement for special notice, ¶3536+), or alter the articles to require board appointments to be approved by the shareholders. The draft new model articles for public companies, however, will contain this requirement (art 20).
> 3. For companies **incorporated on or after 1 October 2007** that adopt Table A, amendments have been made to certain provisions of Table A to correspond with the provisions of the new Companies Act which were in force by that date. regs 78, 79 TA 1985 have been amended for private companies. See ¶9915 for the details of these changes.

2268 Companies can choose whether to modify this power **in** their **articles**, for example by allowing both the board and the shareholders to exercise it, by permitting a class of shareholders to appoint a nominee director, or by delegating it to the board altogether. If the power is delegated solely to the board, shareholders cannot, in the ordinary course of things, exercise the power (but see ¶3130+ for where the power may revert back to them). If a company's **articles** are **silent** on the matter, the shareholders have an inherent power to appoint directors (*Woolf v East Nigel Gold Mining Company* (1905) 21 TLR 660).

Appointment by the shareholders

2270 Shareholders can make appointments to fill a vacancy, add to the board or reappoint a director retiring by rotation. The appointment will be **made at a** general meeting, or by written resolution. The candidate will be **nominated by** either:
– a shareholder who is qualified to vote at the meeting (reg 76 TA 1985, and see ¶3815+ for who can vote); or
– the directors.

In either case, **notice** of the meeting must be accompanied by notice of the proposed resolution to appoint, specifying the details which would appear on the register of directors in respect of the candidate (reg 77 TA 1985). These details are his: name, any former name, usual residential address (unless he has obtained a confidentiality order, ¶3907), nationality, business occupation, any previous directorships held in the last 5 years, and date of birth (s 289 CA 1985). If the candidate is a shareholder's suggestion, the shareholder must first give notice to the company of the (reg 76 TA 1985):
– proposed appointment;
– details which would need to be entered on the register; and
– written confirmation from the candidate of his willingness to be appointed.

The notice can be sent in hard copy, electronic form or in any other agreed form. The methods of communicating with companies are discussed at ¶3628 in the context of shareholders requisitioning meetings.

The **time limits** for the different types of notice as set out in the legislation and Table A are somewhat confusing as a result of the various requirements which apply. They are summarised in the table below, but in most cases the shareholders will have to notify the company of the proposed appointment between 28 and 35 clear days before the meeting. The company will have to give the shareholders at least 21 clear days' notice of both the meeting and the proposed resolution to appoint the director.

Candidate recommended by	Notice of proposed appointment to company	Notice of meeting [2,3]	Notice of proposed resolution [2,3]
Shareholder(s)	Between 14 and 35 clear days before meeting [1]	At least 21 clear days before meeting [4]	Between 14 and 28 days before meeting [5]
Directors	n/a		

Note:
1. Although TA 1985 requires shareholders to give the company between 14 and 35 clear days' notice, statute requires them to give the company special notice of resolutions to appoint directors as replacements for other directors (¶3536+). Therefore, in some cases it will be necessary to comply with both requirements, so shareholders will only have a window of between 28 and 35 clear days before the meeting.
2. To be sent to those entitled to notice of a meeting, see ¶3692+.
3. To comply with special notice requirements, the company will either have to send notice of the resolution to the shareholders with the meeting notice, or advertise the resolution in a suitable newspaper at least 14 days before the meeting (s 312 CA 2006). It also allows all meetings other than public company AGMs to be called on 14 clear days' notice. However, Table A requires 21 clear days' notice to be given of a meeting to consider a resolution appointing a director. Therefore, where a company is governed by Table A, notice of the proposed resolution will have to be sent with the meeting notice at least 21 clear days in advance.
4. reg 38 TA 1985. If company is not governed by Table A, follow articles; if articles are silent, 21 clear days' notice will have to be given of a public company AGM or 14 clear days' notice of a general meeting. Transitional measures applying only to companies incorporated on or after 1 October 2007 delete this requirement, so that the appropriate period of notice depends on whether the resolution is to be considered at a general meeting (14 clear days) or a public company's AGM (21 clear days) (regs 9, 20 SI 2007/2541).
5. Although Table A allows notice of the resolution to be given between 7 and 28 days before the meeting, the legislation requires the company to give the shareholders at least 14 days' notice of the resolution, reducing this window.

MEMO POINTS 1. The draft **new model articles** will not set out a similar procedure for appointing directors.
2. The **new Companies Act** will require slightly different information about directors to be registered, see ¶3896+. These provisions are expected to come into force by 1 October 2009.
3. For companies **incorporated on or after 1 October 2007** that adopt Table A, amendments have been made to certain provisions of Table A to correspond with the provisions of the new Companies Act which were in force by that date. regs 76, 77 TA 1985 have been altered for private companies. See ¶9915 for the details of these changes.

2271

The **appointment** will be **made by** the shareholders by ordinary resolution (reg 78 TA 1985). Companies can also set out their own procedures in their articles, for example, for a class of shareholders to appoint a nominee director. If a company's **articles are silent** as to how the shareholders should exercise their power to appoint directors, it can be done by ordinary resolution, subject to any restrictions imposed by the articles (*Worcester Corsetry Ltd v Witting* [1936] Ch 640).

MEMO POINTS 1. Alternatively, most companies can use the **written resolution** procedure.
2. If shareholders of **public companies** wish to appoint more than one director at one time, they must do so in separate resolutions, unless the shareholders first pass a resolution consenting to the directors being nominated, appointed or their appointments approved in the same resolution (s 160 CA 2006). Without this consent, any resolution dealing with more than one director will be void. There is a minor exception to this, where the directors are specified in the articles, the shareholders can alter the articles by one special resolution even if more than one director will be appointed as a result.
3. The draft **new model articles** will also enable shareholders to appoint directors by ordinary resolution (private companies limited by shares: art 17; public companies: art 19).
4. For companies **incorporated on or after 1 October 2007** that adopt Table A, amendments have been made to certain provisions of Table A to correspond with the provisions of the new Companies Act which were in force by that date. Minor amendments have been made to reg 78 TA 1985 for private companies. See ¶9915 for the details of these changes.

2272

When appointing new directors to office, the company's shareholders (as with the directors) must **act in the interests** of the company as whole and not simply for the benefit of the majority shareholder(s) (*Re H R Harmer Ltd* [1958] 3 All ER 689).

Appointment by the board

2274

The board can fill a vacancy and/or appoint additional directors by board resolution **provided** that (*Channel Collieries Trust Ltd v Dover, St Margaret's and Martin Mill Light Railway Co* [1914] 2 Ch 506):
– the power is not exclusively reserved to the shareholders in the articles; and
– those persons are willing to act as directors.

This power is also included in Table A (reg 79 TA 1985).

Appointment by the board will be **made by** board resolution. Appointments by boards operating under Table A effectively need to be approved by the shareholders at the next AGM, as the directors are required to retire and be re-appointed by the shareholders (reg 73 TA 1985). Only public companies and private companies whose articles specifically require are obliged to hold AGMs. Therefore, a new director will not have to be reappointed in most private companies as there will be no AGM. Shareholders can still remove directors by ordinary resolution if the board makes an appointment of which they do not approve. Alternatively, they could alter the articles to make board appointments subject to shareholder approval. Special rules apply to appointments by the board where it falls below the quorum, see ¶3265+.

> MEMO POINTS 1. Appointments of **alternate directors** by individual directors are dealt with at ¶3438+.
> 2. The draft **new model articles** will also allow boards to appoint directors (private companies limited by shares: art 17; public companies: art 19). Those for public companies will also require board appointments to be confirmed by the shareholders (art 20).
> 3. For companies **incorporated on or after 1 October 2007** that adopt Table A, amendments have been made to certain provisions of Table A to correspond with the provisions of the new Companies Act which were in force by that date. regs 73, 79 TA 1985 have been altered for private companies. See ¶9915 for the details of these changes.

Automatic reappointment

2276 Where a director has retired by rotation (¶2927+) he can be reappointed automatically at the same meeting, provided the shareholders have not:
– replaced him; or
– resolved not to reappoint him.

Appointing a director with unlimited liability

2278 If a company's memorandum states that the liability of its directors, or the managing director, is unlimited, the nomination of a person for that position (whether made by the directors or shareholders) must state that his liability will be unlimited (s 306(2) CA 1985). **Notice** of the unlimited liability also needs to be given to a proposed director by the company's (s 306(3) CA 1985):
– directors;
– secretary;
– managers; or
– promoters.

This ensures that the new director is fully aware of his increased liability.

Failure to include the statement in the proposal or to give notice to the proposed director renders the person at fault liable to a fine and also liable for any damage suffered by the proposed director as a result (s 306(4) CA 1985; ¶9935). It does not, however, affect the validity of the new appointment or the director's unlimited liability.

> MEMO POINTS 1. This also applies to the **appointment of managers**, where the memorandum states that their liability is unlimited. For the meaning of managers, see ¶2181/mp.
> 2. s 306 CA 1985 will be repealed by the **new Companies Act** because the memorandum will no longer contain such information (Sch 16 CA 2006). It is expected that this change will be effective by 1 October 2009.

C. Formalities of appointment

2288 Provisions relating to the formalities of directors' appointments are **found in** both statute and the articles. For appointments made on incorporation, see ¶482.

Each new director must provide **written consent** to his appointment. The **method** by which this is provided depends, for companies governed by Table A, on how the director is appointed. Companies not governed by Table A may make alternative provisions. In every case **Form 288a** must be completed (s 288(2) CA 1985), **signed by** the new director and an existing officer of the company and **filed** at Companies House within 14 days of the appointment. The details of the director's appointment are then entered on the register at Companies House as a matter of public record and advertised in the *Gazette* (ss 1077, 1078 CA 2006).

Appointment by shareholders	Appointment by directors
– Obtain **written notice** from director confirming his willingness to act (reg 76 TA 1985). This notice must accompany notice to shareholders of proposed resolution to appoint director; and – complete **Form** 288a (s 288(2) CA 1985)	Complete **Form** 288a (s 288(2) CA 1985)

MEMO POINTS 1. During the course of the directorship, any **changes** to the details registered at Companies House must be notified to the registrar on Form 288c.
2. The formalities of appointing **alternate directors** are dealt with at ¶3438+. Note that, even for temporary appointments, the same formalities apply to appointing an alternate as they do to appointing any other director.
3. As to whether a **director's residential address** needs to be included on the form, see ¶3907.
4. The **new Companies Act** will require companies to notify Companies House of any change in its directors or the particulars of directors already registered at Companies House (s 167 CA 2006, expected to come into force by 1 October 2009). Notice of a new appointment will have to include his consent to act, as well as the information that is needed to complete the register of directors and the new register of directors' residential addresses (¶3896/mp).
5. The names of Forms 288a and 288c, like the names of other **Companies House forms**, are taken from the section numbers of the legislation. As all of the section numbers will change under the new Companies Act, Companies House proposes to change the names of all of its forms to reflect their function rather than the relevant section number ("Working with Companies House: a consultation on the registrar's rules and related provisions which will apply under the Companies Act 2006"). At the time of writing, the new form names are not yet available.
6. For companies **incorporated on or after 1 October 2007** that adopt Table A, amendments have been made to certain provisions of Table A to correspond with the provisions of the new Companies Act which were in force by that date. reg 76 TA 1985 has been amended for private companies. See ¶9915 for the details of these changes.

2289 As well as the register kept by Companies House, companies must maintain their own **register of directors** (s 288(1) CA 1985). Following a new appointment, this register must be updated with his details. This is usually carried out by the company secretary, but failure to keep or update the register of directors will have consequences for the company and any officer in default (see ¶3894+).

MEMO POINTS The **new Companies Act** will also require companies to keep registers of directors and of their residential addresses, which will have to be updated when a new appointment is made (ss 162-165 CA 2006, expected to come into force by 1 October 2009).

2290 Appointments made at general or board meetings must be **recorded in** the minutes of that meeting in the usual way. A director's appointment at a board or general meeting which has been properly recorded in the minutes is deemed to be valid unless and until it is proved otherwise (ss 249(2), 356 CA 2006). Statute also requires that written resolutions of shareholders are recorded (s 355 CA 2006), and it is good practice for board written resolutions to be recorded as well.

D. Defects in appointment

2300 If the appointment of a director does not comply with any one of the various requirements, or he has been appointed by a body or person who did not have the authority to do so, that director will be a de facto director. Usually, such a director will not realise that there is a defect in his appointment and will continue to act as if he were a properly appointed director.

> **EXAMPLE** Defects in appointment can **arise where** any of the requirements in statute or the articles are not complied with, such as:
> 1. The articles require that directors hold a certain number of shares before they can be appointed (¶2254+). A director has been appointed but he does not in fact have the relevant shareholding.
> 2. The company has appointed a director, but Form 288a has not been filed at Companies House (¶2288+).

2301 If it is discovered that a director has not been appointed properly, or he does not meet the qualifying conditions for his appointment, his **acts on behalf of the company** will nevertheless be valid (s 161 CA 2006; reg 92 TA 1985). This includes his actions in relation to shareholders as well as third party transactions (*Dawson v African Consolidated Land and Trading Co* [1898] 1 Ch 6). This provision ensures that neither the company nor those who deal with it will be in a different position just because of a technical defect.

It **does not validate** the acts of a director who was never appointed, such as a shadow or some de facto directors (*Morris v Kanssen* [1946] 1 All ER 586); nor will it validate acts which would have been outside of the authority of a properly appointed director (*Craven-Ellis v Canons Ltd* [1936] 2 All ER 1066).

> **MEMO POINTS** 1. This saving provision does not validate the **defective appointment** itself, nor does it entitle the director in question to receive any **remuneration** arising from his appointment (although if he has performed valuable services for the company, he may be entitled to receive a fair price for those services, see ¶2698/mp).
> 2. The draft **new model articles** will not include an equivalent of reg 92 TA 1985 because the legislation deals with the issue instead (s 191 CA 2006).

2302 A third party may wish to **enforce** the **validation provisions**, for example so that the company cannot avoid an agreement just because it was made by a de facto director. The party in question must act in good faith and, in particular, must not have known of the defect in the appointment at the relevant time (*Channel Collieries Trust Ltd v Dover*, *St Margaret's and Martin Mill Light Railway Co* [1914] 2 Ch 506; *British Asbestos Co Ltd v Boyd* [1903] 2 Ch 439).

SECTION 3

Directors' duties

SECTION OUTLINE	¶¶
I. General duties	2333
A. Duties	2333
Codification of directors' duties in the new Companies Act	2334
1. Act within authority	2348
a. Types of authority	2350
Express actual authority	2352
Implied actual authority	2354
Ostensible authority	2361
Summary	2365
b. Instructions from the company	2368
2. Fiduciary duties	2373
a. Act within powers	2376
b. Promote the company's success	2379
c. Exercise independent judgment	2389
d. Avoid conflicts of interest and duty	2390
e. Account for profits	2398
f. Not misuse company property and/or information	2405
3. Care, skill and diligence	2411
B. Remedies for and consequences of breach of duty	2434
1. Availability of remedies	2438
Action for breach of contract	2446
Action in tort	2448
Action for breach of fiduciary duties	2451
2. Types of remedy	2463
a. Damages	2463
b. Injunctions	2467
c. Account for profits	2471
d. Restitution of property and tracing	2476
e. Removal of the director	2480
f. Consequences on transactions	2483
C. Relief from liability	2494
1. Ratification	2497
2. Relief provided by statute	2505
3. Indemnity and insurance	2512
II. Specific duties	2532
Civil liability	2534
Criminal liability	2536
A. Management duties	2548
1. General	2548
2. Act within limitations	2554
3. Substantial property transactions	2567
4. Liability for defrauding creditors	2577
5. Liability for company cheques etc	2580
B. Employment duties	2590
1. Health and safety	2590
2. Other employment duties	2596
a. Have regard to employee interests	2596
b. Immigration	2598
C. VAT	2606
D. Insolvency	2612

2317 Directors' duties derive from a number of **sources**. Companies can tailor them by imposing specific duties in a director's service contract as well as setting out those applicable to the board in the articles of association (¶3137+). Underlying such specific duties are those imposed on directors by common law and statute. These duties apply to all directors and are classed as:
– **general duties**, which used to be imposed by common law only, but some have been codified by the new Companies Act. The consequences of breach of these duties have not changed; and
– **specific duties**, which are those significant statutory duties and liabilities that directors may find themselves subject to when running their companies.

> MEMO POINTS   Companies can also be subject to **regulatory supervision**. Regulatory bodies may have the power to investigate companies' conduct, publish reports on them and impose sanctions, which can affect directors personally as well as their companies. Company investigations by the CIB are dealt with at ¶7195+.

2318 Since a limited company is treated as a separate legal entity having its own rights and duties, a director is generally not held **liable** for the company's debts and defaults, but he will be personally liable for particular breaches of the duties imposed on him by common law, statute or his service contract.

There are a number of remedies available in the event of a breach of the directors' general duties, and the action chosen will depend largely upon the nature and extent of the damage suffered, rather than the duty which has been breached. Therefore, these duties and remedies have been discussed as separate topics, with opportunities for relief from liability concluding the discussion of general duties. In contrast, in the case of breach of the specific statutory duties, the liabilities and reliefs are dependent on the terms of the statutory provision which sets out the duty. Therefore, these remedies and reliefs are discussed together with the duty to which they apply.

2319 Directors should consider their actions in the light of their duties as a whole, and remember that more than one duty may apply. Usually, the duties **overlap and work together**, for example, if a director uses knowledge he has gained from his position to enter into a transaction in the same line of business as his company and keeps the resulting profit, he will be in breach of his duties: not to misuse company information, to promote the company's success, to avoid conflicts of interest and duty and to account to the company for his profit. Similarly, breach of a director's specific statutory duties will usually indicate a failure to promote the company's success and/or to exercise care, skill and diligence in performing his functions.

Directors may find themselves in a situation where to follow **one duty breaches another**. For example, if shareholders instruct a director to take action which is not in the interests of the company, the director should weigh up the circumstances and if he decides, honestly and in good faith, not to obey his instructions, he is likely to be relieved from liability.

To whom do directors owe these duties?

2321 A director's **overriding duty** is owed to the company rather than to individual shareholders (*Percival v Wright* [1902] 2 Ch 421). Indeed, the new Companies Act specifically states that the directors' general duties codified in the new Act are owed by a director to his company (s 170 CA 2006; see ¶2334+ for a discussion of these duties).

2322 Directors of a holding company do not owe their duties to a **subsidiary**, unless they are also directors of the subsidiary (*Lindgren v L & P Estates Co Ltd* [1968] 1 All ER 917).

There are also circumstances in which directors will owe duties to **persons other than the company**, such as its employees or other third parties (for example, suppliers, creditors and customers). See ¶2451+ for when directors may owe fiduciary duties to the shareholders and others; and ¶7439+ for duties owed to others in insolvency.

2323 **In practice**, most small companies are owned and run by the same individuals, and so many breaches of duty can be ratified by the company, or are simply not challenged. Most of the cases on this topic have arisen where a company changes hands, new directors are appointed or it becomes insolvent, and it is the new shareholders or directors, or the insolvency practitioners, who institute proceedings to remedy directors' breaches of duty as a way of recovering the company's property and/or swelling its assets.

However, this is not to say that directors can disregard their duties, because there are serious consequences of breach of duty for the director in addition to the detriment caused to the company. Further and as a result of the proposed changes to company law and a number of high-profile cases relating to directors mismanaging companies, directors, shareholders and third parties dealing with directors will be increasingly aware of the standard that directors are expected to achieve.

I. General duties

A. Duties

A director's general duties arise from his position as agent of the company. They fall into **three categories** as follows:
- the duty to act within his authority;
- fiduciary duties; and
- the duty to exercise care, skill and diligence in performing his duties and functions.

The first duty is the same as for commercial agents. Fiduciary duties are imposed upon directors to monitor their ability to deal with the company's property. The duty to exercise care, skill and diligence derives from directors' negligence cases imposing higher standards on directors than on other agents because of their relationship with the company.

2333

Codification of directors' duties in the new Companies Act

Owing to the disparate sources, it can often be difficult for a director to ascertain exactly what his general duties are. High-profile cases relating to corporate misconduct have highlighted the issue, and the White Paper on company law reform concluded that the law on directors' duties and standards of care was largely inaccessible to non-lawyers.

2334

Therefore, the **new Companies Act** sets out directors' main general duties that were originally found in case law to ensure that they, shareholders and those who deal with companies are clear as to what these duties are and the general standard that directors are expected to achieve. The new Act states that these "general duties" should be interpreted and applied in the same way as the common law and equitable rules on which they are based, having regard to the same principles (s 170 CA 2006). Therefore, the existing case law remains relevant. The consequences of breach also follow the common law and equitable rules. With the exception of the duty to exercise reasonable care, skill and diligence, the duties are regarded as fiduciary (s 178 CA 2006). The new Act preserves the shareholders' control over the directors' conduct by retaining their ability to give prior authority for breach of duty, ensuring that the duties are not too restrictive (s 180 CA 2006).

2335

The duties may **overlap** in any given situation, and directors will be expected to comply with all applicable duties, with some logical exceptions (for example, a director will only have to promote the company's success to the extent that he acts within the constitution and other decisions, and the obligation to avoid conflicts will not apply to those which have already been disclosed to the board) (s 179 CA 2006). Further, compliance with these duties does not allow a director to breach any other legal prohibition or requirement. The duties work in tandem with other requirements made of directors, for example, the board can only approve a loan to a director if it is likely to promote the company's success. Companies can impose more onerous duties on their directors, but they cannot dilute those set out in the new Act.

At the time of writing, not all of the duties are **in force**. Therefore, those duties that are not yet in force are discussed in the memo points to their equivalent common law duties.

2337 The general duties **apply to** all directors, irrespective of any other duties or obligations contained in their service contracts. At the time of writing, only the first four general duties are current law, with the implementation date for the remaining provisions still to be announced. The table below summarises the principal duties, and cross-refers to the relevant paragraphs in which the law as it currently stands is explained, with the forthcoming changes noted in the memo points.

	Duty	Reference (CA 2006)	¶¶
1	**To act within their powers** – Act in accordance with the constitution (including any decision properly taken by the shareholders) – Exercise powers for their proper purpose	s 171	¶2376+
2	**To promote the company's success** – Act in a way which the director believes in good faith will promote the company's success for benefit of the shareholders as a whole [1] – Relevant factors to consider: long and short term consequences; interests of employees; the need to foster business relationships; the impact on the community and the environment; the need to maintain a business reputation; and the need to act fairly as between the shareholders	s 172	¶2379+
3	**To exercise independent judgment** – Except where the constitution or a valid decision of the company allows, e.g. by authorised delegation	s 173	¶2389
4	**To exercise reasonable care, skill and diligence** Exercise the same care, skill and diligence as a reasonably diligent person who has: – the general knowledge, skill and experience which may reasonably be expected of director in his position (objective benchmark); and – the general knowledge, skill and experience which that director actually possesses (subjective benchmark)	s 174	¶2411+
5	**To avoid conflicts of interest** – Covers all actual and potential conflicts between a director's interests and his company's, except those relating to transactions/arrangements with the company (which must be disclosed to the board under separate rules (see 7 and 8 below) – Shareholders can authorise the directors to proceed regardless of a conflict (s 180 CA 2006). In addition, the articles can allow the non-interested directors on the board to authorise an interested director to act despite his conflict [2] – There will be no breach of duty if the situation cannot reasonably be regarded as giving rise to a conflict	s 175 [3]	¶2390/mp
6	**Not to accept a benefit (including bribes) from third parties as a result of his office** A director can only accept a benefit if: – the company has authorised him to do so (s 181 CA 2006); or – acceptance cannot reasonably be regarded as creating a conflict of interest	s 176 [3]	¶2398/mp
7	**To disclose his interest in a proposed transaction/arrangement** See ¶3310	s 177 [3]	¶3308+
8	**To disclose his interest in an existing transaction/arrangement** See ¶3310	s 182 [3]	¶3308+

Note:
1. This duty to act for the shareholders' benefit is subject to the company's purposes (e.g. a company set up for charitable purposes will be obliged to benefit others) and to the requirements on the directors to consider creditors' interests in certain circumstances (e.g. where the company's solvency is in danger).
2. In the case of private companies, if articles do not specifically prevent this, the board will be able to do so; whereas public companies' articles will have to allow board to authorise an interested director to act expressly. In either case, the conflicted director will not be able to vote or count in the quorum on a resolution to allow him to act.
3. Not yet in force. The implementation date for these provisions is yet to be announced at the time of writing.

1. Act within authority

2348 A director must **obey** the company's **instructions** without departing from them, unless the company gives him the discretion to do so (*Fraser v BN Furman (Productions) Ltd* [1967] 3 All ER 57). This common law duty remains unchanged by the new Companies Act, although the new fiduciary duty to act within his powers is clearly related (see ¶2376+). Directors are also still under a specific statutory duty to act within the limits of the memorandum, which is discussed with other statutory duties at ¶2554+ but should be read in conjunction with this common law duty.

a. Types of authority

2350 A director can possess different types of authority to act on the company's behalf. "**Actual authority**", as the term implies, simply means that it is clear to a third party that the director has the authority to act on behalf of the company in relation to the relevant matter. This authority can be given expressly to him, or it can be implied from his position. "**Ostensible authority**" arises where he has been held out by the company as having the requisite authority when, in reality, he has no actual authority.

> MEMO POINTS 1. A **third party** wishing to **enforce a transaction** he has entered into with a company acting through a director must demonstrate that the director has the correct authority to do so. While he can look at the circumstances to check that the director has one of the types of authority described below, it can be difficult for him to make sure that the authority was properly delegated to the director by the board or the company in the first place. In appropriate circumstances, such a third party could include other directors of the company (provided they have played no part in bringing about the defect in question; *Smith v Henniker-Major & Co* [2002] 2 BCLC 655) and shareholders (provided they can show that they were "dealing with the company" rather than just acting as shareholders; *EIC Services Ltd v Phipps* [2005] 1 All ER 338, in which shareholders could not validate an unauthorised issue of bonus shares).
> Limitations on the **validity of the directors' authority** may arise because:
> – the board itself did not have the power to bind the company in that manner and so could not have delegated authority to do so to the director;
> – the board's ability to delegate the authority was curtailed by the memorandum, articles, a shareholder resolution or agreement; or
> – the board did not follow the correct procedures (e.g. the meeting was inquorate) when delegating the authority, thus rendering it invalid.
> Since it would be unfair to allow companies to avoid their contractual obligations as a result of such defects (over which the third party had no control), a third party may still enforce the transaction provided he dealt with the company in good faith (s 35A CA 1985; *Royal British Bank v Turquand* [1843-60] All ER Rep 435). This also means that, as long as a third party checks that the director has the requisite authority, he is not obliged to carry out further investigations into whether the board could delegate it to him (s 35B CA 1985). However, this does not allow the third party to turn a blind eye to suspicious circumstances which indicate that the authority is invalid, as he must deal in good faith; indeed, if he receives company property knowing that the director or board acted outside of his/its authority, he is liable as a constructive trustee to return it to the company (ss 35(3), 35A(5) CA 1985). In the case of procedural defects, such as an inquorate meeting delegating authority to a director, a third party is also prevented from enforcing the transaction if he had actual or constructive knowledge of the defect. Therefore, many parties to significant transactions insist on being provided with evidence of the director's authority.
> The enforcement and avoidance of transactions entered into in breach of a director's duties is discussed generally at ¶2483+.
> 2. The **new Companies Act** will restate ss 35A, 35B CA 1985 (s 40 CA 2006, expected to come into force by 1 October 2009).

Express actual authority

2352 Express actual authority can be **acquired** by:
a. a board resolution empowering a director to act on its behalf (this is the most usual method);
b. the articles of the company providing that one director can exercise a broad range of powers on behalf of the company (e.g. a managing director);
c. a shareholder special resolution directing the board to authorise a director to act on behalf of the company in a particular way; or

d. the shareholders appointing a director to transact certain business on behalf of the company.

A third party dealing with a director may require **evidence** of his authority to act, usually in the form of a copy or minute of the board resolution.

Implied actual authority

2354 Implied actual authority derives from the director's position and **status** within the company. If it is reasonable for a third party to assume that he has authority to act for the company in a certain way because of this position, authority can be implied. This protects third parties from being left with unenforceable agreements with a company simply because its director was unusually restricted in his ability to act.

> MEMO POINTS   Implied actual authority can also attach to **agents other than directors**, for example if a person is the company's "sales agent", a third party dealing with him can assume that he has authority to deal with the matters usually within a sales agent's remit, unless the circumstances indicate that this is not the case.

2355 Surprisingly little authority can be conferred on **ordinary directors** in this way. Acts for which they usually have implied actual authority are confined to **everyday managerial tasks**, such as:
– writing letters on the company's behalf;
– signing cheques;
– hiring junior personnel;
– ordering equipment;
– making pension and insurance arrangements;
– dealing with the company's professional advisers, such as accountants and lawyers; and
– sealing documents with the secretary as the other signatory (if the company has a seal).

These administrative acts are unlikely to cause any dispute as to their validity. More **significant activities** such as borrowing money on behalf of the company, selling its assets or making major purchases (e.g. of land) are not within the implied authority of an ordinary director.

2356 Implied authority cannot be attributed to a director just because he has a **title**, unless the title is in common business use with a generally understood scope of office, such as managing or finance director. Authority can be implied in the case of a **de facto director**, commensurate with the type of director he purports to be. The position of **chairman** of the board, however, will not imply any authority to deal with third parties in addition to that of ordinary directors, as it is merely an internal administrative position (*Hely-Hutchinson v Brayhead Ltd* [1967] 3 All ER 98).

2357 Whether authority to bind the company in a particular way can be implied will depend on the circumstances of each case (*Bishopsgate Investment Management Ltd v Maxwell (No 2)* [1994] 1 All ER 261).

> EXAMPLE
> 1. An **ordinary director** of B Ltd was appointed as chairman and also carried out the duties of a **de facto managing director**. Over a number of months he carried out transactions within the remit of a managing director without obtaining consent from the board and the board had made no attempt to prevent him from doing so. He then entered into a transaction with a third party on the company's behalf, which involved agreeing to make certain repayments to that third party and indemnifying him against loss. The board refused to honour the company's obligations under the transaction. The court held that there was no express actual authority and there was no implied actual authority arising from the director's role as chairman. However, there was implied actual authority derived from his role as de facto managing director and so the company was bound by the transaction (*Hely-Hutchinson v Brayhead Ltd* [1967] 3 All ER 98).
> 2. EHM Co had no formally appointed officers, but three individuals purported to act as **ordinary directors**. A person calling himself the company secretary instructed the company's bank to pay cheques signed by these individuals, and provided a copy of a "resolution" to that effect. The company exhausted its bank account and was wound up. The bank was not liable to account to the liquidator for the sums paid out, despite the individuals having no authority to sign the cheques because they were not directors. The court reasoned that if the bank had looked at the company's memorandum and articles and visited its premises, it would still have concluded that the three individuals had the status of directors and, therefore, that they had implied actual authority to carry out such administrative tasks (*Mahony v East Holyford Mining Co* [1874-90] All ER Rep 427).

Whether authority is implied can also depend on **who is trying to establish or challenge a director's authority** because that person cannot assert that a director has implied authority if he knows or ought to know that the director did not. For example, a managing director was not allowed to rely on his implied authority to commence litigation in the company's name when the powers of management were vested in the board as a whole (*Mitchell & Hobbs (UK) Ltd v Mill* [1996] 2 BCLC 102). The challenge to the managing director's actions in this case was an internal one, and clearly both the managing director and shareholders knew that it was a decision that should have been made by the board. By contrast, a third party dealing with a managing director could have assumed that he had extensive authority (actual and ostensible) to act on that company's behalf.

Ostensible authority

Even if a director has no actual (express or implied) authority to act on the company's behalf in a particular way, he can be said to have ostensible, or apparent, authority if the company makes representations to that effect to the third party. Ostensible authority **can be used to** establish authority where no actual authority exists, or to extend the director's actual authority to additional acts (*Hely-Hutchinson v Brayhead Ltd* [1967] 3 All ER 98; *First Energy (UK) Ltd v Hungarian International Bank* [1993] BCLC 1409). This prevents a company evading its obligations to a third party who had been told that its director had authority to bind the company.

To **establish** that a director has ostensible authority, the third party must demonstrate that (*Freeman and Lockyer v Buckhurst Park Properties (Mangal) Ltd* [1964] 1 All ER 630):

a. a representation that he had authority to enter into that type of contract on behalf of the company was made to the third party;

b. the representation was made by a person or persons who had actual authority to manage the business of the company (this representation cannot therefore have been made by the director in question); and

c. the third party was induced by this representation to enter into the contract, i.e. he relied on it.

> MEMO POINTS   The case sets out a fourth criterion for a third party to establish, namely that the company's memorandum and articles allowed it to enter into a contract of the kind sought to be enforced, or to delegate authority to do so. However, this is obsolete now that a **third party** can rely on statutory provisions to **enforce the contract**, ¶2350/mp.

The most common way of **making the representation** is to appoint the director to a particular office, such as managing director, without expressly delegating any powers to him but allowing him to carry out the activities associated with that office (or at least not preventing him from doing so) (*Freeman and Lockyer v Buckhurst Park Properties (Mangal) Ltd* [1964] 1 All ER 630). However, it is not sufficient merely to appoint a person as an ordinary director to give rise to ostensible authority, without further representation(s) that he has additional authority.

If the third party is aware of any **circumstances** which would prevent the director from having authority or which would limit that authority, he cannot claim to have relied on the director's ostensible authority (*Rolled Steel Products (Holdings) Ltd v British Steel & Corp* [1985] 3 All ER 52). Whether a third party can be said to have been aware of such circumstances will depend upon the facts. If, for example, the director is entering into a particularly **unusual transaction**, the third party cannot rely on the director's ostensible authority and must check with the company that the proposed transaction is valid.

> EXAMPLE
> 1. Where a director paid cheques made out to the company into his own bank account, this was enough to put the bank on notice that the **transactions were unusual** and it should have checked with the company that the director had authority to pay the cheques in before allowing him to do so instead of relying on his ostensible authority (*A L Underwood Ltd v Bank of Liverpool* [1924] All ER Rep 230).
> 2. A deputy managing director of DC Ltd, Mr T, signed undertakings and acknowledgements of DC Ltd and its holding company DG Ltd's indebtedness to a third party (in substantial sums) without actual authority. The liquidator of the third party subsequently sought to rely on these letters. Mr T appeared to have ostensible authority to sign the letters, arising out of a course of dealing with the third party in which DC Ltd acquiesced. However, owing to the **suspicious circumstances** of which the court found that the third party was aware (which included the director acting in breach of his fiduciary duties for his own benefit rather than the company's, the extremely onerous nature of the

documents and the fact that signing the documents was not in the usual course of business), he did not act in good faith by failing to check Mr T's authority and therefore was not entitled to rely on Mr T's ostensible authority to bind the company (*Hopkins v TL Dallas Group Ltd* [2005] 1 BCLC 543).

Summary

2365 The following flowchart illustrates how to **determine whether or not** a director has **authority** to bind the company.

Flowchart scenario:

Mr X wants to enter into a contract with A Ltd. He deals with Mr B who acts on A Ltd's behalf. To work out whether Mr B has the authority to bind A Ltd, Mr X should ask himself the following questions:

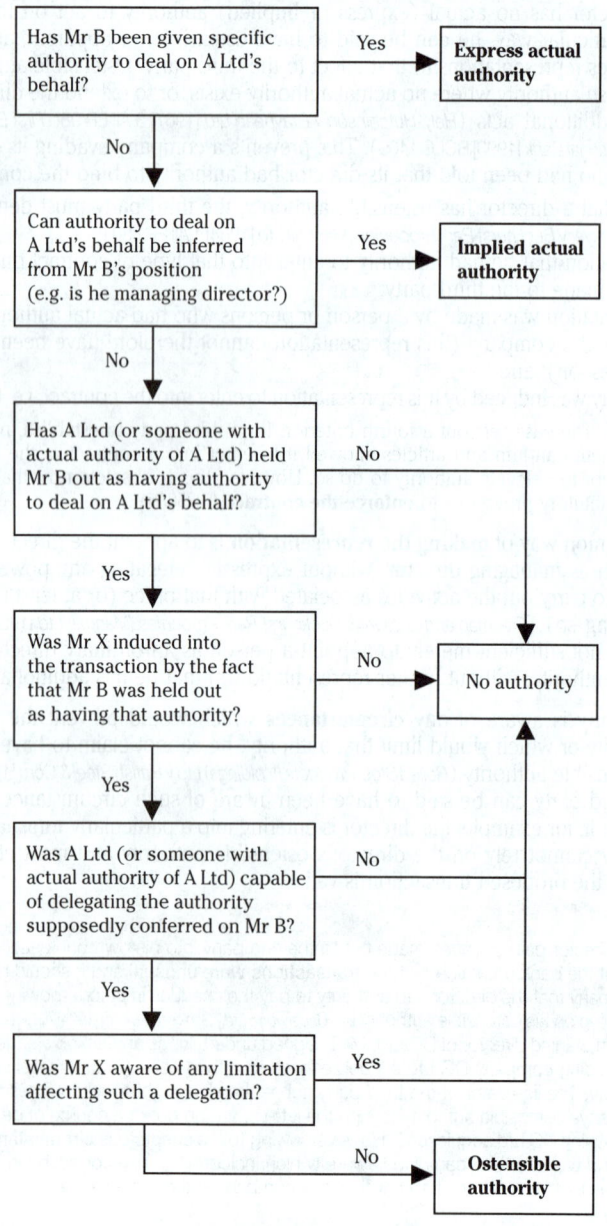

b. Instructions from the company

A director may have **vague** or **unclear** instructions, or **no specific instructions** at all, in which case he will discharge his duty to act within his authority by following a reasonable course of action in what he believes to be the company's best interests. Directors are usually granted a wide discretion in the company's articles to act on its behalf. In exercising his discretion, a director must always work within the boundaries his powers as set out in the memorandum, articles, shareholder resolutions and agreements. As long he acts within these powers when acting on vague or non-existent instructions, he will not be in breach of this duty.

If the directors obey the instructions of the shareholders, they will not usually be liable for breach of duty even if the decision is **commercially unsound** (*Multinational Gas and Petrochemical Company v Multinational Gas and Petrochemical Services Ltd* [1983] 2 All ER 563). However, directors cannot expect illegal acts to be excused on this basis (e.g. wrongful or fraudulent trading or other statutory breaches).

2368

2. Fiduciary duties

A "**fiduciary**" **is** someone who has undertaken to act for or on behalf of another in circumstances which give rise to a relationship of trust and confidence (*Bristol and West Building Society v Mothew (t/a Stapley & Co)* [1996] 4 All ER 698).

Since they are their company's agents, directors **occupy a fiduciary position** towards the company (*Imperial Mercantile Credit Association v Coleman* (1873) LR 6 HL 189): the directors have control over the company's property, the company (their principal) has placed trust and confidence in them to deal with that property properly on its behalf and gives them the power to do so. Fiduciary duties are imposed on directors by the law of equity to prevent them from exercising their powers to the detriment of the company, or otherwise abusing their position.

The general directors' duties set out in the **new Companies Act** are treated as fiduciary duties, with the exception of the duty to exercise reasonable care, skill and diligence (s 178 CA 2006). Therefore, they are discussed below.

> MEMO POINTS 1. Fiduciary duties are distinct from and more far-reaching than the duty of fidelity which applies to all **employees** and therefore all employed directors.
> 2. Since the agency relationship arises between directors and the company, fiduciary duties are primarily **owed to** the company. Fiduciary duties are **not owed to** individual shareholders or creditors (*Multinational Gas and Petrochemical Company v Multinational Gas and Petrochemical Services Ltd* [1983] 2 All ER 563), unless a special relationship has arisen between the parties (see ¶2451+).

2373

Fiduciary duties may continue **after the directorship ends**. For example, directors cannot resign and then take advantage of a business opportunity fostered by his company (see ¶2396+).

> MEMO POINTS The **new Companies Act** specifically states that the duties to avoid conflicts of interest and not to accept benefits from third parties continue to apply to a director once he has left office (s 170 CA 2006). Although this section is in force, the implementation date for the sections containing the actual duties is yet to be announced at the time of writing (ss 175, 176 CA 2006).

2374

A **de facto director** is subject to the same fiduciary duties as a de jure director, although the position of a **shadow director** depends upon the circumstances of the case. For instance, if a shadow director did not deal with the company's assets directly, and did not claim to have the right to do so, fiduciary duties in relation to the property could not be imposed on him (*Ultraframe (UK) Ltd v Fielding* [2005] EWHC 1638 (Ch)).

2375

a. Act within powers

Directors must act in accordance with the company's constitution and only exercise their powers for the purposes for which they are conferred (s 171 CA 2006). This duty, codified in the new Companies Act, was part of the common law fiduciary duty on directors to act

2376

honestly and in good faith in the interests of the company and for a proper purpose. The same case law is still to be used in interpreting the codified duty, and so is discussed below (s 170 CA 2006).

This duty is closely **linked to** directors' statutory duty to act within the limitations of the memorandum (this is contained in the Companies Act 1985 and has not yet been repealed, see ¶2554+) as well as their common law duty to act within their authority (see ¶2348+).

2377 To judge whether a director has exercised his powers for their **proper purposes**, firstly the relevant power must be examined in each case, together with any limitations placed on it, and then the question of whether the dominant purpose for which it was exercised was a proper one must be considered (*Howard Smith Ltd v Ampol Petroleum Ltd* [1974] 1 All ER 1126).

Although this question depends upon analysing what the directors believed at the time, it is subject to objective analysis by the court. It is therefore possible for the directors to act for an improper purpose, even if they believed that they were acting in good faith and in the interests of the company (see example 1 at ¶2387).

> EXAMPLE
> 1. The duty can be breached by using company **assets** for purposes other than those intended, e.g. using company money to pay an unauthorised commission (*Re Faure Electric Accumulator Co* (1888) 40 Ch D 141).
> 2. The duty can be breached where the motive for the decision or transaction is to confer an unauthorised **benefit** on **third parties**, e.g. subjecting company property to a charge for the benefit of a parent company (*Charterbridge Corporation Ltd v Lloyds Bank Ltd* [1969] 2 All ER 1185).

b. Promote the company's success

2379 Directors must act in a way that they consider, in good faith, would be most likely to promote the success of the company for the benefit of the shareholders as a whole (s 172(1) CA 2006). This codified general duty, together with the one to act within their powers, is the equivalent of the common law directors' duty to **act honestly and in good faith** in exercising their powers in what they consider to be the **interests of the company** and for a proper purpose (*Re Smith & Fawcett Ltd* [1942] 1 All ER 542). This was described as directors' "fundamental duty" (*Item Software (UK) Ltd v Fassihi* [2005] 2 BCLC 91).

Guidance on how to apply this duty can be found in both the new legislation and the previous case law (s 170 CA 2006).

2380 The legislation sets out certain **factors** for directors **to consider** when making a decision (s 172(1) CA 2006):
– the likely long-term consequences of the decision;
– the interests of the company's employees;
– the need to foster business relationships (with customers, suppliers, etc) and to maintain a reputation for good business conduct;
– the impact of the decision on the community and environment; and
– the need to act fairly between different shareholders.

This is not an exhaustive list of matters for directors to consider; it merely sets out the basic factors that should play a part in company decision making (*Duties of Company Directors: Ministerial Statements*, June 2007). Directors cannot assume that because they appear to have run through the list, they will automatically comply with the duty. Decision making is not a box-ticking exercise; directors must **give proper consideration** to these, and any other relevant, issues. These matters are subsidiary to the company's overall purpose, since it would not be possible for directors to make decisions that benefited all interested groups all the time. For example, a decision to make employees redundant would clearly not be in the employees' interests, but may well be in the interests of the company as a whole.

The drafting of this provision of the new Companies Act was controversial because there were concerns that it would place an increased burden on directors by requiring them to investigate additional matters when making decisions and to **record** their conclusions on each of the above factors for every decision. However, the Government has made it clear that the list is not intended to change the way directors make decisions (*Duties of Company Directors: Ministerial Statements*, June 2007). These should be the sort of factors directors consider when making decisions anyway, and there is no additional requirement to prove that each factor was looked at. This is not to say that directors do not have to keep proper records of their decisions. Especially where a decision is significant or controversial, or where it will have a serious impact on one of the factors listed above, it would be good practice for the board to record its conclusions on the relevant factors in the minutes. This will help to justify the board's position if a dispute arises.

Components

Honesty and good faith (or, "bona fides") can be difficult to judge, and will depend upon the circumstances. Lack of honesty and good faith is often demonstrated by the directors acting for their own benefit. The court set out a test comprising three questions which it considered helpful in trying to determine whether a director had adhered to the common law version of this duty, which will still be useful in interpreting the codified duty (*Rolled Steel Products (Holdings) Ltd v British Steel & Corp* [1985] 3 All ER 52):
– Is the transaction reasonably incidental to the company's business?
– Was the transaction entered into in good faith?
– Was it entered into for the benefit and to promote the prosperity of the company?

The court has given further **guidance** on approaching whether the directors acted according to this duty (*Howard Smith Ltd v Ampol Petroleum Ltd* [1974] 1 All ER 1126):
– look at the powers expressed in the memorandum, articles, shareholder resolutions and agreements;
– consider them in the context of contemporary business conditions and the usual limits on powers; and
– look at the substantial purpose for which the power was exercised. Was this a proper purpose?

2382

> EXAMPLE
> 1. A company was subject to two competing **takeover bids**. The directors had made the lower bid, and they advised the shareholders to reject the higher one. The court held that the directors should have given the shareholders all of the facts behind both bids so that the shareholders could make up their own minds as to which to accept. Not to do so showed a lack of good faith and resulted in unfair prejudice to the shareholders (*Re a Company (No 008699 of 1985)* [1986] BCLC 382).
> 2. The directors of V Ltd proposed to **increase the share capital** of the company for a rights issue of shares. If the 49% shareholder could not afford to purchase his portion of the issue, his shareholding would be diluted to 10%. The court granted an injunction to restrain the directors from following this course of action, as they were motivated by a desire to benefit their own position and not that of the company (*Pennell, Sutton and Moraybell Securities Ltd v Venida Investments Ltd*, 25/7/74, unreported).
> 3. A contrasting case concerned a company which was under an **obligation to issue shares** (pursuant to an option agreement, which was enforced by a court order for specific performance) and the directors (who were also shareholders) had given an undertaking to court to use their best endeavours to obtain listing for the shares. The Stock Exchange required the share issue to be subject to shareholder consent at a general meeting, and the circular sent out regarding the meeting made no recommendation either way, leaving the decision to the shareholders. The court refused to restrain the director/shareholders from voting against the resolution because, as shareholders, they were entitled to vote as they chose on the resolution (even if they voted in their own interests and not those of the company). On the facts, however, the court ordered that the circular should be re-issued because it did not comply with the necessary requirements as the lack of a recommendation showed that the directors were not using their best endeavours to obtain listing (*Northern Counties Securities Ltd v Jackson & Steeple Ltd* [1974] 2 All ER 625).

The "**success of the company**" does not necessarily mean its profitability. For most commercial companies, success will be measured in terms of a long-term increase in value, but the concept of success will be different for each company, depending on what the shareholders collectively want the company to achieve (*Duties of Company Directors: Ministerial Statements*, June 2007). The directors can determine the company's purposes by looking at the company's constitution, shareholder decisions and any other relevant information

2383

(e.g. policy documents). For companies such as charities and community interest companies, the measure of success may be entirely altruistic. Therefore, if the company's purposes include those for the benefit of others, the directors should adapt this duty accordingly rather than just acting for the benefit of the shareholders (s 172(2) CA 2006).

2384 This duty must be exercised **for the benefit of** the shareholders as a whole, or for the benefit of others if the company's purposes so state (s 172(1), (2) CA 2006). This may involve balancing the conflicting interests of different shareholders, for example.

If **different groups are affected** by a decision, the directors must act fairly and strike a balance between their interests (*Henry v Great Northern Railway Co* (1857) 1 De G & J 606). The key to such a balancing act is that the directors remain free to exercise their judgment in the best interests of the company, and are not obliged or persuaded to act for one group or another. If the directors have made an objective decision which happens to favour one group over another, they will not be in breach of this duty (*Boulting v Association of Cinematograph and Allied Technicians* [1963] 1 All ER 716). On the other hand, if the interests of the company have been **subordinated** to those of the directors, the directors will be in breach of duty even if there is no evidence of dishonesty or of the directors having personally benefited from the decision (*Re W & M Roith Ltd* [1967] 1 All ER 427).

EXAMPLE Where groups of shareholders were **treated differently** on an allotment of shares, the court found that there was no unfairness because the power to allot shares was vested in the directors for them to exercise fairly, which does not necessarily mean equally (*Mutual Life Insurance Co of New York v The Rank Organisation Ltd* [1985] BCLC 11).

2385 If the company is **insolvent** (or is in danger of becoming insolvent), the interests of the creditors become the interests of the company (s 172(3) CA 2006; *Dawson International plc v Coats Patons plc* [1990] BCLC 560). However, the directors still need to act in the best interests of the company as a whole, and must not focus on the interests of individual creditors (*Re Horsley & Weight Ltd* [1982] 3 All ER 1045).

The duty as a whole

2387 Whether a director has complied with this duty is a **subjective** question, depending upon a director's judgment. If he can show that he engaged the company in a particular transaction honestly, believing that it was beneficial to the company, then the court will usually be satisfied that the director acted within this duty, even if on the facts or with the benefit of hindsight the transaction was not in the best interests of the company. It is not the court's job to make commercial decisions for the company. Therefore, if a course of action was one of a number of reasonable options open to a company, the court will not interfere in the decision simply because a section of the company disagrees with it (*Howard Smith Ltd v Ampol Petroleum Ltd* [1974] 1 All ER 1126).

However, the director's belief must be reasonable in the circumstances. The court will not tolerate a reckless, fraudulent or irrational transaction which is not genuinely in the best interests of the company simply because a director claims to have believed that it was in the company's interests.

EXAMPLE
1. The directors of C Ltd, faced with a **takeover bid**, decided honestly and in good faith that it was not in the best interests of the company because the proposed change in the business would upset the employees. The directors exercised their power to allot shares to build up the number of votes against the takeover. Although the directors believed that they were acting in the best interests of the company, they were held to be in breach of their fiduciary duty because they had exercised their power to allot shares for a collateral purpose, i.e. to manipulate the spread of voting (*Hogg v Cramphorn Ltd* [1966] 3 All ER 420).
2. As part of this duty, a director must **disclose his own wrongdoings** to the company (*Item Software (UK) Ltd v Fassihi* [2005] 2 BCLC 91).

c. Exercise independent judgment

2389 A director must exercise independent judgment (s 173(1) CA 2006). Generally speaking, this means that he **cannot allow others to** influence his decisions or to make decisions for him. However, a strict interpretation of this rule would make managing a company very difficult, so various exceptions apply to make it much more practical.

A director **will not breach** this duty if he:

a. acts in accordance with an **agreement** entered into by the company which restricts the exercise of the directors' discretion (s 173(2) CA 2006). For example, the company may have entered into a joint venture agreement that prevents the directors from allotting shares for a certain period;

b. acts in a way authorised by the company's constitution (s 173(2) CA 2006). Most articles allow directors to **delegate** their functions to others, but if they are silent on the matter, the shareholders can authorise specific delegation by special resolution (see ¶3404+ for a full discussion of delegation of directors' powers). Delegation of a director's office may also be permitted. It is common for articles to permit directors to appoint alternates; authority to assign a director's office is also possible but less common. However, since a director is appointed personally, he cannot delegate his appointment altogether. If an unauthorised delegation is made, not only will the director breach this duty, but the delegation itself will be void; or

c. relies on the **advice** or work of others in making his decisions (*Duties of Company Directors: Ministerial Statements*, June 2007). This allows directors to seek professional advice from solicitors and accountants, for example, and base their decisions on it. However, directors must still exercise independent judgment, so a director cannot evade this duty by simply following advice from others blindly.

d. Avoid conflicts of interest and duty

2390 Directors are under a duty to avoid any conflict between their own interests and duties and those of the company. It would appear that putting himself in a position of **potential** conflict will not in itself fall foul of this duty, provided that if the situation develops into an actual conflict of interest, he acts appropriately.

> EXAMPLE
> 1. A director wants to sell his own land to the company: his interests (e.g. to get the best price) are likely to conflict with the company's.
> 2. A director of A Ltd takes up a directorship of B Ltd: the duties he owes to the two companies may conflict, especially if the companies operate in the same field.
> 3. A director enters into a transaction with a third party to which the company is not a party, but has a specific interest, e.g. it is pursuing that business opportunity as well (*Regal (Hastings) Ltd v Gulliver* [1967] 2 AC 134).
> 4. The company enters into a transaction with someone connected to the director, e.g. a family member.

MEMO POINTS The **new Companies Act** will codify this duty (s 175 CA 2006; the implementation date for this provision is yet to be announced at the time of writing). The scope of the codified duty will encompass the common law duty to avoid conflicts of interest and duty as well as that not to misuse company property or information. The statutory duty is widely drafted: directors will have to avoid situations in which they have, or could have, a direct or indirect interest or duty that conflicts, or may conflict, with the interests of the company. Therefore, unlike the current common law duty, potential conflicts are specifically covered. Conflicts of interest arising out of transactions or arrangements of the company will be dealt with under separate provisions (¶3308+). There will be a common sense exception to this duty so that directors in situations that cannot reasonably be regarded as giving rise to a conflict of interest will not breach the duty. In addition, the board will be able to authorise a director to act despite a conflict, provided that:
– in the case of a private company, there is nothing in the articles stopping it from doing so; or
– in the case of a public company, the articles allow it to do so.
An interested director will not be able to count in the quorum or the voting on a resolution to authorise him to act despite his conflict.

Common conflict situations

2392 Breach of this duty has arisen particularly where a director has pursued for his own benefit a **business opportunity** in which his company has a specific interest. The duty is not reduced by the fact that the company would not have chosen to pursue the business opportunity, unless there was an actual independent decision by the board to that effect (*Industrial Development Consultants Ltd v Cooley* [1972] 2 All ER 162; *Kingsley IT Consulting Ltd v McIntosh* [2006] All ER (D) 237 (Feb)). Nor is it reduced by the fact that the company could not have pursued the business opportunity, even if it had wanted to (e.g. because it had insufficient funds) (*Regal (Hastings) Ltd v Gulliver* [1967] 2 AC 134).

> EXAMPLE
> **Conflict**
> 1. If a director carries out work for a third party which the company could have done, he will have breached this duty to the company and will be liable to account for any profit he has made as a result (*Industrial Development Consultants Ltd v Cooley*, above).
> 2. If a director fails to inform his company of a particular business opportunity which it could pursue, this would strongly indicate a breach of duty (*CMS Dolphin Ltd v Simonet* [2001] 2 BCLC 704).
>
> **No conflict**
> A director was held not to have breached his fiduciary duties to his company, despite arranging to work for the company's principal client during his notice period. He had not sought work for the client, and did not start working for it until after his resignation from the company took effect. He had resigned because his relationship with the other director and shareholder had broken down completely and his wife had been made redundant from the company. There was no evidence of disloyalty or conflict of interest, or that he had resigned in order to obtain the client's work for himself. The client had, in fact, approached the director and offered him the work because it wanted to ensure continuity of service for its own clients. The Court of Appeal stressed that this case, as with all breach of fiduciary duties cases, was decided on its particular facts and that a similar case had not been before the courts before (*Foster Bryant Surveying Ltd v Bryant and another* [2007] EWCA Civ 200).

2393 Conflicts also frequently arise where a **director** is on the board of **more than one group company**. Although this is not automatically a conflict situation, directors must be careful to separate out the interests of the different companies and not put the interests of one group company (e.g. the holding company) over another (e.g. the subsidiary) (*Bell v Lever Bros Ltd* [1932] AC 161; *Scottish Co-operative Wholesale Society Ltd v Meyer* [1958] 3 All ER 66).

Nominee directors can be particularly susceptible to such conflicts.

2394 It should be noted that if a director is **also a shareholder**, when he is acting in that capacity he is permitted to vote as he wishes at general meetings and can therefore put his own interests before the company's (¶3824+).

> MEMO POINTS Directors used to have a statutory duty to **disclose** their **interests in shares and debentures** in the company, but the relevant provisions were repealed on 6 April 2007 when some of the new Companies Act was brought into force.

Managing a conflict situation

2396 A director can usually manage a conflict situation by undertaking a combination of the following **actions**:
– declaring his interest;
– not voting on the matter on which he is conflicted;
– taking the other directors' advice on how he should handle the situation;
– accounting to the company for any profit he makes; and/or
– (in extreme cases, and where he does so in good faith) resigning from office.

It is common for a director, after full disclosure of his position, to be able to **obtain consent** from the company to act in certain circumstances where a conflict would arise. Such permission can be set out in the company's articles (¶3308+) or be given on a case by case basis by shareholder resolution. On the other hand, a company may wish to **strengthen the duty**, for example, by specifically preventing a director from acting for another company in his service contract or the articles.

2397 In conflict situations, a director cannot necessarily avoid the conflict by tendering his **resignation** (*Industrial Development Consultants Ltd v Cooley* [1972] 2 All ER 162). **Former directors** must not take advantage of a business opportunity which the company was actively pursuing if this was their motivation for resigning, for example, by keeping the conflict secret.

This is balanced by the doctrine against **restraint of trade**, under which those former directors who were also employees are permitted to use their own skill and knowledge (including, for example, commercial information learned during the directorship) for their own benefit in competition with the company once the employment relationship has ended. This overlaps with the duty not to misuse company property and information (¶2405+).

> EXAMPLE
> 1. Messrs DA, M, WA and S were directors of BMT Ltd. They **planned to leave** the company to **set up a rival business**, MIT Ltd. Mr DA left first, and advertised for staff for MIT Ltd. The others resigned shortly afterwards. Mr DA was not in breach of duty in leaving, setting up a rival business and inviting employees to join him. The others were in breach of duty for not disclosing to BMT Ltd that a rival business was trying to poach its staff, and for not reporting each other's breaches of duty in their complicity with the plan (*British Midland Tool Ltd v Midland International Tooling Ltd* [2003] 2 BCLC 523).
> 2. Mr U was director of IEF Ltd. He resigned because he was dissatisfied with IEF Ltd. He established a business in the same field, and acquired work which IEF Ltd had previously undertaken. Mr U was not in breach of duty because IEF Ltd had not been actively seeking repeat business from that particular source and his **resignation** was not motivated by a desire to take that opportunity for himself. Nor was he in breach for using his knowledge about the industry after his resignation – to hold otherwise would have breached the **restraint of trade** principle (*Island Export Finance Ltd v Umunna* [1986] BCLC 460).

> MEMO POINTS 1. The judge in *British Midland Tool Ltd v Midland International Tooling Ltd* (above) was of the opinion that a director should resign once he has irrevocably resolved to engage in a competing business and takes **preparatory steps** towards doing so without informing his company. However, in a recent judgment it was commented, obiter, that this view was probably too prescriptive since the point at which preparations for setting up a rival business become unlawful will turn on the facts of each case (*Shepherds Investments Ltd v Walters* [2006] EWHC 836 (Ch); see ¶2472 for more on this case).
> 2. The codified duty under the **new Companies Act** will specifically apply to former directors (s 170(2) CA 2006).

e. Account for profits

2398 The general rule is that a director must account to the company for any profits he makes, and is sometimes referred to as the "fair dealing" rule. This is an **automatic** duty, and is imposed even if the director has acted honestly in obtaining the profit and/or the company has allowed him to make (but not to keep) it. Undisclosed profits are known as "**secret profits**", and must be accounted for. Directors who disclose their profits may be permitted by the shareholders to retain them.

> MEMO POINTS 1. A director becomes a **constructive trustee** over any profit he makes, holding it for the benefit of the company. For the consequences of this, see ¶2451+.
> 2. The **new Companies Act** will codify this duty (s 176 CA 2006; the implementation date for this provision is yet to be announced at the time of writing). Directors will not be able to accept a benefit from a third party (i.e. a person other than the company) either because he is a director or because of him doing, or not doing, something as a director if to do so could give rise to a conflict of interest. This will not include payments for services to the company, for example where a director is paid by his company's holding company. The word "benefit" is wide enough to encompass non-financial benefits. It will apply to former as well as current directors (s 170(2) CA 2006).

2399 The duty **applies to** profits arising from a director's transactions with the company, as well as from transactions to which his company is not a party (*Regal (Hastings) Ltd v Gulliver* [1942] 1 All ER 378). This will be the case even if the company would not have been able to benefit from the transaction itself.

In order for the liability to account to arise, the **profit** must be attributable to the director's office in some way, whether by carrying out his duties and functions or through knowledge he has acquired from holding office (*Regal (Hastings) Ltd v Gulliver* [1942] 1 All ER 378). This liability even applies to directors' **remuneration**: any remuneration not authorised by the company will have to be accounted for to the company (*Guinness plc v Saunders* [1990] 1 All ER 652).

> EXAMPLE
> 1. A director had to account for a profit made directly from his **knowledge of confidential information** about his company's affairs, even though he made it in good faith (*Boardman v Phipps* [1966] 3 All ER 721).
> 2. A director was authorised by the board of his company to enter into certain contracts, but he received a **secret commission** for which he had to account (*Boston Deep Sea Fishing and Ice Co v Ansell* (1888) 39 Ch D 339).
> 3. Directors had to account for a **secret financial reward** which they received from the purchaser of their company's business in return for ensuring that the shareholders consented to the sale (*General Exchange Bank v Horner* (1870) LR 9 Eq 480).
> 4. If directors receive a **bribe** from shareholders to act in a particular way, they must account for it to the company (*International Sales & Agencies Ltd v Marcus* [1982] 3 All ER 551).
> 5. The managing director of a building company was an architect. The company failed to obtain a contract, but the potential client was impressed with the managing director and wanted to instruct him to do the work. The managing director **resigned** from the company and then went to work for the client. He was held liable to account to the company for his "profit" because he had breached his fiduciary duty by not disclosing the true situation to his company (*Industrial Development Consultants Ltd v Cooley* [1972] 2 All ER 162).

Permission

2401 As with conflicts of interest, a director can obtain **prior consent** from the company to make a profit. Often companies' articles allow directors to keep such benefits once they have been disclosed to the board (see ¶3308+ for the position under Table A). Otherwise, the shareholders may permit directors in advance to keep their profit by ordinary resolution on a case by case basis, following full disclosure to a general meeting.

If a director has **already gained a profit**, he must make a full disclosure to a general meeting so that the shareholders may resolve to ratify his actions (provided the act was not unlawful, ¶2497+). The shareholders may also resolve to allow him to keep his profit. This additional resolution to relieve the director from his duty to account is crucial. Without it, he will still be liable to account, even if his company has ratified his conduct (*Industrial Development Consultants Ltd v Cooley* [1972] 2 All ER 162). Clearly, if a director follows this route, he risks the shareholders refusing to ratify his actions and remaining liable.

> MEMO POINTS The company's consent or approval **cannot be inferred** and the director is under an obligation to obtain it actively (*British Racing Drivers' Club Ltd v Hextall Erskine & Co (a firm)* [1996] 3 All ER 667).

f. Not misuse company property and/or information

2405 Directors are under a duty to apply **company funds** for lawful purposes. There is an overlap between this duty and those to avoid conflicts of interest and not to make a profit in particular, although misapplication of company funds can amount to a breach of duty by itself in the absence of a conflict or a profit.

> MEMO POINTS Under the **new Companies Act**, this duty will fall within the codified duty to avoid conflicts of interest (see ¶2390/mp) will specifically include the exploitation of property, information and opportunities (s 175 CA 2006; the implementation date for this provision is yet to be announced at the time of writing).

2406 The same principle applies to use of **company information**. If a director uses confidential company information to, for example, deal in the company's shares, he will be in breach of this duty. The case law does not make clear the extent to which different levels of information (confidential information, trade information etc) are covered by this duty. It is likely that information acquired by the director from his office will be protected, which is consistent with the duty not to make a profit from his office.

> EXAMPLE
> 1. Where directors **paid interest and dividends** out of company funds when the company had not made a profit, the payment was in breach of trust because the company could not afford it even though it was technically permitted by the articles (*Re Sharpe*, *Re Bennett*, *Masonic and General Life Assurance Co v Sharpe* [1892] 1 Ch 154).
> 2. Mr C, a shareholder of S Ltd, appointed **nominee directors** to the board to authorise a loan from the company to himself so he could buy shares from other shareholders. The nominees had acted in breach of trust as the company's property was in their hands for the benefit of the company and not one particular shareholder (*Selangor United Rubber Estates Ltd v Cradock (a bankrupt) (No 3)* [1968] 2 All ER 1073).
> 3. A board which authorised a **compensation payment** to a director for loss of his office without the consent of the shareholders acted in breach of duty (*Wallersteiner v Moir* [1974] 3 All ER 217).
> 4. Directors who **sold company assets** at a large discount were in breach of this duty (*Re New Travellers' Chambers Ltd* [1895] 1 Ch 395).
> 5. Mr B was a director of Eden Project Ltd. He registered "The Eden Project" as a **trade mark** in his own name, knowing that it would be vital to EP Ltd's business. He had registered the trade mark in breach of his fiduciary duties and was ordered to assign it to EP Ltd (*Ball v Eden Project Ltd* [2002] 1 BCLC 313).
> 6. A director who resigned and then tried to take advantage of a **business opportunity** fostered by the company had misused company property as well as knowingly acting when he had a conflict of interest. He was liable to account for his profits to the company (*CMS Dolphin Ltd v Simonet* [2001] 2 BCLC 704).
> 7. On the other hand, a director was held not to have breached his fiduciary duties to his company, despite arranging to **work for the company's principal client** during his notice period. He had not sought work from the client, and did not start working for it until after his resignation from the company had taken effect. He had resigned because his relationship with the other director and shareholder had broken down completely and his wife had been made redundant from the company. There was no evidence of disloyalty or conflict of interest, or that he had resigned in order to obtain the client's work for himself. The client had, in fact, approached the director and offered him the work because it wanted to ensure continuity of service for its own clients. The Court of Appeal stressed that this case, as with all breach of fiduciary duties cases, was decided on its particular facts and that a similar case had not been before the courts before (*Foster Bryant Surveying Ltd v Bryant and another* [2007] EWCA Civ 200).

3. Care, skill and diligence

2411 Directors are obliged to exercise reasonable care, skill and diligence (s 174 CA 2006). They owe this duty to their companies because they are carrying out (or claiming to be able to carry out) particular functions with a certain degree of competence for the benefit of others. This duty has been codified, but unlike the other directors' general duties in the new Companies Act, it is not classed as a fiduciary duty. Breach of this duty (i.e. failure to do the job properly) will give rise to a claim in **negligence** against the director for damages to compensate the company for the consequences of his acts or omissions.

The **basis of this duty** arises from the director's assumed responsibility for managing the affairs or property of the company and is not dependent on his service contract, although an executive director may also have this duty expressly set out there (*Henderson v Merrett Syndicates Ltd* [1994] 3 All ER 506). As with the other codified general duties, previous case law in this area can still be relied on in interpreting this duty (s 170 CA 2006).

> MEMO POINTS This codified duty is based on the director's common law duty in tort, and is expressed to be owed to the company (s 170 CA 2006). It is still possible for directors to **owe** the common law duty **to other persons**, wherever the tortious relationship arises, see ¶2448.

2412 A **director is expected to** exercise the care, skill and diligence that would be exercised by a reasonably diligent person with the general knowledge, skill and experience (s 174(2) CA 2006):
– that may reasonably be expected of a person in his position; and
– that he actually has.

This enables the courts to set an **objective** benchmark that a director must meet, but is flexible enough to be applied to diverse directors of different types of company. A director is expected to meet the standards appropriate to his role in his particular type of company. For example, the knowledge, skills and experience expected of a person in the position of a director of a small family business will be different from those expected of the finance director of a multi-national company, which will be different again from those expected of a non-executive director on the board of the same company. The **subjective** element of the test means that directors are also judged by a higher standard if they possess particular knowledge, skills or experience. For example, it is only fair that if a director is also a qualified accountant, this should be taken into account when judging his competency. The test is cumulative; both the subjective and the objective standard must be met (*Duties of Company Directors: Ministerial Statements*, June 2007).

> EXAMPLE Messrs S, P and H were directors of D Ltd. Mr S was making unauthorised loans. Messrs P and H were not as involved in the business as Mr S on a day to day level and claimed to be unaware of Mr S's conduct. However, because Mr P was a chartered **accountant** and Mr H had extensive accountancy experience, the court held that a higher standard of skill and care could be expected from them and they were liable for breach of this duty (*Dorchester Finance Co Ltd v Stebbing (1977)* [1989] BCLC 498).

2414 A director is **not expected to** hold any particular skills or qualifications, especially in areas in which the company would usually instruct an external expert, such as finance, the law or human resources (*Re Brazilian Rubber Plantations and Estates Ltd* [1911] 1 Ch 425; *Re Macro (Ipswich) Ltd*, *Re Earliba Finance Co Ltd*, *Macro v Thompson* [1994] 2 BCLC 354).

If the directors cannot manage any aspect of the company effectively, they should engage external **advisers**. However, in doing so they must maintain their independence and only follow advice to the extent that it is in the company's interests to do so.

> MEMO POINTS It is always open to the shareholders to **dismiss** a director from office if they feel that he does not have the necessary qualities (¶2946+).

2416 The requirement for diligence necessitates active participation in the affairs of the company. Directors should **attend** enough **board meetings** to ensure that they have an adequate understanding of the company, any relevant issues and the performance of other directors and staff (note that a director's service contract may impose a more onerous duty).

It is acceptable for a director to **rely on other directors**, office-holders and employees for information as to what is happening in the company (see example 1 below). However, he must properly consider the reliability of both the information he is provided with, and of the people giving that information (*Norman v Theodore Goddard (a firm)* [1991] BCLC 1028).

> EXAMPLE
> 1. A director of a bank was found not to have breached his duty to act with skill and care in failing to discover his managing director's fraud. It was considered reasonable for him to have **relied upon** the advice and judgment of the managing director in the absence of any reason to question his integrity (*Dovey v Cory* [1901] AC 477).
> 2. A director who voted in favour of making a payment for brokerage/commission **without enquiring** about the details as to why the payment was being made was found liable for breach of his duty to exercise reasonable skill and care. The payment was in relation to fraudulently raising shares on the market (*Re Railway and General Light Improvement Co*, *Marzetti's Case* (1880) 42 LT 206).

2417 Where it is reasonable for him to do so, he may **delegate** his powers. If he does so, he is expected to supervise his delegate (¶3404+).

2418 Although a director will not be liable for the **acts or omissions of** his **co-directors** or other officers solely by virtue of his position, he will be liable if he participates in the wrong. In some cases, directors are clearly involved in causing damage to the company. In less obvious cases, the threshold at which it is deemed that a director participated in the wrong is very low. This might involve signing board meeting minutes which approve, for example, a misapplication of company property or signing a cheque for what turns out to be an unauthorised payment.

B. Remedies for and consequences of breach of duty

2434 Directors' general duties overlap to a certain extent, as do their remedies. The **remedy** sought can depend on the circumstances of the director in default (e.g. does he have the funds to make him worth suing? This will not prevent a court from finding him liable, but will impact on the claimant's ability to enforce the judgment successfully) and the attitude of the company or third party trying to take action following a breach (e.g. the company may want to ratify the wrongful act or avoid the unauthorised transaction, or the third party may want to enforce the unauthorised agreement). The company may decide that the most effective solution is to dismiss the director, as an alternative "self-help" remedy or in combination with others (¶2067+, ¶2100+).

A director may be **relieved** from liability by the court or the company (¶2494+). **Insurance** or an **indemnity** may also be available to cushion the blow to the director and/or the company.

The remedies and reliefs available for breaches of **specific statutory duties**, on the other hand, depend entirely on the duty breached and so are dealt with per duty at ¶2532+.

1. Availability of remedies

2438 Civil remedies for breach of general duties are principally **available to** the company, although third parties may also have a cause of action in respect of certain breaches.

A director will often be in breach of more than one general duty, enabling the company or third party to pursue a variety of remedies. The table below (¶2440) summarises the remedies available for each breach of duty. The different **types of action** available are discussed generally below, and then **each remedy** available for breach of a general duty is dealt with in turn.

2439 Usually, the company or third party (the "**claimant**") will be able to **apply to the court** for a combination of remedies. If the claim is successful, the court will decide which of the remedies will adequately compensate the claimant or protect it from further harm. The claimant will only be **allowed to recover** the value of its loss. If the director continues to be in breach, it may be appropriate for the court to award an injunction to prevent the breach from continuing. A claimant will therefore usually word its application in terms to allow the court to choose between appropriate remedies so that it stands the best chance of recovering its loss.

Normally, an **individual** director (the "**defendant**") will be liable for breach of his duties. If the claimant believes that more than one director is in default, proceedings can be brought against them as joint defendants and they can be made **jointly and severally liable**. Similarly, if the claimant has brought proceedings against one director (e.g. because he seems to be the most solvent), that director can join others into the proceedings to obtain a **contribution** from them in respect of their share of the liability.

2440 This table **summarises** the remedies available for breaches, the liability of the directors and their opportunities for relief from liability.

Breach of duty	Remedy	To whom remedy available	Liability of director	Relief from liability
Contract claims				
Duty to act within authority	– Damages for loss; – account for profits; – injunction; – remove director; and/or – avoid/enforce transaction	– Company[1] – Third parties	– Account for profits/pay damages; – obey injunction; and/or – lose job	– Statutory relief – Ratification
Tort claims				
Negligence/ breach of duty of care, skill and diligence	– Damages; – injunction; – remove director; and/or – avoid/enforce transaction	– Company[1] – Third party	– Pay damages; – obey injunction; and/or – lose job	– Statutory relief – Ratification
Claims for breach of fiduciary duties				
Duty to act within powers				
Duty to promote the success of the company	– Account for profits; – tracing/restitution; – injunction; – avoid/enforce transaction; and/or – remove director	Company[1,2]	– Account for profits; – return property; – obey injunction; and/or – lose job	
Duty to exercise independent judgment				
Duty to avoid conflicts of interest and duty				– Statutory relief – Equitable bars – Ratification
Duty to account for profits	– Account for profits; – tracing/restitution; – injunction; and/or – remove director	Company[1,2]	– Account for profits; – obey injunction; and/or – lose job	
Misuse of company property/ information	– Account for profits/benefit/loss to company; – tracing/restitution; – injunction; – avoid/enforce transaction; and/or – remove director	Company[1,2]	– Account for profits; – return property; – obey injunction; and/or – lose job	

Note:
1. If the company does not take action against the director in breach, or abandons a claim, a shareholder may be able to commence or continue it as a **derivative claim** (see ¶7127+).
2. **Third parties** (usually individual shareholders) may be able to bring a claim for breach of fiduciary duty if the circumstances allow (¶2451+).

Time limits

The right of action against a director is subject to statutory time limits.

2442

Type of claim	Limitation period	Time limit starts to run	Reference (Limitation Act 1980)
Breach of contract[1]	6 years	From breach	s 5
Action in tort	6 years[3]	From wrongful act/omission	s 2
Breach of fiduciary duty[2]	6 years	From breach	s 21(3)

Note:
1. If the action is to **recover land**, the time limit is 12 years (s 15 Limitation Act 1980). The time limit is also 12 years if the contract was signed as a deed or under seal (s 8 Limitation Act 1980).
2. There is no time limit on an action to **recover trust property** from a trustee resulting from a trustee's fraud (s 21(1) Limitation Act 1980).
3. Except for actions for **personal injury**, for which there is a shorter limitation period of 3 years from the date on which the cause of action accrued or the date on which the injured person knew he had a cause of action, if later (s 11 Limitation Act 1980).

Which remedy?

The remedies a claimant pursues will depend upon:
- what damage he has sustained or what the consequences of the breach are;
- the result he wishes to achieve; and
- what remedies are available for the breach in question.

2444

The table below illustrates which remedies address which consequences of breach. Naturally, a claimant may have sustained more than one consequence.

Consequence of breach	Remedy
Financial loss	– Damages
Loss of asset	– Restitution
Profit or other financial gain to director	Account for profit
Director continues to cause loss/make gain	Injunction
Company is party to unauthorised contract	– Avoid – Ratify
Third party wants to bind company to unauthorised contract	Enforce

Action for breach of contract

The **right to sue** in contract depends upon a contractual relationship between the claimant and the defendant.

2446

An implied contract exists between the **company** and the director as a result of the director's position as the company's agent. Breach of a director's general duties enables the company to pursue a contractual claim against him for breach of both this implied contract and (usually) his service contract (¶2678+).

A **third party** will usually have a contractual relationship with the company rather than the director. However, when a director represents himself as being able to contract with a third party on the company's behalf, it results in an implied collateral contract between them, known as a "warranty of authority". Directors may be liable to third parties for breach of this warranty if they enter into a transaction without the proper authority to do so (*Hely-Hutchinson v Brayhead Ltd* [1967] 3 All ER 98). A third party will have to resort to this remedy if he cannot enforce the contract with the company, or does not wish to, for example, because the company has become insolvent since the contract was entered into (¶2350/mp). The third party is usually better off enforcing the contract and then suing the company for breach if it is unable to perform its obligations.

The **remedies** for breach of contract (depending on the circumstances: damages, accounting for profit, injunction and avoiding or enforcing the transaction) are discussed at ¶2463+.

> MEMO POINTS   Where the company could take action against a director for breach of contract, but it does not or it abandons a claim once it has been commenced, a shareholder may be able to commence or continue it as a **derivative claim** (see ¶7127+).

Action in tort

2448 An action in tort is available to a party who has suffered loss as a result of a director's breach of his **duty to exercise care, skill and diligence** (in other words, **negligence**). Although this duty has been codified into statute, the consequences of breach have not changed (s 178 CA 2006). The remedy sought will usually be damages.

Such an action is distinct from breach of contract since it does not rely on a contractual link between the director and the claimant. Rather, it **relies upon** the claimant establishing that the director owed him a duty of care and that the director breached that duty thereby causing him damage. The codified duty of care, skill and diligence is stated to be owed to the company, and therefore can be enforced by the company (s 170(1) CA 2006). However, a duty of skill and care can also be owed by a director to other persons, including individual shareholders, under the general laws of negligence. This is far less common than the director owing the duty to the company, but may arise where he has assured a shareholder that he will pursue a particular business opportunity and the shareholder suffers loss as a result of his failure to do so, for example. A claim can therefore be made by any person to whom the director owed such a duty, which can be a third party as well as the company, depending on the circumstances.

> MEMO POINTS   1. An action in respect of a director's negligent performance of his **service contract** can be brought by the company in tort and/or contract.
> 2. Directors can be held liable for **other tortious acts** in running a company, such as defamation and fraudulent misrepresentation. For example, a director was found guilty of the tort of deceit for signing a framework agreement as his company's managing director. The agreement included provisions as to payment by his company to a supplier which he knew the company could not keep and the company never complied with its payment obligations. The director's activities and those of his company were so closely mingled that they could not be separated. He had made almost all of the representations about his company's credit to the supplier, doing so both personally and procuring the company to make the representations. He was therefore personally liable to the supplier for the loss it suffered as a result of this deceit (*Contex Drouzbha Ltd v Wiseman and another* [2006] EWHC 2708 (QB)).
> 3. Where the company could take action against a director for breach of contract, but it does not or it abandons a claim once it has been commenced, a shareholder may be able to commence or continue it as a **derivative claim** (see ¶7127+).

2449 If a tortious claim arises against a director from his actions (or omissions) in performance of his duties, the **company** may be held **vicariously liable**, ensuring that it is responsible for any harm caused by its business operations. This benefits claimants because the company is often in a better position to pay damages than the director. Vicarious liability arises due to the director's status as employee and/or agent where the wrongful act was:
– authorised by the company;
– ratified by the company; or
– carried out in the course of the director's work.

Therefore, before ratifying a tortious act by a director, a company must ascertain whether or not it could become liable to a third party as a result.

Nevertheless, the **director** may still be **personally liable** for his actions. For example, where a managing director made a fraudulent representation on behalf of his company to a bank to obtain payment under a letter of credit, he argued that since he made the representation on the company's behalf, he should not be personally liable. The court held that although the director's actions could be attributed to the company by virtue of his agency relationship, it did not relieve him of his personal liability for knowingly making the fraudulent representation. Both he and the company (along with other parties involved) were liable (*Standard Chartered Bank v Pakistan National Shipping Corp* [2003] 1 BCLC 244).

Action for breach of fiduciary duties

If a director has acted in breach of his fiduciary duties, specific **equitable remedies** will be available to the company, depending on the breach in question:
- accounting for profits;
- tracing; and
- restitution.

Although some of the fiduciary duties have already been codified, the consequences of breach have not changed (s 178 CA 2006).

These duties are **enforceable by** the company because they rely on the existence of a fiduciary relationship between it and the director. A third party will only be able to bring a claim if the director assumed a fiduciary responsibility towards him over and above his usual relationship with that third party. This is not usual, but may occur between, for instance, a director and an individual shareholder or class of shareholders, allowing him/them to claim against the director.

> EXAMPLE Where a director agreed to act as **agent for the shareholders** in negotiating a takeover bid, he was under a duty to give them impartial advice about the rival bids. The shareholders had this special relationship with the director and could bring a claim against the director in their own names (*Re a Company (No 008699 of 1985)* [1986] BCLC 382).

> MEMO POINTS A director's fiduciary duties **cannot be enforced by** a fellow director because they are owed to the company (*Lee v Chou Wen Hsien* [1985] BCLC 45).

> MEMO POINTS Where the company could take action against a director for breach of contract, but it does not or it abandons a claim once it has been commenced, a shareholder may be able to commence or continue it as a **derivative claim** (see ¶7127+).

Basis of equitable remedies

The **aim** of equitable remedies is to deal fairly with the parties and, as far as possible, restore the situation between them to what it was before the breach. Therefore, if a director has misused company property (e.g. by giving a company car to his friend), the court will require him to return it to the company if possible. It does not matter that he acted in good faith and did not commit a fraud (*Regal (Hastings) Ltd v Gulliver* [1942] 1 All ER 378). This is known as "restitution".

To help the court re-create the parties' previous situation, directors who gain a profit or benefit in breach of their fiduciary duties, or who misuse company property or information become "**constructive trustees**" over the property in question (whether money, assets or information).

This **automatic trust** ensures that **directors** are still under a duty to the company to deal with that property only for its benefit, and enables the court to return it to the company even if it has changed hands (e.g. been sold on) or been converted into something else (e.g. used to purchase something). This is known as "tracing". The trust also means that the director has to account for any **interest or further gain** he makes on the profit, and he can be sued for the additional sum if he does not (*International Sales & Agencies Ltd v Marcus* [1982] 3 All ER 551).

> MEMO POINTS 1. He can also be held liable for the tort of conversion if he **uses the money to purchase** something, for example, as well as committing theft (as the money belongs to the company).
> 2. The court can **relieve** a **constructive trustee from liability** if he acted honestly and reasonably and ought fairly to be excused (s 61 Trustee Act 1925). This overlaps with the companies provision, which directors are more likely to rely on (¶2505+).

It is more difficult to deem a **third party** to be a **constructive trustee** than a director. A third party will only be subject to an equitable remedy if he received the property from the director knowing (or being able to know) that it was acquired in breach of fiduciary duties and he was not acting in good faith in doing so.

> MEMO POINTS The rules which validate a transaction entered into beyond the company's powers in the memorandum or the board's power to bind the company or authorise others to do so are

relevant here (¶2350/mp). If a transaction falls into these categories, it will not be invalid (and the **third party** will **not** be fixed as a **trustee**) simply because the third party knew or could have found out that the transaction was unauthorised. In such cases, the good faith (or otherwise) of the third party will be key.

Bars to equitable remedies

2456 A number of factors can intervene to prevent the re-creation of the parties' previous positions. The **basic principle** is one of fairness: if something has occurred to render it more unfair (on the director, the company or a third party) for the company to obtain an equitable remedy than for it not to do so, the court will not make the order. Situations which may occur in claims against directors include where:
a. the position of the parties has **changed**, e.g. an asset of the company has been sold to a third party who acted in good faith, paid for it and could not have known that the asset actually belonged to the company;
b. the company **delayed** too much before pursuing the director (known as the doctrine of "laches");
c. the company has had a hand in the wrongdoing (sometimes referred to as the need for "**clean hands**"); or
d. the company has **ratified** the director's acts and allowed him to keep the property in question.

These situations are referred to as "**equitable bars**". The court will look at all of the facts and decide upon the fairest way of resolving the situation in the circumstances.

Other remedies

2458 Other remedies available for a breach of fiduciary duty are applying for an **injunction** and **removing the director**. A transaction entered into in breach of fiduciary duties may be **voidable** by the company or enforced by a third party. Breach of one or more fiduciary duties often also encompasses other breaches, so a claimant can apply for additional remedies attached to those breaches.

2. Types of remedy

a. Damages

2463 Damages are available in **claims for** breach of contract and the duty of skill and care (negligence). They can be **claimed by** the company and third parties. The **aim** of this remedy is to compensate the claimant for his loss, and therefore depends upon the circumstances of each case. Clearly, no damages will be awarded if the claimant has not suffered any loss.

2464 Generally speaking, the damages recoverable depend on whether the action arises in tort or in contract. Any damages which are awarded in an action in **tort** should put the company (or other innocent party) back into the position it would have been in if the director had not breached his duty. **Contractual** damages should put the parties forward into the position they would have been in had the contract been properly performed. In **both cases**, the damage suffered must not be too indirect or remote a consequence of the breach, and the claimant will be expected to mitigate his loss as far as possible.

Usually, the **amount of damages** a successful claimant is awarded will be the value of his loss, after taking factors such as mitigation into account. If no loss has been sustained, only nominal damages will be awarded (recognising that the claimant has technically won the case, but compensation is not necessary).

MEMO POINTS Just because a company has suffered loss at the hands of its director's breach of fiduciary duty, a shareholder cannot claim any "**reflective loss**" he has suffered as a result (*Johnson v Gore Wood & Co (a firm)* [2001] 1 All ER 481). For example, the diminution in the market value of his shares or a likely reduction in dividends would not be recoverable where that loss is not personal to the shareholder, but is purely reflective of the company's loss (*Gardner v Parker* [2004] EWCA Civ 781). However, where the company suffers loss but has no cause of action to recover it, a shareholder who has suffered loss (even diminution in the value of his shares) can sue in respect of it if he has a cause of action (*Perry v Day* [2004] EWHC 1398 (Ch)).

b. Injunctions

An injunction is a type of **court order** prohibiting someone from doing something (a restrictive injunction) or requiring them to do something (a mandatory injunction). The former type will be the most common in this context as it can prevent the director committing the breach, although mandatory injunctions can also be sought (e.g. to compel a director to return confidential documents).

A claimant may ask for an injunction in **claims arising out of** any of the breaches listed in the table at ¶2440.

Courts can be reluctant to grant injunctive relief because it has serious consequences for the defendant. An injunction will only be **available if**:
– damages would not be an adequate remedy; and
– the damage is continuing or could recur; or
– the breach is threatened but has not yet occurred.

For example, if a director is misusing company property for his own benefit and refuses to return it to the company, the court can order him to stop his wrongful conduct as well as to return the property.

The **timing** of an injunction application can be crucial. If the breach is ongoing and damage continues to be sustained, applications often need to be made quickly and heard without the court considering all the circumstances. In order to balance the interests of the two parties in such situations, the court can order an interim (i.e. temporary) injunction. The case can then be heard in full at a later date, when the court will decide whether the injunction should stand or not and/or whether another remedy should be awarded. The courts can also impose **conditions** on both sides when granting an injunction.

2467

2468

c. Account for profits

A director can be required to account for any profits he has made at the company's expense in **claims for** breach of his service contract and the duties:
– to act within his authority;
– to act within his powers;
– to promote the success of the company;
– to exercise independent judgment;
– to avoid conflicts of interest and duty;
– to account for profits; and
– not to misuse company property/information.

This is the usual remedy for breaches of fiduciary duties, and can be **claimed by** the company (*Murad v Al-Saraj* [2005] EWCA Civ 959).

MEMO POINTS A **third party** may claim this remedy in special circumstances (¶2451+).

This is an equitable remedy with the **aim** of being fair to all parties and to deter directors from profiting from breaches of fiduciary duties. A director will be liable to account for profits (or other unjust enrichment) regardless of whether or not a loss has in fact been suffered by the company. For example, a director who has obtained a contract for work for himself in breach of his duties will usually have to account to his company for any profit, even if the company itself would not have been awarded the contract (also see example 5 at ¶2399).

2471

2472

EXAMPLE

1. Mr S was a director of CD, a property development company. In his capacity as director, he became aware of an opportunity to develop Craven Cottage Football Stadium. Without revealing this opportunity to CD, he set up another company, FRP Ltd, and proceeded to undertake the project. The court found that Mr S and FRP Ltd were both liable to account to CD. Mr S had acted in clear conflict with CD's interests by not disclosing the opportunity to CD; it was irrelevant whether CD would or could have pursued the project. FRP Ltd was liable to account because it was aware of Mr S's breach by virtue of his 49% shareholding in FRP Ltd (albeit indirectly) and had therefore acted as an accessory to the breach and it was unconscionable for it to retain the benefit (*Crown Dilmun v Sutton* [2004] 1 BCLC 468).

2. The M sisters and Mr A entered into a joint venture to acquire a hotel, each contributing £500,000 (profits to be split equally, and capital gains on the sale of the hotel to be divided equally between the M sisters and Mr A). The hotel was acquired for £3.6m and sold for a profit of £2m; Mr A managed the hotel in the interim. The court found that Mr A had breached his fiduciary duties to the M sisters:
– by failing to disclose the real purchase price of the hotel (he told them it cost £4.1m) and the fact that his contribution was not paid in cash but as a set-off between himself and the seller; and
– for taking a £369,000 commission from the seller.
Had Mr A made the disclosure, the M sisters would probably still have entered into the joint venture with him, but on different terms. The court held that Mr A should account for all profits made, except his remuneration for managing the hotel (as an allowance could be made for his skill and work) and the balance of his £500,000 (as it was an expense of the acquisition). (In a dissenting judgment, Clarke LJ considered that the rule should be more flexible to account for circumstances such as the fact that the M sisters could not have entered into the transaction at all without Mr A, to allow him to retain some profit) (*Murad v Al-Saraj* [2005] EWCA Civ 959).

3. SSF plc was an open-ended investment company, managed by SI Ltd. Mr S was a de facto director of SI Ltd. SI Ltd was in turn advised on its investment policy for SSF plc by SF Ltd, of which Mr W and Mr H were directors. SSF plc's two subsidiaries invested in US traded life policies and UK traded endowment policies. From May 2003, Messrs S, W and H formulated an idea to establish a new fund investing in whole life policies. They took preparatory steps such as putting together a draft business plan, identifying a proposed administrator and banker, and making financial predictions. In August 2003 they instructed a solicitor and went on to prepare the Offering Memorandum, approach third parties regarding services such as auditing and market making as well as approaching potential investors. Two companies were incorporated in October 2003, an open-ended investment company and a company to be its manager and adviser. The defendant directors resigned from SI Ltd and SF Ltd at different times: Mr S in September 2003, Mr H in October 2003 and Mr W in May 2004.
The court found that from the time when Messrs S, W and H consulted solicitors with a view to establishing the business, they had formed an irrevocable intention to set up a competing business and knew that it would be reasonably regarded as competing with SF Ltd and SI Ltd. Since they continued to take steps to set up the business without disclosing their activities and intentions to, and without the consent of, SF Ltd and SI Ltd, they were in breach of their fiduciary duties to those companies. SF Ltd and SI Ltd were entitled to an account of profits accordingly (*Shepherds Investments Ltd v Walters* [2006] EWHC 836 (Ch)).

MEMO POINTS If a director makes a profit from acting improperly during his office **after the directorship has ended** for which he would have been accountable had he still been a director, then he can be held liable to account for his profit (*Island Export Finance Ltd v Umunna* [1986] BCLC 460, although in this case the court found that, on the facts, the director was not in breach of duty).

2473 The remedy is not automatic. The court may decide that it is **not appropriate** if, for example, the company has not suffered any loss (*Derek Randall Enterprises Ltd (in liquidation) v Randall* [1991] BCLC 379), or the director has acted for the benefit of the company but at the same time gained a profit or personal advantage (*Boardman v Phipps* [1966] 3 All ER 721).

It is also **not available** if the company fails to exercise its right to rescind a contract first, or the equitable bars discussed at ¶2456 prevent the company from claiming it (*Hely-Hutchinson v Brayhead Ltd* [1967] 3 All ER 98).

d. Restitution of property and tracing

2476 This remedy can be **available** in cases of breach of fiduciary duty. Whereas accounting for profits is a personal remedy against the director in question, tracing and restitution works against the property itself. It allows the company to recover the property from either the director or a third party and can be applied to money and profit as well as to tangible assets.

In some cases, it may **not be available** either because the property never belonged to the company, or it cannot be identified. For example:
a. the profit gained by the directors derives from a contract the company was not a party to, or it was a bribe (as in *Lister & Co v Stubbs* (1890) 45 Ch D 1), in which case, the personal remedy of accounting for profits is appropriate; or
b. a third party has purchased the property without knowing (or being able to know) that it actually belonged to the company (*Selangor United Rubber Estates Ltd v Cradock (a bankrupt) (No 3)* [1968] 2 All ER 1073).

The other equitable bars discussed at ¶2456 will also apply.

> MEMO POINTS The case of *Lister & Co v Stubbs*, above, held that a director who has accepted **bribes** is in the position of a debtor to the company, rather than a trustee holding the bribe for the company's benefit. However, a Privy Council decision doubted this decision, stating that a proprietary remedy (i.e. one available for breach of trust, such as restitution/tracing) was appropriate to ensure that the bribed director could not benefit from his actions (*Attorney General for Hong Kong v Reid* [1994] 1 All ER 1). The Privy Council case could not overrule *Lister & Co v Stubbs* and so this decision is still binding, although the court has recently indicated that it would prefer to follow the Privy Council (but on the facts of the particular case this was not necessary; *Daraydan Holdings Ltd v Solland International Ltd* [2005] 4 All ER 73).

2477 **Restitution** can be made where the original property can be identified and returned.

Tracing is used where the original property is not identifiable in itself but it can be identified in another asset. For example, if the proceeds of a company share sale are used to buy a house, the other asset can be **clearly identified** and the house (or proceeds from its sale) can be returned to the company. If the original property has been mixed up in a bank account or used towards the purchase of something which is **not clearly identifiable**, then, unless the director is able to distinguish between his property and the company's, the whole of the mixed property will be treated as being recoverable (*Re Tilley's Will Trusts, Burgin v Croad* [1967] 2 All ER 303). This does not allow the company to claim all of the mixed asset; it will be able to claim money to the value of that misappropriated, together with the interest that would have accrued on that sum alone.

> EXAMPLE
> 1. Mr A, a director of X Ltd, has misappropriated company property by giving a company car to his friend, Mr B. Mr B knew that Mr A was in breach of his duties to the company in doing so and assisted Mr A in covering up his use of the car (e.g. by lying to X Ltd when questioned about it).
> a. **Restitution**: Mr B is a constructive trustee of the car and is liable to return it to X Ltd.
> b. **Tracing**: If Mr B has sold it on to another third party, who pays for it and has no knowledge of the fact that the car belongs to X Ltd, X Ltd cannot recover the car itself. However, the proceeds of the sale are identifiable in Mr B's bank account. X Ltd can recover these monies.
>
> 2. Mr Z, a director of C Ltd, enters into a contract with a third party in breach of his fiduciary duties to C Ltd since it was a contract which C Ltd was trying to win. Mr Z is paid for this work by the third party.
> a. **Restitution**: The payment is **clearly identifiable** because Mr Z has put it in a separate bank account. C Ltd can recover the payment together with any interest on it.
> b. **Tracing**: The money was paid into Mr Z's normal bank account and has been mixed with his own money, so is **not identifiable**. The whole fund is treated as being held on trust for C Ltd until C Ltd has recovered the value of the payment (plus interest).
> c. **Tracing**: The money was **used to buy** a car. The trust is imposed upon the car and C Ltd is entitled to it. If Mr Z contributed some of his own money to the purchase, the car will have to be sold and the proceeds distributed accordingly.

e. Removal of the director

2480 **Shareholders** have a **right** to remove a director from office. They do not have to give any **reasons** for doing so, and so this right can be used as a remedy for any of the breaches discussed here.

Removing a director from office may not necessarily **terminate his employment**, and so if he is also an employee the shareholders should instruct the directors to terminate his service contract. Breach of duty will usually entitle the company to terminate the service contract, although this will depend on the circumstances so the company's potential liability under employment law must be taken into account (¶2983+, ¶2986).

f. Consequences on transactions

2483 If a director has entered into a transaction in breach of any of his duties, he will have done so in breach of his authority. Such transactions can be vulnerable to being declared void **by the company** (e.g. *Bamford v Bamford* [1969] 1 All ER 969, which concerned a breach of fiduciary duty).

The company can also choose to enforce such a transaction by **ratifying** it. **Illegal transactions**, on the other hand, such as those entered into fraudulently or in breach of a specific statutory prohibition, are automatically void.

2484 Third parties can enforce transactions which are technically unauthorised because the validity of the director's authority to enter into them on the company's behalf can be challenged (¶2350/mp). To protect the shareholders in situations which are particularly prejudicial to them, the legislation allows them to avoid and prevent transactions involving the **directors dealing with** and receiving a benefit from the **company** through unauthorised:
– contracts (¶2559+);
– loans (¶2804+); and
– substantial property transactions (¶2567+).

At the time of writing, directors are still subject to an additional duty to act within the powers of the memorandum, and special rules apply where this duty has been breached (¶2554+).

C. Relief from liability

2494 Companies may choose to relieve their directors from liability to the company by ratifying their wrongful acts. Alternatively, a director may be able to make use of statutory relief if the court agrees that he acted honestly and reasonably in the circumstances.

Further, statutory duties often include specific relief and exceptions from liability.

1. Ratification

2497 The **company** may choose to waive a director's liability by subsequently ratifying his improper actions. This will apply to most breaches of duty and occurs commonly in smaller owner-managed companies where the directors are also shareholders. Ratification will relieve the director of liability to the company, but will not affect his liability to a third party, and may even render the company vicariously liable to a third party for a director's wrongdoing.

The shareholders **can ratify** a director's negligence, default, breach of duty or breach of trust in relation to the company (s 239(1) CA 2006). Such a decision must either be taken unanimously by the shareholders or by ordinary resolution (or another type of resolution if required, e.g. by statute or the articles) (s 239(2), (6) CA 2006). If a unanimous decision is not taken, the vote of the director concerned (where he is also a shareholder) and any shareholders connected to him cannot be counted, although they may still attend the meeting and count in the quorum (s 239(4) CA 2006). Similarly, if a written resolution on the matter is not unanimous, the director's vote (if he is a shareholder) and that of any shareholders connected to him must be discounted (s 239(3) CA 2006).

Shareholders can also ratify the following acts under separate rules (s 239(7) CA 2006):
– those which are outside the company's powers by special resolution (s 35(3) CA 1985, a provision which is expected to be repealed by 1 October 2009); and
– the board's or individual directors' (or other agents') acts outside of their powers but within the memorandum by ordinary resolution (*Grant v United Kingdom Switchback Railways Co* (1888) 40 Ch D 135).

MEMO POINTS 1. This provision of the new Companies Act came into force on **1 October 2007** and enables shareholders to ratify directors' conduct which occurred on or after that date. In the case of directors' conduct before then, shareholders can still ratify acts which are outside of the company's power by special resolution and those outside of the directors' power by ordinary resolution.
s 35(3) CA 1985 is expected to be repealed by 1 October 2009, but acts within the company's powers but beyond the individual's will still be ratifiable by ordinary resolution.
2. The statutory provisions (in both the 1985 and 2006 Acts) allowing shareholders to ratify these acts and omissions only apply to directors. Therefore, if the shareholders want to ratify the acts or omissions of **another officer** which was outside of his own powers, but within those of the company, they can do so by ordinary resolution.

The **board** can no longer ratify directors' acts (s 239(1), (2) CA 2006). However, it can (if it has the power to do so) still control proceedings brought by the directors on behalf of the company against a director or other person by deciding not to sue, or to settle or release such a claim (s 239(6) CA 2006).

MEMO POINTS The board can still ratify the acts of **other officers or agents** if the act in question would have been within the board's powers.

The **company cannot ratify** illegal or fraudulent acts. Illegal acts include those in breach of the legislation, such as declaring unlawful dividends (*Bairstow v Queens Moat Houses plc* [2001] 2 BCLC 531). Fraudulent acts in this context include fraud on the minority by directors' abuse or misuse of powers (such as cases giving rise to remedies of last resort, see ¶2100+). This is to preserve the power of minority shareholders to object to such treatment, as they would otherwise be overruled by the majority (who may comprise the directors at fault), who can pass the necessary resolution without them (see examples below). If the company is **insolvent**, or is in danger of becoming insolvent, the shareholders cannot ratify a breach of duty or unauthorised act, because the creditors' interests supersede those of the shareholders (*West Mercia Safetywear Ltd (in liquidation) v Dodd* [1988] BCLC 250).

The **board cannot ratify** breaches of duty or other acts outside the scope of its own authority.

EXAMPLE
Ratification allowed:
1. Incidentally making a secret profit (*Regal (Hastings) Ltd v Gulliver* [1942] 1 All ER 378).
2. Failure in skill and care (*Pavlides v Jensen* [1956] 2 All ER 518).
3. Directors exercising their powers for a collateral purpose in good faith (*Bamford v Bamford* [1969] 1 All ER 969).

Ratification not allowed:
1. Abuse of individual shareholders' rights, such as refusing to register a share transfer in bad faith (*Re Smith & Fawcett Ltd* [1942] 1 All ER 542).
2. Fraudulent or dishonest acts (*Mason v Harris* (1879) 11 Ch D 97).
3. Fraud on minority shareholders. In a case in which the director/shareholders had appropriated a contract for their own benefit which the company was pursuing, the company was not allowed to ratify the act because this would result in a fraud on the non-director minority shareholders (*Cook v Deeks* [1916] 1 AC 554).

To obtain ratification, the director must make a full and frank disclosure of the circumstances and consequences of the breach so that the company can make an informed decision.

The wrongful act can then be **ratified by** the appropriate type of resolution. However, ratification can be implied if the unauthorised decision has been acted upon by the board or the company, provided it is an action capable of ratification (board: ¶3297+; shareholders: ¶3590+).

2. Relief provided by statute

2505 A director may be able to rely on statutory relief from liability in **proceedings for** (s 727 CA 1985):
– negligence;
– default;
– breach of duty; or
– breach of trust.

This **includes** breach of the general duties discussed above, as well as those statutory duties imposed by the Companies Act 1985 which give rise to civil liability (*Re Duckwari plc (No 2), Duckwari plc v Offerventure Ltd (No 2)* [1997] 2 BCLC 729). A director can apply for such relief as soon as he is aware that he may be sued (s 727 (2) CA 1985).

Where a duty is codified in the **new Companies Act**, and that provision is in force, directors can also apply for relief from liability (s 1157 CA 2006). This provision for relief is slightly wider, as it allows the applicant to apply for relief in advance where a claim is likely to be made against him (s 1157(2) CA 2006).

> MEMO POINTS 1. Both statutory reliefs also apply to **any other officer** of a company and its **auditor**.
> 2. In any situation in which a director has become a **trustee** of property, e.g. where he is a constructive trustee of the company's property, the court can relieve him from liability if he acted honestly and reasonably and ought fairly to be excused (s 61 Trustee Act 1925). This overlaps with the provision for relief in companies legislation and so will not often be relied upon by directors.

2506 Case law based on the Companies Act 1985 provision gives **guidance** as to how the court will assess applications for relief. The new Companies Act requires the same elements to be shown, so these cases are likely to be helpful in interpreting the new provision where it applies as well.

If the court accepts that the director has acted honestly, reasonably, and with regard to all the circumstances of the case he ought fairly to be excused for the wrongful act, it may relieve him from liability. All three **requirements** must be satisfied (*Re Queensway Systems Ltd* [2006] EWHC 2496 (Ch)). The relief awarded may be whole or partial, and the court can impose terms on it.

The **test** used to assess a director's honesty and reasonableness is whether the director was acting in a way in which an individual dealing with his own affairs with reasonable care and caution could be expected to act (*Re D'Jan of London Ltd, Copp v D'Jan* [1994] 1 BCLC 561).

2507 Whether relief is granted is at the discretion of the court and there are no general rules which can be laid down as to the **circumstances** in which relief will be given. The provision can be particularly useful where there are one or more "innocent" directors who have no knowledge of their fellow directors' breaches, or where the shareholders of a company have instructed a director to act in a way which breaches his duties.

> EXAMPLE
> 1. A nominee director obeyed shareholders' instructions without considering his wider agency duties to the company. Although he acted honestly, he was not granted relief because he did not act reasonably in breaching his duties (*Selangor United Rubber Estates Ltd v Cradock (a bankrupt) (No 3)* [1968] 2 All ER 1073).
> 2. Relief is unlikely to be given at the expense of the company's creditors (*Inn Spirit Ltd v Burns* [2002] 2 BCLC 780).
> 3. Relief will not usually be granted if it would result in a director retaining benefits which he would not have received were he not in default (*Re Marini Ltd* [2004] BCC 172).
> 4. A director was not relieved from liability to repay unauthorised loans to or for the benefit of her and her husband (also a director). Although her husband committed the breaches, she knew what he was doing and could have stopped him, but did not. She acted honestly, insofar as she was ignorant of her duties as a director and the law restricting loans to directors. However, she could

> not be said to have acted reasonably nor would it be fair to excuse her because of her ignorance. She was held jointly and severally liable with her husband to repay the unauthorised loans (Re Queensway Systems Ltd [2006] EWHC 2496 (Ch)).

3. Indemnity and insurance

Directors

A company's articles (or any other contract with the company) **cannot automatically exempt** any director from liability for (s 232 CA 2006):
– negligence;
– default;
– breach of duty; or
– breach of trust.

This is why such decisions are ratified on a case by case basis where possible, ¶2497+ above.

> MEMO POINTS The provisions of the new Companies Act relating to indemnity came into force on 1 October 2007. They **apply to** provisions made by companies to indemnify their directors on or after that date. Provisions made before that date continue to be governed by the old rules, which are effectively the same (s 309A, 309B, 309C CA 1985; paras 15, 16 Sch 3 SI 2007/2194).

2512

However, companies can offer **limited indemnities** to their directors and directors of associated companies. Such indemnities cannot cover liability incurred by a director (s 234 CA 2006):
– to his company;
– to a company associated with his company;
– to pay a fine in criminal proceedings;
– to pay a fine or other sum as a result of any regulatory non-compliance;
– in defending any criminal proceedings in which he is convicted;
– in defending civil proceedings brought against him by his company or a company associated with it in which judgment is made against him; or
– in making an unsuccessful application to court for statutory relief from liability.

2513

Broadly, this **enables a company to** indemnify a director for liabilities to third parties, and for the costs of successfully defending proceedings against him. Such indemnities are referred to as "qualifying third party indemnities", and an example of one for the costs of successful defences and applications for relief is found in Table A (reg 118 TA 1985).

Qualifying third party indemnities must be **disclosed** in the directors' report accompanying the accounts (s 236 CA 2006; ¶4245+). The shareholders are also entitled to inspect these indemnities, or written memoranda of their terms if they are not in writing, in the same way as minutes of shareholder meetings (s 238 CA 2006; see ¶3869). To this end, companies are obliged to retain a copy of any indemnity or memorandum of terms at the registered office or another permitted location (either where the register of shareholders is kept or at the company's principal place of business, as long as they are located in the same part of the UK as the registered office (para 16 Sch 3 SI 2007/2194)) while the indemnity is in force and for at least 1 year after its termination or expiry (s 237 CA 2006). A company can charge 10p per 500 words or part of 500 words for copies of the indemnities or memoranda, plus the reasonable costs of sending the copies out (reg 4 SI 2007/2612). Failure to keep the indemnities or their terms as required or to allow inspection or permit copies to be taken renders any officer in default liable to a fine (¶9935).

> MEMO POINTS 1. A company cannot indemnify its director for an unsuccessful **application for relief** under the provisions relating to the acquisition of shares by an innocent nominee (s 144(3), (4) CA 1985; restated at s 661(3), (4) CA 2006, expected to come into force by 1 October 2009), as well as an unsuccessful application under the general relief from liability provisions (¶2505+ above).
> 2. Companies which are **trustees of occupational pension schemes** may also indemnify their directors against liability for the company's activities as trustee, as long as the indemnity does not include (s 235 CA 2006):
> – liability for a fine in criminal proceedings or for any regulatory breach; or
> – the cost of unsuccessfully defending criminal proceedings.

This is known as a "qualifying pension scheme indemnity". The same retention and inspection rules apply.

3. The draft **new model articles** will contain a qualifying third party indemnity (private companies limited by shares: art 53; public companies: art 85).

4. Draft regulations have been published under the new Companies Act which will allow companies to keep their records, including copies of qualifying indemnities, at the registered office or at one alternative **location** that is situated in the same part of the UK as the registered office (reg 5 draft Companies (Company Records and Fees) Regulations 2007). This part of the draft regulations is likely to come into force by 1 October 2009, when it will replace the transitional provisions in SI 2007/2194. For the proposed regulations on how a person can inspect company records, see ¶2669/mp.

5. The reference for the **copying** fee will change but the actual fee will remain the same when replacement regulations come into force (likely to be by 1 October 2009) (reg 19 draft Companies (Company Records and Fees) Regulations 2007). Copies will be able to be provided in hard copy or electronic form, as requested, but companies will not have to present the copies in a different way to that in which they are kept (regs 11-13 draft Companies (Company Records and Fees) Regulations 2007).

2514 A company's articles can **reduce the effect of**, or **relieve** directors from, certain duties to which they would otherwise be subject (for example, by allowing a director to have a conflict of interest provided it has been disclosed, ¶3308+).

> MEMO POINTS   It is common for directors' liability to be limited in their **service contracts** to gross negligence, so that they are only liable for their own intentional or reckless acts and omissions. Although this can be effective in terms of contractual liability, if the director is sued in tort for negligence, such a clause will have no effect (*Kuwait Asia Bank EC v National Mutual Life Nominees Ltd* [1990] 3 All ER 404). The director could also be sued separately for breach of duty (*Henderson v Merrett Syndicates Ltd* [1994] 3 All ER 506).

2515 A company can purchase and maintain liability **insurance** for its directors for any type of liability, including those for which an indemnity is not permitted (s 233 CA 2006). Cover can be provided either to individual directors (and officers) or to the company itself as reimbursement for any indemnity it has lawfully provided to its directors.

However, insurance **cannot be obtained** in respect of acts which would be contrary to public policy (for example, fraud, dishonesty or malicious conduct, or indemnity for civil or criminal penalties imposed by the courts).

> MEMO POINTS   The draft **new model articles** will also enable companies to purchase and maintain insurance for the benefit of its officers (private companies limited by shares: art 54; public companies: art 86).

Other officers

2517 There are no equivalent statutory **restrictions** on exempting or indemnifying other officers of the company from such liability. The indemnity contained in Table A covers other officers as well (reg 118 TA 1985). **Auditors**' liability is dealt with at ¶4301+. Liability insurance can also be maintained in respect of other officers.

> MEMO POINTS   The provisions in the draft **new model articles** relating to indemnities will only apply to directors (private companies limited by shares: art 53; public companies: art 85). Therefore, companies wishing to be able to indemnify other officers will have to alter these provisions. The draft new model articles will allow companies to purchase and maintain liability insurance for the benefit of officers and other employees (private companies limited by shares: art 54; public companies: art 86).

II. Specific duties

2532 Statute imposes many different duties on directors, breach of which can result in civil and/or criminal liability, depending on the provision in question. The duties have been grouped here according to the field to which they relate, with the different types of liability and relief (where available) specified in each case. These duties are from the Companies Acts and other legislation.

Breaches of specific statutory duties often involve a breach of a director's general duties as well, and may also lead to the director being disqualified (see ¶3012).

Civil liability

If a director breaches a statutory duty which imposes civil liability, there are usually specific consequences set out in the relevant provision. Commonly, he will be liable to account to the company or to pay damages for any loss.

He may be able to apply for statutory **relief** from liability, and/or take advantage of any relief provision attached to that particular duty.

2534

Criminal liability

Statute imposes numerous criminal penalties on company officers, mainly relating to record keeping and filing obligations. A comprehensive table of such duties under the Companies Acts 1985 and 2006, the Business Names Act 1985, the Insolvency Act 1986 and the Company Directors Disqualification Act 1986 is included in the table at ¶9935, which notes the various penalties which can be imposed. The duties discussed here are those which are not dealt with elsewhere and which impose significant liability and/or will commonly affect directors.

Criminal liability usually requires that a criminal act has been committed with **intent**, although some criminal offences render the offender liable even if he did not intend his actions or omissions to result in the criminal act. These are known as "strict liability" offences.

2536

A **director** who commits a crime (including criminal offences under the Companies Act) will generally be liable for his own actions (e.g. theft of company property, false accounting) and could face a fine and/or imprisonment. He may also be ordered to yield up the proceeds of his crime. Companies Act offences impose strict liability on the company, but its officer will be in default if he:
– knowingly and wilfully authorises or permits the relevant breach in the case of an offence under CA 1985 (s 730A CA 1985; para 13 Sch 4 SI 2007/2194); or
– authorises, permits, participates in, or fails to take all reasonable steps to prevent, the breach in question in the case of an offence under CA 2006 where the provision setting out the duty and consequences of breach is already in force (s 1121 CA 2006). A corporate director will only commit an offence in respect of the company as an officer in default if one of its own officers is in default (s 1122 CA 2006). If this is the case, both the company and its officer will be liable.

In order to make directors more accountable for their actions and omissions, the new Companies Act only places liability on officers in default, rather than on the company and any officer in default, for many offences.

2537

MEMO POINTS 1. Companies Act offences usually apply to **other officers**, which include secretaries and managers as well as directors.
2. Certain offences committed by a company under CA 1985 as a result of a director's consent, connivance or neglect are to be **attributed** to that director as well as to the company, including (s 733 CA 1985):
– failure by an outgoing auditor to make a statement to the company (¶4340); and
– various breaches relating to company investigations: obstructing persons with a right to enter premises, whether with a warrant or not (¶7216; ¶7240);
– unauthorised disclosure of information obtained during an investigation (¶7212+); and
– destroying etc documents and giving false information (¶7211).
Other officers of the company, and the shareholders if they manage the company, who bring about these offences in the same way are also liable.

The **company** can be found liable for breach of Companies Act offences and may be **liable to** a fine or to hand over the proceeds of crime. The company's intent to commit these offences does not have to be proved, as they are strict liability offences.

2538

For a company to be convicted of other offences which do not impose strict liability, the actions and intent of the company's officers and other managers will be examined in order to establish the necessary intention to commit the offence (for example, in the case of gross negligence manslaughter and the new statutory offence of corporate manslaughter which is expected to come into force in April 2008 (see ¶7179+). This will render the company, not the board, liable for the offence, but a director may still be liable himself and/or be held liable for conspiring with the company to commit an offence.

If a director commits an offence whilst he is carrying out his duties as a director or employee, the company can be held to be **vicariously liable** for his acts.

A. Management duties

1. General

2548 Statute imposes many duties on directors, mostly relating to housekeeping matters such as **filing and record keeping**. These duties are too numerous to discuss here, so they are listed, together with their criminal penalties and cross-references to any further discussion, in the table at ¶9935.

> *MEMO POINTS* It should be noted that the vast majority of these penalties also apply to **other officers**. The table at ¶9935 states who can be liable for each offence.

2549 The following significant managerial duties are imposed on directors:

Duty	¶¶
To act within the powers of memorandum	¶2554+
To disclose interests in contracts with the company	¶3308+
To disclose certain matters in the annual accounts	¶4245+
To disclose and obtain approval for payments made to directors for loss of office	¶2962+
To disclose directors' service contracts over 2 years long to the shareholders	¶2655+
To obtain shareholder approval of substantial property transactions	¶2567+
To observe the rules on loans to directors	¶2804+
Not to breach a disqualification order/undertaking	¶3070+

2. Act within limitations

2554 Directors' common law duty to act within their authority is discussed at ¶2348+. Although third parties can enforce transactions entered into with the company outside of the **authority of its memorandum**, directors still have a statutory duty to act within the limitations on their powers expressed in the memorandum (s 35(3) CA 1985).

This duty is closely **linked to** directors' general duty to act within his powers (this is a duty codified in the Companies Act 2006 which is already in force, see ¶2376+) as well as their common law duty to act within their authority (see ¶2348+). Since the new codified duty has the same effect, this duty will be repealed by the new Companies Act in due course.

> *MEMO POINTS* Under the **new Companies Act**, companies' powers will not have to be set out in their memoranda. In fact, the new Act will provide that companies' actions will not be able to be questioned on the ground of lack of capacity because of anything in their constitutions, and that, as far as a person dealing in good faith with a company is concerned, the directors' power to bind the company is deemed to be free of limitations under its constitution (ss 39, 40 CA 2006, expected to come into force by 1 October 2009). Having said that, directors will continue to be

under a duty to act within any such limitations (i.e. to act within their powers) and so will be liable to the company for any default in this respect (s 171 CA 2006, which is already in force).

Consequence of breach on company's actions

Statute protects **third parties** from the consequences of the company acting outside of the powers in its memorandum (for example, their transaction being rendered unenforceable) by stating that such acts will still be valid (s 35 CA 1985). For example, if the memorandum limits the company's power to borrow to a certain amount and it exceeds that limit, it cannot later challenge the validity of the loan on the ground that the transaction was entered into outside of the memorandum's powers. Therefore, a party to a transaction with a company is not required to check whether the transaction is authorised by the company's memorandum (s 35B CA 1985).

2555

Shareholders can apply to court to **prevent** a company from entering into a transaction which was not authorised by the memorandum, provided the company is not required to carry out the act by a pre-existing legal obligation (s 35(2) CA 1985). For this reason, most parties to significant transactions with a company (e.g. banks and parties to acquisitions, mergers, guarantees) will still check that a company's memorandum covers the transaction, and may require a company to change its memorandum if it does not.

MEMO POINTS The extent of this protection is **limited** to matters dealt with in the company's memorandum. Therefore, if it has breached a statutory prohibition or restriction on a transaction, this section will not render the transaction valid. Similarly, this provision does not validate transactions which can be set aside in certain circumstances for other reasons, notably those which can be challenged when the company goes into insolvency (¶7808+).

Liability

A director who breaches his duty to act within the limitations of the company's powers set out in the memorandum will incur liability as appropriate in the circumstances. For example, if he has caused loss to the company, he will be liable to pay damages in compensation; if he has made a personal gain from his actions, he will have to account to the company for it.

2556

MEMO POINTS 1. If a director breaches the **limitations** set out **in the articles** or in the **terms of the delegation** of powers to him by the board, he will be in breach of his common law duty to act within his authority or his codified general duty to act within his powers, with similar consequences (¶2376+; ¶2348+).
2. The **transaction** itself is vulnerable to being set aside if the directors acted outside their authority. Enforcement is dealt with at ¶2350/mp.
3. If a **third party** has received company property knowing that the directors or board acted outside of their powers, that third party can become a **constructive trustee** of the property and may be liable to return it to the company (ss 35(3), 35A(5) CA 1985). If the shareholders are willing to excuse a third party of this liability following an act which was outside of the company's memorandum, they must pass a separate special resolution to that effect (s 35(3) CA 1985). If the act was within the company's powers, but outside of the board's or director's powers, the shareholders may ratify it by ordinary resolution.

s 35(3) CA 1985 is expected to be repealed by 1 October 2009 and there will not be an exact equivalent in the **new Companies Act**, although directors are obliged to act within their powers (see ¶2376+). Instead, as far as a person dealing in good faith with the company is concerned, the directors' power to bind the company will be deemed to be free of limitations under its constitution and a person will not be acting in bad faith just because he knows that the act in question is beyond the directors' powers (s 40 CA 2006, expected to come into force by 1 October 2009).

Relief

If shareholders wish to **excuse the directors** from their liability under this section, they must pass a separate special resolution to that effect (s 35(3) CA 1985). The director(s) should make a full and frank disclosure of the circumstances to enable the shareholders to pass a valid resolution.

2557

MEMO POINTS Even when this provision has been repealed, the shareholders will still be able to ratify such a breach under the **new Companies Act**, see ¶2497/mp.

Contracts between a company and its director

2559 The legislation makes specific provision for the situation in which a director (of the company or its holding company) enters into a contract with the company, and in doing so the board has **exceeded** any of its **powers** set out in the memorandum, articles or shareholder resolution(s).

> MEMO POINTS The **new Companies Act** will include an equivalent provision (s41 CA 2006, expected to come into force by 1 October 2009).

Consequences on the transaction

2560 The **shareholders** have the power to declare such a transaction void if (s 322A CA 1985):
a. it was entered into with:
– a director of the company;
– a director of the company's holding company;
– a person connected to any such director; or
– a company associated with any such director; and
b. the board has exceeded any limitation on its powers under the company's constitution in entering into it. This includes limitations on the company's powers in the memorandum, the board's power to bind the company and authorise others to do so (in the memorandum, articles and shareholder resolutions and agreements) as well as procedural requirements to ensure valid decision making.

> MEMO POINTS 1. A transaction **cannot be declared void** in certain circumstances, where (s 322A(5) CA 1985):
> – restitution (of money or other assets the subject of the transaction) is not possible;
> – the company is indemnified for any loss or damage arising out of the transaction;
> – a person who is not a party to the original transaction but who has paid, acted in good faith and was not aware of the board exceeding its powers would be affected if the original transaction is declared void (e.g. a subsequent purchaser); or
> – the shareholders have ratified the transaction in a general meeting.
> 2. **Shadow directors** are not included within this section. **Alternate directors** are included, unless they are not acting as directors in entering into the transaction (*Playcorp Pty Ltd v Shaw* (1993) 10 ACSR 212). The definitions of **connected persons** and **associated companies** are explained at ¶9930.

2561 **Third parties** in this situation can apply to the court for a declaration as to the **status of the contract** (s 322A(7) CA 1985). The court has the power to affirm, sever or set aside the transaction, taking into account all of the circumstances to arrive at the fairest decision for all concerned. Case law has indicated that the principal purpose of the provision is to protect companies against the directors entering into such transactions to the company's detriment and the directors' benefit, and so this is something the court will look for, although its discretion is so wide that its absence will not preclude a declaration being made (*Re Torvale Group Ltd* [1999] 2 BCLC 605).

Director's liability

2562 Whether the shareholders exercise their right to declare the contract void or not, the director is still liable in the following ways (s 322A(3) CA 1985):
– to **account** to the company for any gain (whether made directly or indirectly) he has received from the transaction; and
– to **indemnify** the company for any loss or damage which results from the transaction.

> MEMO POINTS 1. Although these liabilities are not expressed in the legislation as being **joint and several** (between different directors involved) or as taking effect **cumulatively**, this is implied because a company cannot recover the same loss twice. Therefore, if a director has accounted for all of the profit he made out of an offending transaction, there will be no need for him to indemnify the company; if he has accounted for some of his profits, he will only have to indemnify the company for the remainder.
> 2. A director can be **liable concurrently** under this section and **other statutory or common law provisions** for the same act (e.g. misapplying company funds, or failure to account for profits) (s 322A(4) CA 1985). Although the company would not be able to recover its loss more than once,

proceeding against the director under different provisions can widen the scope of the remedies available to the company. For example, this statutory provision does not allow for restitution or tracing, but they may be available at common law.

The shareholders may be willing to **ratify the act** in question (s 322A(5)(d) CA 1985; and see ¶2497+ for where and how ratification is possible).

2563

Connected persons/associated companies

This provision also **applies to** contracts between the company and persons connected to directors or companies associated with them which are outside of the company's powers in its memorandum. Connected persons and associated companies are defined at ¶9930.

2564

In such cases, the connected person or associated company is also **liable** to account and/or indemnify the company for its loss (s 322A(3) CA 1985). They will be exempted from liability if they can show that they were not aware of the board exceeding its powers at the time the transaction was entered into (s 322A(6) CA 1985).

3. Substantial property transactions

All directors are **prohibited from** entering into a "substantial property transaction" with the company unless the shareholders consent by ordinary resolution (s 190 CA 2006). Shareholder approval must either be obtained before the transaction or arrangement is entered into, or the transaction or arrangement must be conditional on approval being obtained. The ordinary resolution can be passed at a meeting or by written resolution.

2567

Transactions included in this prohibition are arrangements between the company and:
– its director;
– a director of its holding company; or
– a person connected to either its director or a director of its holding company,
in which the company acquires or disposes of a non-cash asset over a certain value.

Some transactions or arrangements are **not included**:
– where a director receives anything to which he is entitled under his service contract (s 190(6) CA 2006);
– where a director receives anything in compensation for loss of office (s 190(6) CA 2006);
– those between the company and a person in his capacity as a shareholder (rather than his capacity as a director) (s 192 CA 2006);
– those between the company and its wholly-owned subsidiary (s 192 CA 2006);
– those between two wholly-owned subsidiaries of the same company (s 192 CA 2006);
– those where the company is in compulsory liquidation, CVL or administration (s 193 CA 2006); and
– where the director or his connected person carries out the transaction on a recognised investment exchange through an independent broker (s 194 CA 2006).

<u>MEMO POINTS</u> 1. The definition of "**connected persons**" is complicated and discussed in detail at ¶9930.
2. A **non-cash asset** includes any interest in property other than cash. If an arrangement involves more than one non-cash asset, or there are a series of arrangements, they are to be added together to see if they pass the threshold or not (s 190(5) CA 2006).
3. "**Transactions**" is to be interpreted widely to include contracts and less formal arrangements.
4. If the transaction is with a **director** of the company's **holding company** (or his connected person), it is the shareholders of the holding company who need to give prior consent to the transaction (s 320(1) CA 1985).
5. In relation to the CA 1985 provisions, the court allowed **shareholder consent** to a substantial property transaction to be given informally by a sole shareholder, applying the "*Duomatic*" principle (*NBH Ltd v Hoare* [2006] EWHC 73 (Ch); and see ¶3590+ for a discussion of shareholders' informal agreement).
6. These provisions of the new Companies Act only apply to transactions or arrangements entered into on or after 1 October 2007. If the transaction or arrangement was entered into **before 1 October 2007**, the old rules still apply (para 7 Sch 3 SI 2007/2194). The basic prohibition is the same, except that shareholders must give their prior consent to the arrangement or transaction (s 320(1)

CA 1985). In addition, there is no provision for several non-cash assets or a series of arrangements to be aggregated to see if they should require approval, and payments under service contracts and for loss of office are not exempted. The old rules apply where a company is in administration but not if it is in compulsory or creditors' voluntary liquidation. Otherwise, the same exceptions apply (s 321 CA 1985).

If a transaction or arrangement was approved before 1 October 2007 but entered into afterwards, the approving resolution is still effective as long as it complies with the new Act.

2568 This prohibition only applies if the **value of the non-cash asset** at the date the transaction is entered into is either (s 191 CA 2006, as amended by para 10 Sch 1 SI 2007/2194):
– more than 10% of the company's asset value and more than £5,000; or
– more than £100,000.

For these purposes, the company's net asset value is either (s 191(3) CA 2006):
– the net asset value in the most recent statutory accounts (if they have been prepared); or
– the amount of the company's called-up share capital (if no accounts have been prepared).

MEMO POINTS 1. A transaction covered by this prohibition will usually also need to be **disclosed** in the annual accounts (¶2897).
2. The "**statutory accounts**" are those prepared under CA 1985 until the provisions of the new Companies Act dealing with accounts come into force on 6 April 2008 (applying to financial years commenced on or after 6 April 2008) (para 10 Sch 1 SI 2007/2194).
3. If the **old rules** apply, approval is required for substantial property transactions worth over at least £2,000 which also amount to 10% of the company's asset value or over £100,000 (s 320(2) CA 1985). The net asset value is determined in the same way.

Consequences and liability

2570 If a director has entered into an unauthorised substantial property transaction, there are consequences on both the transaction itself and the director (or his connected person).

The **transaction** will be voidable by the shareholders, i.e. they can choose whether or not to let it stand (s 195(2) CA 2006). If the shareholders **declare it to be void** (also referred to as it being "set aside"), the parties must be returned to the positions they were in before the transaction, i.e. the asset must be returned to the seller and the purchase price to the buyer. The transaction **cannot be declared void** if:
a. restitution of the asset in question is not possible, e.g. because it no longer exists;
b. the company has already been indemnified in respect of its loss by another party;
c. a third party who has paid for it without knowing (or being able to know) of the director's breach would be unfairly affected by allowing the transaction to be set aside; or
d. the company (or the holding company, as appropriate) has ratified the transaction at a general meeting within a reasonable time of the transaction (s 196 CA 2006).

MEMO POINTS If the **old rules** apply, the consequences on the transaction are the same (s 322 CA 1985).

2571 Regardless of whether the shareholders have been able to avoid the transaction, the **director**, his connected person, and any director of the company who authorised the transaction or arrangement are **liable** to (s 195(3) CA 2006):
– account for any gain he has made from the transaction, either directly or indirectly; and
– indemnify the company for any loss it has suffered as a result (jointly and severally with any other director or connected person liable).

If the director's actions have breached any of his other duties, that liability also still stands (s 195(8) CA 2006).

A connected person or director authorising the transaction will **not** be **liable** if he can show that at the time of the transaction he was not aware of the circumstances giving rise to the contravention (s 195(7) CA 2006). A director will not be liable in respect of a transaction between the company and his connected person if he can show that he took all reasonable steps to ensure compliance (s 195(6) CA 2006).

MEMO POINTS If the **old rules** apply, the consequences for directors and connected persons are the same (s 322 CA 1985).

4. Liability for defrauding creditors

2577

If a business is carried on with the intention of defrauding creditors, or for any other fraudulent purpose, every director who knows he is a party to carrying on business in that way is guilty of an offence (s 993 CA 2006). He will be **liable** to imprisonment and/or a fine (¶9935). Note that the maximum term of imprisonment that can be incurred for this offence has been increased to 10 years to bring it into line with similar dishonesty offences under other legislation.

Comment: This specific Companies Act offence is separate from the much **wider statutory offence of fraud** contained in the Fraud Act 2006. This sets out various ways in which fraud and some associated offences (such as possessing articles for use in frauds) can be committed. The main offence of fraud can be committed in three ways:
– by false representation (s 2 Fraud Act 2006);
– by failing to disclose information contrary to a legal obligation to do so (s 3 Fraud Act 2006); and
– by abuse of position (s 4 Fraud Act 2006).
The offences can be committed by companies as well as individuals. In addition, if a company commits one of the offences with the consent or connivance of a director or other officer (including those purporting to be officers), that individual will also be guilty of the offence (s 12 Fraud Act 2006).

MEMO POINTS 1. This is separate from any liability for the insolvency offence of **fraudulent trading** (¶7443+).
2. This offence also applies to **other officers** and any other person (e.g. a shareholder) who was knowingly a party to the offence.
3. This section of the new Companies Act only came into force on **1 October 2007**. However, it applies to offences committed before that date as well (para 46 Sch 3 SI 2007/2194). If the offence occurred before 15 January 2007, the maximum term of imprisonment is still 7 years.

5. Liability for company cheques etc

2580

A director can be personally liable to pay under a cheque or other order for money or goods authorised or issued by him, if the company's name is not clearly stated on that cheque or document (s 349 CA 1985). He is also liable to a fine (¶9935). This provision also includes bills of exchange, promissory notes and endorsements.

EXAMPLE Mr F and Mr L were directors of PC Ltd. They provided FCG Srl with 3 post-dated cheques in respect of goods supplied. The company's name did not appear correctly on the cheques, omitting "Limited" or "Ltd". The first cheque was presented and dishonoured; FCG Srl concluded that there was no point in presenting the other cheques and commenced proceedings for payment. Mr F and Mr L were liable on the first cheque as it had been dishonoured; and since the bank would have been entitled to do the same with the others because the company's name did not appear correctly on them, they were personally liable in respect of them as well (*Fiorentino Comm Giuseppe Srl v Farnessi* [2005] 2 All ER 737).

MEMO POINTS 1. This also applies to **other officers** and any other person acting on behalf of the company.
2. BERR has published draft regulations under the **new Companies Act** requiring companies to include the company's registered name on certain documents, including cheques (draft Companies (Trading Disclosures) Regulations 2008; s 82 CA 2006). Minor discrepancies between the name as registered and as it appears on the document will be allowed, such as the use of lower or upper case letters or punctuation, as long as the discrepancy is not likely to cause confusion (s 85 CA 2006). Contravention of these regulations will prevent the company from bringing any legal action based on the document, and render the company and any defaulting officer liable to a fine (s 83 CA 2006; reg 9 draft Companies (Trading Disclosures) Regulations 2008). The implementation date for these changes is yet to be announced at the time of writing.

B. Employment duties

1. Health and safety

2590 A director may be **personally prosecuted** in respect of certain health and safety offences, if the company has been convicted of the offence first. The relevant offence would have to have been committed by his company with his **consent or connivance** of, or can be attributable to any **neglect** on his part (for example, where a director refuses to authorise expenditure on essential health and safety training) (s 37 HSWA 1974; art 32 SI 2005/1541). Connivance would include deliberately turning a blind eye to health and safety breaches, such as knowing that machinery is being operated dangerously but not taking any action. See ¶7178 for when a company could be liable for health and safety offences.

This type of offence is only **applicable** to directors who have the power to decide corporate policy and strategy (*R v Boal* [1992] BCLC 872).

A **successful prosecution** could result in a fine and/or imprisonment.

> EXAMPLE In *R v Rollco Screw and Rivet Co Ltd* ([1999] 2 Cr App Rep (S) 436), the directors were fined in respect of a serious incident involving asbestos contamination.

> MEMO POINTS 1. For **further details** regarding a company's health and safety requirements, see *Employment Memo*. These are briefly summarised at ¶623.
> 2. The Institute of Directors (IoD) publishes **guidance** for boards on health and safety good practice. At the time of writing, the IoD had consulted on an updated version, which set out four core actions to be taken along with good practice guidelines on how the actions should be effected. The actions are:
> – Planning: complying with the legal requirement for companies with more than five employees to have a written health and safety policy, as well as ensuring that health and safety is a core part of the company's culture, values and performance standards, e.g. having in place effective strategies for communication about health and safety within the company, a regular review procedure, allocating responsibility for health and safety matters and making sure that the issue is regularly addressed by the board.
> – Delivering: by putting the appropriate management systems and practices into place. This includes ensuring that adequate resources are devoted to the issue and that risk assessments are carried out.
> – Monitoring: both incident-led and routine reporting need to form part of a company's monitoring strategy. Companies need to review changes in work practices and procedures to make sure that health and safety issues continue to be addressed, as well as investigating major failures. Companies also need to keep up to date with developments in health and safety regulation and adapt their policies and practices as necessary.
> – Reviewing: health and safety performance should be reviewed by the board on an annual basis (as a minimum).
> The draft guidance stresses the benefits to businesses of dealing with health and safety issues properly, including reducing costs by minimising employee absences and potential legal actions, and improving the company's reputation. It also reminds directors and other officers of their potential personal liability for health and safety breaches, and the fact that directors can be disqualified for conviction of this offence as well (see ¶3012). The IoD proposes to issue a version suitable for smaller companies in due course.
> 3. This duty also applies to **other officers** of the company who are in a position to decide upon health and safety policy.

2591 A company may be liable for **involuntary manslaughter** (i.e. death caused by gross negligence) if a specific director who is sufficiently senior to embody the company can be identified as being guilty (see ¶7175+ for a further discussion of a company's potential liability in this regard). Company directors may also be liable for health and safety offences in respect of the death.

> MEMO POINTS The government has reformed the problematic issue of **corporate manslaughter**. See ¶7179+ for a company's current liability in this regard and an outline of the new Corporate Manslaughter and Corporate Homicide Act 2007, which is expected to come into force in April 2008.

2. Other employment duties

a. Have regard to employee interests

2596 Until 1 October 2007, directors were under a specific duty to have regard to the interests of the company's employees (s 309 CA 1985, now repealed (Sch 2 SI 2007/2194)). This duty has now been absorbed by the directors' general duty to exercise reasonable care, skill and diligence, as part of which directors must consider a number of factors when making decisions, including the impact on the employees (see ¶2411+). As with the duty under CA 1985, the new codified duty is owed to the company and therefore cannot be **enforced by** the employees themselves. Unless the employees are also shareholders, there is little they can do under company law if the directors do not consider their interests and they should rely instead on their rights under employment law.

b. Immigration

2598 It is a criminal offence for an employer to employ an adult (i.e. a person aged 16 or over) who does not have **permission to live and work in the UK** (s 8 Asylum and Immigration Act 1996).

The **penalty** is a fine (of up to £5,000 on a summary conviction or unlimited on indictment), the severity of which will depend on the seriousness of the offence and the employer's financial circumstances. Any officer of the company will be jointly liable with the company if the offence was committed with their consent or as a result of their neglect.

> MEMO POINTS s 8 Asylum and Immigration Act 1996 will be repealed by s 26 Immigration, Asylum and Nationality Act 2006 on a date to be appointed. It will be **replaced by** an offence of employing an adult subject to immigration control who does not have leave to enter or remain in the UK (s 21 Immigration, Asylum and Nationality Act 2006). The penalty for contravention will be imprisonment (of potentially up to 14 years) and/or an unlimited fine. Directors will still be able to be held personally liable (s 22 Immigration, Asylum and Nationality Act 2006). In addition, a company which employs a person over 16 who does not have permission to live and work in the UK will be liable to a civil penalty (s 15 Immigration, Asylum and Nationality Act 2006). A range of other enforcement action will be able to be taken against employers in breach, such as assisting them to comply and draw up an action plan.

C. VAT

2606 A director may be criminally liable to a fine and/or imprisonment for VAT offences, such as fraudulent evasion of VAT, or the production or use of false documents and statements (s 72 Value Added Tax Act 1994). Generally, criminal proceedings are only instigated in respect of serious offences, such as the evasion of over £75,000 in a 3 year period. See *VAT Memo* for further details. VAT fraud could also form the basis of an action against the directors for breach of their duty of good faith to the company (*Fresh n' Clean (Wales) Ltd v Miah* [2006] EWHC 903 (Ch)).

D. Insolvency

2612 If a company is insolvent or is likely to become insolvent, various offences may be committed by a director, requiring him to **contribute to** the company's assets. These offences are summarised here; more detail can be found by following the cross-references.

Offence	Summary	¶¶
Fraudulent trading	A director carries on the company's business during winding up intending to defraud creditors or others, or for any other fraudulent purpose. Could also lead to criminal liability under the parallel offence of defrauding creditors under companies legislation (¶2577).	¶7443+
Wrongful trading	A director fails to take every reasonable step to minimise the potential loss to the company's creditors when he knew, or ought to have concluded, that there was no reasonable prospect that company would avoid insolvent liquidation	¶7449+
Misfeasance	A director has during winding up: – misapplied, retained or became accountable for any of the company's money or property; – been guilty of misfeasance; or – breached any fiduciary or other duty	¶7457+
Transactions which may be set aside	The transaction can be set aside and the director may be liable to make up any loss to the company	¶7808+
Trading under prohibited name	A director involved in a business trading under the name of (or one similar to) a company which has gone into liquidation in last 12 months	¶264+

MEMO POINTS   With the exception of trading under a prohibited name and wrongful trading (which apply to directors and shadow directors only), the above penalties can be imposed on **other officers** and any other person involved in the breach.

SECTION 4

Service contract

2627 Directors do not have to be employees of their companies as well as officers, but it is common for them to enter into a service contract to be employed to provide services beyond the normal duties of their office. Service contracts **benefit** companies and directors by ensuring that both parties are aware of their rights and obligations.

MEMO POINTS   1. A **non-executive director** is usually appointed under a formal letter of appointment setting out his remuneration and the minimum number of board meetings he is expected to attend.
2. A director's **employment status and rights** as an employee, as well as employment contracts in general, are dealt with in *Employment Memo*.

A. Form and content

2635 The service contract will usually be **entered into by** the company whose business the director is appointed to manage, but in certain circumstances it may be appropriate for the director to be employed by another company in the group.

The service contract is usually formalised **in writing**, although it can be oral.

MEMO POINTS   Certain **statutory written particulars** must be provided to the director as an employee **within** 2 months of the start of his employment (s 1 Employment Rights Act 1996). These particulars can be incorporated into his service contract or provided to him separately, for example where his contract is not in writing.

2636 The **terms** of the service contract will be **set by** the board, or a director or committee to which the task has been delegated (reg 84 TA 1985). The service contract must be formulated in the best interests of the company; not to do so may result in a breach of duty by the director(s) who drafted it.

The **provisions of the articles** of association must be considered when setting the terms, because they will override any inconsistent provision in the service contract. The articles will only be incorporated into the director's service contract if this is an express term (*Globalink Telecommunications Ltd v Wilmbury Ltd* [2003] 1 BCLC 145). This is because the articles are a contract between the shareholders and the company, whereas the service contract is between the director and the company.

Note that as well as the **express** terms of the service contract, a director's relationship with the company will also be subject to terms **implied** by:
– common law (for example, fiduciary duties towards the company);
– the employment relationship (for example, the duty of mutual trust and confidence); and
– statute, which sets out general as well as specific duties and liabilities.

> MEMO POINTS 1. A **specimen service contract** is provided at ¶9925.
> 2. Draft **new model articles** under the **new Companies Act** have been published for private companies limited by shares and public companies. They will leave the board to decide what services a director will provide to the company (private companies limited by shares: art 19; public companies: art 22).

2637 Most directors' service contracts will set out their contractual rights and obligations in detail. Specialist advice should be sought since the contract may be subject to detailed **negotiation**, particularly if the director has other interests which could conflict with those of the company.

Key terms

2639 In addition to the usual employment terms and conditions which are found in contracts of employment for general staff, the **terms** below are specifically relevant to directors and will usually be incorporated into the service contract.

Term of appointment

2640 Many service contracts will not be for a fixed term, but will **run from** commencement **until** terminated by either side. Companies or directors looking for stability may wish to include a fixed term in the contract.

The company can enter into a service contract for a **fixed term** of up to and including 2 years without prior approval from the shareholders, or one for a longer period, provided the company can terminate it by giving notice in any circumstances (s 188 CA 2006). For approval of a service contract for a longer fixed term, see ¶2652+.

> MEMO POINTS Where a service contract was **entered into before 1 October 2007**, the old rules still apply, allowing it to be for a fixed term of up to and including 5 years without prior shareholder approval (s 319 CA 1985; para 6 Sch 3 SI 2007/2194).

Job title and place of work

2641 The service contract should set out the director's job title, area(s) of responsibility and place of work. Any specific duties should be included. In certain circumstances, it is advisable for the service contract to contain some **flexibility** as to the director's role and place of work to ensure that the company will not be in breach of contract should it wish to vary these terms, for example by moving the director to a different office. In practice, flexibility clauses should be exercised with caution and after taking specific legal advice.

Duties

2642 The director's **legal obligations** to the company will usually be described in broad terms, reflecting the wide obligations owed by him to the company. These will often include requirements that the director:
– works full-time and devotes the whole of his attention to the company;

- complies with the lawful and reasonable instructions of the board;
- endeavours to promote the company's best interests; and
- does not have any other business interests without the prior consent of the board.

> *MEMO POINTS* Directors owe an **implied duty** to the company to carry out their service contracts with reasonable skill and care. Breach of this implied duty can lead to an action by the company for negligent performance of the service contract. Since this is closely linked to the director's general duty to exercise reasonable care, skill and diligence in running the company, such actions are usually worded in terms of both categories of breach (see ¶2411+).

Remuneration

2643 The service contract will usually specify the director's remuneration package, dealing with his salary, fees as an officer, pension and any other benefits in kind. This is discussed in detail at ¶2696+.

Restrictions on competition

2644 There is an implied duty of fidelity in every employment relationship, which prevents employees from competing with their employer's business or soliciting its customers **during employment**. For clarification and to emphasise the importance of non-competition, the service contract can contain an express clause, setting out the restrictions that the company wishes to impose on the director in respect of potential competition during the directorship.

However, as the duty of fidelity only endures **post-employment** in the case of trade secrets, it is usual to include an express clause in the service contract specifying categories of confidential information and trade secrets (to ensure that the parties are aware of what kind of information is included in these categories) and contractually extending the duty of fidelity to cover confidential information once the employment is terminated. If appropriate, the company may also want to protect its business interests post-employment by including the following **restrictive covenants**:
- non-compete provisions, relating to a prohibited area, specific competitors and/or activities;
- non-solicitation provisions, relating to customers or other employees; and/or
- non-dealing provisions, relating to customers.

Any such post-employment provisions can only provide the company with as much protection as is reasonably necessary. Consequently, they should be sufficiently certain and limit the time and area in which they are effective. To do otherwise may render them uncertain or unreasonable and therefore unenforceable. Since the balance is difficult to get right, specific legal advice should always be sought when drafting restrictive covenants.

2645 It is also important to set out clear provisions regarding the ownership of **intellectual property rights**, particularly if the director is involved in research and development of any kind. The clause should ensure that the company protects its ownership of such rights and that the director is aware of his obligations in this regard.

Termination and dismissal

2646 The service contract should specify:
- any specific **grounds** for dismissal;
- the period of **notice** upon which either party may terminate the director's employment; and
- whether the company is able to make a **payment in lieu of notice** or place the director on "garden leave".

Fixed-term contracts will state the date on which the contract will end.

In practice, termination of employment often, but not always, results in **termination of office** (¶2912+). The exercise of termination provisions requires legal advice to ensure that the company does not expose itself to tribunal claims for unfair, wrongful or constructive dismissal (¶2986).

B. Approval

2652 The **terms** of a director's service contract must usually be approved by the board (although the articles may make other provision, e.g. that the shareholders have to approve all service contracts). The board can delegate this function to a committee or an executive director, such as the managing director (reg 72 TA 1985). The contract will not be binding if it is **not properly approved** (*UK Safety Group Ltd v Heane* [1998] 2 BCLC 208; but see ¶2350/mp for when directors may (rarely) be able to enforce such contracts).

2653 A director may find himself at a board meeting at which his service contract is considered, for example when the contract is up for renewal or variation (e.g. pay rises), in which case his **interest** in his service contract must be **disclosed** to the board (¶3308+).

Each company's articles will provide whether or not the director has the **right to vote** at a meeting regarding the contract. If the company is governed by Table A, he cannot vote or count in the quorum at the meeting (regs 94, 95 TA 1985), unless the shareholders have dis-applied the relevant regulations by ordinary resolution (reg 96 TA 1985).

> MEMO POINTS Under the **new Companies Act**, directors will no longer have to disclose interests in their own service contracts (ss 177, 182 CA 2006; the implementation date for these provisions is yet to be announced at the time of writing).

Contracts for a period of more than 2 years

2655 Directors in a strong bargaining position may negotiate a **fixed-term contract** to give them greater job security. Although shareholders have the right to remove a director from office at any time and for whatever reason (¶2946+), his removal from office is likely to terminate his employment as well, rendering the company liable to a large compensation payment (unless the director was removed because of his fundamental breach of contract). To protect the company from directors negotiating lengthy fixed-term contracts, **prior approval** is specifically required from the shareholders where the contract is for a fixed period of more than 2 years and it (s 188 CA 2006):
– cannot be terminated by the company giving notice during the period; or
– may only be terminated by the company giving notice in specified circumstances.

The 2 years includes any period for which the employment continues otherwise than at the company's instance (i.e. when the company cannot terminate it) as well as any period of notice the company has to give the director of termination.

> MEMO POINTS 1. If the contract is with a **director of the holding company**, the holding company's shareholders must also approve the terms of the service contract (s 188(1) CA 2006).
> 2. For these purposes, a **service contract includes** all contracts under which a director agrees to perform services for the company or its subsidiaries, whether they are directorial services or not, and contracts under which a director is engaged by a third party to perform services for the company or its subsidiaries (s 227 CA 2006).
> 3. If the service contract was entered into **before 1 October 2007**, the old rules still apply, requiring shareholder approval of service contracts for a period longer than 5 years (s 319 CA 1985; para 6 Sch 3 SI 2007/2194). If a contract was approved by the shareholders before 1 October 2007 but entered into afterwards, the shareholder resolution will still be effective as long as it complies with the requirements of the new Act.

2656 Approval is **given by** ordinary resolution. If approval is to be gained **at a general meeting**, the service contract (or a written memorandum of its terms) must be made available for inspection by the shareholders at the registered office at least 15 days before (and including) the date of the meeting. It must also be available at the general meeting itself. If approval is to be obtained **by written resolution**, the document(s) must be sent to the shareholders either with or before the written resolution.

2657 If shareholder approval is **not obtained**, the term referring to the period longer than 2 years will be void, but the rest of the contract will stand. Instead, the service contract will be deemed to be terminable on **reasonable notice** (s 189 CA 2006). Reasonableness is determined by considering all of the circumstances of the case, including the status and remuneration of the director, his age, length of service, and the usual practice in that trade and industry. Under employment law, there are statutory minimum notice periods which will apply, corresponding to an employed director's length of service. In practice, his employment and office will usually end together (see ¶2912+).

> MEMO POINTS   If the **old rules** apply, the consequences of breach are the same (s 319(6) CA 1985).

2658 A company cannot avoid having to obtain shareholder approval by entering into "**rolling**" **service contracts** with a director. For instance, this may occur where a director is employed under a service contract for under 2 years which can only be terminated by the company giving notice in certain circumstances (or cannot be terminated by the company at all) and he enters into a further contract when it has more than six months left to run. In these circumstances, the period of the new service contract is deemed to include the unexpired period of the previous service contract (s 188(4) CA 2006). If the combined duration of the new service contract together with the unexpired term of the previous one is more than 2 years, then shareholder approval is required.

> MEMO POINTS   1. Nor can companies evade the requirement by engaging "independent" directors under a **contract for services** (i.e. those engaged as contractors, rather than as employees) as these contracts are subject to the same rules.
> 2. If the **old rules** apply, a similar restriction is in place (s 319(2) CA 1985).

Signature on behalf of the company

2660 The service contract, once approved, can be signed on behalf of the company, see ¶3486+. Whoever signs the service contract must have **authority** to do so. There is no implied right for a single director (including the managing director) to sign a service contract on behalf of the company.

C. Retention and inspection obligations

2668 Each service contract (or written memorandum of its terms if the contract is not in writing) must be copied and **kept at** (s 228 CA 2006; para 13 Sch 3 SI 2007/2194):
– the company's registered office; or
– the company's principal place of business or the place where the register of shareholders is kept, as long as they are in the same part of the UK in which the company is registered.

Copies of the contracts and memoranda must also be retained for inspection for at least 1 year after they have expired or been terminated.

> MEMO POINTS   1. If they are **not kept at the company's registered office**, the company must notify Companies House of their whereabouts within 14 days using Form 318 (para 13 Sch 3 SI 2007/2194). The name of Form 318, like the names of other Companies House forms, is taken from the section number of the legislation. As all of the section numbers will change under the new Companies Act, Companies House proposes to change the names of all of its forms to reflect their function rather than the relevant section number ("Working with Companies House: a consultation on the registrar's rules and related provisions which will apply under the Companies Act 2006"). At the time of writing, the new form names are not yet available.
> 2. If the contract was **entered into before 1 October 2007**, the old rules still apply (para 13 Sch 3 SI 2007/2194; s 318 CA 1985). They impose the same retention and inspection obligations on the company, except that they do not require the contracts and memoranda to be kept for at least 1 year after their termination or expiration. The old rules also include an exemption to the retention obligations where (s 318(5), (11) CA 1985):
> – the director works wholly or mainly outside the UK, although a copy of the service contract or memorandum should be kept for inspection, stating the terms regarding duration and (if the contract is with the company's subsidiary) the name and place of the subsidiary's incorporation; or
> – the service contract will expire or can be terminated by the company without paying compensation within the next 12 months.
> 3. Draft regulations have been published under the new Companies Act which will allow companies to keep their records, including copies of service contracts, at the registered office or

at one alternative **location** that is situated in the same part of the UK as the registered office (reg 5 draft Companies (Company Records and Fees) Regulations 2007). This part of the draft regulations is likely to come into force by 1 October 2009, when it will replace the transitional provisions in SI 2007/2194. For the proposed regulations on how a person can inspect company records, see ¶2669/mp below.

2669

The contracts and memoranda should be made available (free of charge) for **inspection** by the shareholders (s 229 CA 2006). Any variations must be kept by the company and made available for inspection by the shareholders in the same way. Shareholders are also entitled to a **copy** of the contracts and memoranda at a cost of 10p per 500 words or part of 500 words, plus reasonable delivery costs (reg 4 SI 2007/2612). The company must comply with a request within 7 days of receiving it (s 229(2) CA 2006).

MEMO POINTS 1. Draft regulations under the new Companies Act regarding the inspection and copying of company records have been published. They will require private companies to **make their records available** for inspection for at least 2 hours between 9am and 5pm on a working day to a person who has given notice to the company that they wish to inspect the records (reg 6 draft Companies (Company Records and Fees) Regulations 2007). The notice will either have to be given 10 working days in advance, or 2 working days in advance if notice of a general meeting has been given or a written resolution has been sent to the shareholders for their approval. Public companies will be subject to the same requirements, except that notice will not have to be given that a person wishes to inspect the records (reg 7 draft Companies (Company Records and Fees) Regulations 2007). A company will not have to present the records in a different way to how they are kept, for example a person inspecting records cannot ask to see the records in alphabetical order if they are kept in date order (reg 8 draft Companies (Company Records and Fees) Regulations 2007). The draft regulations will allow a person inspecting the records to make copies of them at the same time (reg 9 draft Companies (Company Records and Fees) Regulations 2007). These regulations are likely to come into force by 1 October 2009.
Until these regulations come into force, companies should allow shareholders to inspect the contracts/memoranda during business hours.
The draft regulations will also restate the fees for providing **copies** when they come into force (reg 19 draft Companies (Company Records and Fees) Regulations 2007). Copies will be able to be provided in hard copy or electronic form, as requested, but the company will not have to present the copies in a different way to that in which the records are kept (regs 11-13 draft Companies (Company Records and Fees) Regulations 2007).
2. If the contract was entered into **before 1 October 2007**, or the request to inspect was made before that date, the old rules apply, which require companies to allow inspection of the documents during business hours (para 13 Sch 3 SI 2007/2194; s 318(7) CA 1985). Under the old rules, companies were not obliged to provide copies of the documents on request.

Breach of these provisions can give rise to the directors in default being held liable (¶9935). If the company has not allowed the contracts/memoranda to be inspected or copied as required, the court can also order it to do so.

2670

MEMO POINTS 1. **Other officers** in breach will also be held liable.
2. If the contract was entered into **before 1 October 2007**, or the breach occurred before that date, the old rules still apply (para 13 Sch 3 SI 2007/2194). They impose liability for breach on the company as well as any officer in default, but the court can only order the company to allow the contracts/memoranda to be inspected (not copied as well) (s 318(8),(9) CA 1985).

D. Breach of service contract

By director

The consequences of breach by the director will usually be set out in the service contract by reference to the company's disciplinary procedure. In addition to (or instead of) removing or disciplining the director, the company may be entitled to pursue him for breach of contract and (¶2434+):
– recover damages;
– obtain an order for the director to account for profits;

2678

– obtain an injunction; or
– avoid an unauthorised transaction entered into by the director.

Further, in cases of **fundamental breach**, the company can treat the contract as discharged and dismiss the director without pay or payment in lieu of notice (known as "summary dismissal") and can also sue for damages. What constitutes a fundamental breach will depend on the facts of each case, including the director's past conduct. Examples include gross misconduct (such as disobedience or dishonesty), serious negligence/incompetence and serious breach of duty. If the breach is **not fundamental**, the company will not be justified in summarily dismissing the director from his employment, and will be liable for wrongful dismissal if it does so (*Wilson v Racher* [1974] IRLR 114). In such cases, the company's remedy will be in damages or withholding the salary of the director (¶2712).

MEMO POINTS 1. A director may be entitled to claim that he has been **unfairly dismissed**. Each case will turn on its own facts, and factors such as whether a disciplinary procedure was followed will be taken into account. See ¶2986 for a summary of unfair dismissal and the other main employment claims.
2. As well as their general duty to exercise care, skill and diligence (¶2411+), directors are under an **implied duty** to exercise skill and care in performing their service contracts.

2679 The company's right to dismiss the director under employment law does not always accord with the shareholders' right to **remove him from office**. The distinction between a director's status as an officer and an employee should be borne in mind. While shareholders have the right to dismiss a director from office, if in doing so they render an employed director unable to fulfil his service contract, the company could be liable under employment law. See ¶2912+ for dismissal of a director (from his employment and from office).

By company

2681 If the service contract is breached by the company, the director is entitled to an appropriate remedy. In the case of a **fundamental breach** (which usually takes the form of the company unilaterally varying the service contract, e.g. reducing the director's salary, varying his working hours or changing his work duties), the director can opt to treat himself as constructively dismissed and seek compensation for wrongful and/or unfair dismissal (¶2986). If he chooses not to leave his employment, or the breach is **not fundamental**, he may be able to obtain:
– damages;
– compensation for arrears of salary or other payment(s) to which he was entitled;
– an injunction ordering the company to/not to carry out a particular action; or
– a declaration of his rights.

SECTION 5

Remuneration

2696 Since most directors are employees as well as officers, they will be remunerated in both capacities. Remuneration is usually **set out** in detail in directors' service contracts.

2697 The appointment of a director to **office** does not automatically entitle him to any remuneration for the performance of his services or reimbursement for any expenses he incurs as a result of his office, sometimes referred to as "directors' fees". He is only **entitled to** remuneration if authorised by the shareholders or, more usually, the company's articles (*Guinness plc v Saunders* [1990] 1 All ER 652; although such a provision in the articles does not constitute a contractual promise to pay, *Hickman v Kent or Romney Marsh Sheep-Breeders' Association* [1914-15] All ER Rep 900). In practice, it is common for the **service contract** to provide that such fees are included in the fixed salary payable to the director for the performance of his duties under his service contract. A non-executive director will, on the other hand, be paid a fee for attending company meetings rather than salary.

If the company has adopted **Table A**, directors will be entitled to be paid whatever fees the shareholders decide upon by ordinary resolution (reg 82 TA 1985). If the resolution does not state the rate at which the fees accrue, it will be on a daily basis.

> MEMO POINTS Draft **new model articles** under the **new Companies Act** have been published for private companies limited by shares and public companies. They will enable the board to fix the directors' remuneration (private companies limited by shares: art 19; public companies: art 22).

If a director receives remuneration that has **not** been properly **authorised**, he will be liable to return it to the company (¶2398+). **2698**

> MEMO POINTS 1. A director who receives unauthorised remuneration for his office may be allowed to keep some or all of it as **compensation** for work done for the company on a quantum meruit basis (i.e. calculated according to what the work was worth); although in *Guinness plc v Saunders* (above), Lord Templeman doubted this could be possible where the articles conferred power to award remuneration on the board and the board had not exercised that power.
> 2. The draft **new model articles** provide that, unless the board decides otherwise, directors do not have to account to the company for any remuneration they receive as directors, officers or employees of the company's subsidiaries or as officers or employees of any other company in which the company is interested (private companies limited by shares: art 19; public companies: art 22).

On the other hand, a director has an **implied right** to be paid **as an employee** in accordance with his contractual terms, provided he is ready and willing to work or he is absent due to illness or other unavoidable circumstances (*Miles v Wakefield Metropolitan District Council* [1987] 1 All ER 1089). Table A enables, but does not oblige, the board to determine a director's remuneration as it sees fit (reg 84 TA 1985). **2699**

> MEMO POINTS 1. **Employment rights** relating to remuneration are discussed in *Employment Memo*. Employed directors are afforded the same employment protection given to any other employees such as the right to **equal pay** and the right to be paid at least the national **minimum wage**.
> 2. The draft **new model articles** will enable the board to fix the directors' remuneration (private companies limited by shares: art 19; public companies: art 22).

Formulating a package

The board usually determines the remuneration package of a director, although the task may be delegated to a committee, or reserved to the shareholders. Table A allows the board to fix remuneration for employment, but the shareholders can determine directors' fees by ordinary resolution (respectively, regs 84, 82 TA 1985). **In practice**, the board will agree a package incorporating both elements along with any others that are appropriate, which the shareholders will approve. **2701**

If the articles specify **how** remuneration is **to be determined**, another method or a different amount to that already agreed cannot be substituted without following the correct approval process (*Guinness plc v Saunders* [1990] 1 All ER 652).

The International Corporate Governance Network, ICGN, publishes **Remuneration Guidelines** to assist companies in formulating remuneration plans which address the need to attract executive talent, while remaining fair and open. The guidelines are based on:
– transparency, so shareholders can access and understand the remuneration plan;
– accountability, by requiring shareholders' approval of remuneration reports; and
– performance, requiring pay and bonuses to be linked to performance goals on a long and/or short term basis as appropriate in the circumstances.

While the guidelines are clearly aimed at larger companies which have the resources to appoint a specific remuneration committee, they are useful reading for companies of any size as they highlight the need for, and give practical advice on how to achieve, an open and clear performance-related remuneration plan. They can be found on the ICGN website.

When **negotiating** a director's remuneration package, the board must keep the best interests of the company in mind and ensure that it can afford to pay the sum agreed. In particular, the board must ensure that a director's remuneration is not excessive. What is regarded as "**excessive**" will vary considerably from company to company, influenced by factors such **2702** as the size of the company and the industry in which it operates. There is no "going rate", as such, for directors (*Secretary of State for Trade and Industry v Van Hengel* [1995] 1 BCLC 545).

Agreeing an excessive remuneration package can **result in**:
a. breach of duty by the directors agreeing to it (¶2379+);
b. the remuneration being challenged by the insolvency practitioner if the company goes into liquidation or administration and the director being required to repay the excessive amount (¶7811+), or the directors agreeing to and/or receiving the remuneration being disqualified if the company enters any type of insolvency (¶3000+); or
c. minority shareholders seeking redress through an application to court on the ground of unfair prejudice (¶2105+).

> EXAMPLE A sole director of a company who awarded himself bonuses and increases in salary at a time when he had been committing numerous breaches of duty as a director (including running a competing business and misappropriating company funds) was liable to account to the company. Given his behaviour, he could not have thought that the payments were justified or in the company's interests, and he could not argue that the shareholders had informally and unanimously approved these payments because he had concealed his conduct from them (*Simply Loans Direct Ltd v Wood and others* [2006] All ER (D) 291 (Jun)).

A. Elements of remuneration

2710 A director's remuneration package is likely to have a mixture of fixed and fluctuating elements and will usually **include** one or more of the following:
– fixed salary;
– directors' fees (usually incorporated into the salary);
– bonus, incentive payments and commission;
– pension;
– other non-cash benefits;
– shares and share options; and
– other payments (for example, lump sums and gratuities).

Fixed salary

2712 A director's service contract will usually set out his fixed salary, with his associated rights and obligations.

The company can **withhold or deduct** sums from his salary if there is a specific term in his service contract which provides for it. In addition, if an employed director is not ready and willing to work or if he declines to perform part of his job, the company is entitled to withhold wages for the period in question without terminating the service contract or having to apply for damages for breach of contract.

2713 There will usually be a specific provision in a director's service contract which will state whether **pay reviews** and **increases** are contractual or discretionary. In exercising its discretion, the company must not act arbitrarily, capriciously or unfairly (*Gardner (F.C.) Ltd v Beresford* [1978] IRLR 63). If the contract is silent, there will be no contractual right to a pay review or increase (*Murco Petroleum Ltd v Forge* [1978] IRLR 50). **Most companies** provide salary reviews on an annual basis with a right to a discretionary increase.

There may be a specific contractual provision allowing for an **automatic** annual increase linked to inflation and calculated by reference to an appropriate index (for example, the retail prices index).

Expenses

2715 Commonly, the service contract will provide for the **reimbursement** of a director's expenses which are incurred in the course of his duties. If the company has adopted Table A, then the directors will be reimbursed for all travelling, hotel and other expenses properly incurred by them during the course of carrying out their directorial duties (reg 83 TA 1985). Alternatively, a company may decide to grant a director a round sum for expenses covering a certain period **in advance**. Shareholder approval is required for the reimbursement or advancement of expenses over a certain amount, see ¶2828.

> MEMO POINTS   The draft **new model articles** will also provide for the reimbursement of directors' expenses (private companies limited by shares: art 20; public companies: art 23).

Bonus, incentive payments and commission

Bonuses, incentive payments and commission are often offered as a reward for performance and/or loyalty, and will usually be in the **form** of additional payments or awards such as share options.

2717

Bonuses are normally **calculated** either on an individual basis and determined by the director's own performance results over the required period, those of his department or the whole company. In contrast, incentive schemes will usually set **targets** which will need to be achieved in a specified period before any payments can be made. Commonly, payments under a commission scheme will vary depending on the **director's performance**. They may be based on a percentage of sales received or on set amounts, such as a fixed amount per sale. Occasionally, a director's salary may be based solely on commission payments, although this is rare.

> MEMO POINTS   "**Long-term incentive schemes**" are distinguished from regular incentive schemes for accounting purposes on the basis that the qualifying targets cannot be fulfilled within a single accounting period.
> Discrimination against a person on the ground of his age is now unlawful (SI 2006/1031). Companies must be careful when drafting long-term incentive schemes not to fall foul of this prohibition, for example, a provision which rewards employees for their length of service without serving as a genuine incentive for the employees to stay with the company may be in breach. Therefore, performance-related targets would be more appropriate.

A service contract must clearly indicate whether any scheme under which a bonus, incentive or commission payment is paid is either **contractual** (where the director has a right to payment, provided he has satisfied express conditions) **or discretionary** (giving the company the freedom to withdraw or replace the terms of the scheme). Companies usually opt for the latter as it gives them more flexibility, although if the discretion is exercised irrationally or perversely, the director will have an action for breach of contract, and may be able to claim constructive dismissal (*Mallone v BPB Industries plc* [2002] EWCA Civ 126).

2718

The service contract must specify **when** any payments will be made and **how** they will be **calculated**. If a director is to be paid a guaranteed minimum payment under any one scheme, then this should also be expressly provided for.

A service contract must also provide for what happens when a director's **employment terminates** before payment under a particular scheme is due. Some companies state that payments will only be made if the director is still employed (and notice has not been given by either side) at the date of payment.

Pension

Most companies' articles include a provision allowing them to provide benefits such as pensions to former directors (such as reg 87 TA 1985). Many companies offer **occupational pension schemes**, also known as retirement benefit schemes, which make tax efficient retirement provision for their employees and directors (if they are "registered schemes"). Alternatively, most companies offer to contribute to their employees' **personal pension schemes**. If there is no suitable pension provision, some companies are obliged to offer access to a **designated stakeholder scheme**. More details on these schemes can be found in *Employment Memo*.

2720

> MEMO POINTS   The draft **new model articles** will also allow companies to make pension arrangements for directors (private companies limited by shares: art 19; public companies: art 22).

Other non-cash benefits

2722 Companies often provide their directors and employees with non-cash benefits, known as **benefits in kind**. Such benefits include the provision of life assurance, directors' liability insurance, a company car, private health care and gym membership. The service contract should specify what non-cash benefits, if any, are to be given to the director and the company should ensure that what is in the service contract corresponds with the company's policies.

Shares and share options

2724 Sometimes a director's service contract will provide that he is entitled to be given, or to purchase, a number of shares in the company, free or for a reduced price. Such shares are known as "employee shares" and special rules apply to them (see ¶847+).

Schemes approved by Revenue and Customs allow the employer to make such shares or options available to the employees with any profits on the shares generally being subject to capital gains tax (CGT) rather than the more expensive income tax and national insurance (NIC), providing certain conditions are met. Corporation tax relief for the costs of the scheme should also be available to the company. However, due to the restrictions inherent in such schemes, many companies prefer to use alternative ways of passing shares to directors.

> MEMO POINTS 1. Directors who have interests in shares or debentures in their company, or a group company, need to make particular **disclosures** to the company (¶3308+).
> 2. For more detail on approved and unapproved schemes, see *Tax Memo*.

2725 The types of approved schemes are summarised below.

Type of scheme	Purpose/features	Reference (ITEPA 2003)
Share incentive plans (SIP)	**Generally**: To provide employees with continuing stake in company valued at up to £7,500 per annum. Certain conditions to be met, e.g. same terms applicable to all. Scheme offers four categories of shares, with different conditions for approval. **Tax**: Income and capital gains tax relief available with different rules applying to each category of shares. Generally, no charge to income tax, provided shares remain in plan for at least 5 years, but if capital receipt on shares within 5 years of acquisition, deemed employment income charge arises. CGT on disposal depends on timing of disposal. Costs to company allowable for corporation tax purposes.	ss 489-515, Sch 2
Enterprise management incentives (EMI)	**Generally**: To recruit/retain key employee. Enables small higher-risk trading companies to grant qualifying share options without income tax consequences. Maximum value of unexercised options per employee is £100,000, with overall maximum value for company of £3 million. **Tax**: No charge to income tax on grant of option. If option is exercised within 10 years at: – at least/more than market value: no charge; or – less than market value (at time option was granted): charge based on difference between market value and amount paid by director for option and shares. Certain disqualifying events result in tax benefits being lost. Disposals chargeable to CGT (taper relief starts on grant of option, which reduces CGT payable). Company should receive corporation tax deduction on exercise of option.	ss 527-541, Sch 5

Type of scheme	Purpose/features	Reference (ITEPA 2003)
Savings-related share option schemes (SRSOS)	**Generally**: Acquisition of shares using funds from savings scheme. Contributions to savings scheme between £10 and £250 per month. Need eligible employees and eligible shares. **Tax**: No charge to income tax on grant of option, increase in value, interest or bonus paid. Only charge to income tax on exercise of option if within 3 years of grant due to takeover. Disposal chargeable to CGT. Costs to company allowable for corporation tax purposes.	ss 516-520, Sch 3
Approved company share option schemes (ACSOP)	**Generally**: Options can be granted to selected individuals as long as aggregate unexercised options do not exceed £30,000. Need eligible employees and eligible shares. **Tax**: Generally no charge to income tax on grant of option or increase in value. Exercise of option is income tax-free provided occurs between 3 and 10 years of grant, or exercise on death or where employee is "good leaver". Disposals chargeable to CGT. Costs to company allowable for corporation tax purposes.	ss 521-526, Sch 4

The **common conditions** for all approved schemes are:

Factor	Requirements
Type of share	Ordinary, fully paid up, non-redeemable
Type of company issuing shares (except EMI scheme)	A company which is either: – quoted on a recognised stock exchange; – controlled by a quoted company; or – not controlled by another company
Restrictions on shares	Minimal restrictions allowed, except restrictions: – imposed on all shares of same class; and – within articles requiring disposal of shares when employees leave employment
Exclusion of employees with material interest	Material interest varies according to type of scheme

Other payments

2727 Companies may decide to make a **one-off lump-sum payment** to a director in particular circumstances, commonly on commencement ("golden hellos"), variation and termination ("golden handshakes") of the service contract. Alternatively, such payments could be made to reward or incentivise directors.

B. Taxation

2735 The tax treatment of remuneration received by an executive director with a service contract is generally the same as that of other employees.

MEMO POINTS 1. The **detail** of the various taxes is dealt with in *Tax Memo*. An employer's obligations relating to all aspects of pay, including pensions, are dealt with in *Employment Memo*.

2. The prohibition on companies making any payment to a director under his service contract which is **tax-free** or which is **calculated by reference** to **income tax rates** was repealed as of 6 April 2007 (SI 2006/3428).

1. National Insurance contributions

2740 Directors' earnings are subject to Class 1 National Insurance contributions (NICs). **Primary contributions** are deducted from the director; **secondary contributions** from the employer, both through the PAYE ("pay as you earn") system. Broadly speaking, NICs are based on a director's earnings (including fees and bonuses) as well as the value of any asset he receives for his employment which can be easily converted into cash (e.g. a physical asset such as gold, investments such as shares, and the benefit of a debt claim). Most benefits which do not fall within this category (e.g. the use of a car) will be caught under Class 1A NICs, which are only payable by the employer.

Directors' NICs are treated differently to other employees' in that the calculation is **based on** the total cumulative annual earnings of the director, rather than on each monthly payment. The NICs can be **deducted on** a monthly account (with the director's consent), but will have to be recalculated at the tax year end and any shortfall paid. NICs can be **calculated by** two methods: based on adapted Revenue and Custom's NIC tables or the exact percentage method, either as for normal employees or using a special method applicable to directors only.

MEMO POINTS 1. Directors' NICs need to be recorded on **forms** P14 (the end of year summary) and P11 (deductions working sheet).
2. If the director continues to work **over the state pension** age (65 in most cases), he is not liable for Class 1 primary contributions. The company, however, must continue to pay Class 1 Secondary and Class 1A NICs for as long as the director is employed.

2. Income tax

2745 Directors will be charged income tax on earnings from their office or employment (s 62(2) ITEPA 2003) if they (s 15 ITEPA 2003):
– are resident or ordinarily resident in the UK; and
– perform their duties wholly in the UK for a UK employer.

A director's income tax liability is **based on** his salary, and most additional benefits he receives. The benefits dealt with below are not comprehensive, but are those likely to be awarded to a director. Benefits received by a director must be **declared to** Revenue and Customs using Form P11D.

Income tax for employed directors is **deducted by** way of the PAYE system, and they are also likely to be subject to self-assessment in relation to any tax which is not deducted at source.

MEMO POINTS Broadly speaking, a director will be treated as being **ordinarily resident** in the UK if:
– he visits the UK and has accommodation here which implies a stay of 3 years or more, e.g. a lease for that period; or
– his visits to the UK average 91 days or more per tax year.

For directors **not resident or not ordinarily resident in the UK**, different rules apply. Earnings received in the UK by directors who are either not resident or not ordinarily resident in the UK but their duties are performed partly in the UK and partly overseas must be apportioned between the two countries (s 25 ITEPA 2003). Where earnings are received in respect of work done abroad:
– by directors who are resident but not ordinarily resident in the UK, regardless of whether the work was done wholly or partly abroad; or
– by non-domiciled directors of an overseas employer,
they are assessed on a remittance basis (i.e. when physically received in the UK) (ss 22, 26 ITEPA 2003).

2746 "**Earnings**" **means** a reward for services (including future services), and for these purposes is **defined as** all salaries, fees, wages, perquisites (i.e. income derived from casual employment in addition to a regular salary) and profits. Therefore, this will include a director's fixed salary, fees and any other payments such as those made under a commission, incentive or bonus scheme. Provided they **arise from** the director's office or employment, they are assessable for tax whether or not they are received from the company (*Hochstrasser (Inspector of Taxes) v Mayes* [1959] 3 All ER 817).

The amount of earnings subject to tax will be **reduced** to take account of necessary travel and subsistence expenses, and other necessary expenses (e.g. subscriptions) incurred wholly and exclusively in the performance of the director's employment (s 336 ITEPA 2003). A company can apply for a dispensation to cover directors' expenses (even in the case of directors with a controlling shareholding), which reduces the administrative burden on both the employer and employee.

> MEMO POINTS 1. Payments such as **lump sum payments** are subject to different rules, which are summarised at ¶2750 below.
> 2. A payment will generally be **deemed not** to be taxable **earnings** where it is made under a contractual right which is outside the scope of the employment or office and/or which is made as a personal gift.

Pension

A new pensions regime came into force on 6 April 2006, and is discussed in detail in *Tax Memo*. The former "approved" schemes which enjoyed tax advantages are now known as "**registered schemes**". There is no minimum contribution required, and no limit on the amount of contributions which can be made to a pension, although only a certain amount will attract tax relief (s 190 FA 2004). The employer's contributions to their employees' registered schemes are still deductible against taxable profits in the period when paid so long as they are paid wholly and exclusively for business purposes (s 196 FA 2004). If contributions exceed £500,000 per annum, a special spreading rule operates. The maximum aggregate contribution on which **tax relief is available** is the higher of £3,600 per tax year and 100% of the employee's earnings (up to £215,000 for 06/07; £225,000 for 07/08). If the cumulative contributions by the employee and employer exceed this amount, the scheme member will be liable to a higher rate tax charge, which will be assessed via his tax return (s 227 FA 2004).

Unregistered schemes, or employer financed retirement benefit schemes, have no such tax advantages.

Lump sum payments

In addition to earnings paid in the normal course of employment, payments may also be made in the form of a lump sum on the commencement, termination or variation of employment. Such payments are often made as **compensation** for the loss or surrender of rights, or for failure to give notice of termination. Alternatively, a lump sum payment may simply be made to **reward** an employee for past or future services. The nature of a lump sum payment will determine whether and how it is taxed. They are taxable as earnings if received in return for services, which will encompass most such payments, for example, a contractual payment in lieu of notice (*EMI Group Electronics Ltd v Coldicott* [1999] STC 803).

General type of lump sum payment	Further detail of type	How taxed	Reference
On commencement of employment	As inducement/in anticipation of future services ("golden hello")	As earnings	*Glantre Engineering Ltd v Goodhand* [1983] 53 TC 165
	Compensation for giving up an advantage in previous employment (rare)	Tax free	*Pritchard v Arundale* [1971] 3 All ER 1011

General type of lump sum payment	Further detail of type	How taxed	Reference
On termination/variation of contract [1]	Contractual payment	As earnings	s 6 ITEPA 2003
	Reward for past services	As earnings	s 6 ITEPA 2003
	Compensation for loss of office	First £30,000 tax free [2, 3] then taxed	s 401 ITEPA 2003
	Following death/injury/disability	Tax free [2]	s 406 ITEPA 2003
	To registered pension scheme	Tax free [2]	s 407 ITEPA 2003
	Relating to periods of foreign service	Tax free [2] or partly tax free, depending on whether meets qualification criteria	ss 413, 414 ITEPA 2003
	Statutory redundancy payment	Tax free, but amount of redundancy payment reduces £30,000 exempt amount [3]	s 309 ITEPA 2003
	Non-statutory redundancy payment	Depends on whether it is compensation for loss of office or reward for past services (see above)	s 401 ITEPA 2003
Payments in lieu of notice	Due to company's breach of contract for failure to give notice	Tax free, but amount reduces £30,000 exempt amount [3]	s 401 ITEPA 2003; *Cerberus Software Ltd v Rowley* [2001] IRLR 160
	Contractual liability	As earnings	s 6 ITEPA 2003
	Discretionary contractual payment	As earnings	*EMI Group Electronics Ltd v Coldicott* [1999] STC 803
	Garden leave	As earnings	s 6 ITEPA 2003
Ex gratia payments [4]	On retirement due to disability or illness, or for termination of employment on employee's death	Not taxed	s 406 ITEPA 2003 Revenue and Customs Statement of Practice 10/81
	Payment treated like a benefit paid from a pension scheme (affects employees nearing retirement age)	Taxed, whether registered scheme or not	–
	Other ex gratia payments on termination	First £30,000 tax free [3] then taxed	–
Restrictive covenants payments	Individual payment made in return for director restricting his future activities	As earnings	s 225 ITEPA 2003
	As part of termination settlement	Tax free as far as payment reaffirms undertakings in service contract, but amount reduces £30,000 exempt amount. [3] If payment is excessive, will be taxed as earnings	Revenue and Customs Statement of Practice 3/96

Note:
1. Company is obliged to **report** any **payments** made over £30,000 to Revenue and Customs by 6 July following the end of the tax year.
2. Qualifying **conditions** apply.
3. £30,000 is a **one-off tax-free amount** per employment (s 404 ITEPA 2003). Therefore, if director receives redundancy payment and another payment in compensation for loss of office, they both go to reduce £30,000.

Non-cash benefits

Non-cash benefits which are provided to a director by virtue of his employment (but not necessarily by his employer) are generally taxable.

2752

> MEMO POINTS 1. Certain benefits are **exempt** (although qualifying criteria may have to be met), for example, relocation costs up to £8,000 (ss 271, 287 ITEPA 2003), a single mobile phone (s 319 ITEPA 2003) and the provision of certain types of childcare (ss 318, 318A ITEPA 2003) are not taxable benefits.
> 2. Directors (and employees) **earning £8,500 or more per annum** are treated differently in respect of the taxation of their non-cash benefits to those earning less than £8,500 per annum (ss 216, 217 ITEPA 2003). Here, the former position only is dealt with.
> Directors (including shadow directors) who **earn less than £8,500** per annum will be treated as if they earned over the threshold if they have a **material interest in the company** (s 216 ITEPA 2003). A material interest is defined as control of more than 5% of the ordinary share capital or, if the company is a close company, if more than 5% of the assets that could be distributed to the director on a notional winding up (s 68 ITEPA 2003).
> The assessment of this **earnings threshold** includes annual salary, all benefits and reimbursed expenses. Contributions to registered pensions or payroll giving schemes can be deducted in calculating the threshold, but employment expenses (including those paid directly by the employer, unless covered by a dispensation) cannot.

The **cash equivalent** of a taxable non-cash benefit is included as income of the director and he will be taxed accordingly. The general principle is that the value of the benefit (or its cash equivalent) is the full cost to the provider. With the exception of car fuel, any **contribution from the director** to the cost of a benefit will reduce its cash equivalent. Certain benefits have **specific valuation rules**; the key ones in relation to directors are described below.

2753

Type of non-cash benefit	Basis of valuation	Reference (ITEPA 2003)
Car	Percentage (not exceeding 35% and determined by car's CO_2 emissions level) of list price of car [1]	ss 114–148
Fuel	Percentage (not exceeding 35% and determined by car's CO_2 emissions level) of fixed sum (£14,400 from 6 April 2003)	ss 149–153
Entertainment	Generally, cost of providing entertainment [2]	s 265
Living accommodation for the directors/their family/household [3]	Annual value of property less rent paid by director. Adjusted if accommodation is used for part of year Additional charge for properties costing more than £75,000	ss 102–113
Ancillary services (e.g. heating, lighting, cleaning, repairs, decoration)	Cost of service to company	ss 201–209
Liability insurance	Generally, cost of providing benefit. Usually claimed as deductible expense of employment	ss 201–209, 346
Interest-free or low-interest loans	Difference between rate of interest actually paid (or part of loan written off) and official rate [4]	ss 173–191
Credit card/vouchers	Cost of providing card/vouchers [5]	ss 73–96A, 266–270A
Shares/share schemes	Generally, difference between value of shares/option and price paid [6] See ¶2725 for summary of rules applicable to different types of scheme	See ¶2725

Note:
1. **Cars** registered before 01/01/98 do not have CO_2 level. Figure is based on engine capacity.
2. Companies can spend up to £150 p.a. (per attendee) tax free on staff **entertainment** (s 264 ITEPA 2003). Business lunches are not taxable.
3. **Accommodation** for this purpose excludes overnight, hotel or board and lodging accommodation. Accommodation provided for reasons of security in order for the director to carry out his duties is not taxable, but is very rare. In this case only, the amount taxable in respect of ancillary services is limited to 10% of the taxable earnings of the director (s 315 ITEPA 2003).
4. **Loans** made on commercial terms by money lending companies are not taxed in this way. See ¶2804+ for the restrictions on companies making loans to their directors.
5. **Credit cards/vouchers** in respect of parking at or near work, or for entertainment or hospitality not provided in recognition of employment (e.g. business lunches) are not taxable.
6. For further detail on these **share schemes**, see Tax Memo.

C. Disclosure of remuneration in the accounts

2761 The accounting disclosure requirements relating to a director's remuneration vary according to the **type of company** for which the director performs his duties (Schs 6, 7A CA 1985), with only the requirements applying to unquoted companies being discussed here.

Comment: Companies' disclosure obligations under the **new Companies Act** will be set out in regulations, with one set for small companies and groups and another for large and medium-sized companies and groups. This separation of the applicable rules should make compliance easier. The accounts provisions of the new Act, and the related regulations, are due to come into force on 6 April 2008 and will apply to financial years starting on or after that date.

1. Disclosure generally

2766 Companies must disclose the following aspects of its directors' remuneration in the notes to the accounts (s 232; Pt I Sch 6 CA 1985):
– emoluments;
– long-term incentive schemes;
– pension schemes;
– compensation for loss of office; and
– share options.
Each of these aspects is expanded upon in turn below.

The **amount to be disclosed** in respect of a particular financial year is the total of all sums receivable by directors during that financial year, even if they have not yet been paid. Generally, the aggregate figures paid to all directors for each aspect of remuneration need to be given, rather than a breakdown of the figures paid to each director. The table at ¶2778 summarises the disclosure requirements for each category of remuneration.

Comment: The provisions of the **new Companies Act** relating to accounts are due to come into force on **6 April 2008**. Under the new Act, regulations will set out what information about directors' remuneration will need to be given in the notes to a company's accounts (s 412 CA 2006). Separate draft regulations have been published for small companies and medium-sized and large companies, which will apply to financial years beginning on or after 6 April 2008. In the case of financial years beginning before this date, the Companies Act 1985 position applies.

Under the new draft regulations, **small companies** will have to disclose the following aspects (paras 2-4 Sch 3 draft Small Companies and Groups (Accounts and Directors' Report) Regulations 2008):
– remuneration paid to directors, including money or assets received or receivable under long-term incentive schemes, and contributions to pension schemes;
– compensation for loss of office; and
– sums paid to third parties in respect of directors' services.
Small companies do not have to include these disclosures in the copy of the accounts filed at Companies House.

Medium-sized and large companies will have to disclose the same aspects in more detail in some cases (paras 1-5 Sch 5 draft Large and Medium-sized Companies and Groups (Accounts and Reports) Regulations 2008).

The new Act will also require all companies to include details of any **advances and credits** granted to a director, as well as any guarantees entered into on his behalf, to be included in the notes to the accounts (s 413 CA 2006).

To determine whether a company has small, medium or large status, see ¶4362+.

MEMO POINTS 1. Companies legislation still uses the term "emoluments", rather than "**earnings**" as used in tax legislation. The new Companies Act will prefer the term "remuneration".

2. If remuneration information (other than the aggregate of gains made by the directors on the exercise of share options) that is required to be disclosed is **readily ascertainable from other information** shown elsewhere in the financial statements, they do not have to be disclosed again.
3. If a payment made to a director **does not relate to a particular reporting period**, it should be reported in the year it is approved for payment (since this is when the liability is created).
4. If the financial statements cover a **period** that is either **less or more than 12 months**, the remuneration disclosed must be in respect of that shorter or longer period.
5. If a director is **appointed during the year**, only the part of his remuneration earned while he was a director needs to be disclosed.

If the total of emoluments and long-term incentive schemes amounts to £200,000 or more, the company must **additionally disclose** how much of it was awarded to the **highest paid director** in that financial year, and (para 2(1), (2) Sch 6 CA 1985):
a. how much of the aggregate company contributions to directors' pensions is attributable to him;
b. if he exercised any share options, a statement to that effect;
c. if any shares were received or receivable by him under a long-term incentive scheme, a statement to that effect; and
d. if his qualifying services (¶2780) are used to calculate his pension benefits, disclose the amount of his accrued pension and the amount of any accrued lump sum.

2767

Comment: If the provisions of the **new Companies Act** apply, only medium-sized and large companies need to include this information if the aggregate of sums received or receivable as remuneration and under long-term incentive schemes equals or exceeds £200,000 (para 2 Sch 5 draft Large and Medium-sized Companies and Groups (Accounts and Reports) Regulations 2008). The details to be disclosed are:
– how much of the total of remuneration and under long-term incentive schemes is attributable to the highest paid director;
– how much of the total contributions to pension schemes is attributable to the highest paid director;
– if his qualifying services are used to calculate his pension benefits, the amount of his accrued pension and the amount of any accrued lump sum; and
– if he has exercised any share options, a statement to that effect and as to whether any shares were received or receivable by him in respect of his qualifying services under a long-term incentive scheme.

MEMO POINTS   This last condition does not apply to benefits accruing under a **money purchase pension scheme** (para 2(2) Sch 6 CA 1985).

Duty of directors

Directors must notify the company of any matter which the company would have to disclose in the accounts (s 232(3) CA 1985). Failure to do so renders the director, other officer or former officer (who held office in the last 5 years) liable to a fine (¶9935).

2769

Comment: When the provisions of the **new Companies Act** come into force on 6 April 2008, only directors and former directors who held office within the previous 5 years will be under an obligation to notify the company of such matters (s 412(5) CA 2006). Failure to do so will render the director or former director liable to a fine (s 412(6) CA 2006).

Group companies

Where a company is a member of a group, only information relating to the directors of the **reporting company** must be disclosed. Therefore, in the consolidated accounts of a parent and its subsidiaries, only payments to the directors of the parent need to be reported. Where directors are paid a single amount for **services to the group**, the board may apportion the salary as appropriate (para 12 Sch 6 CA 1985). If such an allocation is not practicable, this fact should be disclosed.

2771

Comment: Under the **new Companies Act**, group accounts will have to include the same information as individual accounts (except for certain matters which may be treated differently, and directors' remuneration is not one of those matters) (para 2 Sch 6 in both the draft Small Companies and Groups (Accounts and Directors' Report) Regulations 2008 and the draft Large and Medium-sized Companies and Groups (Accounts and Reports) Regulations 2008). However, the new Act will also require companies to disclose details of advances, credits to and guarantees given on behalf of directors (s 413 CA 2006). In the case of group accounts, such transactions will only need to be disclosed if they were made to or on behalf of directors of the parent company, whether by the company or its subsidiary.

Connected persons

2773 It should be noted that the disclosure provisions which are applicable to directors also apply to "connected persons". Therefore, any remuneration received by a person connected to a director must be included in the calculation of that director's remuneration, provided that the amount is not counted twice. The definition of connected persons is explained at ¶9930.

> EXAMPLE
> 1. A is a director of X Ltd. As part of his remuneration package, X Ltd pays his private medical insurance premiums. B, his wife, is also named on the policy and X Ltd pays an additional amount in respect of her premium. B's benefit must be taken into account in the computation of A's emoluments since B is his connected person.
> 2. C and D, husband and wife, are both directors of Z Ltd. They are still connected persons but since the remuneration of each one is disclosed in his/her own right, D's earnings are not taken into account when calculating C's emoluments and vice versa.

Comment: The draft regulations made under the **new Companies Act** will also specify that sums paid to or receivable by a director include those paid to or receivable by his connected persons and any bodies corporate controlled by him (para 6 Sch 3 draft Small Companies and Groups (Accounts and Directors' Report) Regulations 2008; para 7 Sch 5 draft Large and Medium-sized Companies and Groups (Accounts and Reports) Regulations 2008). However, this does not mean that anything needs to be counted twice towards a total sum.

2. Disclosure of particular aspects of remuneration

2778 The table below summarises what must be disclosed in relation to each aspect of remuneration. There follows an explanation of the different factors to be taken into consideration when deciding what should be disclosed and how for each aspect.

Aspect of remuneration	What must be disclosed	Additional information required re. highest paid director
Emoluments	Aggregate paid to all directors	How much of total aggregate of all aspects relates to him
Long term incentive schemes		
Pensions	Company contributions: depends on type of scheme – see table at ¶2784	How much of company's contributions relate to him
	Retirement benefits receivable by current and former directors to extent they exceed entitlements on later of when first eligible and 31/3/97	If qualifying services (¶2780) used to calculate pension benefits and not money purchase scheme, amount of accrued pension and any lump sum
Compensation for loss of office	Aggregate paid to all directors/former directors	n/a
Shares and share options	Number of directors who: – exercised options; and – became entitled to shares under long-term incentive schemes	If he exercised any share options, state that fact. If any shares were received or receivable by him under long-term incentive scheme, state that fact.

> MEMO POINTS See the explanations of the different elements below for the position under the **new Companies Act**.

Emoluments

Emoluments are to be disclosed as the aggregate figure paid to all of the directors.

2780

For these purposes, emoluments **consist of** the following items received by a director for his services (para 1(1) Sch 6 CA 1985):
- fixed salary;
- directors' fees;
- bonuses;
- expense allowances; and
- the value of any non-cash benefits.

The **qualifying services** are those provided (para 1(5) Sch 6 CA 1985):
- as a director of a company or its subsidiaries; and
- otherwise in connection with the management of the affairs of the company or any of its subsidiaries (while a director of the company).

Comment: Where the **new Companies Act** applies to the accounts (see ¶2766), the term "remuneration" will be used instead of "emoluments". For all sizes of company, this will include: salary, fees, bonuses, expenses allowances in so far as they are chargeable to income tax and the value of any non-cash benefits (para 8 Sch 3 draft Small Companies and Groups (Accounts and Directors' Report) Regulations 2008; para 9 Sch 5 draft Large and Medium-sized Companies and Groups (Accounts and Reports) Regulations 2008). It does not include any share options granted to the director or the gains made on them, company contributions to pension schemes or the benefits to which the director is entitled under such schemes, or anything received or receivable by a director under a long-term incentive scheme. "Qualifying services" will mean the same as under the Companies Act 1985 (para 13 Sch 3 draft Small Companies and Groups (Accounts and Directors Report) Regulations 2008; para 15 Sch 5 draft Large and Medium-sized Companies and Groups (Accounts and Reports) Regulations 2008).

MEMO POINTS 1. **Emoluments** for these purposes **do not include** amounts of cash or other advances that a director must repay to the company or any of its subsidiaries. However, if a director is granted a round amount for expenses and this amount is subject to income tax, it will be treated as part of his emoluments. If such payments are not treated as emoluments (and not disclosed in the year in which they were paid) but are subsequently charged to tax, the relevant amount should be included (separately) under emoluments in the accounts when practical to do so (para 11(2) Sch 6 CA 1985).
2. Any amounts which are **paid to or receivable by third parties** for making the services of a director available must be disclosed, including the nature and value of any non-cash benefits provided (para 9(1) Sch 6 CA 1985). The company's subsidiaries are not third parties.
3. Awards under **annual bonus schemes** are included under emoluments, whether payable in cash, shares or any other asset.
If a bonus is awarded in respect of one accounting period but **payment is conditional** upon the director still being employed in a future accounting period, there are two alternative scenarios:
- the condition can be regarded as something upon which the bonus depends, in which case it should be reported in the year it is paid; or
- the bonus can be regarded as having accrued to the director in one year but merely paid during the next, in which case it should be reported in the year in which it accrued.
4. **Lump-sum payments** such as golden hellos are included under emoluments, even though they may not seem to relate to the individual's services as director (para 1(6)(b) Sch 6 CA 1985).
5. Whether a director is providing **qualifying services** is a question of fact. Unless it can be unambiguously shown that a particular payment was made in some other capacity, it should be regarded as a payment for services as a director.

Long-term incentive schemes

The aggregate amounts which are paid under long-term incentive schemes must be disclosed as a distinct category. Long-term incentive schemes are those which award cash or other assets subject to certain **qualifying conditions** (relating to service or performance) that cannot be fulfilled within a single accounting period.

2782

In general, the **amount to be disclosed** includes the value of both cash and non-cash assets.

Comment: Where the **new Companies Act** applies to the accounts (see ¶2766), the aggregate paid under long-term incentive schemes will still have to be disclosed separately. The same definition will apply (paras 2, 9 Sch 3 draft Small Companies and Groups (Accounts and Directors' Report) Regulations 2008; paras 1, 11 Sch 5 draft Large and Medium-sized Companies and Groups (Accounts and Reports) Regulations 2008).

MEMO POINTS 1. Long-term incentive schemes **do not include** (para 1(4) Sch 6 CA 1985):
- bonuses determined by reference to a single year only;
- payments for loss of office and related amounts; or
- retirement benefits.

2. The **amount to be disclosed** excludes share options. If an award is made in shares, it is the number of directors in respect of whose qualifying services the shares were received that must be disclosed.

Pension schemes

2784 The company's contributions to directors' pension schemes and the benefits receivable by current and retired directors must be disclosed separately in the financial statements.

The disclosure **depends upon** the type of pension fund.

Type of scheme[1]	Disclosure
Money purchase	– Contributions paid on behalf of directors; and – number of directors accruing retirement benefits
Final salary	Number of directors accruing retirement benefits
Note: 1. **Hybrid schemes** combining aspects of both types should be categorised according to which type of benefits are most likely at financial year end.	

Comment: If the **new Companies Act** applies to the accounts (see ¶2766), all sizes of company will still have to disclose this information about pension schemes (para 2 Sch 3 draft Small Companies and Groups (Accounts and Directors' Report) Regulations 2008; para 1 Sch 5 draft Large and Medium-sized Companies and Groups (Accounts and Reports) Regulations 2008).

2785 The amount of **retirement benefits** receivable by both current directors and former directors under pension schemes must be disclosed, to the extent that they exceed the amounts the directors were entitled to on the later of (para 7(1) Sch 6 CA 1985):
- when they first became eligible for benefits; and
- 31 March 1997.

Comment: When the **new Companies Act** applies to the accounts (see ¶2766), only large and medium-sized companies will have to make this disclosure (para 3 Sch 5 draft Large and Medium-sized Companies (Accounts and Reports) Regulations 2008).

MEMO POINTS 1. For these purposes, **retirement benefits include** pensions, lump sums, gratuities and other benefits, payable in cash or otherwise. The details of any benefits in kind must be provided in the notes to the financial statements (para 7(3) Sch 6 CA 1985).
2. Amounts paid or receivable under a scheme do **not** have to be **included** in the aggregate figure to the extent that (para 7(2) Sch 6 CA 1985):
- the pension scheme does not require additional funding to make the payments; and
- additional amounts are paid or made available to all members of the scheme entitled to payment at that time on the same basis.

Compensation for loss of office

2787 Companies must disclose the aggregate amount of any compensation given to directors or former directors for loss of office (para 8(1) Sch 6 CA 1985). This includes the value of any non-cash benefits.

Comment: If the **new Companies Act** applies to the accounts (see ¶2766), this will still have to be disclosed (para 3 Sch 3 draft Small Companies and Groups (Accounts and Directors'

Report) Regulations 2008; para 4 Sch 5 draft Large and Medium-sized Companies and Groups (Accounts and Reports) Regulations 2008).

MEMO POINTS 1. If any **non-cash benefits** are included, their valuation must be explained in the notes to the financial statements.
2. This includes payments resulting from a **breach of contract** (e.g. damages, settlements or compromises) (para 8(4) Sch 6 CA 1985).
3. If a director's **pension entitlement is increased** due to him leaving office, it should be disclosed as follows:
– where the increase is made as part of the director's loss of office, the capital cost of the increase; or
– if the increase takes place after a director has already ceased to hold office, it should be disclosed as part of his pension benefits.

Shares and share options

Share options are required to be disclosed as a distinct category, giving the **number of directors** who (para 1(2)(a), (b) Sch 6 CA 1985):
– exercised the share options; and
– became entitled to shares under long-term incentive schemes.

2789

MEMO POINTS Under the **new Companies Act**, only quoted and AIM-listed large and medium-sized companies will need to disclose the amount of gains made by directors on the exercise of share options (para 1 Sch 5 draft Large and Medium-sized Companies and Groups (Accounts and Reports) Regulations 2008).

SECTION 6
Loans to directors

It is relatively common for directors to loan money to their companies to assist with cashflow, or to enter into personal guarantees or secure their companies' debts in some other way. There are, however, **specific restrictions** on the reverse transactions, i.e. directors obtaining loans or similar assistance from their companies, to prevent them from taking advantage of the company's assets for their own personal benefit.

2804

The provisions of the **new Companies Act** relating to loans to directors have come into force. Rather than prohibiting certain types of transaction, as the old rules did, the new Act requires companies to obtain shareholder approval of some transactions. Public companies and their associated companies have to refer more transactions to the shareholders than private companies. The new Act applies to transactions or arrangements entered into on or after 1 October 2007.

The **old rules** still apply to (para 8 Sch 3 SI 2007/2194):
– transactions or arrangements entered into before 1 October 2007; and
– breaches committed before 1 October 2007.

The old rules are still discussed in full to enable companies to determine whether transactions already entered into before this date breach the applicable rules. Further, if a resolution was passed before 1 October 2007 approving a transaction or arrangement under the old rules, it will still be valid provided it complies with the requirements in force at the time.

Since these two systems work in parallel during this **transitional period** while the new Act is being implemented, they are both dealt with below. The focus is on the new rules, with the position under the old rules explained separately as follows:
– summary: ¶2807+
– all companies: restricted transactions, ¶2814;
– public companies and non-relevant private companies: restricted transactions, ¶2821+; and
– all companies: exceptions to the restrictions, ¶2835+.

MEMO POINTS The restrictions on loans to directors specifically cover those to **shadow directors** as well (as applicable: s 330(5) CA 1985; s 223(1) CA 2006).

2805 The new Companies Act imposes **three levels of restrictions** on loans to directors:
- transactions for which all companies must obtain shareholder approval;
- transactions for which just public companies and their associated companies need to obtain approval; and
- transactions which can be made by any type of company without approval.

A company is **associated** with a public company if it is its subsidiary or they are both subsidiaries of the same company (s 256 CA 2006).

Shareholder **approval** should be obtained before the transaction has been entered into. While it can be obtained a reasonable period afterwards, this will only prevent the transaction itself from being declared void, it will not relieve the directors and others involved from being held liable (see ¶2886). An ordinary resolution is required, unless the company's articles demand approval on a higher majority (s 281(3) CA 2006). If the transaction is in favour of a director of the company's holding company, the holding company must approve it as well. In any case, the details of the transaction will have to be provided to the shareholders with the written resolution, or be available at the registered office for at least 15 days before the meeting as well as at the meeting itself. Generally, the details to be provided are:
- the nature of the transaction;
- the amount or value of the transaction and the purpose for which it is required; and
- the extent of the company's liability under any connected transaction.

> **MEMO POINTS** Approval is **not required** if the company is not a UK-registered company or it is a wholly-owned subsidiary of another body corporate. However, if the transaction is in favour of a director of the company's holding company, the holding company will have to approve it.

2806 This table **summarises** the types of transactions to which these restrictions apply, and gives the cross-references to further discussion of the rules.

Type of transaction	Shareholder approval required?	¶¶
Loan	✓	¶2811
Guarantee/security connected with loan	✓	¶2811
Quasi-loan	Public and associated companies only	¶2816
Guarantee/security connected with quasi-loan	Public and associated companies only	¶2816
Loan/quasi-loan to connected person	Public and associated companies only	¶2819
Credit transaction	Public and associated companies only	¶2817
Guarantee/security connected with credit transaction	Public and associated companies only	¶2817
Related arrangement	✓	¶2812; ¶2818
Expenses up to £50,000	✗	¶2828
Loan/quasi-loan/related guarantee or security up to £10,000	✗	¶2830
Credit transaction/related guarantee or security up to £15,000	✗	¶2831
Cost of defending proceedings	✗	¶2829
Cost of dealing with regulatory action/investigation	✗	¶2829
Credit transaction entered into/guarantee or security granted in normal course of business	✗	¶2831
Loan/quasi-loan/credit transaction/related guarantee or security to or regarding an associated body corporate	✗	¶2832
Loan/quasi-loan/related guarantee or security by money-lending company in ordinary course of business	✗	¶2833

Pre-1 October 2007 rules

2807 The Companies Act 1985 provides that **all companies** are subject to a basic prohibition against making loans to directors, and imposes a further level of restriction upon **public companies** and certain related private companies. "**Relevant private companies**" are:
– subsidiaries of public companies;
– subsidiaries of another private company which is itself the subsidiary of a public company; and
– the holding company of a public company.

> **EXAMPLE**
> – B plc is a public company;
> – C Ltd is the private subsidiary of a public company, B plc;
> – D Ltd is the private subsidiary of another private company (C Ltd), which is the subsidiary of a public company, B plc; and
> – A Ltd has a public subsidiary, B plc.
> Therefore, the extra restrictions apply to B plc and the relevant private companies A Ltd, C Ltd and D Ltd.
>
> A Ltd
> |
> B plc
> |
> C Ltd
> |
> D Ltd

Certain transactions which are prohibited for public and relevant private companies by these additional restrictions are not expressly prohibited for other companies. This creates a further category referred to here as "**non-relevant private companies**", which can take advantage of these "extra" permitted transactions.

> **MEMO POINTS** These provisions only apply to companies incorporated in Great Britain, therefore **foreign incorporated companies** (including those incorporated in Northern Ireland) within a group are not subject to the restrictions (although the relevant jurisdiction may impose its own restrictions). So, if B plc was incorporated in France, it could (subject to French law) make a loan to a director of its GB-incorporated parent A Ltd; on the other hand, if B plc was incorporated in GB and A Ltd was French, B plc could not make a loan to a director of A Ltd.

2808 This table **summarises** the types of loan and similar transactions which are permitted and prohibited for non-relevant private and public (and relevant private) companies under the old rules, together with the cross-references to the relevant explanation. If no cross-reference is given, the transaction is permitted because it is not prohibited for that type of company.

Type of transaction	Permitted?	
	For non-relevant private companies	For public companies and relevant private companies
Loans to directors; guarantees and securities relating to loans	✗ ¶2814	✗ ¶2814
Loans to persons connected to directors; guarantees and securities relating to loans	✓	✗ ¶2824
Small loans to directors (under £5,000)	✓ ¶2842	✓ ¶2838
Quasi-loans to directors or connected persons; guarantees and securities relating to quasi-loans	✓	✗ ¶2821
Short term quasi-loans (under £5,000 and repayable within 2 months)	✓	✓ ¶2842
Inter-company loans and quasi-loans	✓	✓ ¶2844
Loans/quasi-loans made by money-lending companies	✓ ¶2839	✓ ¶2839

Type of transaction	Permitted?	
	For non-relevant private companies	For public companies and relevant private companies
Credit transactions to directors and connected persons; guarantees or securities relating to credit transactions	✓	✗ ¶2824
Minor credit transactions (under £10,000); business credit transactions	✓	✓ ¶2843
Transactions in favour of subsidiary and other subsidiaries of same holding company	✓ ¶2840	✓ ¶2840
Transactions in favour of holding companies	✓ ¶2841	✓ ¶2841
Transactions covering directors' expenses	✓ ¶2836	✓ ¶2836
Providing directors funds to meet defence costs	✓ ¶2837	✓ ¶2837
Ancillary arrangements with the effect of a prohibited transaction	✗ ¶2814	✗ ¶2814; ¶2823

A. Restricted transactions

1. All companies

2810 All companies must obtain shareholder approval for some types of transaction. However, there are **exceptions** to this requirement in certain situations, so readers should refer to the summary table at ¶2806 and follow any relevant cross-references to specific exceptions to check whether approval is necessary.

Loans

2811 A company needs shareholder approval to (s 197 CA 2006):
– make a **loan** to its director or a director of its holding company; and
– enter into a **guarantee** or provide any **security** for a loan made by a third party to its director or a director of its holding company.

Related arrangements

2812 Following on from this requirement, other arrangements which would effectively oblige the company to take on a liability which falls within the restriction also need shareholder approval. Such related arrangements are **where** (s 203 CA 2006):
– the company does not enter into the transaction itself, but it assumes or has assigned to it obligations or liabilities which would be prohibited if it had entered into the transaction originally; or
– a third party enters into a transaction with the director that would require consent if the company had entered into it and under which the third party gains a benefit from the company or its associated company.

When seeking shareholder approval for such an arrangement, the following **details** need to be provided to the shareholders:
– the details that would have been disclosed if the company were seeking approval for the transaction to which the arrangement relates (see ¶2805);

– the nature of the arrangement; and
– the extent of the company's liability under the arrangement or any connected transaction.

> EXAMPLE
> 1. Mr Q is a director of S Ltd. Previously, he was a partner in a firm, which lent him £20,000. When he moved jobs, the loan was assigned to S Ltd. This is a restricted related arrangement.
> 2. S Ltd knows that it cannot make a loan to Mr Q. S Ltd has a close working relationship with T Ltd, a company to which it supplies goods. T Ltd offers to loan Mr Q the money instead, on the condition that S Ltd writes off some long-overdue debts owed to it by T Ltd. This is also a restricted related arrangement.

MEMO POINTS "**Arrangements**" has a wider meaning than contractually binding arrangements (for example, oral contracts). It will encompass informal arrangements, such as understandings as to how an agreement will work in practice, or a series of agreements between different parties which have the effect of creating the prohibited obligations. This ensures that agreements structured to evade the prohibitions are caught.
For these purposes, the transaction is treated as having been entered into on the **date** of the arrangement.

Pre-1 October 2007 rules

2814

A company is prohibited from (s 330(2) CA 1985):
– making a **loan** to its director or a director of its holding company; or
– entering into a **guarantee** or providing any **security** for a loan made by a third party to its director or a director of its holding company.

As with the new rules, other transactions which would effectively oblige the company to take on a prohibited obligation are also proscribed. Such **ancillary arrangements** are:
– where the company assumes or has assigned to it obligations or liabilities which would be prohibited if the company had entered into the transaction originally (s 330(6) CA 1985); or
– where the company takes part in an arrangement (between the director and a third party) which would be prohibited if the company had entered into the transaction, where the third party gains a benefit from the company, its holding company or another subsidiary of the same holding company as a result (s 330(7) CA 1985).

MEMO POINTS A **guarantee** includes an indemnity and other similar expressions (s 331(1) CA 1985).

2. Public and associated companies

Loan-like transactions

2816

Public companies and their associated companies (see ¶2805) must obtain shareholder approval of **quasi-loans** to their directors, or directors of their holding companies (s 198 CA 2006). Including quasi-loans in the ambit of the restriction ensures that companies do not evade the requirement for approval of loans by entering into a transaction in a roundabout way.

A "quasi-loan" **occurs where** the company pays an expense of the director, or agrees to reimburse him for an expense, on the condition that the director will repay the company, or he incurs some liability to do so at some point (s 199 CA 2006).

> EXAMPLE
> 1. Mr X is a director of B plc. Mr X is having personal financial problems and cannot meet the monthly mortgage repayments on his house. B plc agrees to pay the mortgage repayments on Mr X's behalf until he is able to do so himself. Mr X agrees that once his cash flow situation has improved, he will repay B plc. This agreement requires approval.
> 2. Mr X is on a business trip, and has use of the company credit card. B plc allows its directors to use the company credit card for non-business purposes, on the condition that the directors repay B plc. Such transactions also require approval.

Also prohibited are **guarantees** given or other **security** entered into by the company in connection with a quasi-loan made by a third party to the company's director or a director of its holding company (s 198 CA 2006).

2817 Public companies and their associated companies cannot enter into **credit transactions** with their directors or directors of their holding companies (s 201 CA 2006). A credit transaction **occurs where** the company (s 202 CA 2006):
– supplies goods or sells land under a hire-purchase or conditional sale agreement;
– leases or hires land or goods in return for periodical payments; or
– disposes of land or supplies goods and services on the understanding that payment (in a lump sum or by instalments) is deferred.

> EXAMPLE
> 1. Mr X is given use of a company car by B plc in the course of his duties. When B plc decides to change its fleet of cars, the company agrees to allow Mr X to buy the car for his own use by making monthly payments to B plc until he has paid the market value of the car. This agreement requires approval.
> 2. Mrs X is a non-executive director of B plc. B plc owns the office building out of which it operates. It rents spare office space to Mrs X from which she runs her separate business. This, too, requires approval.

Also prohibited are **guarantees** given or other **security** entered into by the company in connection with a credit transaction made by a third party with its director or a director of its holding company (s 201 CA 2006).

2818 Public companies and their associated companies must also obtain shareholder approval for **related arrangements** (see ¶2811) to (s 203 CA 2006):
– quasi-loans;
– credit transactions; and
– loans or quasi-loans to persons connected with their directors or the directors of their holding companies.

Connected persons

2819 Public companies and their associated companies cannot evade the requirements to obtain shareholder consent by entering into a restricted transaction in favour of a person connected to the director instead. The **definition** of a "connected person" is complex and explained in full at ¶9930. Briefly, it includes members of the director's family, companies in which he has an interest, trustees of trusts under which he benefits and business partners.

Shareholder approval is required for the following **transactions** between public companies (or their associated companies) and persons connected to their directors or directors of their holding companies (ss 200, 201 CA 2006):
– loans;
– quasi-loans;
– credit transactions; and
– guarantees or other security in connection with a loan, quasi-loan or credit transaction.

Pre-1 October 2007 rules

2821 A public or relevant private company cannot make a **quasi-loan** to its director, or a director of its holding company (s 330(3)(a) CA 1985). Quasi-loan has the same meaning as under the new Act (¶2816). Also prohibited are **guarantees** (including indemnities and similar expressions) given or **other security** entered into by the company in connection with a quasi-loan to its director or the director of its holding company made by a third party (ss 330(3)(c), 331(1) CA 1985).

2822 A public or relevant private company cannot enter into a **credit transaction** with its director or a director of its holding company (s 330(4)(a) CA 1985). "Credit transaction" has the same meaning as under the new Act.

It is also prohibited for a company to enter into a **guarantee** (including indemnities and similar expressions) or to provide any other form of **security** in relation to a credit transaction in favour of its director or a director of its holding company, in which a third party stands as creditor. For example, the company agreeing to stand as a director's guarantor for premises he (personally) leases from a third party.

Ancillary arrangements (¶2814) which would effectively oblige the company to take on these additional prohibited obligations (i.e. relating to connected persons, quasi-loans and credit transactions) are also proscribed by the legislation.

2823

The definition of **connected persons** under the old rules is also explained at ¶9930.

2824

Public companies and relevant private companies cannot enter into the following types of transaction with a person connected to its director or a director of its holding company:
– loans;
– quasi-loans;
– credit transactions;
– guarantees (including indemnities etc) or other security relating to a loan, quasi-loan or credit transaction made by a third party to the connected person; and
– ancillary transactions.

B. Exceptions to the restrictions

Some transactions can be entered into without approval if they do not exceed a certain threshold amount. To calculate this threshold, the **value of a transaction** must be ascertained (s 211 CA 2006).

2826

Transaction	How to value[1]
Loan	Its principal
Quasi-loan	The amount, or maximum amount, the debtor is liable to repay to the company
Guarantee/security	The amount guaranteed or secured
Related arrangement	The value of the transaction to which the arrangement relates
Credit transactions Other transactions not within above categories	Reasonable price which would have been obtainable for land, goods or services in the ordinary course of business on the same terms at the same time
Note: 1. Transactions or arrangements which **cannot be valued** are deemed to be worth over £50,000.	

The value of the transaction usually has to be **aggregated with** the values of any other **relevant transactions** or arrangements, which are other transactions or arrangements entered into previously or at the same time as the transaction in question which did not require shareholder approval (s 210 CA 2006). If a company was a subsidiary of the company entering into the transaction or a subsidiary of that company's holding company at the time of the transaction, but by the time the question arises as to whether the transaction is relevant or not it is not such a subsidiary, the transaction does not have to be aggregated.

2827

The value of a relevant transaction or arrangement is its value as set out above, less the amount by which the debtor's liability has been discharged (s 211(1) CA 2006).

Business expenses

Shareholder approval is not required to meet directors' business expenses, provided the aggregate of the value of the transaction in question and any other relevant transactions and

2828

arrangements does not exceed £50,000 (s 204 CA 2006). Above this threshold, shareholder approval must be obtained.

Defence costs

2829 Companies can meet their directors' (and the directors' of their holding companies) costs in defending **civil or criminal legal proceedings** against them in respect of any alleged negligence, default, breach of duty, breach of trust or application for relief from liability in relation to the company or an associated company, provided the director has to repay those costs if he ultimately loses the proceedings (s 205 CA 2006). A judgment is considered to be final when the time period for appealing against it has expired and no appeal has been made, or where any appeal has been disposed of.

If **regulatory action** is taken against a director of the company or its holding company in relation to the company or an associated company, the company can meet the costs of defending the director against the investigation and any action taken as a result (s 206 CA 2006). There is no need for this to be done on condition that the costs are repaid if the director loses.

Low value transactions

2830 There is no need for shareholder approval to be obtained for small **loans, quasi-loans** or guarantees or other security in relation to such loans (s 207(1) CA 2006). Such a transaction will be "small" if its value, plus the aggregate value of any relevant transactions or arrangements, does not exceed £10,000.

2831 Similarly, small **credit transactions** and guarantees or other security in relation to credit transactions do not necessitate shareholder approval (s 207(2) CA 2006). In this case, the transaction is "small" if its value, plus that of any other relevant transactions or arrangements, does not exceed £15,000.

Credit transactions and related guarantees or other security do not require approval if they are entered in to in the **ordinary course of business** on the usual terms (s 207(3) CA 2006).

Particular types of company

2832 Approval is not required for loans, quasi-loans or credit transactions entered into with **associated companies** or related guarantees or other security entered into for the benefit of associated companies (s 208 CA 2006).

2833 There is also an exception for **money-lending companies**, who do not have to obtain shareholder approval for loans, quasi-loans or related guarantees or other security entered into in the ordinary course of the company's business on the usual terms (s 209 CA 2006). Such companies can also make loans related to buying or improving a director's or employee's home without approval, if the company usually makes such loans and the terms for that director or employee are no more favourable than they would be for another director or employee. A "money-lending company" is one which makes loans, quasi-loans, guarantees and security in the ordinary course of its business.

Pre-1 October 2007 rules

Exceptions applicable to all companies

2835 Some loans and similar transactions are permitted if they are worth less than a certain amount. These **threshold amounts** are to be calculated by aggregating existing loans and loan-like transactions to the director in question.

To **calculate** the relevant **aggregate** amount (s 339 CA 1985):
a. take the value of the transaction in question;
b. add the value of any existing ancillary arrangement (see ¶2814 above) relating to that director which has been entered into by the company/its holding company with the benefit of a relevant exemption; and

c. add the amount outstanding under any other transaction that was also entered into by the company or its subsidiary (or if the loan was made to a director of its holding company, that holding company or any of its subsidiaries) for the benefit of that director using a relevant exemption.

The **values** of the different types of transaction are calculated as summarised below (s 340 CA 1985).

Transaction	How to value[1]
Loan	Its principal
Quasi-loan	Its principal; or the maximum amount the debtor is liable to repay to the company
Guarantee/security	The amount guaranteed or secured
Ancillary transactions	The value of the transaction or arrangement, less any liability discharged
Credit transactions Other transactions not within above categories	The reasonable price which would have been obtainable for the land, goods or services in the ordinary course of business for the same terms at the same time

Note:
1. Transactions or arrangements which **cannot be valued** are deemed to be worth over £100,000.

Companies can pay for and reimburse **expenses** incurred by their directors to enable them to perform their duties, or for the purposes of the company generally, provided (s 337(1) CA 1985):
– the ceiling on the total amount of expenses a company can reimburse is not exceeded; and
– shareholder consent is obtained.

These conditions provide the shareholders with a means of controlling directors' expenses, just as an employer will check his employee's receipts before reimbursing him.

The **maximum** aggregate of relevant amounts permitted is £20,000 (s 337(3) CA 1985). ¶2835 above describes how to calculate the aggregate of relevant amounts and the value of different types of transaction.

The company must obtain **shareholder consent**, complying with the following conditions in order to take advantage of this exemption (s 337(3) CA 1985).

2836

When consent is obtained	Method
Before company meets expense/has reimbursed director	• Director discloses to general meeting[1]: – purpose of expenditure; – amount required from company; and – extent of company's liability under any related transaction; • shareholders approve of company paying expense by ordinary resolution[2]; then • company pays expense/reimburses director
After company has met expense/reimbursed director	• Company pays expense/reimburses director on condition that if shareholders do not consent, director will repay company within 6 months of meeting; • director discloses to general meeting[1]: – purpose of expenditure; – amount required from company; and – extent of company's liability under any related transaction; then • shareholders approve of company paying expense by ordinary resolution[2]

Note:
1. For information to be provided with **notice** of meeting, see ¶3670.
2. If **shareholders do not consent**, in the first situation the company cannot meet expense or reimburse director, and in the second situation, director must repay the company within 6 months of the meeting at which consent was refused. The director's obligation to repay the company still stands after 1 October 2007, even if the 6 months expired before that date (para 10 Sch 3 SI 2007/2194).

In practice, public companies usually rely on shareholder consent after the event by including a resolution in the AGM that directors' expenses be approved because it is administratively less onerous than obtaining consent (prior or subsequent) on a case by case basis. Private companies can obtain shareholder consent by written resolution every year if they do not hold regular general meetings.

2837 A company can provide a director with funds to meet any costs incurred in **defending criminal or civil proceedings** or applying for relief from liability, provided the loan is made on the condition that the money will be repaid if the director's defence or application is not successful (s 337A CA 1985). If the company has already entered into an agreement to pay defence costs before 1 October 2007, it does not have to seek shareholder approval under the new rules to pay them after that date (para 9 Sch 3 SI 2007/2194). If the director has not repaid the costs before 1 October 2007 after being unsuccessful in his defence or application, the obligation still stands (para 11 Sch 3 SI 2007/2194).

2838 If a **loan** made by a company to its director (or the director of its holding company) is **under £5,000**, taken on aggregate with other relevant amounts, it is not prohibited. ¶2835 describes how to calculate the aggregate of relevant amounts and the value of different types of transaction.

> EXAMPLE
> 1. F Ltd wants to lend its director, Mr G, £4,000. F Ltd has already had assigned to it a loan of £1,000 from Mr G's previous employer, £500 of which has been discharged. There are no other relevant amounts to aggregate, therefore, the loan will fall within this exemption.
> 2. As for the situation in 1, except that in addition to the loan and the assignment, F Ltd previously loaned Mr G £3,000, £1,000 of which has been paid off. Since the aggregate amount exceeds £5,000, the loan will not fall within this exemption.
> 3. In this situation, F Ltd wants to lend Mr H, a director of its holding company, E Ltd, £4,000. There are no existing ancillary transactions to take into account, but both F Ltd and I Ltd (which is a subsidiary of the same holding company), have lent money to Mr H in the past. £500 is outstanding to F Ltd and £600 to I Ltd. The aggregate amount exceeds £5,000 and so the loan will not fall within this exemption.

2839 A **money-lending company** may provide a loan or quasi-loan to its director (or person connected to him), or enter into a guarantee in connection with any other loan or quasi-loan (s 338(1) CA 1985), provided that (s 338(3) CA 1985):
a. the company makes the loan etc in question in the ordinary course of its business; and
b. the amount concerned is not greater and the terms are not more favourable than the company would have offered to someone of the same financial standing who had no connection with it.

The **maximum** permitted amount of such a transaction is that it (together with any aggregated relevant amounts) does not exceed £100,000. ¶2835 describes how to calculate the aggregate of relevant amounts and the value of different types of transaction.

> MEMO POINTS 1. An **exception** to condition b. above applies if the company makes a loan to its director, or the director of its holding company (s 338(6) CA 1985):
> – to facilitate the purchase of any **dwelling house and land** to be used as the director's principal residence;
> – to improve the director's principal dwelling house and land; or
> – any loan substituting a loan made for one of those two purposes,
> as long as such loans are usually made by the company to its employees on similar terms.
> 2. A money-lending company **means** one that enters into these transactions in the ordinary course of its business (s 338(2) CA 1985).

2840 The prohibition does not prevent any kind of company from entering into any of the prohibited transactions with a **director of its subsidiary** or another subsidiary of its holding company, as long as the director in question is not also a director of the company giving the loan (or its holding company), and the transaction does not count as an ancillary arrangement (see ¶2814).

> **EXAMPLE**
> Mr Z is a director of L Ltd. K Ltd can make a loan to him without contravening the prohibitions on loans to directors, provided he is not also a director of K Ltd.
> M Ltd could also make a loan to Mr Z.

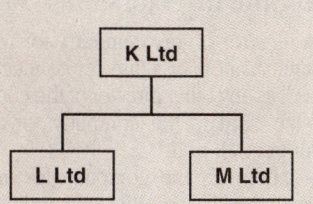

2841 Holding companies are often directors of their subsidiaries. Even so, companies are permitted to enter into the following types of transaction in favour of their holding companies, whether or not the holding company is its director (s 336 CA 1985):
– loans;
– quasi-loans;
– credit transactions, where the company acts as creditor for its holding company; and
– guarantees and other securities in connection with any of the above types of transaction entered into by a third party in favour of the company's holding company.

Exceptions applicable to public and relevant private companies

2842 Public companies and relevant private companies are not prohibited from making **short term** quasi-loans to their directors or to directors of their holding companies if (s 332 CA 1985):
– it must be repaid by the director within 2 months of it being made; and
– the amount outstanding (under this and related quasi-loans) does not exceed £5,000.

> **MEMO POINTS** **Related quasi-loans** are other quasi-loans made to the director by the company or its subsidiary, or if the director is a director of the company's holding company, any other subsidiary as well.

2843 There is an exemption to the prohibition on public companies and relevant private companies entering into credit transactions in the case of **minor credit transactions**, where the aggregate of relevant amounts does not exceed £10,000 (s 335(1) CA 1985). ¶2835 describes how to calculate the aggregate of relevant amounts and the value of the different types of transaction.

A further exemption operates for **business credit transactions**, which are entered into in the usual course of the company's business, for a similar amount and on the same terms for that director as would usually apply to a person with no connection with the company (s 335(2) CA 1985).

2844 If a public company or a relevant private company makes an **inter-company loan or quasi-loan** within its group, the loan or quasi-loan and any related guarantees or other security will not be prohibited simply because a director of one member of the group is connected with another (s 333 CA 1985).

> **EXAMPLE** Using the group structure from the example at ¶2807, but Mr X owns 25% of the shares in C Ltd and B plc owns 75%, making C Ltd an associated company to Mr X (i.e. a connected person):
> 1. Mr X is a director of B plc. B plc **loans** money to C Ltd. This transaction would be prohibited as a loan to a connected person, but falls within the inter-company loan exemption.
> 2. Mr X is a director of B plc. B plc pays C Ltd's rent for a period of six months, on the condition that C Ltd repays B plc by a certain date. This transaction would be prohibited as a **quasi-loan** to a connected person, but falls within the inter-company loan exemption.

C. Consequences of entering into prohibited transactions

2880 One of the significant changes the new Companies Act makes to the loans regime is to remove the criminal penalties for breach of the requirements. Civil penalties can still be incurred by the parties involved. However, if the breach occurred before 1 October 2007, the old rules still apply and both civil and criminal penalties can arise.

On the directors

2882 A director of **any company** for whom a transaction was entered into without the necessary authorisation, or a director connected to a person for whom the transaction was entered into, as well as any other director of the company who authorised it are liable to (s 213(3), (4) CA 2006):
– account to the company for any gain he has made from the transactions (directly or indirectly); and
– indemnify the company for any resulting loss or damage. This obligation is joint and several with any other person liable.

A director who is potentially liable in this way because a restricted transaction was entered into for a person connected to him can defend proceedings against him by showing that he did not know of the circumstances constituting contravention at the time at which the transaction was entered into (s 213(7) CA 2006).

A director does not necessarily have to have authorised the breach actively to be held liable.

> EXAMPLE A director who knowingly allowed his company to make prohibited loans to a co-director on a regular basis was treated as having authorised each loan, even though he did not have actual knowledge of every one at the time. Therefore, he was jointly and severally liable with the director to whom the loans had been made to indemnify the company for its loss. In addition, by not trying to end the practice of making prohibited loans and by failing to call in the outstanding amounts, he was in breach of his fiduciary duty to the company. He was also held liable to account to the company for the difference between what could have been recovered at the date he should have sought repayment of the loans and what was currently recoverable from his co-director (*Neville and another v Krikorian and others* [2006] EWCA Civ 943).

> MEMO POINTS A transaction is considered to have been **made "for"** a director in the circumstances set out in the table below (s 212 CA 2006).

Type of transaction	Made for a director if
Loan/quasi-loan	Made to him
Credit transaction	Goods/services/land was sold/supplied to him
Guarantee/security	Entered into in relation to loan/quasi-loan made to him, or credit transaction made for him
Related arrangement	Transaction to which arrangement relates was made for him

Pre-1 October 2007 rules

2883 **Any director** for whom the prohibited transaction was made and any director who authorised the transaction is liable to account to the company for any gain and to indemnify the company for its loss (jointly and severally with any other person liable) (s 341(2) CA 1985). A transaction was "made for" a person in the same ways as described at ¶2882/mp, with the addition of any other transactions for the supply or transfer of goods, services or land and made for a director if the goods, services or land were/was supplied or transferred to him (s 331(9) CA 1985). The term "related arrangement" should be read as "ancillary arrangement".

A **director of a public company**, or **relevant private company**, who authorises, permits or procures the company to enter into a prohibited transaction is guilty of a criminal offence, and liable to imprisonment and/or a fine (s 342(1), (3) CA 1985; see ¶9935). To be guilty, he must have known or had reasonable cause to believe that the company was in breach.

On connected persons

2884 A connected person **for whom** a restricted **transaction** was **entered into** without the necessary authorisation is also liable to account to the company for his gain, and to indemnify the company for its loss (s 213(3), (4) CA 2006).

A connected person has two potential **defences** to this liability:
a. if he can show that he took all reasonable steps to ensure that the company complied with the rules (s 213(6) CA 2006); or
b. if he can show that, at the time the prohibited transaction was entered into, he did not know of the circumstances constituting the contravention (e.g. he did not know that the

loan came from the company, or he did not know that the person connected to him was a director of that company) (s 213(7) CA 2006).

> MEMO POINTS   The same definitions as above (¶2882/mp) apply to ascertain whether the transaction was entered into "**for**" **a connected person**.

Pre-1 October 2007 rules

Connected persons for whom a prohibited transaction was entered into are also liable in the same way under the old rules (s 341(2) CA 1985). The same defences apply (s 341(4), (5) CA 1985). A connected person may also be criminally liable as a person who procured the breach (¶2888). **2885**

On the transaction

If **any company** has entered into a transaction without the necessary authorisation, the **shareholders** can declare it to be void (s 213(2) CA 2006). This allows them to rescind the contract and recover whatever money or assets the company has lost as a result of the transaction (see ¶2476+). **2886**

This is **not possible if**:
– restitution of the money or asset is not possible;
– the company has been indemnified for its loss and damage (e.g. by the directors);
– a third party, who has given financial consideration in good faith without knowing about the contravention, would be affected by the transaction being avoided; or
– the company or its holding company (depending on which authorising resolution had not been obtained) has given retrospective approval for the transaction in question within a reasonable time of it being entered into.

In which case, the shareholders will have to rely on the directors or connected persons accounting to or indemnifying the company in order to rectify the breach.

Pre-1 October 2007 rules

If a company has entered into a prohibited transaction, the shareholders can also declare the transaction to be void under the old rules (s 341(1) CA 1985). The same exceptions apply, except for the last one as the old rules did not allow for retrospective consent for a prohibited transaction to be obtained. **2887**

Criminal offences: pre-1 October 2007 rules

There are two additional consequences of entering into a prohibited transaction under the old rules, which apply to public companies and relevant private companies. **2888**

Such a **company** which entered into a prohibited transaction is guilty of a criminal offence and liable to a fine (s 342(2) CA 1985; see ¶9935). It can defend the prosecution if it can show that at the time the transaction was entered into, it did not know of the relevant circumstances (e.g. it did not know that a person to whom a loan was made was connected to one of its directors) (s 342(5) CA 1985).

A **person** (connected or unconnected) who procures a public company or relevant private company to enter into a prohibited transaction is guilty of a criminal offence and liable to imprisonment and/or a fine (s 342(3) CA 1985; see ¶9935). To be guilty, he must have known or have had reasonable cause to believe that the company was contravening the prohibition.

D. Disclosure of loans in the accounts

Companies are required to disclose most loans and similar transactions made to directors in their accounts (Pts II, III Sch 6 CA 1985). The transactions to which the requirement applies are **summarised** in the table below. They must be disclosed (whether they are prohibited or **2897** not) if they were made for a person who was a director of the company, its holding company or a connected person during the financial year to which the accounts relate.

The requirements to disclose loans etc have been adapted to refer to the provisions in the new Act in respect of transactions and arrangements entered into on or after 1 October 2007 (Pts II, III Sch 6 CA 1985, as amended by para 6 Sch 4 SI 2007/2194).

All companies [1, 2]	Public and associated companies
Loans to directors of company/holding company	Quasi-loans to directors of company/holding company
Guarantee or other security related to such loan	Loans/quasi-loans to persons connected to director of company/holding company
Assignments that would amount to loan/guarantee	Guarantees/security for loans/quasi-loans to directors/holding companies/connected persons
Ancillary transactions that would amount to loan/guarantee	Credit transactions for directors/holding companies/connected persons
–	Guarantee/security for credit transactions
–	Ancillary transactions

Note:
1. **Also to be disclosed** are agreements to enter into such transactions, and other loans or arrangements entered into by the company in which a person who was a director of it/its holding company had an interest. Holding companies must also disclose transactions entered into by its subsidiaries.
2. There are various **exceptions**, notably "other arrangements" between group companies in the ordinary course of business on the usual terms, and where the aggregate of credit transactions etc for that person does not exceed £5,000.

Comment: The provisions of the **new Companies Act** relating to accounts are due to come into force on **6 April 2008**, and are expected to apply for financial years commencing on or after this date. Under the new Act, details of any advances and credits granted to a director, as well as any guarantees entered into on his behalf, will have to be included in the notes to the accounts (s 413 CA 2006). For an advance or credit, the company will have to show:
– its amount;
– the interest rate;
– its main conditions; and
– any amounts that have been repaid.

In the case of guarantees, the company will have to reveal the main terms, the maximum liability that could be incurred by the company and any amount paid or incurred by the company under the guarantee.

A parent company preparing group accounts will have to include details of these transactions entered into by itself and its subsidiaries.

SECTION 7

Termination

2912 A director's **office** can be terminated by the company, the director himself or automatically. This depends largely on the articles of the company in question. Here, the position discussed is that set out in Table A, together with suggestions for alternative or additional provisions where appropriate.

Termination of a director's **service contract** (i.e. his employment) is a separate matter. Although removing a director from office will usually mean that his service contract is also terminated, it will not necessarily relieve the company from the consequences of terminating that contract. In practice, companies will need to ensure that a director's office and employment end together. For example, if his office endures beyond his employment, he may still have authority to act on the company's behalf, sign contracts, incur expenses and so on.

A. Termination of office

1. Resignation

2920 Usually, the **articles deal** with what is to happen in the event that a director resigns from office. Table A provides that his office is to be vacated automatically if he resigns by giving notice to the company, so a resignation will take effect without the board or company having to accept it (reg 81(d) TA 1985). There is no restriction in Table A as to when a director may resign.

If the **articles do not deal** with whether a director's office is vacated automatically on resignation, for the sake of clarity, the company should accept the director's resignation before it takes effect. This also applies where a different method of resignation is used, for example if the articles specify that resignation is effective upon written notice to the company but a director resigns orally, that resignation will be effective when it is accepted by the company (*Latchford Premier Cinema Ltd v Ennion* [1931] 2 Ch 409).

> MEMO POINTS 1. A valid resignation from office may still be in **breach** of a director's **service contract**, rendering him liable to pay damages to the company (¶2678+).
> 2. Draft **new model articles** under the **new Companies Act** have been published for private companies limited by shares and public companies. They will state that a director's notice of resignation will terminate his office when it takes effect in accordance with its terms (which could be, for example, when the notice states that it will take effect, or when the board accepts it if the articles or service contract provide for this) (private companies limited by shares: art 18; public companies: art 21).

2. Retirement

2925 In the context of directors, the term "retirement" is used to **refer to** both:
– a director retiring at the end of his working life. This may be due to an age limit imposed by the company (see ¶2930 below) or when the director chooses, in which case he will simply resign (see ¶2920 above); and
– leaving the board because the articles require him to do so at a certain stage (not necessarily due to his age).

By rotation

2927 The position discussed here is that in Table A. However, it is common for companies to substitute their **own provisions**, so that directors are not obliged to retire in this way. Alternatively, the provisions may be modified so that only certain directors have to retire by rotation.

Table A provides that directors, **except for** those appointed to an executive position or managing directors, must retire by rotation (regs 73, 84 TA 1985). This **occurs at** AGMs, and so private companies no longer have to follow this procedure, even if the articles still contain the relevant retirement provisions. However, if a company's articles also expressly require it to hold AGMs, it will have to comply with any such retirement procedure (setting out the retirement procedure in the articles is not enough in itself to require the company to hold AGMs; a specific provision is needed) (para 32 Sch 3 SI 2007/2194). Therefore, the retirement by rotation provision will only **apply to** public companies and private companies with articles that require them to hold AGMs.

At the company's **first AGM**, all directors to which the requirement applies are obliged to retire from office. At **subsequent AGMs**, one-third (or the number nearest to one-third) of the directors subject to the provision are obliged to retire. If there is only one director, he must retire. The **directors who are to retire** should be those who have been in office the longest since their appointment (or their last reappointment following retirement by rotation) (reg 74 TA 1985). If there are too many directors appointed (or reappointed) on a given day, lots should be drawn to determine who should retire. Alternatively, the shareholders may have passed an ordinary resolution setting out the order in which any additional directors (i.e. those not appointed to fill a vacancy) are to retire (reg 78 TA 1985).

MEMO POINTS   The draft **new model articles** for private companies limited by shares will not require directors to retire by rotation. Those for public companies will oblige all of the directors to retire at the first AGM (art 20). At each subsequent AGM, only those who have been appointed by the directors since the last AGM and those who were not appointed at one of the preceding two AGMs will have to retire by rotation. Directors who do retire by rotation will have to offer themselves for reappointment by the shareholders, unless they want to retire entirely.
Transitional measures which only apply to **private companies incorporated on or after 1 October 2007** that adopt Table A remove the requirement for directors to retire by rotation (regs 13-18 SI 2007/2541).

2928 Once the relevant directors have retired, the **company** has the following **options**. It can:
– fill the vacancy with another director (see ¶2230+ for how to appoint a different director);
– resolve to reappoint the director;
– resolve not to fill the vacancy; or
– take no action, in which case the retiring director is deemed to have been reappointed (reg 75 TA 1985).

A director must be willing to be **reappointed** (regs 75, 79 TA 1985). If a director is **not reappointed** (whether by resolution or the deemed provision), he will hold office until someone has been appointed in his place, or if no replacement is made, until the end of the AGM.

Comment: In practice, where the retirement by rotation provisions are included they do not usually result in a change in directors because if an alternative appointment is not put forward and the shareholders do not object to the director's reappointment, the director who retired is automatically reappointed.

MEMO POINTS   1. Under the draft **new model articles**, public company directors are not automatically reappointed if the shareholders take no action (art 20). If he is not reappointed, the director will no longer hold office.
2. Transitional measures which only apply to **private companies incorporated on or after 1 October 2007** that adopt Table A remove the requirement for directors to retire by rotation (regs 13-18 SI 2007/2541).

Due to an age limit

2930 **Private companies** may impose age limits upon directors in their articles, in which case the relevant provisions ought to be followed; Table A imposes no such requirement. There is no longer a requirement for public company directors over the age of 70 to retire, as this was repealed on 1 April 2007 (SI 2006/3428).

MEMO POINTS   1. Under legislation brought into force on 1 October 2006 to tackle **age discrimination**, new retirement rules apply to both private and public companies (SI 2006/1031; see ¶2246/mp). Companies can set retirement ages at or above 65, and can also set ages below 65 if this can be objectively justified (which is highly unlikely in the case of most companies). The rules apply to office-holders as well as employees, therefore they will cover retirement ages set for any type of director. When a director reaches the retirement age, companies will be obliged to follow a fair procedure in relation to his retirement and to consider any request from him to work beyond that age.
2. The draft **new model articles** will allow directors to retire when notice of their retirement takes effect (private companies limited by shares: reg 18; public companies: reg 23). In the case of public companies, directors will still have to give their contractual period of notice.

3. Removal

2936 A director will be removed if the company does not want him to continue in office for some reason. The company usually provides for this to happen automatically on certain events, and additionally the shareholders have the right to remove a director for any reason and at any time. Usually, this will be the result of some disagreement with the director, or wrongdoing by him.

a. Automatic

2939 The legislation provides that a director will automatically lose office in some situations, and a company's **articles** usually extend these situations to include more.

Event	Reference
Director ceases to hold office under any provision of Companies Act or is prohibited from holding office by law:	reg 81(a) TA 1985
– **disqualification** (¶3000+);	s 13 CDDA 1986
– **bankruptcy** or making arrangement/ composition with creditors (¶3012); or	s 11 CDDA 1986; reg 81(b) TA 1985
– director fails to acquire or ceases to hold necessary **shares** to **qualify** him to hold office (¶2254+)	s 291 CA 1985
Director suffers from **mental incapacity**[1]	reg 81(c) TA 1985
Director **resigns** from office by notice to company (¶2920)	reg 81(d) TA 1985
Director is **convicted** of indictable offence	Common additional provisions in articles
Director reaches certain **age** (¶2246+)	
Director holds any other office for **profit**	
Director commits certain **breaches of duty**, e.g. personally profits from a contract entered into by the company	
Note: 1. Director is automatically removed if **mental incapacity** results in: – admittance to hospital following application for treatment under the Mental Health Act 1983; – court order is made for his detention; or – court order is made for the appointment of a receiver or similar person to exercise power over his property or affairs. The legislation regarding mental incapacity has been altered recently. The part of the Mental Capacity Act 2005 dealing with the appointment of deputies came into force on 1 October 2007. Under the previous legislation (the Mental Health Act 1983), deputies were called "receivers" and could be appointed to exercise the same powers on behalf of a mentally incapacitated person. Any receivers appointed under the old legislation will be treated as deputies, with the same functions as they had before (Sch 5 Mental Capacity Act 2005). The parts of the Mental Health Act 1983 dealing with compulsory admission to hospital and guardianship and with patients subject to criminal proceedings or under sentence are still in force, as amended by the Mental Health Act 2007. However, Table A has not yet been amended to reflect these changes.	

MEMO POINTS   The draft **new model articles** will provide for a director's office to terminate automatically when (private companies limited by shares: art 18; public companies: art 21):
– he ceases to be a director under companies legislation or any other law (e.g. disqualification);
– a bankruptcy order is made against him, or he makes a composition with his creditors (e.g. he enters into an individual voluntary arrangement);
– he is certified as being physically or mentally incapable of acting as a director and is likely to remain so for more than 3 months; or
– a court order is made preventing him from exercising any powers or rights that he would usually have due to his mental health.

2940 Although the vacation of office in the above situations is automatic and cannot be waived by the board, if the **circumstances change** so he is able to act again, there is nothing preventing him from being reappointed by the company or the board (see ¶2266+).

b. By the board

2943 The board cannot usually remove a director from office on its own initiative. If the board feels that a director should not remain in office, it has a number of **options**:
a. try to persuade him to resign;
b. terminate his employment if he is an employee, which will usually force him out of the company (although the company will be exposed to employment claims as a result if it does not follow the correct procedure, ¶2986);
c. call a shareholder meeting to resolve to remove him; or
d. outvote him on the board (it may need to appoint additional directors to do so), thus reducing his power as a director.

Table A allows the board to dismiss a director by board resolution if he has been voluntarily absent from board meetings for longer than 6 months (reg 81(e) TA 1985). A company may wish to include other similar triggers for removal in its own articles.

> MEMO POINTS   The draft **new model articles** for public companies will enable the board to remove a director by giving him notice to that effect signed by all of the directors (art 21). Those for private companies will not include such a provision.

c. By shareholders

2946 Regardless of any provision in the articles or the director's service contract, shareholders have the **right** to remove a director by ordinary resolution (s 168 CA 2006; s 303(1) CA 1985). The relevant provision of the new Companies Act came into force on 1 October 2007, and the new procedure will apply where the company receives notice from the shareholders that they wish to remove a director on or after that date. There may be a few cases in which the company received notice before that date but has not yet completed the procedure. In these cases, the old rules still apply (see the memo points below).

Procedure

2948 **Shareholders** must give **special notice** of an ordinary resolution to remove a director (and to appoint somebody in his place) (s 168 CA 2006). The special notice procedure is dealt with at ¶3536+. It cannot be replaced by using a written resolution (s 288(2) CA 2006).

On receipt of the special notice, the **company** must **send a copy** to the director concerned straight away (s 169 CA 2006). The **director** may then make **written representations** of a reasonable length to the company and request that it circulates them to the shareholders. If the director does so, the **company** must state that the director has made representations in the notice of the meeting and send a copy of them to all of the shareholders who received the notice. If the representations were received by the company too late for this to happen, the director can require them to be read out at the meeting.

The **director** is entitled to **speak at the meeting** at which the resolution is considered.

> MEMO POINTS   1. Such written representations do not need to be circulated or read out at the meeting if the company or another aggrieved person satisfies the court that the **right is being abused**. In the case of such an application, there are slightly different rules as to the service of the claim form. The claimant must serve the application on the company (if it is not the claimant) and on the director concerned (para 10 CPR PD 49). If service is not possible, the claimant must provide evidence to the court that he has otherwise notified the company and the relevant director of his application.
> 2. To **circumvent** the required **procedure**, companies sometimes provide for an alternative procedure in their articles, e.g. by special resolution. However, shareholders will still be able to use the ordinary resolution and special notice procedure if they wish.
> 3. Shareholders must also give special notice of the resolution to the company under the **old rules** (s 303(2) CA 1985). Directors have equivalent rights to have their written representations circulated or read out at the meeting, and to attend and speak (s 304 CA 1985).

Director/shareholder voting at the meeting

2950 There is no **restriction** on the director concerned voting on the resolution if he is also a shareholder; nor is there any requirement for him to use his vote in the best interests of the company, since he is voting in his capacity as shareholder (¶3824+).

A company's articles may provide that such a director/shareholder has **increased voting rights** when voting on his own removal as director (*Bushell v Faith* [1970] 1 All ER 53). This sort of provision is sometimes found in the articles of family-run companies, to prevent personal disputes affecting how the company is run.

> EXAMPLE   100 shares had been allotted to each of the defendant and his two sisters. The articles provided that on a resolution to remove a director, each share held by that director should be worth three votes, instead of one. The sisters were unable to remove him as a director using their statutory right as shareholders, because he defeated the motion by 300 votes to their 200 (*Bushell v Faith*, above).

> *MEMO POINTS* Depending upon the distribution of shares and the amount of additional votes the director has, such a provision will not always be successful in defeating a resolution to remove the director. If the articles contain an increased voting rights provision which is likely to defeat the resolution, the shareholders could resolve to **change the articles** to remove it. However, the ability to do this will depend upon the drafting of the provision; if it is drafted so that the director also has weighted voting on a resolution to alter the provision, the shareholders may not be successful.

Consequences of removing a director in this way

2952

The legislation preserves the right of a director who has been removed in this way to receive **compensation or damages** for termination of his appointment (s 168(5) CA 2006). Such a dismissal could also give rise to a claim for **unfair prejudice** by the director if he is also a minority shareholder (¶2105+).

A director may also be able to petition for the company's **winding up** on the grounds that it would be "just and equitable" to do so in the case of small family businesses or quasi-partnerships (*Ebrahimi v Westbourne Galleries Ltd* [1972] 2 All ER 492; ¶2133+).

> *MEMO POINTS* Under the **old rules**, the director's rights to compensation are also preserved (s 303(5) CA 1985).

4. Administrative requirements

2957

When a director is removed from office, Form 288b must be **filed at** Companies House within 14 days of the director vacating his office. Companies House will then advertise the change in the *Gazette* (ss 1077, 1078 CA 2006).

The **details** required on the form are:
– the date of termination;
– the name of the director vacating office; and
– his date of birth (unless a corporate director).

The form must be **signed by** a serving director or secretary.

The **registers** of directors and directors' interests will also need to be updated, and the resignation/retirement/removal recorded in the **minutes** of the relevant meeting.

> *MEMO POINTS* 1. The **new Companies Act** will require the removal of a director to be notified to Companies House within 14 days as a change in the company's directors (s 167 CA 2006, expected to come into force by 1 October 2009).
> 2. The name of Form 288b, like the names of other **Companies House forms**, is taken from the section number of the legislation. As all of the section numbers will change under the new Companies Act, Companies House proposes to change the names of all of its forms to reflect their function rather than the relevant section number ("Working with Companies House: a consultation on the registrar's rules and related provisions which will apply under the Companies Act 2006"). At the time of writing, the new form names are not yet available.

5. Compensation for loss of office

2962

A director who is removed from office may be entitled to damages for breach of contract (¶2986), and those who retire may be awarded a sum in recognition of their services.

The provisions of the new Companies Act in relation to payments and transfers of property for loss of office came into force on 1 October 2007, and **apply to** retirement or loss of office on or after that date (para 12 Sch 3 SI 2007/2194). If a resolution was passed approving such a payment or transfer before that date, it will remain valid as long as it complies with the rules in force at the time. Where the director ceased to hold office before 1 October 2007, the old rules apply. These are discussed in the memo points below because they will still be relevant in some cases.

There are **three categories** of payments in compensation for loss of office which must be approved by the shareholders (ss 217-219 CA 2006):

2964

1. payment as compensation for loss of office as a director;

2. payments made in connection with a transfer of the whole or part of the company's (or its subsidiary's) undertaking or property; and

3. payments made in connection with a transfer of the company's or its subsidiary's shares resulting from a takeover bid.

Payments falling into these categories **include** those:
– for loss of another office or employment in connection with the management of the company or one of its subsidiaries, while a director or on ceasing to be a director of the company;
– for or in connection with retirement from office as a director;
– for retirement from another office or employment in connection with the management of the company or one of its subsidiaries, while a director or on ceasing to be a director of the company;
– in the form of cash and/or non-cash benefits;
– made to persons connected to the director;
– made to third parties at the request or for the benefit of the director or a person connected to him; and
– made by the company, at its request or on its behalf.

> MEMO POINTS 1. Where a payment within **category 2 or 3** is made when a director is to cease to hold his office or employment and he is either paid more for his shares than he should have been or he is given valuable consideration by a person other than the company, that excess or consideration is taken as being a payment for the loss of his office (s 216 CA 2006). A payment is also deemed to fall within category 2 or 3, as appropriate, if the arrangement under which it was made was entered into as part of an agreement for the transfer in question, or within 1 year before or 2 years after that agreement (ss 218(5), 219(7) CA 2006). Either the company that is the subject of the transfer or the person to whom the transfer was made must be privy to the arrangement. This prevents payments being made by a circuitous route in order to avoid the requirement for consent.
> 2. See ¶2750 for how such payments are to be **taxed**, and ¶2787 for their disclosure in the **accounts**.
> 3. Under the **old rules**, companies cannot make payments to directors in consideration of their loss of or retirement from office without disclosing the details of the payment to the shareholders and obtaining their approval for it (s 312 CA 1985). Any such payments made in connection with a transfer of all or part of the company's undertaking or property also require approval (s 313 CA 1985). If a director is to receive such a payment in connection with a transfer of the company's shares resulting from a takeover, he must ensure that details of the payment are included in the notice of the offer given to shareholders (s 314 CA 1985).

2965 There are some **exceptions** to this requirement: (ss 220, 221 CA 2006):
– pensions for past services;
– payments consequent on legal obligations unrelated to the event giving rise to the director's loss of office or retirement, such as wages due to the director, including damages for breach of such obligations;
– settlements and compromises relating to termination of the director's office or employment; and
– small payments by the company or its subsidiaries of up to £200.

> MEMO POINTS Under the **old rules**, payments by way of pension or genuine damages for breach of contract do not require approval (s 316 CA 1985).

2966 A payment must be **authorised by** ordinary resolution, unless the company's articles require a higher majority to approve the transaction (s 281(3) CA 2006). The resolution can be passed at a meeting or using the written resolution procedure, but in either case the same details must be made available to the shareholders beforehand (below).

Usually, just the approval of the company's own shareholders is required. The approval of other shareholders is required in the following situations:
– a payment to a director of the company's holding company requires the consent of the holding company's shareholders as well as the company's (s 217(2) CA 2006);
– a payment in connection with the transfer of all or part of a subsidiary's undertaking or property requires the consent of the subsidiary's shareholders as well as the company's (s 218(2) CA 2006); and
– a payment in connection with the transfer of shares in a subsidiary requires the consent of the holders of the shares to which the bid relates and holders of any other shares in the same class, whether in the company or its subsidiary (s 219(1), (2) CA 2006).

However, approval is not required if the company in question is not UK-registered, or it is the wholly-owned subsidiary of another body corporate.

Details of the proposed payment, including its amount, must be made available to the shareholders (ss 217(3), 218(3), 219(3) CA 2006). If the resolution is to be passed using the written procedure, this information must be circulated to the shareholders with or before the resolution. If the resolution is to be passed at a meeting, the information must be made available to shareholders at the registered office for at least 15 days before the meeting as well as at the meeting itself.

2968

Failure to obtain approval will result in the payment being held on trust (either for the company, the company whose undertaking or property was transferred or the persons who have transferred their shares) and any director who authorises the payment will be jointly and severally liable to indemnify the company for its loss (s 222 CA 2006).

> MEMO POINTS   Under the **old rules**, failure to disclose and obtain approval for a payment renders the payment unlawful (s 312 CA 1985). In the case of a payment made in connection with a transfer of a company's undertaking and property, the sum received by the director is also held on trust for the company (s 313(2) CA 1985). In the case of a payment in connection with a transfer of shares resulting from a takeover offer, the director who should have ensured that the details were given to the shareholders and any other person the director instructed to do so are liable to a fine (s 314(3) CA 1985). In addition, the director holds any payment received by him on trust for the persons who have sold their shares as a result of the offer (s 315 CA 1985).

B. Termination of service contract

A director who is also an employee will usually have a service contract (¶2627+). In the absence of a contract, the court will imply an employment relationship if the circumstances support its existence.

2977

If a director is removed from office, his employment will often also be terminated. His contract may expressly provide that his employment depends upon his status as a director. Usually, his **duties in office and as an employee** are dependent on each other, and if he does not carry out either type, he will be in breach of his service contract. However, in some cases a director could still continue as an employee of the company once he has been removed from office.

> EXAMPLE
> 1. Mr X was a full-time executive director of A Ltd; he also had a service contract. His daily duties comprised managing and running the company as a director. Once his office was terminated, he was not able to fulfil his service contract and so this also terminated.
> 2. Mr Z was a full-time executive director of C Ltd; he was also employed as a sales manager, with a service contract. C Ltd is a small family business which designs and manufactures wooden furniture, run by Mr Z and his three brothers. Once his office was terminated, he was still able to fulfil his duties as sales manager and so his service contract was not terminated (although it may have needed to be varied).

> MEMO POINTS   See *Employment Memo* for an explanation of how an **employment relationship** can be **implied** and a more detailed discussion of termination of employment.

Resignation

If an employed director resigns, he must ensure that he gives the correct **period of notice**, which is usually specified in his service contract. If the contract does not stipulate a notice period, or there is no service contract, he will have to give the relevant minimum statutory period (which depends upon his length of service).

2979

If a **director gives no**, or too little, **notice**, he will be in breach of contract which may lead to the company applying for a remedy against him. Usually, the company will be anxious to protect its position by seeking injunctive relief, for example:

- to enforce a garden leave provision in the contract so that the director cannot start work for a new company straight away; and/or
- to enforce restrictive covenants in the contract.

The director may also be liable to pay damages to his employer, although it is not generally worth the company pursuing this remedy.

A director's service contract will usually specify the required **form** of resignation, for example, in writing. If the contract does not deal with this, there are no legal requirements as to the form: it can be communicated in writing, orally or by conduct (e.g. by the director simply not returning to work). However, a director who relies on communicating his resignation by conduct is likely to be in breach of the requirement to give notice.

In practice, there is no need for a resignation to be **accepted** before it is effective, although this formality usually occurs.

Retirement

2981 The retirement process has been **reformed** by the Employment Equality (Age) Regulations 2006, known as the "Age Discrimination Regulations", which came into force on 1 October 2006 (SI 2006/1031). Companies can still set a contractual retirement age in the director's service contract, or a normal retirement age for its employees generally. However, the retirement age must not be lower than the default age of 65, unless this can be objectively justified (which will not be possible in the vast majority of cases, as the justification has to relate to the person's ability to do the job, e.g. his physical fitness would be relevant to a physically demanding role). Whether a company sets a retirement age, or relies on the default age, it will no longer be able to retire its directors early or automatically (ss 98ZA, 98ZC, 98ZG Employment Rights Act 1996). Instead, companies will have to follow a fair retirement **process**, which involves informing the director of his right to request to work beyond the retirement age and considering any such request that is made (Sch 6 SI 2006/1031). Retirement will not constitute unfair dismissal if the director has reached the retirement age, the correct procedural requirements have been followed and the dismissal is the result of a genuine retirement.

Removal

2983 Dismissal is also usually provided for in the service contract, which may set out particular **grounds** in addition to the **discipline and grievance policy** that should be followed (usually by reference to a separate document). Companies must ensure that dismissals are lawful and fair; otherwise the director may have a tribunal claim (¶2986).

A company is entitled to dismiss summarily (i.e. **without notice**) a director from his employment for a fundamental breach (e.g. gross misconduct). The service contract may well set out additional circumstances in which he can be dismissed without notice (for example, if he holds office in a rival company). See the table at ¶2986 below for the consequences of dismissing a director without notice when the company was not entitled to do so.

A company may dismiss a director **with notice**, if this is justified in the circumstances. The company must comply with any contractual notice period (which can be express or implied), or the statutory minimum if there is no such contractual period. The statutory minimum depends upon the director's length of service.

> MEMO POINTS   There are minimum statutory requirements relating to any **dismissal**, **disciplinary action** or **grievance** (ss 29-34, Sch 2-4 Employment Act 2002; SI 2004/752). Compliance with the minimum statutory requirements as well as observance of the best practice principles laid down by the ACAS Code of Practice on disciplinary and grievance procedures is important, as failure can affect the fairness of a dismissal and the amount of compensation to which the director is entitled if he brings a claim, amongst other things. These requirements are discussed in detail in *Employment Memo*.

2984 Depending on the circumstances of the dismissal, the director may be entitled to a **payment on termination**, whether statutory, contractual or discretionary.

If a company has to make employees (including employed directors) **redundant** on a cessation of business or if employees are transferred to another business, it (or its parent) is permitted to award termination payments to those employees affected (s 719 CA 1985). Sanction for such a payment is required. A payment in respect of employees can be **approved by** either the board or shareholders in accordance with any requirements set out in the company's memorandum or articles. If there is no provision, the shareholders must approve the payment by ordinary resolution. Such payments can be made even if they are not in the best interests of the company, but they must be **paid out of** distributable profits (see ¶1612+) if paid before the company is wound up.

MEMO POINTS   This power will be retained in the **new Companies Act** (s 247 CA 2006, expected to come into force by 1 October 2009).

Termination in breach of service contract

2986

If a director's employment has been terminated in breach of his service contract, or his implied employment rights, he will usually be entitled to make a claim for (principally) damages. Similarly, if the director left his employment in breach, for example, by not giving adequate notice, the company will be entitled to apply for relief. Breach of service contract by the director and company was discussed at ¶2678+.

These matters are dealt with in detail in *Employment Memo*. The main claims available are summarised below.

Type of claim	Eligibility	Justification/defence	Consequences
Claims by the director[1]			
Wrongful dismissal	– No minimum period of continuous employment required; and – director was dismissed in breach of contract (e.g. no or insufficient notice)	– Summary dismissal for fundamental breach; – fixed term expired; – director resigned (unless it was constructive dismissal); or – frustration of contract (e.g. director imprisoned/serious or prolonged illness[2])	Compensation
Unfair dismissal	– 1 year's continuous employment (although some dismissals, e.g. because of pregnancy or due to whistleblowing, are automatically unfair so no qualifying period necessary); and – director was dismissed	Fairness on grounds of: – director's capability/qualifications; – his conduct; – retirement; – redundancy; – to continue employment would be a statutory breach; or – another substantial reason (e.g. where dismissal resulted from automatic termination of office in situations stated in articles). Also, company's response was reasonable (e.g. adhered to a reasonable disciplinary policy and minimum statutory procedure).	Compensation; reinstatement/ re-engagement
Constructive dismissal	– Fundamental breach of service contract by company (e.g. unilateral change of terms); and – claim is for wrongful/unfair dismissal as appropriate	– As for wrongful/unfair dismissal; – director accepted breach (delay in claim/ continuing to work); or – no breach	As for wrongful/unfair dismissal

Type of claim	Eligibility	Justification/defence	Consequences
Redundancy payment	2 years' continuous employment. Redundancy can occur on grounds of: – job redundancy (e.g. company ceased trading); – place of work redundancy (e.g. branch where director worked closed); or – employee redundancy (e.g. company has too many directors).	Company has to rebut the presumption of redundancy, e.g. by showing director was dismissed for misconduct. Director can lose right to redundancy payment if he refused offer of suitable alternative employment.	Redundancy pay
Claims by the company			
Breach of service contract[3]	– Director was in breach; and – company suffered damage as result	Director can show constructive dismissal or other breach by company	– Injunction, e.g. to enforce restrictive covenant after contract ends, or enforce garden leave provision; and/or – damages, e.g. for notice period/as indemnity for loss caused by his negligence

Note:
1. Depending on the circumstances of the dismissal, a director may have other separate claims, for example, for discrimination or equal pay.
2. Although regard should be had to the Disability Discrimination Act 1995.
3. The circumstances giving rise to claims for breach of service contract often also give rise to claims against the director for **breach of duty**, which widens the scope of remedies sought against him (¶2434+).

SECTION 8

Disqualification

3000 The court has the **power** to disqualify a person from acting as a director on a variety of **grounds**, the most common of which are persistent failure to comply with filing requirements and that of unfitness. Disqualification proceedings can be **triggered by** a number of circumstances, principally:
– the director appearing before the court on another matter which can lead to disqualification;
– following the report from an insolvency practitioner regarding the directors of an insolvent company; and
– investigation under companies legislation.

The **purpose** of disqualification is chiefly to protect the public, although there is also a strong element of punishment. Not only are the director's freedoms curtailed, but breach of the order or undertaking also has serious consequences. However, in some situations a disqualified director may apply for leave of the court to act as a director of specified companies.

MEMO POINTS Disqualification is **governed by** its own legislation, the Company Directors Disqualification Act 1986 (CDDA 1986), together with its own procedural rules (see ¶3042 below).

A. General concepts

The **effect of disqualification** goes beyond a prohibition on acting as a company director. A disqualification order or undertaking prevents the director from engaging in the following activities without leave of the court (s 1(1)(a) CDDA 1986):
– being a director of any company;
– acting as a receiver of a company's property; and
– being concerned or taking part in (directly or indirectly) the promotion, formation or management of a company.

This ensures that a disqualified director cannot evade the prohibition by managing the company as an employee rather than a director, or by directing the business as a shadow director, for example. Since the focus here is on directors and companies, references are made to being "disqualified as a director", but readers should bear in mind that the scope is in fact wider.

3008

MEMO POINTS 1. He is not allowed to act as an **insolvency practitioner** either (s 1(1)(b) CDDA 1986). The court cannot give a disqualified person leave to act in this capacity.
2. A disqualified person is **also prohibited from** holding quasi-directorial positions in limited liability partnerships (reg 4(2) SI 2001/1090), building societies (s 22A CDDA 1986), incorporated friendly societies (s 22B CDDA 1986), NHS foundation trusts (s 22C CDDA 1986), and acting as trustees of charitable trusts (s 72(1)(f) Charities Act 1993).
3. Disqualification on the ground of **bankruptcy** does not include a prohibition on acting as receiver of a company's property or as an insolvency practitioner (although the latter is prohibited by s 390 IA 1986).
4. The **new Companies Act** will enable the secretary of state to extend the UK disqualification regime to those disqualified abroad (ss 1182-1191 CA 2006, expected to come into force by 1 October 2009).

Who can be disqualified?

The legislation covers **directors** "by whatever name called", and so includes (s 22(4) CDDA 1986):
a. de facto directors, and directors who are referred to within their company as managers, governors and other alternative titles;
b. shadow directors on the grounds of:
– unfitness;
– public interest;
– competition breaches;
– bankruptcy;
– breach of an administration order; and
– companies and insolvency legislation offences; and
c. corporate directors, including companies and other bodies corporate acting as directors.

3010

MEMO POINTS For most of the grounds for disqualification, "**company**" **means** a company incorporated in Great Britain, and any company capable of being wound up under the insolvency legislation, which includes unregistered and overseas companies with a sufficient connection with GB (¶7362+; ¶7592). For applications on the **ground of bankruptcy**, it includes companies incorporated in GB, unregistered companies (including insolvent partnerships) and foreign companies which have an established place of business in GB.

Grounds for and length of disqualification

The grounds for disqualification and when they arise are described in the table below. Depending on the ground in question, the court may have a **discretion** whether or not to disqualify a director in the circumstances of the case. If the court does decide to (or has to) disqualify him it will usually have to determine the **period** of disqualification within prescribed boundaries, although for certain grounds the period automatically corresponds to the offence in question.

3012

The **concept of unfitness** arises in three cases: the grounds of unfitness, public interest and competition law. Although there is only one "ground of unfitness", the concept is used to judge directors' conduct in all three cases in combination with different factors:
– ground of unfitness: company insolvency and unfitness;
– ground of public interest: company investigation and unfitness; and
– ground of breach of competition law: breach of competition law and unfitness.

Here, to avoid confusion between the ground and the concept, the phrase "ground of unfitness" is used when referring to the ground.

Grounds of disqualification	Circumstances in which they arise	Court has discretion?	Period	Reference
Persistent breach of **filing requirements** in companies legislation	Breach of obligation to keep accounting records is most common reason for disqualification. Persistent default can be conclusively proved: – if in breach 3 times in last 5 years; – on conviction of offence for failing to comply; or – if default order made in relation to particular provisions [1]	✓	Max 5 years	s 3 CDDA 1986
Unfitness	Director of company when it was insolvent and conduct renders him unfit Case law on interpretation of unfitness is discussed below	✗	Min 2 years max 15 years	s 6 CDDA 1986
Public interest	Order can be made if, following a company investigation (¶7195+), court is satisfied that director's conduct renders him unfit	✓	Max 15 years	s 8 CDDA 1986
Breach of **competition** law	Director breached competition law and conduct makes him unfit	✗	Max 15 years	s 9A CDDA 1986
Fraud or fraudulent trading **in winding up** [2]	Court can make order where it appears director engaged in fraudulent trading or fraud during winding up (NB: director does not have to have been convicted of offence)	✓	Max 15 years	s 4 CDDA 1986
Wrongful/ fraudulent trading	If director has been found guilty of wrongful/fraudulent trading court can make order on own initiative, or on application	✓	Max 15 years	s 10 CDDA1986
Conviction of **indictable offence** relating to company	For example, insider dealing. Order can be made where appropriate, whether indictable offence was actually tried summarily or on indictment	✓	Max 15 years (max 5 years if case heard summarily)	s 2 CDDA 1986
Conviction of **summary offence** under companies legislation relating to filing requirements	Order can be made if in last 5 years director has been convicted of at least 3 default orders for breaches of these requirements	✓	Max 5 years	s 5 CDDA1986
Company with **prohibited name** (¶264+)	Director of insolvent company cannot act as director of company with same or similar name	n/a – automatic on insolvency	5 years	s 216 IA 1986

Grounds of disqualification	Circumstances in which they arise	Court has discretion?	Period	Reference
Bankruptcy order is made against director	Personal bankruptcy of director	n/a – automatic on bankruptcy	Period of bankruptcy order	s 11 CDDA 1986
Failure to pay under county court **administration order**	On failure to pay, court can revoke administration order and disqualify director	✓	Max 1 year	s 12 CDDA 1986; s 429 IA 1986

Note:
1. **Relevant default orders** are those requiring the company to file its accounts, prepare revised accounts or make its annual return (s 3(3)(b) CDDA 1986). Also included is an order to a liquidator, receiver or manager to make a return, where company is insolvent.
2. The **fraudulent trading** offence is now contained in the new Companies Act, so this provision of CDDA 1986 has been updated (s 4 CDDA 1986 as amended by para 46 Sch 4 SI 2007/2194).

Where the court is able to determine the **period of disqualification**, it will take into account all of the circumstances, in particular the culpability of the director. Each case will be decided on its own facts, and therefore disqualification periods awarded in other cases are not necessarily indicative of what the court will order (*Re NCG Trading*, *Mansell v Official Receiver* [2004] All ER (D) 351 (Oct)).

Although the courts look at each case on its merits and have been reluctant to set general precedents as to what behaviour will lead to particular periods of disqualification, the Court of Appeal has endorsed the categories put forward by the official receiver in cases for disqualification on the ground of unfitness (*Re Sevenoaks Stationers (Retail) Ltd* [1991] 3 All ER 578):
– 2-5 years: where the court must disqualify the director, but the case is not relatively serious enough to warrant doing so for longer;
– 6-10 years: for serious cases that are not in the top bracket; and
– over 10 years: for the most serious cases, for example where a director has been disqualified before.

These are, of course, very broad guidelines and only deal with disqualification on one ground. There are many cases, decided on their own facts, which illustrate the penalties imposed in different circumstances.

3013

EXAMPLE
1. A director who was convicted of failing to maintain a book of accounts was ordered to pay a £1,000 fine and disqualified for **1 year** (*R v Victory* [1999] 2 Cr App Rep (S) 102).
2. A director who was found guilty in the magistrates' court of companies and insolvency legislation offences (duty to keep accounting records (s 221 CA 1985) and duty to co-operate with a liquidator (s 235 IA 1986)) was disqualified for **5 years** as well as being sentenced to **80 hours community punishment** (DTI/CIB press release; company: James Electrical Ltd).
3. Three directors of the same company were disqualified for different periods to reflect their experience and culpability: one director was disqualified for **6 years** because he had retained money due to the Crown, continued to trade when the company was insolvent, misused company bank accounts and did not keep adequate accounting records; the others were only disqualified for **3 years** owing to their lack of skill and experience (*Re Richborough Furniture Ltd* [1996] 1 BCLC 507).
4. A person who accepted appointment as a nominee director of 1,313 UK companies was disqualified for **12 years** (*Re Oldham Vehicle Contracts Ltd*, *Official Receiver v Vass* [1999] BCC 516).
5. Two directors were disqualified for the maximum period of **15 years** because they had procured their company to acquire the business of a partnership, knowing the partnership to be hopelessly insolvent and knowing that their company had no prospect of honestly discharging the partnership's huge liabilities. In their defence, they denied any dishonesty and argued that since they were not accountants themselves, they had relied on experts (including another director who was an accountant). However, the court asserted that every director had a duty to the company to inform himself about its affairs and supervise the business along with the other directors. These were inescapable personal responsibilities. The court found that on the facts of the case, the two directors had actual knowledge of, or had deliberately turned a blind eye to, all of the matters relied on by the secretary of state as amounting to unfitness. They would each be disqualified for the maximum period of 15 years (*Re Vintage Hallmark plc*, *Secretary of State for Trade and Industry v Grove and Gunter* [2006] EWHC 2761 (Ch)).

> *MEMO POINTS* An appellate court should only **alter a period of disqualification** imposed by a lower court if it is satisfied that it is right and fair to do so because the period was significantly too long or the lower court did not take, or could not have taken, relevant factors into account (*Warren v Secretary of State for Trade and Industry* [2006] All ER (D) 147 (Jun)).

B. The concept of unfitness

3021 The court is required to decide whether a director's conduct renders him unfit to act as a director where the case rests on the grounds of **unfitness**, the **public interest** or breach of **competition** law.

Unfitness is not a defined concept, so that, in keeping with the purpose of disqualification, it can be applied where appropriate in the circumstances. It can therefore be difficult to determine exactly **what constitutes unfitness**, but the legislation lists matters to be taken into consideration and existing case law gives an indication as to how the courts react to different situations. In some cases, such as those involving dishonesty and clearly commercially detrimental conduct, unfitness will not be difficult to establish. In other more borderline cases, the court will balance the need for public protection against the scope of the disqualification legislation; directors will not be disqualified for every minor breach of duty.

Ground of unfitness

3023 On this ground, the court is obliged to consider specific **factors** (s 9(1) CDDA 1986). It is not precluded from considering additional matters (for example, a director's failure to co-operate with the FSA's inquiries, *Ghassemian v Secretary of State for Trade and Industry* [2006] EWHC 1715 (Com)), but it must look at these issues in the context of the director's conduct as a whole.

These factors must be considered in relation to each company with which the application deals (Pt I Sch 1 CDDA 1986):

a. **misfeasance** or **breach of duty** (fiduciary or other) by the director;

b. **misapplication** or **retention** by him of the company's **money or property**, or other circumstances requiring him to account to the company (see ¶2398+);

c. the director's responsibility for the company entering into any **transaction defrauding creditors** (see ¶7826+); and

d. the extent of the director's responsibility for the company's **failure to comply with companies legislation** provisions dealing with:
- keeping, preparing, approval and signature of accounts (¶4185+);
- the duty to make annual returns (¶4060+);
- the duty to register charges (¶4636+); and
- the registers of shareholders, directors and secretaries (¶3888+).

3024 Further factors relating to the company's **insolvency** must also be taken into consideration (Pt II Sch 1 CDDA 1986):

a. the director's responsibility for the company's insolvency;

b. his responsibility for the company's failure to supply any goods or services which have been paid for;

c. his responsibility for the company entering into a transaction liable to be set aside (¶7808+);

d. his responsibility for the directors failing to comply with their duty to call the creditors' meeting required to place the company into CVL (¶8448+); and

e. his failure to comply with insolvency legislation obligations relating to:
- the statement of affairs in administration (¶8861+), administrative receivership (¶8861+), CVL (¶8440+) or compulsory liquidation (¶8127+);
- his duty to attend the creditors' meeting required to place the company into CVL (¶8448+);
- delivering up company property (¶8170); and
- co-operating with the liquidator (which is the same as the duty to co-operate with the official receiver described at ¶8121).

MEMO POINTS   In relation to a **LLP**, the extent of the member's responsibility for events leading to him or another member being made liable to contribute to the LLP's assets will also be considered (s 214A IA 1986).

The court's approach

The court must be persuaded that the director is unfit to act as a director based on his conduct on the balance of probabilities, i.e. the **burden of proof** is the civil rather than criminal one. Evidence of a director's **past unfitness** to the necessary level can prove present unfitness, unless the director can satisfy the court otherwise (*Re Polly Peck International plc (No 2), Secretary of State for Trade and Industry v Ellis* [1994] 1 BCLC 574), although simply asserting that the conduct is unlikely to be repeated will not be enough to persuade the court not to disqualify him (*Secretary of State for Trade and Industry v Gray* [1995] 1 BCLC 276). Past conduct will also be relevant where a director who is already subject to a disqualification order applies for leave to act as a director.

3025

There are numerous cases regarding whether a director's conduct renders him unfit or not. Here, the categories of conduct have been extracted to illustrate the sort of behaviour the courts have found to render a director **unfit** to act, although it should be remembered that each case will be judged on its own facts and merits.

3026

> EXAMPLE **Failure to act**
> 1. Failure to stop trading when company insolvent. The director argued that he was unaware of the financial position of the company (*Re Park House Properties Ltd* [1997] 2 BCLC 530).
> 2. A totally inactive non-executive director (*Re Kaytech International plc, Secretary of State for Trade and Industry v Kaczer* [1999] 2 BCLC 351).
> 3. A director relying on the advice of another director without exercising his own judgment (*Re Bradcrown Ltd, Official Receiver v Ireland* [2001] 1 BCLC 547).
> **Financial conduct**
> 4. Directors' policy of paying receipts towards the company overdraft and trade creditors in preference to the (then) Inland Revenue and other creditors (*Re Structural Concrete Ltd, Secretary of State v Barnes* [2001] BCC 578).
> 5. False invoicing and evading VAT (*Official Receiver v Doshi* [2001] 2 BCLC 235).
> 6. In a company which gave financial assistance in breach of companies legislation (¶5557+), the director concerned was a corporate financier and failed to spot the financial assistance in the accounts (*Re Continental Assurance Co of London plc, Secretary of State for Trade and Industry v Burrows* [1997] 1 BCLC 48).
> 7. Fixing salaries of directors with no regard to the accounts or the creditors' interests (*Secretary of State for Trade and Industry v Van Hengel* [1995] 1 BCLC 545).
> **Failure to comply with administrative matters**
> 8. Failure to keep a book of accounts (*R v Victory* [1999] 2 Cr App Rep (S) 102).
> **Dishonesty**
> 9. Trading for personal gain through a succession of failed companies (*Re City Investment Centres Ltd* [1992] BCLC 956).

MEMO POINTS   The secretary of state is entitled to apply to disqualify a director on the ground of unfitness even if the director has been found not guilty in respect of **criminal charges** brought against him **on the same facts**. This would be so even if the criminal charges and the allegations of unfitness in support of the disqualification application were identical (*Secretary of State for Trade and Industry v Carr* [2006] EWHC 2110 (Ch)). This is because criminal and disqualification proceedings differ, as follows:
– the standard of proof in disqualification proceedings is the civil standard, although the more serious the allegation, the more convincing the evidence required to overcome the unlikelihood of what is alleged; and
– the rules as to the admissibility of evidence are different. For example, in disqualification proceedings on the grounds of unfitness, any CIB inspector's report is admissible as evidence of any fact stated in it (s 441(1) CA 1985).

The director's conduct usually has to be dishonest, markedly incompetent or lacking in commercial probity to be serious **enough to warrant disqualification** for unfitness. The judgment as to whether or not a director's conduct renders him unfit clearly involves an assessment of the director's behaviour in the circumstances, and it is open to the court to decide that, on the facts, his conduct does not render him unfit.

3027

> **EXAMPLE**
> 1. Where a director had carried out an **unofficial liquidation** in the expectation that the creditors would be paid in full when more money came into the company, he was found not to be unfit because he had acted for respectable commercial reasons, even though the plan had been very risky (*Re Deaduck Ltd (in liquidation)*, *Baker v Secretary of State for Trade and Industry* [2000] 1 BCLC 148).
> 2. The courts have accepted that, in appropriate circumstances, it can be in the company's and creditors' interests for directors to allow their companies to **trade at a loss in anticipation of future profits** (*Secretary of State for Trade and Industry v Gash* [1997] 1 BCLC 341).
> 3. Where the directors of two furniture companies **used customer deposits as working capital** following the withdrawal of one of their lenders in order to carry on trading for 4 months (they had received **legal advice** that it was acceptable, although not ideal, to do so as long as there was a reasonable expectation that the company could avoid insolvent liquidation), the court did not disqualify them on the ground of unfitness (*Re Uno plc and World of Leather plc*, *Secretary of State for Trade and Industry v Gill* [2004] EWHC 933 (Ch)).

3028 If it is established that the director's conduct renders him unfit (and the company's insolvency has also been proved), the court must make an **order** disqualifying him. The court has a discretion to set the **period** of disqualification within certain limits, so it is able to reflect any mitigating circumstances in the length of disqualification imposed.

Ground of public interest

3030 Cases brought on the ground of the public interest must follow an investigation into the company (¶7195+). The **court's approach** to determining the director's unfitness will be the same as for cases brought on the ground of unfitness, but it is only obliged to take into account the **factors** listed at ¶3023 since the company is not insolvent (s 9(1) CDDA 1986). The court has a discretion to make the **order**, so even if it is proved that the director is unfit it may decide not to disqualify him on the facts of the case. If it does decide to disqualify him, it can set the **period** of disqualification within the stated limits to reflect the seriousness of the case.

Ground of breach of competition law

3032 On this ground, the applicant must show that the director's company breached competition law (either UK or EU) and that his conduct as a director renders him unfit to be concerned in company management (s 9A CDDA 1986). Unfitness is judged by looking at (s 9A(5), (6) CDDA 1986):
– whether his conduct **contributed** to the breach of competition law;
– where he did not contribute to the breach, whether he could have **prevented** it, or ought to have known that the company was in breach; and
– his **conduct** in relation to any other breach of competition law.

If the breach of competition law and unfitness are established, the court must make an **order**. It can set the **period** of disqualification up to the stated maximum, according to the facts of the case.

C. Procedure

3042 Applications for disqualification are **governed by** various rules, as well as the Company Directors Disqualification Act 1986 (CDDA 1986), and there is a large body of case law which gives guidance as to their interpretation in different situations. The discussion here is confined to the main stages of the procedure and obligations upon each party.

> **MEMO POINTS** 1. The **rules** are: the Insolvent Companies (Reports on Conduct of Directors) Rules 1996 (SI 1996/1909 as amended), the Insolvent Companies (Disqualification of Unfit Directors) Proceedings Rules 1987 (SI 1987/2023 as amended), and the Civil Procedure Rules (particularly Practice Direction: Directors' Disqualification Proceedings). The ambit of SI 1987/2023 has recently been expanded to include other applications under CDDA 1986 besides applications for disqualification orders (by SI 2007/1906). These include applications:
> – for leave to commence proceedings after the time limit has expired (¶3047);

– to enforce the duty of a liquidator, administrator or administrative receiver of the company to provide information regarding the director's conduct (¶8166, ¶8856, ¶9377);
– for variation of a disqualification undertaking (¶3072); and
– for leave to act as a director (¶3074+).
However, other than stipulating the form of the applications, the rest of these rules just apply to applications for disqualification orders.

SI 1996/1909 and SI 1987/2023 are part of the **Insolvency Service's review and consolidation** of insolvency-related statutory instruments, ¶7364/mp. The Insolvency Service proposes to merge them into one set of "Disqualification Rules". The Insolvency Service expects the new Rules to come into force in April 2008, but at the time of writing a draft is not yet available.

2. The CPR Practice Direction: Directors' Disqualification Proceedings (referred to here as the "CPR Disqualification PD") sets out the procedure. It is available from the Ministry of Justice's website, and contains the **forms** required for each stage of the procedure.

3043 The person making the application is referred to as the **applicant**. The person against whom the order is sought is the **respondent**, or defendant. Orders can be obtained against persons other than directors, but since the focus here is on directors, the respondent/defendant is referred to as the director.

Applicants

3045 The persons able to apply for a director to be disqualified differ according to the ground relied upon. This table summarises the relevant **applicants and courts** to which the application should be made, depending on the ground for disqualification.

Grounds for disqualification	Who can make the application?	Court	Reference
Persistent breach of **filing requirements** in companies legislation [1]	– Secretary of state; – official receiver; – liquidator; or – past or present shareholder [2] or creditor of the company in relation to whom director committed offence	Court with jurisdiction to wind up any company to which offence/default relates	s 3 CDDA 1986
Unfitness	– Secretary of state; or – official receiver [3]	Court with jurisdiction to wind company up [4]	ss 6, 7 CDDA 1986
Public interest	– Secretary of state	High Court	s 8 CDDA 1986
Breach of **competition** law	– Office of Fair Trading; or – authorised regulators [5]	High Court	s 9A CDDA 1986
Fraud or fraudulent trading in winding up [1]	– Secretary of state; – official receiver; – liquidator; or – past or present shareholder [2] or creditor of the company in relation to whom director committed offence	Court with jurisdiction to wind up any company to which offence/default relates	s 4 CDDA 1986
Wrongful/fraudulent trading	Order made on Court's initiative [6]	Court which made declaration of wrongful/fraudulent trading	s 10 CDDA 1986
Conviction of **indictable offence** relating to company [1]	– Secretary of state; – official receiver; – liquidator; or – past or present shareholder [2] or creditor of the company in relation to whom director committed offence	– Court with jurisdiction to wind up company to which offence related; – court by which person was convicted; or – if summary conviction, any other magistrates' court in same local justice area	s 2 CDDA 1986

Grounds for disqualification	Who can make the application?	Court	Reference
Conviction of **summary offence** under companies legislation relating to filing requirements	Order made on court's initiative[6]	– Court by which he is convicted; or – any other magistrates' court in same local justice area	s 5 CDDA 1986
Company with **prohibited name**	Automatic	Automatic (court with jurisdiction to wind company up has jurisdiction for any application for leave to act)	s 216 IA 1986
Bankruptcy order is made against director	Automatic	Court which adjudged him bankrupt	s 11 CDDA 1986
Failure to pay under county court **administration order**	Order made on Court's initiative[6]	Court which revoked administration order	s 12 CDDA 1986

Note:
1. In relation to which director has committed, or is alleged to have committed, an **offence or default** (s 16(2) CDDA 1986).
The fraudulent trading offence is now contained in the new Companies Act, so this provision of CDDA has been updated (s 4 CDDA 1986 as amended by para 46 Sch 4 SI 2007/2194).
2. It is rare for **shareholder** to make such an application as he must establish that he has a legitimate personal interest in the relief sought, which is unusual.
3. Applications are made by **official receiver** if defendant was a director of company wound up by the court and the secretary of state directs the official receiver to apply.
4. The court retains jurisdiction in disqualification proceedings where the company has been dissolved after the conclusion of the insolvency procedure (*Secretary of State for Trade and Industry v Arnold and Hopley* [2007] EWHC 1933).
5. The following bodies are **authorised regulators** for these purposes, in relation to their sector (s 9E CDDA 1986): the Office of Communications, the Gas and Electricity Markets Authority, the Water Services Regulation Authority, the Office of Rail Regulation, and the Civil Aviation Authority.
6. The **court** can make an order on its **own initiative** if the director is before the court on the matter in question and it is appropriate to make such an order.

Pre-application considerations

3047 A person applying for a disqualification order must give at least 10 days **notice of** his **intention** to do so to the director against whom the order is sought (s 16(1) CDDA 1986), although failure to give the full length of notice will not necessarily prejudice the application (*Re Cedac Ltd*, *Secretary of State for Trade and Industry v Langridge* [1991] BCLC 543).

> MEMO POINTS In cases brought on the **ground of unfitness**, the application must be made within the **time limit** of 2 years of the company becoming insolvent (s 7(2) CDDA 1986). Leave may be granted to serve the application out of time, provided there are justifiable reasons for the delay and the director will not be unfairly prejudiced (*Secretary of State for Trade and Industry v Davies* [1996] 4 All ER 289). The commencement of insolvency depends upon the procedure in question.

Applications and evidence

3049 The applicant must use a "**claim form**"; an example of which is set out in the CPR Disqualification PD.

Applications to court should always be worded carefully, but the court will not necessarily be tied to the specific words used.

> EXAMPLE A director appealed against his disqualification because the application had alleged that he had "caused" false invoices to be raised, but judgment was given on the basis that he had "allowed" them to happen. The appeal was rejected because allegations in a civil case can change at the court's discretion without a formal application being necessary (unlike criminal indictments). If the court is satisfied that the director knows and understands the allegations and will not suffer injustice, it can allow such a change in wording. In this case, the court considered that there was a fine line between "causing" and "allowing", and that the alternative word was first raised months before the substantive hearing, giving the director ample opportunity to address it in his evidence. Therefore, he had understood the allegations and had suffered no injustice as a result of the change (*Kappler v Secretary of State for Trade and Industry* [2006] EWHC 3694).

> MEMO POINTS   The claim form used to be called an "**originating summons**", and readers may see that term still used elsewhere.

Together with this application, the applicant must file his **supporting evidence** at court. The evidence usually comprises one or more affidavits, with supporting documents exhibited, or it may comprise the official receiver's report (evidence is dealt with by rr 3, 6 SI 1987/2023 and para 9 CPR Disqualification PD). **Expert evidence** can be relied on in disqualification applications (*Secretary of State for Trade and Industry v Aaron and others*, unreported, High Court 7 June 2007):
– it can provide assistance to the court on questions of fact, such as where it is necessary for the court to understand the company's specialist product or business. However, it should not be necessary for expert opinion on the director's fitness to be presented to the court, as the court is capable of making this assessment;
– the affidavit should deal with the details of each allegation and only refer to an expert's reports on specific matters. The affidavit should not state that the allegations are "set out in the report";
– the question of expert witnesses should be raised as early as possible in the proceedings so that the need for them can be assessed and discouraged if appropriate; and
– parties in complex cases should draw up a list of any points on which they both agree at an early stage.
A copy of the claim form and evidence must be **served on** the director.

3050

> MEMO POINTS   1. Where a person has been **questioned by the secretary of state** under his powers in **insolvency** legislation during an investigation into a potential offence, his answers can be used in disqualification proceedings but not in criminal proceedings (ss 218, 219 IA 1986). Similarly, the transcripts and notes from **interviews** or **private examinations** conducted under insolvency legislation are admissible (*Re Keypak Homecare Ltd* [1990] BCLC 440; respectively ss 235, 236 IA 1986). Certain evidence collected during an investigation into the company can also be used in evidence in disqualification proceedings (¶7210, ¶7225, ¶7232).
> 2. If the application is brought on the **ground of unfitness** while the company was insolvent, the applicant does not have to prove that the company was in fact insolvent if the company is/was in administration or administrative receivership, but if the company is/was in liquidation he will have to show that this occurred at a time when the company's assets were insufficient to meet its debts and the expenses of the liquidation (s 6(2)(a) CDDA 1986).
> 3. The **opinion of the liquidator** (or any other expert witness) as to whether the director's conduct justifies disqualification is relevant. Affidavits or witness statements including such information should separate out the direct evidence relied upon from the inferences of fact that the court is being asked to make (*Re Pinemoor Ltd* [1997] BCC 708).

Director's response

Firstly, the director must file an **acknowledgement** of service at court within 14 days of service of the claim form upon him.

3052

Secondly, he must file at court any affidavit **evidence** he wishes the court to consider in opposition to the application within 28 days of the date of service of the claim form upon him. For example, evidence from an independent accounting **expert** may be put forward by the director challenging the liquidator's conclusions. Evidence of his fitness or good **character**, though, is not admissible either in his defence or as mitigation.

He can require the applicant to **disclose** the **insolvency practitioner's report** which usually triggers the application to help him establish the basis of the allegations and identify any inconsistencies or additional matters which may assist his defence (Part 3 CPR). The secretary of state will usually assist in disclosing the **documents** in the possession of the insolvency practitioner.

3053

If the director needs to rely on the company's **bank records** in his defence, he can apply to the court for disclosure of them from the bank (Bankers Books (Evidence) Act 1879). The bank may resist giving general disclosure of all records relating to the company, in which case an order for disclosure of defined material can be made (r 31.17(3) CPR; *Re Howglen Ltd* [2001] 2 BCLC 695).

Applicant's reply to response

3055 The applicant must file at court any **further evidence** in reply to the director's response within 14 days from receipt of the director's response.

The hearing

3057 The initial hearing must be fixed for a **date within** 8 weeks from the issue of the claim form (r 7(1) SI 1987/2023; para 10.1 CPR Disqualification PD). It will be heard in open court before a registrar. At this hearing, the registrar will:
– determine the case; or
– give directions (for the management of the case, e.g. inspection of documents) and adjourn the hearing to a later date. The registrar will give reasons for any adjournment and may refer the matter to a judge for trial.

3058 **At the hearing** at which the case is determined, if the applicant is the secretary of state, the official receiver, the OFT (or another authorised regulator, ¶3045) or the liquidator, he must appear and draw the court's attention to any matters which appear to him to be relevant, and to give evidence (s 16(3) CDDA 1986).

The director may also appear and give evidence (s 16(1) CDDA 1986).

The court will weigh up the evidence and decide whether, on the balance of probabilities, a disqualification order should be made and for what period (where there is a discretion).

Stay/striking out of proceedings

3060 Usually, a stay of the proceedings arises where the director agrees to give a disqualification **undertaking** to the court (¶3072).

If **other proceedings** dealing with the **same matters** are under way (whether criminal or civil), the disqualification proceedings can be stayed or struck out. For example, disqualification proceedings on the ground of unfitness might be stayed to await the outcome of criminal proceedings under which the court could make a disqualification order on its own initiative (*Secretary of State for Trade and Industry v Rayna, Re Cedarwood Productions Ltd, Re Inter City Print and Finishing Ltd* [2001] 2 BCLC 48, in which it was held that the civil proceedings could be restored after the directors had been disqualified in the criminal proceedings, because the basis of disqualification was different in each set of proceedings).

An application, defence or other statement of case can be **struck out** if it appears to the court that (r 3.4 CPR):
– it is an abuse of the court's process or is likely in another way to prevent the matter from being dealt with fairly; or
– there has been a failure to comply with a court order or CPR rule or practice direction.

The court will only impose this drastic penalty if it is appropriate in the circumstances, as it is one of a number of sanctions for default open to the court, including costs orders against the defaulting party (*Biguzzi v Rank Leisure plc* [1999] 4 All ER 934).

> MEMO POINTS **Abuse of process** is difficult to establish. For example, the fact that a director is subject to two sets of proceedings based on the same action will not in itself be enough to prove abuse of process, without further evidence of the applicant behaving in an oppressive manner (*Re Migration Services International Ltd, Official Receiver v Webster* [2000] 1 BCLC 666).

D. Disqualification orders and undertakings

3070 A disqualification **order** will state:
– that the director is disqualified from acting in all of the capacities detailed at ¶3008;
– whether leave has been granted to act, and under what conditions; and
– the period for which the order is effective.

> MEMO POINTS   The court can make an order in the **director's absence** in the case of disqualification on the ground of unfitness, public interest or breach of competition law, in which case it may be set aside or varied later on such terms as the court sees fit (r 8 SI 1987/2023).

3071 The order **starts** 21 days after it is made, unless it states otherwise (s 1(2) CDDA 1986). The 21-day period can be **extended or shortened** at the discretion of the court. The time may be extended if, for example, the director was not present at the hearing, in which case it will begin 21 days after service of the order upon him (Re Travel Mondial (UK) Ltd [1991] BCLC 120), or to allow the director to hand over the management of his company to somebody else (Re T & D Services (Timber Preservation & Damp Proofing Contractors) Ltd [1990] BCC 592).

If the director is **already subject to** an order or undertaking, the periods during which the old and new orders/undertakings are effective run concurrently.

3072 The court can accept **disqualification undertakings** instead of making an order where a director is disqualified on the grounds of unfitness or public interest (ss 1A, 7(2A), 8(2A) CDDA 1986). Disqualification undertakings can also be accepted by the OFT (or other authorised regulator, ¶3045) in disqualifications on the ground of competition breaches (s 9B CA 1985).

The undertaking will be in the same **terms** as the order (and the same maximum and minimum time periods apply), and **leave to act** can be granted, with any necessary conditions attached (see ¶3074+ below). Undertakings cannot be set aside, but they can be **varied** by the court following an application by the person subject to it (s 8A(1) CDDA 1986), and the court can reduce the disqualification period, or declare that the order ceases to be in force. In order for an undertaking to cease to be in force, the court must be satisfied either that there is a public interest reason for doing so that outweighs the importance of holding the director to his agreement, or that the applicant has established sufficient grounds that would have discharged a private law contract (Re INS Realisations Ltd [2006] EWHC 135 (Ch)).

EXAMPLE
1. In a case in which proceedings were commenced against a husband and wife in the public interest, the wife gave an undertaking in respect of her alleged unfit conduct (inactivity). Proceedings were withdrawn against the husband, who had allegedly caused the company's insolvency. The court used its power to shorten the wife's undertaking so that it ceased to be in force because there was no longer any public interest in its existence (Re INS Realisations Ltd [2006] EWHC 135 (Ch)).
2. A director had given a disqualification undertaking, after making an unsuccessful application for judicial review of the decision to commence proceedings and an unsuccessful application to have the proceedings dismissed because they had taken an excessive length of time (9 years at this point). After giving the undertaking, he applied to the European Court of Human Rights (ECHR) for relief on the basis that the disqualification proceedings violated his right to a fair trial because they had taken too long. The ECHR upheld his complaint and awarded him damages. The director then applied to have the undertaking set aside. Although it had expired by this time, he felt that it continued to prejudice his career. The court refused to set the undertaking aside, on the ground that (amongst other things) the ECHR's decision was only based on the time it took to conclude the proceedings. It did not find, and it could not be implied, that there could not still have been a fair trial of the disqualification application despite the delay (Eastaway v Secretary of State for Trade and Industry [2007] EWCA Civ 425).

Again, the secretary of state or the OFT (or relevant authorised regulator) must appear at the application for variation of the order to bring any relevant information to the court's attention.

Most directors subject to disqualification proceedings choose to give an undertaking where possible. The main **advantage** of agreeing an undertaking rather than having to go through a disqualification hearing is the costs saving. It also has the benefit of the director's and company's affairs not being analysed at a public hearing, although the disqualification undertaking and any leave to act will still appear on the **public register**.

> MEMO POINTS   1. Undertakings **may be accepted**, in exceptional circumstances, in disqualification proceedings on **other grounds**, for example where the director could not attend court for medical reasons (Re Home Assured Corporation plc [1996] BCC 297).
> 2. If disqualification **proceedings** are already **in progress** when the undertaking is given, they will be stayed.

Leave of the court to act as a director

3074 Directors can **apply** to court for leave to act despite being subject to a disqualification order or undertaking. It is fairly common to do so, and, if granted, it enables a disqualified director to make a living as a director while still being restricted in his activities by the court. Applications can be made during existing disqualification proceedings (by application notice), or at any time when the order or undertaking is in force (by Part 8 claim form).

The application should be **made to** the relevant court as set out in the table at ¶3045.

> MEMO POINTS 1. The **procedure** is dealt with in paras 20-23 CPR Disqualification PD.
> 2. Leave cannot be granted to act as an **insolvency practitioner**.

3075 The secretary of state must **appear at the hearing** of the application to draw any relevant information to the court's attention, give evidence and/or call witnesses as necessary (s 17(5) CDDA 1986).

> MEMO POINTS 1. In the case of applications relating to **competition** law disqualification orders and undertakings, this will be undertaken by the OFT or relevant authorised regulator (¶3045; s 17(6), (7) CDDA 1986).
> 2. If the director is disqualified on the ground of being **bankrupt**, he must serve notice of his intention to apply for leave to act on the official receiver (s 11(3) CDDA 1986). The official receiver is then under an obligation to attend the hearing and oppose it if he feels that it would not be in the public interest for leave to be granted.

3076 The court will balance the protection of the public against the need for the applicant to act as a director. In each case, the court will weigh up the circumstances and will only **grant leave** to act if there is a genuine need and the public will be adequately protected.

> EXAMPLE
> 1. A sole director was not granted leave to act, since he had previously run several **one-man companies**, all of which had gone into liquidation (*Re Britannia Home Centres Ltd* [2001] 2 BCLC 63).
> 2. A director who had been disqualified for trading two companies whilst insolvent, and for using a prohibited name, was not granted leave to run a third company. He had argued that he should be granted leave because the **company would not survive** without him, but the public interest was more important than the company and so the court refused his application (*Secretary of State for Trade and Industry v Barnett* [1998] 2 BCLC 64).

3077 If leave is granted, the court will impose **conditions** on giving leave to act as a director. Common conditions are:
– only being able to act in relation to a named company;
– restricting his capacity (e.g. not being allowed to have sole responsibility for financial decisions or record keeping);
– only being allowed to act for a particular purpose (e.g. to sell or wind up the company);
– requiring an element of supervision from fellow directors (e.g. not being allowed to act on a board comprising fewer than a specified number of directors, or requiring that a director with financial expertise is appointed); and/or
– having to produce accounts to the court at specified intervals (e.g. each quarter).

The conditions will be different in each case, and will depend upon the circumstances of the company and the reasons for disqualification in the first place. The more **narrowly defined** the leave sought, the more likely a director's application is to be granted, for example, the courts will require the director to specify which company or companies he wants to direct.

3078 If leave to act despite a disqualification order or undertaking is granted, the appropriate details are recorded on the disqualified directors **register** kept at Companies House (s 18(1)(c), (d) CDDA 1986).

Register

3080 This is kept by the secretary of state (s 18 CDDA 1986), and can be **accessed by** the public through Companies House.

It **contains** details of:
- disqualification orders;
- disqualification undertakings; and
- applications for leave to act which have been granted, together with any conditions placed upon them.

The details will be **removed** from the register when the order or undertaking expires.

> MEMO POINTS   The secretary of state has published **rules** concerning disclosure of disqualification information (SI 2001/967). These rules form part of the Insolvency Service's review and consolidation of insolvency-related statutory instruments, ¶3042/mp.

Breach of an order or undertaking

Due to the wording of a disqualification order or undertaking, a person will be **in breach if** he: **3082**
- acts as a director;
- acts as a receiver of a company's property;
- acts as an insolvency practitioner; or
- is (directly or indirectly) concerned or takes part in the promotion, formation or management of a company.

> MEMO POINTS   Due to the wording of the last condition, a disqualified person will almost certainly breach his order or undertaking if he acts as a **secretary** or **other officer** of the company without leave.

Breach of an order or undertaking results in **criminal penalties** of (s 13 CDDA 1986; ¶9935): **3083**
- up to 2 years imprisonment and/or a fine, on conviction on indictment; or
- up to 6 months imprisonment and/or a fine, on summary conviction.

> MEMO POINTS   If the order or undertaking related to a **corporate director**, the company will be liable to the appropriate fine, and any officer (or member, in the case of bodies corporate managed by their members) who consented or connived in the commission of the offence or whose neglect led to the offence will be punished individually as above (s 14 CDDA 1986).

In addition, a person who acts in breach of a disqualification order or undertaking is **liable for** the relevant **debts of the company** (s 15(1) CDDA 1986). This also applies to any person who, although not disqualified himself, acted on the instructions of a person he knew to be disqualified. The **relevant debts** will be those that the company incurred when the disqualified person was involved in its management, or when the non-disqualified person was taking instructions from him (s 15(3) CDDA 1986). A director in default of his order or undertaking is jointly and severally liable for these debts with the company and any other person liable for them (s 15(2) CDDA 1986). This offers a creditor the right to pursue a director in breach directly for the debt, and allows the company to obtain a contribution from the director if it is sued by the creditor. It does not give the company the right to sue the director for the amount owed to the creditor (Sharma v Yardley [2005] EWHC 3076 (Ch)). **3084**

CHAPTER 9

Company management and decision making

OUTLINE

SECTION 1 **Management roles**	3118
A Directors and shareholders	3130
B Others involved in company management	3184
C Corporate governance	3199

SECTION 2 **Board decisions**	3217
I Decisions taken at board meetings	3222
A Convening a board meeting	3234
Notice	3236
Informal meetings	3242
B Conduct at a board meeting	3252
1 Attendance	3254
2 Voting	3268
3 Chairman	3274
4 Secretary	3279
5 Adjournments	3281
II Decisions not taken at meetings	3291
III Directors' interests	3308
A Obligation to disclose interests in contracts	3317
1 Who makes the disclosure?	3320
2 What is to be disclosed?	3324
3 Timing of the disclosure	3328
B Consequences of having an interest	3341
C Consequences of not disclosing interests	3367
D Specific duty to disclose interests in shares/debentures	3379
E Additional disclosure obligations	3392
IV Delegation of powers	3404
1 Committees	3408
2 Managing and executive directors	3425
3 Non-directors	3432

4 Alternate directors	3438
5 Assignees	3450
V Sole directors	3460
VI Administrative requirements	3473
1 Minutes	3473
2 Filing requirements	3480
3 Entering into contracts	3486

SECTION 3 **Shareholder decisions**	3513
I Resolutions	3523
A Types of resolution at meetings	3526
1 Ordinary resolutions	3530
Resolutions to appoint and remove directors and auditors	3536
2 Extraordinary resolutions	3544
3 Special resolutions	3553
4 Elective resolutions	3562
B Resolution procedures without meetings	3577
1 Formal written resolutions	3580
2 Informal unanimous agreement	3590
C Summary of resolution requirements	3600
II How to convene and conduct meetings	3610
A Calling a general meeting	3620
1 Directors	3622
2 Shareholders	3625
3 Auditors	3632
4 The court	3635
B Notice	3646
1 Content	3650
2 Notice period	3675
3 Service of notice	3687

C	Holding a general meeting	3711
1	Chairman	3716
2	Attendance	3724
	a Proxies	3727
	b Corporate representatives	3743
	c Minimum attendance ("quorum")	3746
	d Comparison of attendees' rights	3755
3	Adjournments	3760
D	Specific types of meeting	3772
1	Public company Annual General Meetings (AGMs)	3777
2	Class meetings	3794
E	Summary of meetings	3800
III	**Voting**	3810
A	Who can vote?	3815
B	Methods of voting	3836
1	Show of hands	3838
2	Poll voting	3842
3	Postal and electronic voting	3852
IV	**Administrative requirements**	3862
1	Minutes of meetings and resolutions	3864
2	Filing requirements	3871
3	Timeline: shareholder meetings	3873

SECTION 4	**Company registers**	3888
A	Register of directors and secretaries	3894
B	Register of shareholders	3915
1	General rules	3918
2	Single shareholder companies	3943
3	Overseas branch registers	3948
C	Register of directors' interests	3958
D	Register of charges	3975
E	Public company's register of interests in shares	3990
F	Non-statutory registers	4000
G	Inspection and copying rights and fees	4019
H	Rectification of company registers	4027

SECTION 5	**Companies House**	4040
A	Filing requirements	4048
B	The annual return	4060
C	Submitting documents to Companies House	4069
D	Searching the register	4090

3110 The individual roles and responsibilities of the shareholders and directors were examined at ¶2000+ and ¶2160+ respectively. The different ways in which companies make and record their decisions through these bodies is discussed here, looking firstly at the **division of responsibilities** between the directors, shareholders and others involved, and secondly how they work together to run a company. Then, the various legal and administrative requirements relating to the **decisions** of directors and shareholders are dealt with in detail. The **administrative and record keeping** aspects to company decision making are important components of effective management; the secretary, whose role is largely administrative, is dealt with at ¶4115+.

Many of these matters will be dealt with in a company's **articles of association**. Where relevant, this chapter looks at the position as set out in Table A. For companies still governed by Table A 1948, significant differences to Table A are highlighted and readers can also refer to the comparison tables at ¶9920+. Always check a company's own articles of association for any departures from the position in Table A.

The **new Companies Act** will revolutionise the decision making process in **private companies**. The most significant of these changes is improving the written resolution procedure so that decisions can be made with the same level of shareholder support as at a meeting. The new Act also removes unnecessary aspects of decision making, such as AGMs. Many of these provisions are already in force. Draft new model articles under the new Act have been published and are likely to come into force by 1 October 2009 for companies incorporated on or after that date. Those for private companies limited by shares are significantly different to Table A, focusing principally on board decisions. As far as **public companies** are concerned, the new Act does not have such a large impact on decision making, and the draft new model articles are more comparable to Table A. Forthcoming changes are discussed within each topic, as relevant.

MEMO POINTS   In order to bridge the gap between the provisions of the new Act that are already in force and Table A, transitional **amendments** have been made **to Table A** (SI 2007/2541 and SI 2007/2826). For example, the requirement for an extraordinary resolution has been changed to a special resolution, and references to AGMs have been removed for private companies. These transitional articles apply to companies incorporated on or after 1 October 2007, although companies incorporated before this date may wish to make similar amendments to their own articles in order to take full advantage of the legislative changes. Different amendments have been made for private and public companies. The version of Table A reproduced at ¶9915 reflects the amendments. It is likely that further transitional amendments will be made to Table A for companies incorporated on or after 6 April 2008 to reflect the legislative changes due to come into force on that date.

SECTION 1
Management roles

3118 A company is an artificial legal person and therefore the individuals involved in it must undertake its management by making decisions and taking action on its behalf. **Shareholders** comprise "the company": it is their investment that enables the company to exist, so it follows that they should have control over how it is run. The **directors** are there to manage the day to day business of the company: they are the agents of the company and stand in the position of fiduciaries as they are handling the company's property on its behalf. Between them, the shareholders and directors undertake the management responsibilities of a company.

A company often assigns management functions to individuals who are not on the board of directors. **Auditors** play an important role in the management of a company, as do certain **employees** and others.

3119 It is important that company management is clearly divided between the board and the shareholders, as clarity about their responsibilities helps to prevent internal disputes. The principal **management powers** are **found in** a company's articles. Additional powers are set out in statute and can be supplemented by instructions from the shareholders to directors through special resolutions. These documents are all a matter of public record, ensuring that third parties also know that when they deal with a board, it is empowered to make decisions on the company's behalf. Directors are obliged to act within the authority given to them (¶2348+). Setting out the management roles in this way also enables shareholders and third parties to know what they can do when management powers have been abused or exceeded.

3120 Different managerial structures suit different types of company; therefore companies are able to **tailor the roles** according to their needs. For instance, a small family-run company will often make no distinction between the roles of shareholders and directors because the same individuals will fill both roles. In larger companies, the shareholders and directors will usually be different people with different interests. The shareholders' involvement in the company is more likely to be purely financial, and they will leave management matters to the board. Even in such companies, shareholders will want to retain ultimate control over the board to protect their investment, and large companies often appoint independent non-executive directors as objective figures on the board to ensure that the company is managed properly for the shareholders.

A. Directors and shareholders

3130 A company acts through and is run by **two bodies**, or organs: the directors and the shareholders. The directors are collectively known as the "board". The two bodies **work together** to run the company by the shareholders delegating the day to day management powers to the board, but reserving certain important powers to themselves to retain ultimate control.

There is a practical **need for** these two bodies. Numerous decisions need to be made in the course of the day to day running of a company. Although shareholders comprise the company, it is impractical to expect them to be able to, or want to, meet every time such a decision has to be made. Shareholders become involved in a company to make an investment and maybe have a say in significant matters which may affect the company's future. They do not want to deal with daily management matters such as recruitment, or working out the annual office budget. Therefore, they delegate these responsibilities to the board, whilst retaining a measure of ultimate control.

This need for two bodies to run a company is reflected in the statutory **requirement** for every private company to have at least one director (¶2230). Statute only gives a loose definition of a director, and does not define his role. This is left up to each individual company.

> MEMO POINTS 1. **Public companies** must appoint at least two directors (s 154 CA 2006).
> 2. The **new Companies Act** will require every company to have at least one director who is an individual (as opposed to a company), to ensure that its management is more transparent and accountable (s 155 CA 2006; the implementation date for this provision is yet to be announced at the time of writing).

3131 The **key distinction** between the two bodies lies in their different duties and liabilities. A director, as the company's agent and fiduciary, acts on its behalf using the powers given to him by the company. He owes a number of duties to it which arise out of this position and it follows that he is liable to the company for any breaches of those duties (¶2317+). A shareholder, by contrast, can largely exercise his powers (for example, to vote) in his own interests. A shareholder's liability is limited to the amount of his investment, provided his actions are consistent with his position as shareholder and do not stray into the directors' territory (¶2010, ¶3173). This gives him the incentive to take on a quasi-supervisory management role, only stepping in when the board has abused or exceeded its powers.

In **small companies** where the shareholders and directors are the same individuals, it may seem pointless to distinguish between an individual acting as a director and as a shareholder. However, the difference between the liabilities of the two roles should encourage such individuals to be sure of the capacity in which they are acting: shareholders who carry out the functions of directors may be made subject to the same liabilities (see ¶3173). Companies legislation thus ensures that somebody is responsible for directorial duties and liabilities, even if no director has been formally appointed.

3132 The roles of and relationship between the two bodies are principally **defined in** a company's **articles** of association. The articles give the board its standing instructions from the shareholders and set out the nature and extent of its managerial powers (*Automatic Self-Cleansing Filter Syndicate Co v Cunninghame* [1906] 2 Ch 34). Although the articles are a contract between the shareholders and the company (and not the directors, see ¶372+), directors take on their office subject to the articles and the shareholders are entitled to expect their directors to comply with them (*Guinness plc v Saunders* [1990] All ER 652). The articles usually also give the shareholders the power to instruct the board on managerial matters by **special resolution**.

Statute sets out certain managerial powers reserved to the shareholders which cannot be delegated to the board. Again, this helps to maintain the distinction between the roles of the two bodies.

Shareholders can also agree to delegate certain matters to the board in a **shareholders' agreement**. For example, the shareholders could include a provision that the board should decide whether the company can enter into litigation (as in the case of *Breckland Group Holdings Ltd v Suffolk Properties Ltd* [1989] BCLC 100). See ¶2086+ for commentary on shareholders' agreements and how to vary them.

3133 The **new Companies Act** aims to be more practical in how it provides for the shareholders to control the board. It will remove the need for shareholder approval of certain board decisions, to lift the administrative burden that such rubber-stamping entails. For example, if a private company has only one class of shares, it will not need the prior authority of its shareholders to allot shares (s 550 CA 2006, expected to come into force by 1 October 2009). While this seems to reduce the shareholders' power, they will benefit from more practical changes in their favour which will allow them to call the board to account. For example, the new Act has introduced a statutory derivative action procedure, which shareholders can follow if directors breach their duties (¶7127+); directors are required to consider how their decisions will promote the company's success, including the effect on shareholders (¶2379+); and they will have to give reasons for refusing to register a share transfer (s 771 CA 2006, due to come into force on 6 April 2008). Companies should therefore consider the changes, discussed within the relevant topics, and assess how they will impact on their management, in particular the changes that will need to be made to their articles and procedures generally.

1. The board

Companies can express the delegation of managerial powers to the board in whatever way they see fit. Most companies adopt the Table A provision or similar, which states that the **directors can exercise** "all of the powers of the company" (reg 70 TA 1985). This power is a collective one to be **exercised by** the board as a whole, rather than by individual directors (*Re Landhurst Leasing plc* [1999] 1 BCLC 286).

3137

The **powers of the company** are set out in the company's memorandum of association and are usually drafted as widely as possible to cover all activities in which the company may need to engage. Therefore, the general management power of the board is typically very wide, encompassing any decisions necessary to the day to day management of the company, as well as the power to enter into specific transactions, such as borrowing money and granting security over the company's assets, depending upon the terms of the memorandum. Companies grant such wide and loosely defined management powers to the board to ensure that it can run the company effectively without having to refer to the shareholders too frequently. Shareholders are usually content to leave the exercise of those powers to the directors.

> MEMO POINTS 1. If the company only has a **sole director**, that director's actions and the board's amount to the same thing. For the special requirements relating to sole directors, see ¶3460+.
> 2. Draft **new model articles** under the **new Companies Act** have been published for private companies limited by shares and public companies. They both contain substantially the same provisions (arts 2, 3). As far as existing memoranda are concerned, once the new Companies Act comes into force, any objects will be treated as if they are contained in the articles (s 28 CA 2006, expected to come into force by 1 October 2009).

There may be circumstances in which the shareholders want to **limit the board's powers**. Although Table A allows the board to exercise all of the powers of the company, this is made secondary to (reg 70 TA 1985):
– the powers reserved to the shareholders in the legislation (see ¶3149);
– any provisions of the company's memorandum and articles which may limit or place conditions on the board's management power; and
– any instructions received from the shareholders in the form of a special resolution.

3138

Therefore, in order to ascertain the scope of its power, the board must identify the shareholders' powers as well as any limitations on their own. Shareholders can restrict the board's powers further by altering the articles of the company (or indeed by altering the broad powers of the company as expressed in the memorandum), or by giving instructions to the board by special resolution (if permitted by the articles). Both of these possibilities are discussed at ¶3157+.

The general spirit of the articles, as well as its precise terms, must be taken into account; **case law** has identified certain **restrictions** on the board's powers of management, based on the interpretation of the relevant company's articles.

> EXAMPLE
> 1. Where a company's articles stated that the directors were to manage the "business of the company", the court found that fixing their own remuneration was not within that power and the question should have been referred to the shareholders in a general meeting (*Foster v Foster* [1916] 1 Ch 532).
> 2. Where a board gave assurances to the executors of a deceased shareholder that certain formalities in the articles would not be followed regarding the transfer of shares (something which the shareholders should have decided), the court held that the board's powers to manage the company did not include giving non-binding assurances on behalf of the shareholders (*Re Benfield Greig Group*

plc, Nugent v Benfield Greig Group plc [2000] 2 BCLC 488 subsequently reversed by the Court of Appeal on another point ([2002] 1 BCLC 65)).

Specific powers

3140 The **shareholders can give** the board more specific management powers by inserting them into the articles, or by giving (or removing) a specific power to the board by special resolution. This is necessary because the board cannot undertake tasks which are outside of its general management powers without the authorisation of the shareholders. The **scope** of such specific powers will depend upon the terms of the special resolution or alteration to the articles.

Table A gives the board a number of specific powers which can be exercised without further reference to or approval by the shareholders. Note that these powers may be restricted or may require certain conditions to be fulfilled before they are exercised; readers are referred to the paragraphs relating to each power for further information.

Power relating to	Type of power	Reference (TA 1985)[1]	¶¶
Day to day management	Appoint and remove alternate directors	reg 65	¶3438+
	Appoint company agents	reg 71	¶3432+
	Delegate board's powers and functions	reg 72	¶3404+
	Appoint new directors	reg 79 [2]	¶2274
	Appoint directors to executive positions, including managing director	reg 84	¶3425+
	Provide benefits, pensions etc to directors	reg 87	¶2710+
	Call board meetings and regulate their own proceedings	reg 88	¶3222+
	Appoint chairman of the board	reg 91	¶3274+
	Appoint and remove secretary	reg 99	¶4151+
	Give authority to use company seal	reg 101	¶3490
Shares	Exercise liens on shares	regs 8-10	¶1227+
	Make and deal with calls on shares, including forfeiting shares	regs 12, 15, 17-22	¶1205+
	Deal with share transfers, whether transfers are registered or not	regs 23, 24, 26	¶1827+
	Deal with fractions of shares	reg 33	¶1317/mp
	Pay interim dividends	reg 103	¶1665
	Once shareholders have declared dividend to be paid out of a distribution of assets, settle distribution details where difficulties arise, such as issuing fractional certificates	reg 105	n/a
Shareholders	Call general meetings	reg 37 [2]	¶3622+
	Nominate director as chairman of general meetings	reg 42	¶3719+
	Attend and speak at general meetings	reg 44	¶3724
	Deal with proxy forms	reg 62	¶3727+

Note:
1. Many of these provisions will be different where a company adopts the **new model articles**. Readers should follow the relevant cross-references for further details.
2. For companies **incorporated on or after 1 October 2007** that adopt Table A, amendments have been made to certain provisions of Table A to correspond with the provisions of the new Companies Act which were in force by that date. Different amendments have been made for private and public companies. See ¶9915 for the details of these changes.

3141 Where **statute** requires the directors to have the authority of the shareholders to exercise a power, the articles or the appropriate resolution (as required by statute) must permit the directors to do so. Common examples of this are the requirements for authority to:

– allot shares, which the shareholders can authorise directors to do either generally for a certain period of time, or on a case by case basis (¶921+); and
– disapply pre-emption rights (¶940+).

> MEMO POINTS The **new Companies Act** will not require private companies with only one class of shares to obtain the shareholders' authority to allot shares (s 550 CA 2006, expected to come into force by 1 October 2009).

2. The shareholders

Generally speaking, shareholders **do not retain** any of the day to day management powers of the company because they have delegated them to the board. It is possible for shareholders to **retain** some general management powers of the company by the way in which they structure the articles, or by using their ability to direct the board by special resolution. However, shareholders would be unwise to retain too much managerial power since this could render them liable to the same duties and liabilities as directors (¶3173). If a shareholder is keen to be involved in the management of a company, he should seek to be appointed as a director rather than blur the boundary between the two roles.

3146

Although shareholders do not have any general managerial powers reserved to them in the same way as the board, they do retain ultimate **control over** the composition of the board itself. This allows shareholders to remove a director who is not managing the company effectively enough, or to appoint a new director to shift the balance of power on the board if the articles or circumstances allow (¶2946+, ¶2270+).

Specific powers

Specific powers are **reserved to the shareholders** in the legislation. Companies can also choose to give shareholders control over further matters in the articles, either specifically or by allowing the shareholders to give instructions to the board by special resolution.

3148

The **legislation** specifically states that the following matters are to be decided by the shareholders at a general meeting. These powers cannot be relinquished altogether by the shareholders, although some of them can be delegated to or shared with the board.

3149

Matter	Does the power have to be exercised by the shareholders?	Reference[1]	¶¶
Remove a director	No[2] – shareholders can permit directors to exercise as well	s 168 CA 2006	¶2946+
Authorise the directors to allot shares	No – shareholders can permit directors to exercise (for a period of time)	s 80 CA 1985	¶921+
Disapply pre-emption rights	No – shareholders can delegate to directors	s 95(2) CA 1985	¶940+
Alter the memorandum and articles of association	Yes	ss 4, 9 CA 1985	¶410 +, ¶450+
Change the name of the company	Yes	s 28(1) CA 1985	¶273+
Increase or reduce the share capital of the company	Yes	ss 121, 135 CA 1985	¶900 +, ¶1435+
Remove an auditor	No[2]	s 391(1) CA 1985	¶4343+
Voluntarily wind the company up	Yes	s 84 IA 1986	¶8438 +, ¶8604+

Note:
1. Some of these provisions will be altered by the **new Companies Act**, and all of the references will change. Readers should follow the relevant cross-references for further details.
2. If an ordinary resolution to remove a director or auditor is to be considered at a general meeting, special notice needs to be given, see ¶3530+.

3150 The powers reserved to shareholders in a company's **articles** will vary according to the extent to which a company has adopted Table A. **Table A** stipulates that some management matters are to be decided by shareholders, which can be divided into three broad categories:

Category	Type of power	Reference (TA 1985)[1]	¶¶
Financial decisions	Increase, consolidate or divide share capital, subdivide shares or cancel unallotted shares by ordinary resolution	reg 32	¶900+, ¶1312+
	Reduce share capital, capital redemption reserve or share premium account by special resolution	reg 34	¶1435+
	Purchase company's own shares	reg 35	¶1337+
	Declare dividends	regs 102, 105	¶1660+
	Authorise capitalisation of profits	reg 110	¶1013+
Control over the directors	Fix minimum and maximum numbers of directors	reg 64	¶2230, ¶2231
	Appoint director	reg 78 [2]	¶2266+
	Decide directors' fees	reg 82	¶2696+
	Suspend or relax restrictions on directors voting if they are interested in resolution	reg 96	¶3308+
Directors' failure to exercise their powers	Call general meeting if not enough directors in UK to do so	reg 37 [2]	¶3630
	Nominate chairman of general meeting if director cannot/will not chair meeting	reg 43	¶3719

Note:
1. Some of these provisions will be different where a company adopts the **new model articles** under the **new Companies Act**. Readers should follow the relevant cross-references for further details.
2. For companies **incorporated on or after 1 October 2007** that adopt Table A, amendments have been made to certain provisions of Table A to correspond with the provisions of the new Companies Act which were in force by that date. Different amendments have been made for private and public companies. See ¶9915 for the details of these changes.

3151 Any **restrictions** on the shareholders' specific powers will be found in the articles, special resolution or shareholders' agreement, as applicable. For conditions or limits on the statutory powers, readers should follow the relevant cross-references noted in the table at ¶3149.

Power to instruct the board

3152 Shareholders will usually be content to leave the management decisions up to the directors. Even so, the articles may give them the power to give instructions to the board by **special resolution** (reg 70 TA 1985). This power to direct the board by special resolution is an important one, giving the shareholders ultimate control over the company's management. For instance, shareholders may wish to use this power if they do not agree with the board on a particular course of action, or they do not believe that the directors are being pro-active enough in managing the company.

There is no restriction on what these instructions may concern. Shareholders can employ this power for the **purpose** of increasing or restricting both the board's and their own powers by instructing the board:
– to do something (e.g. enter into a particular contract or type of contract);
– not to do something (e.g. prohibiting the board from entering into a contract);
– that the shareholders will deal with a matter which would usually be within the powers of the board; or
– that the board should deal with something that would usually be decided by the shareholders (provided that the decision is not one reserved exclusively to shareholders by statute, see ¶3149 above).

Shareholders must be sure to use this power only when appropriate, as over-use may lead to adverse consequences for them (see ¶3173).

MEMO POINTS 1. For companies still governed by **Table A 1948**, the business of the company is to be managed by the directors, subject to regulations (as far as they do not contradict the articles) prescribed by the company in general meeting (reg 80 TA 1948). Case law held that such regulations had to be in the form of special resolutions. Therefore, companies governed by Table A 1948 are subject to the same principles as those governed by Table A 1985.
2. The procedure for **passing a special resolution** is found at ¶3553+; written resolutions at ¶3577+; and convening a shareholder meeting at ¶3610+.
3. The draft **new model articles** will contain a power for shareholders to direct the board by special resolution (art 3).

3. Altering the balance of power

3157

Shareholders are able to alter the managerial powers assigned to both themselves and the board. **The board** cannot shift the balance of power between itself and the shareholders, nor can it change the details of any powers delegated to it or reserved to the shareholders. The board may, however, be able to determine how its managerial functions are to be carried out by delegating responsibility for particular matters to individuals or committees, depending upon the terms of the articles (see ¶3404+).

Managerial powers are commonly **altered when** the company changes in some way.

EXAMPLE
1. A company which was originally set up as a family business with a small number of director/shareholders needs to bring in an external shareholder to provide additional funds. The external shareholder has no position on the board, unlike the other shareholders, and is likely to want to ensure that his investment is protected. He could retain some managerial control by requiring that the board consults the shareholders on all matters of a particular nature (e.g. all transactions concerning land, or all transactions over a certain value).
2. A company may decide to expand into new areas of business and may need additional managerial powers to reflect this change.
3. The shareholders are dissatisfied with the way in which the board is running the company, for example, they feel that it is not being pro-active enough in seeking out new business opportunities, or they disagree with a particular policy which it has introduced.

3158

The **powers which can be changed** are those contained in the company's articles of association, including instructions given to the directors by way of special resolution. Any powers set out in a shareholders' agreement can also be changed (see ¶2086+). The shareholders' powers set out in legislation **cannot be altered**, although some of them can be delegated to the board (¶3149). Changing the articles or an existing special resolution requires a special resolution, and so is a matter of public record. It is worth noting that changing the balance of power will not be effective retrospectively (reg 70 TA 1985). Therefore, any **decision** which has **already been made** by the directors will stand, provided it was within their powers at the time. Directors' duty to act within their authority is discussed at ¶2348+.

MEMO POINTS The equivalent provision in the draft **new model articles** is in art 3.

3159

There are two principal **methods** of changing the managerial powers. The method used may depend on the type of change to be made:
– a permanent or long-term change, especially one of a general nature, will usually be made by altering the **articles**; and
– an ad hoc or specific change will usually be made by instructing the board by **special resolution**.

The power to instruct the board by special resolution is dependent upon the terms of the articles; if such a power is absent, the shareholders would have to rely on their statutory power to change the articles (either to include this power, or to change the management power in question directly (¶450+)). If the board wants to make a decision which is reserved to the shareholders, it should obtain prior authorisation by special resolution. If the board seeks authorisation from the shareholders after the event (i.e. ratification of their action), this can usually be given by ordinary resolution (see ¶2497+).

There is a further method, which would effectively increase or curb the board's powers of management. Altering the powers of the company in the **memorandum** would in turn change the board's ability to exercise those powers, where the articles allow the directors to exercise all of the powers of the company (as is the case for companies operating under Table A). However, this would increase or restrict the powers of the company as a whole, not just the directors' managerial powers. The procedure for changing the memorandum is described at ¶410+. There is a mechanism whereby certain shareholders or debenture holders can object to a resolution to alter the objects clause, which may be an additional obstacle to using this method.

4. Failure to exercise powers properly

3164 Under **normal circumstances**, once powers have been delegated to the board, the shareholders cannot then exercise those powers themselves. Therefore, if the shareholders were to attempt to pay interim dividends (reg 103 TA 1985) or make a loan (within reg 70 TA 1985), their action could be declared void by the court as being inconsistent with the delegation of management powers to the board (*Scott v Scott* [1943] 1 All ER 582).

Nor can shareholders **complain to the court** simply because the board has made a decision with which they disagree: the general rule is that the court will not interfere with the running of a company, although the circumstances may entitle the shareholder to apply for a "remedy of last resort" (¶2100+). Shareholders will not be permitted to pass a resolution overriding a decision validly made by the directors.

> EXAMPLE A shareholders' agreement stated that any court proceedings commenced by the company had to be approved by at least two directors, each representing a different group of shareholders, but proceedings were commenced in the name of the company by the two directors representing only one group (also the majority shareholder). The full board would not adopt the proceedings, and the court held that the shareholders had no power to override that board decision and adopt the action through a general meeting. The act was outside of the two directors' powers because they needed the consent of the other director, and was outside the shareholder's powers because it was a decision reserved to the directors. Whereas the board could have authorised the subsequent adoption of the proceedings but it did not; the shareholders in a general meeting did not have the power to do so (*Breckland Group Holdings Ltd v Suffolk Properties Ltd* [1989] BCLC 100).

When the board cannot exercise its powers

3166 Shareholders may be able to assume control of the company in very limited situations where the board is incapable of exercising its powers. In such situations, the **shareholders** have a **residual power** to step in to resolve the problem through general meetings (*Barron v Potter* [1914] 1 Ch 895).

Examples of the **types of situations** in which shareholders may exercise this residual power have arisen through case law, where:
a. the board was **deadlocked** (*Barron v Potter* [1914] 1 Ch 895). In this case, a decision taken at a general meeting was effective to exercise the managerial powers;
b. a **quorum** of the board could not be achieved (*Foster v Foster* [1916] 1 Ch 532);
c. there were **no directors** to carry out the business of the company (*Alexander Ward & Co Ltd v Samyang Navigation Co Ltd* [1975] 2 All ER 424). In this case, a shareholder commenced debt recovery proceedings on behalf of his company. The court held that this was within the company's powers, and since there were no directors to take the action for the company, it was appropriate for the shareholder to do so instead; and
d. the directors were **unable to vote** because they had interests in the matter which prevented them from doing so (*Grant v United Kingdom Switchback Railways Co* (1888) 40 Ch D 135). Under the current Table A, the shareholders would be able to suspend or relax these restrictions on voting.

The shareholders' **usual course of action** to resolve the problem would be to: **3167**
– remove a director from office (¶2946+); and/or
– appoint a new director (¶2266+).

The shareholders **could also** commence litigation on behalf of the company, although this may give rise to issues as to which body is entitled to commence and control proceedings (see ¶7124+, ¶7126+).

> MEMO POINTS   Where power reverts back to the shareholders in this way, they are **acting on their own behalf** as an organ of the company, i.e. they act as principal, not agent (*Northern Counties Securities Ltd v Jackson & Steeple Ltd* [1974] 2 All ER 625).

This residual power of the shareholders **derives from** case law, with certain important aspects being codified into the legislation (notably, the shareholders' power to remove a director). Case law has held that even where a company's articles do not give shareholders the power to appoint directors, they can still do so in circumstances where the board is incapable of acting (*Barron v Potter* [1914] 1 Ch 895). **3168**

Once the shareholders have **resolved the problem**, which prevented a competent board from acting, power automatically reverts back to the board. **3169**

Powers abused or exceeded

Consequences for directors

Directors who act outside of the powers delegated to them, either by abusing or exceeding those powers, **risk** serious consequences: **3171**
– personal liability for breach of duty, e.g. accounting for profits (¶2317+);
– statutory fines and/or imprisonment, depending on the breach (¶9935);
– disqualification from acting as a director (¶3000+); and
– removal from office by the shareholders (¶2946+).

These consequences could still arise where directors **follow shareholders' instructions**, whether received through special resolutions or otherwise, without regard to their usual duties. This could arise where the shareholders' wishes and the best interests of the company clash. **3172**

> EXAMPLE   A Ltd set up a subsidiary for a particular purpose, B Ltd, in which A Ltd held the majority of shares and installed three nominee directors on its board (comprising a majority on the board). A Ltd subsequently had no further use for B Ltd and introduced policies intentionally detrimental to B Ltd so that it would be forced to cease business. The nominee directors followed the policies of A Ltd and did not inform their fellow directors of B Ltd about A Ltd's plans, although this was clearly to the detriment of B Ltd. The court held that the nominee directors still owed the same duties to B Ltd as the independent directors, and they were in breach of those duties by acting as they did (*Scottish Co-operative Wholesale Society Ltd v Meyer* [1958] 3 All ER 66).

Similarly, if the company is (or is about to become) **insolvent**, the directors need to bear in mind the interests of creditors when acting upon instructions from the shareholders, who are likely to be acting in their own interests in this situation (*West Mercia Safetywear Ltd (in liquidation) v Dodd* [1988] BCLC 250; ¶2385). In such cases, the board will have to weigh up whether it is in the best interests of the company as a whole (taking into account the interests of shareholders and creditors) to follow the special resolution.

The reason for any **deviation from** the shareholders' instructions should be carefully recorded in the board minutes and/or a resolution, to protect the directors if the shareholders challenge their decision.

Consequences for shareholders

Shareholders who seek to exceed their powers and take on a more directorial role will find themselves open to the same **consequences** as the directors. Therefore, if shareholders use their power to instruct the directors by special resolution regularly, they must bear in mind that their actions may cause them to be: **3173**
– de facto directors, due to their conduct in assuming a managerial role (¶2210); or
– shadow directors, because the directors are used to following their instructions (¶2212+).

If the intent of any instructions to the directors by special resolution was to **defraud creditors**, the shareholders could be liable under insolvency legislation (e.g. for fraudulent trading or misfeasance) or under companies legislation (¶2577), whether or not their conduct actually rendered them de facto or shadow directors.

Consequences on contracts

3174 Contracts which are entered into by a board acting outside of its powers can be affected in different ways, depending on the seriousness of the breach and the action the parties decide to take (¶2483+).

B. Others involved in company management

3184 It is common for companies to involve people who are not shareholders or directors in the management of a company. Auditors and employees are the usual examples, along with external agents such as management consultants, which are often employed by larger companies.

Auditors

3186 Auditors perform an important function in monitoring a company's **financial** health, which is often indicative of how well a company is managed. Auditors are dealt with in detail at ¶4290+.

Employees

3188 It is usual, especially in larger companies, for directors to delegate managerial functions to non-directors employed as managers by the company. The **aim** is to free up the board's time so that it can concentrate on wider commercial issues, while the manager deals with the day to day running of the office. Further delegation is often made to employees who are not necessarily designated as managers, for example because they have particular expertise, such as experience in negotiating sales contracts.

An employee can be **given a managerial role** through delegation by the board, which should also be reflected in his employment contract (¶3432+). The employee/manager will be **answerable to** the board only; the shareholders have no power to interfere in employment matters.

3189 If an employee is given a management role, he usually still has the **status** of an employee rather than a director. However, if his management functions are so extensive that he effectively carries out the work of a director, or if the board is used to following his instructions, he could be deemed to be a de facto director by virtue of his conduct or become a shadow director (see ¶2210, ¶2212+).

C. Corporate governance

3199 The governance of **all types of company** is not comprehensively codified in statute or regulation. Provisions governing the conduct of directors (and so the management of their companies) are found in a variety of sources: statute, regulations and common law (see ¶2160+, ¶3217+). This has led to a somewhat confusing position, making it difficult for directors to be sure of their duties towards their company. The **new Companies Act** sets out these duties to clarify the position, although it does not intend to give a comprehensive statement of all of a director's duties (see ¶2337 for a summary of these duties). At the time of writing, most but not all of these provisions are in force.

All companies are required to provide their shareholders with certain information about the company's performance in their annual **accounts**. These requirements are dealt with at ¶4185+.

> MEMO POINTS 1. There is a system of best practice for the governance of **listed companies** set out in the Combined Code appended to the Listing Rules of the Stock Exchange. This is referred to as "self-regulation", as the Code has been devised and is policed by the City. Non-listed companies, especially large ones, can use the Combined Code as guidance because it serves as a useful benchmark of corporate governance. For example, they may want to adopt elements of the Code appropriate to their situation, such as appointing non-executive directors, putting continued training for directors in place and being open with shareholders about management practices.
> 2. The **European Commission** has produced an "Action Plan on Company Law and Corporate Governance" which intends, among other things, to improve the transparency and accountability of corporate governance across the EU (European Commission Communication to the Council and the European Parliament: *Modernising Company Law and Enhancing Corporate Governance in the European Union – A Plan to Move Forward* 21.5.2003, COM (2003) 284 final). The EC favours a "light touch" approach in this area, encouraging the convergence of governance codes of the different member states, considering best practice at the European Corporate Governance Forum and issuing Commission Recommendations. It continues to work and consult on a number of projects, including plans to introduce a European Private Company Statute to facilitate cross-border business, establishing a common framework for business registers and investigating how European company law can be simplified.

General principles

3202

The **concept** of "**corporate governance**" essentially refers to the system(s) by which directors are monitored in their management of a company. Companies legislation provides for the board of directors to be given broad powers of management, but ultimately to submit to the control of the company (see ¶3118+).

In managing a company, directors must **act in the interests of** the company, which primarily means acting for the benefit of the shareholders (and the creditors, where the company's solvency is at issue, see ¶2385, ¶7312), but they will also have to consider the interests of the employees (e.g. in a redundancy situation) and creditors, as well as customers and suppliers on a practical level. This duty has been codified as the duty to promote the company's success, see ¶2379+. It is usually down to the shareholders to decide whether or not to take action against directors who are in breach of their duties towards the company.

Directors are bound by their **duties and liabilities** to the company (¶2317+), as well as by their service contracts (¶2627+) and statutory duties, such as to disclose any conflicting interests (¶3308+). There are numerous **record keeping obligations** imposed on companies which also assist in ensuring and monitoring effective management, comprising:
– minutes of meetings (board: ¶3473+; shareholder: ¶3864+);
– company registers (¶3888+);
– accounts (¶4185+); and
– filing certain information at Companies House (¶9900).

External bodies also play a part in monitoring the effective management of a company. The role of auditors is discussed at ¶4290+. Bodies such as the CIB (¶7195+), Companies House (¶4040+) and specialist regulatory organisations such as the Competition Commission all play a part in monitoring the different aspects of corporate management.

Political donations

3204

Statute specifically restricts a **company's ability to make** political donations (ss 362-379 CA 2006). This restriction **applies to** the following types of payment made (or contracts entered into to make such payments) on or after 1 October 2007 (para 41 Sch 3 SI 2007/2194):
a. donations to political parties and political organisations; and
b. expenditure incurred in:
– preparing, publishing or disseminating material which could reasonably be regarded as supporting a political party or organisation; or
– expenditure on other activities which could reasonably be regarded in the same way, or which could influence voters.

A company can only make donations to a registered political party or other EU political organisation without the express authorisation of its shareholders if they amount to £5,000 or less in each 12-month period (s 378 CA 2006). Note that this de minimis allowance is not worded widely enough to include political expenditure. If **authorisation** is required, it must (ss 367, 368 CA 2006):
– be obtained before a donation is made or expenditure incurred;
– be in the form of an ordinary resolution (unless the articles require a different type of resolution to be used, s 281 CA 2006);
– specify the type of spending being authorised (i.e. political donations to a party or independent candidate, political donations to a political organisation, or political expenditure). The resolution should not be more specific than this, for example it should not state to which political party donations can be made; and
– set limits on the amount which can be spent in the next 4 years (or shorter period specified by the articles or the directors, if the articles allow them to do so).

This requirement for authorisation mirrors the Companies Act 1985 provisions, so many companies will already have authorising resolutions in place. Such resolutions will still be valid, so there is no need for companies to pass a new resolution under the Companies Act 2006 until their existing resolutions expire (unless they wish to include independent election candidates in the authorisation, see memo point 3 below) (para 42 Sch 3 SI 2007/2194).

A donation or payment cannot be authorised or ratified after the event. If the directors have made a donation or payment **without authorisation**, they are liable to repay the amount spent, plus interest and damages for any loss suffered by the company (369 CA 2006; interest must be paid at a rate of 8% per annum, reg 2 SI 2007/2242). A director can apply to the court for relief from liability for breach of this restriction (¶2505+). Shareholders can take court action in the name of the company against the directors to recover these sums, in addition to their rights to commence derivative proceedings (ss 370–373 CA 2006; for derivative proceedings, see ¶7127+).

> MEMO POINTS 1. Payments made or expenditure incurred **before 1 October 2007** can be authorised by an ordinary resolution or another type of resolution required by the articles that requires a higher majority of approval (s 347C CA 1985).
> If a resolution was passed before 1 October 2007 to approve donations made or expenditure incurred on or after this date, it is treated as complying with the new provision (s 367 CA 2006), and will therefore still be valid, even though it does not set out the categories of donations/expenditure as required (para 42 Sch 3 SI 2007/2194).
> 2. If the company is a subsidiary of a UK-registered **holding company** (which is not itself the subsidiary of another company), the spending must also be authorised by the shareholders of that holding company (s 366 CA 2006). However, if the company is a wholly-owned subsidiary, only the holding company's shareholders need to provide authorisation. A holding company's resolution can authorise the same type of spending by all of its subsidiaries; if it does not cover all subsidiaries, the resolution will have to specify the type of spending and permitted maximum amount for each one within the resolution (s 367 CA 2006). If a donation or payment is made without authorisation, the directors of the holding company will only be jointly and severally liable with the directors of the company which made the donation or payment if they did not take reasonable steps to prevent the donation or payment being made (s 369 CA 2006).
> 3. The new Companies Act also widens the scope of these provisions further to include donations to, or expenditure in relation to, **independent election candidates** (ss 364, 365 CA 2006). However, to give companies time to pass new resolutions to take this new addition into account, the provisions will only come into force regarding independent election candidates from 1 October 2008.
> 4. These **restrictions do not apply** to: donations to trade unions (with the exception of a trade union's political fund), subscriptions for membership to trade associations or donations to all-party parliamentary groups (ss 374, 375, 376 CA 2006). This means that companies can allow employees paid leave to deal with trade union matters, for example, without needing authorisation. Regulations also exempt "political expenditure" by newspapers and other publishing and media companies in the normal course of their business from these restrictions, so that they do not need authorisation from their shareholders to report the news (SI 2007/2081).
> The Companies Act 1985 provisions used to require overseas subsidiaries of a UK parent to obtain authorisation as well as UK-based ones. The new Companies Act does not do so.
> 5. For the **disclosure** of political donations and expenditure in the directors' report to the accounts, see ¶4247.

SECTION 2

Board decisions

SECTION OUTLINE	¶¶
I Decisions taken at board meetings	3222
Board resolutions	3224
A. Convening a board meeting	3234
Notice	3236
Informal meetings	3242
B. Conduct at a board meeting	3252
1. Attendance	3254
a. Tele-/video-conference meetings	3255
b. Quorum	3258
2. Voting	3268
3. Chairman	3274
4. Secretary	3279
5. Adjournments	3281
II Decisions not taken at meetings	3291
Written board resolutions	3293
Unanimous agreement	3297
III Directors' interests	3308
A. Obligation to disclose interests in contracts	3317
1. Who makes the disclosure?	3320
2. What is to be disclosed?	3324
3. Timing of the disclosure	3328
B. Consequences of having an interest	3341
1. Disclosure of interests generally under Table A	3343
2. Companies which depart from Table A	3356
C. Consequences of not disclosing interests	3367
D. Specific duty to disclose interests in shares/debentures	3379
E. Additional disclosure obligations	3392
IV Delegation of powers	3404
1. Committees	3408
2. Managing and executive directors	3425
3. Non-directors	3432
4. Alternate directors	3438
5. Assignees	3450
V Sole directors	3460
VI Administrative requirements	3473
1. Minutes	3473
2. Filing requirements	3480
3. Entering into contracts	3486

3217 It is the responsibility of the directors to manage their companies on a day to day basis. Although some significant decisions must be taken, or at least approved, by the company in a shareholder meeting, the directors are empowered to take most decisions that arise. The duties and liabilities of the directors as individuals are examined at ¶2317+; the power of the board as opposed to that of the shareholders was discussed above at ¶3118+. Here, the decisions taken by the board within the scope of its power and authority are discussed.

Primarily, the board exercises its powers and makes decisions by way of **board resolutions**. These can be passed either at board meetings or, if the articles of a company permit, without meetings by written resolution. There is also some scope for board decisions to be made in a less formal manner. Board resolutions can be **used to** take any decision within the powers of the board, whether relating to the day to day management of the company or to specific transactions. They are often made by the whole board, but boards can also **delegate** their powers and decision making functions to committees.

Disclosure of **directors' interests** is vital to the ability of a board to function when a potential conflict of interests arises, but it will not affect every board meeting or decision.

> MEMO POINTS   It is important that the proper procedures are followed when making decisions at a meeting or otherwise, to ensure the validity of the board's decisions. However, **third parties** are protected from companies being able to claim that contracts are unenforceable against them due to some technical default, such as the meeting at which authority to enter into a contract on the company's behalf was delegated to a director being inquorate. These contracts are still enforceable against the company, preventing companies being able to benefit from their own **procedural errors** (¶2350/mp).

I. Decisions taken at board meetings

3222 The **procedures** surrounding board meetings are less stringent than those for shareholder meetings. However, there are still certain requirements which must be adhered to in order to ensure the validity of decisions taken at board meetings. The procedures are usually **found in** the articles, and the position discussed here is that set out in Table A. Individual companies may modify the provisions of Table A, and so the articles need to be read carefully to check whether a company departs from this position.

> MEMO POINTS   The **new Companies Act** will also leave much of the regulation of board meetings to the articles. Draft **new model articles** under the new Act have been published for private companies limited by shares and public companies. They contain various provisions concerning board meetings, which are highlighted as necessary in the paragraphs below.

Board resolutions

3224 There are no statutory provisions setting out the **form, content** or **notice requirements** for board resolutions. A company's articles may provide for this, but it will usually be left to the board. Table A simply provides that board resolutions can be **passed by** a majority of votes (reg 88 TA 1985). However, board meeting minutes must be kept, forming a record of all board resolutions (¶3473+).

Although there are no specific requirements for board resolutions, directors should bear in mind that if they resolve to **call a shareholder meeting**, they will need to take account of the provisions relating to the type of resolution to be proposed at that meeting when determining the wording and timing of the notice to be sent to shareholders (¶3610+).

Resolutions will be **recorded in** the minute book. Some board resolutions have to be **filed** at Companies House (see ¶3480+), but most do not.

> MEMO POINTS   The draft **new model articles** for **private companies** limited by shares will also leave the question of board resolutions relatively open. They will provide that board resolutions can be passed on a majority of votes or unanimously at a meeting, or by written resolution (art 6). The articles are practical, recognising that many boards operate on an informal but unanimous basis. Therefore, boards will either be able to make decisions unanimously (art 7) or by majority (art 8), in which case they need to consider additional issues not relevant to unanimous decisions, such as interested directors (art 14), the quorum (art 11), a chairman (art 12) and a casting vote (art 13). It will be open to directors to make any rules they see fit about how they make decisions (art 16).
> The draft new model articles for **public companies** will be more traditional, providing for decisions to be made on a majority at a meeting (arts 6, 12) or unanimously in writing (art 17). Public company directors will also be able to make any rules they see fit about how decisions are made (art 18).

A. Convening a board meeting

3234 The **procedure** for convening, or calling, board meetings is **found in** a company's articles. Table A allows directors to regulate their own meetings, or "proceedings", as they see fit (reg 88 TA 1985). Individual companies may modify or replace Table A in their own articles, and the board may impose formal requirements (provided these do not contradict the articles) through board resolutions.

There are no statutory or regulatory requirements stating **how often** board meetings are to be held. Instead, directors are obliged by their various duties to act in the best interests of the company, among other things, and therefore will have to call a board meeting as often as is necessary to ensure effective management. A board may resolve to hold board meetings at certain intervals, or a company may require its board to do so in the articles. Usually, the board will meet at regular intervals to consider routine business, and will hold additional meetings as required.

Board meetings are usually **summoned by** the directors. The secretary must summon a board meeting on the instructions of a director, but cannot do so on his own initiative; by contrast, a director can call a meeting whenever he sees fit (reg 88 TA 1985; and see ¶3279 for the secretary's role in board meetings).

> MEMO POINTS The draft **new model articles** will also allow the board the freedom to dictate how decisions should be made at this level (private companies limited by shares: art 16; public companies: art 18). Any director will be able to call a board meeting by giving reasonable notice (not necessarily in writing) to all directors (private companies limited by shares: art 9; public companies: art 7). Public company secretaries will have to call a meeting if a director so requests, and if a private company chooses to have a secretary a director can call a meeting by authorising the secretary to send notice of it to the directors.

Notice

3236 The notice can be sent to the directors using any of the **methods** available for companies to communicate with others (s 1144, Sch 5 CA 2006). Notices and other communications to be sent by companies must be in hard copy, electronic form, on a website or in any other form agreed with the recipient, which gives companies the freedom to arrange for notice of board meetings to be given orally, for example. These methods are discussed at ¶3695+ in the context of giving notice of shareholder meetings. There are no specific requirements in Table A or the legislation as to the **form** of a board meeting notice; it does not even have to be in writing (reg 111 TA 1985).

The notice should at least set out the **location**, **time** and **date** of the board meeting in order to give the directors a reasonable opportunity of attending. There is no requirement in Table A or statute for the business of the meeting to be set out in the notice. However, it is advisable to give some form of **agenda** to enable the directors to prepare properly for the meeting and therefore discharge their duty to exercise due care, skill and diligence in running the company (¶2411+).

> MEMO POINTS The draft **new model articles** will state that notice of board meetings does not have to be in writing (private companies limited by shares: art 9; public companies: art 7).

Notice period

3237 There is no **requirement** in Table A or the legislation to give a particular period of notice of a board meeting; nor do any specific board resolutions require a defined notice period. Unless the company's articles or a previous board resolution state otherwise, "reasonable" notice of a board meeting needs to be given.

What is reasonable will depend on the company's usual practice and the circumstances of the meeting. In the case of most small limited companies with only a handful of directors, notice of just a few hours should suffice, provided all directors are given a reasonable opportunity to attend. A director of a company governed by Table A cannot veto the convening of a meeting because the **timing is inconvenient** to him.

> **EXAMPLE** Notice of a board meeting was sent to the directors almost one month before the meeting but the date was subsequently queried. A fax was then sent to the unavailable director the evening before the meeting confirming the original timing. The court held that the meeting was convened on reasonable notice because the original notice was given weeks before the meeting (*Colin Gwyer & Associates Ltd v London Wharf (Limehouse) Ltd* [2003] 2 BCLC 153).

> **MEMO POINTS** The draft **new model articles** will require directors to choose a date and time for a board meeting that will enable as many directors as practicable to participate, taking the urgency of the decisions to be taken into account (private companies limited by shares: art 9; public companies: art 7). The articles for public companies go on to state that reasonableness depends on the circumstances.

Entitlement to receive notice

3238 Notice must be **given to** all of the current directors of the company.

A director has no power to waive his right to receive notice of a board meeting (*Young v Ladies' Imperial Club* [1920] 2 KB 523). If a director appoints an **alternate director** and gives him the right to receive notice, the company should still give notice to the appointing director as well, to prevent any potential challenge to the validity of the meeting, unless the articles state otherwise.

The only **exception** to the requirement that all directors must receive notice of a board meeting in Table A is where a director is not in the UK when the notices are sent out (reg 88 TA 1985).

> **MEMO POINTS** The draft **new model articles** will require notice to be given to all directors, unless it is not practicable to do so or a director has waived his entitlement to notice (private companies limited by shares: art 9; public companies: art 7). A director will be able to waive his entitlement to notice by giving the company 7 days' notice to that effect before or after the meeting.

Failure to give notice properly

3239 Failure to give notice **to all directors** is an irregularity that renders the business decided at the board meeting invalid (*Re Oriental Gas Ltd* [2000] 1 BCLC 209). This is the case even if those directors who attended comprised a quorum. However, in such a situation the procedural irregularity can be ratified by all of the directors consenting to the meeting being held without notice (¶3242 below).

In addition, if **a director** who was willing and able to attend a board meeting is excluded, he can apply to the court for an injunction to prevent it from happening again (*Hayes v Bristol Plant Hire Ltd* [1957] 1 All ER 685). If notice was given to **some directors**, but not all of them, and the directors who attend the board meeting try to reverse a decision of a previous valid board meeting, that attempt will be void (*Re Homer District Consolidated Gold Mines*, ex parte Smith (1888) 39 Ch D 546).

3240 Even if notice was sent to a director but **not received** by him, it will be deemed to have been served on him 48 hours after it was posted or sent electronically to him (provided the company can prove that it was posted/sent properly) (s 1147 CA 2006). Table A reflects this deemed service period, but companies often replace it with alternatives appropriate to the method of sending (e.g. 24 hours for first class post) (reg 115 TA 1985). However, the company will not be able to rely on the provision if it is unreasonable to do so, for example where the notice was actually sent by second class post or there has been a postal strike (*Bradman v Trinity Estates plc* [1989] BCLC 757). Companies may also wish to include a specific provision mirroring that for shareholder meeting notices, to ensure that the board meeting is valid even if a director does not receive a notice which has been sent to him (see s 313 CA 2006 and reg 39 TA 1985).

3241 Any **objections** to the manner in which a board meeting is convened must be raised as soon as possible. If an irregularity has occurred in convening a board meeting, for example too short notice was given to the directors, the court will not intervene if the decision taken at the meeting has subsequently been acted upon, because the company will have impliedly ratified the decision.

Informal meetings

3242 It is possible for board meetings to be held informally, for example **without notice**, provided all directors consent. It is important that even those directors who do not attend the meeting consent to it being held without notice, or without any one or more of the formalities set out in the articles or in board resolutions. It is advisable to keep a **record** of all of the directors' consents to a meeting held in this way to prevent any potential dispute later on.

Such informal meetings still need to have a **quorum** in order to be conducted validly.

> *MEMO POINTS* Even those who attend an informal meeting **must intend** for there to be a meeting of the board. A casual meeting of the directors cannot later be called a board meeting if one of the directors denies that a meeting took place. For example in one case, two directors claimed that an informal meeting had been held on the platform of a train station as the third director alighted from a train, but the third director successfully argued that he did not intend for this casual gathering to be treated as a board meeting (*Barron v Potter* [1914] 1 Ch 895).

B. Conduct at a board meeting

3252 The conduct at board meetings will be **governed by** the company's articles. Table A permits directors to regulate their own proceedings as they see fit (reg 88 TA 1985), and also contains provisions relating to the quorum and chairman as specific issues. The board may decide to make further provisions by board resolution. Individual companies may modify, add to or exclude these provisions and directors should check the articles to see whether any specific procedural rules apply. **Disclosure of directors' interests** is also pertinent to the conduct of board meetings, but is dealt with separately at ¶3308+ because the provisions may not affect every board meeting. Here, the basic position relevant to all meetings is addressed.

> *MEMO POINTS* The draft **new model articles** for private companies limited by shares will also enable the board to set out further rules regarding decision making (art 16). They will distinguish between decisions made unanimously and those made by the majority, so that the provisions relating to interested directors, the quorum, chairman and a casting vote will only apply to majority decisions. The draft new model articles for public companies will make no such distinction, but they will allow the board to set out its own rules regarding decision making (art 18).

1. Attendance

3254 All directors are **entitled to** attend board meetings. A director cannot be excluded from attending, although he may be excluded from voting (*Pulbrook v Richmond Consolidated Mining Co* (1878) 9 Ch D 610; ¶3268+). **Alternate directors** and their ability to attend board meetings are dealt with at ¶3438+.

a. Tele-/video-conference meetings

3255 There is no statutory or regulatory provision allowing or prohibiting board meetings conducted via telephone or video link. It is common for companies' articles to **allow** such meetings to take place. The articles should state that if a director participates in a meeting in this way (or even if he makes his views known to the meeting by another method, such as in a telephone call, or by fax or email) then the meeting is to be treated as if it was duly called and held with him present. They may also provide that the director present by tele-/video-conference can count in the **quorum** for the meeting, provided he can participate fully (i.e. speak and be heard by the others present and vice versa).

> *MEMO POINTS* 1. Unless the articles of a company specifically permit, a **series of one-to-one telephone calls** made to various directors in lieu of a meeting would probably not count as a valid meeting, as it is too far removed from the common understanding of a "meeting".

2. The draft **new model articles** are drafted widely to allow directors not present at a meeting to communicate with and participate in it by any means, although they do not specifically deal with tele-/video-conference meetings (private companies limited by shares: art 10; public companies: art 8).

3256 If the articles do **not allow** board meetings to be held with a director in attendance by tele-/video-conference and a meeting was held in this way, the consent of all directors entitled to receive notice (i.e. those absent as well as those present) should be obtained in order to ensure the validity of the meeting (¶3242). It would be preferable to amend the articles to allow board meetings to be held in this way to avoid any potential challenge (¶450+).

In any event, the **minutes** of a telephone/video meeting should be circulated to all attendees to ensure that the directors agree that they reflect the proceedings correctly.

b. Quorum

3258 The quorum is the **minimum number** of directors required to **attend** a board meeting in order for it to proceed validly to business. Note that a quorum is necessary at **every stage** of the meeting, i.e. for each resolution. Directors' eligibility to count in the quorum may well change during a meeting, so the chairman must ensure that the quorum is maintained throughout, otherwise some resolutions may be invalid.

3259 The quorum is usually **specified** in the articles. Companies governed by Table A need to have a quorum of two, unless the directors set it at another figure (reg 89 TA 1985). However, even where the quorum is specified, if the company has consistently held and relied on its board meetings where a **lower number** of directors acted as a quorum, the court will not usually declare its resolutions invalid, as the board will have changed the quorum by its conduct (¶3297+).

Comment: A quorum is not enough in itself for the meeting to be valid; there must first be **a properly called meeting**. For example, even if the articles of a company stipulate that the quorum for a board meeting is two, two of the directors of that company cannot just decide to pursue a course of action without convening a proper meeting. This is the case even if those two directors would, in reality, be the only directors who would attend a board meeting.

MEMO POINTS The draft **new model articles** will mirror this provision for private companies' majority board decisions and public companies board decisions (private companies limited by shares: art 11; public companies: art 9).

3260 Where the quorum is **not specified**, it will either be the number of directors considered as the quorum by the established practice of the board (*Re Tavistock Ironworks Co, Lyster's Case* (1867) LR 4 Eq 233), or a majority of the directors, if there is no established practice (*Re Regent's Canal Iron Co* [1867] WN 79). However, if authority to do something has been delegated to a number of people, e.g. a **committee**, with no specified quorum, all of those people will form the quorum as they must exercise their authority together (*Brown v Andrew* (1849) 18 LJQB 153).

3261 If a company is structured in order to maintain a certain **balance of power** between different groups, for example where a company splits its shareholding into classes of shares, the quorum requirements are often drafted in the articles to reflect this arrangement.

EXAMPLE X Ltd has divided its shareholding into 50 ordinary A shares and 50 ordinary B shares. The business is run by two families, the Adams family who hold the A shares, and the Brown family who hold the B shares. The company has been structured so that each family has an equal say in management. To reflect this on the board, the articles stipulate that the quorum required for board meetings is two directors: one appointed by the holders of the ordinary A shares and one appointed by the holders of the ordinary B shares.

Who can count in the quorum?

3262 A director can only count in the quorum if he is **competent** to do so under the articles. Therefore, a director of a company governed by Table A who has a material interest in the resolution cannot count in the quorum (¶3341+). See ¶3438+ for when **alternate directors** can be counted. Individual companies' articles may contain further **restrictions**. Case law has also commented obiter that a director must be acting within his fiduciary duties to count in the quorum (*Colin Gwyer & Associates Ltd v London Wharf (Limehouse) Ltd* [2003] 2 BCLC 153).

A company cannot **evade** these **restrictions** by artificially arranging the business so that a quorum is always present. If a transaction is truly one transaction, it cannot be divided into two simply so that a quorum can be maintained (*Re North Eastern Insurance Co Ltd* [1919] 1 Ch 198). However, companies governed by Table A can split a resolution to appoint two or more directors to offices or employments within the company into separate resolutions concerning each director, so that the directors can count in the quorum on all resolutions except the one concerning themselves (reg 97 TA 1985).

> MEMO POINTS The draft **new model articles** will not allow directors who have an interest in the matter being decided to count in the quorum (private companies limited by shares: art 14; public companies: art 15). They will not contain an equivalent provision regarding resolutions to appoint directors.

For there to be a quorate meeting, the directors in the quorum must all be **willing to participate** in the meeting, and not just physically be in the same place (*Glatzer & Warwick Shipping Ltd v Bradston Ltd, Re "Ocean Enterprise"* [1997] 1 Lloyd's Rep 449). However, the court may look at the motives of a director for not participating. For example, it will not allow a director to refuse to attend a board meeting in order to frustrate the quorum to prevent valid share transfers from being registered (*Re Sticky Fingers Restaurant Ltd* [1992] BCLC 84).

3263

Lack of quorum

In the absence of a quorum at a board meeting, the meeting is invalid and **any resolutions** passed at that meeting will also be invalid. If a quorum is not achieved for a **particular resolution** only, that resolution is invalid but the rest will stand. This may arise where, for example, a director forming part of the quorum has a material interest in the resolution, which precludes him from counting for that resolution. However, parties contracting with the company are usually protected from the transaction being rendered invalid by such a procedural error affecting the authorising board resolution, see ¶2350/mp.

3264

Despite the fact that a resolution passed at an inquorate meeting is invalid, it may be capable of being **ratified**. This can be done expressly by the shareholders in a general meeting, by the directors in a board meeting (see ¶2497+) or impliedly by conduct (board: ¶3297+; shareholders: ¶3590+). For example, a valid board meeting approving the minutes of an earlier meeting which record that an invalid resolution was properly passed would have the effect of ratifying that resolution (*Municipal Mutual Insurance Ltd v Harrop* [1998] 2 BCLC 540).

Where the board falls below the quorum

It may be that the number of directors sitting on the board falls below the number of directors required to comprise a quorum at meetings, for instance due to **resignation**, **disqualification** or **death**. The articles usually provide that if the number of directors on the board falls below the quorum, the remaining directors can only continue to act to increase the number of directors to the required level or to call a shareholder meeting (e.g. reg 90 TA 1985). Alternatively, the articles may allow the remaining director(s) to carry on acting for any purposes (¶3460+), or in limited cases the management may revert to the shareholders (¶3166+).

3265

> MEMO POINTS 1. The Table A provision allowing directors to continue to act does not permit a **board which has never been quorate** to act. The words "continuing directors" show that the board had to be competent at one stage and then fall below the required quorum level (*Re Sly, Spink & Co* [1911] 2 Ch 430).
> 2. The draft **new model articles** for private companies limited by shares will allow the board to act if a quorum has been set and there are too few directors, but only to appoint further directors or to enable the shareholders to do so (private companies limited by shares: art 11; public companies: art 10).

3266 In Table A, the number of directors required for a **quorum and the minimum number of directors** are both two (regs 89, 64 TA 1985). A discrepancy between these requirements may arise where companies depart from Table A. For example, a company may provide for a minimum number of directors of four, but state that two directors can form a quorum. In such cases, if the total number of directors fell to below four, the continuing directors could only hold a quorate board meeting to fill the vacancy on the board or call a shareholder meeting (*Re Scottish Petroleum Co* (1883) 23 Ch D 413). They could not act for any other purposes until a validly constituted board was achieved.

2. Voting

Entitlement to vote

3268 The **starting point** is that all directors are entitled to vote.

This can be **modified** in the company's articles. For example, a company which divides its directors into different types may limit a sales director to voting on matters concerning his field of expertise, while allowing the governing directors to vote on every matter. Or, if a board of directors is designed to represent different classes of shareholders (as in the example at ¶3261), the articles may provide that directors representing one block of shareholders cannot vote on a resolution to fill a vacancy in the directors representing the other block.

> MEMO POINTS The draft **new model articles** for public companies will set out the basic criteria for voting, allowing one director one vote and preventing his vote from counting if he is interested in the matter in hand (arts 12, 15). Those for private companies will not set out any basic criteria, although they will prevent a director's vote from counting in a majority decision if he is interested (art 14).

3269 There are restrictions in Table A on a director's entitlement to vote if he has an **interest in the matter** under consideration, including a resolution regarding his own appointment to an office or employment within the company (¶3308+).

> MEMO POINTS Case law has also commented obiter that a director's vote should not be counted if he is **acting outside his fiduciary duties** (*Colin Gwyer & Associates Ltd v London Wharf (Limehouse) Ltd* [2003] 2 BCLC 153). In this case, the company in question was a single purpose company holding the head lease of a building, the tenants of which were also the shareholders. Proceedings were commenced against a tenant/shareholder for breach of its covenants under the lease. This tenant/shareholder had a nominee director on the board. The board met to resolve to settle the claim with the tenant/shareholder (the nominee director and one other being present at the meeting). Other tenant/shareholders objected to the settlement, arguing that it was not in the best interests of the company and was for an improper purpose. The court held that the directors were in breach of their fiduciary duties, commenting that it followed that they should not have been counted in the quorum or entitled to vote. Although this is not a procedural rule as such, it complements directors' fiduciary duties and it would be prudent for an interested director not to vote in such circumstances, or at least for the board to record in the minutes why it considered that it was appropriate for him to vote.

3270 A prohibition on a director from voting on a particular matter at a board meeting will not prevent him, **if he also holds shares** in the company, from voting on that matter at a general meeting as a shareholder (provided he is not prevented as a shareholder from voting on other grounds, see ¶3815+).

3271 Any **dispute** as to a director's entitlement to vote will be decided by the chairman, unless the dispute is about the chairman's own entitlement to vote (reg 98 TA 1985). Companies may wish to include a provision in their articles stating what will happen if there is a dispute about the chairman's right to vote (there is no such provision in Table A).

How to vote

3272 Usually, **each director has** one vote on each resolution, and the voting is conducted on a show of hands.

A resolution is usually **carried by** a simple majority of those directors present and voting (reg 88 TA 1985), although the articles may well modify the position. If the vote is tied, the chairman often has the casting vote (¶3276). If the articles are silent as to the majority required, the directors must act unanimously (*Perrott & Perrott Ltd v Stephenson* [1934] Ch 171).

3. Chairman

3274 The articles of a company usually permit the board to elect a chairman. Table A allows the directors to **appoint** a chairman and to **terminate** that appointment (reg 91 TA 1985). It also provides that if the appointed chairman cannot or will not chair a board meeting, they can appoint a **substitute** chairman in his place. The chairman of the board is often the chairman at shareholder meetings as well (for example, reg 42 TA 1985).

The articles can also place a **time limit** on the duration of the appointment, although Table A does not do this. The position of chairman is distinct from a director's office: there is no automatic right for him to be chairman for as long as he is a director, unless the articles expressly provide for this (*Foster v Foster* [1916] 1 Ch 532).

> MEMO POINTS   The draft **new model articles** will enable boards to appoint a chairman (for majority decision making in the case of private companies and decision making in the case of public companies) and to replace him if he is still absent 10 minutes after the meeting was due to start (private companies limited by shares: art 12; public companies: art 11).

3275 The chairman of the board largely has the same general **role and powers** as the chairman of a shareholder meeting (¶3716+). He has the power to resolve any question as to a director's right to vote, unless the query concerns his own right to vote (reg 98 TA 1985). Companies may wish to include a provision in their articles stating what will happen if there is a dispute about the chairman's right to vote (there is no such provision in Table A).

The chairman's decision on any matter will, however, be **invalid if** (*Byng v London Life Association* [1989] 1 All ER 560):
– the decision was taken in bad faith;
– he fails to take relevant factors into account;
– he takes irrelevant factors into account; or
– he reaches a conclusion that no reasonable chairman could reach.

> MEMO POINTS   The draft **new model articles** will give the chairman the right to determine any question as to whether a director is interested in the matter in hand and therefore precluded from voting (private companies limited by shares: art 14; public companies: art 15).

3276 The articles usually state that the chairman has the **casting vote** where votes on a resolution are tied (e.g. reg 88 TA 1985). If the articles are silent on this point, he has no common law right to a casting vote (*Nell v Longbottom* [1894] 1 QB 767).

> MEMO POINTS   The draft **new model articles** for private companies limited by shares will allow the board to assign the casting vote to any director it wishes (art 13). Those for public companies will give the chairman the casting vote (art 13).

3277 Holding the office of chairman does not give a director any automatic power or authority to **enter into contracts** on behalf of the company without the sanction of the board. He still needs either specific authority to do so (*Bell Houses Ltd v City Wall Properties Ltd* [1966] 2 All ER 674), or authority implied by the conduct of the board and the circumstances of the case (*Hely-Hutchinson v Brayhead Ltd* [1967] 3 All ER 98). Directors' authority is discussed in detail at ¶2348+.

4. Secretary

3279 The secretary has no automatic right to **attend** board meetings, but will frequently do so in order to advise the board on administrative or compliance matters, or to take the minutes of the meeting. See ¶4115+ for further discussion on a secretary's general **role, duties and liabilities**.

The secretary will often prepare an **agenda** of the meeting to guide the chairman and the board through the business, although there is no obligation to do so. Unless the articles state otherwise, the board can deal with the business at a board meeting in any order it chooses (*Re Cawley & Co* (1889) 42 Ch D 209).

The secretary will often be instructed to carry out **administrative tasks** following a board meeting, such as filing documents or sending out the notices of a general meeting.

The secretary is not authorised to **exercise the board's powers**, unless permitted by the board. For example, when a secretary sent out notices convening a general shareholder meeting without the authorisation of the board, the proceedings at the general meeting were invalid (*Re State of Wyoming Syndicate* [1901] 2 Ch 431).

Comment: From 6 April 2008, private companies will no longer be obliged to have a secretary when the relevant provisions of the **new Companies Act** come into force (see ¶4116).

5. Adjournments

3281 There are no statutory or regulatory provisions relating to the **procedure** for adjourning board meetings, although a company's articles may set out express requirements. In the absence of any express provisions, board meetings can be adjourned as necessary. In doing so, the chairman and directors must bear their fiduciary duties in mind, especially their duty to act in the company's best interests. Case law has held that it is not necessary to give notice of an adjourned board meeting (*Wills v Murray* (1850) 4 Exch 843). Logically, this will only apply if the date and time of the adjourned meeting was determined at the original meeting, otherwise the directors will not know when next to attend.

If a **resolution** is passed at an adjourned board meeting, it is treated as having been passed on the date of the adjourned, and not the original, meeting (s 381 CA 1985).

II. Decisions not taken at meetings

3291 It is common, especially in smaller companies, for directors not to hold formal board meetings in the usual course of managing the company. Depending on the provisions of the company's articles, the board may be permitted to take their decisions by **written resolution**. This method still formally records the decisions taken by the board, but does not require them to meet face to face, and so will be particularly useful where the directors are scattered geographically, or where too few decisions need to be taken to warrant a board meeting.

A less formal method of decision making is by the **unanimous agreement** of all directors on the board. Decisions made in this way are potentially open to challenge as they are less likely to be recorded, and it can depend upon the circumstances of each case as to whether or not agreement can be inferred.

Written board resolutions

3293 Written resolutions are a common means of making board decisions as they obviate the need to call a meeting and are therefore more convenient. There is no statutory provision allowing directors to use a written resolution **procedure**; it is usually found instead in a company's articles.

A written resolution procedure can be **used instead of** both board and committee meetings by companies governed by Table A (reg 93 TA 1985). The written resolution is **carried by** the signatures of all directors who are entitled to receive notice of the board or committee meeting which the written resolution replaces. The signatures do not all have to appear on the same document, so that individual directors can sign separate copies of the resolution and return them to the company, as long as all of the copies take substantially the same form.

Alternate directors can sign on behalf of their appointor, or the appointor can sign instead, but both signatures cannot be put to the same resolution (reg 93 TA 1985).

MEMO POINTS The draft **new model articles** for **private companies** limited by shares will not set out a specific written board resolution procedure, but they do set out some basic rules for making decisions without a meeting. Unanimous decisions will be able to be made by the directors communicating their agreement to each other by any means, including by signing a copy the resolution (art 7). For majority decisions not made at a meeting, the director who is aware of the need to make the decision will have to make all other directors aware of the need for it, and the directors must have a reasonable opportunity to communicate their views to each other (art 8). Then, if a majority of the directors indicate that they agree to the decision, the resolution will be passed. A written record of all resolutions, whether made at a meeting or not, will have to be kept for at least 10 years (art 15).

The draft new model articles for **public companies** will set out a board written resolution procedure, which will require unanimity (arts 16, 17). Notices of written resolutions can be circulated to the board by a director or the secretary on a director's instructions, indicating what the resolution is and the deadline for agreeing to it. All directors will have to sign the resolution, or a copy of it, in order for it to be passed successfully. So as not to be too restrictive, a resolution can be passed even if some directors sign it after the time by which the notice states it must be agreed to. Again, a record of all written resolutions will have to be kept for at least 10 years.

3294 The written resolution provision in Table A does not override the requirement for a **quorum**. For example, if the articles of a company require a quorum of two, a written resolution signed by one director will not be valid, even if the other director is not entitled to receive notice of the meeting because he is outside the UK (*Davidson & Begg Antiques Ltd v Davidson* [1997] BCC 77). However, in the circumstances of the case the company may be prevented by equity, or "estopped", from denying the validity of the resolution because it has gone on to accept the decision, either expressly or impliedly (*Hood Sailmakers v Axford* [1996] 4 All ER 830).

3295 Companies operating under Table A cannot use a written resolution to pass a resolution regarding a contract in which **a director has an interest**, since an interested director is entitled to receive notice but not to vote (unless he falls within some exceptions) and so would not be able to sign the resolution (reg 94 TA 1985; for directors' interests generally, see ¶3308+). Therefore, unanimity could not be achieved.

Written resolutions are particularly common where a company is governed by a **sole director** (¶3460+). Such companies will have to ensure that their articles allow directors to count in the quorum and vote if they have an interest for the sole director to be able to take such decisions.

MEMO POINTS The **draft new model articles** will prevent the votes of interested directors from counting on most matters (in the case of a private company limited by shares, on majority votes only) (private companies limited by shares: art 14; public companies: art 15).

Unanimous agreement

3297 Although the normal rule is that the acts of a company's board must be authorised by resolutions passed at duly convened board meetings, case law permits directors to take decisions **without formal resolutions** where they act unanimously (*Re Bonelli's Telegraph Co, Collie's Claim* (1871) LR 12 Eq 246).

Unanimity can be **communicated by** directors expressly or impliedly. A director's agreement would be implied if, for example, he was aware of the decision to be made and he either took action supporting the decision, or took no steps to prevent it (e.g. by failing to make his dissent known to the other directors).

Informal acquiescence by the board in an unauthorised contract entered into by one of the directors on behalf of the company can ratify the contract (*Charterhouse Investment Trust Ltd v Tempest Diesels Ltd* [1986] BCLC 1). In a case concerning the variation of a director's service contract, the details of the proposed variation were sent to all of the directors but only authorised by the non-executive directors (the company's articles required the whole board to authorise the amendment). However, the amendment was effective because the other directors had been given the opportunity to object and did not. The decision was within the powers of the directors, and they had informally and unanimously approved it (*Runciman v Walter Runciman plc* [1992] BCLC 1084).

> MEMO POINTS   The draft **new model articles** for private companies limited by shares will not require board decisions to be made at meetings, whether they are to be made unanimously or by a majority (arts 6-8). Those for public companies will be more restrictive, stating that decisions must be made at a meeting or by written resolution (art 6).

3298 As with informal board meetings (¶3242), it is advisable to keep a **written record** of any such informal "resolutions". This will enable the board to produce evidence of the decision taken and the fact that it was unanimous. See ¶2497+ for the ratification of invalid resolutions.

> MEMO POINTS   The draft **new model articles** for private companies limited by shares will require all decisions, however made, to be recorded and kept for at least 10 years (art 15). Those for public companies will not allow informal decisions to be made.

III. Directors' interests

3308 Directors, as part of their **fiduciary duties**, are under an obligation not to allow their own interests to conflict with those of the company and to account for any profits they make, discussed at ¶2390+. If a director puts himself in a position of conflict, the **court can intervene** to set aside the transaction without looking into whether the director breached his other duties: the existence of a conflict is sufficient. Therefore, even a contract which is in fact in the best interests of the company can be set aside if a conflict exists.

If this rule was applied strictly, it would cause companies substantial difficulties. For example, many small companies are run by families, and the directors often employ other family members in the company, or contract work out to them. This would inevitably place a director in a position of conflict. He must engage the best person for the job, but is also likely to be influenced by a desire to benefit his relative by employing him.

3309 Statute and the articles attempt to strike a reasonable balance by modifying the equitable rule. **Statute** seeks to protect companies by ensuring that directors are candid about their interests in contracts (the statutory rule applies to *any* contractual interests, not just conflicting ones) and that they make a formal declaration of those interests to the board.

In the **articles**, each company can decide on the consequences of a director having an interest, i.e. whether its directors can vote and count in the quorum. Table A represents a compromise position, which allows directors to act provided they disclose any material contractual and non-contractual interests (discussed at ¶3341+). Companies can change this as appropriate.

Directors must remember that even if the articles permit them to vote and count in the quorum on a matter in which they are interested, they are still bound by their **other duties** to the company (¶2317+). They must still act in a way that they consider, in good faith, would be most likely to promote the success of the company for the benefit of the shareholders as a whole (*Colin Gwyer & Associates Ltd v London Wharf (Limehouse) Ltd* [2003] 2 BCLC 153. See ¶2379+ for more on this duty. This duty is the codified version of the common law duty to act honestly and in good faith in the best interests of the company, upon which this case is based), and are subject to the consequences of breach of duty if they do not. Directors must also bear in mind that they have **additional obligations** to disclose certain matters to the shareholders.

3310 Although the **new Companies Act** repealed the requirement for directors to disclose their interests in shares and debentures on 6 April 2007, it will still require directors to disclose their other interests. Most of the provisions concerning directors came into force on 1 October 2007, but those concerning directors' interests have not yet been implemented.

While making the obligation more workable, for example by allowing directors to make the disclosure otherwise than in a meeting, it will (rather unhelpfully) divide the duty into:
– declaring **interests in proposed transactions and arrangements**, which is to be treated as a fiduciary duty (s 177 CA 2006; the implementation date for this provision is yet to be announced at the time of writing); and
– declaring **interests in existing transactions and arrangements**, which is treated as a statutory duty (s 182 CA 2006, expected to come into force by 1 October 2009).

Transactions and arrangements are not defined. These two duties will be mutually exclusive, so there will be no need to declare an interest in an existing transaction if it was declared when the transaction was proposed. Therefore, the second duty should mainly be used by new directors and those who acquire an interest after the transaction or arrangement has been entered into.

Either type of **declaration** will be able to be made at a board meeting, in writing (s 184 CA 2006, expected to come into force by 1 October 2009), or by general notice (whereby the director declares that he will be interested in any transaction or arrangement with a particular company, firm or person, s 185 CA 2006, expected to come into force by 1 October 2009). A director will be expected to **declare all interests, unless**:
– he is not aware of the interest, transaction or arrangement;
– the interest cannot reasonably be regarded as giving rise to a conflict;
– the other directors are already aware of his interest; or
– it concerns the terms of his service contract, which are to be considered by the board or a committee.

An interest in a proposed transaction or arrangement will have to be declared before the company enters into it; existing interests will have to be declared as soon as is reasonably practicable. Once an interest has been declared, the director will have to make a further disclosure if his first one proves to be or becomes inaccurate or incomplete.

As for the statutory **consequences of breach**, the two will be dealt with differently:
– interests in proposed transactions or arrangements: treated as breach of a fiduciary duty (see ¶2451+), except that the transaction or arrangement will not be liable to be set aside and will not require the company's consent, unless the articles provide otherwise; and
– interests in existing transactions: breach will be a criminal offence, giving rise to a fine (s 183 CA 2006, expected to come into force by 1 October 2009).

The **consequences of having an interest** will still depend on the company's articles. Draft new model articles have been published for private companies limited by shares and public companies. They will prevent a director from participating in the decision making process (e.g. counting in the quorum) and prevent his vote from being counted if he is interested in the matter, unless (private companies limited by shares: art 14; public companies: art 15):
– the shareholders disapply this restriction by ordinary resolution;
– the interest cannot reasonably be regarded as giving rise to a conflict of interest; or
– his interest only arises because he has given or been given a guarantee, security or indemnity in respect of the company's or its subsidiaries' obligations.

> MEMO POINTS   If a company only has **one director when it should have more than one**, the sole director will have to declare any interests in existing transactions or arrangements in writing, and his declaration will be deemed to form part of the minutes of the next proper board meeting (s 186 CA 2006, expected to come into force by 1 October 2009).

A. Obligation to disclose interests in contracts

3317

Statute requires directors to declare their interests in any contracts or proposed contracts at board meetings.

A company's **articles** cannot override or dilute this statutory requirement. They can, however, add to them by setting out **procedural matters**, or by dealing with aspects not addressed in the legislation.

Table A contains provisions connected to directors' duty to disclose their interests, mainly relating to the **consequences** of a director having a material interest (¶3341+). These regulations are often excluded or altered by individual companies. If the Table A provisions apply, directors should consider them carefully, as they effectively place an additional disclosure obligation on them.

> MEMO POINTS For the changes in this area under the **new Companies Act**, see ¶3310.

1. Who makes the disclosure?

3320 The statutory disclosure must be made by the **directors present at the meeting** at which the contract or proposed contract is discussed. Clearly, a director who is not at the meeting will neither be involved in the discussion about the contract in which he is interested, nor will he vote on the resolution. However, if a director who has previously been absent from board meetings, and therefore has not disclosed his interest, subsequently attends a meeting at which the contract is discussed further, he must ensure that he discloses his interest at the first opportunity.

Newly appointed directors are not under a specific obligation to declare their pre-existing interests, but they usually do so at the first board meeting after their appointment, since the definition of "contract" is wide enough to include those not discussed at a particular meeting (¶3324).

3321 **Shadow directors** are specifically brought within the statutory obligation, and must also make the disclosure (s 317(8) CA 1985). However, shadow directors may not have the right to attend board meetings, and are therefore required to declare their interests in writing to the board. If a shadow director gives specific notice of an interest (¶3329), it is to be minuted as if it had been declared at the relevant board meeting; if it is a general notice (¶3330), it is to be minuted as being declared at the next meeting after the notice was given (s 382(3) CA 1985).

The methods by which information can be sent to a company are discussed at ¶3628, in the context of shareholders requiring the company to hold a meeting.

> MEMO POINTS Under the **new Companies Act**, shadow directors will still be expected to disclose their interests. A specific requirement is imposed on them in the case of existing transactions or arrangements, which mirrors the CA 1985 provisions by requiring the disclosure to be made in writing (s 187 CA 2006). In the case of interests in proposed transactions or arrangements, the new Act will state that this and other general duties imposed on directors will apply to shadow directors as the equitable rules do (s 170 CA 2006). Therefore, shadow directors will still have to disclose their interests. See ¶3310 for the implementation of the directors' interests provisions.

3322 The obligation also applies to a **sole director** even though he cannot have a meeting with himself in the conventional sense of the word (s 317(2) CA 1985). He must make the declaration to himself or to the secretary, if the secretary attends the meeting (*Neptune (Vehicle Washing Equipment) Ltd v Fitzgerald* [1995] 3 All ER 811). At a "meeting" on his own (i.e. without the secretary) he would simply have to record his declaration in the minutes. The fact that the declaration is minuted will be proof that it was made should there be any dispute. Due to the consequences of disclosure (discussed at ¶3341+), companies wishing to allow a sole director to act in matters in which he is interested should amend their articles as outlined in the table at ¶3463.

2. What is to be disclosed?

Meaning of "contract"

3324 The word "contract" **includes** any transactions or arrangements made or entered into by the company on or after 22 December 1980 (s 317(5) CA 1985). It includes any loans, quasi-loans, credit transactions, guarantees or security made by the company for a director or a person connected to him. The statutory definition of a "**connected person**" is complicated and is set out at ¶9930. Consideration of his **service contract** is a common example of a contract in which a director would have an interest.

Directors are still required to make the disclosure whether the contract is **proposed or completed**. For example, a director may have been absent from the meetings at which the contract in which he was interested was discussed, or he may have been appointed after the contract was entered into. Case law has also considered that the duty to disclose an interest is general enough to extend to contracts or proposed contracts which are **not considered at the meeting** (*Neptune (Vehicle Washing Equipment) Ltd v Fitzgerald* [1995] 3 All ER 811).

Meaning of "interest"

A director has to disclose any **direct or indirect** interest. There is no statutory definition of "interest", although usually it will comprise some external and/or personal connection between the director and the transaction and/or another party to the transaction. For example, a director of two separate companies may find that his duties to each company conflict, and this would need to be disclosed (to the boards of both companies). In a case concerning articles which permitted directors to participate in decisions in which they were "in any way interested", the court found that this encompassed not just personal interests, but also where the director owed a **duty conflicting** with those of the company (*Movitex Ltd v Bulfield* [1988] BCLC 104).

3325

The **details** a director has to disclose depend on the circumstances. He has to give full information about his interest to enable the other directors to ascertain what his interest is and how far it goes (*Movitex Ltd v Bulfield* [1988] BCLC 104).

3326

Even **if the other directors already know** that he has an interest, the disclosure must still be made at a board meeting. The requirement will still apply where the director acquires only a **nominal benefit** from the interest (*Todd v Robinson* (1885) 14 QBD 739).

3. Timing of the disclosure

Statute requires the disclosure to be made at a **board meeting** (s 317(2) CA 1985), and therefore a disclosure cannot be made in writing to the other directors (unless the disclosure is made by a shadow director, see ¶3321).

3328

The disclosure must be made to a full board meeting; declaration in a **committee** meeting is not sufficient (*Guinness plc v Saunders* [1990] All ER 652).

Interest in a specific contract

The board meeting at which the director makes his disclosure depends upon whether he is making a specific or a general disclosure. A director can disclose his interest in a specific contract by simply informing the board of his interest, giving the necessary details as to its nature, extent and circumstances as outlined at ¶3326.

3329

He must disclose an interest in a **proposed contract** at the first board meeting at which the contract is considered (s 317(2) CA 1985). Alternatively, if a director was not interested in a proposed contract when the board first considered it but he subsequently acquires an interest, he must make the disclosure at the first board meeting after he became interested.

If a director becomes interested in a **contract after it has been made**, or is appointed to the board after the contract has been completed, he should declare his interest at the first board meeting after his interest arises, or the first one a newly appointed director attends.

Interest in contracts generally

If a director will have an interest in all contracts the company enters into **with another company, firm or person** connected with the director, he can disclose his interest by way

3330

of a general notice (s317(3)CA 1985). The director will then not have to give notice each time such a contract is considered. The general notice can be given (s317(4)CA 1985):
– at a board meeting; or
– in between board meetings, as long as the director takes reasonable steps to ensure that the general notice is considered at the board meeting after it was given.

Form of disclosure

3331 There are no statutory requirements as to the form in which directors must make their declaration to the board (other than shadow directors, who must make it in writing (¶3321)). It is advisable for companies to keep a written **record** of interests as evidence of compliance and for future reference. Declarations of interests will at least be recorded in the minutes of board meetings.

B. Consequences of having an interest

3341 Although statute sets out an obligation and procedure which directors must follow in order to disclose their interests (and provides for the consequences of not doing so, ¶3367+), it does not specify the consequences of having an interest. This is left to companies to deal with in their **articles** if required. Table A provides for two main consequences of a director having a material interest: firstly, he will be allowed to continue to act as a director; secondly, he will not be permitted to vote or count in the quorum on a resolution concerning the matter in which he is interested. The interests with which Table A is concerned are **not just contractual**.

However, companies often choose to adopt their **own disclosure consequences** instead of those set out in Table A. It can cause companies, particularly smaller ones, difficulties to exclude directors with interests from voting and counting in the quorum. In addition, the Table A provisions are complicated, not least because the "interests" referred to are defined differently to those in the legislation. Companies should therefore decide what consequences would be appropriate for them and use, adapt or reject the Table A provisions as required.

MEMO POINTS For the changes in this area under the **new Companies Act**, see ¶3310.

1. Disclosure of interests generally under Table A

3343 Table A allows a director to **continue to act** even if he has his own interests, provided he has disclosed the nature and extent of any material interest to the board (reg 85 TA 1985). This is not an obligation to disclose as such, but if a director wishes to be able to continue to act, he must make the relevant disclosure.

In most cases, an interest will need to be disclosed under both statute and Table A. If a director is in any **doubt** as to whether he should disclose an interest, it would be prudent for him to make the disclosure to the board to ensure that he is able to act under the articles and to fulfil his statutory disclosure duty. If an interest has to be disclosed under both statute and the articles, there is no requirement for the director to make the same disclosure twice.

3344 The Table A provision **differs from the statutory requirement** to disclose interests in two ways:
a. it refers to material interests only: therefore, a director may have to disclose his interest to the board under the statutory provision, but not under the articles if he considers that it is not material; and
b. it is not restricted to contractual interests: therefore, a director may have to make a disclosure under the articles but not statute because the interest is not in a "contract" (as defined at ¶3324).

There is no definition of what would constitute a "**material**" **interest**, but case law can give some guidance on this point, describing it as one which is capable of influencing a director's judgment in a business sense (*Re Coltness Iron Co Ltd* 1951 SLT 344). It has also been contrasted with a trivial or insignificant interest (*Duke of Westminster v Birrane* [1995] 3 All ER 416).

Since **non-contractual interests** are included in the Table A provisions, disclosure extends to situations in which directors have a personal connection with someone else within their company or owe a duty to another company, for example, because they are its director or employee.

There is no stipulation under the Table A disclosure provision as to **when** directors must make their disclosure. They do, however, have to disclose their interests "to the directors" and so making the disclosure at a board meeting would fulfil the requirement (reg 85 TA 1985). Since the timing or manner of disclosure is not specified, directors could also make the disclosure in writing to the board. Table A disclosure is therefore not limited to those directors present at a meeting.

3345

> EXAMPLE Mr A, a director of A Ltd, also becomes a director of B Ltd, a company which operates in the same field of business as A Ltd. Even if Mr A does not attend A Ltd's board meetings for a period of time, he will have to disclose his interest in B Ltd to the A Ltd board and vice versa if he wants to continue to act as director of either company.

Table A reflects the statutory provisions allowing a director to give **general notice** of an interest in any transactions or arrangements with specific persons or a class of persons to allow him to act despite his material interests (reg 86(a) TA 1985). Disclosure under the articles can also be made on a **case by case** basis.

3346

Consequences for directors

Table A **permits** directors with an interest to continue to act as director of the company and to have that interest (reg 85 TA 1985). This is expressed to be "subject to the Act", i.e. the statutory obligation to disclose interests still applies. Table A permits a director to be:
a. a party to or interested in a transaction or arrangement with the company or in which the company is interested; and
b. involved in a company or body corporate which the company promotes or is interested in, including being a director or employee of that other company,
provided the director has disclosed the nature and extent of any material interest. The director will then not have to account to the company for any profits he makes out of his interest, nor can any contract in which he has such an interest be avoided because of that interest (two consequences which may otherwise apply, see ¶2317+).
This allowance seems to **contradict** the established equitable rules which apply to directors against self-dealing and conflicts of interest. However, it is generally accepted that shareholders may decide that it would be beneficial to allow directors to have these interests. Shareholders can always decide not to include the relevant provisions of Table A in their own articles if they are not appropriate.

3347

A director is not prevented from acting if he has an **interest of which he is unaware**, provided it would be unreasonable to expect him to have any knowledge of it (reg 86(b) TA 1985). This practical approach gives directors some leeway in disclosures made under the articles, but they must note that it only applies to interests of which they have "no knowledge" *and* where "it is unreasonable to expect [them] to have any knowledge". Therefore, a director cannot evade the requirement by turning a blind eye to any interests he might have.

3348

Consequences for the board meeting

Once a director has declared an interest to the board, he must then check whether or not he has the **right to vote** on the matter.

Regardless of whether or not a director has disclosed his interest, Table A prevents him from voting on a resolution concerning a matter in which he has an **interest or duty** which is "**material**" and **conflicts**, or may conflict, with the interests of the company (reg 94 TA 1985).

3350

The interests referred to in this article include not only those of a director, but also any **persons connected** to the director, as both direct and indirect interests are specifically included (see ¶9930). Note that this provision encompasses interests *and* duties, making it wider than the statutory obligation to disclose.

> EXAMPLE
> 1. Mr A is a director of A Ltd, which is governed by Table A. The board is considering entering into a lease of a building which is owned by Mr A personally. He has disclosed his interest in the proposed contract to the board under his statutory obligation. His interest is material (it may influence his judgment; it cannot be described as insignificant; the completion of this contract will result in his personal gain), and therefore he is prevented under Table A from voting on the matter and counting in the quorum (¶3353).
> 2. Mr A is also a director of B Ltd, a subsidiary of A Ltd which operates in the same market. At a board meeting of A Ltd, business opportunities are discussed which may be attractive to both A Ltd and B Ltd. Mr A has disclosed his interest under Table A to enable him to continue to act for A Ltd despite his directorship of B Ltd. However, his duty to and interest in B Ltd may conflict with that to A Ltd in this discussion, and therefore Table A prevents him from voting or counting in the quorum on any resolution arising out of the discussion (¶3353).

A director who is a bare trustee (a trusteeship which imposes no duties other than that to hand the trust property to the beneficiary when required), will not have a **conflict** with the company in the absence of other factors which would give rise to a conflict (*Cowan de Groot Properties Ltd v Eagle Trust plc* [1992] 4 All ER 700). For further discussion on whether a matter conflicts with the interests of the company, see ¶2390+.

3351 An **alternate director** is prohibited from voting if his appointor or a person connected to his appointor has a relevant interest (reg 94 TA 1985).

3352 There are a number of **exceptions** to this restriction on directors' ability to vote, which will encompass many of the situations in which a director will find himself (reg 94 TA 1985):
a. the resolution concerns the director receiving a guarantee, security or indemnity relating to money lent to the company or any of its subsidiaries, or a liability incurred by him for the benefit of the company or any of it subsidiaries;
b. the resolution concerns giving a guarantee, security or indemnity to a third party relating to an obligation of the company or any of its subsidiaries, where the director has assumed partial or full responsibility for that obligation;
c. the director's interest has occurred because he has subscribed or agreed to subscribe for shares, debentures or securities in the company or any of its subsidiaries, or because he is or intends to be involved in the underwriting or sub-underwriting of an offer of shares, debentures or securities by the company or any of its subsidiaries for subscription, purchase or exchange; or
d. the resolution concerns a retirement benefits scheme which is approved, or is conditional upon approval, by Revenue and Customs.

3353 If a director has any such material and conflicting (direct or indirect) interest or duty, not only can he not vote, but he cannot count in the **quorum** either (reg 95 TA 1985; ¶3258+).

This restriction also applies to an **alternate director** whose appointor, or a person connected with his appointor, has an interest.

3354 Directors are specifically prohibited by Table A from voting or counting in the quorum on a resolution regarding their **own appointment** to an office or employment within the company (e.g. as chairman or to a committee) (reg 97 TA 1985). Evidently, this is a matter in which a director has an interest.

2. Companies which depart from Table A

3356 The restrictions on a director acting when he is interested in the matter contained in Table A can be **relaxed** by an ordinary resolution of the shareholders at a general meeting (reg 96 TA 1985). Alternatively, the articles can be **amended** by a special resolution if a more long term change is required (¶450+).

If a company has not adopted Table A, the consequences of a director having an interest will depend upon its particular articles. If a company has alternative articles which are **silent** as to the consequences of a director having disclosed an interest, no restrictions apply. However, the directors will have to pay particular attention to the equitable rules as to whether they can act in matters in which they are interested and/or have a conflict.

3357

C. Consequences of not disclosing interests

Failure to disclose an interest in accordance with the statutory obligation renders the non-compliant directors liable to a fine (s 317(7) CA 1985; ¶9935).

3367

It will not render the **contract** itself invalid (*Guinness plc v Saunders* [1990] All ER 652), nor will it usually give rise to an action for damages (*Movitex Ltd v Bulfield* [1988] BCLC 104), but it may make it vulnerable to being set aside. However, where a director had fraudulently concealed his failure to disclose his interest, he was found to have been under a duty to disclose the failure itself and was liable to pay damages to the company (*Item Software (UK) Ltd v Fassihi* [2003] 2 BCLC 1, affirmed on this point on appeal ([2005] 2 BCLC 91)). The contract may need further approval at board or shareholder level, or it may be invalid because it is in breach of the directors' other duties towards the company (e.g. to act in the company's best interests).

    MEMO POINTS   For the changes in this area under the **new Companies Act**, see ¶3310.

If a director's **interest is obvious**, such as the interest of a director in increasing the notice period in his own service contract, failure to disclose an interest could be treated as a mere technicality (*Runciman v Walter Runciman plc* [1992] BCLC 1084). If an **interest is common to all** directors and this fact is known to all of them, the court would be unlikely to find that there was a breach of the statutory provision if a formal declaration had not been made (*Lee Panavision Ltd v Lee Lighting Ltd* [1992] BCLC 22).

3368

In such cases, non-disclosure could not be relied upon as a ground for setting aside the contract or for an unfair prejudice action (*Re BSB Holdings Ltd (No. 2)* [1996] 1 BCLC 155). However, the court has stressed that the fact that an interest is obvious does not excuse non-disclosure, but in the particular circumstances of a case it may be unjust to allow the company initially to accept the decision (or fail to object), and then subsequently seek to set it aside. Directors should, no matter how obvious, always disclose their interests in accordance with the legislation. Just because a contract is not set aside does not mean that the director will not be liable to a fine for non-compliance.

If the articles, like Table A, require disclosure as a prerequisite to allowing a director to benefit from deals done between him and the company, and the director does not make the relevant disclosures but still retains the benefit, he will be in **breach of his duties**. Therefore, the contract will be voidable at the option of the company, and the director will be liable to account for any profit he has gained. However, if the company affirms the contract, or does not take any action to avoid it, the contract will be upheld (*Hely-Hutchinson v Brayhead Ltd* [1967] 3 All ER 98). See ¶2350/mp for when **third parties** can enforce such a contract.

3369

D. Specific duty to disclose interests in shares/debentures

Directors are no longer under an obligation to disclose any personal interest they have in the shares in or debentures of their companies or related companies. This requirement was repealed by the new Companies Act on 6 April 2007 (s 1295, Sch 16 CA 2006; Sch 4 SI 2006/3428).

3379

E. Additional disclosure obligations

3392 In addition to the statutory provision to disclose interests to the board, and any provisions the articles may make in this regard, directors have to make other disclosures of their interests. See ¶3888+ for matters to be disclosed in a company's registers and ¶4185+ for those to be disclosed in the accounts. The legislation also requires directors to disclose certain transactions **to the shareholders** (and in some cases obtain approval for them as well). The articles of a company may reserve further matters to be disclosed to and/or approved by the shareholders in general meetings.

For instance, statute requires directors to disclose the following matters to the shareholders:
– the terms of a director's service contract for a fixed term of over 2 years (¶2655+);
– any compensation received by a director for loss of office, or any other payment received in connection with retirement from office as a director (¶2962+);
– the details of any substantial property transactions entered into between a director and the company (¶2567+); and
– the details of a scheme of arrangement (¶6500+).

> MEMO POINTS As part of a director's duty to act in a way that he considers, in good faith, would be most likely to promote the success of the company for the benefit of the shareholders as a whole (see ¶2379+), he must **disclose** his **own wrongdoing** to the company as well as that of any other director of which he is aware (*Item Software (UK) Ltd v Fassihi* [2005] 2 BCLC 91). He is also expected to **disclose any profits** he makes from his office, as these should be accounted for to the company (although the company may allow the director to keep them).
> A director may also have to **disclose information to** the **Panel on Takeovers and Mergers** in the case of public company takeovers (¶6685+).

IV. Delegation of powers

3404 Although the power to manage the company rests with the board as a whole, it can delegate its powers and functions in a number of ways. The **purpose** of delegation is to facilitate smooth company management, so that functions can be carried out more efficiently without requiring the whole board to meet every time a decision has to be made.

Any **power** of the board or individual directors to delegate is **found in** the company's articles. Directors are agents of the company (¶2185), a personal appointment which cannot be delegated without express permission from the company. Therefore, unless a company's articles contain powers of delegation, directors must perform their duties and functions themselves. It is usual to find delegation provisions in the articles.

Delegation of the board's powers and functions to committees is dealt with first, followed by the different types of delegation to various individuals. Such delegations are **made by** the board, except for delegation to alternate directors and assignees, which are made by individual directors.

> MEMO POINTS 1. It is important that the proper procedures are followed when delegating authority to committees or individuals. However, **third parties** are protected from companies being able to claim that contracts are unenforceable against them due to some technical default, such as the board acting outside of the powers in the memorandum, or making a delegation in breach of limitations on its powers of delegation imposed by the company. These contracts are still enforceable against the company, preventing companies being able to avoid obligations under a contract because of their own errors and defaults (¶2350/mp).
> 2. Draft **new model articles** under the **new Companies Act** have been published for private companies limited by shares and public companies. They will allow directors to delegate their functions to another person or committee by any means, including by power of attorney (for powers of attorney, see ¶3496) (art 4). They will be able to impose whatever terms and conditions are appropriate on the delegation, for example limiting it to certain powers or exercising powers

in relation to a certain territory. They will also be able to authorise sub-delegation. The directors will also be able to alter or revoke the delegation or its terms at any time. A committee's decision making process will follow the procedure for the board set out in the articles, unless specific rules are included for committees (art 5).

1. Committees

A board may wish to delegate some of its powers to a committee because, for example, some of the directors have **expertise** in a particular field and/or as a matter of **convenience**. Large companies often have committees relating to remuneration, audit, nomination and share allotment which are permanently appointed or "standing" committees, and meet as and when these issues arise. Committees could also be established for a specific period of time, for example to negotiate a transaction on behalf of the company, or to deal with a particular issue such as fundraising.

3408

Authority to establish committees

For the board to be able to delegate its powers to a committee there must be an **express provision** in its articles giving that authority. It is usual for articles to do so, and also to allow the board to make regulations governing the proceedings of committees.

3410

Boards of companies governed by Table A have the power to delegate any of their powers to a committee, and to impose conditions on the delegation (reg 72 TA 1985). Powers can be delegated by the board to committees so that only the committee can exercise the power(s) in question, or so that either the board or the committee can do so. The articles may set out more detailed provisions relating to the **scope of** a committee's **powers**, and/or such matters may be left to the directors' discretion to deal with in "terms of reference".

Although the articles might not place any **restrictions** on the board's power to delegate, case law has established that delegation would not be appropriate in particular circumstances, for example, if it is exercised to exclude a director from participating in the management of the company (*Trounce and Wakefield v NCF Kaiapoi Ltd* [1985] 2 NZCLC 99, 422). This is the case even if the director who was excluded was or may have been in a position of conflict. However, if the board can show it would not have been in the company's interests to include the director in the committee, then it may not have acted improperly in setting up the committee to exclude him. Therefore, in exercising their power to delegate, as with the exercise of any power, the directors must have regard to their fiduciary and other duties (¶2317+).

3411

Membership

The board can usually choose **how many** directors form each committee. Table A allows the committee to comprise one or more persons (reg 72 TA 1985). For example, a company may delegate any financial and accounting responsibilities to a finance director alone, or to a finance committee. Even if a company's articles do not contain this provision, a committee can still comprise only one director (*Re Fireproof Doors Ltd* [1916] 2 Ch 142).

3413

There is no restriction on the **type of director** permitted to sit on committees. Therefore, the board may delegate functions to a non-executive director alone or appoint him to a committee, in contrast to the delegation power described below which applies only to the managing director and other executive directors. The board may be able to appoint **non-directors** to a committee, if the articles allow. Table A only allows directors to sit on committees. Non-directors may still attend meetings, e.g. in an advisory capacity, but are not eligible to vote.

A company's articles may set out **further criteria** for the appointment of committee members, although Table A does not. Standing committees (such as the audit or remuneration committees) often comprise named directors, while other committees (such as those set up to negotiate and complete a particular contract) are frequently defined by the number of directors required (e.g. "any two directors"). Companies' articles could also define membership of different committees by expertise or experience, e.g. by requiring that at least one chartered accountant sits on the audit committee.

Scope of committee's powers

3415 The **board resolution** which establishes the committee should make its scope, status and function absolutely clear. Companies can prepare "**terms of reference**" approved by board resolution, which set out in detail any requirements for membership of the committee, its duties, the extent of its powers, how often it should meet, how it should report back to the board and so on. Alternatively, such details could be addressed in the **articles**, although terms of reference give the board more flexibility to deal with the needs of each committee separately and have the advantage of not being in the public domain.

Boards of companies governed by Table A can **impose conditions** on committees and **alter the terms** of the delegation as they see fit (reg 72 TA 1985).

3416 A decision taken by a committee **beyond** the scope of **its powers**, or that has been expressly reserved to the board as a whole, can affect the company and third parties (¶2348+). It will not usually bind the **company** unless it is subsequently ratified by the board or shareholders. For example, it has been held that where the articles vest authority for entering into directors' service contracts in the board, a service contract authorised by the chief executive alone did not bind the company (*UK Safety Group Ltd v Heane* [1998] 2 BCLC 208). Similarly, in another case where a committee authorised the payment of additional remuneration to a director, a power reserved to the board, that decision was invalid (*Guinness plc v Saunders* [1990] 1 All ER 652). The court stated that remuneration would have to be specifically delegated to a committee if this was the intention, and could not fall within a general delegation provision (such as reg 72 TA 1985).

> MEMO POINTS A **third party** dealing with one or more directors on behalf of a company is entitled to assume that they have the necessary authority to do so, provided that the third party is acting in good faith (¶2350/mp).

Meetings

3418 Table A stipulates that the articles will apply to the proceedings of a committee with two or more members in the same way as they apply to board meetings, subject to any conditions placed on the committee by the board (reg 72 TA 1985). Therefore, unless the conditions state otherwise, the **conduct** of a committee meeting should be the same as for a board meeting (see ¶3252+). For example, the committee members can appoint one of their number to chair the committee (reg 91 TA 1985).

Minutes of committee meetings must be kept in the same way as for board meetings (¶3473+). Companies governed by Table A must keep their committee meeting minutes in a book reserved for that purpose, along with a list of the names of the directors on the committee (reg 100 TA 1985).

Duration

3420 Boards of companies governed by Table A have the power to **revoke** or **alter** any delegation to a committee (reg 72 TA 1985), enabling them to withdraw the delegation altogether, or to shorten or extend any time period for which the committee was established. The board resolution or terms of reference creating the committee may have established an **expiry date** for the committee. In the absence of an expiry date, the board will have to pass another board resolution to suspend or revoke the delegated authority.

2. Managing and executive directors

3425 The board can usually appoint directors to the posts of managing or other executive directors. As with delegation to committees, **authority** for this must be granted in the articles. Table A permits the appointment of managing or other executive directors and the delegation of appropriate powers to them (respectively, regs 84, 72 TA 1985). For example, a managing director might be delegated control of the office budget, the ability to employ staff and the power to enter into routine contracts on behalf of the company, amongst other things.

MEMO POINTS   The draft **new model articles** will not contain any specific provisions enabling the appointment of managing or executive directors. However, the general delegation provisions will be wide enough to encompass these roles.

3426 Delegation to a managing or executive director takes place under the same **conditions** as delegation to a committee, and is subject to the same provision of Table A (reg 72 TA 1985). This gives the board flexibility as to what powers and duties are delegated, how long for and the terms under which the delegation is made, as well as the ability to alter or revoke the delegation as necessary.

These titles are not legally defined, and so the appointment of a director to the position of managing director or another directorial title does not in itself give him any **additional powers**: any powers to be exercised by him must be specifically delegated to him (*Mitchell & Hobbs (UK) Ltd v Mill* [1996] 2 BCLC 102). For example, just because a director is given the title "finance director", he does not automatically have control over the company's finances, the authority to sign off the accounts and so on.

MEMO POINTS   There is nothing to prevent companies from giving directorial titles, e.g. "sales director", to **non-directors**. Here, delegation to directors appointed under companies legislation only is discussed; for non-directors, see ¶3432+.

3427 It is advisable for boards to be as specific as possible in making these delegations so that the managing or executive director's role is clear. The board is permitted by Table A to enter into **agreements** with any such director governing his activities outside the usual scope of a director's duties, and to remunerate him accordingly (reg 84 TA 1985).

As far as the managing or executive director is concerned, a **service contract** affords him the best protection (see ¶2627+). This has the advantage to the company of clearly defining that director's role and remuneration, whereas uncertainty can arise from simply relying on the board's powers in the articles to determine matters such as remuneration.

EXAMPLE   The managing director of a company was appointed and certain functions delegated to him, and the articles provided that he would receive such remuneration as the board agreed. The company went into liquidation before the board had come to a decision about his remuneration, and the managing director was not able to claim remuneration for the work he had already carried out (*Re Richmond Gate Property Co Ltd* [1964] 3 All ER 936).

3. Non-directors

3432 The board's powers and/or functions can only be delegated to non-directors if **permitted** by the articles. A company may wish to do so if an employee has expertise in a particular area but does not want to be appointed as a director. For example, the board may want to delegate responsibility for entering into sales contracts to an employee who has more experience of this area than any of the directors on the board. Table A does not include such a delegation, but a company may alter the articles to allow its board to do so if appropriate and/or it could include such powers in the employee's service contract.

Comment: The delegation of the board's powers and functions is a **separate** matter **from** the delegation of more administrative tasks, which will occur on a daily basis. For example, the directors will regularly delegate tasks to employees such as placing routine stationery orders on an informal basis.

3433 Proper delegation to a non-director is not in breach of the directors' **duty to exercise care, skill and diligence** (see ¶2411+). However, an ill-considered or inappropriate delegation to a non-director would be in breach of the directors' duties.

The board must be sure to supervise any non-director to whom powers have been delegated, and to act on any indication that the non-director falls below par in performing his duties. Although the board is entitled to assume that the delegate is competent to carry out the delegated tasks where a proper delegation has been made, the court has held that delegation does not absolve the directors from their **duty to supervise** (*Re City Equitable Fire Insurance Co Ltd* [1925] Ch 407; *Re Barings plc (No 5)* [1999] 1 BCLC 433). The nature and extent of the supervision will

4. Alternate directors

3438 As agents of the company, directors are personally appointed and must perform their functions and duties themselves. If specifically permitted to do so in the articles, they may be able to delegate their functions and duties to another person.

An alternate director is a person who stands in the place of a director. Appointment is **made by** an individual director, rather than the board as a whole. An alternate is **usually appointed when** a director cannot fulfil his duties for a period of time, for example if he is out of the country or absent due to illness.

> MEMO POINTS   The draft **new model articles** for private companies limited by shares will not specifically provide for the appointment of alternates, but the general delegation provisions are wide enough to allow a director to delegate all of his functions to another person. Those for public companies will deal with appointing alternates (arts 24-26). Alternates will be subject to the same rights (unless the articles state otherwise), duties, liabilities and restrictions as their appointors, but will be responsible for their own acts and omissions. The new model articles will provide for their appointments to terminate in two additional circumstances: when their appointors die; and if anything happens in relation to them that would end their appointors' office if it happened to the appointors.

Appointment

3440 Directors may be **permitted** to appoint alternates if their company's articles make specific provision. However, there is no statutory right to do so. Table A allows directors to appoint as an alternate (reg 65 TA 1985):
– another director; or
– another person approved by board resolution.

An alternate director cannot himself appoint an alternate.

A director can appoint an alternate **by** signing and giving notice of the appointment to the company, or by any other method approved by the board (reg 68 TA 1985). If the chosen alternate is not already a director of the company, the appointment will also have to be approved by board resolution.

Rights

3442 An alternate director is entitled to **receive notice** of meetings as well as his appointor, provided the alternate is in the UK at the time (reg 66 TA 1985).

An alternate can also **attend** all board and committee meetings at which his appointor is not present but was entitled to attend (reg 66 TA 1985). He can be counted in the **quorum** in place of his absent appointor (reg 89 TA 1985). Any restrictions on a director counting in the quorum will also apply to his alternate (see example below).

An alternate has the right to **vote** in the place of his absent appointor (reg 66 TA 1985), including signing a written resolution on his behalf (¶3293+). If an alternate is also a director in his own right, he will have two votes on a resolution at a board meeting: one on behalf of his appointor, and one in his own right (reg 88 TA 1985). This is subject to the usual provisions regarding a director's eligibility to vote. If his appointor has an interest in a contract under discussion which precludes him from voting at a board meeting, then the alternate cannot do so either on his behalf (reg 94 TA 1985).

> EXAMPLE   Mr A and Mr X are directors of B Ltd. Mr A appoints Mr X as his alternate to take his place at a board meeting which he cannot attend himself. B Ltd's articles are in the form of Table A without amendment. The board meeting discusses a proposed contract in which Mr A has a material interest, but Mr X does not. All relevant interests have been disclosed.

> On the resolution to consider the proposed contract Mr X counts in the quorum, and votes once because:
> – Mr X as Mr A's alternate cannot count in the quorum or vote because Mr A's interest in the matter prevents him from doing so; but
> – Mr X can count in the quorum and vote in his own right as director because he does not have an interest that prevents him from doing so.
>
> On the other, unrelated, resolutions Mr X counts in the quorum, and votes twice because:
> – Mr X as Mr A's alternate can count in the quorum and vote; and
> – Mr X can also count in the quorum and vote in his own right as director.

Duties and liabilities

An alternate must perform any **functions** and duties of his appointor, for example, executing documents, sitting on any committees and undertaking any other tasks delegated to the appointor.

3444

An alternate is deemed to have the **status** of director for all purposes (reg 69 TA 1985). Table A expressly states that he is not the agent of the appointor, which means that the alternate is fully liable for his own acts and omissions whilst acting as an alternate (see ¶2317+). He is only liable to the company for his acts and omissions whilst acting in the capacity of alternate director; where the alternate is not acting as a director of the company, he has no legal status, powers or duties in relation to the company (*Playcorp Pty Ltd v Shaw* (1993) 10 ACSR 212).

3445

Since an alternate is deemed to be a director, he will be subject to all of the other **requirements** of directors in the legislation and articles, as well as the common law duties and liabilities. Alternates are usually other directors of the same company who will already have complied with these requirements because of the administrative burden involved in what is usually a temporary appointment. These statutory requirements include:
– registering with Companies House and being entered into the company's own statutory books (¶2288+);
– being included in the particulars of directors on the company's letterhead (¶585);
– restrictions on being compensated for loss of office (¶2962+);
– disclosing interests in contracts to the board (¶3308+);
– the prohibition on the company on entering into substantial property transactions involving a director or his connected person (¶2567+);
– the restriction on loans etc to directors and their connected persons (¶2804+); and
– disclosing certain issues in the company accounts (¶4209+).

Remuneration

An alternate director is not entitled to any remuneration for his services as an alternate director under Table A. This is therefore a matter to be agreed between the alternate and his appointor, unless a company makes alternative provision in its articles.

3447

Termination

The appointing director has the right under Table A to **remove** his alternate (reg 65 TA 1985). In order to do so, the appointing director must give notice to the company signed by him, or use any other method approved by the board (reg 68 TA 1985).

3448

The alternate's appointment will **automatically cease** when his appointor's directorship comes to an end, except where the appointor has to retire by rotation and is reappointed at the same general meeting (reg 67 TA 1985; and see ¶2927+).

5. Assignees

Assignment of a director's office is rare, but can be **permitted** by the articles. A director might assign his office if he knows that he will be absent for a long period, or if his company's articles do not permit the appointment of alternates, for example. The assignee will step into

3450

the shoes of the director, and take over his powers and liabilities subject to the terms of the assignment.

Table A does not provide for directors to assign their offices. If the articles make such a provision, they may also specify the **circumstances** under which an assignment can be made (e.g. in the case of absence for an unknown length of time, or absence of over one year), to whom the assignment can be made (e.g. whether non-directors are included), as well as any other relevant conditions.

Any assignment is **only valid if** it is approved by the shareholders by special resolution (s 308 CA 1985).

MEMO POINTS The **new Companies Act** will repeal s 308 CA 1985.

V. Sole directors

3460 Although the default position set out in Table A provides that companies must have a minimum of two directors, private companies are **permitted** by the legislation to have only one director (reg 64 TA 1985; s 154 CA 2006). If a company has a sole director, there are a small number of additional requirements and modifications which are necessary to ensure that the board can still function effectively.

MEMO POINTS 1. **Public companies** must have at least 2 directors (s 154 CA 2006). There used to be an exception for public companies incorporated before 1929, which were allowed to have only one director, but this was repealed when the relevant provision of the new Companies Act came into force on 1 October 2007.
2. The draft **new model articles** under the new Companies Act do not set a minimum number of directors. The **new Companies Act** will require all companies to have at least one director who is an individual to make sure that at least one real person will be accountable for the board's actions (s 155 CA 2006; the implementation date for this provision is yet to be announced at the time of writing).

3461 The legislation ensures that even if a company has only one director, **at least two legal persons** are involved in running the company. Therefore, a sole director cannot also be the secretary of the company (s 283(2) CA 1985). Following on from this, statute provides that (s 283(4) CA 1985):
– the secretary of the company cannot be a body corporate of which the sole director of the company is also the sole director; and
– a body corporate cannot be the sole director of the company where its own sole director is also the secretary of the company.

EXAMPLE
1. Mr A is the sole director of ABC Ltd. He cannot also be the secretary of ABC Ltd.
2. Mr A is the sole director of both ABC Ltd and XYZ Ltd. XYZ Ltd cannot be the secretary of ABC Ltd, just as ABC Ltd cannot be the secretary of XYZ Ltd.
3. Mr A is the secretary of ABC Ltd and the sole director of XYZ Ltd. XYZ Ltd cannot be the sole director of ABC Ltd.

Comment: This provision is expected to be repealed on 6 April 2008 when the relevant provisions of the **new Companies Act** regarding secretaries come into force.

3462 A sole director is subject to the same **duties and liabilities** as any other director (¶2317+).

He also **comprises the board** of the company on his own. He should be careful when acting on behalf of the company to issue any business communications in the name of the board or the company in order to avoid any confusion between him acting as an individual and him as the board and/or the company. A sole director could experience problems in this area if, for example:
– his authority to carry out an act on behalf of the board or the company is questioned (¶2348+);

– there is a question over whether he should be personally liable for an act (¶2317+); or
– the shareholders refuse to ratify his decisions (¶2497+).

A sole director should still have a **service contract** (¶2627+), even if he is also the sole shareholder in the company. This helps to separate him as an individual from the company as a legal person (*Lee v Lee's Air Farming* [1961] 1 AC 12).

Companies having a sole director must ensure that certain **provisions of their articles** reflect this fact to enable the sole director to run the company. The following provisions of Table A will have to be modified.

3463

Provision in Table A[1]	Reference (TA 1985)	Amendment to be made	How to amend
Minimum number of directors is two	reg 64	Reduce minimum number of directors to one	– Special resolution altering articles; or – ordinary resolution agreeing to reduce minimum number of directors to one
Directors can exercise all of company powers	reg 70	Sole director (or "directors or sole director", if companies want to leave it open) can exercise all of company powers (or restricted as appropriate)	Special resolution altering articles
Quorum for board meetings is two directors	reg 89	Reduce quorum to one	Special resolution altering articles
If number of directors falls below quorum, continuing director(s) can only act to fill vacancies or call general meeting	reg 90	If quorum provision above is not altered, companies need to change regulation to enable sole director to exercise all company powers (or restricted as appropriate) if number of directors falls below quorum. This would be used by companies which have more than one director usually, but would be happy to be directed by a sole director if necessary	Special resolution altering articles
Director with interest cannot vote, except in certain cases	reg 94	If sole director is likely to have interests other than Table A exceptions (¶3341+), change articles to allow sole director to vote and count in quorum[2]	– Ordinary resolution to suspend or relax restriction. Can be general or specific (reg 96 TA 1985); or – special resolution to alter articles
Director with interest cannot count in quorum on that matter	reg 95	Sole director can count in quorum whether or not he is interested	Special resolution altering articles

Note:
1. Private companies which want to have a sole director and which adopt the **new model articles** will need to amend them since they refer to "directors" generally, so "director or sole director" might be more suitable. The provisions relating to the quorum and interests will only apply to majority decisions, and so will not have to be altered.
2. Sole director will still have to **declare** his **interest** as the statutory requirements cannot be altered or avoided (¶3308+).

VI. Administrative requirements

1. Minutes

3473 Minutes of board meetings must be **taken** and **kept** for at least 10 years (s 248 CA 2006). The minutes can be kept in hard copy or electronic form, and arranged as the directors see fit (s 1135 CA 2006). If the minutes are not kept in bound books, the company must take adequate steps to guard against (and to facilitate the discovery of) falsification (s 1138 CA 2006).

Taking minutes of the meeting usually falls to the **secretary**, although this is not an obligation. It is important that whoever takes the minutes does so carefully and thoroughly as they constitute evidence of the proceedings at the meeting.

Where a **contract** has been entered into between the company and its **director who is also its sole shareholder**, there is a special requirement to ensure that a written memorandum of the terms of the contract is recorded in the minutes of the first board meeting after the contract has been entered into (s 231 CA 2006). This does not apply to contracts:
– in writing; or
– in the ordinary course of business.

Failure to comply will not affect the validity of the contracts, but will render every officer in default liable to a fine (¶9935).

See ¶3418 for minutes of **committee** meetings.

> MEMO POINTS ss 248, 231 CA 2006 came into force on 1 October 2007 and **apply to** meetings held and contracts entered into on or after that date (para 14 Sch 3 SI 2007/2194). Meetings held and contracts entered into before that date are governed by the old rules, which require minutes of board meetings to be kept in a book for that purpose (s 382 CA 1985) and records of contracts to be kept in the same way as the new rules (s 322B CA 1985).
>
> Draft **new model articles** under the new Act have been published for private companies limited by shares and public companies. Those for private companies will require written records of all board decisions to be kept for at least 10 years (art 15), and those for public companies will require records of written board resolution to be kept for at least 10 years as well, relying on the statutory provision for the retention of the records of decisions made at meetings (art 17). "Written records" includes those kept in electronic form.

3474 Unlike the minutes of shareholder meetings, the shareholders have no automatic right to **inspect** board meeting minutes, so this is left to the company's discretion. However, if an **auditor** makes a request to inspect the board minutes, the directors must allow him to do so (s 389A CA 1985; restated at s 499 CA 2006 as of 6 April 2008).

3475 Minutes of board meetings entered into the minute book and signed by the chairman of that meeting, or of the following meeting, constitute **primary evidence** of the proceedings at that board meeting (s 249 CA 2006). This means that the meeting will be deemed to have been duly held and convened, unless the contrary is proved (for example, by evidence showing that no board meeting took place (Re Oriental Gas Ltd [2000] BCLC 209)). All appointments made at the meeting are deemed to be valid once the minutes have been signed by the relevant chairman. If a **dispute** arises over what was discussed or decided at a meeting, there is also a presumption that a matter was not brought before the board if there is no reference to it in the minutes (which can be rebutted by evidence to the contrary).

Other evidence of proceedings can be put forward **in the absence of minutes** (Re Pyle Works (No 2) [1891] 1 Ch 173). For example, if the company books show that a transaction has taken place which would have required a board resolution, e.g. a forfeiture of shares is recorded, the court can assume that such a resolution was validly passed (Re North Hallenbeagle Mining Co, Knight's Case (1867) LR 2 Ch App 321; Re Fireproof Doors Ltd [1916] 2 Ch 142).

3476 **Failure** to keep minutes in accordance with these statutory provisions renders the officers in default liable to a fine (s 248 CA 2006; ¶9935).

2. Filing requirements

3480 Board resolutions do not have to be filed at Companies House, except for the following **specific resolutions** which must be filed within 15 days of being passed (ss 29, 30 CA 2006):
a. a resolution to alter the memorandum of a public company, e.g. so it no longer states that it is public, following a cancellation of shares forfeited or surrendered to, or acquired by, the company or shares acquired by a third party in which the company has an interest (s 147(2) CA 1985, amended by para 1 Sch 4 SI 2007/2194);
b. a resolution for the re-registration of an old public company as a public company (s 2(3) CC(CP)A 1985, amended by para 38 Sch 4 SI 2007/2194); and
c. a resolution allowing title to shares to be evidenced and transferred without written evidence of title (reg 16(8A) SI 2001/3755, inserted by para 97 Sch 4 SI 2007/2194).

Failure to file these resolutions by the deadline renders the company and any officer in default liable to a fine (s 30 CA 2006; ¶9935).

In addition, if a board passes a resolution to change its company's name in response to a direction from the secretary of state that the company which was exempt from having to have the word "limited" in its name is no longer exempt, it has to notify Companies House so that it can be issued with a certificate of incorporation on change of name (s 31(2A) CA 1985, inserted by para 1 Sch 4 SI 2007/2194).

> *MEMO POINTS* 1. An "**old public company**" is a company in existence before 22 December 1980, or in the process of being incorporated on that date, which would not have been classed as a private company under the old companies legislation and has not since re-registered as a private or public company (s 1 CC(CP)A 1985).
> 2. When the relevant provisions of the **new Companies Act** come into force, board resolution a. above will still have to be registered (s 64 CA 2006; expected to come into force by 1 October 2009). A board resolution to re-register as a private company following a cancellation of shares will have to be registered (s 664 CA 2006, expected to come into force by 1 October 2009). The new Act also provides for regulations to be made regarding the evidence and transfer of shares not in writing, and any resolution required by these regulations will also have to be registered (s 790 CA 2006, due to come into force on 6 April 2008).

3481 There may be **specific company paperwork** which has been approved or completed at the board meeting which will require filing. Common examples are Forms 288a and 288b relating to the appointment and resignation of secretaries and directors. Or, the board meeting may follow a shareholder meeting which gave rise to filing requirements, and the directors may instruct the secretary to carry this out. Usually, the last item on the agenda is to instruct the secretary to complete and file any necessary paperwork, and to update the company registers as required.

> *MEMO POINTS* The names of these forms, like the names of other **Companies House forms**, are taken from the relevant section number of the legislation. As all of the section numbers will change under the new Companies Act, Companies House proposes to change the names of all of its forms to reflect their function rather than the relevant section number ("Working with Companies House: a consultation on the registrar's rules and related provisions which will apply under the Companies Act 2006"). At the time of writing, the new form names are not yet available.

3. Entering into contracts

3486 The business at board meetings commonly includes authorising individual directors and other agents to bind the company by entering into contracts on its behalf. These directors and agents must ensure that the contract is entered into correctly.

A company can enter into a contract under seal or by a person acting on its behalf (whether his authority is express or implied) (s 36 CA 1985). If any additional **formalities** apply to the type of contract in question, they must also be followed, for example a contract for the sale of land must be made in writing and signed by the parties and so a duly authorised officer of the company must sign on its behalf (s 2 Law of Property (Miscellaneous Provisions) Act 1989). Companies should also ensure that their internal procedures are complied with, for example particular types of contract may require a board or shareholder resolution to authorise or ratify them.

Comment: From 6 April 2008, when the relevant provision of the **new Companies Act** comes into force, a document will be validly executed (whether by signature or seal, as a deed or a contract) if it has been signed on the company's behalf by two authorised signatories, or by one director in the presence of a witness who attests the signature (s 44 CA 2006). Directors and company secretaries will be the designated authorised signatories. This change is to enable private companies which choose not to have a secretary to be able to execute documents. As a result, companies will need to adapt their current signature clauses to take these changes into account.

MEMO POINTS   1. Additional formalities apply if the **sole shareholder** in the company is also a director (¶3473).
Public companies must have a trading certificate before they do business, including entering into contracts (¶510+).
2. An agent's ability to enter into contracts on the company's behalf includes **oral contracts**, provided that such a contract would be binding on an individual (e.g. an oral contract for the sale of land would not bind an individual and so cannot bind a company either).
3. A company's ability to enter into **contracts prior to** its **incorporation** is discussed at ¶345+.

Signing documents

3488   If a contract is **signed by** two directors or a director and the company secretary, it is deemed to have been executed by the company itself (s 36A(4) CA 1985).

A contract is still validly executed by the company if signed by persons purporting to be officers of the company when they are not, as long as the purchaser, lessee or mortgagee (or other person acquiring an interest in land) has paid and acts in good faith (s 36A(6) CA 1985).

> EXAMPLE   Contract execution clause:
> Signed by [name of director]
> For and on behalf of A Ltd ....
>
> Signed by [name of director/secretary]
> For and on behalf of A Ltd ....

MEMO POINTS   If the director or secretary of the company is a company itself, documents can be signed by an individual authorised by that **corporate director or secretary** to sign on its behalf (s 36A(7), (8) CA 1985).

Sealing documents

3490   Companies do not usually require documents to be executed under seal; indeed, companies do not have to have a seal at all (s 36A(3) CA 1985). Where a company does have a seal, a document can be executed simply by the company **affixing** it, although the company's articles will usually require this to be **evidenced by** two directors or a director and the secretary (s 36A(2) CA 1985). If Table A applies, the seal can only be used with the **authority** of the board (and the board may delegate this power to a committee), which can also make alternative provisions about how the seal should be witnessed (reg 101 TA 1985). When a document has been executed under seal, it should be recorded in the seal book.

MEMO POINTS   If a company has a seal, it must have the **name of the company** legibly engraved on it (s 350 CA 1985). Failure to do so confers liability on the company and on any officer who uses or authorises the use of the defective seal (¶9935).

Executing deeds

3492   If it is clear from the document that the company intends it to be executed as a deed, it is deemed to be a deed when it is executed (s 36AA CA 1985). Like a contract, a deed can be executed by two directors or a director and the company secretary signing it, or by affixing the company's seal.

> **EXAMPLE** Deed execution clause (signing):
> Executed as a deed and
> delivered on the date first above
> by A Ltd acting by:
>
> ....
> Mr X (Director)
>
> ....
> Mr Y (Director/secretary)

Authenticating documents

A document may have to be authenticated, or certified, for example where it has to be: **3494**
– filed at Companies House;
– used as evidence in a court case; or
– provided to a party dealing with the company as confirmation that a particular act has been carried out.
The board can delegate **authority** to do this to a director, the company secretary or another person.

Powers of attorney

Directors can appoint attorneys to carry out their functions, including executing documents **3496**
on behalf of the company. A power of attorney can be confined to **specified acts**, or it can give a **general power** to act on the director's behalf. If an attorney is to be able to execute a deed instead of a director, his power of attorney must have been executed as a deed. Statute specifically enables directors to appoint attorneys to execute deeds on the company's behalf outside the UK (s 38 CA 1985).

If an attorney is authorised to **sell an interest in land** on behalf of the company, he can do so by signing the company's name in the presence of at least one witness (s 74 LPA 1925). Oddly, the attorney's name or the fact that he is an agent for the company does not have to be included, although it would be prudent to do so in case any dispute arises.

> **MEMO POINTS** 1. The law in this area has recently changed as a result of the relevant parts of the Mental Capacity Act 2005 coming into force on 1 October 2007. Briefly, there are now four **types of power of attorney**:
> – ordinary: by which a person gives his attorney the power to deal with specific or general matters for a period of time. These are the most relevant to business situations, for example a director could appoint an attorney to sit on the board in his place, make decisions and sign documents on his behalf if he knew that he was going to be absent for a number of months. Alternatively, he could appoint an alternate director (see ¶3438+);
> – trustee: similar to an ordinary power of attorney but specifically used for trusts;
> – enduring: by which a person appoints another to look after his financial and legal affairs in the event that he cannot do so himself because of mental incapacity. It has not been possible to grant an enduring power of attorney since 1 October 2007; and
> – lasting: the new version of an enduring power of attorney. There are two types: one dealing with personal welfare (e.g. decisions relating to medical treatment) and one dealing with property and affairs.
> 2. The **new Companies Act** will allow companies to appoint an attorney in writing to execute deeds and other documents on its behalf, whether in the UK or abroad (s 47 CA 2006, expected to come into force by 1 October 2009).

Cheques etc

If a cheque, bill of exchange, promissory note or other such document is made in the **3498**
company's name or on its behalf by a person acting under its authority, it will be deemed to be valid (s 37 CA 1985). The agent can sign the company's name or his own (at the same time indicating that he acts as the company's agent, otherwise he will be personally liable, ¶2580). Usually, the words "for and on behalf of X Ltd" are used.

> **MEMO POINTS** The **new Companies Act** will restate this provision (s 52 CA 2006, expected to come into force by 1 October 2009).

SECTION 3

Shareholder decisions

SECTION OUTLINE	¶¶
I Resolutions	3523
A. Types of resolution at meetings	3526
1. Ordinary resolutions	3530
Resolutions to appoint and remove directors and auditors	3536
2. Extraordinary resolutions	3544
3. Special resolutions	3553
4. Elective resolutions	3562
B. Resolution procedures without meetings	3577
1. Formal written resolutions	3580
2. Informal unanimous agreement	3590
C. Summary table of resolutions	3600
II How to convene and conduct meetings	3610
A. Calling a general meeting	3620
1. Directors	3622
2. Shareholders	3625
3. Auditors	3632
4. The court	3635
B. Notice	3646
1. Content	3650
a. General requirements	3651
b. Requirements for different types of resolution	3656
c. Documents to be provided with the notice or before meetings	3660
2. Notice period	3675
3. Service of notice	3687
a. Who can serve notice?	3689
b. Who can receive notice?	3692
c. Methods of service	3695
d. When notice is served	3704
C. Holding a general meeting	3711
1. Chairman	3716
2. Attendance	3724
a. Proxies	3727
b. Corporate representatives	3743
c. Minimum attendance ("quorum")	3746
d. Comparison of attendees' rights	3755
3. Adjournments	3760
D. Specific types of meeting	3772
1. Public company Annual General Meetings (AGMs)	3777
2. Class meetings	3794
E. Summary of meetings	3800
III Voting	3810
A. Who can vote?	3815
B. Methods of voting	3836
1. Show of hands	3838
2. Poll voting	3842
3. Postal and electronic voting	3852
IV Administrative requirements	3862
1. Minutes of meetings and resolutions	3864
2. Filing requirements	3871
3. Timeline: shareholder meetings	3873

3513 The important role shareholders play in the **management** of companies has already been discussed in contrast with that of the board (¶3130+). Shareholders' power to approve or reject **key decisions**, such as the appointment of company officers, gives them ultimate control as a group over the company (these key decisions are summarised in the table at ¶2074).

3514 Here, the different **issues** that will be decided by the shareholders and the **methods** by which those decisions can be made are explored. Decisions of shareholders are made by way of resolution. Clearly some decisions of the company are more significant than others, e.g. because they affect the company's constitution or the shareholders' rights, and therefore statute specifies that these decisions have to be taken in the form of particular resolutions. The **types of resolution** are discussed below. Generally, the bigger the impact of the decision on the company, the more stringent the requirements of the resolution. It is important that decisions are made in the correct format, as failure to do so may invalidate the resolution.

Companies can choose whether to take the vast majority of its decisions at a **meeting** or using a **written resolution procedure**. A company's decision as to which method to use will depend on factors such as: the number and location of shareholders; whether the company needs to hold a meeting to comply with another obligation; whether or not the business to be discussed is contentious. As written resolutions require the unanimous approval of shareholders, the procedure can only be used for non-contentious business. It is often used by smaller companies.

A company's articles of association will usually deal with the **procedural** aspects of shareholder meetings and decision making. The statutory provisions and those in Table A 1985 are discussed here, as they set out the default position. These references need to be read together with the articles of the company in question, which may well modify the position set out in Table A.

3515 The decision making process is being streamlined by the **new Companies Act**, which has been drafted with the needs of the modern company in mind. The changes give more flexibility in management and decision making, particularly to private companies, which will ease the administrative burden and help to save time and money.

The **changes** which have been and will be made by the new Act are discussed within each relevant topic. The most significant changes are:
– the "elective regime" will become the norm for private companies, for example private companies no longer need to hold AGMs;
– written resolutions will be more widely used. The process is now more practical since there is a deadline by which resolutions must be passed, and the requirement for unanimity has been removed;
– resolutions in general have been simplified: statute now only requires decisions to be made by ordinary or special resolution (with the exception of one elective resolution), and the notice period for all resolutions to be decided at meetings is now the same;
– companies have greater freedom in how to communicate with their shareholders and others. This will speed up the decision making process by allowing notices, written resolutions and other information to be circulated electronically; and
– proxies can now count towards a quorum at a meeting and vote on a show of hands. These enhanced proxy rights will make the use of proxies, and therefore shareholder meetings, more effective.

These changes recognise the needs of, and constraints on, companies today and aim to reduce the administrative burden on them.

I. Resolutions

3523 Resolutions are the means by which a company makes its decisions. There are four types of resolution altogether, although two of them are being phased out. Resolutions can be taken either at shareholder meetings or using a written procedure. The table at ¶3600 summarises the various requirements of each resolution and gives an at-a-glance look at the written resolution procedure.

A. Types of resolution at meetings

3526 There are currently four **types** of resolution by which shareholders can make decisions at meetings. The most common resolution passed at shareholder meetings is the ordinary resolution. Ordinary resolutions represent the **default position**; although there are some ordinary resolutions required by statute, they are largely used when statute or the articles do not require the resolution to be in another form (s 281 CA 2006). Special resolutions are used in specific situations. Elective resolutions are being phased out as the new Companies Act is implemented, and there is currently only one remaining decision for which this form needs to be used. Extraordinary resolutions have already been abolished in statute, but companies' articles may still require decisions to be taken in this form, and so they are still discussed below.

1. Ordinary resolutions

3530 Ordinary resolutions are generally used for **routine business** of the company for which it is not necessary to give the shareholders added protection by requiring a greater level of consent.

3531 **Matters** to be put to an ordinary resolution can be stipulated in the legislation, but it is generally used to decide questions which do not have to be decided by special resolution (i.e. it is the default form of resolution). Anything that statute or the articles state has to be approved "by the shareholders in a general meeting" requires an ordinary resolution (s 281(3) CA 2006). Therefore, it is not possible to give an exhaustive list of ordinary resolutions. The vast majority of decisions which can be taken by ordinary resolution can be taken by special resolution instead (s 282(5) CA 2006). However, there are a few decisions which the legislation requires to be taken by ordinary resolution:
– establishing/renewing the directors' authority to allot shares (see ¶921+);
– fixing the auditor's remuneration, or agreeing how it should be fixed (s 492 CA 2006);
– removing an auditor from office (see ¶4343+);
– obtaining a public company's shareholders' approval to the transfer of a non-cash asset (see ¶1175);
– reconverting stock to shares (s 620 CA 2006); and
– approving the articles of a company formed as a result of a merger or division (ss 912, 928 CA 2006).

A company's articles may require other matters to be passed by special resolution instead.

> *MEMO POINTS* Under the **new Companies Act**, a resolution establishing or renewing a director's authority to allot shares will be able to be passed as an ordinary resolution, but will not have to be (s 551 CA 2006, expected to come into force by 1 October 2009). However, the requirement will be relaxed in other ways because a private company with only one class of shares will not have to have the shareholders' authority to allot (s 550 CA 2006, expected to come into force by 1 October 2009). A resolution to remove an auditor will still have to be an ordinary resolution (s 510 CA 2006, due to come into force on 6 April 2008).

3532 The specific wording of an ordinary resolution does not have to be included in the **notice** of the meeting, but enough detail has to be given to enable the shareholders to have notice of the general business to be considered (s 311 CA 2006). It is advisable to include at least the draft wording of the resolution, to prevent the validity of the decision being challenged (¶3650+). There are new rules setting out how companies can communicate with shareholders and others, which include **sending** notices of resolutions. They allow notices to be sent in hard copy, electronic form, via a website or in any other agreed form, depending on the shareholders' consent. They are discussed at ¶3695+ in the context of sending notices of meetings to shareholders.

There is no minimum **period** of notice required for ordinary resolutions, and so the length of notice given will depend upon the type of meeting being held (¶3675+). However, note that for certain resolutions, **special notice** is required (¶3536+).

3533 An ordinary resolution can be **carried by** a simple majority of the shareholders present (personally or by proxy) and voting at the meeting (i.e. a majority in the number of votes taken on a show of hands, or more than 50% of the votes if taken on a poll) (s 282 CA 2006).

3534 Only certain ordinary resolutions need to be **filed** at Companies House:
a. within 15 days of being passed (ss 29, 30 CA 2006):
– giving authority to the directors to allot shares (s 80 CA 1985, as amended by para 1 Sch 4 SI 2007/2194);
– authorising a market purchase of the company's own shares (s 166(7) CA 1985, as amended by para 1 Sch 4 SI 2007/2194);
– to wind the company up (s 84 IA 1986, as amended by para 39 Sch 4 SI 2007/2194);
– to revoke a board resolution to allow non-written evidence of title to company's shares (reg 16 SI 2001/3755, as amended by para 97 Sch 4 SI 2007/2194); and
– all resolutions or agreements binding all of a class of shareholder where unanimous consent of class has not been obtained must be filed; and
b. an ordinary resolution to remove auditor requires filing within 14 days of being passed (s 391 CA 1985).
Failure to do so renders the company and any officers in default liable to a fine (s 30 CA 2006; ¶9935).

Comment: The **new Companies Act** will also require an ordinary resolution to remove an auditor to be filed at Companies House within 14 days (s 512 CA 2006, due to come into force on 6 April 2008).

Resolutions to appoint and remove directors and auditors

3536 "**Special notice**" given **by a shareholder to the company** of an ordinary resolution is to be distinguished from notice of meetings generally, which is given by the company to the shareholders (see ¶3646+). Special notice has to be given to a company if the shareholders want any of the following **matters** to be considered at a meeting:
– removing a director (s 168 CA 2006);
– removing an auditor before the end of his term, or appointing a new auditor (other than a retiring auditor) (s 391A CA 1985); and
– appointing an auditor to a "casual vacancy" (s 388 CA 1985; ¶4336+).

Comment: From 6 April 2008, the **new Companies Act** will require special notice to be given when removing an auditor before the end of his term or filling a vacancy that has arisen because an appointment was not made when it should have been (ss 511, 515 CA 2006).

3537 If a **shareholder** wants to move any of the above resolutions, he must **give notice** to the company of his intention to do so at least 28 clear days before a meeting, otherwise the resolution will not be effective (ss 312, 360 CA 2006). In practice, a shareholder will send the special notice to the company, which will then prompt the directors either to call a meeting, or to save the resolution for a scheduled meeting. If the directors do not do so, the shareholder may be able to requisition a meeting (¶3626+). Unless a company gives its shareholders longer than the statutory minimum notice of meetings (see ¶3675+), a shareholder will not be able to wait to receive notice of a meeting before submitting a special notice to the company, because he will be out of time. Notice can be sent to the company in hard copy, electronic form or any other agreed form. The methods of sending documents to companies are discussed at ¶3628 in the context of shareholders requisitioning a meeting.

A company cannot thwart a shareholder's right to move a resolution which requires special notice by holding a meeting within 28 days of receiving the shareholder's notice of the resolution. If a company does this, the resolution can still be moved at the meeting, as full special notice will be deemed to have been given (s 312(4) CA 2006).

3538 When a **company receives** special notice of resolutions to remove a director or remove or appoint an auditor, it must send a copy of the special notice to the director(s) or (proposed) auditor(s) concerned straight away (s 169 CA 2006; ss 388, 391A CA 1985), including to a retiring auditor where an appointment arises out of his retirement. For the directors'/auditors' rights in these circumstances, see ¶2946+; ¶4339+.

The **company** will then **give notice** of the resolution to the shareholders along with the notice of the meeting itself. If this is not practicable (for example, because the notice of the meeting has already been printed or sent), notice of the of the resolution is to be given at least 14 clear days before the meeting by advertising in a suitable newspaper (i.e. one with adequate circulation to reach the company's shareholders), or by any other method that is set out in the company's articles of association (ss 312(3), 360 CA 2006).

Comment: The **new Companies Act** will also require the notice to be sent to the relevant auditor straight away (ss 511, 515 CA 2006, due to come into force on 6 April 2008).

3539 The **intention** of the requirement for special notice is to ensure that shareholders, as well as the director or auditor concerned, receive adequate notice of the resolution. The requirement attempts to balance the right of the shareholders to remove company directors and auditors with those officers' rights to justify their position at the shareholder meeting.

Comment: The special notice requirement does not in itself give a shareholder the **right to call a meeting** or have an item placed on the agenda; it is merely a particular procedure attached to these resolutions. If a shareholder wants to move such a resolution at a meeting, he must first rely on his right either to have a resolution circulated, to requisition a meeting, or the company's articles of association for the right to have the item or resolution considered, and then give special notice of the resolution to the company (*Pedley v Inland Waterways Association Ltd* [1977] 1 All ER 209; see ¶3780+ and ¶3626+ for an explanation of shareholders' powers to requisition meetings and resolutions).

2. Extraordinary resolutions

3544 The **new Companies Act** removes the need for extraordinary resolutions by only requiring decisions to be made by ordinary or special resolution. Statute used to require an extraordinary resolution in three cases, which have been updated as follows:
– approving a variation of class rights: this now requires a special resolution (s 125(2) CA 1985, amended by para 2 Sch 4 SI 2007/2194; ¶1270+);
– entering into CVL: this power has been repealed (para 39 Sch 4 SI 2007/2194). However, shareholders can still agree to enter into CVL in other ways (¶8438); and
– authorising a liquidator to pay any class of creditor in full and compromise creditors' claims and liabilities in an MVL: this now requires a special resolution (s 165(2) IA 1986, amended by para 41 Sch 4 SI 2007/2194; ¶8515).

Although statute does not now call on shareholders to use extraordinary resolutions, a company's **articles** (or another contract, such as a shareholders' agreement) may still do so (para 23 Sch 3 SI 2007/2194). If this is the case, the resolution must comply with the former statutory requirements. For example, Table A states that the company can authorise a liquidator to distribute the company's assets to the shareholders by extraordinary resolution (reg 117 TA 1985). For the sake of simplicity, companies may wish to alter their articles to reflect the new statutory position.

MEMO POINTS 1. If a company's **articles** or another contract require an extraordinary resolution for a particular decision, the company must comply with the following:
– any extraordinary resolution set out in the notice of the meeting has to be labelled as such (s 378(1) CA 1985). The notice does not have to include the actual terms of the resolution, but its "entire substance" does have to be given (¶3650+). Notice can be sent to the shareholders in hard copy, electronic form, via a website or in any other agreed form under new rules governing how companies communicate with their shareholders and others. They are discussed at ¶3695+ in the context of sending notices of meetings to shareholders;
– there is no minimum period of notice that needs to be given of an extraordinary resolution, so the notice given will depend upon whether it is to be considered at a general meeting or a public company AGM (¶3675+);
– in order to carry an extraordinary resolution, at least 75% of shareholders at the meeting who are entitled to vote and do so must vote in its favour (s 378(1) CA 1985); and

– extraordinary resolutions still need to be filed at Companies House (s 380(4)(b) CA 1985) is still in force; Sch 2 SI 2007/2194 as amended by SI 2007/2607).
2. Transitional amendments to Table A apply for **companies incorporated on or after 1 October 2007** that adopt Table A, so that a special resolution is required instead of an extraordinary resolution to authorise a liquidator to distribute assets to the shareholders (reg 117 TA 1985 as amended by reg 7 SI 2007/2194).

3. Special resolutions

Statute requires a number of specific decisions to be made by special resolution. There are numerous such decisions, many obscure and rarely used, and so an exhaustive list is not given here. If a special resolution is required for a decision dealt with in this book, it is noted where relevant. The decisions are often those affecting the **company's constitution**, e.g. to change its name or articles, and are therefore important enough to require a larger majority than an ordinary resolution.

3553

Common matters to be decided by special resolution include:
– alteration of the objects clause in the company's memorandum (ss 4, 5, 6 CA 1985);
– alteration of the articles of association (s 9 CA 1985);
– change of company name (s 28 CA 1985);
– ratification of the board's acts which exceed the limitations set out in the memorandum (s 35 CA 1985);
– reduction of share capital (s 135 CA 1985);
– disapplication of pre-emption rights (s 95 CA 1985);
– re-registration as a different type of company (ss 43, 48, 51, 53 CA 1985);
– financial assistance resolutions (s 155 CA 1985);
– approval of off-market purchases by a company of its own shares or of a contingent purchase contract (ss 164, 165 CA 1985);
– compulsory winding up resolution (s 122 IA 1986); and
– voluntary winding up resolution (s 84(1)(b) IA 1986).
A company's articles can require **other matters** to be decided by special resolution.

3554

> MEMO POINTS The **new Companies Act** will still require the following matters to be decided by special resolution (these provisions are expected to come into force by 1 October 2009):
> – alteration of the articles (s 21 CA 2006);
> – change of company name (s 77 CA 2006);
> – reduction of share capital (s 641 CA 2006);
> – re-registration as a different type of company (ss 90, 97, 105 CA 2006); and
> – approval of off-market purchases of a company's own shares or a contingent purchase contract (s 694 CA 2006).
> The memorandum will no longer define the scope of the company's powers, and financial assistance will not be prohibited for private companies so there will be no need for the whitewash procedure (the implementation date for this change is yet to be announced at the time of writing). The winding up resolutions mentioned here will still have to be in the form of special resolutions.

The text of a special resolution must be included in the **notice** of the meeting, and the intention to propose it as a special resolution must be stated (s 283 CA 2006). Once such a statement has been included in the notice, the decision must be made by special resolution. Notice can be **sent** to the shareholders in hard copy, electronic form, via a website or in any other agreed form. The methods of sending documents to shareholders are discussed at ¶3695+ in the context of sending notices of meetings to shareholders.

3555

There is no minimum **period** of notice required for ordinary resolutions, and so the length of notice given will depend upon the type of meeting being held (¶3675+).

A special resolution will be **carried by** at least 75% of shareholders present (personally or by proxy) at the meeting who are entitled to vote and do so (s 283(4), (5) CA 2006).

3556

3557 Special resolutions must be **filed** at Companies House within 15 days of being passed (ss 29, 30 CA 2006). Failure to do so renders the company and any officers in default liable to a fine (¶9935).

> MEMO POINTS Decisions that are still required to be made in this format by CA 1985 have been amended so that they must be filed under the new Companies Act (para 1 Sch 4 SI 2007/2194).

4. Elective resolutions

3562 Elective resolutions used to be used by private companies to simplify their administration, for example by opting out of the requirement to hold an AGM every year. The **new Companies Act** has removed the need for private companies to do this by making the "elective regime" the norm. There is only one remaining elective resolution: to give the directors authority to allot shares for more than 5 years. This is discussed below. Otherwise, the current "elective" matters have been changed as follows:
– all companies will have to circulate their accounts among the shareholders, but only public companies will have to lay them before a general meeting (see ¶4261+);
– only public companies are required to hold AGMs (s 336 CA 2006);
– private companies can consent to shorter notice of a general meeting if 90% agree, unless the articles require more (up to 95%) (s 307 CA 2006). For the position for public companies, see ¶3681/mp; and
– auditors will have to be appointed for each financial year, unless the directors conclude that audited accounts are unlikely to be required (private company limited by shares: s 485 CA 2006, which is already in force; public companies: s 489 CA 2006, due to come into force on 6 April 2008).

3563 The only remaining **matter** which requires an elective resolution is to give the directors authority to allot shares for more than 5 years (s 379A(1)(a) CA 1985). This is expected to be replaced by provisions allowing directors of private companies with only one class of shares to allot shares without the shareholders' authority, unless their articles state otherwise (s 550 CA 2006, expected to come into force by 1 October 2009). Other companies will be able to authorise their directors to allot (generally or on a case by case basis) for up to 5 years, either by ordinary resolution or in the articles (s 551 CA 2006, also expected to come into force by 1 October 2009). A resolution renewing authority to allot will be able to be in the form of an ordinary resolution, even if it will amend the articles.

3564 **Notice** of an elective resolution to give the directors authority to allot shares for more than 5 years must be given to all shareholders entitled to attend and vote at the meeting. The notice must label the elective resolution as such, and set out its terms (¶3650+). Notice can be sent in hard copy, electronic form, via a website or in any other agreed form. The methods of sending documents to shareholders are discussed at ¶3695+ in the context of sending notices of meetings to shareholders.

21 **days**' notice in writing (which includes electronic communication) must be given (s 379A(2) CA 1985). If all of the shareholders entitled to attend and vote at the meeting consent, the meeting may be held on **short notice** (s 379A(2A) CA 1985).

3565 **Carrying** the elective resolution requires the unanimous approval of all shareholders entitled to attend and vote at the meeting, whether they attend in person or by their proxy (s 379A(2) CA 1985). This is in contrast to other types of resolution, which only require the approval of a certain percentage of the voting shareholders who are actually present at the meeting. The written resolution procedure cannot be used to pass this elective resolution (¶3580+).

3566 In order to protect shareholders' rights, the elective resolution can be **revoked** at any time by ordinary resolution, which has the effect of requiring the company to comply with the relevant statutory requirement again (s 379A(3) CA 1985; see ¶921+). If a private company becomes a public company, the elective resolution is automatically revoked (s 379A(4) CA 1985).

The elective resolution and any ordinary resolution revoking it has to be **filed** at Companies House within 15 days of being passed (s 380(4)(bb) CA 1985 is still in force; Sch 2 SI 2007/2194 as amended by SI 2007/2607). Failure to do so renders the company and any officers in default liable to a fine (¶9935).

3567

B. Resolution procedures without meetings

Convening and holding meetings can be costly in terms of both time and money, so companies often opt to pass resolutions without holding a meeting by using written resolutions. The **main advantage** of using a written resolution procedure is that it is often a simpler, cheaper and more efficient method of making decisions. The provisions of the new Companies Act which set out the written resolution procedure for private companies are now in force, making it easier for private companies to take advantage of this method of decision making (see ¶3581+ below).

3577

Any type of company can use a **formal** written resolution procedure: although the statutory procedure is restricted to private companies, any company may set out an alternative procedure in its articles. The statutory procedure used to require all of the shareholders to agree to a written resolution, and it was thought that any procedure set out in the articles had to require at least the same level of consent. However, now that the statutory procedure mirrors the majorities required to pass resolutions at meetings, written resolution procedures will probably be able to do the same (as long as they still meet these minimum consent levels).

In addition to these formal procedures, companies may still rely on the more **informal** common law principle that if all of the shareholders are in agreement, a resolution is valid, whether the correct procedure was followed or not (¶3590+).

1. Formal written resolutions

Private companies are permitted by statute to make decisions by written resolution rather than having to hold a meeting (s 288 CA 2006). They can use the **statutory** written resolution procedure to pass resolutions required by statute even if their articles expressly prohibit written resolutions (s 300 CA 2006). If the articles of a company provide for an **alternative** written resolution procedure, it has the choice as to whether to proceed under the articles or statute (for example, see reg 53 TA 1985). **Public companies** cannot use the statutory procedure, although they may provide for a written resolution procedure in their articles.

3580

> MEMO POINTS 1. The draft **new model articles** under the new Companies Act do not set out an alternative written resolution procedure for private companies because the statutory procedure now provides a very practical and workable option. A written resolution procedure is not set out in the draft new model articles for public companies either, so public companies wishing to adopt the new form articles should consider whether they should include such a process.
> 2. Transitional amendments to Table A applying to **companies incorporated on or after 1 October 2007** that adopt Table A delete reg 53 TA 1985 (reg 6 SI 2007/2541).

Statutory procedure

The statutory written resolution procedure changed on 1 October 2007, when the relevant provisions of the new Companies Act came into force. It is now a more practical process and can be used more frequently as it no longer requires unanimity. It **can be used** by all private companies, and cannot be excluded by a company's articles (ss 288, 300 CA 2006). It even applies retrospectively, so that pre-existing provisions in any statute requiring shareholder resolutions are deemed to allow them to be passed in writing. As with the old procedure, it **cannot be used** are to remove directors and to remove/replace auditors, because these decisions require special notice to be given to the company (¶3536+). As a transitional measure, private companies cannot use written resolutions to give the directors

3581

authority to allot shares for more than 5 years either (s 288(2)(c) CA 2006, inserted by para 13 Sch 1 SI 2007/2194. This still requires an elective resolution, see ¶3562+). Otherwise, written resolutions are available and will be treated as if passed at a general or class meeting as appropriate.

Proposal

3582 Written resolutions can be proposed by the board or the shareholders (ss 291, 292 CA 2006). If the **board** wishes to put a written resolution to the shareholders, it will simply circulate it as described below (¶3583).

Shareholders with 5% of the total voting rights on the resolution can also request the board to circulate a written resolution (the articles can reduce this threshold). The request can be sent electronically or in hard copy, and the requesting shareholder(s) can include a statement of up to 1,000 words to be circulated with it. The resolution and statement must be circulated by the directors within 21 days of the request, unless it would be ineffective as a resolution, defamatory, frivolous or vexatious, or unless an application has been made to court complaining that the shareholders' power is being abused (ss 292, 293, 295 CA 2006). The written resolution and statement will not have to be circulated until the requesting shareholders have covered the costs of doing so, or the company has resolved to excuse them (s 294 CA 2006).

Circulation

3583 A written resolution and any shareholders' statement must be circulated to all **eligible shareholders**, i.e. those who are able to vote on the date of circulation (and at the time of circulation, if shares change hands on the same day) (ss 289, 291, 293 CA 2006). One copy can be circulated, if this would not cause too much of a delay (this is only a realistic option in very small companies, e.g. where all of the shareholders are members of the same family), or a copy can be sent to each eligible shareholder in hard copy or electronic **form**, or it can be posted on a website. As well as the terms of the resolution, a statement must be included explaining how to agree to it and by what date. A special resolution must be labelled as such (s 283 CA 2006). If the company includes an electronic address on the documents it sends out, the shareholders can communicate with the company regarding the resolution via that address (s 298 CA 2006).

Certain statutory provisions require **additional information** to be provided to shareholders with the notice of a meeting or at the meeting itself (see ¶3660+). If these decisions are to be taken by written resolution, the same information needs to be sent to the shareholders so that they are not put at a disadvantage

A copy of the written resolution and any related information must also be sent to the company's **auditor** (s 390 CA 1985; para 4 Sch 4 SI 2007/2194).

Comment: The **new Companies Act** will also enable the company's auditor to receive the same information as the shareholders (s 502 CA 2006, due to come into force on 6 April 2008).

Passing the resolution

3584 A shareholder will **agree** to the resolution when the company receives from him an authenticated document identifying the resolution and indicating his agreement (whether in hard copy or electronic form) (s 296 CA 2006). Once given, a shareholders' agreement will not be able to be revoked. The resolution is **passed when** the requisite majority is achieved:
– for a written ordinary resolution, a simple majority (s 282 CA 2006); or
– for a written special resolution, a majority of 75% or more (s 283 CA 2006).

A shareholder has one vote for every share (or for every £10-worth of stock he holds); if the company does not have a share capital, each member will have one vote (s 284 CA 2006).

The new procedure introduces a deadline of 28 days from the date of circulation, by which the resolution must be passed (s 297 CA 2006). If the written resolution and statement are made available to the shareholders on a website, they will have to remain on the website until the end of this period (s 299 CA 2006).

3585 Written resolutions have to be **filed** at Companies House within 15 days, if they contain a special resolution or any other resolution which would have to be filed if it was not passed as a written resolution (ss 29, 30 CA 2006). Failure to do so renders the company and any officers in default liable to a fine (¶9935).

A record of all written resolutions must also be kept by the company, see ¶3866.

Alternative procedure in the articles

3586 **Any company** (public or private) may provide for an alternative written resolution procedure to be set out in its articles. An alternative procedure in the articles may simply be less formal than the statutory procedure, for example by not requiring the written resolution to be sent to the auditor (see reg 53 TA 1985), or it may provide for a more convenient process.

Despite their exclusion from the statutory procedure, there is nothing prohibiting public companies from including a written resolution procedure in their articles. The practicality of such a procedure is another matter, as public companies will often have too many shareholders to be able to rely on them all agreeing and remembering to return their resolutions for the process to be effective.

Comment: Draft **new model articles** under the new Act have been published for private companies limited by shares and public companies. They will not contain an alternative written resolution procedure. Since the new statutory procedure is far more practical than the old one, there will be little need for private companies to set out their own procedures, although public companies will still have to do so if they wish to use written resolutions because the statutory procedure does not apply to them.

MEMO POINTS Transitional amendments to Table A applying to **companies incorporated on or after 1 October 2007** that adopt Table A delete reg 53 TA 1985 (reg 6 SI 2007/2541).

3587 To **avoid** any **potential conflict**, the company should make any alternative procedure as specific as possible. For example, if the company wants to provide for email resolutions, it should have in place an appropriate method of verifying the identity of the shareholders, e.g. electronic signatures. Further, once a written resolution has been passed when the company receives the last signature, the secretary should circulate a minute to all shareholders confirming that the resolution has been passed. This sort of procedure could work well for small companies, but may cause more administrative difficulties in larger companies.

If a company chooses to use an alternative procedure set out in its articles, it should state on the written resolution that the procedure in the articles applies to avoid uncertainty and unwarranted challenges to the resolution.

3588 It has been held in some circumstances that the legislative formalities attached to certain resolutions should not be evaded, presumably because those requirements offer the shareholders and/or creditors a degree of protection. To guard against any challenge to a written resolution, where the **resolution** would usually **require a particular procedure** in the legislation, it would be best practice to hold a meeting and pass the resolution in accordance with that procedure, or at least to use the statutory written resolution procedure. For example, since neither the statutory nor the informal written resolution procedures can be used to remove and/or replace a director or an auditor, a written resolution procedure in the articles could be challenged if used in these circumstances.

It has also been held that a written resolution procedure contained in the articles should not have been used to approve the reduction of a company's share capital and cancellation of its share premium account, because the settled practice was to require the formalities of a special resolution (*Re Barry Artist Ltd* [1985] 1 WLR 1305). Although the statutory procedure supersedes this case as far as private companies are concerned because it allows any resolutions (other than those to remove/replace directors or auditors) to be passed as written resolutions, it may still provide guidance for **public companies**. This might indicate a reluctance to accept a written resolution in lieu of a particular procedure laid down by statute, although, in reality, the court is unlikely to reject such a written resolution only on the grounds of it being written, since it is used to accepting written resolutions in the same circumstances from private companies.

Written resolutions have to be **filed** at Companies House within 15 days, if they contain a special resolution or any other resolution which would have to be filed if it was not passed as a written resolution (ss 29, 30 CA 2006). Failure to do so renders the company and any officers in default liable to a fine (¶9935).

A record of all written resolutions must also be kept by the company, see ¶3866.

2. Informal unanimous agreement

3590 If all of a company's shareholders are in agreement, the validity of a decision cannot subsequently be challenged even if the correct procedure was not followed. The new Companies Act specifically preserves this common law rule (s 281 CA 2006). This is commonly referred to as the "*Duomatic*" **principle**, after the leading case (*Re Duomatic Ltd* [1969] 1 All ER 161). This **fallback position** permits a company to hold a meeting on short notice with the consent of all shareholders, or pass a resolution unanimously, even if the correct procedure for passing the resolution or holding the meeting has not been followed. This applies even for specific types of resolution, for example a special resolution to change a company's articles (*Cane v Jones* [1981] 1 All ER 533).

3591 Each shareholder's **consent** does not have to be obtained at a meeting, or even at the same time. For example, the unanimous consent of the shareholders to a transaction which was within the company's powers but not the directors' was held to bind the company although the assents to the transaction were not obtained together in a meeting (*Cane v Jones* [1981] 1 All ER 533). The principle also applies to decisions contained in shareholders' agreements, which may be signed by shareholders separately as they join the company (*Euro Brokers Holdings Ltd v Monecor* [2003] 1 BCLC 506).

Actual consents are required (*Re D'Jan of London Ltd, Copp v D'Jan* [1994] 1 BCLC 561), but acquiescence with knowledge of a decision may be tantamount to consent (*Re Home Treat Ltd* [1991] BCLC 705).

MEMO POINTS 1. The assent of **non-voting shareholders** is not required (*Re Duomatic Ltd* [1969] 1 All ER 161).
2. The rule also applies if all of the shareholders of a **class of shares** pass a resolution that would otherwise have been considered at a class meeting (*Re Torvale Group Ltd* [1999] 2 BCLC 605).

3592 There are **limits** to the extent of the principle of informal unanimous consent. A company cannot use it to make a decision which involves the legitimate concerns of non-members, such as a resolution to remove a director or auditor. The court has held that the statutory mechanisms concerning the purchase of a company's own shares are there not just for the benefit of the current shareholders, but also for future shareholders and the creditors. This would indicate that informal unanimous consent should not be relied upon for decisions concerning these groups either.

The principle is also subject to certain requirements regarding, and restrictions on, **who can vote**. For instance, an informal resolution to buy back shares was held to be void because it (*Re R W Peak (Kings Lynn) Ltd* [1998] 1 BCLC 193; ¶1337+):
– reduced the protection for creditors of having a formal procedure;
– was in breach of the statutory provisions requiring the contract to be approved in advance; and
– was not agreed to unanimously because the shareholder whose shares were the subject of the resolution could not take part in the vote.

Decisions made in this way have to be **filed** at Companies House within 15 days if they amount to a special resolution or any other resolution which would have to be filed if it was not passed as a written resolution (ss 29, 30 CA 2006). Failure to do so renders the company and any officers in default liable to a fine (¶9935).

A record of all written resolutions must also be kept by the company, see ¶3866.

C. Summary of resolution requirements

3600

Type of resolution	Procedure	Notice	How to pass	Filing requirements
Ordinary Used for: – resolutions that do not have to be special resolutions – resolutions at ¶3531	Meeting	Needs to contain enough detail to inform the shareholders of the general business of the meeting, rather than the full text Period depends on type of meeting: – general/class: 14 days – plc AGM: 21 days. Note that certain resolutions require special notice (¶3536+)	50+% of those present and voting	Only certain ordinary resolutions need to be filed at Companies House, see ¶3534
	Statutory written	Terms of resolution and an explanation of how to agree to it and by when	50+% of eligible shareholders Resolution must be passed within 28 days of circulation	
Special	Meeting	Needs to contain full text of the resolution and state that it is a special resolution Period depends on type of meeting: – general/class: 14 days – plc AGM: 21 days	75% of those present and voting	Needs to be filed at Companies House within 15 days of being passed
	Statutory written	Terms of resolution, the fact that it is a special resolution and an explanation of how to agree to it and by when	75% of eligible shareholders Resolution must be passed within 28 days of circulation	
Elective Only used to give directors authority to allot shares for more than 5 years [1]	Meeting	Terms of resolution and the fact that it is an elective resolution Period: 21 days, unless short notice agreed to by the shareholders	All shareholders entitled to attend and vote at the meeting	Needs to be filed at Companies House within 15 days of being passed

Note:
1. An elective resolution will not be necessary for this decision when the relevant provisions of the new Companies Act come into force, which is expected to be by 1 October 2009 (¶3563).

II. How to convene and conduct meetings

Types of meeting

3610 Shareholder meetings take **three forms**:
– general meetings are used for any business to be decided by all of the shareholders entitled to vote;
– annual general meetings (AGMs) only have to be held by public companies every year; and
– class meetings are held where a decision only needs to be made by the holders of one class of shares.

Now that the provisions of the new Companies Act regarding meetings and resolutions have come into force, shareholder meetings are likely to become less common. **Private companies** will be able to use the new statutory written resolution procedure, which allows the vast majority of resolutions to be passed in writing on the same majorities as at a meeting (see ¶3580+). This will greatly reduce the need for the shareholders to meet at all. However, companies may well still want to hold general meetings as a way of keeping in touch with the shareholders and making them feel involved in company management, particularly as private companies are no longer obliged to hold AGMs.

Public companies, on the other hand do still have to hold AGMs (see ¶3777+). They will not be able to use the new statutory written resolution procedure either (although they will still be able to include an alternative written resolution procedure in their articles if they wish, see ¶3586+), and so most public companies will continue to hold general meetings as and when the need arises.

Comment: The **term** "general meeting" is preferred here to "extraordinary general meeting" or "EGM" because general meetings are now the norm for private companies, so there is no need to distinguish between extraordinary and annual meetings as far as they are concerned. This term is also consistent with the new Companies Act. Readers may still see the terms "extraordinary general meeting" and "EGM" used in other sources, including companies' articles (for example, Table A defines an EGM as a meeting of the shareholders which is not an AGM or a class meeting, reg 36 TA 1985). They should be read as referring to a general meeting.

MEMO POINTS Transitional amendments to Table A apply to **companies incorporated on or after 1 October 2007** that adopt Table A only, deleting reg 36 TA 1985 (reg 4 SI 2007/2541).

3611 Shareholders with a certain class of shares hold **class meetings** to make decisions which only affect them. For example, the articles of the company or the document setting out the terms of those shares may require a meeting to be held in particular circumstances, or the rights of those shareholders may need to be altered (see ¶3794+).

3612 The discussion of the **procedures** relating to general meetings follows that for a general meeting. General meetings are the most common type of meeting as private companies do not have to hold AGMs. Even public companies may have to hold general meetings between AGMs. Only companies whose shares are divided into classes need to hold class meetings when an issue arises that only concerns that class. In most cases, the procedures are the same, but any specific rules for the different types of meeting are highlighted as necessary.

A. Calling a general meeting

General meetings are usually called, or "**convened**", by the directors **when** the board needs to consult or obtain the approval of the shareholders for a particular matter, or at the shareholders' request (¶3626+). The legislation also gives shareholders the right to call meetings directly in certain situations, as well as setting out a "fallback" position enabling the court to call a meeting where necessary.

3620

1. Directors

On their own initiative

Meetings are usually called by the directors on their own initiative (and they now have a statutory power to do so, s 302 CA 2006). A meeting must be convened by a properly constituted board with the authority of the directors. The directors will decide **when and where** to convene the shareholder meeting at a board meeting, where they will also determine the wording of the notice and the resolutions to be considered.

3622

> MEMO POINTS Directors of **public companies** are **obliged to call** a general meeting if the company's net assets fall to half, or less than half, of its called-up share capital (s 142 CA 1985; ¶7441). This provision will be restated in the **new Companies Act** (s 656 CA 2006, expected to come into force by 1 October 2009).

The court can intervene regarding the date of the meeting if the directors' discretion has been **improperly exercised**, for example by calling the meeting deliberately early to prevent new transferees of shares from exercising their voting rights, rather than waiting until they have been duly registered (*Cannon v Trask* (1875) LR 20 Eq 669).

3623

When prompted by shareholders or auditors

The directors can be prompted to call a meeting following a shareholders' or auditor's **requisition** for a meeting (¶3626+, ¶3632). On receipt of the requisition the directors must convene (as opposed to "hold") a general meeting "forthwith", which has been held to mean "as soon as reasonably practicable" (*Re Windward Island (Enterprises) UK Ltd* [1983] BCLC 293). **Statute** gives the directors a maximum of 21 days from receipt of a requisition by the shareholders or a resigning auditor within which to **convene** the meeting (respectively, s 304 CA 2006, s 392A CA 1985). If the directors then fail to **hold** the general meeting within 28 days of the notice, they will be deemed to have convened the meeting improperly.

3624

If the company is governed by **Table A**, a meeting requisitioned by the shareholders in this way cannot be **held** later than 8 weeks after the company receives the requisition (reg 37 TA 1985). The discrepancy between the statutory and regulatory time limits (i.e. 7 weeks in the legislation and 8 in Table A between receiving the requisition and holding the meeting) seems to be without reason. To avoid any allegations that a requisitioned meeting was convened improperly, directors should ensure that they comply with the shorter statutory limit.

Comment: From 6 April 2008, the **new Companies Act** will impose the same statutory deadlines on the board convening a meeting at the request of a resigning auditor (s 518 CA 2006).

> MEMO POINTS 1. Directors can usually be **prevented from calling a meeting** altogether by a court injunction in appropriate cases, but it has been held that it would not be appropriate to do so where the directors are calling a general meeting following a shareholders' requisition (*Cumbrian Newspapers Group Ltd v Cumberland and Westmorland Herald Newspaper and Printing Co Ltd* [1986] 2 All ER 816).
> 2. Draft **new model articles** under the new Act have been published for private companies limited by shares and public companies. They will not contain any provisions comparable to those in Table A.

3. Transitional amendments to Table A apply to **companies incorporated on or after 1 October 2007** that adopt Table A, and they remove this discrepancy in the deadline for holding a requisitioned meeting. Instead, the directors must call a general meeting in accordance with the statutory deadline (reg 5 SI 2007/2541).

2. Shareholders

3625 Shareholders have the statutory right to require the directors to hold a general meeting by way of a formal written request, or **requisition**. They used to be able to call a general meeting directly, although this right has now been repealed.

Company required to hold a general meeting by the shareholders

3626 The articles of a company cannot override the shareholders' right to requisition a general meeting. The request must be **made by** a shareholder or group of shareholders (s 303 CA 2006):
– with the right to vote at general meetings; and
– holding 10% of the total paid-up share capital which carries voting rights.
This percentage is reduced to 5% if the company has not held a general meeting at which the shareholders had the right to circulate a resolution (which they might have, for example, because they had requisitioned that meeting) in the preceding 12 months.

> MEMO POINTS 1. For companies **without a share capital**, qualifying shareholders must hold at least 10% (or 5% in the same circumstances as for companies with a share capital) of the voting rights (s 303 CA 2006).
> 2. There is a question as to whether shares should be counted as qualifying where the **voting rights are suspended**, for instance because calls on the shares are in arrears or following the death of a shareholder (regs 31, 57 TA 1985). To err on the side of caution, companies should assume that such shares do not count as qualifying, as technically they do not carry voting rights at the time of the requisition.

3627 The requisition can be in hard copy or electronic **form**. It must **contain** (s 303 CA 2006):
– a description of the general business to be dealt with at the meeting; and
– the text of any resolutions to be proposed.

It is important that the requisition is worded carefully, as only business stated in the requisition can be dealt with at the meeting. A resolution cannot be put to the meeting if it would be ineffective, or it is defamatory, frivolous or vexatious. However, if the requisition states the objects, rather than the precise wording of a resolution, and those objects can be achieved by a shareholder resolution, the directors have to call the meeting to consider the resolution (*Rose v McGivern* [1998] 2 BCLC 593).

The requisition has to be **signed by** each requisitionist (or authenticated, if in electronic form). The signatures do not all have to appear on the same document, so the requisitionists can sign and send their copy of the request to the company individually. If the requisition forms separate documents, they do not all have to be identical provided the sense of the documents is the same (*Fruit and Vegetable Growers' Association Ltd v Kekewich* [1912] 2 Ch 52). In the case of jointly held shares, the requisition needs to be signed by all joint shareholders (*Patent Wood Keg Syndicate Ltd v Pearse* [1906] WN 164).

The requisition can be **sent** to the company following the new rules for communicating with companies explained below.

The **cost** of the shareholders' requisition is to be borne by the shareholders, unless the company resolves otherwise.

3628 The new Companies Act allows for shareholders and others to communicate with companies in different ways, for example by email. A requisition for a general meeting and any other document that needs to be **sent** to a company can be sent in hard copy, electronic form or by any other agreed method (s 1144, Sch 4 CA 2006).

Method	Company's consent required?	Address for service	Deemed to have been delivered[1]
Hard copy[2] delivered by hand or sent by post	No	– Address specified for the purpose – Company's registered office – Other service address authorised under companies legislation	Sent by post: 48 hours after posted (and it was properly addressed, prepaid and posted)
Electronic form sent electronically (e.g. email or fax) or by post (e.g. CD ROM)	Yes[3]	– Address specified for the purpose – Deemed address[3]	– Sent electronically: 48 hours after sent (and it was properly addressed) – Sent by post: 48 hours after posted (and it was properly addressed, prepaid and posted)
Other agreed form	Yes	As specified	–

Note:
1. s 1147 CA 2006.
2. Paper copy, or similar form capable of being read with the naked eye (s 1168 CA 2006).
3. Company can consent generally or specifically to a document being sent electronically (e.g. in the articles) or it can be deemed to have agreed by statute. Company is deemed to have consented to receiving electronic communications about a general meeting or proxies at the meeting, or about a written resolution, if it included an electronic address (e.g. email address or fax number) on the relevant document (ss 298, 333 CA 2006). Any such communications must be sent to that address. If it accepts electronic communications, the company should make it clear to shareholders and other senders that any communications containing a virus will be rejected, but that the sender will be informed where possible (ICSA guidance note number 160207).

MEMO POINTS   These rules for sending information to a company **apply to** any information sent by any person. If another statutory provision stipulates how a document should be sent to a company, and these requirements contradict the new rules, the other statutory provision should be followed instead (s 1143 CA 2006).

Directors must call a requisitioned meeting within 21 days of receiving the requisition, and the meeting must be held within 28 days of their notice (s 304 CA 2006, although see ¶3624 for where the articles set out alternative deadlines).

The requisitioning shareholder(s) can call the meeting directly if the **directors fail** (s 305 CA 2006):
– to call it within 21 days of receiving the shareholder requisition;
– to include any resolution specified in the requisition in the notice of the meeting (as long as the resolution is not ineffective, defamatory, frivolous or vexatious); or
– in the case of a special resolution, to include the required information in the notice.

Requisitionists holding more than half of the voting rights of the original requisitioning shareholders can convene the meeting, following the procedure the directors would use as far as possible. The meeting should be held within 3 months from the expiry of the directors' 21-day deadline.

The shareholders must be reimbursed for any reasonable **expenses** of calling the meeting by the company out of the fees or remuneration of the directors who failed to call the meeting. As well as being able to call the meeting themselves, the shareholders concerned may have an action for **unfair prejudice** (*McGuinness v Bremner plc* [1988] BCLC 673; see ¶2105+ for a discussion of this type of action).

3629

Shareholders' ability to call the meeting directly

Shareholders no longer have the right to call a meeting without asking the directors to do so first (Sch 2 SI 2007/2194 repealed s 370 CA 1985). However, there is nothing to prevent a company from including it in its **articles**, for example the draft new model articles for public companies will enable shareholders to call a general meeting for the limited purpose of appointing more directors if there are fewer than two directors at the time (art 27).

3630

3. Auditors

3632 Where an auditor has **resigned** he can include with his resignation a requisition that the directors convene a general meeting straight away so that the shareholders or creditors can consider the circumstances of his resignation (s 392A CA 1985). He can also require the directors to circulate a statement of the circumstances connected with his resignation to the shareholders (either before the requisitioned general meeting or before the AGM at which his office would have expired) (¶4341+).

Failure to call or hold a general meeting requisitioned by a resigning auditor renders every director who failed to take all reasonable steps to ensure that the meeting was convened guilty of an offence and liable to a fine (¶9935).

Comment: The **new Companies Act** will also give resigning auditors this power (s 518 CA 2006, due to come into force on 6 April 2008).

4. The court

3635 If it has been **impracticable** to call a meeting, or it would be impracticable to conduct it properly, the court can order that a meeting takes place, and it can also give directions as to how the meeting is convened and/or conducted (s 306 CA 2006). Each case will be considered on its own facts and merits. If the court makes an order to allow a meeting to take place, it is not a comment on the conduct of the parties; any alleged wrongdoing by the directors should be resolved in **other proceedings** (e.g. unfair prejudice proceedings).

EXAMPLE
1. The court can order that the meeting is only attended by the company's executive committee, and the other shareholders have to vote by postal ballot, in order to avoid **disruption** and **intimidation** (*Re British Union for the Abolition of Vivisection* [1995] 2 BCLC 1).
2. The shares in OP Ltd were held 51%-49% by director-shareholders A and B respectively. A tried to remove B as a director, but B refused to attend meetings, rendering them inquorate so the resolution could not be considered. The court held that A, as a majority shareholder, had a statutory right to remove a director by ordinary resolution, and the **quorum requirement** could not be used by B as a right of veto. It therefore ordered that the meeting could be held with a quorum of one (*Re Opera Photographic Ltd* [1989] 1 WLR 634). Shareholders will not be allowed to use the quorum provisions to prevent the majority from exercising its rights (*Union Music Ltd v Watson* [2003] 1 BCLC 453; in this case, the quorum provisions were set out in a shareholders' agreement).
3. On the other hand, the court has refused to interfere where the different classes of shareholder had freely entered into a **prior agreement** which provided for a particular quorum at general meetings because the rights of classes of shareholders which have been agreed should not be overturned (*Lipe Ltd v Leyland DAF Ltd* [1994] 1 BCLC 84).
4. Mr M (a 0.5% shareholder) applied to the court for an order that a meeting be summoned to consider resolutions to replace the current board and dismiss any new directors that may have been appointed by the board before the meeting. The court would not order a meeting to be held because, on the facts, it was **practicable** to either call or conduct the meeting. The court would not allow a shareholder to use a court order to circumvent the need to give any as-yet unascertained new directors special notice of their proposed removal. Any such directors could be removed at a later meeting if necessary (*Monnington v Easier plc* [1995] EWHC 2578 (Ch)).
5. Where there has been a **deadlock** between the shareholders, the court has refused to use its powers to make directions at a meeting to alter the balance of power. In the case of a two-shareholder company, the court decided that as the shareholders had chosen to divide the shares equally, they would have considered the possibility of deadlock and must have seen it as a form of protection to prevent the company taking decisions of which one shareholder or the other did not approve (*Ross v Telford* [1998] 1 BCLC 82).
6. The court may also order the timing of the meeting to fit in with any **other proceedings** (*Re Woven Rugs* [2002] 1 BCLC 324).

Procedure

3636 The **court** may make an order on its own initiative or on **application** by either a director or any shareholder who would have been entitled to vote at the meeting (s 306 CA 2006). The application should be made by way of claim form (¶7143+).

B. Notice

3646 A company is required to notify its shareholders, and other people entitled to notice, that a meeting of the company will take place. As well as giving the shareholders the practical details (such as when and where the meeting will be held), the notice gives them the opportunity to consider what business is going to be discussed. The shareholder can then decide whether he wants to attend and whether he wishes to exercise any rights in relation to the meeting, such as appointing a proxy or circulating a statement.

There are a surprising number of factors which must be taken into consideration when giving notice of a meeting. Both the legislation and Table A (or the company's articles in an alternative form) lay down various requirements as to the **form** of the notice. These requirements increase depending on what type of resolution is to be considered, for example it may be a resolution that requires particular treatment in the notice, and/or the company may have to send out additional information with the notice. The **timing** of the notice is also important, as a meeting called on insufficient notice will be invalid, negating any resolutions passed at it. A company must ensure that it gets the timing right, according to the resolutions to be passed, and that the notice is **served** correctly.

1. Content

3650 Generally speaking, notices must **comply** strictly with the statutory provisions under which they are issued. For example, if a notice is given of a resolution to proceed under a particular section of the legislation, it must clearly state that this is the case by referring to the relevant provision (*Re Stearic Acid Co Ltd* (1863) 2 New Rep 544, concerning the appointment of a liquidator).

a. General requirements

3651 As a minimum, notices of meetings should contain the following **information** (s 311 CA 2006):
– the date, time and place of the meeting; and
– the general nature of the business to be considered.

The requirement to state the general business for the meeting to discuss is subject to the company's articles, which may require more specific information to be provided or, on the other hand, may permit the notice to include no such information. Table A mirrors the new statutory provision (reg 38 TA 1985).

> MEMO POINTS 1. In the case of a **public company** holding an **AGM**, the notice must also state that the meeting is an AGM (s 337 CA 2006).
> 2. For companies **incorporated on or after 1 October 2007** that adopt Table A, amendments have been made to certain provisions of Table A to correspond with the provisions of the new Companies Act which were in force by that date. reg 38 TA 1985 has been amended in different ways for private and for public companies. See ¶9915 for the details of these changes.

3652 The notice needs to give sufficient **information about the business** to be considered at the meeting to enable the shareholders to know what decisions are to be made (*Young v South Africa & Australian Exploration and Development Syndicate* [1896] 2 Ch 268). This complements any requirements to give the wording of particular resolutions (¶3656+ below). Only resolutions which are within the scope of the notice can be included in the business at the meeting. There is no comprehensive guidance as to what will be sufficient information, but case law has clarified some areas:
a. if a notice is clear enough to give reasonable notice of the business to be considered, then the decision will not be invalidated because the notice does not specifically set out all of the details of that business (*Re London and Mediterranean Bank, Wright's Case* (1868) LR 12 Eq 335n); and
b. if the notice comprises several items of business and one of them is beyond the company's powers or ineffective for another reason, the other items will only be invalid if they depend upon the ultra vires item (*Re Willaire Systems plc* [1987] BCLC 67).

> MEMO POINTS Companies incorporated before 1 July 1985 and still operating under **Table A 1948** will divide the business to be considered into "ordinary" and "special" business. What constitutes special business will be specified in the articles. Table A 1948 provides that **special business** is any business apart from:
> – declaring dividends;
> – considering accounts, balance sheets and the reports of the directors and auditors;
> – electing directors in place of those retiring; and
> – appointing auditors and deciding on their remuneration.
> All of these matters are designated ordinary business and would usually be considered at an AGM, although a company's articles could alter these definitions.
> Table A 1948 required the general nature of any special business to be included in the notice of a meeting. Although there is no equivalent requirement for ordinary business, it is the practice to include the items of ordinary business in the notice as well, for example, by giving the names of those directors who are retiring and/or being re-elected. This ties in with the requirement to give sufficient information regarding the business to be considered at the meeting in the notice, and would guard against shareholders challenging decisions made at a meeting because insufficient details of the business had been given.

3653 **Amendments** to the resolutions or business to be considered at the meeting can be made, provided the amendment would not affect the shareholders' decision as to whether or not to attend the meeting. For example, if notice is given of a resolution to approve a director's remuneration, the amount to be paid to the director can be reduced at the meeting, but not increased. If a company's articles distinguish between ordinary and special business (like Table A 1948, see above), amendments to ordinary business are only permitted if the amended resolution would still be classified as ordinary business.

3654 Business transacted on **insufficient notice**, or business that is significantly **different** from that notified is invalid. Note that only those items of business not properly notified will be invalidated; the rest of the business will stand. Minor **errors or irregularities** will not render a notice invalid.

If insufficient notice of the business to be considered has been given, **a shareholder can** apply to the court to restrain the company from acting on the relevant resolution(s) (*MacConnell v E Prill & Co Ltd* [1916] 2 Ch 57). If any challenge is raised regarding the adequacy of the notice, the court will look at any circular as well as the notice itself to see whether proper notice of the business had been given (¶3660+; *Re Moorgate Mercantile Holdings Ltd* [1980] 1 All ER 40). If a notice is misleading, the court can either restrain the meeting from being held until proper notice has been given, or prevent the directors from acting on the resolutions (*Baillie v Oriental Telephone and Electric Co Ltd* [1915] 1 Ch 503).

b. Requirements for different types of resolution

3656 The general rules discussed above apply to **ordinary resolutions**. They do not have to be set out in full in the notice, as long as sufficient information is given to enable the shareholders to ascertain the business to be considered. Ordinary resolutions can be **amended** at the meeting within the scope of the information given in the notice.

3657 If the meeting is to consider a **special resolution**, the notice must (s 283 CA 2006):
– include the text of the resolution; and
– state that it is intended to be passed as a special resolution.

For an **elective** resolution, the **terms** of the resolution also need to be specified in the notice (¶3562+). The terms of an **extraordinary** or **special** resolution do not have to be set out, but the notice must contain the "entire substance" of the resolution, because the resolution passed must be that in the notice. Only **amendments** of grammatical or clerical errors, or rewording the resolution in a more formal manner, are permitted (*Re Moorgate Mercantile Holdings Ltd* [1980] 1 All ER 40; s 378(1), (2) CA 1985). Other amendments can only be made with the consent of all shareholders (or all shareholders of the class if the resolution is to be passed at a class meeting).

> **EXAMPLE**
> 1. A notice states that a special resolution to alter or replace the articles is to be considered at the meeting and advises shareholders that the new or altered articles are available for inspection at the registered office. This does not give shareholders the entire substance of the special resolution: notice of the specific changes needs to be given to the shareholders.
> 2. In a case where a special resolution to reduce the premium share capital account was to be moved, the notice of the special resolution stated that the account would be cancelled, but the resolution passed at the meeting was to reduce the share premium account to £321.17 (*Re Moorgate Mercantile Holdings Ltd*, above). This was the amount attributable to a recent share issue, which could not be treated as lost, as could the rest of the account, when it came to applying to the court to confirm the cancellation of the share premium account (¶1435+). The court held that the resolution passed at the meeting was not valid, because it was not the same, or substantially the same, as the resolution in the notice.
> 3. On the other hand, a special resolution to appoint a liquidator was held to be valid, although the name of the liquidator in the notice was different to the one in the resolution passed at the meeting (*Re Trench Tubeless Tyre Co, Bethell v Trench Tubeless Tyre Co* [1900] 1 Ch 408). In this case, it seems that the substance of the resolution was to appoint a liquidator, not who that liquidator would be.

c. Documents to be provided with the notice or before meetings

Companies are required to include **proxy statements** in their notices of meetings (¶3732+). **3660**

If a **director has an interest** in passing a resolution, he must give full disclosure of that **3661** interest in the notice of the meeting, as it may affect the way in which the shareholders vote (*Normandy v Ind Coope & Co Ltd* [1908] 1 Ch 84; see ¶3308+ for a discussion of directors' interests).

If the meeting has been called to discuss **non-routine business**, the directors will often send **3662** out a **circular** along with the notice, which gives more detail of the business to be considered. This gives the directors the opportunity to lobby the shareholders about the resolutions, and to answer any points raised in a shareholder statement. Directors must be sure only to lobby the shareholders to vote in a particular way if it is in the company's best interests, not just the directors' (*Peel v London & NW Railway Co* [1907] 1 Ch 5).

Shareholders' statements

Shareholders have the right to require the company to circulate a statement before a **general** **3663** **meeting** to the other shareholders regarding any matter to be considered at the meeting (s 314(1) CA 2006). This right is an important one, enabling a shareholder to make his views known in advance of the meeting, lobby support from other shareholders, or have his say whether or not he can attend. Although it is important, the right as expressed in the Companies Act 1985 was rarely used in practice because shareholders had to bear the cost of circulation, which could be considerable in a large company. This problem has been tackled in the new Companies Act, which allows the company to pay the costs instead (see ¶3666 below).

In the case of a public company **AGM**, shareholders have a similar right to circulate a resolution to be moved at the forthcoming meeting, see ¶3780+.

> **MEMO POINTS** The provisions of the new Companies Act dealing with shareholders' statements have been in force since 1 October 2007. However, if a **request** was made to a private company to circulate a statement **under CA 1985** and the company has not complied with it when it should have done, it is still under an obligation to hold an AGM under CA 1985, presumably to ensure that the shareholders have an opportunity to raise their point at a meeting (para 29 Sch 3 SI 2007/2194). See ¶3777+ for AGMs.

Either: **3664**
– a shareholder or shareholders holding at least 5% of the total voting rights of all of the shareholders with the right to vote either on the resolution in question, or at the meeting if the statement does not concern a particular resolution; or
– at least 100 shareholders holding shares to the average value per shareholder of at least £100,

can requisition the company to circulate a statement in relation to any resolution or matter to be considered at any meeting (s 314(2), (3) CA 2006). The statement cannot be longer than 1,000 words.

The requisition can be **sent** to the company in hard copy or electronic form (s 314(4) CA 2006). The rules governing communicating with companies are discussed at ¶3628 in the context of shareholders requisitioning a meeting.

> MEMO POINTS If a shareholder's qualification to circulate a statement is **challenged** because the currency in which the shares are issued is not sterling, the court can determine the appropriate date and rate of interest in order to judge the requisitionists' standing (*Re Scandinavian Bank Group plc* [1987] 2 All ER 70).

3666 The company **has to circulate** a shareholder's statement if (s 315, 316 CA 2006):
– a copy signed by all of the requisitionists is deposited at the registered office of the company at least 1 week (calculated in clear days, s 360 CA 2006) before the meeting; and
– a reasonably sufficient sum to cover the expense of the company circulating the statement is deposited or tendered with the statement, unless the company has already resolved that the requisitioning shareholders should not bear this cost.

The company **does not have to circulate** the statement if:
– the request does not meet the statutory requirements;
– where the costs of circulation have not been met, where the requisitioning shareholders must pay them; or
– the company or another aggrieved person satisfies the court that the right is being abused (s 317 CA 2006). On such an application, the court has the power to order the requisitioning shareholders to pay the company's costs, even if they are not a party to the application.

> MEMO POINTS If the meeting in question is a **public company's AGM** and the request was received before the end of the company's preceding financial year, the requisitioning shareholder(s) will not have to bear the costs of circulation, whether or not the company so resolves (s 316 CA 2006).

3667 The statements are to be **served** on the shareholders entitled to receive notice of the meeting in the same manner as the notices themselves. This can be in hard copy, electronic form, via a website or in any other agreed form (see ¶3695+). They should be served at the same time as the notice for the meeting, or if that is not possible, as soon as practicable thereafter. **Failure** to comply renders every officer of the company who is in default liable to a fine (s 315 CA 2006; ¶9935).

Auditors' statements

3668 Where an auditor **resigns**, he can require the company to circulate a statement (of reasonable length) regarding the circumstances connected with his resignation to the shareholders, either (s 392A CA 1985):
– before a meeting he has requisitioned (¶3632); or
– before the general meeting at which his term of office would have expired (¶4336+).

See ¶3628 for the methods by which the auditor can send his statement to the company (a discussion of methods of communication in the context of shareholders requisitioning meetings). Unless the statement is received too late, the **company is to serve a copy** of it on the shareholders to whom notice of the meeting is or was sent. The statement can be sent using the same methods as the notice itself, see ¶3695+. The **notice** itself must point out to the shareholders that the statement has been made, if it was received before the notice was served. If the statement is received by the company after notice of the meeting has been sent out, the auditor can require that the statement is read out at the meeting (s 392A(6) CA 1985).

The company **does not have to circulate** the statement if it or another aggrieved person satisfies the court that the auditor is using the right to publicise defamatory material (s 392(7) CA 1985). On such an application, the court has the power to order the auditor to pay all or part of the company's costs, even if he is not a party to the application.

Comment: The **new Companies Act** will also give auditors this right (s 518 CA 2006, due to come into force on 6 April 2008).

Summary of documents and statements

Certain **statutory provisions require** additional information to be provided to the shareholders together with the notice of the meeting or at the meeting itself. These documents must also be sent to the shareholders where the written resolution procedure is used instead of a meeting (¶3577+).

3670

Type of resolution	Documents required	How/when the documents are to be available	Reference [1]
Special resolution to **disapply pre-emption rights** or special resolution to renew resolution to do so ¶940+	Written statement from directors setting out: – reasons for recommending the disapplication; – amount to be paid to company; and – directors' justification of amount	Sent to shareholders with notice	s 95 CA 1985 [2]
Special resolution to **approve financial assistance** ¶5557+	Directors' statutory declaration, with auditors' report	Available for inspection by shareholders at meeting	ss 155, 156, 157 CA 1985 [3]
Special resolution to: – authorise terms of proposed contract for **off-market purchase of company's own shares**; – vary contingent purchase contract; or – authorise release of company's rights under approved contract ¶1383+	Copy of contract, or memorandum of terms (if contract not in writing)	– Available for inspection at registered office at least 15 days before meeting; and – available at meeting	ss 164, 165, 167 CA 1985 [4]
Special resolution to authorise **payment out of capital** by private company to **redeem or purchase own shares** ¶1400+	Statutory declaration of directors regarding payment out of capital, with auditors' report	Available for inspection at meeting	ss 173, 174 CA 1985 [5]
Ordinary resolution to authorise terms of **director's service contract** lasting more than 2 years ¶2655+	Written memorandum of proposed agreement	– Available for inspection at registered office at least 15 days before meeting; and – available at meeting	s 188 CA 2006
Ordinary resolution to authorise a **"loan" to a director**, where authorisation is necessary ¶2804+	Statement detailing: – nature of the transaction; – amount and purpose of the "loan"; and – extent of the company's liability under any connected transaction	– Available for inspection at registered office at least 15 days before meeting; and – available at meeting	ss 197, 198, 200, 201, 203 CA 2006
Public **company's accounts** laid before general meeting [6] ¶4273+	Copy of: – company accounts (balance sheet and profit & loss account); – auditor's report; and – directors' report	To be sent to all shareholders (including preferential shareholders), debenture holders and others entitled to receive notice at least 21 days before meeting [7]	ss 238, 241, 252 CA 1985

Type of resolution	Documents required	How/when the documents are to be available	Reference [1]
Any	Shareholder's statement ¶3663+	Sent out to shareholders with notice of meeting, or as soon as practicable thereafter	s 315 CA 2006
Any	Auditor's statement ¶3668	Sent out with notice of meeting. Notice points out that statement has been made. If statement received too late, read out at meeting	s 392A CA 1985

Note:
1. Under the **new Companies Act**, the relevant references for provisions not yet in force will be:
– disapply pre-emption rights: s 571 CA 2006, expected to come into force by 1 October 2009;
– approve financial assistance: this will no longer be applicable. See ¶5557/mp;
– off-market purchase of own shares: ss 694-700 CA 2006, expected to come into force by 1 October 2009;
– payment out of capital to redeem/purchase own shares: s 718 CA 2006, expected to come into force by 1 October 2009;
– accounts: ss 423, 424 CA 2006, due to come into force on 6 April 2008;
– auditor's statement: s 518 CA 2006, due to come into force on 6 April 2008.
2. For **written resolutions**, the reference is s 300A CA 2006.
3. For written resolutions, the reference is s 300B CA 2006.
4. For written resolutions, the reference is s 300C CA 2006.
5. For written resolutions, the reference is s 300D CA 2006.
6. **Private companies** also have to circulate their accounts amongst the shareholders, but this is not tied to laying them before an AGM because this is no longer a requirement of a private company (see ¶4265+).
7. Copy of accounts must be sent to **all shareholders**, whether or not they have right to receive notice, attend or vote at meeting.

2. Notice period

3675 Working out the correct notice period for general meetings has been made much easier by the new Companies Act as it now just depends on the type of meeting (ss 307, 360 CA 2006):
– general meetings of private and public companies: 14 clear days; or
– public company AGMs: 21 clear days.

Unless a company's articles stipulate otherwise, the type of resolution will not affect the length of notice under the new Act.

Comment: If the meeting is to consider an **elective resolution** to give the directors authority to allot shares for more than 5 years (the only remaining elective resolution), 21 clear days' notice of the resolution must be given (¶3564).

3676 Companies can give **alternative notice periods** if the shareholders agree. **Longer** notice periods can be set out in the articles, either for meetings in general or which only apply when certain matters are to be considered at a meeting (s 307 CA 2006). For example, Table A stipulates that no more than 28 clear days' notice of the intention to appoint or reappoint a director (other than a director retiring by rotation) can be given (reg 77 TA 1985). **Shorter** notice periods can also be given, see ¶3681+ below.

MEMO POINTS 1. The draft **new model articles** will not contain an equivalent provision.
2. Transitional amendments to Table A which apply to **private companies incorporated on or after 1 October 2007** that adopt Table A omit the words "other than a director retiring by rotation" from reg 77 TA 1985 (reg 15 SI 2007/2541).

3677 The timeline at ¶3873 illustrates the **chronology** of events leading up to and following a meeting, including when notices are to be served.

Calculating notice

3679 Notice of a general meeting must be calculated on "clear days", which means that the day on which the notice was served and the day of the meeting cannot be counted (s 360

CA 2006). Table A also requires notice to be given based on "clear days" (regs 1, 38 TA 1985). A "day" has been held to mean from midnight to midnight (*Mercantile Investment & General Trust Co v International Co of Mexico* [1893] 1 Ch 484n).

Therefore, calculating notice is not as simple as counting forward the statutory minimum number of days from the date on which the notice was sent out. Notices must also be sent out sufficiently early in order to account for deemed service as well as the notion of clear days (¶3704).

> EXAMPLE A private limited company proposes to hold a general meeting on the 30th of the month. It must give the shareholders at least 14 clear days' notice.
> The notices will need to be sent out to the shareholders by post on the 13th of the month, at the latest. They are then deemed to have been served on the 15th. The 15th and the 30th cannot be included in the calculation, to allow for the "clear days" rule. The shareholders are given exactly the minimum of 14 clear days' notice of the meeting on the 30th.

MEMO POINTS 1. This rules **also applies to** (s 360 CA 2006):
– giving special notice of a resolution (¶3536+);
– circulating a shareholders' statement and calculating when the expenses of doing so have to be submitted to the company (¶3663+); and
– circulating a shareholder resolution before a public company AGM and calculating when the expenses of doing so have to be submitted to the company (¶3780+).
2. For companies **incorporated on or after 1 October 2007** that adopt Table A, amendments have been made to certain provisions of Table A to correspond with the provisions of the new Companies Act which were in force by that date. reg 38 TA 1985 has been amended in different ways for private and for public companies. See ¶9915 for the details of these changes.

Shareholder agreement to shorter notice

3681

Companies are only permitted to call a meeting on shorter notice than the statutory minimum with a certain level of shareholder consent (s 307 CA 2006).

In the case of **private companies**, a majority in number of the shareholders who together hold at least 90% of the nominal value of the shares which carry the right to attend general meetings and vote can agree to hold a general meeting on shorter notice. A company's articles may require a higher percentage, up to a maximum of 95%. Table A requires the agreement of this maximum (reg 38 TA 1985).

Public companies, on the other hand must obtain the consent of a majority in number of their shareholders who together hold at least 95% in the nominal value of the shares which carry the right to attend and vote at general meetings.

The shareholders can **unanimously** consent to a meeting being called on short notice, dispensing with the need for the company to concern itself with achieving the relevant threshold (see ¶3590+). Alternatively, private companies can use the written resolution procedure rather than calling a general meeting. See ¶3785 for the short notice requirements for public company **AGMs**.

MEMO POINTS 1. For companies **without a share capital**, the requisite consent to short notice can be achieved by a majority in number of members with voting rights at the meeting (s 307 CA 2006; reg 38 TA 1985).
2. Transitional amendments to Table A applying to **private companies incorporated on or after 1 October 2007** that adopt Table A reduce the threshold for consent to short notice to the statutory 90% (reg 9 SI 2007/2541).

3682

Consents to short notice of a meeting are usually obtained **in writing**, to avoid any future dispute as to the validity of the business at the meeting on the ground of inadequate notice. They can be submitted in electronic form, like any other communication to a company, see ¶3628. If a company accepts consents in electronic format, it should retain them in a secure manner (e.g. print them out and file them in the usual way) and have in place a way of verifying the identity of the shareholders (e.g. a unique identification number for each shareholder, or electronic signatures).

3. Service of notice

3687 Notice of general meetings must be given either in hard copy, electronic form or on a website (s 308 CA 2006). However, because the former legislation required the **method** of service to be set out in the company's articles of association, many companies will be restricted as to which method they can use (s 370 CA 1985, now repealed). Therefore, companies may wish to alter their articles to give them more flexibility.

a. Who can serve notice?

3689 The **secretary** or **director** issuing notice needs the authority of the board to do so. For example, where a secretary issued notice of a meeting without the board's authority, the notice was invalid (Re Haycroft Gold Reduction and Mining Company Ltd [1900] 2 Ch 230). Nevertheless, the board can subsequently ratify a notice issued without authority (Hooper v Kerr, Stuart & Co (1900) 83 LT 729).

3690 The articles may allow **shareholders** to call a meeting directly, in which case they would give notice in the same way as the directors or follow any special requirements set out in the articles.

b. Who can receive notice?

3692 The legislation requires notice to be **sent to**:
– shareholders (s 310 CA 2006);
– shareholders' beneficiaries, personal representatives or trustees in bankruptcy, following death or bankruptcy (Sch 5 CA 2006; reg 38 TA 1985);
– directors (s 310 CA 2006; reg 44 TA 1985); and
– auditors (s 390 CA 1985).

However, this right is subject to the articles, so companies can **restrict** it if they wish. For example, Table A makes the shareholders' right to receive notice subject to any restrictions attached to the shares (reg 38 TA 1985). The terms on which shares are issued may also restrict this right, for example, preference shares usually prevent the shareholder from receiving notice of meetings, unless the meeting concerns that type of shares. The articles or terms of issue may provide that non-voting shareholders do not have the right to receive notice of meetings, as well as excluding their rights to attend and vote. If the articles or terms of a share issue do not preclude the right to receive notice, a shareholder will be entitled to do so, even though he may not be entitled to attend and/or vote at the meeting. Similarly, if a shareholder has only been suspended from being able to vote, he is still entitled to receive notice (¶3815+).

Equally, companies may wish to **extend** the right to others, for example to proxies or corporate representatives.

Comment: The **new Companies Act** will still give auditors the right to receive notice (s 502 CA 2006, due to come into force on 6 April 2008).

MEMO POINTS 1. If **shares** are **held jointly**, the notice can be sent to both/all joint shareholders or to the shareholder named first in the register (para 16 Sch 5 CA 2006). However, this is subject to the articles, so companies governed by Table A must send it to the first-named shareholder (reg 112 TA 1985).
2. **Debenture holders** secured by a floating charge which was issued **prior to 1 December 1947** are entitled to receive notice where there is a special resolution to alter the objects clause in the memorandum (s 5 CA 1985).
3. The **draft new model articles** for private companies limited by shares will not deal with giving notice of shareholder meetings. Those for public companies will relieve a company from sending notice to a shareholder if two consecutive documents are undelivered within 12 months (art 80). In order to revive the right, the shareholder will have to provide a valid address for the register

of shareholders, or give the necessary consents and information to receive the information in electronic form.

4. For companies **incorporated on or after 1 October 2007** that adopt Table A, amendments have been made to certain provisions of Table A to correspond with the provisions of the new Companies Act which were in force by that date. reg 38 TA 1985 has been amended in different ways for private and for public companies. See ¶9915 for the details of these changes.

3693 A **beneficiary**, **personal representative** or **trustee in bankruptcy** of a shareholder will only have the right to receive notice if he provides an address for service to the company (para 17 Sch 5 CA 2006). If he does not do so, the company can send notices to the shareholder's address as if his death or bankruptcy had not occurred. A company's articles can alter this rule, but Table A does not (regs 38, 116 TA 1985).

Table A also provides that a company only has to serve notice on a **shareholder living outside the UK** if he provides an address for service within the UK, or an address for notice to be served by electronic communication (reg 112 TA 1985).

> MEMO POINTS 1. If a shareholder is in **enemy-occupied territories**, he has no right to receive notice (Re The Anglo-International Bank Ltd [1943] 2 All ER 88).
> 2. The draft **new model articles** for private companies limited by shares will not contain equivalent rules about giving notice of shareholder meetings. Those for public companies will relieve a company from having to give notice to any shareholder who does not notify it of their current contact details (art 80).
> 3. For companies **incorporated on or after 1 October 2007** that adopt Table A, amendments have been made to certain provisions of Table A to correspond with the provisions of the new Companies Act which were in force by that date. reg 38 TA 1985 has been amended in different ways for private and for public companies. See ¶9915 for the details of these changes.

c. Methods of service

3695 The new Companies Act introduced more modern communication rules so that companies, shareholders and others who deal with companies can benefit from faster and more efficient methods of communication if they wish (SI 2006/3428). The **rules apply to** any situation in which a company communicates with its shareholders and other people, not just to giving notice of meetings (s 1144; Sch 5 CA 2006). Here, in the context of giving notice of shareholder meetings, it is assumed that the recipient is a shareholder although the rules apply to other recipients as well. Any differences are highlighted in the memo points.

Notice of meetings must be given to all those entitled to receive it either in hard copy, electronic form or on a website (s 308 CA 2006). Whatever method of communication is used, the same information must be provided (¶3650+).

In **other situations**, the company can communicate with shareholders and others in hard copy, electronic form, via a website or by any other method agreed with the recipient (in which case, the information will be validly supplied to the recipient if it is sent as agreed, para 15 Sch 5 CA 2006).

> MEMO POINTS **Guidance** on the communication rules has been published by the Institute of Chartered Secretaries and Administrators, ICSA. It focuses on communication between companies and shareholders and sets out a number of best practice points, which are highlighted below where relevant. The full guidance note: "ICSA Guidance on Electronic Communications with Shareholders 2007" (ref. 160207) is available on ICSA's website.

Hard copy

3696 Notices in hard copy are usually **served by** first class post, but second class post or a form of recorded delivery can also be used (see ¶3704 for when notices are deemed to have been served).

The correct **address** for service is (para 4 Sch 5 CA 2006):
– an address specified for the purpose by the recipient;
– for shareholders, their address recorded in the register of shareholders;
– for other companies (e.g. corporate shareholders), their registered office;

– for directors, their address recorded in the register of directors; and
– any other address authorised by companies legislation.

If none of these options applies, it can be sent to the recipient's last address known to the company. Alternatively, a notice can simply be handed to the recipient (para 3 Sch 5 CA 2006).

If a document is **served electronically or via a website** instead, a shareholder or debenture holder is entitled to ask for a hard copy of it (s 1145 CA 2006). This is the case even if he specifically consented to receiving the document in that other form. Companies must provide a hard copy within 21 days of the shareholder's request, and cannot charge a fee for the hard copy. Failure to comply will render the company and any officer in default liable to a fine.

> MEMO POINTS A document is in **hard copy** if it is a paper copy or similar form capable of being read with the naked eye (s 1168 CA 2006). A document is sent "**by post**" if it is posted in a pre-paid envelope (para 3 Sch 5 CA 2006).

Electronic form

3697 Service of the notice by electronic communication includes **email, fax** and **CD ROM** (s 1168 CA 2006).

To use any of these methods, each shareholder must **consent** to receive information in that form (either specifically or generally) and provide an address for service (paras 6, 7 Sch 5 CA 2006). To obtain these consents, the company can send out **invitations** to agree to receive information electronically. Invitations should (ICSA guidance note number 160207):
– be sent to all shareholders on equal terms; and
– give details of any software or hardware requirements, including instructions as to how to download free software.

The shareholders can accept this invitation and give an appropriate address for service, or reject it (actively, or by not responding) and continue to receive hard copies. A shareholder can withdraw his consent at any time and revert to receiving information in hard copy.

ICSA recommends that if notices are **delivered by email**, the email system should be set up so that a record of the emails sent can be kept as proof of service. Similarly, the fax transmission log should be kept if notices are **sent by fax**. If the company receives any failed transmission messages (using fax or email), and cannot successfully re-send the message, then a hard copy of the notice should be sent out within 48 hours (an automatic "out of office" email does not count as a failed transmission message). However, the company will not always receive a failed transmission report, so it should make it clear to shareholders that its obligation to provide the information is satisfied when it sends the information and it cannot be responsible for any failure in transmission beyond its control.

If the information is on a CD ROM or another electronic format which requires **service by post**, the company needs to send it to the same address it would send hard copies to (see ¶3696 above).

> MEMO POINTS 1. A company could also communicate with the recipient by **telephone** or **text message**. Again, proper records should be kept, for example ICSA's guidance recommends that if notices are delivered by telephone, careful records are kept of those contacted and the date and time of the call.
> 2. Unlike website communications, shareholders cannot be **deemed to agree** to receive information electronically. However, where a company has included an electronic address in the following documents, it is deemed to consent to receiving information using that address about the relevant matter:
> – a written resolution or document accompanying a written resolution (see ¶3581+);
> – notice of a meeting (see 3650+); and
> – proxy instruments or invitations (see ¶3732+, ¶3734+).
> The company must therefore ensure that it does not include an electronic address if it does not wish to receive communications in this way.
> 3. A shareholder's **address for service** of electronic communications must not be entered on the register of shareholders or any other document which is open to public inspection (ICSA guidance note number 160207).
> 4. Companies should, of course, ensure that electronic communications are **virus**-free, as far as is reasonably practicable.

Via a website

3698 Alternatively, and subject to the shareholders agreeing, notices can be posted on a website and the shareholders and other recipients notified when the information is available (ss 308, 309, 1144, Sch 5 CA 2006).

Obtaining consent

3699 In order to obtain the shareholders' consent, whether actual or deemed, the company will send out an **invitation** to agree to website communications.

Shareholders can **respond** by:
– giving their consent to receiving information via a website and providing an address to which the notification that the information is available can be sent;
– informing the company that they do not want to receive information in that way; or
– ignoring the invitation. However, if they do not respond, they may be taken as consenting (¶3700 below).

Shareholders can **change their minds** at any time and ask to receive hard copies or electronic communications instead. ICSA recommends that the website includes a facility for shareholders to do this (or explains how to do so if such a facility is not available) (ICSA guidance note number 160207).

If a shareholder **does not agree** to receiving website communications, the company must not pester him into giving his consent. In fact, if a shareholder has been invited to consent more than once in any 12-month period, he will not be deemed to consent to website communications if he does not respond (para 10 Sch 5 CA 2006). Of course, his actual consent could be obtained within that period, but ICSA recommends that where a shareholder does not wish to receive information via a website, he should not be invited to do so more than once in any 12-month period.

> MEMO POINTS As with **invitations** to receive information electronically, when asking for consent to receive website communications, ICSA recommends that the invitations:
> – are sent to all shareholders on equal terms; and
> – give details of any software or hardware requirements, including instructions as to how to download free software.

3700 Ideally, the **positive consent** of each shareholder should be obtained individually to notice being given in this way. However, website communication is likely to be mostly used by companies with a large number of shareholders, as they will benefit from the greatest cost and administrative savings, and it may be difficult for them to obtain the positive consent of every shareholder. Therefore, companies can obtain shareholders' "**deemed consent**" as well as their actual consent. A shareholder will be deemed to have consented to receiving notice via a website if (para 10 Sch 5 CA 2006):
– the company's articles provide, or the shareholders resolve, for notice to be posted in this manner (any such resolution will have to be filed at Companies House within 15 days (s 380 CA 1985; ss 29, 30 CA 2006));
– the shareholder has been asked individually to agree to receiving notice via a website; and
– he has not responded to that request for at least 28 days.

ICSA recommends that this deadline is not interpreted strictly, so that if a shareholder's request to receive information in hard copy is received just after the deadline, deemed consent cannot be inferred (ICSA guidance note number 160207). In any event, a shareholder can **revoke** his deemed consent at any time by asking to receive information in another form.

> MEMO POINTS Where a company is sending information to a **non-shareholder**, it can only do so via a website if that person consents. Non-shareholders' consent cannot be obtained to receiving information via a website using the "deemed" method, with the exception of **debenture holders** to whom a similar procedure applies (para 11 Sch 5 CA 2006).

Making the information available

3701 Shareholders must be **notified** that the notice is available on the website. This notification must include (para 13 Sch 5 CA 2006):
- the fact that the information is available, or the date from which it will be available;
- the address of the website;
- the location of the information on the website; and
- how the document can be accessed.

ICSA recommends that any email notifications include a link to the notice and to any online voting facility, to make it as easy as possible for shareholders to access the information (ICSA guidance note number 160207).

It should be sent to the address for each recipient to which the company sends other communications, in electronic or hard copy form as appropriate. Therefore, particularly where a company is relying on a shareholder's deemed consent, it may have to send the notification in hard copy to the shareholder's postal address. Notice is taken to have been given on the date on which the shareholders were notified that it was available, or on the date on which it was posted on the website, if later.

The notice itself has to be in a **form** that is legible by the naked eye, and capable of being copied (e.g. printed out) (para 12 Sch 5 CA 2006). The notice must be **available for** the whole notice period (unless the website is unavailable for some of the period due to technical difficulties which were out of the company's control) (para 14 Sch 5 CA 2006).

> MEMO POINTS In the case of information being posted on a website to which **no notice period applies**, it must be available for at least 28 days.

Consequences of not serving notice properly

3703 **Failure** to serve notice correctly will invalidate the meeting and the business decided there (*Smyth v Darley* (1849) 2 HL Cas 789). However, companies are allowed some leeway in that if notice is **accidentally** not given to one or more persons entitled to receive it, decisions at the meeting will still be valid (s 313 CA 2006, which applies where notice of the meeting was given on or after 1 October 2007 (para 28 Sch 3 SI 2007/2194)). A company's articles can exclude this allowance, but Table A actually includes a similar provision (reg 39 TA 1985). A company can only rely on this exception if it does not know that the notice was not served (i.e. the company does not have the opportunity to rectify the situation). For example, where a notice was sent recorded delivery, but a failed delivery notice had been sent to the company, it could not rely on the exception (which was the one included in Table A) to excuse non-service, as it knew that the notice had not been delivered in the first place (*Re Thundercrest Ltd* [1995] 1 BCLC 117).

In many cases, it is practical for companies to rely on a **deemed service** provision in its articles (see ¶3704 below). It saves the company the expense of using recorded deliveries, or the time of chasing up fax or email receipts. On the other hand, if the company wishes to ensure a good or full attendance at the meeting, it would be sensible to use a form of communication which enables the company to be sure that all shareholders have received the notice.

d. When notice is served

3704 Notice is **deemed to have been served** 48 hours after it has been posted or sent electronically (not including non-working days) (s 1147 CA 2006). In the case of notices published on a website, service is deemed to have occurred when the information is made available on the website, or when the recipient received notice that the information was available, if later (para 13 Sch 5 CA 2006).

Alternative deemed service times can be agreed, for example companies' own articles often amend the period to 24 hours after posting or sending. ICSA recommends that where a company sends information by email, it amends its articles so the information is deemed to have been served on the day it was sent (ICSA guidance note number 160207). If it is unreasonable to expect that delivery actually occurred within the stated period, the company cannot rely on its deemed delivery provision. For example, in the case of a postal strike (*Bradman v Trinity Estates plc* [1989] BCLC 757), or where the notices are sent by second class post (in which case, the minimum deemed delivery period is 48 hours). It is good practice for companies to keep a record of when notices are "sent", by whatever method, to ensure that the notice period is calculated correctly (¶3675+).

C. Holding a general meeting

The conduct of the proceedings at a shareholder meeting is largely **governed by** the articles, although the basic requirements are set out in legislation. Attendance is a vital issue. Companies need to ensure that all shareholders entitled to attend are given the opportunity to do so to enable them to exercise their rights. Particular attention must be paid to the quorum, as this affects the meeting's validity. The chairman plays a key role, as his main responsibility is to oversee and direct the meeting. He is dealt with first of all, as this is the first matter addressed at any meeting. Attendance is then discussed, followed by the principles and procedures relating to adjournment.

3711

1. Chairman

It is the chairman's **role** to direct the proceedings at the meeting. He has authority to decide all questions arising at meetings in the first instance, although this may be challenged subsequently by a shareholder (*Henderson v Bank of Australasia* (1890) 45 Ch D 330). Generally, the chairman has to:

a. ensure that the business is dealt with efficiently;
b. preserve order at the meeting;
c. adjourn the meeting if order cannot be maintained (see ¶3760+ for the chairman's duties regarding adjournment);
d. resolve any questions as to a shareholder's entitlement to vote (reg 58 TA 1985; this is also be included in the draft new model articles, private companies limited by shares: art 43; public companies: art 34);
e. act reasonably and in good faith (e.g. only adjourn the meeting as long as necessary, *John v Rees* [1969] 2 All ER 274);
f. ascertain the true sense of the meeting (e.g. by requiring a poll to be taken if it appears that the voting would go differently, *The Second Consolidated Trust Ltd v Ceylon Amalgamated Tea & Rubber Estates Ltd* [1943] 2 All ER 567; and see ¶3843);
g. ensure that the discussions on each matter remain reasonable, and end each discussion once it has been debated fairly, giving the shareholders an opportunity to be heard; and
h. dissolve the meeting when all business has been dealt with.

3716

If a **resolution** to be considered by the meeting has been **proposed by the directors**, the chairman will usually introduce it to the meeting. If a resolution has been put forward **by the shareholders**, the chairman should appoint an appropriate shareholder to propose it to the meeting. Although it is common for each resolution to be proposed and seconded, this is not a requirement.

3717

Appointment

Unless the articles of the company provide otherwise, any shareholder at the meeting can be appointed as chairman by ordinary resolution (s 319 CA 2006). This includes proxy-holders (s 328 CA 2006). The articles will often specify **who can be chairman** of the meeting. For example, Table A provides that the chairman of the board, or any other director nominated by the board in the absence of a board chairman, will be the chairman of a general meeting

3719

(reg 42 TA 1985). If he is not present or willing to act 15 minutes from the time the meeting was due to begin, the directors present should elect another director to be chairman. If there is only one director present, he will be the chairman. If there is no director willing to act as chairman, or no director present at the meeting, then the shareholders present and entitled to vote should elect one of their number to be chairman (reg 43 TA 1985).

If there is a vote among the shareholders to elect a chairman, and an **objection** arises as to the qualification of a shareholder to vote which is resolved by a person who has appointed himself as chairman (rather than being appointed by the meeting), that decision may be open to challenge subsequently in the courts (*Re Bradford Investments plc* [1991] BCLC 224; ¶3815+).

> MEMO POINTS   The draft **new model articles** will provide that the board chairman will chair general meetings, unless he does not attend within 10 minutes from the designated start time of the meeting, in which case any remaining directors (or the shareholders, if there are no directors present) must appoint a new chairman (private companies limited by shares: art 39; public companies: art 30).

2. Attendance

3724 Subject to any restrictions in the articles and/or the terms of the shares, **shareholders** can attend, speak and vote at a meeting. This applies to corporate representatives as well as proxies, although in the case of proxies the right to speak and vote is sometimes restricted.

Shareholders are entitled to **speak** at meetings. Minority shareholders are as entitled to speak as the others, but once they have had a fair opportunity to be heard, the chairman can close the discussion and put the matter to a vote with the sanction of the meeting (*Wall v London & Northern Assets Corpn* [1898] 2 Ch 469).

Other **non-voting parties** who can attend are directors (reg 44 TA 1985) and auditors (in certain circumstances: ¶4299, ¶4342, ¶4345). This gives shareholders the opportunity to put questions to the directors and auditors regarding the business in hand, although the directors do not have to respond to questions where it would not be in the company's best interests to do so.

It usually falls to the company secretary to keep a **record** of the attendees at the meeting. This will be recorded in the minutes and ensures that the correct shareholders are counted in the quorum.

> MEMO POINTS   1. Case law has held that a class of shareholders with **no voting rights** cannot attend general meetings unless the articles allow (*Re Mackenzie & Co Ltd* [1916-17] All ER 1018).
> 2. The draft **new model articles** will also allow directors to participate in shareholder meetings, as well as other people permitted by the chairman to do so (private companies limited by shares: art 40; public companies: art 31).

3725 As with the entitlement to receive notice, the articles or the terms of a share issue can **restrict or preclude** certain shareholders or classes of shareholder from being able to attend meetings. Holders of non-voting shares, for example, may commonly be prevented from attending meetings. A shareholder whose voting rights have been suspended may also be prevented from attending (¶3815+).

a. Proxies

3727 A proxy is a person **appointed by** a shareholder to attend, speak and vote at the meeting on his behalf. Shareholders, including corporate shareholders, have a statutory right to appoint a proxy (s 324 CA 2006; *Re Indian Zoedone Co* (1884) 26 Ch D 70).

The rights described below are those set out in the legislation, but a company's articles may confer more extensive rights on shareholders and proxies (s 331 CA 2006). The appointing shareholder empower the proxy to exercise any or all of his rights, so can restrict the proxy's rights as appropriate, for example by only appointing him to vote on a particular resolution.

Comment: The proxy is the **person** appointed; the **document** appointing the proxy is referred to as the instrument, appointment or form (the draft new model articles will refer to the document as a "proxy notice"). This terminology is different from proxies in an insolvency situation (¶8349+)

> MEMO POINTS The articles could also permit a shareholder who lives outside the UK or who is abroad for a period of time to appoint an **attorney** to attend one particular meeting or all meetings and vote in his place.

The articles of a company will usually contain detailed provisions regarding proxies. Subject to the articles, anybody **can be a proxy**. He may, but does not have to, be a shareholder or a director.

3729

A shareholder can appoint **more than one proxy** (s 324 CA 2006; Table A includes a similar provision: reg 59 TA 1985). Theoretically, he could appoint one for each share he holds although this would be highly unusual. The ability to appoint more than one proxy may, however, be useful where a shareholder holds shares on behalf of different groups, for example.

> MEMO POINTS If a company's share capital is divided into **stock**, a shareholder can appoint a proxy for each bundle of £10 (or multiple of £10) worth of stock held by him (s 324 CA 2006).

Rights of proxies

The legislation gives proxies the right to **attend**, count in the quorum and **speak** at meetings, as well as to **vote** (by whatever method) (ss 318, 324 CA 2006). The shareholder appointing the proxy can qualify the rights to attend, speak and vote as he sees fit. For example, he may not want to give the proxy the right to speak at the meeting, or he may want to appoint a proxy to vote only on a specific resolution. A company's articles may well set out additional rights.

3730

> MEMO POINTS The draft **new model articles** will allow a shareholder to retain his right to attend, speak and vote even when he has appointed a proxy (private companies limited by shares: art 46; public companies: art 38).

A proxy is his appointor's agent and so he **owes a duty** to act in a way to give effect to his appointor's wishes (*Cousins v International Brick Co Ltd* [1931] 2 Ch 90). This allows the proxy to vote even where amendments have been made to a resolution at the meeting. Without this leeway, proxies would be unable to follow their instructions to vote for or against a resolution once it has been amended because it would be different to the one contained in the notice of the meeting given to the shareholder, which formed the basis of his instructions.

3731

Proxy statements in notices of meetings

Every **notice** of a meeting must contain a statement that a shareholder entitled to attend and vote at the meeting may appoint a proxy to do so in his place (s 325 CA 2006). As well as explaining the shareholder's statutory rights, the notice must set out any more extensive rights granted by the articles to appoint more than one proxy (e.g. to appoint more than one proxy per share). **Failure** to comply with this requirement renders any officers in default liable to a fine (¶9935).

3732

> MEMO POINTS If the company includes an email or other **electronic address** in its proxy statement, it will be deemed to have consented to receive any document or information relating to the meeting at that address (s 333 CA 2006). For the methods by which shareholders and others can communicate with a company generally, see ¶3628.

The company may send out **invitations** to appoint a particular person or persons as proxy (s 326 CA 2006). This will commonly be a director who will be present at the meeting. If such invitations are sent out, they must be sent **to all** of the shareholders. If invitations are only sent **to some** of the shareholders, every officer in default is liable to a fine (¶9935).

3733

Alternatively, a company can provide a shareholder with an appointment form naming a proxy, or a list of those willing to act as proxy, **on request**, without having to distribute it to all of the shareholders, as long as the same form or list is distributed to all shareholders entitled to vote if they ask for it.

> MEMO POINTS If the company includes an email or other **electronic address** in a proxy invitation, it will be deemed to have consented to receive any document or information relating to the meeting at that address (s 333 CA 2006). For the methods by which shareholders and others can communicate with a company generally, see ¶3628.

Proxy appointment forms

3734 Private and unlisted public companies are not obliged by statute to send out proxy appointment forms (unlike the proxy statements, which are compulsory), although it may be in the company's interests to do so because it increases the likelihood of holding a quorate meeting by making it as easy as possible for shareholders to appoint proxies (¶3746+). A **sample** proxy appointment form is contained in Table A (reg 60 TA 1985). Since directors are permitted to promote policies which are in the company's best interests, they can recover from the company the cost of sending out proxy appointment forms together with pre-paid envelopes for their return in order to increase the likelihood of proxies being appointed.

The form will usually provide for **two-way voting** (i.e. allowing the appointing shareholder to instruct the proxy to vote for or against the resolution(s)). The form should also enable the appointor to add any other instructions to his proxy, e.g. to abstain on a particular matter, to ask a certain question, or to specify how the proxy should vote if a resolution is altered. If the appointment is in electronic form, there should be a space or a text box for the appointor to add this information.

There may already be a **named proxy** on the form (subject to the rules regarding proxy invitations, above), but the appointing shareholder still has the right to nominate his own proxy (reg 61 TA 1985).

> MEMO POINTS 1. Where a company **gives notice** of the general meeting to shareholders **via a website** but has to notify certain shareholders in hard copy that the material is available on the website, ICSA recommends that personalised proxy appointment forms are included with the notification (ICSA guidance note number 160207; see ¶3698+ for how to give notice in this way).
> 2. The draft **new model articles** will not set out sample forms. They will, however, stipulate the contents of the notice required to appoint a proxy (called a "proxy notice" in these articles) and will allow companies to draw up specific forms for the purpose (private companies limited by shares: art 45; public companies: art 37). Unless the shareholder states otherwise in the proxy notice, it will be assumed that the proxy has a discretion as to how to vote.
> 3. Transitional amendments to Table A which apply to **companies incorporated on or after 1 October 2007** that adopt Table A remove references in the sample proxy form to annual and extraordinary meetings for private companies (replacing them with references to "general meetings"), and to extraordinary meetings for public companies (regs 11, 12, 21, 22 SI 2007/2541).

3735 Proxy appointments are usually **in writing**. They can be sent to a company in hard copy, electronic form or any other form agreed between the shareholder and the company (e.g. verbally). See ¶3628 for how shareholders may communicate with their companies.

3736 Table A permits the proxy appointment to be **executed** on behalf of the shareholder as well as by the shareholder himself (reg 60 TA 1985). If the appointment is made in writing or by electronic communication, Table A stipulates that the authority (e.g. power of attorney) under which the appointment was executed on behalf of the shareholder, or a copy of it, must be sent to the company with the proxy appointment (reg 62 TA 1985).

If the articles provide for proxy appointments to be made by means other than in writing (for example, by telephone), the articles should specify when and how the authority under which the appointment is executed should be lodged with the company for inspection.

> MEMO POINTS 1. The draft **new model articles** will not allow a proxy appointment to be executed on a shareholder's behalf. Instead, they specifically require that it is signed by or on behalf of the appointing shareholder, or authenticated in another manner acceptable to the directors (private companies limited by shares: art 45; public companies: art 37).
> 2. Transitional amendments to Table A which apply to **companies incorporated on or after 1 October 2007** that adopt Table A remove references in the sample proxy forms (regs 60, 61 TA 1985) to annual and extraordinary meetings for private companies (replacing them with references to "general meetings"), and to extraordinary meetings for public companies (regs 11, 12, 21, 22 SI 2007/2541).

3737 If the proxy appointment form **does not comply** with any mandatory requirements, the appointment is invalid and the proxy cannot be permitted by the chairman to vote. For example, if the articles require the appointment to be witnessed and it has not been, it will be invalid (*Harben v Phillips* (1883) 23 Ch D 14). On the other hand, a proxy form is not invalidated simply because it contains a misprint or mistake, such as spelling errors (*Oliver v Dalgleish* [1963] 3 All ER 330). The forms are not subject to stamp duty.

Delivery of proxy forms

The articles usually state **when** proxy appointments have to be delivered to, or lodged with, the company. However, the legislation sets out the earliest deadlines allowed, and if the articles require proxy appointments to be delivered any sooner, those provisions will be void. These minimum periods are (s 327 CA 2006):
– for proxies appointed to attend, speak and/or vote at a meeting or adjourned meeting: not more than 48 hours before the meeting; and
– for proxies appointed to vote on a poll which is taken more than 48 hours after it was demanded: not more than 24 hours before the poll is taken.

In calculating these periods, non-working days are not to be counted.

Table A mirrors these provisions, also requiring appointments for a poll not taken straight away but taken within 48 hours of the demand to be delivered at the meeting at which the poll is demanded (reg 62 TA 1985).

3738

MEMO POINTS 1. Where a company **gives notice** of the general meeting to shareholders **via a website**, ICSA recommends that the deadlines for delivering proxy appointments to the company are made clear in any notification that general meeting material is available on the website (ICSA guidance note number 160207; see ¶3698+ for giving notice in this way).
2. The **new Companies Act** will also stipulate that the articles cannot require forms appointing proxies to vote on a poll taken within 48 hours of the demand for a poll to be submitted before the poll is demanded (s 327(2)(c) CA 2006). This subsection was not brought into force with the rest of the section on 1 October 2007 and the implementation date is yet to be announced at the time of writing (art 2 SI 2007/2194). However, companies governed by Table A will have to comply with this limit anyway. The draft **new model articles** for public companies will mirror these deadlines (art 38), but those for private companies limited by shares will not include any deadlines.

If the **articles do not provide** for proxy appointments to be lodged before a meeting or poll, the proxy form does not have to be sent to the company prior to the meeting, and will be effective provided it is lodged at the meeting before the proxy casts a vote (*Re Philip Alexander Securities & Futures Ltd (in administration)* [1999] 1 BCLC 124).

3739

Revocation of appointments

Subject to the terms of any agreement between the appointing shareholder and the proxy, a proxy appointment can be revoked by the shareholder at any **time** before the meeting. **Notice** of termination of the appointment must be received by the company before the commencement of the meeting if it is to prevent him from counting in the quorum, acting as chairman or demanding a poll (s 330 CA 2006). If the notice of termination is to prevent his vote from counting, it must be received by the company before the meeting, adjourned meeting or poll (in the case of a poll taken more than 48 hours after it was demanded). As with the delivery of proxy appointment forms, earlier deadlines can be set, up to a maximum of 48 hours before the meeting or adjourned meeting, or up to 24 hours before a poll held more than 48 hours after it was demanded. These time periods cannot include non-working days.

3741

Table A provides that a proxy appointment can be terminated at any time before the meeting (or before the time set for the poll) by lodging notice of the revocation at the registered office (or other place named by the articles for the lodgement of proxy appointments) (reg 63 TA 1985).

Despite any provisions stipulating that the revocation must be given before the meeting, the shareholder retains the right to attend. Where the proxy also attends the meeting in person and **no notice** of revocation has been submitted to the company, the shareholder will still be entitled to vote in his own right. If both the shareholder and proxy vote, only the vote cast first will be counted.

> **MEMO POINTS** The **new Companies Act** will also prevent the articles from settling a deadline earlier than when the poll is demanded for a vote taken on a poll within 48 hours (s 330(6)(c) CA 2006; art 2 SI 2007/2194). This subsection was not brought into force with the rest of the section on 1 October 2007.

b. Corporate representatives

3743 If a corporation holds shares or voting rights in a company, it can be represented at a meeting by a person or persons **authorised by** the board of the corporation to attend and vote on its behalf (s 323 CA 2006), or by another governing body (for example, a liquidator; *Hillman v Crystal Bowl Amusements Ltd* [1973] 1 All ER 379).

A corporate representative can exercise all of the **powers** the corporate shareholder could exercise if it were a natural person, including attending, speaking and voting at meetings. Corporate representatives have the same right to appoint proxies to attend in their place as shareholders do.

A corporate shareholder can **appoint more than one** representative if it wishes. Each representative will be entitled to exercise all of the corporate shareholder's powers. However, to avoid confusion, if they exercise the same power differently, the power is treated as not having been exercised. Therefore, it is important that the corporate shareholder's board briefs the representatives properly as to how to exercised the corporate shareholder's powers on its behalf.

> **EXAMPLE** X Ltd holds shares in K Ltd. It appoints Mr A and Mr B as its corporate representatives. When K Ltd holds a general meeting, Mr A and Mr B are both entitled to attend, speak and vote at the meeting. On the first resolution, which is decided on a show of hands, Mr A and Mr B both vote in favour. X Ltd is treated as having cast its vote in favour of the resolution. On the second resolution, also taken on a show of hands, Mr A votes for and Mr B against it. X Ltd is treated as not having voted because its representatives exercised X Ltd's powers differently.

3744 The articles will usually set out the **procedure** for appointing corporate representatives and revoking their appointments. A director, secretary or other authorised representative of the company can usually require a corporate representative to provide **evidence** of his authority to attend the meeting on behalf of the corporate shareholder, for example a certified copy of the board resolution appointing him. Table A provides that the appointment of a corporate representative can be **revoked** at any time before the meeting or poll by lodging notice of the revocation at the registered office of the company (or other place stated in the articles) (reg 63 TA 1985).

c. Minimum attendance

3746 "**Quorum**" is the term used to refer to the minimum number of shareholders required at the meeting in order for it to proceed validly to business.

Note that a quorum is required to be **present when** the meeting considers each resolution. Shareholders' ability to count in the quorum may change during the meeting, for example, where a resolution on which some shareholders are precluded from voting is considered and the articles prevent a shareholder who cannot vote from counting in the quorum as well. Therefore, the chairman must check that a quorum is present for each resolution.

Forming a quorum

3747 Unless the articles of the company provide otherwise, two "qualifying persons" **comprise** a quorum for the meeting (s 318 CA 2006). A "qualifying person" is:
– an individual shareholder;
– a corporate representative (if a corporate shareholder has appointed more than one representative, only one of its representatives will count); or
– a proxy appointed by a shareholder for that meeting (if a shareholder has appointed more than one proxy, only one of his proxies will count).

This is a change from the position under the Companies Act 1985, which did not allow proxies to count in the quorum. For this reason, a company's articles usually specify that shareholders present in person or by proxy to count in the quorum, and Table A specifically enables both proxies and corporate representatives to count (reg 40 TA 1985).

The legislation does not stipulate that the shareholders comprising the quorum have to be **able to vote**, whereas Table A does. In practice, there would be little point in having only shareholders who could not vote present at a meeting, but, subject to the company's articles, a meeting could still usefully take place with two shareholders forming a quorum where only one of them could vote. If, like Table A, the articles stipulate that only shareholders entitled to vote can count in the quorum, the chairman should ensure that the attendees are checked against the register of shareholders so that those who cannot vote are not counted in the quorum (reg 40 TA 1985).

> MEMO POINTS 1. In the case of companies with a **sole shareholder**, one qualifying person can comprise a quorum. The quorum at a **class meeting** is usually specified in the articles or the terms attached to the class of shares.
> 2. Companies incorporated before 22 December 1980 and which are still governed by **Table A 1948**, have a quorum requirement of three shareholders present in person, and if a quorum is still not present half an hour from the time the meeting was due to start, the number of shareholders present will comprise a quorum (reg 54 TA 1948).
> 3. Like the legislation, **Table A** enables two persons to form the quorum. Transitional amendments which apply to **private companies incorporated on or after 1 October 2007** only disapply this quorum in the case of companies with a single shareholder (reg 10 SI 2007/2541).
> 4. The draft **new model articles** do not require an alternative quorum to that set out in the legislation (private companies limited by shares: art 38; public companies: art 29).

3748 Directors, auditors and any other non-shareholder attendees **do not count** in the quorum. If other non-shareholders attend a meeting of the company, their presence does not invalidate the proceedings, provided they do not take part (Re Quinn & National Catholic Benefit and Thrift Society's Arbitration [1921] 2 Ch 318). If the articles of a company require personal attendance at meetings by shareholders, an attorney attending in person is not sufficient (M Harris Ltd, Petitioners 1956 SC 207). Although, if a shareholder holds shares in his own right and on behalf of someone else as trustee, he counts as two shareholders for the quorum because he holds the shares in two capacities (Neil McLeod & Sons Ltd, Petitioners 1967 SC 16).

Counting a quorum

3749 Shareholders may still be counted in the quorum even if they are **not all in the same room**, provided that they can participate in the meeting, for example via audio-visual links. In a case where the audio-visual links to two overflow rooms did not work, and the meeting was conducted by passing messages between the main room and the overflow rooms, the court held that this did not successfully allow all shareholders present to participate (Byng v London Life Association [1989] 1 All ER 560). The court left open the question as to whether a valid meeting would be convened if every shareholder was in a separate place linked together by audio-visual connections, which could be a possibility at meetings of small companies.

3750 Once the meeting has begun, **shareholders can leave** without affecting the proceedings, provided that the number of shareholders left does not fall below the quorum (Re Hartley Baird Ltd [1954] 3 All ER 695). If the meeting is quorate at the beginning, but during the course of the meeting the number of shareholders **falls below the quorum** then the meeting should be adjourned (reg 41 TA 1985).

Lack of quorum

3752 If half an hour after the time the meeting was due to start a quorum is still **not present**, Table A provides that the meeting will be adjourned to the same time and place the following week, or to another time and place decided upon by the directors (reg 41 TA 1985). Although Table A does not state that the directors can determine the day, it is suggested that they may do so as this is consistent with the power to decide upon a different time and place.

The articles of a company may provide that if a quorum is still not present after a certain time, then the shareholders who are present will be a quorum.

> MEMO POINTS The draft **new model articles** contain an equivalent provision (private companies limited by shares: art 41; public companies: art 32).

3753 If a meeting is **inquorate**, the resolutions carried at the meeting will be invalid.

d. Comparison of attendees' rights

3755

Right/action	Shareholders[1]	Proxies	Corporate representatives	¶¶
Receive notice of meeting	✓	✗	✗	¶3692+
Attend meeting	✓ Subject to restrictions	✓ Subject to same restrictions as appointor – i.e. if appointor cannot attend, neither can his proxy – and any other restrictions in appointment form	✓ Subject to same restrictions as shareholder he represents	¶3724+
Count in quorum	✓ Articles may restrict, e.g. by stating shareholder has to have right to vote	✓ Subject to same restrictions as appointor he represents	✓ Subject to same restrictions as shareholder he represents	¶3746+
Speak at meeting	✓	✓ Subject to any restrictions in appointment form	✓	¶3724+
Vote:	Subject to voting restrictions	Subject to same restrictions as appointor, and any in appointment form	Subject to same restrictions as shareholder he represents	¶3810+
1. On a show of hands	1. ✓	1. ✓	1. ✓	
2. On poll	2. ✓	2. ✓	2. ✓	
Freedom of vote	✓ Complete freedom as to how to exercise vote, **unless** he is a nominee/trustee/bankrupt/transferor where the transfer is not yet registered, who must vote as instructed or in beneficial holder's best interests	✗ Must vote as instructed	✗ Must vote in accordance with authority	¶3824+
Demand a poll	✓ If qualifies, i.e. – 2 shareholders with the right to vote; or – 1 shareholder holding 10% of the paid up share capital and entitled to vote	✓ If appointor would qualify	✓ If shareholder he represents would qualify	¶3842+

Right/action	Shareholders[1]	Proxies	Corporate representatives	¶¶
Appoint a representative to attend	✓ Proxy – can appoint more than one; corporate representative – if corporate shareholder (can appoint more than one)	✗	✓ Corporate representative can appoint proxy to attend in his place	¶3727+ ¶3743+
Proof of entitlements	Name entered on register of shareholders	Proxy appointment form lodged with company	Evidence (e.g. copy board resolution of corporate shareholder he represents) submitted to company	¶3915+ ¶3727+ ¶3743+
Revocation of appointment	n/a But rights can be suspended or restricted	✓ By notice to company before meeting or poll	✓ By notice to company before meeting or poll	¶3727+ ¶3743+

Note:
1. "Shareholders" **includes**: beneficiaries on death or bankruptcy; authorised representatives such as trustees, nominees, receivers; and transferors of shares where transfer has not yet been registered.

3. Adjournments

3760 If a meeting is adjourned, it is initially convened at the time, date and place specified in the notice, but then all or part of the meeting is reconvened and held at another date, time and/or place. This may be **necessary if**, for instance, the meeting is or becomes inquorate, or it is disrupted, or a shareholder requires an adjournment to consider a resolution. If valid notice of a meeting has been given, it cannot then be cancelled or postponed if, for example, it becomes apparent that the timing is inconvenient; the meeting must be convened as per the notice and then adjourned (*Smith v Paringa Mines Ltd* [1906] 2 Ch 193).

3761 An adjourned meeting is a continuation of the original meeting; it is not a new meeting with new business. Therefore, when the meeting is **reconvened**, the articles usually provide that only business which was due to take place at the original meeting may be considered. **Resolutions passed** at an adjourned meeting (i.e. when it reconvenes) are treated as being passed on the date of the reconvened meeting, not the date of the original meeting (s 332 CA 2006).

3762 The articles of association usually provide for adjournments of meetings. The **chairman** may adjourn a meeting with the consent, or at the direction, of the shareholders (reg 45 TA 1985). If the articles give the chairman a discretion to decide whether or not to adjourn the meeting, he must exercise the power in good faith, and may refuse to adjourn the meeting even if the shareholders demand an adjournment (*Salisbury Gold Mining Co v Hathorn* [1897] AC 268). If the articles of the company do not give the chairman a specific power to adjourn the meeting, it can be adjourned on an **ordinary resolution** (*National Dwellings Society v Sykes* [1894] 3 Ch 159).

> MEMO POINTS The draft **new model articles** will allow a meeting to be adjourned if the meeting consents or if it directs the chairman to adjourn by way of ordinary resolution, or if it appears to the chairman that it is necessary to do so to ensure the participants' safety or the meeting's proper conduct (private companies limited by shares: art 41; public companies: art 32).

3763 In addition to any power given to the chairman in the articles to adjourn the meeting, if the provisions of the articles prove to be impossible to follow (such as there being no quorum so the meeting cannot pass a valid ordinary resolution) then the chairman has a **residual common law power** to adjourn a meeting, regardless of whether the articles give him a discretion to do so.

The chairman is **entitled to exercise** this common law power if it is necessary to give all shareholders entitled to vote a reasonable opportunity to do so. The chairman can only take this decision if it is impossible for him to ascertain the wishes of the meeting. He must:
– exercise this power in good faith;
– only consider reasonable factors in coming to his decision; and
– not come to a decision which no reasonable chairman could have made.
Otherwise his decision is invalid.

> EXAMPLE The venue booked for a general meeting of LLA was too small for the meeting. The chairman adjourned the meeting to a larger venue the same afternoon, seeing that the proceedings were impracticable. The court held that the chairman had not considered two important factors in coming to his decision: the adjournment would prejudice those who could not attend in the afternoon because it would be too late for them to appoint proxies; and it would have been feasible to adjourn the meeting to a later date, or to dissolve it and call another at a later date, because the contract to be considered did not have to be finalised for some months. This would have enabled members to attend or to appoint proxies to attend the later meeting. Therefore, the resolution passed at the reconvened meeting was invalid (*Byng v London Life Association* [1989] 1 All ER 560).
> The company was limited by guarantee, hence the references here to members rather than shareholders. This does not affect the case's relevance to shareholders.

The reconvened meeting

3764 **Notice** of a meeting to be reconvened following an adjournment does not need to be given if the meeting takes place fewer than 14 days after the original meeting. Otherwise, 7 clear days' notice needs to be given, stating the time and place of the reconvened meeting (reg 45 TA 1985).

Notice of the adjourned meeting can be **sent** in the same way as notice of the original meeting (¶3695+).

> MEMO POINTS The new **draft model articles** will include equivalent rules about giving notice of reconvened meetings (private companies limited by shares: art 41; public companies: art 32).

D. Specific types of meeting

3772 Having examined the procedures and issues applicable to meetings in the context of general meetings, the specific requirements and procedures which apply to public company **AGMs** and **class meetings** are considered here.

1. Public company Annual General Meetings (AGMs)

3777 An AGM is distinct from other types of shareholder meeting in that there is a **statutory obligation** on public companies to hold an AGM each year, and **notice** to the shareholders must clearly state that the meeting is an AGM (ss 336, 337 CA 2006). Otherwise, there is no practical difference between an AGM and a general meeting: the same business can be considered and the same shareholders can attend.

3778 **Private companies** are no longer required to hold AGMs by statute. This change has been introduced because it was considered an unnecessary administrative and economic burden on private companies. In any event, many private companies opted out of holding AGMs by passing an elective resolution to that effect. However, some private companies may still wish to hold AGMs because they provide a structure to the company year and enable shareholders to feel involved in the running of the company, as well as providing a useful opportunity to deal with housekeeping and other matters together. Private companies can still hold general meetings on an annual basis if they wish (in which case, they should set out the relevant procedure in the articles), but they will not be statutory AGMs. Therefore, the company will be able to deal with whatever matters it wishes at these meetings and the officers will not commit an offence if they fail to hold one. If a private company's memorandum or articles require it to hold AGMs, it must continue to do so (para 32 Sch 3 SI 2007/2194).

> MEMO POINTS 1. These provisions of the new Companies Act have been in force since 1 October 2007. However, there are two situations in which a **private company must hold an AGM**:
> – if the company had opted out of holding AGMs, but the shareholders requisitioned one before 1 October 2007, an AGM must still be held in accordance with CA 1985 (unless the company would not have to do so under CA 1985 because the requisition does not comply with the requirements) (para 34 Sch 3 SI 2007/2194); and
> – if a request was made to a private company to circulate a shareholders' statement under CA 1985 and the company has not complied with it when it should have done, it is still under an obligation to hold an AGM under CA 1985, presumably to ensure that the shareholders have an opportunity to raise their point at a meeting (para 29 Sch 3 SI 2007/2194). See ¶3663+ for shareholders' statements.
> 2. Transitional amendments to Table A applying to **private companies incorporated on or after 1 October 2007** that adopt Table A mean that it does not deal with AGMs for private companies (reg 9 SI 2007/2541).

Table A and the legislation do not prescribe what sort of **business** has to be considered at an AGM, although individual companies' articles may well do so. Shareholders can submit resolutions to the company to be considered at an AGM. The usual items considered at AGMs are those that arise on a yearly basis, such as:
– the re-appointment of the directors, where this is required by the articles (¶2274, ¶2927+);
– the re-appointment of auditors (¶4336+);
– laying the accounts before the shareholders (¶4273+);
– proposing a dividend for the approval of the shareholders (¶1663);
– the renewal of the directors' authority to allot shares (¶925+); and
– the waiver of shareholders' pre-emption rights on allotment (¶958+).

3779

> MEMO POINTS Companies incorporated before 1 July 1985 and still operating under **Table A 1948** will divide its business at meetings into "ordinary" and "special" business. The ordinary business will usually be addressed in AGMs. See ¶3652/mp for a discussion of ordinary and special business.

a. Shareholder resolutions at an AGM

Either:
– a shareholder or shareholders holding at least 5% of the total voting rights of all the shareholders with the right to vote at the next AGM; or
– at least 100 shareholders holding shares to the average value per shareholder of at least £100,
can **requisition** a public company to give notice of any resolution which may properly be moved at the AGM (s 338 CA 2006). This works in tandem with the right to circulate a statement in relation to a matter to be considered at any meeting, including an AGM (¶3663+).

3780

The resolution can only be sent to the company in hard copy or electronic form (and not in another form agreed with the company, unlike many other documents). Sending documents to a company is discussed at ¶3628 in the context of shareholders requisitioning a general meeting.

> MEMO POINTS If a shareholder's qualification is **challenged** because the currency in which the shares are issued is not sterling, the court will determine the appropriate date and rate of interest to judge whether or not the requisitionists have adequate standing (*Re Scandinavian Bank Group plc* [1987] 2 All ER 70).

The company is only **bound to circulate** a shareholder resolution if a copy signed by all of the requisitionists is received by the company either (s 338 CA 2006):
– at least 6 weeks (calculated in clear days, s 360 CA 2006) before the AGM; or
– by the time notice of the meeting has been given, if notice is given later than 6 weeks before the meeting.

3781

The **expense** of circulating such resolutions is to be met by the requisitioning shareholders, unless (s 340 CA 2006):
– their request is made before the end of the financial year preceding the AGM; or
– the company resolves that the requisitionists should not have to meet the expenses.

If the requisitionists do have to pay for the resolution to be circulated, they must provide a sum reasonably sufficient to cover the cost with the requisition. If they do not, the company is not bound to circulate it.

The resolution should be **served** on the shareholders entitled to receive notice of the meeting in hard copy, electronic form, via a website or using another agreed method (see ¶3695+ for the rules on companies sending information to shareholders and others). Any other shareholders are entitled to receive notice of the general effect of the resolution. These notices are to be served at the same time as the notice of the meeting or, if that is not possible, as soon as practicable after that.

Failure to circulate a resolution renders every officer of the company who is in default liable to a fine (s 339 CA 2006; ¶9935).

b. Obligation to hold AGMs

3783 As a transitional measure, existing public companies must calculate the timing of their **first AGM after 1 October 2007** under the old rules (s 366 CA 1985; para 35 Sch 3 SI 2007/2194):
– a public company incorporated before 1 October 2007 that has not yet held its first AGM after incorporation must hold it within 18 months of incorporation; or
– a public company that has already held its first AGM after incorporation must hold its AGM within 15 months of the previous one.

If a public company is **newly incorporated** (or an existing company converts to a public company) on or after 1 October 2007, it must hold its AGM within 7 months from its accounting reference date (s 336(1) CA 2006, amended by para 15 Sch 1 SI 2007/2194). This is also the case for an existing public company that has **already held an AGM after 1 October 2007**.

When the transitional period expires, public companies will have to hold an AGM within 6 months of the company's accounting reference date (at the time of writing, it is not yet known for how long the transitional arrangements will be in place). If the company changes its accounting reference date or shortens its accounting reference period, it will comply with the requirement by holding an AGM within 3 months of giving notice of the change to Companies House. Failure to do so within the requisite period will render every officer in default liable to a fine (s 336 CA 2006). Holding a general meeting within the period will not satisfy the requirement to hold an AGM.

3784 Subject to statute and the articles, directors can choose **when and where** to hold an AGM. They must exercise this discretion in good faith (*Cannon v Trask* (1875) LR 20 Eq 669, in which an AGM was called early to prevent new transferees of shares who were opposed to the board from attending and voting).

3785 At least 21 clear days' **notice** must be given of an AGM (ss 307, 360 CA 2006; reg 38 TA 1985). See ¶3646+ for notices of meetings generally. AGMs can only be held on **shorter notice** with the consent of all shareholders entitled to attend and vote at the meeting (s 337 CA 2006; reg 38 TA 1985).

As well as complying with the usual requirements as to its **contents**, the notice must clearly state that the meeting is an AGM (s 337 CA 2006; reg 38 TA 1985).

The notice can be **served** in hard copy, electronic form or via a website (see ¶3695+).

Failure to hold an AGM

3788 If a public company fails to hold an AGM as obliged by the legislation, every officer of the company in default is liable to a fine (s 336 CA 2006; ¶9935).

> MEMO POINTS Under the old legislation, shareholders could **apply to the secretary of state** for an order that an AGM must be held (s 367 CA 1985, now repealed). This power was repealed when the relevant provisions of the new Companies Act came into force on 1 October 2007. However, if an application was made to the secretary of state in respect of a public company before that date, an order may still be made (para 35 Sch 3 SI 2007/2194). Otherwise, this power cannot be relied upon.

2. Class Meetings

3794 Class meetings are **usually called** to vary the rights attached to a particular class of shares (¶1270+), but can also be called to consider any matter which only concerns one class of shareholder. Class meetings are attended by the shareholders of the class of shares specified in the notice of the meeting. As with other meetings, other non-voting parties (e.g. directors, auditors) can attend and speak at a class meeting, but cannot vote or count in the quorum.

Holding a class meeting

3795 Class meetings are usually held separately from general meetings, but could be held within a general meeting provided that only members of that class voted and there was no objection to the meeting being conducted in this way (*Carruth v Imperial Chemical Industries Ltd* [1937] 2 All ER 422).

The **procedure** for convening a class meeting is usually set out in the articles of the company, or the document setting out the conditions attached to the class of shares. It is normally the same as, or similar to, that for general meetings and will be subject to the articles, as well as various statutory provisions which apply to class meetings in the same way as they do to other types of meeting (with any necessary modifications), notably (ss 334, 335 CA 2006):
– notice to be given to shareholders (¶3646+);
– quorum requirements (¶3746+);
– chairman of the meeting (¶3716+);
– proxies (¶3727+);
– corporate representatives (¶3743+); and
– the circulation of shareholders' statements (¶3663+).

Only the following provisions specifically do not apply to class meetings:
– shareholders' power to require the directors to call a meeting (¶3626+); and
– the court's power to order a meeting (¶3635+).

Other provisions have to be modified where a class meeting is held to **vary rights attached to a class of shares**:
– the quorum is at least two persons holding at least one third of the nominal value of the issued shares of the relevant class (or voting rights of that class, if the company does not have a share capital). In the case of an adjourned meeting, at least one person in the relevant class can form the quorum; and
– any person in the relevant class at the meeting can demand a poll.

> MEMO POINTS 1. Instruments creating **debentures** often set out similar procedures for meetings of debenture holders as the company has for class meetings.
> 2. Only reasonable notice is required of a **meeting of subscribers** (*John Morley Building Co v Barras* [1891] 2 Ch 386), therefore the notice requirements of Table A do not apply.

3796 Shareholders holding the type of shares which are the subject of the meeting are **entitled to attend** (subject to any restrictions attached to the type of shares). If a class of shares does not have voting rights attached to them, those shareholders would only be able to meet to vary their rights, in which case they can attend and vote.

The **quorum** required for a class meeting will usually be specified in the articles or the conditions attached to that class of shares.

If all of the shares of a particular class are held by a **sole shareholder**, a resolution passed by that shareholder in relation to that class of shares will be deemed to have been passed at a class meeting (*East v Bennett Bros Ltd* [1911] 1 Ch 163). This is consistent with the unanimous agreement rule and the provisions relating to decision making in sole shareholder companies (¶3590+, ¶3868).

MEMO POINTS   If the company was registered before 22 December 1980 and still operates under **Table A 1948**, all of the provisions of Table A relating to general meetings also apply to class meetings, except that the quorum for class meetings is at least two persons (or their proxies) holding one third of the issued shares in that class, and any shareholder or proxy can demand a poll (reg 4 TA 1948).

E. Summary of meetings

3800

Type of meeting	When to call	Who can call	Notice	Short notice?
Public company's AGM [1] ¶3777+	Within 6 months of accounting reference date [2]	Directors	21 clear days' notice. Must state meeting is an AGM	Yes – unanimous consent of all shareholders
General meeting [3] ¶3620+, ¶3646+, ¶3711+	– When necessary; and – when requisitioned	– Directors; – shareholders; and – court	14 clear days' notice	Yes: – private company: with consent of 90% of shareholders (or up to 95% if articles stipulate) – public company: with consent of 95% of shareholders
Class Meeting [3] ¶3794+	When necessary	– Directors; and – class shareholders	As for general meeting	As for general meeting

Note:
1. **Private companies** can still hold AGMs if their articles require. The procedure for doing so should be set out in the articles.
2. This is **subject to** transitional arrangements which apply while the new Companies Act is being implemented, see ¶3783.
3. For either a public or a private company.

III. Voting

3810   As well as making sure that the meeting is convened and conducted properly, companies must follow the rules relating to voting to ensure that the decisions taken at the meeting are valid. All participants in the meeting need to be aware of their voting rights. The chairman and/or secretary at the meeting play an important role in this by checking that those who vote are **entitled** to do so, and the chairman will decide when voting should take place and by which **method**.

A. Who can vote?

Primarily, the **person entitled** to vote is the shareholder whose name is on the register (¶3915+), or his duly appointed proxy or corporate representative. This will be subject to any restrictions in the articles and/or terms of issue of the shares, as well as any order made in respect of those shares.

3815

In the case of **jointly held shares**, the vote of the shareholder whose name appears first on the register of shareholders is counted (s 286 CA 2006). A company's articles can change this rule; Table A mirrors it (reg 55 TA 1985). If joint shareholders hold two or more shares, they can register their names in a different order for each share so that both of them have the opportunity to vote (Burns v Siemens Brothers Dynamo Works [1919] 1 Ch 225).

3816

The company is not concerned with any **third party interests** in the shares, which can arise because of a mortgage, trust or nomineeship. The person entered on the register is entitled to vote at the meeting, and how that vote is exercised depends upon any agreement between the shareholder and the third party. Case law has established the position in relation to different kinds of third party interests:
a. a **bare trustee** or **nominee** must vote as directed and if he has no instructions, he must vote in the best interests of his appointor (Kirby v Wilkins [1929] 2 Ch 444);
b. where shares have been transferred and paid for, but the transfer not yet registered, the **transferor** (i.e. the person transferring the shares) must vote at the direction of, or in the best interests of, the transferee (i.e. the person receiving the shares) (Lyle & Scott Ltd v Scott's Trustees [1959] 2 All ER 661; see ¶1829+). While the whole purchase price is unpaid, the transferor can still vote as he sees fit, but this is subject to the fiduciary duties he owes as a trustee towards the transferee (Michaels v Harley House (Marylebone) Ltd [1999] 1 All ER 356); and
c. a **bankrupt** must vote as directed by his trustee in bankruptcy (Morgan v Gray [1953] 1 All ER 213).

> MEMO POINTS 1. **Public companies** can require persons who have (or have within the previous three years) invested in the company for details of their own and any **third party interests** in the company's shares and other relevant information (¶2042+). If that person fails to do so, the company can apply to the court for an order suspending the rights attached to those shares. The articles of **private companies** sometimes contain a similar provision, enabling the company to suspend the rights attached to the shares if the shareholder does not comply with such a request.
> 2. Table A provides that if an order has been made because of a shareholder's **mental incapacity** (whether that order has been made by a court in the UK or elsewhere), that shareholder can vote through his deputy (formerly known as a receiver) or other authorised person on a show of hands, or on a poll (where he can also vote by proxy) (reg 56 TA 1985). Evidence of the relevant person's authority to vote on behalf of the shareholder needs to be lodged with the company at the same place as specified for proxy appointments in the articles (if nowhere is specified, this will be the registered office of the company), at least 48 hours before the meeting or adjourned meeting. The vote cannot be exercised unless evidence of the authority has been deposited.
> The draft **new model articles** will not include such a provision.

Companies can set out a procedure for dealing with any **objections** to a shareholder's entitlement to vote in their articles (s 287 CA 2006). Table A requires any objection to be raised at the meeting (reg 58 TA 1985). The chairman will decide whether a shareholder's vote is valid, and his decision is final. Any objections raised after the meeting will not be considered. Further, the court has held that because proxy forms are lodged 48 hours before the meeting, there is ample time to examine their validity and so objections to proxies' entitlement to vote will not be accepted after the meeting either (Marx v Estates & General Investments Ltd [1975] 3 All ER 1064; reg 62 TA 1985).

3817

> MEMO POINTS The draft **new model articles** include a similar provision to Table A (private companies limited by shares: art 43; public companies: art 34).

The extent of voting rights

The **normal rules** depend upon how the resolution is put to the vote (s 284 CA 2006):
– on a show of hands (see ¶3838+): one vote per shareholder present in person or by proxy;

3819

– on a poll (see ¶3842+): one vote per share or £10-worth of stock;
– by written resolution (see ¶3581+): one vote per share or £10-worth of stock.

A company's articles can set out **alternative** voting rights. Table A provides that each shareholder has one vote on a show of hands, and on a poll each share carries one vote (reg 54 TA 1985). The articles may also mirror the terms of a share issue by varying the voting rights attached to particular shares, for example, preference shares often have no voting rights (¶780+).

MEMO POINTS 1. The default position in relation to **companies not having a share capital** is that each member has one vote, regardless of how the resolution is decided (s 284 CA 2006).
2. The **Table A provision** applicable to most companies does not allow proxies to vote on a show of hands. However, transitional measures which only apply to companies incorporated on or after 1 October 2007 that adopt Table A amend reg 54 TA 1985 to allow proxies to vote on a show of hands (reg 4 SI 2007/2826).

3820 A company's articles or the terms of issue of its shares may provide that, in specified circumstances, a shareholder's voting rights are **increased**. A common example is a clause known as a "*Bushell v Faith* **clause**" which entitles a director to an increased vote on a resolution to remove him from office. This comes from a case in which the articles of the company provided that a director/shareholder's votes would be multiplied by three on a poll in any resolution to remove him from office (Bushell v Faith [1970] 1 All ER 53; ¶2950).

3821 Voting rights can also be **restricted** by statute, the articles or the terms of issue of the shares. For example, in the case of a special resolution to approve the off-market purchase of the company's own shares, the holders of the shares in question cannot vote (¶1387+). If a shareholder has a mixture of shares, some of which are the subject of the resolution, he cannot vote on a show of hands but can vote on a poll only using the voting rights attached to the shares which are not the subject of the resolution.

A shareholder holding **non-voting shares** may not vote on any resolution, and cannot complain about resolutions passed by the other shareholders even if they affect his shares, unless it amounts to a variation of his class rights (Re Barrow Haematite Steel Co (1888) 39 Ch D 582, a case relating to preference shares).

3822 It is possible, although not very common, for a shareholder's voting rights to be **suspended**.

The articles of association can provide for voting rights to be suspended **by the company** in specific circumstances. For instance, a company may prevent a particular shareholder from attending meetings and/or from voting if he has not paid all of the money due for his shares (e.g. reg 57 TA 1985). Unless the articles state otherwise, if a shareholder has paid for some but not all of his shares, he will only lose the voting rights attached to those shares which remain unpaid.

Voting rights can also be suspended **by the secretary of state or the court** making an order to that effect (see ¶2043, ¶7241). Such an order has a wider effect than just suspending the voting rights attached to specific shares; it also provides that the shares cannot be transferred and that no issues or payment may be made in respect of those shares (other than in a liquidation) (s 454 CA 1985). It is an offence for a person or the company to contravene such restrictions placed on shares (s 455 CA 1985; ¶9935).

MEMO POINTS Draft **new model articles** under the **new Companies Act** have been published for private companies limited by shares and public companies. Those for public companies will also prevent shareholders exercising the voting rights attached to shares which they have not paid for in full (art 40).

Shareholder's right to vote as he wishes

3824 A shareholder's vote is his **personal property** and, subject to the articles of the company or the terms of any other agreement to the contrary (e.g. in a shareholders' agreement), he may vote as he wishes even if this is not in the best interests of the company (Pender v Lushington (1877) 6 Ch D 70).

3825 If a **director is also a shareholder** of the company, his right to vote as he sees fit does not put him in a conflict position because his actions as a director and as a shareholder are separate (see ¶2390+). Even if the company has given an undertaking to the court that the directors would call a general meeting and recommend that the shareholders approve a particular resolution, the director as shareholder may still vote against that resolution if he sees fit (Northern Counties Securities Ltd v Jackson & Steeple Ltd [1974] 2 All ER 625).

3826 If a **decision** of the company is **challenged**, the court will therefore not look at the personal motives of the shareholders in their voting, but if a minority of shareholders has been suppressed by an improper or corrupt influence, it may intervene (Re London & Mercantile Discount Co (1865) LR 1 Eq 277). For example, the court has intervened where the resolution passed was to prevent the investigation of fraud committed by those voting, and where the resolution had the effect of depriving the minority of its share of the company's assets (respectively, Atwool v Merryweather (1867) LR 5 Eq 464n; Menier v Hooper's Telegraph Works (1874) LR 9 Ch App 350). The court has also overturned a shareholder resolution ratifying an allotment of shares for improper purposes because it would have had an inequitable effect on the minority shareholder (Clemens v Clemens Bros Ltd [1976] 2 All ER 268). These are the sorts of situations that may give rise to an action by minority shareholders for relief from unfair prejudice (see ¶2105+).

The court will only grant an injunction to **prevent** a **shareholder voting** in an extreme case. For example, the court granted such an injunction on an application to prevent two controlling shareholders from voting, because they were opposed to a resolution to approve a restructuring agreement to keep the company afloat (Standard Chartered Bank v Walker [1992] BCLC 603). The court judged that this was an extreme case because failure to approve the restructuring would:
– result in the company being wound up because it was in so much debt; and
– destroy the property (i.e. shares in the company) over which the banks had charges, damaging both the company and its funders.

B. Methods of voting

3836 A company's **articles** of association can govern which method of voting is to be used. For instance, some companies provide that all votes are to be decided on a poll, as it can be a fairer method of determining a resolution. Usually, particularly in smaller companies where the division of shares is often more straight-forward, a vote on a show of hands suffices, and is much quicker and more convenient to carry out. Although a company's articles may exclude the use of voting on a show of hands, they cannot exclude voting on a poll except in very limited circumstances.

1. Show of hands

3838 A company's articles will normally specify whether and when votes are to be taken on a show of hands. Votes are usually cast in this way to start with (reg 46 TA 1985).

Subject to any rights and restrictions attached to shares, a show of hands **entitles** each shareholder (or its/his corporate representative or proxy) to one vote. Therefore, if a shareholder with more than one share wishes to spread his vote by voting differently in respect of different shares or if he wants to increase his voting power, he will have to appoint proxies in respect of different shares or bundles of shares. This would be unusual, but may be appropriate where a person holds shares on behalf of different beneficial owners who are best served by voting in different ways, for example a trustee who holds shares on behalf of various beneficiaries. The same result could be achieved by appointing nominees or proxies; although appointing proxies would be easier and can be done in respect of just a particular meeting or resolution.

MEMO POINTS A company cannot reduce the weight of a **proxy's vote** on a show of hands as compared to his appointor if he were present and voting (s 285 CA 2006). This applies whether the shareholder has appointed one or more proxies.
It is possible to appoint **more than one nominee or proxy**, as long as the shareholder has more than one share (nominees: ¶2034+; proxies: ¶3727+).

3839 Unless a poll is demanded, the chairman's declaration that a resolution has been carried or lost is conclusive proof of the **result of the vote**, as is a proper entry of the declaration in the minutes of the meeting (s 320 CA 2006; reg 47 TA 1985; see ¶3864+ for taking minutes of meetings). The percentages of votes for and against the resolution do not have to be recorded. If the votes are tied, the articles often give the chairman the casting vote (reg 50 TA 1985).

MEMO POINTS 1. The draft **new model articles** will also give the chairman the casting vote (private companies limited by shares: art 42; public companies: art 33).
2. Transitional measures which only apply to **companies incorporated on or after 1 October 2007** that adopt Table A omit reg 50 TA 1985 (reg 3 SI 2007/2826).

3840 **Proxies** can vote on a show of hands, unless the company's articles state otherwise (s 284 CA 2006). However, if a shareholder present at the meeting is also acting as proxy for another shareholder, he cannot cast his own vote and that of his proxy appointor at the same time, because each person can only vote once on a show of hands and the chairman cannot ascertain how many votes his hand is intended to convey (*Ernest v Loma Gold Mines* [1896] 2 Ch 572). In order to cast his own and his appointor's votes, that shareholder/proxy would have to demand a poll (if he qualifies to do so). Although the articles may prevent proxies from voting on a show of hands altogether, they cannot dilute the weight of a proxy's vote on a show of hands as compared to his appointor if he were present and voting (s 285 CA 2006). This applies whether the shareholder has appointed one or more proxies. If a shareholder has appointed more than one proxy (¶3729), each proxy can use the voting rights attached to the shares in respect of which he was appointed.

Corporate representatives may vote on a show of hands.

2. Poll voting

3842 The vote will be taken by poll if this is demanded before the show of hands or on declaration of its result, or where the articles provide that voting will take place by poll (reg 46 TA 1985). If the poll is demanded after the vote has been taken on a show of hands, the result on the show of hands will not stand (s 320 CA 2006).

In a poll, subject to the articles, shareholders are **entitled** to one vote per share (s 284 CA 2006). A poll might be held if there is deadlock on a show of hands, or where a fairer result could be achieved on a poll (e.g. because the spread of shareholdings amongst the shareholders is uneven or because a shareholder present at the meeting is also a proxy for someone else). There is no requirement to give reasons for demanding or holding a vote on a poll, and there is no restriction on the circumstances in which such a vote can be held.

MEMO POINTS 1. For companies **without a share capital**, each member is entitled to one vote unless the articles state otherwise (s 284 CA 2006). If a company has **converted its shares into stock**, shareholders have one vote per bundle of £10-worth of stock unless the articles state otherwise.
2. The draft **new model articles** will set out when voting is to be taken on a poll (private companies limited by shares: art 44; public companies: art 35).

Who can demand a poll

3843 Table A enables a poll to be **demanded by** (reg 46 TA 1985):
– the chairman;
– at least two shareholders with the right to vote; or
– at least one shareholder with 10% of the paid up share capital on shares entitled to vote.

The **chairman's right** to demand a poll is not personal to him. It must be exercised only if it is necessary to make sense of the meeting or to enable the meeting to carry on for the purposes for which it was convened (*The Second Consolidated Trust Ltd v Ceylon Amalgamated Tea & Rubber Estates Ltd* [1943] 2 All ER 567). For instance, if a shareholder with several shares has appointed more than one proxy in order to increase his voting power on a show of hands, the chairman should call a poll in order to achieve a fairer outcome (ICSA guidance note 071017).

Polls can also be demanded by **proxies** subject to the same qualifications as their appointors, because the proxy appointment is deemed authority to do so (s 329 CA 2006).

> MEMO POINTS 1. If the resolution to be voted upon is a special resolution to approve the **purchase or redemption of the company's own shares**, any shareholder or his proxy can demand a poll (ss 164, 165, 167, 174 CA 1985; ¶1337+).
> 2. In the case of a **company without a share capital**, at least one member with 10% of the voting rights present at the meeting can demand a poll.
> 3. The draft **new model articles** will set out the same rights to demand a poll, as well as allowing directors to do so (private companies limited by shares: art 44; public companies: art 35).

The articles of association of a company can only **restrict the right** to demand a poll where the decision under consideration is: the election of a chairman for the meeting; or, whether to adjourn the meeting. Even then, the poll may still be demanded on those questions by:
– 5 or more shareholders with the right to vote on the resolution; or
– shareholders holding 10% of the value of the paid-up shares entitled to attend and vote on the resolution.

3844

If the articles of a company restrict the right to demand a poll any further, including a demand made by a proxy, the provision is void (s 321 CA 2006).

> MEMO POINTS The threshold for companies **without a share capital** is members representing 10% of the voting rights on that resolution.

Withdrawal of demand

A demand for a poll can be withdrawn before the poll is taken, with the consent of the chairman (reg 48 TA 1985). If the demand is withdrawn, it is treated as never having been made and any previous vote on a show of hands will be valid.

3845

> MEMO POINTS The draft **new model articles** will allow demands for polls to be withdrawn if they are made before the poll is taken and the chairman consents (private companies limited by shares: art 44; public companies: art 35).

Voting

Subject to any rights and restrictions attached to the shares, **one vote** is counted for each share held by a shareholder. If a shareholder is entitled to **more than one vote**, he does not have to use all of his votes, or use all of his votes in the same way (s 322 CA 2006). This provision can be useful to trustees or nominees acting for a group of beneficiaries with different interests, as it enables them to spread their voting to reflect those interests.

3846

Since shareholders can appoint **proxies** to exercise all or any of their rights, they can vote on a poll, subject to any restrictions contained in the company's articles (ss 284, 324 CA 2006; reg 59 TA 1985 permits proxies to vote on a poll). See ¶3738+ for the deadlines by which proxy appointment forms need to be submitted before a poll so that a proxy can vote.

Table A allows the chairman to direct **how the poll** is taken, for example, whether the poll can be taken at the time or needs to be delayed, whether votes are to be recorded on poll cards or simply noted down by the secretary (reg 49 TA 1985). He may appoint shareholders or non-shareholders as scrutineers, and he can fix a time and place for announcing the outcome. There is no rule that votes taken on a poll are confidential (*Haarhaus & Co v Law Debenture Trust Corp plc* [1988] BCLC 640).

3847

> MEMO POINTS The draft **new model articles** will contain an equivalent provision (private companies limited by shares: art 44; public companies: art 36).

3848 If the votes are **tied**, the chairman only has the casting vote if stated in the articles. Table A gives the chairman the casting vote (reg 50 TA 1985).

> MEMO POINTS   1. The draft **new model articles** will give the chairman the casting vote (private companies limited by shares: art 42; public companies: art 33).
> 2. Transitional measures which only apply to **companies incorporated on or after 1 October 2007** that adopt Table A omit reg 50 TA 1985 (reg 3 SI 2007/2826).

Timing of poll

3849 Votes on a poll can be taken **at the same meeting** at which they were demanded. However, particularly in larger companies, it is common for polls to be taken later to make the necessary administrative arrangements, such as checking how many votes each shareholder is entitled to and appointing scrutineers to count the votes.

A poll demanded on most matters may be taken **at a later time and place** as the chairman directs, up to 30 days later (reg 51 TA 1985). As with the chairman's right to demand a poll, his right to ascertain the time and place is invalid if he exercises it in bad faith or if he fails to consider relevant factors (*Byng v London Life Association* [1989] 1 All ER 560). If the time and place for the poll are agreed upon at the meeting, there is no need to give notice to the shareholders. Otherwise, at least 7 clear days' notice must be given (reg 52 TA 1985). This gives shareholders enough advance notice to appoint proxies if necessary.

A poll concerning the **election of a chairman or** the **adjournment** of the meeting is to be taken straight away (reg 51 TA 1985). If it is impossible to take the poll straight away, the resumption of the meeting on a later date is treated as a continuation of the original meeting; therefore proxy appointments submitted 48 hours before the original meeting are valid (*Jackson v Hamlyn* [1953] 1 All ER 887).

> MEMO POINTS   The draft **new model articles** for public companies will contain an equivalent provision (art 36). Those for private companies limited by shares require a poll to be taken immediately and as the chairman directs (art 44).

3850 **After the poll** on the matter demanded, the meeting returns to any other business to be considered, voting in the usual way (reg 51 TA 1985).

> MEMO POINTS   The draft **new model articles** for public companies will contain an equivalent provision (art 36).

3. Postal and electronic voting

3852 Votes may be cast by post or electronically, if the **articles** of a company provide for this. Table A does not include such a provision. Companies need to consider the practicalities of such a method, for example, how to verify the identity of the shareholder (e.g. by electronic signature, a witnessed signature on paper, a personal identification number). If a company does employ such an alternative voting method, it should clearly set out how to vote in the notice of the meeting in whatever form it is given (ICSA guidance note number 160207).

For example, postal votes could be submitted following a meeting at which a poll was demanded but where voting on the poll was postponed to be carried out by post. Voting by email may be a useful option where the meeting is taking place via video-conference, or companies may be able to provide web-conferencing facilities with electronic voting. Or, a large company may have access to electronic voting facilities whereby shareholders can cast their vote via a keypad at their seat in the meeting room. However, when using these alternative methods, companies need to consider whether they are actually making the decision by written resolution and therefore need to comply with the requisite formalities (¶3580+). For instance, if no meeting took place, and the company invites shareholders to vote on a matter "by post" or by email, it would in fact be proposing a written resolution.

IV. Administrative requirements

3862 The **secretary** usually sees to the administrative requirements of meetings. The procedure and paperwork required in giving notice of meetings has already been discussed (¶3646+). It is a statutory requirement to **keep records** of meetings and resolutions. The various **registers** which are to be kept by a company are dealt with separately at ¶3888+.

Comment: From 6 April 2008, when the relevant provisions of the **new Companies Act** come into force, private companies will no longer be required to have a secretary (see ¶4116). If a company chooses not to have a secretary, it should ensure that it allocates responsibility for administrative matters to another person.

1. Minutes of meetings and resolutions

3864 Companies are **obliged** to keep minutes of all general and class meetings (ss 355, 359 CA 2006). Failure to do so renders every officer in default liable to a fine (¶9935).

The main **purpose** of minutes is to provide evidence of a company's proceedings: minutes signed by a director or the secretary are primary evidence that the meeting was duly convened, held and conducted, and that any appointments at the meeting were duly made, unless the contrary can be shown (s 356 CA 2006). For example, minutes were not proof of a meeting where it was shown that the meeting had not in fact taken place (*Glatzer & Warwick Shipping Ltd v Bradston Ltd, Re "Ocean Enterprise"* [1997] 1 Lloyds Rep 449). Draft minutes can be accepted as evidence of the meeting provided that the meeting dealt with the business as the draft sets out (*R v Kingston Crown Court* [2001] 4 All ER 721). The articles of a company may provide that the minutes of a meeting are conclusive evidence of the proceedings and their accuracy cannot be challenged unless they are fraudulent or erroneous (*Kerr v John Mottram Ltd* [1940] Ch 657).

3866 **Resolutions passed at meetings** must be recorded in the minutes (s 355 CA 2006). This will form part of the record of the meeting itself. Records also have to be kept of **written resolutions** and other resolutions not made at meetings.

These records constitute primary **evidence** that the resolution was duly passed if they appear to be signed by a director or the secretary (s 356 CA 2006). Where a vote has been taken on a show of hands, a record of the chairman's declaration of the result in the minutes is conclusive proof of the result of the vote, without the percentages or numbers voting for or against being recorded, even if a specific threshold must be reached to carry the resolution (s 320 CA 2006; reg 47 TA 1985). If any resolution is challenged, the burden of proof will be on the party contending that the decision was not duly passed to prove otherwise (*Ayre v Skelsey's Adamant Cement Co* (1905) 21 TLR 464).

Procedure

3867 Minutes are usually **taken** during the meeting by the company secretary and **written up** afterwards. Minutes need to be written up within a reasonable period of time in order to be valid (*Toms v Cinema Trust Co Ltd* [1915] WN 28).

The requirements as to the **form** in which the minutes have to be kept are flexible. Traditionally, company records were kept in bound books, but they can now be kept in hard copy or electronic form, as long as the information is readily accessible (s 1135 CA 2006). The records can be arranged as the directors see fit. The advantage of using bound books was that the records were protected against falsification because it is fairly obvious if a page has been added or removed. If another hard copy or electronic form is used, the company must take adequate precautions against the records being falsified, and make sure that there is a system in place to discover any falsification that does occur (s 1138 CA 2006). Most electronic documents record when modifications have been made. Failure to keep the records in a proper form or to protect them against falsification renders every office in default liable to a fine (¶9935).

Minutes should be **signed by** a director or the secretary so that the record stands as evidence of the resolutions and proceedings. It is usual for the chairman of the meeting or of the next meeting to do this. Any amendments should be dealt with at the next meeting and can be made by hand and initialled by the chairman when he signs the minutes, or amended in the electronic version. Amendments should not be made once the minutes have been signed.

Minutes of meetings and records of resolutions must be **kept for** at least 10 years from the date of the meeting, resolution or decision (s 355 CA 2006). Companies should therefore ensure that their document retention policy facilitates this.

3868 Private companies with a **sole shareholder** are to keep a written record, either in the form of minutes or a written resolution, of any decision taken by that shareholder (s 357 CA 2006). This is the equivalent for a sole shareholder company of obtaining unanimous consent for resolutions of all shareholders. **Failure** to record decisions will not invalidate the decision, but it will render the sole shareholder liable to a fine (¶9935).

Inspection

3869 The shareholder meeting minutes and records of resolutions should be **kept at** the registered office of the company and be available for inspection by any shareholder without charge (s 358 CA 2006). This applies to all such records made in the last 10 years. An advantage to keeping minutes in electronic form is that they can be accessed remotely from other locations as well.

Inspection should be **permitted** for at least two hours every business day between the hours of 9am and 5pm (reg 3 SI 1991/1998). A shareholder can be charged for copies of minutes (the charge is currently 10p per 500 words or part of 500 words copied, plus the reasonable costs of sending the copies out (reg 4 SI 2007/2612)).

If the company **fails** to allow inspection or provide copies, every officer in default is liable to a fine (s 358 CA 2006; ¶9935). The court can order the immediate inspection of the records, or that the copies requested are provided to the shareholders.

> MEMO POINTS 1. Under new regulations likely to come into force by 1 October 2009, private companies will have to **allow inspection** of their records between 9am and 5pm on a working day specified by a person asking to inspect them (reg 6 draft Company (Company Records and Fees) Regulations 2007). That person will have to give the company 2 working days' notice that he wants to inspect the records during the notice period for a meeting or during the period for agreeing to a written resolution. At all other times, he will have to give 10 working days' notice. Public companies will still have to allow inspection for at least 2 hours of every working day between 9am and 5pm (reg 7 draft Company (Company Records and Fees) Regulations 2007). When allowing inspection, the company is not obliged to present the information in any particular way (e.g. a person inspecting records cannot ask for them to be arranged into subject matter when they are arranged in date order) (reg 8 draft Company (Company Records and Fees) Regulations 2007). A person inspecting the records will be able to copy them, but the company does not have to assist him in doing so (e.g. the person can take a longhand copy of a record, but the company does not have to go to the expense of photocopying it for him. If he wants a photocopy, the person will have to ask the company for one, for which he will be charged) (reg 9 draft Company (Company Records and Fees) Regulations 2007).
> 2. Under new regulations likely to come into force by 1 October 2009, the reference for the fee for **copying** the minutes will change to reg 19 draft Companies (Company Records and Fees) Regulations 2007. The fee itself will remain the same. Copies will be able to be provided in hard or electronic form, as requested, but the company will not have to change the order in which the records are kept (regs 11-13 draft Companies (Company Records and Fees) Regulations 2007).
> 3. Draft regulations published by BERR propose to allow a company to **keep records at** a single alternative location within the same part of the UK as the registered office (i.e. England and Wales, Wales or Scotland) (reg 5 draft Companies (Company Records and Fees) Regulations 2007). This part of the draft regulations is not likely to come into force until 1 October 2009. When this alternative is available, the company will have to notify Companies House of the location of its records, and of any change in that location, within 14 days of any change. This will not be necessary if the records have always been kept at the company's registered office.

Failure to give notice to Companies House within the time period where appropriate will render every officer in default liable to a fine.

2. Filing requirements

3871

Certain resolutions need to be filed at Companies House within a particular period of being passed, whether at a meeting or by written resolution. The **time limits** for filing **resolutions** are (ss 29, 30 CA 2006; s 380 CA 1985, so far as it is still in force: SI 2007/2194 and SI 2007/2607):
– ordinary resolutions: only certain ones need to be filed, see ¶3534;
– special resolutions: within 15 days of being passed;
– extraordinary resolutions: within 15 days of being passed (see ¶3544); and
– elective resolution to give directors the authority to allot shares for more than 5 years: within 15 days of being passed.

As well as these main resolutions, certain resolutions or agreements also need to be filed within 15 days:
– those that should have been passed as special or extraordinary resolutions;
– those that were agreed to unanimously that should have been passed in a particular way;
– those that bind all of the shareholders in a class, but that were not agreed to by all of them; and
– any other resolutions or agreements required to be filed by statute.

Other business conducted at the meeting may give rise to filing obligations, for example the appointment of a director needs to be recorded at Companies House by filing Form 288a. See ¶9900 for a list of forms that have to be filed at Companies House and details of the relevant circumstances and deadlines.

The role of **Companies House** is looked at in detail in ¶4040+.

> MEMO POINTS   The name of Form 288a, like other **Companies House forms**, is taken from the relevant section number in the legislation. As all of the section numbers will change under the new Companies Act, Companies House proposes to change the names of all of its forms to reflect their function rather than the relevant section number ("Working with Companies House: a consultation on the registrar's rules and related provisions which will apply under the Companies Act 2006"). At the time of writing, the new form names are not yet available.

3. Timeline: shareholder meetings

3873

Day[1]	Action	¶¶
- 48	Company receives **shareholder requisition** for general meeting (company has maximum of 21 days from receipt of requisition within which to give notice of meeting; notice can be for maximum of 28 days)	¶3626+
- 43	Plc receives **shareholder resolution** for AGM: it gives notice of resolution to other shareholders if notice of AGM has already been sent	¶3780+
- 29	Company receives **special notice** of ordinary resolution if required: it gives copy of special notice to director/auditor concerned	¶3536+
- 27	Company sends notice of general meeting on **shareholder requisition** [2]	¶3626+, ¶3646+
- 22	Company sends **notice** of AGM/elective resolution at general meeting [2]	¶3785, ¶3564
	Public company sends **accounts** to shareholders to lay before meeting [3]	¶4273+
- 15	Company sends **notice of general meeting** [2], including details of any resolution on **special notice**, if applicable	¶3646+, ¶3536+
	Documents to be made available at registered office, depending on resolution: documents concerning the off-market purchase of the company's own shares; details of loans to directors; and director's service contract	¶3660+
	Company sends notice of intention to **appoint/reappoint director** (minimum of 14 days', maximum of 28 days' notice)	¶2270+

Day[1]	Action	¶¶
-8	Company receives **shareholder statement**: company circulates statement	¶3663+
-2	**Proxy appointments** deposited with company	¶3738+
M	Meeting	¶3711+
	Documents to be available at meeting: statutory declaration and auditor's report regarding financial assistance; copy of contract for the off-market purchase of company's own shares; statutory declaration and auditor's report regarding payment out of capital for redemption or purchase of company's own shares; director's service contract; details of loans to directors to be approved	¶3660+
+1	Write up **minutes** of meeting/resolutions within reasonable time	¶3862+
+6	If meeting has been **adjourned for 14 days** or more, send notice of adjourned meeting 7 clear days in advance	¶3764
+13	If meeting has been **adjourned for fewer than 14 days**, there is no need to give notice	¶3760+
+14	Deadline for **filing** ordinary resolution to **remove an auditor**	¶3534
+15	Deadline for **filing** most resolutions [4]	¶3600
+23	If **poll** was postponed at meeting, but not fixed, give 7 days' notice	¶3842+
+30	**Poll** can be held up to 30 days after meeting [5]	¶3842+

Note:
1. Days shown take into account the concept of "**clear days**" where necessary. Companies will have to adjust the times as required depending on when notices are deemed to be received under their chosen method of communication.
2. Where applicable, **documents** to be sent out **with the notice** are: directors' statement regarding disapplication of pre-emption rights, any auditor's statement and shareholders' statements (as well as details of any shareholder resolutions to be considered at a public company AGM, notice of which must have been received by now).
3. Only public companies will have to lay accounts before the shareholders from **6 April 2008** (¶4273+). However, all companies will still be required to circulate them (¶4261+).
4. If the meeting is **adjourned**, or a vote is taken on a **poll at a later date**, and the resolution which requires filing is passed at a later date, the deadline for filing is 15 days after the resolution has been passed.
5. **Proxy appointments** for a poll must be delivered to the company not more than 24 hours before the poll, unless the poll is taken within 48 hours of the demand, in which case they must be delivered when the poll is demanded (¶3738).

SECTION 4

Company registers

3888 In addition to the records of meetings and resolutions discussed at ¶3862+ and ¶3473+, companies keep a number of registers as a record of the individuals or corporations involved in their management and of significant transactions. **Statute** imposes an obligation upon companies to keep some of the registers, such as the register of shareholders and the register of directors and secretaries, and others, such as the register of allotments, are kept by companies as a matter of **best practice**.

3889 The registers, also known as a company's "statutory books", are usually **maintained by** the company secretary, although this is not necessarily the case. Where the legislation imposes an obligation upon companies to keep a particular register, any penalties for non-compliance apply to both the company and every officer of the company who is in default. Therefore, directors should not merely assume that the secretary will deal with updating the registers, unless he has agreed or been instructed to do so.

Company registers were traditionally **kept in** bound books. Statutory registers are allowed to be kept in other formats, e.g. looseleaf binder or on computer, provided they can be reproduced in a legible form (ss 722, 723 CA 1985). There are no specific requirements as to the format of non-statutory registers. Therefore, a register can be kept on a computer system, as long as it can be printed out. If a register is kept in a format other than in a bound book, statute requires that "adequate precautions" are taken against its falsification. Failure to do so renders the company and any officer in default liable to a fine (¶9935). The legislation does not give any guidance as to what measures would be "adequate", but sensible precautions would include password-protecting computer records and ensuring that the company's computer system is reasonably safe from unwanted external access. In the case of looseleaf binders, the records could be kept locked away, accessible only to certain persons (while, of course, allowing for inspection and copying as required by statute and/or the articles).

Comment: From **6 April 2008**, private companies will no longer be obliged to have a secretary (see ¶4116). If a private company takes advantage of this relaxation in the rules, it must ensure that someone else is given responsibility for maintaining the company's registers.

> MEMO POINTS The **new Companies Act** will be more flexible in allowing company records to be kept in hard or electronic form (s1135 CA 2006). If kept in electronic form, they will still have to be able to be reproduced as hard copy. If bound books are not used, the company will have to both guard against falsification and facilitate the discovery of falsification (s1138 CA 2006). Failure to comply will render any officer in default liable to a fine. Company registers will usually have to be kept at the company's registered office, although the secretary of state will be able to make regulations allowing certain registers to be kept elsewhere (s1136 CA 2006). These provisions apply when the relevant provisions of the new Companies Act come into force in relation to each register; this is noted as relevant in the paragraphs below.

A. Register of directors and secretaries

Every company must keep a register of directors and secretaries (s 288 CA 1985). In practice, these are two separate registers, two sections in a looseleaf register or two electronic documents. The register is to be **kept at** the registered office of the company.   **3894**

Failure to keep the register, or keeping an incorrect register, renders the company and any officer in default liable to a fine (¶9935).

> MEMO POINTS Under the **new Companies Act**, all companies will have to keep a register of directors (s162 CA 2006). Public companies and private companies which choose to have a secretary will still have to keep a register of secretaries (s275 CA 2006). Failure to comply with either requirement will render the company and any officer in default liable to a fine. The provisions relating to the registers of directors and secretaries are expected to come into force by 1 October 2009.
> Both registers will be able to be kept at (ss 162, 275, 1136 CA 2006; reg 5 Companies (Company Records and Fees) Regulations 2007):
> – the registered office; or
> – another location that is situated in the same part of the UK as the registered office.

Contents

Register of directors

The **information** to be recorded in the register of directors where the director is an **individual** is (s 289 CA 1985):   **3896**
– name;
– any former name;
– usual residential address;
– nationality;
– business occupation (if applicable);
– details of any other directorships held by him at the time of entry into the register or any time in the last five years; and
– date of birth.

See ¶3907 below for where the register will not contain all of this information.

> **MEMO POINTS** The information required to be kept on the register under the **new Companies Act** will change. Only the following will be required (ss 163, 164 CA 2006, expected to come into force by 1 October 2009):
> **a.** for an individual:
> – name;
> – any former name;
> – a service address;
> – the country, state or part of the UK in which he is usually resident;
> – nationality;
> – business occupation (if applicable); and
> – date of birth; or
> **b.** for corporate directors and firms:
> – corporate or firm name;
> – registered or principal office; and
> – particulars of the register on which it appears and its registration number (e.g. for companies incorporated in England and Wales, this will be Companies House and its company registration number). Non-EEA companies to which the First Company Law Directive does not apply will have to state the form of the company, the law by which it is governed and any register on which it appears, together with its identification number.
>
> These changes are designed to protect directors from having to disclose their home addresses on the public register at Companies House. Instead, the service address could be the company's registered office, the director's solicitor's or any other address (including his residential address, if he wishes). However, the company will have to keep a **new register of directors' residential addresses**, so that directors can be traced by the authorities if necessary, for example when they are in breach of their obligations (s 165 CA 2006, expected to come into force by 1 October 2009). If a director's residential address is the same as the service address given in the register of directors, the entry will be able to state this fact (unless the company's registered office is his home address and he states "the company's registered office" as his service address, in which case the address will have to be given). Failure to comply will render the company and every officer in default liable to a fine.

3897 The **name** of an individual director means his forename and surname. If a director has a title, e.g. Lord, the title can be entered instead of, or as well as, the forename and surname.

> **EXAMPLE**
> John Smith
> Sir (John) Smith
> Lord of Smithfield
> Lord Smith of Smithfield
> John Smith, Lord of Smithfield

The **former name** of an individual director does not include a:
– woman's maiden name;
– name used before the director's 18th birthday;
– name used by the director more than 20 years ago; or
– name used by a peer, or person with another British title, before he adopted the title.

If a director is a **corporation or Scottish firm**, the register must contain the corporate or firm name and registered or principal office.

> **MEMO POINTS** Under the **new Companies Act**, a former name will not have to be given if it was used (s 163 CA 2006, expected to come into force by 1 October 2009):
> – before the director's 16th birthday;
> – more than 20 years ago; or
> – by a peer or other titled person before he adopted the title.

3898 **Other directorships** do not have to be entered on the register if the other company is dormant or in the same group as the company.

Former directorships only have to be disclosed if the director held the office within the last five years. As with current directorships, previous offices held do not have to be entered on the register if the other company was dormant or in the same group as the company.

For the purposes of the register, a **shadow director** is deemed to be a director and therefore his details must also be included (s 288(6) CA 1985).

Register of secretaries

The **information** to be recorded in the register of secretaries where the secretary is an **individual** is (s 290 CA 1985):
– name;
– former name; and
– usual residential address.

> MEMO POINTS The same information will have to be recorded on public companies' register of secretaries under the **new Companies Act**, except that the secretary may give an address for service rather than his residential address (s 277 CA 2006, expected to come into force by 1 October 2009).

3899

If the company has **joint secretaries**, the information must be entered into the register in respect of each joint secretary.

3900

If the secretary is a **corporation or Scottish firm**, the register must contain the corporate or firm name and registered or principal office. In the case of any **other firm** (partnership), the particulars of each partner should be registered as joint secretaries.

> MEMO POINTS Under the **new Companies Act**, additional information about corporate secretaries/firms will be required (s 278 CA 2006, expected to come into force by 1 October 2009). They will have to give particulars of the register on which they appear and their registration number (e.g. for companies incorporated in England and Wales, this will be Companies House and its company registration number). Non-EEA companies to which the First Company Law Directive does not apply will have to state the form of the company, the law by which it is governed and any register on which it appears, together with its identification number. If a partnership holds the office, the details of the partnership as if it was a legal person will be required, rather than the details of each partner.

Changes and additions to the register

The company must **notify** Companies House within 14 days of any change to the register of directors and secretaries. This applies both where officers of the company are appointed and resign, and where the details regarding the officer change (e.g. a change of address). See ¶479+ for how to notify Companies House of the first director(s) and secretary on formation of a company.

3902

Failure to do so renders the company and any officer in default liable to a fine (¶9935).

> MEMO POINTS Changes to the registers of directors and secretaries will also have to be notified to Companies House within 14 days under the **new Companies Act** (ss 167, 276 CA 2006, expected to come into force by 1 October 2009). This will include notifying Companies House of changes to the register of directors' residential addresses. Changes regarding shadow directors will not have to be notified.

The following **forms** are to be used to notify Companies House of a change in the register:

3903

Type of change	Form	Deadline for filing
New director or secretary appointed	288a	14 days from change
End of director's or secretary's appointment	288b	
Change in details for any director or secretary (e.g. change of name, address)	288c	

> MEMO POINTS The names of these forms, like other **Companies House forms**, are taken from the relevant section number in the legislation. As all of the section numbers will change under the new Companies Act, Companies House proposes to change the names of all of its forms to reflect their function rather than the relevant section number ("Working with Companies House: a consultation on the registrar's rules and related provisions which will apply under the Companies Act 2006"). At the time of writing, the new form names are not yet available.

3904 Where an officer is **appointed**, the form notifying Companies House of the appointment must include that officer's signature as evidence of his willingness to take up the appointment.

Inspection

3906 The register of directors and secretaries can be inspected by any shareholder without charge (s 288(3) CA 1985). Others may also inspect the register, on payment of a fee (the fees are set out in the table at ¶4019). Companies must have the register **available** for inspection for at least two hours between 9am and 5pm on each business day (reg 3 SI 1991/1998). A "**business day**" is Monday to Friday, excluding bank holidays.

The legislation does not provide for a right of shareholders or others to take **copies** of the register. However, when making it available for inspection, a company must allow the person carrying out the inspection to copy the register by taking notes or a transcript (reg 3 SI 1991/1998).

Failure to permit inspection renders the company and every officer in default liable to a fine (¶9935).

> MEMO POINTS   Under the **new Companies Act**, the registers of directors and secretaries (where applicable) will have to be open for inspection by any shareholder without charge, and by any other person for a fee (ss 162, 275 CA 2006, expected to come into force by 1 October 2009). Failure to do so will render the company and any officer in default liable to a fine. For the proposed regulations on how a person can inspect company records, see ¶3869/mp.

Confidentiality orders

3907 Unlike shareholders, directors are currently required to have their usual **residential addresses** entered on the register. As this information is available to the public, it has led directors to be exposed to intimidation and violence, for example, from animal rights campaigners. Directors can apply to the secretary of state for a confidentiality order, so that this information cannot be disclosed by the company or by Companies House. It is only held by Companies House on a restricted register, to which only certain bodies such as the police and the FSA have access (ss 723B, 723C CA 1985; s 1087 CA 2006; ¶4090).

> MEMO POINTS   Under the **new Companies Act**, directors will have the right to give service addresses instead of their residential addresses for display on the public record. Only certain bodies and credit reference agencies will be able to access their residential addresses on the new register of directors' residential addresses (see ¶3896). Draft regulations under the new Act have been published, which enable directors who do not wish their residential addresses to be disclosed to credit reference agencies, or whose residential addresses are already on the register (whether filed under the old rules, or as a service address under the new ones) to apply to Companies House for the address not to be made available for public inspection (draft Companies (Particulars of Usual Residential Address) Regulations 2008, likely to come into force by 1 October 2009). Former directors will also be able to make such an application if the information was placed on the register on or after 1 January 2003. Such applications will be able to be made in similar circumstances as an application for a confidentiality order.

B. Register of shareholders

3915 Every company must keep a register of shareholders (s 352 CA 1985). The register must record members other than shareholders, for example in the case of a company limited by guarantee and not by shares. References here are to shareholders rather than members, unless statute requires specific references to members. The term "members" generally includes shareholders, although note that a person can be a shareholder without being a member if he holds a share warrant (¶1902/mp). For a fuller discussion of who can be a shareholder, see ¶2020+ and ¶1902/mp.

1. General rules

Contents

3918 It is vital that the register of shareholders is maintained accurately as its contents are primary **evidence** of all matters which the legislation requires or allows to be contained in it. For example, unless it can be proved otherwise, the register is proof of the names of all of the shareholders. The legislation requires the register of shareholders to contain the following **information** for each shareholder (s 352 CA 1985):
a. his name;
b. his postal address;
c. the date on which he was registered;
d. the date on which he ceased to be a shareholder;
e. how many shares are held by him (and which particular shares, if they are distinguished, e.g. by individual numbers);
f. if the company divides its shares into different classes, what class(es) he holds and how many; and
g. the amount paid up on his shares.

> MEMO POINTS 1. Where a company **does not have a share capital**, but has more than one class of members, the class to which that member belongs is to be entered in the register instead of points e. f. and g. above.
> 2. Where a company has **converted** any of its **shares into stock** and notified Companies House accordingly (¶1312/mp), the amount and class of the stock held by a member is to be entered into the register instead of points e. f. and g. above.
> 3. The **new Companies Act** will require the same information to be recorded (s 113 CA 2006, expected to come into force by 1 October 2009).

3919 If shares are **held** by two or more persons **jointly**, the shareholders are entitled to have their names entered on the register in whatever order they want (*Re TH Saunders & Co Ltd* [1908] 1 Ch 415). Since only the vote of the first-named shareholder is counted, joint shareholders may wish to enter their names in a different order for each share if they hold more than one, to allow the vote of each one of them to count (*Burns v Siemens Brothers Dynamo Works* [1919] 1 Ch 225).

> MEMO POINTS The **new Companies Act** will require the names of each joint holder to be included (s 113 CA 2006, expected to come into force by 1 October 2009). Again, only the first-named shareholder's vote will count.

3920 The **address** of the shareholder does not have to be his residential address (unlike directors and secretaries), but does have to be a postal address (which includes a post office box address).

3921 A transferee of shares (i.e. a purchaser or recipient) is entitled to rely on the entries in the register and the share certificate as evidence of the **amount paid up** on the shares he purchases.

If the shares have been paid for using **non-cash consideration** (e.g. an asset or services) the register should state that they are paid up to the extent of the value of that consideration, even though no money has changed hands (*Re Anglesea Colliery Co* (1866) LR 2 Eq 379).

3922 **Failure** to comply with these record keeping obligations renders the company and every officer in default liable to a fine (¶9935). The limitation period, which is the date after which proceedings cannot be brought, for actions arising out of the company making or deleting any entry in its register of shareholders is 20 years after the entry or deletion, assuming that the action is not already barred by another limitation period which applies to the case (s 352(7) CA 1985).

> MEMO POINTS The **new Companies Act** will reduce this limitation period to 10 years (s 128 CA 2006, expected to come into force by 1 October 2009).

Special cases

3923 It is not necessary for companies to enter the details of any **trust** over the shares on the register of shareholders (s 360 CA 1985). This means that the company is not obliged to take account of equitable third party interests in its shares when dealing with them. Therefore, the name of the trustee will be entered in the register and the company can deal with him as if he was the beneficial owner. How the trustee deals with the shares for the beneficiary is a matter between them. This rule also prevents third parties from alleging that the company itself is in the position of trustee to them in relation to the shares.

> MEMO POINTS This will be restated in the **new Companies Act** (s 126 CA 2006, expected to come into force by 1 October 2009).

3924 The legislation sets out particular requirements for entry in the register where a company issues **share warrants** (¶1902/mp). The name of the bearer, or holder, of the share warrant is not entered on the register of shareholders. If the company does enter the bearer's name on the register, it is responsible for any loss suffered by any person as a result.

If a warrant is **issued**, the company is to (s 355 CA 1985):
– strike out the name of the shareholder entered in the register as holding the shares specified in the warrant, as if that shareholder had ceased to be a shareholder;
– enter the fact that a share warrant has been issued;
– enter a statement of the shares in the warrant, e.g. identifying them by a number if the company assigns numbers to its shares; and
– enter the date of the issue of the share warrant.

If the share warrant is **surrendered** for cancellation, the shareholder can have his name entered in the register again, subject to the company's articles. The date of surrender of the share warrant is also to be entered on the register.

> MEMO POINTS This will be restated in the **new Companies Act** (s 122 CA 2006, expected to come into force by 1 October 2009).

Form

3925 Although the register of shareholders is usually kept in **paper** form, it can be kept in "non-legible" form, e.g. on a computer or other **electronic** method of recording the information. If the register is kept in "non-legible" form, the company must notify Companies House of this fact by filing Form 353a.

> MEMO POINTS The name of Form 353a, like other **Companies House forms**, is taken from the relevant section number in the legislation. As all of the section numbers will change under the new Companies Act, Companies House proposes to change the names of all of its forms to reflect their function rather than the relevant section number ("Working with Companies House: a consultation on the registrar's rules and related provisions which will apply under the Companies Act 2006"). At the time of writing, the new form names are not yet available.

3926 If a company has **more than 50 shareholders**, it must keep an **index** of the names of the shareholders in the same place as the register (s 354 CA 1985). The index must contain sufficient information to enable the corresponding entry in the register of shareholders to be found. Any joint shareholders of the company must be listed separately. Any changes to the register itself must also be made to the index, if necessary, within 14 days of the alteration being made to the register.

If the register itself can act as an index, because the shareholders are ordered alphabetically rather than chronologically for example, the company does not have to keep a separate index as well.

Any **failure** by the company in respect of its index requirements renders the company and every officer in default liable to a fine (s 354(4) CA 1985; ¶9935). If the register is kept by another person who fails to keep the index with the register, he is also liable to a fine as if he were an officer of the company in default (s 357 CA 1985).

> MEMO POINTS The **new Companies Act** will contain the same requirements regarding the index, except that only the company and any officer in default will be liable to a fine in the case of breach (s 115 CA 2006, expected to come into force by 1 October 2009).

Location

3928

The register of shareholders usually has to be kept at the company's registered office (s 353 CA 1985). It may only be kept at another office of the company if it is actually maintained at that other office. Companies frequently instruct someone outside of the company to maintain the register, such as an accountant or solicitor. In such cases, the register can be kept at the office of that person.

If the register is **not kept at the registered office**, or if the location of the register **changes** (including where the register was kept outside the registered office and then returns to the registered office), the company must notify Companies House using Form 353 within 14 days of the change. Companies registered in England and Wales cannot keep their register outside of England and Wales. Similarly, companies registered in Scotland must keep their registers in Scotland.

Failure to do so renders the company and every officer in default liable to a fine. If the register is kept by another person, and he fails to notify the registrar of a change in the register's location, he is liable to a fine as if he were an officer of the company in default (s 357 CA 1985; ¶9935).

> MEMO POINTS 1. The **new Companies Act** will require the register and index to be kept at: (ss 114, 115, 1136 CA 2006; reg 5 draft Companies (Company Records and Fees) Regulations 2007; all expected to come into force by 1 October 2009):
> – the company's registered office; or
> – another location that is situated in the same part of the UK as the registered office.
> Unless the register has always been kept at the registered office, Companies House will have to be notified within 14 days of any change. Failure to do so will render the company and any officer in default liable to a fine.
> 2. The name of Form 353, like other **Companies House forms**, is taken from the relevant section number in the legislation. As all of the section numbers will change under the new Companies Act, Companies House proposes to change the names of all of its forms to reflect their function rather than the relevant section number ("Working with Companies House: a consultation on the registrar's rules and related provisions which will apply under the Companies Act 2006"). At the time of writing, the new form names are not yet available.

Inspection

3930

The register and its index (if applicable) must be open to any shareholder for inspection without charge (s 116 CA 2006). The register of shareholders must be **available** for inspection for at least two hours between 9am and 5pm on each business day (reg 3 SI 1991/1998). Non-shareholders may also inspect the register, but the company is entitled to charge them a fee for doing so (the fees are set out in the table at ¶4019).

Both shareholders and non-shareholders can also request a **copy** of the register or index, or part of it. The company is entitled to charge both shareholders and non-shareholders for any copies provided (the fees are set out in the table at ¶4019). In addition to this, when a person is inspecting the register and/or index, a company must permit him to copy it by taking notes or a transcript (reg 3 SI 1991/1998).

Comment: Where a request to inspect or copy is made on or after **1 October 2007** and the company has been obliged to submit an annual return with a return date (see ¶4061) of 1 October 2007 or later, the new rules under the new Companies Act apply (para 2 Sch 3 SI 2007/2194). If a request was submitted before that date, or the company has not yet had to submit such an annual return, the old rules under the Companies Act 1985 apply. However, for these purposes, the effect of the two sets of rules is the same (however, see memo point below for further proposed changes).

> MEMO POINTS 1. A company may **close its register** of shareholders for a maximum of 30 days in each calendar year (s 358 CA 1985). The company must advertise the fact that it is closing the register in a newspaper which is circulated in the area of the company's registered office. The new Companies Act will repeal this provision (Sch 16 CA 2006). Until this repeal is brought into force, shareholders and others cannot inspect or obtain copies of the register when it is closed (para 2 Sch 1 SI 2007/2194).

2. Draft regulations under the **new Companies Act** published by BERR propose to ease the administrative burden on private companies by only requiring them to make their records available for inspection for 2 hours between 9am and 5pm on a working day on request (reg 6 draft Companies (Company Records and Fees) Regulations 2007, likely to come into force by 1 October 2009). Any person who wants to inspect the register will usually have to give the company 10 working days' notice. However, if he wishes to inspect it during the notice period for a meeting or during the period allowed for passing a written resolution, he can give only 2 working days' notice.

3931 A **request to inspect/copy** the register must state the purpose for which the information is to be used, as well as their name and address (and the name of an individual who is responsible for the request, in the case of a request from an organisation) (s 116 CA 2006). They also have to give details of any third party to which the information will be passed and for what purpose it will be used. It is an offence to make a misleading, false or deceptive request, rendering the person in default liable to imprisonment and/or a fine (s 119 CA 2006).

To inspect or obtain copies of part of the register, the shareholder or other person making the request must ask for it in terms of the information on the register. For example, he could ask for all entries for shareholders whose surnames begin with a C. The company does not have to extract entries according to, or even group them by (reg 4 SI 1991/1998):
– the location of the shareholders' addresses;
– gender;
– nationality;
– legal status (i.e. whether a shareholder is a corporate shareholder or not); or
– size of holding.

MEMO POINTS Under the **old rules**, a person requesting to inspect or copy the register does not have to give any reasons to the company for doing so (*Holland v Dickson* (1888) 37 Ch D 669).

3932 Once the company has received a request to inspect or copy the register or index, it must **comply** within 5 working days.

However, if it believes that the **request has not been made for a proper purpose**, it can apply to court (s 117 CA 2006). The court will be able to order the company not to comply with the request (and, if necessary, any similar requests) as well as ordering the person making the request to pay the company's costs. Guidance on this "proper purpose test" has been published by ICSA (guidance note number 080607). It remains to be seen how the court will interpret "proper purposes", but it is hoped that this will better protect shareholders from intimidation and unwanted junk mail.

Failure to comply with a proper request will render the company and every officer in default liable to a fine (s 118 CA 2006). It will be an offence for a person receiving the information to do/not to do anything that results in the information being passed on and used for improper purposes (s 119 CA 2006). Conviction of this offence will result in imprisonment and/or a fine.

MEMO POINTS 1. If the **old rules** apply, the company must send any copies out within 10 days of the request (s 356 CA 1985). A company must usually allow access to the register, even to a person who is hostile to the company. If it refuses to do so, the person denied access can apply to the court for an order allowing him to inspect or copy the register. If the court finds that the company denied that person access for a good reason in the company's best interests, it will not make such an order. If it finds for the person seeking access to the register, the court can place "relevant and reasonable" conditions on disclosure to address the company's concerns about the purposes for which the information may be used, or accept a suitable undertaking by the company to make the relevant disclosure voluntarily instead of making an order (*Pelling v Families Need Fathers Ltd* [2002] 2 All ER 440).
Otherwise, any **refusal** by the company to allow access to the register and index or to provide copies when requested, renders the company and every officer in default liable to a fine (s 356 CA 1985; ¶9935). If the register is kept by a person other than the company (e.g. a solicitor or accountant), and that person does not allow the register to be inspected or does not provide copies when requested, he is also liable to a fine as if he was an officer of the company in default (s 357 CA 1985).
2. Under the **new Companies Act**, when the company provides the information requested, it will have to inform the person of when the register was last updated (s 120 CA 2006, expected to come into force by 1 October 2009). If the register has been updated but the changes have not been

followed through on the index, the company must inform the person of this as well. Failure to do so will render the company and every officer in default liable to a fine.

3933 The requirement to allow the register to be inspected and copied ceases if a **company goes into liquidation** (*Re Kent Coalfields Syndicate* [1898] 1 QB 754). The liquidator will take custody of the register of shareholders.

3934 The right of inspection is widely used by research and marketing organisations. Unfortunately, this means that most of the requests for inspection or copies are not for purposes connected with the company or the shareholders' interests. Shareholders are afforded some protection from **unwanted marketing** in that they are not required to have their residential addresses entered on the register. Shareholders can rely on their rights under data protection legislation to prevent processing of their personal data which is "likely to cause unwarranted and substantial damage or distress" (s 10 Data Protection Act 1998).

Shareholders concerned about receiving direct marketing (or, "junk mail") are entitled to prevent unwanted use of their details under data protection legislation, by serving notices on businesses who are using or who are likely to use the information for direct marketing (s 11 Data Protection Act 1998). The Direct Marketing Authority also offers some protection through its preference schemes with which individuals can register to ensure that their details are not used by direct marketing businesses. For more information on data protection and direct marketing, visit the Information Commissioner's website.

Retention

3936 The required information must be **kept for** at least 20 years after a person has ceased to be a shareholder of the company (s 352(6) CA 1985).

> MEMO POINTS The **new Companies Act** will require this information to be removed after 10 years (s 121 CA 2006, expected to come into force by 1 October 2009).

2. Single shareholder companies

3943 If a company has, or its membership falls to, only one shareholder it must make an entry in the register of shareholders with the name and address of the sole shareholder stating (s 352A CA 1985):
– that the company has only one member; and
– the date on which this occurred.

If the number of shareholders **rises above one** again, a statement that the company has ceased to be a company with only one member and the date which this took place must be added to the entry.

Failure to comply with these requirements renders the company and any officer in default liable to a fine (¶9935).

> MEMO POINTS The **new Companies Act** will repeat these requirements, as well as requiring a company incorporated with only one shareholder to include a statement of that fact in its register of shareholders (s 123 CA 2006, expected to come into force by 1 October 2009). This will only apply to limited companies, so if an unlimited company with one member re-registers as a limited company, it will have to add this statement to its register.

3. Overseas branch registers

UK companies with overseas branch

3948 A UK company with a branch (¶145+) in **specified countries and territories** may keep an "overseas branch register", which is a register of those shareholders of the company who are resident in the country in which that branch operates (s 362 CA 1985). The overseas branch register is deemed to be a part of the company's register of shareholders, which is known as the "principal register" in this context (para 2 Sch 14 CA 1985).

> MEMO POINTS 1. Overseas branch registers were known as "**dominion registers**" under the Companies Act 1948, and "**colonial registers**" under the 1929 Act. Any references to these registers in old company articles are to be read as references to overseas branch registers.
> 2. The **new Companies Act** will also allow companies to keep an overseas branch register as part of its "main register" (ss 129, 131 CA 2006, expected to come into force by 1 October 2009).

3949 Branch offices in these countries and territories may keep an overseas branch register (Pt I Sch 14 CA 1985):

- Bangladesh
- Cyprus
- Dominica
- The Gambia
- Ghana
- Guyana
- Hong Kong
- India
- Kenya
- Kiribati
- Lesotho
- Malawi
- Malaysia
- Malta
- Nigeria
- Northern Ireland
- Pakistan
- Republic of Ireland
- Seychelles
- Sierra Leone
- Singapore
- South Africa
- Sri Lanka
- Swaziland
- Trinidad and Tobago
- Uganda
- Zimbabwe
- Any part of Her Majesty's dominions/overseas territories outside the UK, Channel Islands and the Isle of Man, currently:
  – Anguilla;
  – Bermuda;
  – British Antarctic Territory;
  – British Indian Ocean Territory;
  – British Virgin Islands;
  – Cayman Islands;
  – Falkland Islands;
  – Gibraltar;
  – Montserrat;
  – St Helena, Ascension Island and Tristan da Cunha;
  – Turk and Caicos Islands;
  – Pitcairn Island;
  – South Georgia and South Sandwich Islands; and
  – Sovereign Base Areas on Cyprus.

> MEMO POINTS The **new Companies Act** will contain the same list, replacing "Northern Ireland" and "Republic of Ireland" with "Ireland" (s 129 CA 2006, expected to come into force by 1 October 2009).

3950 A company which keeps an overseas branch register is to **give notice** to Companies House, using Form 362 (or Form 362(a) if the register is kept in a "non-legible" format) (para 1 Sch 14 CA 1985):
– of where that overseas register is kept;
– of any change in its location; and
– if the company ceases to hold a branch register.

The form is to be sent to Companies House within 14 days of either: the opening of the branch office, the change in location or the discontinuance of the register. **Failure** to comply with this requirement renders the company and every officer in default liable to a fine (¶9935).

An overseas branch register is required to be kept in the same manner as the principal register. An up-to-date **duplicate** of the overseas branch register is to be kept at the same place as the company's principal register in GB (para 4 Sch 14 CA 1985). To this end, companies are to send to the registered office a copy of every entry in the overseas branch register as soon as possible after it has been made. Failure to comply with these rules renders the company and every officer or agent who holds the overseas branch register and is in default liable to a fine (¶9935).

Other than the duplicate register held by the company, any **transactions of shares** noted in an overseas branch register should only be recorded in that register, to avoid any confusion. Shares on the overseas branch register are to be distinguished from those on the principal register: an instrument of transfer of shares registered in an overseas branch register is a transfer of property situated outside the UK.

The company can **cease to hold** an overseas branch register, in which case the entries should be transferred to another overseas branch register, or to the principal register. If the overseas register is **closed** for a period of up to 30 days, an advertisement of that fact is to be circulated in a newspaper local to the branch office.

The courts of the countries or territories in which the overseas branch registers are kept have **jurisdiction** to deal with matters such as rectifying the register and ordering inspection and copying to take place, provided the local law of that country or territory makes comparable provision for companies to keep and maintain registers of shareholders to UK legislation (and it did so immediately before the UK legislation came into effect) (para 3(2) Sch 14 CA 1985).

> MEMO POINTS 1. The **new Companies Act** will make similar provisions, except that agents will not be liable for default (ss 130-135 CA 2006, expected to come into force by 1 October 2009).
> 2. The name of Form 362, like other **Companies House forms**, is taken from the relevant section number in the legislation. As all of the section numbers will change under the new Companies Act, Companies House proposes to change the names of all of its forms to reflect their function rather than the relevant section number ("Working with Companies House: a consultation on the registrar's rules and related provisions which will apply under the Companies Act 2006"). At the time of writing, the new form names are not yet available.

Overseas companies with a branch in the UK

3952 If the local law of an overseas country allows a company incorporated in that country to keep a register of shareholders resident in Great Britain, similar provisions to overseas branch registers apply with regard to (para 9 Sch 14 CA 1985):
– keeping the register at the registered office;
– inspecting and copying the register; and
– rectifying the register.

This applies to the countries and territories listed at ¶3949, as well as Botswana, Zambia and Tonga, and any country which is under the protection or administration of the UK under the trusteeship system of the UN.

C. Register of directors' interests

3958 Companies used to be obliged to keep a register of directors' interests in **shares and debentures** which have been notified to the company by the director. However, since 6 April 2007, directors have not been required to disclose their interests in shares or debentures, so companies no longer need to maintain this register (s 1177, Sch 16 CA 2006; Sch 4 SI 2006/3428).

D. Register of charges

Internal register

3975 Companies are required to keep a register of charges **containing** details of any fixed or floating charges over its undertaking or property (s 407 CA 1985). Note that the company's internal register must include details of all charges, whereas that kept by Companies House only has to deal with certain ones (see ¶3979+ below).

The entry in relation to each charge is to state:
– a short description of the property charged;
– the amount of the charge; and
– the name(s) of the person(s) entitled under the charge, except in the case of securities to bearer.

The company is to **keep copies** of each charge instrument which has to be registered at Companies House (¶3979).

Failure to enter a charge in the register renders the officer of the company in default liable to a fine (¶9935).

> MEMO POINTS   The **new Companies Act** will also require companies to record this information in its register of charges and keep copies of the charge instruments (ss 875, 876 CA 2006, expected to come into force by 1 October 2009).

Location

3976 The company's register of charges is to be kept at its registered office (s 407 CA 1985).

> MEMO POINTS   The **new Companies Act** will allow the register to be kept at the registered office or another single alternative location that is in the same part of the UK as the registered office (s 877 CA 2006; reg 5 draft Companies (Company Records and Fees) Regulations 2007; both expected to come into force by 1 October 2009).

Inspection

3977 The register and copy charge instruments are to be **available** for inspection at the registered office of the company for at least two hours each business day. Shareholders and creditors of the company can inspect the register without paying any fee, and any other person can inspect it for payment of a maximum fee of 5p per inspection (s 408 CA 1985).

The legislation does not provide a right for shareholders or non-shareholders to take **copies** of the register, but the register kept at Companies House will contain the same information, and copies of that register can be obtained by anybody (¶4019).

> MEMO POINTS   These inspection provisions will be restated in the **new Companies Act** (s 877 CA 2006, expected to come into force by 1 October 2009). For the proposed regulations on how a person can inspect company records, see ¶3869/mp.

3978 **Failure** to permit any person to inspect the register or the copies of the charge instruments renders each officer in default liable to a fine (¶9935). Further, the court can make an order for the register or copies of the charge instruments to be inspected if the company refuses access (s 408 CA 1985).

> MEMO POINTS   The **new Companies Act** will also contain these consequences of failure to comply, except that the company will also be liable for any default (s 877 CA 2006, expected to come into force by 1 October 2009).

Register kept at Companies House

3979 A separate register of charges is kept for each company at Companies House **containing** details of those charges a company is required to register (s 401 CA 1985). The registration of charges is dealt with at ¶4636+, including:
– what types of charges have to be registered;
– the timing of registration;
– the information required by Companies House;
– overseas issues; and
– the consequences of failing to register a charge.

> MEMO POINTS   1. Another type of charge which has to be notified to Companies House for entry in the register is the **appointment of a receiver** or manager (s 405 CA 1985; ¶9195+). Companies House must be notified of such an appointment by the person who obtained the order or made the appointment, within 7 days of the order or appointment. An entry will then be made on the register of charges at Companies House. This alerts other creditors to the position. Any **failure** to inform the registrar of the appointment renders the person in default liable to a fine (¶9935). Companies House must also be notified when a receiver or manager ceases to act.
> 2. The **new Companies Act** will also require charges to be registered at Companies House (ss 869-874 CA 2006, expected to come into force by 1 October 2009). Draft regulations under the new Act have been published setting out the details of charges which have to be filed at Companies House (draft Companies (Prescribed Particulars of Company Charges) Regulations 2007).

Different **forms** are required by Companies House, depending on the information to be registered: **3980**

Information to be given to Companies House	Form	Reference (CA 1985)
Mortgage/charge to be entered on register	395	s 395
Charge securing series of debentures	397	s 397
Issue of secured debentures in series	397a	s 397
Charge over property in Scotland/Northern Ireland which has been registered in that jurisdiction	398	s 398
Mortgage/charge attached to acquired property	400	s 400
Satisfaction of charge in full/part	403a	s 403
Property/undertaking subject to charge has been released from it	403b	s 403
Property/undertaking subject to charge has been sold	403b	s 403
Appointment of receiver/manager	405(1)	s 405
Receiver/manager ceasing to act	405(2)	s 405

MEMO POINTS The names of these forms, like other **Companies House forms**, are taken from the relevant section numbers in the legislation. As all of the section numbers will change under the new Companies Act, Companies House proposes to change the names of all of its forms to reflect their function rather than the relevant section number ("Working with Companies House: a consultation on the registrar's rules and related provisions which will apply under the Companies Act 2006"). At the time of writing, the new form names are not yet available.

Once a charge has been filed at Companies House, the registrar issues a **certificate** to that effect. The certificate is conclusive evidence that the charge was correctly filed and registered. If a debenture or series of debentures is secured, a copy of the certificate of the relevant charge(s) is to be endorsed on the debenture or series of debenture stock (s 402 CA 1985). **3981**

The register of charges at Companies House is open to **inspection** by anybody. This protects those dealing with the company, such as customers and creditors, by making public the extent of a company's encumbered assets (i.e. those subject to the security, which will not be available to the company's general creditors on insolvency). Copies of the register can also be ordered from Companies House by anybody (¶4090). **3982**

The register is kept up to date by the company notifying Companies House if the **charge is paid off**, or "satisfied", on the relevant form (¶3980). Any information communicated to Companies House regarding the satisfaction and release of a charge must be correct, and the form requires a director to make a "statutory declaration" to verify it. Making a statutory declaration is tantamount to giving evidence in court, and if a director makes a statement which he knows is false, or does not believe to be true, he is liable to imprisonment and/or a fine (¶9935). The register will be amended to reflect the fact that all or part of the charge has been satisfied, or that part of the property which was the subject of the charge has either been released from the charge, or has been sold by the company.

E. Public company's register of interests in shares

Shareholders in public companies used to be obliged to disclose their interests in shares automatically, and these interests had to be recorded in a register. Now that the relevant provisions of the new Companies Act have come into force, public company shareholders will only have to disclose their interests on request (¶2042+). A register of interests in shares will have to be kept, recording any information disclosed to it under these provisions (s 808 CA 2006). **3990**

3991 Within 3 days of receiving the **information** requested from a person who has or has had an interest in the company's shares, the company must note on the register against the relevant shareholder's name (s 808 CA 2006):
- the fact that a request was made and the date on which it was made; and
- the information provided in compliance with the request.

Failure to do so will render the company and any officer liable to a fine (¶9935).

3992 Public companies will have to keep an **index** of the names on the register of interests in shares to allow the information on the register to be found easily, unless the register is already ordered as an index (s 810 CA 2006). The index must be kept with the register and updated within 10 days of any alteration to the register. Failure to comply with the provisions relating to the index will render the company and any officers in default liable to a fine (¶9935).

3993 The register and index must be **kept at** the company's registered office, or any other place permitted in regulations (ss 809, 810 CA 2006). Unless the register has always been kept at the registered office, the company will have to notify Companies House of its location and any change. Failure to comply will render the company and any officer in default liable to a fine (¶9935).

> MEMO POINTS Draft regulations have been published under the **new Companies Act** which will allow companies to keep their register of interests in shares at the registered office or at one alternative location that is situated in the same part of the UK as the registered office (reg 5 draft Companies (Company Records and Fees) Regulations 2007). This part of the draft regulations is likely to come into force by 1 October 2009. For the proposed regulations on how a person can inspect company records, see ¶3869/mp.

3994 Any person can **inspect** the register and any index without charge (s 811 CA 2006), although the company can charge for **copies** of any entry in the register. The fees for these copies will be set out in regulations in due course; in the meantime, it is assumed that the fees applicable to copying the register under the Companies Act 1985 still apply.

Failure by the company to comply with its obligations relating to the inspection of the register and index and taking copies of the register renders it and any officer in default liable to a fine (s 813 CA 2006; ¶9935).

> MEMO POINTS The **new Companies Act** also sets out a procedure for requesting the right to inspect or copy the register, but its implementation has been postponed (the date is yet to be announced at the time of writing). A person requesting the right to do so must give the company his name and address (and the name of an individual responsible for the request if it comes from an organisation), stating the purpose for which the information will be used. If it will be passed on to other parties, the same details must be given regarding those parties and their use of the information (s 811(4) CA 2006). The company will have to either comply with the request or refuse to do so on the ground that it was not made for a proper purpose (s 812 CA 2006). A person whose request is refused can apply to court, notifying the company. The company then has to notify, as far as possible, the people whose information will be disclosed if it has to comply with the request. The court can also order the company not to disclose the information, and not to comply with any similar request in the future. It is an offence for a person making a request to make a misleading, false or deceptive statement in it, or to do or not do anything that results in the information being disclosed to a third party who uses it for an improper purpose (s 814 CA 2006). Conviction of either offence renders that person liable to imprisonment and/or a fine.

3995 An entry in the register can only be **removed** if:
- it is more than 6 years old (s 816 CA 2006); or
- it consists of incorrect information about a third party (s 817 CA 2006).

If an entry is incorrectly removed, it must be restored as soon as is reasonably practicable (s 815 CA 2006).

Failure to comply with the provisions relating to removal of entries renders the company and any officer in default liable to a fine (¶9935).

> MEMO POINTS An entry can also be **changed** to reflect an alteration in certain types of share acquisition agreement, on application by a party to the agreement (s 818 CA 2006; the relevant types of share acquisition agreement are defined at s 824 CA 2006).

3996 The register must be **kept for** 6 years after a company ceases to be a public company (s 819 CA 2006). Contravention renders the company and any officers in default liable to a fine (¶9935).

F. Non-statutory registers

4000 Most companies keep additional registers to those required by statute which record the movement of shares and debentures in the company and contracts to which it has agreed. This is a matter of **good record keeping and management**, and makes it easier to prepare other documents, especially the register of shareholders and the annual return.

Register of share applications and allotments

4002 This usually **contains** details of each application and allotment such as the name of the applicant or allottee, when it was made and how many shares it concerned. Applications for shares do not have to be in a particular form. They are usually made in writing, and in the case of public companies making an offer to the public are often made by way of a pre-printed application form. There is no statutory requirement to keep a formal record of applications and allotments, but it can be a useful tool for the company, for example by showing who the latest shareholders are, which can assist in complying with other record keeping obligations.

Since there is no statutory requirement to keep these records, there is no automatic right of the shareholders or anybody else to **inspect** or obtain copies of the register. A company may provide for such a right in its articles: Table A enables shareholders to inspect non-statutory documents if the company passes an ordinary resolution to that effect (reg 109 TA 1985).

> *MEMO POINTS* Draft **new model articles** under the **new Companies Act** have been published. They will allow shareholders, in addition to their statutory rights to inspect certain registers and records, to inspect the company's accounts and other records if the board allows or the company passes an ordinary resolution to that effect (private companies limited by shares: art 51; public companies: art 83) but those for private companies limited by shares will not. BERR has published draft regulations under the new Act, which deal with when inspection of company records will be able to occur and how much the company can charge for copies (draft Companies (Company Records and Fees) Regulations 2007). These are explained further at ¶3869/mp in the context of shareholder meeting minutes.

Register of share transfers

4004 A company may keep a register of transfers of its shares for the same reasons as the register of applications and allotments. It assists with the preparation of the annual return as it gives an at-a-glance record of the latest changes in the company's membership. The register will usually **contain** the details of each transfer (when, how much, and from and to whom), and may record the details of the relevant certificates issued by the company.

As with the register of applications and allotments, there is no automatic right of **inspection**, although a company's articles may provide for shareholders and others to inspect it (such as reg 109 TA 1985).

> *MEMO POINTS* The draft **new model articles** will allow shareholders, in addition to their statutory rights to inspect certain registers and records, to inspect the company's accounts and other records if the board allows or the company passes an ordinary resolution to that effect (private companies limited by shares: art 51; public companies: art 83) but those for private companies limited by shares will not. BERR has published draft regulations under the new Act, which deal with when inspection of company records will be able to occur (draft Companies (Company Records and Fees) Regulations 2007). These are explained further at ¶3869/mp in the context of shareholder meeting minutes.

Register of debenture holders

4006 Companies usually keep a record of debenture holders so it can see what payments are to be made to which holders and when. Although there is no obligation to keep such a register, where a company does so, similar rules to the other registers apply as to the register's **location** (s 190 CA 1985). The register is to be kept at a company's registered office, or at whichever company office the register is made up at, or at the office of some other person who maintains the register. The register's location must be notified to Companies House using Form 190, or Form 190a if the register is kept in a digital format, on its creation or a change in location. A company registered in England and Wales is not permitted to keep its register in Scotland, and vice versa.

A company must **notify** Companies House of the whereabouts of the register and any duplicate, unless the register has always been kept at the registered office. If it is kept somewhere other than the registered office, the address must be included in the annual return (s 364(1) CA 1985).

Comment: The **new Companies Act** includes similar rules regarding registers of debenture holders, due to come into force on 6 April 2008, except that the register will have to be kept at the registered office or another place permitted by regulations (ss 743-748 CA 2006).

> MEMO POINTS 1. Draft regulations under the new Act propose to allow companies to keep their records in a single alternative **location** within the same part of the UK as the registered office (reg 5 draft Companies (Company Records and Fees) Regulations 2007, likely to come into force by 1 October 2009).
> 2. The name of Form 190, like other **Companies House forms**, is taken from the relevant section number in the legislation. As all of the section numbers will change under the new Companies Act, Companies House proposes to change the names of all of its forms to reflect their function rather than the relevant section number ("Working with Companies House: a consultation on the registrar's rules and related provisions which will apply under the Companies Act 2006"). At the time of writing, the new form names are not yet available.

4007 Similar rights of **inspection** also apply to the register of debenture holders as to statutory registers (s 191 CA 1985). Shareholders are to be allowed to inspect the register without charge, and non-shareholders can do so for a fee (the fees are set out in the table at ¶4019). The register is to be available for inspection for at least two hours between the hours of 9am and 5pm on each business day (reg 3 SI 1991/1998).

Copies must be provided to any shareholder or non-shareholder on request, and upon payment of a fee (the fees for copies of the register itself are set out in the table at ¶4019). In addition to obtaining copies of the register itself, a debenture holder may request a copy of any **trust deed** securing the issue of his debentures, subject to a fee of 10p per 100 words or part of 100 words copied (Sch 2 SI 1991/1998).

When a person is inspecting the register or has requested copies of it, the company does not have to **extract entries** according to, or even group them by (reg 4 SI 1991/1998):
– the location of the shareholders' addresses;
– gender;
– nationality;
– legal status (i.e. whether a shareholder is a corporate shareholder or not); or
– size of holding.

Failure to allow inspection or to provide copies renders the company and any officer in default liable to a fine (s 191(4) CA 1985; ¶9935).

Comment: As with other registers, under the **new Companies Act**, a person requesting inspection/copies of the register of debenture holders will have to give his name and address (and the name of an individual responsible for the request if an organisation makes it) and give the purpose for which the information will be used (s 744 CA 2006, due to come into force on 6 April 2008). If the information will be passed on to a third party, he will also have to give the third party's details and purpose for which the information will be used as well. The company will either have to comply with the request or apply to court on the ground that the information will not be used for a proper purpose (s 745 CA 2006, due to come into force on 6 April 2008). The person making the request will commit an offence if he includes misleading, false or deceptive information in his request or if he does/fails to do anything that results in the information being passed on to a third party which uses it improperly (s 747 CA 2006, due to come into force on 6 April 2008). Conviction will result in imprisonment and/or a fine.

> MEMO POINTS   Draft regulations under the new Act propose to allow private companies to only make their records available for **inspection** between 9am and 5 pm on a working day on request (reg 6 draft Companies (Company Records and Fees) Regulations 2007, likely to come into force by 1 October 2009). A request will be able to be made on 10 working days' notice, unless it is made during the notice period for a meeting or the period within which a written resolution can be agreed, in which case only 2 working days' notice needs to be given. Public companies will still be expected to have their records available for inspection for at least 2 hours between 9am and 5 pm on business days (reg 7 draft Companies (Company Records and Fees) Regulations 2007, likely to come into force by 1 October 2009). Companies will be able to charge 10p per 500 words or part of 500 words for **copies** of trust deeds, plus the reasonable costs of sending copies out from 6 April 2008 (reg 16 draft Companies (Company Records and Fees) Regulations 2007). Copies will be able to be provided in hard copy or electronic form, as requested (regs 11-13 draft Companies (Company Records and Fees) Regulations 2007, likely to come into force by 1 Octobr 2009).

4008 The register may be **closed** for a period not exceeding 30 days in any one calendar year, if the articles, debentures, stock certificates or trust deed make provision for this.

4009 As with the register of shareholders, there is a 20 year **limitation period**, after which no claims may be brought in respect of the company making or failing to make entries in the register. The period runs from the entry, or failure to make the entry, and is subject to any lesser period of limitation affecting the claim (s 353(7) CA 1985).

Comment: Under the **new Companies Act**, the limitation period will be 10 years (s 748 CA 2006, due to come into force on 6 April 2008).

Book of executed documents

4011 Companies usually keep a record of all documents executed by the company as a **deed** or affixed with the company **seal** (if applicable). For most companies, the record will simply comprise the meeting minutes approving the execution of the document. If a company enters into many transactions requiring the execution of documents as deeds, it is advisable to keep a separate "seal book" or "book of executed documents" in which all executions are recorded and the book is produced to the meeting for approval (and this fact noted in the minutes of the meeting and in the book). This enables companies to keep track of how many deeds it has entered into, and to **control** the execution of onerous contracts.

G. Inspection and copying rights and fees

4019 The rights to inspect the various company registers differ, as do the applicable charges. This table summarises the position in relation to each register, distinguishing between the rights of shareholders and non-shareholders. The final row, "CH", indicates whether or not there is a register of the same information kept at Companies House, which will be available for inspection by shareholders and non-shareholders alike on payment of a fee (¶4040+). At the time of writing, the fees are set out in SI 1991/1998 and SI 2007/2612, although these regulations will be superseded as more of the new Companies Act is implemented and some of the fees will change (see the notes to the table).

	Director	Secretary	Share-holders	Charges	Plc's interests in shares	Debenture holders	Shares – application allotment & transfer
Shareholders							
Inspect	✓	✓	✓	✓	✓	✓	Only if articles provide
– charge	✗	✗	✗	✗	✗	✗	
Copy	✗	✗	✓	✗	✓	✓	
– charge	n/a	n/a	Up to 5 entries: £1; up to the next 95 entries: £30; up to the next 900 entries: £30; up to the next 99,000 entries: £30; up to the rest of the register: £30 [1]	n/a	Up to 5 entries: £1; up to the next 95 entries: £30; up to the next 900 entries: £30; up to the next 99,000 entries: £30; up to the rest of the register: £30 [1]	Up to 100 entries: £2.50; next 1,000 entries or part thereof: £20; each batch of 1,000 entries or part thereof after that: £15 [2]	
Non-shareholders							
Inspect	✓	✓	✓	✓	✓	✓	Only if articles provide
– charge	£2.50 p/hour or part hour [3]	£2.50 p/hour or part hour [3]	£3.50 p/hour or part hour [3]	Up to 5p per inspection	✗	£2.50 p/hour or part hour [4]	
Copy	✗	✗	✓	✗	✓	✓	
– charge	n/a	n/a	Up to 5 entries: £1; up to the next 95 entries: £30; up to the next 900 entries: £30; up to the next 99,000 entries: £30; up to the rest of the register: £30 [1]	n/a	Up to 5 entries: £1; up to the next 95 entries: £30; up to the next 900 entries: £30; up to the next 99,000 entries: £30; up to the rest of the register: £30 [1]	Up to 100 entries: £2.50; next 1,000 entries or part thereof: £20; each batch of 1,000 entries or part thereof after that – £15 [2]	
CH	✓	✓	✗	✓	✗	✗	✗

Note:
1. Plus the reasonable costs of sending the copies out.
By 1 October 2009, the fee structure is expected to change to (draft Companies (Company Records and Fees) Regulations 2007):
– up to 10 entries: £1;
– next 90 entries or part thereof: £10;
– next 900 entries or part thereof: £20;
– next 49,000 entries or part thereof: £40;
– the rest of the register or part thereof: £40; plus
– reasonable costs of sending the copies.
2. On 6 April 2008, the fee structure will change as set out in note 1 above.
3. By 1 October 2009, the fee will be £3.50 per hour or part of an hour (draft Companies (Company Records and Fees) Regulations 2007).
4. On 6 April 2008, the fee will change to £3.50 per hour or part of an hour (draft Companies (Company Records and Fees) Regulations 2007).

H. Rectification of company registers

Register of shareholders

4027 Statute enables the court to rectify the register in the case of **certain inaccuracies** (s 359 CA 1985):
– the name of a person is wrongly entered in the register;
– the name of a person is wrongly omitted from the register; or
– a person's name is not removed from the register when he ceases to be a shareholder, or there is unnecessary delay in doing so.

> MEMO POINTS The court will retain this power under the **new Companies Act** (s 125 CA 2006, expected to come into force by 1 October 2009).

4028 The person aggrieved by the inaccurate entry or omission, any shareholder of the company or the company itself can **apply to the court** to rectify the register. A Part 8 claim form should be used to make the application (CPR PD 49).

The court has a **discretion** whether or not to make the order, and also has the discretion to order the company to pay damages to the aggrieved party for any harm caused by the error. If the court makes an order for rectification it will also order the company to notify Companies House of the change(s) in order to comply with the legislation. The court's statutory power to rectify the register of shareholders includes resolving any dispute regarding the shares (s 359(3) CA 1985; *Re Hoicrest Ltd*, *Keene v Martin* [2000] 1 BCLC 194).

> MEMO POINTS 1. The court will **not allow** the register to be rectified if, for example, a person who wants his name removed has dealt with the shares as if he owned them (e.g. if he has voted at meetings or accepted dividends).
> 2. The court also has the power to allow a liquidator to rectify the register of shareholders for the same reasons as above, after a **winding up** order has been made against a company (s 148 IA 1986; ¶7863).
> 3. If a **transfer** has proved to be **invalid**, the transferor has a prima facie right to have the register rectified so that his name is restored (*Smith v Charles Building Services Ltd* [2006] All ER (D) 120 (Jan)). It is then for the transferee to prove that rectification should not occur, e.g. if the transferor's original entry on the register was procured improperly.

Register of charges at Companies House

4030 On application by the company or another interested person, the court can **make an order to** (s 404 CA 1985):
– correct an omission or mis-statement on the register of charges kept at Companies House; or
– extend the period within which a charge is to be registered.

To make such an order, the court must be satisfied that the mistake:
– was accidental;
– was not for a reason which could prejudice the creditors or shareholders in any way; or
– can be duly justified in some other way.

In making the order, the court can impose any terms it sees fit.

Case law has indicated that the **court's power** to rectify the register of charges **does not extend to** removing information accidentally included on the forms submitted to Companies House. In a case in which schedules containing personal information were attached to the forms registering the charges, the court held that its powers were restricted to entries on the face of the register. The forms did not comprise part of the charges and could not be removed (*igroup v Ocwen* [2003] 4 All ER 1063).

> MEMO POINTS The court will still have its power to rectify the register under the **new Companies Act** (s 873 CA 2006, expected to come into force by 1 October 2009). The registrar will also have a new power to remove information from any register which was given to Companies House but not required, after notifying the person or company concerned (s 1094 CA 2006, expected to come into force by 1 October 2009).

SECTION 5

Companies House

4040 The legislation requires companies to file certain documents at Companies House which are kept on the **register of companies** maintained by the registrar of companies. As companies deal with the registrar through Companies House, references are made here to filing a document at Companies House rather than with the registrar of companies, but the two terms are essentially synonymous.

The occasions which give rise to filing requirements are discussed under the relevant topics, and the relevant forms, procedures and filing requirements can also be found with their topic. Here, the **function** of Companies House is dealt with, followed by general **information and advice** about filing documents with Companies House. The only document to be filed which is dealt with in any detail here is the **annual return** because it is a document which has to be submitted annually rather than being triggered by an event within the company.

Status, organisation and functions

4042 Companies House is an executive agency of BERR. The registrar of companies for England and Wales is **based in** Cardiff, and is also the chief executive of Companies House. The registrar of companies for Scotland is based in Edinburgh. See ¶9905 for their respective contact details.

All limited companies are registered at Companies House. The regime for registering companies is prescribed in legislation (principally the Companies Acts and related legislation such as the Insolvency Act 1986). Companies House states that its functions are to:
– incorporate and dissolve limited companies;
– examine and store company information delivered to Companies House under the legislation; and
– make that information available to the public.

A. Filing requirements

4048 The legislation requires companies to file numerous forms and documents with Companies House over the course of its life. There are **specific** requirements relating to individual forms and documents, which are dealt with under each relevant topic.

The legislation also sets out **general** requirements as to filing forms and documents with Companies House, with which companies have to comply in order for their documents to be placed on the register. When a document is sent to Companies House in hard copy, it is scanned and kept electronically. Therefore, the **purpose** of these requirements is to ensure that the documents are legible and will remain so once they are scanned.

Companies House can **reject documents** which do not meet the requirements, by returning them to the company with a notice specifying the problem and stating that an acceptable copy must be delivered within 14 days (s 706 CA 1985). If an acceptable copy is not sent within the time limit, Companies House is entitled to treat the document as never having been delivered. This could, depending on the document in question, leave the officers of the company open to late filing penalties or penalties for failure to file the document (see ¶9935). If documents are submitted to Companies House electronically, these problems will not arise. However, Companies House can still reject documents that appear not to have been completed correctly (e.g. missing information) or which are not accompanied by the correct paperwork or fee.

4049 Documents delivered under the companies and insolvency legislation can be submitted in **Welsh** by companies with a registered office in Wales (s 1104 CA 2006, as amended by SI 2006/3428 to incorporate transitional arrangements). Such documents (with some exceptions, e.g. pre-printed Welsh forms, see Companies House website for full details) must be accompanied by a certified translation in English. Certain documents (agreements affecting a company's constitution, copy group accounts, charge instruments and contracts which have to be filed under s 88 (2)(b)(i) CA 1985) can be filed in **other languages**, with translations in English (s 1105 CA 2006; SI 2006/3429). In all other cases, documents are to be submitted in English (s 1103 CA 2006). Important information such as constitutional documents, accounts and information about directors (for a full list, see s 1078 CA 2006) can be filed with a translation in any of the official languages of the EU (SI 2006/3429). This will be useful where a company is part of an international group, for example.

MEMO POINTS Draft regulations under the **new Companies Act** have been published which will allow certain important documents relating to Welsh companies to be filed in Welsh without an English translation (draft Companies (Registrar of Companies) Regulations 2008, likely to come into force by 1 October 2009). They also provide for a small number of documents to be filed in other languages with English translations.

4050 Companies House's requirements for the **quality of documents** and forms submitted are as follows:

Requirement	Reference
Registered number of company in prominent position on document	s 706 CA 1985
Paper: – A4 size; – plain white with matt finish; and – between 80 and 100gsm in weight	Companies House guidance
Text: – black ink or type; – clear, legible writing; – bold lettering; – at least 1.8mm high; – characters of uniform density; and – line width at least 0.25mm	
General layout: – portrait format (as opposed to landscape); – good margin around all edges (at least 10mm); – do not send carbon copies; – do not use dot-matrix printers; – if photocopy is sent, ensure it is clear, as grey shading on photocopies can prevent scanning; – company number in top right-hand corner of first page; – no pictures (e.g. in accounts), although line graphs are now acceptable; and – unbound documents only	

MEMO POINTS The **new Companies Act** will also allow Companies House to specify its requirements for the documents submitted (s 1068 CA 2006). This provision was brought into force as far as is necessary to give effect to other provisions of the new Act on 1 January 2007 (SI 2006/3428). Therefore, Companies House's requirements apply to all documents, whether filed under CA 1985 or CA 2006. In its July 2007 consultation paper "Working with Companies House: a consultation document on the Registrar's rules and related provisions which will apply under the Companies Act 2006", Companies House indicated that the same basic rules will apply to most classes of documents.

4051 The various **resolutions** that need to be filed are listed at ¶3600 for shareholder resolutions and ¶3480 for directors' resolutions. Generally speaking, resolutions must be in a printed form, or some other approved form. Resolutions are usually signed by a director, secretary or the chairman of the meeting. If a **written resolution** needs to be submitted to Companies House, it must be headed "written resolution" and signed by all of the shareholders (or directors, as appropriate).

> **MEMO POINTS** In a consultation paper on the effect of the new Companies Act on Companies House procedures, Companies House proposed to introduce rules setting out the **format** of resolutions altering the articles and how they should be **authenticated** ("Working with Companies House: a consultation on the registrar's rules and related provisions which will apply under the Companies Act 2006"). At the time of writing, these rules had not yet been published.

4052 Companies House will accept documents which have been signed using **automatically generated signatures** (e.g. by a stamp or computer). Companies House accepts such signatures in good faith, but the documents must still have been given due consideration and approved by the signatory. Documents submitted electronically (see ¶4069+) are authenticated by way of a code.

If a **certified copy** of a document is required by Companies House, the document can be verified by the signature of a director, secretary or other authorised officer (s 41 CA 1985). Companies House can stipulate the persons from whom it will accept certified copies (s 1111 CA 2006).

> **EXAMPLE** Certified a true copy
>
> _____ (signature)
> Director/secretary/authorised officer [*state which*]
> Dated this   day of   200

Filing periods

4053 There are various **statutory deadlines** for filing forms and documents at Companies House. By way of a summary, the table at ¶9900 sets out the periods for the different documents together with cross-references to the relevant topic for further information.

B. The annual return

4060 The annual return, or "**Form 363a**" is a document that must be submitted by every company to Companies House annually. Its **purpose** is to provide Companies House with a summary of specified information about the company at a particular point in time. Although it contains information which is repeated in other company forms (for example, the details of directors, secretaries and the registered office) the annual return also lists the shareholders of a company and their respective shareholdings. Together with the annual accounts, the annual return provides a useful overview of a company's situation at a given point in time.

It is a **statutory obligation** for all companies to deliver annual returns on time and in the prescribed form (s 363(1) CA 1985). A company's director(s) and secretary must ensure compliance and that the form is an accurate reflection of the company's position at the date to which it is made up. **Failure** to do so renders the company liable to a fine (s 363(3) CA 1985; ¶9935). The company's directors and secretary are also liable unless they can show that they took all reasonable steps to avoid the breach (s 363(4) CA 1985).

> **MEMO POINTS** 1. Under the **new Companies Act**, companies will still be obliged to file annual returns (s 854 CA 2006, expected to come into force by 1 October 2009). Failure to do so will render the company, its directors and secretary (in the case of a public company or a private company with a secretary) and any other officer liable to a fine (s 858 CA 2006, expected to come into force by 1 October 2009).
> 2. The name of Form 363a, like the names of other **Companies House forms**, is taken from the section number of the legislation. As all of the section numbers will change under the new Companies Act, Companies House proposes to change the names of all of its forms to reflect their function rather than the relevant section number ("Working with Companies House: a consultation on the registrar's rules and related provisions which will apply under the Companies Act 2006"). At the time of writing, the new form names are not yet available.

Deadline

4061 Annual returns have to be submitted within 28 days of the "**return date**", or "**made-up date**" (these terms refer to the same date; the former is used in the legislation and the latter by

Companies House. Here, only the term "return date" is used to avoid any confusion). The return date appears on each annual return form and is either the anniversary of the (s 363(1) CA 1985):
– company's incorporation; or
– return date of the last annual return registered at Companies House.

Completing the form

The annual return must **contain** (ss 364, 364A CA 1985):

4062

a. the registered office address;
b. the type of company;
c. the principal business activities of the company;
d. the name and address of the secretary;
e. the name and address of each director, and in the case of directors who are individuals (as opposed to other companies or partnerships), his nationality, date of birth and business occupation;
f. the location of the register of shareholders and/or debentures, if not at the registered office;
g. the total number of issued shares at the return date;
h. the aggregate nominal value of the issued shares at the return date;
i. if the company divides its shares into classes, the nature of each class and the total number and aggregate nominal value of the issued shares in each class at the return date;
j. a list of the names and addresses of each shareholder at the return date, including those shareholders who have ceased to be a shareholder since the return was made up (or since incorporation in the case of a first annual return). The list should be in alphabetical order, or else indexed so that the names can be found easily;
k. the number of shares (of each class) held by each shareholder at the return date; and
l. the number of shares transferred since the last annual return (or since incorporation in the case of a first annual return) by each person who has ceased to be a shareholder, together with the dates of registration of the transfers.

> MEMO POINTS 1. The requirements at g. h. i. k. and l. in the list only apply to companies which have a share capital. **Companies without a share capital** still need to give details of their membership.
> 2. The **nominal value** of shares means the total face value of the shares, not taking any premium into account.
> 3. There will be some differences in the required contents of the annual return under the **new Companies Act** (ss 855, 856 CA 2006, expected to come into force by 1 October 2009):
> – only public companies and private companies with secretaries will have to provide information about their secretaries;
> – the information required about directors, secretaries and shareholders will be prescribed by regulations (see below); and
> – the statement of capital will have to state the number of shares (rather than issued shares, since the distinction between authorised and issued shares will not longer exist) and the amount paid up and how much is unpaid on the shares (as well as the other information listed above).
> Draft regulations under the new Act have been published setting out the information that will have to be included in the annual return (draft Companies (Annual Return and Service Addresses) Regulations 2007, which are drafted to amend the new Companies Act to include this information. They are also likely to come into force by 1 October 2009):
> – shareholders: the names of all current shareholders and all those who ceased to be a shareholder since the date of the last return; the number and class of any shares transferred since the date of the last return and the date of any such transfers; and the number and class of any shares transferred since the date of the last return and the date of any such transfers;
> – directors (not including shadow directors): their names and any former names; their service addresses (this may be the company's registered office address); the countries or states in which they are usually resident; their nationalities; their business occupations; and their dates of birth;
> – secretaries: their names and addresses for service;
> – if the company keeps its records at a location other than the company's registered office, the address of the alternative location; and
> – the voting rights attached to different classes of shares.
> The type of company and business activities will still have to be specified using the same classifications.

4063 The company's **type** and principal **business activities** are categorised into codes. The list of business activity codes is too long to reproduce here, and can be found on the Companies House website. The types of company are categorised as follows (para 5 Sch 3 SI 1990/1766):

Type of company	Code
Public limited company	T1
Private company limited by shares	T2
Private company limited by guarantee without share capital	T3
Private company limited by shares exempted from having to have "limited" as part of its name (s 30 CA 1985)	T4
Private company limited by guarantee exempted from having to have "limited" as part of its name (s 30 CA 1985)	T5
Private unlimited company with share capital	T6
Private unlimited company without share capital	T7

> **MEMO POINTS** Companies required to deliver annual returns as a company incorporated in the **Channel Islands** or the **Isle of Man** or an **unregistered company** (ss 699, 718 CA 1985) should give the type of company according to the category which the directors believe is most appropriate in their circumstances.

4064 The required **details of individual officers** are their forename, surname and usual residential address (s 364(4)(a) CA 1985). If an individual is titled, this title can be given as well as or instead of his forename and surname (s 364(5) CA 1985). In the case of **corporations** or **Scottish firms**, the corporate or firm name and the address of its registered or principal office should be given (s 364(4)(b) CA 1985). If all of the partners in a firm are joint secretaries, the name and principal office of the firm can be given instead of the names and addresses of each partner (s 364(6) CA 1985).

> **MEMO POINTS** The details of officers required under the **new Companies Act** will be set out in regulations, the draft of which has been published and is outlined at ¶4062/mp (draft Companies (Annual Return and Service Address) Regulations 2007). However, directors will be able to give an address for service, in common with the requirements for the register of directors (see ¶3896/mp).

4065 A **full list of shareholders** only has to be given with the first annual return after incorporation and then once every three years (s 364A(6) CA 1985). In the interim period, companies only have to give the details of new shareholders, or persons ceasing to be shareholders, and of any shares transferred since the date of the last annual return (for companies with large shareholder lists, it may be easier to submit a full list with each annual return). Companies can submit their shareholder lists in an **alternative format**, e.g. on CD ROM, with the prior consent of Companies House.

If a company has an **overseas register** (see ¶3948+), the details on that register need to be included in its annual return. If the copies of entries on the overseas register have not been received by the company prior to the return date of the annual return, those details will have to be included in the following annual return (s 364A CA 1985).

> **MEMO POINTS** 1. If any of the company's shares have been converted from shares into **stock**, the annual return should give the details relating to the stock, giving the amount of the stock instead of the number and nominal value of the shares (s 364A CA 1985).
> 2. This will also be the case under the **new Companies Act** (s 856 CA 2006, expected to come into force by 1 October 2009).

4066 The annual return is a summary of information about the company; it is not a method of informing Companies House about **changes in the company** which are required to be notified by statute. Companies House will not accept an ordinary annual return (i.e. on Form 363a) that records different information to that on the register, unless the company has notified it of the change using the correct statutory form.

Changes in information contained in the annual return which must also be notified on other statutory forms/documents are:

Event	Form	¶¶
Change of company name	Authorising resolution	¶273+
Change of registered office	287	¶570
Appointment of director or secretary	288a	¶2288+, ¶4151+
End of director's or secretary's appointment	288b	¶2920+, ¶4158+
Change of details of officer, e.g. address	288c	¶3902+
Change of address of where register of shareholders is kept	353	¶3928
Change of address of where register of debenture holders is kept	190	¶4006+
Allotment of new shares	88(2)	¶1086+
Consolidation, division, sub-division, redemption or cancellation of shares	122	¶1314+, ¶1374+, ¶1312/mp
Conversion or re-conversion of stock into shares	122	¶1312/mp
Increase in nominal capital	123, plus authorising resolution	¶900+
Rights attached to allotted shares which are not stated in memorandum and articles	128(1), plus authorising resolution	¶915
Variation of rights to allotted shares which are not stated in memorandum or articles	128(3), plus the authorising resolution	¶915, ¶1288+
Assignment of new name to any class of share other than by amendment of memorandum or articles	128(4), plus authorising resolution	¶1288+
Company purchasing its own shares	169	¶1383+

MEMO POINTS   The names of these forms, like other **Companies House forms**, are taken from the relevant section numbers in the legislation. As all of the section numbers will change under the new Companies Act, Companies House proposes to change the names of all of its forms to reflect their function rather than the relevant section number ("Working with Companies House: a consultation on the registrar's rules and related provisions which will apply under the Companies Act 2006"). At the time of writing, the new form names are not yet available.

Companies House also now sends companies a "**shuttle**" form, "**Form 363s**", which contains the information submitted on the previous annual return for companies to amend if certain details have changed. Paper shuttle forms do not include a list of the company's shareholders any more, so this information will have to be provided by the company, even if it has already filed a paper Form 88(2) informing Companies House of an allotment of shares. Companies which file their annual returns electronically will not be affected, as their information is updated automatically by the Companies House system.

The shuttle form can be used to inform Companies House of **certain changes**:
– in the registered office;
– in the address at which the register of shareholders and/or debenture holders is kept;
– in the principal business activities of the company;
– in the details of company officers and shareholders, e.g. address; and
– the fact and date that an officer resigned.

Even with the shuttle annual return, there are separate forms which must be used to inform Companies House of other changes (see above), such as the appointment of a new company

4067

officer, the allotment of new shares by the company, or a change in the company's total nominal capital.

4068 Companies have the **choice** as to whether to amend the shuttle form or complete and return a new annual return (Form 363a). The forms can be obtained on request from Companies House, downloaded from its website or from statutory form software packages.

C. Submitting documents to Companies House

4069 Documents can be submitted to Companies House by **hand** or **post**, or **electronically**. Note that Companies House **does not accept** delivery of statutory documents by fax.

There are two methods of submitting documents electronically to Companies House, see ¶4074+ below. Most documents can be delivered electronically; readers should check the website for the up-to-date list. Companies House encourages companies to use an electronic method because of the speed of processing (Companies House can process 95% of electronically filed documents within 24 hours, as opposed to around 8 to 10 days for documents submitted in hard copy) and increased security when compared to postal filing.

4070 Companies with their registered office **in England and Wales** should send their documents to the Cardiff office for filing (this can be done via the London office). Those with registered offices **in Scotland** should use the Edinburgh office.

Companies incorporated outside the UK and Gibraltar but which have a **branch office** in Great Britain should send documents for filing to the Cardiff or Edinburgh offices, depending on where their branch is based (s 695A CA 1985). Companies incorporated in the **Channel Islands** or the **Isle of Man** should also register any necessary documents with the relevant office if they have established a place of business in England and Wales or Scotland, or both (s 699 CA 1985).

By hand/post

4072 Documents can be delivered to the **Companies House offices** in Cardiff, London or Edinburgh **by hand** (see ¶9905 for the addresses of the respective offices). Documents can be delivered to these offices outside of working hours, although only the Cardiff office is manned during evenings and weekends and able to provide proof of delivery outside of office hours.

If documents are delivered **by post**, Companies House makes it clear that it does not accept **delay** in transit as a sufficient reason to waive a penalty. Therefore, documents must be sent in plenty of time before a deadline, and a reliable delivery service used. If a document is sent close to the deadline, companies should use a guaranteed delivery service.

Companies House will **acknowledge receipt** of documents if a self-addressed envelope is provided. Usually, a copy of the covering letter enclosing the documents is included, and Companies House is requested to endorse and return it to the company. Companies can also check their own records regularly to ensure that documents have been placed on the register.

Electronic filing

4074 Documents can be submitted to Companies House via **email**, using their **software filing** service. Most common company forms can be filed electronically, and the list is growing; check Companies House's website for the up-to-date list.

Companies need to have suitable software and computing facilities, and to register with Companies House to use this service. When a company registers, it needs to notify Companies House of its authentication code and the details of the officers or other authorised persons who will be responsible for presenting the documents. This replaces the **signatures** on the documents. A group of companies can use the same code. There are further security measures for incorporation documents and appointments of directors enabling Companies House to verify that the directors have consented to act. The form must contain three items of personal information provided by the new officer (officers can choose from: place of birth, telephone number, national insurance number, passport number, mother's maiden name, father's forename, eye colour). For incorporations, either three pieces of personal information can be given, or a six-digit code can be used by prior arrangement with Companies House.

The **WebFiling** service allows certain documents to be submitted to Companies House via their website. Companies must register for the service. Again, the documents are **signed by** way of an authentication code, and there is also an additional security code to be used when filing via the internet.

4075

Some companies have fallen prey to "**company hijacking**", whereby a person not involved with the company illegally changes certain company details, such as its registered office and directors, and uses the company's name to trade. With either electronic or web filing, companies can sign up to an anti-hijacking service with Companies House, known as "**PROOF**". Companies which do so will only be able to submit changes of their registered office, directors and other pertinent details electronically, to prevent unauthorised persons from doing so by post.

4076

> MEMO POINTS   For example, Companies House has warned its customers that fraudsters had contacted some customers posing as Companies House, asking for WebFiling authentication codes in order to hijack the companies. Companies House will not ask for such information over the telephone, so companies should report any similar bogus calls to Companies House.

Contact details

The Companies House contact details for filing, general communication and queries are set out at ¶9905.

4078

Correcting mistakes on the register

Generally speaking, Companies House has no power to remove a document from the register once it has been registered. If a company realises that there is a mistake or omission on the document, it should contact Companies House straight away; if it has been received but **not yet entered** on the register, the document can usually be returned. If, on the other hand, the document has **already been entered** on the register, the company will have to submit a correct copy, clearly marked "amended", together with a covering letter explaining what mistake has been made and requesting that the amended copy is placed on the register. The amended document will appear on the register together with the original. Companies House recommends that those wishing to have a document removed from the register seek legal advice, as it may be necessary to apply to court for a declaration that the document is a nullity.

4080

It is only possible to apply to court for an order to **rectify the register of charges or shareholders** maintained by Companies House (¶4027+).

> MEMO POINTS   Under the **new Companies Act**, the register at Companies House will be able to be changed in various ways (these powers are expected to come into force by 1 October 2009):
> – Companies House will be able to correct a document if it is incomplete or internally inconsistent (s 1075 CA 2006). Companies House will consult the company and obtain its consent before exercising this power;
> – if any information on the register appears to be inconsistent with other information, Companies House can require the company to provide a replacement document or additional information (s 1093 CA 2006);
> – Companies House can remove information that should not have been included in a document (s 1094 CA 2006);
> – under draft regulations, Companies House will have the power to annotate the register to explain any misleading or confusing documents (draft Companies (Registrar of Companies) Regulations 2008);

– Companies House will be able to accept a replacement document where the original did not comply with the requirements for delivery to Companies House or it contained unnecessary material (s 1076 CA 2006);
– certain information (to do with the registered office, directors, secretaries or registered service addresses) will be able to be rectified if it is inaccurate or it derives from anything that is invalid or ineffective (including a decision of the company made without authority) (s 1095 CA 2006). An application to correct the information must be made by the person who submitted the document concerned, or the company or individual to which the information relates (draft Companies (Registrar of Companies) Regulations 2008); and
– the court will be able to order Companies House to remove any information from the register that is inaccurate or derives from anything that is invalid or ineffective (s 1096 CA 2006).

If any information is corrected, removed or replaced, Companies House will have to annotate the register so that a person inspecting it will be able to find out the date and nature of the change (s 1081 CA 2006).

D. Searching the register

4090 The register of company information maintained at Companies House is open to the public; anyone can **inspect** it and request **copies** of any part of it (ss 1085, 1086 CA 2006).

Certain **information** is **not available** to the public, such as directors' residential addresses where a confidentiality order is in place (¶3907), the contents of charge documents submitted as part of a company's registration obligations (¶4636+) and any email addresses, passwords etc in a document for the purposes of filing it electronically at Companies House (s 1087 CA 2006). The secretary of state can make regulations enabling people to apply to Companies House to have their addresses made unavailable to the public, which will be useful for directors whose residential addresses are currently on the register (s 1088 CA 2006).

Searches of the register are usually carried out **on-line** through one of two websites. **Companies House Direct** is a subscriber service, charging to access the register. Documents can be downloaded or requested by post and are provided individually, in groups (e.g. mortgage documents), or reports (e.g. giving current company appointments and general company information). The charges differ depending on what is ordered. Companies can also sign up to the "Monitor" service, which will notify them of specified changes to filed information about certain companies on request.

The **Companies House website** provides free basic company information (such as registered office, name, number, date of incorporation and so on) via its "WebCheck" service for which users do not have to register. Additional information, such as annual accounts and returns, can be purchased over the internet with charges being made per purchase.

General information about companies can also be obtained from Companies House on **DVD ROM**. The DVDs are updated monthly, and can be purchased as a one-off or on subscription. There is also a DVD ROM released each year containing general information on all companies which have been dissolved or have changed their name in the last 20 years.

Before the register was available on-line, company searches were carried out on **microfiche**. The microfiches are up-to-date to 31 December 2002. These archive microfiches can be ordered on-line through Companies House Direct or by contacting Companies House.

Searches can also be carried out though **company search agencies** which deal with Companies House on behalf of companies and other persons wishing to search the register.

MEMO POINTS Under the **new Companies Act**, any person will also be able to inspect the index of company names kept at Companies House (ss 1099, 1100 CA 2006, expected to come into force by 1 October 2009).

CHAPTER 10
Company secretary

OUTLINE	¶¶
1 Who can be a company secretary? 4120	Advisory 4146
2 Legal status and liabilities 4129	4 From appointment to removal 4151
As an agent 4131	Appointment 4151
As an officer....................................... 4136	Service contract 4156
3 Functions in practice 4142	Termination 4158
Administrative 4144	

4115 Directors perform the principal duties of management, while the company secretary is mainly **responsible for** the company's administration. At the time of writing, all **companies are obliged** to have a company secretary to ensure that there are always two legal persons running a company, which helps to protect it from fraud and bad management (s 283(1) CA 1985). However, this will change from 6 April 2008, as outlined below.

There is no statutory **definition** of a company secretary, allowing each company to tailor the office to its own needs. In a **small company**, the secretary's role may be purely administrative, comprising filing documents at Companies House and maintaining the internal books and registers. On the other hand, a **large company** is likely to need its secretary to fulfil a more managerial and advisory role, performing tasks such as organising meetings, heading a team of administrative staff and advising directors on their legal obligations, as well as performing administrative duties.

   MEMO POINTS   **Table A defines** the secretary as "the secretary of the company or any other person appointed to perform the duties of the secretary of the company" (reg 1 TA 1985).

4116 The **new Companies Act** will abolish the obligation for private companies to have a secretary as of 6 April 2008 (s 270 CA 2006). Instead, **private companies** will be allowed to be managed by a minimum of one director, as long as he is an individual (ss 154, 155 CA 2006; the former is already in force, but the implementation of the latter is yet to be announced). This recognises that the obligation to have a secretary imposes a financial and managerial burden on small private companies, many of which outsource the role to a firm of solicitors, accountants or a company secretarial services agency, when a director could perform the same functions. If a private company chooses not to have a secretary, documents which would have been sent to or served on the company by sending them to or serving them on the secretary can be sent to or served on the company instead, and anything addressed to the secretary will be taken to have been sent to or served on the company (s 270(3) CA 2006). Similarly, anything that would have been done by or to the secretary can be done by or to a director or another person authorised by the board. To avoid any confusion, the company should remove references to the office of company secretary from its articles and other company paperwork, and allocate responsibility for company filing and other duties undertaken by the secretary to others.

Public companies will still have to have a company secretary, and the secretary of state will be able to order those which do not to remedy the situation (ss 271, 272 CA 2006, due to come into force on 6 April 2008).

1. Who can be a company secretary?

4120 There are few prescribed rules on who can be a company secretary. As with directorships, the office can be held by individuals, partnerships and companies, with some specific restrictions which are summarised in the table below.

Type	Can be secretary?	Reference
Individual	✓	s 290(1) CA 1985 [1]
Company [2, 3]	✓	s 290(1) CA 1985 [4]
Partnership	✓	s 290(1) CA 1985 [4]
Directors	✓	s 284 CA 1985 [5]
Sole director (whether individual or corporate director)	✗	¶3460+
Auditor	✗	s 27(1) CA 1989
Person disqualified from acting as a director	✗	¶4121

Note:
1. By 1 October 2009, s 277 CA 2006 will set out the particulars required to be registered for individual secretaries.
2. **Company includes** companies incorporated outside Great Britain.
3. There are currently restrictions on **companies** being secretaries which relate to **sole directors** (see ¶3460+).
4. By 1 October 2009, s 278 CA 2006 will set out the particulars required to be registered for secretaries which are corporations or firms.
5. From 6 April 2008, s 280 CA 2006 will allow a person to act as director and secretary.

4121 A **disqualified person** will generally not be able to act as a secretary because of the prohibition in the order or undertaking on him being concerned or taking part in the formation, promotion or management of a company.

He may be able to act as secretary in the few cases where his functions are simply administrative form-filling on the board's instructions. However, it will depend on the court's interpretation of what constitutes being concerned with or **taking part in** the **management** of a company. This has been construed widely, to include any internal or external involvement in the conduct of a company's affairs. It is not necessary for a person to be involved in a company's "central management and direction" to take part in its management (*Drew v Lord Advocate* 1995 SCCR 647), although his role should involve a degree of decision making (*Commissioner of Corporate Affairs v Bracht* (1989) 7 ACLC 40, an Australian case concerning similar provisions to s 11 CDDA 1986, by which a bankrupt is disqualified). Therefore, normal secretarial responsibilities for making decisions relating to administration, such as hiring staff or procuring services for the office, would breach an order or undertaking. If there is any doubt, the disqualified person should apply to court for leave to act or the company should appoint another secretary (¶3074+).

4122 **In practice**, the appointment will depend very much on the type of company. In **small companies**, because the administrative needs of the company are relatively narrow, one of the directors (provided he is not the sole director, see ¶3460+) or another employee often takes on the office of secretary as well. Alternatively, it is often contracted out to a firm of solicitors or accountants, or to a company secretarial services agency. By contrast, the secretary of a **large company** will probably need to be employed full-time and will be appointed because of his experience and expertise.

Companies may also establish their own **conditions**, for example, that the secretary must normally retire at a certain age, hold shares or possess some professional experience (whether by previously holding a similar office or having a professional qualification). These requirements could be stipulated in the articles, service contract or merely be a requirement of the recruitment process.

Comment: The restrictions on a sole director acting as company secretary are expected to be repealed on 6 April 2008. The **new Companies Act** allows private companies to be governed by only one director, provided he is an individual (ss 154, 155 CA 2006, the former is already in force, while the implementation date for the latter is yet to be announced). This provides sufficient security for companies and those dealing with them, as it ensures that an identifiable individual is responsible for the company. Public companies will have to have two directors in any case, at least one of which will have to be an individual.

> MEMO POINTS 1. Company secretaries can qualify as **chartered secretaries** through the Institute of Chartered Secretaries and Administrators ("ICSA"). ICSA publishes a number of guidance notes on company management, including one on the role of the secretary. These notes can be found on its website.
> 2. The comments at ¶2251 relating to the **mental capacity** of directors are relevant to secretaries, as they also have to consent to hold office. However, Table A does not provide for the office of secretary to be vacated automatically if its holder becomes of unsound mind.
> 3. There is no requirement for the secretary's **nationality** to be declared, unlike directors' (¶2250), but if a secretary is **resident abroad**, he should ensure that he is able to discharge his duties effectively (¶4131).
> 4. In setting a **retirement age**, companies must ensure that they do not breach the provisions of the Employment Equality (Age) Regulations 2006, known as the "Age Discrimination Regulations" (SI 2006/1031). The Age Discrimination Regulations effectively prevent companies from setting a retirement age lower than 65, and require them to consider requests to work beyond whatever age is set (see ¶2981). Companies must also make sure that they do not place **conditions on appointment** that discriminate against one age group or another, for example requiring a particular level of experience could discriminate against a younger person who has different but equally valid qualifications/experience for the job. The Age Discrimination Regulations apply to office holders as well as employees. This topic is discussed in detail in *Employment Memo*.

Public companies

4124

Directors of public companies are under an **obligation** to ensure that their secretary (s 286 CA 1985):
a. appears to have the necessary knowledge and experience to perform the role properly; and
b. possesses one of the following types of experience:
– he was the secretary of another public company for at least 3 out of the 5 years prior to his appointment;
– he is a member of a specified relevant body;
– he is a UK barrister or solicitor; or
– he appears to be capable of the job because of his experience or membership of another body.

Comment: The **new Companies Act** restates these qualification requirements, except that it does not include holding office on 22 December 1980 as relevant experience for being a public company secretary (see memo point below) (s 273 CA 2006). This provision will come into force on 6 April 2008.

> MEMO POINTS 1. The **specified relevant bodies** are: the Institute of Chartered Accountants in England and Wales; the Institute of Chartered Accountants of Scotland; the Chartered Association of Certified Accountants; the Institute of Chartered Accountants in Ireland; the Institute of Chartered Secretaries and Administrators; the Institute of Cost and Management Accountants; and the Chartered Institute of Public Finance and Accountancy.
> 2. Another **acceptable** type of **experience** is that he was the company's secretary, assistant or deputy secretary on 22 December 1980 and has held office since that date.

2. Legal status and liabilities

4129

A secretary's duties and liabilities principally **derive from** his status as officer, agent and employee of the company, each of which carries its own legal duties. His status as employee is dealt with in *Employment Memo*. The secretary's duties and functions should be set out **in writing**, whether in his service contract or another agreed document. Failure to comply with many of the statutory duties set out in companies legislation renders the company and any director, secretary or other officer at fault liable, and so clarity as to who is responsible for such tasks is advisable.

A company can **indemnify** its secretary against liability arising from his office, and it can also purchase and maintain liability **insurance** in respect of its secretary (¶2517).

As an agent

4131 Like the directors, the secretary acts as the company's agent. This means that similar agency **duties** are imposed on him by common law as are imposed on directors by statute and case law (¶2333+):
– to act within his authority;
– to adhere to his fiduciary duties; and
– to carry out his role with skill and care.

A secretary will be **liable** in the same way as the directors for his own acts and defaults (see ¶2434+). Since the secretary's role is more administrative than managerial, he is less likely to find himself in breach of these duties, and any errors or breaches are more likely to be corrected. Nevertheless, secretaries must abide by their duties to ensure the smooth running of the company and avoid the serious liabilities that a breach could entail.

> MEMO POINTS A secretary will not usually be liable for a **director's defaults**, even if he knew about them (*Joint Stock Discount Co v Brown* (1869) LR 8 Eq 376).

Power to bind company

4132 As an agent, the secretary has the power to bind the company (¶2348+).

In particular, he has ostensible authority to carry out **administrative acts** on behalf of the company, extending to signing contracts dealing with these matters on the company's behalf (e.g. employing junior staff). Therefore, even if a company does not specify the scope of its secretary's duties and functions, he will have the authority to bind the company in administrative matters.

> EXAMPLE The secretary of FFF Ltd ordered hire cars in the company's name, stating that they were for business use. In fact, FFF Ltd was not aware of the transactions and the secretary used the cars personally. When the hire company sued FFF Ltd for payment, the court ordered FFF Ltd to pay. It held that a company secretary had ostensible authority to make representations and enter into contracts on behalf of his company in relation to its day to day administration; therefore, this contract had not been entered into outside of the secretary's authority and was binding on the company (*Panorama Developments (Guildford) Ltd v Fidelis Furnishing Fabrics Ltd* [1971] 3 All ER 16).

> MEMO POINTS 1. This ostensible authority does not extend to matters specifically reserved to **other officers** (e.g. sending out notices of general meetings). For authority to undertake such tasks, specific delegation is required.
> 2. A company secretary also has the power to **execute documents** with a director and authenticate documents on his own (¶3486+).

4133 The secretary may also be given **further authority** to bind the company in the following situations:

a. he may have specific authority **delegated** to him by the board to enter into contracts and otherwise act on the company's behalf. This gives him express actual authority to bind the company, and will be more common to those secretaries who are actively involved in management; and

b. he may have implied actual authority to bind the company if his and the company's **actions over a period of time** support this. For example, if the board has allowed (or, at least, has not objected to) the secretary dealing with certain contracts over a period of time, he will have such authority.

Relief from liability

4134 Owing to the administrative nature of the secretary's usual duties and functions, if he has acted outside of his authority or breached his agency duties, his acts will usually be capable of **ratification** by the board (either by board resolution or conduct; see ¶2497+). For example, if the secretary calls a general meeting without being instructed to do so by the board (a matter within the board's powers but not the secretary's), the notice will be invalid. However, the board can ratify the notice as it was within its power to call the meeting. The shareholders may also be able to ratify the secretary's actions by ordinary resolution.

Like the directors, a company secretary may apply for **statutory relief** from liability for breach of his duties (¶2505+).

As an officer

4136 The legislation imposes **liability** on secretaries for numerous breaches of (mainly) administrative requirements as officers of the company. The table at ¶9935 sets out these duties with their relevant liabilities and cross-references to further discussions of each duty. A **secretary** will be **in default if** he:
– knowingly and wilfully authorises or permits the relevant breach in the case of an offence under CA 1985 (s 730A CA 1985; para 13 Sch 4 SI 2007/2194); or
– authorises, permits, participates in, or fails to take all reasonable steps to prevent, the breach in question in the case of an offence under CA 2006 where the provision setting out the duty and consequences of breach is already in force (s 1121 CA 2006). A corporate secretary will only commit an offence in respect of the company as an officer in default if one of its own officers is in default (s 1122 CA 2006). If this is the case, both the company and its officer will be liable.

4137 A secretary may be **relieved from liability** for breach of these duties either by the general statutory provision for those Companies Act duties which carry civil liability (¶2505+), or by a specific relief attached to the duty in question.

3. Functions in practice

4142 It is not possible to give a definitive list of the duties and functions expected of a secretary, as his responsibilities will depend upon the type of company for which he works. The common **administrative tasks** are listed in the table below, of which any combination may be carried out by a secretary. This list is applicable to secretaries of any size of company, although in a large private or public company they are likely to be delegated to an assistant or deputy secretary, or to an employee supervised by the secretary. The **advisory functions** listed are more likely to apply to secretaries of large companies, particularly public companies. In such companies, not only does the secretary fulfil an important administrative role, but he will also be expected to assist the board with legal, accounting and other compliance matters.

MEMO POINTS Secretaries of any sized company, but particularly those undertaking a more advisory role, must be careful not to fall into the role of a **shadow director** (¶2212+). Those who do will be held liable for any breaches as if they were directors, and may be disqualified on the same grounds (¶2434+, ¶3000+).

Administrative

4144 The company secretary is usually expected to perform the tasks summarised in the table below.

Type of administrative duty	Examples	¶¶
Statutory filing requirements	– Annual returns; – company accounts; and – other company forms	See ¶9900 for table of forms to be filed at Companies House and their deadlines
Company registers	– Updating registers; – keeping them in their proper location; and – arranging inspection and copies	See ¶3888+ for requirements relating to registers
Meetings	– Convening meetings (board and shareholder) on board's instructions; and – producing paperwork: notices, agendas, documents for inspection	¶3222+ – board meetings ¶3610+ – shareholder meetings
Minute books	– Taking minutes at board and shareholder meetings; – arranging for books to be signed; and – arranging inspection	¶3473+ – board meetings ¶3862+ – shareholder meetings

Type of administrative duty	Examples	¶¶
Communicating with shareholders	– Notices; – reports; and – dividend payments	See references in "Meetings" row above ¶1660+
Company signs and stationery	– Ensuring company name appears at registered office; and – ensuring correct details appear on company stationery, contracts etc	¶585
Share transfers[1]	– Certifying transfers; and – issuing share certificates	¶1827+
Group companies	Maintaining record of group structure	¶194+
Insurance, pensions etc	Arranging company's insurances, pensions etc	-
Company seal	– Keeping seal secure; and – maintaining register of sealed documents	¶3490 ¶4011

Note:
1. **Large public companies** often employ a professional share registrar to undertake these duties.

Advisory

4146 If a secretary takes on further advisory responsibilities, he will be expected to keep up to date on **best practice** and advise the directors on a number of technical areas, commonly:
– compliance with the memorandum and articles, and drafting any necessary amendments;
– legal compliance by the company and directors; and
– corporate governance.

The secretary may also be actively involved in **assisting** the company's **accountants and auditor** prepare the annual accounts and report, and he will assist in the **due diligence** exercise and preparation of documents if the company is involved in an acquisition or disposal (¶5652+).

Such secretaries should have a relevant professional qualification and/or experience, even though only secretaries of **public companies** are obliged to do so by the legislation (¶4124).

---

4. From appointment to removal

Appointment

4151 When a company is first incorporated, the formalities of appointing the **first secretary** are different to those for subsequent appointments (see ¶482).

The **procedure** for making appointments **during a company's life** is as follows:
a. the secretary is usually appointed by the directors at a board meeting (or by written resolution) (reg 99 TA 1985); and
b. his consent to act is given by him signing Form 288a, which must be filed at Companies House within 14 days of the appointment so that his appointment can be entered on the register as a matter of public record (see ¶3899+ for the details required to be entered on the form) (s 288(2) CA 1985).

> *MEMO POINTS* 1. If the power to appoint a secretary is granted to the directors in the articles, the **shareholders** cannot do so except by altering the articles (¶450+) or giving instructions to the board by special resolution (¶3152). The articles may provide for the shareholders to make the appointment, but this would be unusual.
> 2. During the course of the secretary holding office, Companies House must be notified within 14 days of any **change** to his registered **details** using Form 288c. The **new Companies Act** will also require companies to notify Companies House if there is any change to its register of secretaries (s 276 CA 2006, expected to come into force by 1 October 2009).

3. Draft **new model articles** under the **new Companies Act** have been published for private companies limited by shares and public companies. They will not set out the procedure for appointing secretaries. However, this is within the board's powers to manage the company and so it will still be able to do so, unless the articles are altered to require the secretary to be appointed by the shareholders.

4. The names of these forms, like the names of other **Companies House forms**, are taken from the section number of the legislation. As all of the section numbers will change under the new Companies Act, Companies House proposes to change the names of all of its forms to reflect their function rather than the relevant section number ("Working with Companies House: a consultation on the registrar's rules and related provisions which will apply under the Companies Act 2006"). At the time of writing, the new form names are not yet available.

As well as the register kept by Companies House, companies must maintain their own **register of secretaries** (s 288(1) CA 1985). A new secretary's first task is usually to update this register with his details (¶3894+). **Failure** to keep or update the register renders the company and any officer in default liable to a fine (¶9935).

Appointments will be **recorded** in the board meeting minutes in the usual way (¶3473+).

> MEMO POINTS The **new Companies Act** will also oblige companies to keep a register of their secretaries (s 275 CA 2006, expected to come into force by 1 October 2009).

4152

More than one secretary

Joint secretaries can be appointed (s 290(1) CA 1985). This can be useful if a partnership (e.g. a firm of solicitors) holds office, or if the role needs to be split between two people (e.g. due to the volume of work or likely absences). If two or more individuals are appointed as joint secretaries, their details will have to be recorded separately, but if all of the partners in a firm are joint secretaries, the details of the firm can be entered on the register as if it was a legal person.

In practice, since there are no prescribed duties of a secretary, there is nothing to prevent a company from appointing one company secretary, whose name appears on the register, when in fact the duties are performed by more than one person or a team supervised by the secretary.

Comment: The **new Companies Act** will also allow joint secretaries to be appointed (ss 273, 275, 276 CA 2006; s 273 is due to come into force on 6 April 2008, but ss 275, 276 are expected to come into force by 1 October 2009).

4153

The legislation also envisages the roles of **assistant** and **deputy secretaries**, although it does not set out any requirements as to who can undertake these roles, or what qualifications they must have. Again, these roles will be useful for larger companies where there is too much work involved for one person. There are no applicable registration requirements in the legislation.

Comment: The **new Companies Act** also provides for assistant and deputy secretaries, without setting out any requirements for their appointment or roles (s 274 CA 2006, due to come into force on 6 April 2008).

4154

Failure to appoint a secretary

If there is no company secretary, the **duties** of that office can be **carried out by** (s 283(3) CA 1985):
− any assistant or deputy secretary; or
− any other officer authorised by the board, if there is no assistant or deputy secretary.

Reliance on this provision should only be a temporary measure between appointments, as the company must comply with its obligation to have a secretary.

Comment: Under the provisions of **new Companies Act** due to come into force on 6 April 2008, the secretary's functions in a private company which chooses not to have a secretary will be able to be carried out by any director or other person authorised by the board (s 270 CA 2006). If a public company does not have a secretary, the secretary of state will be able to direct the company to remedy the situation (s 272 CA 2006). If the company fails to comply with these directions, it and every officer in default will be guilty of an offence. If the office

4155

is vacant (in either a private company with a secretary or a public company), any assistant or deputy, or other authorised officer, will still be able to carry out the secretary's duties (s 274 CA 2006).

Service contract

4156 If the office requires the secretary to work regularly full- or part-time in the company, he will usually have a service contract. The **terms** of the service contract will be set by the board, including the term of office and remuneration (reg 99 TA 1985). They will be similar to those in a director's service contract (¶2627+).

The board will also **approve** the contract, which will then be **signed by** the secretary and an authorised person on behalf of the company.

> MEMO POINTS 1. There is no need for secretaries' service contracts with any particular fixed term to be **approved** by the shareholders, nor do they have to be available for **inspection**.
> 2. Where the secretary is employed by the company to perform a full- or part-time role, his **remuneration** will usually comprise a fixed salary, together with other elements as appropriate. See ¶2710+ for a discussion of the different elements comprising a director's salary, which will be relevant to a secretary. The taxation of the various elements is then dealt with at ¶2735+. There is no requirement to disclose a secretary's salary separately in the company accounts.
> 3. The draft **new model articles** will not contain any provisions concerning company secretaries.

4157 Clearly, a secretary has to abide by the terms of his service contract (as does the company). The discussion at ¶2678+ relating to the consequences for the company and a director of a **breach** of service contract is also relevant here.

Termination

4158 Like a director, a secretary usually has a **dual role** of officer and employee. It will be possible to remove him from office while his employment continues, but the two will often end together. The discussion at ¶2977+ relating to the termination of a director's **service contract** is also relevant to secretaries. Here, removal from office and disqualification are considered only in so far as they apply to secretaries.

Removal from office

4159 The secretary can **resign** from office. The resignation will usually be given in writing and accepted by the board before it takes effect. The articles may extend any age limit imposed on directors to the secretary as well, in which case, he will normally **retire** at the stated age. The board has the power to **remove** the secretary from office by board resolution (reg 99 TA 1985).

Table A does not set out a procedure for resignation, nor does it stipulate a retirement age for secretaries of any type of company. In setting a retirement age and in dealing with a secretary at retirement, companies must ensure that they do not breach the Age Discrimination Regulations (¶2981). Unlike directors, there is no provision in Table A for the secretary's office to be **automatically vacated** when certain events occur, but the directors will usually remove the secretary in similar circumstances: if he is disqualified, made bankrupt, becomes mentally incapable of performing his duties, or is absent from his duties for a length of time.

> MEMO POINTS The draft **new model articles** will not contain any provisions regarding secretaries.

4160 When a secretary is removed from office, Form 288b must be **filed** at Companies House within 14 days to enable the register to be updated (s 288(2) CA 1985). The name of the secretary, the date of termination of his office and his date of birth (unless the secretary is a company) must be entered on the form, and it must be **signed by** a serving director or secretary. The internal **register** of secretaries will also need to be updated, and the resignation/ retirement/removal recorded in the **minutes** of the relevant meeting.

> MEMO POINTS 1. The name of Form 288b, like the names of other **Companies House forms**, is taken from the section number of the legislation. As all of the section numbers will change under the new Companies Act, Companies House proposes to change the names of all of its forms to reflect their function rather than the relevant section number ("Working with Companies House:

a consultation on the registrar's rules and related provisions which will apply under the Companies Act 2006"). At the time of writing, the new form names are not yet available.

2. The **new Companies Act** will also oblige companies to notify Companies House when a secretary is removed from office (s 276 CA 2006, expected to come into force by 1 October 2009).

Disqualification

4161 A company secretary may be disqualified **on the grounds of** (¶3012+):
– bankruptcy;
– breach of an administration order;
– breach of company filing requirements;
– fraud;
– wrongful or fraudulent trading; and
– conviction for a company-related indictable or summary offence.

4162 If a **company has been disqualified** (for its conduct as a corporate director, ¶3010) and it breaches the order or undertaking, the secretary of the disqualified company is also liable for the breach if he had a hand in the company committing that offence (whether by consenting to or conniving in it, or because the offence was committed due to his neglect) (s 14 CDDA 1986).

MEMO POINTS This also applies to **other officers** of the company in default.

CHAPTER 11

Company accounts

OUTLINE ¶¶

A	Record keeping obligations	4195		Filing at Companies House	4278
B	Annual accounts	4209	C	Audit	4290
1	A financial year	4217	1	Role of auditor	4295
2	Financial statements	4226	2	Auditor's report	4312
3	Directors' report	4245	3	Appointment and termination	4336
4	Circulation	4261	D	Special cases	4356
	Board approval and signature	4263	1	Small and medium-sized companies	4360
	Publication	4265	2	Groups	4382
	Laying before general meeting	4273	3	Dormant companies	4407

Companies have an obligation to keep adequate financial **records**, which are used to prepare the company's **annual accounts** for a financial year. A company's annual accounts give a summary of the financial affairs of the company. They must be prepared in accordance with legislation and accounting standards. The financial statements consist of a balance sheet and profit and loss account, together with notes to those financial statements.

4185

The financial statements must be accompanied by a **directors' report** (sometimes referred to as an "annual report"). The accounts of most companies must be independently **audited**; only small and dormant companies are exempt from this requirement.

A company's annual accounts, directors' report and auditor's report (if relevant) must be **circulated** to its shareholders and **filed** at Companies House. The public availability of financial information about a company is a price which must be paid for the benefit of limited liability.

Special rules apply to:
– **small and medium-sized** companies;
– **groups**; and
– **dormant** companies.

Comment: The **new Companies Act** will repeal and restate most of the statutory provisions regarding accounts and audit. Some changes to this topic have already come into force, to fit in with the abolition of AGMs for private companies. However, most of the new provisions and related regulations will come into force on **6 April 2008** and apply to financial years commencing on or after that date. Any differences between the current and proposed new provisions are highlighted in the text below, and where the new Act simply restates the current law, the future statutory reference is given.

A. Record keeping obligations

What records must be kept?

4195 **All companies** are required to keep minimum accounting records which show and explain the company's transactions.

The records to be kept must be **sufficient to** disclose the company's financial position with reasonable accuracy at any time, as well as giving a "true and fair view" of its financial affairs (¶4228). The records must also be sufficient to enable the directors to ensure that any statutory annual accounts will comply with legal requirements (¶4226+) (s 221(1) CA 1985; restated at s 386(1) CA 2006 as of 6 April 2008).

There are few statutory prescriptions as to exactly what records are required. The only specifications are that the accounting records **must contain** day to day entries of the company's receipts and expenditure and a record of its assets and liabilities. If the company deals in goods, the accounting records must also contain statements of the stock held at the end of each financial year. Except for goods sold by way of ordinary retail trade, the accounting records of a company which deals in goods must also contain a statement of all of the goods sold and purchased, identifying the goods, buyers and sellers in each case (s 221(2), (3) CA 1985; restated at s 386(3), (4) CA 2006 as of 6 April 2008).

> MEMO POINTS 1. Record keeping obligations also apply to a **parent company with a subsidiary undertaking** that is not a company and so not subject to the above record keeping obligations. The parent company must take reasonable steps to secure that the subsidiary undertaking keeps whatever accounting records are necessary to enable the parent's directors to ensure that any statutory annual accounts will comply with the legal requirements (s 221(4) CA 1985; restated at s 386(5) CA 2006 as of 6 April 2008).
> 2. If a company **fails** to keep the correct type of accounting records, every officer in default is guilty of a criminal offence unless he shows that he acted honestly and that, in the circumstances of the company's business, the default was excusable (s 221(5) CA 1985; restated at s 387 CA 2006 as of 6 April 2008; ¶9935).

Inspection of records

4197 Accounting records must be **kept at** the company's registered office or another location which the directors think is suitable (s 222(1) CA 1985; restated at s 388(1) CA 2006 as of 6 April 2008).

> MEMO POINTS 1. If the accounting records are **kept outside of GB**, accounts and returns with respect to the business must be also kept at a place within GB. Those accounts and returns must disclose, with reasonable accuracy, the financial position of the business in question at intervals of not more than 6 months. They must also enable the directors to ensure that any statutory accounts are prepared in accordance with legal requirements (s 222(2), (3) CA 1985; restated at s 388(2), (3) CA 2006 as of 6 April 2008, but "GB" will be replaced with "UK" because the **new Companies Act** also covers Northern Ireland).
> 2. If a company **fails** to keep accounting records at the correct location, or fails to send them there, every officer in default is guilty of a criminal offence unless he shows that he acted honestly and that, in the circumstances of the company's business, the default was excusable (s 222(4) CA 1985; restated at s 389(1), (2) CA 2006 as of 6 April 2008).

4198 Accounting records must be **kept for** 3 years (in the case of a private company) and 6 years (in the case of a public company) from the date on which they are made (s 222(5) CA 1985; restated at s 388(4) CA 2006 as of 6 April 2008).

> MEMO POINTS 1. The period of retention is longer for **tax purposes**. For example, for corporation tax purposes, a company must keep records until the latest of the following:
> – 6 years from the end of the accounting period to which they relate;
> – the date on which Revenue and Customs no longer have the power to enquire into the tax return; or
> – the date on which an enquiry into the return is completed.

2. An officer is guilty of a criminal offence if he **fails** to take all reasonable steps to secure compliance of these, or intentionally causes default by the company (s 222(6) CA 1985; restated at s 389(3), (4) CA 2006 as of 6 April 2008; ¶9935).

Accounting records must be available at all times for **inspection by** the company's officers (s 222(1) CA 1985; restated at s 388(1) CA 2006 as of 6 April 2008). The statutory provision does not enable an officer to enforce his right to inspect if the company refuses to allow him access to the records. However, the same right exists at common law, which an officer can rely on to apply to court for an order compelling the company to allow him to inspect the records (*Oxford Legal Group Ltd v Sibbasbridge Services plc and Millar* [2007] EWHC 2265).

It should be noted that the company's shareholders are not entitled to inspect the accounts.

4199

B. Annual accounts

Companies are required to prepare annual accounts for each **financial year** (¶4217+). A financial year varies from company to company and is not necessarily a calendar year (January to December) or a tax year (April to March).

4209

The format and content of a company's annual accounts is underpinned by an extensive **regulatory framework** (¶4211+). Although most companies choose to prepare their accounts under the Companies Act 1985 (known as "Companies Act accounts"), they can prepare them under international accounting standards instead (known as "IAS accounts").

Company accounts consist of various **financial statements** which allow a reader to assess the financial position of the company (¶4226+). For companies preparing Companies Act accounts, there is a difference between its **statutory accounts** and the accounts which it must prepare to comply with wider accounting standards. Its statutory accounts consist solely of the profit and loss account and balance sheet, together with notes to those financial statements. The accounting standards also require a company to prepare a cash-flow statement and a statement of total recognised gains and losses (STRGL).

Company accounts must also be accompanied by a **directors' report** for that financial year (¶4245+). The accounts of larger companies must be audited and accompanied by an **auditor's report** (¶4312+).

Statutory accounts must be **approved** by the board of directors and laid before the shareholders, together with the directors' report and any auditor's report. Those documents must then be filed at Companies House (¶4261+).

The following explanation gives an **overview** of the general requirements relating to statutory company accounts. Reference should be made to *Accountancy and Financial Reporting Memo* for a wider and more detailed consideration of accounting standards and practice.

Regulatory framework

The preparation of annual accounts is required by company law. However, in the UK, the principles by which company accounts should be prepared, referred to as **Generally Accepted Accounting Principles (GAAP)**, are derived from a number of sources (some are mandatory, while others are merely advisory).

4211

Mandatory sources of UK GAAP include:
a. the requirements of the Companies Act 1985 (which will be restated in the new Companies Act when the relevant provisions come into force); and
b. accounting standards, which are:
– Financial Reporting Standards (FRSs) issued or adopted by the Accounting Standards Board (ASB);
– Statements of Standard Accounting Practice (SSAPs) also issued or adopted by the ASB; and
– Abstracts issued by the ASB's Urgent Issues Task Force (UITF).

Advisory sources of UK GAAP include:
- Financial Reporting Exposure Drafts (FREDs) issued by the ASB in advance of an FRS, which should be followed unless they contradict an existing FRS;
- Statement of Principles for Financial Reporting issued by the ASB; and
- statements and recommendations from professional or industrial bodies, e.g. Statements of Recommended Practice (SORPs), Technical Releases and accounting recommendations from the Institute of Chartered Accountants of England and Wales (ICAEW).

> MEMO POINTS The Financial Reporting Review Panel (FRRP) is the UK's corporate reporting and governance regulator. It is empowered to **review** the annual accounts and directors' reports of:
> - public limited companies;
> - companies within a group headed by a public limited company;
> - large private companies (i.e. not qualifying as small or medium-sized);
> - private companies within a large group; and
> - any issuer of listed securities that is incorporated or otherwise formed in the UK.
> It selects accounts from companies carrying on all types of business, with particular focus on certain sectors such as retail and telecommunications. It can also select accounts to review in response to complaints and referrals. When reviewing the accounts and reports, the FRRP will look at:
> - whether the accounts and reports comply with the requirements of companies legislation and the applicable accounting standards. It will only look at whether the business review complies with the ASB's non-mandatory guidance "Reporting statement: operating and financial review" if the company states that it has voluntarily complied with that statement; and
> - whether the business review in the directors' report is consistent with the accounts and any other material in the annual report, and whether it is balanced and comprehensive.
> If it discovers any breach of the legislation, the FRRP can require the accounts or reports to be voluntarily revised by the company. If the company refuses to do so, the FRRP has the power to apply to court for an order that they are revised (s 245B CA 1985; restated at s 456 CA 2006 as of 6 April 2008), although it has not yet had to resort to this as companies have always voluntarily changed their defective accounts.

4212 Given the global marketplace, accounting in the UK is increasingly being influenced by international practices. The International Accounting Standards Board (IASB) issues and adopts **international accounting standards** such as:
- International Accounting Standards (IASs);
- International Financial Reporting Standards (IFRSs); and
- interpretations (SIC-IFRIC interpretations).

The IASB is currently working extensively with national standard setters to achieve global convergence and reflect international practice. The process of **convergence** has been accelerated in the EU by the EU regulation on the application of international accounting standards (EC Regulation 1606/2002) which requires all EU listed companies to prepare their consolidated accounts in conformity with international accounting standards for financial years beginning on or after 1 January 2005. Since that date, non-listed companies have also been free to **choose** whether to adopt international accounting standards or to continue to prepare their accounts in accordance with UK GAAP.

In the UK, the ASB's intention is to bring UK GAAP into line with IFRS. In October 2006, following consultation, the ASB announced that it would not continue to follow a phased convergence approach. Instead, it will issue new IFRS-based UK accounting standards, which will become mandatory on a single date. That date is currently estimated to be financial years beginning on or after 1 January 2009. The actual date will be governed by the outcome and timings of the IASB's proposals. It is likely that the ASB will follow a two-tier approach to financial reporting, the higher tier (of listed companies and publicly accountable bodies) will apply IFRS and the lower tier potentially and ideally will be based on the IASB's SME project. The ASB has said this will depend upon the whether or not the IASB's proposals will be suitable for the UK's needs. At the time of writing, a response to the Exposure Draft has not yet been published.

> MEMO POINTS 1. Under AIM rules, all **AIM parent companies** incorporated in the UK are required to present their consolidated annual accounts for financial periods commencing on or after 1 January 2007 in accordance with IFRS. The Financial Reporting Council (FRC) has published guidance on the implementation of IFRSs by UK AIM companies, which is available on their website.

2. A **revised IAS 1** was issued in September 2007, but is only effective for financial years commencing on or after 1 January 2009 (although earlier adoption is permitted).

1. A financial year

Company directors are required to prepare accounts for each financial year (s 226(1) CA 1985; restated at s 394 CA 2006 as of 6 April 2008). In general, a company's "financial year" is the **length** of its accounting reference period. A company's first financial year begins with its date of incorporation. Each subsequent financial year begins with the day immediately following the end of the previous financial year. All financial years end on the last date of the company's accounting reference period, although the directors can instead pick an end date of up to 7 days before or after the end of the accounting reference period (s 223 CA 1985; restated at s 390 CA 2006 as of 6 April 2008).

4217

> MEMO POINTS   Unless there are good reasons not to, the directors of a **parent company** must ensure that the financial year of its subsidiary undertakings coincides with the parent company's own financial year (s 223(5) CA 1985; restated at s 390 CA 2006 as of 6 April 2008). If the undertaking is not a company, a financial year is any period in respect of which a profit and loss account is required to be made up for that undertaking (e.g. by the undertaking's constitution or law of establishment). It does not matter if that period is not actually a year.

A company's **accounting reference period** is determined according to its accounting reference date. This date is set when the company is incorporated, although it is possible to change it (see below). For all new incorporations, the company's accounting reference date is automatically set at the last day of the month of incorporation. A company's first accounting reference period must be from the date of incorporation to an accounting reference date which is within a period of between 6 and 18 months. All subsequent accounting reference periods will be from one accounting reference date to the next. The period will therefore be 12 months, unless the accounting reference date is changed.

4218

> EXAMPLE   A Ltd is incorporated on 6 September 2007. Its accounting reference date is automatically set at 30 September. Its first accounting reference period is from 6 September 2007 to 30 September 2008. Its first financial year is from 6 September 2007 to any date between 23 September and 7 October 2008.
> Its subsequent accounting reference periods will run from 30 September to 30 September the following year. Its subsequent financial years will run from the date the previous financial year ended to any date between 23 September and 7 October the following year.

Change of accounting reference period

A company can change its accounting reference date so as to **shorten or extend** either its current or the immediately previous accounting reference period (s 225(1), (2) CA 1985; restated at s 392 CA 2006 as of 6 April 2008). However, an accounting reference period **cannot be extended beyond** 18 months unless the company is in administration (s 225(6) CA 1985; restated at s 392 CA 2006 as of 6 April 2008).

4220

A company cannot change a period for which the **accounts are already overdue**, i.e. if the time allowed for laying and delivering accounts and reports in relation to that period has expired (see ¶4261+) (s 225(5) CA 1985; restated at s 392 CA 2006 as of 6 April 2008).

There are restrictions on the **number of times a company can extend** its accounting reference period. An extension cannot be made more than once in 5 years unless the company (ss 225(4), 701(3) CA 1985; restated at s 392 CA 2006 as of 6 April 2008):
– is a subsidiary or parent of another EEA undertaking and the change is being made so that the accounting reference date of the company coincides with the accounting reference date of the other EEA undertaking;
– is in administration;
– has the approval of the secretary of state (a copy of the approval must be provided to Companies House); or
– is an overseas company.

4221 The **procedure** for changing a company's accounting reference date is straightforward. The decision can be made by board resolution, then the company should file Form 225 at Companies House. The change will become effective upon filing the form.

> MEMO POINTS The name of Form 225, like the names of other **Companies House forms**, is taken from the section number of the legislation. As all of the section numbers will change under the new Companies Act, Companies House proposes to change the names of all of its forms to reflect their function rather than the relevant section number ("Working with Companies House: a consultation on the registrar's rules and related provisions which will apply under the Companies Act 2006"). At the time of writing, the new form names are not yet available.

2. Financial statements

4226 Most unlisted companies prepare their accounts in accordance with the Companies Act 1985 ("Companies Act accounts"), although they can choose to prepare their accounts under international accounting standards instead ("IAS accounts") (s 226(2) CA 1985; restated at s 395 CA 2006 as of 6 April 2008).

Companies Act accounts consist of a balance sheet; a profit and loss account; and specific additional information which must be provided in the notes to the accounts. In addition, companies which prepare Companies Act accounts must comply with the wider requirements of UK GAAP. This involves the preparation of two further primary financial statements: a cash-flow statement and a statement of total recognised gains and losses (STRGL). These latter two financial statements do not form part of the company's statutory accounts (which must be filed at Companies House, see ¶4278+).

IAS accounts consist of a balance sheet; an income statement; a statement of changes in equity; a cash-flow statement; and certain additional information which must be provided in the notes to the accounts.

> MEMO POINTS 1. Under the **EC Directive on annual accounts** (EC Directive 2006/46), which must be implemented by 5 September 2008, material off-balance sheet arrangements and related party transactions will need to be presented in company accounts. Large companies will have to provide information on these two topics in the notes to their accounts (s 410A CA 2006 as inserted by the draft Companies Act 2006 (Accounts and Reports) (Amendment) Regulations 2008; para 72 Sch 1 draft Large and Medium-sized Companies and Groups (Accounts and Reports) Regulations 2008). Medium-sized companies will only have to state the nature and purpose of any off-balance sheet arrangements (s 410A CA 2006; reg 4 draft Large and Medium-sized Companies and Groups (Accounts and Reports) Regulations 2008).
> 2. Under the **new Companies Act**, the detail of the form and content of the balance sheet and profit and loss account, as well as the information which must be provided in the notes to the accounts, will be set out in regulations. Two sets of draft regulations have been published: one just for small companies and one for both medium-sized and large companies. The drafts largely restate the Companies Act 1985 requirements, but the separation of the rules into the different sizes of companies should make compliance easier.

General principles

True and fair view

4228 One of the most important general principles in UK accounting is that the financial statements of a company must give a "true and fair view" of its financial affairs (s 226A(2) CA 1985). A similar principle applies in international accounting standards, which require "fair presentation" (IAS 1(13)).

Generally, compliance with accounting standards will ensure a true and fair view/fair presentation. However, in some circumstances, such compliance may not give readers a proper appreciation of a company's financial statements. In order to satisfy the true and fair requirement, the company may need to provide additional information or depart from an accounting provision, to the extent necessary to give a true and fair view (s 226A(4), (5) CA 1985; restated at s 396(5) CA 2006 as of 6 April 2008). Such a departure is known as a "**true and fair override**" and is only permitted in exceptional circumstances. Where a company uses a true and fair override, the particulars of the departure, the reasons for it and its effect must be given in a note to the accounts (s 226A(6), para 15 Sch 4 CA 1985; restated at s 396(5) CA 2006 as of 6 April 2008). Further guidance as to exercise of the true and fair override is given by FRS 18 "Accounting policies" and in IAS 1(17), (18).

Comment: The **new Companies Act** will contain a new statutory duty on the directors to only approve statutory accounts which present a true and fair view of the company's financial affairs and, if the accounts are audited, the auditor will have to have regard to this duty (s 393 CA 2006, due to come into force on 6 April 2008).

Going concern

All financial statements are prepared on the **presumption** that the business is a going concern, unless there is a reason why that presumption should not apply (for example, because the directors have no realistic alternative but to cease trading or liquidate the entity) (para 10 Sch 4 CA 1985; FRS 18(21); IAS 1(23)). This means that all assets and liabilities are recorded at amounts that are expected to be recovered or discharged in the normal course of business.

4229

Comment: This will be restated in the regulations under the **new Companies Act** which set out the content of companies' accounts, and are due to come into force on 6 April 2008 (para 11 Sch 1 in both the draft Large and Medium-sized Companies and Groups (Accounts and Reports) Regulations 2008 and the draft Small Companies and Groups (Accounts and Directors' Report) Regulations 2008).

> MEMO POINTS There is a slight **discrepancy between UK GAAP and international accounting standards** as to when the going concern presumption can be rebutted. Under UK GAAP, the going concern basis should be disregarded only when the business either has actually ceased trading or is in the process of liquidation, or the directors have no realistic alternative but to do so (FRS 18(23)). Under international accounting standards, the going concern basis can be disregarded when the directors intend either to liquidate the entity or to cease trading, or have no realistic alternative but to do so (IAS 1(23)).

If the business is **no longer a going concern**, the financial statements should reflect the amounts recoverable from a quick sale or scrap, that is their "break-up value". Fixed and long-term assets and liabilities should be reclassified as current assets and liabilities, and provisions should be created in respect of anticipated further losses expected to be incurred to the date of termination of the business.

4230

Consistency

In many areas of financial reporting, companies can choose which **accounting policies** to apply in preparing their financial statements. However, once chosen, those accounting policies must be applied consistently within the same accounts as from one financial year to the next (para 11 Sch 4 CA 1985, restated at para 12 Sch 1 in both sets of draft regulations as of 6 April 2008; FRS 18; IAS 1(27)).

4231

Consistency is an aid to **comparability**, enabling a person reading the financial statements to evaluate the financial performance of the entity over time and to compare its performance to that of other entities. Consequently, financial statements must also disclose comparative figures for the previous financial year (para 4 Sch 4 CA 1985, restated at para 7 Sch 1 in both sets of draft regulations as of 6 April 2008; IAS 1(36)).

Comment: The concept of consistency does not preclude **changes to accounting policies** where the changes are appropriate and of benefit to readers (for example, when a new accounting standard is introduced whose treatment of certain items may differ from those employed by the entity). Similarly, the nature of an entity's operations or activities may change, making established accounting policies obsolete.

Prudence

Companies are required to use a prudent basis in determining the amount of any item included in its financial statements (para 12 Sch 4 CA 1985; restated at para 13 Sch 1 in both

4232

sets of draft regulations as of 6 April 2008). Two factors play an integral part in the concept of a prudent basis:
– only **profits** that have been **realised** at the balance sheet date should be included in the profit and loss account; and
– all **known liabilities and losses** relating to the current or previous financial years (that have either already arisen or are likely to arise) must be taken into account in the financial statements.

Accruals basis

4233 The accruals basis of accounting holds that revenue and costs should be taken into account as they are earned or accrued, rather than when their cash value is received or paid. It is a long-accepted accounting principle that financial statements, apart from cash-flow information, should be prepared on an accruals basis (para 13 Sch 4 CA 1985, restated at para 14 Sch 1 in both sets of draft regulations as of 6 April 2008; FRS 18; IAS 1(25)).

Separate valuation

4234 The notion of separate valuation is that in determining the aggregate amount of any item in a financial statement, each individual asset or liability making up that item should be determined separately (para 14 Sch 4 CA 1985; restated at para 15 Sch 1 in both sets of draft regulations as of 6 April 2008).

Balance sheet

4236 Every company must prepare a balance sheet which gives a true and fair view/fair presentation of a company's state of affairs at the end of its financial year. A balance sheet is essentially a snapshot of the company's assets and liabilities on a particular date (the last date of the financial year).

There are some differences in the presentational requirements for a balance sheet between Companies Act accounts and IAS accounts.

Comment: Under the **new Companies Act**, the detail of the form and content of the balance sheet, as well as the information which must be provided in the notes to the accounts, will be set out in regulations. Two sets of draft regulations have been published: one for just small companies and one for both medium-sized and large companies. The drafts largely restate the Companies Act 1985 requirements, but the separation of the rules into the different sizes of companies should make compliance easier.

Companies Act balance sheet

4237 Companies can chose one of two balance sheet formats under the Companies Act 1985 (para 8 Sch 4 CA 1985). Format 1, shown below, which is the more popular, is a vertical format. Format 2 is a horizontal format.

It should be noted that the formats do not specify where the "balance" should be struck. The norm is to strike a balance for net assets (after item J in the format below) which equals the aggregate of the capital and reserves (item K). In practice, the numbered items are not usually shown on the face of the balance sheet but are aggregated under the relevant asset heading (e.g. "intangible assets"). The analysis of the numbered items is instead included in the notes to the accounts.

Comment: Under the **new Companies Act**, the balance sheet formats will be set out in regulations which are due to come into force on 6 April 2008 (para 1 Sch 1 in both the draft Large and Medium-sized Companies and Groups (Accounts and Reports) Regulations 2008 and the draft Small Companies and Groups (Accounts and Directors' Report) Regulations 2008). The format for large and medium-sized companies is the same, but that for small companies includes simplified sub-headings because small companies benefit from certain exemptions (see ¶4366+).

		Balance Sheet: Format 1	
A	Called up share capital not paid [1]		
B	Fixed assets		
B-I		Intangible assets	
	1	Development costs	
	2	Concessions, patents, licences, trade marks and similar rights and assets [2]	
	3	Goodwill [3]	
	4	Payments on account	
B-II		Tangible assets	
	1	Land and buildings	
	2	Plant and machinery	
	3	Fixtures, fittings, tools and equipment	
	4	Payments on account and assets in course of construction	
B-III		Investments	
	1	Shares in group undertakings	
	2	Loans to group undertakings	
	3	Participating interests	
	4	Loans to undertakings in which the company has a participating interest	
	5	Other investments other than loans	
	6	Other loans	
	7	Own shares [4]	
C	Current assets		
C-I		Stocks	
	1	Raw materials and consumables	
	2	Work in progress	
	3	Finished goods/goods for resale	
	4	Payments on account	
C-II		Debtors [5]	
	1	Trade debtors	
	2	Amounts owed by group undertakings	
	3	Amounts owed by undertaking in which the company has a participating interest	
	4	Other debtors	
	5	Called up share capital not paid [1]	
	6	Prepayments and accrued income [6]	
C-III		Investments	
	1	Shares in group undertakings	
	2	Own shares [4]	
	3	Other investments	
C-IV		Cash at bank and in hand	
D	Prepayments and accrued income [6]		
E	Creditors: amounts falling due within one year		
	1	Debenture loans [7]	
	2	Bank loans and overdrafts [8]	
	3	Payments received on account	
	4	Trade creditors	
	5	Bills of exchange payable	
	6	Amounts owed to group undertakings	

Balance Sheet: Format 1

	7	Amounts owed to undertakings in which the company has a participatory interest
	8	Other creditors including taxation and social security [9]
	9	Accruals and deferred income [10]
F		**Net current assets (liabilities)** [11]
G		**Total assets less current liabilities**
H		**Creditors: amounts falling due after more than one year**
	1	Debenture loans [7]
	2	Bank loans and overdrafts
	3	Payments received on account [8]
	4	Trade creditors
	5	Bills of exchange payable
	6	Amounts owed to group undertakings
	7	Amounts owed to undertakings in which the company has a participating interest
	8	Other creditors including taxation and social security [9]
	9	Accruals and deferred income [10]
I		**Provisions for liabilities**
	1	Pensions and similar obligations
	2	Taxation, including deferred taxation
	3	Other provisions
J		**Accruals and deferred income** [10]
K		**Capital and reserves**
K-I		Called up share capital [12]
K-II		Share premium account
K-III		Revaluation reserve
K-IV		Other reserves
	1	Capital redemption reserve
	2	Reserve for own shares
	3	Reserves provided for by the articles of association
	4	Other reserves
K-V		Profit and loss account

Note:
1. Called up but unpaid share capital may be shown at either position (A or C-II-5).
2. Concessions, patents, licences, trade marks, etc should only be included in the company's balance sheet under this item if they were created internally by the company or acquired for valuable consideration (and are not required to be shown under goodwill).
3. Goodwill should only be included if acquired for valuable consideration.
4. The nominal value of any own shares should be shown separately.
5. Debtors falling due after more than 1 year should be shown separately for each item under debtors.
6. Prepayments and accrued income may be shown at either position (C-II-6 or D).
7. Debenture loans: the amount of any convertible loans should be shown separately.
8. Payments received on account of orders must be shown for each item where not shown as a deduction from stocks.
9. The amount for creditors in respect of taxation and social security must be shown separately from the amounts for other creditors.
10. Accruals and deferred income may be shown at either position J or at one of positions E9 and H9.
11. Net current assets (liabilities) should include amounts shown under "prepayments and accrued income".
12. Called up share capital: the amount of allotted share capital and called up share capital which has been paid up should be shown separately.

IAS balance sheet

A balance sheet prepared under international accounting standards does not have to be presented in a particular **format**. The format normally seen in the UK (above) is therefore acceptable.

Instead of prescribing a format, international accounting standards require a company to classify its items, separating **current and non-current** assets and liabilities (IAS 1(51)). They also set out **minimum disclosures** which must appear on the face of the balance sheet (IAS 1(68)). These are set out in the table below. Other items should be presented on the face of the balance sheet when this is relevant to an understanding of the entity's position (e.g. the total assets held for sale) (IAS 1(69)). Further sub-classification of the items may be required under the relevant IFRSs if the amounts are material.

4239

	Balance sheet: minimum disclosures
1	Property, plant and equipment
2	Investment property
3	Intangible assets
4	Financial assets (excluding items shown under 5, 8 and 9)
5	Investments accounted for under the equity method
6	Biological assets
7	Inventories
8	Trade and other receivables
9	Cash and cash equivalents
10	Trade and other payables
11	Provisions
12	Financial liabilities (excluding items shown under 10 and 11)
13	Liabilities and assets for current tax (as defined in IAS 12)
14	Deferred tax liabilities and deferred tax assets (as defined in IAS 12)
15	Minority interests
16	Issued capital and reserves[1]

Note:
1. The following disclosures are required under issued share capital and reserves (IAS 1(76)):
 – authorised, issued and fully paid, and issued but not fully paid share capital;
 – nominal value of share capital;
 – reconciliation of shares at the beginning and end of the financial year;
 – description of rights, preferences and restrictions;
 – treasury shares, shares held by subsidiaries and associates;
 – shares to be issued under options or contracts; and
 – a description of the nature and purpose of each reserve.

Profit and loss account

Every company must prepare a profit and loss account which gives a true and fair view/fair presentation of a company's profit or loss for the financial year. A profit and loss account is essentially a summary of the income and expenses of the company over the length of the financial year. In international accounting standards, the profit and loss account is known as an "income statement".

4241

There are some differences in the presentational requirements between Companies Act accounts and IAS accounts.

Comment: Under the **new Companies Act**, the detail of the form and content of the profit and loss account, as well as the information which must be provided in the notes to the accounts, will be set out in regulations. Two sets of draft regulations have been published: one just for small companies and one for both medium-sized and large companies. The drafts largely restate the Companies Act 1985 requirements, but the separation of the rules into the different sizes of companies should make compliance easier.

Companies Act profit and loss account

4242 Companies can choose one of four different **formats** for its profit and loss account which are set out in the Companies Act 1985 (para 8 Sch 4 CA 1985). Those formats are supplemented by FRS 3 "Reporting financial performance", which introduces a range of additional disclosures.

The most common format is **Format 1**, shown below. This format discloses the company's cost of sales and gross profit and classifies expenditure in terms of administration and distribution costs.

Comment: Under the **new Companies Act**, the profit and loss account formats will be set out in regulations which are due to come into force on 6 April 2008 (para 1 Sch 1 in both the draft Large and Medium-sized Companies and Groups (Accounts and Reports) Regulations 2008 and the draft Small Companies and Groups (Accounts and Directors' Report) Regulations 2008). The regulations also set out four formats; Format 1 shown below is the same, except that "Operating profits and loss" is omitted.

Profit and loss account: Format 1 (incorporating the requirements of FRS 3)
Turnover
Cost of sales [1]
Gross profit or loss
Distribution costs [1]
Administration costs [1]
Other operating income
Operating profit and loss [1]
Profits or losses on the sale or termination of an operation [2]
Cost of a fundamental reorganisation or restructuring [2]
Profits or losses on disposals of fixed assets [2]
Income from shares in group undertakings
Income from participating interests
Income from other fixed asset investments [3]
Other interest receivable and similar income [3]
Amounts written off investments
Interest payable and similar charges [4]
Profit or loss on ordinary activities before taxation [5]
Tax on profit and loss on ordinary activities
Profit or loss on ordinary activities after taxation
Extraordinary income
Extraordinary charges
Extraordinary profit or loss
Tax on extraordinary profit or loss
Other taxes not shown under the above items
Profit or loss for the financial year
Dividends paid and proposed [5]
Amounts set aside or proposed to be set aside to, or withdrawn or proposed to be withdrawn from, reserves [5]

Note:
1. The amounts under these items must be stated after taking into account any necessary provisions for depreciation or diminution in value of assets.
2. Not part of Format 1 but required by FRS 3.
3. Income and interest derived from group undertakings should be shown separately from income and interest derived from other sources.
4. The amount payable to group undertakings should be shown separately.
5. Not part of Format 1 but required by Companies Act 1985 (para 3 Sch 4 CA 1985; restated at para 3 Sch 1 in both sets of draft regulations as of 6 April 2008).

Any detail supporting these key disclosures is normally given in the **notes** to the accounts (including, in particular, the amount of any provisions for depreciation and diminution in value of tangible and intangible fixed assets). In addition, the notes must contain a considerable number of other disclosures as required by the Companies Act 1985, FRS 3 and other accounting standards and pronouncements.

Comment: Under the **new Companies Act**, the information which will have to be provided in the notes to the accounts will be set out in regulations. Two sets of draft regulations have been published: one just for small companies and one for both medium-sized and large companies. The drafts largely restate the Companies Act 1985 requirements, but the separation of the rules into the different sizes of companies should make compliance easier.

4243

IAS income statement

The **format** of an IAS income statement is more flexible than a Companies Act profit and loss account. Expenses can be analysed by function (e.g. cost of sales, distribution costs, administrative costs etc), as with Format 1 under the Companies Act 1985, or by nature (e.g. staff costs, depreciation etc), as with Format 2 under the Companies Act 1985 (IAS 1(88)). If the income statement classifies items by function, additional information on the nature of the expense must be disclosed (IAS 1(93)).

Instead of a prescribed format, as with the balance sheet, international accounting standards specify the **minimum disclosures** which must appear on the face of the income statement. These are set out in the table below. Additional items may be needed to fairly present the entity's financial results or if they are material (IAS 1(87)).

4244

	Income statement: minimum disclosures
1	Revenue
2	Finance costs
3	Share of the profit or loss of associates and joint ventures accounted for using the equity method
4	Total net profit or loss from discontinued operations comprising: – post-tax profit or loss of discontinued operations; and – post-tax gain or loss recognised on the disposal of the assets or disposal group(s) constituting the discontinued operations
5	Tax expenses
6	Profit or loss

3. Directors' report

The accounts for each financial year must be accompanied by a directors' report, also known as the "**annual report**" (ss 234, 262 CA 1985). Recent legislation has changed the requirements (SI 2005/1011). **Large and medium-sized companies** are required to produce an "enhanced" directors' report, containing more information than was previously the case (ss 234ZZA, 234ZZB, Sch 7 CA 1985). Large companies have to provide more information than medium-sized ones (s 246A(2A) CA 1985). **Small companies** do not have to produce an "enhanced" report, but their directors' report must still contain some minimum disclosures (s 246(4) CA 1985). The definitions of small and medium-sized companies are considered at ¶4360+.

4245

There was a great deal of publicity and media interest surrounding the directors' **narrative reporting** requirements under the **new Companies Act** when it received Royal Assent in November 2006. Narrative reporting simply means explaining in words what the accounts show in terms of the events and actions of the company over the relevant accounting period. Under the 1985 Act, large and medium-sized companies must provide narrative reporting on their activities through the "business review" part of the directors' report. The new Companies Act largely restates the directors' report requirements as of 6 April 2008 as far as unquoted companies are concerned (ss 415-419 CA 2006), setting out the details in regulations. The new Act's provision setting out the obligation to include the business review (¶4252) and its

4246

contents is already in force and applies to financial years commencing on or after 1 October 2007 (s 417 CA 2006, para 43 Sch 3 SI 2007/2194).

In some respects, the new provisions are more favourable as there is a new "**safe-harbour**" clause under which directors will not have to disclose information about impending developments or matters in the course of negotiation if the disclosure would, in their opinion, be seriously prejudicial to the interests of the company (s 417(10) CA 2006, already in force).

On the other hand, another provision in the Act, also already in force, makes the **directors liable** to the company if they knowingly include a false or misleading statement in their report (see ¶4258).

Comment: The **business review** provision of the new Companies Act has come into force ahead of the other accounts provisions, which are due to come into force on 6 April 2008. Therefore, the references in s 417 CA 2006 to the size of a company have been amended for the time being to refer to the CA 1985 thresholds (see ¶4362+) (para 16 Sch 1 SI 2007/2194).

Most of the publicity has been connected with the increased reporting requirements for **quoted companies**. These will have to provide more information about (s 417(5) CA 2006, already in force):
– the main trends and factors likely to affect the future development, performance and position of the company's business;
– environmental matters (including the impact of the company's business on the environment), the company's employees, and social and community issues, including information about any policies of the company in relation to those matters and the effectiveness of those policies; and
– information about persons with whom the company has contractual or other arrangements which are essential to the business of the company, unless disclosure of information about a person would be seriously prejudicial to him and contrary to the public interest.

Disclosure by all companies

4247   Every directors' report must state the matters set out in the table below.

Disclosure	Reference (CA 1985)	New reference [1]
Principal activities of the company and its subsidiaries during the year. These activities will be the various classes of business in which the company operates.	s 234ZZA(1)(b)	s 416(1) CA 2006
Names of any persons who were **directors** during the financial year [2]	s 234ZZA(1)(a)	s 416(1) CA 2006
Amount and recipient of **political donations or expenditure** by the company or any of its subsidiaries to any political party or political organisation in the EU, including the UK (providing the donations and expenditure exceed £200 in total), and any contributions of whatever amount to a non-EU political party [3]	para 3, Sch 7	small: paras 2, 3 Sch 5 large/medium-sized: paras 3, 4 Sch 7
Amount and purpose of any **charitable donations** exceeding £200 given by the company or any of its subsidiaries [4]	para 5, Sch 7	small: para 4 Sch 5 large/medium-sized: para 5 Sch 7
Any **acquisitions** by the company **of its own shares**, including: – the number and nominal value of shares acquired; – if purchased, the aggregate consideration paid for the shares and the reasons for the purchase; – the maximum and nominal value of shares acquired or charged during the year; – the number and nominal value of any acquired shares which were subsequently disposed of in the year; and – if disposed of for money or money's worth, the amount or value of the consideration received	paras 7, 8, Sch 7	small: para 6 Sch 5 large/medium-sized: paras 8, 9 Sch 7

Disclosure	Reference (CA 1985)	New reference[1]
Where the average number of persons employed by the company in each week of the financial year exceeds 250, a description of the company's policy regarding the **employment of disabled persons** (i.e. appointment, training, career development and promotion)[5]	para 9, Sch 7	small: para 5 Sch 5 large/medium-sized: para 10 Sch 7

Note:
1. These provisions are due to come into force on **6 April 2008** and will apply to financial years commencing on or after that date. "Small" references are to the draft Small Companies and Groups (Accounts and Directors' Report) Regulations 2008; "Large/medium-sized" references are to the draft Large and Medium-sized Companies and Groups (Accounts and Reports) Regulations 2008.
2. It is also conventional to state:
 – the dates of any appointments or resignations of directors during the financial year;
 – details of any appointments or resignations since the end of the financial year; and
 – which directors are due to retire at the next AGM and whether they offer themselves for re-election.
3. When the regulations under the new Companies Act come into force, this threshold will increase to £2,000, and from 1 October 2008 will include donations to independent election candidates.
4. When the regulations under the new Companies Act come into force, this threshold will increase to £2,000.
5. Although unlikely, it is possible for a company to have more than 250 employees and qualify as a small company or medium-sized company, see ¶4362+.

Directors' interests

4249

Companies used to be required to disclose information about their directors' interests in shares or debentures in the accounts. However, this obligation was repealed on 6 April 2007, along with the requirements for directors to disclose these interests to their companies and for companies to maintain a register of these disclosures (art 5 Sch 2 SI 2007/1093).

Audited companies

4251

The directors' report of companies which have their accounts audited (see ¶4290) must contain a **statement** that, in the case of each director at the time when the report is approved (¶4263) (s 234ZA(2) CA 1985; restated at s 418 CA 2006 as of 6 April 2008):
a. so far as the director is aware, there is no relevant audit information (meaning information needed by the company's auditor in connection with preparing his report) of which the auditor is unaware; and
b. the director has taken all steps he ought to have taken in order to make himself aware of any relevant audit information and to establish that the auditor is aware of that information.

If the directors' report contains a **false statement**, every director who knew that the statement was false, or was reckless as to whether it was false, and failed to take reasonable steps to prevent the report from being approved, is guilty of an offence (s 234ZA(6) CA 1985; restated at s 418(5), (6) CA 2006 as of 6 April 2008; ¶9935).

> MEMO POINTS In order for a director to take all the necessary steps he should, as a minimum, make enquiries of his fellow directors and of the company's auditor. The enquiries, and any other steps he may take, will be considered against the backdrop of his **duty to exercise care, skill and diligence** (s 234ZA(4)(5) CA 1985; restated at s 418(4) CA 2006 as of 6 April 2008). When determining whether an individual director has complied with this duty, two standards will be considered: the knowledge, skill and experience that may reasonably be expected of a person carrying out his functions (the so-called "objective standard") and the knowledge, skill and experience which that director in fact has (the so-called "subjective standard"). For more on the duty to exercise care, skill and diligence, see ¶2411+.

Additional disclosures by large and medium-sized companies

4252

The additional information which must be contained in the "enhanced" directors' report of large and medium-sized companies is set out in the table below.

Disclosure	Reference (CA 1985)	New reference[1]
Business review[2]: – a fair review of the company's business, being a balanced and comprehensive analysis of the development and performance of the company's business during the financial year and its position at the end of that year, consistent with the business' size and complexity; – must contain a description of the principal risks and uncertainties facing the company; – should include financial key performance indicators (i.e. factors that measure the development, performance or position of the company's business)[3]	–	s 417 CA 2006
Amount (if any) of the directors' recommended **dividend payment**	s 234ZZA(1)(c)	s 416(3) CA 2006
Where significant, the difference between the market **value of the company's land and buildings** and the value at which they are included in the balance sheet	para 1 Sch 7	para 2 Sch 7
Where necessary for the assessment of the assets, liabilities, financial position and profit or loss of the company, an explanation of the company's **use of financial instruments**, including an indication of its financial risk management objectives and policies and its exposure to price, credit, liquidity and cash flow risks	para 5A Sch 7	para 6 Sch 7
Particulars of any important **events** affecting the company which have occurred **since the end of the financial year**	para 6(1)(a) Sch 7	para 7 Sch 7
Indication of the likely **future developments** in the business of the company	para 6(1)(b) Sch 7	para 7 Sch 7
Indication of the activities, if any, of the company in the field of **research and development**	para 6(1)(c) Sch 7	para 7 Sch 7
Indication of the existence of any **overseas branches** (see ¶145 for definition of branch)[4]	para 6(1)(d) Sch 7	para 7 Sch 7
Where the average number of persons employed by the company in each week of the financial year exceeds 250, a statement describing the action that has been taken to introduce, maintain or develop **employee participation** (information, consultation and encouraging involvement through employees' share schemes or other means)	para 11 Sch 7	para 11 Sch 7
Creditor payment policy[5] including: – whether it is the company's policy to follow any code or standard on payment practice and if so, the name of the code or standard and the place where copies can be obtained; – whether it is the company's policy to settle the terms of payment with suppliers prior to each transaction; – what is the policy in respect of suppliers not fitting within the above two categories; and – the average number of days taken to settle trade creditors. If different policies apply to different suppliers or classes of suppliers, the suppliers to which the different policies apply should be identified.	para 12 Sch 7	para 12 Sch 7

Note:
1. These provisions are due to come into force on **6 April 2008** and will apply to financial years commencing on or after that date, with the exception of the business review provision, which came into force on **1 October 2007** and applies to financial years commencing on or after that date. References to Schedule 7 are to Schedule 7 of the draft Large and Medium-sized Companies and Groups (Accounts and Reports) Regulations 2008.
2. Guidance on the use of key performance indicators is contained in paras 75-77 of Reporting Statement "Operating and Financial Review" issued by the ASB. In the main, this non-mandatory guidance applies only to listed companies who choose to produce an OFR in addition to the enhanced directors' report. However, BERR has stated that the guidance on key performance indicators is also applicable to non-listed large and medium-sized companies.
3. Previously, medium-sized companies which prepared IAS accounts rather than Companies Act accounts (¶4226) had to include non-financial key performance indicators in their business review report (s 246A(1) CA 1985). This anomaly has not been restated in the new Companies Act: medium-sized companies do not have to use non-financial key performance indicators regardless of the basis upon which they prepare their accounts (s 417(7) CA 2006).
4. Disclosure of overseas branches does not apply to unlimited companies.
5. Disclosure of the creditor payment policy only applies to public companies, or large companies which are members of a group the parent of which is a public company.

Additional disclosures by large companies

The "enhanced" directors' report of non-listed large companies must also include, in the business review, analysis using **non-financial key performance indicators**. These would include information relating to environmental and employee matters (s 417(6) CA 2006).

4254

> MEMO POINTS 1. Although **medium-sized companies** are not required to include non-financial key performance indicators in their directors' report (s 417(7) CA 2006), BERR encourages such companies to report on these issues voluntarily in recognition of the benefits such disclosure brings to the operation of the business.
> 2. The Department for Environment, Food and Rural Affairs has published **guidance** on the use of environmental key performance indicators which can be downloaded from its website (*www.defra.gov.uk*).
> 3. The business review provision of the **new Companies Act** has come into force ahead of the other accounts provisions, which are due to come into force on 6 April 2008. Therefore, the references in s 417 CA 2006 to the size of a company have been amended for the time being to refer to the CA 1985 thresholds (see para 16 Sch 1 SI 2007/2194).

Directors' liability

Under requirements contained in the **new Companies Act** which apply to reports first sent to shareholders on or after 20 January 2007 (art 3(1)(c), para 3 Sch 5 SI 2006/3428), a director is liable to **compensate** his company for any loss suffered by it as a result of (s 463 CA 2006):
– any untrue or misleading statement in a directors' report, provided the director knew the statement was untrue or misleading or was reckless as to whether it was untrue or misleading; or
– the omission from a report of anything required to be included in it, provided the director knew the omission was a dishonest concealment of a material fact.

This provision does not allow third parties to make claims against the directors; the directors are only liable to the company (s 463(4) CA 2006).

4258

In addition, if the directors' report does not comply with the statutory requirements, every director who:
– knew that it did not comply or was reckless as to whether it complied; and
– failed to take all reasonable steps to secure compliance,
is guilty of a **criminal offence** punishable by a fine (s 234(5) CA 1985; restated at s 415 CA 2006 as of 6 April 2008; ¶9935).

4259

---

4. Circulation

A company's statutory annual accounts, together with the directors' report must be **approved** by the board. Those documents, together with the auditor's report (if applicable), must then be:
– **published**;
– **laid** before the shareholders; and
– **filed** at Companies House.

4261

It should be noted that, for companies preparing Companies Act accounts, there is a difference between its **statutory accounts** and the accounts which it must prepare to comply with wider accounting standards. Its statutory accounts consist solely of the profit and loss account and balance sheet, together with notes to those financial statements. The accounting standards also require a company to prepare a cash flow statement and a statement of total recognised gains and losses.

Comment: **Private companies** are no longer required to lay their accounts before a general meeting (¶4273+), although they do still have to publish and circulate them. The changes to private companies' obligations in this respect **apply** to financial years starting on or after 1 October 2007.

Board approval and signature

A company's statutory **annual accounts** and its **directors' report** must be approved by the board and signed on its behalf by a director or the company secretary. The name of the

4263

signatory must be stated on every copy of the directors' report. The accounts must be signed at the bottom of the company's balance sheet and the name of the signatory must be stated on every copy of the balance sheet (ss 233, 234A CA 1985; restated at ss 414, 419 CA 2006 as of 6 April 2008).

If the board approves **accounts which do not comply** with the legislative requirements, every director who is a party to their approval and knows that they do not comply, or is reckless as to whether they comply, is guilty of an offence (s 233(5) CA 1985; restated at s 414 CA 2006 as of 6 April 2008; ¶9935). Further, if an **unsigned** copy of the balance sheet or directors' report is circulated, published or issued, the company and every officer in default is guilty of an offence (ss 233(6), 234A(4) CA 1985; restated at ss 414, 419 CA 2006 as of 6 April 2008; ¶9935).

Publication

Mandatory publication

4265 A copy of the following documents must be **sent to** every shareholder (and also to every debenture holder or any other person entitled to receive notice of general meetings) (s 238(1), (2) CA 1985; restated at s 423 CA 2006 as of 6 April 2008):
- the company's **statutory annual accounts**;
- the **directors' report**; and
- the **auditor's report** (if relevant).

> MEMO POINTS 1. Copies need **not be sent to** a shareholder or debenture holder who is not entitled to receive notice of general meetings, if the company is unaware of his address (s 238(2)(a) CA 1985). Under the new Companies Act, a company will only have to send accounts and reports to persons for whom they have a current address (s 423(2), (3) CA 2006 as of 6 April 2008).
> 2. In the case of **joint shareholders or debenture holders**, copies must generally be sent to each holder. However, if neither holder is entitled to receive notice of general meetings, copies need only be sent to one of them. If some of the joint holders are entitled to receive notice, copies need only be sent to those holders (s 238(2)(b), (c) CA 1985). Under the new Companies Act, copies will need to be sent to every joint holder, or to the holder whose name appears first in the register of shareholders, provided the company has a current address for him (s 423, para 16 Sch 5 CA 2006 as of 6 April 2008).
> 3. In the case of a **company limited by guarantee** or an **unlimited company** without share capital, copies should only be sent to members, debenture holders or other persons entitled to receive notice of general meetings (s 238(3) CA 1985; restated at s 423(4) CA 2006 as of 6 April 2008).
> 4. Companies whose accounts have been audited are permitted to send **summary financial statements** instead of the full reports and accounts, provided the auditor has expressed a positive opinion as to the consistency of the summary with the full accounts (s 251 CA 1985; SI 1995/2092; SI 2005/2281). The summary can only be sent to those persons who have chosen to receive it by either:
> – giving an express notification of their wish to the company; or
> – failing to respond to an opportunity to elect to receive the full accounts.
> An entitled person can choose to continue receiving the company's full accounts if he prefers, and he remains entitled to request a copy of the full accounts even if he has chosen to receive the summary.
> The summary must include a summary auditor's report but not a summary directors' report (although information on dividends paid and proposed must instead be included as a note to the summary profit and loss account).
> The directors are liable for any false or misleading statement in the summary financial statements, so far as it is derived from their report, in the same way that they would be for such a statement in the report itself (see ¶4258). An example of an auditor's report is available from the Auditing Practices Board (Bulletin 2007/1, published in January 2007).
> Under the **new Companies Act**, the provisions relating to summary financial statements will be set out in regulations (ss 426, 427 CA 2006 as of 6 April 2008). The draft Companies (Summary Financial Statement) Regulations 2008 essentially set out the same provisions with necessary changes corresponding to the new Act, such as replacing references to the memorandum with the constitution. The final version of the regulations is expected to come into force on 6 April 2008, applying to financial years commencing on or after that date, and will replace the current regulations.

4266 The documents can be **sent by** any of the following methods (s 1144(2), Sch 5 CA 2006):
– personal delivery or post;
– electronic communication (e.g. email), provided the recipient has given the company an appropriate address for that purpose;

– publishing them onto a website, provided the recipients have consented to this method of service. The recipients must be notified that the documents have been published, the address of the website, the place on that website where the documents may be accessed and how they may be accessed. For example, the recipients could all be emailed a web link with an access password; or
– any other method agreed between the company and shareholder.

For details of the new communication provisions, which apply to any communications by a company to its shareholders, see ¶3695+, where they are discussed in the context of giving notice of a shareholder meeting.

A **private company** must send the documents out by the following deadline (s 238A(1) CA 1985, inserted by para 3 Sch 4 SI 2007/2194; s 235(1) CA 1985, as amended by para 3 Sch 4 SI 2007/2194):
– by the end of the period for delivering accounts to Companies House (¶4279+); or
– if the company actually delivers them sooner, by the date on which this occurs.

4267

A **public company** must send the documents out at least 21 days before they are laid before the general meeting (see ¶4273+; s 238A(2) CA 1985). However, if all of the shareholders entitled to vote at the meeting approve, the documents can be sent out later (s 238A(3) CA 1985).

If a company **fails to send** the documents, the company and every officer in default is guilty of an offence (s 238(5) CA 1985 as amended by para 3 Sch 4 SI 2007/2194; restated at s 425 CA 2006 as of 6 April 2008; ¶9935).

Comment: Under the **new Companies Act**, the position for private and public companies will remain the same (s 424 CA 2006, due to come into force on 6 April 2008).

Additional copies

In addition to the mandatory copies to which they are entitled (¶4265+), a company's **shareholder or debenture holder** is entitled to demand one further copy of the (s 239 CA 1985; restated at s 431 CA 2006 as of 6 April 2008):
– last annual accounts;
– last directors' report; and
– the auditor's report on those documents (if relevant).

4268

The company must meet such a demand **within** 7 days. It **cannot charge** for the additional copies.

The documents can be **sent** using any of the methods referred to at ¶4266.

If the company **fails to send** a copy on demand, the company and every officer in default is guilty of an offence (¶9935).

Voluntary publication

A company can of course choose to publish its statutory and/or non-statutory accounts to any other persons. A company will be **treated as having "published"** its accounts if it publishes, issues or circulates them, or otherwise makes them available for public inspection, in a way which invites the public to read them.

4269

If a company chooses to publish its **statutory accounts**, they must always be accompanied by either the auditor's report or the accountant's report which confirms that the company falls within the audit exemption (¶4290) (s 240(1) CA 1985).

4270

Comment: Under the **new Companies Act**, a company that is exempt from audit will no longer need to attach an accountant's report to its accounts (s 434 CA 2006, due to come into force on 6 April 2008).

> MEMO POINTS A company which is required to prepare **group accounts** cannot publish its individual statutory accounts without also publishing its group statutory accounts (s 240(2) CA 1985; restated at s 434 CA 2006 as of 6 April 2008).

If a company chooses to publish any **non-statutory accounts** (such as an interim report), they must not be published with the relevant auditor's report or accountant's report. Instead,

4271

they must be published with a **statement** indicating (s 240(3) CA 1985; restated at s 435 CA 2006 as of 6 April 2008):
– that they are not the company's statutory accounts;
– whether any statutory accounts for that financial year have been filed at Companies House; and
– whether the statutory accounts are accompanied by an auditor's report or accountant's report, and whether the relevant report is qualified or unqualified.

Comment: Under the **new Companies Act**, a company which is exempt from audit will not need to refer to an accountant's report (s 435 CA 2006, due to come into force on 6 April 2008).

MEMO POINTS 1. If the statutory accounts are accompanied by an auditor's report, the statement with the non-statutory accounts **must also state** whether:
– the report is qualified or unqualified;
– the auditor drew attention to any matters short of qualifying the report;
– the auditor considered that the accounting records or returns were inadequate or did not agree with the accounts; or
– the report states that the auditor failed to obtain necessary information and explanations.
2. If an **unlimited company** which does not have to file its statutory accounts (see ¶4278/mp) publishes non-statutory accounts, instead of stating whether any statutory accounts have been filed, the statement should say that the company is exempt from the requirement to file statutory accounts (s 254(4) CA 1985; restated at s 448 CA 2006 as of 6 April 2008).
3. If the company **contravenes any requirement** relating to the voluntary publication of its accounts, the company and any officer in default is guilty of an offence (s 240(6) CA 1985; restated at s 435 CA 2006 as of 6 April 2008; ¶9935).

Laying accounts before general meeting

4273 A **public company's** annual accounts, directors' report and auditor's report (if relevant) must be laid before a general meeting of the company's shareholders (s 241 CA 1985 as amended by Sch 2 SI 2007/2194). "Laying" simply **means** presenting those accounts to the shareholders; the accounts do not have to be approved by them. Since the laying of accounts is an annual event, it generally **occurs at** the company's annual general meeting.

Failure to lay accounts and reports is a criminal offence, rendering the directors in default liable to a fine (s 241(2) CA 1985; ¶9935). A director can defend such a charge by proving that he took all reasonable steps to secure compliance with the requirements, although not on the basis that the documents were never prepared (s 241(3), (4) CA 1985).

For financial years commencing on or after 1 October 2007, **private companies** are no longer required to lay their accounts before the shareholders (Sch 2, para 49 Sch 3 SI 2007/2194). This transitional measure has been brought into force ahead of the implementation of the relevant provisions of the new Companies Act, which will only impose this requirement on public companies (s 437 CA 2006, due to come into force on 6 April 2008). As a result of this change, the associated provisions allowing private companies to opt out of the requirement have also been repealed.

Time period

4275 The time period for laying the accounts before the shareholders is the same as that for filing them at Companies House (¶4279). Although the legislation does not require it, they are usually laid before the shareholders, then filed at Companies House.

Filing at Companies House

4278 Companies must file their statutory **annual accounts, directors' report and auditor's report** (if relevant) at Companies House (s 242(1) CA 1985; restated at s 446 CA 2006 as of 6 April 2008). Any documents not in English (or Welsh for companies whose registered office is in Wales) must be accompanied by an English translation.

MEMO POINTS **Small and medium-sized companies** may prepare and file "abbreviated accounts" instead (see ¶4360+).
Dormant companies may file dormant company accounts instead (see ¶4407+).

Unlimited companies need only file accounts if, during the period covered by the accounts, the company was a subsidiary or parent of a limited undertaking (s 254 CA 1985; restated at s 448 CA 2006 as of 6 April 2008).

The **time period** for filing accounts at Companies House is strict: **4279**
– for a **private company**, the documents must be filed within 10 months of the end of the relevant accounting reference period (¶4217+); and
– for a **public company**, the time period is 7 months from the end of the relevant accounting period (s 244(1) CA 1985).

If the documents relate to the company's **first financial year** and the accounting reference period is more than 12 months, the period for filing is the longer of (s 244(2) CA 1985):
– 22 months (for a private company) or 19 months (for a public company) from the date of incorporation; or
– 3 months from the end of the accounting reference period.

If the **accounting reference period is shortened** (¶4220), the period for the laying of documents is the longer of:
– the last date for filing the accounts calculated by reference to the new accounting reference date; or
– 3 months from the date that Form 225 (change of accounting reference date) was filed.

Note that there is a particular **definition of a month** in this context (*Dodds v Walker* [1981] 2 All ER 609; *Registrar of Companies v Radio-Tech Engineering Ltd* [2004] BCC 277). A period of months after a given date ends on the corresponding date in the appropriate month. For example, 10 months after 30 September 2006 is 30 July 2007, not 31 July. Similarly, 10 months after 28 February 2006 is 28 December 2007, not 31 December. However, if there is no corresponding date, the last day of the month will apply. For example, 10 months after 30 April 2007 is 28 February 2008. There is no relaxation of the rule if the last date falls on a Sunday or a bank holiday: the documents must be posted in time to arrive before the deadline.

> EXAMPLE
> 1. A Ltd's accounting reference date is 31 December. It has prepared accounts for the financial year from 1 January to 31 December 2007. The last date for the laying of its accounts and reports is 31 October 2008 (i.e. 10 months after 31 December 2006).
> 2. Suppose that on 1 September 2008, A Ltd changed its accounting reference date to 30 September, effective from the previous accounting reference period. Its accounting reference period for 2007 would therefore be shortened so that it ran from 1 January to 30 September 2007. The last date for laying its accounts for that year would now be 1 December 2008 (i.e. 3 months after the change of accounting reference date).
> 3. B plc's accounting reference date is also 31 December and it too has prepared accounts for the financial year from 1 January to 31 December 2007. The last date for the laying of its accounts and reports is 31 July 2008 (i.e. 7 months after 31 December 2007).
> 4. C Ltd was incorporated on 6 July 2007. Its accounting reference date was automatically set to 31 July. Its first accounting reference period is from 6 July 2007 to 31 July 2008 and it prepares accounts for that period. The last date for the laying of its accounts is 6 May 2009 (i.e. 22 months after 6 July 2007).
> 5. D plc is also incorporated on 6 July 2006 but it immediately changes its accounting reference date to 30 November. Its first accounting reference period therefore runs from 6 July 2007 to 30 November 2008. The last date for laying its accounts for that period would be 28 February 2009 (i.e. 3 months after 30 November 2008).

Comment: Under the **new Companies Act**, the period for filing accounts will be reduced to 9 months from the end of the relevant accounting period for private companies, and 6 months for public companies. In addition, the "corresponding date rule" laid down in *Dodds v Walker* ([1981] 2 All ER 609) will be reversed. This means that, for example, 6 months from 30th June will be 31st December (ss 442, 443 CA 2006, due to come into force on 6 April 2008).

The time period can be **extended** only if there is a special reason for doing so (for example, there has been an unforeseen event which was outside the control of the company and its directors). The application must be made before the expiry of the original allowed period. It must be in writing, addressed to the secretary of state and give a full explanation as to

4280

why an extension is being sought. There is no obligation on the secretary of state to grant an extension (s 244(5) CA 1985; restated at s 442(5) CA 2006 as of 6 April 2008).

4281 The **consequences of failing to file** accounts can be serious. At a minimum, there is an automatic **civil fine**, payable by the company, for late filing (s 242A CA 1985). The fine is levied by Companies House. The amount of the fine in each case is set out in the table below.

Length of delay	Private company	Public company
3 months or less	£100	£500
More than 3 months up to 6 months	£250	£1,000
More than 6 months up to 12 months	£500	£2,000
More than 12 months	£1,000	£5,000

In addition to the fine, every director will be guilty of a **criminal offence** for which they may be prosecuted (¶9935) (s 242(2) CA 1985; restated at s 451 CA 2006 as of 6 April 2008). A director can defend such a prosecution on the basis that he took all reasonable steps to secure the filing of the accounts and reports before the end of the relevant time period allowed for the filing (s 242(4) CA 1985; restated at s 451 CA 2006 as of April 2008).

If a company persistently fails to file accounts it may be **wound up** on the grounds of public interest on a petition by the secretary of state (¶7626+) and/or the directors may be **disqualified** (¶3000+).

Comment: Under the **new Companies Act**, the amount of the penalty will be set out in regulations (s 453 CA 2006). The draft Companies (Late Filing Penalties) Regulations 2007 are expected to increase the fines as summarised below to take account of inflation between 1992 and 2007 (reg 4).

Length of delay	Private company	Public company
1 month or less	£150	£750
More than 1 month up to 3 months	£375	£1,500
More than 3 months up to 6 months	£750	£3,000
More than 6 months	£1,500	£7,500

Given the fact that the deadline for filing accounts will be shorter under the new Act (see ¶4279 above), Companies House intends to give companies a chance to get used to the new regime before imposing the updated penalties. Therefore, these penalties will apply to accounts delivered late on or after 1 February 2009, giving companies a 10-month window after the regulations come into force on 6 April 2008 to arrange filing (reg 2 draft Companies (Late Filing Penalties) Regulations 2007). However, the old fines will still apply during this period. For accounts filed on or after 1 February 2009, the new fines will apply whether or not the accounts are filed under the new Act.

The regulations will also introduce a "repeat offender penalty", whereby the fine will be doubled if a company files its accounts late for 2 years in succession. This penalty will only be imposed where a company has failed to file two sets of accounts under the new Act, so will not arise until early 2011.

C. Audit

4290 Generally speaking, the annual accounts of all companies must be independently audited (which means that they are independently verified). However, **small companies** can claim exemption from audit (see ¶4372+) as can **dormant companies** (see ¶4410+).

Auditors are professionally qualified persons from the accountancy field, usually acting through the firm of accountants which employs them. Their **role** is an important one with particular rights and duties (¶4295+). They have liabilities to the company, its shareholders and others who have, or may have, a stake in the company (¶4301+). There are also strict disclosure requirements on the services and remuneration of auditors and their associates, which apply to all accounts for financial years beginning on or after 1 October 2005 (¶4305+).

Once an auditor has carried out the audit, he must prepare an **auditor's report**, which accompanies the annual accounts and directors' report (¶4312+). The most important part of the report is the auditor's opinion on the financial statements.

Since auditors have an important role in ensuring the integrity of the company's public financial information, there are special rules for their **appointment** and the **termination** of that appointment (¶4336+).

> MEMO POINTS   A **new EC Directive on the audit** of company accounts, published on 9 June 2006, will have to be implemented into UK law by 29 June 2008 (EC Directive 2006/43). The directive's main provisions are as follows:
> **a.** statutory auditor and **audit firm** are separately defined, and many of the new provisions deal specifically with audit firms;
> **b.** each statutory auditor and audit firm will have to be identified in an **electronic public register**. For audit firms, the register will show the number of statutory auditors employed by, or associated with it, the owners and management of the firm, and information on any network of which it is a member;
> **c.** a statutory auditor or audit firm will have to be **independent** from the audited entity, and appointment procedures will have to ensure that this is the case;
> **d.** statutory audits will have to be carried out in accordance with **international standards on auditing**;
> **e.** statutory auditors and audit firms will have to be subject to a system of **quality assurance** that is subject to public supervision. Member states will have to organise systems of investigations and sanctions, which will have to provide for appropriate public disclosures;
> **f.** each member state will have to designate **supervisory authorities** responsible for approval, registration, quality assurance, inspection and discipline; and
> **g.** it will only be possible to dismiss the statutory auditor or audit firm if there is a significant reason why the statutory auditor cannot finalise the audit. The reasons for **dismissal or resignation** will have to be disclosed to the relevant supervisory authorities.
> The Directive will be **implemented** in the UK via regulations under the new Companies Act, one amending the new Act to deal with regulating the audit profession in accordance with the Directive (draft Statutory Auditors and Third Country Auditors Regulations 2007) and one delegating the secretary of state's functions under the new Act in respect of supervision the profession to the Professional Oversight Board (draft Statutory Auditors (Delegation of Functions etc) Order 2008). Where relevant, these provisions are referred to below. The regulations will come into force on 6 April 2008.

1. Role of auditor

Rights and duties

4295 Auditors are **responsible for investigating** whether (s 237(1) CA 1985; restated at s 498 CA 2006 as of 6 April 2008):
– proper accounting records have been kept by the company;
– proper returns adequate for the audit have been received from branches not visited by them; and
– the company's individual accounts are in agreement with its accounting records and returns.

4296 In order that auditors may carry out their investigations, they have the **right to access** the company's books, accounts and vouchers at any time, whether that information is held in paper or electronic form (s 389A(1)(a) CA 1985; restated at s 499 CA 2006 as of 6 April 2008).

4297 Auditors also have the **right to question** any of the following people who must give whatever information or explanations the auditors think necessary to perform their duties as auditors (s 389A(1), (2), (3) CA 1985; restated at s 499 CA 2006 as of 6 April 2008):
– any officer or employee of the company;
– any person holding or accountable for any of the company's books, accounts or vouchers; and
– any subsidiary undertakings, their officers, employees, auditors or persons in possession of or accountable for the subsidiary's books, accounts or vouchers.

The auditors can also question a person who fell into any of the above categories at a time to which the information or explanations they require relate (such as a former director or previous accountants).

MEMO POINTS Where a company has a **subsidiary undertaking which is not a body corporate incorporated in GB**, if required, the parent company must take all reasonable steps to obtain the information or explanations which the auditor requires from the subsidiary, its officers, employees, auditor or persons holding or accountable for the subsidiary's books, accounts or vouchers (s 389A(5) CA 1985; restated at s 500 CA 2006 as of 6 April 2008 in respect of subsidiary undertakings not incorporated in the UK, rather than in GB because the new Act will apply to Northern Ireland as well). A parent company which fails to take these steps, and every officer of it who is in default, is guilty of an offence (s 389B(4) CA 1985; restated at s 501 CA 2006 as of 6 April 2008; ¶9935).

4298 A person who knowingly or recklessly gives any materially **misleading, false or deceptive information** or explanations to an auditor is guilty of a criminal offence (s 389B(1) CA 1985; restated at s 501 CA 2006 as of 6 April 2008; ¶9935). Similarly, a person whom an auditor is entitled to question but who **refuses or delays in giving information** or explanations is guilty of a criminal offence (although he can defend the charge on the basis that it was not reasonably practicable for him to provide the required information or explanations) (s 389B(2), (3) CA 1985; restated at s 501 CA 2006 as of 6 April 2008; ¶9935). Further, the auditor retains the **right to apply for an injunction** to enforce his rights to access information and question people (s 389B(5) CA 1985; restated at s 501 CA 2006 as of 6 April 2008).

MEMO POINTS A statement given to auditors in response to their questions cannot be used as **evidence in any criminal proceedings** against the person giving the statement, except for those offences mentioned immediately above (s 389A(6) CA 1985; restated at s 499 CA 2006 as of 6 April 2008). Further, a person does not have to disclose information which would be subject to **legal professional privilege** in a High Court claim (s 389A(7) CA 1985; restated at s 499 CA 2006 as of 6 April 2008).

4299 Auditors have the right to receive notices of and **attend general meetings** of the shareholders. They also have the right to be heard at any general meeting they attend on any part of the business of the meeting which concerns them as auditors. Where the company has appointed a firm of auditors, the right to attend or be heard can be exercised by any individual representative who has been authorised by it in writing (s 390 CA 1985; restated at s 502 CA 2006 as of 6 April 2008).

Liabilities

4301 Professionals must exercise a **standard of care** in accordance with the proper practice accepted in the opinion of a body of responsible and skilled practitioners in that field (*Bolam v Friern Barnet Hospital Management Committee* [1957] 2 All ER 118). As far as auditors are concerned, that standard is as set out in current accounting and auditing standards, although the court will also hear the expert evidence of other auditors (*Lloyd Cheyham & Co Ltd v Littlejohn & Co* [1987] BCLC 303). If they fail to exercise the requisite standard of care, auditors may be found liable for negligence or breach of an implied term in their contract of engagement to take reasonable skill and care.

Comment: The **new Companies Act** creates a new criminal offence in relation to inaccurate auditor's reports, which will come into force on 6 April 2008. The offence is committed by any individual eligible to be a statutory auditor who knowingly or recklessly (s 507 CA 2006):
– causes a report to include anything that is misleading, false or deceptive; or

– causes it to omit a statement that the accounts do not agree with accounting records or returns, that necessary information and explanations were not obtained, or that the directors wrongly took advantage of an exemption from the obligation to prepare group accounts.

> MEMO POINTS Auditors must always bear the possibility of **fraud** in mind. They should not take information at face value, but maintain an attitude of professional scepticism throughout the audit. It is likely that any failure by the auditors to detect such a fundamental defect in the accounts will be treated as a failure to meet the necessary standard of care (IAS 240).

One of the problematic issues in this area is the **persons who may bring a claim** against the auditor. A breach of contract claim may only be brought by persons with a contractual relationship with the auditor and in most cases this is likely to be only the company. Other parties who rely on the accounts such as individual shareholders, creditors, potential investors and persons acquiring shares, may only succeed in a claim against a company's auditor if they can show that the auditor owed them a duty of care.

4302

It is now settled law that auditors only owe a **duty of care** to the company and the shareholders as a whole (*Caparo Industries plc v Dickman* [1990] 1 All ER 568). This is because, according to the House of Lords, the purpose of the audit is to give the shareholders sufficient reliable information on the company's affairs so as to enable them to exercise their powers to scrutinise and control the company's management. Accordingly, a proximity of relationship, leading to a duty of care, can only be established between an auditor and the persons who use his report for the purpose for which it was intended.

4303

As far as other parties are concerned, a duty of care will only be owed if a contractual or other special relationship can be established. For example, auditors who separately confirm their opinion to a third party could be held to have a duty of care to him (*ADT Ltd v BDO Binder Hamlyn* [1996] BCC 808). Lenders often seek to establish a special relationship by asserting reliance on the audited accounts of a company in loan documentation. For this reason, auditors often include an express **limitation of liability** in their reports (see ¶4312+).

> EXAMPLE
> MAN AG purchased the entire issued share capital of ERF plc from WS Ltd, relying upon financial information which was later found to have been falsified by ERF plc's financial controller. MAN AG brought a claim against F Ltd (which had taken over WS Ltd). F Ltd joined ERF plc's auditors, Ernst & Young, in the claim as defendants on the basis that their failure to detect the false accounting and/or to report their concerns about the financial controller breached their duty of care to WS Ltd.
> The claim against F Ltd was successful, but the court decided that Ernst & Young did not owe WS Ltd a duty of care. Aspects of the audit had been negligent, but this was only actionable by ERF plc. WS Ltd had not been able to show that the audit statement had been specifically communicated to it for a reason beyond the statutory purposes, and so Ernst & Young did not owe it a duty of care beyond the duty it already owed to WS Ltd as a shareholder of ERF plc. WS Ltd could not rely on this duty of care because it was owed to the shareholders as a group and their loss was merely reflective of ERF plc's (see ¶2464) (*MAN AG v Freightliner Ltd* [2005] EWHC 2347 (Comm)).

Comment: Under the **new Companies Act**, a "liability limitation agreement" (that is, an agreement that seeks to limit the liability of an auditor to his client company) will be effective provided it is fair and reasonable and approved by an ordinary resolution of the shareholders. Such agreements will have to be disclosed, either in the annual accounts or directors' report. The agreement will only be valid in relation to one financial year and so will have to be renewed each year. The shareholders will have the right to terminate the agreement by ordinary resolution (ss 534-538 CA 2006, due to come into force on 6 April 2008). The terms of these agreements are not likely to be dictated, unless in practice they have an adverse effect, for example on competition ("Companies Act 2006 – a consultative document" (February 2007)). For a general discussion of these issues, in the context of directors to whom they also apply, see ¶2512+.

> MEMO POINTS Companies cannot **exempt** an auditor employed by it from liability for negligence, default, breach of duty or breach of trust in relation to the company (s 310 CA 1985). This applies whether or not the auditor is an officer of the company. It cannot **indemnify** such an auditor from liability either, except in relation to the costs of successfully defending civil or criminal proceedings or making a successful application for relief from liability. Table A contains such a

provision (reg 118 TA 1985). Although unusual, a company may, however, maintain **insurance** for an auditor against liability for negligence, default, breach of duty or breach of trust.

Disclosure of services and remuneration

4305 In recent years, following global financial scandals such as Enron, the independence of auditors who also carry out both **audit and non-audit work** for a company has been called into question. As a result, there are stricter disclosure requirements on the services and remuneration of auditors and their associates, which apply to all accounts for financial years beginning on or after 1 October 2005 (s 390B CA 1985; SI 2005/2417; restated at s 494 CA 2006 as of 6 April 2008).

Comment: For financial years beginning on or after **6 April 2008**, new regulations regarding disclosure will apply (draft Companies (Disclosure of Auditor Remuneration and Liability Limitation Agreements) Regulations 2007). In addition to the information that must be disclosed about auditors' remuneration, if a company has entered into a liability limitation agreement, it must disclose the principal terms of the agreement and the date on which it was approved by the shareholders (or the date on which approval was waived, an option open to private companies) in notes to the accounts (reg 8 draft Companies (Disclosure of Auditor Remuneration and Liability Limitation Agreements) Regulations 2007). For financial years beginning before 6 April 2008, SI 2005/2417 still applies.

> MEMO POINTS **Guidance**, published in October 2006, is available from the ICAEW on the disclosure of auditor remuneration for the audit of accounts and other (non-audit) services (Tech 06/06).

Small or medium-sized company

4306 The notes to the annual accounts of a small or medium-sized company (¶4362+), must disclose the amount of any **remuneration** receivable by the company's auditor **for auditing** the accounts. If the company has appointed more than one person or firm as auditor during the period to which the accounts relate, a separate disclosure is required in respect of each person. Where the remuneration includes benefits in kind, the notes must also disclose the nature and estimated monetary value of the benefits (reg 3 SI 2005/2417).

Comment: This will still be the case under the new regulations from **6 April 2008** (reg 4 draft Companies (Disclosure of Auditor Remuneration and Liability Limitation Agreements) Regulations 2007). The Professional Oversight Board will also be able to require information about the remuneration of **medium-sized companies**' auditors to be provided in respect of non-auditing services, tax advice and other services not disclosed.

Large companies

4307 The disclosure requirements for large companies are more extensive. As well as the disclosures which apply to small and medium-sized companies, the notes to the accounts of large companies must disclose any **remuneration** receivable by the auditor, or his associate, at any time during the period to which the accounts relate, for the supply of **non-audit services** to the company or its associates (reg 4 SI 2005/2417; restated at reg 5 draft Companies (Disclosure of Auditor Remuneration and Liability Limitation Agreements) Regulations 2007 as of 6 April 2008). **Separate disclosure** is required of each of the following non-audit services (where a service falls into more than one category, it should be treated as falling within the one which is listed first) (Sch 2 SI 2005/2417; restated at Sch 2 draft Companies (Disclosure of Auditor Remuneration and Liability Limitation Agreements) Regulations 2007 as of 6 April 2008):
– the auditing of accounts of associates of the company pursuant to legislation (including foreign laws);
– other services supplied pursuant to such legislation;
– other services relating to taxation;
– services relating to information technology;
– internal audit services;
– valuation and actuarial services;
– services relating to litigation;

– services relating to recruitment and remuneration;
– services relating to corporate finance transactions entered into or proposed to be entered into by or on behalf of the company or any of its associates; and
– all other services.

> MEMO POINTS 1. Eligible **large groups** should set out the remuneration of the auditor and their associates for non-audit work as if all the undertakings included in the consolidation were a single company. The individual accounts of the relevant parent company and subsidiaries included in the consolidation should state that the information is contained in the group accounts (reg 5 SI 2005/2417; restated at reg 6 draft Companies (Disclosure of Auditor Remuneration and Liability Limitation Agreements) Regulations 2007 as of 6 April 2008).
> 2. The **auditor is obliged to inform** the company's directors of the remuneration he and his associates were entitled to receive for non-audit work so that it can be included in the notes to the accounts (reg 6 SI 2005/2417; restated at reg 7 draft Companies (Disclosure of Auditor Remuneration and Liability Limitation Agreements) Regulations 2007 as of 6 April 2008).

4308

There is a detailed definition of an "**associate**" for these purposes, which in part depends upon whether the auditor is a partnership or corporate body (Sch 1 SI 2005/2417; restated at Sch 1 draft Companies (Disclosure of Auditor Remuneration and Liability Limitation Agreements) Regulations 2007 as of 6 April 2008).

The following are associates **of the auditor**, regardless of whether the auditor is a partnership or a corporate body:
a. any person controlled by the auditor or an associate of the auditor, except where that control is as a result of the controller acting:
– as an insolvency practitioner; or
– in the capacity of receiver or manager of the property of a corporate body; or
b. any person who, or group of persons acting together which, has control of the auditor;
c. any person using a trading name which is the same or similar to a trading name used by the auditor, if the auditor uses that name with the intention of creating the impression of a connection between them and that other person; and
d. any person who is party to an arrangement with the auditor, with or without any other person, under which costs, profits, quality control, business strategy or significant professional resources are shared.

The following are considered to be an associate of an **auditor which is a partnership**:
– any other partnership which has a partner in common with the company's auditor;
– any partner in the company's auditor;
– any corporate body which is in the same group as a corporate body which is a partner in the auditor or in a partnership which has a partner in common with the auditor; and
– any corporate body of which a partner in the auditor is a director.

The following are considered to be an associate of an **auditor which is a corporate body**:
– any other corporate body which has a director in common with the auditor;
– any director of the auditor;
– any corporate body which is in the same group as a corporate body which is a director of, or has a director in common with, the auditor;
– any partnership in which a director of the auditor is a partner;
– any corporate body which is in the same group as the auditor; and
– any partnership in which any such corporate body which is in the same group as the auditor is a partner.

> MEMO POINTS For these purposes, "**partner**" includes a member of a limited liability partnership and "**partnership**" includes a limited liability partnership and a partnership constituted under foreign law.

2. Auditor's report

The auditor's report should be **headed** "Independent Auditors' Report to the Members of [*name of company*]" (APB Bulletin 2001/2) and divided into the following four sections (SAS 600):
– an **introduction**;

4312

- a headed section dealing with the **respective responsibilities of directors and auditors**;
- a headed section dealing with the **basis of the audit opinion**; and
- a headed section expressing the auditor's **opinions**.

4313 Auditors should not express an opinion on financial statements until they have been approved by the directors. Furthermore, the report should be **signed and dated** on the same date. Auditors should not backdate an audit report. The report may be signed in the name of the auditor's firm, the name of the individual auditor or both. Usually, the signature is that of the firm because it assumes responsibility for the audit. For the purposes of identification, the report normally includes the location of the auditor's office. Where appropriate, his status as registered auditor is also stated (s 236 CA 1985).

Comment: Under the **new Companies Act**, where the auditor is a firm, the report will have to be signed by an individual at that firm who is the **"senior statutory auditor"**. This is a person identified as such under standards to be issued by the European Commission, or guidance issued by the secretary of state or a body appointed by him. The senior statutory auditor will not be subject to any increased exposure to liability (ss 503, 504 CA 2006, due to come into force on 6 April 2008).

The auditor will still have to be **named in every published copy** of the report and the copy filed at Companies House. Where the auditor is an audit firm, the senior statutory auditor will also have to be named. This will not apply where the company passes a resolution to omit the name because it considers that there are reasonable grounds that this would create or be likely to create a serious risk that the auditor, senior statutory auditor or any other person, would be subject to violence or intimidation (such as where the audited company is involved in testing on animals). Where the auditor is not named for this reason, the company will have given notice of the resolution to the secretary of state, stating the name and registered number of the company, the financial year of the company to which the report relates, and the name of the auditor and, if appropriate, the senior statutory auditor. A statement that such a resolution has been passed and delivered to the secretary of state will have to be included in every published copy of the report instead (ss 505, 506 CA 2006, due to come into force on 6 April 2008)

> MEMO POINTS   If a copy of the auditor's report is circulated, published or issued **without a statement of the names** of the auditor, the company and every officer in default is guilty of an offence (s 236(4) CA 1985, restated at s 505 CA 2006 as of 6 April 2008; ¶9935).

4314 **Guidance** on the preparation of an auditor's report is provided by the International Standard on Auditing (UK and Ireland) 700, Auditor's Reports on Financial Statements in Great Britain and Northern Ireland (APB Bulletin 2006/6), which also contains examples of reports, and Statement on Auditing Standards 600 (SAS 600). They are all are issued by the Auditing Practices Board.

Introduction to report

Identification of financial statements

4316 Since the financial statements of a company may contain financial information beyond the company's statutory accounts (e.g. in the directors' report or a chairman's statement), it is important that the auditors identify the statements to which their opinion refers. In the past, this has been done by the use of **page numbers**. However, since more and more companies are publishing their financial statements in electronic form, auditors are increasingly referring to the individual components of the financial statements **by name**. The financial statements have to be identified by name if they are published on a website not in "PDF" format.

4317 Auditors have no responsibility for other information beyond being satisfied that it is not inconsistent with the financial statements or otherwise misleading.

Limitation of liability

4318 Given the potential liability of auditors, it is becoming increasingly common for an auditor to include an express limitation of liability in the introduction to his report. The relevant paragraph usually states that responsibility of the auditor for his audit is limited to the company and its shareholders as a body. See ¶4301+ on auditors' liability and the effectiveness of a limitation of liability agreement.

Small and medium-sized companies

In the case of small and medium-sized companies that prepare financial statements in accordance with FRSSE (¶4367), the auditor should refer to this fact in the introductory paragraph of his report. He can also, but need not, draw attention to such a company's exemption from the requirement to present a cash flow statement.

4319

Respective responsibilities of directors and auditors

A separate section of the report, appropriately headed, should distinguish between the responsibilities of the auditor and the directors. The **distinction** would be expressed clearly by including the following (APB Bulletin 2006/6):
– a statement that the financial statements are the responsibility of the directors, together with a description of these responsibilities or a reference to them if they appear elsewhere in the financial statements or accompanying information; and
– a statement that the auditor's responsibility is to express an opinion on the financial statements.

4321

Basis of audit opinion

In a separate section of the report, the auditor is required to explain the basis of his opinion by including the following:

a. a statement as to their **compliance** or otherwise with Auditing Standards, together the reasons for any departure from them;
b. a statement that the **audit process** includes:
– examining, on a test basis, evidence relevant to the amounts and disclosures in the financial statements;
– assessing the significant estimates and judgments made by the directors in preparing the financial statements;
– considering whether the accounting policies are appropriate to the company's circumstances, consistently applied and adequately disclosed;
c. a statement that he planned and performed the audit so as to obtain reasonable assurance that the financial statements are free from **material misstatement**, whether caused by fraud or other irregularity or error, and that he has evaluated the overall presentation of the financial statements; and
d. a statement that the audit provides a **reasonable basis** for the opinion.

If warranted by the circumstances, an additional paragraph should be added to refer to a fundamental uncertainty, or draw attention to any **other matters** the auditor may regard as important to a proper understanding of the basis of his opinion (e.g. a material post-balance sheet event).

4323

Opinion

The opinion paragraph should clearly indicate the financial reporting framework used to prepare the financial statements (including identifying the country of origin of the financial reporting framework when it is not International Accounting Standards). It should also state the auditor's opinion as to whether (s 235(1B), (2) CA 1985; restated at s 495 CA 2006 as of 6 April 2008):
– the financial statements give a **true and fair view** of the state of affairs of the company as at the end of its financial year and of its profit or loss for the financial year;
– the **accounts have been properly prepared** in accordance with statutory requirements; and
– the information given in the directors' report is consistent with the accounts (see ISA 720 (Revised) issued by the ASB on 10 April 2006).

4325

4326 The opinion must also **draw attention to the following particular failures** by the company (s 237 CA 1985; restated at s 498 CA 2006 as of 6 April 2008):
– proper accounting records have not been kept;
– proper returns adequate for the audit have not been received from branches not visited by the auditor;
– the accounts are not in agreement with the accounting records and returns;
– the auditor has failed to obtain all the information and explanations which, to the best of his knowledge and belief, are necessary for the purposes of his audit;
– the annual accounts do not disclose information relating to directors' emoluments, benefits, loans or transactions (as required by the legislation, see ¶2766+ and ¶2897); and/or
– the company has taken advantage of the exemption for small and medium-sized groups from the need to prepare group accounts and, in the auditor's opinion, it was not entitled to do so.

If the auditor is satisfied that these matters have been complied with, there is no need for it to refer to them.

4327 Where the auditor has no material concerns, the opinion is "**unqualified**". However, the auditor must express a "**qualified**" opinion, "**adverse**" opinion or "**disclaimer**" of opinion where any of the following matters have a material effect on the financial statements:
– the statements do not give a true and fair view;
– there has been a limitation on the scope of the auditor's examination; or
– there is a disagreement between the auditor and the directors about the treatment or disclosure of a matter in the financial statements.

Unqualified opinion

4328 An opinion is referred to as "unqualified" when the auditor states that in his opinion the accounts give a **true and fair view** of the state of affairs of the company and that they have been properly prepared in accordance with all relevant legislation and accounting standards.

Qualified opinion

4329 An opinion is referred to as "qualified" when the directors state that in their opinion the accounts give a **true and fair view except for certain material matters** on which the auditors have reservations. A reservation is material if its omission or misstatement would reasonably influence the decisions of a user of the financial statements. The reservations must be fully explained, either in the opinion or by reference to a note to the accounts, if that note contains adequate information to allow readers to fully appreciate the situation.

> *MEMO POINTS* The FRRP (see ¶4211/mp) wants to secure early **notification of published qualified audit reports** because they are a clear indication that the accounts may not have been prepared properly. Then, corrected information can be put out promptly. In 2007, the FRRP consulted on a proposal for registered audit firms to voluntarily disclose any qualified audit report in relation to a company within the FRRP's remit. At the time of writing, the results of this consultation have not been published.

Adverse opinion

4330 An adverse opinion is issued when the effect of a disagreement between the auditor and the directors about the treatment or disclosure of a matter in the financial statements is so material and pervasive that the auditor feels that the financial statements are seriously misleading. In this event, they are required to express the opinion that the **financial statements do not give a true and fair view**.

Disclaimer of opinion

4331 A disclaimer of opinion is expressed when there has been a limitation on the scope of the auditor's work and the possible effect of that limitation is so material and pervasive that the auditor has **not been able to obtain sufficient evidence to form an opinion**. The report should explain the nature of the limitation (in the "basis of opinion" section) and clearly state (in the "opinion" section) that he is unable to express an opinion on the financial statements.

3. Appointment and termination

Appointment

All companies must appoint an auditor, except for small companies and dormant companies (which are **exempt** from the requirement to audit their accounts, see ¶4372+ and ¶4410+ respectively).

In the case of either type of company, an auditor's **remuneration** will be fixed by the shareholders, directors or secretary of state, depending on who appointed him (s 390A CA 1985; restated at s 492 CA 2006 as of 6 April 2008). See ¶4305+ for the requirement to disclose an auditor's remuneration and services.

4336

> MEMO POINTS The **references** for companies' obligation to appoint an auditor, unless they are exempt from doing so, are complicated during this implementation phase for the new Companies Act:
> – for private companies: s 485 CA 2006 in respect of financial years beginning on or after 1 October 2007. For earlier financial years, the same provision as for public companies applies; and
> – public companies s 384 CA 1985 as amended by para 8 Sch 4 SI 2007/2194. This will be restated at s 489 CA 2006 as of 6 April 2008.

Where a **private company** has to appoint an auditor for a financial year, it must do so within 28 days of (s 485(2) CA 2006 as amended by para 17 Sch 1 SI 2007/2194):
– the end of the time allowed for delivering accounts and reports to Companies House (see ¶4279+); or
– the day on which the company circulated the accounts and reports to the shareholders, if earlier (see ¶4265+).

4337

The auditor can be **appointed by** the **directors** at certain times (s 485(3) CA 2006):
– before the company's first deadline for appointing an auditor;
– after a period during which the company was exempt from needing to appoint an auditor; or
– to fill a casual vacancy.

Otherwise, the **shareholders** must do so, including where the directors have failed to make an appointment (s 485(4) CA 2006). An ordinary resolution can be used.

An auditor will **stay in office** until it is terminated, see ¶4339+ (s 487 CA 2006).

Comment: These provisions of the new Companies Act came into force on **1 October 2007** and apply to financial years beginning on or after that date.

> MEMO POINTS The **secretary of state** has a default **power to appoint** an auditor where the company fails to do so (s 486 CA 2006). The company must notify the secretary of state of its failure within 1 week, otherwise the company and every officer in default is liable to a fine.

A **public company** that has to appoint an auditor must do so at the meeting at which the accounts and reports are laid before the shareholders (usually its AGM) (s 385(2) CA 1985; restated at s 489(2) CA 2006 as of 6 April 2008).

4338

The company's first auditor can be **appointed by** the **directors** before the first accounts are laid (s 385(3) CA 1985; restated at s 489(3) CA 2006 as of 6 April 2008). The directors can also appoint an auditor in the same situations as a private company (above). In other situations, the **shareholders** must appoint the auditor at the appropriate meeting, and they can do so by ordinary resolution.

An auditor will **hold office until** the end of the next meeting at which the accounts and reports are laid or he is removed, see ¶4339+ (s 385(2) CA 1985; s 491 CA 2006 as of 6 April 2008).

> MEMO POINTS 1. "**Special notice**" is required (see ¶3536+) for a public company's shareholder resolution to (s 388(3) CA 1985):
> – fill a casual vacancy; or

– renew the appointment of an auditor who was appointed by the directors to fill a casual vacancy.

These provisions are not restated in the **new Companies Act**. Special notice will only be required to remove or to fail to reappoint an auditor.

2. The **secretary of state** also has a default **power to appoint** an auditor of a public company where the company fails to do so (s 387 CA 1985; restated at s 490 CA 2006 as of 6 April 2008). Again, the company must notify the secretary of state of its failure within 1 week.

Termination of appointment

4339 The auditor's appointment may be **terminated by**:
– his resignation;
– his removal; or
– the non-renewal of his appointment.

Since the auditor has the role of independent scrutineer, if he ceases to hold office because of circumstances which are relevant to the integrity of the company's finances, this must be brought to the attention of the company's shareholders and creditors.

Auditor's statement

4340 Where an auditor ceases to hold office, for whatever **reason**, he must make a statement of any **circumstances** connected with him ceasing to hold office, which he considers should be brought to the attention of the shareholders or creditors of the company (for example, any financial impropriety in the company). If, as is usually the case, the auditor considers that there are no such circumstances, the statement should state this fact. The statement must be **deposited at** the company's registered office (s 394(1) CA 1985; restated at s 519 CA 2006 as of 6 April 2008).

There is no particular **form** for the statement; the usual practice is for the auditor to provide it in the form of a letter to the company on his firm's headed notepaper. The **time** for depositing the statement depends upon the reason for the auditor ceasing to hold office.

Reason for ceasing to hold office	Time period for depositing statement
Resignation	With notice of resignation
Failure to seek re-appointment	Less than 14 days before end of time allowed for next appointment
Any other case	Within 14 days of ceasing to hold office

MEMO POINTS 1. If the **statement refers to circumstances** which the auditor considers should be brought to the attention of the shareholders or creditors, the company must, within 14 days of receipt, **send a copy to** every person who is entitled to a copy of the accounts. The auditor must send a copy of his statement to Companies House between 21 and 28 days after depositing the statement at the company's registered office, unless the company has applied to court with an objection to the statement (s 394(3), (5) CA 1985; restated at ss 520, 521 CA 2006 as of 6 April 2008). The **company can object to the statement** on the grounds that the auditor is using it to secure needless publicity for defamatory matter, by making an application to court within 14 days of receipt. The company must notify the auditor if it makes such an application (s 394(3), (4) CA 1985; restated at s 520 CA 2006 as of 6 April 2008). If the court agrees with the company, it must direct that copies of the statement need not be sent out, and it may direct that the company's costs should be paid by the auditor in whole or in part. In that case, the company must send a statement setting out the effects of the order to every person entitled to copies of the accounts (s 394(6) CA 1985; restated at s 520 CA 2006 as of 6 April 2008). If the court does not agree with the company, the company must send out the statements and notify the auditor of the court's decision. The auditor must send a copy of his statement to Companies House within 7 days of receiving notification of the court's decision (s 394(7) CA 1985; restated at s 521 CA 2006 as of 6 April 2008).

2. An auditor ceasing to hold office who **does not provide a statement** is guilty of a criminal offence. This charge can be defended on the basis that the auditor took all reasonable steps and exercised all due diligence to avoid commission of the offence. Actions can be taken against unincorporated bodies (e.g. partnerships) and against individuals for a corporate body's default. If a company defaults in this respect, the company and every officer is guilty of an offence (s 394A CA 1985; restated at ss 519, 520 CA 2006 as of 6 April 2008; ¶9935).

3. Under the **new Companies Act**, both an auditor who has resigned or has been dismissed and the company for which he has ceased to act will also have to send a copy of his leaving statement to an appropriate audit authority. For non-listed companies, or where there is no major public interest in the audit, the appropriate audit authority will be the auditor's supervisory body and the timing requirement will be set by each such body (ss 522-525 CA 2006 as of 6 April 2008).

Resignation

An auditor is permitted to resign from office by sending a written **notice to** that effect to the company's registered office. The resignation can **take effect from** the date of the notice, or on any later date specified in the notice. A resignation cannot operate retrospectively. A company must **file a copy** of the resignation notice at Companies House within 14 days (s 392 CA 1985; restated at s 516 CA 2006 as of 6 April 2008). Failure to do so is a criminal offence by the company and every officer in default (¶9935).

4341

A resignation is not effective unless it is accompanied by an **auditor's statement** (¶4340), which must be deposited at the same time (ss 392, 394(2) CA 1985; restated at s 519 CA 2006 as of 6 April 2008). The usual practice is for the resignation and statement to be set out in the same letter.

4342

In the rare case where the auditor's **statement sets out circumstances** which he believes should be brought to the attention of the company's shareholders and creditors, the resigning auditor has **three further rights** (s 392A CA 1985; restated at s 518 CA 2006 as of 6 April 2008):
– the right to requisition a general meeting;
– the right to attend a general meeting and be heard on any business concerning the auditor; and
– the right to request that a written statement of the circumstances connected with the resignation be circulated before, or read out at, a general meeting.

> MEMO POINTS 1. The auditor's **requisition of a general meeting** for the purpose of receiving and considering the auditor's explanation of the circumstances connected with his resignation must be deposited with his resignation. The directors must convene a meeting within 21 days of the requisition, and cannot give more than 28 days' notice. The last date for a meeting called by the directors is therefore 49 days after the requisition. Failure to convene a meeting is a criminal offence (¶9935) (s 392A(2), (5) CA 1985; restated at s 518 CA 2006 as of 6 April 2008).
> 2. The resigned auditor is entitled to **attend the following meetings** as if he were still the company's appointed auditor (see ¶4299) (s 392A(8) CA 1985; restated at s 518 CA 2006 as of 6 April 2008):
> – a requisitioned general meeting;
> – the general meeting at which his term of office would have expired; or
> – the general meeting at which the vacancy caused by his resignation will be filled.
> 3. The auditor is entitled to request that the company circulates **a written statement** (of a reasonable length) of the circumstances connected with his resignation to the shareholders before any of the meetings which he is entitled to attend. Providing the statement is received in time, the company must refer to it in the notice of the relevant meeting and send a copy to every person entitled to notice of the meeting. If the statement is not sent out, the auditor can require it to be read out at the meeting. The company, or any other aggrieved party (e.g. a director) can, however, object to the statement being circulated or read out on the ground that the auditor is abusing his rights to secure needless publicity for defamatory matter. The objection must be made applying to court and if the court agrees with the applicant, it may also order that the company's costs on the application should be paid wholly or partly by the auditor (s 392A(3), (4), (6), (7) CA 1985; restated at s 518 CA 2006 as of 6 April 2008).

Removal

An auditor can be removed from office at any time **by the shareholders** passing an ordinary resolution to that effect (s 391(1) CA 1985; restated at s 510 CA 2006 as of 6 April 2008). Any resolution to remove an auditor requires "**special notice**" (see ¶3536+).

4343

> MEMO POINTS The auditor proposed to be removed is entitled to make **written representations** to the company, and can request that the representations be circulated to the company's shareholders. As long as the representations are received in time, the company must refer to them in the notice of the relevant meeting and send a copy to every person entitled to notice of the meeting. If the representations are not sent out, the auditor can require them to be read out at the meeting. The company, or any other aggrieved party (e.g. a director) can, however, object to the representations being circulated or read out on the ground that the auditors are abusing

their rights to secure needless publicity for defamatory matter. The objection must be made by applying to court and if the court agrees with the applicant, it may also order that the company's costs of the application should be paid wholly or partly by the auditor (s 391A CA 1985; restated at s 511 CA 2006 as of 6 April 2008).

4344 The company must **notify** Companies House of a resolution to remove an auditor within 14 days of it being passed by filing Form 391. Failure to file the form is a criminal offence by the company and every officer who is in default (s 391(2) CA 1985; restated at s 512 CA 2006 as of 6 April 2008; ¶9935).

> MEMO POINTS   The name of Form 391, like the names of other **Companies House forms**, is taken from the section number of the legislation. As all of the section numbers will change under the new Companies Act, Companies House proposes to change the names of all of its forms to reflect their function rather than the relevant section number ("Working with Companies House: a consultation on the registrar's rules and related provisions which will apply under the Companies Act 2006"). At the time of writing, the new form names are not yet available.

4345 Although an auditor can be removed notwithstanding any agreement between him and the company, the auditor will still be entitled to **claim any compensation or damages** payable in respect of the termination of his appointment (s 391 CA 1985; restated at s 513 CA 2006 as of 6 April 2008). For example, the auditor could claim payment for any work which he had not yet invoiced.

In addition, the removed auditor will be entitled to **attend the following meetings**, and be heard on any matters concerning the auditor, as if he were still the company's appointed auditor (¶4299):
– the general meeting at which his term of office would have expired; or
– the general meeting at which the vacancy caused by his resignation will be filled.

Comment: Under the **new Companies Act**, if an auditor is removed from office because he disagreed with the company on a professional matter (i.e. regarding accounting treatments or audit procedures) or for another **improper reason**, a shareholder will be able to apply to court for an order remedying the situation on the ground that the company has been conducted in an unfairly prejudicial manner (s 994 CA 2006 as amended by reg 34 draft Statutory Auditors and Third Country Auditors Regulations 2007, due to come into force on 6 April 2008). See ¶2105+ for the procedure.

Non-renewal of appointment

4346 An auditor's appointment runs for a financial year, unless it is terminated early. Companies will usually reappoint the same auditor year after year if there is no reason to change.

If a **private company** does not actively reappoint an auditor by the time the period for appointing auditors has expired (see ¶4337), the auditor is usually deemed to have been reappointed (s 487 CA 2006). However, the company will actively have to reappoint an auditor:
– who was appointed by the directors (unless the company has already passed an elective resolution to dispense with the need to appoint auditors each year, para 44 Sch 3 SI 2007/2194 (a transitional measure that will be revoked in due course)); or
– if the articles require.

Automatic reappointment can be prevented by:
– 5% of the shareholders holding the total voting rights (or a lower percentage specified in the articles) giving notice to the company that the auditor should not be reappointed automatically (s 488 CA 2006). The notice must be in hard copy of electronic form, signed by each shareholder and received by the company before the end of the accounting period for which the auditor held office; or
– the directors resolving that no auditor should be appointed for the financial year.

Auditors of **public companies** must be actively reappointed (s 385(2) CA 1985; restated at s 491 CA 2006 as of 6 April 2008).

In the case of all companies, **special notice** is required of a resolution which has the effect of not renewing the appointment of an auditor and appointing a new auditor in his place (see ¶3536+).

MEMO POINTS The retiring auditor has the same rights as an auditor who is being removed from office to make **written representations** to the company (see ¶4343+).

D. Special cases

4356

Special rules **apply to** the accounts of:
- small and medium-sized companies;
- groups; and
- dormant companies.

MEMO POINTS Special rules also apply to the accounts and audit of particular types of company. For example, **charities** meeting the small companies threshold are exempt from audit requirements if their auditors prepare a special report for the members (ss 249A, 249B CA 1985). For more on charities, and the requirements applicable to other special types of company, see *Accountancy and Financial Reporting Memo*.

1. Small and medium-sized companies

Small and medium-sized companies can **choose** to take advantage of certain **exemptions** from the general accounting and audit requirements. However, companies can choose to continue preparing their financial statements under the rules applying to larger companies if they wish. This is usual if they are part of a group or if, due to anticipated growth, they do not expect to be able to take advantage of the exemption in the future.

4360

Small companies can prepare shorter form accounts for submission to shareholders and abbreviated accounts for filing at Companies House. Certain small companies are also exempted from the requirement to have their accounts audited.

The only exemption available to **medium-sized companies** is that they can prepare abbreviated accounts for filing at Companies House.

MEMO POINTS See ¶4212 for the development of **new** IFRS-based **accounting standards** for small and medium-sized companies.

Determining small and medium status

A company is **ineligible** for small or medium status if, at any time during the relevant financial year, it is a public company or another company in its group is a public company or another corporate body which may lawfully offer its shares or debentures to the public (s 247A CA 1985; restated at s 384 CA 2006 as of 6 April 2008).

4362

MEMO POINTS For financial years ending before 31 December 2006, the following companies, or groups containing the following companies, are also ineligible for small company status (SI 2006/2782):
- companies permitted to carry on "regulated activities" by the FSA; or
- insurance companies.

In order to be treated as small or medium-sized, a company must meet any two of the **size limit conditions** set out in the table below (s 247(3) CA 1985).

4363

Condition	Small company limits	Medium-sized company limits
Maximum **turnover** (adjusted proportionately if the period is not a full year)	£5.6m	£22.8m
Maximum **balance sheet total** (i.e. total assets before the deduction of liabilities)	£2.8m	£11.4m
Maximum average number of **employees** for the year (determined on a monthly basis)	50	250

Comment: These limits are currently restated in the new Companies Act (ss 382, 465 CA 2006). However, the thresholds are expected to be **increased** as follows for financial years beginning on or after **6 April 2008** (draft Companies Act (Accounts and Reports) (Amendments) Regulations 2008):
– small companies: £6.5 million turnover; £3.26 million balance sheet total; and
– medium-sized companies: £25.9 million turnover; £12.9 million balance sheet total.
The employee thresholds are not expected to change.

4364 For its **first financial year**, a company will qualify as small or medium-sized if it meets any two of the size limits in that year. For **subsequent years**, it will qualify provided it satisfies any two of the size limit conditions in both the year in question and the preceding year. If a company qualifies as small or medium-sized in one year, it will continue to be treated as one in the following year, even if it fails to satisfy the conditions in that year. However, if it does not satisfy any two of the size limit conditions in the year after that, it will not qualify in that third year (s 247(1), (2) CA 1985; restated at ss 382, 465 CA 2006 as of 6 April 2008).

Exemptions for small companies

Shorter form accounts

4366 Small companies are entitled to prepare shorter form accounts for **presentation to their shareholders** (s 246 CA 1985; restated at s 444 CA 2006 as of 6 April 2008). These accounts use a **simplified format of the balance sheet** and require fewer supplementary disclosures (Sch 8 CA 1985, which will be restated in the draft Small Companies and Groups (Accounts and Directors' Report) Regulations 2008).

4367 Small companies may also choose to apply the **Financial Reporting Standard for Smaller Entities** (FRSSE) instead of normal accounting standards. This reduces further the level of supplementary disclosures that the company would otherwise have to make in its accounts. FRSSE still requires a small company to prepare a statement of total recognised gains and losses, although a separate statement is not required if its only recognised gains and losses are already reflected in the profit and loss account. FRSSE recommends, but does not require, small companies to prepare a cash-flow statement.

MEMO POINTS The ASB introduced a **new FRSSE** which is effective for accounting periods beginning on or after 1 January 2007.

4368 The **directors' report** of a small company is less detailed than those of medium-sized or large companies (see ¶4247).

Abbreviated accounts

4369 Small companies may take advantage of the exemptions to prepare abbreviated accounts for **filing at Companies House** (s 246(5) CA 1985; restated at s 444 CA 2006 as of 6 April 2008). Companies do not always take advantage of this exemption, even when it is available, as usually they are happy to file shorter form accounts. Abbreviated accounts are often filed for reasons of business confidentiality.

4370 The **levels of disclosure** in abbreviated accounts are even less onerous than those required for shorter form accounts (Schs 5, 6 CA 1985). Abbreviated accounts need not contain a profit and loss account or a directors' report. A simplified format of the balance sheet applies, in which the debtors and creditors who are due after more than one year are disclosed in the notes (Sch 8A CA 1985). Further, the balance sheet must contain a prominent statement that the accounts have been prepared under the abbreviated account's provisions (s 246(8) CA 1985). Abbreviated accounts are not required to give a true and fair view or comply with the disclosure requirements of accounting standards, including FRSSE.

Comment: Under the **new Companies Act**, from 6 April 2008, the abbreviated balance sheet will have to contain a prominent statement that it has been prepared under the "small companies regime" (s 414(3) CA 2006). The contents of the abbreviated balance sheet will be set out in regulations (Sch 4 draft Small Companies and Groups (Accounts and Directors' Report) Regulations 2008).

Where the company qualified for, but has not taken advantage of, the exemption from audit, the abbreviated accounts must also be accompanied by a **special auditor's report** stating that the company is entitled to prepare abbreviated accounts and they have been properly prepared (s 247B CA 1985; restated at s 449 CA 2006 as of 6 April 2008). The APB has published guidance on the preparation of this report, entitled "The Special Auditor's Report on Abbreviated Accounts in the United Kingdom" (Bulletin 2006/3), and an example of such a report (Bulletin 2007/1, published in January 2007).

4371

Audit exemption

A small company is exempt from the requirement to have its accounts audited if (s 249A CA 1985; restated at s 477 CA 2006 as of 6 April 2008):
– its **turnover** is £5.6 million or less; and
– its **balance sheet total** (i.e. gross assets) is £2.8 million or less.

4372

Comment: These thresholds are expected to be **increased** for financial years beginning on or after 6 April 2008 to (reg 5 draft Companies Act 2006 (Accounts and Reports) (Amendment) Regulations 2008):
– turnover: £6.5 million; and
– balance sheet total: £3.26 million.

However, any shareholder or group of shareholders holding at least 10% of the nominal value of any class of the company's issued share capital can require it to obtain an audit. The **audit requisition** should be made in writing and deposited at the company's registered office not later than 1 month after the end of the financial year in respect of which the audit is required (s 249B(2) CA 1985; restated at s 476 CA 2006 as of 6 April 2008).

4373

Where a company has taken advantage of the audit exemption, its balance sheet must include a **directors' statement** above their signatures to the effect that (s 249B(4) CA 1985; restated at s 476 CA 2006 as of 6 April 2008):
– the company was entitled to exemption from audit;
– the shareholders have not requisitioned an audit for the year in question; and
– the directors acknowledge their responsibilities for ensuring that the company keeps accounting records and prepares accounts which give a true and fair view and which otherwise comply with all legislative requirements.

4374

Exemptions for medium-sized companies

Medium-sized companies are entitled to fewer exemptions than small companies. They are only entitled to prepare **abbreviated accounts** for filing at Companies House. The abbreviated accounts of medium-sized companies are different from those for small companies. The normal requirements apply to the balance sheet and notes to the financial statements. However, the following exemptions apply (s 246A CA 1985):
– the **profit and loss account** can aggregate turnover, cost of sales, gross profit or loss, and other operating income and show them as one item labelled "gross profit or loss"; and
– the **directors' report** need not include non-financial key performance indicators in the business review (see ¶4247+).

4376

Comment: Under the **new Companies Act**, the contents of the abbreviated accounts of medium-sized companies will be set out in regulations, combining various categories in the profit and loss accounts and exempting them from having to give particulars of their turnover (s 425 CA 2006; reg 4 draft Large and Medium-sized Companies and Groups (Accounts and Reports) Regulations 2008).

As with small companies, the abbreviated accounts of a medium-sized company must be accompanied by a **special auditor's report** (see ¶4371).

4377

2. Groups

4382 A group is not recognised as a separate legal person, but it can report financial information as a single entity. Each individual undertaking within a group has its own obligation to maintain accounting records and produce individual financial statements. Group accounts, also known as "**consolidated accounts**", consist of the financial statements of the individual undertakings that comprise the group, which are added together before making a number of consolidation adjustments. The structure of groups, including the **definitions** of parent and subsidiary undertakings, are considered at ¶213+.

Subject to the **exceptions** at ¶4384+, group accounts must be **prepared by** any company which is a parent undertaking at the end of a financial year (s 227(1) CA 1985; restated at s 399 CA 2006 as of 6 April 2008). These accounts are in addition to the parent's individual accounts.

The **format and content** of group accounts will depend upon the basis upon which they are prepared (see ¶4394+). As with individual accounts, non-listed companies can choose to prepare group accounts in accordance with the Companies Act 1985 (known as "Companies Act group accounts") or in accordance with international accounting standards (known as "IAS group accounts") (s 227(3) CA 1985; restated at s 403 CA 2006 as of 6 April 2008). However, except where there are good reasons for not doing so, the directors of a parent company must secure that the individual accounts of the parent and subsidiaries are all prepared using the same financial reporting framework (s 227C CA 1985; restated at s 407 CA 2006 as of 6 April 2008).

Group accounts must be accompanied by a "**group directors' report**" relating to the parent and subsidiaries included in the consolidation. A group directors' report may, where appropriate, give greater emphasis to the matters that are significant to those undertakings, taken as a whole (s 234(2), (3) CA 1985; restated at s 415 CA 2006 as of 6 April 2008).

Group accounts are subject to the same **audit** requirements as individual accounts (see ¶4290+) and must be **circulated** to shareholders of the parent company and **filed** at Companies House in the same way as individual accounts (see ¶4261+). This is because the definition of "annual accounts", to which the audit, circulation and filing requirements apply, includes both individual and group accounts (s 262(1) CA 1985; restated at s 471 CA 2006 as of 6 April 2008).

Exemptions from group accounts

4384 Group accounts may not be required for a financial year in the following cases:
– the **parent is itself a subsidiary** undertaking included in the accounts of a larger group;
– the parent heads a group which qualifies as a **small or medium-sized group**; or
– all **subsidiary** companies within the group are **exempt from consolidation**.

A parent company which is not required to prepare group accounts must make certain **disclosures** relating to its subsidiaries in the notes to its individual accounts.

Parent included in accounts of larger group

4385 A parent company may be **exempt** from the requirement to prepare group accounts if it is a subsidiary and its immediate parent (ss 228(1), 228A(1) CA 1985; restated at ss 400, 401 CA 2006 as of 6 April 2008):
– holds all of its shares; or
– holds more than half of its shares, and the company has not received notice from the shareholders (who either hold more than half of the shares not held by the company's immediate parent, or who hold at least 5% of the company's total shares) within 6 months of the financial year end requesting group accounts to be prepared.

4386 For the company to benefit from the exemption, the following conditions must be met (ss 228(2), 228A(2) CA 1985; restated at ss 400, 401 CA 2006 as of 6 April 2008):
– the company must be included in the consolidated accounts of the parent of its wider group that are drawn up to the same date or an earlier date in the same financial year;

COMPANY ACCOUNTS 537

– if the parent of the group is within the EEA, the consolidated group accounts must be drawn up and audited, and the parent's annual report must be drawn up under the Seventh Company Law Directive (EEC Directive 349/1983) or in accordance with international accounting standards. If the parent is not within the EEA, the consolidated group accounts and annual report must be drawn up under the Seventh Company Law Directive (EEC Directive 349/1983) or in an equivalent manner, and the accounts must be audited in accordance with the local law of the parent company;
– in its own individual accounts, the company must disclose: the fact that it is exempt from preparing group accounts; the name of the parent company; where the parent company was incorporated if it was not incorporated in GB; and the address of the parent company's principal place of business if it is unincorporated;
– the company must deliver copies of the consolidated group accounts and parent company's annual report to Companies House within the deadline for filing its own individual accounts, including a translation if the documents are not in English.

> MEMO POINTS   The ASB has published **guidance on** when the group accounts of a non-EEA parent company will meet the requirement for "**equivalence**" with the EU Seventh Directive (UITF Abstract 43). The guidance can be downloaded from the ASB's website.

Small or medium-sized groups

A parent company is exempt from the requirement to prepare group accounts for a financial year if the group headed by that company qualifies as a small or medium-sized group (s 248(1) CA 1985).

4387

Comment: Under the **new Companies Act**, the exemption from the preparation of group accounts by parent companies heading medium-sized groups will be abolished from 6 April 2008. The parent companies of all groups, except small ones, will have to prepare group accounts (s 399 CA 2006).

> MEMO POINTS   1. A group is **ineligible** for small or medium-sized status if any of its members is (s 248(2) CA 1985; restated at s 478 CA 2006 as of 6 April 2008):
> – a public company or other corporate body which is lawfully entitled to offer its shares or debentures to the public;
> – an undertaking authorised to carry on "regulated activities" by the FSA; or
> – an insurance company.
> Note that a group consists of a parent and its subsidiaries. Therefore, whether or not the parent of the company claiming exemption falls into the above categories is irrelevant in determining small or medium-sized group status.
> 2. If a company has taken advantage of the exemption for small and medium-sized groups when in the auditor's opinion it was not entitled to do so, the **auditor's report** must state that fact (s 237(4A) CA 1985; restated at s 498 CA 2006 as of 6 April 2008).

In order to be treated as small or medium-sized, the group must meet any two of the **size limit conditions** set out in the table below (s 249(3) CA 1985; restated at ss 383, 466 CA 2006 as of 6 April 2008).

4388

Condition	Small group limits[1]	Medium-sized group limits[1]
Maximum aggregate **turnover** (adjusted proportionately if the period is not a full year)	£5.6m net or £6.72m gross	£22.8m net or £27.36m gross
Maximum aggregate **balance sheet total** (i.e. total assets before the deduction of liabilities)	£2.8m net or £3.36m gross	£11.4m net or £13.68m gross
Maximum aggregate average number of **employees** for the year (determined on a monthly basis)	50	250

Note:
1. "**Net**" means with the set-offs and other adjustment required in the presentation of group accounts and "**gross**" means without those set-offs and adjustments. A company can satisfy the relevant requirement on the basis of either the net or gross figure.

Comment: These thresholds are expected to be **increased** affecting financial years beginning on or after 6 April 2008 to (regs 3, 4 draft Companies Act 2006 (Accounts and Reports) (Amendment) Regulations 2008):
– small groups: £6.5 million net or £7.8 million gross turnover; £3.26 million net or £3.9 million gross balance sheet total; and
– medium-sized groups: £25.9 million net or £31.1 million gross turnover; £12.9 million net or £15.5 million gross balance sheet total.
The thresholds for the numbers of employees are not expected to change.

4389 For a parent company's **first financial year**, a group will qualify as small or medium-sized if it meets any two of the size limits in that year. For **subsequent years**, it will qualify provided it satisfies any two of the size limit conditions in both the year in question and the preceding year. If a group qualifies as small or medium-sized in one year, it will continue to be treated as one in the following year, even if it fails to satisfy the conditions in that year. However, if it does not satisfy any two of the size limit conditions in the year after that, then it will not qualify in that third year (s 249(1), (2) CA 1985; restated at ss 383, 466 CA 2006 as of 6 April 2008).

Subsidiaries excluded from consolidation

4390 Subsidiaries may be excluded from consolidation in Companies Act group accounts in the following cases (s 229(2), (3) CA 1985; restated at s 405 CA 2006 as of 6 April 2008):
– the inclusion of the subsidiary is **not material** for the purpose of giving a true and fair view (although two or more subsidiaries may only be excluded if they are not material taken together);
– **severe long-term restrictions** substantially hinder the exercise of the rights of the parent company over the assets or management of the subsidiary;
– the **information** necessary for the preparation of group accounts **cannot be obtained** without disproportionate expense or undue delay; or
– the interest of the parent company is held exclusively with a view to **subsequent resale**.

4391 Where all of a parent's subsidiaries could be excluded from consolidation in Companies Act group accounts, the parent is exempt from the requirement to prepare group accounts (s 229(5) CA 1985; restated at s 402 CA 2006 as of 6 April 2008).

Disclosures in individual accounts of exempt companies

4392 The individual accounts of parent companies which are exempt from the requirement to prepare group accounts must include the following information (s 231; Pt I, Sch 5 CA 1985):
– the **reason** why the company is exempt from the requirement to prepare group accounts and if the reason is that all subsidiaries are excluded from consolidation, the reason why each subsidiary is excluded;
– the **name** of each subsidiary and the country of incorporation if not in GB;
– the **shareholdings** in each subsidiary, identifying the class and proportion of the nominal value of the shares of that class represented by the holdings;
– the aggregate amount of the **capital and reserves** as at the end of the financial year, and the **profit and loss** for that year, of each subsidiary;
– the number, description and amount of **shares held by or on behalf of its subsidiaries**; and
– details of any **other significant holdings** in undertakings which are not subsidiaries (significant is defined as 20% or more of the nominal value of any share class or where the balance sheet value of the holding exceeds 20% of the company's total assets).

Comment: Under the **new Companies Act**, the information which will have to be included in the individual accounts of exempt parent companies will be set out in regulations (reg 7, Pt 1 Sch 4 draft Large and Medium-sized Companies and Groups (Accounts and Reports) Regulations 2008; reg 4, Sch 2 draft Small Companies and Groups (Accounts and Directors' Report) Regulations 2008).

Form and content of group accounts

Companies Act group accounts **comprise** a consolidated balance sheet and consolidated profit and loss account that give a true and fair view of the state of affairs of the undertakings included in the consolidation as a whole (s 227A(1), (2) CA 1985; restated at s 404 CA 2006 as of 6 April 2008). Wider accounting standards also require the preparation of a consolidated cash-flow statement and consolidated statement of total recognised gains and losses. Generally speaking, the financial statements for all subsidiary undertakings included in the consolidation should be prepared to the same **financial year** as that of the parent (s 223(5) CA 1985; restated at s 390 CA 2006 as of 6 April 2008). The group accounts will therefore normally take its figures from the financial statements of the subsidiaries for the relevant year. **4394**

The **format** of group accounts must match, so far as is practicable, the format of individual accounts as if the undertakings included in the consolidation were a single company (para 1 Sch 4A CA 1985). The consolidated balance sheet and profit and loss account will therefore look much the same as the balance sheet and profit and loss account of an individual company (see ¶4226+). **4395**

Comment: Under the **new Companies Act**, the format of group accounts will be set out in regulations (Sch 6 in both the draft Large and Medium-sized Companies and Groups (Accounts and Reports) Regulations 2008 and draft Small Companies and Groups (Accounts and Directors' Report) Regulations 2008).

The consolidated financial statements must incorporate in full the information contained in the individual accounts of the undertakings included in the consolidation, subject to the following **adjustments** (Sch 4A CA 1985): **4396**
– elimination of group transactions;
– adjustments to bring the basis of valuing the assets and liabilities of subsidiaries into line with the basis used in the group accounts;
– adjustments where an undertaking becomes a subsidiary of the parent in the financial year in question (i.e. acquisition and merger accounting) (see ¶6900+);
– minority interests (i.e. shares in subsidiaries included in the consolidation not held by the parent or its other subsidiaries) must be shown on the face of the balance sheet and profit and loss account; and
– proportional consolidation of joint venture companies.

Comment: Under the **new Companies Act**, the adjustments to the group accounts will be set out in regulations (Sch 6 in both the draft Large and Medium-sized Companies and Groups (Accounts and Reports) Regulations 2008 and draft Small Companies and Groups (Accounts and Directors' Report) Regulations 2008).

Any **differences of accounting rules**, and the reasons for them, as between a parent company's individual accounts for a financial year and its group accounts must be disclosed in a note to the group accounts (para 4 Sch 4A CA 1985). **4397**

Comment: Under the **new Companies Act**, the contents of the notes to group accounts will be set out in regulations (para 4 Sch 6 in both the draft Large and Medium-sized Companies and Groups (Accounts and Reports) Regulations 2008 and draft Small Companies and Groups (Accounts and Directors' Report) Regulations 2008).

3. Dormant companies

A company is **considered to be "dormant"** during any financial year in which it has no significant accounting transactions (s 249AA(4) CA 1985; restated at s 1169 CA 2006 as of 6 April 2008). This means that the company must not have entered a transaction in its accounting records except (s 249AA(5), (6) CA 1985; restated at s 1169 CA 2006 as of 6 April 2008): **4407**
– as a result of the subscriber shares being issued;
– a fee paid to Companies House for a change of name;

– a fee paid to Companies House for re-registration from private company to public or vice versa;
– a penalty paid to Companies House for failing to deliver accounts on time; or
– a fee paid to Companies House with the company's annual return.

> *MEMO POINTS* A company will **not be treated as dormant** if, at any time in the financial year in question, the company was authorised to carry on "regulated activities" by the FSA or was an insurance company.

4408 The directors can decide to keep a company dormant for a number of **reasons**, for example:
– to protect a company name;
– to hold an asset or intellectual property (e.g. as nominee); or
– as a property management company set up as a vehicle to own the head lease or freehold of a property.

Audit exemption

4410 A company which has been **dormant since its formation** is exempt from audit. A company which **used to trade** but has been dormant since the end of the previous financial year is also exempt from audit, provided it does not have to prepare group accounts for that year and qualifies as a small company (or would have qualified but for the fact it was ineligible for small company status) (see ¶4362+) (s 249AA(1), (2) CA 1975; restated at s 480 CA 2006 as of 6 April 2008).

4411 However, as with small companies which are exempt from audit, any shareholder or group of shareholders holding at least 10% of the nominal value of any class of the dormant company's issued share capital, can **requisition an audit** (see ¶4373).

4412 As with small companies, where a dormant company has taken advantage of the audit exemption, its balance sheet must include a **directors' statement** above the directors signature (see ¶4374).

Dormant company accounts

4414 A dormant company is not exempt from preparing and filing accounts. Accounts must be prepared and filed within the usual time period, even where the dormant company has remained dormant for a number of years, or has never traded.

4415 Dormant private companies nearly always take advantage of the option to file **abbreviated accounts** available to small companies (see ¶4369+). Therefore, dormant companies usually only file a balance sheet at Companies House. Although not part of the abbreviated accounts, a directors' report and, where a company traded in the previous financial year, a profit and loss account, must still be circulated to shareholders.

4416 There is no special **format** for dormant company accounts, although the financial statements are likely to be much simpler since many items will have no entries. Companies House publishes a standard form for dormant company accounts, called Form DCA, available to download from the Companies House website. This form is only suitable for companies limited by shares which are not subsidiaries and which have been dormant since incorporation.

CHAPTER 12

Company finance

OUTLINE

SECTION 1 **Debt finance** 4504	Group company guarantee 4700
	C Other types of security 4714
I Types of debt 4515	1 Lien 4714
A Short-term debt 4515	2 Pledge 4720
B Term loan funding 4535	3 Commercial security 4727
C Loan agreements 4545	4 Security for judgment debts 4739
II Types of security 4562	III Procedure 4755
A Mortgages and charges 4574	1 Capacity 4755
1 Legal mortgage 4587	2 Power of directors 4762
2 Equitable mortgage 4596	3 Creation of borrowing and security 4767
3 Fixed charge 4603	Security over family home 4769
4 Floating charge 4610	
5 Mortgages and charges over different assets 4618	SECTION 2 **Private equity finance** 4800
6 Registration 4636	
7 Satisfaction and release 4656	A Overview 4805
8 Enforcement 4663	1 Suitability of company 4807
9 Lender's rights against third parties 4672	2 Private equity investors 4809
Priority agreements 4676	3 Procedure 4816
10 Subordination 4680	B Financial promotions 4825
B Guarantees 4696	C Prospectuses 4845
Personal guarantee 4698	

4500

Most companies at some point need more money than they receive as revenue, whether for the day to day running of their business, or for major capital expenditure such as buying new premises. The ways in which a company obtains this extra money is known as "financing".

The most common way in which companies obtain new finance is through **debt** (loans, overdrafts etc). The lender in turn often requires some security for repayment, over and above the borrower's promise that the debt will be repaid. Unlawful financial assistance may occur where a company borrows money or gives security in relation to the financing of an acquisition of shares in itself or its holding company (see ¶5557+).

Another, more unusual, type of financing is through an offer by the company to an investor who pays money in return for an issue of new shares. This is known as "equity finance". Share offers as a source of finance are more common for companies with shares that can be traded on a public market (e.g. the London Stock Exchange or AIM), but unlisted companies may also raise finance by this method. Where the shares are in an unlisted company, this type of financing is known as "**private equity finance**". There are detailed and strict regulatory requirements that govern offers of shares.

External financing, that is finance from sources outside of the company, is dealt with here. However, many smaller companies are internally financed by their directors.

4501 An effort has been made to explain terms and to minimise the use of jargon but unfortunately no discussion of corporate finance can avoid it completely. Reference can also be made to the glossary at ¶9940.

SECTION 1

Debt finance

4504 The **type of debt** (¶4515+) that a company will require depends upon why it needs to borrow. Borrowing that finances the day to day running of the business is known as "working capital". Working capital is typically financed by flexible, short-term debt such as overdraft arrangements. Medium to long-term debt is known as "term loan funding". This is normally used to finance capital expenditure, such as the purchase of new machinery.

When a lender advances money, it usually requires some way of recouping the money owed to it should the borrower not fulfil its obligations. The arrangement which gives the lender this protection is known as "security". There are many **types of security** (¶4562+), most of which involve the lender taking an interest over the borrower's assets. This is known as "direct security" and the two most common examples are a mortgage and a charge. Instead of direct security, the lender can take a guarantee from a suitable third party who will be liable to repay the loan if the borrower does not. This is known as "collateral security". Other types of security can arise by the borrower depositing an item with the lender, through commercial arrangements with suppliers or through a court order.

Companies do not automatically have the capacity to borrow or grant security; they must be empowered to do so by their memorandum and articles. The **procedure** itself is relatively straightforward and usually led by the lender. The advance of money and the taking of security usually occur at the same time although, if a lender has advanced money to the borrower before, security may already be in place. Security put in place after an advance is liable to be set aside during insolvency (see ¶4612).

I. Types of debt

A. Short-term debt

1. Bank facilities

Overdraft facility

4515 When a company needs to borrow working capital for the day to day running of its business, it usually relies on an overdraft facility. An overdraft is an **arrangement between** a company and its bank under which the company is permitted to **borrow up to** a particular maximum limit on a specific bank account. This will usually be the company's main trading account and, as part of the overdraft arrangement, the company will be required to pay all trade receipts into that account. The actual amount borrowed by the company through its overdraft will therefore fluctuate over time and sometimes a company may not be overdrawn at all.

4516 An overdraft is an "**on-demand**" facility. This means that the borrower will be permitted to borrow up to the overdraft limit but the amount borrowed is **immediately repayable** on the bank's demand. This is the key difference between an overdraft and a term loan (described at ¶4535). A borrower wholly reliant on its overdraft facility is therefore in a particularly vulnerable position if the bank withdraws its support.

4517 The bank will set a company's **overdraft limit** based on the company's financial record. Overdraft limits can be changed and most banks will them limits at least annually if not more frequently. As part of the review process, a bank will usually require the borrower to provide it with regular financial reports.

4518 A combination of regular financial reporting, reviewable overdraft limits and the prospect of immediate repayment means that a company's **bank** often has a high degree of **control** and influence over its business.

Revolving credit facility

4520 A more formal facility for working capital is a "revolving credit facility". Under this facility, subject to a minimum draw-down level, the borrower is permitted to draw down, repay and re-draw money up to the limit of the facility during a set period (known as the "commitment period"). All of the outstanding borrowings become **repayable** at the end of the commitment period. The borrower is therefore able to use the facility to meet its business requirements but will not incur excess borrowings. The advantage of this over an overdraft is that the borrowings are not repayable on demand. A revolving credit facility is a "**committed facility**" because the lender is committed to making the advance.

2. Arrangements with suppliers

4525 As well as bank facilities, companies often rely on **trade credit** from their suppliers to assist short-term cash flow. This means that suppliers agree to a delay between them delivering the goods or services and receiving payment. Sometimes, the credit is offered as part of the supplier's standard terms (e.g. payment within 30 days of delivery). Other times, a particular credit agreement may be reached between company and supplier (e.g. a maximum credit limit with the oldest orders having to be paid first). It is unusual for a company's trade creditors to take **security** over the company's assets. Instead, suppliers normally rely on the fact that a company needs to maintain a good credit record for trading purposes.

Sometimes, companies enter into commercial arrangements with suppliers that have the effect of borrowing and security although the legal structure is quite different (see ¶4727+).

B. Term loan funding

4535 When a company needs to finance its capital expenditure, such as buying new machinery, it will usually obtain a "term loan". This is a loan which is **repayable on** particular dates or on the occurrence of particular events. Common types are:
– "bullet repayments", where the loan must be repaid in one lump sum; and
– "amortisation", where payments are made in equal instalments at regular intervals according to a repayment plan. If the last instalment is larger than the previous ones, it is called a "balloon repayment".

The loan is usually **advanced** to the borrower in one lump sum or over a short period of time, but sometimes the advance occurs in stages. For example, if the borrower is constructing new premises, a sum may be advanced as each phase of the construction begins. Where a loan is advanced in stages, the borrower and lender are said to have entered into a "facility arrangement". Such loans are "committed" facilities because the lender is committed to making the advance, subject to the company meeting certain pre-agreed conditions.

A term loan is normally obtained from **one lender** but sometimes, in order to spread the risk of a very high value loan, the loan will be provided by a **group of lenders**. A loan from a group of lenders is called a "syndicated loan".

C. Loan agreements

4545 The terms of a loan agreement will vary depending upon the type of loan. A committed facility is likely to be more complex than an on-demand facility as it must deal with the conditions that have to be satisfied before the advance will be made and the circumstances in which it must be repaid. A loan agreement, particularly in respect of a committed facility is usually referred to as a "**facility agreement**". The main provisions that will be found in a committed facility agreement are:
– the details of the loan facility;
– conditions precedent;
– representations and warranties;
– covenants; and
– events of default.

Loan facility details

4546 The facility **agreement will set out**:
– the purpose of the facility;
– the sum which the lender is making available under the facility (known as the "principal");
– when draw-down can take place; and
– the terms of repayment.

The lender will also expect to make a commercial return on the agreement. The **lender's return** will usually be made up of one or more of the following:
– an up-front arrangement fee;
– periodic fees charged during the life of the facility;
– a commitment commission payable on any unused part of the facility; and/or
– interest on the amount advanced.

The facility agreement will normally have clauses to protect the lender's return, for example, early repayment penalties.

Conditions precedent

4547 These are the conditions that must be satisfied before the lender will make the advance. These will vary from case to case and could be numerous if the facility is intended to be used to finance a complex transaction.

Representations and warranties

4548 These are statements of fact upon which the lender is relying to make the advance. They will relate both to **legal matters** (e.g. that the borrower has the power and authority to enter into the agreement) and **commercial matters** (e.g. the financial position of the borrower). If the loan is to be advanced in stages, the representations are usually repeated at each stage so the borrower will have to ensure that the representations are true each time it draws down on the facility.

Covenants

4549 These are the borrower's obligations and commonly include positive covenants (which are promises to take certain action) and negative covenants (which are promises to refrain from certain actions unless the lender gives its consent).

Common **positive covenants** include:
– to keep financial performance within particular parameters;
– to provide financial information to the lender at regular intervals;
– to comply with all laws, pay taxes punctually and maintain the usual insurances; and
– to comply with certain financial covenants.

Common **negative covenants** include:
– not to dispose of material assets or the whole or any part of the business; and
– not to increase borrowings, grant any further security or enter into agreements which have the same effect (e.g. sale and leaseback agreements). This is known as a "negative pledge" clause.

4550 Another common covenant, particularly if the borrowing is unsecured, is a "**pari passu**" covenant. This requires the borrower to ensure that its obligations under the facility agreement will rank equally and rateably with the present and future obligations of the borrower. For example, if A Ltd borrowed £100,000 from Bank B and £50,000 from Bank C, the loans would rank pari passu if they had to be repaid at an equal rate. This is intended to protect the unsecured lender from other creditors taking priority if the company goes into liquidation.

4551 In the event of a **breach of any covenant**, the lender will have a breach of contract claim against the borrower (or possibly a claim against a subsequent lender for inducing the borrower to breach its contract). Lenders should be aware that a negative pledge clause or a pari passu covenant is not a substitute for security as neither gives the lender enforceable proprietary rights over the assets of the borrower (these are rights which are enforceable against third parties).

Events of default

4552 These are the events that would trigger the lender's right to early repayment. **Common** events of default include:
– non-payment of any amounts due to the lender;
– insolvency related events (e.g. steps towards winding up the borrower);
– litigation-related events leading to enforcement against the borrower's assets (e.g. bailiffs being appointed);
– any representation in the facility agreement being untrue; and
– any breach of the covenants in the facility agreement.

II. Types of security

4562 When a lender advances money, it usually needs some protection or assurance that it will be able to recoup the amount owed to it should the borrower not fulfil its obligations (known as "default"). The arrangement which gives the lender this protection or assurance is known as "security".

The terminology used in this area can be confusing, particularly because terms are not used consistently. The term "security" here **means** an arrangement which secures a financial obligation. This should not be confused with the use of the term in the context of investments where it means shares, stock or bonds.

4563 The two **most common types** of security are a "mortgage" and a "charge" (¶4574+). These are direct securities which involve the lender taking an interest in some or all of the borrower's assets. The assets over which the security is taken are known as "secured assets" (or to be more specific, "mortgaged assets" or "charged assets", as appropriate).

Instead of direct security, a lender can enter into an agreement with a third party which allows it to sue another person if the borrower defaults. This is known as collateral security, the most common of which is a guarantee (¶4696+).

Other **less common types** of security can arise through:
– the borrower depositing an asset or title deeds to an asset with the lender. For example, a pledge (¶4720+) or a lien (¶4714+);
– commercial arrangements which have the economic effect of borrowing and security, although they are not strictly security. Such arrangements are commonly referred to as "commercial security" and include retention of title clauses, invoice finance and leasing arrangements (¶4727+); or
– a court order granted in favour of a person who has won a court case and is owed money by the person who lost the case (¶4739+).

4564 The lender's primary concern when taking security is its **strength** and **value**. Security over assets is considered to be better than a guarantee. This is because security over assets gives the lender rights over something of value. By contrast, a guarantee simply gives the lender an extra person to sue and is only worth as much as the person giving it. Where the lender takes security over assets, it will want to ensure that the asset is worth at least as much as the amount secured on it and that its value will be preserved, for example, by ensuring that the borrower is not able to dispose of it.

However, it is not always possible for the lender to take whichever form of security it wishes. This will depend upon a number of factors including:
– the bargaining positions of the lender and borrower;
– the amount of borrowing being secured;
– whether the borrower has already given security over its assets; and
– the type of asset being secured.

A. Mortgages and charges

4574 Mortgages and charges are security arrangements which give the lender an interest over the assets of the borrower, although the borrower continues to possess and use them. The **lender's interest** is a proprietary one (which means that it is enforceable against third parties) as opposed to merely contractual (which means that it would only be enforceable against the other party to the contract, i.e. the borrower).

> MEMO POINTS 1. In most cases, the secured assets belong to the borrower. However, where a **group of companies** is involved and the borrower does not have sufficient assets, the lender will take security over the assets of another company in the group or over the assets of the entire group. In this case, the lender must be careful to avoid "structural subordination" (see ¶4683) and the company giving the security must ensure that this is in its own best interests to do so.
> 2. If the borrower is a **small company**, without a long trading history or new to a lender, security will sometimes be taken over the **assets of its directors**. The consent of family members is often required and lenders must be careful to ensure that their consent is obtained fairly (see ¶4769+).

4575 In most cases, in order for a mortgage or charge to be completely enforceable it will need to be **registered** with Companies House (¶4637+). A record of the security will also have to be kept by the company in its "register of charges" (¶3975+). A mortgage or charge over some assets may also have to be registered on other public registers (¶4653).

4576 Once created, the mortgage or charge will **remain in place until** it is (¶4656+):
– satisfied, i.e. the borrower fulfils its obligations;
– released, i.e. the borrower's obligations remain outstanding but the lender agrees that the security no longer applies; or
– enforced, i.e. the borrower defaults and the lender realises the value of the security.

4577 It is of course open to a borrower to borrow from multiple lenders. Its ability to do so will depend largely upon the security it can offer them. It is possible for more than one security to be created over the same assets but then the issue of **priority** arises, meaning the order in which lenders have first claim to the asset (¶4672+). Sometimes, multiple lenders and the borrower will contractually agree to a different order of priority to the one which would apply under the usual legal principles, or one lender will agree to **subordinate** its debt (this means that the lender agrees that its debt will be repaid after other debts) (¶4680+). If the borrower becomes insolvent, there are special rules about the priority of security holders over other creditors of the borrower (see ¶7975+).

Distinction between mortgage and charge

4578 Although similar, there is in fact a legal distinction between the two types of security. A **charge** gives the lender the right to resort to the charged asset in the event of the borrower's default. It does not involve a transfer of title in the asset to the lender nor does it give the lender the right to take possession of the asset. Strictly speaking, all charges are equitable in nature. A charge can be **fixed** on a particular asset or **floating** over a class of assets. The distinction is important if the borrower goes into liquidation or administration because a fixed charge takes priority over preferential creditors and floating charges (see liquidation: ¶7975+; administration: ¶8936+).

4579 A **mortgage** goes further than a charge and actually transfers title in the asset to the lender: legal title in the case of a **legal** mortgage, or equitable title in the case of an **equitable** mortgage. The transfer is made with the implied condition that title will be transferred back to the borrower once it has fulfilled its obligations. This condition is known as the "equity of redemption". The transfer of title gives the lender greater security than a charge as it inhibits the borrower from dealing with the asset.

> MEMO POINTS A mortgage must be **distinguished from** an absolute **sale**. Under a mortgage, if the borrower defaults and the secured asset is sold by the lender for more than the amount owed to it, it must give the excess to the borrower. If the sale is at a loss, the borrower is liable to repay any amount still owed to the lender. By contrast, under a sale, the seller is not entitled to have the asset returned if it pays the money back to the buyer, and the buyer can keep the profit or must bear any loss when it sells the asset on (*Welsh Development Agency v Export Finance Co Ltd* [1992] BCLC 148). A question mark may arise over a sale under which the seller has the right to repurchase the asset, as this is similar to the borrower's right to have the asset transferred back to it. A right to repurchase alone does not turn a sale into a mortgage so a standard **sale and repurchase** agreement or **sale and leaseback** agreement is not treated as a mortgage (*Orion Finance Ltd v Crown Financial Management Ltd* [1996] 2 BCLC 78).

4580 The **distinction** between a mortgage and charge is **blurred in practice** because the steps that are taken by a lender to control charged assets and/or prevent a subsequent lender from taking priority are the same as those to create an equitable mortgage. In addition, the terms are often used interchangeably by legal practitioners. Company law practitioners tend to use the term "charge" to describe both mortgages and charges. However, the term "mortgage" is used in property law, while in insolvency law the generic term "security" is used throughout (respectively, s 205(1)(xvi) LPA 1925; s 248 IA 1986). The text below uses the terms in their strict sense.

Debentures

4581 The term "debenture" is often used in the commercial world to cover various **lending scenarios**. In effect, it can be thought of as a glorified "IOU". It is used in company law to mean bonds sold by a company to raise money (direct debt financing). However, it is also used in the context of secured lending from a bank or other institution (indirect debt financing). The security could be a mortgage or a charge or both.

This can include, for example, where a lender takes a legal mortgage over some assets, an equitable mortgage over others, a fixed charge over others and a floating charge over the rest. There is usually a sweeper clause to ensure that all of the assets of the borrower come within the ambit of the security. This clause states that the lender takes a floating charge over "all of the assets and undertaking" of the borrower.

> *MEMO POINTS* The **legal definition** of "debenture" is notoriously difficult to pin down (*Knightsbridge Estates Trust v Byrne* [1940] 2 All ER 401). Although it is used to describe security taken over various assets of a company, it can include any document that either creates or acknowledges a debt. Companies legislation sets out a definition of the term, in the context of direct debt financing, that includes "debenture stock, bonds and any other securities of a company, whether or not constituting a charge on the assets of the company" (s 744 CA 1985; restated at s 738 CA 2006 as of 6 April 2008). However, the term is, as we have seen, used more widely than statute suggests.

Pitfalls

4583 Before taking a mortgage or charge, a lender should be aware of the potential pitfalls:
- the **transaction may be challenged** and set aside in the event of the borrower's insolvency (see ¶7808+); and/or
- if the transaction is connected with the acquisition of shares, it may be treated as unlawful **financial assistance** (see ¶5557+).

1. Legal mortgage

4587 The essential **characteristic** of a legal mortgage is that legal title to the mortgaged asset is transferred to the lender subject to the equity of redemption. This is the borrower's right to have the asset transferred back to it upon satisfaction of the secured obligations.

4588 A legal mortgage is the best **level of security** because the transfer of legal title effectively prevents the borrower from dealing with the asset any further and ensures that the lender has complete control over it in the event of enforcement.

4589 A legal mortgage is not always **suitable**. Firstly, it is only possible if the borrower holds legal and beneficial title to the asset at the time the security interest is created. It is therefore not possible to create a legal mortgage over future assets, nor can one be created over assets which are only beneficially owned. Secondly, taking legal and beneficial title to an asset may have adverse consequences for the lender and borrower. For example, a legal mortgage over shares may result in the company whose shares are being mortgaged becoming the subsidiary of the lender, which would have tax and accounting implications.

4590 A legal mortgage is **created by** assigning (i.e. transferring) title in the mortgaged asset to the lender subject to the equity of redemption. This is sometimes referred to as an "assignment by way of security".

There are no particular assignment **formalities** for most assets, other than that the transfer must usually occur at the time (and not just be an agreement to transfer the asset) and that the transferor holds the legal title to the asset at the time of the transfer. Therefore, an assignment can even take place orally, although this clearly is not desirable as the parties will want the opportunity to set out the terms of the mortgage and record their agreement in writing for future reference (*Newlove v Shrewsbury* (1888) 21 QBD 41). Some assets do, however, require particular assignment formalities, such as freehold and leasehold property (see ¶4620), shares (see ¶1865+) and "book debts".

> *MEMO POINTS* The right to claim payment for the supply of goods and services, is collectively known as a company's **book debts**. This right is an asset of the company and can be sold, mortgaged and otherwise dealt with like the company's other assets. In order to assign items such as book debts, the assignment document must (s 136 LPA 1925):
> - be in writing and signed by the borrower (it is not necessary to execute it as a deed);
> - state that the assignment is absolute and not by way of charge (although this does not prevent the document from specifying that the asset will be reassigned to the borrower upon it satisfying its obligations); and
> - be notified in writing to any person against whom the borrower would have had a claim (e.g. if the assignment was of a debt owed to the borrower, notice would have to be given to the debtor).
> See ¶4626+ for the particular issues concerning security over book debts.

4591 If the parties **fail to comply with** the necessary **formalities** then the legal mortgage will take effect as an equitable mortgage.

2. Equitable mortgage

4596 An equitable mortgage **arises when** only the equitable title in the mortgaged asset is transferred to the lender.

This will normally occur when the lender and borrower enter into an agreement to create a legal mortgage but do not comply with the formalities of creation (i.e. the **legal mortgage is not perfected**). This can occur by mistake (for example, because the lender and borrower think they have complied with the formalities but in fact have not). Alternatively, the agreement may relate to the borrower's future assets (and the lender and borrower intend to complete the formalities once the borrower actually owns the assets). It follows that if the formalities are never properly completed, the legal mortgage will never be perfected and will continue to operate as an equitable mortgage.

In rarer cases, an equitable mortgage can occur when it is the specific **intention** of the lender and borrower that only equitable title will transfer, for example, because the borrower only has an equitable interest in the asset, or the asset is one that is only recognised in equity (e.g. the benefits of a trust fund).

4597 An **advantage** of the fact that legal title is not transferred is that an equitable mortgage can be taken over future property and property which is only owned beneficially. Further, an equitable mortgage may avoid any adverse consequences that could arise from a transfer of the legal title (although sometimes even an equitable interest in the mortgaged asset could be problematic for the lender).

4598 An equitable mortgage does not give the same **level of security** as a legal mortgage because legal title to the asset remains with the borrower who could theoretically sell it on. If the equitable mortgage was intentional, the mortgage document will normally contain contractual restrictions on this but they are only enforceable against the borrower. The lender's right to enforce its equitable interest against third parties, such as a buyer of the asset, will depend upon whether that third party was aware of it (see ¶4672+).

3. Fixed charge

4603 The **characteristics** of a fixed charge are similar to an equitable mortgage but, instead of transferring equitable title in an asset to the lender, the lender has the right to use that asset if the borrower defaults (*Re Charge Card Services Ltd* [1987] BCLC 17).

The charge "fixes" or attaches to the charged asset so that the borrower is not able to deal with it or transfer it to a third party without the lender's consent. Since a fixed charge prevents the borrower from dealing with the asset, it is only **appropriate for** more permanent assets, such as property, or assets which can be controlled by the lender.

4604 A key feature of a fixed charge is that the **lender** must be able to, and must actually, exercise sufficient **control** over the charged asset. Control can be exercised through the contractual provisions of the charging document or, if title to the asset comprises deeds, by lodging the title deeds with the lender.

> **MEMO POINTS** 1. A fixed charge can give the **borrower** limited **freedom** to deal with the charged asset. For example, the borrower could be permitted to remain in occupation of charged buildings (*Re Atlantic Computer Systems plc (No 1)* [1991] BCLC 606). However, it would be inconsistent with a fixed charge for the borrower to be completely free to deal with the asset in the course of its business. For example, the freedom to sell and buy office equipment used in the business would be inconsistent with a fixed charge over that equipment (*Re G E Tunbridge Ltd* [1995] 1 BCLC 34) and the freedom to use escrow money in the ordinary course of business would be inconsistent with a fixed charge over that money (*Re ASRS Establishment Ltd* [2000] 2 BCLC 631).

2. If assets are charged by **lodging title deeds** with the lender, the charge is known as a "charge by deposit of title deeds" and the charging document is sometimes referred to as a "memorandum of deposit" instead of a fixed charge. However, title deeds are becoming a thing of the past since the title to most land is now registered.

4605 In theory, a fixed charge does not give the same **level of security** as an equitable mortgage because the lender needs the borrower (or failing that, the court) to take some action to realise the value of the charged asset. In practice, the charge document usually contains provisions similar to those found in an equitable mortgage such as:
– a "further assurance clause" that the borrower will execute all documents required to vest title to the asset in the lender, his nominees or a purchaser; and
– a power of attorney in favour of the lender so that he can execute those documents if the borrower fails to do so (in which case the charge document must be executed as a deed).

> MEMO POINTS Sometimes lenders will go further so that if an asset is already in existence, the borrower is required to execute the necessary assignment documents in "**escrow**". Under this arrangement, the lender keeps the undated executed documents assigning the asset, but the assignment is only completed (i.e. the documents are dated and the assignment takes effect) if the borrower defaults.

4. Floating charge

4610 The essential **characteristic** of a floating charge is that it gives the lender an equitable interest over a class of assets, the components of which, in the ordinary course of the borrower's business, change from time to time. The charge "floats" over the class and only "fixes" upon the actual assets in that class in certain circumstances (known as "crystallisation"). Until the charge crystallises, the borrower is free to deal with the assets in that class in the ordinary course of its business (*Re Yorkshire Woolcombers' Association Ltd* [1903] 2 Ch 284). After crystallisation, the charge takes effect as a fixed charge on the assets in the charged class.

4611 A floating charge is required for a **class of assets** which by its nature would make it impractical for a lender to exercise the degree of control necessary for a fixed charge. The classic example of a class of assets over which only a floating charge is practical is stock in trade. Since the charge floats over a class of assets which is constantly changing, the charge is usually expressed to be over both present and future assets in the particular class although a charge over just future assets or just present assets could still take effect as a floating charge (*Re Bond Worth Ltd* [1979] 3 All ER 919).

> MEMO POINTS The courts take a "substance over form" approach to **interpreting charge documents**. Therefore, a charge that is labelled as a fixed charge may actually take effect as a floating charge depending upon the characteristics of the charge (*National Westminster Bank plc v Spectrum Plus Ltd* [2005] 2 BCLC 269). Equally, a charge described as floating could take effect as a fixed charge if it prevents the borrower from dealing with the assets without the lender's permission (*The Russell-Cooke Trust Co v Elliott and others* [2007] EWHC 1443 (Ch)). Similarly, a document may be deemed to take effect as a charge even if the word "charge" is not used in the charging document (*Re Bond Worth Ltd* [1979] 3 All ER 919).

4612 A floating charge should always be created at the same time as or before the advance from the lender to the borrower. This is because in the event of the **borrower's insolvency** a floating charge created after the advance would not be enforceable if the borrower goes into liquidation or administration within a certain time period (see ¶7836+).

4613 A floating charge **crystallises** by operation of the law or in the circumstances contractually agreed to by the lender and borrower in the charging document.

By **operation of the law**, a floating charge will crystallise automatically upon:
– the winding up of the borrower, whether or not this is an event of default (*Re Crompton & Co Ltd* [1914] 1 Ch 954);
– the appointment of an administrator or administrative receiver by or on behalf of the lender (*Evans v Rival Granite Quarries Ltd* [1910] 2 KB 979);
– the lender taking possession of the borrower's assets by way of a court order (*Biggerstaff v Rowatt's Wharf Ltd* [1896] 2 Ch 93);

– the borrower disposing of all or substantially all of its assets so that it cannot carry on its business (*Hubbuck v Helms* (1887) 56 LJ Ch 536); or
– the borrower ceasing to carry on its business (rather than ceasing to be a going concern) (*Re Woodroffes (Musical Instruments) Ltd* [1985] 2 All ER 908).

Common **contractual reasons** for the crystallisation of a floating charge are:
– the borrower failing to repay money;
– the creation of a subsequent charge over the charged assets;
– the crystallisation of another charge; and
– the lender serving notice on the borrower under specific circumstances (e.g. upon a breach by the borrower of its obligations under the facility agreement).

5. Mortgages and charges over different assets

The type of mortgage or charge which a lender will take depends largely upon the type of asset over which security is to be taken.

4618

A **legal mortgage** can only be taken over a specific asset which is in existence at the time of the charge. The asset must also be capable of and suitable for assignment to the lender. The complications involved in transferring legal title mean that legal mortgages are generally only used for freehold and leasehold property.

An **equitable mortgage** can be taken over other specific assets which are capable of and suitable for assignment but usually a **fixed charge** will be sufficient for the lender in such situations. A fixed charge will generally also be taken over specific future assets or those which are not capable of or suitable for assignment to the lender, provided the assets are ones over which the lender can exercise control.

A **floating charge** will be taken over any other assets or classes of assets, particularly those with which the borrower must be able to deal in the ordinary course of its business.

The table below is a **summary** of which mortgage or charge is likely to be taken over the usual assets of a trading company. Further commentary can be found by following the cross-references to other paragraphs.

4619

Charged asset	Legal mortgage	Equitable mortgage/ fixed charge	Floating charge	¶¶
Freehold and leasehold property that is: – held by borrower at time of charge; or – acquired after creation of charge	✓	✓		¶4620+
Fixed plant and machinery that are: – fixtures; or – not fixtures	✓	✓		¶4622+
Moveable tangible assets (e.g. loose plant and machinery, vehicles etc)			✓	¶4625
Stock			✓	-
Work in progress			✓	-
Goodwill		✓		-
Book debts			✓	¶4626+
Cash		✓		¶4632
Shares (of another company)	✓	✓		¶1915+

Freehold and leasehold property

A lender will normally take a legal mortgage over **existing** freehold or leasehold property because, unlike other assets, a legal mortgage can be created over such property without the need to formally assign legal title to the lender. The problems of assigning and acquiring

4620

legal title to the property are therefore avoided. The lender will not actually take legal title to the property but, in the case of freehold property, its security interest will last for 3,000 years and, in the case of leasehold property, its security interest will last for 1 day less than the length of the borrower's lease (s 87 LPA 1925). In order to create such a legal mortgage, the security document must expressly state that the property is being "charged by way of a legal mortgage" and should be executed as a deed (s 1(2)(c), 52 LPA 1925).

4621 **Future** freehold or leasehold property will usually be subject to a fixed charge.

Fixed plant and machinery

4622 In the case of fixed plant and machinery, it is important to determine whether or not the asset is a "**fixture**". Fixtures are treated as part of the property to which they are attached and therefore come within any security over that property. Plant and machinery will be treated as "fixtures" if they are annexed to land or buildings (for example, attached by cement or screws) and the purpose of the annexation is to bring about a permanent improvement in the land or building. An asset will not be a fixture if it is going to be removed in the future or if the purpose of the annexation is only to assist in the use of the land or building. For example, plant and machinery bolted to a factory floor are likely to be fixtures but those that are free-standing are not.

4623 Particular care must be taken to ensure that **assets belonging to a third party** (for example, on hire-purchase) do not amount to a fixture as they could come within a mortgage over the relevant land or building. If they do, the lender's interest could take priority over the third party's which would cause problems for both the company and the third party. In case of doubt, the lender should be asked for a written acknowledgement that the asset will not be treated as a fixture.

4624 If the fixed plant and machinery is **not a fixture**, it will usually be subject to a fixed charge although it could be subject to a chattel mortgage (see ¶4625 below).

Moveable tangible assets

4625 Normally, a company will need to be able to deal with its moveable tangible assets in the course of its business and so such assets will be subject to a **floating charge**. However, where the asset is particularly valuable or has a more permanent nature, the lender may take a legal mortgage. This is sometimes known as a "**chattel mortgage**".

Book debts

4626 "Book debts" is an accounting **term which refers to** money owed to a business which would be recorded in its books of account, such as for trade sales. Generally speaking, the book debts of a company are constantly changing. A company usually needs to be able to collect its debts and use the proceeds in the course of its business (although it may not need to do so in respect of a specific book debt). A company that is not able to do so will be deprived of its cash flow. It is perhaps worth saying at this stage that there is no distinction in law between an uncollected book debt and the proceeds once collected, even though the nature of the asset has changed from a receivable into cash. This is because the right to collect a debt is worth nothing without the right to use the proceeds and it does not make commercial sense to separate the two (*Agnew v Commissioners for Inland Revenue, Re Brumark* [2001] 2 BCLC 188).

The type of security which a lender may take depends upon whether it wishes to take security over **specific book debts** (such as money owed to the borrower as a result of one particular order) or over the borrower's **general book debts**.

Specific book debts

4627 It is possible for a lender to take a legal mortgage or equitable mortgage/fixed charge over a specific book debt. A **legal mortgage** requires a legal assignment of the debt to the lender. This would require notice of the assignment to be given to the debtor, who would have to pay the lender instead of the company. Although perhaps appropriate if a small number of debts were being assigned, a legal assignment would be commercially impractical for a large number of book debts. The lender would incur administrative costs by having to collect the debts of the company and the company's line of credit with its creditors (for example, its suppliers) would be damaged.

As a result, an **equitable mortgage** (which requires an equitable assignment of the debt) or a **fixed charge** could be more appropriate. Under an equitable assignment, the debtor continues to pay the company, which has to account to the lender for the proceeds. The debtor only has to be notified of the assignment when the company is in default. The mortgage document should give the company authority to collect the debts on behalf of the lender and require the company to hold the proceeds on trust for the lender.

General book debts

Case law has determined that a **fixed charge** can be created over fluctuating book debts (whether or not they are actually entered in the books of the borrower) only in very narrow circumstances (*National Westminster Bank plc v Spectrum Plus Ltd, Re Spectrum Plus Ltd* [2005] 2 BCLC 269). In order to create a fixed charge, the company must be:
– prohibited from disposing of book debts before they are collected;
– required to collect book debts on behalf of the lender; and
– required to pay the proceeds of all book debts into a bank account over which the lender has control or pay them to the lender (to reduce the company's outstanding debt to it).

Any charge over book debts which does not satisfy these criteria will operate as a **floating charge** regardless of the terminology used in the charging document.

4628

The key to creating a fixed charge is the lender's control over the proceeds of the book debts. A **bank lender** can only demonstrate the necessary control if the bank account into which the proceeds are paid is "blocked", that is to say the borrower is unable to draw from the account without the permission of the lender (*National Westminster Bank plc v Spectrum Plus Ltd, Re Spectrum Plus Ltd* [2005] 2 BCLC 269). However, this would clearly restrict the borrower's cash flow, perhaps to the extent that it is unable to do business effectively. Alternatively, the proceeds of the book debts could be paid into an operating account (i.e. one on which the borrower can draw without permission) which is "swept" regularly (maybe even on a daily basis) so that funds in excess of a certain amount are transferred into a blocked account.

4629

> MEMO POINTS   The House of Lords' decision in *National Westminster Bank plc v Spectrum Plus Ltd* overturned more than 25 years-worth of bank practice and is now the "last word" on charges over book debts. Previously, all that was required was for the proceeds to be paid into a designated account at the lender bank. The borrower was then permitted to draw on that bank account and use the money for the purposes of its trade (*Siebe Gorman & Co Ltd v Barclays Bank Ltd* [1979] 2 Lloyd's Rep 142). However, the House of Lords decided that this was inconsistent with the characteristics of a fixed charge.
> The **reversal of the law** was expected to have a significant impact on bank security arrangements. Any bank charges over book debts which pre-date the House of Lords' decision are unlikely to meet the new test and so are likely to take effect as floating charges instead of fixed ones (with the consequence that they will not rank as highly in the event of the borrower's insolvency, see ¶7977+). Banks are not able to cure the defect by altering the practical arrangements (for example, by requiring the borrower to pay collected book debts into a blocked account); a new charging document is required (*Re Beam Tube Products Ltd* [2006] EWHC 486 (Ch)). This raises issues as to what consideration for the new security is given, unless the lender advances further funds or the borrower is already in default. Even with consideration, the new security may be vulnerable to being set aside as a preference (¶7819+) or a voidable floating charge if the consideration has already been given (¶7836+).
> However, the commercial reality is that little has changed as far as ordinary lending is concerned and banks accept that a floating charge over book debts is as good a security as they can get. Arrangements such as requiring the borrower to pay the proceeds of book debts into a blocked account and factoring debts are unsuitable in most circumstances because they are too impractical and administratively onerous for both the lender and the borrower. Therefore, unless the lending is particularly risky or complex, banks have not tended to insist on creating a fixed charge over book debts. Fixed charges over general book debts are therefore likely to become less common in practice.

4630 Demonstrating control is even more difficult when the **lender is not a bank**. A non-bank lender must exercise actual control over the designated bank account into which the book debts are to be paid (for example, by taking a fixed charge over the bank account). Again, this is likely to be impractical. If the borrower is permitted to pay the proceeds of its book debts into an ordinary bank account which operates without restrictions, the charge will take effect as a floating charge (*Re Brightlife Ltd* [1986] BCLC 418). Further, as mentioned above, it is not possible to split the uncollected book debts from their proceeds and create a fixed equitable charge over uncollected book debts and a floating charge over the proceeds (this practice was approved by the Court of Appeal in *Re New Bullas Trading Ltd* ([1994] 1 BCLC 449) but that case was overturned by *National Westminster Bank plc v Spectrum Plus Ltd, Re Spectrum Plus Ltd* ([2005] 2 BCLC 269)).

4631 As a result of the difficulties in demonstrating control, the usual practice is for lenders who do not want to take a floating charge to enter into an **invoice discounting** or **debt factoring** arrangement with the company rather than take a fixed charge over book debts (see ¶4730+).

Cash

4632 Security **over cash** is usually created by depositing the cash in a designated bank account. This creates a debt of the same amount due from the bank to the company over which the lender can take an equitable mortgage or a fixed charge.

6. Registration

4636 Following their creation, nearly all mortgages and charges must be registered at **Companies House**. In addition, mortgages or charges over particular assets should be registered on **other public registers** which are maintained for those assets.

A record of all mortgages and charges affecting the assets or undertaking of a company (whether or not they are of a type which must be registered at Companies House or on any other register) must also be kept by the company in its "**register of charges**" (see ¶3975+).

a. Companies House

4637 The **purpose** of the requirement to register charges at Companies House is to give persons dealing with the company notice of any prior interests over its assets. The requirement is more than procedural; a **failure to register** a mortgage or charge which should be registered will affect its enforceability (see ¶4647+).

> MEMO POINTS The Law Commission has reviewed the law that governs the registration of mortgages and charges. It published its final report on 31 August 2005 entitled "Company Security Interests" in which it **recommends** replacing the current scheme with an online "notice-filing" system. Filings would be made by the secured party without the need for legal expertise, registrations could be made in advance and the 21-day limit would be removed. The classes of security interests that require filing would be extended to cover commercial security interests such as factoring arrangements. It also recommends clarifying the priority rules for competing security interests and providing effective remedies for all secured parties. At the time of writing, BERR has not yet published a response to this consultation. The **new Companies Act** restates the current registration regime and does not include any of the Law Commission's proposals. The provisions of the new Act relating to the registration of charges are expected to come into force by 1 October 2009.

Which types of security must be registered?

4638 All **floating charges** (whether over all or part of a company's undertaking or assets) must be registered at Companies House. The table below sets out which **other mortgages and charges** have to be registered, by the type of asset.

Asset	Registration of mortgage or fixed charge at Companies House? (s 396(1) CA 1985)
Freehold and leasehold property:	
– land	✓
– rent or other periodic income	✗
– other interest in land	✓
Fixed plant and machinery	✓[1]
Moveable tangible assets:	
– ship (or any share in a ship)	✓
– aircraft	✓
– any other asset	✓[1]
Book debts	✓
Stock	✗[2]
Work in progress	✗[2]
Goodwill	✓
Intellectual property[3]	✓
Cash	✗[4]
Shares (in another company)	✗[4]

Note:
1. A charge that was created or evidenced by a document which, if executed by an individual, would require registration as a **bill of sale**, must be registered at Companies House. A bill of sale is a document which transfers ownership of a personal asset. If an individual transfers personal assets to another but retains possession of those assets, the bill of sale must be registered with the High Court (s 8 Bills of Sale Act 1878). The formalities of court registration are so strict that such bills of sale for individuals are rarely seen in practice. In the case of a company, it is arguable that a fixed charge over tangible assets falls within the category of charges that would require registration as a bill of sale.
2. In practice, a floating charge would be taken over these assets and so the security would be have to be registered on that basis.
3. This means any patent, trade mark, registered design, copyright, design right or any licence under those rights.
4. Security over "**financial collateral**" (which includes cash credited to an account and shares in a company) does not have to be registered where (reg 4(4) SI 2003/3226):
– the security giver and holder are non-natural persons (e.g. companies);
– the arrangement is evidenced in writing; and
– the lender takes possession or control of the asset.
However, lenders sometimes still register a mortgage or charge over shares as there is uncertainty as to whether dividends payable on those shares amount to a book debt (owed by the company to its shareholder). Similarly, in practice, a mortgage or charge over cash deposits is also often registered as those deposits may also be treated as a book debt (owed by the bank to the depositor).

MEMO POINTS 1. In addition, the following unusual mortgages or charges must also be registered (s 396(1) CA 1985):
– over the borrower's **uncalled share capital**;
– over **unpaid shareholder calls**; and
– to secure any **issue of debentures**.
These provisions are restated in the **new Companies Act** (s 860(7) CA 2006, expected to come into force by 1 October 2009).

Deadline

Any mortgage or charge that requires registration must be registered at Companies House **within** 21 days after the date of its creation (s 395(1) CA 1985; restated at s 870 CA 2006 by 1 October 2009). For example, a charge created on 1 January must be registered by 22 January. Note that weekends and bank holidays are included in calculating the 21-day period so, if the final date for registration falls on such a day, the document should be delivered by the last preceding working day.

MEMO POINTS 1. An **extension of time** for registration can only be obtained by an application to court which has absolute discretion to grant it if (s 404 CA 1985; restated at s 873 CA 2006 by 1 October 2009):
– the failure to register was accidental or inadvertent or due to some other sufficient cause and would not prejudice the creditors or shareholders of the company; or
– it is otherwise just and equitable to grant the extension.

If the extension is granted, it will usually be on the condition that registration will not affect the rights acquired by any third parties in the period between the date on which the mortgage or charge was created and actual registration, and that the company can apply to court to cancel the extension if it is wound up before a particular date. If the company is under threat of liquidation or administration, an additional condition that the liquidator or administrator can challenge the late registration will usually be included (*Barclays Bank plc v Stuart Landon Ltd* [2001] 2 BCLC 316). Unless there are exceptional circumstances, an extension will **not be granted** after the commencement of a winding up as this would prejudice the rights of unsecured creditors (*Re R M Arnold & Co Ltd* [1984] BCLC 535). The usual practice is that Companies House will register the mortgage or charge following an extension, but will not issue a certificate of registration until it is clear that the extension will not be revoked. However, once issued, even if mistakenly, the mortgage or charge will take priority in accordance with the order that authorised its registration, as the certificate is conclusive evidence of registration (see ¶4641) (*Re Top Marques Car Rental Ltd* [2006] EWHC 109 (Ch)).

2. The **date of creation** is the date the mortgage or charge comes into effect. This is usually the date upon which the document is properly executed by the borrower. If the document is held in escrow, the mortgage or charge is normally created when the escrow conditions are fulfilled (*Terrapin International Ltd v IRC* [1976] 2 All ER 461). However, there is at least one case in which the court held that the date of execution was the date of delivery subject to escrow (*Alan Estates Ltd v W G Stores Ltd* [1981] 3 All ER 481). To be on the safe side, lenders should calculate the 21-day period from the earliest of these dates.

3. A mortgage or charge over **future assets** comes into effect upon execution of the document, not when the assets actually come within the ambit of the security (*Independent Automatic Sales Ltd v Knowles & Foster* [1962] 3 All ER 27).

4. An **agreement to create a mortgage or charge** contingent upon the occurrence of a particular event need not be registered until the event occurs and the security is actually created (*William v Burlington Investments Ltd* (1977) 121 SJ 424). In contrast, an unconditional agreement to create a mortgage or charge must be registered as the lender acquires an immediate equitable charge on the subject matter (*Swiss Bank Corp v Lloyds Bank Ltd* [1980] 2 All ER 419).

Who must register?

4640 The primary obligation to register a mortgage or charge rests with the company but any interested person can present one for registration (s 399 CA 1985; restated at s 860(2) CA 2006 by 1 October 2009). In practice, registration is usually carried out by the lender as it is most concerned with the mortgage's or charge's enforceability.

> MEMO POINTS   Under the **new Companies Act**, if the mortgage or charge is registered by someone other than the company, the company will have to reimburse him for any Companies House fees (s 860(3) CA 2006, expected to come into force by 1 October 2009).

How to register?

4641 A mortgage or charge is registered by **filing**:
– Form 395;
– the original mortgage or charge document (or a copy in the case of overseas property); and
– a fee of £13.

Companies House will date stamp the original document upon receipt of a correct filing. It will therefore always be clear on the face of the document whether it has been properly registered or not. Later (and perhaps not within the 21-day timescale), Companies House will issue a certificate of registration and return the original document to the person who presented it for registration. This certificate is conclusive evidence that the mortgage or charge has been properly registered (s 401(2) CA 1985; restated at s 869(6) CA 2006 by 1 October 2009).

> MEMO POINTS   The name of Form 395, like the names of other **Companies House forms**, is taken from the section number of the legislation. As all of the section numbers will change under the new Companies Act, Companies House proposes to change the names of all of its forms to reflect their function rather than the relevant section number ("Working with Companies House: a consultation on the registrar's rules and related provisions which will apply under the Companies Act 2006"). At the time of writing, the new form names are not yet available.

Form 395

It is extremely important that Form 395 is completed correctly as otherwise Companies House will reject the application for registration. The documents will then have to be corrected and re-filed, still within the original 21-day timescale; Companies House does not have the discretion to give extensions of time for this or any other reason.

4642

Form 395 requires the following **information**:
– the borrower's company number;
– the borrower's company name;
– the date the mortgage or charge was created;
– a description of the instrument;
– the name and address of the lender(s);
– short particulars of the property charged/mortgaged including any negative pledge; and
– particulars of any commission, allowance and discounts.

The form must be **dated and signed** on behalf of the company, mortgage holder or charge holder. The most common reason for Companies House to reject a form is because it has not been signed and dated.

> MEMO POINTS 1. If a **mistake** is discovered following registration, the Companies House record can only be corrected by an application to court. The procedure is the same as for extensions of time for registration (see ¶4639).
> 2. Under the **new Companies Act**, the following details will have to be registered at Companies House (s 860(1) CA 2006; reg 2 draft Companies (Prescribed Particulars of Company Charges) Regulations 2007):
> – the date of creation of the charge;
> – a description of the instrument creating or evidencing the charge;
> – the amount secured by the charge;
> – the name and address of the person entitled to the charge; and
> – brief details of the property charged.
> The new form will of course require the borrower's company name and number as well. These changes are expected to come into force by 1 October 2009.

Overseas issues

In the case of English and Welsh registered companies, if the security is created in the UK but the **secured assets are outside the UK**, the security can still be registered at Companies House although the security may also need to be registered in the place where the assets are situated for it to be enforceable (s 398(3) CA 1985; restated at s 866(2) CA 2006 by 1 October 2009).

4643

If the secured assets are outside of the UK and the **security is created outside the UK**, the original security document need not be sent to Companies House; a verified copy will be sufficient. Further, the deadline for registration will be extended by the amount of time that post will take to reach the UK from the place where the security was created (s 398(1), (2) CA 1985; restated at ss 866(1), 870(1)(b) CA 2006 by 1 October 2009).

> MEMO POINTS If the secured assets are in **Scotland** or **Northern Ireland** and the security is registered in that jurisdiction, it will be deemed to have been duly registered in England and Wales upon the filing of a verified copy of the security document and Form 398 (s 398(4) CA 1985; restated at s 867 CA 2006 by 1 October 2009). As with other Companies House forms, the name of this form is likely to be changed to reflect its purpose rather than the section number of the legislation. At the time of writing, the new form names are not yet available.

A mortgage or charge **over assets** in England and Wales **of an overseas company** with an established place of business in England and Wales is subject to the same rules on registration, whether the borrower has registered its branch or is a "Slavenburg company" (that is an overseas company which has not registered in England and Wales). As usual, **failure to register** the security will render it void as against an administrator, liquidator or any creditor of the borrower even in the event of a foreign winding up. The prudent course of action is therefore to register a mortgage or charge over the assets of an overseas company in the normal way, whether or not the assets are actually situated in England and Wales at the time the security is created. If the security is not registered and the assets subsequently become situated in England and Wales, it will not be enforceable and the lender will be out of

4644

time to register it (s 409 CA 1985; *N V Slavenburg's Bank v Intercontinental Natural Resources Ltd* [1980] 1 All ER 955).

> MEMO POINTS 1. If the overseas company has registered in England and Wales, **Companies House** will register the mortgage or charge against that company. Otherwise, Companies House keeps a list known as the "Slavenburg Index" of mortgages and charges registered against Slavenburg companies.
> 2. The **new Companies Act** envisages that the regime for the registration of mortgages and charges over the UK assets of registered overseas companies will be set out in regulations (s 1052 CA 2006). At the time of writing, no regulations or draft regulations have yet been published.

Property acquired subject to a mortgage or charge

4645 Where a company acquires an asset that is subject to a mortgage or charge that must be registered, the company must **re-register** the mortgage or charge against its own name **within** 21 days of acquiring the property by filing (s 400(1), (2) CA 1985; restated at ss 862, 870(2) CA 2006 by 1 October 2009):
– Form 400; and
– a certified copy of the mortgage or charge document.

If the asset is situated in, and the mortgage or charge was created outside of, GB, the deadline is extended by the amount of time that post would take to reach the UK (s 400(3) CA 1985; restated at s 870(2)(b) CA 2006 by 1 October 2009).

> MEMO POINTS 1. Under the **new Companies Act**, the same details as for a normal charge will have to be registered at Companies House (see ¶4642/mp above), plus the date of the acquisition of the property subject to the mortgage or charge (s 862(1) CA 2006; expected to come into force by 1 October 2009; reg 4 draft Companies (Prescribed Particulars of Company Charges) Regulations 2007).
> 2. The name of Form 400, like the names of other **Companies House forms**, is taken from the section number of the legislation. As all of the section numbers will change under the new Companies Act, Companies House proposes to change the names of all of its forms to reflect their function rather than the relevant section number ("Working with Companies House: a consultation on the registrar's rules and related provisions which will apply under the Companies Act 2006"). At the time of writing, the new form names are not yet available.

4646 **Failure to re-register** the mortgage or charge does not affect its enforceability. However, the acquiring company and every officer of it who is in default is liable to a fine (s 400(4) CA 1985; restated at s 862(4), (5) CA 2006 by 1 October 2009; ¶9635).

Failure to register

4647 Failing to register a mortgage or charge which should be registered within the required timescale has consequences for:
– the enforceability of the security;
– the enforceability of the debt; and
– the borrower and its officers.

Enforceability of security

4648 A mortgage or charge which should be registered but is not cannot be enforced **against an administrator, liquidator or any creditor** of the borrower (s 395(1) CA 1985; restated at s 874(1) CA 2006 by 1 October 2009). Its effectiveness is therefore greatly reduced in the event of the borrower's insolvency or in the event of any creditor taking enforcement action against the secured assets. Further, the mortgage or charge cannot be enforced in priority to a subsequent mortgage or charge which is properly registered, even if the later secured party was aware of the earlier unregistered security (*Re Monolithic Building Co* [1914-15] All ER Rep 249).

> MEMO POINTS The reference to administrator and liquidator **includes** the borrower when it is in administration or liquidation and the reference to creditor is to a creditor who claims some sort of proprietary interest in the secured asset (*Smith (Administrator of Cosslett (Contractors) Ltd) v Bridgend County Borough Council* [2002] 1 All ER 292).

4649 A failure to register is not completely fatal to enforceability. The mortgage or charge is still enforceable as against the borrower (when it is not in administration or liquidation) and an administrator or liquidator cannot challenge the enforcement if it is completed before the commencement of the administration or liquidation (*Independent Automatic Sales Ltd v Knowles & Foster* [1962] 3 All ER 27; see ¶7903+, ¶8818+). In the unlikely event that the secured assets remain intact after administration or after all monies have been paid out in a liquidation, they will continue to be subject to the unregistered security (*Smith (Administrator of Cosslett (Contractors) Ltd) v Bridgend County Borough Council* [2002] 1 All ER 292).

Enforceability of debt

The enforceability of the debt underlying the mortgage or charge is not affected by a failure to register. This means that the borrower still has an obligation to repay the debt. In fact, if the security becomes void for want of registration, the money secured by it immediately becomes payable (s 395(2) CA 1985; restated at s 874(3) CA 2006 by 1 October 2009).

4650

Liability of borrower and its officers

In addition to the effect on enforceability, the borrower, or any officer of the borrower who fails to register a security within the required timescale is subject to a fine (s 399(3) CA 1985; restated at s 860(4), (5) CA 2006 by 1 October 2009; ¶9935).

4651

b. Other public registers

As set out in the table below, in addition to registration at Companies House, **mortgages or charges over particular assets** should also be registered on other public registers which are maintained for those assets. This records the lender's interest in the asset and ensures that it will bind any third party who deals with the asset in the future (such as a purchaser or subsequent security holder).

4653

Asset	Other register
Freehold or leasehold property	Land Register [1]
Ship	Registry of Shipping and Seamen [2]
Aircraft	Register of Aircraft Mortgages [3]
Patent	Patents Register [4]
Trade mark	Trade Marks Register [4]
Registered design right	Design Rights Register [4]

Note:
1. Maintained by the **Land Registry** which publishes a comprehensive range of guidance leaflets (*www.landreg.gov.uk*). The charge will be recorded against the registered number of the land in question.
2. Maintained by the **Maritime and Coastguard Agency** (*www.mcga.gov.uk*).
3. Maintained by the **Civil Aviation Authority** (*www.caa.co.uk*).
4. Maintained by the **UK Intellectual Property Office** (*www.ipo.gov.uk*).

7. Satisfaction and release

When the borrower fulfils its obligations, the lender usually has no further need for the mortgage or charge. The security is then said to be "**satisfied**". Sometimes, the borrower may need to sell property over which a lender has a security interest. In these circumstances, the borrower will need the lender to "**release**" the property from the mortgage or charge so that it can be sold free of the lender's interest.

4656

Although there is no requirement to do so, it is good practice for the borrower to **notify Companies House** when a mortgage or charge has been partly or wholly satisfied or released so that the public record is up to date. The appropriate form should be filed at Companies House in order to notify it of the satisfaction or release of a registered security interest:
– Form 403a, if the security has been satisfied in full or in part; or
– Form 403b, if an asset has been released from a registered security.

4657

4658 > MEMO POINTS   The names of these forms, like the names of other **Companies House forms**, are taken from the section number of the legislation. As all of the section numbers will change under the new Companies Act, Companies House proposes to change the names of all of its forms to reflect their function rather than the relevant section number ("Working with Companies House: a consultation on the registrar's rules and related provisions which will apply under the Companies Act 2006"). At the time of writing, the new form names are not yet available.

The lender does not have to sign the forms or consent to the process. Instead, the forms contain a **statutory declaration** by an officer of the borrower that the mortgage or charge has been satisfied or the asset has been released. Any person who knowingly and wilfully makes a false statutory declaration will be guilty of a criminal offence and subject to imprisonment of up to 2 years (s 5 Perjury Act 1911). Further, any person who files a declaration which he knows or believes to be false is liable to imprisonment, a fine or both (s 403(2A) CA 1985; ¶9935).

> MEMO POINTS   These provisions are restated in the **new Companies Act** (s 872 CA 2006, expected to come into force by 1 October 2009). However, it is not yet known whether the content of the Companies House forms will change. In other areas, such as on the formation of a company, the statutory declaration will be replaced by a "statement of compliance" by the directors and it may be that the same change is also adopted in this area.

8. Enforcement

4663   A mortgage or charge gives the lender the right to have recourse to the secured assets in the event of the borrower's default. Enforcement is the process by which the lender exercises this right. The purpose of enforcement is for the lender to recoup the money owed to it by realising the value of the secured assets.

Before taking enforcement action, the lender should consider whether an informal arrangement with the borrower may be more appropriate (see ¶7323+). Further, the lender does not have to enforce its mortgage or charge: it can sue the borrower for breach of contract instead.

If the lender does decide to take **formal enforcement action** and has a floating charge over the whole or substantially the whole of the borrower's property, it will be able to institute insolvency proceedings out of court by appointing:
– an **administrator**, if it is the holder of a "qualifying floating charge" (see ¶8690+); or
– an **administrative receiver**, if the floating charge was created before 15 September 2003 (see ¶9195+).

Other security holders will normally exercise their contractual power, assuming one is contained in the mortgage or charge document, to appoint an **ordinary receiver** (¶9195+). This prevents them from incurring personal liability towards the borrower in relation to the enforcement.

If this power is not available, a lender can exercise its **power of sale**, or in rare cases, foreclose. **Foreclosure** is normally the last resort for lenders with a mortgage or charge over freehold or leasehold property.

> MEMO POINTS   The holder of a mortgage or charge over land also has the power to appoint an **LPA receiver** to collect income from the secured land instead of selling it (see ¶9228).

Power of sale

4664   The lender's power to sell the secured assets in the event of the borrower's default must be **contained in** the mortgage or charge document. Provided the mortgage or charge document is executed as a deed, this power is implied when the secured loan becomes due (s 101 LPA 1925). It is usual for the underlying loan document to contain a term to the effect that the whole balance becomes due if just one repayment is missed or if the borrower otherwise breaches the terms of the loan, so that this power is implied at the earliest possible stage.

A lender can exercise its implied power of sale in the following **circumstances** (s 103 LPA 1925):
- the borrower has failed to pay the secured debt after receiving 3 months' notice;
- interest is 2 months' in arrears; or
- there has been another breach of the deed other than one relating to repayment of the principal debt or interest.

As well as, or instead of, the above circumstances, the mortgage or charge document will usually specify that the power of sale is exercisable as soon as the borrower defaults in making any payments. This means that, in practice, a lender does not have to give notice to the borrower or wait for any length of time before exercising its power of sale.

4665

> MEMO POINTS 1. The lender has a duty to **obtain the market value** of the secured asset at the time of enforcement but does not have to wait until the market improves to get the best possible price (*Cuckmere Brick Co Ltd v Mutual Finance Ltd* [1971] 2 All ER 633).
> 2. The lender cannot **sell the secured asset to** itself or to its trustee or agent (*Martinson v Clowes* (1882) 21 Ch D 857). However, the lender may sell to a company in which it is interested (e.g. as a shareholder or a director) provided the sale is made in good faith and the lender takes reasonable precautions to obtain the best price reasonably obtainable at the time. Where the lender has a large interest in the purchasing company, a heavy onus lies on it to show that it acted fairly to the borrower and used its best endeavours to obtain that price (*Tse Kwong Lam v Wong Chit Sen* [1983] 3 All ER 54).

The **proceeds of sale** must be **used for** the following purposes and in the following order (s 105 LPA 1925):
1. discharge any prior incumbrances over the secured assets (e.g. a charge which takes priority);
2. pay all costs properly incurred by the lender incidental to the sale or any attempted sale;
3. pay the money, interest and costs owed under the mortgage or charge; and
4. pay any surplus to the borrower (and until then the lender holds the money on trust for the borrower).

4666

If the proceeds of sale are **not enough to satisfy the secured debt**, the lender can sue the borrower for the shortfall (*Gordon Grant and Co Ltd v Boos* [1926] AC 781). The security holder has 12 years from the date of sale to sue for any shortfall in the principal debt, but only 6 years to sue for interest (*Bristol & West plc v Bartlett* [2002] 4 All ER 544). If the borrower is insolvent, the lender will become an unsecured creditor for the amount of the debt still outstanding.

Foreclosure

Foreclosure is the process by which a lender becomes the absolute owner of a mortgaged or charged property. It is only **available for** mortgages or charges over freehold or leasehold property (ss 88(2), 89(2) LPA 1925). It is not often used in practice because the lender will lose the right to claim any money still owed to it if the value of the asset falls short of the borrower's debt, unless the lender is prepared and able to return the asset (*Kinnaird v Trollope* (1888) 39 Ch D 636).

4667

In order **to obtain foreclosure**, the lender must first obtain an order of "foreclosure nisi" from the court. This is an interim order which will give the borrower a set period of time to repay the money owed. If it fails to do so, the lender can go back to court and obtain an order for "foreclosure absolute" which finalises the lender's absolute ownership of the property. As part of the action for foreclosure, a lender can request the court to direct a sale of the secured property (s 91(2) LPA 1925).

9. Lender's rights against third parties

A mortgage or charge gives the lender a proprietary right over the secured asset. This means that the right is enforceable against third parties; the right is over the asset not just over the borrower. The lender's rights may sometimes have to compete with the rights of third parties, for example, if another lender has taken security over the same asset or if the asset has been sold or given to another person. If this occurs, the issue of whose interest takes **priority** will

4672

arise. This is important because the person with priority can enforce their rights over the secured assets first and is therefore more likely to realise any value from them.

MEMO POINTS   The issue of priority will also arise if the **borrower becomes insolvent** because then security holders take priority over unsecured creditors. At this time, whether a charge is fixed or floating is particularly pertinent. This is because fixed charge holders take priority over preferential creditors (such as payments due to employees) who in turn take priority over floating charge holders. Further, a percentage of floating charge assets are ring-fenced for unsecured creditors. For more on priority during insolvency, see ¶7975+ (liquidation); ¶8922+ (administration); ¶9321+ (receivership).

4673 The **general rule** is that the first legal interest takes priority over subsequent interests. The first equitable interest takes priority over the interests of all subsequent persons, except for a person acting in good faith who gave some consideration for his interest (for example, by buying it) and who did not have notice of the prior equitable interest.

4674 **Legal mortgage** holders therefore take priority over any subsequent person who acquires an interest in the asset. By contrast, an **equitable mortgage or charge holder** will only take priority over someone if he had notice of the security holder's interest. A person will be deemed to have notice of any mortgage or charge registered at Companies House or on any other public register. Therefore, in practice, the holders of the first registered mortgage or charge over an asset will take priority over any person who subsequently claims an interest in the asset.

MEMO POINTS   However, it is possible for the first-registered charge to be **prevented from having priority** over a subsequently registered charge, if the parties had an understanding that the second charge would take priority, as happened in a recent case (*Scottish & Newcastle plc v Lancashire Mortgage Corporation Ltd* [2007] EWCA Civ 684). LMC and S&N both took charges over the same house; LMC's charge was executed first but registered second. The charges were registered at HM Land Registry, and the relevant legislation gave priority to the first-registered charge (s 29 Land Registration Act 1925, now repealed but s 48 Land Registration Act 2002 includes an equivalent provision). The court found that S&N knew that LMC expected priority and benefited from that expectation because part of the monies owing to it were paid off with the loan LMC made to the debtor. S&N's passive acquiescence was enough to give rise to proprietary estoppel, preventing it from insisting on its priority over LMC.

4675 Except in the case of freehold and leasehold property, it is not possible to create more than one legal mortgage over the **same asset** because of the requirement to assign legal title to the lender. Equitable mortgages or charges over the same assets take priority in the order of creation.

Priority agreements

4676 In practice, if a borrower borrows from **multiple lenders**, the lenders will agree priorities between themselves by way of a priority agreement. This is a purely contractual arrangement between the lenders as to how the proceeds of a sale of the secured assets will be distributed on enforcement of any of their securities (although conventionally the borrower may also be required to execute the agreement). Best practice is to execute the priority agreement as a deed.

4677 Priority agreements are quite **usual when** a company is being **financed** by more than one lender **for different purposes**. For example, if one lender is providing term loan funding and another an overdraft facility, the first lender will usually take priority over particular fixed assets and the second will usually take priority over other assets. A priority agreement is also usual where there is some **doubt as to priority of payment**. For example, if a first charge secures a fluctuating overdraft, the first lender may want to ensure that it takes priority over subsequent lenders in respect of any increases to the overdraft facility after subsequent charges are registered. Similarly, if a first charge does not have a limit on the amount of borrowing it secures, a subsequent lender may wish to place a ceiling on the amount that the first lender can recover so that the subsequent lender can be sure of how much property will remain against which it can enforce its security.

10. Subordination

What is subordination?

Where one lender agrees that the debt owed to it should be repaid after debts owed to the other lender(s) the arrangement is known as a "postponement" or "subordination". The borrower as well as the lenders will be a party to the contract which is known as an "inter-creditor agreement". The lender whose debt has been subordinated is known as the "junior creditor" and its debt is referred to as the "junior debt". The other lender(s) are known as the "senior creditor(s)" and their debt is referred to as the "senior debt". A middle-ranking lender (that is one whose debt has been subordinated to a senior creditor but not to a junior creditor) is known as a "mezzanine creditor" and its debt is referred to as the "mezzanine debt".

4680

A subordination can be a "turnover subordination" or a "conditional subordination". A **turnover subordination** provides that any money received by the junior creditor up to the level of the senior debt will belong to the senior creditor. A turnover subordination can either be a "trust turnover subordination", under which the junior creditor holds any money it receives on trust for the senior creditor, or a "contractual turnover subordination" under which the junior creditor agrees to pay any money it receives to the senior creditor.

4683

A **conditional subordination** (also known as "contingent" or "flawed debt" subordination) provides that payment of the junior debt is conditional upon payment in full of the senior debt.

> MEMO POINTS "**Structural subordination**" is where a debt is inadvertently subordinated because of a group structure. It occurs when a lender takes security over the assets of a group holding company but the value of the group resides in its trading subsidiaries whose assets are secured to other lenders. In the event of a winding up, the group holding company (as a shareholder) will be paid after the subsidiaries' secured and unsecured creditors. A lender who enforces security held over the holding company's shareholding in its subsidiaries will be in the same position. The funds available to pay the lender from the assets of subsidiaries will therefore be limited to what is left after all of the subsidiaries' creditors have been paid. In effect, the lender will have become subordinated to the subsidiaries' creditors. In order to avoid structural subordination, a lender should take security over the assets of subsidiaries as well as the holding company.

Why subordinate?

A **junior creditor** may agree to have its debt subordinated because it will obtain a higher rate of return on its loan. Alternatively, the junior creditor may be connected to the borrower (for example, it may be its parent company or main supplier) and may need to agree to the subordination in order to secure external funding so that the borrower can continue to trade.

4684

From the **borrower's point of view**, subordination will increase the likelihood of the senior lender agreeing to advance money and the amount of money that it is prepared to advance. Subordination is therefore usual where a borrower needs to maximise its borrowing capacity.

Subordination is often a feature of highly leveraged transactions (these are ones with a high debt to equity ratio). Examples are the financing of an asset acquisition (such as the purchase of another company, business or property), which is known as "**acquisition finance**", and of a project (such as a property development), which is known as "**project finance**". Some lenders specialise in providing subordinated debt, known as "**mezzanine financing**".

4685

Inter-creditor agreement

An inter-creditor agreement sets out the terms of the subordination. The **effect** is that the junior creditor is not able to demand repayment of the junior debt or enforce its security, even if it is entitled to do so under its loan documentation, and any payment received by the junior creditor will be applied towards the senior debt.

4686

MEMO POINTS   A separate subordination agreement is not necessarily required where the **junior creditor is connected to** the **borrower**. For example, suppose Bank A were lending money to Mr B so he could purchase the share capital of C Ltd and, immediately following completion of the acquisition, Bank A and Mr B were going to lend working capital to C Ltd. The loan agreement between Bank A and Mr B could contain a covenant that Mr B would not accept loan repayments from C Ltd until Bank A's loan had been repaid in full and the loan agreement between Bank A and C Ltd could contain a covenant that C Ltd would not repay Mr B's loan before it repaid Bank A's loan.

4687 The main provisions of an inter-creditor are as follows:
a. undertakings by the borrower not to pay the junior debt or create or amend any security in relation to that debt;
b. undertakings by the junior creditor not to demand or seek payment of the junior debt or to enforce, create, or amend any security in relation to that debt;
c. permitted payments by the borrower to the junior creditor (usually limited to interest, expenses and any payment to which the senior creditor gives its prior written consent);
d. the treatment of **non-permitted payments** to the junior creditor (i.e. that they will be turned over to the senior creditor, and perhaps held by the junior creditor on trust for the senior creditor, see ¶4683);
e. priority between the junior and senior creditors' security (i.e. that the senior creditor's security will rank ahead of the junior creditor's and that any proceeds from enforcement of the junior creditor's security will be applied firstly in payment of the senior debt and secondly in payment of the junior debt);
f. in the event of the **borrower's insolvency**, that the senior creditor is authorised to claim for and exercise all rights of representation in respect of the junior debt;
g. confirmation that the **borrower's actions**, if they have the consent of the senior creditor or are required under the senior creditor's loan documentation, will be deemed not to breach the junior creditor's loan documentation;
h. representations and warranties by the borrower that it has the capacity and authorisation to enter into the agreement;
i. representations and warranties by the junior creditor that only it is entitled to enforce the junior debt and that it has provided the senior creditor with full copies of all of the terms relating to that debt; and
j. confirmation that the subordination will remain **in force until** the senior debt has been fully discharged and that the senior creditor is not obliged to advance any further money to the borrower, notwithstanding any other event (e.g: when the senior or junior creditor had notice of any security held by the other; the appointment of a liquidator, administrator or receiver in relation to the borrower; or any unenforceability of the senior security).

Effect of insolvency

4688 One of the difficult aspects of subordination is the effect of the insolvency of either the borrower or the junior creditor, which depends upon how the subordination agreement has been drafted.

Determining solvency of borrower

4689 The junior debt will normally have to be taken into account in determining the insolvency of the borrower. However, if the borrower is likely to be insolvent under the cash-flow or balance sheet insolvency tests (see ¶7600+), a carefully drafted **conditional subordination** (which for example provides for the junior debt to be payable only if the borrower is solvent) may mean that the junior debt need not be taken into account.

Borrower's insolvency

4690 The second issue is what happens if the borrower does become insolvent? **Is the liquidator bound by the subordination** agreement? The short answer is yes; case law has decided that both trust subordinations and contractual subordinations are binding on the borrower's liquidator (*Re Maxwell Communications Corp plc (No 2)* [1994] 1 All ER 737). This has been confirmed by the Court of Appeal, which held that the creditors of an insolvent borrower were bound by the consequences of a subordination agreement just as the borrower and its members would have been if it had remained solvent (*Squires v AIG Europe (UK) Ltd* [2006] EWCA Civ 7).

> **MEMO POINTS** Subordinations are an exception to the **pari passu principle** in insolvency law which states that the debts of the borrower rank equally and if its assets are insufficient to meet its debts, the creditors must receive an equal proportion of the money due to them (see ¶8054+). The general rule is that it is not possible to contract out of the pari passu principle (*British Eagle International Airlines Ltd v Compagnie Nationale Air France* [1975] 2 All ER 390) but the cases noted above have decided that this does not apply to subordinations. A word of caution however, as some cases have tended towards the position that it is not possible to contract out of the pari passu principle unless a security or trust interest has been created (*Re Lewis's of Leicester Ltd* [1995] 1 BCLC 428). If this line of reasoning is followed, trust subordinations will bind a liquidator but contractual subordinations will not.

4691 What is the **effect of the liquidator being bound** by the subordination agreement? The answer depends on the type of subordination.

Under a **turnover subordination**, both the senior and junior creditor will receive a dividend from the liquidator but since the junior creditor's dividend will be turned over to the senior creditor, the senior creditor will receive a "double dividend".

Under a **conditional subordination**, the junior creditor may not receive a dividend until all of the borrower's creditors have been paid. This is because under the pari passu principle, the liquidator is obliged to pay the borrower's ordinary creditors on an equal basis, so the senior debt will be repaid at the same rate as the other debts of the borrower and the junior debt will not become payable until that occurs. This will not be a problem if the senior and junior debts are both secured as they will take priority over the unsecured creditors.

> **MEMO POINTS** Assuming the **debts are secured**, a secondary problem could arise if the senior debt is secured by a floating charge and the junior debt by a fixed charge. By subordinating the junior debt, the fixed charge will rank behind the floating charge and therefore both will rank behind the borrower's preferential creditors.

Junior creditor's insolvency

4692 The third issue is the position of the senior creditor in the event of the junior creditor's insolvency. The senior creditor is not affected under a **conditional subordination** because the junior debt would not have become due and so the junior creditor would not have received any money from the borrower which properly belonged to the senior creditor. In contrast, under a turnover subordination, the junior creditor may have received money before it became insolvent which it should have turned over to the senior creditor. Under a **contractual turnover subordination**, the senior creditor would rank as an unsecured creditor in respect of any money received by the junior creditor from the borrower. However, under a **trust turnover subordination**, the senior creditor would have a proprietary interest in the money received by the junior creditor and would therefore take priority over the junior creditor's unsecured creditors.

Cross-debts owed by junior creditor

4693 If the borrower and junior creditor are connected, there may be cross-debts owed by the junior creditor to the borrower. For example, if the junior creditor was a director and the borrower was his company, it is possible for the company to have made loans to the director as well as vice versa. The borrower has the right to set off any cross-debts against the debts it owes to the junior creditor. The **borrower's right of set-off** when it is solvent can be contractually limited by the subordination agreement; however, if the borrower becomes insolvent, the liquidator must set off those debts and the parties cannot contract out of this provision (r 4.90 IR 1986).

A **trust turnover subordination** will avoid this effect because the subordination will take effect as an equitable assignment to the senior creditor of the right to receive payment of the junior debt. The connection between the debt and cross-debt will therefore be broken and no right of set-off off will arise.

A **conditional subordination** or **contractual turnover subordination** will not be sufficient to break the connection because in both cases, the debt will still be owed to the junior creditor and the cross-debt will still be owed to the borrower. A liquidator is required to take account of all sums owing between the two parties, whether or not due and whether or not payment is conditional.

B. Guarantees

4696 A guarantee can be **defined as** a promise to perform the obligations of a person if that person fails to perform them itself. In the context of borrowing, the obligations of the borrower to repay the lender can be guaranteed by a third party who is known as the "guarantor". The main agreement is between the borrower and lender; the guarantee is a side or collateral agreement. If the borrower fails to perform its obligation, the lender has the option of calling in the guarantee. In effect, a guarantee gives the lender an extra person to sue.

A guarantee is a contractual right (enforceable against the guarantor only) rather than a proprietary one (enforceable against the guarantor's property). It is therefore not a like-for-like substitute for a mortgage or charge. A guarantee is usually demanded by a lender when the borrower has few assets (so a mortgage or charge cannot be taken). Sometimes, the guarantee itself is secured upon the assets of the guarantor.

> MEMO POINTS Guarantees must be carefully **drafted** to ensure that all of the obligations intended to be guaranteed (and only those obligations) are covered. For example, where a parent company guaranteed its obligations under a joint venture agreement, this included its obligations under a facility letter although they were not specifically referred to in the joint venture agreement, because it was clear that the subsidiary's obligations had to be interpreted in the light of both documents (*Wolsey Securities Ltd v Abbeygate Management Services Ltd* [2007] EWCA Civ 423).

4697 Since guarantees are collateral to a main agreement, there is usually some connection between the guarantor and borrower. The two most common situations in which a company's borrowings are guaranteed are:
– a **personal guarantee** of the company's borrowings by one or more of its directors; and
– a company guaranteeing the borrowings of another company in its group, known as a **group company guarantee**.

Personal guarantee

4698 A personal guarantee of a company's borrowings by one or more of its **directors** is often required by banks, particularly in the case of a small company which does not have a long trading history or which is new to the bank. The guarantee will usually be for all money owed by the company to the bank but will have a cap. Directors' personal guarantees of £30,000 or more are not uncommon.

4699 Since personal guarantees can involve substantial liabilities, the courts have been anxious to protect the innocent or naïve individual from giving a guarantee without understanding the significance of what he is doing. Accordingly, a personal guarantee could be **unenforceable if the guarantor**:
– was subject to undue influence (*Barclays Bank plc v O'Brien* [1993] 4 All ER 417); or
– did not fully understand the terms of the agreement (*Saunders v Anglia Building Society* [1970] 3 All ER 961).

As a result, banks always require personal guarantors to take **independent legal advice** before signing a guarantee and the legal adviser is usually required to countersign the document to confirm that he has given the appropriate legal advice (see ¶4769).

Group company guarantee

4700 A guarantee from a company in the same group as the borrower is **often required if** the borrower does not have sufficient assets over which the lender can take security. Even if security is being taken, a guarantee from a high profile group company can be attractive to a lender because if the borrower defaults, the threat of the guarantor's loss of reputation can sometimes be as effective as the threat that a lender may enforce its security against the borrower.

4701 Whenever a company considers guaranteeing the borrowings of another, the directors of the guarantor must always be sure that the guarantee is of **benefit to the guarantor** (as opposed to of benefit to the group) or they may be in breach of their duty to act in their company's best interests.

> *MEMO POINTS* 1. The same considerations apply if the **guarantee is secured or** if the assets of one company are used to **secure** the **borrowings of another company** in the group.
> 2. The guarantor must also have the **capacity** and **power** to enter into the guarantee (¶4755+).

4702 It would be best for the directors to **consider the interests of the guarantor and borrower separately**, but this is not necessary. In the absence of actual separate consideration, the proper test is whether an intelligent and honest man in the position of a director of the company concerned, could, in all of the circumstances, have reasonably believed that the transaction was for the benefit of the company (*Charterbridge Corporation Ltd v Lloyds Bank Ltd* [1969] 2 All ER 1185). In practice, the board of the guarantor should separately approve the guarantee and record the reasons why it was thought to be in the guarantor's interests.

4703 Where a **parent company guarantees** the borrowings of its subsidiary, it is arguable that the guarantee is of benefit to the parent company due to its interest in the subsidiary.

The guarantor's directors may find it more difficult to show that the guarantor has benefited where a **subsidiary guarantees** the borrowings of its parent company or another subsidiary in the same group. However, benefit to the guarantor could be shown, for example, if it relied on the parent company or other subsidiary for day to day management, working capital, skills or trading premises.

It is unlikely that the directors will be able to show benefit to the guarantor where it and the borrower are connected in some way (for example, if they have common directors) but are **not** actually **part of the same group**.

C. Other types of security

1. Lien

Legal lien

4714 There are two main types of lien. A legal lien (also known as a "**possessory lien**") is the right of a creditor to retain an asset belonging to a debtor until the debt has been paid. However, it gives no automatic rights to the creditor other than the right to possession so, for example, the creditor is not able to sell the asset to satisfy the debt. Instead, the lien is a tool to persuade the debtor to repay the debt rather than actually providing a remedy should it fail to do so. A legal lien most often arises when a service has been performed but not paid for and can be distinguished from other legal security interests because the asset comes into the creditor's possession for a reason other than to provide security.

Most legal liens arise under common law from general custom. The classic **examples** of common law liens are the "skilled workman's lien" (for example, a mechanic's right to retain possession of a repaired vehicle until he has been paid for the repairs) and a solicitor's right to retain his client's papers until payment. Liens can also arise under statute, in which case the creditor's rights depend on the wording of the statute. For example, a seller of goods has a right to retain possession of them until he has been paid (s 41 Sale of Goods Act 1979).

Equitable lien

4715 By contrast, an equitable lien does not rely on the creditor's possession of the asset. Instead, the lien gives the creditor the right to apply to court to have an asset that is in the possession of the debtor realised and the proceeds paid to him to satisfy the debt. It arises in favour of an **unpaid seller** under the equitable principle that a person who has obtained an asset under a contract that requires payment is not entitled to keep it without payment of the price. For example, a seller of land has an equitable lien over that land until he is paid in full.

2. Pledge

4720 A pledge is the delivery of possession of an asset to a creditor as security for repayment of a debt, although the debtor retains ownership. It is similar to a legal lien in that the creditor retains possession of a debtor's asset until repayment, but the key differences are that:
– the asset is delivered to the creditor with the intention of providing him with security; and
– the creditor has the right to sell the asset if repayment does not occur.

> MEMO POINTS A pledge can **arise under** common law, in which case the right of sale can be exercised upon notice to the debtor. The length of notice will depend upon the circumstances. In order to avoid uncertainty, a **letter of pledge** (sometimes called a memorandum of deposit) is usually agreed between the creditor and debtor. This document sets out the terms on which the pledged item is to be held and in particular when and how the right of sale can be exercised.

4721 Since a pledge requires delivery, only **moveable assets** can be pledged. As well as the usual tangible assets (such as goods in a warehouse), this includes paper assets closely linked with their document of title (such as bearer cheques or securities).

4722 **Delivery** can be actual or constructive (which means that it can be deemed to have occurred by the action taken). For example, delivery of goods in a warehouse could occur by the debtor handing over the keys to the warehouse.

3. Commercial security

4727 "Commercial security" is a loose term used to describe commercial arrangements which, although not strictly security, have the effect of protecting a creditor from default by the debtor. The **common feature** of such arrangements is that the creditor owns the asset rather than the debtor. As a result, the debtor cannot use the asset as security for borrowing and the asset is not available to the debtor's creditors in the event of its insolvency. Some common commercial security arrangements are explained below.

Retention of title

4728 Contracts for the **supply of goods** sometimes contain a "retention of title" clause. This is a clause that specifies that ownership of the supplied goods remains with the supplier until it has been paid in full, even though the buyer has possession of the goods. It is often used when goods are supplied on credit. In order for the right to be of value, the supplier must have the right to enter the buyer's premises to reclaim the goods and the buyer must be obliged to store them separately so the supplier can identify them.

4729 A retention of title provision can be strengthened by the following clauses in the contract:
– an "**all monies clause**" under which the supplier retains title not only until the supplied goods are paid for but until all other monies due to the supplier from the buyer are paid;
– a "**proceeds of sale clause**" under which the supplier is entitled to trace his title into the proceeds of sale if the goods are sold on to a third party; and/or

– a "**mixed goods clause**" under which, if the goods are incorporated into other goods, the supplier is entitled to trace his title into those goods.

Invoice finance

For many companies, their largest asset is their right to be paid for outstanding invoices. Invoice finance is an arrangement which allows a company to get an immediate **cash advance on its invoices** as they are issued. It is a relatively common way for companies that supply goods or services on credit to raise money.

Invoice finance can be arranged through most banks, but there are also companies which specialise in it. The commercial effect is similar to a fixed charge over book debts but invoice finance arrangements do not have to be **registered** at Companies House.

There are two types of invoice finance: debt factoring and invoice discounting.

Debt factoring

Under this arrangement, a company assigns the right to be paid on its invoices to a factoring company. The factor will also be responsible for debt collection and sales ledger administration.

In return, the factor will pay the company 80-90% of each invoice's value, usually within 24 hours of issue. The balance, less charges, is paid when the factor receives payment of the invoice from the end customer.

The main **risk** associated with invoice finance is that the customer will fail to pay. This risk can either be retained by the company (known as recourse factoring) or passed onto the factor (known as non-recourse factoring). In recourse factoring, the factor will expect the company to reimburse the advance on an invoice which not paid. In non-recourse factoring, the factor takes out credit insurance to cover the risk of bad debts. The cost of the insurance is passed onto the company.

There are usually two **charges** for debt factoring:
– a service fee which is calculated as a percentage of the total invoice value, to cover the costs of debt collection, sales ledger administration and, if appropriate, the risk of bad debts; and
– a percentage discount on the cash advance which is similar to the interest rate charged on loans.

Since the factor is responsible for debt collection, the arrangement is **disclosed** to customers who are directed to pay the factor rather than the company.

Invoice discounting

This arrangement is the same as debt factoring, but the company retains responsibility for debt collection and sales ledger administration. It is therefore more **appropriate for** larger companies which can afford the staff and systems to manage these services in-house.

Like debt factoring, there are usually two **charges** for invoice discounting:
– an administration fee which is either a flat fee or a percentage of the total invoice value; and
– a percentage discount on the cash advance which is similar to the interest rate charged on loans.

Since the company is responsible for debt collection, the arrangement is **not disclosed** to customers.

Leasing arrangements

Leasing arrangements provide alternative ways for a company to finance the **acquisition of an asset**. Under such arrangements, the asset is owned by a finance company (the lessor) which leases the asset to the company which actually wishes to use the asset (the lessee). The lessee pays instalments that, over the life of the lease, add up to the cost of the asset plus a return on the capital for the lessor. The commercial effect of the leasing arrangement is similar to a loan secured on the asset in question in that the lessee has possession and use of the asset and has to make regular payments to the lessor.

4734 Under a **finance lease**, the asset is bought from a seller by the lessor instead of the lessee. At the end of the lease, the lessor will sell the asset for its residual value.

4735 A **hire-purchase agreement** is a special type of leasing arrangement which gives the lessee the option to purchase the asset at the end of the lease period. A **conditional sale** agreement is similar, but it contractually commits the buyer to buy the goods from the outset, even though the price is paid in instalments. The advantage of hire purchase is that the buyer of the goods cannot validly pass ownership to a third party before he has paid the total amount due to the seller under the agreement.

4736 A **sale and lease back** is similar to a finance lease but, instead of the lessor buying the asset from the seller, the asset is first bought by the lessee, then sold to the lessor who then leases the asset back to the lessee. The lessee therefore gets a cash lump sum on the sale to the lessor which can be used to pay for the asset if the lessee has just bought it. The lessee continues to be able to use the asset even though it has technically sold it. Sometimes, at the end of the lease term, the lessee can buy the asset back for a nominal amount. This is known as a **sale and repurchase** or a "repo agreement".

4. Security for judgment debts

4739 Where a person (the judgment creditor) obtains a court judgment against another (the judgment debtor) for payment of a sum of money (the judgment debt), he can enforce that judgment by way of a "charging order" or a "third party debt order". Like commercially agreed security interests, both of these orders enable the judgment creditor to appropriate an asset of the judgment debtor in whole or partial satisfaction of the judgment debt.

Charging order

4740 A charging order **imposes a charge** over a specific asset of the judgment debtor in favour of the judgment creditor to secure payment of the judgment debt (s 1 Charging Orders Act 1979).

A "**charging order nisi**" (i.e. an interim charging order) is **made upon** a court application by the judgment creditor without notice to the judgment debtor. The charging order is made "absolute" (i.e. final) at a later hearing when the court hears arguments from both sides. Until the order is made absolute it is liable to be set aside, for example on an application by a liquidator in a compulsory liquidation (*Re Roberts Petroleum Ltd v Bernard Kenny Ltd (in liquidation)* [1983] 1 All ER 564). If the order is made "**absolute**", the order operates and is enforceable as if it were a fixed equitable charge created from the date of the order nisi (s 3 Charging Orders Act 1979). However, a charging order does not have to be **registered** at Companies House (*Re Overseas Aviation Engineering (GB) Ltd* [1962] 3 All ER 12).

Third party debt order

4741 A third party debt order (formerly known as a "garnishee order") enables a judgment creditor to claim money which is due to the judgment debtor from a third party. It is most commonly used to get money deposited at a bank or building society.

As with a charging order, an **interim third party debt order** is made upon a court application by the judgment creditor without notice to the judgment debtor but the **final third party debt order** will not be made until a later hearing. The judgment creditor is able to claim the money only after the final order has been made. The order is void against a liquidator if the money is not paid before the commencement of the winding up.

III. Procedure

1. Capacity

In the past, before the creation of any borrowing or security, the capacity of the borrower to enter into the transaction would first be established. In order **to determine capacity**, it is necessary to examine the memorandum of the borrower and establish that one of the following conditions is satisfied, namely that the borrowing and security are:
– within the objects of the borrower;
– reasonably incidental to the objects of the borrower; or
– within the express powers of the borrower.

If the **borrower did not have capacity**, the transaction could have been void (i.e. "ultra vires"), rendering the lender's security unenforceable.

> MEMO POINTS Under the **new Companies Act**, companies will not have to specify their objects but they will be able to restrict them by provisions in their articles if they wish (see ¶399). Companies with unspecified objects will have unrestricted objects and powers. When the provisions of the new Act dealing with the company's constitution come into force (expected to be by 1 October 2009), any objects set out in an existing company's memorandum will be treated as if they were included in its articles (s 28 CA 2006). It remains to be seen whether lenders will continue to insist on certain objects (such as the power to borrow) being included in the articles before they will lend a company money.

4755

The potential effect of a lack of capacity on innocent **third parties**, such as lenders, has been mitigated by legislation. A lender is protected where the directors have agreed to enter the contract even if there are no relevant powers in the memorandum or articles (ss 35(1), 35A CA 1985). The lender is entitled to assume that the power of the directors to limit the company is unfettered and it is not obliged to consult the memorandum or articles (s 35B CA 1985). It may even be protected where there is no decision by the whole board, provided at least one director made the decision (*Smith v Henniker-Major & Co* [2002] 2 BCLC 655). In short, lenders and other third parties will usually be able to enforce loan agreements and/or security documents that have been created without capacity. However, a vigilant lender would still wish to see the board minutes that authorise the company entering into the loan.

> MEMO POINTS Under the **new Companies Act**, it will not be possible to challenge the validity of a company's act on the ground that it lacked capacity because of a provision in its constitution (s 39 CA 2006, expected to come into force by 1 October 2009).

4756

The **directors** in question could be in breach of their duties to the company if they acted beyond their powers, and therefore liable to the company for any loss (see ¶2434+). A **shareholder** could restrain an act beyond the company's powers if he was aware of it before the contract was signed (s 35A(4) CA 1985; restated at s 40(4) CA 2006 by 1 October 2009).

These provisions do not protect a transaction where the third party is a director or a connected person (s 35A(6) CA 1985; restated at s 41 CA 2006 by 1 October 2009).

4757

2. Power of directors

The borrowing and security must be within the powers of the directors. The creation of borrowing and the granting of security comes within the general management powers conferred on the directors by the articles. For most companies, this power is unrestricted (see reg 70 TA 1985).

> MEMO POINTS 1. Some company's articles contain a **limit on borrowing** (e.g. reg 79 TA 1948) and/or restrictions on guaranteeing the borrowings of third parties. If there are such limits or restrictions, a shareholder resolution to approve the transaction will be required.

4762

2. Draft **new model articles** for private companies limited by shares and public companies under the **new Companies Act** have been published. These give the directors general management powers which may only be restricted by a shareholder resolution (arts 2, 3 in both sets of draft articles). In addition, the new Act itself provides that, in relation to a person who deals with a company in good faith, the director's power to bind the company, or authorise others to do so, is free of any limitations under the company's constitution (s 40(1) CA 2006, expected to come into force by 1 October 2009).

3. Creation of borrowing and security

4767 Once the capacity and power of the borrower has been established, the creation of the borrowing and security is a purely **contractual process** and usually led by the lender. Once the documentation has been finalised, it is usual for a board meeting of the borrower to be held at which the documents are approved and a particular director or directors are given authority to execute them for the company. The advance of money and the taking of security usually occur at the same time but security may already be in place if a lender has advanced money to the company before.

4768 Where **institutional lenders** are involved, a preliminary offer to advance money is followed by a period of investigation by the lender, both into the financial position of the company and its legal capacity to borrow and offer security. In more complex or high value cases, the lender will use external solicitors. The lender (or its solicitor) will also send the borrower (or its solicitor) the loan and security documentation. Often there is little scope for the borrower to negotiate amendments as institutional lenders insist on the use of their standard forms.

The lender will **make the advance** (known as "draw down") once:
– its investigation has been satisfactorily completed;
– the documents have been properly executed; and
– the conditions precedent have been met.

Security over family home

4769 Personal guarantees are sometimes secured by the lender taking a mortgage over the director's own assets, most usually his house. Particular problems can arise when the asset to be mortgaged is a family home because the consent of the director's spouse or other adult family members who live there is required. As with the giving of personal guarantees (¶4698+), the courts have been anxious to **protect vulnerable family members** from giving consent without fully understanding the consequences of their actions. Case law has determined that protection should be given to anyone who places their trust and confidence in relation to financial matters in the director. The most frequent cases involve a husband and wife or co-habitees, but the protection has also been extended to other family members such as elderly parents (*Avon Finance Co Ltd v Bridger* [1985] 2 All ER 281).

4770 A vulnerable person has the right to apply to court to have the **security set aside if** his consent was obtained (*Barclays Bank plc v O'Brien* [1993] 4 All ER 417):
– by the undue influence of the director;
– by misrepresentation on the part of the director; or
– by some other actionable wrong.

This right is **enforceable against the lender if** it had notice of the wrong action. A lender who takes security over a family home knowing that the consent of a vulnerable person (which specifically includes a spouse) has been procured is deemed to have such notice. This is because there is no financial advantage to the person whose consent has been procured and there is a high risk in transactions of this kind that some kind of wrong has been committed (*CIBC Mortgages plc v Pitt* [1993] 4 All ER 433). Therefore, on the face of it, the lender will always run the risk of its security being set aside in the future.

4771 However, the courts have also understood that a law designed to protect the vulnerable must not go so far as to make the family home unacceptable to lenders as security. Case law has determined that a lender will not be deemed to have notice of the wrong action if it has taken steps to inquire about the circumstances in which the consent was given.

The **steps which the lender must take** are to (*Barclays Bank plc v O'Brien* [1993] 4 All ER 417):
– meet the vulnerable person without the director being present;
– warn the person at the meeting of their potential liability and the risks they are running; and
– recommend that the person takes independent legal advice. If the lender is aware of additional circumstances which make it highly likely that the person is not giving their consent freely, the lender should insist that he takes independent legal advice.

Directors should therefore expect any adult who has an interest in the family home, or other property being offered as security, to be interviewed by the bank and be required to take **independent legal advice**. The onus is on the bank to take steps to check directly with the vulnerable person the name of the solicitor he wishes to act for him and the bank must provide the solicitor with the financial information that he needs for the purpose of giving the advice (*Royal Bank of Scotland plc v Etridge (No 2)* [2001] 4 All ER 449).

4772

The advice which solicitors must give has been clearly set out in case law (*Royal Bank of Scotland plc v Etridge (No 2)* [2001] 4 All ER 449) and includes **advice relating to**:
– the nature of the documents and the practical consequences this will have for that person;
– the seriousness of the risks involved;
– the purpose of the facility;
– the amount of the facility; and
– the fact that the amount and terms of the facility may be changed without reference to that person.

4773

Solicitors must meet the relevant person in a **face to face meeting**, without the presence of the person whose obligations are being secured. Solicitors could be acting for both the vulnerable person and the person whose obligations are being secured. However, in advising the vulnerable person the solicitor may have a conflict of interest. If there is a real risk that other interests may inhibit the solicitor's advice to the vulnerable person, he must cease to act.

The lender will require a **certificate** of confirmation from the solicitor that the vulnerable person has been properly advised as a pre-condition to completion of the transaction.

SECTION 2

Private equity finance

Equity finance can be **defined as** money received by a company from investors in exchange for it issuing them with shares. Where the company is unlisted, this is known as "private equity finance".

4800

In Europe, private equity finance is synonymous with "**venture capital**". In the USA, "venture capital" refers only to investment in early stage or expanding companies and "private equity" refers to investment in later stage companies, or to fund a management buy-out or buy-in (see ¶6040+).

General share issues are discussed at ¶889+. This section discusses share issues to investors previously unconnected with the issuing company for the sole or main purpose of raising finance.

Private equity finance is subject to two important regulatory regimes:
– the **financial promotions** regime (¶4825+); and
– the **prospectus** regime (¶4845+).

A. Overview

4805 Private equity finance is still relatively uncommon when compared to debt finance. However, this type of investment is currently extremely popular and unlisted companies are finding themselves increasingly exposed to private equity investors.

Private equity covers a broad range of investments, including:
– investment in start-up and entrepreneurial companies, commonly referred to as venture capital;
– investment in existing companies being bought out by management, commonly referred to as management buy-outs; and
– high value acquisitions involving a large element of debt, commonly referred to as leveraged buy-outs. These often involve the delisting of quoted companies, known as public to private deals.

It is this last category that attracts attention and bad press because these deals often involve large high-profile companies. In 2007, private equity hit the headlines because it was the subject of a parliamentary enquiry by the Treasury Select Committee. Three main criticisms were levelled at this type of investment:
– it is perceived as enjoying unfair tax advantages;
– it has a destabilising effect on the country's economy; and
– the lack of transparency in these sort of deals.

However, it is generally recognised that investment in start-ups and entrepreneurial companies, and management buy-outs (discussed at ¶6040+) makes a positive contribution to business. This type of private equity is more common and more likely to affect small and medium-sized companies, and so is focused on here.

MEMO POINTS Detailed information about obtaining private equity finance can be obtained from the **British Private Equity and Venture Capital Association**.

1. Suitability of company

4807 Private equity finance is not suitable for all types of company. In general, it is more suitable for **entrepreneurial** companies, as opposed to companies which are run to maintain the director/shareholders' standard of living or a family business which will be passed onto the next generation.

This is because a private equity investor will expect to be able to realise its investment in the medium term. So, a company will usually only be able to find investment if it is potentially **high-growth** (meaning that it will increase in value relatively quickly, usually within about 5 years). As a result, private equity investment is traditionally attracted to certain high-growth sectors, such as telecoms, media and technology.

In addition, the investor will expect an **exit strategy** to be in place, typically, either a sale of the company or flotation on a public market. Private equity finance is therefore usually only appropriate when a company intends to develop in this way.

2. Private equity investors

4809 Private equity investors can broadly be divided into **four categories**:
– business angel;
– venture capitalist;
– corporate venturer; and
  private equity firm.

Business angel

A business angel is a **high net worth individual** who invests in start-up or early stage companies. Business angels usually organise themselves into networks to find appropriate investment opportunities. They may invest individually or as part of a group (known as a "syndicate"). Individual business angels usually **invest between** £10,000 and £750,000 but higher levels of investment could be available through a syndicate. In addition to their money, many business angels also make their own skills and contacts available to the company. Further information can be obtained from the **British Business Angels Association**.

4810

Venture capitalist

A venture capitalist is a **company** which specialises in investing its own money into unlisted companies. They are usually known by their acronym, VC. Similar to business angels, venture capitalists often actively participate in the companies in which they invest and will usually require board representation in return for introducing new partners, suppliers and customers to the company. Venture capitalists usually have a higher **minimum level of investment** compared to business angels, typically around £750,000.

4811

Private equity firms

A private equity firm is one which specialises in investing in unlisted companies. In contrast to venture capitalists, they obtain money for investment from external sources, normally institutional investors such as pension funds and insurance companies.

4812

These external **sources of funds** may be structured in different ways, which could limit the type of company in which the private equity firm may invest. Many private equity funds are structured as limited partnerships for a fixed term of 10 years. The fund will be invested for the period of the fixed term and, at the end, the original investors will have to be repaid their investment plus any additional returns.

Funds may also be structured as quoted **Venture and Development Capital Investment Trusts** (VDCITs) or **Venture Capital Trusts** (VCTs). VCTs are a government initiative designed to make private equity investment more attractive to private investors by giving them tax incentives. There are restrictions on the types of company in which a VCT may invest (see *Tax Memo* for further details).

Corporate venturers

A corporate venturer is a large company which invests in smaller companies **within the same sector**. The larger company is able to provide the smaller company with access to developed marketing and distribution channels, as well as its technical skills and expertise. In return, as well as a return on its financial investment, the large company will gain access to new technology and research and development in areas related to its operations. Indeed corporate venturers often expect to enter into exclusive licensing or distribution agreements with the smaller company.

4813

Corporate venturing is encouraged by the government by way of the **Corporate Venturing Scheme** (CVS) which gives the corporate venturer various tax incentives. Further information on CVSs can be found in *Tax Memo*.

3. Procedure

A company can seek private equity finance **directly** from potential investors. However, because of the financial promotions regime (see below) it normally **engages an agent** to act as an intermediary. There are many corporate finance firms which specialise in finding private equity finance.

4816

If the company is seeking finance from a **range of investors**, firstly, it or its agent will have to prepare a "private placing memorandum" or "**information memorandum**" which will set

4817

out detailed information about the issuer and the shares on offer. The information will be similar to that found in a prospectus and will include:
- a summary;
- a description of the issuing company's business;
- an explanation of its current financial position;
- details of its financing plans;
- details of the share structure and shares being offered;
- taxation implications;
- any pre-conditions (e.g. shareholder approvals); and
- the subscription and acceptance procedure.

4818 Where the shares are being placed with a **single investor** (e.g. a venture capitalist), the issuing company and investor will normally negotiate directly with each other. A single investor will normally expect board representation and may even specify the rights which should attach to the shares being issued. The terms agreed between the issuing company and investor will normally be set out in a "**subscription agreement**".

> MEMO POINTS **Other documents** which may be necessary are:
> - new articles to reflect the new share structure and class rights of the new shares;
> - new directors' service agreements (¶2627+); and/or
> - a shareholders' agreement (¶2086+).

4819 Following the initial contact between the company/agent and the investors, there will be a period of **investigation** by the investors. If the investors decide to take up the shares being offered, the intermediary will normally send them a simple application form and close the offer period. As with a usual share issue, the investors will be required to pay for the shares for which they have agreed to subscribe and they will be issued with share certificates.

B. Financial promotions

4825 A person must not, in the course of business, make a financial promotion (that is, communicate an invitation or inducement to engage in investment activity) unless (s 21 FSMA 2000):
- he is an authorised person; or
- the content of the communication is approved by an authorised person.

"**Investment activity**" covers a broad range of activities including the acquisition and disposal of shares (Sch 1 SI 2005/1529). Therefore, all share issues and offers are potentially subject to the financial promotions regime.

> MEMO POINTS 1. The communication must be made "**in the course of business**". However, it is not necessary for the person to be engaged in financial services business.
> 2. The communication can be made in any **form** (e.g. written document, advertisement, unsolicited or solicited telephone call, online etc).
> 3. Where the communication originates from **outside the UK**, the financial promotions regime only applies if the communication is capable of having an effect in the UK (s 21(3) FSMA 2000). Where the communication originates in the UK, the regime does not apply to communications made to, and directed only at, persons outside the UK (reg 12 SI 2005/1529). If the communication is in the form of a prospectus that has been approved by the proper authority in **another EEA state** and "passported" out to the UK (see ¶4875+), it will not breach the restrictions on financial promotions (SI 2005/1529 as amended by SI 2007/2615).

Exemptions

4827 There are many exemptions from the financial promotion regime, principally (SI 2005/1529):
- communications by a company to its **own shareholders** or creditors (reg 43);
- **intra-group** communications (reg 45);

– communications between connected individuals in connection with a **sale of a controlling interest in a company** (reg 62);
– communications in connection with **takeovers of unlisted companies** (provided the target's shares have not been listed at any time in the previous 10 years) (regs 63-66);
– communications made between **participants in a joint enterprise** in connection with or for the purpose of that joint enterprise (reg 39);
– communications made and directed only at **investment professionals** (reg 19); and
– communications to certified **high net worth individuals** or **sophisticated investors** (regs 48, 50).

Approval

If no exception applies, the communication must be made or approved by a **person authorised by the FSA**. In practice, this means that the offer document will either need to be:
– issued by an authorised firm (e.g. corporate finance advisers) on behalf of its client company; or
– issued by the company, provided the offer document states that it has been approved by an authorised firm.

In order to obtain authorisation, a person or firm must apply to the FSA. If their application is accepted, they are bound by the FSA's Conduct of Business Rules.

4829

Breach

A person who makes an unauthorised financial promotion is guilty of a **criminal offence** subject to a maximum penalty of 2 years' imprisonment and an unlimited fine (s 25 FSMA 2000).

The criminal offence can be defended on the basis that the person:
– believed on reasonable grounds that the content of the communication was prepared or approved by an authorised person; or
– took all reasonable precautions and exercised all due diligence to avoid committing the offence.

4831

In addition, any agreement entered into on the basis of the unauthorised financial promotion will be **unenforceable** (s 30 FSMA 2000). The person who entered into the agreement is entitled to be reimbursed for any money or assets transferred by him under the agreement, and to damages for any loss incurred by him in the transfer.

4832

Finally, a company which makes unauthorised financial promotions could be **wound up** by the court on the grounds of public interest (see ¶7626+) (*Re UK-Euro Group plc* [2006] EWHC 2102 (Ch)).

4833

C. Prospectuses

In certain circumstances, an offer to issue shares must be made by a prospectus which has been **approved by** the UK Listing Authority (part of the FSA). This is a detailed document setting out information about the company and the offer so that investors can make an informed decision as to whether or not to accept the issue.

4845

The circumstances in which a prospectus is required and the contents of that document are set out in the **Prospectus Rules**. These are published by the UKLA and are available to download from the FSA's website.

> *MEMO POINTS* The Prospectus Rules **came into force on** 1 July 2005 and, together with the Prospectus Regulations 2005 (SI 2005/1433), implement the EU Prospectus Directive (EC Directive 2003/71) and the EU Prospectus Regulation (EC Regulation 809/2004). They replace the Public Offers of Securities Regulations 1995 (SI 1995/1537).

The Committee of European Securities Regulators (CESR) has published answers to frequently asked questions on the Prospectus Directive, which can be found on its website *www.cesr-eu.org*.

Scope

4850 The Prospectus Rules apply to **public offers of transferable securities** (including shares) by listed and unlisted companies. A public offer is widely defined as a communication to persons "in any form, and by any means".

Exemptions

4855 The main exemptions from the requirement to publish a prospectus are (s 85 FSMA 2000, rr 1.2.2, 1.2.3 Prospectus Rules):
– private placements to **less than 100 persons** in each EU member state;
– **bonus issues**;
– **stock dividends**;
– **employee shares** (if the employer's securities are already listed);
– **takeovers and mergers** (see ¶6675+);
– offers to **qualified investors** (including small and medium-sized enterprises who can "self-certify" that they satisfy the qualifying criteria); and
– where the offer requires a person accepting it to pay a **minimum consideration** of €50,000.

Contents

4860 The prospectus must be in a form which is comprehensible and easy to analyse, and must set out the **information necessary** to enable investors to make an informed assessment of (s 87A FSMA 2000):
– the assets and liabilities, financial position, profits and losses, and prospects of the issuer (and any guarantor); and
– the rights attaching to the transferable securities.

4862 Prospectuses can take one of two **formats**:
a. a **single** document containing all the required information divided into the following parts:
– a table of contents;
– a summary which briefly and in non-technical language conveys the essential characteristics of, and risks associated with, the issuer, any guarantor and the securities; and
– specified information appropriate for the issue as set out in the Prospectus Rules; or
b. a **three-part** document comprising:
– a registration document (which is valid for securities' issues in the next 12 months);
– a securities note which sets out information relating to the securities being issued; and
– a summary setting out information about the issuer and the risks involved.

> MEMO POINTS The directors of the issuer are only **responsible** for prospectuses for equity shares, warrants or options to subscribe for its equity shares and certain other transferable securities (r 5.5 Prospectus Rules).

4864 If, before the offer closes, a significant new factor, material mistake or inaccuracy arises relating to the information included in the prospectus, a **supplementary prospectus** containing details of the new factor, mistake or inaccuracy must be submitted to the UKLA for its approval (s 87G FSMA 2000).

4865 The UKLA has published a factsheet with **guidance for unlisted companies** on the drafting and approval of prospectuses under the Prospectus Directive (UKLA Factsheet No. 3 (April 2006)). It covers:
– how a prospectus should be submitted for approval;
– the format of the prospectus;
– what historical financial information is required; and
– the contents of the prospectus.
A copy can be downloaded from the FSA's website.

MEMO POINTS The ICAEW has published **guidance for accountants** who prepare reports for inclusion in or in connection with prospectuses and for auditors whose audit report on the company's accounts is to be included, or referred to, in a prospectus (AAF TECH 02/06). The guidance can be downloaded from the ICAEW's website.

Withdrawal rights

4870

A person who has accepted an offer set out in a prospectus may withdraw his acceptance if the prospectus does not set out the final offer price or amount of securities to be offered to the public (and does not set out the criteria or conditions by which those figures will be determined). The right to withdraw subsists for up to 2 days after the relevant information has been provided to the UKLA. Any person who has accepted the offer may also withdraw his acceptance up to 2 days after publication of a supplementary prospectus (s 87Q FSMA 2000).

Passport rights

4875

A prospectus approved by the UKLA benefits from a "European passport". This means that it may be used for public offers in all other EU countries, subject to notification to the relevant authority in the other country and translation into the local language if this is required by that authority.

Guidance on the UKLA's passporting in and passporting out procedure is available in UKLA Factsheet No. 4 (October 2006) which can be downloaded from the FSA's website. Further information can also be obtained from the UKLA's helpdesk on 020 7066 8333.

4876

In order to **passport out** a prospectus approved by the UKLA, the issuer should submit a written request for a "certificate of approval" by **email** to *LTAdmin@fsa.gov.uk*. Attached to the email should be:

a. a **request letter** from the issuer setting out the name and date of the document to be passported, the jurisdiction to which the passport should be sent, contact details for the person with whom the UKLA should correspond and confirmation that "no significant new factor, material mistake or inaccuracy has arisen" since the date the prospectus was approved if it is not passported on the day of approval;
b. the **prospectus or supplement** to be passported. Note that a registration document or a securities note cannot be passported on its own. Similarly, a supplementary prospectus can only be passported if the original prospectus has previously be passported out;
c. translations of the summary. This is required for all equity prospectuses or retail debt prospectuses, except ones being passported to Luxembourg, Austria or the Netherlands. These jurisdictions accept prospectuses in English; and
d. documents incorporated by reference for prospectuses passported to Germany only.

4877

In order to **passport in** a prospectus approved by a member state other than the UK, the issuer should contact the home competent authority which approved the prospectus and follow their procedures. The home competent authority will email the UKLA attaching the approved prospectus and a certificate of approval. The UKLA will provide a confirmation of receipt within 24 hours. A list of all documents passported into the UK can be viewed on the UKLA's website at *www.fsa.gov.uk/Pages/Doing/UKLA/index.shtml*.

CHAPTER 13

Buying and selling a company

OUTLINE

Introduction		5200
Overview		5202

SECTION 1 Preparation 5207

A	The seller	5212
1	Preparing the target	5212
2	Marketing	5219
	a Introduction by an intermediary	5225
	Information memorandum	5227
	Data room	5229
	b Auction	5235
3	Confidentiality	5244
	Confidentiality agreement	5245
	Control of information	5247
B	The buyer	5258
	Identifying potential targets	5261
	Evaluating potential targets	5262
	Approaching the potential target	5264

SECTION 2 Deal structure 5280

I	Asset or share sale	5280
	What is a share sale?	5281
	What is an asset sale?	5282
	Choosing between shares and assets	5283
A	Taxation of asset sales	5290
1	Seller	5291
	Corporation tax	5291
	Passing sale proceeds to shareholders	5292
2	Buyer	5297
	Stamp duty land tax	5298
3	Apportionment	5314
4	VAT	5321
B	Taxation of share sales	5335
1	Individual seller	5338
	a Capital gains tax	5343
	b Deferral of capital gains tax	5354
2	Corporate seller	5361

	Substantial shareholding exemption	5362
3	Tax clearances	5367
4	Buyer	5378
C	Comparison of other factors	5390
1	Transaction process	5392
2	Post-completion liabilities	5395
II	Price	5410
A	Valuation of target	5415
B	Form of consideration	5426
1	Shares in the buyer	5427
2	Loan notes	5437
C	Payment structure	5460
1	Deferred consideration	5463
	a Earn-outs	5465
	b Security for payment	5468
	c Tax consequences	5472
2	Net asset value adjustment	5480
3	Retention	5489
III	Competition law implications	5505
A	UK merger control	5507
B	EU merger control	5520
IV	Heads of agreement	5529
A	Non-contractual provisions	5532
B	Contractual provisions	5535
C	Format	5540

SECTION 3 Financing the purchase 5550

	Financial assistance in share acquisitions	5557
1	General prohibition	5565
	What constitutes financial assistance?	5569
	Purpose of assistance	5575
	Exceptions to the prohibition	5579
2	Whitewash procedure	5586
	a Pre-conditions	5593
	Type of company	5594

Net asset requirement	5595
b Directors' statutory declaration	5600
c Auditor's report	5609
d Shareholders' approval	5613
e Companies House filing	5620
f Timing of assistance	5622
g Summary timeline	5625
3 Breach	5630
Consequences for transaction	5631
Consequences for company and its officers	5634
Consequences for other parties	5638

SECTION 4 Investigation of target 5652

A Questioning the seller	5656
1 Guidance for managing process	5659
2 Typical questions	5669
B Searches of public registers	5695
Property searches	5696
Intellectual property searches	5703
Insolvency searches	5704
C Surveys and inspections of property	5708

SECTION 5 Negotiation of documents 5720

I Share sale and purchase agreement	5725
Clauses and schedules	5725
1 Parties	5728
2 Recitals	5729
3 Interpretation	5730
4 Agreement to buy and sell	5731
5 Conditions	5732
6 Post-completion restrictions on seller	5735
7 Boiler plate clauses	5740
8 Signature	5741
II Asset sale and purchase agreement	5750
Clauses and schedules	5750
1 Agreement to buy and sell	5751
2 Stock	5756
3 Contracts	5758
4 Properties	5764
5 Debtors, creditors and liabilities	5766
6 Employees	5771
7 VAT	5787
III Allocation of risk	5800

A Protection for buyer	5807
1 Overview of warranties and indemnities	5809
What is a warranty?	5809
What is an indemnity?	5812
What risks do they cover?	5814
When are they both used?	5817
2 Who is liable?	5822
3 Remedies	5826
a Damages	5827
b Rescission	5838
4 Effect of seller's knowledge	5845
5 Effect of buyer's knowledge	5847
6 Joint and several liability	5852
7 Security for claims	5858
8 Date of application	5864
9 Defined terms	5871
B Protection for seller	5890
1 Disclosure letter	5892
a General disclosures	5895
b Specific disclosures	5907
c Disclosure bundle	5913
2 Seller limitation provisions	5918
Claim period	5920
Maximum claim value	5922
Minimum claim value	5923
Double recovery	5924
3 Buyer's warranties	5929
IV Other documents	5945
A Share sales	5945
1 Tax deed	5945
2 Employment documents	5963
3 Deed of contribution	5975
B Asset sales	5985
Deed of assignment	5988

SECTION 6 Exchange and completion 6005

1 Document list	6012
2 Post-completion	6020

SECTION 7 Management buy-out 6040

Investigation of target and warranties	6042
Financing	6043
Management team	6048

Introduction

5200

The buying and selling of companies is commonplace. Frequently, a sale happens as a result of **strategic planning** by the shareholders so that they can realise the value of their shares at the optimum price. However, a sale or purchase may also arise as a result of a company's desire to:
– diversify;
– expand; or
– concentrate on its key operations.

This chapter looks at sales and purchases **by private contract** which effectively result in a change in ownership of the company or its business. The sale and purchase can be structured as a share sale or an asset sale. The company whose shares or assets are being sold is referred to as the "**target**".

Where a purchase of shares is proposed and the target has many shareholders, the purchase is normally carried out by way of a **takeover** offer. Further, where the target is a **public company**, or a private company whose shares have been subject to public dealing or which has issued a prospectus in the previous 10 years, the transaction will be subject to regulation by the Panel on Takeover and Mergers. Takeovers and acquisitions of such companies are dealt with in detail at ¶6675+.

In most cases, the seller and buyer will be unconnected, and that is the assumption here. Sometimes, the buyer will already be involved in the management of the business. **Management buy-outs**, as this type of purchase is called, are dealt with at ¶6040+. **Group reorganisations** are dealt with separately at ¶6405+.

Overview

5202

The key to obtaining the optimum result in any sale or purchase is **preparation** (¶5207+), even before the seller has identified a buyer or the buyer has identified a target. The next step is, of course, finding the right buyer or target, as appropriate. Even at this early stage, the parties, particularly the seller, should be thinking about how to maintain **confidentiality** (¶5244+). An information leak could be disastrous for the target's business and could threaten negotiations. In order to maintain confidentiality, the deal would usually be given a code name, e.g. Project Nicholas.

Once the protagonists (seller, buyer and target) have been identified, the **structure of the deal** will have to be agreed. A sale and purchase can be carried out in one of two ways (¶5280+):
– **share based**, involving the sale and purchase of the shares of the company which carries on the business; or
– **asset based**, involving the sale and purchase of the goodwill and assets used in connection with the business.

Most importantly, the parties will have to agree on a **price**, the form of payment and the payment structure (¶5410+). Larger transactions may have **competition law** implications (¶5505+). Once these matters have been agreed in principle, they are often put into writing, in a document known as the "**heads of agreement**" (¶5529+).

Parallel to initial negotiations with the seller, the buyer will need to consider how it proposes to **finance the purchase** (¶5550+). If the transaction is share based, both parties will need to consider whether the target could be giving **financial assistance for the share acquisition** (¶5557+). Such financial assistance is unlawful unless one of the exceptions applies. The **new Companies Act** will remove this restriction for private companies (at the time of writing, the implementation date for this change is yet to be announced).

The transaction will then begin in earnest. The first stage is for the buyer to **investigate the target** (¶5652). This process is known as "due diligence". The depth of the investigation will depend upon:
– the level of the buyer's existing knowledge of the business;
– the value of the deal; and
– the complexity of the target's business operations.

Once most of the investigation has been completed, the parties will proceed to **negotiation**. The main contract between the parties is the **sale and purchase agreement** (¶5720+), the format of which is slightly different depending upon whether the deal is a share or asset sale. The bulk of both types of sale and purchase agreement is taken up with warranties which **allocate risk** between the buyer and the seller (¶5800+).

Lower value and/or simple transactions tend to have shorter, less detailed documentation in order to limit expenditure on professional fees. High value and/or complex transactions will have a substantial number of additional documents, which will vary according to the type of acquisition/disposal.

Once the documents are in an agreed form, the contracts will need to be exchanged and completion of the sale and purchase will have to take place (¶6005+). **Exchange** is shorthand for the process by which contracts are signed and exchanged (so that each party is holding an original signed by the other). This is the time when the contract becomes binding on the parties. **Completion** is the date when the actual sale and purchase takes place. A further date, known as the "effective date", may be involved. This is the date upon which the transfer of the business becomes effective. It is more usual to find this in asset sales.

Although a **gap** between exchange and completion is common in property transactions, in corporate transactions a **simultaneous** exchange and completion is usually preferable. However, a gap is sometimes contemplated when the parties are anxious to procure a binding commitment (for example, so that an announcement can be made to the financial press) but certain matters are still outstanding (such as tax clearances or third party consents).

Exchange and completion usually occur at a face-to-face **completion meeting** between the seller, buyer and their legal advisers. Where the acquisition is being financed by a bank, the bank's representatives and their legal advisers may also be present.

There are various practical, administrative and contractual matters which must be dealt with **post-completion** (¶6020+).

SECTION 1

Preparation

5207 Preparation is vital in order to obtain the maximum benefit from a sale or purchase. The seller should begin preparing for a sale even before a buyer has been found. Similarly, a buyer should begin preparation before a target has been found. A smooth transaction will have real **benefits** for both seller and buyer because it will minimise:
– professional fees;
– time spent on the transaction, so that the business is disrupted as little as possible; and
– friction between the seller and buyer, especially if a post-completion relationship is envisaged.

A. The seller

1. Preparing the target

5212 The main task of a seller will be to arrange the target's affairs so that it is ready for sale. At a minimum, this will involve some "housekeeping". Sometimes, a pre-sale reorganisation may be required (see ¶6405+).

5213 **Good housekeeping** makes a target more attractive to a buyer because:
- the legal and financial risks of the business are lowered; and
- the buyer will find it easier to carry on the business after the sale.

In addition, the seller will find that good preparation will have an **impact upon the price**. A buyer will seek to obtain the target for the best possible price, and in doing so will look for matters that could potentially affect its value. If the target's business is poorly organised (for example, if paperwork cannot be found), the buyer will not be able to verify key issues and therefore may not be prepared to pay as much as the seller may think the target is worth.

5214 The seller should therefore ensure that the business is properly organised and on a sound legal footing before marketing it for sale. In particular, it should make sure that:
- **business records** (particularly financial records and company registers) are properly maintained from incorporation;
- **insurance** policies are continuous and easily evidenced in writing;
- **terms and conditions of service/sale** appropriate to the nature of the business are professionally drafted and updated, and a record of all terms and conditions used by the business are kept in an easily accessible manner;
- the business' **major contracts** with customers and suppliers are evidenced in writing, and full signed and dated copies are kept in an easily accessible manner;
- any **intellectual property** owned or used by the business is evidenced in writing, particularly where it is its primary asset, and the business is able to demonstrate that it has been proactive in protecting its intellectual property;
- details of any **real estate** owned or occupied by the business are kept up to date and any disputes affecting the property have been rectified. These records should also demonstrate that the seller has complied with all statutory obligations (e.g. planning permission);
- **computer system and data** records (including details of copyright and licences) are maintained; and
- **employee** records (including employment contracts and handbooks) are maintained. It should be possible to demonstrate a clear and consistent method for dealing with staff.

2. Marketing

5219 Finding a buyer can be difficult, especially for private companies, which are not permitted to offer their shares to the public. A seller and buyer may be **known to each** other through trade connections. For example, the target and the buyer may be competitors or one may be a major supplier or customer of the other. Otherwise, the two main methods of finding suitable buyers are:
- **introduction by an intermediary**; or
- through an **auction**.

The marketing of companies, even through intermediaries, is usually quite informal. However, if economic conditions are right, and the extra costs involved warrant it, some companies can benefit from being auctioned. The marketing of a company through an auction is a more structured process and far less common.

5220 In a share sale, the marketers and sellers of a company should be careful to avoid making an unauthorised **financial promotion** (see ¶4825+). This increased cost of regulatory compliance is one potential disadvantage of share sales.

a. Introduction by an intermediary

5225 Sellers often use intermediaries to find or make contact with potential buyers. The intermediary may be:
- a **professional adviser** (e.g. an accountant) who has contacts in the target's business field and who will expect to be retained as an adviser on the deal; or
- an **agent** who specialises in buying and selling companies. The agent's fee will typically be a percentage of the price, payable on completion of the sale.

5226 The use of an intermediary may assist the seller in maintaining confidentiality, as it will not have to make direct contact with potential buyers. Thus, a seller may use an intermediary to make the **initial approach** to a buyer which the seller already has in mind. The intermediary's initial approach will usually be on a no-names basis (meaning that the intermediary will not reveal the name of the seller), with only basic details of the target being revealed.

If the potential buyer expresses an interest, the intermediary will usually procure that it signs a **confidentiality agreement** (see ¶5245). Usually the buyer's advisers will send a written **information request** to the seller. This lists the information which the buyer's advisers wish to see in order to take the first steps in evaluating the value and liabilities of the target. The seller's advisers usually respond by sending a bundle of documents and other information. This process is discussed at ¶5656+. However, in some deals, such as where there are several potential **buyers in competition** with each other, a more formal process involving an information memorandum and data room will be set up in addition to the usual questions and answers.

Information memorandum

5227 In order to market the company, the professional or agent will sometimes prepare an "information memorandum". This is effectively a sales brochure setting out information which will enable a potential buyer to evaluate the target and decide whether or not to make an offer to purchase it. The information memorandum usually contains:
– a **description** of the target's business, its current operations, location, markets, products and history;
– an explanation of the **purpose** of the sale and the preferred **structure**;
– figures relating to past and current **financial performance**, and trading and profit projections;
– a breakdown of major **customers** and **suppliers**;
– information on the business' trading premises and other **property holdings**; and
– information on the **management** and **employee** structure.

5228 The **accuracy** of the information is clearly important. Any inaccuracies should be kept to a minimum so that the seller is not disadvantaged during the sale process. If the information is **inaccurate**:
– professional fees will increase because a buyer will be particularly careful in verifying information through the due diligence process;
– the seller's management costs will increase as it will have to provide the same information again and clarify any inaccuracies in the information already given to the buyer;
– the buyer will have an excuse to re-open negotiations on price and the deal structure;
– a buyer who has relied upon inaccurate representations and suffers loss may be able to claim damages for misrepresentation (see ¶5830); and
– the seller may be in breach of financial promotion regulations leading to criminal sanctions (see ¶4831+).

> MEMO POINTS It should be remembered that the seller may be required to **warrant the accuracy** of the information in the sale and purchase agreement (¶5815). Although normally resisted during negotiations, if this warranty is accepted, the information will have to be verified and appropriate disclosures made in respect of any inaccuracies.

Data room

5229 A data room is a room at the seller's solicitor's or accountant's office where **more detailed information and documents** regarding the target are kept for inspection by potential buyers.

The **benefit** for the buyer is that it is better able to assess the target, spot potential liabilities and therefore make a realistic offer. The benefit for the seller is that the selected buyer's investigation of the target could be limited to an inspection of the data room documents. The seller will also benefit from a smoother transaction as there are unlikely to be any surprises during negotiations.

> MEMO POINTS For the effect of a data room on the **warranties** in the sale and purchase agreement, see ¶5847+.

5230 In order to maintain confidentiality, the use of a data room is usually controlled through **data room rules** to which the buyer must agree beforehand. For example, it is usual for:
– photocopying and dictation to be limited;
– access to be limited to the buyer and a certain number of its (usually named) representatives and/or professional advisers;
– the room to be open for a specified limited period (to maintain confidentiality between different potential buyers); and/or
– limits to be placed on the number of times a person may enter and leave the room.

Some of the more unnecessarily restrictive rules are usually disregarded in practice.

b. Auction

5235 In the **rare circumstance** of a target with numerous potential buyers and no particular business issues, a sale by auction may be appropriate to achieve the highest possible price.

Process

5236 The auction is normally structured so that buyers are **filtered** out at each stage of the bid process. The successful buyer at the end of the process will be the one prepared to pay the highest price and purchase on the best possible terms the seller can achieve.

5237 The **first stage** of the process is for the bidders (i.e. the potential buyers) to be given information and draft contractual documents, after signing a confidentiality agreement. The bidders will be given a limited amount of time to consider the information and respond, indicating whether they are still interested in acquiring the business. They will usually be asked to provide an indicative price for the business and frequently will be asked to mark up the first draft of the sale and purchase agreement. This enables the seller, not only to evaluate the price which it is likely to receive for the business but, also to consider the potential risks that are associated with any bid.

5238 The seller will then select bidders to move to the **next stage** of the auction. At this stage, the bidders will be given access to the data room, perhaps meet the target's management, and see the seller's response to their contractual amendments. Bidders will be required to submit their final offers by a specified deadline.

5239 Once the date for submission of final offers has elapsed, the seller will consider the offers made to it and decide which one to **accept**. After this time, the negotiation process will be the same as if there had always been just one buyer, except that the buyer is likely to have less bargaining power as the seller will usually have other interested parties should negotiations with the preferred bidder break down.

3. Confidentiality

5244 Confidentiality is extremely important throughout a transaction. **Confidential information** relevant to a company sale and purchase can broadly be split into the following categories:
– the fact that the target is for sale;
– information about the target's business (e.g. its customer list, accounting information, details of key employees, etc);
– details of the negotiations; and
– the terms of the final contract.

A **leak** of confidential information can be costly in business terms because it can:
– give competitors an advantage;
– cause uncertainty for suppliers, customers, creditors and/or employees of the target who may make moves to protect their position to the detriment of the target business; and/or
– lead to a weakened negotiation position.

In order to **protect** confidential information from disclosure, the buyer will normally be required to sign a confidentiality agreement and the seller must take steps to control the flow of information. Confidentiality is also aided by using a code name for the deal, to minimise the risk of the target's identity being inadvertently revealed.

Confidentiality agreement

5245 Confidential information is protected from disclosure under **common law** but such a claim is difficult to prove and the available remedies may not be effective. As a result, sellers usually prefer to rely upon a **contractual** confidentiality obligation. Thus potential buyers should be required to sign a confidentiality agreement (also known as a non-disclosure agreement) before any information is released to them (perhaps even including the seller's identity).

5246 A confidentiality agreement will normally contain the following **provisions**:
a. a **description** of the proposed transaction;
b. a wide **definition** of "confidential information";
c. **undertakings** by the buyer:
– to keep the confidential information secure and private;
– only to use confidential information for the purposes of evaluating the proposed transaction;
– not to disclose confidential information other than to specified individuals (usually professional advisers and particular representatives of the buyer) who have been notified of the confidential nature of the information and who have also agreed to keep that information confidential;
– not to make copies of the confidential information;
– not to announce or disclose the existence of negotiations or the terms of the proposed transaction without the seller's consent; and
– to return confidential information on demand;
d. **restrictive covenants** preventing the buyer from soliciting the target's customers, suppliers or employees;
e. the right of the seller to bring **injunctive proceedings** against the buyer for breach of the agreement; and
f. specifying to whom and how **requests for confidential information** should be made.

In order to make the agreement **legally binding**, a benefit and a burden need to be included. This could be the buyer being given access to the information and the seller allowing it. Alternatively, it the buyer could pay a nominal sum to the seller, e.g. £1, or the agreement could be signed in the form of a deed.

If the **buyer is part of a group**, either all the group companies should sign the agreement or the parent company should sign. The agreement should state that it will procure that its subsidiaries comply with the undertakings in the agreement.

Control of information

5247 Although a confidentiality agreement can help to focus the buyer's mind and provide an avenue for redress should a breach of confidentiality occur, in reality it is often expensive to enforce and, if breached, the damage has probably already been done. The control of information to **prevent a breach** of confidentiality is therefore usually a more effective tool.

5248 Controlling information is a practical business. **Steps** which a seller can take include:
– ensuring that a record is kept of what information has been disclosed, to whom and when;
– sending documents out with a covering letter marked "private and confidential" so that it is only opened by the intended recipient; and
– asking for written acknowledgement of receipt.

> MEMO POINTS A seller may wish to **restrict disclosure** of confidential business information until after exchange of contracts, but a buyer is extremely unlikely to make a contractual commitment to the purchase without full disclosure having been made. For this reason, particularly sensitive business information (for example, the detail of intellectual property rights) is sometimes disclosed later in negotiations, when a level of trust has built between the parties and there is greater certainty that the deal is going to proceed to completion.

B. The buyer

The first step for the buyer is to determine the **purpose of the acquisition**. A buyer may be looking for an acquisition for a number of reasons, for example, to:
– increase market share;
– enter new markets;
– take over a rival;
– increase profitability;
– acquire new products or technology;
– invest in a sound business; or
– secure a supply chain or distribution network.

5258

Once the purpose of the acquisition has been established, the buyer should prepare a list of **business criteria** that the target needs to fulfil in order to achieve that purpose, such as those relating to its:
– market;
– geographical area;
– product range;
– management team; and
– financial performance.

5259

The buyer will also have to decide how much it can afford to pay and be realistic about the targets that can be found within that budget. **Finance options** are discussed more fully at ¶5550+.

There are three aspects to **finding a suitable acquisition target**:
– identifying potential targets;
– evaluating them against the buyer's business criteria; and
– approaching a target.

5260

Identifying potential targets

Potential targets can be identified through the **buyer's own knowledge** of the industry and market. Alternatively, a buyer could use an **intermediary** such as a business broker or accountancy firm. An intermediary may have a suitable company for sale on its books or it can act as a finder and "sound out" potential sellers. The internet is becoming an increasingly common way to find an acquisition target (for example, see *www.companiesforsale.uk.com* or *www.businessesforsale.com*).

5261

Evaluating potential targets

Once potential targets have been identified, they should be evaluated against the buyer's business criteria. In order to make this evaluation, the buyer will need to **gather information** about the target. It is possible to do this by way of a company or business search without approaching the seller directly.

5262

A **company search** (see ¶4090+) will reveal information registered at Companies House including:
– the target's statutory accounts (profit and loss account and balance sheet);
– the target's share structure, the rights attaching to those shares and any restrictions on transfer (which can be found in the target's articles);
– details of the target's directors; and
– details of any security granted over the target's assets.

Wider business information can be found by obtaining a report from a **credit and business reference agency**, for example, Experian (*www.uk.experian.com*), ICC (*www.icc.co.uk*) or D & B Small Business Centre (*www.do-business.net*).

Care should be taken when considering information acquired through searches as some information may be **out of date**. For example:
- private companies have up to 10 months after the end of their accounting period within which to file accounts and so a company's public accounting information may be up to 22 months old; and
- shareholder information is only submitted on a company's annual return and so may be up to 12 months old.

> MEMO POINTS   See ¶4279 for the deadlines for filing accounts under the **new Companies Act**.

5263 An **intermediary** may be able to provide further information if the target is being marketed, although minimal information is likely to be released until the intermediary is assured that the buyer is serious (¶5225) and confidentiality has been assured (¶5244).

Approaching potential targets

5264 After carrying out an initial evaluation, a buyer should have a choice of potential targets to approach. Careful thought should be given about **to whom** the approach should be made. If the target is not part of a group, the majority shareholder would be the usual person to approach. If the target is a subsidiary, an approach to the appropriate director of the parent company may be more fruitful than an approach to a director of the target itself.

5265 The approach can be **made by** the buyer directly or by an intermediary, although if the seller is to take the approach seriously he will expect contact with the buyer fairly early in the process. The initial meeting can be planned (for example, by setting up a face-to-face meeting or telephone call) or the approach can be made in a more informal setting (for example, at a business event).

5266 The buyer will generally only be able to proceed if its approach is received favourably. In a share sale where there are several **shareholders**, all of them will usually have to agree to the sale.

> MEMO POINTS   In a share sale, it is not necessarily fatal to the sale if **some** of the target's shareholders **do not consent**. If the buyer makes a takeover offer which is accepted by more than 90% of the target's shareholders, it may be able to "squeeze-out" the remaining minority shareholders (¶6930+). Further, in limited circumstances, the shares of a public company may be acquired by way of a hostile takeover (see ¶6675+).

SECTION 2

Deal structure

I. Asset or share sale

5280 A company sale and purchase can be structured in one of two ways:
- a share sale and purchase; or
- an asset sale and purchase.

Although the transaction procedure will be similar in both cases, the two types of transaction are fundamentally different in concept.

What is a share sale?

5281 In a share sale, the buyer purchases 100% of the shares of the company. The **subject** of the sale is the company's shares and the **seller** is the shareholder. Following the sale, the target company (and its customers) may see no changes apart from the identity of the target's shareholder; the underlying assets and liabilities of the business will continue to be owned by the target company. The purchase will have no direct effect on the **buyer**, except that its balance sheet will reflect the value of its share investment.

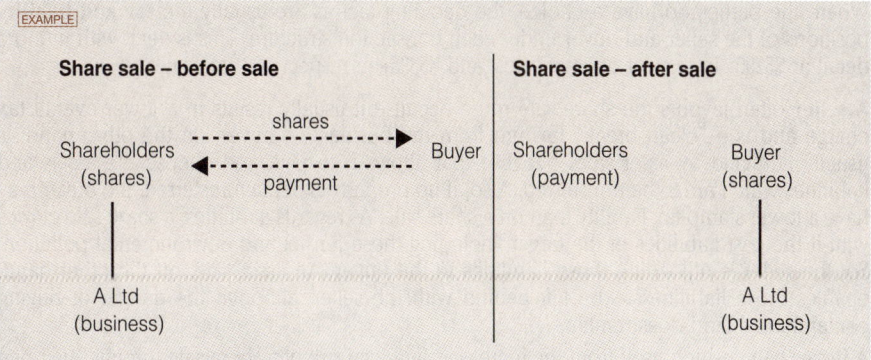

What is an asset sale?

In an asset sale, the **seller** is the target company itself and the **subject** of the sale is the tangible and intangible assets of its business, described as its "undertaking and assets" (including its goodwill, property, plant and machinery, contracts with customers etc). Thus, the identity of the person operating the target's business will change from the seller to the buyer, and the **buyer** will see the transferred assets (and any transferred liabilities) incorporated directly into its balance sheet.

5282

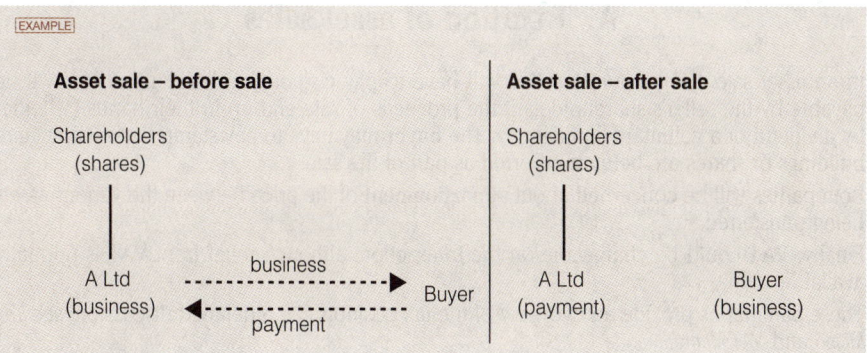

Choosing between shares and assets

No choice

In most cases, the parties will need to choose between a share sale and an asset sale. However sometimes, the transaction will have to be structured as an asset sale. This will happen, for example:
a. if it is a **sale by liquidators, administrators** or **administrative receivers**;
b. where there are **dissenting minority shareholders** and so 100% of the target's shares cannot be sold to the buyer (although, if the buyer acquires 90% of the target's shares it may be able to rely on its "squeeze-out" rights, see ¶6930+);
c. **only part of the company's business is being sold**, for example, if one company operates two different businesses (although, the business to be sold could be hived down (¶6415+) into a new company and the shares in the new company sold to the buyer instead); or
d. the business is being operated by a **sole trader or partnership**, not a company with shares. (The discussion below relating to asset sales assumes a corporate seller, although

5283

there would be little difference from the buyer's perspective if the target were a sole trader or partnership.)

Choice

5284 Where the parties do have a choice, the deciding factors are usually the **tax and liability** positions of the seller and buyer under each transaction structure. This is dealt with in more detail at ¶5290+ in respect of asset sales, and ¶5335+ in respect of share sales.

5285 A **seller** often favours the share sale route because it usually results in a lower overall tax charge and is a "clean break" for him from the business. A buyer, on the other hand, is usually attracted by asset sales because that allows it to pick and choose the assets and liabilities which are to be transferred. Also, if no property is being transferred, the buyer may have a lower stamp tax liability than on a share sale. As regards liabilities, a share sale carries with it the past liabilities of the target, including those for tax and environmental pollution. So, the seller is offloading those liabilities to the buyer. An asset sale, on the other hand, enables those liabilities to be left behind with the seller, although the danger of buying contaminated land does remain.

A **buyer** can cushion itself from the increased financial risk of a share sale through the price it negotiates and by including appropriate warranties and indemnities in the sale and purchase agreement. In addition, in a share sale, the buyer benefits from the fact that disruption to the business will be minimised and the transaction is likely to be smoother. The tension between the two is therefore normally resolved in favour of the seller, so most deals are structured as share sales, where there is a choice.

A. Taxation of asset sales

5290 In an asset sale, the corporate **seller** will have to pay corporation tax. Further tax will be payable by the seller's shareholders if the proceeds of sale end up in their hands (whether by dividend or a voluntary liquidation). The **buyer** may have to pay stamp taxes if any land, buildings or shares are being transferred as part of the sale.

Both parties will be concerned about **apportionment** of the price between the various assets being transferred.

Finally, **VAT** could be chargeable on the transaction, although relief from VAT is normally available.

These paragraphs provide an overview of the tax position. For a detailed discussion, see *Tax Memo* and *VAT Memo*.

1. Seller

Corporation tax

5291 A corporate seller will have to pay corporation tax on any capital gain arising on the assets sold. However, the tax charge could be mitigated by the availability of tax losses and certain reliefs. Those most applicable to an asset sale by a company are:
– the use of **trading and capital losses**;
– the availability of **roll-over relief**, where the gain from the sale of qualifying assets is rolled over into other business assets; and
– the availability of **investment relief**, where the gain is invested in corporate venturing scheme shares.

Corporate sellers should also consider the effect on **capital allowances**.

See *Tax Memo* for further detail.

Passing sale proceeds to shareholders

5292

Where the whole of a company's business and assets are sold, all that is left is a company with a "cash pot". There are three main ways in which the proceeds can be put into the hands of the shareholders, all of which would result in the shareholders having to pay a certain amount of tax on their receipt. This **double charge to tax** is one of the main reasons for the unpopularity of asset sales amongst owner-managed companies.

The two ways for the shareholders to obtain the proceeds are:
– the shareholders could be paid a **cash dividend** resulting in an income tax charge if the shareholder is an individual (see ¶1780+); or
– the company could be **liquidated** or **dissolved** so that any surplus cash would be distributed to the shareholders, resulting in a receipt of capital rather than income.

2. Buyer

The buyer will have to pay:
– **stamp duty land tax** in respect of any consideration it pays for the company's land and buildings; and
– **stamp duty** in respect of any consideration it pays for any share investments held by the company (although this is rare in practice) (see ¶1875+).

5297

> MEMO POINTS The buyer's major tax issue on an acquisition of assets used to be **stamp duty**. From 1 December 2003, stamp duty on property was replaced with stamp duty land tax, and stamp duty on transfers of other assets was essentially abolished. However, stamp duty is still payable in respect of transfers of shares, see ¶1875+

Stamp duty land tax

Stamp duty land tax (SDLT) **applies to** all transactions involving the acquisition of a chargeable interest in land in the UK. It is irrelevant whether the parties to the transaction are present or resident in the UK, whether the transaction is completed in the UK or overseas and however the transaction is effected (by a legal document, by a court order, orally etc).

5298

After completion of the sale and purchase agreement in which the company's property is transferred to the buyer, the buyer will have to:
– report it to Revenue and Customs, if it is a **notifiable transaction**; and
– pay any **tax due** within 30 days of completion.

5299

Revenue and Customs have various investigative and assessment powers to ensure that SDLT is being reported and paid. Further detail can be found in *Tax Memo*.

> MEMO POINTS As an anti-avoidance measure, if a contract is substantially performed before it is fully completed, a charge to SDLT will arise at the time of **substantial performance** rather than on completion. "Substantial performance" is not defined but Revenue and Customs have stated that they will treat a contract as being substantially performed if:
> – 90% or more of the consideration has been paid;
> – the buyer has taken possession of the property; or
> – the buyer is entitled to receive rents or profits from the property.
> A contract can be treated as substantially performed even if it is conditional, although if the condition is not satisfied, the SDLT paid can be reclaimed. SDLT can also be reclaimed if the contract is subsequently rescinded or annulled.
> Where substantial performance occurs before completion, both events are notifiable transactions.

Reporting of notifiable transaction

Within 30 days of completion (or substantial performance if this was before completion), a completed **land transaction return**, signed by the buyer, must be delivered to Revenue and Customs in respect of each notifiable transaction. Each return must include a self-assessment of SDLT liability. Payment of any SDLT due (see ¶5307+) must be made within 30 days of completion (or substantial performance, if sooner).

5300

> **MEMO POINTS** A transaction is **notifiable** if it is:
> **a.** the **transfer** of a freehold or leasehold interest (save for the transfer of residential property where the total consideration is less than £1,000);
> **b.** the **assignment of a lease** of 7 years or more which results in an SDLT charge of at least 1% of the consideration (even if none is actually payable because a relief is available);
> **c.** the **grant of a lease** for a term of:
> – 7 years or more in return for a chargeable consideration;
> – less than 7 years which results in an SDLT charge (even if none is actually payable because a relief is available); or
> **d.** any **other transaction** where SDLT of at least 1% of the consideration is due (or would be but for the availability of a relief).
> Some transactions are exempt but these will not generally be relevant in an arm's length business sale for value.

5301 The land transaction return must be made on Form SDLT1 (and other supplementary forms). These forms are not straightforward so will generally be **completed by** the buyer's solicitor. Each Form SDLT1 has a payslip at the end with a unique transaction reference number. This number must be entered on any supplementary forms. As a result, forms cannot be downloaded and photocopies are not accepted.

5302 The return can be completed by hand or on-screen. Forms for completion **by hand** are available from the Revenue and Customs orderline (0845 302 1472). Forms can be completed **on-screen**, in one of the following ways:
– online at the Revenue and Customs website (*www.hmrc.gov.uk/so/online/menu.htm*); or
– using an electronic substitute return form from an approved supplier. Some of these suppliers also allow the form to be filed online. A list of approved suppliers is posted on the Revenue and Customs website.

All returns have a **unique transaction reference number**. This is pre-printed on forms obtained from Revenue and Customs. For online filing using the Revenue and Customs website, this reference number is generated automatically when a fully completed form is submitted. For other on-screen methods, a reference number can be taken from a pre-printed individual payslip. Individual payslips are available from the Revenue and Customs orderline on the telephone number above.

Payment after online filing should ideally be made electronically quoting the reference number. Otherwise, the reference number will need to be written on the back of the cheque when sending the SDLT payment.

5303 The following **forms** are relevant for SDLT.

Form	Purpose
SDLT1	Primary return form, which must be completed for all notifiable transactions
SDLT2	Supplementary form, which must be completed where there are more than two sellers or buyers
SDLT3	Supplementary form, which must be completed only where additional information is required to identify the property or the transaction involves more than one property
SDLT4v2	Supplementary form, which must be completed when additional information is required about the transaction (e.g. when the interest purchased is non-residential; the buyer is a company; or, where the interest acquired is part of a business sale agreement)

SDLT6 is a booklet entitled "How to complete your land transaction return" and contains **guidance notes** on completing these forms.

Sample forms (to view only) and the guidance notes are available on the Revenue and Customs website.

5304 If the buyer **fails to submit a return** within 30 days of completion or substantial performance, a flat-rate penalty of £100 will be charged if the return is delivered within 3 months of the filing date, and £200 in all other cases. If the return is still outstanding 12 months after the filing date, a tax-related penalty will be charged. This will not exceed the tax due. In addition, a daily penalty of up to £60 per day may be imposed if the buyer fails to respond to a notice demanding submission of a return.

If the buyer submits an **incomplete or incorrect return**, it will not be processed. Instead, Revenue and Customs will usually send the buyer an SDLT8 letter which will explain why the return was not acceptable. The buyer should return the letter with the required information within the 30-day filing period as otherwise a late filing penalty will be levied.

5305

> MEMO POINTS A tax-related penalty (not exceeding the tax due) may be imposed if the buyer **fraudulently or negligently** makes an incorrect return, or discovers that a submitted return is incorrect and does not correct the error without unreasonable delay. Further, a person (including an adviser) who is **knowingly** involved in the fraudulent evasion of SDLT is guilty of a criminal offence punishable by imprisonment and/or a fine. Similarly, a person (including an adviser) who knowingly assists in the preparation of an incorrect return may be subject to a penalty of up to £3,000.

If the **return is properly submitted**, Revenue and Customs will provide the buyer with a land transaction return certificate (SDLT5). The certificate is only evidence that a return has been submitted; Revenue and Customs can enquire into the validity of a return and the amount of duty paid even after the certificate has been issued.

5306

> MEMO POINTS The land transaction return certificate is required to register the property transfer with the Land Registry. If no land transaction return is required, the buyer will need to provide the Land Registry with a **self-certificate**. The self-certification must be made on Form SDLT60. An SDLT60 can also be used to avoid completing a land transaction return where a **short-term lease** is granted in favour of the buyer. Whether or not a return is required in these circumstances is calculated by reference to the net present value of the lease. There is an online calculator on the Revenue and Customs website which will calculate this value. SDLT 68 Guidance Notes provides guidance on completing Form SDLT 60.

Calculation of SDLT due

SDLT is payable on the **chargeable consideration** which the buyer paid for the property. In an asset sale (where a freehold or leasehold interest has been transferred or where a lease has been assigned), the chargeable consideration will be the **amount paid** for the property. This will be apparent from the way in which the consideration has been **apportioned** between the property and other assets (see ¶5314+). The consideration should be apportioned on a just and equitable basis and professional valuations may be required to support the apportionment.

5307

> MEMO POINTS 1. Where some of the consideration is **deferred**, the chargeable consideration is the total amount payable. There is no reduction for the delay in payment.
> 2. Where the consideration is **contingent** on an event, for example, the grant of planning permission, the consideration is based on the assumption that the amount relating to the contingency will be paid. Where the consideration is **uncertain or unascertained**, the chargeable consideration will be based on a reasonable estimate of the amount that will be paid.
> Once the actual amount of consideration is established, an **adjustment** will be made. Any overpayment of SDLT can be reclaimed, and if more SDLT is payable, a return and the extra tax must be submitted within 30 days of when the actual consideration is established.
> The buyer can apply to Revenue and Customs to **defer payment of SDLT** on any unascertainable or uncertain consideration which is payable more than 6 months after completion.
> 3. Sometimes, instead of selling the company's premises to the buyer, the seller will **grant the buyer a lease** of those premises. This allows the seller to retain a capital asset (i.e. the property) and obtain an income from it (i.e. rent from the buyer). The calculation of the chargeable consideration for the grant of a lease is complicated as it depends upon the premium paid by the buyer for the lease and rent that will be paid under it. See *Tax Memo* for further details.

The charge to SDLT is based on a **slab system**. This means that when the chargeable consideration exceeds a rate threshold, the higher rate applies to the whole consideration. The **rate** depends on whether the property is residential or non-residential, as the table below demonstrates.

5308

% [1]	Residential property [1,2]	Non-residential or mixed use property [1]
0	£0 – £125,000	£0 – £150,000
1	over £125,000 – £250,000	over £150,000 – £250,000
3	over £250,000 – £500,000	over £250,000 – £500,000
4	over £500,000	over £500,000

Note:
1. These rates and bands apply to transactions completed on or after 23 March 2006.
2. A **residential property** is:
– one which is used as, or is suitable for use as, a dwelling; and
– land that forms part of the garden or grounds, and any outbuildings of a dwelling.
A dwelling includes most residential accommodation but not children's homes, residential care homes, hospitals or hospices, prisons, or hotels, inns or similar establishments.
Where a building is not in use, the use for which it is most suitable will override any others.
The residential or non-residential status of the property on purchase is the critical factor, not the buyer's intended use after purchase.

EXAMPLE Mr A buys two residential properties. Property B costs £100,000 and property C costs £450,000. There is no SDLT charge on B as the consideration is below £125,000. The SDLT charge on C is £13,500 (3% of £450,000).

5309 There are several reliefs from SDLT (see *Tax Memo*). The reliefs most likely to be of relevance in an asset sale are:
a. group relief, which is available on transfers of property between companies where one is the 75% subsidiary of the other, or both are 75% subsidiaries of a third company;
b. reconstruction relief, which is available if the property is being transferred under a scheme of reconstruction (see ¶6530+) in exchange for shares; and
c. acquisition relief, which is available where the property is being bought as part of a business and at least 90% of the total consideration is being paid in shares. Under acquisition relief, the rate of tax is reduced to 0.5%.

3. Apportionment

5314 In an asset sale, even though many separate assets are being transferred to the buyer, usually the parties negotiate a global price, known as the "**consideration**". One of the most important issues, in terms of the tax impact, is the way in which the consideration is to be apportioned amongst the various assets being sold.

5315 Apportionment figures are usually agreed between the parties' accountants. Apportionment is not an exact science and there is some degree of leeway. The buyer and seller will have different objectives and the final apportionment is likely to represent a **compromise** between their two positions.

5316 The way in which the consideration has been apportioned is usually set out in the sale and purchase agreement. This serves both as a contractual commitment between the buyer and seller, and as **evidence to Revenue and Customs** who will generally accept the agreed apportionment, provided it is commercially realistic. Revenue and Customs do, however, have the power to reallocate the consideration and will exercise this power if the apportionment is artificial and purely designed to avoid tax, for example, if a clearly valuable freehold property is allocated only nominal consideration.

4. VAT

5321 When a business and its assets are sold, no VAT will be chargeable so long as the sale qualifies as a "**transfer of a going concern**". The sale of part of a business can be treated as a transfer of a going concern, if that part is capable of being operated separately as a business.

The sale and purchase agreement will normally set out the VAT position in an asset sale and provide for what should happen if Revenue and Customs disagree so that VAT becomes chargeable on all or some of the assets (¶5787).

These paragraphs provide an overview of this topic. For a detailed discussion, see *VAT Memo*.

> MEMO POINTS 1. If the **seller ceases to be registered for VAT** following the sale, a deemed supply is made of all goods still held by it at that time and VAT will be chargeable on the value of those goods (para 8 Sch 4 VATA 1994).
> 2. The seller will usually keep the VAT **records**, but must make certain information available to the buyer. However, if the buyer takes over the seller's VAT registration (which is rare), the seller will have to pass its records to the buyer, unless Revenue and Customs allows the seller to keep them (s 49(2A) VATA 1994).

It is important to establish whether or not the conditions for transfer as a going concern have been met because the VAT rules are compulsory.

5322

If **VAT is charged** when it should not have been:
– the buyer will not be able to reclaim this amount as input tax because there was no taxable supply; and
– the seller will have to cancel any tax invoice issued and provide the buyer with a refund of the VAT charged.

If **VAT is not charged** when it should have been, the seller will have to account for the correct amount of VAT out of the consideration it received.

> MEMO POINTS Revenue and Customs may allow the buyer to make an **input tax recovery** if they are satisfied that the VAT has been reported on the seller's return and has been paid. However, this is entirely discretionary and certainly should not be relied upon.

Conditions for transfer as going concern

The conditions which must be fulfilled in order for the sale to be treated as a transfer as a going concern are:

5323

a. assets:
– the transferred assets must be intended for use by the buyer in a similar business to the one carried on by the seller;

b. business activities and trading:
– the business must be a going concern at the time of transfer (this means that it must be an operating business but it does not necessarily have to be commercially viable);
– the buyer must acquire the business, not just its capital assets;
– there must be no significant break in trading, either before or after the transfer; and
– the buyer must operate the business, with the result that immediately consecutive transfers do not qualify (e.g. if A transfers to B, who immediately transfers to C, neither transfer will qualify);

c. VAT registration:
– if the seller is registered for VAT, the buyer must also either be registered, be required to compulsorily register or be accepted for voluntary registration; or
– if the seller is not registered for VAT, there is no requirement for the buyer to be registered.

> MEMO POINTS It is possible for the seller to **transfer** its **VAT registration number** to the buyer but this does not generally occur in arm's length sales between unconnected persons (see ¶5788/mp).

Transfer involving land and buildings

To be treated as a transfer of a going concern, the buyer will have to comply with **further conditions** if the sale includes land and buildings which:
– are under 3 years old, still under construction or civil engineering works (these are normally standard-rated for VAT purposes); or
– would normally be exempt from VAT but the seller has elected to waive that exemption (this is commonly referred to as "opting to tax").

5324

In those two circumstances, the buyer must **opt to tax** the property. If it does not, the seller must charge VAT on the price for the property, even though the rest of the transfer qualifies as a transfer as a going concern.

> MEMO POINTS The buyer's **option to tax** can be **disapplied** by Revenue and Customs as a result of an anti-avoidance measure. The anti-avoidance measure only has effect where the properties are occupied for something other than wholly or mainly taxable business purposes and where

the land or building is a capital item for the purposes of the VAT Capital Goods Scheme (see *VAT Memo* for details).

5325 Where the buyer must opt to tax, by the time of the transfer, the buyer will need to have:
– **notified Revenue and Customs** of its election to opt to tax;
– **notified the seller** in writing that the election in respect of that property has been maintained; and
– made a **declaration to the seller** that its option will not be disapplied by the anti-avoidance provisions.

The seller is responsible for applying the correct VAT treatment and may be required to support its decision by Revenue and Customs. The seller should therefore obtain a copy of the buyer's notification to Revenue and Customs in order to satisfy itself that the buyer's election has been put in place in time.

MEMO POINTS The **notification to Revenue and Customs** should be made either on Form VAT 1614 (available to download from the Revenue and Customs' website) or by letter setting out the same information as is required to complete the form. If the buyer is registering for VAT at the same time as exercising the option to tax, the form or letter should be sent to its local VAT Registration Unit. Otherwise, the form or letter should be submitted to Revenue and Customs' Option to Tax National Unit in Glasgow (the address is on the form).

B. Taxation of share sales

5335 In a share sale, **individual selling shareholders** will have to pay capital gains tax, and a **corporate selling shareholder** will have to pay corporation tax, on any increase in the value of the shares since they acquired them. The calculation is basically the same in both cases but the tax reliefs are different, in particular, companies do not benefit from taper relief. In some cases, the sellers will need to obtain **advance tax clearance** from Revenue and Customs to confirm that the tax relief they are hoping to claim will apply.

A **buyer** on the other hand will have to pay stamp duty on the value of the purchase price.

These paragraphs provide an overview of the tax position. For a detailed discussion, see *Tax Memo* and *VAT Memo*.

1. Individual seller

5338 An individual shareholder will have to pay **capital gains tax** on any increase in the value of his shares between when he acquired them and the sale. This increase is known as the "chargeable gain".

The basic chargeable **gain is reduced by**:
– indexation allowance (if the shares were held by him before April 1998);
– taper relief;
– loss relief; and
– the annual exemption.

Tax is payable on this reduced amount.

However, an individual could **defer payment of tax by**:
– utilising Enterprise Investment Scheme (EIS) deferral relief; or
– taking paper consideration (see ¶5426+).

Comment: The explanation below is a **general overview only**. For example, there are complex rules for calculating the chargeable gain if shares of the same class were acquired at different times for different prices. In addition, other reliefs may be available depending upon individual circumstances. A detailed explanation of capital gains tax can be found in *Tax Memo*.

MEMO POINTS The Finance Bill before parliament at the time of writing proposes to **withdraw** indexation allowance and taper relief.

a. Capital gains tax

Basic calculation

The first step in calculating the chargeable gain is to deduct "allowable expenditure" from the "disposal proceeds".

The **allowable expenditure** (also known as the "base cost") is the price paid for the shares on acquisition plus the incidental costs of acquisition.

The **disposal proceeds** is the value of the consideration being paid for the shares in the sale minus the incidental costs of sale. If the sale is being made at an arm's length to an unconnected buyer, the value of the consideration will be the actual consideration received. If the sale is not being made at arm's length or if the consideration cannot be valued (which may be the case if the shares are being exchanged for other shares), the value will be the open market value of the shares which have been sold.

5343

> EXAMPLE Mr A bought his shares in X Ltd for £30,000 in January 1991 (which was their market value at that time). At the time Mr A spent £1,000 on professional fees. In January 2008, Mr A sold his shares in an arm's length sale for £500,000. He spent £2,000 on advertising the sale of his shares and £13,000 on professional fees.
>
> | | | £ | £ |
> |---|---|---:|---:|
> | Proceeds of sale | | | 500,000 |
> | Less: Incidental costs of disposal | | | (15,000) |
> | | | | 485,000 |
> | Less base cost: | Acquisition cost | 30,000 | |
> | | Other allowable costs | 1,000 | |
> | | | | (31,000) |
> | Basic gain | | | 454,000 |

> MEMO POINTS **Incidental costs** are those incurred wholly and exclusively for the purposes of the acquisition or sale and include:
> – fees, commission or remuneration paid to a surveyor, valuer, auctioneer, accountant, agent or legal adviser;
> – costs of transfer, including stamp duty; and
> – advertising to find a buyer or seller.

Indexation allowance

The basic gain is then "indexed" by adding an indexation allowance. Indexation allowance aims to take account of inflation between acquisition and disposal by **increasing the base cost** in line with the retail price index (RPI) that is published by the government. This has the effect of reducing the chargeable gain.

For individuals, indexation is calculated **from** the month of acquisition (or 31 March 1982, if the shares had been acquired before then and the market value on 31 March 1982 was higher than the acquisition cost) **to** 5 April 1998. After that period, taper relief applies.

5344

> EXAMPLE Continuing the previous example, assume RPI in January 1991 was 105.3 and in April 1998 was 162.6.
>
> | | £ |
> |---|---:|
> | Unindexed gain | 454,000 |
> | Less indexation allowance: | |
> | January 1991 to April 1998 | |
> | $\dfrac{(162.6 - 105.3)}{105.3} = 0.544 \times 31,000 = 16,869$ | (16,869) |
> | Indexed gain | 437,131 |

> MEMO POINTS 1. Where the seller is a company, indexation allowance is available to the date of the sale rather than just to April 1998. A **corporate seller** cannot take advantage of taper relief.
> 2. The Finance Bill before parliament at the time of writing proposes to **withdraw** indexation allowance for assets acquired before 6 April 1998 and to withdraw taper relief.

Loss relief

5345 An individual can reduce his indexed chargeable gain by setting it off against any "**allowable losses**". An allowable loss is the amount by which, on the disposal of an asset, the allowable expenditure exceeds the disposal proceeds. For example, the seller may have sold an investment and made a loss on that sale.

The following allowable losses can be set off against a chargeable gain on a share sale:
– those incurred in the same tax year as the share sale (known as "**current year relief**");
– those incurred in previous tax years to the extent that they have not already been utilised (known as "**carry forward relief**"); or
– if the shareholder dies in the 3 tax years after the sale, those incurred in the year of death (known as "**carry back relief**").

EXAMPLE Continuing the previous example, assume that in January 2008, Mr A sold some antiques at a price of £10,000 (disposal proceeds) which he had bought for £47,131 (allowable expenditure). His allowable loss on that sale was £37,131.

	£
Indexed gain	437,131
Less allowable losses: current year relief	(37,131)
Gain before taper relief	400,000

MEMO POINTS The **maximum** amount of allowable loss that can be set off against a chargeable gain is **restricted** to the amount required to reduce the chargeable gain (before taper relief) to the level of the annual exemption. Where the chargeable gain is already less than the annual exemption, no losses may be utilised.

Taper relief

5346 Once the indexed gain has been calculated and loss relief applied, individuals must apply taper relief. Taper relief determines the **proportion of a chargeable gain that will be taxed**, based on the number of complete years that the shares have been held. The longer the shares have been held, the smaller the percentage of the gain that will be taxed. For a higher rate tax-payer, this can reduce the effective rate of tax from the headline capital gains tax rate of 40% down to as little as 10%.

The percentage by which the chargeable gain will be reduced depends upon whether the shares are "business assets" or "non-business assets". As the table below demonstrates, establishing that the shares are "business assets" is extremely beneficial to the seller.

Number of complete years shares held	Business assets Percentage of gain chargeable (%) - disposals after 5/4/02	Non-business assets Percentage of gain chargeable (%) - disposals after 5/4/98
0	100	100
1	50	100
2	25	100
3	25	95
4	25	90
5	25	85
6	25	80
7	25	75
8	25	70
9	25	65
10 +	25	60

MEMO POINTS The Finance Bill before parliament at the time of writing proposes to **withdraw** taper relief.

Business or non-business asset

5347 Shares are treated as a business asset if the target company is a trading company, or the holding company in a trading group. A **trading company** is a company carrying on trading activities which do not include any substantial activities other than those trading activities. There are special rules for joint venture companies. Therefore a special purpose vehicle, such as a property holding company, would not qualify as a business asset.

In addition, one or more of the following **other conditions** must be met:
– the company is unlisted;
– the seller is an officer or employee (full-time or otherwise) of the company or a connected company; or
– at least 5% of the voting rights in the company are exercisable by the seller.

Shares in a **non-trading company** will be treated as a business asset if the seller is an officer or employee of the company and does not have the rights to more than 10% of the issued shares, voting rights or rights to distributions.

EXAMPLE Continuing the previous example, assuming that X Ltd is an unlisted trading company, Mr A will qualify for business asset taper relief having held his shares for over two years.

	£
Gain before taper relief	400,000
Gain after taper relief @ 25%	100,000

Annual exemption

An individual is only liable to capital gains tax for a tax year in which his aggregate chargeable gains (after indexation, loss relief and taper relief) exceed the annual exemption. If an individual's gains for a tax year are below this amount, no capital gains tax is payable. However, the unused exemption cannot be carried forward and set off against future gains. The annual exemption for 2007/08 is £9,200.

5348

EXAMPLE Continuing the previous example, assume Mr A had no other chargeable gains in the year 2007/2008:

	£
Gain after taper relief	100,000
Less: Annual exemption	(9,200)
Taxable gain	90,800

Tax rates

Capital gains are taxed as though they were the top slice of the individual's income for the tax year. The **rate of tax** payable will therefore depend upon the individual's total taxable income. It must be remembered that the tax payable, although calculated according to income tax bands, is actually capital gains tax.

5349

Capital gains tax rate [1]	Tax bands	Bands for 2007/08 [2]
10%	Starting rate band	£0 – £2,230
20%	Lower and basic rate band	£2,231 – £34,600
40%	Higher rate band	over £34,600

Note:
1. These rates have been effective since 6 April 2000.
2. These are the income tax bands set by the government and usually change every April. They were last updated on 6 April 2007.

EXAMPLE Continuing the previous example, Mr A's total taxable gain for 2007/08 is £90,800 and his total taxable income for the year is £30,150.

		Income £	Capital Gains £
Starting rate band	(£0 – £2,230)	2,230	-
Lower/basic rate band	(£2,231 – £34,600)	28,000	4,370
Higher rate band	(£34,601 +)	-	86,430
		30,230	90,800

The capital gains tax due is therefore calculated as follows:
£4,370 @ 20%	874
£86,430 @ 40%	34,572
Total	35,446

b. Deferral of capital gains tax

5354 There are several capital gains tax reliefs under which an individual could **defer payment of tax**. Those most likely to be relevant in a share sale are:
- Enterprise Investment Scheme (EIS) deferral relief; or
- roll-over relief and hold-over relief available when the seller is paid by way of shares or loan notes, rather than cash (see ¶5426+).

Enterprise Investment Scheme (EIS) deferral relief

5355 EIS is a scheme intended to **encourage investment in smaller companies**, thereby making it easier for them to raise finance through share issues. That encouragement takes the form of tax incentives for the investor. One such incentive is that an individual is able to defer a chargeable gain by investing the gain in shares which are eligible for EIS deferral relief. In other words, a seller can delay payment of capital gains tax by subscribing for eligible shares. Gains that are deferred into eligible shares will become taxable only when the EIS shares are sold. It is at this stage that the gain is said to have "crystallised".

> MEMO POINTS 1. From 19 July 2007, a company **must not raise over** £2 million in total from CVS, EIS and VCT schemes in the 12 months ending on the date of the relevant investment. See *Tax Memo* for detail of all of these schemes.
> 2. The gain will **crystallise early** if the shareholder ceases to be resident or ordinarily resident in the UK within 5 years of subscribing for the EIS shares or if the EIS shares cease to be eligible (i.e. if the on-going conditions discussed below are breached).
> 3. The **amount of gain eligible for deferral** is the gain after all reliefs have been claimed, except taper relief. **Taper relief** is calculated when the gain crystallises but is generally calculated in respect to the ownership period of the original shares in target. There is therefore generally no effect on the amount of taper relief which can be claimed in respect of the gain. (The Finance Bill before parliament at the time of writing proposes to withdraw taper relief.)
> 4. EIS deferral **relief** may be claimed as if the EIS subscription was made on the date the fund closed. For funds that closed on or after 6 October 2006, the fund must be 90% invested within 12 months after closure. For funds that closed on or before 5 October 2006, the fund must have been 90% invested within 6 months after closure.

5356 The **conditions** for obtaining EIS deferral relief are summarised in the table below:

	Conditions
Eligible shares	– New, ordinary shares (preferential or redeemable shares are not eligible) – Cash subscription
EIS company	– Unquoted – Must have fewer than 50 full-time employees at the date on which the relevant shares or securities are issued[1] – Must not have raised more than £2 million in total from CVS, EIS and VCT schemes in the 12 months ending on the date of the relevant investment[2] – Not the target whose shares have been sold, and not in the same group as the target – Immediately before eligible shares are issued, aggregate assets (without deducting liabilities) do not exceed £7 million, and immediately after issue they do not exceed £8 million[3] – Cannot control any company, other than 51% subsidiaries, and must not be controlled by or be a 51% subsidiary of another company – Is preparing to, or does, carry on a qualifying trade[4] – Uses money raised from eligible share issue to finance a qualifying trade, or research and development which is expected to lead to a qualifying trade[4]

	Conditions
Seller	Resident and ordinarily resident in the UK at both the date on which he disposed of the shares in target company and the date he acquired the EIS shares
Timing	Eligible shares acquired within 1 year before and 3 years after the seller disposed of his shares in target company

Note:
1. This change took effect from 6 April 2007, although it does not apply to EIS shares issued before 19 July 2007 (the date on which the FA 2007 received royal assent). Previously, there was no limit on the number of employees.
2. This took effect from 6 April 2007, but does not apply to EIS shares issued before 19 July 2007. If the limit of £2 million is exceeded, none of the shares or securities within the issue that caused the breach will qualify for the relief.
3. These limits took effect from 6 April 2006. The previous limits were £15 million immediately before the investment and £16 million immediately afterwards. The change therefore substantially restricts the availability of this scheme.
4. A **qualifying trade** is a trade carried on wholly or mainly in the UK on a commercial basis, with a view to the realisation of profit. The trade will not qualify if more than 20% involves certain non-qualifying activities including:
– property dealing and development;
– financial, legal or accountancy services;
– leasing or hiring goods; or
– operating or managing hotels, nursing homes and residential care homes.
A qualifying trade may also be carried on by subsidiaries that are:
– 100% subsidiaries of direct 90% subsidiaries; or
– 90% subsidiaries of direct 100% subsidiaries.
It is also possible to effect a transfer within a group of a qualifying trade of exploiting relevant tangible assets.

5357 EIS deferral relief must be claimed by the seller in writing. The **claim** must be accompanied by a certificate of eligibility from the EIS company (Form EIS 3). The claim must specify the amount of gain to be deferred so, for example, the individual could leave sufficient chargeable gains to utilise losses or the annual exemption. The time limit for claims is 5 years from 31 January following the tax year in which the sale of the target's shares occurred.

2. Corporate seller

5361 A corporate seller may have to pay **corporation tax** on the chargeable gains it makes as a result of it selling its shares in a subsidiary.

The calculation of the gain upon which tax may be paid is the same as for an individual except that indexation allowance is applied up to the date of the sale; taper relief does not apply to corporate sellers (¶5338).

In addition, different loss reliefs and allowances are available for companies. Those most applicable to a share sale by a company are:
– exemption from tax for gains on disposals of **substantial shareholdings** (¶5362);
– the use of **trading and capital losses**;
– the availability of **investment relief**, where the gain is invested in corporate venturing scheme shares; and
– taking **paper consideration** (see ¶5426+).

A corporate seller will also have to consider the tax consequences of the **target leaving the seller's group**. For example, tax charges may arise in respect of intra-group transfers in the previous 6 years and a decision will need to be made about whether any tax losses of the target will be utilised.

Further details on all of these topics can be found in *Tax Memo*.

Substantial shareholding exemption

5362 A gain on a disposal of shares by a company will be exempt from tax if all of the following qualifying conditions are met:
a. substantial shareholding: the corporate seller must, at the time of the disposal, have a holding of 10% or more of the ordinary share capital of the target, which also carries an entitlement to 10% or more of the profits available for distribution and assets on a winding up;

b. period of ownership: the corporate seller must have held its substantial shareholding for a continuous 12 month period beginning not more than 2 years prior to the sale; and
c. qualifying companies: the corporate seller and target must have been either stand alone trading companies or members of a 51% trading group throughout the 12-month qualifying period of ownership and after the date of disposal.

These conditions must either:
– be satisfied at the time of disposal; or
– have been satisfied had the disposal taken place up to 2 years earlier.

> MEMO POINTS 1. If the corporate seller cannot satisfy the above requirements but another group company can, then the disposal will be treated as if made by the **other group company** and will therefore qualify for the exemption from capital gains tax.
> 2. The **2 year "look back"** is not available if the corporate seller was not a trading company after the disposal (unless the reason it was not a trading company after the disposal was because it was being or was about to be wound up).
> 3. If the **target company does not trade** immediately after the date of the disposal, the 2 year look back exemption is only available if, at some time during the 2 year period, the target company was controlled by either the corporate seller (and connected persons) or a group company of the corporate seller.

3. Tax clearances

5367 In particular cases set out in tax legislation, the seller is able to apply to Revenue and Customs for **confirmation** that a particular tax liability will not arise as a consequence of a proposed transaction. This is known as a "tax clearance".

Tax clearance, if it is available and appropriate to the transaction, should always be obtained **in advance** of completion. Clearance cannot be given retrospectively and if it has not been obtained, there is a danger that a tax liability will arise.

Requirement for clearance

5368 In the context of a share sale to an unconnected party, tax clearances will generally be required where some or all of the consideration is being paid in **shares or loan notes** (¶5426+).

5369 The two relevant tax clearances are confirmation from Revenue and Customs that it accepts that:
a. an issue by the buyer of shares in itself in **exchange for shares** in the target company will be effected for bona fide commercial reasons and does not form part of a scheme or arrangement of which the main purpose, or one of the main purposes, is avoidance of liability to capital gains tax or corporation tax (clearance under s 138 TCGA 1992); and
b. the **transaction in securities** will be carried out for bona fide commercial reasons and does not have as its main object, or one of its main objects, to enable tax advantages to be obtained (clearance under s 707 ICTA 1988).

> MEMO POINTS 1. In a share sale, provided certain conditions are fulfilled, a **share exchange** (i.e. payment of consideration by way of shares or loan notes) could give the seller a tax advantage (see ¶5428+). The **purpose of obtaining tax clearance** is to ensure that those conditions will be fulfilled and the tax advantage will be obtained. In an exchange of shares for loan notes, tax clearance will not be given if the seller intends to become non-UK tax resident before he redeems the loan notes, thereby avoiding the payment of capital gains tax altogether. The court has held that the main purpose of such a scheme would be to avoid tax (*Snell v Commissioners for HMRC* [2006] EWHC 3350 (Ch)).
> 2. Where a **transaction in securities** gives a person a tax advantage, Revenue and Customs will make adjustments to counteract the advantage, unless the transaction was carried out for bona fide commercial reasons and did not have as its main object, or one of its main objects, to enable tax advantages to be obtained (s 703 ICTA 1988). The **purpose of obtaining tax clearance** is to ensure that such an adjustment will not be made. Certain transactions in securities will automatically

be reviewed by Revenue and Customs as being of a type which could be challenged and it is therefore prudent to obtain advance tax clearance in those cases. The transactions include:
– a merger of two or more unlisted companies in which shares or securities form all or part of the consideration;
– a sale of shares to a company in which the seller has a substantial interest;
– a company reconstruction in which some or all of the shareholders in the original company retain an interest in the second company; and
– the transfer or sale by a company of its assets or business to another company having some or all of the same shareholders followed by the liquidation of the company whose assets/business have been acquired, or the sale of shares in either company.

Application for clearance

5370 An application for tax clearance for a transaction in securities and/or a share exchange should be made in writing by way of a **single letter**. The letter is normally drafted by the seller's tax adviser. Only one application is required, regardless of the number of clearances being asked for in respect of the transaction or series of transactions. The same person at Revenue and Customs will deal with each of the clearances and a single response will be given.

> MEMO POINTS There is no particular **form of letter** required but it must fully and accurately disclose all facts and considerations material to the decision, or the clearance will be void. The top of the letter should specify which clearances are being requested. The letter itself should contain details of the transaction so that Revenue and Customs can determine whether or not to grant clearance. Usually the letter will set out:
> – the name, address and tax district of the sellers, buyer and target;
> – the current shareholdings and the changes that will occur as a result of the proposed transaction; and
> – an outline of the transaction and in particular, the proposed consideration and payment structure.

5371 Applications should be **sent to**:
Clearance & Counteraction Team, Anti-Avoidance Group Intelligence
First Floor
22 Kingsway
London
WC2B 6NR

Applications can also be made **by fax** (to 020 7438 4409) **or by email** (to *reconstructions @hmrc.gsi.gov.uk*) in which case a hard copy should not be sent in the post.

A **market sensitive** application (that is one containing information that could affect the price of a listed company and/or the financial affairs of a well known individual) should be addressed to the Team Leader (who should be warned by telephone on 020 7438 6585 before market sensitive information is faxed or emailed to him).

An acknowledgement of receipt will only be sent in respect of applications which are expected to take more than a few days to deal with. Any general **enquiries** or those regarding the progress of an application can be made by telephone to 020 7438 8355.

5372 Within 30 days of receipt of the application, Revenue and Customs must either:
– notify the applicant of their **decision**; or
– require the applicant to provide **further information** so that they can make their decision.

If further information is requested, it must be provided within 30 days (or such longer period as Revenue and Customs allow), or Revenue and Customs need not proceed further with the application. Once the further information has been supplied, Revenue and Customs then have another 30 days within which to notify the applicant of their decision or to require further information. Tax clearance applications should therefore be submitted in good time so that completion is not delayed.

5373 A **revised application** will have to be submitted if, during negotiations, the proposed transaction changes so that the original application does not fully and accurately disclose all the material facts and circumstances. As a result, the tax clearance application is usually only made once negotiations on the main structure of the deal have been concluded. The possibility of changes to the deal affecting the seller's tax clearance is often used as a **negotiating tool** by him to resist last minute alterations by the buyer.

4. Buyer

5378 The buyer will have to pay **stamp duty** on the amount of consideration paid for the purchase (see ¶1875+ for a more general discussion about stamp duty on share transfers). Stamp duty is charged at 0.5% of the total purchase price, rounded up to the nearest £5.

The key issue in a share sale is valuing the purchase price. Where the price is to be paid **in cash**, the value will be self-evident. Where the price is to be paid **in another form** (e.g. shares or loan notes, see ¶5426+), stamp duty will have to be paid on the value of the consideration.

> MEMO POINTS 1. The value of **unquoted shares** is the open market value, being the price that a willing buyer would pay to a willing seller in a private sale on arm's length terms. The valuation is made with the assumption that the prospective buyer has all the information that a prudent buyer might reasonably require and will take into account any restrictions on the transfer of shares.
> 2. The value of **quoted shares** is the lower of:
> – the lower of the two prices quoted in the Stock Exchange Daily Official List for the completion date, plus a quarter of the difference between the two prices; and
> – the average of the highest and lowest prices recorded for normal bargains on that date.
> 3. The value of a **loan note** is the amount payable under the loan note instrument.

5379 Where some **payment is deferred** (¶5463+), the total value of the payment expected to be made in the 20 years following completion needs to be taken into account. This is reduced to 12 years where payments are due for the duration of an individual's life. There is no discount on the amount of stamp duty for the delay in payment of the consideration (s 56 Stamp Act 1891).

Where the **price is contingent** on a future event and unascertainable (for example, on an earn-out), the following rules apply (*Underground Electric Railways Co of London Ltd v IRC* [1906] AC 21; *Coventry City Council v IRC* [1979] Ch 14; *LM Tenancies 1 plc v IRC* [1996] STC 880):
– if the maximum price is ascertainable, then that maximum is the value for stamp duty purposes (e.g. 10% of profits for the first 4 years subject to a maximum of £100,000);
– if the maximum is unascertainable but the minimum price can be ascertained, then that minimum is the value for stamp duty purposes (e.g. £50,000 plus an increase for inflation for the first 18 months); and
– if neither the minimum nor maximum are ascertainable but a basic figure is stated which may be reduced or increased depending on circumstances, that basic figure is deemed to be the value for stamp duty purposes (e.g. £300,000 plus 5% of profits or minus 5% of losses for the first 12 months).

A fixed duty of £5 is due in respect of any other element of the price.

> EXAMPLE Mr A sells his shares in B Ltd to Mrs C for £100,000 plus 10% of the profits for the first year. The consideration for stamp duty purposes is £100,000 and duty of £500 is due. A further fixed duty of £5 is due in respect of the unascertainable consideration, regardless of the amount of consideration eventually paid.

> MEMO POINTS Where the amount of **consideration is subject to variation**, pending completion accounts (see ¶5480+), Revenue and Customs operate a "wait & see" policy. Under this policy, documents can be provisionally stamped, using the initial consideration (or the buyer's estimate of the consideration), provided Revenue and Customs receive an undertaking to resubmit the documents, with any additional duty and interest, when the final figure is known. If the documents are submitted for stamping by an adviser, the undertaking must come from the adviser. If the documents are submitted by the buyer, the buyer must give the undertaking but the cheque can be drawn from the adviser's client account (para 4.317 Stamp Taxes Manual).

C. Comparison of other factors

As well as the tax implications, the parties will need to consider the impact that a sale of shares or a sale of assets will have on:
- the smoothness (and thereby the cost and speed) of the **transaction process**; and
- where the risk for the business' **liabilities** will lie following completion.

5390

1. Transaction process

5392

Factor	¶¶	Sale of assets	Sale of shares
Number of assets to transfer	–	**Each asset** of the business has to be transferred and so further steps may have to be taken to ensure that the buyer takes title to, or the benefit of, a particular asset. For example, the consent of third parties may be required (e.g. the landlord's consent to assignment of a lease). The transaction is therefore more complex and could be subject to external delays	The sale involves only **one asset**, the shares, so the entire business can be transferred in one transaction
Employees	¶5771+	Employees of the business are given **extra rights** by legislation, commonly referred to as "TUPE", which adds a layer of formality to the transfer process and can result in costly liabilities for the seller and buyer if not followed properly	In most circumstances, TUPE does not apply and so the employees have **no extra rights**[1]
Buyer's investigation	¶5652+	The buyer can concentrate its investigation on the **particular assets** being purchased, which has the effect of limiting due diligence and streamlining warranties. This could save some time and expense	The buyer will need to investigate **all aspects of the company** and so extensive due diligence and full warranties are likely to be required which could add to the time and cost of the transaction
Partial sale	¶6405+	The seller can transfer part of its business **without** the need for a **pre-sale reorganisation**	The whole company is transferred so a **pre-sale reorganisation will be required** if only part of the company's business is being transferred
Financial promotions regulation	¶4825+	The restriction on financial promotions is **not likely to apply** to an asset sale	Financial services regulation **may apply**. The buyer and its advisors will need to ensure that their actions are not prohibited
Financial assistance by target	¶5557+	The buyer **is permitted** to use the business to finance its purchase e.g. by borrowing on the security of a transferred property	The target **is prohibited** from giving any financial assistance to either buyer or seller, unless it is a private company, in which case it must comply with the "whitewash" procedure. The prohibition on private companies providing financial assistance will be abolished in due course (¶5557/mp).

Note:
1. Where a subsidiary company is sold to a new parent pursuant to a share sale and that new parent company takes over control of the subsidiary's activities, the subsidiary's business has in fact been transferred to the new parent company. In these circumstances, TUPE can apply (*Millam v The Print Factory (London) 1991 Limited* [2007] EWCA Civ 322).

2. Post-completion liabilities

5395

	Sale of assets	Sale of shares
Buyer	The buyer can cherry **pick the assets** which it wants and specifically **exclude liabilities** from the transfer	The buyer must **take all of the liabilities** of the business. However, the financial risk to the buyer for known liabilities can be minimised by passing liability back to the seller through indemnities in the sale and purchase agreement
Seller	The seller will **retain liabilities**, for example, to third parties and for tax. The sale will therefore not operate as a "clean break"	The sellers **do not retain any liabilities** in respect of the business, other than those specifically agreed in the contract with the buyer. The sale therefore operates as a "clean break" for them

II. Price

5410 Agreeing on a price is often the most difficult aspect of structuring a deal. There are three main factors which interact here which are each dealt with below:
– **valuation** of the target;
– the **form of consideration**; and
– the **payment structure**.

A seller may be willing to accept a lower price where the payment is made in cash on completion. A buyer may be willing to pay a higher price if most of the payment is deferred or is calculated by reference to actual profits earned by the business after completion.

5411 In a **share sale**, the agreed value will need to be divided between each share class, depending upon the rights attaching to each class. Ordinary shares are generally the most valuable as the voting rights they carry lead to control of the company. The value attributable to a share class will need to be divided pro rata amongst the issued shares in that class. It is therefore not possible to pay one shareholder more per share than another, if they hold the same class of shares.

In an **asset sale**, the agreed value will need to be apportioned between the assets being transferred (¶5314+).

A. Valuation of target

5415 The value of the target will depend on a wide variety of **factors** including:
– the prevailing market conditions;
– its current, past and projected financial performance;
– its assets and liabilities; and
– the opportunities for growth and development.

At a certain level, valuation is a subjective science and both buyer and seller may have to move from their positions to meet the expectations of the other. In the end, a company is only worth as much as a buyer is willing to pay for it: the so-called "true value".

Valuation methods

There are numerous methods which can be used to value a company. Most valuation methods are based on either asset value or income value. An **asset valuation** treats the target's business as a collection of marketable assets and values each one separately to give a total valuation. Such valuations are common for a company that is to stop trading or is an investment or holding company. An **income valuation** considers the company to be an investment and bases the valuation on the return that the buyer expects to receive. This is usually appropriate for a trading company that is being sold as a going concern.

5416

Earnings multiplier

One of the most common **income valuation methods** is the "earnings multiplier". There are many variations on how this method is applied but the basic principle is the same. An estimate is made of the target's projected earnings and this is multiplied by a risk factor.

5417

Clearly much depends upon how **projected earnings** are calculated and the multiplier used. "Earnings before interest and tax" (i.e. pre-tax profits with interest payments on debts added back) is a well known accounting concept and an estimate of next year's figure is often a preferred starting point for the earnings against which the multiplier is to be applied.

5418

Commentators believe that the **appropriate multiplier** is typically between two and five, perhaps less if the company has few tangible assets and perhaps more if it is particularly attractive. This multiple represents the buyer getting its investment back from profits within two or five years, which is an annual return on the buyer's investment of between 50% and 20%. This is typically the return that a buyer will expect on making an investment in small to medium–sized private company; the riskier its business, the higher the expected rate of return. "Rule of thumb" multipliers appropriate to a particular market based on the sale of comparable companies are sometimes published in the financial press, but care should be taken when applying market multiples to a business which varies from the average.

5419

In addition to a multiple of earnings, some credit is usually given for the company's assets which are often considered to have a value separate from that of the company. So, for example, the **net asset value** of the company is often added to the multiple of earnings (which is why a net asset value adjustment to the price may be built into the price structure, see ¶5480+). Care must be taken not to double-count assets. For example, if the value of a company's property is added to the earnings multiplier, market rent should be deducted as an expense of the business when calculating earnings.

5420

Other valuation methods

Other valuation methods include:
a. balance sheet method, where a target is worth no more than the value of its net assets. This could be appropriate for a company that is losing money (although not one with a profit potential, for example, because it holds a patent ripe for exploitation);
b. cash-flow method, which bases the valuation on how much of a loan the company's cash-flow will support, usually based on a relatively short loan term of about 5 years. The valuation will change depending on interest rate conditions (low interest rates will result in a higher valuation) and the buyer's borrowing power; and
c. value of specific intangible assets, where the value is based on the cost to the buyer of creating the company's intangible assets. For example, a company's most valuable asset may be its customer list. If the cost to the buyer of finding a customer is £100 then it may value a company with a ready-made customer list at £90 per customer. The price will typically be adjusted to compensate the buyer should customers leave within a certain period after the sale. This valuation method could be used where the intangible asset is unlikely to be affected by the company changing hands, for example, insurance brokers or employment agencies.

5421

B. Form of consideration

5426 The payment which a seller receives under the contract is known as "consideration". Consideration is usually paid in **cash**, although sometimes it can wholly or partly be paid in **shares** in the buyer or **loan notes**. This is known as "paper consideration".

In a share sale, paper consideration can result in **tax benefits and risks** for the sellers. There are also tax benefits in paper consideration in an asset sale for non-corporate sellers.

1. Shares in the buyer

5427 A corporate buyer will sometimes offer to issue shares to the seller in partial satisfaction of the consideration for the sale. The effect is that the **seller continues to have an interest** in the business as a shareholder of the buyer. This could be attractive where the seller is going to maintain his connection to the company, for example as an employee, but this effect would not attract a seller who wants an outright sale, as his main objective is to realise the value of the business.

Consideration in the form of shares could also be attractive if the **buyer's shares are listed**. The seller can quickly and easily realise the value of his shareholding, and perhaps make a gain if the shares rise in value. There is of course a degree of speculation involved, but the risk to the seller of decreasing share values can be minimised by the buyer agreeing to issue further shares should values fall below an agreed level. Thought will need to be given to applicable stock exchange and listing rules as well as market conditions (for example, there may be restrictions on the seller disposing of the newly issued shares, so as to maintain an orderly market).

Tax consequences

5428 Taking shares instead of cash can have tax benefits for the seller because a type of "**roll-over relief**" will be available, which delays when the seller has to pay tax.

In a share sale, where the sale shares are exchanged for shares in the buyer, the share exchange is not treated as a disposal of the sale shares. Instead, the shares of the buyer are treated as having been acquired by the seller at the same time and at the same cost as the sale shares. In other words, the new shares "stand in the shoes" of the original sale shares (s 135 TCGA 1992). The gain upon which the seller will pay tax will be calculated and become payable only when the seller eventually disposes of his new shares in the buyer.

5430 This relief is subject to certain **conditions**. If the seller holds more than 5% of the target's shares, the exchange must have been made "for bona fide commercial reasons and must not form part of a scheme for the avoidance of capital gains tax" (s 137 TCGA 1992). Sellers are strongly advised to obtain **advance tax clearance** from Revenue and Customs for reassurance that this condition has been fulfilled (see ¶5367+).

> MEMO POINTS 1. The **other conditions** which will usually be fulfilled on the sale of a company anyway are that:
> – the buyer must hold more than 25% of the ordinary share capital of the target, either before or as a result of the exchange; or
> – the exchange must be made as a result of a general offer to the target's shareholders which had been made on the condition that the buyer will control the target.
> 2. In a recent case, involving an exchange of shares for loan notes, the court held that this type of **roll over relief is not available** if, at the time of exchange, the seller intends to become non-UK tax resident before he redeems the loan notes, thereby avoiding the payment of capital gains tax altogether. The court has held that the main purpose of such a scheme would be to avoid tax (*Snell v Commissioners for HMRC* [2006] EWHC 3350 (Ch)). By analogy, on an exchange of shares, the relief is not likely to be available if the seller intends to become non-UK tax resident before selling the shares which has received from the buyer.

5431 An individual selling shareholder will need to carefully consider the **interaction between roll-over relief and taper relief** (which does not apply to companies). In particular, he will need to ensure that the shares in the buyer continue to qualify for business asset taper relief (see ¶5346+). If the shares in the buyer only qualify for non-business asset taper relief, the total gain when he sells the shares in the buyer will be apportioned between the two elements. Since business asset taper relief is more advantageous than non-business asset taper relief, the amount of relief applicable to the gain will be diluted.

If the seller already qualifies for full business asset taper relief on the sale shares and he wishes to take paper consideration, he is advised to take QCBs instead (¶5439), unless there is a particular commercial reason for him to take shares in the buyer. This will prevent his business asset taper relief from being diluted.

If the seller does not qualify for full business asset taper relief, there may be an advantage to taking shares in the buyer in order to keep the taper relief clock running.

> MEMO POINTS 1. The seller could obtain **contractual protection** from the risk of the buyer's shares not qualifying as business assets by inserting clauses in the sale and purchase agreement, for example, to prevent the buyer from changing its trading status. However, restrictions on its post-completion activities are likely to be unattractive to the buyer.
> 2. The Finance Bill before parliament at the time of writing proposes to **withdraw** taper relief.

2. Loan notes

5437 Loan notes are a form of "**debt security**" under which the issuer (the buyer) agrees to pay the holder (the seller) the value of the note at a specified future date. At a simple level, they are a business "IOU". By issuing loan notes, the buyer effectively borrows some of the consideration from the seller. Loan notes are issued for their tax benefits (¶5440+) which are only available on a share sale. As a result, loan notes are **not appropriate for asset sales**. Loan notes are issued in accordance with terms set out in a document known as a "loan note instrument".

5438 Since loan notes are effectively a way of deferring payment of the consideration, the buyer's ability to pay on the loan notes is always an issue. **Security** for payment in the form of a charge or guarantee should always be considered (see ¶5468+).

5439 There are two types of loan notes, **qualifying corporate bonds (QCBs)** and **non-qualifying corporate bonds (non-QCBs)**. The terms of the loan note instrument will determine whether it is a QCB or a non-QCB.

The main requirements for **QCB status** are that:
– the debt must represent a "normal commercial loan";
– the loan note must not carry any special conversion rights that would entitle the holder to receive in excess of a reasonable return; and
– the loan note must be expressed in sterling and must not be capable of being converted into another currency.

As a result of these requirements, there are generally two clauses which are inserted into the loan note instrument to ensure **non-QCB status**, if required:
– a "foreign currency clause" so that the note is capable of being converted into a currency other than sterling; and/or
– a right to subscribe for further loan notes.

Tax consequences

5440 If the buyer needs to borrow money from the seller, why not have a simple loan agreement between the buyer and seller or have a straightforward deferred consideration payment structure; **why should the buyer issue loan notes**? The answer, as ever, is tax driven. Under a loan back to the buyer or a deferred payment structure, the seller will be taxed on the full consideration, even though he had loaned some of it straight back to the buyer or not received all of it at completion. This could have obvious cash flow implications (see ¶5472+). Both QCBs and non-QCBs delay when the seller has to pay tax, but in different ways.

Non-QCBs

5441 Where shares are exchanged for non-QCBs, the seller could benefit from "**roll-over relief**", as he would if he had received shares in the buyer (¶5428+). This is because non-QCBs will be treated as "securities" (i.e. akin to shares and stock) if they are a "marketable commodity". In order to ensure that they achieve that status, the loan notes must at least be transferable. Care should be taken if the loan note gives the issuer (i.e. the buyer) the right of set-off, for example, in respect of money owed to it for a warranty claim, as this is likely to threaten the "marketability" status of the loan note.

As with consideration in the form of shares in the buyer, individuals will need to consider the **interaction with taper relief** and if full business asset taper relief has been achieved, QCBs should be taken instead. (The Finance Bill before parliament at the time of writing proposes to withdraw taper relief.)

> MEMO POINTS   In an exchange of shares for loan notes, **roll-over relief will not be available** if the seller intends to become non-UK tax resident before he redeems the loan notes, thereby avoiding the payment of capital gains tax altogether. The court has held that the main purpose of such a scheme would be to avoid tax (*Snell v Commissioners for HMRC* [2006] EWHC 3350 (Ch)).

QCBs

5442 Where shares are exchanged for QCBs, the gain made on the sale of the seller's shares is calculated at the time of the sale but only becomes payable when the loan note is paid (that is to say the gain is "**held over**"). The advantage is that the seller's tax liability is frozen and his business asset taper relief is not at risk of being diluted. The disadvantage is that the seller will have to pay that liability regardless of whether or not he obtains the full value of the loan note. This is one of the reasons why QCBs are usually secured, most commonly by a bank guarantee (see ¶5468+). (The Finance Bill before parliament at the time of writing proposes to withdraw taper relief.)

C. Payment structure

5460 Whatever the form of consideration, it is unusual for all of it to be paid on completion. Most payment structures incorporate some type of **deferred consideration**, either:
– where the amount of the consideration is certain at completion but payment is made in **instalments** after completion; or
– where the consideration is uncertain at completion and is calculated by reference to the performance of the target following completion. This is known as an "**earn-out**".

In addition, most share sales incorporate a **net asset value adjustment**, where the buyer is refunded part of the consideration, or the seller is paid more, depending on whether the net asset value of the target company on completion is less or more than the expected amount.

Finally, in both share and asset sales, most buyers insist upon a **retention**, where some of the cash consideration is retained by the buyer as a contingency against potential liabilities.

1. Deferred consideration

5463 As the name suggests, deferred consideration broadly refers to any consideration that is paid after, rather than at the same time as, completion of the sale and purchase. The consideration could be **certain** at completion, but simply payable in instalments, or it could be **uncertain**, because it depends upon the performance of the target after completion. Unascertainable consideration calculated in this way is known as an "**earn-out**". In both cases, the seller will need to:
– ensure that it has **security** for the future consideration; and
– consider the **tax consequences** of the deferral.

a. Earn-outs

In an earn-out, part or all of the consideration is calculated by reference to the financial **performance of the target after completion**. For example, the earn-out may specify that the seller will be paid four times the first year's profits, or a sliding scale could be employed so that the seller can choose whether to take four times profit in year 1, three times profit in year 2 or two times profit in year 3. Earn-outs are a particularly popular method of incentivising a seller who is going to maintain his involvement in the target after completion.

5465

With earn-outs, the devil is in the detail. The important points to be specified in the sale and purchase agreement are:
a. the **chosen performance indicator**, e.g. profit, turnover etc, including the exact way in which it is to be calculated. There will often be a difference in the way in which the seller and buyer prepare their accounts and so the accounting treatment should be specified, such as the method by which depreciation of assets is calculated;
b. over what **period** the earn-out is to operate. For example, profit in the 12 to 24 months after completion, or turnover in the 2 years immediately following completion;
c. limits on the buyer's and target's activities that could affect the earn-out, e.g. incurring extraordinary expenditure, paying dividends or taking out loans. The buyer will usually resist any attempt to restrict its freedom to deal with the target after completion and even if the buyer accepts limits in principle, there will be a tension between the buyer's desire to take long-term decisions for itself and its group, and the seller's desire to maximise the earn-out over the shorter earn-out period. The amount of protection that the seller will be able to secure will therefore depend upon the negotiating strengths of the two parties; and
d. the procedure for calculation. Usually the buyer's accountants will calculate the figure and then the seller (or his accountant) will have the right to agree or disagree with the calculation within a set period of time. In the event of disagreement, the matter is usually put to an independent accountant for expert determination. Once the figure has been agreed, the earn-out clauses should specify when and how the earn-out will be payable (e.g. cash, loan notes etc).

5466

b. Security for payment

As the shares or assets, as appropriate, will be transferred at completion, if any part of the consideration is deferred or calculated by reference to an earn-out, the seller should consider whether he requires security from the buyer to ensure that it will meet future payments. Whether or not security is necessary will depend upon the **creditworthiness of the buyer**. For example, security is likely to be an issue where the buyer is a company which has just been incorporated to act as an acquisition vehicle and has no trading history or assets of its own.

5468

The best form of security, if required, is for the seller to take a **charge** over the buyer's assets (see ¶4574+). However, this is quite an extreme measure and will be resisted by a corporate buyer as it will restrict its borrowing capacity. An acceptable compromise is usually for a more creditworthy and solvent third party to be a signatory to the sale and purchase agreement and **guarantee** the buyer's obligations under that document or **procure** that the buyer fulfils particular obligations (see ¶4696+). If the buyer is part of a group, the guarantor is usually its immediate or ultimate parent. If the buyer is a single company, the guarantors are usually the individual major shareholders. As an alternative to a third party guarantee, a bank guarantee could be obtained. On a more practical level, the seller should investigate how the purchase is being financed to assure himself of the buyer's ability to pay (see ¶5550+).

5469

> MEMO POINTS 1. The seller should ensure that he carries out a **company search** on any corporate guarantor to check that it has the capacity to enter into the agreement, and a winding up petition search to check that it is not at risk of being liquidated. A **bankruptcy search** is advisable for individual guarantors to make sure that they have not been declared bankrupt. See ¶5695+ for more information on searches. **Credit reports** can be obtained from credit reference agencies (see ¶5262).

2. When incorporating a guarantee into an agreement, care should be taken in the **drafting** to ensure that the guarantee covers all potential payments. For example, if it is intended for the guarantee to cover payments due under a separate agreement (such as a loan agreement) that other agreement must be incorporated into the guarantee clause (*Wolsey Securities Ltd v Abbeygate Management Services (Hampton) Limited* [2006] EWCA Civ 423).

3. An **agreement to procure compliance** with a contract term is more than an administrative burden; it has the same legal effect as a guarantee. This means that, for example, if the third party agrees to procure that the buyer pays the deferred consideration and the buyer then fails to do so, the third party is liable in place of the buyer (*Nearfield Ltd v Lincoln Nominees Ltd* [2006] EWHC 2421 (Ch)).

c. Tax consequences

5472 One of the most problematic effects of deferred consideration is the impact on the seller's **cash-flow**. Cash-flow may be affected because the seller may have to pay tax on his gains before he received all of the consideration.

Where an earn-out is **payable in shares or loan notes**, the tax treatment at ¶5428+ (shares) and ¶5440+ (loan notes) must also be considered. Where the earn-out is payable partly in shares and partly in cash, the elements must be treated separately.

Ascertainable deferred consideration

5473 Where the deferred consideration is ascertainable, whether or not it is subject to adjustments, the gain upon which the seller must pay **tax is calculated by** reference to the whole consideration (s 48 TCGA 1992). There is no discount or allowance for the fact that the seller has not received all of the consideration or the risk that he may not. This can cause real difficulties where the seller cannot meet his tax liability out of the consideration received at completion.

EXAMPLE On 1 March 2007, Mr A sells his shares in B Ltd for £100,000 payable at completion and £500,000 payable on 1 March 2009. His capital gains tax liability could be up to £240,000 (40% of £600,000). This will be payable in January 2008 (i.e. when his tax liability for the tax year 06/07 becomes due), before he has received the rest of the consideration.

MEMO POINTS There are however two factors which can **mitigate** this effect:
– where the consideration is payable over a period of 18 months, Revenue and Customs have the discretion to allow tax to be paid by instalments where the seller would otherwise suffer undue hardship (s 280 TCGA 1992); and
– if the seller does not in fact receive the full amount of the deferred consideration, the tax liability will be recalculated and any overpayment will be refunded (s 48 TCGA 1992).

Unascertainable consideration

5474 If the deferred consideration is of a "wholly uncertain and unascertainable amount", the gain upon which the seller will pay **tax is calculated by** reference to the market value of their right to receive the unascertainable consideration (*Marren v Ingles* [1980] 3 All ER 95). Valuing the right to receive consideration is difficult in practice. Revenue and Customs may accept a low valuation where the future profitability of the company is in doubt but not if, on the past performance of the company, the seller looks likely to achieve the earn-out. Thus, if the value of the right to receive an earn-out is sufficiently high, the seller may again have a problem with cash-flow.

5475 The second problem with earn-outs is that, if the actual **earn-out** is **less than the value** attributed to it, the seller will not get a refund of the tax overpayment. However, if the **earn-out exceeds the value** attributed to it, the seller will have to pay tax on the excess.

MEMO POINTS The seemingly unfair tax treatment of an earn-out is **because** the right to receive further unascertainable consideration is treated as an asset of the seller and he is deemed to have disposed of that asset when the further consideration is paid (*Marren v Ingles* [1980] 3 All ER 95). Thus, he will be taxed under the usual tax regime if he makes a **capital gain on** that **disposal** (i.e. if the actual consideration exceeds the value that was given to his right to receive it). However, if the seller makes a **capital loss on** that **disposal** (i.e. if the actual consideration is less than the value that was given to his right), he will not get any relief from the fact that he paid tax on a higher amount than he actually received. This is because capital losses cannot be carried back and set off against capital gains made in previous accounting periods. The loss could be carried forward, but this is only useful if the seller expects to make capital gains in the future.

EXAMPLE Mr B sells his company for £200,000 payable on completion and further consideration of 20% of profit for the next 5 years, payable at the end of that period. The earn-out right is valued at £500,000. Assuming a base cost of £100,000 (including indexation and other allowances), Mr B's capital gain is £600,000. His tax liability is therefore up to £240,000 (40% x £600,000). 5 years later, Mr B receives his earn-out and is treated as having disposed of his right to receive it.

a. Assume Mr B's **earn-out is more than expected** at £750,000. His base cost was £500,000 and discounting indexation and other allowances, he has made a capital gain of £250,000 upon which he must pay capital gains tax.
b. Assume Mr B's **earn-out is less than expected** at £400,000. His base cost was again £500,000 and discounting indexation and other allowances, he has made a capital loss of £100,000. In effect, he has paid tax on a gain of £100,000 which he did not actually make. He cannot carry back this loss to set it off against the gain he made 5 years ago when he sold the company.
Assume 2 years later, Mr B sells some antique chairs and makes a capital gain of £150,000. He can set off the capital loss from the earn-out against this gain. He therefore only has to pay tax on a gain of £50,000.

---

2. Net asset value adjustment

5480 A net asset value adjustment is a common feature of **share sales**. A downward or upward adjustment to the consideration is made if the net asset value of the company at completion is below or above an agreed amount. Usually, the adjustment is operated on a pound for pound basis. This means that the consideration is adjusted downwards by £1 for every £1 of any shortfall, or upwards by £1 for every £1 of any excess.

Normally, the parties agree to a **cushion** before the adjustment takes effect. For example, if the net asset value was expected to be £100,000, the seller and buyer could agree that the adjustment would only be made if the actual value was below £90,000 or above £110,000. If, for example, the actual value was either £85,000 or £115,000, whether the adjustment would then operate on the whole amount of the shortfall/excess (i.e. £15,000), or just the amount below/above the cushion (i.e. £5,000), as well as the amount of the cushion itself, is a matter of negotiation.

5481 The seller and buyer will usually have an idea of the expected **net asset value figure** fairly early in the negotiations. Indeed, some pre-sale tax planning measures may be taken to reduce the net assets of the company. For example, if the company has a lot of cash, it may be more tax efficient for the seller to take a pre-sale dividend rather than for the buyer to pay for cash.

The **final figure** for insertion into the sale and purchase agreement is usually provided by the seller's accountant close to completion so that it is as accurate as possible. This reduces the likelihood of an adjustment. The buyer is likely to reopen negotiations on price and/or the payment structure if the final figure is much lower than expected at the beginning of negotiations.

Completion accounts

5482 In order to determine whether an adjustment is necessary, a balance sheet of the target company as at the date of completion must be **prepared after completion**. This process is often referred to as preparation of the "completion accounts" or the "completion balance sheet". Since it has a more detailed knowledge of the target up to completion, the completion accounts are normally **prepared by** the seller's accountant (who in practice will usually also have been the target's accountant) within a specified period of time, with the buyer and its accountant having the right to agree or disagree with them, again within a set period of time.

Completion accounts and the net asset value adjustment are usually completed fairly quickly after completion, usually **within** 3 to 6 months. In the rare event of disagreement which cannot be resolved between the parties, the matter is usually put to an independent accountant for expert determination.

5483 In order to compare like with like, the completion accounts should be prepared on the basis of UK GAAP and the same **accounting principles** as the target's accounts were when it was under the control of the seller. To avoid any misunderstandings, any unusual accounting treatments are normally specified in the sale and purchase agreement.

It is also advisable for the sale and purchase agreement to specify in which order the accounting treatments should be applied. In deciding how an item in the completion accounts should be treated, firstly the parties should look to the accounting policies specified in the sale and purchase agreement. If the matter is not dealt with there, the item should be treated as it was in previous accounts of the target. Finally, if the item is new, it should be treated in accordance with UK GAAP.

Tax consequences

5484 Ordinarily, the seller would have to pay capital gains tax on the full (unadjusted) consideration. This could result in an **overpayment of tax** where there was a shortfall in the net asset value as the seller would have paid tax on more consideration than was left in his hands in the end. In order to avoid this effect, the **definition of consideration** in the sale and purchase agreement should specify that the consideration will be adjusted by the net asset value provisions. The agreement should not state that the seller will refund some of the consideration to the buyer. This is because, if the adjustment operates as a refund, the seller will be treated for tax purposes as having received the higher amount of consideration.

3. Retention

5489 A retention, as the name suggests, is a holding back by the buyer of part of the consideration in order to meet the potential liabilities of the seller to the buyer. If the seller agrees to a retention, there are three issues to consider which are dealt with in more detail below:
– what **liabilities** can be met by the retention;
– the **amount** of the retention; and
– the length of the retention **period**.

5490 Normal practice is for the retention to be held in an **escrow account** in the joint names of the buyer's and seller's solicitors. The solicitors should ensure that the escrow account provisions in the sale and purchase agreement specify that the retention (or part of it) is only to be released upon the joint written instructions of the buyer and seller. It is not for the solicitors to say whether the retention release provisions in the sale and purchase agreement have been satisfied.

5491 The **tax consequences** of a retention are the same as those of accepting ascertainable deferred consideration (see ¶5473). This is because a retention has the same effect as deferred consideration, albeit that under a retention the money has nominally been paid to the seller and retained by the buyer under particular conditions, whereas deferred consideration has yet to be paid to the seller.

Liabilities to be met out of retention

5492 A retention is generally only requested by the buyer to meet **known potential liabilities**, for example, a possible net asset value shortfall or a specific indemnity claim. However, an aggressive buyer may push for a retention to cover **warranty claims**. Even if this was not the original purpose of the retention, once a retention for another purpose has been agreed, a buyer will often argue that it should cover warranty and indemnity claims on the basis that it is illogical for it to have to recover damages from the seller when those damages could be met out of the retention. In principle, this is also logical from the seller's point of view, as he would not have to meet the claim out of his own pocket.

5493 If the retention is used to meet warranty and indemnity claims, the seller should insist that it can only be used to meet "**certain**" **claims** so that the buyer is not able to delay release of the retention on spurious grounds. The drafting of this can be tricky: what amounts to "certain"? An acceptable compromise is usually if full details of a warranty claim with more than a 50% chance of success is brought to the seller's attention in writing by the buyer within the retention period (the percentage chance of success to be determined by a barrister with appropriate experience agreed by the parties or nominated by the Bar Council). Even then, it would not be fair for all of the retention to be held back if the retention far exceeded the value of the claim. The drafting could allow for the retention to be released in stages, for example, for only so much of the retention as was necessary to meet the claim to be held back and the remainder paid over to the seller.

Thought should also be given to the interplay between the retention and the **de minimis provisions** (see ¶5923). For example, if the retention was less that the minimum aggregate warranty claim value, there would be little point in allowing the retention to be set off against warranty claims.

5494

Amount of retention

Generally, between 5% and 15% of the total consideration is thought to be a reasonable retention but this will **vary depending upon**:
– how much cash the seller is getting on completion. If most of the consideration is deferred or is in paper form, the seller is likely only to agree to a lower percentage so that the cash in their hand on the day of completion is not disproportionately diminished; and
– what liabilities the retention is intended to cover. If the retention is to cover potential known liabilities, then it is usually possible to estimate their extent and fix the retention at an appropriate figure.

5495

Retention period

The length of the retention period will largely **depend upon the main purpose** of the retention. For example, if the main purpose is to meet a possible net asset value shortfall, the retention period would normally be until the completion accounts are finalised. If the main purpose is a bit more open ended, the length of the retention period is far more open to negotiation but some attempt should be made to estimate the time it will take for potential liabilities to surface.

5496

III. Competition law implications

Laws to prevent anti-competitive mergers between businesses exist at UK and EU level and they will need to be considered before negotiations are too far advanced. These laws will only be of concern for businesses with a **high turnover** or a **dominant market position**.

The following is an outline of the main provisions. Further detailed guidance can be obtained from the Office of Fair Trading (OFT) (see ¶9905).

5505

A. UK merger control

The UK merger control provisions **apply when** the EU merger control provisions do not (see ¶5520+). Under the UK provisions, the OFT should refer a merger to the Competition Commission for **further investigation if** it believes:
– a "relevant merger" situation has or will be created; and
– the merger has resulted in a "substantial lessening of competition" within a market for goods or services in the UK.

5507

Relevant merger

5508 A merger for these purposes is an arrangement whereby two or more enterprises **cease to be distinct** (for example, by being brought under common ownership or control). Therefore, both a sale of shares and a sale of assets will be caught by the provisions.

The merger must also meet the **threshold** requirements, which are that:
– the UK turnover of the target enterprise exceeds £70 million; or
– the enterprises supply or acquire similar goods or services and, as a result of the merger, together supply or acquire at least 25% of those goods or services in the UK (or a substantial part of it).

Substantial lessening of competition

5509 A merger may be expected to lead to a substantial lessening of competition when it is expected to **weaken rivalry** between competing businesses to such an extent that customers would be harmed. This may come about, for example, through reduced product choice, or because prices could be raised profitably, output could be reduced and/or product quality or innovation could be reduced.

The **test for reference** will be met if the OFT has a reasonably held belief that, on the basis of the evidence available to it, there is at least a significant prospect that a merger may be expected to lessen competition substantially. This test is lower than that applied by the Competition Commission when determining whether the merger has substantially lessened competition because the OFT acts as a "first-phase screen".

OFT action

5510 The OFT can only make a reference **before or within** 4 months of the merger taking place. The only exception is if the merger takes place without being made public or without the OFT being informed. In that circumstance, the 4 months will run from the date upon which a public announcement is made or the OFT is informed.

5511 The parties are not required to **notify the OFT** of a relevant merger (except in certain public interest cases). However, most mergers will come to the OFT's attention through the department's monitoring of the media. If the Competition Commission finds that the **merger is anti-competitive**, it can order the parties to undo the transaction. Given the drastic and costly consequences of an adverse ruling, in practice, if the transaction is capable of being referred, the parties and their advisers should make an early approach to the OFT.

> MEMO POINTS It used to be possible to approach the OFT for confidential **guidance** and/or informal **advice**. However, in April 2006, the OFT suspended its provision of confidential guidance. The OFT now only considers applications for informal advice in respect of confidential transactions where there is a good faith intention to proceed and where its duty to refer to the Competition Commission is a genuine issue. The OFT is in the process of drafting further guidance to clarify the long-term position on this service which is anticipated to be published in early 2008. The current transitional provisions are published on the OFT's website. These changes do not affect pre-notification contacts, which are aimed at expediting smooth handling of public cases.

5512 A **fee** of £15,000, £30,000 or £45,000, depending upon the turnover of the enterprise being acquired, must be paid to the OFT in respect of all relevant mergers, regardless of whether or not they are referred to the Competition Commission.

B. EU merger control

5520 The EU merger control provisions apply to mergers (referred to as "concentrations" in the legislation) with a "**community dimension**" (EC Regulation 139/2004).

> MEMO POINTS On 10 July 2007, the EU Commission adopted a new consolidated Commission Jurisdictional Notice on the application of this regulation to EU merger control provisions in company sales (IP/07/1043). This notice replaces the following previous notices:

- Notice on the concept of concentration;
- Notice on the concept of full-function joint ventures;
- Notice on the concept of undertakings concerned; and
- Notice on the calculation of turnover.

The consolidation was undertaken in order to make the notice more "user friendly" and to enable companies to establish more easily whether or not the EU Commission is competent to review a proposed transaction.

5521 Unless each of the undertakings concerned in the merger achieves more than two-thirds of its total EU turnover within one member state, a merger will be deemed to have a community dimension when one of the following two **thresholds** are met (art 2 EC Regulation 139/2004):

a.
- the combined total worldwide turnover of all the undertakings concerned is more than €5 billion; and
- the total EU turnover of at least two of those undertakings is more than €250 million;

or

b.
- the combined total worldwide turnover of all the undertakings concerned is at least €2.5 billion;
- in each of at least three member states, the combined total turnover of all those undertakings is at least €100 million;
- in each of the three member states referred to above, at least two of the undertakings involved have a total turnover of at least €25million; and
- the total EU turnover of at least two of the undertakings is more than €100 million.

5522 A merger with a community dimension must be **notified to** the European Commission **within** 1 week after the conclusion of the agreement, the announcement of a public bid or acquisition of a controlling interest (whichever occurs first). The notification should be made on **Form CO** which can be obtained from the European Commission website (see ¶9905), a copy of which will automatically be forwarded to the OFT.

5523 A **merger cannot be implemented unless** the Commission gives clearance, except in the case of public bids or where the Commission has given special permission (i.e. has granted a derogation). The Commission has 1 month from receipt of the notification to decide whether the merger falls within the scope of the merger regulations.

5524 If the Commission has serious doubts about the merger's compatibility with the Common Market, it will normally open proceedings to initiate a full **investigation**. This will be carried out with the co-operation of the OFT. The **OFT** therefore encourages parties involved in an EU merger to bring this directly to its attention at the earliest possible stage, in addition to the mandatory notification requirement to the Commission.

IV. Heads of agreement

5529 Once an outline agreement has been reached on the price structure, the commercial terms of the deal can be put into writing. This document is commonly referred to as "heads of agreement" or "**heads of terms**", often shortened to "the heads".

5530 The **purpose** of the heads is to summarise the main terms of the deal. In addition, putting the agreed terms into writing has the advantage of flushing out any areas of misunderstanding between the parties. It is useful to spend some time getting the wording right as reference will be made to the heads throughout negotiations, particularly by advisers, in order to determine the intentions of the parties. It is difficult, without good reason, to reopen negotiations on something which has been agreed in the heads. However, the parties should avoid getting bogged down in detailed negotiations when the substantive issues will be dealt with in negotiations on the sale and purchase agreement itself.

A. Non-contractual provisions

5532 It is important to remember that, except for the matters referred to below, the heads of agreement should only be a **statement of intent**, not a legally binding contract. The actual contract will be the final version of the sale and purchase agreement. To ensure that the heads do not create a contractual commitment, a clause in the document should state that, except for specified clauses, it is not intended to bind the parties in contract.

To reiterate the position of the heads as a statement of intent, it will normally state that the buyer's intention to **purchase is subject to** satisfactory completion of "due diligence", that is an investigation of the target (¶5652+).

B. Contractual provisions

5535 As well as setting out the outline commercial terms, the heads often contain two clauses which are intended to create a contractual commitment. They are:
– to give the buyer a period of exclusivity; and
– to protect a party from wasted costs if the other pulls out of negotiations.

Exclusivity

5536 The buyer will often request a period of exclusivity in which the seller agrees not to approach or negotiate with any other potential buyers. This can also be **beneficial** for the seller as it will encourage a serious buyer to move quickly and ensure that the deal is progressed, if not completed, by the end of the exclusivity period. A **disadvantage** is that, if negotiations do not appear to be going well, the seller will not be able to line up another potential buyer as a back up.

A period of exclusivity can be agreed regardless of whether the parties also agree heads of agreement.

Wasted costs

5537 An agreement by one party to pay the costs of the other, should it **pull out of negotiations**, is sometimes included in heads of agreement in order to give the parties protection from wasted costs. Whether or not a party accepts this clause should be considered carefully. At the very least, the clause should be **reciprocal** (i.e. the seller will pay the buyer if the seller pulls out, and the buyer will pay the seller if the buyer pulls out). However, this does not guarantee a level playing field; a plc buyer is likely to retain more expensive advisers and therefore have far higher costs than the seller of a family owned company. A seller or buyer may find that he cannot afford to pull out of a bad deal. Some balance can be brought back by specifying that costs will only be payable if a party pulls out **without good cause**. For example, the buyer may wish to pull out if due diligence reveals a large liability (good cause) or if his funding falls through (bad cause). The drafting of the clause clearly needs to be considered carefully.

C. Format

5540 There is no particular format which the document should take. Some buyers issue a **letter** for the seller to countersign; sometimes the document looks more like a **contract** between the buyer and seller. Although the heads of agreement may be drafted by lawyers, they are often drafted by the parties, who are in the best position to summarise the main terms of the deal. However, it is advisable for the document to be reviewed by lawyers before signature.

SECTION 3

Financing the purchase

5550 Before the deal can be done, obviously, the buyer must be able to fund the purchase. A **buyer** has three **main funding options**:
- cash reserves;
- bank borrowing (also known as "acquisition finance") (¶4535+); and/or
- equity finance (¶4800+).

In addition, for cash flow purposes, a buyer may prefer to offer deferred consideration (¶5463+) or paper consideration (¶5426+), instead of cash.

5551 Financing the purchase is mainly the buyer's concern, but the seller should reassure himself that the buyer has this in hand. The **seller** may wish to take more of an interest (including reviewing any finance documents, such as bank loan and security agreements) if the price structure involves an element of deferred consideration and there is a concern as to whether the buyer is able to meet that future liability. (The sellers will have a breach of contract claim against the buyer if it fails to pay, but it will be of little use if the buyer is insolvent.) The seller may find it prudent to take some sort of security for payment (see ¶5468+).

5552 In a **share sale**, if the buyer intends to fund the purchase through bank borrowing, very often, the bank will expect to take security over the assets of the target. This will amount to unlawful "**financial assistance**", a topic which is developed fully below. Under the new Companies Act, private companies will be allowed to give financial assistance. Until this change comes into force (the date of which is yet to be announced at the time of writing), private companies can give financial assistance if they comply with the "whitewash procedure" (¶5586+) or the transaction falls within one of the other less common exceptions (¶5579+). It is normal practice for the buyer's solicitors to prepare the whitewash documents as it is for the benefit of their clients. The seller's solicitors normally only review the whitewash documents if a seller is staying on as a director or taking subordinated security.

Financial assistance in share acquisitions

5557 There are strict **statutory restrictions** on the ability of a target company or any of its subsidiaries to give financial assistance for the purpose of an acquisition of shares in the target company.

The restrictions amount to a **general prohibition** on the giving of financial assistance with very specific exceptions. The most useful exception is that private companies can give financial assistance if they satisfy certain pre-conditions and comply with a certain procedure, known as the "**whitewash**" procedure. The consequences of a **breach** and giving unlawful financial assistance are severe, most notably, the transaction is void and unenforceable.

The statutory provisions are relatively loosely drafted (perhaps surprising given the severity of the consequences of breach). This has led to much judicial interpretation of them and uncertainty as to their application. The **result in practice** is that all parties to any transaction which involves a transfer of shares must be alive to the possibility of financial assistance. If there is any doubt, financial assistance should be assumed and (if no other exception applies) either the whitewash procedure should be followed or the transaction should be restructured. It is in the interests of both parties to the transaction to ensure that there is no breach.

Case law has emphasised the importance of directors obtaining **independent professional advice** (both legal and accountancy) (*Belmont Finance Corporation Ltd v Williams Furniture Ltd (No 2) [1980] 1 All ER 393*). Professional advisers should ensure that their client is fully informed of the legal position and of any doubts over the validity of the proposed transaction or they may be found guilty of negligence (e.g. *Hill v Mullis & Peake [1999] BCC 325*).

> MEMO POINTS   The **new Companies Act** will abolish the prohibition on a private company giving financial assistance for the acquisition of its own shares or the shares of its private holding company. As a consequence, the "whitewash procedure" will not be required and those provisions will be repealed. The implementation date for this change is yet to be announced at the time of writing.
> The prohibition will continue to apply to assistance given by a public company or its subsidiaries for the acquisition of the public company's shares (s 678(1) CA 2006, expected to come into force on 1 October 2009). The prohibition will also continue to apply to assistance given by a public subsidiary company for the acquisition of shares in its private holding company (s 679(1) CA 2006, expected to come into force on 1 October 2009).

1. General prohibition

5565 Subject to a number of exceptions, the most important of which is the whitewash procedure for private companies (see ¶5586+), it is generally prohibited for a company to give financial assistance for the purpose of an acquisition of its own shares. In a group structure, a subsidiary cannot give financial assistance for the purpose of an acquisition of shares in its holding company, but a holding company can give financial assistance for the acquisition of shares in its subsidiary (s 151(1), (2) CA 1985; restated for public companies at s 678(1) CA 2006 by 1 October 2009).

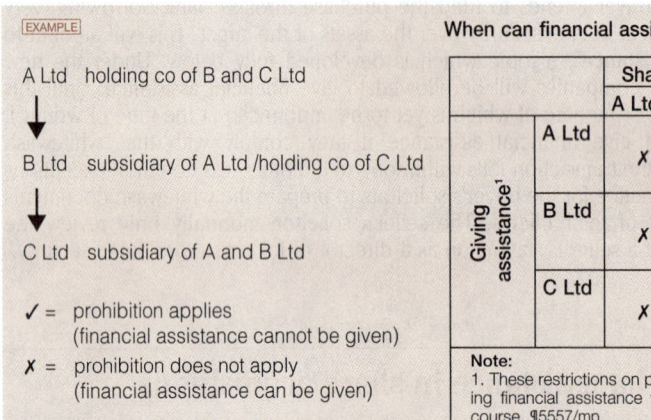

> MEMO POINTS   See ¶199+ for the **definitions** of subsidiary and holding company.

5566 The **prohibition applies** regardless of (*Chaston v SWP Group plc [2003] 1 BCLC 675*):
– the form of the acquisition (e.g. a purchase, a subscription for new shares or a share exchange);
– to whom the assistance is given (e.g. a buyer or seller or any of their subsidiaries, associated companies or nominees, or even the company itself); and
– whether the assistance was given directly or indirectly.

5567 The prohibition applies to assistance given **before or at the same time as the acquisition**. "Pre-transactional" assistance is covered, even though a person may only be proposing to acquire the shares and no acquisition may ultimately take place. The distinction between "pre-transactional" assistance and a company merely preparing itself for sale is uncertain, particularly when a definite buyer is on the scene.

5568 Assistance given **after the acquisition** is prohibited if it reduces or discharges a liability that was incurred for the purpose of the acquisition. A person may incur a liability for the purpose of an acquisition by changing his financial position, and that liability could be reduced or discharged by the company wholly or partly restoring the person's financial position to what it was before the acquisition took place (s 152(3) CA 1985; restated for public companies at s 679(3) CA 2006 by 1 October 2009).

MEMO POINTS   Where the assistance is given after the acquisition, the prohibition will only apply if the target is a public company at the time that the assistance is given. Accordingly, the prohibition will not apply where the target has re-registered as a private company since the shares were acquired and is a private company at the time the assistance is given. However, the prohibition will apply where the target was a private company at the time the shares were acquired, but has re-registered as a public company at the time the assistance is given (s 152(3)(b) CA 1985; restated for public companies at s 679(3) CA 2006 by 1 October 2009).

What constitutes financial assistance?

5569 There are five main **categories of financial assistance** (s 152(1) CA 1985; restated for public companies at s 677(1) CA 2006 by 1 October 2009):
– financial assistance by way of a gift (which could include a sale at an undervalue or the acquisition of an asset at an overvalue);
– financial assistance by way of a release, waiver, guarantee, security or indemnity (except for an indemnity against the company's own neglect or default);
– financial assistance by way of a loan (or the novation of the loan) of or assignment of rights arising under a loan);
– any other financial assistance given by a company with no or negative net assets; or
– any other financial assistance which reduces the net assets of a company to a material extent (see below).

EXAMPLE   **Typical examples** of unlawful financial assistance are:
1. The buyer borrows the purchase money and those borrowings are secured on the assets of the target.
2. At the buyer's and the seller's request, the target sells assets at an undervalue or for deferred consideration to make it more attractive for sale.
3. The target pays some of the consideration for the sale, e.g:
– the target loans the purchase money to the buyer;
– following the acquisition, the target pays a dividend to the buyer which repays the purchase money; or
– the target pays a bonus to the seller (who is also a director of the target) which exceeds the value of his services.
4. Following the sale, the target (which is now a subsidiary of the buyer) enters into a group banking arrangement so that the buyer's borrowings (including the acquisition debt) are secured on the assets of the target.
5. The target pays the transactional costs of the buyer or the seller (e.g. legal or accountancy fees).

MEMO POINTS   Financial assistance **also includes** any agreement under which any of the obligations of the person giving the assistance are to be fulfilled before the obligations of the other party to the agreement are fulfilled (or by way of the novation of or the assignment of rights arising under such an agreement) (s 152 CA 1985; restated for public companies at s 677 CA 2006 by 1 October 2009). This catches agreements which are similar to loans such as credit or deferred payment agreements. For example, if the target gave assistance by selling an asset but payment did not have to be made until a future date, that would be an agreement where the obligations of the company giving assistance had to be fulfilled before the obligations of the other party to the agreement.

5570 The final category is a catch-all so that assistance which results in a **material reduction in a company's positive net assets** will be caught even if it does not fall into any of the previous discrete categories. If there is no reduction and none of the other categories is relevant, then the prohibition will not apply.

5571 For the two final categories of financial assistance, a company's **net asset figure equals** its actual total assets less its actual total liabilities (including contingent or prospective liabilities) not just those assets and liabilities recorded in the accounts or their book value (s 152(2)

CA 1985; restated for public companies at s 677(2) CA 2006 by 1 October 2009). The date upon which the affect on net assets should be assessed is that on which the assistance is given. Where the assistance consists of the assumption of a liability to make payments in the future, the date on which the assistance is given is that on which the liability is assumed and not when any payment becomes due *(Parlett v Guppys (Bridport) Ltd [1996] 2 BCLC 34)*. The calculation of a company's assets and liabilities depends upon general accounting principles (see *Accountancy and Financial Reporting Memo*).

> MEMO POINTS If a reduction has occurred, whether it is **material or not** is a question of degree dependent upon the facts of the particular case and the court has declined to set out a general rule on the matter *(Parlett v Guppys (Bridport) Ltd [1996] 2 BCLC 34)*.

5572 The term "**financial assistance**" is not **defined** by statute. Case law has determined that the term conveys a commercial concept and does not have a technical legal meaning. What matters is the commercial substance of the transaction *(Charterhouse Investment Trust Ltd v Tempest Diesels Ltd [1986] BCLC 1)*. It is also necessary for assistance, in the nature of aid or help, to be given to someone; it is not "assistance" to give someone something to which they are already entitled *(MT Realisations Ltd (in liquidation) v Digital Equipment Co Ltd [2003] 2 BCLC 117)*. For example, the repayment of a debt which is properly due is not financial assistance *(Anglo Petroleum Ltd v TFB (Mortgages) Ltd [2007] EWCA Civ 456)*. If money in some shape or form is involved, then the assistance will be "financial" *(Armour Hick Northern Ltd v Armour Trust Ltd [1980] 3 All ER 833)*.

5573 The **test** is one of "**commercial reality**" *(Charterhouse Investment Trust Ltd v Tempest Diesels Ltd [1986] BCLC 1)*. The court will examine the transaction as a whole to see who gained the financial advantage. However, it is not necessary for the company giving the assistance to suffer a detriment, so for example a loan repayable with interest would benefit the company that made the loan but would still constitute financial assistance. The only case where a disadvantage to the company is required is when the assistance results in a material reduction in the company's net assets *(Chaston v SWP Group plc [2003] 1 BCLC 675)*.

5574 One grey area is when an **inducement to enter into a share transaction** constitutes financial assistance. On the one hand, a company can give covenants and warranties for the purpose of a share acquisition *(Barclays Bank plc v British & Commonwealth Holdings plc [1996] 1 BCLC 1)*, but on the other hand it cannot pay the fees of solicitors or other advisers *(Chaston v SWP Group plc [2003] 1 BCLC 675)*. However, payment fees of the buyer paying an agent who introduced the seller to the shares does not constitute financial assistance *(Corporate Development Partners LLC v E-Relationship Marketing Ltd [2007] EWHC 436)*.

> EXAMPLE **No financial assistance**
> MTR Ltd was a loss-making insolvent subsidiary company funded by its parent, DEC Ltd, to the tune of about £8m. MTI Ltd bought the shares of MTR Ltd for £1 and at the same time agreed to pay £6.5m for an assignment to it of the £8m loan, the price to be paid in instalments. Following the sale and assignment, MTI Ltd could not meet the price instalments due to DEC Ltd. The payments were rescheduled so that all sums payable from DEC Ltd's group to MTR Ltd would be paid to DEC Ltd and reduce the outstanding instalments. The court decided the commercial realities of the arrangement did not involve financial assistance. Before the rescheduling, DEC Ltd's group would have paid the money it owed to MTR Ltd, which would have paid money to MTI Ltd to repay the £8m loan. MTI Ltd would have paid the money back to DEC Ltd for the loan assignment. All the rescheduling did was short-circuit this position *(MT Realisations Ltd (in liquidation) v Digital Equipment Co Ltd [2003] 2 BCLC 117)*.
>
> **Financial assistance**
> DRC Ltd, a subsidiary of DRCH Ltd, paid accountants' fees for work they carried out to assist SWP plc's due diligence exercise during negotiations between the shareholders of DRCH Ltd for the sale of their shares to SWP plc. The court decided that as a commercial matter, financial assistance was given. The accountants received payment for their services and both buyer and sellers were relieved of the obligation to pay for this service themselves. The assistance was clearly financial, even though it had no impact on the share price paid by SWP plc *(Chaston v SWP Group plc [2003] 1 BCLC 675)*.

Purpose of assistance

The prohibition will not apply where the assistance is given **for one purpose** only and that purpose is not the acquisition of shares.

5575

> EXAMPLE Mrs D, Mr EB and Mr PB were partners in a residential care home business run from a property known as "The Mount". The business was operated through a company of which they were all shareholders and directors but The Mount was owned by them individually. The local authority subsequently cancelled the business' care home registration because Mr EB was charged with assault and Mr EB and Mr PB had failed to disclose spent convictions. In order to prevent permanent de-registration, Mr EB and Mr PB agreed to transfer their shares in the company to Mrs D, Mrs D gave up her interest in The Mount to Mr EB and Mr PB, who in turn granted the company a 21 year lease of that property. The rent charged to the company was £29,000 per annum in excess of market rent and it was alleged that this amounted to unlawful financial assistance. The court decided that the financial assistance had not been given for the purpose of the acquisition. Mrs D's purpose in agreeing to the onerous lease was to secure the premises for the company as it needed a lease of The Mount if it was going to continue in business. The company entering into the lease was in connection with the acquisition but not for the purpose of it (*Dyment v Boyden* [2005] 1 BCLC 163).

Where the assistance is given **for a number of purposes**, one of which is the share acquisition, it will be permitted in two situations (s 153(2) CA 1985; restated for public companies at s 678(4) CA 2006 by 1 October 2009):
– the principal purpose of the assistance is not for the acquisition or, in other words, the acquisition is a subsidiary purpose; or
– the acquisition is an incidental part of some larger purpose of the company giving the assistance.

5576

In both cases, the assistance must be given in **good faith in the interests of the company** giving it (a duty that, for directors, has recently been re-termed "to promote the company's success" (see ¶2379+), but the effect is the same). This means that those responsible for procuring that the company provides the assistance must act in the genuine belief that it is being done in the company's interest (*Brady v Brady* [1988] 2 All ER 617). Financial assistance given by an insolvent company is not in the interests of the company as the interests of the creditors would be disadvantaged (*Plaut v Steiner* (1989) 5 BCC 352). Where intra-group assistance is proposed, the interests of the individual company giving the assistance should be considered and the directors should ensure that this is recorded in board minutes.

5577

It is important in this context to **distinguish between "purpose" and "reason"**. "Purpose" is the object of the transaction and must be considered from the point of view of the company giving the assistance, not the person receiving the assistance. "Reason" is why the transaction is being carried out. The ultimate reason for the financial assistance may, and in most cases probably will, be more important than the transaction itself. For example, if a buyer proposes to finance his purchase using the company's own funds, the reason for the assistance could be because the company was failing and a change of management was required. However, this "more important" reason does not constitute a "larger purpose"; the purpose of the assistance remains that of enabling the shares to be acquired. The financial or commercial advantages flowing from the acquisition are a by-product of that, rather than an independent purpose (*Brady v Brady* [1988] 2 All ER 617).

5578

> EXAMPLE
> **1.** A family run group of companies reached a deadlock in management. A complicated scheme of reorganisation was implemented so that one side of the business would be split from the other. At the end of the reorganisation, one side of the business was headed by M Ltd (with subsidiary B Ltd) and the other by A Ltd. M Ltd owed £341,838 to A Ltd for the transfer to it of B Ltd. The last stage of the reorganisation involved a transfer of assets from B Ltd to A Ltd to satisfy the debt owed by M Ltd which clearly amounted to financial assistance. The court decided that the resolution of the management deadlock was merely the result of the scheme, not the purpose. The only purpose of B Ltd transferring assets to A Ltd was to pay for the shares of B Ltd to vest in M Ltd. The acquisition was not a mere incident of the scheme devised to break the deadlock. It was the essence of the scheme itself and the object which the scheme set out to achieve (*Brady v Brady* [1988] 2 All ER 617).

2. DRC Ltd, a subsidiary of DRCH Ltd, paid accountants' fees for work they carried out to assist SWP plc's due diligence exercise during negotiations between the shareholders of DRCH Ltd for the sale of their shares to SWP plc. The court decided that the liability to pay the accountants' fees was incurred for the purpose of the acquisition by SWP plc of DRCH Ltd's shares. It was irrelevant that the directors of DRC Ltd were motivated by the best interests of their company; this was a reason for their acts not a purpose in itself (*Chaston v SWP Group plc* [2003] 1 BCLC 675).

Exceptions to the prohibition

5579 The most important exception to the general prohibition is that a private company can give financial assistance, provided it complies with a certain procedure which is commonly referred to as the "**whitewash procedure**" (see ¶5586+).

> MEMO POINTS **Foreign companies** and foreign subsidiaries (i.e. those incorporated outside Great Britain) are permitted to give financial assistance without restriction (*Arab Bank plc v Mercantile Holdings Ltd* [1994] 1 BCLC 330; ss 735, 736 CA 1985).

5580 The **other exceptions** are set out in the table below with a reference to other parts of the book where further information about each exception can be found (s 153(3)-(4) CA 1985; restated for public companies at ss 681, 682 CA 2006 by 1 October 2009).

Exception	¶¶
Lawful dividend payment	¶1603+
Assistance relating to the acquisition of shares by employees or their families [1, 2]	-
Redemption of shares or a purchase by the company of its own shares [3]	¶1337+
Allotment of bonus shares (but not the paying up of already allotted bonus shares)	¶1013
Court confirmed reduction in share capital	¶1435+
Assistance given under a court approved scheme of arrangement with the company's creditors and shareholders (i.e. a scheme of arrangement)	¶6500+
Assistance given under an arrangement with the company's liquidator in a voluntary winding up to accept shares as consideration for the sale of property (i.e. a section 110 reorganisation)	¶6465+
Distribution of assets (including cash) to shareholders in the course of the company's liquidation	¶8087+
Assistance given under any company voluntary arrangement between the company and its creditors which is binding on the creditors	¶9435+
Where lending money is part of the ordinary business of the company and the assistance is given in the ordinary course of business [2]	-

Note:
1. The assistance must fall within one of the following categories:
– assistance by a company for the purposes of its **employees' share scheme** (see ¶847+) if the assistance is given in good faith and is in the interests of the company;
– assistance by a company or any of its subsidiaries to enable or facilitate **transactions between bona fide employees** or former employees of any company in the group or their families (spouses, civil partners, surviving spouses, surviving civil partners, children or stepchildren under 18 years) so that any of those people could acquire the beneficial ownership of shares in the company; or
– a company making a **loan to** its **employees** (other than directors) in good faith with a view to enabling them to acquire beneficial ownership of fully paid shares in itself or its holding company.
2. Where the assistance is being given by a **public company**, this exception only applies if its net assets are not reduced, or, the assistance is provided out of distributable profits (the relevant definitions are those discussed at ¶5595+).
3. This exception had been thought to apply to any assistance given for the purpose of a **redemption or own share purchase**. However, obiter comments by Arden LJ in *Chaston v SWP Group plc* ([2003] 1 BCLC 675) have cast doubt on this interpretation. In that case, Arden LJ gave the grant of security by a company to secure a borrowing raised to purchase its own shares as an example of a company giving financial assistance to itself. It may therefore be prudent to assume that the exception only applies to a payment by the company for a redemption or own share purchase.

5581 Even **if one of the exceptions applies**, financial assistance can only be given lawfully if:
a. it is within the **company's objects and powers** as set out in its memorandum and articles of association. This will not be a problem for most companies as the power to give assistance or the type of assistance proposed is usually listed as a specific object and comes within the general management powers of the directors. However, a company operating under Table

A 1948 that was registered on or before 2 December 1981 will need to amend its articles as they specifically restrict its ability to give financial assistance (reg 10 TA 1948); and
b. it is likely to **promote the success of the company** giving the assistance, so that the directors are not in breach of their fiduciary duties (see ¶2373+).

Consideration should also be given to whether the assistance amounts to an unauthorised **distribution to shareholders** (see ¶1603+), or an **avoidable transaction** under insolvency law, such as a preference or a transaction at an undervalue (see ¶7808+).

If none of the exceptions applies, the consequences of breaching the prohibition and giving unlawful financial assistance are set out at ¶5630+. **5582**

2. Whitewash procedure

Subject to certain **pre-conditions**, the whitewash procedure is a statutory process available to private companies which legitimises financial assistance given by them. **5586**

> MEMO POINTS The **new Companies Act** will abolish the prohibition on a private company giving financial assistance for the acquisition of its own shares or the shares of its private holding company. As a consequence, the "whitewash procedure" will not be required and those provisions will be repealed. The implementation date for this change is yet to be announced at the time of writing.
>
> The prohibition will continue to apply to assistance given by a public company or its subsidiaries for the acquisition of the public company's shares and for assistance given by a public company subsidiary for the acquisition of shares in its private holding company. However, the whitewash procedure will not be available for such transactions.

The whitewash procedure involves **three stages** for the company giving the assistance (and in certain situations, its holding companies) as follows: **5587**
– all the directors must make a statutory declaration, giving particulars of the assistance and an opinion regarding the solvency of the company in the next 12 months;
– the auditor must prepare a report supporting the statutory declaration; and
– the shareholders must pass a special resolution to approve the assistance, unless it is being given by a wholly-owned subsidiary.

Once the stages have been completed, the documents should be filed at Companies House and the assistance must be given within restricted time limits. A **summary timeline** of the process can be found at ¶5625.

The procedure must be followed before the assistance is given; it cannot be applied retrospectively to ratify unlawful assistance that has already been given. If the **procedure is not correctly followed**, the assistance will not have been "whitewashed" and all of the consequences of breaching the statutory prohibition will follow (see ¶5630+). Non-compliance with the whitewash procedures cannot be waived by the unanimous consent of the shareholders (Re S H & Co (Realisations) 1990 Ltd [1993] BCLC 1309). **5588**

a. Pre-conditions

The whitewash procedure is only available if: **5593**
– the company giving and receiving the assistance is of the **right type**;
– the company giving the assistance meets the **net asset requirement**; and
– the assistance is within the **company's objects and powers** and is likely to **promote its success** (see ¶5581).

Type of company

The whitewash procedure is **available to** a private company so that it can give financial assistance for the acquisition of its own shares or those of its private holding company as long as there is no intermediate public company in the group. (The whitewash procedure is **5594** not necessary for private holding companies giving financial assistance for the acquisition of shares in their subsidiaries, as this is not prohibited in any case, see ¶5565.)

The whitewash procedure is **not available** to (s 155(1), (3) CA 1985):
– a public company;
– a private company which is a subsidiary of a public company where the assistance is for the acquisition of shares in the public company; or
– a private company which is a subsidiary of a public company which in turn is a subsidiary of a private company, where the assistance is for the acquisition of shares in the ultimate private holding company.

Note that since the assistance can be given after the acquisition, an acquirer of shares in a public company could **re-register it as a private company**, comply with the whitewash procedure and then give assistance to discharge a liability incurred during the acquisition.

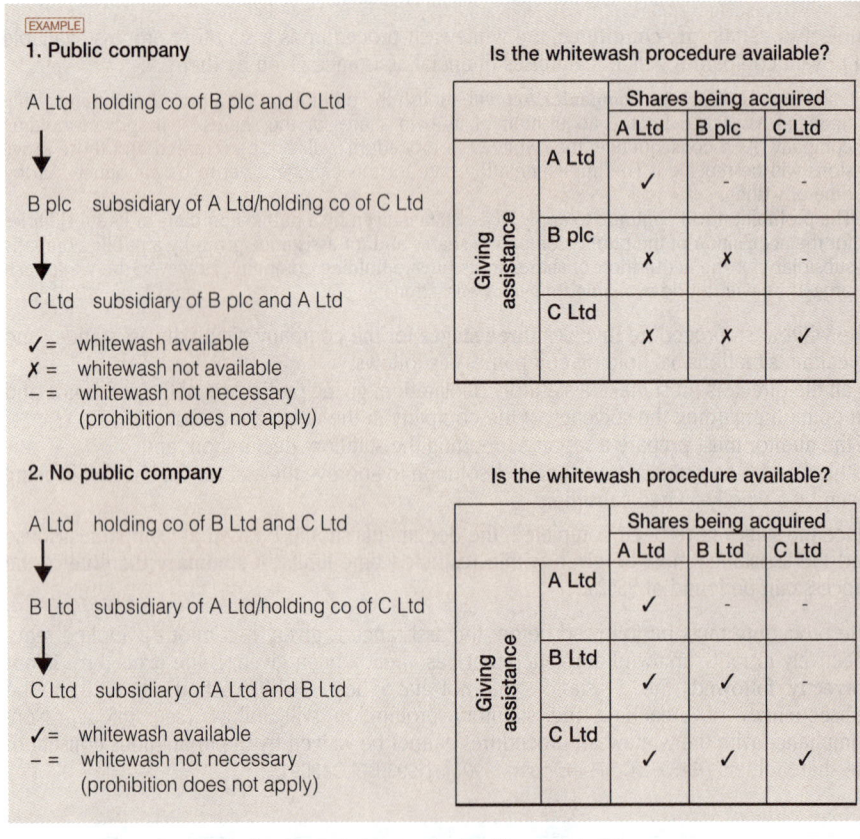

MEMO POINTS See ¶199+ for the **definitions** of subsidiary and holding company.

Net asset requirement

5595 The whitewash procedure can only be used if the company giving the assistance has positive net assets and (s 155(2) CA 1985):
– they are **not reduced** by giving the assistance; **or**
– to the extent that they are reduced, there are **sufficient distributable profits** to cover the reduction.

The reason for this requirement is to ensure that the creditors of the company are not disadvantaged. Either the assistance does not impact upon the net assets of the company or it only impacts upon the part that could have been distributed to the shareholders.

5596 In the context of the whitewash procedure, "**net assets**" **means** total assets less total liabilities, taking into account the assets and liabilities (including contingent or prospective liabilities) recorded in the company's accounting records immediately before the financial assistance is given (s 154(2) CA 1985). The assets and liabilities must therefore be accorded their book value. "**Distributable profits**" are the profits which a company is allowed to distribute by way of a dividend to its shareholders (see ¶1612+). If the assistance will reduce net assets, the company must have enough distributable profits to cover that part of the assistance (so that the shareholders rather than the creditors will be affected).

5597 In practice, **accountancy advice** should be obtained if there is any concern about the impact on net assets. In most cases, a lender will require the company's auditor to produce a non-statutory report confirming that net assets are not reduced or that any reduction is covered by distributable profits. Guidance to auditors as to the provision of such non-statutory reports can be found in the ICAEW technical release entitled "Financial assistance for acquisition of a company's own shares: non-statutory reports to bankers by auditors" (FRAG 26/94, September 1994). The court will usually rely on expert accountancy evidence to determine whether net assets have been reduced or that any reduction is covered by distributable profits, but will be free to decide which evidence it prefers in the event of a conflict between experts (*Hill v Mullis & Peake* [1999] BCC 325).

b. Directors' statutory declaration

Who makes the declaration?

5600 The directors of the company giving the assistance must make a statutory declaration, giving particulars of the assistance and confirming the solvency of the company.

Where the assistance is being given by a **group** company for the acquisition of shares in a holding company, the statutory declaration must also be made by the directors of the company whose shares are being acquired and any intermediate holding company (ss 155(6), 156(1), (2) CA 1985). A separate declaration will be needed for each company; all of the directors must make the declaration.

EXAMPLE

A Ltd holding co of B and C Ltd
↓
B Ltd subsidiary of A Ltd/holding co of C Ltd
↓
C Ltd subsidiary of A and B Ltd

– = prohibition does not apply

Which company's directors must make declaration?

Giving assistance	Shares being acquired		
	A Ltd	B Ltd	C Ltd
A Ltd	A Ltd	-	-
B Ltd	A Ltd B Ltd	B Ltd	-
C Ltd	A Ltd B Ltd C Ltd	B Ltd C Ltd	C Ltd

MEMO POINTS 1. The legislation does not specify whether the directors must all sign one declaration. This could be an issue where the **directors cannot meet** at the same time to swear the same declaration. Companies House prefers a single declaration but it will accept more than one declaration if they are all in exactly the same form, have been sworn on the same date and are filed together.
2. See ¶199+ for the **definitions** of subsidiary and holding company.

5601 If the directors are going to change following the sale and purchase then the usual practice is for the **new directors** to be appointed before the assistance is given so that they can make the declaration. This is so that the old directors can avoid the personal liability that they would otherwise incur (as to which see ¶5605+). However, care should be taken that the appointment of new directors is not a sham and that the new directors are properly informed as to the state of the company's affairs (*Re In A Flap Envelope Co Ltd* [2004] 1 BCLC 64). Similarly, if the directors of a company are to remain in office after a sale, they should be properly informed about the buyer's plans for the company so that they are able to make a declaration regarding the company's prospects in the following 12 months.

EXAMPLE Mr J was the sole director of IAFEC Ltd who proposed to give financial assistance to L Ltd. On the day of the whitewash procedure, Mr J resigned as sole director and Mr R (a director of L Ltd) was appointed in his place. Mr R made the statutory declaration, resigned and Mr J was re-appointed as sole director on the same day. The court decided that there was no period of time in which, in reality, it could be said that Mr R was a director and Mr J was not. The appointment and resignations were therefore a sham. Since Mr J did not cease to be a de facto director, the statutory declaration was not made by all the directors and so was invalid (Re In A Flap Envelope Co Ltd [2004] 1 BCLC 64).

Forms

5602 Where a company is giving financial assistance for the acquisition of shares in itself, the directors should make their statutory declaration on Form 155(6)a. Where the assistance is being given by a **group company** for the acquisition of shares in a holding company, Form 155(6)a should be used by the directors of the company proposing to give assistance, and Form 155(6)b should be used by the directors of its holding companies.

EXAMPLE

A Ltd — holding co of B and C Ltd
↓
B Ltd — subsidiary of A Ltd/ holding co of C Ltd
↓
C Ltd — subsidiary of A and B Ltd

– = prohibition does not apply

Which form?

Giving assistance		Shares being acquired		
		A Ltd	B Ltd	C Ltd
	A Ltd	A Ltd – 155(6)a	–	–
	B Ltd	A Ltd – 155(6)b B Ltd – 155(6)a	B Ltd – 155(6)a	–
	C Ltd	A Ltd – 155(6)b B Ltd – 155(6)b C Ltd – 155(6)a	B Ltd – 155(6)b C Ltd – 155(6)a	C Ltd – 155(6)a

MEMO POINTS 1. It is not strictly necessary to use the Companies House forms as long as the statutory declaration contains all the same information (Re NL Electrical, Ghosh v 3i plc [1994] 1 BCLC 22). However, the company may have problems filing a statutory declaration made in an **alternative format** and so use of the Companies House forms is strongly recommended.
2. See ¶199+ for the **definitions** of subsidiary and holding company.
3. The names of Forms 155(6)(a) and 155(6)(b), like the names of other **Companies House forms**, are taken from the section numbers of the legislation. As all of the section numbers will change under the new Companies Act, Companies House proposes to change the names of all of its forms to reflect their function rather than the relevant section number ("Working with Companies House: a consultation on the registrar's rules and related provisions which will apply under the Companies Act 2006"). At the time of writing, the new form names are not yet available.

5603 The declaration must be sworn in front of a solicitor, Commissioner for Oaths, Notary Public or Justice of the Peace. The following **information** is required to complete the forms:
– name and company number of the company whose directors are making the declaration;
– full names and addresses of the directors;
– whether the company's business is banking, insurance or some other business;
– name of the company giving the assistance and name of the company whose shares are being acquired, if different;
– whether the assistance is for the purpose of either an acquisition, or reducing or discharging a liability incurred for the purpose of an acquisition;
– number and class of shares being acquired;
– full name and address of the person to whom assistance is being given. If the recipient is a company, the registered office address should be stated;

- the form of the assistance (e.g. a loan, charge, guarantee etc). Full details should be given (*Re S H & Co (Realisations) 1990 Ltd* [1993] BCLC 1309);
- name of the person who will or has acquired the shares;
- the principal terms upon which the assistance will be given;
- the amount of cash to be transferred to the assisted person in pounds;
- the value of any asset to be transferred to the assisted person in pounds;
- the date on which the assistance is to be given; and
- a declaration of the solvency of the company in the form set out below.

> EXAMPLE **Declaration of solvency:**
> I/We have formed the opinion, as regards the company's initial situation immediately following the date on which the assistance is proposed to be given, that there will be no ground on which it could then be found to be unable to pay its debts.
> *either*
> (a) I/We have formed the opinion that the company will be able to pay its debts as they fall due during the year immediately following that date.
> *or*
> (b) It is intended to commence the winding up of the company within 12 months of that date, and I/we have formed the opinion that the company will be able to pay its debts in full within 12 months of the commencement of the winding up.

In forming their **opinion** as to whether or not the company would be unable to pay its debts, the directors must apply the same **test** as under insolvency law (see ¶7600, ¶7601). The directors must therefore be able to ascertain the extent of the financial assistance. This may mean that the assistance has to be subject to a maximum. For example, if the financial assistance is in the form of a guarantee, the directors will not know the extent of the company's liability under that guarantee unless a cap is put on it.

Defective declaration

The **directors incur personal liability** when they make a declaration. A director who makes a declaration without having reasonable grounds for the opinion expressed in it is liable to imprisonment, a fine or both (s 156(7) CA 1985; ¶9935). A director who makes a false declaration may be disqualified from being a director if he made it without exercising any independent judgment, for example, by only relying upon the judgment of professional advisers (*Re Bradcrown Ltd, Official Receiver v Ireland* [2001] 1 BCLC 547). The directors could also be sued by the company for breaching their statutory duties to act within their powers (s 171 CA 2006), to exercise reasonable care, skill and diligence (s 174 CA 2006), and to promote the success of the company (s 172 CA 2006). This could particularly apply where the declaration has been made by new directors (see ¶5601). However, if the directors had reasonable grounds for their opinion, they will not be liable if that opinion turns out to have been wrong.

An inaccurate declaration may affect the **validity of the whitewash** procedure. The deciding factor appears to be the degree of inaccuracy, for example, an obvious error will not affect the declaration. Instead the courts have decided that the declaration should be judged objectively, reading it as a whole.

> EXAMPLE
> **Whitewash valid**
> 1. J Ltd received financial assistance for its purchase of shares in HT Ltd. The statutory declaration was deficient in two ways; firstly, it named J Ltd and others as receiving the financial assistance when the assistance was only received by J Ltd and, secondly, it did not indicate the amount of cash to be transferred to the assisted person. The court decided that the first deficiency was not a true defect because other parties could have received the assistance even though in this particular instance they had not. The second deficiency was a true defect but the declaration did make clear elsewhere the amount being lent to J Ltd in cash. Bearing in mind the severe consequences of deciding that the declaration was invalid and having regard to the declaration as a whole, there was sufficient compliance with the statutory requirements to treat the declaration as valid (*Re Hill & Tyler Ltd (in administration), Harlow v Loveday* [2005] 1 BCLC 41).

2. R Ltd bought shares in SH Ltd partly financed by a loan from N Ltd. Following the purchase, N Ltd and SH Ltd entered into a debenture under which SH Ltd agreed to repay the loan, charged its assets to N Ltd as security for N Ltd's loan and guaranteed R Ltd's loan repayments. The statutory declaration stated that a debenture had been granted but did not state which property had been charged, the kind of charge granted or that a guarantee had been given. The court decided that, although the case was close to the line, the declaration reasonably and fairly described the particulars of the form and the principal terms of the financial assistance. It was therefore sufficient to satisfy the statutory requirements. However, in future, solicitors should err on the side of caution and include a full form of particulars (*Re S H & Co (Realisations) 1990 Ltd* [1993] BCLC 1309).

Whitewash invalidated
3. Mr J was the sole director of IAFEC Ltd who proposed to give financial assistance to L Ltd. On the day of the whitewash procedure, Mr J resigned as sole director and Mr R (a director of L Ltd) was appointed in his place. Mr R made the statutory declaration, resigned and Mr J was re-appointed as sole director on the same day. The court decided that both Mr R and Mr J should have made the statutory declaration (see example ¶5601) but even if they had, it would not have been valid because neither Mr R nor Mr J had properly informed themselves of the company's state of affairs. There was no evidence that Mr R knew anything of IAFEC Ltd's financial affairs nor that Mr J had made any enquiries into the company's financial standing (*Re In A Flap Envelope Co Ltd* [2004] 1 BCLC 64).

c. Auditor's report

5609 The auditor of each company whose directors have made a statutory declaration must prepare a report, which must be **annexed to** the relevant declaration.

In the case of the target, there is nearly always an issue as to **which auditor** will prepare the report, the old auditor (i.e. the seller's) or the new auditor (i.e. the buyer's). In practice, the report is usually prepared by the new auditor. It is therefore necessary for the old auditor to resign and the new auditor be appointed earlier in the completion meeting, before the directors' make their statutory declaration and before the matter is formally put to the shareholders.

The report must be **addressed to** the directors of the relevant company and should be in the **form** set out below (APB Bulletin 2007/1).

> EXAMPLE Sample report
>
> **Report of the independent auditor to the directors of A Ltd pursuant to section 156(4) of the Companies Act 1985**
>
> We report on the attached statutory declaration of the directors dated [*insert date*], prepared pursuant to the Companies Act 1985, in connection with the proposal that [*insert name of company giving assistance*] should give financial assistance for the purchase of [*insert number and class*] shares of [*insert name of company's whose shares are being purchased*].
>
> Basis of opinion
> We have enquired into the state of the company's affairs in order to review the bases for the statutory declaration.
>
> Opinion
> We are not aware of anything to indicate that the opinion expressed by the directors in their statutory declaration as to any of the matters mentioned in section 156(2) of the Companies Act 1985 is unreasonable in all the circumstances.
>
> [*Signed*]
> Registered auditor
> [*Address*]
> [*Date – same as directors' statutory declaration*]

> MEMO POINTS There is no alternative position for **companies below the audit threshold**. It appears therefore that such companies will have to appoint an auditor for the purpose of providing the report.

Defective report

5610 A **false** auditor's **report**, for example if the auditor has not in fact enquired into the state of the company, will invalidate the whitewash procedure (*Re In a Flap Envelope Co Ltd* [2004] 1 BCLC 64). A **negligent report** may not have the same effect. However, in both cases, the auditor could be sued by the company for negligence or for dishonestly participating in a breach by the directors of their duty to exercise their powers for a proper purpose (*Caparo Industries plc v Dickman* [1990] 1 All ER 568; *Royal Brunei Airlines Sdn Bhd v Tan* [1995] 3 All ER 97). This is because the auditor owes a duty of care to the company. It is not clear whether the directors would also have a claim against the auditor in this situation.

d. Shareholders' approval

5613 Where a company is giving financial assistance for the acquisition of shares in itself, the shareholders must approve that assistance by way of a special resolution (s 155(4) CA 1985).

Where the assistance is being given by a **group company** for the acquisition of shares in a holding company, no special resolution is required where the assistance is being given by a wholly owned subsidiary. If the assistance is not being given by a wholly owned subsidiary, a special resolution is required from the shareholders of the company giving the assistance, the company whose shares are being acquired, and any intermediate holding company (unless it is a wholly owned subsidiary) (s 155(5) CA 1985).

EXAMPLE

1. Subsidiary not wholly owned

A Ltd   holding co of B and C Ltd
↓
B Ltd   subsidiary of A Ltd (not wholly owned)/ holding co of C Ltd
↓
C Ltd   subsidiary of A and B Ltd (not wholly owned by B Ltd)

– = prohibition does not apply

Which company's shareholders must pass special resolution?

Giving assistance	Shares being acquired		
	A Ltd	B Ltd	C Ltd
A Ltd	A Ltd	-	-
B Ltd	A Ltd B Ltd	B Ltd	-
C Ltd	A Ltd B Ltd C Ltd	B Ltd C Ltd	C Ltd

2. Subsidiary wholly owned

A Ltd   holding co of B and C Ltd
↓
B Ltd   wholly owned subsidiary of A Ltd/ holding co of C Ltd
↓
C Ltd   subsidiary of B Ltd (not wholly owned) and C Ltd

✗ = special resolution not required
– = prohibition does not apply

Which company's shareholders must pass special resolution?

Giving assistance	Shares being acquired		
	A Ltd	B Ltd	C Ltd
A Ltd	A Ltd	-	-
B Ltd	✗	✗	-
C Ltd	A Ltd C Ltd	C Ltd	C Ltd

MEMO POINTS   See ¶199 for **definitions** of subsidiary, holding company and wholly owned subsidiary.

5614 The special resolution must be passed on the **date** of the directors' statutory declaration or within the following week (s 157(1) CA 1985). This requirement can be problematic in terms of timing because of the **notice requirements** for a shareholder meeting. In order to circumvent this problem, where possible, the written resolution procedure is used in practice (¶3580+) and the resolution is passed on the date of the statutory declaration. If the written resolution procedure cannot be used, the majority shareholders could consent to short notice and the resolution could be passed at a meeting instead (¶3681+). If neither of these options is available, the shareholder meeting must be convened before the statutory declaration and the date of the declaration must be arranged to fit in with the date of the meeting.

5615 A copy of the directors' declaration together with the annexed auditor's report must be **available for inspection** at the meeting at which the resolution is passed, otherwise the resolution is not effective (s 157(4) CA 1985).

> MEMO POINTS   If the written resolution procedure is used, instead of the documents being available for inspection at the shareholder meeting, they must be **supplied to each shareholder** before or at the same time as the resolution is supplied to him for signature (para 4 Sch 15A CA 1985).

Shareholder objection

5616 One or more **shareholders holding** 10% or more of the company's issued share capital (by nominal value) who voted against the resolution or who did not consent to it can apply to court for the cancellation of the resolution (s 157(2)(a) CA 1985). If there is more than one objector, they can appoint one of themselves to make the application for all of them. The appointment must be in writing.

Comment: In practice, it is usual for unanimous shareholder consent to be procured. A bank funder would not be comfortable with providing finance for the acquisition if there was a possibility that the whitewash could be challenged by a minority shareholder.

5617 The **procedure for an application to object to a resolution** is as follows (ss 54, 157(3) CA 1985):
a. the application must be made within 28 days of the resolution being passed;
b. once the company has been notified of the application, it must immediately file Form 157 at Companies House;
c. at the hearing of the application, the court must make an order either to cancel or confirm the resolution. The court also has the discretion to make any other order, including for the purchase of the dissenting shareholders' shares by a third party and/or the company;
d. a copy of the court's order will be provided to all the parties and the company must file an office copy at Companies House within 15 days of the date of the order (or any longer period that the court specifies); and
e. if the court order makes an alteration to the memorandum or articles, the effect is the same as if the alteration had been made by special resolution and the usual filing requirements apply (see ¶410+, ¶450+). If the court does not order a change to the memorandum and articles, one cannot be made unless court authorisation is obtained.

> MEMO POINTS   The name of Form 157, like the names of other **Companies House forms**, is taken from the section number of the legislation. As all of the section numbers will change under the new Companies Act, Companies House proposes to change the names of all of its forms to reflect their function rather than the relevant section number ("Working with Companies House: a consultation on the registrar's rules and related provisions which will apply under the Companies Act 2006"). At the time of writing, the new form names are not yet available.

5618 Any company or officer who **fails to file** Form 157 or the court order is liable to a fine (¶9935).

e.   Companies House filing

5620 The directors' statutory declaration, auditor's report and shareholder resolution must be filed at Companies House **within** 15 days of the resolution being passed. If a special resolution is not required, the statutory declaration and auditors' report must be filed at Companies House within 15 days of the declaration being made (s 155(5) CA 1985 as amended by para 1 Sch 4 SI 2007/2194).

If the company **fails to file** the documents within the required time, the company and every officer in default is liable to a fine and a daily default fine (¶9935) but the whitewash procedure is not invalidated (*Re NL Electrical*, *Ghosh v 3i plc* [1994] BCLC 22).

f. Timing of assistance

First date by which assistance can be given

If every required **resolution is passed unanimously** by all shareholders entitled to vote at general meetings of the company (not just those who did actually vote), the assistance can be given immediately after the last resolution is passed.

However, **if one or more shareholders did not vote or voted against** the assistance, the company has to wait for 4 weeks after the date on which the special resolution was passed before giving the assistance to see if an application to object to the resolution is filed. If more than one company had to pass a special resolution and total unanimity was not achieved by them all, the company giving the assistance has to wait 4 weeks after the date on which the last resolution was passed (s 158(2) CA 1985).

If an application to object to the resolution is filed, unless the court orders otherwise, the assistance cannot be given until the court has made its final decision (s 158(3) CA 1985).

Because of this delay and the potential uncertainty caused by dissenting shareholders, **in practice** a unanimous shareholder decision is always procured, by way of a written resolution if this is possible (see ¶5614).

5622

> MEMO POINTS   The 4-week delay is only triggered by a dissenting shareholder with voting rights, although the right to object to the resolution extends to **non-voting** shareholders. In practice therefore, if all the voting shareholders approve the resolution and the assistance is given immediately, a non-voting shareholder will find it difficult to object. He will still have the right to file an application, but it is submitted that the court will be more inclined to approve a resolution that has already been acted upon; if the application had merit, it would perhaps make an order for the purchase of the non-voting shares.

Last date by which assistance must be given

In all cases, the assistance must be given **within** 8 weeks of the date on which the directors made their statutory declaration. If the directors of more than one company have made a declaration, the assistance must be given within 8 weeks of the date on which the earliest of the declarations is made. There is no automatic extension to this time limit if an application to object to the resolution is filed, but the court can order to extend the time limit and will generally do so if the resolution has been upheld and an extension is required (s 158(4) CA 1985).

5624

> MEMO POINTS   Where the **assistance takes the form of** the **incurrence of an obligation** it does not matter that performance of the obligation could occur outside of the time limit. For example, if A Ltd gives assistance in the form of a guarantee, A Ltd must enter into the guarantee within 8 weeks even if the guarantee is not called upon until much later.

g. Summary timeline

5625

Day	Stage		
-22	Call shareholder meeting (if written resolution or consent to short notice cannot be obtained)		
-7	Directors' statutory declaration Auditors' report		
0	Pass shareholder resolution		
	Unanimous by all shareholders	Not unanimous and/or not all shareholders consent but no objection	Objection
	First day for assistance	-	-
+ 8	Companies House filings (if no shareholder resolution required)		
+ 15	Companies House filings (if shareholder resolution required)		
+ 28	-	First day for assistance	Deadline for court application. No assistance until court order.
+ 49	Last day for assistance	Last day for assistance	Last day for assistance (unless court orders extension)

3. Breach

5630 The consequences of giving unlawful financial assistance are severe for:
- the transaction;
- the company and its officers; and
- other involved parties.

> **MEMO POINTS** Where a company gives unlawful financial assistance, it may **release** its directors and the recipient of the assistance **from liability** provided it does not jeopardise the solvency of the company or cause loss to creditors. The release must be approved unanimously by the company's shareholders (*Cox v Cox* [2006] EWHC 1077 (Ch)).

Consequences for transaction

5631 It is illegal to give financial assistance in breach of the prohibition. Unlawful financial assistance is therefore **void** and any agreements that support it will have no effect and be **unenforceable**. For example:
- if the target has lent money to the buyer, it will not be able to recover the loan under the loan agreement; or
- if a lender has taken security over the target's assets, it will not be able to enforce that security.

This effect applies equally to **innocent parties** who may not have given or received the assistance themselves. For example, a lender will not be able to enforce its security for a loan to a target which in turn used that money to give unlawful financial assistance (even if the loan itself is enforceable) (*Re Hill & Tyler Ltd (in administration)*, *Harlow v Loveday* [2005] 1 BCLC 41). However, the repayment of a debt which is properly due and unrelated to the acquisition is not financial assistance (*Anglo Petroleum Ltd v TFB (Mortgages) Ltd* [2007] EWCA Civ 456).

> **MEMO POINTS** Even though the agreements will be rendered unenforceable, it may be possible for a lender to **recover loan money** through the principle of restitution.

5632 It is possible to **sever the illegal part** of the transaction from the remainder. The effect on the wider transaction could therefore be limited. For example, a share sale agreement would be enforceable even though an ancillary loan or security agreement was not (*Carney v Herbert* [1985] BCLC 140).

However, it is not possible for an unlawful agreement to be partly enforceable. For example, security which partly secures money used to give unlawful financial assistance and partly secures other lawful lending will be wholly unenforceable. It is not possible to say that it could be enforced as far as the lawful lending was concerned but not enforced as far as the unlawful financial assistance was concerned (*Re Hill & Tyler Ltd (in administration)*, *Harlow v Loveday* [2005] 1 BCLC 41).

> EXAMPLE
>
> **1. Severance possible**
> Mr H sold his shares in A Ltd to I Ltd, a company controlled by Mr C. The parties agreed that I Ltd would pay for the shares in instalments, Mr C would guaranteed those payments should I Ltd default and payment would further be secured by mortgages over the property of A Ltd's subsidiary. The court decided that the mortgage constituted unlawful financial assistance. However, it was severable from the remainder of the transaction because the mortgage was ancillary to the overall transaction and its elimination would not affect the sale of the shares. The fact that Mr H might have refused to enter into the transaction unless the mortgage had been granted was not a relevant factor in determining its severability. Mr H was therefore entitled to enforce the share sale agreement against I Ltd and the guarantee against Mr C (*Carney v Herbert* [1985] BCLC 140).
>
> **2. Severance not possible**
> The shares of HT Ltd were purchased by J Ltd, a new company specially formed for that purpose by Mr L. J Ltd was loaned £150,000 by Mr L, partly to finance the purchase and partly to provide working capital. That loan was secured by a written guarantee and a debenture from HT Ltd in favour of Mr L. Mr L subsequently made two further advances to J Ltd to provide working capital, of £30,000 and £20,000. These advances were also secured by the guarantee and debenture (which applied to "all monies" advanced). The court decided that the guarantee and debenture would have amounted to unlawful financial assistance (if the whitewash had not been complied with). Accordingly, those agreements would have been void and wholly unenforceable. In the absence of severance (which was not possible on the facts), it could not be said that the guarantee and debenture could be unenforceable as to the advance which was used to finance the share purchase but enforceable as to the other advances which were unconnected with the acquisition (*Re Hill & Tyler Ltd (in administration)*, *Harlow v Loveday* [2005] 1 BCLC 41).

5633 A potentially unlawful **agreement** which **could be performed lawfully** will not be void. This is because where an agreement could be performed in a number of ways, the court will presume that the parties will carry it out lawfully. So, for example, an agreement to give financial assistance will be enforceable if the parties comply with the whitewash procedure before the actual assistance is given (*Brady v Brady* [1988] 2 All ER 617).

Consequences for company and its officers

5634 The directors of a company which gives unlawful financial assistance are in **breach of their fiduciary duties** and their statutory duty to exercise care, skill and diligence (s 178 CA 2006). They could therefore be sued by the company, its liquidator or, in some cases, by a shareholder, for recovery of any loss to the company. For example, if a company unlawfully paid the legal and accountancy fees of the buyer and seller in a share sale, the directors could be sued for repayment of those fees (*Chaston v SWP Group plc* [2003] 1 BCLC 675). See ¶2434+ for breach of fiduciary duties and ¶7126+ for actions by shareholders.

> MEMO POINTS 1. As an alternative to an action for breach of fiduciary duties, the directors could be sued for the **tort of conspiracy**, i.e. that the directors have acted together to effect an unlawful purpose which resulted in damage to the company (*Belmont Finance Corporation Ltd v Williams Furniture Ltd (No 2)* [1980] 1 All ER 393).
> 2. A director's breach of the financial assistance provisions will also be taken into account if an action for **disqualification** is brought against him on the ground of unfitness (¶3021+).

5635 If the company is subsequently wound up, the officers or any person who has taken part in the promotion, formation or management of the company could be held liable for **misfeasance** and required to account for the money and contribute to the assets of the company (see ¶7457+).

5636 Breach of the financial assistance provisions also carries severe statutory **criminal penalties** for the company and its officers. Any company that gives unlawful financial assistance is liable to be fined. In addition, any officer of the company is liable to imprisonment and/or a fine (s 151(3) CA 1985). See ¶9935 for details of the maximum imprisonment term and fine.

> MEMO POINTS Under the **new Companies Act**, if a public company breaches the financial assistance provisions the company and its officers will also face severe statutory penalties. The company will be liable for a fine and any officer of the company in default will be liable to imprisonment, a fine, or both (s 680(2) CA 2006, expected to come into force by 1 October 2009).

5637 There are additional consequences for a **public company** that gives financial assistance so a person can acquire its shares and the company has a beneficial interest in the shares. The company must cancel the shares and diminish its share capital by the nominal value of the cancelled shares within 1 year of the acquisition unless it has previously transferred the shares or its interest in them. If the effect of the cancellation is to take the company's allotted share capital below the authorised minimum for public companies, the company must apply for re-registration as a private company, stating the effect of the cancellation. The company and the shareholder are not permitted to exercise any voting rights in the shares (s 146 CA 1985). The same applies to a **private company which re-registers as a public company**, except that instead of having to cancel the shares within 1 year of acquisition, the company must cancel them within 1 year of re-registration (s 148 CA 1985).

> MEMO POINTS These provisions are expected to be repealed by 1 October 2009. Whilst the prohibition on giving financial assistance is to be retained for public companies under the new Act, there are no equivalent provisions in the **new Companies Act**. Public companies will be prohibited from providing post-acquisition assistance, but if a public company re-registers as a private company after the acquisition of its shares, this prohibition will be lifted (s 678(3) CA 2006, expected to come into force by 1 October 2009). However, if a post-acquisition assistance is given by a private company which then re-registers as a public company after the acquisition of its shares, the prohibition will still apply

Consequences for other parties

5638 Any **person who receives** unlawful financial assistance with the knowledge that it was given in breach of the directors' fiduciary duties may be liable to return the money or property under the principle of "knowing receipt". The test is whether the party's knowledge makes it unconscionable for him to retain the benefit of the receipt (*Bank of Credit and Commerce International (Overseas) Ltd v Akindele* [2004] 4 All ER 221). This can place lenders in a difficult position. For example, if a loan to a buyer is repaid out of the target company's funds, the lender could be liable to repay the money if it had knowledge of the source of the repayments.

5639 Any **person who dishonestly assists** the directors in committing the breach of their fiduciary duties could be liable to make good the company's loss (*Royal Brunei Airlines Sdn Bhd v Tan* [1995] 2 AC 378). Unlike liability for "knowing receipt", there is no need for the party to have received the assistance himself. The key to establishing liability is dishonesty. The actions must have been dishonest by the standards of ordinary people and the dishonest party must have known that his actions breached those standards (*Twinsectra Ltd v Yardley* [2002] 2 All ER 377).

SECTION 4

Investigation of target

5652 The buyer will have made an initial investigation into the target before negotiations have even begun, to determine whether or not it is suitable for purchase (see ¶5258+). Once the buyer and sellers are ready to move forward into negotiations, the buyer will need to carry out a thorough investigation of the target. This process of investigation is known as "**due diligence**".

5653 The **purpose** of due diligence is twofold. Firstly, it aims to draw out information that will help the buyer understand the business so that it is able to take it over from completion. Secondly, it aims to draw out areas of financial or legal risk which could be costly to the buyer. Some questions are therefore quite technical in nature and will need specialist input. For example, it is usual for tax specialists to examine the target's tax status, for property law specialists to examine the target's property holdings and for employment law specialists to examine the target's employment situation.

5654 The due diligence exercise is usually **carried out by** advisers; normally, the buyer's accountants carry out the financial due diligence and its solicitors carry out the legal due diligence. Each adviser will liaise with his counterpart acting for the seller. In **high value transactions**, the buyer's advisers will prepare a due diligence report for their client to explain what issues were investigated, the results of that investigation and the extent of any discovered liabilities. In **smaller value transactions**, it may be more cost effective for the buyer and seller to manage the process themselves. However, they should make sure that they keep their advisers informed, for example, by copying any direct correspondence between themselves to their respective solicitors (including copies of any enclosures).

Most of the information will be found out by **questioning** the seller (see ¶5656+). In addition, the buyer will carry out **searches of public registers** (see ¶5695+).

A. Questioning the seller

5656 The formal investigation is carried out using a **question and answer** format. The seller will usually be asked to respond to a lengthy questionnaire with supplemental questions being asked if necessary. This is normally coupled with a more informal investigation carried out by the buyer and/or its advisers **visiting the target's premises** and finding out information about the business "on the ground".

Guidance for managing the process and a review of the **typical questions** are considered below.

5657 Before the seller releases any information in relation to the due diligence exercise, it should ensure that the information will be kept confidential and will not be abused by the buyer should the sale not proceed. Issues relating to **confidentiality**, such as confidentiality agreements and how to control the flow of information, should be dealt with at the pre-sale stage of the process (see ¶5244+). In addition, the seller should be ready to explain the new faces which the target's staff, suppliers and customers will inevitably see at the business.

1. Guidance for managing the process

5659 Due diligence generates a great deal of paperwork. It is therefore extremely important that the process is managed effectively in order to:
– maintain confidentiality;
– minimise disruption; and
– ease the disclosure process (¶5892+).
Some guidance for ensuring a more efficient due diligence exercise are given below.

Written questions and answers

5660 A seller should always insist that questions from or on behalf of the buyer are put in writing. Similarly, a buyer should insist on written answers to its questions. Furthermore, the seller and buyer should keep a copy of the questionnaire, any follow up questions, the answers and any documents that accompanied them. **Without a written record**, it is very easy to forget what information was given and when. This can lead to disagreements during negotiations. A written record will also make the disclosure process far easier as much of the information will already be to hand.

Dated documents

5661 If questions and answers are dated, it is easier to determine when the information has become out of date. This will assist during the disclosure process.

Use of standard questionnaires

5662 Solicitors and accountants usually have a standard due diligence questionnaire, but these can be frustrating for the seller if the questions are not appropriate for the target. The buyer and its advisers should review, and if necessary **amend**, their standard questionnaire before sending it out to the seller and its advisers.

Copy documents

5663 The seller will invariably need to provide copies of important documents such as leases or major supply contracts. No original documents should be handed over at this stage except for the statutory books of the target, which the buyer will need to inspect and then return. It is quite easy for **mistakes** to be made when photocopying, but a quick check to make sure that a full legible copy of any requested document has been supplied will reduce the need to provide repeat copies. In particular, the seller should watch out for **double-sided documents**, such as contracts with the terms and conditions in small print on the back. The seller should avoid **writing on the copies** as the buyer will normally expect "clean" documents.

Answers

5664 The due diligence process can be extremely time-consuming for both seller and buyer. Unfortunately, there are no short cuts; the seller will need to answer all the questions as fully as possible. If a question is not understood, the seller should ask his advisers to explain what is required. If an answer is unclear or throws up new issues, the buyer will normally ask **supplemental questions** until it has a satisfactory and complete answer. Having said that, there is no need to repeat information; if a question asks for information that has already been given, the seller should refer the buyer to the relevant previous answer. If a question would take a disproportionate amount of time and effort to answer, the seller should ask the buyer to waive the question. If a question is **not relevant** to the business, for example where the buyer asks for details of manufacturing operations but there is none, the seller will give a "nil response".

Some questions will inevitably take time to answer but the seller should avoid holding back answers until the whole questionnaire has been completed. A buyer will normally prefer to receive the **answers in stages**. So, once a reasonable number of questions have been answered, the seller should send these on and simply mark which are to follow. This keeps the process moving and gives the transaction the momentum it needs.

2. Typical questions

5669 Due diligence can be extremely wide ranging. Typically, it will cover the **topics** listed in the table below, in the order in which they are usually found in a standard due diligence questionnaire. Some topics are only relevant to one of share or asset sales and these are also indicated in the table.

Topic [1]	¶¶
Constitution of target company [2]	¶5670
Target business	¶5671
The seller [3]	¶5672
Accounts	¶5673
Financing	¶5674+
Taxation [4]	¶5678
Property	¶5679

Topic[1]	¶¶
Environmental matters	¶5680
Tangible assets	¶5681
Intellectual property	¶5682
Information technology	¶5683
Trading matters	¶5684
Litigation	¶5685
Employees	¶5686
Data protection	¶5687
Health and safety	¶5688
Insurance	¶5689
Pensions	¶5690
Competition	¶5691

Note:
1. In an asset sale, questions should be restricted to those relating to the business and assets being purchased.
2. Usually not relevant in an asset sale.
3. Questions about the seller are usually only required if the seller is a company.
4. Usually not relevant in an asset sale.

Constitution

5670

Questions about the constitution of the target company are only relevant to **share sales**. They give the buyer essential **information about** the legal structure of the target and its subsidiaries, which the buyer will check against the results of its company search. The following information is usually required:
– a copy of the certificate of incorporation, any certificate of incorporation on change of name, memorandum and articles, any shareholder resolutions and any shareholder agreements;
– share capital information, e.g. the amount authorised, issued and paid up, share classes and denominations;
– shareholder information, e.g. names and addresses, number of shares held by each person and whether or not the shares are held on trust;
– names and addresses of the directors and secretary;
– the accounting reference date;
– where the statutory and minute books may be inspected;
– details of any share option agreements; and
– similar details about the target's subsidiaries.

Business

5671

The buyer will need general **information about** the target, whether by way of an asset or share purchase. More detailed trading information is usually requested later in the questionnaire. The following information is usually required:
– description of the business;
– details of any change in the nature of the business;
– copies of sales and marketing literature; and
– details of all current business opportunities and any that are at risk because of the negotiations to change control of the target.

The seller

5672

In a sale by a **corporate seller**, the buyer will need company **information about** the seller to make sure it has the capacity to sell the target. The following information is usually required:
– details of shareholders and their shareholdings, directors and secretary;

– a copy of the memorandum and articles and any shareholder or similar agreement under which consent to the sale is required from a third party; and
– a chart of the corporate group to which the seller belongs showing its legal structure and the way in which its business is organised.

Accounts

5673 Accounts information is obviously important to the buyer so that it can assess the financial health of the target but also to make sure that the target has complied with its legal obligations in this area. The seller should therefore expect **information about** the target's accounts to be requested under both the financial and legal due diligence. The following information is usually required:
– audited accounts for the last 3 years;
– management accounts since the last audited accounts; and
– current business plans, budgets, forecasts and the underlying assumptions.

Finance

5674 In a share sale, the financial liabilities of the target will go with the sale. It is therefore extremely important that the buyer has **information about** the way in which the target is financed. In an asset sale, the questions need to be more tailored to bring out information about any encumbrances on the particular assets being transferred.

The following information is usually required:
– details of all bank accounts including current balances;
– copies of all banking arrangements including facility letters;
– copies of all debt instruments, e.g. debenture stock, loan notes etc;
– copies of all invoice discounting and debt factoring arrangements;
– details and copies of all security documents relating to the target or its subsidiaries, e.g. mortgages, charges or debentures;
– copies of any guarantees or indemnities given by the target or its subsidiaries;
– details of any grants or allowances made to the target or its subsidiaries over the last 6 years;
– details of any capital commitments;
– copies of any lease, rental, hire-purchase, credit or similar agreement;
– details of intra-group debts and contingent liabilities;
– a list of aged debtors marking those considered bad or doubtful; and
– details of any credit agreements with customers.

Release of security

5675 In most sales, the information questionnaire will reveal bank security (e.g. mortgages, charges or debentures). In an asset sale, any security over the assets to be transferred will have to be released before completion. In a share sale, the buyer may require any security over the underlying assets of the target to be released as it will want to put its own financial arrangements in place. This will involve some **liaison** with the relevant bank or building society.

5676 If the **lender is still owed money**, it will not release its security, but it will often confirm that a release will be given when it has been repaid (for example, as is the case where a property is being sold that still has an outstanding mortgage). The buyer may then agree to complete the purchase without obtaining the releases, if the seller's solicitor gives the buyer's solicitor an undertaking to obtain a release immediately after completion. In order to comply with this undertaking, the seller's solicitor will need to obtain an up to date redemption statement from the lender and agree with the seller that the lender should be repaid from the purchase price payable on completion, before the balance is transferred onto the seller.

5677 Even if a release is not required, at the very least, before completion, the seller should be asked to obtain written confirmation from the holder of any floating charge that the charge has not crystallised (see ¶4610+). This is known as a "**certificate of non-crystallisation**" but is normally just a letter of confirmation from the bank to the seller. The buyer should request that it be obtained immediately before completion so as to be as up to date as possible.

Taxation

In a **share sale**, **information about** the target's tax history is important to the buyer, as the tax liabilities will go with the target. Revenue and Customs' investigations can go back 6 years and this is why the buyer normally concentrates on this period. Previous dealings with Revenue and Customs (or the Inland Revenue and Customs & Excise, before the organisations were integrated) are relevant, as a history of disputes may indicate that the tax affairs of the target are under particular scrutiny by tax authorities.

The following information is normally requested:
– a copy of the last 6 years' tax computations and assessments;
– the status of all tax computations and assessments and details of any matters unresolved with Revenue and Customs or other taxation authorities;
– details of all past disputes with Revenue and Customs or other taxation authorities;
– details of all VAT (including details of any VAT group), PAYE and NICs arrangements and any potential liabilities; and
– details of tax losses and available or utilised reliefs.

5678

Property

The buyer will need to have **information about** all property (i.e. land and buildings) in which the target has an interest or which it needs to operate the business, whether that property is owned, rented, occupied or just used by the target. In an asset sale, detailed information is only required in respect of property that is being transferred. The following information is normally requested:
– address of each property and the legal basis upon which it is occupied;
– a description of the use of each property and a list of all occupiers;
– a copy of a plan of each property;
– official copy entries of the title to any freehold or long leasehold property which is registered at the Land Registry (or an abstract of title for any non-registered freehold or long leasehold property);
– copies of leases, sub-leases, tenancies and licences under which any property is held or sub-let to third parties;
– details of all rents, service charges and other outgoings in relation to each of the properties, stating which are due by the seller or target and which are due to the seller or target, specifying any which are overdue and any review of the level of rent which is outstanding;
– confirmation as to whether or not an option to tax for VAT purposes has been made (see ¶5324);
– copies of all licences to assign, licences to sub-let, licences for alterations, licences for change of user, assignments, side letters, deeds of variation, rent review memoranda, guarantees or warranties;
– details of any property development carried out by the seller or target and copies of all planning permissions, building regulation approvals and fire certificates relating to each of the properties;
– a copy of any valuations;
– details of any rights benefiting the property over other land or rights granted over each property in favour of other parties;
– details of any notices received from the local authority or other government department; and
– details of any disputes relating to any of the properties.

> [MEMO POINTS] The seller is unlikely to give any assurances about the **physical state or condition** of the property and the buyer is likely to need a structural survey.

5679

Environment

Environmental matters have become increasingly regulated in recent years. A buyer will need **information about** any activities undertaken by the business and/or at its premises that could result in environmental liability. Liability for contaminated land could be of concern, particularly with the growth in development of brownfield sites. Again, for asset sales, this information is normally only relevant to the extent that land or buildings are being transfer-

5680

red to the buyer, but the buyer should be careful to ensure that the target has not previously occupied a property for a potentially contaminative use.

The following information is usually requested:
- details of environmental licences or permits;
- details of all processes on site;
- details of waste and any other substances handled by the target;
- a copy of any environmental policy, consent, approval, audit or survey;
- a copy of any waste management agreement with external suppliers;
- details of any actual or potential complaints, notices, investigations, claims or prosecutions relating to environmental matters by the public, adjoining landowners, environmental organisations, local authority, Environment Agency, other government department or similar body;
- any insurance claim relating to environmental matters;
- details of any known or suspected contamination in, on or under any property in which the target has or had an interest; and
- previous uses of any property or land in which the target has an interest.

Tangible assets

5681 The phrase "tangible assets" refers to the physical assets of the target, for example, plant and machinery and company cars. Computer systems are usually dealt with separately (see ¶5683). Tangible assets are often a vital component of the target business, especially a manufacturing one. As well as drawing out **information about** the assets held by the target, the buyer will need to find out if there are assets which the target uses but does not own as they will be an additional cost to the buyer. In an asset sale, questions should only be asked about the specific assets being sold to the buyer.

The following information is usually requested:
- details of all tangible assets owned and/or used in the business stating which are owned by the target, which are owned by a third party and which are shared with third parties;
- in relation to all fixed assets owned by the target, details of the acquisition costs, written down value and estimated realisable value;
- details of any major items of capital equipment purchased in the last 3 years or contracted to be or proposed to be purchased;
- details of any tangible assets which will become obsolete or otherwise need replacing in the next 3 years; and
- details of any significant repairs to plant and equipment in the last 3 years and any expected repairs in the next 3 years.

Intellectual property

5682 The buyer will need **information about** the business' "hard" intellectual property, such as patents, registered designs and trademarks, as well as "soft" intellectual property, such as copyright or confidential information. All businesses will have some intellectual property, and it will be a valuable business asset in many cases. The buyer will need to determine what intellectual property is used in the business, and the legal basis of that use.

The following information is usually requested:
- details of all intellectual property (patents, registered designs, copyright, trademarks, business/trading/brand names, technical information, know-how etc) owned and/or used by the target and an explanation of each one's significance;
- a list of any pending patent, registered design or trademark applications;
- a list of all internet domain names owned and/or used by the target, specifying which are registered to the target and which are used under licence, and supplying copy registration or licence documents as appropriate;
- a copy of the licence agreement in respect of intellectual property used, but not owned by the target, or if there is no licence agreement, an explanation of the terms upon which the target is entitled to use the intellectual property;

– a list of all third parties which use intellectual property owned by the target and a copy of each one's licence agreement, or if there is no licence agreement, an explanation of the terms upon which the third party is entitled to use the target's intellectual property;
– details of any matter of which the seller may be aware that may affect the validity or registration of any intellectual property owned or used by the target;
– details of any dispute relating to any intellectual property owned or used by the target;
– details of any third party, apart from those licensed to use it, and key personnel to whom intellectual property information has been disclosed; and
– details of the target's confidentiality arrangements.

Information technology

Information technology is an important part of most businesses. A buyer will need **information about** the target's computer and other communication systems (e.g. telephone) to ensure their integrity, as well as making sure that all software licences are in place. The following information is usually requested:
– a list of all hardware used by the target and their location, specifying which are owned by the target and providing a copy of the leasing document or other arrangements for use in respect of hardware owned by a third party;
– details of any hardware which needs or is likely to need replacing in the next 2 years;
– a list of all software used by the target, specifying which are owned by the target and providing a copy of the licence agreements;
– in relation to any software owned by the target, details of who developed the software and to the extent it was developed by non-employees, a copy of the agreement between the developer and the target under which all rights to the software were assigned to the target;
– details of the maintenance and service arrangements for the target's information technology systems, including a copy of any agreements with external suppliers; and
– details of the target's disaster recovery plan and a copy of any relevant documents.

5683

Trading matters

Information about the target's trading practices is usually crucial to the buyer. It is here that the buyer will get a real understanding of the business, its position in the market and its prospects. It is also here that the buyer is likely to find significant areas of business risk, for example, because contracts with major suppliers and/or customers have not been put into place. The following information is usually requested:
– details and copies of any material, long-term, onerous or unusual contracts or commitments;
– details and copies of all licences and authorisations necessary to carry on the business;
– details and copies of all standard terms and conditions under which the target supplies goods/services;
– a list of any customers to whom different terms and conditions apply and a copy of the terms applicable to them;
– details and copies of contracts made with major customers and suppliers (usually specified as being those accounting for more than 5% of sales or supplies) for the last 3 years and the value of sales or supplies (as applicable) attributable to them;
– details of any major customer or supplier lost in the last 3 years or likely to be lost in the next 2 years and the reason or likely reason for that loss;
– details of any current or past dispute with any major customer or supplier;
– details and copies of any contract or commitment with a third party for distribution, agency, franchise, research and development, joint venture, partnership, profit-sharing or other similar arrangement;
– details of any intra-group trading arrangements;
– details of any current or past formal or informal agreements or tacit arrangements with competitors (¶5691);
– details of any current negotiations which could lead to any of the above types of arrangement; and

5684

– details of any agreements or arrangements which may be affected by a change of control of the target following the sale to the buyer.

Litigation

5685 The buyer will need **information about** any litigation or potential litigation involving the target as these could result in significant liabilities, even if the target is likely to succeed in the case. The litigation could have a knock-on effect on the goodwill of the business, and, in a share sale, those liabilities would go with the target. The following information is usually requested:
– details of any litigation (including court proceedings, arbitration, expert determination or other non-judicial dispute resolution procedure) in which the target has been involved in the last 3 years, the current status of that litigation and copies of significant statements of case;
– details of any dispute or set of circumstances which may lead to litigation; and
– details of any investigation or decision of any court, government or quasi-government department, regulatory authority or other similar body in relation to the target.

Employees

5686 The buyer will need extremely detailed **information about** the target's employees and employment practices, particularly so that the buyer can understand its potential liabilities in this respect. In an **asset sale**, employee information is even more important because of the protection employees may receive under TUPE (see ¶5771+). However, personal information about employees is protected from disclosure under data protection law. The seller should therefore ensure that individuals cannot be identified from the disclosed information. At the very least, information should be disclosed anonymously, for example, by assigning each employee a number.

The following information will usually be requested:
– details about each employee (date of birth, start date, job description and department, normal working hours, salary, overtime, commission or bonus, benefits, notice period, disciplinary record, whether permanent, fixed-term, full-time or part-time);
– details of any consultants or agency workers and a copy of the relevant consultancy or agency agreement;
– details of any employee seconded by or to the target;
– copies of all service agreements, contracts of employment, collective agreements, agreements with trade unions and documents confirming compliance with the Working Time Regulations 1998;
– details and copies of all employment policies, specifying which are contractual and which are non-contractual;
– details of any share option or profit sharing scheme;
– details of any redundancy proposals and any enhanced redundancy rights;
– details of any person whose employment was terminated in the previous 6 months, whether by the employer or employee, and the reason for the termination;
– details of all grievances, negotiations or disputes with or claims brought by or against employees, employee representatives or trade unions;
– details of any suspensions in the last 12 months;
– details of any personal commitment to any employee;
– details of pension arrangements (see ¶5690); and
– details of any consultation with employees or employees' representatives regarding the proposed sale.

Caution needs to be exercised where a subsidiary company is sold to a new parent company pursuant to a share sale and that parent company takes over control of the subsidiary's activities, because it could be held that the subsidiary's business has been transferred to the new parent company. Accordingly, the provisions of TUPE will apply (*Millam v The Print Factory (London) 1991 Limited* [2007] EWCA Civ 322).

> MEMO POINTS   In an **asset sale** which amounts to a TUPE transfer (see ¶5771+), the seller is required to notify the buyer of "**employee liability information**". This includes information about:
> – the identity and age of employees;
> – their statements of terms and conditions of employment;
> – any disciplinary proceedings or grievances issued in the last 2 years;
> – any legal action brought by employees against the seller in the last 2 years;
> – any legal action which the seller has reasonable grounds to believe may be brought by an employee; and
> – any collective agreement which will have effect after the transfer.
> The seller has to notify the buyer in writing of any change in the information. Notification may be given in more than one instalment and can be given indirectly, through a third party. It should be provided at least 14 days before the transfer or, if special circumstances make this not reasonably practicable, as soon as reasonably practicable thereafter. Failure to provide the information enables the buyer to bring a claim against the seller (in an employment tribunal) for such compensation as is just and equitable in all the circumstances. The tribunal will have regard to any loss sustained by the buyer and the terms of any contract between the seller and buyer under which the seller may be liable to pay the buyer for failure to provide such information. There is a minimum award of £500 for each employee for whom the information was not provided, unless the tribunal considers it just and equitable to award a lesser sum (regs 11, 12 SI 2006/246).

Data protection

5687

The buyer will need **information about** the steps the target has taken to ensure that it is data protection compliant, as non-compliance can lead to fines and, in a share sale, this liability will go with the target. However, even in an asset sale, data protection compliance is of particular importance to a business with a valuable database, as the Information Commissioner has the power to order the destruction of data which has been compiled, or used, in breach of data protection regulations. The following information is usually requested:
– a copy of the target's registration with the Information Commissioner;
– details of any data protection and/or document retention policy, including a copy of any written policy;
– a description of the types of personal data held by the target and how that data is processed;
– details of any subject access requests and/or complaints by individuals about data held by the target;
– details of any investigation by the Information Commissioner; and
– details of data protection measures taken in respect of personal data transferred out of the European Union.

Health and safety

5688

As with data protection, the buyer of any business will need **information about** the steps the target has taken to ensure it complies with health and safety regulations. However, health and safety will be more of an issue in manufacturing or other risky business areas where the likelihood of injury is greater. More specific questions may need to be asked depending upon the type of business being purchased. The following information is normally requested:
– a copy of the target's health and safety policy and an explanation of its implementation (including individual health and safety responsibilities, health and safety committees, risk assessments, reporting, recording and investigation procedures, fire protection procedures, use of hazardous material procedures, first aid procedure, training and monitoring);
– a copy of any health and safety agreements, audits or reports;
– a copy of the target's accident book entries for the last 3 years;
– details of any investigation by or notices received from any local authority, government department or the Health & Safety Executive;
– details of any actual (whether or not outstanding) or potential claim, prosecution or complaint concerning health and safety issues;
– details of any insurance claim related to health and safety issues;
– details of all materials used or present at any of the target's premises; and
– details of any construction work carried out by the business.

Insurance

5689 The buyer will want to review **information about** the insurance policies which the company has in place. It will want confirmation that all necessary insurances have been maintained, as well as details and copies of them, specifying the nature and amount of cover, the premium, any excess and next renewal date. In order to assess the scope of the cover, a buyer will usually ask for details of all insurance arrangements in place relating to:
- property owned or rented by the company;
- professional indemnity;
- directors' and officers' liability;
- product liability; and
- product recall.

A buyer will usually ask for details of any insurance claims made in the last 12 months, together with details of any outstanding and potential claims. It is good practice for the buyer to investigate the solvency of the insurance providers before taking over any contracts. In an asset sale, the buyer will want to establish whether or not the existing policies may be assigned or novated to it. If the policies do not allow for this, it will have to arrange its own insurance cover.

Pensions

5690 If the target operates a pension scheme, it will usually transfer upon completion. In order to understand the obligations and liabilities which the buyer will be taking on board, the buyer will need **information about** the scheme, especially so that it can review the extent to which the transfer may trigger an employer debt. On a transfer, debt is triggered when the target company ceases to participate in the pension scheme (ss 75, 75A Pensions Act 1995). If the buyer choses not to continue with the scheme, it will have to make good any deficiencies in any salary-related schemes. The buyer will want to review the following details:
- the pension scheme itself (e.g. trust deeds, rules, handbooks);
- information about the employees in the scheme (e.g. sex, date of birth, date of joining the scheme, current pensionable salary and additional benefits or contributions made;
- the latest actuarial valuation and the trustees' annual report;
- the employer's contribution rates and any proposed changes;
- any ex-gratia or unregistered pension arrangements;
- confirmation that the scheme is a registered pension scheme, together with a copy of the contracting-out certificate;
- any special early retirement provisions or promises made which may lead to enhanced early retirement benefits on redundancy; and
- whether clearance has been obtained from the Pensions Regulator to confirm that the sale will not result in the issuance of a contribution notice or financial support direction, under which the buyer would incur financial liabilities for the scheme.

> MEMO POINTS The **Pensions Regulator** published **guidance** on obtaining clearance in April 2005 and, at the time of writing, has published a draft updated version for consultation. This new draft sets out the central principles that the Regulator expects all trustees and employers to follow when they are involved in corporate transactions. It also gives guidance on identifying when a detrimental event occurs and how to apply for clearance. The main aim of the guidance is to protect the benefits of scheme members. It therefore encourages mitigation (that is, taking action to minimise the effects on the pension scheme) and negotiation where a detrimental effect on the pension scheme is anticipated, even if the parties have no intention of applying for clearance. The draft guidance can be freely downloaded from the Pensions Regulator's website (*www.thepensionsregulator.gov.uk*).

Competition

5691 Depending on the size of the target and the nature of its business, a buyer may request **information about** the target company's compliance with competition law:
- whether the transfer will become subject, if at all, to UK merger control (¶5507+) or EU merger control (¶5520+);

– whether the company is a monopolist, in a market with few players or part of an industry which has a bad reputation for compliance with competition law;
– whether contracts entered into with competitors, customers, suppliers, agents, distributors, licensees, franchisees and joint venture partners contain restrictive provisions that could infringe competition laws;
– whether the relevant competition authorities have been notified of any contracts which do contain provisions that infringe competition laws and the relevant clearances or comfort letters have been obtained; and
– whether the company is under investigation by competition authorities or has previously been under investigation.

B. Searches of public registers

There are several searches which the buyer will be able to carry out in order to find or confirm information about the seller and the underlying assets. In every case, each party should carry out a **Companies House search** in respect of any other company involved in the transaction (such as the seller, buyer, guarantor and, in a share sale, the target and its subsidiaries) (see ¶4090). **Other searches** relating to particular assets are:
– property searches;
– intellectual property searches; and
– insolvency searches.

5695

> MEMO POINTS   If the transaction involves **competition concerns**, a search should be made of the "Register of Orders and Undertakings" and the "Competition Act 1998 Public Register" held by the Office of Fair Trading. Free online searches can be carried out on the OFT's website.

Property searches

There are three searches which the buyer may need to carry out in respect of any property to be transferred:
– a local authority search;
– a land registry search; and
– a search of the land charges register.

5696

> MEMO POINTS   **Other searches** may be appropriate if the land is of a special type or in an area subject to particular environmental risks. For example:
> – a commons registration search, if the land could be common land;
> – an environmental search;
> – a drainage search;
> – an agricultural land search, if the property is agricultural land; or
> – a coal mining search, if the property is in a current or former coal mining area.

Local authority search

A local authority search will **reveal** certain burdens on the property which would not be discovered by inspecting the title deeds or visiting the property (such as conservation orders, smoke control orders etc) as well as other matters affecting the property (such as planning permissions, road building schemes etc).

5697

> MEMO POINTS   A local authority search actually comprises two searches. One is of the "**local land charges register**" which reveals burdens which must be registered by the local authority (e.g. conservation orders). The other is a **questionnaire** to various local authority departments about actions which they have taken that will bind someone who buys a property (e.g. road building schemes, enforcement notices for breaches of planning legislation).

A local authority search can be **made by** post or in person. A separate search will be required in respect of each property. A **postal search** is made by sending completed Forms LLC1 and CON29 in duplicate (with two copies of a plan showing the property outlined in red) to the

5698

local authority in which the property is situated. The cost is usually between £150 and £250, but will vary from authority to authority. Results usually take 2 or 3 weeks to arrive and include an "official certificate of search" which guarantees the results. The search may need to be renewed nearer to completion to ensure it is up to date, although this is generally only an issue where bank funding secured by a mortgage is being obtained (a search is generally regarded as out of date if it is more than 3 months old at completion). Alternatively, if time is short, a **personal search** could be carried out by a visit to the local authority offices. The results will not be as comprehensive as a postal search and are not guaranteed.

Land registry

5699 A search of the land register maintained by the Land Registry will **reveal** the owner of any registered freehold and leasehold land interests, and any encumbrances on the title, such as a mortgage.

5700 An official copy (also known as the "**office copy**") of the Land Register in respect of a property, together with a property plan, can be obtained by post. The search should be made on Form OC1 and costs £6 for the register and £6 for the plan.

In an asset sale, a few days before exchange, an application for an **official search** with priority should also be made. The application should be made in duplicate on Form OS1 (if the whole property is being transferred) or Form OS2 (if only part of the property is being transferred). The application will need to be accompanied by two copies of a plan showing the property outlined in red. The application should be sent to the District Land Registry in which the property is situated. The cost of each search is £6.

Further details, and free copies of all Land Registry forms, can be found on the Land Registry website.

MEMO POINTS 1. An official search on Form OS1 or OS2 will give 30 days' **priority**. A person with priority will not be affected by changes to the register during the period of priority. Official searches with priority are only available if the person searching has a protectable interest (i.e. the person is purchasing, leasing or taking a charge over the property). The buyer in an asset sale is purchasing the property and so has a protectable interest. The buyer in a share sale is not purchasing the property; it is purchasing the company which owns the property. It therefore does not have a protectable interest.
2. Land registry searches can also be carried out **by fax, telephone or online**. The person carrying out the search can either be registered for this service or he can pay with a credit/debit card. Alternatively, the search can be carried out in person at the Land Registry Customer Information Centre. The cost of each online search is £3 instead of the usual £6. Further detail can be found on the Land Registry website.

Land charges department

5701 If any freehold property to be transferred is unregistered, the buyer should carry out a search at the Land Charges Department of the Land Registry. The Land Charges Department does not record actual ownership of unregistered land; title should be deduced from the seller's title deeds. However, a search at this department will **reveal** persons with an interest in unregistered land (e.g. rights of way, matrimonial rights etc) which may not be apparent from the title deeds and which would bind a purchaser. If the person being searched against is an individual, it will also reveal any bankruptcy entries.

5702 The search is carried out **against the owners' names**, rather than the property address, for the period that the person owned the property. This means that a search will be needed against the name of the seller, any previous names of the seller (for example, if the company changed its name) and any previous owners of the property (these names should be apparent from the title deeds). The search is **made by** post on Form K15 and sent to the Land Charges Department of the Land Registry at Plymouth. Up to six names may be searched against in each search. The cost of a search is £2 per name.

MEMO POINTS 1. The results of the search are given by way of a certificate. A buyer will be protected for 15 days after the date of the certificate. This means that any entry made on the Land Charges Department's register during the **period of protection**, but before the purchase is completed, will not affect the buyer. To avoid any doubt, the certificate will state the date on which the period of protection will end.

2. Searches at the Land Charges Department can also be carried out **by fax, telephone or online**. The person carrying out the search can either be registered for this service or can pay with a credit/debit card. Alternatively, the search can be carried out in person at the Land Charges Department Customer Information Centre. Further detail can be found on the Land Registry website.

Intellectual property searches

The UK Intellectual Property Office keeps records of **registered** intellectual property rights. A search should be made of:
- the patents database, in respect of any patents;
- the trade marks database, in respect of any registered trademarks; and
- the designs database, in respect of any registered designs.

Free searches can be carried out online at the UK Intellectual Property Office website. More detailed information can be found out by employing specialist search agents (including those at the UK Intellectual Property Office itself). Detailed search fees will vary from agent to agent.

5703

> MEMO POINTS Information about **unregistered** rights cannot be found by carrying out independent searches, so the buyer should ensure that the seller is required to provide details of these rights (¶5682). The common unregistered rights relevant to a business are:
> - copyright, which can be relevant to any written material, for example correspondence, manuals, lists of customers, industrial drawings, artwork, diagrams, software, and also to artistic material such as music, films, and recordings; and
> - database right, which would usually be most relevant to lists of information, e.g. lists of customers.

Insolvency searches

A bankruptcy search should be carried out in respect of any party who is **an individual**. Bankruptcy entries for individuals are kept by the Land Charges Department of the Land Registry (see ¶5701+). An application for a "bankruptcy only" search can be made on Form K16 in the same way as a full search. Alternatively, a bankruptcy and individual voluntary arrangement search can be made on-line through the Insolvency Service website free of charge.

5704

If the party is a **company**, a search at **Companies House** will reveal whether or not the company is involved in insolvency proceedings (¶4090). However, a search at Companies House will not reveal a winding up petition which has been presented to the court but has not yet been heard. Since a winding up dates from the date upon which the petition was presented, rather than the date on which the winding up order was made, it is important to discover whether any petitions are pending. This can be done by searching the **Central Registry of Winding Up Petitions**. The Central Registry may be searched in person at the Companies Court General Office at the Royal Courts of Justice in London, or by telephone on 0906 7540043 (a premium rate number).

5705

For both **individuals and companies**, a search can be made of the **Registry of Judgments, Orders and Fines**. This will reveal:
- county court judgments in the previous 6 years;
- administration orders in the previous 6 years;
- child support agency orders in the previous 6 years;
- high court judgments since 4 April 2006; and
- fines registered by local judgment area for convictions in the previous 5 years.

Searches can be made by post, online or in person and cost between £8 and £30 per name, depending upon the extent of the search. See *www.registry-trust.org.uk* for further details.

Credit reference agencies can be approached if a more comprehensive credit record is required (see ¶5262).

5706

C. Surveys and inspections of property

5708 For any sizeable acquisition which involves buying land and/or buildings, it is important for the property to be properly inspected. This could take the form of a structural survey of a building, including checking the services.

For land holdings, a **surveyor** should check the property, paying particular attention to the following issues:
– Do the boundaries comply with the plans?
– Is there adequate access to the site?
– Are any of the neighbouring properties likely to cause any problems (e.g. an industrial site which causes noise or smell problems)?

Environmental issues may also necessitate a site inspection. Is there any evidence of the site having been used for industrial processes in the past, and therefore a possibility of pollution still existing? If the target is engaged in any form of industrial activity, does it have all of the permits and licences for the activities actually taking place on site? This could be something as mundane as having an oil storage tank for the heating plant for a factory, storing waste products, or having a surface water discharge to a nearby stream. Again, the condition of neighbouring sites can also be relevant, as there could be polluting activities undertaken there which could affect the condition of the target's site.

SECTION 5

Negotiation of documents

5720 Once the bulk of the due diligence has been completed, the parties can move onto negotiating the contractual documents. The main document which will embody the agreement between the parties is the **sale and purchase agreement**. The **length** of the document will vary depending upon the complexity and value of the transaction. An agreement for a low-value simple transaction will probably be under 20 pages, whereas agreements for higher-value complex transactions are often several hundred pages in length. A clause by clause analysis of the share sale and purchase agreement and asset sale and purchase agreement can be found at ¶5725+ and ¶5750+ respectively.

In the absence of any contractual provisions to the contrary, the risk of the purchase will fall on the buyer (for example, if after completion the buyer discovered that the business did not actually own some of its assets, it would have no recourse to the seller). Much of the sale and purchase agreement is therefore concerned with **allocation of risk** (see ¶5800+). The buyer normally attempts to pass risk back to the seller through warranties and indemnities in the sale and purchase agreement, and the seller normally limits how much risk it will take on through preparing a disclosure letter in answer to the warranties and inserting "seller limitation provisions" into the sale and purchase agreement.

5721 It is now usual practice for the **buyer to prepare** the first draft of the agreement. This is because the bulk of the agreement deals with allocation of risk, which is the buyer's concern. The seller will consider the draft, make the amendments he requires and return it to the buyer. The buyer will in turn consider the amendments, re-amend the draft and return it to the seller. There will usually be numerous meetings between the parties to resolve their differences. The document will continue to be discussed until it is in an agreed form.

5722 **Other documents** are often necessary apart from the sale and purchase agreement and disclosure letter. These will depend upon whether the transaction is a sale of shares or a sale of assets and will vary from transaction to transaction.

The most common substantive ancillary documents in a **sale of shares** (see ¶5945+) are:
- the tax deed (although this is sometimes included as a schedule to the sale and purchase agreement);
- employment documents; and
- a deed of contribution.

The most common substantive ancillary document in a **sale of assets** is the deed of assignment (see ¶5985+).

Other documents upon which there is unlikely to be any substantive negotiation will also need to be prepared (e.g. board minutes, stock transfer forms for share sales etc). A **full list of documentation** is included in the completion checklist at ¶6012+.

I. Share sale and purchase agreement

Clauses and schedules

The share sale and purchase agreement is normally divided into the **sections/clauses** listed in the table below and further information can be found at the relevant paragraph references.

5725

Section/clause	¶¶
Parties	¶5728
Recitals	¶5729
Interpretation	¶5730
Agreement to buy and sell	¶5731
Consideration: – form – payment structure	 ¶5426+ ¶5460+
Conditions	¶5732+
Completion	¶6005+
Warranties and indemnities: – general – buyer's clauses – seller's clauses	 ¶5800+ ¶5807+ ¶5890+
Post-completion restrictions on seller	¶5735+
Boiler plate clauses	¶5740
Signature	¶5741+

The agreement is also likely to have a number of **schedules**, for example:
- a schedule of information to identify the target company (i.e. its name, registered office, share capital, accounting reference date etc);
- where there are multiple sellers, a schedule of information to identify each of them (i.e. their names, addresses and the number and class of shares held by each of them);
- a list of warranties (¶5814+);
- where the consideration is to be calculated by reference to an earn-out, a schedule setting out the earn-out provisions (¶5465+);
- where the consideration is subject to a net asset value adjustment, a schedule setting out provisions for the preparation of completion accounts (¶5480+); and
- a tax covenant, if a separate tax deed is not going to be signed (¶5945+).

5726

It should be noted that only one version of the contract will be prepared and signed, regardless of the number of sellers. **Multiple sellers** will therefore need to co-ordinate between themselves to ensure that they are all happy with the negotiated document. Usually, the day to day negotiations are handled by the major shareholder(s) as they have the biggest stake

5727

in the negotiations. Minority shareholders are usually kept abreast of progress and then brought into play once the document is nearing an agreed form so that they can give the final "sign off".

1. Parties

5728 The parties to the agreement are the **persons who have agreed to be bound** by it and will ultimately sign it. They will be the seller and the buyer at least. Other parties, if appropriate, can include:
– additional warrantors (see ¶5822); and/or
– the guarantor (see ¶5468+) (usually the parent company of the buyer or seller, as the circumstances of the deal require).

2. Recitals

5729 The purpose of the recitals is to set out **background information** regarding the transaction and to make explicit the parties' intention to sell and purchase the target's shares in accordance with the terms of the agreement. Although a traditional component of the contract, in fact the recitals have no legal effect. Older style contracts would indulge in lengthy recitals but the modern practice is for recitals to be omitted in case they conflict with the substantive provisions of the agreement.

3. Interpretation

5730 The first clause of the agreement usually deals with:
– **definitions** of terms used in the agreement (normally listed alphabetically for ease of reference); and
– **other statements of interpretation** (e.g. that references to one gender include the other).

The definitions need to be looked at closely as they will affect the meaning of the remainder of the agreement. Clearly, there is only a need to define terms to the extent they are used in the agreement. Where clauses are deleted (either from a precedent agreement or during negotiations), the defined terms should be reviewed and any unnecessary definitions removed.

4. Agreement to buy and sell

5731 The next clause is usually an agreement by the seller to sell and the buyer to buy the target's shares, on the terms set out in the agreement, with "**full title guarantee**". This short but important clause describes the entire transaction in a nutshell.

The words "full title guarantee" are statutory (ss 2, 3(1) Law of Property (Miscellaneous Provisions) Act 1994). When they are used, they imply that the seller has made certain promises about his ownership of the shares. These promises are known as "**covenants of title**". The covenants of title implied by full title guarantee are that:
– the seller has the right to dispose of his shares;
– the seller will at his own cost do all that he reasonably can to give the buyer the title to the shares which he is purporting to sell; and
– the shares are free from all charges and encumbrances, whether monetary or not, and from all other rights exercisable by third parties (except for those which the seller does not and could not reasonably be expected to know about).

It is possible for the parties to agree to **vary** these **covenants of title**. Sometimes, the buyer will try to extend the covenants so that the seller is liable for charges, encumbrances and third party rights which it did not and could not reasonably be expected to know about. However, this is normally resisted by the seller.

> MEMO POINTS 1. It is possible to convey property by giving "**limited title guarantee**". This implies more limited covenants of title and should not be accepted in a normal negotiated sale and purchase of shares.
> 2. Before the statutory covenants of title came into force, the agreement used to state that the seller sold as "**legal and beneficial owners**". This wording can still be found in older agreements but is no longer appropriate.

5. Conditions

The conditions are the matters that must be **satisfied after the contracts have been signed** and exchanged in order for the buyer to proceed with completion of the purchase. In other words, although the parties have been contractually bound to sell and purchase the shares, completion of that sale and purchase is dependant upon the conditions being fulfilled.

5732

Conditions lead to a **gap between exchange and completion** (see ¶5865), which can involve:
– difficulties if circumstances change between exchange and completion;
– difficulties in determining whether the conditions have been fulfilled; and
– increased costs involved in drafting and negotiating extra provisions in the sale and purchase agreement.

As a result, conditional sale and purchase agreements are avoided in practice, whenever possible.

The **type of condition**, if required, can be a general one, for example, obtaining relevant tax clearances (¶5367+). Normally, however, they are much more transaction-specific, for example:
– reaching a particular target (such as finishing the development of a new product);
– winning a particular contract; or
– obtaining the consent of a particular third party (e.g. from a major supplier or customer who could terminate their contract with the company on a change of control).

5733

Some **drafting points** to consider if the agreement is to be conditional are:
– to draft the conditions clearly so that there is no room for debate as to whether or not they have been fulfilled;
– to set a long stop date. This is the last date by which the conditions can be fulfilled. Without a long stop date, the agreement could be void for uncertainty;
– to set out what will happen if the conditions are not fulfilled by the long stop date. Normally, the parties are entitled to walk away with no liabilities. Sometimes, however, it is possible to negotiate that the party at fault must contribute towards the other's costs.

5734

6. Post-completion restrictions on sellers

Sale and purchase agreements usually contain clauses which restrict the seller's activities after completion. Their **purpose** is to protect the target's goodwill and prevent the seller from undermining the buyer's investment in the company. There are normally three types of restrictions:
– "**restrictive covenants**" limit the seller's post-completion business activities;
– **confidentiality** provisions to prevent the seller from using or disclosing the target's confidential information; and
– **change of name** covenants require a corporate seller to change its company name (if it is similar to the target's name) and not use the target's company or trading name in the future.

5735

> MEMO POINTS In the case of a **corporate seller**, the buyer may require the individuals behind the company to be joined as a party to the sale and purchase agreement and enter into the same post-completion restrictions. The buyer's protection could be completely undermined if, for example, the majority shareholder of a corporate seller simply carried on the prohibited activities in his own name or under the guise of a new company.

Restrictive covenants

5736 Restrictive covenants are usually expressed to prevent the seller from:
- competing with the target's business ("**non-competition**");
- soliciting the target's customers ("**non-solicitation**");
- dealing with the target's customers if approached by them ("**non-dealing**");
- interfering with the target's relationship with its suppliers ("**non-interference**"); and
- soliciting or employing the target's employees ("**non-poaching**").

5737 Restrictive covenants can only be enforced if they are **reasonable**, i.e. they only go as far as necessary to protect the interests of the parties. This means that they must protect a legitimate business interest and be no wider than is necessary to protect that interest. What is reasonable will vary from transaction to transaction and so the covenants should always be tailored to the target. As a minimum, each covenant should:
- be limited as to its **duration** (e.g. a covenant of more than 1 or 2 years would probably not be reasonable);
- relate to the **business of the target** as it is at completion (e.g. it would not be reasonable to prevent the seller from soliciting new customers); and
- be limited as to **geographical area** (e.g. if the target's business is local, it would not be reasonable to prevent the seller from setting up in competition anywhere in the country).

5738 A restrictive covenant agreed to in the context of the sale of a company for an arm's length price is much more likely to be upheld by a court than one imposed on an individual, e.g. an employee leaving to go to a new job. A restrictive covenant **affecting an individual** could restrict that individual from earning their living. In contrast, a restrictive covenant **affecting a business** which has been bought for a large sum of money would be viewed as protecting that investment. In general, the burden is on the buyer to demonstrate that the covenant is reasonable.

5739 A judge will not rewrite an **unreasonable** covenant so as to make it reasonable, and therefore enforceable, nor will he enforce a restriction in more limited terms than those imposed by the covenant agreed between the parties (*J A Mont (UK) Ltd v Mills* [1993] IRLR 172). However, where one clause contains several restrictions, the court may consider the reasonableness of each clause separately. Any unreasonable clauses could then be struck out, without affecting the enforceability of the remaining restrictions. This is known as the "**blue pencil test**". To facilitate its application, normal practice is to deal with each type of restriction in a separate and distinct clause.

7. Boiler plate clauses

5740 "Boiler plate" clauses are found at the end of most contracts. They are important in their effect but **rarely contentious**.

Boiler plate clauses are fairly self explanatory. The most common ones are:
- **entire agreement**: states that the terms of the sale and purchase agreement represent the whole agreement between the parties and supersede all previous agreements or understandings between them;
- **variation**: states that any variation to the agreement must be made in writing and signed by all the parties;
- **waiver**: states that any waiver by one party of another party's obligations must be made in writing and that a failure by a party to enforce its rights is not deemed to be a waiver of those rights;
- **further assurance**: states that every party will do all of the acts necessary to give effect to the agreement;
- **continuing obligations**: states that the obligations of the parties under the agreement will continue notwithstanding completion;
- **assignment**: states that the rights and obligations under the agreement are personal to the parties and may not be assigned or transferred to another person;

- **announcements**: states that no announcement about the transaction is to be made without the consent of the other parties;
- **costs**: states that each party is to bear its own costs in relation to the transaction;
- **notices**: states the method by which notices under the agreement should be served and gives the name, address, fax number and email address of the person on whom notices should be served on behalf of each party (assuming that notices can be communicated by post, fax and email); and
- **applicable law and jurisdiction**: states that the agreement is governed under English law and that the parties submit to the exclusive jurisdiction of the English courts.

> MEMO POINTS 1. The **entire agreement** clause must also state that it does not exclude liability for fraudulent misrepresentation. This is because, otherwise, the clause would be unreasonable under statute and therefore unenforceable, which could leave the seller open to misrepresentation claims in respect of information provided during negotiations (*Thomas Witter Ltd v TBP Industries Ltd* [1996] 2 All ER 573; s 3 Misrepresentation Act 1967).
> 2. The purpose of an entire agreement clause is to prevent the introduction of a new term into the agreement, or creating a side contract, thereby changing the contents of the sale and purchase agreement. The clause will therefore not prevent the court from hearing evidence regarding **pre-contractual negotiations** in order to ascertain the meaning of a term in the agreement (*Proforce Recruit Ltd v The Rugby Group Ltd* [2006] EWCA Civ 69).
> 3. One **consequence of the buyer not being able to assign** the agreement is that if the buyer transfers its shares to another party, the new buyer will not have the benefit of the seller's warranties. If the buyer has such a transfer in mind, it may try to negotiate the ability to assign the benefit of the warranties. This will usually be resisted by the seller because his agreement is with the buyer alone. However, the seller may agree for the buyer to be able to assign to another company in the buyer's group. This would at least allow the buyer to transfer the target's shares as part of a group reorganisation and still keep the benefit of the warranties.
> 4. It is particularly important that the parties pay their own costs. If the parties' **costs are met by the target**, this will amount to financial assistance and the whole transaction could be void (see ¶5574).

8. Signature

5741 The agreement must be **signed by** all the parties. So, for example, one selling shareholder cannot sign on behalf of all the shareholders.

> MEMO POINTS If a **signatory is unavailable**, it is possible for another person to be given a power of attorney to sign the agreement instead.

5742 The **form of signature** depends upon whether or not the agreement is to take effect as a **deed**, which is more formal than an ordinary **contract**. The most significant aspect of the agreement taking effect as a deed is that, subject to its other terms, the parties have 12 years to bring a claim (instead of 6 years for ordinary contracts). Thus, the agreement should take effect as a deed if any of the warranty claim periods exceed 6 years from completion (see ¶5920+).

> MEMO POINTS The other main difference between deeds and ordinary contracts is that an ordinary contractual obligation must be supported by consideration, which is not necessary if the obligation is contained in a document that has been executed as a deed. Perhaps overcautiously, sale and purchase agreements are sometimes executed as deeds in order to avoid problems of **lack of consideration** for a particular obligation (e.g. the post-completion restrictions on the sellers).

Contract

5743 The example shows how the document should be signed if it is to take effect as an ordinary contract. Signature by an individual and by a company are illustrated.

> EXAMPLE
>
> Signed by .... Signed by [name of director] ....
> [name of
> individual]   Signed by [name of director/ ....
>   secretary]

Deed

5744 The example shows how the document should be signed if it is to take effect as a deed. Signature by an individual and by a company are illustrated (although the company's articles of association may contain further requirements, for example, relating to the company fixing its common seal).

EXAMPLE

Executed as a deed and delivered on the date first above by [name of individual] in the presence of:	))))	Executed as a deed and delivered on the date first above by X Ltd acting by:
Witness signature Witness name Witness address Witness occupation	....	.... Director .... Director/Secretary

MEMO POINTS 1. A deed is not effective until it is **delivered** but there is a presumption that a deed entered into by a company is delivered on execution (s 36A(5) CA 1985; restated at s 46(2) CA 2006 by 1 October 2009). The form of signature should therefore make it clear that the deed is not deemed to be delivered (i.e. the sale and purchase agreement is not intended to create binding obligations) until it has been dated (which will happen at the completion meeting or when the agreement is released from escrow).

2. Under the **new Companies Act** a document will be validly executed by a company if it has been signed on its behalf by two authorised signatories (which are the directors and the company secretary), or by a director in the presence of a witness who attests the signature (s 44 CA 2006, due to come into force on 6 April 2008).

II. Asset sale and purchase agreement

Clauses and schedules

5750 The asset sale and purchase agreement is normally divided into the **sections/clauses** listed in the table below and further information can be found at the relevant paragraph references. Some of the sections/clauses mirror those found in a share sale and purchase agreement and so the reference is to that agreement.

Section/clause	¶¶
Parties	¶5728
Recitals	¶5729
Interpretation	¶5730
Agreement to buy and sell	¶5751+
Consideration − form − payment structure − apportionment (although this may be set out in a schedule, see below)	 ¶5426+ ¶5460+ ¶5314+
Conditions	¶5732+
Completion	¶6005+
Stock	¶5756+
Contracts	¶5758+
Properties	¶5764+
Debtors, creditors and liabilities	¶5766+

Section/clause	¶¶
Employees	¶5771+
VAT	¶5787+
Warranties and indemnities: – general – buyer's clauses – seller's clauses	¶5800+ ¶5807+ ¶5890+
Post-completion restrictions on seller	¶5735+
Boiler plate clauses	¶5740
Signature	¶5741+

The agreement is also likely to have a number of **schedules**, for example:
- to set out details of the assets which are being transferred (e.g. freehold and leasehold properties, including any tenancies or other encumbrances to which they may be subject; a list of contracts; a list of tangible assets etc) and a list of assets which are excluded from the sale (see ¶5754);
- to set out how the consideration has been apportioned (see ¶5314+);
- a list of warranties (see ¶5814+);
- details of the employees which are transferring to the buyer with the business (¶5771+); and
- details of the transfer of pension arrangements.

1. Agreement to buy and sell

The clause which contains the agreement to buy and sell also sets out:
- the date upon which the sale and purchase will take effect (known as the "**effective date**"); and
- the **subject of the sale and purchase** (i.e. the business and assets).

5751

   MEMO POINTS   The clause should specify that the seller sells with "full title guarantee" as this implies certain **covenants of title** in relation to the assets being transferred (see ¶5731). Further covenants of title will be implied by statute in respect of goods, such as plant, machinery and stock (ss 12-14 Sale of Goods Act 1979). These are:
- an undertaking that the seller has title to the goods;
- that any goods sold by description (e.g. an inventory) correspond to that description; and
- that the goods are of satisfactory quality and fit for their purpose.

The seller can exclude these covenants (other than the undertaking as to title) so far as it is reasonable to do so (s 6 Unfair Contract Terms Act 1977). A buyer on the other hand will supplement these covenants through the warranties (e.g. by a warranty that the plant and machinery are in good condition and fit for their purpose).

Effective date

The effective date is sometimes the date of completion but often it is another date which is convenient for the parties. The **importance** of the effective date is that this is when the benefit and burden of the business will transfer to the buyer.

5752

   EXAMPLE   A Ltd is proposing to sell its business to B Ltd. A Ltd's financial year ends on 31 December. The parties exchange and complete the agreement on 24 December 2007, before the Christmas break, but the agreement specifies that the effective date is 31 December 2007, to coincide with A Ltd's year end.

The practice has arisen for the effective date to be any date, before or after exchange and completion. However, there could be concerns where the effective date **pre-dates exchange and completion** because:
- the parties cannot pass title to assets from an earlier date;
- the seller cannot be deemed to have carried on the business as agent or on trust for the buyer from an earlier date since an agency or trust cannot be created retrospectively; and

5753

— Revenue and Customs will treat the business' income up to completion as belonging to the seller, whatever the terms of the sale and purchase agreement.

If the parties were working towards an earlier effective date, the agreement to buy and sell should take effect as at completion and the parties should instead **rely on** an **apportionment** of the business' receipts and outgoings as at the effective date (see ¶5766+).

Subject of sale and purchase

5754 The subject of the sale and purchase is usually broken down into its **constituent parts** so that there is as much certainty as possible as to what the buyer is taking. These are normally the:
- business as a going concern (to comply with VAT rules, see ¶5321+);
- goodwill;
- properties;
- stock;
- benefit of the contracts;
- tangible assets; and
- intellectual property rights.

A **sweeper sub-clause**, referring to all other assets owned by the seller in connection with the business other than the "excluded assets", makes sure that all of the necessary business and assets are passed to the buyer.

> MEMO POINTS **Definitions** for "business", each of the separately listed assets and the "excluded assets" will need to be included in the "interpretation" clause. The "**excluded assets**" are normally listed in a schedule to the agreement and generally include the business' book debts, cash in hand and any amounts recoverable in respect of taxation attributable to periods ended on or before the effective date. Other transaction-specific assets could also be excluded from the sale, for example, the business' property could be excluded because the buyer already has suitable trading premises.

5755 The seller will generally need to **compile lists and details** of all of these assets so that they can be listed in schedules to the sale and purchase agreement, for example:
- details of all freehold and leasehold property;
- a list of the business' tangible assets (e.g. plant and machinery); and
- a list of all contracts (e.g. sales contracts, contracts with suppliers, rental agreements).

This can involve considerable effort on the part of the seller, particularly if the business is large, fragmented over several sites or does not have stringent document control procedures.

2. Stock

5756 The **value** of stock, or work-in-progress, is usually left outstanding at completion because it generally cannot be determined until a stock take or reconciliation has been done. Instead, the sale and purchase agreement will usually set out provisions for the stock or work-in-progress to be valued as at the effective date and paid for separately.

> MEMO POINTS In a **small business sale**, if it is possible for the stock take to be done in one day, the value of the stock can simply be written into the sale and purchase agreement just before completion. There is then no need to for the agreement to contain relatively complicated stock valuation provisions.

5757 The provisions in the sale and purchase agreement will need to deal with:
- the **basis of the valuation**, including how to value partly finished, obsolete or slow-to-sell goods;
- the **timing** of the valuation, which should generally be as quickly as practicable after completion; and
- that in the event of **disagreement**, the matter should be referred to an independent accountant for expert determination.

In practice, the seller and buyer will usually carry out a **physical stock take** together.

3. Contracts

5758 The business' contracts (except for employment contracts which are treated differently, see ¶5771+) are an asset which must be **transferred** from the seller to the buyer. Contracts can be transferred by way of assignment or by novation.

5759 In an **assignment**, the seller transfers its rights and obligations under the business' contracts to the buyer. The seller cannot assign its obligations under a contract (known as the "**burden**" of the contract) without the consent of the other party to the contract. However, unless the contract specifies that consent is required, the seller can assign its rights under it (known as the "**benefit**" of the contract) without the consent of the other party. In order to perfect an assignment of the benefit, so that the buyer is able to enforce it directly against the third party, the buyer must give the third party written **notice** of the assignment (s 136 Law of Property Act 1925). Even if the third party's consent is required, the only parties to the assignment are the seller and the buyer. An assignment of the business' contracts can therefore be dealt with in the sale and purchase agreement.

5760 In a **novation**, the existing contract operates as though it had always been made between the other party and the buyer. The other party must be a party to the novation and so a separate novation agreement between the seller, buyer and third party is required for each novated contract. In practice, the third party is just as likely to require a **new contract** with the buyer, rather than a novation of the existing contract with the seller.

5761 Sometimes, the third party's consent to an assignment or novation **cannot be obtained before completion**, for example, because:
– the third party has no incentive to conform to the seller and buyer's timetable;
– the third party may be reluctant to deal with an unknown buyer, as opposed to a seller with whom it has had an ongoing relationship; or
– the seller and buyer may wish to keep the transaction confidential until the parties are contractually bound to proceed with the sale and purchase (i.e. until exchange).

The sale and purchase agreement must therefore deal with contracts:
– which are assignable (either without consent or because consent has already been obtained);
– where the consent of the third party is required, but will be obtained after exchange; and
– where the consent of the third party is required, but is refused.

5762 The **agreement will normally state that**:
– the buyer will perform the obligations and assume the benefits under the business' contracts as at the effective date;
– the seller will assign all contracts to the buyer which are capable of being assigned;
– the seller and buyer will use their reasonable endeavours to obtain the consent of the third party to a contract to an assignment or novation, where this is required; and
– if consent from the third party is required, unless and until that consent is given, the contract will not be treated as assigned to the buyer (which would be a breach of that contract). Instead, the seller will hold the contract on trust by for the buyer who will perform the contract on the seller's behalf and will indemnify the seller in respect of its actions. In turn, the seller will direct that payments should be made to the buyer and pay over any payments it erroneously receives.

> MEMO POINTS Both parties should be aware that the term "**reasonable endeavours**" does not require either party to sacrifice its own commercial interests, except where the contract specifically requires certain steps to be taken in order to use reasonable endeavours. The term **best endeavours** places a more onerous burden on the party concerned that "reasonable endeavours" (*Rhodia International Holdings Ltd v Huntsman International LLC* [2007] EWHC 292 (Comm)).

5763 In practice, most **routine or minor contracts** (e.g. for utility services, leases of photocopiers, telephone systems etc) are not formally assigned. The third party service provider in such cases will generally be unconcerned by the business transfer, provided the buyer continues to make its payments on time. An informal notice to them will normally be sufficient.

On the other hand, the business' **significant contracts**, for example, with trade suppliers or customers, will need to be assigned or novated in accordance with their terms. Where the third party's consent is required, the buyer and seller will normally agree on an informal basis when and how to approach that party and some three-way negotiation may be required. If the contract is an important one, the buyer may require consent to be obtained before the sale and purchase agreement is signed, or make completion conditional upon obtaining such consent (see ¶5732+).

4. Properties

5764 The business' properties, whether owned or leased, are another asset which must be transferred to the buyer by the seller. A **schedule** to the sale and purchase agreement **will normally set out**:
– details of the freehold and leasehold properties;
– details of any tenancies and other encumbrances to which they are subject; and
– the terms of sale, which are essentially the same as would normally apply if just a property were being transferred (e.g. the Standard Commercial Property Conditions (2nd edition) with any required modifications).

> MEMO POINTS 1. As part of its investigation, the buyer will need to carry out **property searches and surveys** (¶5696+, ¶5708) which may need to be refreshed close to completion (see ¶5899+).
> 2. See ¶5815 for the effect on **warranties**.

5765 **Leases** are a type of contract and will need to be assigned to the buyer (see ¶5758+). A lease will normally specify that it is not to be assigned without the **landlord's consent**, which the landlord is not permitted to unreasonably withhold or delay (s 1(3) Landlord and Tenant Act 1988).

In practice, obtaining consent can take time, perhaps because there is no particular incentive for the landlord to move quickly. The buyer will normally require the landlord's consent to be **obtained before** exchange (although it is possible for this to be a condition of completion instead (see ¶5732+)). It is therefore advisable for the seller to approach the landlord for consent as early as possible in negotiations. The landlord will normally charge a fee for giving its consent. In a business sale, these costs are normally absorbed by the seller, but there is nothing to prevent the seller negotiating a contribution from the buyer.

> MEMO POINTS 1. Normally the landlord will need to be provided with evidence that the buyer will be a "good" tenant. Unqualified **references** from the buyer's bank, current or past landlord, accountant and trade reference will normally be sufficient. If the buyer is unable to provide adequate references (e.g. because it is a newly incorporated company), the landlord will normally require a bank or individual guarantee and/or a rent deposit.
> 2. **Leases granted on or after 1 January 1996** may require the seller to enter into an "Authorised Guarantee Agreement" under which the seller guarantees the performance by the buyer of the tenant's obligations under the lease.

5. Debtors, creditors and liabilities

5766 The business' **debtors and creditors** will normally be **apportioned** as at the effective date so that:
– **money owed to** the seller in connection with the business, before the effective date belongs to the seller, and after the effective date belongs to the buyer; and
– **money owed by** the seller in connection with the business, before the effective date is to be paid by the seller, and after the effective date is to be paid by the buyer.

Further, a **reconciliation** in respect of any accrued charges or payment will have to be made after completion.

5767 The **reason that debts are apportioned** rather than sold to the buyer is that they represent uncollected cash. The buyer is unlikely to pay the face value of these debts, but instead will expect a discount to take into account the costs of collection and the risk that some of the debts will prove bad or doubtful. Further, if the business' debts are assigned to the buyer, notice of that assignment will have to be given to the debtors. This could cause anxiety amongst some debtors resulting in defaults or at least a reluctance to continue trading with the business.

> MEMO POINTS If the business' credit control employees transfer to the buyer, the sale and purchase agreement usually specifies that the **buyer** is to act **as the seller's collection agent** in respect of debts owed to the business for the period before the effective date. This is because the debtors will be used to dealing with particular people and so the collection of debts is likely to be easier if this continues. The buyer may charge a fee for this function.

5768 The **reason that creditors** of the business **are apportioned** rather than transferred to the buyer is that the buyer does not usually want to fulfil liabilities which it did not personally incur. It may not be fully aware of the circumstances in which the liability arose and, by accepting the liability, it would open itself to an unnecessary risk. In addition, the seller may not be comfortable with transferring the liabilities. This is because, as far as the person to whom the debt or other liability is owed, responsibility for paying the debt or discharging the liability remains with the seller. The seller will therefore normally want to remain in control and ensure that the debt is paid or liability discharged so that the third party cannot bring a claim against the seller in the future.

5769 So far as **other liabilities** are concerned, in an asset sale, the buyer will only take on liabilities if it chooses to do so. The sale and purchase agreement will therefore normally expressly state that the business' liabilities (other than those specified) will remain with the seller who will indemnify the buyer against them.

> MEMO POINTS Even if the buyer does not expressly choose to do so, it will **take on liabilities** under the business' employment contracts, environmental liabilities and liabilities under contracts that have been transferred to it.

5770 A particular concern is usually **product or service liability** claims brought by customers in respect of products or services supplied by the seller before the transfer. Normally, the sale and purchase agreement will expressly state that this liability remains with the seller. In order to protect the buyer's commercial interests, the seller will normally be required to report any such claims to the buyer and not to take any steps which would damage the buyer's interests (such as admitting that a product was faulty) unless the buyer has consented.

Where the seller has disposed of its whole business, it may find it difficult to maintain an **after-sales service**. Therefore, the sale and purchase agreement may provide for this to be carried out by the buyer, at the seller's expense.

6. Employees

5771 Under regulations, known as "**TUPE**" (Transfer of Undertakings (Protection of Employment) Regulations 2006 SI 2006/246), employees of the business have extra rights which **protect** their **employment**. The basic effect of these rights is that, where TUPE applies, the buyer must take over the seller's employees, if they are employed in the transferring business, on the same terms and conditions as the seller employed them. The buyer effectively steps into the seller's shoes, as if the buyer had always been the employees' employer.

In addition, TUPE imposes obligations on the seller and buyer to **inform and consult** with the appropriate representatives of affected employees before the transfer takes place.

For a detailed examination of all aspects of TUPE, see *Employment Memo*.

> MEMO POINTS In a **share sale**, the identity of the employer does not change; the employees remain employed by the target company and so TUPE does not usually apply (usually, evidence of assets or employees being transferred is required, which does not tend to happen in share sales). To apply TUPE in these circumstances would have the effect of piercing the corporate veil, which cannot be done simply because a group of companies is operated as a single economic entity. However, TUPE can apply in a share sale if the new owners take over control of the company's activities. For example, where a subsidiary company was sold to a new parent company and that new parent took over control of the subsidiary's activities (e.g. it operated the payroll for the subsidiary and had control of its day to day activities) the court found that there

had been a transfer of the company's day to day activities to the new parent company and so TUPE applied (*Millam v The Print Factory (London) 1991 Ltd* [2007] EWCA Civ 322). In this case, the court stated that the corporate veil had not been pierced: instead of the group being organised so that it looked as if the parent carried on the subsidiary's activities for policy reasons, the subsidiary did not actually carry on the activities at all.

5772 It is not possible to contract out of TUPE, i.e. the employees cannot agree to waive their rights, but the seller and buyer can come to a **contractual agreement** as to who should bear the cost of any TUPE liabilities. This is normally dealt with in the sale and purchase agreement.

5773 Within 1 month after the transfer, the employees whose employment has been transferred to the buyer must be **notified** in writing of the change in the identity of their employer and the date upon which his or her continuous period of employment with the buyer began (s 4(6) Employment Rights Act 1996).

> MEMO POINTS   The date upon which an employee's **continuous period of employment** began is important for calculating various employment rights. The basic rule is that there is continuity of employment from the start of employment until that particular employment ends. However, TUPE does not break continuity, so for example, if an employee started with X Ltd on 1 January 2008 and transferred to Y Ltd under TUPE on 1 July 2008, his continuous employment began on 1 January 2008.

5774 Complex case law has developed to determine whether or not a business has transferred and when the transfer took place, but there is usually no dispute on these matters in a business sale. It is normally quite clear that a business has transferred as that is the very essence of the agreement. The **date of transfer** is usually set out in the sale and purchase agreement (i.e. the "effective date", see ¶5752+).

Protection of employment

5775 The rights which protect the employment of the employees are summarised in the table below and developed further underneath it.

	Effect of right	Liability
Contract of employment	Automatically transfers to buyer	Buyer liable for all pre- and post-transfer liabilities in relation to employment
Changes to terms and conditions of employment	Ineffective, if changes made by reason of the transfer or a reason connected with the transfer that is not an "economic, technical or organisational reason" entailing changes in the workforce ("ETO reason")	Buyer liable for damages for differences between old and new terms
Dismissal	Automatic unfair dismissal if reason is transfer or a reason connected with transfer that is not ETO reason	Buyer liable for pre- and post-transfer dismissals (unless ETO defence applies)

Contract of employment

5776 All the seller's rights, powers, duties and liabilities under or in connection with the employment contracts of employees employed in the business (including the seller's obligations in respect of the employees' contractual rights such as pay, benefits, holiday entitlement etc) **automatically transfer** to the buyer (reg 4(2)(a) SI 2006/246). The **buyer**, not the seller, **will be liable** to the employees after the transfer, and any act or omission of the seller before the transfer in respect of the employees will be deemed to have been an act or omission of the buyer (reg 4(2)(b) SI 2006/246). So, for example, if the seller owed wages to the employees before the transfer, the employees must claim their unpaid wages from the buyer after the transfer.

MEMO POINTS Old age, invalidity or survivor benefits under an **occupational pension scheme** do not transfer under TUPE (reg 10 SI 2006/246), although other benefits under the scheme, such as enhanced redundancy entitlements or early retirement benefits, do transfer (*Beckmann v Dynamco Whicheloe Macfarlane Ltd* [2002] IRLR 578; *Martin v South Bank University* [2004] IRLR 74). For private sector employees who would have been entitled to an occupational pension scheme before the transfer, the buyer does, however, have to provide an alternative scheme (a defined benefit (i.e. final salary), money purchase or stakeholder scheme where the buyer matches the employee's contributions up to a maximum of 6% of salary) (ss 257, 258 Pensions Act 2004; SI 2005/649).

A seller's obligation to make contributions to an employee's **personal pension scheme** (whether an individual or group scheme) will transfer to the buyer as these do not fall within the definition of "occupational pension scheme" (s 1 Pension Schemes Act 1993).

Changes to terms and conditions

5777 The buyer can agree contractual variations with the transferred employees provided the sole or principal reason for the variation is not the transfer but an ETO reason connected with the transfer (reg 4(5) SI 2006/246). An "**ETO reason**" is an "economic, technical or organisational reason entailing changes in the workforce", such as a genuine redundancy or business reorganisation.

This definition can present practical difficulties. For example, the buyer cannot **harmonise the terms** of transferring employees with those of existing employees: the desire to achieve harmonisation is deemed to be by reason of the transfer itself and is not an ETO reason.

If the changes are not disadvantageous to the employees, buyers usually take a pragmatic approach and implement changes in the expectation that few, if any, employees are likely to complain.

MEMO POINTS Where the **transfer** took place **before 6 April 2006**, changes to a transferred employee's terms and conditions of employment that are made for a reason connected with the transfer will be legally ineffective, even if the employee has agreed to the variation (*Wilson v St Helens Borough Council* [1998] IRLR 706) and even if the variation is to the employee's advantage (*Foreningen af Arbejdsledere i Danmark v Daddy's Dance Hall A/S* [1988] IRLR 315).

5778 Where a transfer involves or would involve a **substantial change in working conditions** to the material detriment of a transferring employee, he has the statutory right to treat his contract of employment as terminated and he will be treated as having been dismissed (reg 4(9) SI 2006/246). However, the employee cannot make a claim for payment in lieu of a notice period to which he was entitled under his contract (reg 4(10) SI 2006/246).

This right is separate from the employee's common law right to claim **constructive dismissal** because his employer had made substantial detrimental changes to his terms of employment which amounted to a fundamental or repudiatory breach of contract (e.g. reducing salary or benefits) (reg 4(11) SI 2006/246).

The statutory right is easier to claim because it is not necessary to show that the substantial detrimental change amounts to a fundamental or repudiatory breach.

MEMO POINTS Only the common law remedy was available to employees for **transfers** which took place **before 6 April 2006**.

Dismissal

5779 A dismissal will be **automatically unfair** if the sole or principal reason for it is the transfer itself or a reason connected with the transfer that is not an ETO reason (reg 7(1) SI 2006/246).

If, however, the sole or principal reason is not the transfer itself but is a reason connected with the transfer that is an ETO reason, the dismissal will be **potentially fair**, subject to the normal test of reasonableness under unfair dismissal legislation (see *Employment Memo*). The dismissal will be treated as having been either for redundancy, if the appropriate test of redundancy is met, or for some other substantial reason (reg 7(3)(b) SI 2006/246). The employer will have to show that he acted reasonably in all the circumstances in treating the reason as a fair reason for dismissal to avoid liability. This may require the employer to consider alternatives to dismissal and to consult with the employee.

Liability for the dismissal of transferring employees will **transfer to the buyer** so that it becomes liable for both pre- and post-transfer dismissals, unless there is an ETO defence.

> MEMO POINTS   The **liability** for a pre-transfer dismissal by the seller will **not transfer to the buyer** if the seller had an ETO defence. However, it should be noted that the seller will not succeed in an ETO defence where it dismisses employees at the buyer's request to achieve a sale or make the business more attractive (*Wheeler v (1) Patel (2) J Golding Group of Companies* [1987] IRLR 211). Therefore, if the buyer needs to dismiss transferring employees, it should do so itself after the transfer so that it can rely on its own ETO defence.

Information and consultation

5780 The seller (in respect of its own employees) and the buyer (in respect of its own employees) have an obligation to inform and consult with the **appropriate representatives** of the employees that will be affected by the business transfer. An overview of the process is at ¶5784.

> MEMO POINTS   1. The appropriate representatives must be **elected by** the affected employees and must themselves be affected employees as at the election date. The employer should make arrangements to ensure that the election is fair and that the number of representatives to be elected will sufficiently represent the affected employees' interests.
> If the affected employees **fail to elect representatives**, the employer has to give (in writing) each affected employee the information which it would otherwise have been required to give to the elected representatives. There is no duty to consult if such a failure to elect occurs.
> In practice, elections are rarely carried out where **small numbers of employees** are concerned. Instead, the seller and buyer will normally inform each affected employee and consult individually where this is necessary.
> 2. Additional duties to consult with employees on an ongoing basis, including in relation to a proposed transfer, are imposed on UK businesses. These obligations apply to businesses with 100 or more employees, and from 6 April 2008 they will apply to businesses with 50 or more employees (SI 2004/3426). (See *Employment Law Memo* for further details).

Obligation to inform

5781 The seller and buyer each have an obligation to inform their own employees' representatives of (reg 13 SI 2006/246):
a. the **fact** that a transfer is to take place, **when** approximately it will take place and the **reason** for it (but it is not obliged to justify the transfer or discuss its merits);
b. the legal, economic and social **implications of the transfer** for any affected employees, which may include an explanation of the legal effect in relation to employment contracts, collective agreements and statutory rights, the impact on pay and benefits, and any relocation plans; and
c. the **measures** which it envisages it will take, in connection with the transfer, in relation to any affected employees (or, if no measures are envisaged, confirmation of that fact). In addition, the seller must inform its employees' representatives of the measures which the buyer envisages it will take (or, if no measures are envisaged, confirmation of that fact). The buyer must provide the seller with such information as will allow it to comply with this obligation.

The seller and buyer are not able to circumvent this obligation by pleading that the transaction is **commercially sensitive** or must be kept confidential.

Obligation to consult

5782 The seller and buyer have an obligation to consult with their own employees' representatives only if they envisage they will be **taking measures** in relation to the affected employees. This means that the seller will not have to consult if it does not envisage taking any measures, nor does it have to consult if the buyer envisages taking measures. The buyer is not obliged to consult with the representatives of the transferring employees before the transfer as it does not yet employ the employees.

> MEMO POINTS   If consultation is required, there is no obligation to agree with any requests made during the consultation process. However, the consultation must be meaningful **with a view to seeking agreement** to the intended measures (reg 13(6) SI 2006/246). The employer must consider any representations made by the appropriate representatives, reply to them and give reasons for rejecting any of them.

Timing

The **information** must be provided long enough before the transfer to enable consultation to take place (whether or not the obligation to consult exists). The timing will depend upon the number of employees, their location and the complexity of the transaction but at least 2 to 4 weeks before the transfer will be normally be appropriate.

If the employer is also obliged to **consult**, the process should begin before the sale and purchase agreement is signed so that it can respond to any representations raised.

5783

Overview

Informing and consulting with appropriate representatives (or individual employees if there are no appropriate representatives) will run alongside the negotiations between the seller and buyer, as the flowchart below demonstrates. These duties should not be forgotten in the rush towards completing the deal.

5784

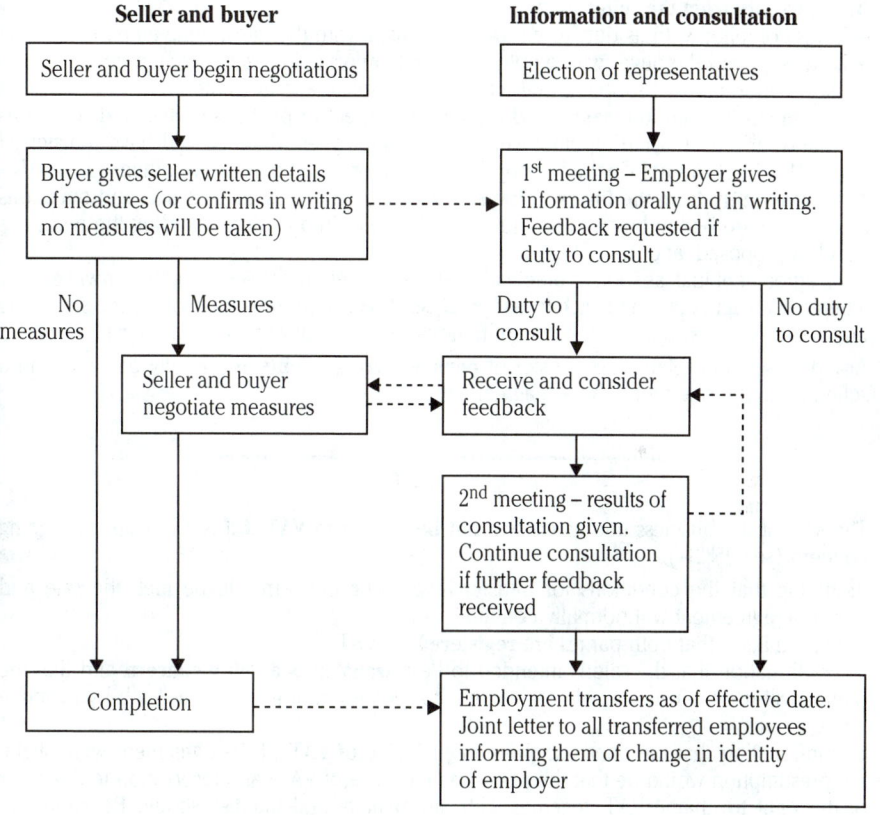

Failure to inform and consult

An employee can bring a claim for failure to inform and consult and an employment tribunal can order the employer to **pay up to** 13 weeks' pay per employee (uncapped) (regs 15(7), (8), 16(3) SI 2006/246). The seller may be able to defend a claim on the basis that it was not reasonably practicable for it to inform and consult with its employees because the buyer had failed to provide it with the necessary information (the seller must have chased the buyer for that information).

For transfers **on or after 6 April 2006**, the buyer and seller can be made jointly and severally liable for an award of compensation made by an employment tribunal (reg 15(9) SI 2006/246). Employees may therefore bring proceedings against either the buyer or seller or, as is more likely, both.

5785

> MEMO POINTS   Where the transfer took place **before 6 April 2006**, it was held that liability to pay compensation for failure to inform and consult would transfer from the seller to the buyer (even where the failure to consult was not the buyer's fault) (*Alamo Group (Europe) Ltd v Tucker* [2003] IRLR 266). This was contrary to a previous decision in which the court held that liability stayed with the seller on the basis that if the award transferred there would be no incentive on the seller to comply with its obligations (*TGWU v McKinnon* [2001] ICR 1281). Without a decision from a higher court, the decision in the more recent case (i.e. *Alamo*) was preferred.

Contractual provisions

5786 Since TUPE can result in many employment related liabilities, which could be borne by the party not at fault, the practice has arisen for the sale and purchase agreement to include various contractual provisions to apportion any TUPE liabilities between the seller and buyer. The usual contractual provisions are as follows:

a. an **acknowledgement** that TUPE applies to the transfer and that the employment of the employees named in a schedule to the sale and purchase agreement has transferred to the buyer;

b. a **warranty from the seller** that:
– it has complied with its duty to inform and consult with the transferring employees;
– it has supplied the buyer with employee liability information (see ¶5686); and
– all the information it supplied to the buyer is complete and accurate;

c. an **indemnity from the seller to the buyer** in respect of pre-transfer acts and omissions in relation to the transferring employees or any employees which should have transferred under TUPE but did not (including any failure to inform and consult with them);

d. an **indemnity from the buyer to the seller** in respect of post-transfer acts and omissions and any failure by the buyer to provide the seller with information regarding the measures which it proposed; and

e. an agreement that, as soon as practicable after completion, the seller and buyer will deliver a **letter** in an agreed form **to each transferred employee**, informing them of the transfer to the buyer and the date upon which their continuous employment with the buyer began.

Any provisions in relation to transfer of **pension arrangements** are usually dealt with in a schedule to the sale and purchase agreement.

7. VAT

5787 The sale of the business and assets will **not be subject to VAT if** it is a transfer as a going concern (see ¶5321+).

Assuming that the conditions for transfer as a going concern will be met, the sale and purchase agreement will normally contain:

a. confirmation that both parties are **registered** for VAT;

b. confirmation that the sale is intended to be a **transfer as a going concern** and that the parties will use their reasonable endeavours to secure that it is treated as such by Revenue and Customs;

c. confirmation that the purchase **price is exclusive of VAT** (if the agreement were silent, the presumption would be that the price was inclusive of VAT) and reservation to the seller of the right to charge VAT, together with any penalty and interest, should Revenue and Customs subsequently hold that VAT should have been charged; and

d. a **warranty** from the seller that it has not elected to waive exemption from VAT in respect of any property being transferred. If, unusually, the seller has elected to waive the exemption, this warranty would be replaced by a warranty from the buyer that it too has elected to waive the exemption and that his option to tax will not be disapplied by anti-avoidance provisions (see ¶5324).

5788 From September 2007, the seller has been required to keep the business' **VAT records** for 6 years from the date of the transfer (s 100 FA 2007). However, the seller is under a duty to provide the buyer with sufficient information to enable it to comply with ongoing reporting commitments. Revenue and Customs is also under a duty to provide the buyer with any information which they hold for this purpose.

So that the buyer can comply with its reporting obligations, the sale and purchase agreement should expressly give the buyer the free **right to access** to the business' financial records (relating to the period before the sale) and require the seller to transfer them to the buyer 6 years after the transfer date.

> **MEMO POINTS** In an arm's length transaction, the buyer will normally have a different **VAT registration number** from the seller. In a connected transaction (e.g. between group companies), the buyer may wish to take over the seller's VAT registration number. In doing so, the buyer will assume responsibility for submitting any tax returns due at the date of the transfer and for accounting for any continuing VAT liability. An application to transfer the seller's VAT registration number must be made jointly by the buyer and seller on Form VAT 68, available from a local VAT office. However, if the buyer takes over the seller's VAT registration number (which is rare), the seller will have to pass the business records to the buyer unless Revenue and Customs gives permission for the seller to keep the records (s 100 FA 2007).

If the business is transferred as a going concern and the **seller** is not going to continue trading in another capacity, it will need to **cancel** its **VAT registration**. Cancellation should be notified to Revenue and Customs using Form VAT 7 within 30 days of the transfer. This is not necessary where the buyer is taking over the seller's VAT registration number.

If the business is transferred as a going concern, the **buyer** will need to **register for VAT** within 30 days of the business being transferred. See *Tax Memo* for further details.

5789

III. Allocation of risk

Buyer beware

The sale and purchase agreement is a contract between the seller to sell and the buyer to buy the shares or assets, as appropriate. In the absence of any written or oral contractual provisions to the contrary, a buyer purchases at his risk without any recourse to the seller. This general rule is known as "**caveat emptor**" – "buyer beware". This means that:
– there is no legal protection for the buyer's interests; and
– the seller is not obliged to minimise any risks to which a potential buyer may be exposed or to make any statements about the shares/assets to be sold.

5800

However, any **statements by the seller** that are made must not be false or a misrepresentation. Furthermore all **representations** must be full, frank and tell the whole truth. If a statement is made by the seller that **misleads** the buyer, the buyer may be able to rescind the contract and/or recover his losses from the seller by way of an action in **misrepresentation**. However, actions in misrepresentation are difficult and expensive to bring as a result of complex rules and difficulties of proof. Consequently, it is unlikely to be an adequate and/or viable method of protection for a prospective buyer.

5801

> **EXAMPLE** A chemist owns and runs X Ltd, specialising in the production of dyes for paint. During the production process a poisonous liquid is produced which has always been disposed of into the river that runs past the plant. Recent environmental laws mean that it is no longer possible for the poison to be disposed of in the river. X Ltd has not built the necessary disposal facilities and has been warned that it must comply or face a large fine. The chemist decides to ignore the risk because he is about to sell the company to Mr B and does not want to reduce the value of X Ltd by spending its money. Mr B buys all of the shares in X Ltd using stock transfer forms and no other agreement. Soon afterwards X Ltd is fined and is forced to spend £80,000 improving the poison disposal facilities.
>
> 1. Suppose Mr B had not asked the chemist about the disposal of the poison or any potential liabilities. Mr B (through his ownership of X Ltd) would be forced to bear the costs, as in acquiring X Ltd, he took all the associated risks.
> 2. Suppose Mr B did ask the chemist about the disposal of the poison and any potential liabilities and the chemist informed him that the poison was disposed of in the river, but did not tell him about the impact of the changes to the environmental laws upon the company. Mr B would be

> entitled to bring a claim for misrepresentation against the chemist as the chemist misrepresented the company's position by not being full and frank with regard to its potential liabilities. The liability for the costs could then be passed onto the chemist rather than being borne by X Ltd.

MEMO POINTS The caveat emptor rule is more onerous when applied to shares than assets. A **buyer of shares** not only acquires the risks associated with those shares but also those of the company. Further, a change in the ownership of shares does not affect the liabilities of a company, i.e. the liabilities remain with the target and so indirectly pass to the buyer through his ownership of the target's shares. A **buyer of assets** on the other hand, only acquires the risk relating to the assets being purchased. Liability in respect of assets lies with the owner at the time that the liability arose, i.e. existing liabilities remain with the seller.

5802 A **buyer who is paying little** or no consideration may accept the risks associated with having no and/or limited recourse to a seller as the risks are balanced by the low acquisition cost. However, a **buyer paying large sums** of money will wish to minimise his risks as far as possible. This will be of particular concern to a buyer buying in the business and assets of, or shares in, an older well-established trading company, as it is more likely to have acquired increased liabilities because it has traded for longer than a newer or dormant company.

Rebalancing the risk

5803 The **buyer** will usually try to counter the effect of the caveat emptor rule and provide himself with some **protection** from risk by introducing specific contractual provisions into the sale and purchase agreement to re-apportion the risk between the parties. The two types of contractual provision used by a buyer are **warranties and indemnities** (see ¶5807+).

However, as these provisions are designed to put as much of the risk as is possible on the **seller**, the seller in return will want to limit his exposure as far as he is able. He will do so by making **disclosures** against the warranties and introducing specific contractual provisions in the sale and purchase agreement, known collectively as "**seller limitation clauses**" which limit his liability and restrict the buyer's ability to make claims against him (see ¶5890+).

Negotiation process

5804 The process of rebalancing the risk will be done through negotiations, which will result in several drafts of the documents and frequently continues right up until immediately before exchange.

The **buyer** will usually incorporate the warranties and indemnities which it requires into the first draft of the sale and purchase agreement.

The **seller** will as a result carry out a thorough examination of the affairs of his company with his professional advisers to determine what risks would arise from the requested warranties and indemnities. If the due diligence process has been properly managed (see ¶5652+), much of the information will already be to hand. The seller will compile this information into a disclosure letter to the buyer, which will provide the buyer with information affecting the warranties. The seller will also insert seller limitation clauses into the draft sale and purchase agreement. It may also propose amendments to the warranties and indemnities.

In return, the buyer will then consider the seller's amendments to the sale and purchase agreement in the light of the information received in the disclosure letter. It will also consider what information is acceptable for inclusion in the disclosure letter as it will limit his ability to make warranty claims. If a disclosure reveals a previously unknown significant liability, the buyer may renegotiate the purchase price, or seek to include a further indemnity in respect of the liability.

This negotiation will be one of the most **contentious aspects of a transaction** with each party wanting to minimise the risk to which they are exposed. Some risks are most appropriately borne by one of the parties as they have knowledge of a particular event, whilst others will depend on the commercial factors influencing the transaction. The process not only results in protection for the buyer but also encourages the seller to carefully consider the extent of the liabilities to which he is exposing himself and to disclose accordingly. Practically speaking, this detailed method of disclosure may also lead to a re-evaluation of the transaction and/or its purchase price.

A. Protection for buyer

5807 The buyer can minimise his risk by creating contractual obligations with the seller within the sale and purchase agreement known as "**warranties**" and "**indemnities**". Generally speaking, indemnities afford the best protection for the buyer and warranties are a better option (insofar as there is one) for the seller.

1. Overview of warranties and indemnities

What is a warranty?

5809 A warranty is a **contractual statement of fact**, relating to the shares/assets and the business to be sold. It provides an assurance to the buyer as to the state/liabilities of various aspect of the target and its business.

Warranties, if breached, act to **compensate a buyer for** buying something which was not as it was expected to be. If the buyer can demonstrate that there has been a breach of warranty that affects the purchase price, he is entitled to be compensated for the reduction in the value of what he bought. In the case of a share sale, this will be the value of his shares, and in the case of an asset sale, this will be the value of the underlying business and assets (¶5827+).

A warranty may also be a **representation** if it induces the buyer to enter into the sale and purchase agreement in reliance upon it. If such a warranty is false, it will amount to a misrepresentation for which the buyer may be able to claim damages (¶5830). In certain cases, the buyer may even be able to rescind the agreement (¶5838+).

> EXAMPLE A buys 100 shares in X Ltd from B for £1,000. B provides a warranty that there are 100 issued shares in the company. After he has purchased X Ltd, A discovers that there are in fact 102 issued shares in the company; 2 shares were never transferred to B by the subscribers (C and D). Subscriber C is a partner in the firm of solicitors employed to form the company. He executes a stock transfer form transferring his share to A at no cost.
> Subscriber D is an ex-employee who refuses to transfer his share to A. Suppose that the value of A's shares is reduced by 10% as a result, i.e. they are now worth £900.
> A is not able to claim any monies from B in relation to the share owned by Subscriber C as there is no resulting reduction in the value of his shares. He is however able to make a claim for £100 in respect of the share owned by Subscriber D.

5810 Warranties have a second function in that they **encourage the seller to make specific disclosures** of liabilities (¶5907+). The buyer is therefore provided with greater information with which to assess the risks that he is acquiring and to negotiate an appropriate price and protection mechanism.

> EXAMPLE A taxi company is being sold for £150,000. The price was negotiated on the basis that the company owned all the cars it used in the course of its business and so the buyer inserts a warranty to this effect into the share purchase agreement. The sellers disclose that two of the ten cars used by the company are leased from a finance company and there is still £20,000 left to pay on them. The buyer renegotiates the price down to £130,000.

However, disclosures have the effect of watering down the warranties. For example, a warranty could be a sweeping statement to the effect that there is no pollution on a factory site which is being bought as part of the deal. The disclosure by the seller in relation to this could be a report from an environmental scientist to the effect that there is extensive pollution of the site. The net result is that the warranty is largely pointless.

5811 Warranties are usually **contained in** schedules at the end of the sale and purchase agreement and a clause in the main body of the agreement will incorporate them into the contract between the buyer and seller. This clause will normally state that the sellers warrant that the warranties in the schedule are true and accurate both at execution and at completion.

What is an indemnity?

5812 An indemnity is a **contractual promise** in relation to a certain specified risk to compensate the injured party if the risk actually occurs.

Indemnities, if breached, enable the buyer to claim **damages** so that he can be put back into the financial position he would have been in had the relevant event not occurred. This means that the buyer merely needs to show that he has suffered a loss. The damages that he is able to claim will extend to all losses that he has suffered as a result of the breach of the indemnity. A successful claimant will be able to claim not only for a reduction in the value of that which he bought, but also for any expenses or losses that he incurs as a result of the breach.

> EXAMPLE X Ltd decides to buy a restaurant business, but having carried out due diligence on the business, it is concerned that it may be liable to pay compensation to a waitress who fell and injured herself at work. The seller does not believe that she will make a claim for compensation and refuses to reduce the purchase price to take into account this risk.
> The seller does however agree that it should be liable should any compensation be paid to the waitress and agrees to give X Ltd an indemnity to that effect.
> Shortly after X Ltd acquires the business, the waitress successfully brings a claim for £25,000 of damages in respect of her injury. The total cost to X Ltd including its legal fees and loss of earnings (caused when the restaurant was closed for health and safety reasons) is £40,000. X Ltd is entitled to recover £40,000 from the seller as that is the figure that will put it back into the position it would have been in had the waitress' claim not been made.

5813 Indemnities which relate to non-tax matters are usually **contained in** the main body of the sale and purchase agreement. In a share sale, indemnities relating to tax are usually contained in a schedule to the main sale and purchase agreement, or sometimes in a separate tax deed (see ¶5945+). (Tax indemnities are not appropriate for asset sales as the tax liabilities remain with the seller.)

What risks do they cover?

5814 Warranties contain detailed statements which are intended to deal with all areas that may create liability for a buyer. Each will be **tailored to the needs of the buyer** and the perceived risks associated with the acquisition but **balanced against the interests of the sellers**. If a company is relatively simple and/or the value of the transaction small, warranties will tend to be shorter. In high value or complex transactions, the warranties are likely to extend for tens of pages. In either case, the warranties are likely to form the bulk of the agreement.

5815 There are a wide **range of warranties** that may be included within a sale and purchase agreement. Below is a list of those that are commonly found. The list however cannot be exhaustive, as each transaction is unique with its own specific issues and concerns. Warranties normally relate to the same subjects upon which the buyer will have carried out due diligence (¶5652+), that is to say:
– the accuracy of information provided by the seller to the buyer;
– the constitution of the target;
– the capacity and interests of the seller;
– the target's accounts and management accounts;
– the target's finances;
– taxation;
– the target's property holdings;
– compliance with environmental regulations;
– ownership and condition of assets;
– the target's intellectual property rights;
– absence of environmental contamination on the properties;

- the target's computer systems;
- holding of appropriate licences;
- compliance with laws;
- the target's contracts, agreements and trade agreements;
- the target's solvency;
- litigation by or against the target;
- the target's officers and employees;
- compliance with data protection regulations;
- compliance with health and safety;
- the target's insurance policies;
- pension arrangements; and
- compliance with competition requirements.

MEMO POINTS 1. In a share sale, the same warranties should be expressed to apply to the target's **subsidiaries**. If there are no subsidiaries, a warranty to that effect will be sufficient.
2. Sometimes, a buyer may obtain an **accountants' report** on which the seller provides a **global warranty** as to its accuracy. The result is that the warranties, particularly those that relate to the financial and trading affairs of the target company, will be shorter. It allows the buyer to make a decision on the state of the company's affairs using a report produced by its professional advisers, whilst being able to make a warranty claim should it be incorrect. This may significantly reduce the warranty negotiations, but for the seller it results in an onerous warranty without the benefit of examining the effect of each warranty individually and disclosing against them.
3. The allocation of risk would be dealt with differently if only a **property** were being transferred. In a property sale, there are not usually any warranties. Instead, the buyer relies on the seller's answers to the buyer's written enquiries, and if any of those answers are untrue then the buyer will have an action for misrepresentation against the seller. In an asset sale therefore, the seller may be able to argue for less stringent property warranties on the basis that these amount to "extra" protection for the buyer. The argument against full warranties is likely to be even stronger if the property is the business' main asset (e.g. a pub or hotel business).

When are they both used?

It is possible for warranties and indemnities to be used to **cover the same type of risk**. As noted above, in the context of shares, taxation liabilities are dealt with by way of indemnities in the tax deed. However, tax warranties are also contained within the warranties schedule to the sale and purchase agreement. This could equally happen with other types of liability in both asset and share sales.

Over the years, there has been an increase in the use of indemnities in addition to warranties as a result of the due diligence and disclosure processes, by which new risks are identified which had not been appreciated originally. As a result, the buyer may decide not to buy the target company or, conversely, choose to go ahead with the purchase irrespective of the risks. He may also renegotiate the purchase price. But, if the seller refuses to reduce it because the risk is unlikely to result in an actual liability then the buyer may seek an indemnity. Its use in these circumstances is pertinent when potential risks exist that are unlikely to ever happen, but if they did, would be expensive for the target.

5817

EXAMPLE A is buying XYZ Ltd from B and C. A discovers that XYZ Ltd's customer database is not data protection compliant. A is concerned that XYZ Ltd may be fined by the Information Commissioner, or be required to destroy this valuable asset. B and C believe that it is unlikely that the Information Commissioner will take any action against XYZ Ltd and therefore refuse to reduce the purchase but agree to indemnify A and XYZ Ltd should enforcement action be taken.

At first sight, it may seem unnecessary to have the same type of risk covered by a warranty and an indemnity but this is to misunderstand their **respective purposes**. The purpose of a warranty is to retrospectively adjust the purchase price in the event that the circumstances surrounding the sale and purchase (and upon which the original price was based) turn out to be different to those that the buyer expected. The purpose of an indemnity is to compensate the buyer for future specific liabilities. Therefore, sometimes the buyer will insist upon a risk being covered by both a warranty and an indemnity.

5818

2. Who is liable?

5822 The person who gives the warranties and indemnities (that is to say, incurs liability under them) is referred to as "**warrantor**".

5823 In most cases, the warrantor is the seller, or in the case of multiple sellers, all of them. Sometimes, however, the seller(s) or buyer may require either only some of the sellers (in the case of multiple sellers) or someone else connected to the transaction, to act as warrantor(s). For example:
– if one of the sellers of a company's shares is a **venture capitalist** whose sole purpose was to invest in the company and in exchange for taking such risk, it had contractually agreed that it would not provide warranties and indemnities on the company's disposal, the warrantors may be the other sellers only;
– if a seller of shares had **no involvement in the day to day management** of the company but other sellers did, the warrantors may only be the sellers involved in the company's operation; or
– if the **sellers are trustees**, they will not usually give any warranties or indemnities other than warranting ownership and so the warrantors may only be the other sellers or the beneficiaries of the trusts.

The **buyer may seek additional warrantors** because it is concerned that the sellers would be unable to pay the buyer should there be a valid warranty or indemnity claim. For example, if the **seller is a company**, the buyer may wish the majority shareholder or group parent company (if it is a member of a group of companies) to join as a warrantor.

Before accepting replacement warrantors, the buyer should carefully consider whether they have sufficient funds and/or assets to be able to continue to meet a claim for the life of the warranties. If the buyer is concerned about the replacement warrantors, it should consider requiring alternative warrantors or obtaining security for claims (see ¶5858+).

> MEMO POINTS Throughout this section the term **seller** has been used, even in circumstances where the seller is not the warrantor and whether the protection is a warranty or an indemnity.

3. Remedies

5826 In order to make a **successful warranty claim**, a buyer will need to demonstrate that an event has occurred which renders the statement made in a warranty untrue. In order to make a **successful indemnity claim**, the buyer will need to demonstrate that the event against which he is being indemnified against has occurred. The remedy for a breach of warranty or under an indemnity is damages, but the ways in which the damages are calculated are different. Breach of warranty can also result in rescission, but this is rare.

a. Damages

5827 The right to claim **financial compensation**, known as damages, is the more usual remedy for breach of warranty or under an indemnity. This right will be **subject to any limitations or exclusions of liability** in the sale and purchase agreement (e.g. see ¶5918+).

Warranty claim

5828 In a warranty claim, the buyer can claim damages from the seller for:
– breach of contract, which is easier to prove but likely to result in a lower amount of damages; or
– misrepresentation, which is harder to prove but will result in higher damages.

5829 The amount of damages recoverable by the buyer in a **breach of contract** claim is the difference between the actual price and the amount of the reduction in the value of the shares/assets caused by the breach of warranty. No claim may be made for any other losses or costs incurred in making the claim. If a breach of warranty does not affect the value of the shares/assets, a buyer is unable to make a claim under contract. This can cause problems in share sales of private companies because it is often difficult to link the breach to a fall in share value. A buyer will often seek to strengthen its position by including a clause in the sale and purchase agreement which specifies that in a warranty claim, it is entitled to be compensated for its loss on a pound for pound basis (in effect, turning warranties into indemnities, see below). This will naturally be resisted by the seller, although, depending upon the seller's negotiating position, it may have to accept the amendment and instead rely on the seller limitation clauses (¶5918+).

5830

Damages for **misrepresentation** (whether fraudulent, negligent or innocent) can be claimed under statute, but the claim can be defended by the seller on the basis that he believed the warranty was true and had reasonable grounds for that belief (s 2(1) Misrepresentation Act 1967). It is therefore harder for the buyer to succeed in its claim. However, if it does succeed, the amount of damages recoverable by the buyer is the amount of loss it has suffered, so that it can be put in the position it would have been in if the warranty had been true. The buyer is therefore likely to recover more of its losses.

Sometimes, the seller will attempt to include a clause which states that the warranties do not amount to representations and that the statutory remedies for misrepresentation (including rescission, see below) are excluded. **Exclusions of liability for misrepresentation** are subject to a test of reasonableness, and in any event, it is not possible to exclude liability for fraudulent misrepresentations (s 3 Misrepresentation Act 1967; *Thomas Witter Ltd v TBP Industries Ltd* [1996] 2 All ER 573). See ¶5740 for the effect on the "entire agreement" clause.

MEMO POINTS 1. The buyer could also try to claim damages for the **tort of deceit or negligent misstatement**. The amount of damages would be calculated in the same way as for misrepresentation. However, these torts are even harder to prove and so it is usually more convenient to rely on the statutory remedy if tortious damages are being sought.
2. A corporate seller can be vicariously liable for **fraudulent information** provided by an employee (*MAN AG v Freightliner Ltd* [2005] EWHC 2347 (Comm)).

Indemnity claim

Indemnities, if breached, aim at putting the buyer back in the financial position it would have been in had the relevant event not occurred. Thus the only remedy under an indemnity is a claim for damages, but (subject to any agreement to the contrary between the seller and buyer) there is no limit upon the **amount** of damages that a buyer may recover. He may recover any loss that arises as a result of the indemnity claim, including the costs incurred in bringing the claim, on a pound for pound basis. The damages recoverable under an indemnity are therefore much wider than for a breach of contract and it is not necessary for the buyer to demonstrate a link between the liability and the resultant value of the company.

5832

Taxation of damages

As discussed earlier, a seller must pay capital gains tax on the gain it makes on the disposal of its shares or assets (¶5290+). However, a successful breach of warranty or indemnity claim will result in a payment back to the buyer from the seller, so the seller will be left with less of the consideration in his hands. Two questions therefore arise which are dealt with below:
– will the **buyer** have to pay tax on the damages it receives?
– will the **seller** be entitled to set off the damages against his tax liability on the consideration?

5834

The **buyer's potential liability to pay tax on damages** arose out of a case which suggested that the right to damages or an indemnity was a chargeable asset for tax purposes, and that payment under that right was a deemed disposal of that asset. The recipient would therefore have to pay tax on the amount of damages received (*Zim Properties Ltd v Proctor (Inspector of Taxes)* [1985] STC 90). However, by **concession from Revenue and Customs**, damages received under a warranty or indemnity included as one of the terms of a sale and purchase agreement are not immediately subject to tax, but are deducted from the base cost of the assets or shares on a future disposal (ESC D33).

5835

Despite this concession, the buyer will usually insist on a "**grossing up**" clause in the sale and purchase agreement, which passes the risk of any tax liability on the damages onto the sellers. This should pose little problem for the seller, provided he is sure the payment will come within the concession.

The key to **coming within the concession** is that the payment must be received by the buyer and the claim must arise out of the contract. This should not be a problem where the damages are received for a breach of warranty claim as this claim will always be brought by the buyer. However, in a share sale, care should be taken that payments under an indemnity are made to the buyer rather than to the target company (see further the discussion in relation to tax indemnities at ¶5945+).

5836 By the same concession (ESC D33), any payment made by the seller under the warranties or indemnities will result in a retrospective downwards adjustment to the consideration and consequential **adjustment to the capital gains tax payable by the seller**. Again, despite the concession, the sale and purchase agreement will usually expressly state that any money paid to the buyer under a warranty or indemnity claim will be treated as a downward adjustment to the consideration.

b. Rescission

5838 Rescission is the action of **undoing an agreement**. In order to **claim** rescission, the buyer:
– must have relied upon a false statement of fact (i.e. a misrepresentation); and
– must not have affirmed the contract after discovering the breach, for example, by selling some of the assets or declaring a dividend.

5839 The remedy is **only available if** the parties can be put back in the position they were in before they entered into the contract. This may be possible after exchange, if there is a gap between exchange and completion (¶5865), but it is likely to be impossible after completion. The remedy is available under statute (s 2(2) Misrepresentation Act 1967), but it is usually included as an express term of the sale and purchase agreement. This is because there is an argument that, on the wording of the statute, the remedy applies only to representations made before the parties enter into the contract.

5840 Since it is such a severe remedy, the right of rescission is usually **resisted by the seller** by including a clause in the sale and purchase agreement which expressly states that the contract cannot be rescinded. Like other exclusions of liability for misrepresentation, this clause is subject to a test of reasonableness and cannot apply if the rescission is because of a fraudulent misrepresentation (s 3 Misrepresentation Act 1967).

4. Effect of seller's knowledge

5845 A seller may wish to qualify the **warranties** so that they are made either:
– to the best of his knowledge and belief; and/or
– so far as he is aware.

Such qualifications are rarely found in **indemnities** because the seller's knowledge of events does not usually affect a buyer's ability to make an indemnity claim.

The effect of qualifications about the seller's knowledge is to make the success of a warranty claim less certain in that a buyer must prove that the seller had actual knowledge or belief of the circumstances that gave rise to the breach. Because of the duty to disclose imposed on the seller by the disclosure letter, a qualification as to a seller's knowledge, belief or awareness will imply that the **seller has investigated** to the extent that a buyer could reasonably expect him to have done so. A buyer may extend this principle by the inclusion of a clause requiring that the seller makes full enquiry into the subject of the warranty, irrespective of whether or not the seller thought that it was relevant to the buyer. This clause should be drafted carefully so that it applies to all the warranties (*Smolenski v Wheeler* [2006] EWHC 2145 (Ch)).

> **MEMO POINTS** **If a seller is a company**, its deemed knowledge will be that of named individuals such as the directors and senior managers.

5. Effect of buyer's knowledge

As discussed earlier, it is usual for a buyer to investigate the target's affairs before a purchase and so it may well already know about matters that could give rise to a **warranty claim**. However, normal practice is for the buyer to include a clause in the sale and purchase agreement stating that any information gained and not included in the disclosure letter will have no effect on any warranty claim that he may make. This is normally resisted by the seller because it is not "fair" for him to be liable when the buyer was aware of the circumstances and proceeded with the purchase.

5847

This attitude has found sympathy in the case in the example below, which cast doubt on the buyer's ability to exclude his knowledge in this way. The court reasoned that if, before entering into a contract, a buyer has knowledge of information which could result in a warranty claim, that knowledge would make it difficult for the buyer to **demonstrate that he has suffered a loss** as a result of it. This is because the basis of a warranty claim is that the buyer be compensated for the diminution in the purchase price of the company that a breach causes. If he knew of the loss and therefore the effect on the value of the transaction but opted to proceed with the purchase anyway, it is difficult for him to argue that he would have paid less for the company.

5848

> **EXAMPLE** E purchased 100% of the shares in ABC Ltd from Mr and Mrs T who warranted that there were no material circumstances in relation to ABC Ltd which had not been disclosed in the disclosure letter and which if disclosed may have been expected to affect the decision of E to buy all or some of the shares. After completion, E made a warranty claim against Mr and Mrs T as the shares were less valuable than their purchase price as a result of a matter that was not contained within the disclosure letter. Mr and Mrs T successfully argued that E had actual knowledge of the matter that had been omitted and that therefore had based the purchase price taking this into account. As a result, the amount that E would have paid for the shares had not diminished. (*Eurocopy plc v Teesdale* [1992] BCLC 1067).
> The case was decided without a full hearing and so it is possible that another court could come to a different decision, for example, in a case where the parties have a more equal bargaining position.

The buyer will still usually insist on a clause excluding its knowledge, despite the doubt caused by the above case, because the seller is then encouraged to make **full disclosure** in the disclosure letter. Furthermore, it is in the interests of both parties to ensure that there is a clear written set of information limiting the effect of the liabilities so that each party is clearly able to assess the extent of any potential claim.

5849

> **MEMO POINTS** An **exception** to the buyer's knowledge being excluded from affecting the warranties could arise if the seller made information available in a **data room** (see ¶5229+). In that case, the seller will often seek to disclose all matters revealed in the data room documents (in other words, treat the buyer has having knowledge of all matters revealed in them), regardless of whether the buyer actually inspected the document or not.

The buyer's knowledge is not relevant to an **indemnity claim** as the basis of such a claim does not relate to the diminution in value of the shares or assets, but to any actual losses, expenses, costs etc suffered by the buyer.

5850

6. Joint and several liability

The apportionment of liability for a warranty or indemnity claim is an issue where there is **more than one seller**.

5852

Where two or more sellers assume a liability "**severally**", the buyer must make a claim in respect of that liability against each of them separately for the proportionate amount of the claim for which they are liable.

Where two or more sellers assume a liability "**jointly**", the buyer must make a claim in respect of that liability against all of them for the whole amount of the claim.

In order to get the best of both worlds, a buyer is likely to insist that the warranties and indemnities are given by the sellers "**jointly and severally**". This means that a buyer can recover all of the money owed to him from any one or all of the sellers. The **effect** of joint and several liability is to pass the risk of one seller going insolvent, or otherwise being unable to pay a warranty claim, on to the other sellers. It is normally accepted by the sellers because it is fairer for them, the "culpable" sellers, to take the risk than an "innocent" buyer.

> EXAMPLE X, Y and Z own 100% of the shares in ABC Ltd. X owns 50%, Y owns 30% and Z owns 20%. They agree to sell their shares to K. X is a multimillionaire, Y has some personal wealth but Z is in financial difficulties and needs the money received from the sale to pay off his debts. 3 months after completion, K discovers a breach of warranty claim against X, Y and Z for £100,000.
>
> 1. Warranties given severally
> Suppose K had accepted that X, Y and Z were severally liable for warranty claims in proportion to their shareholdings. K therefore separately sues X for £50,000, Y for £30,000 and Z for £20,000. Although K is successful against all of them, he only recovers £50,000 from X and £30,000 from Y. Z is unable to pay and is forced to declare himself bankrupt.
>
> 2. Warranties given jointly
> Suppose K had accepted that X, Y and Z were jointly liable for warranty claims. K successfully sues X, Y and Z together for £100,000. Z is unable to pay so his share of the claim must be met by X and Y. K therefore recovers £60,000 from X and £40,000 from Y.
>
> 3. Warranties given jointly and severally, X remains in the UK
> Suppose K had accepted that X, Y and Z were jointly and severally liable for warranty claims. K decides that it will be easiest to recover the money from X as he is the most solvent. He successfully brings a claim against X, who must pay Y and Z's share of the liabilities. K is therefore able to recover the whole £100,000 from X.
>
> 4. Warranties given jointly and severally, X leaves the UK
> Suppose K had accepted that X, Y and Z were jointly and severally liable for warranty claims but immediately after completion X moves abroad. K decides that it is not worth suing X (as he is out of the jurisdiction) or Z (as he is unlikely to be able to pay). He successfully brings a claim against Y, who must pay X and Z's share of the liabilities. K is therefore able to recover the whole £100,000 from Y.

5853 If the buyer does not claim from all the sellers, the sellers that have been forced to pay more than their fair share can claim a **contribution** from the non-paying sellers under special statutory provisions (s 1 Civil Liability (Contributions) Act 1978). However, the statutory provisions are complex and there is a risk that the contribution would not be calculated in the way that the sellers would like. Consequently, it is common for the sellers to enter into a "**deed of contribution**". This is a contract between the sellers only, which sets out the proportions in which they should bear liability for claims under the sale and purchase agreement (see ¶5975+).

Of course, the right to claim a contribution is only of use if the non-paying sellers are solvent and have not left the jurisdiction. Some shareholders may be willing to accept this risk, perhaps because they are all part of one family. Some multiple sellers, for example those who are unconnected to each other, may wish to protect themselves from the insolvency of other sellers by setting up a **private retention fund**, for example, by depositing a proportion of their sale proceeds with one seller to be held under trust for all of them.

7. Security for claims

5858 As with any other type of contractual obligation, if there is an actionable breach of warranty and/or indemnity, the buyer will need to make a claim. It may be **difficult for the buyer to recover** the damages because the sellers may:
– have left the country;
– have no money or assets;
– have been declared bankrupt/gone into liquidation; or
– seek to delay payment by contesting the claim.

> **MEMO POINTS** It is sometimes difficult for the buyer to assess the risk of these matters occurring as there may be a substantial **delay** between completion of the sale and the time at which the warranty claim arises, during which period the circumstances of the seller could have altered dramatically. For example, a seller of shares who is going to remain an employee of the target following completion may appear to be a low risk at the time of completion; he will be solvent, having just received the consideration for the sale and as an employee, he will be in the country and the recipient of ongoing funds. However, a year later, the same seller could have left his employment and moved himself and his money off-shore.

5859 In order to ensure that it is able to rely on the warranties and indemnities as comfort for the risks taken by him in acquiring the company, a buyer may require that the seller provide him with security for payment. This may take the form of:
– a **retention**, where money is retained either an escrow account or held by the buyer's solicitors subject to the terms of an undertaking, usually requiring the consent of both parties before monies can be released (see ¶5489+); or
– **additional warrantors**, which will give the buyer an extra person to sue in the event of a warranty claim (see ¶5822+).

> **MEMO POINTS** Although the best form of security would be a **charge or mortgage** over the seller's assets, these are rarely given to the buyer of a business or shares as protection for warranty claims. This could possibly be because the risk is rather remote as: firstly, a warranty claim has to arise; secondly, the buyer has to show that the seller is liable; and thirdly, the seller has to fail to pay.

8. Date of application

Warranties

5864 It is usual for warranties to become effective and be deemed to have been made at completion. This means that the seller promises that each statement is **true as at completion**. For example, if the warranty is "no employee of the company has resigned", the warranty would still be true, even if an employee resigned the day after completion.

Gap between exchange and completion

5865 The situation is more complex when there is a gap between exchange and completion because the agreement is conditional (¶5732+). In order to protect itself from a **change of circumstances** between exchange and completion (when the seller will have control of the company), the buyer will usually insist on the **warranties** being made at exchange and then **repeated** at completion. This means that the seller must promise that the warranties are true and accurate on exchange (i.e. the date on which the agreement is signed), as well as on completion (i.e. the date on which title to the shares or assets transfers to the buyer). If circumstances have changed, the seller could be liable for breach of warranty. In order to avoid this liability, the seller may need to prepare a **second disclosure letter** to update his disclosures. This will obviously result in extra costs for both parties.

> **MEMO POINTS** As an alternative to the warranties being repeated on completion, the buyer may prefer to put **restrictions on the target's activities** between exchange and completion (e.g. preventing the seller from taking any steps outside the ordinary course of business, increasing borrowing, entering into any major contracts etc.). This does not give the buyer as much protection as repeating the warranties, but may be sensible where the buyer is going to be involved in the target's business before completion. In those circumstances, the buyer will have a degree of control over the target (which will lower the risk of an unforeseen increase in the target's liabilities before completion). Indeed, the seller may not agree to repeat the warranties as this would result in him taking the risk for decisions which have been taken in collaboration with the buyer.

Indemnities

5866 The date of application is not relevant to indemnities. The indemnity becomes enforceable at completion, along with the other terms of the contract. However, unlike warranties, which look to the past, it relates to **future** losses that the buyer may incur in relation to a specified event. The seller's obligation to indemnify the buyer is therefore ongoing and will continue for the life of the contract, or for whatever shorter period the parties may have agreed and specified in the indemnity or sale and purchase agreement (e.g. in the seller limitation clauses, see ¶5918+).

9. Defined terms

5871 As warranties and indemnities are contentious, it is particularly important that the terms used in them are **concise and certain**. As a result, there will be a number of defined terms which are only used in the warranties and indemnities. For example, the warranties will usually refer to the target's "intellectual property" and this term will need to be given a precise definition. The **buyer** will wish to ensure that the definitions contained in the warranties and indemnities are as wide as possible so as to ensure that all potential liabilities are covered whilst still maintaining certainty. A **seller** will however seek to limit the extent of the defined terms and thus his potential liability.

5872 The other important definitions are the terms "Warranties" and "Indemnities" themselves, although sometimes the term "Warranties" is defined to include the indemnities.

> EXAMPLE Warranties means the obligations, warranties, representations and undertakings of the Warrantors contained in this agreement, including without limitation the warranties in Schedule X.

This means that both the warranties and any other obligations will be subject to the limitations in the seller limitation clauses. This may result in a cap on the claim value and/or a lower limitation period being imposed. A **seller** would benefit from the definition being drawn this widely whereas a **buyer** would prefer to restrict the definition to just the warranties.

B. Protection for seller

5890 Frequently, the contractual protection for the buyer offered by warranties and indemnities is too extensive to be commercially acceptable to the seller. As a result, the seller will seek to limit his risk through:
– the **disclosure letter** (¶5892+), in which the seller informs the buyer of all the circumstances in which the warranties are untrue, so that no breach of warranty claim can be made by the buyer on those grounds; and
– various clauses in the sale and purchase agreement to limit the amount of and circumstances in which a warranty or indemnity claim may be made. These clauses are together referred to by practitioners as the "**seller limitation provisions**" (¶5918+).

In certain situations, the seller may require the **buyer to provide warranties** (see ¶5929).

> MEMO POINTS The seller may also **amend the warranties and indemnities**, for example, deleting any that are irrelevant to the target. In practice, only minor amendments are generally made to relevant warranties and indemnities (e.g. to make sure that they are not too vague). Normally, the seller relies on the disclosure letter and seller limitation provisions instead.

1. Disclosure letter

5892 The disclosure letter is a document produced by the seller in which he sets out all the **exceptions to the warranties**; that is all the ways in which the warranties are untrue. The document is usually presented in a letter **format**, addressed to the buyer from the seller. The disclosure letter must be **incorporated into the sale and purchase agreement** by specifically stating that the warranties are made subject to the matters disclosed in the disclosure letter.

| MEMO POINTS | The buyer will usually insist that the warranties are subject to matters "**fully and fairly**" **disclosed** in the disclosure letter. This is intended to prevent the seller from incidentally referring to a matter, or obscuring the effect of a disclosure, and asserting that sufficient disclosure has been made. In practical terms, this means that the seller is required to spell out every disclosure. It cannot rely on vague statements or reference to a document, if the matter being disclosed is not apparent from the face of the document.

The disclosure letter has a dual **purpose**. 5893

Firstly, the sale and purchase agreement should state that the seller warrants that the warranties are true, except as disclosed in the disclosure letter. As a result, the buyer is not able to make a breach of warranty claim in respect of disclosed information. The disclosure letter therefore limits the seller's liability under the warranties.

Secondly, such disclosure enables the buyer to better assess the risks to which it is exposed and renegotiate the purchase price if necessary.

The letter will usually be divided into three sections:
- **general disclosures**;
- **specific disclosures**; and
- **the disclosure bundle**, which is an indexed bundle of documents that has been referred to in either the general or the specific disclosures.

a. General disclosures

General disclosures relate to general matters which apply to all the warranties. Whilst they tend to be standard, they may have differing significance according to the transaction. Usually, they relate to: 5895
- documentation that is connected with the transaction;
- various commercial searches;
- the statutory records of the company;
- property searches;
- business reports/plans;
- accounts;
- public records; and
- the actual knowledge of the buyer.

General disclosures are usually very wide and consequently would affect the validity of most of the warranties if accepted without amendment by the buyer. A **buyer** will wish to understand the exact extent of the disclosures on the warranties. If it accepts general disclosures without amendment, many of the warranties will be unenforceable. Conversely, a **seller** will wish to make them as wide and unspecific as possible in order to limit his liability.

Transaction documentation

The **seller** will usually seek to disclose the various agreements between the parties, together with the due diligence bundle and all relevant correspondence between the parties/their advisers. This is normally acceptable to the buyer, provided the disclosed documents are specifically listed and included in the disclosure bundle. The seller must take care that the due diligence information is still up to date. 5896

Commercial searches

The commercial searches may include anything that would be revealed by a search of: 5897
- Companies House;
- the Central Registry for Winding Up Petitions in England and Wales;
- the Office of Fair Trading;
- the Consumer Credit Registry;
- any intellectual property registry in England; and
- any other public registry.

A seller will wish to make **general reference** to the searches because this makes the disclosure wider. Conversely, for certainty, a buyer will insist that all such searches are **specifically listed** and apply as at a specified **date**. In any event, a buyer will need to ensure that it has obtained and considered each of the searches that are disclosed. As wide disclosure creates uncertainty, it is arguably in the interests of both parties for the searches to be listed and date-specific.

Statutory records

5898 It is usual for all minutes and the statutory books of the target company and its group of companies (in a share sale) or the seller (in an asset sale) to be disclosed. This general disclosure will have the effect of substantially reducing the warranties in relation to ownership and records. The added benefit from the **seller's** point of view is that it avoids the need to disclose minor errors in the statutory records, of which there are likely to be many. It is therefore important that the **buyer** has reviewed the books carefully, as they will be evidence of the ownership and the manner in which the target has been conducted. A buyer may wish to limit disclosure to certain aspects of the books and/or the target company's recent history.

Property searches

5899 General property disclosures are usually made of anything that would be revealed by:
a. an inspection of:
- the deeds of any relevant properties;
- planning consents;
- building or by-law approvals;
- the formal enquiries between the parties; and
- the properties themselves; and

b. searches of:
- any relevant local authority;
- the Land Charges Department of HM Land Registry;
- HM Land Registry;
- the Commons Register;
- the Environmental Agency; and
- commercial site databases, such as Landmark.

Clearly, this general disclosure is only relevant to the extent that the sale includes land and buildings and as such will substantially reduce the effectiveness of the property warranties. As with the commercial searches, a **seller** will be keen to disclose the potential contents of all searches, as this will remove the need to disclose individually against the warranties. A **buyer**, on the other hand, will usually seek to limit the disclosure to specific searches carried out on a specified date (see ¶5696+). However, the buyer's negotiating position is slightly weaker because the items referred to in the general disclosure are usually all that it would have to rely on if it had purchased the property alone (warranties are not generally given in property transactions).

Business reports/plans

5900 Any business plan prepared in relation to the target company or its group of companies is normally disclosed to the buyer. Such a plan will usually relate to the future running of the business based on the seller's ideas but is unlikely to adequately explain all of the rationale behind the assumptions upon which it is based. Any report will deal with a wide variety of the issues affecting the business and may therefore impact on a wide range of warranties.

A **seller** will prefer to disclose the whole report, but the **buyer** is unlikely to accept it, as in so doing he would accept disclosure based on assumptions of which he may not be fully aware. The usual **compromise** is for the seller to opt to disclose certain aspects of it against specific warranties.

Accounts

The target company's accounts will usually have been shown to the buyer during the due diligence exercise. Normally, they will have been used to establish the value and viability of the target. A **seller** will usually argue that the accounts should be disclosed, as the buyer has had adequate time to examine them during the due diligence process and to assess them in relation to the operation and the value of the target. From a **buyer's** point of view, it will be important that it is able to rely on the accounts, hence the large number of warranties relating to them as they form the basis of its assessment of the viability of its acquisition. As a result, it will be wary of accepting wide disclosure of the accounts as this would will have the effect of invalidating most of the accounts and some tax warranties. The usual **compromise** is for the last 3 years' accounts (auditor's and directors' statement, profit and loss account, balance sheet and notes) to be generally disclosed. The buyer may also accept a general disclosure of the latest management accounts if it has had an opportunity to inspect them.

5901

Public domain

The **seller** will usually try to disclose generally any matter that is in the public domain, i.e. any matter that is not private to the target. This general disclosure acts as a "sweeper" for the seller in case he fails to specifically disclose something which was common knowledge. For example, if the target were in the telecommunications industry and the government had announced its intention to re-nationalise the telecommunications network. However, a **buyer** will usually object to such a disclosure, as not only is it very wide, but it is impossible to establish and prove what it encompasses.

5902

Buyer's knowledge

During the negotiation process, the buyer will have gained considerable information in relation to the target company. Some will have been provided in writing, however, other information will have been provided verbally. The **seller** will wish to ensure that all information provided to the buyer is considered as disclosed. A buyer is unlikely to accept this, as it cannot be expected to remember all information provided. However, it will usually accept that information provided in specific documents, and included in the disclosure bundle, are within its knowledge. A buyer should be aware that, despite this limitation on the disclosure, it may not be able to bring a warranty claim in respect of a matter that was within its actual knowledge (see ¶5847+).

5903

---

b. Specific disclosures

In addition to the general disclosures, the seller will also need to disclose specific matters that **relate to specific warranties**. The specific disclosures can be quite lengthy, depending upon the complexity of the business being sold.

5907

> EXAMPLE A is selling J Ltd to B. Two months before completion, J Ltd dismissed an employee, Jane Smith, for gross misconduct. The sale and purchase agreement contains the following warranty:
>
> Warranty X   No employee of J Ltd has had their employment terminated in the 4 months before completion.
>
> The disclosure letter will therefore need to contain the following specific disclosure:
>
> Disclosure X   Jane Smith was dismissed for gross misconduct on [date].

The seller will usually **preface the specific disclosures** with a statement that any specific disclosure, although made against a specific warranty, should be treated as being disclosed against all the warranties. This is usually acceptable to the buyer provided that the disclosures themselves are detailed enough for him to understand which warranties are affected by them.

5908

A seller will also sometimes try to preface the specific disclosures with a statement that the whole of any document referred to in the specific disclosures is also deemed to be disclosed, regardless of whether or not it has been included in the disclosure bundle. This is never acceptable to a buyer as it cannot assess the impact that a disclosed document will have on the warranties without actually seeing it.

5909 In a **share sale**, if the **target has subsidiaries**, disclosures will need to be made in respect of each of them. If there are numerous subsidiaries and therefore several specific disclosures per warranty, it may be clearer to divide the disclosure letter so that the disclosures relating to each company are separated.

c. Disclosure bundle

5913 The term "disclosure bundle" **refers to** the documents which the seller has disclosed against the warranties. An index to the disclosure bundle will usually be attached as a schedule to the disclosure letter. The bundle is usually incorporated into the disclosure letter by means of a statement that the documents in the bundle are deemed to be disclosed against the warranties in their entirety.

The disclosure bundle will **contain** many of the documents provided during the due diligence process and is likely to be lengthy. A seller will prefer to have as comprehensive a disclosure bundle as possible by including all the documents provided to the buyer in due diligence. A buyer will prefer to restrict the documents to those to which the disclosures refer, as this will demonstrate the relevance of each document to the warranties.

EXAMPLE

Warranty Y	J Ltd does not use any intellectual property in respect of which any third party has any right, title or interest.
Disclosure Y	J Ltd's computer system uses software under licence from Microsoft. A copy of the licence is at document Z of the disclosure bundle.

---

2. Seller limitation provisions

5918 In addition to disclosure, a seller will seek to introduce a number of clauses **in the sale and purchase agreement** to further limit his liability. These clauses are collectively referred to as the "seller limitation provisions", or sometimes the "vendor protection provisions". They usually relate to the value of, and circumstances in which, claims may be made. As they will reflect the bargaining positions of the parties and relevant facts surrounding the purchase, they will be specific to each individual transaction.

Usually the seller limitation provisions will only limit the seller's liability for warranty claims. However, if the seller has a strong bargaining position, he may be able to extend the scope of the provisions so that they also limit his liability for claims under the indemnities.

The usual **provisions**:
– limit the time within which a claim may be made;
– limit claims to those that are made whilst the buyers remain in ownership;
– limit the aggregate maximum claim value;
– limit the minimum claim value;
– prevent "double recovery"; and
– where there are multiple sellers, limit each seller's liability to a several basis (see ¶5852+).

Claim period

5920 The claim period is the length of time within which the buyer can bring a claim against the seller for breach of warranty or under the indemnities. The **statutory claim period** depends upon how the document containing the warranties and/or indemnities has been signed (see ¶5741+). If the document is signed as a **contract**, the period will be 6 years from breach, but if it is executed as a **deed**, the claim period is extended to 12 years from the date of breach (ss 5, 8 Limitation Act 1980). Any document which specifies a claim period beyond 6 years should be executed as a deed, as it is unclear whether it is possible to contractually extend the claim period beyond that which is contained in statute. It is however possible to shorten the claim period by agreement between the parties.

Generally, the **seller** will wish to limit the claim period, as the longer it is, the greater the chance of a breach occurring and a consequential claim arising. Conversely, the **buyer** will wish to extend the claim period for as long as possible.

5921

Commercially, the eventual result will depend on the bargaining position of the parties but, on average, the buyer will **normally agree to** limit the claim period to:
– about 3 years after completion in respect of claims under the **non-tax warranties**, so that the buyer is able to prepare 2 years worth of accounts, as most claims will have arisen by then; and
– about 7 years after completion in respect of claims under the **tax warranties and tax deed**, as Revenue and Customs may make an assessment up to 6 years after the end of financial year (extended to 20 years if fraudulent or negligent conduct is involved).

The seller is likely to want the claim period for non-tax matters to also apply to the **non-tax indemnities**. However, a buyer is unlikely to agree to this as those indemnities are intended to protect him from a specific risk identified during the due diligence/disclosure process. The buyer will normally press for the non-tax indemnities to be excluded from the limit altogether or for a longer claim period to apply instead.

> EXAMPLE X purchases A Ltd from Y on 31 May 2007. A Ltd's financial year ends on 31 March. X and Y agree that the claim period in respect of:
> – tax warranties and tax deed will expire at 5pm on 31 March 2014 (6 years from 31 March 2008 which is the end of the financial year in which completion occurred); and
> – non-tax warranties will expire at 5pm on 30 September 2010 (2 years from 31 March 2008 plus 6 months to finalise the accounts for the financial year ending on 31 March 2010).

MEMO POINTS It is also necessary to decide what should happen within the claim period. It is unusual for the buyer to be required to issue court proceedings. Normally, it is only required to serve **written notice of the claim** on the seller. The notice does not have to particularise the buyer's claim unless the sale and purchase agreement requires this (*Forrest v Glasser* [2006] EWCA Civ 1086). There is also usually a clause which requires the buyer to issue court proceedings within 12 months of notifying the seller of a claim. This allows enough time for the parties to negotiate a settlement but ensures that if one cannot be reached, the buyer must either drop its claim or pursue it through the courts.

Maximum claim value

It is usual for a maximum to be set on the **aggregate value of claims** for which the seller may be liable. This is normally the price the buyer is going to pay (so the buyer cannot recover more than what he paid for the company in the first place). However, this is not always an acceptable compromise, for example:
– if there are multiple sellers and they are not all warrantors, the warrantors may wish to set the maximum claim value at the amount of consideration which they will receive rather than the amount which all of the sellers together will receive; or
– if the target is insolvent and being sold for nominal consideration, the buyer will wish to set the maximum claim value at a much higher figure.

5922

The **seller** will normally seek to apply this limit to all claims under the sale and purchase agreement, whether for breach of warranty or under an indemnity. He will also normally want the limit to apply to the value of the claim together with all costs and expenses incurred by the buyer in bringing it. The **buyer** will normally seek to restrict the limit to warranty claims only (so that other claims do not have a maximum claim value) and will want the limit to apply only to the value of the claim so that it can claim its costs and expenses on top.

Minimum claim value

As costs associated with claims are expensive, it is usual for a clause limiting the minimum claim value to be included to prevent the buyer from making frivolous or minor claims. This clause is known as the "**de minimis**" provision and can take the following **forms**:

5923

– setting a level below which claims are disregarded; and/or
– preventing claims from being brought until they exceed an aggregate amount, after which time all the claims pending can be brought.

The seller of course will wish to set the thresholds as high as possible and the buyer will wish to set them as low as possible. The reasonable compromise generally depends upon the amount of consideration being paid. Something around 0.5% of the purchase price for the level below which claims are disregarded and 3% for the aggregate amount which must be reached before a claim can be brought are generally considered to be acceptable.

Double recovery

5924 Sometimes a buyer can also recover losses arising from breach of warranty and/or indemnity **from a third party** (for example, by suing a supplier for breach of contract or under an insurance policy). A buyer will wish to retain its right to claim against the seller or the third party, if applicable, as this will provide it with greater choice and more chance of recovering all its losses. But a seller will wish to force the buyer to pursue the third party and only be liable if the buyer is unable to recover its losses. A compromise may be to enable the buyer to recover from the seller, but to give the seller the **right to recover** from third parties on the target company's behalf. In these circumstances, the buyer will wish to have a level of control over proceedings to ensure that the seller protects the target company. Alternatively, the seller may have the right to force the buyer to **litigate** at the seller's cost and pay over any monies recovered to the seller.

3. Buyer's warranties

5929 The buyer may give the seller warranties as to:
a. its **capacity** to enter into the agreement. This is common practice in the USA. Although it appears reasonable that the buyer should warrant to the seller that it is able to enter into the agreement, such warranties are rare in the UK; or
b. its **business**, for example, where some of the consideration is being paid in the form of shares in the buyer.

IV. Other documents

A. Share sales

1. Tax deed

5945 The tax deed is a document which deals exclusively with the apportionment of the target company's tax liabilities. The **essence** of the document is that the seller agrees to indemnify the buyer against any tax liabilities of the target referable to the period before completion. The result is that these will be payable by the seller, rather than the target or the buyer.

Some particular issues to consider when negotiating the tax deed are:
– the **form** of the indemnity;
– whether the indemnity should extend to liabilities attributable to a "**combination of events**";
– whether the indemnity should extend to the target losing any **available tax reliefs**;
– who should have **conduct of claims** against and negotiations with Revenue and Customs; and
– a **limitation** of the seller's liability.

> MEMO POINTS Where the target is part of a **group**, it will be important to consider any group arrangements, e.g. group relief surrenders and VAT groups. See *Tax Memo* for further details.

Form of indemnity

Historically, the requirement for a **separate document** arose because: **5947**
– the buyer wished to be indemnified against pre-transfer tax liabilities, rather than rely on the tax warranties in the sale and purchase agreement, as it is easier to recover damages under an indemnity (see ¶5826+);
– the tax liabilities had to be borne by the target, not the buyer, so it was more straightforward if payments under the indemnity were made directly to the target. As a result, the parties to the indemnity were the sellers and the target; and
– the target could not give any consideration for the indemnity as this would amount to unlawful financial assistance (¶5569+). A separate document executed as a deed was thought to avoid the suggestion that consideration had passed from the target to the seller (documents executed as a deed are enforceable without consideration, see ¶5741+).

However, changes to the way indemnity payments are taxed (see ¶5834+) mean that the indemnity must now be in favour of the buyer (although still in respect of the tax liabilities of the target) and **payment** must be **to the buyer** rather than the target. **5948**

> MEMO POINTS Revenue and Customs guidance confirms that the buyer may direct that the **payment** be made **to the target** itself, and the payment will still be treated as having been made to the buyer (Revenue and Customs Manual CG13045).

The parties to the indemnity are therefore now the seller and the buyer, that is, the same as the parties to the sale and purchase agreement. As a result, a separate tax deed is no longer necessary and it is becoming increasingly common for the terms to be **incorporated into the sale and purchase agreement**, usually in a schedule. Where the indemnity is incorporated into the sale and purchase agreement, it is referred to as the "**tax covenant**". Nevertheless, a separate tax deed is also quite typical. **5949**

> MEMO POINTS As well as payments being made to the buyer, Revenue and Customs require the indemnity to be "included as one of the terms of a contract of purchase and sale" (ESC D33). Some practitioners interpreted this as meaning that the indemnity had to be included in the sale and purchase agreement itself. However, Revenue and Customs guidance confirms that it does not distinguish between payments made under an indemnity contained in the sale and purchase agreement as opposed to an indemnity contained in a separate document as part of the overall terms of an agreement for sale (Revenue and Customs Manual CG13042). As a result, a **separate tax deed** between the sellers and buyer is just as effective for tax purposes as a tax covenant incorporated into the sale and purchase agreement, provided (as it should do) that the sale and purchase agreement specifies that execution of the tax deed is a condition of completion.

Combination of events

The buyer will naturally want to draw the indemnity as widely as possible. One common device is to extend the scope of the indemnity to include liabilities that arise after completion, but as a result of a combination of events, some occurring **before completion** (when the target was in the control of the seller) and some occurring **after completion** (when the target was in the control of the buyer). **5950**

> MEMO POINTS The extension of the indemnity to include a combination of pre- and post-completion events is sometimes **explicit** but sometimes the indemnity is **implicitly** extended by drafting which simply refers to liabilities incurred wholly "or partly" as a result of pre-completion acts or omissions.

The seller should **object** to the indemnity being extended in this way. Clearly, it is not fair for the seller to have to indemnify the buyer in respect of post-completion matters which are within the buyer's control. On the other hand, it is not fair for the target to incur an unexpected tax liability after completion which was triggered by a pre-completion event which was within the seller's control. **5951**

5952 The normal **compromise** is that the seller will indemnify the buyer for a combination of pre- and post-completion events when:
– the pre-completion event was outside the target's ordinary course of business; and
– the post-completion event was within the target's ordinary course of business.

Availability of tax reliefs

5953 Again, in an effort to extend the scope of the indemnity, the buyer will often draft the indemnity so it covers the withdrawal or loss of any grant, allowance or relief from taxation which would otherwise have been available. This appears straightforward where a **relief** has been **taken into account** when preparing the target's accounts; if that relief subsequently becomes unavailable, then the target will have further tax to pay which was not expected and the seller will have to pay that extra liability under the indemnity.

However, the seller may question why he should have to underwrite the availability of **further reliefs** (for example, if the target has surplus losses), particularly if the availability of a particular relief has not been taken into account when deciding on the overall consideration.

5954 The buyer is normally only **indemnified** against a loss of a tax relief in three **circumstances**:
– where the target's accounts show the repayment of taxation as an asset and that repayment is lost;
– where the availability of a tax relief has been taken into account when preparing the target's accounts and the loss of that relief would adversely affect another provision in the accounts; and
– where a relief referable to the period after completion is used to set off tax payable on profits arising before completion and, if the relief had not been applied, the seller would have been liable under the indemnity in any event.

Conduct of claims

5955 Consideration should be given as to who should have conduct of a claim where there is a **dispute with Revenue and Customs**. Where a tax assessment is likely to result in liability for the seller under the tax deed/covenant, the seller will often wish to have the final say in dealings with Revenue and Customs. However, the buyer is likely to resist this because it will not want the target to enter into protracted negotiations with Revenue and Customs as this could potentially damage the relationship between the buyer's group and the tax authorities.

5956 It is difficult to draft appropriate provisions which give the seller control of claims but equally allow the buyer to protect its relationship with Revenue and Customs. In the end, the party with the greater **negotiating power** will usually succeed in retaining conduct of claims, with the other party being able to give it reasonable instructions.

Limitation of liability

5957 The liability of the seller under the tax deed/covenant is usually subject to the **same limitations as the tax warranties** such as the maximum and minimum claim limits, the claim period etc (see ¶5918+). However, the terms of the **disclosure letter** (¶5892+) will not usually apply, so the seller will still be liable even if a tax liability is brought to the buyer's attention.

> MEMO POINTS If the indemnity is in a **separate tax deed**, there is usually no need to repeat the clauses. The tax deed will normally just incorporate the necessary clauses from the sale and purchase agreement by reference to that document.

2. Employment documents

5963 The buyer is likely to envisage a **change of personnel** at the target following completion of the share sale. This must be carried out carefully with due regard to the employees' employment rights (see *Employment Memo*).

Changes are most likely to be made at board level and in many share sales where the **directors** are also shareholders, they are usually quite happy to comply with the buyer's requirements. At the very least, the buyer will normally require that the directors **resign** from their position on the board at completion so that it can appoint its own directors instead (see ¶6005+).

If the directors work for the target, they will also be employees with all the usual employment rights, including the right not to be unfairly dismissed. Therefore, if their employment is also going to be brought to an end at completion, they may be requested to sign a **compromise agreement** (see below). A cautious buyer may request that the directors sign compromise agreements even if they are just resigning from their position on the board, but continuing to work for the target, so as to avoid a claim for constructive dismissal.

If the directors are continuing in their positions or continuing as employees, they will normally have to enter into **new service agreements** so that their terms and conditions of employment are harmonised with those of the buyer and the new directors of the target. See ¶2627+ for more on directors' service agreements and ¶9925 for a sample agreement.

5964

Compromise agreement

A compromise agreement is a **special contract** between an employee and its employer under which the employee agrees to waive a number of his employment rights.

5965

Employment rights can be contractual (that is, particular to that employee's contract of employment) or arise under common law, but most are statutory (such as the right not to be unfairly dismissed). An agreement in which the employee waives his **contractual rights** does not have to take any particular form. However, with the exception of employment tribunal claims which are settled via ACAS, any agreement under which an employee waives his **statutory rights** must comply with a number of statutory conditions in order for it to be valid.

> MEMO POINTS   If, as would usually be the case, the compromise agreement was intended to prevent an employee from bringing **both contractual and statutory** employment claims, the agreement must comply with the statutory conditions.

The **conditions** for a valid compromise agreement relate to:
– the form of the agreement;
– the particularisation of the claim being compromised;
– reference to statutory conditions; and
– the employee having received legal advice.

5966

Form

The agreement must be in **writing**.

5967

Particularisation of claim

The agreement must relate to particular claims. A blanket agreement (for example, one which says it is "in full and final settlement of all claims which the employee has or may have against its employer") will not be effective. The **main claim** which a director/employee would have is that he was unfairly dismissed on completion (this would be the case even if he "resigned" as that resignation was forced by the buyer).

5968

> MEMO POINTS   It is not sufficient to simply list all the possible statutory claims in a compromise agreement. If the compromise agreement is of a particular claim raised which is not yet the subject of proceedings (as would normally be the case in an share sale), it is **good practice** for the particulars of the nature of the allegations, and of the statute under which they are made, or the common law basis of the alleged claim, to be inserted in the agreement in the form of a brief factual and legal description. It is **not good practice** to use a standard form of agreement which simply contains a list of examples of statutory claims, further to a general clause that the agreement is in full and final settlement of all claims. The agreement should be tailored to the individual circumstances otherwise it will not be effective. For example, where an employee is a fulltime permanent employee, it will not be appropriate to include references to fixed-term or parttime employees' rights (*University of East London v Hinton* [2005] ICR 1260).

Reference to statutory conditions

5969 The compromise agreement must state that the statutory conditions regulating compromise agreements have been complied with. This means that the specific statutory reference must be stated in the agreement (for example, where an unfair dismissal claim is being compromised, the agreement must state that it complies with s 203(2)(f) Employment Rights Act 1996) (*Lunt v Merseyside Tech Ltd* [1999] IRLR 458).

Legal advice

5970 The employee must obtain advice from a "**relevant independent adviser**" as to the terms and effect of the agreement and, in particular, its effect on the employee's ability to pursue his rights before a tribunal. The agreement must identify the adviser, who will normally be required to sign a declaration that he qualifies as a "relevant independent adviser". A qualified lawyer (including a solicitor holding a current practising certificate) will fulfil the requirements provided that he or his firm is not also acting for the employer.

In the case of a share sale, the **selling shareholder's solicitor** will usually be able to act as the relevant independent adviser if the shareholders are also the directors. If a director is not also a shareholder, he will need to obtain independent legal advice from another firm of solicitors.

> MEMO POINTS It is usual practice for the employer (i.e. the target) to contribute towards the **costs of the employee** having to obtain legal advice. However, in the context of a share sale, in order to avoid problems of financial assistance, it is recommended that those costs are borne by the seller rather than the target.

3. Deed of contribution

5975 A deed of contribution is necessary when there are **multiple sellers or warrantors** who have joint and several liabilities under the sale and purchase agreement (see ¶5852+) but wish to apportion liability amongst themselves in a different way. The effect is that:
– for the buyer, the sellers' liability to it is as set out in the sale and purchase agreement; and
– for the sellers, their liability to each other is as set out in the deed of contribution.

5976 The deed of contribution will normally **set out**:
– the proportion of a claim under the sale and purchase agreement for which each seller will be liable;
– that if a seller pays more than its due proportion (e.g. because the buyer has brought a claim against that seller alone), it has the right to be reimbursed by the other sellers;
– that each seller warrants to the others that he has made full disclosure of all matters known to him in the disclosure letter, and that he agrees to indemnify the other sellers against their costs if he is in breach of that warranty;
– what action should be taken in the event of a claim by the buyer against any of the sellers; and
– how liability should be distributed if one or more of the sellers is declared bankrupt (e.g. that his liability should be equally divided amongst the other sellers).

B. Asset sales

5985 In an asset sale, legal and beneficial title to each of the business' **assets must be transferred** to the buyer (see ¶1829+ for an explanation as to the difference between legal and beneficial ownership).

5986 The legal and beneficial title to **physical assets** (e.g. plant and machinery and stock) owned by the seller can be transferred **by delivery**. For those assets, therefore, there is no need for any document other than the sale and purchase agreement.

The transfer of a **freehold or leasehold land interest** requires execution of a separate document. If the land interest is registered, it can only be transferred using a **transfer form** prescribed by the Land Registry. Form TP1 is required if part of a registered title is transferred and Form TR1 is required if the whole of a registered title is being transferred. If the land interest is unregistered, the document does not have to be in a prescribed form but if the interest is registrable, it will have to be registered after the sale using Form FR1.

Deed of assignment

In the case of the business' intangible assets, legal and beneficial title will need to be formally transferred by way of an assignment. Assignment of the **business' contracts** is normally incorporated into the sale and purchase agreement (see ¶5758+). However, the usual practice is for separate deeds of assignment to be executed for:
– **goodwill**; and
– each registered **intellectual property** right (that is a patent, registered design right or registered trade mark) so that this shorter document can be presented to the UK Intellectual Property Office for registration of the transfer (see ¶6020+).

A deed of assignment is a short document. An explanation of the **usual provisions** found in the document is set out in the table below.

Section/clause	Provision
Parties	The parties to the assignment will be the seller (known as the "assignor") and the buyer (known as the "assignee")
Recitals	That the assignment is being made pursuant to the sale and purchase of the relevant business and assets
Definitions	A definition of the asset being assigned. In the case of goodwill, this is given the same definition as in the sale and purchase agreement. In the case of a registered intellectual property right, a full description of the right, including the registration number should be given.
Assignment	That the assignor agrees to assign the relevant asset to the assignee absolutely. An "absolute" assignment in writing is required by statute (s 136 LPA 1925).
Execution	The assignment should be executed as a deed (see ¶5741+)

SECTION 6

Exchange and completion

"**Exchange**" is shorthand for the signature and exchange of contracts, which is when the parties become contractually bound to the terms of the agreement. Originally, each party would sign an identical copy of the agreement and physically exchange their copy for the other party's. Each party would then hold a copy that had been signed by the other. The practice now is for all parties to sign identical copies so that each party has a copy that has been signed by all the parties. As a result, "exchange" is now sometimes referred to as "**signing**".

"**Completion**" is when the sale and purchase of the shares or assets actually occurs. In the USA this is referred to as "**closing**" and that term is becoming increasingly popular in the UK.

In a sale of shares and a sale of assets, exchange and completion usually occurs at the same time, at a **completion meeting** attended by the parties and their legal advisers. This is referred to as a **simultaneous** exchange and completion. A meeting allows for any last minute amendments to documents to be finalised before signature and for the various board and shareholder meetings to be held. Towards the end of negotiations, a face-to-face meeting between all of the parties and their advisers is usually the only way to resolve outstanding, and sometimes crucial, issues. Unfortunately, this means that the meetings have a tendency to take several hours, sometimes extending late into the night. This can be avoided by proper planning (for example, by ensuring that as many documents as possible are in their agreed form before the meeting), but given the numbers of documents involved, even just signing them can take a considerable amount of time.

In a conditional agreement (see ¶5732+), there will be a **gap** between exchange and completion. This will normally entail **two meetings**, an exchange meeting and a completion meeting. The exchange meeting will normally be the substantive meeting as this is when the parties will become contractually bound. The completion meeting will then simply involve the formalities of transfer.

6007 The **mechanics** of exchange and completion are set out in a clause in the sale and purchase agreement, including:
– where each meeting will occur;
– what documents will be handed over by the seller;
– how the buyer will pay any consideration due;
– what other documents will need to be executed by the parties; and
– what matters will need to be dealt with by way of a board meeting of the target.

1. Document list

6012 Before the exchange or completion meeting, it is often useful for the parties to prepare a document list setting out who has responsibility for the preparation of each document. Each document will have to be in a **form which is agreed** by all the parties.

A suggested document list is given below, although of course not all of the documents will be relevant for every transaction. The list below assumes that the preliminary documents (information memorandum, heads of agreement, confidentiality agreement and due diligence questionnaire) have already been prepared.

Documents for signature

6013

Document	Responsibility
Sale and purchase agreement	Buyer
Disclosure letter	Seller
Tax deed	Buyer
Deed of assignment	Buyer
Board minutes of buyer – to approve purchase	Buyer
Board minutes of buyer's corporate guarantor – to approve guarantee	Buyer
Board minutes of corporate seller – to approve sale – to approve change of name	Seller
Board minutes of target company – to approve transfer of shares – to accept resignation of old directors and secretary – to appoint new directors and secretary – to change auditors – to change accounting reference date – to change registered office	Buyer or seller
Written resolution of shareholders of target company – to approve change of name	Seller
Loan note instrument	Seller

Document	Responsibility
Letters of resignation – from exiting directors/ company secretary	Buyer or seller
Letter of resignation – from auditor including statement that there are no circumstances connected with them ceasing to hold office which they consider should be brought to the attention of the target's members or creditors (s 394 CA 1985; restated at s 519 CA 2006 as of 6 April 2008).	Seller
Compromise agreements – between target and exiting directors/employees	Buyer
Service agreements – for retained directors	Buyer
Voting powers of attorney [1] – appointing buyer as attorney of seller to exercise voting rights of shares being transferred until transfer registered by target	Buyer
Signing powers of attorney – appointing main seller as attorney of other sellers to sign documents at meeting in their absence	Seller
Stock transfer forms	Buyer or seller
Deed of indemnity – for any lost share certificates	Seller
Companies House forms [2]: – Form 288a (appointment of director/secretary) – Form 288b (removal of director/secretary) – Form 287 (change of registered office) – Form 225 (change of accounting reference date)	Buyer
Buyer's finance documents: – Facility agreement – Debenture – Companies House Form M395 [2] – Directors' statutory declaration for purposes of financial assistance "whitewash" – Auditor's report on directors' statutory declaration – Shareholder resolution to approve financial assistance	Buyer
Press release	Buyer and seller

Note:
1. **A power of attorney** from each seller to the buyer is required so that the buyer is empowered to exercise the voting rights attached to the sale shares until the share transfer is registered in the target's statutory register (following payment of stamp duty). This is because legal ownership of the shares does not transfer to the buyer until that moment (see ¶1830).
2. The name of Forms 288a, 288b, 286, 225 and M395, like the names of other **Companies House forms**, are taken from the section number of the legislation. As all of the section numbers will change under the new Companies Act, Companies House proposes to change the names of all of its forms to reflect their function rather than the relevant section number ("Working with Companies House: a consultation on the registrar's rules and related provisions which will apply under the Companies Act 2006"). At the time of writing, the new form names are not yet available.

Documents to be handed to buyer

6014

Share sale	Asset sale
Share certificates for sale shares	Third party consents
Statutory books and company seal of target	Leases/property title documents
Leases/property title documents	Bank security releases
Bank balances at close of business on the date before completion	–
Bank security releases/certificate of non-crystallisation	–
Cheque books	–
Bank mandate form	–

2. Post-completion

6020 Following completion, the buyer and seller will need to deal with:
- the practicalities of handing over the business;
- administrative matters; and
- post-completion obligations under the sale and purchase agreement.

Practical matters

6021 The buyer will need to **take possession** of the business which it has just purchased (whether by way of a share sale or an asset sale). For example, the buyer will need to be given all relevant keys to buildings, filing cabinets etc, and passwords to the IT systems. In an asset sale, that process may be more complex as the buyer may have to **move assets and documents** from the seller's premises to its own. There will certainly need to be some co-operation between the seller and buyer in this respect.

An important consideration for the buyer is to make sure that **insurances** are in place. This will certainly be required in an asset sale, but may also be required in a share sale if the target's assets were covered under the seller's group insurance policy.

Administrative matters

6022 The buyer and seller will also have to deal with any **Companies House filings** in respect of themselves. In a share sale, the buyer will be responsible for the filings in respect of the target (see ¶4069+).

6023 The buyer will need to pay **stamp taxes** within 30 days of completion. Stamp duty on share transfers is dealt with at ¶1875+. On an asset sale, stamp duty land tax will be payable if the sale includes property (see ¶5298+).

Asset sale: registration of transfers

6024 In an asset sale, the identity of the owner of the various assets transferred will change from the seller to the buyer. The buyer will need to register that it is the new owner of assets, if ownership is recorded on **public registers**.

6025 A transfer of a freehold or registered leasehold **land** interest, or the grant of a lease for a term of more than 7 years, must be registered at the Land Registry (s 4(1)(c) Land Registration Act 2002; check with the Land Registry for details).

6026 A transfer of **intellectual property** consisting of a UK patent, registered design right or registered trade mark must be registered with the UK Intellectual Property Office within 6 months of the transfer. The table below sets out the appropriate form in each case and any fee payable. All of the forms must be signed by the buyer and seller (or their representatives). Alternatively, the UK Intellectual Property Office will accept other documents as proof that the transfer has taken place, for example, the deed of assignment. The forms can be downloaded, free of charge, from the UK Intellectual Property Office website.

Intellectual property right	Form	Fee
Patent	PF21/77	none
Registered design right	DF12A	none
Registered trade mark	TM16	£50 per form

MEMO POINTS If the transfer is **not registered** with the UK Intellectual Property Office within 6 months of it taking place, the buyer will not be entitled to damages for any infringement of the intellectual property right between the date of the transfer and the date of registration.

Contractual obligations

6027 The most common post-completion obligation is for the buyer and seller to agree **completion accounts**. This could arise where:
- the consideration is calculated by reference to an earn-out (¶5465+);

– in a share sale, there is a net asset value adjustment (¶5480+); or
– in an asset sale, if a stock valuation is necessary (¶5756+).

Other post-completion obligations include the calculation of an earn-out or the issue of loan notes. It is helpful to **diarise deadlines**, some of which may be years from completion, so that they are not forgotten.

SECTION 7

Management buy-out

A management buy-out, commonly referred to as an "MBO", is a particular type of purchase whereby the individuals involved in the day to day running of a company buy it from its owners. This may occur **because**:
– the owners wish to dispose of the company and the managers wish to acquire it so that their employment is secured; or
– the managers wish to own the company in which they work and are so fundamental to the operation of the business that the owners risk losing the value of the company should the managers leave their employment.

6040

> MEMO POINTS   A **management buy-in**, or "MBI", is where a pre-assembled management team with no current connection to the target buys a company. An MBI will generally follow the same process as an arm's length transaction, although some of the arrangements between the management team and their funder may be similar to those found in an MBO (see ¶6043+).

An MBO will generally follow the **same process** as a sale to an unconnected party **except** in relation to the following:
– investigation of target and warranties;
– financing; and
– the management team.

6041

Investigation of target and warranties

The investigation of the target in an MBO is normally **not as extensive** as the investigation in a sale to an unconnected party, because the management will already have most of the information about the target's operations. The investigation is therefore normally concentrated on aspects of the target over which the management did not have control, for example, financing, accounts etc.

6042

Prior knowledge of the target's operations will also have an impact upon the warranties. The seller will normally **resist giving full warranties** because it will not want to take the risk for a breach which the management either caused or knew about. The usual compromise is for the seller to give warranties on matters which were within its control and for the management to take the risk on matters which were within its control.

The warranty position will also be of interest to the management's funders, and this is considered below.

Financing

Management buy-outs are usually **funded by** a bank and/or venture capitalist (see ¶4809+), as the management will rarely have the necessary cash. The funder will usually have to lend money for the purchase and on-going working capital for trading purposes after completion and so will have a high financial stake in the transaction. In return, the funder will usually expect the management to put some of its own assets at risk and give personal guarantees for the borrowing. If the management does not have sufficient realisable assets, the funder will usually expect some level of cash investment.

6043

6044 It is usual for the funder to take extra steps to **minimise its risk**. In particular, the funder will usually:
a. undertake its own due diligence;
b. require that the management provides the funder with warranties relating to the target so that the funder will have a mirror claim should there be a breach of warranty; and
c. require that the benefit of the main sale and purchase agreement is capable of being freely assigned from the management (as buyer) to the funder. This would allow the funder to bring a claim directly against the seller, in the event of a breach of warranty. The funder can therefore avoid being engaged in litigation with the management, which could be detrimental to their relationship and to the on-going business. As a result, funders are often reluctant to accept less than full warranties in the sale and purchase agreement.

6045 If a venture capital firm is used, the **venture capitalist** will expect to take shares in the target so that it has an equity investment in the business' growth. Normally, a new company will be incorporated to act as an acquisition vehicle and both the management and the venture capital company will be shareholders in this new company. A shareholders' agreement relating to the new acquisition vehicle, similar to one found for a joint venture company (see ¶6550+) will set out the relationship between the management and the venture capitalist. Most importantly, the agreement should set out the envisaged exit strategy (for example, flotation on the stock market or sale to a third party).

6046 Since the management will not usually have enough **security for their funding**, the funder will normally take security over the target's business. Where the MBO is proceeding as a share sale, this will result in the target giving financial assistance for the acquisition of its shares (¶5557+). This will be unlawful unless the target complies with the whitewash procedure (¶5586+).

> MEMO POINTS   When the relevant provisions of the **new Companies Act** come into force, financial assistance will no longer be prohibited for most private companies (¶5557+). Therefore, the whitewash procedure will not be required. The implementation date for this change is yet to be announced at the time of writing.

6047 One of the **whitewash** requirements is for the directors of the target to give a statutory declaration regarding the financial stability of the target in the 12 months after completion (¶5600+). This can result in a timing problem. The declaration should properly be made by the new directors (i.e. the management) so that they, and not the old directors, take the risk for the declaration. However, the new directors will not be appointed until funding has been given and the deal completes, yet funding will not be given until the financial assistance is whitewashed, which in turn requires the statutory declaration.

In practice, the whitewash and completion of the deal will take place at the same **completion meeting** where events should occur in the following order:
– at a board meeting of the target, the old directors resign and the new directors are appointed with immediate effect;
– the board meeting whitewashes the financial assistance (which includes the new directors making the required statutory declaration);
– the board meeting then breaks to allow for the sale and purchase to be completed; and
– finally, the target's board meeting resumes to approve the share transfers and any other changes required as result of completion.

The "risk" to the seller of the new directors being appointed before completion therefore becomes only theoretical.

Management team

6048 The management team is a key element of an MBO. The first step is for the team to ensure that it does not put its position in the target at risk. As employees, the management has **duties** of confidentiality and of fidelity and loyalty to their employer. If the individuals are also directors, they have additional duties to act with care, skill and diligence and to promote the company's success. An MBO could result in a **conflict of interests**. An early approach to the target's shareholders/parent is advisable, although in many cases the MBO will have been positively encouraged by them.

6049 As the key element to the transaction, the management team should be prepared to commit to the target for at least 3 to 5 years after completion. Their **continued involvement** in the target will be a requirement of funding as the funders will be investing in the people behind the MBO just as much as the target. The documentation (for example, finance documents, shareholders' agreement and individual service agreements) will reflect this, giving incentives for the management's continued involvement and disincentives for an early exit.

The medium-term aim of the MBO management team is often to float the company on the Stock Exchange or Alternative Investment Market, with a view to selling their shares for a significant personal profit.

CHAPTER 14

Corporate restructuring and development

OUTLINE

		¶¶
SECTION 1 Reorganisations		6405
A Hive-down		6415
1 Procedure		6420
2 Tax consequences		6429
B Share for share exchange		6453
C Section 110 reorganisation		6465
1 Procedure		6472
2 Rights of objectors		6488
D Scheme of arrangement		6500
1 General procedure		6507
2 Reconstruction or amalgamation		6530
SECTION 2 Joint ventures		6550
A Joint venture company (JVC)		6560
B Preliminary issues		6568
1 Relationship between JVC and participants		6568
2 Competition law		6583
3 Pre-contractual documents		6591
C Key JVC documents		6600
1 Shareholders' agreement		6600
2 Articles of association		6630
D Taxation		6640
1 Group relief		6641
2 Consortium relief		6650
E Accounting treatment		6655
SECTION 3 Takeovers		6675
I Public company takeovers		6685
Financial services regulation		6686
Prospectus requirements		6687
Takeover Directive		6688
A The Panel on Takeovers and Mergers		6700
1 Function		6705

		¶¶
2 Decision making and appeals		6710
The Panel		6710
The Panel Executive		6712
The Code Committee		6716
Hearings Committee		6717
Takeover Appeal Board		6723
3 Powers		6729
B The takeover process		6745
Summary		6746
1 Scope of the Code		6755
Application of the Code		6755
Code waiver		6760
Definitions		6765
2 Pre-offer considerations		6776
a Preparation		6776
b Secrecy		6778
c Announcements		6780
d Pre-offer share dealing		6787
Effect on bidder's offer		6787
Stakebuilding		6790
Restrictions on persons with confidential information		6793
Irrevocable undertakings		6794
e Approaching the target		6798
3 Offer		6805
a Mandatory cash offer		6805
b Voluntary offer		6815
c Timetable		6827
d Alterations		6835
Extensions		6835
Revisions		6838
4 Conduct of the parties		6850
a Share dealing during offer period		6850
b Disclosure requirements		6860
c Frustrating tactics		6865
d Provision of information		6872
Equality		6873
Accuracy		6876
Responsibility		6879
Offer document		6881
Target board's circular		6882

Profit forecasts and asset valuations	6884	2 Takeover offer	6936
e Advertisements and telephone campaigns	6890	B Bidder's "squeeze-out" right	6945
5 Consequences of offer	6900	C Minority shareholders' "sell-out" right	6965
a Successful offer	6900	**III Takeover by scheme of arrangement**	**6985**
b Unsuccessful offer	6915	A Advantages	6990
II Compulsory acquisition	**6930**	B Disadvantages	6995
A Scope of provisions	6935	C Types of scheme	7000
1 Target	6935		

6400 A company's **needs change** over time, depending on a variety of factors, including:
- the type of business it runs;
- the market within which it operates;
- the economic climate (both in the UK and globally);
- the management and consequential direction of the business; and
- the resources it has available to it.

Therefore, a company's directors and managers should regularly review their strategy and may consider a number of options to help to achieve the aims of the business and its owners.

An internal **reorganisation** may be necessary so that the structure of the company or group and its business(es) suits future plans (¶6405+).

Where the development of a business requires the input of two or more companies, but the participants wish to retain their separate identities, a **joint venture** may be the best course of action (¶6550+).

One of the most common corporate development options involving an external party is an **acquisition** (that is, the purchase of a company) or a **disposal** (that is, the sale of a company). The buying and selling of companies through private contract is considered in detail at ¶5200+. Where the acquisition is carried out by way of a public offer to all of the shareholders of a company to buy their shares, the transaction is called a "**takeover**" (¶6675+). Usually, only public companies are subject to takeovers. Sometimes, the term "**merger**" is used to describe an acquisition or a takeover. This implies that the purchasing company and the target company are of equal size or commercial standing. There is however no distinction in procedure; the purchasing company will still either complete an acquisition or a takeover, as appropriate.

SECTION 1

Reorganisations

6405 A company or group may need to reorganise its shareholding or business operations for various **reasons**. For example:
- in preparation for sale to an external party;
- because the separation of diverse businesses would have tax or accounting benefits;
- to protect certain assets such as intellectual property;
- to separate a loss-making operation of a company from the rest of it; or
- to resolve a deadlock in an owner-managed company.

6406 There are several **mechanisms** by which a reorganisation can be achieved and more than one may be required. The main mechanisms considered below are:
- hive-down;
- share for share exchange;

– section 110 reorganisation; and
– court approved scheme of arrangement.

A reorganisation is essentially a contractual **process**. However, that process can be complex because of the need to ensure parity of share values, adequate consideration for the various transfers and to minimise the tax consequences. In addition, the administrative burden may be significant if there are more than a few companies and/or individual minority shareholders are involved (e.g. through formal or informal employee share schemes) because of the need to ensure that all parties commit to the reorganisation. It is therefore important that the reorganisation is planned from start to finish before any steps are taken to implement it.

6407

A. Hive-down

A hive-down is a **transfer by** a company of the whole or part of its business **down to** a wholly-owned subsidiary, usually referred to as the "hive-down company". The transfer will therefore generally operate in the same way as an asset sale (¶5280+), with some special considerations due to the connection between the parties.

6415

A hive-down may be carried out for a variety of **reasons**, for example:
– to separate two parts of a company's business for accounting and tax purposes;
– in preparation for an intended sale of the hived-down business to an external party so that the shares in the hived-down company can be sold instead of the assets of the hived-down business;
– as part, or in expectation, of insolvency proceedings, so that the hived-down business can be preserved as a going concern in a "clean" subsidiary. The shares in the subsidiary can then be offered for sale to an external party, who will take the business free from the liabilities of the insolvent parent company; or
– to separate a loss-making business so its liabilities do not affect the profit-making parts of the group (this is usually in conjunction with the eventual dissolution or sale of the loss-making part of the business).

6416

As each company is a separate legal person, the hived-down business cannot be gratuitously transferred to the subsidiary. The **consideration** for a hive-down is usually paid in one of two ways:
– by the hive-down company issuing shares to the parent. The shares in the hive-down company, by definition, reflect the value of the hived-down business and preserve the previous ownership position; or
– by the value of the business, as certified by an accountant, being left as a debt outstanding from the hive-down company to the parent.

6417

The result is that the parent converts one asset (i.e. the business) into another (i.e. debt or shares) of equal value.

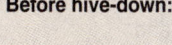 A Ltd runs two businesses, a haulage business and a drinks business. It wants to separate its businesses for accounting and tax purposes. The decision is made to hive down the drinks business. B Ltd, a new wholly-owned subsidiary of A Ltd is formed. The drinks business is transferred to B Ltd at its market value which is £100,000. The consideration for the transfer is left as a debt due to A Ltd from B Ltd.

MEMO POINTS   In a hive-down **during insolvency**, if the hive-down company is to be sold to a third party, the **consideration** is normally set as the "fair value" to be determined by the insolvency practitioner and is left as a debt outstanding from the hive-down company to the insolvent parent company. The fair value is set after it has been agreed with the third party, who, as part of the sale and purchase, will advance sufficient funds to the hive-down company so that it can settle the inter-company debt.

1. Procedure

6420 A hive-down is essentially an **asset sale** from a parent to a wholly-owned subsidiary (see ¶5280+) but there are some variations due to the fact that the parties are connected to each other.

The **hive-down company** may be an existing subsidiary of the parent, but in most situations (including in a hive-down during insolvency), it will be a newly incorporated company. Incorporation of a new company is considered at ¶474+. The various practical arrangements when setting up a new trading company will also have to be dealt with (e.g. VAT registration, opening bank accounts, taking out insurances, applying for any necessary business licences etc).

6421 The **hive-down agreement** will essentially follow the format of an asset sale and purchase agreement (see ¶5750+). However, the following additional issues should be considered in a hive-down:

a. unlike in an arm's length sale, the hive-down company will not take on the **liabilities** of the parent, as the purpose is to ensure that the hive-down company is "clean". In addition, the hive-down company may need to be excluded from the parent's security for its banking facility. The bank's consent would be needed for this;

b. if the hive-down is taking place early in receivership or administration, it is usual for the **effective date** to be set as the date the receiver or administrator was appointed. All trade since that date is then deemed to be that of the hive-down company, which is convenient for accounting purposes; and

c. the level of **warranties** may not be as detailed. In the case of a hive-down during insolvency, a liquidator, receiver or administrator will not give any warranties.

6422 The usual **TUPE** rules apply to a hive-down where the **parent company is solvent** (see ¶5771+).

However, new TUPE rules apply where the **parent company is insolvent**. These came into force for transfers of undertakings (including hive-downs) which take place on or after 6 April 2006 (SI 2006/246). Under the new rules:

a. TUPE **does not apply** when the parent company is subject to insolvency proceedings which have been instituted with a view to the liquidation of the company's assets and are under the supervision of an insolvency practitioner (reg 8(7) SI 2006/246). According to government guidelines, this means that TUPE will not apply if the parent company is in compulsory liquidation or creditors' voluntary liquidation;

b. TUPE **applies subject to two modifications** when the parent company is subject to "relevant insolvency proceedings". This is defined as any insolvency proceedings under the supervision of an insolvency practitioner which have not been opened with a view to the liquidation of the company's assets (reg 8(6) SI 2006/246). According to government guidelines, this means that the modified TUPE applies if the parent company is in administration, administrative receivership or is subject to a company voluntary arrangement; and

c. TUPE **applies as usual** in all other cases. According to government guidelines, this is if the parent company is in a members' voluntary liquidation or receivership (other than administrative receivership).

MEMO POINTS   The **two modifications** which apply when the parent company is subject to "relevant insolvency proceedings" are that:

a. certain **pre-existing debts** owed by the parent company to relevant employees (including statutory redundancy pay, arrears of pay, payment in lieu of notice, holiday pay and the basic award compensation for unfair dismissal) will not pass to the hive-down company. Instead, the relevant employees will be entitled to claim these payments from the secretary of state through the National

Insurance fund (reg 8(3) SI 2006/246; this only applies where insolvency proceedings have commenced before the transfer, *Secretary of State for Trade and Industry v Slater and others*, EAT case 0119/07); and
b. the parent company, hive-down company or insolvency practitioner will be able to agree **variations to the terms and conditions** of employment with employee representatives (including reducing pay) (reg 9 SI 2006/246).

6424 Both the parent and the hive-down company should approve the hive-down at a formal board meeting. Each **director** of each company should:
– confirm that the hive-down is likely to **promote the success** of the relevant company (¶2379+);
– check the articles of the relevant company to ensure that he will count in the **quorum** for a board meeting and that he will be able to vote on resolutions in which he has an interest;
– consider whether the hive-down amounts to a **substantial property transaction** and therefore requires shareholder approval (¶2567+); and
– if he is also a director or shareholder of the other company, **declare his interest** in the transaction at the board meeting to approve the hive-down (¶3317+).

2. Tax consequences

6429 A hive-down can result in the following tax consequences:
– **trading losses** of the transferor can be utilised by the hive-down company (¶6430+);
– the transfer of assets to the hive-down company will be treated as a **no gain/no loss disposal**, so no corporation tax charge will arise on any chargeable gain. However, the charge will crystallise if the hive-down company leaves the group (¶6433+); and
– relief from **stamp taxes** is normally available, but this may be withdrawn if the hive-down company later leaves the group (¶6436+).
In addition, as with asset sales to an external party, the transfer will not be subject to **VAT**, provided the conditions for a transfer as a going concern are satisfied (see ¶5321+).

Trading losses

6430 Any unused trading losses within the transferred trade can be **transferred to** and utilised by the hive-down company, but only against activities of the transferred trade (s 343(3) ICTA 1988). If the transferee company is already carrying on a different trade before the hive-down, it will be necessary to "stream" the profits and losses from each activity to calculate the extent to which brought forward losses can be utilised.
Losses of the trade transferred arising in subsequent periods cannot be carried back to a period before the transfer.

6431 This provision is **conditional upon** the parent having at least a 75% beneficial interest in the hive-down company (ss 343(1), 344(1)-(3) ICTA 1988). The parent will not have such an interest if either:
– a binding contract exists for the sale of the shares in the hive-down company (*Wood Preservation Ltd v Prior* [1969] 1 All ER 364); or
– the parent is in liquidation, as it then ceases to be the beneficial owner of its assets, including its shares in the hive-down company (*Ayerst (Inspector of Taxes) v C & K (Construction) Ltd* [1975] 2 All ER 537).
It is therefore important that the hive-down occurs before either of these two events.

6432 The hive-down company's entitlement to claim loss relief will not be affected by a subsequent **change in control**, for example, by way of a share sale to an external party. However, the relief may be denied if, within 3 years of the change in control, there is a major **change in** the **nature or conduct** of the hived-down business (s 768 ICTA 1988).
Revenue and Customs guidance on what they consider to be a major change, with a number of examples, is available (SP 10/91).

MEMO POINTS 1. The **relief** will be **restricted** where the amount of "relevant liabilities" exceeds the value of "relevant assets". In such a case, the excess of liabilities will be deducted from the losses which may be carried forward by the hive-down company (s 343(4) ICTA 1988). The effect is that, where the whole business of the parent is being hived down, the hive-down company has to take over the parent's liabilities in order to utilise the parent's trading losses.

2. Where the hive-down company is able to claim loss relief, it also takes over the parent's **capital allowances** position as if it had been carrying on the hived-down business since the parent began to do so, and as if everything done to or by the parent had been done to or by the hive-down company (s 343(2) ICTA 1988).

No gain/no loss disposal

6433 The transfer of assets from a parent to a hive-down company qualifies as a transfer of chargeable assets within a 75% chargeable gains group. Such transfers are no gain/no loss disposals, which means that the disposing company (i.e. the parent) is deemed to sell each chargeable asset of the hived-down business at a price which gives rise to neither a gain nor a loss. This is known as an **intra-group transfer** and the treatment is mandatory (s 171 TCGA 1992).

6434 If the parent sells its shares in the hive-down company to an external party within 6 years of the hive-down, the chargeable gains may crystallise. This is known as a "**degrouping charge**" (s 179 TCGA 1992). The hive-down company will be deemed to have sold, and immediately reacquired, the asset at its market value on the date of the intra-group transfer, but the gain will be chargeable at the start of the accounting period in which the hive-down company left the parent's group.

> MEMO POINTS However, the degrouping charge **does not apply to** a transfer of assets from one associated company to another where both cease to be members of a group at the same time (s 170(3) TCGA 1992). Two or more companies are associated if they would form a group by themselves (s 179(10) TCGA 1992). This could occur in a complex hive-down involving different members of a group transferring assets (including shares) to the hive-down company so that it becomes the parent of its own group. All such intra-group transfers would be treated as no gain/no loss disposals but, in the event of the shares in the hive-down company being sold to an external party, the associated companies' exemption could mean that the degrouping charge does not apply. The associated companies' exemption will only apply if the transferring company and hive-down company are associated both when they leave the group and when the no gain/no loss disposal occurred (*Johnston Publishing (North) Ltd v HMRC Commissioners* [2007] EWHC 512 (Ch)).

6435 An **external buyer** of the hive-down company's entire issued share capital will naturally wish to have **protection** from the potential degrouping charge. The parent may be required to give an indemnity in respect of such a liability or to accept a reduction in the purchase price.

Alternatively, the parent can agree with the external buyer that it (or a company in its group) will make a **joint election** with the hive-down company that the gain or allowable loss accruing on the deemed sale (or such part specified in the election) should be treated as accruing to the parent (or other group company) and not the hive-down company. There is no particular form for the election; it must simply be made in writing to an officer of the Board of Revenue and Customs no later than 2 years after the end of the accounting period of the hive-down company in which the deemed sale fell (s 179A TCGA 1992).

Where an election is made, the parent (or other group company) can claim for **roll-over relief of the degrouping charge** (s 179B TCGA 1992). As a result, a joint election may be preferable to an indemnity or reduction in the purchase price.

Stamp taxes

6436 Where one of the hived-down assets includes land or buildings, a liability to **stamp duty land tax** could arise (¶5298+). However, **group relief** from stamp duty land tax will normally be available (¶6437+).

›Where one of the hived-down assets includes shares, a liability to **stamp duty** could arise (¶1875+). However, **associated companies' relief** from stamp duty will normally be available (¶6441+).

The availability of both of these **reliefs is restricted** if there is a change in control of the hive-down company. The timing of the transaction will therefore need to be considered carefully where the hive-down is being carried out with the intention of selling the hive-down company to an external party.

SDLT Group relief

Intra-group transfers of property (including the grant of a lease) are **exempt** from stamp duty land tax (s 62, Sch 7 FA 2003). For these purposes, companies are members of the same group if one is the 75% subsidiary of the other or both are 75% subsidiaries of a third company.

6437

Group **relief will be available**, not only in a traditional hive-down where property is transferred from a parent to a new wholly-owned subsidiary, but also where:
– another 75% subsidiary of the parent transfers property to the hive-down company; or
– the parent or other 75% subsidiary retains the property and grants the hive-down company a lease instead.

6438

Group **relief will not be available** where arrangements are in place at the effective date of the transaction, as a result of which any of the following apply (para 2 Sch 7 FA 2003):
a. a person has, or could obtain, **control** of the hive-down company, but not the transferring company;
b. the **consideration** is to be provided or received (directly or indirectly) by a person other than a group company (e.g. where the hive-down consideration is to be left as an inter-company debt due to the parent and arrangements are in place for that debt to be met by an external party who intends to buy the shares in the hive-down company);
c. the transferring company and the hive-down company are to cease being members of the same **group** because the hive-down company is to cease being a 75% subsidiary of the transferring company or their mutual parent;
d. (from 17 March 2004) there is a **transfer of rights** under a contract to another group company; or
e. (from 20 July 2005) the acquisition does **not take place for bona fide commercial reasons**, and forms part of a scheme to avoid liability to tax.

6439

Group **relief will be withdrawn** where, following a successful claim, the hive-down company ceases to be a member of the same group as the transferring company either within 3 years of the hive-down, or as a result of arrangements made during the 3 years after the hive-down (para 3 Sch 7 FA 2003).

The **exceptions** are if the hive-down company ceases to be in the same group (para 4 Sch 7 FA 2003):
– because the transferring company has left the group;
– by reason of anything done in the course of the winding up of the transferring company; or
– where there is an acquisition of shares in the hive-down company in relation to which stamp duty acquisition relief (¶6454) applies and the hive-down company leaves the group as a result.

From 19 May 2005, an **anti-avoidance rule** applies to stop chains of transfers, which were being used to circumvent the withdrawal of relief (para 4A Sch 7 FA 2003). Essentially, property which was transferred within the group more than once could avoid stamp duty land tax, because only the immediate transfer was taken into account. The new provision means that all previous transfers which have occurred in the 3 years before the change of control of the last transferee (which leaves the group) are taken into account. Transfers where no relief (group, reconstruction or acquisition) has been claimed are ignored for this purpose.

Where the relief is withdrawn and the resulting tax is not paid within 6 months, Revenue and Customs can **recover the unpaid tax** from the transferring company, another group company or a controlling director.

6440

Associated companies relief

A transfer of shareholdings between associated companies is **exempt** from ad valorem stamp duty (s 42 FA 1930). Two companies are associated for these purposes if one is a 75% subsidiary of the other or both are 75% subsidiaries of another company.

This will include a traditional hive-down from a parent to a new wholly-owned subsidiary, provided the parent is the beneficial owner of 75% of the hive-down company. However, the parent will not be the beneficial owner, and therefore the **relief will not be available**, if:
– there are arrangements in existence for any person to obtain control of the hive-down company but not the parent; or
– the parent is in liquidation.

6441

6442 Further, the **relief will be denied** if the transfer is made in connection with an arrangement whereby (s 27(3) FA 1967):
– the consideration is provided, or received directly or indirectly, by a person outside the group. This will include where the hive-down consideration is to be left as an inter-company debt due to the parent and arrangements are in place for that debt to be met by an external party who intends to buy the shares in the hive-down company;
– the parent or hive-down company are no longer to be part of the same group; or
– the shares being transferred were previously transferred to the parent by a person outside of the group.

6443 Where applicable, the relief must be **claimed** and the stock transfer form adjudicated to confirm that no stamp duty is payable. The adjudication request must be accompanied by a statutory declaration setting out the grounds for claiming relief and giving assurance that the statutory provisions have not been breached.

B. Share for share exchange

6453 A share for share exchange involves the shareholders of a company transferring their shares to another company in return for shares in that second company. The result is that the original company will become the wholly-owned subsidiary of the second company. The transfer therefore operates as a **share sale** with the price being paid entirely in shares, rather than cash (see ¶5426+). The share exchange agreement is essentially the same as a share sale and purchase agreement (see ¶5725+).

Such "pure" share for share exchanges are a useful method of restructuring companies under **common ownership** to bring them within one group, for example, so that both companies can be sold to an external party.

EXAMPLE The Smith family are the shareholders in two companies; A Ltd, which manufactures windows and B Ltd, which sells windows. A buyer is interested in both companies. The Smith family wish to bring both companies within the same group to streamline the sale. They therefore sell their shares in B Ltd to A Ltd in return for further shares in A Ltd of equivalent value. As a result, B Ltd becomes the wholly-owned subsidiary of A Ltd. Now, the buyer need only purchase the shares in A Ltd and it will obtain control of both companies.

Before share exchange:

Smith family

A Ltd (manufacture)   B Ltd (sales)

After share exchange:

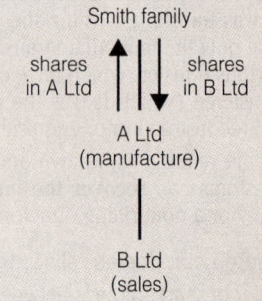

Stamp duty

6454 Stamp duty is normally payable on a transfer of shares (¶1875+), but **acquisition relief** may be available on a share for share exchange (s 77 FA 1986).

The **conditions** for acquisition relief are that:
– the share capital of the target company must consist of the same classes of shares in the same proportion as the share capital of the acquiring company;

– after the exchange, each of the shareholders that held shares in the target company must hold the same (or nearly the same) proportion of shares of the same class in the acquiring company. This means that the share structure of both companies must either be identical or as identical as is practically possible; and
– the transfer must be effected for bona fide commercial reasons and not as part of any scheme or arrangement which has as its main purpose, or one of them, the avoidance of tax. This condition will be satisfied if tax clearance has been obtained (see ¶5367+).

C. Section 110 reorganisation

6465 A section 110 reorganisation (known by the section number of the relevant legislation) takes advantage of a statutory mechanism which enables a company or group to completely **separate two or more businesses** (s 110 IA 1986). The reorganisation essentially involves the transfer of the businesses to new companies and the voluntary liquidation of the original company. It remains a popular way for solvent companies or groups (often family-owned and in a state of management deadlock) to demerge their businesses so that they each become controlled by a different group of shareholders and managers.

Advantages

6466 The two main advantages of such a reorganisation are:
a. if the appropriate special resolutions are passed, it is **binding** on all of the shareholders (s 110(5) IA 1986). The scheme can therefore be implemented by those holding 75% or more of the company's voting share capital (the percentage required to pass a special resolution) although there is protection for any dissenting shareholders (¶6488+); and
b. no court approval is required, provided the liquidation can proceed as a members' voluntary liquidation or the liquidation committee approves the reorganisation in a creditors' voluntary liquidation (¶6481).

Disadvantages

6467 This type of reorganisation has two main disadvantages:
a. it involves a **liquidation** which, depending upon the circumstances of the company being liquidated, can be expensive and time consuming and could result in creditor involvement. This effect can be minimised by a pre-liquidation reorganisation so that the company being liquidated is a new holding company without a trading history (¶6475+); and
b. the various transfers involved in the reorganisation must be done under contract rather than by the court vesting assets in the shareholders (as under a court approved scheme of arrangement, ¶6500+) which will have **tax consequences**. These can be minimised by obtaining tax clearances; relief from stamp taxes may also be available.

1. Procedure

6472 The reorganisation process can be complex and so it is useful to take an **example**. In the example below, A Ltd is a trading company, the shareholders of which are the Smith family and the Jones family who all hold ordinary shares. A Ltd originally operated a haulage business but in time expanded to include the manufacture and sale of soft drinks. The two businesses are, in substance, operated separately. Smith family and Jones family have reached a deadlock in management and a decision is taken to demerge the businesses. Smith family will take the haulage business and Jones family will take the drinks business.

At the start of the reorganisation, the company structure looks like this:

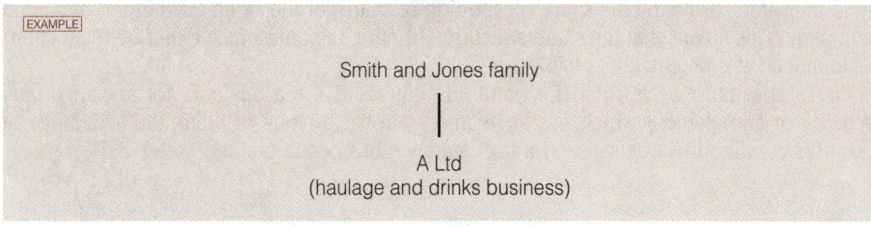

6473 The basic **steps** for the whole reorganisation are as follows, and are discussed in further detail below:

Step 1: A reorganisation of the businesses into a pyramid group structure. The apex of the pyramid is a non-trading holding company. At the base of the pyramid are its immediate wholly-owned subsidiaries, each owning one of the businesses that is to be demerged. The form of this reorganisation will vary depending upon the existing structure of the company or group. In order to avoid the disadvantages of liquidating the original trading company, a new holding company is inserted into the structure. This "clean" holding company will be liquidated instead.

Step 2: A reorganisation of the holding company's share capital so that each group of shareholders holds different classes of shares.

Step 3: The formation of new companies to which each of the businesses will be transferred.

Step 4: The voluntary liquidation of the holding company. As part of the liquidation, the liquidator is authorised to transfer the subsidiaries to the new companies in exchange for shares in those new companies being distributed to each group of shareholders. The two businesses will therefore be demerged.

Step 5: Completion of the liquidation of the holding company which removes the only remaining link between the groups of shareholders and the demerged businesses.

6474 The **essence of the scheme** is that during the course of the winding up, the liquidator transfers the haulage business to one company in return for shares in that company being distributed to the Smith family, and transfers the drinks business to another company in return for shares in that other company being distributed to the Jones family. The result is that the shareholdings of the Smith and Jones families, and the two businesses, are split.

Step 1: Reorganisation into pyramid group structure

Step 1a: Hive down business

6475 A new wholly-owned subsidiary of A Ltd is formed, B Ltd (¶474+). The haulage business is hived down to B Ltd with the assets being transferred at their market value. The consideration for the transfer is satisfied by B Ltd issuing shares of an appropriate value to A Ltd (¶6417). The drinks business remains in A Ltd.

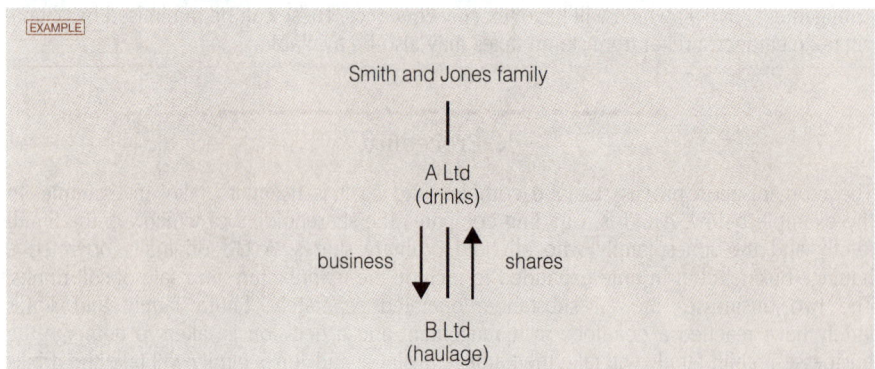

Step 1b: New holding company

A new holding company, H Ltd, is formed by the Smith and Jones families who hold their shares in H Ltd in exactly the same proportion as their shareholdings in A Ltd. The Smith and Jones families enter into an agreement with H Ltd to exchange all their shares in A Ltd for equivalent shareholdings in H Ltd (¶6453). The result is that A Ltd becomes the wholly-owned subsidiary of H Ltd whose shares are held in the same proportions as A Ltd's shares were held.

6476

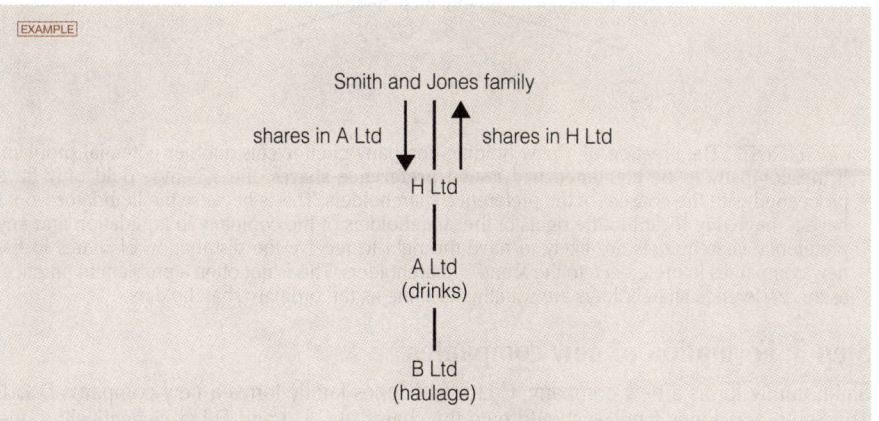

EXAMPLE

Step 1c: Restructure

A Ltd declares a dividend payable to H Ltd which is satisfied by a distribution of assets, namely A Ltd's shareholding in B Ltd (¶1710+). If A Ltd does not have enough distributable profits or if the tax payable on the distribution is prohibitive, its shareholding in B Ltd can be sold to H Ltd and the value of that shareholding left as an inter-company debt owed from H Ltd to A Ltd. The result is that H Ltd becomes the immediate holding company of both A Ltd and B Ltd.

6477

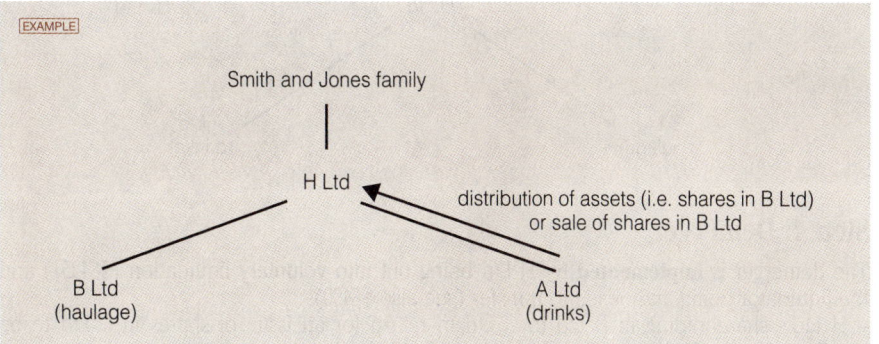

EXAMPLE

Step 2: Reorganisation of H Ltd's share capital

The share capital of H Ltd is altered by dividing its ordinary share capital into X ordinary shares and Y ordinary shares. The share rights of the new shares are specified as follows:
– the X shares will confer an exclusive right in the profits of B Ltd, any surplus of assets in the winding up of B Ltd, and the exclusive right to appoint the directors of B Ltd; and
– the Y shares will have the same rights in relation to A Ltd.

All the shares held by the Smith family are converted into X ordinary shares and the shares held by the Jones family are converted into Y ordinary shares.

6478

EXAMPLE

```
            Smith family      Jones family
            (X shares)        (Y shares)
                    \        /
                     \      /
                      H Ltd
                     /      \
                    /        \
            B Ltd              A Ltd
           (haulage)          (drinks)
```

MEMO POINTS The creation of a new holding company circumvents another potential problem. If the company to be liquidated had issued **preference shares**, the scheme could only have proceeded with the consent of the preference shareholders. This is because the liquidator would have to have due regard to the rights of the shareholders of the company in liquidation and any preference shareholders are likely to have the right to receive the distribution of shares in the new companies in preference to the X and Y shareholders. This is not often a problem in practice, as the preference shareholders are usually the same as the ordinary shareholders.

Step 3: Formation of new companies

6479   Smith family forms a new company, C Ltd, and Jones family forms a new company, D Ltd. The Smith and Jones families should own the shares in C Ltd and D Ltd respectively in the same proportion as they hold their shares in H Ltd. Both C Ltd and D Ltd should have substantial unissued share capital.

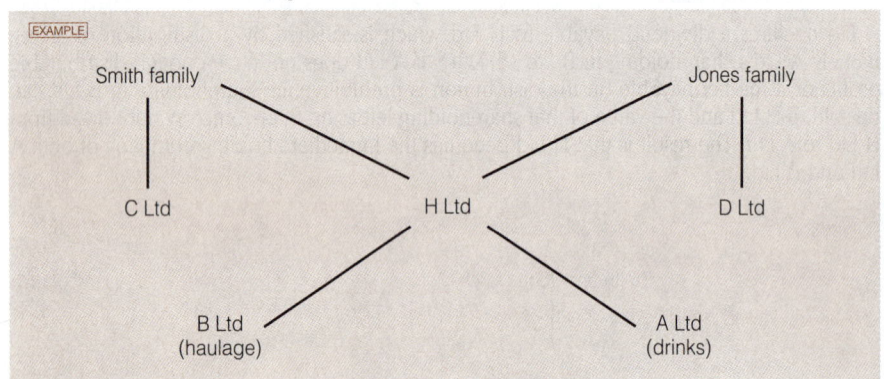

Step 4: Demerger

6480   The demerger is **implemented by** H Ltd being put into voluntary liquidation (¶8425+) and the liquidator being authorised to transfer (see also ¶8490):
– H Ltd's shareholding in B Ltd to C Ltd in return for an issue of shares in C Ltd to be distributed to the X shareholders (that is, the Smith family); and
– H Ltd's shareholding in A Ltd to D Ltd in return for an issue of shares in D Ltd to be distributed to the Y shareholders (that is, the Jones family).

The result is that B Ltd becomes a wholly-owned subsidiary of C Ltd, and A Ltd becomes a wholly-owned subsidiary of D Ltd.

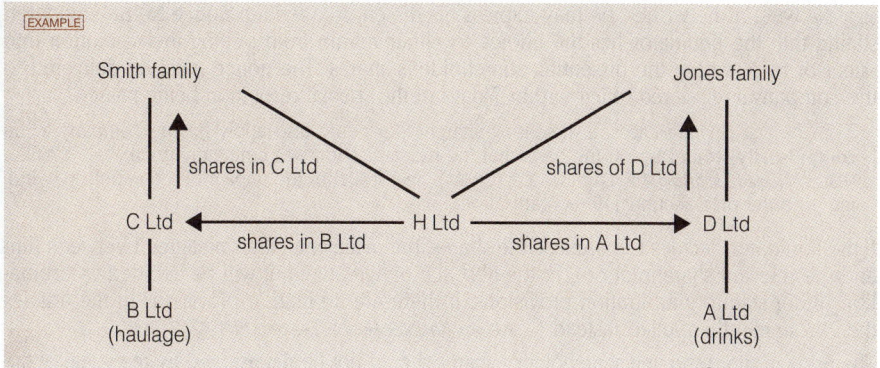

The **liquidator** can be given authority to carry out the reorganisation before, after or at the same time as the resolution to enter voluntary liquidation or to appoint a liquidator (s 110(6) IA 1986). If H Ltd is in members' voluntary liquidation then the liquidator can be authorised by a special resolution of the shareholders (¶8557+). If H Ltd is in creditors' voluntary liquidation then the authorisation must come from the court or the liquidation committee (s 110(3) IA 1986; see ¶7380+ for making applications to court in insolvency proceedings, ¶8547+ for the liquidation committee in a CVL).

6481

Once the authorisation has been received, the liquidator will put the reorganisation into effect by entering into **sale agreements** with C Ltd and D Ltd respectively. The agreements can, and normally will, provide that the shares will be allotted directly to the Smith and Jones families rather than being distributed to them by the liquidator. The Smith and Jones families would normally be asked to claim their right to an allotment of the new shares by returning an appropriate notice to the liquidator. It is possible to set a time limit by which the Smith and Jones families must accept the new shares. If a shareholder misses a deadline either through negligence or accident, he cannot compel C or D Ltd, as appropriate, to allot the shares to him (*Burdett-Coutts v True Blue (Hannan's) Gold Mine* [1899] 2 Ch 616).

6482

Step 5: Liquidation completed

The liquidation of H Ltd is then completed following the usual rules for a voluntary liquidation. After completion of the liquidation and dissolution of H Ltd, the two sides of the business will have completely demerged.

6483

EXAMPLE

```
     Smith family              Jones family
          |                         |
        C Ltd                     D Ltd
          |                         |
        B Ltd                     A Ltd
      (haulage)                  (drinks)
```

2. Rights of objectors

Dissenting shareholders

Any shareholder who did not vote in favour of the special resolution that authorised the liquidator to accept shares in return for a transfer of assets is given some statutory protection

6488

(s 111 IA 1986). If he wishes, he may express his dissent in a written **notice to** the liquidator, stating that the liquidator has the choice to either refrain from putting the resolution into effect or to purchase the dissenting shareholder's shares. The notice must be delivered to the company's registered office **within** 7 days of the special resolution being passed.

> MEMO POINTS In rare cases, a dissenting shareholder could also apply for the company to be **compulsorily wound up** on the basis that the reorganisation was eminently unfair (see ¶7602+) (*Re Consolidated South Rand Mines Deep Ltd* [1909] 1 Ch 491). See ¶6491 for the impact of a compulsory winding up order on a section 110 reorganisation.

6489 If the liquidator decides to purchase the shares, the **price** can either be agreed between him and the relevant shareholder or, in the absence of agreement, it will be decided by arbitration under statutory arbitration provisions. If there are arbitration provisions in the articles then these can be applied instead (*Llewellyn v Kasintoe Rubber Estates Ltd* [1914] 2 Ch 670).

The price of the dissenting shareholder's shares should not be **determined by** the value of the shares he would have received if he had participated in the reorganisation. Instead, his shares will be valued as a proportion of the net asset value of the company in liquidation (*Re Mysore West Gold Mining Company* (1889) 42 Ch D 535). The shareholder will have access to some financial information about the company (such as the statement of affairs filed at Companies House) so that he can see whether the price offered to him is fair (¶8440+; see also ¶8530, ¶8645).

6490 If the liquidator does decide to purchase the shares, the price must be **paid before** the company is dissolved and the money can be **raised by** the liquidator in any manner approved by special resolution (s 111(3) IA 1986).

Creditors

6491 Creditors can **prove in the liquidation** of the company in the normal way (see ¶8030+). However, this right is not of much use if the reorganisation has put the assets of the company out of their reach and the value of those assets has been transferred to the shareholders. Disadvantaged creditors do not have the right to prevent the reorganisation as such but they can apply to court to place the company into compulsory liquidation (see ¶7587+). If a **compulsory winding up** order is made by the court within a year of the special resolution that authorised the liquidator to accept shares in return for a transfer of assets, the reorganisation can only proceed with the consent of the court (s 110(6) IA 1986).

D. Scheme of arrangement

6500 A scheme of arrangement is a statutory **procedure** by which court approval can be obtained for any proposed compromise or arrangement between a company and its shareholders (or any class of shareholders). It is also commonly known as a **section 425 scheme** after the section number of the relevant legislation. If the scheme is approved by the court and at least 75% of the shareholders in each class, the arrangement is binding on all of the shareholders and the company (s 425 CA 1985; restated at s 899 CA 2006, due to come into force on 6 April 2008). Special rules apply if the scheme is a **reconstruction or amalgamation** (see ¶6530+).

> MEMO POINTS The same mechanism can be used to obtain court approval for any compromise or arrangement between a company and its **creditors**, in which case all the references to shareholders should be read as references to creditors. In order for the scheme to be binding on the creditors, it must be approved by at least 75% of each class of creditors. Schemes of arrangement are therefore sometimes used as an alternative to insolvency proceedings so that a company restructures its debts, e.g. by way of a debt for equity swap, or during a liquidation or administration as part of the relevant insolvency practitioner's powers.

6501 A scheme of arrangement is not a reorganisation procedure as such. Instead, it is a way in which a proposed transaction or series of transactions between a company and its shareholders can be sanctioned by the court thereby preventing it from being challenged in the future (*Barclays Bank plc v British & Commonwealth Holdings plc* [1996] 1 BCLC 1).

The **scope** of the statutory provision is extremely wide as the term "arrangement" has no specific definition. The scheme does not have to alter the existing rights between the company and its shareholders; instead it can alter the rights of the shareholders as against another party (*Re T & N Ltd* [2006] EWHC 1447 (Ch)). Unanimous consent is not a requirement (*Re Cape plc* [2006] EWHC 1316 (Ch)).

So, a scheme of arrangement can be **used to** bring about almost any kind of merger, demerger or internal reorganisation and can involve external parties. In practice, schemes of arrangement are usually used when it would be difficult or impossible:
– to obtain contractual agreement to the reorganisation from all the shareholders; and/or
– to carry out the proposed transactions under general company law (for example, a redenomination of issued share capital, see ¶1325+).

Schemes of arrangement are also used where the bidder in a public company takeover wishes to purchase 100% of the target's shares (¶6985+).

That is not to say that a scheme of arrangement is a procedure of last resort; it can be used even if the reorganisation could have been carried out using another procedure (such as a reduction of capital or the "squeeze-out" of minority shareholders) (*Re National Bank Ltd* [1966] 1 All ER 1006).

The **minimum requirements** are that the company must be a party to the arrangement and there must be some element of give and take, meaning that the shareholders must achieve some benefit in agreeing to the arrangement (*Re NFU Development Trust Ltd* [1973] 1 All ER 135). In addition, the company must be confident that a court will form the view that at least 75% of each class of shareholders would be reasonably likely to accept the proposed arrangement.

6502

1. General procedure

The **basic steps** required to implement a scheme of arrangement are as follows:
a. the company or any shareholder should **apply to court** for an order that a meeting of shareholders (or class of shareholders) is called. If the company is in liquidation or administration, the liquidator or administrator should also be a party to the court application;
b. if the court agrees, it will order that the appropriate **shareholder meetings** are held. If 75% of the shareholders (or class of shareholders) present and voting at the meetings agree to the arrangement and it is also **approved by the court**, then it is binding on all of the shareholders (or all of the class in question) and on the company. If the company is in liquidation, it is binding on the liquidator and contributories; and
c. for the scheme to have effect, a copy of the **court order must be filed** at Companies House. A copy must also be attached to every copy of the company's memorandum issued after the court order has been made.

6507

> MEMO POINTS The court procedure for creditors' schemes is subject to a **practice direction**, the principles of which have been treated below as also applying to shareholder schemes (*Practice Statement* [2002] 3 All ER 96).

Application to court

The application is usually **made to** the Companies Court (which is part of the Chancery Division of the High Court). It should be in the **form** of a Part 8 claim form, asking for (para 7 CPR PD 49):
– directions for convening a meeting of creditors and/or shareholders (as appropriate);
– the court's sanction for the compromise or arrangement, if it is approved at the meeting(s), and a direction for a further court hearing for this purpose; and
– a direction that the claimant (i.e. the company, or its liquidator or administrator) files at court a copy of the report by the chairman of the meeting(s).

See ¶7143+ for more on how to make court applications.

6508

MEMO POINTS Applications can also be made to a **county court** if that court has jurisdiction to wind up the company, i.e. if the company's paid up share capital is £120,000 or less. However, county court applications are rare in practice because of the specialist judges available at the Companies Court.

6509 The application is usually **made by** the company (or the liquidator or administrator if the company is in liquidation or administration) but can also be made by a shareholder if he has the support of the company. The scheme must have the approval of the company either through the board or by way of an ordinary shareholder resolution (*Re Savoy Hotel Ltd* [1981] 3 All ER 646). There is no need for a defendant to be named unless the court so orders (para 7 CPR PD 49).

6510 The application must be supported by a **witness statement** from a director (or the liquidator or administrator, as appropriate) giving the necessary statutory information about the company as well as the terms of the proposed compromise or arrangement (para 7 CPR PD 49). The witness statement should explain the scheme, its purpose and any relevant facts. It should also specify which meetings are required, where they will be held, a nomination for who should be chairman and the wording of any advertisement which is required (for example, in national newspapers). The circular to shareholders and/or creditors and the scheme itself must be attached to the witness statement.

6511 The applicant should take all reasonable steps to give **notice** of the application and initial hearing date to any person affected by the scheme specifying (*Practice Statement* [2002] 3 All ER 96):
– that the scheme has been proposed;
– the purpose of the scheme; and
– the shareholder meetings which the applicant thinks will be required and their composition.

However, the court has recognised that time pressures may make this impractical in some situations (*Re Marconi Corporation plc and Re Marconi plc* [2003] All ER (D) 362 (Mar)).

First court hearing

6512 An application to the Companies Court will first be heard by the registrar. The **purpose** of this first hearing is to consider the jurisdiction of the court to approve the scheme. The court will not at this stage consider the fairness of the scheme with a view to deciding whether or not to sanction it (*Re Telewest Communications plc (No 1)* [2005] 1 BCLC 752).

MEMO POINTS The court has jurisdiction to sanction a scheme which contains provisions for the company to **change the scheme** itself or any agreements or documents entered into to put the scheme into effect. However, in most cases, the court is unlikely to exercise this jurisdiction. This is because the court and the company's shareholders will normally need to know with clarity and certainty the terms of the arrangement and how they will be affected. Where the scheme could be changed by the company, there is the obvious possibility that the shareholders would be happy with the scheme in its original form but not as subsequently changed. The court may exercise its jurisdiction in unusual circumstances, where the provisions relating to future changes also contain a mechanism to protect shareholders (*Re Cape plc* [2006] EWHC 1316 (Ch)).

6513 One of the registrar's main tasks will be to consider the constitution of the **classes of shareholder** and whether one or more meetings should be convened. Responsibility for ensuring that the correct class meetings are called falls on the applicant and it should bring to the attention of the court at the earliest opportunity any issues which may arise relating to the constitution of the meetings or which may affect the conduct of those meetings (*Practice Statement* [2002] 3 All ER 96).

MEMO POINTS Where a company proposes a scheme of arrangement with **creditors**, it is sometimes impossible for the company to assemble a comprehensive and reliable list of those affected by the scheme. In such cases, all reasonable steps must be taken to bring the proposed scheme and meetings to the attention of those who will be affected by it (*Re T & N Ltd* [2006] EWHC 1447 (Ch)).

6514 **Different meetings** for different classes will be required if there are significant dissimilarities in their rights (either before or after the arrangement is put into effect) (*Sovereign Life Assurance Co v Dodd* [1892] 2 QB 573).

In order to avoid giving a minority group the right of veto, those whose rights are sufficiently similar to the rights of others so that they can properly consult together will be required to attend **one meeting** (*Re Hawk Insurance Company Ltd* [2001] 2 BCLC 480). However, even where there is one meeting, the court can order that the votes for and against the scheme be recorded and it can take the effect of the votes of the different groups on the overall result into account when exercising its discretion as to whether or not to sanction the scheme (*Re Cape plc* [2006] EWHC 1316 (Ch)).

> MEMO POINTS   In considering whether there are significant dissimilarities between the rights of shareholders before and after the scheme is put into effect, it is essential to identify the **correct comparator** (*Re T & N Ltd* [2006] EWHC 1447 (Ch)):
> – where the scheme is proposed as an alternative to an insolvent liquidation, the shareholders' rights under the scheme should be compared to their rights in an insolvent liquidation;
> – where the company is solvent and will continue in business, their rights under the scheme should be compared to their rights against the company as a continuing entity; and
> – where the scheme is concerned with tortious claims against an insurer, the claimants' rights under the scheme should be compared to their rights in litigation.

6515 The registrar will **not agree to call** the required meetings if there would be no point in doing so (for example, if shareholder opposition was so great that the court reasonably believes that the necessary majority would not be obtained).

If the registrar **does agree to call** the required meetings, he will decide upon the form of any advertisements, meeting notices and the form of proxies (although if another valid form of proxy is used by a shareholder, that shareholder will not forfeit his right to have his proxy counted at the meeting) (*Re Dorman Long and Co Ltd* [1933] All ER Rep 460).

> MEMO POINTS   When giving directions regarding notices of meetings, it is open to the court to direct which **documents** should be **sent to the shareholders**. In a complicated scheme, the court may direct that the more complex and formal documents should only be sent if requested, and that a copy of the scheme itself need not be included (*Re T & N Ltd* [2006] EWHC 1447 (Ch)).

Call shareholder meetings

6516 The shareholder meetings should be **called by** the company in accordance with the registrar's order. If they are not, there is a real risk that the application will be rejected when it is heard by the court again.

Normally, the court will require at least 21 clear days' **notice** of the meeting to be given to the affected shareholders. No notice is required to be given to shareholders who are unaffected by the scheme (for example, in an insolvent company, shareholders whose shares have no value) (*Re Oceanic Steam Navigation Co Ltd* [1938] 3 All ER 740).

> MEMO POINTS   1. In the case of a **creditors' scheme**, notice need not be given to subordinated creditors where their debts will not be affected (*Re British and Commonwealth Holdings plc (No 3)* [1992] BCLC 322; *Re Maxwell Communications Corp plc (No 2)* [1994] 1 All ER 737).
> 2. The legislation expressly requires a scheme of arrangement to be approved by a "meeting" of shareholders or creditors, as appropriate. The conventional legal meaning of meeting in this context is an assembly or coming together of two or more persons (which could occur remotely, for example, by telephone). As an exception, where a class comprises only one person, a meeting attended by that person or his proxy satisfies the statutory requirement. In fact, in that case, it is not essential to convene a meeting because the person may individually consent to the scheme (for example, by signing a resolution to that effect). However, a meeting will not satisfy the legislative requirements if it is attended by only one person (or his proxy) and there is no evidence that he is the only person in his class (*Re Altitude Scaffolding Ltd, Re T & N Ltd* [2006] EWHC 1401 (Ch)).

6517 An **explanatory statement** must be sent with every notice. The statement must set out (s 426(2) CA 1985; restated at s 897(2) CA 2006, as of 6 April 2008):
– the effect of the compromise or arrangement;
– any material interests of the directors of the company (whether in their capacity as directors, shareholders or any other capacity); and
– the effect of the compromise or arrangement on the directors' interests in so far as it is different from the effect on other interests.

The directors have a duty to notify the company of their material interests in this regard. Any director who fails to do so is liable to a fine (s 426(7) CA 1985; restated at s 898 CA 2006, as of 6 April 2008; ¶9935).

MEMO POINTS 1. If the **notice is given by advertisement**, the advertisement must contain the explanatory statement or notification of a place where the shareholders entitled to attend the meeting may obtain copies, which must be supplied free of charge (s 426(3), (5) CA 1985; restated at s 897(4) CA 2006, as of 6 April 2008). If the advertisement does not conform to these requirements, a new meeting may have to be held with the proper notice even where no prejudice has been suffered (*Scottish Eastern Investment Trust Ltd, Petitioners* 1966 SLT 285). A copy of the newspaper which carried the relevant advertisement should be filed with the court.
2. If the compromise or arrangement affects the rights of **debenture holders**, the statement must also state the material interests of the trustees of any deed for securing the issue of debentures and explain any effect the compromise or arrangement would have on those interests, in so far as it was different from the effect on other interests (s 426(4) CA 1985; restated at s 897(3) CA 2006, as of 6 April 2008). The trustees have a duty to notify the company of their material interests or be liable to a fine (s 426(7) CA 1985; restated at s 898 CA 2006, as of 6 April 2008).
3. If the scheme is being used to effect a **takeover** to which the City Code on Takeovers and Mergers applies, the statement must also comply with the requirements of the City Code (see ¶6872+).

6518 If the company **fails to send** an appropriate explanatory statement with each notice, the company and every officer in default is liable to be fined (unless that failure was due to a director refusing to supply the necessary particulars of his interests) (s 426(6) CA 1985; restated at s 897 CA 2006, as of 6 April 2008; ¶9935).

For the consequences of a **change in circumstances** between sending the explanatory statement and the meeting, see ¶1479.

MEMO POINTS For these purposes only, "**officer**" includes a liquidator or administrator of the company and a trustee of a deed securing the issue of debentures of the company (s 426(6) CA 1985; restated at s 897(6) CA 2006, as of 6 April 2008).

Hold shareholder meetings

6519 The scheme must be voted upon by the shareholders at each class meeting. The vote must be on a poll; a show of hands is not permitted. The **required majority** is 75% of the nominal share value of those attending in person or by proxy (s 425(2) CA 1985; restated at s 899(1) CA 2006, as of 6 April 2008). As far as possible, the class meetings should be kept separate from each other, although the presence of other classes would not necessarily be fatal to the scheme (*Carruth v Imperial Chemical Industries Ltd* [1937] 2 All ER 422).

6520 The **chairman** of the meetings should keep a note of:
– the number and value of the holders of each class of shares who were present in person and by proxy at each meeting;
– the number and value of the shareholders in each class who voted for and against the scheme, distinguishing votes in person and by proxy;
– the number and value of shareholders present who did not vote; and
– particulars of any proxies rejected by the chairman and the reason for the rejection.
This information should be included in the chairman's **report to the court** on the conduct and result of the meeting. The report should also have a copy of the scheme attached to it signed by the chairman for identification purposes.

Second court hearing

6521 Unless it decided that it would not sanction the scheme at the first hearing, the court will have given **directions** for a further hearing to take place once the shareholder meeting (and any creditors' meeting) has been held. The parties should follow the court's directions as to how this second hearing should take place and the information that should be put before the court.

The second hearing will usually take place in chambers (which is not open to the public, unlike hearings in open court). Any **shareholder who objects** to the scheme should give notice of his opposition at the relevant class meeting and appear at the second court hearing to present his objections to the judge. A shareholder who has not objected earlier will still be able to do so at the second court hearing, but he will have to show the court that he had a good reason for not raising the issue earlier (*Practice Statement* [2002] 3 All ER 96). Any shareholder who fails to present his objections at the second court hearing will not be entitled to appeal the court's decision (or will only be entitled to appeal if he first obtains leave to appeal, i.e. the court's prior consent) (*Re Securities Insurance Co* [1894] 2 Ch 410).

6522

> MEMO POINTS 1. A shareholder **cannot object** to a scheme simply on the basis that it could have been implemented under another statutory procedure.
> 2. A shareholder needs to have strong **evidence** to persuade the court not to sanction a scheme on the basis that more votes had been cast against the scheme than had been recorded by the chairman, or on the basis that one of the shareholders had a particular financial interest in the scheme (*Re Linton Park plc* [2005] All ER (D) 174 (Nov)).

The court has absolute **discretion** as to whether or not to sanction the scheme. The **test** which it will apply is an objective one, namely, whether the scheme is one which an intelligent and honest man, who is a member of the class concerned and acting in respect of his interest, might reasonably approve (*Re Dorman Long and Co Ltd* [1933] All ER Rep 460).

6523

In practice, unless a shareholder proves otherwise, this test will be **satisfied where** the appropriate meetings have been properly convened and the necessary majority of shareholders has approved the scheme, having received a full explanation of its effects. The accuracy and contents of the explanatory statement are therefore particularly important.

> MEMO POINTS Regardless of shareholder approval, a court **cannot sanction** a scheme that is outside of the powers of the company (for example, if it contemplates actions outside of the company's objects). If necessary, the memorandum should be changed before the court hearing (see ¶410+). Nor can it sanction a scheme that would otherwise be unlawful (for example, it cannot agree to issue shares at a discount). However, a scheme which would be unlawful if effected by contract between the parties (for example, because it contained an unfair contract term) could be approved by the court. This is because a scheme of arrangement does not constitute a contract or a notice (*Re Cape plc* [2006] EWHC 1316 (Ch)).

The court will generally impose **conditions** on a scheme which could have been carried out as a section 110 reorganisation or which involves the transfer of a business in return for shares being issued directly to the shareholders (s 427(3)(e) CA 1985; restated at s 900 CA 2006, as of 6 April 2008). Those conditions are for the protection of any shareholders who objected to the scheme and will be equivalent to the protection enjoyed by dissenting shareholders under a section 110 reorganisation (see ¶6488+).

6524

Companies House filing

The court's order will only be effective once a copy of it has been filed at Companies House (s 425 CA 1985; restated at s 899(4) CA 2006, as of 6 April 2008).

6525

A copy of the order must also be attached to every copy of the company's memorandum that is issued after the order has been made. Any company or officer in default of this requirement is liable to be fined (see ¶9935).

Comment: As of 6 April 2008, when the relevant provisions of the **new Companies Act** come into force, instead of the court order being attached to every copy of the company's memorandum, it will have to be attached to every copy of the company's articles (s 901(3) CA 2006). However, since the provisions abolishing the memorandum are not expected to come into force until 1 October 2009, transitional provisions are likely to apply extending this requirement until that date. Otherwise, this requirement will remain the same (s 901 CA 2006).

> MEMO POINTS If the company **does not have a memorandum** then the copy of the court order must be attached to the document that constitutes the company or defines its constitution.

2. Reconstruction or amalgamation

6530 In addition to the normal rules for schemes of arrangement, the **court** has **special powers** where a scheme is proposed for, or in connection with, a reconstruction or amalgamation and, as part of the scheme, the whole or part of any company's business or assets is to be transferred to another company (s 427 CA 1985; restated at s 900 CA 2006, as of 6 April 2008).

Complex additional rules apply if a scheme of arrangement for the purpose of a reconstruction or amalgamation involves the **merger or division of a public company** (see ¶6536+).

> MEMO POINTS These powers are only **available where** the companies concerned are formed and registered in England, Wales or Scotland, unless the reconstruction or amalgamation involves a merger or division of public companies, in which case they are also available to companies formed and registered in Northern Ireland (ss 427(6), 427A(6) CA 1985). The provisions in the **new Companies Act** will apply to all UK-registered companies.

Definitions

6531 There is no statutory definition of the terms "amalgamation" or "reconstruction" and although they are used in both company and tax legislation, they are commercial, not legal, terms (*Re South African Supply and Cold Storage Co* [1904] 2 Ch 268). The terms have, however, been considered judicially and although the cases were decided in their own legislative contexts, the judges' remarks in each case point towards a single meaning of both terms (*Re Mytravel Group plc* [2005] 2 BCLC 123).

Reconstruction

6532 A reconstruction denotes the transfer of an undertaking or part of the undertaking of an existing company to a new company with shareholders who are substantially the same persons in the new company as in the old company (*Brooklands Selangor Holdings Ltd v IRC* [1970] 2 All ER 76). In other words, **substantially the same business** must be carried on by **substantially the same persons** (*Re South African Supply and Cold Storage Co* [1904] 2 Ch 268). The scheme cannot involve a sale of the businesses to an outsider; that would be a mere sale.

It is not vital that all of the assets or the liabilities of the business should be transferred in order for it to be substantially the same before and after the scheme, but **merely transferring assets** without actually transferring the business is unlikely to be sufficient (*Re South African Supply and Cold Storage Co* [1904] 2 Ch 268).

Whether the shareholders are substantially the same is a matter of fact but the relevant comparison to make is between the **nominal value of the shareholdings** before and after the transfer (*Brooklands Selangor Holdings Ltd v IRC* [1970] 2 All ER 76).

> EXAMPLE The majority shareholder in BSR Ltd wanted the company to continue trading but a number of minority shareholders wanted its assets to be realised. To meet both groups' requirements, a scheme of arrangement was carried out with court approval. Under the scheme, part of BSR Ltd's business was transferred to a new subsidiary called BSH Ltd, all the shares in BSR Ltd were vested in the majority shareholder and all the shares in BSH Ltd were vested in the minority shareholders. The court decided that the scheme was not a reconstruction because a substantial change in the shareholders had occurred. Although the shareholders in the new company (BSH Ltd) consisted of the vast majority by number of the shareholders in the old company (BSR Ltd), they represented only approximately 50% by nominal value (*Brooklands Selangor Holdings Ltd v IRC* [1970] 2 All ER 76).

> MEMO POINTS A reconstruction can involve the reconstruction of a single company into **two or more successor companies** (*Fallon v Fellows (Inspector of Taxes)* [2001] STC 1409). However, a reconstruction is not the same as a **partition** (i.e. where the business of a company is divided between its shareholders) (*Brooklands Selangor Holdings Ltd v IRC* [1970] 2 All ER 76). If a company or group wishes to partition its businesses, the appropriate mechanism is a section 110 reorganisation (see ¶6465+).

Amalgamation

6533 An amalgamation denotes a **merging** of substantially two or more existing undertakings into one undertaking, the shareholders of each merging company becoming substantially the shareholders in the company which holds the merged undertakings (*Re South African Supply and Cold Storage Co* [1904] 2 Ch 268).

An amalgamation can be **implemented either by** the transfer of two or more undertakings to a new company, or by the transfer of one or more undertakings to an existing company. A popular amalgamation method is a share for share exchange (¶6453+). For example, the amalgamation of A Ltd and B Ltd could be brought about by the issue of shares in A Ltd to the shareholders of B Ltd in exchange for their B Ltd shares, so that B Ltd became the subsidiary of A Ltd (*Crane Fruehauf Ltd v IRC* [1975] 1 All ER 429). However, the purchase or exchange of shares does not, by itself, result in an amalgamation. In order for there to be a true amalgamation, the undertakings of A Ltd and B Ltd must be merged (for example, by a hive up of B Ltd's business to A Ltd (¶6415+) and the liquidation of B Ltd). The court will look at the transaction as a whole to see if a true amalgamation is proposed (*Swithland Investments Ltd v IRC* [1990] STC 448).

Court's powers

Where a scheme for the purpose of an amalgamation or reconstruction involves a transfer of the undertaking or assets of one company, A Ltd, to another company, B Ltd, the **court can order** (s 427(3), (4) CA 1985; restated at s 900(2) CA 2006, as of 6 April 2008):
– the necessary transfer of assets or liabilities so that they vest in B Ltd free from any mortgage or charge;
– the allotting or appropriation by B Ltd of any shares or similar interests which are to be allotted or appropriated by B Ltd under the scheme;
– the continuation by or against B Ltd of any legal proceedings pending by or against A Ltd;
– the dissolution, without liquidation, of A Ltd;
– a provision to be made for any persons who dissent from the scheme; and/or
– any incidental, consequential or supplemental matters that are necessary to ensure that the scheme is carried out fully and effectively.

6534

If the court makes such an order, every company to which the order relates must **file** a copy of it at Companies House within 7 days after it is made (s 427(5) CA 1985; restated at s 900(6) CA 2006, as of 6 April 2008). Any company or officer in default of this requirement is liable to be fined (see ¶9935).

6535

Mergers and divisions of public companies

When do the additional rules apply?

Complex rules apply where an arrangement is proposed for the purpose of, or in connection with, a reconstruction or amalgamation which involves one or more public companies transferring their undertaking, property and liabilities to one or more other companies in **exchange for shares** being received by the shareholders of the transferring companies (s 427A CA 1985; restated at s 902 CA 2006, as of 6 April 2008). These rules implement certain EU directives (EEC Directive 1978/855 and EEC Directive 1982/891) and apply in **three cases**:

Case 1. Where the transfer is by one public company to a pre-existing public company (i.e. other than one formed for the purpose of the scheme).

Case 2. Where the transfer is by two or more public companies (including the company in respect of which the scheme is proposed) to another company (public or private) formed for the purpose of the scheme.

Case 3. Where the transfer is by one public company to two or more companies, each of which is either a pre-existing public company or a company (public or private) formed for the purpose of the scheme.

6536

Comment: The relevant provisions of the **new Companies Act** are due to come into force on 6 April 2008. They will restate the application of special rules to these transactions, as well as the rules themselves. However, the terminology will change. Case 1 will be referred to as a "merger by absorption" and Case 2 will be referred to as a "merger by formation of a new company". These types of transactions are dealt with together as "mergers" (ss 904-918 CA 2006). Case 3 will be dealt with alone as a "division" (ss 919-934 CA 2006).

MEMO POINTS 1. The provisions **do not apply** where the company in respect of which the arrangement is proposed is being wound up (s 427A(4) CA 1985; restated at s 902(3) CA 2006, as of 6 April 2008).
2. The **scheme cannot** involve any shares in the companies to which the transfers are being made being allotted to the transferring companies or their nominee (para 7 Sch 15B CA 1985).
3. Unless 75% by value of the creditors of the transferring company agree, in a **case 3 scheme**, a company to which a transfer is being made will be jointly and severally liable for the total liabilities transferred to all the companies, up to the value of the property less the value of the liabilities transferred to it in particular (para 15 Sch 15B CA 1985; restated at s 940 CA 2006, as of 6 April 2008).
4. The EC Directive on **cross-border mergers** of limited liability companies was due to be implemented on 15 December 2007. The Cross-Border Mergers Regulations will provide a similar framework for cross-border mergers to the structure for domestic mergers described above (SI 2007/2974). The merger will be able to take one of three forms (reg 2 SI 2007/2974):
– merger by absorption;
– merger by absorption of a wholly-owned company; and
– merger by formation of a new company.
As with domestic mergers, a cross-border merger will have to be sanctioned by the shareholders (and the creditors, if the court orders a creditors' meeting to be held) and the court. The process will involve certain filings being made at Companies House (guidance on this has been published by Companies House and is available on its website). The regulations also set out detailed requirements for employee participation.
A UK company in administration will be able to participate in a cross-boarder merger, in which case the administrator's consent will also have to be obtained before the pre-merger steps are taken.
As to whether the Takeover Code applies to a cross-border merger, see ¶6755/mp.

Summary of rules

6537 The full details of the rules are quite complex. To summarise the requirements, the court will only sanction a reconstruction or amalgamation that falls into any of the above cases if:
a. the scheme has been **approved by** 75% by value of each class of shareholder in a pre-existing public company to which a transfer is being made (para 1 Sch 15B CA 1985; restated at ss 907, 922 CA 2006, as of 6 April 2008);
b. the **draft terms** of the proposed scheme have been (para 2 Sch 15B CA 1985; restated at ss 905, 906, 920, 921 CA 2006, due to come into force on 6 April 2008):
– drawn up and adopted by the directors of the transferring companies and any pre-existing companies to which a transfer is being made;
– filed by the directors of each company at Companies House; and
– published by the registrar in the *Gazette* at least 1 month before the shareholder meetings to approve the scheme;
c. a **directors' report** from the directors of the transferring companies and any pre-existing companies to which a transfer is being made has been drawn up which contains the information in the explanatory statement (see ¶6517) and additional specified information;
d. an **expert's report** from an independent auditor containing specified information about the share valuation and ratios has been drawn up on behalf of each transferring company and any pre-existing company to which a transfer is being made; and
e. the draft terms, directors' report, expert's report and up to date company accounts have been available for **inspection by shareholders** for at least 1 month before the shareholder meetings.
These requirements have some specified **exceptions** (paras 10-14 Sch 15B CA 1985; restated at ss 915-918, 931-934 CA 2006, as of 6 April 2008).

MEMO POINTS 1. The **draft terms** must provide specified particulars of the scheme and even more particulars must be provided for case 3 schemes (paras 2, 3 Sch 15B CA 1985; restated at ss 905, 921 CA 2006, as of 6 April 2008). Further, in a case 3 scheme, the directors of each transferring company must **report any material changes** to the property and liabilities being transferred that have occurred between the adoption of the draft terms and the shareholder meeting to its shareholders and to the companies to which the transfer is being made (these companies must in turn report the changes to their shareholder meetings).
2. A **new Directive on mergers and divisions** of public companies amending EEC Directive 1978/855 and EEC Directive 1982/891 has been published (EC Directive 2007/63). The amendments allow companies to complete a merger or division without an expert's report and without inspection of the draft terms, if its shareholders and security holders agree. This brings the merger and division provisions into line with those on cross-border mergers of limited liability companies (EC Directive

2005/56). Member states are expected to bring provisions into force making these changes by 31 December 2008.

6538 If the court sanctions the scheme, it will **fix the date** on which the transfers must be made and the date on which any transferring company will be dissolved (para 9 Sch 15B CA 1985; restated at s 939 CA 2006, as of 6 April 2008).

SECTION 2
Joint ventures

6550 At its most basic, a joint venture is a **co-operation** between two or more parties for a mutual purpose. That purpose could be charitable or commercial; short-term (e.g. developing a property for sale) or long-term (e.g. setting up and running a new business). In a company law context, a joint venture normally refers to a commercial co-operation between two or more parties for mutual profit and that is the sense in which the term will be used here. A joint venture is an attractive prospect in the right circumstances as it allows the participants to combine know-how and resources in the expectation that the sum is better than its parts.

6551 One of the first decisions the participants will have to make is **which business medium** they wish to use to carry on the joint venture. This will vary from case to case. By far the most common choice of business medium for a commercial joint venture is a private company limited by shares, referred to as the **joint venture company** (JVC), or special purpose vehicle (SPV). This is examined in more detail below.

Other choices could include:
– a partnership (¶17+);
– a limited liability partnership (¶77+);
– a limited partnership under the Limited Partnership Act 1907;
– where at least two of the participants are from different EU members states, a European Economic Interest Grouping (EEIG) (¶104+); and
– where the business is to operate in more than one EU member state, a European Company (known as a Societas Europaea, or SE) (¶88+).

> MEMO POINTS Where the joint venture is of a short-term nature, there may be no need to use a different business medium at all. Instead, the parties could govern their dealings entirely by contract, through a **joint venture agreement**. Many of the terms of a joint venture agreement will be similar to those found in the JVC's shareholders' agreement (see ¶6600+). In practice, however, it is usually important for the joint venture to have separate accounts and, for the other reasons outlined at ¶6552 below, a separate company is normally preferable.

6552 There are certain **advantages to using a private limited company** over other business media. In the particular context of a joint venture, the factors to consider are:
a. **limited liability** from the claims of third parties in the event that the JVC fails;
b. a **separate legal personality** so the business can develop in its own name and generate its own goodwill. If appropriate, this could make it easier for the participants to realise the value of the joint venture, e.g. by sale to a third party or listing on a public market. In addition, if the joint venture fails, the participants may find it easier to distance themselves from the failure, both legally and commercially. The disadvantage of a separate identity is that the joint venture will have to be run in the best interests of the JVC, and not those of the participants, although it is rare in practice for these to conflict. Conflict of interest issues are usually most relevant to directors who are on the board of both a participant and the JVC, particularly if there are arm's length contracts between the participant and the JVC (¶6578+); and
c. as a separate company the JVC will have to **file records at Companies House**, which means that some information will be public (e.g. shareholdings, directorships, accounts).

However, there is considerable scope for the private arrangements between the participants to be kept confidential through the shareholders' agreement (¶6600+).

A. Joint venture company (JVC)

6560 Where a joint venture is conducted through a private company limited by shares, the participants become shareholders of the JVC and thereby become co-owners of the enterprise. There are essentially **two choices** for the participants, both of which are examined in further detail. The participants can either:
– incorporate a new company to act as the JVC; or
– use an existing wholly-owned subsidiary of one of the participants.

New company

6561 A newly incorporated company is the most common type of JVC. The participants are each issued with shares in the new company in return for either a transfer of assets or cash, or a mixture of both. Equally, the new company could act as a parent, by the participants transferring shares in their subsidiaries to the new company in exchange for shares.

The main **advantages** of using a new company are that:
– it is "clean", that is to say, it has no trading history or potential liabilities which will impact upon the joint venture; and
– the share structure can be easily set up to meet the needs of the participants.

The main **disadvantages** are that:
– any assets relating to the joint venture which need to be owned by the JVC will have to be transferred to the new company. This could result in tax liabilities; and
– since the company has no trading history, any bank lending may have to be guaranteed by the participants. In practice, the likelihood of this will depend on the bank's view of its own exposure (see ¶6576+).

6562 Incorporation of the new company is usually arranged by one the participants, who will be expected to warrant that the company has been properly incorporated, has never traded and has no liabilities (see ¶6606). These **warranties** are uncontroversial and there should be no problem in giving them. Where the incorporation was arranged by the participant's adviser, the participant may request a **comfort letter** from the adviser to the effect that the warranties being given are true and accurate. This provides a remedy over and above a claim for negligence should there turn out to be a problem with the new company. Advisers should check that their professional indemnity insurance would cover a claim under a comfort letter.

Existing wholly-owned subsidiary

6563 Sometimes, it may be more appropriate to use an existing subsidiary of one of the participants to act as the JVC, for example, the existing subsidiary may own many of the assets which are to be used in the joint venture.

The **other participants** will then need to become shareholders of the existing subsidiary. As with a newly incorporated JVC, this could be achieved through an issue of new shares in exchange for a transfer of assets or cash. Alternatively, shares could be transferred to the others by the participant who is the parent of the proposed JVC. In such a case, the consideration for the transfer would be paid to the parent participant rather than to the JVC itself.

The use of an existing subsidiary requires consideration of the following range of issues:
a. the external participants will usually expect detailed **warranties and indemnities** from the parent participants regarding the business of the proposed JVC so that they are not exposed to pre-joint venture liabilities;

b. any assets held by the proposed JVC which are not required for the joint venture will have to be transferred to another company in the parent participant's group. Since the **transfer of assets** is in connection with the external participant's acquisition of shares in the proposed JVC, there is a possibility that the transfer could amount to unlawful financial assistance (see ¶5557+) and a "whitewash" may be required (see ¶5586+. This will only be necessary until the law changes, the date of which is yet to be announced at the time of writing). In addition, the usual tax considerations when transferring assets within a group will need to be considered;

c. before or at the same time as the issue or transfer of shares to the external participants, the **share structure** of the proposed JVC will need to be altered to meet the requirements of the joint venture. This could involve an alteration of share capital (¶1312+) and the adoption of new articles of association; and

d. the **tax consequences** of the proposed JVC leaving the parent participant's tax group will need to be considered. For example, tax charges may arise in respect of intra-group transfers in the previous 6 years and a decision will need to be made about how any tax losses will be utilised.

B. Preliminary issues

1. Relationship between JVC and participants

The relationship between the JVC and the participants operates on many different levels. The participants:
- are **shareholders** in the JVC (¶6569+);
- provide its **assets** (¶6573+);
- provide its **funding**, at least initially (¶6575+); and
- usually seek to participate in its **commercial decisions and management**, even if they are not involved on a day to day basis (¶6578+).

6568

Shareholders

The participants' holding of **ordinary shares** in the JVC is one of the essential features of a joint venture and many matters regarding how it will be run are set out in the shareholders' agreement which is examined in detail below at ¶6600+.

6569

The **proportion** of shares held by each participant is purely a matter for commercial negotiation. The starting point is usually the value of each participant's contribution, but this is often contentious, particularly if one of the participants is bringing something intangible, such as management skills or contacts, or a piece of commercially untested but potentially promising intellectual property. Often a financially/commercially stronger participant will be able to negotiate a higher proportion of shares relative to its contribution. In some cases, the participants will have equal ordinary shareholdings and, if necessary, any extra contribution by one of them will be compensated in other ways (e.g. through the issue of non-voting redeemable preference shares, licence fees for the use of assets, or the payment of management charges for administrative assistance).

6570

> MEMO POINTS Where there are only **two participants**, a 50/50 shareholding split will ensure that neither will be able to take action without the consent of the other. In practice, the shareholders' agreement will usually provide for what should happen in that circumstance. There are often deadlock provisions (see ¶6625+) but there may also be a casting vote given to one participant, particularly if there are outstanding loan monies due to him (¶6575). Where there are **more than two participants**, each should consider the fact that it could be outvoted by the others together. Minority participants should consider introducing veto rights in relation to important decisions in a shareholders' agreement (see ¶6616).

Share classes

6571 It is also common for **each participant** to hold a different class of ordinary share. This is necessary if the participants are to have rights particular to their shares. If this is the case each participant (or group of participants) will constitute a separate class of shareholder. Class rights can only be altered with the consent of the shareholders in that class (see ¶1270+) and so the rights of the participants, particularly minority shareholders, will be better protected.

6572 Normally, aside from the specific rights, each class will carry **mirror rights** so that on all other matters the participants will rank equally. It is common to find the following specific **class rights**:
– that each class has the right to appoint a director (¶6579);
– that each class' director must be present at any board meeting in order for the meeting to be quorate;
– that a member of each class must be present at any shareholder meeting in order for the meeting to be quorate; and
– that the shareholders of a class will have pre-emption rights over other shareholders in respect of the shares in that class.

Sometimes, especially where one participant is a minority shareholder, a particular class may be given **veto rights** over certain shareholder resolutions (e.g. the appointment of a director or the allotment of shares). In practice, it is far more common to have the veto rights as a contractual right in a shareholders' agreement rather than enhanced voting rights under the articles (¶6616). Where they are included in the articles, such rights should be expressed as enhanced voting rights in respect of a shareholders' vote on the subject in question (the so-called "*Bushell v Faith* clause"), rather than a straightforward power to veto the resolution, which could be seen as a fetter on the company's statutory powers and rights (*Southern Foundries (1926) Ltd v Shirlaw* [1940] 2 All ER 445; *Russell v Northern Bank Development Corp Ltd* [1992] 3 All ER 161).

Assets

6573 The participants will normally have agreed to a joint venture because each has assets (in the widest sense of the word) which can only be exploited to their maximum potential when combined with the assets of the others. For example, one participant may own the intellectual property rights to a new product whereas the other may own the manufacturing plant capable of building it. It is therefore necessary for the participants to **identify which** assets they will be contributing to the joint venture.

6574 The participants will then have to agree how these assets will be made available to the JVC. There are effectively two choices either:
a. the asset is retained by the participant, and **leased or licensed to the JVC**. This is usually the preferred choice when it is agreed that the participant will use the asset in its other operations and it is intended that it will not be for the exclusive use of the JVC. It is important that the terms of the lease or licence are carefully considered. The other participants will need to ensure that they do not give the person granting it the ability to prevent the asset from being used by the JVC. In practice it is usual for the person granting the lease/licence to be able to terminate it in specified circumstances, e.g. if the JVC is the subject of insolvency proceedings or materially breaches the terms of the licence. The JVC (as lease/licence holder) should avoid a time or other limit on use, or a general ability of the person granting the licence to terminate. The JVC may also want to be able to sue or terminate the lease/licence if the asset is shown not to be owned by the grantor; or
b. the asset is **transferred to the JVC**, in exchange for an allotment of shares, or with the consideration left outstanding as a loan payable when the JVC can afford to do so. This can be interest-bearing, but often it carries no interest. There may be tax liabilities on the asset transfer. Broadly speaking, the taxation treatment will depend upon whether or not the JVC is part of the transferring participant's group.

> MEMO POINTS Where the relevant **asset** is actually **held by a participant's subsidiary**, a refinement of option b. is for the participant to transfer its shares in the subsidiary to the JVC. The JVC

thereby becomes the holding company of the relevant subsidiary and is able to put the appropriate intra-group arrangements in place for use of the relevant asset. Consideration will have to be given for the tax consequences of the subsidiary leaving the participant's group.

Funding

From the participants

The JVC may have received some cash from the participants in exchange for it allotting shares to them. The participants will usually ensure that their **capital contributions** are sufficient for the foreseeable future. Additional working capital, if required, is also often provided by way of further capital contributions (i.e. in exchange for a further allotment of shares). Alternatively, further capital can be provided by way of **loans**.

The participants will need to agree on the **amount** of loan or capital each will provide and the circumstances in which further funding will be provided. This is often subject to an overall cap and dependent upon sound financial management, for example, the production of budget forecasts. Commonly, matching funding arrangements are agreed (that is to say, each participant agrees to match the funding of the others).

The manner and extent of funding from participants is usually specifically dealt with in the shareholders' agreement (see ¶6619+).

> MEMO POINTS 1. Where funding is provided by way of capital contributions, particularly if one participant is providing extra funding, the participant often takes **redeemable convertible preference shares**. Such shares are a quasi-loan form of equity (see ¶780+; ¶817+). This participant often has a casting vote until the preference shares are either redeemed or converted.
> 2. Where funding is provided by way of a **loan**, the repayment terms will need to be carefully considered as they could affect the JVC's ability to pay dividends, redeem or pay interest on preference shares or pay licence or lease fees to participants for the use of assets. The JVC directors will also need to ensure that the loan is on competitive terms as the directors must only enter into it if it is likely to promote the company's success. Commercially, it is unusual for the terms to be onerous. A participant may take security in respect of a loan, but this is unusual. In practice, security would only put the participant in a preferable position as compared to ordinary creditors because if, as is likely, the JVC later wanted to borrow from a bank, the bank would require the postponement of the participant's security.

From third parties

The JVC may also wish to obtain **loans** from third parties, such as a bank. If the track record and general standing of the participants is good, the bank is unlikely to insist on its funding being guaranteed by them, and will rely on a **comfort letter** instead.

Less commonly, the bank may insist on its loans being guaranteed by the participants. Where the **guarantee** is provided by more than one participant, the bank will normally insist on being able to pursue any of them for the whole amount outstanding should the guarantee be called in. The participants should therefore consider entering into some form of contribution agreement so that each participant pays a proportionate amount of the liability (¶5975+). In addition, the participants will need to ensure that they are able to give the guarantee under the terms of the security for their existing bank facilities (e.g. by obtaining specific bank consent). This could give rise to practical difficulties, particularly where different banks are involved.

In any event, most shareholders' agreements will **limit the JVC's borrowing capacity** and will require it to obtain the prior consent of the participants before incurring any borrowing (see ¶6616).

Commercial decisions and management

The participants are usually able to exert a level of control over the commercial decisions and management of the JVC by requiring prior **shareholder consent** for certain decisions (see ¶6616).

In addition, the share rights of the participants usually give each of them the ability to **appoint at least one director** to the board of the JVC. The role and duties of the JVC's directors are the same as that of any other company. As a result, particular conflict of interest issues may arise for directors appointed by a participant. Most fundamentally, the directors of the JVC must promote the success of the JVC for the benefit of its shareholders as a whole, not just the person or company that nominated them (see ¶2379+). If the appointed director is unable to act in the best interests of the JVC, he may have to consider resigning.

Directors nominated by the participants may be supplemented by other, **independent, non-executive directors**.

2. Competition law

6583 There are two aspects of UK and EU competition law which need to be considered when a joint venture is being contemplated:
– **merger control** provisions; and
– restrictions against **anti-competitive agreements**.

The local competition laws of any **other jurisdictions** in which the participants operate must also be considered.

Where there are any competition concerns, it is usual for completion of the joint venture to be conditional upon the receipt of any necessary **competition clearances** or consents.

> MEMO POINTS Once the joint venture company has been set up, the participants must ensure that it does not **abuse any dominant position** it may have in the particular market of goods or services in which it operates as this could be a breach of a third limb of UK and EU competition law (s 18 Competition Act 1998, known as the "Chapter II prohibition"; art 82 EC Treaty).

Merger control

6584 Merger control provisions have been considered in the context of buying and selling a company (see ¶5505+).

The **EU merger control** provisions will only apply if the joint venture is "full-function". A JVC will be full-function if it performs on a lasting basis all the functions of an autonomous economic entity. If the JVC simply takes over one specific function within the participants' business activities, for example, sales or research and development, then the EU merger control provisions will not apply. Further guidance on the application of the EU provisions to joint ventures is available in the consolidated Commission Jurisdictional Notice (IP/07/1043).

The **UK merger control** provisions will apply if the EU provisions do not.

Anti-competitive agreements

6585 UK and EU competition law prohibit agreements (s 2 Competition Act 1998; art 81 EC Treaty):
– which may **affect trade** within the UK or between EU member states (as appropriate); and
– which may have as their object or effect, the **prevention, restriction or distortion of competition** within the UK or within the EU common market, or a substantial part of it (as appropriate).

Common restrictions which will come within the ambit of the prohibition are:
– price-fixing agreements;
– non-competition agreements; and
– undertakings in supply contracts between the JVC and participants.

UK competition law is applied and enforced by the OFT. Since 1 May 2004, the OFT, as well as the European Commission, has also had the power to apply and enforce EU competition law. The **OFT guidance** "Agreements and concerted practices" explains these provisions and how the OFT expects them to operate. It is available to download from the OFT's website.

3. Pre-contractual documents

6591 In some respects, a joint venture transaction can appear similar to a company sale or purchase in that it will bring together two or more companies. As a consequence, some of the pre-contractual documents are similar. In particular:

a. a participant seeking potential joint venture partners may prepare an **information memorandum** which describes the deal on offer (see ¶5227+);

b. the participants will need to maintain **confidentiality** during negotiations. This will entail the preparation of a confidentiality agreement and the maintenance of effective document control by each participant (see ¶5244+). In addition, confidentiality will need to be ensured during the period of the joint venture and after its conclusion. This is particularly the case when the joint venture is between participants who would otherwise be competitors. Confidentiality is therefore normally also dealt with in the shareholders' agreement (¶6624);
c. once the deal has been agreed in principle, it is sometimes recorded in a non-binding document known as the "**heads of agreement**" (see ¶5529+). This may also contain contractually binding provisions in which the participants agree to deal with each other exclusively for a limited period and/or to pay the aborted costs of the other participants, should one of them withdraw from negotiations; and
d. some level of informal **investigation**, or "due diligence" is likely to be required in order that each participant can gauge the prospects of the joint venture and the legal and financial position of the other participants (see ¶5652+).

These measures help to protect the parties at this early stage, when they are sharing potentially valuable information before the actual JVC documents are in place.

> EXAMPLE Mr B had an idea for a project to raise money for the acquisition, consolidation and operation of veterinary surgeries and practices through a company to be floated on the Stock Exchange. He approached Mr C to discuss the project with a view to raising finance and Mr C agreed to participate as financier. However, after several months of negotiations with various parties, Mr C teamed up with other joint venturers, found finance for and pursued the project through a JVC without Mr B.
> Mr B claimed breach of contract, or alternatively that Mr C held some of his shares in the JVC on trust for him. Both of these claims were rejected by the court. The agreement between Mr B and Mr C was too vague to amount to an enforceable contract. The constructive trust point failed because there was no suggestion of an arrangement or understanding that Mr C would acquire or try and obtain shares in the JVC on behalf of Mr B, nor that Mr B relied on any such arrangement or understanding. The court did acknowledge that the project was Mr B's idea, that he had done work on it to make it commercially viable and that he had not been paid for what he had contributed in ideas or work. It suggested that the idea should have been protected by a binding contract, or by an action for breach of confidence (which had not been pursued). Payment for work done in anticipation of a contract that is never concluded may have given rise to an implied contract to pay for the work, or to a restitutionary claim for unjust enrichment (but no such claims were made in the case) (*Cayzer v Beddow* [2007] EWCA Civ 644).

C. Key JVC documents

1. Shareholders' agreement

6600 The shareholders' agreement is the most important JVC document as it usually determines the participants' dealings with each other and the JVC. The **main clauses** of a JVC shareholders' agreement are examined below.

6601 A shareholders' agreement is often used to give shareholders protection over and above that in the company's articles. The **advantages** of using a shareholders' agreement instead of including these matters in the articles are:
a. the document can be kept private, whereas the articles have to be filed at Companies House and are therefore available to the public;
b. the shareholders may have direct contractual remedies against the company and the other shareholders, rather than having to rely on derivative actions which can be difficult to establish. This would depend on the circumstances of each case as, in many situations, the other shareholders may still be able to argue that the loss is not recoverable by the aggrieved shareholder as it merely reflects the loss to the company (see ¶2464; ¶7127+); and

c. as with all contracts, all the parties will need to consent in order for it to be amended (unless the agreement itself sets out a mechanism whereby it can be amended with the consent of the majority), whereas the articles can be amended by a 75% majority.

6602 It is important to remember that a shareholders' agreement is a contract between the parties to it. This means that new shareholders will not be bound by its terms. As a consequence, any significant new shareholders should be made to execute a "**deed of adherence**" in which they agree to be bound by the terms of the agreement as if they had been a party to it. Normally, execution of a deed of adherence is a pre-condition to the registration of a share transfer. However, the requirement applies equally to a new participant who is issued with shares. A template deed of adherence is usually attached as a schedule or appendix to the shareholders' agreement.

> MEMO POINTS **Small shareholders**, particularly key employees who acquire a small shareholding as a consequence of exercising options, are often excluded from signing up to a shareholders' agreement (and therefore any deed of adherence) for practical and administrative reasons.

Parties

6603 Clearly, the **participant** shareholders will be parties to the agreement. Where the participant shareholder is a shell or minor subsidiary of the "real" participant, it may be appropriate to obtain **parent company guarantees** in respect of the shareholders' liabilities under the agreement. When incorporating a parent company guarantee into an agreement, care should be taken in the drafting to ensure that the guarantee covers all potential payments (or specifically excludes payments that the guarantee is not supposed to cover).

> EXAMPLE AMS Ltd and WS Ltd entered into a joint venture to construct a block of flats, setting up a subsidiary of AMS Ltd as the JVC. The joint venture was to be funded by loans from a bank and WS Ltd. The facility letter setting out WS Ltd's funding arrangements was annexed to the joint venture agreement between the three companies, which obliged the JVC to repay any money advanced to it by WS Ltd under the facility letter, among other things. AMS Ltd guaranteed the JVC's obligations under the joint venture agreement. The joint venture was not a success and the JVC ended up in liquidation with monies outstanding to WS Ltd.
> WS Ltd claimed under the guarantee. AMS Ltd accepted that it was liable in respect of loan monies advanced by WS Ltd to the JVC, because these were specifically referred to in the joint venture agreement. WS Ltd also claimed that AMS Ltd was liable in respect of management charges debited from the JVC's loan account under the facility letter. These charges were not specifically referred to in the joint venture agreement. AMS Ltd argued that it guaranteed the JVC's obligations under the joint venture agreement, not the facility letter.
> The court held that AMS Ltd was liable for both the loan monies and the management charges. Although they were separate documents, the facility letter was annexed to the joint venture agreement and referred to in it. It was clear that the JVC's obligations had to be interpreted in the light of both documents. The management charges were debited from the JVC's loan account, and the JVC would have been liable to repay the sum due under the account. On the other hand, some of the other charges under the facility letter were found to be excluded from the guarantee (*Wolsey Securities Ltd v Abbeygate Management Services Ltd* [2007] EWCA Civ 423).

> MEMO POINTS Note that some obligations in the agreement (e.g. the confidentiality clause and restrictive covenants) may extend beyond the participants to their "**associates**", which will need to be defined. The associates will not be a party to the agreement, but instead each participant will be required to "procure" that its associates comply with the relevant requirement. If the associates fail to comply, then the participant will be in breach of contract and will have to pay damages calculated by reference to the amount that the associate ought to have paid if it could have been sued. For example, if a participant agreed to procure that its subsidiary repaid a loan and the subsidiary failed to do so, the participant would be liable in place of the subsidiary. An agreement to procure compliance with a contract term is therefore more than an administrative burden; it has the same legal effect as a guarantee (*Nearfield Ltd v Lincoln Nominees Ltd* [2006] EWHC 2421 (Ch)).

6604 It is also usual to find that the **JVC itself** is also a party. Where necessary, this enables the participants to sue the JVC under contract, instead of relying on their statutory rights as shareholders. However, the JVC cannot enter into obligations that restrict the exercise of its statutory powers. For example, it cannot agree to comply with the instructions of a participant with only 20% of the vote, when normally the action would require an ordinary resolution passed by more than 50% of the vote. Therefore, instead of the JVC entering into such obligations, the clause setting out the matters which require shareholder consent (¶6616) is usually drafted so that the participants agree to procure that the JVC does not do any of the matters listed without the appropriate level of consent.

> MEMO POINTS In some cases, the JVC will have, or will be likely to acquire, subsidiaries with which the participants will also want to have a contractual relationship. Accordingly, any existing **subsidiaries of the JVC** will normally be joined as a party to the agreement and the JVC will usually be required to procure the joining of any future subsidiaries.

Completion

6605

Completion of the shareholders' agreement (and therefore the joint venture deal) will usually be conditional upon matters which occur at the same time as the agreement is signed so that there is **no gap between exchange and completion**. For example:
– completion of other collateral agreements (e.g. an asset or share sale agreement, a loan agreement, directors' service contracts);
– the passing of any relevant board and shareholder resolutions (e.g. change of name resolutions, allotment of shares); and
– the participants subscribing for their relevant shareholdings in exchange for the agreed consideration.

Occasionally, completion is conditional upon transaction-specific matters such as the obtaining of relevant tax and competition clearances, or third party consents. Further drafting points arise where conditions have to be satisfied after the agreement is signed so that there is a **gap between exchange and completion** (see ¶5732; ¶5865).

Warranties and indemnities

6606

Warranties and indemnities will be required from the participant "responsible" for the JVC. Where the JVC is **newly incorporated** and the participant was merely responsible for its formation, the warranties will be minimal and uncontroversial (¶6562). Where the JVC was an **existing subsidiary** of one of the participants (¶6563), extensive warranties and indemnities similar to those found in a share sale and purchase agreement may be required (see ¶5814+).

Relationship with articles

6607

It is important that the shareholders' agreement is considered together with the JVC's articles, and that there is **no conflict** between them. In most cases, the articles will require amendment too (see ¶6630+).

Nevertheless, the participants must consider what should happen in the event of **conflict**. Usually, the participants will wish the provisions of the agreement to prevail over the articles as it has been the subject of detailed negotiation. However, an agreement which purports to amend the articles would have to be registered with Companies House (s 29 CA 2006). Therefore, the agreement normally expressly states that it is not intended to be an amendment of the articles but, if necessary, the participants agree to amend them to give effect to the terms of the shareholders' agreement.

The agreement will also normally state that the participants agree to **exercise their voting rights** to ensure that the articles are complied with. This provides the participants with a contractual remedy should a participant fail to comply with the articles, rather than relying on derivative actions which may be difficult to establish.

6608

Share transfers

6609

Most JVCs have restrictions on share transfers since the individual participants/shareholders are required for the success of the joint venture and each has made a personal commitment to the project. The level of restriction will vary from joint venture to joint venture. However, it is usual to find extensive **pre-emption provisions** (see ¶1842+) which mirror those found in the JVC's articles. Alternatively, instead of repeating the share transfer restrictions in the shareholders' agreement, it could simply state that any issue of new shares or transfer of shares must be in accordance with the articles.

6610 It is important that the implications of the share transfer restrictions are properly thought through. For example:
a. should corporate participants be permitted to **transfer shares within their group**? This is usually permitted but often with the proviso that it is done for bona fide tax planning reasons;
b. should individual participants be permitted to **transfer shares to family members or trusts?** Again, this is usually permitted but often with the proviso that it is done for bona fide tax planning reasons;
c. should participants be able to **transfer only part, but not all**, of their shareholding, thereby leading to a diversification of the shareholder base and the potential for minority shareholders to hold the balance of power?
d. if the JVC has different classes of shares, should participants be free to **transfer shares within their class**? If there are several shareholders holding one class, for instance a number of individuals acting in concert, it may be permitted for those shareholders to transfer to another person within, but not outside, the class;
e. should the **consent of all the shareholders be required for a transfer** which would result in a change of control in the JVC?
f. should there be "**drag along**" **rights** which permit a specified majority of shareholders (or in some cases a minority shareholder) to force a sale of the company, including the sale of the shares of the other shareholders? If there are drag along rights it is usual for there to be "**tag along**" **rights** which give the right of the minority shareholders to sell their shares on the same terms as the majority shareholders.

It is usual to find **mandatory transfer provisions** which compel a shareholder to offer its shares for sale to the other shareholders. In the case of a corporate shareholder this is usually in the event of a participant getting into financial difficulties or breaching the agreement. In addition, in the case of an individual this usually also extends to the individual dying, becoming mentally incapacitated, or, if he is an employee or director, breaching his terms of employment or directorship.

6611 Other restrictions often found in JVC shareholders' agreements are:
– a **lock-in**, which prevents the participants from voluntarily disposing of their interest in the JVC's shares for a specified period of time or until a particular event occurs (e.g. a particular profit level is reached). This ensures that the participants are tied into the JVC for a minimum period;
– that a participant will not transfer its shares unless the person to whom the shares are being transferred executes and delivers a **deed of adherence** (¶6602); and
– **restrictive covenants** (¶6624).

6612 Finally, the agreement must deal with the position of a participant which has transferred its shares. Should it be **released from its obligations** and liabilities if the transfer was in accordance with the agreement/articles? The usual compromise is that:
– a participant will not be released from its obligations if the transfer is to another group company, family member or trust. This is because the person to whom the shares have been transferred may not be as solvent as the participant, or may be off-shore;
– where the participant has no interest in any JVC shares following a transfer, it will be released from all obligations except any of an ongoing nature, such as intellectual property and confidentiality obligations and restrictive covenants; and
– where the participant retains an interest in any JVC shares, it will only be released with the consent of the other shareholders.

6613 It is also important to think through the practical effects of a participant leaving the joint venture. How will this **affect other arrangements** such as asset leases, financing or management? The agreement will need to set out whether these arrangements will continue. The negotiations between the participants should result in a compromise between the need for the existing participant to leave the joint venture with as little exposure to risk as possible, and the need for the remaining participants to ensure continuity of the JVC.

Management

6614 Control over the JVC's management is one of the key provisions in the agreement, as this is the practical way in which each participant can protect its interest. Each participant will normally be entitled to **nominate a director** to the JVC's board (see ¶6579). Where each participant has shares of a different class, the right to nominate a director may be expressed as a share right and mirrored in the articles, although often it is only a contractual right under the shareholders' agreement. The agreement will normally specify whether the nominee directors are entitled to any remuneration for their position and that any alternate that they appoint will have to be approved by the board.

6615 It is also usual to see provisions regarding **board meetings**, including:
– the chairman (e.g. who should act and whether he has a casting vote);
– the appropriate quorum (e.g. at least one director nominated by each participant);
– the frequency with which they are held;
– notice provisions (including whether a director who is absent from the UK must be given notice);
– the location;
– the ability to appoint an alternate director (usually, the alternate will be able to vote and count towards the quorum); and
– practical considerations such as whether a board meeting can be held by telephone or video conference.

6616 However, the participants will exercise the highest degree of control through the list of actions which require prior **shareholder consent**, sometimes referred to as "veto rights". The level of consent required will determine the amount of control which may be exercised by a particular participant. Where the unanimous consent of the shareholders is required, even minority shareholders will hold the power of veto. Where 75% of shareholders need to consent, the majority will prevail.

The list of prohibited actions without consent is usually extensive and each participant should ensure that their particular concerns are covered. By way of example, the list usually requires a specific level of shareholder consent for:
– acquiring or disposing of shares, a business or an undertaking;
– borrowing or giving security;
– entering into any material contracts;
– altering the memorandum, articles or share capital;
– making a distribution other than in accordance with an agreed dividend policy;
– incurring any extraordinary capital expenditure;
– appointing directors or high-level employees;
– adopting and altering the budget or business plan;
– altering the auditors, accounting policies or accounting reference date;
– materially changing the nature of the JVC's business;
– disposing of any material assets;
– granting options or pension arrangements; and
– commencing or defending material litigation.

6617 The agreement may also normally set out any **positive ongoing arrangements**. For example, regarding:
– dividend policy;
– VAT registration and tax compliance;
– insurances; and
– protection of key assets such as intellectual property.

Financial reporting

6618 Another important way in which the participants maintain control over their interest in the JVC is through financial reporting. **Regular reporting** may not be necessary if the investment is not material to the participants, or if all of the participants are involved in the management of the JVC. In most cases, however, some degree of reporting is normally required. The participants should ensure that a balance is struck between their ability to access up to date financial information and the JVC being able to conduct its business without unnecessary administrative burdens.

Particular provisions which may be considered are a **budget** agreement mechanism and a requirement to provide each shareholder with regular financial **information** in the form of annual audited accounts and management accounts. The frequency of financial information depends on the size and nature of the JVC; often quarterly management accounts are provided. The agreement also often states who is to act as the **auditor**, the **accounting reference date** and the **accounting policies**.

Funding

6619 The participants will need to consider how the JVC will be financed. The **initial funding** by the participants (by way of loans or a subscription for shares in the JVC in exchange for cash and/or assets) is often sufficient to start with.

6620 If the JVC requires further **funding in the future** it may need to consider raising working capital from bank lending or from the shareholders. However, in many cases, the JVC will require additional working capital from the participants.

If the participants are comfortable with committing to further funding, the agreement will need to specify the necessary **pre-conditions**. When drafting the pre-conditions, the following should be kept in mind:

a. however tight the drafting, opinions on whether the JVC requires further funding are likely to differ. It is therefore usual for the participants to agree that the level of further funding, perhaps subject to an overall cap, has to be consented to by a specified percentage of shareholders or the board of directors. In the event of deadlock, the matter could be referred to an independent accountant. However, this could be difficult in practice as the accountant will be required to determine a question of commercial opinion, where both opinions are potentially equally valid, rather than a matter of fact;

b. there may be agreement on the nature of funding (i.e. by way of loan or capital and, if capital, whether by subscription for ordinary shares or preference shares);

c. the participants should agree on the proportion of funding expected from each of them (e.g. most often in accordance with their percentage shareholdings) and the advance from each participant should be conditional upon the others fulfilling their obligation. Often if one participant does not agree to provide further funding, the terms of the loan or capital are enhanced in favour of the participants who do; and

d. it may be unfair for a participant to provide further funding if the shortfall was caused by another participant breaching the terms of the agreement. The drafting could require the participant at fault to make up the shortfall.

The agreement will also need to set out **when and how** the funding will be provided (e.g. within 1 month of the agreement or determination that funding is required, and either in exchange for non-voting preference shares or in return for loan notes issued under a pre-agreed loan note instrument). This will often be all that is included if the participants are reluctant to agree to commit to an obligation to provide future funding.

6621 As discussed above (see ¶6575+), the participants may take on financial liabilities to third parties (e.g. by guaranteeing the JVC's bank borrowing) which could result in one participant incurring more than its fair share of liability. It is therefore usual to find cross-indemnity and **contribution** clauses in the shareholders' agreement, so that the paying participant is able to claim any overpayment it makes from the others.

Trading with participants

6622 Any supply or service arrangements between any participant and the JVC will need to be **separately recorded** (for example, a lease of property or an agreement for the supply of goods or services).

The shareholders' agreement will normally state that any trading arrangements between the participants and the JVC must be on **arm's length terms**. This reflects the fact that the JVC has its own legal identity. Any trading arrangements on **favourable terms** should be properly documented and the parties should bear the following in mind:

- the tax consequences of the arrangement;
- the duties of the directors of each company to promote the success of his company in the interests of its shareholders as a whole; and
- the risk that a transaction at an undervalue could be set aside on insolvency.

The participants should also consider the ability of the JVC to pursue any of them for a **breach** of any trading arrangements. A participant may be able to prevent the JVC from commencing and pursuing litigation because of his shareholding, the balance of power at board level or the list of actions requiring consent in the shareholders' agreement (see ¶6616). It is therefore usual to find a provision in the shareholders' agreement under which the participants agree not to impede the JVC from pursuing a claim against them.

Protection of business

The participants will need to ensure that the JVC's business is protected from interference by their own activities. This is achieved through the shareholders' agreement containing:
- **confidentiality** undertakings from each of the participants in respect of themselves and their associates (see ¶5245+ for a discussion of confidentiality undertakings, albeit in the context of buying and selling a company); and
- **restrictive covenants** which prevent the participants from competing or interfering with the JVC's business. Careful thought will have to be given as to how the "business" of the JVC is defined to ensure that the obligations are enforceable (see ¶5736+).

> MEMO POINTS It may be more appropriate for these obligations to be given to the JVC rather than to the other participants as it will be easier for the JVC to **prove loss** in the event of breach. On the other hand, where the JVC has suffered the loss, the participants will not be able to recover that loss themselves because of the "proper claimant" principle (see ¶7124+).

Deadlock provisions

At the start of any joint venture, the participants are usually co-operative and confident that their collaboration will be a success. There will be considerable goodwill on both sides and relations between the individuals involved are likely to be good. However, in hoping for the best, the participants must remember to plan for the worst; personalities and priorities change. One such worst case scenario is where the participants are unable or unwilling to make decisions, leaving the JVC in an effective **state of paralysis**. This is normally referred to as "deadlock".

Deadlock provisions must be seen as a last resort, when **relationships** between the participants have **irretrievably broken-down**. Before they are invoked, the participants are usually required to try to negotiate a compromise, sometimes through a mediator. Assuming there is no prospect of agreement, a deadlock can be resolved in a number of ways.

Where the participants each want to carry on the JVC, the agreement can provide for a "**russian roulette**" solution whereby each participant who wishes to carry on with the business despite the deadlock makes a simultaneous sealed offer for the shares of the other participants. The party making the highest offer has the right to purchase the shares of the other participants at the price offered. This is likely to favour the financially strongest participant, although even a financially strong participant is still unlikely to want to pay more than what it considers to be a fair price.

Other solutions are, for example, that:
- the participants are allowed to offer their shares for sale in accordance with the JVC's pre-emption provisions;
- a participant's shares are bought back by the JVC;
- the participants are required to co-operate in a sale of the JVC to a third party; and/or
- the JVC is put into voluntary liquidation.

The **drafting** and practical consequences of each choice must be considered carefully. In some cases, it may be better to offer **alternative options**. For example, that a participant can offer to sell its shares, but if no other participant accepts and the JVC has insufficient funds, a third party should be found to purchase the JVC's entire issued share capital. If no third party can be found within a specified period, the JVC should be put into voluntary liquidation.

MEMO POINTS One alternative to a "russian roulette" clause is a "**Texas shoot-out**" clause. This works as follows. If A wants to leave the JVC, it serves a "buy notice" on B, offering to buy B's shares for a specified price. B then serves a counter notice stating that either (a) it is prepared to sell its own shares to A at the price offered in A's notice, or (b) that it wishes to buy A's interest at a higher price than that offered in A's notice. If both parties want to buy the other's shares, a sealed bid system is used. Obviously, the party making the higher bid takes over the JVC.

Standard clauses

6627 The standard, so-called "boiler plate" clauses are similar to those found in a share sale and purchase agreement (see ¶5740) with some differences, mainly because a JVC deals with an ongoing commercial relationship and a sale and purchase relates to a one-off event. For example, the JVC shareholders' agreement will usually expressly state that no partnership exists between the participants.

2. Articles of association

6630 A company's articles of association are a public document setting out the way in which the company is to be managed. Legislation has prescribed a model set of articles, Table A, which will apply to a company unless the shareholders agree otherwise (see ¶441+).

There will be some areas where **Table A conflicts with** the provisions of the **shareholders' agreement** or where particular provisions are inappropriate for a JVC. The choice is therefore either to exclude and/or amend the parts of Table A which are inappropriate or to exclude the whole of Table A and adopt completely new articles. The latter choice has the advantage of all of the articles being contained in one document, making for easier reading and comparison with the provisions of the shareholders' agreement. However, it is more common to see JVCs with articles which generally include Table A and make amendments where necessary as most of Table A is likely to be suitable.

In either case, the starting point for the JVC's articles is Table A. This will need to be compared to the shareholders' agreement and viewed in light of the participants' intentions so that any areas of conflict are resolved.

MEMO POINTS A new set of model articles prescribed in regulations made under the **new Companies Act** will apply to companies incorporated from October 2009. At the time of writing, they are in draft form. Like Table A, the new model articles will need to be tailored to suit a JVC by excluding or amending certain provisions, or by replacing them altogether. For companies incorporated on or after 1 October 2007, Table A will apply with specific modifications to account for the provisions of the new Act already in force at that time. Different amendments apply depending on whether the company is private limited by shares or public; the changes are noted at ¶9915. Further transitional amendments are likely to be made to take the changes coming into force on 6 April 2008 into account as well.

6631 In addition, the JVC's articles may also have to be amended to include:
– the different **share classes** and their class rights (¶6571+);
– the **issue of new shares**;
– the **share transfer restrictions** and **pre-emption provisions** (see ¶6609+); and
– **drag along** and **tag along** rights.

D. Taxation

6640 There are four main tax issues to consider when setting up a JVC:
– whether the levels of shareholdings in the JVC are such that it belongs to a group of companies;
– the availability of **group loss relief** and **consortium relief** (see ¶6641+, ¶6650+);
– the tax consequences for participants who **transfer assets to the JVC** in exchange for the JVC issuing the participant with shares. Broadly speaking, the taxation treatment will depend upon whether or not the JVC is part of the transferring participant's group; and

- **VAT registration**. Depending upon the participants' shareholdings, the JVC could be part of a participant's group VAT registration. However, since the JVC will then be jointly and severally liable for the group's VAT responsibility, JVC's are usually separately registered. Supplies between the participants and the JVC will therefore be subject to VAT in the usual way.

See *Tax Memo* for further details.

1. Group relief

Group loss relief allows **losses** incurred by a company to be utilised by other companies in the same group, so as to reduce those companies' profits chargeable to corporation tax (s 402 ICTA 1988). The relief must be claimed by the company which wishes to utilise the loss and the company which incurred it must formally consent to surrender that loss.

6641

The following losses are **eligible** for group relief (s 403 ICTA 1988):
– trading losses, including capital allowances;
– non-trading loan relationship deficits;
– charges on income, to the extent that they cannot be used by the surrendering company; and
– Schedule A business losses (i.e. losses arising from an interest in UK land or property), to the extent that they cannot be used by the surrendering company.

Losses may be **surrendered** as follows:
– by a parent company to one or more of its subsidiaries;
– by a subsidiary to its parent; or
– by a subsidiary to its fellow subsidiaries.

Group relief could therefore be particularly useful at the beginning of a joint venture, when the JVC may be loss-making, as it enables a profitable participant (such as the JVC's parent) to utilise those losses.

Conditions

Group relief is available to companies who are members of a **75% group**. For such a group to exist, the parent participant must be beneficially entitled to not less than 75% of the share capital, distributable profits and assets on a winding up. Holdings may be direct or indirect.

6642

EXAMPLE

A Ltd
|
95%
|
B Ltd
|
80%   A Ltd owns (95% x 80%) = 76% of C Ltd
|
C Ltd
| A Ltd owns (95% x 80% x 98%) = 74.5% of D Ltd
| B Ltd owns (80% x 98%) = 78.4% of D Ltd
98%
| There are two 75% groups. A Ltd, B Ltd and C Ltd form one group, and B
D Ltd   Ltd, C Ltd and D Ltd form another

MEMO POINTS   Enforceable **options** granted over shares affect the ownership of the company for group relief purposes and may therefore result in the holding falling below the required level.

As of 1 April 2006, losses have been able to be surrendered by any company in the group which is **resident**, or has a **permanent establishment**, in the UK or an EU member state.

6643

Before this date, group relief was only available between UK resident companies/permanent establishments. Where a company's accounting period straddles 1 April 2006, the period is split into two notional periods.

> MEMO POINTS 1. There are special rules for calculating the amount of relief where the surrendering company is trading via a **UK permanent establishment** or an **overseas permanent establishment** (i.e. resident in the UK but trading overseas) (ss 403D, 403E ICTA 1988). In brief, losses by such companies can only be group relieved if:
> – they are attributable to activities which, if profitable, would be subject to UK corporation tax; and
> – they cannot be offset against the non-UK profits of a third party for the purposes of any foreign taxes.
> Similarly, where a non-UK resident company with a permanent establishment in the UK wishes to utilise another company's losses, those losses can only be set against profits which are subject to UK corporation tax and are not excluded, for example, under a double tax agreement.
> 2. Where the surrendering company is not resident in the UK but is **resident in the EU** or carries on trade via a **permanent establishment in the EU**, the EU losses may only be available for group relief it they meet certain qualifying conditions (see *Tax Memo*) (Sch 18A ICTA 1988). Where these conditions are met, the EU loss must be recalculated in accordance with UK tax rules. If the recalculation produces a loss, that amount is available for surrender. If it produces a profit, no group relief can be surrendered.

6644 Group relief is only available in full where the companies form part of the same group throughout the accounting period. Where **arrangements exist for the sale** of a group company, group relief is only available until the date the arrangements came into force (s 410 ICTA 1988).

> MEMO POINTS The legislation does not define "arrangements". A JVC shareholders' agreement which contains mandatory share transfer provisions upon the occurrence of particular events is **not an arrangement** until one of those events actually occurs (ESC C10). Simple negotiations for the sale of a company do not constitute arrangements until an offer is accepted subject to contract, or on similar terms, e.g. when written heads of agreement are issued. Arrangements can exist even where the sale proves abortive. Similarly, where the disposal requires shareholders' approval, arrangements do not exist until the approval is given, or before the directors become aware that approval will be given (SP 3/93).

Calculation

6645 Losses available for group relief are set off against the profits of the company claiming the relief, assuming that the claimant has already set its own trading losses against its income. Group relief is given after any reliefs of the same or an earlier accounting period, but in priority to any losses carried back from a subsequent period.

> EXAMPLE A Ltd incurs a trading loss of £5,000 and has rental business profits of £17,000. Its profits for group relief purposes are £12,000. It is irrelevant whether a claim for loss relief in respect of the £5,000 is actually made or whether the loss is utilised in another way.

6646 Losses can only be set against profits of the **overlap period**. This is the part of the surrendering company's accounting period which overlaps with the claimant company's accounting period for which both companies were members of the same group (s 403A ICTA 1988).

Where both companies have the **same accounting period**, the whole period will be the overlap period.

Where they have **different accounting periods**, or one of the companies ceases to be a member of the group, losses can only be set against profits of the period which is common to both companies. To calculate the maximum group relief, it is necessary to calculate the loss of the overlap period and the profit of the overlap period. The maximum amount that can be surrendered is the lower of these two figures.

As companies have consecutive accounting periods, the whole loss incurred during the accounting period of the surrendering company will generally be available. However, it may be split between two different accounting periods of the claimant company.

> **EXAMPLE** A Ltd prepares accounts annually to 31 December and has a loss available for group relief of £16,000 for the period ended 31 December 20X4 (it makes a profit in other years). B Ltd prepares accounts annually to 30 June and has profits for the period ended 30 June 20X4 of £15,000 and 30 June 20X5 of £20,000. The maximum group relief is calculated as follows:
>
> | | Start | End | |
> |---|---|---|---|
> | A Ltd AP | 01/01/X4 | 31/12/X4 | |
> | B Ltd AP | 01/07/X3 | 30/06/X4 | |
> | Overlap period 1 | 01/01/X4 | 30/06/X4 | i.e. 6 months |
> | | | | |
> | B Ltd AP | 01/07/X4 | 30/06/X5 | |
> | Overlap period 2 | 01/07/X4 | 31/12/X4 | i.e. 6 months |
>
> A Ltd – eligible loss:
>
> | | | |
> |---|---|---|
> | Overlap period 1 | 6/12 x £16,000 | £8,000 |
> | Overlap period 2 | 6/12 x £16,000 | £8,000 |
>
> B Ltd – eligible profit:
>
> | | | |
> |---|---|---|
> | Overlap period 1 | 6/12 x £15,000 | £7,500 |
> | Overlap period 2 | 6/12 x £20,000 | £10,000 |
>
> Therefore the maximum group relief A Ltd can surrender to B Ltd is:
> £7,500 for the corporation tax period ended 30/06/X4; and
> £8,000 for the corporation tax period ended 30/06/X5

6647 Where the surrendering company is less than 100% owned by the claimant company, as would be the case in a JVC, it is common practice for the claimant company to make a **payment for the group relief surrender**. This compensates minority shareholders who may feel disadvantaged. Payments of up to £1 for every £1 loss surrendered are ignored for tax purposes.

6648 Where a group consists of more than two companies, it may allocate eligible losses to whichever group company it chooses, up to the **maximum group relief** available for each claimant company. Maximum benefit is generally obtained by allocating losses to companies in the following order:
a. those falling in the margin between the small companies' rate and the main rate of corporation tax (to reduce their profits to the small companies' rate threshold);
b. those paying corporation tax at the main rate; and
c. lastly, those paying tax at the small companies' rate.

However, the immediate cashflow advantage of surrendering losses against current year profits must be weighed against the merits of setting the loss against future trading profits which might be taxed at a higher rate.

Claims

6649 Claims for the relief must be **made on** the claimant company's corporation tax return, usually within 12 months of the filing date for the accounting period to which the claim relates. If there has been an enquiry into a return, the time limit is extended until 30 days after the conclusion of the enquiry or any resulting appeal.

The **claim must specify** the surrendering company and the amount claimed, and will be invalid if the amount claimed is greater than the actual loss available. Claims may be made for less than the maximum available. The claim must also state the residence of the claimant or surrendering company.

The surrendering company must notify the Inspector of Taxes of its **consent to the surrender**, no later than the date the claim is made. A copy of the consent notice must accompany the corresponding claim. If the surrendering company is resident in the EU, but not the UK, the notice must be given by the claimant company.

The consent notice should state:
– the claimant company's name;
– its tax district reference;

– the amount of relief surrendered (in the case of EU resident companies and permanent establishments, the EEA tax loss amount must also be specified); and
– the accounting period to which the surrender relates.

> MEMO POINTS 1. Once made, a claim cannot be **amended** but, within the time limits, it may be **withdrawn** and a revised claim submitted.
> 2. If a company has given its **consent to surrender** an amount which subsequently proves to **exceed the total loss available**, it must withdraw its consent within 30 days, submit a consent to a reduced claim and notify the claimant company of the reduction. If the surrendering company is EU resident or is an EU permanent establishment, the requisite notices must be given by the claimant company instead. The affected companies must then amend their corporation tax returns, if possible.
> 3. If the **group relief claimed is excessive** (e.g. because the amount claimed exceeds the loss available and the claimant company cannot amend its return), Revenue and Customs will issue an assessment to recover the tax lost.
> 4. Revenue and Customs may enter into **special arrangements** with a group so that the parent company (or other specified company) may act on behalf of the group members, amending returns as appropriate. The requirement for claims to be accompanied by a copy of the consent notice is waived in this situation. This has considerable administrative advantages for both the group and Revenue and Customs.

2. Consortium relief

6650 In addition, or as an alternative to the JVC belonging to a group with a participant, the corporate participants may form a **consortium** for tax purposes. A consortium exists when up to 20 companies (which in the case of a JVC will be the corporate participants) each own at least 5%, and jointly at least 75%, of the ordinary share capital of another company (which will be the JVC). To qualify, the JVC must be a trading company (which is not a 75% subsidiary of another company), or a holding company directly owning at least 90% of a trading company.

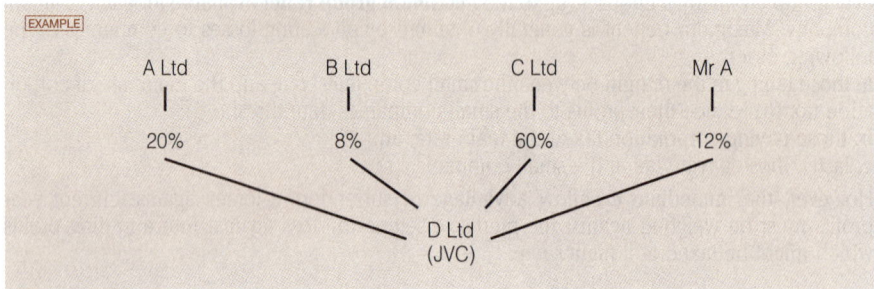

Consortia are entitled to a **modified form of group relief** known as consortium relief. This allows:
– a corporate participant to surrender its losses to the JVC or its 90% trading subsidiary; and
– the JVC or its 90% subsidiary to surrender its losses to the corporate participants.

> MEMO POINTS 1. Consortium relief is only available between companies that are **resident** in the UK or trading in the UK via a permanent establishment. The group relief rules for losses incurred by an EU resident company or an EU permanent establishment do not apply to consortia.
> 2. Both **group relief and consortium relief** may be available where either the JVC or corporate participant has 75% subsidiaries. The general rule is that group relief takes precedence over consortium relief, i.e. losses must first be utilised either notionally or actually under group relief rules and only the balance can be utilised under consortium relief rules. The exception is that if the loss-making company is a group and consortium member, it can surrender its losses in whichever order it chooses.
> 3. When a participant is both a **group member and consortium member**, it can act as a link company. This means that any losses which can be surrendered to it under consortium relief can be used by the participant itself or by its fellow group members. Similarly, any loss it incurs which is eligible for group relief can be surrendered to the JVC. This may be of benefit where the participant has insufficient profits to absorb the loss or pays tax at a lower rate than the JVC.

The **calculation** of consortium relief is the same as group relief, with equivalent restrictions for companies joining or leaving the consortium during a accounting period. However, the calculation is modified to take account of the holding of each corporate participant. Where the JVC (or its 90% trading subsidiary) incurs the loss, the loss may be surrendered in proportion to the participant's interest in the JVC. Where the participant incurs the loss, the loss can be surrendered in proportion to its interest in the profits of the JVC.

6651

> EXAMPLE A Ltd is a JVC and B Ltd a participant with a 30% interest. Both companies prepare accounts to 31 December. During a full accounting period, one of the companies makes a profit of £15,000 and one a loss of £12,000.
>
> If A Ltd incurred the loss, the maximum eligible for consortium relief would be:
> Interest x JVC loss   30% x £12,000   £3,600
>
> If B Ltd incurred the loss, the maximum eligible for consortium relief would be:
> Interest x JVC profit   30% x £15,000   £4,500

It is therefore important to correctly identify the **level of the participant's interest**. In most cases, this will simply be its percentage of ordinary shareholding. However, where the shareholding has varied through the accounting period, the appropriate percentage is the average holding over that period. Where the JVC has different issued share classes, the member's interest is taken to be the lowest of the following percentages:
– ordinary share capital held;
– entitlement to distributable assets on a winding up; and
– entitlement to distributable profits.

6652

Claims for consortium relief are made in the same way as for group relief (see ¶6649+).

6653

E. Accounting treatment

The accounting treatment of a JVC by the participants depends upon whether the JVC is deemed to be:
– a **subsidiary**;
– an **associate**; or
– a **joint venture**.

The explanations here are only a summary. A detailed explanation of the three types of treatment can be found in *Accountancy and Financial Reporting Memo*.

6655

Classification

The primary factor to differentiate between a subsidiary, associate and joint venture is the level of the participant's **control**. If a participant has overall control over the JVC then a parent/subsidiary relationship will exist. If a participant's influence over the JVC is not so dominant, then an associate or joint venture relationship may exist. The other relevant criteria are the degree of the participant's **involvement** in the JVC's operations and finances, and the participant's **long-term intentions**.

The table below is a **summary** of how the JVC should be classified.

6656

Arrangement	Nature of relationship	¶¶	Reference
Subsidiary	Participant controls JVC [1]	¶4382+	FRS 2; s 258 CA 1985 [2]
Associate	Participant holds a participating interest and has a significant influence but does not control JVC [3]	¶6657+	FRS 9/IAS 28; s 260 CA 1985 [4]; para 20 Sch 4A CA 1985 [4]
Joint venture	Participant holds long-term interest and shares joint control [5] under a contractual arrangement		FRS 9/IAS 31 [4]

Note:
1. See ¶194+ for the different types of **control** which give rise to a subsidiary relationship.
2. This will be restated in the **new Companies Act** (s 1162 CA 2006, which comes into force when necessary as various provisions which include the terms "parent" and "subsidiary" come into force).
3. In broad terms, the participant will be presumed to hold a **participating interest** and have a **significant influence** if it holds 20% or more of the JVC. The presumption of a participating interest can be rebutted if the participant's interest is neither long-term nor for the purpose of securing a contribution to the participant's activities. Under FRS 9, the participant must also exercise a significant influence by being actively involved and influential in the policy and strategic decisions of the JVC. The presumption of significant influence will be rebutted if these criteria are not met. Note that under IAS 28, the key issue is the existence of significant influence; there is no need for the participant to actually exercise that influence.
4. Under the **new Companies Act**, these provisions will be set out in regulations. Two sets of draft regulations have been published: one for small companies and one for medium-sized and large companies (see ¶4362+ for an explanation of these classifications), and are expected to apply to financial years starting on or after 6 April 2008. They allow JVCs which are managed by the company and another company outside of its group to be included in the company's group accounts and to be classified as "joint ventures" (para 18 Sch 6 in both the draft Small Companies and Groups (Accounts and Directors' Report) Regulations 2008 and the draft Large and Medium-sized Companies and Groups (Accounts and Reports) Regulations 2008). An "associated undertaking" is one in which the company has a participating interest and a significant influence over its operating and financial policy, but that is not a subsidiary or a JVC (para 19 Sch 6 of both sets of draft regulations).
5. The participant will be deemed to **jointly control** a venture with other participants if none of the participants alone can control the JVC but all together can do so, and decisions on financial and operating policy essential to the activities, economic performance and financial position of the JVC require each participant's consent. Where a participant **does not share joint control** (even if the other participants do), its interest in the JVC is merely an investment and should be accounted for as such.

Accounting for associates and joint ventures

6657 The accounting treatment for associates and joint ventures is broadly similar, but there are some differences in the presentation of information in the consolidated accounts.

Participant's individual financial statements

6658 Where the participant **does not prepare consolidated financial statements**, its individual financial statements should present the relevant amounts for the JVC by either (FRS 9(48)):
– preparing a separate set of financial statements; or
– disclosing the relevant amounts, together with the effects of including them, in the notes to its own financial statements.

Investing entities that are exempt from preparing consolidated financial statements, or would be if they had subsidiaries, are exempt from this requirement.

Where the participant **does prepare consolidated financial statements**, the participant's interest in the JVC should be treated as fixed asset investments and shown either (FRS 9(21), (26)):
– at cost, less any amounts written off; or
– at valuation.

Any goodwill arising should be separately identified.

Participant's consolidated accounts

6659 In the case of **associates**, the participant's consolidated accounts should include the JVC using the **equity method** of accounting. The objective is to reflect the actual relationship between the participant and JVC. The effect is that:
– the consolidated **profit and loss account** will show the participant's share of the JVC's results (rather than dividends paid to the participant);

– the consolidated **balance sheet** will include information based on the participant's share of the JVC's net assets (rather than the cost or market value of the participant's shareholding); and
– the consolidated **cash flow statement** will include the cash flow between the participant and JVC, including dividends and loans.

Comment: Under the draft regulations published under the **new Companies Act**, associated companies will be able to be included in the participant's consolidated accounts using the equity method (para 21 Sch 6 in both the draft Small Companies and Groups (Accounts and Directors' Report) Regulations 2008 and the draft Large and Medium-sized Companies and Groups (Accounts and Reports) Regulations 2008). These regulations are expected to apply to financial years commencing on or after 6 April 2008.

In the case of **joint ventures**, the participant should use the **gross equity method** of accounting. This is essentially the same as the equity method except that the following information should be presented separately from the group accounts:
– the participant's share of the JVC's turnover in the profit and loss account; and
– the participant's share of the JVC's gross assets and liabilities.

Further, any supplemental information given for the JVC (except for items below profit before tax in the profit and loss account) must be clearly separated from the group accounts and must not be included in the group totals.

6660

Comment: Under the draft regulations published under the **new Companies Act**, joint ventures will be able to be included in the participant's consolidated accounts using the proportional consolidation method (para 18 Sch 6 in both the draft Small Companies and Groups (Accounts and Directors' Report) Regulations 2008 and the draft Large and Medium-sized Companies and Groups (Accounts and Reports) Regulations 2008). These regulations are expected to apply to financial years commencing on or after 6 April 2008. This will allow the participant to apply the usual rules in preparing consolidated accounts, with any necessary adjustments to reflect the proportion of its holding in the joint venture. Companies will have to state the factors on which the management of the joint venture is based and the proportion of the capital of the joint venture held by the participant and other companies included in the consolidated accounts (para 27 Sch 6 the draft Small Companies and Groups (Accounts and Directors' Report) Regulations 2008; para 18 Sch 4 the draft Large and Medium-sized Companies and Groups (Accounts and Reports) Regulations 2008).

SECTION 3

Takeovers

The **definition** of a takeover can be broken down into the following ingredients:
– an attempt by a person, normally a company rather than an individual (known as the "**bidder**");
– to acquire control over a company (known as the "**target**");
– by way of an offer on the same terms to all of the target's shareholders to buy their shares, which they are invited to accept by a particular date (known as the "**takeover offer**").

The target's board can recommend the offer to the target's shareholders (known as a "**recommended** takeover") or it can oppose the takeover (known as a "**hostile** takeover").

6675

> MEMO POINTS In the UK takeover market, the words **merger** and takeover are used interchangeably. "Takeover" implies that the bidder is larger than the target, whereas "merger" implies that the bidder and target are companies of equal size or standing. In both cases, the result is the same. The identities of the target and bidder are unchanged at completion and they continue to exist as separate entities. Where the bidder is a company, the target will become its immediate subsidiary. However, the motive for a takeover may entail some rationalisation of the businesses in order to make them more profitable. Note that "merger" has a particular meaning for accounting purposes (¶6901).

6676 A takeover offer is normally only **issued when** the target is a public company or a private company which has been listed or which has issued a prospectus in the previous 10 years. This is because these companies usually have a diverse shareholder base and it is not possible to negotiate with the shareholders either individually or collectively.

By contrast, where the target is a **private company**, the acquisition is normally achieved through one to one negotiations between the prospective buyer and the target's shareholders. This is because private companies normally have a limited base of shareholders who can negotiate collectively. Such transactions are dealt with in detail at ¶5200+.

A **reverse takeover** is one where the target is larger than the bidder. The result is that the target shareholders become majority shareholders in the bidder.

6677 **Takeovers of public companies**, whether listed or unlisted, are regulated by the City Code on Takeover and Mergers, which is administered by the Panel on Takeovers and Mergers. The public company takeover process is dealt with in further detail at ¶6685+, after an overview of the regulatory framework. In the case of targets with fewer than ten shareholders, the Panel may grant a "Code waiver", that is, agree not to apply the Code to a particular transaction (¶6760+).

6678 After a takeover process has been completed, even if it was successful in gaining control, the bidder is unlikely to have acquired 100% of the target's shares. A bidder can only guarantee achieving **100% control** of a public or private company target either by way of:

a. statutory **compulsory acquisition** provisions: these could apply where, following a takeover offer, the bidder has acquired 90% of the target's shares which it or parties with whom it is acting in concert do not already hold (¶6930+). These provisions give the bidder the right to buy the remaining shares and also give the remaining minority shareholders the right to force the bidder into buying their shares; or

b. a **scheme of arrangement**: this could be available if the takeover is recommended and the bidder has control of over 75% of the target's voting shares, or the support of 75% of the target's shareholders (¶6985+). A scheme of arrangement is therefore an increasingly popular alternative to a formal takeover.

I. Public company takeovers

6685 In order to understand the takeover process, it is first necessary to understand the **regulatory framework**.

Takeovers of listed and unlisted public companies are regulated by the **Panel on Takeovers and Mergers**, the function of which is to ensure the fair conduct of a takeover bid from the point of view of shareholders. It does this by publishing and enforcing the City Code on Takeovers and Mergers.

Other regulatory considerations in a takeover are:
– **financial services** regulation (¶6686);
– **prospectus** requirements (¶6687); and
– **merger control** provisions (¶5505+).

Where the transaction has an **international** dimension, the regulatory environment in other jurisdictions may be relevant. Similarly, there may be specific regulatory considerations depending upon the **industry sector** in which the target operates.

> MEMO POINTS   Where the target or bidder is **admitted onto a public market**, such as the London Stock Exchange, consideration will have to be given to:
> – the rules of the relevant market;
> – additional rules in the Code which are only relevant for companies whose shares are dealt with on a regulated market;

– the criminal offence of insider dealing, which in general only applies to dealings on a regulated market (Pt V Criminal Justice Act 1993); and
– restrictions to prevent market abuse (Pt VIII FSMA 2000).
Listed companies and dealings on public markets are outside the scope of this work and so these issues will not be examined further.

Financial services regulation

Financial services regulation which regulates the making of "financial promotions" is discussed at ¶4825+. For the purposes of takeover activity, it is likely that communications with the target's shareholders (e.g. the offer document, the target board's circular if it recommends the offer, and other announcements, advertisements or telephone campaigns promoting the offer) will constitute a communication to invite or induce an engagement in "**investment activity**" within the meaning of financial services regulation. Such communications must therefore either come within an **exemption** or be approved by an **authorised person**.

6686

Prospectus requirements

There is a requirement to publish a prospectus approved by the UKLA (part of the FSA) when a public company offers transferable securities to the public, even if they are unlisted (see ¶4845+). Therefore, the **prospectus regime will** be likely to **apply when**:
– the bidder offers its own shares in exchange for shares in the target; or
– the bidder offers transferable loan notes as alternative consideration to a cash offer. An offer of loan notes would fall outside of the prospectus regime if the loan notes included transfer restrictions.

6687

There are some **exemptions** available to the requirement to produce a prospectus, one of which is in connection with takeovers and mergers. Guidance on this exemption was provided by the UKLA in *List!* (Issue No. 10, June 2005). Where transferable securities are offered in connection with a takeover or merger, there is no requirement to produce a prospectus if a document is available containing information regarded by the UKLA as being equivalent to a prospectus. A bidder therefore has the choice of whether to prepare a prospectus or an equivalent document. A prospectus benefits from "passport provisions" (this means that the document will be approved for sending to the target's shareholders throughout the EU) which do not apply to equivalent documents. However, this benefit is probably outweighed by the statutory right for shareholders to be able to withdraw their acceptances to prospectus offers, which goes beyond the withdrawal rights in the City Code. It is therefore likely that bidders will use an equivalent document rather than a prospectus.

See ¶6990 for the application of the prospectus regime to a takeover by way of a scheme of arrangement.

Takeover Directive

The European Directive on Takeover Bids (the "Takeover Directive") (EC Directive 2004/25) had to be implemented into the national law of member states by 20 May 2006.

6688

The Directive was **fully implemented** when the relevant provisions of the new Companies Act came into force on 6 April 2007 (ss 942-992 CA 2006; SI 2007/1093). As with the City Code, these provisions apply to unlisted and listed public companies, and to certain private companies (see ¶6755+).

In addition to the legislative changes, the Panel has made related **changes to the Code**, which have also been in force since 6 April 2007.

> MEMO POINTS 1. The new Companies Act has also made changes to the statutory **compulsory acquisition** procedures (see ¶6930+).
> 2. The provisions of the new Companies Act dealing with takeovers also apply to takeovers of **unregistered companies** which have shares traded on a regulated market (SI 2007/318).

A. The Panel on Takeovers and Mergers

6700 The Panel on Takeovers and Mergers is an independent body, designated to act as the supervisory authority to regulate takeovers in the UK. Its main **functions** are to issue and administer the City Code on Takeovers and Mergers and to supervise and regulate takeovers and other matters to which the Code applies. Membership of the Panel is drawn from the UK's major financial and business institutions.

Day to day **decisions** regarding the application of the Code are made by the Panel Executive. Disciplinary decisions regarding sanctions for breach of the Code are made by the Hearings Committee. **Appeals** from the Panel Executive are also heard by the Hearings Committee and appeals from the Hearings Committee are heard by the Takeover Appeal Board, an independent tribunal. In practice, recourse to the courts is limited.

1. Function

6705 The Panel's **function is** to ensure the fair and orderly conduct of a takeover bid from the point of view of shareholders by administering the City Code on Takeovers and Mergers. Its functions are now conferred on it by the new Companies Act (s 942 CA 2006).

The Panel's **function is not** to consider:
– the financial or commercial implications of a takeover. These decisions are for the target and its shareholders; or
– whether the takeover is in the public interest, for example, whether the takeover would restrict competition. These issues are for the government and other regulatory bodies, for example, the Office of Fair Trading, the CIB, the Competition Commission or the European Commission.

2. Decision making and appeals

The Panel

6710 The Panel comprises a Chairman, up to two Deputy Chairmen and up to twenty other members, all of whom are appointed by the Panel. The remainder of the **membership** is nominated by various financial and securities related associations and bodies (e.g. the Association of British Insurers, the Confederation of British Industry and the Institute of Chartered Accountants in England and Wales).

6711 The day to day work of the Panel is carried out through the Panel Executive (¶6712+). Publication and review of the Code is carried out through the Code Committee (¶6716). Appeals from the Panel Executive and disciplinary proceedings are heard by the Hearings Committee (¶6717+).

The Panel assumes overall **responsibility** for the policy, financing and administration of the Panel's functions and for the functioning and operation of the Code. It is directly responsible for those matters not dealt with through one of the Panel's committees (Intro para 4(a) City Code).

The Panel Executive

6712 The Panel Executive is headed by the Director General, usually an investment banker on secondment, who is an officer of the Panel. The Executive is independent of the Panel and although it has some permanent **members**, many are on secondments from banks and leading law and accountancy firms.

6713 The Panel has delegated **responsibility for** day to day decisions regarding the application of the Code to the Panel Executive. The Executive monitors every takeover and checks that all documents and announcements issued, and actions taken, comply with the Code.

The Executive is available for consultation before or during a takeover transaction (Intro para 6 City Code). **6714**

The Executive's general **guidance** on interpretation of the Code can be sought and it handles many such queries. Guidance can also be sought in relation to a specific issue on a "no names" basis, where the person seeking the guidance does not disclose to the Executive the names of the companies concerned (to preserve commercial confidentiality). In either case, the guidance is not binding.

The Executive can also be asked for a **ruling** based upon the particular facts of a case. If the Executive is able to hear the views of all the parties involved, it will give an **unconditional** ruling as to the basis on which the parties can proceed to minimise the risk of breaching the Code. An unconditional ruling is binding on those who are made aware of it unless and until overturned by the Hearings Committee or the Takeover Appeal Board (s 945 CA 2006).

If the Executive is not able to hear the views of the other parties, it may give a **conditional** ruling, which could be varied or set aside when the other parties' views are known. Persons who are made aware of a conditional ruling have to comply with it.

In addition to giving rulings at the requires of a party, the Executive may give rulings on its own initiative.

Appeals from rulings of the Executive are heard by the Hearings Committee (¶6717+). **6715**

[MEMO POINTS] As a separate issue from appealing against its rulings, **complaints** about the Executive's service can be referred to the Panel's Complaints Office. Details of how to make a complaint can be found on the Panel's website.

The Code Committee

The Panel has delegated **responsibility for** reviewing the Code to the Code Committee (Intro para 4(b) City Code). The Code Committee will, where appropriate, issue amendments to the substantive provisions of the Code. Usually, the Code Committee will publish a consultation paper before any such amendments are made. A copy of past and current consultations, and the response to them, can be viewed on the Panel's website. **6716**

Membership of the Code Committee is drawn from the Panel.

Hearings Committee

The Hearings Committee comprises the Chairman of the Panel, up to two Deputy Chairmen and up to eight other **members** designated by the Panel (Intro para 4(c) City Code). **6717**

Its **function** is to (Intro para 7(a) City Code):
– review rulings of the Executive;
– hear disciplinary proceedings instituted by the Executive when the Executive thinks there has been a breach of the Code; and
– hear any particularly unusual, important or difficult matters referred to it by the Executive.

The Hearings Committee's **proceedings** are informal and normally in private (Intro para 7(c) City Code). Its quorum is five (including the Chairman). Each party usually presents his case in person and, although each can be legally represented, this is not usual. The parties should briefly present their case in writing beforehand. At the hearing, the parties can call on witnesses if necessary, with the consent of the Chairman. The parties will normally be able to hear and review all of the evidence before the Committee, but the disclosure of evidence can be restricted in exceptional cases, for example, if it is commercially sensitive. The Committee will provide a reasoned decision to the parties as soon as practicable after the hearing. The decision will normally be published by way of a Panel Statement on the Panel's website. **6718**

Any party to a hearing before the Hearings Committee (or any person denied permission to be a party) may **appeal** to the Takeover Appeal Board against any ruling of the Hearings Committee or its chairman (including in respect of procedural directions). **6719**

Notice of the appeal must be given within the time period stipulated by the Committee or its chairman. If no time period is stipulated, notice must be given within 2 business days of the receipt in writing of the Hearings Committee's, or Chairman's, ruling (Intro para 7(e) City Code).

Takeover Appeal Board

6723 Appeals from the Hearings Committee are heard by an independent body known as the Takeover Appeal Board (Intro para 8 City Code). The Takeover Appeal Board is **headed by** a Chairman who is appointed by the Master of the Rolls and will usually have previously held high judicial office. The remainder of the Board is appointed by the Chairman.

Appeal hearings are generally conducted in the same way as Hearings Committee hearings, using the Board's Rules, which are available on its website. The quorum for an appeal hearing is three, but the Board hearing an appeal will usually comprise at least five members.

The Board is able to confirm, vary, set aside, annul or replace a ruling by the Hearings Committee. Having come to a **decision**, the Board will remit the matter back to the Hearings Committee, with such directions (if any) as it considers appropriate to give effect to its decision (Intro para 8(c) City Code). The Board's decision will be provided in writing to the parties as soon as practicable and will usually be published in a public statement as well.

6724 The Panel's decisions are subject to **judicial review** by the courts. However, in practice the courts are reluctant to interfere with a decision and will generally limit themselves to reviewing the decision making process once the bid has been concluded (R v Panel on Takeovers and Mergers, ex parte Datafin plc [1987] 1 All ER 564). As a consequence, tactical litigation (that is, legal proceedings taken by parties to a bid with a view to frustrating or hampering the bid or the target's defence) is not currently a feature of UK takeover practice.

There was a risk that **tactical litigation** would have increased upon implementation of the Takeover Directive (¶6688) as, once the Panel and Code were given statutory force, the parties to a bid could have brought civil litigation actions based on the interpretation or application of the Code. Tactical litigation is seen as undesirable because it can deny the shareholders of the target the opportunity of deciding upon the merits of the bid and can be costly and time-consuming, prolonging uncertainty in the market. Therefore, the following provisions were included in the new Companies Act to **avoid** tactical litigation:
– rights of action for breach of statutory duty are excluded (s 956 CA 2006);
– transactions are not capable of being set aside by reason of a breach of the Code or failure to comply with a Panel ruling (transactions can still be set aside in cases of misrepresentation or fraud) (s 956 CA 2006);
– parties are bound by a ruling, unless reviewed by the Hearings Committee or successfully appealed to the Appeal Board (s 945 CA 2006);
– no party other than the Panel is entitled to apply to court for an order to enforce Panel rule-based requirements or requirements for the disclosure of documents or information (s 955 CA 2006); and
– the Panel and those involved with it are immune from liability (except if they have acted in bad faith or where the immunity would contravene the Human Rights Act 1998) (s 961 CA 2006).

3. Powers

6729 The Panel is the **supervisory authority** to regulate takeovers under the Takeover Directive (¶6688). This means that it has statutory authority and compliance with its rulings is a legal requirement for all companies involved in a takeover to which the Code applies (s 942 CA 2006).

> MEMO POINTS **Until 6 April 2007**, when the relevant provision of the new Companies Act came into force, the Panel operated as a peer review system, on the basis of consent amongst professionals working in the field of takeovers and supported by statute-backed organisations.

Information gathering

6730

The Panel obtains information regarding takeovers from the parties to the transaction and their advisers. The Code places a specific **disclosure obligation** on persons dealing with the Panel to disclose to it any information known to them that is relevant to the matter being considered (and to correct or update that information if it changes). The is subject to legal professional privilege. Where a matter has been determined by the Panel and a person becomes aware that the information they supplied to the Panel was incorrect, incomplete or misleading, the person has to contact the Panel promptly to correct the position (Intro para 9(a) City Code; s 947 CA 2006). The Panel has the power to require any person to provide it with any documents or information that are reasonably required in connection with the exercise of its functions, subject to legal professional privilege (Intro para 9(b) City Code; s 947 CA 2006). It will do so by issuing a notice setting out the information required, how it should be verified and by what date it must be supplied. Failure to comply is a breach of the Code.

In practice it is usually extremely difficult to circumvent the Panel by not reporting information, as it also obtains **information from**:
– the financial press;
– the London Stock Exchange's computerised systems for the surveillance of markets and dealings, to which it has direct access;
– advisers, who are required to co-operate with the Panel in its investigations by the FSA and certain professional bodies; and
– a mutual exchange of information with other regulatory bodies such as the FSA and the CIB. The Panel is a designated authority under the Companies Act 1985 and the Financial Services and Markets Act 2000 to receive regulatory information.

Enforcing the code

6731

The Panel has various **powers** to enforce the Code, which it will use where necessary to remedy a particular breach (Intro para 10 City Code). In many cases, disciplinary action will be more appropriate, in which case it will rely on those measures instead or as well (see ¶6732 below). The Panel has the following powers to enforce the code (Intro para 10 City Code):
– to give a **direction** preventing a person from breaching the Code (including on an interim basis whilst the matter is awaiting determination by the Panel) or to ensure compliance with the Code (s 946 CA 2006);
– in the case of breaches of rr 6, 9, 11, 14, 15, 16 or 35.3 of the Code, to require the **payment of compensation** and interest to the holder or former holders of securities in the target to ensure that they receive whatever amount they would have been entitled to receive had the relevant Rule been complied with (s 954 CA 2006);
– to apply to court for an order to secure compliance with a Panel ruling or request for documents or information (s 955 CA 2006). Failure by a person to comply with a resulting court order is contempt of court; and
– a breach of the Rules relating to the offer and response documents (i.e. rr 24, 25, 27 (as far as it requires the offer or circular to be updated), 30.1, 30.2, 32.1 and 32.6A) constitutes an offence, rendering the person in default liable to a fine (s 953 CA 2006).

> MEMO POINTS   Breach of a rule-based requirement does not give rise to a right of action for **breach of statutory duty** (s 956 CA 2006). This is one of the measures included in the new Companies Act to prevent tactical litigation, see ¶6724.

Disciplinary powers

6732

In addition to its powers to enforce the Code, the Panel can ensure compliance with its decisions through a range of less formal sanctions (Intro para 11 City Code):
– **private censure**;
– **public censure**. Public criticism by the Panel during the course of a takeover bid is likely to damage the bidder's prospects of success, as shareholders are likely to treat documents which have been publicly criticised by the Panel with suspicion. Further, public criticism by the Panel of a professional involved in a takeover is likely to lead to a loss of professional standing;

– the suspension or withdrawal of an exemption, approval or other **special status** which the Panel has granted to the person;
– **reporting** the offender's conduct **to another regulatory authority** for it to take action (e.g. the CIB, the FSA, Stock Exchange or a relevant professional body). Most professionals working in the takeover market rely on FSA authorisation to carry on their business. FSA enforcement action against an authorised person found to be in breach of the Code could include public censure, fines, the removal of authorisation, the imposition of injunctions and orders for restitution. In addition, the CIB could take breaches of the Code into account in the course of an investigation into the conduct of a company or its directors; and
– the Panel can prevent a transgressor from having recourse to professional advice by triggering "**cold-shouldering**" procedures by the FSA and certain professional bodies. These prohibit their members from acting for a person in a transaction that is subject to the Code.

B. The takeover process

6745 The public company process is governed by the **City Code on Takeovers and Mergers** ("the Code") which sets out the way in which takeovers should be conducted.

A **summary** of the most important provisions of the Code is given below, followed by a detailed examination of:
a. the **scope** of the Code (¶6755+), including the type of companies and transactions to which the Code applies, how to gain exemption from it (known as a "Code waiver"), and some important definitions used in it;
b. the **pre-offer considerations** (¶6776+), including the requirement for absolute secrecy until the bid is announced, when pre-offer announcements must be made and the effect of pre-offer share dealing;
c. the **offer process** (¶6805+), including when a mandatory offer must be made, how to make a voluntary offer and the offer timetable;
d. the rules governing the **conduct of the parties** during an offer (¶6850+), including the effect of share dealing during the offer period, important disclosure requirements for most shareholders, a restriction on the use of frustrating tactics by the target's board and the requirements regarding the provision of information to shareholders; and
e. finally, a look at the **consequences** of the two outcomes of a takeover offer (¶6900+), namely a successful offer and an unsuccessful offer.

Summary

6746 The spirit of the Code is enshrined in six General Principles which are statements of the accepted standards of commercial behaviour. The General Principles are expanded upon by 38 Rules which also govern specific aspects of takeover procedure. A **key feature** of the Code is its flexibility and the Panel's ability to apply it to new situations as they arise. Copies of the full Code can be bought from the Panel or downloaded from its website.

The **general principles** of the City Code are:
– all holders of shares of the same class in the target company must be treated equally;
– the holders of those shares must have enough time and information to enable them to make an informed decision about the bid;
– the board of the target company must act in the interests of the company as a whole, and must allow the shareholders to make a decision about the bid;
– there must be no false markets created and therefore no distortion of the markets as a whole;
– the party making the bid must not announce it unless it has the cash to satisfy any cash component of the offer; and
– in running its business the target must not be handicapped by the bid for any longer than is reasonably necessary

The most **important provisions** of the Code are summarised in the table below.

Subject	Summary	¶¶	Reference (City Code)
Equality between shareholders	– Equal treatment of target's shareholders by bidder	–	GP 1
	– No favourable terms for selected shareholders	¶6788	r 16
	– All shareholders should be provided with the same information, except for confidential information passed by target to bidder	¶6873+	r 20.1
Making an offer	Announcement of the offer should only take place if bidder can and will continue to be able to implement it. Responsibility for this also rests with bidder's financial adviser	¶6816+	r 2.5
Mandatory cash offer	When a person or group acquires shares carrying 30% or more of the voting rights of company, a mandatory cash offer must be made to all remaining shareholders at the highest price it paid for those shares in the previous 12 months	¶6805+	r 9
Cash alternative	Even if the bidder is offering its own shares as consideration, a cash alternative must be made available to holders of a particular class of shares, at least at the highest price paid by bidder, if it acquires shares of that class for cash: – during offer period; or – during offer period or previous 12 months, where those shares carry 10% or more of the voting rights of that class of shares	¶6854	r 11.1
Increase offer	If the bidder acquires target's shares at a higher price than offered, the offer must be increased to at least that price	¶6853	r 6.2
Provision of information	– Target's shareholders must be given sufficient information to make an informed decision	¶6872+	GP 2, r 23
	– Target's board must appoint an independent adviser to give his opinion on the offer. The views of the target's board and the adviser must be circulated to target's shareholders	¶6882+	rr 3.1, 25.1
	– Documents sent to the shareholders or advertisements published in connection with the offer must include a statement of responsibility for its contents from each of the directors of target and, if appropriate, each of the directors of bidder	¶6879+	r 19.2
	– Parties must endeavour to prevent the creation of a false market or uncertainty. Misleading, inaccurate or unsubstantiated statements in documents or media must be publicly corrected immediately	¶6876+	GP 4, rr 19.1, 19.3
	– Profit forecasts and asset valuations must comply with specific standards and must be reported on by professional advisers	¶6884	rr 28, 29
Disclosure of share dealings	Share dealings during the offer period are permitted but there are strict disclosure requirements which apply to most shareholders (not just the bidder)	¶6860+	r 8
Frustrating tactics	Target's directors may not take action to frustrate a bona fide takeover offer unless they have the shareholders' consent	¶6865+	GP 3, r 21
Timetable	Offer process must be carried out within the Code's timetable	¶6827	rr 30-34

1. Scope of the Code

Application of the Code

6755 The Code applies to transactions where the **target** is any one of the following types of company (Intro para 3(a) City Code):
- listed and unlisted public companies;
- private companies, if their shares had been listed or otherwise subject to public dealing at any time in the previous 10 years, or they have issued a prospectus in the 10 years prior to the date of an announcement; and
- European Companies (¶88+).

The transaction will only come within the Panel's jurisdiction if the target is **resident** in the UK, Channel Islands or Isle of Man. As far as unlisted companies are concerned, the Panel will consider a company to be resident if it is incorporated, and has its place of central management, in one of those jurisdictions. Both limbs of the test must be satisfied for the Code to apply.

Comment: Although the Code applies to takeovers of companies in the **Channel Islands** and the **Isle of Man**, it does not have statutory force in these areas (unless and until legislation to that effect is passed, s 965 CA 2006). Therefore, the Code must be followed, but the Panel cannot invoke its statutory powers in relation to such takeovers.

> MEMO POINTS The Panel **shares jurisdiction** with its counterpart authority in another EU member state where the target is (Intro para 3(a) City Code):
> - a UK incorporated company listed on a regulated market in another member state;
> - incorporated in another member state but listed only on a UK regulated market; or
> - in certain circumstances, incorporated in another member state and listed on regulated markets in more than one member state including the UK.
>
> The Panel has published guidance on the circumstances in which the Code will apply to a **cross-border merger** (see ¶6536/mp; Practice Statement 18 of 2007). Broadly, these are where the Code applies to at least one transferor company in a merger by absorption or a merger by formation of a new company. Parties should consult the Executive at an early stage when considering entering into any cross-border merger that may be subject to the Code.
>
> Further, where the **target is listed** on a UK, Channel Islands or Isle of Man regulated market (currently, these are certain markets operated by the London Stock Exchange and virt-x, and CISX in Guernsey, but not AIM or the PLUS Markets Group), it is not necessary for the company's place of central management to also be within the jurisdiction. Any offer for such a company will be covered by the Code if it has its registered office in the UK, Channel Islands or Isle of Man. If the company's securities are traded in the same member state as its registered office, the regulator of that member state has sole jurisdiction.

6756 The Code applies to all takeover and merger **transactions** where control over a relevant target is being sought or consolidated, including (Intro para 3(b) City Code):
- new share issues;
- partial offers (e.g. to minority shareholders);
- share capital reorganisations;
- an offer by a parent for shares in a subsidiary; and
- statutory mergers and Court approved schemes of arrangement.

The Code does not apply to offers for non-voting, non-equity shares unless the bidder already holds such shares when it makes an offer (r 15 City Code).

Code waiver

6760 Under an established procedure, the Executive may agree that the Code will not be applied to a transaction (known as a "Code waiver") **when** the target has ten shareholders or fewer and it would be inappropriate or unduly onerous to apply the Code. The Executive will not grant a Code Waiver unless it is satisfied that all the shareholders have had their rights under the Code fully explained to them and agree to the waiver. The Executive's practice in relation to Code waivers is set out in the "Note to advisers in relation to Code waivers", which is available on the Panel's website.

A waiver from the Panel is the only way to disapply the Code. A company and its shareholders cannot **contract out** of the Code, for example, by including a provision to that effect in the company's articles.

> MEMO POINTS   1. For these purposes, "**shareholders**" **includes** anyone who holds shares (in any class), options, warrants or other rights to apply for equity share capital.
> 2. The waiver is transaction specific. It is not possible to obtain a waiver in respect of all **future transactions** relating to the target.

The **procedure** for obtaining a Code waiver is as follows:

6761

Step	Action
1	The target's advisers should contact the Executive and obtain preliminary consent to a waiver
2	If the Executive agrees, the advisers should amend the template Code waiver letter to take account of the particular transaction. The template explains the information which needs to be included. The draft Code waiver letter should then be sent to the Executive for its approval
3	Once approved, the Code waiver letter should be sent to all of the target's shareholders. The shareholders must be given at least 7 days to consider the terms of the letter and seek independent financial or legal advice before counter-signing it. The signature of the registered shareholder is normally required; signature under a power of attorney is not normally acceptable
4	Once the shareholders have signed and returned their Code waiver letters, the advisers should send them all to the Executive. The Code waiver will only be granted once it has original letters signed by all the shareholders. Faxed copies are not acceptable
5	Once the Executive has received all of the original signed Code waiver letters, it will contact the advisers by telephone to confirm that the Code waiver has been granted

A copy of the **Code waiver letter** can be downloaded from the Panel's website.

Definitions

Acting in concert

In many of the rules detailed below, the Code places obligations on persons "acting in concert" with the bidder, also known as "concert parties". The **general definition** of "acting in concert" is persons who, under a formal or informal agreement or understanding, co-operate to obtain or consolidate control of a company or to frustrate the successful outcome of an offer for a company.

6765

A person or group of persons will be treated as having **control** of a company if they hold a total of at least 30% of the company's voting shares, regardless of whether or not their holdings give them control in reality.

A person and each of its **affiliated persons** are deemed to be acting in concert with each other.

6766

> MEMO POINTS   An "affiliated person" is any undertaking in respect of which any person:
> – has a majority of the shareholders' or members' voting rights;
> – is a shareholder or member and at the same time has the right to appoint or remove a majority of the directors on the board;
> – is a shareholder or member and alone controls a majority of the shareholders' or members' voting rights pursuant to an agreement entered into with other shareholders or members; or
> – has the power to exercise, or actually exercises, dominant influence or control.
> A person's rights as regards voting, appointment or removal will include the rights of any other affiliated person, and those of any person or entity acting on his behalf or on behalf of another affiliated person.

6767 In addition, there is a **presumption** that the following categories of persons are acting in concert with others in the same category.

Category	Persons in category
A	A company, its parent, subsidiaries and fellow subsidiaries and their associated companies (for this purpose, ownership or control of 20% of a company's equity share capital is the test for associated company status)
B	A company, its directors, their close relatives and related family trusts
C	A company, its pension funds and the pension funds of any company in category A
D	A fund manager with any investment company, unit trust or other person whose investments the fund manager manages on a discretionary basis in respect of the relevant investment accounts [1]
E	A connected adviser [2], its client and the bidder or target (if the client is acting in concert with the bidder or with the target's directors) and persons controlling, controlled by or under the same control as the adviser [1]
F	Directors of a company which is subject to an offer or where the directors have reason to believe a bona fide offer for their company may be imminent

Note:
1. **Fund managers and traders** can apply to the Panel for exempt status and will then not be included in this category.
2. A **connected adviser** is the corporate broker to the bidder or target and any adviser to:
– the bidder or target;
– any person who is acting in concert with the bidder or target (where that advice is in relation to the offer or in relation to the reason why that person is treated as a concert party); or
– a category a. associate of the bidder or target (see ¶6770+ below).

[MEMO POINTS] 1. Where a cash alternative offer has been underwritten, the terms of the **underwriting agreement** may amount to an agreement or understanding between the underwriter and bidder within the meaning of acting in concert. In cases of doubt, the Panel should be consulted.
2. **Standstill agreements** may be relevant and the Panel should be consulted in cases of doubt. A standstill agreement is an agreement between a company, or its directors, and a shareholder which restrict the shareholder or directors from either offering for, or accepting an offer for, the company's shares or from increasing or reducing shareholdings.
3. **Consortium investors** will normally be treated as acting in concert with the bidder. Where an investor is part of a larger organisation, the Panel should be consulted to establish whether other parts of the organisation will also be regarded as acting in concert.
4. A person giving **irrevocable commitments** to accept or not accept an offer will generally not be treated as acting in concert with the bidder or target as appropriate. The Panel will reconsider the position if the person giving the commitment acquires an interest in more shares or if the terms of the commitment give the bidder or target:
– the conditional or absolute right to exercise or direct the exercise of the voting rights attaching to the shares; or
– general control of them.

Associate

6770 The **general definition** of "associate" is all persons (whether or not they are acting in concert) who directly or indirectly own or deal in the shares of a bidder or the target company and who, in addition to their normal interest as shareholders, have a commercial, financial or personal interest or potential interest in the outcome of the offer.

6771 There is a **presumption** that the following persons will be treated as an associate of the bidder or target:
a. the bidder or target's parent, subsidiaries and fellow subsidiaries of the same parent and their associated companies (for this purpose ownership or control of 20% of a company's equity share capital is the test for associated company status);
b. connected advisers and persons controlling, controlled by or under the same control as connected advisers;
c. the bidder or target's directors, or the directors of any other company in category a, together with close relatives and related trusts;
d. the pension fund of a bidder, the target or any company in category a;

e. any investment company, unit trust or other person whose investments an associate manages on a discretionary basis in respect of the relevant investment accounts;
f. an employee benefit trust of a bidder or the target or any company in category a;
g. a person who owns more than 5% of a class of relevant securities; and
h. a company having a material trading arrangement with a bidder or the target.

2. Pre-offer considerations

a. Preparation

6776 The bidder must ensure that it has carried out all necessary preparations **before announcing** its bid because once the offer has been announced it can only be withdrawn in limited circumstances. This is because:
– an offer which is not implemented could create a false market in the target's shares or could be seen as misleading shareholders (GP 4 City Code);
– the announcement of an offer should only take place if the bidder can and will continue to be able to implement the offer. Responsibility for ensuring this also rests with the bidder's financial advisers (r 2.5 City Code).

Before announcing its offer, the bidder will therefore need to have:
– appointed its advisers;
– conducted its due diligence; and
– ensured that it has adequate finances in place to complete the offer.

b. Secrecy

6778 Secrecy before an announcement is made is extremely important (r 2.1 City Code). **Confidential information**, especially price-sensitive information, regarding an offer or a prospective offer may only be passed to another person if it is necessary to do so and if that other person is made aware of the need for secrecy. Advisers are expected to **warn** their clients of the importance of secrecy and security at the beginning of discussions. All persons in possession of confidential information must take the necessary steps to **minimise leaks**, in particular, when proof printing documents prior to an announcement. Specialist firms of secure printers are often used.

c. Announcements

6780 An announcement is required in the following circumstances:
a. a firm intention without pre-conditions to make an **offer has been notified** to the target's board (¶6816+);
b. the requirement to make a **mandatory cash offer** has been triggered (see ¶6805+);
c. the target is the subject of **rumour and speculation** (or in the case of a listed target, there is an untoward movement in its share price):
– before an approach to the target's board has been made;
– after an approach to the target's board has been made, where that rumour and speculation (or movement in share price) is reasonably likely to be as a result of the bidder's actions; or
– when a bidder is being sought for shareholdings which together carry more than 30% of the voting rights of the target, or the target's board is seeking a bidder;
d. negotiations or discussions are about to **extend** beyond those who "need to know" in the companies concerned and their advisers; or
e. a **bidder is being sought** for shareholdings which together carry more than 30% of the voting rights of the target, or the target's board is seeking a bidder and the number of potential buyers or bidders is about to be increased to include more than a very restricted number of people.

MEMO POINTS It is advisable to **consult with the Panel** as to whether an announcement is required and particularly:
- whether any rumour, speculation or movements in share price trigger the announcement requirement; and
- when extending negotiations or discussions (for example, in order to arrange financing) to seek irrevocable undertakings to accept an offer once it is made, or to organise a consortium to make the offer.

6781 If an announcement is required prior to the bidder approaching the board of the target, **responsibility** for it rests with the bidder. After an approach has been made, responsibility for an announcement rests with the target's board (r 2.3 City Code).

6782 In the case of situations a. and b, an **announcement of a firm intention** to make an offer is required (see ¶6817 for further details, including to whom a copy of the announcement must be sent).

In the case of situations c, d. and e, where an announcement is required but the bidder is not ready to make a firm offer, a brief **announcement** that **talks are taking place** (there is no need to name the potential bidder) or that a potential bidder is considering making an offer will be sufficient. Except with the consent of the Panel, the brief announcement should also include a summary of the disclosure provisions (see ¶6860+) (r 2.4(a) City Code). A copy of all such announcements must be sent by the target to its shareholders and to the Panel (r 2.6(a) City Code).

In either case, the first announcement will trigger the **start of the offer period** (see ¶6827).

6783 Any time after the announcement of a possible offer, where the potential bidder has been named, the target can ask the Panel to make a "**put up or shut up**" order (r 2.4(b) City Code). This is a mechanism whereby the Panel imposes a time-limit within which the bidder must either make a firm announcement or state that it does not intend to make an offer. A statement that a potential bidder does not intend to make an offer effectively prevents it from making an offer in the following 6 months, and from stakebuilding more than a 30% shareholding in the target unless there is a material change in circumstances. Put up or shut up orders are therefore an extremely useful method of dealing with uncertainty by putting pressure on bidders to formalise a bid.

MEMO POINTS The specific restrictions are that within 6 months of the **statement of intention not to make an offer**, neither the bidder, nor any person who acted in concert with it, nor any person who is subsequently acting in concert with either of them, may (r 2.8 City Code):
- announce an offer or possible offer for the target, including a partial offer under which the bidder could acquire 30% or more of the target's voting rights;
- acquire shares in the target if that would result in the bidder having to make a mandatory offer for the remaining shares (see ¶6805+);
- acquire any shares or rights over shares if they, together with shares or rights acquired by persons acting in concert with the bidder, would in aggregate carry 30% or more of the target's voting rights;
- make any statement which raises or confirms the possibility that an offer may be made for the target; or
- take any steps in connection with a possible offer for the target where knowledge of the possible offer might be extended beyond those who "need to know" in the bidder and its immediate advisers.

d. Pre-offer share dealing

Effect on bidder's offer

6787 The bidder is not prohibited from dealing in the target's shares before it has made a firm offer. However, it should bear in mind that the offer, when made, must be on no less favourable terms than the terms upon which it, or a party with which it is acting in concert, **acquires shares in the 3 months before the offer**. The Panel may extend this time period if it considers that this is necessary for the equal treatment of shareholders (r 6.1 City Code).

6788 When an offer is a reasonable possibility, the bidder or persons acting in concert with it cannot deal in the target's shares if there is an agreement to purchase shares which contains **favourable conditions** which it is not intending to make available to all of the target's shareholders on a subsequent offer (r 16 City Code).

Stakebuilding

6790 There are rules to **prevent** a person from stakebuilding when they hold 50% or less of the voting rights in a company (r 5.1 City Code). Specifically:
– when a person or any person acting in concert with him holds shares or rights over shares which together carry less than 30% of the voting rights in a company, the person may not acquire shares or rights which will take the combined holding to 30% or more of the voting rights; and
– when a person holds shares or rights over shares which together carry between 30% and 50% of the voting rights of a company, it may not acquire any further voting rights.

> MEMO POINTS For these purposes, the **acquisition** of new shares, shares under a share option scheme, subscription, conversion or option rights, and the exercise of options over existing shares are not counted. However, new shares acquired as a result of the exercise of a subscription, conversion or option right are counted (r 5.1 City Code notes 3 and 4).

6791 There are, however, some **exceptions** to the rule against stakebuilding (r 5.2 City Code). These exceptions allow an acquisition:
a. at any time from a single shareholder, if that is the only acquisition within a 7-day period (unless a firm unconditional offer has been announced). This exception can only be used once, until an offer is made and lapses (r 5.3 City Code);
b. immediately before the person makes a firm announcement which is to be recommended by the target's board and the acquisition is conditional upon the announcement;
c. after a firm unconditional offer has been announced and one of the following conditions is met:
– the acquisition is approved by the target's board;
– the offer has been recommended (even if the recommendation is withdrawn);
– the first closing date has passed and the merger control regulations are not relevant; or
– the offer is completely unconditional;
d. made through the acceptance of a takeover offer; or
e. by a person and his concert parties who already hold 30% of a company's voting rights if their acquisitions over 12 months are not more than 1% of a company's voting shares and their percentage holding does not exceed the highest percentage holding in the previous 12 months. Effectively, although the person and its concert parties can acquire up to 1% of a company's voting shares, it must sell at least the same amount so that its average holding does not increase.

6792 An acquisition of shares under one of these exceptions may well trigger the requirement to make a **mandatory offer** (see ¶6805+), in which case an immediate announcement of the offer must be made (r 5.2 City Code note 2).

> MEMO POINTS 1. An acquisition from a **single shareholder** must be **disclosed** to the company, a regulatory information service (a list of which can be found in Appendix 3 to the Listing Rules) and the Panel no later than 12 noon on the business day following the acquisition (r 5.4 City Code).
> 2. The stakebuilding restrictions do not apply to the receipt of **gifts**. If a person receives a gift of shares which takes his holding of voting shares to 30% or more, he must consult the Panel. He will not normally be required to make a mandatory offer but, after receipt of the gift, will be subject to the usual rules (r 5.1 City Code note 9).

Restrictions on persons with confidential information

6793 Any person (other than the potential bidder) who is in possession of confidential price-sensitive information concerning an offer or possible offer is **prohibited from** (r 4.1 City Code):
– dealing in securities (e.g. shares, options or derivatives) of the target except where the proposed offer is not price-sensitive in relation to those securities;
– dealing in securities of the bidder except where the proposed offer is not price-sensitive in relation to those securities; and
– recommending anyone else to deal in the relevant securities.

This prohibition applies **in addition to** restrictions on insider dealing and market abuse provisions in financial services regulations (see ¶6685+).

Irrevocable undertakings

6794 Where the bidder is proposing to contact shareholders with a view to seeking an **irrevocable undertaking** from them to accept the offer if it is made, it must consult the Panel in advance (r 4.3 City Code). The Panel will wish to be satisfied that the shareholder being approached will be provided with adequate information and a realistic opportunity to consider whether the commitment should be given, including obtaining independent advice. The bidder's financial adviser will be responsible for ensuring compliance with all relevant regulatory requirements.

6795 The bidder should ensure that **no consideration** is provided to a shareholder for giving an irrevocable undertaking. This is because the bidder is prohibited from entering into arrangements where the acceptance of an offer by some shareholders is subject to more favourable conditions than the general offer (r 16 City Code). Shares acquired under the irrevocable undertakings will count towards meeting the threshold for the bidder's compulsory acquisition rights (see ¶6937).

e. Approaching the target

6798 The bidder must put its offer forward at **first instance** to the target's board or their advisers and the identity of the ultimate bidder must be disclosed at the outset (r 1 City Code). When approached, the board is entitled to assume that the bidder is, or will be, in a position to fully implement the offer.

In practice, in the case of a **hostile** takeover, the approach is likely to consist of a telephone call to the target's chairman immediately before the announcement of a firm offer is made. Where a **recommended** takeover is being sought, the approach will be made relatively early with a view to securing the board's agreement.

3. Offer

a. Mandatory cash offer

6805 A mandatory offer for the shares of a company must be **made by** any person **when** he acquires, together with persons acting in concert with him (r 9.1 City Code):
– shares which carry 30% or more of that company's voting rights; or
– further voting shares where they already hold between 30% and 50% of the company's voting shares.

The offer must generally be **made to** the holders of all other shares, regardless of class.

> MEMO POINTS 1. Offers to **different classes** should be comparable and the Panel should be consulted in advance when different classes are involved.
> 2. In general, the acquisition of convertible securities, warrants, options or other **rights over shares** (e.g. irrevocable undertakings) will not count towards determining whether the mandatory offer provisions have been triggered. However, the exercise of conversion or option rights will count, as will the taking of an option. To be on the safe side, the Panel should be consulted in advance of the acquisition (r 9.1 City Code note 11).
> 3. Any **increase in the voting rights** of the bidder, and persons acting in concert with it, will be treated as an acquisition for the purposes of deciding whether the mandatory offer provisions have been triggered (r 37.1 City Code). This includes an increase through the target redeeming or purchasing its own shares.

6806 The mandatory offer must be **in cash** or include a cash alternative. The cash **price** must be at least as high as the highest price paid by the bidder, or any person acting in concert with it, for shares of that class during the offer period and in the 12 months before the announcement of the mandatory offer (r 9.5(a) City Code).

If, after a mandatory offer announcement has been made for shares of a particular class, the bidder or its concert parties acquire any interest in shares of that class, the offer price must be increased to at least the highest price paid for those shares (r 9.5(b) City Code).

If the bidder considers that it should not pay the highest price, it can apply to the Panel which has the discretion to **adjust the price**. Factors which the Panel may take into account include (r 9.5 City Code note 3):
- the size and timing of the relevant purchases;
- the attitude of the target's board;
- from whom the shares have been purchased at a high price;
- the number of shares purchased in the preceding 12 months;
- if an offer is required in order to enable a company in serious financial difficulty to be rescued;
- if an offer is required after a person acquired shares by way of a gift (see r 5.1 City Code note 9); and
- if an offer is required as a result of an increase in voting rights following a share redemption or own share purchase (see r 37.1 City Code).

Announcement

An announcement that an obligation to make a mandatory offer has been incurred must be made **immediately upon** an acquisition of shares which gives rise to the obligation. The announcement cannot be delayed whilst information is obtained: any further information can be the subject of a later announcement (r 2.2 City Code). An announcement of a possible offer (¶6782) is not permitted in such cases.

The **contents and consequences** of making a firm announcement are considered below at ¶6817+. In addition, announcement of a mandatory offer must also include confirmation from the bidder's financial adviser or another appropriate third party that the bidder has sufficient resources to satisfy full acceptance of the offer.

6807

> MEMO POINTS   Prime **responsibility** to make the offer rests with the person whose acquisition triggers the mandatory offer provisions. However, where that person is not the principal member of the group acting in concert, the obligation may also attach to the principal member or members instead (r 9.2 City Code).

Conditions

Mandatory offers must be conditional only upon the bidder receiving **acceptances** which will give it, together with its concert parties, more than 50% of the voting rights in the target. If the bidder and its concert parties already hold 50% of the voting rights, the offer must be unconditional (r 9.3 City Code). The Panel will normally only consider a dispensation from this rule under exceptional circumstances (r 9.3 City Code note 3).

6808

> MEMO POINTS   Since the offer is mandatory, **pre-conditions** to making the offer are irrelevant. If the offer is **referred to merger control authorities** (i.e. the Competition Commission or European Commission), or they initiate proceedings, the offer will lapse. The offer must include a statement to this effect. The reference or the initiation of proceedings must occur before the later of either the first closing date or the date on which the offer becomes or is declared unconditional as to acceptances. However, the offer must be reinstated if the merger is approved later (rr 9.4, 12.1 City Code).

Dispensation

It is possible to apply to the Panel for a dispensation from the requirement to make a mandatory offer in any one of the following six circumstances (r 9 City Code notes on dispensations):
- the proposal is **approved by a poll vote** of the target's independent shareholders (known as the "whitewash"). Early consultation with the Panel is essential in this case. Guidance on the procedure to be followed to obtain the Panel waiver is set out in Appendix 1 to the Code;
- the obligation has arisen as a result of a lender taking or enforcing **security for a loan**;
- the target is in such a serious financial position that the only way it can be saved is by an **urgent rescue operation**;
- the obligation to make a mandatory offer has been incurred due to an **inadvertent mistake**, provided sufficient shares are sold within a limited period to unconnected persons

6809

to take the shareholder, together with any concert parties, below the 30% threshold. The Panel should be consulted on the exercise of the voting rights attached to the shares prior to sell-down; or
– persons holding **50% or more** of the target's voting shares state in writing that they **would not accept** a mandatory offer if made, or one other person already holds 50% or more of the target's voting shares.

> MEMO POINTS 1. Where provisions would have been triggered as a result of a **lender enforcing its security**, the Panel will not normally require an offer if sufficient shares (i.e. to take the holding below 30%) are sold within a limited period to persons unconnected with the lender. At any time before sufficient shares are sold, or if the holding in excess of 29.9% is temporary, the lender must consult the Panel as to its ability to exercise the voting rights attaching to its shares. Where arrangements are made involving the transfer of voting rights to a lender, the Panel will need to be convinced that the arrangements are necessary to preserve the lender's security and the security was not given at a time when the lender had reason to believe that enforcement was likely. Following enforcement, a receiver, liquidator or administrator will not be required to make an offer when he takes control of 30% or more of the shares, but the mandatory offer rules will apply to anyone who buys shares from him.
> 2. Dispensation on the grounds of an **urgent rescue operation** will only be granted if approval for the rescue operation by a vote of independent shareholders is obtained as soon as possible after the rescue operation is carried out, or if some other protection for independent shareholders is provided which the Panel considers satisfactory in the circumstances. If neither of these criteria is fulfilled, a mandatory offer will be required but the Panel may adjust the price in appropriate circumstance (see ¶6806).

b. Voluntary offer

6815 When a bidder makes a voluntary offer, it is generally free to set the **consideration** at whatever level it wishes, subject to:
– the overriding principle that the target's shareholders are treated equally (GP 1 City Code); and
– compliance with the rules on share dealing before or during the offer (respectively, ¶6787+, ¶6850+).

Announcement

6816 A voluntary offer must be announced **immediately after** a firm and unconditional intention to make an offer has been notified to the target's board, irrespective of its views on the offer (r 2.2 City Code). In addition, a bidder may be forced into making an offer by the target obtaining a "put up or shut up" order from the Panel (see ¶6783).

A bidder should only announce a firm intention to make an offer after the most careful and responsible consideration. Such an announcement should only be made when the bidder has every reason to believe it can and will continue to be able to implement the offer. Responsibility for ensuring this also rests with the bidder's financial advisers (r 2.5 City Code).

6817 **Announcement of a firm intention** must set out (r 2.5 City Code):
– the terms of the offer;
– the identity of the bidder;
– all conditions to which the offer is subject;
– details of shares in the target currently held by the bidder and its concert parties, as well as any shares over which they have obtained irrevocable undertakings, options or other rights of purchase;
– details of any derivative linked to securities in the target and entered into by the bidder or its concert parties;
– details of any agreement relating to any pre-conditions or conditions to the offer, including any break fees payable;
– details of any arrangement with the bidder, the target or their associates to induce or refrain from dealing in the target's shares; and

– a summary of the disclosure requirements in the form approved by the Panel (available to download from the Panel's website).

> **MEMO POINTS** 1. Promptly after **publication** of an announcement of a firm intention (regardless of whether it was preceded by announcement of a possible offer) (r 2.6 City Code):
> – the target must send a copy of the announcement to its shareholders and to the Panel; and
> – both the bidder and target must make that announcement readily available to their employees' representatives or, where there are no such representatives, to the employees themselves.
> Where necessary, the bidder and target will be required to explain the implications of the announcement.
> As an alternative to sending the full announcement, both bidder and target can send a circular summarising the terms and conditions of the offer, including a summary of the disclosure provisions available to download from the Panel's website. However, where a circular is sent, the full text of the announcement must readily and promptly be made available to the shareholders and employees' representatives or employees, for example, by placing it on a website.
> 2. Where the **offer is for cash**, or includes an element of cash, the announcement must also include confirmation from the bidder's financial adviser or other appropriate third party that the bidder has sufficient resources to satisfy full acceptance of the offer (r 2.5(c) City Code).

6818

The **consequences** of a firm announcement are serious and binding. Once a firm announcement has been made, the bidder is expected to proceed with posting the offer document unless (r 2.7 City Code):
– a pre-condition to making the offer can be invoked;
– a condition to the offer could be invoked if it were made;
– a competitor has posted a higher offer; or
– the Panel gives its consent to the offer not being made because the target has frustrated the offer with the approval of its shareholders.

Pre-conditions

The bidder must consult the Panel **before** it makes **an announcement** if it intends to include in it any pre-conditions to making the offer. Pre-conditions should not be subjective and their fulfilment should not be solely in the hands of the directors of the bidder or target company (r 13.1 City Code).

6819

The only pre-conditions to making a voluntary offer which are permitted without the Panel's consent relate to the fulfilment of **regulatory requirements**, specifically (rr 13.2, 13.3 City Code):
– if merger control provisions are relevant, that there is no reference to the Competition Commission or initiation of proceedings or referral by the European Commission and that any decision by the merger control authorities is satisfactory to the bidder; and
– that any other material official authorisation or regulatory clearance is obtained (where the offer is recommended or where the Panel is satisfied that the authorisation or clearance cannot be obtained within the Code's timetable).

Financial pre-conditions, such as the ability to secure funding, will not normally be accepted. The Panel may allow such a pre-condition in exceptional cases, for example where, due to the likely period required to obtain any necessary official authorisation or clearance, it is not reasonable for the bidder to maintain committed finance throughout the offer period. In such cases, the financial pre-condition must be satisfied (or waived), or the offer must be withdrawn, within 21 days after the satisfaction (or waiver) of any other pre-conditions. In addition, the bidder and its financial adviser must confirm in writing to the Panel, before the announcement of the offer, that they are not aware of any reason why the bidder would be unable to satisfy the financing pre-condition within that 21-day period (r 13.3 City Code notes).

> **MEMO POINTS** Where the **offer is for cash**, or includes an element of cash, and the bidder proposes to finance it by an issue of new securities, any conditions required as a matter of law or regulatory requirement will have to be included in the offer (r 13.3 City Code note). Such conditions will not be waivable and the Panel will have to be consulted in advance. The conditions which the Panel will normally consider necessary for such purposes include:
> – the passing of any necessary resolutions; and
> – where the new securities are to be publicly traded, an appropriate listing or admission to trading condition.

Conditions

6820 The bidder is given some more leeway in setting conditions to the offer itself. As with the mandatory offer, the offer must normally be conditional upon the bidder receiving acceptances which will give it, together with its concert parties, more than 50% of the voting rights in the target (r 10 City Code). In practice, the bidder will often wish to acquire 100% of the shares and if this is the case it will make the offer conditional upon a 90% acceptance level as this will allow it to invoke the statutory compulsory acquisition provisions (see ¶6945+). There are detailed rules for calculating whether the **acceptance condition** has been satisfied (r 10 City Code notes).

6821 Unlike a mandatory offer, the bidder is also permitted to set **other conditions**, provided they are not entirely subjective, or the fulfilment of the conditions is not entirely in the bidder's hands (r 13.1 City Code). As with pre-conditions (¶6819), an offer must not normally be made subject to a condition relating to **financing** (r 13.3 City Code note).

It is therefore usual to find **transaction specific** conditions (e.g. that shareholders' approval is obtained) in addition to the following common conditions:
– since the last audited accounts, there has been no material adverse change in the target's business, financial or trading position;
– there are no change of control provisions in the target's main contracts which will be invoked; and
– the target is not and will not be materially affected by any litigation.

> MEMO POINTS The current finance agreements of the target are usually replaced by arrangements with the bidder's financiers and if this is the case a **change of control** clause in those agreements will be irrelevant. It is therefore often more important that key commercial contracts are not terminated following a change of control. Commonly, the bidder will contact any important suppliers and customers during the due diligence process to obtain assurances that this is the case.

Invoking pre-conditions and conditions

6822 In order to maintain stability in the market, even if an offer is subject to conditions, or the making of an offer is subject to pre-conditions, the Code requires bidders or potential bidders to **use all reasonable efforts** to ensure that the conditions are satisfied (r 13.4(b) City Code).

Further, a bidder should not invoke any condition or pre-condition which would result in the offer not proceeding, being withdrawn or lapsing, unless the circumstances are of **material significance** to the bidder in the context of the offer (r 13.4(a) City Code). A target should not invoke, or cause or permit the bidder to invoke, any condition unless the circumstances which give rise to the right to invoke the condition are of material significance to the target's shareholders in the context of the offer (r 13.5 City Code). If the target cannot invoke or cause or permit the bidder to invoke a condition, the Panel may instead determine that the accepting shareholders should have the right to withdraw their acceptances (r 13.5 City Code note 2).

c. Timetable

6827 The Code imposes a strict timetable on the offer process. This seeks to minimise disruption to the market and the target and bidder's operations, whilst giving shareholders adequate time to consider the bid. The timetable is set out in the table below.

The **offer period starts** when a possible offer announcement or firm announcement is made. An announcement that shares carrying 30% or more of the voting rights of a company are for sale or that a board is seeking potential bidders for the company will be treated as a possible offer announcement. The **offer period finishes** on the later of the first closing date or the date when the offer becomes or is declared unconditional as to acceptances or lapses.

Day	Action	Explanation	Reference (City Code)
– 28	Firm announcement	–	–
0	Posting of offer document	Offer document must normally be posted to the target's shareholders within 28 days of a firm announcement (¶6881)	r 30.1(a)
		At the same time, or before, a copy must be sent to the Panel	r 19.7
		At the same time, both the bidder and target must make the offer document readily available to their employees' representatives, or if there are none, to their employees	r 30.1(b)
		At the same time, the bidder must put the offer document on display and announce that the offer document has been posted and where it can be inspected	r 30.1(a)
14	Target board's circular	Target board must give the shareholders its views on the offer as soon as practicable after the publication of the announcement and at least within 14 days (¶6882+). At the same time, the target board should make its circular readily and promptly available to its employees' representatives, or if there are none, to the employees themselves. At the same time, the target board must put the circular on display and announce that it has been posted and where it can be inspected	r 30.2
21	First possible closing date	Offer must initially be open for at least 21 days, although the bidder can announce an extension (¶6835+)	rr 31.1, 31.2
35	Earliest acceptance closing date	An offer must be kept open for at least 14 days after it becomes unconditional as to acceptances. Therefore, if offer becomes unconditional as to acceptances by the first closing date, Day 35 is the first day the offer may close	r 31.4
39	Last date for material announcements by target	Other than with the Panel's prior consent, the target's board is not permitted to make any material announcements after Day 39 (e.g. trading results, profit or dividend forecasts, asset valuations or proposals for dividend payments, material acquisition or disposal). Such announcements are usually used to defend a hostile takeover	r 31.9
42	Satisfaction of conditions (except acceptance)	All conditions must be fulfilled, or the offer must lapse, within 21 days of the first closing date or the date the offer becomes or is declared unconditional as to acceptances, whichever is the later. Day 42 is therefore the last day for satisfaction of all conditions if the offer becomes unconditional as to acceptances by the first closing date	r 31.7
42	Withdrawal of acceptances	Any shareholder may withdraw his acceptance of an offer if it has not become unconditional as to acceptances within 21 days after the first closing date. The right to withdraw lasts up to the earlier of either: – the offer becoming or being declared unconditional as to acceptances; or – 1pm on the final day for fulfilment of the acceptance condition This allows shareholders to move to a competitive bidder if they wish	r 34

Day	Action	Explanation	Reference (City Code)
46	Last date for revisions	Offer must be open for at least 14 days following date on which revised offer document is posted. Therefore, no revised offer can be posted in the 14 days before final date offer can become or be declared unconditional as to acceptances (¶6838+)	r 32.1
60	Final day for fulfilment of acceptance condition	Offer (revised or not) may not become or be declared unconditional as to acceptances after midnight on the 60th day after the initial offer document was posted. The Panel can extend this deadline in some circumstances (see ¶6835+). The last time for acceptances as set out in the offer document must be no later than 1pm on the final day (or any earlier date beyond which the bidder has stated the offer will not be extended). An announcement as to whether or not the acceptance condition has been fulfilled must be made by 5pm on the final day (or any earlier date beyond which the bidder has stated the offer will not be extended)	r 31.6
81	Last date for satisfaction of all conditions	See Day 42. Day 81 is the last date for satisfaction of all conditions if the offer is declared unconditional as to acceptances on the final day	r 31.7
95	Last date for payment	If an offer succeeds, except with the Panel's consent, consideration must be posted to the shareholders within 14 days of the later of: – the first closing date; – the date offer becomes or is declared wholly unconditional; and – the date of receipt of a complete acceptance. Therefore, if the last conditions are not satisfied or waived until Day 81, Day 95 is the latest date for payment	r 31.8
95	Last date for return of documents	If an offer lapses, all documents of title and other documents lodged with the acceptances must be returned within 14 days of the offer lapsing	r 31.10

Announcement of acceptance levels

6830 An announcement of acceptance levels must be **made by** 8am on the business day after the day on which (r 17.1 City Code):
– the offer is due to expire;
– the offer becomes or is declared unconditional as to acceptances; or
– the offer is revised or extended (¶6835+).

The **announcement must state** both the total number and percentage levels of each class of shares and the rights over each class of shares:
– for which acceptances have been received;
– held before the start of the offer period; and
– acquired or agreed to be acquired during the offer period.

6831 If, having announced that the offer is unconditional as to acceptances, the bidder then **fails to make an announcement** of acceptance levels by 3.30pm on the relevant day, any shareholder who has accepted the offer is permitted to withdraw that acceptance at any time during the next 8 days. After 8 days, assuming the bidder still has sufficient acceptances, it may confirm that the offer is still unconditional as to acceptances. Provided that the bidder then makes an announcement of acceptance levels, no more shareholders may withdraw their acceptances. The bidder must then keep the offer open for 14 days from the date of confirmation (r 17.2 City Code).

d. Alterations

Extensions

6835 A bidder may wish to extend the time limit for shareholders to accept its offer if it does not achieve the desired level of acceptances by the specified closing date. There is no obligation on a bidder to grant extensions (r 31.1 City Code) but it may do so provided that neither it nor its advisers have made a "**no extension statement**", i.e. a statement that the offer will not be open for acceptance beyond a particular date unless it is unconditional as to acceptances.

> MEMO POINTS 1. An **accidental** no extension statement must be immediately withdrawn or the bidder will be bound by it (r 31.5 City Code).
> 2. The bidder can reserve the **right to set aside** a no extension statement if specific circumstances arise (e.g. if the offer is recommended). The document in which the no extension statement is made must contain a prominent reference to such a reservation, and any subsequent reference to the no extension statement must also make reference to the reservation (r 31.5 City Code note 2).

6836 There are two types of extension which the bidder may grant. It may either (r 31.2 City Code):
– announce a **new closing date**, following which a further extension can be granted; or
– if the offer is already unconditional as to acceptances, announce that the offer is **open until further notice**, in which case the shareholders who have not accepted must be given at least 14 days' notice in writing before the offer is closed.

6837 In both cases, the final day for acceptances cannot be **extended beyond Day 60** (see timetable at ¶6827) unless the Panel gives permission. The Panel will normally only give permission if (r 31.6 City Code):
– there is a competitive bidder;
– the target's board consents;
– the target's board has made a material announcement after Day 39;
– the bidder's receiving agent needs an extension in order to have time to certify the number of acceptances;
– the parties are dealing with the Competition Commission or the European Commission; or
– the Panel has introduced withdrawal rights (see ¶6822).

> MEMO POINTS If the offer remains open for acceptances beyond **Day 70**, shareholders who have not accepted the offer must also be given at least 14 days' further notice in writing before the offer is closed (r 31.2 City Code).

Revisions

6838 A bidder may wish to revise its offer voluntarily (for example, if a competitive offer looks likely). However, the bidder may be required to revise its offer if it deals in the target's shares during the offer period, outside of the offer.

> MEMO POINTS If the bidder revises its offer, it must send out a **revised offer document** (drawn up in the same way as the offer document, ¶6881) (r 32.1 City Code). In response, the target's board must post a **circular** containing its opinion on the revised offer (in the same manner as it would respond to an offer document, ¶6882+) (r 32.6 City Code). Both the bidder and the target are permitted to cross-refer to previous documents.
> As with the original offer document and circular, the bidder and target board must (rr 32.1, 32.6, 32.7 City Code):
> – make the revised offer document or circular, as appropriate, readily and promptly available to their respective employee representatives or, where there are no such representatives, to the employees themselves; and
> – put the offer document or circular, as appropriate, on display and announce that it has been posted and where it can be inspected.

6839 In particular, a revised offer will normally be **required** if (r 32.1 City Code note 2):
– the bidder, or any person acting in concert with it, buys shares at above the offer price (¶6853);
– it becomes obliged to provide a cash alternative or securities alternative (¶6854, ¶6855); or
– it becomes obliged to make or increase a mandatory cash offer (¶6805+).

> **MEMO POINTS** 1. All shareholders who accepted the original offer must be entitled to the **revised consideration** (r 32.3 City Code).
> 2. The bidder may only impose **new conditions** if they are necessary to implement an increased or improved offer (r 32.4 City Code).
> 3. In the case of **competitive bidders**, the Panel will normally require revised offers to be published in accordance with an auction procedure, the terms of which will be determined by the Panel (r 32.5 City Code).

6840 A revision is **not permitted**:
– in the 14 days before the last date on which an offer can become unconditional as to acceptances (see timetable at ¶6827); or
– if it or its advisers have made a "**no increase statement**", i.e. a statement that the offer will not be increased (r 32.2 City Code).

> **MEMO POINTS** 1. An **accidental** no increase statement must be immediately withdrawn or the bidder will be bound by it (r 32.2 City Code).
> 2. The bidder can reserve the **right to set aside** a no increase statement if specific circumstances arise (e.g. if a competitive offer is made). The document in which the no increase statement is made must contain a prominent reference to such a reservation, and any subsequent reference to the no increase statement must also make reference to the reservation (r 32.2 City Code note 2).

4. Conduct of the parties

a. Share dealing during offer period

Restrictions on the bidder

6850 A bidder, and its concert parties, can **continue to deal** in a target's shares during the offer period provided any favourable conditions attached to the deal are available to all of the target's shareholders (r 16 City Code). In hostile takeovers, the rules against stakebuilding may apply during the offer period and so restrict share dealing (see ¶6790+).

6851 Although the bidder is generally still able to deal in the target's shares during the offer period, there are **specific provisions for when**:
– the target's shares are sold;
– shares are bought for a higher price than the current offer price;
– shares are bought for cash; and
– shares are bought in exchange for securities.

In addition, immediately after a purchase of the target company's shares by a bidder or any person acting in concert with it, an appropriate **announcement** must be made by the bidder. Whenever practicable, the announcement should also state the number of shares purchased and the price paid (r 7.1 City Code).

Sale of shares

6852 The bidder and its concert parties can **only sell shares if** (r 4.2 City Code):
– the sale is at the value of the offer or higher;
– it has the Panel's prior consent (which will not be given if the offer is a mandatory one); and
– at least 24 hours' public notice has been given that such sales may be made.

After the bidder or its concert parties announce that sales may be made, they may not make any further purchases and the offer can only be revised with the Panel's consent, which will only be given in exceptional circumstances.

Shares bought at higher price

6853 If the bidder or its concert parties buy shares at above the then current offer price between making an announcement of a firm bid and when the offer closes for acceptances, the bidder must **increase its offer to** at least the highest price paid for the shares. An announcement that the offer is going to be revised must be made by the bidder immediately after the purchase. The normal rules regarding revisions will apply (¶6838+) (r 6.2 City Code).

Shares bought for cash

A cash offer must be made, or **cash alternative offered**, for shares in a particular class if a bidder or its concert parties buys shares in the target for cash either (r 11.1 City Code):
– at any time during the offer period; or
– during the offer period and in the previous 12 months and those shares together carry 10% or more of the voting rights in that class of shares.
The cash offer or alternative must be at the highest price paid in the relevant period.

6854

> MEMO POINTS   Shares acquired in **exchange for securities** either during or in the 12 months before the start of the offer period will be treated as having been acquired for cash on the basis of the value of the securities at the time of the purchase. But, the obligation to provide a cash alternative will not arise if the seller must hold the securities he received until either the offer has lapsed or the offer consideration has been posted to the accepting shareholders (r 11.1 City Code note 5).

Shares bought in exchange for securities

If a bidder, or any person acting in concert with it, buys shares which carry 10% or more of the voting rights in a share class during the offer period and in the previous 3 months in exchange for securities, the bidder will have to **offer the same securities** to all other holders of shares in that class (r 11.2 City Code). In practice this means it will have to offer securities to the same value but not necessarily the same number. In addition, if it has made more than one purchase in exchange for securities it must offer the same securities at the highest value at which it made a previous purchase.

6855

> MEMO POINTS   The bidder will also have an obligation to offer **cash or a cash alternative** (see ¶6854) unless the seller is required to hold the securities he received until either the offer has lapsed or the offer consideration has been posted to the accepting shareholders (r 11.2 City Code).

Restrictions on the target

Apart from exempt market makers, the target's **financial advisers or corporate broker** (or any person controlled by or controlling them) are not permitted to (r 4.4 City Code):
– buy or deal in the target's shares, derivatives or options;
– lend money to any person so they can buy or deal in the target's shares, derivatives or options (unless the loan is provided in the ordinary course of business, on normal commercial terms to someone with whom they have an established customer relationship); or
– enter into any arrangement which may be an inducement to a person to keep, deal or refrain from dealing in the target's shares.

6856

---

b. Disclosure requirements

The Code requires **dealings in** "relevant securities" **during** the offer period to be disclosed to the Panel (r 8 City Code). "Relevant securities" broadly equate to any shares or securities in the target and, where any part of the consideration for the offer is shares in the bidder, the bidder (r 8 City Code note 2). The disclosure requirements apply equally to dealings in relevant securities of unlisted public companies and of private companies to which the Code applies (r 8 City Code note 11).

6860

The **Disclosure Table** on the Panel's website should be consulted in this regard as it lists:
– all targets in an offer period;
– all bidders and named potential bidders; and
– all classes of relevant securities.

The disclosure requirements apply to **dealings by the following persons**:
– the bidder, target and any of their associates; and
– any person who is (or will be as a result of the deal) directly or indirectly interested in 1% or more of any class of relevant securities.

> MEMO POINTS 1. The bidder, target and any of their associates must also disclose the details of any **irrevocable undertaking or letter of intent** procured during the offer period. Any person who gives such an undertaking or letter but later realises that he will not be able to comply with it, or does not intend to comply with it, must promptly announce an update of the position. Alternatively, he can notify the Panel and the bidder or target (as appropriate) who will then have to make the announcement (r 8.4 City Code).
> 2. A person will be treated as having an **interest in securities** if he:
> – own them;
> – controls them;
> – has a call option or written put option in respect of them; or
> – has a long derivative referenced to them.

6861 Except for dealings by a person with a 1% interest, disclosure must be made **no later than** 12 noon on the business day following the date of the transaction. Disclosure by a person with a 1% interest must be made no later than 3.30pm on the business day following the date of the transaction (r 8 City Code note 3).

Dealings should be **disclosed to** a regulatory information service (a list of which can be found in Appendix 3 to the Listing Rules) by fax or electronic delivery. A copy must also be sent to the Panel's Market Surveillance Unit by fax or by email (see ¶9905) (r 8 City Code note 4).

Specimen **disclosure forms** are available from the Panel's website (r 8 City Code note 5).

Since the disclosure requirements apply to a potentially wide group of shareholders, a **summary** of the disclosure provisions must be sent with the offer document (¶6881).

c. Frustrating tactics

6865 Frustrating, or defensive, tactics are **actions by** the target's directors which are designed to prevent or discourage a takeover. The ability of the target's directors to employ such tactics is restricted by the Code and is subject to the general principle that once an offer has been notified to the board or the board has reason to believe that an offer is imminent, it should not, without the approval of the shareholders, take any action which would prevent the shareholders from considering a bona fide offer (GP 3 City Code).

In addition, the directors should be mindful of their duty to promote the success of the company (see ¶6882).

6866 Intentionally frustrating tactics are normally only a feature of hostile takeovers. Nevertheless, in both a recommended and a hostile takeover, from the time an offer has been made or the target's board has reason to believe that a bona fide offer may be imminent, the **following actions must be approved by** an ordinary resolution of the target's shareholders in a general meeting (r 21 City Code):
– the issue of any authorised share capital;
– the creation or issue of any securities carrying conversion or subscription rights (or an agreement to create or issue securities of that type);
– the sale, disposal or acquisition of a material amount of assets (or an agreement to sell, dispose or acquire those assets);
– entering into contracts outside the ordinary course of business; and
– one which may result in any offer or bona fide possible offer being frustrated or in shareholders being denied the opportunity to decide on its merit.

The Panel should be consulted in advance when there are any **doubts** as to whether the approval of the shareholders is required (r 21 City Code note 3). The Panel will normally **waive the requirement** to obtain shareholder consent if the proposed action is acceptable to the bidder (r 21.1 City Code note 1).

MEMO POINTS 1. The Panel's **consent to proceed without** shareholder **approval** will be required where the proposed action is in pursuance of an earlier contract or another pre-existing obligation, or where the action has already been partly or fully implemented, or is in the ordinary course of business (r21.1 City Code).
2. The Panel will normally **waive the requirement for** a shareholder **meeting** where the holders of more than 50% of the voting rights state in writing that they approve the action proposed and would vote in favour of any resolution to that effect proposed at a general meeting (r21.1 City Code note 10).

In addition to obtaining shareholder consent for the above actions, the Panel considers that the declaration and payment of an **interim dividend** by the target outside the normal course could effectively frustrate an offer and so the target and its advisers must consult the Panel in advance of declaring such a dividend (r21 City Code note 3).

6867

d. Provision of information

The Code requirements regarding the provision of information supplements other regulatory requirements (see ¶6685+). The general rule is that **sufficient information** must be given to the shareholders, in good time, so that they can make an informed decision regarding the advantages or disadvantages of an offer. No relevant information should be withheld from them. The bidder's obligation towards the target's shareholders is no less than its obligations towards its own shareholders (r23 City Code).

6872

Subsequent documents sent to the target's shareholders must contain details of any **material changes** in the information previously published or, if there have been no such changes, a statement to that effect (r27.1 City Code).

Copies of all documents and announcements bearing on an offer must at the time of release be **lodged with** the Panel and the advisers to all other parties to the offer (r19.7 City Code).

MEMO POINTS Information does not have to be provided, and documents do not have to be sent, **outside the EEA** where there is a significant risk of civil, regulatory or criminal exposure and this cannot be avoided by making minor amendments to the information or documents. The exception applies to information or documents to be sent to shareholders and employees' representatives or employees. However, this is subject to the proviso that, on the date the information is to be provided, less than 3% of the target's shares are registered to shareholders located in the relevant jurisdiction, or less than 3% of the employees are located there, as appropriate. The Panel also has a discretion to grant an individual dispensation in cases where the 3% threshold does not apply (r30.3 City Code).

Equality

Equality of information to **shareholders** is one of the most important provisions of the Code. Information about all companies involved in an offer must be made equally available to all of the target's shareholders as nearly as possible at the same time and in the same manner. This does not apply to confidential information given by the target company to a bona fide potential bidder, or vice versa (GP1 City Code; r20.1 City Code).

6873

The Code also requires equality of information between **competitive bidders** or potential bidders. Any information, including particulars of shares, given to one bidder must, on request, be given promptly to another bidder or bona fide potential bidder, even if an offer from the other bidder is less welcome (r20.2 City Code). It is ultimately for the shareholders to determine the relative merits of each bid.

6874

Where the offer or potential offer is a management buy-out, the bidder or potential bidder must, on request, promptly provide the target's independent directors or advisers with all of the information which it has provided to its own financiers or potential financiers (r20.3 City Code).

6875

Accuracy

In addition to other regulatory requirements (particularly those under financial services regulations, see ¶6686), the Code also places a high degree of importance on the quality of the

6876

information provided during a takeover. All documents, advertisements or statements must be prepared to the highest **standards** of care and accuracy and the information given must be adequately and fairly represented (r 19.1 City Code). This rule applies whether the information is issued by the company itself or by an adviser on its behalf.

MEMO POINTS The Panel considers that financial **advisers** and any relevant public relations advisers are responsible for guiding their clients with regard to the release of information during the course of an offer. Comment should be avoided on future profits and prospects, asset values and the likelihood of an offer being revised. In appropriate circumstances, the Panel may require a statement of retraction (r 19.1 City Code note 1).

6877 Information must be **presented** in a straightforward manner using unambiguous language. In particular:
– the sources for facts must be clearly stated;
– quotations must only be used where the board is prepared to corroborate or substantiate them and the responsibility statement is included (see ¶6879). Quotations should not be used out of context and details of the origin must be included; and
– pictorial representations, charts, graph and diagrams must be to scale.

MEMO POINTS The Panel should be consulted in advance before any party makes a **merger benefit statement** (i.e. a quantified statement about the expected financial benefits of a proposed takeover or merger). Further information may need to be provided upon the making of such a statement (r 19.1 City Code note 8).

6878 In addition, even if factually accurate, the person involved in an offer and their advisers must take care not to issue a **statement which may mislead** shareholders and the market or may create uncertainty (r 19.3 City Code). This particularly applies to:
– a statement from the bidder that it **may improve** upon its offer without quantifying the improvement and committing itself to the improvement. Such statements are prohibited;
– a "**holding statement**", i.e. where the bidder states that it is considering its position in the light of new developments or where a potential competing bidder states that it is considering making an offer. The Panel must be consulted in advance of making such a statement as it is not permissible for it to remain unclarified for more than a limited period of time; and
– statements **about the level of support** from shareholders, which will have to be verified to the Panel's satisfaction.

Responsibility

6879 The **responsibility statement** required by the Code is a familiar component of offer documentation. Each document issued to shareholders, or an advertisement published in connection with an offer, must state that the directors of the target and/or, where appropriate, the bidder "accept responsibility for the information contained in the document or advertisement and that, to the best of their knowledge and belief (having taken all reasonable care to ensure that such is the case), the information contained in the document or advertisement is in accordance with the facts and, where appropriate, that it does not omit anything likely to affect the import of such information" (r 19.2(a) City Code).

The responsibility statement **does not have to be included**:
– in product or company advertisements which do not relate to the offer;
– on notices relating to court schemes; or
– in an advertisement which only reproduces information already published in a circular which included a responsibility statement.

MEMO POINTS 1. All of the directors will have to make the statement, even if the actual preparation of the document or advertisement has been **delegated** to a committee of the board (r 19.2 City Code note 1).
2. The Panel's consent is required if any **director is to be excluded** from taking responsibility and it will only be given in exceptional circumstances. If consent is given, the reasons for any exclusion will have to be stated in the document or advertisement (r 19.2(b) City Code).
3. A **qualified responsibility statement** will be permitted where a company issues information about another company when it is made clear that the information has been compiled from published sources. In such cases, the issuing directors only have to take responsibility for the correctness and fairness of the reproduction or presentation (r 19.2 City Code note 3).

4. The Panel should be consulted if the **bidder** is **under** the ultimate **control** of other persons. The Panel will normally require other persons (e.g. the directors of the parent company) to take responsibility for documents or advertisements issued by or on behalf of the bidder (r 19.2 City Code note 6).

6880 The **effect** of the responsibility statement is that, if the information to which the statement refers is inaccurate and misleading, the directors making it could be liable for negligent misstatement (*Hedley Byrne & Co Ltd v Heller & Partners Ltd* [1963] 2 All ER 575). The liability will arise where the document or advertisement includes a misstatement and:
– the person making the claim is one whom the directors should have reasonably foreseen would have suffered loss;
– there is a sufficiently proximate relationship between the directors and the person making the claim;
– it is fair, just and reasonable for the directors to be liable; and
– the loss suffered by the person making the claim was caused by his reliance upon the misstatement.

Any shareholders to whom the offer documents are sent are likely to fulfil these requirements. However, the liability could extend to others (e.g. purchasers of shares who rely upon published information) (*Possfund Custodian Trustee Ltd v Diamond* [1996] 2 BCLC 665).

Offer document

6881 The Code sets out a detailed list of information which must be included in the offer document issued by the bidder and reference to the particular provisions of the Code should be made in each case (r 24 City Code). A summary of the principal information which must be included in the offer document is set out in the table below.

Subject	Summary
Administrative	– The **date** on which the document is despatched – A **warning statement** at the head of the document on the following terms: "If you are in doubt about this offer you should consult an independent financial adviser authorised under the Financial Services and Markets Act 2000" – If the document includes a recommendation or opinion of a **financial adviser**, unless actually issued by the adviser, a statement that the adviser has given and not withdrawn his consent to the inclusion of the recommendation or opinion – The **national law** which will govern contracts concluded between the bidder and the target's shareholders
Offer and acceptance	– Details of each class of **shares** in respect of which the offer is being made, including whether they will be transferred with or without a dividend, and the maximum and minimum percentages of those shares which the bidder undertakes to acquire – The **terms of the offer**, including the consideration offered for each class of security, the total consideration offered and the way in which the consideration is to be paid – Acceptance **procedures** and the particulars of all documents required for a valid acceptance – The **time** allowed for acceptance of the offer and any alternative offer – All **conditions** (including normal conditions relating to acceptances, listing and increase of capital) to which the offer is subject – The **compensation** (if any) offered for the removal of shareholders' rights
Information to assess value of offer	– If either the shares to which the offer relates or the shares being offered as consideration are **listed**, the middle market quotations for the previous 6 months – If either the shares to which the offer relates or the shares being offered as consideration are **not listed**, any information available as to the number and price of transactions which have taken place in the previous 6 months, or a statement that no such transactions have taken place – If the document includes a **price comparison** between the offer and previous prices of the target's shares, a prominent comparison between the offer and the price on the last business day before start of the offer period – If the offer includes an element of **cash**, confirmation by an appropriate third party (e.g. the bidder's bank or financial adviser) that the bidder has the available resources to satisfy the offer in full

Subject	Summary
Bidder's intentions for target	– The bidder's intentions regarding the future of the **target's business** and redeployment of the target's fixed assets – The bidder's **strategic plans** for the target and their likely repercussions on employment and the locations of the target's places of business – The bidder's intentions regarding the continued **employment** of employees of the target and its subsidiaries, including any material change in the conditions of employment – The bidder's long-term **commercial justification** for the proposed offer – Details of any person to whom shares acquired under the offer will ultimately be transferred
Information about bidder	– The **name and address** of the bidder and, if appropriate, the person making the offer on behalf of the bidder – Detailed financial information about the bidder (where the **bidder is listed** on the London Stock Exchange or on AIM) – Detailed financial information about the bidder, disclosure of the identity of persons who control the bidder, and any other information which the Panel requires (where the **bidder is not listed** on the London Stock Exchange or on AIM) – Details of **shareholdings** in the target and any **share dealings** in the last 12 months by the bidder, its directors and persons acting in concert with it, or a statement that there are no shareholdings and/or have been no share dealings – Details of the bidder's concert parties and, to the extent that it is known, the target's concert parties, if the target's shareholders need details of that party in order to reach a properly informed decision on the offer – The bidder's intentions regarding the future of the **bidder's business** in so far as it is affected by the offer – The bidder's **strategic plans** for itself and their likely repercussions on employment and the locations of the bidder's places of business, in so far as they are affected by the offer – The bidder's intentions regarding the continued **employment** of employees of the bidder and its subsidiaries, including any material change in the conditions of employment, in so far as they are affected by the offer
Disclosure of relevant arrangements	– Details of any agreement to invoke or not invoke a **condition** to the bidder's offer – Details of any **irrevocable undertakings** – Details of how the offer is to be **financed** (the main lenders or arrangers of finance must be named) and a statement that either a payment or security for the lending will not be secured upon the target's business, or, if it is proposed that the target's assets will be used as security for the finance being provided, a description of the proposed arrangements – Details of any **agreements connected to the offer** between the bidder or any person acting in concert with it and any of the directors, recent directors, shareholders or recent shareholders of the target
Explanation of Code provisions	– A summary of the **disclosure obligations** on share dealing in the form approved by the Panel (available to download from its website) – Mention of the rules regarding the **counting of acceptances** (a reference to Notes 4-7 on Rule 10 will be sufficient) – Details of the Code timetable (¶6827) – Details of Code rules on **announcements of acceptance levels** (¶6830+) – If relevant, when the bidder or target may **invoke a condition** to the offer (¶6822)

Further information if securities exchange offer	– Full particulars of the securities being offered including the rights attaching to them
	– Details of the first **dividend** or interest payment
	– Details of how the securities will **rank** for dividends/interest, capital and redemption
	– Statement indicating the **effect of acceptance** on:
	  – the capital and income position of the target's shareholders;
	  – the bidder's assets, profits and business; and
	  – the emoluments of the bidder's directors (or a statement that there will be no effect)
	– If the bidder's securities are **not listed**, a statement as to whether a listing is to be sought for the securities and an estimate of the value of the securities by an appropriate adviser

MEMO POINTS   At the same time or before posting the offer document, a **copy** must be **sent to the Panel** (r 19.7 City Code). At the same time, as posting, it must be made readily available to the bidder's employees' representatives, or to the employees themselves if there are no representatives (r 30.1 (b) City Code). In addition, it must be put on display and the bidder must announce that it has been posted and where it can be inspected (r 30.1 (a) City Code).

Target board's circular

The target board must obtain **independent advice** on the offer (r 3.1 City Code). It must communicate the substance of that advice to its shareholders and at the same time **circulate its own views** on the offer to the target's shareholders (r 25.1 City Code). Where the target board's circular includes the recommendation or opinion of a financial adviser, it must include a statement that the adviser has given and not withdrawn his consent, unless the circular was issued by that adviser (r 25.1 City Code).

6882

MEMO POINTS   1. Directors who are also shareholders must still be careful to **promote the success of the target** and must be prepared to explain their decisions in public. Shareholders of a company that is effectively controlled by a board must accept that the attitude of their board will be decisive in any offer (r 25.1 City Code note 1). A director with a **conflict of interest** (e.g. in a management buy-out where the director will have a continuing role) should not be joined with the board in the expression of its views. The nature of the conflict should be explained to shareholders (r 25.1 City Code notes 3 and 4).
2. Where the target's **board is split**, the target must also circulate the views of the minority (r 25.1 City Code note 2).
3. At the same time as posting its circular to its shareholders, the target's board must also (r 30.2 City Code):
– make it readily and promptly available to its employees' representatives or, where there are none, the employees themselves; and
– put it on display and announce that the circular has been posted and where it can be inspected.

The target board's first major circular advising shareholders of the offer should include the following provisions (r 25 City Code):
– **comments upon the bidder's statements** in the offer document regarding its intentions towards the target's business and its employees;
– the **effect** of implementation of the offer on all the target's interests, including employment;
– the **bidder's strategic plans** for the target and their likely repercussions on employment and the locations of the target's places of business, as set out in the offer document;
– details of certain **shareholdings** (generally to demonstrate shareholdings of the directors and their associates in the target and, in the case of a securities exchange offer, the bidder);
– whether the **directors intend to accept or reject** the offer in respect of their own shareholdings;
– details of all current **service contracts** of any director or proposed director of the target or its subsidiaries, and details of any service contracts replaced or amended in the previous 6 months;
– details of any **arrangement with the bidder**, the target or their associates to induce or refrain from dealing in the target's shares;
– details of certain **material contracts and documents** (e.g. any irrevocable undertakings and contracts outside the ordinary course of business); and
– all known material **changes in the financial or trading position** of the target since its last published accounts, or a statement that there are no known material changes.

6883

MEMO POINTS   The target board's circular must have appended a separate **opinion from the representatives of its employees** on the effects of the offer on employment, provided that the opinion is received in good time before publication of the circular (r 30.2 City Code). There is, however, no requirement for the target to consult with them. "In good time" means "in sufficient time to publish it with the target board's circular". If, as sometimes happens with a recommended offer, the announcement, offer document and target board's circular are published on the same day so that there is no time for the opinion of employee representatives to be appended, there is no requirement on the target board to circulate the opinion when it does become available.

Profit forecasts and asset valuations

6884 The Code lays out special rules to deal with profit forecasts and asset valuations so that any such figures will not mislead shareholders. In general:
a. the forecast or valuation must be **made by** a properly qualified person. Forecasts must be examined and reported on by the auditors or consultant accountants and any financial adviser mentioned in the document (r 28.3 City Code). Valuations must be supported by the opinion of a named independent valuer who is appropriately qualified given the nature of the asset (r 29.1 City Code);
b. the **assumptions** upon which the forecast is based (r 28.2 City Code) and the basis of the valuation (r 29.2 City Code) must be clearly stated;
c. any **potential tax liabilities** must be stated:
– in the case of a profit forecast before taxation, together with any extraordinary items and minority interests; and
– in the case of a valuation, those that would arise if the assets were sold at the amount of the valuation together with a comment as to the likelihood of such a liability crystallising; and
d. the report or opinion must be included in the document containing the forecast or valuation (as appropriate) together with a statement that those making the report or giving their opinion have given and not withdrawn their consent to the **publication**.

> MEMO POINTS 1. The following will be **treated as a profit forecast** by the Panel (r 28.6 City Code):
> – a statement which imposes a minimum or maximum threshold on the likely profits of a particular period, even if no figures are used (e.g. "profits will be somewhat higher than last year");
> – an estimate of profit for a period that has already expired;
> – unaudited profit figures published during an offer period; and
> – a forecast which relates to a limited period (e.g. the next quarter).
> Dividend forecasts will generally **not be treated as a profit forecast**.
> Profit warranties, earnings enhancement and merger benefit statements published in connection with an offer **may be treated as a profit forecast** and the Panel should be consulted in advance in such cases.
> 2. "**Assets**" include land, buildings, plant and machinery, as well as other assets (e.g. stocks, ships, TV rental contracts and the individual parts of a business). Where other assets are involved the Panel should be consulted in advance (r 29.1(a) City Code).

e. Advertisements and telephone campaigns

6890 In addition to other regulatory requirements, particularly those under financial services regulations (¶6686), the Code imposes restrictions on the use of advertisements and telephone campaigns during a takeover.

6891 **Advertisements** must either be approved by the Panel or fall within one of a number of permitted categories (such as product or corporate advertisements, or advertisements which must be published under other legislation) (r 19.4 City Code). This applies regardless of the medium in which the advertisement is to appear.

Copies of advertisements and any material released to the media (including notes to editors) must at the time of release be **lodged with the Panel** and the advisers to all other parties to the offer. This type of material must not be released to the media under an embargo (r 19.7 City Code).

> MEMO POINTS The Panel's prior consent must be obtained where any document is to be issued using **non-print media** such as television, videos, audio tapes etc, even if it does not amount to an advertisement (r 19.1 City Code note 6).

6892 Shareholders may not be pressurised and must be encouraged to consult with their professional advisers when they are contacted by telephone. **Telephone campaigns** may only be conducted by staff of the financial adviser, who are fully aware of the Code's requirements (r 19.5 City Code). Where this is impossible, the Panel may give its consent to others making the call provided that certain protections are put into place (e.g. the financial adviser briefing the caller in advance, and use of a script which has been approved by the Panel) (r 19.5 City Code note 1).

Callers may only quote **previously published information** which is still accurate and not misleading when it is quoted. Where new information is inadvertently given to some shareholders, it must immediately be made generally available to the other shareholders (r 19.5 City Code note 2). This is to preserve the general principle of equality of information between shareholders.

The Panel should be consulted in advance if a telephone campaign is to be conducted with a view to obtaining **irrevocable undertakings**. In some circumstances, the Panel may allow the disclosure of information about a proposed offer which has not been publicly announced (r 19.5 City Code note 3).

5. Consequences of offer

a. Successful offer

Accounting implications

Upon a successful takeover, the bidder will usually become the parent company and the target will become its subsidiary. There are **two accounting options** when the bidder's group prepares its consolidated financial statement: merger accounting or acquisition accounting (Sch 4A CA 1985; FRS 6). An overview of the two options is given below. Further details, including when use of one or other of the options is mandatory, can be found in *Accountancy and Financial Reporting Memo*.

6900

Comment: Under the **new Companies Act**, accounting requirements will be set out in regulations. Two sets of draft regulations have been published: one for small companies and one for medium-sized and large companies (see ¶4362+ for an explanation of these classifications), and are expected to apply to financial years starting on or after 6 April 2008. They will also allow groups to choose between the merger and acquisition accounting methods (Sch 6 in both the draft Small Companies and Groups (Accounts and Directors' Report) Regulations 2008 and the draft Large and Medium-sized Companies and Groups (Accounts and Reports) Regulations 2008).

Merger accounting

Merger accounting treats the bidder and target as separate businesses as though they were continuing as before, only now jointly owned and managed. The **effect** of merger accounting is that the target is treated as if it had always been part of the bidder's group. For example:
– the target's assets and liabilities are included in the group financial statements at the value recorded in the target's financial statements (subject to any adjustments for group accounting policy);
– the target's profits and cash flows are included in the group's financial statement for the entire financial year in which the takeover occurred; and
– no goodwill arises.

6901

Merger accounting is **compulsory when** the takeover qualifies as a true merger. The criteria for determining whether the takeover qualifies as a merger include that:
– the bidder holds at least 90% of shares in the target carrying a right to participate in distributions; and
– at least 90% of the shares were acquired by way of a share exchange.

Acquisition accounting

Acquisition accounting focuses on the bidder who has gained control over another company, i.e. the target. The **effect** is that the group's consolidated accounts principally show the results of the target only from the date that the bidder acquires control over it. For example:
– the target's assets and liabilities are included in the group financial statements at their fair values as at the date of acquisition;

6902

– the target's profits and cash flows may be brought into the group financial statements only from the date of acquisition; and
– the difference between the bidder's acquisition cost and the fair value of the target's net assets must be recorded as goodwill.

Acquisition accounting should be **used when** the merger accounting requirements are not met.

Minority shareholders

6903 In many takeovers, the bidder will not have acquired 100% control of the company pursuant to the initial offer. Some shareholders may refuse to accept the offer, whereas others may simply fail to respond. In this case the bidder will be left with some minority shareholders in the target. The **impact** of the minority will depend upon:
– the class of shares (e.g. preferential shareholders may inhibit the bidder's intentions as to dividend payments; ordinary shareholders may impact upon the bidder's voting power); and
– the size of their shareholding.

For further detail on the rights of minority shareholders, see ¶2067+.

6904 If the bidder has achieved a level of 90% acceptances from the shareholders to whom the offer is made, it will be able to take advantage of statutory **compulsory acquisition** provisions. Conversely, if the bidder holds at least 90% of the voting rights in the target, the minority shareholders may be able to take advantage of statutory compulsory acquisition provisions which operate in their favour. See ¶6930+ for further details.

6905 If the bidder and its concert parties hold more than 50% of the voting rights of the target, they may not within 6 months of the closure of the offer make a **second offer** to, or acquire shares from, any shareholder in the target on better terms than those available under the offer (r 35.3 City Code).

b. Unsuccessful offer

6915 Where an offer does not become wholly unconditional but instead is withdrawn or lapses, the Code effectively imposes a 12-month ban on another takeover bid by the same party (r 35.1 City Code). The **ban applies to** the bidder and to any person who acted in concert with it in the course of the offer or subsequently acted in concert with any of them.

The **prohibited actions** are:
– announcing an offer or possible offer for the target (including a partial offer which could result in the bidder holding 30% or more voting rights of the target);
– making an acquisition that would trigger the requirement to make a mandatory offer for the target's shares (see ¶6805+);
– making a statement which raises or confirms the possibility that an offer might be made for the target; or
– taking any steps in connection with a possible offer for the target where knowledge of the possible offer might extend beyond those who "need to know" in the bidder and its immediate advisers.

6916 The **Panel will waive** this rule in very limited circumstances such as if a new competitive offer is made, material regulatory requirements have been fulfilled or the new offer is recommended by the board (where the bidder was prevented from altering its original offer as a result of a no increase or no extension statement) (r 35.1 City Code note (a)).

II. Compulsory acquisition

In most successful takeovers, the bidder is unlikely to gain control over 100% of the target's shares. Some minority shareholders may refuse to accept the offer and others may just fail to respond. Where the bidder has acquired at least 90% control, statutory compulsory acquisition provisions (ss 974-991 CA 2006):
– give it the right to acquire the minority shareholdings (known as "**squeeze-out**"); and
– give the minority shareholders the right to require the bidder to purchase their shares (known as "**sell-out**").

6930

A. Scope of provisions

1. Target

The compulsory acquisition provisions apply to takeovers of all types of company recognised under companies legislation. They therefore apply whether the target is a public or a private company.

6935

2. Takeover offer

In order to take advantage of the provisions, a takeover offer must have been made. This is **defined as** an offer to acquire all the shares in the target, or all the shares in a particular class in the target, except for shares already held by the bidder.

The offer must put forward the same **terms** to all the shareholders in each class of shares to which the offer relates (s 974 CA 2006). For example, if the target has issued ordinary and preference shares and the bidder makes an offer for all of the issued shares, different terms can apply to the ordinary and preference shareholders, but all of the ordinary shareholders must be offered the same terms and all of the preference shareholders must be offered the same terms.

6936

MEMO POINTS 1. An offer falls within the **definition** of a takeover offer even when (s 978 CA 2006):
– there are some shareholders who will be unable to accept it because of restrictions in the country in which the shareholder resides; or
– the offer is not communicated to a shareholder without an address in the UK in order to avoid contravening the law of another country, as long as either the offer itself is published in the *Gazette* or a notice is published in the *Gazette* stating that a copy of the offer document can be obtained from a place in the EEA or on a website.
In addition, an offer is treated as having been made on the same **terms** if different consideration is offered for shares in the same class which have been allotted at different times because the earlier allotted shares are entitled to a dividend but the later allotted shares are not. The difference in the consideration must reflect the difference in dividend entitlement only (s 976(2) CA 2006)
2. In practice, the offer will usually have included **consideration alternatives** (e.g. cash, shares or a combination of cash and shares). Where the same consideration alternatives were not offered to all the shareholders, the variation to the form of consideration must have been made because a non-UK law precluded an offer of the consideration specified in the offer, or only would have allowed it after the bidder had complied with conditions with which it could not comply or which it found unduly onerous. Such an offer is still treated as having been made on the same terms, provided the shareholders received consideration of substantially the same value (s 976(3) CA 2006).
3. **Convertible securities** are treated as shares if they are convertible into or entitle the holder to apply for shares (s 989(1) CA 2006). The bidder can therefore make a separate offer for them and the compulsory acquisition provisions will apply to that offer. However, where an offer is made

for shares, any **conversion or option rights** (i.e. the right to opt for shares to be issued) is not treated as coming within the offer (s 989(2) CA 2006). This means that any shares acquired by shareholders under conversion or option rights after the date of the offer will not be subject to the offer. The result is that the bidder may fail to reach the required threshold, or may fall below the threshold after reaching it because of further conversions or the exercise of further options. The bidder should ensure that its offer extends to shares which may be issued under conversions or options and should carefully consider the impact of any such outstanding rights.

Shares that the bidder has contracted to acquire

6937 For these purposes, shares will be **treated as** "already held by the bidder" if they are shares which it has contracted (conditionally or unconditionally) to acquire (s 975(1) CA 2006). This does not include where a shareholder is bound to accept the takeover offer when it is made if no or negligible consideration has been provided by the bidder other than a promise to make the offer (for example, shares which will be acquired under irrevocable undertakings from the target's directors) (s 975(2) CA 2006).

The effect is that shares which the bidder already holds, or which it has contracted to acquire will not be counted in the takeover offer. On the other hand, shares held by other persons, including shares in respect of which irrevocable undertakings have been obtained, will be treated as being part of the takeover offer.

Shares held by bidder's associate

6938 Shares that an associate of the bidder holds or has contracted to acquire, whether at the date of the offer or subsequently, are not treated as shares to which the offer relates, even if the offer extends to such shares. Such shares are therefore not counted as being within the takeover offer (s 977(2) CA 2006).

The **definition** of associate for these purposes is quite complex (s 988 CA 2006). It means:
– where the bidder is an individual, his spouse or civil partner and any minor child or stepchild;
– a holding company, subsidiary or fellow subsidiary of the bidder;
– a nominee of the bidder, holding company, subsidiary or fellow subsidiary;
– any company in which the bidder is substantially interested; and
– any person who is, or is the nominee of someone who is, a party to an agreement with the bidder to acquire an interest in shares included in the takeover offer on terms which include an obligation or restriction on any of the parties with respect to the use, retention or disposal of their interest in the relevant shares.

> MEMO POINTS A bidder is deemed to have a **substantial interest** in a company if:
> – the company or its directors are accustomed to act in accordance with the bidder's directions or instructions; or
> – the bidder is entitled to exercise or control the exercise of a third or more of the voting power at the company's general meetings.

B. Bidder's "squeeze-out" right

6945 Where a bidder makes a takeover offer and does not acquire all of the shares to which that offer relates, it may have a statutory right to acquire the remaining shares. This is referred to as the bidder's "squeeze-out" right.

Availability of right

6946 This right is available when the bidder has unconditionally acquired or contracted to acquire both 90% by **value** of the shares to which the offer relates and 90% of the **voting rights** carried by those shares (unless the shares are non-voting). If the offer relates to different classes of shares, then both thresholds must be reached in relation to each class (s 979(1)-(3) CA 2006).

Where an offer includes all or any shares which are allotted subsequently, in deciding whether the 90% threshold has been reached, the bidder only needs to consider the shares which have been allotted **at the time** it exercises its "squeeze-out" right (s 979(5)-(7) CA 2006). If more shares are subsequently allotted which take the percentage of acceptances received below the 90% threshold, the squeeze-out notices already served are not invalidated. However, the bidder will not be able to serve further "squeeze-out" notices until he reaches the 90% threshold again.

The bidder's **pre-offer shareholding**, including shares which it had contracted to acquire before the offer, is not counted for these purposes (see ¶6937). This means that the bidder must acquire 90% of the shares held by other people, not 90% of the total shares.

> MEMO POINTS 1. If the offer relates to **different classes** of shares, the right is triggered in any class in which the bidder acquires 90% or more in value of the shares and 90% or more of the voting rights in that class (s 979(4) CA 2006). For example, if the offer relates to ordinary and preference shares and the bidder acquires 94% of the ordinary shares which it has offered to purchase and 75% of the preference shares, it will only be able to compulsorily acquire the remaining ordinary shares.
> 2. During the offer period, the bidder may **acquire shares other than through acceptances** of the takeover offer, or its **associate** (¶6938) may acquire or contract to acquire the shares instead. These shares will only be counted towards meeting the threshold if the consideration paid for them does not exceed the value of the consideration specified in the terms of the offer or the terms of the offer are revised to match or exceed the consideration paid (s 979(8)-(10) CA 2006).
> 3. In the case of **joint bidders**, joint acquisitions through acceptances of the offer and joint or separate acquisitions other than through acceptances of the offer, will be considered in determining whether the threshold has been met (s 987 CA 2006).

Exercising the right

6949 If the takeover is subject to the City Code on Takeovers and Mergers, the bidder must have reached the threshold **within** 3 months of the last day on which the offer can be accepted (s 980(2) CA 2006). In the case of takeovers not subject to the City Code (e.g. most private company takeovers), notice will have to be given within 6 months after the date of the offer if that is earlier.

> MEMO POINTS Where the threshold is not met because the bidder has **not been able to trace** one or more of the **shareholders** after making reasonable enquiries, and with those shares the bidder would have met the threshold, the bidder can apply to court for an order authorising it to exercise its right to buy the remaining shares. The court must be satisfied that the consideration offered is fair and reasonable and that the order is just and equitable having regard in particular to the number of shareholders who have been traced but who have not accepted the offer (s 986(9), (10) CA 2006).

6950 If the bidder wishes to exercise its right, it must give **notice to the shareholder** (on Form 980(1)). Once notice has been given, the bidder is entitled and bound to acquire the relevant shares on the same terms as the offer.

When the bidder gives the **first notice** in relation to an offer, it must also send a copy of it to the target together with a statutory declaration (on Form 980dec) stating that the conditions for the giving of the notice are satisfied (s 980(4) CA 2006). Where the bidder is a company, the statutory declaration must be signed by a director (s 980(5) CA 2006).

> MEMO POINTS 1. In the case of **joint bidders**, the notice may be given by only one of them but the statutory declaration must be made by all of them (s 987(5), (6) CA 2006).
> 2. A bidder who **fails to send a copy** of its first notice and the statutory declaration to the target, or makes a declaration knowing that it is false or without having reasonable grounds for believing it is true, will be liable to imprisonment and/or a fine (s 980(6), (8) CA 2006). A person can defend this charge on the basis that he took reasonable steps to secure compliance with the requirement (s 980(7) CA 2006).
> 3. The names of these forms, like the other **Companies House forms**, are taken from the section number of the legislation. As all of the section numbers will change under the new Companies Act, Companies House proposes to change the names of all of its forms to reflect their function

instead ("Working with Companies House: a consultation on the registrar's rules and related provisions which will apply under the Companies Act 2006"). Although the names of these forms have already been updated, they are likely to be renamed again in due course. At the time of writing, the new form names are not yet available.

6951 The bidder's **notice** to the minority shareholders should be **given by** (reg 4 SI 1987/752 as amended by SI 2007/1093):
- personal delivery;
- post, sent by recorded delivery; or
- advertisement in the *Gazette* or as required by the articles, in respect of the holder of share warrants.

If the bidder is a company it can also give notice:
- in electronic form;
- by means of a website; or
- in any other way agreed with the intended recipient.

See ¶3695+ for details of how companies can communicate with shareholders, explained in the context of giving notice of shareholder meetings.

6952 If the offer gives the shareholder a **choice of consideration**, the notice should (s 981(3) CA 2006):
- give particulars of the choice;
- state that the shareholder has 6 weeks from the date of the notice to indicate his choice in writing, and the address to which the shareholder should send his decision; and
- state which consideration will apply in default of the shareholder making a choice.

> MEMO POINTS If the bidder is **no longer able to provide** any non-cash consideration, or a third party was to provide the consideration and that third party is no longer bound or able to provide it, the consideration will be taken to consist of an equivalent cash amount as at the date of the notice (s 981(5) CA 2006).

Completion

6953 Completion of the purchase will take place 6 weeks **after** the date of the notice. At that time, the bidder must send to the company a copy of the **notice** it has given to each shareholder (s 981(6) CA 2006). The notice must be accompanied by a completed stock transfer form executed on behalf of the shareholder by a person nominated by the bidder. On receipt of the stock transfer form, the company must register the bidder as the holder of those shares (s 981(7) CA 2006).

> MEMO POINTS Where the shares are not registered but are transferable by the delivery of **share warrants**, instead of a stock transfer form, a copy of the notice sent to the company must be accompanied by a statement to that effect. On receipt of the statement, the share warrants in issue will become void and the company must issue replacement warrants to the bidder (s 981(8) CA 2006).

6954 At the same time as sending the company a copy of the relevant notice, the bidder must pay or transfer the relevant **consideration** to the company (s 981(6) CA 2006). If the consideration consists of shares or securities, they must be allotted to the company (s 981(6) CA 2006). The company will hold the consideration it receives on trust for the relevant shareholder and must pay it, and any dividend, interest or other sums accruing from the consideration, into a separate interest bearing bank account (ss 981(9), 982 CA 2006).

If the **shareholder** entitled to the consideration **cannot be found** after 12 years of making reasonable enquiries at reasonable intervals, or if the company is wound up in that time, the consideration and any sums accruing from it must be paid into court (s 982(4), (5) CA 2006). The expenses of making enquiries can be paid out of the consideration held on behalf of the person whom the company is attempting to locate (s 982(9) CA 2006).

Shareholder objection

6955 A minority shareholder who receives notice from a bidder that it intends to compulsorily acquire his shares may **apply to court** for an order that the bidder is not entitled to acquire his shares or for an order that the terms of the acquisition are different from those in the takeover offer (s 986(1) CA 2006).

The application must be made **within** 6 weeks of the date on which the notice was given. The applicant must notify the bidder of his application, who in turn must notify any shareholder who is being squeezed out or who is exercising his rights of sell-out, and is not a party to the application (s 986(6), (7) CA 2006).

When an application is made, completion is suspended until the court has made its **decision** (s 986(2) CA 2006). The court cannot reduce the consideration below that offered in the bid, although it can order that higher consideration must be paid in exceptional circumstances (s 986(4) CA 2006). The court will not order the shareholder to pay costs and expenses unless there is some culpable conduct on his part (for example, if the application was unnecessary, improper or vexatious, or he was guilty of unreasonable delay or conduct in the proceedings) (s 986(5) CA 2006).

C. Minority shareholders' "sell-out" right

Where a bidder makes a takeover offer and does not acquire all the shares to which that offer relates, the remaining shareholders have the right to require the bidder to buy their shares. This is known as the minority shareholders' "sell out" right.

6965

Availability of right

This right is available when the bidder has unconditionally acquired or contracted to acquire both 90% by **value** of the shares to which the offer relates and 90% of the **voting rights** carried by those shares (unless the shares are non-voting) (s 983(1)-(3) CA 2006).

6966

The bidder does not have to purchase the minority shareholders' shares unless it actually acquires, or unconditionally contracts to acquire, 90% or more of the shares by the end of the **period** within which the sell-out rights can be exercised. This prevents the bidder from being forced to buy the minority shareholders' shares when conditions remain unfulfilled and the bidder does not actually acquire 90% of the shares.

In contrast to the bidder's "squeeze-out rights", the bidder's **pre-offer shareholding** in the target and any acquisitions during the offer period by it or its associates (regardless of price) count for the purposes of deciding whether or not the threshold has been met. The right is therefore available when the bidder reaches 90% of the total shares rather than 90% of the shares held by other people.

> MEMO POINTS 1. If the offer relates to **different classes** of shares, the right is triggered in any class in which the bidder acquires 90% or more in value of the shares and 90% or more of the voting rights in that class (s 983(4) CA 2006). For example, if the offer relates to ordinary and preference shares and the bidder acquires 94% of the ordinary shares which it has offered to purchase and 75% of the preference shares, it will only have to acquire the remaining ordinary shares.
> 2. In the case of **joint bidders**, joint acquisitions through acceptances of the offer and joint or separate acquisitions other than through acceptances of the offer, will be considered in determining whether the threshold has been met (s 987(2) CA 2006).

Once the threshold is met, the bidder must give **notice to the remaining shareholders** that their right has been triggered (s 984(3) CA 2006). Notice must be given on Form 984 and must be sent within 1 month of the threshold being met. If the notice is sent during the offer period, it must state that the offer is still open for acceptance.

6967

The notice may specify a period **within** which the shareholders can exercise their right, but that period must be at least 3 months after the last day for acceptance of the offer, or 3 months after the date of the bidder's notice (s 984(2) CA 2006).

Where there is a **choice of consideration**, the notice must provide the same information as if the company were exercising its right to compulsorily acquire the shares (see ¶6952) (s 985(3) CA 2006).

Notice need **not be given** if the company has already given notice that it intends to compulsorily acquire the shares (s 984(4) CA 2006).

> MEMO POINTS 1. If the bidder **fails to give notice** to the shareholders when it is obliged to, it (and every officer in default, if the bidder is a company) will be liable to a fine and a daily default fine for continued contravention (¶9935) (s 984(5), (7) CA 2006). A person can defend this charge on the basis that he took reasonable steps to secure compliance with the requirement (s 984(6) CA 2006).
> 2. The name of Form 984, like the other **Companies House forms**, is taken from the section number of the legislation. As all of the section numbers will change under the new Companies Act, Companies House proposes to change the names of all of its forms to reflect their function instead ("Working with Companies House: a consultation on the registrar's rules and related provisions which will apply under the Companies Act 2006"). Although the names of these forms have already been updated, they are likely to be renamed again in due course. At the time of writing, the new form names are not yet available.

6968 The shareholder must **exercise his right by** means of a written notice addressed to the bidder but no particular form is required. This notice can be sent to the company in hard copy, electronic form or another agreed form (see ¶3628), as well as via a website if the shareholder is a company (see ¶3695 +).

6969 Where a shareholder exercises his sell-out right, the bidder becomes bound to acquire the shareholder's shares on the **terms** of the offer or on such other terms as may be agreed (s 985(2) CA 2006). If the bidder and shareholder **cannot agree** terms, either of them may apply to court for it to settle the terms as it thinks fit (s 986(3) CA 2006). The shareholder applicant must promptly notify the bidder if he makes an application to court. A bidder who is notified of a shareholder's application or who applies to court itself must notify any shareholder who is being squeezed out or who is exercising his rights of sell-out, and is not a party to the application (s 986(6)-(8) CA 2006).

The **court** cannot reduce the consideration below that offered in the bid, although it can order that higher consideration must be paid in exceptional circumstances (s 986(4) CA 2006). The court will not order the shareholder to pay costs and expenses unless there was some culpable conduct on his part (e.g. the application was unnecessary, improper or vexatious, or he was guilty of unreasonable delay or conduct in the proceedings) (s 986(5) CA 2006).

III. Takeover by scheme of arrangement

6985 Instead of making a takeover offer, or after an offer has been made, a takeover of the shares of a **private or public company** can be achieved using a court approved scheme of arrangement (Re National Bank Ltd [1966] 1 All ER 1006). The mechanics of a scheme of arrangement are dealt with in further detail at ¶6500+.

Recent **adaptations to the City Code**, effective from 14 January 2008, specifically address takeovers by scheme of arrangement (Takeover Panel Instrument 2007/1). A new Appendix 7 sets out particular rules that should be followed in the case of such a takeover, and various amendments have been made to the provisions of the Code itself (e.g. to the definitions and timescales) so that the Code can be applied more easily to schemes. The new Appendix also specifies which provisions of the Code do not apply to takeovers by scheme of arrangement. In certain cases, such as where the target board does not support the scheme, the Executive must still be consulted on how the Code should apply.

> MEMO POINTS The revised Code **applies to** transactions announced (see ¶6816+) on or after 14 January 2008. The Executive should be consulted about the application of the Code to transactions that straddle this implementation date. As a result of these amendments, the Executive has announced that it intends to withdraw Practice Statement 14 of 2005 (which deals with schemes of arrangement) in due course.

A. Advantages

The main advantages of a scheme of arrangement over a normal takeover are: **6990**
– the scheme can **bind 100% of shareholders** with only 75% of shareholder approval, whereas a straightforward takeover requires 90% of shareholders (excluding the shares already held by the bidder or parties with which it is acting in concert) to agree before the remaining 10% can be compulsorily acquired;
– a cancellation scheme (see ¶7000) will **avoid stamp duty** because there is no transfer of shares whereas in a straightforward takeover, the bidder will need to pay stamp duty on the shares transferred to it; and
– it is likely that if the scheme involves the issue of transferable securities by the bidder, the prospectus regime (¶6687) will not apply.

Comment: Schemes of arrangement are not expressly excluded from the **prospectus regime**. However, the common view among practitioners is that the issue of transferable securities as part of a scheme of arrangement does not fall within the regime because there is no offer which enables shareholders to buy or subscribe for securities. Instead, there is a court procedure under which shareholders are asked to vote on and approve an arrangement. The UKLA has stated that whether this view is correct or not is a matter of law, and ultimately for the courts to decide. However, it is inclined to agree that the common view is correct (*List!* – Issue no 10, June 2005).

B. Disadvantages

The main disadvantages of a scheme of arrangement over a normal takeover are: **6995**
– the **time and expense** of court involvement (although the expense may be cancelled out by the stamp duty saving);
– the target and its directors have **control** over the process rather than the bidder (although it is possible for the bidder and target to enter into a merger agreement which requires the target to implement the scheme according to the terms of the agreement);
– the **scheme can be withdrawn** once the process has commenced which gives shareholders less certainty; and
– the possible danger of **irrevocable undertakings** from the target's directors. In a recommended takeover offer, it is usual for the directors of the target to give irrevocable undertakings to accept the offer if the 90% compulsory acquisition threshold is reached. The shareholdings of persons who have given such undertakings count towards the 90% threshold. In a scheme of arrangement, 75% approval from each class of shareholder is required. It is, however, possible that shareholders who have given irrevocable undertakings constitute a separate class. A separate class meeting would then be required for all of the other shareholders and it may be much more difficult to secure the 75% majority from them in isolation.

C. Types of scheme

There are two main types of schemes by which a takeover could be implemented: **7000**
– a cancellation scheme; or
– a transfer scheme.

A **cancellation scheme** involves the bidder paying the target shareholders to agree to a cancellation of their issued shares. The amount of cancelled share capital is transferred to a new reserve (usually called the "cancellation reserve") which is then capitalised by using it to pay for new shares issued to the bidder. A cancellation scheme must comply with additional procedures because it is also a reduction of share capital (see ¶1435+).

A **transfer scheme** is a straightforward transfer of shares from the target's shareholders to the bidder in exchange for the bidder paying the shareholders some form of consideration (e.g. cash or shares in the bidder).

CHAPTER 15
Litigation and investigations

OUTLINE ¶¶

A	Civil proceedings	7118
1	Using the company's name in litigation	7124
2	Using a shareholder's name in litigation	7126
	On his own behalf	7126
	On the company's behalf	7127
3	Control of litigation	7134
4	Procedures	7139
	a Applications under companies legislation	7143
	b Other types of action	7162
B	Criminal proceedings	7175
1	Against a company	7176
2	Against an officer	7183
3	Procedure	7184
C	CIB investigations	7195
1	General investigations into a company's conduct and affairs	7206
	a Investigators	7208
	b Inspectors	7219
	c Consequences of an investigation	7231
2	Investigations into specific aspects of a company	7237
	Ownership	7239
	Suspected criminal activity discovered during liquidation	7247
	To assist overseas authorities	7250

A company is a distinct legal entity from its shareholders and the board, and so it may find itself subject to **civil or criminal proceedings** in a number of situations. A company may also need to commence civil proceedings against another person, for example to recover money owed to it. In many such proceedings, the division between the company and its officers or shareholders can be unclear because the company must act through these agents. **Directors** are most likely to face legal proceedings against them individually due to their hands-on involvement with the company's management and the numerous obligations attached to their office; these duties and liabilities are discussed at ¶2317+. As individuals, **shareholders** may need to take action against the company (see ¶2067+, ¶2100+). In certain circumstances, they may be able to take action in their own names which should properly be taken by the company. These are called "derivative actions" and are discussed at ¶7127+.

A company may also be subject to an **investigation** by the Companies Investigation Branch (CIB), which is part of the Insolvency Service. These investigations are fact-finding exercises to determine whether or not there are grounds for taking action against the company, its officers or shareholders for wrongdoing (such as winding the company up, reporting it or its officers for criminal offences or taking action against the directors for breach of duty). Therefore, the object of the CIB's investigations is not to determine liability or guilt. Investigators or inspectors will be authorised to take steps such as inspecting company documents, interviewing officers and entering the company's premises in order to obtain the information needed to decide whether any further action should be taken.

7115

A. Civil proceedings

7118 A company may have to **commence or defend** ordinary civil legal proceedings for a number of **reasons**, contract disputes being a common cause of such action. It is also obliged by companies legislation to refer to court in relation to a number of matters, such as reducing its share capital. It may also have to commence or defend proceedings relating to the conduct of the company or its directors (for example, actions for unfair prejudice or actions against directors for breach of statutory duty).

Once it has been established that a claim exists, one of the first decisions to make is **whether action can and should be taken** in the company's name. As well as the commercial and financial implications of litigation, other factors may influence a company's ability to go to court, for example:

a. if the dispute arises out of a contract, the company may have to take certain steps (for example, serving particular notices on the other party and using an alternative dispute resolution procedure) before it can take court action; or

b. if the company is in liquidation or another insolvency procedure, its ability to take and defend legal action is severely curtailed (see the summary table at ¶7350).

MEMO POINTS   The **new Companies Act** aims to reduce unnecessary company procedures. Therefore, by 1 October 2009, private companies limited by shares will not have to apply to court to obtain approval of a reduction of capital (see ¶1469/mp), although they will still be able to do so if they wish.

7119 Civil proceedings are principally **governed by** the Civil Procedure Rules ("CPR"), the aim of which is to deal with claims justly by (r 1.1 CPR):

a. ensuring that the parties are on an equal footing;
b. saving expense;
c. dealing with cases in ways which are proportionate to:
– the amount of money involved;
– the importance of the case;
– the complexity of the issues; and
– the financial position of each party;
d. ensuring that cases are dealt with expeditiously and fairly; and
e. allotting an appropriate share of the court's resources to each case, taking into account the need to allot resources to other cases.

This is known as the "**overriding objective**", and must be borne in mind when conducting civil proceedings.

The text of the CPR can be found on the Ministry of Justice website.

1. Using the company's name in litigation

7124 A company is a legal entity in its own right and so can sue in its corporate name to redress a wrong done to it or to recover money or damages due to it (s 13 CA 1985; restated at s 16 CA 2006 by 1 October 2009). This is known as the "**proper claimant principle**". Similarly, proceedings can be commenced against the company in its corporate name.

Legal action may only be commenced in the company's name with the **consent of** the company; in companies governed by Table A, this authority is part of the general management power delegated to the board (reg 70 TA 1985; which an individual director cannot exercise on his own, *Mitchell & Hobbs (UK) Ltd v Mill* [1996] 2 BCLC 102). It is possible for proceedings to be commenced by a majority of the shareholders even if the directors object (*Pender v Lushington* (1877) 6 Ch D 70).

If unwanted legal action has been commenced **without** the proper **authority**, the company can apply to have its name struck out of the proceedings. This should be done as soon as possible. Alternatively, the company can ratify the decision if it supports the unauthorised action and wishes to continue with the claim (*Alexander Ward & Co Ltd v Samyang Navigation Co Ltd* [1975] 2 All ER 424).

EXAMPLE The proper claimant principle is part of the "**rule in *Foss v Harbottle***", which takes its name from the leading case in this area (*Foss v Harbottle* (1843) 2 Hare 461). In this case, two of the shareholders, Mr F and another, alleged that certain directors (including Mr H) had been making secret profits and that all of the directors were in breach of their fiduciary duties by allowing the company to enter into fraudulent transactions. The two shareholders commenced proceedings in their own names and on behalf of the other shareholders except the defendants. However, the court would not let the action proceed because the company was a legal entity in its own right, not just an association of individual shareholders, and was the proper plaintiff (now called a claimant) in the proceedings.

The other two principles forming the rule in *Foss v Harbottle* are that:
– generally, the court will not interfere with the internal management of a company; and
– the shareholders cannot sue to correct an irregularity or informality in company procedure where the act would otherwise be within the company's powers and the intention of the shareholders is clear.

MEMO POINTS 1. If the company **changes** its **name** during the proceedings, the new name must be used on the relevant documents with the old name in brackets to avoid any confusion.
2. **Insolvency practitioners** can take legal action in the company's name where the company is subject to a formal insolvency procedure.
3. Draft **new model articles** under the new Companies Act have been published for private companies limited by shares and public companies. Both sets of new model articles will include an equivalent of reg 70 TA 1985 (art 2).

In normal circumstances, a company and the individuals running it are treated as being entirely separate with their own rights and liabilities, so if a company is sued it must comply with any order against it, whereas if an individual is sued judgment is imposed on him rather than his company. However, it is possible for a party to argue that the **company** itself **is a mere façade**, used to disguise the fact that (usually) the company has been established to evade either limitations on conduct imposed by law or the rights of third parties to relief (*Adams v Cape Industries plc* [1991] 1 All ER 929). In such circumstances, which are rare and difficult to establish, the court will look behind the concept of the company being a separate legal person in its own right and can give judgment against the individuals involved and/or the façade company as appropriate, including orders for costs. This is called "**piercing the corporate veil**".

7125

EXAMPLE
1. Where a company was used as a front for laundering the proceeds of drug-trafficking, the corporate veil could be pierced so that assets held by the company (property and money in the bank) could be counted as the defendant's property and made subject to restraint and receivership orders under the Drug Trafficking Act 1994 pending confiscation proceedings (*Crown Prosecution Service v Compton and others* [2002] EWCA Civ 1720).
2. An individual transferred property into the name of a company he had set up in order to avoid an action for specific performance to transfer the property to the claimant, which was being brought against him personally. The court found that the company was a sham and was being used as a device to avoid justice and so it made an order for specific performance against the company (*Jones v Lipman* [1962] 1 All ER 442).
3. Mr S was a director of T AB and controlled I Ltd. He extracted money without authority from T AB in breach of his fiduciary duties and paid it into I Ltd. The court was entitled to pierce the corporate veil because I Ltd had been used as a device by Mr S to conceal the true facts, and it could treat the receipt by I Ltd of the money as receipt by Mr S and order him to account for the money to T AB (*Trustor AB v Smallbone (No 2)* [2001] 3 All ER 987).

MEMO POINTS It is also possible to pierce the corporate veil in **group company** situations, although this is also very difficult to establish. For example, a claimant could not have a defendant company substituted for another company in its group simply because the defendant company no longer had sufficient assets as a result of the group assets being restructured, in the absence of some impropriety or sham in the restructuring (*Ord v Belhaven Pubs Ltd* [1998] 2 BCLC 447). Similarly, the corporate veil cannot be pierced because a group has been structured so that particular liabilities fall on particular companies (*Adams v Cape Industries plc*, above).

2. Using a shareholder's name in litigation

On his own behalf

7126 A shareholder can commence proceedings in his own name where his **individual rights** have been affected (*Edwards v Halliwell* [1950] 2 All ER 1064). However, he will not be able to claim for any **reflective loss** he has suffered as a result of a wrong done to the company (see ¶2464/mp).

On the company's behalf

7127 As an **exception to the proper claimant principle**, proceedings that should be commenced in the company's name (because the company suffered the wrong) can be commenced in the name of a shareholder or a group of shareholders.

These claims are known as "**derivative claims**" because the individual derives his right of action from the company. Whether a claim is a true derivative claim or whether alternative action should be taken instead (for example, for unfair prejudice; ¶2105+) will depend entirely on the circumstances of the case.

This area was reformed when the relevant provisions of the new Companies Act came into force on 1 October 2007 (ss 260-264 CA 2006). Until then, derivative claims were governed by common law. The right to bring a derivative claim and the procedure for doing so are now set out in statute and the CPR. Therefore, any claims commenced on or after 1 October 2007 must be brought under the new statutory provisions.

> MEMO POINTS   If a claimant had applied for permission to continue his derivative claim **before 1 October 2007**, the common law position will continue to apply to that claim. As a transitional measure, if the claim was commenced on or after 1 October 2007 but the acts or omissions complained of occurred before this date, the statutory rules will apply to the claim but the court will only allow the claim to continue if it would have been able to do so under the common law rules (para 20 Sch 3 SI 2007/2194; see ¶7130/mp for the criteria that were applied in these cases).

7128 The new statutory provisions cover the most common **situation** in which a shareholder may need to bring a derivative claim, that is where the company has a right of action against a director for his (actual or proposed) negligence, default, breach of duty or breach of trust (s 260 CA 2006). The claim does not necessarily have to be brought against the director (it could be brought against a person who has benefited from the act or omission complained of as well as or instead of the director) and the claim can still be pursued even if the director has not benefited from his wrongdoing.

The **conditions** for bringing a derivative claim under statute are that:
– the claimant is a shareholder of the company. This is widely defined to include those to whom shares have been automatically transferred or transmitted, e.g. on the shareholder's death or bankruptcy, and those who were not shareholders when the cause of action arose (this is because the cause of action belongs to the company, not individual shareholders);
– the cause of action is vested in the company; and
– relief must be sought for the company's benefit and not the shareholder's.

Comment: There has been **concern** that this new derivative right will substantially increase the amount of shareholder litigation because it allows action to be taken against directors and third parties and it potentially enables an individual to obtain shares in a company after the event in order to bring a claim (e.g. an environmental action group could obtain a single share in a company and then bring a derivative claim against the directors for breach of their duty to promote the success of the company (which obliges the directors to consider the impact of the company's operations on the environment, amongst other things)). However, the explanatory notes to the new Act indicate that the courts should exercise their discretion to refuse permission to proceed (see ¶7130 below) robustly to ensure that only genuine claims continue. For example, it states that claims will only be allowed to proceed against third parties in limited circumstances where the third party was somehow involved in or at least aware of the director's breach, such as knowingly receiving property transferred in breach of trust (para 494, Explanatory Notes to CA 2006). As with any litigation, shareholders taking action under this provision will incur costs even if their claim is thrown out at the first stage, which should be a strong deterrent to shareholders bringing baseless claims.

MEMO POINTS 1. Derivative claims may also be brought in **other situations** under the new Act, but only where a shareholder has applied to the court for relief from unfair prejudice (see ¶2105+). As part of its discretion to make any order that is appropriate in the circumstances, the court can order that proceedings are commenced in the name and on behalf of the company by any person, including a shareholder (s 996 CA 2006). In which case, there is no need for the shareholder to apply to the court for permission to continue with the claim as this order replaces the first stage in the derivative claim procedure.
2. By way of background information, a derivative claim under the **common law** could be brought where the company's consent to commence proceedings could not be obtained and this was considered to be a fraud on the minority. This depended on the circumstances of each case, but the common law established that the following situations were likely to represent a "fraud on the minority" and could therefore be brought as derivative claims:
a. the act complained of was fraudulent, oppressive, ultra vires or criminal (*Edwards v Halliwell* [1950] 2 All ER 1064; *Cockburn v Newbridge Sanitary Steam Laundry Co Ltd and Llewellyn* [1915] 1 IR 237);
b. the wrongdoers had the majority of votes and were therefore able to block consent to take court action (*Prudential Assurance Co Ltd v Newman Industries Ltd (No 2)* [1982] 1 All ER 354); or
c. the company was carrying, or proposing to carry, out an action with the consent of a majority of the shareholders when a greater level of consent was required (e.g. a special resolution was necessary, *Baillie v Oriental Telephone and Electric Co Ltd* [1915] 1 Ch 503).

In order to prevent shareholders from taking advantage of the right to take derivative action in inappropriate circumstances, the **procedure** for these claims has a built in "filter" stage that requires the shareholder to apply to court for permission to proceed with his claim (ss 260-264 CA 2006). The procedure is set out in the CPR, and is summarised in the following flowchart (rr 19.9-19.9F CPR; CPR PD 19C).

7130

```
┌─────────────────────────────────────┐
│ Claimant issues claim form and files│
│ application notice for permission   │
│ to continue with claim [1,4]        │
└─────────────────────────────────────┘
                  ↓
┌─────────────────────────────────────┐
│ Claimant to notify company of claim │
│         and application [2]         │
└─────────────────────────────────────┘
                  ↓
┌─────────────────────────────────────┐
│ Claimant to file witness statement  │
│ at court confirming company was     │
│              notified               │
└─────────────────────────────────────┘
                  ↓
┌─────────────────────────────────────┐
│   Paper hearing of application      │
│   for permission to continue [3]    │
└─────────────────────────────────────┘
                  ↓
            Permission granted?
          Y ←            → N
              ↓
  Court gives directions      Appeal? → N → Derivative action cannot proceed
              ↓                  ↓ Y
  Directions complied with,   Request hearing within 7 days
  e.g. defence filed          and notify company
              ↓                  ↓
  Hearing of claim [4]        Oral hearing [3]
                                 ↓
                            Permission granted?
                          Y ←            → N
                                        ↓
                          Derivative action cannot proceed
```

Note:
1. The **claim form** must be headed "derivative claim" and the company should be named as a defendant to the action.
2. **Copies** of all of the documents filed at court must be included with the notice, together with a copy of s 263(1)-(4) CA 2006 which sets out the factors the court will take into account when making its decision. The court can allow the claimant to **delay** notifying the company of the claim if it is satisfied that it would be likely to jeopardise part of the remedy sought. If the claimant wants to apply to court for permission to delay notification, he should do so at the same time as submitting the claim form and application for permission to continue to court (or as soon as possible after that). He does not have to give notice of the application to delay notification to the company.

3. A **paper hearing** means that the judge (either a Chancery Division High Court judge if the claim was issued in the High Court, or a circuit judge if it was issued in the county court) will decide whether the derivative claim should be allowed to proceed on the basis of the papers filed at court without the parties being present.

In deciding whether or not the claim should be allowed to continue (whether at the initial paper hearing, or at an oral appeal hearing), the judge will look at the following **factors** (s 263 CA 2006):
– whether the shareholder is acting in good faith;
– the importance that a person acting in accordance with the duty to promote the success of the company would attach to continuing the claim;
– whether the act or omission giving rise to the cause of action could (and would be likely to) be authorised or ratified by the company;
– whether the company has decided not to pursue the claim;
– whether the act or omission gives the shareholder the right to pursue court action in his own right instead; and
– evidence of the views of other shareholders without a personal interest in the claim. Normally, the decision will be made without representations (written in the case of the paper hearing, and in person in the case of the oral second hearing) from the company. If the company decides to make representations to court without being invited to do so, it will not usually be allowed to recover its costs of doing so.

The claim will not be allowed to continue if:
– a person acting in accordance with the duty to promote the success of the company would not pursue it; or
– if the act or omission complained has been authorised or ratified by the company.

4. The court has the power to order the company to indemnify the claimant for his **costs** of bringing the claim (including the costs incurred in making the application for permission to continue). The claimant should state that he wants such an order to be made on his claim form.

MEMO POINTS 1. This procedure **applies to** derivative actions:
– brought by a shareholder;
– taken over by a shareholder after the company has already commenced proceedings;
– that arise during the course of other proceedings; and
– that are not taken under the new Companies Act (against bodies corporate to which the new Act's provisions do not apply, or against trade unions).

The procedure **does not apply to** a derivative action that is taken as part of the remedy awarded by the court for relief from unfair prejudice (see ¶2105+). This is because permission to commence a derivative action is given by the court in the order made in the unfair prejudice proceedings, so there is no need for the "filter" stage.

2. The filter stage was also a feature of the **common law** procedure (which still applies if proceedings were commenced before 1 October 2007, or if they were commenced after this date but the actions or omissions complained of took place before then). The court considered the following criteria when deciding whether or not to allow a derivative action to proceed:
– whether the shareholder was acting for the benefit of the company and in respect of wrongs done to the company (*Nurcombe v Nurcombe* [1985] 1 All ER 65; *Barrett v Duckett* [1995] 1 BCLC 243);
– whether the shareholder had participated in the wrong complained of (*Mumbray v Lapper* [2005] EWHC 1152 (Ch));
– whether there was an appropriate alternative remedy, for example a liquidator could investigate and pursue any claim necessary if a winding up petition has been presented (*Barret v Duckett*, above); and
– the importance that a person acting in accordance with a duty to promote the success of the company would attach to continuing the claim.

3. Control of litigation

The **board** will usually have the authority to control legal proceedings taken by the company, for example instructing and liaising with legal representation and taking responsibility for signing court documents on behalf of the company. In most companies, this will be incorporated in the board's general management power, although it will depend upon the company's articles (reg 70 TA 1985). The board may delegate responsibility for litigation to a particular director or senior employee, such as an in-house lawyer in a large company. If the claim is not brought in the company's name, the representing **shareholder** will control the litigation.

It is usually necessary to instruct a **solicitor** to advise on and handle the claim, and for a **barrister** or a solicitor with the right to be heard in court (called "rights of audience") to

7134

represent the company in court. If proceedings are commenced in or transferred to the High Court, the company must have legal representation.

> MEMO POINTS   The draft **new model articles** will contain an equivalent provision (art 2 for both private companies limited by shares and public companies).

4. Procedures

7139 The court places a great deal of importance upon the **conduct of the parties** when a claim is brought before it. Its "**pre-action protocols**" set out the steps it expects parties to have taken before they resort to court action in all cases (the CPR Practice Direction – Protocols) and in specific types of claims (for example, the Pre-Action Protocol for Construction and Engineering Disputes). Generally speaking, the protocols require the parties to set out their arguments and demands clearly to each other and attempt to resolve their dispute before asking the court to intervene. Parties are expected to consider an alternative dispute resolution procedure, such as mediation, prior to going to court. If they do not try to avoid taking court action, the court can impose costs penalties on those in default.

Many **applications** made **under companies legislation** are not based on disputes; they seek the court's permission for or confirmation of a particular course of action instead. In these cases, pre-action steps such as mediation are not appropriate, although the parties must still conduct their claim or application in accordance with the overriding objective (¶7119).

> MEMO POINTS   In February 2007, the Civil Justice Council published a public consultation on its **proposal to consolidate** the nine existing pre-action protocols, which often reiterate the same steps and principles, into just one to cover all potential claims. Although the consultation closed in April 2007, the Civil Justice Council's response had not yet been published at the time of writing.

7140 Whether an application is made under companies legislation or not, the claimant may be required to provide **security for costs**. This protects the defendant from being drawn into court proceedings which it may win but in which it is unlikely to recover its costs because the claimant company cannot afford to pay them. This will be a particular issue where proceedings have been issued by an insolvency practitioner appointed in relation to the claimant company (¶7803+).

> MEMO POINTS   1. An **application** for security for costs can be made against a company **under** either companies legislation (s 726 CA 1985, expected to be repealed by 1 October 2009) or the Civil Procedure Rules (rr 25.12, 25.13 CPR).
> 2. s 726 CA 1985 is expected to be repealed by 1 October 2009. There will be no replacement provision in the **new Companies Act**. However, this will make no real difference because a court will still be able to order security for costs to be paid under the CPR.

a. Applications under companies legislation

7143 **Applications** under companies legislation can be **made to** either the county court or the High Court. If proceedings are commenced in the High Court, a company must instruct a solicitor to act on its behalf; this is not necessary, but is often appropriate, for proceedings in the county court.

Applications to the **High Court** under companies and insolvency legislation are made to the Companies Court, which is part of the Chancery Division of the High Court. Proceedings are issued in the Companies Court General Office and usually dealt with by a registrar. Further information on the detailed procedure and practice of such claims can be found in the HM Courts Service's guidance on the Chancery Division on its website.

> MEMO POINTS   Action can be taken against a company for **breach** of the various **statutory duties** imposed upon it by companies legislation. These offences and their penalties are set out at ¶9935. Proceedings will be commenced by the secretary of state. However, most of these actions are criminal rather than civil.

Form of application

7146 Before the CPR was updated in October 2007, several applications under companies legislation had to be made by **petition**. Now, there is only one type of application that needs to be made in this form (an application for relief from unfair prejudice (¶2105+)). Therefore, applications to court under companies legislation will usually be by Part 8 **claim form**, although some applications may be required to be made in another form (e.g. normal claim form) by the CPR or legislation (para 5 CPR PD 49).

7147 Most company-related applications must be made by way of a "**Part 8 claim form**" (that is, made following the claim procedure set out in Part 8 CPR).

This type of claim form must give the following **information** (r 8.2 CPR; Part 8 claim form):
a. that Part 8 CPR applies to the application;
b. the question that the claimant wishes the court to decide or the remedy he seeks and his legal basis for doing so;
c. that the claim is made under the Companies Act 1985 or 2006 (or other legislation, as appropriate);
d. the claimant's name, and if he is making the application in a representative capacity, what that capacity is;
e. the defendant's name, and if he is being sued in a representative capacity, what that capacity is;
f. the details of the claim; and
g. whether the claim includes any issues under the Human Rights Act 1998.

EXAMPLE
Title of proceedings on the claim form:
"In the matter of the Companies Act 2006 [plus any other statute under which the claim is made] And in the matter of Re X Ltd, company registration number 0012345"

Claim forms must be **verified by** a statement of truth, made by either the claimant (in the case of a company, it will be made by the person authorised to control the proceedings) or his solicitor (Part 22 CPR).

MEMO POINTS   The **name of the court** to which the application is to be made should be entered in the top right-hand corner of the claim form. The **claim number** should be left blank by the claimant as this will be allocated by the court.

7148 The claim form must be **filed** at court together with the correct **fee** (which depends on the application in question, see the HM Courts Service website or speak to the court in which the application is to be filed for details). The claimant should file enough copies for:
– the court;
– one to be returned to it; and
– enough for service on the defendant(s) (¶7152). If the court is to effect service, it will keep the relevant copies. If the claimant is to serve the claim form on the defendants, the court will return these copies as well.

The court will then **issue the claim** by stamping it with the date of issue and assigning a claim number to it.

Unlike normal claim forms, the claimant cannot file more detailed particulars of claim after the claim form, but if he has supporting **written evidence** (for example, witness statements) he can file it with the claim form (para 7 CPR PD 8).

Part 8 procedure

7151 The "Part 8 procedure" is a **streamlined** version of the usual **claim procedure** in the civil courts, and must be used for applications made under companies legislation, unless the CPR or legislation states otherwise (para 5 CPR PD 49). Much of the usual procedure will apply, together with some special **requirements**. The summary table at ¶7165 illustrates the progress of the petition procedure.

> **MEMO POINTS** The practice direction sets out **special procedural rules** for certain types of application:
> - for access by the authorities to company documents where a criminal offence is suspected (paras 6, 15 CPR PD 49; ¶7185);
> - for sanction of a scheme of arrangement (para 7 CPR PD 49; ¶6507+);
> - to prevent a statement from being circulated because the right to do so is being abused (para 11 CPR PD 49; ¶2948, ¶3582, ¶3627, ¶3666, ¶4340+);
> - to enforce a director's liability for making unauthorised political donations or incurring unauthorised political expenditure (para 12 CPR PD 49; ¶3204);
> - to enforce the City Code on Takeovers and Mergers (para 13 CPR PD 49; ¶6731); and
> - for approval of a reduction of capital (para 19 CPR PD 49; ¶1484).

7152 Once a claim has been issued, it is the claimant's responsibility to **serve** the claim form and any supporting evidence on the defendant (para 20 CPR PD 49). This must be done within at least 4 months of issue (r 7.5 CPR). If any other documents need to be served on the defendant during the course of the proceedings, it is the claimant who must do so rather than the court.

Where documents must be **served on a company**, the serving party can choose a number of methods.

Method of service[1]	Deemed date of service	Reference (CPR)
Personal service: leaving document with person holding a senior position in the company (i.e. officer, manager, treasurer or chief executive)	Date service effected	r 6.4(4); para 6 CPR PD 6
Posting first class	On second day after posted	r 6.7
Leaving document at company's premises	Day after document left	r 6.7
By DX	On second day after put in document exchange	r 6.7
By fax[2]	On day transmitted, if transmitted before 4pm on a business day. Otherwise, next business day after transmitted.	r 6.7
By other electronic communication (e.g. email)[2]	On second day after transmitted	r 6.7

Note:
1. The correct **address for service** is either a company's principal office (not necessarily its registered office) or any place of business within the jurisdiction which has a real connection with the claim, unless its registered office is specified as proper address for service (r 6.5 CPR).
Companies legislation also makes alternative provisions for service of documents on companies, although the Civil Procedure Rules offer more options (s 1139 CA 2006 or s 725 CA 1985, depending on the legislation governing the application). If the application is made under the 1985 Act, a document can be left at or sent to the company's registered office or principal place of business (with a copy being sent to the registered office). If the application is made under the 2006 Act, it can only be left at the registered office.
2. Both parties must agree in writing to serving documents by **electronic communication** and provide relevant fax number, email address or other electronic identification for that purpose (para 3.1 CPR PD 6). If the fax number, email address or other identification is included on a party's solicitor's headed paper, or in a statement of case or response to a claim filed at court, it will be taken that the party has consented to service to that number, address or identification. The serving party should check whether there are any limitations on the form of documents or size of attachments that the recipient can receive (para 3.2 CPR PD 6).

After serving the claim form, the claimant must file a certificate of service at court within 7 days (r 6.14 CPR).

> **MEMO POINTS** There are particular rules on **serving** documents **on an overseas company**, the details of which are outside the scope of this discussion. Broadly speaking, the serving party can choose between serving the document:
> - at the address registered at Companies House as its place of business within Great Britain (s 695(1) CA 1985 or s 1139 CA 2006, depending on whether the documents are to be served under the 1985 or 2006 Act);

– on the person registered at Companies House as the authorised person for accepting service, where the company has a branch in Great Britain (s 694A CA 1985 or s 1139 CA 2006, depending on whether the documents are to be served under the 1985 or 2006 Act); or
– in accordance with the CPR (see Part 6 CPR and CPR PD 6B).

The defendant must then file and serve his **acknowledgement of service**, together with any written evidence he has in **defence** of the claim, within a further 14 days of service of the claim form (rr 8.3, 8.5 CPR). This deadline can be extended by agreement between the parties as notified to the court (r 2.11 CPR). If the defendant does not file an acknowledgement of service, he may not participate in the hearing (although he may still attend) (r 8.4 CPR).

7153

Once the defendant's evidence has been filed at court and served on the **claimant**, the claimant has 14 days to file and serve any **evidence in reply** (r 8.5 CPR). This deadline can also be extended by agreement as notified to the court.

Part 8 claims are automatically **allocated to** the multi-track, giving the court a wide discretion to make any appropriate **directions** regarding the case, and obviating the requirement for the parties to file allocation questionnaires (r 8.9 CPR). The court may give such directions (with or without summoning the parties to a case management conference) once the claim form has been issued, including fixing a hearing date and the deadlines for disclosing documents, which the parties must follow (Part 29 CPR).

7154

At least 8 weeks before the hearing date, the parties will be required to file a **pre-trial checklist**, or listing questionnaire. This will be sent to them by the court and must be returned by the deadline set in the court's directions. The court may summon a pre-trial review to discuss the next steps, and will set (or confirm) the hearing date and timetable leading up to it (for example, stipulating when the trial bundles need to be prepared).

Comment: The court may order a company to **disclose** any documents relevant to the case, including those kept in electronic format. Companies should ensure that they have a proper procedure for the retention of such documents (including correspondence by email) and their retrieval so that they will be able to comply with an order for disclosure (as well as it being a matter of good business practice). In appropriate circumstances, the courts can impose costs penalties on parties which fail to comply with these orders.

Part 8 claims are sometimes decided without a **hearing** (para 6.3 CPR PD 8). If a hearing is necessary, it will usually only take one day, depending upon how complex the matter is. Both parties are given the opportunity to present their case and evidence to the court (para 8 CPR PD 8). Alternatively, the court may give further directions for the management of the case at the hearing, for example where the parties have not complied with their disclosure obligations meaning that the case cannot be heard.

7155

If the case is heard in full, the court will usually give its **judgment** at the end of the hearing, although if the matter is complex it may adjourn and deliver its judgment at a later date.

The CPR sets out detailed rules about **costs** (Parts 43-48 CPR). Generally speaking, the unsuccessful party is required to pay the other party's costs. However, the court will take the circumstances of the case into account, such as the conduct of the parties before and during the proceedings, and may make a different order as appropriate in the circumstances (e.g. ordering that each party bears its own costs or even that the successful party pays the other party's costs).

7156

EXAMPLE Mr S was a shareholder and director of GR Ltd. He was also a consultant for the firm of solicitors which was instructed by GR Ltd in its claim (GR Ltd had purchased the claim from a third party). The court criticised Mr S's conduct of the case, finding that he had been dishonest and had intimidated one of the defendant's witnesses. At first instance, Mr S was ordered to pay all of the costs of the litigation. On appeal, Mr S argued that the order should not stand because his genuine belief in the claim had not been questioned. The Court of Appeal rejected this, stating that a lack of good faith was not a condition for an order for a third party to pay costs; the key factor was that he was the real party for whose benefit the litigation had been pursued. Mr S had controlled the litigation and, whether or not he believed in the claim, all of the costs had been caused by his dishonesty and impropriety (*Goodwood Recoveries Ltd v Breen* [2006] 2 All ER 533).

Once the court has decided who should pay the costs of the proceedings, it has to work out **how much** is due. One of three methods can be used:
- it can be calculated according to basic figures set out in the rules, known as "**fixed costs**". This basis is used for particular types of straightforward cases, such as debt recovery;
- a **summary assessment** can be carried out, for which the parties will have to submit a statement of costs which briefly sets out the costs they have incurred. Instead of asking the court to assess the costs, the parties can agree a figure; or
- a **detailed assessment** can be carried out, for which the parties will have to submit a bill of costs. This is a more in-depth assessment than a summary one, and will usually be used in complex cases where there is disagreement between the parties as to the reasonableness of the costs incurred. A detailed assessment is carried out at a separate hearing presided over by a costs officer. Preparing a detailed assessment can, in itself, be a costly business, so the parties often reach agreement instead.

There are **two levels** of costs award that the court can make where a summary or a detailed assessment is carried out:
- that costs are paid on the **standard basis**, which is the usual award. This means that the court will look at the statement or bill of costs and only order the other party to pay those that are proportionate and reasonably incurred. If there is any doubt as to whether an item should be allowed, it is construed in the paying party's favour. Reasonable and proportionate solicitor's/barrister's fees will be allowed, but these will be worked out according to standard rates tables (which set out the rates that the court considers reasonable for a solicitor or barrister of different levels of experience in London and outside London; this can be found on the HM Courts Service website) rather than the rates actually charged by the legal representative; or
- that costs are paid on the **indemnity basis**, which means that the paying party must pay the costs that the other party actually incurred (except where an item is unreasonable). If there is any doubt as to whether an item should be allowed, it is construed in the recipient's favour. This order will only be made where there has been some wrongdoing by the paying party and the court wants to show its strong disapproval of his conduct. Therefore, this type of costs order is difficult to obtain (see for example *Re Realstar Ltd* [2007] All ER (D) 171 (Aug)).

EXAMPLE A firm of chartered accountants sued two client companies (which were connected) together for non payment of its fees. The companies in turn issued a counterclaim for professional negligence against the firm. During an adjournment of the trial, the directors put the companies into administration. The directors were added to the proceedings as defendants, on the basis that they had controlled and funded the litigation. The judge found that the counterclaim for professional negligence was baseless and should not have been brought. The companies were therefore ordered to pay the firm's costs on the indemnity basis. In addition, one of the directors (who the court found to be an evasive and untruthful witness, and who had controlled and managed the companies' counterclaim throughout) was made personally liable for these costs, jointly and severally with the companies. Since the companies were in administration, it is likely that the director would have had to pay the bulk of the costs (*Chantrey Vellacott v The Convergence Group plc and others* [2007] EWHC 1774 (Ch)).

Summary

7157

Stage	Responsibility of	Deadline[1]	¶¶
File claim form and claimant's evidence at court	Claimant	-	¶7147+
Issue claim form	Court	-	¶7148
Serve claim form and evidence on defendant	Claimant	Within 4 months of issue	¶7152
File certificate of service at court	Claimant	Within 7 days of service	¶7152

Stage	Responsibility of	Deadline[1]	¶¶
File acknowledgement of service at court with any written evidence in defence	Defendant	Within 14 days of service of claim form	¶7153
File and serve evidence in reply	Claimant	Within 14 days of service of defendant's evidence	¶7153
Comply with court's directions (including pre-trial checklist)	Claimant and defendant	Any deadlines will be specified by court	¶7154
Hearing (if applicable)	-	-	¶7155

Note:
1. Most **deadlines** can be **extended** by agreement between the parties notified in writing to the court (r 2.11 CPR).

Petition procedure

7159

The CPR does not set out how applications made by petition should proceed. There used to be a requirement for the petitioner to apply for **directions** on the conduct of the case, but this has not been included in the new practice direction on applications under companies legislation that has been in effect since 1 October 2007. However, the court has wide case management powers under Part 3 CPR, so it would still be appropriate to apply for directions if the court does not give them on its own initiative.

b. Other types of action

7162

A company can sue and be sued in its own right, since it is a distinct legal entity. Therefore, it may find itself subject to an action for breach of **contract** or commission of a **tort**. A company can only act through its agents, such as directors and employees; although it will be these individuals who commit the acts or omissions in question, if they do so in the course of their agency or employment, the company can be held liable. However, if the company can show that the individual was acting entirely under his own influence, it will not be held liable.

Similarly, a company can sue others for a breach of contract or a tort committed against it.

> MEMO POINTS   In the case of a **public company**, fair and accurate reports of company meetings are privileged and cannot form the basis of a defamation action, provided they are not made with malice (s 15, para 13 Sch 1 Defamation Act 1996). The same applies to publishing copies or extracts of documents sent to a public company's shareholders which:
> – have been issued by the board or the company's auditors, or have been circulated by a shareholder in accordance with a statutory right; and
> – relate to the appointment, resignation, retirement or dismissal of directors.

Procedure

7164

Generally speaking, if a claim is worth under £15,000, it must be **commenced in** the county court (unless it is a claim for damages in respect of personal injuries, in which case the figure is £50,000); otherwise, the claimant may choose to commence proceedings in the High Court (para 2 CPR PD 7). If proceedings are commenced in the High Court, a company must instruct a solicitor to act on its behalf. This is not necessary, but often appropriate, for proceedings in the county court.

Claims other than those brought under companies legislation usually follow the normal claims **procedure** (Part 7 CPR; unless it is another special type of claim for which the Part 8 procedure is used, see ¶7151+ above). The claim form usually sets out the basic information about the claim and the relief sought, with further details about the claim being provided in the particulars of claim. In simpler cases, the details of the claim may be included in the claim form itself. Both the claim form and the particulars of claim must be verified by a statement of truth.

7165 The procedure for normal claims can be **summarised** as follows.

Stage	Responsibility of	Deadline[1]	Reference (CPR)
File claim form at court	Claimant	-	Part 7
Issue claim form	Court	-	Part 7
Serve claim form on defendant	Claimant or court	Within 4 months of issue [2]	r 7.5; Part 6; see ¶7152 for service on a company
File certificate of service at court	Claimant, if served claim form on defendant [3]	Within 7 days of service of claim form on defendant	r 6.14
File particulars of claim at court and serve on defendant (if not already served with claim form)	Claimant	14 days after service of claim form	r 7.4; Part 16
File acknowledgement of service at court (optional, but increases time for preparing defence [4])	Defendant	14 days after service of claim form/particulars of claim (if served later than claim form)	Part 10
File defence at court and serve on claimant [4]	Defendant	– If filed acknowledgement of service, 28 days after service of claim form/particulars (if served later than claim form); or – if have not filed acknowledgement of service, 14 days after service of claim form/particulars (if served later than claim form)	Part 15
File reply to defence at court and serve on defendant	Claimant	With allocation questionnaire (see row below)	r 15.8
File allocation questionnaires at court [5]	Claimant and defendant	By deadline specified by court (which will be at least 14 days after court has served questionnaires)	r 26.3
Comply with court's directions (e.g. exchange of witness statements, disclosure of evidence etc)	Claimant and defendant	Any deadlines will be specified by court	Parts 26-33
Hearing	-	-	Part 39

Note:
1. Most **deadlines** can be **extended** by agreement between the parties notified in writing to the court (r 2.11 CPR).
2. To **extend** this deadline, parties can either agree an extension in writing using the general extension provision (r 2.11 CPR), or apply to court for an order (r 7.6 CPR) (*Thomas v The Home Office* [2006] EWCA Civ 1355).
3. If **court served** the **claim form**, there is no need to file certificate of service. Instead, court will send notice to claimant stating when claim form was deemed to have been served (r 6.14 CPR).
4. However, if the defendant **fails** to serve an acknowledgement of service or a defence within 14 days of service of the claim form, the claimant will be entitled to apply for default judgment (provided default judgment is allowed for the type of claim in question) (r 10.2 CPR; r 15.3 CPR; Part 12 CPR).
5. On the basis of the allocation questionnaire and the type of case, the court will allocate the claim to a track (Part 26 CPR). The "**small claims track**" is generally used for financial claims worth up to £5,000 (or personal injury claims worth up to £1,000). The "**fast track**" is for claims which do not fall within the small claims track, but are worth up to £15,000. The "**multi-track**" is for all other claims, and therefore the more complicated and valuable claims follow this track. Each track has its own rules for case management, which are tailored to the likely complexity of each type of case: small claims track, Part 27; fast track, Part 28; multi-track, Part 29.

B. Criminal proceedings

As well as the numerous **criminal penalties** for which a company can be liable under companies and insolvency legislation (which are set out in the table at ¶9935), it is possible for a company to be held liable for other **common law and statutory offences**. Its officers may also be held personally liable for committing company-related crimes.

1. Against a company

A company **can be** criminally **liable** either:
a. vicariously, for the acts of its employees and agents. This is usually the case for statutory offences (which often impose strict liability, such as many offences under companies legislation, as well as others, such as road traffic offences), although it is applicable to some common law offences as well, for example public nuisance; or
b. in its own right. A company can be liable for a "strict liability" offence, which does not require the perpetrator to have intended to commit the offence, avoiding the problem of proving the state of mind of the company. It can also be convicted of common law offences which do require an intention to commit the crime if it can be shown that a person or persons acting as "the directing mind of the company", such as the board or a manager, had the requisite intent. This is known as the "identification principle" (*R v ICR Haulage Ltd* [1944] 1 All ER 691).

It can be difficult to establish a company's liability using the **identification principle**, especially in the case of a large company with a complex management structure and this has led to changes in the way in which companies can be held liable for manslaughter (see ¶7179+ below). The company's liability is usually confined to the acts of its directors and other superior officers who have management responsibilities, although the company can be liable for the actions of the directors' delegates acting within their authority if the directors have delegated their management functions (*Tesco Supermarkets Ltd v Nattrass* [1971] 2 All ER 127; *Esseden Engineering Company v Maile* [1982] RTR 260). However, the individual states of mind of a number of directors or officers cannot be added together to ascribe liability to the company (*R v P & O European Ferries (Dover) Ltd* [1990] 93 Cr App R 72). The court will look at all of the circumstances, taking into account the extent to which the person is in control of the company's business (or part of it) as well as looking at his position within the company, so that a person will not be the directing mind of the company if, in fact, he has little autonomy within it (*R v Andrews Weatherfoil Ltd* [1972] 1 All ER 65).

Although there are many different crimes for which companies can be held liable, two of the **most common** are health and safety and environmental offences, so these are discussed below (respectively, ¶7178, ¶7182). The issue of corporate manslaughter has been well publicised recently due to the anticipated implementation of new legislation on this topic in April 2008. An outline of a company's liability for manslaughter is also below at ¶7179+.

A company **cannot be** held **liable** for crimes which:
– are only punishable by imprisonment (*R v ICR Haulage Ltd* [1944] 1 All ER 691); or
– can only be committed by a natural person, such as rape.

Health and safety offences

The commonest form of criminal liability encountered by companies arises under health and safety law. There are **general duties** on companies as employers (and others in charge of work premises) to safeguard the health and safety of their employees and of the general public (ss 2-4 HSWA 1974). The company is expected to comply "so far as is reasonably practicable" (information on this standard is provided by the Health and Safety Executive (HSE)). The most authoritative guidance on applying the statutory duties to specific work situations is given in the Approved Codes of Practice (ACOPs). These are approved by the Health and

Safety Commission (HSC), which oversees the HSE (s 16 HSWA 1974). The general duties are fleshed out by regulations, e.g. the Management of Health and Safety at Work Regulations (SI 1992/3242). Other regulations deal with specific areas of work activity, e.g. the Personal Protective Equipment at Work Regulations 1992.

Health and safety law is primarily **enforced by** the HSE, with local authorities playing a secondary role. In a prosecution, breach of a provision in an ACOP is taken as proof of a relevant allegation (s 17 HSWA 1974). On a practical level, the HSE enforces the law by inspecting workplaces and it can issue (ss 21-23 HSWA 1974):
– improvement notices, which specify work that needs to be done to rectify an unsafe situation and a time limit for doing so; and
– prohibition notices, which require the company to cease its activities until the unsafe situation is remedied.

The **penalties** for breach of health and safety law can be heavy. Breach of a duty renders the company liable to a fine of up to £20,000 on summary conviction, or an unlimited fine on indictment (s 33 HSWA 1974). The court will take into account several factors when determining the level of the fine, including the size of the company, the seriousness of the breach, whether the breach occurred with a view to a profit and the degree of danger involved (R v Howe & Co (Engineers) Ltd [1999] 2 Cr App R (S) 37). By way of an example, the highest fines imposed so far for one incident have been for the Hatfield rail crash, for which Network Rail was fined £3.5 million and Balfour Beatty was fined £7.5 million in 2006. Breach of a prohibition or improvement notice gives rise to a fine, as well as the person(s) responsible being liable to imprisonment. A director, manager or other officer of a company can be prosecuted personally if their company has been convicted of an offence under the legislation (see ¶2590).

> MEMO POINTS 1. There is also a complimentary **duty on employees** to take reasonable care of their own health and safety and that of others (s 7 HSWA 1974).
> 2. The HSE also publishes other **guidance** material on many of the regulations, including advisory leaflets, information on analysing for hazardous substances, and advisory DVDs.
> 3. The **Health and Safety (Offences) Bill** is currently before parliament. It proposes to extend the maximum fine of £20,000 on summary conviction to offences under health and safety regulations and other offences which are seen as comparable to breach of the general duties. It also proposes to make imprisonment available as a punishment for more health and safety breaches.
> 4. Further **detail** on health and safety compliance can be found in *Employment Memo*.

Manslaughter

Pre-6 April 2008

7179 The law governing how companies can be held liable for manslaughter will **change** significantly when a new statutory offence of "corporate manslaughter" is introduced in April 2008. The reasons for this change and an explanation of the new law follow at ¶7180, ¶7181.

For offences which were committed before 6 April 2008, a company can be held liable for the offence of **gross negligence manslaughter** where (R v Adomako [1994] 3 All ER 79):
– the company owed a duty of care to the deceased; and
– the breach of that duty was the substantial cause of his death, or the breach was so grossly negligent as to show such a disregard for the deceased's life that it warrants criminal punishment.

Since the company itself cannot commit the acts or omissions which led to the victim's death, an individual (or group of individuals, such as the board) that embodies the company must be guilty of the victim's manslaughter under the identification principle (¶7176). A grossly negligent breach would include, for example, indifference to an obvious risk. The **punishment** for a successful prosecution is a fine for the company and usually imprisonment for the guilty individual(s).

7180 One of the main **reasons for reform** in this area is that public opinion has favoured a specific avenue of prosecution for corporate manslaughter. Although successful prosecutions have been brought against individuals for manslaughter, against individuals and companies for breaches of health and safety law and companies have been sued in the civil courts for negligence, prosecutions against companies for gross negligence manslaughter fail or are not pursued because of the difficulty in applying the identification principle. Take, for example, the Paddington rail crash. Although the health and safety cases against Thames Trains and Railtrack revealed serious failings in management and practice (so much so that the £2 million fine imposed on Thames Trains in 2004 set a record at the time. In March 2007, Railtrack was fined £4 million for its part in the disaster), the CPS decided that there was not enough evidence to charge either company with gross negligence manslaughter.

The main problem with such cases is that even where an individual at fault can be identified, it is extremely difficult to show that he was the "directing mind" of the company, especially in large companies with complex management structures. Therefore, in the cases where there is arguably the greatest public interest in seeing justice done, such as public transport disasters, companies are perceived as literally getting away with murder.

Post-6 April 2008

The Corporate Manslaughter and Corporate Homicide Act 2007 (CMCHA 2007) will introduce an **offence** of corporate manslaughter (called corporate homicide in Scotland). A company will be guilty of this new offence if the way in which its activities are managed or organised (s 1 CMCHA 2007):
– causes a person's death; and
– amounts to a gross breach of a relevant duty of care owed by the company to the deceased.

The offence will **apply to** companies, as well as other bodies, such as certain government departments, police forces and other employers (including partnerships). The majority of the new Act is due to come into force on 6 April 2008 and will apply to offences committed on or after this date (s 27(3) CMCHA 2007). The new statutory offence will only replace the common law offence of gross negligence manslaughter in so far as it applies to companies and other bodies liable under the Act. In appropriate cases, individuals, such as directors, will still be able to be held personally liable for gross negligence manslaughter and prosecutions under health and safety legislation will still be able to be brought against both companies and individuals.

The offence will be **punishable** on indictment, rendering defendant companies liable to a fine (s 1(6) CMCHA 2007). The sentencing guidelines have not yet been drafted at the time of writing, but the courts are expected to consider similar factors as they do in cases of fatal health and safety breaches when they set the level of the fine (see ¶7178 above). There is, of course, no other punishment that can be levied against a company, but there is concern that this will not have the deterrent effect that imprisoning senior management figures would have. However, the court will also be able to impose other types of punishment that should be a deterrent to others:
– "remedial orders" to ensure that the company remedies the breach, any other cause of the death and/or any other health and safety deficiency (s 9 CMCHA 2007); and
– "publicity orders" to make sure that a company's conviction and punishment are made public (s 10 CMCHA 2007; this power is expected to be implemented in the autumn of 2008 to allow for further consultation on how this new punishment should be imposed).

Comment: As well as the provisions relating to publicity orders, the application of the duty of care to **death in custody** will also be brought into force later than the rest of the Act. Death in custody proved to be an extremely contentious issue while the legislation was passing through parliament. The compromise reached was to include duties of care owed to those in custody within the scope of the offence, but to delay the application of the legislation to death in custody. It is expected to be brought within the scope of the Act in about 3 years' time.

7181

MEMO POINTS 1. The Ministry of Justice has published **guidance** on the new Act: "A guide to the Corporate Manslaughter and Corporate Homicide Act 2007" (October 2007). This can be found on the Ministry of Justice's website.
2. A **parent company** cannot be convicted for a breach by its subsidiary. All companies have their own separate legal identity, so each company in a group would be prosecuted separately where appropriate (Ministry of Justice guidance).

Environmental offences

7182 A company can be criminally liable for environmental matters. Breaches of the relevant requirements can range from lack of a permit, failure to comply with the terms of an environmental permit, or simply contravention of environmental law, e.g. by causing too much noise. Typical **types of activity** which require a permit are:
– dealing with waste, including carrying it (SI 1994/1056);
– operating an industrial or agricultural process which requires authorisation under Pollution Prevention and Control (which are processes that, generally, discharge industrial pollutants to air and/or water) (SI 2000/1973); and
– discharging waste water, including into a sewer (s 118 Water Industry Act 1991) or into a watercourse (s 85 Water Resources Act 1991).

A common type of environmental liability is causing too much noise, dust or smell. This can give rise to criminal liability as statutory nuisance (s 79 Environmental Protection Act 1990; Anti Social Behaviour Act 2003). This type of problem could occur with any business premises, not just industrial ones.

> MEMO POINTS Environmental breaches could also constitute common law nuisance which is a tort giving rise to **civil liability**, so a company find itself both criminally and civilly liable.

2. Against an officer

7183 A **company's officers** will generally be liable for their own criminal acts, for example theft of company property (company-related criminal offences commonly affecting directors and other officers are discussed at ¶2536+). Where two or more directors of a company have worked together to commit a fraud, the company itself will usually be charged with **conspiracy** as well (unless the company is a victim of the fraud). If there is only one directing mind of the company (see ¶7176), there is no action for conspiracy, although both the individual and the company may still be charged with the principal offence.

Usually, where companies legislation imposes strict liability on the company, its officer will be liable if he:
– knowingly and wilfully authorises or permits the relevant breach in the case of an offence under the 1985 Act (s 730A CA 1985; para 13 Sch 4 SI 2007/2194); or
– authorises, permits, participates in or fails to take all reasonable steps to prevent the breach in the case of an offence under the 2006 Act where the provision setting out the duty and consequences of breach is already in force (s 1121 CA 2006). A corporate officer will only commit an offence in respect of the company as an officer in default if one of its own officers is in default (s 1122 CA 2006). If this is the case, both the company and its officer will be liable.

> MEMO POINTS Where the **company is guilty** of certain statutory offences, an **officer** (or shareholder, if the company is managed by its shareholders) can also be **held liable** for the offence if it was committed with his consent, connivance or neglect. These offences include (s 733 CA 1985):
> – failure by an outgoing auditor to make a statement to the company (¶4340); and
> – various breaches relating to company investigations: obstructing a person with the right to enter the company's premises, whether with a warrant or not (¶7216; ¶7240); unauthorised disclosure of information obtained during an investigation (¶7212+); and destroying documents and giving false information (¶7211).

3. Procedure

7184 Criminal procedure is **governed by** the Criminal Procedure Rules, which can be found on the Ministry of Justice website. Criminal offences fall into different categories, depending on their seriousness:
– **summary offences**, which are only dealt with in the magistrates' court (for the less serious);

– **indictable offences**, which are only dealt with in the crown court (for the more serious); and
– offences which are **triable either way**, which can be tried in either type of court as appropriate.

A summary offence under the Companies Acts must be **prosecuted within** 3 years of the commission of the offence and within 12 months of the director of public prosecutions or secretary of state deciding that there is enough evidence to prosecute (s 731 CA 1985 or s 1128 CA 2006, depending on which Act applies to the offence). This applies to prosecutions of companies, their officers and other potentially liable individuals.

MEMO POINTS **Authority** of the secretary of state or director of public prosecutions is required for public authorities **to prosecute** a company or individual for some specific statutory offences (s 732 CA 1985 or s 1126(2) CA 2006, depending on which Act applies to the offence).

Where it is reasonably suspected that an individual has committed an **offence relating to the management** of the company's affairs whilst holding office and evidence relating to the offence may be found in books or papers under the company's control, the court can allow the secretary of state, director of public prosecutions or chief of police to have **access to** that **information** (s 721 CA 1985 or s 1132 CA 2006, depending on which Act applies to the offence).

7185

MEMO POINTS **Special rules** apply to these applications. Notice of the application does not need to be given to an individual against whom an order is sought and there is no requirement to serve a claim form upon him (offence under s 721 CA 2006: para 6 CPR PD 49; offence under s 1132 CA 2006: para 15 CPR PD 49).

Very broadly, the **stages** to a criminal prosecution are as follows:

7186

```
Proceedings commenced:
charge or summons
          │
          ▼
Magistrates' court:
• summary offence: tried
• offence triable either way: mode of trial hearing
  (case then either tried by magistrates or committed
  to crown court)
• indictable offence: sent to crown court
          │
          ▼
Crown court: trial of indictable
offences and either way offences
committed to crown court
```

C. CIB investigations

The secretary of state for trade and industry is given extensive powers under companies legislation to investigate the affairs and conduct of companies. The **purpose** of these investigations is to determine whether further action, such as criminal proceedings, disqualifying the directors or winding the company up, should be taken; it is not in itself a judicial process. In practice, this **power** is **exercised by** the Companies Investigation Branch ("CIB") of the Insolvency Service.

7195

A company may also be subject to investigations by other regulatory bodies which supervise aspects of its business, for example, Revenue and Customs, the Serious Fraud Office, the Competition Commission or the Financial Services Authority.

> **MEMO POINTS** CIB investigations are one of the few topics that will remain in the Companies Act 1985. The **new Companies Act** has made some changes to the existing provisions, which came into force on 1 October 2007 and are noted where relevant.

7196 CIB investigations are usually **triggered by** complaints or requests for investigations from:
- members of the public (via the CIB's section of the Insolvency Service website);
- regulatory bodies with authority over the company;
- the company itself; or
- the company's shareholders.

Usually, the investigation will be a general one into the company's conduct and affairs, looking for evidence of alleged fraud, for example. More specific investigations can be undertaken, for example looking at the company's ownership, but these are far less common.

Investigations are usually **carried out by** CIB officials known as investigators, although in the most serious cases professionally qualified inspectors will do so. If the investigators or inspectors uncover wrongdoing, there can be serious **consequences** for the company and its officers.

Pre-investigation stage

7199 The CIB will usually make **informal enquiries** before deciding whether or not a full investigation is necessary. This involves interviewing persons involved in the company on an informal basis. Individuals who co-operate with the CIB in this way will not breach their **confidentiality** obligations if the disclosure is (s 448A CA 1985):
a. made voluntarily;
b. one which he would be required to make if the company was being investigated (which does not include disclosures made in breach of legal professional privilege, ¶7210/mp);
c. made in good faith in the belief that it will assist the secretary of state in his investigatory functions and does not exceed what is required (for example, it is not made maliciously); and
d. not prohibited by law (e.g. the Data Protection Act 1998) or by the duty of confidentiality owed by a lawyer or banker to his client.

The aim of this protection is to encourage individuals to co-operate with the CIB at this early stage so that it can make an informed decision as to whether or not to proceed with the investigation.

> **MEMO POINTS** Any information obtained at this preliminary stage cannot form the **basis of a winding up petition** in the public interest on the just and equitable ground (s 124A(1)(a) IA 1986). However, information obtained during the course of any ensuing investigation can be used in this way (¶7231+).

Decision to investigate

7200 The CIB **will** only **investigate** a company if:
- there is a good reason for doing so (i.e. there are reasonable grounds to suspect serious misconduct or material irregularity in the company's affairs);
- an investigation is likely to have a useful result; and
- it is in the public interest to do so.

It has a discretion as to whether to act on a complaint, and will not give the complainant its reasons for taking action or not. If it does investigate, the CIB will not usually tell the complainant the outcome of the investigation because it will be confidential; he will only find out if legal action is taken against the company, when the proceedings are a matter of public record.

If the CIB concludes that there are sufficient grounds for an investigation, whether from informal enquiries or not, the company will be subject to:
- a general investigation by investigators or inspectors; or
- an investigation into a specific matter.

It is possible to **challenge** the CIB's decision to investigate a company through the judicial review procedure. However, such an action is difficult to establish (particularly if the CIB does not disclose the complaint on which the decision is based on public interest grounds), since the applicant has to prove that the decision was not made in good faith, or that it was made frivolously or vexatiously.

7201 The CIB **will not investigate**:
a. a company in compulsory liquidation, as the official receiver undertakes this task (¶8120+);
b. where there are appropriate civil remedies available to the complainant (for example, an action for recovery of a debt), unless there are special circumstances such as evidence of fraud;
c. where the issue relates to the internal management of the company (because there is no public interest in such an investigation); or
d. where the matter should be dealt with by another body, for example the FSA where the company is in the financial services industry or Trading Standards where the complaint relates to the company's goods or services. Where appropriate, the CIB will pass a complaint to a body which is in a better position to investigate.

1. General investigations into a company's conduct and affairs

7206 CIB investigations are either **carried out by** investigators or inspectors. The usual course is to instruct investigators because, although they have fewer powers than inspectors, they usually provide the most cost-effective way of investigating the company and obtaining the information needed to take the matter forward, where appropriate.

a. Investigators

7208 Investigators can be **appointed** by the secretary of state to gather information about a company's affairs. Although this is a less formal procedure than appointing inspectors, it can have the same **outcome** because the information obtained can be used to wind the company up, disqualify its directors and commence criminal proceedings. Investigators are usually CIB employees, keeping the costs of the investigation down by not incurring the fees of external professionals.

Powers

Obtaining information

7210 The investigators can be authorised by the secretary of state to require the company or any other person (usually the company's officers, but the authorisation can extend to any other person, e.g. customers of the company) to **produce documents** and **provide information** to them (s 447 CA 1985). This encompasses documents in any form, including electronic, and the investigators can take copies of the information away. This requirement will not affect any lien over the documents.

If required to provide information, an individual must answer an investigator's questions. Any statement made can be **used in evidence** against him in **civil proceedings** (s 447A(1) CA 1985). On the other hand, if **criminal proceedings** are later commenced against the interviewee (other than for perjury or providing false information to the investigators or the secretary of state, see ¶7211 below), his responses cannot be used in evidence against him nor can any questions be asked during those proceedings about them (s 447A(2), (3) CA 1985). This clearly limits the usefulness of taking such statements where criminal proceedings are envisaged. However, evidence acquired other than in such statements can be used, for example, information in company documents acquired during the investigation.

MEMO POINTS 1. Information does not have to be disclosed where it is protected by **legal professional privilege** or it is confidential **banking information** (s 452 CA 1985). However, a lawyer can be required to disclose the name and address of his client.
2. The **secretary of state** can also **require** the company to produce documents and provide information directly, although it is more usual to do so through the investigators.
3. Since directors' **disqualification proceedings** are not criminal proceedings, this restriction on the use of interviewees' statements in evidence does not apply.

7211 **Failure to comply** with a request for information or documents can result in action for contempt of court, which is punishable by a fine and/or imprisonment. It is an offence for a person to provide a materially **false statement** knowingly or recklessly, punishable in the same way (s 451 CA 1985; ¶9935).

It is also an offence for an officer of the company to **destroy, mutilate or falsify** (or make a false entry in) a **document** affecting or relating to the company's property or affairs, or to part with, alter or make an omission in such a document (s 450 CA 1985). The term "document" includes information recorded in any form (e.g. electronically). It is also an offence to be privy to another person carrying out any of these actions. These offences are punishable by imprisonment and/or a fine. However, an officer who destroyed, mutilated or falsified (or made a false entry in) a document, or was privy to another person doing so, is not guilty of an offence if he can prove that he had no intention of concealing the company's affairs or defeating the law.

Disclosure of information obtained

7212 **Generally** speaking, any information obtained during an investigation remains confidential and cannot be disclosed to another party (s 449 CA 1985). This applies to information whether it is obtained:
– during pre-investigation enquiries;
– by requiring persons to produce documents or give information; or
– by gaining access to the company's premises.

There are, however, certain **exceptions**:
a. there is no prohibition on disclosure where the information is or has already been available to the public from another source (s 449(9) CA 1985);
b. information can be disclosed to specified persons (usually bodies carrying out public functions, or regulators) for specified reasons connected with that person's official functions, for example to (Schs 15C, 15D CA 1985):
– the director of public prosecutions or the police with a view to commencing criminal proceedings;
– the secretary of state for business, enterprise and regulatory reform with a view to commencing disqualification proceedings;
– the FSA for the purpose of an investigation under the Financial Services and Markets Act 2000; or
– the secretary of state or the Treasury to enable them to exercise their functions under companies or insolvency legislation; and
c. disclosures can be made to other investigators or inspectors (s 451A CA 1985).

Even in these circumstances, disclosure is not permitted where it would breach the Data Protection Act 1998 (s 449(11) CA 1985).

7213 Making an **unauthorised disclosure** is an offence, punishable by imprisonment and/or a fine (¶9935).

Access to premises

7214 An investigator has the power to enter any premises which he believes are wholly or partly **used for** the purposes of the company's business (s 453A CA 1985). From a practical point of view, this makes it easier for the investigators to obtain documents and information (and to judge whether or not those involved in the company are co-operating fully with them), and also enables them to witness the workings of the company first hand; this power does not enable the investigators to search for documents, nor can they remove anything from the premises.

When he **enters** the premises, an investigator must (s 453B CA 1985):
– do so during trading hours;
– produce his identification and evidence of the secretary of state's authority; and
– provide an appropriate person at the premises with a written statement of his powers and of the rights and obligations of the company, occupier of the premises and other persons present.

He can be **accompanied by** appropriate staff, such as secretarial or information technology personnel, who must also produce identification on entry.

Once on the premises, he can **remain** there for as long as is necessary to materially assist him in his investigations (and as long as is reasonable, e.g. he cannot stay during unsociable hours). He can return another day or at a more reasonable time, as long as he still has the necessary grounds to gain entry to the premises.

> MEMO POINTS   An **appropriate person** is an officer of the company, or an employee if an officer is not present (s 453B(8) CA 1985). Where neither is present, and it appears that the company is not the sole occupant of the premises, the investigator can leave the written statement with any other person who appears to occupy the premises or otherwise be in charge of them (s 453B(9) CA 1985). If there is **no appropriate person** to whom the investigator can give his written statement, he must give notice to the company of this fact, the time of the visit and the information about his powers and the rights and obligations of the company required in the statement as soon as is reasonably practicable (s 453B(5) CA 1985).

7215 After the visit, the investigator must prepare a **written record** of it, and give a copy to the company and any other occupier of the premises on request (s 453B(6) CA 1985). The information obtained as a result of exercising this power can form the basis of a winding up petition in the public interest on the just and equitable ground or an application to disqualify a director on the ground of unfitness.

7216 If **entry is refused**, the investigator will have to obtain a search warrant (s 448 CA 1985), but any person who intentionally obstructs an investigator or a member of his staff (¶9935):
– is guilty of an offence and liable to a fine (s 453A(5) CA 1985); and
– may be held liable for contempt of court (which is punishable by imprisonment and/or a fine) if the investigator certifies that person's obstruction to the court (s 453C CA 1985).

If a warrant is obtained, it is also an offence to prevent the investigator from exercising it (s 448(7) CA 1985; ¶9935).

b. Inspectors

7219 By contrast with investigators, inspectors can only be appointed in particular circumstances and are **rare** due to the effectiveness of the investigators' powers to obtain the information required by the CIB to assess whether or not further action must be taken. Inspectors have extensive powers to investigate the company's conduct and affairs, and will then report on their findings to the CIB. A team of inspectors will comprise relevant professionals; usually, a senior barrister and a partner in a leading accountancy firm will be appointed in each case.

The **offences** discussed at ¶7211 above relating to providing false statements to investigators and destroying company documents also apply to investigations by inspectors.

The **costs** of investigations by inspectors are initially met by the secretary of state, but he can recoup them from the company or any individuals in default involved with the company (s 439 CA 1985).

> MEMO POINTS   The **new Companies Act** has widened the secretary of state's powers to control inspections. As well as having more control over the appointment of inspectors (see ¶7221 below), he can:
> – give directions on the inspectors' report, such as what it should cover, the form or manner in which it should be made and the date to which it should be made up (s 446A CA 1985); and
> – terminate an inspection, depending on the circumstances (s 446B CA 1985).
>
> These new powers **apply** where an inspector was appointed on or after 1 October 2007 (para 48 Sch 3 SI 2007/2194).

Appointment

7221 Inspectors can only be appointed in appropriate **circumstances**, such as those which indicate that (s 432(2) CA 1985):
a. the company's affairs are being, or have been, conducted:
– with the intent to defraud creditors or any other person;

– for a fraudulent or unlawful purpose; or
– in a way that is unfairly prejudicial to some shareholders;
b. an act or omission of the company (including proposed acts and omissions) is or would be unfairly prejudicial;
c. the company was formed for a fraudulent or unlawful purpose;
d. those concerned with the company's formation or management have been guilty of fraud, misfeasance or other misconduct; or
e. the shareholders have not been given all of the information they can expect regarding the company's affairs.

A **company** or a certain number of its shareholders (either shareholders holding at least 10% of the issued shares, or at least 200 shareholders) can apply to the secretary of state for the appointment of inspectors (s 431 CA 1985). However, this rarely occurs in practice because a complaint can be made to the CIB without the need for such formalities, which could result in investigators being instructed to examine the company instead.

The **court** can also order that an inspection is carried out on its own initiative (for example, where it is dealing with proceedings against directors for breach of duty, it may order an investigation into any apparent criminal activity within the company), in which case inspectors must be appointed (s 432(1) CA 1985).

> MEMO POINTS 1. In the case of **companies without a share capital**, at least 20% of the company's members can make the application.
> 2. The **new Companies Act** has given the secretary of state new powers to manage the appointment of inspectors as follows (inserted by ss 1036, 1037 CA 2006):
> – in order to resign, an inspector must give notice to the secretary of state (s 446C CA 1985);
> – the secretary of state can revoke an inspector's appointment by giving him written notice to that effect (s 446C CA 1985);
> – the secretary of state can appoint a replacement for an inspector who has resigned, whose appointment has been revoked, or who has died (s 446D CA 1985); and
> – the secretary of state can require a former inspector to provide him or another inspector with any documents (including those not in hard copy) he has relating to an inspection (s 446E CA 1985). These new powers **apply** where an inspector was appointed on or after 1 October 2007 (para 48 Sch 3 SI 2007/2194).

Powers

Obtaining information

7223 The company's **officers and agents**, including those who no longer hold office and professional agents such as lawyers, bankers and auditors, are under a **duty to co-operate** with the inspectors by (s 434 CA 1985):
– producing all documents relating to the company (this includes information recorded in any form, e.g. electronic);
– attending the inspectors when required; and
– assisting the inspectors as far as they are reasonably able to do so.

The inspectors can extend this duty to **other persons** they consider may be in possession of information relevant to the investigation.

To **reinforce** these duties, the inspectors can also examine any person under oath and obtain a warrant to enter and search premises if they suspect that all of the relevant information has not been disclosed (ss 434(3), 448 CA 1985).

> MEMO POINTS Information does not have to be disclosed where it is protected by **legal professional privilege** or it is confidential **banking information** (s 452 CA 1985). However, a lawyer can be required to disclose the name and address of his client.

7224 **Failure to co-operate** with the inspectors can render the officer, agent or other person liable as if he had committed contempt of court (for which a person can be imprisoned and/or fined) (s 436 CA 1985).

7225 Where a person is **interviewed** by the inspectors, they will usually be provided with a transcript of their evidence so that they can address any erroneous or misleading information. If the inspectors have any criticisms of the interviewee they will usually put them to him to allow him to make any further representations before including them in the report. The inspectors are not under any duty to do this, although they must act fairly and therefore will give interviewees the chance to respond before criticising them in their report and they must, of course, respect the interviewees' human rights (*Re Pergamon Press Ltd* [1970] 3 All ER 535; *Maxwell v Department for Trade and Industry* [1974] 2 All ER 122).

It is sensible for witnesses to take the time to review these transcripts because they may be used as **evidence** in subsequent related **civil litigation** (*Soden v Burns*, *R v Secretary of State for Trade and Industry, ex parte Soden* [1996] 2 BCLC 636). On the other hand, if **criminal proceedings** are later commenced against the interviewee (other than for perjury), his responses cannot be used in evidence against him nor can any questions be asked during those proceedings about them (s 434(5A) CA 1985). This clearly limits the usefulness of taking such statements where criminal proceedings are envisaged. However, evidence acquired other than in such statements can be used, for example information in company documents acquired during the inspection and the contents of the inspectors' report.

> MEMO POINTS Since directors' **disqualification proceedings** are not criminal proceedings, this restriction on the use of interviewees' statements in evidence does not apply.

The secretary of state can also require the company or any person to **produce documents** and **provide information** (s 447(2) CA 1985). This is discussed further in the context of investigators above (¶7210+).

7226

Investigating connected companies

Inspectors also have the power to investigate other companies in the immediate group of the company subject to the main investigation if they consider that it is necessary to do so (s 433 CA 1985). The company's **holding company**, **subsidiary** and any other **subsidiary of its holding company** can be investigated in this way. The inspectors' findings relating to the connected companies can only be included in their report to the extent that they are relevant to the main investigation.

7227

Access to premises

The provisions described above relating to investigators gaining access to premises also apply to inspectors (¶7214+).

7228

---

c. Consequences of an investigation

If the investigation reveals that the complaint was unfounded or there is not a good enough public interest reason to continue with the investigation, **no action** will be taken. The CIB may take **informal action** where it appears that the case is not serious enough to warrant more formal action being taken, such as setting out improvements which the company should make in the light of the investigation, or giving it a written warning containing steps it must take if it is to avoid more **formal action**.

7231

Any wrongdoing which is uncovered will be:
a. disclosed to another body to take appropriate action (¶7212);
b. followed up with further investigations into potential criminal offences by the secretary of state, e.g. for defrauding creditors (¶2577) or theft;
c. used to form the basis of a winding up petition in the public interest on the ground that it is just and equitable to wind the company up (¶7626+), particularly where the company obtains investment or advance payments from the public; and/or
d. used to commence disqualification proceedings against one or more directors (*Re Samuel Sherman plc* [1991] 1 WLR 1070; ¶3000+).

7232

If the investigation was carried out by inspectors, the report is admissible as evidence in any proceedings, including disqualification proceedings (s 441 CA 1985). They can also be published at the discretion of the CIB (s 437 CA 1985); it is the CIB's policy to publish such reports about public companies if it is in the public interest to do so.

> **EXAMPLE**
> 1. TI Ltd trained publicans in how to run a pub and claimed to be able to give them a placement in a pub of their choice at the end of their training in return for fees of between £4,000 and £5,000. However, the training was poor and the placements were not of the promised standard and sometimes did not exist. The company also failed to maintain proper accounting records and to file its accounts and annual returns. The secretary of state had TI Ltd wound up in the public interest ((then) DTI press release; company: Tudor Inns Ltd).
> 2. Trading standards received 796 complaints about B & C plc in less than 18 months, regarding their aggressive sales tactics. They cold-called businesses offering to send reports on management and HR matters on a 21-day free review, without making it clear that the customer would be charged up to £400 if the report was not returned within that period. Following investigation, the managing director was disqualified for 13 years, two other directors gave undertakings not to act as directors for 6 years each, and a fourth director undertook not to do so for 5 years. The company was wound up in the public interest ((then) DTI press release; company: Berger & Co plc).
> 3. Mr A's company carried on business as an insurance broker, becoming a broker for Lloyds. It entered into CVL when Lloyds' floating charge over it crystallised. During the investigation that followed, evidence came to light that the company had carried on a practice of inflating the premiums negotiated with Lloyds. The secretary of state applied for Mr A to be disqualified as a director on the grounds that he knew that this practice was fraudulent, and as a result he was in breach of his fiduciary duties to act honestly in the company's best interests (now known as the duty to promote the company's success) and not to make and keep a secret profit. The court disqualified him for 9 years (a period which reflected the seriousness of his conduct and the amount of secret profit which had been made) (Re J A Chapman & Co Ltd, Secretary of State for Trade and Industry v Amiss [2003] 2 BCLC 206).

2. Investigations into specific aspects of a company

7237 The CIB also has the power to investigate more specific aspects of a company if necessary, as well as assisting overseas authorities by investigating a company in this country and passing its findings on to them (such as where a company or group is being investigated abroad for fraud). Such investigations are rare.

Ownership

7239 Where there is a good reason to do so, the secretary of state can **appoint inspectors** to investigate the ownership of any company to identify those interested in its shares and able to control or influence it (s 442 CA 1985). Such investigations can follow a request to the CIB (for instance, in a public company where the information has not been provided in response to a request for information about share interests, see ¶2042+), or a more formal application by the company or a certain number of shareholders (s 442(3) CA 1985). The terms of the inspectors' appointments can set out the scope of the investigation, confining it to matters connected with specific shares or debentures for example, and will exclude any matter that is not reasonable to investigate.

If it is **not** necessary to **appoint inspectors**, but there is still a good reason to investigate the company's ownership, the secretary of state can require any person he reasonably believes to have relevant information about present or past interests in shares or debentures, including the names and addresses of those interested and/or their representatives, to disclose it to him (s 444(1) CA 1985). The secretary of state will not appoint inspectors where the request to do so is vexatious.

7240 Inspectors have the same **powers** when investigating a company's ownership as they do in a general investigation as regards:
– obtaining documents and information from those interested in the company (¶7210+); and
– investigating a connected company (¶7227).

The inspectors' powers to obtain documents are reinforced by their ability to apply for a warrant to enter and search premises if they believe that all of the necessary documents have not been disclosed (s 448 CA 1985). **Failure to co-operate** with the inspectors or obstructing their exercise of a warrant renders the person in default liable to imprisonment and/or a fine and can lead to prosecution for contempt of court (ss 436, 444(3), 448(7) CA 1985; ¶¶9935). It is also an offence to destroy a document (described at ¶7211).

At the end of the investigation, the inspectors will prepare a **report** for the CIB, which may be published in full or with certain elements removed (ss 437, 443(3) CA 1985).

> MEMO POINTS   Information does not have to be disclosed where it is protected by **legal professional privilege** or it is confidential **banking information** (s 452 CA 1985). However, a lawyer can be required to disclose the name and address of his client.
> The **disclosure** provisions noted at ¶7212+ in the context of general investigations also apply to documents and information obtained in relation to the ownership of shares.

7241 The secretary of state can order that the **shares** or debentures under investigation are **frozen**, if there are difficulties in ascertaining their ownership (s 445 CA 1985). The registered holders of the shares are prevented from dealing with them (for example, transferring them or exercising their voting rights) until they reveal the true owners (s 454 CA 1985). The restrictions can be relaxed where they would unfairly affect a third party's rights, but can only be lifted with the consent of the court or the secretary of state (ss 445(1A), 456, 457 CA 1985).

Suspected criminal activity discovered during liquidation

7247 The CIB can investigate a company following a report from the company's liquidator or the official receiver that he suspects a past or present officer of the company, or one of its current shareholders, of committing a criminal offence (ss 218, 219 IA 1986). Such investigations are analogous to those carried out by inspectors.

To assist overseas authorities

7250 The CIB can also carry out investigations in this country following a request from a foreign regulatory authority (ss 82-91 CA 1989). If it decides to assist the overseas authority as requested, it has similar **powers** to those in a domestic investigation by inspectors to obtain documents and information.

CHAPTER 16

Introduction to corporate insolvency

OUTLINE	¶¶

SECTION 1 **The company in financial difficulties** .. 7312		2 Notices... 7404
		3 Time limits..................................... 7412
		C Insolvency practitioners................. 7422
A Informal solutions............................ 7323		D Directors' liabilities 7439
B Formal solutions 7334		1 Fraudulent trading 7443
Liquidation/winding up...................... 7335		2 Wrongful trading 7449
Administration 7338		3 Misfeasance 7457
Receivership 7340		4 Other personal liability................... 7461
Voluntary arrangements 7342		5 Criminal liability 7464
C Summary table 7350		
		SECTION 3 **After insolvency** 7475
SECTION 2 **General principles** .. 7360		A Entering further insolvency procedures 7481
		B Dissolution and striking off............. 7491
A Jurisdiction and legislation 7362		1 Dissolution following liquidation 7497
1 Domestic law.................................. 7364		2 Application to be struck off............ 7502
2 European law................................. 7366		3 Struck off automatically 7516
3 Cross-border insolvencies.............. 7375		4 Dissolution by the court................. 7525
B Applications and procedural matters 7380		C Restoration to the register 7534
1 Court applications.......................... 7380		

Companies with financial problems face a number of difficult **decisions** about the best course of action to take. Can the company's financial situation be turned around and, if so, how? Should the company enter into a formal insolvency procedure? Could the directors be facing personal liability? A company stands the best chance of recovery if it recognises its financial problems early on and takes appropriate steps to resolve them before its creditors take matters into their own hands. Given the complexity of the decisions and the seriousness of their consequences, the company should seek professional advice from a solicitor, insolvency practitioner or accountant.

7300

Here, the **main considerations** to be taken into account are addressed, although the options available to each company will depend upon its particular circumstances. **Procedures and principles** applicable to insolvency proceedings in general are discussed first, followed by the fate of a company **after** it has undergone a **formal insolvency** procedure. Included in this discussion are methods of dissolving and striking a company off the register at Companies House, and restoring it to the register again, which (although commonly linked to insolvency) may also apply to a company which has not undergone a formal insolvency procedure. The subsequent chapters each deal with an insolvency procedure in detail. Many aspects of these procedures overlap and so the reader will be referred, where necessary, to a full explanation of a topic discussed in the context of another procedure. Where this is the case, any specific differences between the treatment of the different procedures are highlighted in the memo points to the text.

7301 It is important to distinguish between the common **concept of "insolvency"**, which refers to the state of a company's finances, and the legal concept, which refers to the state of a company to which certain legal procedures apply. Although the two concepts are often found together because the legal procedures are designed to deal with companies in financial difficulties, the two are not necessarily dependent on one another. Therefore, a company which is **financially "insolvent"**, in that it cannot pay its debts as they fall due or its liabilities outweigh its assets, is not "**in insolvency**" **in the legal sense** until it or a third party initiates a formal insolvency procedure. Similarly, there are many situations in which the insolvency procedures can be applied when a company is financially solvent, for example, as a pre-emptive move to prevent its finances deteriorating further, or because it is being wound up in the public interest.

Legally speaking, a **company enters insolvency when** it enters into one of the following procedures:
– liquidation (compulsory or voluntary);
– administration;
– receivership (administrative or ordinary); or
– a company voluntary arrangement ("CVA").

Each of these procedures is discussed in detail in the subsequent chapters, and compared below at ¶7350.

7302 The courts can deal with insolvency proceedings in relation to the following **types of companies**:
a. companies incorporated under companies legislation (s 117 IA 1986);
b. unregistered English or Welsh companies, including partnerships (ss 220-229, 420 IA 1986; SI 1994/2421);
c. foreign companies, which may be subject to insolvency procedures in this jurisdiction:
– under the EC Insolvency Regulation (¶7366+);
– by being wound up as an unregistered company; or
– because jurisdiction can be established on the basis that there is a sufficient connection between the company and England and Wales, and there is a reasonable prospect of its creditors benefiting from a winding up (*Re Allobrogia Steamship Corpn* [1978] 3 All ER 423).

For a discussion of the court's jurisdiction and applicable legislation and Rules, see ¶7362+.

> MEMO POINTS   The winding up of **unregistered companies** and **partnerships** is not dealt with here. There are also separate insolvency provisions relating to **individuals**, including **sole traders**, who can be subject to bankruptcy, bankruptcy restrictions or administration orders or undertakings, or individual voluntary arrangements ("IVAs").

SECTION 1

The company in financial difficulties

7312 A company faced with financial difficulties has a number of **options** to pursue, depending on what it aims to achieve, how serious its financial position is and how co-operative its creditors are willing to be. The company's **directors** are under various duties to act properly and responsibly in relation to the company, which includes reacting to its financial situation appropriately. In addition, directors are under a specific duty to minimise the potential loss to the company's creditors in the event of its insolvency. Once the company is of "doubtful solvency", their primary duty is no longer owed to the company; they have to put the creditors' interests first (*Colin Gwyer & Associates Ltd v London Wharf (Limehouse) Ltd* [2003] 2 BCLC 153). Given the directors' potential personal liability and disqualification for not taking appropriate action, they should seek the advice of a corporate recovery professional at the earliest opportunity. Directors' duties to the company in general are discussed at ¶2317+, and their duties and liabilities in insolvency situations are discussed below at ¶7439+. The appropriate course of action will always depend upon the company's particular circumstances.

7313 As well as the various solutions to the company's financial problems, the principal **broader issues** directors need to consider are as follows:
- should the company cease trading?
- have the directors' actions given rise to any criminal liabilities?
- could the directors' actions have rendered them liable to contribute to the company's assets or any of its debts?
- is the company under any contractual liability to notify others of its insolvency, and/or do other parties have particular rights when the company becomes insolvent (e.g. to terminate a contract)?
- what obligations does the company have towards its employees?
- should any of the directors resign?

7314 Although insolvency procedures themselves do not usually terminate the **contracts** to which a company is a party, most commercial contracts will contain a provision by which the contract either automatically **terminates** if one of the parties becomes financially insolvent or enters into an insolvency procedure, or it gives the other party the right to terminate in those situations. Where the company is in financial difficulties, the directors will therefore need to review the company's contracts carefully and check whether they are under any **obligation to inform** the other parties of its insolvency. Failure to do so will usually entitle the other party to a remedy, including a right to terminate the contract where the failure is deemed to be an act of default under the contract. If the contract in question is a security document, the security holder may be prompted to use any right he has to place the company into administration or receivership.

The **effects of** each type of **insolvency procedure** on contracts to which the company is a party are discussed within the relevant topics.

7315 Any company with **employees** will also be subject to a number of duties to them as a matter of course and its directors must take their interests into account when making any important decision (¶2379+). Where the company is in financial difficulties, the board must bear in mind the company's duties to the employees when making decisions about its future. For example, if the directors decide that it is appropriate to rationalise the business and close part of it down, it must follow appropriate redundancy and dismissal procedures. The company must consider its potential liabilities for unfair and wrongful dismissals, as well as for redundancy payments. Following the proper procedures will help to minimise the company's liabilities. For more information regarding the company's employment duties and liabilities, see *Employment Memo*.

> MEMO POINTS **Consultation requirements** are imposed by the EU Information and Consultation Directive (EC Directive 2002/14), which requires employers to consult with employees before taking important business decisions, particularly where these affect employee rights. The Directive is being implemented in stages, depending on the size of the employer's organisation. The first stage, for employers with more than 150 employees, was implemented on 6 April 2005, followed by employers with 100 or more employees on 6 April 2007. It will apply to employers with 50 or more employees from 6 April 2008.

A. Informal solutions

7323 Before looking at the more formal insolvency procedures, which often result in a worse outcome for all concerned, it is advisable for a company to examine its existing affairs to see whether the **business** can be streamlined and made **more profitable**. This could simply be a matter of putting more efficient management procedures in place, or it may involve closing certain parts of the business. If the company has more serious financial problems, it may be able to resolve its financial difficulties by **disposing of** part of its **business or assets** and applying the sale proceeds to pay off its debts. For example, where one division of the business is particularly unprofitable, it could be closed down and the assets sold off, or, where the business is basically sound, a buyer may be willing to purchase all or part of it as a going concern. Company sales are discussed at ¶5200+.

If the company does not wish to carry on trading and has enough assets to meet all of its liabilities, it may wish to cease to trade, realise its assets and pay off its debts itself. Once the creditors have been paid off, the company may distribute the surplus amongst the shareholders, although doing so through a members' voluntary winding up is usually more tax-efficient. Such an **informal winding down** is only a realistic option where the company's assets are greater than its liabilities; otherwise, a formal liquidation will usually be required to ensure that the creditors are dealt with fairly.

7324 A company may be in a position to obtain **further funding**, for example where the business is basically sound but is suffering from a temporary cash-flow problem. The methods by which companies can obtain additional funding are discussed at ¶4500+. Companies in this situation will usually have to grant security for the funding, and may have to agree to less favourable terms than they would otherwise, since they are in a weaker bargaining position. On the other hand, if an existing creditor provides extra funding, he may be less inclined to place the company into a formal insolvency procedure because his chances of fully recovering the debts owed to him are usually maximised if the company continues to trade.

7325 The company may be able to **agree with** its **creditors** that they will:
a. not take action against the company to recover their debts for a certain period of time (i.e. an informal moratorium); and/or
b. accept a lesser amount in payment of their debts according to a certain timetable (i.e. compromise their claims).

This effectively amounts to an informal CVA. The **advantage** of such an informal agreement is that the parties can agree the terms between them, as the agreement will be governed by the law of contract. However, it does **depend upon** the co-operation and goodwill of all of the company's creditors, because a creditor who does not agree to the moratorium could still take action such as enforcing his debt or appointing a receiver (depending on the terms of any security in his favour), jeopardising the position of the other creditors. If the company cannot obtain the agreement of all of its creditors, it would be better for it to enter into a CVA so that dissenting creditors can be bound, and the company may be eligible for the added protection of a pre-CVA moratorium.

7326 If a company has not traded for a period of time, it may be **struck off** the register at Companies House and dissolved without being wound up first (¶7491+). If the company applies to be struck off, it should ensure that it has no assets to realise and distribute and that there are no outstanding claims against it, otherwise the striking off can be prevented or the company may be restored to the register after it has been dissolved. The company may also be struck off for inactivity by Companies House.

B. Formal solutions

7334 The different insolvency procedures are each discussed in detail in the subsequent chapters. Here, each procedure is **summarised**, together with the situations in which it is generally most suitable.

Liquidation/winding up

7335 This is the procedure whereby a company's assets are sold as far as possible and the proceeds used to pay off its creditors. Any surplus funds after all of its debts have been satisfied are paid to its shareholders (who are known as "contributories", see ¶7863). At the end of the process, the company is dissolved and ceases to exist. Therefore this procedure is generally used where the company is in **serious financial difficulties** and there is no other way of effecting an orderly realisation and fair distribution of the assets. Alternatively, it can be used where those involved in the company simply wish to **cease trading** and close the business down.

Liquidation is a highly **regulated** procedure, particularly compulsory liquidation. It **aims** to deal with all creditors fairly, although it is very unlikely that any of them will be paid in full (except in an MVL), and achieve an orderly winding up of the company's affairs. The **liquidator** steps in and takes control of the company, managing its business, selling its assets and distributing the proceeds to the creditors and shareholders.

There are **three types** of liquidation: **7336**

a. compulsory (¶7570+): in which a petition is presented to the court by any one of a number of persons, including creditors, following which the court will make a winding up order if appropriate. The liquidation is effected by a liquidator, who can be the official receiver or an independent insolvency practitioner. In any compulsory liquidation, the official receiver also investigates the conduct of the company and its officers prior to the liquidation;

b. creditors' voluntary, or CVL (¶8437+): in which the shareholders resolve to wind the company up voluntarily. Under this procedure, the court has less influence (although it still has ultimate control). The liquidation is conducted by the liquidator, with the creditors playing a significant role. This type of voluntary liquidation is usually relied upon where the company is insolvent; and

c. members' (i.e. shareholders') **voluntary**, or MVL (¶8594+): this is similar to a CVL, except that the shareholders have more influence. Since the company must be solvent to enter into this procedure, the creditors will be paid in full and do not need to control the liquidation. This procedure is usually relied upon where those involved in the company decide that they wish to end the business.

Administration

Administration has a more positive **aim**: to rescue the company from its financial troubles so that it can carry on business afterwards. It can therefore be relied upon by companies which are in financial difficulties, but where the **business** is still **commercially sound** and has a good prospect of trading successfully once the administration is over. Alternatively, it is used instead of, or prior to, liquidation in cases where a better realisation for creditors can be obtained by the company trading for a time under the administrator's supervision. There are three statutory purposes of an administration, one of which must be chosen as the aim of the procedure in each case: **7338**

– rescuing the company as a going concern;

– achieving a better result than would be achieved if the company were placed into liquidation; or

– realising the company's property to distribute to one or more secured and/or preferential creditors.

The **administrator** takes over the company's business for a relatively short period of time, reforming it and selling off such assets as are necessary to achieve the purpose of the administration. He is given a wide range of powers, which are similar to a liquidator's although he uses them to achieve a different goal. Given these extensive powers, the process is highly **regulated** and the creditors are involved in it. However, generally speaking, it is quicker and more cost-effective than a liquidation and can have a more positive outcome. Administrators can be appointed by various persons making an application to court, or out of court by the company, its board or holders of certain floating charges.

Receivership

The ability to appoint a receiver is a specific **method of enforcement** available to security holders, where their security provides for it or they have a statutory right to use it. Receivers can also be appointed by the court. Receivership is usually relied upon where the **company** **7340** has **defaulted** on its repayments under the loan attached to the security in question. The receiver steps in to take control of the secured assets and realise them in order to discharge the secured debt. The difference between receivership and other types of insolvency procedures is that a receivership is conducted for the benefit of the specific security holder and not the creditors as a whole. Receivership can be extremely detrimental to the company and its creditors, as the receiver usually has to realise its key assets, damaging the company's goodwill and making it difficult for it to carry on business afterwards. Therefore, many companies have to go into liquidation following receivership.

There are **two types** of receiver:

a. administrative receivers (¶9237+): who are appointed under a specific type of security which has been granted over all, or substantially all, of the company's assets. This form of receivership is highly regulated because the administrative receiver takes control of all of the secured assets, which effectively comprise the whole of the company, in much the same way as a liquidator or administrator. Due to reforms in the law, this type of receivership is being phased out in favour of administration because it is perceived as giving the security holder an unfair advantage over other creditors; and

b. ordinary receivers (¶9239): who are appointed under security instruments or a statutory power over a specific asset or assets. Ordinary receivership relies mainly on contractual powers and duties set out in the security document and the receiver's appointment or statutory powers contained in other legislation, rather than on insolvency legislation and the Rules (although there is some overall insolvency regulation). Such a receivership is less detrimental to the company, although if the receiver realises key assets or parts of the business the company may have no option but to go into liquidation afterwards.

Voluntary arrangements

7342 A company voluntary arrangement ("CVA") is an **agreement** between the company and its creditors, whereby the creditors grant the company a period of tolerance in return for the company undertaking to repay its debts to the extent agreed with the creditors. The **aim** is to rescue the company from its financial troubles so that it can carry on trading successfully afterwards. Creditors are only likely to agree to this course of action where their prospects of recovery are reasonable (i.e. better than in liquidation or administration) and the company has a good prospect of carrying on business in the future.

The **advantage** of this process over those discussed above is that a voluntary arrangement is very flexible; since it is governed by the terms agreed between the parties, it can be tailored to the company's individual circumstances. Many companies will be able to take advantage of the pre-CVA moratorium, which prevents dissenting creditors taking action against it before the CVA becomes binding. A formal CVA can bind a certain amount of dissenting or unknown creditors, unlike informal arrangements, and an insolvency practitioner (the "**nominee**" before the arrangement is approved; the "**supervisor**" afterwards) implements the arrangement. However, there is a certain amount of **regulation** which needs to be adhered to, such as the basic criteria that the arrangement must meet and the formal process which must be followed to enter into the arrangement.

C. Summary table

7350 This table summarises and compares the main features of each type of formal insolvency procedure, and informal solutions in general. Broadly speaking, the **advantages** of the formal procedures are:

a. an independent professional conducts the procedure;

b. the parties are clear as to where they stand and an impartial, orderly and fair process is followed; and

c. the procedures enable differing levels of court involvement, for example where a dispute or question arises or the parties are not satisfied with the insolvency practitioner's conduct.

On the other hand, such procedures have certain **disadvantages**, for example:
- inflexibility and a certain lack of control by the company and its creditors;
- if the company wants to continue to trade afterwards, the stigma of insolvency can make it difficult to regain goodwill; and
- one insolvency procedure often leads to dissolution or another type of procedure.

Other specific advantages and disadvantages of the various procedures are highlighted below.

	Purpose	Initiated by	Conducted by	Other features
Compulsory liquidation	To wind up insolvent company; realise and distribute its assets in a fair and orderly manner	– Creditors; – contributories; – board; – company; or – secretary of state	– Official receiver; – liquidator; – liquidation committee; and – creditors	– All creditors dealt with; – creditors involved in procedure; – investigation into conduct of company; – liquidator can increase assets by challenging transactions; – moratorium, ¶7697+, ¶7746+; – creditors rarely paid in full; and – shareholders rarely receive distribution
Creditors' voluntary liquidation (CVL)	To allow insolvent company to wind itself up without court proceedings	Creditors and shareholders	– Liquidator; – liquidation committee; and – creditors	– All creditors dealt with; – creditors involved in procedure; – liquidator can increase assets by challenging transactions; – moratorium, ¶8465+, but creditor can petition for compulsory liquidation; and – shareholders rarely receive distribution
Members' voluntary liquidation (MVL)	To allow solvent company to wind itself up without court proceedings	Board and shareholders	– Liquidator; and – shareholders	– All creditors dealt with; – shareholders involved in procedure; – liquidator can increase assets by challenging transactions; – moratorium, ¶8623, but creditor can petition for compulsory liquidation; – if company becomes insolvent, can be converted to CVL; and – shareholders usually receive distribution
Administration	To rescue company as going concern/ achieve better result for creditors than in liquidation/ realise property for secured or preferential creditors	Court application: – company; – board; – creditors; – liquidator; or – supervisor Out of court: – qualifying floating charge holder; [1] – company; or – board	– Administrator; – creditors' committee; and – creditors	– Timetable encourages quick resolution; – company can often continue trading; – administrator can increase assets by challenging transactions; and – moratorium, ¶8813+

	Purpose	Initiated by	Conducted by	Other features
Administrative receivership	To recover money owed to secured creditor	Floating charge holder[2]	Administrative receiver	– No formal moratorium, but creditor taking action will only be able to recover his claim out of assets not dealt with by administrative receiver; – other creditors not taken into account; – company can rarely carry on trading afterwards; and – other creditors and shareholders usually left with nothing
Ordinary receivership	To recover money owed to secured creditor	Security holder with right (contractual/ statutory) to appoint receiver	Receiver	– Company can carry on trading afterwards; – no formal moratorium, but creditor taking action will only be able to recover his claim out of assets not dealt with by receiver; and – other creditors not taken into account
Voluntary arrangement (CVA)	To resolve company's financial problems by agreement with creditors	– Board; – liquidator; or – administrator	– Nominee before proposal approved; – supervisor afterwards; and – directors	– Flexibility because terms agreed between company and creditors; – can bind unknown and dissenting creditors; – company can carry on trading afterwards; and – company may be eligible for moratorium prior to approval of proposals, ¶9466+; during CVA, terms usually include moratorium
Informal solutions	To resolve company's financial difficulties and preserve goodwill	– Company/board; and/or – creditors	– Company; and – creditors	– Flexibility; – avoid stigma of insolvency; – moratorium, if provided for in agreement; – lack of regulation can produce unfair result on creditors not party to agreement; and – not carried out by independent professional

Note:
1. Whose charge was created on or after 15/09/03.
2. Whose charge was created before 15/09/03.

SECTION 2
General principles

There are various matters which are relevant to insolvency procedures as a whole and so are dealt with here: governing **legislation and jurisdiction**, **applications** and **other procedures** which apply in all formal insolvency procedures, and the general rules relating to **insolvency practitioners**.

Directors' liabilities are also discussed here. Although many of the liabilities only arise in a liquidation, directors need to be aware of them whenever their company is in financial trouble because other insolvency procedures can lead to liquidation, and a company cannot always predict when a third party will present a petition against it.

7360

A. Jurisdiction and legislation

Insolvency proceedings can be **dealt with by** the High Court or county courts. If proceedings are commenced in the wrong court (i.e. one with inappropriate jurisdiction, rather than one with no jurisdiction at all), they will not be invalidated, but can be (s 118 IA 1986; r 7.12 IR 1986):
– dealt with by the inappropriate court;
– transferred to the correct court; or
– struck out.

7362

The **High Court** can **wind up** any company registered in England and Wales, including companies with no share capital (s 117 IA 1986; r 7.47 IR 1986). The High Court's jurisdiction is exercised through:
– the Companies Court, which is part of the Chancery Division at the High Court in London; or
– certain District Registries, namely Birmingham, Bristol, Cardiff, Leeds, Liverpool, Manchester, Newcastle upon Tyne and Preston.

County courts can only **wind up** companies with (s 117 IA 1986):
– a paid up share capital which does not exceed £120,000; and
– a registered office in the relevant district.

Not all county courts have insolvency jurisdiction; readers should check the HM Courts Service website or contact the relevant county court directly. County courts have the same powers in relation to insolvency matters as the High Court (s 117(5) IA 1986). Matters in county court proceedings may be referred to the High Court where all of the parties or one of the parties and the judge consider it appropriate to do so (s 119 IA 1986).

In proceedings within **other insolvency procedures**, the court's jurisdiction is the same as that for winding up.

7363

1. Domestic law

Insolvency procedures are **governed by** the Insolvency Act 1986 ("IA 1986"), which sets out the main principles, powers and obligations, and the Insolvency Rules 1986 (SI 1986/1925, referred to as "IR 1986"), which focus on the various processes and administrative matters in more detail. Any references in the text to the Insolvency Rules 1986 are to "the Rules". Both the legislation and Rules have been amended and references to specific provisions are to the amended versions. Where the amendments are significant, such as in the case of the reformed administration regime or the addition of the pre-CVA moratorium, the changes are discussed in more detail in the introductory comments to the relevant topic.

In addition, the Insolvency Service, the section of BERR which deals with insolvency matters, publishes various forms of **guidance** for insolvency practitioners and the general public.

7364

References to the "Technical Manual" and *Dear IP* are to such guidance, which can be found on the Insolvency Service's website.

> **MEMO POINTS** The Insolvency Service is currently **reviewing the Rules**, together with related statutory instruments, with the aim of consolidating and modernising them.
> The re-drafted Rules will be divided into parts, like the current Rules. Parts 1-6 will deal with matters which are specific to particular procedures; the rest set out the Rules relating to topics which are common to most procedures. Most of the Rules grouped into the "common parts" will apply to all procedures except for CVAs and IVAs. The parts will be arranged as follows:
> – Part 1: Company Voluntary Arrangements;
> – Part 2: Administration procedure;
> – Part 3: Administrative receivership;
> – Part 4: Companies winding up;
> – Part 5: Individual voluntary arrangements;
> – Part 6: Bankruptcy;
> – Part 7: Common part – claims by and distributions to creditors;
> – Part 8: Common part – court rules in proceedings under the Act or the Rules;
> – Part 9: Common part – creditors' and liquidation committee;
> – Part 10: Common part – disclaimer;
> – Part 11: Common part – EC Regulation;
> – Part 12: Common part – insolvency register;
> – Part 13: Common part – meetings;
> – Part 14: Common part – proxies and company representation;
> – Part 15: Common part – public examination;
> – Part 16: Common part – remuneration and reporting to creditors;
> – Part 17: Common part – special manager;
> – Part 18: Miscellaneous and general;
> – Part 19: Interpretation; and
> – Schedules.
> Some changes will also have to be made to the Insolvency Act 1986 to reflect the new Rules. The Insolvency Service has issued a public consultation document setting out these changes ("A consultation document on changes to the Insolvency Act 1986 and the Company Directors Disqualification Act 1986 to be made by a Legislative Reform Order for the modernisation and streamlining of insolvency procedures" (September 2007)). The proposals are noted where relevant. Broadly, the key changes that are being proposed will:
> – make the exchange of information easier, for example by allowing insolvency practitioners to make information available on a website;
> – reduce the cost and administrative burden of providing information where this is not necessary, for example by allowing creditors to opt in to receiving updates rather than requiring insolvency practitioners to send them to every creditor whether they read them or not, and by removing the requirement on liquidators to hold annual meetings; and
> – replace affidavits with witness statements.
> To allow for this consultation process to take place, the **anticipated commencement** of the new Rules has been postponed to October 2008, although some of the smaller statutory instruments within the review will still come into force in April 2008. At the time of writing, a draft of the new Rules has not yet been published. Readers should check the online updates and newsletters for developments.

2. European law

7366 The EC Regulation on Insolvency Proceedings (EC Regulation 1346/2000), referred to here as the "EC Insolvency Regulation", **provides for** mutual recognition of insolvency proceedings and co-operation between the courts and insolvency practitioners within the EC (regs 16, 31 EC Insolvency Reg). It will be **relevant where** a company operates in more than one member state and is or will be subject to an insolvency procedure commenced on or after 31 May 2002, when the EC Insolvency Regulation came into force.

Although the EC Insolvency Regulation is stated to **apply to** "collective insolvency proceedings which contain the partial or total divestment of a debtor and the appointment of a liquidator", a wider group of insolvency procedures than liquidation is permitted in main proceedings, but not in secondary proceedings (see ¶7369+ below). It **does not apply to** receiverships (whether administrative or ordinary) because they are not "collective proceedings"; members' voluntary liquidations and winding up orders based on the just and equitable ground are not included either because the company is not insolvent in these cases.

References to a "**member state liquidator**" are to the insolvency practitioner with conduct of the proceedings, whether he is in fact a liquidator or not (e.g. if the main proceedings are an administration, the administrator is the "member state liquidator"). Where member state liquidators have rights in relation to the different insolvency procedures described in the subsequent chapters, such as the right to attend meetings, this is noted as relevant.

The EC Insolvency Regulation applies to all **member states** except for Denmark. At the time of writing, the member states are: Austria, Belgium, Bulgaria, Cyprus, the Czech Republic, Denmark, Estonia, Finland, France, Germany, Greece, Hungary, Ireland, Italy, Latvia, Lithuania, Luxembourg, Malta, the Netherlands, Poland, Portugal, Romania, Slovakia, Slovenia, Spain, Sweden and the United Kingdom. The EC Insolvency Regulation also applies to Gibraltar (art 299(4) EC Treaty). The duty to co-operate and the fact that main proceedings are automatically recognised in the other member states enables **cross-border insolvencies** to be conducted more efficiently than under the provision for co-operation in domestic insolvency legislation, see ¶7376.

MEMO POINTS   The **Cross-Border Insolvency Regulations 2006** (SI 2006/1030) significantly overlap with the EC Insolvency Regulation in their aims and approach, for example allowing for complementary "main" proceedings in one jurisdiction with "non-main" ones in others, although the regulations will be of use where the debtor, creditor or assets are located outside of the EU (¶7377). In the event of a conflict between the EC Insolvency Regulation and the regulations, the former will prevail (art 10 EC Treaty).

Main proceedings

The EC Insolvency Regulation allows for insolvency procedures to be opened in different member states in relation to a company at the same time. The main proceedings must be **commenced in** the member state in which the company's "centre of main interests" is situated. These proceedings will be recognised automatically across all member states, so that the relevant insolvency practitioner can exercise his extensive powers in relation to the company's assets even if they are located in another member state (unless secondary proceedings are opened in another member state, in which case his powers are curtailed, see ¶7369+ below) (reg 17 EC Insolvency Reg).

7367

The following **types of UK insolvency procedures** can be commenced as main proceedings (Annex A, EC Insolvency Reg):
– compulsory liquidation (except for winding up orders made purely on the just and equitable ground);
– creditors' voluntary liquidation (with the court's confirmation, see ¶8459+);
– administration; and
– company voluntary arrangements.

These procedures are commenced in the usual way, indicating in the relevant document (e.g. petition, administration application etc) that the EC Insolvency Regulation applies and that these are the main proceedings. The types of main proceedings in each member state are listed at Annex A to the EC Insolvency Regulation, which is amended from time to time to include changes by member states to their procedures and new member states entering the EU.

A company's "**centre of main interests**" (or, COMI) is presumed to be the country in which its registered office is situated, unless it can be proved otherwise (reg 3(1) EC Insolvency Reg). It should be the place from which the company administers its interests on a regular basis and which is ascertainable by third parties (recital 13 EC Insolvency Reg). The centre of main interests is not further defined and it is left to the national courts to decide whether main proceedings should be commenced in their jurisdiction in the circumstances of each case. If it can be shown that a company's centre of main interests is within the EU, main proceedings can be commenced here even if the company was incorporated outside the EU. This prevents companies deliberately being incorporated outside the EU to avoid the member states' insolvency procedures.

7368

> **EXAMPLE**
> 1. An administration application made against a company incorporated in Delaware, USA, was granted on the basis that its centre of main interests was in England and it therefore fell within the EC Insolvency Regulation (enabling an administration order to be made under the then s 8(7) IA 1986, now para 111, Sch B1 IA 1986) because the company had never traded in the USA and its operations were almost exclusively carried out in England (*Re BRAC Rent-a-Car International Inc* [2003] 2 All ER 201).
> 2. The C & A Group was a global company supplying automotive components, with its head office in Michigan, USA and its European headquarters in Germany. The American section of the company went into Chapter 11 bankruptcy; subsequently administration applications were made in respect of the 24 European companies in its group. Between the American company filing for bankruptcy and the applications being made, the European companies' management was changed so that it was carried out from the UK. Since functions such as IT, human resources, sales, engineering design and pooled bank accounts were all located here and strategic and financial issues were dealt with in England, the court was satisfied that the centre of main interests of all of the European companies was the UK and administration orders were made accordingly (*Re Collins & Aikman Corporation Group* [2005] EWHC 1754 (Ch)).

MEMO POINTS A **subsidiary's** centre of main interests is not determined by the location of its **parent** company's registered office, even if economic decisions are made by the parent company. The presumption is still that the centre of main interests is in the same member state as the company's own registered office, unless it is clear to a third party that this is not the case (*Re Eurofood IFSC Ltd* (C-341/04), in which the internal workings of the parent-subsidiary relationship could not rebut this presumption).

Secondary proceedings

7369 Another set of secondary, or territorial, proceedings can be **opened in** another member state in which the company has an "establishment" (reg 3(2) EC Insolvency Reg). Only a compulsory or creditors' voluntary liquidation (with the court's confirmation, see ¶8459+) can be commenced as secondary proceedings, and its effect is **limited to** the assets within that jurisdiction. The fact that main proceedings have been opened in relation to the company will serve as proof of its insolvency for opening secondary proceedings (reg 3(3) EC Insolvency Reg). Secondary proceedings can be **opened by** the insolvency practitioner in the main proceedings as well as those usually able to place the company into compulsory or creditors' voluntary liquidation (reg 29 EC Insolvency Reg; in the case of secondary proceedings opened in other member states, those able to commence the procedures in Annex B in the relevant country will be able to do so (Annex B is amended from time to time to include changes by member states to their procedures and new member states entering the EU)). Procedures are commenced in the usual way, indicating in the winding up petition that the EC Insolvency Regulation applies and that these are the secondary proceedings for a compulsory liquidation. In the case of a CVL, it will also be commenced in the usual way, but the liquidator will then have to apply to court for the procedure to be confirmed as the secondary proceedings.

A company has an **establishment** within a member state if it is a place in which it carries out a "non-transitory economic activity with human means and goods" (reg 2(h) EC Insolvency Reg). Although the fact that a company has assets in a member state is (in itself) insufficient, a company with an office, branch or manned warehouse, for example, can be said to have an establishment in that country.

> **EXAMPLE**
> 1. Z SARL is a manufacturing company with limited liability incorporated in France. However, its centre of main interests is in England, where its principal factory, most of its workforce and administrative centre are located. It also has a warehouse in Germany, from which its products are distributed around Europe. English main insolvency proceedings (i.e. compulsory liquidation, CVL, administration or CVA) can be commenced against Z SARL in England, applying English insolvency law. In order to protect the company's assets in Germany, the English insolvency practitioner can open secondary proceedings there, under German insolvency law (either das Konkursverfahren or das Gesamtvollstreckungsverfahren, i.e. the German corporate insolvency procedures listed in Annex B to the EC Insolvency Regulation), because the company has an "establishment" there. Alternatively, a German creditor, for example, entitled to commence such a procedure may open secondary proceedings in Germany in relation to the German assets.

> **2.** An English company, A Ltd, has its centre of main interests in France and has been placed into liquidation judiciaire (i.e. one of the procedures specified in Annex A). It also runs an office in England, which has assets worth realising. The French liquidator can open secondary proceedings in England (compulsory liquidation or CVL) to recover those assets, as can the persons entitled to commence these procedures in England.

MEMO POINTS Secondary proceedings can only be **opened before main proceedings** where (reg 3(4) EC Insolvency Reg):
– main proceedings cannot be opened owing to the law of the member state in which the company has its centre of main interests; or
– a creditor whose domicile, habitual residence or registered office is in the member state in which the company has an establishment, or whose claim arises out of the operation of that establishment, so requests.

The relevant **insolvency practitioner in** the **main proceedings** has wide powers in relation to any secondary proceedings, as well as being able to commence them. He can: **7370**
a. suspend the realisation process in secondary proceedings (reg 33 EC Insolvency Reg);
b. propose a rescue plan or composition in secondary proceedings, enabling him to convert the liquidation into an administration or CVA (reg 34 EC Insolvency Reg); and
c. request that pre-existing secondary proceedings are converted into liquidation (reg 37 EC Insolvency Reg).
However, he cannot deal with the company's assets in the member state in which the secondary proceedings have been opened. The insolvency practitioners in the different procedures must **co-operate** with each other and share information, especially where it is relevant to the other's procedure (reg 31 EC Insolvency Reg).

Applicable law

Generally speaking, the law applicable to the proceedings, whether **main or secondary**, is the law of the state in which they were opened (regs 4, 28 EC Insolvency Reg). However, there are situations in which the law of another member state will apply, for example where parties or property are in that member state (see regs 5-15 EC Insolvency Reg). **7371**

Creditors

Creditors in other member states can prove their **claims** in procedures to which the EC Insolvency Regulation applies (whether main or secondary) (reg 32 EC Insolvency Reg). When the procedures are commenced, the insolvency practitioner must inform all known creditors who have their habitual residence, domicile or registered office in a member state other than the one in which the procedures were opened of the following (reg 40 EC Insolvency Reg): **7372**
– the procedure;
– their right to claim; and
– the relevant deadlines for doing so.

All such creditors can submit a claim to the insolvency practitioner in writing (reg 39 EC Insolvency Reg). The insolvency practitioner's notice should be in all of the official **languages** of the EU (Sch A EC Insolvency Reg), but the creditor can submit his claim in his own language and may be required to provide a translation into the language of the member state in which the procedure is conducted (reg 42 EC Insolvency Reg).

In addition, **insolvency practitioners** in main and secondary proceedings can submit claims in other procedures as if they were creditors, including claims proved for by creditors in their own procedures (although if two claims are submitted in respect of the same debt, only one will be admitted, r 11.3 IR 1986) (reg 32 EC Insolvency Reg).

3. Cross-border insolvencies

Cross-border insolvencies are relatively rare, but the lack of co-ordination between the laws and procedures in different jurisdictions has tended to complicate those that do arise. Beyond the scope of the EC Insolvency Regulation, there are two sets of **rules** governing such insolvencies. **7375**

MEMO POINTS   An **overseas company** with a **branch in GB** must make certain filings at Companies House if it is subject to insolvency proceedings (¶180).

7376 The Insolvency Act provides for cross-border judicial **co-operation** where a request has been received from a court in a **designated country** (s 426 IA 1986). If the other country involved is an EU member state other than Denmark, the EC Insolvency Regulation provides for far more extensive co-operation and that regulation must be preferred where there is any conflict between it and domestic legislation (art 10 EC Treaty). Where the country in question is not a member state, this provision may still be relied upon. The designated countries are: Anguilla, Australia, the Bahamas, Bermuda, Botswana, Brunei Darussalam, Canada, the Cayman Islands, the Falkland Islands, Gibraltar, Guernsey, Hong Kong, the Republic of Ireland, Malaysia, Montserrat, New Zealand, the Republic of South Africa, St Helena, Turks and Caicos Islands, Tuvalu and the British Virgin Islands (SI 1986/2123; SI 1989/2409; SI 1996/253; SI 1998/2766). The Insolvency Act also provides for automatic co-operation between courts in the different parts of the British Isles, i.e. England and Wales, Scotland, Northern Ireland, the Channel Islands and the Isle of Man.

In the case of cross-border insolvencies with countries which are **not designated countries** or member states (and Denmark), individual protocols can be drawn up for co-operation on a case by case basis (see the International Insolvency Institute website). However, with the implementation of the Cross-Border Insolvency Regulations, such requests for co-operation, or individual protocols, will be even less frequent.

7377 The Cross-Border Insolvency Regulations 2006 (SI 2006/1030, which came into force on 4 April 2006) aim to address the complications that arise in cross-border insolvencies by implementing the United Nations Commission on International Trade Law's ("**UNCITRAL**") **Model Law** on cross-border insolvency. The regulations provide a transparent method of dealing with insolvency issues which may arise in foreign jurisdictions, including provisions which encourage co-operation between insolvency practitioners, protect and allow for the realisation of a debtor's assets abroad, and enable enforcement action to be taken and remedies to be sought in different countries. They allow foreign insolvency representatives to initiate insolvency proceedings in this country where the debtor is subject to a foreign procedure, and give that representative the right to participate in the proceedings here. Similarly to the EC Insolvency Regulation, foreign proceedings are deemed to be "main" or "non-main", giving the foreign representative different levels of rights in proceedings in this country. In the case of main proceedings, for instance, a moratorium can be imposed on the local creditors' and the debtor's actions while arrangements are made for the reorganisation of the debtor's assets. However, it is important to note that, unless the court orders otherwise, the recognition of foreign proceedings does not prevent local creditors from starting or continuing with insolvency proceedings here.

Applications under the regulations will be dealt with by the Chancery Division of the High Court and District Registries with insolvency jurisdiction. If a foreign representative has been appointed in relation to a company registered in Great Britain, or with a branch here, he will have to **file** Form ML7 at Companies House.

There are many parallels between the Cross-Border Insolvency Regulations and the EC Insolvency Regulation, although the regulations are not confined to insolvencies in **EU member states** and will therefore constitute complementary rules. Where both the EC Insolvency Regulation and the regulations apply, the EC Insolvency Regulation takes precedence in the case of a conflict within the EU (art 3, Sch 1 SI 2006/1030). Several **countries**, including the USA and New Zealand, have implemented the Model Law into their own insolvency law, with Canada and Australia intending to do so; the government anticipates that requests for co-operation will principally come from these countries. The other countries which have already adopted the Model Law are: Japan, Mexico, the Republic of South Africa, Poland, Romania, the British Virgin Islands, Serbia, Montenegro, Colombia and Eritrea.

B. Applications and procedural matters

1. Court applications

7380 Where the company is in a formal insolvency procedure, the legislation and Rules provide for certain parties to make applications to court on a number of **different matters**, from seeking directions to challenging decisions. The Rules set out general provisions applicable to such applications. These are **summarised** below, and should be read together with the discussion relating to the application in question for any specific requirements.

> MEMO POINTS The **Civil Procedure Rules**, which govern civil court proceedings, apply to insolvency proceedings as well, but only insofar as they do not contradict the Rules. There is also a CPR Practice Direction which deals specifically with insolvency matters ("the CPR Insolvency PD"). Insolvency proceedings are automatically allocated to the multi-track, and so the provisions in the CPR relating to allocation questionnaires and track allocation do not apply (r 7.51 IR 1986).

7381 The general application provisions described below are **not relevant to** (r 7.1 IR 1986):
– petitions for winding up (¶7587+);
– applications for administration orders (¶8721+); or
– applications relating to transactions defrauding creditors (¶7826+), which must be made by claim form.

Making an application

7382 There are **two types** of insolvency application (r 7.2 IR 1986):
– originating applications, which are made in procedures not already before the court; and
– ordinary applications, which are made within procedures already before the court.

Therefore, applications made relating to compulsory liquidations should be by way of ordinary applications, but in voluntary liquidations each application should be made by originating application because the liquidation is not already being dealt with by the court.

7383 Every application must contain certain basic **information** (r 7.3 IR 1986):
– the names of the parties;
– the relief, order or directions sought;
– who will be served with the application;
– who must be given notice of the application according to the legislation and/or Rules; and
– the applicant's address for service.

7384 The application must be **filed** at court, with one copy plus enough extra copies for each of the persons required to be served with the application (r 7.4 IR 1986).

7385 The court will usually fix a **venue** for the hearing at this stage so that the application can be served on the parties together with details of the venue. In insolvency proceedings, the "venue" of a hearing is its date, time and place (r 13.6 IR 1986).

7386 The court will usually return the copies of the application for **service** endorsed with the venue to the applicant, who must then serve a copy on each respondent named in the application, plus any other person upon whom it must be served (r 7.4 IR 1986). Usually, 14 days' notice needs to be given, although the court has a wide discretion to give other directions as to service.

If the legislation or Rules provide for the **hearing** to be "**without notice**", the court can hear the application without anybody else having to be served. The term "ex parte" is still used in parts of the legislation and Rules to refer to such applications, although it has been replaced by "without notice" since the Civil Procedure Rules reformed civil applications (r 0.2 IR 1986). In cases of urgency, the court may allow an application which usually requires notice to be heard without notice (in exceptional circumstances only, since this deprives the other parties of their right to attend and be heard at the hearing), or on a **shorter notice** period (r 7.4(6) IR 1986).

Evidence

7388 Evidence must usually be given by **affidavit or witness statement** verified by a statement of truth, unless the legislation, Rules or court stipulates otherwise (r 7.7 IR 1986). Witness statements replaced affidavits in non-insolvency civil proceedings under the Civil Procedure Rules, although parties to insolvency proceedings can choose whether to use an affidavit or a witness statement in most cases (r 7.57 IR 1986). However, the following evidence must be presented in the form of an affidavit:

a. verification of the statement of affairs in compulsory liquidation and administrative receivership (rr 4.33, 3.4 IR 1986);

b. verification of the accounts submitted to the official receiver in compulsory liquidation (r 4.39 IR 1986);

c. verification of further information to the statement of affairs or accounts submitted to the official receiver in compulsory liquidation (r 4.42 IR 1986);

d. verification of accounts in CVL (r 4.40 IR 1986);

e. where a proof of debt is required to be submitted in the form of an affidavit in liquidation (rr 4.73, 4.77 IR 1986); and

f. evidence relating to public examinations (rr 9.3, 9.4 IR 1986).

The affidavit or witness statement can be **made by** a party to the application, i.e. the applicant or respondent, or any other person who has direct knowledge of the matter, such as their solicitor (r 7.8 IR 1986). A creditor's affidavit of debt may be sworn in front of his own solicitor (usually, it must be witnessed by an independent solicitor or notary) (r 7.57 IR 1986).

An applicant's affidavit or witness statement must be **filed** at court and **served** on the respondent at least 14 days before the hearing, while a respondent must submit his evidence in opposition to court and serve a copy on the applicant at least 7 days before the hearing (r 7.8 IR 1986). The legislation or Rules relating to the specific application may also require the evidence to be served on other persons.

> MEMO POINTS 1. An affidavit or witness statement **made by** the relevant **insolvency practitioner or official receiver** must state the capacity in which he makes the statement, the position he holds and his work address (r 7.57 IR 1986). As an alternative form of evidence, the court will accept reports as if they were affidavits if they are made by the official receiver or his deputy, or by an administrator, liquidator, provisional liquidator or special manager where the application does not involve other parties and the court does not order otherwise (r 7.9 IR 1986).
>
> 2. As part of the Insolvency Service's review of secondary legislation (see ¶7364/mp), it is taking the opportunity to make alterations to the primary legislation either where it is necessary to support the new Rules or to remove unnecessary administrative burdens. The Service proposes to remove the requirement for certain documents to be verified by **affidavit** in insolvency procedures (proposal 5, "A consultation document on changes to the Insolvency Act 1986 and the Company Directors Disqualification Act 1986 to be made by a Legislative Reform Order for the modernisation and streamlining of insolvency procedures" (September 2007)). Since the reform of civil procedures generally in 1998, affidavits in other types of procedures have been replaced by witness statements, which do not have to be sworn/affirmed by a solicitor/commissioner for oaths/notary. Therefore, this change will reduce the cost and time involved in preparing these documents. At the time of writing, the consultation is still open. If this proposal is accepted, the changes are likely to be implemented from 1 October 2008.

7389 In addition to presenting evidence by affidavit or witness statement, the court can order that a deponent appears in person to be **cross-examined** on his written evidence (r 7.7 IR 1986). If he does not attend, his affidavit cannot be used in evidence without the court's permission.

The hearing

7390 The application will usually be heard by a **registrar**, unless he considers that the matter should be decided by a judge or the application requests relief that he is not authorised to grant (r 7.6 IR 1986). The registrar usually deals with applications in chambers, i.e. in private. If referred to a judge, he will either determine the application or refer it back to the registrar with directions as to how to proceed.

Some applications can only be dealt with by a **judge**, so there is no need for it to be sent to the registrar first. The judge will usually deal with applications in open court, i.e. in public,

although he can also do so in chambers. The following applications will be dealt with directly by a judge (para 5 CPR Insolvency PD):
a. petitions to wind a company up;
b. public examinations;
c. applications for urgent interim relief, such as avoiding a disposition of company property between a winding up petition being presented and an order being made (¶7674+);
d. applications to restrain a winding up petition being presented or advertised;
e. applications to appoint a provisional liquidator;
f. applications for an administration order, an interim order relating to it and for directions relating to an order or to vary or discharge it (including to convert it into liquidation);
g. where a CVA has been approved, applications to stay a winding up order, terminate an administrator's appointment or for directions generally;
h. appeals from county court or registrars' decisions; and
i. applications to imprison a person for contempt of court.
In the Companies Court at the High Court the **court manager**, or in District Registries the **district judge**, can deal with the following applications:
a. to extend or shorten deadlines relating to winding up;
b. for substituted service of winding up petitions;
c. to withdraw a winding up petition;
d. to substitute a petitioner on a winding up petition;
e. to transfer proceedings from the High Court to the county court; and
f. the following applications by the official receiver:
– for limited disclosure of a statement of affairs;
– for relief from duties imposed by the Rules; and
– for permission to give notice of a meeting by advertisement only.

Attendance

The hearing, whether in chambers or in open court, can be attended by any creditor or contributory of the company in question (r 7.53 IR 1986). An attendee must **provide** written confirmation to the court of his status, and may attend in person or be represented by his solicitor. He may also request that he is **given notice** of any step in the proceedings. However, he must bear the cost of his involvement in the proceedings himself, and if the court considers that he has caused the company to incur additional costs he may be ordered to pay those as well. If he does not pay, his right to attend and be kept informed of the proceedings will be suspended. If it is more convenient, for example where there are many creditors and contributories, the court can nominate representatives from each group to attend and receive notice. If more than one representative is appointed for one group, they cannot instruct separate solicitors.

7391

MEMO POINTS For these purposes, a **member state liquidator** is deemed to be a creditor and so can attend hearings (r 7.53 IR 1986).

Orders

Any order made by the court can be **enforced** as if it were a judgment (r 7.19 IR 1986). Orders made in one county court can be enforced by another, even if it does not have jurisdiction in insolvency proceedings.

7392

Appeals

Any court with insolvency jurisdiction (¶7362+) can **review, rescind or vary** any order it has made in insolvency proceedings (r 7.47 IR 1986).

7393

Appeals of decisions of the county court or a High Court registrar are **heard by** a single judge of the High Court, with no requirement to obtain leave for the appeal (r 7.47(2) IR 1986). Further appeals can be made to the Court of Appeal, but only with its leave or that of the High Court judge. High Court judges' decisions can be appealed directly to the Court of Appeal, with the consent of the judge or Court of Appeal. Appeals can only succeed if the previous decision was based upon an error of law or principle, and new evidence can only be relied upon if it was not available at the previous hearing (*Re Industrial and Commercial Securities plc* (1989) 5 BCC 320).

> *MEMO POINTS* 1. A **decision of** the **official receiver or secretary of state** must be appealed within 28 days of the appellant being notified of the decision (r 7.50 IR 1986).
> 2. The court has clarified that this power **only applies to** orders made in the exercise of a court's insolvency jurisdiction (*Eastaway v Secretary of State for Trade and Industry* [2007] EWCA Civ 425). Therefore, it does not apply to applications to vary or set aside disqualification orders or undertakings.

7394 The power to **review** should only be used where there has been a change in circumstances and/or new information has come to light which was not before the original court (*Re R S & M Engineering Co Ltd*, *Mond v Hammond Suddards (a firm) (No 2)* [1999] 2 BCLC 485).

An application to **rescind** a winding up order must be made within 7 days of the order by a party able to appear at the petition hearing, although the court may extend this deadline (rr 7.47, 12.9 IR 1986; ¶7718+).

Costs

7395 The general rules regarding costs in legal proceedings are set out in the Civil Procedure Rules (parts 43, 44, 45, 47, 48 CPR apply to insolvency proceedings). Where the costs are to be paid out of the company's assets, they should either be **agreed** with the insolvency practitioner or **decided** by detailed assessment. If the parties cannot agree, the insolvency practitioner will apply to court for an assessment (r 7.34 IR 1986; Part 47 CPR deals with detailed assessment of costs). Even where the parties agree the costs, a liquidation or creditors' committee can insist on them being subject to detailed assessment.

Witnesses in court proceedings are usually allowed their costs and expenses (i.e. travel and subsistence), although a company officer who is under examination or appearing at another hearing relating to his insolvent company will not usually be allowed his costs (r 7.41 IR 1986). A petitioner is not usually classed as a witness, but may be allowed similar costs.

A person may **apply** for his costs to be paid **after** the **proceedings** have finished by applying to the court and serving a sealed copy of his application on the relevant insolvency practitioner (and the official receiver if the company is in compulsory winding up) (r 7.40 IR 1986). The court must be satisfied that the application could not have been made during the proceedings.

> *MEMO POINTS* It is rare for an **insolvency practitioner** or the official receiver to be made **personally liable** for costs, but the court can so direct if appropriate (r 7.39 IR 1986).

Record keeping

7398 The **court** keeps a **record** of all insolvency proceedings, which contains their history, decisions and any interim steps (r 7.27 IR 1986). They will not contain any sensitive information, such as affidavit or witness statement evidence.

The following persons have the **right to inspect** the court's file at reasonable times (r 7.31 IR 1986):
– the responsible insolvency practitioner;
– an authorised officer of the Insolvency Service;
– a creditor of the company in question who has provided written confirmation of his status;
– any director or other officer, or former director/officer, of the company in question; and
– any shareholder of the company, or contributory where it is in liquidation.

Any **other person** can apply to inspect the records of court proceedings but the registrar can decide not to allow it if he considers that the applicant wants to inspect them for an improper purpose (r 7.28 IR 1986; for example, where a business wanted to search the court's records regularly so that it could then sell the information on to customers, *Re Creditnet Ltd* [1996] 2 BCLC 133. However, in a subsequent decision which did not refer to *Re Creditnet Ltd*, the court found that as long as such a company could do no more than an individual would be able to do in respect of a named debtor, there should be no objection, *Re Austintel Ltd* [1997] 1 BCLC 233). This decision can be appealed to a judge, but no further.

Another way in which the right to inspect may be **restricted** is for the court to direct that certain documents, or parts of them, can only be inspected with leave on the application of the responsible insolvency practitioner, official receiver or any other interested party (r7.31(5) IR 1986). This may happen if a document contains commercially sensitive information, for example. A person prevented from inspecting a document by such an application can still apply to the court for leave to do so (*Astor Chemicals Ltd v Synthetic Technology Ltd* [1990] BCLC 1). Inspection of the statement of affairs and any affidavit of concurrence may also be prevented if an order for **limited disclosure** is in force (compulsory liquidation: ¶8133; administration: ¶8871; administrative receivership: ¶9378).

MEMO POINTS   1. A **member state liquidator** in main proceedings is deemed to be a creditor for these purposes (r7.64 IR 1986).
2. The court will also keep a record of all *Gazette* **notices and newspaper advertisements** published in relation to an insolvency procedure (r7.32 IR 1986).

If a person is permitted, or has the right, to inspect the court file, he or his solicitor can request office **copies** to be provided to him, although the court will make a charge for this (rr 7.61, 12.15 IR 1986).

7399

2. Notices

The legislation and Rules require notices to be given in a number of situations, whether in respect of applications to court, meetings or action by the insolvency practitioner such as distributing dividends. Certain **general provisions** apply to all notices in insolvency proceedings, although the particular requirements of each type of notice should also be followed.

7404

MEMO POINTS   As part of the Insolvency Service's review of secondary legislation (see ¶7364/mp), it is taking the opportunity to make alterations to the primary legislation either where it is necessary to support the new Rules or to remove unnecessary administrative burdens. The Service has put forward several proposals relating to insolvency practitioners **communicating with creditors and other interested parties** (proposal 1, "A consultation document on changes to the Insolvency Act 1986 and the Company Directors Disqualification Act 1986 to be made by a Legislative Reform Order for the modernisation and streamlining of insolvency procedures" (September 2007)):
– to remove the requirement for insolvency practitioners to send information to all known creditors at various stages in the procedure. Generally speaking, most creditors just want to know how much of their debt will be repaid and have no interest in the general progress of the procedure. This requirement therefore creates a heavy but unnecessary financial and administrative burden. It will be replaced by a system allowing creditors who do wish to be kept up to date to "opt in" to receiving information from the insolvency practitioner;
– to allow any documents or information that must be "written" or "in writing" to be sent electronically (unless the document has to be served personally); and
– to allow insolvency practitioners to provide information to creditors and shareholders by sending a link to a website where the information can be found.
At the time of writing, the consultation is still open. If these proposals are accepted, the changes are likely to be implemented from 1 October 2008.

Service is generally the **responsibility of** the parties and will not be undertaken by the court (para 1.3 CPR Insolvency PD). Notices must be given **in writing** unless the court, Rules or legislation provides otherwise (r 12.4 IR 1986). Any other specific requirements as to notice (such as its contents) depend upon the type of notice in question. Where notice is required of the venue of a hearing, it can be given by serving a copy of the application which has been sealed by the court as it will be endorsed with this information (r 13.3 IR 1986). The notice can be **sent** together, or combined, **with** any other document which must be sent to that person at the same time (r 12.14 IR 1986).

7405

Service can be accomplished using a number of different **methods** (rr 6.2, 6.4 CPR; rr 12.10, 12.11 IR 1986):
a. personal service, i.e. giving it directly to the individual or to a person holding a senior position within a company to be served;

7406

b. post (first or second class); or
c. hand delivery to an address given for service.

If served **by post**, the following rules apply (r 12.10 IR 1986):
a. it must be in an envelope addressed to the person to be served at their last known address, and can be pre-paid first or second class;
b. if it is sent by first class post, it is treated as being served on the second day after it was posted unless it can be proved otherwise;
c. if it is sent by second class post, it is treated as being served on the fourth day after it was posted unless it can be proved otherwise; and
d. the date of posting is taken as the date of the post-mark, unless it can be proved otherwise.

If a document is served **personally** or **by hand** after 5pm on a business day or on a weekend or bank holiday, it will be treated as if it was served on the next business day (r 6.7 CPR).

If the person to be served has stipulated that notice is to be **given to** his **solicitor**, notice can be served on that solicitor instead; otherwise solicitors have no implied authority to accept service (r 13.4 IR 1986).

> MEMO POINTS 1. Where **no address for service** has been given, the default address to be used is set out in detail in the Civil Procedure Rules, and is essentially the last known residential address for an individual or place of business for a business (r 6.5(6) CPR).
> 2. Where the person to be served is **out of the jurisdiction**, an application to court must be made for directions (r 12.12 IR 1986). Directions are not required where it is a member state liquidator who needs to be served. This Rule does not, however, apply to **notices of meetings**. The court has interpreted the wording as relating to documents in court proceedings only, and stated that it would not be a good use of the court's time for it to have to give directions every time notice of a meeting had to be served out of the jurisdiction (*Re T & N Ltd* [2006] EWHC 842 (Ch)). On the other hand, the Rules relating to the service of documents by post and the application of the CPR to the service of documents (i.e. rr 12.10, 12.11 IR 1986) do apply to notices of meetings, as they are drafted in more general terms.

7407 Where a **certificate of service** is required, it must state the method used and the date upon which service was effected (r 6.10 CPR). The person required to give notice or someone instructed by him to do so can certify service, either in a separate document to, or endorsed on a copy of, the notice (r 12.4 IR 1986). If notice is given by an insolvency practitioner or the official receiver, he can prove service by certifying that it was posted properly.

7408 Insolvency legislation requires certain notices to be **advertised in the *Gazette*** so that they are formally brought to the attention of the general public. The *Gazette* is the official publication in which statutory notices on various matters, including parliamentary, planning and public finance as well as company and insolvency matters, are advertised. In the case of companies registered in England and Wales, the appropriate publication is the *London Gazette*; there are also *Edinburgh* and *Belfast Gazettes* for companies registered in Scotland and Northern Ireland respectively (rr 13.1, 13.13 IR 1986; s 744 CA 1985).

3. Time limits

7412 Generally, time limits set out in the Rules are to be calculated based on **clear days**, e.g. not counting the day on which notice of a meeting was served nor the day on which the meeting is held (r 2.8 CPR; r 12.9 IR 1986).

Where a time limit is to be counted in "**business days**", it is calculated excluding:
– the days specified in the rule (e.g. service of the petition, advertisement and the day of the hearing, as applicable) (r 2.8 CPR; r 12.9 IR 1986); and
– weekends, Christmas Day, Good Friday and bank holidays (except for Scottish bank holidays which are not shared with England and Wales) (r 13.13(1) IR 1986).

Time limits for compliance with a requirement in the Rules can be **extended or shortened** by the court (r 3.1 CPR; r 12.9 IR 1986). In the case of winding up deadlines, those in the legislation can also be extended (r 4.3 IR 1986).

> **EXAMPLE** Calculating the minimum time period (7 business days) required between advertisement of a winding up petition and the hearing (¶7647) can be illustrated as follows:

Date	Event	Day counted?
Tues 23	Petition advertised	✗
Wed 24	-	✓
Thurs 26	-	✓
Fri 27	-	✓
Sat 28	Weekend	✗
Sun 29	Weekend	✗
Mon 30	-	✓
Tues 31	-	✓
Wed 1	-	✓
Thurs 2	-	✓
Fri 3	Hearing	✗

C. Insolvency practitioners

An "insolvency practitioner" is **defined as** a person qualified to act as a liquidator, provisional liquidator, administrator, administrative receiver and nominee/supervisor of a company (s 388 IA 1986). Receivers are often insolvency practitioners, although this is not a requirement; for example, an appropriate receiver of land could be a professional such as a chartered surveyor, in view of his expertise in dealing with that type of property.

Qualification

Qualification as an insolvency practitioner comprises the following elements (s 390 IA 1986):
– he must be an individual, not a corporate entity or a firm;
– he must be authorised to act as an insolvency practitioner; and
– there must be security in force for the performance of his functions.

A person **cannot act** as an insolvency practitioner where:
a. he is an undischarged bankrupt (including where he is subject to a bankruptcy restrictions order);
b. he is subject to a disqualification order or undertaking preventing him from acting as a director or being involved in the management of a company; or
c. he lacks the mental capacity to act (within the meaning of the Mental Capacity Act 2005).
It is an offence for a person (other than the official receiver) to act as an insolvency practitioner **without** the correct **qualifications** or when he is not permitted to act (s 389 IA 1986; ¶9935).

> **MEMO POINTS** A person acting as a **nominee or supervisor** of a company subject to a CVA, does not commit an offence provided he is authorised to act because of his membership of a recognised body (see ¶7424 below), he has the correct security in force and does not fall within the categories of persons not permitted to act as above (s 389A IA 1986).

Most insolvency practitioners are **authorised** to act as a result of their membership of one of the professional bodies recognised by the secretary of state for that purpose (SI 1986/1764):
– The Chartered Association of Certified Accountants;
– The Insolvency Practitioners Association;
– The Institute of Chartered Accountants in England and Wales;
– The Institute of Chartered Accountants in Ireland;
– The Institute of Chartered Accountants in Scotland;
– The Law Society; and
– The Law Society of Scotland.

7422

7423

7424

Alternatively, an individual can apply directly to the secretary of state (or any other competent authority designated by him) for authorisation, which will be awarded if he meets the correct criteria (regs 6-11 SI 2005/524).

> **MEMO POINTS** As well as authorising insolvency practitioners to act, these bodies regulate the **practitioners' conduct** through their own rules and disciplinary procedures. Insolvency practitioners must also follow the Insolvency Service's "Guide to Professional Conduct and Ethics" which can be found on the Service's website. It focuses on five key ethical principles: integrity, objectivity, competence, due skill and courtesy, and is designed to assist practitioners in identifying threats to these principles and put in place appropriate safeguards to combat them. The guide is adopted by the regulatory bodies and therefore applies to their members along with the bodies' own ethical codes, but it also applies to practitioners who are authorised individually by the secretary of state. The Joint Insolvency Committee ("JIC") recently consulted on an updated and revised ethical guide. The consultation closed in July 2007, but at the time of writing, the JIC had not yet published its response or a further draft of the code.

7425 Every insolvency practitioner is required to ensure that there is adequate financial **security** in place to cover the proper exercise of his functions for each of his cases (s 390(3) IA 1986). The security comprises a **bond**, by which a surety undertakes to be jointly and severally liable with the insolvency practitioner for losses caused by the insolvency practitioner's fraud or dishonesty, or that of another person with whom the insolvency practitioner connived, up to (reg 12, Sch 2 SI 2005/524):
a. a "penalty sum" at least equal to the value of the insolvent company's assets, as estimated by the insolvency practitioner at the date of his appointment in the case (not including any charged assets to the extent of their security, or any assets held on trust to which the company is not entitled beneficially). The minimum penalty sum is £5,000; the maximum £5,000,000; plus
b. up to £250,000 if the penalty sum is insufficient.
A **limit** of £25,000,000 or more may be placed on the aggregate that will be met out of all of the bonds relating to one insolvency practitioner, and the bond may state that all claims must be made within a particular time limit. For further details relating to the security, see SI 2005/524.

> **MEMO POINTS** In the case of a **nominee or supervisor** of a voluntary arrangement, the "penalty sum" must be equal to the value of the assets subject to the arrangement (Sch 2 SI 2005/524).

General record-keeping obligations

7426 In addition to the specific record-keeping and disclosure obligations applicable in each type of procedure, insolvency practitioners are required to keep general records of each case in which they act, which their professional body and the secretary of state may **inspect** (regs 13, 14, 15, Sch 3 SI 2005/524). The secretary of state can also access the practice records held by an individual practitioner, his employer or the firm of which he is a partner (reg 16 SI 2005/524).

Taking action against insolvency practitioners

7427 If a person involved in an insolvency procedure is **not satisfied with** the insolvency practitioner's **conduct** of the case, he has a number of avenues of redress:
a. complain directly to the insolvency practitioner concerned;
b. complain to the insolvency practitioner's professional body, or to the Insolvency Service if the insolvency practitioner was authorised directly by the secretary of state. Each professional body has its own complaints process, and reference should be made to the relevant body. The insolvency practitioner should give the name of his body when asked, or the practitioners' register at the Insolvency Service can be searched on its website; or
c. where the insolvency practitioner has committed a particular breach, take court action against him if the complainant has the right to do so.

Breach of specific duties

7428 Insolvency practitioners can be sued for **misfeasance**, which is discussed below in the context of directors (¶7457+). This is a summary procedure, providing a reasonably quick

and straightforward method of taking action against an insolvency practitioner. Action can be taken against insolvency practitioners for breach of a number of duties relating to **different types of procedures**, which are discussed as follows:
- liquidation, ¶8234+;
- administration, ¶9016+;
- receivership, ¶9392+; and
- voluntary arrangements, ¶9544.

They are also subject to various **filing and administrative duties**, e.g. to give notices and place advertisements, which are found in the relevant topics of the different types of procedures. Failure to comply with such requirements often renders the insolvency practitioner liable to a fine.

Breach of general duties

An insolvency practitioner's general duties can also give rise to liability, which a person wishing to take action against him may rely on because, for example, one of the simpler routes does not give him an appropriate remedy or his claim does not fall within one of the relevant categories.

7429

The insolvency practitioner is usually an **agent** of the company, although his agency differs from the normal commercial agency relationship in that he controls the actions of his principal. His status as agent will afford him protection against personal liability. For example, an insolvency practitioner is only likely to be found personally liable for statements made about a company's affairs if they were made fraudulently or if he assumed personal responsibility for them, since they will usually have been made by him as the company's agent (*Williams v Natural Life Health Foods Ltd* [1998] 1 BCLC 690, a case concerning directors as agents).

Although insolvency practitioners are professionals engaged to perform a service, it is not common for them to be sued for **professional negligence** (*Harmony Carpets v Chaffin-Laird* [2000] BCC 893, a case regarding an individual voluntary arrangement). This is because a duty of care to a particular claimant, such as a creditor, cannot usually be established. However, it may be appropriate in the circumstances to hold the insolvency practitioner to an equitable duty of care (*Medforth v Blake* [1999] 3 All ER 97, in which a receiver breached his equitable duty of care to manage the company's business profitably).

As **officers of the court**, insolvency practitioners are under a common law duty to conduct themselves honourably, for example by honouring assurances, and not to take advantage of or insist on their legal rights if the circumstances and justice require (known as "the rule in *ex parte James*" after the authoritative case *Re Condon, ex parte James* (1874) 9 Ch App 609).

Insolvency practitioners are also **fiduciaries**, for example, if they act despite a conflict of interest they can be removed from office (*Re Corbenstoke Ltd (No 2)* [1990] BCLC 60, in which the company's liquidator was also the trustee in bankruptcy of one of the company's creditors, putting him in a conflicted position). However, an insolvency practitioner does not owe a specific fiduciary duty to the creditors (*Mahomed v Morris* [2000] 2 BCLC 536).

> MEMO POINTS   A **duty of care** can only be established to an individual creditor in exceptional circumstances (*A & J Fabrications Ltd v Grant Thornton* [1998] 2 BCLC 227, in which a creditor had chosen the liquidator and agreed to pay his fees up to £5,000).

D. Directors' liabilities

Directors owe many duties to a company, which are discussed in detail at ¶2317+. Very broadly speaking, they comprise agency, fiduciary, common law and statutory duties. Directors also owe specific duties when the company is in insolvency, and can be made subject to certain liabilities. The **specific duties and liabilities** are summarised at ¶7461 and discussed within the individual procedures; here, the discussion focuses on the directors' more **general liabilities** connected with their conduct leading up to insolvency.

7439

7440 When their companies experience financial problems, directors are faced with difficult decisions, particularly in the light of the liability that can be imposed upon them for making the wrong ones. Since every company's situation will be different, directors should seek professional advice tailored to their needs. Although the offences of **wrongful** and **fraudulent trading** only apply to a company in liquidation, directors whose companies are in financial difficulties need to consider them no matter which route they propose taking. Any insolvency procedure can lead to liquidation; for example where an administration can no longer achieve its aims, or where a pre-CVA moratorium ends without the CVA having been approved. **Misfeasance** can apply where the company is in liquidation or administration, although proceedings can also be taken in respect of conduct prior to these procedures. It is useful to look at these duties and liabilities together since they give an overview of the general management duties of the directors of a company in insolvency, as opposed to their specific duties, such as co-operating with the insolvency practitioner.

Directors must also remember that their conduct may cause them to be **disqualified** (¶3000+). Being found liable for fraudulent or wrongful trading can be grounds for disqualification in themselves, but a director can also be disqualified if the company is insolvent and his conduct renders him unfit to be a director. A number of factors must be taken into account, such as the director's responsibility for the company's insolvency, any misfeasance committed by him and any specific failures such as not co-operating with a liquidator. A list of these factors is at ¶3023+, together with a full discussion of disqualification on the ground of unfitness.

7441 In the case of a **public company**, as soon as its **net assets fall** to half or less of the company's called-up share capital, the directors must convene a general meeting to consider what action, if any, needs to be taken to deal with the situation (s 142 CA 1985; restated at s 656 CA 2006 by 1 October 2009). The directors must summon the meeting within 28 days of knowing of the company's net asset position for a date within 56 days of acquiring that knowledge. Knowingly and wilfully failing to summon the meeting as required, or permitting the failure, renders a director liable to a fine (¶9935).

1. Fraudulent trading

7443 A person **commits** fraudulent trading **if** (s 213 IA 1986):
a. any business of the company is carried on:
– with the intent to defraud creditors (whether of the company or any other person); or
– for any fraudulent purpose;
b. that person was knowingly a party to the business being carried on in that manner; and
c. the company is then wound up.

Directors are most likely to be **liable** under this provision, although action can be taken against any person involved in carrying on the company's business, for example a creditor who received payment when he knew that the business could only be carried on with the intent to defraud creditors (*Re Gerald Cooper Chemicals Ltd* [1978] 2 All ER 49). Knowingly being a party to the fraudulent trading includes deliberately ignoring a clear breach (*Re Bank of Credit and Commerce International SA (No 15), Morris v Bank of India* [2005] 2 BCLC 328).

> MEMO POINTS 1. Note that, unlike wrongful trading, below, the company only has to be in liquidation, it does not have to be **insolvent**.
> 2. This offence is separate from that of **defrauding creditors** (sometimes also called fraudulent trading) under companies legislation, see ¶2577.

7444 For these purposes, carrying on a business requires the person in question to take **positive steps**, for example a secretary or financial adviser who failed to bring the company's financial position to the attention of the directors was not liable for fraudulent trading (*Re Maidstone Building Provisions Ltd* [1971] 3 All ER 363). It can, however, comprise carrying out just one transaction (*Re Gerald Cooper Chemicals Ltd* [1978] 2 All ER 49).

The intent to defraud requires **dishonesty**. This intent cannot be separated from the element of carrying on business, so if an individual creditor has been defrauded without the business having been conducted fraudulently, his remedy lies under general law and not fraudulent trading (*Morphitis v Bernasconi* [2003] 2 BCLC 53).

> **EXAMPLE**
> 1. A person who ordered goods when he knew that there was no reasonable prospect of the supplier being paid when the debt became due, or shortly afterwards, had the requisite intent to defraud (*R v Grantham* [1984] BCLC 270).
> 2. Having the intention to prefer one creditor over another, in the knowledge (or with the reasonable suspicion) that the company would not have enough assets to pay its creditors in full is not enough to constitute fraudulent trading (*Re Sarflax Ltd* [1979] 1 All ER 529).

MEMO POINTS 1. The **creditors prejudiced** by the person's actions can include potential, future and contingent creditors (*R v Smith* [1996] 2 BCLC 109).
2. In a case in which a liquidator sought fraudulent trading declarations relating to transactions carried out in the period **between presentation of the petition** against a company **and the order being made**, the court held that the company had not carried on business as the transactions were automatically void (see ¶7674+; no applications had been made to court to validate the transactions). The transactions in question were therefore incapable of amounting to fraudulent trading (*Carman v The Cronos Group SA* [2005] EWHC 2403 (Ch)).

An **application** for a declaration of fraudulent trading must be **made by** a liquidator. The **court** has the **power** to (ss 213, 215 IA 1986):
a. order the persons found to carry on fraudulent trading to contribute to the company's assets as appropriate in the circumstances;
b. impose a charge on any debt owed by the company to the fraudulent trader (including his assignee or someone acting on his behalf) and provide for the enforcement of that charge; and/or
c. order that any debt owed by the company to the fraudulent trader (including his assignee or someone acting on his behalf) is deferred so that it is only repaid after all of the company's other debts, plus interest, have been met.

Any such **order** is for the **benefit of** the creditors as a whole, not individuals, and is unlikely to exceed the amount of credit obtained whilst trading fraudulently, although it may be increased where the person is particularly blameworthy. For example, a director's seriously fraudulent conduct, ranging from book-keeping irregularities and forging cheques to defrauding the VAT authorities, rendered him liable to make up the company's deficiency to its creditors plus interest from the commencement of his company's liquidation (*Re L Todd (Swanscombe) Ltd* [1990] BCLC 454).
In addition, a declaration of fraudulent trading against a director can trigger **disqualification** (¶3000+).

MEMO POINTS 1. **Insurance** policies will exclude fraud and therefore a director will not be able to rely on his liability insurance to meet fraudulent trading penalties. Nor will he be able to obtain statutory **relief from liability** (¶2505+; *Re Produce Marketing Consortium Ltd* (1989) 5 BCC 569).
2. Any **payments** made into the company's assets as a **result of** such an **order** do not fall within the property of the company subject to a floating charge over the company's present and future assets (*Re Oasis Merchandising Services Ltd (in liquidation), Ward v Aitken* [1997] 1 BCLC 689).

There is a separate **criminal offence** in companies legislation, whereby every person (whether a director or not) who was knowingly a party to carrying on a business with the intention of defrauding creditors, or for any other fraudulent purpose, is guilty of an offence (s 458 CA 1985). This does not rely on the company being in liquidation or any other insolvency procedure. A person found guilty of this offence will be **liable** to imprisonment and/or a fine (see ¶9935).

7445

7446

2. Wrongful trading

It can be difficult for a liquidator to prove the positive steps and fraudulent intent required to establish that a person should be liable for fraudulent trading. Wrongful trading catches directors who have **negligently mis-managed** their business, but whose behaviour falls short of actual dishonesty, for instance, they have failed to monitor it properly and failed to take appropriate

7449

action. This provision combines a subjective and objective test for detecting default, so that the director's own behaviour is examined against the benchmark of the objective "reasonable" director. Although liability for wrongful trading is generally easier to prove than that for fraudulent trading, it is narrower in that it only **applies to** directors (including shadow directors). Again, it is an action which can only be brought by a liquidator.

Although the legislation labels this liability "wrongful **trading**", there is no requirement for the director to cause the company to trade, unlike an action for fraudulent trading.

7450 A director can be held **liable** for wrongful trading **if** (s 214 IA 1986):
a. the company is in insolvent liquidation;
b. before the company went into liquidation, the director knew, or ought to have known, that there was no reasonable prospect of the company avoiding insolvent liquidation;
c. he was a director at that time; and
d. he did not take every step he should have done to minimise the loss to the company's creditors.

MEMO POINTS The **limitation period** for bringing a wrongful trading action against a director is 6 years from the date of the company going into liquidation (s 9(1) Limitation Act 1980).

Establishing liability

7451 The company's **insolvency** in liquidation is judged using the "balance-sheet test", so that a director can only be held liable where the company's liabilities outweigh its assets (s 214(6) IA 1986). This is to prevent directors being liable where the company is merely cash-flow insolvent, since the creditors should be paid in full in the liquidation if its assets are still greater than its liabilities and therefore will not have suffered any loss as a result of the directors' actions. In such a situation, it is the shareholders who are more likely to suffer, and they may be able to pursue the director(s) for a specific breach of duty (see ¶2434+) or misfeasance (¶7457+).

Further, the company must have suffered **loss**, i.e. it must be in a worse position when it went into insolvent liquidation than it would otherwise have been in if the directors had taken the appropriate action (Re Marini Ltd [2004] BCC 172).

7452 To assist in the difficult task of proving what the director knew or ought to have known about the company's financial position and what action he should have taken in the circumstances, the legislation sets out a combined subjective and objective method of testing the director's actions. The director's knowledge, conclusions he should have reached and action is **judged against** the general knowledge, skill and experience of (s 214(4) IA 1986):
– a person carrying out the same functions as are carried out by that director in the company (objective element); and
– the director in question (subjective element).

The test sets a basic **benchmark** by which the director is judged, but if he actually possesses a higher level of knowledge, skill and experience, he will be judged by that higher standard. The focus on the particular functions of the director ensures that the test is tailored to each case, so that a finance director is judged against what is expected of someone in that position and a director who is not expected to be actively involved in the company's management, for example a non-executive director, will be judged by an appropriately lower standard. A fuller discussion of this test with examples is found at ¶2411+, as it is also the test applied to actions against directors for breach of their general duty to exercise care, skill and diligence in running their companies.

The question of whether the director knew or ought to have concluded that the company had no reasonable **prospect** of **avoiding insolvent liquidation** can be a difficult one to resolve. The court will look at a number of factors as relevant in each case, such as:
a. the financial information which was available to the director and that which should have been available to him (Re Produce Marketing Consortium Ltd (No 2) [1989] BCLC 520);
b. the attitude of the creditors who were aware of the company's financial position; and
c. the professional advice received by the director regarding the company's position.

The **timing** of the director knowing that insolvent liquidation could not be avoided is clearly important in assessing the extent of his liability, as the longer he was engaged in wrongful trading, the more culpable he will be.

> **EXAMPLE**
> 1. The court considered that the directors had the requisite knowledge that the company had no reasonable prospect of avoiding insolvency at the latest when their accountants advised them that this was the case and that they could be liable for wrongful trading, although on the facts they were found to have known about the company's financial position earlier (*Re Purpoint Ltd* [1991] BCLC 491).
> 2. The court held that directors, who were too inexperienced to carry out their roles in the business, had the requisite knowledge from the time when the company's creditors exerted clear pressure on the company (*Re DKG Contractors Ltd* [1990] BCC 903).
> 3. RGO Ltd was incorporated in 1996 and had always traded at a loss. However, it had the prospect of additional funding, parts of which were paid to it between April and September 1998 by Mr S. Mr S gave assurances in September 1998 that he would obtain further funding for the company, but he did not fulfil his promise. The company went into CVL in June 1999. The court found that the directors of RGO Ltd had a reasonable belief that the company would obtain further funding until October 1998 when the money did not materialise. They ought to have concluded at that point that the company could not avoid insolvent liquidation, which should have outweighed their faith in Mr S. They were therefore liable for wrongful trading from October 1998 (*Re The Rod Gunner Organisation Ltd, Rubin v Gunner* [2004] 2 BCLC 110).

7453 A director can **defend** an action for wrongful trading by showing that he took all steps that a reasonably diligent person would have taken in order to minimise the potential loss to the creditors (s 214(3) IA 1986). The reasons for the company's liquidation will be relevant here, as they will influence the appropriate action in the circumstances. Broadly speaking, the court will look for **action such as**:
a. informing the creditors of the company's financial position;
b. considering appropriate insolvency procedures;
c. consulting professional advisers;
d. the board regularly reviewing up to date financial information;
e. considering cutbacks, for example in non-contractual benefits offered to directors and employees, closing down part of the business and making redundancies; and
f. considering resignation.

A director can choose to **resign** his office at any time, even if it would be detrimental to the company for him to do so (*CMS Dolphin Ltd v Simonet* [2001] 2 BCLC 704). It may be that he is under a duty to resign, if this is in the company's best interests. He cannot resign simply to escape liability for his actions, for example, the statutory liabilities usually specify that directors and former directors can be made liable, and common law liabilities apply to the person's status at the time of the action or omission rather than that at the time of the hearing. However, if a director has realised that the company is unlikely to be able to avoid insolvent liquidation and he has voted on the board for the company to take all reasonable steps to minimise the creditors' losses but the other directors refuse to take such action, he should either (*Secretary of State for Trade and Industry v Gash* [1997] 1 BCLC 341):
– resign, to minimise his liability for wrongful trading; or
– remain in office if he thinks that he can influence the other directors to cease trading or otherwise minimise the creditors' losses.

Consequences

7454 If the **court** concludes that the director is liable for wrongful trading, it **can** (ss 214, 215 IA 1986):
a. order him to contribute to the company's assets as appropriate in the circumstances;
b. impose a charge on any debt owed by the company to the wrongful trader (including his assignee or someone acting on his behalf) and provide for the enforcement of that charge; and/or
c. order that any debt owed by the company to the wrongful trader (including his assignee or someone acting on his behalf) is deferred so that it is only repaid after all of the company's other debts, plus interest, have been met.

The court can set the required **contributions** to reflect the level of culpability of the different directors. For example, a director who resigned because the rest of the board refused to take action to minimise the creditors' loss will be less blameworthy than those who remained on the board and took no action or made the creditors' position worse. Again, the contribution to the company's assets is for the benefit of the creditors as a whole and not individuals.

In addition, a declaration of wrongful trading against a director can trigger **disqualification** (¶3000+).

> MEMO POINTS 1. A director may be able to rely on an **insurance** policy to cover his liability for wrongful trading, depending on its terms. A director cannot obtain statutory **relief from liability** for wrongful trading (*Re Produce Marketing Consortium Ltd* (1989) 5 BCC 569).
> 2. Any **payments** made into the company's assets as a **result of** such an **order** do not fall within the property of the company subject to a floating charge over the company's present and future assets (*Re Oasis Merchandising Services Ltd (in liquidation), Ward v Aitken* [1997] 1 BCLC 689).

3. Misfeasance

7457 Statute provides for a **summary method** of pursuing those involved in the company for various **breaches of duty**, under a provision for liability for "misfeasance". Effectively, it is a simpler method of taking action against the directors and others where the company is in liquidation for breaches such as misapplication of the company's property (whether before or during the liquidation). **Action** can be taken **against** (s 212(1) IA 1986):
– a director or other officer;
– a liquidator of the company;
– an administrative receiver of the company; or
– any other person who is or has been involved in the company's promotion, formation or management, for example a supervisor of a voluntary arrangement, shadow director or receiver.

If the company is in administration, the administrator can be sued for misfeasance (para 75 Sch B1 IA 1986).

The **application** can be made **by** (liquidation: s 212(3) IA 1986):
– a liquidator;
– the official receiver;
– a creditor; or
– a contributory, with leave of the court.

> MEMO POINTS 1. If a **liquidator** has already obtained his **release**, leave of the court is required to bring an action against him (s 212(4) IA 1986).
> As regards a **contributory obtaining leave** of the court to take action, he will not be allowed to sue in his individual capacity for loss suffered by the company. If he sues for his own loss, he must be able to show that it is not too remote from the defendant's actions (*Johnson v Gore Wood & Co (a firm)* [2001] 1 All ER 481, a case against an insolvency practitioner).
> 2. An application in relation to an **administrator** or former administrator's conduct can be made by a creditor or contributory, the company's liquidator or administrator, or the official receiver (para 75 Sch B1 IA 1986). If the administrator has already been discharged from liability, an application can only be made with the court's permission.

7458 "Misfeasance" covers a broad **range of misdemeanours** affecting the company:
– misapplication of any of the company's money or other property;
– retention of any money or other property;
– otherwise becoming accountable for any money or other property;
– breach of fiduciary duties;
– breach of other duties, including a common law duty of care; and
– other misfeasance.

The company must have suffered **loss** as a result of the director's (or other person's) actions.

> EXAMPLE
> **Misfeasance**
> 1. Granting a preference (*Re Mercia Safetywear Ltd v Dodd* (1988) 4 BCC 30).
> 2. Directors making gifts of the company's property for no proper trading purpose (*Re Barton Manufacturing Co Ltd* [1999] 1 BCLC 740).

> 3. A liquidator who allows the company to trade without the requisite sanction, especially when the company's assets should have been realised quickly (*Re Centralcrest Engineering Ltd, IRC v Nelmes* [2000] BCC 727).
>
> **No loss to company**
> 4. A director received an allegedly secret commission from his company. However, on the day before the company went into liquidation, he paid this sum into the company's bank account to reduce its indebtedness to the bank. The court held that the director's liability to the company had been discharged when he paid the money over and there was no longer any misfeasance case to answer (*Re Derek Randall Enterprises Ltd, Derek Randall Enterprises Ltd (in liquidation) v Randall* [1991] BCLC 379).

Misfeasance **does not cover** contractual claims, and cannot be used if the company has been dissolved (respectively, *Re Etic Ltd* [1928] Ch 861; *Re Lewis & Smart Ltd* [1954] 2 All ER 19).

The **court** can **order** a person found liable for misfeasance to (liquidation: s 212(3) IA 1986; administration: para 75 Sch B1 IA 1986):
- repay, restore or account for the misapplied property; or
- contribute to the company's assets by way of compensation.

Unlike fraudulent and wrongful trading, the statutory **relief from liability** can be applied in appropriate cases (¶2505+).

7459

4. Other personal liability

Directors are subject to a number of **specific duties** which arise when the company enters into a **specific insolvency procedure**, some of which relate back to their behaviour prior to the procedure. This table summarises those duties and their associated liabilities, which are discussed further where indicated.

7461

Duty/event giving rise to liability	Associated liability	Applicable in			
		L[1]	A	AR	R	CVA
Co-operate with insolvency practitioner, including making statement of affairs when required, ¶8120+; ¶8855+	Fine. Summoned to court to provide information etc. Order to comply with insolvency practitioner's request.	✓	✓	✓		[2]
Disposition of company property after petition presented, ¶7674+	May have to make good loss caused by disposition	✓[3]				
Transaction prior to insolvency challenged, ¶7808+	May have to make good loss caused by transaction	✓	✓	[4]	[4]	[4]
To contribute as contributory, ¶7863+	Contribute amount of liability	✓				
Director found to be unfit as a director, ¶3000+	Disqualified as director following insolvency practitioner's report to secretary of state	✓	✓	✓	[5]	[5]
Director found to have committed criminal offence, ¶8120+	Prosecuted following insolvency practitioner's report to secretary of state	✓	[5]	[5]	[5]	[5]

Key: L – liquidation
A – administration
AR – administrative receivership
R – receivership
CVA – company voluntary arrangement

Note:
1. Director also under duty to present **petition** once **board resolves** to do so, even if he voted against resolution/ was not present (*Re Equiticorp International plc* [1989] BCLC 597).
2. Unless the liquidator or administrator is the **nominee**, in which case, the directors do have to co-operate with him.
3. Compulsory liquidations **only** (s 127(1) IA 1986).
4. Provisions relating to **transactions defrauding creditors** applicable where company is in all types of insolvency procedure as well as where company is not insolvent (¶7826+).
5. However, just because insolvency practitioner is not under specific duty to report such matters to secretary of state does not mean directors cannot be disqualified and/or prosecuted through usual channels.

7462 Directors can also be held personally liable **for the company's obligations** in a number of specific circumstances:
a. loans to directors, ¶2804+;
b. substantial property transactions involving directors, ¶2567+;
c. torts committed by the company which the director authorised or for which he has taken responsibility (*Williams v Natural Life Health Foods Ltd* [1998] 1 BCLC 690); and
d. company's breach of insolvency legislation (s 432 IA 1986).

5. Criminal liability

7464 Insolvency legislation imposes specific criminal offences on directors or other officers of a company if they deal with the company's property in particular ways during or prior to **liquidation**. Although these offences only apply in a liquidation, directors must be aware of them whenever their company is in financial difficulties since other insolvency procedures may lead to liquidation, or they may get no warning of a creditor presenting a petition against the company. If found guilty, the director or other person will be liable to a fine and/or imprisonment (¶9935).

Offence	Timing	Defence	Reference (IA 1986)
Conceal company's property worth over £500	After commencement of liquidation or in preceding 12 months	No intent to defraud	s 206 [1,2]
Conceal company's debts		No intent to defraud	
Fraudulently remove company's property worth over £500		No statutory defence	
– Conceal, destroy, mutilate or falsify any book/paper affecting or relating to company's property/affairs; or – be privy to someone else doing so		No intent to conceal company's affairs or defeat law	
– Make false entry in such book/paper; or – be privy to someone else doing so		No intent to conceal company's affairs or defeat law	
– Fraudulently part with, alter or make omission in, any document relating to company's property/affairs; or – be privy to someone else doing so		No statutory defence	
– Pawn, pledge or dispose of company's property (other than in usual course of business) which was obtained on credit and has not been paid for; or – taking property knowing it was obtained on credit and not paid for		No intent to defraud	
Give away, transfer, grant charge over, cause or connive in levying execution against company's property	Within 5 years before liquidation	No intent to defraud creditors	s 207
Conceal/remove any part of company's property	After, or in the 2 months before, unsatisfied judgment/order for payment obtained against company	No intent to defraud creditors	

Note:
1. "Officer" includes a **shadow director**.
2. Directors also commit an offence if they engage in similar conduct during a **pre-CVA moratorium** (¶9487).

There are further offences relating to the directors' and other officers' conduct **during liquidation**, which are discussed within that topic:
- criminal misconduct during winding up, ¶7781;
- falsification of company's books (also applies to contributories), ¶8170;
- making omissions from statements relating to the company's affairs, ¶8169;
- making false representations to creditors, ¶8169; and
- re-using the company's name, ¶264+.

7465

SECTION 3

After insolvency

A **company's fate** at the conclusion of an insolvency procedure usually falls into one of three categories:
- its fortunes are revived and it can carry on trading;
- it is placed into another insolvency procedure; or
- it has no assets left and must be dissolved.

7475

If the company **carries on trading**, it will probably have to work hard to restore goodwill with its creditors and customers, for example it may find that suppliers impose more stringent credit terms. The insolvency procedure should prompt the board to review its management and financial procedures and policies, and it may be necessary to change key personnel. Such actions will assist in persuading those dealing with the company that it is back on track. Alternatively, it may need to be placed into **another insolvency procedure**, usually because the insolvency practitioner feels that it is appropriate, but others such as creditors and the company itself may also be able to do so.

7476

If the company needs to be **dissolved**, it will cease to exist. This will occur if a liquidation is not converted into another procedure and may occur where another procedure has left the company with no assets. Dissolution is discussed at ¶7491+ below.

A. Entering further insolvency procedures

A company is usually placed into a subsequent insolvency procedure because the responsible insolvency practitioner considers that it will be better suited to the company's position, but it can be initiated by others in some situations, e.g. the board, creditors or the company itself. The table below summarises the **situations** in which a company can move from one insolvency procedure to another. This does not deal with situations in which a period of time has passed between one procedure finishing and the next one beginning; there are specific restrictions on administration and CVAs being entered into in such circumstances and reference should be made to the relevant discussions on entering these procedures.

7481

To: From:	Liquidation	Administration	Receivership	CVA
Liquidation	Official receiver can petition for compulsory liquidation when company is in voluntary liquidation	Liquidator or qualifying floating charge holder can apply for administration order	Receiver can be appointed, but unlikely to take on appointment because he is not company's agent (therefore open to personal liability) and liquidator has possession of assets	Liquidator can propose CVA, but company cannot obtain pre-CVA moratorium
Administration	Court can terminate administrator's appointment on petition on public interest grounds or by FSA. Administrator can convert administration into voluntary winding up; special rules apply to the liquidation. Member State liquidator can convert into liquidation	–	Ordinary receiver can only be appointed with consent of court or administrator	Administrator can propose CVA, but company cannot obtain pre-CVA moratorium
Receivership	Administrative receiver can petition for compulsory winding up. Ordinary receiver can petition on ground that company cannot pay its debts	Administration order can be applied for if person who appointed administrative receiver consents or court doubts validity of security under which he was appointed. Administrator can be appointed out of court; if ordinary/LPA receiver is in office, he can be required to leave by administrator	Second receiver can be appointed	CVA can be proposed, but company cannot obtain pre-CVA moratorium if it is in administrative receivership
CVA	Supervisor can petition for compulsory winding up. Creditor can petition where moratorium ends without CVA being approved. Member state liquidator can convert into liquidation	Supervisor can apply for administration order. Administrator can be appointed out of court, with leave of court, provided company did not have pre-CVA moratorium	Ordinary receiver can only be appointed with leave of court. Administrative receiver can only be appointed if company is not eligible for pre-CVA moratorium	Another CVA can be proposed but company cannot obtain pre-CVA moratorium if it is already in CVA or another pre-CVA moratorium has ended in previous 12 months

B. Dissolution and striking off

7491 The **final stage** in a company's liquidation is dissolution, when its name is taken off the register at Companies House, any remaining property in it passes to the Crown and it ceases to exist. Companies can also be struck off the register and dissolved in other situations, some of which will be appropriate where the company is in financial difficulties or has emerged from an insolvency procedure. For comparison purposes and the sake of convenience, these situations are all dealt with here even though not all of them are dependent on the company having been in insolvency.

The **different methods** of dissolution are:

Method	Situation	¶¶
Dissolution following liquidation	Where liquidator has realised and distributed as many of company's assets as possible, whether in compulsory/voluntary liquidation	¶7497
Private company applies to be struck off register	Where company no longer wishes to trade, e.g. directors in small company want to retire and there is nobody to replace them, or company has carried out an informal winding down and wishes to cease trading	¶7502+
Companies House strikes company off register	Company does not appear to be in business, e.g. it has not complied with filing obligations	¶7516+
Dissolved by court	As part of scheme of reconstruction or amalgamation (¶6530+)	¶7525

7492 When a company is dissolved, its **property** and any other rights (whether actually vested in the company, held on trust for it or in the possession of another person in another way) are deemed to belong to the Crown (s 654 CA 1985). This is referred to as "**bona vacantia**" property. The Crown can disclaim property which has vested in it in this way by filing notice of its intention to do so at Companies House, which will then advertise the notice in the *Gazette* (s 656 CA 1985). If this happens, the property is treated as if it was disclaimed by a liquidator (s 657 CA 1985; ¶7917+). If a **company is restored** to the register after its property has been disposed of by the Crown, the Crown must pay an amount equal to the consideration it received for the property, or the value of the property at the date of the disposition if it was given away (s 655 CA 1985). Therefore, if a company had assets when it was dissolved, it is still worth restoring to the register to realise and distribute the assets for the benefit of the creditors or shareholders entitled.

MEMO POINTS 1. If the company is situated in a relevant area, its property will belong to the **Duchy of Lancaster** or the **Duke of Cornwall** instead of the Crown.
2. The **new Companies Act** will largely restate these provisions (ss 1012-1019, 1034 CA 2006, expected to come into force by 1 October 2009). In addition, instead of stating that the effect of Crown disclaimer is the same as a liquidator's disclaimer, the effects will be set out directly in the new Act.

1. Dissolution following liquidation

7497 The liquidation of a company is usually ended by the liquidator, who will carry out the final steps required and file the relevant documents at Companies House, triggering the company's dissolution. Depending on the type of liquidation, the dissolution process is started in one of the following ways.

Type of liquidation	Ended by	Documents filed at Companies House	Companies House action	¶¶
Compulsory	Liquidator (including official receiver acting as liquidator)	– Liquidator's final report; and – copy resolutions from final meeting on Form 4.43	– Register documents; and – dissolve company after 3 months[1]	¶8393+
	Official receiver	Application for early dissolution	– Register application; and – dissolve company after 3 months[1]	¶8396+
CVL or MVL	Liquidator	– Liquidator's account; – return confirming final meeting held; and – copy of any special resolution	– Register documents; – advertise in *Gazette*; and – dissolve company after 3 months of return being registered[2]	CVL: ¶8579; MVL: ¶8665

Note:
1. This period can be **extended** in compulsory liquidation by the secretary of state on the application of the official receiver or any other person who appears to him to be interested (ss 202, 203, 205 IA 1986).
2. In the case of a voluntary liquidation, the liquidator or any other interested person can apply to the court for this period to be **extended** (s 201 IA 1986).

2. Application to be struck off

7502 A private company can apply to Companies House to be struck off the register. This would be **appropriate where**, for example, the company has carried out an informal winding down of its business, or where it is no longer required. Since creditors and others can prevent the company being struck off, it cannot rely on this as a way of avoiding insolvency procedures where they would be more appropriate.

> MEMO POINTS 1. This procedure is not available to **public companies** (s 652A CA 1985).
> 2. Under the **new Companies Act**, public companies will be able to apply to be struck off voluntarily (s 1003 CA 2006, expected to come into force by 1 October 2009). Otherwise, the voluntary striking off procedure will be restated in the new Act (ss 1003-1011 CA 2006, expected to come into force by 1 October 2009).

Conditions

7503 A company must comply with certain conditions to make an application to be struck off. Within the 3 months before the application has been made, it **must not** have (s 652B CA 1985):
a. changed its name;
b. traded or otherwise carried on business;
c. disposed of any property or rights (other than as a gift) which it had for the purpose of disposing of or gaining from in the normal course of its business before it ceased to trade or otherwise carry on business; or
d. carried out any other activity, except one necessary to make the application, conclude the company's business or comply with a statutory requirement or the secretary of state's directions.

A company is not counted as "trading" if it pays off any of its debts incurred during the course of its business during this period.

> EXAMPLE A Ltd, a drinks manufacturer, intends to make an application to be struck off the register. It ceased to trade more than 3 months before the application was made. It can go ahead with the application as long as it does not sell its drinks within the 3 month period, although it can sell its delivery vans, bottling machine and warehouse, as it did not hold them for the purpose of disposing of them in the usual course of its business.

An **application cannot be made** where (s 652B CA 1985):
a. the company is in liquidation, including where a petition has been presented but not heard;
b. the company is in administration, including where an administration application has been made but not heard, or a notice of intention to appoint an administrator out of court has been filed at court but an administrator has not yet been appointed or the notice has not yet expired;
c. a receiver has been appointed over the company's property;
d. the company is subject to a CVA; or
e. an application has been made to court for approval of a compromise or arrangement between the company and its creditors and shareholders, which has not yet been concluded (¶6500+).

Application process

Before making the application, the board should close down the business as much as possible, for example by closing the bank account and selling or giving away the company's assets. It should also inform the persons who deal with the company (listed at ¶7507), as they will be able to object to the application: making sure that there will be no objections in advance will ensure that the process runs smoothly.

The application must be in **Form** 652a, signed by:
– the sole director;
– both directors, if there are only two; or
– the majority of directors, if there are more than two.

It should be **sent to** Companies House, together with the appropriate fee. Companies House will file the application, so that it appears on the company's public file. It will also notify the company of the application at its registered office (to ensure that the application has not been made fraudulently by a third party) and place an **advertisement** in the *Gazette* inviting interested parties to object (s 652A CA 1985).

> MEMO POINTS   The name of Form 652a, like the names of other **Companies House forms**, is taken from the section number of the legislation. As all of the section numbers will change under the new Companies Act, Companies House proposes to change the names of all of its forms to reflect their function rather than the relevant section number ("Working with Companies House: a consultation on the registrar's rules and related provisions which will apply under the Companies Act 2006"). At the time of writing, the new form names are not yet available.

The board must **notify** the following persons of the application within 7 days of sending it to Companies House, by sending them a copy (s 652B(6) CA 1985):
a. the shareholders;
b. the creditors, including contingent and prospective creditors (e.g. landlord, Revenue and Customs);
c. the employees;
d. the mangers or trustees of any employee pension fund; and
e. any directors who did not sign the application.

If any new persons in the list come to light after this deadline, the board must send them a copy of the application within 7 days (s 652C(2) CA 1985). If the company is registered for VAT, it must also notify the relevant VAT office.

A director must **withdraw the application** straight away if any of the following occurs before the application is dealt with (s 652C(4), (5) CA 1985):
a. the company carries out any of the activities which preclude an application being made, listed at ¶7503 above; or
b. the company enters into any of the insolvency procedures at ¶7504 above, or makes a compromise or arrangement with its creditors and shareholders.

The withdrawal must be sent to Companies House on **Form** 652c, which can be signed by any director.

> MEMO POINTS The name of Form 652c, like the names of other **Companies House forms**, is taken from the section number of the legislation. As all of the section numbers will change under the new Companies Act, Companies House proposes to change the names of all of its forms to reflect their function rather than the relevant section number ("Working with Companies House: a consultation on the registrar's rules and related provisions which will apply under the Companies Act 2006"). At the time of writing, the new form names are not yet available.

7509 Persons interested in the company may **object** to it being struck off the register by setting out their reasons in writing and sending them, along with any supporting evidence, to Companies House. A person may object for a number of **reasons**, including:
– the company does not comply with the conditions for making the application;
– some of the interested parties have not been informed of the application by the board;
– any of the declarations on the application are false;
– legal action is being taken against the company; or
– the directors have committed an offence.

If **no objections** have been received at the end of at least 3 months from the date of Companies House's advertisement, the company will receive confirmation that it has been struck off the register, together with the proposed date of dissolution. Companies House will place a further **advertisement** in the *Gazette* of this fact and when this is published, the company is dissolved (s 652A(4), (5) CA 1985).

Liability

7510 A number of **offences** can be committed by the directors connected with applications for their companies to be struck off, which can render them liable to a fine and/or imprisonment, as well as being a ground for disqualification (¶9935).

Offence	Defence	Reference (CA 1985)
Making application when company has carried out prohibited activities	Director did not know, and could not reasonably have known, about facts constituting breach	
Making application when company is subject to insolvency procedure or compromise/arrangement with creditors and shareholders		
Failing to provide copies of application to the persons listed at ¶7507 within 7 days	Director took all reasonable steps to perform duty	s 652E
Failing to provide copies of application to new persons within 7 days	Director was not aware of application at time or took all reasonable steps to perform duty	
Not withdrawing application straight away when required		
Failure to provide copies of application to persons (existing or new) listed at ¶7507 within 7 days, with intent of concealing application from that person	No statutory defence	
Knowingly or recklessly giving false information to Companies House in connection with application to strike off	No statutory defence	s 652F
Knowingly or recklessly making application purporting to be under s 652A CA 1985, but which is not	No statutory defence	

7511 Even after the company has been struck off and dissolved, the liability of the **directors, managers and shareholders** continues and can be enforced as if the company had not been struck off (s 652A(6) CA 1985). Also, a company can still be **wound up** when it has been dissolved, although this would be rare (but it could occur if, for instance, there are substantial calls owing on shares and other debts which could be collected and distributed to outstanding creditors, or transactions which could be challenged to create assets for the company) since the company will usually have no assets (s 652A(7) CA 1985).

3. Struck off automatically

Companies House can strike a company off the register on its own initiative in **two circumstances**:
– where the company appears to have ceased to operate; and
– where the company is in liquidation but no liquidator is acting or the company's affairs have been wound up but the liquidator has not initiated dissolution.

> **MEMO POINTS** The automatic striking off provisions will be restated in the **new Companies Act** (ss 1000-1002 CA 2006, expected to come into force by 1 October 2009).

Company no longer in business

Companies House will usually be alerted to the fact that a company is not in business when it has failed on successive occasions to file its regular annual accounts and returns, or when mail it has sent to the company has been returned as undelivered. In such circumstances, Companies House will follow this **procedure** (s 652 CA 1985):
a. write to the company asking whether it is in business or operation;
b. if no reply is received within 1 month, send another letter by registered post within 14 days, which refers to the first letter and warns the company that it will be struck off if it does not reply within 1 month;
c. if no reply is received within 1 month, or the company informs Companies House that it has ceased business or operation, Companies House will:
– place a notice in the *Gazette*; and
– send notice to the company that it will be struck off the register and dissolved within 3 months, unless Companies House is informed of a good reason not to do so; and
d. if the deadline elapses and no good reason has been given for the company not to be struck off, Companies House will place a further notice in the *Gazette*, on publication of which the company is dissolved.

Company in liquidation

Companies House can strike a company off the register if it is in liquidation and (s 652(4) CA 1985):
– it appears that there is **no liquidator** acting; or
– the liquidation appears to have been concluded, but the **liquidator** has **not filed** any **returns** for 6 consecutive months.

In either circumstance, Companies House will follow this **procedure**:
a. place a notice in the *Gazette*;
b. send notice to the company that it will be struck off the register and dissolved within 3 months, unless Companies House is informed of a good reason not to do so; and
c. if the deadline elapses and no good reason has been given for the company not to be struck off, Companies House will place a further notice in the *Gazette*, on publication of which the company is dissolved.

Liability

As with a voluntary application to be struck off, even after the company has been dissolved, the liability of the **directors, managers and shareholders** continues and can be enforced as if the company had not been struck off (s 652(6) CA 1985). Also, a company can still be **wound up** when it has been dissolved, although this would be rare (but it could occur if, for instance, there are substantial calls owing on shares and other debts which could be collected and distributed to outstanding creditors, or transactions which could be challenged to create assets for the company) since the company will have no assets.

4. Dissolution by the court

Schemes for a **company's reconstruction or amalgamation** are discussed at ¶6530+. Where such a scheme involves a transfer of the undertaking or assets of one company to another,

C. Restoration to the register

7534 Although a company ceases to exist when it is struck off the register and dissolved, it is possible for it to be restored to the register after dissolution. This is to **protect** the rights of persons dealing with the company, allowing, for example, a person to bring a claim against the company which employed him for personal injury when his claim only came to light after the company has been dissolved (in reality, the claim will be met by the company's employers' liability insurers). This has been useful in claims for industrial diseases such as asbestosis where it may be many years before the patient's symptoms become apparent. Alternatively, a company can be restored simply because it should not have been struck off for a technical reason, such as failing to notify the correct parties of an application to strike off, or because an asset was overlooked during liquidation and can still be distributed. This prevents companies taking advantage of the striking-off procedure to avoid their responsibilities.

7535 The **method of restoration** depends upon how the company was struck off:

Dissolved/struck off	Method of restoration	Reference (CA 1985)
Following liquidation	Apply to have dissolution declared void	s 651
Following voluntary application to strike off	Apply for restoration	s 653
Struck off by Companies House	Apply for restoration	s 653
Following court dissolution	Apply to have dissolution declared void	s 651

MEMO POINTS The **new Companies Act** will introduce a new type of restoration to deal with cases in which a company has been automatically struck off the register when it should not have been. In all other cases, an application for restoration will be able to be made to court, replacing the current system which uses two types of application (to have a dissolution declared void and for restoration to the register) to do the same thing (ss 1029-1032 CA 2006, expected to come into force by 1 October 2009; ¶7541/mp).

The new "**administrative restoration**" **procedure** will aim to restore a company quickly and simply where it should not have been struck off, by avoiding a court application altogether (ss 1024-1028 CA 2006, expected to come into force by 1 October 2009). A former director or shareholder will be able to apply directly to Companies House within 6 years of the company's dissolution to have it restored to the register. To qualify for restoration:
– the company will have had to have been carrying on business when it was struck off;
– the Crown will have to consent in writing to the restoration if any of the company's property vested as bona vacantia. The applicant will have to pay the Crown's costs of dealing with the property and application if this is the case; and
– the applicant will have to update Companies House's records and pay any outstanding penalties (no penalties for failing to file accounts will accrue while the company is dissolved, although there may be outstanding penalties from before that time).
The application will have to be accompanied by a statement of compliance that the applicant has the requisite standing and the company qualifies for restoration. Restoration will take effect as of the date on which Companies House notifies the applicant of its decision, and the company will be treated as if it had never been dissolved or struck off. The court will be able to make directions to restore the position of the company and other parties so that they are not prejudiced by the dissolution. If Companies House refuses to restore a company to the register, the applicant will be able to apply to court for restoration within 28 days (s 1030 CA 2006, expected to come into force by 1 October 2009).
The new Companies Act will also specify that a restored company (whether via a court application or the administrative procedure) will have the same **name** and company registration number

as it did before it was dissolved (s 1033 CA 2006, expected to come into force by 1 October 2009). However, if another company has taken that name since dissolution, the restored company will be directed to change its name.

Declaring dissolution void

An **application** can be **made by** the company's liquidator or any other interested person (s 651 CA 1985). It must usually be made within 2 years of the company's dissolution, but this deadline can be waived where the applicant needs to make a claim against the company for damages for:
– personal injuries (including claims for funeral expenses under s 1(2)(c) Law Reform (Miscellaneous Provisions) Act 1934); or
– a fatal accident (under the Fatal Accidents Act 1976).

The applicant must establish an "**interest**" in the application, although he does not have to have a strong link with the company to do so (*Stanhope Pension Trust Ltd v Registrar of Companies* [1994] 1 BCLC 628).

7537

> MEMO POINTS   Under the **new Companies Act**, applications to have a dissolution declared void will be replaced by applications for restoration to the register.

The application must be made to court in the **form** of a Part 8 claim form (para 5 CPR PD 49). The claim form must be **served on** Companies House's solicitor (i.e. the treasury solicitor or the solicitor to the relevant Duchy) and Companies House. Once the claim has been filed at court, the court will notify the applicant of a hearing date. The applicant must give Companies House at least 10 days' notice of the hearing.

7538

The court will require an **affidavit** or **witness statement** containing a statement of truth stating that:
a. the claim form has been properly served;
b. Companies House's solicitor has no objection to the restoration of the company (which should be provided in acknowledgement of the claim form), along with a copy of the letter;
c. details about the company:
– when it was incorporated;
– the nature of its objects;
– its shareholders and officers;
– its trading activity, and when it stopped trading, if at all; and
– comments regarding the company's solvency;
d. an explanation of any failure to comply with Companies House filing requirements;
e. details of the dissolution; and
f. any other information pertinent to the reasons for making the application.

The following copy **documents** should be **attached**:
– Companies House's solicitor's letter confirming he has no objection to the company's restoration;
– the company's certificate of incorporation; and
– the company's memorandum and articles.

Companies House will usually **require** that the company's file is brought up to date at least 5 days before the hearing, i.e. any missing annual accounts and returns should be filed, and any irregularities in the company's structure should be corrected.

> MEMO POINTS   The Insolvency Service has proposed that **affidavits** are replaced by witness statements (see ¶7388). This change is likely to be implemented from 1 October 2008.

In deciding whether to make the **order**, the court will look at whether the purpose of the application is to achieve one of the usual purposes of restoring the company, such as taking legal action against it or distributing a left-over asset. If any proposed legal action against the company is statute-barred (i.e. the limitation time period within which the action must be brought has expired), it will only be restored if the applicant can show that he has grounds for disapplying the limitation period (under s 33 Limitation Act 1980; *Re Philip Powis Ltd* [1997] 2 BCLC 481).

7539

If an order is made, its **effect** is to treat the company as if it had not been dissolved, allowing action to be taken against it (s 651(1) CA 1985). If appropriate, the court can order that the time between the company's dissolution and the order shall not be counted in calculating the limitation period for action against the company (s 651(6) CA 1985; *Smith v White Knight Laundry Ltd* [2001] 2 BCLC 206).

The applicant must **send a copy** of the order to Companies House within 7 days; failure to do so renders him liable to a fine (s 651(3) CA 1985; ¶9935).

7540 The applicant is usually required to pay Companies House's **costs**, as well as any late filing penalties (¶9935).

Restoring company to register

7541 The **application** differs depending on whether the company was struck off voluntarily or by Companies House. The provisions noted above in relation to applications to declare a dissolution void regarding the form of the application, service and affidavit or witness statement evidence also apply here (¶7538).

Struck off	Applicants	Grounds	Deadline	Reference (CA 1985)
Voluntarily	– Persons listed at ¶7507 above who should have been notified of application; or – secretary of state	– Person entitled to notice of application was not notified; – company was not eligible to make application either because it carried on business etc, or it was subject to an insolvency procedure or compromise/arrangement with creditors and shareholders; or – another fair reason to restore company	20 years from advertisement in *Gazette* that company was struck off	s 653(2B), (2D)
By Companies House	– Shareholder; – creditor; or – secretary of state	– Company was carrying on business/operation when it was struck off; or – another fair reason to restore company. For secretary of state's application, it must be in public interest to restore company.		s 653(1), (2)

> **MEMO POINTS** Under the **new Companies Act**, the restoration procedure will be simplified (ss 1029-1032 CA 2006, expected to come into force by 1 October 2009). Where a company has been dissolved following winding up, administration, automatic striking off by Companies House or voluntary striking off, an application will be able to be made to the court for restoration by:
> – the secretary of state;
> – a former director;
> – a person interested in the same land in which the company had a superior or derivative interest, or which was subject to rights vested in the company or benefited from obligations owed by the company;
> – a person with a contractual relationship with the company;
> – a person with a potential legal claim against the company;
> – the manager or trustee of a pension fund established for the benefit of the company's employees;
> – a former shareholder or his personal representative;
> – a creditor;
> – a former liquidator;
> – a person entitled to notice of a voluntary striking off application, where one was made; and
> – any other person the court considers to have an interest.
> The application will have to be made within 6 years of the dissolution of the company in normal circumstances, however there will be no time limit on applications relating to personal injury claims. As with current applications, the court will have the discretion to direct that the time

during which the company was dissolved will not count towards the limitation period of the underlying claim.

The court will be able to restore a company which was in business when it was struck off automatically, where it was struck off voluntarily at a time when it did not meet the necessary criteria, or where it is just to do so in any other case. If the court grants the application, restoration will be effective from the time when the court gives notice to Companies House. Companies House will then publish a notice of the restoration in the *Gazette*. The company will be treated as if it had never been struck off, and the court can give directions to ensure that the company and other parties dealing with it are not prejudiced by its dissolution, including directions to update the company's file at Companies House and to pay Companies House's and the Crown's costs of dealing with the application.

7542

If an **order** is made, an office copy must be sent to Companies House. On receipt of this, the company is restored to the register and treated as if it had not been struck off (s 653(3) CA 1985). The court can also make any appropriate order to put the company and those associated with it back in the position they would have been in had the company not been struck off. For example, if the company was struck off because it was in breach of its filing obligations, the court can order that it makes up its missing annual accounts and returns.

The applicant is usually required to pay Companies House's **costs**, as well as any late filing penalties (¶9935).

> MEMO POINTS   A significant effect of the company being treated as if it had not been struck off is that the **contracts** to which it was a party when it was struck off continue (*Orchidway Properties Ltd v Fairlight Commercial Ltd* (2002) LTL 4/7/02). Although contracts are frustrated when a company is dissolved, if the company is subsequently restored, the frustration is deemed not to have occurred. Therefore if the company was struck off as a result of a voluntary application, this does not constitute a repudiatory breach of the contract (since it is reversible and therefore does not prevent a company performing its obligations under the contract). On the other hand, the other party can serve effective notice of its contractual obligations on the company, and if the company then fails to perform, a repudiatory breach will occur.

CHAPTER 17

Compulsory liquidation

OUTLINE

	¶¶
Summary of compulsory and voluntary liquidation procedures	7572

SECTION 1 Obtaining the order ... 7585

A	Presenting the petition	7587
1	Circumstances	7592
	a Unable to pay debts	7593
	b Just and equitable	7602
	c Other grounds	7608
2	Petitioners	7616
	a Creditors	7617
	b Contributories	7619
	c The company	7623
	d The board	7624
	e Insolvency practitioners	7625
	f Official petitioners	7626
	g Grounds available to different petitioners	7629
3	Procedure	7634
	a Where petitioner is not a contributory	7636
	b Where petitioner is a contributory	7656
B	Consequences of presenting a petition	7672
1	Dispositions of company property	7674
2	Transfers of shares and changes in shareholders' status	7683
3	Provisional liquidators	7686
4	Effect of petition on other proceedings	7697
5	Striking out the petition	7705
C	The petition hearing	7718
1	Opposition	7719
2	Court's powers	7721
3	Costs	7723
4	The winding up order	7729
5	Appeals	7734
6	Staying winding up proceedings	7736
D	Consequences of a winding up order	7746

SECTION 2 Dealing with the company's assets ... 7772

I	Collection	7779
A	Carrying on business	7791
B	Increasing assets	7803
1	Challenging dubious transactions	7808
	a Transactions at an undervalue	7811
	b Preferences	7819
	c Transactions defrauding creditors	7826
	d Floating charges	7836
	e Extortionate credit transactions	7842
2	Other litigation	7850
C	Money owed by contributories	7863
1	Who is a contributory?	7863
2	Recovery of debts from contributories	7869
II	Selling the assets	7893
1	Particular types of assets	7901
2	Assets not realised by the liquidator	7914
	a Onerous property	7917
	b Contracts	7928
III	Distribution	7945
A	Costs and expenses of winding up	7956
1	Costs of realising secured assets	7956
2	Other expenses of winding up	7957
	a Order of priority	7958
	b Particular costs and expenses	7961
B	Creditors	7975
1	Secured creditors	7977
	a General principles	7978
	b Submitting a proof	7984
	c Interest	7989
	d Fixed charges	7990
	e Floating charges	7992
2	Other creditors	8003
	a Provable debts	8005
	b How to prove debts	8030
	c Distributions to creditors	8042

Preferential creditors	8044
Unsecured creditors	8053
Deferred creditors	8066
d Creditors who are also debtors of the company	8072
C Contributories	8087
D Distribution summary	8101

SECTION 3 Investigations into the company 8117

A	Official receiver: investigations into conduct	8120
1	Statement of affairs	8127
2	Accounts	8138
3	Any other information	8144
B	Liquidator: investigations into the company's affairs	8165

SECTION 4 Persons with conduct of the liquidation 8192

A	Liquidator	8195
1	Appointment	8200
2	Powers, duties and liabilities	8215
	a Summary table	8216
	b Control of the liquidator	8217
	c Providing information	8227

	d Financial and administrative matters	8231
	e Challenging the liquidator	8234
3	Remuneration	8242
4	Termination	8250
	a Resignation	8251
	b Removal	8254
	c Automatic	8263
	d Release	8264
	e Replacement	8267
B	Official receiver	8277
C	Liquidation committee	8292
1	General rules	8294
	a Establishment	8296
	b Supervising the liquidator	8302
	c Meetings	8307
	d Changes to the committee	8314
2	Rules where the liquidation immediately follows administration	8322
D	Creditors' and contributories' meetings	8335
1	Summoning meetings	8335
2	Conduct of meetings	8345
3	Administrative matters	8365
E	Special managers	8375

SECTION 5 Conclusion of the liquidation 8393

7570 Compulsory liquidation, or compulsory winding up, is the most draconian of the formal insolvency procedures, with its **aim** of selling off as many of the company's assets as possible in order to repay its debts. Unless the liquidation is converted into another insolvency procedure (see ¶7481), it will **result** in the company being dissolved. Therefore, compulsory liquidation is usually **initiated by** the company's creditors, although other groups of people involved in the company, including the company itself and its board, can also do so. It is often used as a last resort after other ways of dealing with the company's financial difficulties (whether informal or formal solutions, ¶7323+, ¶7334+) have been tried, because creditors are very unlikely to recover all of their debts in this insolvency procedure. It can also be used as a means of investigating and punishing wrongdoing in the company, since the company's affairs and management are investigated thoroughly and action can be taken against the directors and others involved.

Compulsory liquidation differs from other insolvency procedures in the level of control exercised over it through the legislation and Rules and by the court. A **liquidator** usually takes control of the company itself and has wide powers to deal with its assets in order to achieve the purpose of the liquidation. Due to the serious consequences of liquidation on the company and those dealing with it, the liquidator's powers are themselves controlled by corresponding duties and liabilities. The **official receiver** also has an important role in any compulsory liquidation, which is to investigate the conduct of the company and report any wrongdoing (see ¶8120+). He will usually be appointed as liquidator when the company is first placed into compulsory liquidation, but most liquidations will be handed over to an insolvency practitioner while the official receiver conducts his separate investigations.

COMPULSORY LIQUIDATION

This flowchart summarises and compares the compulsory and voluntary liquidation **procedures**. It shows that although the entry routes are different, the liquidator's functions, conduct and result of the liquidation itself are largely the same, with the official receiver's investigatory functions being confined to compulsory liquidation.

Other procedures (principally, voluntary liquidation and administration) share common elements with this insolvency procedure, therefore readers will find **memo points** noting similarities and differences between compulsory liquidation and other procedures within various topics. These are only relevant to those readers interested in the other procedures which **cross-refer** to compulsory liquidation.

The **terms** "liquidation" and "winding up" are synonymous, although "liquidation" is preferred here, where the context allows.

Summary of compulsory and voluntary liquidation procedures

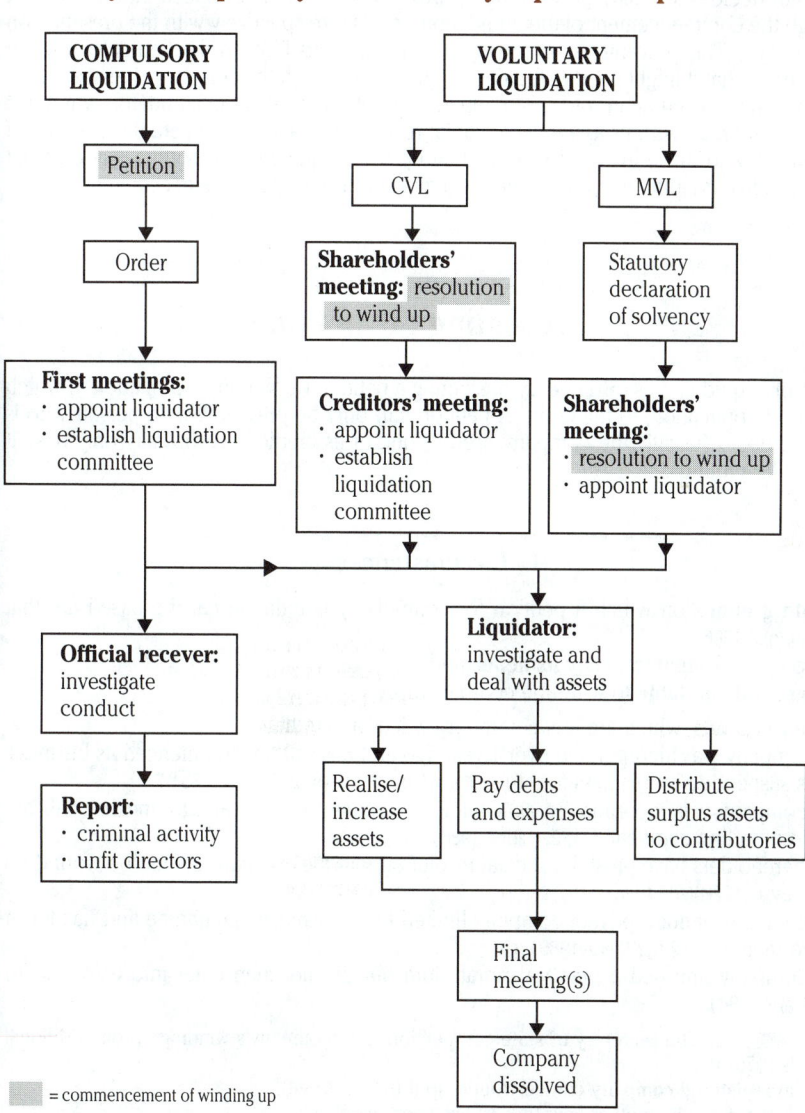

SECTION 1
Obtaining the order

7585 A company is compulsorily wound up by a court order, which is applied for by submitting a **petition** to court. The petition must rely on one of the specified **grounds**, and can only be **made by** certain categories of people. Once the petition has been presented, there is a period during which the company's activities are restricted to a certain degree, and in some cases a provisional liquidator will be appointed to control the company until an order is made. The petition is then considered by the court at a **hearing**, at which the different parties concerned have the opportunity to express their views.

If the court decides to make the winding up **order**, the company is placed into liquidation (although the commencement of the liquidation begins retrospectively with the presentation of the petition. This prevents the company putting its assets beyond the liquidator's reach once it knows that it might go into liquidation, ¶7747). Although the company does not cease to exist when the winding up order is made, control of it passes to the liquidator, who must investigate and **deal with** its **assets**. The official receiver will also **investigate** the conduct of the company and those involved in it leading up to its liquidation, reporting any criminal activities and/or conduct warranting the disqualification of directors as necessary.

A. Presenting the petition

7587 Compulsory liquidation is **initiated by** presenting a petition (a "winding up petition"), which is a form of application, to the court. A petition can only be presented by a person who is eligible to do so (usually the company itself or one of its creditors), who may only base it on particular grounds.

1. Circumstances

7592 The **main grounds** on which a petition for compulsory liquidation can be based are that (s 122(1)(f), (g) IA 1986):
– the company is **unable to pay its debts**; and
– it is **just and equitable** to wind the company up.

The **other grounds**, which are less commonly relied on, are that:
a. the company was incorporated over 1 year ago and has still not commenced its business, or it has suspended its business for at least a whole year (s 122(1)(d) IA 1986);
b. the company was incorporated as a public company over 1 year ago and has still not obtained a trading certificate (s 122(1)(b) IA 1986);
c. the shareholders have passed a special resolution that the company should be wound up in this way (s 122(1)(a) IA 1986);
d. the company is not a private company limited by shares or by guarantee and has fewer than two members (s 122(1)(e) IA 1986); or
e. the company imposed a pre-CVA moratorium but did not then enter into CVA (¶9466) (s 122(1)(fa) IA 1986).

> MEMO POINTS 1. The **secretary of state** can petition for a company's winding up on additional grounds (¶7626+).
> 2. An **unregistered company** can be wound up if (s 221(5) IA 1986):
> – it was registered in another country and has been dissolved;
> – it has ceased business;
> – it is only carrying on business to wind its affairs up;

– it is unable to pay its debts; or
– it is just and equitable to wind the company up.
3. Persons carrying out "**regulated activities**" in contravention of FSMA 2000 can be wound up on specific grounds (s 367 FSMA 2000).

a. Unable to pay debts

There are **four methods** by which it can be shown that a company is unable to pay its debts. The petitioner can provide **evidence** that (s 123 IA 1986):
– he has served a statutory demand for a debt of over £750 on the company, which the company neglected to pay by the deadline;
– he has unsuccessfully attempted to enforce a judgment debt;
– the company cannot pay its debts as they fall due; or
– the company's liabilities outweigh its assets.

7593

Which method is used will depend on the circumstances. For instance, if a creditor has obtained an order in other court proceedings for the company to pay him a certain sum, and he has attempted to enforce the judgment debt without success, he has a clear route to winding the company up. Similarly, serving a statutory demand is a clear-cut way of establishing that a company is unable to pay its debts as they fall due. However, it may be inappropriate to use a statutory demand, in case it gives the company advance warning that it may be wound up. This could leave the petitioning creditor with a reduced chance of recovery because a large creditor (such as a bank) has extended its security over other assets, or the company has dissipated its assets, for example.

A creditor should not try to wind a company up on this ground on the basis of a genuinely **disputed debt**, otherwise his petition is liable to be struck out (¶7705+; Re a Company [1984] 3 All ER 78). In such cases, the appropriate course is for the parties to resolve the dispute, whether between themselves or by commencing other legal proceedings as the circumstances require.

MEMO POINTS 1. A petition cannot be based on a **debt** which is **statute barred** because the petitioner is no longer a creditor of the company. However, an exception is made in cases of judgment debts, since presenting a winding up petition does not count as "bringing an action" upon a judgment debt (Ridgeway Motors (Isleworth) Ltd v ALTS Ltd [2005] 2 BCLC 61).
2. The **minimum value** of £750 is expected to be increased to £1,500 from October 2008 as part of the Insolvency Service's review of the law (see ¶7364/mp).

Statutory demands

If a company **owes a creditor more than** £750, that creditor can serve a statutory demand for payment (s 123(1)(a) IA 1986).

7594

It must be made in the standard **form**, Form 4.1, and contain the following **details** (rr 4.5, 4.6 IR 1986):
– the amount of the debt and how it arose;
– if the amount claimed includes any interest or other charge which was not previously notified to the debtor, the basis of the demand must be explained. The amount claimed must not be more than the debt (plus interest and charges) accrued at the date of the demand;
– the purpose of the demand;
– the fact that if the demand is not satisfied, the creditor may petition for the company's winding up;
– the time limit for payment of the debt (21 days from service on the company);
– the methods of compliance open to the company;
– contact details for a named person whom the company can contact about the debt;
– the date of the demand; and
– the signature of a person authorised to make the demand on the creditor's behalf (e.g. a director, other authorised officer or solicitor).

MEMO POINTS 1. If the statutory demand contains **errors** or is **defective** in some way, it will remain valid until set aside by the court (Re a Debtor (No 001 of 1987, Lancaster) [1989] 2 All ER 46; Khan v Breezevale SARL, Re a Debtor (No 106 of 1992) [1996] BPIR 190. These cases concern statutory demands against individuals rather than companies, but in the absence of any reported cases on this point specifically relating to demands against companies, the bankruptcy position is likely to apply). An ineffective statutory demand can still be used as evidence of the company's inability to pay its debts as they fall due (see ¶7600 below).

As with winding up petitions, statutory demands should not be used as a tactical move in a dispute, for example to force an alleged debtor to pay despite a genuine dispute over the debt, or to establish liability. The court will **set aside** a **statutory demand** in such circumstances, for example:
– where there is a genuine dispute over the debt (*Re Janeash Ltd* [1990] BCC 250);
– where the statutory demand was used to decide whether or not the company presenting the demand was entitled to dismiss its director summarily (*Ashworth v Newnote Ltd* [2007] EWCA Civ 793); or
– where a statutory demand was based on compensation for harassment, where neither the harassment nor the company's liability for it had been established (*Re Rare Ltd* [2007] All ER (D) 381 (Jun)). The same criteria are applied when the court considers whether to restrain presentation of a petition (¶7641) or whether to strike a petition out (¶7705+).

2. The **minimum value** of £750 is expected to be increased to £1,500 from October 2008 as part of the Insolvency Service's review of the law (see ¶7364/mp).

7595 The **debtor** must be the company which owes the debt to the creditor. It does not have to be insolvent. In fact, persistent failure to pay the debt without good reason may in itself indicate that the company is unable to do so, justifying a demand for payment under threat of liquidation (*Cornhill Insurance plc v Improvement Services Ltd* [1986] BCLC 26).

A **creditor** making the statutory demand must be able to discharge the debt, so that once it is paid, the company is not under any further obligation to the creditor in relation to it. Most creditors would be able to do so, although an equitable assignee of part of a debt, for example, could not (*Re Steel Wing Co* [1920] All ER Rep 292).

7596 The demand must be based on a **debt** which is:
– for a liquidated sum;
– absolutely due and payable; and
– not contingent on any event (*JSF Finance & Currency Exchange Co Ltd v Akma Solutions Inc* [2001] 2 BCLC 307).

A creditor can make a statutory demand for an undisputed **portion of a debt**, even if another part is genuinely disputed by the company (*Re a Company (No 008122 of 1989), ex parte Trans Continental Insurance Services Ltd* [1990] BCLC 697). The same principles apply to any **deductions** made from the sum claimed, for example, if the creditor reduces the demand by what he owes (or might owe) the company, this must also be for a liquidated sum (*Re Humberstone Jersey Ltd* [1977] LS Gaz R 711, where it was held that a reduction could not be made for unliquidated damages claimed by the company for the creditor's alleged breach of contract).

MEMO POINTS 1. If the debt is due in a **foreign currency**, it can be expressed in that currency (*Re a Debtor (No 051-SD-1991), ex parte Richie Bros Auctioneers v Debtor* [1993] 2 All ER 40; a case concerning bankruptcy, but the judge specifically stated that the same would be true of corporate insolvency cases as well). However, the pounds sterling equivalent must also be stated (r 4.91(2) IR 1986).

2. Whether a debt is due and payable is not necessarily straight-forward. Regardless of whether liabilities under a guarantee are expressed to be **payable "on demand"**, if the guarantors are actually primary obligors then liability is not contingent on a demand being made (*Bradford Old Bank Ltd v Sutcliffe* [1918] 2 KB 833; *MS Fashions Ltd v Bank of Credit and Commerce International SA (in liquidation) (No 2)* [1993] 3 All ER 789). The guarantee must be interpreted according to its real meaning. Simply stating that the liabilities are payable "on demand" does not override the guarantors' status as primary obligors if that is how the rest of the guarantee treats them. Therefore, it is possible for a statutory demand to be issued without a demand for payment being made first under the guarantee (*TS & S Global Ltd v Fithian-Franks and others* [2007] EWHC 1401 (Ch)).

On the other hand, if a demand under the guarantee is properly required to render the liability due and payable, a statutory demand will not constitute that demand because it serves an entirely different purpose (*TS & S Global Ltd v Fithian-Franks and others*, above).

7597 The statutory demand must be **served** on the company by leaving it at the registered office. The case law has been contradictory as to whether or not it can be served by post, but it has been held that if the creditor can prove that the demand was delivered, it will have been served properly (*Re a Company (No 008790 of 1990)* [1991] BCLC 561). **In practice**, most solicitors use "process servers", who are agents specialising in serving documents and provide a witness statement to prove that they did (or did not) serve the demand.

MEMO POINTS If the **company does not have a registered office**, the statutory demand can be served at its actual office (*Re Fortune Copper Mining Co* (1871) LR 10 Eq 390).

If the **company does not pay** its debt within 21 days of service, it is deemed to be unable to do so and the creditor can petition for its winding up. This period is calculated clear of the day on which the demand was served and that on which the petition will be presented.

7598

EXAMPLE If a statutory demand is served on A Ltd on 1 March, the earliest the winding up petition can be presented if A Ltd fails to pay is 23 March.

The company must have "neglected" to pay the debt demanded, that is failed or omitted to pay without a good reason; therefore a refusal to pay on the basis of a substantial dispute over the debt does not entitle the creditor to present a petition.

Enforcement of judgment debts

If the **creditor** has previously obtained a **judgment in its favour** ordering the company to pay a certain sum, and the company does not or is unable to pay on enforcement, it will be deemed to be unable to pay its debts and the creditor can petition to wind it up (s 123(1)(b) IA 1986). To establish this ground, the execution must actually be carried out; it is not enough for the enforcement officer to report that he could not gain access to the premises (*Re a Debtor (No 340 of 1992), ex parte the Debtor v First National Commercial Bank plc* [1996] 2 All ER 211). A petition can still be presented on these grounds even if the judgment is under appeal, or the company has a counterclaim (*Re Amalgamated Properties of Rhodesia (1913) Ltd* [1917] 2 Ch 115; *Re Douglas (Griggs) Engineering Ltd* [1963] 1 All ER 498).

7599

MEMO POINTS **Enforcement officers** were previously known as "sheriffs" (s 99, Sch 7 Courts Act 2003).

Unable to pay debts as they fall due

If a company cannot pay its debts as they fall due, it is presumed to be insolvent and can be wound up; this is known as "**cash-flow** insolvency", or the "cash-flow test" (s 123(1)(e) IA 1986). It can be difficult for a creditor who only has access to the information at Companies House to obtain financial information about the company, so this test allows him to rely on more accessible factual information, such as the fact that the company has not paid one or more creditors without good reason.

7600

If the company can **prove** that **it can pay its debts**, it will be able to rebut the presumption of insolvency that arises in these circumstances (*Re Bradford Tramways Co* (1876) 4 Ch D 18). Even if the company can only pay up with the help of loans, it is still seen as able to pay its debts for these purposes.

The company's ability to pay its debts is **judged at** the time of the petition. The fact that it may be able to pay its debts once its assets are realised is irrelevant (*Re European Life Assurance Society* (1869) LR 9 Eq 122). The court will also only look at the debts due and demanded at that time, rather than looking at the wider financial position of the company.

EXAMPLE
1. **Non-payment of interest** due, without explanation (*Re Richbell Strategic Holdings Ltd* [1997] 2 BCLC 429).
2. A company which persistently and deliberately **does not pay** its debts **until** it is **compelled** to do so (*Re a Company* [1986] BCLC 261).
3. A company's directors told a creditor there were **no assets** against which execution could be carried out (*Re Douglas (Griggs) Engineering Ltd* [1962] 1 All ER 498).
4. There are **outstanding judgments** against the company and **several creditors** demanding payment (*Re Tweeds Garages Ltd* [1962] 1 All ER 121).

Company's liabilities outweigh its assets

The company will be deemed to be unable to pay its debts if it can be shown that its assets are worth less than its total liabilities (s 123(2) IA 1986). This method is known as "**balance sheet** insolvency", or the "balance sheet test", and can be difficult for a creditor to establish without access to the company's books and records.

7601

"**Assets**" are given a wide definition for these purposes, with both existing and probable assets being taken into account (*Re Capital Annuities Ltd* [1978] 3 All ER 704). However, "**probable**" assets do not include those which the company hopes to acquire without some legal right to do so (although the fact that a company is likely to acquire assets before its liabilities fall due may persuade the court to use its discretion not to order a winding up (*Byblos Bank SAL v Al-Khudhairy* [1987] BCLC 232)). Similarly, **prospective and contingent liabilities** can also be taken into account if they are likely to become current liabilities (*Re a Company* [1986] BCLC 261).

MEMO POINTS 1. The company's subscribed but **uncalled capital** can be taken into account as an **asset**, although evidence of a shareholder's own insolvency may counteract this (*Re European Life Assurance Society* (1869) LR 9 Eq 122).
2. A **contingent liability** is one which arises from an existing legal obligation but depends upon an event happening, which may or may not occur (*Stonegate Securities Ltd v Gregory* [1980] 1 All ER 241). A **prospective liability** is a possible liability under an existing contract, not potential liabilities that the company may incur in the future. For example, a company may be obliged by a contract to purchase shares in a new company if that new company is incorporated and starts to trade (a contingent liability); or a company may have prospective liabilities under a supply contract if the goods it supplies are defective. However, the fact that a company will incur liabilities by entering into contracts or otherwise carrying on its business in the future is not to be taken into account for these purposes.

b. Just and equitable

7602 This ground for winding up has been deliberately left open to the courts to interpret, so that is does not become confined to a particular set of **circumstances**. Therefore, each case is assessed on its own facts. Examples of successful petitions are given below to illustrate the situations in which this ground can be relied on (although it should be noted that this is not a "closed list", *Re St Piran Ltd* [1981] 3 All ER 270). The court's judgment is **based on** the circumstances at the date of the hearing, rather than that of the petition (*Re Fildes Bros Ltd* [1970] 1 All ER 923). Therefore, the petitioner must bear in mind that the company's circumstances may have changed since he presented his petition.

EXAMPLE
1. Oppressive management and misconduct
a. The company's affairs were being conducted in bad faith, because the directors had failed to hold general meetings, produce accounts, appoint auditors and recommend a dividend, all in order to acquire the shareholders' shares at a bargain (*Loch v John Blackwood Ltd* [1924] All ER Rep 200).
b. The company was established on the basis of a relationship of mutual trust and confidence between the shareholders, which had broken down irreparably (*Re Zinotty Properties Ltd* [1984] 3 All ER 754).
c. A director/shareholder of the company was wrongfully removed as a director and chairman (*Tay Bok Choon v Tahansan Sdn Bhd* [1987] BCLC 472).
d. The directors failed, on several occasions, to recommend reasonable dividends despite the company's profitability (*Re a Company (No 000370 of 1987), ex parte Glossop* [1988] BCLC 570).
e. The company failed to pay a creditor on a number of occasions, and it was also in the best interests of the other creditors to wind it up (*Re a Company* [1986] BCLC 261).

2. Company without a purpose
a. The company's articles provided that it would be wound up when a particular event occurred, and that event happened, e.g. a single purpose vehicle (*Re American Pioneer Leather Co* [1918] 1 Ch 556).
b. The main object for which the company was formed became impracticable (*Re Eastern Telegraph Co Ltd* [1947] 2 All ER 104).

3. Illegality
a. The company was formed (or was being carried on) for a fraudulent purpose (*Re Thomas Edward Brinsmead & Sons* [1895-9] All ER Rep Ext 1861).
b. The company's affairs were to be investigated (*Re Peruvian Amazon Co Ltd* (1913) 29 TLR 384).

7603 Since the court's decision rests on the circumstances of the case, usually evidenced by setting one party's version of events against another's, **petitioners** are likely to rely on a ground which is more straightforward to establish, if possible. It is often, but by no means exclusively, shareholders who have to resort to using this ground.

The petitioner's **conduct** will be taken into account because the court assesses each case on an equitable basis. The equitable principle which requires the petitioner to come to court with "clean hands" applies. Therefore, if the petitioner's own misconduct caused the dispute or he had previously acquiesced in the conduct about which he now complains, the court will not grant his petition (*Vujnovich v Vujnovich* [1990] BCLC 227; *Re Fildes Bros Ltd* [1970] 1 All ER 923). However, even if his conduct contributed in some way to the breakdown, he may still be able to obtain the order if he can show that the respondent's conduct was the substantial cause (*Re RA Noble & Sons (Clothing) Ltd* [1983] BCLC 273).

This ground is also discussed in the context of a **shareholder remedy** of last resort (¶2100+), which deals with circumstances such as those illustrated in examples 1b-d. above. Where a shareholder seeks compulsory liquidation on this ground, the circumstances may be similar to those in which he may petition for unfair prejudice. The fact that he has an alternative course of action will not prevent the court from ordering the company's winding up, unless he is acting unreasonably in not seeking another remedy (s 125(2) IA 1986). However, winding up should not be used routinely as an alternative to unfair prejudice. Shareholders should only present a petition if they genuinely want to wind the company up (para 1 CPR PD 49B).

A **contingent creditor** may petition for a company's winding up on this ground, in which case the court will assess whether he has a sufficient interest in the company to render it just and equitable that it is wound up. He will have to show that it will be unable to pay its debts when the contingent debt becomes due (*Re a Company (No 003028 of 1987)* [1988] BCLC 282).

c. Other grounds

Public company with no trading certificate

Public companies' requirement to have a trading certificate was discussed at ¶510+. Petitions on this ground can be **presented by** the secretary of state (s 124(4) IA 1986).

7608

Not trading for 1 year

This ground is not often relied upon because companies usually prefer to ask Companies House to strike it off the register if it has ceased trading (¶7502+). The **petitioner must establish** that the company has not traded for 1 year, which can be difficult given the breadth of most companies' objects. For example, the order will not be made if:
a. the company's objects allow it to be a non-trading company;
b. it has only ceased business in part (e.g. ceased to operate in one area but not in others), unless that part was substantially the whole of the company's business (*Re Kronand Metal Co* [1899] WN 14); or
c. the company itself ceases business, but it is or becomes the parent of a company which continues to trade (*Re Eastern Telegraph Co Ltd* [1947] 2 All ER 104).

The **court** will **consider** the good faith of the directors and shareholders, and will take account of the majority of the shareholders' wishes (*Re Capital Fire Insurance Association* (1882) 21 Ch D 209; *Re Tomlin Patent Horse Shoe Co Ltd* (1886) 55 LT 314).

If non-trading is established, the court then has a discretion whether or not to make the order in the **circumstances**. For example, if it can be shown that there was a good reason for not trading and the company is likely to (re)commence its business the court may decide not to make the order (*Re Capital Fire Insurance Association* (1883) 24 Ch D 408).

7609

Shareholder special resolution

This is not a common ground for a compulsory liquidation because shareholders are more likely to wind the company up voluntarily (see ¶8425+). The shareholders might have to put the company into compulsory liquidation if the directors are not prepared or able to make the statutory declaration of solvency required for an MVL, or the creditors will not support a CVL. Alternatively, they may choose to do so in order to initiate an investigation into the

7610

company's affairs by the official receiver, where they suspect that the company has not been managed properly (see ¶8120+).

If the shareholders **cannot pass a special resolution** because fewer than 75% are in favour, they can pass an ordinary resolution to wind the company up compulsorily on other grounds (see table at ¶7629).

Not enough shareholders/members

7611 Public and unlimited private companies can be wound up if they have fewer than two shareholders, so that the remaining shareholder can avoid incurring personal liability under companies legislation (s 24(1) CA 1985). Again, this ground is not common since it only applies to a relatively narrow range of companies. Insolvency legislation uses the term "**member**" rather than shareholder in relation to this ground, and **defines** it in slightly wider terms than companies legislation. As well as the subscribers to the memorandum and every other person who agrees to be a member whose name is in the company's register, insolvency legislation includes those to whom shares are transferred or transmitted. Therefore, a transferee whose name is not yet in the register of shareholders, or a personal representative or trustee in bankruptcy who has not chosen to have his name on the register, is included in this definition.

> MEMO POINTS 1. **Private limited companies** (by shares or guarantee) can be wound up for having no shareholders or members on the ground that it would be just and equitable.
> 2. In the case of a **transferee**, a proper instrument of transfer (executed and delivered to the transferee or company) will be required as evidence of membership; an agreement to transfer will not suffice (*Re Quickdome Ltd* [1988] BCLC 370, a case on s 459 CA 1985, a provision in companies legislation which extends the definition of "member" in the same way).
> 3. s 24 CA 1985 is likely to be repealed by 1 October 2009, when most of the provisions of the **new Companies Act** relating to shareholders are expected to come into force. The new Act will allow all companies to be formed with just one shareholder (s 7 CA 2006, expected to come into force by 1 October 2009).

Pre-CVA moratorium ends without voluntary arrangement

7612 Certain companies are eligible for a moratorium prior to entering into a CVA (¶9466+). To prevent a company from taking advantage of this freeze on action against it, if the moratorium ends without a CVA proposal having been approved, a creditor can petition for the company's compulsory liquidation.

2. Petitioners

7616 The legislation provides an exhaustive list of **who may present a petition** (s 124(1) IA 1986; *Re William Hockley, Ltd* [1962] 1 All ER 111). A person may fall into more than one category, for example he may be both a creditor and a contributory, but the capacity in which he petitions can affect the grounds on which the petition can be based as well as the procedure to be followed (since there is a different procedure for contributories' petitions). If a petitioner has a choice of capacity, he will choose the one with the most convenient procedure, or the one which allows him to proceed on whichever ground he finds it easiest to prove (for example, a creditor can use a statutory demand). The table at ¶7629 summarises the grounds upon which each type of petitioner can rely.

a. Creditors

7617 Creditors can present a winding up petition against the debtor company on any of the **grounds** detailed above, although they will usually do so on the ground that the company cannot pay its debts. As a **general rule**, an unpaid creditor is entitled to a winding up order as of right, although this is always subject to the court's power to exercise its discretion (*Re Sklan Ltd* [1961] 2 All ER 680; *Re P & J Macrae Ltd* [1961] 1 All ER 302). If the creditor is entitled to present the petition and the company cannot pay its debts, an order will usually be made; the burden is on the company to establish why it should not (*Re Lummus Agricultural Services Ltd* [2001] 1 BCLC 137).

A creditor is a person to whom a debt is owed (the meaning of "debt" for the purposes of insolvency legislation is set out at ¶9941). Although "creditor" is not **defined** in the legislation, case law illustrates which creditors have been **permitted** to petition in addition to the usual meaning of the word.

> EXAMPLE
> 1. A secured creditor. Even if he has appointed an administrative receiver, he does not have to wait until the conclusion of the administrative receivership (*Re Leigh Estates (UK) Ltd* [1994] BCC 292).
> 2. A person to whom a debt (or part of a debt (*Re Steel Wing Co* [1920] All ER Rep 292)) has been assigned, whether in law or in equity (*Re a Company (No 003624 of 2002)* [2002] All ER (D) 274 (Dec)).
> 3. A person who has been awarded judgment for a claim for unliquidated damages (*Re Pen-y-van Colliery Co* (1877) 6 Ch D 477).

Petitions have also been permitted from **contingent and prospective creditors**. A contingent creditor is one whose debt will only become due when a particular event happens (and that event may or may not occur). A prospective creditor is one whose debt will become due in the future, either on a fixed date or on a date which will be determined by reference to future events (*Stonegate Securities Ltd v Gregory* [1980] 1 All ER 241).

If the petitioning creditor's debt has been paid before the petition is presented, he will **not** **7618** be **permitted** to proceed with the petition (*Re William Hockley, Ltd* [1962] 1 All ER 111). Similarly, if the debt is paid by the company after the petition has been presented, the court will dismiss the petition unless another creditor agrees to be substituted for the original petitioner (¶7650). Further examples of where petitions have not been permitted are set out below.

> EXAMPLE
> 1. The creditor's debt is substantially disputed (*Re Fitness Centre (South East) Ltd* [1986] BCLC 518).
> 2. The creditor's claim was statute-barred when he presented the petition (*Re a Debtor (No 050A-SD-1995)* [1997] 1 BCLC 280); unless based on a judgment debt (*Ridgeway Motors (Isleworth) Ltd v ALTS Ltd* [2005] 2 BCLC 61).
> 3. The petitioner's claim arises out of an illegal (*Re South Wales Atlantic Steamship Co* (1875) 2 Ch D 763) or ultra vires (*Re National Permanent Benefit Building Society, ex parte Williamson* (1869) 5 Ch App 309) transaction.
> 4. The petitioner is a debenture stock holder who does not have a direct covenant with the company (*Re Dunderland Iron Ore Co Ltd* [1909] 1 Ch 446).

If a petitioner's **debt** is **less than £750** the court will usually reject the petition, unless:
– it is unopposed;
– it is based on a judgment debt;
– it is supported by other creditors; or
– there are other special circumstances.
However, if the petition is based on a **statutory demand**, the debt must be at least £750.

---

b. Contributories

A contributory is **defined** as "every person liable to contribute to the assets of a company in **7619** the event of its being wound up" (for a full definition, see ¶7863+). Unlike creditors, contributories are not entitled to wind up an insolvent company as of right, unless there are special circumstances (*Re Norwich Yarn Co* (1850) 12 Beav 366). Therefore, contributories must meet certain **eligibility criteria** in order to be able to present a petition.

Shareholders

Shareholders can present a petition against the company on most **grounds**. They usually **7620** rely on the ground that it would be just and equitable to wind the company up where they decide to place it into compulsory liquidation, although it would often be more advantageous for them to seek a voluntary liquidation (¶8425+).

A shareholder **may** only **present a petition** as a contributory of the company **if** (s 124(2) IA 1986):
a. the shares in respect of which he is a contributory have been held by him for at least 6 out of the 18 months preceding the presentation of the petition, or he has received the shares following the death of a former shareholder; or
b. in the case of an unlimited company, there are fewer than two members.

Clearly, in the latter case the appropriate **ground** will be that the company has fewer than two members. In the former case, the contributory can present the petition on a number of grounds (see table at ¶7629 below), but the most usual is the just and equitable ground.

There is an exception to these restrictions on presenting a petition where a **former shareholder** is liable to contribute to the company's assets as a result of the company redeeming or purchasing its own shares back from him using a payment out of its capital. Such a former shareholder may only petition for the company's winding up as a contributory on the **grounds** that (s 124(3) IA 1986):
- the company is unable to pay its debts; or
- it is just and equitable that the company should be wound up.

Since a shareholder is generally only liable to contribute the amount unpaid on his shares, a holder of **fully paid shares** will not usually be allowed to present a petition, unless he can prove that he will have an interest in the liquidation because the company is solvent and there will be enough surplus assets for distribution among the shareholders (*Re Martin Coulter Enterprises Ltd* [1988] BCLC 12). A shareholder who is **in arrears with calls** will not usually be allowed to present a petition either, but if he is permitted to do so he will usually be required to pay the amount of unpaid calls into court (*Re Crystal Reef Gold Mining Co* [1892] 1 Ch 408).

> MEMO POINTS 1. A **bankrupt contributory shareholder's** trustee in bankruptcy can petition as a contributory if his name has been on the register of shareholders for the requisite length of time (*Re H L Bolton Engineering Co Ltd* [1956] 1 All ER 799). If not, the bankrupt can petition on the instructions of his trustee in bankruptcy (*Re K/9 Meat Supplies (Guildford) Ltd* [1966] 3 All ER 320). A **dead contributory shareholder's** personal representatives may petition as contributories (s 81 IA 1986).
> 2. A holder of **fully paid shares** will not have to prove the company's solvency and a surplus of assets where:
> – the petition is presented on the ground that it would be just and equitable to wind the company up because the company has failed to supply accounts and other information, and it is therefore not possible for the shareholder to prove the company's financial position;
> – the petition alleges that the affairs of the company require investigation, the result of which is likely to create a surplus of assets (*Re Newman and Howard Ltd* [1961] 2 All ER 495); or
> – the petition is presented on the ground that the number of shareholders has fallen below two (i.e. in the case of public or unlimited companies).

Directors

7621 Directors can also be contributories of the company, but will only be able to petition in this capacity where they are **former directors** liable to contribute because they authorised the company to redeem or purchase its own shares using a payment out of its capital when it was not reasonable to do so (¶1337+). Such a former director may only petition for the company's winding up as a contributory on the **grounds** that (s 124(3) IA 1986):
- the company is unable to pay its debts; or
- it is just and equitable that the company should be wound up.

If a director does not qualify as a contributory for these purposes, or if he wishes to present a petition on another ground, he must do so as part of the board (below), or in his capacity as a creditor or a shareholder/contributory if applicable.

> MEMO POINTS Although directors of **unlimited companies** are also contributories (¶7863+), they will only be able to present a petition as a contributory if they are a former director in the same situation described above.

---

c. The company

7623 The company has the power to present a petition to the court for its own compulsory liquidation by:
- **ordinary resolution** on the grounds listed in the table at ¶7629; or
- **special resolution** (although this is rare, see ¶7610).

If the company is already subject to another type of insolvency procedure, a petition by the relevant insolvency practitioner must be in the name of the company in some circumstances (¶7625 below).

d. The board

7624 The board has the power to present a winding up petition against the company by **board resolution**. Once the resolution has been passed, it is the duty of all of the directors (even those who did not attend the meeting, or who voted against the resolution) to implement it (*Re Equiticorp International plc* [1989] BCLC 597, a case concerning an old administration but the wording of the relevant legislative provision is comparable). Once a valid resolution has been passed, any director may present the petition on behalf of the board.

e. Insolvency practitioners

7625 Where a **company** is already **subject to another type of insolvency procedure**, the relevant insolvency practitioner can petition for its winding up:
a. the official receiver, where the company is already being wound up voluntarily;
b. an administrator (s 14 IA 1986);
c. an administrative receiver (s 42 IA 1986);
d. an ordinary receiver, if the terms of the security under which he was appointed or his appointment specifically authorise him to do so, or if the court is prepared to accept that the ability to present a petition is part of his power under the security to protect the company's assets (*Re Emmadart Ltd* [1979] 1 All ER 599). A receiver appointed by the court cannot present a petition on behalf of the company (*Parsons v Sovereign Bank of Canada* [1913] AC 160);
e. the supervisor of a voluntary arrangement, whether the CVA is "dead or alive" (*Re Arthur Rathbone Kitchens Ltd* [1997] 2 BCLC 280; s 7(4)(b) IA 1986); or
f. a liquidator or temporary administrator in EC insolvency proceedings (¶7366+).

MEMO POINTS   An **administrator's** or **supervisor's** petition is treated as if it was presented by a contributory (r 4.7(9) IR 1986; see ¶7656+). In addition, a petition made by the administrator must be made in the name of the company by its administrator and include an application that the administrator's appointment is terminated (r 4.7(7) IR 1986; ¶9141).

f. Official petitioners

7626 The **secretary of state** can present a winding up petition against a company on the **grounds** that:
a. it is in the public interest (s 124A IA 1986). He can base his petition on information obtained:
– as part of a CIB investigation (¶7195+);
– in a report by inspectors made under their powers in the FSMA 2000;
– following a request for information or documents under the FSMA 2000 (ss 165, 171-173, 175 FSMA 2000);
– as part of an investigation into fraud under the Criminal Justice Act 1987 (s 2 Criminal Justice Act 1987); or
– through assisting overseas regulatory authorities (s 89 CA 1989);
b. it is an old public company (as defined by the CC(CP)A 1985) (s 122(1)(c) IA 1986); and
c. it was incorporated as a public company over 1 year ago but has not yet obtained a trading certificate.

7627 The company does not necessarily have to act unlawfully for a petition on the **public interest** ground to succeed (*Re Senator Hanseatische Verwaltungsgesellschaft mbH* [1996] 2 BCLC 562). The secretary of state has the discretion to petition if it seems to him, in the circumstances, that it is in the public interest for the company to be wound up.

EXAMPLE
Winding up order made
1. Companies operating illegal trading schemes under the Fair Trading Act 1973 (*Re Delfin International (SA) Ltd, Re Delfin Marketing (UK) Ltd* [2000] 1 BCLC 71).
2. A company which was set up to receive income from housing benefit but was badly mismanaged (*Secretary of State for Trade and Industry v Leyton Housing Trustees Ltd* [2000] 2 BCLC 808).

3. A company acting as a company formation agent which established companies for foreign investors in such a way as to conceal the identities of the persons running them (*Re London Citylink Ltd* [2005] All ER (D) 188 (Dec)).
4. A company which failed to keep proper accounting records and failed to co-operate with a CIB investigation. Other factors contributing to its winding up included a lack of transparency in its affairs and confusion between its affairs and those of its director/owners and their other companies (*Re Atlantic Properties Ltd* [2006] EWHC 610 (Ch)).

Winding up order not made
5. Telephone canvassing companies (*Re a Company (No 005669 of 1998)* [2000] 1 BCLC 427).

MEMO POINTS 1. The secretary of state **cannot petition** on the public interest ground if the company is already being wound up by the court (s 124A(2) IA 1986).
2. The court may still wind the company up even if the **part of the business** which was not in the public interest has been **removed or ceased**, e.g. to illustrate its disapproval at the way in which the company was run (*Re Walter L Jacob & Co Ltd* [1989] BCLC 345; *Re Equity & Provident Ltd* [2002] 2 BCLC 78).

7628 **Other official petitioners** are:
– the FSA (s 367 FSMA 2000);
– the attorney general, for charitable companies (s 63 Charities Act 1993);
– a magistrates' court officer authorised to enforce fines imposed by that court (s 124(1) IA 1986; power to enforce fines contained in the Magistrates' Courts Act 1980); and
– the regulator of CICs can present a winding up petition against a CIC on the ground that it is just and equitable for it to be wound up (s 124(4A) IA 1986; s 50 Companies (Audit, Investigations and Community Enterprise) Act 2004).

g. Grounds available to different petitioners

7629 This table **summarises** the principal petitioners and the grounds on which they can wind a company up.

Ground of petition	Who can petition?				
	CR	Contributory[1]		Co	Board	Sos
		S/h	D			
Company unable to pay debts	✓	✓	✓	✓[2]	✓	
Just and equitable	✓	✓	✓	✓[2]	✓	
Company has not traded for 1 year	✓	✓		✓[2]	✓	
Public company with no trading certificate	✓	✓		✓[2]	✓	✓
Company limited by shares or guarantee with fewer than 2 shareholders/members	✓	✓		✓[2]	✓	
Shareholder special resolution				✓		
Pre-CVA moratorium ends with no CVA in place	✓					
Public interest						✓
Old public company						✓

Key: CR: creditor
S/h: shareholder
D: director
Co: company
Sos: secretary of state

Note:
1. Contributory **shareholders** and **directors** can only present petitions if they fall within certain categories, see ¶7619+.
2. Shareholder ordinary **resolution** required.

3. Procedure

The procedure to be followed **depends upon** whether the petitioner has presented the petition as a contributory or not. The correct procedures must be followed; otherwise the petition risks being dismissed by the court. Here, the procedure for non-contributory petitions is dealt with first as it is the most common and some aspects of it are also a feature of contributory petitions.

a. Where petitioner is not a contributory

Form

A petition presented by a non-contributory must be in **Form 4.2**, with appropriate variations where the circumstances require (r 12.7(2) IR 1986). One form should be used per company, although interrelated petitions can proceed together (*Re a Company* [1984] BCLC 307).

The form requires the petitioner to insert the following **details**:
a. of the company:
– name;
– company registration number;
– date of incorporation;
– registered office address;
– nominal capital, its composition and how much is paid up;
– principal objects stated in the memorandum; and
– whether the company is an insurance undertaking;
b. the petitioner's full name and address;
c. the title of the court to which the petition is presented;
d. the ground(s) upon which the petition is based; and
e. whether the EC Insolvency Regulation affects the proceedings (see ¶7366+).

It is essential that the petitioner sets out the **ground**(s) on which his petition is based, otherwise his petition may be dismissed and he may be ordered to pay costs (*Re Wear Engine Works Co* [1874-80] All ER Rep Ext 1889). He must elaborate on the grounds, setting out the **reasons** for his allegations; a simple statement that the company is insolvent and unable to pay its debts, for example, will not suffice (*Securum Finance Ltd v Camswell Ltd* [1994] BCC 434). For the effect of mistakes in the petition, see ¶7732.

> MEMO POINTS 1. Where the **petition follows an administration or a CVA**, and it contains a request to appoint the relevant insolvency practitioner from those proceedings as liquidator (respectively, ¶9141, ¶9557), the proposed liquidator must file a report at court at least 2 days before the return date on the petition. The report must state (s 140 IA 1986; r 4.7(10) IR 1986):
> – when he notified the creditors of his intention to be appointed as liquidator (this must have been at least 10 days before the report was filed); and
> – the details of any responses to his notification, including any objections.
> 2. Under the **new Companies Act**, companies will have unlimited objects unless they are specifically restricted by the articles (s 31 CA 2006, expected to come into force by 1 October 2009). Therefore, Form 4.2 is likely to be amended in due course.

Verifying the petition

The petition must be verified by an **affidavit**, by which the petitioner (or his representative) confirms that the statements in the petition are true, or that they are true to the best of his knowledge, information and belief (r 4.12(1) IR 1986). It must also state whether the EC Insolvency Regulation applies and, if so, whether the proceedings will be main or secondary (¶7366+). As an **alternative** to the affidavit, a witness statement verified by a statement of truth may be used (r 7.57(5) IR 1986). This is the modern equivalent of an affidavit and is used in most other types of court procedures. Here, references are to affidavits, as this is consistent with the legislation and rules, but they include witness statements.

The affidavit can be **made by** (r 4.12(4) IR 1986):
– the petitioner (or one of them, if there are two or more);
– a company officer or solicitor, or some other person concerned in the matters giving rise to the petition; or
– some other person who is authorised to make the affidavit and has knowledge of the relevant matters.

Where the affidavit is made by someone other than the petitioner, he must specify the capacity in which he makes the affidavit and how he has knowledge of the relevant matters. For example, the petitioner's solicitor will state that he has the requisite knowledge through his conduct of the file.

The petition must be **exhibited to** the affidavit (r 4.12(3) IR 1986). If one affidavit is used to verify **several petitions**, the name of each company and the statements relied on by the petitioner must be stated in relation to each one. A copy of the affidavit must be filed with each petition (r 4.12(7) IR 1986).

> MEMO POINTS As part of the Insolvency Service's review of secondary legislation (see ¶7364/mp), it is taking the opportunity to make alterations to the primary legislation either where it is necessary to support the new Rules or to remove unnecessary administrative burdens. The Service proposes to remove the requirement for certain documents to be verified by **affidavit** in insolvency procedures (proposal 5, "A consultation document on changes to the Insolvency Act 1986 and the Company Directors Disqualification Act 1986 to be made by a Legislative Reform Order for the modernisation and streamlining of insolvency procedures" (September 2007)). Since the reform of civil procedures generally in 1998, affidavits in other types of procedures have been replaced by witness statements, which do not have to be sworn/affirmed by a solicitor/commissioner for oaths/notary. Therefore, this change will reduce the cost and administrative time involved in preparing these documents. At the time of writing, the consultation is still open. If this proposal is accepted, the changes are likely to be implemented from 1 October 2008.

7638 The **purpose** of the affidavit is to provide evidence of the truth of the statements in the petition to the court (r 4.12(6) IR 1986), even where the statements comprise hearsay (Re ABC Coupler and Engineering Co Ltd (No 2) [1962] 3 All ER 68). However, since the affidavit provides "prima facie" evidence, it can be rebutted by contrary evidence.

> MEMO POINTS **Additional affidavits** should be filed in the following circumstances because evidence of further matters is required:
> – an allegation of fraud is made (Re London and Hull Soap Works Ltd [1907] WN 254);
> – the petition is based on an allegation that the affairs of the company should be investigated (Re S A Hawken Ltd [1950] 2 All ER 408); or
> – the petition is based on the just and equitable ground but does not set out all of the facts (Re W R Willcocks & Co Ltd [1973] 2 All ER 93).
> Where such an affidavit is filed, **notice** of it should be given to the company to prevent the company applying for an adjournment to respond to the additional affidavit, delaying the petition.

Presenting the petition to court

7639 When the petition is **filed** by post or by hand at the relevant court, it is said to have been "presented" (r 4.7 IR 1986). The court will only accept the petition if the following **items** are presented together:
a. the original petition;
b. the correct number of copies of the petition (see below);
c. the affidavit verifying the petition;
d. the correct fee (currently, £670 deposit plus £190 court fee);
e. the receipt for the deposit, unless a suitable alternative arrangement has been made (see below); and
f. a letter signed by the petitioner (if he is acting in person) or by/on behalf of his solicitor (if he is not) which specifies:
– exactly what the court is being asked to do;
– enclosing the documents listed above; and
– enclosing a stamped addressed envelope (of a suitable size) for the return of documents to him (either the documents above where the petition is not accepted, or the petition once it has been processed and returned by the court).

Additional **copies of the petition** need to be provided as summarised below.

Situation[1]	Purpose	Reference
Every petition	Exhibit to affidavit	r 4.12(3) IR 1986
Petitioner is not company	Service on company	r 4.7(3) IR 1986
Company in: – voluntary liquidation – administration – administrative receivership – CVA	Service on relevant insolvency practitioner	r 4.7(4) IR 1986
Member state liquidator appointed in main proceedings	Service on member state liquidator	¶7366+

Note:
1. If the company is (or was) an **authorised deposit-taker** (r 13.12A IR 1986) and the petitioner is not the FSA, a copy also needs to be included for service on the FSA (r 4.7(4) IR 1986).

A **deposit** of £670 must be paid to the court at which the petition is presented, usually at a separate fees desk (reg 6(1) SI 2004/593). A receipt will be issued, which must be presented to the court along with the petition and documents listed above. The deposit is **used as** security for the fee that the official receiver receives for carrying out his duties when a winding up order is made, and is passed on to him by the court.

On receiving a petition together with all the relevant items, the **court** will then (r 4.7(5)-(6) IR 1986):
– seal each copy of the petition (i.e. stamp it with the court seal);
– add to each copy the time, date and place of the hearing (known as the "return date"); and
– return (either by post or in person) the copies to the petitioner or his solicitor.

MEMO POINTS **Alternatively**, if the petitioner has made another suitable arrangement for paying the **deposit** to the official receiver, the secretary of state will give written notice to the court of this, which is acceptable in place of the receipt as long as the notice has not been revoked (e.g. because the fee has not in fact been paid) (r 4.7(2)-(2B) IR 1986).

7640

Restraining presentation

The **court** has the **power** to restrain a petitioner from presenting his petition in order to prevent an abuse of process of the court (*Bryanston Finance Ltd v de Vries (No 2)* [1976] 1 All ER 25; *Re Portedge Ltd* [1997] BCC 23/*RWH Enterprises Ltd v Portedge Ltd* [1998] BCC 556 on appeal).

7641

> EXAMPLE A petitioner served a statutory demand on a company in respect of money which she alleged it owed her as compensation for harassment that she claimed to have suffered from one of its employees. The court restrained her from presenting a petition against the company, finding that the service of the statutory demand was an extreme abuse of process because:
> – the debt was genuinely disputed: the alleged harassment was under investigation by the police, but there was no evidence that the employee or the company had been found liable to her for it; and
> – the petitioner was not even a creditor of the company because she had not proved that the company was liable (vicariously or otherwise) for the alleged civil wrong. She was therefore not entitled to present a petition (*Re Rare Ltd* [2007] All ER (D) 381 (Jun)).

Further examples of abusive petitions are given at ¶7705+, in the context of when the court will strike out a petition after it has been presented.

Such an **application**, usually made by the company itself, should be made by originating application on **Form** 7.1 directly to the judge (para 5.1(3) CPR Insolvency PD). The **evidence** presented to the court must be strong enough to show that the petition is likely to fail.

Serving the petition

A sealed copy of the petition must be **served on** the company at its registered office (unless, of course, the company has presented a petition against itself). Service is **effected by** handing the petition to a person at the registered office who (r 4.8(3) IR 1986):
– confirms he is an officer or employee of the company, or he holds such a position to the best of the server's knowledge, information and belief; or
– confirms that he is authorised to accept service of documents on the company's behalf.

7644

If there is no such person available, the petition may be left at the registered office in a way in which it is likely to reach a person at the office (e.g. posting it through the letterbox). Therefore, it is necessary for the petitioner, or his agent, to attend the registered office (he can only leave it at the office if there is nobody there to accept service, and therefore must be there to check this first). For this reason, most petitioners use an agent known as a "**process server**" to serve the petition.

The **registered office** is the place last notified to Companies House as such (r 4.8(1)-(2) IR 1986). If service at the registered office is not practicable (e.g. the building is boarded up), the company has **no registered office** or is an unregistered company, the petition may be served at the company's last known principal place of business in a way in which it is likely to reach a person attending at the office (r 4.8(4) IR 1986). Alternatively, it can be served on a director, secretary or manager of the company wherever that person may be (e.g. at home).

If **service is not possible**, for example if the petition cannot be delivered to or left at the registered office and there is no other known address for the company or its officers, the petitioner must apply to the court for directions. He can make the application without notice to any other parties, giving evidence by affidavit as to what steps have been taken to comply with the service requirements and why they have been unsuccessful (r 4.8(6)-(7) IR 1986). The court may approve another method of service, known as "substituted service", (such as delivery to the registered office address and advertisement in the *Gazette*, to give the company a reasonable opportunity of knowing about the petition) or make alternative directions.

> **MEMO POINTS** 1. If the petition is to be served on an **overseas company**, it can be served on the person notified to Companies House as authorised to accept service on behalf of the company, by leaving it at or sending it to the address provided (ss 691, 695 CA 1985). If this is not possible, the petition can be left at or sent to any of the company's places of business in GB. For the changes under the new Companies Act to the registration of overseas companies, see ¶140.
> 2. The Insolvency Service has proposed that **affidavits** are replaced by witness statements (see ¶7637). This change is likely to be implemented on 1 October 2008.

7645 Service is **proved** to the court by affidavit in Form 4.4 (if served at the registered office) or 4.5 (if not, or if served on an overseas company), specifying how service was effected. If a process server has been used, he usually provides the affidavit. A sealed copy of the petition must be **exhibited** to the affidavit (r 4.9 IR 1986). If substituted service was ordered, a sealed copy of the relevant order must also be exhibited. The affidavit and exhibit(s) must be **filed** at court immediately after service (r 4.9 IR 1986). Again, a witness statement may be used instead of an affidavit (r 7.57(5), (7) IR 1986).

> **MEMO POINTS** The Insolvency Service has proposed that **affidavits** are replaced by witness statements (see ¶7637). This change is likely to be implemented on 1 October 2008.

Providing copies to other parties

7646 The petitioner is also required to **send** a copy of the petition **to** the relevant insolvency practitioner, if he knows that the company is subject to another type of insolvency procedure (including to a member state liquidator, if applicable, ¶7366+). It must be sent on the first business day after the petition was served on the company (r 4.10 IR 1986), and may be sent by post (r 13.3 IR 1986; ¶7404+).

In addition, the petitioner must provide a copy of the petition to a director, contributory or creditor of the company within 2 clear days of a **request** to do so (r 4.13 IR 1986). A fee of 15p per A4 or A5 page and 30p per A3 page is payable by the person making the request (r 13.11 IR 1986).

Advertising the petition

7647 Usually, the petition must be **advertised in** the *Gazette* (r 4.11(1) IR 1986), although the court may direct otherwise (e.g. that it is advertised in another named newspaper, r 4.11(3) IR 1986). The **purpose** of requiring an advertisement in the *Gazette* is to ensure that those entitled to appear and be heard at the petition hearing have the chance to do so (*Secretary of State for Trade and Industry v North West Holdings plc* [1999] 1 BCLC 425). Petitioners sometimes also advertise the petition in a local newspaper to encourage support for the petition, although care must be taken not to do so abusively (e.g. by pre-empting the decision of the court before it has heard the petition) as the court has the power to dismiss the petition as a result of such action.

The advertisement in the *Gazette* must be in the correct **form**, Form 4.6, which specifies:
– the company's name and registered number;
– its registered office, principal place of business (if unregistered) or address at which service of the petition was effected (if an overseas company);
– the petitioner's name and address;
– if the petitioner is the company, its registered office (or principal place of business if unregistered);
– the date of presentation of the petition;
– where the hearing will take place;
– the petitioner's solicitor's name and address (if applicable); and
– a statement that any person intending to attend the hearing (in support or opposition) must notify the petitioner (see ¶7653+).

The *Gazette* charges a fee of (currently) £36.80 for the advertisement, which includes a copy of the published advertisement.

The **timing** of the advertisement depends upon whether the petitioner is the company or not.

Petitioner is the company	Petitioner is not the company
At least 7 business days (¶7412) before the hearing	– A minimum of 7 business days after petition served on company; and – at least 7 business days before the hearing

The 7-day delay after service on the company enables it to **restrain advertisement** before the petition is made public if it has grounds for disputing the petition (*Re Signland Ltd* [1982] 2 All ER 609). This is done by an ex parte application for an injunction so that advertisement can be restrained until the dispute is heard by the court.

7648 If the petition is **not properly advertised**, the court may dismiss it (r 4.11(5) IR 1986). The court is unlikely to dismiss the petition if the error was not the petitioner's fault, for example where the wrong address for service was given by Companies House, resulting in the petition being advertised before the company was served (*Re Garton (Western) Ltd* [1989] BCLC 304), rather it will grant an adjournment to enable the Rules to be followed.

7649 Once the advertisement has been published, it must be **filed** at the court as soon as possible, even if the advertisement is defective (e.g. the timing is wrong or it contains errors) or the petitioner decides not to pursue the petition (para 2.2 CPR Insolvency PD). At the latest, a copy of the advertisement must be filed with the certificate of compliance (¶7652 below).

Withdrawing the petition and substituting petitioners

7650 The petitioner may wish to withdraw the petition, for example if his debt has been paid. If the petition has **not yet** been **advertised**, he must apply (without notice to the other parties) for leave of the court at least 5 clear days before the hearing date. If:
– the petitioner has not received any notices from other parties (supporting or opposing the petition); and
– the company consents to the withdrawal,
then the court can allow the petitioner to withdraw his petition, with costs to be agreed between the parties (r 4.15 IR 1986).

If the petition has been **advertised**, the application for withdrawal must be made at the hearing to enable other creditors to be substituted as petitioner. The court has a wide discretion to **substitute** another **creditor**, and will usually do so if (r 4.19 IR 1986):
a. he would have had the right to present a petition;
b. he wants to prosecute the petition; and

c. the petitioner:
- is not entitled to present the petition;
- failed to advertise the petition within the time limit;
- consents to withdrawing his petition; or
- appears at the hearing, but does not apply for the order set out in his petition.

The application to be substituted is usually made orally at the hearing.

If **substitution** is **ordered**, the court usually directs that the petition and affidavit are amended and re-served on the company. It may also have to be re-advertised, for example if the original petition was not advertised, or where a contributory's petition is taken over by a creditor (Re Creative Handbook Ltd [1985] BCLC 1).

The **new petitioner** should review the petition proceedings and ensure that the Rules have been complied with. If they have not, he should effect compliance (applying for an adjournment of the petition hearing if necessary).

MEMO POINTS 1. If the petitioner withdraws his petition because his **debt has been paid**, but another creditor is substituted, the petitioner is at risk of having to repay the amount received as a voidable disposition of company property after a petition has been presented (¶7674+; Re Square 3 Ltd [2006] All ER (D) 280 (May)).

2. If the **petitioner consents, or** has **failed to advertise in time**, the substitution order can be made at any time (including before the hearing). The applicant should obtain written confirmation from the petitioner that the petition was not advertised and he does not wish to continue as petitioner, which can be produced at court. Alternatively, he could make the petitioner the respondent to his application so that he can confirm this in person to the court.

3. An **assignee of the debt** on which the petition is based can be substituted as petitioner, unless the assignment only took place for that person could acquire the petition (Perak Pioneer Ltd v Petroliam Nasional Bhd [1986] AC 849).

4. The court may also substitute a **member state liquidator** as petitioner if he wishes to take over the petition, on such terms as the court sees fit (r 4.19(2A) IR 1986).

Compliance with the Rules

7652 The petitioner must ensure that the Rules have been complied with, and he must file a **certificate** of compliance in Form 4.7 with the court (r 4.14 IR 1986). The **deadline** for doing so depends upon which court is hearing the petition:
- county court: at least 5 clear days before the petition is heard (r 4.14 IR 1986); or
- High Court: by 4.30pm on the Friday before the hearing (para 3.1 CPR Insolvency PD).

The certificate **states** the dates of:
- presentation;
- the hearing;
- service on the company (if applicable); and
- advertisement.

A copy of the advertisement must be filed at court with the certificate. **Failure** to submit a correct certificate can lead to the court dismissing the petition (r 4.14(4) IR 1986).

Third parties intending to appear at the hearing

7653 Any person intending to appear at the hearing must **notify** the petitioner in Form 4.9, stating (r 4.16 IR 1986):
- his name, address and telephone number;
- the contact details of any specified person authorised to speak on his behalf;
- whether he intends to support or oppose the petition; and
- the amount and nature of his debt.

The notice can be **sent to** the petitioner at the address on the court file or in the advertisement, or to his solicitor (r 4.16(3) IR 1986). It must reach the petitioner by at least 4pm on the business day before the hearing (or adjourned hearing, if appropriate) (r 4.16(4) IR 1986).

A person who **fails** to give notice can only appear at the hearing with the court's leave (r 4.16(5) IR 1986). Leave will usually be granted, provided the person in question undertakes that he will not seek an order for his costs of appearing at the hearing (this undertaking will be discharged once the petition is granted or dismissed).

The **petitioner** must prepare a **list** in Form 4.10 of those who have given notice of their intention to appear, stating:
– their names, addresses and solicitors (if known); and
– whether they intend to oppose or support the petition.

The petitioner must hand this list to the court before the hearing begins (r 4.17 IR 1986). Where the court allows extra persons to appear at the hearing, their names should be added to the list by hand.

7654

b. Where petitioner is a contributory

There is a different procedure for the presentation of contributories' petitions. An administrator's or supervisor's petition is treated as if it was presented by a contributory and so should also follow this form and procedure (r 4.7(9) IR 1986). The most common category of contributories comprises the shareholders, but there are others; those eligible to present a petition are discussed at ¶7619+.

7656

Form

The petition must be in Form 4.14, **specifying** the ground(s) on which it is made (r 4.22(1) IR 1986). The petition requires the same information as a non-contributory's petition (¶7636). It must also state whether the petitioner would object to an order being made during the proceedings for the avoidance of any of the following transactions occurring between the presentation of the petition and any winding up order (¶7674+, ¶7683; paras 2-6 CPR PD 49B):
– dispositions of the company's property;
– transfers of its shares; or
– changes in the status of its membership.

7657

Contributories will not usually object to such orders, since they preserve the assets available to them in the liquidation. However, if, for example, they feel it would be beneficial for the company to keep trading, or to complete a transaction, they would lodge an objection. If a contributory does object, his affidavit must state his reasons for doing so. If he would consent to such an order in a modified form, the petition must set out the form of the order he would accept, and the affidavit must state his reasons for the modification. The court will balance the advantages and disadvantages of allowing the disposition to proceed.

> MEMO POINTS If the **petitioner** has stated that he consents to an order (modified or not) but then **changes his mind** before the hearing, he must notify the company and can apply for an order directing that an avoidance order shall not be made (or shall only be made as modified).

There is no requirement to file an affidavit **verifying**, or any other **evidence in support** of, the petition. However, where the petitioner objects to an avoidance order being made, or only consents to a modified order, he must give a short written statement of his reasons in accordance with CPR PD 49B (see ¶7657 above).

7658

Presenting the petition to court

The petition is presented when it is **filed** at the relevant court together with (r 4.22(1), (1A) IR 1986):
a. one copy for service;
b. the correct fee (currently, £670 deposit plus £190 court fee);
c. the receipt for the deposit (see ¶7640); and
d. if the petition is presented by post, a letter signed by the petitioner (if unrepresented) or by or on behalf of his solicitor stating:
– what the court is being asked to do;
– enclosing the required documents; and

7659

- enclosing a stamped addressed envelope (of the appropriate size) for the return of documents to the petitioner or his solicitor.

The **court** will then (r 4.22 IR 1986):
- fix a date for a directions hearing to be attended by the petitioner and company; and
- return a sealed copy of the petition for service stating the date and time of that hearing.

Serving the petition

7660 The petitioner must serve a sealed copy of the petition **on the company** at least 14 clear days before the return day (r 4.22(4) IR 1986). Service can be effected in a number of different **ways** (r 6.2 CPR):

a. personally, by leaving it with a senior person at the company, or the company's solicitor (if he has informed the petitioner that he is authorised to accept service on the company's behalf). If the document is served out of business hours (i.e. after 5pm, at the weekend or on a bank holiday) it will be deemed to be served on the next business day (r 6.7 CPR);

b. first class post, in which case it will be deemed to have been served on the second business day after it was posted (taken as the postmarked date), unless there is evidence to the contrary (r 12.10 IR 1986);

c. second class post, as above, except it is deemed to have been served on the fourth business day after posting;

d. leaving the petition at the address for service;

e. document exchange;

f. fax; or

g. any other method permitted by the court.

The correct **address for service** is the company's principal office, or any place of business within the jurisdiction that has a real connection with the petition (r 6.5 CPR).

> MEMO POINTS If a **member state liquidator** has been appointed in relation to the company in main proceedings, the petitioner must also send a copy of the petition to him (r 4.22(5) IR 1986).

The directions hearing

7661 The court will give directions on the following **issues** at the directions hearing (r 4.23(1) IR 1986):
- service of the petition;
- whether particulars of claim and a defence are required;
- how to proceed with the petition generally;
- whether and how the petition is to be advertised (in this context, advertisement is usually in a regular newspaper rather than the *Gazette*);
- how any evidence is to be presented at the hearing (e.g. by affidavit or orally; how deponents of affidavits should be cross-examined; what matters should be dealt with in evidence); and
- any other related matter.

> MEMO POINTS If the petition is **advertised** or an advertisement arranged **before directions** are given, the petition may be struck out as an abuse of process (*Re Doreen Boards Ltd* [1996] 1 BCLC 501).

Third parties intending to appear at the hearing

7662 The following provisions relating to non-contributory petitions apply to contributory petitions as well, see ¶7653+:
- **notification** by third parties of their intention to appear at the hearing; and
- the requirement of the petitioner to provide the court with a **list** of such persons.

B. Consequences of presenting a petition

The date the petition is presented is significant because, if an order is made, the **commencement of the liquidation** operates retrospectively from this date (s 129(2) IA 1986). Although a company is not in liquidation until an order has been made by the court, the consequences of presentation have a significant impact on how the company is managed between presentation and the hearing, since the focus must now be on the creditors' interests rather than the shareholders'. Case law has clarified that presentation occurs when the petition is delivered to court, not when the court issues it (*Re Blights Builders Ltd* [2007] All ER (D) 147 (Jan)).

Any **dispositions of the company's property**, including **transfers of shares**, made during this period can be recovered or prevented, to maximise the assets available for distribution to the creditors (¶7674+, ¶7683). Although this only affects a company once an order has been made, it is discussed here because the company and those dealing with it need to be aware of the potential consequences of entering into such transactions before an order is made. A company's activities will be restricted even further if a **provisional liquidator** is appointed (¶7686+). The commencement of the liquidation also has an impact on other matters (summarised at ¶7747), including **other legal proceedings** in which a company is or becomes involved, which can be stayed or restrained during this period (discussed at ¶7697+).

In view of these serious consequences of presentation, the court has a wide discretion to **strike out a petition** where it should not have been presented (¶7705+).

7672

> MEMO POINTS 1. The deemed date of commencement of winding up is different where (s 129(1), (1A) IA 1986):
> – the **company resolves** to be wound up voluntarily and then a petition is presented, in which case it commences on the date of the resolution; and
> – the court treats an **application** for an **administration** order as a winding up petition, in which case it commences on the date of the order.
> 2. Although **other methods** of preserving a company's assets may be available using the court's powers to grant interim relief, the court will be reluctant use these powers unless there is a convincing reason why the methods of preserving the company's assets described below are not suitable. For example, where a petitioner had obtained **freezing orders** against the assets of a third party, the court held that a provisional liquidator should have been appointed instead. He could have ensured that any claims against the third parties were pursued as appropriate and in all of the creditors' interests (*HM Revenue & Customs v Egleton and others* [2006] EWHC 2313 (Ch)). However, since the petition hearing was less than a week away from the hearing at which the freezing orders were challenged, the court allowed them to remain in place in the exceptional circumstances of the case (otherwise the petitioner would have simply appointed a provisional liquidator who would have applied for the same orders to be made again).

1. Dispositions of company property

Any disposition (or, **disposal**) of the company's property after a petition has been presented is void, unless the court orders otherwise (s 127(1) IA 1986). Although the wording of the provision is wide enough to extend to dispositions after a winding up order has been made, case law has established that it only **operates** between presentation of the petition and the order (*Re Oriental Bank Corpn, ex parte Guillemin* (1884) 28 Ch D 634).

The wide definition of "property" for insolvency purposes is set out at ¶9941. There is no statutory **definition** of a disposition, but given that the purpose of the provision is to prevent the company from dissipating its assets before the order is made, case law has interpreted the term widely to include any transaction by which the company reduces its rights in relation to an asset (such as giving up its contractual rights, or presenting a post-dated cheque to a creditor). It includes dispositions of the company's property made by a third party or indirectly in some other way. If there is any **doubt** as to whether the disposition will

7674

be allowed or not, it is prudent to apply to the court before the transaction is entered into for a prior validating order.

The **petitioning creditor** must bear in mind that if he accepts payment of his debt after the petition has been presented but before the order, he risks having to repay the money to the company as a result of this power.

> MEMO POINTS   An exception to this provision operates where dispositions are made by an **administrator** while a **winding up petition** is **suspended** (s 127(2) IA 1986).

7675 The **application** can be made by the company or any other interested person (including a shareholder, even if he is not a party to the disposition (*Re Argentum Reductions (UK) Ltd* [1975] 1 All ER 608)). It should usually be made to the registrar or district judge. **Notice** that the application has been made must be given to (*Practice note – validation orders*, issued by the Chancellor of the High Court on 11 January 2007):
– the petitioning creditor and any substitute petitioner (see ¶7650);
– if the company is already subject to another type of insolvency procedure, the relevant insolvency practitioner; and
– any creditor who has given notice of his intention to appear at the petition hearing.

The application should be supported by written **evidence** in the form of an affidavit or witness statement made by a director or other officer of the company, and should be accompanied by a draft of the order sought. The evidence should set out:
– when and to whom notice has been given of the application;
– the company's registered office and nominal paid up share capital;
– a summary of the circumstances leading up to the petition and how the company became aware that a petition had been presented;
– whether the petition debt is admitted or disputed, with a summary of any dispute;
– full details of the company's financial position (including details of its assets and liabilities), supported by documents such as the latest filed accounts or an estimated statement of affairs, and a cash flow forecast and profit and loss projection for the period for which the order is sought;
– details of the dispositions or payments in respect of which an order is sought (including details of any property involved, with an independent valuation), and the reasons for making them; and
– details of any consents obtained from the persons with notice of the application.

Opposition to such an application commonly comes from the petitioner, the creditors or shareholders.

> MEMO POINTS   The Insolvency Service has proposed that **affidavits** are replaced by witness statements (see ¶7637). This change is likely to be implemented on 1 October 2008.

7676 Orders can be made to **validate dispositions**, for example, it is common for the court to allow a company to pay money in and out of its bank account and to dispose of its property for proper value in the ordinary course of its business, where the company needs to trade during this interim period. In considering whether to make an order **in advance** of a disposition or **retrospectively**, the court will consider the same factors. Clearly, obtaining prior approval is a safer route, as it obviates the risk of the disposition being rendered void. The company will usually be forced to apply for such an order in advance of any dispositions because banks often freeze a company's bank account once they learn that a petition has been presented, preventing any business being conducted.

Factors taken into consideration by the court

7677 The court will need to be satisfied that the company is either solvent and able to pay its debts as they fall due, or that a particular transaction or series of transactions will be beneficial to or will not prejudice the interests of all of the unsecured creditors as a class. It will consider a number of factors when deciding whether to validate a disposition or to declare it void (*Re Gray's Inn Construction Co Ltd* [1980] 1 All ER 814; *Denney v John Hudson & Co Ltd* [1992] BCLC 901; *Re Fairway Graphics Ltd* [1991] BCLC 468).

The starting point is that the assets of the company at the commencement of the liquidation are to be distributed among the **unsecured creditors** pari passu (i.e. at the same rate, so that each one receives a proportion of the assets commensurate with his debt). However, the court recognises that it may be in the creditors' interests that the company is allowed to make certain distributions between the presentation of the petition and the winding up order being made. The interests of the unsecured creditors are key. For instance, the court will not allow the payment in full of one unsecured creditor when the others will only receive a dividend in the winding up, unless it would benefit the creditors as a whole to pay that creditor off (such as where the business can only continue to trade if it pays for certain goods). Similarly, the sale of an asset at full market value will not disadvantage the unsecured creditors as the same net amount will be available for distribution.

Generally, **if the company is solvent** the interests of the creditors will not carry such weight because their position is less likely to be disadvantaged by any disposition (although the disposition may be prevented to protect the shareholders' position in appropriate cases, see example 1g. below).

The court will usually validate a disposition that was **made in good faith** when the parties were unaware of the petition (unless there was an intention to give an advantage to the disponee over the other creditors, see ¶7819+).

EXAMPLE
1. Dispositions void/not allowed to proceed
a. Payment using the company's cash (*Re Liverpool Civil Service Association, ex parte Greenwood* (1874) 9 Ch App 511).
b. Creating a charge over the company's property (*Re Park Ward & Co Ltd* [1926] Ch 828).
c. Selling any part of the company's property (*Re Flint* [1993] Ch 319).
d. Paying a creditor out of the company's bank account, whether the account is in credit or overdraft (*Hollicourt (Contracts) Ltd (in liquidation) v Bank of Ireland* [2001] 1 All ER 289).
e. Paying money into the company's bank account, which is in overdraft. This is a disposition in favour of the bank (*Re Gray's Inn Construction Co Ltd* [1980] 1 All ER 814) (however, if a payment is made into an account which is in credit, the position is currently unclear).
f. Spending money defending an unfair prejudice application while the company is subject to a creditor's petition (*Re Crossmore Electrical and Civil Engineering Ltd* [1989] BCLC 137).
g. Making payments out of the company's bank account while the company is subject to a public interest winding up petition, even if the company is solvent (here, the petition was based on concern for the shareholders and any dispositions may have worsened their position in the winding up (*Re a Company (No 007130 of 1998)* [2000] 1 BCLC 582)).
h. Where the company's solvency is in doubt and an application for a validation order is opposed by the petitioner (*Re a Company (No 007523 of 1986)* [1987] BCLC 200).

2. Dispositions valid/allowed to proceed
a. Paying to a charge holder the proceeds of sale of the asset over which he had the charge, since the charge holder already has a beneficial interest in the property and is only receiving that to which he is entitled (*Re Margart Pty Ltd, Hamilton v Westpac Banking Corp* [1985] BCLC 314).
b. Dealings with a company's property by its receiver (*Sowman v David Samuel Trust Ltd* [1978] 1 All ER 616).
c. An unconditional contract for the sale of property which was entered into before the petition was presented (although any variation in its terms, or waiving or confirming a conditional contract will probably be a disposition, *Re French's (Wine Bar) Ltd* [1987] BCLC 499).
d. Spending money defending the winding up petition (*Re Crossmore Electrical and Civil Engineering Ltd*, above).
e. Spend money in relation to litigation where the company is solvent (here, the litigation related to a proposed management buy-out) (*Re a Company (No 005685 of 1988), ex parte Schwarcz* [1989] BCLC 424).

If the court decides that the disposition is **void**, it will order the property to be returned and/or the director or other person making the disposition (e.g. the company's bank) to make good any loss to the company. The property will then form part of the company's assets again, ready for realisation and distribution by the liquidator. If the court **validates** a disposition, it will make an order to that effect (the standard form validating order can be found at para 7 CPR PD 49B).

7678

MEMO POINTS If the company has made a payment to discharge a **secured debt**, and this is declared void, the creditor's security will be resurrected.

2. Transfers of shares and changes in shareholders' status

7683 The statutory provision preventing dispositions of the company's property (¶7674+) also applies to any transfers of shares and changes in shareholders' status which occur after the petition is presented, rendering them **void** unless the court orders otherwise (s 127 IA 1986). Unlike the dispositions of property, this **applies** after the winding up order has been made as well. The court will not usually allow a transfer of shares to go ahead, except in exceptional circumstances. If the transfer is not allowed to be registered, the transferee will be in the position of any other transferee whose name has not yet been entered in the register (¶2032/mp), so he may (through the transferor) assert his right to any payment made in respect of the shares, and can be held liable by the transferor for any calls. If the transfer is validated, the transferee becomes a present member and the transferor a past member for the purposes of deciding who is a contributory (*Re National Bank of Wales, Taylor, Phillips and Rickards' Cases* [1897] 1 Ch 298).

3. Provisional liquidators

7686 A provisional liquidator is **usually appointed** after the petition has been presented if there is a danger of the company's assets being dissipated, or where the company's affairs need to be investigated as soon as possible. This prevents those involved in running the company from taking advantage of the time delay between the presentation of the petition and the hearing. The appointment of a provisional liquidator effectively prevents the company from dealing with its assets or continuing its business, and therefore an appointment will only be made in appropriate circumstances. If other measures would be adequate to preserve the status quo, they should be used instead (*Constantinidis v JGL Trading Pty* [1995] 17 ACSR 625).

Appointment

7687 A provisional liquidator is one **appointed** by the court **during** the period after presentation of the petition but before the winding up order has been made (s 135(1) IA 1986). This serious step is usually only taken where there is a need to protect creditors or the public.

> EXAMPLE
> 1. The assets were in danger of being dissipated (*Re Marseilles Extension Railway and Land Co* (1867) LR 4 Eq 692).
> 2. The company was clearly insolvent (*Re Railway Finance Co Ltd* (1886) 35 Beav 473).
> 3. Appropriate regulatory authorities intended to investigate the company's affairs (*Re Forum Underwriting Ltd* [2002] All ER (D) 106 (Dec)).
> 4. The company's business was in breach of the Fair Trading Act 1973 and was an unlawful lottery. It was therefore a virtual certainty that a winding up order would be made at the petition hearing. The company's assets needed to be protected and further unlawful activities prevented (*Re Treasure Traders Corporation Ltd* [2005] EWHC 2774 (Ch)).

Although the appointment of a provisional liquidator is not intended to pre-empt the winding up order, the **court will look for** a good case for the company being wound up because of the potentially detrimental effects on the company if the appointment is made (*Re Highfield Commodities Ltd* [1984] 3 All ER 884; *Re Forrester & Lamego Ltd* [1997] 2 BCLC 155). Instead of appointing a provisional liquidator, the court may accept appropriate undertakings from the company and the individuals who run it, for example, from a managing director/shareholder not to carry out any or certain business before the petition hearing (*Re Forrester & Lamego Ltd*, above).

Application

7688 The application for the appointment of a provisional liquidator can be **made by** (r 4.25(1) IR 1986):
– the petitioner;
– a creditor;
– a contributory;
– the company;
– the secretary of state;

– a temporary administrator (i.e. one appointed under reg 38 EC Insolvency Reg);
– a member state liquidator appointed in main proceedings under the EC Insolvency Regulation; or
– any person who would be able to present a winding up petition against the company under any legislation.

The application should follow the **procedure** for applications in insolvency proceedings explained at ¶7380+. The company should be made respondent to the application, although it may be made without notice in urgent cases (in which case, the applicant will usually be required to give an undertaking to the court to abide by any order for damages it may make in the company's favour, known as a "cross-undertaking in damages").

The application must be **supported by** an affidavit stating (r 4.25(2) IR 1986):
a. the grounds on which the provisional liquidator should be appointed;
b. if the proposed provisional liquidator is not the official receiver, confirmation that he has consented to act and is qualified to do so (to the best of the applicant's belief);
c. whether or not the official receiver has been informed and supplied with a copy of the application;
d. whether the applicant is aware of a liquidator, administrator or administrative receiver acting in relation to the company, or that it is subject to a proposed or actual CVA; and
e. the applicant's estimate of the value of assets over which the provisional liquidator is to be appointed.

Copies of the application and supporting affidavit must be sent to the official receiver in sufficient time to enable him to attend the hearing, at which he can make any appropriate representations (r 4.25(3) IR 1986).

MEMO POINTS A **witness statement** can be used as an alternative to an affidavit (r 7.57(5), (7) IR 1986). The Insolvency Service has proposed that affidavits are replaced by witness statements (see ¶7637). This change is likely to be implemented on 1 October 2008.

Court order

The court can make an order for the appointment of a provisional liquidator on whatever terms it thinks fit (r 4.25(4) IR 1986). The order will be in Form 4.15, specifying the functions he is to undertake in relation to the company's affairs (r 4.26(1) IR 1986). **Notice** of the appointment must be given by the court to the official receiver (and to the provisional liquidator, if he is not the official receiver) on Form 4.14A (r 4.25A IR 1986).

7689

The court usually **appoints** the official receiver as provisional liquidator, facilitating a smooth transition into winding up (if an order is made), since the official receiver is commonly the initial liquidator until another appointment is made (s 135(2) IA 1986). Another qualified insolvency practitioner can be appointed instead (ss 135(2), 230(4), 388 IA 1986), for example where:
– the winding up petition is combined with an application for relief from unfair prejudice;
– the winding up petition is by an administrator, who can become the provisional liquidator; or
– the company's assets are outside of the jurisdiction.

If the official receiver is to be appointed, the applicant must **deposit** a sum specified by the court to cover the official receiver's remuneration and expenses before the order is issued (r 4.27(1) IR 1986). If this sum is inadequate, the court can order the applicant to deposit more. The deposit must be paid to the official receiver within 2 clear days of the court's order, otherwise the order can be discharged (r 4.27(2) IR 1986). If a winding up order is subsequently made, the provisional liquidator is paid out of the company's assets (and the deposit, to the extent that the assets are insufficient). If there are sufficient assets, the deposit will be refunded to the applicant out of the company's assets according to the order of priority (r 4.27(3) IR 1986; ¶7958).

As soon as the order is made, the **court will send** three sealed copies to the person appointed (and one to the official receiver if he is not appointed), who will send a copy to each of (r 4.26(3) IR 1986):
– the company, or the company's liquidator if it is already in voluntary liquidation; and
– Companies House, with Form 4.15A.

If an administrative receiver is acting in relation to the company, the court will also send a copy to him (r 4.26(2) IR 1986).

Consequences of appointment

7690 The appointment of a provisional liquidator has various effects which differ from the usual course of events between the presentation of a winding up petition and the hearing. The **directors** cannot continue to exercise most of their powers in terms of managing the company (Re Mawcon Ltd [1969] 1 All ER 188). However, they are able to instruct lawyers in matters connected with the insolvency proceedings with which the provisional liquidator will not deal, such as opposing the petition and appealing against an order (Re National Employers Mutual General Insurance Association Ltd (in liquidation) [1995] 1 BCLC 232). The powers and authority of any other **agents** of the company also cease once the agent has received notification of the provisional liquidator's appointment (Pacific and General Insurance Co Ltd v Hazell [1997] BCC 400).

Legal actions and proceedings cannot be commenced or continued against the company without leave of the court, and will be subject to any conditions which the court may impose, as if a winding up order had been made (s 130(2) IA 1986, see ¶7757). The rules relating to **enforcement** once an order has been made (¶7903+) also apply where a provisional liquidator is appointed.

MEMO POINTS Any **defects in** a provisional liquidator's **appointment or qualification** will not invalidate his acts as liquidator (s 232 IA 1986).

Duties and powers

7691 Once in office, it is the provisional liquidator's duty to take control of the company's **assets** and any chose in action (such as a right to collect debts) to which the company is or appears to be entitled (s 144 IA 1986).

Although a provisional liquidator's powers and responsibilities are not prescribed by legislation or the Rules, the court will usually **limit his powers** to taking possession of and protecting the assets, in accordance with his purpose of preserving the position of the creditors (s 135(5) IA 1986). This power includes closing offices and dismissing staff, if this is necessary to preserve assets (Re Union Accident Insurance Co Ltd [1972] 1 All ER 1105). The court may, if appropriate, grant the provisional liquidator the power to dispose of assets (Re Goodwill Merchant Financial Services Ltd [2001] 1 BCLC 259). A provisional liquidator also has the power to apply to court for the appointment of a special manager, where it would be in the interests of the creditors, contributories or shareholders to have another person managing the company's business or property, or where it is required due to the nature of the business or property (¶8375+).

In **exercising** whatever **powers** are granted to him, the provisional liquidator must act in the interests of the company and the creditors. His powers and liabilities also include those of other insolvency practitioners, to:
– require the supply of public utilities to the company (s 233 IA 1986); and
– obtain information about the company (¶8169+).

MEMO POINTS 1. A provisional liquidator is probably not subject to the obligations relating to how liquidators **deal with the company's money or records**, etc (SI 1994/2507; ¶8232+), as these apply where the company is "being wound up" (which applies from the order, Re Christonette International Ltd [1982] 3 All ER 225), not "in the course of winding up" (which would apply from the petition being presented).
2. As with a liquidator, **liens** over the company's books, records and papers are not generally enforceable against a provisional liquidator, unless they are over title documents (¶8017).

Termination

7692 The provisional liquidator's appointment can be terminated **by** an order of the court on application by the provisional liquidator, or by any of the persons entitled to apply for his appointment (s 172(2) IA 1986; r 4.31 IR 1986; ¶7688 above). This usually occurs when the petition is dismissed or the winding up order made, although there is no restriction on when the appointment can be terminated. The provisional liquidator must vacate his office if he ceases to be qualified to act (s 172(5) IA 1986).

The court will determine when the provisional liquidator's **release** is effective, following an application by him (s 174(5) IA 1986). From that time on, he is released from liability for his acts and omissions during office, except that he can still be sued for misfeasance (s 174(6) IA 1986; ¶7457+).

4. Effect of petition on other proceedings

It may be that a company subject to a winding up petition is also subject to other court proceedings, for example a breach of contract claim or enforcement action. Since such disputes can often be resolved during the course of the winding up (for example, the liquidator has the power to settle claims against the company, ¶8216), the **court** has the **power** to stay or restrain proceedings (s 126 IA 1986). This has the **effect** of suspending the action against the company until a further application is made to lift the stay. This can be used in respect of proceedings or actions commenced before or after the petition has been presented; once the winding up order has been made, separate rules apply to commencing proceedings against the company (¶7757).

7697

Applications to stay or restrain proceedings

The application can be **made by**:
- the company;
- any creditor; or
- any contributory,

at any **time** between the presentation of the petition and a winding up order being made. The application should be **made to**:

a. the High Court or Court of Appeal for proceedings in those courts (where the proceedings can be stayed); or

b. the court with jurisdiction to wind the company up for any other action or proceeding against the company (where the proceedings or action can be restrained).

The application **procedure** is described at ¶7380+.

The phrase "**action or proceeding**" is widely construed to include:
- civil claims;
- executions and sales of property subject to an order made before presentation of the petition;
- distress actions; and
- criminal proceedings.

7698

> MEMO POINTS 1. If the company is in **voluntary liquidation**, an application can be made to stay existing litigation once the resolution to wind up has been passed. In such a case, the **application** can be **made by** the liquidator or any contributory asking the court to exercise its power to stay the proceedings (s 112 IA 1986; ¶8523+).
> 2. Actions or proceedings against **unregistered companies** subject to a winding up petition can also be stayed or restrained, as can those against **companies formed under** s 680 CA 1985 (ss 126(2), 227 IA 1986). The equivalent of s 680 CA 1985 under the new Companies Act (s 1040 CA 2006) is expected to come into force by 1 October 2009.

The **court will consider** all the circumstances and base its decision as to whether to stay or restrain the non-insolvency proceedings on what would be fair in each particular case. Often, if the action concerns a disputed debt, it is better for all concerned for the action to proceed so the issue can be resolved (*Cook v "X" Chair Patents Co Ltd* [1959] 3 All ER 906).

7699

> MEMO POINTS If the proceedings are **inter-connected**, or the company is involved in proceedings **against another party** (e.g. in a group action as claimants or defendants), the court will usually allow the proceedings to continue because of the risk of prejudice to the other parties involved in allowing a stay (*Re Rio Grande Do Sul SS Co* (1877) 5 Ch D 282; *New Cap Reinsurance Corp Ltd v HIH Casualty & General Insurance Ltd* [2002] 2 BCLC 228).

Enforcement proceedings

In the case of enforcement proceedings, the court's decision depends on the type of remedy pursued by the creditor. **Execution**, for example, will usually be restrained so that creditors

7700

can be treated equally in the distribution of the company's assets (*Bowkett v Fullers United Electric Works Ltd* [1923] 1 KB 160). On the other hand, if an action to **distrain goods** was commenced before the petition was presented, the court will not usually restrain it (*Re Bellaglade Ltd* [1977] 1 All ER 319 (landlord's distress); *Re Memco Engineering Ltd* [1985] 3 All ER 267 (Crown's statutory right of distress)). Similarly, **secured creditors** will not be denied their right of enforcement. See ¶7903+ for the liquidator's ability to deal with assets which are affected by enforcement proceedings once a winding up order has been made.

5. Striking out the petition

Grounds

7705 If a petition is an **abuse** of the **process of the court**, it can be struck out on the application of the company before the hearing (see ¶7641 for restraining such a petition before it is presented). The court has a wide discretion to take such action, with case law identifying particular areas in which petitions have been struck out.

7706 If there is a genuine and substantial **dispute over the debt** which forms the basis of the petition, the court will usually strike the petition out because it will not tolerate the use of liquidation as a form of debt collection. Such a matter should be resolved in separate proceedings. However, the court will look at all of the circumstances and exercise its discretion accordingly. For example, it can decide whether or not the dispute is substantial (*Re UK (Aid) Ltd, GlaxoSmithKline Export Ltd v UK (Aid) Ltd* [2003] 2 BCLC 351), or that the petition should proceed despite the dispute because it would be unfair to dismiss it in the circumstances (*Alipour v Ary, Re a Company (No 002180 of 1996)* [1997] 1 BCLC 557). Further, if the debtor company's counterclaim matches or exceeds the amount of the debt in the petition or statutory demand, the petition will not be allowed to proceed (*Re a Company (No 004298 of 2006)* [2006] All ER (D) 277 (Jun), in which a petition was restrained from presentation but the same principle applies to striking out).

EXAMPLE
1. Petition struck out
Where the petition was an abuse of process, even if:
– it had already been advertised and there may be other creditors with undisputed debts who wish to appear at the petition hearing (those creditors may present a petition against the company themselves) (*Re a Company (No 010656 of 1990)* [1991] BCLC 464); or
– the company is insolvent (*Mann v Goldstein* [1968] 2 All ER 769).

2. Petition not struck out
a. The undisputed part of the debt is worth more than £750 (*Re Pendigo Ltd* [1996] 2 BCLC 64).
b. The petitioner can show that he has an arguable case and striking out the petition will deprive him of a remedy (*Re Claybridge Shipping Co SA (1981)* [1997] 1 BCLC 572, where the company was foreign but only had assets in the UK, which were likely to be dissipated if the petition was not allowed to proceed).
c. A contributory's petition was allowed to proceed, despite a dispute as to his eligibility to present it, because dismissing it would leave him without a remedy, whereas the company could argue its case at the petition hearing (*Alipour v Ary*, above).

Petitions have also been struck out because they were **unsatisfactory** in some way.

EXAMPLE
3. Petition struck out
a. It contained a misrepresentation (*Re a Company* [1974] 1 All ER 256).
b. It was presented by someone who did not meet the relevant conditions, e.g. a contributory whose name should have been but was not on the register of shareholders.
c. The petitioner had commenced other, inconsistent, proceedings, and so the petition was pointless (*Re a Company (No 003028 of 1987)* [1988] BCLC 282).
d. The petition was bound to fail (*Re a Company (No 005685 of 1988), ex parte Schwarcz (No 2)* [1989] BCLC 427).
e. The petition was based upon a dishonoured cheque, which had been re-presented (because the re-presentation of a cheque amounts to conditional payment and suspends the petitioner's right to sue/wind up) (*Re a Company (No 001259 of 1991), ex parte Medialite Ltd* [1991] BCLC 594).

f. The petitioner's conduct was intended to put undue pressure on the company, e.g. where the petition was faxed to the company's bankers on the same day as it was presented (*Re a Company (No 013925 of 1991), ex parte Roussell* [1992] BCLC 562), or where the petitioner telephoned other creditors to tell them about the petition both before and after presentation (*Re Doreen Boards Ltd* [1996] 1 BCLC 501). However, in some circumstances, such as where there is no dispute about the debt and the company is insolvent, notifying other parties of the petition may not constitute undue pressure (*SN Group plc v Barclays Bank plc* [1993] BCC 506).

g. The petition was misleading in that it failed to disclose a dispute about the amount of the debt, and stated that there was no evidence (*Re MCI WorldCom Ltd* [2003] 1 BCLC 330).

4. Petition not struck out
The petition contained incorrect information, which was not material to it (*Re IT Parts Ltd* [2005] All ER (D) 122 (Dec)).

If a **petition** was **not brought in good faith**, the court may strike it out, although this is relatively rare.

EXAMPLE
5. Petition struck out
The petition was presented to gain a private advantage (*Re a Company* [1983] BCLC 492).

6. Petition not struck out
a. The petition was presented to obtain payment of debt, but pursued with personal hostility and/or an ulterior motive (*Re a Company (No 006273 of 1992)* [1993] BCLC 131).
b. The petitioner had obtained judgment for a sum which was being paid off in instalments. An instalment cheque was not honoured, and the petitioner presented a winding up petition. However, when the instalment was paid, the petitioner refused to withdraw petition before costs in the previous proceedings were agreed (*Re a Company (No 004601 of 1997)* [1998] 2 BCLC 111).

Procedure

The **application** to strike the petition out should be **made** as soon as possible after presentation, so that the company may also obtain an injunction restraining its advertisement. The **procedure** for applying to strike out follows that for other insolvency applications, explained at ¶7380+.

7708

If an order striking the petition out is made for abuse of process, the court may well order the petitioner to pay the company's **costs** on the indemnity basis, so that the company is reimbursed for the real costs it incurred during the proceedings (*Re a Company (No 002507 of 2003)* [2003] 2 BCLC 346). A solicitor or barrister may be ordered to pay "wasted costs" personally in cases of wrongdoing (s 51 Supreme Court Act 1981). This is to discourage petitioners and their legal advisers from abusing the winding up procedure, and to demonstrate the court's strong disapproval by punishing those who do.

MEMO POINTS The company may also have grounds for suing the petitioner for the tort of **malicious presentation of a petition**. Such an action should be brought as a separate civil action, not within the insolvency proceedings (*Partizan Ltd v O J Kilkenny & Co Ltd* [1998] 1 BCLC 157).

C. The petition hearing

The **venue** of the petition hearing, i.e. its date, time and place, will be stated on the petition returned by the court. The petition will be **heard by** the registrar or district judge in the first instance, who may refer appropriate cases to a judge. The hearing will be **attended by** the petitioner and the company, who are entitled to be heard. If other persons wish to appear, they must notify the petitioner in advance (¶7653+).

7718

MEMO POINTS A **provisional liquidator** is not usually entitled to be heard at the petition hearing (*Re General International Agency Co Ltd* (1865) 55 ER 1065).

1. Opposition

7719 Winding up petitions can be opposed on various **grounds** by the different **parties** involved. The court will give weight to any opposing arguments depending upon the party and circumstances in question.

Opposing party	Common grounds for opposition	Comments	Reference
Company	Dispute over debt on which petition is based	Company will usually apply to have petition struck out	¶7705+; *Re James Millward & Co Ltd* [1940] 1 All ER 347
	Company has a cross-claim that: – is genuine/substantial – exceeds petitioner's debt – company has not been able to litigate on	Court will usually dismiss petition	*Re Bayoil SA, Seawind Tankers Corpn v Bayoil SA* [1999] 1 All ER 374
Creditor	Often argue against winding up if would get better realisation of debt via another route, e.g. CVA, administration or allowing company to trade out of difficulties	Court will usually attach great weight to views of majority of creditors[1], although this is not the deciding factor	*Re P & J Macrae Ltd* [1961] 1 All ER 302; *Re Southard & Co Ltd* [1979] 3 All ER 556
Secured creditor[2]	As creditor, above	Same weight usually attached to views regarding unsecured portion of debt as to unsecured creditors	-
	Oppose petition where his security (and therefore priority over unsecured creditors on distribution of the company's assets) is at risk	If petitioner's argument against the security appears substantial, less weight will be given to opposition of secured creditors whose security is attacked	-
Contributory	Often opposes petition to protect investment, hoping company can trade out of difficulties or agree CVA	Court will attach less weight to contributories' views than those of unsecured creditors. Contributory must establish there will be assets to distribute to him in liquidation. Company does not have to oppose petition as well	*Re Camburn Petroleum Products Ltd* [1979] 3 All ER 297; *Re Rodencroft Ltd*, *Re WG Birch Developments Ltd*, *Re H-M Birch Ltd* [2004] 3 All ER 56

Note:
1. Where the company is **already in voluntary liquidation** and the majority of creditors wants this to continue, the minority must establish why the winding up order should be made. On the other hand, if the company is **not already in voluntary liquidation** and the majority does not want the order to be made, it must show the court why an order should not be made (*Re Television Parlour plc* (1987) 4 BCC 95).
2. If security does not cover whole debt, **secured creditor** is unsecured for shortfall and can be heard.

2. Court's powers

7721 The court will hear and consider the arguments of the petitioner, company and any other person who has given notice of his appearance (or been given leave to appear), as well as examining the evidence before it. On hearing the petition, it has the power to (s 125(1) IA 1986):
– **dismiss** the petition;
– **adjourn** the hearing (conditionally or unconditionally);

- make an **interim order**; or
- make any **other order** it thinks fit.

Adjournments are common, for example to allow the company to raise money or restructure its business, or to allow the parties to gather evidence. When allowing an adjournment, the court may impose costs conditions on the parties (*Re a Company (No 005448 of 1996), Re a Company (No 005449 of 1996), Re Commercial Guarantee Ltd* [1998] 1 BCLC 98). The court will not, however, permit repeated or excessively long adjournments (*Re Boston Timber Fabrications Ltd* [1984] BCLC 328).

The court has a complete **discretion** as to whether to make a winding up order (*Re Southard & Co Ltd* [1979] 3 All ER 556), although there are a number of **principles** it will follow when exercising this discretion:
a. if the **debt is unpaid** and the **company is insolvent**, the petitioning creditor is entitled to a winding up order (unless there are very strong grounds to persuade the court otherwise) (*Re Camburn Petroleum Products Ltd* [1979] 3 All ER 297);
b. if the petition is based on the "**just and equitable**" ground, the court will exercise its discretion on the merits of the case;
c. the court will take account of the **public interest** and **commercial morality**, for example, it can order that the company's affairs be investigated if there is strong evidence that this is necessary, despite opposition from the company's creditors (*Re E Bishop & Sons Ltd* [1900] 2 Ch 254);
d. if the **company has no assets**, the court must decide whether it is just and equitable to make a winding up order (e.g. to allow the company's affairs to be investigated, *Bell Group Finance (Pty) Ltd (in liquidation) v Bell Group (UK) Holdings Ltd* [1996] 1 BCLC 304); and
e. it can consider the **wishes of creditors or contributories**, if these are substantiated by evidence, and can direct that meetings of creditors or contributories be held to ascertain those wishes, with directions as to their conduct (s 195(1) IA 1986). However, the court is not obliged to do so, and can come to its own conclusions even if these are opposed by the majority at a meeting (*Re Bank of Credit and Commerce International SA* [1993] BCLC 1490). Examples of this are where:
- the majority view is clearly wrong (*Re Vuma Ltd* [1960] 3 All ER 629);
- one person has a controlling influence (*Re Medical Battery Co* [1894] 1 Ch 444); or
- the opposing creditor was connected with the company (e.g. a contributory or director), the court would not give as much weight to his view as to those of others (*Re Lummus Agricultural Services Ltd* [2001] 1 BCLC 137).

7722

3. Costs

The **court** has an absolute **discretion** as to what orders it makes for payment of the parties' costs in the proceedings. The usual course is summarised in the table below, with pertinent examples of where the court has not followed these rules highlighted in the notes to the table.

7723

Outcome of hearing	General rule		Reference
	Costs of	Paid	
Winding up order made[1]	Petitioner	Out of company's assets	r 4.218 IR 1986
	Company		
	Creditors (as group)		
	Contributories (as group)		
	Second petitioner	Out of company's assets, but only up to time he learned of earlier petition	*Re Sheringham Development Co Ltd* [1893] WN 5
	Original petitioner who has been substituted	Out of company's assets, but only costs relating to obtaining order (e.g. presenting/advertising), not costs of preparing or appearing	*Re Esal (Commodities) Ltd* [1985] BCLC 450
	Other party appearing	By himself	*Re Humber Ironworks Co* (1866) LR 2 Eq 15

Outcome of hearing	General rule		Reference
	Costs of	Paid	
Petition dismissed [2, 3]	Company	By petitioner	*Re Cannon Screen Entertainment Ltd* [1989] BCLC 660
	Creditors (as group)		
	Contributories (as group)		

Note:
1. Court **deviated from general rules** when winding up **order made** where:
– creditors and contributories appearing used same solicitors as petitioner, company or each other: not entitled to separate costs (*Re Brighton Marine Palace and Pier Co Ltd* (1897) 41 Sol Jo 257; *Re Silberhütte Supply Co Ltd* [1910] WN 81);
– even if creditor's petition is successful, he may have to pay some of his own costs, for example where company was already in voluntary liquidation and petitioner included irrelevant matters in petition for tactical reasons (*Re A & N Thermo Products Ltd* [1963] 3 All ER 721); and
– on successful contributory's petition, opposing contributories may be ordered to pay costs, so that successful contributory does not have to do so (indirectly, by costs coming out of assets, reducing amount available to contributories on distribution).
2. Common situations in which the court is likely to **deviate from general rules** when petition has been **dismissed** are where:
– judgment/undisputed creditor's petition is dismissed because of majority opposition, he will not usually be ordered to pay costs, unless petition was unreasonable (*Re Sklan Ltd* [1961] 2 All ER 680);
– company has paid petitioner's debt without provision as to costs, court will usually order company to pay costs (*Re Shusella Ltd* [1983] BCLC 505). However, if petitioner has not complied with Rules (e.g. not advertised the petition) he will not receive order for his costs, and should therefore either obtain payment of debt plus costs, or advertise petition;
– petition is based on default judgment (i.e. one awarded because company did not respond to court action) which is then set aside, company can still be ordered to pay petitioner's costs if petition is dismissed provided petitioner was not at fault (*Re Lanaghan Bros Ltd* [1977] 1 All ER 265); and
– where the court disapproves of the company's behaviour towards the petitioner, company can be ordered to pay his costs to encourage it to comply with its obligations in future (*Re a Company* [1986] BCLC 261).
3. If **petition is withdrawn**, petitioner will have to pay one set of costs to those supporting and one to those opposing the petition (*Re British Electric Street Tramways* [1903] 1 Ch 725).

MEMO POINTS   On an **unsuccessful petition** by the **secretary of state** on the ground of public interest, the court will not usually order him to pay costs if the petition was properly presented. However, he must continually and objectively review the situation, and if he goes ahead with an inappropriate petition, he may be ordered to pay costs from the date of the relevant change of circumstances (*Re Xyllyx plc (No 2)* [1992] BCLC 378).

7724 The company usually has to meet the remuneration and fees of a **provisional liquidator** or **special manager**, even where the petition is dismissed, although the court has a discretion to order otherwise (*Re Secure and Provide plc* [1992] BCC 405).

Assessment

7725 Costs are usually assessed on the **standard basis**, which means that the party who is awarded costs will not be reimbursed for all he has spent on the application, but he will receive what the court sees as reasonable. For example, the party will have paid his solicitor a certain rate per hour, but the court is unlikely to order costs at that rate, rather it will refer to standard tables of reasonable rates for the region, which are available on the HM Courts Service website. Therefore, there can be a significant discrepancy between the costs awarded by the court and the costs actually incurred by the party (which he is still liable to pay to his legal team). Solicitors must advise their clients about costs when they first accept instructions and at regular intervals throughout the case.

The court can award costs on the **indemnity basis**, by which the actual costs incurred are ordered to be paid. It is, however, very difficult to persuade the court that the indemnity basis should be applied (see for example *Re Realstar Ltd* [2007] All ER (D) 171 (Aug)).

For more on costs in litigation, see ¶7156.

Payment

7726 The costs are **usually paid out of** the company's assets, and rank above creditors in the order of priority (¶7958), although the court has the power to make a different order.

The court can make a direct order for costs against a **third party**, where appropriate in the light of his conduct or the circumstances (*Aiden Shipping Co Ltd v Interbulk Ltd, The Vimeira* [1986] 2 All ER 409; r 48.2 CPR). For example, such orders have been made against:
– directors of the company (*Re Aurum Marketing Ltd* [2000] 2 BCLC 645);

– a holding company which funded a subsidiary's opposition to a petition (*Stocznia Gdanska SA v Latreefers Inc (No 2)* [2001] 2 BCLC 116); and
– an associated company which benefited from the company's business because of the way in which the directors ran the company (*Re Brackland Magazines Ltd* [1994] 1 BCLC 190).

How and whether the court exercises its discretion in this way depends entirely on all the circumstances of the case in question. A director who mounts opposition to a petition through the company will not be personally liable for costs if he genuinely believes that the company has a defence and it is in its best interests to oppose the petition, unless there are other reasons to make such an order (*Re Northwest Holdings plc, Secretary of State for Trade and Industry v Backhouse* [2001] 1 BCLC 468). **Public interest petitions** brought by the secretary of state are more likely to involve this sort of order because, amongst other things, the reputation of the individuals involved in the company is often at stake and so they are likely to fund opposition to the petition themselves.

MEMO POINTS 1. Alternatively, the court may order that the **order of priority is altered** and the costs are deferred to payment of the unsecured creditors, known as a "Bathampton order" after the authoritative case (*Re Bathampton Properties Ltd* [1976] 3 All ER 200). This type of order would also be appropriate in cases where one of the parties is at fault in some way, but is less common now that courts can make orders against third parties, since costs deferred to payment to the creditors are less likely to be paid (simply because the pool of assets is not big enough) and, if they are paid, the assets available to contributories are further reduced.
2. The court can also order **solicitors and barristers** to pay "wasted costs" personally, where justified in the circumstances (s 51 Supreme Court Act 1981; *Re Merc Property Ltd* [1999] 2 BCLC 286).

4. The winding up order

7729 Once the order has been made, the court notifies the official receiver (r 4.20(1) IR 1986) and an individual official receiver is assigned to the case. The order must be settled (i.e. drawn up) by the court in **Form** 4.11. The **parties** to the proceedings must leave all documents needed to draw up the order at court (effectively, counsel's papers) no later than the business day after the petition hearing (r 4.20(2) IR 1986). It is not usually necessary for any of the parties to attend court to settle the order, although an appointment to do so can be made by the court (r 4.20(3) IR 1986).

Once settled, the **court** will **send** three sealed copies of the order to the official receiver (r 4.21 IR 1986), who will then:
– serve a sealed copy on the company;
– forward a copy to Companies House; and
– advertise the order in the *Gazette* and in another newspaper of his choice.

Mistakes and defects

7730 The court has the power to **rescind or vary** a winding up order (r 7.47 IR 1986), even if it has already been settled (*Re Calmex Ltd* [1989] 1 All ER 485). The court's power can be used, for example, to correct a mistake in the winding up order (*Re Brian Sheridan Cars Ltd* [1996] 1 BCLC 327).

7731 An **application** for **rescission** of a winding up order must be made by (para 7 CPR Insolvency PD):
– a creditor;
– a contributory; or
– the company jointly with a creditor or contributory,
within 7 clear days of the order being made (r 7.47(4) IR 1986). This **time limit** can be extended if appropriate. The application does not have to be in a particular **form**, but must be supported by written **evidence**, including evidence of the assets and liabilities of the company (para 7 CPR Insolvency PD). However, if the winding up order was not opposed, a statement of the circumstances can be submitted by the applicant's legal adviser instead. **Notice** of the application must be given to the official receiver; any person intending to appear at the hearing must notify the applicant (see ¶7653+).

> **EXAMPLE**
> **Rescission granted**:
> 1. To allow proposals for a voluntary arrangement to be put to the creditors (*Re Dollar Land (Feltham) Ltd* [1995] 2 BCLC 370).
> 2. The company was wound up by mistake (the time limit for applying for rescission was extended in this case) (*Re Calmex Ltd* [1989] 1 All ER 485).
> 3. The company knew nothing of the winding up proceedings because it had moved but its registered office had accidentally not been changed (*Re Virgo Systems Ltd* [1990] BCLC 34).
> 4. The district judge had refused to grant an adjournment of the petition to allow the company time to pay the petitioner, but the petitioner's debt and costs were later paid by the company out of funds loaned to it by its owner (*HM Customs & Excise v Tony Newcombe Ltd* [2003] EWHC 2083 (Ch)).

MEMO POINTS If the **application** is **unsuccessful**, the **costs** of the petitioning creditor, supporting creditors and official receiver are usually ordered to be paid by the creditor/contributory who made or joined the application (so that they are not taken out of the company's assets).

7732 If it is discovered that the **petition contained errors** after the winding up order has been made, an application for leave to amend it must be made to the court manager in the High Court (or the district judge in the county court). The order can be altered if the error does not affect it, for example a minor mistake in the company's name (provided this does not mean that the company subject to the order can be confused with another). On the other hand, a more substantial mistake may result in the order being rescinded, for example if the registered office was incorrect, a director or shareholder of the company will probably be able to claim that he was not aware of the petition because it was not correctly served.

5. Appeals

7734 The **court** to which the appellant appeals depends upon where the order was made in the first place (see ¶7393).

The appeal can be **made by** any party who appeared at the petition hearing, although others may also do so with leave of the court (*Re Fall Silkstone Colliery Co* (1876) 1 Ch D 38; *Re Securities Insurance Co* [1894] 2 Ch 410). If the company is the appellant, the appeal is conducted by the directors, not the liquidator. The application must be in the form of an ordinary application, following the usual procedure for civil appeals (¶7382+; Part 52 CPR).

While the **appeal process** is **under way**, the court will usually stay the advertisement of the winding up order, but not the winding up itself (*Re A & B C Chewing Gum Ltd* [1975] 1 All ER 1017).

If the company is the appellant, the directors conducting the appeal may be personally liable for **costs** if the appeal fails, so that the company's assets are not reduced (*Re Consolidated South Rand Mines Deep Ltd* [1909] 1 Ch 491; ¶7726). Therefore, the Court of Appeal may require security for costs to be provided at the beginning or during the appeal process (r 25.15 CPR; s 726(1) CA 1985).

MEMO POINTS s 726 CA 1985 is expected to be repealed by 1 October 2009. There will be no replacement provision in the **new Companies Act**. However, this will make no real difference because a court will still be able to order security for costs to be paid under the CPR.

6. Staying winding up proceedings

7736 At any time after the order has been made, the **court** has the **power** to stay the winding up proceedings (s 147 IA 1986). An **application** for a stay can be **made by**:
– the liquidator or official receiver;
– any creditor; or
– any contributory.

The **procedure** follows that for other applications in insolvency proceedings (¶7380+).

In exercising its discretion to use this power, the **court will look at** the commercial morality of granting a stay. For example, it will usually want to see appropriate proposals for satisfying all creditors as well as the liquidator's and shareholders' consent to the stay (*Re Lowston Ltd*

[1991] BCLC 570). On the other hand, if there is evidence of misfeasance or the need to investigate the company's conduct further, a stay will not be granted (*Re Telescriptor Syndicate Ltd* [1903] 2 Ch 174). If a stay is granted, the court can impose whatever **conditions** it sees fit, including imposing a time limit on the stay.

> MEMO POINTS Such an application can also be made by the liquidator or any creditor or contributory in a **voluntary liquidation** (s 112 IA 1986; ¶8523+).

D. Consequences of a winding up order

7746 A winding up order is **made in favour of** all creditors and contributories of the company, even though it was presented by one and may not have been supported by all (s 130(4) IA 1986). This means that, subject to the order of priorities in which the company's assets will be distributed, no creditor or contributory will be favoured over another. The order marks certain **changes in the company's status**, as well as that of the individuals involved with it, and affects dealings with the company's property. The management of the company is taken out of the hands of the directors and taken over by the official receiver or liquidator (¶8192+).

Commencement of winding up

7747 The order itself does not signify the date for the commencement of winding up, as this is retrospectively fixed at the date of the presentation of the petition (¶7672). Although the company cannot be said to be in liquidation until the order has been made, "relating back" to the date of presentation prevents companies from dissipating their assets before the official receiver or liquidator is appointed to safeguard and deal with those assets. This date is significant as regards the matters set out in the table.

Topic	¶¶
Liquidator's ability to deal with company's assets	¶7779+
Assets subject to enforcement proceedings	¶7903+
Challenging certain transactions: – Transactions at an undervalue – Preferences – Floating charges – Extortionate credit transactions	¶7811+ ¶7819+ ¶7836+ ¶7842+
Who is a contributory?	¶7863+
The costs that can be paid out of the company's assets as expenses of the winding up	¶7957+
Provable debts Calculating interest on debts	¶8005+ ¶8021+

> MEMO POINTS In a **voluntary liquidation**, the winding up commences when the resolution to wind up is passed (s 86 IA 1986).

Company

7748 A company subject to a winding up order remains a **legal entity** in its own right until dissolution. However, although the **property** and assets held by it when the winding up order is made remain vested in the company, it is deemed to hold that property on trust for the creditors to the extent of their debts and so is not beneficially entitled to it any more (*Re Anglo-Moravian Hungarian Junction Rly Co, ex parte Watkin* (1875) 1 Ch D 130; *Ayerst (Inspector of Taxes) v C & K (Construction) Ltd* [1975] 2 All ER 537).

> MEMO POINTS The court can order that a company's **property vests in the liquidator**, although this is not usually necessary (s 145(1) IA 1986).

7749 The winding up order takes precedence over any of the company's **articles** which are inconsistent with insolvency legislation. This particularly affects those articles dealing with the company's property, such as the right to inspect the company's books and records as well as other rights, like an article restricting the company's ability to make calls on shares (*Newton v Anglo-Australian Investment Co, Debenture-holders* [1895] AC 244; *Re Yorkshire Fibre Co* (1870) LR 9 Eq 650).

7750 The fact that an order has been made must be **publicised** by including a statement that the company is being wound up on all of the company's websites as well as any invoices, orders for goods, business letters and order forms in hard copy, electronic form or any other form, which include the company's name, and which are issued (s 188(1) IA 1986):
– by or on behalf of the company;
– by a liquidator; or
– by a receiver or manager of the company's property.

Failure to comply renders the officer of the company, liquidator, or any receiver or manager who knowingly and wilfully permitted the default liable to a fine (¶9935).

> MEMO POINTS The statement's inclusion on a company's websites and order forms became a requirement as of January 2007, following the implementation of amendments to the First Company Law Directive (by EC Directive 2003/58). The requirement applies to companies already in liquidation at that time as well as those entering liquidation subsequently.

7751 Usually, the **company's business** will be ended when the order is made. However, the liquidator can continue the business if it would be beneficial to the winding up and he has the requisite consent (¶7791+). Therefore, **contracts** which are still ongoing to which the company is a party are not automatically terminated when the order is made, and the company and other parties are still obliged to perform their obligations under them. However, this will depend on the terms of each contract. Many contracts include a clause to the effect that they will terminate if one party becomes insolvent. The liquidator can choose to carry out a contract on the company's behalf or to declare that he cannot do so, in which case third parties can treat the contract as having been breached by the company and claim damages (*Telsen Electric Co Ltd v J J Eastick & Sons* [1936] 3 All ER 266). It is possible for the third party to apply for an order for specific performance against the company. However, this is a difficult remedy to obtain as the applicant must show that damages would not be adequate, and so such cases are usually confined to contracts relating to the sale of land (*Re Coregrange Ltd* [1984] BCLC 453). A contract cannot be enforced against the liquidator personally unless he has adopted it. See ¶7914+ for the liquidator's powers to deal with contracts.

The commencement of the liquidation results in the end of the company's accounting period for **corporation tax** purposes and the beginning of a new one (s 12 ICTA 1988). Each successive period of 12 months is a separate accounting period, until the completion of the liquidation. Since the company also ceases to be the beneficial owner of its assets, any subsidiaries cease to be members of the same group for most corporation tax purposes, such as the surrender of group relief for losses (ss 402-413 ICTA 1988). However, for **capital gains** purposes, there is no chargeable disposal to the liquidator and the group relationship endures even where the court has made an order vesting the assets in the liquidator (ss 8, 170 TCGA 1992; s 145(1) IA 1986). For **VAT** purposes, the commencement of liquidation of a member of a VAT group may result in its removal from the group and re-registration in its own name. If the liquidation relates to the representative member of a VAT group, all members of the group will be automatically de-registered and each solvent member that continues to trade will be automatically re-registered. Insolvent members of the group that continue to trade can apply to be re-registered as well. Group VAT treatment may be allowed on a case by case basis, but the companies will have to act quickly to avoid de-registration.

Directors

7752 When a winding up order is made against a company, the directors' **powers to act** on the company's behalf cease and so they are no longer able to run the company, although they are able to appeal against the winding up order (*Re Mawcon Ltd* [1969] 1 All ER 188; *Re Union Accident*

Insurance Co Ltd [1972] 1 All ER 1105). Despite this, their **office** does not automatically terminate, and so a director wishing to step down must still resign in the usual way (*Madrid Bank Ltd v Bayley* (1866) LR 2 QB 37; ¶2912+). Their fiduciary duties to the company also survive the withdrawal of their power to act (*Condliffe and Hilton v Sheingold* [2007] EWCA Civ 1043).

Directors have **new duties** imposed on them when the order is made. They can also incur personal **liability** and/or may be disqualified because of their conduct leading up to the order.

Duty/liability specific to insolvency	¶¶
Duty to co-operate	¶8120+, ¶8169+
Liability to contribute to company's assets	¶7863+
Liability as a result of certain transactions being challenged	¶7808+
Liability as a result of disposing of company property after petition presented	¶7674+
Liability for company's obligations: – loans to directors – tort committed by company but authorised by or responsibility of director [1] – company's breach of insolvency legislation [2]	¶2804+
Fraudulent trading	¶7443+
Wrongful trading	¶7449+
Misfeasance	¶7457+
Disqualification	¶3000+
Criminal liabilities: – concealing/disposing of/falsifying company property/debts/books – fraud during/prior to winding up – misconduct during winding up – destruction/falsification of books – making omissions from any statement relating to company's affairs – making false representations to creditors – re-using company's name	¶7464 ¶7464 ¶7781 ¶8170 ¶8169 ¶8169 ¶264+
Note: 1. *Williams v Natural Life Health Foods Ltd* [1998] 1 BCLC 690. 2. s 432 IA 1986.	

Shareholders

7753 The effect of the petition on **transfers of shares** still operates once the winding up order has been made (¶7683).

Employees and agents

7754 When a winding up order is published, the company's employees' **contracts** are automatically terminated, giving rise to wrongful dismissal claims (*Re Oriental Bank Corpn, MacDowall's Case* (1886) 32 Ch D 366). However, if the liquidator wants to carry on the business of the company, he can waive the dismissals so that the contracts remain in force (*Re English Joint Stock Bank, ex parte Harding* (1867) LR 3 Eq 341). This waiver may be implied by the liquidator carrying on business and allowing the workers' employment to continue (*MacDowall's Case*, above). Employees' claims in relation to dismissal are summarised at ¶2986 (see *Employment Memo* for a full discussion). The principal **claims arising** when the company goes into liquidation will be for wrongful dismissal and redundancy. Such claims can be brought against a company in liquidation, and a successful claimant will have to prove in the liquidation for any damages awarded.

Employees who are **owed money by the company** are treated as preferential creditors for particular debts, and will be able to claim a certain amount as a "guaranteed debt" from the secretary of state (¶8045). In the absence of any special circumstances, they are otherwise treated as ordinary unsecured creditors.

> MEMO POINTS If the liquidator transfers all or part of the company's undertaking, **TUPE** may apply. The new TUPE regulations, which came into force on 6 April 2006, no longer contain an exception in relation to hive-downs (SI 2006/246). See ¶6415+ for hive-downs, ¶6422 for the application of TUPE in insolvency hive-downs and *Employment Memo* for the effect of TUPE generally.

7755 The **authority of any agents** to act on behalf of the company is terminated as soon as notice of the winding up order is received by them (*Pacific and General Insurance Co Ltd v Hazell* [1997] BCC 400). If a provisional liquidator was appointed before the order was made, notice of his appointment would have already terminated any agents' authorities.

Other legal proceedings

7757 Any **existing legal proceedings** against the company are automatically stayed when a winding up order is made, and can only continue with leave of the court (s 130(2) IA 1986). This is in contrast to the position after the petition has been presented, where the company, a creditor or contributory must apply to the court for a stay or restraint (¶7697+). However, the factors involved in the court's decision whether or not to grant leave to proceed are similar at both stages (see ¶7850+). Where **new proceedings** are contemplated, prior authorisation of the court should also be sought. In some cases, the court has given retrospective leave after proceedings were commenced against a company in liquidation, although this is entirely a matter for the court's discretion and therefore third parties should not rely on obtaining leave in this way (*Re Linkrealm Ltd* [1998] BCC 478, in which the court followed a bankruptcy authority rather than previous liquidation case law). The effect of the winding up order on **creditors enforcing their debts** is discussed at ¶7903+.

> MEMO POINTS If proceedings are **brought by the company**, the defendant may file a cross-claim for liquidated or unliquidated damages up to the value of the company's claim without leave of the court, so as to reduce or extinguish the claim; any further claim requires leave of the court in the usual way (*Langley Constructions (Brixham) Ltd v Wells* [1969] 2 All ER 46).

SECTION 2
Dealing with the company's assets

7772 The **liquidator's general functions** in a compulsory liquidation are to collect, realise and distribute the company's assets. Although these functions follow a chronological pattern for dealing with a particular asset, in reality the liquidator will be carrying out all of these functions simultaneously in most liquidations as there will be many types of asset to deal with, some of which will be more complicated than others. The liquidator does not, therefore, have to wait until he has realised all of the assets before he can start distributing them, rather he must make distributions as and when possible. This enables the creditors to minimise their losses and the amount of interest accruing on their debts during the liquidation.

Usually, these functions will be **undertaken by** a liquidator appointed for the purpose. At the same time, the official receiver undertakes his investigations into the conduct of the company leading up to the liquidation (¶8120+). However, in some cases, usually where a company has no or few assets, a liquidator will not be appointed and the official receiver will deal with the company's assets as well as carrying out his investigations into its conduct. In such cases, all references to the liquidator in the context of dealing with the assets should be read as referring to the "official receiver acting as liquidator". The roles played by the liquidator and official receiver in the conduct of the liquidation are discussed at ¶8192+.

7773 To enable him to deal with the company's assets efficiently, the liquidator is given a wide range of **powers**; a table of these powers can be found at ¶8216. Their exercise is **controlled** in a number of ways, principally:
– by the need for sanction from the court or liquidation committee before exercising certain powers;
– by the court; and
– by a number of duties imposed on the liquidator.

A discussion of the liquidator's powers, duties and liabilities can be found at ¶8215+.

7774 The company remains its own legal personality, separate from the liquidator, during liquidation and is still the legal owner of its assets, unless an order is made vesting them in the liquidator (s 145 IA 1986; this is not common). However, the **liquidator** is **entitled to deal with** the **assets** for the benefit of the liquidation, because the company has lost the beneficial ownership of them in favour of its creditors (*Ayerst (Inspector of Taxes) v C & K (Construction) Ltd* [1975] 2 All ER 537). The liquidator can deal with the assets owned by the company at the commencement of the liquidation, as well as those assets acquired by the company during its course, with some restrictions (¶7901+).

I. Collection

7779 The liquidator must take possession of the company's **assets**, including tangible property and intangible choses in action (i.e. legal rights, such as the right to claim a debt from a third party) to which the company is or appears to be entitled (s 144(1) IA 1986). Therefore, he will have to collect any money owed to the company by its debtors, including its shareholders and other contributories. On a practical level, collecting the assets will involve the liquidator taking steps such as:
– examining the statement of affairs (¶8127+);
– taking a detailed inventory of all assets on the company's premises;
– examining company documents and questioning its officers and employees as to ownership of the assets;
– labelling the assets and either physically removing them from the premises, or changing the locks to protect them for the benefit of the liquidation; and
– making sure that the assets are properly insured.

The liquidator must look in particular at ways of increasing the company's assets, for example by taking action to recover assets which have been dissipated in order to evade the liquidator's control, or by carrying on trading for a period of time.

MEMO POINTS In a **voluntary liquidation**, there is no statutory equivalent of the liquidator's duty to take possession of the company's assets, but since his purpose is to wind the company's affairs up and distribute its assets, he must take possession of them (ss 91, 100 IA 1986).

7781 Any **director** or other officer (past or present) who does any of the following in relation to the company's assets commits a **criminal offence** (s 208 IA 1986):
a. does not, to the best of his knowledge and belief, reveal all of the company's property to the liquidator, or inform him of how, when, to whom and for how much any of it was disposed of other than in the usual course of business;
b. does not deliver any part of the company's property and all books and papers in his custody or under his control to the liquidator, or in accordance with the liquidator's instructions, as required;
c. does not inform the liquidator as soon as is practicable that he believes that a creditor has proved for a debt which is false;
d. prevents any book or paper relating to the company's property or affairs from being produced after the commencement of the winding up; or
e. tries to account for any part of the company's property by inventing losses or expenses.
He will be deemed to have committed the offence if he did so at any creditors' meeting in the 12 months prior to the commencement of the liquidation.

A director or officer can **defend** prosecution for a. and b. if he can prove that he did not intend to defraud, and it is a defence to e. to prove that he did not intend to conceal the state of the company's affairs or defeat the law. If found **guilty** of any of these offences, the director or other officer is liable to imprisonment and/or a fine (¶9935).

A. Carrying on business

7791 The liquidator has the **power** to carry on the company's business for a period during the winding up, although it is not common since goodwill rapidly depletes once a company goes into liquidation. However, he may need to use this power, for example:
– to sell the business (or part of it) as a going concern;
– to complete a particular deal which will be beneficial to the company; or
– because he can achieve a better realisation of the assets over a period of time.

Due to the potential risk to creditors, he needs the **consent** of the court or the liquidation committee to do this (¶8218), which will only be given for a specified (and usually short) period of time (*Re Wreck Recovery and Salvage Co* [1874-80] All ER Rep 755). The court will usually grant permission if it is convinced that the liquidator genuinely and reasonably considers it necessary for the company's successful liquidation. The burden is on any person objecting to the proposed action to show that this is not the case (*Re Great Eastern Electric Co Ltd* [1941] 1 All ER 409). The court will not allow the business to be continued for the purposes of carrying out a financial reconstruction or in the hope that the company will make a profit (*Re Wreck Recovery and Salvage Co*, above; *Re Great Eastern Electric Co Ltd*, above).

7792 **Debts incurred** by the company continuing to trade usually qualify as expenses of the liquidation (and can therefore be paid in priority to other unsecured debts) (*Re S Davis & Co Ltd* [1945] Ch 402). Otherwise, they are provable in the usual way (¶8030+), with special rules for tax (¶7964) and rent (¶7965) incurred after the commencement of the liquidation.

7793 If the liquidator **fails to obtain consent**, he may be liable to reimburse the company for any losses sustained as a result of the continued trading or his misfeasance, particularly if it was unreasonable to allow the company to trade (*Re Centralcrest Engineering Ltd*, *IRC v Nelmes* [2000] BCC 727, in which the liquidator was ordered to reimburse £120,000 to the company). If the liquidator exceeds his powers, for example by entering into contracts which are not necessary for the liquidation, he may be liable for breach of his warranty of authority. The burden is on the person alleging the breach to prove his case against the liquidator (*Hire Purchase Furnishing Co v Richens* (1887) 20 QBD 387).

B. Increasing assets

7803 As well as identifying and collecting all of the assets which belong to the company, the liquidator must ascertain whether there are any opportunities to increase the company's assets, and take appropriate **action** for the benefit of the liquidation. To this end, he will start with the statement of affairs and use his powers to obtain company documents and other information (¶8117+). This could result in him taking various types of action to:
– reverse and avoid the effects of transactions depriving the company and therefore its creditors of assets;
– commence or defend legal proceedings in the company's name; and
– pursue the officers to compensate for their wrongdoing (¶7439+).

1. Challenging dubious transactions

7808 Statute gives the court wide powers to reverse the effect of certain transactions entered into by a company during the period leading up to its insolvency. This **prevents** directors and others involved in company management from putting assets out of the reach of the liquidator, or favouring one creditor over the others. When such a transaction is challenged, the **court can** order (among other things, depending on the type of transaction) that the position between the company and the third party is restored, so that any asset sold must be returned to the company, for example. Therefore, when a liquidator assumes conduct of a liquidation, he will look very closely at the transactions entered into by the company prior to its insolvency, as a successful action can increase the pool of assets available to meet creditors' claims.

Applications challenging these transactions are usually **made by** the liquidator, except for transactions defrauding creditors, which can be made in a wider range of circumstances (¶7826+). A transaction may fall within more than one category, so the liquidator may choose to make his application in the alternative (although he cannot recover twice for one transaction), for example he may apply for relief on the basis that the transaction was a preference and/or an extortionate credit transaction. The liquidator needs the consent of the court or the liquidation committee before using these recovery processes (para 3A Sch 4 IA 1986). Applications can also be made by a person involved in the transaction, for example a director who benefited from an alleged preference, for a declaration that the transaction is valid. The procedure for making applications relating to insolvency procedures is discussed at ¶7380+.

The liquidator may still, if appropriate in the circumstances, pursue **other legal action** based on the same facts, such as imposing personal liabilities on directors (e.g. for wrongful or fraudulent trading).

MEMO POINTS 1. The provisions described below all apply to companies in liquidation (compulsory or voluntary) and **administration**. Therefore, if a company is in administration, the administrator will make the application and the timing of the transaction must relate to the commencement of the administration. The avoidance of transactions defrauding creditors has wider application (see ¶7826+).
2. Note that any **charge** which should be **registered** will be void against the liquidator or administrator and creditors if it was not registered before the company went into liquidation or administration (¶4648+).

Summary table

The following **transactions** may be challenged. This table provides a summary of the key elements only; further discussion is found by following the relevant cross-reference.

7809

Type of transaction	Definition	Other party to transaction	Timing of transaction	¶¶
Transaction at an undervalue	– Gift; or – company receives significantly less consideration than asset/transaction is worth	– Any – If connected, presumption of insolvency	– 2 years before commencement of liquidation/administration; and – company insolvent at time or became insolvent as result	¶7811+
Preference	Act/omission that puts other party in better position than he would otherwise have been in during company's insolvency	– Creditor/surety/guarantor – If connected, relevant time extended	– Company insolvent at time or became insolvent as result; and – 6 months before commencement of liquidation/administration; or – extended to 2 years if preference given to connected person	¶7819+
Transaction defrauding creditors	Transaction at undervalue that is for purpose of putting assets out of claimant's reach or prejudicing his interests	Any	Any	¶7826+

Type of transaction	Definition	Other party to transaction	Timing of transaction	¶¶
Floating charges	Charge created as a floating charge after consideration for it was paid to company	– Any – If connected, relevant time extended – If not connected, company's insolvency required to avoid floating charge	– 1 year before commencement of liquidation/ administration (only if company was unable to pay debts at time or became unable to pay debts because of transaction which charge secured); – if charge created in favour of connected person, 2 years (regardless of company's solvency); or – between administration application and order or between filing notice of intent to appoint administrator and appointment	¶7836+
Extortionate credit transaction	Provision of credit to company for grossly exorbitant payments or terms that grossly contravene fair dealing principles	Any	3 years before commencement of liquidation/ administration	¶7842+

a. Transactions at an undervalue

7811 When a company is in financial difficulties, the directors will often try to dissipate its assets, by:
– giving them away or selling them to a connected person for nominal consideration to prevent them being realised for the benefit of the creditors; or
– selling them at less than their true value to obtain cash quickly to pay off the most pressing creditors.
In either case, the creditors of the company lose out when it goes into liquidation, since the pot of assets available to the liquidator has been reduced. Therefore, the liquidator is allowed to recover such assets or their proceeds of sale in appropriate circumstances, unless the transaction falls within one of the exceptions (¶7815).

Definitions

7812 A transaction at an undervalue is defined as one in which the company (s 238(4) IA 1986):
a. makes a **gift** to another person, or enters into a transaction with another person on terms which do not provide for the company to receive any consideration; or
b. enters into a transaction with another person for consideration which is significantly **less** (in terms of money or money's worth) in value than the **consideration** provided by the company.
In assessing the **value** of the consideration, the court will take all of the circumstances into account and base its judgment on the value at the date of entry into the transaction. If the consideration is precarious and speculative, the person relying on that consideration (i.e. the person defending the claim) must establish its value (*Phillips and another v Brewin Dolphin Bell Lawrie and another* [2001] UKHL 2).

EXAMPLE If the following transactions were entered into within the "relevant time" (see ¶7813 below) before A Ltd entered into liquidation, the liquidator could challenge them as transactions at an undervalue.
1. A Ltd has surplus stock which it cannot sell. It gives this stock to B Ltd, another subsidiary of A Ltd's holding company which operates in the same industry, to sell to B Ltd's customers. A Ltd has received no consideration.
2. A Ltd sells a car, worth £6,000, to a third party for £2,000. A Ltd has received significantly less consideration for the car than it is worth.

Granting security over the company's assets will not usually count as a transaction at an undervalue: it does not deplete the company's assets or reduce their value because the loss of the right to deal with the assets is not capable of financial valuation (*Re M C Bacon Ltd* [1990] BCLC 324). This allows companies in financial difficulties to try to avoid formal insolvency with the support of banks and other creditors. However, since each case will be different, the court will still assess the circumstances like any other transaction, taking into account factors such as the security holder's right to rely on his security and take priority over other creditors to see if any consideration was given (*Hill v Spread Trustee Company* [2006] EWCA Civ 542, a bankruptcy case based on a similar provision). In any event, a balance must be struck so that the pari passu principle between creditors is not upset, therefore security granted with an intention to prefer one creditor over the others can be challenged as a preference instead (¶7819+).

7813

The liquidator can only challenge transactions entered into at the "**relevant time**", which has two principal elements:
a. the transaction must have been entered into within the 2 years before the commencement of the liquidation (¶7672); and
b. the company must have been insolvent at the time, or have become insolvent as a result of the transaction.

Insolvency is judged in the same way as a petition presented on the ground that the company is unable to pay its debts, therefore this provision cannot usually be used in a solvent winding up (¶7593+). The company is deemed to be insolvent for these purposes if:
– either the balance sheet or cash-flow test is satisfied; or
– the transaction was entered into with a connected person. In this case, the presumption of insolvency is rebuttable (s 240(2) IA 1986).

A "**connected person**" for these purposes is one who is (s 249 IA 1986):
– a director;
– a shadow director;
– an associate of a director or shadow director; or
– an associate of the company.

"**Associate**" is defined at ¶7895, but is broadly:
a. a relative, business partner, employer or employee, or a company under his or his and his associate's control (to be an associate of an individual); or
b. under the same control as the company (to be an associate of a company).

Therefore, an employee is not "connected" to his employer company simply because he is an employee.

EXAMPLE In the example above, transaction 1 is between connected persons, since A Ltd and B Ltd are under the same control. It will be presumed that the company is insolvent at the time, or became insolvent because, of the transaction unless the contrary is proved.
In transaction 2, the liquidator will have to prove the company's insolvency because the other party is not connected to A Ltd.

MEMO POINTS If the company is in **administration**, or was in **administration immediately before liquidation**, the relevant time is the 2 years before the application for an administration order was made, a notice of intention to appoint an administrator out of court was filed or, if an administrator was appointed in another way, when his appointment took effect. The company does not have to be or become insolvent if the transaction was entered into after the application was made or notice of intention filed.

Exceptions

7815 Even if the transaction in question meets all of the above criteria, it will be **protected** if (s 238(5) IA 1986):
– the company entered into it in good faith for the purpose of carrying on its business; and
– there were reasonable grounds for believing that the company would benefit from the transaction at the time.

Therefore, the court will look at the **motives** of the directors and others in control of the company, in particular whether there was any intention to keep assets out of the creditors' hands.

The purpose of **carrying on** the **business** of the company can include any purpose for which the company was established (which will be set out in its memorandum), and is therefore wider than the more common concept of the "usual course of business" which refers to its usual, everyday activities. However, it is confined to the business of the company in question, for example, where payments by various companies in a group had been made to keep the group's overdraft within its limits, this was not accepted by the court as being in good faith for the purpose of the company's business (*Re Barton Manufacturing Co Ltd* [1999] 1 BCLC 740).

The second factor of **reasonableness** constitutes an objective test, whereby the court will look at what a reasonable board would have done in those circumstances. The court will consider whether or not the perceived benefit to the company (which does not have to be financial in nature) justifies the "undervalue" of the transaction.

Consequences

7816 The **court** has a wide **power** to restore the position (as far as is practicable) to what it would have been had the transaction at an undervalue not taken place, by making whatever order it thinks fit (s 238(3) IA 1986). Without limiting the court to making the **suggested orders**, the legislation sets out several specific orders that can be made to help to restore the position of the parties (s 241(1) IA 1986):
a. property transferred out of the company can be vested in it again;
b. any proceeds of the sale of property transferred out of the company can be vested in it;
c. any security granted by the company can be released or discharged;
d. a person receiving any benefit from the company can pay the sums directed by the court straight to the liquidator;
e. where a person's obligations under any security or guarantee were released or discharged, the security or guarantee can be revived or new ones imposed;
f. security for the discharge of any obligation imposed by the order can be provided for with the same priority as that discharged or released; and
g. any person whose property is vested in the company, or on whom obligations are imposed, can be allowed to prove in the liquidation for any debts or liabilities which arose from, or were released or discharged by, the transaction.

> MEMO POINTS The court can also make **persons** and **property out of the jurisdiction** subject to an order (*Re Paramount Airways Ltd* [1992] 3 All ER 1).

7817 Such orders may have a serious effect on **third parties** to the transaction. They can still be bound by an order, even though they were not originally a party to the transaction. However, third parties to the transaction are **protected** where they have given value for the transaction in good faith. If this is the case, the order cannot (s 241(2) IA 1986):
– prejudice any interest he has in property acquired from someone other than the company; and
– require him to pay a sum to the liquidator, unless he was a party to the transaction.

The onus is on the third party to show that this is not the case if he is to avoid the effects of any order (s 241(2A) IA 1986).

7818 The court's power to restore the position between the parties does not affect the liquidator's ability to apply for **other** appropriate **remedies** (s 241(4) IA 1986), for example:
a. imposing liability on directors (¶7439+);

b. obtaining a freezing or search order to ensure that assets are not compromised during the proceedings; or
c. applying for relief from an extortionate credit transaction (¶7842+).

b. Preferences

Directors threatened by the prospect of formal insolvency may be tempted to improve the position of a creditor in return for his continued support, by ensuring that he has a better chance of recovering his debt (for example, by paying him off ahead of other creditors or granting or increasing his security). Directors are particularly likely to want to improve the position of connected creditors, such as themselves, once they realise that insolvency proceedings are likely. Since the rest of the creditors are disadvantaged by such action, the liquidator has the power to challenge preferential treatment so that the balance between the creditors can be restored.

7819

Definitions

There are several elements to the definition of a preference (s 239 IA 1986):
a. the **other party**: must be one of the company's creditors, or a surety or guarantor for its debts or other liabilities;
b. an **action/omission**: the company must do or fail to do something or have something done or not done to it which has the effect of putting the other party in a better position when the company goes into insolvent liquidation;
c. intention: the company must have been influenced by a desire to put the other party in that better position; and
d. timing: the preference must have been given at the relevant time.

7820

> EXAMPLE If the following transactions were entered into within the "relevant time" (see ¶7822 below) before A Ltd enters winding up, the liquidator could challenge them as preferences.
> 1. A Ltd pays the debt of an unsecured creditor. This puts him in a better position than he would otherwise have been in when A Ltd goes into liquidation, since he has been paid in priority to the other creditors (including any secured creditors) instead of in the usual order (see ¶7945). This would also apply if A Ltd had partly paid off his debt.
> 2. A Ltd grants security for an existing and previously unsecured debt. Again, this strengthens the former unsecured creditor's position in the event of the company's insolvency as he will now be repaid as a secured creditor in priority to the unsecured creditors. This would also apply if A Ltd increased the security of a partly secured creditor to cover his unsecured debt.

In addition to intending to carry out the act (or permit the omission), the company must have been influenced by a **desire to prefer** that creditor, surety or guarantor. This is a step further than simply having the desire to carry out the act which constitutes the preference. It will be rare for evidence of this desire to be available (for example, in board minutes), and so the liquidator will invite the court to infer it from the circumstances. He must show that the desire existed on the balance of probabilities, and that it **influenced** the company to take the action (or permit the omission). It does not have to be the only, or even the most significant, factor influencing the company's decision. So, a company succumbing to commercial pressure from a lender did not have the necessary desire to prefer, as the company had little option if it wanted to continue trading (*Re M C Bacon Ltd*, below).

7821

> EXAMPLE When MCB Ltd was in financial difficulties, it granted debentures to its bank in return for further support. The liquidator challenged the transaction as a preference. The judge in that case stressed that the company must have positively desired to improve its creditor's position in the event of its own insolvent liquidation for the debentures to be set aside. He found that the parties were only motivated by "proper commercial considerations" and although the bank's position was actually improved in the company's insolvency, this was not a consequence desired by the company so as to influence its decision to grant the debentures (*Re M C Bacon Ltd* [1990] BCLC 324).

If the preference is given to a person **connected** (see above, ¶7813) with the company at the time, it is presumed that the company was influenced by the desire to put him in a better position. For example, it is common for a director to lend money to or act as guarantor for his company and it will be assumed that any preferential treatment was intended to improve his position. The burden of proof is reversed so that the connected person must prove that the company was not so influenced, and the relevant time period within which the transaction must have occurred is also extended (below).

EXAMPLE FM Ltd, a magazine publishing company, was in financial difficulties and trying to negotiate the sale of its best-selling title. It already had an overdraft facility with the bank, guaranteed by its director, Mr F. Mr F also granted a loan to FM Ltd, which was secured by a debenture. The court found that the company had not been motivated by a desire to prefer Mr F in granting him the debenture; rather, the transaction was motivated by the genuine commercial need to keep the business going during the negotiations in order to receive a fair price for the best-selling title, and the need to raise money from a source other than the bank (*Re Fairway Magazines Ltd, Fairbairn v Hartigan* [1993] BCLC 643).

7822 The "**relevant time**" within which the preference was given depends upon whether the other party was connected to the company or not (s 240 IA 1986):
a. if the preference was granted to:
– an unconnected person, the relevant time is the 6 months before the commencement of the liquidation; or
– a connected person, the relevant time is the 2 years before the commencement of the liquidation; and
b. the company must have been insolvent at the time, or have become insolvent as a result of the transaction (see ¶7813 above).

MEMO POINTS If the company is in **administration**, or was in **administration immediately before liquidation**, the relevant time is the 6 months or 2 years before the application for an administration order was made, a notice of intention to appoint an administrator out of court was filed or, if an administrator was appointed in another way, when his appointment took effect. The company does not have to be or become insolvent if the preference was granted after the application was made or notice filed.

Consequences

7823 The **court** has a wide **power** to restore the position (as far as practicable) to what it would have been had the preference not been granted, by making whatever order it thinks fit (s 239(3) IA 1986). The same provisions noted above regarding transactions at an undervalue apply to preferences as regards (¶7816+):
– the suggested orders which can be made;
– the position of third parties who have given value in good faith; and
– the other remedies available.

c. Transactions defrauding creditors

7826 Transactions defrauding creditors are similar to transactions at an undervalue, and one transaction may fall into both categories. The key difference is the additional element of the purpose or motive of defrauding creditors, which is lacking in the purely factual definition of a transaction at an undervalue. Transactions defrauding creditors have a wider application in terms of:
– the situations in which they apply;
– the lack of a time period within which the transaction must have occurred to be challenged; and
– who can apply.

Definitions

7827 A transaction defrauding creditors can be defined as one which (s 423(1), (2) IA 1986):
a. is at an undervalue; and

b. was entered into for the **purpose** of:
– putting assets beyond the reach of someone who has made or may make a claim against the company; or
– prejudicing the interests of a person in relation to his claim.

> EXAMPLE A Ltd and B Ltd, both controlled by Mr A and Mr B, each owned a unit on a business estate. They later transferred the units to another company, C Ltd, controlled by the same persons. The property management company sued C Ltd for failure to pay the service charge. During the proceedings, the units were transferred to D Ltd (also under the same control). Judgment was awarded against C and D Ltd. Between judgment and the costs assessment, the units were transferred to E and F Ltd for no consideration. The management company succeeded in having the transfers set aside as transactions defrauding creditors and the court made charging orders over the units to secure payment of the judgment and costs (*Beckenham MC Ltd v Centralex Ltd* [2004] 2 BCLC 764).

> MEMO POINTS The **definition** of **transaction at an undervalue** is substantially the same as set out above (¶7812+), with the addition of transactions entered into with another party in consideration of marriage or the formation of a civil partnership. Clearly, this is not a category which will often apply to companies, but since the marriage or civil partnership does not have to be between the parties to the transaction, it conceivably could arise in some situations.

When assessing whether the **purpose of the transaction** was to put assets beyond the reach of creditors, the court will look for it being the real and substantial purpose (i.e. the main purpose, rather than just a consequence) (*Inland Revenue Commissioners v Hashmi* [2002] 2 BCLC 489). Defrauding creditors does not have to be the only purpose (*Re Brabon, Treharne v Brabon* [2001] 1 BCLC 11). The motives of the other party to the transaction are not relevant (*Moon v Franklin* [1996] BPIR 196). Each case will be judged on its own particular facts.

7828

> EXAMPLE
> 1. A transaction can still be classed as defrauding creditors even if there was no dishonest intention behind it (*Arbuthnot Leasing International Ltd v Havelet Leasing Ltd (No 2)* [1990] BCC 636).
> 2. Where a claimant obtained judgment against a company in civil proceedings, which went into receivership almost immediately meaning that the claimant received nothing, his claim for relief from a transaction defrauding creditors was rejected as it was misconceived (*Dora v Simper* [2000] 2 BCLC 561).

Application

Applications for relief from the effects of transactions defrauding creditors can be made whether or not the company is subject to insolvency proceedings, although they are most **commonly made** in connection with transactions at an undervalue and preferences. If the company is subject to insolvency proceedings, the application should be made in accordance with the Rules; if not, it should follow the CPR. An application can be **made by** a number of specified persons, depending on the company's circumstances, although the application will always be treated as being made on behalf of every victim to ensure that they are all treated equally (s 424 IA 1986).

7829

Company's situation	Applicant(s)[1,2]
In liquidation	– Official receiver – liquidator; or – victim of transaction, with court's permission
In administration	– Official receiver – administrator; or – victim of transaction, with court's permission
Subject to a CVA	– Supervisor; or – victim of transaction
Any other situation	Victim of transaction

Note:
1. A "**victim of the transaction**" is a person who is (or is capable of being) prejudiced by the transaction (s 424(2) IA 1986).
2. The **FSA** can also apply for relief if the company was carrying out an activity regulated by the FSA at the time the transaction was entered into and the transaction was part of a regulated activity (s 375 FSMA 2000). Again, the application is taken to be made on behalf of all of the victims of the transaction.

7830 There is no **relevant time** within which a transaction must have occurred for it to be challenged as a transaction defrauding creditors.

Consequences

7831 If the **court** finds that a transaction defrauding creditors has taken place, it has a wide discretion to make whatever **order** it sees fit to (s 423 IA 1986):
– restore the position as if the transaction had not been entered into; and
– protect the interests of the victim(s) of the transaction.

The legislation goes on to give examples of possible orders, similar to those listed at ¶7816 (s 425 IA 1986). Again, innocent **third parties** to the transaction are afforded some protection (as described at ¶7817; s 425(2) IA 1986).

d. Floating charges

7836 Floating charges are dealt with generally at ¶4610+. They provide lenders with valuable security, as they can be used to secure intangible and fluctuating assets which cannot be made subject to fixed charges. Large lenders, such as banks, often take fixed and floating charges over the whole of a company, its assets and undertaking, which can leave unsecured creditors with nothing in a liquidation, or just a ring-fenced portion of the assets subject to the floating charge (¶7992+). Floating charges created in the period immediately before the winding up can be challenged to the extent that value for the charge (e.g. the loan from the floating charge holder) was paid before it was created, preventing a previously partly secured or unsecured creditor from improving his position in the liquidation. However, there does not have to be an application by the liquidator. If the statutory criteria are met, the floating charge is automatically invalid.

Definitions

7837 A **floating charge** is defined as one **created** as such. This means that it may be avoided even if it has crystallised under its terms by the time the company is in liquidation or administration (s 251 IA 1986). For the treatment of floating charges in liquidation generally, see ¶7992+.

7838 To be avoided, a floating charge must have been created within the **relevant time** period, which differs depending on the person in whose favour the charge was made. A floating charge can be avoided if it was created (s 245(3), (4) IA 1986):
a. in favour of a person who is **not connected** with the company within the 12 months before the commencement of the liquidation, if the company:
– was unable to pay its debts (¶7593+) at the time; or
– became unable to pay its debts as a result of the transaction secured by the floating charge;
b. in favour of a **connected** person (¶7813) within the 2 years before the commencement of the winding up, regardless of the company's solvency.

> MEMO POINTS   In the case of a company in **administration**, there are two **additional relevant time periods** within which floating charges can also be challenged (regardless of the person in whose favour the charge was created):
> – between an application for an administration order and the order being made; or
> – between a notice of intention to appoint an administrator and the appointment being made.
> References above to the "commencement of the liquidation" should be read as being to the "**onset of insolvency**", which is defined as (s 245(5) IA 1986):
> – where an administration order has been made, the date of the administration application;
> – where an administrator has been appointed out of court, the date on which the notice is filed; and
> – in any other case, the date on which the appointment of the administrator takes effect.

Consequences

7839 The effect of a floating charge being avoided is to **prevent** the charge holder from benefiting from the charge in the liquidation. The other terms of the charge are valid, therefore the company is still liable to repay the principal and interest secured, and the charge holder can prove in the liquidation for the sums owing to him.

Since the terms of the charge are not invalidated retrospectively, if the **company has already paid off** the charge holder, or the **charge holder has enforced** his security, the liquidator cannot interfere with these transactions to recover the money or assets (*Re Parkes Garage (Swadlincote) Ltd* [1929] 1 Ch 139; *Power v Sharp Investments Ltd* [1994] 1 BCLC 111).

7840 The **extent** to which the effects of a floating charge created at the relevant time can be avoided is limited. The aggregate of the value of the following sums **cannot be avoided** (s 245(2) IA 1986):
a. as much of the consideration for the creation of the floating charge which comprises money paid or goods or services supplied to the company at the time of, or after, its creation;
b. as much of the consideration which comprises the discharge or reduction of any debt of the company at the time of, or after, the creation of the charge; and
c. the amount of any interest payable on a. or b. under any agreement under which money, goods or services were received or debts discharged or reduced.

Therefore, in respect of these sums, the charge holder will retain the benefit of his charge, principally his priority over the other creditors. It will be noted that credit is only given for money, goods and services received by the company; other receivables such as land or debts are not included.

> EXAMPLE   A Ltd is in financial difficulties. The bank already holds a fixed charge over A Ltd's assets securing a substantial loan. However, the bank is concerned that this fixed charge does not provide adequate security. In return for continuing this loan and providing overdraft facilities of up to £30,000, A Ltd grants the bank a floating charge over the rest of the company's assets and undertaking. A Ltd enters into winding up within 12 months. At that time, A Ltd has drawn on £20,000-worth of the available overdraft facilities since the creation of the floating charge, therefore the floating charge will be valid as far as it secures that amount. The rest of it can be avoided by the liquidator, preventing the bank from bolstering its fixed charge.

e. Extortionate credit transactions

7842 A company in financial difficulties will not be in a strong bargaining position when it comes to obtaining credit, making it easier for creditors to impose terms which are unfavourable from the company's perspective. In order to be avoided as an extortionate credit transaction, the terms must be extremely unreasonable. This allows creditors to protect their position as necessary, without enabling them to take undue advantage of such companies. There is very little case law on this area, so it seems that the provisions are rarely used.

Definitions

7843 An extortionate credit transaction can be defined as (s 244(3) IA 1986):
a. credit transaction: a transaction to which the company is a party by which it is provided with credit; and
b. extortionate: where the terms, considering the risk to the party providing the credit:
– require grossly exorbitant payments to be made for the credit; or
– otherwise grossly contravene the ordinary principles of fair dealing.
The transaction is presumed to be extortionate unless the contrary is proved, although there is no test which determines whether or not a transaction meets the "extortionate" criteria.

7844 Such a transaction can be challenged if it was entered into within the **relevant time**, being the 3 years ending with the commencement of the liquidation (s 244(2) IA 1986).

> MEMO POINTS   In the case of a company in **administration**, the **relevant time** period is the 3 years ending with the company entering administration (¶8808).

Consequences

7845 Where an extortionate credit transaction has been entered into within the relevant time, the **court** will make an appropriate **order**, which may include any combination of the following (s 244(4) IA 1986):
– setting aside all or part of the transaction;

- varying the terms of the transaction or any security held in connection with it;
- requiring a party to the transaction to hand over any sums received by him to the liquidator;
- requiring a party to the transaction to hand over any property held by him as security for the transaction to the liquidator; and
- directing any person(s) to account to any other(s) for any sums necessary.

An extortionate credit transaction may also constitute a **transaction at an undervalue**, in which case the court can make an appropriate order (¶7816+).

2. Other litigation

7850 The liquidator may consider that it is in the company's interests to either **commence or continue litigation** between the company and another party. The company may be the claimant or defendant to any type of litigation, for example, claims for breach of contract, personal injury or injunctions to prevent the company carrying out certain acts. Commencing or taking over litigation can be **expensive** and therefore the liquidator may only do so if there is a real prospect of success and the cost and time involved would result in a benefit to the liquidation (¶7961+). For example, he must not defend a valid claim to which the company has no real defence (*General Share and Trust Co v Wetley Brick & Pottery Co* (1882) 20 Ch D 260). **Alternatively**, the liquidator could settle the matter out of court, if appropriate, and admit any compromised claim instead (which can be proved for in the liquidation).

From the point of view of **litigation** taken **against the company**, the presentation of the petition and the order being made affect whether or not the proceedings are allowed to continue or be commenced (see ¶7697+ and ¶7757 respectively). The position is summarised below, whether the company is the claimant or the defendant.

MEMO POINTS For the position in a **voluntary liquidation**, see ¶8469+.

7851 Since litigation could potentially reduce the funds available for distribution, or create an inequality between the company's creditors, certain **requirements** must be met in different situations.

Type of litigation		Requirements	Reference
New:	Company is claimant	- Liquidator needs sanction of court or liquidation committee - Any counterclaim against company needs leave of court to proceed - Defendant can apply for security for costs from company	¶8218; s 130(2) IA 1986; s 726 CA 1985[1]
	Company is defendant	- Liquidator needs sanction of court or liquidation committee - Claimant needs leave of court to bring proceedings	¶8218; s 130(2) IA 1986
Existing:	Company is claimant	- Liquidator can choose whether or not to continue with claim - Defendant can apply for security for costs from company	s 726(1) CA 1985[1]
	Company is defendant	- Company/creditors/contributories can apply for stay of proceedings between presentation of petition and order - Automatic stay when order made - Claimant needs leave of court to continue proceedings	¶7698+; ¶7757; s 130(2) IA 1986
Note: 1. s 726 CA 1985 is expected to be repealed by 1 October 2009. There will be no replacement provision in the **new Companies Act**. However, this will make no real difference because a court will still be able to order security for costs to be paid under the CPR (r 25.15 CPR).			

7852 Generally speaking, where the **court's permission** is **required** to commence or continue litigation against a company in liquidation, it will not be granted. However, the court will always look at the circumstances and may give its consent to proceedings in appropriate cases.

EXAMPLE
1. A **secured creditor** will generally be allowed to commence or continue proceedings if necessary to realise or enforce his security (*Re Pound & Hutchins* (1889) 42 Ch D 402).
2. Litigation was allowed to proceed against a company in liquidation for the **specific performance** of a contract for the sale of land, since land is a unique asset and cannot be adequately replaced by financial compensation (*Thames Plate Glass Co v Land & Sea Telegraph Construction Co* (1871) 6 Ch App 643).

MEMO POINTS The **general rules** regarding insolvency **applications** can be found at ¶7380+.

7853 Rather than resorting to litigation, potential claimants can present their claim to the **liquidator** and ask him to **admit** it, saving both parties time, resources and expense. Unless there is a genuine dispute as to the validity of the claim and it is worth defending, the liquidator will usually admit the claim (placing a value on it) and allow the claimant to submit a proof for a certain amount. The claimant then stands as an unsecured creditor, and any dispute as to the value placed on the claim by the liquidator can be resolved following the appropriate process (¶8040).

In certain cases, however, this will not be possible as the claimant has to **establish** the company's **liability**, for example, a claimant with a personal injury claim will still have to establish that the company was liable for his injuries before he can claim from the company's insurance company (¶8016).

C. Money owed by contributories

1. Who is a contributory?

7863 Insolvency law uses the **term** "contributories" to refer to a company's shareholders. Shareholders are liable to contribute to the company's assets if it is wound up, up to the amount owing on their shares. Even shareholders who have fully paid up any calls on their shares are called contributories because they were liable to contribute but have discharged that liability (*Re Anglesea Colliery Co* (1866) 1 Ch App 555). Most shareholders will fall into this category. Contributories have certain **rights** where their company is in liquidation, for example to present a petition, participate in meetings and receive a distribution. These rights apply to all shareholders.

When the liquidator collects in the company's assets, he can only require **contributions from** those who owe money to the company (s 79 IA 1986). These are:
– shareholders with unpaid calls on their shares; and
– certain other people who are liable to contribute in specific (and not very common) circumstances.

The liquidator's first source of information will therefore be the register of shareholders, but he must look beyond it (e.g. by making sure that the changes in shareholdings are up to date), and he may have to rectify the register with the court's consent (r 4.196 IR 1986).

MEMO POINTS 1. In a **voluntary liquidation**, liquidators can also apply to the court to have the register corrected, but since there is no requirement for them to draw up a formal list of contributories it is not usually necessary at this stage (s 112 IA 1986; ¶8523+). Instead, it can wait until an application is made to court for sanction to transfer the shares in question (*Re Onward Building Society* [1891] 2 QB 463).
2. Contributories commit a **criminal offence** if they interfere with any of the company's books, papers or securities. This offence is described in relation to directors at ¶8170.

7864 Contributories **liable to contribute** to the company's assets are:

Category [1]	Liability [2]	Reference (IA 1986)
Current **shareholder** [3, 4]	Up to amount unpaid on shares in respect of which he is a shareholder	s 74(2)(d)
Former shareholder, who ceased to hold shares within 1 year of commencement of liquidation (¶7672)	– Up to amount unpaid on shares in respect of which he is a shareholder – Only liable to contribute if existing shareholders cannot satisfy their contributions – No liability for debts or liabilities incurred after ceased to be a shareholder – Amount he received for shares if they were redeemed or purchased by company out of its capital, and if company's assets and other contributions are not enough to meet debts, liabilities and expenses of liquidation (liable jointly and severally with director) (¶1337+)	s 74(2)(d) s 74(2)(c) s 74(2)(b) s 76(3)
Other former shareholders	No liability	s 74(2)(a)
Current **director**	Amount paid to former shareholder if he signed statutory declaration authorising redemption or purchase of shares by company out of its capital, and if company's assets and other contributions are not enough to meet debts, liabilities and expenses of liquidation (liable jointly and severally with former shareholder) (¶1337+)	s 76(3)
Current director or manager with unlimited liability	• Only liable to contribute if: – court deems it necessary to satisfy company's debts, liabilities and expenses of liquidation; or – company's articles require • Liability to contribute as if he were member of unlimited company [4]	s 75(2)(c) s 75(1)
Former director or manager with unlimited liability who ceased to hold office within 1 year of commencement of liquidation	– Liability to contribute as if he were member of unlimited company [4] – No liability re. debts or liabilities incurred after he ceased to hold office	s 75(1) s 75(2)(b)
Other former director or manager with unlimited liability	– Generally, no liability – Amount paid to former shareholder if he signed statutory declaration authorising redemption or purchase of shares by company out of its capital, and if company's assets and other contributions are not enough to meet debts, liabilities and expenses of liquidation (liable jointly and severally with former shareholder) (¶1337+)	s 75(2)(a) s 76(3)

Note:
1. Personal representative/beneficiary becomes liable to contribute in place of **dead shareholder** (s 81 IA 1986). Similarly, **bankrupt shareholder's** trustee in bankruptcy steps into his shoes (s 82 IA 1986).
2. Shareholder's **liability** to contribute to company's assets may be **restricted** in insurance policy or other contract (s 74(2)(e) IA 1986).
3. In a **company limited by guarantee**, members are liable to contribute amount undertaken by them (stated in memorandum) (s 74(3) IA 1986). If company limited by guarantee also has share capital, they will be liable to pay any sums unpaid on their shares as well.
4. In an **unlimited company**, members must contribute as much as necessary to meet company's debts and liabilities and expenses of liquidation (s 74(1) IA 1986).
Where an **unlimited company re-registers as limited** (whether public or private) and winding up commences within 3 years, any person who was member when it re-registered is liable to contribute to debts and liabilities incurred before re-registration (s 77(2) IA 1986). If no current members were members at time of re-registration, member at that time (whether he was a current or former member at that time) is still liable to contribute, even if current members have satisfied all of their contributions. This will not apply if contributing member ceased to be member over 1 year before commencement of liquidation (ss 74(2)(a), 77(3) IA 1986).
Where a **limited company** has **re-registered as unlimited**, past members of company at time of application to re-register are not liable to contribute to company's assets any more than they would be if company had not re-registered (i.e. see former shareholders, above).

2. Recovery of debts from contributories

The liquidator's first step is to make a **list** of the **contributories** as soon as possible after his appointment, so that he knows to whom any surplus must be distributed and also so that calls can be made as a way of increasing the assets (r 4.196 IR 1986). This is a duty which statute imposes on the court, but the court delegates it to the liquidator (s 148(1) IA 1986; r 4.195 IR 1986). This list enables the liquidator to make calls on the correct shareholders, and gives the shareholders the chance to challenge their inclusion on the list as contributories. In the rare cases where there are non-shareholding contributories, the liquidator will claim the appropriate amount owed.

7869

He will draw up two lists of shareholder contributories in order to identify those liable to contribute and those to whom a distribution will be made if there are enough assets, as follows:
– "**A**" **list**: all shareholders of the company at the commencement of the winding up; and
– "**B**" **list**: all past shareholders of the company who ceased to be shareholders during the preceding year (except for fully paid up shareholders, since they have no liability to contribute and will not have any right to a distribution).

7870

The liquidator will only make calls on those on the "B" list who are liable to contribute if the "A" list contributories are unable to satisfy their contributions (*Re Apex Film Distributors* [1960] 1 All ER 152).

Comment: Current holders of **fully paid shares** should ensure that they are on the "A" list even though they are not liable to contribute, because if a return of capital is possible it is distributed amongst those on the list (¶8087+).

> MEMO POINTS In a **voluntary liquidation**, the liquidator has the same power to make the list of contributories (s 165(4) IA 1986).

The list must take the prescribed form and once it has been drawn up, the liquidator must **notify** everyone on the list (rr 4.197, 4.198 IR 1986):
– of the capacity in which he is included;
– of the number of shares or the interest for which he is included;
– of how many of the shares or how much of the interest has been called and paid up;
– that his inclusion on the list may result in any uncalled capital being called up; and
– that he has 21 days from the date of the notice within which to object to any inclusion or omission on the list.

7871

If he receives an **objection**, the liquidator has 14 days to consider it and notify the objector that the list has been altered or the objection rejected. This notice must also inform the objector of his right to apply to court for the list to be altered within 21 days (r 4.199 IR 1986). The liquidator can **alter** or **add to** the list after it has been settled, provided he gives notice to the affected shareholder(s) (r 4.200 IR 1986). The court can **waive** the requirement to list the contributories if it considers that it will not be necessary to make calls on shares or adjust the contributories' rights, for example, where the share capital is fully paid up.

> MEMO POINTS The rules relating to the list of contributories do not apply in a **voluntary liquidation**. There is no equivalent procedure regarding the notification of, and objection to, a person's inclusion on the list, since it is primarily made for the liquidator's own use. However, as a matter of good practice, the liquidator will usually follow the same procedure. If a person objects to being classed as a contributory, he can defend the claim made against him when the liquidator demands payment, or apply to court to be removed from the list (s 112 IA 1986; ¶8523+).

Making calls

The court's power to make calls on shares is also delegated to the liquidator, but he must still obtain leave of the court or sanction of the liquidation committee to use it (s 150 IA 1986; r 4.202 IR 1986). In practice, there is usually little money to collect from the shareholders since most shares are paid up on issue. The calls are **made against** the names on the liquidator's

7872

list, who can be required to contribute any money needed to satisfy the company's debts and liabilities as well as the costs, charges and expenses of the liquidation, up **to the extent of** each contributory's liability. The calls can be calculated to compensate for the probability that some contributories will fail (wholly or partly) to pay.

The **company's debts and liabilities** which the calls are intended to meet do not have to be established before a call is made. Therefore, if the liquidator's assessment of the liquidation at an early stage indicates that the calls will be needed to pay the creditors, he should call up the full amount owed (Re Barned's Banking Co Ltd (1867) 36 LJ Ch 215).

In making calls, the liquidator is not bound by any **shareholders'** or other **agreement** with the company regarding calls (Newton v Anglo-Australian Investment Co, Debenture-Holders [1895] AC 244). Similarly, any relevant provisions in the company's **articles** do not apply (Re Welsh Flannel and Tweed Co (1875) LR 20 Eq 360).

> MEMO POINTS 1. The liquidator has the same power to make calls in a **voluntary liquidation**, although there is no need for him to obtain sanction to do so (s 165(4) IA 1986).
> 2. Where a **contributory** is **bankrupt**, the liquidator can prove for the estimated liability to future calls as well as any sums owing on previous calls in the bankruptcy on the company's behalf (s 82 IA 1986).

Obtaining sanction

7873 The liquidator can obtain sanction to make calls from the **liquidation committee** by calling a meeting, giving at least 7 days' notice which contains a statement of the proposed amount of the call and its purpose, to each committee member (s 160(2) IA 1986; r 4.203 IR 1986). Alternatively, he can apply to the **court** for sanction by filing an ex parte application with a supporting affidavit in Form 4.56, stating the amount of the proposed call and the contributories on whom it will be made (r 4.204 IR 1986). The court can direct that notice of the order is given to the contributories or that it is publicly advertised. If the liquidation committee has improperly refused to sanction a call, the liquidator can apply to the court to have its decision overturned (Re North Eastern Insurance Co Ltd (1915) 85 LJ Ch 751).

The liquidator **does not need sanction** to enforce calls previously made by the directors, which have not yet been paid (Westmoreland Green and Blue Slate Co v Feilden [1891] 3 Ch 15). This option would be preferred over the simpler one of making new calls if interest has accrued on overdue calls.

> MEMO POINTS 1. In the case of a **voluntary liquidation**, the liquidator does not need sanction of the liquidation committee or court (s 165(4) IA 1986).
> 2. The Insolvency Service has proposed that **affidavits** are replaced by witness statements (see ¶7637). This change is likely to be implemented on 1 October 2008.

Notice of calls due

7874 Once sanctioned, notice of the call must be **given to** all contributories affected on Form 4.58, stating (r 4.205 IR 1986):
– the amount (or balance) due from him; and
– whether the court or the liquidation committee sanctioned the call.

> MEMO POINTS In the case of a **voluntary liquidation**, the notice requirements do not apply, although clearly the liquidator will have to inform contributories that calls have been made and how much is owed by each one (r 4.1 IR 1986).

Payment of calls

7875 There are no specific rules prescribing the **method** of payment, although the court can authorise the liquidator to accept payment of calls in instalments (Re Law Guarantee Trust and Accident Society Ltd (1910) 26 TLR 565).

7876 The question of whether contributories can **set off** monies owed to them against calls made has been addressed in a mixture of the legislation and case law, and so the position depends upon the circumstances.

Situation	Is set-off possible against calls?	Reference
Limited company being wound up; solvent contributory	Contributory cannot set off debts or dividends due to him against calls, whether calls made before or during liquidation. He cannot receive distribution until his calls are fully paid up, except where the creditors have been paid in full (below)	*Re West of England Bank, ex parte Brown* (1879) 12 Ch D 823
Insolvent contributory	– Individual: can set off debt against calls – Company: same as for solvent contributories	para 8 Sch 4 IA 1986; *Re Auriferous Properties Ltd* [1898] 1 Ch 691; *Re Leeds and Hanley Theatres of Varieties Ltd* [1904] 2 Ch 45
Deceased contributory	Set-off likely as situation is comparable to bankrupt individual's	s 34, Pt 1 Sch 1 Administration of Estates Act 1925; *Re McMahon, Fuller v McMahon* [1900] 1 Ch 173
Unlimited company being wound up	Calls are not made in the liquidation, so liquidator must recover debts due from contributories by applying to court. Set-off of debt relating to independent dealing is allowed, but not any money due as dividend or profit as member Debts can be set off against calls made before, but not during, winding up	*Re West of England and South Wales District Bank, ex parte Branwhite* (1879) 48 LJ Ch 463
Contributory is director with unlimited liability	Position is same as for members of unlimited company	s 149(2)(b) IA 1986
Creditors paid in full	Calls may be set off against debts due to contributories, although if contributory proved for his debt, he will already have been paid	ss 74(2), 149(3) IA 1986; *Re Compania de Electricidad de la Provincia de Buenos Aires Ltd* [1978] 3 All ER 668

If the **contributories do not pay** up their calls, the liquidator can apply to the court for an order enforcing this obligation, known as a "balance order" (r 4.205(2) IR 1986; s 150 IA 1986). If enforcement action is taken, statutory interest can be awarded on the amount due (s 35A Supreme Court Act 1981; *Re Overend, Gurney & Co, ex parte Linlott* (1867) LR 4 Eq 184). Further, the court can cause a contributory to be arrested if it can be shown that (either before or after a winding up order is made) he plans to leave the jurisdiction or remove or hide any of his property in order to avoid paying up his calls (s 158 IA 1986). His books, papers and moveable property can also be seized.

7877

MEMO POINTS   In the case of the liquidation of an **unregistered company** or a **voluntary liquidation**, the liquidator can also apply to court to enforce unpaid calls (respectively, ss 299(1), 112 IA 1986 (¶8523+)).

Recouping sums owed in capacity as shareholders

The legislation gives liquidators the power to apply to the court for an order for a contributory to pay any debt owed by him to the company in his capacity as shareholder, **other than calls** (s 149 IA 1986). Since the debt must be owed as a shareholder, the power is restricted in practice to sums such as improperly paid dividends, as it cannot be used to recover ordinary debts (*Re Marlborough Club Co* (1868) LR 5 Eq 365). In some circumstances, it may also be used to recover sums paid to the contributories by the liquidator.

7878

EXAMPLE
1. A liquidator took action to challenge the distribution of unlawful dividends to shareholders (¶1730+) in order to increase the company's assets (*It's a Wrap (UK) Ltd v Gula* [2006] EWCA Civ 544).
2. A Ltd went into voluntary liquidation. The only shareholders were the administrators of the estate of Mrs W (who were Mr W and another individual). Mr W claimed that he should receive the assets

of A Ltd, on the grounds that his wife had been his nominee and he had in fact provided all of the company's capital. The liquidator paid him a substantial amount, as a refund to a contributory. The company's income was assessed to super-tax, and the special commissioners deemed that the company's income should be the shareholders', and served a notice of assessment in the company's name on Mr W regarding the income he had received. When Mr W did not pay, a notice of charge was served on the company. The liquidator had distributed all of the company's assets without making provision for this bill. The Crown applied for an order compelling Mr W to repay the liquidator the amount owed to the Crown under the tax bill (*Re Aidall Ltd* [1932] All ER Rep 296; in *Butler v Broadhead* [1974] 2 All ER 401, the court held that the then equivalent of s 149 IA 1986 was applied in *Re Aidall Ltd*).

MEMO POINTS   In the case of a **voluntary liquidation**, the liquidator can also apply to the court to recoup sums owed by contributories (s 112 IA 1986; ¶8523+).

II. Selling the assets

7893 Once the assets have been identified and secured, the liquidator will have to **liquidate**, or realise, them (i.e. turn them into cash) to distribute amongst the creditors and contributories. This may not be possible in the case of some assets, such as perishable goods like food, but in most cases the liquidator will be able to sell the company's assets individually or as a whole. The liquidator must ensure that he obtains the highest **price** for the assets, and so may have to obtain professional valuations. He will usually achieve the best price if he is able to sell the company's business as a going concern, since he is able to sell the tangible assets together with the intangible ones, such as goodwill. In some cases, it may be appropriate to distribute the assets themselves to the creditors or shareholders (¶7914).

Since the liquidator is an officer of the court, it is a criminal offence (contempt of court) for a person to interfere with his possession of the company's assets. If a **person** has a **claim over an asset**, he must assert it through the proper channels by bringing it to the liquidator's attention and referring the matter to the court if a dispute arises.

MEMO POINTS   In a **voluntary liquidation**, the liquidator is not an officer of the court. Therefore, he will need to apply to the court for delivery up of an asset in the possession of another person, or for an injunction to restrain a person from interfering with it.

Liquidator's power to sell

7894 Although the liquidator has the power to sell the company's property without the sanction of the liquidation committee or the court, he **cannot sell** the rights and powers that enable him to deal with that property. For example, he cannot assign his right to take legal proceedings to render a disposition of the company's property or transfer of its shares void (*Re Ayala Holdings Ltd (No 2)* [1996] 1 BCLC 467). Nor can he sell an asset on terms other than those which apply to the company, for instance he could not assign a lease which contained a covenant against assignment, without the landlord's consent (*Re Farrow's Bank Ltd* [1921] 2 Ch 164).

The liquidator may be **unable to sell** an asset, or may find that the company is subject to an onerous **contract** under which it is obliged to perform cumbersome or expensive obligations, or will not make a profit. In such circumstances, he can disclaim the property, releasing the company from its obligations. This procedure is dealt with below (¶7917+). Even if a contract is not onerous, the liquidator can declare that the company is unable to perform its obligations (¶7928+).

MEMO POINTS   1. Although a liquidator cannot assign his own legal rights to take action, he can **assign** the company's **causes of action**. However, he must ensure that he takes legal advice on the value of the potential claims, otherwise his decision may be challenged (*Ultraframe (UK) Limited v Rigby* [2005] EWCA Civ 276; see ¶8219+, ¶8234+ for a discussion on challenging a liquidator's decisions).
2. See ¶8490 for a liquidator's power to accept shares in consideration for assets in a **voluntary liquidation**.

Sales to connected persons

If the liquidator sells to a person **connected to** the **company**, he is obliged to inform the liquidation committee (unless he is the official receiver acting as liquidator) (s 167(2) IA 1986). A person is connected to the company for these purposes if he is (s 249 IA 1986):
- the director or shadow director of the company; or
- their associate (defined below) or an associate of the company.

If he sells to a **member of the liquidation committee** (past or present) or his associate, prior sanction will be required (¶8298+).

If he sells to **his own associate**, any person interested in the transaction can apply to the court to have it set aside and order the liquidator to compensate the company for any loss suffered as a result (r 4.149 IR 1986), unless the liquidator obtained:
- prior consent of the court; or
- full value for the transaction, and was unaware that the other party was his associate.

A is an associate of B if (s 435 IA 1986):
a. he is B's spouse or civil partner;
b. B's relative;
c. he is B's spouse's or civil partner's relative;
d. he is the spouse or civil partner of a relative of B or B's spouse or civil partner;
e. he is B's business partner, in which case he is also an associate of B's spouse, civil partner or relative;
f. he is B's employer or employee (for these purposes, employees include company officers, whether or not they are technically employed); or
g. A is a company of which B has control, or shares the control with his associates.

However, this rule will not prevent the liquidator from passing the property to an associate as a result of legal or equitable rules relating to trust property or fiduciary obligations (e.g. if the liquidator's associate is the beneficiary of a trust over the company's assets) (r 4.149(3) IR 1986).

<u>MEMO POINTS</u> 1. A **trustee** is an associate of the beneficiaries of the trust (or persons who may benefit from the trust by the trustee exercising his powers in relation to it) and their associates. A **company** (A Ltd) is an associate of another company (B Ltd) if:
- the same person has control (i.e. the directors usually follow his instructions, or he controls one third of the voting rights) of A Ltd and B Ltd, or the controller of A Ltd's associate controls B Ltd, or they control B Ltd together; or
- A Ltd and B Ltd are controlled by the same group, or by what could be regarded as the same group, of persons.

A **relative** is a lineal ancestor or descendant, brother/sister, aunt/uncle, nephew/niece, including half-blood, adopted, step and illegitimate relations. Spouses and civil partners include former and reputed spouses and civil partners.
2. In a **voluntary liquidation**, the liquidator must follow the same procedure when selling to a connected person (s 165(6) IA 1986). A sale to his associate can be challenged in the same way (r 4.149 IR 1986).

Financial requirements

The liquidator is obliged to **deal with** the **money** received in the course of the liquidation in a particular manner. It must be paid in full into the Insolvency Services Account, which is kept by the secretary of state with the Bank of England, following specific rules (ss 403-409 IA 1986; reg 5 SI 1994/2507). If sums are deposited which do not need to be used immediately in the winding up, they can be invested in government securities at the liquidator's request (reg 9 SI 1994/2507). If the liquidator needs the company to carry on trading, he can apply to the secretary of state for permission to open a "local bank account", which he can pay into and withdraw from up to a specified limit, for practical purposes (reg 6 SI 1994/2507).

<u>MEMO POINTS</u> 1. In a **voluntary liquidation**, the liquidator does not have to maintain a local bank account for trading purposes, because he is not required to pay all of the money he receives into the Insolvency Services Account (reg 6 SI 1994/2507). Rather, he can make payments into the account as necessary (reg 5(2) SI 1994/2507).
2. As part of the Insolvency Service's review of secondary legislation (see ¶7364/mp), it is taking the opportunity to make alterations to the primary legislation either where it is necessary to support the new Rules or to remove unnecessary administrative burdens. The Service **proposes to remove** the

need for monies in insolvency proceedings to be paid into and out of the Insolvency Services Account at the Bank of England (proposal 7, "A consultation document on changes to the Insolvency Act 1986 and the Company Directors Disqualification Act 1986 to be made by a Legislative Reform Order for the modernisation and streamlining of insolvency procedures" (September 2007)). Since 2004, the Bank of England has concentrated its operations on maintaining monetary and financial stability and only provides banking facilities to the Insolvency Service. Therefore, allowing the Insolvency Services Account to be held elsewhere will mean that the Bank of England will not have to incur the cost of providing these facilities just to the Service. At the time of writing, the consultation is still open. If this proposal is accepted, the changes are likely to be implemented from 1 October 2008.

1. Particular types of assets

7901 The liquidator's ability to realise certain categories of asset is restricted, as outlined below. There are particular rules on dealing with **secured assets**, which affect how the proceeds are distributed and are therefore dealt with under that wider topic at ¶7977+.

Goods

7902 Goods in the company's possession which are subject to a valid **retention of title** claim (¶9940) are not available to the liquidator, because they do not belong to the company, unless the liquidator pays for them in full.

Liens, on the other hand, over books, records and papers of the company are not generally enforceable against the liquidator, unless they are over title documents (¶8017).

Assets subject to enforcement actions

7903 Outside the context of liquidation, a judgment creditor of the company is permitted to enforce his judgment, usually by way of:
– **execution order**: seizing and selling the company's goods (distress is a contractual version, usually used by landlords for non-payment of rent);
– **charging order**: obtaining a charge on the debtor's land or other securities to protect the debt; or
– **third party debt order**: requiring a third party who owes money to the company to pay that money directly to the creditor (for example, by ordering the debtor's bank to pay the creditor out of the debtor's bank account).

Court orders for enforcement actions fall within the definition of security and therefore a **liquidator's ability to deal with** such goods is limited (*Re Printing & Numerical Registering Co* (1878) 8 Ch D 535), and depends upon the stage which the enforcement proceedings have reached at the commencement of the liquidation (¶7672).

> MEMO POINTS   Usually, the commencement of a **voluntary liquidation** is the date of the resolution, but if the creditor had notice of a meeting at which a resolution for voluntary liquidation is proposed, the date he had notice is taken as the date of the commencement of the liquidation (s 183(2)(a) IA 1986).

Effect of winding up at different stages of enforcement

7904 Enforcement **started after** the commencement of the liquidation is void, and therefore will not prevent the liquidator from dealing with the assets in the usual way (s 128 IA 1986).

7905 If enforcement has been **completed before** the commencement of the liquidation, the liquidator cannot recover those funds or assets for the benefit of the liquidation (s 183 IA 1986). For these purposes, enforcement is "**completed**" where:
– execution against goods (including distress): the goods have been seized and sold, or a charging order absolute has been made;
– attachment against land: the land has been seized, a receiver has been appointed or a charging order absolute has been made; and
– attachment of debts: payment of the debt has been received by the creditor, or a third party debt order absolute has been made.

7906 If such enforcement has been issued, but **not completed**, **before** the commencement of liquidation, the creditor will have to account to the liquidator for sums received after that date (s 183 IA 1986). In addition, he will not be able to continue with any execution or attachment procedures already begun. If the creditor had already received money to satisfy the debt (fully or partially) before the commencement of the liquidation, he can keep it (*Re Andrew, Official Receiver v Standard Range & Foundry Co Ltd (No 2)* [1936] 3 All ER 450; *Re Caribbean Products (Yam Importers) Ltd* [1966] 1 All ER 181).

This **restriction** is **qualified** as follows:
a. it can be **set aside by the court**, on whatever terms it thinks fit (s 183(2) IA 1986). However, because such an order would favour one creditor over the others, the court will only do so in special circumstances (*Re Caribbean Products (Yam Importers) Ltd*, above);
b. the liquidator is not allowed to recover assets of the company which have been **bought** in good faith **by a third party** from an enforcement or similar officer (s 183(2) IA 1986); and
c. it does not apply to **distress by a landlord**, whereby he has seized the goods of his tenant to secure payment of rent arrears. If the tenant then fails to pay, the landlord can sell the goods and retain the proceeds up to the amount he is owed (*Re Bellaglade Ltd* [1977] 1 All ER 319). However, distress cannot be levied after winding up has commenced (s 128 IA 1986).

> MEMO POINTS A number of **duties** are imposed on **enforcement officers** relating to executions begun but not completed when liquidation is commenced, the details of which are outside the scope of this book (s 184 IA 1986). Broadly, when they receive notice that a winding up order has been made or provisional liquidator appointed (or, in the case of a voluntary liquidation, a resolution for winding up has been passed):
> – they must deliver any goods seized or money received in satisfaction of the debt to the liquidator (the enforcement officer's costs comprise a first charge over the goods or money, which the liquidator must satisfy); and
> – if the judgment is worth over £500 and goods are sold or money paid to the enforcement officer to avoid a sale, the enforcement officer must retain the balance (after he has deducted his costs) for 14 days so that any liquidation commenced in that period can be notified to him and the money dealt with accordingly.
> The court can set aside the liquidator's rights under this provision in favour of a creditor.

Assets subject to trusts and other equitable claims

7907 Assets held on trust by the company for a third party, or those to which a third party has a better equitable or proprietary claim, are **generally** not available to the liquidator. However, the liquidator may be able to gain access to such assets, if:
– the trust has been created as a preference (¶7819+); or
– the court uses its discretion to order that assets held by the company on trust for a third party must be applied to pay the liquidator's costs and charges (*Re Berkeley Applegate (Investment Consultants) Ltd* [1988] 3 All ER 71).

If the **trust** was created over the assets **by way of security**, the rules relating to secured assets apply (¶7977+).

7908 The company's **pension scheme** is often one of the most complex assets with which the liquidator has to deal. The consequences of the company's insolvency on a pension scheme operated by it will depend on the scheme's trust deed or rules. The scheme is often wound up.

If the pension scheme is **in surplus**, the scheme rules usually provide for the surplus to be used, in whole or in part, to increase the members' entitlements at the discretion of the scheme trustees and/or employer. Such a discretion conferred on the employer will be exercised by the independent trustee of the scheme (ss 22, 23, 25, 26 Pensions Act 1995; the liquidator is obliged to ensure that at least one of the trustees is independent). Any surplus not used in this way, or where the rules do not allow for it, will be paid to the employer. However, the surplus may end up being held on trust for the benefit of the contributors to the scheme and/or as bona vacantia property, depending on the rules of the scheme in question (¶9940; *David v Richards and Wallington Industries Ltd* [1991] 2 All ER 563). In some circumstances, the liquidator may even be able to apply surplus funds to pay creditors.

If, on the other hand, the scheme is **in deficit**, the amount of the deficit is treated as a non-preferential debt owed by the employer to the scheme (s 75 Pensions Act 1995).

Proceeds of crime

7909 The liquidator will not be able to deal with assets in relation to which:
– a **restraint order** was made; or
– an **enforcement receiver**, **enforcement administrator** or **director's receiver** was appointed,
before the company went into liquidation (s 426 Proceeds of Crime Act 2002). If such a step is taken after the company enters liquidation, the court's powers over assets connected with criminal activities cannot be exercised if it would interfere with the liquidator paying the expenses of the liquidation and making distributions to creditors.

If the company has made a **tainted gift**, insolvency proceedings cannot be taken in relation to those assets as a transaction at an undervalue, preference or transaction defrauding creditors, as long as one of the steps listed above has been taken (s 427 Proceeds of Crime Act 2002).

An **insolvency practitioner** who deals with such property when he was not entitled to do so will not be **liable** for any loss or damage caused by his actions, provided he reasonably believed that he was entitled to take the action he did and he did not act negligently (ss 432, 433 Proceeds of Crime Act 2002).

2. Assets not realised by the liquidator

7914 Most assets will be realised by the liquidator for the benefit of the liquidation. However, there are two categories of assets in particular which can be, but are not always, realised:
– **onerous property**: this is difficult to realise and often imposes long-term obligations on the company, which cannot be fulfilled while the company is in liquidation and therefore must be released; and
– **contracts**: these can be rescinded by the liquidator or by the other parties to the contract, for example because the contract cannot be fulfilled by the company in liquidation.

Further, unrealised assets may be distributed, where appropriate and with the necessary consent. Assets can only be used to **repay creditors** if they cannot be readily or advantageously sold by the liquidator, for example because of the nature of the assets or other special circumstances (r 4.183 IR 1986). The liquidator needs the permission of the liquidation committee to distribute assets to creditors, and may do so according to the assets' estimated value. The liquidator may also be able to **distribute** unrealised assets **to the shareholders**, if this is allowed by the company's articles. Table A permits the liquidator to do so, if authorised by an extraordinary resolution of the shareholders (reg 117 TA 1985).

> MEMO POINTS 1. In a **voluntary liquidation**, the liquidator has the additional option of distributing shares and other interests in a purchaser company to the shareholders instead of cash (¶8490). The provision allowing the liquidator to repay the creditors using unrealised assets does not apply in an **MVL** because there should be no need for it in a solvent liquidation.
> 2. Although **extraordinary resolutions** are no longer required under statute, if a company's articles still require certain decisions to be made using this form of resolution then the company will have to comply, see ¶3544. For companies incorporated on or after 1 October 2007 that adopt Table A, this requirement is amended so that reg 117 TA 1985 calls for a special resolution instead (reg 7 SI 2007/2541).

a. Onerous property

7917 The liquidator can free the company from certain long-term or onerous obligations, to enable him to conclude the liquidation within a reasonable period of time, by "**disclaiming**" it. The **most common type of property** disclaimed by the liquidator is a lease, since a company which is no longer in business has no need for its premises, but the lease to which it is subject may impose obligations on the company for years to come. If the liquidator is unable (or if it would not be cost- and/or time-effective) to assign the lease, he can disclaim it instead. The liquidator does not need the **sanction** of the court or liquidation committee to exercise his power of disclaimer, but any person aggrieved by his decision can challenge it through the court (which will usually only interfere if the liquidator's decision was made in bad faith or was unreasonable, ¶8234+).

This **power applies to** any (s 178(3) IA 1986):
- unprofitable contracts;
- property which is unsaleable or difficult to sell;
- property which imposes a financial liability on the company; or
- property which requires the company to perform any other onerous act.

"**Property**" is widely defined for insolvency purposes (¶9941).

7918

Procedure

The **liquidator** can disclaim property at any **time** during the liquidation, even if he has already exercised any rights of ownership over it, for example by using it, taking possession of it or selling it (s 178(2) IA 1986).

However, this can put **other persons interested** in the same property, such as landlords, sub-tenants and guarantors, at a disadvantage because they cannot deal with it as they wish. Therefore, such a person can require the liquidator to decide whether to disclaim property by sending him a "notice to elect" in Form 4.54, by personal delivery or registered post (s 178(5) IA 1986; r 4.191 IR 1986). If the liquidator has not served a notice of disclaimer within 28 days from receiving the notice to elect, he cannot disclaim that property.

7919

If the liquidator decides to disclaim an asset, the procedure is as follows:

7920

Party	Action	Details	Timing	Reference
Liquidator	Files notice of disclaimer at court	Form 4.53 needs to contain enough information about property so it can be identified	– Any time during the liquidation; or – within 28 days of notice to elect	r 4.187 IR 1986; s 178(2) IA 1986
Court	Returns notice to liquidator endorsed with date of filing	Date endorsed = "date of disclaimer"	n/a	r 4.187 IR 1986
Liquidator	Gives notice to other parties and notifies court of recipients	Copies to: – every person claiming an interest in property; and – every person under liability regarding property that will not be released by the disclaimer (see ¶7922+)	Within 7 days of receiving endorsed notice from court	r 4.188 IR 1986
		If leasehold property, also copies to every person claiming under company as underlessee or mortgagee		
		If unprofitable contract, also copies to parties and every person with an interest in it		
		Also copies to any person liquidator subsequently realises should have had notice as above, unless: – liquidator is satisfied person is aware of disclaimer and its date; or – court orders that notice to that person is not necessary	As soon as liquidator realises person should have been notified	r 4.88 IR 1986
		Also copies to any person liquidator thinks should be notified for public interest or other reasons	At any time	r 4.189 IR 1986

Party	Action	Details	Timing	Reference
Interested party	Apply for vesting order	See ¶7924+	Within 3 months of earliest of: – applicant being aware of disclaimer; or – applicant receiving notice	r 4.194 IR 1986

Effect of disclaimer

7922 When the liquidator disclaims onerous property, the **company** is released from its rights, interests and liabilities in respect of the property in question (s 178(4) IA 1986); a disclaimer only affects the rights, interests and liabilities of **other persons** so far as it is necessary to release the company. Any person suffering loss or damage as a result of the disclaimer becomes a creditor of the company and can prove in the winding up (s 178(6) IA 1986).

The further effects of disclaimer on real property depend upon the type of land in question:
a. freehold land becomes bona vacantia property; and
b. leasehold land, either:
– if the **company is** the **original lessee** the leased land reverts to the landlord, who gets immediate possession and is no longer entitled to future rent; or
– if the **company is** an **assignee** of a lease created before 1/1/96 the leased land reverts to the original lessee, who will be liable to the landlord for any breaches even if they were committed by the company as assignee (unless the covenant in question is a "real covenant" (i.e. concerning the land itself) in which case the company can still be liable). The original lessee will be able to prove in the liquidation if he has rights of indemnity against the company. Otherwise, he will have to claim against the person to whom he assigned the lease, and the claim will be passed along the chain of assignees until the penultimate assignee to the company proves in the liquidation. If the lease was created on or after 1/1/96, any previous assignees are automatically released from their liabilities on assignment, therefore when the company is released from its liabilities under the lease, the landlord has to prove for any loss or damage suffered. This different treatment is due to the effect of the Landlord and Tenant (Covenants) Act 1995, which changed the way in which lease obligations could be enforced when a lease has been assigned.

7923 If a lease has been continued for the benefit of the liquidation, and in the case of all other disclaimed property, the disclaimer is **effective from** the date endorsed on the notice of disclaimer by the court (s 178(4) IA 1986; Re HH Realisations Ltd (1975) 31 P & CR 249, a case under the old statutory provisions).

In the case of leasehold land where the **lease** has **not** been **continued** for the benefit of the liquidation, a disclaimer is effective when all persons claiming under the company as underlessee or mortgagee have been served with notice, and (s 179 IA 1986):
– no applications for a vesting order (see below) have been made within 14 days of the last notice being received: or
– such an application has been made, but the court has directed the disclaimer to proceed.

MEMO POINTS   Disclaimer of a lease will not release a **surety** of the lessee or assignees, but the landlord cannot both take possession of the property and claim rent from the surety (Hindcastle Ltd v Barbara Attenborough Associates Ltd [1996] 1 All ER 737; Active Estates Ltd v Parness [2002] EWHC 893 (Ch)).

Ownership of disclaimed property

7924 Once a liquidator has disclaimed any of the company's property, a person who has either an interest in that property or is subject to liabilities which are not discharged by the disclaimer can apply to the court for a "**vesting order**" (s 181 IA 1986). A vesting order transfers the

legal ownership of the disclaimed property to another person. That person does not necessarily have to be the applicant (for example, a landlord can ask the court to vest a lease in a sub-lessee), but must be a person who is either:
– entitled to the property (or the trustee of such a person); or
– subject to liabilities regarding the property which are not discharged by the disclaimer (or the trustee of such a person), if it would be a fair way of compensating him for his liabilities.

Application

7925 The application for a vesting order must be **made within** 3 months of the applicant being aware of the disclaimer or receiving a copy of the liquidator's notice, whichever is earlier (r 4.194 IR 1986). The application must be filed at court together with an affidavit stating:
– whether he makes the application as someone with an interest or a liability in the disclaimed property;
– the date on which he became aware of the disclaimer or received a copy of the liquidator's notice;
– the grounds for his application; and
– the order he wants the court to make.

The court will notify the applicant of the hearing's date, time and place, and the applicant must **give notice to** the liquidator of the hearing, together with a copy of his application and affidavit, at least 7 clear days before the hearing. The court may require that notice of the hearing and application is also given to other parties. Once the court has made its order, it will send copies to the liquidator and applicant.

The **general rules** concerning insolvency applications can be found at ¶7380+.

> MEMO POINTS   The Insolvency Service has proposed that **affidavits** are replaced by witness statements (see ¶7637). This change is likely to be implemented on 1 October 2008.

Orders

7926 The order vests the property in the person chosen by the court, without the need for any additional transfer or assignment (s 181(6) IA 1986).

> MEMO POINTS   When the property vests in any person (including the Crown), any **rentcharge** (¶9940) due on the property is only payable by him when he takes possession or control, or is in occupation, of it (s 180 IA 1986).

7927 If the application asks the court to vest **leasehold property** in an underlessee or mortgagee, it can only do so on the basis of the same liabilities and obligations:
– as the company at the commencement of the liquidation; or
– to which he would have been subject if the lease had been assigned to him at the commencement of the liquidation.

If the underlessee or mortgagee **refuses to take** the **property** on these terms, the court will terminate his proprietary interest. If nobody will accept the lease on these terms, the court can vest the property in any person liable to perform the lessee's covenants (s 182(3) IA 1986).

Since the application also suspends the effect of disclaimer over any leasehold property, an order concerning such property must re-activate the disclaimer (s 179 IA 1986).

b. Contracts

7928 When a company goes into liquidation, it will usually be a party to a number of contracts. The liquidation will not in itself constitute a breach by the company of any unperformed contracts (unless their terms provide otherwise), and so the **other parties** to the contracts cannot refuse to perform their obligations because of the company's position (*British Wagon Co and Parkgate Wagon Co v Lea & Co* (1880) 5 QBD 149). Unless the liquidator causes the company to carry on trading for the benefit of the liquidation, the company is unlikely to be able to comply with them. This can leave the other parties in a difficult position, for example, they may be obliged to carry out work with little prospect of being paid. There are a number of ways in which the other party can **seek redress**.

7929 If the **company does not perform** its obligations under the contract, the other party will usually be able to sue for breach of contract. It is common to find terms in commercial contracts which provide for termination on one party's insolvency, determining the parties' claims against each other at that point. Otherwise, the liquidator can declare that he is unable to perform the contracts, which will be treated as a breach entitling the other party to claim damages (*Telsen Electric Co Ltd v J J Eastick & Sons* [1936] 3 All ER 266).

In rare circumstances, the other party may be able to obtain an order for **specific performance** of a contract, for example where the contract concerned land (*Re Coregrange Ltd* [1984] BCLC 453).

7930 As an alternative to suing the company for breach of contract, which may not be cost- or time-effective, the legislation allows a person who is interested in a contract to apply to the court to have it **rescinded** (s 186 IA 1986). This will also be useful for the liquidator where the remaining obligations under the contract fall to the other party (for example, where the company had paid for services which the other party has not yet performed). The liquidator can defend such an application on the basis that the obligations of the company will be carried out in full. If the court orders the contract to be rescinded, it can order either party to pay damages to the other for non-performance of the contract as is fair in the circumstances, and if the company is ordered to pay damages to another party, they can be proved for in the winding up.

III. Distribution

7945 The proceeds of realising the assets must be used to discharge the company's liabilities. Broadly speaking, distributions of assets not subject to a fixed charge must be made in a **fixed order**, to:
a. discharge the expenses of the liquidation;
b. meet the creditors' claims in the following order:
– preferential creditors (who, if not fully paid out of the unsecured assets are paid out of the non-ring-fenced portion of any assets secured by a floating charge);
– unsecured creditors (who, if not fully paid out of the unsecured assets are paid out of the ring-fenced portion of any assets secured by a floating charge); and
– deferred creditors; and
c. pay any surplus to the contributories.

Assets subject to a **fixed charge** must be applied to discharge the costs of realising those assets and then the debt for which they are secured; any surplus may be applied to the company's other liabilities in the fixed order. The liquidator is required to deal with **floating charges** in a particular way, to ensure some distribution to unsecured creditors, which is discussed at ¶7992+. The order of distribution is illustrated by way of a **flowchart** at ¶8101+, which is followed by worked examples following through two different scenarios.

MEMO POINTS The **new Companies Act** will allow the liquidator to pay the general expenses of the liquidation out of the company's assets, including those subject to floating charges. See ¶7997.

7946 If the liquidator **mistakenly makes a distribution** to discharge a liability which the company does not owe, he can apply to the court for directions as to how to remedy the error, or enter into a compromise or arrangement with the creditors and shareholders, if he can obtain the relevant sanction (s 167(3) IA 1986; ¶8215+). If the mistake cannot be remedied, the liquidator may be held personally liable, if it can be shown that the mistake was made negligently, recklessly or intentionally (*Re Home and Colonial Insurance Co Ltd* [1929] All ER Rep 231), or that the liquidator should have sought the court's directions before making the payment (e.g. where there was doubt as to whether the company was liable).

A. Costs and expenses of winding up

1. Cost of realising secured assets

7956

A secured creditor's options on liquidation of the debtor company are discussed at ¶7977+. Secured assets can be **realised by the charge holder**, in which case he must bear any costs of realisation himself. If the **liquidator realises** the assets, the proceeds must be applied to discharge the costs of realisation before the debt for which they were secured is paid off. In the case of a floating charge, these costs are met out of the non ring-fenced portion of assets.

If the secured **debt cannot be paid in full** with the remaining proceeds of the relevant assets, the creditor can prove for the unsecured balance. On the other hand, if there is a **surplus** left over after the debt has been paid off in full, it is added to the general pot of assets to meet the expenses of the liquidation and other creditors' claims.

2. Other expenses of winding up

7957

The general body of unsecured assets is to be used to meet the expenses of the liquidation, including the remuneration of the liquidator, before any other claims (*Re Salters Hall School Ltd (in liquidation), Merrygold v Horton* [1998] 1 BCLC 401). The Rules lay down an **order of priority** in which the expenses must be paid, which can only be altered by court order where the company's assets are insufficient to meet those expenses so that the court decides which expenses should be paid out of the assets and which should not (s 156 IA 1986).

As a result, a **liquidator's decisions** as to whether to pursue a particular course of action in the liquidation have to take into account whether or not he will be able to recoup his expenses (both in terms of whether there will be sufficient assets and whether those expenses would be payable as "expenses of the liquidation"), and whether it would be a proper use of the company's money. If a liquidator decides to pursue a particular course of action, he does not have to have sufficient money in hand. He can incur the expenses on the anticipation of the increased assets meeting them, or he can obtain funding from the unsecured creditors who will benefit from the proposed action (*Re Demaglass Ltd, Lewis v Dempster* [2003] 1 BCLC 412). If he is in any doubt, he should seek guidance from the court as to whether the proposed costs would fall into one of the categories of "expenses of the liquidation".

> MEMO POINTS The court can also be asked to exercise its power to alter the order in which expenses are paid in a **voluntary liquidation** (s 112 IA 1986; ¶8523+).

a. Order of priority

7958

The expenses of the winding up must be paid out of the company's assets in the following order (r 4.218(1) IR 1986).

Rank[1]	Expense
1	• Official receiver/liquidator incurred in: – preserving, realising or getting in company's assets; and – conduct of legal proceedings (in own name or company's) • Employing shorthand writer (as ordered by the court) for a public examination carried out by official receiver • Holding modified public examination on official receiver's application
2	Other expenses or disbursements of official receiver (or under his authority), including those arising because he has carried on company's business

Rank[1]	Expense
3	– Fees payable under fees orders for making applications and presenting petitions in insolvency matters, including those payable to official receiver, except those for performing his general duties (ss 414-415A IA 1986) – Any remuneration payable to official receiver
4	– Fees payable under fees orders to official receiver for performing his general duties (ss 414-415A IA 1986) – Repayable deposit lodged under fees order for such fees
5	Cost of security provided by provisional liquidator, liquidator or special manager
6	Provisional liquidator's remuneration
7	Deposit lodged on application for provisional liquidator to be appointed
8	Petitioner's costs and those of other persons appearing on the petition whose costs were allowed by court
9	Special manager's remuneration
10	Costs of person employed or authorised to assist in preparing statement of affairs or accounts (¶8129)
11	Any allowance made towards costs by court on application to be released from obligation to submit statement of affairs or for extension of time
12	Costs of employing shorthand writer other than in 1 above
13	Liquidator's disbursements (including travelling costs of members of liquidation committee where liquidator has allowed reimbursement; not including corporation tax incurred in 16 below)
14	Remuneration/emoluments of person employed by liquidator to perform services for company (as required/authorised by IA 1986 or IR 1986)
15	Liquidator's remuneration, up to amount payable to official receiver under Sch 6 IA 1986
16	Corporation tax on chargeable gains accruing on realisation of company's asset (whether realised by liquidator, secured creditor, receiver or manager)
17	Remainder (if any) of liquidator's remuneration
18	Any other expenses of liquidator properly chargeable in carrying out his functions

Note:
1. These provisions apply where the liquidation commenced on or after **1/1/03** (SI 2002/2712). Where winding up was commenced **before** this date the unamended Rule applies.

MEMO POINTS   The same order of priority applies in a **CVL**. However, since an **MVL** must be a solvent winding up, an order of priority is not necessary because all of the expenses and liabilities can be met by the company's assets (r 4.1 IR 1986).

7959 If the company has been subject to **another** type of **insolvency proceeding** immediately **prior** to the compulsory liquidation, the expenses are dealt with as follows:
a. the costs of a preceding voluntary liquidation (including the costs of preliminary steps such as calling and holding the meeting, *Re A V Sorge & Co Ltd* [1986] BCLC 490) and that liquidator's remuneration rank first (r 4.219 IR 1986); and
b. the company's assets may be subject to a charge to pay the expenses and relevant insolvency practitioner's remuneration in the case of a preceding administration, receivership or CVA (respectively: para 99 Sch B1 IA 1986; ss 37(4), 45(2) IA 1986; rr 1.23, 4.21A IR 1986).

b. Particular costs and expenses

Litigation

7961 The costs of litigation commenced or defended by the liquidator on the company's behalf are normally paid as an expense of the liquidation.

The liquidator's ability to recover the costs of commencing or defending legal proceedings as an expense of the liquidation depends on whether the winding up commenced before or after 1 January 2003, owing to the amendments to the order of priority which came into force on that date. If the **liquidation** was **commenced after 1 January 2003**, he can recover the costs of both successful and unsuccessful litigation at rank 1 in the table at ¶7958 above, and any costs or expenses which do not strictly fall into these categories can be recovered under the final catch-all category at rank 18.

The rules relating to the costs of litigation as an expense of the liquidation do not affect the **court's power to order costs** to be paid by any party to litigation, including ordering that costs be paid by the company or the liquidator (r 4.220(2) IR 1986). Nor do they affect the right of any party who wins on costs. For example, if the liquidator is ordered to pay a proportion of the costs of another party to the litigation, that party can enforce that order, irrespective of whether the liquidator can recover his costs as an expense of the liquidation.

MEMO POINTS 1. These provisions were brought in to clarify the position which had arisen through case law, and which still applies to liquidations commenced **before 1 January 2003**. Readers interested in these liquidations should refer to these key **cases**: *Re M C Bacon Ltd (No 2)* [1990] BCLC 607; *Re R S & M Engineering Co Ltd, Mond v Hammond Suddards (a firm) (No 2)* [1999] 2 BCLC 485; and *Re Floor Fourteen Ltd, Lewis v Commissioner of Inland Revenue* [2001] 3 All ER 499.
2. See ¶7997 for **proposed changes** to how the costs of litigation can be paid out of the company's assets.

If there are **insufficient assets** in the company to sustain litigation, the liquidator may have to seek financial help from third parties (but in doing so he must be careful to avoid agreements that are illegal under the law relating to maintenance and champerty).

7963

If the **liquidator** has **acted improperly** in commencing or defending the proceedings or during the course of the litigation, the court has the power to order him to pay costs personally (s 51(1) Supreme Court Act 1981; *Aiden Shipping Co Ltd v Interbulk Ltd, The Vimeira* [1986] 2 All ER 409).

Tax

Any tax liabilities which arose **before the liquidation** will be dealt with as unsecured claims with no preferential status. The Crown may set off a tax refund owed by one government department against tax owed to another department. See ¶7751 for the effect of the commencement of the winding up on tax matters.

7964

Liabilities arising **during the liquidation** are dealt with in different ways, principally:
a. corporation tax: liability to corporation tax arises on profits made during liquidation (s 8 ICTA 1988). The liquidator will only usually be liable for them if the company in question was incorporated outside the UK, in which case he will seek to be reimbursed by the company (s 108 Taxes Management Act 1970). Corporation tax is treated as a disbursement of the liquidator, within rank 13 of the order of priority for the expenses of the winding up (see ¶7958 above), except for corporation tax on chargeable gains on the realisation of an asset, which falls within rank 16 (*Re Toshoku Finance UK plc (in liquidation)* [2002] 3 All ER 961). In the final year of the liquidation, the liquidator can make an assessment for tax before the end of the company's accounting period at the rate of tax set for the previous financial year, if not fixed or proposed specifically (s 342 ICTA 1988);
b. VAT: the company is still viewed as the taxable person whilst in liquidation, but Revenue and Customs will deal with the liquidator, who must make the VAT returns and account for VAT collected by the company. He must notify the local VAT office of his appointment within 21 days (reg 9 SI 1995/2518). A VAT registered company should remain so, as long as the company's business is continued and/or assets are being realised. Otherwise, the company ceases to be a taxable person (para 8 Sch 4 VATA 1994); and
c. other taxes: the liquidator should ensure that the company continues to comply with its other taxation obligations, such as PAYE and NICs. If the company's property is occupied, rates due after the commencement of liquidation are payable as an expense of the liquidation. On the other hand, rates (or instalments of rates) due before then will have to be proved for in the usual way. Council tax may be payable where the company is the owner of an empty dwelling, and is treated in a similar way (s 6 Local Government Finance Act 1992).

Rent

7965 If the company remains in possession of leased property during the liquidation because the liquidator has permission to continue to trade, the rent accruing after the commencement of the liquidation is usually payable as an expense of the winding up (*Re ABC Coupler and Engineering Co Ltd (No 3)* [1970] 1 All ER 650). Rent accruing due in other circumstances must be proved for in the liquidation (¶8013+).

B. Creditors

7975 Creditors are **treated** differently, **depending on** whether or not their debts are secured, and on the type of security they hold. Before he can make any distributions, the liquidator must **identify** all of the company's creditors, categorise them and ascertain the value of their claims against the company by examining the statement of affairs and creditors' proofs, and by conducting his own investigations, such as questioning officers and employees and looking at the company's books and records (¶8165+). Liquidators must take positive action to identify the creditors, so they often contact potential creditors individually and advertise the need to submit proofs in suitable newspapers (i.e. those with adequate circulation to reach the company's creditors), as well as doing so before declaring the first dividend (¶8055).

The position of **secured creditors** is dealt with first, followed by other creditors, who may be **preferential, ordinary or deferred unsecured creditors**.

1. Secured creditors

7977 A secured creditor is **defined as** a creditor of the company who holds a mortgage, charge, lien or other security over property of the company in respect of his debt (s 248 IA 1986). Security must comprise a proprietary or possessory interest over the property, and **includes**:
a. express agreements to give security, such as a mortgage or other charge instrument;
b. security given impliedly (whether under contract or automatically by law), such as a vendor's or solicitor's lien;
c. statutory security, such as an enforcement officer's charge over goods;
d. security arising as a result of a court order, for example an execution, charging or third party debt order;
e. guarantees given by directors or others in respect of the company's debts which are specifically secured; and
f. security over the property of third parties (e.g. group companies) for the company's debts (*Re Rushton (a bankrupt), ex parte National Westminster Bank Ltd v Official Receiver* [1971] 2 All ER 937).

Security does **not include** the rights of a legal owner under a hire-purchase, conditional sale, chattel leasing or retention of title agreement, nor does it include guarantees by third parties of the company's indebtedness, unless they are specifically secured (*Re Printing & Numerical Registering Co* (1878) 8 Ch D 535). If a creditor's debt is secured over assets belonging to a person other than the company, he will not be a secured creditor for the purposes of the company's liquidation. **Unregistered mortgages and charges** will usually be void against the liquidator (¶4647+).

a. General principles

7978 Secured creditors are not obliged to **prove** in the liquidation, and will only have to do so if their security is not sufficient to cover the debt owed to them. The creditor will submit a proof of debt, stating how much is owed to him and what proportion of the debt is secured, proving for any unsecured part (rr 4.75(1), 4.88(1) IR 1986). He will probably have to estimate the

value of his security, and may alter it at a later date (¶7985+), adjusting any unsecured portion accordingly. In practice, secured creditors will often submit a proof even if they do not anticipate that their security will fall short, as this ensures that the liquidator is aware of their claim to the assets and enables them to alter their proof should the value of the secured assets decline, as well as giving them the option of having their security redeemed by the liquidator. They will also need to consider the implications of submitting a proof on the interest they can claim (¶7989).

Whether or not they prove in the winding up, secured creditors can **choose to** rely on their security or surrender it.

MEMO POINTS If a secured creditor's claim is **partly preferential**, he can apply any proceeds from the realisation of his security to the non-preferential part of his claim and prove for the preferential part (*Re William Hall (Contractors) Ltd* [1967] 2 All ER 1150).

Relying on security

Most secured creditors will rely on their security as it gives them priority over the other creditors in having their debts paid off. They may do so **independently of the liquidator** and realise their secured assets by selling them or taking whatever enforcement action is available with the court's consent, if necessary (¶7757). The **costs** of realisation fall to the secured creditor, who will effectively pay them out of the proceeds of sale. If he has already submitted a proof, he must amend it so that the net amount realised replaces the estimated value and the unsecured balance is adjusted accordingly (r 4.99 IR 1986). If he has not already submitted a proof, he may have to do so if the proceeds of the secured assets did not pay off the debt in full.

7979

Secured creditors will often look to the **liquidator** to **redeem** their security for them, since the liquidator will have the tools for realising the assets at his disposal. In such a case, the creditor will need to have submitted a proof (even if there is no unsecured part of the debt for which he needs to prove).

7980

If redemption is **initiated by the liquidator**, he will notify the secured creditor that he intends to redeem the security at the value in the proof 28 days from the notice. The creditor then has the opportunity to revalue the security within 21 clear days (or longer, if the liquidator allows) and the liquidator will have to redeem it at the new value (r 4.97 IR 1986).

Alternatively, the **secured creditor** can give a written notice to the liquidator at any time, requiring him to elect whether to redeem the security or not at the value placed on it at the time of the notice; the liquidator then has 6 months to exercise his power or decide against it.

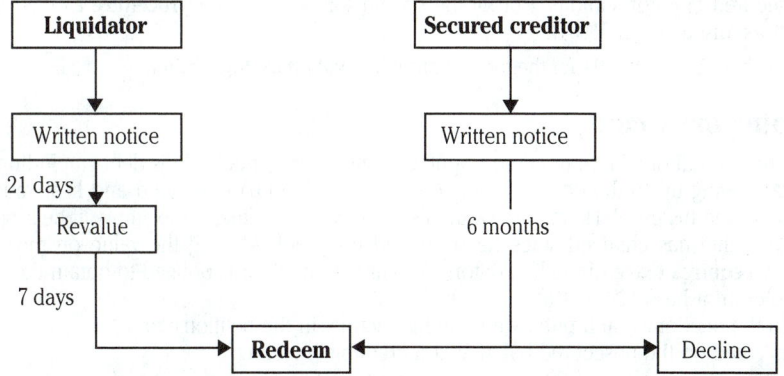

If the liquidator redeems a secured creditor's security, whether following notice from the creditor or not, the **costs** of realisation and transferring the proceeds to the creditor are payable out of the assets.

7981

Surrendering security

7982 A secured creditor can surrender his security and prove for the whole debt (r 4.88(2) IR 1986). He can do so **voluntarily** by informing the liquidator. Since secured creditors are generally in a much better position as regards distributions than unsecured creditors, this is not common, but examples of where this may occur are given below.

> EXAMPLE
> 1. A holding company is a secured creditor of its subsidiary, which is in liquidation. The holding company and subsidiary operate in the same sector and have many suppliers in common, who are unsecured creditors of the subsidiary. By surrendering its security and becoming an unsecured creditor as well, the holding company can preserve its relationship with the suppliers for the benefit of its own continuing business.
> 2. A secured creditor has a floating charge over certain of the company's assets. However, the assets are not worth enough to repay him and, owing to their nature, will be very expensive to realise. The charge holder surrenders his security because, taking into account the value of the unsecured assets and distributions that have to be made before the unsecured creditors, he has a chance of receiving a higher dividend as an unsecured creditor.

7983 However, he may also **impliedly** surrender his security by failing to disclose it on his proof of debt form (r 4.96 IR 1986). He may apply to the court for relief, but it will not be granted where:
– he has simply made a mistake about the value of the security;
– he deliberately omitted to disclose it on his proof; or
– the company has changed its position on the basis that no security was being claimed (*Re Safety Explosives Ltd* [1904] 1 Ch 226).

If the court does grant relief, it can allow the proof form to be amended accordingly.

> MEMO POINTS 1. In a **voluntary liquidation**, the proof does not have to be in a particular form. However, liquidators often send out proofs in the same form as for compulsory liquidations so they get all of the information they need. If a secured creditor omits to disclose his security on such a proof form, he will still impliedly surrender it unless he can show that his omission was inadvertent or due to an honest mistake (*LCP Retail Ltd v Segal* [2006] EWHC 2087 (Ch)).
> 2. The Rules relating to surrender of security, redemption of security by the liquidator and testing the security's value (rr 4.96-4.98 IR 1986) do not affect the **rights of third parties** protected by the **EC Insolvency Regulation** (reg 5 EC Insolvency Reg; see ¶7366+ for a discussion of the EC Insolvency Regulation generally).

b. Submitting a proof

7984 If a secured creditor submits a proof, he should follow the same **procedure** as unsecured creditors, discussed at ¶8030+.

> MEMO POINTS See ¶8491+ for the form of proof in a **voluntary liquidation**.

Valuing the security

7985 A secured creditor will be required to put a **value** on how much of his debt (including any interest owing up to the commencement of the winding up) is secured and how much is unsecured in his proof. He may **re-value** his security at any time, for example, if he suspects that its value has changed since he submitted his proof. Altering the value on the proof usually **requires leave** of the liquidator, although the creditor is obliged to obtain the leave of the court if he (r 4.95 IR 1986):
– was the petitioner (and put a value on his security in the petition); or
– has voted on the unsecured balance at a creditors' meeting.

If his unsecured claim is reduced after a **dividend** has been **declared**, the creditor must immediately repay any amount he has received over that to which he would have been entitled (r 11.9 IR 1986). If his unsecured claim is increased by the revaluation, he is entitled to receive a top-up out of any money the liquidator has available for paying the next dividend to unsecured creditors before that further dividend is paid.

MEMO POINTS In a **voluntary liquidation**, a secured creditor can alter his proof with the leave of the liquidator or the court in any situation (r 4.95(2) IR 1986).

7986 A **creditor** who **fails to comply** with any of the Rules relating to the valuation of securities can be disqualified (wholly or partly) by the court from participating in dividends (r 11.10 IR 1986).

7987 The liquidator can **test** any **valuation** of a security if he is not satisfied with it, by requiring any property comprised in the security to be offered for sale (r 4.98 IR 1986). If the terms of sale cannot be agreed, they may be set by the court. If the sale occurs by auction, both the liquidator (on the company's behalf) and creditor may attend the auction and bid for the property in question.

c. Interest

7989 Interest accruing **before** the **commencement of** the **liquidation** is provable as part of the debt. If the secured creditor has not submitted a proof, he can still apply the proceeds of realising his security to paying off pre-liquidation interest.

A secured creditor's right to receive interest on his debts **after the commencement of** the **liquidation** differs according to whether or not he submits a proof. If he **does not prove**, he is entitled to apply the proceeds of realising his security to the principal, costs and interest, including interest accruing after the commencement of liquidation, in full (*Re Joint Stock Discount Co, Warrant Finance Co's Case* (1870) 39 LJ Ch 417). If he **does prove** in the liquidation, on the other hand, he cannot apply the proceeds of realising his security towards interest accruing after the commencement of the liquidation, although profits made from the security since then can be used to pay off the interest accruing in the same period (*Re London, Windsor and Greenwich Hotels Co, Quartermaine's Case* [1892] 1 Ch 639).

d. Fixed charges

7990 Assets which are secured by a valid fixed charge at the commencement of the liquidation are usually only **available to meet** the debts and liabilities in respect of which they have been secured (and the costs of their realisation), not the costs of the liquidation or any of the company's liabilities. However, the secured assets can be made available if:
– the secured creditor surrenders his security;
– the liquidator is able to obtain their release, for example by establishing that the charge was not valid; or
– there is a surplus remaining after the costs of realisation and secured creditor's debt and interest have been paid off.

e. Floating charges

7992 Floating charges created on or after 15 September 2003 must be treated in a particular way by the liquidator. The assets subject to the charge are divided into **two funds** to be used to meet different claims:
a. a "ring-fenced" portion, which can be used to pay off the unsecured creditors before the floating charge holder, if the unsecured assets are insufficient; and
b. a "non ring-fenced" portion, which can be used to pay off the preferential creditors before the floating charge holder, if the unsecured assets are insufficient.

For these purposes, a floating charge is one created as a floating charge, so that those which have crystallised before the commencement of the liquidation are still caught, but those which were intended as fixed charges are not (s 251 IA 1986; *Re Portbase (Clothing) Ltd, Mond v Taylor* [1993] 3 All ER 829).

7993 The **flowchart** and **examples** at ¶8101+ illustrate how the preferential and unsecured creditors can be paid out of the non ring-fenced and ring-fenced portions of the assets subject to a floating charge.

"Ring-fenced" fund

7994 If a floating charge was **created on or after 15 September 2003**, a certain portion (the "prescribed part") of the "net property" comprising the floating charge must be ring-fenced by the liquidator and set aside to pay the unsecured creditors if the unsecured assets are insufficient to do so (s 176A IA 1986). The prescribed part can only be used to repay the floating charge holder once the unsecured creditors have been paid in full.

The following **definitions** apply here:
a. "prescribed part" (SI 2003/2097): between £10,000 and £600,000, calculated as follows:
– 50% of an amount of the company's net property up to £10,000; plus
– 20% of any remaining net property over £10,000; and
b. "net property" (s 176A(6) IA 1986): the amount of its property which would be available for the satisfaction of holders of debentures or floating charges created by the company.

7995 The liquidator **does not have to ring-fence** a sum for the unsecured creditors if (s 176A(3)-(5) IA 1986):
a. the company's net property is less than the "prescribed minimum" of £10,000 and the liquidator considers that the costs of distributing to the unsecured creditors would outweigh the benefits of doing so;
b. the obligation is disapplied by a CVA or compromise or other arrangement with the creditors and shareholders (¶6500+); or
c. the liquidator is excused from doing so by an order of the court on the ground that the cost of distributing to the unsecured creditors would outweigh the benefits.

> MEMO POINTS If the liquidator **applies** to court to be **excused from ring-fencing** a sum for the unsecured creditors, his application must be in the correct form supported by evidence (r 7.3A IR 1986). He is only obliged to give **notice** of the application to any other insolvency practitioner acting in relation to the company, including a member state liquidator (r 7.4A IR 1986). If the application is successful, the liquidator must (s 176A(5) IA 1986; r 12.22 IR 1986):
> – send a copy of the order to the company;
> – send a copy to Companies House with Form 12.1; and
> – (unless the court directed otherwise) send a copy of the order to every creditor of whose claim and address he is aware; or
> – advertise the order in an appropriate newspaper so that it comes to the unsecured creditors' attention, if the court allows.

Non "ring-fenced" fund

7997 If the unsecured assets are insufficient to pay the preferential creditors in full, the non ring-fenced portion of the assets subject to the floating charge can be used to do so. These assets are not to be applied to pay the expenses of the liquidation as well, except for costs incurred in preserving or realising the assets under the floating charge (*Re Leyland Daf Ltd, Buchler v Talbot* [2004] 1 All ER 1289). The floating charge holder then ranks ahead of the unsecured creditors once the preferential debts have been paid.

> MEMO POINTS The **new Companies Act** will insert a provision into IA 1986 (at s 176ZA IA 1986) that the expenses of the liquidation shall be paid out of the company's assets (including those subject to floating charges) in priority to unsecured creditors and floating charge holders, which will deliberately reverse part of the decision in *Re Leyland Daf Ltd*, above (s 1282 CA 2006, due to come into force on 6 April 2008). The logic behind this is that collective insolvency procedures should be funded by all creditors, including floating charge holders.
> The new Act recognises that this may be unduly harsh on floating charge holders and so allows regulations to be made restricting the expenses that can be met to those agreed by the charge holder or the court. At the time of writing, the Insolvency Service's proposals on this issue are out to **consultation**. It proposes to make changes to the Insolvency Rules so that:
> – the expenses of the liquidation should also be payable out of the proceeds of any litigation that the liquidator has the power to bring or defend; and

– where the assets of the company available to meet the general pool of creditors' claims are not sufficient to meet the expenses of the liquidation, the expenses should be able to be paid out of floating charge assets in priority to the claims of the floating charge holder. However, if the expenses to be met are related to litigation, the liquidator will have to obtain the floating charge holder's approval. If the charge holder is the defendant in the litigation, or he refuses his consent, the liquidator will be able to apply to court instead. A new form for seeking consent is set out in the consultation.

The new Rules, if approved by the consultation, are expected to come into force on 6 April 2008, applying to liquidations commenced on or after that date.

2. Other creditors

Creditors **claim** in the liquidation **by** "proving" for their debts (whether in writing or not); the **document** by which they are required to establish their claims is called a "proof" (r 4.73(3) IR 1986).

8003

a. Provable debts

Debts are widely defined in the Rules as (r 13.12 IR 1986):
a. any debt or liability to which the company is subject at the date on which it goes into liquidation;
b. any debt or liability to which the company may become subject after that date because of any obligation incurred before it went into liquidation; and
c. any provable interest (see ¶8021+ below).

Therefore, this generally **encompasses** all debts, whether (rr 12.3, 13.12 IR 1986):
– present or future;
– certain or contingent;
– ascertained or sounding in damages (which would only be fixed when the claim is heard); or
– fixed/liquidated or capable of being fixed by rules or by opinion.

A "**liability**" is defined as a liability to pay money or money's worth, including statutory liabilities and those incurred by breaches of trust, contract, tort, bailment or a liability to make a restitution.

8005

> MEMO POINTS 1. The definition of "debt" contained in the Rules has been amended to reflect recent case law so that **victims of a company's negligence** can still claim in its liquidation even if they have not yet suffered any damage (Re T & N Ltd [2005] All ER (D) 211 (Dec), a case which concerned potential claims against group companies for asbestos-related personal injuries which were likely to occur in the future but had not yet come to light (due to the nature of the disease caused by asbestos exposure); SI 2006/1272). This will assist people who have, due to the company's negligence, contracted an illness that does not manifest its symptoms for some time. A liability in tort is now provable in liquidation or administration if (rr 12.3, 13.12(2) IR 1986):
> – the cause of action had accrued at the date on which the company entered liquidation or administration; or
> – all of the elements required to establish the cause of action existed at the date on which the company entered liquidation or administration, except for the actionable damage.
> This change applies to liquidations entered into on or after 1 June 2006, either by a resolution being passed or a petition being presented on or after that date (reg 3 SI 2006/1272). However, the change will not apply if the company has entered liquidation:
> – because a preceding administration which was commenced before 1 June 2006 was converted into voluntary liquidation; or
> – on a winding up petition where an immediately preceding administration or voluntary liquidation was commenced before that date.
> The change also applies to **administrations** entered into on or after 1 June 2006, except where the administration application was filed or an immediately preceding liquidation (compulsory or voluntary) was commenced before that date.
> 2. Obligations under a confiscation order (made under s 1 Drug Trafficking Offences Act 1986, s 71 Criminal Justice Act 1988 or Pts 2-4 Proceeds of Crime Act 2002) are **not provable**. There are certain other types of

debts which are not provable either as a matter of public policy or by statute, for example debts arising out of an illegal transaction (r 12.3(3) IR 1986).

3. Certain debts are **provable**, **but** distributions to the relevant creditors are **deferred** until all other debts have been paid in full with interest (¶8066).

8006 Provable debts are usually **determined at the date** of the commencement of the liquidation but, owing to the wide definitions of debts and liabilities, the debt does not have to be due at that date as long as the liability or obligation giving rise to the debt existed at that time. **Debts payable in the future** can be the subject of a proof, but will be reduced according to a set formula for dividend purposes (¶8059), with any shortfall being made up as a deferred debt if there are sufficient funds.

If the company was in **administration** immediately **before** the liquidation, such debts can be proved for until the company entered into administration.

Specific types of claim

Future and contingent debts

8007 Future and contingent debts are provable, but their **value** will be estimated by the liquidator once the proof has been submitted, until their actual value becomes known (¶8036+). If their value is not known when the liquidator pays a dividend to the unsecured creditors, the dividend is calculated according to a set formula (¶8059).

Unliquidated claims

8008 In the case of unliquidated claims, the liquidator will also estimate the value of the debt when the proof is submitted. Commonly, the company will breach **contracts** to which it is a party on entering into liquidation, which, together with liability for contractual damages arising before the commencement of the liquidation, are provable unliquidated debts (see ¶7928+ for a wider discussion on the effect of liquidation on contracts). The law relating to contractual damages applies, so that the damage must have been within the contemplation of the parties at the time of the contract and the claimant must mitigate his loss. If there is a dispute as to its amount, the court will value it as at the date of the commencement of the liquidation (*Re British American Continental Bank Ltd* [1922] 2 Ch 575).

In the case of claims in **tort**, if the cause of action (even if the actionable damage has not yet occurred, see ¶8005/mp) arose before the commencement of liquidation, an unliquidated claim can be proved for in the liquidation.

Judgment debts

8009 Creditors with judgment debts or claims which have been **compromised** with the company before the commencement of the liquidation can prove in the winding up. Judgment debts can be rejected if there was no consideration for the debt or it was improperly obtained, for example where a judgment was obtained by fraud or collusion, or it would not have been made had the proper judicial process been followed (*Re Menastar Finance Ltd (in liquidation), Menastar Ltd v Simon* [2003] 1 BCLC 338).

Expiry of limitation period

8010 **Generally**, debts which are statute barred at the commencement of the liquidation are not provable in the winding up, since the right to claim the debt has "expired" and the person claiming it is no longer a creditor. If the debt is not statute barred at that time but becomes barred before the creditor submits his proof, the debt can still be proved for (*Re General Rolling Stock Co, Joint Stock Discount Co's Claim* (1872) 7 Ch App 646). A **judgment debt**, on the other hand, can be proved for even if more than 6 years have passed between the judgment and the commencement of the liquidation, because a judgment creditor remains a creditor in a broader sense; he is only prevented from taking certain actions based on the judgment after 6 years (*Ridgeway Motors (Isleworth) Ltd v ALTS Ltd* [2005] 2 BCLC 61).

> MEMO POINTS In a **solvent voluntary liquidation**, statute barred debts can only be proved for if the contributories agree (*Re Art Reproduction Co Ltd* [1951] 2 All ER 984).

Money owed to shareholders

8011

Any money owed by the company to its shareholders as **dividends**, **profits** or **other debts** arising out of their capacity as shareholders (e.g. claims arising out of the memorandum and articles, and other claims arising out of companies legislation) is deemed not to be a debt of the company in liquidation and therefore cannot be the subject of a proof (s 74(2) IA 1986). However, the liquidator should still be notified of such monies owing because they will be taken into account when assessing how much of a distribution should be made to shareholders, and will effectively be treated as a deferred debt, in that they will be assessed in the same way as any other debt and paid before the surplus is distributed to the shareholders (¶8066).

Employees' claims

8012

Employees can have a number of types of claim against a company in liquidation, mainly arising from the automatic termination of their service contracts when the winding up order is made:
- **preferential claims** for some remuneration owed and accrued holiday pay (see ¶8044+);
- **guaranteed debts**, which the employee can claim from the secretary of state, where his employment was terminated because of the liquidation (¶8044+). There are also rights in some circumstances to have pension contributions made up (s 124 Pension Schemes Act 1993); and
- **unsecured claims** for wrongful or unfair dismissal or redundancy pay arising in other circumstances (although many will be recoverable from the secretary of state under b).

> MEMO POINTS 1. A **retired employee** can prove for the capital value of his pension, if it is a contractual entitlement, but not if it was gratuitous (*Re Profits and Income Insurance Co* [1929] 1 Ch 262; *Re Birkbeck Permanent Benefit Building Society* [1913] 1 Ch 400).
> 2. However, awards made under employment legislation after the company enters liquidation will not be provable because the debt arises too late (¶8005+), even if the acts complained of took place before the liquidation (*Day v Haine and another* [2007] All ER (D) 298 (Oct)).

Landlords' claims

8013

Landlords can prove for **rent** due up to the commencement of the liquidation (r 4.92 IR 1986). If subsequent rent is not payable as an expense of the liquidation, the landlord may have to prove as an unsecured creditor. There are two possible scenarios:
a. the **company is still the lessee**. The liquidator will usually:
- sell the lease;
- surrender the lease with the landlord's agreement, allowing the landlord to prove in the liquidation for his loss (i.e. future rent and liability on the covenants); or
- disclaim the lease (¶7917+).
If the liquidator takes no such action, the landlord can prove for all accrued rent and any other sums due, and notify the liquidator of the future obligation to pay rent. He cannot prove for future rent, but must wait for it to become due each time (*Re Park Air Services plc* [1999] 1 All ER 673); or
b. the **company has assigned the lease**. The landlord must prove for a contingent claim based on the difference in value of the lease with and without the benefit of the company's covenants (*Re House Property and Investment Co Ltd* [1953] 2 All ER 1525).

> MEMO POINTS If the company is in **administration**, rent and other periodical payments which had fallen due when the company entered administration can be the subject of a proof (r 2.87 IR 1986). If the company entered administration part way through a rent period, the creditor can prove for the amount that would have been due up to that date, as if the debt accrued daily.
> Where an **administration immediately preceded** the liquidation, periodical payments due up until the company entered administration only can be the subject of a proof (r 4.92 IR 1986). Where a **liquidation immediately preceded** an administration, only periodical payments due at the commencement of the liquidation can be proved for in the administration.

8014

The lease may give the landlord the **right of forfeiture** (also called a right of re-entry) on his tenant's liquidation. This right can be lost if waived by the landlord, which he can do by taking any action inconsistent with it after he has had notice of the liquidation. Examples of such action are negotiating the surrender of the lease, or serving a notice on the liquidator to elect to disclaim the lease (for these purposes, having notice of the winding up from the advertisement in the *Gazette* (whether or not he had seen it) is not sufficient, *Official Custodian for Charities v Parway Estates Developments Ltd* [1984] 3 All ER 679). There are statutory restrictions on the right of forfeiture, which (in general terms) allow tenants under leases of certain types of property to apply for relief from forfeiture in the 12 months after the commencement of the liquidation (s 146(9), (10) Law of Property Act 1925; s 1 Law of Property (Amendment) Act 1929). After that, the tenant is not entitled to relief, but any assignee of the lessee, sub-tenant or mortgagee retains the right. Generally, if the landlord has the right of **forfeiture for non-payment of rent** it will not be affected by liquidation, nor will the tenant's right to relief on paying up the arrears of unpaid rent (*Re Brompton Securities Ltd (No 2)* [1988] 3 All ER 677).

Insured liabilities

8016 A creditor may have a right against the company's insurers if his claim is a **liability** for which the company held **third party insurance**, which is commonly held by companies in respect of negligence and defective product claims, for example. If so, the company's rights to claim against the insurer are automatically transferred to and vested in the creditor on commencement of the liquidation, whether the liability was incurred before or after that date (s 1 Third Parties (Rights Against Insurers) Act 1930). However, the company's liability must still be established in proceedings against it rather than the insurer (*Bradley v Eagle Star Insurance Co Ltd* [1989] 1 All ER 961). Creditors can therefore obtain disclosure of relevant documentation before commencing proceedings to establish liability (*Re OT Computers (in administration)* [2004] 2 BCLC 682).

> MEMO POINTS This does not apply to a company which is **voluntarily wound up** for the purposes of **reconstructing** or **amalgamating** with another company (s 1(6) Third Parties (Rights Against Insurers) Act 1930).

Professional fees

8017 Fees incurred **in connection with** the **liquidation** are payable as an expense of the liquidation (¶7957+). **Solicitors**' fees not incurred in advising the company or liquidator, or otherwise in connection with putting the company into liquidation can be proved for in the liquidation (a solicitor does not have to have submitted a signed bill in order to prove for his debt, *Re Woods, ex parte Ditton* (1880) 13 Ch D 318).

Professional liens, which a solicitor or accountant may have over particular documents in their possession belonging to their clients, may not be enforceable once the company is in liquidation if their exercise would deprive the liquidator of possession of the documents in question. This is because a lien over the company's books, records or papers is not usually enforceable against a liquidator (s 246(2) IA 1986). A lien arising over any other type of property will not be affected by this provision, but may be **affected** as follows:
a. a lien cannot be exercised over documents which are required by statute or the articles of association to be kept at the registered office of the company or another specified place (*Re Capital Fire Insurance Association* (1883) 24 Ch D 408);
b. any assets acquired by a solicitor (or other professional adviser) after the commencement of the liquidation must be delivered to the liquidator (*Re Capital Fire Insurance Association* (1883) 24 Ch D 408);
c. a solicitor has a lien on a fund recovered as a result of his work for the client company, whether before or after the liquidation, for his costs of that work and the work involved in establishing his claim against the liquidator (*Re Meter Cabs Ltd* [1911] 2 Ch 557). He can also obtain a charging order over that fund (s 73 Solicitors Act 1974); and
d. the lien can be lost by taking action contrary to it, such as proving in the liquidation without valuing or referring to the lien (*Re Carter, Carter v Carter* (1885) 55 LJ Ch 230).

Assigned debts

8018 A debt which has been assigned can form the basis of a proof by the **assignee** for the full amount of the debt, even where he bought it at a discount (*Re Humber Ironworks Co* (1869) LR 8 Eq 122, in which the debt was assigned to a contributory). If the **assignor** has already submitted a proof, the assignee should submit his own and require the liquidator to substitute it for that of the assignor (*Re Frost, ex parte Official Receiver* [1899] 2 QB 50).

Property held by the company on trust

8019 If the creditor claims that the company holds his **property** on trust, he does not have a claim in the liquidation as trust assets are not available to the liquidator. However, if the **benefit of a debt** owed by the company is held on trust, the beneficial owner or the trustee can prove in the liquidation for that debt, although they cannot both do so due to the rule against double proof (see ¶8024) (*Re Bank of Credit and Commerce International SA (No 7)* [1994] 1 BCLC 455).

Debts in foreign currencies

Debts in foreign currencies must be **converted** into sterling at the date of the commencement of the liquidation for the purposes of the winding up. The applicable rate is the middle exchange rate on the London Foreign Exchange Market at the close of business on that day (referred to as "the official rate"; if there is no such rate for the day in question, it will be determined by the court) (r 4.91 IR 1986). Any **dividends** will be **paid** to the creditor in sterling based on that converted proof (*Re Lines Bros Ltd* [1982] 2 All ER 183). If the creditor receives less than his full debt as a result of the conversion, the liquidator may make up any shortfall out of any surplus assets before these are distributed to the shareholders (¶8066).

8020

> MEMO POINTS If the company is in **administration**, the relevant reference in the Rules is different (r 2.84 IR 1986).

If an **administration immediately preceded** the liquidation, the sterling value of the debt is calculated from the date the company entered into administration (r 4.91 IR 1986). Similarly, if a **liquidation immediately preceded** an administration, it is calculated from the commencement of the liquidation (r 2.86 IR 1986).

Interest

Any interest on a debt is provable to the extent that it **accrued before** the commencement of the **liquidation** (r 4.93(1) IR 1986). The interest can arise:
a. due to the terms of a contract;
b. due to the Late Payment of Commercial Debts (Interest) Act 1998;
c. where the debt arises out of a written instrument specifying that it is due at a particular time, interest will be due for the period between when the debt became due and the commencement of the liquidation (r 4.93(3) IR 1986); or
d. where a demand for payment was made, giving notice that interest would be payable from the date of demand to the date of payment, interest will be due for the period between the demand and the commencement of the liquidation (r 4.93(4), (5) IR 1986).

8021

In the case of c. or d. the **rate** of interest is that set out in statute at the commencement of the liquidation (s 17 Judgments Act 1838).

> MEMO POINTS If an **administration immediately preceded** the liquidation, interest can be claimed up to the date on which the company entered administration.

Any interest **accruing after** the company entered into **liquidation** is not provable (r 4.93(1) IR 1986). However, the interest still needs to be calculated (from the later of when the company went into liquidation, or when the debt became overdue), since any surplus remaining after the proved debts have been paid must be used to pay interest for this period before being distributed to the shareholders (s 189 IA 1986). Any interest paid under this provision ranks equally, even if the debts to which it accrued did not. The interest is **calculated** as either:
– the statutory rate at the commencement of the liquidation (s 17 Judgments Act 1838); or
– the rate applicable to that debt were it not for the liquidation.

8022

Multiple claimants

Only one dividend can be paid out in respect of what is substantially the same debt, i.e. the liquidator can only distribute up to the amount owed, although he may do so in instalments, or interim dividends (*Re Oriental Commercial Bank, ex parte European Bank* (1871) 7 Ch App 99). This is known as the "**rule against double proof**" and is generally applicable where both a creditor and guarantor (or surety) prove in the winding up. However, it also applies where the company owes money to two or more creditors jointly and severally, or where the legal and beneficial interests in the debt are owned by separate parties.

8024

The effect of the rule is as follows, where the **whole** of the **debt** has been **guaranteed**:
a. the creditor cannot prove in the liquidation for the debt and also claim from the guarantor;
b. if the guarantor pays the creditor in full, he can then prove in the liquidation;

c. the guarantor can prove in the liquidation even if he has not paid the creditor (as long as the creditor has not himself proved), although if the creditor then proves, his proof will replace the guarantor's (*The Liverpool (No 2)* [1960] 3 All ER 307); and
d. if the guarantor has limited his liability, he cannot prove as long as any part of the debt is outstanding, even if he has paid up the amount for which he is liable (*Barclays Bank Ltd v TOSG Trust Fund Ltd* [1984] BCLC 1).

If only **part of the debt** has been **guaranteed**, the guarantor can pay the creditor the guaranteed part and then prove for it in the liquidation.

MEMO POINTS 1. Where the **guarantor** is **prevented from proving**, he may not set off the amount of his claim against any other sums which are due from him to the company (*Re Fenton, ex parte Fenton Textile Association Ltd* [1931] 1 Ch 85).
2. In the case of **administrations**, the Rules specifically state that dividend payments cannot be made more than once in respect of the same debt (r 2.96(3) IR 1986).

8025 In cases in which the debt is owed by the company and **another debtor**, the creditor can claim it from each one until he has received the full amount owing to him, including interest, provided he deducts any payments received or dividends declared from his proof (*Re Amalgamated Investment and Property Co Ltd* [1984] 3 All ER 272).

b. How to prove debts

8030 Generally, creditors must submit their claims to the liquidator in writing on **Form** 4.25, or a substantially similar document, signed by or on behalf of the creditor (r 4.73 IR 1986). This is referred to as the "proof of debt", or "**proof**". A creditor can ask the liquidator to send him the relevant form (r 4.74 IR 1986).

Creditors are not generally under any obligation to prove by a particular **deadline**, except where (¶8055):
a. the liquidator has published his intention to declare a dividend to creditors who have submitted their proofs by a particular date; or
b. the court has set a date by which the creditors must prove to be able to participate in a particular dividend.

In such cases, any creditor failing to prove by the deadline will not be able to participate in the relevant dividend, but will still be able to submit a proof at a later stage to benefit from any further distributions (¶8056).

MEMO POINTS The procedure for proving in a **voluntary liquidation** is described at ¶8491+.

Form

8032 The proof must contain the following **information** (r 4.75 IR 1986):
– the creditor's name, address and company registration number (if applicable);
– his total claim, including VAT, at the commencement of the liquidation;
– whether or not that figure includes any outstanding uncapitalised interest;
– details of how and when the debt arose;
– details of any security held, the date it was given and its estimated value;
– details of any reservation of title arising in respect of the goods to which the debt refers; and
– the name, address and authority of the signatory of the proof (if not the creditor).

The creditor must specify the documents by which he can **substantiate his claim** but does not have to submit them with the proof; the liquidator, chairman or other convenor of any meeting can require them to be produced at any time. However, any proof submitted for money owed on a negotiable instrument such as a cheque, bill of exchange or promissory note must be accompanied by the instrument or a certified copy of it, unless the liquidator allows otherwise (r 4.87 IR 1986).

MEMO POINTS 1. If the winding up **follows** immediately on from an **administration**, a creditor proving in the administration is deemed to have proved in the liquidation (r 4.73(8) IR 1986).
2. If any trade or other **discounts**, except for discounts for immediate, early or cash settlement, would have been available to the company were it not for the liquidation, they must be deducted from the creditor's claim (r 4.89 IR 1986).

The liquidator can require a proof to be **verified** by an "affidavit of debt", on Form 4.26 or **8033**
a substantially similar document, which can be sworn before the creditor's own solicitor
(rr 4.77(2), 7.57(3) IR 1986). The liquidator will usually require such verification where he is in
doubt as to the value of the claim, or whether he should admit it, particularly if he is
considering rejecting a proof which has been submitted informally.

> MEMO POINTS Unlike many insolvency affidavits, the affidavit of debt cannot be made in the form
> of a **witness statement** instead (r 7.57(6) IR 1986).
> The Insolvency Service has proposed that **affidavits** are replaced by witness statements (see
> ¶7637). This change is likely to be implemented on 1 October 2008.

Cost

Generally, creditors bear the **cost of proving** their debts, although the court can order other- **8035**
wise. Any costs incurred by the liquidator in estimating the quantum of claims are payable
as an expense of the liquidation (r 4.78 IR 1986).

Consideration of proofs

The liquidator must **examine** all proofs submitted to him and, in relation to each one, can **8036**
(r 4.82 IR 1986):
– **admit** all of it for a dividend;
– admit part of it for a dividend; or
– **reject** all of it.

He must assess the validity of the grounds for each debt being proved, and may be liable
for misfeasance if he does not (¶7457+; *Re Home and Colonial Insurance Co Ltd* [1929] All ER Rep 231).
He will also:
– categorise the debts (i.e. secured, preferential, ordinary unsecured or deferred) to deal
with accordingly;
– consider whether set-off applies to the debt to calculate the sum for which the proof is
admitted; and
– determine to what extent the creditor should be permitted to vote at a creditors' meeting
(¶8354+).

When deciding whether or not to admit a proof, the liquidator is obliged to make use of any
defence to the claim available to the company, even if it is a technical or commercially unreasonable one (*Re Home and Colonial Insurance Co Ltd* [1929] All ER Rep 231). If he does not, he may be
personally liable to reimburse the company for any amount paid in respect of the claim.
However, this is subject to the liquidator's general duty not to take advantage of his legal rights
where it would be unfair of him to do so, and the court can order any enrichment to the
company as a result of such a decision to be repaid (*Re Condon, ex parte James* (1874) 9 Ch App 609,
known as "the rule in *ex parte James*"). A proof can be rejected because it is an **abuse of
process**, if it is based on a claim which has already been raised and rejected in other proceedings, for example a claim for wrongful dismissal (*Re Thomas Christy Ltd (in liquidation)* [1994] 2 BCLC 527).

If the proof is wholly or partially **rejected**, the liquidator must send a written statement **8037**
explaining the reasons for its rejection to the creditor as soon as he has made his decision.

In the case of **unliquidated, future or contingent debts**, the liquidator has to estimate the **8038**
value of the debt (r 4.86(1) IR 1986). The creditor can amend his proof at any time during the
liquidation, for example, he can prove for the full amount if his contingent claim becomes
ascertained (*Stanhope Pension Trust Ltd v Registrar of Companies* [1994] 1 BCLC 628). The liquidator can
also revise his estimate, informing the creditor accordingly. However, any previous distributions of the company's assets cannot be disturbed, so the creditor may have missed the
opportunity to prove in full if the assets have already been distributed.

Alteration of proofs

A proof can be **withdrawn** or **varied** at any time by agreement between the creditor and **8039**
liquidator (r 4.84 IR 1986). The liquidator also has the power to **compromise** claims, with the
sanction of the court or the liquidation committee (¶8215+).

If a proof was **wrongly admitted or** its value **should be reduced**, the liquidator (or any creditor, if he will not to do so) can apply to the court for an appropriate order (r 4.85 IR 1986). Notice of the hearing's date, time and place, once fixed by the court, must be given by the applicant to the creditor whose proof is at issue (and to the liquidator, if he is not the applicant). The applicant needs to show, on the balance of probabilities, that the proof should be expunged or reduced (*Re Globe Legal Services Ltd* [2002] BCC 858). If a proof is expunged or reduced, the creditor affected can keep any dividend already received by him; however if it has been reduced, he will not receive any further dividend until he has returned any overpaid dividends already received (*Re Browne, ex parte Official Receiver v Thompson* [1960] 2 A ER 625).

Challenging the liquidator's decision

8040 If a **creditor** disagrees with the liquidator's decision in dealing with his proof, he can **appeal** to the court to have it reversed or varied within 21 clear days of receiving the liquidator's statement that the whole or part of his claim has been rejected (r 4.83(1) IR 1986). The liquidator can bring any matter to the court's attention which is relevant to the consideration of the proof, even if he did not include it in his statement to the creditor (*Re Thomas Christy Ltd (in liquidation)* [1984] 2 BCLC 527). If the official receiver is acting as liquidator, he will not be liable for the costs of the application incurred by any person (r 4.83(6) IR 1986). Any other liquidator will only be so liable if the court orders.

Any **other creditor** or any **contributory** may also **appeal** to the court following a decision by the liquidator to admit or reject any proof, within 21 clear days of being aware of that decision.

Access to proofs

8041 The proofs can be **inspected** at reasonable times on business days by (r 4.79 IR 1986; ¶7412):
– creditors who have submitted proofs which have not been entirely rejected;
– contributories; and
– persons acting for such creditors and contributories.

Any person inspecting the proofs may take copies on payment of a fee of 15p per A4 or A5 page and 30p per A3 page (r 13.11 IR 1986). A creditor (and a member state liquidator in the main proceedings) can also **require** the liquidator to send him a **list of creditors** and the amounts of their respective debts, provided a statement of affairs has not already been filed at court or Companies House (r 12.17 IR 1986). The liquidator can charge the same fee as for copying inspected proofs. It is a criminal offence for a person to pretend to be entitled to obtain such a list or inspect proofs (r 12.18 IR 1986; ¶9935).

c. Distributions to creditors

8042 **When** the liquidator has collected in and realised sufficient assets of the company, is able to estimate the expenses of the liquidation and has identified the creditors and their claims (or at least can estimate them), he will make distributions to the creditors. This is a continuing process, running along side realisation of the assets (i.e. the liquidator does not have to wait until he has realised all of the assets). In a straightforward liquidation of a small company, the liquidator may just declare **one dividend**, whereas in larger and more complex liquidations, where it is likely to take some time to deal with the company's assets properly, he may declare a number of **interim dividends** before the **final one**.

Preferential debts must be paid in full before any dividend is payable to ordinary creditors. If there are sufficient assets remaining, the liquidator will then distribute dividends to the body of **unsecured** creditors. Finally, the **deferred** creditors will be paid in order if there are any surplus funds.

Preferential creditors

8044 Certain debts, known as "preferential debts", are to be paid out of the company's assets **in priority** to all others (s 175 IA 1986). They rank equally among themselves, so that if the company's assets are insufficient to meet all of the preferential debts, they each receive the same proportion of their debt. Dividends are declared and paid to preferential creditors in the same way as ordinary creditors, with any appropriate alterations to the procedure (r 11.12 IR 1986; ¶8053+).

> MEMO POINTS Preferential creditors can also be paid out of assets secured by a floating charge **before** the company goes into **liquidation**, where the charge holder takes possession of any of the property subject to the charge (s 196 CA 1985; restated at s 754 CA 2006, due to come into force on 6 April 2008). An example of such a case was where a debenture holder (whose rights were secured by a floating charge) had entered into an agreement with the company whereby he would receive consideration in two tranches, one on signature of the agreement and one at a later date. He also took an assignment of book debts from the company's subsidiaries. The company went into voluntary liquidation between payment of the two tranches. The court held that the preferential creditors were entitled to be paid out of the consideration paid both before and after the company entered liquidation (s 196 CA 1985; s 175 IA 1986). However, the assignment of the book debts would not be caught, since the debenture holder had not taken possession of assets within his floating charge, unlike the payments to him which were in realisation of his security and therefore caught by the relevant statutory provisions (Re Oval 1742 Ltd (in creditors' voluntary liquidation), Customs and Excise Commissioners v Royal Bank of Scotland [2006] All ER (D) 57 (Nov)).

Eligible debts

The **categories** of preferential debts have been significantly reduced following legislative reform, which abolished the preferential status of debts owed to the Crown (most notably, taxes) (s 251 Enterprise Act 2002). The amended position is discussed here; where the liquidation commenced before 15 September 2003, readers should refer to the old position.

8045

Now, preferential debts (in order of priority) are:
a. sums owing to **occupational pension schemes** and state scheme premiums (i.e. sums to which Sch 4 Pension Schemes Act 1993 applies) (para 8 Sch 6 IA 1986); and
b. the following sums due to **employees**:
– **remuneration** due to current and former employees in respect of up to 4 months before the relevant date (¶8046), up to a maximum of £800 (para 9 Sch 6 IA 1986; art 4 SI 1986/1996);
– accrued **holiday pay** due to a former employee in respect of any period up to the relevant date (para 10 Sch 6 IA 1986);
– any advances made by third parties towards remuneration or accrued holiday pay for the relevant periods; and
– payments ordered to be paid by the company to **reservists**, and payments due as a result of the company's default in that respect, up to a maximum of £800 (Reserve Forces (Safeguard of Employment) Act 1985; para 12 Sch 6 IA 1986; art 4 SI 1986/1996).

Since it may take some time for the liquidator to pay the preferential debts, the secretary of state will pay certain **guaranteed debts**, on application of the employee up to the statutory maximum (£310 per week as of 1 February 2007, but it changes every year (SI 2006/3045)) to protect the employees from undue hardship (ss 182-186 Employment Rights Act 1996). The secretary of state will meet the following debts:
– arrears of pay for up to 8 weeks;
– statutory notice payments;
– up to 6 weeks' holiday pay accruing in the 12 months up to the company's insolvency; and
– the basic unfair dismissal award.

If the secretary of state makes a payment out under these provisions, he is subrogated to the preferential rights of the employee in the liquidation (s 189 Employment Rights Act 1996).

> MEMO POINTS 1. A **third category** of preferential debts comprises any EC levies on, or surcharges for, **coal and steel** production (para 15A Sch 6 IA 1986).
> 2. The **liquidator's decision** as to whether a claim is preferential or not can be **challenged** in the same way as his decisions on whether to reject a proof (¶8040).

Preferential debts are assessed at the "**relevant date**", which will be the date of the winding up order in most cases of straightforward compulsory liquidation. Statute provides for the situations set out in the following table (s 387 (3) IA 1986).

8046

	Situation	Relevant date
1	Compulsory liquidation (which does not fall into 2 or 4 below) without preceding voluntary liquidation	First appointment of provisional liquidator, or if none, date of winding up order
2	Compulsory liquidation ordered immediately following administration	Date company entered into administration (¶8808)
3	Administration converted into voluntary liquidation (¶9142) and case is not within 1, 2, 4 or 5	
4	Administration converted into compulsory liquidation under EC Insolvency Regulation (¶7366+)	
5	Order made deeming company to have passed resolution for voluntary liquidation following conversion of administration into liquidation under EC Insolvency Regulation	
6	Any other case	Date resolution to wind up passed

Insufficient unsecured assets

8047 If the preferential creditors are **not paid in full** out of unsecured assets, they are entitled to be paid out of any property:

a. comprising the **non ring-fenced** fund of assets subject to a **floating charge** in preference to the floating charge holder, but not property comprised in any fixed charge even if it was created by the same document as the floating charge (¶7992+); and

b. over which a person, usually a landlord, has **exercised a right of distress** in the 3 months before the winding up order (¶7903+). Such assets or their proceeds of sale are subject to a charge for the benefit of the company to be used to meet the preferential debts as far as the company's own assets are insufficient to do so (s 176(2) IA 1986).

The floating charge holder or person who distrained on the goods then effectively ranks as a postponed preferential creditor in respect of that amount, i.e. he is entitled to be repaid once the preferential debts listed above have been discharged, but before the general body of unsecured creditors (s 176(3) IA 1986).

Mixed proofs

8048 The liquidator must discharge these preferential debts before dealing with the unsecured creditors. If a creditor's claim is **partly preferential**, such as an employee who has a claim for accrued holiday pay and remuneration as well as an unsecured debt, he will be able to prove as an unsecured creditor for the non-preferential part. A secured creditor with a partly preferential claim may realise his security and apply the proceeds towards discharging the non-preferential part of his debt, proving for the preferential portion (*Re William Hall (Contractors) Ltd* [1967] 2 All ER 1150). However, if a creditor is able to set off a sum against a partly preferential, partly non-preferential claim, he must do so rateably (*Re Unit 2 Windows Ltd* [1985] 3 All ER 647).

Unsecured creditors

8053 The liquidator is under a **duty to declare and distribute dividends** to creditors in respect of the debts for which they have proved, whenever he has enough funds in the liquidation, once he has taken into account:

– his estimate of the expenses of the liquidation (r 4.180(1) IR 1986);
– debts which he considers may be due to creditors who have not been able to prove in the winding up because of where they live (r 4.182(1) IR 1986);
– any debts which are the subject of claims which have not yet been determined; and
– disputed proofs and claims.

This ensures that the liquidator will still have enough funds to meet these liabilities if or when they arise after the dividend has been paid.

"**Creditors**", for the purposes of declaring dividends, are those creditors of the company of whom the liquidator is aware, or who are identified in the company's statement of affairs, including a member state liquidator where one is appointed (r 11.1(2), (3) IR 1986).

The **general rule** is that the creditors must be **dealt with pari passu**. This means that they rank equally, so that if the company's assets are insufficient to meet its debts, the creditors receive a ratable proportion of the money due to them (r 4.181(1) IR 1986). This principle is supported by the statutory provisions which enable the liquidator to swell the company's assets, for example, by recouping preferences, transactions at an undervalue and certain floating charges, to prevent the company putting some creditors at an advantage over others close to the commencement of the liquidation (¶7808+).

8054

However, important **exceptions** mean that, in effect, distributions to creditors (other than secured creditors, who are paid out of the proceeds of their secured assets) are made according to the following **order of priority**, so that certain creditors are paid out of the company's assets before others:
a. expenses of the winding up; and
b. creditors' claims in the following order:
– preferential creditors (who, if not fully paid out of the unsecured assets are paid out of the non ring-fenced portion of any assets secured by a floating charge);
– unsecured creditors (who, if not fully paid out of the unsecured assets are paid out of the ring-fenced portion of any assets secured by a floating charge); and
– deferred creditors.
Any surplus is paid to the contributories.

The order of distribution is illustrated by way of a **flowchart** at ¶8101, followed by examples. Within each category of (and subdivision within) creditors and contributories, distributions are made pari passu, so that if there is not enough to satisfy each level in full, they will receive a ratable dividend out of the assets available.

A creditor can agree with the company to **subordinate his debt**, so that he is not paid until the other creditors to whom he agreed to give priority have been paid in full (*Re Maxwell Communications Corp plc (No 2)* [1994] 1 All ER 737). For the effect of insolvency on subordination agreements, see ¶4688+.

MEMO POINTS   The general pari passu principle also applies to a **voluntary liquidation** (s 107 IA 1986).

Notice

Before declaring a dividend, the liquidator must give notice of his intention to do so to (r 11.2(1) IR 1986):
– all creditors whose addresses he knows, who have not yet proved their debts; and
– a member state liquidator, where one is appointed.

8055

In the case of a **first dividend**, he must also advertise his intention to declare it (usually, in a newspaper with appropriate circulation), unless he has already invited creditors to prove by public advertisement (r 11.2(1A) IR 1986).

The notice or advertisement must **state**:
a. the deadline, or "last date for proving", by which the creditors must prove to be able to participate in the dividend, which must be at least 21 days from the date of the notice;
b. that the liquidator intends to declare the dividend within 4 months of the last date for proving; and
c. whether the dividend is interim or final.

MEMO POINTS   1. The **court** also has the **power** to set a date (or dates) by which the creditors must prove to be able to participate in the dividend (s 153 IA 1986). This also applies in a voluntary liquidation (s 112 IA 1986; ¶8523+).
2. In an **MVL**, the liquidator must advertise that he intends to make a distribution to creditors in any newspaper he thinks is most appropriate for bringing it to their attention (r 4.182A IR 1986). The advertisement must contain the same information as outlined above.

Considering proofs for participation in dividends

Within 7 days from the last date for proving, the **liquidator** must **admit or reject** (wholly or partially) all proofs submitted to him, or make any provision he thinks necessary (for example, where it is a disputed debt) (r 11.3 IR 1986).

8056

The liquidator is only obliged to pay dividends in respect of proven debts, although he may deal with **late proofs** at his discretion (r 4.180(1) IR 1986). However, if a creditor proves his debt after the dividend has been declared, he cannot participate in that dividend itself, but is entitled to a payment in respect of it out of the money available for a further dividend before it is applied to that dividend (r 4.182(2) IR 1986). If, however, a creditor submits his proof after all of the assets have been distributed, he will, generally, lose the right to any sort of dividend. Such a creditor may try to establish that the liquidator was in breach of his overriding duty to collect in the company's assets and apply them in the discharge of its liabilities and is therefore liable to the creditor (¶8215+). To protect himself from such claims, the liquidator can apply to court for an order barring future claims after a particular date from any creditor (s 153 IA 1986).

> MEMO POINTS In an **MVL**, the liquidator also has a discretion to deal with late proofs (r 4.182A(3) IR 1986). If the creditor submits his proof or increases the amount for which he is proving after the last date for proving, he cannot participate in the forthcoming dividend (or cannot receive an increased dividend), but he is entitled to be paid out of any money available for a further dividend (r 4.182A(4) IR 1986).
>
> In a **voluntary liquidation**, the liquidator can also apply to court to bar future claims (s 112 IA 1986; ¶8523+).

Dividend not declared

8057 The dividend can be **postponed or cancelled** if, within 4 months from the last date for proving (r 11.4 IR 1986):
– a rejected creditor applies to court to reverse or vary the liquidator's decision; or
– any other application is made to court for the liquidator's decision in relation to a proof to be reversed or varied, for the proof to be expunged, or for the amount claimed to be reduced.

> EXAMPLE The liquidators of L Ltd had declared a "first and final" dividend. MS Ltd's proof had been rejected and it applied to court challenging the liquidators' decision. However, MS Ltd did not serve notice of its application on the liquidators on time. Therefore, when the liquidators sent notices of the declaration and cheques to the known creditors, they did not know about MS Ltd's challenge. When they learned about the application, they stopped the cheques and informed the creditors that the dividend would be postponed. Ultimately, MS Ltd's debt was paid, leaving the liquidators unable to meet the other creditors' claims in full.
> The court held that the liquidators were entitled to postpone or cancel a dividend at any time prior to payment, as long as they did so within 4 months of the deadline for proving debts (*Lomax Leisure Ltd (in liquidation) v Miller and Bramston* [2007] EWHC 2508 (Ch)). This case concerned an MVL, but the same provisions are applicable to other types of liquidation.

Declaring a dividend

8058 Otherwise, the liquidator must declare the dividend **within** 4 months of the last date for proving (r 11.5 IR 1986). If an application to reverse or vary the liquidator's decision is pending, the liquidator must have the leave of the court to declare the dividend, and he must make any provision relating to the proof at issue as directed by the court.

Once declared, he must give **notice** to the creditors of (rr 4.180(3), 11.6 IR 1986):
a. the amounts realised from the sale of assets, broken down into how much has been realised from particular assets as far as possible;
b. payments made in his conduct of the liquidation;
c. if applicable, what provisions he has made for unsettled claims and what funds have been retained for particular purposes;
d. the total amount to be distributed, and the rate of the dividend;
e. how the dividend will be distributed;
f. enough further details of the company, its assets and affairs so that they can understand the calculation of the dividend and how it will be distributed; and
g. whether, and if so when, any further dividend is expected to be declared.

> MEMO POINTS In the case of an **MVL**, the notice does not have to contain the information at f. in the list (since r 4.180 does not apply, r 4.1 IR 1986).

If a **future or contingent debt** is still unascertained when a dividend is declared, the amount of his admitted proof is **reduced by** a percentage for the purposes of calculating the dividend only (r 11.13 IR 1986):

8059

$$\frac{X}{1.05^n}$$

Key:

X: value of admitted proof.

n: period beginning with the relevant date and ending with date on which payment of creditor's debt would have been due, expressed in years and months in decimalised form.
Relevant date: the date company went into liquidation. If liquidation was immediately preceded by an administration, the date company went into administration.

This ensures that the creditor does not benefit from having his debt repaid early, at the other creditors' expense.

> MEMO POINTS   This formula and the related Rule were **revised by** provisions which came **into force on** 1 April 2005. The position here applies to liquidations entered into on or after this date (SI 2005/527). Readers interested in prior liquidations should refer to the unamended Rule.
> This formula also applies to future or contingent debts proved for in **administration**, in which case the relevant date is that on which the company entered administration (or where the administration was immediately preceded by liquidation, the date on which the company entered liquidation) (r 2.105 IR 1986).

In addition or as an **alternative** to a financial dividend, the liquidator can divide any property of the company's between the company's creditors according to its estimated value, if the property cannot be sold either due to its nature or other special circumstances (r 4.183 IR 1986). The liquidator needs sanction from the liquidation committee to do this.

8060

> MEMO POINTS   This provision does not apply to **MVLs** (r 4.1 IR 1986).

Final dividend

When the **liquidator** has **realised all** of the company's **assets**, or as many as can be realised in a cost- and time-effective manner, he must give notice that he is (r 4.186 IR 1986):
– declaring a final dividend; or
– will not be declaring any further (or any) dividends.

8062

Notice of a final dividend must give the same information required of notices of other dividends (¶8055) and require that any claims against the assets are established by a specified deadline. The notice of no (further) dividends must also give this deadline, as well as stating that no funds have been realised, or that the funds realised have been used to meet the expenses of the liquidation (r 11.7 IR 1986). The deadline in either case may be postponed by the court on application by any person, but otherwise, the liquidator is required to pay any outstanding expenses of the liquidation out of the assets and declare and distribute any final dividend (r 4.186(4) IR 1986). In dealing with the final dividend, he only has to take account of those debts already proved.

> MEMO POINTS   In an **MVL**, the liquidator only has to take account of proved debts, and the notice given to the creditors must state that any creditors who have not proved by the deadline cannot participate in the dividend (r 4.182A(5), (6) IR 1986).

Payment

Payment is made by cheque or payable order (also referred to as "payment instruments") prepared by the Insolvency Service and sent to the liquidator to pass on to the creditors (reg 8 SI 1994/2507). Payment may be sent out with the notice of the declaration of dividends, and it can be sent by post or another way agreed with the creditor (r 11.6 IR 1986). Alternatively, it can be collected by the creditor from the liquidator. Any **unclaimed or undelivered** payment instruments must be sent to the Insolvency Service when the liquidator vacates office, endorsed as "cancelled" (reg 8 SI 1994/2507).

8063

> MEMO POINTS   1. Payment will only be made once in respect of the same debt, and if both a **creditor and member state liquidator** have proved in respect of the **same debt**, only the creditor (or his assignee, if he has given notice that he has assigned the debt) will be paid (r 11.3(3), (4) IR 1986).
> 2. A creditor is entitled to **assign** his dividend to another person, in which case he must give notice to the liquidator specifying the name and address of the assignee (r 11.11 IR 1986).

8064 3. In a **voluntary liquidation**, the liquidator draws up cheques himself, unless the funds are in the insolvency services account, in which case he needs to apply to the secretary of state to have them paid to him first (reg 8 SI 1994/2507).

8064 If the **liquidator refuses to pay** a dividend, the court can order him to pay it plus interest on the dividend and the costs of the application to court in appropriate circumstances, all out of his own pocket (r 4.182(3) IR 1986).

MEMO POINTS Such an application can also be made in a **voluntary liquidation** (s 112 IA 1986; ¶8523+).

Deferred creditors

8066 Certain claims can only be **paid after** all other creditors have been paid in full in the following order:
a. payment making up any discount on a future or contingent debt (¶8059);
b. any interest accruing after the commencement of the liquidation (s 189(2) IA 1986);
c. a restitution order made following a breach of obligations under the FSMA 2000 in respect of specific profits made as a result of the breach (s 382(1)(a) FSMA 2000 only, and not if the order is made under that provision and s 382(1)(b) FSMA 2000 together);
d. a claim which has to be postponed under insolvency or other legislation, such as loans made to a partner in a partnership in return for a share in the profits (s 3 Partnership Act 1890);
e. any **money owed to shareholders** in their capacity as shareholders, for example by way of dividends or profits (¶8011);
f. if the company decided before the liquidation to put aside a **sum for** the benefit of **employees** in case the business was wound up or transferred (s 719 CA 1985), the liquidator can apply this fund accordingly with the further sanction of the company (by ordinary resolution, unless the memorandum or articles requires another type) after its liabilities have been satisfied (s 187 IA 1986). Any creditor or contributory can apply to the court with respect to this power; and
g. if a **foreign currency creditor** has received less than his full debt, for example because of the exchange rate applied, the liquidator may have to make up the discrepancy before paying any surplus over to the contributories (Re Lines Bros Ltd [1982] 2 All ER 183).

MEMO POINTS The provision of the **new Companies Act** allowing companies to make payments to employees on a cessation or transfer of the business was due to come into force on 1 October 2007, but its implementation was revoked (art 4 SI 2007/2607). Therefore, the CA 1985 provision (s 719 CA 1985) is expected to remain in force until 1 October 2009. There are consequential amendments to s 187 IA 1986 set out in the original commencement order (para 42 Sch 4 SI 2007/2194) which would have been necessary if the implementation had gone ahead in 2007. Although these amendments were not revoked by SI 2007/2607, they are no longer necessary.

d. Creditors who are also debtors of the company

8072 If transactions and other "**mutual dealings**" before the liquidation between a creditor proving in the liquidation and the company resulted in debts owing and credits standing to each party when the company goes into liquidation, the sums due from one party can be **set off** against the sums due from the other (r 4.90 IR 1986). There are many cases commenting on different permutations of this basic rule, but the general position is summarised here.

EXAMPLE A Ltd, a drinks manufacturer, is in liquidation. Before the winding up order was made, A Ltd traded with sole trader B, who provided glass bottles to A Ltd and also recycled used and broken glass bottles from A Ltd. When the winding up order was made, A Ltd owed £1,200 to B for the supply of glass bottles. However, B owed £300 to A Ltd for bottles supplied to him for recycling by A Ltd. B's debt to A Ltd is automatically set off against A Ltd's debt to B, leaving B with a balance of £900 for which he has to prove in the liquidation.

MEMO POINTS The Rules relating to set off were **revised by** provisions which came **into force on** 1 April 2005. The position here applies to liquidations entered into on or after this date (SI 2005/527). Readers interested in prior liquidations should refer to the unamended Rule (i.e. r 4.90 IR 1986).

8073 Set-off is mandatory (i.e. the parties cannot agree in advance that should one of them become insolvent, the set-off rules will not apply) and **automatic**, so a creditor does not have to prove for his debt before he can set off any sums owed to him by the company. Once the claims have been set off against each other, the creditor can prove for any net balance, or the company can claim any sums owing from the debtor, as appropriate. Since the cross-claims between the parties are extinguished in this way, a particular cross-claim of one party cannot be assigned to a third party, although any net balance can be assigned (*Stein v Blake* [1995] 2 All ER 961).

Claims which can be set off

A **claim against the company** must be provable; the company needs a right to make a pecuniary demand to be able to set off its **claim against a creditor**. Therefore, a right to appropriate the creditor's property in its control or a right to be discharged from liabilities owed to the creditor cannot be set off, even though they may have financial worth. The sum due to or from the company can be set off whether it is:
a. payable currently or in the future;
b. due under a certain or contingent obligation; or
c. for a fixed or liquidated amount or an amount capable of being ascertained by fixed rules or opinion. If the debt is not for a fixed value, the liquidator can estimate it in the same way as he estimates proofs (¶8038).

The formula set out at ¶8059 is applied to any future or contingent debts owed to or by the company to calculate the amount of set-off applicable.

8075

EXAMPLE
1. A creditor's secured debt can be set off against the company's unsecured debt (*MS Fashions Ltd v Bank of Credit and Commerce International SA (in liquidation) (No 2)* [1993] 3 All ER 769).
2. A money claim cannot be set off against the value of goods held, unless those goods have been entrusted to the recipient specifically to sell, in which case they are tantamount to cash (*Eberle's Hotels & Restaurant Co Ltd v Jonas* (1887) 18 QBD 459; *Rolls Razor Ltd v Cox* [1967] 1 All ER 397).
3. If money has been paid over to one party for a specific purpose, it cannot be applied for another purpose if it would amount to a misappropriation of the funds to do so, and even once that purpose has been achieved, the owner's consent is required to apply it in setting off monies owed (*Carreras Rothmans Ltd v Freeman Mathews Treasure Ltd (in liquidation)* [1985] 1 All ER 155).

The concept of **mutuality** is an important one, and is judged on an objective basis so that the parties cannot simply agree that their dealings are mutual. Mutuality does not mean that the claims which are set off against each other have to be connected; the claims may be independent, but each party must be clearly and beneficially entitled to his claim(s), which must be owed between the same parties in the same right. For example, claims by third parties cannot be brought into the set-off (*Re Bank of Credit and Commerce International SA (No 8)* [1998] 1 BCLC 68). If one or both of the parties is claiming to be able to set off a beneficial interest, he needs to be able to produce clear proof of his entitlement (*Bank of Credit and Commerce International SA (in liquidation) v Al-Saud* [1997] 1 BCLC 457).

Contingent debts owed by the company to the creditor may be set off, based on the estimated value of the creditor's proof, since they can be proved for in the liquidation. However, a contingent debt owed by the creditor to the company cannot be used by the liquidator to set off sums owed by the company, and the creditor can prove in full for the amount he is owed (*MS Fashions Ltd v Bank of Credit and Commerce International SA (in liquidation) (No 2)*, above). Debts between the **Crown** and the company may be set off (s 434 IA 1986; *Re West End Networks Ltd (in liquidation), Secretary of State for Trade and Industry v Frid* [2004] 2 All ER 1042). For the treatment of **partly preferential debts** and set-off, see ¶8048.

Claims which cannot be set off

Set-off is not permitted in respect of sums due if (r 4.90(2) IR 1986):
– the creditor of the company was aware that a **petition** was pending against the company when the obligation giving rise to the debt was incurred;
– the obligation arose during the course of an immediately preceding **administration**;
– the liquidation immediately follows on from an administration and the obligation arose when the creditor knew that an application for an administration order was pending or a person had given notice of his intention to appoint an administrator; or
– the creditor acquired the debt by entering into an **assignment** during liquidation, a preceding administration or when the creditor had notice of the winding up petition, a preceding administration application or a notice of intention to appoint an administrator.

8077

MEMO POINTS   In the case of a **CVL**, the creditor will not be allowed to set off sums due if he was aware that a creditors' meeting had been called to place the company into CVL.

C. Contributories

8087 The contributories are last in the order of distribution of the company's assets, and so rarely receive any distribution in a liquidation. If there is a surplus, the liquidator **will usually distribute** it in money form, although he may also be able to distribute actual surplus assets (reg 117 TA 1985). Table A requires the liquidator to obtain consent of the company by extraordinary resolution to do this. This power will be useful for distributing assets whose financial value is obvious, such as shares and securities, but the liquidator may also value and distribute other assets in the same way.

When assessing **who is entitled** to participate in the distribution, the liquidator's first point of reference will be the list of contributories, which is based on the register of shareholders (¶7863+). Non-shareholding contributories and others are not usually entitled to receive a distribution, although a company's articles may specifically provide otherwise.

MEMO POINTS   1. In the case of the **death of a shareholder**, the holder of the grant of probate or letters of administration for the estate can be recognised as the shareholder (although personal representatives under a foreign grant of administration will not usually be recognised unless they have obtained English letters of administration as well, or the articles of the company allow, *New York Breweries Co v A-G* [1899] AC 62).
2. The liquidator may distribute surplus assets to an **equitable shareholder** (i.e. a transferee of shares who is not yet registered), even though the transfer of shares to him has not yet been registered by the company. There is no need for the liquidator to insist on the equitable shareholder perfecting his title by getting it registered (*Re Baku Consolidated Oilfields Ltd* [1994] 1 BCLC 173).
3. Although **extraordinary resolutions** are no longer required under statute, if a company's articles still require certain decisions to be made using this form of resolution then the company will have to comply, see ¶3544. For companies incorporated on or after 1 October 2007 that adopt Table A, amendments have been made to be consistent with the new Act so this decision must be made by special resolution instead (reg 7 SI 2007/2541 amending reg 117 TA 1985). However, these changes do not apply to companies incorporated before 1 October 2007 unless they have altered their articles separately.

Entitlement to surplus assets

8088 The contributories' entitlement to any surplus assets is **dependent upon** the provisions in the company's memorandum and articles relating to distributions in insolvency (provisions relating to how dividends should be distributed while the company is trading do not affect these distributions, *Re Driffield Gas Light Co* [1898] 1 Ch 451). Table A does not alter the basic position described below, although individual companies' articles may do and therefore must be consulted. The company may even have provided that the contributories cannot share in the distribution at all, although it must state what is to happen to any surplus assets for such a provision to be effective (*Re Merchant Navy Supply Association Ltd* [1947] 1 All ER 894).

The default position is for distributions to be made pari passu, and if a company wants a different method to be applied it must expressly set out the alternative.

EXAMPLE   In a case in which the company had not altered its memorandum correctly to dictate different classes of shareholders' rights to participate in surplus assets on winding up, the court applied the principle that if a company's memorandum does not indicate otherwise, shareholders should participate pari passu. The court would not admit extrinsic evidence to show that differential rights were intended. If such evidence could not be admissible for interpreting or implying a term into a company's articles, it could be admitted even less in respect of a company's memorandum. Although the company's articles set out differential rights on a winding up, it was clear from the relevant local statute that such rights must be expressed in the memorandum (*Clarke and others v HSBC Bank Middle East and others* [2006] UKPC 31, a Privy Council case concerning a Bahamian company, which, although not binding on English courts, does have persuasive authority).

Before the liquidator can distribute any surplus to the contributories, he must **adjust their rights** so that any distributions are made on an equal footing between them all (s 154 IA 1986;

This is a power of the court which has been delegated to the liquidator, s 160 IA 1986). This involves making calls on any shares which are still partly paid and ensuring that any other debts due to or from the contributories to the company are paid (¶7872+).

MEMO POINTS In a **voluntary liquidation**, the liquidator must also distribute the surplus assets to the contributories according to their rights and interests in the company (s 107 IA 1986). He also has the power to adjust the rights of the contributories (s 165(5) IA 1986).

Making distributions

The **basic position** is that the surplus assets will be distributed pari passu, according to the nominal value of the shares held by each contributory. Where **some shares** have been **paid up more** than others:
– the contributories who have paid more will receive the difference between the amount they have paid up and how much the others have paid up, together with any interest accruing on the amount they have paid up (if it carries interest) (*Re Wakefield Rolling Stock Co* [1892] 3 Ch 165; *Re Driffield Gas Light Co* [1898] 1 Ch 451);
– then all contributories will be repaid the amount actually paid up on their shares; and
– then any surplus will be divided rateably according to the nominal value of their shares.

Another common situation in which the distribution is made differently is where the company has issued **preference shares**. Subject to the interpretation of all of the relevant provisions in the memorandum and articles:
a. a preference as to the repayment of paid-up **capital** will usually mean that the preferential shareholder will be repaid first, but the ordinary shareholders alone will be entitled to share in any surplus once their own capital has been repaid (*Scottish Insurance Corp Ltd v Wilsons and Clyde Coal Co Ltd* [1949] 1 All ER 1068); and
b. a preference as to dividends will not usually entitle the preferential shareholder to recoup any arrears or deficiency in his **dividend** (as it was dependent on the dividend being declared by the directors). However, if the articles are worded so that any profits belong to the shareholders whether or not dividends have actually been declared, he will be able to do so (*Re Crichton's Oil Co* [1900-3] All ER Rep Ext 1378). On the other hand, if preferential shareholders are entitled to a fixed cumulative preferential dividend and to rank preferentially for dividends and capital, it is implied that this is the case in liquidation and so preferential shareholders are entitled to any arrears (*Re Wharfedale Brewery Co Ltd* [1952] 2 All ER 635).
For a further discussion of a return of capital to preference shareholders, see ¶833+.

MEMO POINTS The relevant statutory provision only refers to shareholders' rights being varied by the **articles** of association, although the **memorandum** can do so as well (s 107 IA 1986). This provision is only specifically related to voluntary liquidations, although it also applies to compulsory liquidations by analogy (*Liverpool and District Hospital for Diseases of the Heart v A-G* [1981] 1 All ER 994).

8089

The liquidator must obtain the **court's consent** to make a distribution to the contributories (s 154 IA 1986, r 4.221 IR 1986). If an order is made, the liquidator will inform each of the persons who will receive part of the surplus of the rate of return per share and whether he expects to be able to make any other returns (r 4.222 IR 1986). The payments will be sent to the contributories by post, unless another method is agreed.

If a liquidator makes an **unauthorised distribution**, he can be ordered to meet the claims of any outstanding unpaid creditors (see ¶7457+). A contributory receiving a distribution that he knows has been made without the liquidator having made provision for outstanding creditors may be liable to return it (s 149(1) IA 1986).

MEMO POINTS In a **voluntary liquidation**, the liquidator does not require the consent of the court to make distributions to the shareholders (s 107 IA 1986).

8090

Tax consequences

Distributions to contributories in respect of the share capital are classed for tax purposes as "**capital distributions**" and treated as consideration for a disposal of an interest in the shares (s 122 TCGA 1992). If more than one distribution is made, the contributory is treated as making a partial disposal of his shares on each distribution (other than the last) (s 42 TCGA 1992, *Statement of Practice D3*). This also applies if assets are distributed to the contributories instead of cash, and the company is treated as having disposed of the asset at its market value (s 17 TCGA 1992).

8091

D. Distribution summary

8101 The following **flowchart** summarises the way in which a company's secured and unsecured assets are distributed to its creditors and contributories in a set order.

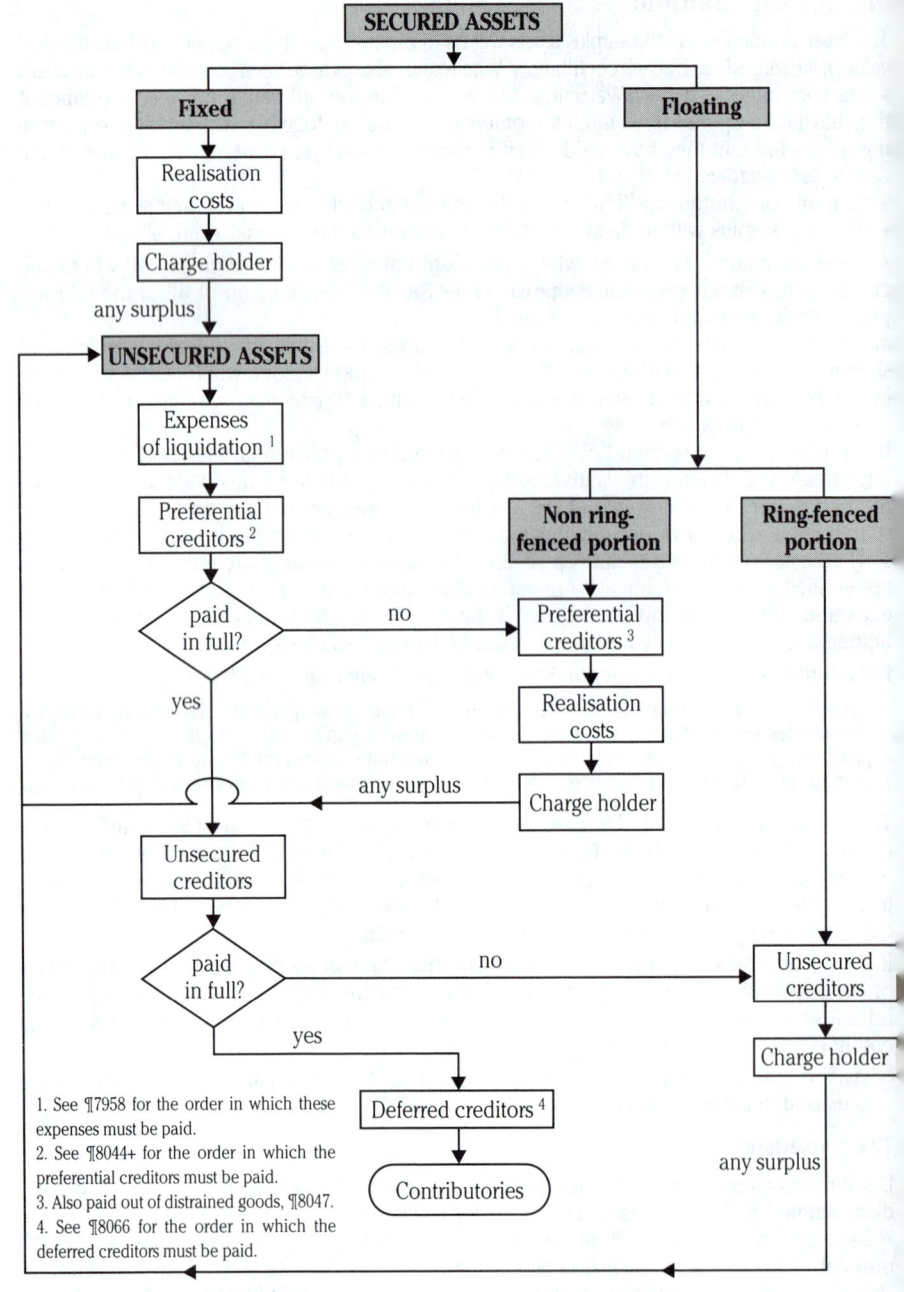

1. See ¶7958 for the order in which these expenses must be paid.
2. See ¶8044+ for the order in which the preferential creditors must be paid.
3. Also paid out of distrained goods, ¶8047.
4. See ¶8066 for the order in which the deferred creditors must be paid.

The following examples illustrate **how to use the flowchart**.

8102

> EXAMPLE
>
> **1. Insufficient assets to repay all creditors**
> Jones & Black Ltd is in liquidation. Its **total assets** are worth £100,000. The expenses of the winding up amount to £20,000, and its debts are as follows:
>
> | | |
> |---|---|
> | bank | £60,000 |
> | employees | £1,000 |
> | unsecured creditors | £30,000 |
> | deferred creditors | £4,000 |
>
> The bank holds a fixed and floating charge over certain of the company's assets as security for its debt. Once liquidated, the assets subject to the fixed charge are worth £60,000, and those subject to the floating charge are worth £15,000 (of the assets subject to the floating charge, the liquidator ring-fences £6,000). Therefore, £75,000 of the company's assets are **secured**, and £25,000 are **unsecured**. They can be distributed as follows:
> a. With the proceeds of the assets subject to the **fixed charge**, the liquidator can pay the realisation costs, which amount to £9,000, as well as £51,000 of the bank's debt. At this stage, the bank is still owed £9,000, and there is no surplus left over from distributing the assets subject to the fixed charge available to add to the unsecured assets to meet the other claims.
> b. Out of the unsecured assets, the **expenses of the liquidation** (£20,000) are paid first. The nature of the employees' claims fall within the definition of **preferential debts**, and so they are paid next.
> c. Since the preferential debts have been paid in full, the **non ring-fenced** portion of the assets secured by the **floating charge** (£9,000) can be applied to the costs of realising those assets (£1,000) and the rest paid to the bank. The bank is now owed £1,000. There is no surplus in the ring-fenced portion to feed back into the pot of unsecured assets.
> d. Only £4,000 of unsecured assets are available to meet the **unsecured creditors'** claims (which now includes the bank for £1,000), which would give them a dividend of 13p in the £1. Since they are not paid in full, they are entitled to be paid out of the **ring-fenced** portion of the assets subject to the **floating charge** (£6,000), which increases their dividend to 33p in the £1, but does not leave any surplus to meet the rest of the bank's debt or to pay the deferred creditors. A distribution cannot be made to the contributories.
>
> **2. Sufficient assets to repay all creditors**
> If the company's **total assets** were worth £140,000 (again, £60,000 are subject to the fixed charge and £15,000 to the floating charge; £65,000 are unsecured), the liquidator would distribute them as follows:
> a. As in 1
> b. As in 1
> c. As in 1
> d. £44,000 of unsecured assets are available to meet the **unsecured creditors'** claims (£30,000), enabling them to be paid in full. Therefore, the **ring-fenced** portion of the assets subject to the **floating charge** (£6,000) is not required to meet the unsecured creditors' claims, and can be used to pay the bank. There is a surplus of £5,000, which is added to the remaining unsecured assets, leaving a total of £19,000 left to distribute.
> e. The **deferred creditors** (£4,000) can be paid in full, leaving a surplus of £15,000 to be distributed to the **contributories**.

SECTION 3

Investigations into the company

Every company in compulsory liquidation must have its **conduct** investigated **by the official receiver**. This may be the deciding factor in opting for this form of winding up over another insolvency procedure, where there is a choice. For example, if those involved in the company suspect that a director has been engaged in conduct that renders him unfit to hold office, or even is criminal, this will automatically be investigated when the company goes into compulsory liquidation. It may also be a deciding factor at the petition hearing if the court is choosing between applications for different procedures (*Re Dollarland (Manhattan) Ltd*

8117

[2005] All ER (D) 371 (Nov)). Companies in any sort of liquidation must have their **affairs** investigated **by** the **liquidator** so that he can identify all of the company's assets in order to collect, realise and distribute them. If he uncovers evidence of any conduct worthy of disqualification or criminal prosecution in the course of his investigations, he is also under a duty to report it.

Investigations into the company during liquidation are separate from investigations which can be carried out during the company's life and may result in it being wound up in the public interest (dealt with at ¶7195+).

A. Official receiver: investigations into conduct

8120 The official receiver's duty to investigate **applies to** every company which is subject to a winding up order made by the court. He must examine (s 132(1) IA 1986):
– any failure of the company, and its causes; and
– the company generally, as regards its promotion, formation, business, dealings and affairs.

This duty is phrased in wide terms with the **aim** of ensuring that all aspects of the company and the reasons for its liquidation are investigated. To assist him in this, he can require any liquidator with conduct of the liquidation to provide him with information.

8121 The official receiver is given a number of **powers** so that he can carry out his investigations, most of which enable him to obtain information from those involved in running the company. To assist in these investigations, those **individuals** (listed in the table below) are under a **duty** to (s 235 IA 1986):
– provide the official receiver with whatever information he reasonably requests concerning the company and its promotion, formation, business, affairs or property; and
– attend the official receiver as reasonably required.

This is known as the "**duty to co-operate**". Once the company has gone into liquidation, the official receiver can require these individuals to co-operate at any time.

Persons	Any time limit on past involvement?
Company officers	No
Those who took part in company's formation	Within 1 year before winding up order
Employees (including under contract for services) who official receiver thinks are capable of giving required information	Within 1 year before winding up order
Officers/employees of corporate officer of company	Corporate officer must have held office within 1 year before winding up order

Failure to comply with this duty renders the individual liable to a fine, and the official receiver could resort to other ways of obtaining the information from those individuals, including summoning them to be examined by the court (in public or in private) (s 235(5) IA 1986; ¶9935).

Consequences of investigation

8122 Once the official receiver has concluded his investigations, he will **report to** the **court** on any matters he thinks should be drawn to its attention. If such a report is made, it is primary evidence of the matters with which it deals (s 132(2) IA 1986).

The official receiver is also under a duty to **report to** the **secretary of state** any:
– **directors** of the company who appear to him to be unfit to be involved in the management of a company (s 7(3) CDDA 1986); and
– **officers** (past and present) and **shareholders** who appear to him to be guilty of a criminal offence (s 218 IA 1986).

The secretary of state will then take the appropriate action, for example, commencing disqualification proceedings against a director (ss 218, 219 IA 1986).

1. Statement of affairs

8127 To assist him in his investigations, the official receiver can require the directors (or other persons listed in the table at ¶8121 if necessary) to provide a "statement of affairs" (s 131 IA 1986). This is discretionary, and the official receiver can require a statement to be made whether the company is solvent or insolvent (r 4.32 IR 1986).

Instead of requiring each person involved in the company to make individual statements of affairs, the official receiver can ask additional deponents (from the same categories listed in the table above) to confirm that they agree with another's statement of affairs by submitting an **affidavit of concurrence** (r 4.33(3) IR 1986). This affidavit will state that the deponent agrees with the statement of affairs; if there are particular matters with which he does not agree or does not have the necessary knowledge to agree, he must identify these matters and qualify his affidavit accordingly.

MEMO POINTS 1. The official receiver can require a statement to be made after a **provisional liquidator** has been appointed as well as when a winding up order has been made.
2. For a discussion of the statement of affairs in a **CVL**, see ¶8440+. The statutory declaration of solvency required in an **MVL** must be accompanied by a statement of assets and liabilities (¶8610+).
3. The Insolvency Service has proposed that **affidavits** are replaced by witness statements (see ¶7637). This change is likely to be implemented on 1 October 2008.

8128 The official receiver's **requisition** must be in Form 4.16, which informs the recipient of (r 4.32(4) IR 1986):
– the names and addresses of any other persons required to make a statement;
– the time within which the statement must be delivered to the official receiver (within 21 days of the day after he received the notice, s 131(4) IA 1986);
– the penalty for failure to comply with the requisition; and
– his duty to co-operate with the official receiver (¶8121).

Preparing the statement

8129 The statement of affairs must be in Form 4.17, which requires the following **information** (s 131(2) IA 1986):
– the particulars of the company's assets, debts and liabilities;
– the names and addresses of the company's creditors;
– details of any securities held by creditors, including the dates on which they were given; and
– any other information required by the official receiver.

The deponent can ask the official receiver for instructions as to **how to prepare** the statement and for the necessary form (r 4.32(5) IR 1986).

If the deponent needs **assistance** in preparing the required document, the official receiver can (r 4.37 IR 1986):
– employ someone to help him, the costs of which will be met out of the company's assets as an expense of the liquidation; or
– at the deponent's request, allow him to employ someone to assist and grant an allowance towards the costs of doing so, also to be paid as an expense of the liquidation.

If the deponent submits such a request to the official receiver, he must provide the name of a person or firm whose assistance he seeks, together with an estimate of the costs involved. If the official receiver approves, he will only allow the deponent to use that person or firm, and can impose conditions on their access to the company's books and records (e.g. by dictating the dates/times). Obtaining assistance to make the statement or affidavit of concurrence does not relieve the deponent from, or dilute, his obligations regarding the statement. If he is able to make the statement of affairs or an affidavit of concurrence **without assistance**, he must bear any costs of doing so himself.

The statement must be **verified by** affidavit, which is included in Form 4.17 and can be sworn in front of the official receiver, his deputy, an Insolvency Service officer or court officer authorised to do so (unlike other affidavits, which need to be sworn in front of a solicitor, notary, commissioner for oaths, etc) (s 131 IA 1986; r 4.33 IR 1986).

MEMO POINTS   Unlike most other insolvency affidavits, the statement of affairs cannot be verified by a **witness statement** as an alternative to an affidavit, nor can the affidavit of concurrence (r 7.57(6) IR 1986).

The Insolvency Service has proposed that affidavits are replaced by witness statements (see ¶7637). This change is likely to be implemented on 1 October 2008.

8130 Where a person required to make a statement of affairs **fails** to do so, the official receiver can apply to the court for an order enforcing the requirement (r 7.20 IR 1986). He should use this remedy rather than apply for a public examination (*Re Wallace Smith Trust Co Ltd* [1992] BCC 707).

Release from duty to make statement

8131 A person requested to make a statement can be released from his duty to do so in appropriate cases, for example where he does not have the relevant knowledge to make the statement (s 131 IA 1986). The official receiver can release a person from this obligation at his **discretion** or on that individual's **request** (r 4.36 IR 1986).

If he refuses an individual's request for release, the individual can **apply to court** (s 131(5) IA 1986). The application will be dismissed at a preliminary stage if the individual has had the opportunity to attend court (on 7 clear days' notice) and cannot show sufficient cause for his application (r 4.36 IR 1986). If the application is not dismissed, the court will notify the applicant of the venue (i.e. the date, time and place) for his case. At least 14 clear days before the hearing, the applicant must **send to the official receiver**:
– a notice stating the venue of the hearing;
– a copy of the application; and
– any evidence he intends to raise in favour of his application.

The official receiver is entitled to attend and be heard at the hearing, and/or may file a written report of relevant matters which he believes should be brought to the court's attention. If he files such a report, he must send a copy of it to the applicant at least 5 clear days before the hearing. Once the court has heard all the evidence and decided the application, sealed copies of any **order** will be sent to the applicant and the official receiver. The applicant's **costs** must be met by him; he will not receive any contribution out of the company's assets, unless the court orders otherwise.

Submitting the statement

8132 The **deadline** for delivering the statement of affairs to the official receiver is 21 days from the day after the requisition notice was received by the deponent (s 131(4) IA 1986). The deponent who made the affidavit (or one of them, if it was made by more than one person) must **deliver** to the official receiver (r 4.33 IR 1986):
– the statement of affairs; and
– a verified copy (i.e. the copy attached to and verified by the affidavit).

In the case of affidavits of concurrence, the deponent must deliver the original, plus one copy, to the official receiver within the same timescale.

EXAMPLE   Mr X, a director of XYZ Ltd, received a requisition notice to make a statement of affairs on 1 March. He must deliver his statement with a verified copy to the official receiver by 22 March.

The official receiver can, at his discretion or the request of a deponent, **extend the deadline** for submitting the statement of affairs (s 131 IA 1986; r 4.36 IR 1986). If he refuses to do so, the deponent can apply to the court for an extension of time, following the same procedure outlined above for applying to be released from the obligation to make a statement.

8133 The official receiver will then **file** the verified copy of the statement of affairs and any affidavits of concurrence at court (r 4.33 IR 1986) and **send** a summary to the creditors and contributories (¶8280+).

As a record of the liquidation, the statement of affairs is open to public **inspection**. However, if there is any information in the statement which the official receiver thinks may prejudice the conduct of the liquidation, he may apply to court for an order of **limited disclosure** (r 4.35 IR 1986). The court can then order that the statement should not be filed, or that it should be filed separately and not be open to inspection without leave of the court.

2. Accounts

8138 The official receiver can also require any of the **individuals** listed in the table at ¶8121 to provide him with the company's accounts (s 235 IA 1986). He can **specify** what he needs in terms of (r 4.39 IR 1986):
a. the nature of the accounts (e.g. audited, management, provisional, etc);
b. the date to which they are made up; and
c. the period to which they relate, from:
– up to 3 years before the winding up petition was presented;
– an earlier date to which audited accounts of the company were last prepared; or
– an earlier period (if he has obtained an order from the court).

The accounts must be **verified by** affidavit, if required by the official receiver. The provisions relating to the **costs** of preparing a statement of affairs and obtaining **assistance** also apply to providing accounts to the official receiver (¶8129).

> MEMO POINTS 1. In a **CVL**, the liquidator can exercise this power to obtain accounts (r 4.40 IR 1986). If he needs access to accounts which are from an earlier period, he can apply to the court for an appropriate order (s 112 IA 1986; ¶8523+). The liquidator must obtain the sanction of the liquidation committee (if there is one) to allow an individual to obtain assistance to prepare the accounts and have the costs (or part of them) met out of the assets (r 4.41 IR 1986). The individual's request must contain an estimate of the costs and name the person or firm he intends to use.
> 2. The Insolvency Service has proposed that **affidavits** are replaced by witness statements (see ¶7637). This change is likely to be implemented on 1 October 2008.

8139 The **deadline** for submitting accounts is 21 days from the request (unlike the statement of affairs and affidavit of concurrence, the rules do not specify that the 21 days start from the day after receipt of the request), or whatever longer period the official receiver allows. However, time limits set out in the Rules are calculated in clear days, giving the individual extra time. The individual must **deliver** two copies of the accounts (each with an affidavit, if required); the official receiver then **files** one copy at court.

> EXAMPLE Mr X, a director of XYZ Ltd (in liquidation), received a requisition notice to submit specified accounts verified by affidavit on 1 March. He must deliver two copies of the accounts and affidavit to the official receiver by 23 March.

> MEMO POINTS In a **CVL**, the deadline is the same. However, only one copy needs to be submitted to the liquidator since the accounts do not have to be filed at court (r 4.40 IR 1986).

3. Any other information

8144 Further to the powers to require information about the company's affairs and accounts, the official receiver can require any of the **persons** who have made a statement of affairs, affidavit of concurrence or have submitted accounts, to provide any further **information in writing** (which may also have to be verified by affidavit) explaining or modifying these documents (r 4.42 IR 1986). Two copies of the information (and affidavit, if required) must be submitted to the official receiver within 21 clear days of the request (or longer, if the official receiver allows), one of which will be filed by him at court.

> MEMO POINTS Unlike most other insolvency affidavits, the information cannot be verified by a **witness statement** as an alternative to an affidavit (r 7.57(6) IR 1986).
> The Insolvency Service has proposed that **affidavits** are replaced by witness statements (see ¶7637). This change is likely to be implemented on 1 October 2008.

8145 The official receiver also has extensive powers to obtain information on any matter he requires relating to the company from certain individuals **by public and private examination**. The official receiver can require a private examination of certain individuals whether or not he is acting as liquidator. This method is dealt with at ¶8172+, since it is also a tool commonly used by liquidators in investigating the company's affairs. Public examination, on the other hand, is only available to the official receiver investigating the company's affairs and so is dealt with below.

Public examination

8146 A public examination is an interview conducted in open court under oath to ascertain matters relating to the liquidation of the company. It is **useful where** the official receiver feels that the company's officers are not co-operating as fully and honestly as they should with his investigation. However, it is not used frequently in practice because the official receiver can rely on simpler methods of obtaining information via the statement of affairs, accounts and informally interviewing those involved with the company who have a duty to co-operate with him. Therefore, public examination tends to be **used to** obtain evidence of delinquent conduct of those involved with the company. It has a wider application than the alternative private examination, since:
– creditors can attend;
– it is held in open court; and
– the examinee cannot rely on the privilege against self-incrimination.

> MEMO POINTS A liquidator in a **voluntary liquidation** can apply to the court for a public examination (s 112 IA 1986 (¶8523+); *Re Campbell Coverings Ltd (No 2)* [1954] 1 All ER 222).

Possible examinees

8147 The following **individuals** can be required to submit to public examination (s 133(1) IA 1986):
a. past and present officers of the company;
b. any liquidator or administrator of the company, or receiver or manager of its property; or
c. any other person who is or was concerned with or has taken part in the promotion, formation or management of the company.

This applies whether or not the person in question is a British subject, and whether or not he is in the jurisdiction. If necessary the order can be served on him abroad (r 12.12(3) IR 1986).

If the individual falls within one of these categories the application for an order for public examination will be granted, unless there are no questions which the court could properly ask him (which would be rare) (*Re Casterbridge Properties Ltd (in liquidation)* [2003] 4 All ER 1041). If the official receiver claims that a person falls within category c. above, that person can apply for the order to be rescinded on the ground that he does not properly fall within that category (r 4.211(4) IR 1986).

Obtaining the order

8148 The official receiver can **apply to the court** for a public examination if he thinks it necessary, and he must do so on the request of (s 133(2) IA 1986):
– half (by value) of the company's creditors; or
– three-quarters (by value) of the company's contributories.

A **requisition** from creditors or contributories must be made in writing, giving the following details (r 4.213 IR 1986):
a. the name of the proposed examinee, his relationship with the company and why he should be examined; and

b. unless the requisitionist meets the relevant threshold requirement alone, he must provide details of:
– the supporting creditors, the value of each of their debts and written confirmation from each of them that they support the requisition; or
– the supporting contributories, each of their respective values and written confirmation from each of them that they support the requisition.

The official receiver must apply to court within 28 days of receiving the request or, if he thinks the request is unreasonable in the circumstances, he can apply to the court for an order relieving him of this obligation and the court will decide whether or not the application should go ahead.

If the application was made on the official receiver's own initiative, the court will **order** that the examinee submits to a public examination (s 133(3) IA 1986). To prevent unfounded requests for public examination, if the application stemmed from a requisition by the creditors or contributories, the court will first assess whether a public examination is justified. **8149**

A copy of the order for the individual to attend court to be examined must be **served on him** straight away (r 4.211(1) IR 1986). The official receiver will also give at least 14 days' **notice of the hearing** to (r 4.212 IR 1986):
– any liquidator or special manager; and
– every creditor and contributory known to the official receiver (unless the court orders otherwise).

The official receiver may also **advertise** the public examination in one or more newspaper(s) at least 14 days before the hearing, which will give other potential creditors and contributories the chance to attend the examination. He must not advertise the examination within 7 days of the order being served on the individual, unless the court orders otherwise, in case the examinee applies to have the order rescinded.

At the examination

The individual will swear an oath, and then he must answer all questions put to him by the court, or which the court allows to be asked by others present (r 4.215 IR 1986). The **questions can be asked by** (s 133(4) IA 1986): **8150**
– the official receiver;
– the company's liquidator;
– any special manager appointed over the company's business or property;
– any creditor who has submitted his proof in the winding up; and
– any contributory.

The questioners can appear by their legal or other authorised representative (r 4.215 IR 1986).

The examinee can be **questioned on** a wide range of matters relating to (s 133(3) IA 1986): **8151**
– the promotion, formation or management of the company;
– the conduct of the company's business and affairs; or
– his dealings in relation to the company.

He must give the best **answers** possible, referring to documentary records if necessary. He cannot refuse to answer because he thinks the court knows the answer already, or because he does not have access to the relevant documents (*Re Richbell Strategic Holdings Ltd (in liquidation) (No 2)* [2000] 2 BCLC 794). The individual can employ his own solicitor (and barrister, if he wishes) to ask him questions at the examination to qualify or explain his answers to the questions put to him (r 4.215 IR 1986).

The individual in question may be subject to **criminal proceedings** related to the insolvency, such as fraud, and in these circumstances the court can adjourn the examination if it considers that to continue would prejudice the fair trial of the criminal matter (r 4.215 IR 1986). The privilege against self-incrimination is not available to a person being examined in this way, and so the individual cannot refuse to answer questions on the basis that to do so might incriminate him in other proceedings (*Re Bishopsgate Investment Management Ltd* [1992] BCC 222). The written record of the examination can be used as evidence in other proceedings (¶8155).

8152 The court can **adjourn an examination** where necessary, either to another specified place and time, or generally (r 4.216 IR 1986). If the examination has been adjourned, it can be resumed on the application of the official receiver or the individual to be examined. If the individual makes such an application, he may be required to pay the costs of sending out notices to the requisite people by paying the required sum to the official receiver in advance.

Non-attendance

8153 If the **individual** is **unable** to undergo public examination because of a physical or mental impairment, the court can order the examination to be stayed, or modify the conduct of the examination to accommodate that person's needs (r 4.214 IR 1986). An application for such a stay or modification must be made to the court by:
– the official receiver;
– a friend or relative of the individual of whom the court approves as a proper person to apply; or
– any court-appointed person who represents, or manages the property of, the individual.

If the **application** is **not** made **by the official receiver**, he (and the liquidator, if the official receiver is not acting as liquidator) must be given at least 7 clear days' notice, and may require the applicant to provide a deposit for the expenses of any modified examination before an order can be made. The application also needs to be supported by a registered doctor's affidavit regarding the individual's mental and physical condition (unless the individual lacks capacity within the meaning of the Mental Capacity Act 2005). An application made **by the official receiver** can be made without notice to the other parties, and supported by evidence in the form of a report to the court by the official receiver.

> MEMO POINTS The Insolvency Service has proposed that **affidavits** are replaced by witness statements (see ¶7637). This change is likely to be implemented on 1 October 2008.

8154 **Failure to attend** a public examination without a reasonable excuse is contempt of court (s 134 IA 1986). The court can order an individual's arrest and the seizure of any documents, money or goods in his possession, both for actual failure to attend and if there are reasonable grounds for suspecting that he will abscond in order to avoid or delay the examination.

Administrative matters

8155 Afterwards, the individual will be asked to sign a **written record** of the examination and verify it by affidavit (r 4.215 IR 1986). This record can be used as evidence against the individual in any proceedings (r 4.215(5) IR 1986).

> MEMO POINTS The Insolvency Service has proposed that **affidavits** are replaced by witness statements (see ¶7637). This change is likely to be implemented on 1 October 2008.

8156 The **costs** of the examination are usually met out of the company's assets. However, the requisitionist(s) may be required to provide a deposit to the official receiver, out of which the court can order some of the expenses to be paid (rr 4.213, 4.217 IR 1986). This helps to prevent unnecessary requisitions for public examination by creditors or contributories.

B. Liquidator: investigations into the company's affairs

8165 The liquidator's role in investigating the company's affairs is principally **to determine** the company's assets and liabilities so that he can deal with them. This also involves looking closely at any potential actions (e.g. transactions at an undervalue, preferences and other legal action) which could result in the assets being increased. If, during the course of his investigations, he uncovers conduct which renders a person unfit to be a director or criminally liable, he must report it to the proper authorities.

His investigations will usually involve the following **steps**:
– questioning company officers (including former directors who held office up to 3 years before the liquidation) and senior employees;
– examining the company's books and comparing them to the information recorded at Companies House;
– examining the company's charges register and charge documents, checking the validity of the charges; and
– safeguarding and examining the company's records, paying particular attention to the accounts and looking for any discrepancies and transactions with persons connected to or companies associated with the company (particularly directors, who often attempt to reduce their liability to the company just before it becomes insolvent).

The liquidator will begin his investigation as soon as possible after his appointment, and the process is often commenced by the official receiver before a liquidator takes up office. The liquidator will invite the creditors and liquidation committee to bring any matters they feel require investigation to his attention.

MEMO POINTS **Statement of Insolvency Practice** 2 deals with the liquidator's investigations into a company's affairs.

Reporting duties

Although the liquidator does not have to report any **directors** he thinks should be **disqualified** (this duty falls on the official receiver, ¶8122), he is required to do the following on request (s 7(4) CDDA 1986):
a. provide the official receiver or secretary of state with information regarding a person's conduct as director of the company; and
b. allow the official receiver or secretary of state to inspect any of the company's books, papers and other records which are relevant to that person's conduct as a director.

8166

MEMO POINTS In the case of a **voluntary liquidation**, the liquidator must report any directors who appear to be unfit to the secretary of state, as well as providing information to the official receiver or secretary of state (s 7(3) CDDA 1986). An unintended consequence of the changes to the administration regime to allow administrations to be converted to voluntary liquidations is that where this occurs and the administrator becomes the liquidator, the same insolvency practitioner is obliged to filed the report twice and in many cases they are identical. As part of the Insolvency Service's review of secondary legislation (see ¶7364/mp), it is taking the opportunity to make alterations to the primary legislation either where it is necessary to support the new Rules or to remove unnecessary administrative burdens. The Service proposes to alter this obligation so that where a report has already been filed in respect of the company when it was in administration, the liquidator (if he is the same insolvency practitioner) does not have to file a second one unless there are additional matters to report (proposal 6 "A consultation document on changes to the Insolvency Act 1986 and the Company Directors Disqualification Act 1986 to be made by a Legislative Reform Order for the modernisation and streamlining of insolvency procedures" (September 2007)). At the time of writing, the consultation is still open. If this proposal is accepted, the changes are likely to be implemented from 1 October 2008.

The liquidator is under a duty to report any **officer** (past or present) or **shareholder** to the official receiver who appears to him to have committed any **criminal offence** in relation to the company (s 218 IA 1986). If it appears to the court that an offence has been committed by an officer of the company, it can order the liquidator to report it to the secretary of state. The specific criminal offences, which can be committed by officers (and sometimes others as well, such as contributories) when the company is in or prior to liquidation, are summarised at ¶7464+.

8167

MEMO POINTS 1. In the case of a **voluntary liquidation**, the liquidator must report any apparent criminal offence committed by officers or shareholders directly to the secretary of state, since the official receiver does not act (s 218(4) IA 1986). He must also co-operate with the secretary of state's investigation by giving him access to documents and providing facilities for inspecting and copying them.
2. The liquidator must also report to the **FSA** any company which appears to be carrying on a "**regulated activity**" in contravention of the general prohibition (s 370 FSMA 2000).

Obtaining information about the company

8169 The officers and other **individuals** involved in the company are under the same **duty to co-operate** with the liquidator as they are in relation to the official receiver (¶8121).

Any past or present officer commits an **offence** for which he can be fined and/or imprisoned if he:
– has made any material **omission from any statement** relating to the **company's affairs** with the intention to defraud (s 210 IA 1986); or
– makes any **false representations** or commits any other **fraud** for the purposes of obtaining the creditors' consent to an agreement relating to the company's affairs or liquidation (s 211 IA 1986).

If he has done so prior to the winding up, he is deemed to have committed the offence (¶9935).

8170 The liquidator can order any person who has any of the company's **money**, **property**, **books** or **papers** in his possession to deliver them to him (s 234 IA 1986). If the liquidator has seized property which does not in fact belong to the company (although he reasonably believed that he could deal with it at the time), he will not be liable for any loss or damage caused by the seizure, unless caused by his negligence. He also has a lien over the property or its proceeds of sale for his expenses in dealing with it. This is a power ascribed to the court by statute, which has been delegated to the liquidator (r 4.185 IR 1986).

An officer or contributory commits an **offence** if he does any of the following with the intent to defraud or deceive (s 209 IA 1986):
– destroys, mutilates, changes or falsifies any of the company's books, papers or securities; or
– makes (or is privy to someone else making) any false or fraudulent entry in any register, accounts book or other company document.

Committing this offence renders him liable to a fine and/or imprisonment (¶9935).

Private examination

8172 If, however, such people do not co-operate voluntarily, or the liquidator suspects that they are not providing all of the information they should, he can apply to the court for a private examination of them and others who may have relevant information (s 236 IA 1986). A private examination can **comprise** a combination of:
– answering questions;
– preparing an affidavit; and
– delivering documents.

This procedure is often relied on by liquidators, and is particularly useful where they are trying to obtain information about transactions in which the company was involved leading up to liquidation and where they are considering commencing or continuing litigation for the benefit of the liquidation.

The court **can examine** any:
– of the company's officers;
– alleged debtor of the company;
– person known or suspected to be in possession of any of the company's property; and
– person the court thinks is capable of providing information regarding the company's promotion, formation, business, dealings, affairs and property.

This last category is very wide, and can even include creditors (*Re Sasea Finance Ltd* [1998] 1 BCLC 559).

> MEMO POINTS 1. Private examination is also available to the **official receiver**, whether or not he is acting as liquidator.
> 2. The case law is inconsistent as to whether it is possible to compel a **person living abroad** to submit to private examination. In *Re Seagull Manufacturing Co Ltd (in liquidation)* ([1993] 2 All ER 980), it was commented that an order compelling private examination cannot be served abroad. However,

in *Re McIssac, Petitioner, Joint Liquidators of First Tokyo Index Trust Ltd* ([1994] BCC 410), a Scottish case, it was allowed.
3. Private examination is also available to **administrators** and **administrative receivers** where a company is in those procedures. References here to liquidators, the official receiver and office-holders should be read as being to the administrator or administrative receiver as relevant.
4. The Insolvency Service has proposed that **affidavits** are replaced by witness statements (see ¶7637). This change is likely to be implemented on 1 October 2008.

The **application** must be in writing, setting out the (r 9.2 IR 1986): **8173**
a. grounds on which it is made;
b. identity of the proposed examinee; and
c. purpose(s) of the examination, i.e:
– to appear before court;
– to clarify or give additional information about any matter in dispute;
– the production of documents; or
– to make an affidavit.

The liquidator must **satisfy the court that** the order requested is reasonable and will assist in the beneficial liquidation of the company, but it will usually be granted unless the examination would be oppressive on the examinee or an abuse of process (*Re Atlantic Computers plc* [1998] BCC 200; *Re British and Commonwealth Holdings plc (No 2)* [1992] BCLC 314). However, an order in a solvent liquidation would be unusual (*Re Galileo Group Ltd* [1998] 1 All ER 545).

The application may be made **without notice** to the proposed examinee if there is a good reason, for example where there is a danger of documents disappearing or another urgent need for the examination (r 9.4 IR 1986; *Re Maxwell Communications Corpn plc (No 3)* [1995] 1 BCLC 521; *Re PFTZM Ltd (in liquidation)* [1995] 2 BCLC 354).

The **court can order** the examinee to (r 9.3 IR 1986): **8174**

Action required	Further information given in the order
Submit affidavit or written answers to questions to court	– Matters with which affidavit must deal, usually based on written questions, or "interrogatories", submitted in writing by liquidator (s 237(4) IA 1986); and – deadline for submission to court
Produce any documents in his possession or control	– Specify documents (i.e. books, papers, other records); – deadline; and – how he is to comply
Appear before court	– Date (at least 14 days from date of order), time and place

The examinee must **attend** an examination in person, but he may bring his own legal representative(s) with him at his own expense if he wishes (r 9.4 IR 1986). The examination will usually be held before a registrar, unless the matter is referred to a judge (r 7.6 IR 1986). He can be asked any **questions** that the court allows **by** the liquidator or his representative (r 9.4 IR 1986). Questions may also be directed to him through the liquidator by: **8175**
– other professional office-holders who would have been able to apply for the examination (e.g. the official receiver); and
– where the application was based upon information supplied by a creditor, that creditor.

The examinee's legal representative can ask him questions (as permitted by the court) to give him the opportunity to explain or qualify any answers given by him, as well as being able to make representations to the court on his behalf. If the examinee was ordered to clarify or give further information on certain matters, the court will direct him as to which questions he should answer, and may require him to give his answers in an affidavit.

A **written record** will be kept of the examination, which must be read and signed by the examinee. Usually, this record, as well as any affidavit or written answers to questions, will not be filed at court and can only be **inspected by** the liquidator or other office-holder who would have been able to apply for the examination (r 9.5 IR 1986). However, the court may direct that it should be filed or grant leave to others to inspect the written documents as appropriate in the circumstances. **8176**

> **EXAMPLE**
> 1. Auditors can be allowed to inspect the documents, with certain confidential passages redacted if appropriate (*Re British and Commonwealth Holdings plc (Nos 1 and 2)* [1992] 2 All ER 801).
> 2. The Serious Fraud Office can be granted access to documents obtained as a result of private examination to assist in their investigations (*Re Arrows Ltd (No 4)* [1994] 3 All ER 814).

8177 After the examinee has complied with the order, the liquidator can apply to court for a **further order** for the examinee to hand over any material and any sums owed to the company on the basis of evidence gathered as a result of the private examination (s 237 IA 1986).

SECTION 4

Persons with conduct of the liquidation

8192 A company's winding up is principally conducted by the **liquidator**, who manages the day to day business of collecting, realising and distributing the company's assets. These functions can also be carried out by the **official receiver** acting as liquidator if a separate liquidator is not appointed, and his role in this regard is discussed here. Whether or not he acts as liquidator, the official receiver plays a specific role in investigating the conduct of every company leading up to its insolvency, which is discussed at ¶8120+.

Since the liquidation of a company has a serious impact on its **creditors**, they are given a supervisory role to play in its conduct. They have the most involvement through their elected members on the **liquidation committee**, which must be referred to by the liquidator on a number of matters, including sanctioning the exercise of certain of his powers. The **general body of creditors** will also be consulted from time to time by the liquidator and the court, and has ultimate control over the liquidator in its ability to remove him from office (¶8255+). Creditors also have the right to access certain information about the liquidation (¶8227+).

The **contributories** also take on a supervisory role, albeit to a lesser extent. There may be contributory members sitting on the **liquidation committee**, and if the creditors are paid in full, the contributories can take over the committee since only they have an interest in the liquidation from that point onwards. The **general body of contributories** can also be consulted by the liquidator and the court, and have access to certain information about the liquidation.

If the business of the company being wound up is particularly complex and specialised, the liquidator can appoint a **special manager**, who has relevant expertise, to assist him in conducting the liquidation.

A. Liquidator

8195 It is the liquidator who puts the winding up order into effect by collecting, realising and distributing the assets of the company to its creditors and contributories. His **investigations** into the company's business and his **dealings with** its **assets** are discussed at ¶8165+ and ¶7772+. His extensive powers in relation to the company are supervised and controlled by the other persons with conduct of the liquidation, namely the liquidation committee, creditors, contributories and the court. They have various powers to deal with his **appointment**, the exercise of his **powers** whilst in office, his **remuneration** and the **termination** of his office.

The **official receiver** can also **act as liquidator**, but will generally only do so if the company in question has no or few assets to realise and distribute. If the official receiver is acting in this capacity, his powers, duties and liabilities are the same as an independent liquidator's, but specific features of this office are discussed at ¶8277+.

1. Appointment

Other than the official receiver, a liquidator must be **qualified** and **authorised** to act as an insolvency practitioner (s 230(3) IA 1986). Authorisation is either granted via one of seven recognised professional bodies or by the secretary of state directly. The Insolvency Service website has a database of authorised insolvency practitioners which can be accessed by members of the public. Local official receivers can also provide a list of practitioners in the area. Although there are differences in their methods of appointment, the same duties and powers apply whether the role is filled by the official receiver or an insolvency practitioner.

8200

If the **official receiver** is acting as liquidator, his appointment operates automatically when the winding up order is made, unless the court appoints a named insolvency practitioner at the petition hearing. **Insolvency practitioners**, on the other hand, can be appointed as liquidators of the company in a number of different ways:
– when the winding up order is made;
– by the creditors and contributories; and
– by the secretary of state.

8201

Once an appointment has been made, **actions** by the person acting as liquidator are not carried out in his own name, but **in the name of** (s 163 IA 1986):
– "the liquidator"; or
– "the official receiver as liquidator".

The position of liquidator can be filled by one or more persons. If **joint liquidators** are appointed (by the same procedure as single liquidators), the appointment must state whether their actions can be carried out by them individually, or whether they have to be undertaken by them all (s 231 IA 1986).

MEMO POINTS 1. Any **defects** in his **appointment** or qualification will not invalidate a liquidator's acts (s 232 IA 1986).
2. The liquidator must not **solicit votes** or proxies to ensure his appointment. If he does so, the court can prevent his remuneration being paid out of the company's assets, and the liquidator or any other person who attempted to use **bribes** to ensure the appointment is liable to a fine (r 4.150 IR 1986; s 164 IA 1986; ¶9935).
3. The appointment of the liquidator in a **voluntary liquidation** is dealt with separately at ¶8508+.

When winding up order made

If the liquidation immediately **follows** an **administration** or **CVA**, the court may appoint the administrator or supervisor to act as the liquidator in the winding up (s 140 IA 1986). This power is limited, as only these individuals may be appointed at this time. In **other situations**, the official receiver takes on the conduct of the liquidation and a liquidator is appointed in the usual way.

8203

The administrator or supervisor must file a **notice** at court confirming that he is a qualified insolvency practitioner and that he consents to act, before the court will issue its order appointing him (r 4.102 IR 1986). The appointment **takes effect** at the date of the order, which will be in Form 4.29 or 4.30 (in the case of joint liquidators) and sent in duplicate to the official receiver, who will then send the sealed copy to the appointed liquidator. The new liquidator must then give **notice** of his appointment to:
– all of the company's creditors and contributories (or, at least those of whom he is aware at this stage) within 28 days of the order. The court may allow him to advertise his appointment as an alternative to giving individual notices; and
– Companies House, on Form 4.31 (r 4.106 IR 1986).

MEMO POINTS 1. The **notice** or **advertisement** must state whether meetings of creditors and contributories (or just creditors) will be called to set up a liquidation committee, and, if not, that the creditors have the right to require him to do so (r 4.102 IR 1986).

2. Where an **administrator** is appointed as liquidator in this way, and he becomes aware of **additional creditors** which were not brought to his attention during the administration, he must send them a copy of any report or statement sent to the other creditors during the administration, stating that it is sent to them under r 4.49A IR 1986.

By creditors and contributories

Summoning the meetings

8204 Where the **official receiver is the liquidator** of the company, he is under a duty to consider whether to summon meetings of the creditors and contributories for them to appoint a liquidator in his place (s 136(5) IA 1986). These **meetings** are **known as** (r 4.50 IR 1986):
– "the first meeting of creditors";
– "the first meeting of contributories"; and
– (together) "the first meetings in the liquidation".

He must decide whether to exercise his power to call these meetings within 12 weeks of the winding up order and if he decides not to do so, he must notify the court, creditors and contributories of his decision within that timeframe.

8205 If he decides to **summon** the **meetings himself**, he must fix the venue (i.e. the date, time and place) for each meeting to be held not more than 4 months after the winding up order was made (r 4.50 IR 1986).

Even if he decides not to summon the meetings himself, he is obliged to do so if **requested** (at any time) by one-quarter in value of the creditors. The creditors must be informed of this right when the official receiver notifies them that he is not going to call a meeting (s 136(6) IA 1986). A creditor's request must be in Form 4.21 and be sent to the official receiver with (r 4.57 IR 1986):
– a list of creditors agreeing with the request;
– the amount of those creditors' respective claims;
– written confirmation of their agreement; and
– a statement of the purpose of the proposed meeting (see ¶8207 below).

If the requisitioning creditor's claim alone comprises one-quarter of the value of all creditors, he does not have to give the details of other creditors agreeing with the request.

The **official receiver must** then (r 4.50 IR 1986):
– withdraw any previous notice given by him stating that he will not call the meetings;
– fix a venue for each meeting for not more than 3 months after he receives the request; and
– give notice of the meetings as summarised in the table below.

8206 However the meeting is called, **notice** must be given to the following persons (r 4.50 IR 1986).

Notice of	Notice to	Specifying	Deadline
First meetings in liquidation	Court	Venue (i.e. the date, time and place of the meeting)	As soon as venue fixed
	Public: advertised in newspaper		Reasonable time before meeting to enable people to attend
First meeting of creditors	Creditors known to official receiver or identified in statement of affairs	– Venue; and – deadline (max 4 days before meeting) by which proofs of debt and proxies have to be submitted	At least 21 days before relevant meeting
First meeting of contributories	Every person who seems to be contributory	– Venue; and – deadline (max 4 days before meeting) by which proxies have to be submitted	

Conduct and business

The **procedure** at the first meetings in the liquidation is the same as for other meetings during the liquidation, discussed at ¶8335+. On the other hand, the business which can be discussed is more restricted, with slight differences as to the **resolutions** that can be considered by the two meetings (r 4.52 IR 1986).

8207

Resolution	First meeting of creditors	First meeting of contributories
To appoint named person(s) as (joint) liquidator(s)	✓	✓
To establish liquidation committee	✓	✓
To settle terms of liquidator's remuneration or defer decision (unless liquidation committee established)	✓	
If joint liquidators appointed, to specify whether acts are to be done by one/all of them	✓	✓
To authorise expenses of meetings to be expenses of liquidation, if meeting requisitioned by creditors	✓	
To adjourn meeting for up to 3 weeks	✓	✓
To appoint official receiver as liquidator		
Any other resolutions chairman thinks appropriate for special reasons	✓	✓

Both creditors and contributories can **nominate** a named insolvency practitioner to be the **liquidator**, but the creditors' choice has precedence (s 139 IA 1986). If the creditors do not make a nomination, the contributories' nominee will be appointed. On the other hand, if the two meetings have nominated **different liquidators**, any creditor or contributory can apply to the court (within 7 days of the creditors' nomination) for an order appointing:
– the contributories' choice instead of, or jointly with, the creditors'; or
– a different liquidator.

8208

The requirements relating to notices noted above (¶8206) also apply where the court appoints a liquidator in these circumstances. If, on the other hand, **no liquidator is appointed** at meetings called by the official receiver, he must consider whether to refer the matter to the secretary of state (s 137 IA 1986).

MEMO POINTS Normally, resolutions at creditors' and contributories' meetings are passed by a simple majority (¶8354+; ¶8357). Special rules apply to **voting** on resolutions to appoint a liquidator where **more than one nomination** is made (¶8359).

Administrative requirements

The **nominated person** must then confirm in writing that (r 4.100 IR 1986):
– he is an insolvency practitioner duly qualified to act as the company's liquidator; and
– he consents to act.

8209

The chairman of the meeting can then **certify the appointment**, which is valid from that date, and send a copy to the official receiver (if the official receiver is not the chairman), who must then send copies to the court and the new liquidator. The liquidator then has to **advertise** his appointment in an appropriate newspaper so that it is brought to the attention of the company's creditors and contributories, and file a notice of his appointment at Companies House (r 4.106 IR 1986).

The **official receiver** must then **hand over** conduct of the liquidation to the liquidator by giving him (r 4.107 IR 1986):
– possession of the company's assets;
– a copy of any report he has made to the creditors and contributories (¶8280+); and
– any other information he considers necessary to enable the liquidator to discharge his duties effectively.

On handover, the liquidator must settle the official receiver's **expenses** and discharge any guarantees given by him, or undertake to do so out of the first realisation of the company's assets.

> MEMO POINTS If the **liquidator** was **appointed by the court** because the meetings could not agree on the appointment, he must submit confirmation of his qualification and consent to act to the court (r4.102 IR 1986). The court will send two copies of the order to the official receiver, who will seal one and send it to the liquidator. The liquidator must give notice to the creditors and contributories of his appointment within 28 days, or advertise it as above. In the notice or advertisement, he must state whether he intends to summon meetings to establish a liquidation committee; if not, the notice or advertisement must inform the creditors of their right to require him to call such meetings.

By secretary of state

8210 If the official receiver is acting as liquidator, he can apply to the secretary of state to have someone appointed in his place at any time (s 137 IA 1986). The secretary of state has the **discretion** whether or not to make an appointment. However, the creditors' wishes will be carried out unless there is a good reason not to (e.g. the creditors cannot agree, but the company's assets are in jeopardy so the estate would benefit from a liquidator being appointed as soon as possible). The official receiver must consult the creditors and ensure that the proposed liquidator is qualified and willing to act. If he appoints a liquidator, two copies of the certificate of appointment will be sent to the official receiver, who must file one at court and send the other to the new liquidator (r4.104 IR 1986). The appointment **takes effect** on the date on the certificate.

The new liquidator must then **notify** all of the company's creditors and contributories (or, at least those of whom he is aware) of his appointment (s 137 IA 1986). Although there is no statutory **deadline**, best practice requires the liquidator to do so within 28 days of his appointment, in common with appointments at the same time as the winding up order (para 4, chapter 3, *Dear IP*). If he wishes to **advertise** his appointment in a newspaper instead of giving individual notices, he must obtain the consent and directions of the court (although he could advertise as well as giving individual notices, if the expense of doing so is justified and proportionate). The notice or advertisement must state whether meetings of creditors and contributories (or just creditors) will be called to set up a liquidation committee, and, if not, that the creditors have the right to require him to do so (s 137(5) IA 1986).

2. Powers, duties and liabilities

8215 The **aim** of a liquidator's powers, duties and liabilities is to reinforce his primary function which, in the case of a compulsory liquidation, is set out in statute as (s 143(1) IA 1986): "to secure that the assets of the company are got in, realised and distributed to the company's creditors and, if there is a surplus, to the persons entitled to it."

Collecting in the company's assets to discharge its liabilities is a duty imposed on the court by statute, which it has delegated to the liquidator (s 148 IA 1986; r4.179 IR 1986). The liquidator also fulfils an important role in keeping the court, creditors and contributories informed about the conduct of the liquidation. These administrative and reporting duties are discussed below (¶8227+).

a. Summary table

8216 To enable the liquidator to fulfil his statutory duties, he is granted wide-ranging **powers** (particularly so in the case of the last power listed below, by which the liquidator can do anything else necessary in the liquidation), some of which require the sanction of the liquidation committee or the court before they can be exercised.

Power	Sanction required?	Reference
Carry on company's business for benefit of winding up	Yes – of court or liquidation committee	para 5 Sch 4 IA 1986
Bring legal proceedings for: – fraudulent trading; – wrongful trading; – transactions at an undervalue; – preferences; and – transactions defrauding creditors	Yes – of court or liquidation committee	para 3A Sch 4 IA 1986
Bring or defend other legal proceedings in company's name	Yes – of court or liquidation committee	para 4 Sch 4 IA 1986
Summon persons for private examination	Yes – court must grant application	s 236 IA 1986
Make calls on shares	Yes – of court or liquidation committee	s 160(2) IA 1986
Pay any class of creditors in full	Yes – of court or liquidation committee	para 1 Sch 4 IA 1986
Make a compromise or arrangement: – with any creditor(s) (or those claiming to be creditors)[1]; or – by which company may be rendered liable	Yes – of court or liquidation committee	para 2 Sch 4 IA 1986
Compromise: • any of the following between company and a contributory, debtor or other person with liability to company[2]: – calls (and liabilities to calls); – debts (and liabilities capable of resulting in debts); or – claims (present/future, certain/ contingent), and to take security for their discharge and give complete discharge in respect of any of them; and • any questions relating to or affecting company assets	Yes – of court or liquidation committee	para 3 Sch 4 IA 1986
Distribute unrealised assets to creditors	Yes – of liquidation committee	r 4.183 IR 1986
Sell company property to member (or his associate) of liquidation committee	Yes – of court or liquidation committee	r 4.170 IR 1986
Distribute unrealised assets to contributories	Yes – of shareholders by extraordinary resolution[3]	reg 117 TA 1985
Sell company property to liquidator's associate	No – but transaction can be set aside	s 167 IA 1986
Dispose of any of company property to person connected with it (¶7895)	No – but notify liquidation committee if liquidator is not official receiver	s 167(2) IA 1986
Instruct solicitors	No – but notify liquidation committee if liquidator is not official receiver	s 167(2) IA 1986
Sell any of company's property as a whole or in parcels, by: – public auction; or – private contract	No	para 6 Sch 4 IA 1986
Act and execute deeds, receipts and other documents (using company's seal where necessary) in company's name and on its behalf	No	para 7 Sch 4 IA 1986
Raise security on company's assets, such as where liquidator is carrying on company's business to sell as a going concern	No	para 10 Sch 4 IA 1986

Power	Sanction required?	Reference
Draw, accept, make and endorse any bill of exchange or promissory note in company's name and on its behalf (so company is liable), e.g. to draw cheque on company's bank account	No	para 9 Sch 4 IA 1986
Appoint an agent to carry out any acts he is unable to do himself [4], e.g. accountants, bankers	No	para 12 Sch 4 IA 1986
Prove, rank, claim and receive dividends in any contributory's bankruptcy/insolvency	No	para 8 Sch 4 IA 1986
Take out letters of administration to any deceased contributory's estate and take any action necessary for obtaining money due from estate to company	No	para 11 Sch 4 IA 1986
Summon creditors' and contributories' meetings to ascertain their wishes (he can also be requisitioned to do so, ¶8336+)	No	s 168(2) IA 1986
Use his discretion in managing assets and distributing them amongst creditors (subject to any legislative restrictions)	No	s 168(4) IA 1986
Require supply of public utilities to company (provided he personally guarantees the payment of bills)	No	s 233 IA 1986
Obtain documentation	No – except where application to court is necessary	s 234 IA 1986
Disclaim property	No but court procedure to follow	s 178 IA 1986
Do all other things necessary to wind up company's affairs and distribute its assets	No	para 13 Sch 4 IA 1986

Note:
1. This power is used to compromise with **individual creditors**. If a compromise is made with **all of the creditors** the liquidator should apply for a formal scheme of arrangement (¶6500+), unless each creditor consents (*Re British and Commonwealth Holdings plc (No 3)* [1992] BCLC 322).
2. As part of the Insolvency Service's review of secondary legislation (see ¶7364/mp), it is taking the opportunity to make alterations to the primary legislation either where it is necessary to support the new Rules or to remove unnecessary administrative burdens. The Service proposes to remove the requirement for liquidators to obtain sanction to make decisions about the **settlement of claims owing to the company** (proposal 2, "A consultation document on changes to the Insolvency Act 1986 and the Company Directors Disqualification Act 1986 to be made by a Legislative Reform Order for the modernisation and streamlining of insolvency procedures" (September 2007)). The requirement for sanction to exercise certain powers is left over from the time when the insolvency profession was not regulated. As this is no longer the case, insolvency practitioners are best placed to make such decisions. At the time of writing, the consultation is still open. If this proposal is accepted, the changes are likely to be implemented from 1 October 2008.
3. Although **extraordinary resolutions** are no longer required under statute, if a company's articles still require certain decisions to be made using this form of resolution then the company will have to comply, see ¶3544. For companies incorporated on or after 1 October 2007 that adopt Table A, amendments have been made to be consistent with the new Companies Act so this decision must be made by special resolution instead (reg 7 SI 2007/2541 amending reg 117 TA 1985). However, these changes do not apply to companies incorporated before 1 October 2007 unless they have altered their articles separately.
4. However, the liquidator must continue to exercise his **discretion** himself even where an agent is appointed (*Re Great Eastern Electric Co Ltd* [1941] 1 All ER 409). Even joint liquidators cannot delegate their powers generally to one of them, unless their terms of appointment allow.

MEMO POINTS For a liquidator's powers in a **voluntary liquidation**, see ¶8515+.

b. Control of the liquidator

8217 The liquidator's extensive powers to deal with the company's business and assets are subject to a number of controls. The most significant powers require the **sanction** of the liquidation committee or the court. The **liquidation committee** also supervises the general conduct of the liquidation (¶8302+). Particular issues can be referred to the **court** if necessary. In addition, the liquidator is subject to the **general duties** that are attached to his office and profession. Sometimes, when a liquidator fails to do his job properly, the best course of action may be to remove him from office (¶8254+).

Sanction for use of powers

Where sanction is required, whether from the liquidation committee, creditors' meeting or the court, it must be specific, rather than a blanket consent for the liquidator to exercise a power or powers (r 4.184(1) IR 1986). In considering **whether to sanction** the use of any of the powers, the **court** will consider all of the facts and reach its own conclusions. The liquidator's views will carry considerable weight, but the court will not assume that his wishes should prevail over those of the creditors and contributories (*Re Greenhaven Motors Ltd* [1999] 1 BCLC 635). It may be appropriate for the court to require meetings of creditors and contributories to be held so that their wishes can be ascertained (¶8335).

8218

If the liquidator acts **without consent**, the court or liquidation committee can ratify his actions if satisfied that he acted as a matter of urgency and he has requested sanction promptly (r 4.184(2) IR 1986). Lack of consent will not prejudice any person who dealt with the liquidator in good faith and paid for the property in question. In exercising these powers, the liquidator's role is analogous to that of the company's agent, as he is acting on behalf of the company without incurring personal liability (*Stead, Hazel & Co v Cooper* [1933] All ER Rep 770). However, like any other agent, if he acts negligently or outside of his authority he may incur **personal liability**. If appropriate in the circumstances, the court can indemnify the liquidator even if he has acted without sanction.

EXAMPLE A liquidator instructed a solicitor (which used to require the consent of the liquidation committee) to recover a debt without sanction, because he had learned that the debtor might become insolvent soon and had to act quickly to recover the money. The court could not give consent for this retrospectively, but could allow the liquidator to pay the solicitor's bill out of the company's assets because he had acted reasonably and for the benefit of the liquidation (*Re Associated Travel Leisure and Services Ltd (in liquidation)* [1978] 2 All ER 273).

MEMO POINTS This Rule (r 4.184 IR 1986) does not apply in the case of **voluntary liquidations**, although sanction is still required for the exercise of certain powers (¶8515).

Control of the court

As well as the requirement for the court's consent in certain cases, the **exercise of** these **powers** is subject to the control of the court in three different ways.

8219

MEMO POINTS 1. Further, where the liquidator exercises those **powers delegated** to him **by the court**, he does so as an officer of the court and so is subject to its control (s 160(1) IA 1986). These powers are:
– collecting the company's assets to discharge its liabilities (¶8215);
– summoning meetings of creditors and contributories (¶8335);
– ordering a person in possession of the company's money, property, books or papers to hand them over (¶8170);
– making a list of contributories (¶7869);
– making calls on shares (¶7872); and
– adjusting the shareholders' rights (¶8088).
2. In the case of a **voluntary liquidation**, the liquidator, a creditor or contributory can apply to the court regarding the exercise of the liquidator's powers (s 112 IA 1986; ¶8523+).

Firstly, any **creditor or contributory** can apply to court for directions regarding the exercise or proposed exercise of the liquidator's powers contained in Schedule 4 to the Act (these are most of the powers set out in the table at ¶8216 above; s 167(3) IA 1986). A contributory must establish that he has a substantial chance of receiving assets in the liquidation (*Re Barings plc (No 7)* [2002] 1 BCLC 401). In contrast to the court's approach when considering whether to sanction the use of any powers, it will usually only intervene if the liquidator exercised (or proposes to exercise) his powers fraudulently, in bad faith or unreasonably (*Re Greenhaven Motors Ltd* [1999] 1 BCLC 635).

8220

If an **application** is made **by a contributory**, the court's approach depends upon whether the decision in question was one:
a. for which the liquidator **needs court approval**, in which case a contributory is entitled to make the application and the court will judge the decision or proposed decision on its merits, giving weight to the liquidator's view (r 7.54 IR 1986); or

b. that the **liquidator** could **take independently**, in which case a contributory is likely to have to establish that he has a financial interest in the liquidation in order to make an application. In such a case, the court will generally only interfere with the liquidator's decision if it was taken in bad faith or was so perverse that no reasonable and properly advised liquidator could have taken it (*Re Edennote Ltd, Tottenham Hotspur plc v Ryman* [1996] 2 BCLC 389). If the court does not interfere with the decision, the applicant may be able to sue the liquidator in negligence, if he can establish a duty of care (although if the liquidator has taken legal advice, this will usually satisfy any duty).

8221 Secondly, any **other person** who is aggrieved by the liquidator's actions or decisions can apply to the court, which may confirm, reverse or alter the act or decision and make any other directions as appropriate (s 168(5) IA 1986). This provision is wider than that allowing creditors and contributories to apply to the court regarding the liquidator's exercise of his powers, since any person may apply provided he is legitimately affected and has no other redress (*Re Hans Place Ltd (in liquidation)* [1993] BCLC 768, in which the original lessee was allowed to apply after the liquidator had disclaimed the company's under-lease). However, it has been held that the applicant must be directly affected by the liquidator's exercise of the power, for example, a third party who is denied the chance to buy an asset as a result of the liquidator's actions cannot apply (*Mahomed v Morris* [2000] 2 BCLC 536).

8222 Thirdly, the **liquidator** can apply to court for directions (s 168(3) IA 1986), but he should only do so where there is real doubt as to the correct course of action (*Re Hinchley Island Hotel Ltd, Craig v Humberclyde Industrial Finance Group Ltd* [1998] 2 BCLC 526).

8223 If the **liquidator** has **failed to comply** with any of his duties to file, deliver or make up any document (including accounts and returns) or to give any notice, a creditor or contributory can apply to the court for enforcement of the relevant duty (s 170 IA 1986). The consequences of failing to comply with the order can be serious for the liquidator, for example, he could be imprisoned for contempt of court (*Re Allan Ellis (Transport and Packing) Services Ltd* (1989) 5 BCC 835, in which the liquidator was imprisoned for 9 months).

General duties

8224 The office of liquidator, like that of director, spans a number of different **roles**:
– **agent**: the liquidator generally administers the company's estate using his powers as its agent, for example, selling the company's assets on its behalf or employing a solicitor. In doing so, he does not incur personal liability (*Stewart v Engel* [2000] 2 BCLC 528);
– **officer of the court** (s 160 IA 1986): therefore, he is responsible to the court in performing his duties and anybody interfering with the liquidator is in contempt of court and can be punished accordingly (s 167(3) IA 1986);
– **officer of the company**: this is generally the case, but not in every situation, for example a liquidator is an officer for the purposes of obtaining statutory relief from liability, but statute deals with officers and liquidators as separate categories for the purposes of misfeasance (*Re X Co Ltd* [1907] 2 Ch 92; ¶2505+; ¶7457+); and
– **fiduciary**: therefore, similar duties and liabilities apply to liquidators as to directors.

> MEMO POINTS 1. Although liquidators have been described as being **trustees** for the creditors as a whole, this is only true in so far as the property of the company can only be used or disposed of for the benefit of the creditors (*Re Oriental Inland Steam Co, ex parte Scinde Rly Co* (1874) 9 Ch App 557; *Ayerst (Inspector of Taxes) v C & K (Construction) Ltd* [1975] 2 All ER 537). Although a high standard of care is expected of them, liquidators are not subject to the same duties and liabilities as trustees.
> 2. In the case of a **voluntary liquidation**, the liquidator is not an officer of the court, although the court still has control of the winding up since matters and disputes can be referred to it for determination (s 112 IA 1986; ¶8523+).

8225 Therefore, his actions are also governed by other more general duties, which **arise out of** his office and the various roles he plays in the liquidation.

COMPULSORY LIQUIDATION

Duty	Imposed by virtue of	Reference
Act with an appropriate degree of skill and care	Position as company's agent	*Re Home and Colonial Insurance Co Ltd* [1929] All ER Rep 231
Exercise his discretion personally	Position as company's agent	*Re Scotch Granite Co* (1867) 17 LT 533
Act for a proper purpose	Fiduciary position	*Re LR Gertzenstein Ltd* [1936] 3 All ER 341
Avoid conflicts of interest and duty	Fiduciary position	*Re Llynvi and Tondu Co* (1889) 6 TLR 11
Not fetter his discretion	Fiduciary position	*Re Scotch Granite Co* (1867) 17 LT 533
Treat all classes of claimant fairly and equally	Fiduciary position	*Re Exchange Securities & Commodities Ltd* [1983] BCLC 186
Act in interests of creditors and contributories generally (not individual creditors and contributories)	Fiduciary position	*Leon v York-O-Matic Ltd* [1966] 3 All ER 277
Not to profit from his office (and account to company if he makes secret profit)	Fiduciary position	*Re LR Gertzenstein Ltd* [1936] 3 All ER 341; *Silkstone and Haigh Moor Coal Co v Edey* [1900] 1 Ch 167
Act in good faith	– Fiduciary position – Position as officer of court	*Leon v York-O-Matic Ltd* [1966] 3 All ER 277
Act impartially and independently	– Fiduciary position – Position as officer of court	*Re Lubin, Rosen and Associates Ltd* [1975] 1 All ER 577; *Re Rubber and Produce Investment Trust* [1915] 1 Ch 382
Not take advantage of his legal rights, if circumstances and justice require	Position as officer of court	*Re Condon, ex parte James* (1874) 9 Ch App 609

c. Providing information

To the creditors and contributories

The liquidator has various duties to **report to** the liquidation committee, which are dealt with at ¶8304+.

8227

Creditors and contributories can have the same access to the **records of the insolvency proceedings** as other persons (¶8230 below).

> MEMO POINTS As part of the Insolvency Service's review of secondary legislation (see ¶7364/mp), it is taking the opportunity to make alterations to the primary legislation either where it is necessary to support the new Rules or to remove unnecessary administrative burdens. The Service proposes to remove the requirement for insolvency practitioners to **send information to all known creditors** at various stages in the procedure (proposal 1, "A consultation document on changes to the Insolvency Act 1986 and the Company Directors Disqualification Act 1986 to be made by a Legislative Reform Order for the modernisation and streamlining of insolvency procedures" (September 2007)). Generally speaking, most creditors just want to know how much of their debt will be repaid and have no interest in the general progress of the procedure. This requirement therefore creates a heavy but unnecessary financial and administrative burden. It will be replaced by a system allowing creditors who do wish to be kept up to date to "opt in" to receiving information from the insolvency practitioner. The consultation also includes proposals to allow information to be exchanged using electronic communication where the recipient agrees, and for insolvency practitioners to make information available via a website.
> At the time of writing, the consultation is still open. If these proposals are accepted, the changes are likely to be implemented from 1 October 2008.

8228 The creditors and contributories are entitled to apply to the court for an order allowing them to inspect the **company's books and papers** (s 155 IA 1986). Case law has restricted the application of this provision as follows.

> EXAMPLE
> 1. It can only be used to give creditors and contributories documents in the **possession of the company**, and (obiter) it can only be used for the **purposes of** the liquidation (Re North Brazilian Sugar Factories (1887) 37 Ch D 83).
> 2. It cannot be used to give a director access to information to help him prepare a **defence** to criminal charges, as this is entirely outside the purposes of the liquidation. Nor can he use it to resist a claim against him by the company, as this would be detrimental to the liquidation (Re DPR Futures Ltd [1989] BCLC 634).
> 3. It does not apply to information passed between the liquidator and the Insolvency Service, e.g. regarding the potential disqualification of directors (Re W & A Glaser Ltd [1994] BCC 199).
> 4. It can be used to ascertain whether the **liquidator** has carried out his **duties** properly, e.g. where he has potentially wasted company assets by pursuing litigation with no prospect of success (Re Movitex Ltd [1992] 2 All ER 264).

It is a criminal **offence** for a person to pretend to be entitled to inspect any document as a creditor or contributory (r 12.18 IR 1986; ¶9935).

MEMO POINTS In a **voluntary liquidation**, such an application can also be made (s 112 IA 1986; ¶8523+).

To others

8229 So that the **liquidation** is generally **publicised**, the liquidator must ensure that the following documents (whether in hard copy, electronic form or any other form) issued on the company's or his behalf, or on which the company's name appears, state that the company is being wound up (s 188 IA 1986):
– invoices;
– order forms;
– orders for goods; and
– business letters.

This information must also appear on all of the company's websites. **Failure** to do so renders the liquidator (and any other officer, receiver or manager of the company who authorised or permitted the default to occur) liable to a fine (¶9935).

MEMO POINTS The statement's inclusion on a company's websites and order forms became a requirement as of January 2007, following the implementation of amendments to the First Company Law Directive (by EC Directive 2003/58). The requirement applies to companies already in liquidation at that time as well as those entering liquidation subsequently.

8230 The court's **records of the insolvency proceedings** are generally open to public inspection, on application to the court (which may, in its discretion, decide that it is not appropriate to allow access) (¶7398+). The legislation and Rules also provide for interested parties to have access to documents relating to the liquidation (for example, the liquidation committee). The liquidator may **deny access** to his records if he considers that (r 12.13 IR 1986):
– a document should be treated as confidential; or
– disclosing a document would be detrimental to the interests of the creditors, shareholders or contributories.

He may not prevent the inspection of **proofs** and **proxies**. If the liquidator denies access, a member of the committee can apply to the court, which can overrule or confirm his decision, as well as placing conditions on any access granted.

A liquidator may disclose the **company's books and papers** to a third party to do something that does not affect the assets directly, provided they are not privileged or confidential (Re Acli Metals (London) Ltd [1989] BCLC 749). This does not entitle them to inspect the documents which are not in the company's possession (Re North Brazilian Sugar Factories (1887) 37 Ch D 83).

d. Financial and administrative matters

8231 Where the **company** is **not wound up within 1 year** from the commencement of the liquidation, the liquidator must file a statement of his receipts and payments (Form 4.68) at Companies House at regular intervals until the conclusion of the liquidation (s 192 IA 1986).

The **statement** must **contain** (see the guidance notes attached to Form 4.68):
a. details of realisations of assets existing at the commencement of the liquidation, including any balance in the company's bank account, book debts and calls collected by the liquidator, property sold and interest received on any investments;
b. details of disbursements, including all payments to creditors and contributories as well as payments of costs, charges and expenses;
c. details of any investments made;
d. if the liquidator carries on the company's business for the benefit of the liquidation, he must include the totals of the receipts and payments of the trading account in his statement; and
e. as well as entering payments to creditors and contributories in the disbursements, the liquidator must provide separate accounts showing the amount of each creditor's claim and the dividends paid to each creditor and contributory.

The liquidator must submit his **first** such **statement** within 30 days of the first anniversary of the commencement of the liquidation (r 4.223 IR 1986). **After that**, the statements must be filed at Companies House every 6 months until the liquidation is concluded. His **last statement** must be submitted at the conclusion of the liquidation. A final statement is not required if the return submitted after the final meeting (¶8393+) is filed first and shows that there are no unclaimed assets or funds in the liquidator's hands. Instead, a copy of that return must be sent by the liquidator to the secretary of state.

If the liquidator **fails** to comply with these obligations, he is liable to a fine (s 192(2) IA 1986; ¶9935).

MEMO POINTS This Rule (i.e r 4.223 IR 1986) does not apply in an **MVL**, although the statutory requirement to file the statement of receipts and payments does.

8232 The liquidator is obliged to keep separate **financial records** for each company in respect of which he acts, which he must submit to the liquidation committee for inspection when required to do so (reg 10 SI 1994/2507). If he has carried on the business of the company for any period of time, he must keep **trading accounts** (reg 12 SI 1994/2507). The liquidator must submit his financial records and accounts to the secretary of state at the conclusion of the liquidation, but the secretary of state can also require the liquidator to produce them, and any other books and records, at any time (regs 14, 15 SI 1994/2507).

If requested by any:
– creditor;
– contributory; or
– director,
the liquidator must, within 14 days, supply a statement of his **receipts and payments** for the period of 1 year ending with the latest anniversary of his appointment (reg 11 SI 1994/2507).

The liquidator must **hand over** the financial records and trading accounts to any successor as soon as possible after the new appointment is made (unless he has vacated office because the liquidation is complete for practical purposes and the official receiver takes over, in which case he will only have to deliver them to the official receiver on request) (reg 13 SI 1994/2507). If there is no successor, he must **retain** the financial records and trading accounts (including those he has inherited from a predecessor) for 6 years following his vacation of office.

MEMO POINTS The obligations to keep separate financial records and trading accounts for the company do not apply in a **voluntary liquidation** (i.e. regs 10, 12 SI 1994/2507). However, the liquidator does have an additional duty to report financial matters to the secretary of state (¶8535).

8233 The liquidator can deal with the **company's books, papers** and other **records** as he sees fit, which includes selling, destroying or disposing of them in any other way during his conduct of the liquidation, or when he vacates office (reg 16 SI 1994/2507). Unless the liquidator is the official receiver, he needs the permission of the official receiver to do this.

If the liquidator is replaced, he must **hand over** the company's books, papers and records to his successor (¶8267).

[MEMO POINTS] In a **voluntary liquidation**, the last liquidator can destroy or dispose of the company's books, papers and other records 1 year after it has been dissolved, but he cannot do so during the winding up (reg 16 SI 1994/2507).

e. Challenging the liquidator

8234 In addition to challenging specific decisions of the liquidator, a person who has suffered damage as a result of the liquidator's actions may be able to commence proceedings against him.

Summary remedy

8235 Insolvency legislation provides a general "summary remedy" against delinquent liquidators for the breaches most likely to arise from their actions under the heading "**misfeasance**". Action for misfeasance can also be taken against other persons, such as directors, and is dealt with at ¶7457+.

Other claims

8236 A liquidator may be subject to other claims, in the same way as any other person providing a service and/or acting as agent. The most common claims are summarised in the table below.

Generally, claims against a liquidator cannot be **brought by** a **contributory** in his individual capacity if the loss was suffered by the company (*Johnson v Gore Wood & Co (a firm)* [2001] 1 All ER 481). Even if he has suffered a personal loss, he will not have a claim if the company has also suffered loss. For example, if the liquidator failed to realise an asset for the benefit of the liquidation, the company as a whole has lost the benefit of that revenue and the contributory has also lost the potential distribution. On the other hand, if the liquidator simply failed to make a distribution to him, the contributory can claim in his own name. The logic behind this is that if the company has suffered loss, a claim should be brought for the benefit of the company, whereas a claim brought by the contributory would only benefit him (*Re Lewis & Smart Ltd* [1954] 2 All ER 19).

Type of claim	Comments	Reference
Negligence	Liquidator does not usually owe a duty of care to individual creditors [1] Liquidator's negligence can be a factor in some statutory duties, which state he is only liable if negligent [2]	-
Negligent misstatement and misrepresentations	Without fraud or assumption of personal liability, statements made by liquidator about company's affairs are made as agent and therefore he is not likely to incur personal liability	*Williams v Natural Life Health Foods Ltd* [1998] 1 BCLC 690
	Statements made while liquidator acts as an officer of court will not give rise to personal liability [3]	*Mond v Hyde* [1998] 2 BCLC 340
Trespass/conversion	If liquidator deals with assets belonging to third party, he could be liable for the torts of trespass (by seizing asset) and conversion (if he realises it) [2,4]	s 234(3), (4) IA 1986
	Liquidator has lien over property or proceeds of sale for his expenses incurred in seizing or disposing of it	s 234(3), (4) IA 1986
	Liquidator's protection appears to be confined to tangible assets (e.g. it does not extend to book debts and other intangible property)	*Welsh Development Agency v Export Finance Co Ltd* [1992] BCLC 148

Type of claim	Comments	Reference
Breach of contract	Liquidator contracts on company's behalf as agent, and therefore will not incur personal liability as long as he acts within his authority	*Stewart v Engel* [2000] BCLC 528

Note:
1. However, there are **circumstances** in which a liquidator **can owe** such a **duty of care** to an individual creditor if he is in a position of trust and confidence to that person beyond his usual relationship with the creditors. For example, where a creditor had selected liquidator and agreed to pay the liquidator's expenses up to £5,000 (*A & J Fabrications Ltd v Grant Thornton* [1998] 2 BCLC 227).
2. Such statutory provisions include liability for dealing with:
– an asset which does not belong to company (¶8170); and
– property subject to enforcement as proceeds of crime (¶7909).
3. Liquidator is not officer of court in **voluntary liquidation**.
4. For example, if liquidator is aware of third party's claim to asset, it may be negligent of him not to apply to court to determine ownership (if he has sufficient time) before he deals with it.

8237 Once a liquidator's **appointment** has **terminated** and he has obtained his release, he is generally not liable for his actions or omissions during office (although the court may grant permission to take action against the liquidator, see ¶7457+).

3. Remuneration

How much?

8242 The liquidator's remuneration is usually **fixed by** the liquidation committee with reference to either (r 4.127 IR 1986):
– a percentage of the value of the assets realised and/or distributed; or
– the time spent by the liquidator and his staff in conducting the liquidation.

The committee must **decide** which method to use, taking into account:
– the complexity of the case;
– any exceptional responsibilities which the liquidator has to undertake;
– the effectiveness of the liquidator's conduct of the liquidation; and
– the value and nature of the assets with which he has to deal.

In the absence of a liquidation committee, this decision will be made at a creditors' meeting. If **no decision** is reached, the liquidator can calculate his remuneration by using a formula set out in the Rules, which is based on the value of the assets realised and distributions made (r 4.127A, Sch 6 IR 1986).

> **MEMO POINTS** 1. In a **CVL**, the same rules apply as to how the remuneration is fixed. In an **MVL**, the liquidator's remuneration is fixed by reference to the same factors, but it must be approved by the shareholders in a general meeting. If his remuneration is not agreed in this way, it is calculated using a formula set out in the Rules based on the value of the assets realised and the distributions made (r 4.148B IR 1986).
> 2. **Joint liquidators** must decide between them how the remuneration is to be apportioned, and can refer to the court, liquidation committee or meeting of creditors for resolution of any disagreement (r 4.128 IR 1986). In a **CVL**, the liquidation committee or creditors can decide this issue (r 4.128(2) IR 1986); in an **MVL**, the shareholders can do so (r 4.148A(5) IR 1986).
> 3. The remuneration of the **official receiver** acting as liquidator is worked out according to particular regulations (reg 35 SI 1994/2507).

8243 If the liquidator considers that the amount fixed is **too low**, he can:
a. ask the creditors to increase it by resolution, where it was fixed by the liquidation committee (r 4.129 IR 1986); or
b. apply to court for an order increasing it, where it was fixed by the liquidation committee, creditors or the default formula (r 4.130 IR 1986). He must give the members of the liquidation committee (or the creditors, if there is no committee) at least 14 days' notice to give them the opportunity to appear or be represented at the hearing.

Conversely, the creditors may consider that the remuneration agreed upon is **too high**, in which case one quarter in value of them can apply to court for an order that it be reduced (r 4.131 IR 1986). The court may dismiss the application, if no sufficient cause is shown for the reduction (and the applicant has had the chance to appear before the court to justify his application). Otherwise, the court will fix a venue (i.e. the date, time and place) for the hearing. The applicant must send a notice of the venue and a copy of the application and any supporting evidence to the liquidator at least 14 clear days before the hearing. The costs of such a hearing usually have to be borne by the applicant.

MEMO POINTS In an **MVL**, if the liquidator considers that his remuneration is too low, he can apply to the court to have it increased (r4.148A(6) IR 1986). He must give the contributories 14 days notice to give them the opportunity to appear or be represented at the hearing.

Realising secured assets

8244 If the liquidator realises assets on behalf of a secured creditor, he is entitled to **remuneration based on** the assets realised (for fixed charges and mortgages) or the assets realised and distributions made (for floating charges) (r 4.127B, Sch 6 IR 1986).

MEMO POINTS This also applies to **voluntary liquidations** (rr 4.1, 4.148A IR 1986).

Payment when the liquidator leaves office

8245 A liquidator whose **office is terminated** is entitled to be **paid** his remuneration out of the company's assets (as long as it has been properly fixed, as detailed above). He will be required to **return** his remuneration if it later transpires that the company does not have sufficient assets to pay the other expenses of the liquidation ranking above the liquidator's remuneration (¶7958). He can challenge this by applying to court for an order allowing him to retain it, if he can show that he should be entitled to do so (s 156 IA 1986; *Re Salters Hall School Ltd (in liquidation)*, *Merrygold v Horton* [1998] 1 BCLC 401). He can also apply to the Insolvency Service for the reimbursement of all necessary disbursements and expenses incurred through his conduct of the liquidation out of any residue of the company's money in the Insolvency Service's Account (reg 7 SI 1994/2507).

If the liquidator is **replaced** by another insolvency practitioner or the official receiver, he is entitled to be reimbursed for any disbursements and expenses (not already repaid) out of any funds available (reg 7 SI 1994/2507).

MEMO POINTS A liquidator in a **voluntary winding up** can also challenge having to return his remuneration (s 112 IA 1986; ¶8523+).

4. Termination

8250 There are various **methods** by which a liquidator's appointment can be terminated, either voluntarily, at the insistence of others or by operation of law. The **liquidator's** prime **concern** when his appointment is terminated is to obtain his release, since this will prevent him from being held liable for his acts and omissions during the conduct of the liquidation (¶8264+).

a. Resignation

8251 The **situations** in which a liquidator is allowed to resign are limited to (s 172(6) IA 1986; r 4.108 IR 1986):
– ill-health;
– where he intends to cease practising as an insolvency practitioner;
– where there is a conflict of interest or a change in his personal circumstances which prevents or hampers the discharge of his duties; or
– where he is one of joint liquidators and he and the other(s) think that it is no longer necessary for that number of joint liquidators to continue in office.

The liquidator must **notify** the **official receiver** of his intention to resign, inform him when the creditors' meeting relating to the resignation will be (this notice must be given at least 21 days before any meeting) and give details of any outstanding property of the company's which has not been fully dealt with (r 4.137 IR 1986).

MEMO POINTS In a **voluntary liquidation**, the official receiver does not have to be notified of the liquidator's intention to resign. (In the case of an **MVL**, the relevant reference in the Rules to the above provisions is r 4.142(3), (4) IR 1986.)

COMPULSORY LIQUIDATION 971

8252 The liquidator must **submit** his **resignation to** a meeting of creditors, which was called for that purpose.

The **notice** of the meeting must state its purpose, inform the creditors of the consequences of his release from office (¶8264+), and summarise accounting information relating to the liquidation (r 4.108 IR 1986). A copy must also be sent to the official receiver.

> MEMO POINTS In an **MVL**, the liquidator can submit his resignation to a meeting of the shareholders (r 4.142(1) IR 1986). The notice of the meeting is just required to state the purpose of the meeting.

8253 The following **resolutions** will be considered at the meeting, with the **consequences** noted where relevant:

Resolution	Passed?	Consequences and administrative steps	Reference
To accept liquidator's resignation	✓[1]	– Chairman to send copy resolution and certificate to official receiver within 3 days. – Form 4.32 to be given to resigning liquidator after meeting – Liquidator to send copy Form 4.32 to official receiver with copy of account sent to creditors with notice of meeting – Official receiver to file Form 4.32 at court	r 4.109 IR 1986
	✗[2]	None required, but liquidator may apply to court for leave to resign. Any order (Form 4.34) can give directions on matters resulting from resignation and set a date from which the liquidator's release is effective. Court gives liquidator 2 copies, one of which he sends to official receiver; liquidator gives court and official receiver notice of resignation in Form 4.36	r 4.111 IR 1986
To appoint new liquidator	✓[3]	– Chairman to send copy resolution and certificate of appointment (complying with formalities for appointments by creditors) to official receiver within 3 days – Advertisement of new liquidator's appointment must state that his predecessor resigned and has been released (if applicable)	r 4.109 IR 1986; ¶8209; r 4.112 IR 1986
	✗[4]	No liquidator appointed: conduct of liquidation reverts to official receiver	¶8278
To give resigning liquidator his release	✓[5]	Liquidator released	¶8264+
	✗[6]	– Chairman to send copy resolution to official receiver within 3 days – Liquidator applies to the secretary of state for his release	r 4.109 IR 1986

Note:
1. In **CVL**, if resolution is passed, liquidator must file notice of his resignation at Companies House in Form 4.40 (r 4.110 IR 1986). In **MVL**, there is no need for meeting to accept resignation, but he must file the notice at Companies House after meeting (r 4.142(5) IR 1986).
2. If liquidator has to apply to court for leave to resign in **voluntary liquidation**, two copies of the order are sent to the liquidator, who files one at Companies House (r 4.111(2), (4) IR 1986).
3. In **voluntary liquidation**, chairman must send certificate of appointment directly to new liquidator (r 4.110 IR 1986). In **MVL**, advertisement of new liquidator's appointment only has to state that predecessor resigned (r 4.142(6) IR 1986).
4. In **voluntary liquidation**, official receiver does not take over conduct of liquidation where there is a vacancy; see ¶8508+ for how vacancy is filled.
5. In **MVL**, there is no need for meeting to resolve to release liquidator.
6. In **CVL**, chairman does not have to send copy of resolution not to release liquidator to official receiver.

> MEMO POINTS Where **no quorum** is present at the meeting of creditors, it is deemed that:
> – the meeting was held;
> – the resolution to accept the liquidator's resignation was passed; and
> – the creditors did not resolve against the liquidator obtaining his release.
> The person who would have been chairman were the meeting quorate will sign a written statement to the effect that the quorum was not achieved and the liquidator can resign (r 4.108 IR 1986). If there is no quorum at a meeting of shareholders called to accept the liquidator's resignation in an **MVL**, the meeting is deemed to have been held (r 4.142(4A) IR 1986). This is because it is not necessary for the meeting to accept the liquidator's resignation or grant him his release.

b. Removal

8254 The liquidator can be removed from office in **three ways**, by (s 172 IA 1986):
- a general meeting of creditors summoned for that purpose;
- order of the court; or
- direction of the secretary of state, if appointed by him.

> MEMO POINTS A **provisional liquidator** can only be removed by the court (¶7692).

By meeting of creditors

8255 Creditors' meetings in general are discussed at ¶8335+. In most cases, there are no special **requirements** for calling a creditors' meeting to remove a liquidator, however, in certain cases, such a meeting can only be held if (s 172 IA 1986):
- the court directs (in which case, the provisions regarding the court's directions described below apply); or
- the meeting is requested by at least one quarter (in value) of the creditors.

These cases are where:
- the official receiver is the liquidator, except where he occupies that role during a vacancy following the departure of a liquidator who was nominated by the creditors or contributories;
- the liquidator was appointed by the court, except where the liquidation follows an administration or CVA; or
- the liquidator was appointed by the secretary of state.

> MEMO POINTS For removal of the liquidator by a meeting in the case of a **voluntary liquidation**, see ¶8539+.

8256 The creditors' power to **summon** a meeting generally is discussed at ¶8336+. A meeting to remove the liquidator can be summoned in the same way, except that the **notice** must state that this is one of the purposes of the meeting and draw the creditors' attention to the consequences of releasing the liquidator (¶8264+; r 4.113 IR 1986). A copy of the notice must also be sent to the official receiver. Where such a meeting is summoned (or proposed to be summoned), the **court** (on application by any creditor) can give **directions** as to (r 4.115 IR 1986):
- how it should be summoned;
- proxies;
- the conduct of the meeting; and
- any other matter which the court thinks is in need of control.

8257 Usually, at creditors' meetings, the liquidator or his nominee is the **chairman**, but in the case of meetings called to remove the liquidator any other person may be appointed chairman (r 4.113 IR 1986). If, however, the liquidator or his nominee is the chairman at such a meeting, he cannot **adjourn** it without the consent of at least 50% (in value) of all of the creditors present (in person or by proxy) and entitled to vote at the meeting.

The following **resolutions** will be considered at the meeting, with the **consequences** noted where relevant:

Resolution	Passed?	Consequences and administrative steps	Reference
To remove liquidator	✓	– Chairman to send copy resolution and certificate (Form 4.37) to official receiver within 3 days – Official receiver to file certificate at court	r 4.113 IR 1986
	✗	Liquidator remains in office	-
To appoint new liquidator	✓	– Chairman to send copy resolution and certificate of appointment (complying with formalities for appointments by creditors) to official receiver within 3 days – Advertisement of new liquidator's appointment must state that his predecessor was removed and has been released (if applicable)	r 4.113 IR 1986; ¶8209; r 4.118 IR 1986
	✗	No liquidator: conduct of liquidation reverts to official receiver	¶8278

Resolution	Passed?	Consequences and administrative steps	Reference
To give removed liquidator his release	✓	Liquidator released	¶8264+
	✗	– Chairman to send copy resolution to official receiver within 3 days – Liquidator applies to secretary of state for release	r 4.113 IR 1986

By the court

The legislation states that a liquidator can be removed by the court, but does not go on to set out **who may apply** (s 172(2) IA 1986). However, case law has stated that the applicant must have a legitimate interest in the liquidator's removal.

8258

> EXAMPLE
>
> 1. A **contributory** in an insolvent liquidation was not permitted to apply for the liquidator's removal because there would be no funds available to distribute to him and so he did not have a legitimate interest (*Re Corbenstoke Ltd (No 2)* [1990] BCLC 60; in this case, the applicant was a contributory and a creditor so his application was allowed to proceed in his capacity as creditor (below)).
> 2. A **debtor** was not permitted to apply for the liquidator's removal (*Deloitte & Touche AG v Johnson* [2000] 1 BCLC 485).

The statutory provision does not give any specific **circumstances** in which the court can remove a liquidator in this way, although in the light of the previous drafting of the provision, and that of the comparable provision relating to voluntary liquidation, it is considered that a liquidator will be removed "on cause shown", i.e. where, for whatever reason, the liquidator cannot fulfil his functions and duties (*Re A & C Supplies Ltd* [1998] 1 BCLC 603). The "cause" will be considered in the light of the real, substantial and honest interests of the liquidation and the purpose for which the liquidator was appointed (*Re Buildlead Ltd, Quicksons (South and West) Ltd v Katz* [2003] 4 All ER 864).

> EXAMPLE
>
> **Liquidator removed**:
> 1. A liquidator who had a **conflict of interest** because he was a director and debtor of the company and also a trustee in bankruptcy to a creditor was removed by the court (*Re Corbenstoke Ltd* (No 2), above).
> 2. A liquidator who **failed to carry out** his **duties** as **pro-actively** as he should have done was removed by the court (*Re Keypak Homecare Ltd* [1987] BCLC 409; a voluntary liquidation case).
> 3. A liquidator was removed by the court due to his **misconduct** and **unfitness** to act as a liquidator (*Re Sir John Moore Gold Mining Co* (1879) 12 Ch D 325; a voluntary liquidation case).
>
> **Liquidator not removed**:
> 4. Joint liquidators were appointed over a company in liquidation. The applicant asked them to investigate particular matters, but he was not satisfied with their actions. The court would not remove them from office because the **applicant had not shown** that they were not independent or that they had been inactive, and it would have been too expensive and disruptive to replace them (*AMP Enterprises Ltd v Hoffman* [2003] 1 BCLC 319; a voluntary liquidation case).

MEMO POINTS In a **voluntary liquidation**, the liquidator can be removed by the court under two provisions (ss 108, 171(2) IA 1986). The first provision states that the liquidator can be removed "on cause shown", and since this approach is adopted when removing him under the other provision, the considerations are the same.

The court may **dismiss** the **application**, if no sufficient cause is shown for the liquidator's removal and the applicant has had the chance to appear before the court to justify his application (r 4.119 IR 1986).

8259

MEMO POINTS This also applies in a **CVL** (r 4.120 IR 1986) and an **MVL** (r 4.143 IR 1986).

Otherwise, the court will fix the **hearing** (r 4.119 IR 1986). The applicant must send a notice of the date, time and place of the hearing and a copy of the application and any supporting evidence to the liquidator and official receiver at least 14 clear days before the hearing. The **costs** of such a hearing cannot usually be met out of the company's assets, and the court may require the applicant to make a deposit or provide security for the liquidator's costs before the hearing.

8260

If the **liquidator is removed**, the court can make any directions it thinks are necessary and will send copies of the order (in Form 4.39) to the liquidator and official receiver. The court may also appoint a new liquidator (in which case, the same procedural steps must be followed as in ¶8209).

> MEMO POINTS This also applies in a **CVL** (r4.120 IR 1986) and an **MVL** (r4.143 IR 1986), except that in a voluntary liquidation the court will send two copies of the order to the liquidator, who must send one of them to Companies House with a notice that he has ceased to act.

By the secretary of state

8261 A liquidator appointed by the secretary of state (¶8210) can be removed by him (s 172(4) IA 1986). Before the secretary of state removes the liquidator from office, he must **inform** the liquidator and official receiver of (r4.123 IR 1986):
– his decision;
– the reasons for his decision; and
– a time period within which the liquidator can make representations to him against the decision.

If he decides to remove the liquidator, he must send **notices** to that effect to the court, liquidator and official receiver. The court has the power to make a similar order giving any necessary directions, as if it had removed the liquidator.

> MEMO POINTS There is no equivalent of this provision for a **voluntary liquidation**, as the secretary of state cannot appoint a liquidator.

c. Automatic

8263 The liquidator's office will automatically be terminated in the following situations:
a. where a **final meeting** has been held at which the liquidator has given his report on the completion of the winding up (¶8393+). The liquidator vacates office when he has given notice to the court and Companies House that the meeting has been held and of the outcome of any resolutions (s 172(8) IA 1986);
b. if he **ceases to be qualified** as an insolvency practitioner (this ground does not apply to the official receiver acting as liquidator) (s 172(5) IA 1986); and
c. on the **death** of the liquidator (other than the official receiver). Notice of his death must be given to the official receiver by (r4.132 IR 1986):
– his personal representatives;
– a partner in his firm (who is also an insolvency practitioner or a member of a body authorising insolvency practitioners); or
– any other person who produces the death certificate.

The official receiver will then notify the court to set a date for the **release** of the liquidator.

> MEMO POINTS In the case of a **voluntary liquidation**, the liquidator also automatically vacates office:
> – following a final meeting, in which case the notice only has to be given to Companies House (s 171(6) IA 1986);
> – when he ceases to be qualified (s 171(4) IA 1986); and
> – when he dies (CVL: notice of the death must be given to Companies House and the liquidation committee, or a member of it (r4.133 IR 1986); MVL: notice of the death must be given to Companies House and the directors (r4.145 IR 1986)).

d. Release

8264 When the liquidator obtains his release, he is **discharged from** all liability in respect of any of his acts or omissions in the liquidation and in relation to his conduct as liquidator generally (s 174(6) IA 1986). However, this does not prevent him from being held liable for misfeasance (¶7457+).

> MEMO POINTS This applies in a **voluntary liquidation** as well (s 173 IA 1986).

The time from which the **release is effective** depends on who the liquidator was and how his office was terminated.

8265

Who was liquidator	How office terminated		Release effective	Reference[1]
Liquidator	Resignation[2]	Accepted by creditors' meeting which did not resolve against releasing him	When official receiver files notice of resignation at court[3]	s 174(4) IA 1986; r 4.121 IR 1986
		Accepted by creditors' meeting which resolved against releasing him	Following application by former liquidator to secretary of state, when secretary of state determines[4]	
	Removal[5]	By meeting of creditors which did not resolve against releasing him	When notice given to court that liquidator ceased to hold office[6]	s 174(4) IA 1986
		By meeting of creditors which resolved against releasing him	Following application by former liquidator to secretary of state, when secretary of state determines[4]	
		By court		
		By secretary of state[7]		
	Automatically[8]	Ceased to act as insolvency practitioner		
		Final meeting which did not resolve against releasing him	When liquidator files notice at court and Companies House	s 174(4) IA 1986
		Final meeting which resolved against releasing him	Following application by former liquidator to secretary of state, when secretary of state determines[4]	s 174(4) IA 1986
		Death	When notice given to court that liquidator ceased to hold office[9]	
Official receiver acting as liquidator	Replacement	Meeting of creditors or contributories nominated replacement	When official receiver notifies court he has been replaced	s 174(2) IA 1986
		Secretary of state replaced him		
		Court replaced him	When court determines	
	Automatically	Notified secretary of state that winding up is complete	When secretary of state determines[10]	s 174(3) IA 1986
Provisional liquidator	Removal	By court order (¶7692)	Following application by former provisional liquidator, when court determines	s 174(5) IA 1986

Note:
1. In **voluntary liquidation**, relevant statutory reference is s 173(2) IA 1986, and Rules reference is: CVL: r 4.122 IR 1986; MVL: r 4.144 IR 1986.
2. In **MVL**, there is no need for meeting of shareholders to resolve to release liquidator.
3. In **voluntary liquidation**, liquidator files notice of own resignation at Companies House.
4. Where **liquidator** is released by **secretary of state**, secretary of state must send certificate of release to official receiver, who will file it at court (r 4.121 IR 1986). Copy will be sent to former liquidator.
5. In **MVL**, meeting of shareholders can remove liquidator, and there is no need for it to resolve to replace him. Liquidator can also be removed when winding up order is made against company, in which case liquidator must apply to secretary of state for release.
6. In **voluntary liquidation**, notice that liquidator has ceased to hold office must be given to Companies House.
7. Liquidator in **voluntary liquidation** cannot be removed by secretary of state.
8. In **voluntary liquidation**, liquidator's release is effective as soon as he has vacated office after final meeting.
9. Notice of liquidator's death must be given to Companies House in **voluntary winding up**.
10. **Secretary of state** will notify court that he has released **official receiver**, as well as giving summary of official receiver's receipts and payments (r 4.124(3) IR 1986).

e. Replacement

8267 The **official receiver** becomes the liquidator of the company if a vacancy is created by a liquidator's retirement, removal or automatic vacation of office (s 136 IA 1986). A **new liquidator** can be appointed by:
– the creditors' meeting called to accept his resignation or remove him (rr 4.109, 4.113 IR 1986);
– the secretary of state if requested to do so by the official receiver (s 137 IA 1986); or
– the court. Although the court does not have a statutory power to do so where it has removed the liquidator, it has been held that this falls within its general powers to make any necessary directions (*Re A & C Supplies Ltd* [1998] 1 BCLC 603).

If the liquidator's office has been terminated because he has resigned, been removed or ceased to be qualified, he must **give his successor** (r 4.138 IR 1986):
– the company's assets (less the expenses of the liquidation (including his remuneration, ¶8245) and any distributions made by him);
– the records of the liquidation, including correspondence, proofs and other papers; and
– the company's books, records and other papers.

The liquidator must also **send the Insolvency Service** any valid unclaimed or undelivered dividend payment instruments or returns to contributories, endorsed with the word "cancelled" (reg 8 SI 1994/2507). See ¶8232 for dealing with the financial records on vacation of office.

MEMO POINTS 1. If there is a **vacancy** in the office of liquidator during a **voluntary liquidation**, the official receiver does not step in. See ¶8508+ for how such a vacancy is filled.
2. In a **voluntary liquidation**, the liquidator must also **hand over** the same items (CVL: r 4.138 IR 1986; MVL: r 4.148 IR 1986).

B. Official receiver

8277 The **role** of official receiver is a statutory office, created by insolvency legislation (ss 399-401 IA 1986). There are currently 38 official receivers attached either to the High Court or county courts with winding up jurisdiction, who work within teams comprising deputy official receivers and supporting staff (¶7362+). They are civil servants who operate under the ultimate direction of the secretary of state for business, enterprise & regulatory reform since his department (BERR) has overall responsibility for the management of insolvency matters in England and Wales. However, they usually act on the instructions and guidance of the head of the Insolvency Service, the inspector general. Consistent with the legislation and Rules, the term "official receiver" is used to refer to the individual official receivers collectively.

8278 The official receiver **acts as liquidator** of the company when the order is first made and holds that position until an insolvency practitioner is appointed as liquidator, unless a particular insolvency practitioner was appointed when the order was made (s 136(2) IA 1986; ¶8203). He also steps into the role if there is a vacancy during the course of the liquidation (s 136(3) IA 1986). The official receiver may continue to act as liquidator until the end of the liquidation, particularly if the case is suitable for early dissolution (¶8396+) or the company has few assets, but he will usually pass the liquidation on to a liquidator when there are assets and other issues to deal with. The official receiver's **functions, activities and powers** as liquidator are the same as a liquidator's, so they are discussed together at ¶8215+ (references to the liquidator should be read as being to "the official receiver acting as liquidator").

The official receiver's other function is to **investigate the conduct** of the company and its affairs, and to report any matters of concern to the court and secretary of state. This role is discussed at ¶8120+.

The matters relating to the official receiver which are not specific to his performance of either of these two roles are discussed here.

Immediate procedural steps

When the **winding up order** is **made**, the court will give notice of it to the official receiver straight away (r 4.20 IR 1986). Once it has been drawn up, the court will send three sealed copies to the official receiver, who must then send one copy each to (r 4.21 IR 1986):
– the company at its registered office (or last known principal place of business if it has no registered office); and
– Companies House (s 130 IA 1986).

The official receiver must **advertise** the order by:
a. placing the appropriate notice in the *Gazette*; and
b. advertising in another newspaper chosen by him. This advertisement should reach as many of the company's potential creditors or contributories as possible, and so the newspaper with the largest circulation in the local area is usually chosen, although if the company's business operates across the country, the order can be advertised in an appropriate national newspaper.

In addition to advertising, the official receiver will usually **notify** a number of **other people** and organisations, as appropriate in the circumstances, of the winding up order. This helps him to gather information about the company, its business and the assets and liabilities with which he has to deal. Common examples are:
– suppliers and third party owners of goods;
– holders of charges over the company's assets;
– banks, credit and charge card companies;
– any insolvency practitioner who already acts in respect of the company;
– High Court Enforcement Officers, to prevent execution against the company's assets;
– if the company is a party to any other legal proceedings, the relevant court and parties;
– employees and administrators of employee pension schemes;
– Revenue and Customs;
– insurers;
– landlord; and
– any regulatory bodies relevant to the company's business.

8279

Reporting to creditors and contributories

The official receiver has two main **obligations** to report to creditors and contributories, as set out below. These duties may be **restricted** where:
– the court, on his application, relieves him of the duty to report, or authorises him to do so in another way (r 4.47 IR 1986); or
– the liquidation proceedings are stayed (r 4.48 IR 1986).

8280

Initial report

The official receiver must send a report which sets out the company's affairs to creditors and contributories at least once after the winding up order has been made (r 4.43 IR 1986). The report must **state**:
– an estimate of the portion of the company's assets which can be put aside for the unsecured creditors;
– an estimate of the value of the company's net property; and
– whether the official receiver or liquidator intends to apply for an order excusing him from ring-fencing a portion of the assets subject to a floating charge to pay the unsecured creditors (¶7992+).

The estimates do not have to include any information that could seriously prejudice the commercial interests of the company, and if they are excluded on this ground the report must contain a statement to that effect (r 4.43(1A) IR 1986).

8281

> MEMO POINTS **Creditors mean**, in the context of the official receiver's reporting obligations, those of the company known to the official receiver, or those identified in the statement of affairs where one has been submitted (r 4.44 IR 1986).

Report on the company's affairs

8282 If a **statement of affairs** has been **filed** at court (¶8127+), the official receiver must send a summary of the statement to the creditors and contributories (r 4.45 IR 1986). He must also provide any additional explanations or modifications given by the deponent, and any of his own observations regarding the statement or the affairs of the company in general, as necessary.

If a **statement of affairs** has **not** been **made**, the official receiver must send to the creditors and contributories a summary of the company's affairs (to the extent of his knowledge) and any other observations he has on it or the affairs of the company in general as soon as possible after he or the court has dispensed with the requirement for a statement of affairs (r 4.46 IR 1986).

The official receiver is not required to provide such a summary to the creditors and contributories if he has already reported to them and he considers that there are no additional matters that need to be brought to their attention (rr 4.45, 4.46 IR 1986).

If an order for **limited disclosure** of the statement has been obtained, the official receiver may not have to disclose certain parts of the statement or summary, depending on the terms of the order.

A copy of any report or summary given to the creditors and contributories must be **filed** at court.

C. Liquidation committee

8292 The liquidation committee's **main function** is to assist and supervise the liquidator in dealing with the company's assets for the benefit of the liquidation. It performs a particularly useful role in large and complex liquidations, enabling the liquidator to obtain information and advice about the company and its affairs.

The **general rules** discussed below apply to all liquidation committees; the **special rules** applying to establishing a liquidation committee where the liquidation immediately follows administration are at ¶8322+.

1. General rules

8294 Liquidation committees are **usually** only **found** where a liquidator is winding the company up, although they are not obligatory.

If the **official receiver** acts as liquidator, a committee can be established, but is not necessary, as its functions fall to the secretary of state, who allows the official receiver to carry them out (s 141(5) IA 1986; r 4.172(2) IR 1986).

8295 If there is **no liquidation committee** at any time during the winding up and the official receiver is not acting as liquidator, the committee's functions are carried out by the secretary of state (s 141(4) IA 1986). In this case, the provisions requiring the liquidator to give notice and report to the committee do not apply, although the secretary of state retains the committee's right to request such information (r 4.172(1) IR 1986).

> MEMO POINTS This only applies to a compulsory liquidation; for the position in a **CVL**, see ¶8548+.

a. Establishment

8296 The liquidation committee can be established **by** separate meetings of the creditors and contributories which (s 141(1), (2) IA 1986):
– were called to appoint the liquidator (¶8204+); or

– are summoned by the liquidator for the purpose, either on his initiative or at the creditors' request (¶8335+).

If the **creditors' meeting does not appoint** a committee the contributories' meeting can appoint a member to apply to court for an order to summon another creditors' meeting to establish a committee (r 4.154 IR 1986). If the creditors still do not appoint a committee, the contributories may do so. If it is the contributories' meeting which resolves against a committee while the creditors' meeting was in favour of it, or does not resolve to appoint one, the committee should be set up unless the court orders otherwise (s 141(3) IA 1986).

MEMO POINTS   For the initial establishment of a liquidation committee in a **CVL**, see ¶8548+.

Membership

The **composition** of the committee must be as follows (rr 4.152, 4.154 IR 1986): **8297**
– between three and five creditors elected by the creditors' meeting; and
– if it is a "solvent winding up" and the contributories' meeting decides to elect members of the committee, up to three contributories elected by them; or
– if the contributories' meeting established the committee because the creditors' meeting did not, between three and five contributories elected by them.

The members are **called** "creditor members" and "contributory members" as applicable. A member cannot sit on the committee as both a creditor and a contributory.

A creditor **cannot be a member** of the committee if (r 4.152 IR 1986):
– his debt is fully secured;
– he has not lodged a proof of his debt; or
– his proof has been disallowed for the purposes of voting, distributions or dividends.

A **body corporate** can be a member, provided it acts by a representative.

MEMO POINTS   1. For these purposes, a "**solvent winding up**" is one in which the company was wound up on a ground other than inability to pay its debts (r 4.151 IR 1986; ¶7592+).
2. **Additional members** can sit on the committee: a representative of the FSA (s 371 FSMA 2000) and a representative of the Financial Services Compensation Scheme manager (s 215 FSMA 2000).

Restrictions on dealings by members and their associates

Committee members and their associates are restricted in their ability to enter into transactions resulting in them benefiting from the company's estate, because membership of the committee puts them in a **fiduciary position** from which they cannot make a profit (Re F T Hawkins & Co Ltd [1952] 2 All ER 467). The persons affected by this restriction are (r 4.170 IR 1986): **8298**
– the current committee members;
– their representatives;
– associates (¶7895) of members or their representatives; and
– former committee members who sat on the committee within the preceding 12 months.

Such a person may not enter into a **transaction**, which results in him:
– receiving payment for services given or goods supplied in connection with the liquidation;
– obtaining any profit from the liquidation; or
– acquiring any asset which forms part of the company's estate,
without prior **sanction** of the court or the liquidation committee (and the liquidation committee is satisfied that full disclosure has been given and the person will give full value for the transaction). When the liquidation committee considers the resolution, a member or representative cannot vote if he is to participate (directly or indirectly) in the transaction. Alternatively, if such a person had to enter into a restricted transaction as a matter of urgency or to perform a contract which was entered into before the company went into liquidation, he can obtain retrospective leave from the court (provided he applies without delay). The costs of such an application cannot be paid out of the company's assets, unless the court orders otherwise.

If **sanction** is **not obtained**, any person interested can apply to the court to set the transaction aside and make any other order that is appropriate in the circumstances (for example, requiring a person to whom the restriction applies to account for any profit made). If the **8299** restricted person who breached these rules is an associate of a committee member or representative, the court will not make such an order if it is satisfied that he was not aware that entering into the transaction without sanction was not permitted.

Formalities of establishment

8300 The **consent** of the elected members (which can be given by their proxies or corporate representatives, unless the terms of their appointment state otherwise) can be obtained at or after the meeting. The establishment of the **committee** is **effective when** the liquidator issues a certificate of its due constitution, once the minimum number of members has consented to act. If further members consent to act after the certificate has been issued, the liquidator must issue an amended certificate.

The certificate (and any subsequent amended certificates) must be **filed** at court by the liquidator.

> MEMO POINTS 1. In the case of a **CVL**, the certificate and any amended certificates must be filed at Companies House, rather than at court (r 4.153(6), (8) IR 1986).
> 2. The liquidator usually **chairs** the meetings of creditors and contributories (¶8345+). If he does not, the chairman must notify the liquidator of the resolution and give him the names and addresses of the persons elected as members so that he can prepare the certificate (r 4.153 IR 1986).

8301 If there is a **defect** in the **formalities** of establishing the committee or the appointment, election or qualification of any member or representative, the acts of the committee remain valid (r 4.172A IR 1986).

b. Supervising the liquidator

8302 The liquidation committee supervises the liquidator in that he is required to seek its **consent for** the exercise of some of his powers, as well as being under a duty to keep the committee **informed** on certain matters. It may also fix his **remuneration** (¶8242), and check the fees paid to solicitors and other agents by requiring these costs to be assessed (r 7.34 IR 1986).

Sanction for use of powers

8303 One of the liquidation committee's functions is to sanction the liquidator's use of **certain powers**. The liquidator must obtain the **consent** of the liquidation committee to (Sch 4, s 160(2) IA 1986; rr 4.183, 4.170 IR 1986):
a. carry on the company's business for the benefit of the liquidation;
b. bring or defend legal proceedings in the company's name;
c. pay any class of creditors in full;
d. make a compromise or arrangement either with any creditors, or as a result of which the company may incur liabilities;
e. compromise and discharge (and take security for the discharge of) claims, debts and calls between the company and a contributory;
f. compromise any questions relating to or affecting the assets of the company;
g. bring legal proceedings for fraudulent and wrongful trading, transactions at an undervalue, preferences and transactions defrauding creditors;
h. make calls on shares;
i. distribute unrealised assets to creditors; and
j. sell company property to a member of the liquidation committee or his associate.

See ¶8216 for a full list of the liquidator's powers.

The factors to be taken into consideration when deciding whether or not to sanction the liquidator's actions are discussed at ¶8218.

The **court** can override the liquidation committee's decision in appropriate cases, but this does not give the liquidator the right to apply to the court for sanction over the liquidation committee's head as a way of avoiding their refusal to sanction his proposed action (*Re North Eastern Insurance Co Ltd* (1915) 85 LJ Ch 751; *Re Consolidated Diesel Engine Manufacturers Ltd* [1915] 1 Ch 192).

MEMO POINTS   In a **CVL**, it is not necessary for the liquidator to obtain the sanction of the liquidation committee to exercise the powers at a. and b.

Access to information

The **liquidator** must **report** to the committee on a number of matters: **8304**
a. if the committee is set up more than 28 days after the liquidator has been appointed, he must provide it with a **summary of his actions** since appointment (r 4.155 IR 1986). He must also answer any questions regarding his conduct. If a member joins the committee at a later stage, he is only entitled to request a summary report of the conduct of the liquidation so far;
b. he must inform the committee on **matters** which are **of concern** to it regarding the liquidation. The committee can leave it to the liquidator's discretion to decide which matters he informs it of, and/or tell him that it wants him to report on specified issues, although the liquidator will not have to do so if he considers that (r 4.155 IR 1986):
– their request is unreasonable or frivolous;
– the cost of doing so would outweigh the importance of the information; or
– there are not sufficient assets to enable him to comply with the request;
c. the liquidator must send a written report to each member setting out the **general progress** of the liquidation and any other matters of which he considers the committee should be informed (r 4.168 IR 1986). The committee can request the liquidator to do this (but cannot do so more than once in any 2-month period), and if it does not, the liquidator must report once every 6 months; and
d. the liquidator must inform the committee if he intends to **exercise** his **powers** to:
– instruct a solicitor to advise in the liquidation; or
– dispose of any of the company's property to a person connected with it.

MEMO POINTS   In a **CVL**, the liquidator does not have to notify the committee of the matters listed at d.

The liquidation committee is entitled to access to the **liquidator's records**, subject to the same exceptions as requests for access from other parties (see ¶8230). **8305**

If the committee is dissatisfied with the liquidator's **financial records**, it may inform the secretary of state, giving details of its objections, who may then take such action as he sees fit (reg 10 SI 1994/2507).

MEMO POINTS   1. The liquidator does not have to disclose to the committee any reports he makes to the official receiver (or, if the official receiver acts as liquidator, to the secretary of state) regarding the **directors' conduct** (¶8122, ¶8166+; Re W & A Glaser Ltd [1994] BCC 199).
2. The committee cannot complain about the liquidator's financial records to the secretary of state in a **CVL**.

c. Meetings

The liquidator will usually **call** meetings of the liquidation committee. He must call the first meeting within 3 months of the later of his appointment or the committee's establishment (r 4.156 IR 1986). Subsequent meetings will either be called: **8307**
a. on his own initiative;
b. at the request of a creditor member (in which case it must be held within 21 days of the liquidator receiving the request); or
c. on a specific date previously fixed by a resolution of the liquidation committee.

The liquidator must give 7 days' **notice** of the date, time and place of the meeting to every member (or his representative) for the meeting to be valid, unless a member has waived this requirement. Such a waiver can be given either at or before the meeting in question.

Attendance

Members can be **represented** on the committee by another person specifically authorised for that purpose (r 4.159 IR 1986). The representative must have a letter of authority to act (the **8308**

authority may be general or specific, e.g. to attend a particular meeting) signed by or on behalf of the committee member. This can be in the form of a **proxy** or a **corporate representative** appointment which deals with creditors' or contributories' meetings, unless the terms of the appointment preclude liquidation committee meetings. The terms governing his appointment are a matter to be agreed between him and his appointor. The chairman of the meeting can inspect any letters of authority and exclude a representative from the meeting if he is not validly appointed. Assuming the representative's authority is valid, he can attend and vote at the meeting on behalf of his appointor. If the representative signs any document on the member's behalf, he must state that he is doing so underneath his signature.

A **representative cannot**:
a. be:
– a body corporate;
– a disqualified director;
– an undischarged bankrupt; or
– a person who is subject to a bankruptcy restrictions order (including an interim order) or undertaking;
b. represent more than one committee member at the same meeting; or
c. act as a committee member in his own right and as a representative for someone else at the same time.

Otherwise, the **general rules** for **proxy-holders** and corporate representatives are the same as for creditors' and contributories' meetings at ¶8349+.

8309 Any reasonable **travel expenses** of the committee members or their representatives attending the meeting or carrying out other committee business are payable out of the company's assets as an expense of the liquidation (r 4.169 IR 1986).

Conduct of the meeting

8310 The **chairman** must be the liquidator, or a person nominated by him to act who is either another qualified insolvency practitioner or an experienced employee of the liquidator or his firm (r 4.157 IR 1986).

The **quorum** for a liquidation committee meeting is two creditor members present or represented (r 4.158(1) IR 1986). If there are no creditor members, the quorum is two contributory members present or represented (*Sharpe v Dawes* (1876) 2 QBD 26).

MEMO POINTS In the case of a **CVL**, the quorum for a liquidation committee meeting is any two members present or represented at the meeting (r 4.158(2) IR 1986).

Voting

8311 **Resolutions** at the meeting are passed by simple majority of the creditor members present or represented (r 4.165 IR 1986); each member has one vote. The contributory members' votes must still be recorded, but only count towards the vote if there are just contributory members on the committee (either because the committee was formed by the contributories or because the creditors have been paid in full and are no longer entitled to vote). Each resolution passed at the meeting must be **recorded** in writing (either separately or within the minutes), and the record signed by the chairman and kept with the other records of the liquidation (r 4.166(2) IR 1986).

MEMO POINTS In the case of a **CVL**, each member has one vote (whether he is present or represented), and the resolution is passed when a majority at the meeting votes in its favour (r 4.166 IR 1986). As in a compulsory liquidation, a written record (signed by the chairman) must be kept of each resolution with the records of the liquidation.

8312 **Written resolutions** can be used instead of calling a meeting each time a decision needs to be made (r 4.167 IR 1986). The liquidator must send a copy of the proposed resolution(s) (set out so that agreement and dissent can be indicated for each one) to each committee member or his representative. A committee member can, within 7 business days of the liquidator sending out the written resolutions, require him to call a meeting to consider them

(¶7412). Assuming no such request is received, the resolution will be passed when the liquidator has received written confirmation of the agreement of a majority of the members.

d. Changes to the committee

A person's membership of the liquidation committee can be **terminated by**:

8314

Method		Reference (IR 1986)
Resignation	Written notice to liquidator	r 4.160
Automatic termination	– Member's bankruptcy: trustee in bankruptcy becomes member instead – Absence from 3 consecutive meetings (unless members resolve not to remove him at third meeting) – Creditor member ceases to be/is discovered never to have been creditor	r 4.161
Removal	By resolution of creditors' or contributories' meetings, as applicable to type of member. 14 days' notice of resolution must have been given before meeting	r 4.162

Vacancies on the liquidation committee are dealt with as follows:

8315

Position on committee vacated by	Replaced by[1]	Method of appointment	Reference (IR 1986)
Creditor member	Another creditor	– By liquidator, with consent of majority of other creditor members; or – by creditors' meeting[2]; and – new member consents	r 4.163
Contributory member	Another contributory	– By liquidator, with consent of majority of other contributory members; or – by contributories' meeting[2,3]; and – new member consents	r 4.164

Note:
1. Vacancy does **not** have to be **filled** if (creditors: r 4.163 IR 1986; contributories: r 4.171 IR 1986):
– number of remaining creditor or contributory members (as applicable) is above minimum; and
– liquidator and remaining creditor or contributory members (as applicable) agree not to do so.
2. At least 14 days' **notice** of resolution needs to be given. If liquidator is not **chairman** at the meeting, chairman needs to notify liquidator of the appointment.
3. In **CVL**, if contributory members fill vacancy, creditor members can resolve that appointee should not become member. Court can overturn decision, or appoint another person to fill vacancy.

Where the composition of the committee changes after the initial members have consented to act, the **liquidator must inform** the court (or Companies House, in the case of a CVL) of the changes (¶8300).

Even if there is a **defect** in the appointment, election or qualifications of any member of the committee (or a representative), the acts of the liquidation committee remain valid (r 4.172A IR 1986).

8316

Creditors paid in full

Any **creditor members** of the liquidation committee automatically cease to be members when the liquidator files a certificate (Form 4.50) at court that the creditors have been paid in full, with interest (r 4.171 IR 1986). The liquidation **committee exists** as long as there are still at least three contributory members, or until a contributories' meeting resolves to abolish it. Contributories can fill vacancies on the committee (up to a maximum of five contributory members) as summarised above, and the committee can continue to act as if it comprised creditor members. If the number of contributories on the committee falls below three, it

8317

cannot act. The committee will automatically cease to exist if more than 28 days have passed since the liquidator issued his certificate that the creditors were paid in full and no, or too few, contributory members are appointed.

MEMO POINTS In the case of a **CVL**, the certificate confirming that the creditors have been paid in full must be filed at Companies House (r 4.171(3) IR 1986).

2. Rules where the liquidation immediately follows administration

8322 Different rules apply to the **establishment** of a liquidation committee if:
– the winding up order was made on an application for the termination of an administration by the administrator (¶9141, ¶9164+); and
– the court appointed the administrator as liquidator when the order was made.

MEMO POINTS In a **CVL** which **immediately follows** an **administration**, the creditors' committee also automatically becomes the liquidation committee (s 101 IA 1986). See ¶9142+ for a summary of the other differences in such a CVL.

8323 If a **creditors' committee** was established in the administration (¶9060+), it automatically becomes the liquidation committee (r 4.174 IR 1986).

However, this will not occur if the committee comprised fewer than three members when the court appointed the administrator as liquidator. The **number of members** on the committee can change when the winding up order is made, because any creditors' committee members whose debts are fully secured cannot sit on a liquidation committee. The liquidation committee can comprise between three and five creditors elected by the creditors' meeting which established the creditors' committee in the administration, or which has been summoned by the liquidator for the purpose (r 4.175 IR 1986). If the winding up is a solvent one, the liquidator must summon a contributories' meeting on 21 days' notice to elect any contributory members (up to three).

Every member must **consent** to act (or continue to act) as a committee member (r 4.176 IR 1986).

8324 Once the minimum number of members has confirmed its consent, the liquidator can issue and file at court a **certificate** of the committee's continuance (Form 4.52). The committee can act from the date of issue. The certificate must also state whether the liquidator has called a meeting of contributories and whether it elected any contributory members. If some members consent after the liquidator has issued his certificate, he must issue an amended certificate (which also has to be filed at court, also Form 4.52). Any change in membership at a later date must be reported to the court on Form 4.49.

8325 The liquidator must **report to the committee** on his actions since the winding up order was made as soon as possible after he has issued his certificate (r 4.177 IR 1986). A member joining the committee at a later date can only ask the liquidator to provide him with a summary report. The members of the committee have access to the liquidator's records as described at ¶8304+.

D. Creditors' and contributories' meetings

1. Summoning meetings

8335 Meetings of creditors and contributories can be **summoned by** different parties for various **reasons**.

Meeting called by	Purpose	Reference
Court	Ascertain wishes of creditors and contributories in any matter relating to winding up Weight of views depends upon: – creditors: value of debt; and – contributories: number of votes or company's articles Court can appoint chairman, who must report back to court	s 195 IA 1986
Liquidator [1]	To ascertain wishes of creditors and contributories [2]: – on own initiative; or – at the request of creditors or contributories	¶8336+
	To accept resignation, grant release and replace liquidator	¶8252+
	To provide them with requested information	¶8336+
	To fix remuneration if liquidation committee does not do so (or there is no committee)	¶8242+
	Final meeting of creditors when the winding up is, for practical purposes, complete	¶8393+
Official receiver	To appoint liquidator: – on own initiative; or – at creditors' request	¶8204+

Note:
1. In a **CVL**, the creditors have more influence, so liquidator will consult them more regularly (see ¶8555+); in an **MVL**, liquidator must consult shareholders (¶8645+).
2. Liquidator's power to summon meetings is one of the court's powers delegated to him (s 195 IA 1986; r 4.54(1) IR 1986).

Requests for meetings by creditors and contributories

8336 There are no specific **grounds** on which creditors and contributories can request a meeting, but they will usually do so to obtain information from the liquidator, or to remove and replace him. Although the legislation states that the liquidator must comply with the request, if there was a good reason for **not calling** a meeting (e.g. because it would be a pointless exercise) the court is unlikely to interfere with his decision, unless he has exceeded his powers or acted fraudulently or unreasonably (*Harold M Pitman & Co v Top Business Systems (Nottingham) Ltd* [1984] BCLC 593). The court may also instruct a liquidator not to comply with a request, even if it was made properly (*Re Barings plc (No 6)*, *Hamilton v Law Debenture Trustees Ltd* [2001] 2 BCLC 159).

MEMO POINTS In the case of a **CVL**, the contributories cannot request a meeting (r 4.57(4) IR 1986).

8337 A request for a meeting of the creditors and/or contributories must either be in the **form** of (s 168(2) IA 1986):
– a resolution by the appropriate meeting; or
– a written request by 10% in value of the creditors or contributories (as applicable).

A request by the **creditors** must be made on Form 4.21 and sent to the liquidator with (r 4.57 IR 1986):
a. a statement of the purpose of the proposed meeting; and
b. a list of the creditors agreeing with the request, details of their claims and written confirmation from them of their consent (this is not required if the requisitioning creditor's claim is sufficient on its own).

A request by **contributories** for a meeting must be on Form 4.24, giving the same information as a creditors' request but giving details of consenting contributories instead.

MEMO POINTS Special rules apply to requests by the **creditors** to summon a meeting to **remove** the **liquidator** (compulsory liquidation: ¶8255+; voluntary liquidation: ¶8539+).

8338 A person (creditor or contributory) requiring the liquidator to hold a meeting is expected to bear the **costs** of summoning and holding it, and he must deposit security for the expenses with the liquidator before his request needs to be acted upon (r 4.61 IR 1986). A creditors' meeting may then resolve that its expenses, and those of any contributories' meeting requested at the same time, must be met out of the company's assets as an expense of the liquidation. The contributories' meeting can pass a similar resolution, but its expenses are deferred to the right of the creditors to be paid in full with interest. Any deposit not used to meet the expenses of a meeting will be returned.

Notices

8339 Notices of meetings must be given at least 21 days beforehand (notices of the first meetings are dealt with at ¶8206) (rr 4.57, 4.54 IR 1986). They must be given **to** all **creditors and contributories** known as such to the liquidator, in Form 4.22 for creditors' meetings and Form 4.23 for contributories' meetings, specifying (r 4.54 IR 1986):
– the purpose of the meeting; and
– the venue (i.e. the date, time and place) at which proxies must be lodged (and, in the case of creditors, proofs as well) in order for the attendees to be entitled to vote at the meeting. The specified venue can be up to 4 days before the meeting.

Proxy forms must be sent out with the notice, in Form 8.4, and **proof** of debt forms are usually sent out as well (r 4.60(3) IR 1986). The notices can be **served** personally or by post (¶7406) and may also be advertised in a newspaper if the liquidator sees fit or the court so orders (the court can also order that the notice is served by public advertisement instead of individually, taking into account the relative costs of the two methods, the amount of assets available and the extent of the creditors' or contributories' interests, r 4.59 IR 1986).

When deciding on the **venue for meetings**, the liquidator must consider the convenience of the attendees (other than the chairman) (r 4.60 IR 1986). The meeting must be summoned for a time between 10am and 4pm on a business day (¶7412), unless the court allows it to be held at a different time.

> MEMO POINTS 1. In the case of a **CVL**, the notice must state the venue at which the creditors, if they are not attending in person, must lodge their proxies so that the proxies can vote (r 4.54(5) IR 1986). Proxies in **voluntary liquidations** are on Form 8.5.
> 2. As part of the Insolvency Service's review of secondary legislation (see ¶7364/mp), it is taking the opportunity to make alterations to the primary legislation either where it is necessary to support the new Rules or to remove unnecessary administrative burdens. The Service proposes to remove the requirement for insolvency practitioners to send information to all known creditors at various stages in the procedure, including **notices of creditors' meetings** (proposal 1, "A consultation document on changes to the Insolvency Act 1986 and the Company Directors Disqualification Act 1986 to be made by a Legislative Reform Order for the modernisation and streamlining of insolvency procedures" (September 2007)). Generally speaking, most creditors just want to know how much of their debt will be repaid and have no interest in the general progress of the procedure. This requirement therefore creates a heavy but unnecessary financial and administrative burden. It will be replaced by a system allowing creditors who do wish to be kept up to date to "opt in" to receiving information from the insolvency practitioner. The consultation paper also proposes to allow insolvency practitioners to:
> – send information, including notices of meetings using electronic communication where the recipient agrees;
> – make information available via a website; and
> – hold meetings of shareholders and creditors by whatever means appropriate in the circumstances. This would allow meetings to be held over the internet, for example, or via a mixture of media.
> At the time of writing, the consultation is still open. If these proposals are accepted, the changes are likely to be implemented from 1 October 2008.

8340 The liquidator must also give at least 21 days' notice of a meeting **to** those company **officers and employees** he thinks necessary (r 4.58 IR 1986). The notice can either give them the opportunity to attend, or it can require their attendance. Notice can be given to (s 235(3) IA 1986):
– past or present officers;
– those who took part in the formation of the company within 1 year before the company went into liquidation;
– employees, including former employees who were employed within 1 year before the company went into liquidation; and

– past (within 1 year before company went into liquidation) and present officers and employees of a company holding office in the company in liquidation.

Similarly, **if** the **meeting is adjourned**, the chairman must notify any of those people he thinks necessary who were not at the meeting itself (r 4.58 IR 1986). If the creditors or contributories want to question an employee or officer of the company who is not present, the chairman can adjourn the meeting so that he can attend when it is reconvened. The chairman has a discretion to decide what questions the attendees can put to any officer or employee.

Such a person wishing to **attend** the meeting (whether or not he has been given notice) must give reasonable notice of his intention to do so. The chairman has a discretion to decide whether or not they can attend and participate in the meeting.

2. Conduct of meetings

Chairman

The chairman will **usually be** the liquidator (or his nominee), but if the official receiver convened the meeting, he (or his nominee) will chair it (r 4.55 IR 1986). A nomination by the official receiver must be in writing, unless the nominee is another official receiver or deputy official receiver. A liquidator's nominee must either be a qualified insolvency practitioner or an experienced employee of the liquidator's firm.

8345

If there is **no** one at the meeting to act as **chairman**, an attendee who is entitled to vote can appoint any person to be chairman, with the consent of the other attendees entitled to vote. If an agreement cannot be reached, the meeting is adjourned to the same time and place the following week (or the next business day after that, if that day is not a business day) (r 4.65 IR 1986).

> MEMO POINTS   In the case of a **CVL**, the liquidator or his nominee will be the chairman at the meeting (r 4.56 IR 1986). This is the case except at a meeting to resolve to enter into a CVL, whether from an MVL or not (¶8443+, ¶8448+).

As well as having **control** of the meeting, the chairman can decide whether to admit creditors' proofs for the purposes of allowing them to vote (¶8354+).

8346

He is often **appointed as proxy** for members who cannot attend. If his proxy requires him to vote for a particular resolution (a "special proxy") but no other member proposes that resolution, he must propose it himself unless there is a good reason for not doing so (r 4.64 IR 1986). If he does not propose the resolution, he must inform his principal of his reasons straight after the meeting.

The chairman may **suspend** a **meeting** for up to 1 hour (he can only do this once during each meeting) (r 4.65 IR 1986). He can also **adjourn** the meeting to an appropriate time and place at his discretion, and must do so if the meeting so resolves (but see ¶8257 for the special rule relating to adjournment where a resolution to remove the liquidator is proposed). In addition to the chairman's wide discretion, the Rules set out further situations in which the meeting may be adjourned if necessary, where:
– a quorum is not present 30 minutes after the meeting was due to start;
– the attendees wish to question an officer or employee who is not present at the meeting; and
– an agreement cannot be reached as to who chairs the meeting.

8347

Proofs and proxies lodged up to midday on the business day prior to an adjourned meeting can be used at an adjourned meeting (¶7412).

Attendance

A creditors' or contributories' meeting must be quorate to proceed to business. The **quorum** depends on the type of meeting (r 12.4A IR 1986):

8348

Type of meeting	Quorum
Creditors'	At least one creditor entitled to vote
Contributories'	– At least two contributories entitled to vote; or – if there is only one contributory entitled to vote, he can form a quorum alone

The quorum can be reached by the relevant number of persons attending in person or by proxy, and includes attendance by a corporate representative. If a **quorum is not present** 30 minutes from when the meeting was due to start, the chairman may adjourn the meeting to an appropriate time and place (r 4.65 IR 1986). It may be that the meeting is quorate by the **chairman attending on his own** (because he can be nominated as a member's proxy) or the chairman and one other person. In such a situation, if the chairman is aware of other people who would be entitled to vote at the meeting (e.g. because he has received proofs from them), he must wait at least 15 minutes beyond the scheduled commencement of the meeting before allowing it to proceed to business (r 12.4A IR 1986).

Proxies and proxy-holders

8349 A contributory or creditor entitled to attend the meeting (the "principal") **can appoint** a person over 18 to do so in his place (the "proxy-holder") (r 8.1 IR 1986); the appointment forms themselves are called "proxies". Only one proxy-holder can be appointed at any one time per contributory or creditor, although the principal may give alternative names on his form, in case one or more choices is unavailable. Often, the chairman of the meeting is chosen as a proxy-holder, since he will definitely be able to attend the meeting and (as an insolvency practitioner or experienced employee of an insolvency practice) can be trusted to vote sensibly and impartially where the terms of the proxy give him a discretion to do so. If the chairman is given a proxy for a particular meeting, he must accept the appointment, and if someone else acts as chairman at the meeting, the new chairman takes over the proxy appointment (r 8.3 IR 1986).

> MEMO POINTS   If the **official receiver** is appointed as proxy-holder, his deputy or any other official receiver can act in his place, as can another officer in the Insolvency Service who is authorised in writing by the official receiver to do so (r 8.3 IR 1986).

8350 Proxy **appointment forms** will be sent out with the notice of the meeting, which must leave the name of the proxy-holder blank so that the principal has a free choice (r 8.2 IR 1986). Principals must use the form accompanying the notice, or a form substantially similar to it, otherwise their appointments will not be valid. The principal, or someone on his behalf (stating the nature of his authority), must sign the form. The proxy-holder could be authorised to sign on behalf of the principal.

To be valid, the proxy must be **lodged** in accordance with the instructions given in the notice of the meeting. A proxy appointment sent by fax is valid (*IRC v Conbeer* [1996] BCC 189).

8351 A proxy-holder is **appointed to** attend, speak, propose resolutions and vote or abstain at meetings for his principal, either according to specific instructions or at his discretion. He can propose any resolution that he would be entitled to vote on if it was proposed by someone else (r 8.3 IR 1986). If the instructions do not deal with a resolution put forward at the meeting the proxy-holder can vote as he sees fit, unless the terms of the proxy state otherwise. A proxy given in respect of a particular meeting can be used at any **adjournment** of that meeting.

A proxy-holder **cannot vote** on any resolution which would result in him or his associate receiving any funds from the company's estate (directly or indirectly), unless the terms of the proxy instruct him to vote in that way (r 8.6 IR 1986). If the proxy-holder was authorised by the principal to sign the proxy on his behalf and the terms instructed him to vote on such a resolution, he can only do so if he produces the written authorisation from the principal.

> MEMO POINTS   If a proxy-holder is instructed to act for or against a nomination on a resolution to **appoint a liquidator**, that instruction applies to a resolution to appoint that person jointly with another, unless the proxy specifically states otherwise (r 8.3 IR 1986).

After the meeting, the proxy forms used for voting must be **kept by** the chairman (and passed on to the liquidator, if the liquidator did not act as chairman at the meeting) (r 8.4 IR 1986). The liquidator must allow the proxies to be **inspected** at reasonable times on business days by (r 8.5 IR 1986):
- the creditors (for proxies used at a creditors' meeting);
- the contributories (for proxies used at a contributories' meeting); and
- the directors of the company (who can inspect either type of proxy).

In addition, any person attending a meeting is entitled to inspect the proxies for that meeting, along with related documents (most significantly proofs), which were given following the notice of the meeting. It is a criminal **offence** for a person to pretend to be entitled to inspect any document as a creditor or contributory (r 12.18 IR 1986; ¶9935).

8352

If a person is appointed as a company's **corporate representative**, the company does not have to submit a proxy to enable the representative to attend the meeting on its behalf (r 8.7 IR 1986). Instead, the corporate representative must produce a copy of the resolution giving him authority to act (either a sealed or certified copy) to the chairman of the meeting.

8353

Voting

Creditors

A creditor **can only vote** at a creditors' meeting **if** (r 4.67 IR 1986):
- he has lodged a valid proof of debt, which has been admitted for the purposes of enabling him to vote (¶8030+); and
- where he has appointed a proxy to vote on his behalf, the form has been lodged correctly and by the deadline stated in the notice.

8354

The **number of votes** ascribed to each creditor depends upon the value of his debt and he is entitled to vote once in respect of each debt on each resolution. Therefore, a creditor will only be allowed to vote in respect of an unliquidated or unascertained debt if the chairman agrees to put a value on it for the purposes of voting. Secured creditors can only vote in respect of the unsecured portion of their debt; if they are fully secured, they cannot vote (r 4.67 IR 1986). Conceivably, a creditor could split his vote, for example voting in favour with £x and against with £y, provided the sums add up to the value for which his debt has been admitted (*Re Polly Peck International plc* [1991] BCC 503, a case regarding administration which is likely to apply to liquidation as well due to the similarity of the relevant Rules).

8355

The chairman has the power to **admit or reject proofs** in whole or in part for voting purposes at the meeting (r 4.70 IR 1986). If he is in doubt over whether to admit a proof, he must mark it as "objected to" and allow the creditor to vote at the meeting, although the vote may subsequently be declared invalid if the chairman later rejects the proof.

MEMO POINTS 1. The court can declare that the creditors, or a class of creditors, are entitled to vote at creditors' meetings **without having to prove their debts** (r 4.67(2) IR 1986). This is, however, rare.
2. In a **CVL**, the liquidator can, in his discretion, **allow** a creditor **to vote** even if he has not proved his debt, where he is satisfied that the creditor did not prove due to circumstances out of his control (r 4.68 IR 1986).
3. A **member state liquidator** is entitled to vote at creditors' meetings where the liquidator admits for voting purposes a proof of a debt claimed to be owed to the creditors in the proceedings in which the member state liquidator acts (r 4.67(1)(a) IR 1986). A **creditor** who lodges a proof in the liquidation and also **claims in other proceedings** can only vote in his capacity as creditor (not as a claimant in other proceedings) at the meeting (r 4.67(7) IR 1986). If a creditor claims in more than one set of other proceedings, and more than one member state liquidator seeks to vote as a result of that claim, the member state liquidator in the main proceedings is entitled to exercise the vote (whether or not the creditor claims in the main proceedings) (r 4.67(8) IR 1986; see ¶7366+ for the relevant definitions).
4. A **creditor secured by** a **bill of exchange or promissory note** can only vote in respect of his debt if he (r 4.67(5) IR 1986):
- treats the liabilities on the bill or note of any person whose liability precedes the company's liability as security for those amounts (unless the person liable has gone into liquidation or personal bankruptcy); and

– estimates the value of the security and deducts it from his claim for the purposes of being able to vote.
5. A **liquidator** (or his partners or employees) cannot **vote** in person or by proxy on any resolution which deals with his remuneration or conduct (r 4.63 IR 1986).

8356 Creditors can **appeal** any of the **chairman's decisions** about proofs or voting (including where an "objected to" proof is later declared invalid). The court will consider whether the claim can be established and in what amount on the evidence presented to it, and can order another meeting to be called, or make another appropriate order. The chairman is not liable for the costs of such an application, unless the court orders otherwise (and if the chairman is the official receiver or his nominee, he will not be so liable). **Alternatively**, a creditor who is aggrieved by the chairman's decision as to his entitlement to vote may be entitled to require a meeting to be summoned to remove the liquidator (¶8255+). This might be a faster and more cost effective way of resolving the dispute as the new liquidator will then assess his proof (*Re Inside Sport Ltd (in liquidation)* [2000] 1 BCLC 302).

> MEMO POINTS   In a **CVL**, a creditor who objects to the liquidator's decision regarding his entitlement to vote could, as additional courses of action to appealing the decision:
> – petition for the compulsory liquidation of the company (which would be a matter for the court to decide taking into account all of the circumstances, so the creditor should have good reasons for taking this course of action, particularly if most of the creditors are still in favour of a voluntary liquidation); or
> – apply to the court for an order that his debt be admitted at the value he placed on it in his proof under the court's general power to determine issues arising in a voluntary liquidation (s 112 IA 1986; ¶8523+).

Contributories

8357 The **value** of the contributories' votes depends upon the company's articles (r 4.63 IR 1986). This is usually the same as at general meetings, but the articles may provide for particular rules to apply to contributories' meetings in insolvency (¶3810+; r 4.69 IR 1986).

Resolutions

8359 Resolutions are **passed by** a majority in value of creditors or contributories present and voting (r 4.63 IR 1986).
Special rules apply to two types of resolution (r 4.63 IR 1986):
a. appointment of a liquidator. If two nominations are made, the one with the support of a majority in value of those present and entitled to vote is appointed. If three or more are nominated, any one of them with a clear majority over the others together is appointed. The chairman must continue to put the decision to a vote until there is a clear majority in either scenario (disregarding each time the candidate who received the least support and anyone who withdraws), or he can propose a resolution that joint liquidators be appointed; and
b. those affecting the **liquidator's remuneration or conduct** (current, proposed or former). The votes of the:
– liquidator;
– other person(s) the subject of the resolution; and
– their associates (¶7895)
do not count. This is the case whether the vote was cast as a creditor, contributory or proxy-holder (unless the proxy appointment specifically instructed him how to vote, ¶8351).

> MEMO POINTS   In the case of a **CVL**, where two nominations are made for the appointment of a liquidator, the one with the majority of support from those attending the meeting (personally or by proxy) is appointed (r 4.63(2), (2A) IR 1986).

3. Administrative matters

8365 The chairman must cause **minutes** of each meeting to be taken and kept, recording all resolutions which were passed at the meeting (r 4.71 IR 1986). The minutes must be signed by the chairman and kept with the liquidation records. Once signed, the minutes are prima facie evidence that the meeting was correctly convened and held, the business was properly conducted and any resolutions were duly passed (r 12.5 IR 1986). A **list of attendees** must also be made and kept (r 4.71 IR 1986). The chairman must ensure that the particulars of any **resolutions** passed at the meeting are filed at court within 21 days of the meeting.

> MEMO POINTS   In the case of a **CVL**, there is no obligation on the liquidator to file the resolutions at court (r 4.71(4) IR 1986).

E. Special managers

The liquidator, provisional liquidator or official receiver can apply to court for the appointment of a special manager where another person is required to manage the company's business or property for the following **reasons** (s 177(2) IA 1986):
- it is necessary due to the nature of the company's business or property; or
- it would be in the interests of its creditors, contributories or members.

Such an appointment is usually **required where** the company's business is highly specialised or complex, for example an insurance company. The liquidator can recommend a person to fill the role; he does not have to be an insolvency practitioner, but will have to have suitable experience (a special manager is often an accountant who is also an insolvency practitioner). Depending on the nature of the company in question, the appointment of another type of specialist may be more appropriate.

8375

Appointment

The **application** must be accompanied by a report setting out the reasons for the application and the liquidator's estimate of the assets over which the special manager will be appointed (r 4.206 IR 1986). The application can be made at any stage of the liquidation, including between presentation of the petition and the winding up order being made.

If the court grants the application, its **order** appointing the special manger will be in Form 4.60 and will specify the duration of the appointment in terms of:
- a period of time;
- termination in specific circumstances; or
- running until a further order by the court.

The court will also fix the special manager's **remuneration**. It can **renew** his appointment by making an appropriate order.

8376

> MEMO POINTS   The acts of a special manager are valid, despite any **defect in his appointment** or qualifications (r 4.206(6) IR 1986).

Powers and duties

The **court can give** the special manager whatever powers it sees fit, including specifying that any of the legislative provisions relating to liquidators or provisional liquidators will apply to him as well (s 177 IA 1986). Usually, the special manager will carry on the day to day management of the company, reporting to the liquidator and following his instructions. He must act within the powers prescribed for him by the court in the order appointing him, and if he needs to act beyond those powers, the liquidator must apply on his behalf for leave of the court.

The special manager must submit **accounts** detailing his receipts and payments to the liquidator for approval, who will then add them to his own accounts (r 4.209 IR 1986).

8377

Termination

A special manager's appointment can be terminated in **three ways** (r 4.210 IR 1986):
a. by the dismissal of the winding up petition;

8378

b. if a provisional liquidator is in office and is dismissed without a winding up order being made; or
c. by order of the court following an application by the liquidator, if:
- the liquidator believes that the special manager is no longer necessary or profitable; or
- the creditors have requested, by resolution, that the appointment be terminated.

> MEMO POINTS   In the case of a **CVL**, only ground c. above is available as a means of terminating a special manager's appointment (r 4.210(1) IR 1986).

SECTION 5

Conclusion of the liquidation

By liquidator

8393 When it appears to the liquidator that the liquidation is for practical purposes complete, he must summon a **final meeting** of the company's creditors to (s 146(1) IA 1986):
- receive his final report; and
- determine whether he should be released (see ¶8264+).

He can summon the final meeting at the same time as giving notice of any final distribution of the company's property. However, if the final meeting is summoned for an earlier date, it must be adjourned until the liquidator is able to report to the meeting that the liquidation is complete (s 146(2) IA 1986). He must give **notice** of the final meeting as follows (r 4.125 IR 1986):
- to all creditors of whom he is aware, at least 28 days' before the meeting; and
- advertise the meeting in the *Gazette* at least 1 month before the meeting.

This ensures that even those creditors of whom the liquidator was not aware have the opportunity to attend.

At the meeting, the liquidator's **report** must give financial details in the form of (r 4.125 IR 1986):
- a summary of his receipts and payments;
- a statement that he has reconciled his account with that held by the secretary of state; and
- the amount paid to unsecured creditors out of the sum ring-fenced for that purpose (¶7992+).

The creditors can question the liquidator on any matter in his report. They can also resolve against granting him his release.

8394 **After** the **final meeting**, the liquidator must send a copy of his report and Form 4.42 to the court, which informs it (r 4.125 IR 1986):
- that the meeting has been held; and
- whether he was granted his release.

A copy of this notice must also be sent to the secretary of state, and the liquidator must notify Companies House of the resolutions on Form 4.43. If the **meeting** was **not quorate**, he must inform the court accordingly and the meeting is then deemed to have been held and the creditors are deemed not to have resolved against granting the liquidator his release.

> MEMO POINTS   The court can **relieve** the liquidator of any of the **procedural duties** detailed above (i.e. those in r 4.125 IR 1986), or allow him to fulfil them in a different way. The court's decision will depend upon the cost of carrying out the duty, the amount of assets available and the extent of the creditors' and contributories' interests (r 4.125A IR 1986).

8395 As soon as the liquidator has given notice to the court and Companies House, he **vacates office** (s 172(8) IA 1986). He must then deliver to the official receiver any of the company's papers, books and records which have not already been disposed of during the liquidation (r 4.138(3) IR 1986). For how the liquidator is released, see ¶8264+.

By official receiver

8396 The official receiver can apply to Companies House for the **early dissolution** of a company in respect of which he acts as liquidator, if his investigations reveal that (s 202(2) IA 1986):
– the realisable assets of the company are insufficient to cover the expenses of the liquidation; and
– the affairs of the company do not require any further investigation.

He must give at least 28 days' **notice** to the creditors, contributories and any administrative receiver of his intention to make the application. He is then relieved from carrying out any of the duties imposed on him relating to the company, other than to make the application (s 202(4) IA 1986).

Once the notice has been served, any creditor or contributory, administrative receiver or the official receiver can **apply** to the secretary of state **for directions** on the grounds that (s 203 IA 1986):
– the realisable assets of the company are sufficient to cover the expenses of the winding up;
– the affairs of the company do require further investigation; or
– early dissolution would be inappropriate for some other reason.

The secretary of state may give directions for the winding up of the company to continue, if appropriate in the circumstances. He will give the applicant two copies of the directions, one of which must be sent to Companies House (s 202 IA 1986; r 4.224 IR 1986). If the applicant fails to do so within 7 days of the directions being given, he is liable to a fine (s 203 (5), (6) IA 1986; ¶9935). The secretary of state's decision can be **appealed** by applying to court, and any decision on appeal must also be filed, with Form 4.69, at Companies House within 7 days of the decision by the successful party in the appeal (s 203 IA 1986; r 4.225 IR 1986).

Unless such directions are given, the registrar registers the application when he receives it and, if no objection is made, the **company is dissolved** after 3 months. This deadline can be deferred by the secretary of state, on the application of the official receiver or any other interested person before the 3 months expire (ss 202, 203 IA 1986).

8397 If **early dissolution is not possible**, but the official receiver remains the liquidator, he can give notice to the court that the winding up is "for practical purposes complete" in the same way as a liquidator can when the **winding up is at an end**, ¶8393.

Dissolution of the company

8398 Once notice from the liquidator or official receiver that the winding up is complete has been registered at Companies House (i.e. any case other than early dissolution by the official receiver), the registrar of companies will place an **advertisement** in the *Gazette* (ss 1077, 1078 CA 2006). The company is automatically dissolved after 3 months, unless an objection is made (s 205 IA 1986). This **period** can be extended by the secretary of state on application of any person who appears to be interested; a decision which can be appealed to the court. Any person who obtains an extension or successfully appeals the secretary of state's decision must file a copy of the direction or order at Companies House. Failure to do so renders him liable to a fine (¶9935).

Dissolution is discussed in **more detail** at ¶7491+, including what happens to any assets left in the company at the time and how the dissolution can be declared void in appropriate circumstances.

CHAPTER 18

Voluntary liquidation

OUTLINE ¶¶

SECTION 1 **Creditors' voluntary liquidation**	8437
A Entering liquidation	8438
1 Procedure	8439
a Statement of affairs	8440
b Shareholders' meeting	8443
c Creditors' meeting	8448
d Administrative requirements	8457
e Summary	8458
f Special cases	8459
2 Effect of winding up resolution	8465
3 Staying winding up proceedings	8479
B Dealing with the company's assets	8489
C Persons with conduct of the liquidation	8502
1 Liquidator	8507
a Appointment	8508
b Powers, duties and liabilities	8514
c Remuneration	8537
d Termination	8538
2 Liquidation committee	8547
3 Creditors' and shareholders' meetings	8555
4 Financial Services Authority	8563
D Conclusion of the liquidation	8573
SECTION 2 **Members' voluntary liquidation**	8594
A Entering liquidation	8604
1 Procedure	8609
2 Effect of winding up resolution	8623
B Dealing with the company's assets	8633
C Persons with conduct of the liquidation	8643
Liquidator	8644
Shareholders' meetings	8645
Creditors' meeting where company becomes insolvent	8648
Financial Services Authority	8652
D Conclusion of the liquidation	8662

If the company and creditors agree that liquidation is the best option for the company, they can choose to place it into **voluntary liquidation** rather than a less flexible **compulsory liquidation**. Broadly speaking, voluntary liquidations are resolved more quickly, amicably and less expensively than compulsory liquidations. However, a creditor cannot bring about a voluntary liquidation without the support of the shareholders (or, at least, the support of the majority required to pass the resolution), and so he will have to petition for compulsory liquidation if the shareholders are not in agreement.

8425

Once in voluntary liquidation, the company can still be placed into compulsory liquidation by a creditor or contributory's petition to court (¶7587+). Any contributory pursuing this route will have to convince the court that his interests will be prejudiced if the voluntary liquidation continues if his petition is to succeed.

There are **two types** of voluntary liquidation, neither of which is dependent upon the company's insolvency: creditors' (**CVL**) and members' (**MVL**). In a CVL, the creditors and shareholders of the company both have a hand in the conduct of the winding up, although the creditors have more control: since the company is usually insolvent, they get a greater say in the decisions which will affect how much of a recovery they will make. By contrast, a company can only enter into an MVL if its directors are prepared to make a declaration of solvency. Since the creditors will therefore make a full recovery, the liquidator does not

8426

consult them in his conduct of the liquidation. Instead, he looks to the shareholders, whose eventual distribution will depend upon his decisions.

8427 Most of the topics covered in the context of compulsory liquidation are also applicable to voluntary liquidation. Where this is the case, the reader can find the relevant subject by following the appropriate **cross-references** in the text or tables provided. The discussions within compulsory liquidation to which the reader is referred apply equally to voluntary liquidation, with the following specific issues noted in the **memo points**:
– differences in the law or procedures discussed;
– alternative references applicable to voluntary liquidation where the law and/or procedures are the same; and
– specific differences and/or references in the case of either a CVL or an MVL.

Readers should look for the bold text in the memo points, as applicable: voluntary liquidation, CVL, or MVL.

Where there are **specific topics** in their own right which are **only applicable to voluntary liquidations**, they are discussed here. Similarly, the reader may be referred from the MVL section to the discussion of topics applicable to both types of voluntary liquidation in the CVL section.

The **terms** "liquidation" and "winding up" are essentially synonymous, although "liquidation" is preferred here where the context allows. The concept of "contributories" is still relevant in voluntary liquidations (see ¶7863+ for a full definition of this term). Although contributories are most commonly shareholders, references here to shareholders are not synonymous with contributories; for example, the company's decision to enter into voluntary liquidation is taken at a shareholders' meeting, not a contributories' meeting. However, the legislation and Rules still set out various provisions applicable to contributories in voluntary liquidations, so these terms are used specifically to refer to one group or another.

SECTION 1

Creditors' voluntary liquidation

8437 Despite the name, a company can only enter into a CVL if its shareholders so resolve. Once the resolution has been passed, however, its creditors are the driving force behind the liquidation, as they can appoint their choice of liquidator over that of the shareholders and establish a liquidation committee to supervise him. The shareholders are still involved, but the process is designed to give the creditors more control.

A company does not have to meet any particular criteria to enter into a CVL, nor does it have to give its **reasons** for doing so. It will often occur as a result of continued pressure from the company's creditors as a group, perhaps following an unsuccessful informal or formal voluntary arrangement.

A. Entering liquidation

8438 A company can be wound up voluntarily on **two grounds**, when (s 84(1) IA 1986 as amended by para 39 Sch 4 SI 2007/2194):
a. the shareholders resolve by special resolution that it should be wound up voluntarily; or
b. a fixed term for the duration of the company has expired, or another specified event which signifies that it should be dissolved has occurred, and the shareholders resolve that the company should be wound up voluntarily.

The first ground can be relied on when a company intends to go into either CVL or MVL (¶8604). The second ground is rare as few companies are set up with a defined end date;

even if they are, the company often decides to carry on business beyond that time. If it is relied upon, the type of resolution required will depend upon the terms (usually in the memorandum and/or articles) in question.

Comment: Until 1 October 2007, shareholders could also resolve by **extraordinary resolution** that the company could not continue business because of its liabilities and that it was advisable to wind it up. However, the new Companies Act has abolished extraordinary resolutions, and so this option has been removed to be consistent with the new law (para 39 Sch 4 SI 2007/2194). The same effect can still be achieved by passing the special resolution instead, which requires the same majority.

1. Procedure

In a voluntary winding up, the procedural **steps** for entering into liquidation are **taken by** the company acting through its board, which is required to call both a shareholders' and a creditors' meeting; there is no court involvement. As a result, the procedure is simple and relatively quick, as the **timeline** at ¶8458 illustrates.

8439

The **procedure differs** in two cases, **where** (¶8459+):
- the EC Insolvency Regulation applies; and
- an administration is converted into a CVL.

a. Statement of affairs

The board is required to prepare a statement of affairs in Form 4.19, describing the financial state of the company (s 99 IA 1986). The statement is usually **prepared before** the shareholders' meeting, although it can be prepared at any time until the creditors' meeting since it only has to be produced at that point (r 4.34(4) IR 1986). The statement can reflect the company's position at a date up to 14 clear days before the shareholders' resolution to wind it up.

8440

The statement must include the following **information** (s 99(2) IA 1986):
- particulars of the company's assets, debts and liabilities;
- the names and addresses of the company's creditors; and
- the securities held by the creditors and the dates on which they were granted.

The statement must be **verified by** affidavit, which is included on the form, by some or all of the directors. A witness statement cannot be used instead.

> MEMO POINTS   As part of the Insolvency Service's review of secondary legislation (see ¶7364/mp), it is taking the opportunity to make alterations to the primary legislation either where it is necessary to support the new Rules or to remove unnecessary administrative burdens. The Service proposes to remove the requirement for certain documents to be verified by **affidavit** in insolvency procedures (proposal 5, "A consultation document on changes to the Insolvency Act 1986 and the Company Directors Disqualification Act 1986 to be made by a Legislative Reform Order for the modernisation and streamlining of insolvency procedures" (September 2007)). Since the reform of civil procedures generally in 1998, affidavits in other types of procedures have been replaced by witness statements, which do not have to be sworn/affirmed by a solicitor/commissioner for oaths/notary. Therefore, this change will reduce the cost and administrative time involved in preparing these documents. At the time of writing, the consultation is still open. If this proposal is accepted, the changes are likely to be implemented from 1 October 2008.

The reasonable and necessary **expenses** of preparing the statement of affairs are an expense of the winding up to be met out of the company's assets (r 4.38 IR 1986). If any such expenses have been **paid before** the **creditors' meeting**, the director chairing the meeting must inform the creditors how much has been paid and to whom. If a liquidator has been appointed before the creditors' meeting (see ¶8447 below), he may make such a payment, but:
- if there is a liquidation committee, he must give it 7 days' notice of his intention to do so; and
- if the payment is to be made to the liquidator or his associate, he needs the consent of the liquidation committee, the creditors or the court.

8441

8442 If the directors **fail** to produce a statement in the correct form at the creditors' meeting, they are guilty of an offence and liable to a fine (s 99(3) IA 1986; ¶9935).

Any past or present officer commits an offence for which he can be fined and/or imprisoned if he (¶9935):
a. has made any material **omission from any statement** relating to the company's affairs, unless he had no intention to defraud (s 210 IA 1986); or
b. makes any **false representations** or commits any other **fraud** for the purposes of obtaining the creditors' consent to an agreement relating to the company's affairs or the liquidation (s 211 IA 1986).

If he has done so prior to the liquidation, he is deemed to have committed an offence.

b. Shareholders' meeting

8443 The next stage is for the company to be **placed into liquidation** by the shareholders resolving to do so at a meeting. The meeting also gives them the chance to appoint members to any liquidation committee that the creditors may establish, and also to appoint a liquidator (although such an appointment may be overruled by the creditors).

As an **alternative to** calling a **meeting**, the board could circulate written resolutions to the shareholders instead (¶3580+).

Calling the meeting

8444 The process will be **initiated by** the board, which will have to call the meeting. The board can be required to call a meeting by the shareholders. The procedure for calling meetings is described in detail at ¶3620+. The board must ensure that it gives the correct period of **notice**, which will be 14 clear days' notice for a general meeting (special resolutions no longer require a longer period of notice. If, unusually, the decision is to be taken at a public company AGM, 21 clear days' notice will have to be given). Alternatively, the meeting may be held on short notice with the correct level of shareholder consent. As well as giving the requisite notice to the shareholders, the directors must give 5 days' notice of the meeting to any holders of qualifying floating charges (¶8779) created on or after 15 September 2003 (s 84(2A) IA 1986).

Conduct

8445 The **general** conduct of the meeting is the same as any other shareholders' meeting (¶3711+). However, **attendance** by one shareholder cannot constitute a valid general meeting for the purpose of appointing a liquidator, unless the company is a private company with only one shareholder (*Re London Flats Ltd* [1969] 2 All ER 744).

Business

8446 The **resolutions** which will be considered at the meeting are:
– a special resolution to wind the company up (unless the company is being wound up following a specified trigger event, and another type is required) (s 84(1) IA 1986);
– an ordinary resolution to nominate a liquidator; and
– an ordinary resolution to nominate up to five members to sit on the liquidation committee (¶8547+).

8447 The formalities of **appointing** a **liquidator** are dealt with at ¶8508+. In the run-up to a voluntary liquidation, the company usually seeks advice from an insolvency practitioner. If the company then decides to go into voluntary liquidation, the shareholders will often appoint that insolvency practitioner as liquidator. However, the creditors may wish to appoint a liquidator who has had no previous dealings with the company to ensure independence, and they will be able to do so at their meeting (¶8454). If the creditors' meeting is not held on the same day, the directors must provide the liquidator appointed by the shareholders with a copy of their statement of affairs, either straight after his nomination or as soon as the statement has been made (r 4.34A IR 1986).

Any **liquidator** appointed at this stage has limited **powers** to act until after the creditors' meeting. He must obtain the sanction of the court to exercise any of his powers (¶8515), other than those to (s 166(2) IA 1986):
– take the company's property into his custody or control (including property to which the company appears to be entitled);
– dispose of perishable and other goods, the value of which will diminish if they are not dealt with immediately (e.g. seasonal goods); and
– protect the company's assets.

Therefore, if a quick sale of the business is required, the creditors' meeting should be held on the same day, or the liquidator should apply to court straight away for sanction for his proposed actions. If the liquidator exercises any powers other than those listed above without sanction, he is liable to a fine (s 166(7) IA 1986; ¶9935).

> MEMO POINTS If **more than one liquidator** is **nominated**, the voting procedure is the same as at a creditors' meeting (¶8454).
> If **joint liquidators** are **appointed**, the meeting should stipulate by ordinary resolution how the powers are to be divided between them (s 231 IA 1986).

c. Creditors' meeting

The creditors' meeting is the final stage of entering voluntary winding up. The company is technically already in liquidation as a result of the shareholders' resolution, but the liquidator cannot yet exercise most of his powers. Therefore, the creditors' meeting is **usually held on the same day** as the shareholders' meeting. The board's statement of affairs will be produced at the meeting, giving the creditors the relevant financial information about the company and an estimate of their chances of recovery.

8448

Calling the meeting

The board must call a meeting of the creditors **to be held** up to 14 days after the shareholders' meeting, although it is usually held on the same day (s 98(1) IA 1986). The **notice** must state (r 4.51(2) IR 1986; s 98(2) IA 1986):
a. the company's name and registered number;
b. the venue (i.e. the date, time and place) for the meeting;
c. the time (from 12 noon on the business day before the meeting) by which proxies must be lodged to entitle the proxy-holder to vote at the meeting; and
d. either:
– the name and address of a qualified insolvency practitioner who will provide the creditors with such information about the company's affairs as the creditors reasonably require before the meeting, free of charge; or
– a place local to the company's principal place of business where a list of the company's creditors will be available for inspection free of charge during the 2 business days before the meeting.

8449

Proxy forms must be sent out with the notice, in Form 8.5, and **proof** of debt forms are usually sent out as well (r 4.60(3) IR 1986). There is no requirement to state a deadline by which proofs have to be submitted before the meeting, but since the creditors can only vote if their proofs have been admitted, they should submit them to the liquidator in advance.

Notice must be **sent to** the creditors at least 7 days before the meeting, by post or personal service, unless the court has ordered that notice should only be given by public advertisement and not individual notices (r 4.59 IR 1986). It must also be **advertised** in the *Gazette* and in at least two local newspapers.

> MEMO POINTS 1. The **local newspapers** (and **place** at which the list of creditors will be available) chosen should be circulated (or, be) in the locality where the company's principal place of business in Great Britain has been during the 6 months prior to notice of the shareholders' meeting being sent out (s 98 IA 1986). If the shareholders resolved to wind the company up by written resolution, the period should be calculated according to the date of the resolution. If the company's principal place of business has moved within that period, the advertisement must be given in all relevant localities. If the company's principal place of business was not in Great Britain during that period, the advertisements must be given in the locality of the registered office.

2. As part of the Insolvency Service's review of secondary legislation (see ¶7364/mp), it is taking the opportunity to make alterations to the primary legislation either where it is necessary to support the new Rules or to remove unnecessary administrative burdens. The Service **proposes to remove** the requirements:
– for the creditors' meeting to be **advertised** in local newspapers (proposal 3, "A consultation document on changes to the Insolvency Act 1986 and the Company Directors Disqualification Act 1986 to be made by a Legislative Reform Order for the modernisation and streamlining of insolvency procedures" (September 2007)). Currently, this requirement means that the cost of advertising has to be incurred, whether or not the liquidator is aware of all of the company's creditors and whether or not the advertisements in the local newspapers are likely to come to the creditors' attention. Therefore, these advertisements are thought to be ineffective. The requirement will be replaced with a discretion to publicise the meeting if necessary to attract the attention of additional creditors by whatever means the liquidator feels would be most effective (for example, a notice could be placed on the company's own website). The obligation to advertise in the *Gazette* will remain, as this is an effective way of reaching creditors (for example, banks carry out regular searches of the *Gazette* to check for any notices about their customers); and
– for the notice to be delivered **by post**, so that it can be sent electronically instead where the recipients agree (proposal 1).
At the time of writing, the consultation is still open. If these proposals are accepted, the changes are likely to be implemented from 1 October 2008.
3. This short deadline for submitting proxies does not have to be given where the winding up **immediately followed** an **administration** (r4.1 IR 1986). Instead, the usual deadline of up to 4 days before the meeting will be given (¶8339).

8450 It is an offence for the company to **fail to comply** with most of the requirements regarding the contents of the notice, giving rise to liability for a fine (s 98(6) IA 1986; ¶9935). The liquidator is under a duty to apply to the court within 7 days of his appointment, or of him becoming aware of the failure if earlier, to ask for directions as to how the default should be remedied (s 166 IA 1986). If he fails to do so, he is also liable to a fine (¶9935). Despite the mandatory wording of the legislative provision, it has been held that the liquidator can decide that it is not necessary to apply for directions (Re Salcombe Hotel Development Co Ltd [1991] BCLC 44). For example, it is possible for the creditors present at the meeting to waive the requirement for notice to ensure that the resolution to wind up is valid (Re Oxted Motor Co [1921] 3 KB 32).

Failure to state the venue and time for **lodging proofs and proxies** in the notice is not an offence but will affect the validity of the meeting.

Conduct

8451 The board must appoint one of the directors to be the **chairman** of the creditors' meeting (s 99 IA 1986). If he fails to attend and preside at the meeting, he is guilty of an offence and liable to a fine, but those present at the meeting can elect another chairman and proceed with the meeting (Re Salcombe Hotel Development Co Ltd [1991] BCLC 44; ¶9935).

8452 At the meeting, the board must produce the **statement of affairs** to the creditors (s 99 IA 1986). Failure to do so is an offence and gives rise to the liquidator's obligation to apply to the court for directions (¶8450 above; ¶9935). At least one director will be at the meeting (as chairman), enabling the creditors to ask questions about the statement and the conduct of the company's affairs in general, although it is usual for all of the directors to attend. If the statement of affairs is **not up to date**, the board must also report to the meeting (orally or in writing) on any material transactions which have occurred between the date to which the statement is made up and the date of the meeting (r 4.53B IR 1986). This report must be recorded in the minutes of the meeting.

If a **liquidator** has **already** been **appointed**, he must attend the creditors' meeting and report to it on any exercise of his powers (s 166 IA 1986; failure to do so renders him liable to a fine, ¶9935). Such a liquidator will usually lead the meeting, although not as chairman, explaining the proceedings and his proposals for conducting the liquidation.

Business

8453 Next, the following **resolutions** can be considered (rr 4.52(1), 4.53 IR 1986):
a. to appoint a named insolvency practitioner (but not the official receiver) as liquidator, or more than one as joint liquidators;

b. to establish a liquidation committee;
c. if a liquidation committee is not set up, to specify the liquidator's remuneration or to defer this decision;
d. if joint liquidators are appointed, to determine whether acts are to be done by one or both/all of them;
e. to adjourn the meeting for up to 3 weeks; and
f. any other resolution, which the chairman considers appropriate for special reasons.

The rules for **voting** at creditors' meetings are dealt with at ¶8354+.

> MEMO POINTS 1. If the CVL immediately **follows** an **administration** (para 83(3) Sch B1 IA 1986), this restricted list of permitted resolutions does not apply (r 4.1(6) IR 1986).
> 2. If **joint liquidators** are appointed, the meeting should stipulate how the powers are to be divided between them (s 231 IA 1986).
> 3. If the **shareholders' meeting** was **adjourned**, the creditors' meeting can go ahead before the shareholders' meeting is reconvened, but the **resolutions** passed by the creditors will not **take effect** until after the shareholders' meeting (r 4.53A IR 1986).

Even if the shareholders have already **appointed** a **liquidator**, the creditors can still put their own nomination forward, for example if they feel the need to appoint an independent liquidator who has not previously advised the company. If this happens, the creditors' choice prevails, unless a director, shareholder or creditor of the company applies to court within 7 days of the nomination asking for an order that (s 100 IA 1986):
– the shareholders' choice is appointed instead of, or jointly with, the creditors' choice; or
– a different liquidator altogether is appointed.

8454

If **one nomination** is put forward, the meeting will be asked to vote for/against his appointment. Similarly, in a contest between **two nominees**, the meeting will vote for/against each one and the person who gains the most support will be appointed (provided he is supported by over 50% of those present, i.e. enough to pass an ordinary resolution) (r 4.63(1) IR 1986). If **more than two** nominations are put forward, the voters will vote for their favoured candidate, rather than for and against each one. One nominee must attain more of the votes than the others put together in order to be appointed; if there is no such majority, the chairman will continue taking votes (excluding any nominee who withdraws and the one who received the fewest votes on the last vote) until one has a majority over the others or two or more are appointed jointly.

Creditors usually decide to **establish** a **liquidation committee**, in which case they can appoint up to five persons to sit on it (s 101 IA 1986). The functions and procedures of the liquidation committee are discussed at ¶8547+. If the shareholders appointed committee members at their meeting, they will also join the liquidation committee.

8455

Costs

The **reasonable expenses** of calling, advertising and holding a creditors' meeting can be met out of the assets of the company as an expense of the liquidation (r 4.62 IR 1986). If money is paid out of the assets **before the creditors' meeting**, the chairman must inform the creditors of how much has been paid and to whom. A liquidator can make such a payment, provided he gives at least 7 days' notice of his intention to do so to the liquidation committee, if one has already been appointed at this stage by the shareholders. Any **payment to** the **liquidator** himself or an associate of his can only be made with the sanction of the liquidation committee, creditors or the court.

8456

> MEMO POINTS These provisions do not apply if the CVL immediately **follows** an **administration** (para 83(3) Sch B1 IA 1986).

d. Administrative requirements

After the **shareholders' meeting**, the company must:
– file a copy of the resolution to wind up at Companies House within 15 days of it being passed (s 84(3) IA 1986); and
– advertise the resolution in the *Gazette* within 14 days of it being passed (s 85(1) IA 1986).

8457

The liquidator must, within 14 days of his appointment (s 109(1) IA 1986; SI 1985/854):
- file a notice of his appointment at Companies House; and
- advertise his appointment in the *Gazette*.

Failure to comply with these requirements renders the company and every officer in default liable to a fine (ss 85(2), 109(2) IA 1986; s 30(2) CA 2006; ¶9935). For these purposes, the liquidator is included as an officer of the company (s 85(2) IA 1986; s 30(4) CA 2006).

After the **creditors' meeting**, the board must deliver the statement of affairs to the new liquidator, who must file it at Companies House within 7 days (r 4.34 IR 1986). See ¶8530 for the information which the liquidator must give to creditors within 28 days of the meeting.

> MEMO POINTS The Insolvency Service has clarified that a liquidator must still file notice of his appointment where an **administration** has been **converted into a CVL** (¶9142; para 4, chapter 12, *Dear IP*). However, it is reviewing whether the requirement is necessary and any change in the law will be made as part of the wider review of the Rules (¶7364/mp).

e. Summary

8458 The following **timeline** illustrates the steps that must be taken to place a company into CVL, and when they must occur in relation to the shareholders' meeting, which is marked "**M**". A more detailed timeline of the events surrounding a shareholders' meeting is found at ¶3873. The deadlines by which events must occur are used here, although the creditors' and shareholders' meetings can be held on the same day, in which case, the preparatory steps for the creditors' meeting must be taken at the correct times in advance of both meetings.

Day	Event
-18	Send out notice of shareholders' meeting [1]
-15	Prepare statement of affairs
-8	Send notice of shareholders' meeting to qualifying floating charge holders [1]
M	Shareholders' meeting: – resolution to wind company up; [2] – appoint liquidator; and – appoint shareholder members of liquidation committee
+ 7	Send notice of creditors' meeting. Advertisements appear in *Gazette* and local newspapers.
+ 12	If creditors have not been given the name of an insolvency practitioner who can provide information about the company's affairs, a list of creditors must be made available for inspection until creditors' meeting
+ 13	12 noon onwards: creditors' proxies to be lodged
+ 14	Creditors' meeting: – review statement of affairs; – appoint liquidator; and – establish liquidation committee. After meeting: hand over statement of affairs to liquidator. Advertise shareholders' resolution in *Gazette*.
+ 15	File shareholders' resolution at Companies House
+ 21	Liquidator files statement of affairs at Companies House
+ 28	Liquidator: [3] – files notice of appointment at Companies House; and – advertises appointment in *Gazette*

Note:
1. Assuming notices are sent out by 1st class post, so service is deemed on 2nd day after posting (r 12.10 IR 1986; ¶3704).
2. This marks commencement of liquidation.
3. If shareholders' appointment of liquidator was not overturned at creditors' meeting, liquidator must do this within 14 days of his appointment.

f. Special cases

Application of EC Insolvency Regulation

8459

The EC Insolvency Regulation is discussed at ¶7366+. If a CVL is to be the **main or secondary proceedings**, it needs to be confirmed by the court after the resolutions to place the company into CVL have been passed. The CVL will need to be the main proceedings where a company has assets and/or business interests in other member states, as it will give the liquidator the power to recover and realise them even though they are situated abroad. If main proceedings have already been commenced against the company in another member state, the CVL will have to be confirmed as the secondary proceedings. While the CVL will largely be conducted as usual, the liquidator will have a duty to co-operate and share information with the liquidator of the main proceedings, who will also have certain rights to influence the secondary proceedings. In addition, the creditors' position is improved if the CVL is the main or secondary proceedings, as they will be entitled to make a claim in related proceedings in other member states as well (although they can only recover up to the amount of their debt).

<u>MEMO POINTS</u> A CVL can also be confirmed where it has been **converted from** an **administration** (r 7.62(8) IR 1986).

The liquidator will make an **application** to court without notice to any other parties, attaching a copy of the shareholders' resolution, evidence of his appointment and a copy of the statement of affairs laid before the creditors' meeting (r 7.62 IR 1986). The court can then confirm the CVL by sealing the application. Once confirmed, the liquidator must **notify** any member state liquidator in the main proceedings and all known creditors who have their habitual residence, domicile or registered office in another member state (see ¶7372).

8460

Administration converted into CVL

8461

An administration can be converted into a CVL without the need for a statement of affairs and shareholders' and creditors' meetings. Instead, the administrator converts the procedure by filing the relevant documents at court and serving certain parties with the correct notices. This **method** and a summary of the **different provisions** relating to the conduct of a CVL commenced in this way are discussed at ¶9142+.

2. Effect of winding up resolution

A voluntary liquidation **begins when** the resolution to wind the company up is passed (s 86 IA 1986). This is referred to as the **commencement of the liquidation**, and signals many changes in the company's activities and powers, affecting those involved in its management. It is particularly significant in relation to specific proceedings which challenge transactions entered into in the run-up to the liquidation (see ¶7808+).

8465

If the shareholders' **meeting** was **adjourned** before the resolution to wind up could be approved, the liquidation still begins on the date the resolution is passed and not on the date of the original meeting (s 332 CA 2006).

<u>MEMO POINTS</u> If the company resolved to wind the company up voluntarily and **then** a **petition is presented**, the liquidation still commences on the date of the resolution (s 129(1) IA 1986).

Company's business and assets

8466

Once the resolution has been passed, the company must **cease to** carry on its business, except to the extent that is necessary for the liquidation to be completed (s 87 IA 1986). The company remains a legal entity in its own right and its **corporate powers** are valid until it is dissolved, so that, for example, its **property** remains vested in its name. However, the creditors become entitled to the benefit of that property by virtue of an automatic statutory trust that is imposed when the resolution is passed, and so the property must be dealt with in their interests (*Ayerst (Inspector of Taxes) v C & K (Construction) Ltd* [1975] 2 All ER 537).

> MEMO POINTS The liquidator can apply to have all or part of the company's **property vested in** him instead, although this is not usually necessary (ss 112, 145 IA 1986).

8467 The liquidation will not in itself constitute a breach by the company of any **contracts**, unless their terms state otherwise, and so the other parties to the contracts cannot refuse to perform their obligations just because the company is in liquidation (*British Wagon Co and Parkgate Wagon Co v Lea & Co* (1880) 5 QBD 149). However, if the liquidator declares that he is unable to perform the contracts, this is treated as a breach entitling the other party to claim damages (*Telsen Electric Co Ltd v J J Eastick & Sons* [1936] 3 All ER 266). In rare circumstances, the other party may be able to obtain an order for specific performance of a contract (for example, where the contract concerns land) (*Re Coregrange Ltd* [1984] BCLC 453). A contract cannot be enforced against the liquidator personally unless he has adopted it. See ¶7914+ for the liquidator's power to deal with contracts to minimise the company's liabilities.

Any **transfers of shares** made after the commencement of a voluntary liquidation are void, except those made to, or with the consent of, the liquidator (s 88 IA 1986).

8468 The fact that the company is in liquidation must be **publicised** by adding a statement to that effect to all of the company's websites and any invoices, orders for goods, order forms and business letters which bear the company's name and are issued (s 188(1) IA 1986):
– by or on behalf of the company;
– by a liquidator; or
– by a receiver or manager of the company's property.

Failure to comply renders the officer of the company, liquidator, receiver or manager who knowingly and wilfully permitted the default liable to a fine (¶9935).

> MEMO POINTS The statement's inclusion on a company's websites and order forms became a requirement as of January 2007, following the implementation of amendments to the First Company Law Directive (by EC Directive 2003/58). The requirement applies to companies already in liquidation at that time as well as those entering liquidation subsequently.

Litigation

8469 Once the company is in voluntary winding up, its **ability to commence and defend** litigation is affected.

Type of litigation	Requirements/powers	Reference
Company is claimant	– Liquidator does not need sanction – Counterclaim does not need leave of court – Defendant can apply for security for costs	¶8514+ s 726 CA 1985 [1]
Company is defendant	– Claimant does not need leave of court – Liquidator/creditor/contributory can apply to restrain or stay proceedings – Liquidator has power to compromise claims with sanction (CVL: of court/liquidation committee; MVL: of shareholders)	¶8514+ s 112 IA 1986

Note:
1. s 726 CA 1985 is expected to be repealed by 1 October 2009. There will be no replacement provision in the **new Companies Act**. However, this will make no real difference because a court will still be able to order security for costs to be paid under the CPR (r 25.15 CPR).

8470 As regards **enforcement action** taken after the commencement of the liquidation, see ¶7903+.

Constitution

8471 Once the resolution is passed, any provisions in the company's **articles** of association which are inconsistent with insolvency legislation cease to have effect. For example, provisions restricting the ability to make calls on shares and those relating to the inspection of the company's books are commonly affected.

Directors

8472 The resolution does not terminate the directors' office, although they do not automatically have the power to act once the **liquidator** has been **appointed** (s 103 IA 1986). They can be permitted to continue to exercise their powers by the liquidation committee (or by the creditors, if there is no liquidation committee).

On the other hand if a **liquidator** has **not** been **appointed**, the directors can only exercise most of their powers with the consent of the court. They can only perform the following actions without such consent (s 114 IA 1986):
– complying with the provisions relating to creditors' meetings (¶8448+) and preparing the statement of affairs (¶8440+);
– disposing of perishable and other goods, the value of which will diminish if they are not immediately disposed of (e.g. seasonal goods); and
– protecting the company's assets.

If a director **acts without consent**, he is liable to a fine (¶9935). Further, if he has entered into a transaction without consent, the transaction itself will be invalid unless the third party dealt with the director in good faith without notice of the restrictions on his powers (such as where the resolution has not been registered or advertised and the third party has no way of finding out that the company is in voluntary liquidation, *Re a Company (No 006341 of 1992), ex parte B Ltd* [1994] 1 BCLC 225).

MEMO POINTS In an **MVL**, the directors remain in office once the **liquidator** has been **appointed**, but their powers cease (s 91(2) IA 1986). They can be given permission to exercise certain powers during the MVL by the liquidator or the shareholders (by ordinary resolution). If no liquidator has been appointed, they must also apply to the court or only act within the restricted powers described at b. and c. in the list above.

Employees

8473 The survival of the employees' **contracts** will depend on the circumstances. The terms of the contracts may state that cessation of the business, or a resolution to wind up, constitutes repudiation of the contract by the employer. If not, the contracts will be terminated when the liquidator is appointed, unless the liquidator decides to continue the company's business for a period. See ¶8830/mp for the implications of selling the business as a going concern or making employees redundant. Employees' claims are summarised at ¶2986 (see *Employment Memo* for a full discussion). The principal **claims arising** when the company goes into liquidation will be for wrongful dismissal (for termination without notice) and redundancy. Such claims can be brought against a company in liquidation, and a successful claimant will have to prove in the liquidation for any damages awarded.

Employees who are **owed money by the company** are treated as preferential creditors for particular debts, and will be able to claim a certain amount as a "guaranteed debt" from the secretary of state (¶8045+). In the absence of any special circumstances, they are otherwise treated as ordinary unsecured creditors.

MEMO POINTS If all or part of a company's undertaking is transferred, **TUPE** may apply. The new TUPE regulations which came into force on 6 April 2006 do not contain an exception in relation to hive-downs, unlike the old regulations (SI 2006/246). See ¶6415+ for hive-downs, ¶6422 for the application of TUPE in insolvency hive-downs and *Employment Memo* for the effect of TUPE generally.

Other agents

8474 The authority of the company's agents will be terminated automatically when they have notice of the resolution (*Re Oriental Bank Corpn, ex parte Guillemin* (1884) 28 Ch D 634).

3. Staying winding up proceedings

8479 The court has the power to stay the winding up proceedings in the same way as in a compulsory liquidation (see ¶7736). Where the company is in voluntary liquidation, the **application** must be made under the provision enabling the court to exercise the powers available to it in a compulsory liquidation (s 112 IA 1986).

B. Dealing with the company's assets

8489 Most of the discussion at ¶7772+ relating to dealing with the company's assets when it is in compulsory liquidation is also applicable in a voluntary liquidation, with the exception of:
– the liquidator's additional power in voluntary liquidation to accept shares as consideration for a transfer of the company's assets; and
– the form in which debts have to be proved,
which are dealt with below.

A table of broad **cross-references** is given below. There are some specific matters and differences pertinent to a voluntary liquidation, which are highlighted in the **memo points** to the topics discussed in the context of a compulsory liquidation. Readers will find the following type of information in these memo points:
– where the discussion is the same for a voluntary liquidation but the references are different, the alternative references are provided;
– any procedural or legal differences which need to be followed in a voluntary liquidation; and
– any differences which just apply to either a CVL or an MVL.

Topic			¶¶
Collection	Carrying on business		¶7791+
	Increasing assets:		
	• Challenging certain transactions:	– transactions at an undervalue	¶7811+
		– preferences	¶7819+
		– transactions defrauding creditors	¶7826+
		– floating charges	¶7836+
		– extortionate credit transactions	¶7842+
	• Other litigation (but see also ¶8469)		¶7850+
	Money owed by **contributories**:		
	– Definition of contributory		¶7863+
	– Recovery of debts		¶7869+
Realisation	• Liquidator's **power to sell** in general		¶7894+
	• Particular types of assets		¶7901+
	• **Assets not realised** by the liquidator:	– onerous property	¶7917+
		– contracts	¶7928+
Distribution	Costs and expenses of liquidation		¶7956
			¶7957+
	Secured creditors		¶7977+
	Unsecured creditors:		
	– Provable debts		¶8005+
	– How to prove debts (except the form of the proof, see ¶8492 below)		¶8030+
	– **Preferential creditors**		¶8044+
	– Ordinary unsecured creditors		¶8053+
	– **Deferred creditors**		¶8066+
	Creditors who are also debtors of the company/**set-off**		¶8072+
	Shareholders/contributories		¶8087+
	Summary illustration of distribution process		¶8101+

Accepting shares as consideration for company's assets

8490 The liquidator in a voluntary winding up is given more **flexibility** as to how he makes distributions to the shareholders. As well as distributing cash and assets, he can:
a. accept shares, policies, or other similar interests as consideration, in whole or in part, of a transfer or sale of all or part of the company's business (s 110(2) IA 1986); or

b. enter into an agreement which enables the shareholders of the company to participate in the profits of, or receive another benefit from, the purchaser company (s 110(4) IA 1986).

The interests or the benefit of the agreement can be "distributed" to the company's shareholders instead of, or as well as, the proceeds of realisation. To take either course of action, he must have the **sanction** of the liquidation committee or the court.

This power is **usually used in** solvent liquidations, particularly reconstructions and mergers because it gives the shareholders of the company being wound up a stake in the purchaser company. The process is commonly referred to as a "**section 110 reorganisation**", after the relevant statutory reference, and is dealt with in detail at ¶6465+.

MEMO POINTS In an **MVL**, the liquidator needs the sanction of the shareholders in the form of a special resolution (s 110(3) IA 1986). A shareholder who did not vote in favour of the resolution has the opportunity to object to the proposed action, by submitting a written objection addressed to the liquidator and leaving it at the company's registered office within 7 days of the resolution being approved (s 111 IA 1986). Such an objection can require the liquidator not to carry out the proposed action or to purchase the shareholder's interest (at a price to be agreed between the parties, or determined at arbitration).

How to prove debts

The procedure for proving debts in a voluntary liquidation is less formal than in a compulsory liquidation, although the **terminology** is the same:
– a creditor making a claim "proves" for it, whether in writing or not; and
– the document by which he seeks to establish his claim is the "proof".

8491

The liquidator may, but is not obliged to, **require** the **creditors** who wish to recover their debts to submit their claims in writing to him (r 4.73(2) IR 1986). Clearly, it is easier from an administrative point of view for the liquidator if he does so.

MEMO POINTS If the liquidation follows immediately on from an **administration**, a creditor who proved in the administration is taken as having proved in the liquidation as well (r 4.73(8) IR 1986).

Form

The **proof** can be in any form (r 4.73(6) IR 1986). There are no stipulations as to the **information** that must be included in it, although the liquidator can require the creditor to supply (r 4.76 IR 1986):
– any of the information required in a proof in a compulsory liquidation; and/or
– any other documentary or other evidence.

8492

In practice, the liquidator will usually need this information in order to consider the proof properly, and so will often send out proofs in the same form as in a compulsory liquidation. Creditors must submit all of the information required in the proof, otherwise they could suffer the same consequences as they would if the company were in compulsory liquidation, e.g. being deemed to surrender their security (*LCP Retail Ltd v Segal* [2006] EWHC 2087 (Ch)). The convener or chairman of a meeting can also ask for the information listed above.

The liquidator can require that the claim is verified by an **affidavit**, using the "affidavit of debt form" (Form 4.26) or a substantially similar document.

MEMO POINTS The Insolvency Service has proposed that **affidavits** are replaced by witness statements (see ¶8440). This change is likely to be implemented from 1 October 2008.

C. Persons with conduct of the liquidation

A voluntary liquidation is largely conducted by the same persons as a compulsory liquidation, with the exception that the official receiver is not involved. Therefore, the liquidation is carried out by the **liquidator** under the supervision of the **liquidation committee** and having regard to the wishes of the **creditors and shareholders**. Depending on the nature of the company's business, a **special manager** (¶8375+) can be appointed, and/or the **FSA**

8502

may have specific powers during the liquidation. The **court** has ultimate control over the proceedings (¶8521+).

1. Liquidator

8507 As in a compulsory liquidation, the liquidator is **responsible for** dealing with the company's assets, paying off its liabilities and distributing any surplus assets to its shareholders (s 165 IA 1986). He must refer to the liquidation committee on a number of matters, and is always subject to the ultimate control of the court.

Whilst the **appointment** of the liquidator in a voluntary winding up is specific to this type of procedure, the treatment of the liquidator's **powers, duties and liabilities**, **remuneration** and **termination** in a compulsory and voluntary liquidation are similar. Readers are therefore referred to the relevant topics within compulsory liquidation as necessary, with aspects specific to voluntary liquidation being dealt with here.

a. Appointment

8508 A liquidator must be **qualified** and **authorised** to act as an insolvency practitioner (s 230(3) IA 1986). Authorisation is either granted by one of seven recognised professional bodies or the secretary of state. The Insolvency Service website has a database of authorised practitioners which can be accessed by members of the public, or local official receivers can provide a list of practitioners in the area.

A liquidator can be appointed to act in a particular liquidation in a number of different ways. Principally, the creditors and shareholders will do so in a voluntary liquidation, with the court stepping in to make an appointment where they cannot agree or fail to fill a vacancy. **More than one liquidator** can be appointed to act in a single liquidation, in which case their terms of appointment must make it clear whether the joint liquidators can carry out their activities individually or whether they must act together at all times (s 231 IA 1986).

By creditors' or shareholders' meetings

8509 The **first liquidator** will be appointed at the first meetings of creditors and shareholders (see ¶8443+, ¶8448+ for how the first meetings are convened and conducted).

Where there is a **vacancy** in the office of liquidator, a creditors' meeting can be held to fill it (s 104 IA 1986). Such a meeting can be summoned by a continuing liquidator or, if there is nobody in office at all, any creditor (r 4.101A IR 1986). The procedure to be followed at the meeting is the same as for other meetings (¶8557+).

> *MEMO POINTS* In an **MVL**, the **first liquidator** is appointed by the shareholders at the general meeting at which they resolve to wind the company up. Any **vacancy** in the office of liquidator can be filled by a meeting of shareholders, summoned by any contributory or continuing liquidator (s 92 IA 1986). The conduct of the meeting will be governed by the company's articles, or as directed by the court following an application by any contributory or continuing liquidator.

Administrative requirements

8510 The person appointed as liquidator by the shareholders' or creditors' meeting must provide the chairman with a **statement** that he (r 4.101(2) IR 1986):
– is an insolvency practitioner;
– is duly qualified under the legislation; and
– consents to act.

The **chairman** must then **certify** the appointment (on Form 4.27 for a single liquidator; Form 4.28 for joint liquidators) and send the certificate to the liquidator. The chairman must also be satisfied that the appointed liquidator has enough **security** (¶7425) to be able to perform his duties properly (r 12.8 IR 1986). It is not necessary to do this for a liquidator who was appointed by the shareholders but replaced by the creditors on the same day (r 4.101(3),(4) IR 1986).

MEMO POINTS 1. If the CVL **follows** immediately on from an **administration**, these rules do not apply (r 4.2(5) IR 1986).
2. The liquidator's statement and certificate of appointment are also necessary in an **MVL** (r 4.139 IR 1986).
3. A prospective liquidator must not attempt to gain his appointment by **solicitation** or **bribery** (¶8201/mp).

The liquidator must, within 14 days of his appointment (s 109(1) IA 1986; SI 1985/854): **8511**
– **file** notice of his appointment on Form 600 at Companies House; and
– **advertise** notice of his appointment in the *Gazette* on Form 600a.
Failure to comply with these requirements is an offence, giving rise to liability for a fine.

The liquidator must also give **notice** of his appointment in appropriate newspapers to bring it to the attention of the company's creditors and contributories (r 4.106 IR 1986), except where he was appointed by the shareholders and replaced on the same day by the creditors (r 4.106(2) IR 1986). The costs of doing so can be reimbursed as an expense of the liquidation.

MEMO POINTS 1. In the case of an **MVL**, the liquidator must, within 28 days of his appointment, give notice of it to all creditors of whom he is aware (r 4.139(4) IR 1986).
2. These provisions do not apply if the CVL immediately **follows** an **administration** (para 83(3) Sch B1 IA 1986).
3. The names of these forms, like the names of other **Companies House forms**, are taken from the section numbers of the legislation. As all of the section numbers will change under the new Companies Act, Companies House proposes to change the names of all of its forms to reflect their function rather than the relevant section number ("Working with Companies House: a consultation on the registrar's rules and related provisions which will apply under the Companies Act 2006"). At the time of writing, the new form names are not yet available.

By court

The court may be required to appoint a liquidator where, in a CVL, the shareholders' and **8512**
creditors' meetings cannot agree on the appointment of the **first liquidator** (¶8443+; ¶8448+),
or where there is a **vacancy** for whatever reason (s 108 IA 1986).

Before the court can issue its order appointing a liquidator, the prospective liquidator must **8513**
file a written **statement** (Form 4.30) at court confirming that he (r 4.103 IR 1986):
– is an insolvency practitioner duly qualified to act as the company's liquidator; and
– consents to act.
The liquidator's appointment takes effect when the court seals the order.

The liquidator must then, within 28 days, **notify** all of the company's creditors (of whom he is aware at that time) of his appointment. Alternatively, the court may allow him to **advertise** his appointment.

MEMO POINTS In an **MVL**, the same procedure must be followed (r 4.140 IR 1986), except that there is no specific provision in the Rules allowing the liquidator to advertise instead of sending notices to the creditors. However, it is within the court's powers to allow this, on its own initiative (e.g. when the liquidator is appointed) or on application (s 112 IA 1986, ¶8523+).

b. Powers, duties and liabilities

The liquidator has wide powers to deal with the company's business and assets, and so is **8514**
also subject to associated duties and liabilities, which control the exercise of those powers
(ss 107, 165 IA 1986). The position is very similar to that in a compulsory liquidation; points
specific to voluntary liquidations are dealt with here and readers are referred to relevant
topics elsewhere as necessary.

The liquidator's **powers** are summarised in the table below, with cross-references to any **8515**
wider discussion of the relevant power. Although the powers are largely the same as in a
compulsory winding up, the liquidator needs sanction to exercise his powers on fewer occasions in a voluntary liquidation.

Power	Sanction required?	Reference
Carry on company's business for benefit of winding up	No	para 5 Sch 4 IA 1986; ¶7791+
Bring legal proceedings for: – fraudulent trading; – wrongful trading; – transactions at an undervalue; – preferences; and – transactions defrauding creditors	Yes – of court or liquidation committee[1]	para 3A Sch 4 IA 1986; ¶7443+, ¶7449+, ¶7808+
Bring or defend other legal proceedings in company's name	No	para 4 Sch 4 IA 1986; ¶7803+, ¶8469
Make calls on shares	No	s 165(4) IA 1986; ¶7869+
Summon persons for private examination	Yes – court must grant application	¶8172+
Pay any class of creditors in full	Yes – of court or liquidation committee[1]	para 1 Sch 4 IA 1986
Make a compromise or arrangement: – with any creditor(s) (or those claiming to be creditors)[2]; or – by which company may be rendered liable	Yes – of court or liquidation committee[1]	para 2 Sch 4 IA 1986
Compromise: • any of the following between company and contributory, debtor or other person with liability to company[3]: – calls (and liabilities to calls); – debts (and liabilities capable of resulting in debts); or – claims (present/future, certain/contingent), and to take security for their discharge and give complete discharge in respect of any of them; and • any questions relating to or affecting company assets	Yes – of court or liquidation committee[1]	para 3 Sch 4 IA 1986
Distribute unrealised assets to creditors	Yes – of liquidation committee[1,4]	r 4.183 IR 1986; ¶7914+
Sell company property to member of liquidation committee (or his associate)	Yes – of court or liquidation committee[1,5]	¶8298+
Accept alternative consideration for sale of company's business in form of: – shares or similar interests; or – agreement that shareholders will profit-share in or receive some other benefit from purchaser company	Yes – of court or liquidation committee[1]	¶8490 ¶6465+
Distribute unrealised assets to shareholders	Yes – of shareholders by extraordinary resolution[6]	reg 117 TA 1985; ¶7914+
Sell company property to liquidator's associate	No – but transaction can be set aside	¶7895
Dispose of any of company's property to person connected with it	No – but notify liquidation committee[5]	s 165(6) IA 1986; ¶7895
Sell any of company's property as a whole or in parcels, by public auction or private contract	No	para 6 Sch 4 IA 1986
Act and execute deeds, receipts and other documents (using company's seal where necessary) in name and on behalf of company	No	para 7 Sch 4 IA 1986
Raise security on company's assets, such as where liquidator is carrying on company's business to sell as going concern	No	para 10 Sch 4 IA 1986; ¶7791+

Power	Sanction required?	Reference
Draw, accept, make and endorse any bill of exchange or promissory note in name and on behalf of company (so company is liable), e.g. to draw cheque on company's bank account	No	para 9 Sch 4 IA 1986
Appoint agent to carry out any acts he is unable to do himself[7], e.g. accountants, bankers	No	para 12 Sch 4 IA 1986
Prove, rank, claim and receive dividends in any contributory's bankruptcy/insolvency	No	para 8 Sch 4 IA 1986
Take out letters of administration to any deceased contributory's estate and take any action necessary for obtaining money due from estate to company	No	para 11 Sch 4 IA 1986
Summon creditors' and shareholders' meetings to ascertain their wishes (must do so if requisitioned, ¶8336+)	No	s 165(4) IA 1986
Require supply of public utilities to company (provided personally guarantees payment of bills)	No	s 233 IA 1986
Obtain documentation	No – except where application to court is necessary	¶8169+
Disclaim onerous property	No	¶7917+
Do all other things necessary to wind up company's affairs and distribute its assets	No	para 13 Sch 4 IA 1986

Note:
1. If **no liquidation committee**, creditors' meeting can sanction exercise of liquidator's power (s 165(2) IA 1986). In **MVL**, liquidator's exercise of powers must be sanctioned by special resolution of shareholders in general meeting (s 165(2) IA 1986 as amended by para 41 Sch 4 SI 2007/2194).
2. This power is used to compromise with **individual creditors**, whereas if compromise is made with **all creditors** liquidator should apply for formal scheme of arrangement (¶6500+), unless each creditor consents (Re British and Commonwealth Holdings plc (No 3) [1992] BCLC 322).
3. As part of the Insolvency Service's review of secondary legislation (see ¶7364/mp), it is taking the opportunity to make alterations to the primary legislation either where it is necessary to support the new Rules or to remove unnecessary administrative burdens. The Service proposes to remove the requirement for liquidators to obtain sanction to make decisions about the **settlement of claims owing to the company** (proposal 2, "A consultation document on changes to the Insolvency Act 1986 and the Company Directors Disqualification Act 1986 to be made by a Legislative Reform Order for the modernisation and streamlining of insolvency procedures" (September 2007)). The requirement for sanction to exercise certain powers is left over from the time when the insolvency profession was not regulated. As this is no longer the case, insolvency practitioners are best placed to make such decisions. At the time of writing, the consultation is still open. If this proposal is accepted, the changes are likely to be implemented from 1 October 2008.
4. This Rule is not applicable in **MVL**; since company must be solvent there should be no need to exercise this power.
5. This is not applicable in **MVL**, since there is no liquidation committee. In a **CVL**, if there is no liquidation committee, liquidator does not have to notify another body.
6. Although the new Companies Act has abolished **extraordinary resolutions** in statute, if a company's articles state that certain decisions must be taken in this form, it still has to comply with those provisions, see ¶3544. For companies incorporated on or after 1 October 2007 that adopt Table A, amendments have been made to be consistent with the new Companies Act so this decision must be made by special resolution instead (reg 7 SI 2007/2541 amending reg 117 TA 1985). However, these changes do not apply to companies incorporated before 1 October 2007 unless they have altered their articles separately.
7. However, liquidator must continue to exercise his **discretion** himself even where agent is appointed (Re Great Eastern Electric Co Ltd [1941] 1 All ER 409). Even joint liquidators cannot delegate their powers generally to one of them, unless terms of appointment allow.

8516 If a **liquidator** is **appointed before** the **first creditors' meeting** is held, he needs the sanction of the court to exercise his powers, except those to (s 166(2) IA 1986):
– take the company's property into his custody or control (including property to which the company appears to be entitled);
– dispose of perishable and other goods, the value of which will diminish if they are not dealt with immediately (e.g. seasonal goods); and
– protect the company's assets.

MEMO POINTS This does not apply in an **MVL**.

Investigating the company's affairs

8518 The liquidator's powers and duties in investigating the company's affairs in a voluntary liquidation are very similar to those of the official receiver and liquidator in a compulsory liquidation. The following discussions apply with relevant differences noted in the memo points.

As in a compulsory liquidation, the company's officers, employees and others involved in it are under a **duty to co-operate** with the liquidator as he conducts his investigations (¶8121).

Topic	¶¶
Liquidator's duties to **report**: – directors who should be disqualified because their conduct renders them unfit to hold office; and – officers or shareholders who appear to have committed a criminal offence	¶8166+
Liquidator's power to **obtain information** about the company	¶8169+
Liquidator's power to obtain information from the individuals involved in it: – informally – by public examination – by private examination	¶8144 ¶8146+ ¶8172+
Liquidator's power to require person involved in company to submit accounts [1]	¶8138+
Note: 1. Does not apply in an **MVL**.	

8519 The liquidator in a voluntary winding up has an additional obligation to make a **report to** the **FSA** if it appears that the company is or has been carrying on a regulated activity in contravention of the general prohibition (s 370 FSMA 2000).

Control of the liquidator

8521 The liquidator's extensive powers to deal with the company's business and assets are subject to a number of controls. The most significant powers require the **sanction** of the liquidation committee or the court. The **liquidation committee** also supervises the general conduct of the liquidation, and particular issues can be referred to the **court** if necessary. The court can also remove the liquidator in extreme cases (¶8258+). In addition, the liquidator is subject to the **general duties** that are attached to his office and profession.

> MEMO POINTS By contrast, in an **MVL**, the shareholders exercise control over the liquidator in so far as he must refer to them for sanction to exercise certain powers, see table at ¶8515.

Sanction for use of powers

8522 The table at ¶8515 above indicates **which** of the liquidator's **powers** require the sanction of the court or liquidation committee in order to be exercised. The factors taken into account when deciding **whether** or not **to sanction** the liquidator's actions, and the liquidator's personal liability for **acting without sanction**, are the same as in a compulsory liquidation (¶8218).

Control of the court

8523 Although the liquidator in a voluntary liquidation is not an officer of the court and therefore not subject to the court's control in the same way as in a compulsory liquidation, the court has the power to exercise control over the liquidator's actions when requested to do so (s 112 IA 1986). The **court** can be **asked to** determine any question arising in the liquidation and/or to exercise any power it would be able to exercise if the company was being wound up by the court. If it considers that it would be just and beneficial to the liquidation to grant the application, it will make any order it sees fit, imposing conditions on different parties as necessary.

This wide power enables the court to take whatever **action** it thinks necessary and, more specifically, to exercise control over the liquidation in the same way as it would in a compulsory liquidation. These **powers** are discussed in the context of a compulsory liquidation; important examples are as follows.

Power	¶¶
To correct register of shareholders	¶7863
To remove alleged contributory from liquidator's list of contributories	¶7871
To recover debts owed by shareholders other than calls	¶7878
To bar proofs from creditors being submitted after a certain point	¶8055
To order liquidator to pay dividends if he refuses to do so	¶8064
To order public examination	¶8146+
To interfere in liquidator's exercise or proposed exercise of powers	¶8219+
To allow creditors and contributories to inspect company's books and records	¶8228

An **application** can be **made by**:
- the liquidator, but only where there is real doubt as to his proper course of action;
- any creditor; or
- any contributory.

The applicant must also ensure that this type of application is the **appropriate forum** for his request.

8524

EXAMPLE

1. If the question is best determined in ordinary litigation and there are sufficient funds in the liquidation to sustain such an action, an application under this provision will not be permitted (*Re Stetzel Thompson & Co Ltd* (1988) 4 BCC 74).
2. This type of application cannot be used by an applicant to do something he would not otherwise be able to do, so a creditor was not allowed to ask the court to order a private examination of a director of the company. Firstly, the creditor would not be entitled to do so in a compulsory liquidation, and secondly he was intending to sue the director personally. The court could not allow a private examination to be used to carry out "fishing expeditions" to obtain information to use in separate proceedings (*Re James McHale Automobiles Ltd* [1997] 1 BCLC 273).

As in a compulsory liquidation, if the **liquidator fails to comply** with any of his duties to file, deliver or make up any document (including accounts and returns) or to give any notice, a creditor or contributory can apply to the court for enforcement of the relevant duty (s 170 IA 1986). The consequences of failing to comply with the order can be serious for the liquidator, for example, imprisonment for contempt of court (*Re Allan Ellis (Transport and Packing) Services Ltd* (1989) 5 BCC 835, in which the liquidator was imprisoned for 9 months).

8525

General duties

The liquidator in a voluntary liquidation is subject to the general duties arising from the nature of his appointment as a **fiduciary**, **agent** and **officer** of the company. These duties are discussed at ¶8224+. Unlike in a compulsory liquidation, a liquidator in a voluntary liquidation is not an officer of the court and so those duties which are dependent on this status will not specifically apply to him (*Re T H Knitwear (Wholesale) Ltd* [1988] 1 All ER 860).

8527

The **liquidator's actions** can be **challenged** in a number of ways, which are discussed generally at ¶8234+. A creditor or contributory will also be able to apply to the court to ask it to exercise its powers as if the company was in compulsory liquidation to question and challenge the liquidator's actions (see ¶8523+ above).

8528

Providing information

To creditors and contributories

Within 28 days of the first creditors' meeting, the liquidator must provide the creditors and contributories with (r 4.49(1) IR 1986):
a. a copy or summary of the directors' **statement of affairs**; and

8530

b. a **report** of the proceedings at the creditors' meeting, including (r 4.49(2) IR 1986):
– an estimate of the amount of the company's assets which will have to be ring-fenced (¶7992+);
– an estimate of the value of the net property available to the floating charge holder(s); and
– whether (and, if so, why) the liquidator proposes to apply to court to be excused from ring-fencing the required fund.
However, the liquidator is not required to reveal any information that would seriously prejudice the commercial interests of the company.

> MEMO POINTS 1. The liquidator's initial duties to report to the creditors and contributories apply to creditors' meetings summoned by the liquidator during an **MVL** because the company is insolvent (¶8648+). Otherwise, there is no equivalent duty in an MVL.
> 2. Where an **administration** has been **converted into** a **CVL**, this reporting requirement does not apply because a first meeting of creditors is not necessary. Instead, the administrator must send a copy of his final report in the administration to all creditors once he has converted the procedure (¶9142).
> 3. As part of the Insolvency Service's review of secondary legislation (see ¶7364/mp), it is taking the opportunity to make alterations to the primary legislation either where it is necessary to support the new Rules or to remove unnecessary administrative burdens. The Service proposes to remove the requirement for insolvency practitioners to **send information to all known creditors** at various stages in the procedure (proposal 1, "A consultation document on changes to the Insolvency Act 1986 and the Company Directors Disqualification Act 1986 to be made by a Legislative Reform Order for the modernisation and streamlining of insolvency procedures" (September 2007)). Generally speaking, most creditors just want to know how much of their debt will be repaid and have no interest in the general progress of the procedure. This requirement therefore creates a heavy but unnecessary financial and administrative burden. It will be replaced by a system allowing creditors who do wish to be kept up to date to "opt in" to receiving information from the insolvency practitioner. The consultation also proposes to allow information to be exchanged using electronic communication where the recipient agrees, and for insolvency practitioners to make information available via a website.
> At the time of writing, the consultation is still open. If these proposals are accepted, the changes are likely to be implemented from 1 October 2008.

8531 The creditors and contributories can require the liquidator to send them a free copy of any **statement of receipts and payments** (¶8534 below) filed at Companies House (reg 11(2) SI 1994/2507). The liquidator must comply with this request within 14 days of filing the statement at Companies House or receiving the request, whichever is later.

8532 See ¶8304+ for the liquidator's other duties to report to the **liquidation committee**, and the paragraphs noted at ¶8534 below for his **other duties** to provide information.

8533 It is a criminal **offence** for a person to pretend to be entitled to inspect any document as a creditor or contributory (r 12.18 IR 1986; ¶9935).

To others

8534 The liquidator's duties to provide information to other persons are discussed as follows:
– complying with **general publicity** requirements (¶8468);
– allowing access to the **records of the liquidation** (¶8230); and
– filing a **statement of receipts and payments** at Companies House where the liquidation has been carried on for over 1 year (¶8231).

> MEMO POINTS The liquidator does not have to file a statement of receipts and payments in an MVL.

Financial and administrative matters

8535 Liquidators in voluntary liquidations have an extra duty to **report to the secretary of state** on financial matters. If requested by the secretary of state, a liquidator or former liquidator must provide (reg 17 SI 1994/2507):
a. details of any money in his possession or control representing:
– unclaimed or undistributed assets of the company;

– dividends; or
– other sums due to any person as a shareholder or former shareholder; and

b. any other details required by the secretary of state for the purpose of ascertaining or collecting in any money payable into the Insolvency Services Account.

The information must be certified by the liquidator, if required, and submitted within 14 days of the request.

The liquidator's ability to deal with the **company's books, papers** and **other records** is dealt with at ¶8233.

8536

c. Remuneration

The liquidator's **entitlement** to remuneration and the methods of its **calculation** are dealt with in the context of compulsory liquidation, with relevant differences noted in memo points; see ¶8242+.

8537

d. Termination

Most of the discussion at ¶8250+ concerning the termination of the liquidator's office is applicable to voluntary liquidation, with the exception of his removal at a creditors' meeting, discussed below. Otherwise, readers should refer to:
– **resignation**: ¶8251+;
– **removal**: ¶8254+;
– **automatic vacation of office**: ¶8263; and
– **release** from liabilities: ¶8264+.

Filling vacancies created by such terminations is dealt with at ¶8508+.

8538

Removal by meeting of creditors

Most of the rules governing creditors' meetings in compulsory and voluntary liquidations are dealt with together; see the table of cross-references at ¶8557.

8539

The creditors can remove the liquidator at a meeting summoned for that purpose (s 171(2) IA 1986). If 25% by value of the **creditors request** that such a **meeting** is held, the liquidator is obliged to call it (r 4.114 IR 1986). The **notice** summoning the meeting must state the purpose for which it is being held and the consequences of granting the liquidator his release.

8540

Where such a meeting is summoned (or is proposed to be summoned), any creditor can apply to the court for **directions** as to (r 4.115 IR 1986):
– how it should be summoned;
– proxies;
– the conduct of the meeting; and
– any other matter which the court thinks is in need of control.

> MEMO POINTS   In an **MVL**, the liquidator can be removed by a meeting of the shareholders called for that purpose instead (s 171(2)(a) IA 1986). There is no specific provision in the Rules governing how such a meeting should be requisitioned, therefore the shareholders should follow the usual procedure for requisitioning general meetings, applying to the liquidator instead of the directors (¶3626+). If the liquidator refuses to call a meeting, the shareholders can apply to court (under s 306 CA 2006; see ¶3635+), or the procedure relating to the removal of the liquidator by the court can be followed (¶8258+).

Usually, the liquidator or his nominee will chair creditors' meetings. However, where a meeting has been summoned to remove the liquidator an alternative **chairman** can be appointed (r 4.114 IR 1986). If an alternative is not appointed, the liquidator/nominee will chair the meeting, but he is not allowed to adjourn it without the consent of at least half in value of the creditors present (in person or by proxy) and voting at the meeting.

8541

The following **resolutions** will be considered at the meeting, with the **consequences** noted where relevant.

Resolution	Passed?	Consequences and administrative steps	Reference
To remove liquidator	✓	– Chairman to send certificate of removal to new liquidator (or Companies House if no new liquidator) – New liquidator to file certificate at Companies House	r 4.117 IR 1986
	✗	Liquidator remains in office	-
To appoint new liquidator	✓	– See ¶8509+ – Advertisement of new liquidator's appointment must state his predecessor was removed and has been released (if applicable)	r 4.118 IR 1986
	✗	No liquidator; see ¶8512+	-
To give removed liquidator his release	✓	Liquidator released	¶8264
	✗	Liquidator must apply to secretary of state for release (¶8265)	r 4.122 IR 1986

8542 There is a **special rule** regarding summoning the meeting where the **liquidator** was **appointed by** the **court** (¶8512+). In such a case, a meeting of the creditors can only be held to remove the liquidator where (s 171(3) IA 1986):
– the liquidator agrees;
– the court directs (in which case, the court can also give directions about how the meeting should be summoned and conducted; r 4.115 IR 1986); or
– the meeting is requested by at least 50% (by value) of the creditors.

> MEMO POINTS In the case of an **MVL**, the special rule applies, except that the meeting must be requested by shareholders with at least 50% of the total voting rights at the meeting (s 171(3)(a) IA 1986).

2. Liquidation committee

8547 Most of the issues concerning liquidation committees in a CVL are the same as, or similar to, those in compulsory liquidation. The following exceptions are dealt with below:
– initial establishment; and
– how the functions of a liquidation committee are performed when there is no committee.

The following main topics are found within the context of compulsory liquidation, with any relevant adaptations for a CVL noted in the memo points. References in these discussions to "contributory members" should be read as "shareholder members".

Topic	¶¶
Membership: – eligibility for membership – restrictions on dealings by members and their associates	¶8297 ¶8298+
Supervising the liquidator: – sanction for use of powers – access to information	¶8303 ¶8304+
Meetings: – calling – attendance – conduct – voting	¶8307 ¶8308+ ¶8310 ¶8311+
Changes to liquidation committee	¶8314+

Establishment

It is usual for the liquidation committee to be established **by** the creditors at their first meeting (¶8448+), although they can do so at any subsequent meeting (s 101 IA 1986).

8548

The committee must have at least three members in order to be established (r 4.152(2) IR 1986), but can **comprise** up to (s 101 IA 1986):
a. five people chosen by the creditors ("creditor members"); plus
b. five chosen by the shareholders, either at the meeting at which the resolution to wind up was passed or at any subsequent meeting ("shareholder members").

8549

However, if shareholder members are appointed, the creditors can resolve that those appointees should not sit on the committee; this resolution can only be reversed by the court. The court also has the power, if an application is made, to appoint other people to the committee instead of those mentioned in the resolution.

Once established by the creditors, the committee cannot act until the **formalities of establishment** have been complied with (¶8300+).

> MEMO POINTS 1. The provisions relating to the minimum number of members of the liquidation committee and eligibility do not apply if the CVL immediately **follows** an **administration** (para 83(3) Sch B1 IA 1986).
> 2. **Additional members** of the committee can be:
> – a representative of the FSA (s 371 FSMA 2000); and
> – a representative of the scheme manager (s 215 FSMA 2000).
> Again, these provisions do not apply where the CVL immediately **follows** an **administration**.

No liquidation committee

The liquidation committee has a number of functions, which must be **performed by** others if no committee is appointed:

8550

Function of liquidation committee	If no committee, performed by	Reference
Sanctioning exercise of liquidator's powers that require sanction	Court or creditors	¶8303
Sanctioning liquidator accepting shares in consideration for company's assets	Court	¶8490
Sanctioning continuation of directors' powers	Creditors	¶8472
Reviewing liquidator's financial records and reports	Creditors can review financial records	¶8305
Assessing costs of persons to be paid out of company's assets (such as solicitors' fees)	n/a	r 7.34 IR 1986
Fixing liquidator's remuneration	Creditors	¶8242+

3. Creditors' and shareholders' meetings

Creditors' and shareholders' meetings must be held **annually** so that the liquidator can keep them informed about the conduct of the liquidation. Between these annual meetings, **other meetings** can be called, either by the liquidator or the court to consult the two groups on particular issues, or at the request of the groups themselves to question the liquidator and obtain information about the conduct of the liquidation.

8555

Annual meetings

Aside from the first meetings needed to place the company into voluntary liquidation, the liquidator **must call** a shareholders' meeting and a creditors' meeting within 3 months of the end of (s 105 IA 1986):
– the first year from the commencement of the liquidation; and
– each subsequent year.

8556

The liquidator must lay an account of his acts and dealings and of the conduct of the liquidation in general before the meeting.

If he **fails to comply** with the requirement to hold a meeting or produce the correct documentation, he is liable to a fine (¶9935).

> MEMO POINTS 1. The secretary of state can **extend** the **deadline** within which the liquidator must summon these meetings. This will only happen in appropriate cases, such as where the liquidator anticipates that the final meeting will be called within 6 months, or the liquidation is being held up by (for example) a dispute of which the creditors and shareholders are already aware.
> 2. If the company was **previously in an MVL** and the creditors' meeting resolving to convert it to a CVL was held 3 months or less before the end of the first anniversary of the commencement of the liquidation, the liquidator does not have to hold another creditors' meeting at the end of that year (s 105(4) IA 1986).

Other meetings

8557 Most of the rules relating to the conduct of creditors' meetings are the same in a CVL as in a compulsory liquidation; the discussion relating to contributories' meetings is relevant to shareholders' meetings in a CVL. The table below gives the relevant cross-references to the main topics

Topic	¶¶
Summoning meetings[1]: – who can summon meetings – requests by creditors and contributories – notices	¶8335 ¶8336+ ¶8339+
Conduct: • chairman • attendance • proxies • voting: – creditors – contributories • resolutions	¶8345+ ¶8348 ¶8349+ ¶8354+ ¶8357 ¶8359
Note: 1. Except where the **creditors** wish to call a **meeting to remove** the **liquidator**, in which case see ¶8539+.	

8558 The liquidator can call **creditors' or shareholders' meetings** in order to ascertain their wishes on any issue regarding the liquidation. For example, if there is no liquidation committee, he will require the sanction of the creditors to exercise certain powers (s 165(2)(b) IA 1986; ¶8515).

If necessary, the liquidator can call **general meetings** of the company, either to obtain its sanction, or for any other purpose he sees fit (s 165(4) IA 1986). He only needs the sanction of the company in a few situations, for example if he needs to effect a change to the company (such as its name) in order to sell its business. The procedure is the same as for a company which is not subject to insolvency proceedings (¶3620+).

4. Financial Services Authority

8563 The FSA has certain rights where a **company** which is an "**authorised person**" is being wound up voluntarily (s 365 FSMA 2000). In such a situation, the FSA can:

a. refer questions arising in the liquidation to the court and ask it to exercise any powers it would otherwise have if the company were being wound up compulsorily (i.e. any application under s 112 IA 1986, ¶8523+);

b. be heard at any hearing in court regarding the liquidation;

c. receive copies of any notice or document to be sent to a creditor;

d. send a representative to attend and speak at creditors' and liquidation committee meetings;

e. petition for the company to be wound up by the court; and

f. apply to the court for a meeting to be held if a compromise or arrangement is proposed between the company and its creditors (¶6500+).

D. Conclusion of the liquidation

8573 If the winding up has been completed and all (or as many as possible) of the assets have been realised and distributed, the company will ultimately be **dissolved**. Alternatively, it may be appropriate for the company to enter into **another** type of **insolvency proceeding** (¶7481).

Final meetings

8574 Once the liquidator has wound the company's affairs up, he must **call** final meetings of the creditors and shareholders. If he fails to do so, he is liable to a fine (s 106 IA 1986; ¶9935).

Creditors

8575 **Notice** of the meeting must be:
a. advertised in the *Gazette* at least 1 month in advance, specifying the time, place and object of the meeting (s 106 IA 1986); and
b. given to the creditors who have proved their debts at least 28 days before the meeting (r 4.126 IR 1986).

8576 At the meeting, the liquidator must present his **account of the liquidation**, showing (s 106 IA 1986):
– how the winding up has been conducted;
– how the property has been disposed of; and
– the amount paid to the unsecured creditors out of the ring-fenced portion of any floating charge(s) (r 4.126(4) IR 1986).

The creditors then have the opportunity to **question the liquidator** on the matters raised in the account, and may resolve against giving the liquidator his release if they are not satisfied with his conduct of the liquidation (r 4.126 IR 1986; ¶8264+).

Shareholders

8577 **Notice** of the meeting must be:
– advertised in the *Gazette*, as for the final creditors' meeting (s 106 IA 1986); and
– given to the shareholders in accordance with the company's articles.

The **liquidator** also **presents** his account of the liquidation to the shareholders' meeting, although they have no specific power to question him on the matters raised in it.

Administrative matters

8578 The **liquidator** must **file** at Companies House:
a. within 1 week of the latest meeting (s 106 IA 1986):
– a copy of his account; and
– Form 4.72, stating that the two meetings were held and when (or, as the case may be, that a meeting was summoned but had to be abandoned because a quorum could not be achieved); and
b. a copy of any special resolution passed at the shareholders' meeting, within 15 days of the resolution being passed (ss 29, 30 CA 2006; see ¶3600 for a summary of which other resolutions need to be filed at Companies House).
Failure to do so renders him liable to a fine (¶9935).

Dissolution

8579 Once the relevant documents have been filed at Companies House, the registrar of companies will register them and place an **advertisement** in the *Gazette* (s 201(2) IA 1986; s 1078(2) CA 2006). Three months later, the company is deemed to have been dissolved (s 201 IA 1986). This period can be extended by the court on application by the liquidator or any other interested party; if such an order is obtained, the applicant must file a copy of the order at Companies House (failure to do so renders him liable to a fine; ¶9935).

It is possible to have the dissolution declared **void**; see ¶7537+.

SECTION 2
Members' voluntary liquidation

8594 A members' voluntary liquidation is different to a CVL in two principal respects. The company's **solvency** will be the key factor that determines whether or not it can be voluntarily wound up by its shareholders: before the company can resolve to enter into MVL, the company must be solvent and the board must make a statutory declaration of the company's solvency. If the company proves to be insolvent during the course of the MVL, the proceedings will be converted into a CVL. Secondly, as the name suggests, it is the shareholders who have **control** over the process rather than the creditors, as they appoint and supervise the liquidator as well as resolving to put the company into MVL.

A. Entering liquidation

8604 The shareholders can cause the company to enter into MVL on two of the **grounds** that are available in the case of a CVL, namely (s 84(1) IA 1986):
a. the company resolves by special resolution that it should be wound up voluntarily; or
b. a fixed term for the duration of the company has expired, or a specified event which signifies that it should be dissolved has occurred, and the company resolves to be wound up voluntarily.

In practice, the second ground is not often relied upon; if it is, the type of resolution required will depend on the terms (usually in the memorandum and/or articles) in question.

1. Procedure

8609 The legislation states that the **key difference between** a **CVL and** an **MVL** is the fact that a statutory declaration has been made by the board in the case of an MVL (s 90 IA 1986). This is the first stage in the process for a company entering into MVL, after which only a shareholders' meeting needs to be held and the administrative requirements completed. The process is illustrated by the **timeline** at ¶8617.

If an **administration** is **converted into** an **MVL**, the procedure is different. The statutory declaration of solvency and shareholders' meetings are not required, as the administrator converts the administration by filing the relevant documents at court (¶9142+).

Statutory declaration of solvency

8610 Entering into MVL involves an additional **first step** compared to the CVL procedure. Before the shareholders can pass their resolution, the board must make a statutory declaration of the company's solvency (s 89 IA 1986). This declaration must **state** that:
a. the directors have made a full inquiry into the company's affairs; and
b. as a result of their inquiry, they are of the opinion that the company will be able to pay its debts in full, including interest at the official rate, within a stated period (which must not be more than 12 months from the commencement of the liquidation).

The declaration must be **made before** the resolution to wind up has been passed, up to a maximum of 5 weeks beforehand.

It must be accompanied by a **statement** of the company's **assets and liabilities** made up to the latest practicable date before the declaration was made. Although this statement must be substantially correct, any errors or omissions that do not result in a misleading picture of the company's position will not invalidate the statement or declaration (Re New Millennium Experience Co Ltd [2004] 1 All ER 687).

The declaration must be **made at** a board meeting **by**, as applicable:
– the sole director;
– both directors (if there are only two); or
– a majority of the directors.

> MEMO POINTS   The "**official rate**" of interest is the greater of (s 189 IA 1986):
> – a statutory rate (specified in s 17 Judgments Act 1838) on the date of the commencement of the liquidation; and
> – the rate applicable to that debt normally.

The declaration is tantamount to giving evidence under oath, and therefore the directors must only make the statement after careful consideration. A **director** who does not have reasonable grounds for his opinion that the debts of the company will be paid in full with interest is **liable** to imprisonment and/or an unlimited fine (s 89(4) IA 1986; ¶9935). If the company was unable to pay its debts in full within the time period stated in the declaration, it will be presumed that the director did not have reasonable grounds for his opinion, unless he can prove otherwise (s 89(5) IA 1986). **8611**

Shareholders' meeting

The next stage is for the company to be **placed into liquidation** by the shareholders resolving to do so at a meeting. The shareholders will also **appoint** the **liquidator**; this appointment can only be overridden by the creditors if the MVL is converted into a CVL. **8612**

As an **alternative to** calling a **meeting**, the board could circulate written resolutions to the shareholders (¶3580+).

Calling the meeting

The procedure for entering MVL will usually be **initiated by** the board, which will have to call the meeting. The board can be required to call the meeting by the shareholders, although the process must be collaborative since the shareholders cannot put the company into MVL without the board having first sworn their statutory declaration. The procedure for calling meetings is described in detail at ¶3620+. The board must ensure that it gives the correct period of **notice**: this is now dependent on the type of meeting, rather than the resolution, so general meetings will need 14 clear days' notice (if, unusually, the resolution is to be passed at a public company's AGM, the notice period is 21 clear days' notice) (ss 314, 360 CA 2006). The meeting may still be held on short notice with the correct level of shareholder consent. As well as giving the requisite notice to the shareholders, the directors must give 5 days' notice of the meeting to any holders of qualifying floating charges (¶8779) created on or after 15 September 2003 (s 84(5) IA 1986). **8613**

Conduct

The **general conduct** of the meeting is the same as for any other shareholders' meeting (¶3711+). However, **attendance** by just one shareholder cannot constitute a valid general meeting for the purpose of appointing a liquidator, unless the company is a private company with only one shareholder (Re London Flats Ltd [1969] 2 All ER 744). **8614**

Business

The **resolutions** which will be considered at the meeting are:
– a resolution to wind the company up (s 84(1) IA 1986); and
– an ordinary resolution to nominate a liquidator. **8615**

The formalities of **appointing** a **liquidator** are dealt with at ¶8509+. In addition, the meeting may need or wish to consider:
a. an ordinary resolution to fix the liquidator's remuneration (¶8242+); or

b. an extraordinary resolution to authorise the liquidator to make distributions of the company's assets to the shareholders instead of cash (reg 117 TA 1985).

MEMO POINTS 1. If **more than one liquidator** is **nominated**, the voting procedure is the same as at a creditors' meeting in a CVL (¶8454).
Although there is no express power in the legislation or the Rules to **appoint joint liquidators** in an MVL, the Rules assume that this can occur (e.g. the chairman certifies the appointment of joint liquidators on Form 4.28). If joint liquidators are appointed, the meeting should stipulate by ordinary resolution how their powers are to be divided between them (s 231 IA 1986).
2. Although the new Companies Act has abolished **extraordinary resolutions** in statute, if a company's articles requires certain decisions to be taken in this form, it still has to comply with those provisions, see ¶3544. For companies incorporated on or after 1 October 2007 that adopt Table A, amendments have been made to be consistent with the new Companies Act so this decision must be made by special resolution instead (reg 7 SI 2007/2541 amending reg 117 TA 1985). However, these changes do not apply to companies incorporated before 1 October 2007 unless they have altered their articles separately.

Administrative requirements

8616 The **board** must:
a. file the following documents at Companies House within 15 days of the resolution being passed:
– its statutory declaration (s 89(3) IA 1986); and
– a copy of the resolution to wind the company up (s 84(3) IA 1986); and
b. advertise a notice of the resolution to wind up in the *Gazette* within 14 days of the resolution being passed (s 85(1) IA 1986).

The **liquidator** must, within 14 days of his appointment (s 109(1) IA 1986; SI 1985/854):
– file a notice of his appointment at Companies House; and
– advertise his appointment in the *Gazette*.

Failure to comply with any of these administrative requirements renders the company and every officer in default (or the liquidator, as appropriate) liable to a fine (ss 85(2), 89(6), 109(2) IA 1986; ss 29, 30 CA 2006; ¶9935).

Summary

8617 The following **timeline** illustrates the steps that must be taken to place a company into MVL, and when they must occur in relation to the shareholders' meeting, which is marked "**M**". A more detailed timeline of the events surrounding a shareholders' meeting is found at ¶3873. The deadlines by which events must occur are illustrated.

Day	Event
-35	Board meeting to: – approve statement of assets and liabilities and swear statutory declaration of solvency; and – call shareholder meeting
-18	Send notice of shareholders' meeting to shareholders [1,2]
-8	Send notice of shareholders' meeting to qualifying floating charge holders [2]
M	Shareholders' meeting: – resolution to wind company up [3]; and – appoint liquidator
+ 14	Liquidator: – files notice of appointment at Companies House; and – advertises appointment in *Gazette* Board advertises resolution to wind up in *Gazette*
+ 15	Board files shareholders' resolution and board's statutory declaration at Companies House
Note: 1. Assuming 14 clear days' notice of meeting is required. 2. Assuming notices are sent out by 1st class post, so service is deemed on 2nd day after posting (r 12.10 IR 1986; ¶3704). 3. This marks the commencement of the liquidation.	

2. Effect of winding up resolution

Once the resolution to wind the company up has been passed, the MVL has **commenced** (s 86 IA 1986). This affects many aspects of the company in largely the same way as in a CVL and readers should refer to that discussion, as follows.

8623

Topic	¶¶
Commencement of liquidation	¶8465
Effect on: – company's business and assets	¶8466+
– litigation by and against the company	¶8469+
– company's constitution	¶8471
– directors	¶8472
– employees	¶8473
– other agents	¶8474
Court's power to stay liquidation proceedings	¶8479

B. Dealing with the company's assets

In an MVL, the company's assets are dealt with in the same way as in a CVL. The **table of cross-references** at ¶8489 and the ensuing paragraphs should be consulted to find the relevant topics.

8633

If the **liquidator sells assets** of the company **to** its **director**, or to a director of its holding company, as part of the realisation process, he must check whether the transaction is classed as a "substantial property transaction" requiring the approval of the shareholders in a general meeting. Substantial property transactions are discussed at ¶2567+.

> MEMO POINTS The legislative provision makes a specific exception from the general prohibition for **substantial property transactions** in favour of directors in the case of compulsory liquidations and CVLs (s 193 CA 2006). There is no such exception for transactions undertaken during an MVL, so the rules relating to such transactions must be followed.

C. Persons with conduct of the liquidation

An MVL is largely conducted by the same persons as a CVL, except that there is no liquidation committee. Therefore, the liquidation is carried out by the **liquidator** under the supervision of the **shareholders**. Depending on the nature of the company's business, a **special manager** (¶8375+) can be appointed, and/or the **FSA** may have specific powers during the liquidation. The **court** does not have a great deal of involvement in an MVL, although it does have the power to deal with issues when asked (¶8523+) and to call meetings of creditors and shareholders in order to ascertain their wishes on any matter (¶8335).

8643

Liquidator

The **appointment**, **powers and liabilities** and **remuneration** of the liquidator and **termination** of his office in an MVL are similar to that in a CVL, discussed at ¶8507+; the minor differences applicable to an MVL are highlighted in the memo points.

8644

Shareholders' meetings

After the liquidator, the shareholders have the most **influence over the conduct of an MVL**. They take the place of the liquidation committee in a CVL in sanctioning certain of the

8645

liquidator's actions (¶8515), as well as being consulted and reported to by the liquidator. However, these requirements are more relaxed in an MVL than a CVL or compulsory liquidation. Instead, the shareholders can rely on other provisions to gain **access to information** about the liquidation by:
- requesting certain information (¶8228);
- accessing the records of the liquidation (¶8230); and
- viewing the annual statement of receipts and payments filed at Companies House (¶8231).

Annual meetings

8646 If the MVL is not converted into a CVL, but **takes longer than 12 months**, the liquidator is obliged to call a meeting at the end of the first year from the commencement of the liquidation and then annually until the liquidation has been concluded (s 93(1) IA 1986). The meetings can be held in the 3 months after the end of each year, or a longer period if the secretary of state allows. Since the MVL must be converted into a CVL if the liquidator realises that the company cannot pay its debts within the period stated in the board's declaration (a maximum of 12 months), these annual meetings will only **occur where** the company's debts have been paid off but the liquidator is still dealing with the assets to distribute to the shareholders.

At these meetings, the liquidator must present an **account** of the conduct of the liquidation, including his acts and dealings, during the preceding year.

If the **liquidator fails** to call the annual meetings or lay his account before them, he is liable to a fine (¶9935).

MEMO POINTS As part of the Insolvency Service's review of secondary legislation (see ¶7364/mp), it is taking the opportunity to make alterations to the primary legislation either where it is necessary to support the new Rules or to remove unnecessary administrative burdens. The Service proposes to **remove the requirement** for liquidators to hold annual meetings in MVLs (proposal 4, "A consultation document on changes to the Insolvency Act 1986 and the Company Directors Disqualification Act 1986 to be made by a Legislative Reform Order for the modernisation and streamlining of insolvency procedures" (September 2007)). These meetings are usually poorly attended and serve little purpose, since the liquidator must file his receipts and payments account at Companies House anyway. The meeting is not required for any particular decisions to be made. Shareholders and creditors would still be able to put questions to the liquidator regarding the information in his account, and their rights to challenge the liquidator's actions would remain, so the removal of this requirement is not expected to reduce shareholders' and creditors' involvement in the liquidation. Further, the Service plans to include a requirement in the new Insolvency Rules for liquidators and insolvency practitioners in other procedures to provide progress reports to creditors and shareholders to keep them up to date. At the time of writing, the consultation is still open. If this proposal is accepted, the changes are likely to be implemented from 1 October 2008.

Other meetings

8647 Other shareholders' meetings are held in accordance with the company's articles of association. This topic is discussed in depth at ¶3610+. The liquidator may summon shareholders' meetings to obtain their sanction, or for any other **purpose** he thinks fit (s 165(4) IA 1986). Meetings may be necessary to:
a. remove and replace the liquidator;
b. sanction the exercise the following powers of the liquidator:
- selling assets in return for shares or other interests in another company (¶8490);
- allowing the directors to exercise their powers (¶8472);
- paying a class of creditors in full (¶8515);
- compromising calls, debts and claims with shareholders (¶8515); and
- bringing proceedings concerning fraudulent or wrongful trading, transactions at an undervalue, preferences or transactions defrauding creditors (¶8515);

c. alter the company's memorandum and articles or change its name, for example, in readiness for the business being sold by the liquidator; or
d. consult the shareholders on a proposed course of action.

MEMO POINTS The Insolvency Service proposes to remove the requirement for liquidators to obtain sanction to exercise their power to **compromise claims** against the company, see ¶8515.

Creditors' meeting where company becomes insolvent

If the liquidator decides that the company will not be able to pay its debts with interest within the time stated in the board's statutory declaration, he is obliged to **convert** the **MVL into a CVL** (s 95 IA 1986). This occurs automatically when a creditors' meeting is held.

8648

The liquidator must **summon** this meeting to be held within 28 days of the day after he formed his opinion about the company's financial position, giving the creditors at least 7 days' **notice** by post. He must also advertise the notice in the *Gazette* and at least two local newspapers. In the period before the meeting, he must **provide** the creditors with any **information** about the company's affairs that they reasonably require, free of charge (and the notice of the meeting must state that the liquidator will provide such information).

> MEMO POINTS   As part of the Insolvency Service's review of secondary legislation (see ¶7364/mp), it is taking the opportunity to make alterations to the primary legislation either where it is necessary to support the new Rules or to remove unnecessary administrative burdens. The Service **proposes to remove** the requirements:
> – for the creditors' meeting to be advertised in local newspapers (proposal 3, "A consultation document on changes to the Insolvency Act 1986 and the Company Directors Disqualification Act 1986 to be made by a Legislative Reform Order for the modernisation and streamlining of insolvency procedures" (September 2007)). Currently, this requirement means that the cost of advertising has to be incurred, whether or not the liquidator is aware of all of the company's creditors and whether or not the advertisements in the local newspapers are likely to come to the creditors' attention. Therefore, these advertisements are thought to be ineffective. The requirement will be replaced with a discretion to publicise the meeting if necessary to attract the attention of additional creditors by whatever means the liquidator feels would be most effective (for example, a notice could be placed on the company's own website). The obligation to advertise in the *Gazette* will remain, as this is an effective way of reaching creditors (for example, banks carry out regular searches of the *Gazette* to check for any notices about their customers); and
> – for the notice to be delivered by post, so that it can be sent electronically instead where the recipients agree (proposal 1).
> At the time of writing, the consultation is still open. If these proposals are accepted, the changes are likely to be implemented from 1 October 2008.

The liquidator will **chair** the creditors' meeting, and must present a **statement of affairs** (in Form 4.18) to the meeting, which summarises the company's assets and liabilities and lists its creditors at the date of his opinion.

8649

Otherwise, the **conduct** of the meeting is the same as at a creditors' meeting held for the purposes of the company entering straight into CVL (¶8448+). There is no need for the creditors to pass a **resolution** to convert the winding up, as this occurs automatically. They may wish to appoint a liquidation committee and their own liquidator, overriding the shareholders' choice.

Once the **meeting has been held**, the company is in CVL and is treated as if (s 96 IA 1986):
a. the board's statutory declaration had not been made; and
b. the shareholders' meeting at which it was resolved to put the company into MVL and the creditors' meeting converting it into CVL were the two meetings required to put the company into CVL (see ¶8443+, ¶8448+).

8650

In terms of **administrative requirements**, the statement of affairs and Form 4.20 must be filed at Companies House within 7 days of the meeting (r 4.34 IR 1986), and the liquidator must report to the creditors and contributories within 28 days of the meeting (¶8530+).

> MEMO POINTS   In terms of **compliance with the Rules**, which apply in different ways to CVLs and MVLs, the winding up is treated as a CVL and the CVL Rules must be followed from the date on which the liquidator forms his opinion that the company will not be able to comply with the directors' statutory declaration of solvency (r 4.1(2) IR 1986).

If the **liquidator fails** to comply with any of his obligations relating to the conversion of the MVL into a CVL, he is liable to a fine (s 95(8) IA 1986; ¶9935).

8651

Financial Services Authority

The FSA has certain rights where a company which is an "authorised person" is being wound up voluntarily (¶8563).

8652

D. Conclusion of the liquidation

8662 If the winding up has been completed and all (or as many as possible) of the assets have been realised and distributed, the company will ultimately be **dissolved**. Alternatively, it may be appropriate for it to enter into **another** type of **insolvency procedure** (¶7481).

8663 Once the company has been fully wound up, the liquidator must prepare an **account of the liquidation**, which shows how the company's property has been disposed of and how the liquidation has been conducted in general (Form 4.71; s 94(1) IA 1986).

Final meeting

8664 He must then summon a shareholders' meeting by advertising a **notice** in the *Gazette*, specifying its time, place and object at least 1 month before the meeting (s 94(1), (2) IA 1986). In practice, he will also give the shareholders notice of the meeting in accordance with the company's articles. If he fails to call the meeting, he is liable to a fine (s 94(6) IA 1986; ¶9935).
At the meeting, he must present his account to them and explain it.
After the meeting, he must file at Companies House:
a. within 1 week of the meeting:
– a copy of his account; and
– a return (Form 4.71) confirming either that the meeting was held (and when), or that it had to be abandoned because no quorum was present; and
b. within 15 days of the meeting, a copy of any special resolution passed (ss 29, 30 CA 2006; see ¶3600 for a summary of which other resolutions need to be filed at Companies House).
If he **fails** to comply with these administrative requirements, he is liable to a fine (s 94(4) IA 1986; s 30 CA 2006; ¶9935).

Dissolution

8665 Once the relevant documents have been filed at Companies House, the registrar of companies will register them and place an **advertisement** in the *Gazette* (s 201(2) IA 1986; s 1078(2) CA 2006). Three months after registration of the return, the company is deemed to have been dissolved (s 201 IA 1986). This period can be extended by the court on application by the liquidator or any other interested party; if such an order is obtained, the applicant must file a copy of the order at Companies House (failure to do so renders him liable to a fine; ¶9935).
It is possible to have the dissolution declared **void**; see ¶7537+.

CHAPTER 19
Administration

OUTLINE ¶¶

Summary of administration procedure 8694

SECTION 1 Entering administration 8710

A Court procedure 8721
1 Applicants 8728
2 Procedure 8734
   a Application 8736
   b Hearing 8746
B Out of court procedures 8762
1 By company or its board 8764
2 By qualifying floating charge holder 8777
C Administrative requirements following all appointments 8797
D Effect of administration 8808
1 Moratorium 8813
2 Other consequences 8826

SECTION 2 Managing the company's affairs, business and assets 8845

A Investigation 8855
1 Statement of affairs 8861
2 Proposals 8876
   a Contents 8878
   b Circulation 8882
   c Approval 8885
   d Consequences of creditors' decision ... 8892
B Dealing with the assets 8904
1 Power to sell 8905
2 Assets belonging to third parties 8909
C Distribution 8922
1 Costs and expenses of the administration 8927
2 Secured creditors 8936

3 Other creditors 8948
   a Proving debts 8949
   b Distributions 8963
   Preferential creditors 8965
   Unsecured creditors 8967
   Deferred creditors 8975
   Creditors who are also debtors of the company 8976

SECTION 3 Persons involved in the administration 8992

A Administrator 8995
1 Appointment 8998
2 Powers, duties and liabilities 9010
   Powers: summary table 9011
3 Remuneration 9026
4 Termination 9035
   Resignation 9036
   Removal 9038
   Automatic vacation of office 9040
   Discharge from liability 9042
   Replacement 9044
B Creditors 9057
1 Creditors' committee 9060
2 Creditors in general 9076
C Shareholders 9102
D Financial Services Authority 9112

SECTION 4 Conclusion of the administration 9127

A Purpose of administration achieved ... 9130
B Conversion into liquidation 9141
C Company has no assets 9154
D Other situations 9164

8690 The **aim** of administration is totally different to that of liquidation. Whereas a liquidator's function is to bring a company to an end, the **administrator's job** is to rescue it from financial difficulties so that it can carry on business. He takes over the management of the company and its affairs for a relatively short period of time, usually selling off certain parts of the business so that the company's finances are revived and its business is salvaged (or, at least its assets are salvaged). He has extensive powers to deal with the company's business, affairs and property, including making distributions to creditors (although, unlike in a liquidation, he is not obliged to do so). Throughout the administration, the **company is protected** from most types of legal action against it by a moratorium. This gives companies "breathing space" from creditors' demands so they can put their affairs in order and find the best strategy for resolving their financial problems.

8691 The **law** relating to administration has been substantially **revised** to encourage more companies, especially smaller ones, to make use of the procedure at an early stage, rather than resorting to liquidation when it is too late to salvage the business. The new provisions apply to administrations commencing on or after 15 September 2003, and have a number of **advantages** when compared to the old provisions:

a. the **entry routes** into administration have been expanded, allowing certain floating charge holders to initiate the process out of court, as well as allowing the company and board to do so;

b. the **purposes** for which administration can be used are now more widely phrased and easier to use, since it can only be entered into to achieve one of three purposes (instead of a combination of four under the old provisions);

c. the legislation sets out a default end-date for administrations, so they cannot be carried on indefinitely, as well as a series of **deadlines** to ensure that the administration progresses efficiently;

d. the administrator has a new power to make **distributions** to creditors, improving their position; and

e. modern provisions allow correspondence by email, telephone and other electronic forms, and where a provision requires a person to put something in writing, this can be done by email, fax, etc (para 111 Sch B1 IA 1986).

The position of certain floating charge holders, known as "**qualifying floating charge holders**" (see ¶8779 for the relevant definitions), has been substantially altered under the new regime. They have been given the right to appoint an administrator out of court because their right to appoint administrative receivers was removed by the same amendments to the law (although other floating charge holders may still be able to do so; see ¶9237+). The amendments to the law were intended to encourage the use of administration, since it is a procedure undertaken for the benefit of all creditors, in contrast to administrative receivership which only benefits the appointing charge holder.

The new provisions are contained in Schedule B1 to the IA 1986, with the corresponding Rules in Part II (as amended).

> MEMO POINTS   1. Although an administrator can correspond with creditors and others using electronic means, **email** has been judged not to be a sufficiently certain method of communication for sending statutory notices to creditors, owing to the problems of, for example, having emails blocked and the ease with which creditors can change their email addresses (Re Sporting Options plc [2004] EWHC 3128 (Ch)). However, an administrator can send creditors a short document containing the details of a website where the full notice can be found (it will only be in large administrations that the cost savings of using this method would make it worthwhile).
>
> 2. The **new provisions do not apply** to administrations resulting from administration petitions presented to court before 15 September 2003. Although some such administrations will still exist, most current administrations will be governed by the new provisions. (There were no appointments under the pre-2003 provisions for 2006, the last year for which figures are available.) Therefore, the **old provisions** are not dealt with in this book; readers should consult ss 8-27 IA 1986 and Part II of the Rules in their unamended form.
>
> The old provisions also still apply to certain types of company and partnership, which are outside the scope of this book (reg 3 SI 2003/2093):
>
> – water and sewerage undertakers (i.e. companies appointed under Pt II Ch 1 Water Industry Act 1991);

- protected railway companies (under s 59 Railways Act 1993 and s 19 Channel Tunnel Rail Link Act 1996);
- air traffic companies (s 26 Transport Act 2000);
- public-private partnership companies (s 210 Greater London Authority Act 1999); and
- building societies (s 119 Building Societies Act 1986).

Summary of administration procedure

The flowchart below provides an overview of the administration process, from entry using the court or out of court procedures, to the different end results.

8694

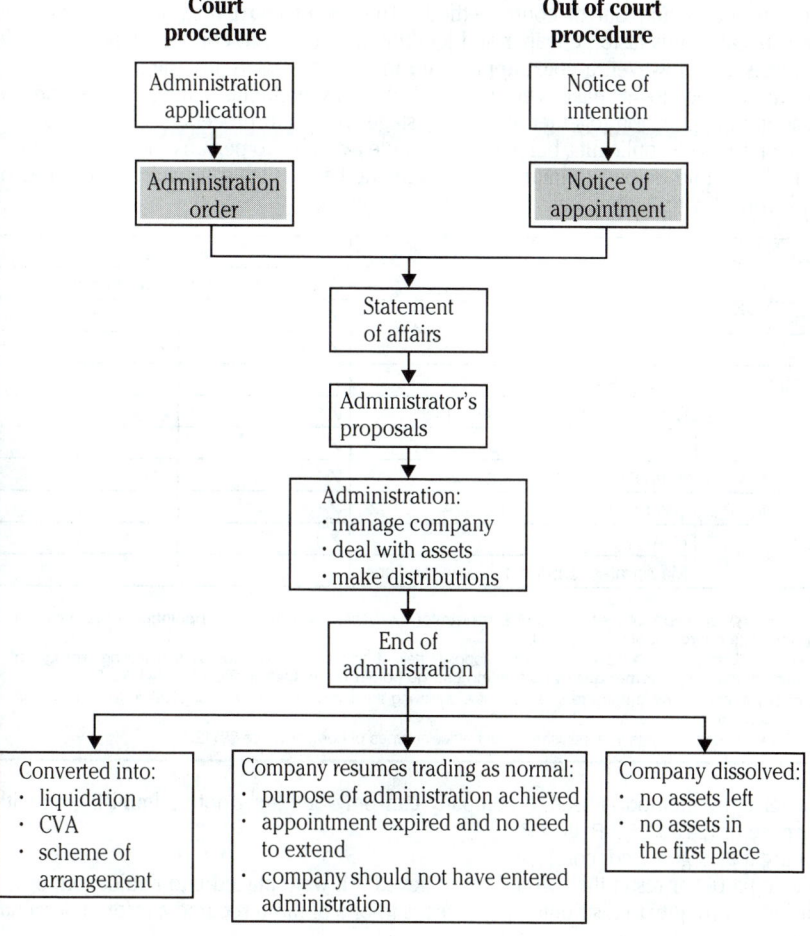

= appointment of administrator begins

SECTION 1
Entering administration

8710 A company can be placed into administration by two **methods**: making an application to court, or appointing an administrator out of court. There are two different ways of making an out of court appointment, depending on whether a qualifying floating charge holder or the company or its board makes the appointment. These categories of person have a choice between the court and out of court methods. The **out of court** method will usually be preferred because it is faster, cheaper and less bureaucratic, with court guidance available where necessary. However, a **court application** may be necessary in a large and complex administration because it makes sense to deal with any preliminary applications and the administration application together at an early stage. The court procedure is dealt with first as it is open to more applicants, being the only route available to persons such as unsecured creditors. The table below summarises which method is available to which categories of person involved with a company.

Person		Method	
		Court application	Out of court
Company		✓	✓
Directors		✓	✓
Creditors [1]	Unsecured	✓	
	Qualifying floating charge holder	✓ [2]	✓
	Other secured creditors	✓	
Liquidator, where company is in liquidation		✓	
Supervisor, where company is subject to a CVA		✓	
Others	FSA [3]	✓	
	Magistrates' court enforcement officer	✓	

Note:
1. Creditors can also appoint their choice of administrator by substituting him for an **appointment** made **by the company** or its **board** out of court (¶9006).
2. Qualifying floating charge holders can also appoint their choice of administrator by substituting him for an **appointment** made **by another qualifying floating charge holder** or **another applicant** (¶8744, ¶9004+).
A **company's insolvency** is not a requirement of a qualifying floating charge holder's application to court, unlike the other applicants' applications.
3. The **FSA** has certain rights in administration of particular types of company, see ¶9112.

8711 Whichever entry method is used, a company can only be placed into administration with the **purpose** of (para 3(1) Sch B1 IA 1986):
– rescuing it as a going concern;
– achieving a better result than would be achieved if it were placed into liquidation; or
– realising its property to distribute the proceeds to one or more secured and/or preferential creditors.

The **preferred purpose** is rescuing the company as a going concern. The "achieving a better result" purpose can only be relied upon if it is not reasonably practicable to rescue the company as a going concern or if a better result would be achieved by not rescuing the company (para 3(3) Sch B1 IA 1986). The "realising its property" purpose can only be relied upon if the other two options are not available and if the interests of the creditors as a whole will not be harmed unnecessarily (para 3(4) Sch B1 IA 1986).

A. Court procedure

The **aim** of an administration order is to revive a company in financial difficulties, ensuring its continued existence if possible. The order will only be granted for one of the three statutory purposes where the company is, or is likely to become, **unable to pay its debts** (except in the case of an application by a qualifying floating charge holder) (para 11 Sch B1 IA 1986). The phrase "unable to pay its debts" has the same meaning as in a liquidation (¶7593+). The order can be obtained by making an application to the court, following the correct procedure. If granted, an administrator is appointed by the court to manage the company with the aim of achieving the selected purpose.

8721

Companies which can be placed into administration

Most **types of company** can be placed into administration, with some specialist exceptions (such as insurance companies) which are not dealt with here (para 9 Sch B1 IA 1986).

8722

> MEMO POINTS As well as limited companies incorporated under companies legislation, companies incorporated in an **EU member state** other than the UK and those incorporated outside of the EU but with a centre of main interests within the EU (except Denmark) can also enter into administration (para 111(1A), (1B) Sch B1 IA 1986). See ¶7366+ for a discussion of European jurisdiction and the definition of a centre of main interests. A company may also be placed into administration under the **EC Insolvency Regulation** if the company's main centre of interests is in the UK, or it is elsewhere but the company has an establishment in the UK (reg 3 EC Insolvency Reg).
> A company which has a principal place of business in **Northern Ireland** can only enter into administration if it also has one in England, Wales or Scotland (para 111A Sch B1 IA 1986).
> There is no express power in insolvency legislation to place an **unregistered company** into administration, but the EC Insolvency Regulation can be used to this effect.
> Administration orders can be made against **foreign companies** at the request of the relevant foreign court (s 426 IA 1986). The secretary of state has the power to provide for the administration of foreign companies, but has not exercised it at the time of writing (s 254 EA 2002). Also, the Cross-Border Insolvency Regulations 2006 create similar powers to the EC Insolvency Regulation as regards certain non-EU member states, see ¶7375+.

Generally, an administration application **cannot be made** in respect of a company which is already in:
- administration (para 7 Sch B1 IA 1986);
- compulsory or voluntary liquidation (para 8 Sch B1 IA 1986); or
- administrative receivership (para 39 Sch B1 IA 1986).

8723

However, there are various important **exceptions** to this:
a. if the company is in **liquidation**, an application can be made by (¶8729):
- a qualifying floating charge holder; or
- a liquidator; and
b. if the company is in **administrative receivership**, an application can be made where (para 39 Sch B1 IA 1986):
- the person who appointed the administrative receiver consents; or
- the court concludes that the security under which the administrative receiver was appointed is likely to be released or discharged as a transaction at an undervalue or a preference, or it is a floating charge which could be avoided if an administration order was made.

1. Applicants

The administration **application** can be **made by**:
- the company (para 12(1) Sch B1 IA 1986);
- its directors (para 12(1) Sch B1 IA 1986);
- one or more of its creditors (whether secured or unsecured, including qualifying floating charge holders) (paras 12(1), 35, 37(2) Sch B1 IA 1986);

8728

- an officer of the magistrates' court, using his powers to enforce fines imposed on the company (i.e. s 87A Magistrates' Court Act 1980) (para 12(1) Sch B1 IA 1986);
- a combination of the above applicants (para 12(1) Sch B1 IA 1986);
- a liquidator of the company (para 38(1) Sch B1 IA 1986);
- a supervisor of a CVA by which the company is bound (s 7(4), para 12(5) Sch B1 IA 1986); or
- the FSA, in certain circumstances (s 359 FSMA 2000).

Individual **shareholders** are not able to apply for an administration order in their capacity as shareholders, because the company must be (or be likely to become) unable to pay its debts and so a shareholder would not be able to establish a sufficient interest in the outcome of the application. The company (i.e. the shareholders as a body) on the other hand has a "sufficient interest" in the administration even if it is insolvent (*Re Land and Property Trust Co plc* [1991] BCLC 845).

If the **directors** make the application, the decision can be taken by a simple majority of the board, even if the company's articles require a higher majority to pass such a resolution (para 105 Sch B1 IA 1986). The board meeting and resolution should be conducted as usual.

Normally, a creditor must base his status on an **undisputed debt**. For example, a creditor's application was refused because he claimed to be a creditor on the basis of an anticipated breach or repudiation of a contract by the company, which could not be described as undisputed (*Re Simoco Digital UK Ltd, Thunderbird Industries LLC v Simoco Digital UK Ltd* [2004] 1 BCLC 541). However, a creditor with a disputed debt may secure permission to present an application, provided that he can demonstrate that he has an arguable case in the dispute and that a sufficient debt is owing to him (*Hammonds (a firm) v Pro-fit USA Ltd* [2007] EWHC 1998 (Ch)).

> MEMO POINTS The **FSA** can apply for an administration order against a company which is or was (s 359 FSMA 2000):
> - an authorised person;
> - an appointed representative; or
> - carrying on a regulated activity in contravention of the general prohibition.
>
> If another person applies to have such a company placed into administration, the FSA has various powers during that administration (¶9112).

8729 Usually, if a **company** is **in liquidation**, an administrator cannot be appointed. However the company's liquidator can apply to have the liquidation (whether voluntary or compulsory) converted into an administration (para 38 Sch B1 IA 1986). A qualifying floating charge holder can also apply for an administration order if the company is in compulsory liquidation (para 37 Sch B1 IA 1986). If the court grants the application in either case, it will also deal with a number of necessary ancillary matters (¶8751).

2. Procedure

8734 The procedural requirements of an administration application **differ** slightly **depending on** which category of person is applying. The procedure is designed to be **quick**, with only 5 days' notice having to be given to persons entitled to attend the hearing, and so it is important that the application and evidence are prepared properly so that the procedure is not delayed.

a. Application

8736 An application for an administration order is made on **Form** 2.1B, which requires the applicant to state (r 2.2(1) IR 1986):
- which provision he is relying on in making the application;
- various basic details about the company (all of which can be obtained from a search of the register at Companies House);
- a statement that the applicant believes that the company is, or is likely to become, unable to pay its debts (unless the applicant is a qualifying floating charge holder);
- whether the EC Insolvency Regulation will apply (¶7366+); and
- the name of the proposed administrator(s).

Depending on the applicant, the application needs to contain certain other **information**:

Applicant	Information required	Reference
All applicants[1]	• Attach Form 2.2B completed by (each) proposed administrator, stating: – his consent to be appointed; – details of any previous professional relationship with company; and – that he believes administration is reasonably likely to achieve its purpose • Attach supporting affidavit	rr 2.3, 2.4 IR 1986
Company	Name and address of company for service (registered office, unless good reason to give another address)	r 2.3(1) IR 1986
Directors	– Name and address of company for service (registered office, unless good reason to give another address); – state that application is being made by directors under para 12(1)(b); and – the application treated as if made by company	r 2.3 (1), (2) IR 1986
Single creditor	Name and address of that creditor for service	r 2.3(3) IR 1986
More than one creditor	– Names of all creditors making application; and – specify one creditor's name and address for service (the application will then be treated as if made by that creditor only)	r 2.3(4) IR 1986
Qualifying floating charge holder – company not in liquidation	– Does not have to state company is or is likely to become unable to pay debts; – state application made under para 35; and – provide enough evidence to satisfy the court he has right to appoint an administrator	para 35 Sch B1 IA 1986
Qualifying floating charge holder – company in liquidation	– State the application is made under para 37; and – details of the liquidation, liquidator and his appointment, together with an explanation of why administration is necessary, plus any other relevant information	para 37 Sch B1 IA 1986; r 2.11 IR 1986

Note:
1. If the **supervisor of a CVA** makes the application, it is treated as if it was being made by the company.

Supporting affidavit

The application must be **supported by** an affidavit (rr 2.2(1), 2.4 IR 1986). A witness statement can be used instead, with the relevant modifications.

8737

The correct **deponent** of the affidavit depends upon the applicant (r 2.2 IR 1986).

Applicant	Deponent
Company	One director or secretary on company's behalf
Directors	One director or secretary on board's behalf
Creditors	Person authorised by all creditors making application. Affidavit must state nature of his authority and means by which he has acquired knowledge on which affidavit is based
Single creditor	Applicant
Supervisor of CVA	As if application made by company

MEMO POINTS   As part of the Insolvency Service's review of secondary legislation (see ¶7364/mp), it is taking the opportunity to make alterations to the primary legislation either where it is necessary to support the new Rules or to remove unnecessary administrative burdens. The Service proposes to remove the requirement for certain documents to be verified by **affidavit** in insolvency procedures (proposal 5, "A consultation document on changes to the Insolvency Act 1986 and the Company Directors Disqualification Act 1986 to be made by a Legislative Reform Order for the modernisation and streamlining of insolvency procedures" (September 2007)). Since the reform of civil procedures generally in 1998, affidavits in other types of procedures have been replaced by witness statements, which do not have to be sworn/affirmed by a solicitor/commissioner for oaths/notary. Therefore, this change will reduce the cost and administrative time involved in preparing these documents. At the time of writing, the consultation is still open. If this proposal is accepted, the changes are likely to be implemented from 1 October 2008.

8738 The following **information** must be included in the affidavit, to the best of the applicant's knowledge and belief (r 2.4 IR 1986):
– a statement of the company's financial position, detailing its assets and liabilities (including contingent and prospective liabilities);
– details of any security known or believed to be held by the creditors, and whether any of that security confers the right to appoint an administrative receiver (and state if an administrative receiver has been appointed);
– details of any other insolvency proceedings to which the company is subject (including any winding up petition(s) presented);
– if more than one administrator is proposed to be appointed, state how their functions are to be divided between them (i.e. whether both/all of them can carry out all of the functions or whether each one is to have specific powers and, if so, what);
– details of any other matters which should be drawn to the court's attention to assist in making its assessment; and
– whether the EC Insolvency Regulation will apply and, if it will, whether these proceedings are to be main or secondary (¶7366+).

If the application is being made by a **qualifying floating charge holder** when the company is not in liquidation, he must also give enough information in his application to satisfy the court that he is entitled to appoint an administrator (r 2.4(3) IR 1986).

If the application is being made when the **company** is **in liquidation** by its liquidator or a qualifying floating charge holder, the applicant must also give the following information (r 2.11(1) IR 1986):
– details of the liquidator and the liquidation;
– his reasons for wanting to convert the proceedings into an administration; and
– any other relevant matters which will assist the court.

A qualifying floating charge holder must also provide evidence of his entitlement to appoint an administrator (r 2.11(2) IR 1986).

8739 If the applicant **does not fully disclose** all of the above matters of which he is aware and the administration order is made, the administrator can later apply for his discharge from liability (*Re Sharps of Truro Ltd* [1990] BCC 94).

Filing at court

8740 The application can be filed at court in person or **by** post. The applicant must **submit** (r 2.5 IR 1986):
– the original application with supporting affidavit and Form 2.2B attached;
– enough copies of the application and attachments to serve on the correct parties (see ¶8743); and
– the fee (currently £150).

Once it has received all of the correct documents, the **court will**:
– endorse the application and copies with the date and time of filing;
– fix the date, time and place for the hearing of the application and endorse it on the application and copies; and
– seal each copy and issue them to the applicant.

8741 **After filing**, it is the applicant's responsibility to (r 2.5(4) IR 1986):
– serve the copies on the correct parties; and
– notify the court in writing of any other insolvency proceedings against the company of which he is aware (including those commenced under the EC Insolvency Regulation).

Consequences of filing

8742 Between making the application and the order taking effect (or the application being dismissed), an **interim moratorium** operates (para 44(1) Sch B1 IA 1986). The **effect** is broadly the same as for a full moratorium, except that references to the need for the administrator's consent do not apply since he has not yet been appointed (see ¶8813+). Therefore, action cannot be taken against the company during this period, except for the following specific actions which only apply to an interim moratorium (para 44(7) Sch B1 IA 1986):
– the presentation of a petition for the company's liquidation, either on the ground of public interest or by the FSA (¶7626+);
– the appointment of an administrator by a qualifying floating charge holder (¶8777+);
– the appointment of an administrative receiver; and
– an administrative receiver exercising his functions.

> MEMO POINTS If an **administrative receiver** is in place when an administration application is made, the interim moratorium does not begin until his appointor has consented to the administration order being made (para 44(6) Sch B1 IA 1986).

Service

8743 As soon as is reasonably practicable after he has made the application, the applicant must serve copies of it (together with attachments) on all of the **persons** listed below as are relevant in the circumstances (para 12(2) Sch B1 IA 1986; rr 2.6(3), 2.7 IR 1986):
– the proposed administrator;
– the company, if it is not the applicant;
– any other person who is or may be entitled to appoint an administrator;
– a person who has appointed an administrative receiver;
– a person who is entitled to appoint an administrative receiver;
– an administrative receiver;
– a person who has petitioned for the company to be wound up;
– a provisional liquidator;
– a supervisor of a CVA;
– a member state liquidator in main proceedings relating to the company;
– an enforcement or other officer charged with execution or another process against the company or its property; and
– a person who has distrained against the company or its property.

The **method** of service is usually delivery (by first class post or in person) to a company's registered office (or principal place of business, if it is not practicable to serve it at the registered office) and to an individual's usual or last known address (r 2.8 IR 1986). The court may direct that service is to be carried out in another manner, in which case those instructions must be followed. If first class post is used, the document is deemed to have been served on the recipient on the second business day after posting.

The **deadline** for service on all of the relevant persons is at least 5 clear days before the application hearing (r 2.8 IR 1986). It is possible for the court to shorten this period (r 12.9 IR 1986) but, since the deadline is so short in the first place, there will be few circumstances in which this would be justified (Re a Company (No 000175 of 1987) [1987] BCLC 467).

Service can be **carried out by** the applicant, his solicitor or another person instructed by them (commonly, a process server) (r 2.8(1) IR 1986).

Qualifying floating charge holder's right to substitute administrator

8744 A qualifying floating charge holder will have the application served on him as a person who is entitled to appoint an administrator. He can **object** to the appointment of the proposed administrator and make his own nomination instead, by filing the following **documents** at court (para 36 Sch B1 IA 1986; r 2.10(1) IR 1986):
– the written consent of any qualifying floating charge holders in priority to him to his objection and nomination;
– Form 2.2B completed by his nominee; and
– evidence to satisfy the court of his entitlement to appoint an administrator.

If he makes such an application, the court must grant it unless it is inappropriate to do so in the particular circumstances of the case (para 36 Sch B1 IA 1986). If the administrator is substituted in this way, the original applicant's **costs** are still payable as an expense of the administration (unless the court orders otherwise) (r 2.10(2) IR 1986).

Affidavit of service

8745 Once the necessary people have been served with a copy of the application and its attachments, the applicant must file an affidavit of service at court **confirming** (r 2.9 IR 1986):
- who has been served;
- the method used; and
- when service was effected.

The affidavit is in **Form** 2.3B, although a witness statement can be used instead (with the appropriate amendments). A sealed copy of the application must be exhibited to the affidavit. The affidavit can be **made by** the applicant or a person instructed by him, such as a solicitor.

The affidavit must be filed at court as soon as is reasonably practicable after service has been effected, with a final **deadline** of at least 1 clear day before the hearing.

> MEMO POINTS The Insolvency Service has proposed that **affidavits** are replaced by witness statements (see ¶8737). This change is likely to be implemented on 1 October 2008.

b. Hearing

8746 The hearing can be **attended by** (r 2.12(1) IR 1986):
- the applicant;
- the company;
- one or more directors;
- the proposed administrator;
- any qualifying floating charge holders;
- an administrative receiver of the company;
- a person who has petitioned for the company's winding up;
- a member state liquidator in main proceedings;
- a supervisor of a CVA; and
- any other person that the court allows.

A **shareholder** is unlikely to be allowed to attend the hearing. Since the company is, or is likely to become, unable to pay its debts, a shareholder will not have a sufficient interest in the outcome of the application to attend (*Re Chelmsford City Football Club (1980) Ltd* [1991] BCC 133, a case decided under the old administration provisions in which the company was obviously insolvent. This can be contrasted with another case (*Re Farnborough-Aircraft.com Ltd* [2002] 2 BCLC 641), in which it was not clear whether the company was insolvent owing to two significantly disparate valuations, and so the shareholders were allowed to appear). However, if the application was made by a qualifying floating charge holder, the company does not have to be insolvent and so a shareholder may be permitted to attend the hearing at the court's discretion.

8747 An administration **application** can be **withdrawn** by the applicant, but he needs the court's permission to do so (para 12(3) Sch B1 IA 1986).

The court's decision

8748 The court must be **satisfied that** the administration is reasonably likely to achieve the stated purpose and that the company is, or is likely to become, unable to pay its debts before it may make the order. It has a complete discretion as to whether or not to make the order (para 11 Sch B1 IA 1986). It will **consider** all of the material circumstances, and may find it appropriate to dismiss the application or make an alternative order. For example, if there is a genuine dispute over a creditor applicant's claim against the company, an order will not usually be made (*Re Simoco Digital UK Ltd*, *Thunderbird Industries LLC v Simoco Digital UK Ltd* [2004] 1 BCLC 541).

In order to show that something is "**reasonably likely**" or "**likely**", the court must be satisfied that it is more probable than not that the company will become unable to pay its debts and that there is a real prospect that the purpose of the administration will be achieved (*Re AA Mutual International Insurance Co Ltd* [2005] 2 BCLC 8). Cases decided under the old regime can still provide some guidance as to **how** the **court will approach** the question of whether the administration is likely to achieve its purpose. The **principal factors** that the courts looked at were:
a. the degree of support that the proposed administration received from the company's creditors, directors and shareholders;
b. how administration compared to liquidation in terms of:
– the likelihood of more money being realised from a sale as a going concern as opposed to on a break-up basis;
– the chances of the company's contracts being continued and being profitable during the administration; and
– cost (in terms of redundancies, for example, as well as purely financial costs) and speed; and
c. the likelihood of the company sustaining continued losses during administration and whether it had sufficient funds to support this form of corporate recovery.

MEMO POINTS   Useful **cases** decided under the old provisions include: *Re Harris Simons Construction Ltd* [1989] BCLC 202, *Re Consumer and Industrial Press Ltd* [1988] BCLC 177 and *Re Imperial Motors (UK) Ltd* [1990] BCLC 29.

The court can come to a number of **possible decisions** at the hearing (para 13 Sch B1 IA 1986). It can: **8749**
a. make an administration order;
b. dismiss the application;
c. adjourn the hearing, either with or without conditions (e.g. to allow the parties the opportunity to inspect further evidence, perhaps requiring certain parties to make disclosures);
d. make an interim order (e.g. restricting the directors' or company's powers, giving the court or an insolvency practitioner the power to exercise its/his discretion). This would be useful where the hearing has been adjourned for a time and, for example, the assets of the company are in danger of being dissipated before the rescheduled hearing;
e. treat the application as a winding up petition and make a winding up order accordingly; or
f. make any other order appropriate in the circumstances.
If the court makes an order under d. or f. above, it will give directions as to how and to whom notice of that order is to be given (r 2.14(3) IR 1986).

Administration order

An administration order will be in **Form** 2.4B (r 2.12(2) IR 1986) and will: **8750**
– order that the company's affairs, business and property are to be managed by the administrator(s) for the period that the order is in force;
– appoint a named insolvency practitioner as the company's administrator (or, more than one as joint administrators);
– state whether the EC Insolvency Regulation applies to the administration;
– set out any further order made by the court;
– set out any order as to costs; and
– state the date from which the administrator's appointment is to have effect.
Once the order has been made, the court will send two sealed copies to the applicant, who must **give notice** of the order to the administrator by sending him one copy as soon as is reasonably practicable (r 2.14 IR 1986).

In the case of an application by the liquidator or a qualifying floating charge holder when the **company** is **in liquidation**, there are a number of additional matters with which the court has to deal if it makes an administration order (paras 37(2), 38(2) Sch B1 IA 1986; r 2.13 IR 1986):   **8751**
– discharge any winding up order;
– specify which powers can be exercised by the administrator;
– remove a liquidator appointed in a voluntary liquidation from office;

- give directions regarding the liquidator's release;
- give directions regarding any indemnity given to the liquidator;
- give directions regarding any assets in the liquidator's possession or control; and
- provide for any other matter, whether regarding the liquidation or not.

Costs

8752 Where an application is successful, the applicant's costs are usually treated as an expense of the administration; otherwise, the costs will be borne by the applicant (r 2.12 IR 1986). The court can also order that the costs of any other person should be paid as an expense of the administration.

B. Out of court procedures

8762 There are **two** out of court **methods** of placing a company into administration: one that can be used by the company and its board and the other by qualifying floating charge holders. The out of court procedures share the same elements, but there are differences in the details and source materials and so they are dealt with separately for clarity. **Companies and their boards** are allowed to make use of the out of court system to encourage them to seek a constructive solution to financial problems at an early stage. Appointments by **qualifying floating charge holders** are a substitute for their inability to appoint administrative receivers following changes in the law (see ¶8691).

1. By company or its board

8764 The company and its board have the **power** to appoint an administrator out of court, although their choice of administrator may be substituted by a creditor (¶9006). The decision is made by shareholder or board resolution, as appropriate. The company and its board can also make use of the administration application procedure through the court, discussed at ¶8721+.

8765 An administrator **cannot be appointed** by the company or its board in the circumstances set out in the table below, some of which will only affect the ability to appoint an administrator if they have occurred in the previous 12 months.

Restriction	Timescale	Reference (Sch B1 IA 1986)
Winding up petition presented but not yet dealt with [1]	n/a	para 25
Administration application made but not yet dealt with	n/a	para 25
Appointment of administrator by company or board (whether out of court or by application to court) has ceased	In the preceding 12 months	para 23
Company is in administration already	n/a	para 7
Company is in liquidation already	n/a	para 8
Administrative receiver is in office	n/a	para 25
Moratorium in respect of company has ended when there is no voluntary arrangement in force	In the preceding 12 months	para 24(1)
Voluntary arrangement in respect of company which had been made during moratorium has ended prematurely	In the preceding 12 months	para 24(2)
Note: 1. Presentation of a petition **occurs when** it is delivered to the court, not when it is issued by the court (*Re Blights Builders Ltd* [2007] All ER (D) 147 (Jan)).		

ADMINISTRATION 1039

<mark>MEMO POINTS</mark> The company or directors intending to appoint an administrator must obtain the **FSA**'s written consent before making the appointment if the company is or was:
– an authorised person;
– an appointed representative; or
– carrying on a regulated activity in contravention of the general prohibition.
A copy of the consent must be attached to any notice of intention to appoint an administrator, or to the notice of appointment if a notice of intention was not necessary (s 362A FSMA 2000).

Notice of intention

The company or its board must give at least 5 days' written **notice** of its intention to appoint an administrator to (para 26(1), (2) Sch B1 IA 1986; r 2.20(2) IR 1986):
– any qualifying floating charge holder with the right to appoint an administrator;
– any person who is or may be entitled to appoint an administrative receiver (¶9237+);
– any enforcement officer charged with the execution or other legal process against the company or its property of which the person giving notice is aware;
– any person who has distrained against the company or its property, of which the person giving notice is aware;
– any supervisor of a voluntary arrangement; and
– the company, if the appointment is by the board.
The notice should be in **Form** 2.8B, identifying the proposed administrator, and **accompanied by** either a copy of the shareholder resolution or a record of the board's decision as appropriate (rr 2.20, 2.22 IR 1986).
If there is **no** person on whom the **notice** needs to be served, the company can file its notice of appointment straight away (a different form is required, ¶8770).

8766

After serving notice on the relevant persons, the company or board must file the following at court as soon as is reasonably practicable (para 27(1), (2) Sch B1 IA 1986; r 2.22 IR 1986):
– a copy of the notice, together with the copy resolution or decision; and
– a statutory declaration made by or on behalf of the company or board.
The **statutory declaration** is part of Form 2.8B, and requires the deponent to state that:
– the company is, or is likely to become, unable to pay its debts;
– the company is not in liquidation; and
– the appointment does not fall within the restrictions listed in the table at ¶8765.
The declaration cannot be made more than 5 days before it is filed at court (r 2.21 IR 1986). If the deponent makes a **false declaration** which he does not reasonably believe to be true, he is liable to a fine (para 27(4) Sch B1 IA 1986; ¶9935).

8767

Consequences of filing notice of intention

This will commence the **interim moratorium**, which will last until either an administrator is appointed or the brief time period within which an appointment can be made (¶8769 below) has expired (para 44(4) Sch B1 IA 1986). The effect of the interim moratorium is described at ¶8742.

8768

Notice of appointment

There is a brief window in which the **appointment can be made** (para 28 Sch B1 IA 1986):
a. between:
– 5 business days after the notice of intention, to give the relevant persons adequate notice; or
– when those persons notified who are or may be entitled to appoint an administrator or an administrative receiver have given their written consent to the appointment; and
b. 10 business days beginning with the date on which the notice of intention was filed at court.

8769

<mark>EXAMPLE</mark> A notice of intention was served and filed at court on Monday 1st. Business days do not include weekends or the days on which the period starts or finishes, and so the appointment can be made between Tuesday 9th at the earliest, and Tuesday 16th at the latest.
If the persons entitled to appoint an administrator or administrative receiver consent in writing prior to Tuesday 9th, the appointment can be made from that earlier date.

8770 The appointment is **made by** way of a notice. The requirements are different, depending on whether a notice of intention was given or not. Both forms require the person making the appointment to give a statutory declaration that the contents of the form are true.

	Notice of intention given (para 29 Sch B1 IA 1986)	No notice of intention given (paras 29, 30 Sch B1 IA 1986)
Notice of appointment	Form 2.9B	Form 2.10B
Statutory declaration [1]	Made by or on behalf of appointor, confirming that: – he is entitled to make appointment; – the appointment is in accordance with new administration provisions; and – statements made and information given in statutory declaration filed with notice of intention remain accurate, as far as deponent is aware	Made by or on behalf of appointor, confirming that: – he is entitled to make appointment; – appointment is in accordance with new administration provisions; – the company is, or is likely to become, unable to pay its debts; – the company is not in liquidation; and – the appointment does not fall within restrictions listed in the table at ¶8765
Attachments	– Administrator's consent in Form 2.2B (¶8736); [2] – consent of all persons to whom notice of intention was given, unless deadline of 5 business days has expired; and – if more than one administrator is being appointed, a statement as to how their powers and functions should be divided	– Administrator's consent in Form 2.2B (¶8736); [2] – copy of resolution to appoint the administrator; and – if more than one administrator is being appointed, a statement as to how their powers and functions should be divided

Note:
1. If deponent makes a **false declaration** that he does not reasonably believe to be true, he is liable to a fine (para 29(7) Sch B1 IA 1986; ¶9935).
2. For the purpose of this statement, the **administrator can rely on** information provided by the directors, unless he has reason to doubt its accuracy (para 29(4) Sch B1 IA 1986).

8771 The **appointment commences when** the notice of appointment has been correctly filed at court (para 31 Sch B1 IA 1986). Therefore, the person appointing the administrator must **notify** his appointee as soon as is reasonably practicable after filing; **failure** to do so renders him liable to a fine (para 32 Sch B1 IA 1986; ¶9935).

> MEMO POINTS If, however, the **company enters administration before** the **notice of appointment** has been filed because of a preceding administration application, the notice of appointment will not be effective and there is no obligation on the company or its board to notify the proposed administrator (para 33 Sch B1 IA 1986).

Invalid appointment

8772 If an appointment is later discovered to be invalid, the court can order the company or board to **indemnify the administrator** against any liability which arises as a result of that invalidity (para 34 Sch B1 IA 1986).

2. By qualifying floating charge holder

8777 Certain floating charge holders have the **right to** appoint an administrator using an out of court procedure, provided they and their charge(s) fall within the definitions below. Such charge holders can also make administration applications to court, and substitute their choice of administrator where an administrator has been appointed (¶8744, ¶9004):
– by a qualifying floating charge holder with a lower priority than him; or
– by the company or its board out of court.

A qualifying floating charge holder **cannot appoint** an administrator out of court if (paras 7, 8, 17 Sch B1 IA 1986):
- the company is in administration;
- the company is in compulsory or voluntary liquidation;
- a provisional liquidator has been appointed; or
- an administrative receiver is in office.

Relevant definitions

A **floating charge** is defined as a charge created as a floating charge (para 111(1) Sch B1 IA 1986), which therefore includes floating charges which have crystallised, but not those created as fixed charges which are floating charges by default because, for example, the assets over which they were created are not suitable (¶4610+).

A floating charge "**qualifies**", i.e. enables the holder to make an administration application, if the instrument by which it was created (para 14(2) Sch B1 IA 1986):
- states that the relevant provision applies to the charge (i.e. para 14 Sch B1 IA 1986);
- purports to give the charge holder the power to appoint an administrator; or
- purports to give the charge holder the power to appoint an administrative receiver (¶9237+).

A charge cannot be relied upon to appoint an administrator if it is **not enforceable** (para 16 Sch B1 IA 1986). However, a floating charge holder can still appoint an administrator if there is a dispute over whether he can enforce his security (*BCPMS (Europe) Ltd v GMAC Commercial Finance plc* [2006] All ER (D) 285 (Feb)).

A person is a qualifying floating **charge holder** if he holds one or more debentures secured by (para 14(3) Sch B1 IA 1986):
- a qualifying floating charge relating to all or substantially all of the company's property;
- several qualifying floating charges which together relate to all or substantially all of the company's property; or
- charges and other forms of security, at least one of which is a qualifying floating charge, which together relate to all or substantially all of the company's property.

Notice of intention

The charge holder must first **give notice to** the holder of any prior qualifying floating charge of his intention to appoint an administrator, using **Form** 2.5B (paras 14, 15, Sch B1 IA 1986; r 2.15 IR 1986). The other charge(s) may have priority over his because they were granted first, or because an agreement has been entered into between the charge holders to vary the order of priorities. Notice must be served at least 2 business days before the appointment; the rules regarding service discussed at ¶8743 apply here.

The other charge holders can give their **written consent** to the proposed appointment by either completing and returning the relevant section of Form 2.5B (r 2.16(4) IR 1986), or each providing written confirmation of (r 2.16(5) IR 1986):
- the name, registered office address and registered number of the company in question;
- the details of his charge, including the date on which it was registered, any financial limit on it or priority agreement in relation to it;
- his name and address;
- the name and address of the charge holder intending to make the appointment;
- the date he received Form 2.5B from that charge holder;
- the name of the proposed administrator(s);
- a statement of his consent to the administrator's appointment; and
- his signature and the date of the statement.

If **no written consent** is received, the charge holder may still go ahead with his appointment but must confirm that he gave the correct notices of intention when he files his notice of appointment at court (see ¶8782+).

The charge holder must **file** his notice of intention in Form 2.5B at court at the same time as he sends it to the prior charge holders (r 2.15 IR 1986).

Consequences of filing notice of intention

8781 Filing the notice at court will commence the **interim moratorium** (para 44 Sch B1 IA 1986). It will last until either:
- the administrator is appointed; or
- 5 business days have passed since the notice was filed at court and no administrator has been appointed.

The **effect** of the interim moratorium is the same as when an administration application has been made (¶8742).

Notice of appointment

8782 Once the 2-day notice period has expired, the charge holder can **file** his notice of appointment at court on **Form** 2.6B (r 2.16(1) IR 1986).

The notice includes a **statutory declaration** to be completed by the charge holder confirming that (para 18(2) Sch B1 IA 1986):
- he is the holder of a qualifying floating charge relating to the company's property;
- the (or each) charge relied on in making the appointment is (or was) enforceable at the date of the appointment; and
- the appointment is made in accordance with the new administration provisions (i.e. Schedule B1).

The statutory declaration cannot be made more than 5 days before Form 2.6B is filed at court (r 2.16(3) IR 1986). If the deponent makes a **false declaration** which he does not reasonably believe to be true, he is liable to a fine (para 18(7) Sch B1 IA 1986; ¶9935).

8783 This notice must be **accompanied by** (r 2.16(2) IR 1986):
a. the administrator's consent to act in Form 2.2B (¶8736);
b. either:
- evidence that the charge holder has served the correct notice on any prior qualifying floating charge holders; or
- copies of their written consent to the charge holder's appointment; and

c. if more than one administrator is to be appointed, a statement as to how their duties and functions are to be divided between them.

If the notice is filed when the court is closed a special procedure must be followed, which is described below (¶8786).

> MEMO POINTS In the case of appointments by charge holders, when the administrators complete **Form 2.2B**, they can rely on information provided by the directors, unless they have reason to doubt the accuracy of that information (para 18(4) Sch B1 IA 1986).

Filing and service

8784 Three copies of the notice of appointment must be **filed at court** (r 2.17 IR 1986). The court will then seal and endorse them with the date and time at which they were filed. It will issue two of the copies to the charge holder, who must **send** one **to the administrator** as soon as is reasonably practicable, since the administrator's appointment commences when the notice of appointment has been filed properly (para 20 Sch B1 IA 1986). This confirms to the administrator exactly when this occurred (para 19 Sch B1 IA 1986). If the charge holder fails to send a notice to the administrator, he is liable to a fine (para 20 Sch B1 IA 1986; ¶9935). If the notice is filed when the court is closed, special rules apply (see ¶8786 below).

Appointment made where administration application pending

8785 If the charge holder appoints an administrator when another applicant has applied to court for an administration order, the charge holder must also **send** a copy of the **notice of appointment to** the applicant and the court to which the application has been made as soon as is reasonably practicable (r 2.18 IR 1986). Failure to do so renders him liable to a fine (para 20 Sch B1 IA 1986; ¶9935).

Appointment made out of business hours

It may be necessary to make an appointment as a matter of urgency when the **court** is **closed**, for example, to prevent the company's assets being taken out of the creditors' reach. In such cases, a **special procedure** must be followed (r 2.19 IR 1986):

a. fax the notice to a designated fax number (found on the Insolvency Service website) on Form 2.7B;

b. obtain a fax **transmission report** showing the time and date of the fax and part or all of the first page of the form from the fax machine used to send the form. The appointment takes effect from this time, and the charge holder must inform the administrator that he has filed the notice as soon as is reasonably practicable;

c. the notice faxed to the court will be forwarded to the relevant court with jurisdiction to be placed on the court file;

d. on the next day that the court is open for business, the charge holder must **file at court**:
– three copies of the notice;
– the relevant supporting documentation;
– the fax transmission report; and
– a statement as to why the notice had to be filed out of hours, including why it would have been damaging to the company and creditors not to have acted in that way; and

e. the **court will** then seal the copies of the notice, endorse them with the date and time of the appointment (according to the fax transmission report) and issue two copies to the charge holder, who must send one to the administrator.

If the charge holder **fails to file** the copies of the notice, supporting documents and fax transmission report at court the next day on which it is open for business, the administrator's appointment ceases.

8786

Invalid appointment

If an appointment is later discovered to be invalid, the court can order the charge holder to **indemnify the administrator** against any resulting liability (para 21 Sch B1 IA 1986).

8787

C. Administrative requirements following all appointments

The administrator is obliged to take a number of administrative steps upon his appointment, mainly to **notify** all of the necessary persons involved with the company of its administration. If he **fails** to comply with any of the requirements set out in the table below, he is liable to a fine (para 46(9) Sch B1 IA 1986; ¶9935).

8797

Requirement	Deadline	Reference
Notify company of appointment using Form 2.12B	As soon as is reasonably practicable	para 46(2) Sch B1 IA 1986
Advertise appointment using Form 2.11B in *Gazette* and one appropriate newspaper to bring it to creditors' attention	As soon as is reasonably practicable	para 46(2) Sch B1 IA 1986; r 2.27 IR 1986
Obtain list of creditors	As soon as is reasonably practicable	para 46(3) Sch B1 IA 1986
Send notice of appointment to every creditor of whom he is aware using Form 2.12B[1]	As soon as is reasonably practicable	para 46(3) Sch B1 IA 1986

Requirement	Deadline	Reference
Send notice of appointment to Companies House [2]	Within 7 days of: – date of order; or – date of receiving notice from charge holder/company/board	para 46(4) Sch B1 IA 1986
Give notice of appointment using Form 2.12B to any of the following, as relevant: [3] – administrative receiver; – person who has presented winding up petition; – provisional liquidator; – supervisor of CVA; – enforcement officer charged with execution or another legal process against company or its property; and – person who has distrained against company or its property	As soon as is reasonably practicable after: – date of order; or – date of receiving notice from charge holder/company/board	para 46(5) Sch B1 IA 1986; r 2.27 IR 1986

Note:
1. The court can direct that this **requirement does not apply** (para 46(7) Sch B1 IA 1986).
2. If administrator has been appointed as **replacement** for another administrator, he must use Form 2.40B (r 2.128 IR 1986).
3. The court can direct that this **requirement does not apply**, or that **different deadline** applies (para 46(7) Sch B1 IA 1986).

8798 The administrator is also required to **publicise** his appointment **during** the **administration** (¶9021).

D. Effect of administration

8808 The company **enters administration when**:
a. the administration **order** states that the administrator's appointment is to take effect. If the order does not specify a date, it is deemed to be the date on which the order was made (para 13(2) Sch B1 IA 1986); or
b. the notice of an appointment **out of court** has been correctly filed at court (paras 19, 31 Sch B1 IA 1986).

When the administrator's appointment takes effect, he must take over the management of the company's business, affairs and property, and he is given extensive powers in this regard. The conduct of the administration is discussed at ¶8992+, and the administrator's powers in particular at ¶9010+. This change in the way in which the company is managed has an impact upon its **officers** and **employees**, as well as **third parties** dealing with it. The administrator's appointment also triggers the **moratorium**, ensuring that the administration can be carried out without the company having to deal with legal action against it.

MEMO POINTS As in a liquidation, the administrator can **challenge certain transactions** which took place before the company went into administration, recovering assets and money that should not have left the company (¶7808+). However, there are different time limits within which such transactions must have taken place for the administrator to be able to mount a challenge. Rather than these limits being calculated backwards from the company's entry into administration (i.e. the appointment of the administrator), they are calculated backwards from the date of the administration application or the filing of the notice of intention (i.e. the date when it was known that the company was likely to go into administration).

1. Moratorium

8813 Since the aim of the administration is to rescue the company's business, or at least its assets, the company is under the **protection** of a moratorium during administration. This means that most types of legal action, including insolvency proceedings, cannot be taken against it, giving it financial certainty (i.e. preventing claims outside of the administration being made) while it attempts to revive its fortunes.

Before the administrator's appointment takes effect, the company benefits from an **interim moratorium** (¶8742). This offers a similar, although not quite as extensive, protection with the aim of ensuring that the company's assets do not "disappear" as soon as the potential administration comes to light. The interim moratorium begins when an administration application or notice of intention to appoint an administrator is filed; it will end when the application is granted or dismissed, a notice of appointment is filed or the deadline for doing so has expired.

Other insolvency proceedings

New proceedings

As a **general rule**, once a company is in administration, it cannot be placed into voluntary or compulsory liquidation (para 42 Sch B1 IA 1986). The minor **exceptions** allow a winding up order to be made in two specific circumstances (para 42(4) Sch B1 IA 1986):
– on the ground of the public interest, including against a Societas Europaea (i.e. a European Company) (¶7626+); and
– by the FSA (s 367 FSMA).

If a petition is presented in either of these two circumstances, the administrator must apply to the court for directions as to how to proceed (¶9014).

Whilst an administrative receiver cannot be appointed, an ordinary receiver may be appointed with the administrator's or the court's consent (para 43(4), (6A) Sch B1 IA 1986). An administration can be **converted** into other types of insolvency proceedings by the administrator (see ¶7481, ¶9141+).

8814

Existing or pending proceedings

Where the company goes into administration when a **winding up petition** has been presented against it, a winding up order will not be made during the administration, but:
a. in the case of an administration order being made by the court, the petition will be dismissed (para 40(1) Sch B1 IA 1986); and
b. if a qualifying floating charge holder has appointed an administrator, the petition will be suspended, unless it is a public interest petition, including one against a Societas Europaea (i.e. a European Company) or a petition by the FSA (para 40(1), (2) Sch B1 IA 1986). The same limited exceptions apply as to the moratorium on new proceedings. Therefore, if a winding up petition has been presented and the company or board want it to go into administration instead, it will have to use the court procedure.

8815

> MEMO POINTS If the **petition is suspended**, the administrator's dealings with the company's property are not at risk of being declared void as a disposition after the petition has been presented (s 127(2) IA 1986; ¶7674+).

For the position where the company is **already subject to another insolvency proceeding**, see:
– court procedure: ¶8723;
– out of court appointment by company or board: ¶8765; or
– out of court appointment by qualifying floating charge holder: ¶8778.

8816

An **administrative receiver** acting in relation to the company must vacate office (para 41(1), (2) Sch B1 IA 1986):
– in the case of an administration order, when the order takes effect; or
– in the case of an appointment out of court, if required to do so by the administrator.

If an **ordinary receiver** of the company's property has been appointed prior to the commencement of the administrator's appointment by either method, he must vacate office if the administrator requires him to do so (para 41(2) Sch B1 IA 1986).

8817

> MEMO POINTS Where an **administrative or ordinary receiver** vacates office under these circumstances, his **remuneration** is charged on and paid out of the company's property in his possession or under his control (para 41(3) Sch B1 IA 1986).

Other types of legal proceedings

8818 The company is also protected against other legal actions during administration. The following legal proceedings **can only be taken** against the company with the **consent** of either the administrator or the court (para 43 Sch B1 IA 1986).

Type of action	Definitions	Reference
– Legal proceedings – Execution – Distress – Other legal processes (permission required to commence and continue)	– Legal proceedings: not just proceedings brought by creditors, e.g. can include criminal proceedings – Legal process: judicial steps only, so will not include taking contractual steps, e.g. exercising right to terminate	para 43(6) Sch B1 IA 1986; Re Rhondda Waste Disposal Co Ltd [2000] All ER (D) 162; Re Olympia & York Canary Wharf Ltd [1993] BCLC 453
Enforcement of security over company's property, including appointing an ordinary receiver	– Security: see ¶9941 – Taking steps to enforce security: need definite act[1] – Property: see ¶9941	para 43(2) Sch B1 IA 1986; Re London Flight Centre (Stansted) Ltd [2002] All ER (D) 52 (Jul)
Repossession of goods in company's possession under hire-purchase agreement[2]	– In the company's possession: includes where goods have been sublet/are in possession of others, e.g. for repair – Hire-purchase agreement: includes conditional sale agreement, chattel-leasing agreement and retention of title agreements – Under hire-purchase agreement: includes where agreement has expired	paras 43(3), 111 Sch B1 IA 1986; Re Atlantic Computer Systems plc (No 1) [1191] BCLC 606; Re David Meek Access Ltd [1994] 1 BCLC 680
Landlord's exercise of right of forfeiture by peaceable re-entry of company's premises	– Landlord: includes any person to whom rent is payable – Forfeiture: see ¶9940	para 43(4) Sch B1 IA 1986

Note:
1. **What is a definite act** depends on the circumstances, e.g. if enforcing a lien, unqualified refusal is required from the lien-holder to return company's assets to constitute taking steps to enforce; but if he just states that unless the administrator consents to enforcement he will apply to court for consent (and does so promptly), the lien-holder is not taking steps to enforce the security. Enforcing security includes appointing a receiver under that security (*Royal Trust Bank v Buchler* [1989] BCLC 130, in which the bank was not allowed to do so).
2. More detailed **definitions** can be found in the Consumer Credit Act 1974.

Obtaining consent to take proceedings

8820 It is preferable for the person intending to take any of the above legal proceedings against the company to obtain permission **from** the **administrator**. As an officer of the court, he should make his decision promptly and give reasons for any refusal. He must balance the effect of granting permission on the company and its unsecured creditors against the effect of refusing permission on the person seeking consent. Generally, if granting permission to take the proposed action will not impede the administrator in achieving the purpose of the administration and the action is reasonable, leave should be granted (*Re Atlantic Computer Systems plc (No 1)* [1991] BCLC 606). The **court** will take a similar approach, usually giving weight to the proprietary interests of the person seeking consent. However, each case depends on its own circumstances, for example the conduct of the parties may be an important factor.

The fact that the company has entered into administration does not stop time running for the purpose of the **limitation period**, whether the action is taken by or against the company (*Re Maxwell Fleet and Facilities Management Ltd (in administration)* [2000] 1 All ER 464). Therefore, if a claim is almost out of time, this would be an argument for allowing the claimant to proceed against the company, rather than denying him a remedy.

MEMO POINTS Various **cases** dealing with the old administration regime have given guidance on the administrator's and court's exercise of their discretion to permit action to be taken against the company, as summarised above. It is likely that the same guidance will apply to the new administration provisions. For more detail, readers should refer to the case of *Re Atlantic Computer Systems plc (No 1)* [1991] BCLC 606 in particular.

An administrator may be held liable in tort for **trespass** or **conversion** if he retains goods to which the owner had an immediate right of possession and has made a lawful demand for delivery, which the administrator has unreasonably refused or with which he otherwise wrongfully interferes (s 1 Torts (Interference with Goods) Act 1977). Further, even if he is not technically liable for conversion, the court can hold him liable as an officer of the court if he **wrongfully retains** goods for purposes other than to perform the administration properly, for example by using them as a bargaining tool (*Barclays Mercantile Business Finance Ltd v Sibec Developments Ltd* [1993] BCLC 1077). In such cases, the court can require the administrator to return the goods to their owner and pay any appropriate damages to compensate for his actions.

8821

2. Other consequences

On the company

The administration does not automatically terminate the directors' offices, although they cannot exercise their **management** power without the consent of the administrator (para 64 Sch B1 IA 1986). The same provision applies to the company as a whole, so the shareholders cannot exercise their management functions without the administrator's consent either. "Management power" is broadly defined to include all management powers which could interfere with the exercise of the administrator's powers, whether statutory or contractual. The administrator can grant general or specific permission to the directors or the company to exercise such powers. As part of the administrator's extensive management powers, he can also appoint and remove directors, and call shareholder meetings (paras 59, 61, 62 Sch B1 IA 1986).

8826

In terms of the company's **statutory filing and reporting** duties, Companies House puts a "stop" on the company's file when it receives notice of an administrator's appointment, until it can ascertain from the administrator whether or not the directors are capable of continuing to comply. This will depend upon the involvement of the directors in the company's management during the administration (i.e. whether they have access to the relevant information). If they can comply with their obligations, the stop is lifted and the filing obligations must be fulfilled as usual. This is a Companies House policy, and therefore its application may differ depending on the circumstances of a particular company. If the directors are in any doubt as to whether their obligations continue in this regard, they should contact the administrator and/or Companies House.

Contracts

Contracts to which the company is a party may **terminate** when it enters administration, if this is an express term of the contract. Otherwise, the contract will remain in force.

8827

Unlike a liquidator, an administrator has no power to disclaim a contract and he cannot simply choose not to perform certain ones. If the **administrator does not perform** the contracts, the other party can:
a. take **action under the contract**, such as issuing notices requiring the administrator to perform it or exercising a right to terminate. Such action does not fall within the definition of "legal processes" prohibited during the moratorium, and so does not require the administrator's or the court's consent (*Re Olympia & York Canary Wharf Ltd* [1993] BCLC 453, an old administration case which is likely to apply to the current regime as well). If the other party is entitled to a payment under the contract, he will have an unsecured claim in the administration; and/or
b. make an **application to court**, with the consent of the administrator or the court (¶8818+), which may result in an order for:
– **damages**, in which case the party will have an unsecured claim against the company. He will not be able to enforce his judgment against the company without the administrator's or the court's consent;

8828

– **specific performance**, compelling the company managed by the administrator to perform the contract. As an equitable remedy, specific performance will only be granted in appropriate circumstances, taking into account factors such as the conduct of the parties and the adequacy of damages as an alternative remedy; or

– an **injunction**, preventing/compelling the administrator from doing/to do something. Again, this is a discretionary remedy and will only be granted in appropriate circumstances.

It must be noted that every case **depends upon** its own facts and in some circumstances the court will allow an administrator not to perform his duties under a contract, e.g. allowing him to retain the use of premises or assets while not having to pay the company's rent or hire charges (*Re Atlantic Computer Systems plc (No 1)* [1991] BCLC 606).

8829 If the **other party does not perform** his obligations under the contract, the administrator can take enforcement proceedings in the company's name. He can also apply for damages, specific performance or other injunctions, or rely on contractual remedies, depending on the terms of the contract in question.

On employees

8830 Employees' contracts do not automatically **terminate** when the company goes into administration. The administrator can adopt their contracts or terminate them subject to the employee's terms and conditions of employment and their protection under employment law. His course of action will depend upon his plans for the administration. If he intends to cause the company to carry on trading, he will clearly need to retain and continue to pay most of the workforce. A summary of remedies available to employees where their contracts are terminated is at ¶2986. The administrator is not personally liable to the employees for sums due under their contacts, but he may have to pay such sums out of the company's assets when he vacates office (¶8928).

> MEMO POINTS 1. **Redundancies** are fairly common where a company enters administration, as the administrator may need to sell off or close down parts of the business (see *Employment Memo* for a detailed discussion of this topic). In addition to the usual consultation obligations during redundancy, where 20 or more redundancies are proposed at the company within 90 days, the administrator, on behalf of the company, is under a duty to consult with employee representatives and notify BERR (ss 188, 195(2) Trade Union and Labour Relations (Consolidation) Act 1992). The duty may also arise where he seeks to vary terms of employment by dismissal and re-engagement. In special circumstances, where it is impracticable to consult, he can take the steps which are reasonable in the circumstances instead, although they fall short of proper consultation. However, the fact that the company is subject to an insolvency procedure in itself is not enough to constitute special circumstances (e.g. *Re Hartlebury Printers Ltd (in liquidation)* [1993] 1 All ER 470).
> 2. If the administrator transfers all or part of the company's undertaking, **TUPE** may apply (SI 2006/246). The new TUPE regulations, which came into force on 6 April 2006, no longer contain an exception in relation to hive-downs.
> See ¶6415+ for hive-downs, ¶6422 for the application of TUPE in insolvency hive-downs and *Employment Memo* for the effect of TUPE generally.

SECTION 2

Managing the company's affairs, business and assets

8845 It is the **administrator's job** to manage the company's affairs, business and assets to achieve the purpose of the administration (see ¶8711). His first step is to **investigate** the company, which he does principally by requiring an officer of the company (or other relevant person) to prepare a statement of affairs for him to analyse. There is no role in administration for the official receiver to investigate the conduct of the company's affairs. However, if the administrator discovers behaviour for which a director should be disqualified, he must report it (¶8856).

In addition to analysing the company's statement of affairs, he must also examine the company's books and records and its list of creditors. He must then prepare his **proposals** for how the administration is to be conducted. If at this stage he concludes that the purpose cannot be achieved, or the company should not have been placed into administration, he must apply for the termination of his appointment (¶9164+). The proposals are then put to the creditors, who may suggest modifications; if they are approved, the administrator must conduct the administration in accordance with them and any directions the court may make. The proposals are not, however, static; they may be revised as the administration progresses.

In implementing his proposals, the administrator will carry on the **management** of the company's business and affairs, so that it continues to trade, perform its contracts and so on. He may **realise** assets belonging to the company and make **distributions** to creditors. Each administration will be different, depending on its circumstances and the individual proposals made. For example, if the company is in a very poor financial state, the only possible purpose of the administration may be to realise the company's property in order to make a distribution to one or more secured and/or preferential creditors, in which case the administrator's actions will be more akin to that of a liquidator. On the other hand, if he aims to rescue the company as a going concern, the administrator will carry on the company's business, but sell off any unprofitable parts of it and/or put improved management and financial procedures in place.

A. Investigation

8855 When the administrator's appointment commences, he will use similar powers to a liquidator and/or official receiver to investigate the company's affairs so that he can prepare his proposals. For example, he will examine the company's books and **records**, question its officers and senior employees, as well as **obtain information** from creditors. The following powers will assist him in his investigations, which are dealt with in the context of compulsory liquidation:
– the duty of those involved in the company to co-operate with the administrator (¶8121);
– his ability to retrieve the company's money, property, books and papers (¶8170); and
– his ability to require an individual involved in the company to submit to private examination (¶8172+).

The prime tool in the administrator's investigation into the company's business and assets is the **statement of affairs**, which must usually be prepared for the administrator by at least one director of the company.

> MEMO POINTS Similar rules apply to preparing a statement of affairs in an **administrative receivership**; if readers are interested in this procedure, they should read references to the "administrator" as to the "administrative receiver", and to "administration" as to "administrative receivership" and note the references and minor differences in procedure highlighted in the memo points.

8856 The administrator fulfils his duty to report on the **conduct of the directors** of the company as part of his investigations into the affairs of the company. He must report to the secretary of state if it appears to him that a director's conduct renders him unfit to be concerned in company management and the company is or has been insolvent (s 7(3) CDDA 1986). In addition, the secretary of state or official receiver may require him (or a former administrator of the company) to report on any person's conduct as director of the company, and to provide and allow inspection of any documents relevant to that person's conduct (s 7(4) CDDA 1986).

> MEMO POINTS 1. The administrator must also **report** the company **to** the **FSA** if it appears to him that it is or has been carrying on a regulated activity in contravention of the prohibition, unless the administration has come about as a result of an administration application by the FSA (s 361 FSMA 2000).
> 2. An unintended consequence of the changes to the law allowing administrations to be converted to voluntary liquidations is that where this occurs and the administrator becomes the liquidator, the same insolvency practitioner is obliged to filed the report twice and in many cases they are identical. As part of the Insolvency Service's review of secondary legislation (see ¶7364/mp), it is taking the opportunity to make alterations to the primary legislation either where

it is necessary to support the new Rules or to remove unnecessary administrative burdens. The Service proposes to **alter this obligation** so that where a report has already been filed in respect of the company when it was in administration, the liquidator (if he is the same insolvency practitioner) does not have to file a second one unless there are additional matters to report (proposal 6 "A consultation document on changes to the Insolvency Act 1986 and the Company Directors Disqualification Act 1986 to be made by a Legislative Reform Order for the modernisation and streamlining of insolvency procedures" (September 2007)). At the time of writing, the consultation is still open. If this proposal is accepted, the changes are likely to be implemented from 1 October 2008.

1. Statement of affairs

Requirement to prepare statement

8861 Once appointed, the administrator must require one of the following **persons** involved in the company **to prepare** a statement of affairs as soon as is reasonably practicable (para 47(3) Sch B1 IA 1986):
– a current or former officer of the company;
– a person who participated in the company's formation in the year before the administration;
– an employee of the company employed during the year prior to the administration; or
– a person who is or was an officer or employee of a corporate officer of the company in the year prior to the administration.

The statement is usually best made by an officer of the company, as he will have access to the relevant information. If a person **fails** to provide the administrator with a statement of affairs when requested, he is liable to a fine (para 48 Sch B1 IA 1986; ¶9935).

> MEMO POINTS An **administrative receiver** is also under a duty to require a statement to be made by the same persons (s 41(1), (3) IA 1986). Likewise, failure to comply leads to a fine (s 47(6) IA 1986; ¶9935).

8862 The administrator will submit his **requisition** in Form 2.13B, giving the following information (r 2.28(3) IR 1986):
– the names and addresses of any other persons to whom such a request has been sent;
– the deadline by which the statement must be delivered (see ¶8869);
– that failure to comply with the request is an offence; and
– that the recipient, along with all of the other persons listed above, is under a duty to co-operate with the administrator (¶8121).

The administrator will also provide the relevant **forms** needed to prepare the statement (r 2.28(4) IR 1986).

> MEMO POINTS An **administrative receiver's** requisition will contain the same information (r 3.3(3) IR 1986) and he will provide the correct form on which to prepare the statement on request (r 3.3(4) IR 1986).

Preparing the statement

8863 The statement itself must be in **Form** 2.14B and give the following **information** (para 47(2) Sch B1 IA 1986; r 2.29(1) IR 1986):
– details of the company's assets and liabilities;
– the names and addresses of the company's creditors;
– details of the security held by each creditor, including the date on which it was granted; and
– details of the company's shareholders.

The statement must be **verified** by a statement of truth, which is included on the form, by the person making the statement (r 2.29(1) IR 1986).

> MEMO POINTS In an **administrative receivership**, the statement must be made in Form 3.2, which requires the same information except for the details of the shareholders. It must be verified by an affidavit (s 47(2) IA 1986; r 3.4 IR 1986).
> The Insolvency Service has proposed that **affidavits** are replaced by witness statements (see ¶8737). This change is likely to be implemented on 1 October 2008.

The reasonable **expenses** of making a statement of affairs will be met by the administrator out of the funds received by him in his conduct of the administration (r 2.32 IR 1986). The administrator's decision to pay, or not to pay, such expenses can be appealed to the court.

8864

> MEMO POINTS   This is also the case in **administrative receivership** (r 3.7 IR 1986).

Release from duty

The **administrator** may release a person from his duty to make a statement, either on his own initiative or at the **request of** any of the persons listed at ¶8861 (para 48(2) Sch B1 IA 1986; r 2.31 IR 1986).

8865

> MEMO POINTS   This is also the case in **administrative receivership**, following the same procedure as outlined below (s 47(5) IA 1986; r 3.6 IR 1986).

If the **administrator refuses** such a request for release, the person affected can apply to court for an appropriate order (para 48(3) Sch B1 IA 1986).

8866

The court can **dismiss** an application if it does not give sufficient cause, although it must first give the applicant 7 clear days' notice of its intention to do so, giving him the opportunity to request a hearing at which he can attend and put his case forward (r 2.31 IR 1986).

If the application is **not dismissed**, the court will notify the applicant of the date, time and place of the hearing. The applicant must give at least 14 clear days' **notice** of the hearing to the administrator, and also provide him with a copy of the application and any evidence on which he intends to rely. The administrator is entitled to submit a written report to the court, bringing any matters to its attention as he thinks appropriate. If he does so, he must send a copy to the applicant at least 5 clear days before the hearing. The administrator is entitled to attend and be heard at the **hearing**, whether or not he has already filed a report. Copies of any order made will be sent to the applicant and the administrator. The applicant's **costs** are usually payable by him personally, unless the court orders otherwise.

Statement of concurrence

In addition to a main statement of affairs, the administrator can require any of the persons listed at ¶8861 to make a "**statement of concurrence**". This states that the deponent agrees with the statement of affairs (r 2.29(2), (5) IR 1986):
a. without qualification; or
b. with qualification on all or certain matters, because he:
– does not agree with the maker of the statement;
– thinks that the statement is erroneous or misleading; or
– cannot agree because he does not have the necessary direct knowledge.

8867

The statement of concurrence must be made using **Form** 2.15B, which includes a verifying statement of truth (r 2.29(2), (6) IR 1986).

The administrator will **inform** the person making the full statement of affairs that a statement of concurrence has been requested and from whom.

> MEMO POINTS   An **administrative receiver** can require these persons to make an affidavit of concurrence relating to the statement of affairs (r 3.4(2) IR 1986). It must be delivered by the deponent to the administrative receiver, with one copy (r 3.4(5) IR 1986).
> The Insolvency Service has proposed that **affidavits** are replaced by witness statements (see ¶8737). This change is likely to be implemented on 1 October 2008.

The reasonable **expenses** of making a statement of concurrence will be met by the administrator out of the funds received by him in his conduct of the administration (r 2.32 IR 1986). The administrator's decision to pay, or not to pay, such expenses can be appealed to the court.

8868

> MEMO POINTS   This is also the case in **administrative receivership** (r 3.7 IR 1986).

Deadlines

The usual deadline for submitting the **statement of affairs** is within 11 days from the day on which the deponent receives the administrator's request (para 48(1) Sch B1 IA 1986). The deponent must deliver (r 2.29(3) IR 1986):

8869

– the statement, plus one copy, to the administrator; and
– a copy of the statement to all persons required to make a statement of concurrence.

The administrator can **extend** the deadline within which the statement must be submitted, either on his own initiative or at the request of any of the persons listed at ¶8861, using the same procedure as for releasing a person from his duty to submit the statement described at ¶8865+ (para 48(2) Sch B1 IA 1986; r 2.31 IR 1986).

A **statement of concurrence** must be submitted within 5 business days from the day on which the deponent receives the statement of affairs (r 2.29(4) IR 1986). The deponent must deliver it, plus one copy, to the administrator. The administrator can also agree to **extend** this deadline.

> MEMO POINTS In an **administrative receivership**, the statement of affairs must be submitted within 21 days of the day after the request (s 47(4) IA 1986). It must be delivered to the administrative receiver by the deponent together with the verifying affidavit, which must have a copy of the statement attached to it (r 3.4(4) IR 1986). The deadline can be extended. There is no deadline stipulated for affidavits of concurrence; the administrative receiver will inform the deponent of when this needs to be submitted.

Administrative requirements

8870 The administrator is required to **file** the statement of affairs and any statement(s) of concurrence at Companies House along with Form 2.16B, unless an order for limited disclosure has been made (r 2.29(7) IR 1986).

> MEMO POINTS In an **administrative receivership**, the statement of affairs and affidavit of concurrence need to be filed along with the report to the creditors, see ¶9378+.

Exception to filing requirements

8871 If the administrator considers that it would prejudice the administration for the statement of affairs to be disclosed, he can apply to the court for an order for **limited disclosure** in relation to all or part of it (r 2.30 IR 1986). An order for limited disclosure will state that the statement, or a specified part of it, should not be filed at Companies House. If such an order is made, the administrator must notify Companies House on Form 2.16B, also sending a copy of the order for the company's file.

If there is a significant **change in circumstances** after an order has been made, which renders the order unnecessary or requires it to be altered, the administrator must apply to the court for the order, or part of it, to be rescinded (r 2.30(7) IR 1986). He must then file the statement of affairs (to the extent permitted by the new order) at Companies House, with Form 2.16B (r 2.30(8) IR 1986). If he has already sent out his proposals for the conduct of the administration (see ¶8876+ below), he must provide the creditors with the statement of affairs as filed at Companies House, or a summary of it (r 2.39(9) IR 1986).

A **creditor** may **obtain disclosure** of all or part of the statement subject to the order, by making an application to court supported by affidavit evidence (r 2.30(4), (5) IR 1986). He must give the administrator at least 3 clear days' notice of the application. The court can order disclosure in appropriate circumstances, placing conditions on it as necessary (r 2.30(6) IR 1986).

> MEMO POINTS The Insolvency Service has proposed that **affidavits** are replaced by witness statements (see ¶8737). This change is likely to be implemented on 1 October 2008.

2. Proposals

8876 Once the administrator has assessed the statement of affairs and completed his other investigations into the company's affairs, he is required to prepare proposals for his conduct of the administration, **setting out** how the purpose of the administration will be achieved (see ¶8711). If he concludes that the purpose cannot be achieved, he must apply to end the administration (¶9164+). The proposals must be approved by the creditors, but the administrator can modify them to address any particular objections (with consent, unless the modification is minor). However, administration normally affords the creditors their best chance of recovery and so they will usually approve the proposals, unless the proposals are unfair or based on poor information.

The **court** may give **directions** to the administrator on any aspect of his management of the company's affairs, business or property (para 68(2) Sch B1 IA 1986). Such directions will (para 68(3) Sch B1 IA 1986):
– be consistent with the administrator's proposals;
– deal with a change in circumstances since the proposals (or revisions to them) were approved; or
– clarify a misunderstanding that has arisen.

Alternatively, directions can be given where there are no proposals because the initial ones have not been approved by the creditors. However the directions arise, the administrator is obliged to comply with them (para 68(2) Sch B1 IA 1986).

a. Contents

The administrator must make a **statement of** his **proposals** as to how the company can achieve the purpose of the administration, which has to be sent to the creditors (para 49 Sch B1 IA 1986). He must state which of the three **purposes** is applicable (¶8711), but if more than one is possible, he can compare the various outcomes so that the creditors can choose which one they wish him to pursue (¶8711; para 5, chapter 1, *Dear IP*).

8878

The statement **must set out** the following **information** (para 49(2) Sch B1 IA 1986; r 2.33(2) IR 1986):
1. details of the relevant court and case number;
2. details of the company, including any trading names;
3. details of the administrator's appointment, including how functions are to be divided between any joint administrators;
4. the names of the directors and secretary and details of any shares they have in the company;
5. an account of how the company went into administration;
6. a copy or summary of any statement of affairs, including any comments on it by the administrator;
7. where an order for limited disclosure has been obtained in relation to a statement of affairs, the administrator must state the fact that it has been made, who provided the statement, the date of the order and the details or a summary of the information not covered by the order;
8. where a full statement of affairs is not provided in the proposals or one has not been made, details of the company's creditors and any security they hold;
9. where no statement of affairs has been made, an explanation as to why this is the case, as well as details of the company's financial position as at the latest practicable date (at least after the company went into administration, unless the court allows otherwise);
10. the proposed basis for calculating the administrator's remuneration;
11. if the administrator does not propose a CVA, an estimate of the company's net property and the fund secured by floating charges that he will be able to ring-fence (to the best of his knowledge and belief), and whether he intends to make an application to be excused from ring-fencing that sum (see ¶7995). If he states that the company has insufficient property to distribute to the unsecured creditors, except for out of a ring-fenced fund, this will affect the creditors required to consent to certain matters during the administration (see ¶8883, ¶8885+, ¶9000, ¶9027+, ¶9042, ¶9090);
12. how the administrator considers that the purpose of the administration can be achieved, and how it will end;
13. if the purpose of the administration is the second or third statutory purpose, why the first and/or second purpose could not be achieved, as applicable;
14. if a CVL is proposed, that the creditors can put forward their own candidate for the office of liquidator, as well as giving details of his candidate;
15. if the administrator did not call a meeting of creditors, his reasons for not doing so;
16. an account of his management of the company, including details of any disposals of assets, and details of how he proposes to continue to manage and finance the business;

8879

17. whether the EC Insolvency Regulation applies, and if so whether the administration constitutes main or secondary proceedings; and

18. any other information the administrator thinks appropriate to enable the creditors to make an informed decision about the proposals.

The statement **can include** proposals for a CVA (¶9448+) or for another form of compromise or arrangement with the creditors or shareholders (such as a statutory scheme of arrangement, see ¶6500+).

> MEMO POINTS 1. The creditors must be given enough **information** in the proposals to enable them to participate in the administration in a meaningful way, supporting the aims of collectivity and transparency (para 5, Chapter 1 *Dear IP*).
> 2. From 15 December 2007, the statement will also be able to include proposals for a **cross-border merger** (see ¶6536/mp; para 73 Sch B1 IA 1986 as amended by reg 65 SI 2007/2974).

8880 The statement **cannot include**:

a. any information which would seriously prejudice the commercial interests of the company if disclosed. If any such information is omitted, the administrator must include a statement to that effect in the proposals (r 2.33(3) IR 1986); or

b. any action which would have any of the following consequences (unless the administrator has the consent of the relevant creditor or the action forms part of a CVA or other compromise or arrangement, which, in themselves, require their consent) (para 73 Sch B1 IA 1986):
– it affects the right of a secured creditor to enforce his security;
– it would result in a preferential debt being paid out of priority; or
– it would result in one preferential creditor being paid less (rateably) than another.

b. Circulation

8882 The administrator must **send** his **proposals** to (para 49(4) Sch B1 IA 1986):

a. Companies House, along with Form 2.17B (r 2.33(1) IR 1986);

b. every creditor of whom he is aware and for whom he has an address, along with an invitation to the initial creditors' meeting (see ¶8885+); and

c. every shareholder of whom he is aware and for whom he has an address. **Alternatively**, he can give notice that he will provide a copy of the proposals to any shareholder who applies to him in writing (para 49(6) Sch B1 IA 1986). In which case, he must advertise the notice in a newspaper so that it is likely to come to the shareholders' attention, specifying the address to which they must write to request a copy (r 2.33(7), (8) IR 1986). The advertisement should be placed as soon as is reasonably practicable after the proposals have been sent to the other relevant people, and not later than 8 weeks after the company went into administration.

> MEMO POINTS Even where the administrator intends to **terminate** the **administration** (whether by an application to court (¶9164+) or by notice that the purposes of the administration have been achieved (¶9130)), he must send a report to all creditors (for whom he has an address) giving them the information at 1–16 in the list at ¶8879 (r 2.33(b) IR 1986).

8883 The administrator's **deadline** for circulating his proposals is within 8 weeks of the company entering into administration, but it should be done as soon as is reasonably practicable (para 49(5) Sch B1 IA 1986). Failure to give notice to the correct people within the deadline renders the administrator liable to a fine (¶9935).

The administrator can obtain an **extension of time** either by applying to court, or with the consent of the creditors (para 49(8) Sch B1 IA 1986). If a **court order** is granted, he must notify the people to whom he must send the proposals as soon as is reasonably practicable after the order has been made (r 2.33(4) IR 1986). The **creditors** can only grant one extension of time for up to 28 days (para 108 Sch B1 IA 1986). They cannot extend a period which has expired or has already been extended by the court. The creditors' consent to the extension can be given individually in writing, or collectively at a creditors' meeting. As the table below demonstrates, the level of consent required from the creditors differs, depending on whether the administrator has stated in the proposals that there are not enough assets to distribute to creditors, other than out of any ring-fenced portion of a floating charge.

	No statement in proposals	Statement in proposals
Consent required	– Each secured creditor; and – if there are unsecured debts, consent of creditors whose debts total over 50% of unsecured debts, not including any creditor who does not respond	• Each secured creditor; or • if administrator thinks he can distribute to preferential creditors: – each secured creditor; and – preferential creditors whose debts total over 50% of preferential debts, not including any creditor who does not respond

c. Approval

The administrator's proposals must be approved by the company's creditors before they can be put into effect. To obtain approval, the administrator has to call an **initial creditors' meeting**, with some minor exceptions (¶8887). As an **alternative** to a meeting, he can gain approval of his proposals by written resolution (discussed at ¶9078+). Even if he chooses this method, the creditors can still require a meeting to be held.

8885

Calling the meeting

Notice of the meeting must be sent to the creditors with the proposals at least 14 days in advance of the meeting, and failure to do so renders the administrator liable to a fine (para 51(1), (5) Sch B1 IA 1986; ¶9935). The administrator must also give notice to any of the company's current or former officers, whose presence at the meeting he requires (r 2.34(2) IR 1986). The meeting must also be **advertised** in the same newspaper in which the administrator's appointment was advertised, as well as in any other appropriate newspaper which will ensure that the meeting is brought to the attention of the creditors (r 2.34(1) IR 1986).

8886

The **date of the meeting** must be within 10 weeks of the company going into administration, but should be held as soon as is reasonably practicable (para 51(2) Sch B1 IA 1986). The administrator may obtain an extension to this **deadline** by (paras 51(4), 107, 108 Sch B1 IA 1986):
a. obtaining the creditors' consent, in the same way as obtaining consent for an extension for circulating the proposals (¶8883); or
b. applying to the court. If the court makes an order, the administrator must notify the same persons to whom he sent the notice of the meeting and proposals using Form 2.18B (r 2.34(3) IR 1986).

Otherwise, **failure** to hold the meeting within the requisite time period renders the administrator liable to a fine (para 51(5) Sch B1 IA 1986; ¶9935).

Administrator does not call meeting

The administrator **does not have to** call an initial creditors' meeting if he considers that the company (para 52 Sch B1 IA 1986):
a. has enough assets to pay all of the creditors in full;
b. does not have enough assets to enable a distribution to be made to the unsecured creditors, other than out of the ring-fenced fund; or
c. cannot be rescued as a going concern, nor would a better result be achieved for the creditors if the company was placed into liquidation (i.e. neither of the first two purposes of the administration can be achieved).

8887

However, to protect the creditors in such a situation, the administrator can be **required to hold** an initial creditors' meeting by those creditors whose debts amount to at least 10% of the company's total debts. They must request a meeting using Form 2.21B within 12 days of the proposals being sent out. The request must include the following information (r 2.37 IR 1986):
– a list of creditors agreeing with the request (unless the requisitioning creditor is owed enough of the company's debts by himself);
– written confirmation of each of their agreement; and
– the purpose of the proposed meeting.

8888

Such a meeting must be held within 28 days of the administrator receiving the request. Although the person submitting the request must pay a deposit to the administrator to cover the **costs** of the meeting, the creditors can resolve at the meeting that these costs should be met out of the company's assets, in which case the deposit will be repaid.

If a **meeting** is **not requisitioned** within the 12-day period, the proposals will be deemed to have been approved (r 2.33 IR 1986).

Conduct and business

8889 The administrator must **present** a copy of his **proposals** to the meeting (para 51(3) Sch B1 IA 1986). The meeting may (para 53 Sch B1 IA 1986):
- approve them as they are presented;
- approve them with modifications; or
- reject them.

The meeting can be **adjourned** once for up to 14 days by the chairman if there are not enough creditors present to approve the proposals with any modifications (r 2.34(4) IR 1986; see ¶9085, ¶9086+). However, the meeting can be adjourned again or for a longer period, if so directed by the court.

Administrative requirements

8890 As soon as is reasonably practicable after the creditors have approved or rejected the proposals, the administrator must **give notice** of their decision as set out in the table below (para 53(2) Sch B1 IA 1986; r 2.46 IR 1986).

Notify	Documents to send
Creditors who received notice of meeting/written resolution	Form 2.23B confirming decision, including details of any approved modifications
Other persons who received copy of proposals (usually shareholders and officers)	
Court	– Copy form 2.23B – Copy proposals considered at meeting
Companies House	
Creditors who did not receive notice of meeting/written resolution (because they came to light later)	

Failure to give notice of the decision to the relevant persons renders the administrator liable to a fine (para 53(3) Sch B1 IA 1986; ¶9935).

d. Consequences of creditors' decision

8892 If the creditors **approved** the administrator's proposals, with or without modifications, the administrator must manage the business, affairs and property of the company in accordance with them (para 68 Sch B1 IA 1986).

8893 If the administrator has reported to court that the creditors have **rejected** the proposals or proposed revisions, it may (para 55(2) Sch B1 IA 1986):
- direct that the administrator's appointment shall cease to have effect from a given time;
- direct that the hearing should be adjourned (with or without conditions);
- make an appropriate interim order;
- where a winding up petition was suspended pending the administration, make an order on that petition; or
- make any other appropriate order.

As there is no Rule specifying how an administrator should apply for his appointment to cease when the creditors reject his proposals, he should follow an analogous Rule (r 2.114 IR 1986, discussed at ¶9164+) and (*Re M L Design Group Ltd* [2006] All ER (D) 75 (Jan)):
– attach a progress report to the application; and
– notify the creditors of the application and that he will ask the court to determine his remuneration.

Revising the proposals

The proposals can be revised, even after they have been approved by the creditors. If a minor revision is needed, the administrator may make the alterations himself, but a substantial alteration requires the consent of a creditors' meeting, giving **notice** of the proposed revision in Form 2.22B to each creditor (para 54(1) Sch B1 IA 1986; r 2.45(2) IR 1986). The administrator must also notify the shareholders of his intended alterations by (para 54(2), (3) Sch B1 IA 1986; r 2.45(3), (4) IR 1986):
a. sending out the statement of the proposed revisions to each shareholder for whom the administrator has an address, within 5 days of sending it to the creditors; or
b. placing an advertisement in an appropriate newspaper, undertaking to send a copy of the proposed changes to any shareholder who requests one in writing. The advertisement must state the address to which they should write.
At the meeting, the administrator must present his statement of proposed revisions, and the creditors can (para 54(5) Sch B1 IA 1986):
– approve them as they are presented;
– approve them with modifications; or
– reject them.
After the meeting, the administrator must give notice of the decision in the same way as he did regarding the original proposals, using Form 2.23B (r 2.46 IR 1986; ¶8890). Failure to do so renders him liable to a fine (para 54(7) Sch B1 IA 1986; ¶9935).
The administrator must then carry out his functions according to the revised proposals.

8894

> MEMO POINTS 1. If the proposed revision is to end the administration and place the company into a **CVL** and the administrator proposes to nominate a liquidator, the revision must state that the creditors can propose another person as liquidator before approving the alterations (r 2.45(2)(g) IR 1986).
> 2. In exceptional cases where the proposals prove to be impractical and there is **no time** to wait for the creditors to approve revisions (e.g. because the company would suffer loss in the meantime), the court can step in to direct the conduct of the administration until the proposals are revised (*Re Smallman Construction Ltd* [1989] BCLC 420).

B. Dealing with the assets

When the administrator takes up his appointment, he must **identify** the company's assets and **take** custody or **control** of all of the property to which the company appears to be entitled (para 67 Sch B1 IA 1986). Unlike a liquidator, the administrator will usually **carry on** the company's **business** during the administration, particularly where the aim is to rescue it as a going concern.

The administrator will also look for opportunities to **increase** the **company's assets**, and can challenge the same types of transactions as a liquidator can (¶7808+). The administrator may also need to take or defend **legal proceedings** on the company's behalf. However, due to the moratorium on proceedings, other parties can only take proceedings against the company with permission (¶8813+). The concept of "contributories" is not generally applicable in administration, although as part of his management powers, the administrator may make calls on unpaid shares and he can retrieve other money owed by shareholders as part of his general collection of the assets. However, where the legislation or Rules specifically refer to contributories, the term has been used here, since contributories are a distinct category of persons (see ¶7863+).

8904

1. Power to sell

8905 When realising the assets, the administrator must take reasonable care to obtain the best **price** for them in the circumstances, including choosing a good time to sell (*Re Charnley Davies Ltd (No 2)* [1990] BCLC 760). He will not be liable if his judgment of the situation proves to be mistaken, unless it was unreasonable and due to an error that a person in his position should not have made. He can sell the company's assets prior to his proposals being approved by the creditors and without the court's direction, if this is appropriate in the circumstances (*Re Transbus International Ltd* [2004] 2 All ER 911).

8906 No matter how or by whom the administrator was appointed, he is an officer of the court (para 5 Sch B1 IA 1986), and a person who attempts to interfere with the exercise of his duties can be prosecuted for contempt of court. This includes retrieving or asserting a **claim over property** in the administrator's possession or control, and so a person in this position must apply to the court for permission to take such action (*Re Exchange Travel (Holdings) Ltd* [1991] BCLC 728). If the administrator has seized property which does not in fact belong to the company (although he reasonably believed that he could deal with it at the time), he will not be liable for any loss or damage caused by the seizure (unless caused by his negligence), and he has a lien over the property or its proceeds of sale for his expenses in dealing with it (s 234 IA 1986).

> MEMO POINTS The limitation on the administrator's **liability** for **dealing with property** which appears to belong to the company is limited to tangible property (*Welsh Development Agency v Export Finance Co Ltd* [1992] BCLC 148; s 234 IA 1986).

Sales to directors

8907 It is common for administrators to sell some or all of the company's assets to the directors, who may wish to carry on the business as another company or in another form. Transactions entered into by administrators used to constitute "**substantial property transactions**" and so required shareholder approval. However, the new Companies Act extended the exception which was applicable to transactions entered into during compulsory liquidation or CVL to administrations as well, so administrators can now bypass this unnecessary administrative step (s 193 CA 2006).

8908 The administrator may "**hive-down**" the company's business into a new company in order to rescue it and allow it to continue as a going concern. See ¶6415+ for a discussion of the transactional process involved in a hive-down.

2. Assets belonging to third parties

8909 An administrator can deal with certain assets which are in the company's possession or control, but which it does not legally own. Special rules apply in administrations to assets secured under different types of charges and to assets leased under hire-purchase agreements (including retention of title agreements), which are dealt with here. Assets subject to **trusts** and other equitable claims can be dealt with in the same way as in a liquidation (¶7907).

There is no equivalent restriction on goods which are the proceeds of crime, nor can an administrator disclaim onerous property. The effect of administration on the company's contracts is discussed at ¶8827+. The moratorium will affect the ability of third parties to take **enforcement** action against the company and its assets (¶8818+).

Secured with a floating charge

8910 Even if property is subject to a floating charge, an administrator can **take action** in relation to it without the permission of the charge holder or the court, including disposing of it, as if there was no floating charge in place (para 70 Sch B1 IA 1986).

If the property is disposed of, the **floating charge holder** is **protected** because the charge is transferred to the property which replaces the charged property (referred to as "acquired property" in the legislation), giving him the same rights over the new property as he had over the old, including any priority he had over other charge holders. Therefore, if the property is sold, the floating charge holder has rights over the purchase price received by the administrator. However, the floating charge holder loses control over the timing of the disposal and there will be no "acquired property" for him to exercise his rights over if the administrator takes action other than disposing of the property.

The administrator may also be obliged to **ring-fence** a portion of assets subject to a floating charge for the benefit of the unsecured creditors (¶7992+).

Secured with other types of security

If the administrator wishes to **dispose of property** which is subject to another type of security (commonly, mortgages, fixed charges and liens), he must apply to the court for permission (para 71 Sch B1 IA 1986). The administrator must give notice of the hearing to the affected security holder as soon as is reasonably practicable after the court has informed him of its date, time and place (r 2.66(2) IR 1986).

8911

The court will only allow the administrator to make the disposal if it is satisfied that this course of action will further the purpose of the administration (para 71(2) Sch B1 IA 1986). To **protect** security holders, the legislation requires that the proceeds of sale are used to discharge the sums secured, including interest and costs (Re ARV Aviation Ltd [1989] BCLC 664), along with any amount the court requires to be added to the proceeds of sale to make them up to the market value (i.e. the price which would be realised in a sale on the open market to a willing vendor) (para 71(3) Sch B1 IA 1986). If the property disposed of was secured by more than one instrument, the proceeds of sale and any additional sum are to be applied according to the order of priorities between the securities (para 71(4) Sch B1 IA 1986).

If an **order** is **made**, the administrator must (r 2.66(4), (5) IR 1986):
– give a sealed copy of any court order obtained to the affected security holder; and
– file a sealed copy of the order, together with Form 2.28B, at Companies House within 14 days.

Failure to file a copy at Companies House without a reasonable excuse gives rise to a fine (¶9935).

> MEMO POINTS **Liens** over the company's books, papers or other records are not enforceable against the administrator (s 246 IA 1986).

Leased or under hire-purchase agreement

The court can also allow the administrator to **dispose** of goods in the company's possession under a hire-purchase agreement (para 72 Sch B1 IA 1986). This includes goods under conditional sale agreements, chattel leasing agreements and **retention of title** agreements (para 111 Sch B1 IA 1986; ¶9940). Again, the administrator must apply to court for permission, which will only be granted if the proposed disposition will further the purpose of the administration. The administrator must notify the lessor of the date, time and place of the hearing as soon as is reasonably practicable after the court has given him that information (r 2.66(2) IR 1986). Otherwise, goods in the company's possession which are subject to such agreements are not available to the administrator, because they do not belong to the company, unless he pays for them in full.

8912

As **protection** for the lessor under the hire-purchase agreement, the net proceeds of the disposal and any additional sum ordered by the court to make up the proceeds to the market value are to be applied to pay off any sums due under the agreement. Therefore, this protection is limited in that the lessor only receives the hire charges under the agreement, and is not compensated for the residual value of the goods. If an **order** is **made**, the administrator must (r 2.66(4), (5) IR 1986):
– give a sealed copy of any court order obtained to the affected lessor; and

– file a sealed copy of the order, together with Form 2.28B, at Companies House within 14 days.

Failure to file a copy at Companies House without a reasonable excuse gives rise to a fine (¶9935).

C. Distribution

8922 An administrator may make distributions to the company's creditors, although this is not the principal aim of the administration (unlike a liquidation) (para 65(1) Sch B1 IA 1986). The administrator does not need the court's permission to make distributions to **secured** or **preferential** creditors, but he does need consent to distribute to **unsecured** creditors, since it is not a power he will usually have to exercise (para 65(3) Sch B1 IA 1986). In addition to his power to make distributions to creditors, the administrator can **make payments** (¶9011):
– necessary for carrying out his functions; and
– which he considers are likely to assist in the achievement of the purpose of the administration.

This gives the administrator considerable freedom to agree compromises and arrangements with individual creditors as well as distributing dividends to them collectively.

1. Costs and expenses of the administration

8927 The Rules list the costs and expenses of the administration that are **payable out of** the company's assets. Other costs and expenses must be met by the party concerned (r 12.2(2) IR 1986), for example:
– applications to court by a creditor will usually have to be paid for by that creditor, unless the court orders otherwise;
– the costs of realising security must be met out of the proceeds of that security; and
– the costs associated with the ring-fenced fund must be met out of that fund.

The following costs and expenses may be met out of the company's assets in the **order of priority** set out in the table below (r 2.67 IR 1986). It is usual for the administrator to discharge such costs and expenses as they arise but he is not under any obligation to do so, because the company is liable for them rather than the administrator (as he is its agent). Payment may be a matter for his discretion in the circumstances, although it would be unusual for him to refuse to pay.

Rank	Cost/expense
1	Costs properly incurred by administrator in performing his functions
2	The cost of any security provided by administrator for his office
3	Where an administration order was made, the costs of applicant and any other person appearing at hearing Where an administrator was appointed out of court, the costs the appointor incurred in making the appointment, and those of other person(s) in giving notice of the intention to appoint the administrator
4	The amount payable to any person employed or authorised to assist in the preparation of statement of affairs/concurrence
5	Any allowance granted by the court towards the costs of an application asking for a release from the obligation to submit a statement of affairs/concurrence
6	Disbursements necessarily incurred by the administrator during administration, including those of creditors' committee/representatives allowed by the administrator (¶¶9069), except payment of corporation tax in 9 below [1]
7	The remuneration/emoluments of any person employed by the administrator to perform services for the company

Rank	Cost/expense
8	The agreed remuneration of the administrator
9	Corporation tax payable on chargeable gains accruing on realisation of any asset, whether the realisation is effected by an administrator, secured creditor or manager appointed to deal with the security

Note:
1. **Rates** payable to the local council in respect of occupied non-domestic property are payable out of the company's assets as an expense of the administration (*Exeter City Council v Bairstow, Martin and Trident Fashions plc* [2007] EWHC 400 (Ch), where the court also indicated that the same principle would apply to unoccupied properties as well).

When the administrator vacates office, the following costs and expenses can be met out of any property which was in his custody or control immediately before he ceased to hold office (para 99(3), (4) Sch B1 IA 1986):
– **debts or liabilities under contracts** entered into by him or his predecessor; and
– his **remuneration and expenses**, as set out in the order of priority above.

The administrator is automatically granted a charge over such assets in relation to these sums, which ranks above any floating charge to which they are subject.

The debts arising out of contracts entered into by the administrator before he ceased to hold office include those under **employment contracts** adopted by him, although **special rules** apply in such cases (para 99(5) Sch B1 IA 1986). The administrator has 14 days from his appointment within which he can take action in relation to the contracts without actually adopting them. This allows him to assess the situation and decide whether or not to keep the employees on. Where contracts are adopted, the administrator is only liable to pay wages or salaries arising since the adoption; any sums arising before the administration are provable (usually preferential) debts. See ¶8830 for the effect of administration on employees generally.

MEMO POINTS **Wages and salary include** holiday pay, sick and other absence pay, sums payable in lieu of holiday entitlement, contributions to occupational pension schemes and sums which would be treated as earnings for social security purposes (para 99(6) Sch B1 IA 1986). The court has held that protective awards (under s 189 Trade Union and Labour Relations (Consolidation) Act 1992), awards of pay in lieu of notice, and payments in respect of wrongful, unfair dismissal and redundancy are not payable in priority to the administrator's remuneration and expenses (*Re Leeds United Association Football Club Ltd* [2007] EWHC 1761 (Ch); *Re Huddersfield Fine Worsteds Ltd (in administration)*, *Krasner v McMath and other appeals* [2005] 4 All ER 886; *Allders Limited (in administration)* [2005] 2 All ER 122).

It has been held that **legal expenses** incurred by an administrator in relation to his duties fall within the category of liabilities arising out of contracts entered into by the administrator (*Re a Company (No 005174 of 1999)* [2000] 1 BCLC 593; an old administration case which is likely to apply to new administrations as well). The expenses of **unsuccessful litigation** can also be treated as an expense of the administration, since the fact that the action did not succeed does not necessarily indicate that the administrator acted improperly in pursuing it (*Re Ciro Citterio Menswear plc (in administration) (No 4)* [2002] All ER (D) 107 (May)).

Although these expenses must usually be paid in the prescribed order of priority, the court can order that they are paid in a **different order**, as it thinks is fair, if there are insufficient assets to meet all of the liabilities (r 2.67(2), (3) IR 1986).

Tax

Since the administrator acts as the company's agent and is discharged from any liability arising out of his actions as administrator when he vacates office, tax liabilities arising **during** the **administration** usually remain those of the company (para 7 ICAEW TR 799: Tax Aspects of the Insolvency Act 1986).

Tax liabilities are dealt with in different ways, principally:
a. corporation tax: when the company enters administration, a new accounting period is deemed to begin (s 12(7ZA) ICTA 1998). In the final year of administration, the administrator can make an assessment for tax before the end of the company's accounting period at the rate of tax set for the previous financial year; if not fixed or proposed specifically (s 342A ICTA

1988). Revenue and Customs do not regard the company's entry into administration as affecting the beneficial ownership of the company's assets or shares. Therefore, the company's status as part of a group does not alter and it can still benefit from group reliefs. However, the administrator's proposals should be examined as they could result in the beneficial ownership of shares being transferred and the company being separated off from its group;
b. VAT: the administrator must notify the company's local VAT office of his appointment within 21 days (reg 9 SI 1995/2518). The company continues to be a taxable person as long as the administrator carries on the company's business. Otherwise, it ceases to be a taxable person and so goods forming part of its assets are deemed to be supplied in the course of its business immediately before the administration, unless (para 8, Sch 4 VATA 1994):
– the business is transferred as a going concern to another taxable person; or
– VAT on the deemed supply would not exceed £1,000; and
c. other taxes: as the administrator becomes the employer, he must operate PAYE and account for income tax and National Insurance contributions deducted from the company's employees.

2. Secured creditors

8936 Once a secured creditor has satisfied the administrator that his security is valid, he must decide **how** he wants **to deal** with it during the administration. This will depend largely upon the administrator's proposals. For example, if the administrator is carrying on the company's business and does not need to realise the assets secured by the charge, the secured creditor may be happy to leave his security in place and continue to deal with the company as before. On the other hand, the administrator may need to release the security or the creditor may want to have his debt repaid during the administration for financial certainty. **Security** is widely **defined** for the purposes of insolvency legislation, as set out at ¶7977.

The following topics relating to secured creditors, which are dealt with in the context of compulsory liquidation, also apply in administration:
– **interest** on secured debts (¶7989);
– **fixed** charges (¶7990); and
– **floating** charges and the ring-fenced fund (¶7992+).

References to the liquidator, liquidation and winding up should be read as references to the administrator and administration respectively.

Secured creditors' entitlement to vote at **creditors' meetings** is discussed at ¶9086+.

8937 When a company enters administration, a secured creditor has a number of **options** open to him. He can (r 2.83 IR 1986):
– realise his security and prove for the unsecured balance;
– surrender his security and prove for the whole debt as an unsecured creditor;
– value his security and prove for the unsecured balance; or
– rely on his security alone.

If a secured creditor's claim is **partly preferential**, he can apply the proceeds of realising his security to the non-preferential part of his debt and prove for the preferential part (*Re William Hall (Contractors) Ltd* [1967] 2 All ER 1150).

8938 A secured creditor can **surrender** his security voluntarily (see ¶7982 for examples of why he may wish to do so), or he may be deemed to have done so by failing to disclose it in his proof (r 2.91(1) IR 1986). However, the creditor can apply to court to be relieved of this consequence if he can establish that the omission of his security in the proof was accidental or an honest mistake. The court may direct that the proof is amended as a result. The creditor will usually have to bear the costs of such an application.

Submitting a proof

8939 If a secured creditor submits a proof, he should follow the same **procedure** as unsecured creditors, which is discussed at ¶8954+.

Valuing security

8940 A secured creditor will have to place a value on his security if he **wishes to prove** for any unsecured balance and does not want to realise his security himself. This involves a degree of estimation, and so the value he places on it may **change** or later appear to be inaccurate. A revaluation requires the permission of the administrator in most cases, although the creditor must seek permission of the court if (r2.90 IR 1986):
– he was the applicant for the administration order or appointor of the administrator and he placed a value on his security in his application or notice of appointment; or
– he has voted in respect of the unsecured balance of his debt.

If the creditor's revaluation results in a reduction in his claim and occurs after a **dividend** has been **declared**, he must repay the excess dividend he received (r2.102(2) IR 1986). If the revaluation increased his claim, he is entitled to receive a top-up to his dividend out of any money the administrator has set aside for the payment of further dividends, in priority to the new dividends being paid to other creditors (r2.102(3) IR 1986). Once the dividend has been declared, however, he is not entitled to disturb it (i.e. he cannot ask the administrator to recalculate his declared dividend before it is paid, as this will affect the other creditors' dividends).

8941 If the **administrator** is **not satisfied** with the value placed on a security, he can require the secured property to be offered for sale, either on agreed terms or as determined by the court (r2.93 IR 1986). If the sale is by auction, the administrator and the creditor can both appear and bid.

8942 If the **creditor breaches** any of the rules relating to valuation or revaluation of securities, the administrator can apply to court to have him wholly or partially disqualified from dividends (r2.103 IR 1986).

Realisation of security

8943 If the **administrator** intends to **realise** the security, he will notify the creditor at least 28 days in advance (r2.92 IR 1986). The creditor has 21 days from the notice (or longer, if the administrator allows) within which to revalue his security so that it will be redeemed at the new value. The creditor can require the administrator to state whether or not he intends to redeem the security, by serving him with notice to that effect. The administrator has 3 months from that notice to exercise his power to redeem it, or to decide not to do so. If the administrator will not redeem the security, the secured creditor can then realise it himself.

If a secured **creditor** submits a proof for the unsecured balance of his debt and subsequently **realises** his security, he must amend his proof, substituting the value he placed on his security with the net amount realised and amending the unsecured balance if necessary (r2.94 IR 1986). This is treated as an amended valuation.

3. Other creditors

8948 Creditors **claim** in the administration **by** "proving" for their debts; the document by which they do so is called a "proof" (r2.72(2) IR 1986). Most debts will be provable, although special rules apply to some types of debt.

a. Proving debts

8949 The vast majority of claims against a company in administration are **provable** as debts (r12.3 IR 1986). The minor exceptions are:
a. claims which are postponed by insolvency or other legislation;
b. obligations arising under a confiscation order (under the Drug Trafficking Offences Act 1986, the Criminal Justice Act 1988 or the Proceeds of Crime Act 2002);

c. restitution claims arising out of a breach of FSMA 2000, by which the person who committed the breach profited, but only where loss has not been suffered by another as a result (i.e. a claim under s 382(1)(a) FSMA 2000 but not s 382(1)(b) FSMA 2000); and
d. specific debts which are not provable under legislation or common law. This includes debts arising out of illegal transactions or gaming contracts.

"Debts" are widely defined by insolvency legislation (see ¶8005).

The Rules do not specifically state that the debts which can be proved are determined **at the time** the company went into administration, but this is likely to be the case as the situation is comparable to proving debts in a liquidation. Debts **payable in the future** can be proved for in the administration, but will be reduced according to a set formula when calculating the dividend, which is discussed at ¶8059 (r 2.89 IR 1986).

8950 The administrator can estimate the value of a debt which is for an **unascertained amount**, for example because it is contingent on an event occurring, and allow the creditor to prove for the estimated amount (r 2.81 IR 1986). If the circumstances change, he can subsequently revise his estimate and inform the relevant creditor that he has done so.

Specific types of debt

8951 There are specific **issues to consider** when proving for the following types of debt, which are dealt with in the context of compulsory liquidation. Any points specific to administration can be found in the memo points to the relevant paragraphs, otherwise the issues are the same as in a liquidation.

Type of debt	¶¶
Unliquidated claims	¶8008
Judgment debts	¶8009
Expiry of limitation period [1]	¶8010
Money owed to shareholders	¶8011
Employees' claims	¶8012
Landlords' claims and other periodical payments	¶8013+
Insured liabilities	¶8016
Professional fees	¶8017
Assigned debts	¶8018
Property held by company on trust	¶8019
Debts in foreign currencies	¶8020
Multiple claimants	¶8024+

Note:
1. For the effect of administration on **limitation periods** which are **still running** when the company goes into administration, see ¶8820.

Interest

8952 Interest which has accrued on a provable debt **before** the **company entered administration** is provable, provided the interest is payable in one of the situations described in the table (r 2.88 IR 1986).

Interest payable due to	Rate of interest
Previous agreement	As agreed
Debt arose due to written instrument and became due at a specified time – interest can be claimed from that time	Statutory rate on date company entered administration (s 17 Judgments Act 1838)
Other situations: only if written demand for payment was made, giving notice that interest would be payable from demand to date of payment	

MEMO POINTS If the company was in **liquidation immediately before the administration**, interest can only be claimed until the company went into liquidation (r 2.88(1) IR 1986).

Although interest accruing **after** the **company entered administration** cannot be included in the proof, it should still be calculated, because any surplus in the company's assets after the proved debts have been paid will be used to pay interest accruing since the company entered administration (r 2.88(7) IR 1986). Even if the debts on which this interest accrues are paid at different levels of priority, the interest itself ranks equally (r 2.88(8) IR 1986). Therefore, if there is not enough of a surplus to pay such interest in full, each creditor will receive a ratable proportion of the sum due to him. The **rate** of interest which will be applied is the highest of (r 2.88(9) IR 1986):
– the statutory rate; and
– the rate which would apply if the company were not in administration.

Procedure for proving debts

A creditor must prove his debt in writing, referred to as his "proof of debt" or "**proof**" (r 2.72 IR 1986).

The proof must be **signed by** or on behalf of the creditor and contain the following **information**:
a. the creditor's name and address;
b. the total amount of his claim on the date on which the company went into administration, minus any payments to him since then, and any sums which can be set off against the debt (¶8976+);
c. whether the claim includes outstanding uncapitalised interest and/or VAT;
d. whether the claim is wholly or partly preferential;
e. details of how and when the debt arose;
f. details of any security held by the creditor, the date on which it was created and the creditor's estimated value of it (see ¶7985+);
g. details of any retention of title claim over any goods to which the debt refers;
h. details of any document(s) which can be used as evidence of the debt. These do not have to be attached at this stage, although the administrator can ask for them to be produced at a later date; and
i. if the proof is signed on behalf of the creditor, the name, address and authority of the signatory.

MEMO POINTS 1. A debt owed on a **negotiable instrument** such as a **cheque**, bill of exchange or promissory note can only be the subject of a proof if the instrument itself, or a certified copy of it, is produced to the administrator (r 2.82 IR 1986). The administrator may waive this requirement.
2. If the company would have been granted a **discount** on any money owed to a creditor, e.g. a trade discount, the proof must reflect that deduction (r 2.84 IR 1986). This does not apply to discounts for early or cash settlement of the debt.

Unlike in a liquidation, there is no specific **form** by which a creditor must prove his debt, although the administrator can require him to verify his proof by affidavit using Form 2.29B, whether or not a written proof has already been lodged (r 2.73 IR 1986).

MEMO POINTS The Insolvency Service has proposed that **affidavits** are replaced by witness statements (see ¶8737). This change is likely to be implemented on 1 October 2008.

Generally, creditors bear the **cost** of proving their debts, although the court can order otherwise (r 2.74 IR 1986). Any costs incurred by the administrator in estimating the quantum of claims are payable as an expense of the administration.

Consideration of proofs

The administrator must examine all proofs submitted to him and, in relation to each one, he can (r 2.77 IR 1986):
– **admit** all of it for a dividend;
– admit part of it for a dividend; or
– **reject** all of it.

He will take similar factors into account when **assessing** the proofs as a liquidator does in a compulsory liquidation (¶8036+).

If the administrator rejects all or part of a proof, he must give his **reasons** for doing so to the creditor in writing as soon as is reasonably practicable.

Alteration of proofs

8958 A proof can be **withdrawn** or the amount of it **varied** at any time by agreement between the creditor and administrator (r 2.79 IR 1986).

8959 If the administrator subsequently thinks that a proof was **wrongly admitted or** that its value **should be reduced**, he (or any creditor, if the administrator will not do so) can apply to the court for the appropriate order (r 2.80 IR 1986). Notice of the date, time and place of the hearing, once fixed by the court, must be given to the affected creditor (and to the administrator, if he is not the applicant) by the applicant. The applicant needs to show, on the balance of probabilities, that the proof should be cancelled or reduced (*Re Globe Legal Services Ltd* [2002] BCC 858; a liquidation case, which is likely to apply to administration given the similarity of the relevant rules).

Challenging the administrator's decision

8960 If the **creditor** disagrees with the administrator's decision in dealing with his proof, he can **appeal** to the court to have the decision reversed or varied within 21 days of receiving the administrator's statement informing him that all or part of his claim has been rejected (r 2.78(1) IR 1986). Any other creditor may also appeal to the court following a decision by the administrator to admit or reject any proof within 21 days of being aware of that decision (r 2.78(1) IR 1986). Once an **application** has been made and the date, time and place of the hearing fixed by the court, the applicant must give **notice** of it to:
– the administrator; and
– the affected creditor, if he is not the applicant.

The administrator will then file a copy of the proof and the reasons for his decision at court (r 2.78(3), (4) IR 1986). He will not be personally liable for the **costs** incurred in the application, unless the court orders otherwise (r 2.78(6) IR 1986).

Access to proofs

8961 The proofs can be **inspected** at reasonable times on business days by (r 2.75 IR 1986):
– creditors who have submitted proofs which have not been entirely rejected;
– contributories; and
– persons acting for such creditors and contributories.

Unlike other documents in his records of the administration, the administrator cannot refuse a request to inspect proofs (r 12.13(4) IR 1986). Any person inspecting the proofs may take copies on payment of a fee of 15p per A4 or A5 page and 30p per A3 page (r 13.11 IR 1986). A creditor (and a member state liquidator in the main proceedings) can also **require** the administrator to send him a **list of creditors** and the amounts of their respective debts, if a statement of affairs has not been filed at court or Companies House (r 12.17 IR 1986). The administrator can charge the same fee as for copying inspected proofs. If a person pretends to be entitled to obtain such a list or inspect proofs he is liable to a fine (r 12.18 IR 1986; ¶9935).

b. Distributions

8963 The general rule is that debts **rank** equally between themselves, except for preferential debts which are paid first (r 2.69 IR 1986). The other creditors are to be paid out of the company's assets in full unless there are not enough assets, in which case they will be paid in ratable proportions of their individual debts.

Preferential creditors

Certain debts, known as "preferential debts", are to be **paid** out of the company's assets **in priority** to all other debts. Broadly speaking, preferential debts are those owing to occupational pension schemes and to employees. They are discussed in detail at ¶8044+ in the context of compulsory liquidation; the same provisions apply in an administration.

8965

> MEMO POINTS   The position discussed is as amended by the Enterprise Act 2002. These changes do not apply where:
> – the administration **followed** immediately on from a **liquidation**, the resolution or petition for which predates 15 September 2003; or
> – the administration **followed** immediately on from a **receivership** in which the receiver was appointed before the same date.
> In such cases, the unamended provisions relating to preferential debts apply (SI 2003/2332).

Unsecured creditors

The administrator needs the **permission** of the court to make a distribution to unsecured, non-preferential creditors (para 65(3) Sch B1 IA 1986). Distributions are made by way of **dividends**.

8967

As an **alternative to a dividend**, the administrator can distribute the company's unrealised assets to the creditors, if (r 2.71 IR 1986):
– the assets in question cannot readily or advantageously be sold, due to their nature or other circumstances; and
– he has the permission of the creditors' committee, or the creditors if there is no committee.

If the **dividend** is intended to be a **sole or final** one, the administrator must ensure that the following liabilities have been met by the last date for proving (r 2.68(3) IR 1986):
– any outstanding expenses of an immediately preceding liquidation or provisional liquidation; and
– any debts, liabilities, remuneration or expenses incurred by a current or former administrator capable of being charged on the company's assets and paid in priority to floating charge holders (see ¶8927+).

8968

Advance notice of dividend

Once he has received the court's directions, the administrator must give 28 days' **notice** of his **intention to declare** and distribute a dividend to the creditors (r 2.95(1) IR 1986). The notice must **state** (r 2.95(3) IR 1986):
a. whether the distribution is to preferential creditors only, or to preferential and unsecured creditors;
b. how much of any qualifying floating charge has been ring-fenced for the benefit of the unsecured creditors if the administrator intends to make a distribution to them (unless the court has ordered that there is no need to ring-fence a portion of the floating charge, see ¶7995);
c. the date by which proofs must be lodged for creditors to take part in the dividend, which is at least 21 days from the date of the notice (the "**last date for proving**");
d. that it is the administrator's intention to make a distribution within 2 months of that date; and
e. whether the proposed dividend is an interim or a final one.

8969

In the case of a notice of intention to distribute a **sole or final dividend**, a creditor who does not prove by the last date for proving loses his chance to participate in the distribution (r 2.68(3) IR 1986).

The notice must be **sent to** all creditors whose addresses are known to the administrator unless he only intends to distribute to preferential creditors, in which case he only has to send it to creditors who he believes have relevant claims (r 2.95(2), (5) IR 1986). As well as sending out this notice, the administrator must **advertise** the need for creditors to prove their debts, and he may not declare a dividend until he has done so (r 2.95(3) IR 1986). If he just intends to make a distribution to preferential creditors, he only needs to advertise if he thinks it is required (r2.95(5) IR 1986).

> MEMO POINTS A copy of the notice must also be sent to a **member state liquidator**, if applicable (r2.95(2) IR 1986).

Dealing with proofs

8970 Within 7 days of the last date for proving, the administrator must deal with the proofs submitted to him, either by **admitting** or **rejecting** them, or by **making provision** in respect of them as he thinks fit (e.g. where he needs to view further evidence before coming to a firm conclusion, he can place an estimated value on the proof for the purpose of the dividend in question and examine the debt further at a later date) (r2.96(1) IR 1986). Usually, the administrator will deal with proofs as and when they are submitted during the course of the administration and so it will only be the ones submitted at this later stage with which he will have to deal. He is not obliged to deal with any received after the last date for proving, although he may do so at his discretion (r2.96 IR 1986).

> MEMO POINTS Payment can only be made once in respect of each debt (i.e. up to the amount of the debt, although smaller interim dividends can be paid), mirroring the common law **rule against double proof** which applies in liquidation (¶8024; r2.96(3) IR 1986).
> If a **creditor and** a **member state liquidator** have both submitted proofs in relation to the same debt, a dividend can only be paid to the creditor, unless he has assigned the debt (r2.96(4) IR 1986).

8971 In **calculating the dividend**, the administrator must make provision for the following items (r2.70(1) IR 1986):
– debts which he considers may not have been proved because the creditors in question have not had time to establish their proofs because of where they live;
– debts which are based on claims which have not yet been determined; and
– disputed proofs and claims.

Notice of dividend

8972 Within 2 months of the last date for proving, the administrator must **declare the dividend** to one or more classes of creditor to whom he gave notice (r2.97 IR 1986). If an appeal to court regarding the administrator's decision is pending, he can only make the declaration with the court's permission.

The administrator must give **notice** of the declaration to all creditors who have proved their debts, as well as to any member state liquidator appointed in relation to the company, **stating** (r2.98 IR 1986):
a. the amount he has raised from the sale of assets, detailing how much is attributable to which asset as far as practicable;
b. what payments he has made in his capacity as administrator;
c. if a distribution is being made to the unsecured creditors, the value of any ring-fenced fund of assets subject to any qualifying floating charge, unless the court has ordered that there is no need to ring-fence the required sum (see ¶7995);
d. what provisions have been made for unsettled claims and what funds have been retained for specific purposes, if any;
e. the total amount of the dividend, and the rate at which it will be paid;
f. how the administrator will distribute the dividend; and
g. whether, and if so when, any further dividend is expected.

Payment

8973 Dividend payments can be made at the same **time** as the notice declaring it, **by** post or some other method agreed with the creditor (r2.99 IR 1986).

A creditor entitled to a dividend can **assign** it, or instruct the administrator to pay it directly, to another person (r2.104 IR 1986). The creditor must give the administrator written notice of the name and address of the person to whom he wishes the payment to be made.

> MEMO POINTS If a **proof** is **increased** after a dividend has been paid, the creditor is entitled to be paid the additional balance that he would have received on the original dividend out of the

money available for any subsequent dividend before that next dividend is paid (r 2.101 IR 1986). If his proof is **decreased**, withdrawn or cancelled after a dividend has been paid, the creditor must repay any overpayment of dividends that he has received.

Similarly, if a **creditor proves** his debt **too late** to participate in the dividend, he is entitled (if his proof is admitted by the administrator) to be paid the dividend he would have received out of the money available for any subsequent dividend before that dividend is paid, unless he has missed the deadline for a sole or final dividend (r 2.70(2) IR 1986).

If the administrator **refuses to pay** a dividend, the court may order him to do so, as well as ordering him to pay interest on it together with the costs of the court proceedings personally where the court deems it appropriate (r 2.70(3) IR 1986). **8974**

Deferred creditors

Certain debts are **paid after** distributions have been made to preferential and unsecured creditors. Such deferred debts are either prescribed by statute or the Rules, or are agreed to be deferred between the parties. They are discussed at ¶8066 in the context of compulsory liquidation. **8975**

Creditors who are also debtors of the company

If pre-administration transactions and other "**mutual dealings**" between a creditor who has submitted a proof and the company resulted in debts owing and credits standing to each party when the company goes into administration, the sums due from one party can be **set off** against the sums due from the other (r 2.85 IR 1986). Only the balance, if any, of the account between the creditor and the company is provable in the administration; if the balance of the account is in the company's favour, the "creditor" must contribute this sum to the company's assets. Set-off **occurs automatically** for the purpose of calculating dividends. **8976**

A sum owing to or from the company **can be set off** whether it is:
– payable currently or in the future;
– due as a result of a certain or contingent obligation; or
– for a fixed or liquidated amount, or capable of being ascertained by fixed rules or opinion.

EXAMPLE   A Ltd, a drinks manufacturer, is in administration. Before the administrator was appointed, A Ltd traded with sole trader B, who provided glass bottles to A Ltd and also recycled used and broken glass bottles from A Ltd. When the administrator was appointed, A Ltd owed £1,200 to B for the supply of glass bottles. However, B owed £300 to A Ltd for bottles supplied to him for recycling by A Ltd. B's debt to A Ltd is automatically set off against A Ltd's debt to B, leaving B with a balance of £900 for which he can prove in the administration.

MEMO POINTS   The Rules relating to set off were **revised by** provisions which came **into force on** 1 April 2005. The position here applies to administrations entered into on or after this date (SI 2005/527). Readers interested in earlier administrations should refer to the unamended Rule (i.e. r 2.85 IR 1986).

Sums due to or from the company **cannot be set off** if (r 2.85(2) IR 1986): **8977**
a. the obligation giving rise to the debt arose after the company entered administration;
b. the other party had notice when the obligation arose that:
– an administration application was pending; or
– notice of intention to appoint an administrator had been given;
c. the obligation arose during an immediately preceding liquidation;
d. the obligation arose prior to an immediately preceding liquidation when the other party had notice that:
– a creditors' meeting had been called to resolve to wind the company up; or
– a winding up petition against the company was pending; or
e. the creditor acquired the debt by entering into an assignment during the administration or a preceding liquidation, or before the administration or preceding liquidation when he had notice of the administration application, notice of intention to appoint an administrator, a preceding winding up petition or a creditors' meeting to resolve to wind up the company.

SECTION 3

Persons involved in the administration

8992 Once the company enters administration, the **administrator** takes over the management of its business and affairs in order to achieve the purpose of the administration. The administrator's role is defined by extensive powers to deal with the company and its assets, and is kept in check by the duties to which he must adhere. He is supervised by the **court**, as well as by the **creditors** through their **meetings** and **committee**. In some cases, the **FSA** may also be involved in the conduct of the administration.

A. Administrator

8995 An administrator is a person **appointed to** manage the company's affairs, business and property (para 1(1) Sch B1 IA 1986). He must be a **qualified** insolvency practitioner, able to act in relation to the company (para 6 Sch B1 IA 1986; ¶7422+).

8996 Even if there is a **defect in** the administrator's **appointment or qualification**, his acts are still valid (para 104 Sch B1 IA 1986). This is likely only to apply to errors or irregularities, rather than enabling the requirements of appointment to be avoided altogether (*Morris v Kanssen* [1946] 1 All ER 586, a case on a similar provision relating to the appointment of directors).

1. Appointment

8998 Three **methods** can be used to appoint an administrator when a company **first** enters administration:
– by order of the court on application by the company, its board or its creditors (among others; see ¶8721+);
– out of court by the company or its board (¶8764+); and
– out of court by the holder of a qualifying floating charge (¶8777+).

Each method is dealt with in detail where indicated as part of the discussion on how the company enters into administration.

For where an administrator is appointed as a **replacement** for one who retires, is removed or whose office is terminated, see ¶9044+.

Duration

8999 The administrator's **appointment expires** on its first anniversary, unless it is extended beyond that time (para 76(1) Sch B1 IA 1986). It is not usual for the administration to expire, since the administrator will apply for its termination if it is concluded sooner (¶9127+), and he will request an extension of his appointment if he needs more time.

9000 The **court** can grant an **extension** for a specific period, provided the administrator is still in office, whether or not his appointment has already been extended (para 77(1)(a) Sch B1 IA 1986). When he applies for an extension, he must submit a progress report to the court which covers the period elapsed since the last progress report was submitted, or the commencement of the administration if none has been filed (r 2.112(1) IR 1986). If an order is granted, the administrator must inform Companies House as soon as is reasonably practicable (para 77(2) Sch B1 IA 1986). Failure to do so gives rise to a fine (para 77(3) Sch B1 IA 1986; ¶9935).

The administrator may also obtain an extension to his time in office of up to 6 months with the consent of the **creditors** (para 78(1), (2) Sch B1 IA 1986). When he seeks their consent, he must send out a progress report which covers the period since his last report, or since the beginning of the administration if it is the first one (r 2.112(2) IR 1986). The creditors' consent can be obtained individually in writing or collectively at a creditors' meeting (para 78(3) Sch B1 IA 1986). As the table below demonstrates, the creditors that are required to consent depends upon whether or not the administrator's proposals stated that there were insufficient assets to distribute to the unsecured creditors other than out of any ring-fenced fund.

	No statement in proposals	Statement in proposals
Consent required	– Each secured creditor; and – if there are unsecured debts, consent of creditors whose debts total over 50% of unsecured debts, not including any creditor who does not respond	• Each secured creditor; or • if administrator thinks he can only distribute to preferential creditors: – each secured creditor; and – preferential creditors whose debts total over 50% of preferential debts, not including any creditor who does not respond

Where the relevant creditors consent to an extension, the administrator must **notify** the court and Companies House using Form 2.31B; **failure** to do so gives rise to a fine (para 78(6) Sch B1 IA 1986; r 2.112(3) IR 1986; ¶9935).

An **extension cannot be obtained** in this way:
– on more than one occasion;
– after the court has granted an extension; or
– after the administrator's term of office has expired.

Number of administrators

9001 It is particularly useful in large and complex administrations to appoint more than one administrator, referred to as "**joint administrators**" (para 100 Sch B1 IA 1986). If joint administrators are appointed, their appointment must state how the functions of the office are to be divided between the individuals, specifying which must be exercised jointly and which by any or all of them (para 100(2) Sch B1 IA 1986).

Usually, joint administrators are **empowered to** exercise all of the functions of their office both individually and jointly and are therefore jointly and severally **responsible** for the conduct of the whole administration; if an administrator commits an offence by failing to carry out a duty, each joint administrator is taken as doing so and they can be prosecuted individually (para 101(4) Sch B1 IA 1986). However, if the terms of the appointment ascribe particular functions to one or more administrators, only he/they are responsible (and liable) for those functions.

Where joint administrators have been appointed, **references** to "the administrator" are to the joint administrators (paras 101, 102 Sch B1 IA 1986). For example, the publicity requirements (¶9021) require all joint administrators to be named.

9002 Even where the company is already in administration, **another administrator** can be appointed to act jointly (i.e. together with) or concurrently (i.e. along side) with the existing administrator(s) (para 103(1) Sch B1 IA 1986). As set out in the table below, the entitlement to make such an additional appointment depends on how the company went into administration in the first place. However, the consent of the current administrator(s) must be obtained in all cases.

Entry into administration	Additional appointment made by
Administration order	Court order on application by: – company; – board; – one/more creditors; – magistrates' court officer under enforcement powers; – a combination of the above; or – administrator
Appointment by qualifying floating charge holder	– Qualifying floating charge holder who made original appointment; or – court order, on application by administrator

Entry into administration	Additional appointment made by
Appointment by company	• Court order, on application by administrator; or • company, with consent of: – all qualifying floating charge holders; or – if charge holders do not consent, the court
Appointment by board	• Court order, on application by administrator; or • board, with consent of: – all qualifying floating charge holders; or – if charge holders do not consent, the court

Where an additional administrator is appointed, the same provisions regarding **notice** and **advertisement** of the appointment apply as to the original appointment (r 2.127 IR 1986; ¶8797). However, the new administrator (whether he is a replacement or an additional appointment) must notify Companies House of his appointment using Form 2.40B (r 2.128 IR 1986).

Substitution of administrator

9003 An appointed administrator can be substituted for another in the **situations** set out below. If such a substitution is made, the same requirements regarding advertising and giving notice of the appointment apply as for a normal appointment (¶8797), except that:
– any forms must clearly state that the administrator is a replacement (r 2.127 IR 1986); and
– the new administrator must notify Companies House of his appointment using Form 2.40B (r 2.128 IR 1986).

By floating charge holder

9004 If an administrator has been appointed **out of court** by a qualifying floating charge holder, the holder of another qualifying floating charge which ranks in priority can apply to the court for the administrator to be replaced by his own choice (para 96(2) Sch B1 IA 1986). One floating charge takes priority over another if it was created first, or if an agreement has been entered into between the charge holders giving it priority (para 96(3) Sch B1 IA 1986).

9005 If an **administration application** has been made to the court by a person who is not a qualifying floating charge holder, such a charge holder can apply to the court to have his choice of administrator appointed instead of the original applicant's (¶8744).

By creditors

9006 If an administrator has been appointed **out of court** by the company or the board and there is no qualifying floating charge in respect of the company's property, the creditors may replace the administrator by passing a resolution at a meeting (para 97(2) Sch B1 IA 1986). For the appointment to be valid, the proposed administrator's written consent to act must be presented to the meeting before the resolution is made (para 97(3) Sch B1 IA 1986).

2. Powers, duties and liabilities

9010 The **administrator's aim** is to achieve one of the following statutory purposes of the administration (para 3(1) Sch B1 IA 1986):
a. to rescue the company as a going concern;
b. to achieve a better result for the company's creditors as a whole than would be likely if the company went into liquidation instead; or
c. to realise the company's property to distribute to one or more secured or preferential creditors.

He does so by **preparing proposals** for the achievement of the purpose and by **managing** the company's affairs, business and property according to those proposals as approved by the creditors, including any revisions (¶8876+). The court may also give directions to the administrator as to how he should perform his functions.

He must perform his functions as quickly and efficiently as is reasonably practicable in order to achieve the stated purpose of the administration (paras 3, 4 Sch B1 IA 1986). The administrator is under a duty to **act for the benefit of** the creditors as a whole, and not any particular creditor (para 3(2) Sch B1 IA 1986).

Powers: summary table

An administrator has **extensive powers** to do "anything necessary or expedient" to manage the company's affairs, business and property (para 59(1) Sch B1 IA 1986). The legislation sets out some specific powers, listed in the table below, but this does not prevent the administrator's powers extending to any that the directors could exercise before the company went into administration (*Denny v Yeldon* [1995] 1 BCLC 560, in which the administrator could change the company's pension scheme). A person who deals with the administrator in good faith, e.g. buying some of the company's assets or entering into any other contract, does not have to check whether the administrator is acting within his powers (para 59(3) Sch B1 IA 1986).

9011

Power	Reference (IA 1986)
Take possession of and collect the company's property and take proceedings to this end [1]	para 1 Sch 1
Sell or dispose of the company's property by public auction or private contract [2]	para 2 Sch 1
Raise or borrow money and grant security for that borrowing over the company's property	para 3 Sch 1
Appoint a professional person, e.g. solicitor/accountant, to assist in his duties [3]	para 4 Sch 1
Bring or defend any action or other legal proceedings in the company's name and on its behalf [1]	para 5 Sch 1
Refer a question affecting the company to arbitration	para 6 Sch 1
Effect and maintain insurances in respect of the company's business and property	para 7 Sch 1
Use the company's seal	para 8 Sch 1
Do all acts and execute any deed, receipt or other document in the company's name and on its behalf	para 9 Sch 1
Draw, accept, make and endorse any bill of exchange or promissory note in the company's name and on its behalf	para 10 Sch 1
Appoint an agent to carry out business which the administrator is unable to do himself or can be more conveniently carried out by an agent	para 11 Sch 1
Employ and dismiss employees	para 11 Sch 1
Do all things necessary to realise the company's property, including carrying out works	para 12 Sch 1
Make any payment necessary or incidental to performing his functions [4, 5]	para 13 Sch 1
Make any payments he considers likely to assist in achieving the purpose of administration [4, 5]	para 66 Sch B1 [7]
Carry on the company's business	para 14 Sch 1
Establish subsidiaries of the company	para 15 Sch 1
Transfer all or part of the company's business and property to its subsidiaries	para 16 Sch 1
Grant or accept surrender of a lease or tenancy of the company's property. Take a lease or tenancy of any property required or convenient for the company's business	para 17 Sch 1
Make arrangement or compromise on behalf of the company [5]	para 18 Sch 1
Call up any of the company's uncalled share capital	para 19 Sch 1
Rank and claim in bankruptcy or insolvency of any of the company's debtors. Receive dividends in any such proceedings. Accede to trust deeds for creditors of any of the company's debtors	para 20 Sch 1
Present or defend a petition for the company's winding up [6]	para 21 Sch 1
Move the company's registered office	para 22 Sch 1

Power	Reference (IA 1986)
Do all other things incidental to exercise of his powers	para 23 Sch 1
Remove or appoint directors	para 61 Sch B1 [7]
Call shareholders' or creditors' meetings	para 62 Sch B1 [7]
Require a supply of public utilities to the company (provided he personally guarantees payment of bills)	s 233
Obtain a court order for delivery up of the company's property in another's possession (¶8170)	s 234
Examine persons required to co-operate with him in private (¶8172+)	s 236

Note:
1. Since the administrator acts as company's agent, any **proceedings** commenced by him will be in the company's name (para 69 Sch B1 IA 1986).
2. This **power to sell** the company's property includes sales before the administrator's proposals have been approved (*Re Transbus International Ltd* [2004] 2 All ER 911). However, if an administration order precludes him taking such action, which would be unusual, he cannot do so.
3. Administrators are sometimes **solicitors** as well. If such an administrator employs his own firm to act on the company's behalf, any costs incurred must be authorised by a creditors' committee, creditors in a meeting or the court (r 2.106(8) IR 1986).
4. See ¶8936+, ¶8948+ for a discussion of an administrator's ability to make **distributions** to creditors.
5. In *Re TXU UK Ltd (in administration)* ([2003] 2 BCLC 341), the court allowed an administrator to **settle** some **potential claims** against the company because it was satisfied that it was likely to benefit creditors (and shareholders, if company proved to be solvent). The judge held that these powers were designed to enable settlements and payments for proper purposes which would benefit administration as a whole, not just specifically to achieve administration's purpose.
6. A **petition** for the company's winding up can be presented by an administrator in the company's name, and any winding up order will be made on discharge of the administration (¶9141+).
7. These powers are not available to an **administrative receiver**.

EXAMPLE The wide extent of administrators' powers can be illustrated by a case involving administration orders made against several European companies as main proceedings under the EC Insolvency Regulation (*Re Collins & Aikman Europe SA and others* [2006] EWHC 1343 (Ch)). The administrators adopted a co-ordinated approach to the various administrations because the companies' businesses had been closely linked. In order to prevent secondary proceedings being opened in other member states and impeding the progress of the administrations, the administrators gave assurances that creditors would be treated in the same way as under their local law when distributions were made. On the administrators' application for directions, the court held that it could allow the administrators to make the distributions as proposed (para 66 Sch B1 IA 1986). It was satisfied from the outcome of the creditors' meetings that the creditors were supportive of the proposals (even those who would be worse off in terms of distributions under local law than English law), in view of the expense, delay and complication of the alternative of converting the UK administrations into CVLs or CVAs, and of opening secondary proceedings in the other member states.

Control of the administrator

9012 The administrator's conduct is **regulated and monitored** in a number of ways, whether by the duties which are imposed upon him by his office or by specific direction of the court. Where an administrator has acted inappropriately, his actions can be challenged (see ¶9016+). Unlike a liquidator, the administrator does not need the permission of the court or creditors to exercise certain powers. However, the **creditors** still have a say in the conduct of the administration because his proposals must be approved by them (¶8876+). The administrator must keep the creditors informed of the administration's progress at regular intervals and the creditors can require him to answer questions about it (¶9076+). In this way, the creditors in an administration can exercise a degree of supervision over the administrator.

General duties

9013 The office of administrator encompasses a number of different **roles**:

a. an **officer of the court**, whether the administrator was appointed in or out of court (para 5 Sch B1 IA 1986);

b. the company's **agent** in performing his functions (para 69 Sch B1 IA 1986). The administrator therefore does not incur personal liability, unless he acts outside of those functions, because he contracts and takes action in the name of the company;

c. an "**officer**" **of the company** for some purposes. For example, like directors, administrators cannot cause the company to engage in activities outside its authority (as set out in its memorandum), and they can apply for the same statutory relief from breach of duty that is available to directors (see ¶2505+); and

d. a **fiduciary**, since he deals with the company's property on behalf of the creditors.

Therefore, his actions are also governed by the more general duties which go with these roles. These duties are summarised in the context of liquidators in the table at ¶8225.

Control of the court

The **administrator** is an officer of the court and therefore subject to its control. He can apply to court for **directions** on any matter relating to his functions (para 63 Sch B1 IA 1986). The court may look at whether a particular course of action or commercial transaction is within the administrator's powers; however, it cannot be asked to make commercial decisions for the administrator, as such matters should be within his expertise (*MTI Trading Systems Ltd v Winter* [1998] BCC 591, a case concerning the old administration provisions which is likely to apply to the new regime as well).

9014

In exceptional circumstances, the court has the power to direct the **conduct of** the **administration** where the proposals, as approved, are impracticable and the matter is too urgent to wait for the creditors to approve revised proposals at a meeting, for example where the company will suffer losses if the court does not step in (*Re Smallman Construction Ltd* [1989] BCLC 420).

A **creditor** or **shareholder** of the company can also apply for the court's **intervention**, where the administrator (para 74(1) Sch B1 IA 1986):
– is, was or proposes acting in a way which would unfairly harm the interests of a creditor or shareholder of the company (either individually or collectively); or
– is not performing his functions as quickly or efficiently as he should in the circumstances.

9015

The administrator's actions can be complained of even if they are within his powers, or he is following a court order which allows him to deal with property subject to security or which has been leased under a hire-purchase agreement (para 74(5) Sch B1 IA 1986; see ¶8911, ¶8912).

On hearing such an application, the **court may** make any order it thinks is appropriate, including granting the relief requested, adjourning the hearing (with or without conditions), making an interim order and dismissing the application (para 74(3) Sch B1 IA 1986). Specific orders relating to the administrator's conduct include (para 74(4) Sch B1 IA 1986):
– regulating the exercise of his functions;
– requiring him to do, or to refrain from doing, a particular thing;
– requiring a creditors' meeting to be held for a particular purpose; and
– ending his appointment.

The **court will not**, however, make an order that would interfere with the implementation of any proposals or revised proposals which were approved more than 28 days before the application was made. Nor will it make an order that will impede a CVA or other compromise or arrangement with shareholders or creditors (para 74(6) Sch B1 IA 1986; ¶6500+).

MEMO POINTS From 15 December 2007, the court will not make an order that would interfere with a **cross-border merger** either (see ¶6536/mp; para 74 Sch B1 IA 1986 as amended by reg 65 SI 2007/2974).

Challenging the administrator

Action can be taken against an administrator for misfeasance and/or general claims in contract or tort (for example, negligence). The appropriate claim will depend upon the circumstances of the case, and they may be pleaded in the alternative. In addition, administrators are subject to **regulation** by their professional body and the Insolvency Service, which can take disciplinary action against them in appropriate cases.

9016

In the case of a breach of fiduciary or other duties, or where an administrator has become liable to account to the company in another way, he can be pursued for **misfeasance**. This is discussed at ¶7457+, as it can also be used as a remedy against other insolvency practitioners and directors.

9017

9018 An administrator may be personally liable in **tort** if he brings about the commission of a tort by the company. For example, where administrators allegedly wrongfully retained goods which had been leased to the company under a hire-purchase agreement, they were not discharged from liability when the administration ended because they still had to answer the claim against them in tort (*Barclays Mercantile Business Finance Ltd v Sibec Developments Ltd* [1993] 2 All ER 195). An administrator is exempt under legislation from certain torts involving dealing with property that he reasonably believes belongs to the company (¶8906), but he may be liable for his own actions or omissions caused by his **negligence** when dealing with such property and in other circumstances. However, a creditor cannot usually sue an administrator personally for breach of a duty of care in negligence or breach of fiduciary duty because the administrator owes a duty of care to the creditors as a whole rather than to individuals, except in exceptional circumstances (*Kyrris v Oldham*, *Royle v Oldham* [2004] 1 BCLC 305; a case regarding a limited partnership in administration). A creditor may be able to bring a claim for misfeasance instead.

Since the administrator acts as the company's agent, he is not personally liable under **contracts** he enters into, as he does so on behalf of the company. However, if he enters into a contract personally or acts outside of his authority as an agent he can be held personally liable (*Barclays Mercantile Business Finance Ltd v Sibec Developments Ltd*, above). As for payment of debts and liabilities arising under contracts entered into by the administrator during the administration, including employment contracts adopted by him, see ¶8928+.

Providing information

To creditors

9019 The administrator is required to make regular **reports to** the **creditors** setting out the progress of the administration (see ¶9076+). This ensures that they are fully informed about the administrator's conduct and actions, and can challenge his decisions if necessary. In addition, the creditors' committee can require him to appear before them to answer questions and provide information about the administration (¶9061), and the creditors in general can request that a meeting is held for any reason, giving them another opportunity to question him (¶9081).

> MEMO POINTS   As part of the Insolvency Service's review of secondary legislation (see ¶7364/mp), it is taking the opportunity to make alterations to the primary legislation either where it is necessary to support the new Rules or to remove unnecessary administrative burdens. The Service proposes to remove the requirement for insolvency practitioners to **send information to all known creditors** at various stages in the procedure (proposal 1, "A consultation document on changes to the Insolvency Act 1986 and the Company Directors Disqualification Act 1986 to be made by a Legislative Reform Order for the modernisation and streamlining of insolvency procedures" (September 2007)). Generally speaking, most creditors just want to know how much of their debt will be repaid and have no interest in the general progress of the procedure. This requirement therefore creates a heavy but unnecessary financial and administrative burden. It will be replaced by a system allowing creditors who do wish to be kept up to date to "opt in" to receiving information from the insolvency practitioner. The consultation also proposes to allow information to be exchanged using electronic communication where the recipient agrees, and for insolvency practitioners to make information available via a website.
> At the time of writing, the consultation is still open. If these proposals are accepted, the changes are likely to be implemented from 1 October 2008.

9020 The administrator is entitled to **refuse** to allow **inspection** of a document forming part of the records of the administration if he considers that (r 12.13 IR 1986):
– it should be treated as confidential; or
– its disclosure would be detrimental to the creditors' or shareholders' interests.

A person seeking to inspect such a document may apply to the court to have the administrator's decision overruled. On any such application, the court may impose conditions on any inspection it allows.

> MEMO POINTS   The administrator cannot refuse access to **proofs or proxies** (r 12.13(4) IR 1986).

To others

The administrator must ensure that those dealing with the company are well aware of the fact that the company is in administration. A statement must be included on every **business document** issued by or on behalf of the company that its affairs, business and property are being managed by the administrator, giving his name (para 45 Sch B1 IA 1986). Business documents include invoices, orders for goods or services and business letters. If the administrator, an officer of the company or the company itself **fail** to comply with, or permit a contravention of, this requirement, they are liable to a fine (¶9935).

9021

From January 2007, companies in liquidation have been required to state the fact that it is in liquidation on **all documents** issued by the company **including** those issued in electronic form, websites and order forms (EC Directive 2003/58). At the time of writing, the government has proposed to apply similar provisions to the administration process. Meanwhile, the Insolvency Service has recommended that, as a matter of good practice, insolvency practitioners should follow the new provisions in administration procedures (*Dear IP* March 2007, Issue No 31). As a result, a statement that the company's affairs, business and property are being managed by the administrator, including his name, should be included on any business documents issued in hard copy, electronic or other form, as well as on all of the company's websites.

At the **end** of the **administration**, if the company is then **wound up** by the court, the administrator must provide the liquidator (and official receiver, if he so requests) with such information about the company's promotion, formation, business, dealings, affairs or property as required, as well as attending the liquidator or official receiver in person as required (s 235 IA 1986).

9022

---

3. Remuneration

An administrator's remuneration is **payable** out of the company's assets, and therefore the creditors are given the opportunity to decide how it is calculated and how much he should be paid. If they do not make this decision, it falls to the court to ensure that the company is fairly treated.

9026

> MEMO POINTS The Rules relating to administrators' remuneration do not specifically include fees incurred for **pre-appointment** services, for example in investigating the company's affairs in anticipation of taking on a case (rr 2.67, 2.106 IR 1986). Although this prevents insolvency practitioners from incurring unnecessary costs at an early stage, legitimate preparatory work will need to be carried out. (It should be noted that expenses incurred in attending an administration application hearing or making an appointment out of court are recoverable as an expense of the administration, but these expenses will not necessarily cover all of the preparatory work done by the administrator (¶8927, ranking at 3 in the table).) Therefore, it may be necessary for the creditors and/or the company to agree to pay such fees separately. It is anticipated that the Rules will be amended to allow necessary pre-appointment fees to be recovered, although at the time of writing such changes have not yet been made.

How much?

The administrator's remuneration is fixed using one of **two methods** (r 2.106(2) IR 1986):
- as a percentage of the value of the property with which he has to deal; or
- according to the time spent by him and his staff in conducting the administration.

9027

Usually, the figure is set by the **creditors' committee**, which must decide on the most appropriate method to use, taking into account (r 2.106(4) IR 1986):
- the complexity of the case;
- any exceptional responsibilities which the administrator has to take on;
- the effectiveness of the administrator's conduct of the administration; and
- the value and nature of the property with which he has to deal.

9028

If there is no creditors' committee, or it does not make a decision, the matter can be referred to a **creditors' meeting** to determine by resolution (r 2.106(5) IR 1986).

If neither the creditors' committee nor meeting fixes his remuneration, the administrator can ask the **court** to do so (r2.106(6) IR 1986).

> MEMO POINTS   1. If the **proposals stated** that there are **not enough assets** to make a distribution to unsecured creditors other than out of any ring-fenced portion of assets secured under a floating charge and there is no creditors' committee (or the committee has not fixed the administrator's remuneration), his remuneration can be fixed with the approval of the following persons, having regard to the same factors as the committee (r2.106(5A) IR 1986):
> – each secured creditor; and
> – if the administrator has made or will make a distribution to preferential creditors, preferential creditors with debts amounting to 50% of the company's preferential debts (not including any creditor who does not respond to the request for approval).
> If his remuneration is not or cannot be fixed in this way, the administrator can apply to court.
> 2. If **joint administrators** have been appointed, they must decide between them how the remuneration should be divided up. If a dispute arises, it can be settled by the creditors' committee creditors in a meeting or by the court (r2.106(7) IR 1986).

Altering remuneration

9029 If the administrator considers that the amount fixed by the creditors' committee is **too low** he can ask for it to be increased by the **creditors** (r2.107 IR 1986). If the proposals stated that there are insufficient assets to distribute to the unsecured creditors other than out of any ring-fenced portion of a floating charge, the resolution must be approved by certain creditors as set out above (¶9028/mp). Unless the administrator's remuneration was fixed by the court in the first place, he can challenge the amount by asking the **court** to increase it (r2.108(1) (1A) IR 1986). He must give at least 14 days' notice of his application to the creditors' committee (or the creditors, if there is no committee) to give them the chance to appear or be represented at the hearing (r2.108(2), (3) IR 1986). The court can order that the costs of any creditors or their representatives appearing at the hearing are payable as an expense of the administration (r2.108(4) IR 1986).

Or, if the creditors consider that the remuneration fixed is **too high**, they may apply to the **court** for an order reducing it (r2.109(1) IR 1986). The applicant creditor must have the support of at least 25% in value of the creditors (including himself). If the court lists the application for a hearing, it will give the applicant notice of its date, time and place. The applicant must then give the administrator at least 14 days' notice of the hearing and provide him with a copy of the application, together with any relevant evidence in support (r2.109(3) IR 1986). If the court considers that there are not sufficient grounds for the remuneration to be reduced it can dismiss the application without a hearing (r2.109(2) IR 1986). It will, however, give the applicant at least 7 days' notice, upon receipt of which he can insist on a hearing being held without notice to the administrator so that he can present his case to the court. Even if the application is successful, the applicant's costs are not usually payable as an expense of the administration, although the court may order otherwise (r2.109(5) IR 1986).

Remuneration on termination of office

9030 Once an administrator has ceased to hold office, his remuneration and expenses are **payable out of** the company's property of which he had custody or control when he left office (para 99 Sch B1 IA 1986). He has a charge on that property for any sums owed to him, which ranks in priority to any floating charges already created, but below the charge relating to the debts and liabilities incurred on contracts entered into by him during the administration. This provision is discussed further at ¶8928.

> MEMO POINTS   A case under the previous administration provisions held that the **limitation period** for claims relating to the administrator's charge over company property for his remuneration and expenses was 12 years (*Re Maxwell Fleet and Facilities Management Ltd (in administration)* [2000] 1 All ER 464). It is likely that this will apply to the current provisions as well.

4. Termination

9035 Where the administrator resigns, is removed or ceases to be an insolvency practitioner, he is under a **duty to deliver** to his replacement (r 2.129 IR 1986):
– the company's assets, after deducting his properly incurred expenses and distributions;
– the records of the administration, including correspondence, proofs and other relevant papers; and
– the company's books, papers and other records.
If he **fails** to do so, he is liable to a fine (¶9935).

Resignation

9036 An administrator can only resign in certain **circumstances** (para 87(1) Sch B1 IA 1986; r 2.119 IR 1986):
– due to ill health;
– because he intends to cease practising as an insolvency practitioner;
– where he is not able to continue in his duties because of a conflict of interest or a change in his personal circumstances; or
– for another reason, with the court's permission.

Before resigning, he must give at least 7 days' **notice** of his intention to resign to the following persons, depending on the circumstances (r 2.120 IR 1986):
a. any continuing administrator, where there has been a joint appointment;
b. any creditors' committee;
c. where there is no continuing administrator and no creditors' committee, the company and its creditors;
d. if the administrator was appointed out of court:
– the appointor; and
– the holders of all qualifying floating charges (however, where the appointment was made by a qualifying floating charge holder, just those ranking in priority to him need to be notified); and
e. any member state liquidator.
The notice must be in **Form** 2.37B.

9037 The **resignation** itself must be in **Form** 2.38B (r 2.121(1) IR 1986). The **method** of the actual resignation depends upon how he was appointed.

Method of appointment	Method of resignation	Reference
By court order	– Notice of resignation filed at court; – Copy to Companies House; and – Copy to all persons to whom notice of intention to resign was sent, up to 5 business days after filed at court	para 87(2) Sch B1 IA 1986; r 2.121 IR 1986
Out of court by company, board or qualifying floating charge holder	• Notice of resignation to appointor; and • Up to 5 business days later: – copy filed at court; – copy to Companies House; and – copy to all persons to whom notice of intention to resign was sent	

Removal

9038 The administrator can be removed from office at any time **by** the court (para 88 Sch B1 IA 1986). There are no defined **grounds** upon which such an application can be made; however, the court is likely to consider similar factors as when it deals with applications to remove liquidators (¶8258+).

There is no prescribed list of suitable **applicants** either, although the court will consider applications from those with an interest in the administration, principally:
– the creditors;
– the company;
– the board;

- any qualifying floating charge holders; and
- any others as appropriate in the circumstances, for example the FSA.

9039 The **application** must state the grounds on which the applicant wishes the administrator to be removed (r 2.122 IR 1986). It must be **served** at least 5 business days before the hearing on:
- the administrator;
- the person who applied for the administration order or who appointed the administrator out of court;
- the company;
- all creditors (including floating charge holders);
- any creditors' committee; and
- any joint administrator.

If an **order to remove** the administrator is made, the applicant must send a copy to:
- the administrator, as soon as is reasonably practicable;
- all persons to whom notice of the application was given, within 5 business days of the order being made;
- Companies House, using Form 2.39B, also within 5 business days of the order being made.

Automatic termination of office

9040 The administrator's office is automatically terminated when he **ceases to be qualified** as an insolvency practitioner (para 89 Sch B1 IA 1986). If this occurs, he must **notify**:
- the court, if he was appointed by an administration order; or
- his appointor, if he was appointed out of court; and
- in either case, Companies House, using Form 2.39B (r 2.123 IR 1986).

If he **fails to notify** the court or his appointor without a reasonable excuse, he is liable to a fine (¶9935).

9041 The office is also automatically terminated if the administrator **dies** (r 2.124 IR 1986). In such a case, the court must be **notified** of the death by:
- another partner in the administrator's firm who is a qualified insolvency practitioner or a member of a recognised body for the authorisation of insolvency practitioners;
- any other person who can produce the death certificate, or a copy of it; or
- if neither of the above, the administrator's personal representatives.

Whoever gives notice to the court must also inform Companies House using Form 2.39B.

Discharge from liability

9042 Unlike a liquidator, an administrator does not have to apply to be discharged from any liability accruing during his office (para 98 Sch B1 IA 1986). The discharge will **take effect** where the administrator:
a. was appointed out of court (by a qualifying floating charge holder, the company or the board), at a time appointed by the creditors' committee or the creditors in a meeting where there is no committee, or another time specified by the court;
b. was appointed under an administration order, at a time specified by the court; or
c. dies, when the notice of his death has been filed at court, or another time specified by the court.

The discharge may be **delayed** or made subject to **conditions** if there is a claim against the administrator.

> EXAMPLE
> 1. An administrator's release was postponed for 2 months to allow the official receiver and creditors to investigate a claim against him (Re Sheridan Securities Ltd (1988) 4 BCC 200).
> 2. An administrator will not be released while there is an outstanding triable claim against him (Barclays Mercantile Business Finance Ltd v Sibec Developments Ltd [1993] 2 All ER 195).
> 3. The court granted an administrator his release, excepting a specific claim against him and any other claim made within 3 months (Re Powerstore (Trading) Ltd, Re Homepower Stores Ltd [1998] 1 All ER 121).
> These cases were decided under the old administration provisions, but are likely to apply to new administrations as well. Under the old provisions, the discharge from liability was referred to as the release.

Even where an administrator has been fully discharged from liability under this provision, action can still be taken against him for **misfeasance**, see ¶7457+.

> MEMO POINTS 1. If the administrator was **appointed out of court and** the proposals stated that there was **insufficient property** in the company for him to make distributions to unsecured creditors except out of any ring-fenced fund secured by a floating charge, a resolution of the creditors' committee or creditors' meeting to discharge the administrator can only be passed with the consent of (para 98(3) Sch B1 IA 1986):
> – each secured creditor; or
> – if a distribution has been, or may be, made to preferential creditors, each secured creditor and those preferential creditors whose debts total more than 50% of the preferential debts of the company and who responded to the request for approval.
> 2. Any **debts or liabilities under contracts** entered into by the administrator on behalf of the company during his appointment are payable out of the company's property of which he had custody or control when he ceased to hold office, and he has a charge over this property in respect of them (see ¶8928+).

Replacement

The **method** of appointing a replacement administrator where a vacancy arises, whether caused by an administrator's death, resignation, removal or ceasing to be qualified, depends upon how the administration was initiated in the first place.

9044

Method of entry into administration	Method of replacement	Reference (Sch B1 IA 1986)
Court order	Application to the court by: – creditors' committee; – the company; [1] – board; [1] – one or more creditors; or [1] – any remaining joint administrator	para 91(1)
Appointment by qualifying floating charge holder	Floating charge holder may appoint replacement [2]	para 92
Appointment by the company	The company may appoint a replacement, provided it has consent of: [2] – each qualifying floating charge holder; or – the court, if such a charge holder does not consent	para 93
Appointment by the board	The board may appoint a replacement, provided it has consent of: [2] – each qualifying floating charge holder; or – the court, if such a charge holder does not consent	para 94

Note:
1. **Applications** can **only be made** by these applicants if (para 91(2) Sch B1 IA 1986):
– there is no creditors' committee;
– the court is satisfied that any remaining joint administrator is not taking steps to arrange replacement; or
– the court is satisfied that there is another good reason why application should be made.
2. If the **administrator** is **not replaced** by an appropriate person, an application can be made to the court by a creditors' committee, the company, the board, one or more creditors or the remaining administrator for an order appointing a replacement (para 95 Sch B1 IA 1986). The court will hear an application if it is satisfied that an appropriate person is not taking reasonable steps to arrange replacement or there is another good reason for application to be made. Such an application must be accompanied by affidavit evidence of the appropriate person's failure to act or other good reason for the application, as well as Form 2.2B (r 2.125(3) IR 1986). The Insolvency Service has proposed that **affidavits** are replaced by witness statements (see ¶8737). This change is likely to be implemented on 1 October 2008.
Administrators appointed out of court by a qualifying floating charge holder, the company or the board can be **substituted** in certain circumstances (¶9003+).

Application to court

If an application to court is required, it should be **accompanied by** a statement by the proposed administrator of his qualification and willingness to act in Form 2.2B (r 2.125(1) IR 1986).

9045

The application must be **served on** (rr 2.6, 2.125(2) IR 1986):
- the original applicant for the administration order;
- the proposed administrator;
- the company, if the application is made by another person;
- any administrative receiver;
- any person whose winding up petition against the company is pending;
- any supervisor of a voluntary arrangement; and
- any member state liquidator.

The **rules for service** are the same as for an application for an administration order, including (r 2.125(5) IR 1986):
- the method of service (¶8743); and
- the need for proof of service (¶8745).

Qualifying floating charge holders also have the right to substitute their choice of replacement administrator (¶8744).

The same persons can attend or be represented at the **hearing** as at an administration application hearing (¶8746; r 2.125(5) IR 1986). If the court makes an **order** appointing the proposed administrator, it will send two sealed copies in Form 2.4B to the applicant, who must then send one of them to the new administrator as soon as is reasonably practicable (r 2.125(5) IR 1986). The costs of the applicant and any others allowed by the court will usually be payable as an expense of the administration (r 2.125(5) IR 1986).

Administrative requirements in all cases

9046 Where a replacement administrator has been appointed, the administrative requirements as to giving **notice** of **and advertising** the appointment (set out in the table at ¶8797) apply as in an initial appointment, except that any forms must clearly state that the administrator is a replacement (r 2.128 IR 1986). However, the new administrator must notify Companies House of his appointment using Form 2.40B (r 2.128 IR 1986).

9047 The **former administrator** must **provide** his replacement with an itemised list of all of the proofs he received as well as the proofs themselves (r 2.76 IR 1986).

B. Creditors

9057 The creditors of a company in administration are **kept informed about** the progress of the **administration** through progress reports and meetings. A creditors' committee may be established, which functions in largely the same way as a liquidation committee, except that the administrator is not required to refer to it for sanction for use of his powers.

1. Creditors' committee

9060 A creditors' committee can be established during an administration to **assist** the administrator in performing his functions and to act as agreed from time to time (r 2.52(1) IR 1986). The committee also **supervises** the administrator, as it can:
a. require him to provide information about the conduct and progress of the administration (¶9061 below);
b. review the adequacy of his security (r 12.8 IR 1986); and
c. require him to have the costs of any person instructed by him (e.g. solicitors) determined by detailed assessment, if they are payable out of the company's assets (r 7.34(2) IR 1986).

> *MEMO POINTS* A creditors' committee can also be established in an **administrative receivership**. Readers interested in such committees should read "administrator" as "administrative receiver" and "administration" as "administrative receivership" and note the references and minor differences highlighted in the memo points.

In an administrative receivership, the creditors' committee is also established to assist the administrative receiver and act on the creditors' behalf (s 49(1) IA 1986; r 3.18 IR 1986). It can also require the administrative receiver to provide information and review his security (r 12.8 IR 1986).

9061 The committee can give the administrator at least 7 days' written notice that it wishes him to attend a meeting to **provide information** about the exercise of his functions (para 57(3) Sch B1 IA 1986). The **notice** must be signed by a majority of committee members or their representatives at that time (r 2.62(1) IR 1986). The meeting must be fixed for a business day by the committee, but the administrator will decide the time and place (r 2.62 IR 1986). The administrator's duty to provide information is subject to his ability to refuse to disclose confidential information (¶9019+).

MEMO POINTS In an **administrative receivership**, the committee can ask the administrative receiver to provide information (s 49(2) IA 1986), using the same procedure (r 3.28 IR 1986).

Establishment

9062 A creditors' committee can be established **by** a resolution of a creditors' meeting (para 57(1) Sch B1 IA 1986). It must comprise between three and five creditors, as elected at that meeting by the highest number of votes on a single ballot (r 2.50(1) IR 1986; Re Polly Peck International plc [1991] BCC 503). Any creditor can be **elected** to sit on the committee, provided:
– his claim has not been rejected for voting purposes (r 2.50(2) IR 1986); and
– he consents (consent may be given on his behalf by his proxy or corporate representative, unless the terms of the proxy or authority state otherwise) (r 2.51(2) IR 1986).

If a creditor is itself a company, it can be elected to sit on the committee through a representative (r 2.50(3) IR 1986).

Once the committee members have been elected and at least three of them have consented to act, the administrator will issue a **certificate** on Form 2.26B as soon as is reasonably practicable, confirming that it was properly constituted (r 2.51(3), (4) IR 1986). The certificate must be filed at Companies House (r 2.51(5) IR 1986). If any remaining original committee members give their consent subsequently, he will issue an amended certificate in the same form and file it at Companies House.

Any **defects** in the **formalities** of establishing the committee, or in the appointment or qualification of any of its members do not render the acts of the committee invalid (r 2.65 IR 1986).

MEMO POINTS Creditors can establish a committee in an **administrative receivership** (s 49(1) IA 1986). The effect of the Rules is the same as in administration, but the references for the following matters are different:
– number on the committee (r 3.16(1) IR 1986);
– requirement for consent to sit on the committee (r 3.17 IR 1986);
– need to certify the committee's establishment (r 3.17 IR 1986); and
– defects in the formalities of establishment (r 3.30A IR 1986).

Meetings

9063 The administrator must **call** a meeting within 6 weeks of the committee being **first established** (r 2.52(3) IR 1986). **Afterwards**, meetings will be held (r 2.52(2), (3) IR 1986):
– when and where the administrator determines;
– if requested by a member or his representative, within 14 days of the administrator receiving that request; or
– on a specified date, determined at the previous meeting.

The administrator must give at least 7 days' **notice** of the meeting and its date, time and place to each member (or his representative, as appropriate), unless a member has waived the need to receive notice (r 2.52(4) IR 1986). A committee member can waive this right either before or at the meeting.

MEMO POINTS An **administrative receiver** must call the first meeting within 3 months of the committee's establishment (r 3.18(3) IR 1986). Subsequent meetings are held on the same basis as in an administration, except that an administrative receiver must call a meeting within 21 days of receiving a request (r 3.18(2), (3) IR 1986). The relevant references regarding notice are rr 3.18, 3.20 IR 1986.

Business and conduct

9064 The administrator or his nominee (who must either be a qualified insolvency practitioner or an experienced employee of the administrator or his firm) will be the **chairman** of the meeting (r 2.53(1) IR 1986). If the meeting was requested by the committee members to question the administrator, the members can appoint one of their number to chair the meeting instead (r 2.62(2) IR 1986). Each member has one **vote**, and a **resolution** is passed when a numerical majority of the members present or represented have voted in favour (r 2.60 IR 1986). Each resolution must be recorded in writing, whether as part of the minutes, or separately, signed by the chairman and placed in the company's minute book.

> MEMO POINTS These provisions apply in **administrative receivership**, with different references:
> – chairman (r 3.19 IR 1986);
> – alternative chairman (r 3.28(3) IR 1986); and
> – voting (r 3.26 IR 1986).

9065 A committee **member** can enter into a transaction or otherwise **deal with** the **company** while he sits on the committee, provided he deals in good faith and for value (r 2.64 IR 1986). An interested person may apply to the court to have a transaction set aside if it appears to contravene this requirement, and the court can order the member to compensate the company for any loss it has suffered as a result of the transaction.

> MEMO POINTS This also applies in an **administrative receivership** (r 3.30 IR 1986).

Attendance

9066 The meeting may validly proceed to business once a **quorum** of at least two members is present or represented, and notice has been duly given to all necessary members (r 2.54 IR 1986).

> MEMO POINTS This also applies in an **administrative receivership** (r 3.20 IR 1986).

9067 A committee member may be **represented** on the committee **by** a person authorised by him in writing for that purpose (r 2.55 IR 1986). A proxy form, authorisation to be a corporate representative or other written authorisation to represent the member can be presented as a letter of authority. The chairman can require an apparent representative to produce his authorisation at a meeting and can exclude him from the meeting if it appears to be invalid.
A member **cannot be represented by**:
– a person who already represents another member on the same committee;
– a body corporate;
– a disqualified director;
– an undischarged bankrupt; or
– a person subject to a bankruptcy restrictions order (or interim order) or undertaking.

The **representative can** attend and speak at the meeting and vote on behalf of his appointor, but he must act according to the terms of his appointment at all times, not in his own right. If he signs a document on behalf of the member, he must state that he is the representative for that member underneath his signature. The terms of his appointment (e.g. the scope of his powers, the method of his removal, etc) are to be agreed between him and the committee member, and are governed by the usual rules relating to agency contracts.

> MEMO POINTS This also applies in an **administrative receivership** (r 3.21 IR 1986).

Decisions made without a meeting

9068 As an alternative to calling a meeting to consider a resolution, decisions can be made by **written resolution**. A written resolution must be **sent to** all members (or their representatives, if appointed for that purpose), and it must be set out so that the member can indicate his agreement or disagreement with each resolution on the copy sent to him (r 2.61 IR 1986). Members are entitled to **require** the administrator to call **a meeting** to consider the resolution(s) within 7 days of the administrator sending them out. If a meeting is not requested, the resolution is deemed to be **passed** when the administrator has received the approval of a majority of the committee members. Any resolution approved in this way must be placed in the company's minute book, together with a note that the creditors' committee's approval was obtained.

> MEMO POINTS   This also applies in an **administrative receivership** (r3.27 IR 1986).

Committee members' expenses

Any reasonable travel expenses incurred by the committee members or their representatives in attending meetings or otherwise carrying out committee business are to be **met by** the administrator as an expense of the administration (r 2.63 IR 1986). However, this is not the case if a meeting not summoned by the administrator is held within 6 weeks of a previous meeting (i.e. it was requested by a member, or held because the committee set the date at the previous meeting).

9069

> MEMO POINTS   Expenses are also reimbursed in an **administrative receivership**, although the exception applies to meetings not called by the administrative receiver within 3 months of a previous meeting (r3.29 IR 1986).

Changes in membership

Membership of the committee can come to an **end** in the ways set out in the table below.

9070

Method of termination	Procedure	Reference (IR 1986)[1]
Resigned	Member submits notice in writing to administrator	r 2.56
Removed	– 14 days' notice of intention to resolve to remove member at creditors' meeting; and – resolution of creditors' meeting	r 2.58
Automatically terminated	– If a member becomes bankrupt, his trustee in bankruptcy automatically replaces him; – a member enters into composition or arrangement with his creditors; – a member is absent from three consecutive meetings, and is not represented (although committee can resolve that his membership should not terminate at the third meeting); or – a member ceases to be, or is found never to have been, a creditor	r 2.57

Note:
1. In the case of **administrative receiverships**, the references are rr 3.22-3.24 IR 1986.

Vacancies on the committee do **not** need to be **filled** if the administrator and a majority of the remaining members so resolve, as long as the committee still comprises the minimum three members (r 2.59 IR 1986). A vacancy can be **filled** by the administrator, with the approval of a majority of the other members and the consent of the creditor nominated. Any changes in the committee's membership must also be notified to Companies House on Form 2.27B (r 2.51(6) IR 1986).

9071

> MEMO POINTS   This is also the case in **administrative receivership** (rr 3.17(5), 3.25 IR 1986).

2. Creditors in general

The administrator must **report to the creditors** on the **progress of** the **administration** at regular intervals, starting 6 months after the beginning of the administration. Subsequent reports must be made for each 6-month period after that, unless an administrator has vacated office, in which case his report must cover the period from the last report made (or from the start of the administration, if there is no previous report) to when the appointment ceased (r 2.47(3) IR 1986).

9076

Each progress report must include the following **information** (r 2.47(1) IR 1986):
– the name of the court dealing with the administration, including the case reference number;
– the company's name, registered office address and registered number;
– the administrator's name, address, date of appointment and, where applicable, the name and address of his appointor, any previous administrators holding office and, where there are joint administrators, how their functions are divided between them;
– details of any extensions to the administrators' initial period of appointment;
– progress made since the last report or the commencement of the administration, as appropriate, including an abstract receipts and payments account for that period;
– details of any outstanding assets to be realised; and
– any other information relevant to the creditors.

> MEMO POINTS 1. Where an **administrator** has **ceased to act**, the receipts and payments account must include a statement regarding the amount paid to unsecured creditors out of any ring-fenced fund of assets secured by a qualifying floating charge.
> 2. The Insolvency Service has proposed to **reduce the requirements** on administrators to report to creditors, see ¶9019.

9077 The administrator must **send** the progress report **to** the creditors, attached to Form 2.24B, within 1 month of the end of the period, unless the court extends the deadline (r 2.47(4), (5) IR 1986). He must also file copies of the report and Form 2.24B at court and Companies House.

Failure to report on the administration's progress to the creditors, the court and Companies House as required renders the administrator liable to a fine (r 2.47(6) IR 1986; ¶9935).

Consulting creditors without a meeting

9078 Instead of calling a creditors' meeting, the administrator can consult and update creditors **by correspondence** (para 58 Sch B1 IA 1986). Even if the administrator is required to hold a meeting by the creditors or the court, he can satisfy this requirement by writing to them instead. This applies equally to consideration of his statement of **proposals** as to other resolutions.

If the administrator wants to put a **resolution** to the creditors in this way, he must send notice of it to every creditor who would be entitled to be notified of a meeting, using Form 2.25B (r 2.48(1) IR 1986). This will state the closing date (at least 14 days after the date of the notice) on which the administrator must receive the creditors' votes by 12 noon, together with their written statements confirming their entitlement to vote (r 2.48(2), (4) IR 1986). The administrator can disregard any votes received without this statement, as well as those cast by creditors who he believes are not entitled to vote (r 2.48(3) IR 1986). For the resolution to be passed, the administrator must receive at least one valid form by the closing date, otherwise he must call a creditors' meeting to consider the resolution (r 2.48(5), (6) IR 1986). He may call a meeting if his proposals or revised proposals are rejected by the creditors in correspondence (r 2.48(8) IR 1986).

9079 If the **creditors want a meeting** to be held, they must require the administrator to summon one within 5 business days of the written resolution or proposals being sent out to them (r 2.48(7) IR 1986). The request must come from a creditor or group of creditors whose debts amount to at least 10% in value of the total debts of the company.

Calling a meeting

9080 The **administrator** can **summon** creditors' meetings during the administration, following particular rules (para 50 Sch B1 IA 1986). Such meetings must be called to consider the administrator's proposals, or any subsequent revision to them, but he may also call a meeting at any time to consult the creditors on any matter, or update them on the progress of the administration (para 62 Sch B1 IA 1986).

The **court** can also **direct** the administrator to hold a creditors' meeting at any time (para 56 Sch B1 IA 1986).

Creditors' request

The **creditors** can **require** the administrator to summon a meeting, whether to consider his proposals where he has not called a meeting, or for any other reason during the administration (para 56 Sch B1 IA 1986). The requisitioning creditors must be owed at least 10% of the company's total debts. The request must be in **Form** 2.21B, giving the following **information** (r 2.37 IR 1986):
– which creditors agree with the request, along with the amount of their debts;
– if more than the requisitioning creditor's debt is needed to make up the required value, written confirmation by each of the other creditors listed that they concur with the request; and
– the purpose of the proposed meeting.

A request for an **initial meeting** must be made within 12 days of the administrator sending out his statement of proposals (r 2.37 IR 1986). The meeting must be held as soon as is reasonably practicable, but at least within 10 weeks of the company entering administration. This deadline can be extended by the court. If **another meeting** is requested during the course of the administration, the administrator must comply within 28 days of receiving the notice (r 2.37 IR 1986). If he fails to call a meeting during the administration as requested, he is liable to a fine (para 56 Sch B1 IA 1986; ¶9935).

The **expenses** of any requisitioned meeting must be met by the requisitioner (r 2.37 IR 1986). The administrator requires a **deposit** in respect of those expenses, and he will not call the meeting until he receives the amount requested. However, the meeting may resolve that the relevant expenses should be paid out of the company's assets, in which case the deposit will be repaid to the requisitioner.

MEMO POINTS   If the administrator has not sent out details of his proposals, and therefore has **not summoned** an **initial meeting**, the creditors can require him to summon one (¶8887+).

9081

Notice

The administrator must **give** at least 14 days' notice of a meeting **to** all creditors known to him with claims against the company at the start of the administration (unless a creditor's claim has been paid in full) (r 2.35(4) IR 1986). The notice period can be **varied**, using the same method described at ¶8886. The notice must be in **Form** 2.20B, accompanied by proxy forms, informing the creditors of the date, time and place of the meeting and how they are entitled to vote. The notices can be **served by** post or personally (r 2.35(2), (4) IR 1986).

9082

Conduct

The **chairman** must be the administrator or his nominee, who must either be a qualified insolvency practitioner himself or an experienced employee in the administrator's firm (r 2.36 IR 1986). If the chairman is not present within 30 minutes of the scheduled start of the meeting, it is automatically adjourned to the same time and place the following week (or the day after, if that day is not a business day) (r 2.35(5) IR 1986).

9083

Other than in the absence of a chairman, a meeting may be **adjourned** once by the chairman for up to 14 days (r 2.35(6) IR 1986). In appropriate circumstances, the court may allow further or longer adjournments. If the meeting is adjourned, the chairman must notify the creditors of the date, time and place of the adjourned meeting as soon as is reasonably practicable (r 2.35(7) IR 1986).

9084

A **quorum** of at least one creditor entitled to vote at the meeting is required for the meeting to proceed to business (r 12.4A(2) IR 1986). That creditor can be present personally, by proxy or by a corporate representative (if the creditor is a company) (r 12.4A(3) IR 1986). Where a meeting is quorate either by just the chairman attending (he is commonly appointed as proxy) or by him plus one other person, and he is aware of one or more other creditors who will be entitled to vote if they attended, the meeting cannot commence until at least 15 minutes after its scheduled start time (r 12.4A(4) IR 1986).

9085

Voting

9086 A **resolution** at a creditors' meeting is **passed** when a majority in value of those present and voting, in person or by proxy, vote in its favour (r 2.43 IR 1986). However, this is qualified by a rule that the resolution is invalid if it is voted against by more than half of the creditors in value:
– who are not connected to the company; and
– to whom notice of the meeting was sent.

This ensures fairness to unconnected creditors, as it prevents connected creditors, such as directors, from dominating proceedings at the meeting. The definition of a connected person for insolvency purposes is discussed at ¶7813.

Entitlement to vote generally

9087 A creditor is entitled to vote at a creditors' meeting (r 2.38(1) IR 1986):
– if he has given **details** of his **claim** to the administrator by 12 noon on the day before the meeting;
– if his **claim** has been **admitted**; and
– if the creditor wishes to use a **proxy**, the form has been lodged with the administrator before the vote is taken (*Re Philip Alexander Securities & Futures Ltd (in administration)* [1999] 1 BCLC 124).

The chairman may allow a creditor to vote who has not complied with the above requirements, if the failure to do so was due to reasons beyond his control (r 2.38(2) IR 1986).

> MEMO POINTS Where a creditor at the meeting has also lodged a claim in other proceedings under the **EC Insolvency Regulation** and a member state liquidator attends the meeting and votes in respect of the same claim, only the creditor's vote will count (r 2.38(7) IR 1986). If more than one member state liquidator attempts to vote in respect of a creditor's claim which has been lodged in more than one other proceeding, the member state liquidator in the main proceedings is entitled to vote, whether or not the creditor has claimed in the main proceedings (r 2.38(8) IR 1986).

9088 The **chairman** has the **power** to admit or reject a claim as regards the creditor's entitlement to vote (r 2.39(1) IR 1986). In doing so, he can ask for any evidence of the claim he needs in order to verify it (r 2.38(3) IR 1986). If he is in doubt as to whether to admit or reject it, he will mark it as "objected to", but allow the creditor to vote at the meeting (r 2.39(3) IR 1986). If the objection to the claim is later sustained, that creditor's vote will subsequently be declared invalid.

A creditor can **appeal** the chairman's decision to the court and, if his appeal is upheld, the court can order another meeting to be summoned, or make another appropriate order (r 2.39(2), (4) IR 1986). If the meeting in question was the initial meeting to consider the administrator's proposals, the appeal must be made within 14 days of the administrator's report to court being delivered (r 2.39(5) IR 1986). The chairman will not be personally liable for the costs of an appeal, unless the court orders otherwise (for example, where he made an incorrect decision negligently or fraudulently) (r 2.39(6) IR 1986).

A creditor cannot vote in respect of a **debt** for an **unliquidated** or **unascertained** amount, unless the chairman agrees to admit an estimated minimum value of the debt for voting purposes at the meeting (r 2.38(5) IR 1986). Where a chairman is required to place a value upon an unascertained or unliquidated debt, he is only required to examine the evidence submitted by the creditor in question, any other creditor or the debtor (*Re Newlands (Seaford) Educational Trust, Chittenden and others v Pepper and others* [2006] EWHC 1511 (Ch)). He is not required to speculate as to its value, nor does he have to investigate the creditor's claim independently of the evidence provided to him. If he concludes that a value higher than £1 should be attributed to the debt, he must do so; otherwise, he can only value the debt at £1.

9089 A creditor's vote is **calculated** depending on the amount of his claim on the date that the company went into administration, minus any payments to him or adjustments due to set-off (¶8976+) (r 2.38(4) IR 1986). It has been held that a creditor may split his vote so that he ascribes a portion for and a portion against a particular resolution where it would be unjust not to allow him to do so, e.g. where his voting entitlement represents different beneficial interests in respect of which he acts as a trustee (*Re Polly Peck International plc* [1992] BCLC 1025). However, in normal circumstances, a creditor cannot vote more than once on a single resolution (r 2.38(6) IR 1986).

Special cases

A **secured creditor** may only vote at a creditors' meeting in respect of any unsecured balance of his debt (r 2.40 IR 1986). However, where the proposals state that the administrator will not be calling an initial meeting because there will be insufficient assets to distribute to unsecured creditors except out of any ring-fenced portion of assets subject to a floating charge, a secured creditor can vote according to the full value of his secured and unsecured debt at any requisitioned meeting (¶8887+).

9090

The owner of goods under a **hire-purchase** or chattel leasing agreement, or the seller under a conditional sale agreement, can vote according to the amount due to him on the date the company entered administration (r 2.42 IR 1986).

9091

If a debt is based on or secured by a **bill of exchange** or **promissory note**, the creditor will only be allowed to vote if he agrees to (r 2.41 IR 1986):
a. treat the liabilities on the bill or note of any person whose liability precedes the company's liability as security for those amounts (unless the person liable has gone into liquidation or bankruptcy); and
b. deduct the estimated value of that security from his claim for the purposes of being entitled to vote.

Administrative requirements

Minutes of the creditors' meeting must be entered into the company's minute book, including the names and addresses of the creditors who attended in person and by proxy (r 2.44 IR 1986). If a creditors' committee has been established, the names and addresses of the committee members must also be noted. The minutes, signed by the chairman, constitute primary evidence of the fact that the meeting was duly convened and held and of the proceedings and resolutions at the meeting (r 12.5 IR 1986).

9092

C. Shareholders

The administrator can also call shareholders' **meetings** (para 62 Sch B1 IA 1986). Since the company often carries on business during the administration, this would be necessary for the usual reasons, as well as where the administrator needs to obtain shareholder consent for matters relating to realising the company's business and/or assets, for example to change its name or articles to prepare it for sale. On the other hand the shareholders may wish to requisition a meeting in order to be updated by the administrator on the progress of the administration.

9102

The meeting is to be summoned and **conducted** according to the articles and companies legislation as if the company were not in administration (see ¶3610+), with the following minor modifications (r 2.49 IR 1986):
a. the administrator is to fix the date, time and place of the meeting with regard to the shareholders' convenience;
b. the administrator or his nominee is the chairman of the meeting. If the chairman is not present within 30 minutes of when the meeting was supposed to start, it is automatically adjourned to the same time and place the following week (or the next day, if that is not a business day); and
c. the chairman must see that minutes of the meeting are entered into the company's minute book.

MEMO POINTS If the **laws of another member state apply** to the meeting, it must be summoned and conducted according the constitution of the company and laws of that member state, with the modifications listed above (r2.49 IR 1986).

D. Financial Services Authority

9112 The FSA has certain **powers** in relation to the administration of (s 362 FSMA 2000):
– an authorised person;
– an appointed representative; or
– a company carrying on a regulated activity in contravention of the general prohibition against such activities.
It is entitled to:
– be heard at any administration application hearing;
– be heard at any other hearing relating to the administration;
– receive any documents sent out to the creditors;
– apply to court, challenging the administrator's conduct on the ground that the creditors have been prejudiced;
– attend meetings of the creditors or their committee and make representations to the meeting; and
– apply to court concerning any compromise or arrangement made with the company's creditors.

SECTION 4

Conclusion of the administration

9127 There are a number of **ways** in which an administration can come to an end, **depending on** its success and the position of the company at the end of it. It may be that the purpose of the administration has been achieved and the company can resume business as usual. On the other hand, it will be appropriate to dissolve the company altogether if the administrator has had to realise and distribute all of its assets. If the company cannot be revived but there are remaining assets to be dealt with, the administration can be converted into a liquidation before it is dissolved.

Some of the **procedures** differ slightly depending on whether the company entered administration through a court application or out of court.

A. Purpose of administration achieved

9130 Where the stated purpose has been achieved, the administration comes to an end in different ways, **depending on** whether or not the company entered administration by court order.

Entry method	Exit method	Administrator's appointment ends	Reference
Administration order	Administrator must: – apply to court; then – file Form 2.33B at Companies House with copy of order and final progress report	When court directs	para 86 Sch B1 IA 1986; r 2.116 IR 1986
Administrator appointed out of court by director, company or qualifying floating charge holder	Administrator must: – file notice (Form 2.32B) and final progress report with Companies House; – file two copies[1] of notice (Form 2.32B) at court, with final progress report and statement that these documents have been sent to Companies House; and – within 5 business days, give notice to every creditor (for whom he has an address), or publish an undertaking to provide the notice to any creditor who so requests[2]	Date and time endorsed on notice by court	para 80 Sch B1 IA 1986; r 2.113 IR 1986

Note:
1. The court will endorse notices with date and time of filing, and return one copy to administrator.
2. If the administrator **fails** to comply, he is liable to a fine (¶9935). If he chooses to **publish** his undertaking to provide notice, he must do so in same newspaper as he published notice of his appointment as well as in the Gazette.

9131 If the **purpose** of the administration **cannot be achieved**, the administrator must apply to court for his appointment to terminate (¶9164+).

B. Conversion into liquidation

Compulsory liquidation

9141 If a petition is presented against the company by a **third party** to wind it up in the public interest (including against a Societas Europaea, i.e. a European Company), or a petition is presented by the **FSA**, the court will either order that the administrator's appointment is to cease or that it should continue pending the petition hearing (para 82(1), (3) Sch B1 IA 1986). The same will occur if a provisional liquidator is appointed following either of these types of winding up petition (para 82(2) Sch B1 IA 1986). If the court orders the administrator to remain in office, it will also specify which of his powers he can continue to exercise, and how the legislative provisions are to be adapted to take account of the petition and any provisional liquidator (para 82(4) Sch B1 IA 1986).

The **administrator** can also **petition** to have the company wound up. The petition must (r 4.7(7) IR 1986):
– state that it is being presented by the company's administrator;
– give the name of the administrator, case number of the administration and its date of commencement; and
– include the application for the administrator's appointment to cease (¶9130+ above).

If the administrator wishes to be **appointed as liquidator**, he must also inform the court of when he notified the creditors of his intention (this must be at least 10 days beforehand) and what their responses were (r 4.7(10) IR 1986). Such a petition will be treated as if it were made by the contributories, and the Rules regarding contributories' petitions apply (¶7656+) (r 4.7(9) IR 1986).

Voluntary liquidation

9142 If the **administrator** is of the opinion that the money due to the secured creditors has been paid to, or set aside for, them and a distribution will be made to the unsecured creditors, he can convert the administration into a voluntary liquidation by filing the following documents at Companies House (para 83 Sch B1 IA 1986; r 2.117(1) IR 1986):
– Form 2.34B; and
– a final progress report, including details of the assets to be dealt with in the liquidation.

As soon as is reasonably practicable, the administrator must then file a copy of the notice at court, and send it to all of the creditors for whom he has an address (para 83(5) Sch B1 IA 1986). A copy of the notice and report must also be sent to every person who received notice of the administrator's appointment (r 2.117(2) IR 1986).

Once Companies House has registered the documents, the **administrator's appointment** is **terminated** and the company will be wound up as if a resolution for its voluntary liquidation had been passed on the day on which the documents were registered (para 83(6) Sch B1 IA 1986).

If a conversion into a voluntary liquidation is anticipated by the administrator, it will form part of his proposals. If the administrator **nominated a liquidator** (often himself) in his proposals or revised proposals, the creditors can nominate their own liquidator during the period between receipt and approval of the proposals. If no liquidator has been nominated in this way, the administrator will be appointed (para 83(7) Sch B1 IA 1986).

An **MVL** would be unusual, as the company will usually just resume trading if it is solvent at the end of the administration, but it may occur if the shareholders wish to exit the company via this route; a **CVL** on the other hand would be more common, as it enables the company to be wound up with the creditors' continued involvement.

Conduct

9143 If the company enters voluntary liquidation in this manner, its conduct is slightly **different** to a usual voluntary liquidation because certain legislative provisions do not apply, or are modified (para 83(8) Sch B1 IA 1986).

Provision	Difference to usual voluntary liquidation	¶¶
Advertising resolution to wind up	Does not apply	CVL: ¶8457; MVL: ¶8616
Date of commencement of winding up	Date of commencement of winding up is date of registration of notice (Form 2.34B), not date on which resolution was passed	CVL: ¶8465; MVL: ¶8623
Statutory declaration of solvency for MVL	Does not apply	¶8610+
First meeting of creditors in CVL	Does not apply	¶8448+
Requirement of liquidator to lay statement of affairs before first meeting of creditors in CVL	Does not apply	¶8452
Creditors' initial appointment of liquidator in CVL	Does not apply	¶8454
Commencement of liquidation where voluntary winding up precedes winding up petition	Date of commencement of winding up is date of registration of notice (Form 2.34B), not date on which resolution was passed	¶8465
Appointment of liquidation committee	Any creditors' committee automatically becomes liquidation committee	¶8548+

Conversion by member state liquidator

9144 Where a member state liquidator has been appointed in relation to the company in **main proceedings outside of the UK**, he can apply to court for the administration to be converted into liquidation (reg 37 EC Insolvency Reg; rr 2.130-2.132 IR 1986; ¶7366+). The application to court must be supported by an affidavit or witness statement, and served on the company and the administrator once it has been filed at court. The court can make any order it thinks fit, including that the company be wound up as if a resolution for voluntary winding up had been passed on any ground. If the court orders that the administration should be converted into a liquidation, it can make any necessary order regarding that conversion.

MEMO POINTS The Insolvency Service has proposed that **affidavits** are replaced by witness statements (see ¶8737). This change is likely to be implemented on 1 October 2008.

C. Company has no assets

If it becomes apparent during the administration that the company has no assets which can be distributed to its creditors, it must be **dissolved** unless the court orders otherwise (para 84 Sch B1 IA 1986). This exit route can be used where the assets of the company have been realised and distributed to the creditors, as well as where the company had no assets in the first place (para 6, chapter 1, *Dear IP*; Re GHE Realisations Ltd (formerly Gatehouse Estates Ltd) [2005] All ER (D) 64 (Nov)). The administrator must submit **Form** 2.35B to Companies House, attaching his final progress report (r 2.118(1) IR 1986). Then, as soon as is reasonably practicable, he must send a copy to:
– the court (para 84(5) Sch B1 IA 1986);
– all creditors for whom he has an address (para 84(5) Sch B1 IA 1986); and
– all other people who received notice of his appointment (r 2.118(2) IR 1986).
Failure to notify the court or the creditors renders him liable to a fine (para 84(9) Sch B1 IA 1986; ¶9935).

9154

Once this form has been registered at Companies House, the administrator's **appointment** is **terminated**. Three months later, the company is deemed to be dissolved unless an application to court has been made by an interested party to (para 84(6), (7) Sch B1 IA 1986):
– extend the 3-month period;
– suspend it; or
– disapply the dissolution altogether.
If such an order is made and the applicant was not the administrator, he must send a copy of the order to the administrator (r 2.118(3) IR 1986). Whether or not the administrator was the applicant, he must notify Companies House using Form 2.36B as soon as is reasonably practicable after he learns of the order (para 84(8) Sch B1 IA 1986).

D. Other situations

Administrator's application

The administrator must apply to court for his appointment to terminate from a specified time where (para 79(2) Sch B1 IA 1986):
– he thinks the **purpose** of the administration **cannot be achieved**;
– he thinks that the **company should not have entered administration**; or
– a **creditors' meeting requires** him to do so.
He can also apply, at his discretion, if the company went into administration as a result of an administration order and he thinks that its purpose has been sufficiently achieved. He can **combine** his application **with** a winding up petition if he thinks that the administration should be converted into compulsory liquidation. Alternatively, he can include proposals for a CVA or scheme of arrangement as part of his application, if this would be an appropriate course of action for the company (Re Olympia & York Canary Wharf Ltd (No 3) [1994] 1 BCLC 702).

9164

If the creditors have not required him to make the application, at least 7 days before he applies to court he must give **notice** to (r 2.114(3) IR 1986):
- the person who applied for the administration order or appointed him; and
- the creditors.

If the application to end the administration is going to be accompanied by a petition to wind the company up, he must also notify the creditors whether he intends to nominate himself as liquidator (see ¶9141, ¶9142+) (r 2.114(4) IR 1986).

9165 Any application must be **accompanied by** (r 2.114 IR 1986):
- a progress report covering the period since the last one, or since the commencement of the administration if none has been made yet;
- a statement by the administrator detailing the steps he thinks the company should take next;
- where he has had to notify the creditors, a statement that he has done so, together with copies of any responses from them; and
- where the creditors have required him to make the application, a statement as to whether or not he agrees that it is necessary.

9166 The **court** may make any **order** it thinks is appropriate, including adjourning the hearing (with or without conditions), dismissing the application, making an interim order or ordering the end of the administration by terminating the administrator's appointment (paras 79, 85 Sch B1 IA 1986). If the court ends the administration, the administrator must notify Companies House using Form 2.33B, attaching a copy of the order and his final progress report (r 2.116 IR 1986). Failure to do so renders him liable to a fine (para 86 Sch B1 IA 1986; r 2.116 IR 1986; ¶9935).

Creditor's application

9167 A creditor can apply to court for the cessation of the administrator's appointment **because** the person who applied for the administration order or appointed the administrator out of court was improperly motivated in doing so (para 81 Sch B1 IA 1986).

A **copy** of the application must be **served on** the administrator and the person who applied for the administration order or appointed the administrator out of court at least 5 business days before the hearing (r 2.115 IR 1986). If the administrator was appointed under a qualifying floating charge, the holder of that charge must also be notified. The persons on whom the application is served can appear at the hearing.

The court may make any **order** it thinks appropriate, including adjourning the hearing (with or without conditions), dismissing the application, making an interim order and terminating the administrator's appointment (para 81(3) Sch B1 IA 1986). Where the appointment is terminated, the court will send a copy of the order to the administrator (r 2.115(3) IR 1986). He must then notify Companies House using Form 2.33B, attaching a copy of the order and his final progress report (r 2.116 IR 1986).

Expiry without extension, or any other circumstances

9168 Where the administrator's appointment expires (whether after an extension or not, ¶8999+), or the administration ends under any other circumstances not already discussed, the administrator must prepare a **final progress report**, which includes a summary of (r 2.110 IR 1986):
- his proposals;
- any significant amendments to or departures from the proposals;
- the steps taken during the administration; and
- the outcome of the administration.

This report, together with Form 2.30B giving notice of the end of the administration, must be **filed** at court as soon as is reasonably practicable, but within 5 business days of the end of the administration at the latest (r 2.111 IR 1986). The administrator must also send the form and final report to Companies House and to all persons who received a copy of his proposals. If he **fails** to comply with these requirements, he is liable to a fine (¶9935).

CHAPTER 20

Receivership

OUTLINE

Summary of receivership procedure 9198

SECTION 1 Entering receivership 9200

A Appointment 9222
1 Ability to appoint a receiver 9222
   a Power to appoint 9224
   b Types of receiver 9236
     Administrative receivers 9237
     Ordinary receivers 9239
2 Methods of appointment 9244
B Effect of receivership 9260

SECTION 2 Dealing with the company's assets 9282

A Collection, preservation and realisation 9304
B Distribution 9321

SECTION 3 The receiver 9343

A Powers 9345
B Duties 9359
1 General duties 9360
2 Providing information 9367
3 Conduct of an administrative receivership 9376
C Liabilities 9392
D Termination of office and conclusion of receivership 9402

9195 Receivership is a **method of enforcement** available to holders of security over a company's assets, whereby a receiver is appointed to take control of those assets and realise them for the benefit of his appointor, discharging the secured debt as far as possible. Therefore, receivers are usually appointed where a company has defaulted on its repayments under a secured loan and the secured creditor is concerned that he will not be paid in full without taking enforcement action.

Receivers are usually professionals (either insolvency practitioners, chartered accountants or other corporate recovery specialists), who can be **appointed by** the court or by the security holder out of court. The focus here is on appointments made out of court, because court-appointed receivers (discussed briefly at ¶9229) are less common and their purpose and powers and the assets available to them are decided upon by the court. On the other hand, out of court appointments depend largely on the terms of the security document in question, although statutory rights to appoint receivers can also be relied upon in some cases.

9196 The two main **types of receiver**, administrative and ordinary receivers, are discussed at ¶9236+. They essentially perform the same function, but there are many **differences** between them, due to the fact that an administrative receiver takes control of most, if not all, of the company's business and assets. As a result, more duties are imposed on him to protect the company and those dealing with it. At the same time, he has extensive powers to deal with the company's assets to enable him to act in relation to a wide and potentially complex range of assets. An ordinary receiver, on the other hand, will be appointed in relation to a specific asset or group of assets, and so he does not require such a wide range of powers.

Terminology

9197 Where a discussion applies to both **types of receiver**, they are referred to as "receivers". The law relating to only one type or the other will be discussed in terms of an "administrative receiver" or an "ordinary receiver", as applicable. Readers may come across references to "managers" or "receiver and managers" in this context. These terms were used to refer to receivers who were akin to administrative receivers prior to that role being introduced by legislation. The term "manager" is not used here, to avoid confusion with a company's ordinary managers.

Receivers can be appointed under a number of different **types of security** (¶9224+). Types of security are discussed at ¶4562+. Where the type is pertinent to the discussion, the specific term will be used, e.g. fixed charge, floating charge, mortgage, etc. Where the discussion applies to all or any type, the generic terms "security", "security document" and "security holder" are used.

References to the "**company**" here are to the debtor, over whose assets the receiver is appointed, although of course the security holder will often also be a company.

Summary of receivership procedure

9198

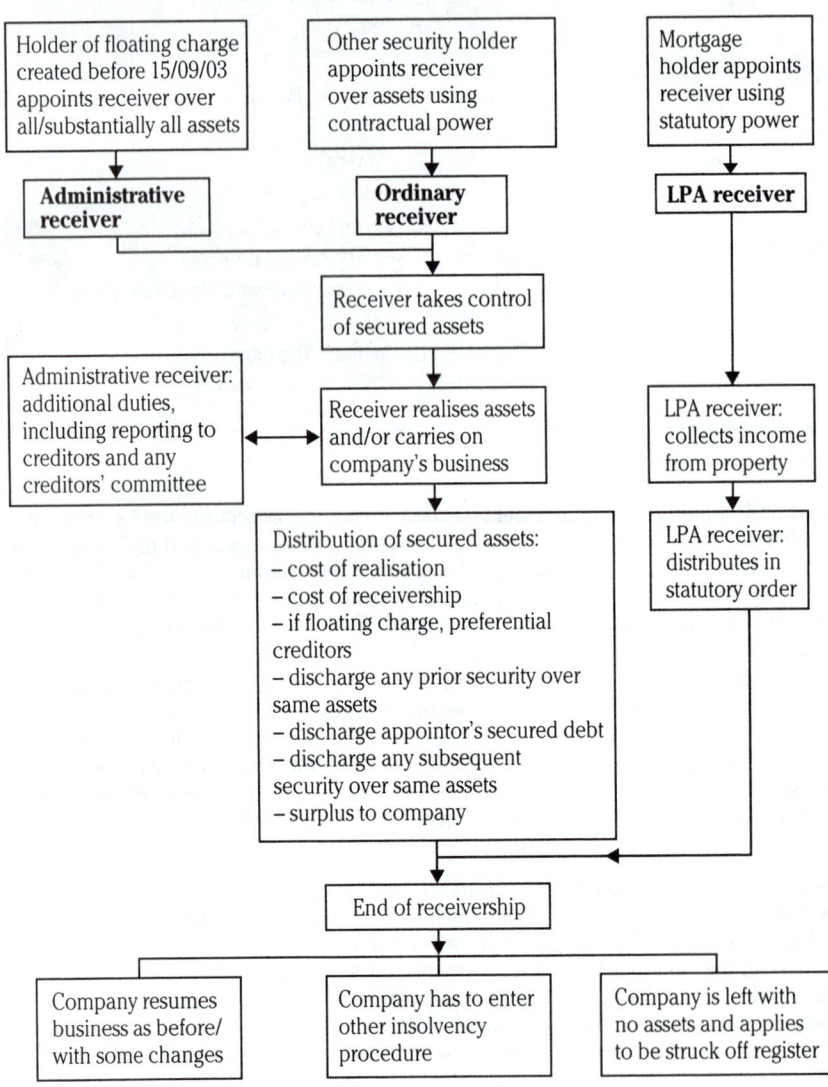

SECTION 1
Entering receivership

9200 The **procedure** for appointing a receiver out of court is usually a straight-forward matter of serving notices on the correct persons (¶9244+). However, **before** an **appointment** is made, a security holder must resolve two important issues, whether:
- receivership is the best solution in the circumstances; and
- he has the right to appoint a receiver.

9211 A security holder considering receivership should look at the pros and cons of the procedure before making an appointment. These will differ in each situation, but the broad **advantages and disadvantages** can be summarised as follows.

Advantages	Disadvantages
• The receiver does not have to take account of **unsecured liabilities** (unless appointed under floating charge, ¶9327), giving a good chance of fully discharging debt. • The security holder can appoint a receiver entirely in his **own interests**, without taking those of the company or unsecured creditors into account. • **Flexibility**: the receiver can carry on all/part of business and/or realise assets to achieve best result for his appointor. • Receivership is principally a **contractual remedy**, allowing the security holder to dictate the terms of appointment, e.g. powers. Procedures are usually practical and straight forward. • Assets are dealt with by an experienced **professional** who is likely to be able to realise them more efficiently than the company or security holder. • Can prevent an **administrator** being appointed by court (¶8723), although cannot prevent an administrator being appointed out of court.	• Some **other securities** over the same assets may rank ahead of the appointor's security and must be paid off first. • The receiver may have to pay off certain **unsecured creditors** to enable the company to continue trading. • Receivership may terminate the company's **contracts**, preventing it from carrying on business and diminishing its value. • The **stigma** of receivership usually diminishes goodwill, resulting in: – a lower price if the business is sold as a going concern; and – difficulties collecting debts and persuading people to carry on doing business with the company. • Some statutory and regulatory **control**, especially of administrative and LPA receivers. The court can give directions regarding the conduct of receivership. • The receiver's **costs and expenses** have priority over the security holder's distributions. • If an **appointment** is **invalid**, the security holder may have to pay damages to the company and indemnify the receiver against any liabilities he incurred as a result of his office (¶9392). • No **moratorium** on other proceedings against the company. Receivership will not generally prevent the company entering or being placed into **liquidation/administration**.

9212 Appointing a receiver is one of a number of remedies likely to be provided for under the terms of the security. However, in the light of the potential disadvantages of receivership, it is advisable for a security holder to consider his **alternative options** before making an appointment. His object will be to recover the secured debt as quickly and cost-effectively as possible, which he may be able to do by:

a. enforcing a covenant to pay in the security document, by taking **legal action** if necessary, for example, where the security holder knows that the company has enough assets, or a guarantor of the debt is able to pay;

b. exercising any **power of sale** or right of **foreclosure** (¶4667);

c. exercising a **right to possession** of the assets, which may be contained in the security document or occurs automatically in the case of legal mortgages and charges over registered land (under which the security holder has an immediate right of possession, whether or not the company is in default);

d. if the company's business is financially sound, it may be best to agree **not** to **enforce** the security for a period of time (i.e. agree to a moratorium) to allow the company to resolve its cash-flow problems, which may involve it realising some of its own assets to repay the security holder. Or, the security holder could use its influence to put pressure on the company (i.e. by threatening to take enforcement action), perhaps insisting that it appoints a supervisory director or manager or requiring the company to consult a corporate recovery professional and follow his guidance; or

e. imposing **another insolvency procedure** on the company, although this will not usually benefit the security holder more than receivership.

A. Appointment

1. Ability to appoint a receiver

9222 The ability to appoint a receiver out of court **depends upon**:
– the type of security held; and
– the terms of that security.

The type of security will also dictate which kind of receiver is appointed.

Appointments may also be made **by the court**. However, given the costs and time it takes to appoint a receiver in this way (which exposes the assets to the danger of being dissipated prior to appointment), it is usually only relied on by those with no contractual or statutory right, or as a means of enforcing criminal or civil penalties.

a. Power to appoint

9224 A security holder must ensure that he has the right to appoint a receiver before he attempts to do so. If the **appointment** is **not valid**, the security holder may be liable to pay damages to the company for the loss it suffered as a result of the appointment, and he may also have to indemnify the receiver for any liability he incurred during his appointment (*Rolled Steel Products (Holdings) Ltd v British Steel & Corp* [1985] 3 All ER 52; s 34 IA 1986).

Depending on the security in question, a receiver can be appointed in relation to any **type of company**. Receivers can also be appointed in relation to limited liability partnerships, with some modifications to the legislative and regulatory provisions.

Contractual power

9225 Usually, ordinary receivers are appointed under specific powers in the relevant **security document**, which could take one of a number of forms, including:
– a legal mortgage over specific land;
– a fixed charge over other assets;
– a floating charge over the company's undertaking, property and assets; and
– a debenture containing a mixture of fixed and floating charges.

Administrative receivers can only be appointed under certain floating charges, see ¶9237+.

9226 Since the power is contractual, the security under which it is to be exercised must itself be **valid**. The following issues, for example, should be considered:
– whether the directors acted within their powers in causing the company to grant the security;
– whether the charge has been properly executed;
– whether the charge has been registered, if required;

RECEIVERSHIP 1099

– whether the charge could be set aside or avoided by a liquidator or administrator who has been or may be appointed; and
– whether the document is legal. For example, it could infringe company law requirements regarding directors disclosing their interests, substantial property transactions or loans to directors.

In addition, the security holder must act in accordance with the **terms of the security**, which may restrict his right to appoint a receiver to particular situations, or impose conditions on it. Therefore, he can only appoint a receiver if this right has arisen under the terms and he has correctly complied with any conditions precedent imposed on that right, such as the service of demands for payment or a notice of default. He must also make the appointment in accordance with any procedures set out in the terms.

The terms of the security usually specify the **circumstances** in which the **power arises**, often on default of the payment or other significant terms, and on insolvency steps being taken against or by the company. The power may arise when the debt becomes due, although the security holder will not usually use it until the company fails to pay or the secured assets are in jeopardy. Unless the parties have agreed otherwise, the debt will be repayable on demand. Once he has demanded repayment, the security holder must allow the company a reasonable (but usually short) time to pay up (Williams & Glyn's Bank Ltd v Barnes [1981] Com LR 205; Cripps (Pharmaceuticals) Ltd v Wickenden [1973] 2 All ER 606). This does not include allowing time to borrow the funds from another source if the company does not have the money to hand. He will then be able to exercise his power to appoint a receiver.

9227

Statutory power

The **principal** statutory **power** to appoint a receiver occurs where (ss 101(1)(iii), 109(1) LPA 1925):
– the security in question is a mortgage or fixed charge over property;
– the secured debt has become due; and
– the security holder has become entitled to exercise his power of sale (see ¶4664+).

9228

A receiver appointed under this power is often referred to as a "**LPA receiver**". The **function** of this type of receiver differs from a contractually appointed receiver, since he can only collect the income from the secured land (unless the security holder delegates additional powers to him). Therefore, he will collect the rent that the company would otherwise have received and pay it over to the security holder, after discharging certain payments. As they are so limited in scope, such appointments are rare in practice, but can be useful if the secured land is unsaleable or if the principal debt does not need to be repaid urgently and the rent would meet the interest repayments.

There are also other, rarely used, statutory powers to appoint receivers.

> MEMO POINTS The security holder can **delegate** his own **powers** under his security to the receiver, to increase the receiver's ability to act. These powers include:
> – selling the secured property (s 101(1)(i) LPA 1925); and
> – leasing the property on statutory terms (s 99 LPA 1925), and accepting the surrender of a lease in order to grant a lease on those terms (s 100 LPA 1925).

Appointments made by the court

A **security holder** may need to **apply** to court to enforce his security if, for example:
a. the security document does not allow a receiver to be appointed in the circumstances which have arisen (for instance, where the secured assets are in jeopardy but the company has not actually defaulted yet, Re London Pressed Hinge Co Ltd [1905] 1 Ch 576; Cryne v Barclays Bank plc [1987] BCLC 548); or
b. the company is resisting the security holder's contractual right of enforcement, or another dispute has arisen.

9229

A receiver will not necessarily be appointed, as the court may be able to grant other, simpler remedies in the circumstances, such as making an execution or charging order. The **court** may also appoint a receiver on its **own initiative**, for example to resolve a partnership dispute, or as a means of equitable execution (s 37 Supreme Court Act 1981).

Any court appointment will usually **take effect from** the date of the order, and the appointment must be **notified** to Companies House within 7 days (s 405 CA 1985; restated at s 871 CA 2006 by 1 October 2009). Failure to do so renders the person obtaining the order liable to a fine (¶9935). If the **company** is already **in compulsory liquidation**, the official receiver may be appointed as receiver (s 32 IA 1986).

The receiver's **powers and duties** will be determined by the court order, although if the court appoints an administrative receiver, he will be able to exercise the powers of this office (¶9347+) in addition to any set out in the order. The court will also fix the receiver's **remuneration** and costs allowance, and may disallow his claims if appropriate in the circumstances, such as where his actions were improper or misguided (*Mellor v Mellor* [1992] 4 All ER 10). A person intending to bring proceedings against a court-appointed receiver because of his actions whilst in office should obtain leave of the court first (*Re Botibol* [1947] 1 All ER 26). A court-appointed receiver's **status** is as an officer of the court, not the agent or trustee of the person who made the application (*Mellor v Mellor*, above), and therefore he can be personally liable for contracts he enters into (although he still has a right of indemnity, see ¶9392).

General restrictions on appointment

9230 An ordinary receiver does not have to be a **qualified** insolvency practitioner, although an administrative receiver does (s 230(2) IA 1986). The following persons **cannot act** as a receiver:
– a body corporate (s 30 IA 1986; see ¶9935 for the penalty for breach of this prohibition);
– an undischarged bankrupt, unless the appointment is made by the court (s 31 IA 1986; see ¶9935 for the penalty for breach of this prohibition); and
– a person disqualified from being involved in the management of a company (¶3000+).

Therefore, it is possible for the security holder or even a director of the company to act as a receiver, although this would be unusual given the liabilities that can accompany the appointment and the expertise required to deal with the secured assets properly (¶9392).

9231 Aside from the restriction on holders of qualifying floating charges created on or after 15 September 2003 appointing administrative receivers (see ¶9238 below), there are further restrictions where the company is already subject to **other insolvency procedures**, summarised in the table below. If a **receiver** is **already in place**, another security holder can still appoint his own receiver. However, it is often only worthwhile where the second security holder has priority over the first or his security relates to different assets, since a receiver must distribute the proceeds of an asset in accordance with the order of priority (¶9321+).

Other insolvency procedure affecting company [1]	Ability to appoint administrative receiver	Ability to appoint ordinary receiver
Administration (¶8813+) [2]	Existing administrative receiver must vacate office. [3] New administrative receiver cannot be appointed.	Existing ordinary receiver must vacate office if administrator requires. [3] New ordinary receiver cannot be appointed without leave of: – court; or – administrator.
CVA (¶9471+)	New administrative receiver cannot be appointed if company has obtained moratorium	New ordinary receiver cannot be appointed without leave of court if company has obtained moratorium

Note:
1. If a company is in **liquidation**, a receiver can still be appointed, although his status as the company's agent is different (¶9361). This may expose him personally to liabilities, and he may have to apply to court for leave to take possession of secured assets if the liquidator refuses to allow him to do so (¶7893).
If the mortgage holder appoints an **LPA receiver when company is insolvent**, he needs the court's permission (s 110 LPA 1925).
2. An **administration application** can be made while the company is in administrative receivership, but only if the administrative receiver consents or if the court considers that the floating charge under which he was appointed can be challenged (para 39 Sch B1 IA 1986). However, an administrative receiver cannot block the **appointment** of an administrator **out of court**.
3. Where an **administrative or ordinary receiver** vacates office in these circumstances, his **remuneration** is charged on and paid out of the company's property in his possession or under his control (para 41 Sch B1 IA 1986).

b. Types of receiver

9236 Broadly speaking, if a security holder was granted a **floating charge** over all, or most of the company's assets before 15 September 2003, he can appoint an administrative receiver. The holders of **other types of security** can appoint an ordinary receiver, using either a contractual right to do so under their security or a statutory power.

Administrative receivers

9237 An administrative receiver is one appointed (s 29(2) IA 1986):
a. by or on behalf of holders of security created as a **floating charge** (whether alone or in combination with other securities); and
b. over the whole, or substantially the **whole**, of the **company's property**.

Both elements must be present together for the receiver to be an administrative receiver, so if, for example, a floating charge holder appoints a receiver over only a few assets, he will actually appoint an ordinary receiver. However, if the receiver would have been appointed over all or substantially all of the assets but cannot because another **receiver** has **already** been **appointed** in relation to some specific assets, the second appointment can still take effect as an administrative receivership.

The fact that the appointment is made under a floating charge is also vital. For example, in a case in which the company had no assets over which a floating charge could be granted but a creditor still obtained a combined fixed charge over its assets and a floating charge over "everything else" (purely to give him rights if another person attempted to appoint an administrator), the court found that a receiver appointed under that security was still an administrative receiver (*Re Croftbell Ltd* [1990] BCLC 844).

> MEMO POINTS There is no statutory definition of **what constitutes "substantially the whole"** of the company's **assets**, nor is there any direct authority in case law. If there is any doubt, the company's circumstances must be examined carefully and an assessment of the assets made on a qualitative as well as a quantitative basis.

9238 Since the Enterprise Act 2002 reformed insolvency law, the ability to appoint an administrative receiver has been severely curtailed. Now, the holder of a **qualifying floating charge** (¶8779) which was created on or after 15 September 2003 cannot appoint an administrative receiver, even if his charge document allows him to do so (s 72A(1) IA 1986). Instead, these charge holders have new rights to appoint an administrator (¶8777+). This change is designed to encourage the use of administration, a procedure carried out for the benefit of all creditors which usually aims to rescue the company. However, since there are many qualifying floating charges created before this date under which administrative receivers can still be appointed, a discussion of administrative receivers is still relevant.

> MEMO POINTS The **prohibition** on holders of qualifying floating charges created on or after 15 September 2003 appointing administrative receivers **does not apply** to appointments under certain specialist agreements or in relation to particular types of company, which are not common (ss 72B-72GA IA 1986).

Ordinary receivers

9239 An ordinary receiver is one who is not appointed as an administrative receiver; he is usually **appointed** in relation to a specific asset or group of assets over which the security holder has a mortgage or charge. Such receivers are sometimes referred to as "LPA receivers", after the statutory power contained in the Law of Property Act 1925 to appoint a receiver (¶9228). In fact, most receivers are not appointed under the statutory power but under the terms of the relevant security.

2. Methods of appointment

9244 The method of appointment is usually **determined by** the security under which the receiver is appointed. Typically, a security holder needs to give the proposed receiver written notice of the appointment, which must be accepted by the receiver within a certain period of time. Following the receiver's acceptance, certain administrative requirements must be complied with.

Notification of proposed appointment

9245 In the case of a **contractual power** to appoint, the security document will usually set out the method of appointment, in which case that procedure should be followed. Usually, the appointment must be in writing. An **LPA receiver** must be appointed in writing by the security holder (s 109(1) LPA 1925).

If **more than one** administrative receiver is appointed by the same security holder, the appointment must specify whether the administrative receivers' acts can be carried out by each one individually or whether they must be carried out by them all acting together (s 231 IA 1986). The division of power between joint receivers might be dictated by the terms of the security document.

9246 The notification of the security holder's proposed appointment must be **sent to** the intended receiver, who may accept or reject it. He does not have to accept in writing, for example, **acceptance** could be given orally or impliedly, as long as it is unequivocal and unconditional.

If an **administrative receiver** does not accept the appointment in writing, he must confirm his acceptance in writing to the appointor within 7 days, stating the time and date he received the notification and the time and date of his acceptance (r 3.1(2), (5) IR 1986). The acceptance and/or confirmation may be given on the administrative receiver's behalf (for example, where the administrative receiver works for a firm of insolvency practitioners or accountants, the firm may well accept or confirm the appointment on his behalf) (r 3.1(4) IR 1986).

9247 A receiver must accept the appointment by the end of the business day after that on which he received the notification, but the **commencement of** his **appointment** is deemed to have occurred when he received the notification (s 33 IA 1986). In the case of a notice to appoint **joint receivers**, both or all of them must accept within the deadline, and their appointment is deemed to have commenced when the notice was received by or on behalf of them all (r 3.1(1) IR 1986). In the case of an **LPA receiver**, the appointment will commence once it has been accepted expressly or impliedly by the receiver.

Administrative requirements

9248 **Notice** of any type of appointment must be filed at Companies House by the appointor within 7 days, using **Form** 405(1) (s 405(1) CA 1985; restated at s 871 CA 2006 by 1 October 2009). Failure to do so renders the appointor liable to a fine (¶9935).

> MEMO POINTS The name of Form 405(1), like the names of other **Companies House forms**, is taken from the section number of the legislation. As all of the section numbers will change under the new Companies Act, Companies House proposes to change the names of all of its forms to reflect their function rather than the relevant section number ("Working with Companies House: a consultation on the registrar's rules and related provisions which will apply under the Companies Act 2006"). At the time of writing, the new form names are not yet available.

9249 If an **administrative receiver** is appointed, he must give **notice** of his appointment to the company straight away, and to all of the company's creditors for whom he has an address, within 28 days of his appointment (s 46(1) IA 1986). This notice must contain the following **information** (r 3.2(2) IR 1986):
– the company's registered number and its name at the date of his appointment;
– any previous names of the company within the 12 months before his appointment;
– any other trading names used by the company in that time;
– his name and address;
– the date of his appointment;
– the name of his appointor and a brief description of the security document under which he was appointed, including its date; and
– a brief description of any of the company's assets over which he is not appointed.

He must also **advertise** a notice in the same form straight after his appointment in the *Gazette* and one other newspaper he thinks is likely to come to the attention of the company's creditors (s 46(1) IA 1986; r 3.2(3), (4) IR 1986).

Failure to comply renders the administrative receiver liable to a fine (s 46(4) IA 1986; ¶9935).

> MEMO POINTS These requirements do not apply to **replacement** or **additional** administrative receivers. In the case of replacement administrative receivers, they do, however, have to comply to the extent that their predecessor(s) did not (s 46(2) IA 1986).

B. Effect of receivership

The effect of receivership on a company will **depend on** the type of receiver appointed and the extent to which he can exercise control over the company's assets and business. For example, if a receiver is appointed under a fixed charge in relation to a specific asset, the company can carry on business as usual except in so far as it cannot deal with that asset or interfere with the receiver's right to do so. Similarly, if an LPA receiver has been appointed, he is entitled to the income from the property in question, but otherwise the board and shareholders can carry on as normal. The management of the company will be affected where a receiver has powers in that regard, usually in an administrative receivership, and the directors may find themselves effectively powerless to act during the procedure.

9260

Company and board

The **directors** remain in office, but they can only exercise their **powers** in so far as they do not infringe on the appointing security holder's position (*Newhart Developments Ltd v Co-operative Commercial Bank Ltd* [1978] 2 All ER 896). The board may also take action on the company's behalf if the receiver will not, including defending a winding up petition. It can also sue a receiver who discharges his duties improperly, although individual shareholders cannot (*Watts v Midland Bank plc* [1986] BCLC 15).

9261

Although the directors will technically still be under a **duty** to prepare and file annual accounts, returns and other documents at Companies House, they will often have to rely on the receiver to supply the relevant information since he will have assumed management of the company. If he refuses to provide them with this information, the directors will usually be able to rely on the statutory defences to liability for breach of the duties in question. See ¶9900 for the various filing requirements and ¶4185+ for the accounting requirements.

In the case of an **administrative receivership**, the company's **management** will be taken over by the administrative receiver. He is under a duty to report to creditors on his conduct because his actions can affect their prospects of recovery, and he must produce information to the creditors' committee when required (*Smiths Ltd v Middleton* [1979] 3 All ER 842; ¶9378+, ¶9382).

9262

Contracts

Pre-receivership

Contracts entered into by the company prior to it entering into receivership will only **terminate** when the receiver is appointed, if this is expressly or impliedly provided for in the contract. The receiver is not personally liable on the contract (for the case of employment contracts, see ¶9266+ below). Although the company's obligations continue once it is in receivership, it may be best in the circumstances for the receiver to refuse to perform the company's obligations and leave the other party to accept its **repudiation** or claim for damages (in which case, the other party will be an unsecured creditor for any damages awarded or agreed). The receiver must, however, act in accordance with his functions and therefore cannot repudiate a contract if it would be detrimental to the realisation of the assets, the goodwill of the company or its future trading prospects (*Airlines Airspares Ltd v Handley Page Ltd* [1970] 1 All ER 29). In some cases, a receiver can be prevented from repudiating a contract, for example, the buyer of land which the company has contracted to sell may be able to obtain an order for specific performance obliging the receiver to transfer it to him (*Freevale Ltd v Metrostore (Holdings) Ltd* [1984] 1 All ER 495).

9263

During receivership

9264 Once the company is in receivership, the receiver is usually empowered to **enter into contracts** as agent for the company. He does, however, incur personal liability on contracts he **adopts** or enters into after he takes up his appointment, unless this is expressly excluded in the contract (s 37 IA 1986 (ordinary receiver); s 44 IA 1986 (administrative receiver)). Although he is entitled to an indemnity out of the company's assets, this is only useful where the company has enough assets to meet these liabilities (¶9392). Any new contracts entered into by the receiver on the company's behalf should make clear that the company is in receivership and that the receiver is acting as the company's receiver and agent. A receiver will exclude his liability under such contracts and avoid giving warranties or making representations as to title and other matters relating to the assets under any contract he enters into on the company's behalf.

> MEMO POINTS The receiver's **indemnity does not cover** liability under contracts entered into without the authority to do so (s 37(3) IA 1986 (ordinary receiver); s 44(3) IA 1986 (administrative receiver)).

9265 If the **secured debt** in relation to which the receiver was appointed was **guaranteed**, the guarantor remains liable under his guarantee as long as this is provided for under its terms (usually, until it is paid off, surrendered or otherwise changed by the security holder's actions) (*China and South Sea Bank Ltd v Tan* [1989] 3 All ER 839).

Employees

9266 A **contract of employment** can be affected by the company entering receivership in a number of ways. A receiver will usually wish to carry on the company's business and so will adopt the employment contracts, making any variations that are necessary. He cannot be deemed to adopt employment contracts within the first 14 days of holding office, but he will usually write to the employees setting out their position and rights. If he wishes to cause the company to carry on trading, he will invariably have to pay them as normal, as he will need their co-operation to keep the business going and preserve as much of the company's goodwill as possible.

Event [1]	Liability (s 37 IA 1986) [2]
Contract adopted	– The receiver cannot adopt contract by doing/omitting to do anything within first 14 days of appointment [3] – The contract can expressly exclude the receiver's liability; otherwise the receiver is personally liable – If the receiver is liable, he can be indemnified out of the company's assets
New contract supersedes old	– The contract can expressly exclude the receiver's liability; otherwise, the receiver is personally liable – If the receiver is liable, he can be indemnified out of the company's assets
Original contract varied	
Contract terminated	The employee is entitled to usual employment remedies (either under his contract, or in statute (see ¶2986)) [4,5]

Note:
1. If all or part of the company's undertaking is transferred, TUPE may apply (SI 2006/246). The new **TUPE** regulations which came into force on 6 April 2006 no longer contain an exception in relation to hive-downs. See ¶6415+ for hive-downs, ¶6422 for the application of TUPE in insolvency hive-downs and *Employment Memo* for the effect of TUPE generally.
2. For **administrative receivers**, reference is s 44 IA 1986, and his liabilities are circumscribed as set out below.
3. Therefore, even where **contracts continue** during this time, the receiver is not personally liable under them.
4. Many sums due to employees under contract or due to employment claims can be claimed from the secretary of state as "**guaranteed debts**" and/or **preferential debts**, see ¶8044+. For these purposes, the appointment of a receiver counts as "insolvency".
5. **Redundancies** are fairly common where a company enters receivership, as a receiver will usually need to sell off or close down parts of the business. The company may still be under a duty to **consult employee representatives** (see *Employment Memo* for a detailed discussion of this topic). In addition to the usual consultation obligations during redundancy, where 20 or more redundancies are proposed within 90 days, the employer company is under duty to consult with employee representatives (ss 188, 195(2) Trade Union and Labour Relations (Consolidation) Act 1992). The duty may also arise where the employer seeks to vary employment terms by dismissal and re-engagement. The employer is also required to notify BERR. In special circumstances, where consultation is impractical, the employer company can take reasonable steps in the circumstances even if this falls short of proper consultation. However, the fact that the company is subject to insolvency proceedings in itself is not enough to constitute special circumstances (e.g. *Re Hartlebury Printers Ltd (in liquidation)* [1993] 1 All ER 470).

In the case of an **administrative receiver** adopting a contract of employment, his liability is limited to wages, salary and contributions to an occupational pension scheme which (s 44(2A) IA 1986):
- relate to services rendered since the adoption of the contract; and
- are incurred while the administrative receiver is in office.

Ordinary receivers, in contrast, do not have the protection of this limited liability and therefore are liable for all sums due under contracts of employment whenever they arose (although they do have a right of indemnity out of the company's assets).

9267

SECTION 2

Dealing with the company's assets

A receiver's primary duty is to discharge his appointor's debt using the assets secured by the security under which he was appointed. The **assets** will be **determined by** the security document, as will the debt. However, in contrast to a liquidation or administration, any interest accruing on the secured debt during receivership can be added to the sum to be discharged and therefore the receiver must ensure that he has an up to date statement of the principal and interest so that he knows **how much** of the secured assets he needs to realise.

Once he is in office, the receiver's **course of action** depends on the circumstances of each company, as well as the powers granted to him. For example, an administrative receiver will usually carry on the company's business because he has control over most, if not all, of its assets and is likely to realise the best price for them if the company's goodwill and reputation are intact as far as possible. However, this will not be true of every case. Although a receiver is under a professional duty to discharge his functions with reasonable skill and care and can be held liable if he does not, he is under no specific obligation to exercise his power of sale or to carry on the company's business (*Re B Johnson & Co (Builders) Ltd* [1955] 2 All ER 775).

9282

Which assets?

The receiver can only deal with the **specific assets** in respect of which he has been appointed. This question can also determine whether or not he is an administrative receiver and therefore subject to a higher level of regulation under insolvency legislation and the Rules (¶9236+). The scope of the receiver's appointment **depends upon**:
- the security document; and
- the wording of the appointment.

Assets can be expressly excluded from the receiver's remit by the terms of the security or the receiver's appointment, which can be useful to prevent him having to deal with assets which are difficult to sell but expensive to maintain, for example land in the process of being developed.

Due to the vulnerability of **assets under a floating charge** (see ¶9288 below), security documents usually impose fixed charges on as many of the company's assets as possible with just the balance being secured by a floating charge. The receiver undertakes a primarily practical exercise of ascertaining which assets are under his control and which are not, although he must also **consider** whether:
a. purported fixed charges could actually be floating (¶4610+, ¶4618+);
b. there are any prior and/or subsequent charges affecting the same assets, of which he needs to take account when dealing with the assets;
c. any of the relevant assets are subject to third party rights (¶9289+);
d. the assets could be affected by a liquidator's or administrator's ability to challenge certain transactions (¶7808+); and
e. this or any other floating charge could be avoided by a liquidator or administrator (¶7836+; only floating charges created up to 2 years before the insolvency can be challenged, so

9283

holders of these charges will not now be able to appoint an administrative receiver, but they could still appoint an ordinary receiver if their charge allows).

9284 Any **securities ranking above** that under which the receiver was appointed must be respected. Therefore, if a receiver is appointed over assets in respect of which the company has granted prior security, he must account to these security holders first (*Re Arauco Co Ltd* (1898) 79 LT 336). A prior security holder's rights in respect of the assets are preserved so that, for instance, he may take possession of the assets or appoint his own receiver. If there are any **subsequent securities**, the receiver must use any surplus left after he has paid his appointor to pay off sums owing to those security holders. An administrative receiver may apply to court for permission to deal with assets, subject to any subsequent security over them (¶9347+).

MEMO POINTS Where there are **other securities**, the receiver will "marshal" the funds to be fair to the other security holders. This means that if the receiver's appointor has a first charge over asset 1 and asset 2, and another security holder has a second charge over asset 1 only, the receiver will try to pay his appointor out of the realisation of asset 2 as far as possible, to enable the other security holder to recover as much as possible out of asset 1.

9285 An **LPA receiver** appointed under the statutory power in respect of mortgaged land is a receiver of the income deriving from that land, or any part of it as specified in the charge (s 101(1)(iii) LPA 1925).

Considerations relating to specific assets

Under fixed charges

9287 A receiver's ability to deal with assets subject to **enforcement action** depends on the timing of the enforcement and his appointment, as well as on the type of enforcement pursued. Assets which are subject to fixed charges will retain their priority over an order for enforcement, enabling the receiver to deal with them as usual, except where a creditor has obtained an injunction against the company preventing it from dealing with the assets pending the court's decision on his claim. If this is the case, the receiver must abide by the injunction or apply to court to have it discharged before dealing with the affected assets. He may be liable for contempt of court if he causes the company to breach the injunction, or does not take reasonable steps to prevent a breach.

Under floating charges

9288 Unlike fixed charges, floating charges do not assign the assets to the charge holder until crystallisation (which will happen when the receiver is appointed, if not before, see ¶4613), and so a floating charge holder may lose priority over these assets to a person taking prior **enforcement action**. The main issues are summarised in the table below.

Type of enforcement action	Timing	Consequences for floating charge
Execution: judgment creditor obtains an order allowing him to seize and sell the company's assets to the value of judgment and costs	Order delivered but no assets seized before receivership	Priority unaffected (*Re London Pressed Hinge Co Ltd* [1905] 1 Ch 576)
	Assets seized but not sold before receivership	
	Assets seized and sold before receivership	Priority lost
Third party debt order: the company's debtor is ordered to pay debt to the judgment creditor instead of the company[1]	Order made absolute but money not paid to judgment creditor before receivership	Priority unaffected (*Norton v Yates* [1906] 1 KB 112)
	Money paid to the judgment creditor before receivership	Priority lost
Charging order: giving the judgment creditor a charge over particular assets	Interim or absolute order made before the receivership	Priority lost

Type of enforcement action	Timing	Consequences for floating charge
Distress: the landlord seizes the tenant's assets in payment of rent arrears [2]	Distress levied and assets sold before or after receivership	Priority lost [3]

Note:
1. The company can only **assign a debt** over which a third party debt order has been made subject to that order (*Galbraith v Grimshaw* [1910] AC 508).
2. A landlord's **right to forfeit** a lease is not affected by the receiver's appointment (indeed, receivership is often cited as a trigger for forfeiture in the lease).
3. A landlord's **right to distrain** on any goods on the premises applies, regardless of to whom the assets belong. If goods belonging to a third party are distrained, the third party must follow a specific procedure to have them released (s 1 Law of Distress Amendment Act 1908).

Other assets

If any of the assets within the floating charge were already subject to **liens**, they are taken by the receiver subject to those liens (*Brunton v Electrical Engineering Corporation* [1892] 1 Ch 434). Liens are discussed further at ¶4714+. Similarly, if an administrative receiver obtains an order to produce documents under a lien as part of his power to investigate the company's affairs, the lien holder must show the documents to the receiver, although he can refuse to hand them over altogether (*Re Aveling Barford Ltd* [1988] 3 All ER 1019).

9289

> MEMO POINTS However, if the **lien arises after** a **winding up petition** has been presented against the company, it will be void unless the court orders otherwise (¶7674+).

Where some of the company's assets are subject to valid **retention of title claims**, the third party with the benefit of those claims can still rely on them against a receiver (¶4728+). Usually, the company will lose any rights it had to deal with the assets, including selling them, when it goes into receivership and will have to return the assets or pay off the debt protected by the claims in order to keep them.

9290

A company's stock-in-trade is often subject to retention of title clauses. If the **company** has itself **sold goods** to third parties, the receiver may still be able to deal with them if title to the assets has not yet passed. For example, if a customer has ordered and paid for goods which have not yet been delivered and title passes on delivery, the receiver will be able to deal with them, leaving the customer with an unsecured claim against the company for non-delivery. On the other hand, if title passed on payment, the receiver is obliged to deliver the goods to the customer, as the assets cannot be subject to any floating charge under which he is appointed.

Where the company is in possession of assets under a **hire-purchase** or similar **agreement**, the receiver cannot deal with the assets any more than the company could under the agreement. The agreement may be drafted to terminate on the company entering receivership.

9291

The receiver cannot deal with assets **held** by the company **on trust** for a third party, unless the trust is a form of security, in which case it is subject to the usual rules regarding priority and registration (*Re Bond Worth Ltd* [1979] 3 All ER 919).

9292

> EXAMPLE
> The following property was held on trust and therefore was out of the receiver's reach:
> 1. Proceeds of factored book debts (*Lloyds and Scottish Finance Ltd v Cyril Lord Carpets Sales Ltd* (1979) [1992] BCLC 609).
> 2. Assets held by the company for another party (the company's principal) as an agent, such as proceeds of the sale of goods sold as an agent (*Triffit Nurseries (a firm) v Salads Etcetera Ltd (in administrative receivership)* [2000] 1 BCLC 761).

Security over all of the company's property does not extend to its statutory **books** and other records (*Re Clyne Tin Plate Co Ltd* (1882) 47 LT 439). Therefore, the company's officers may retain them, and a liquidator may take control of them if the company goes into liquidation.

9293

On the other hand, any **title documents** to the assets in respect of which he has been appointed can be kept and dealt with by the receiver (*Engel v South Metropolitan Brewing and Bottling Co* [1892] 1 Ch 442).

9294 A receiver appointed under a floating charge cannot act in relation to assets which are subject to the following types of **proceeds of crime** orders (s 430 Proceeds of Crime Act 2002):
– a restraint order made before the receiver's appointment; or
– one appointing an enforcement receiver, enforcement administrator or director's receiver.

If an administrative receiver deals with such assets, he is entitled to a lien over the assets or their proceeds for his remuneration and expenses of doing so, and he will only be personally liable if he dealt with them negligently (ss 432, 433 Proceeds of Crime Act 2002).

A. Collection, preservation and realisation

9304 In terms of collecting the assets over which he is appointed, a receiver will usually take the same **practical steps** as a liquidator to protect them for the benefit of his appointor and the other creditors (¶7779). In extreme cases, where the receiver considers that the secured **assets** are **in** particular **danger** of being, or have already been, dissipated, he can petition for the company's liquidation so that the liquidator can use his more extensive powers to protect and increase the assets, especially his powers to challenge transactions entered into prior to liquidation. An ordinary receiver has a common law power to do this (*Re Emmadart Ltd* [1979] 1 All ER 599), while an administrative receiver can rely on his statutory powers (¶9347+). If a winding up order is made, however, prior dispositions of property may be void unless the court orders otherwise, and so the receiver should apply for his dealings with the company's property to stand (¶7674+).

9305 An **administrative receiver** can apply to court to order a person in possession of any of the company's property, books, papers or records, to deliver them to him directly (s 234(1) IA 1986). If he has **seized property** which does not belong to the company (although he reasonably believed that he could deal with it at the time), he will not be liable for any loss or damage caused by the seizure, unless caused by his negligence (s 234(3), (4) IA 1986). He also has a lien over the property or its proceeds of sale for his expenses in dealing with it. See ¶9392 for his liability for wrongfully retaining goods.

9306 An ordinary receiver may be able to cause the company to **carry on trading** for a period, if the security under which he is appointed allows. He will need to be able to exercise the company's management powers, including entering into contracts as the company's agent. An administrative receiver is granted this power by statute, also acting as the company's agent (¶9347+).

Increasing assets

9307 A receiver can take **legal action**, without the company's consent, to recover any of the secured assets which he cannot readily collect (*M Wheeler & Co Ltd v Warren* [1928] Ch 840). Although a receiver cannot **challenge** the same **transactions** as a liquidator or administrator (¶7808+), if any transactions prior to the receivership were entered into beyond the company's powers, or were void or illegal in another way, he can apply to court for the transaction to be set aside or declared void and for the relevant assets or money to be returned to the company. Examples of such transactions are those entered into by the directors in breach of their fiduciary or statutory duties, such as a loan made to a director without following the correct procedure, or a transaction entered into by a director on the company's behalf which was fraudulent or a product of his misfeasance or negligence. In deciding whether to take such action, the receiver must balance the benefit to the receivership against the time and costs involved.

> **EXAMPLE** Dr L, a shareholder, controlled both AB Ltd and P Ltd. AB Ltd owned a piece of land which had been valued at £650,000, but was sold to P Ltd for only £350,000. The receiver of AB Ltd challenged this transaction, and the court held that the sale had been constructed as a roundabout manner of making an unauthorised return of capital to Dr L at a time when the company was in financial difficulties and was therefore not able to use the proper procedure. The directors of AB Ltd were in breach of their fiduciary duties in carrying out the sale at an undervalue, and P Ltd was held liable as a constructive trustee because it was aware of the circumstances of the breach (also being controlled by Dr L). The sale was therefore set aside (*Aveling Barford Ltd v Perion Ltd* [1989] BCLC 626).

9309 **Share capital** usually falls within a debenture comprising fixed and floating charges, and an **administrative receiver** has the power to call up any unpaid share capital (¶9347+). However, he only has the same rights as the company in doing so and therefore must follow any procedures and restrictions set out in the company's articles, except for any requirements to obtain board or shareholder authority (because the power to authorise calls will have been delegated to him by virtue of the security under which he was appointed, if this was validly entered into under the company's memorandum and articles (¶1205+)).

Power to sell

9310 An **ordinary receiver**'s power to sell is usually contained in the security document under which he was appointed. In the absence of a contractual power to sell, only a mortgage holder can sell the secured assets, using his statutory power (s 101 LPA 1925). An **administrative receiver** is granted this power by statute, but the security will usually reiterate it as well (¶9347+).

As part of his common law duty to act with reasonable skill and care, a receiver must consider the **timing and terms** of any sale in relation to how it may affect the realisation achieved. He can sell the property at any time before the security is discharged but, for instance, he may favour deferring the sale of assets which could be improved before sale, such as land which is undergoing development. If the receiver plans to sell the business as a going concern, he will want to retain the goodwill in the company pending the sale and therefore will cause the company to carry on trading. Such a sale may be effected directly to the purchaser or following a hive-down (¶6415+). Alternatively, he may have to sell the assets off separately, meaning that quick sales will be favoured before the company's reputation is damaged too much and before the receiver incurs too many liabilities in retaining the assets.

> **MEMO POINTS** 1. An **LPA receiver** does not have a power of sale, unless it has been specifically delegated to him by his appointor (¶9228). If the mortgage holder or receiver (where the power has been delegated) exercises his power of sale, he can sell the mortgaged property free of encumbrances ranking below his mortgage (ss 101, 104 LPA 1925).
> 2. **Sales to directors** are relatively common in receiverships, as they enable the directors either to purchase the asset for the benefit of the company or to buy elements of the company's business to trade under a different commercial entity. In such cases the rules relating to substantial property transactions may apply (¶2567+).

9311 A receiver cannot usually sell the property with a clean **title**, because it will still be subject to any security over it, including that under which he was appointed. The security usually allows the receiver to convey the legal estate in the company's name, but purchasers will often require either:
– the security holder, who can give good title, to execute the sale; or
– the receiver to give an undertaking that the security will be discharged.
See ¶9347+ for an administrative receiver's ability to apply to the court to sell assets free of other security.

B. Distribution

9321 The receiver's aim is to discharge his appointor's security, paying off the principal and interest owed to him out of the secured assets. Although this comprises the **principal distribution** he is obliged to make, the costs of realisation and the receivership in general also have to be met out of the same funds, as will certain other claims. Aside from distributions required to be made to preferential and unsecured creditors in some circumstances (to whom the usual pari passu principle applies), there is usually only one person, the appointor, to whom a distribution must be made at any one time and so the receiver can distribute to him as much of the proceeds of realisation as is necessary to pay him off in full.

Any **surplus** is to be distributed to subsequent holders of security over the same assets and then to the company. If the **assets are insufficient** to pay the appointor in full, he will have exhausted his security and will be an unsecured creditor for the remainder of his debt. The receiver is under no duty to recover this unsecured portion for him. If two security holders rank equally in relation to the same assets, and the assets are insufficient to pay both off in full, they will only be entitled to be paid off pari passu.

> MEMO POINTS It would be unusual for more than one receiver to be appointed at the same time in respect of the same assets but under different, **equally-ranking charges**, but it is the kind of situation likely to give rise to disputes regarding the conduct of the receivership. The court may appoint a receiver in such a situation to oversee the receiverships and provide an independent assessment of the appropriate course of action (*Bass Breweries Ltd v Delaney* [1994] BCC 851).

9322 The security may set out the **order of priority** in which a receiver must distribute the proceeds of the realised assets, subject to the payment of preferential debts out of the proceeds of a floating charge (¶9326). A typical order of priority will be:
a. the costs of realisation;
b. the costs of the receivership, including the receiver's remuneration;
c. if the receiver was appointed under a floating charge:
– the preferential creditors; followed by
– the unsecured creditors out of any fund ring-fenced for their benefit (¶9327);
d. the appointor's debt (principal and interest to the date of payment);
e. any subsequent charge holders; and
f. any surplus to the company (or its liquidator).

The rights of prior and subsequent security holders are dealt with at ¶9284.

In the case of an **LPA receiver**, statute prescribes the following order of distribution for the proceeds of the income he receives from the mortgaged property (s 109(8) LPA 1925):
a. payment of rents, taxes, rates and outgoings affecting the mortgaged property;
b. payment of annual and other sums and interest on them, which have priority over the mortgage;
c. payment of the LPA receiver's commission, the premium on any insurance payable under the mortgage or legislation, and the cost of any necessary repairs to the property as required by the mortgage holder;
d. payment of the interest under the mortgage;
e. payments towards the principal under the mortgage; and
f. any residue must be paid to the person who would have received the income from the property if the receiver were not appointed (usually the person who granted the mortgage in the first place).

> MEMO POINTS 1. If the **company** is also **in liquidation**, the costs of the liquidation will be met out of the proceeds of realisation before they are applied to the preferential creditors and then the receiver's appointor.
> 2. An **LPA receiver** does not have a power of **sale**, unless it has been delegated to him by his appointor (¶9228). If the property is sold by the receiver under this delegated power or by a person other than the receiver (whether the person who granted the mortgage or the mortgage holder in possession) while a receiver is in office, statute sets out the order in which the proceeds of sale are to be distributed (s 105 LPA 1925; ¶4666).

Specific distributions

Costs and expenses of receivership

9323 The security will usually allow the receiver's appointor to add any costs and expenses reasonably **incurred in enforcing** the **security** to the amount of principal, interest and other sums he is already owed under it. This allows him to recoup any sums paid to the receiver by way of remuneration and other expenses, but not any third party's costs (*Parker-Tweedale v Dunbar Bank plc (No 2)* [1990] 2 All ER 588).

The **remuneration** of receivers appointed under security documents depends upon the terms of the security. It is usually stated to be fixed by the appointor, and will be based on the time spent by the receiver and his staff in dealing with the matter, taking into account the complexity of the case.

Receivers are usually entitled to be paid all of their remuneration, costs and expenses out of the charged assets. They therefore obtain a **contractual indemnity** from their appointor before they accept their appointment to cover:
- their remuneration and expenses; and
- any liabilities incurred during the conduct of the receivership that can properly be paid out of the receivership assets, such as the costs of insuring the assets or taking or defending legal proceedings to protect or increase them.

> MEMO POINTS 1. The court has the power to **review and fix** a receiver's **remuneration** on the application of a liquidator of the company (s 35 IA 1986). If the court decides that the rate awarded so far has been too high, it can require the receiver to repay any excess but will only do so in respect of sums received before the application was made in exceptional circumstances. The receiver may apply to the court for directions regarding his remuneration in the case of a dispute (s 36 IA 1986; *Re Therm-a-Stor Ltd (in administrative receivership), Morris v Lewis* [1996] 3 All ER 228).
> 2. Statute entitles **LPA receivers** to a **commission** in respect of their remuneration and all costs, charges and expenses they incur at a rate of up to 5% of the gross amount of monies received (s 109(6) LPA 1925).

9324 Generally speaking, a **receiver** is not personally liable to meet the company's **tax liabilities**, although in reality he will often take responsibility for accounting to the appropriate authorities for taxes as necessary. Receivership, unlike liquidation and administration, will not bring the company's accounting period to an end.

The tax effects of **administrative receivership** are summarised below:

a. corporation tax: tax on gains made by the receiver dealing with the company's assets is payable by the company. Tax on trading and other profits made by the receiver is also payable by the company, although it is unusual for a company in receivership to make a net profit (s 26(2) TCGA 1992);

b. VAT: the company is still viewed as a taxable person, but Revenue and Customs will deal with the receiver, who must make VAT returns and account for VAT collected by the company (para 8, Sch 4 VATA 1994). VAT returns are to be based on pre- and post-receivership VAT separately. The receiver must notify the local VAT office of his appointment within 21 days if the company is registered for VAT (reg 9 SI 1995/2518; *Sargent v Customs & Excise Comrs* [1995] 2 BCLC 34); and

c. other taxes: since the receiver is the employer, he must operate PAYE and account for any income tax and National Insurance contributions deducted (s 108(3) Taxes Management Act 1970). The company is still liable for rates, unless the receiver has dispossessed the property in question, in which case he becomes liable (*Ratford v Northavon District Council* [1986] 3 All ER 193).

> MEMO POINTS The Rules dealing with the **VAT bad debt** certificates issued by an administrative receiver are no longer relevant since the creditors do not have to show that the company is insolvent any more in order to claim the relief (i.e. rr 3.36, 3.37 IR 1986).

9325 A receiver is not liable for **rent payments** due by a company, whether incurred before or after his appointment (*Hand v Blow* [1901] 2 Ch 721). However, a landlord can rely on his usual remedies for non-payment of rent against a company in receivership, such as distress and forfeiture. Therefore, the receiver will usually have to pay post-receivership rent so the company can carry on business and he can achieve the best realisation of the secured assets.

Preferential creditors

9326 Where the receiver has been appointed under security which was created as a floating charge and the company is not already in liquidation, the preferential debts must be **paid out of** the proceeds of the secured assets in the receiver's hands before the secured debt (principal and interest) (s 40(1), (2) IA 1986). However, any sums paid out in this way can be recouped out of the company's unsecured assets (s 40(3) IA 1986). This provision transfers the risk of the company's assets being insufficient to meet these liabilities from the preferential creditors (who mostly comprise employees) to the security holder. The **categories** of preferential debts are explained at ¶8044+. The "relevant date" for calculating such claims where the company is in receivership is to be taken as the date of the receiver's appointment (s 387(4)(a) IA 1986).

The receiver must pay the preferential creditors in their **order of priority**, and if he makes a distribution to his appointor or other creditors without paying (or without at least reserving a sum to pay) the preferential creditors first, he will be personally liable to them for his breach of statutory duty (*IRC v Goldblatt* [1972] 2 All ER 202, in which a receiver caused the company to carry on business at a loss). Even if the assets subject to the floating charge do not need to be realised, for example where the security comprises fixed and floating charges and the assets secured under the fixed charge are sufficient to meet his appointor's debt, the receiver must still pay the preferential creditors.

> MEMO POINTS   If the **company** then **goes into liquidation**, the assets subject to the floating charge under which the receiver was appointed are not available for paying the costs of the liquidation or further preferential debts, although assets subject to other floating charges are (*Re Leyland Daf Ltd, Buchler v Talbot* [2004] 1 All ER 1289; s 175 IA 1986). However, the **new Companies Act** will reverse this decision (s 1282 CA 2006, due to come into force on 6 April 2008, ¶7997/mp).
> If the **company** was **already in liquidation**, the floating charge will be used to meet liquidation claims and expenses according to the rules discussed at ¶7992+ (because the requirement to pay preferential creditors in the receivership does not apply (s 40(2) IA 1986)). The floating charge holder then ranks above the unsecured creditors in a distribution of the relevant secured assets (*Re Leyland Daf Ltd, Buchler v Talbot,* above).

Unsecured creditors

9327 Where an ordinary receiver is **appointed under** a **floating charge** created on or after 15 September 2003 (this requirement therefore does not apply to administrative receivers), he is required, like liquidators and administrators, to ring-fence a certain proportion of the assets (and their proceeds) to meet the claims of the unsecured creditors before the remainder can be distributed to the charge holder. The receiver can apply to court to be excused from this requirement, and it will not be necessary to ring-fence the fund in certain other circumstances. The topic is explained further at ¶7992+. If the obligation to ring-fence this fund arises, the receiver must make distributions to unsecured creditors accordingly, but if it does not, he has no other duty to distribute funds to them since any surplus assets after he has discharged his appointor's security must be returned to the company.

Any receiver may, as a practical matter, have to pay off certain unsecured creditors such as landlords, employees or important suppliers, if this is necessary to keep the business going.

Creditors who are also debtors of the company

9328 The law relating to **set-off** in a receivership is more restricted than that in liquidation or administration, because it is not automatic and can be contractually excluded (*Hongkong and Shanghai Banking Corporation v Kloeckner & Co AG* [1989] 3 All ER 513). Generally speaking, sums owed by a debtor to the company can be set off against any sums owed to him by the company to reduce or even cancel out a debt, provided there is mutuality between the two parties and the debts arise out of the same or connected contracts. The topic of set-off is discussed further in the context of liquidation, see ¶8072+.

> MEMO POINTS   Like any contractual term, a set-off **provision may be unenforceable** for a number of reasons, for example it may be unfair under the Unfair Contract Terms Act 1977 (*Stewart Gill Ltd v Horatio Myer & Co Ltd* [1992] 2 All ER 257, dealing with a clause excluding set-off in a company's standard terms and conditions, which is common).

SECTION 3

The receiver

9343 Due to the contractual, rather than statutory, nature of a receiver's appointment, his **conduct of the receivership** is governed largely by the terms of the security and his appointment, and so varies in each case. There are, however, general principles which apply to all receivers, as well as specific statutory and regulatory provisions relating to **administrative receivers** only, which render their role similar to that of an administrator in terms of their duties to involve the creditors in the process. **Appointing** a receiver is dealt with at ¶9222+, and his **remuneration** at ¶9323.

A. Powers

9345 An **ordinary receiver**'s powers are defined by the terms of the security document under which he is appointed. An **LPA receiver** has limited statutory powers conferred on him, which can be augmented by additional powers in the security document (ss 103, 109 LPA 1925). Specific and extensive powers are granted to an **administrative receiver**, see ¶9347+ below.

There is no direct authority as to whether a receiver's **powers** are **limited to** actions that the company itself could take under its memorandum, although this is likely to be the case (*Re Home Treat Ltd* [1991] BCLC 705, an administration case on the same point). However, the company can alter the objects clause in its memorandum to give its receiver wider powers if necessary.

> MEMO POINTS Companies incorporated under the **new Companies Act** will have unlimited objects, but restrictions in existing companies' objects will still apply (see ¶419/mp).

9346 A receiver appointed under a security document or his appointor(s) can apply to the **court** for **directions** on any matters relating to the performance of his functions (s 35 IA 1986). For example, many cases have been brought under this provision for directions as to the order of priority in which distributions ought to be made.

Administrative receiver

9347 An administrative receiver is given the same **extensive powers** as an administrator by insolvency legislation (s 42 IA 1986; see ¶9011 for a list of these powers, noting the exceptions which apply to administrative receivers). Nevertheless, these powers are usually repeated in the security document and can be augmented with additional powers. This ensures that even if the appointment cannot take effect as an administrative receivership because it is confined to too few assets, the receiver will still have the powers of an administrative receiver, albeit relating to a narrower field of assets.

9348 A **third party** dealing with an administrative receiver in good faith and for value (i.e. one who does not receive property from him as a gift) does not have to check whether the administrative receiver is acting within his powers in relation to the transaction in question (s 42(3) IA 1986). He is further protected in that the administrative receiver's acts cannot be challenged if there is a defect in his appointment, although this is probably confined to technical or procedural defects rather than substantive ones (s 232 IA 1986).

9349 An administrative receiver also has a specific power to apply to the court for permission to **deal with secured assets** as if they were not charged, provided the security in question (s 43 IA 1986):
– is not held by his appointor; and
– ranks below any security held by his appointor.

He must notify the affected security holder of the date, time and place of the hearing to enable him to attend (r 3.31 IR 1986).

He must satisfy the court that the disposal of the assets in question would **achieve a better realisation** of the company's assets as a whole than would otherwise be achieved. An order would allow the administrative receiver to sell the secured assets free of any encumbrances, i.e. to "overreach" the other security, which is more attractive to a potential purchaser and can assist in achieving a better realisation. Without this permission, the administrative receiver cannot sell free of any security, not even the one under which he was appointed (*Re Real Meat Company Ltd* [1996] BCC 254), and so purchasers often wish to deal directly with the security holder, or to obtain an undertaking from the administrative receiver that he will discharge the security.

If permission is granted, the order will **protect** any **other affected security holders** by providing that their security must be discharged using the net proceeds of the disposal, and if this falls below the amount that should have been realised on the open market, the deficiency will have to be made up. The administrative receiver is required to **file** any order made at Companies House within 14 days, and is liable to a fine if he fails to do so (s 43(5), (6) IA 1986; ¶9935). He must also send a copy to the affected security holder(s) (r 3.31(4) IR 1986).

B. Duties

9359 Compared to liquidators and administrators, **ordinary receivers** have relatively few specific duties, unless they are set out in their appointing security document. However, general duties control their conduct to a great extent, as they must act within the terms of their appointment with the reasonable skill and care expected of someone in their position. This is also true of **administrative receivers**, upon whom additional duties are imposed, commensurate with their greater control over the company's management and assets.

The **terms of security documents** allowing the appointment of a receiver usually state that:
– he is the company's agent;
– the company shall be responsible for his actions and omissions; and
– he has an irrevocable power of attorney.

1. General duties

9360 A receiver's **common law** duties are, broadly (*Medforth v Blake* [1999] 3 All ER 97):
– to act in good faith;
– to cause the secured debt and interest to be paid; and
– to manage the property with due diligence including, where relevant, to carry on the company's business profitably.

A receiver also occupies a **fiduciary** position in relation to his appointor, with the duties that entails (*Gomba Holdings UK Ltd v Minories Finance Ltd* [1989] 1 All ER 261; see ¶2373+ for a discussion of fiduciary duties in the context of directors).

9361 A receiver's **agency** differs from a normal commercial agency, in that the company does not dictate its terms and cannot terminate it. As an agent of the company, he **owes** a **duty to** the company and his appointor, but not to the creditors (*Lathia v Dronsfield Bros Ltd* [1987] BCLC 321). He owes the usual agent's duties, including to act within the scope of his powers, carry out his functions with reasonable skill and care and to account for any profit he makes to his principal (subject, of course, to the terms of the security). He is also entitled to an indemnity for any liabilities he incurs in carrying out his duties (¶9392).

Statute provides that **LPA receivers** and **administrative receivers** are the company's agent (respectively: s 109(2) LPA 1925; s 44 IA 1986). However, most security documents also expressly state that they will be an agent and may set out their powers and liabilities in that respect.

MEMO POINTS If the **company** is **in liquidation**, the receiver's agency ceases, but he will still be able to deal with and sell the charged assets in the name of the company (*Re Henry Pound, Son & Hutchins* (1889) 42 Ch D 402). However, a person buying from the receiver in this situation may prefer to receive title directly from the receiver's appointor. A person buying from an administrative receiver has added protection (¶9348).

If there is **no agency provision** in the security document, an **ordinary receiver** will not be regarded as the company's agent, but could be construed as his appointor's agent or as acting as principal in relation to the company's assets, exposing him to personal liability and making it difficult for him to sell the company's assets.

9362

2. Providing information

Receivers are required to deliver **accounts of receipts and payments** to Companies House at the following intervals.

9367

	Ordinary receivers[1] (s 38 IA 1986)	Administrative receivers[2,3,4] (r 3.32 IR 1986)
Initial accounts	Within 1 month of first anniversary of his appointment	Within 2 months of first anniversary of his appointment
Subsequent accounts	Within 1 month of every 6-month period after that	Within 2 months of every 12-month period after that
Final accounts	Within 1 month of his appointment ceasing	Within 2 months of his appointment ceasing

Note:
1. Companies House may **extend** the 1-month period.
2. The court may **extend** the 2-month period.
3. Copies of the accounts must **also** be **sent to** the company, administrative receiver's appointor and members of any creditors' committee.
4. **Administrative receivers** have other duties to provide information to the creditors in general as well as to any creditors' committee, see ¶9378.

Failure to comply with these requirements renders the receiver liable to a fine (s 38(5) IA 1986; r 3.32(5) IR 1986; ¶9935).

To **publicise** the receivership, a statement that a receiver has been appointed must appear on every one of the following documents which contains the company's name (s 39(1) IA 1986):
– invoices;
– orders for goods; and
– business letters.

9368

Failure to do so renders the company, any officers in default, receiver and liquidator (if applicable) liable to a fine (¶9935).

Since January 2007, companies in liquidation have been required to state the fact that it is in liquidation on **all documents** issued by the company **including** those issued in electronic form, websites and order forms (EC Directive 2003/58). At the time of writing, the Government has proposed to apply similar provisions to the receivership process, but this change has not yet been made. Meanwhile, the Insolvency Service has recommended that, as a matter of good practice, insolvency practitioners should follow the new provisions in receivership procedures (*Dear IP* March 2007, Issue No 31). As a result, a statement that the company's affairs, business and property are being managed by the receiver, including his name, should be included on any business documents issued in hard copy, electronic or other form, as well as on all of the company's websites.

If an **ordinary receiver** appointed under a **floating charge** is required to ring-fence a portion of the assets subject to the charge for the benefit of the unsecured creditors (which will be the case in the same situations that apply to a liquidator, see ¶9327, ¶7992+), he must notify the company's creditors of (r 3.39 IR 1986):
– his appointment;

9369

- his estimate of the assets which should be ring-fenced for the benefit of the unsecured creditors;
- his estimate of the value of the company's net property;
- whether, and if so why, he proposes to apply to court to be excused from ring-fencing the relevant assets (¶7992+); and
- whether he intends to petition for the company's winding up.

The ordinary receiver does not have to reveal any information which could prejudice the commercial interests of the company, although if he does exclude any such information, he must state that he has done so in the notice. If it is not practicable for him to send this report to all of the creditors (e.g. because there are too many of them), he can publish the information in an appropriate newspaper instead. In dealing with any ring-fenced fund, the ordinary receiver must **apply to court** for directions as to how he should make it available to discharge the unsecured debts (r 3.40 IR 1986).

> MEMO POINTS   As part of the Insolvency Service's review of secondary legislation (see ¶7364/mp), it is taking the opportunity to make alterations to the primary legislation either where it is necessary to support the new Rules or to remove unnecessary administrative burdens. The Service proposes to remove the requirement for insolvency practitioners to **send information to all known creditors** at various stages in the procedure (proposal 1, "A consultation document on changes to the Insolvency Act 1986 and the Company Directors Disqualification Act 1986 to be made by a Legislative Reform Order for the modernisation and streamlining of insolvency procedures" (September 2007)). Generally speaking, most creditors just want to know how much of their debt will be repaid and have no interest in the general progress of the procedure. This requirement therefore creates a heavy but unnecessary financial and administrative burden. It will be replaced by a system allowing creditors who do wish to be kept up to date to "opt in" to receiving information from the insolvency practitioner. The consultation also proposes to allow information to be exchanged by electronic communication where the recipient agrees, and for insolvency practitioners to make information available via a website.
>
> At the time of writing, the consultation is still open. If these proposals are accepted, the changes are likely to be implemented from 1 October 2008.

9370 Where a **liquidator is appointed** in respect of the company, he can require the receiver to provide proper accounts of his receipts and payments and pay over any amount which should be paid to the liquidator (s 41 IA 1986). If he fails to do so, the liquidator can apply to the court for an order compelling him to do so (s 41 IA 1986).

At the **end** of an **administrative receivership**, if the company is then wound up by the court, the administrative receiver must, as required (s 235 IA 1986):
- provide the liquidator or official receiver with such information about the company's promotion, formation, business, dealings, affairs or property; and
- attend the liquidator or official receiver in person.

9371 If a **receiver fails** to comply with his duties to make any return, account or other document or to give notice, he can be served with a notice requiring him to do so. If he fails to comply within 14 days of the notice, the court can compel him to correct the breach on application by any shareholder, creditor or Companies House, in addition to paying any fines he has incurred by his failure (s 41 IA 1986).

> MEMO POINTS   The **FSA** can make an application to enforce such duties if the company is or was (s 363 FSMA 2000):
> - an authorised person;
> - an appointment representative; or
> - carrying on a regulated activity in contravention of the prohibition.

3. Conduct of an administrative receivership

9376 The following duties, similar to those to which an administrator is subject, are only imposed upon an administrative receiver. These **extra duties** are required because he has control over a wider range of the company's assets and therefore:
- he needs to make a more thorough investigation of the company's affairs; and
- his actions are more likely to impact on creditors other than his appointor.

He must keep the creditors informed about the progress of the receivership so they can monitor their own chances of recovery and take other action to protect their interests if necessary.

Investigate the company's affairs

The administrative receiver is obliged to conduct a thorough investigation into the company's affairs, and relies on information obtained from directors and others involved in the company who are under a duty to co-operate with him (¶8121) to:
- prepare a **statement of affairs** (¶8861+);
- **deliver** the **company's property** to him (¶8170); and
- submit to **private examination** (¶8172+).

These topics are dealt with elsewhere, because they mirror powers and duties granted to administrators and liquidators, with relevant differences noted in the memo points.

An administrative receiver is under a duty to report on the **conduct of** the **directors** of the company if:
a. it appears to him that a director's conduct renders him unfit to be concerned in company management and the company is or has been insolvent (s 7(3) CDDA 1986); or
b. the secretary of state or official receiver requires (this includes providing and allowing inspection of any documents relevant to a director's conduct) (s 7(4) CDDA 1986).

9377

> MEMO POINTS   The administrative receiver must also **report** the company **to** the **FSA** if it appears to him that it is or has been carrying on a regulated activity without having the necessary authorisation or falling within an exemption from the prohibition (s 364 FSMA 2000).

Reporting to creditors

An administrative receiver is required to produce a report regarding the administrative receivership within 3 months of his appointment (s 48(1) IA 1986). The report must set out the following **information** (s 48(1), (5) IA 1986; r 3.8(5) IR 1986):
a. the events leading up to the administrative receivership, as far as he is aware;
b. his conduct of the administrative receivership in terms of any disposals or proposed disposals of assets and whether he is carrying, or intends to carry, on the business of the company;
c. the debts owed to his appointor(s), broken down into principal and interest;
d. the amounts due to preferential creditors;
e. the amount likely to be available for the payment of other creditors;
f. a summary of the company's affairs and any relevant comments;
g. an estimate of the company's net assets and the value of assets available for ring-fencing for the benefit of the unsecured creditors (see ¶7992+); and
h. whether, and if so why, the administrative receiver intends making an application to court to be excused from having to ring-fence a portion of the company's assets for the benefit of the unsecured creditors (see ¶7992+).

9378

It **does not** have to **include** any information which would seriously prejudice the administrative receiver's ability to carry out his functions, or any part of the statement of affairs which is subject to an order for limited disclosure (s 48(6) IA 1986; r 3.5 IR 1986). If the calculation in g. above omits any information because it would seriously prejudice the commercial interests of the company, the administrative receiver must state that this is the case (r 3.8(6) IR 1986).

> MEMO POINTS   1. Although an administrative receiver is not obliged to ring-fence part of a floating charge for the benefit of unsecured creditors (the obligation only applies to floating charges created on or after 15/09/03, and an administrative receiver can only be appointed under a floating charge created before then), the Rules specifically require him to include the information at g. and h.
> 2. The Insolvency Service has proposed to replace the obligations on insolvency practitioners to **send information to creditors** at different stages with a system allowing creditors to opt in to receiving information instead (¶9369/mp).

Filing

9379 This report must be **sent to**:
– Companies House, together with copies of the statement(s) of affairs and affidavit(s) of concurrence, provided an order for limited disclosure has not been obtained (r 3.8(3) IR 1986);
– all secured creditors for whom he has an address; and
– any trustees for secured creditors.

He must also either send it to all unsecured creditors for whom he has an address, or advertise the fact that he has made the report (in the same newspaper in which the advertisement of his appointment appeared) and send a copy to any unsecured creditor who requests one free of charge (s 48(2) IA 1986; r 3.8(1) IR 1986). He must also do this within 3 months of his appointment.

If the administrative receiver considers that it would prejudice the conduct of the receivership if all or part of the statement of affairs was disclosed, he can apply for an order for limited disclosure so that he does **not have to file** it (or the sensitive part of it) (r 3.5 IR 1986).

> *MEMO POINTS* 1. If the company is in, or goes into, **liquidation**, the administrative receiver must send a copy of the report to the liquidator within 7 days of either: sending the report to Companies House and the secured creditors; or, the liquidator's nomination or appointment (s 48(4) IA 1986). Unless the company goes into liquidation after he has notified the unsecured creditors as well, the administrative receiver is then excused from sending the report to the unsecured creditors or advertising his notice.
> 2. An administrative receiver who was appointed in **addition to** or as a **replacement** for another does not have to prepare this report to creditors, except to the extent that his predecessor failed to do so (s 48(7) IA 1986).
> 3. The Insolvency Service has proposed that **affidavits** are replaced by witness statements (see ¶8737). This change is likely to be implemented from 1 October 2008.

9380 **Failure** to report to Companies House and the creditors in this manner renders the administrative receiver liable to a fine (s 48(8) IA 1986; ¶9935).

Creditors' meeting

9381 The administrative receiver is also required to **present the report to** a meeting of unsecured creditors, which must be called on at least 14 days' notice specifying the purpose of the meeting (s 48(2) IA 1986). This meeting may also establish a creditors' committee.

He can, however apply to court to be **excused from holding** such a meeting, and if he has done so he must state the date, time and place of the court hearing in the report or the advertisement to unsecured creditors to give them the opportunity to attend (r 3.8(2) IR 1986).

Creditors' committee

9382 The main **purpose** of establishing a creditors' committee in an administrative receivership is to obtain information from the administrative receiver to keep the general creditors informed. The committee also supervises the administrative receiver to a certain extent, in requiring information and deciding matters put to them. However, the administrative receiver does not owe a duty to the general creditors, so their decision making capacity is limited to matters about which he wishes to consult them, usually to ensure their support for the administrative receivership and to prevent them from taking action which could impede it.

The **rules** relating to its establishment, membership and conduct are similar to those for creditors' committees in administrations, see ¶9060+ (any relevant differences are noted in the memo points to that discussion).

C. Liabilities

A receiver is open to a number of liabilities, although he will usually ensure that he obtains an indemnity to cover those arising in the proper course of the receivership. The main liabilities can be summarised as follows.

9392

Liability	Relief from liability [1]	Indemnity	Reference
Under contracts adopted or entered into during receivership	Can be expressly excluded in contract	– Statutory – Usually contractual from appointor as well	s 37 IA 1986 (ordinary receivers); s 44 IA 1986 (administrative receivers)
As an agent [2, 3]	If acting within authority, the company is liable If not acting within authority or fails in duties as agent, the receiver is liable	– Contractual (if acting within authority) – Statutory from appointors against liabilities arising because the security or appointment is invalid – Lien over assets in his control re. personal liability (¶9403)	s 34 IA 1986
Misfeasance (the administrative receiver or receiver engaged in management of company only)	Statutory relief can be applied where appropriate	–	¶7457+
Tort – trespass/conversion re. third party goods	Administrative receiver: not liable if he reasonably believed he was entitled to seize or dispose of goods, unless loss or damage was caused by his negligence (s 234(3), (4) IA 1986) [4]	–	Re Botibol [1947] 1 All ER 25; s 1 Torts (Interference with Goods) Act 1977

Note:
1. An **administrative receiver** can apply to court for statutory relief from liability for his negligence, default, or breach of duty or trust, whether in relation to past or future actions (see ¶2505+). Therefore, if the administrative receiver is unsure whether his proposed action is within his powers, he can apply to court for directions and relief from liability before he pursues it.
2. Examples of receivers **breaching agency duties**, including the implied duty to act with due skill and care, are:
– where a receiver does not take reasonable care to obtain market value of secured property, he can be liable to company as well as to other holders of security over the same property (*Burgess v Auger, Burgess v Vanstock Ltd* [1998] 2 BCLC 478);
– not carrying on the company's business profitably and with due diligence (*Medforth v Blake* [1999] 3 All ER 97); and
– negligently causing a loss/reduction in the value of secured assets (*Knight v Lawrence* [1991] BCC 411, in which a receiver failed to a trigger rent review provision in a lease that would have benefited the company).
3. Since the receiver is the company's agent, the **appointor** will not ordinarily be **liable** for the receiver's actions, unless he instructs the receiver to do or not to do something beyond his powers or otherwise interferes in conduct of receivership (*Re American Express International Banking Corp v Hurley* [1985] 3 All ER 564). For example, where receivers took unsuccessful legal action against a person for breach of contract, the court would not order the receivers (rather than the company) to pay the defendant's costs because they were acting as the company's agents (*Dolphin Quays Developments Limited v Mills and others* [2007] EWHC 1180 (Ch)). The defendant should have applied for security for costs at an early stage in the litigation.
4. He even has a **lien** over property/proceeds of its realisation for costs of seizing/disposing of it. This protection is limited to tangible assets (*Welsh Development Agency v Export Finance Co Ltd* [1992] BCLC 148).

D. Termination of office and conclusion of receivership

9402 When the receiver has achieved his aim, i.e. either paid off the money owed to his appointor or exhausted the secured assets in respect of which he was appointed, he will resign and the receivership will come to an end. The receiver's office can be terminated in other ways, but he will usually be replaced by another until the **purpose of** the **receivership** has been **achieved**. Once the receivership has ended, the company may continue to trade as usual. However, it is often the case that the company is left with insufficient assets to carry on its business, and/or that its reputation and goodwill have been eroded to such an extent during the receivership that it is not able to carry on trading. Therefore, liquidation often follows receivership (and, indeed, can be commenced during receivership), or administration if there is a chance of rescuing part or all of the company or if it would achieve a better realisation than a liquidation.

If an ordinary receiver has been appointed under a floating charge and is obliged to ring-fence a portion of the secured assets for the benefit of the unsecured creditors, he may petition for the company's **winding up** on the ground that it is unable to pay its debts (r 3.40 IR 1986; ¶7593+). An administrative receiver can petition for the company's winding up on any appropriate grounds (s 42, Sch 1 IA 1986). For the possibilities of the company being subject to **another insolvency procedure** as well as, or at the end of, ordinary or administrative receivership, see ¶7481.

> MEMO POINTS Where a **liquidator or administrator** is **appointed** to the company, an ordinary receiver must hand over any ring-fenced portion of the floating charge under which he was appointed (r 3.40 IR 1986; ¶9327; ¶7992+).

9403 A receiver must **cease to act** and return the company's property and money **when** he has discharged his appointor's security and paid or made provision for the costs of the receivership, his remuneration and other necessary sums (such as preferential claims). If he **fails** to do so, he may be held liable to the company for trespass (s 1 Torts (Interference with Goods) Act 1977).

He is entitled to a first charge over the company's property which was in his control in respect of his **statutory indemnity** for any liability he incurred under contracts entered into or adopted during the receivership (s 37(4) IA 1986 (ordinary receiver); s 44(3) IA 1986 (administrative receiver)). As an agent, he is also entitled to a lien over assets in his control in respect of any **personal liability** he has incurred in performing his functions properly, unless the lien is defeated because the company has gone into administration or liquidation (*Foxcroft v Wood* (1828) 4 Russ 487; ¶7902).

Ordinary receiver

9404 There are no statutory or regulatory provisions relating to the termination of an ordinary receiver's office. The ability of the appointor to **remove** him from office and replace him without applying to court will usually be provided for in the security. However, matters such as the ordinary receiver's **resignation** and **automatic** vacation of office are not usually dealt with. A right to resign may be implied in the circumstances, otherwise he may need his appointor's consent to do so.

As well as any contractual power by the appointor, a receiver can be **replaced** by:
– the court, on the application of a secured creditor or the appointor (*Re Slogger Automatic Feeder Co Ltd* [1915] 1 Ch 478); and
– a prior security holder appointing his own receiver over the same assets.

The company's books and records must be passed on to any replacement receiver. If a replacement is appointed as soon as possible, the receivership will be continuous, but if there is a delay a new receivership will have begun (*Re White's Mortgage, Public Trustee v White* [1943] 1 All ER 299).

MEMO POINTS 1. An **LPA receiver** can be **removed** by the mortgagee in writing (s 109(5) LPA 1925).
2. An **administrator** can require the receiver to vacate office (para 41(2) Sch B1 IA 1986).

Where an ordinary receiver ceases to act for any reason, he must file an **abstract of receipts and payments** covering the period since the last one (or covering the whole of his appointment if he has not already filed one) at Companies House within 1 month of the end of his appointment (s 38(3) IA 1986). He must also give **notice** of the end of his appointment to Companies House using Form 405(2) (s 405 CA 1985; restated at s 871 CA 2006 by 1 October 2009); failure to do so renders him liable to a fine (¶9935).

9405

MEMO POINTS The name of Form 405(2), like the names of other **Companies House forms**, is taken from the section number of the legislation. As all of the section numbers will change under the new Companies Act, Companies House proposes to change the names of all of its forms to reflect their function rather than the relevant section number ("Working with Companies House: a consultation on the registrar's rules and related provisions which will apply under the Companies Act 2006"). At the time of writing, the new form names are not yet available.

Administrative receiver

An administrative receiver's appointment may be terminated in the following ways, each of which has different **notice** requirements.

9406

Method of termination		Notice requirements	Reference
Resignation[1]		An administrative receiver must give at least 7 days' notice in writing, specifying the date on which his appointment will cease, to: – his appointor; – company (or its liquidator); and – members of any creditors' committee Within 14 days of termination, the administrative receiver must send notice to Companies House[3]	s 45 (1), (4) IA 1986; r 3.33 IR 1986
Removal[2]		Within 14 days of termination, the administrative receiver must send notice to Companies House[3]	s 45(1), (4) IA 1986
Automatic termination	Ceases to be qualified insolvency practitioner	– Company (or its liquidator); and – members of any creditors' committee. Within 14 days of termination, the administrative receiver must send notice to Companies House.[3]	s 45(2), (4) IA 1986; r 3.35(1) IR 1986
	Death	The appointor must give notice as soon as he is aware to – Companies House; – the company (or its liquidator); and – members of any creditors' committee.	r 3.34 IR 1986

Note:
1. If an administrative receiver must resign because an **administration order** has been made, he does not have to give notice (¶8814+).
2. If **administrator** is **appointed out of court**, he can require the administrative receiver to vacate office; if he is appointed by the court, the administrative receiver must vacate office (para 41 Sch B1 IA 1986).
3. **Failure** to do so renders the administrative receiver liable to fine (s 45(5) IA 1986; ¶9935).

An administrative receiver must also file his **abstract of receipts and payments** for the same period as an ordinary receiver at Companies House within 2 months of ceasing to act (r 3.32 IR 1986).

CHAPTER 21
Company voluntary arrangements

OUTLINE	¶¶
Summary of CVA procedure 9439	b Conduct of the meetings 9501
A Entering into a CVA 9445	c Administrative requirements 9512
1 Preparation 9448	d Appeal against the CVA 9513
2 Obtaining a moratorium 9466	B Conduct of a CVA 9526
a Effect 9471	1 Effect of the CVA 9532
b Duration 9490	2 Persons with conduct of the CVA 9541
3 Approving the CVA proposal 9499	3 Conclusion of the CVA 9555
a Notice of the meetings 9500	

9435 A company voluntary arrangement, or CVA, is an **agreement** entered into **between** a company and its creditors, with the aim of restoring the company's financial health. Although the legislation and Rules provide for this type of insolvency procedure, the actual details of each CVA are different because they depend upon the terms agreed between the parties, as appropriate in each company's circumstances. There are certain common **features**, however, which distinguish a CVA from other agreements that a company may enter into with its creditors:

a. the terms must meet some basic criteria and deal with certain issues (¶¶9448+);

b. the implementation of the agreement is supervised by a qualified insolvency practitioner, who usually has wide-ranging authority under the agreement to manage the company during the CVA; and

c. the terms of the CVA are filed at court, enabling those involved to inspect them at any time. The parties can also refer matters to the court, for example, to challenge the supervisor's or directors' actions during the CVA, or to resolve questions and disputes.

The CVA **procedure** is designed to be fast and straight-forward, to enable companies to take the initiative when they are in financial difficulties and to resolve these problems before having to rely on more formal and draconian insolvency procedures. It is, therefore, in the nature of a "rescue" procedure. Broadly speaking, the terms of the CVA are set out in the **proposal**, which is presented to the insolvency practitioner who will implement and conduct the arrangement. If he accepts the appointment, he is referred to as the "nominee" at the preliminary stage before the proposal is approved. The proposal is then put to the creditors and shareholders for their **approval**, under the nominee's supervision. If approved, the nominee becomes the "supervisor" of the CVA and implements the proposal according to its terms.

9436 As a result of **reforms** to the CVA procedure, certain companies can now benefit from a moratorium (i.e. a "freeze" on third parties, notably creditors, taking action against it) in the period between drafting the proposal and its approval. These reforms prevent creditors who are not in favour of the CVA from taking other enforcement or insolvency action against the company, which may have a less even-handed effect on the other creditors and would usually be more detrimental to the company. This **applies to** eligible companies' CVAs in which the nominees accepted their appointments on or after 1 January 2003 (or, in the case of a liquidator or administrator proposing a CVA of which he is the nominee, where he summoned the meetings on or after this date).

The **moratorium procedure** is principally contained in Schedule A1 to IA 1986. Apart from obtaining the moratorium itself, the procedure for entering and implementing the CVA is largely the same with a moratorium as without one. However, many of the references are different. Where this is the case, references applicable to companies which have obtained a moratorium and to those which have not are given separately.

> MEMO POINTS **Prior to the reforms**, unknown creditors at the time of approval were not bound by the CVA and could therefore upset its implementation by taking action against the company or could obtain an unfairly high distribution instead, and shareholders could veto the approval of the proposal. These loopholes hindered the use and effectiveness of CVAs, prompting the changes in the law.

9437 Therefore, there are now two ways in which a company can **enter into a CVA**: one with the benefit of a moratorium and one without. The different routes are illustrated in the summary flowchart of the procedure below. Where a company is **eligible for a moratorium** (¶9467+), it will usually take that option because it is better protected during the vulnerable period between announcing its plans for insolvency proceedings and having those proceedings implemented. However, a company cannot take advantage of this temporary freeze on creditor action and then not approve a CVA at the end of it. This would prejudice its creditors' interests, and so creditors are entitled to present a winding up petition against a company if the moratorium ends without a CVA being in place (¶7612). The moratorium also subjects the directors to specific liabilities (¶9484).

If the company is **not eligible for a moratorium** and is not already subject to other insolvency proceedings, the board may consider it necessary to couple the proposal with an administration application to benefit from the moratorium which arises before an administration order is made. It is also possible for the company to obtain an adjournment of the hearing of a winding up petition against it so that the board can propose a CVA instead, although this clearly runs the risk of liquidation if the CVA is not approved.

There is no restriction on a company entering into a CVA when it is subject to **other insolvency procedures**. A liquidator or administrator has the power to propose a CVA, but if the company is in receivership or another CVA already applies, the board will have to do so. A company can only obtain a pre-CVA moratorium if it is in ordinary receivership, since it will otherwise already have the benefit of restrictions on action being taken against it.

9438 Administration may present a viable **alternative to a CVA**, if approval of the proposal cannot be obtained, for example. It is a more formal procedure, but also aims to revive the company so that it can carry on trading if possible. Depending on the circumstances, it may be advisable for creditors to reject the proposal and opt for administration or liquidation instead, as these procedures allow the insolvency practitioner to challenge more transactions which the company has entered into beforehand (¶7808+) and to take action against the directors (¶7439+). However, in the absence of such wrongdoing, CVAs have the advantage over other proceedings of flexibility, giving the creditors a say in the terms under which they are conducted.

Companies legislation sets out a procedure by which companies can enter into a compromise or scheme of arrangement with its creditors and shareholders (¶6500+). However, this can be complex, requiring separate meetings of the different classes of creditors and approval of the court. Another alternative is for the company to enter into a less formal, contractual arrangement with its creditors, although such a course of action can only be effective with the creditors' full co-operation.

Summary of CVA procedure

9439

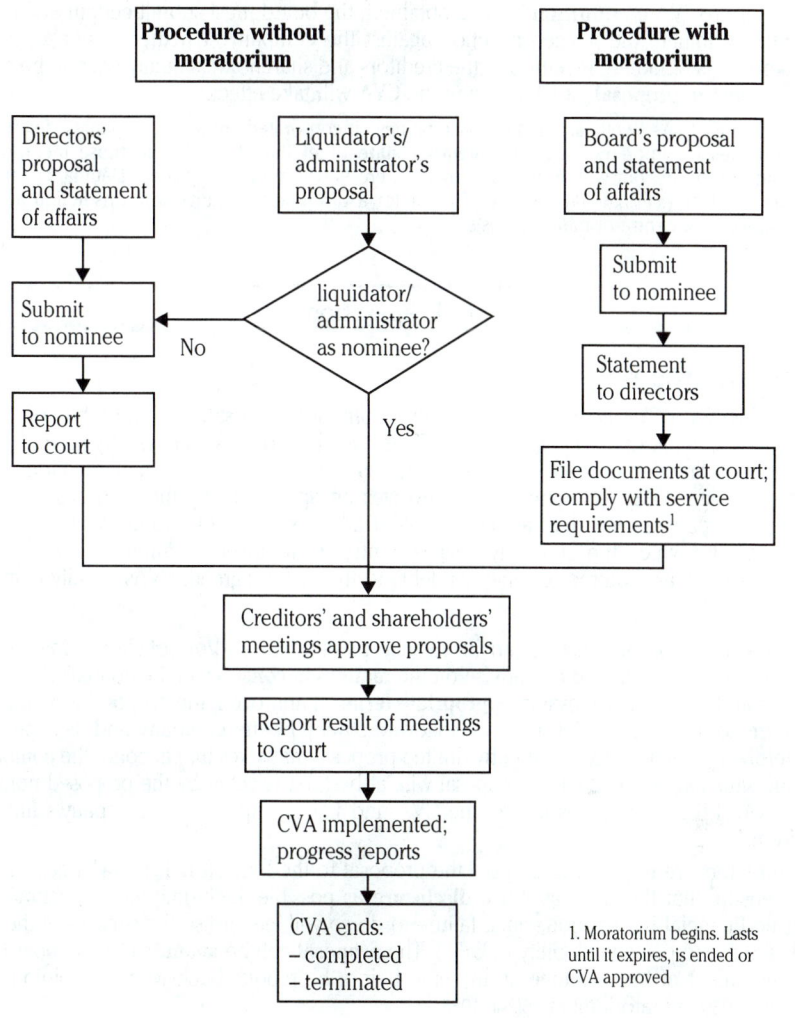

A. Entering into a CVA

A company can enter into a CVA in the ways summarised above. The **first stage** in all procedures is for a proposal to be put together. This is a detailed document containing the proposed terms of the CVA itself, and must therefore be carefully researched and considered, and drafted with professional advice. Where the board makes the proposal, it must also prepare a statement of the company's affairs; this is not necessary if a liquidator or administrator makes the proposal, because a statement will already have been made.

A board's proposal must be submitted to the proposed **nominee**, who will analyse and comment upon it. If he approves of it, he will accept the appointment and report accordingly to the court, or to the board if a moratorium is to be obtained. This is often a formality, since the proposed nominee usually advises the board on its proposal in the first place. A nominee's

9445

report is not required where the proposal was put together by a liquidator or administrator, if the relevant insolvency practitioner will become the nominee.

Then, if a pre-CVA **moratorium** is to be obtained, the board must submit certain documents to court to initiate the freeze on action against the company. Whether or not a pre-CVA moratorium is obtained, meetings of the creditors and shareholders finally need to be called to **approve the proposal**, at which point the CVA will take effect.

> MEMO POINTS   As well as limited companies incorporated under companies legislation, companies incorporated in an **EU member state** other than the UK and those incorporated outside of the EU but with a centre of main interests within the EU (except Denmark) can also propose CVAs (s 1(4), (5), (6) IA 1986). See ¶7366+ for a discussion of European jurisdiction and the definition of a centre of main interests.

1. Preparation

The CVA proposal

9448 A **proposal** for a CVA is one which sets out a composition in satisfaction of the company's debts or a scheme of arrangement of its affairs, which is to be supervised by an insolvency practitioner or other person qualified to act as a nominee/supervisor in relation to the company (s 1 IA 1986). A "composition" involves an agreement by the creditors to accept payment of part of their debt as payment of it all; a "scheme of arrangement" is another agreement by which the company assigns control of its assets to another to realise and distribute them as required to repay its debts to the extent agreed. CVAs usually comprise both elements.

9449 The **board** will usually instruct an insolvency practitioner and/or solicitor before putting together the proposal, who can advise on the **matters to consider** in the company's circumstances and draft the proposal in **appropriate terms**. If approved, the proposal will comprise the terms of the CVA, which must be followed strictly by the company and its supervisor. Therefore, it is vital to have a properly drafted proposal that takes into account the company's unique situation. An inadequate proposal will, at best, be rejected by the proposed nominee or, at worst, cause disputes during the CVA and fail to improve the company's financial position.

The directors are required to prepare the proposal to the best of their knowledge, but they must ensure that they give as **full a disclosure** as possible, including giving accurate and realistic financial information, since failure to do so will jeopardise the success of the CVA and give rise to personal liability (¶9513+). The **proposal** can be **amended** by the board with the agreement of the nominee at any time before he reports back with his opinion on it (r 1.3(3) IR 1986; moratorium: r 1.35(2) IR 1986).

9450 If the company is **in liquidation** or **administration**, the liquidator or administrator can make the proposal instead of the board. They often put themselves forward as the nominee, but are not obliged to do so. There are some differences in the procedure where the liquidator or administrator is to be the nominee, which are noted where relevant.

Considerations

9451 It is important to bear in mind that the proposal will invariably need to go further than the mandatory requirements listed at ¶9453 in order to set out a **workable proposal** and give the creditors and shareholders **enough information** on which to base their decision. For example, the following factors will usually have to be addressed:

a. whether the CVA should be for a fixed period or should terminate when certain targets are reached, as well as provisions for its early termination and the creditors' rights in that event;

b. whether the CVA is dependent on the company obtaining further funding, security or a guarantee from another party or upon a transaction it anticipates entering into;

c. if the company is going to carry on business during the CVA, its business and management plan, together with management accounts and cash-flow projections;

d. the powers of the supervisor to implement the proposal, which may be similar to those of administrators (¶9011) and liquidators (¶8216);
e. restrictions on the creditors taking enforcement and other legal action against the company. Usually, only a short moratorium will be tolerated, during which the company's debts are paid, and/or extra funding or assistance is obtained;
f. provision for the costs of the CVA to be met out of the scheme assets;
g. appropriate indemnities and protection of the supervisor from personal liabilities;
h. whether or not the CVA is to constitute a trust and, if so, who the trustee and beneficiaries will be;
i. whether and, if so, how the CVA can be varied once it has begun. To ensure fairness to all parties, substantial variations should involve a similar procedure to approval of the original proposal, while the power to make minor variations may be delegated to the supervisor;
j. how the supervisor will assess and admit or reject the claims of the creditors (usually using a similar method to proving debts in a liquidation, ¶8030+);
k. if third parties are to be involved, for example to provide funding, how they are to be bound by the CVA; and
l. how any unknown creditors will be dealt with, for example allowing them to be a party to the CVA without disturbing the dividends already declared.

Above all, the proposal must be **open and honest**. If a secret arrangement is entered into with a particular party, this could lead to the company being wound up in the public interest or the proposal being challenged because it is unfairly prejudicial to some parties (¶9513+).

> MEMO POINTS   If there is no express power to **vary the CVA**, it can only be altered with the consent of all creditors entitled to a share in the proceeds of the assets within the CVA (*Raja v Rubin* [1999] 1 BCLC 621).

Mandatory contents

The proposal must contain the following **information** (rr 1.3(2), 1.35 IR 1986):   **9453**
1. why the board considers a CVA to be necessary and why it thinks the creditors should approve the proposal;
2. how long the CVA is proposed to last;
3. as far as the directors are aware:
– the company's assets, together with the estimated value of each one;
– details of any charges over the assets; and
– the extent to which any of the assets are excluded from the CVA;
4. details of any other property within the CVA, including where it has come from and the terms on which it can be included;
5. as far as the directors are aware, details of the company's liabilities and the way in which it proposes to deal with them, i.e. whether and to what extent they will be met, modified, postponed or dealt with in another way, particularly:
– preferential (¶8044+) and secured creditors;
– creditors connected with the company; and
– whether there is a possibility of any of the company's previous transactions being challenged in a liquidation (¶7808+), and if so whether and how the company will be indemnified in respect of these claims;
6. as far as the directors are aware, an estimate of the amount which will be ring-fenced if the company goes into liquidation if the proposal is not accepted, and whether the requirement to ring-fence is disapplied by the CVA (s 176A IA 1986; ¶7992+). In making this estimate, the board does not have to reveal any information which could seriously prejudice the company's commercial interests (r 1.3(4) IR 1986);
7. as far as the directors are aware, an estimate of the company's net property (again, the board does not have to disclose anything which could seriously prejudice the company's commercial interests) (¶7992+);
8. details of any guarantees given for the company's debts, stating whether the guarantors are connected to the company;
9. whether any of the directors or other persons intend to give guarantees for the purposes of the CVA, and whether any security will be given for them;

10. details of any credit facilities which will be arranged, and how these debts will be paid off;
11. how the funds held for the purposes of the CVA are to be dealt with (i.e. in terms of banking and investing them);
12. when distributions to the creditors are anticipated, together with estimates of the amounts;
13. how it is proposed to deal with any creditors bound by the CVA if it was approved in their absence because they did not receive notice of it;
14. how any funds which are intended to be, but are not, distributed to creditors when the CVA ends will be dealt with;
15. how much remuneration and expenses will be paid to the nominee;
16. the name, address and qualification of the proposed supervisor;
17. the supervisor's functions in the CVA;
18. how the supervisor will be remunerated and his expenses paid;
19. whether the EC Insolvency Regulation will apply and, if so, whether the CVA will be the main or secondary proceedings (a CVA can only comprise secondary proceedings if the company was in liquidation (compulsory or CVL) first and the member state liquidator converts it to a CVA; ¶7370); and
20. the address to which the nominee should send his opinion on the proposal and his consent to act.

> MEMO POINTS If the **proposal** is **made by** a **liquidator or administrator**, he must also state whether or not he intends making an application to court to be excused from ring-fencing a proportion of the assets subject to a floating charge for the benefit of the unsecured creditors (¶7995), although he is not obliged to reveal any information which would be prejudicial to the commercial interests of the company as long as he states that he has omitted it on this ground (r1.10 IR 1986). He must add any other information he considers necessary to enable the creditors and shareholders to make an informed decision. An administrator must also provide the names and addresses of the company's preferential creditors, along with the respective amounts of their debts. A liquidator in a compulsory liquidation must send a copy of the proposal to the official receiver along with the name and address of his nominee (r1.12 IR 1986).

9455 The **proposal cannot** be approved if it contains certain provisions, see ¶9504.

Statement of affairs

9456 The statement of affairs is **intended to** supplement and clarify the proposal. It must reflect the company's affairs at a date no earlier than 2 weeks prior to that of the proposal and be in **Form** 1.6, which requires the following **information** (r1.5 IR 1986; moratorium: r1.37 IR 1986):
– a categorised list of the company's assets, together with an estimate of the value of each category;
– details of security over any of the company's assets, including the amount of the secured claim and the date on which the security was created;
– the names and addresses of any preferential creditors, together with the amounts of their respective claims;
– the names and addresses of the company's unsecured creditors, together with the amounts of their respective claims;
– details of debts owed by and to persons connected with the company;
– names and addresses of the company's shareholders, together with their respective shareholdings; and
– any other details required by the nominee to enable him to report to court on the proposal.

The statement must be **certified by** two or more directors (or a director and the secretary) as being correct to the best of their knowledge and belief (r1.5(4) IR 1986; moratorium: r1.37(4) IR 1986).

> MEMO POINTS 1. The nominee may agree to allow the directors to make the statement of affairs up to an **earlier date** (but not earlier than 2 months before the proposal and statement of affairs were delivered to him), giving a written statement of his reasons for doing so to the board (r1.5(3) IR 1986; moratorium: r1.37(3) IR 1986). This statement will have to be submitted to court if the board applies for a moratorium.

2. The relevant date for **calculating preferential claims** is usually the date that the CVA takes effect, although if the company is in liquidation or administration, it is the date of the commencement of the liquidation or the date on which the company entered administration (s 387 IA 1986; respectively, ¶7747; ¶8808).

Submission to nominee

The **proposal** must be **sent to** the nominee (or to a person authorised to accept delivery on his behalf) (r 1.4 IR 1986; moratorium: para 6 Sch A1 IA 1986, r 1.36 IR 1986). The **statement of affairs** can be sent up to 7 clear days after the proposal (r 1.5 IR 1986; moratorium: r 1.37 IR 1986). If the proposal was prepared by the liquidator or administrator, the statement of affairs already prepared in the existing proceedings should be used (r 1.12(5) IR 1986).

Where a moratorium is to be obtained, the **nominee** must confirm receipt of the documents and, if he **consents to act**, he will say so in his response to the board. Where a moratorium is not to be obtained and the nominee consents to act, he will endorse the notice with the date of receipt and confirmation that he accepts the appointment, and return this to the board.

9457

> MEMO POINTS Where the company is in **liquidation or administration**, there is usually no need to submit the proposal, as the relevant insolvency practitioner will be the nominee. However, where the nominee is not the company's liquidator or administrator, the relevant insolvency practitioner must send a copy of the proposal to the nominee, along with a copy of the statement of affairs (rr 1.4(2), 1.12 IR 1986). If the nominee agrees to act, he must endorse the notice with the date of receipt and confirmation that he will take on the appointment and return it to the relevant insolvency practitioner (r 1.4(3) IR 1986).

The **proposal** can be **amended**, with the nominee's consent, at any time up to when the nominee makes his report to court (¶9461 below), for example changes may prove to be necessary as a result of the nominee's investigations into the company's affairs (r 1.3(3) IR 1986; moratorium: r 1.35(2) IR 1986).

9458

Where a moratorium is not to be obtained, and the nominee cannot prepare the report on the basis of the proposal and statement of affairs alone, he can require the directors to give him any **further information** about the company's affairs, including why the company is insolvent or facing insolvency and details of any previous proposals that have been put forward (r 1.6 IR 1986). The board must allow the nominee to have access to the company's books and records. He can also ask for information about the company's current and former officers (who have held office in the last 2 years), specifically whether any of them have been involved in another insolvent company or have been personally bankrupt or have entered into an individual voluntary arrangement with their own creditors.

9459

> MEMO POINTS Where the **proposal** has been made **by** a **liquidator or administrator**, and the nominee is a different insolvency practitioner, he can require the liquidator or administrator to give him further information as described above (r 1.12(5) IR 1986). If the liquidator or administrator is the nominee, the directors and former officers are under a duty to co-operate with their investigations and requests for information in any event (¶8121).

Nominee's response

The nominee will **consider** the **proposal** and statement of affairs carefully before suggesting any modifications or preparing his report. Nominees are advised to look at the following aspects in particular (para 5, *Statement of Insolvency Practice 3*):
– the directors' attitude;
– the prospects of the company being able to follow the terms of the proposal;
– the control which the company will have over its assets during the CVA, as opposed to that of the supervisor;
– the extent to which the restrictions on the company and those dealing with it which would apply if the company was in liquidation are missing from the proposal;
– the fairness of the proposed CVA to the creditors and the company;
– whether the proposed CVA would be a feasible and acceptable alternative to other insolvency proceedings;
– whether the proposal as drafted should be considered by the creditors; and
– the prospects of the CVA succeeding.

9460

9461 The nominee is required to give his **opinion on** the **proposal**, which must contain slightly different information depending on whether the company intends to obtain a moratorium or not. If a moratorium will not be obtained, a report needs to be filed at court. Otherwise, the nominee must send a statement to the board, and the board must file it at court together with the other documents needed to obtain the moratorium (¶9468).

	Contents	Send to	Deadline	Reference
No moratorium	Report: – whether proposal has reasonable prospect of being approved and implemented. If so, give comments on proposal; if not, give reasons; – whether meetings should be held to approve proposal. If so, state date, time and place of meeting; if not, give reasons; and – if extension to deadline for submitting statement of affairs was allowed, give reasons	Court[1] (copy to company)	28 days after receiving notice of proposal	s 2 IA 1986; rr 1.5, 1.7 IR 1986
Moratorium	Statement: – whether proposal has reasonable prospect of being approved and implemented. If so, give comments on proposal; if not, give reasons; – whether company is likely to have enough funds to carry on business as proposed during moratorium. If not, give reasons; – whether meetings should be held to approve proposal. If so, state date, time and place of meeting; if not, give reasons; – if extension to deadline for submitting statement of affairs was allowed, include statement of reasons given to board; and – consent to act, if he accepts the appointment	Board	28 days after receiving proposal	para 6 Sch A1 IA 1986; rr 1.37, 1.38 IR 1986

Note:
1. Report must be **submitted** to court **with** the following documents (r 1.7 IR 1986):
– copy proposal (as amended, if applicable);
– copy summary statement of affairs; and
– nominee's comments on proposal, if applicable.
Court will endorse papers with date of submission and file them. If **nominee fails** to submit report or dies during office, court can replace him with another insolvency practitioner (s 2(4) IA 1986). Applicant must give nominee 7 days' notice of application (unless he is dead) (r 1.8 IR 1986). Replacement nominee must file consent to act and confirmation he is qualified at court before appointment can take effect. For similar provisions in the case of a moratorium, see ¶9475.

MEMO POINTS   Where the **proposal** was prepared **by** the company's **liquidator or administrator**, a report to court is not required, unless a different nominee has been appointed, in which case the report must be made as above.

2. Obtaining a moratorium

9466 Where a company is able to do so, it will usually opt to have a moratorium imposed prior to the CVA coming into effect, as it gives it **protection** against creditor action. The board must do its best to ensure that the proposal is approved, by taking steps such as obtaining proper advice on its contents to ensure that it is fair and workable and making sure that the nominee will not have a reason to terminate the moratorium. If the moratorium ends without the proposal having been agreed, the creditors have an additional ground upon which they can petition to have the company wound up. During the moratorium, the company will also be **restricted** in its actions and supervised by the nominee, and the directors will be subject to specific duties and liabilities.

Eligible companies

Only "**small companies**" can benefit from a moratorium in connection with a CVA. A small company is defined as one which meets at least two of the following criteria (s 247(3) CA 1985):
– its turnover does not exceed £5,600,000;
– its balance sheet total does not exceed £2,800,000; and
– it has no more than 50 employees.

Even if a company meets two of these requirements, it is **not eligible** if:
a. it is a holding company of a group of companies which does not qualify as a small or medium sized group for the full financial year which ended before the application for a moratorium was filed (para 3 Sch A1 IA 1986; ¶4360+);
b. it is ineligible because it is a party to a capital market arrangement or a public private partnership agreement, or it has incurred more than £10 million worth of liabilities under any agreement (paras 2, 4A-C Sch A1 IA 1986; for the interpretation of these terms, see paras 4D-K Sch A1 IA 1986); or
c. it is subject to one of the following types of insolvency procedure (para 4 Sch A1 IA 1986):
– an administration order is in force;
– an administrator appointed out of court by the company or its board has been in office in the preceding 12 months;
– the company is in liquidation;
– a provisional liquidator has been appointed;
– an administrative receiver has been appointed over the company's assets;
– a CVA is already in place in relation to the company;
– the company has obtained a moratorium at any time in the preceding 12 months, which ended without a CVA being in place or a CVA during that time ended prematurely; or
– a CVA proposed by an administrator or liquidator has been entered into.

Comment: The **small company thresholds** are currently restated in the new Companies Act (ss 382, 465 CA 2006). However, they are expected to be increased for financial years beginning on or after **6 April 2008** to £6,500,000 turnover and £3,260,000 balance sheet total (draft Companies Act (Accounts and Reports) (Amendments) Regulations 2008). The employee thresholds will remain the same.

9467

Obtaining the moratorium is a simple matter of the board **filing** the following **documents** at court **within** 3 working days of receiving the nominee's opinion on their proposal (para 7 Sch A1 IA 1986; r 1.39 IR 1986):
– their proposal for the CVA;
– the statement of affairs (Form 1.6);
– a statement that the company is eligible for a moratorium (Form 1.7);
– the nominee's consent to act (Form 1.8);
– the nominee's positive statement of opinion regarding the proposal (Form 1.5);
– four copies of a schedule listing the above documents (Form 1.9);
– if applicable, a copy of the reasons given by the nominee for allowing the statement of affairs to be made up to an earlier date (¶9456/mp); and
– a copy of the nominee's comments regarding the proposal.

The court will stamp the date of filing on the copies of the schedule, which indicates the **beginning of the moratorium**, returning three of the copies to the person filing them (para 8(1) Sch A1 IA 1986; r 1.39(3) IR 1986).

9468

Administrative requirements

The board must then **serve** two of the copies of the stamped schedule on the nominee and one on the company (para 9 Sch A1 IA 1986; r 1.40 IR 1986). Failure to notify the nominee straight away renders the directors liable to imprisonment and/or a fine (¶9935).

9469

The nominee must then (para 10 Sch A1 IA 1986; r 1.40 IR 1986):
a. advertise the start of the moratorium in the *Gazette* and one other newspaper which he thinks is appropriate for bringing it to the attention of the company's creditors; and
b. send notice that the moratorium has started to:
– Companies House;
– any creditor who has presented a petition against the company prior to the beginning of the moratorium, which has not been dismissed or withdrawn;
– any enforcement officer of whom the nominee is aware who is charged with execution or another enforcement action against the company or its property; and
– any person who has distrained against the company or its property.

Failure to advertise the moratorium or give notice of it to Companies House or a petitioning creditor renders the nominee liable to a fine (¶9935).

a. Effect

9471 The **moratorium enables** the company to sort out its affairs and prepare to put the CVA proposal to the creditors and shareholders without worrying about unexpected claims being made against it, or creditors taking aggressive debt recovery measures. To ensure fair dealing with its creditors and customers, certain **restrictions** are placed on the company to prevent it from taking unfair advantage of the moratorium.

Supervision of the company

9472 During the moratorium, the **nominee** is under an obligation to monitor the company's business and affairs to enable him to decide whether or not (para 24 Sch A1 IA 1986):
– the CVA has a reasonable prospect of being approved and implemented; and
– the company has enough funds to enable it to carry on as much of the business as it intends to during the moratorium or CVA.

The directors must provide him with whatever information he needs, on which the nominee is entitled to rely unless he has reason to question the accuracy of it.

If the nominee reaches any of the following conclusions at any time during the moratorium, he must withdraw his consent to act and bring the **moratorium** to an **end** (para 25 Sch A1 IA 1986):
a. the proposed CVA (whether modified or not) does not have a reasonable prospect of being approved or implemented;
b. the company will not have enough funds to continue as much of its business as it intends during the moratorium or CVA;
c. the company was not eligible for a moratorium at the date of filing; or
d. the directors have failed in their duty to provide him with the information he needs to monitor the company during the moratorium.

If he ends the moratorium in this way, he must **notify** the following persons that he has withdrawn his consent to act and why he has done so (para 25(5) Sch A1 IA 1986; r 1.44 IR 1986):
– the court;
– Companies House;
– the company; and
– all creditors of whose claims he is aware.

Failure to do so renders him liable to a fine (¶9935).

9473 The nominee must also look into the **directors'** and other officers' **conduct**, and is obliged to report any apparent criminal activity regarding the moratorium or the CVA to the appropriate authorities (s 7A IA 1986). There are particular criminal offences for which directors can be liable in relation to the moratorium, see ¶9486+, but this obligation to report criminal conduct appears to be wider and so includes a greater range of criminal offences, such as fraud. The nominee must also co-operate with the appropriate authority's investigations, providing it with any information and access to documents it requires. If the offence is prosecuted, the nominee, supervisor and all other officers and agents (including solicitors and bankers) of the company are required to assist in the prosecution as far as is reasonable. Such a report may cause the secretary of state to commence an **investigation** into the **company's affairs** and/or **disqualification** proceedings (¶7195+; ¶3000+).

Challenging the nominee

The nominee's **acts and decisions** during the moratorium can be challenged by any creditor, director, shareholder or other person affected (para 26 Sch A1 IA 1986). An application can be made to court for relief either during or after the moratorium, giving at least 7 clear days' notice to the nominee (r 1.47 IR 1986). The court can confirm, reverse or modify the nominee's act or decision, give him directions or make any other appropriate order, including ending the moratorium.

9474

If it appears that the **company has suffered loss** at the hands of the nominee but it does not intend to make a claim against him, any creditor can apply to court (either during or after the moratorium) for relief, giving at least 7 clear days' notice to the nominee (para 27 Sch A1 IA 1986; r 1.47 IR 1986). Unless the court is satisfied that the nominee acted reasonably in the circumstances, it has a wide power on hearing such an application to order:
– that the company should pursue its claim against the nominee;
– that the creditor can pursue the claim against the nominee on the company's behalf;
– that conditions should apply to the company or creditor pursuing any such claim;
– that the nominee assists in any such claim;
– that the proceeds of any such claim be distributed in a particular way;
– that the moratorium should end; and/or
– another solution or consequential directions as appropriate.

Replacing the nominee

The board may apply to court for the replacement of the nominee in limited **circumstances**, where (para 28 Sch A1 IA 1986):
– he has failed to comply with a duty imposed upon him;
– he has died; or
– it is impracticable or inappropriate (e.g. a conflict of interest has arisen) for him to continue to act.

9475

The board must give the nominee 7 clear days' notice of the **application** (unless he has died, of course) (r 1.45 IR 1986). The nominee may also make the application in the last situation in the list above, giving the board 7 clear days' notice. Like the original nominee, the replacement must be qualified to act, submit his consent to do so to court and notify Companies House and his predecessor (except where he has died) of his appointment (rr 1.45, 1.46 IR 1986).

Restrictions on those dealing with company

During a moratorium, the following steps towards **insolvency proceedings** and **enforcement action** cannot be taken against the company (para 12(1) Sch A1 IA 1986):
a. presenting most types of winding up petition (there are certain exceptions);
b. making an order for the compulsory liquidation of the company;
c. passing a resolution to wind the company up voluntarily;
d. presenting an administration application;
e. appointing an administrator out of court (whether by a floating charge holder, the board or the company);
f. appointing an administrative receiver;
g. exercising a right of forfeiture by peaceable re-entry into premises rented by the company, unless the court has given leave to do so;
h. taking any other steps to enforce any security over the company's property or repossess goods bailed to the company under a hire-purchase agreement, unless the court has given leave to do so; and

9476

i. taking other proceedings, distress, execution or other legal processes against the company or its property, unless leave of the court has been obtained.

If any of the company's property is secured by a **floating charge** which enables the charge holder to give notice to the company that it has **crystallised**, or allowing him to impose restrictions on the company as a result of the moratorium or another event which occurs during the moratorium, the charge holder can only do so once the moratorium has come to an end (para 13 Sch A1 IA 1986). A floating charge holder cannot apply to the court for leave to take steps to enforce his security or take other legal action (g. and h. above) by crystallising his charge.

See below for the enforcement of **security granted** by the company **during** the **moratorium** (¶9479).

> MEMO POINTS Certain types of winding up petition, referred to in the legislation as "**excepted petitions**", can be presented against the company during a moratorium (para 12(4) Sch A1 IA 1986):
> – a public interest petition, including one against a Societas Europaea (i.e. a European Company); and
> – a petition by the FSA on the just and equitable ground.

Restrictions imposed on company

9477 Just as the company is protected from creditor action during the moratorium, **third parties** dealing with it are **protected** from it incurring further indebtedness or otherwise jeopardising the position of the creditors by restrictions being placed on its dealings. Although breach of these restrictions gives rise to the personal liability of those involved, it will not render any transactions void or unenforceable against the company.

Business in general

9478 If the company wishes to call, or shareholders wish to requisition, a **general meeting** other than one to consider the CVA proposal, they must obtain the nominee's or the court's consent (para 12(1) Sch A1 IA 1986). If the court gives leave to hold a meeting, it may impose conditions, for example restricting the business which can be dealt with at the meeting.

9479 The company is **limited** in the amount of **credit** it can obtain from a person who is not aware of the moratorium, including goods bailed to it under hire- and conditional-purchase agreements (para 17 Sch A1 IA 1986). The limit is £250, although this can be varied by the secretary of state (s 417A IA 1986). Failure to comply renders the company and any of its officers in default liable to a fine and/or imprisonment (¶9935).

The company can **grant security** over its assets during the moratorium, but the security can only be enforced if there were reasonable grounds for believing that it would benefit the company at the time it was granted (para 14 Sch A1 IA 1986).

9480 The nominee's name and a statement that the moratorium is in force must appear on all of the following documents issued by or on behalf of the company which mention its name (para 16 Sch A1 IA 1986):
– **invoices**;
– **orders** for goods; and
– **business letters**.

Failure to comply renders the company and any of its officers in default liable to a fine (¶9935).

Payments

9481 The company can only **make payments** towards debts and other liabilities which arose before the moratorium if (para 19 Sch A1 IA 1986):
– it believes that the payment will benefit the company; and
– the moratorium committee (see ¶9493), or the nominee if there is no committee, has approved the payment.

This does not apply to making payments **to security holders** where the company has been able to dispose of the secured assets, see ¶9483 below. In other cases, **failure** to comply with the restriction on payments renders the company and any of its officers in default liable to a fine and/or imprisonment (see ¶9935).

Disposals

The company can dispose of its **property** in the ordinary course of its business, such as selling goods, but otherwise can only do so if (para 18 Sch A1 IA 1986):
- it believes that the disposal will be to its benefit; and
- the moratorium committee (¶9493), or the nominee if there is no committee, has approved the disposal.

Failure to comply renders the company and any of its officers in default liable to a fine and/or imprisonment (¶9935).

> MEMO POINTS If the company disposes of any of its property, transfers its shares or alters the status of any shareholders during the 28 days after the nominee reports the results of the meetings to the court or during the moratorium, the disposition cannot be avoided if the company goes into **liquidation** (see ¶7674+, ¶7683; para 12(2) Sch A1 IA 1986). However, it can be avoided if the company has gone into liquidation as a result of an "excepted petition" (see ¶9476/mp).

If the **property** in question is **secured**, the company can dispose of it as if it were not secured, with the consent of the relevant security holder or the court (para 20 Sch A1 IA 1986). This also applies to disposing of goods bailed to the company under a hire- or conditional-purchase, chattel leasing or retention of title agreement as if the company owned those goods. If consent has been obtained from the court, the company must give notice of the order to the security holder, and send a copy of the order to Companies House within 14 days; failure to do so renders the directors liable to a fine (para 20 Sch A1 IA 1986; r 1.43 IR 1986; ¶9935).

Where the security in question was created as a **floating charge**, the charge holder is protected as he obtains a charge over the proceeds of disposal for the same amount which ranks at the same level of priority as his floating charge (para 20(4) Sch A1 IA 1986). In the case of **other security**, it is a term of the consent to the disposal that (para 20(5), (6) Sch A1 IA 1986):
- its proceeds are used to discharge the sums owed to the security holder; and
- any shortfall between the purchase price obtained and that which would have been obtained by a willing vendor on the open market is made up.

Disposal of secured property **without consent** renders the company and its officers in default liable to a fine and/or imprisonment (para 22 Sch A1 IA 1986; ¶9935).

> MEMO POINTS The company cannot deal with secured property in this way if it is subject to **certain** special **types of charges**, namely market, system or collateral security charges (para 23(1) Sch A1 IA 1986). In addition, if the company enters into any such charge during the moratorium, the company and its officers in default are liable to a fine and/or imprisonment, although the transaction secured by the security and the security itself will not be rendered void or unenforceable (¶9935).

9482

9483

Liability of the directors

During the moratorium, the nominee is only required to supervise the company and investigate the feasibility of the proposed CVA. Therefore, the board carries on **running the company** during this time, under the restrictions on the company's activities set out above. As an added protection to those dealing with the company, the directors can incur specific liability during the moratorium if they do not manage the company properly.

9484

Conduct of the company's affairs

If the board has been, is or proposes, running the company in such a way that is **unfairly prejudicial** to the creditors' or shareholders' interests (either as a whole or relating to particular groups), an affected creditor or shareholder can apply to the court for relief (para 40 Sch A1 IA 1986). Such an application can be made during or after the moratorium. The court has a wide power to grant any **relief** that is appropriate in the circumstances, including:
- regulating the management of the company during the rest of the moratorium;
- requiring the board to stop the action complained of, or to carry out the omission complained of;
- requiring creditors' and/or shareholders' meetings to be held to consider the matters directed by the court; and
- bringing the moratorium to an end.

9485

> MEMO POINTS If the company was **already in administration or compulsory liquidation** when the moratorium started, the administrator or liquidator must make the application (para 40(7), (8) Sch A1 IA 1986).

Criminal offences

9486 A director or other officer commits an offence if he makes a **false representation** or otherwise **fraudulently** acts or fails to act in a particular way in order to obtain a moratorium or an extension of one, whether or not the moratorium or extension was obtained (para 42 Sch A1 IA 1986). This offence is **punishable** by imprisonment and/or a fine (¶9935).

9487 A director, or other officer of the company, will have committed a criminal offence if he carried out any of the following actions relating to the **company's property and records** during the moratorium or within the 12 months prior to the start of it (para 41 Sch A1 IA 1986):
a. concealing over £500-worth of the company's property;
b. fraudulently removing over £500-worth of the company's property;
c. concealing any debt due to or from the company;
d. concealing, destroying, mutilating, falsifying or making any false entry in any book or paper affecting or relating to the company's property or affairs;
e. fraudulently parting with, altering or making any omission in any document relating to the company's property or affairs; or
f. pawning, pledging or disposing of any of the company's property (other than in the ordinary course of business), which has been obtained on credit or not paid for.

An offence is also committed by an officer if he is privy to another officer committing d. or e.

The offence is **punishable** by imprisonment and/or a fine (¶9935). The accused can mount one of two **defences** to a prosecution:
– in the case of a. c. or f. above, proving that he had no intent to defraud; or
– in the case of d. or e. above, proving that he had no intention of concealing the company's state of affairs or to defeat the law.

> MEMO POINTS Where an offence has been committed in relation to f. above, a **person who receives** the **property** in question also commits an offence if he does so knowing that it has been pawned, pledged or disposed of in circumstances which amount to an offence during a moratorium, or would be if a moratorium commenced within the next 12 months (para 41(7) Sch A1 IA 1986).

---

b. Duration

9490 The moratorium **commences on** the date the papers are filed at court, and **lasts until** one of the following events occurs (para 8 Sch A1 IA 1986).

Circumstances	Moratorium ends	Reference (Sch A1 IA 1986)
Meetings of shareholders and creditors are held to consider CVA proposal[1]	On date meetings held	para 8
Meetings of shareholders and creditors summoned but not held for the first time within 28 days of beginning of moratorium[1]	On date meetings were due to be held	para 8
Meetings of shareholders and creditors not summoned within 28 days of beginning of moratorium and no extension has been agreed (i.e. moratorium expires)	28 days after it started	para 8
Adjournment of meeting proposed, but meeting would not approve nominee's costs	Date of meeting	para 32
Moratorium extended	On date extension expires	para 8
Nominee withdraws consent to act	When consent withdrawn	para 8

Circumstances	Moratorium ends	Reference (Sch A1 IA 1986)
Nominee's or directors' actions successfully challenged and court orders termination of moratorium	As ordered by court	para 8
Shareholders' and creditors' meetings decide to terminate moratorium	Date of decision	para 8
None of the above	Date on which decision to approve CVA takes effect	para 8

Note:
1. If meetings were held, or due to be held, on different days, moratorium ends on later of the two dates.

Extension

Where a **meeting** is to be **adjourned** (¶9502+), the moratorium may need to be extended for up to 2 months after the day on which the meetings were held, or the last meeting was held if they were held on different days (para 32 Sch A1 IA 1986). Before the meeting is adjourned, the nominee must inform it of the actions he has taken in monitoring the company during the moratorium and what he will need to do if the moratorium is extended, as well as setting out his costs (both incurred and anticipated). The meeting will then resolve whether or not to approve his anticipated costs for the proposed extension; if it refuses to do so, the moratorium will end. If a replacement nominee has been proposed, he must inform the meeting of the steps he will take to monitor the company during the moratorium, and if the meeting refuses to approve those costs the moratorium will come to an end.

If the meetings extend the moratorium, the nominee must **notify** Companies House and the court, specifying the new expiry date (r 1.41(1) IR 1986; para 34 Sch A1 IA 1986); failure to do so renders him liable to a fine, ¶9935). If extended, the moratorium **lasts until** the expiry of the extension or until the shareholders' and creditors' meetings decide to terminate it (para 32 Sch A1 IA 1986).

MEMO POINTS The secretary of state can **vary** the **maximum period** of the extension.

9491

The moratorium can also be extended **by the court** where an application has been made by a shareholder objecting to the creditors' decision taking precedence over theirs (para 36(5) Sch A1 IA 1986; ¶9505). In such a case, the nominee must notify Companies House, sending it a copy of the order (r 1.41(2) IR 1986; para 34 Sch A1 IA 1986). Failure to do so renders him liable to a fine (¶9935).

9492

If the meeting resolves to extend the moratorium, it can establish a **moratorium committee** to perform whatever functions the meeting decides to delegate to it (para 35 Sch A1 IA 1986). The meeting must first approve an estimate of the costs which will be incurred by the committee in carrying out these functions. Any costs actually incurred by it up to the estimate must be reimbursed by the nominee. The committee will only last as long as the moratorium.

9493

End of moratorium

When the moratorium ends, the **nominee must** (para 11 Sch A1 IA 1986; r 1.42 IR 1986):
a. advertise it in the *Gazette* and one other newspaper he thinks is appropriate to bring it to the attention of the creditors; and
b. give notice of it, specifying the date on which it ended, to:
– Companies House;
– the court;
– the company; and
– all creditors of whom he is aware.

Failure to do so renders him liable to a fine (¶9935).

If a moratorium has **ended without** the **approval** of the proposal, the company can be wound up by a creditor (¶7612).

9494

3. Approving the CVA proposal

9499 The next stage is for **meetings of** the **creditors and shareholders** to consider the proposal, approving, rejecting or modifying it as necessary. Ideally, both meetings should approve it. However if they reach different conclusions, the creditors' decision takes precedence, subject to an appeal process available to the shareholders. Approval will signal the **start of the CVA** and the supervisor's term of office. Most of the issues relating to the supervisor's powers and appointment will be addressed in the proposal, although the meeting may need to consider some matters regarding his remuneration and expenses, and the division of power between any joint supervisors. The meeting may also have to deal with matters relating to the moratorium, such as its extension, where one is in force.

a. Notice of the meetings

9500 The nominee must **summon** the meetings. The venue (i.e. the date, time and place) of the meetings and **notice requirements** differ slightly, depending on whether or not a moratorium has been obtained.

	Venue	Notice requirements			Reference
		Give notice to	Contents	Length of notice	
No moratorium	– At venue stated in report: held 14-28 days after filing[1] – Creditors' meeting first; can be on same day, if not, must be within 7 days of each other	– All creditors and shareholders of whom nominee is aware; and – all officers, plus any who left within last 2 years who nominee requires to attend	– Rules for voting at creditors' meeting (¶9507+); – court at which any report filed; and – attach: proposal, statement of affairs/summary, nominee's comments on proposal, proxy forms	14 days	s 3 IA 1986; rr 1.9, 1.13, 1.16 IR 1986
Moratorium	– At venue stated in report – Must be within 28 days of start of moratorium – Can be on same day/together	All creditors and shareholders of whom nominee is aware	– Rules for voting at creditors' meeting (¶9507+); – court at which moratorium documents filed; and – attach: proposal, statement of affairs/summary, nominee's comments on proposal, list of creditors with amounts owed	14 days	para 29 Sch A1 IA 1986; rr 1.48, 1.53 IR 1986

Note:
1. Unless the **court directs** the meeting to be held at another venue to that stated in the report (s 3(1) IA 1986).
If the **liquidator/administrator** made the proposal and is the nominee, he must summon the meeting at a venue he thinks is suitable (s 3(2) IA 1986).

b. Conduct of the meetings

9501 Creditors and shareholders can **attend** the meetings in person or by proxy. The rules regarding proxies discussed in the context of compulsory liquidations at ¶8349+ apply here. The chairman is often chosen as a proxy, but he is restricted in his ability to vote as a proxy on resolutions dealing with the remuneration or expenses of the nominee/supervisor (¶9508/mp). The chairman may **exclude** any officer of the company from attending all or part of either meeting, even if that person was given notice of it (see above, r 1.16 IR 1986).

The **quorum** for a creditors' meeting is at least one creditor (present or represented) who is entitled to vote (r 12.4A IR 1986). In the case of a shareholders' meeting, the quorum is usually at least two shareholders present or represented, but this depends upon the company's articles. If the quorum is achieved at either meeting by the chairman alone, or with one other person, and the chairman is aware of others intending to attend the meeting, he must wait a further 15 minutes after the meeting was due to start before allowing it to proceed to business.

The nominee, or another insolvency practitioner or an experienced employee in his firm, will be the **chairman** of the meetings (r 1.14 IR 1986).

> MEMO POINTS   As part of the Insolvency Service's review of secondary legislation (see ¶7364/mp), it is taking the opportunity to make alterations to the primary legislation either where it is necessary to support the new Rules or to remove unnecessary administrative burdens. The Service proposes to allow **meetings** in insolvency procedures to be **held by** whatever means are appropriate, for example over the internet (proposal 1, "A consultation document on changes to the Insolvency Act 1986 and the Company Directors Disqualification Act 1986 to be made by a Legislative Reform Order for the modernisation and streamlining of insolvency procedures" (September 2007)). At the time of writing, the consultation is still open. If this proposal is accepted, the changes are likely to be implemented from 1 October 2008.

Adjournments

The meetings can be adjourned **by** the **chairman** for a date up to 14 days after the original meeting or after the moratorium ends (including where the moratorium has been extended) (r 1.21 IR 1986; moratorium: r 1.53 IR 1986). The meeting may be adjourned more than once during that period, but not beyond it. He must adjourn the meeting if the **creditors or shareholders** so resolve. Adjournments are usually required where the proposal needs to be modified and further research needs to be carried out as to the feasibility and consequences of the modifications.

9502

The nominee must **notify** the court that a meeting has been adjourned if the proposal was made by the board. If the company is under a moratorium, the meeting can impose conditions on the adjournment, including:
– requiring the replacement of the nominee with another insolvency practitioner (para 33 Sch A1 IA 1986);
– extending the moratorium (¶9491+); and/or
– establishing a moratorium committee (¶9493).

Any replacement nominee can only act if he files a statement at court confirming his consent to act.

If the **proposal** (whether modified or not) has still **not** been **accepted** by the creditors after an adjournment, it is deemed to have been rejected (r 1.21 IR 1986; moratorium: r 1.53 IR 1986).

9503

Business

The principal business of the meetings is to **consider the proposal**, which creditors and shareholders may approve, reject or modify (s 4(1) IA 1986; moratorium: para 31 Sch A1 IA 1986). Modifications can include a proposal that an insolvency practitioner other than the nominee supervises the CVA (s 4(2) IA 1986; moratorium: para 31 Sch A1 IA 1986). Modifications do not have to take any particular form, although the meeting must understand what the terms of the modified proposal are (*Doorbar v Alltime Securities Ltd* [1995] 1 BCLC 316). Where a moratorium is in place and the board wants to seek approval for its modifications, it must give notice of them to the nominee at least 7 days before the meetings (para 31(7) Sch A1 IA 1986).

9504

The proposal (or modification(s)) **cannot include** certain **terms** (s 4(3), (4) IA 1986; moratorium: para 31 Sch A1 IA 1986):
a. affecting the right of a secured creditor to enforce his security, without that secured creditor's consent;

b. under which a preferential creditor loses his right to receive distributions in priority to other creditors, without his consent;
c. under which the preferential creditors are paid other than pari passu, without the consent of the disadvantaged person(s); or
d. any which prevent the proposal from falling within the definition of a "proposal" (see ¶9448+).

> MEMO POINTS If a **replacement nominee** is approved by the meeting, he must give written confirmation to the chairman that he is qualified and consents to act (r 1.22 IR 1986). If **two or more supervisors** are appointed under one CVA, the creditors can also decide whether they can act individually or whether they must act together (r 1.22 IR 1986).

9505 Although the two meetings can be held separately, the CVA must be **approved by** both meetings (s 4A IA 1986; moratorium: para 36 Sch A1 IA 1986).

However, **if** the **two meetings disagree**, the creditors' decision will take precedence, unless a shareholder applies to court for the shareholders' decision to be implemented instead. A shareholder may make such an application up to 28 days after the creditors' decision, or the shareholders', if taken later. Where the court has ordered that the shareholders' decision prevails, or has made another order as appropriate in the circumstances, the applicant must serve sealed copies of it on the supervisor and the board (by serving a copy on the company at its registered office) (r 1.22A IR 1986; moratorium: para 36 Sch A1 IA 1986). The supervisor or board must then serve notice of it on the creditors and shareholders who were sent notice of the meetings or are affected by the order. The applicant must also file an office copy of the order at Companies House within 7 days.

> MEMO POINTS Where a moratorium has not been obtained and the company in question is regulated by the **FSA**, the FSA is entitled to be heard at the application hearing (s 4A(5) IA 1986).

9506 Where the company has the benefit of a **moratorium**, the following decisions are also only valid if made by both meetings (para 36 Sch A1 IA 1986):
– extending the moratorium;
– ending the moratorium;
– establishing a moratorium committee; and
– approving the nominee's anticipated costs of monitoring the company during an extended moratorium.

The same provisions noted above apply where the two meetings disagree with one another.

Voting: creditors

9507 Every creditor who has received notice of the meeting is **entitled to vote** in the first instance, although the chairman must check each attendee's entitlement at the meeting and admit or reject their claims accordingly (e.g. it may be found that a person is not in fact a creditor because he does not have a valid claim against the company, or that only part of his claim is valid) (rr 1.17, 1.17A IR 1986; moratorium: rr 1.49, 1.50 IR 1986). Establishing who is entitled to vote is critical, not only for a valid approval of the proposal, but also in terms of who is bound by the CVA (¶9526). Creditors whose claims are disputed or defended by the company, or which may be extinguished by set-off, still count as claims for the purposes of voting, and are not to be counted as an unliquidated debt (*Re a Debtor (No 400 IO of 1996)*, *Re a Debtor (No 401 IO of 1996)* [1997] 2 BCLC 144). If the chairman is in doubt as to whether to **admit or reject** a claim, he must mark it as being "objected to" but allow the creditor to vote; if the chairman's objection is sustained after further investigation, the relevant votes will be declared invalid.

The **chairman's decision** can be **challenged** by any creditor or shareholder appealing to court within 28 days of the nominee reporting the result of the meeting to court, which may reverse or vary the decision, or declare the votes to be invalid. The court may also order that another meeting is held, or make another appropriate order, if it is satisfied that the circumstances leading to the appeal caused unfair prejudice or material irregularity. The chairman is not personally liable for the costs of the appeal.

A creditor's **vote does not count** in respect of any claim, or part of it, which (r 1.19 IR 1986; moratorium: r 1.52 IR 1986):
- was not notified to the chairman or convenor of the meeting; or
- is secured or partly secured (although, it is thought that the creditor can vote on the unsecured part, *Re a Debtor (No 031/32/33 of 1993), Calor Gas Ltd v Peircy* [1994] 2 BCLC 321, an IVA case).

If the creditor's claim is **based** or secured **on a bill of exchange** or **promissory note**, he will only be allowed to vote if he agrees to (r 1.19 IR 1986; moratorium: r 1.52 IR 1986):
a. treat any liabilities on the bill or note prior to the company's liability as security for those amounts (unless the person liable has gone into liquidation or personal bankruptcy); and
b. deduct the estimated value of that security from his claim for the purposes of being entitled to vote.

9508

> MEMO POINTS 1. Although these creditors' votes are discounted at the meeting, they still qualify as being "entitled to vote" and so are still **bound by** the terms of the **CVA** if it is approved (¶9526).
> 2. If the company has the benefit of a **moratorium**, a secured creditor's vote is not discounted on a vote regarding extending the moratorium or ending it before the extension is over (r 1.52(3) IR 1986).
> 3. If the **chairman** is **appointed as** a **proxy** for a creditor, as is common, he cannot use the proxy vote to increase or reduce the amount of the nominee's or supervisor's remuneration, unless the terms of the proxy specifically instruct him to vote in that way (r 1.15 IR 1986). If he does so without authorisation, the vote will not count (r 1.19 IR 1986; moratorium: r 1.52 IR 1986).

The **amount of each** creditor's **vote** depends on the debt owed to him at the beginning of the:
- meeting;
- liquidation or administration; or
- moratorium,

as applicable, less any payments which have reduced the amount owing (r 1.17 IR 1986; moratorium: r 1.49 IR 1986). If the creditor's debt is unliquidated or unascertained, he can still vote but the debt will be deemed to have a nominal value of £1, unless the chairman decides otherwise. The chairman is only required to examine the evidence submitted by the creditor in question, any other creditor or the debtor (*Re Newlands (Seaford) Educational Trust, Chittenden and others v Pepper and others* [2006] EWHC 1511 (Ch)). He is not required to speculate as to its value, nor does he have to investigate the creditor's claim independently of the evidence provided to him. If he concludes that a value higher than £1 should be attributed to the debt, he must do so; otherwise, he can only value it at £1.

9509

> MEMO POINTS Where the company is in **liquidation or administration**, the creditor's vote is calculated according to his debt at the date of the commencement of those proceedings (r 1.17 IR 1986).

The majorities required **to pass a resolution** at the creditors' meeting depend upon the resolution in question (r 1.19 IR 1986; moratorium: r 1.52 IR 1986).

9510

Resolution	Majority required
Approve CVA proposal	More than 75% [1]
Approve modifications to CVA proposal	
Extend moratorium	
End moratorium before expiry of extended period	
Any other resolution	More than 50% [1]

Note:
1. The resolution must be approved by the requisite **majority in value** of creditors present (in person or by proxy) and voting.

However, a **resolution cannot be passed** if those voting against it include more than 50% in value of the creditors (r 1.19 IR 1986; moratorium: r 1.52 IR 1986):
- who have had notice of the meeting;
- whose votes are not discounted (¶9508); and
- who are not connected to the company (¶7813).

This prevents creditors connected with the company, such as directors, from dominating the decision making process.

The **chairman's decision** regarding the approval of resolutions can be appealed to the court by any creditor or shareholder in the same way as his decision regarding voting entitlements (r 1.19(7) IR 1986; moratorium: r 1.52(8) IR 1986).

Voting: shareholders

9511 Shareholders' **entitlement to vote** at the meeting to approve the CVA is the same as at a normal general meeting, i.e. in accordance with the company's articles (r 1.18 IR 1986; moratorium: r 1.51 IR 1986; ¶3815+).

A **resolution is passed by** more than 50% in value of the shareholders present (in person or by proxy) voting in its favour, unless the company's articles provide otherwise (r 1.20 IR 1986; moratorium: r 1.53 IR 1986). The value of each shareholder's vote is determined by the articles.

c. Administrative requirements

9512 **Minutes** of the meetings signed by the chairman constitute primary evidence that they were duly convened, held and conducted and that the resolutions were duly passed (r 12.5 IR 1986).

The chairman must send a **report** of the result of the meetings to the court and all persons to whom notice of the meeting(s) was sent (s 4(6) IA 1986, r 1.24 IR 1986; moratorium: para 30(3) Sch A1 IA 1986, r 1.54 IR 1986). The report must deal with the following matters (r 1.24(2) IR 1986):
a. whether the proposal was approved by both meetings or just the creditors;
b. whether any modifications were made to the proposal;
c. what resolutions were presented to each meeting, and the decision on each one;
d. who was present at each meeting, what their individual voting values were and how they voted on each resolution;
e. whether the supervisor considers that the EC Insolvency Regulation applies to the CVA and, if so, whether it constitutes the main or secondary proceedings (a CVA can only comprise secondary proceedings if the company was in liquidation (compulsory or CVL) first and the member state liquidator converted it to a CVA; ¶7370); and
f. any other information he considers should be brought to the court's attention.

The report must be sent to the court within 4 days of the meetings (r 1.24(3) IR 1986). If the proposal was approved, a copy of the report must also be sent to Companies House (r 1.24(5) IR 1986).

d. Appeal against the CVA

9513 After the CVA has been approved, the following persons may apply to court for relief on the grounds that the CVA **unfairly prejudices** the interests of a creditor, shareholder or contributory (see ¶7863+ for a definition of a contributory), or that there has been a **material irregularity** at or concerning the meetings (s 6 IA 1986; moratorium: para 38 Sch A1 IA 1986):
– a person entitled to vote at either of the meetings;
– a person who would have been entitled to vote at the creditors' meeting if he had received notice of it;
– the nominee or his successor; or
– the liquidator or administrator.

Unless such a challenge is mounted, any defects in the formalities of the meetings will not render their decisions invalid (s 6(7) IA 1986; moratorium: para 38(9) Sch A1 IA 1986).

> MEMO POINTS If the company is an authorised person, the **FSA** can also make an application, or be heard at the hearing of another's application (s 356 FSMA 2000).

9514 If a CVA puts a creditor in a less advantageous position than he was in without the CVA, it will be prejudicial towards him. There is no set **test** for judging whether or not that prejudice is unfair, but **unfairness** can generally be assessed by comparing the creditor's position

under the CVA to (*Prudential Assurance Company Ltd and others v PRG Powerhouse Ltd and others* [2007] EWHC 1002 (Ch)):
– the other creditors' positions under the CVA;
– what his position would have been in a liquidation; and
– what his position would have been under a formal scheme of arrangement (see ¶6500+).

"Unfair prejudice" against a creditor will only be found where there is a disproportionate disadvantage to certain creditors compared to the others (i.e. different treatment is not enough in itself). The unfairness must have been **caused by** the terms of the CVA and the interests affected must be those in the creditor's capacity as creditor (*Doorbar v Alltime Securities Ltd (No 2)* [1995] 2 BCLC 513, affirmed [1996] 1 BCLC 487). In the case of a proposal put forward by an administrator or liquidator of the company, which he considers to be fair to the creditors, the court should not speculate about other proposals which might have been put forward by way of comparison, unless it can be shown that he was not acting in good faith or that he was biased towards particular creditors. Instead, the court should look at whether the creditors' interests would be served better by the proposed CVA or by not entering into a CVA (*Sisu Capital Fund Ltd v Tucker* [2005] EWHC 2170 (Ch)).

An "**irregularity**" usually involves a failure to observe the Rules (*Re Sweatfield Ltd* [1997] BCC 744), although it can also include misleading or false information being included in the proposal or statement of affairs (*Re a Debtor (No 087 of 1993) (No 2)* [1996] 1 BCLC 63). To be material, the irregularity must be one which, when considered objectively, affected the outcome of the essential votes taken at the creditors' meeting (*Doorbar v Alltime Securities Ltd (Nos 1 and 2)* [1996] 1 BCLC 487).

9515 Such an **application** must be **made within** 28 days of the nominee reporting the meetings' decisions to court. Alternatively, if the applicant was not given notice of the meeting, he has 28 days from the date on which he became aware that the meeting had taken place, even if this is after the CVA has ended (provided it has not ended prematurely; ¶9555).

9516 The **court** has wide **powers** to revoke or suspend the approval of the CVA and any other decision taken at the meeting, where it is satisfied that the meeting was not held or conducted properly (r 1.25 IR 1986; moratorium: para 38 Sch A1 IA 1986). The court may order that further meetings be held properly to reconsider the original proposal, or that one is held to consider a revised proposal put forward by the board.

The applicant must **serve** copies of any order on (r 1.25(4) IR 1986):
– the supervisor;
– the person(s) who made the proposal;
– the persons required to attend any meeting ordered to be held by the court; and
– Companies House, within 7 days.

Directors' conduct

9517 Where a moratorium has not been obtained and a director or other officer makes a **false representation** or **fraudulently** does or omits to do anything in order to obtain approval of the proposal, he is liable to a fine and/or imprisonment, whether or not the proposal was in fact approved (s 6A IA 1986; ¶9935). This includes making false or fraudulent representations in the proposal and to or before the meeting. See ¶9486 for the equivalent offence where a moratorium has been obtained.

B. Conduct of a CVA

9526 Once the proposal has been approved by both meetings, the CVA **takes effect**. Whether it was approved by both meetings or only by either one of them, it will take effect as if it had been approved by the creditors' meeting (s 5 IA 1986). The CVA will be conducted according to the terms of the proposal (¶9448+).

It **binds** all of the creditors who were entitled to vote at the meeting (regardless of whether or not they did) and those who would have been entitled to vote had they had notice of the meeting (formal or otherwise) (s 5 IA 1986; moratorium: para 37 Sch A1 IA 1986). Creditors are "entitled to vote" for these purposes even if their vote was discounted (¶9508), preventing them from avoiding a CVA by, for example, not disclosing their claim to the chairman (*Re Bradley-Hole (a bankrupt)* [1995] 2 BCLC 163).

> MEMO POINTS If a **creditor** who was bound by the CVA because he would have been entitled to vote at the meeting but was **not given notice** of it has not been paid at the end of the CVA, the company is liable to pay that creditor the amount owed to him under the arrangement (s 5(2A) IA 1986). This does not apply if the CVA ended prematurely, i.e. when it ended it had not been fully implemented regarding all persons bound by it (s 7B IA 1986).

9527 While there is no express **power to vary** a CVA in the legislation or Rules, the terms of the CVA may include one (*Re Broome (a debtor), Thompson v Broome* [1999] 1 BCLC 356, an IVA case). However, such powers should be exercised with care as they could potentially be unfair to creditors subject to the CVA and therefore open to challenge. A supervisor cannot use his power to apply to the court for directions which would have the effect of varying the CVA (*Re Alpa Lightning Ltd* [1997] BPIR 341; ¶9543). If there is no express power to vary the CVA, a variation can still be contractually agreed between all of the parties.

1. Effect of the CVA

On the company

9532 The **assets** within the CVA, which are determined by the terms of the proposal, usually become subject to a trust of which the supervisor is the trustee and the creditors are the beneficiaries to the extent of the amounts to which they are entitled under the CVA. The trust will be effective even if the assets in question are subject to a floating charge, unless the charge crystallised prior to the proposal being approved (*Re Leisure Study Group Ltd* [1994] 2 BCLC 65).

The directors must do all that is required to give the supervisor **possession** of the assets subject to the CVA as soon as it takes effect (r 1.23 IR 1986; moratorium: r 1.54 IR 1986). If the company is in **liquidation or administration** and the liquidator or administrator is not the supervisor, this duty falls on them. Whoever the supervisor is, he must either:
– discharge any outstanding remuneration, costs or disbursements due to the liquidator or administrator once he has possession of the assets; or
– give the liquidator or administrator a written undertaking to do so out of the first realisation of the assets before he takes possession of them.

The liquidator or administrator has a charge over the assets for these sums, subject to the supervisor's costs of realising them.

> MEMO POINTS Whether or not the trust comes to an end if the company then goes into **liquidation** depends upon the terms of the CVA. If the CVA does not deal with what happens to the trust on liquidation, the trust will continue (*Re N T Gallagher & Son Ltd, Shierson v Tomlinson* [2002] 2 BCLC 133). This protects the participants in the CVA from losing the benefit of it because of the actions of a non-CVA creditor, such as those whose debts arose after the CVA was approved. However, if the winding up petition was presented by the supervisor, the trust will not survive (*Davis v Martin-Sklan* [1995] 2 BCLC 483).

9533 As for which **debts** are **included** in the CVA, this will depend upon the terms of the proposal as approved, which will be clear as to most types of debts. There is no specific requirement for debts within a CVA to be provable debts, so the categories of debts could be wider than in other insolvency procedures. For example, the court has held that, by analogy with an arrangement with creditors under companies legislation, persons with contingent claims against the company for negligent exposure to asbestos which may arise in the future could be brought within a CVA (*Re T & N Ltd* [2005] All ER (D) 211 (Dec)). Whether a creditor is bound by the CVA depends on whether he was entitled to vote at the meeting approving the proposal (¶9507+).

Problems of interpretation can arise as to categories such as "**future**" or "**contingent**" liabilities. For example, rent becoming due to a landlord after the CVA takes effect has been held in separate cases to be within an arrangement (*Doorbar v Alltime Securities Ltd* [1995] BCLC 316), and not to be so (*Burford Midland Properties Ltd v Marley Extrusions Ltd* [1995] BCLC 102).

Claims which are **not included** in the CVA survive and can be pursued against the company separately.

If the company is in **liquidation** or **administration**, the court may stay or discharge those proceedings, or give any necessary directions regarding the conduct of them so that the CVA can be implemented (s 5(3) IA 1986). However, the court cannot do so after 28 days from the report of the meeting results being filed at court, or while the approval or implementation of the CVA is being challenged (s 5(4) IA 1986).

9534

If a **winding up petition** against the company was presented before a moratorium, the court must dismiss it (unless it is an "excepted petition", ¶9476/mp) if the 28-day deadline for challenging the meetings' decision has expired and no application has been made (¶9513+; para 37 Sch A1 IA 1986). If an application has been made, the court's action will depend upon the decision it makes.

Challenging the implementation of the CVA

During the CVA, any act, omission or decision of the supervisor can be challenged (s 7(3) IA 1986; moratorium: para 37 Sch A1 IA 1986). The **application** to court for appropriate relief can be **made** by any creditor or other person dissatisfied with the supervisor's conduct. For example, a creditor may challenge the supervisor's decision to reject his claim for participation in the CVA (*Holdenhurst Securities plc v Cohen* [2001] 1 BCLC 460).

9535

Inspection of documents

Any director, shareholder or creditor of the company is entitled to inspect the **court file** at any time (r 1.7(3) IR 1986).

9536

The secretary of state is entitled to inspect the **supervisor's records and accounts** of the CVA and the abstracts/reports referred to at ¶9546+ at any time, and he can require that the records and accounts are audited (r 1.27 IR 1986; moratorium: r 1.54 IR 1986).

2. Persons with conduct of the CVA

The **supervisor** is primarily responsible for the conduct of a CVA, and the exact scope of his powers and duties will be set out in the CVA itself. The **board** may also retain some of its management functions, or may be required to assist the supervisor in running the company during the CVA, under his supervision. There are no provisions governing **creditors**' and **shareholders**' involvement in the process once the proposal has been approved, but meetings may need to be called by the supervisor under the terms of the CVA. For example, if the terms of the CVA are to be varied, the consent of the creditors and shareholders is usually required. In addition, shareholder meetings may need to be held for the usual reasons, following the normal rules (¶3513+).

9541

Supervisor

The **nominee** (or any replacement) **becomes** the supervisor of the CVA once the proposal has been approved (s 7(2) IA 1986; moratorium: para 39 Sch A1 IA 1986). However, the supervisor will be someone other than the nominee if the court has so ordered or modifications were made to the proposal to that effect (¶9504+). **More than one** supervisor may be in office, in which case the creditors can stipulate how the functions of the office are to be apportioned between them.

9542

The supervisor can apply to **court** for **directions** on any matter arising under the CVA (s 7(4) IA 1986; moratorium: para 39 Sch A1 IA 1986). Although the court cannot alter or modify the CVA,

9543

it can give the supervisor directions as to how to interpret and implement it correctly where a term is unclear.

9544 The supervisor's **powers** will be set out in the CVA. In addition, the supervisor has the same power as a liquidator or administrator to require the supply of public utilities to the company, provided he personally guarantees payment of the bills (s 233 IA 1986). He can also challenge transactions defrauding creditors, but not the other types of transaction open to challenge by a liquidator or administrator (¶7826+).

Since the supervisor will normally act as the company's agent, he will not usually incur personal **liability**. However, he can be found liable for misfeasance as a person who is concerned or has taken part in the management of the company (¶7457). He may also be liable in tort, for example for negligence. The general principles summarised in the table at ¶8236 are relevant here.

Appointment

9545 **During the CVA**, a supervisor can be appointed by the court, either as an additional supervisor, to fill a vacancy or to substitute an existing supervisor, where it is appropriate to do so or it is inexpedient, difficult or impracticable for the appointment to be made out of court (s 7(5), (6) IA 1986; moratorium: para 39 Sch A1 IA 1986). The application can be made by any person with a sufficient interest in the matter (such as the supervisor's firm where he had ceased to be a partner, Re A & C Supplies Ltd [1998] 1 BCLC 603).

Record-keeping and disclosure obligations

9546 The supervisor is obliged to keep **accounting records**, including receipts and payments, in the vast majority of cases. Specifically, he must do so where the CVA requires or authorises him to (r 1.26 IR 1986; moratorium: r 1.54 IR 1986):
– carry on the business of the company;
– realise its assets; or
– otherwise administer or dispose of any of its funds.

In such a case, he must submit an **abstract of** his **receipts and payments** in the CVA at least once every 12 months to:
– court;
– Companies House;
– the company;
– all creditors bound by the CVA;
– all shareholders bound by the CVA (unless he has permission not to send it to them); and
– the company's auditors, where it is not in liquidation.

The abstract must either date from the beginning of his appointment, or the end of the period dealt with in the last abstract, as applicable. It must be sent out within 2 months of the end of the period with which it deals.

> MEMO POINTS 1. Where the supervisor is obliged to give notice or provide any document to the court, Companies House or the official receiver under this or any other provision, he must also give notice to any **member state liquidator** (r 1.34 IR 1986).
> 2. As part of the Insolvency Service's review of secondary legislation (see ¶7364/mp), it is taking the opportunity to make alterations to the primary legislation either where it is necessary to support the new Rules or to remove unnecessary administrative burdens. The Service proposes to remove the requirement for insolvency practitioners to **send information to all known creditors** at various stages in the procedure (proposal 1, "A consultation document on changes to the Insolvency Act 1986 and the Company Directors Disqualification Act 1986 to be made by a Legislative Reform Order for the modernisation and streamlining of insolvency procedures" (September 2007)). Generally speaking, most creditors just want to know how much of their debt will be repaid and have no interest in the general progress of the procedure. This requirement therefore creates a heavy but unnecessary financial and administrative burden. It will be replaced by a system allowing creditors who do wish to be kept up to date to "opt in" to receiving information from the insolvency practitioner. The consultation paper also includes proposals to allow information to be exchanged by electronic communication where the recipient agrees, and for insolvency practitioners to provide information to interested parties via a website.

At the time of writing, the consultation is still open. If these proposals are accepted, the changes are likely to be implemented from 1 October 2008.

If he is not obliged to keep accounting records in this way, he must still send out a **progress report** on the efficacy of the CVA to the same persons at least once every 12 months (r 1.26 IR 1986; moratorium: r 1.54 IR 1986).

9547

The supervisor can apply to court for permission (r 1.26 IR 1986; moratorium: r 1.54 IR 1986):
– to **vary** the timing of sending the abstracts/reports;
– **not to send** abstracts/reports to the shareholders; or
– **instead of sending** the abstracts/reports to the shareholders, to advertise that they are available.

9548

Remuneration and expenses

The supervisor **can incur** the following fees, costs, charges and expenses in implementing a CVA (r 1.28 IR 1986; moratorium: r 1.54 IR 1986):
– those allowed by the terms of the CVA, or which would be payable if the company were in liquidation or administration; and
– disbursements and agreed remuneration of the nominee prior to the approval of the proposal.

9549

Directors

The directors' **involvement** in a CVA will depend upon the terms of the arrangement in question. Provided their conduct has not been brought into question, they will often carry on the company's business as usual, albeit under the supervision and instruction of the supervisor, since their inside knowledge and experience can assist him in conducting the CVA successfully. In addition to those which apply when the company is not in an insolvency procedure, directors are subject to the following **liabilities** during a CVA:
– attempting to obtain approval of the proposal by false representation or other fraudulent means (¶9517);
– involvement in a criminal offence relating to the moratorium or CVA (¶9473);
– performing an act or omission during a moratorium, which causes a creditor or shareholder to suffer unfair prejudice (¶9485);
– other criminal activity relating to the moratorium (¶9486+);
– if the liquidator or administrator is also the nominee, failing to co-operate with him (¶8121); and
– involvement in transactions defrauding creditors (¶7826+).

9550

3. Conclusion of the CVA

A CVA can come to an end for a number of **reasons**, commonly:
– its terms usually provide for it to end when certain targets have been reached or at the end of a fixed period;
– when the supervisor believes that the CVA has been successfully implemented or can no longer be achieved; or
– by court order following a challenge to the approval of the CVA or the conduct of the supervisor.

9555

If a CVA is ended (whether by court order or because the supervisor cannot implement it) before it was fully implemented in respect of all persons bound by it, it is referred to as having **ended prematurely** (s 7B IA 1986). This has certain implications for persons bound by the CVA who did not have notice of the meetings to approve the proposal (¶9526).

Once the CVA has been completed or terminated, the supervisor must send **notice** of that fact to all creditors and shareholders bound by it (r 1.29 IR 1986). The notice must include a report which:
– summarises the receipts and payments of the CVA;

9556

– explains any departure from the original proposal;
– if any money was distributed to unsecured creditors out of any ring-fenced fund, how much; and
– if the CVA has been terminated, the reasons for this.

Once the **supervisor** has forwarded copies of this notice and report to the court and Companies House, he can **leave office**.

Conversion into another insolvency procedure

9557 The supervisor of a CVA can (s 7(4)(b) IA 1986):
– petition for the company's **winding up** (¶7636); and
– apply for it to be placed into **administration** (¶8728).

This would be appropriate where the CVA cannot be conducted successfully. An example would be where the company does not have the funds to operate for its duration, but administration or liquidation would be an appropriate alternative, allowing the creditors to recover some of their debts.

9558 Where a **member state liquidator** has been **appointed** in relation to the company **after the CVA** took effect, he can convert the CVA into a winding up if it is in the interests of the creditors in the main proceedings (reg 37 EC Insolvency Reg). The member state liquidator must apply to court for leave to convert the CVA, supporting his application with affidavit evidence, and serve the application and affidavit on the company and the supervisor (rr 1.31, 1.32 IR 1986). The court has the power to make any order as appropriate in the circumstances, including specifying whether the company is to be wound up compulsorily or as if the creditors or shareholders had passed a resolution to do so voluntarily (r 1.33 IR 1986). If the CVA is converted into a liquidation, the costs and expenses of the CVA comprise a first charge over the company's assets in the liquidation.

> MEMO POINTS   As part of the Insolvency Service's review of secondary legislation (see ¶7364/mp), it is taking the opportunity to make alterations to the primary legislation either where it is necessary to support the new Rules or to remove unnecessary administrative burdens. The Service proposes to remove the requirement for certain documents to be verified by **affidavit** in insolvency procedures (proposal 5, "A consultation document on changes to the Insolvency Act 1986 and the Company Directors Disqualification Act 1986 to be made by a Legislative Reform Order for the modernisation and streamlining of insolvency procedures" (September 2007)). Since the reform of civil procedures generally in 1998, affidavits in other types of procedures have been replaced by witness statements, which do not have to be sworn/affirmed by a solicitor/commissioner for oaths/notary. Therefore, this change will reduce the cost and administrative time involved in preparing these documents. At the time of writing, the consultation is still open. If this proposal is accepted, the changes are likely to be implemented from 1 October 2008.

> # Appendix

OUTLINE	¶¶
Companies House forms and filing deadlines	9900
Useful contacts	9905
Table B 1985	9910
Table A 1985	9915
Comparison between Table A 1985 and Table A 1948	9920
Sample director's service contract	9925
Definition of "connected person"	9930
Table of criminal offences	9935

Companies House forms and filing deadlines

This table is arranged in order of the length of the period within which filing is permitted. It does not include details of incorporation documents (see ¶479+), foreign or Scottish forms and documents or forms required to be filed under IA 1986 or IR 1986 (for which, readers should refer to the relevant insolvency topic). **9900**

The **names** of Companies House forms are taken from the relevant section number in the legislation. As all of the section numbers will change under the new Companies Act, Companies House proposes to change the names of all of its forms to reflect their function rather than the relevant section number ("Working with Companies House: a consultation on the registrar's rules and related provisions which will apply under the Companies Act 2006"). At the time of writing, new names for all of the forms are not available.

Form/document	Purpose of form/document	Filing deadline	¶¶
54	Notice of application to court for cancellation of special resolution regarding re-registration	As soon as application is made	¶678
157	Notice of application to court for cancellation of special resolution regarding financial assistance for acquisition of shares	As soon as application is made	¶5617
176	Notice of application to court for cancellation of resolution for redemption or purchase of own shares out of capital	As soon as application is made	¶1418
190	Notice of place where register of debenture holders or duplicate is kept, or change in that place	On change of address	¶4006
190a	Notice of place for inspection of register of debenture holders kept in non-legible form, or change in that place	On change of address	¶4006

Form/document	Purpose of form/document	Filing deadline	¶¶
266(3)	Notice that company no longer wishes to be an investment company	On decision not to be an investment company	-
287	Change in registered office	Change takes effect on delivery of notice to Companies House so it is advisable for companies to file notice as soon as change occurs	¶570
Resolution to change name	Change of name	No deadline, but change will not take effect until form is filed and certificate is issued	¶275
30(5)(c)	Declaration on change of name omitting "limited" from title	File with resolution to change name	¶242
117	Application by public company for trading certificate	No deadline, but company will not be able to do business or borrow before application is made	¶510+
405(2)	Notice of ordinary receiver or manager ceasing to act	On ceasing to act	¶9405
405(1)	Notice of appointment of receiver or manager	7 days	¶9248
288a	Appointment of director/secretary	14 days	¶2288 ¶4151
288b	Termination of director's/secretary's appointment	14 days	¶2957 ¶4160
288c	Change of details of director/secretary	14 days	¶3902+
318	Notice of place where copies of directors' service contracts are kept, or change in that place	14 days	¶2668
353	Notice of place where register of shareholders is kept, or change in that place	14 days	¶3928
353a	Notice of place for inspection of register of shareholders kept in non-legible form, or change in that place	14 days	¶3925
362	Notice of place where overseas branch register is kept, or change in that place or of discontinuance of register	14 days	¶3950
362a	Notice of place for inspection of overseas branch register kept in non-legible form, or change in that place	14 days	¶3950
391	Notice that company has passed ordinary resolution to remove auditor from office	14 days	¶4344
Notice of auditor's resignation	Notice received by company that auditor wishes to resign (s 392 CA 1985)	14 days	¶4341
600	Notice of appointment of liquidator in members' or creditors' voluntary liquidation	14 days	¶8511
6	Notice of cancellation or alteration of objects of company	15 days of either: – court order; or – end of time period for making application to court	¶417+
43(3)	Application by private company for re-registration as public company	15 days	¶666+
43(3)(e)	Declaration of compliance with requirements by private company re-registering as public company	15 days	¶666+

Form/document	Purpose of form/document	Filing deadline	¶¶
49(1)	Application by private company for re-registration as unlimited	15 days	¶681+
49(8)(a)	Shareholders' assent to company being re-registered as unlimited	15 days	¶681+
G49(8)(b)	Statutory declaration by directors of shareholders' assent to re-registration of company as unlimited	15 days	¶681+
51	Application by unlimited company to be re-registered as limited	15 days	¶684+
123	Notice of increase in nominal capital	15 days	¶907
139	Application by public company for re-registration as private company following court order reducing capital	15 days (or as court order directs)	¶1493+
147	Application by public company for re-registration as private company following cancellation of shares and reduction of nominal value of allotted capital	15 days	¶1222
155(6)(a)	Director's declaration regarding financial assistance for acquisition of shares	15 days	¶5602+
155(6)(b)	Holding company directors' declaration regarding financial assistance for acquisition of shares	15 days	¶5602+
173	Director's declaration regarding redemption or purchase of own shares out of capital	15 days	¶1404+
Resolutions to be filed	– Special resolutions and resolutions that should have been passed in this way (s 30 CA 2006)	15 days	¶3553+
	– Extraordinary resolutions and resolutions that should have been passed in this way (s 380 CA 1985 as amended by SI 2007/2607)		¶3544
	– Elective resolutions (s 380 CA 1985 as amended by SI 2007/2607)		¶3562+
	– Ordinary resolutions revoking elective resolutions (s 380 CA 1985 as amended by SI 2007/2607)		¶3566+
	– Ordinary resolution to authorise share allotments (s 80 CA 1985, as amended by para 1 Sch 4 SI 2007/2194)		¶907
	– Ordinary resolution to wind up company voluntarily (s 84 IA 1986, as amended by para 39 Sch 4 SI 2007/2194)		¶8457 ¶8616
	– Board resolution by public company to re-register as private company following cancellation of shares and reduction of nominal value of allotted capital (s 147(2) CA 1985, amended by para 1 Sch 4 SI 2007/2194)		¶1222
	– Board resolution for re-registration of old public company as public company (s 2(3) CC(CP)A 1985, amended by para 38 Sch 4 SI 2007/2194)		–
	– Board resolution to allow non-written evidence of title to company's shares and ordinary resolution revoking it (reg 16 SI 2001/3755, as amended by para 97 Sch 4 SI 2007/2194)		–
	– All resolutions or agreements binding all of a class of shareholder where unanimous consent of class has not been obtained		–
	– Resolutions that were agreed unanimously but should have been passed in a particular way		–

Form/document	Purpose of form/document	Filing deadline	¶¶
395	Particulars of mortgage or charge	21 days	¶4641+
397	Particulars of charge to secure series of debentures	21 days	¶3980
397(a)	Particulars of issue of secured debentures in series	21 days	¶3980
398	Certificate of registration in Scotland or Northern Ireland of charge comprising property there	21 days	¶4643
400	Particulars of mortgage or charge on acquired property	21 days	¶4645
53	Application by public company to be re-registered as private	28 days	¶677
169	Return by company purchasing own shares	28 days	¶1394
363a	Annual return	28 days	¶4060+
363a Sch	List of past and present shareholders for annual return	with annual return	¶4062
363s	Shuttle annual return issued by Companies House	28 days	¶4067
88(2)	Return of allotment of shares	1 month	¶1087
88(3)	Particulars of contract relating to shares allotted as fully or partly paid up not in cash	1 month	¶1087
122	Notice of consolidation, division, sub-division, redemption or cancellation of shares, or conversion/re-conversion of shares into stock	1 month	¶1318 ¶1378 ¶1312
128(1)	Statement of rights attached to allotted shares	1 month	¶915 ¶1087
128(3)	Statement of variation of share rights	1 month	¶915 ¶2086
128(4)	Notice of assignment of name or new name of class of shares	1 month	¶915
129(1)	Statement by company without share capital of rights attached to new class of members	1 month	¶915
129(2)	Statement by company without share capital of variation of members' class rights	1 month	¶915
129(3)	Notice by company without share capital of assignment of name or other designation to class of members	1 month	¶915
984	Notice to non-assenting shareholders	within 1 month of the threshold being met	¶6967
Annual accounts	-	**Private companies**: – Within 10 months of accounting period end; or – If in company's first accounting period which is longer than 12 months, 22 months from date of incorporation, or 3 months from end of first accounting period, whichever expires later[1] **Public companies**: – Within 7 months of accounting period end; or	¶4278+

Form/document	Purpose of form/document	Filing deadline	¶¶
		– If in company's first accounting period which is longer than 12 months, 19 months from date of incorporation, or 3 months from end of first accounting period, whichever expires later[1]	
97	Statement of amount or % of commission payable in connection with subscription of shares	Before payment of commission	¶1238
225	Notice of change of accounting reference date	Any time before period for filing accounts has expired	¶4221
266(1)	Notice of intention to carry on business as investment company	Prior to commencement of investment business	–
403(a)	Declaration of satisfaction in full or in part of mortgage or charge	No deadline	¶4657
403(b)	Declaration that part of property or undertaking which is subject of charge has either been released from charge, or no longer forms part of company's property	No deadline	¶4657
652a	Application to strike company off register	No deadline	¶7506
652c	Withdrawal of application to strike company off register	No deadline	¶7508
–	Board resolution to change company's name after direction from secretary of state that company which was exempt from including "limited" in its name is no longer exempt: notify Companies House so it can issue certificate of incorporation on change of name (s 31(2A) CA 1985, inserted by para 1 Sch 4 SI 2007/2194)	No deadline, but new certificate of incorporation will only be issued when Companies House receives notice	¶242

Note:
1. From 6 April 2008, private companies will have 9 months from the end of their accounting periods, and public companies will have 6 months within which to file their accounts (ss 442, 443 CA 2006).

Useful contacts

9905

Organisation	Contact details	
Companies House	England and Wales: (document filing)	Companies House Crown Way Maindy Cardiff, CF14 3UZ DX 33050
	Scotland: (document filing)	Companies House 37 Castle Terrace Edinburgh, H1 2EB DX ED235 Edinburgh 1
	Companies House Executive Agency 21 Bloomsbury Street London, WC1B 3XD	
	Companies House also runs a contact centre which answers queries relating to statutory documents, filing and related issues on 0870 33 33 636, or email enquiries@companies-house.gov.uk.	
	Statutory forms, guidance and information can be found on the Companies House website: www.companieshouse.gov.uk.	
Revenue and Customs, general information	Revenue and Customs has a number of different contact points depending upon the nature of the enquiry/tax. Detailed information can be found on its website: www.hmrc.gov.uk	
Revenue and Customs, Birmingham Stamp Office	For payment of stamp duty on share transfers: Birmingham Stamp Office 9th Floor City Centre House 30 Union Street Birmingham, B2 4AR DX 15001 Birmingham 1 Telephone: 0845 603 0135 Same day stamping helpline: 0121 616 4513	
Financial Services Authority	25 The North Colonnade Canary Wharf London, E14 5HS Main switchboard: 020 7066 1000 Consumer helpline: 0845 606 1234 Authorised firms' contact centre: 0845 606 9966 Fax: 020 7066 1099 Website: www.fsa.gov.uk	
Courts service	Contact details for all courts can be found on its website: www.hmcourts-service.gov.uk	
Takeover Panel	The Panel on Takeovers and Mergers 10 Paternoster Square London, EC4M 7DY	
	General Enquiries: Telephone: 020 7382 9026 Fax: 020 7236 7005 Website: www.thetakeoverpanel.org.uk	
	Market Surveillance Unit: Telephone: 020 7638 0129 Fax: 020 7236 7013 Email: monitoring@disclosure.org.uk.	

Organisation	Contact details
Regulatory information service	Approved services are listed on the FSA's website at: *www.fsa.gov.uk/Pages/doing/ukla/ris/contact/index.shtml*
Takeover Appeal Board	Address, telephone and fax are the same as for the Takeover Panel. Email: *secretary@thetakeoverappealboard.org.uk* Website: *www.thetakeoverappealboard.org.uk*
Companies Investigations Branch	Companies Investigation Branch Insolvency Service 21 Bloomsbury Street London, WC1B 3QW Email: *vetting.section@berr.gsi.gov.uk* Website: *www.insolvency.gov.uk/cib*
Office of Fair Trading	Office of Fair Trading Fleetbank House 2-6 Salisbury Square London, EC4Y 8JX Main switchboard: 020 7211 8000 General enquiries: 08457 22 44 99 Email: *enquiries@oft.gsi.gov.uk* Website: *www.oft.gov.uk* Copies of leaflets and reports published by the OFT can be downloaded from the website. Orders can also be made by telephone on 0800 389 3158 or by email: *oft@ecgroup.uk.com*
Gazette	The London Gazette PO Box 7923 London, SE1 5ZH Information and advertising: 0870 600 5522 The Edinburgh Gazette 71 Lothian Road Edinburgh, EH3 9AW Information and advertising: 0131 622 1342/0131 659 7032 Subscriptions: 0870 600 5522 Website: *www.gazettes-online.co.uk*
Information Commissioner	Information Commissioner's Office Wycliffe House Water Lane Wilmslow Cheshire, SK9 5AF Switchboard: 01625 545 700 Fax: 01625 524 510 Helpline telephone: 01625 545 745 Notification helpline: 01625 545 740 Website: *www.ico.gov.uk*
Insolvency Service	The Insolvency Service 21 Bloomsbury Street London, WC1B 3QW Public enquiry lines: General insolvency: 0845 602 9848 Redundancy: 0845 145 0004 Website: *www.insolvency.gov.uk* Estate Accounts and Insolvency Practitioner Unit (IPU) is based in Birmingham at: The Insolvency Service Ladywood House 45/6 Stephenson Street Birmingham, B2 4DS General enquiries: 0121 698 4000

Organisation	Contact details
International Insolvency Institute	Website: *www.iiiglobal.org*
Ministry of Justice	Website: *www.justice.gov.uk*
European Commission	Company law and corporate governance website: *ec.europa.eu/internalmarket/ company/indexen.htm*
Land Registry	Website: *www.landregistry.co.uk*
Intellectual Property Office	Website: *www.ipo.gov.uk*
Institute of Chartered Accountants of England and Wales	Website: *www.icaew.co.uk*
Institute of Chartered Secretaries and Administrators	Website: *www.icsa.org.uk*
Accounting Standards Board	Website: *www.frc.org.uk/asb*
Auditing Practices Board	Website: *www.frc.org.uk/apb*
British Venture Capital Association	Website: *www.bvca.co.uk*
British Business Angel Association	Website: *www.bbaa.org.uk*
Office of the Regulator of Community Interest Companies	Website: *www.cicregulator.gov.uk*
Co-operatives[UK]	Website: *www.cooperatives-uk.coop*
International Corporate Governance Network	Website: *www.icgn.org*
Financial Reporting Council	Website: *www.frc.org.uk*

Table B 1985

9910

A PRIVATE COMPANY LIMITED BY SHARES
MEMORANDUM OF ASSOCIATION[1]

1. The company's name is "The South Wales Motor Transport Company cyfyngedig".[2]

2. The company's registered office is to be situated in Wales.

3. The company's objects are the carriage of passengers and goods in motor vehicles between such places as the company may from time to time determine and the doing of all such other things as are incidental or conducive to the attainment of that object.

4. The liability of the members is limited.

5. The company's share capital is £50,000 divided into 50,000 shares of £1 each.

We, the subscribers to this memorandum of association, wish to be formed into a company pursuant to this memorandum; and we agree to take the number of shares shown opposite our respective names.

Names and Addresses of Subscribers	Number of shares taken by each Subscriber
1. Thomas Jones, 138 Mountfield Street, Tredegar.	1
2. Mary Evans, 19 Merthyr Road, Aberystwyth.	1
Total shares taken	2

Dated   19

Witness to the above signatures, Anne Brown, "Woodlands", Fieldside Road, Bryn Mawr.

---

1. See ¶394+ for further information on the memorandum, including how it may be altered to suit the needs of a particular company.
For companies incorporated on or after 1 October 2009, the memorandum will simply state that the subscribers wish to form a company and agree to become shareholders on formation. In the case of a company with share capital, the subscribers will agree to take at least one share each. The memorandum will have to be authenticated by each subscriber (s 8 CA 2006, expected to come into force by 1 October 2009). The form of the memorandum will be set out in regulations (at the time of writing, the regulations are still in draft form: Schs 1, 2 draft Companies (Registration) Regulations 2007 (August 2007 version)).
2. The example used in Table B (SI 1985/805) is of a Welsh company using the Welsh language term "cyfyngedig" meaning "Limited". Companies which state in their memorandum that they are incorporated in England and Wales use the English term "Limited" or its abbreviation "Ltd" instead.

Table A 1985[1]

REGULATIONS FOR MANAGEMENT OF A COMPANY LIMITED BY SHARES

INTERPRETATION

1. In these regulations-

"the Act" means the Companies Act 1985 including any statutory modification or re-enactment thereof *and any provisions of the Companies Act 2006*[2] *for the time being in force.*

"the articles" means the articles of the company.

"clear days" in relation to the period of a notice means that period excluding the day when the notice is given or deemed to be given and the day for which it is given or on which it is to take effect.

"communication" means the same as in the Electronic Communications Act 2000,

"electronic communication" means the same as in the Electronic Communications Act 2000.[3]

"executed" includes any mode of execution.

"office" means the registered office of the company.

"the holder" in relation to shares means the member whose name is entered in the register of members as the holder of the shares.

"the seal" means the common seal of the company.

"secretary" means the secretary of the company or any other person appointed to perform the duties of the secretary of the company, including a joint, assistant or deputy secretary.

"the United Kingdom" means Great Britain and Northern Ireland.

Unless the context otherwise requires, words or expressions contained in these regulations bear the same meaning as in the Act but excluding any statutory modification thereof not in force when these regulations become binding on the company.

SHARE CAPITAL

2. Subject to the provisions of the Act and without prejudice to any rights attached to any existing shares, any share may be issued with such rights or restrictions as the company may by ordinary resolution determine.

3. Subject to the provisions of the Act, shares may be issued which are to be redeemed or are to be liable to be redeemed at the option of the company or the holder on such terms and in such manner as may be provided by the articles.

4. The company may exercise the powers of paying commissions conferred by the Act. Subject to the *provisions*[4] of the Act, any such commission may be satisfied by the payment of cash or by the allotment of fully or partly paid shares or partly in one way and partly in the other.

5. Except as required by law, no person shall be recognised by the company as holding any share upon any trust and (except as otherwise provided by the articles or by law) the company shall not be bound by or recognise any interest in any share except an absolute right to the entirety thereof in the holder.

SHARE CERTIFICATES

6. Every member, upon becoming the holder of any shares, shall be entitled without payment to one certificate for all the shares of each class held by him (and, upon transferring a part of his holding of shares of any class, to a certificate for the balance of such holding) or several certificates each for one or more of his shares upon payment for every certificate after the first of such reasonable sum as the directors may determine. Every certificate shall be sealed with the seal and shall specify the number, class and distinguishing numbers (if any) of the shares to which it relates and the amount or respective amounts paid up thereon. The company shall not be bound to issue more than one certificate for shares held jointly by several persons and delivery of a certificate to one joint holder shall be a sufficient delivery to all of them.

7. If a share certificate is defaced, worn-out, lost or destroyed, it may be renewed on such terms (if any) as to evidence and indemnity and payment of the expenses reasonably incurred by the company in investigating evidence as the directors may determine but otherwise free of charge, and (in the case of defacement or wearing-out) on delivery up of the old certificate.

LIEN

8. The company shall have a first and paramount lien on every share (not being a fully paid share) for all moneys (whether presently payable or not) payable at a fixed time or called in respect of that share. The

directors may at any time declare any share to be wholly or in part exempt from the provisions of this regulation. The company's lien on a share shall extend to any amount payable in respect of it.

9. The company may sell in such manner as the directors determine any shares on which the company has a lien if a sum in respect of which the lien exists is presently payable and is not paid within fourteen clear days after notice has been given to the holder of the share or to the person entitled to it in consequence of the death or bankruptcy of the holder, demanding payment and stating that if the notice is not complied with the shares may be sold.

10. To give effect to a sale the directors may authorise some person to execute an instrument of transfer of the shares sold to, or in accordance with the directions of, the purchaser. The title of the transferee to the shares shall not be affected by any irregularity in or invalidity of the proceedings in reference to the sale.

11. The net proceeds of the sale, after payment of the costs, shall be applied in payment of so much of the sum for which the lien exists as is presently payable, and any residue shall (upon surrender to the company for cancellation of the certificate for the shares sold and subject to a like lien for any moneys not presently payable as existed upon the shares before the sale) be paid to the person entitled to the shares at the date of the sale.

CALLS ON SHARES AND FORFEITURE

12. Subject to the terms of allotment, the directors may make calls upon the members in respect of any moneys unpaid on their shares (whether in respect of nominal value or premium) and each member shall (subject to receiving at least fourteen clear days' notice specifying when and where payment is to be made) pay to the company as required by the notice the amount called on his shares. A call may be required to be paid by instalments. A call may, before receipt by the company of any sum due thereunder, be revoked in whole or part and payment of a call may be postponed in whole or part. A person upon whom a call is made shall remain liable for calls made upon him notwithstanding the subsequent transfer of the shares in respect whereof the call was made.

13. A call shall be deemed to have been made at the time when the resolution of the directors authorising the call was passed.

14. The joint holders of a share shall be jointly and severally liable to pay all calls in respect thereof.

15. If a call remains unpaid after it has become due and payable the person from whom it is due and payable shall pay interest on the amount unpaid from the day it became due and payable until it is paid at the rate fixed by the terms of allotment of the share or in the notice of the call or, if no rate is fixed, at the appropriate rate (as defined by the Act) but the directors may waive payment of the interest wholly or in part.

16. An amount payable in respect of a share on allotment or at any fixed date, whether in respect of nominal value or premium or as an instalment of a call, shall be deemed to be a call and if it is not paid the provisions of the articles shall apply as if that amount had become due and payable by virtue of a call.

17. Subject to the terms of allotment, the directors may make arrangements on the issue of shares for a difference between the holders in the amounts and times of payment of calls on their shares.

18. If a call remains unpaid after it has become due and payable the directors may give to the person from whom it is due not less than fourteen clear days' notice requiring payment of the amount unpaid together with any interest which may have accrued. The notice shall name the place where payment is to be made and shall state that if the notice is not complied with the shares in respect of which the call was made will be liable to be forfeited.

19. If the notice is not complied with any share in respect of which it was given may, before the payment required by the notice has been made, be forfeited by a resolution of the directors and the forfeiture shall include all dividends or other moneys payable in respect of the forfeited shares and not paid before the forfeiture.

20. Subject to the provisions of the Act, a forfeited share may be sold, re-allotted or otherwise disposed of on such terms and in such manner as the directors determine either to the person who was before the forfeiture the holder or to any other person and at any time before sale, re-allotment or other disposition, the forfeiture may be cancelled on such terms as the directors think fit. Where for the purposes of its disposal a forfeited share is to be transferred to any person the directors may authorise some person to execute an instrument of transfer of the share to that person.

21. A person any of whose shares have been forfeited shall cease to be a member in respect of them and shall surrender to the company for cancellation the certificate for the shares forfeited but shall remain liable to the company for all moneys which at the date of forfeiture were presently payable by him to the company in respect of those shares with interest at the rate at which interest was payable on those moneys before the forfeiture or, if no interest was so payable, at the appropriate rate (as defined in the Act) from the date of forfeiture until payment but the directors may waive payment wholly or in part or

enforce payment without any allowance for the value of the shares at the time of forfeiture or for any consideration received on their disposal.

22. A statutory declaration by a director or the secretary that a share has been forfeited on a specified date shall be conclusive evidence of the facts stated in it as against all persons claiming to be entitled to the share and the declaration shall (subject to the execution of an instrument of transfer if necessary) constitute a good title to the share and the person to whom the share is disposed of shall not be bound to see to the application of the consideration, if any, nor shall his title to the share be affected by any irregularity in or invalidity of the proceedings in reference to the forfeiture or disposal of the share.

TRANSFER OF SHARES

23. The instrument of transfer of a share may be in any usual form or in any other form which the directors may approve and shall be executed by or on behalf of the transferor and, unless the share is fully paid, by or on behalf of the transferee.

24. The directors may refuse to register the transfer of a share which is not fully paid to a person of whom they do not approve and they may refuse to register the transfer of a share on which the company has a lien. They may also refuse to register a transfer unless-
(a) it is lodged at the office or at such other place as the directors may appoint and is accompanied by the certificate for the shares to which it relates and such other evidence as the directors may reasonably require to show the right of the transferor to make the transfer;
(b) it is in respect of only one class of shares; and
(c) it is in favour of not more than four transferees.

25. If the directors refuse to register a transfer of a share, they shall within two months after the date on which the transfer was lodged with the company send to the transferee notice of the refusal.

26. The registration of transfers of shares or of transfers of any class of shares may be suspended at such times and for such periods (not exceeding thirty days in any year) as the directors may determine.

27. No fee shall be charged for the registration of any instrument of transfer or other document relating to or affecting the title to any share.

28. The company shall be entitled to retain any instrument of transfer which is registered, but any instrument of transfer which the directors refuse to register shall be returned to the person lodging it when notice of the refusal is given.

TRANSMISSION OF SHARES

29. If a member dies the survivor or survivors where he was a joint holder, and his personal representatives where he was a sole holder or the only survivor of joint holders, shall be the only persons recognised by the company as having any title to his interest; but nothing herein contained shall release the estate of a deceased member from any liability in respect of any share which had been jointly held by him.

30. A person becoming entitled to a share in consequence of the death or bankruptcy of a member may, upon such evidence being produced as the directors may properly require, elect either to become the holder of the share or to have some person nominated by him registered as the transferee. If he elects to become the holder he shall give notice to the company to that effect. If he elects to have another person registered he shall execute an instrument of transfer of the share to that person. All the articles relating to the transfer of shares shall apply to the notice or instrument of transfer as if it were an instrument of transfer executed by the member and the death or bankruptcy of the member had not occurred.

31. A person becoming entitled to a share in consequence of the death or bankruptcy of a member shall have the rights to which he would be entitled if he were the holder of the share, except that he shall not, before being registered as the holder of the share, be entitled in respect of it to attend or vote at any meeting of the company or at any separate meeting of the holders of any class of shares in the company.

ALTERATION OF SHARE CAPITAL

32. The company may by ordinary resolution-
(a) increase its share capital by new shares of such amount as the resolution prescribes;
(b) consolidate and divide all or any of its share capital into shares of larger amount than its existing shares;
(c) subject to the provisions of the Act, sub-divide its shares, or any of them, into shares of smaller amount and the resolution may determine that, as between the shares resulting from the sub-division, any of them may have any preference or advantage as compared with the others; and
(d) cancel shares which, at the date of the passing of the resolution, have not been taken or agreed to be taken by any person and diminish the amount of its share capital by the amount of the shares so cancelled.

33. Whenever as a result of a consolidation of shares any members would become entitled to fractions of a share, the directors may, on behalf of those members, sell the shares representing the fractions for

the best price reasonably obtainable to any person (including, subject to the provisions of the Act, the company) and distribute the net proceeds of sale in due proportion among those members, and the directors may authorise some person to execute an instrument of transfer of the shares to, or in accordance with the directions of, the purchaser. The transferee shall not be bound to see to the application of the purchase money nor shall his title to the shares be affected by any irregularity in or invalidity of the proceedings in reference to the sale.

34. Subject to the provisions of the Act, the company may by special resolution reduce its share capital, any capital redemption reserve and any share premium account in any way.

PURCHASE OF OWN SHARES

35. Subject to the provisions of the Act, the company may purchase its own shares (including any redeemable shares) and, if it is a private company, make a payment in respect of the redemption or purchase of its own shares otherwise than out of distributable profits of the company or the proceeds of a fresh issue of shares.

GENERAL MEETINGS

36.[5]

37. The directors may call general meetings and, on the requisition of members pursuant to the provisions of the Act, shall forthwith proceed to convene a[6] general meeting *in accordance with the provisions of the Act*[7]. If there are not within the United Kingdom sufficient directors to call a general meeting, any director or any member of the company may call a general meeting.

NOTICE OF GENERAL MEETINGS

38.[8] General meetings shall be called by at least fourteen clear days' notice but a general meeting may be called by shorter notice if it is so agreed[9] by a majority in number of the members having a right to attend and vote being a majority together holding not less than ninety[10] per cent in nominal value of the shares giving that right.

The notice shall specify the time and place of the meeting and the general nature of the business to be transacted[11].

Subject to the provisions of the articles and to any restrictions imposed on any shares, the notice shall be given to all the members, to all persons entitled to a share in consequence of the death or bankruptcy of a member and to the directors and auditors.

39. The accidental omission to give notice of a meeting to, or the non-receipt of notice of a meeting by, any person entitled to receive notice shall not invalidate the proceedings at that meeting.

PROCEEDINGS AT GENERAL MEETINGS

40. No business shall be transacted at any meeting unless a quorum is present. *Save in the case of a company with a single member*[12] two persons entitled to vote upon the business to be transacted, each being a member or a proxy for a member or a duly authorised representative of a corporation, shall be a quorum.
SI 2007/2541 deleted "Subject as aforesaid, a director who retires at an annual general meeting may, if willing to act, be reappointed. If he is not reappointed, he shall retain office until the meeting appoints someone in his place, or if it does not do so, until the end of the meeting" for private companies only. The regulation still applies for public companies.

41. If such a quorum is not present within half an hour from the time appointed for the meeting, or if during a meeting such a quorum ceases to be present, the meeting shall stand adjourned to the same day in the next week at the same time and place or *to*[13] such time and place as the directors may determine.

42. The chairman, if any, of the board of directors or in his absence some other director nominated by the directors shall preside as chairman of the meeting, but if neither the chairman nor such other director (if any) be present within fifteen minutes after the time appointed for holding the meeting and willing to act, the directors present shall elect one of their number to be chairman and, if there is only one director present and willing to act, he shall be chairman.

43. If no director is willing to act as chairman, or if no director is present within fifteen minutes after the time appointed for holding the meeting, the members present and entitled to vote shall choose one of their number to be chairman.

44. A director shall, notwithstanding that he is not a member, be entitled to attend and speak at any general meeting and at any separate meeting of the holders of any class of shares in the company.

45. The chairman may, with the consent of a meeting at which a quorum is present (and shall if so directed by the meeting), adjourn the meeting from time to time and from place to place, but no business shall be transacted at an adjourned meeting other than business which might properly have been transacted at the meeting had the adjournment not taken place. When a meeting is adjourned for fourteen

days or more, at least seven clear days' notice shall be given specifying the time and place of the adjourned meeting and the general nature of the business to be transacted. Otherwise, it shall not be necessary to give any such notice.

46. A resolution put to the vote of a meeting shall be decided on a show of hands unless before, or on the declaration of the result of, the show of hands a poll is duly demanded. Subject to the provisions of the Act, a poll may be demanded-
(a) by the chairman; or
(b) by at least two members having the right to vote at the meeting; or
(c) by a member or members representing not less than one-tenth of the total voting rights of all the members having the right to vote at the meeting; or
(d) by a member or members holding shares conferring a right to vote at the meeting being shares on which an aggregate sum has been paid up equal to not less than one-tenth of the total sum paid up on all the shares conferring that right;
and a demand by a person as proxy for a member shall be the same as a demand by the member.

47. Unless a poll is duly demanded a declaration by the chairman that a resolution has been carried or carried unanimously, or by a particular majority, or lost, or not carried by a particular majority and an entry to that effect in the minutes of the meeting shall be conclusive evidence of the fact without proof of the number or proportion of the votes recorded in favour of or against the resolution.

48. The demand for a poll may, before the poll is taken, be withdrawn but only with the consent of the chairman and a demand so withdrawn shall not be taken to have invalidated the result of a show of hands declared before the demand was made.

49. A poll shall be taken as the chairman directs and he may appoint scrutineers (who need not be members) and fix a time and place for declaring the result of the poll. The result of the poll shall be deemed to be the resolution of the meeting at which the poll was demanded.

50. [14]

51. A poll demanded on the election of a chairman or on a question of adjournment shall be taken forthwith. A poll demanded on any other question shall be taken either forthwith or at such time and place as the chairman directs not being more than thirty days after the poll is demanded. The demand for a poll shall not prevent the continuance of a meeting for the transaction of any business other than the question on which the poll was demanded. If a poll is demanded before the declaration of the result of a show of hands and the demand is duly withdrawn, the meeting shall continue as if the demand had not been made.

52. No notice need be given of a poll not taken forthwith if the time and place at which it is to be taken are announced at the meeting at which it is demanded. In any other case at least seven clear days' notice shall be given specifying the time and place at which the poll is to be taken.

53. [15]

VOTES OF MEMBERS

54. Subject to any rights or restrictions attached to any shares, on a show of hands every member who (being an individual) is present in person *or by proxy* [16] or (being a corporation) is present by a duly authorised representative *or by proxy* [17], *unless the proxy (in either case) or the representative is* [18] himself a member entitled to vote, shall have one vote and on a poll every member shall have one vote for every share of which he is the holder.

55. In the case of joint holders the vote of the senior who tenders a vote, whether in person or by proxy, shall be accepted to the exclusion of the votes of the other joint holders; and seniority shall be determined by the order in which the names of the holders stand in the register of members.

56. A member in respect of whom an order has been made by any court having jurisdiction (whether in the United Kingdom or elsewhere) in matters concerning mental disorder may vote, whether on a show of hands or on a poll, by his receiver, curator bonis or other person authorised in that behalf appointed by that court, and any such receiver, curator bonis or other person may, on a poll, vote by proxy. Evidence to the satisfaction of the directors of the authority of the person claiming to exercise the right to vote shall be deposited at the office, or at such other place as is specified in accordance with the articles for the deposit of instruments of proxy, not less than 48 hours before the time appointed for holding the meeting or adjourned meeting at which the right to vote is to be exercised and in default the right to vote shall not be exercisable. [19]

57. No member shall vote at any general meeting or at any separate meeting of the holders of any class of shares in the company, either in person or by proxy, in respect of any share held by him unless all moneys presently payable by him in respect of that share have been paid.

58. No objection shall be raised to the qualification of any voter except at the meeting or adjourned meeting at which the vote objected to is tendered, and every vote not disallowed at the meeting shall be valid. Any objection made in due time shall be referred to the chairman whose decision shall be final and conclusive.

59. On a poll votes may be given either personally or by proxy. A member may appoint more than one proxy to attend on the same occasion.

60. *The appointment of*[20] a proxy shall be executed by or on behalf of the appointor and shall be in the following form (or in a form as near thereto as circumstances allow or in any other form which is usual or which the directors may approve)-

"_____ PLC/Limited

I/We, _____, of _____, being a member/members of the above-named company, hereby appoint _____ of _____, or failing him, _____ of _____, as my/our proxy to vote in my/our name[s] and on my/our behalf at the [21] general meeting of the company to be held on _____ 19___, and at any adjournment thereof.
Signed on _____ 19___" [22]

61. Where it is desired to afford members an opportunity of instructing the proxy how he shall act the *appointment of*[23] a proxy shall be in the following form (or in a form as near thereto as circumstances allow or in any other form which is usual or which the directors may approve)-

"_____ PLC/Limited

I/We, _____, of _____, being a member/members of the above-named company, hereby appoint _____ of _____, or failing him, _____ of _____, as my/our proxy to vote in my/our name[s] and on my/our behalf at the [24] general meeting of the company, to be held on _____ 19___, and at any adjournment thereof.

This form is to be used in respect of the resolutions mentioned below as follows:
Resolution No. 1 *for *against
Resolution No. 2 *for *against.

* Strike out whichever is not desired.

Unless otherwise instructed, the proxy may vote as he thinks fit or abstain from voting.

Signed this ___ day of _____ 19___" [25]

62. *The appointment of*[26] a proxy and any authority under which it is executed or a copy of such authority certified notarially or in some other way approved by the directors may –
(a) *in the case of an instrument in writing*[27] be deposited at the office or at such other place within the United Kingdom as is specified in the notice convening the meeting or in any instrument of proxy sent out by the company in relation to the meeting not less than 48 hours before the time for holding the meeting or adjourned meeting at which the person named in the instrument proposes to vote; or
(aa) *in the case of an appointment contained in an electronic communication, where an address has been specified for the purpose of receiving electronic communications-*
(i) in the notice convening the meeting, or
(ii) in any instrument of proxy sent out by the company in relation to the meeting, or
(iii) in any invitation contained in an electronic communication to appoint a proxy issued by the company in relation to the meeting,
be received at such address not less than 48 hours before the time for holding the meeting or adjourned meeting at which the person named in the appointment proposes to vote;[28]
(b) in the case of a poll taken more than 48 hours after it is demanded, be deposited *or received*[29] as aforesaid after the poll has been demanded and not less than 24 hours before the time appointed for the taking of the poll; or
(c) where the poll is not taken forthwith but is taken not more than 48 hours after it was demanded, be delivered at the meeting at which the poll was demanded to the chairman or to the secretary or to any director;
and an appointment of proxy which is not deposited, delivered or *received*[30] in a manner so permitted shall be invalid. *In this regulation and the next, "address", in relation to electronic communications, includes any number or address used for the purposes of such communications.*[31]

63. A vote given or poll demanded by proxy or by the duly authorised representative of a corporation shall be valid notwithstanding the previous determination of the authority of the person voting or demanding a poll unless notice of the determination was received by the company at the office or at such other place at which the instrument of proxy was duly deposited *or, where the appointment of the proxy was contained in an electronic communication, at the address at which such appointment was duly received*[32] before the commencement of the meeting or adjourned meeting at which the vote is given or the poll demanded or (in the case of a poll taken otherwise than on the same day as the meeting or adjourned meeting) the time appointed for taking the poll.

NUMBER OF DIRECTORS

64. Unless otherwise determined by ordinary resolution, the number of directors (other than alternate directors) shall not be subject to any maximum but shall be not less than two.

ALTERNATE DIRECTORS

65. Any director (other than an alternate director) may appoint any other director, or any other person approved by resolution of the directors and willing to act, to be an alternate director and may remove from office an alternate director so appointed by him.

66. An alternate director shall be entitled to receive notice of all meetings of directors and of all meetings of committees of directors of which his appointor is a member, to attend and vote at any such meeting at which the director appointing him is not personally present, and generally to perform all the functions of his appointor as a director in his absence but shall not be entitled to receive any remuneration from the company for his services as an alternate director. But it shall not be necessary to give notice of such a meeting to an alternate director who is absent from the United Kingdom.

67. An alternate director shall cease to be an alternate director if his appointor ceases to be a director; but, if a director retires by rotation or otherwise but is reappointed or deemed to have been reappointed at the meeting at which he retires, any appointment of an alternate director made by him which was in force immediately prior to his retirement shall continue after his reappointment.

68. Any appointment or removal of an alternate director shall be by notice to the company signed by the director making or revoking the appointment or in any other manner approved by the directors.

69. Save as otherwise provided in the articles, an alternate director shall be deemed for all purposes to be a director and shall alone be responsible for his own acts and defaults and he shall not be deemed to be the agent of the director appointing him.

POWER OF DIRECTORS

70. Subject to the provisions of the Act, the memorandum and the articles and to any directions given by special resolution, the business of the company shall be managed by the directors who may exercise all the powers of the company. No alteration of the memorandum or articles and no such direction shall invalidate any prior act of the directors which would have been valid if that alteration had not been made or that direction had not been given. The powers given by this regulation shall not be limited by any special power given to the directors by the articles and a meeting of directors at which a quorum is present may exercise all powers exercisable by the directors.

71. The directors may, by power of attorney or otherwise, appoint any person to be the agent of the company for such purposes and on such conditions as they determine, including authority for the agent to delegate all or any of his powers.

DELEGATION OF DIRECTORS' POWERS

72. The directors may delegate any of their powers to any committee consisting of one or more directors. They may also delegate to any managing director or any director holding any other executive office such of their powers as they consider desirable to be exercised by him. Any such delegation may be made subject to any conditions the directors may impose, and either collaterally with or to the exclusion of their own powers and may be revoked or altered. Subject to any such conditions, the proceedings of a committee with two or more members shall be governed by the articles regulating the proceedings of directors so far as they are capable of applying.

APPOINTMENT AND RETIREMENT OF DIRECTORS

73.[33]

74.[34]

75.[35]

76. No person[36] shall be appointed or reappointed a director at any general meeting unless-
(a) he is recommended by the directors; or
(b) not less than fourteen nor more than thirty-five clear days before the date appointed for the meeting, notice executed by a member qualified to vote at the meeting has been given to the company of the intention to propose that person for appointment or reappointment stating the particulars which would, if he were so appointed or reappointed, be required to be included in the company's register of directors together with notice executed by that person of his willingness to be appointed or reappointed.

77. Not less than seven nor more than twenty-eight clear days before the date appointed for holding a general meeting notice shall be given to all who are entitled to receive notice of the meeting of any person[37] who is recommended by the directors for appointment or reappointment as a director at the

meeting or in respect of whom notice has been duly given to the company of the intention to propose him at the meeting for appointment or reappointment as a director. The notice shall give the particulars of that person which would, if he were so appointed or reappointed, be required to be included in the company's register of directors.

78.[38] The company may by ordinary resolution appoint a person who is willing to act to be a director either to fill a vacancy or as an additional director and may also determine the rotation in which any additional directors are to retire.

79. The directors may appoint a person who is willing to act to be a director, either to fill a vacancy or as an additional director, provided that the appointment does not cause the number of directors to exceed any number fixed by or in accordance with the articles as the maximum number of directors.[39]

80.[40]

DISQUALIFICATION AND REMOVAL OF DIRECTORS

81. The office of a director shall be vacated if-
(a) he ceases to be a director by virtue of any provision of the Act or he becomes prohibited by law from being a director; or
(b) he becomes bankrupt or makes any arrangement or composition with his creditors generally; or
(c) he is, or may be, suffering from mental disorder and either-
(i) he is admitted to hospital in pursuance of an application for admission for treatment under the Mental Health Act 1983 or, in Scotland, an application for admission under the Mental Health (Scotland) Act 1960, or
(ii) an order is made by a court having jurisdiction (whether in the United Kingdom or elsewhere) in matters concerning mental disorder for his detention or for the appointment of a receiver, curator bonis or other person to exercise powers[41] with respect to his property or affairs; or
(d) he resigns his office by notice to the company; or
(e) he shall for more than six consecutive months have been absent without permission of the directors from meetings of directors held during that period and the directors resolve that his office be vacated.

REMUNERATION OF DIRECTORS

82. The directors shall be entitled to such remuneration as the company may by ordinary resolution determine and, unless the resolution provides otherwise, the remuneration shall be deemed to accrue from day to day.

DIRECTORS' EXPENSES

83. The directors may be paid all travelling, hotel, and other expenses properly incurred by them in connection with their attendance at meetings of directors or committees of directors or general meetings or separate meetings of the holders of any class of shares or of debentures of the company or otherwise in connection with the discharge of their duties.

DIRECTORS' APPOINTMENTS AND INTERESTS

84. Subject to the provisions of the Act, the directors may appoint one or more of their number to the office of managing director or to any other executive office under the company and may enter into an agreement or arrangement with any director for his employment by the company or for the provision by him of any services outside the scope of the ordinary duties of a director. Any such appointment, agreement or arrangement may be made upon such terms as the directors determine and they may remunerate any such director for his services as they think fit. Any appointment of a director to an executive office shall terminate if he ceases to be a director but without prejudice to any claim to damages for breach of the contract of service between the director and the company. A managing director and a director holding any other executive office shall not be subject to retirement by rotation.

85. Subject to the provisions of the Act, and provided that he has disclosed to the directors the nature and extent of any material interest of his, a director notwithstanding his office-
(a) may be a party to, or otherwise interested in, any transaction or arrangement with the company or in which the company is otherwise interested;
(b) may be a director or other officer of, or employed by, or a party to any transaction or arrangement with, or otherwise interested in, any body corporate promoted by the company or in which the company is otherwise interested; and
(c) shall not, by reason of his office, be accountable to the company for any benefit which he derives from any such office or employment or from any such transaction or arrangement or from any interest in any such body corporate and no such transaction or arrangement shall be liable to be avoided on the ground of any such interest or benefit.

86. For the purposes of regulation 85-
(a) a general notice given to the directors that a director is to be regarded as having an interest of the nature and extent specified in the notice in any transaction or arrangement in which a specified person or class of persons is interested shall be deemed to be a disclosure that the director has an interest in any such transaction of the nature and extent so specified; and
(b) an interest of which a director has no knowledge and of which it is unreasonable to expect him to have knowledge shall not be treated as an interest of his.

DIRECTORS' GRATUITIES AND PENSIONS

87. The directors may provide benefits, whether by the payment of gratuities or pensions or by insurance or otherwise, for any director who has held but no longer holds any executive office or employment with the company or with any body corporate which is or has been a subsidiary of the company or a predecessor in business of the company or of any subsidiary, and for any member of his family (including a spouse and a former spouse) or any person who is or was dependent on him, and may (as well before as after he ceases to hold such office or employment) contribute to any fund and pay premiums for the purchase or provision of any such benefit.

PROCEEDINGS OF DIRECTORS

88. Subject to the provisions of the articles, the directors may regulate their proceedings as they think fit. A director may, and the secretary at the request of a director shall, call a meeting of the directors. It shall not be necessary to give notice of a meeting to a director who is absent from the United Kingdom. Questions arising at a meeting shall be decided by a majority of votes. In the case of an equality of votes, the chairman shall have a second or casting vote. A director who is also an alternate director shall be entitled in the absence of his appointor to a separate vote on behalf of his appointor in addition to his own vote.

89. The quorum for the transaction of the business of the directors may be fixed by the directors and unless so fixed at any other number shall be two. A person who holds office only as an alternate director shall, if his appointor is not present, be counted in the quorum.

90. The continuing directors or a sole continuing director may act notwithstanding any vacancies in their number, but, if the number of directors is less than the number fixed as the quorum, the continuing directors or director may act only for the purpose of filling vacancies or of calling a general meeting.

91. The directors may appoint one of their number to be the chairman of the board of directors and may at any time remove him from that office. Unless he is unwilling to do so, the director so appointed shall preside at every meeting of the directors at which he is present. But if there is no director holding that office, or if the director holding it is unwilling to preside or is not present within five minutes after the time appointed for the meeting, the directors present may appoint one of their number to be chairman of the meeting.

92. All acts done by a meeting of directors, or a committee of directors, or by a person acting as a director shall, notwithstanding that it be afterwards discovered that there was a defect in the appointment of any director or that any of them were disqualified from holding office, or had vacated office, or were not entitled to vote, be as valid as if every such person had been duly appointed and was qualified and had continued to be a director and had been entitled to vote.

93. A resolution in writing signed by all the directors entitled to receive notice of a meeting of directors or of a committee of directors shall be as valid and effectual as if it had been passed at a meeting of directors or (as the case may be) a committee of directors duly convened and held and may consist of several documents in the like form each signed by one or more directors; but a resolution signed by an alternate director need not also be signed by his appointor and, if it is signed by a director who has appointed an alternate director, it need not be signed by the alternate director in that capacity.

94. Save as otherwise provided by the articles, a director shall not vote at a meeting of directors or of a committee of directors on any resolution concerning a matter in which he has, directly or indirectly, an interest or duty which is material and which conflicts or may conflict with the interests of the company unless his interest or duty arises only because the case falls within one or more of the following para graphs-
(a) the resolution relates to the giving to him of a guarantee, security, or indemnity in respect of money lent to, or an obligation incurred by him for the benefit of, the company or any of its subsidiaries;
(b) the resolution relates to the giving to a third party of a guarantee, security, or indemnity in respect of an obligation of the company or any of its subsidiaries for which the director has assumed responsibility in whole or in part and whether alone or jointly with others under a guarantee or indemnity or by the giving of security;
(c) his interest arises by virtue of his subscribing or agreeing to subscribe for any shares, debentures or other securities of the company or any of its subsidiaries, or by virtue of his being, or intending to become, a participant in the underwriting or sub-underwriting of an offer of any such shares, debentures, or other securities by the company or any of its subsidiaries for subscription, purchase or exchange;

(d) the resolution relates in any way to a retirement benefits scheme which has been approved, or is conditional upon approval, by the Board of Inland Revenue for taxation purposes.

For the purposes of this regulation, an interest of a person who is, for any purpose of the Act (excluding any statutory modification thereof not in force when this regulation becomes binding on the company), connected with a director shall be treated as an interest of the director and, in relation to an alternate director, an interest of his appointor shall be treated as an interest of the alternate director without prejudice to any interest which the alternate director has otherwise.

95. A director shall not be counted in the quorum present at a meeting in relation to a resolution on which he is not entitled to vote.

96. The company may by ordinary resolution suspend or relax to any extent, either generally or in respect of any particular matter, any provision of the articles prohibiting a director from voting at a meeting of directors or of a committee of directors.

97. Where proposals are under consideration concerning the appointment of two or more directors to offices or employments with the company or any body corporate in which the company is interested the proposals may be divided and considered in relation to each director separately and (provided he is not for another reason precluded from voting) each of the directors concerned shall be entitled to vote and be counted in the quorum in respect of each resolution except that concerning his own appointment.

98. If a question arises at a meeting of directors or of a committee of directors as to the right of a director to vote, the question may, before the conclusion of the meeting, be referred to the chairman of the meeting and his ruling in relation to any director other than himself shall be final and conclusive.

SECRETARY

99. Subject to the provisions of the Act, the secretary shall be appointed by the directors for such term, at such remuneration and upon such conditions as they may think fit; and any secretary so appointed may be removed by them.

MINUTES

100. The directors shall cause minutes to be made in books kept for the purpose-
(a) of all appointments of officers made by the directors; and
(b) of all proceedings at meetings of the company, of the holders of any class of shares in the company, and of the directors, and of committees of directors, including the names of the directors present at each such meeting.

THE SEAL

101. The seal shall only be used by the authority of the directors or of a committee of directors authorised by the directors. The directors may determine who shall sign any instrument to which the seal is affixed and unless otherwise so determined it shall be signed by a director and by the secretary or by a second director.

DIVIDENDS

102. Subject to the provisions of the Act, the company may by ordinary resolution declare dividends in accordance with the respective rights of the members, but no dividend shall exceed the amount recommended by the directors.

103. Subject to the provisions of the Act, the directors may pay interim dividends if it appears to them that they are justified by the profits of the company available for distribution. If the share capital is divided into different classes, the directors may pay interim dividends on shares which confer deferred or non-preferred rights with regard to dividend as well as on shares which confer preferential rights with regard to dividend, but no interim dividend shall be paid on shares carrying deferred or non-preferred rights if, at the time of payment, any preferential dividend is in arrear. The directors may also pay at intervals settled by them any dividend payable at a fixed rate if it appears to them that the profits available for distribution justify the payment. Provided the directors act in good faith they shall not incur any liability to the holders of shares conferring preferred rights for any loss they may suffer by the lawful payment of an interim dividend on any shares having deferred or non-preferred rights.

104. Except as otherwise provided by the rights attached to shares, all dividends shall be declared and paid according to the amounts paid up on the shares on which the dividend is paid. All dividends shall be apportioned and paid proportionately to the amounts paid up on the shares during any portion or portions of the period in respect of which the dividend is paid; but, if any share is issued on terms providing that it shall rank for dividend as from a particular date, that share shall rank for dividend accordingly.

105. A general meeting declaring a dividend may, upon the recommendation of the directors, direct that it shall be satisfied wholly or partly by the distribution of assets and, where any difficulty arises in regard to the distribution, the directors may settle the same and in particular may issue fractional certificates and

fix the value for distribution of any assets and may determine that cash shall be paid to any member upon the footing of the value so fixed in order to adjust the rights of members and may vest any assets in trustees.

106. Any dividend or other moneys payable in respect of a share may be paid by cheque sent by post to the registered address of the person entitled or, if two or more persons are the holders of the share or are jointly entitled to it by reason of the death or bankruptcy of the holder, to the registered address of that one of those persons who is first named in the register of members or to such person and to such address as the person or persons entitled may in writing direct. Every cheque shall be made payable to the order of the person or persons entitled or to such other person as the person or persons entitled may in writing direct and payment of the cheque shall be a good discharge to the company. Any joint holder or other person jointly entitled to a share as aforesaid may give receipts for any dividend or other moneys payable in respect of the share.

107. No dividend or other moneys payable in respect of a share shall bear interest against the company unless otherwise provided by the rights attached to the share.

108. Any dividend which has remained unclaimed for twelve years from the date when it became due for payment shall, if the directors so resolve, be forfeited and cease to remain owing by the company.

ACCOUNTS

109. No member shall (as such) have any right of inspecting any accounting records or other book or document of the company except as conferred by statute or authorised by the directors or by ordinary resolution of the company.

CAPITALISATION OF PROFITS

110. The directors may with the authority of an ordinary resolution of the company-
(a) subject as hereinafter provided, resolve to capitalise any undivided profits of the company not required for paying any preferential dividend (whether or not they are available for distribution) or any sum standing to the credit of the company's share premium account or capital redemption reserve;
(b) appropriate the sum resolved to be capitalised to the members who would have been entitled to it if it were distributed by way of dividend and in the same proportions and apply such sum on their behalf either in or towards paying up the amounts, if any, for the time being unpaid on any shares held by them respectively, or in paying up in full unissued shares or debentures of the company of a nominal amount equal to that sum, and allot the shares or debentures credited as fully paid to those members, or as they may direct, in those proportions, or partly in one way and partly in the other: but the share premium account, the capital redemption reserve, and any profits which are not available for distribution may, for the purposes of this regulation, only be applied in paying up unissued shares to be allotted to members credited as fully paid;
(c) make such provision by the issue of fractional certificates or by payment in cash or otherwise as they determine in the case of shares or debentures becoming distributable under this regulation in fractions; and
(d) authorise any person to enter on behalf of all the members concerned into an agreement with the company providing for the allotment to them respectively, credited as fully paid, of any shares or debentures to which they are entitled upon such capitalisation, any agreement made under such authority being binding on all such members.

NOTICES

111. *Any notice to be given to or by any person pursuant to the articles (other than a notice calling a meeting of the directors) shall be in writing or shall be given using electronic communications to an address for the time being notified for that purpose to the person giving the notice.*

In this regulation, "address", in relation to electronic communications, includes any number or address used for the purposes of such communications. [42]

112. The company may give any notice to a member either personally or by sending it by post in a prepaid envelope addressed to the member at his registered address or by leaving it at that address *or by giving it using electronic communications to an address for the time being notified to the company by the member* [43]. In the case of joint holders of a share, all notices shall be given to the joint holder whose name stands first in the register of members in respect of the joint holding and notice so given shall be sufficient notice to all joint holders. A member whose registered address is not within the United Kingdom and who gives to the company an address within the United kingdom at which notices may be given to him, *or an address to which notices may be sent using electronic communications*, [44] shall be entitled to have notice given to him at that address, but otherwise no such member shall be entitled to receive any notice from the company. *In this regulation and the next, "address", in relation to electronic communications, includes any number or address used for the purposes of such communications.* [45]

113. A member present, either in person or by proxy, at any meeting of the company or of the holders of any class of shares in the company shall be deemed to have received notice of the meeting and, where requisite, of the purposes for which it was called.

114. Every person who becomes entitled to a share shall be bound by any notice in respect of that share which, before his name is entered in the register of members, has been duly given to a person from whom he derives his title.

115. Proof that an envelope containing a notice was properly addressed, prepaid and posted shall be conclusive evidence that the notice was given. *Proof that a notice contained in an electronic communication was sent in accordance with guidance issued by the Institute of Chartered Secretaries and Administrators shall be conclusive evidence that the notice was given.* [46] A notice shall [47] be deemed to be given at the expiration of 48 hours after the envelope containing it was posted *or, in the case of a notice contained in an electronic communication, at the expiration of 48 hours after the time it was sent.* [48]

116. A notice may be given by the company to the persons entitled to a share in consequence of the death or bankruptcy of a member by sending or delivering it, in any manner authorised by the articles for the giving of notice to a member, addressed to them by name, or by the title of representatives of the deceased, or trustee of the bankrupt or by any like description at the address, if any, within the United Kingdom supplied for that purpose by the persons claiming to be so entitled. Until such an address has been supplied, a notice may be given in any manner in which it might have been given if the death or bankruptcy had not occurred.

WINDING UP

117. If the company is wound up, the liquidator may, with the sanction of a special [49] resolution of the company and any other sanction required by the Act, divide among the members in specie the whole or any part of the assets of the company and may, for that purpose, value any assets and determine how the division shall be carried out as between the members or different classes of members. The liquidator may, with the like sanction, vest the whole or any part of the assets in trustees upon such trusts for the benefit of the members as he with the like sanction determines, but no member shall be compelled to accept any assets upon which there is a liability.

INDEMNITY

118. Subject to the provisions of the Act but without prejudice to any indemnity to which a director may otherwise be entitled, every director or other officer or auditor of the company shall be indemnified out of the assets of the company against any liability incurred by him in defending any proceedings, whether civil or criminal, in which judgment is given in his favour or in which he is acquitted or in connection with any application in which relief is granted to him by the court from liability for negligence, default, breach of duty or breach of trust in relation to the affairs of the company.

---

1. As amended by SI 1985/1052 (in force on 01/08/85), SI 2000/3373 (in force on 22/12/00), SI 2007/2541 and SI 2007/2826 (both in force on 01/10/07). Amendments to Table A are not retrospective, therefore companies adopting Table A provisions before any relevant amendments came into force which have not updated their articles cannot rely on them. Each amendment has been marked to enable readers to check whether it applies. TA 1985 itself came into force on 01/07/85 (SI 1985/805); companies adopting Table A provisions before that date should consult the appropriate old form of Table A (usually TA 1948). Note that the version of Table A reproduced here incorporates transitional amendments made to reflect provisions of the new Companies Act that came into force on 1 October 2007 (SI 2007/2541 and SI 2007/2607). Some of the amendments are different for private companies and public companies: the text sets out Table A as it applies to private companies, with differences for public companies explained in the notes.
See ¶435+ for further information on Table A, including how it may be altered to suit the needs of a particular company. Companies incorporated on or after 1 October 2009 will be able to adopt model articles under the new Companies Act. There will be separate model articles for private companies limited by shares, public companies and private companies limited by guarantee. These new model articles are in draft form at the time of writing (draft Companies (Model Articles) Regulations 2007, available on the BERR website).
2. Inserted by SI 2007/2541.
3. Inserted by SI 2000/3373.
4. Inserted by SI 1985/1052, replacing the word "provision".
5. SI 2007/2541 deleted "All general meetings other than annual general meetings shall be called extraordinary general meetings".
6. SI 2007/2541, replacing the words "an extraordinary".
7. SI 2007/2541, replacing the words "for a date not later than eight weeks after receipt of the requisition".
8. SI 2007/2541 deleted "An annual general meeting and an extraordinary general meeting called for the passing of a special resolution or a resolution appointing a person as a director shall be called by at least twenty-one clear days' notice. All other extraordinary" for private companies only. For public companies, SI 2007/2541 changed this text to: "An annual general meeting shall be called by at least twenty-one clear days' notice. All other".
9. SI 2007/2541 deleted "(a) in the case of an annual general meeting, by all the members entitled to attend and vote thereat; and (b) in the case of any other meeting" for private companies only. The wording still applies for public companies.
10. SI 2007/2541 deleted the word "five" for private companies only. The wording still applies for public companies.

11. SI 2007/2541 deleted the words "and, in the case of an annual general meeting, shall specify the meeting as such" for private companies only. The wording still applies for public companies.
12. Inserted by SI 2007/2541 for private companies only.
13. Inserted by SI 1985/1052.
14. SI 2007/2826 deleted "In the case of an equality of votes, whether on a show of hands or on a poll, the chairman shall be entitled to a casting vote in addition to any other vote he may have".
15. SI 2007/2541 deleted "A resolution in writing executed by or on behalf of each member who would have been entitled to vote upon it if it had been proposed at a general meeting at which he was present shall be as effectual as if it had been passed at a general meeting duly convened and held and may consist of several instruments in the like form each executed by or on behalf of one or more members".
16. Inserted by SI 2007/2826.
17. Inserted by SI 2007/2826.
18. Inserted by SI 2007/2826, replacing the words "not being".
19. The legislation regarding mental incapacity has been altered recently. The part of the Mental Capacity Act 2005 dealing with the appointment of deputies came into force on 1 October 2007. People appointed by the court to act on a mentally incapacitated person's behalf are now known as "deputies". However, Table A has not yet been amended to reflect these changes.
20. Inserted by SI 2000/3373, replacing the words "An instrument appointing". SI 2000/3373 also deleted the words "in writing," after "a proxy shall be" in the first sentence.
21. SI 2007/2541 deleted the words "annual/extraordinary" for private companies only. For public companies, the words "any other" replace "extraordinary".
22. The date on the proxy form has not been updated, but it should now refer to the relevant 20___ date.
23. Inserted by SI 2000/3373, replacing the words "instrument appointing".
24. SI 2007/2541 deleted the words "annual/extraordinary" for private companies only. For public companies, the words "any other" replace "extraordinary".
25. The date on the proxy form has not been updated, but it should now refer to the relevant 20___ date.
26. Inserted by SI 2000/3373, replacing the words "The instrument appointing".
27. Inserted by SI 2000/3373.
28. Inserted by SI 2000/3373.
29. Inserted by SI 2000/3373.
30. Inserted by SI 2000/3373, replacing the words "and an instrument of proxy which is not deposited or delivered".
31. Inserted by SI 2000/3373.
32. Inserted by SI 2000/3373.
33. SI 2007/2541 deleted "At the first annual general meeting all the directors shall retire from office, and at every subsequent annual general meeting one-third of the directors who are subject to retirement by rotation or, if their number is not three or a multiple of three, the number nearest to one-third shall retire from office; but, if there is only one director who is subject to retirement by rotation, he shall retire" for private companies only. The regulation still applies for public companies.
34. SI 2007/2541 deleted "Subject to the provisions of the Act, the directors to retire by rotation shall be those who have been longest in office since their last appointment or reappointment, but as between persons who became or were last reappointed directors on the same day those to retire shall (unless they otherwise agree among themselves) be determined by lot" for private companies only. The regulation still applies for public companies.
35. SI 2007/2541 deleted "If the company, at the meeting at which a director retires by rotation, does not fill the vacancy the retiring director shall, if willing to act, be deemed to have been reappointed unless at the meeting it is resolved not to fill the vacancy or unless a resolution for the reappointment of the director is put to the meeting and lost" for private companies only. The regulation still applies for public companies.
36. SI 2007/2541 deleted "other than a director retiring by rotation" for private companies only. The wording still applies for public companies.
37. SI 2007/2541 deleted "(other than a director retiring by rotation at the meeting)" for private companies only. The wording still applies for public companies.
38. SI 2007/2541 deleted "Subject as aforesaid," for private companies only. The wording still applies for public companies.
39. SI 2007/2541 deleted "A director so appointed shall hold office only until the next following annual general meeting and shall not be taken into account in determining the directors who are to retire by rotation at the meeting. If not reappointed at such annual general meeting, he shall vacate office at the conclusion thereof" for private companies only. The wording still applies for public companies.
40. SI 2007/2541 deleted "Subject as aforesaid, a director who retires at an annual general meeting may, if willing to act, be reappointed. If he is not reappointed, he shall retain office until the meeting appoints someone in his place, or if it does not do so, until the end of the meeting" for private companies only. The regulation still applies to public companies.
41. The legislation regarding mental incapacity has been altered recently. The part of the Mental Capacity Act 2005 dealing with the appointment of deputies came into force on 1 October 2007. People appointed by the court to act on a mentally incapacitated person's behalf are now known as "deputies". However, Table A has not yet been amended to reflect these changes.
42. Inserted by SI 2000/3373, replacing the words "Any notice to be given to or by any person pursuant to the articles shall be in writing except that a notice calling a meeting of the directors need not be in writing."
43. Inserted by SI 2000/3373.
44. Inserted by SI 2000/3373.
45. Inserted by SI 2000/3373. Note that contrary to the inserted words, there is no reference to "address" in the next regulation (i.e. regulation 113).
46. Inserted by SI 2000/3373. The relevant guidance is "ICSA Guidance on Electronic Communications with Shareholders 2007" (reference number 160207).
47. The words "unless the contrary is proved" were deleted by SI 1985/1052.
48. Inserted by SI 2000/3373.
49. Inserted by SI 2007/2541, replacing the words "an extraordinary".

Comparison between Table A 1985 and Table A 1948

9920

Table 1 at ¶9922 is a comparison between Table A 1985 (as amended, including the amendments made on 1 October 2007) and Table A 1948 (as amended). The final column highlights in what way, if any, the Table A 1948 provisions differ from the Table A 1985 provisions. The purpose of the table is to bring these differences to the attention of readers who are familiar with the now commonplace standard Table A 1985 provision.

There are also various provisions within Table A 1948 which have no equivalent in Table A 1985. In some cases, but not all, this is because the relevant Table A 1948 provision was given statutory force within the Companies Act 1985 and so there was no need to also include it within Table A 1985. Table 2 at ¶9923 lists these missing provisions and highlights whether or not they now have a statutory equivalent, giving cross-references to the relevant text.

Table 1

9922

Table A 1985 reg.	Subject matter	Equivalent Table A 1948 reg.	Differences in Table A 1948 provision
INTERPRETATION			
1	Definitions	1	Fewer definitions
SHARE CAPITAL			
2	Shares may be issued with such rights as the company may by ordinary resolution determine	2	Substantially same provision
3	Power to issue redeemable shares	3	Companies registered before 3 December 1981 only authorised to issue redeemable preference shares
4	Power to pay commission	6	Maximum commission of 10% of price at which shares are issued
5	Company not to recognise holding of shares on trust etc	7	Substantially same provision
SHARE CERTIFICATES			
6	Issue of share certificates	8	Substantially same provision
7	Replacement of share certificates	9	Substantially same provision
LIEN			
8	Company has first lien on all shares not being fully paid for all moneys payable on those shares	11	For companies registered before 3 December 1981, lien extended to all moneys payable by shareholder or his estate to company
9	Company may sell shares upon which it has a lien if not fully paid up after demand	12	Substantially same provision
10	Power of directors to execute transfer instrument on sale	13	Substantially same provision
11	Application of proceeds of sale	14	Remainder of proceeds of sale may be paid to person entitled to shares at date of sale without surrender of share certificate

Table A 1985 reg.	Subject matter	Equivalent Table A 1948 reg.	Differences in Table A 1948 provision
CALLS ON SHARES AND FORFEITURE			
12	Power to make calls	15	Call may not exceed quarter of nominal value of share or be payable within 1 month from date for payment of immediately preceding call
13	Call deemed to be made at time of directors resolution	16	Substantially same provision
14	Joint shareholders' liability for calls	17	Substantially same provision
15	Interest on unpaid calls	18	Maximum interest rate of 5% per annum
16	Amount payable in respect of shares deemed to be a call	19	Substantially same provision
17	Power to make different arrangements for calls on a share issue	20	Substantially same provision
18	Notice of unpaid calls	33-34	Substantially same provision
19	Forfeiture of shares where notice has been given	35	Dividends or other moneys payable in respect of forfeited shares, but not paid before forfeiture, not also expressly forfeited
20	Power to sell, re-allot etc forfeited shares	36	Substantially same provision
21	Effect of forfeiture on shareholder	37	Shareholder's liability to pay interest on unpaid call does not expressly continue after forfeiture
22	Statutory declaration of director or secretary constitutes good title to forfeited shares	38	Substantially same provision
TRANSFER OF SHARES			
23	Form of instrument of transfer of shares	22-23	Instrument of transfer must be executed by transferor and transferee
24	Power of directors to refuse to register transfer of shares	24-25	Company also has right to charge a fee of up to 2s 6d to register transfer but no right to refuse registration of transfer in favour of more than four transferees
25	Refusal to register transfer to be notified within 2 months	26	Substantially same provision
26	Power to suspend registration of transfer of shares	27	Substantially same provision
27	No fee to be charged for registering document of title	25, 28	Company has right to charge a fee of up to 2s 6d to register documents affecting title
28	Power to retain instrument of transfer which is registered/obligation to return instrument of transfer which is not registered	n/a	No equivalent provision

Table A 1985 reg.	Subject matter	Equivalent Table A 1948 reg.	Differences in Table A 1948 provision
TRANSMISSION OF SHARES			
29	Transmission of shares of deceased shareholder	29	Substantially same provision
30	Registration as shareholder of person entitled by death or bankruptcy	30-31	Substantially same provision
31	Rights of person entitled by death or bankruptcy	32	Directors also have power to require person entitled on death or bankruptcy either to elect to be registered or to transfer share and if he does not, directors may withhold payment of dividends or other moneys payable in respect of share
ALTERATION OF SHARE CAPITAL			
32	Power to increase, consolidate, subdivide share capital and cancel unissued shares	44-45	Substantially same provision
33	Procedures relating to alteration of share capital	n/a	No equivalent provision
34	Power to reduce share capital, capital redemption reserve and share premium account	46	Substantially same provision
PURCHASE OF OWN SHARES			
35	Power to purchase own shares; private company power to pay otherwise than out of distributable profits	n/a	No equivalent provision
GENERAL MEETINGS			
36	Now deleted (SI 2007/2541)	48	All meetings (except AGM) called extraordinary general meetings
37	Power to call general meetings. Deadline now deleted because it is in CA 2006	49	Substantially same provision
NOTICE OF GENERAL MEETINGS			
38	Length of notice (now different for public and private companies); matters to be specified in notice; persons to whom notice should be given	50, 134	Notice of general meetings needs to be given to directors
39	Effect of accidental omission of notice to, or non-receipt by, entitled person	51	Substantially same provision
PROCEEDINGS AT GENERAL MEETINGS			
40	Quorum at general meetings, unless single shareholder private company	53	For companies registered before 22 December 1980, quorum is three shareholders present in person. No provision for single shareholder private company
41	Adjournment of meeting where quorum not present	54	For companies registered before 22 December 1980, if quorum is not present at adjourned meeting within half an hour of appointed time, shareholders present will constitute quorum

Table A 1985 reg.	Subject matter	Equivalent Table A 1948 reg.	Differences in Table A 1948 provision
42	Chairman of general meetings nominated/elected by directors	55	Substantially same provision
43	Shareholders' power to choose chairman	56	Substantially same provision
44	Directors' right to attend and speak at general and class meetings	n/a	No equivalent provision
45	Adjournment of general meetings	57	Notice of adjourned meeting, in manner of the notice for original meeting, need only be given if adjournment is for 30 days or more
46	Voting by show of hands; right to demand poll	58, 72	For companies registered before 22 December 1980, three shareholders present in person or proxy (whether or not they had right to vote) can demand a poll
47	On a show of hands, chairman's declaration of results of vote sufficient evidence	58	Substantially same provision
48	Withdrawal of demand for poll	58	Demand for poll may be withdrawn without chairman's consent
49	Chairman to fix procedure for poll	59	Substantially same provision
50	Now deleted (SI 2007/2541)	60	Chairman's casting vote
51	Time of poll	61	Time of poll on questions other than election of chairman and adjournment entirely at chairman's discretion
52	Notice of poll	n/a	No equivalent provision
53	Now deleted (SI 2007/2541)	73A	Written resolution by shareholders. Only applicable to companies registered on or after 22 December 1980
VOTES OF MEMBERS			
54	One vote per shareholder (including proxies) on show of hands; one vote per share on a poll	62, 74	Substantially same provision, except proxies are not included on a show of hands
55	Votes by joint holders	63	Substantially same provision
56	Votes by shareholders with a mental disorder	64	No requirement for person exercising vote of shareholder with mental disorder to deposit evidence of his authority at least 48 hours before the meeting
57	Share only counted in vote if all moneys payable on it have been paid	65	Substantially same provision
58	Objections to qualification of a voter	66	Substantially same provision
59	Right to appoint a proxy	67	Shareholder does not have right to appoint more than one proxy to attend on the same occasion

APPENDIX 1175

Table A 1985 reg.	Subject matter	Equivalent Table A 1948 reg.	Differences in Table A 1948 provision
60	Form of proxy appointment: only refers to general meetings for private companies; refers to AGMs and other general meetings for public companies	68, 70	Substantially same provision, but no differences between public and private companies
61	Form of proxy appointment with voting instructions: only refers to general meetings for private companies; refers to AGMs and other general meetings for public companies	71	Substantially same provision, but no difference between public and private companies
62	Delivery of form of proxy	69	No power to deliver appointment by electronic communication
63	Notice of termination of proxy appointment	73	Substantially same provision
NUMBER OF DIRECTORS			
64	Minimum number of directors	75, 94	Number and names of first directors fixed by subscribers. Number may be increased or reduced by ordinary resolution. No automatic minimum or maximum number.
ALTERNATE DIRECTORS			
65	Power to appoint and remove alternate director	n/a	No equivalent provision
66	Rights of alternate director	n/a	No equivalent provision
67	Consequences of appointor ceasing to be a director	n/a	No equivalent provision
68	Notice of appointment or removal	n/a	No equivalent provision
69	Alternate director is director not agent	n/a	No equivalent provision
POWER OF DIRECTORS			
70	Directors' general management power	80	Substantially same provision
71	Directors' power to appoint agents	81	Substantially same provision
DELEGATION OF DIRECTORS' POWERS			
72	Directors' power to delegate to committee or executive directors	102-104	Substantially same provision
APPOINTMENT AND RETIREMENT OF DIRECTORS			
73	Public companies only: number of directors to retire by rotation at AGMs	89	Substantially same provision. Applies to all companies.
74	Public companies only: longest-serving directors to retire by rotation	90	Substantially same provision. Applies to all companies.
75	Public companies only: reappointment of retired directors	92	Substantially same provision. Applies to all companies.
76	Appointment of director (for public companies only: other than one retiring by rotation)	93	Notice of shareholder's intention to propose another person as director must be left between 3 and 21 days before date of relevant meeting

Table A 1985 reg.	Subject matter	Equivalent Table A 1948 reg.	Differences in Table A 1948 provision
77	Notice of proposed appointment of any person recommended by directors (for public companies only: other than one retiring by rotation)	n/a	No equivalent provision
78	Shareholders' right to appoint directors	97	Substantially same provision
79	Directors' power to appoint directors (for public companies only: including the requirement for them to retire by rotation)	95	Substantially same provision, but the newly appointed director must retire at the next AGM for reappointment by the shareholders in all companies
80	Public companies only: re-appointment of retiring directors	91	Substantially same provision. Applies to all companies.
DISQUALIFICATION AND REMOVAL OF DIRECTORS			
81	Vacation of office of director	88	Substantially same provision
REMUNERATION OF DIRECTORS			
82	Remuneration set by ordinary resolution	76	Substantially same provision
DIRECTORS' EXPENSES			
83	Right to expenses incurred in attendance at meeting or discharge of duties	76	Substantially same provision
DIRECTORS' APPOINTMENTS AND INTERESTS			
84	Managing and executive directors	107-109	No power to appoint other executive directors
85-86	Directors' interests in company transactions or arrangements	78, 84(1), 84(3)	Director's entitlement to be interested in company transactions/arrangements not expressly subject to disclosure of those interests
DIRECTORS' GRATUITIES AND PENSIONS			
87	Right to pay gratuities and/or pension to directors and their family/dependents	87	Substantially same provision
PROCEEDINGS OF DIRECTORS			
88	Procedure for board meetings	98	Substantially same provision
89	Quorum at board meetings	99	Substantially same provision
90	Power of directors when below quorum	100	Substantially same provision
91	Chairman of board meetings	101	Substantially same provision
92	Defective appointments	105	Substantially same provision
93	Written resolution of directors	106	Written resolution not expressly available to committee of directors
94	Conflicted directors ineligible to vote	84(2)	Director eligible to vote on contract or arrangement with another company in which he is interested as an officer or shareholder
95	Director not entitled to vote not counted in quorum	84(2)	Substantially same provision

Table A 1985 reg.	Subject matter	Equivalent Table A 1948 reg.	Differences in Table A 1948 provision
96	Suspension of prohibition against voting when conflicted	84(2)	Substantially same provision
97	Composite resolutions for appointment of directors	84(4)	Substantially same provision
98	Chairman to resolve questions of directors' entitlement to vote	n/a	No equivalent provision
SECRETARY			
99	Appointment, remuneration and removal of secretary	110	Substantially same provision
MINUTES			
100	Directors' responsibility to keep minutes	86	Substantially same provision
THE SEAL			
101	Use of company seal	113	Substantially same provision
DIVIDENDS			
102	Declaration of dividends	114	Substantially same provision
103	Interim dividends	115	No express provisions dealing with interim dividends where share capital is divided into different classes, or with payment of fixed dividends
104	Calculation of dividends	118	Substantially same provision
105	Payment of dividend by way of distribution of assets	120	Substantially same provision
106	Payment of dividends	121	Substantially same provision
107	No interest on dividends	122	Substantially same provision
108	Unclaimed dividends	n/a	No equivalent provision
ACCOUNTS			
109	No right of shareholders to inspect company books	125	Substantially same provision
CAPITALISATION OF PROFITS			
110	Power to capitalise profits	128-129	Companies incorporated before 22 December 1980 may only capitalise distributable profits and reserve accounts. Share premium account and capital redemption reserve may only be used to fully pay up bonus shares to be issued to existing shareholders. Companies incorporated on or after 22 December 1980 may also capitalise non-distributable profits and reserve accounts (regardless of whether or not they are required for paying any preferential dividend). Share premium account, capital redemption reserve and non-distributable profits and reserve accounts may only be used to fully pay up bonus shares to be allotted to existing shareholders.

Table A 1985 reg.	Subject matter	Equivalent Table A 1948 reg.	Differences in Table A 1948 provision
NOTICES			
111	Notices in writing or using electronic communication	n/a	No equivalent provision
112	Procedure for giving notice	131, 132	Substantially same provision
113	Shareholder present at meeting deemed to have received notice	n/a	No equivalent provision
114	Notice given to previous shareholder binding on subsequent title holder	n/a	No equivalent provision
115	Proof of notice; deemed notice	131	Notice of meeting deemed to be given 24 hours after posting, and in the case of other notices, when letter would be delivered in the ordinary course of post
116	Notice to person entitled on death or bankruptcy	133	Substantially same provision
WINDING UP			
117	Division of assets on winding up (now requiring special resolution)	135	Substantially same provision, but requires extraordinary resolution
INDEMNITY			
118	Officers and auditor indemnified against certain legal expenses	136	Substantially same provision

Table 2

Table A 1948 reg.	Subject matter	¶¶
4-5	Variation of class rights	¶1270+
10	Prohibition on giving financial assistance – only applicable to companies registered before 3 December 1981	¶5557+
21	Directors may pay interest of up to 5% per annum on advances from shareholders in respect of moneys uncalled and unpaid upon shares	n/a
40-43	Conversion of shares into stock	¶1312
47	Requirements relating to holding AGM	¶3777+
52	Special business at general meetings	n/a
77	Company entitled to fix shareholding qualification for directors	n/a
79	Borrowing powers subject to limits	n/a
82	Official seal for use abroad	n/a
83	Keeping dominion register	n/a
84(5)	Director may act by himself, or his firm, in professional capacity for company, except as auditor	n/a
85	Directors to determine manner in which cheques, receipts etc are signed, drawn, accepted etc	n/a
96	Shareholders' right to remove director by ordinary resolution	¶2946+
111-112	Sole director may not act as secretary	¶3461
116	Dividends may only be paid out of profits – only for companies registered before 22 December 1980	¶1610+
117	Before recommending dividend, directors entitled to set aside out of profits a reserve for use in company's business or investment, or carry forward profits which they think prudent not to distribute	n/a – but directors are still entitled to do so
119	Right to deduct from dividend sums payable by a shareholder to company in relation to his shares	n/a
123, 124, 126, 127	Duty to keep accounting records, prepare annual accounts, circulate them and lay them before shareholders	¶4195+, ¶4209+
130	Appointment and duties of auditors – only companies registered before 27 January 1968	¶4290+

Sample director's service contract

9925 The following sample service contract is intended to be **used as a starting point**. Whilst it provides example clauses and guidance for drafting key terms for a director, it **should be tailored** to reflect the requirements of the employer company and its articles of association. The service contract should also be consistent with other documents, such as company policies.

As service contracts are **often subject to detailed negotiation**, specialist legal advice should also be sought.

* Clauses marked with an asterisk indicate that the information is required to be provided as part of the employer's obligation to give certain written particulars within 2 months of the start of the director's employment (s 1 Employment Rights Act 1996).

[SUBJECT TO CONTRACT] [1]

This Agreement is made on [date] between:

(1) * [the Company] whose registered office is at [address] (the "Company") and

(2) * [Employee] of [address] (the "Director").

This Agreement sets out the terms on which the Director will serve the Company.

1. Definition and interpretation

In this Agreement:

1.1. "the Board" means the board of directors for the time being of the Company;

1.2. "Company Clients" means any person, firm or company who was at the Termination Date and/or at any time during the [number] months prior to the Termination Date a customer or client of, or in the habit of doing business with, the Company or any other Group Company and in respect of which the Director had dealings, whether directly or indirectly;

1.3. "Confidential Information" includes but is not limited to client or trade secrets and confidential or commercial information relating to the organisation, business, finances, clients, customers, dealings and affairs of the Company and other Group Companies [define confidential information further, if possible];

1.4. "the Employment" means the employment governed by this Agreement;

1.5. "the Group" means the Company and all of its holding or subsidiary companies (as defined in section 1159 of the Companies Act 2006) [2];

1.6. "Group Company" means a member of the Group [2];

1.7. "Incapacity" means any illness, injury, accident or other similar cause which prevents the Director from carrying out his duties under this Agreement;

1.8. "Intellectual Property Rights" means all rights in and to intellectual property in the UK and internationally including without limitation patents, trade marks, copyright, design rights and rights in databases whether or not any of the above are registered and including applications for registration of any of them;

1.9. "Inventions" means all inventions, works and information including, without limitation, discoveries, designs, databases, ideas, methods, programs, diagrams and reports (and any drafts thereof) made or discovered by the Director (alone or with others) in connection with the Employment or relating to or capable of being used in those parts of the businesses of the Company or any Group Company in which the Director is involved;

1.10. "Termination Date" means the date of termination of the Employment;

1.11. words importing one gender include all other genders and words importing the singular include the plural and vice versa;

1.12. references to any statutory provisions include any modifications or re-enactments of those provisions;

1.13. the clause headings do not form part of this Agreement and shall not be taken into account in its construction or interpretation.

2. * **Term of employment**[3]

2.1. Subject to the conditions set out in clause [2.2] below being fulfilled, the Employment will commence on [date]. [The Director's period of continuous employment began on [date]] OR [No employment with a previous employer counts as continuous employment with the Company].

2.2. The conditions to which clause [2.1] refers are as follows:

[list any conditions, e.g. satisfactory medical, references, work permit etc].

2.3. Subject to the Company's right to terminate in accordance with clause [21], the Employment will continue until terminated by either party giving not less than [number] months' notice in writing to the other.

OR

Subject to the Company's right to terminate in accordance with clause [21], the Employment will continue for an initial fixed-term of [initial term], after which it may be terminated by either party giving not less than [number] months' notice in writing to the other.

OR

Subject to the Company's right to terminate in accordance with clause [21], the Employment will be for a fixed-term of [period], expiring on [date], but may be terminated prior to that date by either party giving not less than [number] months' notice in writing to the other [, to expire at any time on or after [date]].

2.4. [The Company reserves the right, at its sole and absolute discretion, to pay salary (at the rate set out in clause [7.1]) in lieu of any required period of notice (whether given by the Director or the Company), less any deductions the Company is required to make by law.]

2.5. [In any event, the Director's normal retirement age is [age]]. [4]

2.6. [If the Director shall cease by reason of his own act or default to be a director of the Company he shall be deemed to be in breach of this Agreement and the Employment shall immediately terminate.]

3. * **Duties**[5]

3.1. The Director will serve the Company in the capacity of [insert job title] and will carry out such duties as the Board may from time to time direct. The Director accepts that the Company may in its discretion require him to perform other duties or tasks outside the scope of his normal duties or to perform his duties for the Company or any Group Company in conjunction with another member of the Board and the Director agrees to perform those duties or undertake those tasks as if they were specifically required under this Agreement.

3.2. The Director agrees that he will:

3.2.1. devote all of his time, attention and skill to the Employment;

3.2.2. properly perform his duties and exercise his powers;

3.2.3. accept such offices or directorships as may reasonably be required by the Board;

3.2.4. comply with the proper and reasonable directions of the Board and all rules and regulations issued by the Company;

3.2.5. use his best endeavours to promote, develop and extend the business, interests and reputation of the Group; and

3.2.6. promptly disclose to the Board any information that comes into his possession which adversely affects the Company or the Group.

3.3. The Director will keep the Board promptly and fully informed (in writing if so requested) of his conduct of the [business, finances or affairs] of the Company or any Group Company.

3.4. The Company may appoint another person to act jointly with the Director.

3.5. The Company may, with the Director's consent (which will not be unreasonably withheld), require him to perform duties for any Group Company [, and may transfer the Employment to any such company].

4. * **Place of work**

4.1. The Director's usual place of employment is [address] [although from time to time and at the absolute discretion of the Board the Director may be required on reasonable prior notice to work at [specify other locations] on a temporary or permanent basis].

4.2. The Director may be required at the absolute discretion of the Board to undertake travel within the United Kingdom and internationally from time to time for the proper performance of his duties.

4.3. [The Director may also be required at the absolute discretion of the Board to live and work in [location outside UK]. Further details are provided [in clause [5] below] [details of any relocation policy] OR [Unless otherwise agreed with the Board, the Director will not be required to live and work outside the United Kingdom.]

5. * **[Work outside the UK]**

[It is anticipated that the Director's posting to [location] will be for [period] [, subject to the absolute discretion of the Company to change the period of his posting.] During that time the Director's salary will be paid in [specify currency] and the Director will additionally be entitled to [additional remuneration or benefits, if any]. At the end of the posting, [specify terms and conditions relating to return to UK]].

6. * **Hours of work**

6.1. The Company's normal hours of work are from [time] to [time] [Monday to Friday]. The Director will comply with such hours and will also work any further hours as may from time to time become necessary in order to perform his duties to the satisfaction of the Board. He will not be entitled to receive any additional remuneration for work done outside his normal hours of work.

6.2. [The Working Time Regulations 1998 (the "Regulations") prohibit employees from exceeding the average weekly limit on working time (48 hours per week) unless they have agreed that the limit will not apply to them. The Director therefore agrees that this limit will not apply to him. This agreement will apply indefinitely, subject to the Director giving the Company [period of notice – up to 3 months] written notice that he withdraws his agreement]

OR

[The parties acknowledge that the Director has autonomous decision-taking powers and that he is able to determine the duration of his own working time, and that, as a result, the exemptions available in Regulation 20 of the Working Time Regulations 1998 (the "Regulations") will apply].

7. * **Salary [and Bonus]**

7.1. The Director will be paid a salary of £[amount] per annum subject to deductions for tax and NICs, payable by [method of payment] [interval of payment] on or about [time of payment]. Salary will accrue from day to day and will be inclusive of any directors' fees payable to the Director by the Company or any Group Company.

7.2. Salary will be reviewed annually by the Board on or around [date] in each year. [There is no obligation on the Board to increase the level of the Director's salary at a review. The Board reserves the right to decrease salary at a review if deemed appropriate.] Any increase awarded in one year will not create any right or entitlement or set any precedent in relation to subsequent years. Any revision to the Director's salary will take effect from [date/period after review].

7.3. [The Director may be eligible to participate in the Company's [discretionary] bonus scheme, subject to the rules of that scheme from time to time in force. [insert any conditions to eligibility] [The decision to award a bonus in any given year and the amount of any such bonus is at the Company's absolute discretion. Payment of a bonus in a particular bonus year will not create any right or entitlement to a bonus in any subsequent bonus years]].

7.4. The Director authorises the Company at any time during the Employment or in any event on the termination of the Employment, howsoever arising, to deduct from the Director's salary payment and any sums reimbursable to the Director by the Company any amount from time to time which the Director owes to the Company (or any Group Company) including but not limited to any outstanding loans, advances, payments for excess holiday and overpayment of wages and the Director expressly consents to any such deductions pursuant to Part II of the Employment Rights Act 1996.

8. Other benefits

8.1. * Pension

[The Director will be eligible to join the Company's [non-contributory/ contributory] pension scheme [on commencement of the Employment/after completing [*number*] weeks'/ months' service], subject to the rules of the scheme from time to time in force].

OR

[The Company does not operate a pension scheme in relation to the Employment. The Company will pay contributions to the Director's personal pension arrangements at the rate of [*amount of contributions*], subject to any applicable Revenue and Customs requirements].

* A contracting-out certificate in relation to the [State Earnings Related Pension Scheme (SERPS)]/[State Second Pension] [is]/[is not] in force in respect of the Employment.

8.2. Permanent health insurance

Subject to the Company's right to terminate the Employment, if the Director complies with any eligibility or other conditions imposed by the Company or by the relevant insurance provider, the Director may be eligible to receive payments under the Company's permanent health insurance arrangements. The terms and level of such cover will be in accordance with the Company's policy from time to time in force.

The Company reserves the right to cease to offer permanent health insurance or to substitute another provider, or to alter the benefits available to the Director under, or the terms and conditions of, any scheme or schemes at any time and no compensation will be paid to the Director. The Company will not be liable in the event of any failure by or refusal from any provider or providers to provide cover or any application of any conditions or limitations to the benefit or benefits by any provider or providers.

8.3. Private medical cover

The Director [and his spouse/partner and minor children] will, subject to meeting any conditions or eligibility criteria imposed by the insurance provider and subject to the rules of any such scheme from time to time in force, be eligible for such free private medical insurance as the Company may from time to time arrange.

The Company reserves the right to cease to offer private medical insurance or to substitute another provider, or to alter the benefits available to the Director under, or the terms and conditions of, any scheme or schemes at any time and no compensation will be paid to the Director. The Company will not be liable in the event of any failure by or refusal from any provider or providers to provide cover or any application of any conditions or limitations to the benefit or benefits by any provider or providers.

8.4. Company car

The Director will be eligible to participate in the Company's company car scheme, subject to the rules of the scheme from time to time in force. Participation is conditional on the Director having and retaining a valid full UK driving licence.

8.5. Share schemes

The Director may be eligible to participate in the Company's share scheme arrangements from time to time in force. Details of such arrangements will be provided separately.

8.6. Other (e.g. professional subscriptions)

[*insert details*]

9. Expenses

The Company shall reimburse the Director (against production of satisfactory receipts) all reasonable travelling, hotel and other expenses properly incurred by him in the performance of his duties.

[Any credit or charge card provided to the Director by the Company must only be used for expenses properly incurred by him in the performance of the duties of the Employment.]

10. * Annual leave

The leave year runs from [date] to [date]. The Director is entitled, in addition to English and Welsh [or Scottish] bank and public holidays, to [number] days' paid holiday in each holiday year, accruing on a [daily] basis.

The Director's entitlement will be pro-rated in the year of joining and leaving the Company.

The Director must obtain the Board's prior approval to the dates on which he proposes to take his holiday.

On the termination of the Employment, the Director will be entitled to a payment in lieu of any accrued but untaken holiday. [The Director will not accrue any contractual holiday entitlement during any period of notice (given by [the Company] or the Director), save that the Director's entitlement to annual leave pursuant to the Regulations shall continue to accrue during such period]. If, on the termination of the Employment, the Director has taken holidays in excess of his entitlement, the Company may deduct from his final salary payment an amount equal to the gross salary paid to him in respect of such holidays and the Director expressly consents to any such deductions.

11. * Sickness absence

11.1. If the Director is absent from work due to Incapacity, he (or someone on his behalf) must notify the Company on the first day of absence. If the absence due to Incapacity lasts 7 calendar days or less, the Director must complete a self-certification form on his return to work. For absences lasting more than 7 calendar days, the Director must produce a medical certificate from his doctor stating the reason for his absence. The Director must keep the Company regularly informed of his absence and likely duration of his absence. Further medical certificates are required for each further [week] of absence due to Incapacity. [Failure to notify the Company of his absence may render the Director subject to disciplinary action and may also bar him from receiving sick pay.]

11.2. Subject to the Company's right to terminate the Employment under clauses [2] and [21] of this Agreement and the Director's compliance with this clause [11], the Director will be paid salary (inclusive of any Statutory Sick Pay (SSP)) [and provided all contractual benefits] during absence due to his Incapacity for a total of [period] in any period of 12 months. [Thereafter any further payment in respect of absence due to the Director's Incapacity will be at the sole discretion of the Company].

11.3. Any payments to which the Director is entitled under any social security scheme (whether or not claimed by the Director) may be deducted from any sick pay paid to the Director by the Company.

11.4. If the Incapacity is caused by the fault of a third party in respect of which compensation for loss of [salary] under this Agreement is or may be recovered, the Director will, if required by the Board, repay to the Company any money it has paid to him as [salary] for the same period of absence.

[11.5. The Company at all times reserves the right to withhold, discontinue or request repayment of any contractual sick pay if:

11.5.1 the Director fails to follow the Company's absence procedure;

11.5.2. the Company is satisfied that there has been an abuse of the sick pay arrangements or misrepresentation of the Director's health; or

11.5.3. the Director behaves in a way likely to delay, hinder or impede recovery.]

12. Medical examination

The Company may require the Director to undergo a medical examination by a medical practitioner appointed or approved by the Company and the Director authorises that medical practitioner to disclose to the Company [and its advisers] the results of the examination and discuss with it [or them] any matters arising from the examination which might impair the proper performance of the Director's duties.

13. * Collective agreements

[There are no collective agreements which affect the terms and conditions of the Director's employment].

14. Directorships

14.1. Any office or directorship held by the Director is subject to the articles of association of that company. In the case of any conflict between the articles and this Agreement, the articles will prevail.

14.2. The Director will not, without the consent of the Company, resign any office or directorship held by him, and will not do or omit to do anything that would provide grounds for his disqualification as a director of any Group Company.

14.3. The Director will resign from any office or directorship held in the Company and any Group Company and all other companies of which he shall have been appointed as a director by any member of the Group, if so requested by the Board.

14.4. If the Director fails to comply with clause [14.3] above, the Company is hereby appointed to act as the Director's attorney to execute any document or do anything in his name necessary to effect his resignation. If there is any doubt as to whether such a document or action has been executed or carried out within the authority conferred by this clause, a certificate in writing signed by any director or the secretary of the Company will be conclusive evidence that such is the case. [6]

15. Outside interests

15.1. The Director will disclose in writing to the Board all his interests in any business (apart for any interest in a Group Company) throughout the Employment.

15.2. Subject to clause [15.3] below, during the Employment (including without limitation any period of garden leave), the Director will not, without the prior written consent of the Board or except as a representative of the Company, be engaged, concerned, or interested, directly or indirectly, in the conduct of any other business of a similar nature to or which competes with that of the Company (or any Group Company) [or which is a supplier or customer of the Company (or any Group Company)].

15.3. The Director may hold or be interested in shares or other securities of any company [which are listed or quoted on any recognised stock exchange or dealt on the Alternative Investments Market] provided that the interest of the Director in such shares or other securities does not extend to more than [5%] of the total amount of such shares or securities.

16. Dealings in securities

The Director will comply (and will procure that his spouse/partner and minor children comply) with all applicable rules of law (including, in particular, Part V of the Criminal Justice Act 1993), Stock Exchange codes, rules and regulations, and all rules, policies and codes of conduct of the Company as issued from time to time in relation to the holding of and dealing in shares, debentures or other securities.

17. Confidentiality

17.1. The Director acknowledges that during the course of the Employment, he will have access to and is likely to obtain Confidential Information.

17.2. Without prejudice to any common law duties owed to the Company, the Director agrees that he will not, during or after the Employment, except as authorised by the Company or as required by law or his duties, use, divulge or disclose to any person, firm or organisation, any Confidential Information which may come to his knowledge during the Employment. The Director further agrees to use his best endeavours to prevent the unauthorised use or disclosure of such information.

17.3. This restriction will not apply to information which becomes public (other than through unauthorised disclosure by the Director), and is not intended to exclude or restrict his right to make a protected disclosure under the Public Interest Disclosure Act 1998.

17.4. The Director is likely to obtain Confidential Information belonging to or relating to other Group Companies. The Director will treat such information as falling within the terms of clauses [17.2 and 17.3] above, and those clauses will apply with any necessary amendment to such information. The Director will, at the Company's request, enter into an agreement or undertaking with other Group Companies in the same terms as clauses [17.2 and 17.3] above.

17.5. Unless it is [an expressly agreed] part of the Director's duties, the Director will not, without the prior written consent of the Board, communicate with any press, radio or television representative on any issue relating to the business or affairs of the Company or any Group Company or to any officers, employees, customers or clients of any such company.

18. **Return of company property**

On the termination of the Employment howsoever arising or at the Company's specific request, the Director will immediately return to the Company all property belonging or relating to any Group Company that is in his possession or under his control. For the avoidance of doubt, this includes (but is not limited to) [the Director's company car, keys, security cards, *list other property*], and all documents, records, correspondence, papers and other materials (and any copies thereof), whether in hard copy or in electronic or machine readable form, made or kept by, or provided to, the Director during the Employment. The Director must not retain any copies or extracts of such material.

19. **Intellectual Property**

19.1. The Director will promptly communicate full details of any Inventions to the Company. All Intellectual Property Rights in the Inventions will belong to the Company or the appropriate Group Company, as the case may be.

19.2. The Director will not disclose or exploit any Invention unless authorised by the Company or in the proper performance of his duties.

19.3. The Director hereby assigns to the Company or any other Group Company as appropriate to the extent allowed by law all his existing and future rights (including Intellectual Property Rights), title and interests in all Inventions.

19.4. To the extent that any right in such Inventions may not be assigned to the Company or other Group Company, the Director will hold all such rights on trust for the Company.

19.5. In any event, at the request and expense of the Company, the Director will give it all information and assistance as may be necessary to enable the Company effectively to exploit the Intellectual Property Rights, and will execute all documents and do all things which may be necessary to vest all such rights in the Company (or as it may direct) as legal and beneficial owner and to secure appropriate protection for all such rights anywhere in the world.

19.6. The Director hereby irrevocably appoints the Company as the Director's attorney to take any action in his name and execute any document on his behalf for the purpose of giving to the Company (or its nominee) the full benefit of the provisions of this clause. If there is any doubt as to whether such a document or action has been executed or carried out within the authority conferred by this clause, a certificate in writing signed by any director or the secretary of the Company will be conclusive evidence that such is the case. [6]

19.7. The Director waives all of his moral rights (as defined in the Copyright, Designs and Patents Act 1988) and any corresponding foreign rights in respect of all Inventions where the Intellectual Property Rights belong to the Company or appropriate Group Company by virtue of this clause, to the extent that such waiver is permitted by law.

19.8. The Director will promptly notify the Company in writing if he becomes aware of any infringement or suspected infringement of any Intellectual Property Rights in any Invention.

19.9. Rights and obligations under this clause will survive the termination of the Employment in respect of Inventions made during the Employment and will be binding on the Director's personal representatives.

20.* **Discipline and grievances**

The Company's disciplinary rules and disciplinary and grievance procedures as set out in the Staff Handbook from time to time apply to the Director.

21. **Termination and suspension of employment**

21.1. **Termination for long-term incapacity**

If the Director is absent for a total period of [*period*] (including Saturdays, Sundays and public holidays) in any period of 12 months due to Incapacity, the Company may terminate the Employment [immediately by written notice] OR [by giving the Director [*shorter period of notice than clause [2.3]*]. [⁷]

21.2. **Summary termination**

The Employment may be terminated immediately without notice [or payment in lieu of notice] if the Director:

21.2.1. is guilty of any gross misconduct or conducts himself (in connection with the Employment or otherwise) in a way which is detrimental to the Company or any Group Company;

21.2.2. commits a serious or persistent breach or non-observance of his obligations under this Agreement or has failed to perform his duties to the standard required by the Board;

21.2.3. does not comply within a reasonable time with any lawful order or direction given to him by the Board;

21.2.4. becomes bankrupt or makes any arrangement or composition with his creditors or has a receiving order made against him;

21.2.5. is guilty of insider dealing or of dishonesty or is convicted of an offence (other than a motoring offence not resulting in imprisonment);

21.2.6. is disqualified from being a director of a company;

21.2.7. ceases to be a director of the Company or a Group Company without the consent of the [Board/ Company/Group Company];

21.2.8. by his actions or omissions brings the name or reputation of the Company or any Group Company into disrepute or prejudices the interests of the business of the Company or any Group Company;

21.2.9. fails to comply in any material respect with any policy of the Company or any Group Company; or

21.2.10. becomes of unsound mind.

[*this list should be consistent with policies on disciplinary matters*]

This list is intended as a guide and is non-exhaustive.

If the Employment is terminated in accordance with this clause [21], the Director will have no claim for damages or any other remedy against the Company by reason of such termination.

21.3. On the termination of the Employment for any reason or if the Director shall cease for any reason to be a director of the Company, the Director shall if so requested by the Company resign immediately without compensation from his office as director of the Company, all other companies of which he is a director within the Group, and all other companies of which he shall have been appointed as a director by any member of the Group.

21.4. The Company reserves the right at any time to suspend the Director on full pay [and contractual benefits] from the performance of some or all of his duties under this Agreement in connection with any investigation or matter with which he is involved for such period as the Company in its absolute discretion shall decide.

21.5. During any such period referred to in clause [21.4]:

21.5.1. the Director shall, if requested by the Company, refrain from contacting or communicating with [employees, customers, clients and professional contacts] of the Company or any Group Company;

21.5.2. the Company shall be entitled to make such announcements or statements to [employees, customers, clients and professional contacts] of the Company or any Group Company concerning the Director as the Company in its absolute discretion shall decide; and

21.5.3. the Company shall be under no obligation to provide any work for the Director and the Director shall continue to be bound by the express and implied duties of the Employment.

22. Reconstruction or amalgamation

If the Employment is terminated by reason of the liquidation of the Company in order to effect its reconstruction or amalgamation, the Director will have no claim against the Company provided that he is offered employment with the company or undertaking resulting from the reconstruction or amalgamation on terms and conditions that are no less favourable to him than the terms of this Agreement.

23. Garden leave

[Once notice to terminate the Employment has been given by either party in accordance with clause [2.3] of this Agreement,] OR [During the last [number] months of the [initial fixed-term/fixed-term,] or if the Director resigns without giving the required period of notice and the Company does not accept that resignation, the following provisions will apply for [such period as the Company in its absolute discretion may decide/a maximum period of [period]]:

23.1. the Company will not be obliged to provide the Director with any work or require him to perform any duties or may require him to perform such specific duties as are expressly assigned to him by the Company for such period as the Company in its absolute discretion may decide;

23.2. the Company may exclude the Director from its premises or the premises of any other Group Company and may require him not to be involved in the business of such companies;

23.3. the Director's salary and all contractual benefits [excluding any bonus] will continue to be paid or provided;

23.4. the Director will remain bound by his obligations under this Agreement and, in particular, by clause [15];

23.5. the Director will return all of the Company's property including without limitation all Confidential Information;

23.6. the Company may require the Director not to have any contact or communication with any of its [employees, customers, clients, or professional contacts] in relation to the business of the Company or any Group Company;

23.7. the Company may make such announcements or statements to any of the [employees, customers, clients, or professional contacts] of the Company or any Group Company or any other third parties concerning the Director as it in its absolute discretion may decide;

23.8. the Company may require the Director immediately to resign without claim for compensation from any office which he holds in the Company or any Group Company. If he fails to do so, the Director hereby irrevocably appoints the Company to be his attorney to execute any document or do anything in his name necessary to effect his resignation. [[6]]

[The Company reserves the right to require the Director to take holiday which is accrued up to the commencement of garden leave and which will accrue to the date the Employment terminates during the period of garden leave on such day or days as the Company may specify. No contractual holiday entitlement shall accrue during such period, save that the Director's entitlement to annual leave pursuant to the Regulations shall continue to accrue during such period.]

[At the end of any period of garden leave imposed, the Company may make a payment in lieu of the balance of [any required period of notice (whether given by the Director or the Company)] OR [the initial fixed-term/fixed-term], less any deductions the Company is required to make by law.]

24. Post-termination restrictive covenants

24.1 During the Employment, the Director is likely to obtain trade secrets and confidential information and personal knowledge of and influence over the Group's clients, customers and employees. As a result, the Director agrees to observe the following restrictive covenants after the Termination Date. [8]

24.1.1. The Director covenants that he will not, for a period of [*period*] from the Termination Date [(less any period of garden leave served under clause [23])] and within [*insert geographical area of restriction*], on his own account or for or with any other person, directly or indirectly carry on or be engaged in any activity or business which is or is intended to be in competition with the business of the Company or any Group Company which was carried on by such company at the Termination Date and with which the Director was concerned or connected at any time during the [*number*] months prior to the Termination Date.

24.1.2. The Director covenants that he will not, for a period of [*period*] from the Termination Date [(less any period of garden leave imposed by the Company)], in competition with the Company or any other Group Company, on his own behalf or for or with any other person, directly or indirectly seek orders from or solicit the custom of Company Clients.

24.1.3. The Director covenants that he will not, for a period of [*period*] from the Termination Date [(less any period of garden leave imposed by the Company)], in competition with the Company or any other Group Company, on his own behalf or for or with any other person, directly or indirectly deal or otherwise do business with Company Clients.

24.1.4. The Director covenants that he will not, for a period of [*period*] from the Termination Date [(less any period of garden leave imposed by the Company)], in competition with the Company or any other Group Company, on his own behalf or for or with any other person, directly or indirectly entice or try to entice away from the Company or any other Group Company any person who was at the Termination Date and/or any time during the [*number*] months prior to the Termination Date [a senior or key employee, director, *list class of employee*] of such a company and with whom the Director had worked closely at any time during that period.

24.1.5. The Director shall at the request of the Company enter into a direct agreement or undertaking with any other Group Company by which he will accept restrictive covenants corresponding to the restrictive covenants contained in this clause [24]. The Director acknowledges that the provisions of this clause [24] constitute severable undertakings given for the benefit of the Company and all other Group Companies and may be enforced by the Company on its own behalf or on behalf of any other Group Company.

24.1.6. Before accepting any employment, appointment or engagement with any third party either during the Employment or at any time during the period of [*period*] after the Termination Date, the Director shall draw the provisions of this clause [24] to the attention of such third party.

24.1.7. [Each of the covenants set out above is entirely separate and independent of the others and is considered and accepted by the parties [each of whom has taken legal advice] to be reasonable and necessary for the protection of the legitimate interests of the Company and the Group Companies. If any covenant or part thereof shall be found void, invalid or unenforceable by any court of competent jurisdiction, but would be valid if some words were deleted, such covenants shall apply with such modification as may be necessary to make it valid and effective.]

24.1.8. [In the event of any covenant or part thereof being declared void, invalid or unenforceable by any court of competent jurisdiction, all other covenants or parts thereof shall remain in full force and effect and shall not be affected.]

24.1.9. After the Termination Date, the Director will not without the consent of the Company represent himself still to be connected in any way with the Company or any Group Company.

25. Data protection

In relation to Personal Data and Sensitive Personal Data (as defined by the Data Protection Act 1998) provided by the Director to the Company, the Director gives his consent to the holding and processing of that data for all purposes relating to the Employment. In particular, the Director agrees that the Company can hold and process Personal and Sensitive Personal Data in order to pay and review his remuneration and other benefits, provide and administer any such benefits, provide information to professional advisers and to legal and regulatory authorities such as Revenue and Customs and the Contributions Agency, administer and maintain personnel records (including sickness and other absence records), carry out performance reviews, provide information to potential purchasers of the Company or the business area in which the Director works, give references to future employers, and transfer Personal and Sensitive Personal Data concerning the Director to a country outside the EEA.

26. Notices

Notices may be given by letter or fax. Notices to the Company must be addressed to [its registered office] for the time being. Notices to the Director must be given to him personally or sent to his last known address. Any notice sent by letter or fax will be deemed to have been given at the time at which the letter or fax would be delivered in the ordinary course of post or transmission. A notice delivered by hand is given on delivery.

27. Statutory particulars

This Agreement contains the written particulars of employment which the Company is obliged to provide the Director under the Employment Rights Act 1996.

28. Miscellaneous

28.1. This Agreement will be governed by and interpreted in accordance with English law. The Company and the Director submit to the exclusive jurisdiction of the English Courts and Tribunals in relation to any claim or matter arising in connection with this Agreement.

28.2. This Agreement supersedes any previous oral or written agreement between the Company and the Director in relation to the matters dealt within it. It contains the whole agreement between the Company and the Director relating to the Employment as at the date of the Agreement, except for any terms implied by law that cannot be excluded by the agreement of the parties.

28.3. The Director cannot assign this Agreement to anyone else.

28.4. [This Agreement may only be modified by the written agreement of the parties] OR [The Company reserves the right to vary or amend these terms and conditions on giving not less than [*number*] weeks' prior written notice to the Director].

EXECUTED as a DEED [6] [9] by
[*the Company*] acting by
Director
Director/Secretary

EXECUTED as a DEED [6] [9]by
[*the Director*]
in the presence of:
[*signature of witness*]
Name
Address
Occupation

MEMO POINTS 1. If the service agreement is the **subject of negotiation**, it is advisable to head the drafts "subject to contract" to indicate that final agreement has not yet been reached. Once it has been agreed (and prior to the execution of the agreement), the heading should be removed.
2. The Company may be part of a **group of companies**. If this is the case, consideration should be given to the Director's involvement with other group companies and the implications for drafting the agreement. The definitions used must be tailored as appropriate, for example, to include other subsidiaries of the same holding company if necessary.
3. If a director's service contract is for a **fixed term of more than 2 years**, shareholder approval must be obtained, see ¶2655+.
4. Following the introduction of **age discrimination legislation** in October 2006, most employers can now only set retirement ages within their organisation at or above 65 (this is a default retirement age, to be reviewed in 2011). If a company wishes to set a retirement age of below 65, this will need to be justified. Companies should note that, even if a normal retirement age is set out in the contract, they will still need to follow through a fair retirement procedure in order to avoid liability for unfair dismissal, which includes considering requests by employees to work beyond their normal retirement age. See ¶2246/mp for the relevance of these regulations to directors specifically, and *Employment Memo* for a detailed discussion.
5. As well as their contractual duties to the company, directors are also subject to a number of **duties** imposed by common law and statute, see ¶2317+.
6. As drafted, the service agreement contains **powers of attorney** in favour of the Company to allow it to effect the resignation of the Director's directorships and to execute any documents or take any necessary action to vest intellectual property rights in the Company. In order to be valid, a power of attorney must be executed as a deed.
7. Although this clause is useful, companies should ensure that they also comply, where relevant, with **disability discrimination legislation**, including the duty to make reasonable adjustments in relation to a disabled person (see *Employment Memo* for a detailed discussion).
8. **Post-termination restrictive covenants** are, in principle, void and unenforceable because they seek to restrict an individual's freedom to earn a living and use his skill and knowledge. However, such covenants may be enforceable if the Company has legitimate business interests to protect and the restraint is no wider than necessary to protect those interests. Restrictive covenants must therefore be carefully drafted. They should correspond with the circumstances of the individual company and director (for example, terms such as "customers", "clients" and "key employees" should not be generalised but instead be defined and tailored to the business) and should be reviewed on a regular basis to meet the ongoing needs of the company.
9. Agreements which are executed as a deed on behalf of a company **need to be signed either by** two directors or one director and the company secretary; those executed by an individual need to be witnessed by an independent person.

Definition of "connected person"

9930 To ensure that **directors** act independently and in the company's interests, rather than their own, companies legislation imposes a number of **restrictions** on how they deal with their companies, whether preventing them from entering into certain transactions or obliging them to disclose their dealings. To prevent directors from circumventing these measures, which protect shareholders, they are often extended to persons connected to the directors. The statutory definition of a connected person is complex and designed to include personal relationships and other companies in which a director is interested. It can be broken down into **two elements**:
– the basic definition of persons connected to a director; and
– a further definition, which describes which companies are connected to the director.

This table summarises the **topics** for which the definition is relevant. Although not all of these topics are yet governed by the new Companies Act, the definitions of "connected persons" and related terms are now set out in the new Act.

Topic	¶¶
Disclosing interests at board meetings	¶3317+, ¶3367+
Substantial property transactions	¶2567+
Contracts between company and its director	¶2559+
Disclosure of directors' remuneration in company accounts	¶2761+
Loans to directors	¶2804+
Payments for loss of office	¶2962+
Shareholder ratification of director's wrongdoing	¶2497+

MEMO POINTS 1. A connected "**person**" refers to a legal person and therefore can include companies.
2. The definition of connected persons explained here is that set out in companies legislation. For an explanation of "connected persons" under **insolvency** legislation, see ¶7895.

Connected persons

9931 A person is connected to a director if he/it is not also a director of the same company and he/it falls into any of the categories set out in the table (s 253 CA 2006).

	Categories of connected persons [1]
1	The director's spouse, civil partner, or person with whom he lives as a partner (whether of a different sex or the same sex) in an enduring family relationship [2, 3]
2	– The director's child or step-child (of any age); and – any children or step-children of the director's partner (who are under 18 and who live with the director)
3	The director's parents
4	A company connected with the director [4]
5	The trustee of a trust of which the director or numbers 1-4 are beneficiaries or can otherwise benefit from the trustee exercising his powers under the trust [5]
6	A person acting as a business partner of the director, or of numbers 1-5 [6]

Note:
1. For all of these categories of connected person, a "**director**" includes a shadow director (s 223(1) CA 2006). For these purposes, however, a company is not a shadow director of its subsidiary merely because its subsidiary's directors are accustomed to acting in accordance with its directions/instructions (s 251 CA 2006). In other circumstances this may mean the company is a shadow director (¶2212+).
2. **Former** spouses, civil partners and partners are not specifically included.
3. The term "**partner**" carries its usual meaning, and so cannot include other relatives with whom the director lives such as grandparents, siblings, nieces, nephews, aunts or uncles.
4. A **company means** any "body corporate", see ¶9940. "Connected" is defined at ¶9932 below.
5. A **trustee** can be a company. This does not include a trustee of an employee share/pension scheme.

6. Also included is a **firm** which is a legal person (e.g. a Scottish firm) in which:
- the director is a partner;
- a partner in the firm is connected to the director under numbers 1-5; or
- a partner in the firm is another firm of which the director or his connected person is a partner.

Connected companies

In order to ascertain whether or not a company is connected to a director, the legislation looks at the percentage of shares or voting rights controlled by the director and/or his connected person in that company. There are two aspects to consider:
- the **interests** that the director or his connected person has in the shares; and
- the extent to which the director or his connected person can **control** the shares.

Each is examined in turn below, followed by examples.

When ascertaining whether or not a director or his connected person has or can control an interest in shares:

a. the interests or control of the director and his connected person(s) can be taken together. If a company is a director's connected person, its interests are only added to his for calculating interests or control of interests if the company is also a trustee or partner (see numbers 5 and 6 in the table at ¶9931 above) (s 254(6)(a) CA 2006); and

b. the legislation only takes into account equity share capital in these calculations (defined at ¶727). In this table, references to "shares" or "share capital" are references to equity share capital.

In the explanations below, Mr X is a director of Y Ltd; the issue is whether or not A Ltd is connected to Mr X, or whether or not he has or controls an interest in A Ltd's shares.

9932

> MEMO POINTS 1. The definitions of "**company**" and "**director**" in the note to the table at ¶9931 above also apply here. Interests in **shares** include interests in **debentures** (para 1(2) Sch 1 CA 2006).
> 2. A **trustee** of a trust of which a company associated with a director is a beneficiary is not connected to the director for the purposes of calculating the director's and his connected persons' interests in or control over shares, unless there is another factor to connect him (s 254(6)(b) CA 2006).

A Ltd is associated with Mr X if he and/or his connected person(s) is **interested** in a nominal value of at least 20% of its shares (s 254(2)(a) CA 2006).

When ascertaining whether or not Mr X and/or his connected person has an interest, the following **rules** apply:

Rule	Reference (Sch 1 CA 2006)
Situations in which Mr X/connected person **has an interest** include: – any interest of any kind; – where shares cannot be identified; – joint interests; – entering into a contract to purchase shares; – where he is not the registered holder but is entitled to exercise any right under the shares, or controlled the exercise of such a right; [1] – where he is a beneficiary of a trust which comprises shares in A Ltd; and – except where his interest arises under a trust, where he has the right (whether conditional or not) to acquire an interest or to call for the delivery of the shares to him or to his order, or where he is under an obligation (whether conditional or not) to acquire an interest	para 2(1) para 2(3) para 2(4) para 3(1) para 4(1) para 6(1) para 3(2)
Where another company ("B Ltd") has interest in shares in A Ltd, and: – B Ltd or its directors are accustomed to acting in accordance with Mr X's/connected person's instructions; or – Mr X/connected person is entitled to exercise, or control the exercise of, more than half of the voting power of B Ltd (see number 2 below for when a person exercises control over voting power), then Mr X/connected person **has an interest** in shares of A Ltd	para 5

Rule	Reference (Sch 1 CA 2006)
Situations in which Mr X/connected person **does not have an interest** include where: – he has an interest in reversion or remainder in trust property comprising A Ltd's shares and is entitled to receive income from that trust property during his/another's lifetime; – he holds the shares as a bare/custodian trustee; and – his shares have been delivered to his order in fulfilment of a contract or right to call for their delivery (or they have failed to be so delivered), or where his right to call for delivery of the shares has lapsed	para 6(2) para 6(3) para 3(4)
Note: 1. **Controlling exercise of a right** includes where a person (para 4(2) Sch 1 CA 2006): – has another right which would entitle him to control exercise of that right, e.g. an option; or – is under obligation which would entitle him to control its exercise. It does not include where the person has been appointed as proxy or corporate representative (para 4(3) Sch 1 CA 2006).	

MEMO POINTS 1. **Certain special interests** are ignored for these purposes (para 6(4), (5) Sch 1 CA 2006).
2. **Restrictions on** the exercise of any **rights** connected with the interest in shares are not to be taken into account (para 2(2) Sch 1 CA 2006).

A Ltd is also associated with Mr X if he and/or his connected person is entitled or able to exercise **control** over more than 20% of the voting power at a general meeting of A Ltd (s 254(2)(b) CA 2006).

When ascertaining whether or not Mr X or his connected person has an interest, voting power:
a. includes that exercised by another company under Mr X's control (s 254(4) CA 2006); and
b. is treated as being exercisable by Mr X or his connected person if (para 5(2) Sch 1 CA 2006):
– he exercises, or controls the exercise of, more than half of the voting power at general meetings of another company ("B Ltd"); and
– B Ltd exercises, or controls the exercise of, any voting power at A Ltd's general meetings.

Mr X is **deemed to control** A Ltd if the share capital in which he or his connected person is interested, or the voting power over which he or his connected person has control, amounts to more than half **when taken together** with that of his (other) connected persons and fellow directors of Y Ltd (s 255 CA 2006).

9933 Although the above rules seem complicated, in most cases it will be clear that an individual is connected to a director by virtue of the relationship between them. It can be more difficult to work out whether a company is connected to a director. The examples below illustrate some of the more common situations in which a company will be connected to a director.

EXAMPLE **Basic scenario**: Mr X is a director of Y Ltd. He also holds 21% of the share capital in B Ltd, and 5% in A Ltd. B Ltd holds 15% of the share capital in A Ltd:

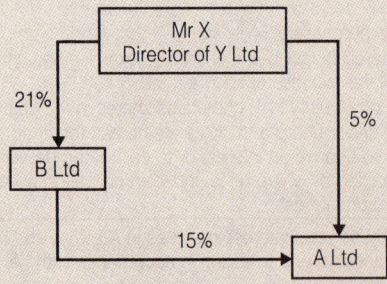

1. Mr X's shareholding in B Ltd means that B Ltd is connected to Mr X. He is not directly connected to A Ltd because he only holds 5% of its shares. Nor is he indirectly connected to A Ltd through his control of B Ltd, because he controls less than half of the voting power in B Ltd.

2. Supposing the scenario is as above, except that Mr X holds 51% of the share capital in B Ltd. B Ltd is still connected to Mr X. Mr X is not directly connected to A Ltd as his own shareholding still stands at 5%, but he is now indirectly connected because he controls more than half of the voting rights in B Ltd and B Ltd controls some of the voting power in A Ltd.

3. If Mr X holds 5% of the share capital in A Ltd, and Mrs X holds 25% of the share capital in A Ltd. A Ltd is connected to Mr X because his and his wife's interests in the shares together comprise more than 20%.

4. Say that the shareholdings in A Ltd are as follows: Mr X still holds 5%; Ms Z, his partner, holds 10%; his son (aged 16) holds 5%; Ms Z's daughter (aged 19) also holds 5%; and a fellow director of Y Ltd, Mr Y, holds 31%. Mr X and his connected persons do not have a sufficient interest in or control of A Ltd directly. However, Mr X is deemed to have control of A Ltd because: (1) he is interested in the share capital or entitled to exercise part of the voting power at a general meeting of A Ltd; and (2) Mr X, his partner, his son and Mr Y together control more than half of the voting power of A Ltd. Ms Z's daughter is not taken into account as a connected person because she is Mr X's partner's daughter and is over 18 (if she was under 18 she would be a connected person; if she was Mr X's daughter she would be a connected person regardless of her age).

Table of criminal offences

The table below lists criminal offences under the following pieces of legislation which are referred to in *Company Law Memo*:
– Companies Act 1985 or Companies Act 2006 where it is in force;
– Insolvency Act 1986;
– Company Directors Disqualification Act 1986;
– Business Names Act 1985; and
– Insolvency Rules 1986.

¶¶	Reference	Persons liable and general nature of offence[1]	Mode of prosecution[2]	Punishment[3]	Daily default fine[4]	Changes under the Companies Act 2006 (where applicable)[5]
¶417+	s 6(3) CA 1985	**Company/officer**: failing to deliver relevant documents to Companies House following alteration of objects	Summary	Fine (1/5th of statutory maximum)	1/50th of statutory maximum	To be repealed by 1 October 2009
¶485	s 12(3B) CA 1985	**Deponent**: making statement of compliance re. company's incorporation documents which he knows to be false or does not believe to be true	Indictment / Summary	2 years and/or fine / 6 months and/or fine (statutory maximum)	–	Restated at s 1112 CA 2006 by 1 October 2009
¶451	s 18(3) CA 1985	**Company/officer**: failing to register change in memorandum/articles	Summary	Fine (1/5th of statutory maximum)	1/50th of statutory maximum	Equivalent offence re. articles only: Fine (level 3) and daily default fine (1/10th of level 3) under s 26 CA 2006 by 1 October 2009.
¶374	s 19(2) CA 1985	**Company/officer**: failing to send copy of memorandum/articles to shareholder when requested	Summary	Fine (1/5th of statutory maximum)	–	Persons liable: officer Fine (level 3) under s 32(4) CA 2006 by 1 October 2009
¶410	s 20(2) CA 1985	**Company/officer**: issuing out-of-date copy of memorandum	Summary	Fine (1/5th of statutory maximum for each occasion)	–	To be repealed by 1 October 2009
¶278	s 28(5) CA 1985	**Company/officer**: failing to change name on direction of secretary of state	Summary	Fine (1/5th of statutory maximum)	1/50th of statutory maximum	Fine (level 3) and daily default fine (1/10th of level 3) under s 68(6) CA 2006 by 1 October 2009
¶242/mp	s 30(5C) CA 1985	**Deponent**: making statement re. company limited by guarantee to be excused from using "ltd" in name, which he knows to be false or does not believe to be true	Indictment / Summary	2 years and/or fine / 6 months and/or fine (statutory maximum)	–	Restated at s 1112 CA 2006 by 1 October 2009
¶242/mp	s 31(5) CA 1985	**Company/officer**: altering memorandum/articles, so ceasing to be exempt from having "limited" as part of its name	Summary	Fine (statutory maximum)	1/10th of statutory maximum	Fine (level 5) and daily default fine (1/10th of level 5) under s 63(3) CA 2006 by 1 October 2009

APPENDIX 1197

¶¶	Reference	Persons liable and general nature of offence[1]	Mode of prosecution[2]	Punishment[3]	Daily default fine[4]	Changes under the Companies Act 2006 (where applicable)[5]
¶242/mp	s 31(6) CA 1985	**Company/officer:** failing to change name on secretary of state's direction to include "limited" (or Welsh equivalent)	Summary	Fine (1/5th of statutory maximum)	1/50th of statutory maximum	Fine (level 5) and daily default fine (1/10th of level 5) under s 64(6) CA 2006 by 1 October 2009
¶278	s 32(4) CA 1985	**Company/officer:** failing to comply with secretary of state's direction to change name on grounds that it is misleading	Summary	Fine (1/5th of statutory maximum)	1/50th of statutory maximum	Fine (level 3) and daily default fine (1/10th of level 3) under s 76(6) CA 2006 by 1 October 2009
¶249	s 33 CA 1985	**Person/company/officer:** trading under misleading name	Summary	Fine (1/5th of statutory maximum)	1/50th of statutory maximum	Fine (level 3) and daily default fine (1/10th of level 3) under s 1197(7) CA 2006 by 1 October 2009
¶249	s 34 CA 1985	**Person/company/officer:** trading or carrying on business with improper use of "limited"	Summary	Fine (1/5th of statutory maximum)	1/50th of statutory maximum	Fine (level 3) and daily default fine (1/10th of level 3) under s 1197(7) CA 2006 by 1 October 2009
¶249	s 34A CA 1985	**Person/company/officer:** trading with improper use of "community interest company"	Summary	Fine (level 3)	1/10th of level 3 on standard scale	Fine (level 3) and daily default fine (1/10th of level 3) under s 1197(7) CA 2006 by 1 October 2009
¶667/mp	s 43(3B) CA 1985	**Officers:** making statement re. re-registering as plc, which he knows to be false or does not believe to be true	Indictment Summary	2 years and/or fine 6 months and/or fine (statutory maximum)	—	Restated at s 1112 CA 2006 by 1 October 2009
¶682	s 49(8B) CA 1985	**Person:** making statement re. registering limited company as unlimited which he knows to be false or does not believe to be true	Indictment Summary	2 years and/or fine 6 months and/or fine (statutory maximum)	—	Restated at s 1112 CA 2006 by 1 October 2009
¶678	s 54(10) CA 1985	**Company/officers:** plc failing to give notice or copy of court order re. shareholder objection to re-registering as private company to Companies House	Summary	Fine (1/5th of statutory maximum)	1/50th of statutory maximum	Fine (level 3) and daily default fine (1/10th of level 3) under s 99(5) CA 2006 by 1 October 2009

APPENDIX

¶¶	Reference	Persons liable and general nature of offence[1]	Mode of prosecution[2]	Punishment[3]	Daily default fine[4]	Changes under the Companies Act 2006 (where applicable)[5]
¶933	s 80(9) CA 1985	**Directors**: exercising company's power of allotment without required authority	Indictment	Fine	—	Restated at s 549(5) CA 2006 by 1 October 2009
			Summary	Fine (statutory maximum)		
¶992	s 81(2) CA 1985	**Company/officers**: private limited company offering shares to public, or allotting shares with a view to their being so offered	Indictment	Fine	—	To be repealed on 6 April 2008
			Summary	Fine (statutory maximum)		
¶978	s 95(6) CA 1985	**Person**: knowingly/recklessly authorising/permitting misleading, false or deceptive material in statement by directors re. disapplication of pre-emption rights	Indictment	2 years and/or fine	—	Penalty on summary conviction in England and Wales will be 12 months' imprisonment and/or fine (statutory maximum) under s 572(3) CA 2006 by 1 October 2009. Punishment on indictment restated.
			Summary	6 months and/or fine (statutory maximum)		
¶1238/mp	s 97(4) CA 1985	**Company/officer**: failing to deliver form disclosing amount/rate of share commission to Companies House	Summary	Fine (1/5th of statutory maximum)	—	To be repealed by 1 October 2009
¶1159	s 110(2) CA 1985	**Officer**: making misleading, false or deceptive statement in connection with valuation of non-cash consideration for shares	Indictment	2 years and/or fine	—	Penalty on summary conviction in England and Wales will be 12 months and/or statutory maximum fine under s 1153(4) CA 2006 by 1 October 2009. Punishment on indictment restated.
			Summary	6 months and/or fine (statutory maximum)		
¶1166	s 111(3) CA 1985	**Officer**: failing to deliver copy of asset valuation report to Companies House	Indictment	Fine	1/10th of statutory maximum	Restated at s 597(4) CA 2006 by 1 October 2009
			Summary	Fine (statutory maximum)		
¶1180	s 111(4) CA 1985	**Company/officer**: failing to deliver copy of resolution re. transfer of asset as consideration for allotment of shares to Companies House	Summary	Fine (1/5th of statutory maximum)	1/50th of statutory maximum	Fine (level 3) and daily default fine (1/10th of level 3) under s 602(3) CA 2006 by 1 October 2009
¶1189	s 114 CA 1985	**Company/officers**: contravening restrictions on non-cash consideration for shares	Indictment	Fine	—	Restated at s 590(2) CA 2006 by 1 October 2009
			Summary	Fine (statutory maximum)		

¶¶	Reference	Persons liable and general nature of offence[1]	Mode of prosecution[2]	Punishment[3]	Daily default fine[4]	Changes under the Companies Act 2006 (where applicable)[5]
¶512	s 117(7) CA 1985	**Company/officer**: plc doing business or exercising borrowing powers in contravention on minimum share capital requirements	Indictment	Fine	–	Restated at s 767(2) CA 2006 as of 6 April 2008
			Summary	Fine (statutory maximum)		
¶511	s 117(7A) CA 1985	**Officer**: making statement re. plc's share capital, which he knows to be false or does not believe to be true	Indictment	2 years and/or fine	–	Restated at s 1112 CA 2006 by 1 October 2009
			Summary	6 months and/or fine (statutory maximum)		
¶1320	s 122(2) CA 1985	**Company/officer**: failing to give notice of reorganisation of share capital to Companies House	Summary	Fine (1/5th of statutory maximum)	1/50th of statutory maximum	Fine (level 3) and daily default fine (1/10th of level 3) under s 619(5) CA 2006 by 1 October 2009
¶909	s 123(4) CA 1985	**Company/officer**: failing to give notice of increase of share capital to Companies House	Summary	Fine (1/5th of statutory maximum)	1/50th of statutory maximum	To be repealed by 1 October 2009
¶1300	s 127(5) CA 1985	**Company/officer**: failing to forward copy of court order re. cancellation of resolution varying shareholders' rights to Companies House	Summary	Fine (1/5th of statutory maximum)	1/50th of statutory maximum	Fine (level 3) and daily default fine (1/10th of level 3) under s 635(3) CA 2006 by 1 October 2009
¶915	s 128(5) CA 1985	**Company/officer**: failing to send particulars of shares carrying special rights to Companies House	Summary	Fine (1/5th of statutory maximum)	1/50th of statutory maximum	Persons liable: officer. Conviction on indictment: fine; summary conviction: fine and daily default fine (1/10th statutory maximum), under s 557(2) CA 2006 by 1 October 2009
¶915	s 129(4) CA 1985	**Company/officer**: failing to send statement of newly created class rights in company without share capital to Companies House	Summary	Fine (1/5th of statutory maximum)	1/50th of statutory maximum	Fine (level 3) and daily default fine (1/10th of level 3) under s 638(3) CA 2006 by 1 October 2009

¶¶	Reference	Persons liable and general nature of offence[1]	Mode of prosecution[2]	Punishment[3]	Daily default fine[4]	Changes under the Companies Act 2006 (where applicable)[5]
¶1486	s 141 CA 1985	**Officer**: concealing name of creditor entitled to object to reduction of capital/wilfully misrepresenting nature or amount of debt or claim/aiding, abetting or being privy to another person doing so	Indictment	Fine	—	Restated at s 647(2) CA 2006 by 1 October 2009
			Summary	Fine (statutory maximum)		
¶7441	s 142(2) CA 1985	**Director**: authorising or permitting non-compliance with section 142 (requirement to convene company meeting to consider serious loss of capital)	Indictment	Fine	—	Restated at s 656(5) CA 2006 by 1 October 2009
			Summary	Fine (statutory maximum)		
¶1339	s 143(2) CA 1985	**Company/officer**: acquiring its own shares in breach of restrictions	Indictment	Company: fine Officer: 2 years and/or fine	—	Penalty on summary conviction in England and Wales will be 12 months' imprisonment and/or fine (statutory maximum) under s 658(3) CA 2006 by 1 October 2009. Punishment on indictment restated.
			Summary	Company: fine (statutory maximum) Officer: 6 months and/or fine (statutory maximum)		
¶1222	s 149(2) CA 1985	**Company/officer**: company failing to cancel its own shares, acquired by itself, or failing to apply for re-registration as private company, as required by section 146(2)	Summary	Fine (1/5th of statutory maximum)	1/50th of statutory maximum	Fine (level 3) and daily default fine (1/10th of level 3) under s 667(3) CA 2006 by 1 October 2009
¶5636	s 151(3) CA 1985	**Company/officer**: company giving financial assistance towards acquisition of its own shares	Indictment	Company: fine Officer: 2 years and/or a fine	—	Public companies only. Penalty on summary conviction in England and Wales will be 12 months' imprisonment and/or fine (statutory maximum) under s 680(2) CA 2006 by 1 October 2009. Punishment on indictment restated.
			Summary	Company: Fine (statutory maximum) Officer: 6 months and/or fine (statutory maximum)		

¶¶	Reference	Persons liable and general nature of offence[1]	Mode of prosecution[2]	Punishment[3]	Daily default fine[4]	Changes under the Companies Act 2006 (where applicable)[5]
¶5620	s 156(6) CA 1985	**Company/officer:** company failing to register statutory declaration or statement under section 155 (whitewash procedure for financial assistance)	Summary	Fine (statutory maximum)	1/50th of statutory maximum	Date of repeal to be announced at the time of writing.
¶5605	s 156(7) CA 1985	**Director:** making statutory declaration or statement under section 155, without having reasonable grounds for opinion expressed in it	Indictment	2 years and/or fine	–	Date of repeal to be announced at the time of writing.
			Summary	6 months and/or fine (statutory maximum)		
¶1394	s 169(6) CA 1985	**Officer:** Default in delivering to registrar the return required by section 169 (disclosure by company of purchase of own shares)	Indictment	Fine	1/10th of statutory maximum	Restated at s 707(7) CA 2006 by 1 October 2009
			Summary	Fine (statutory maximum)		
¶1395	s 169(7) CA 1985	**Company/officer:** failing to keep copy of contract etc at registered office; refusing to allow inspection	Summary	Fine (1/5th of statutory maximum)	1/50th of statutory maximum	Fine (level 3) and daily default fine (1/10th of level 3) under s 703(2) CA 2006 by 1 October 2009
¶1407	s 173(6) CA 1985	**Director:** making statutory declaration under section 173 (redemption/ purchase of company's shares out of capital) without having reasonable grounds for opinion expressed in the declaration	Indictment	2 years and/or fine	–	Penalty on summary conviction in England and Wales will be 12 months' imprisonment and/or fine (statutory maximum) under s 715(2) CA 2006 by 1 October 2009
			Summary	6 months and/or fine (statutory maximum)		
¶1415	s 175(7) CA 1985	**Company/officer:** refusal of inspection of statutory declaration and auditors' report under section 173 etc	Summary	Fine (1/5th of statutory maximum)	1/50th of statutory maximum	Fine (level 3) and daily default fine (1/10th of level 3) under s 720(6) CA 2006 by 1 October 2009

¶¶	Reference	Persons liable and general nature of offence[1]	Mode of prosecution[2]	Punishment[3]	Daily default fine[4] (where applicable)	Changes under the new Companies Act (where applicable)[5]
¶1418	s 176(4) CA 1985	**Company/officer**: company failing to give notice to registrar of application to court under section 176, or to register court order	Summary	Fine (1/5th of statutory maximum)	1/50th of statutory maximum	Fine (level 3) and daily default fine (1/10th of level 3) under s 722(5) CA 2006 by 1 October 2009
¶1896	s 183(6) CA 1985	**Company/officer**: company failing to send notice of refusal to register a transfer of shares or debentures	Summary	Fine (1/5th of statutory maximum)	1/50th of statutory maximum	Fine (level 3) and daily default fine (1/10th of level 3) under s 771(4) CA 2006 as of 6 April 2008
¶1910	s 185(5) CA 1985	**Company/officer**: default in compliance with section 185(1) (certificates to be made ready following allotment or transfer of shares etc)	Summary	Fine (1/5th of statutory maximum)	1/50th of statutory maximum	Persons liable: officer. Fine (level 3) and daily default fine (1/10th of level 3) under s 776(6) CA 2006 as of 6 April 2008
¶4007	s 191(4) CA 1985	**Company/officer**: refusal of inspection or copy of register of debenture-holders	Summary	Fine (1/5th of statutory maximum)	1/50th of statutory maximum	Fine (level 3) and daily default fine (1/10th of level 3) under s 746(2) CA 2006 as of 6 April 2008
¶4195	s 221(5) or 222(4) CA 1985	**Officer**: company failing to keep accounting records	Indictment	2 years and/or fine	–	Penalty on summary conviction in England and Wales will be 12 months' imprisonment and/or fine (statutory maximum) under ss 387(3), 389(4) CA 2006 as of 6 April 2008. Punishment on indictment restated
			Summary	6 months and/or fine (statutory maximum)		
¶4198	s 222(6) CA 1985	**Officer**: failing to secure compliance with, or intentionally causing default under, section 222(5) (preservation of accounting records for requisite number of years)	Indictment	2 years and/or fine	–	Penalty on summary conviction in England and Wales will be 12 months' imprisonment and/or fine (statutory maximum) under s 389(4) CA 2006 as of 6 April 2008. Punishment on indictment restated
			Summary	6 months and/or fine (statutory maximum)		
¶2769	s 232(4) CA 1985	**Director/officer**: default in giving notice of matters relating to himself for purposes of Schedule 6, Part I (disclosure of remuneration in accounts)	Summary	Fine (1/5th of statutory maximum)	–	Persons liable: director/former director. Fine (level 3) under s 412(6) CA 2006 as of 6 April 2008
¶4263	s 233(5) CA 1985	**Director**: approving defective accounts	Indictment	Fine	–	Restated at s 414(5) CA 2006 as of 6 April 2008
			Summary	Fine (statutory maximum)		

¶¶	Reference	Persons liable and general nature of offence [1]	Mode of prosecution [2]	Punishment [3]	Daily default fine [4] (where applicable)	Changes under the new Companies Act (where applicable) [5]
¶4263	s 233(6) CA 1985	**Company/officer**: laying or delivery of unsigned balance sheet; circulating copies of balance sheet without signatures	Summary	Fine (1/5th of statutory maximum)	–	Persons liable: director. Conviction on indictment: fine; summary conviction: fine (statutory maximum) under s 414(5) CA 2006 as of 6 April 2008
¶4245+	s 234(5) CA 1985	**Director**: non-compliance with Part VII, as to directors' report and its content	Indictment	Fine	–	Restated at s 415(5) CA 2006 as of 6 April 2008
			Summary	Fine (statutory maximum)		
¶4251	s 234ZA(6) CA 1985	**Director**: making a statement in a directors' report as mentioned in section 234ZA(2) which is false	Indictment	2 years and/or fine	–	Restated at s 418(6) CA 2006 as of 6 April 2008
			Summary	12 months and/or fine (statutory maximum)		
¶4263	s 234A(4) CA 1985	**Company/officer**: laying, circulating or delivering directors' report without required signature	Summary	Fine (1/5th of statutory maximum)	–	Persons liable: directors. Conviction on indictment: fine; summary conviction: fine (statutory maximum) under s 419(5) CA 2006 as of 6 April 2008
¶4313	s 236(4) CA 1985	**Company/officer**: laying, circulating or delivering auditors' report without required signature	Summary	Fine (1/5th of statutory maximum)	–	Fine (level 3) under s 505(4) CA 2006 as of 6 April 2008
¶4267	s 238(5) CA 1985	**Company/officer**: failing to send company's annual accounts, directors' report and auditors' report to those entitled to receive them	Indictment	Fine	–	Restated at s 425(2) CA 2006 as of 6 April 2008
			Summary	Fine (statutory maximum)		
¶4268	s 239(3) CA 1985	**Company/officer**: failing to supply copy of accounts and reports to shareholder on his demand	Summary	Fine (1/5th of statutory maximum)	1/50th of statutory maximum	Fine (level 3) and daily default fine (1/10th of level 3) under s 431(4) CA 2006 as of 6 April 2008
¶4271	s 240(6) CA 1985	**Company/officer**: failure to comply with requirements in connection with publication of accounts	Summary	Fine (statutory maximum)	–	Fine (level 3) and daily default fine (1/10th of level 3) under s 435(6) CA 2006 as of 6 April 2008
¶4273	s 241(2) or s 242(2) CA 1985	**Director**: in default as regards duty to lay and deliver company's annual accounts, directors' report and auditors' report (public companies only)	Summary	Fine (statutory maximum)	1/10th of statutory maximum	Fine (level 5) and daily default fine (1/10th of level 5) under s 438(4) CA 2006 as of 6 April 2008

¶¶	Reference	Persons liable and general nature of offence [1]	Mode of prosecution [2]	Punishment [3]	Daily default fine [4] (where applicable)	Changes under the new Companies Act (where applicable) [5]
¶3894+	s 288(4) CA 1985	**Company/officer**: failing to keep register of directors and secretaries/ keeping incorrect or out of date register/refusing inspection of register	Summary	Fine (statutory maximum)	1/10th of statutory maximum	Fine (level 5) and daily default fine (1/10th of level 5) under s 162(7) CA 2006 (register of directors) and s 275(7) CA 2006 (register of secretaries) by 1 October 2009
¶2255	s 291(5) CA 1985	**Director**: acting as director without having requisite share qualification	Summary	Fine (1/5th of statutory maximum)	1/50th of statutory maximum	Expected to be repealed by 1 October 2009
¶585	s 305(3) CA 1985	**Company/officer**: default in complying with section 305 (directors' names to appear on company correspondence etc)	Summary	Fine (1/5th of statutory maximum)	–	Fine (level 3) and daily default fine (1/10th level 3) under reg 9 draft Companies (Trading Disclosures) Regulations 2008, the implementation date for which is yet to be announced at the time of writing
¶2278	s 306(4) CA 1985	**Person**: failure to state in nomination that liability of proposed director/manager is unlimited/failure to give notice of that fact to person accepting office	Indictment	Fine [6]	–	To be repealed by 1 October 2009
			Summary	Fine (statutory maximum) [6]		
¶3367	s 317(7) CA 1985	**Director**: failing to disclose interest in contract	Indictment	Fine	–	Restated at s 183 CA 2006, the implementation date for which is yet to be announced at the time of writing
			Summary	Fine (statutory maximum)		
¶2670	s 228(6) CA 2006	**Company/officer**: failing to have directors' service contracts open to inspection/refusing inspection/failing to notify change in location to Companies House	Summary	Fine (level 3)	1/10th of level 3	Provision in force
¶3476	s 248(4) CA 2006	**Company/officer**: terms of unwritten contract between sole member of a private company limited by shares or by guarantee and company not set out in a written memorandum or recorded in minutes of a directors' meeting	Summary	Fine (level 3)	1/10th of level 3	Provision in force

¶¶	Reference	Persons liable and general nature of offence [1]	Mode of prosecution [2]	Punishment [3]	Daily default fine [4] (where applicable)	Changes under the new Companies Act (where applicable) [5]
¶259+	s 348(2) CA 1985	**Company/officer:** failing to paint, affix name; failing to keep it painted or affixed	Summary	Fine (1/5th of statutory maximum)	1/50th of statutory maximum (for failure to keep the name painted or affixed)	Fine (level 3) and daily default fine (1/10th level 3) under reg 9 draft Companies (Trading Disclosures) Regulations 2008, the implementation date for which is yet to be announced at the time of writing
¶259+	s 349(2) CA 1985	**Company:** failing to have name on business correspondence, invoices, etc	Summary	Fine (1/5th of statutory maximum)	–	Fine (level 3) and daily default fine (1/10th level 3) under reg 9 draft Companies (Trading Disclosures) Regulations 2008, the implementation date for which is yet to be announced at the time of writing
¶259+	s 349(3) CA 1985	**Officer:** issuing business letter or document or website not bearing company's name	Summary	Fine (1/5th of statutory maximum)	–	Fine (level 3) and daily default fine (1/10th level 3) under reg 9 draft Companies (Trading Disclosures) Regulations 2008, the implementation date for which is yet to be announced at the time of writing
¶2580	s 349(4) CA 1985	**Officer:** signing cheque, bill of exchange etc on which company's name not mentioned	Summary	Fine (1/5th of statutory maximum) [7]	–	No equivalent offence, but failure to include name on cheque will be offence, reg 9 draft Companies (Trading Disclosures) Regulations 2008, the implementation date for which is yet to be announced at the time of writing
¶3490/mp	s 350(1) CA 1985	**Company:** failing to have its name engraved on company seal	Summary	Fine (1/5th of statutory maximum)	–	Persons liable: company/officer. Fine (level 3) under s 45(5) CA 2006 by 1 October 2009
¶3490/mp	s 350(2) CA 1985	**Officer:** using/authorising use of seal without company's name engraved on it	Summary	Fine (1/5th of statutory maximum)	–	Fine (level 3) under s 45(5) CA 2006 by 1 October 2009
¶585	s 351(5)(a) CA 1985	**Company:** failing to comply with section 351(1), (2) (matters to be stated on business correspondence etc)	Summary	Fine (1/5th of statutory maximum)	–	Fine (level 3) and daily default fine (1/10th level 3) under reg 9 draft Companies (Trading Disclosures) Regulations 2008, the implementation date for which is yet to be announced at the time of writing

¶¶	Reference	Persons liable and general nature of offence[1]	Mode of prosecution[2]	Punishment[3]	Daily default fine[4] (where applicable)	Changes under the new Companies Act (where applicable)[5]
¶585	s 351(5)(b) CA 1985	**Officer/agent**: issuing, or authorising issue of, business document not complying with those subsections	Summary	Fine (1/5th of statutory maximum)	–	Fine (level 3) and daily default fine (1/10th level 3) under reg 9 draft Companies (Trading Disclosures) Regulations 2008, the implementation date for which is yet to be announced at the time of writing
¶3922	s 352(5) CA 1985	**Company/officer**: failure to keep register of shareholders/failure to keep in correct form	Summary	Fine (1/5th of statutory maximum)	1/50th of statutory maximum	Fine (level 3) and daily default fine (1/10th of level 3), under s 113(8) CA 2006 by 1 October 2009
¶3943	s 352A(3) CA 1985	**Company/officer**: failing to make statement that company has only one shareholder in register of shareholders	Summary	Fine (Level 2)	1/10th of level 2	Fine (level 3) and daily default fine (1/10th of level 3) under s 123(5) CA 2006 by 1 October 2009
¶3928	s 353(4) CA 1985	**Company/officer**: failing to send notice of location of register of shareholders to Companies House	Summary	Fine (1/5th of statutory maximum)	1/50th of statutory maximum	Fine (level 3) and daily default fine (1/10th of level 3) under s 114(6) CA 2006 by 1 October 2009
¶3926	s 354(4) CA 1985	**Company/officer**: failing to keep index of shareholders	Summary	Fine (1/5th of statutory maximum)	1/50th of statutory maximum	Fine (level 3) and daily default fine (1/10th of level 3) under s 115(6) CA 2006 by 1 October 2009
¶3932	s 356(5) CA 1985	**Company/officer**: refusing to allow inspection/provide copies of shareholders' register	Summary	Fine (1/5th of statutory maximum)	–	Fine (level 3) and daily default fine (1/10th of level 3) under s 118(2) CA 2006. Provision in force as of 1 October 2007 but only applies once a company has filed an annual return made up to a date after 30 September 2007
¶4060	s 363(3), (4) CA 1985	**Company/director/secretary**: failing to make annual return	Summary	Fine (statutory maximum)	1/10th of statutory maximum	Persons liable: company/director/secretary (if applicable)/other officer. Fine (level 5) and daily default fine (1/10th of level 5) under s 858(2) CA 2006 by 1 October 2009. Officer not in default initially can commit offence for continued contravention

¶¶	Reference	Persons liable and general nature of offence[1]	Mode of prosecution[2]	Punishment[3]	Daily default fine[4] (where applicable)	Changes proposed by the new Companies Act (where applicable)[5]
¶3788	s 336(4) CA 2006	**Officer:** public company failing to hold AGM	Indictment	Fine	–	Provision in force
			Summary	Fine (statutory maximum)		
¶3732	s 325(4) CA 2006	**Officer:** failure to include proxy statement in notices of meetings	Summary	Fine (level 3)	–	Provision in force
¶3733	s 326(4) CA 2006	**Officer:** authorising/permitting issue of irregular proxy invitations	Summary	Fine (level 3)	–	Provision in force
¶3781	s 339(5) CA 2006	**Officer:** failing to comply with requirements re. circulation of shareholder resolutions	Indictment	Fine	–	Provision in force
			Summary	Fine (statutory maximum)		
¶3480 ¶3600	s 380(5) CA 1985	**Company/officer:** failing to file certain resolutions at Companies House	Summary	Fine (1/5th of statutory maximum)	1/50th of statutory maximum	Fine (level 3) and daily default fine (1/10th of level 3) under s 30 CA 2006 by 1 October 2009
¶451	s 380(6) CA 1985	**Officer:** failing to include copy of resolution which has to be filed at Companies House in articles, failing to forward copy to shareholder on request	Summary	Fine (1/5th of statutory maximum) (for each occasion on which copies are issued or, as the case may be, requested)	–	Fine (level 3) for each occasion under s 36(4) CA 2006 by 1 October 2009
¶3476 ¶3864	ss 248(4), 355(4), 359 CA 2006	**Officer:** failing to keep minutes of shareholder, class and board meetings	Summary	Fine (level 3)	1/10th of level 3	Provisions in force
¶3868	s 357(5) CA 2006	**Sole shareholder:** failing to provide company with written record of decision	Summary	Fine (level 2)	–	Provision in force
¶3869	s 358(6) CA 2006	**Officer:** refusing inspection/copies of minutes of general meeting	Summary	Fine (level 3)	1/10th of level 3	Provision in force

APPENDIX

¶¶	Reference	Persons liable and general nature of offence[1]	Mode of prosecution[2]	Punishment[3]	Daily default fine[4] (where applicable)	Changes proposed by the new Companies Act (where applicable)[5]
¶4337+	Private companies: s 486(4) CA 2006; public companies: s 387(2) CA 1985	**Company/officer:** failing to give secretary of state notice of non-appointment of auditors	Summary	Private companies: fine (level 3) Public companies: fine (1/5th of statutory maximum)	Private companies: 1/10th of level 3 Public companies: 1/50th of statutory minimum	Private companies: provision in force Public companies: fine (level 3) and daily default fine 1/10th of level 3) under s 490(4) CA 2006 as of 6 April 2008
¶4298	s 389B(1) CA 1985	**Person:** making false, misleading or deceptive statement to auditor	Indictment	2 years and/or fine	–	Restated at s 501(2) CA 2006 as of 6 April 2008
			Summary	12 months and/or fine (statutory maximum)		
¶4298	s 389B(2) CA 1985	**Person:** failure to provide information or explanations to auditor	Summary	Fine (level 3)	–	Restated at s 501(3), (5) CA 2006 as of 6 April 2008
¶4297	s 389B(4) CA 1985	**Parent company:** failing to obtain from subsidiary undertaking information for purposes of audit	Summary	Fine (level 3)	–	Restated at s 501(3), (5) CA 2006 as of 6 April 2008
¶4344	s 391(2) CA 1985	**Company/officer:** failing to give notice to registrar of removal of auditor	Summary	Fine (1/5th of statutory maximum)	1/50th of statutory maximum	Fine (level 3) and daily default fine (1/10th of level 3) under s 512(3) CA 2006 as of 6 April 2008
¶4341	s 392(3) CA 1985	**Company/officer:** failing to forward notice of auditor's resignation to registrar	Indictment	Fine	1/10th of statutory maximum	Restated at s 517(3) CA 2006 as of 6 April 2008
			Summary	Fine (statutory maximum)		
¶4342	s 392A(5) CA 1985	**Director:** failing to convene meeting requisitioned by resigning auditor	Indictment	Fine	–	Restated at s 518(7) CA 2006 as of 6 April 2008
			Summary	Fine (statutory maximum)		
¶4340	s 394A(1) CA 1985	**Auditor:** ceasing to hold office and failing to deposit statement as to circumstances	Indictment	Fine	–	Restated at s 519(7) CA 2006 as of 6 April 2008
			Summary	Fine (statutory maximum)		

¶¶	Reference	Persons liable and general nature of offence[1]	Mode of prosecution[2]	Punishment[3]	Daily default fine[4] (where applicable)	Changes proposed by the new Companies Act (where applicable)[5]
¶4340	s 394A(4) CA 1985	**Officer:** failing to comply with requirements as to statement of person ceasing to hold office as auditor	Indictment Summary	Fine Fine (statutory maximum)	1/10th of statutory maximum	No daily default fine under s 520(8) CA 2006 as of 6 April 2008
¶4651	s 399(3) CA 1985	**Company/officer:** failing to file at Companies House particulars of charge created by it, or of issue of debentures which requires registration	Indictment Summary	Fine Fine (statutory maximum)	1/10th of statutory maximum	No daily default fine under s 860(5) CA 2006 by 1 October 2009
¶4646	s 400(4) CA 1985	**Company/officer:** failing to file at Companies House particulars of charge on property acquired	Indictment Summary	Fine Fine (statutory maximum)	1/10th of statutory maximum	No daily default fine under s 862(5) CA 2006 by 1 October 2009
¶4658	s 403(2A) CA 1985	**Person:** making false statement under section 403(1A) which he knows to be false or does not believe to be true	Indictment Summary	2 years and/or fine 6 months and/or fine (statutory maximum)	–	Restated at s 1112 CA 2006 by 1 October 2009
¶9229 ¶9248 ¶9405	s 405(4) CA 1985	**Person obtaining order/appointor:** failing to notify Companies House of appointment of receiver or manager, or of his ceasing to act	Summary	Fine (1/5th of statutory maximum)	1/50th of statutory maximum	Fine (level 3) and daily default fine (1/10th of level 3) under s 871(5) CA 2006 by 1 October 2009
¶3975	s 407(3) CA 1985	**Officer:** authorising or permitting omission from company register of charges	Indictment Summary	Fine Fine (statutory maximum)	–	Restated at s 876(4) CA 2006 by 1 October 2009
¶3978	s 408(3) CA 1985	**Officer:** refusing inspection of charging instrument, or of register of charges	Summary	Fine (1/5th of statutory maximum)	1/50th of statutory maximum	Persons liable: company/officer. Fine (level 3) and daily default fine (1/10th of level 3) under s 877(6) CA 2006 by 1 October 2009
¶6525	s 425(4) CA 1985	**Company/officer:** failing to annex to memorandum court order sanctioning compromise or arrangement with creditors	Summary	Fine (1/5th of statutory maximum)	–	Fine (level 3) under s 901(6) CA 2006 (annexed to articles rather than memorandum) as of 6 April 2008

APPENDIX

¶¶	Reference	Persons liable and general nature of offence[1]	Mode of prosecution[2]	Punishment[3]	Daily default fine[4] (where applicable)	Changes proposed by the new Companies Act (where applicable)[5]
¶6518	s 426(6) CA 1985	**Company/officer:** failing to comply with requirements of section 426 (information to shareholders and creditors about compromise or arrangement)	Indictment	Fine	–	Restated under s 897(8) CA 2006 as of 6 April 2008
			Summary	Fine (statutory maximum)	–	
¶6517	s 426(7) CA 1985	**Director or trustee for debenture holders:** failing to give notice to company of matters necessary for purposes of section 426	Summary	Fine (1/5th of statutory maximum)	–	Fine (level 3) under s 898(3) CA 2006 as of 6 April 2008
¶6535	s 427(5) CA 1985	**Company/officer:** failure to deliver to registrar office copy of court order under section 427 (company reconstruction or amalgamation)	Summary	Fine (1/5th of statutory maximum)	1/50th of statutory maximum	Fine (level 3) and daily default fine (1/10th of level 3) under s 900(8) CA 2006 as of 6 April 2008
¶6950	s 980(8) CA 2006	**Bidder:** failing to send copy of notice or making statutory declaration knowing it to be false etc	Indictment	2 years and/or fine	–	Provision in force
			Summary	12 months and/or fine (statutory maximum)	1/50th of statutory maximum	
¶6967	s 984(7) CA 2006	**Bidder:** failing to give notice of rights to minority shareholder	Indictment	Fine	–	Provision in force
			Summary	Fine (statutory maximum)	1/50th of statutory maximum	
¶7240	s444(4) CA 1985, para 1 Sch 3 CA 2006	**Person:** failing to give secretary of state information about interests in shares/giving false information	Indictment	2 years and/or fine	–	Amendment in force
			Summary	12 months and/or fine (statutory maximum)	1/50th of statutory maximum	
¶7240 ¶7216	s 448(7A) CA 1985, para 2 Sch 3 CA 2006	**Person:** obstructing exercise of warrant	Indictment	Fine	–	Amendment in force
			Summary	Fine (statutory maximum)	–	
¶7213	s 449(6A) CA 1985, para 3 Sch 3 CA 2006	**Person:** wrongful disclosure of information obtained during investigation	Indictment	2 years and/or fine	–	Amendment in force
			Summary	12 months and/or fine (statutory maximum)		

APPENDIX 1211

¶¶	Reference	Persons liable and general nature of offence[1]	Mode of prosecution[2]	Punishment[3]	Daily default fine[4] (where applicable)	Changes proposed by the new Companies Act (where applicable)[5]
¶7211	s 450(3) CA 1985, para 4 Sch 3 CA 2006	**Officer**: destroying/mutilating/falsifying company documents/making false entries/parting with/altering/making omissions from such documents	Indictment Summary	7 years and/or fine 12 months and/or fine (statutory maximum)	–	Amendment in force
¶7211	s 451(2) CA 1985, para 5 Sch 3 CA 2006	**Person**: providing false information in response to request for information in company investigation	Indictment Summary	2 years and/or fine 12 months and/or fine (statutory maximum)	–	Amendment in force
¶7216	s 453A(5A) CA 1985, para 6 Sch 3 CA 2006	**Person**: obstructing investigator's access to premises	Indictment Summary	Fine Fine (statutory maximum)	–	Amendment in force
¶3822	s 455(1) CA 1985, para 7 Sch 3 CA 2006	**Person**: contravening restrictions placed on shares	Indictment Summary	Fine Fine (statutory maximum)	–	Amendment in force
¶3822	s 455(2A) CA 1985, para 7 Sch 3 CA 2006	**Company/officer**: issuing shares in contravention of restrictions	Indictment Summary	Fine Fine (statutory maximum)	–	Amendment in force
¶2577	s 993(3) CA 2006	**Person**: being party to carrying on business with intent to defraud creditors	Indictment Summary	10 years and/or fine[8] 12 months and/or fine (statutory maximum)	–	Provision in force
¶2128	s 998(4) CA 2006	**Company/officer**: failure to register office copy of court order under Part XVII altering, or giving leave to alter, company's constitution	Summary	Fine (level 3)	1/10th of level 3	Provision in force
¶7539	s 65(3) CA 1985	**Applicant**: failing to register order declaring company's dissolution void at Companies House	Summary	Fine (1/5th of statutory maximum)	1/50th of statutory maximum	To be repealed by 1 October 2009

APPENDIX

¶¶	Reference	Persons liable and general nature of offence[1]	Mode of prosecution[2]	Punishment[3]	Daily default fine[4] (where applicable)	Changes proposed by the new Companies Act (where applicable)[5]
¶7510	s 652E(1) CA 1985	**Director**: breaching requirements re. application to have company struck off	Indictment	Fine	–	Persons liable: person. Otherwise restated at s 1004(7) CA 2006 by 1 October 2009
			Summary	Fine (statutory maximum)		
¶7510	s 652E(2) CA 1985	**Director**: failing to provide required people with copy of application to strike off with intent to conceal it	Indictment	7 years and/or fine	–	Penalty on summary conviction in England and Wales will be 12 months' imprisonment and/or fine (statutory maximum) under s 1006(7), s 1007(7) CA 2006 by 1 October 2009
			Summary	6 months and/or fine (statutory maximum)		
¶7510	s 652F(1) CA 1985	**Person**: giving false information in connection with application to strike off	Indictment	Fine	–	Restated at s 1112 CA 2006 by 1 October 2009
			Summary	Fine (statutory maximum)		
¶7510	s 652F(2) CA 1985	**Person**: making false application to strike off	Indictment	Fine	–	Restated at s 1112 CA 2006 by 1 October 2009
			Summary	Fine (statutory maximum)		
¶153 ¶165 ¶169 ¶183	s 697(1) CA 1985	**Overseas company/officer/agent**: failing to comply with any of sections 691 to 693 or 696 (registration, filing and stationery requirements)	Summary	Fine (1/5th of statutory maximum)	1/50th of statutory maximum (for continuing offences)	Provisions re. overseas companies will be set out in regulations in due course
¶158	s 697(2) CA 1985	**Overseas company/officer/agent**: contravening section 694(6) (use of unacceptable name)	Indictment	Fine	1/10th of statutory maximum	Provisions re. overseas companies will be set out in regulations in due course
			Summary	Fine (statutory maximum)		
¶146	s 697(3) CA 1985	**Overseas company/officer/agent**: failing to comply with requirements re. registration of branch	Summary	Fine (1/5th level 5)	£100 (for continuing offences)	Provisions re. overseas companies will be set out in regulations in due course

APPENDIX 1213

¶¶	Reference	Persons liable and general nature of offence[1]	Mode of prosecution[2]	Punishment[3]	Daily default fine[4] (where applicable)	Changes proposed by the new Companies Act (where applicable)[5]
¶174	s 703(1) CA 1985	**Overseas company/person:** failing to comply with requirements as to accounts and reports	Indictment	Fine	1/10th of statutory maximum	Provisions re. overseas companies will be set out in regulations in due course
			Summary	Fine (statutory maximum)		
¶180	s 703R(1) CA 1985	**Company/officer:** failing to register winding up/other insolvency proceedings	Indictment	Fine	£100	Provisions re. overseas companies will be set out in regulations in due course
			Summary	Fine (statutory maximum)		
¶180	s 703R(2) CA 1985	**Liquidator:** failing to register appointment, termination of winding up or striking-off of company	Indictment	Fine	£100	Provisions re. overseas companies will be set out in regulations in due course
			Summary	Fine (statutory maximum)		
¶3867	s 1138(3) CA 2006	**Officer:** failing to comply take precautions against falsification of company books/records etc	Summary	Fine (level 3)	1/10th of level 3	Provision in force
¶3950	para 1(3), Pt II, Sch 14 CA 1985	**Company/officer:** failing to give notice of location of overseas branch register etc	Summary	Fine (1/5th of statutory maximum)	1/50th of statutory maximum	Fine (level 3) and daily default fine (1/10th of level 3) under s 130(3) CA 2006 by 1 October 2009
¶3950	para 4(2), Pt II, Sch 14 CA 1985	**Company/officer/agent:** failing to send copies of entries in overseas branch register to registered office in GB, or to keep a duplicate of overseas branch register in GB	Summary	Fine (1/5th of statutory maximum)	1/50th of statutory maximum	Persons liable: company/officer. Fine (level 3) and daily default fine (1/10th of level 3), under s 132(4) CA 2006 by 1 October 2009
¶173	para 5, Pt I, Sch 21D CA 1985	**Overseas company/person:** failing to deliver accounting documents	Indictment	Fine	£100	Provisions re. overseas companies will be set out in regulations in due course
			Summary	Fine (statutory maximum)		
¶174	para 13, Pt I, Sch 21D CA 1985	**Overseas company/person:** failing to deliver accounts and reports	Indictment	Fine	£100	Provisions re. overseas companies will be set out in regulations in due course
			Summary	Fine (statutory maximum)		
¶2043	s 795(3) CA 2006	**Person:** failure to comply with request for disclosure of interests in shares in plc	Indictment	2 years and/or fine	–	Provision in force
			Summary	12 months and/or fine (statutory maximum)		

¶¶	Reference	Persons liable and general nature of offence[1]	Mode of prosecution[2]	Punishment[3]	Daily default fine[4] (where applicable)	Changes proposed by the new Companies Act (where applicable)[5]
¶2043	s 798(4) CA 2006	**Person:** breaches order imposing restrictions on shares	Indictment	Fine	–	Provision in force
		Company/officer: issuing shares in breach of restrictions order	Summary	Fine (statutory maximum)		
¶2044	s 804(3) CA 2006	**Officer:** failure to act on shareholders' request to obtain disclosure of interests in shares	Indictment	Fine	–	Provision in force
			Summary	Fine (statutory maximum)		
¶2044	s 806(2) CA 2006	**Company/officer:** failure to notify Companies House location of reports to shareholders on investigations into shares	Summary	Fine (level 3)	1/10th of level 3	Provision in force
¶2044	s 806(4) CA 2006	**Officer:** failure to report to shareholders on investigations into shares or to comply with other provisions re. reports	Indictment	Fine	–	Provision in force
			Summary	Fine (statutory maximum)		
¶2044	s 807(4) CA 2006	**Company/officer:** failure to allow report to be inspected/copied	Summary	Fine (level 3)	1/10th level 3	Provision in force
¶3991	s 808(6) CA 2006	**Company/officer:** failure to keep/maintain register of interests in shares of plc	Summary	Fine (level 3)	1/10th level 3	Provision in force
¶3993	s 809(5) CA 2006	**Company/officer:** failure to keep register of interests in shares of plc available for inspection or notify Companies House of its location	Summary	Fine (level 3)	1/10th level 3	Provision in force
¶3992, ¶3993	s 810(6) CA 2006	**Company/officer:** failure to maintain index of register of interests in shares of plc, keep it with register and allow inspection of it	Summary	Fine (level 3)	1/10th level 3	Provision in force
¶3994	s 813(2) CA 2006	**Company/officer:** failure to allow inspection/copies of register of interests in shares of plc following valid request	Summary	Fine (level 3)	1/10th level 3	Provision in force
¶3994	s 814(3) CA 2006	**Person:** making false/misleading/deceptive request to inspect/copy register Disclosing information to person not included in request, or failing to prevent such disclosure	Indictment	2 years and/or fine	–	Provision in force
			Summary	12 months and/or fine (statutory maximum)		

¶¶	Reference	Persons liable and general nature of offence[1]	Mode of prosecution[2]	Punishment[3]	Daily default fine[4] (where applicable)	Changes proposed by the new Companies Act (where applicable)[5]
¶3995	s 815(4) CA 2006	**Company/officer:** unauthorised removal of entry from register	Summary	Fine (level 3)	1/10th level 3	Provision in force
¶3996	s 819(3) CA 2006	**Company/officer:** failure to keep register and index for 6 years after ceased to be plc	Summary	Fine (level 3)	1/10th level 3	Provision in force
¶9517	s 6A(1) IA 1986	**Officer:** false representation/fraud to obtain shareholders'/creditors' approval of proposed CVA	Indictment	7 years and/or fine	–	–
			Summary	6 months and/or fine (statutory maximum)		
¶9230	s 30 IA 1986	**Body corporate:** acting as receiver	Indictment	Fine	–	–
			Summary	Fine (statutory maximum)		
¶9230	s 31 IA 1986	**Bankrupt:** acting as receiver	Indictment	2 years and/or fine	–	–
			Summary	6 months and/or fine (statutory maximum)		
¶9367	s 38(5) IA 1986	**Receiver:** failing to deliver accounts to Companies House	Summary	Fine (1/5th of statutory maximum)	1/50th of statutory maximum	–
¶9368	s 39(2) IA 1986	**Company/officer/liquidator/receiver:** failing to state in correspondence that receiver appointed	Summary	Fine (1/5th of statutory maximum)	–	–
¶9349	s 43(6) IA 1986	**Administrative receiver:** failing to file office copy of order permitting disposal of charged property	Summary	Fine (1/5th of statutory maximum)	1/50th of statutory maximum	–
¶9406	s 45(5) IA 1986	**Administrative receiver:** failing to file notice of vacation of office	Summary	Fine (1/5th of statutory maximum)	1/50th of statutory maximum	–
¶9249	s 46(4) IA 1986	**Administrative receiver:** failing to give notice of his appointment	Summary	Fine (1/5th of statutory maximum)	1/50th of statutory maximum	–
¶8861/mp	s 47(6) IA 1986	**Person involved in company:** failing to make/submit statement of affairs in administrative receivership	Indictment	Fine	1/10th of statutory maximum	–
			Summary	Fine (statutory maximum)		
¶9380	s 48(8) IA 1986	**Administrative receiver:** failing to report to Companies House and creditors properly	Summary	Fine (1/5th of statutory maximum)	1/50th of statutory maximum	–

¶¶	Reference	Persons liable and general nature of offence[1]	Mode of prosecution[2]	Punishment[3]	Daily default fine[4] (where applicable)	Changes proposed by the new Companies Act (where applicable)[5]
¶8457	s 85(2) IA 1986	**Company/officer/liquidator**: failing to give notice in *Gazette* of voluntary winding up resolution	Summary	Fine (1/5th of statutory maximum)	1/50th of statutory maximum	–
¶8611	s 89(4) IA 1986	**Director**: making statutory declaration of company's solvency in MVL without reasonable grounds for opinion	Indictment	2 years and/or fine	–	–
			Summary	6 months and/or fine (statutory maximum)		
¶8616	s 89(6) IA 1986	**Company/officer**: statutory declaration of solvency for voluntary liquidation not delivered to Companies House within time limit	Summary	Fine (1/5th of statutory maximum)	1/50th of statutory maximum	–
¶8646	s 93(3) IA 1986	**Liquidator**: failing to summon general meeting at year end in MVL	Summary	Fine (1/5th of statutory maximum)	–	–
¶8664	s 94(4) IA 1986	**Liquidator**: failing to send copy account of winding up and return of final meeting to Companies House in MVL	Summary	Fine (1/5th of statutory maximum)	1/50th of statutory maximum	–
¶8664	s 94(6) IA 1986	**Liquidator**: failing to call final meeting in MVL	Summary	Fine (1/5th of statutory maximum)	–	–
¶8651	s 95(8) IA 1986	**Liquidator**: failing to call creditors' meeting to convert MVL to CVL and/or comply with related requirements	Summary	Fine (statutory maximum)	–	–
¶8450	s 98(6) IA 1986	**Company**: failing to summon and give notice of creditors' meeting to place company into CVL properly	Indictment	Fine	–	–
			Summary	Fine (statutory maximum)		
¶8451+	s 99(3) IA 1986	**Director**: failing to present required statement to meeting to place company into CVL	Indictment	Fine	–	–
		Director appointed to preside at meeting: failing to attend/preside	Summary	Fine (statutory maximum)		
¶8556	s 105(3) IA 1986	**Liquidator**: failing to summon general meeting and creditors' meeting at year end in CVL/failing to produce correct documents at meeting	Summary	Fine (1/5th of statutory maximum)	–	–

¶¶	Reference	Persons liable and general nature of offence[1]	Mode of prosecution[2]	Punishment[3]	Daily default fine[4] (where applicable)	Changes proposed by the new Companies Act (where applicable)[5]
¶8578	s 106(4) IA 1986	**Liquidator:** failing to send account of CVL and return of final meetings to Companies House	Summary	Fine (1/5th of statutory maximum)	1/50th of statutory maximum	–
¶8574+	s 106(6) IA 1986	**Liquidator:** failing to call final meeting of company or creditors in CVL	Summary	Fine (1/5th of statutory maximum)	–	–
¶8616	s 109(2) IA 1986	**Liquidator:** failing to publish notice of appointment in MVL	Summary	Fine (1/5th of statutory maximum)	1/50th of statutory maximum	–
¶8472	s 114(4) IA 1986	**Director:** exercise their powers without sanction or permitted reason when no liquidator appointed in voluntary liquidation	Summary	Fine (statutory maximum)	–	–
¶8130	s 131(7) IA 1986	**Person involved with company:** failing to make/submit statement of affairs when required to do so by liquidator in compulsory liquidation	Indictment	Fine	1/10th of statutory maximum	–
			Summary	Fine (statutory maximum)		
¶8201	s 164 IA 1986	**Liquidator/other person:** giving/offering etc corrupt inducement affecting appointment of liquidator	Indictment	Fine	–	–
			Summary	Fine (statutory maximum)		
¶8447 ¶8452	s 166(7) IA 1986	**Liquidator:** exercising powers without sanction or permitted reason before creditors' meeting held, or liquidator failing to report to creditors' meeting on exercise of powers before meeting in CVL, or failing to apply to court for directions re. default under this provision	Summary	Fine (statutory maximum)	–	–
¶8229 ¶8468	s 188(2) IA 1986	**Company/officer/liquidator/receiver:** failing to comply with publicity requirements on stationery re. liquidation	Summary	Fine (1/5th of statutory maximum)	–	–
¶8231	s 192(2) IA 1986	**Liquidator:** failing to notify Companies House of progress of liquidation	Summary	Fine (1/5th of statutory maximum)	1/50th of statutory maximum	–

¶¶	Reference	Persons liable and general nature of offence[1]	Mode of prosecution[2]	Punishment[3]	Daily default fine[4] (where applicable)	Changes proposed by the new Companies Act (where applicable)[5]
¶8579 ¶8665	s 201(4) IA 1986	**Liquidator/other interested applicant**: failure to deliver copy court order deferring dissolution to Companies House in voluntary liquidation	Summary	Fine (1/5th of statutory maximum)	1/50th of statutory maximum	–
¶8396	s 203(6) IA 1986	**Official receiver/creditor/ contributory/administrative receiver**: failing to deliver copy directions or result of appeal against early dissolution to Companies House	Summary	Fine (1/5th of statutory maximum)	1/50th of statutory maximum	–
¶8398	s 205(7) IA 1986	**Interested applicant**: failing to deliver copy secretary of state's directions or order deferring dissolution to Companies House	Summary	Fine (1/5th of statutory maximum)	1/50th of statutory maximum	–
¶7464	s 206(1) IA 1986	**Past/present officer**: fraud etc prior to liquidation	Indictment Summary	7 years and/or fine 6 months and/or fine (statutory maximum)	–	–
¶7464	s 206(2) IA 1986	**Past/present officer**: being privy to fraud in anticipation of liquidation; fraud/being privy to fraud after commencement of liquidation	Indictment Summary	7 years and/or fine 6 months and/or fine (statutory maximum)	–	–
¶7464	s 206(5) IA 1986	**Person**: taking pawn/pledge or otherwise receiving company property prior to liquidation	Indictment Summary	7 years and/or fine 6 months and/or fine (statutory maximum)	–	–
¶7464	s 207 IA 1986	**Current officer**: entering into transaction in fraud of creditors	Indictment Summary	2 years and/or fine 6 months and/or fine (statutory maximum)	–	–
¶7781	s 208 IA 1986	**Past/present officer**: misconduct re. company's assets during liquidation	Indictment Summary	7 years and/or fine 6 months and/or fine (statutory maximum)	–	–

¶¶	Reference	Persons liable and general nature of offence[1]	Mode of prosecution[2]	Punishment[3]	Daily default fine[4] (where applicable)	Changes proposed by the new Companies Act (where applicable)[5]
¶8170	s 209 IA 1986	**Officer/ contributory**: destroying/ falsifying etc company books during liquidation	Indictment	7 years and/or fine	–	–
			Summary	6 months and/or fine (statutory maximum)		
¶8169 ¶8442	s 210 IA 1986	**Past/present officer**: making material omission from statement of affairs during winding up	Indictment	7 years and/or fine	–	–
			Summary	6 months and/or fine (statutory maximum)		
¶8169 ¶8442	s 211 IA 1986	**Past/present officer**: false representation/fraud to obtain creditors' approval of agreement re. winding up	Indictment	7 years and/or fine	–	–
			Summary	6 months and/or fine (statutory maximum)		
¶264+	s 216(4) IA 1986	**Director**: contravening restrictions re. re-use of company in insolvent liquidation's name	Indictment	2 years and/or fine	–	–
			Summary	6 months and/or fine (statutory maximum)		
¶8121	s 235(5) IA 1986	**Person involved with company**: failing to co-operate with relevant insolvency practitioner	Indictment	Fine	–	–
			Summary	Fine (statutory maximum)		
¶7423	s 389 IA 1986	**Person**: acting as insolvency practitioner when not qualified	Indictment	2 years and/or fine	–	–
			Summary	6 months and/or fine (statutory maximum)		
¶9469	para 9(2), Sch A1 IA 1986	**Director**: failing to notify nominee of beginning of moratorium prior to CVA	Indictment	2 years and/or fine	–	–
			Summary	6 months and/or fine (statutory maximum)		
¶9469	para 10(3), Sch A1 IA 1986	**Nominee**: failing to advertise or notify beginning of moratorium prior to CVA	Summary	Fine (1/5th of statutory maximum)	–	–
¶9494	para 11(2), Sch A1 IA 1986	**Nominee**: failing to advertise or notify end of moratorium prior to CVA	Summary	Fine (1/5th of statutory maximum)	–	–
¶9480	para 16(2), Sch A1 IA 1986	**Company/officer**: failing to state on stationery etc that moratorium in force prior to CVA	Summary	Fine (1/5th of statutory maximum)	–	–

¶¶	Reference	Persons liable and general nature of offence [1]	Mode of prosecution [2]	Punishment [3]	Daily default fine [4] (where applicable)	Changes proposed by the new Companies Act (where applicable) [5]
¶9479	para 17(3)(a), Sch A1 IA 1986	**Company**: obtaining credit without disclosing moratorium prior to CVA	Indictment	Fine	–	–
			Summary	Fine (statutory maximum)		
¶9479	para 17(3)(b), Sch A1 IA 1986	**Officer**: obtaining credit for company without disclosing moratorium prior to CVA	Indictment	2 years and/or fine	–	–
			Summary	6 months and/or fine (statutory maximum)		
¶9482	para 18(3)(a), Sch A1 IA 1986	**Company**: disposing of property without proper reason/sanction	Indictment	Fine	–	–
			Summary	Fine (statutory maximum)		
¶9482	para 18(3)(b), Sch A1 IA 1986	**Officer**: authorising/permitting such disposal of company property	Indictment	2 years and/or fine	–	–
			Summary	6 months and/or fine (statutory maximum)		
¶9481	para 19(3)(a), Sch A1 IA 1986	**Company**: making payments re. liabilities existing before start of moratorium	Indictment	Fine	–	–
			Summary	Fine (statutory maximum)		
¶9481	para 19(3)(b), Sch A1 IA 1986	**Officer**: authorising/permitting such payment	Indictment	2 years and/or fine	–	–
			Summary	6 months and/or fine (statutory maximum)		
¶9483	para 20(9), Sch A1 IA 1986	**Director**: failing to send court order permitting disposal of secured/hire-purchase property to Companies House	Summary	Fine (1/5th of statutory maximum)	–	–
¶9483	para 22(1), Sch A1 IA 1986	**Company**: disposing of charged/hire-purchase property	Indictment	Fine	–	–
			Summary	Fine (statutory maximum)		
¶9483	para 22(2), Sch A1 IA 1986	**Officer**: authorising/permitting such disposal	Indictment	2 years and/or fine	–	–
			Summary	6 months and/or fine (statutory maximum)		

¶¶	Reference	Persons liable and general nature of offence[1]	Mode of prosecution[2]	Punishment[3]	Daily default fine[4] (where applicable)	Changes proposed by the new Companies Act (where applicable)[5]
¶9483/mp	para 23(1)(a), Sch A1 IA 1986	**Company:** entering into market contract etc	Indictment	Fine	–	–
			Summary	Fine (statutory maximum)		
¶9483/mp	para 23(1)(b), Sch A1 IA 1986	**Officer:** authorising/permitting company to enter into market contract etc	Indictment	2 years and/or fine	–	–
			Summary	6 months and/or fine (statutory maximum)		
¶9472	para 25(6), Sch A1 IA 1986	**Nominee:** failing to give notice of withdrawal of consent to act	Summary	Fine (1/5th of statutory maximum)	–	–
¶9491 ¶9492	para 34(3), Sch A1 IA 1986	**Nominee:** failing to give notice of extension of moratorium prior to CVA to Companies House and court	Summary	Fine (1/5th of statutory maximum)	–	–
¶9487	para 41(2), Sch A1 IA 1986	**Officer:** fraud/privity to fraud in anticipation of moratorium prior to CVA	Indictment	7 years and/or fine	–	–
			Summary	6 months and/or fine (statutory maximum)		
¶9487	para 41(3), Sch A1 IA 1986	**Officer:** fraud/privity to fraud during moratorium prior to CVA	Indictment	7 years and/or fine	–	–
			Summary	6 months and/or fine (statutory maximum)		
¶9487	para 41(7), Sch A1 IA 1986	**Person:** knowingly taking in pawn/pledge or otherwise receiving company property during/prior to moratorium prior to CVA	Indictment	7 years and/or fine	–	–
			Summary	6 months and/or fine (statutory maximum)		
¶9486	para 42(1), Sch A1 IA 1986	**Officer:** false representation/fraud to obtain/extend moratorium prior to CVA	Indictment	7 years and/or fine	–	–
			Summary	6 months and/or fine (statutory maximum)		
¶8782	para 18(7), Sch B1 IA 1986	**Floating charge holder:** making false statement in statutory declaration appointing administrator	Indictment	2 years and/or fine	–	–
			Summary	6 months and/or fine (statutory maximum)		

¶¶	Reference	Persons liable and general nature of offence[1]	Mode of prosecution[2]	Punishment[3]	Daily default fine[4] (where applicable)	Changes proposed by the new Companies Act (where applicable)[5]
¶8784	para 20, Sch B1 IA 1986	**Floating charge holder**: failing to notify administrator or others of commencement of appointment	Indictment Summary	2 years and/or fine 6 months and/or fine (statutory maximum)	1/10th of statutory maximum	–
¶8767	para 27(4), Sch B1 IA 1986	**Deponent**: making false statement in statutory declaration re. notice of intention to appoint administrator by company/board	Indictment Summary	2 years and/or fine 6 months and/or fine (statutory maximum)	–	–
¶8770	para 29(7), Sch B1 IA 1986	**Deponent**: making false statement in statutory declaration re. administrator appointed by company/board	Indictment Summary	2 years and/or fine 6 months and/or fine (statutory maximum)	–	–
¶8771	para 32, Sch B1 IA 1986	**Company/board**: failing to notify administrator of commencement of appointment	Indictment Summary	2 years and/or fine 6 months and/or fine (statutory maximum)	1/10th of statutory maximum	–
¶9021	para 45(2), Sch B1 IA 1986	**Administrator/company/officer**: failing to state in business document that administrator appointed	Summary	Fine (1/5th of statutory maximum)	–	–
¶8797	para 46(9), Sch B1 IA 1986	**Administrator**: failing to give notice of appointment	Summary	Fine (1/5th of statutory maximum)	1/50th of statutory maximum	–
¶8861	para 48(4), Sch B1 IA 1986	**Person involved with company**: failing to make statement of affairs in administration	Indictment Summary	Fine Fine (statutory maximum)	1/10th of statutory maximum	–
¶8883	para 49(7), Sch B1 IA 1986	**Administrator**: failing to send out statement of proposals	Summary	Fine (1/5th of statutory maximum)	1/50th of statutory maximum	–
¶8886	para 51(5), Sch B1 IA 1986	**Administrator**: failing to arrange initial creditors' meeting	Summary	Fine (1/5th of statutory maximum)	1/50th of statutory maximum	–

¶¶	Reference	Persons liable and general nature of offence[1]	Mode of prosecution[2]	Punishment[3]	Daily default fine[4] (where applicable)	Changes proposed by the new Companies Act (where applicable)[5]
¶8890	para 53(3), Sch B1 IA 1986	**Administrator:** failing to report decision at initial creditors' meeting	Summary	Fine (1/5th of statutory maximum)	1/50th of statutory maximum	–
¶8894	para 54(7), Sch B1 IA 1986	**Administrator:** failing to report decision taken at creditors' meeting summoned to consider revised proposal	Summary	Fine (1/5th of statutory maximum)	1/50th of statutory maximum	–
¶9081	para 56(2), Sch B1 IA 1986	**Administrator:** failing to summon creditors' meeting when required	Summary	Fine (1/5th of statutory maximum)	1/50th of statutory maximum	–
¶8911	para 71(6), Sch B1 IA 1986	**Administrator:** failing to file court order allowing disposal of charged property at Companies House	Summary	Fine (1/5th of statutory maximum)	1/50th of statutory maximum	–
¶8912	para 72(5), Sch B1 IA 1986	**Administrator:** failing to file court order allowing disposal of hire-purchase property at Companies House	Summary	Fine (1/5th of statutory maximum)	1/50th of statutory maximum	–
¶9000	para 77(3), Sch B1 IA 1986	**Administrator:** failing to notify Companies House of automatic end of administration	Summary	Fine (1/5th of statutory maximum)	1/50th of statutory maximum	–
¶9000	para 78(6), Sch B1 IA 1986	**Administrator:** failing to give notice of extension by consent of term of office	Summary	Fine (1/5th of statutory maximum)	1/50th of statutory maximum	–
¶9130	para 80(6), Sch B1 IA 1986	**Administrator:** failing to give notice of termination of administration where objective achieved	Summary	Fine (1/5th of statutory maximum)	1/50th of statutory maximum	–
¶9154	para 84(9), Sch B1 IA 1986	**Administrator:** failing to comply with provisions where company must be dissolved	Summary	Fine (1/5th of statutory maximum)	1/50th of statutory maximum	–
¶9166	para 86(3), Sch B1 IA 1986	**Administrator:** failing to notify Companies House where court terminates administration	Summary	Fine (1/5th of statutory maximum)	1/50th of statutory maximum	–

¶¶	Reference	Persons liable and general nature of offence[1]	Mode of prosecution[2]	Punishment[3]	Daily default fine[4] (where applicable)	Changes proposed by the new Companies Act (where applicable)[5]
¶9040	para 89(3), Sch B1 IA 1986	**Administrator:** failing to give notice to appointor on ceasing to be qualified	Summary	Fine (1/5th of statutory maximum)	1/50th of statutory maximum	–
¶3083	s 13 CDDA 1986	**Person:** contravention of disqualification order or undertaking. Undischarged bankrupt acting as director or involved in promotion, formation or management of company.	Indictment Summary	2 years and/or fine 6 months and/or fine (statutory maximum)	–	–
¶291	ss 2, 7 BNA 1985	**Person:** use of restricted business name without approval	Summary	Fine (1/50th of statutory maximum)	1/50th of statutory maximum	–
¶297	ss 4, 7 BNA 1985	**Person:** failure to disclose business name	Summary	Fine (1/50th of statutory maximum)	1/50th of statutory maximum	–
¶9077	r 2.47(6) IR 1986	**Administrator:** failing to report on administration's progress to creditors, court and Companies House	Summary	Fine (1/5th of statutory maximum)	1/50th of statutory maximum	–
¶9168	r 2.111(3) IR 1986	**Administrator:** failing to file notice of automatic end of administration at court	Summary	Fine (1/5th of statutory maximum)	1/50th of statutory maximum	–
¶9035	r 2.129(2) IR 1986	**Administrator:** failing to hand over records etc to replacement	Summary	Fine (1/5th of statutory maximum)	1/50th of statutory maximum	–
¶9367	r 3.32(5) IR 1986	**Administrative receiver:** failing to file accounts of receipts and payments at Companies House	Summary	Fine (1/5th of statutory maximum)	1/50th of statutory maximum	–
see appropriate topic	r 12.18 IR 1986	**Person:** pretending to be entitled to inspect any document during liquidation, when inspection limited to creditors, shareholders and/or contributories	Indictment Summary	2 years and/or a fine 6 months and/or a fine (statutory maximum)	–	–

Note:
1. Many of these offences may be committed by the company and/or an "**officer in default**". An officer is in default if he:
– knowingly and wilfully authorises or permits the relevant breach in the case of an offence under CA 1985; para 13 Sch 4 SI 2007/2194); or
– authorises, permits, participates in, or fails to take all reasonable steps to prevent, the breach in question in the case of an offence under CA 2006 where the provision setting out the duty and consequences of breach is already in force (s 1121 CA 2006). A corporate director will only commit an offence in respect of the company as an officer in default if one of its own officers is in default (s 1122 CA 2006). If this is the case, both the company and its officer will be liable.

2. Criminal offences are classified as: summary, indictable or triable either way. **Summary offences** are less serious and can only be tried in the magistrates' court, where a relatively low fine or short term of imprisonment can be imposed on conviction. **Indictable offences** are more serious and can only be tried by the Crown Court, where a jury will determine the case and the judge can impose heavier penalties on conviction. None of the offences above is only triable on indictment, although many are **triable either way**. These cases can be tried at the magistrates' or the Crown Court, depending on a number of factors including the seriousness and the wishes of the defendant (e.g. defendants are sometimes advised that they have a better chance of being acquitted by a jury, and so it is worth opting for a Crown Court trial even if the potential penalties are harsher). A mode of trial hearing at the magistrates' court determines how the case will be heard, after which either the magistrates will deal with the matter or it will be committed to the Crown Court for trial.
Summary proceedings for any offence may be taken against a company at any place at which it has a place of business, and against any other person at any place at which he is for the time being. An offence may only be tried by a magistrates' court in England and Wales if it is laid within 3 years of the commission of the offence, and within 12 months of sufficient evidence to justify the offence, in their opinion, coming before the DPP or secretary of state (s 731 CA 1985; restated at s 1128 CA 2006).

3. This column shows the **maximum punishment** which may be imposed on conviction, whether on indictment or summarily. References to a period of years or months is to a term of imprisonment of that duration (s 730(3) CA 1985). The **standard scale** for fines imposed on summary conviction of an offence is set at the following levels (ss 32, 143 Magistrates' Courts Act 1982, s 17 Criminal Justice Act 1991):
Level 1: £200
Level 2: £500
Level 3: £1,000
Level 4: £2,500
Level 5: £5,000 (**statutory maximum**)

4. The daily default fine, where applicable, is the penalty payable for a **second or subsequent summary conviction** of the offence for each day on which the contravention continued (instead of the penalty specified in the fifth column of the Appendix for that additional offence) (s 730(4) CA 1985). The **new Companies Act** will slightly alter the definition so that the daily default fine is the maximum, rather than prescribed, daily penalty (s 1125 CA 2006).

5. The proposed changes will not operate retrospectively, i.e. offences committed before the changes come into effect will be subject to the current/old penalties. Extensions to the maximum imprisonment on summary conviction from 6 months to 12 months will only take effect upon commencement of s 154(1) Criminal Justice Act 2003, which extends the powers of magistrates' courts in England and Wales to impose sentences of imprisonment on summary conviction (s 1131 CA 2006). At the time of writing, the implementation date is yet to be announced.

6. Person in default also liable for loss suffered by director/manager accepting appointment as a result of failure to give notice of unlimited liability.

7. Officer also liable to pay under that cheque/other document.

8. This section of the new Companies Act only came into force on 1 October 2007 but it applies to offences committed before that date as well (para 46 Sch 3 SI 2007/2194). If the offence occurred before 15 January 2007, the maximum term of imprisonment is still 7 years.

Glossary

General terms

9940

Word or phrase	Meaning
Action	A legal right that can be pursued in a civil court
Agent	A person appointed by another (a principal) to act on his behalf, e.g. to negotiate a contract. A company must act through agents (mainly the directors).
Assignee	The person to whom a legal right is transferred under an assignment
Assignment	The transfer of a legal right from one person to another, e.g. the right to recover a debt; the benefit of shares
Assignor	The person who transfers a legal right to another under an assignment
Attachment of earnings order	An order of the court for the recovery of a sum due under a judgment, i.e. a judgment debt, directly from the debtor's earnings (usually in instalments). This was previously known as a "garnishee order".
Beneficial owner	See "Equitable owner"
Beneficiary	A person who is entitled to benefit from and enforce a trust. Also a person who benefits from a will.
Bill of exchange	The most common example is a cheque. It is written and signed by an account holder, the "drawer". It is an order to a bank, the "drawee", requiring the bank to pay a specified sum of money to a named person, the "payee" (alternatively, it could be made out to the "bearer" of the cheque, i.e. whoever presents it for payment). Cheques today are normally non-transferable, i.e. the original payee cannot sign it over to another person who can then present it for payment, as the words "account payee" are printed on cheques. However, other types of bill of exchange would usually be transferable. The bill may also be "negotiable", i.e. early payment of a post-dated bill can be obtained by accepting a lower payment.
Bill of sale	A document transferring legal ownership of goods from one person to another. If conditional as security for a debt, it constitutes a mortgage over the goods. If absolute, full ownership is transferred.
Body corporate	A company. The term includes companies incorporated within and outside of Great Britain, but not corporations sole or partnerships that are not regarded as bodies corporate by their governing legislation (s 740 CA 1985 or s 1173 CA 2006). A body corporate is a legal person.
Bona fide	Good faith
Bona vacantia	Unowned property. It includes property still owned by a company when it is dissolved and in other situations in which it ceases to be owned, e.g. when it has been disclaimed by a liquidator. It passes to the Crown, Duchy of Lancaster or Duke of Cornwall.
Charging order	An order awarded by the court securing a judgment debtor's property against payment of the judgment debt and interest
Chattel	An item of personal property. It includes any property other than freehold or leasehold land.
Chose in action	A right that can be enforced by legal action, e.g. the right to recover a debt
Claimant	A person who brings a civil claim in court

Word or phrase	Meaning
Clear days	A period of time worked out without counting the day on which the thing in question started and finished. For example, if 14 clear days' notice needs to be given of a meeting, the days on which the notice is given and the meeting is held are not counted towards the period.
Condition precedent	A condition in a contract which must be met before the contract can come into effect
Consideration	The price paid to a person in return for them agreeing to be subject to an obligation in a contract. The price is usually in the form of money, although it could be in another form.
Constructive notice	A legal device by which a person is deemed to know something, even though he does not actually know it, because the circumstances are such that he should have known it (e.g. when information was available on a public register)
Constructive trustee	A legal device by which a person is deemed to be a trustee, even though he was not explicitly made one, because the circumstances are such that he should be in that position (e.g. when he receives goods which he is required to pay for but does not)
Conversion	A tort in which a person treats someone else's property as their own
Corporation	A company. The term includes companies incorporated within and outside of Great Britain, but not corporations sole or Scottish firms (s 740 CA 1985 or s 1173 CA 2006). A corporation is a legal person.
Corporation sole	A legal entity, usually church-related or a political office. It is a company that only ever consists of one member at a time. That member holds a particular office and any property held by the corporation sole passes on to his successor to the office if the member dies, retires or resigns. Examples include the Public Trustee, the Secretary of State for Employment and the Archbishop of Canterbury.
Covenant	A promise in a contract to do or not to do something
Damages	Financial compensation which the court orders should be paid to the successful party in litigation
Deed	A special type of written contract which is signed and witnessed in accordance with particular rules. Unlike normal contracts, it is binding even if there is no consideration. The limitation period within which any civil action must be brought relating to it is 12 years (for normal contracts, the limitation period is 6 years).
Defamation	Making public untrue written or oral statements about a person which harm his character. Such a written or broadcast statement is known as libel; an oral statement is called slander.
Defendant	The person against whom a civil or criminal claim is brought in court
Derivative action	Legal proceedings that should be in the company's name because the company has suffered the wrong, but are commenced in a shareholder's name instead because the company will not do so. A common example is where the company has suffered as a result of a director's breach of duty but will not or cannot take action against the director (e.g. because he controls decision making). This area has recently been reformed (see ¶7127+).
De facto	"In fact". The term means something which does not have lawful authority, but still exists in reality. For example, a de facto director is one who has not been appointed properly (or who has officially left office) but who still acts as and claims to be a director of the company.
De jure	"By law". The term means something that has lawful authority. For example, a de jure director is one who has been validly appointed to the office.
Distress	The seizure of goods as security for the performance of an obligation, e.g. a landlord distraining a tenant's goods to the value of rent arrears

Word or phrase	Meaning
Equitable owner	A person who has an interest in property, but that interest does not include legal title to the property. Equitable ownership arises when the legal and equitable (or, beneficial) titles to property become separated. An example is where property is held on trust, in which case the legal title is held by the trustee and the equitable title by the beneficiary.
Equity	1. The legal concept of fairness. 2. Shares with voting and dividend rights.
Escrow	When a contract is signed but kept pending before coming into effect. In effect, it is in "cold storage".
Estoppel	A rule of evidence or law which prevents (or "estops") a person from relying on facts he alleges to exist or a statement he has made. In contract law, the equitable rule of promissory estoppel applies where A promises B that he will not enforce his rights under the contract, preventing him from doing so in future if B has relied on that promise.
Execute	Signing a contract and having it come into effect
Ex parte	Legal proceedings of which one party has not received notice and so is not present or represented at the hearing, now referred to as "without notice" proceedings. For example, applications for interim injunctions sometimes have to be made "ex parte" because the conduct complained of causes continuing damage to the claimant and needs to be stopped urgently. In case citations, the phrase is sometimes used to indicate that proceedings were taken on someone's behalf, e.g. *Re X Ltd, ex parte Smith*.
Fiduciary	A person in a position of trust and confidence with respect to another person, who must therefore act in that person's interest, e.g. a trustee. For a director's position as fiduciary to the company, see ¶2373+.
First instance	Refers to the first full hearing of a case, usually in the county court or High Court. Used to distinguish between the judgments at this level and those on appeal.
Forfeiture	The loss of property or a right due to breach of an undertaking or an offence. For example, leases often allow the landlord to terminate (or "forfeit") the lease for breach of covenant.
Fraud	Intentional deception, usually resulting in the victim suffering financial damage. Fraud can be both a civil (tortious) and a criminal offence.
Freehold	Land or buildings which are not owned by anyone else
Gazette	The official publication in which statutory notices on various matters, including parliament, planning and public finance as well as company and insolvency matters, are advertised. In the case of companies registered in England and Wales, the appropriate publication is the *London Gazette*; there are also *Edinburgh* and *Belfast Gazettes* for companies registered in Scotland and Northern Ireland, respectively.
Indemnity	In a contract, a promise by one party to pay all of the costs and expenses of another which are incurred as a result of a particular event
Injunction	An order by a court that a person does or does not do something, or stops doing something
Interest	1. A legal right to or over something. 2. When money is borrowed, the extra amount (calculated as a percentage of the original loan) which must be repaid to the lender.
Intra vires	A decision or action which is within the limits of the powers conferred on a company
Judgment creditor	A person who has won a court action and to whom the court has ordered money should be paid
Judgment debtor	A person who has lost a court action and who the court has ordered to pay money to the judgment creditor
Leasehold	Land or buildings which are owned under a lease, with the landlord owning the freehold

Word or phrase	Meaning
Legal person	Includes both a natural person (i.e. a human being) and entities recognised as having a legal personality because they are subject to and benefit from legal rights and duties (known as "juristic persons"). A company is such an entity.
Lessee	The person to whom a lease is granted
Lessor	The person by whom a lease is granted, also known as the landlord if he owns the freehold
Limitation period	The period of time within which a civil action can be brought (principally set out in the Limitation Act 1980)
Liquidated sum	A definite amount of money
Listed company	Any company the shares of which are listed on the official list of the London Stock Exchange or dealt with on a regulated market. Often used as synonym for quoted company.
Litigation	The process of taking legal action through the courts
Minor	Someone who is not able to enter into a contract, or other legal arrangement, because of his age. In the UK, the age of legal capacity is 18 years.
Mortgagee	A person in whose favour a mortgage is granted, e.g. a bank
Mortgagor	A person who gives a mortgage over his property to someone else, i.e. a borrower
New Companies Act	The Companies Act 2006 (CA 2006) is in the process of reforming company law by replacing the vast majority of CA 1985. Although it received Royal Assent (i.e. approval of the final text) on 8 November 2006, it is coming into force in phases. Many provisions are already in force, and so references in the text are given to these provisions as current law. There are two principal implementation phases remaining: one on 6 April 2008 and the last one is likely to be by 1 October 2009. Provisions coming into force on 6 April 2008 are highlighted in comments, and those likely to come into force by 1 October 2009 are dealt with in memo points. The updates and newsletters will keep readers informed of the implementation phases after publication.
New model articles	Companies' articles of association will need to be changed to reflect the new Companies Act once it is fully in force. The Government has published draft new model articles for private companies limited by shares, private companies limited by guarantee and public companies in the draft Companies (Model Articles) Regulations 2007. Since the text of the new model articles has not yet been finalised, the references given in this work are to these drafts. This work focuses on companies limited by shares, so only references to the draft new model articles for private companies limited by shares and public companies are given. The new model articles will work much like Table A does now, forming the default articles of association of companies incorporated under CA 2006 on or after 1 October 2009. Companies incorporated before this date can adopt the new model articles if they wish, and if they do not do so they will at least need to review their existing articles and consider making appropriate changes to reflect the new law. Table A has been amended to reflect some of the changes brought into force on 1 October 2007. Different changes have been made for private companies and public companies. The amended Table A applies to companies incorporated on or after 1 October 2007. The version of Table A reproduced at ¶9915 incorporates the amendments, with the former wording set out in the notes. Further transitional amendments may also be made as of 6 April 2008, in which case they will be addressed in the updates.
Novation	A contract entered into to replace an existing contract. It may be between the same parties, or introduce new or substitute existing parties. For example, it is used instead of an assignment where the benefit and the burden of the contract need to be transferred to another party (since only a benefit can be transferred by way of assignment).

Word or phrase	Meaning
Obiter (dictum)	A comment made during a judgment, which is not essential to the decision of the case. It therefore does not create a binding precedent on cases which follow, but it may be cited as being persuasive guidance.
Officer	Includes a director, secretary and manager of a body corporate (s 744 CA 1985 or s 1173 CA 2006)
Officer in default	Companies legislation imposes liability for statutory breaches on companies and any of their officers in default. However, the definition of an "officer in default" depends upon whether the offence in question is set out in CA 1985 or the provisions of CA 2006 which are in force: – for offences under CA 1985, an officer is in default if he knowingly and wilfully authorises or permits the relevant breach (s 730A CA 1985; para 13 Sch 4 SI 2007/2194); and – for offences under CA 2006, an officer is in default if he authorises, permits, participates in or fails to take all reasonable steps to prevent the relevant breach (s 1121 CA 2006). A corporate officer is only in default if one of its own individual officers is also in default (s 1122 CA 2006), in which case both the company and its officers will be liable.
Pari passu	"In equal amounts". Usually used to refer to the distribution of something (e.g. dividends) to a group (e.g. creditors or shareholders) equally and without preference between them.
Per curiam	A comment made by the court as a whole, rather than one judge in particular. It is usually on a point of general principle, not necessarily to the point of the case in question.
Power of attorney	The law in this area has recently changed. Briefly, there are now four types of power of attorney: – ordinary: by which a person gives his attorney the power to deal with specific or general matters for a period of time. These are the most relevant to business situations, for example a director could appoint an attorney to sit on the board in his place, make decisions and sign documents on his behalf if he knew that he was going to be absent for a number of months. Alternatively, he could appoint an alternate director (see ¶3438+); – trustee: similar to an ordinary power of attorney but specifically used for trusts; – enduring: by which a person appoints another to look after his financial and legal affairs in the event that he cannot do so himself because of mental incapacity. It has not been possible to grant an enduring power of attorney since 1 October 2007; and – lasting: the new version of an enduring power of attorney. There are two types: one dealing with personal welfare (e.g. decisions relating to medical treatment) and one dealing with property and affairs.
Principal	The person on behalf of whom an agent acts
Pro rata	In proportion
Proceeding	A court action
Promissory note	An unconditional written and signed promise by A to B to pay a sum of money to B (or another person specified by B) on demand or at a fixed time. It is negotiable (i.e. it can be transferred simply by handing it over to another party, who is then entitled to enforce it in his own name).
Proxy	A person who is entitled to stand in the place of his appointor, for example to attend and vote at a meeting on behalf of a shareholder
Quorum	The minimum number of people required for a meeting to proceed validly
Quoted company	A company whose equity share capital is included in the official list of the London Stock Exchange, an EEA State, or is admitted to dealing on either the New York Stock Exchange or Nasdaq. Often used as a synonym for listed company.
Remedy	The possible penalties if a person successfully brings a civil court claim against another (e.g. damages)

Word or phrase	Meaning
Rentcharge	A sum regarding land due to a person who is not the owner and has no legal interest in it. Most rentcharges will cease on 21 July 2037, or 60 years after they first became payable (s 3 Rentcharges Act 1977).
Repeal	To revoke a legislative provision expressly in legislation
Restate	To state a legislative provision again, or to word it in a new way, in new legislation
Restrictive covenant	A promise in a contract not to compete with a company's business or interfere with its customers, employees or suppliers
Retention of title	A term in a contract for the sale of goods which stipulates that legal ownership of the goods will not pass to the buyer until the goods have been paid for in full (or until the buyer has discharged all of his liabilities to the seller). This, together with related contractual provisions, allows the seller to recover the goods if the buyer has possession of them and then does not pay. Also known as "reservation of title".
Specific performance	An order of the court that a person carries out the terms of a contract. This is a rare remedy, reserved for cases in which damages would not suffice, e.g. to compel a person who has agreed to sell land to transfer it.
Statute barred	A claim is said to be "Statute barred" if its limitation period has expired
Statutory books	The records and registers that a company is required to keep by law, including its minutes of meetings
Subscriber	A person who agrees to take shares in a company on its formation by signing the memorandum
Third party debt order	An order of the court enabling a judgment creditor to obtain payment of a judgment debt directly from a person who owes money to the judgment debtor. It is most commonly used to order a bank to pay money held in the debtor's bank account to the creditor.
Time barred	See "Statute barred"
Tort	A wrong which causes harm to a person that is legally recognised as entitling the wronged party to bring a civil claim against the person who has wronged him (e.g. negligence, defamation, negligent misrepresentation, deceit)
Transferee	A person to whom something is transferred
Transferor	A person who transfers something
Trespass	Unauthorised temporary use or possession of someone else's property
Trust	An arrangement by which a settlor transfers property to a trustee who keeps and deals with it in accordance with the terms of the trust for the benefit of one or more persons entitled to enforce the trust (beneficiaries)
Trustee	The person to whom property is transferred under a trust, who must keep and deal with that property in accordance with the terms of the trust for the benefit of one or more beneficiaries. He owes fiduciary duties to the beneficiaries, and is answerable to the court. He has legal ownership but is not the equitable owner (this is the beneficiary). Trusts can impose varying degrees of specific duties on a trustee, e.g. a bare or simple trustee only has to hand over the trust property to the beneficiary when he requires. See also Constructive trustee.
Ultra vires	A decision or action which is beyond the limits of the powers conferred on a company. In most cases, only relevant now to actions by shareholders.
Unliquidated sum	An unspecified amount of money
Void	Invalid
Voidable	Able to be invalidated
Warranty	A statement of fact in a sale and purchase contract by a seller to a buyer about the property being sold as at the time of sale. If the warranty turns out to be untrue, the buyer is entitled to damages.

Insolvency terms

Word or phrase	Meaning
Affidavit	A sworn written statement used to support certain applications to court, or as evidence. In general court procedure, affidavits have been largely replaced by witness statements, although they are still used for certain insolvency and company applications and to verify documents such as the statement of affairs. Affidavits are likely to be phased out by October 2008, see ¶7388.
Debt	In relation to a company's liquidation or administration (r 13.12 IR 1986): – any debt or liability to which the company is subject when it goes into liquidation or administration; – any debt or liability to which the company may become subject after it enters liquidation or administration due to an obligation incurred before that date; and – any provable interest. The debt or liability can be present or future, certain or contingent, fixed or liquidated, capable of being fixed in accordance with rules or opinion. Liability includes one to pay money or money's worth, whether under statute, for breach of trust, contract, tort, bailment or an obligation to make restitution.
Disclaimer	The refusal or renunciation of a right, a claim or property. A liquidator can disclaim certain "onerous property".
Moratorium	A temporary prohibition or suspension of legal action against a company
Property	Includes (s 436 IA 1986): a. money; b. goods; c. things in action; d. land; e. every description of property wherever situated; and f. all obligations and interests arising out of or incidental to property, whether: – present or future; or – vested or contingent
Security	Any mortgage, charge, lien or other security (s 248 IA 1986)
Trustee in bankruptcy	The insolvency practitioner in whom a bankrupt's property is vested for the benefit of the bankrupt's creditors when the bankruptcy order is made. He must collect and sell the assets and distribute them amongst the creditors, much like a liquidator.

9941

The numbers refer to paragraphs and the plus sign (+) indicates that the entry covers a number of paragraphs.

A

Abbreviation:
Company name: 47, 242+

Abstract:
Of receipts and payments
 Administration: 9076
 Receivership: 9405
 Administrative receivership: 9406
 CVA: 9536, 9546+
Of title: 5679

Abuse of process:
Directors' disqualification proceedings: 3060
Liquidation:
 Obtaining information: 8173
 Rejection of proof: 8036
 Restraining winding up petition: 7641
 Striking out winding up petition: 7661, 7705+

Accommodation: See Benefits (Director's, Non-cash)

Account for profits:
Duty to:
 Director's: 2398+
 Liquidator's: 8225
 Liquidation committee member's: 8299
 Administrator's: 9013
 Receiver's: 9361
Remedy:
 For breach of duty: 2471+
 For passing off/trade mark infringement: 310
 When director contracts with company: 2562
 For breach of service contact: 2678

Account of receipts and payments:
Receivership: 9367+

Account of the liquidation:
CVL: 8576, 8577
MVL: 8663+

Accountant:
Appointment: 580
Acting as share valuer: 1855
Report on accounts: 4270, 4290+
Shadow director: 2212
Liquidation:
 Fee: 8017
 Lien: 8017
Administration:
 Fee: 8951
 Lien: 8909
See also Adviser

Accounting policy:
Acquisition: 6902
Merger: 6901
Consistency: 4231

Accounting records: 4195+
Failure to keep: 4195, 4326

Accounting reference period: 4218
Change: 4220+
End of: 4275

Accounting standard:
Distributable profits: 1615

Accounts:
Main entry: 4185+
Laying before shareholders:
 Notice of meeting: 3670

Accounts (continued)
For purposes of distribution:
  Main entry: 1620+
  Initial and interim: 1630+
  Management: 1632
  Fraudulent: 1758
  Improperly prepared: 1744
Own share purchase/redemption:
  Disclosure of redeemable shares: 772
  Capital payment: 1402
  Directors' report: 1367
Sale of company:
  Completion accounts: 5482+
  Disclosure of target's: 5901
  Investigation of target: 5673
Other business vehicle:
  Community Interest Company: 66
  European Economic Interest Grouping: 116
  Joint venture company: 6618, 6655+
  Limited liability partnership: 79, 81
  Overseas company: 172+
Compulsory liquidation:
  Liquidator to keep: 8232
  Official receiver's power to request: 8138+
CVL:
  Liquidator's power to request: 8138
  Deadline for: 8139
Disclosure of directors':
  Remuneration: 2778+
  Loans: 2897
Doctrine of capital maintenance: 727
See also Group (Accounts)

Accruals:
Basis of accounting: 4233

Acknowledgement of service:
Disqualification proceedings: 3052
Part 8 claim form: 7153
Non-Part 8 application: 7165

Acquisition: See Sale of company

Acting in concert:
Definition: 6765+

Actual authority: See Authority (Types)

Address:
Registered office: 482, 570
Electronic: 3628, 3697
See also Residential address

Adjournment of meeting:
Board: 3281
Shareholder: 3760+
  Poll vote: 3849

Adjournment of meeting (continued)
Compulsory liquidation:
  Meetings: 8340, 8347, 8351
  Creditors removing liquidator: 8257
Voluntary liquidation:
  First shareholders' meeting: 8465
CVL: 8453, 8557
Administration:
  Creditors': 8889, 9084
CVA: 9502+

Adjudication:
Transfer instrument:
  Stamp duty: 1877

Administration:
Main entry: 8690+
Prodecure flowchart: 8694
Summary: 7338
Accounting reference period: 4220
Before liquidation:
  Debt in foreign currency: 8020
  Expenses: 7959
  Rent: 8013
Before winding up petition: 7636
Converted to liquidation: 9141, 9142+, 9144
After liquidation:
  Debt in foreign currency: 8020
  Interest: 8952
  Rent: 8013
Appointment of receiver during: 9231
Pre-CVA moratorium: 9476
CVA:
  Effect of CVA on: 9534
  Proposed during: 9450
  Submission of proposals during: 9457

Administration application: 8721+

Administration order: 8750+

Administrative receiver:
Definition: 9237+
Appointment: 9244+
  Defect: 9348
  Crystallisation of floating charge: 4613
  Restrictions during pre-CVA moratorium: 9476
Misfeasance: 7457+, 9392
Powers: 9345+
Company's assets:
  Possession of: 9305, 9377
  Secured: 9349
Sale of company by: 5283
Employees: 9267
Private examination: 9377
Statement of affairs/concurrence: 8861+

Administrative receiver *(continued)*
Creditors' committee: 9060+
Report to creditors: 9378+
Administration:
 Appointment of administrator: 8765, 8766
 Administration application: 8742, 8743, 8746

Administrative receivership:
Conduct of: 9376+
Procedure flowchart: 9198
Summary: 7340
Company in administration: 8723, 8778, 8814+

Administrator:
Main entry: 8995+
Administration application hearing: 8746
Appointment: 8710+
 Crystallisation of floating charge: 4613
 Additional administrator: 9002
Consent to act: 8736, 8770, 8783
Officer of court: 8906
Transaction defrauding creditors: 7829
Reporting directors' conduct: 8856
Misfeasance: 7457+
Tort: 8821
Contracts: 8827+
Proposals: 8876+
Managing company: 8845+
Powers:
 Summary table: 9011
Directions from court: 8876
Statement of affairs/concurrence: 8861+
Private examination: 8855
Public examination: 8147
Company's assets: 8904+
 Require delivery of from individual: 8855
 Secured: 8909+
Sale of company by: 5283
Security:
 Realisation: 8943
 Re-valuation: 8940
 Secured creditors: 8936+
 Unregistered: 4658+
Creditors:
 Reporting to/consulting: 9076+
 Distributing to unsecured: 8967
Proof of debt:
 Application to reduce/expunge: 8959
 Consideration of: 8957+, 8970+
Dividend refused: 8974
Creditors' committee: 9061
Creditors' meeting:
 First: 8885+
 Subsequent: 9080+

Administrator *(continued)*
Shareholders' meeting: 9102
End administration: 9164+
Dissolution: 9154
Presenting winding up petition: 9141
Pre-CVA moratorium: 9485
CVA:
 Proposal: 9450, 9453, 9459, 9461, 9500
 Company's assets: 9532
See also Joint administrators

Advance corporation tax: 1795

Adviser:
Reliance upon:
 To pay dividend: 1758+
 To manage company: 2414
 To whitewash financial assistance: 5605
Liability:
 For unlawful financial assistance: 5557
 As shadow director: 2212
 For fraudulent trading: 7444
For compromise agreement: 5970
In takeover:
 Acting in concert with client: 6765+
 Associated with client: 6770+
 Responsibilities: 6776, 6778, 6794, 6816
 Confirmation of bidder's finances: 6807, 6817
 Dealings in shares: 6856
 Information provided by: 6876
 Telephone campaigns by: 6891

Affidavit:
Meaning: 9941
To support:
 Stop notice: 1951
 Director's disqualification: 3050, 3052
Insolvency generally: 7388
Liquidation:
 Public examination: 8154
 Appointment of provisional liquidator: 7688
Compulsory liquidation:
 Verify non-contributory winding up petition: 7637+
 Verify accounts: 8138
 Verify proof: 8033
 Verify statement of affairs: 8129
 Affidavit of concurrence: 8127+
Voluntary liquidation:
 Proof of debt: 8492
CVL:
 Statement of affairs: 8440
Administration:
 Proof of debt: 8955
 Application: 8737+, 8745
Administrative receivership:
 Statement of affairs: 8863
See also Witness statement

Agent:
Meaning: 9940
Authority of: 2350+
For company:
  Director: 2185, 2333+
  Secretary: 4131+
  Formation: 350
  Sales and marketing: 638+
  Insolvency practitioner: 7429
  Liquidator: 8218, 8224+
  Administrator: 9013
  Receiver: 9361+, 9392
For lender:
  Sale of secured asset: 4664
For partnership: 17
For limited liability partnership: 79
Formation of company: 546
Sale of company:
  Use of to search for target: 5261
  Use of to sell business: 5225
Searching Companies House: 4090
Liquidation:
  Effect of liquidation on: 7755, 8474
  Effect of appointment of provisional liquidator on: 7690

AGM: See Annual general meeting

Aircraft:
Mortgage or charge over: 4638, 4653

Allotment: 889+
See also Issue of shares

Allotted share capital: 714

Alternate director:
Main entry: 3438+
Categories of director: 2208
Board meeting:
  Notice of: 3238
  Directors' interests and quorum: 3353
  Directors' interests and voting: 3351
Written resolutions: 3293
Contract with company: 2559+
Financial assistance:
  Statutory declaration: 5601

Amalgamation:
Scheme of arrangement for: 6530+
  Dissolution by court: 7525
Transfer of share in:
  Stamp duty: 1877

Announcement:
Takeover of public company: 6780+

Annual CIC report: 64+

Annual general meeting:
Main entry: 3777+
Directors' retirement by rotation: 2927+
Dividend declaration: 1663, 1665
Laying of accounts: 4273+
During CVL: 8556
See also General meeting, Shareholder meeting

Annual meeting:
CVL: 8556
MVL: 8646

Annual report: See Directors' report

Annual return: 4060+
Shuttle: 4067+

Anti-competitive: See Competition law

Anti-trust: See Competition law

Apparent authority: See Authority (Types)

Appeal:
Against:
  Decision of company names adjudicator: 278
  Reduction of share capital: 1490
  Scheme of arrangement: 6522
  Decision of Panel Executive: 6715
  Decision of Hearings Committee: 6719
Insolvency generally: 7393+
Liquidation:
  Against winding up order: 7734
  Against liquidator's remuneration: 8243
  Against liquidator's decision on proof: 8040, 8057, 8356
Compulsory liquidation:
  Against dissolution: 8396, 8398
Administration:
  Against decision on entitlement to vote: 9088
  Against decision on proof: 8960

Application for registration: 524+

Application to court:
Main entry: 7139+
Not under CA 1985: 7164+
Under CA 1985: 7143+
  Cancel variation of class rights: 1297+
  Objection to auditor's statement: 4340
  Extension of time to register security: 4639
  Correct mistake at Companies House: 4642
  Objection to whitewash of financial assistance: 5617
  Approve scheme of arrangement: 6508+
Insolvency matters: 7380+
  Repay unlawful dividend: 1746

Application to court *(continued)*
Disqualification order: 3042+
Officers' indemnity for: 2513

Appointment:
Director:
  Main entry: 2266+
  Directors' interests: 3354
  Fixed term: 2640
  Joint venture company: 6579
  By shareholders: 3166+
  Unlimited company: 2278
Alternate director: 3438+
Secretary: 4151+
Chairman:
  Of board: 3274
  Of shareholder meeting: 3719
Auditor: 4336+
  Special notice of resolution: 3536+
Banker: 580
Agent: 638+
CIB inspectors: 7221
CIB investigators: 7208
Distributor: 640
Liquidator:
  Compulsory liquidation: 8200+, 8359
  Voluntary liquidation: 8508+
  At shareholders' meeting to enter into CVL: 8359, 8445
  At creditors' meeting to enter into CVL: 8359, 8453+
  At creditors' meeting to convert MVL to CVL: 8649
  MVL: 8615
Official receiver acting as liquidator: 8201
Provisional liquidator: 7687+
Special manager: 8375+
Administrator:
  Main entry: 8998+
  Administrative requirements: 8797+
  By court: 8721+
  Out of court: 8762+
  Out of court and costs: 8927
Receiver: 9222+
Administrative receiver: 9222+
Supervisor: 9545

Apportionment:
Shares:
  Calls on: 1209
  Dividends on: 1676
  Rights issue: 1042+
  Bonus issue: 1033
Share capital:
  Sub-division: 1317
  Loss of: 1439, 1453

Apportionment *(continued)*
Sale of company:
  Consideration: 5314+
  Debtors and creditors: 5766+
  Income and receipts: 5753

Arbitrator:
Pre-emption offer: 1855

Arrangement:
Loans to directors: 2814
See also Scheme of arrangement

Articles:
Main entry: 435+
Table A 1985: 9915
Effect of: 372+
Changes to: 450+
  If sole director: 3463
Relationship with:
  Memorandum: 373
  Shareholders' agreement: 2083
  Director's service contract: 2636
Power:
  Distribution: 1639
  Dividend: 1674
  Financial assistance: 5581
  Calls: 1207+
  Forfeiture: 1219+
  Management: 3157+
  Consolidate/sub-divide share capital: 1317
  Own share purchase: 1385
  Commission on share subscription: 1238
  Redemption: 1374
  Reduce share capital: 1472
  Capitalise profits/reserves: 1027
Shareholders:
  Rights and remedies: 2067+
  Relationship with company governed by: 2082+
  Written resolution: 3586+
  Entitlement to copy: 374
Transfer of shares:
  In breach of: 1888
  Restriction on: 1836+
  Discretion to refuse registration: 1891+
Lien over shares: 1227+
Class rights:
  Variation procedure: 1288
  Variations specified: 1280
Pre-emption rights:
  Alternative: 942
  Statutory: 960+
  Waiver: 973
Joint venture company:
  Main entry: 6630+
  Relationship with shareholders' agreement: 6607+
Community Interest Company: 71

Articles (continued)
Liquidation:
 Effect on: 7872, 7749, 8471
Draft new model articles: 9940

Asset lock:
Community Interest Company: 65+

Assignee/assignor:
Meaning: 9940
Proof of debt:
 Liquidation: 8018
 Administration: 8951

Assignment:
Meaning: 9940
Contract for sale of assets: 5758+
Mortgage: 4590
Director's office: 3450

Assistant secretary: 4154

Associate:
Definition:
 Associate of auditor: 4308
 Takeover offer: 6770+, 6938
 Liquidation: 7895
See also Connected person

Associated company:
Generally, See Connected company
Loans to directors: 2805, 2832

Association:
Unincorporated: 24
Run as company limited by guarantee: 52

Attorney general:
Compulsory liquidation: 7628

Auction:
Of business: 5235+

Audit:
Main entry: 4290+
Directors' report: 4251
Public company:
 Initial accounts: 1634
 Valuation report on allotment: 1158+

Auditor:
Rights and duties:
 Main entry: 4295+
 Inspection of board meeting minutes: 3474
 Copy of shareholder written resolution: 3583
Liability:
 Main entry: 4301+
 Limitation: 4318
 Statutory relief: 2505+

Auditor (continued)
Opinion: 4325+
Remuneration: 4305+
Provision of non-audit services: 4305+
Shareholder meeting:
 Attendance: 3724, 4339+
 Notice: 3692+, 4299
 Requisition: 3632+
Management of company:
 Role: 3186
 Ability to be director: 2244
 Ability to be secretary: 4120
Pre-emption offer:
 Valuation: 1852+
CVA:
 Receive progress report: 9546+
See also Appointment, Termination, Auditor's report, Audit

Auditor's report:
Main entry: 4312+
Administrative requirements:
 Delivery to shareholders: 4265+
 Laying before shareholders: 4273+
 Publication: 4269+
 Filing: 4278+
Special:
 Small company: 4371
 Medium-sized company: 4377
Financial assistance:
 Veracity of directors' statutory declaration: 5609+
 Net asset position: 5597
Own share purchase/redemption:
 Out of capital: 1409+

Authorised share capital:
Meaning: 712
Alteration: 900+

Authority:
Types:
 Flowchart: 2365
 Actual express: 2352
 Actual implied: 2354+
 Ostensible: 2361+
Of director:
 Main entry: 2348+
 Limited in memorandum: 2554+
 Remedy for acting outside authority: 2438+
Of board: 3137+
Of board committee: 3415+
Of secretary: 4131+
To commence litigation: 7124+
Liquidation:
 Of liquidator: 8200
 Liquidator acting without: 8218

B

Balance sheet:
Main entry: 4236+
Statutory accounts: 4209
Consolidated: 4394+
Events since balance sheet date:
    Directors' report: 4252
    Distribution: 1641
Commission payment on share subscription: 1238
Premium on allotment: 1250
Small company: 4366
Dormant company: 4412

Balance sheet test:
Insolvency: 7601
See also Cash-flow test

Bank facility agreement: See Loan agreement

Bank guarantee:
Reduction of share capital: 1459

Bank records:
Use of in disqualification proceedings: 3053
Disclosure during:
    CIB inspection: 7223
    CIB investigation: 7210

Banker:
Appointment: 580

Bankrupt:
Shareholder:
    Ability to be: 2020+
    Voting: 3816
    Pre-emption provisions: 1845
    Transmission of shares: 1976+
    Liability as contributory: 7863+
    Ability to petition for compulsory liquidation: 7620
Director: 2245
Disqualification: 3012
    Leave to act: 3074+
Insolvency practitioner: 7423
Insolvency and calls: 7872+
Receiver: 9230

Bankruptcy:
Search on sale of company: 5704+
Liquidator's power to prove in contributory's: 8216
Administrator's power to prove in debtor's: 9011

Bare trustee:
Directors' interests: 3350

Bathampton order:
Costs of winding up order: 7726
Costs of appeal against winding up order: 7734

Beneficial title: See Equitable (Title to shares)

Beneficiary:
Meaning: 9940
Shareholder's:
    Transfer of shares to: 1964+
    Stamp duty: 1876
    Notice of shareholder meeting: 3692+
Of right to claim debt owed by company:
    Liquidation: 8019
    Administration: 8951

Benefits:
Director's:
    Non-cash: 2722
    Tax: 2752+
    Disclosure in accounts: 2778+
Tax:
    Transfer of asset to employee: 1771, 1785
    Participator of close company: 1805

Bill of exchange:
Meaning: 9940
Proof of debt:
    Compulsory liquidation: 8032
    Administration: 8954
Creditor voting:
    Compulsory liquidation: 8355
    CVL: 8557
    Administration: 9091
    CVA: 9508

Board:
Management:
    Powers: 3137+
    Role: 3118+
Accounts:
    Approval: 4263
    Change accounting reference period: 4221
Borrowing and security: 4767+
Director:
    Appointing: 2274+
    Removing: 2943
Litigation:
    Authority to commence: 7124+
    Control: 7134
Shares:
    Calls: 1208
    Forfeit: 1221
    Interim dividend: 1665
    Refusal to register transfer: 1888+

Board *(continued)*
Subsidiary: 199+
Takeover offer: 6882
Delegation of powers: 3404+
Deadlocked: 3166+
No directors: 3166+
Ratification: 2497+
Sole director: 3462
Compulsory winding up petition: 7624
CVL:
   Creditors' meeting to enter into: 8449+
   Statement of affairs: 8440+, 8457
MVL:
   Shareholders' meeting to enter into: 8613, 8616
   Statutory declaration of solvency: 8610+
Administrator:
   Court appointment: 8721+
   Out of court appointment: 8764+
   Application to remove: 9038+
   Application to replace: 9044+
Pre-CVA moratorium:
   Administrative requirements: 9469
   Effect on: 9471+
CVA:
   Proposal: 9448+, 9457+
   Statement of affairs: 9456

Board meeting:
Main entry: 3217+
Cannot exercise powers: 3166+
First: 590
Joint venture company: 6615

Board resolution: See Resolution (Board)

Boiler plate clauses:
Sale and purchase agreement: 5740

Bona fide: See Good faith

Bona vacantia:
Meaning: 9940
On dissolution: 7492

Bonus payment:
Director's remuneration: 2717+
To employee: 1681

Bonus dividend: 1666

Bonus issue:
Main entry: 1013+
Distribution:
   Definition: 1603
   Non-qualifying: 1775
Capitalise unrealised profit: 1615
Financial assistance: 5579+

Bonus issue *(continued)*
Convertible preference share: 824
Prospectus Rules: 4855
Public company: 1153

Bonus share:
Allotment:
   Capital redemption reserve: 1360
   Share premium account: 1247
   Statutory pre-emption rights: 946
Distribution: 1612
Right to decline: 1031
Capitalisation: 1029

Book debts:
Charge over: 4626+
   Registration: 4638
Sale and purchase agreement: 5766+

Book of executed documents: 4011

Borrower:
Company's ability to be: 4755+
Mortgage or charge:
   Over shares: 1927+
   Registration: 4640
Enforcement:
   Security: 4663+
   Unregistered mortgage or charge: 4658+
Guarantor of: 4696+
Insolvency of and subordination: 4688+

Branch:
Overseas company:
   Registration: 145
   Disclosure in directors' report: 4252
   Change registration to place of business: 183
   Closure/move: 184
   Register of shareholders in UK: 3952
Overseas register and annual return: 4065
UK company overseas: 3948+
European company: 88

Breach of directors' duties:
Remedies for: 2434+
Consequences on transactions/contracts: 2483+
Relief from liability: 2494+
Time limits for action: 2442
See also Director (Duties)

Brokerage fee: 1237

Business angel: 4810

Business day:
Inspection of company registers: 3906
Insolvency matters: 7412

INDEX C 1243

Business name: See Name (Business)

Business types: 1+
Comparison table: 130

Buy: See Sale of company, Sale of goods, Transfer of assets, Transfer of shares

Buy back: See Own share purchase

C

Called-up share capital:
Meaning: 716
On balance sheet: 4237

Calls: See Shareholder calls

Cancellation: See Share capital (cancellation)

Capital: See Reduction of share capital, Return of capital, Share capital, Venture capital

Capital gains tax:
Tax rates: 5349
Annual exemption: 5348
Deferral of: 5354+
Loss relief: 5345
Taper relief:
    Main entry: 5346+
    Loan note consideration: 5441
    Share for share exchange: 5431
Bonus issue: 1037
Loan capitalisation: 1058
Indexation allowance: 5344
Sale of shares by individual: 5338+

Capital maintenance: See Doctrine of capital maintenance

Capital redemption reserve:
Main entry: 1360+
On balance sheet: 4237
Distribution: 1612
Bonus issue: 1029
Own share purchase/redemption: 1351
Reduction: 1435+
Cancellation: 1445
Repayment: 1445
Transfer to reserve account: 1445

Capitalisation: See Bonus share, Loan (Capitalisation)

Car: See Benefits (Director's, Non-cash)

Care, skill and diligence:
Director's duty:
    Main entry: 2411+
    Paying dividend: 1641
    Damages remedy: 2463+
    Injunction remedy: 2467+
    Breach by payment of unlawful distribution: 1742
    Provision of information to auditor: 4251
Delegation to non-director: 3433

Cash:
Balance sheet: 4237
Mortgage or charge over: 4632, 4638
Security over: 4632

Cash dividend: 1708

Cash-flow statement:
Statutory accounts: 4209

Cash-flow test:
Insolvency: 7600
See also Balance sheet test

CCJ: See County court judgment

CD ROM: See Electronic (Communication)

Centre of main interests:
Under EC Insolvency Reg: 7368

Certificate of incorporation:
Formation: 495
Change of name: 273+
Conversion from private to public company: 666
Conversion from public to private company: 679

Certification:
Transfer of share: 1904

Certified copy:
Documents submitted to Companies House: 4052

Chairman:
Board meeting: 3274+
    Implied authority to act on company's behalf: 2354+
Shareholder meeting: 3716+
    Resolution to appoint: 3849
    Right to speak: 3724
    Adjourn: 3760+
    Demand poll: 3843+
Class meeting in scheme of arrangement: 6520

Compulsory liquidation:
    Creditors' meeting to remove liquidator: 8257

Chairman (continued)
Creditors'/contributories' meetings: 8345+, 8348, 8365

Liquidation committee: 8300, 8310

Voluntary liquidation and meeting to appoint liquidator: 8510

CVL:
Creditors' meeting to enter into: 8451
Creditors' meeting to remove liquidator: 8541
Creditors'/contributories' meetings: 8557

MVL and creditors' meeting where company insolvent: 8649

Administration:
Creditors' committee: 9064
Creditors' meeting: 9083, 9088

Administrative receivership and creditors' committee: 9064

CVA:
Appealing decision re. creditors' ability to vote: 9507
Appointed as proxy: 9508
Shareholders'/creditors' meetings to approve proposals: 9501, 9512

Change of control:
Of voting rights:
Effect of own share purchase/redemption: 1351
Effect of mortgage/charge: 1926+

Of company:
Conditions of sale: 5733, 6821
Effect on group relief: 6440
Joint venture: 6610

Charge:
Main entry: 4574+

Distinguished from mortgage: 4578+

Over shares:
Main entry: 1915
Effect on subsidiary relationship: 204+
Registration: 4638

Sale of company: 5469

Registration:
Certificate from Companies House: 3981+
Over property of overseas company: 177
Over property of Slavenburg company: 177
Agreement to create: 4639
At Companies House: 3979+, 4637+
Companies House register and rectification: 4030
Company's internal register: 3975+

Satisfaction and release: 4656+
Companies House register: 3979+

Enforcement: 4663+

Holder's right to foreclose: 4667

Unregistered charge: 4647+

Administration: 8911

Relying on in liquidation, See Security

Charge by deposit of deeds: See Fixed charge

Charging order:
Meaning: 9940
Over shares: 1952
Judgment debt: 4740
Liquidation:
Assets subject of: 7903+
Receivership:
Assets subject of: 9288

Charitable donations:
Disclosure in directors' report: 4247

Charity:
Company:
Limited by guarantee: 52
Community Interest Company: 62, 72
Compulsory liquidation: 7628
Unincorporated association: 24

Chartered director: 2253

Chartered secretary: 4122

Chattel lease:
Administration:
Assets subject to: 8912
Creditor voting at creditors' meeting: 9091

Chattel mortgage: 4625

Cheque:
Company name on: 259+
Signature: 3498
Director's liability: 2580
Proof of debt:
Compulsory liquidation: 8032
Administration: 8954
See also Bill of exchange

Child:
As connected person: 848, 989, 3379, 5580, 6938, 9930+
Director's duty to disclose interest in shares/debentures: 3379
See also Minor

CIB inspection: See CIB investigation

CIB investigation:
Main entry: 7195+
Inspectors: 7219+
Investigators: 7208+
Restriction on transfer of shares during: 1836
Assist overseas authority: 7250

CIB investigation (continued)
Criminal activity discovered during liquidation: 7247
Ownership of shares: 7239+
Share dealings by directors: 7244

CIC: See Community Interest Company

Circular:
From board to shareholders:
  On allotment: 1079
  On takeover of public company: 6882+
  Re. shareholder meeting: 3654, 3662

City Code on Takeovers and Mergers:
Summary: 6746
Application:
  Generally: 6755+
  Conversion from public to private company: 675
  Takeover by scheme of arrangement: 6985+
Code waiver: 6760+
Sanctions for breach: 6730
See also Takeover (Public company), Panel on Takeovers and Mergers

Civil partner:
As connected person: 848, 989, 3379, 5580, 6938, 7895, 9930+

Civil partnership:
Transfer of shares in consideration: 1876
Transactions defrauding creditors: 7827

Civil Procedure Rules: See CPR

Civil proceedings: 7118+

Claim form:
Disqualification application: 3049+
Non-Part 8: 7165
Part 8, See Part 8

Class:
Definition: 1273
Shares:
  Main entry: 740+
  Created by pre-emption rights: 970
  Pre-emption rights on allotment: 962
  Payment of dividend on: 1678+
  Transfer by different instruments: 1866
  Transfer by same instrument: 1891
  Reduction of share capital: 1448+
  Takeover offer: 6936
  In joint venture company: 6571+, 6610
Right:
  Definition: 1275
  Variation: 812, 1270+
  Statement of on allotment: 914+
  Shareholders' agreement: 2087

Class (continued)
Meetings:
  Main entry: 3794+
  To approve scheme of arrangement: 6513+, 6516+, 6519+

Clear days: 3679, 7412, 9940

Close company: 1805

Closing: See Completion

Club:
Run as company limited by guarantee: 52

Coal:
Preferential debt:
  Liquidation: 8045
  Administration: 8965

Combined code: 2204, 3199

Commission:
Subscription for shares: 1237+
Director's remuneration: 2717+

Committee:
Board: 3408+
  Meeting: 3418
See also Creditors' committee, Liquidation committee

Communication with company: 3628, 3695+

Community group:
Run as unincorporated association: 24

Community Interest Company: 62+
Compulsory liquidation:
  Regulator's ability to petition: 7628

Community interest test: 70

Companies Act (New, 2006): 9940

Companies court:
Companies Act applications: 7143
  Insolvency applications: 7390
  Reduction of share capital: 1485, 1488
  Scheme of arrangement: 6512+

Companies House:
Main entry: 4040+
Search:
  Name: 247
  Sale of company: 5262, 5695, 5897
Filing:
  Summary table of forms and deadlines: 9900
  Board resolutions: 3480
  Elective resolutions: 3567
  Extraordinary resolutions: 3544

Companies House (continued)
Ordinary resolutions: 3600
Shareholder written resolution: 3585
Special resolutions: 3557
Formation: 479+
Accounts: 4278+
Auditors' report: 4278+
Directors' report: 4278+
Annual return: 4060+

Striking off company automatically: 7516+

Companies Investigations Branch:
See CIB investigation

Company hijacking: 4076

Company limited by guarantee:
Main entry: 52
Member:
Liability generally: 2010
Liability to contribute in insolvency: 7863+
Name: 242
Memorandum: 399
Share capital: 700
Accounts: 4265
See also Company without share capital

Company limited by shares:
Comparison with sole trader/partnership: 130

Company name: See Name (Company)

Company search:
At Companies House: 4090
Sale of company: 5262, 5695, 5897

Company voluntary arrangement:
See CVA

Company without share capital:
Shareholder meeting:
Demanding poll: 3844
Proxy statement in notice: 3732
Requisition: 3626
Shareholder calling: 3630
Short notice: 3681
Voting: 3819
Voting by poll: 3842
Register of shareholders: 3918
Annual return: 4062
See also Company limited by guarantee, Unlimited company, Community Interest Company

Compensation:
Commercial agents: 639
Director's loss of office:
Main entry: 2962+
Disclosure in accounts: 2778+
Tax: 2750

Compensation (continued)
Auditor's loss of office: 4345+
Breach of City Code: 6731
See also Damages, Lump-sum payment

Competition law:
Generally: 651
Sale of company: 5505+, 5691
Director's service contract: 2644+
Disqualification as director for breach:
General: 3012, 3032
Leave to act: 3075
Joint venture: 6583+

Completion:
Sale of company:
Main entry: 6005+
Effective date: 5752+
Conditional: 5732+
Gap between exchange and: 5732, 5865
Takeover offer and squeeze-out rights: 6953

Compromise agreement: 5965+

Compulsory liquidation:
Main entry: 7570+
Procedure flowchart: 7572
Summary: 7335+
Commencement of winding up: 7672, 7747
Reorganisation under s 110 IA 1986: 6465+
Shareholder remedy: 2100+
After administration: 8032
Appointment of receiver during: 9229

Compulsory winding up: See Compulsory liquidation

Conditional sale agreement:
Credit transaction: 2817, 2822, 2824, 2831, 2833, 2843
Sale of company: 5732+
Assets subject to:
Liquidation: 7977
Administration: 8818, 8912, 9091
CVA: 9479

Confidentiality:
Information: 645
Director's residential address: 3907
Sale of company:
Main entry: 5244+
Data room: 5230
During investigation of target: 5657
Marketing of company for sale: 5226
Sale and purchase agreement: 5735+

Confidentiality *(continued)*
Takeover of public company:
  General: 6793
  Offer: 6778
Joint venture: 6591, 6624
CIB investigation: 7212+
  Pre-investigation stage: 7199

Conflict of interest:
Director's duty to avoid:
  Main entry: 2390+
  Account for profits remedy: 2471+
  Injunction remedy: 2467+
  Restitution/tracing remedy: 2476+
Managing conflict situation: 2396+
Management buy-out: 6048
Joint venture: 6552, 6579
Liquidation:
  Liquidator's duty to avoid: 8225
  Liquidator resigns: 8251+
Administration:
  Administrator's duty to avoid: 9013
  Administrator resigns: 9036
Pre-CVA moratorium:
  Replacement of nominee: 9475

Connected company:
Meaning: 9930+
CIB inspection: 7227
Contract with director: 2559+
Insolvency:
  Meaning: 7813
  Mortgage over shares: 1928
See also Associated company, Connected person

Connected person:
Meaning: 9930+
Contract between company and its director: 2559+
Directors' interests:
  In contracts/other matters: 3317+
  In shares/debentures: 3379+
Director's remuneration: 2773
Distribution of assets: 1711
Loans to directors: 2819, 2824
Own share purchase: 1372
Substantial property transaction: 2567+
Insolvency:
  Mortgage over shares: 1928
  Sale to by liquidator: 7895+
  Transactions which can be challenged: 7813

Consideration:
Meaning: 9940
Cash: 1123

Consideration *(continued)*
Non-cash:
  Definition: 1124
  Statutory pre-emption rights on allotment: 946
Sale of shares:
  Stamp duty: 1875+, 5378+
Sale of company:
  Main entry: 5410+
  Apportionment: 5314+
Takeover:
  Exercise of sell-out rights: 6966
  Exercise of squeeze-out rights: 6952
Takeover of public company: 6852+
  Mandatory cash offer: 6805+
Hive-down: 6417
Loan capitalisation: 1056
Incorporation of business: 557
Allotment of shares, See Payment

Consolidated accounts: See Group (Accounts)

Conspiracy:
Officer and company: 7183

Constitution:
Main entry: 367+
Sale of company: 5670
Unincorporated association: 24
European company: 91

Constructive dismissal: See Dismissal (Constructive)

Constructive trustee:
Meaning: 9940
Director: 2350, 2398, 2452+, 2476+
Shareholder: 1731
Relief from liability: 2505
Third party: 2556

Contingent debt:
Liquidation:
  Calculation of dividend: 8059
  Discount: 8066
  Estimate value: 8038
  Set-off: 8075
Administration:
  Calculation of dividend: 8059
  Discount: 8975
  Proving: 8950
  Set-off: 8976
CVA: 9533

Contingent liability:
Balance sheet test of insolvency: 7601

Contract:
Pre-incorporation: 356+
Formalities: 3486+
Sales and marketing: 628+
Action/remedies for breach: 2446, 7162+
Between company and director: 2559+
  Also sole shareholder: 3473
Directors' interests in:
  Meaning: 3324
  Disclosure: 3317+
Effect of financial difficulties/insolvency proceedings: 7314
Liquidation:
  Breach of contract and proof of debt: 8008
  Insured claim: 8016
Compulsory liquidation: 7928+
  Effect of compulsory winding up order: 7751
  Claim against liquidator: 8236+
  Employees' contracts: 7754
Voluntary liquidation:
  Effect of resolution to wind up: 8467
  Employees' contracts: 8473
Administration:
  Effect of administration: 8827+
  Administrator's debts/liabilities: 8928, 9018
  Breach and proof of unliquidated debt: 8951
  Insured claim: 8951
Receivership:
  Effect of receivership: 9263+
  Employees' contracts: 9266+
  Receiver's liability: 9392

Contributories' meeting:
Compulsory liquidation: 8335+
  First meeting: 8204+
CVL: 8555+

Contributory:
Main entry: 7863+
List: 7869+
Public examination: 8150
Liquidation:
  Liquidator's duty to act in interests: 8225
  Appeal liquidator's decision re. proof: 8040
  Remove liquidator: 8258
Compulsory liquidation:
  Ability to petition: 7619+
  Access to information: 8227+
  Destruction of company books etc: 8170
  Election to liquidation committee: 8297+, 8315
  Establishment of liquidation committee: 8296
  First meeting to appoint liquidator: 8204+
  Fraudulent entry in company document: 8170
  Inspection of proxy forms: 8352
  Liquidator's exercise of powers: 8219+
  Nominate different liquidator from creditors: 8208
  Official receiver's reports: 8280+

Contributory *(continued)*
  Opposing winding up petition: 7719
  Prevent early dissolution: 8396
  Requisition contributories' meeting: 8336+
  Requisition public examination: 8148
  Staying proceedings: 7736
  Voting at contributories' meeting: 8357
Voluntary liquidation:
  Liquidator's duties: 8525
  Statement of affairs and report: 8530
CVL:
  Inspection of proxy forms: 8557
  Requisition contributories' meeting: 8336
  Voting at contributories' meeting: 8557
  Statement of receipts and payments: 8531
MVL:
  Compromise with: 8647
Administration:
  Administrator to act in interests: 9013
  Inspection of proofs: 8961
CVA:
  Challenging proposal: 9513+

Contributory member:
Liquidation committee:
  Compulsory liquidation: 8297+
  CVL: 8548+
  Membership terminated: 8314
  Restrictions on dealings by members: 8298+

Control: See Change of control

Conversion:
From private to public company: 662+
From public to private company: 673+
Into European Company: 98
Into Community Interest Company: 72
Shares:
  Convertible preference shares: 822+
  Redeemable shares: 763
Tort:
  Meaning: 9940
  Liquidator's liability: 8236+
  Administrator's liability: 8821
  Receiver's liability: 9392

Co-operative: 29
Industrial provident society: 121

Copyright: 645
Mortgage or charge over: 4638

Corporate:
Director:
  Ability to be: 2241+
  Breach of disqualification order/undertaking: 3083
  Disqualification: 3010
Secretary: 4120

Corporate *(continued)*
Shareholder: 2026+
Receiver: 9230
Liability for criminal offence: 2536+, 7176+
See also Corporate representative

Corporate governance: 3199+

Corporate manslaughter: 7179+

Corporate representative:
Shareholder meeting:
  Main entry: 3743+
  Voting on show of hands: 3840
Liquidation committee meetings: 8308
Creditors'/contributories' meeting:
  Compulsory liquidation: 8353
  CVL: 8557

Corporate veil:
Piercing of: 7125
Shares allotted for non-cash consideration: 946
Use of company name after liquidation: 270

Corporate venturer: 4813

Corporation:
Ability to be director: 2241+

Corporation tax:
Distribution: 1795
Profit:
  Income from distributions: 1790
  Own share purchase: 1370+
Sale of assets: 5291
Sale of shares: 5361+
Close company: 1805
Liquidation: 7751, 7964
Administration: 8927, 8931
Receivership: 9324

Costs:
Sale of company:
  Paid by target, whether financial assistance: 5574
  Wasted costs agreement: 5537
Litigation: 7156
  Security for costs: 7140
Insolvency applications: 7395
Liquidation:
  Litigation: 7961+
  Proving debt: 8035
  Public examination: 8156
Compulsory liquidation:
  Challenge winding up order: 7731, 7734
  Requisitioned creditors'/contributories' meeting: 8338
  Winding up petition: 7723+

Costs *(continued)*
CVL:
  Creditors' meeting to enter into CVL: 8456
  Requisitioned creditors' meeting: 8557
Administration:
  Administration application: 8752
  Creditor's application to court: 8927
  Dealing with ring-fenced fund: 8927
  Proving debts: 8956
  Realising security: 8927, 8938
Receivership: 9323+
See also Expenses

County court:
Companies Act applications: 7143
Non-Companies Act applications: 7164
Jurisdiction in insolvency proceedings: 7362+

County court judgment:
Search on sale of company: 5706

Coupon rate: 787

Court:
Applications generally: 7118+
Company management: 3164+
Calling shareholder meeting: 3635+
Shareholder voting: 3826
Dividend policy: 1675
Reduction of share capital: 1483+
Insolvency applications: 7380+
Record of insolvency proceedings: 7398+
Removing liquidator: 8258+
Compulsory liquidation:
  Liquidator's powers requiring sanction: 8216, 8217+
  Overturn liquidation committee decision: 8303
Voluntary liquidation:
  Alternative consideration for company's assets: 8490
  Appointing liquidator: 8512+
CVL:
  No liquidation committee: 8550
  Overturn liquidation committee decision: 8303
Administration:
  Administrator's remuneration: 9028
  Consideration of administration application: 8748+
  Directions: 8876
  Distribution to unsecured creditors: 8967
  Extending administrator's appointment: 9000
  Filing administration application: 8740+
  Method of entering into: 8721+
  Replacement of administrator: 9044+
  Re-valuation of security: 8940
Appointment of receiver: 9222, 9229

Court manager:
Insolvency applications: 7390

Covenants:
Meaning: 9940
Loan agreement:
　Main entry: 4549+
　Event of default: 4552
See also Restrictive covenants

CPR:
Main entry: 7119
Insolvency matters: 7380

Credit:
Suppliers: 4525
Pre-CVA moratorium: 9479

Credit transaction:
To director: 2817, 2822, 2824, 2831, 2833, 2843

Creditor:
Balance sheet: 4237
Charges:
　Inspection of register: 3977+
　Unregistered: 4658+
Lien: 4714+
Policy of payment: 4252
Reduction of share capital:
　Non-statutory protection: 1458
　Statutory protection: 1486
　Objection: 1488
Reorganisation under s 110 IA 1986: 6491
Sale of assets: 5766+
Subordination:
　Senior, junior and mezzanine: 4680, 4692
EC Insolvency Reg: 7372
Public examination: 8146+
Liquidation:
　Action against company for insured liability: 8016
　Distribution: 7975+, 8053+, 8101+
　Liquidator's duty to act in interests: 8225
　Official receiver's reports to: 8280+
　Multiple for same debt: 8024+, 8063
　Set-off: 8072+
Compulsory liquidation:
　Ability to petition: 7617+
　Access to information: 8227+
　Appoint liquidator: 8204+
　Election to liquidation committee: 8297+, 8315
　Inspection of proxy forms: 8352
　Liquidator resigning: 8252+
　Liquidator's exercise of powers: 8219+
　Nominate different liquidator to contributories: 8208
　Opposing winding up petition: 7719
　Prevent early dissolution: 8396

Creditor (continued)
　Remove liquidator: 8255+
　Requisition creditors' meeting: 8205, 8336+
　Stay proceedings: 7736
　Voting: 8354+
Voluntary liquidation:
　Company's assets: 8466
CVL:
　EC Insolvency Reg: 8459+
　Final meeting: 8576
　Inspection of proxy forms: 8557
　Liquidator resigns: 8538, 8253
　No liquidation committee: 8550
　Remove liquidator: 8540
　Requisition creditors' meeting: 8557
　Statement of affairs and report: 8530
　Statement of receipts and payments: 8531
　Voting: 8557
MVL:
　Statement of affairs/report: 8530, 8650
Administration:
　Generally: 9057+
　Ability to place company into: 8710
　Action against company for insured liability: 8951
　Administrator's duty to act in interests: 9010, 9013
　Administrator's remuneration: 9029
　Administration application: 8728
　Challenge administrator: 9015
　Costs of application to court: 8927
　Disclosure of statement of affairs/concurrence: 8871
　Election to creditors' committee: 9062
　End administration: 9167
　Entitlement to information: 9019+
　Inspection of proofs: 8961
　Notice of administrator's resignation: 9036
　Notice of dividend: 8969, 8972
　Proposals: 8882+, 8889, 8892+
　Remove administrator: 9038+
　Replace administrator: 9044+
　Request list of creditors: 8961
　Request meeting: 8888, 9079, 9081
　Set-off: 8976+
　Substitute administrator: 9003+
Receivership:
　Set-off: 9328
Administrative receivership:
　Election to creditors' committee: 9062
　Entitlement to information: 9378+
Pre-CVA moratorium:
　Challenge nominee's decisions: 9474
　Unfair prejudice: 9485
CVA:
　Challenge implementation: 9535
　Challenge proposal: 9513+
　Inspection of documents: 9536
　Progress report: 9547
　Voting: 9507+
　Whether bound: 9526

Creditor *(continued)*
See also Defraud creditors, Lender, Proof of debt, Preferential creditor, Secured creditor, Unsecured creditor

Creditor member:
Liquidation committee:
　Compulsory liquidation: 8297+
　CVL: 8549
　Membership terminated: 8314
　Restrictions on dealings: 8298+

Creditors' committee:
Main entry: 9060+
Administrator:
　Discharge from liability: 9042
　Notice of resignation: 9036
　Remuneration: 9028
Liquidation follows administration: 8322+
Administrative receivership: 9060+, 9382

Creditors' meeting:
Compulsory liquidation:
　Main entry: 8335+
　First meeting: 8204+
CVL:
　Main entry: 8555+
　Appoint liquidator: 8509+
　Entering into: 8448+
　Final meeting: 8575+
　Liquidator's report of first meeting: 8530
　Remove liquidator: 8539+
MVL:
　Where company insolvent: 8530, 8648+
Administration:
　Main entry: 9080+
　Administrator's power to call: 9011
　Administrator's remuneration: 9028
　Approving proposals: 8885+
　End administration: 9164+
　Establishment of liquidation committee: 9062
Administrative receivership: 9062, 9381
CVA:
　Approving proposals: 9499+

Creditors' voluntary liquidation: See CVL

Criminal offence:
Under CA 1985/2006: 9935
Under IA 1986: 9935
Under CDDA 1986: 9935
Under BNA 1985: 9935
Under IR 1986: 9935
Company's liability: 7175+
Director's liability:
　Company-related criminal offences: 2536+
　Pre-liquidation: 7464
　During liquidation: 7465

Criminal offence *(continued)*
Disqualification as a director:
　For conviction of: 3012
Compulsory liquidation:
　Liquidator's duty to report: 8167
　Liquidator's power to deal with proceeds: 7909
Voluntary liquidation:
　Liquidator's duty to report: 8167

Criminal Procedure Rules: 7184

Criminal proceedings:
Main entry: 7175+
Public examination: 8151

Cross-claim: See Set-off

Crown court: 7184+, 9935

Cum dividend: 1703

Cumulative dividend: 793

Currency:
Liquidation:
　Exchange rate and deferred debt: 8066
　Proof of debt in foreign currency: 8020
Administration:
　Exchange rate and deferred debt: 8975
　Proof of debt in foreign currency: 8020
Share capital, See Share capital (Redenomination)

Current assets:
Balance sheet: 4237

CVA:
Main entry: 9435+
Procedure flowchart: 9439
Summary: 7342
Commencement: 9526
Financial assistance for acquisition of shares: 5579
Before liquidation:
　Non-contributory winding up petition: 7636
　Conversion: 9557+
　Expenses of: 7959
Before administration:
　Conversion: 9557
　When CVA with moratorium ended prematurely: 8765
After administration: 8880
Appointment of receiver during: 9231

CVL:
Main entry: 8437+
Procedure flowchart: 7572
Summary: 7335+
As opposed to MVL and references to: 8426+

CVL (continued)
Timeline summary of entering into CVL: 8458
Commencement of winding up: 8465
Before compulsory liquidation and expenses: 7959
After administration:
  Conversion: 8461

D

Damages:
Meaning: 9940
Remedy for:
  Breach of directors' duties: 2463+
  Breach of indemnity claim in sale of company: 5827+
  Breach of warranty claim in sale of company: 5827+
  Breach/delay in share issue: 1099
  Directors' refusal of consent for transfer of shares: 1837
  Failure re. own share purchase/redemption of shares: 1427+

Data protection: 656+
Investigation on sale of company: 5687
Of shareholder's details: 3934

Data room: 5229+

Database:
Intellectual property rights: 645+

De facto director:
Categories of director: 2210
Fiduciary duties: 2375
Implied authority to act on company's behalf: 2354+
Disqualification as director: 3010

De jure director:
Categories of director: 2198

Deadlock:
Board: 3166+
  Registration of share transfer: 1892
Joint venture: 6625+
Reorganisation: 6405+
Shareholders: 3635+
  Poll vote: 3842+
  Remedies: 2100+

Debenture:
Meaning of: 4581+
Holder:
  Alter objects in memorandum: 418, 3692
  Class meeting: 3795
  Notice of shareholder meeting: 3692

Debenture (continued)
  Receive company accounts: 4265, 4268
  Register: 4006+
Companies House's register of charges: 3958+
See also Charge, Fixed charge, Floating charge, Mortgage

Debt:
Finance: 4504+
Senior, junior and mezzanine: 4680
Factoring, See Invoice finance
Between company and shareholder:
  Calls: 1217
  Dividend: 1690+
Insolvency definition: 8005, 9941
Liquidation:
  Incurred while liquidator carries on business: 7792
  Owed by company and another debtor: 8025
  Owed to company by shareholder: 7878
  Provable: 8005+
  Subordinated: 8054
  Use of company name after, director's liability: 270
Compulsory liquidation:
  Basis of statutory demand: 7596
Administration:
  Provable: 8949+
CVA: 9533
See also Proof of debt

Debtor:
Balance sheet: 4237
Liquidation:
  Also creditor: 8072+, 8489, 8633
  Private examination: 8172+
  Remove liquidator: 8258
Administration:
  Private examination: 8855
Receivership:
  Also creditor: 9328
Administrative receivership:
  Private examination: 9377
See also Borrower

Deceased:
Shareholder:
  Distribution to in liquidation: 8087
  Personal representative's liability as contributory: 7863+
  Personal representatives petitioning for compulsory liquidation: 7620
  Pre-emption provisions: 1845
  Transfer of shares to beneficiary and stamp duty: 1876
  Transmission of shares: 1964+
Liquidator: 8263

Deceased *(continued)*
Administrator: 9041, 9042
Administrative receiver: 9406
Nominee: 9475

Decision:
Shareholder without meeting: 3577+
Board without meeting: 3291+
Informal/unanimous agreement:
  Shareholders: 3590+
  Board: 3242, 3297+
Ratification of unauthorised decision: 2497+
See also Board meeting, Shareholder meeting, Written resolution

Decision making: 3110+

Deed:
Execution of: 3492
Director's service contract: 9925
Sale and purchase agreement: 5742, 5744
Share transfer instrument: 1868

Deed of adherence:
Shareholders' agreement:
  Joint venture: 6602
  New shareholders: 2089

Deed of assignment: 5988

Deed of contribution: 5853, 5975+

Deed of settlement: See Articles

Deemed service:
In court proceedings: 7152
In insolvency proceedings: 7406
Notice of shareholder meeting: 3679, 3703, 3704

De facto:
Meaning: 9940
Director: 2210

Defamation:
Meaning: 9940
Action/litigation: 7162
Auditor statement: 3668, 4340+
Shareholder statement/resolution: 3627, 3663
Director statement: 2948

Defence:
Company's ability to mount:
  Generally: 7118
  In liquidation: 7961+, 8216, 8469, 8515
  In administration: 9011
Director:
  Costs of successful: 2513, 2829, 2837
  To disqualification application: 3052+

Defence *(continued)*
  To fraudulent trading: 7445
  To wrongful trading: 7453
To employment claim: 2986, 5779, 5785
To offences re.:
  Accounts: 173, 174, 4273, 4280, 4298
  Insolvency: 7464, 7781, 9487
  Loans to directors: 2884, 2888
  Purchase/redemption of own shares: 1407
  Striking off: 7510
  Takeovers: 6951, 6966
To Part 8 claim: 7153
  Reply: 7153
To non-Part 8 claim: 7165
  Reply: 7165
To passing-off/trade mark infringement action: 311

Deferred creditor:
Liquidation: 8066
Administration: 8975

Deferred share: 877

Defraud creditors:
Companies Act offence: 2577, 7446
Insolvency and transaction defrauding creditors: 7826+

De jure:
Meaning: 9940
Director: 2198

Dematerialised shares: See Shares (Paperless holding)

Demerger:
Distribution of assets: 1711
Scheme of arrangement for reconstruction or amalgamation: 6530+
See also Reorganisation (Section 110 IA 1986)

Denomination:
Share capital: 709
See also Share capital (Redenomination)

Deputy:
Director's: 2251, 2939
Shareholder's: 1980
Secretary: 4154

Derivative action/claim: 7127+, 9940

Design right:
Main entry: 645+
Database: 5703, 5897
Mortgage or charge over: 4638, 4653
Transfer: 6026

Designated members:
Limited liability partnership: 79

Director:
Main entry: 2160+

Also shareholder:
Contract with company: 3473
Freedom to transfer shares: 1836
Termination of appointment: 1845

Borrowing and security:
Creation of: 4757, 4762, 4767+
Personal guarantee: 4698+
Security over own assets: 4574, 4769+

Company struck off:
Liabilities: 7510+, 7519

Delegation: 3404+

Dividends and distributions:
Distribution of assets: 1711
Fixed dividend: 1678
Interim dividend: 1665
Liability: 1742+, 1758+
Preference shares: 789, 1679
Recommendation: 1663
Shareholders' liability to: 1734

Duties:
Main entry: 2317+
When alloting shares: 929
When obtaining valuation for non-cash consideration: 1124
When paying dividend: 1641
Public company's net assets: 7441

European Company: 93

Financial assistance:
Statutory declaration: 5600+, 5615
Liability: 5634+

Formation:
Requirements: 464, 482

Joint venture: 6614+

Liabilities:
Generally, See Director (Duties)
In insolvency, See Director (Insolvency liabilities)

Loans to:
Summary tables: 2806, 2808

Payment, See Remuneration

Powers:
Delegation: 3438+, 3450, 3496
General remedies for abuse: 3171+
Unfair prejudice remedy for abuse: 2110

Register:
Information required: 3896+
Residential address: 3896, 3907

Relief from liability: 2494+
For unlawful distribution: 7154+

Removal/resignation/retirement: 2912+

Secretary:
Ability to be: 4120
Appointing: 4151

Director (continued)

Shareholder meeting:
Calling: 3622+
Notice: 3689, 3692+
Right to attend: 3724
Right to speak: 3724
Right to vote: 3270, 3825

Shares:
Authority to allot: 921+
Calls on: 1210, 1217
Commission on allotment: 1238
Consent for transfer: 1837
Pre-emption rights on allotment: 964
Registration of share transfer instrument: 1857, 1888+

Takeover of public company:
Frustrating tactics of target: 6865+
Irrevocable undertaking: 6794+

Unlimited liability: 464, 2278

Insolvency liabilities:
Generally: 7439+
Statutory: 7752
To contribute: 7863+

Liquidation:
Criminal offences: 7464+, 7781
Effect of appointment of provisional liquidator: 7690
Use of company name after: 264+

Compulsory liquidation:
Ability to petition: 7621
Effect: 7752
Inspection of proxy forms: 8352
Reporting unfit director: 8122
Reporting criminal offence: 8167

Voluntary liquidation:
Reporting unfit directors: 8166
Reporting criminal offence: 8167

CVL:
Effect: 8472
Inspection of proxy forms: 8557

Administration:
Ability to place company into: 8710
Appointed/removed by administrator: 9011
Attending administration application hearing: 8746
Effect: 8826
Reporting directors' conduct: 8856
Sale to: 8907+

Receivership:
Effect: 9261+
Sale to: 9310

Administrative receivership:
Reporting director's conduct: 9377

Pre-CVA moratorium:
Criminal offences: 9486+
Effect: 9484+
Reporting director's conduct: 9473

CVA:
Approving proposal: 9517
Company's assets: 9532

Director (continued)
Inspection of documents: 9536
Role during: 9550

See also Alternate director, Appointment, Authority, Benefits, Board, Board meeting, Directors' interests, Directors' report, Disqualification, Fiduciary duties, Management buy-out, Remuneration, Resignation, Service contract, Termination

Directors' interests:
Main entry: 3308+

Sole director:
Changes to articles: 3463

Consequences:
Main entry: 3341+
Shareholders' power to make decision instead: 3166

In shares:
Main entry: 3379+
Register: 3958+
Directors' report/notes to accounts: 4249+
CIB investigation: 7244

In resolution:
Disclosure in notice of shareholder meeting: 3661

See also, Substantial property transaction

Directors' report:
Main entry: 4245+

Board approval: 4263

Business review: 4252+

Shareholders:
Delivery to: 4265+
Laying before: 4273+

Publication with accounts: 4269+

Filing: 4278+

Abbreviated accounts:
Medium-sized company: 4376
Small company: 4370

Group: 4382

Own share purchase or redemption: 1367

Small company: 4368

Disabled persons:
Disclosure in directors' report: 4247

Discharge:
Administrator: 9042

See also Release

Disclaim: See Onerous property

Disclosure:
Name:
Company: 259+
Business: 296+

Commission on subscription for shares: 1238

Disclosure (continued)
Confidential information: 5245+
Director to shareholders: 3392+
Director's remuneration: 2761+
Directors' report: 4247+
Director's wrongdoing: 2387
During CIB inspection: 7223+
During CIB investigation: 7210+
Loans to directors: 2897
Own share purchase/redemption: 1367

Sale of company:
Letter: 5892+
Restricted: 5247+
Effect on warranty claim: 5847+

Takeover of public company:
Share dealings: 6860+

Compulsory liquidation:
Statement of affairs/affidavit of concurrence: 8133

Administration:
Statement of affairs/concurrence: 8871

Administrative receivership:
Report to creditors: 9379

See also Directors' interests

Discount:
Allotment of shares: 1121

Shares:
Commission on subscription: 1238
Valuation for pre-emption offer: 1853

Proof of debt:
Compulsory liquidation: 8032
Administration: 8954

Dismissal:
Director: 2983+
Breach of service contract by company: 2681
Breach of service contract by director: 2678+

Constructive: 2986, 5964

Unfair: 2981, 2986
Sale of company: 5775, 5779+
Hive-down: 6422
Insolvency: 7315, 8012, 8045, 8928

Redundancy:
Director: 2750, 2981, 2986
Sale of company: 5686, 5771+
Insolvency: 6422, 7315, 7754, 8012, 8473, 8830, 8928, 9266

Wrongful:
Director: 2986
Insolvency: 7315, 7754, 8012, 8473

See also Quasi-partnership, Termination

Disposal:
Compulsory liquidation:
After petition presented: 7674+
Statement in contributory's petition: 7657

Disposal *(continued)*
Administration:
  Of assets belonging to third parties: 8909+
Pre-CVA moratorium:
  Restrictions during: 9482+
See also Sale of company

Disqualification:
Main entry: 3000+
Director:
  Allotment for improper purpose: 935
  Financial assistance: 5605
Secretary: 4121, 4161+
Order:
  Meaning and effect: 3070+
  Breach: 3082+
  Leave to act as a director: 3074+
Undertaking:
  Meaning and effect: 3072
Effect on ability to be insolvency practitioner: 3008, 7423, 9230

Dissolution:
Main entry: 7491+
Restoration: 7534+
Sale of company: 5292
Void: 7537+
Partnership: 19
Community Interest Company: 65
Compulsory liquidation:
  Generally: 8398
  Early dissolution: 8396+
CVL: 8579
MVL: 8665
Administration: 9154

Distress:
Meaning: 9940
Liquidation: 7903, 7904+, 8047, 8470
Compulsory liquidation: 7700
Administration: 8818, 8965
  Distrainer's right to notice of administrator's appointment: 8743, 8766, 8797
Receivership: 9288
Pre-CVA moratorium: 9469, 9476

Distributable profits:
Main entry: 1612+
Bonus issue: 1029
Date of dividend: 1694
Insufficient to make distribution: 1728+
Financial assistance using: 5595
Own share purchase/redemption:
  Use for: 1356

Distributable profits *(continued)*
  Transferred to capital redemption reserve: 1361, 1363
Preferential dividend: 789
See also Non-distributable profits, Profit, Profit and loss account

Distribution:
Definition:
  General: 1603
  Tax: 1771
Of profits:
  Main entry: 1600+
  Flowchart: 1650
Bonus shares:
  Tax: 1037
  Non-qualifying distribution: 1775
Own share purchase/redemption: 1369
Liquidation:
  Main entry: 7945+
  Summary chart: 8101
  Order of priority: 7958+
  Based on proof in foreign currency: 8020
  Effect on secured creditor's proof: 7985+
Administration:
  Main entry: 8922+
  Proof of debt in foreign currency: 8020
  Proof of debt owed to shareholder: 8951
  Effect on secured creditor's proof: 8940
  Secured creditor: 8936+
Receivership:
  Main entry: 9321+
See also Dividend, Pari passu

Distribution in specie: See Distribution of assets

Distribution of assets:
Main entry: 1710+
To employee: 1785
Compulsory liquidation: 8087
Voluntary liquidation: 8515
See also Pari passu

Distributor: 640

District judge:
Insolvency applications: 7390

Dividend:
Main entry: 1600+
Declaration and payment:
  Main entry: 1660+
  Summary table: 1722
  Shareholder denied: 2111
  As financial assistance: 5579+
  Before own share purchase/redemption: 1428
  After sale of company and assets: 5292

Dividend *(continued)*
During takeover offer period: 6867
By joint venture company: 6617

On preference share:
Cumulative/Non-cumulative: 793
Fixed: 790
Arrears: 796+, 805+, 812, 1450
Right to: 786+
Participating preference share: 837

On other share class:
Ordinary share: 743+
Deferred share: 877
Non-voting share: 750

On shares:
Forfeited: 1221
Transferred: 1831
Transmitted: 1964
Mortgaged: 1929

Unlawful distributions: 1728+

Disclosure:
Directors' report: 4252

Community Interest Company: 65

See also Distributable profits, Distribution

Division: See Demerger

Divorce:
Former spouse: 9931
Transfer of share in consideration:
Stamp duty: 1876

Doctrine of capital maintenance:
Main entry: 703+
Changes to share capital: 1310
Effect on own share purchase: 1337
Effect on payment of distributions to shareholders: 1610
Effect on reduction of share capital: 1458
See also Financial assistance, Own share purchase, Redeemable shares, Reduction of share capital, Share premium account

Document:
Authenticated/certified by company: 3494
Disclosure:
During CIB inspection: 7223+
Of company's details on: 259+, 585
Of liquidation on company's: 7750, 8229, 8468
Of administration on company's: 9021
Of receivership on company's: 9368
Of pre-CVA moratorium on company's: 9480

CIB investigation:
Destruction, falsification etc: 7211
Disclosure during: 7210+

Filing at Companies House, See Companies House

Document *(continued)*
Liquidation:
Liability re.: 7464+
Record of executed documents: 4011

Domain name: See Name

Domicile:
Company's:
Change: 415
Disclosure: 585
Filing: 415
Memorandum: 399
Director's: 2745
EC Insolvency Reg: 7369, 7372, 8460

Dominant influence:
Parent over subsidiary: 214

Dominant position:
Abuse: 651

Donation: See Political donation

Dormant company:
Definition: 4407+
Accounts: 4414+
Audit: 4410

Due diligence: See Investigation (Acquisition target)

"Duomatic" principle: 3590+

Duty of care:
Conduct of valuation: 1855
Director: 2448
See also Care, skill and diligence
Insolvency practitioners: 7429
Misfeasance (for breach of): 7457+
Liquidator: 8236
Administrator: 9018
See also Negligence, Tort

E

Early dissolution:
Compulsory liquidation: 8396+

Earnings:
Meaning of for income tax purposes: 2746

EC company law action plan:
Proposed directive on shareholders' rights: 2074

EEIG: See European Economic Interest Grouping

Either way offence: 7184

EGM: See General meeting, Shareholder meeting

Elective resolution:
Main entry: 3562+
Notice of shareholder meeting: 3656+
Director's authority to allot shares: 923

Electronic:
Communication:
  Notice of shareholder meeting: 3695+, 3764
  Proxy appointment form: 3735
  With company: 3628, 3695+
Filing:
  At Companies House: 4074+
Incorporation: 505
Signature:
  Documents to be filed at Companies House: 4052
Voting:
  At shareholder meeting: 3852

Email: See Electronic (Communication)

Emoluments: See Remuneration

Employee:
Management role: 3184+
Formation: 618
Disabled persons: 4247
Health and safety: 623, 2590+
Immigration: 2598
Intellectual property: 646
Interests taken into account by director: 2596
Participation:
  Disclosure in directors' report: 4252
Remuneration: 2699
Shares:
  Main entry: 847+
  Financial assistance: 5579+
  Bonus issue: 1037
  Offer of: 986+
  Transfer on termination of employment: 1845, 1854
  Prospectus Rules: 4855
Distribution of assets to:
  Tax: 1785, 8091 (by liquidator)
Also director:
  General: 2187
  Service contract: 2627+
  Written employment terms: 2627
Sale of company:
  Consideration of employees' rights: 5390+
  Investigation of target: 5686
  Protection of employment: 5771+
European company: 95+

Employee *(continued)*
Community Interest Company: 70
Insolvency:
  Effect on: 7315
Liquidation:
  Deferred debt: 8066
  Duty to co-operate with liquidator: 8169
  Preferential debts: 8045+
  Private examination: 8172+
  Proof of debt owed to employee: 8012
  Providing information: 8144
Compulsory liquidation:
  Effect on: 7754
  Duty to co-operate with official receiver: 8121
  Notice of creditors' and contributories' meetings: 8340
  Providing accounts: 8138+
  Statement of affairs: 8127+
Voluntary liquidation:
  Effect on: 8473
CVL:
  Notice of creditors' and contributories' meetings: 8557
  Providing accounts: 8138
Administration:
  Effect on: 8830
  Administrator's power to deal with: 9011
  Deferred debt: 8975
  Duty to co-operate with administrator: 8855
  Preferential debts: 8965
  Proof of debt owed to employee: 8951
  Statement of affairs: 8861+
  Statement of concurrence: 8867+
Receivership:
  Effect on: 9266+
Administrative receivership:
  Duty to co-operate with administrative receiver: 9377
  Private examination: 9377
  Statement of affairs: 8861+
  Statement of concurrence: 8867+
See also Dismissal

Employee share scheme:
Main entry: 848+
Allotment of shares:
  Director's authority: 921
  Public company: 1137
  Pre-emption rights: 946
Directors: 2724+, 2789
Issue of shares:
  Financial promotions on: 998
Share capital:
  Public company: 510

Employee-owned business: 29

Employers' liability insurance: See Insurance

Enforcement:
Effect of winding up petition: 7700
Effect of winding up resolution: 7903+
Liquidation: 7903+
Administration: 8818
Receivership: 9287+
Pre-CVA moratorium: 9476
See also Charge, Execution, Floating charge, Judgment debt, Mortgage, Secured creditor

Enforcement officer:
Liquidation: 7906
Administration:
   Placing company into: 8710, 8728
   Right to receive notice of intention to appoint administrator: 8766

Enterprise Investment Scheme: 5355+

Entertainment:
Part of director's remuneration, See Benefits (Director's, Non-cash)

Environment:
Criminal offences: 7182
Directors' duty to consider: 2379+
Investigation on sale of company: 5680
Licence: 623

Equitable:
Remedies for breach of fiduciary duties: 2451+
Treatment of shareholders in reduction of share capital: 1448+
Mortgage:
   Assets which can be subject to: 4618+
   Characteristics: 4596+
   Over shares: 1938+ (Formalities), 1945+ (Priority between lenders)
   Priority over other security: 4674+
   Right of foreclosure: 4667
Shareholder, See Transferee
Title to shares:
   Meaning: 1829
   Effect of share certificate: 1902
   Notice to company: 1950+
   Transfer: 1830
   Transfer and pre-emption provisions: 1847, 1857

Equity:
Meaning: 9940
Finance: 4800+
Share capital: 727

Escrow Account: 5489+

Establishment:
Under EC Insolvency Reg: 7369

European company: 88+

European Economic Interest Grouping: 104+

European passport: 4875+

Evidence:
Disqualification applications: 3050, 3052+, 3055
Obtained in CIB investigation: 7210+, 7225
Part 8 proceedings: 7148, 7153
Non-Part 8 proceedings: 7165
Insolvency applications: 7388+

Ex dividend: 1703

Ex gratia payment: See Lump-sum payment

Excepted petition: 9476

Exchange:
Contract on sale of company: 6005+

Execution:
Contracts: 3488, 5743
Deeds: 3492, 5744
Enforcement action:
   Liquidation: 7599, 7697+, 7700, 7903+, 7977
   Administration: 8818
   Receivership: 9229, 9288
   Pre-CVA moratorium: 9476
Record of: 4011
See also Transfer instrument, Witness

Executive director:
Main entry: 3425+
Categories of director: 2200+
Implied authority to act on company's behalf: 2354+

Ex parte:
Meaning: 9940
James, rule in: 7429, 8036, 8225

Expenses:
Director's:
   Main entry: 2715
   Requirement for approval: 2828, 2836
   Disclosure in accounts: 2778+
Share premium account: 1247
Liquidation:
   Main entry: 7956+
   Liquidation committee members: 8309
   Requisitioned creditors'/contributories' meeting: 8338
Compulsory liquidation:
   Order of priority: 7958+
   Statement of affairs: 8129

Expenses *(continued)*
CVL:
   Order of priority: 7958
   Statement of affairs: 8441
MVL:
   Order of priority: 7958
Administration:
   Main entry: 8927+
   Order of priority: 8927, 8930
   Creditors' meeting requisitioned by creditors: 9081
   Statement of affairs: 8864
   Statement of concurrence: 8868
Receivership: 9323+
Administrative receivership:
   Statement of affairs: 8864
   Statement of concurrence: 8868
CVA: 9549

Expert:
Valuation of shares for pre-emption offer: 1855
Valuation of non-cash asset transferred by shareholder to public company: 1178
Valuation of non-cash consideration for allotment by public company: 1158

Extortionate credit transaction: 7842+

Extraordinary dividend: 1666

Extraordinary general meeting: See General meeting, Shareholder meeting

Extraordinary resolution:
Main entry: 3544+
Notice of meeting: 3656+
Liquidation:
   To voluntarily wind company up: 8438
   Sanction distribution of property to shareholders: 8087

F

Factoring: See Invoice finance

Fair review report:
Directors' report: 4252

False representation:
During:
   Liquidation: 8169
   Pre-CVA moratorium: 9486
In CVA proposal: 9517
In statement of affairs in CVL: 8442
See also Misrepresentation

Fax:
Requisition of shareholder meeting: 3627+

Fax *(continued)*
Serving notice of shareholder meeting: 3697
Submitting documents to Companies House: 4069

Fees:
Of professionals instructed:
   Liquidation: 8017
   Administration: 8951
See also Remuneration

Fiduciary:
Meaning: 2373, 9940
Director: 2186, 2373+
Holding and subsidiary companies: 203
Liquidator: 8224+
Administrator: 9013
Receiver: 9360

Fiduciary duties:
Director:
   Main entry: 2186, 2373+
   Allotment for proper purpose: 929
   Breach by unlawful distribution: 1742
   Breach by unlawful financial assistance: 5634+
   Breach in whitewash of financial assistance: 5605
   Remedies for breach by: 2451+
   Voting when in breach: 3269+
Liquidator:
   Compulsory liquidation: 8244+
   Voluntary liquidation: 8527
Liquidation committee member: 8298
Administrator: 9013, 9017, 9018
Receiver: 9360

Filing: See Companies House

Final dividend: 1663

Final meeting:
Compulsory liquidation: 8393+
Termination of liquidator's office: 8263
Voluntary liquidation: 8574+

Final report:
Compulsory liquidation: 8393
Administration: 9168

Finance:
Own share purchase or redemption: 1356+
Of company, See Funding

Financial adviser: See Adviser

Financial assistance:
Main entry: 5557+
Commission on subscription for shares: 1238

INDEX   F   1261

Financial assistance *(continued)*
Consideration for allotment of shares: 1125
Distribution:
    Liability of shareholder: 1730
    Unauthorised: 5581
Effect of insolvency: 5581
Effect on distributable profits: 1626, 1631
Sale of company: 5390+
When taking security: 4583
Joint venture company: 6563

Financial promotion:
Share issue: 4825+
Sale of company:
    Factor to consider: 5390+
    Marketing: 5220
Takeover of public company: 998

Financial records:
Compulsory liquidation: 8232
Liquidation committee objection to: 8305
See also Accounts (Compulsory liquidation, CVL), Records (Accounting)

Financial report:
Voluntary liquidation: 8535

Financial Services Authority:
Breach of City Code on Takeovers and Mergers: 6730
Compulsory liquidation: 7628, 7639, 7829, 8167, 8297
Voluntary liquidation: 8563
Administration: 8710, 8728, 8765, 8856, 9038+, 9112, 9141
Administrative receiver: 9377
CVA: 9513+

Financial statements:
Main entry: 4226+
Notes to: 4209
See also Balance sheet, Profit and loss account

Financial year:
Main entry: 4217+
Disclosing subsequent events in directors' report: 4252
Distinguished from calendar and tax year: 4209
Previous year's figures in financial statements: 4231
Balance sheet at end of, See Balance sheet

Fixed assets:
On balance sheet: 4237

Fixed charge:
Characteristics: 4603+
Assets over which it can be taken: 4618+
Over book debts: 4626+
Over shares: 1917
Registration at Companies House: 4637+
Liquidation:
    Distribution out of assets: 7990
    Remuneration of liquidator for realisation: 8244
Administration: 8936
Receivership: 9287
Pre-CVA moratorium: 9483
See also Floating charge

Fixed dividend:
Right: 1678+
Preference share: 790

Fixture:
Security over: 4622+

Floating charge:
Characteristics: 4610+
Assets over which it can be taken: 4618+
Crystallisation: 4613
    Certificate of non-crystallisation in sale of company: 5677
Enforcement: 4663
Registration at Companies House: 4637+
Challenging:
    In insolvency: 7836+
Liquidation:
    Distribution out of assets: 7992+
    Paying preferential creditors: 8047
    Remuneration of liquidator: 8244
CVL:
    Notice of meeting to enter into: 8444
MVL:
    Notice of meeting to enter into: 8613
Administration:
    Generally: 8936+
    Administration application: 8728+, 8738, 8751
    Administration application hearing: 8746
    Appointment of administrator out of court by qualifying holder: 8742, 8777+
    Assets: 8910
    Definition of qualifying floating charge: 8779
    Holder placing company into: 8710
    Notice of administrator's intention to resign: 9036
    Notice of intention to appoint administrator: 8766, 8780
    Preferential creditors: 8965
    Removing administrator: 9038+
    Replacing administrator: 9044
    Substituting administrator: 8744, 9003+
Receivership: 9236+, 9288

Floating charge (continued)
Ordinary receivership:
Ring-fence: 9327, 9369+
Administrative receivership:
Holder placing company into: 8691, 9237+
Ring-fence: 9327, 9378+
Pre-CVA moratorium: 9476, 9483
See also Fixed charge

Foreclosure: 4667

Foreign company:
Loans to director: 2807
Whether can be subject to insolvency proceedings: 7302, 8722, 9445
See also Overseas company

Forfeiture:
Meaning: 9940
Main entry: 1219+
Lease:
Lessee in liquidation: 8014
Lessee in administration: 8951, 8818
Lessee in pre-CVA moratorium: 9476
Unclaimed dividend: 1692

Form 2.1B:
Administration application: 8736+

Form 2.2B:
Administrator's consent to be appointed: 8770, 8783

Form 2.3B:
Confirmation of service of administration application: 8745

Form 2.4B:
Administration order: 8750

Form 2.5B:
Charge holder's notice to other charge holders of intention to appoint administrator: 8780+

Form 2.6B:
Charge holder's notice of appointment of administrator: 8782+

Form 2.8B:
Company/board's notice of intention to appoint administrator: 8766+

Form 2.9B:
Company/board's notice of intention to appoint administrator: 8770

Form 2.10B:
Company/board's notice of intention to appoint administrator: 8770

Form 2.21B:
Creditor requisition for meeting: 9081

Form 2.29B:
Affidavit of proof of debt: 8955

Form 4.1: See Statutory demand

Form 4.2:
Non-contributory's petition to wind up: 7636

Form 4.14:
Contributory's petition to wind up: 7656+

Form 4.19: See Statement of affairs (CVL)

Form 4.25: See Proof of debt (Liquidation)

Form 288a:
Appointment of director: 2288
Appointment of secretary: 4151

Form 288b:
Removal of director: 2957
Removal of secretary: 4160

Form 288c:
Change to particulars of director: 2288
Change to particulars of secretary: 4151

Form 363a: See Annual return

Form 363s: See Annual return (Shuttle)

Form 395:
Registration of mortgage/charge at Companies House: 4642

Formation:
Of company:
Main entry: 340+
Incorporation of business: 550+
For joint venture: 6560+
For purposes of hive-down: 6420
Documents to file at Companies House: 479
Fees payable to Companies House: 480
Agent's liabilities: 350
European company: 98
European Economic Interest Grouping: 112+
Limited liability partnership: 83
Community Interest Company: 69+
Choice of business vehicle comparison table: 130
Liquidation:
Individual involved to co-operate with liquidator: 8169
Individual involved to provide further information: 8144

Formation *(continued)*
Compulsory liquidation:
Individual involved to co-operate with official receiver: 8121
Individual involved to make statement of affairs: 8127+
Individual involved to provide accounts: 8138+
CVL:
Individual involved to provide accounts 8138
Administration:
Individual involved to co-operate with administrator: 8855
Individual involved to prepare statement: 8861+ (affairs), 8867+ (concurrence)
Administrative receivership:
Individual involved to co-operate with administrative receiver: 9377
Individual involved to prepare statement: 8861+ (affairs), 8867+ (concurrence)

Franked investment income: 1790

Foss v Harbottle, rule in: 7124+

Fraud:
Meaning: 9940
Defrauding creditors: 2577, 7446
Disqualification as a director: 3012
Evasion of VAT: 2606
On the minority: 7128
Insolvency practitioner: 7425, 7429
Liquidation: 7464, 7626, 7638, 7826+, 7909, 8169 (compulsory liquidation), 8170, 8442 (CVL)
Pre-CVA moratorium: 9486

Fraudulent misrepresentation:
Action/litigation: 7162

Fraudulent trading:
Main entry: 7443+
Disqualification as a director: 3012

Fuel: See Benefits (Director's, Non-cash)

Full title guarantee:
Meaning: 5731

Funding:
Shareholders' agreement: 2087
Bonus issue: 1018
Issue of preference shares: 781
Business acquisition: 5550+
Joint venture company: 6619+
Management buy-out: 6043+
Target of sale of company: 5674+
Of company, See Finance

Future debt:
Liquidation:
Calculation of dividend: 8059
Discount as deferred debt: 8066
Estimating value: 8038
Set-off: 8075
Voluntary liquidation: 8056, 8489
Administration:
Calculation of dividend: 8059
Discount as deferred debt: 8975
Proof of debt: 8949
Set-off: 8976
CVA: 9533

G

GAAP:
UK:
Convergence with IFRS: 4212
Sources: 4211

Garden leave:
Payment to director:
Income tax: 2750

General meeting:
Minimum notice period: 3675+
CVL: 8558
MVL:
Removing liquidator: 8540
See also Shareholder meeting

Generally accepted accounting principles: See GAAP

Gift:
Shares:
Main entry: 1827
Breach of pre-emption provisions: 1858
Stamp duty: 1876
Financial assistance for acquisition of shares: 5569

Going concern:
Basis for preparation of accounts: 4229
Rescue company as: 8711
See also Transfer as a going concern

Golden handshake: See Lump-sum payment

Golden hello: See Lump-sum payment

Golden share: See Master share

Good faith:
Change to articles: 450

Good faith *(continued)*
Director's duty to act in: See Promote the company's success
Liquidator's duty to act in good faith: 8225
Administrator's duty to act in good faith: 9013
Receiver's duty to act in good faith: 9360

Goods:
Financial records of company dealing in: 4195

Goodwill:
Name: 305+
Company name infringing: 247
Mortgage or charge over: 4638

Grant of representation: 1967

Gross misconduct:
Employee and valuation of shares for pre-emption offer: 1854

Group:
Main entry: 194+
Accounts:
　Main entry: 4382+
　Definition of parent and subsidiary undertaking: 213+
　Distribution by reference to: 1621, 1744
Confidentiality agreement: 5246
Directors' report: 4382
Disclosure of director's remuneration in company accounts: 2771
Dividend:
　Inter-group: 1615
Financial assistance: 5565, 5577
　Whitewash procedure: 5594
　Whitewash by wholly owned subsidiary: 5613
Guarantee: 4700
Piercing the corporate veil: 7125
Security over assets: 4574+
Transfer of shares within:
　Stamp duty: 1877
　Of joint venture company: 6610
Transfer of assets within:
　Effect on distributable profits: 1615
　And definition of distribution for tax purposes: 1771
　Prior to sale of shares: 5361

Group relief:
Stamp duty: 5309
Whether distribution for tax purposes: 1771

Guarantee:
Main entry: 4696+
Sale of company: 5469
Loans to directors: 2816, 2817, 2821, 2822

Guarantee *(continued)*
Joint venture: 6603
Secured by family home: 4769+
Company, See Company limited by guarantee

Guaranteed debt:
Liquidation:
　Employee: 8012
　Employees' preferential debts: 8045
　Proof of: 8024
Administration:
　Employee: 8951
　Employees' preferential debts: 8965
Receivership: 9265

Guarantor:
Sale of company: 5728
Proof of guaranteed debt in liquidation: 8024

H

Hard copy:
Sending information to company in: 3628
Company sending information in: 3696

Heads of agreement:
Sale of company: 5529+
Joint venture: 6591

Health and safety:
Main entry: 623, 7178
Breach of requirements: 2590+
Investigation on sale of company: 5688

Hearing:
Disqualification: 3057+
Part 8 claim: 7155
Non-part 8 claim: 7165
Panel on Takeovers and Mergers: 6710+
Reduction of share capital: 1488+
Scheme of arrangement: 6512+, 6521+
Unfair prejudice application: 2120
Insolvency applications: 7380+
Winding up petition: 7718+
Administration application: 8746+

High court:
CA 1985 applications: 7143
Non-CA 1985 applications: 7164
Insolvency proceedings: 7362+

Hire-purchase:
Liquidation: 7977

Hire-purchase (continued)
Administration:
  Assets under agreement: 8912
  Creditor voting at creditors' meeting: 9091
  Effect of company entering into: 8818
Receivership: 9291
See also Lease

Hive-down:
Main entry: 6415+
Sale of company: 5283
Effect on employees:
  Compulsory liquidation: 7754
  Voluntary liquidation: 8473
  Administration: 8830
  Receivership: 9266

Holding company:
Definition: 199+
Loans to directors: 2804+
Liability as shadow director: 2213
Director's service contract with company's holding company: 2655+
Acquisition of shares in subsidiary: 5565
Subsidiary holding shares in: 2028
Guarantee: 4700+
See also Parent Company

Holiday pay:
Employees' preferential debts:
  Liquidation: 8045
  Administration: 8965

Honesty:
Director's duty to act honestly, See Promote the company's success

Human rights:
Interviewee's during CIB investigation: 7225
Transfer of shares and pre-emption rights: 1842

Husband: See Spouse

I

Incentive schemes:
Director's remuneration: 2717+
Disclosure of director's remuneration in company accounts: 2778+
See also Employee share scheme

Income statement:
International accounting standards: 4244

Income tax:
On distributions: 1780+

Income tax (continued)
Bonus issue: 1037
Director's remuneration: 2745+

Incorporated business:
Definition and contrast with unincorporated: 1
Main types: 39
Table of comparison with unincorporated business: 130

Incorporation: See Formation

Indemnity:
Meaning: 9940
Director's against liability: 2512+
Acquisition of shares and financial assistance: 5569
Sale of company:
  Main entry: 5800+
  Minimise risk to buyer: 5395
  Retention for claim: 5492+
Receiver's: 9323, 9403
Against tax liabilities, See Tax deed

Independence:
Director's duty to exercise independent judgment: 2389
  Account for profits remedy: 2471+
  Injunction remedy: 2467+
  Restitution/tracing remedy: 2476+
Liquidator's duty to exercise discretion personally and not to fetter: 8225
Administrator's duty to exercise discretion personally and not to fetter: 9013

Independent election candidate: See Political donation

Indictable offence: 7184, 9935

Individual:
Insolvency proceedings: 7302
Liquidation:
  Duty to co-operate with liquidator: 8169
  Duty to provide further information: 8144
  Private examination: 8172+
  Public examination: 8147
Compulsory liquidation:
  Duty to co-operate with official receiver: 8121
  Duty to deliver company's property to liquidator: 8170
  Duty to make statement of affairs: 8127+, 8131
  Duty to provide accounts: 8138+
  Liquidator's exercise of powers: 8221
  Notice of creditors' and contributories' meetings: 8340
CVL:
  Duty to provide accounts: 8138

Individual *(continued)*
  Notice of creditors' and contributories' meetings: 8557
Administration:
  Duty to co-operate with administrator: 8855
  Duty to deliver company's property to administrator: 8855
  Duty to prepare statement: 8861+ (affairs), 8867+ (concurrence)
  Duty to submit to private examination: 8855
Administrative receivership:
  Duty to co-operate with administrative receiver: 8855
  Duty to deliver company's property to administrative receiver: 8855
  Duty to prepare statement: 8861+ (affairs), 8867+ (concurrence)
  Private examination: 9377+
CVA:
  Challenge nominee's decisions during pre-CVA moratorium: 9474
  Challenge implementation: 9535

Industrial and provident society:
Main entry: 121
Co-operative: 29

Information:
Director's duty not to misuse: 2405+
  Account for profits remedy: 2471+
  Injunction remedy2467+
  Restitution/tracing remedy: 2476+

Information memorandum:
Joint venture: 6591
Private placing: 4812
Sale of company: 5227+

Information technology:
Sale of company: 5683
See also Electronic

Inheritance:
Shares and stamp duty: 1876

Inheritance tax:
Own share purchase: 1798

Initial accounts: See Accounts

Injunction:
Meaning: 9940
Remedy for breach of directors' duties: 2467+
Auditor's right to access information: 4298
Pre-emption provisions: 1857

Insider dealing:
Interests in shares in public companies: 2042+

Insolvency:
Summary table:
  Comparison of different procedures: 7350
  Converting one insolvency procedure to another: 7481
Terms generally: 7301
Balance sheet test: 7601
Cash-flow test: 7600
Types of company which can be subject to proceedings: 7302
UK legislative framework: 7364
Court's jurisdiction: 7362+
Cross-border jurisdiction: 7366+, 7375+
Foreign companies.
  Incorporated in EU member state: 7366+, 7676
  Incorporated elsewhere: 7375+
Overseas company:
  With GB branch: 180
  Filing requirements: 180
After paying dividend: 1641
Before formal insolvency proceedings: 7312+
Director:
  Liabilities generally: 7439+
  Liability for unlawful distribution: 1746
  Disqualification: 3023+
EC legislation: 7366+
Financial assistance: 5577
Of borrower:
  Challenging security: 7808+
  Subordination: 4688+
  Floating chargeholder: 4612
  Default in loan agreement: 4552
  Mortgage over shares: 1930
Of shareholder:
  Transfer of shares: 1842, 1845, 1854
Searches on sale of company: 5704+
See also Administration, Administrative receivership, Compulsory liquidation, CVA, CVL, Liquidation, MVL, Receivership, Voluntary liquidation

Insolvency practitioner:
Main entry: 7422+
Disqualification: 3008
  Leave to act: 3074
Liability as shadow director: 2212
Liability for costs in insolvency applications: 7395
Power to litigate in company's name: 7124
Compulsory liquidation:
  Ability to petition: 7625

Insolvency Service:
Guidance: 7364
Complaints re. insolvency practitioners: 7427
Database of insolvency practitioners: 8200

Inspection:
By CIB, See CIB Investigation
Accounting records: 4197+
Companies House information:
 Main entry: 4090+
 Register of charges: 3982
Company registers:
 Summary table: 4019
 Interests in shares: 3994
 Charges: 3977+
 Directors and secretaries: 3906
 Directors' interests: 3967
 Director's residential address: 3907
 Shareholders: 3930+
Minutes:
 Board meeting: 3474
 Shareholder meeting: 3869
Service contract:
 Director's: 2668+
 Secretary's: 4156
Court record of insolvency proceedings: 7398+
Insolvency practitioner's records: 7426
Liquidation:
 Proof of debt: 8041
 Company's books and papers: 8228
 Liquidator's records: 8305
 Records of liquidation: 8230
Compulsory liquidation:
 Proxy forms: 8352
 Statement of affairs: 8133
CVL:
 Proxy forms: 8557
Administration:
 Proof of debt: 9020
 Proxies: 9020
 Records of administration: 9019+
 Proof of debt: 8961
CVA:
 Documents: 9536

Inspector:
CIB inspection: 7219+

Insurance:
Policies of company: 613
Director against liability: 2515
Auditor against liability: 4303
Investigation on sale of company: 5689
Fraudulent trading: 7445
Wrongful trading: 7454
Creditor's claim against company:
 Liquidation: 8016
 Administration: 8951

Intellectual property:
Summary table: 645
Business name: 286

Intellectual property *(continued)*
Company name: 247
Target of sale of company:
 Investigation: 5682
 Searches against: 5703
 Disclosure of searches: 5899
Protection:
 Generally: 646
 By reorganisation: 6405+
Mortgage or charge over: 4638, 4653
Transfer: 6026
See also Copyright, Design right, Trade mark and Patent

Inter-company loan: 2844

Interest:
Meaning: 9940
Community Interest Company: 65
Discounted share: 1121, 1187
Loan:
 Generally: 4546
 When treated as distribution: 1771
Unpaid calls: 1217
Unpaid dividend: 1692
Liquidation:
 Secured debts: 7989
 Proving for interest: 8021+
 Deferred debt: 8066
MVL: 8610
Administration:
 Secured debts: 8936
 Proving for interest: 8952+
 Deferred debt: 8975

Interests:
Director's duty to act in company's, See Promote the company's success
In shares:
 Provision of information to company: 3816
 Voting: 3816
 Public company and disclosure: 2042+
 CIB inspection: 7239+
Employees:
 Director's duty to have regard to: 2596
Contributories:
 Liquidator's duty to act in: 8225
Creditors:
 Liquidator's duty to act in: 8225
 Administrator's duty to act in: 9013
See also Directors' interests; for Unfair prejudice to shareholders' interests, see Unfair prejudice

Interim accounts: See Accounts

Interim dividend:
Main entry: 1665

Interim dividend *(continued)*
Review of board decision: 1694
Satisfied by distribution of assets: 1710

International accounting standards:
Main entry: 4212
Accounts prepared under: 4226

Internet:
Method of serving notice of shareholder meeting: 3698+
Method of company sending information generally: 3698+

Interview:
In insolvency and disqualification proceedings: 3050

Investigation:
Acquisition target:
   Main entry: 5652+
   Summary table of typical topics: 5669
   Seller's consideration of: 5390+
   Searches of public registers: 5695+
   Searches of public registers, disclosure: 5897
   In management buy-out: 6042
On joint venture: 6591
By CIB: 7195+
By Panel on Takeovers and Mergers: 6731
Company's affairs:
   Compulsory liquidation: 8117+
   Voluntary liquidation: 8518+
   Administration: 8855+
   Administrative receivership: 9377
   Pre-CVA moratorium: 9472+

Investigator:
CIB investigation: 7208+

Invoice:
Disclosure:
   Company name: 259+
   Liquidation: 8229, 8468
   Administration: 9021
   Receivership: 9368
   Pre-CVA moratorium: 9480
Discounting, See Invoice finance

Invoice finance:
Main entry: 4730
Instead of fixed charge over book debts: 4631

Irrevocable undertaking:
Alternative to shareholders' agreement: 2086
Accept takeover offer: 6794+

Issue of shares:
Main entry: 889+
Pre-issue checklist: 1070

Issue of shares *(continued)*
Procedure:
   Generally: 1068+
   Flowchart: 1081
Purpose: 4800+
Distinction from allotment:
   Generally: 889
   Relevance on bonus issue: 1030
Delay failure: 1097+
Dividend: 1702
Redeemable shares: 763+
Reorganisation under section 110 IA 1986: 6480+
Own share purchase or redemption: 1356, 1361, 1364
During takeover offer: 6866
See also Bonus issue, Rights issue

Issued share capital:
Meaning: 714

J

Joint administrators:
Main entry: 9001+
Division of responsibility: 8879
Duties: 9013
Notice of intention to resign: 9036
Remuneration: 9028
Replacement: 9044+

Joint and several liability:
Allotment at a discount: 1121
Loans to directors: 2882
Partnership: 18
Public company:
   Entering into transaction without trading certificate: 512
   Only one shareholder: 2015
Use of company name after liquidation: 270
Warrantors in sale of company: 5852+, 5975+

Joint liquidators:
Appointment:
   Compulsory liquidation: 8201
   Voluntary liquidation: 8508
   CVL at creditors' meeting: 8453
   CVL at shareholders' meeting: 8447
   MVL: 8615
Remuneration: 8242
Resignation: 8251+

Joint receivers:
Appointment: 9247

Joint secretaries: 4153
Joint shareholders:
Capacity: 2048
Death: 1964
Pre-emption rights on allotment: 950
Register: 3919, 3926
Shareholder calls: 1209
Voting: 3816, 3584 (written resolution)

Joint venture:
Main entry: 6550+
Financial promotions: 4827
Agreement, See Shareholders' agreement

Judge:
Insolvency applications: 7390

Judgment debt:
Proof of debt:
  Liquidation: 8009
  Administration: 8951
Winding up petition to enforce: 7599
See also Enforcement

Just and equitable:
Ground for compulsory liquidation: 7602+
  As shareholder remedy: 2133+

K

Key performance indicators:
Directors' report:
  Medium-sized company: 4252
  Large company: 4254

L

Land charges:
Search on sale of company:
  Investigation purposes: 5701+
  Disclosure: 5899

Land registry:
Search on sale of company:
  Investigation purposes: 5699+
  Disclosure: 5899

Land transaction return:
Stamp duty land tax: 5300+

Landlord:
Proof of debt:
  Liquidation: 8013+
  Administration: 8951

Landlord *(continued)*
Sale of company: 5765
See also Distress, Onerous property

Large company:
Directors' report: 4245+
Remuneration of auditors: 4307

Lawyer: See Adviser, Solicitor

Lease:
Assets: 4733+
Land and buildings:
  SDLT: 5298+
  Assignment: 5765
Liquidation:
  Disclaimer: 7917+
Administrator's power to enter into: 9011
See also Distress, Onerous property

Legal mortgage:
Characteristics: 4587+
Assets over which it can be taken: 4618+
Over shares:
  Formalities: 1934
  Priority: 1945+
Priority: 4673+
Foreclosure: 4667
See also Mortgage

Legal title:
Meaning: 1829
Shares:
  Transfers generally: 1830
  Transfer on legal mortgage: 4587+
  Registration of transfer instrument: 1882
  Share certificate as evidence: 1902, 1906

Lender:
Auditor's duty of care: 4303
Liability for unlawful financial assistance: 5638+
See also Loan, Secured creditor

Lessee:
Meaning: 9940
Insolvency of:
  Landlord proving for rent: 8013+

Letter:
From company:
  Disclosure of company information: 585
  Disclosure of compulsory liquidation: 8229
  Disclosure of voluntary liquidation: 8468
  Disclosure of administration: 9021
  Disclosure of receivership: 9368
  Disclosure of pre-CVA moratorium: 9480
See also Hard copy

Letter of administration:
Liquidation:
  Distribution to contributories: 8087
  Liquidator's power to take out: 8216, 8515
Transmission of shares: 1967

Licence:
Environmental: 623

Lien:
Main entry: 4714+
Over shares:
  Main entry: 1227+
  Registration of share transfer instrument: 1891
  Priority over mortgage: 1943
Assets subject to:
  Liquidation: 7691, 7902, 8017
  Administration: 8911
  Receivership: 9289
Professionals':
  Liquidation: 8017
  Administration: 8951

Limitation of liability:
Standard terms and conditions: 633
Auditors: 4303, 4318

Limitation period:
Meaning: 9940
Generally: 2442
Shareholder calls: 1217
Unpaid dividend: 1691
Liquidation: 8010
Administration: 8820, 8951

Limited liability partnership:
Main entry: 77+
Ability to be director: 2242
Distinguished from partnership: 17
Disqualification as member: 3010, 3024

Limited partnership: 17

Limited title guarantee: 5731

Liquidation:
Summary:
  Of process: 7335+
  Challengeable transactions: 7809
  Distributions: 8101
  Procedure flowchart: 7572
Charging order: 4740
Contract for future payment on allotment: 1118
Dissolution: 7497
Dividend:
  Arrears: 805+
  Unpaid: 1691+

Liquidation (continued)
Financial assistance:
  Distribution of assets: 5579
  Misfeasance: 5635
Floating charge: 4613
Overseas company: 180
Own share purchase followed by: 1407, 1427
Preference shares:
  Right to capital following: 803+
  Use in anticipation of MVL: 830
  Voting on resolution for: 812
Redemption followed by: 1407, 1427
Sale of company followed by: 5292
Section 110 IA 1986 reorganisation: 6465+
Third party debt order: 4741
Unregistered mortgage/charge: 4644, 4648+
Use of company name after: 264+
Administration followed by:
  Generally: 9141, 9142+
  Appointment of liquidator: 8203
  Proving for interest: 8021
  Proving for rent: 8013
  Liquidation committee: 8322+
  Proof of debt in foreign currency: 8020
Administration when company in:
  Generally: 8723
  Appointment of administrator: 8765, 8778
During administration: 8814+
During receivership:
  Effect on receiver's agency: 9361
  Appointment of receiver: 9231
  Application of floating charge assets: 9326
  Expenses of liquidation: 9322
During administrative receivership: 9379
CVA followed by:
  Appointment of liquidator: 8203
During CVA:
  Proposal: 9450
  Effect on liquidation: 9534
  Submission of proposals to nominee: 9457
See also Compulsory liquidation, CVA, CVL, MVL, Voluntary liquidation

Liquidation committee:
Meetings: 8307+
Compulsory liquidation:
  Main entry: 8292+
  Sanction of liquidator's powers: 7791+, 8303, 8216, 8217+
  Consent to liquidator making calls on shares: 7873
  Fixing liquidator's remuneration: 8242+
Compulsory liquidation:
  Inspection of financial records: 8232
CVL:
  Main entry: 8547+

Liquidation committee *(continued)*
  Sanction of liquidator's powers: 8303, 8489, 8490, 8515
  Consent to liquidator making calls on shares: 7873
  Established by creditors' meeting: 8455
  Fixing liquidator's remuneration: 8242+

Liquidator:
Acting without sanction: 8218
After administration:
  Obtaining information: 9022
Appeal:
  Decision on proofs: 8040
  Decision on preferential debts: 8045
Application:
  Alter proofs: 8039
  Private examination: 8172+
  Relief from transaction defrauding creditors: 7829
Charging order: 4740
Dealing with proofs: 8036+, 8056
Distribution:
  To shareholders: 8090
  To creditors: 8053+
Financial obligations: 7896
Misfeasance: 7457+
Power:
  Challenge pre-insolvency transactions: 7808+
  Deal with company's assets: 7772+, 8215+
  Deal with company records: 8233
  Distribute unrealised assets: 7914
  Test valuation of security: 7987
Public examination:
  Asking questions at: 8150
  Of liquidator: 8147
Reporting activities of directors/shareholders: 8166+
Sale of company: 5283
Section 110 IA 1986 reorganisation: 6465+
Third party debt order: 4741
Unregistered mortgage/charge: 4644, 4658+
Compulsory liquidation:
  Main entry: 8195+
  Appoint special manager: 8375+
  Final meeting: 8393+
  Investigation into company's affairs: 8165+
  Supervision by liquidation committee: 8302+
  Stay of proceedings: 7736
  Summary table of powers: 8216
  Voting: 8355, 8359
Voluntary liquidation:
  Main entry: 8507+
  Investigation into company's affairs: 8518+
  Power to offer alternative consideration on sale of assets: 8490
  Hand over to successor: 8267

Liquidator *(continued)*
  Publicise liquidation: 8468
  Summary table of powers: 8515
CVL:
  Appointment: 8457
  Calling meetings: 8558
  Calling final meetings: 8574+
  Conversion of MVL to CVL: 8648+
  Creditors' meeting to enter into CVL: 8448+
  EC Insolvency Reg: 8459+
  Supervision by liquidation committee: 8302+
  Power to request accounts: 8138
  Powers to act between shareholders'/creditors' meeting: 8447
  Voting: 8355, 8359
MVL:
  Account of winding up: 8646
  Appointment: 8616
  Company insolvent: 8648
  Final shareholders' meeting: 8664
  Power to sell to directors: 8633
Administration:
  Placing company into: 8710, 8728+, 8738, 8751+
Receivership:
  Power to require receiver to provide information: 9370+
  Receiver's remuneration: 9323
CVA:
  Company's assets: 9532
  Pre-CVA moratorium: 9485
  Proposal by: 9450, 9453, 9459, 9461
  Summoning meetings: 9500
See also Joint liquidators, Provisional liquidator

Listed company: 9940

Listing questionnaire:
Part 8 procedure: 7154

Litigation:
Meaning: 9940
Main entry: 7115+
Investigation of on sale of company: 5685
Compulsory liquidation: 7757+, 7850+
Voluntary liquidation: 8469+
Administration: 8818+, 9011
Receivership: 9307+

LLP: See Limited liability partnership

Loan:
To company: 4504+
To director: 2804+
To Community Interest Company:
  Cap on interest rate: 65
To joint venture company: 6575+
Capitalisation: 1053+

Loan (continued)
Financial assistance:
    When constitutes: 5569
    When irrecoverable: 5631+
For purpose of acquisition: 5550+
See also Charge, Guarantee, Mortgage, Security, Subordination

Loan agreement:
Main entry: 4545+
Restriction on reduction of share capital: 1460
Restriction on distribution: 1639

Loan capital: See Redeemable shares

Loan notes:
Consideration for sale of company:
    Main entry: 5437+
    Tax clearance: 5368+

Local authority:
Search on sale of company:
    Process and procedure: 5697+
    Disclosure: 5899

Loss:
Accumulated realised:
    Meaning: 1613+
    Of public company: 1647
After period of accounts: 1641
Surrender, See Tax (Reliefs, Group loss relief)

LPA receiver:
Definition: 9239, 9228
Appointment: 9231, 9245+
Company's agent: 9361
Dealing with company's assets: 9285
Power to sell assets: 9310
Distribution: 9322
Powers: 9345
Removal: 9404

Lump-sum payment:
To director:
    Remuneration: 2727
    Income tax: 2750

M

Made-up date:
For annual return: 4061

Magistrates' court:
Directors' disqualification jurisdiction: 3045

Magistrates' court (continued)
Officer:
    Appointing administrator: 8728, 9002
    Presenting winding up petition: 7628
Prosecution in: 7184+, 9935

Main proceedings:
EC Insolvency Reg: 7367+
CVL: 8459+
Convert administration to liquidation: 9144
Convert CVL to liquidation: 9558

Management:
Company:
    Main entry: 3110+
    Effect of shareholders' agreement: 2086+
    Effect of preference shares: 781
Partnership: 18
Unincorporated association: 24
Limited liability partnership: 79+
European company: 92+
European Economic Interest Grouping: 107+
Joint venture company: 6614+
Co-operative: 29
Industrial provident society: 121

Management accounts: See Accounts (For purposes of distribution)

Management buy-out/buy-in: 6040+

Manager:
Status: 2181, 2184
Liability:
    For Companies Act offences: 2537
    Company struck off by application: 7511
    Company struck off by Companies House: 7519
    Unlimited: 464, 2278
Disqualification: 3010
European Economic Interest Grouping: 107

Managing director:
Main entry: 3425+
Authority: 2354+

Manslaughter: 2591, 7179+

Market share:
Competition implications: 651, 5505+

Market value:
Definition: 1115
Action affecting: 1279
Pre-emption offer:
    Fair value: 1853
    Discount: 1854

Marketing:
Company for sale: 5219+
See also Sale of goods

Marriage:
Transfer of shares in consideration: 1876
Transactions defrauding creditors: 7827
See also Spouse

Master share: 860+

Medium-sized company:
Definition: 4362
Abbreviated accounts: 4376+
Directors' report: 4245+
Remuneration of auditors: 4306

Medium-sized group:
Definition: 4388
Preparation of group accounts: 4387+

Member:
Distinguished from shareholder: 2000
Company limited by guarantee:
    Liability: 52
    Liability during insolvency: 7863+
European Economic Interest Grouping: 106
Limited liability partnership: 79+
Unincorporated association: 24
Unlimited company: 57, 2012, 7863+, 7876

Member state liquidator:
Main entry: 7366
Ability to attend insolvency application hearing: 7391
Substitution for another petitioner: 7650
Voting at creditors' meetings: 8355
Administration:
    Attending administration application hearing: 8746
    Converting into liquidation: 9144
    Creditor proved same debt: 8970
    Notice of administrator's intention to resign: 9036
    Notice of dividend: 8972
    Notice of intention to declare dividend: 8969
    Request list of creditors: 8961
CVA:
    Converting into liquidation: 9558

Members' voluntary liquidation: See MVL

Memorandum:
Main entry: 394+
Under CA 2006: 519
Effect and overlap with articles: 372+

Memorandum *(continued)*
Capacity to create borrowing or security: 4755+
Change:
    Effect on management powers: 3159+
    Procedure: 410+
Community Interest Company: 71
Director's duty to act within terms: 2554+
Disclosure of company name in: 259+
Entitlement to copy: 374
Restriction on distribution: 1639
Right to dividend under: 1674
Source of shareholders' rights and remedies: 2079+
Varying class right contained in: 1288

Memorandum of deposit: 4604

Mental capacity:
Director: 2251, 2939
Secretary: 4122
Shareholder:
    Voting: 3816
    Trigger of pre-emption provisions: 1845
    Transmission of shares: 1980
Public examination in liquidation: 8153

Merger:
Allotment pursuant to: 1250+
Competition controls:
    Main entry: 5505+
    Joint venture: 6584
Forming European company: 98
Public company:
    Valuation of consideration for allotment: 1153
    Scheme of arrangement: 6530+
See also Sale of company, Takeover, Accounting policy

Minor:
Meaning: 9940
Ability to be shareholder: 2022
Ability to be director: 2246
See also Child

Minority shareholder remedies: See Shareholder (Minority)

Minutes:
Board meeting: 3473+
Committee meeting: 3418
Shareholder meeting: 3864+
Creditors' and contributory meetings in liquidation: 8365
Creditors' meeting in administration: 9092
Shareholders' and creditors' meeting in CVA: 9512

Misfeasance:
Main entry: 7457+
Disqualification as director: 3023
Liquidator: 7793, 8036, 8235, 8264
Administrator: 9016+, 9042
Receiver: 9392
Supervisor of CVA: 9544

Misrepresentation:
Allotment: 1098
Sale of company:
 Damages: 5828+
 Rescission: 5838+
 Exclusion of liability: 5730, 5840
Liquidation:
 By liquidator: 8236+
 By use of company name after: 265
See also False representation

Misuse of company property/ information:
Director's duty:
 Main entry: 2405+
 Injunction remedy for breach: 2467+
 Account for profits remedy for breach: 2471+
 Restitution/tracing remedy for breach: 2476+
 Disqualification: 3023

Model articles:
Meaning: 9940

Model law: 7377

Money lending company: 2833

Moral right: 645

Moratorium:
Meaning: 9941
Compulsory liquidation:
 Between presentation of petition and winding up order: 7697+
 After winding up order made: 7757
Compulsory liquidation:
 On litigation: 7850+
Voluntary liquidation: 8469+
Administration:
 Main entry: 8813+
 Interim moratorium: 8742, 8768, 8781
 Pre-CVA moratorium ended: 8765
Pre-CVA:
 Main entry: 9466+
 Availability: 9436
 Decisions by creditors' and shareholders' meetings: 9506
 Committee: 9493
 Ground for compulsory liquidation: 7612

Mortgage:
Main entry: 4574+
Distinguished from charge: 4578+
Registration:
 Register of charges: 3975+
 At Companies House: 4637+
 Overseas/Slavenburg company: 177, 4644
Release/satisfaction: 4656+
Enforcement: 4663+
Priority: 4672+
Subordination: 4687+
Over shares:
 Main entry: 1915+
 Subsidiary relationship: 204
Realisation in liquidation: 7977+, 8244
Assets subject to in administration: 8911
See also Charge, Legal mortgage, Equitable (Mortgage) and Security

Mortgagee:
Meaning: 9940
See also Lender

Mortgagor:
Meaning: 9940
See also Borrower

Mutual dealings: See Set-off

Mutual society: See Industrial and provident society

MVL:
Main entry: 8594+
Procedure flowchart: 7572
Summary: 7335+
Summary timeline: 8617
Distinguished from CVL: 8426+
Commencement of winding up: 8623
Staying proceedings: 8479
Expenses where before compulsory liquidation: 7959
Converted into CVL: 8648+

N

Name:
Company:
 Main entry: 240+
 In memorandum: 399
 Change: 273+
 Change on sale of company: 5735
 Use of in litigation: 7124+
 Director's use of same name after insolvency: 264+, 3012

Name *(continued)*
Business: 285+
Partnership: 17
Limited liability partnership: 83
Overseas company: 158
Community Interest Company: 69
European Economic Interest Grouping: 108
Internet domain: 645

National Insurance contributions:
Company's obligations: 608
Director's remuneration: 2740
Payment on benefits in kind: 1785
Administration: 8931
Receivership: 9324

Nationality:
Director: 2250
Secretary: 4122

Negligence:
Action by or against company for: 7162+
Directors: 2411+, 2448, 7127+
Auditors: 4301
Insolvency practitioner: 7429
Liquidator: 8170, 8218, 8220, 8236+
Administrator: 8906, 9016+
Receiver: 9305, 9392
Supervisor of CVA: 9544
See also Tort; for Director, See Care, skill and diligence

Negligent misstatement: 1410, 5830, 6880, 8236

Negotiable instrument:
Proof of debt:
  Compulsory liquidation: 8032
  Administration: 8954

Net assets:
Adjustment to consideration on sale of company: 5480+
Balance sheet: 4237
Doctrine of capital maintenance: 703+
Financial assistance:
  Company with no or negative: 5569
  Reduced by material amount: 5569+
  Whitewash: 5595+
Public company and distribution: 1645+

New Companies Act:
Meaning: 9940

New model articles:
Meaning: 9940

NIC: See National Insurance contributions

Nil-paid shares: See Shares (Nil or partly paid)

No gain/no loss disposal: 6433+

Nominal share capital: See Authorised share capital

Nominal value:
Definition: 1115
Allotment for less than: 1121
Unpaid: 1205+
Reduction: 1438
Effect on right to dividend: 1676

Nominee:
Director:
  Main entry: 2206
  Conflicts of interest: 2390+
Shareholder:
  Capacity: 2032+
  Voting: 3816
  Before registration of share transfer: 1831
  Stamp duty on share transfers: 1877
  Subsidiary relationship: 203
  Unfair prejudice: 2117
  Objection to variation of class rights: 1297
Pre-CVA moratorium:
  Supervision of company: 9472+
  Duty to report directors' conduct: 9473
  Replacement: 9475
  End of moratorium: 9494
CVA:
  Qualification: 7423
  Consent to act: 9457
  Financial bond: 7425
  Review of proposals: 9445, 9457+
  Summoning meetings to approve proposal: 9500
  Replacement: 9504

Non-cumulative dividend: 793

Non-director:
Main entry: 3432+
Directorial title: 3426
Membership of committee: 3413
With managerial role: 3188+

Non-distributable profits: 1025, 1027, 1029

Non-equity share capital: 727

Non-executive director:
Main entry: 2204
Appointment: 2627

Non-QCBs: See Non-qualifying corporate bonds

Non-qualifying corporate bonds:
5437+

Non-qualifying distribution:
Meaning: 1775
Tax credit: 1782
Corporation tax calculation: 1790
Notification to Revenue and Customs: 1796

Non-voting share: 749+, 3821

Notice:
Board meeting:
　Main entry: 3236+
　To alternate director: 3442
Shareholder meeting:
　Main entry: 3646+
　Proxy statement: 3732
　Reconvened after adjournment: 3764
AGM:
　Main entry: 3785
　Shareholder resolutions: 3781
Class meeting:
　Main entry: 3795
　Scheme of arrangement: 6516+
Ordinary resolution: 3532
Special resolution: 3555
Elective resolution: 3564
Extraordinary resolution: 3544
Shares:
　Calls: 1208
　Exercise of lien: 1228
　Forfeiture: 1221
　Mortgage over: 1920
　Refusal to register transfer: 1896+
　Statutory pre-emption offer: 950+
Transmission: 1969+, 1977
Of company's constitution: 367
Disqualification application: 3047
Own share purchase/redemption out of capital: 1414
Takeover offer:
　Shareholder exercising sell-out rights: 6966
　Bidder exercising squeeze-out rights: 6951
Insolvency: 7404+
Liquidation:
　Dividend: 8055, 8058, 8062
Compulsory liquidation:
　First meetings: 8206
　Meetings generally: 8339+

Notice (continued)
　Creditors' meeting to remove liquidator: 8256
　Final meeting: 8393
　Early dissolution: 8396
CVL:
　Meetings to enter CVL: 8444, 8449+
　Meetings generally: 8557
　Creditors' meeting to remove liquidator: 8540
　Final meetings: 8575, 8577
MVL:
　Meeting to enter into MVL: 8613
　Creditors' meeting if insolvent: 8648
　Final meeting: 8664
Administration:
　Appointment of administrator by company: 8766+
　Appointment of administrator by floating charge holder: 8780+
　Approval of proposals: 8886, 8890
　Creditors' committee meeting: 9063
　Creditors' meeting: 9082
　Dividend: 8969, 8972
　End of administration: 9130
　Intention of administrator to resign: 9036
　Request information from administrator: 9061
　Revised proposals: 8894
Pre-CVA moratorium: 9469
CVA:
　Meetings to approve proposals: 9499+
　End of CVA: 9556
Receivership:
　Appointment of receiver: 9246, 9248+

Novation:
Meaning: 9940
Pre-incorporation contract: 357
Contracts on sale of assets: 5758+

Number:
Company:
　Given on formation: 495
　Disclosure: 585
Directors: 2230+
Secretaries: 4116, 4153+
Share: 709
Shareholders: 2012+

O

Obey instructions:
Director's duty:
　Main entry: 2348+
　If vague or commercially unsound: 2368

Objects:
Of company: 399
Change: 417

Offence: See Criminal offence

Offer: See Public offer, Takeover

Officer:
Meaning: 9940
Director: 2184
Secretary: 4136+
Entitlement to inspect accounting records: 4199
Liability:
  Breach of disqualification order or undertaking: 3082
  Breach of immigration requirements: 2598
  Company cheques: 2580
  Criminal: 2536+, 7183, 7464+, 8122, 8167, 9935
  Defrauding creditors: 2577
  In default (meaning): 9940
  Insolvency: 7439+
  Misfeasance: 7457+
  Statutory relief: 2505+
  Indemnity insurance: 2515, 2517
Liquidation:
  Duty to co-operate with liquidator: 8169+
  Duty to provide further information: 8144
  Private examination: 8172+
  Public examination: 8147
Compulsory liquidation:
  Duty to co-operate with official receiver: 8121
  Destruction of company books, papers, securities: 8170
  Duty to make statement of affairs: 8127+
  Release from duty to make statement of affairs: 8131
  Duty to provide accounts: 8138+
  Fraudulent entry in register, accounts, company document: 8170
  Notice of creditors' and contributories' meetings: 8340
  Liquidator as officer: 8224+
Voluntary liquidation:
  Duty to publicise liquidation: 8468
  Liquidator as officer: 8523, 8527
CVL:
  Duty to co-operate with liquidator: 8518
Administration:
  Duty to prepare statement of affairs: 8861+
  Duty to cooperate with administrator: 8855
  Duty to prepare statement of concurrence: 8867+
  Administrator as officer: 8906, 9013, 9014
Administrative receivership:
  Duty to prepare statement of affairs: 8861+
  Duty to prepare statement of concurrence: 8867+
CVA:
  Attendance at shareholders'/creditors' meetings to approve proposals: 9501

Official receiver:
Main entry: 8277+

Official receiver *(continued)*
Appointment:
  As liquidator: 8195+
  As receiver: 9229
  As proxy: 8349
Remuneration: 8242
Compulsory liquidation:
  Application for appointment of special manager: 8375+
  Application for early dissolution: 8396+
  Application for relief from transaction defrauding creditors: 7829
  Application to stay proceedings: 7736
  Entitlement to information following administration: 9022
  Investigation into conduct of company: 8120+
  Power to deal with company's assets: 7772
  Private examination: 8172+
  Public examination: 8146+
  Statement of affairs: 8127+
  Release as liquidator: 8264+
  Hand over conduct of liquidation to liquidator: 8209
  Obligation to consider appointment of liquidator: 8204+
  Power to request accounts: 8138+
Voluntary liquidation: 8502
Administrative receivership:
  Reporting director's conduct to: 9377

Off-market purchase: See Own share purchase

Off-the-shelf company:
Main entry: 546+
First board meeting: 590

Onerous property: 7917+

Order:
Insolvency applications: 7392
For goods:
  Statement of compulsory liquidation: 8229
  Statement of voluntary liquidation: 8468
  Statement of administration: 9021
  Statement of receivership: 9368
  Statement of pre-CVA: 9480
Disqualification, See Disqualification (Order)

Ordinary application: 7382+

Ordinary business: 3652

Ordinary receiver:
Definition: 9239
Appointment: 9245+
Liability for contract of employment: 9267
Powers: 9345

Ordinary resolution:
Main entry: 3530+

Ordinary resolution *(continued)*
Special notice: 3536+
Contents of notice of meeting: 3656+

Ordinary shares:
Main entry: 743+
Conversion into redeemable shares: 1445
Dividend:
    Payment before preferential dividend: 1679
    Payment amongst different classes: 1681
Reduction of share capital:
    Pay off: 1450
    Apportionment of loss: 1453
Joint venture company: 6569+

Originating summons: 3049

Originating application: 7382+, 7641

Overseas company:
Main entry: 140+
Branch:
    Annual return: 4065
    Disclosure in directors' report: 4252
    Register: 3948+
Change to accounting reference period: 4220
Registration of mortgage/charge: 4644
Pre-incorporation contracts: 356
Service of documents in litigation: 7152
Serving of winding up petition on: 7644
Insolvency:
    Branch: 180
    Cross-border: 7366+, 7375
Administration: 8710

Overseas director: 2250

Own share purchase:
Main entry: 1337+
Procedure:
    Off-market purchase: 1383+
    Out of capital: 1400+
    Summary table: 1424
Contract:
    Advance approval: 1387+
    Variation/release/assignment: 1392, 1626, 1631
    Kept at registered office: 1395
    Failure to perform: 1427+
Whether distribution: 1603, 1771
Disclosure in director's report: 4247
Financed out of distributable profits:
    Effect on distributable profits: 1612, 1626, 1631
Whether financial assistance: 5580
Liability to repay unlawful payment: 1730
Taxation of payment: 1798

P

Paid up share capital:
Meaning: 718
Reduction: 1445

Panel on Takeovers and Mergers:
Main entry: 6700+
Panel Executive: 6715+
Code Committee: 6719
Decision making and appeals: 6710+
Powers: 6729+

Paper copy: See Hard copy

Par value: See Nominal value

Parent company:
Definition: 194, 213+
Group accounts: 4382+
Individual accounts:
    Disclosures if exempt from group accounts: 4392
Financial year:
    Coincide with subsidiary's: 4217
Non-company subsidiary undertaking: 4195
Sale of company:
    Warrantor: 5823
Joint venture company:
    Guarantee: 6603
See also Holding company

Pari passu:
Meaning: 9940
Shares: 740
Covenant in loan agreement: 4550
Insolvency:
    Subordination agreement: 4690
    Distributions to creditors: 8054

Part 8:
Claim form: 7146+
    Service: 7152+
Application procedure: 7151+
    Summary table: 7157

Participating interest: 214

Participator:
Close company: 1771, 1805

Particulars of claim:
Part 8 application: 7148
Non-Part 8 application: 7164+

Partnership:
Main entry: 17+

Partnership *(continued)*
Ability to be secretary: 4120
Conversion to limited company: 550+
Comparison to limited company: 130
Sale of business: 5283
Insolvency proceedings: 7302
See also Limited liability partnership, Limited partnership

Passing off: 305+, 645

Passport rights: 4875+

Patent:
Summary: 645
Mortgage or charge over: 4638, 4653
Registration of transfer: 6026
Assignment: 5988+
Office:
  Search of on sale of company: 5703
  Disclosure of search of on sale of company: 5897
See also Intellectual property

PAYE:
Main entry: 608
Director's remuneration: 2745
In liquidation: 7964
In administration: 8931
In receivership: 9324

Payment:
Allotment:
  Generally: 1110+
  Public company: 1135+
Dividend: 1660+
Own share purchase:
  Main entry: 1356+
  Entering into contingent contract: 1390
  Variation or release of contract: 1392
Redemption: 1356+
Shareholder calls: 1208+
Pre-CVA moratorium:
  Restrictions during: 9481
In lieu of notice, See Lump-sum payment

Payment instrument: 8063

Pension:
Director's: 2720
  Income tax: 2748
  Disclosure in company accounts: 2778+
Investigation on sale of company: 5690
Occupational pension scheme:
  Preferential debt in liquidation: 8045
  Preferential debt in administration: 8928

Pension *(continued)*
Liquidator's power to deal: 7908
Transfer under TUPE: 5776

Permissible capital payment:
Meaning: 1357
Capital redemption reserve:
  Amount transferred: 1361, 1365, 1366

Personal administration order: 3012

Personal representative:
Deceased shareholder:
  Ability to hold shares: 2032+
  Application for unfair prejudice: 2105
  Distribution in liquidation: 8087
  Liability in company's insolvency: 7863+
  Notice of exercise of lien: 1228
  Notice of pre-emption rights on allotment: 950+
  Petition for compulsory liquidation: 7620
  Transmission of shares to: 1964+
Deceased liquidator: 8263
Deceased administrator: 9041

Petition:
Court procedure: 7146, 7159
Unfair prejudice: 2105+
Winding up, See Winding up petition

Petitioner:
For company's liquidation:
  Main entry: 7616+
  Summary: 7629
  Attendance at administration application hearing: 8746

Phoenix company: 264+

Piercing the corporate veil: 270, 1337, 7125

Place of business:
Overseas company:
  Registration: 151+
  Change registration to branch: 183
  Closure or move: 184

Plant and machinery:
Mortgage or charge over: 4622+, 4638
Sale:
  Investigation: 5681
  Transfer by delivery: 5986

Pledge: 4720+

Political activity:
Community Interest Company: 62+

Political donation:
Corporate governance: 3204
Disclosure of in directors' report: 4247

Poll voting:
Shareholder meeting: 3842+
Scheme of arrangement: 6519
Dispensation from mandatory takeover offer: 6809

Post:
Communicating with company by: 3628, 3695+

Postal voting: 3852

Powers:
Director's duty to act within: 2376+, 2554+
Account for profits remedy: 2471+
Injuction remedy: 2467+
Restitution/tracing remedy: 2476+

Power of attorney:
Meaning: 9940
By director: 3496
On sale of company: 6013
Receiver: 9359

Pre-CVA moratorium: See Moratorium (Pre-CVA)

Pre-emption rights:
Allotment: 940+
Mortgage over shares: 1922
Transfer of shares:
 Main entry: 1842+
 Own share purchase: 1385
 Registration of transfer if in breach: 1888
 Triggered by election by personal representatives: 1972

Preference: 7819+

Preference shares:
Main entry: 780+
Convertible: 822+
Participating: 829+
Redeemable: 817+
Statutory pre-emption rights on allotment: 946
Bonus issue: 1018
Distribution in liquidation: 8089
Dividend: 1679
Reduction of share capital:
 Apportionment of loss: 1453
 Pay off: 1450+
Section 110 IA 1986 reorganisation: 6478

Preferential creditor:
Liquidation:
 Main entry: 8044+
 Partly secured: 7978
 Employees: 8012

Preferential creditor (continued)
Administration:
 Main entry: 8965
 Determining administrator's remuneration: 9028
 Determining discharge of administrator from liability: 9042
 Partly secured: 8937
Receivership: 9326
CVA: 9456

Pre-incorporation acts: 345+

Premium:
Definition: 1115
Allotment for less than maximum: 1121
Transfer to shareholder premium account: 1245+
Shareholder calls: 1205+

Price-fixing: 651, 6585

Priority:
Subordination: 4680
Mortgage or charge:
 Registered over unregistered: 4658+
 Between security holders: 4672+
 Over shares 1943+

Private equity: 4800+

Private examination:
Liquidation: 8172+
Administration: 9011
Administrative receivership: 9377
Use of evidence in disqualification proceedings: 3050

Privilege:
Disclosure of information during CIB:
 Investigation: 7210
 Inspection: 7223

Probate:
Transmission of shares: 1967

Proceeds of crime:
Director's liability: 2537
Company's liability: 2538
Liquidation: 7909, 8236
Administration: 8909, 8949
Receivership: 9294

Product liability insurance: 613

Profit:
Realised:
 Meaning: 1613+

Profit (continued)
Public company distribution: 1647
Profit and loss account: 4232

European Economic Interest Grouping: 116
Forecast in takeover of public company: 6884
Industrial and provident society: 121
Limited liability partnership: 80
Partnership: 18
Available for distribution, See Distributable profits
Chargeable to corporation tax, See Corporation tax
See also Account for profits

Profit and loss account:
Main entry: 4241+
Statutory accounts: 4209
Abbreviated accounts:
Small company: 4370
Medium-sized company: 4376
Balance sheet: 4237
Consolidated: 4394+
Deficit:
Elimination of by reduction of share capital: 1438

Promissory note:
Meaning: 9940
Proof of debt:
Compulsory liquidation: 9032
Administration: 8954
Voting at creditors' meeting:
Compulsory liquidation: 8355
CVL: 8355
Administration: 9091
CVA: 9508

Promote the company's success: 2379+
Account for profits remedy: 2471+
Injunction remedy: 2467+
Restitution/tracing remedy: 2476+

Promotor:
Role in company formation: 345+
Disclosure of benefit or fee: 511
Disqualification: 3008, 3082+
Notice of unlimited liability: 464

Proof of debt:
Liquidation:
Secured creditor: 7978+
Unsecured creditor: 8003+
Rule against double proof: 8024
Last date for proving: 8055, 8056
Late: 8056
Voting at creditors' meeting: 8354+

Proof of debt (continued)
Compulsory liquidation:
Procedure: 8030+
Form sent out with notice of creditors' and contributories' meetings: 8339
Voluntary liquidation: 8491+
CVL:
Forms sent out with notice of creditors' meeting: 8449
Administration:
Main entry: 8954+
Changed/withdrawn/expunged before payment of dividend: 8973
Information passed on by outgoing administrator: 9047

Proper claimant principle: 7124

Proper purpose:
Allotment of shares: 929, 935
Director's duty to act for: 2376+, 2379+
Liquidator's duty to act for: 8225
Administrator's duty to act for: 8225, 9013

Property:
Director's duty not to misuse: 2405+
Account for profits remedy: 2471+
Injuction remedy: 2467+
Restitution/tracing remedy: 2476+
Sale:
Disclosure of searches: 5899
Investigation by buyer: 5679
Provisions in sale and purchase agreement: 5764+
Registration: 6025
Searches: 5696+
Stamp duty land tax: 5298+
Transfer form: 5987
VAT: 5324+
Mortgage or charge:
Registration: 4638, 4653
Registration if acquired subject to: 4645
Over family home: 4769+

Proposals:
Administration:
Main entry: 8876+
Modification: 8894
CVA:
Main entry: 9448+
Approval: 9499+
Deemed rejection: 9503
Modification: 9504
Rejection: 9504
Appeal against approval: 9513+

Prospective liability: 7601

Prospectus:
Share issue:
 Main entry: 4845+
 Exemptions for unlisted company: 995
Scheme of arrangement: 6990
Takeover of public company: 6687

Protected payment: See Guaranteed debt

Provisional liquidator:
Main entry: 7686+
Attendance at winding up petition hearing: 7718
Statement of affairs: 8127
Compulsory liquidation:
 Removal: 8254
 Termination of office and release: 8264+
 Application for appointment of special manager: 8375+
Administration: 8778

Proxy:
Meaning: 9940
Shareholder meeting:
 Main entry: 3727+
 Voting on show of hands: 3840
 Demand poll: 3843+
 Voting on poll: 3846
Liquidation committee meetings: 8308
Compulsory liquidation:
 Creditors' and contributories' meeting: 8349
 Form: 8339
 Chairman appointed as: 8346
CVL:
 Generally: 8557
 Form: 8449
Administration:
 Creditors' committee meetings: 9067
 Creditors' meetings: 9082, 9085, 9086, 9087
Receivership:
 Creditors' committee meetings: 9062, 9067, 9082, 9085, 9086+, 9092
CVA:
 Shareholders'/creditors' meetings: 9501, 9508, 9510, 9511

Public company:
AGM: 3777+
Defamation: 7162
Directors:
 Continue in office past retirement age: 3536
 Loans to: 2804+
 Minimum number: 464, 2230, 3460
 Non-executive: 2204
 Resolution to appoint more than one: 2271
Distribution:
 Interim and initial accounts: 1633+
 Net assets: 1645+

Public company *(continued)*
Financial assistance:
 Unavailability of whitewash: 5594
 Unlawful: 5637
Memorandum: 399
Net assets fall: 720, 7441
Own share purchase:
 Approval of contract: 1390
 Disclosure of payment: 1394
 Minimum requirements: 1385
Promotor: 351
Secretary: 4124
Share capital:
 Denomination: 709
 Minimum: 510, 720
 Reduction: 1490, 1494
Shareholders:
 Proxy's right to speak at meeting: 3730
 Written resolution: 3580+
 Transfer of non-cash asset: 1171+
Shares:
 Payment for allotment: 1135+
 Charge over: 1916
 Lien over: 1227
 Forfeiture: 1219, 1222
 Disclosure of interest: 2042+
 Register of interest: 3990+
Subscribers: 463
Trading certificate:
 Formation: 510+
 Failure to obtain: 512, 7608
Private company:
 Comparison with: 47
 Conversion into: 673+
 Conversion from: 662+
Listed company:
 Distinguished from: 47
Company limited by guarantee: 52
Unlimited company: 57
Strike off: 7502
See also Takeover

Public examination: 8146+

Public interest:
Disqualification as director: 3012, 3030
Winding up in: 7626+

Public liability insurance: 613

Public offer:
Shares:
 By private company: 986+
 Commission payments: 1237+
See also Takeover

Purchase: See Sale of company, Sale of goods, Transfer of assets, Transfer of shares

Q

QCBs: See Qualifying corporate bonds

Qualification:
Director: 2241+
Insolvency practitioner: 7423+
Liquidator: 8200
   Ceasing to be qualified: 8263
Administrator: 8995+
   Ceasing to be qualified: 9040
Receiver: 9230
   Ceasing to be qualified: 9406

Qualification shares: 1836, 2254

Qualifying corporate bonds: 5437+

Qualifying distribution:
Meaning: 1775
Tax credit: 1780+
Corporation tax: 1790

Qualifying floating charge: See Floating charge (Administration)

Quasi-loan:
To director: 2816, 2821, 2826, 2832, 2835, 2841, 2897
To holding company: 2841

Quasi-partnership:
Remedies for breakdown: 2100+, 7127+
Shareholders' agreement: 2086

Quorum:
Meaning: 9940
Board meeting:
   Main entry: 3258+
   Alternate director: 3442
   Directors' interests: 3353
   Sole director: 3463
   Tele-/Video-conference: 3255+
   Written resolution: 3294
Shareholder meeting:
   Main entry: 3746+
   CVL: 8445, 8253
   MVL: 8253
   CVA: 9501
Class meeting: 3796
Contributories' meeting: 8348, 8253
Creditors' committee meeting: 9066
Creditors' meeting:
   Liquidation: 8348, 8253
   Administration: 9085
   CVA: 9501
Liquidation committee meeting: 8310

Quoted company: 9940

R

Ratchet: 824

Rates:
Liquidation: 7964
Receivership: 9324
See also Interest

Ratification:
Main entry: 2497+
Pre-incorporation contract: 357
Of unlawful distribution: 1754+
Liquidator's acts: 8218

Receipt: 259+

Receiver:
Main entry: 9343+
Types: 9236+
Dealing with company's assets: 9282+
Expenses: 9323
Liability for contracts: 9263+
Misfeasance: 7457+
Multiple: 9321
Power to sell assets: 9310+
Court-appointed: 9229
Registration of appointment: 3979+
Mental incapacity, See Deputy
See also Administrative receiver, Ordinary receiver, Joint receivers

Receivership:
Main entry: 9195+
Procedure flowchart: 9198
Summary: 7340
Before liquidation: 7959
Before administration: 8817

Reconstruction:
Definition: 6532
Relief from stamp duty land tax: 5309
Scheme of arrangement:
   Generally: 6530+
   Dissolution: 7525
Group, See Reorganisation

Record date: 1703

Records:
Accounting: 4195+
Retention:
   Generally: 656+
   Tax and accounting: 605, 4198

Records (continued)
VAT: 5788
See also Minutes, Register

Rectification:
Articles: 379
Register:
 Main entry: 4027+
 Allotment in breach of pre-emption rights: 979
 At Companies House: 4030, 4080
 Liability of directors for cost: 1898

Redeemable shares:
Main entry: 760+
Bonus issue: 1018
Purchase: 1338
Redemption:
 Main entry: 1337+
 Terms and manner: 768+
 Summary table: 1424
 Whether distribution: 1603
 Whether financial assistance: 5580
 Whether variation of class rights: 1279
 Bonus shares: 1775, 1782
 Liability to repay unlawful payment: 1730

Redenomination: See Share capital (Redenomination)

Reduction of share capital:
Main entry: 1435+
Summary and checklist: 1500
Increase distributable profits: 1615
Whether distribution: 1603
Whether financial assistance: 5580
Whether variation of class right: 1279
Loss written off: 1612
Redenominate share capital: 1327
Return of capital: 803+
Consolidate/sub-divide share capital: 1317

Redundancy:
Hive-down: 6422
Payment to director: 2750, 2983+
Sale of company: 5686, 5771+
Remedy: 2986
Compulsory liquidation: 7754, 8012
Voluntary liquidation: 8473
Administration: 8830, 8928
Receivership: 9266

Reflective loss:
Main entry: 2464
Shareholders' agreement: 6601
Claim against auditors: 4303

Register:
Main entry: 3888+
Disclosure in sale of company: 5898

Register of charges:
Company's internal register: 3975+
Companies House register: 3979+
Rectification: 4030
Registration of mortgage or charge: 4636+

Register of debenture holders: 4006+

Register of directors: 3894+

Register of directors' interests: 3958

Register of directors' residential addresses: 3896, 3902, 3907

Register of disqualified directors: 3080

Register of interests in shares: 3990+

Register of secretaries: 3894+

Register of share applications and allotments: 4002

Register of share transfers:
Main entry: 4004
Transfer of shares: 1883

Register of shareholders:
Main entry: 3915+
Update:
 Consolidation or sub-division of share capital: 1318
 Own share purchase: 1395
 Redemption: 1378
Allotment: 1086
Transfer of shares:
 Registration: 1883, 2057
 Effect of registration on title to shares: 1830
Personal representative: 1964+
Trustee in bankruptcy: 1976
Mental incapacity of shareholder: 1980
Rectification: 4027+
Liquidation:
 Liquidator's power to correct: 7863

Registered design right: 645

Registered office:
Formation: 482
Disclosure: 585
Change: 570
Accounting records kept at: 4197

Registered office *(continued)*
Director's service contract kept at: 2668+
Own share purchase contract kept at: 1395

Registrar:
Insolvency applications to court: 7390
Reduction of share capital: 1485+
Scheme of arrangement: 6512+

Registrar of Companies: See Companies House

Registration:
Mortgage/charge: 4636+
Overseas company:
  Branch: 145+
  Established place of business: 151+
Transfer of shares:
  Main entry: 1882+
  Breach of pre-emption provisions: 1857
  Effect of refusal on mortgage: 1922
  Effect on priority of mortgages: 1945+
  Forged transfer instrument: 1870
  Irregularity in transfer instrument: 1869
  Production of share certificate: 1904
VAT: 607
  Transfer on sale of company: 5788
Health and safety: 623
See also Articles, Formation, Memorandum, Number

Release:
Mortgage/charge: 4656+
Liquidator: 8264+
Provisional liquidator: 7692
See also Discharge

Relevant private company:
Loan to director: 2807

Removal:
Director:
  From office: 2936+
  From employment/service contract: 2983+
  To enable board to function: 3166+
  Special notice of resolution: 3536+
Auditor:
  From office: 4343+
  Special notice of resolution: 3536+
Secretary: 4159+
Liquidator:
  Liquidation: 8254+
  Release: 8264+
  Voluntary liquidation: 8538+
Liquidation committee member: 8314
Administrator: 9038+
Ordinary receiver: 9404

Removal *(continued)*
LPA receiver: 9404
Administrative receiver: 9406

Remuneration:
Director:
  Main entry: 2696+
  Alternate: 3447
  In shareholders' agreement: 2087
  Unauthorised: 2398+
  Disclosure in accounts: 2778+
  Disclosure in CIC report: 66
Secretary: 4156
Auditor:
  Disclosure: 4305+
Employees:
  By way of dividend: 1681
  Claim in liquidation: 8012, 8045
  Claim in administration: 8928, 8965
  Claim in receivership: 9326
Liquidator: 8242+
Special manager: 8376
Administrator: 9026+
Receiver: 9323
  Appointed by court: 9229
  Vacation of office on administration: 8817
Nominee of CVA: 9453
Supervisor of CVA: 9549

Renominalisation: See Share capital (renominalisation)

Rent:
Expenses:
  Liquidation: 7965
  Receivership: 9325
Proof of debt:
  Liquidation: 8013+
  Administration: 8951

Rentcharge:
Meaning: 9940
Insolvency: 7926

Reorganisation:
Main entry: 6405+
Group:
  Allotment pursuant to: 1252
Share capital:
  Convertible preference shares: 824
Loss written off on: 1612
Pre-sale: 5212
Section 110 IA 1986:
  Main entry: 6465+
  Summary: 6473+
  Whether financial assistance: 5580

Report:
Insolvency practitioner:
  Use in disqualification proceedings: 3053
Official receiver:
  To creditors/contributories: 8280+

Reporting requirements: See Companies House

Representation:
Loan agreement: 4548
Inter-creditor agreement: 4687
Sale of company:
  Information memorandum: 5228
  Overlap with warranty: 5809
See also False representation, Fraudulent misrepresentation, Misrepresentation

Requisition:
Shareholder meeting: 3624, 3626+, 3632
Shareholder resolution at AGM: 3780+
Shareholder statement before meeting: 3663+

Re-registration: See Conversion

Rescission:
Main entry: 5838+
Loan to director: 2886
Insolvency: 7393
Winding up order: 7394, 7730+

Research and development:
Disclosure of in directors' report: 4252

Reserve capital: 1205

Reserves:
Balance sheet: 4237
Public company's undistributable: 1646

Residence:
Director: 2250
Secretary: 4122
Target of takeover: 6755+

Residential address:
Director: 3896, 3902, 3907, 4064, 4090
Secretary: 3899, 3920, 4064
Shareholder: 3920, 3934

Resignation:
Director:
  Generally: 2920
  Conflict of interest: 2396+
  From employment/service contract: 2979
  On sale of company: 5963+
Secretary: 4159+

Resignation *(continued)*
Auditor: 4341+
Liquidator:
  Main entry: 8251+
  Release: 8264+
Liquidation committee member: 8314
Administrator: 9036+
Ordinary receiver: 9404
Administrative receiver: 9406

Resolution:
Board:
  Main entry: 3224
  Filing requirements: 3480
Shareholder:
  Main entry: 3523+
  Summary table: 3600
  Filing requirements: 3871
  Minutes: 3866
  Where meeting adjourned: 3760+
Filing at Companies House: 4051
Liquidation committee: 8311+
Compulsory liquidation:
  First meetings: 8207
  Meetings generally: 8359, 8365
  Appoint/remove/release liquidator: 8208, 8253, 8257
Voluntary liquidation:
  Enter into: 8438+
CVL:
  Enter into: 8446, 8453+
  Effect of resolution to wind up: 8465+
  Meetings generally: 8557
  Appoint liquidator: 8508+, 8541
  Remove/release liquidator: 8541
  Filing requirements: 8457
MVL:
  Enter into: 8604, 8615
  Effect of resolution to wind up: 8623
  Appoint liquidator: 8615
Administration:
  Appoint administrator out of court: 8764+
  Creditors' committee meetings: 9064
  Creditors' meeting: 9086
Administrative receivership:
  Creditors' committee meetings: 9064
CVA:
  Creditors' meeting: 9510
  Shareholders' meeting: 9511

Restitution: 2476+

Restitution order:
Under FSMA 2000: 8066

Restraint of trade:
Doctrine against: 2396+, 5738+

Restraint order: 7909

Restrictive covenants:
Meaning: 9940
Director's service contract: 2644
Confidentiality agreement: 5246
Sale of company: 5735+
Joint venture agreement: 6624
Payments relating to: 2750

Restructuring: See Reorganisation

Retention:
Accounting records: 4198
Company records: 3743, 3869
Director's service contract: 2668+
Documents: 656+
Register of shareholders: 3936+
Sale of company: 5489+, 5859
Tax records: 605, 4198
Financial records and trading accounts:
  Liquidation: 8232
Proxy forms:
  Liquidation: 8352

Retention of title:
Meaning: 9940
Main entry: 4728+
Standard terms and conditions: 633
Goods subject to:
  Liquidator's power to deal: 7902
  Administrator's power to deal: 8912
  Receiver's power to deal: 9290

Retirement:
Director:
  From office: 2925+
  From employment/service contract: 2981
Secretary: 4159+

Retirement benefit: See Pension

Return date: 4061

Return of capital:
Right:
  Ordinary shares: 743+
  Non-voting shares: 750
  Preference shares: 803+
  Participating preference shares: 833+
Right:
  Deferred shares: 877
Reduction of share capital: 1450+

Rights issue:
Main entry: 1042+
Effect on convertible preference share: 824
Allotment at less than market value: 1121

Ring-fence:
Liquidation: 7992+
Administration: 8910, 8927
Receivership: 9327, 9369+

Rule against double proof:
Liquidation: 8024
Administration: 8970

S

Salary: See Remuneration

Sale and leaseback:
Meaning of: 4736
Distinguished from mortgage: 4579

Sale and repurchase:
Meaning of: 4736
Distinguished from mortgage: 4579

Sale of assets: See Transfer of assets, Sale of company

Sale of company:
Main entry: 5200+
Comparison table:
  Between sale of shares and sale of assets: 5392
Document checklist for completion: 6013+
Pre-sale reorganisation: 6405+
See also Hive-down

Sale of goods:
Main entry: 628+
Agency agreement: 638+
Distribution agreement: 640
Retention of title: 4728+
Terms and conditions:
  Standard: 633
  Investigation on sale of company: 5684

Sale of shares: See Transfer of shares, Sale of company

Same day incorporation: 500

Scheme of arrangement:
Main entry: 6500+
Whether financial assistance: 5580
Redenominate share capital: 1327
Takeover: 6985+
Stamp duty: 1877
Variation of class rights: 1289
When preferable to reduction of share capital: 1440

Scrip dividend: See Stock dividend

Scrip issue: See Bonus issue

SE: See European company

Seal: 3490

Search warrant:
CIB investigation: 7216

Secondary proceedings:
Meaning: 7369+
CVL: 8459+
CVA: 9453, 9512

Secret profit:
Director's duty:
   Main entry: 2398+
   Injunction as remedy for breach: 2467+
   Account for profits as remedy for breach: 2471+
   Restitution/tracing as remedy for breach: 2476+
Liquidator's duty: 8225
Administrator's duty: 9013

Secretary:
Main entry: 4115+
Company formation:
   Details to be provided: 482, 525
   Minimum number: 464
Role at board meetings: 3279
Notice of shareholder meeting: 3689
Disqualification order or undertaking: 3082
Register of secretaries: 3899+
Remuneration in shareholders' agreement: 2087
Registration of share transfer: 1889
Ability to be director: 2244
Assistant/deputy: 4154
Joint: 4153

Secretary of state:
Power:
   Require company to hold AGM: 3788
   Suspend shareholder's voting rights: 3822
Compulsory liquidation:
   Power to petition: 7626+
   Action following official receiver's report: 8122
   Application to extend period before dissolution: 8398
   Appointment of liquidator: 8210
   Early dissolution application: 8396
   Objection to liquidator's financial records: 8305
   Removal of liquidator: 8261
Voluntary liquidation: 8535
Administration: 8856

Secretary of state *(continued)*
Administrative receivership: 9377
CVA: 9536
Power to investigate companies, See CIB investigation

Section 110 reorganisation: See Reorganisation (Section 110 IA 1986)

Section 700 accounts: 174

Secured assets:
Liquidation:
   Cost of realisation: 7956
   Remuneration of liquidator for realisation of: 8244
Administration:
   Administrator dealing with: 8911
   Required to be sold by administrator: 8941
Administrative receivership: 9349
Pre-CVA moratorium: 9483

Secured creditor:
Liquidation: 7977+
Administration:
   Main entry: 8936+
   Ability to place company into: 8710
   Determining administrator's remuneration: 9028
   Determining discharge of administrator from liability: 9042
   Voting at creditors' meeting: 9090
Receivership:
   As enforcement method: 9195+
CVA:
   Vote at creditors' meeting: 9508
See also Lender

Security:
Meaning: 9941
Main entry: 4562+
Financial assistance:
   Whether constitutes: 5569
   Unlawful: 5631+
Loan to director: 2816+, 2821+
Management buy-out: 6046+
Sale of company:
   Breach of warranty claim: 5858+
   Consideration: 5468+
   Investigation: 5674+
Liquidation:
   Realisation: 7979+
   Surrender: 7982+
   Value: 7985+
Administration:
   Realisation: 8943
   Costs of realising: 8927

Security *(continued)*

Receivership:
  Additional security: 9284
  Company's books subject to security: 9293
  Contractual power to appoint receiver: 9225+
  Statutory power to appoint receiver: 9228

Pre-CVA moratorium: 9479

See also Mortgage, Charge

Security for costs: 7140

Company in liquidation: 7734, 7851, 8260, 8469

Servant: 1158

Service:

Documents/information by company: 3695+
Documents/information to company: 3628
Part 8 claim form: 7152
Non-Part 8 claim form: 7165
Notice of pre-emption rights on allotment: 951
Notice of board meetings: 3240
Notice of shareholder meetings: 3687+
Notice in insolvency matters generally: 7404+
Statutory demand: 7597
Non-contributory winding up petition: 7644+
Contributory winding up petition: 7660
Administration:
  Administration application: 8741, 8743+
  Application by creditor to end administration: 9167

Service contract:

Director's:
  Main entry: 2627+
  Sample: 9925
  Limitation of liability: 2514
  Termination: 2977+
  Breach: 2986
  On sale of company: 5964
Secretary's: 4156+

Set-off:

Unpaid dividends against unpaid calls: 1691
On repayment of unlawful distribution: 1743
Limited by subordination agreement: 4693
Liquidation:
  Main entry: 8072+
  Guarantor cannot prove: 8024
  Liquidator dealing with proofs: 8036
Administration: 8976+
Receivership: 9328

Shadow ACT: 1795

Shadow director:

Main entry: 2212+
Contract with company: 2559+

Shadow director *(continued)*

Disclosure of directors' interests: 3321
Disqualification as director: 3010
Disclosure of interest in shares/debentures: 3379+
Fiduciary duties: 2375
Misfeasance: 7457+
Use of company name after liquidation: 264+

Share capital:

Main entry: 700+
Alteration:
  Main entry: 1310+
  Summary chart: 1310
  Undertaking not to: 901
  Joint venture company: 6563
Authorised: 399, 712
Cancellation:
  Unissued: 1312
  Issued: 1445
  Forfeiture: 1222
  Effect on class rights: 1279
  Public company: 1152
Consolidation: 1314+
Disclosure on business letter or order form: 585
Effect of own share purchase or redemption: 1351
Redenomination: 1325+
  Reduction of share capital: 1445
  Scheme of arrangement: 6501
Renominalisation: 1326
Sub-division: 1314+
Mortgage or charge over uncalled: 4638
Public company: 510, 720
Company limited by guarantee: 52
Unlimited company: 57
European company: 90

See also Issue of shares, Shares, Stock, Reduction of share capital

Share certificate:

Main entry: 1902+
Allotment:
  Failure to send to allottee: 1099
  Requirement: 1086
Delivery to transferee:
  Trigger pre-emption provisions: 1848
  Transfer of shares: 1869
Deposit with lender: 1938
Forged transfer instrument: 1870
Registration of share transfer instrument: 1883
Return:
  Forfeiture: 1223
  Consolidation/sub-division of share capital: 1318

Share certificate *(continued)*
    Exercise of lien: 1229
    Own share purchase: 1395
    Redemption: 1378

Share class: See Class (Shares)

Share for share exchange:

Main entry: 6453+

Roll-over relief: 5428+

Stamp duty: 1877

Tax clearance: 5368+

Share options:

Allotment:
    Directors' authority: 921
    Statutory pre-emption rights: 945

Director's remuneration:
    Main entry: 2724+
    Disclosure: 2778+

Reduction of share capital: 1461

Share premium account:

Main entry: 1245+

Balance sheet: 4237

Capitalisation of in bonus issue: 1029

Own share purchase or redemption: 1351

Reduction:
    Main entry: 1435+
    Cancellation/repayment/transfer to reserve account: 1445

Share schemes:

Employee: 847+

HM Revenue and Customs approved: 2724+

Share warrant:

Main entry: 1902

Register of shareholders: 3924

Shareholder:

Main entry: 2000+

Summary table of rights and remedies: 2074

Liability:
    Company struck off register: 7511, 7519
    To pay for shares: 1119

Management powers:
    Main entry: 3146+
    Changes: 3157+
    Exceed: 3173
    Power to change board's: 3152+, 3157+
    Power to exercise board's: 3166+
    Role: 3118+

Shareholder meeting:
    Calling: 3630
    Notice: 3690, 3692+
    Proxy: 3727+
    Quorum: 3747+

Shareholder *(continued)*
    Requisition: 3625+
    Right to attend: 3724+
    Right to circulate statement before: 3663+
    Right to demand poll: 3843+
    Voting: 3815+

Sole shareholder: 2014+

Accounts:
    Delivery: 4265+
    Approval: 4273+
    Inspection: 4199

AGM:
    Right to put resolution: 3780+

Allotment:
    Pre-emption rights: 940+
    Unauthorised: 933

Articles: 379, 384

Auditor's duty of care towards: 4302+

Class rights:
    Objection to variation: 1297+
    Weighted voting rights: 1275
    Attendance at class meetings: 3796

Contributory: 7863+
    Distribution to: 8087+

Death:
    Stamp duty: 1876
    Transmission of shares: 1964+

Director:
    Ability to be: 2244
    Appointment: 2270+
    Approving expenses of: 2828, 2836
    Approving service contract of: 2655+
    Owing duties to: 2321+
    Prevent unauthorised transaction by: 2555
    Ratify unauthorised transaction by: 2497+
    Removal from office: 2946+

Dividend:
    Approval of interim: 1665
    Creation of debt: 1690+
    Declaration: 1663
    Right to: 1674+
    Unlawful: 1730+, 1754+
    Taxation: 1769+

Dormant company: 4411

Financial assistance:
    Approval of whitewash: 5613+

Forfeiture: 1219, 1223+

Inspection of registers:
    Register of charges: 3977+
    Register of directors and secretaries: 3906
    Register of directors' interests: 3967
    Register of shareholders: 3930+

Joint venture company:
    Generally: 6569+
    Consent to actions: 6616
    Funding: 6575+
    Management: 6578+
    Shareholders' agreement: 6600+
    Transfer of shares: 6609+

Shareholder (continued)

Litigation:
  Control: 7134+
  In company's name: 7124+
  In own name: 7126+

Minority:
  Rights and remedies generally: 2074
  Power under shareholders' agreement: 2086
  Objection to sale of company: 5283
  Objection to whitewash of financial assistance: 5616+
  Objection to conversion from public to private company: 678
  Objection to change of objects: 417
  Objection to scheme of arrangement: 6522+
  Objection to section 110 IA 1986 reorganisation: 6488+
  Valuation of shares for pre-emption offer: 1853
  Unfair prejudice: 2105+
  Winding up company: 2133+

Public company:
  Liability on allotment for non-cash consideration: 1185+
  Transfer of non-cash asset: 1171+
  Disclosure of interest: 2042+
  Failure to disclose interest: 1836

Secretary:
  Appointment: 4151
  Service contract: 4156

Takeover:
  Approval of frustrating tactics: 6865+
  Effect on minority: 6903+
  Irrevocable undertaking: 6794+
  Provision of information: 6872+
  Squeeze-out/sell-out rights: 6930+

Liquidation:
  Claim against liquidator: 8236
  Debts owed to shareholders: 8066
  Distribution to contributory: 8087+
  Proof of debt: 8011
  Report criminal activity of: 8122, 8167

Compulsory liquidation:
  Effect of order: 7753
  Petition: 7620
  Special resolution to wind up: 7610

MVL:
  Resolution to enter: 8604

Administration:
  Appointing administrator: 8764+
  Administration application hearing: 8746
  Challenging administrator's powers: 9015
  Copy of proposals: 8882+
  Debts owed to: 8951
  Shareholders' meeting: 9102

Pre-CVA moratorium:
  Challenging nominee's decisions: 9474
  Effect on: 9471+
  Extending: 9492
  Unfair prejudice: 9485

CVA:
  Challenging proposal: 9513+

Shareholder (continued)

  Inspection of documents: 9536
  Objecting to creditors' decision taking precedence: 9505
  Provision of information to: 9546+

See also Joint shareholders, Shareholder meeting, Shares, Transfer of shares, Unfair prejudice

Shareholder calls:

Main entry: 1205+
Liability to pay on forfeiture: 1223
Mortgage or charge over: 4638
Liquidator's power to make: 7872+
Administrator's power to make: 9011
Administrative receiver's power to make: 9309

Shareholder meeting:

Main entry: 3610+
Summary table: 3800
Summary timeline of events: 3873
Summary table of documents and statements to be circulated before meeting: 3670
Summary table of rights of attendees: 3755
Administrative requirements: 3862+
Personal representatives: 1964
Conduct: 3711+
Minimum attendance, See Quorum
Compulsory liquidation: 8335+
CVL:
  Main entry: 8555+
  Enter into: 8443+
  Appoint liquidator: 8509
  Final: 8577
MVL:
  Main entry: 8645+
  Enter into: 8612+
  Sanction of liquidator accepting alternative consideration: 8490
  Appoint liquidator: 8509+
  Remove liquidator: 8540
  Final: 8664
Administration:
  Main entry: 9102
  Administrator's power to call: 9011
Pre-CVA moratorium: 9478
CVA:
  Approve proposals: 9499+
  Disagree with creditors' meeting: 9505

Shareholder resolution: See Resolution (Shareholder)

Shareholders' agreement:

Main entry: 2086+

Shareholders' agreement *(continued)*
Breach:
  Discount valuation of shares for pre-emption offer: 1854
  Trigger of pre-emption provisions: 1845
Calls on shares in insolvency: 7872
Dividend:
  Right to: 1674
  Restrictions: 1639
Joint venture: 6600+
Pre-emption rights:
  Alternative: 942
  Waiver: 973
Restrict ability to change articles: 452
Source of rights and remedies: 2079+

Shares:
Main entry: 700+
CIB investigation:
  Into dealings by directors: 7244
  Into ownership: 7239+
Consideration for sale of company:
  Main entry: 5426+
  Tax clearance: 5368+
Directors':
  Qualification shares: 1836, 2254+
  Authority to allot: 921+
  Remuneration: 2752+, 2724+, 2778+
Fully paid:
  Definition: 1117
  Form of transfer instrument: 1865
Nil or partly paid:
  Definition: 1117
  Dividend: 1676
  Company's lien: 1227
  Forfeiture: 1219+
  Form of transfer instrument: 1865
  Liability of mortgagee: 1920
  Refusal of registration of share transfer instrument: 1891
  Rights and liability: 1119
  Shareholder calls: 1205+
  Extinguishing or reducing liability to pay: 1445
Paperless holding: 1828
Register:
  Of applications and allotments: 4002
  Of transfers: 4004
  Of mortgages and charges: 3975+, 4636
Trust over: 3923
Voting rights:
  Increased: 3820
  Restricted: 3821
  Suspended: 3822
See also Allotment, Bonus issue, Class (Shares), Directors' interests (In shares), Deferred shares, Employee (Shares), Issue of shares, Ordinary shares, Master share, Mortgage (Over shares), Non-voting shares, Preference shares, Redeema-

Shares *(continued)*
ble shares, Rights issue, Transfer of shares, Transmission, Subscriber (Shares)

Shelf company: See Off-the-shelf company

Ship: 4638, 4653

Show of hands: 3838+

Sign:
At place of business:
  Main entry: 585
  Overseas company: 168

Single shareholder company: 2014+
See also Sole shareholder

Skill and care
Director's duty, See Care, skill and diligence
Employee's duty: 2417+
Liquidator's duty: 8225
Administrator's duty: 9013
Receiver's duty: 9282

Slavenburg company: 177, 4644

Small company:
Definition: 4362+
Abbreviated accounts: 4369+
Audit: 4372
CVA: 9467
Director's report: 4368, 4245+
Distribution: 1795
Remuneration of auditors: 4306
Short form accounts: 4366

Small group:
Definition: 4388
Group accounts: 4387+

Social enterprise: 62

Social responsibility: 2087

Societas europaea: See European company

Sole director:
Main entry: 3460+
Written resolutions: 3295
Disclosure of directors' interests: 3322
Ability to be secretary: 4120

Sole shareholder:
Also director and contract with company: 3473
Shareholder meeting:
  Quorum: 3747
  Minutes: 3868

Sole shareholder *(continued)*
Register of shareholders: 3943
See also Single shareholder company

Sole trader:
Main entry: 12+
Conversion to limited company: 550+
Sale of business: 5283
Table of comparison with company limited by shares: 130
Insolvency proceedings: 7302

Solicitor:
Advice:
    Litigation: 7134
    Security over family home: 4773
    Personal guarantee: 4699
    Compromise agreement: 5970
Shadow director: 2212
Liability to pay costs of winding up petition: 7726
Lien: 4714
Liquidation: 8017
Administration:
    Lien: 8909
    Fee: 8951
    Administrator's power to instruct: 9011

Special business: 3652

Special dividend: 1666

Special manager:
Main entry: 8375+
Public examination: 8150

Special notice:
Main entry: 3536+
Remove/replace director: 2946+
Auditor:
    Remove: 4343
    Not renew appointment: 4346+

Special proxy: 8346

Special resolution:
Main entry: 3553+
Approve:
    Own share purchase contract: 1387+
    Payment out of capital: 1412
    Reduction of share capital: 1481
    Section 110 IA 1986 reorganisation: 6481
    Whitewash of financial assistance: 5613+
Change:
    Articles: 451
    Company name: 275
    Objects: 417
    Board's management powers: 3152+, 3157+

Special resolution *(continued)*
Notice of meeting:
    Contents: 7656+
    Document to accompany: 3670
Conversion from:
    Private to public company: 665
    Public to private company: 676
Enter into compulsory liquidation: 7610
Enter into voluntary winding up: 8438
MVL:
    Sanction liquidator's power to accept alternative consideration: 8490

Specific performance:
Meaning: 9940
Remedy:
    Breach by liquidator of company's contract: 8467
    Failure to complete own share purchase: 1427
    Failure to redeem shares: 1427
    Directors' refuse to register transfer of shares: 1837

Spouse:
As connected person: 848, 989, 3379, 5580, 6938, 7895, 9930+
Disclosing interest in shares/debentures: 3379

Stakebuilding: 6790+

Stamp duty:
Main entry: 1875+
Acquisition relief: 6454
Associated companies relief: 6441+
Allotment of shares: 1087
Own share purchase: 1394
Reduction of share capital: 1440
Sale of company: 5378+
Transfer of shares:
    Unpaid: 1888
    Transfer instrument must be chargeable to: 1869

Stamp duty land tax:
Main entry: 5297+
Group relief: 6437+

Stamp duty reserve tax: 1875

Statement of affairs:
Compulsory liquidation: 8127+
CVL:
    Enter into: 8440+
    Presented to creditors' meeting: 8452
    After creditors' meeting: 8457
    Liquidator to provide to creditors and contributories: 8530

Statement of affairs (continued)
MVL:
Liquidator to provide to creditors: 8530, 8649
Administration: 8861+, 8927
Administrative receivership: 8861+
CVA: 9456

Statement of compliance: 536

Statement of assets and liabilities: 8610+

Statement of concurrence: 8867+, 8927

Statement of receipts and payments:
Compulsory liquidation: 8231+, 8377
CVL: 8531, 8533

Stationery:
Disclosure of:
Company information: 259+, 585
Liquidation: 8229, 8468
Administration: 9021
Receivership: 9368
Pre-CVA moratorium: 9480
Overseas company: 169

Statutory books: 9940
See also Minutes, Records, Register

Statute barred: 9940

Statutory declaration:
Formation: 485
Disposal of forfeited shares: 1222
Before own share purchase/redemption out of capital: 1404+
Whitewash of financial assistance:
By directors: 5600+
Delivery to shareholders: 5615
MVL: 8610+

Statutory demand: 7594+

Steel: 8045

Stock:
In company: 709
Balance sheet: 4237
Conversion of shares into:
Ability of company: 1312
Authority: 1317
Information to be entered in register of shareholders: 3918
Entry in annual return: 4065
Mortgage or charge over: 4611, 4638
Sale of assets: 5756
Statement of in financial records: 4195

Stock dividend:
Main entry: 1714
Taxation: 1771
Prospectus: 4855

Stock transfer form: See Transfer instrument

Stop notice: 1951

Strict liability: 2536

Striking off:
Main entry: 7491+
Restoration to register: 7534+

Sub-division: See Share capital

Subordination:
Main entry: 4680+
Structural:
Meaning: 4683
Security over assets of group: 4574
Insolvency: 4690

Subscriber:
Definition: 2010, 9940
Additional: 2055
Effect of becoming: 405
Notice of meeting: 3795
Memorandum: 399, 519
Minimum number: 463, 2012
Minor's ability to be: 2022
Shares:
Rights of: 872
Public company: 1148
Pre-emption rights: 946

Subscription:
Allotment of right to:
Director's authority to grant: 921
Statutory pre-emption rights: 945
Price: 1115

Subsidiary:
Definition: 199+
Undertaking: 213+
Wholly-owned: 208
Accounts:
Consolidation in group accounts: 4382
Exclusion from consolidation in group accounts: 4390
Created by mortgage over shares: 1928
Director:
Duties to: 2321+
Loans to: 2832, 2840, 2841

Subsidiary *(continued)*
- **Financial assistance:**
  - Acquisition of shares in holding company: 5565
  - By wholly-owned: 5613
- **Financial year:** 4217
- **Holding shares in parent:** 2028
- **Joint venture company:** 6563
- **Sale of:**
  - Corporation tax: 5361+
  - Disclosure: 5909
- **Administrator's power to establish:** 9011

Substantial property transaction:
- **Main entry:** 2567+
- **Allotment for non-cash consideration:** 1070
- **Own share purchase:** 1385
- **Distribution of assets:** 1711
- **Hive-down:** 6424
- **Incorporation of business:** 552+
- **MVL:** 8633
- **Administration:** 8907
- **Receivership:** 9310

Summary offence: 7184, 9935

Supervisor:
- **CVA:**
  - Main entry: 9542+
  - More than one: 9504
  - Qualification: 7423
  - Financial bond: 7425
  - Ability to deal with company's assets: 9532+
  - Duty to give notice of end: 9556
  - Ability to convert into other proceedings: 9557
- **Misfeasance:** 7457+
- **Application:**
  - Challenge transaction defrauding creditors: 7829
- **Administration:**
  - Ability to place company into: 8710
  - Application to place company into: 8728
  - Attending application hearing: 8746
  - Notice of intention to appoint administrator: 8766

Surrender:
- **Of security:**
  - Liquidation: 7982+
  - Administration: 8937+

T

Table A:
- **Main entry:** 441+
- **Common changes to in articles:** 443
- **Community Interest Company:** 71

Table A *(continued)*
- **Table A 1985:** 9915
- **Comparison between Table A 1985 and 1948:** 9920

Takeover:
- **Public company:**
  - Main entry: 6675+
  - Regulatory framework: 6685+
  - Takeover Directive: 6688+
- **Compulsory acquisition following:** 6930+
- **Scheme of arrangement:** 6501+, 6985+
- **Financial promotions:** 4827
- **Prospectus Rules:** 4855

See also City Code on Takeovers and Mergers, Panel on Takeovers and Mergers

Target:
- **Acquisition:**
  - Public company: 5200
  - Preparation: 5212+
  - Search: 5260+

Tax:
- **Main entry:** 605+
- **Director's remuneration:** 2735+
- **Distribution:**
  - Main entry: 1769+
  - Assets: 1711
- **VAT evasion:** 2606
- **Sale of company:**
  - Assets: 5290+
  - Shares: 5335+
  - Damages for breach of warranty or indemnity: 5834+
  - Deferred consideration: 5472+
  - Earn out: 5474+
  - Investigation: 5678
  - Indemnity: 5945+
  - Consideration in form of loan notes: 5440+
  - Consideration in form of shares: 5428+
  - Retention: 5491
  - Tax clearance: 5367+
- **Other transactions:**
  - Hive-down: 6429
  - Loan capitalisation: 1058
  - Mortgage over shares: 1928
  - Own share purchase or redemption: 1369+
  - Bonus issue: 1037
  - Incorporation of business: 553+
- **Reliefs:**
  - Group loss relief: 6641+
  - Consortium relief: 6650+
  - Gift relief: 558+
  - Incorporation relief: 554
  - Taper relief: 555, 557, 2725, 5346+
- **Other types of business vehicle:**
  - Joint venture company: 6640+, 6561, 6563
  - Sole trader: 12

Tax *(continued)*
Unincorporated association: 24
Partnership: 17
Limited liability partnership: 77
European Economic Interest Grouping: 116

Liquidation:
Compulsory winding up order: 7751
Distribution to shareholders: 8091
Meeting tax liabilities: 7964

Administration: 8931

Receivership: 9324

Tax clearance:
Sale of company: 5367+

Own share purchase or redemption:
Availability: 1369
Notification to Revenue and Customs: 1396
Capital treatment: 1798

Tax covenant: See Tax Deed

Tax credit: 1780+

Tax deed:
Main entry: 5945+
Maximum claim period: 5921

Tele-conference:
Board meeting: 3255+
Shareholder meeting: 3749

Tenant:
Landlord proving for rent:
Liquidation: 8013+
Administration: 8951

Termination:
Director:
Office/employment: 2912+
Employment/service contract: 2977+
Alternate: 3448

Chairman of board: 3274
Secretary: 4158+
Auditor: 4339+
Partnership: 19
Liquidator:
Compulsory liquidation: 8245, 8250+
Voluntary liquidation: 8538+

Membership of liquidation committee: 8314
Provisional liquidator: 7692
Special manager: 8378
Administrator: 9030, 9035+
Receiver: 9402+

Terms and conditions: 633

Terms of reference: 3415

Territorial proceedings: See Secondary proceedings

Third party:
Action against director for breach of contract: 2446
Director's duties to: 2321+
Enforcing transaction: 2554+, 2350
Liability for unfair prejudice: 2128
Transaction at an undervalue/preference: 7817

Third party debt order:
Meaning: 9940
Main entry: 4741
Assets subject to:
Liquidator's power to deal: 7903+
Receiver's power to deal: 9288

Title documents:
Receiver's power to deal: 9293

Tort:
Meaning: 9940
Action for: 7162+
Remedies for: 2448+
Liquidation:
Proof of debt: 8008
Liability of liquidator: 8236+
Administration:
Liability of administrator: 8821, 9018
Receivership:
Liability of receiver: 9392

See also Conversion, Defamation, Negligence, Negligent misstatement, Trespass

Tracing: 2476+

Trade mark:
Main entry: 645
Database search:
Disclosure: 5897
Method: 5703
Infringement: 305+
Mortgage or charge over: 4638, 4653
Assignment: 5988, 6026

Trading name: See Name (Business)

Trading certificate: 510+

Trading losses:
Utilisation of by hive-down company: 6430+

Transaction:
Between company and its director: 2559+
Breach of director's duty: 2483
Challenged on insolvency: 7808+
Illegal: 2483

Transaction (continued)
Prohibited: 2880+
Unauthorised:
 Outside authority of memorandum: 2554+
 Ratified: 2497+
See also Substantial property transaction

Transaction defrauding creditors:
Main entry: 7826+
Disqualification as a director: 3023

Transaction at an undervalue: 7811+

Transfer as a going concern:
VAT: 5321+
Liquidator's power to: 8216, 8515
Administrator's power to: 8908
Receiver's power to: 9310
See also Hive-down, Sale of company, Transfer of shares

Transfer by way of security: See Mortgage

Transfer instrument:
Main entry: 1865+
Executed by transferor: 1848
Executed by personal representatives: 1969+
Execution of blank: 1939
Forged: 1906
Registration: 1882+, 1946+

Transfer of assets:
At an undervalue:
 Taxation: 1771
 Distribution: 1605
 Before liquidation/administration: 7811+
Intra-group:
 Effect on distributable profits: 1615
 Taxation: 1771
Crystallisation of floating charge: 4613
During takeover offer period: 6866
Special dividend on: 1666
Community Interest Company: 65, 66
See also Sale of company

Transfer of company: See Sale of company

Transfer of shares:
Main entry: 1827+
Between declaration and payment of dividend: 1702+
Liability for shareholder call: 1209
After forfeiture: 1222
After exercise of lien: 1229

Transfer of shares (continued)
Financial promotions: 4825+
Public company takeover:
 Before offer period: 6787+
 During offer period: 6850+
 Disclosure: 6860+
Joint venture company: 6609+
Compulsory liquidation: 7683
Voluntary liquidation: 8467

Transferee:
Meaning: 1825, 9940
Distribution to equitable shareholder in liquidation: 8087
Entitlement to registration of transfer: 1867
Entitlement to share certificate: 1909+
Share transfer instrument:
 Execution: 1868
 Limit on number: 1866, 1891
 Risk of refusal to register: 1897
Transfer not yet registered:
 Rights: 1831
 Voting: 3816

Transferor:
Meaning: 1825, 9940
Share transfer instrument:
 Execution: 1866
 Withdrawal/revocation: 1867
Transfer not yet registered:
 Rights: 1831
 Voting: 3816

Transformation: See Conversion

Transmission: 1962+

Treasury shares: 740
Cancellation: 1395, 1435

Trespass:
Meaning: 9940
Liquidator's liability: 8236+
Administrator's liability: 8821
Receiver's liability: 9392, 9403

Trigger event:
Pre-emption rights on transfer of shares:
 Main entry: 1845+
 Election by personal representative: 1972

True and fair view: 4228

Trust:
Meaning: 9940
Over shares: 2032+, 3923
Over assets when company in:
 Liquidation: 7907+, 8019+

Trust *(continued)*
 Administration: 8909, 8951
 Receivership: 9292
 CVA: 9532

Trust account: 1459

Trustee:
Meaning: 9940
As connected person: 9930+
Gift of shares: 1830
Sale of secured asset to lender's: 4664
Shareholder: 2032+
 Voting: 3816
Transfer not yet registered: 1831
Unincorporated association: 24
Warrantor in sale of company: 5823
Liquidation:
 Right to claim debt owed by company: 8019
 Liquidator: 8224
Administration:
 Right to claim debt owed by company: 8951
Constructive, See Constructive trustee

Trustee in bankruptcy:
Meaning: 9940
Ability to:
 Apply for unfair prejudice remedy: 2105
 Be shareholder: 2032+
 Petition for compulsory liquidation: 7620
Liability in company's insolvency: 7863+
Notice:
 Exercise by company of lien over shares: 1228
 Pre-emption rights on allotment: 950+
Transmission of shares: 1976+

TUPE:
Sale of company: 5392, 5771+
Hive-down: 6422
Insolvency:
 Compulsory liquidation: 7754
 Voluntary liquidation: 8473
 Administration: 8830
 Receivership: 9266

U

Uncalled share capital: 716

Uncertified shares: See Shares (Paperless holding)

Undertaking:
Consideration for allotment of shares:
 Main entry: 1148
 Enforceability: 1190+

Undertaking *(continued)*
Not to refuse to register transfer of shares: 1923
Not to alter share capital: 901
Disqualification, See Disqualification undertaking

Underwriter:
Commission: 1237+

Unfair dismissal:
Claim: 2981, 2986
Sale of company: 5775, 5779+
Hive-down: 6422
Insolvency: 7315, 8012, 8045, 8928

Unfair prejudice:
Main entry: 2105+
Allotment:
 For improper purpose: 935
 For non-cash consideration: 946
 In breach of pre-emption rights: 979
Appointment of non-independent valuer of shares: 1852
Community Interest Company: 72
Dividend policy: 1675
Removal of pre-emption provisions: 1842
Rights issue: 1044
Shareholder calls: 1210
Variation of class rights: 1297+
Pre-CVA moratorium: 9485
CVA: 9513+

Unfitness:
Director's disqualification: 3021+
 Ground: 3012

Unincorporated association: 24
Co-operative: 29

Unincorporated business:
Definition: 1
Main types: 8+
Table of comparison with incorporated business: 130

Unlimited company:
Generally: 57
Accounts:
 Delivery to: 4265
 Filing at Companies House: 4278
 Publication of non-statutory: 4271
Liability of director/manager as contributory: 7863+
Notice of shareholder meeting: 3675
Redeemable shares: 760

Unlimited company *(continued)*
Share capital:
  Generally: 700
  Changes: 1310
  Reduction: 1436
  Statement: 712
Shareholders' liability: 2010
Subscribers: 463

Unliquidated debt:
Liquidation: 8008
  Estimating value: 8038
  Voting at creditors' meeting: 8355
Administration: 8951
  Voting at creditors' meeting: 9088

Unregistered company:
Insolvency proceedings: 7302
Grounds for compulsory liquidation: 7592
Placing into administration: 8722

Unsecured creditor:
Liquidation:
  Ability to present winding up petition: 7617+
  Distribution: 8053+
  Employee: 8012
Administration:
  Ability to place company into: 8710
  Distribution: 8967+
  Employee: 8012
Receivership:
  Distribution: 9327

V

Valuation:
Aggregate item in financial statement: 4234
Consideration on sale of shares: 5378+
Distributed asset: 1712
Distribution for tax purposes: 1773
Distribution of asset to employee: 1785
Duty of care of valuer: 1855
Land and buildings: 4252
Non-cash asset transferred by shareholder: 1177+
Non-cash consideration for allotment:
  Private company: 1124
  Public company: 1152+
Sale of company:
  Stock: 5756+
  Target: 5415+
  Unascertainable consideration: 5474+
Shares:
  For pre-emption offer: 1852+
  In unfair prejudice claim: 2124+
Takeover: 6884

Value Added Tax: See VAT

VAT:
Incorporation of business: 553
Evasion: 2606
Hive-down: 6429
Joint venture company: 6640
Registration: 607
Sale of company: 5321+, 5787+
Liquidation: 7964
Administration: 8931
Receivership: 9324

Venture capital:
Main entry: 4800+
Management buy-out: 6045
Offer of shares: 986+
Sale of company: 5823

Venture capitalist: 4811

Venue:
Insolvency proceedings: 7385

Vesting order:
Liquidator:
  Compulsory liquidation: 7774
  Voluntary liquidation: 8466
Onerous property disclaimed in liquidation: 7924+

Vicarious liability:
Company for director's criminal acts: 2538, 7176
Company for director's negligence: 2449

Vide-conference:
Board meeting: 3255+
Shareholder meeting: 3749

Voluntary arrangement:
Insolvency procedure, See CVA

Voluntary group:
Unincorporated association: 24

Voluntary liquidation:
Main entry: 8425+
Procedure flowchart: 7572
Summary: 7335
Reorganisation under section 110 IA 1986: 6465+
See also CVL, Liquidation, MVL

Voluntary winding up: See Voluntary liquidation, CVL, Liquidation, MVL

Voting:

Board meeting:
　Generally: 3268+
　Alternate director: 3442
　When director has interest: 3350+

Shareholder meeting: 3810+

Shareholder written resolution: 3580+

Bankrupt: 2024

Enhanced/increased: 3820
　Director/shareholder: 2950
　Joint venture: 6572
　Purpose of allotment: 929
　Whether class right: 1275

Joint venture company:
　Generally: 6572
　Compliance with articles: 6608
　Deadlock: 6625+

Own share purchase:
　Approve contract: 1389
　Approve payment out of capital: 1412
　Effect: 1351

Right:
　After transfer of shares: 1831
　Deferred shares: 877
　Master share: 861
　Suspension: 3626, 3816, 3822
　Corporate representative: 3743
　Death of shareholder: 1964
　Mortgage over shares: 1928
　Non-voting shares: 750
　Ordinary shares: 743+
　Preference shares: 812
　Proxy: 3730

Shareholders' agreement: 2088

Subsidiary relationship: 199+

Written resolution: 3584

Compulsory liquidation:
　Creditors'/contributories' meeting: 8354+
　Liquidation committee meeting: 8311+

CVL:
　Creditors'/contributories' meeting: 8354+
　Liquidation committee meeting: 8311

Administration:
　Creditors' committee meeting: 9064
　Creditors' meeting: 9086+

Administrative receivership:
　Creditors' committee meeting: 9064

CVA:
　Creditors' meeting: 9507+
　Shareholders' meeting: 9511

Voting trust:

Alternative to shareholders' agreement: 2086

Vouchers:

Part of director's remuneration, See Benefits

W

Waiver:

City Code on Takeovers and Mergers: 6760+

Financial assistance:
　Form of: 5569
　Shareholders' failure to follow whitewash: 5588

Payment of distribution: 1754+

Payment of interest on unpaid call: 1217

Pre-emption rights:
　Allotment: 973+
　Mortgage over shares: 1923
　Transfer of shares: 1844

Right to dividend: 1682

Warrantor:

Sale of company: 5822+
　Party to sale and purchase agreement: 5728
　Joint and several liability: 5852+
　Additional: 5822+, 5859

Warranty:

Meaning: 9940

Inter-creditor agreement: 4687

Joint venture company: 6562, 6563, 6606

Loan agreement: 4548

Management buy-out: 6042

Sale of company:
　Main entry: 5800+
　Meaning: 5809+
　By buyer: 5929
　Financial assistance: 5574
　Retention for claim: 5492
　Accuracy of information memorandum: 5228
　Claim, double recovery of: 5924
　Claim, maximum claim value: 5922
　Claim, minimum claim value: 5923
　Disclosure letter: 5892+
　Effect of buyer's knowledge: 5847+
　Effect of gap between exchange and completion: 5865
　Effect of seller's knowledge: 5845
　Limits to: 5890+
　Maximum claim period: 5920
　Remedy for breach: 5826+
　Security for breach: 5858+
　Seller limitation provisions: 5918+
　Range of risks: 5814+

Web filing:

Companies House: 4074+

Website:

Company giving information via: 3698+

Disclosure of:
　Company information: 259+, 585
　Liquidation: 8229, 8468

Notice of shareholder meeting: 3698+

Welsh:
Filing at Companies House: 4049
Translation of company name: 242

Whitewash:
Financial assistance:
   Main entry: 5586+
   Summary timeline: 5625
Takeover of public company:
   Dispensation from mandatory offer rule: 6809

Wife: See Spouse

Winding up: See Liquidation

Winding up hearing:
Main entry: 7718+
Notice of attendance: 7653+, 7662

Winding up order:
Main entry: 7729+
Appeal: 7734
Appointment of liquidator: 8203
Court's decision: 7721+
Official receiver's initial action following: 8279

Winding up petition:
Main entry: 7585+
Contributory petition filing checklist: 7659
Non-contributory petition filing checklist: 7639+
After own share purchase or redemption: 1407
Based on CIB investigation: 7199
Company entering administration: 8815
Presentation:
   After administration application filed at court: 8742
   After resolution to wind up: 8465
   Before pre-CVA moratorium: 9534
   By administrator: 9011, 9141
   By receiver: 7625, 9304
   During administration: 9141
   During CVA: 9557
   During pre-CVA moratorium: 9476
   During voluntary liquidation: 7625
Search and sale of company: 5704+
Shareholder remedy: 2133+
Striking out: 7705+
Summary of petitioners: 7629

Winding up resolution:
CVL: 8438+
MVL: 8604+
Pre-CVA moratorium: 9476

Witness:
Documents generally: 3486+, 5741

Witness *(continued)*
To memorandum: 399
To execution of share transfer instrument: 1868
To share certificate: 1909
Insolvency applications: 7395
See also Evidence

Witness statement:
Reduction of share capital: 1484
Scheme of arrangement: 6510
Insolvency applications: 7388+
Compulsory liquidation: 8033
Non-contributory winding up petition: 7637+
Provisional liquidator: 7688
Administration:
   Confirming service of application: 8745
   Supporting application: 8737+
See also Affidavit, Evidence

Work in progress:
Mortgage or charge over: 4638

Written resolution:
Board: 3293+
Shareholder:
   Main entry: 3580+
   Alter authorised share capital: 904
   Approve own share purchase contract: 1389
   Approve own share purchase or redemption out of capital: 1412
   Approve reduction of share capital: 1481
   Approve whitewash of financial assistance: 5614
   Change articles: 451
   Consolidate or sub-divide share capital: 1317
   Declare final dividend: 1663
   Director's service contract over 5 years: 2655+
   During compulsory liquidation: 8312
   During CVL: 8443
   During MVL: 8612
Minutes of shareholder meeting: 3866
Filing at Companies House: 4051
Administration:
   Creditors in general: 9078
   Creditors to approve proposals: 8885

Wrongful dismissal:
Claim: 2986
Insolvency: 7315, 7754, 8012, 8473

Wrongful retention of goods:
Administrator's liability: 8821, 9018

Wrongful trading:
Main entry: 7449+
Ground for disqualification as a director: 3012, 7454

Composition réalisée par NORD COMPO

PRINTED IN FRANCE BY HÉRISSEY (CPI GROUP)
27092 EVREUX CEDEX 9

Dépôt légal : 2008
N° d'impression : 107029